Webster's New World™ Dictionary

VICTORIA NEUFELDT
Editor in Chief

ANDREW N. SPARKS
Project Editor

WARNER BOOKS

A Time Warner Company

Webster's New World Dictionary. Warner Books Paperback Edition.

This dictionary is based on and includes material from
Webster's New World Dictionary,
Third College Edition, copyright © 1988

Published by Webster's New World Dictionaries, A Division of Simon & Schuster, Inc.

Dictionary Editorial Offices: New World Dictionaries, 850 Euclid Avenue, Cleveland, Ohio 44114

Distributed by Warner Books.

Warner Books, Inc.
1271 Avenue of the Americas
New York, N.Y. 10020

A Time Warner Company

Manufactured in the United States of America

First Warner Books Printing: August, 1990

25 24 23 22 21

FOREWORD

This new dictionary is the Third Edition of what has long been the most widely used paperback dictionary in the country. Based on the recently published Third College Edition of *Webster's New World Dictionary*, this new dictionary was prepared by the same staff that produced the Third College Edition.

Like its predecessor, this dictionary is designed for those who want a small and handy, dependable, up-to-date reference. Although the word list is smaller and the definitions are shorter, they have been prepared with the same care and lexicographical expertise as that devoted to the preparation of the parent College Edition.

The vocabulary entered has been chosen for its usefulness in everyday, practical situations, as for the person reading a periodical or book on the way to work or school, or writing a report or a college composition away from easy access to larger reference works. Thus, in addition to the general vocabulary, this book includes common prefixes and suffixes, abbreviations and acronyms, and geographical and biographical names, all in a single alphabetical listing.

Of particular help to both native speakers of English unsure about fine distinctions and people for whom English is still a secondary language, are the large number of idiomatic expressions included, the many illustrative phrases, designed to clarify meaning and show typical context, the usage labels and phrases to help the user choose the appropriate word for a given situation, and the etymologies, which not only add information about the history of a word but also serve to enhance one's understanding of current meanings and connotations. Also useful as well as attractive are the line drawings supplementing many definitions.

The reader is urged to read the Guide to the Dictionary, beginning on page v, for a clear explanation of the information found in this dictionary.

Although much is new for this book, including the redesigned page, much remains the same. Users of former editions need not fear that what they loved about the old book will be gone from the new. It still bears the stamp of its first and principal author, David Guralnik (now retired), who established the high standard of the New World family of dictionaries.

The creation of this edition was carried out under the able lexicographical guidance of Senior Editor Andrew Sparks, a long-time member of the New World staff.

Victoria Neufeldt
Editor in Chief

DICTIONARY STAFF

Editor in Chief

Victoria Neufeldt

Project Editor

Andrew N. Sparks

Editorial Staff

Jonathan Goldman
Andra Kalnins
Fernando de Mello Vianna
James E. Naso
Katherine Goidich Soltis
Donald Stewart
Stephen P. Teresi

Administrative, Data Processing, and Clerical Staff

Laura J. Borovac
Alisa Murray
Cynthia M. Sadonick
Betty Dziedzic Thompson

Proofreading and Data Inputting

Mark Kmetzko
Paulette Kovelan
Shirley M. Miller

Citation Readers

Joan Felice
Batya Jundef
Patricia Nash

GUIDE TO THE USE OF THIS DICTIONARY

I. THE MAIN ENTRY WORD

A. *Arrangement of Entries*—All main entries, including single words, hyphenated and unhyphenated compounds, proper names, prefixes, suffixes, and abbreviations, are listed in strict alphabetical order and are set in large, boldface type.

a[2] (ə; *stressed,* ā) ***adj.*** . . .
a-[2] *prefix* . . .
a or **a.** **1** about **2** acre(s) . . .
aard·vark (ärd′värk′) ***n.*** . . .
Aar·on (er′ən) *Bible* . . .
ab- ⟦L⟧ *prefix* . . .
AB **1** Alberta (Canada) **2** Bachelor of Arts . . .
a·back (ə bak′) ***adv.*** [Archaic] backward . . . **—taken aback** startled . . .

Note that in biographical entries only the last, or family, name has been considered in alphabetization, but when two or more persons have the same family name, they have been arranged within the entry block in alphabetical order by first names.

John·son (jän′sən) **1** **An·drew** . . . **2** **Lyn·don Baines** . . . **3** **Samuel** . . .

Idiomatic phrases listed after a main entry have also been entered alphabetically within each group.

fly[1] (flī) ***vi.*** . . . **—fly into** . . . **—let fly (at)** . . . **—on the fly** . . .

B. *Variant Spellings & Forms*—When variant spellings of a word are some distance apart alphabetically, the definition appears with the spelling most frequently used, and the other spellings are cross-referred to this entry. If two commonly used variant spellings are alphabetically close to each other, they are entered as a joint boldface entry, but the order of entry does not necessarily indicate that the form entered first is "more correct," or is to be given preference.

the·a·ter or **the·a·tre** (thē′ə tər) ***n.*** . . .

If a variant spelling or spellings are alphabetically close to the prevailing spelling, they are given at the end of the entry block in small boldface.

par·af·fin . . . ***n.*** . . . Also **par′af·fine** . . .

C. *Cross-references*—When an entry is cross-referred to another term that has the same meaning but is more frequently used, the entry cross-referred to is usually in small capitals.

an·aes·the·si·a . . . ***n.*** ANESTHESIA . . .

D. *Homographs*—Main entries that are spelled alike but are different in meaning and origin, as **bat** (a club), **bat** (the animal), and **bat** (to wink), are given separate entry and are marked by superscript numbers following the boldface spellings.

bat[1] . . . ***n.*** . . .
bat[2] . . . ***n.*** . . .
bat[3] . . . ***vt.*** . . .

E. *Foreign Terms*—Foreign words and phrases encountered with some frequency in English but not completely naturalized are set in boldface italic type. The user of the dictionary is thus signaled that such terms are usually printed in italics or underlined in writing.

bon·jour (bōn zhoor′) ***interj., n.*** ⟦Fr⟧ . . .

F. *Prefixes, Suffixes, & Combining Forms*—Prefixes and initial combining forms are indicated by a hyphen following the entry form.

hemi- . . . *prefix* half . . .

Suffixes and terminal combining forms are indicated by a hyphen preceding the entry form.

-a·ble . . . *suffix* **1** that can . . .

The abundance of these forms, whose syllabification and pronunciation can be determined from the words containing them, makes it possible for the reader to understand and pronounce countless complex terms not entered in the dictionary but formed with affixes and words that are entered.

G. ***Word Division***—The word divisions (or syllabifications) used in this dictionary are those in general use.

The parts of entry words are separated by heavy, centered periods or sometimes by stress marks.

fun·da·men·tal (fun'də ment''l) ***adj.*** . . .
coun'ter·rev'o·lu'tion ***n.*** . . .

II. PRONUNCIATION

A. ***Introduction***—The pronunciations given in this dictionary are those used by good speakers of American English. Many words of the language occur in everyday speech. Good speakers do not always pronounce these words in the same way. Because the various pronunciations are widely used by good speakers, however, the pronunciations must be considered as acceptable pronunciations.

B. ***Key to Pronunciation***

Symbol	*Key Words*	*Symbol*	*Key Words*
ə	a in ago	f	fit, if
	e in over		
	i in sanity	g	get, tag
	o in comply		
	u in focus	h	he, ahead
a	at, gas		
ā	ate, day	i	is, lid
ä	car, father	ī	ice, high
b	bed, tab	j	joy, agile
ch	chin, march	k	kid, take
d	dip, wad	l	lid, sail
e	end, ten		
ē	eve, be	m	met, aim
n	no, pan	t	top, sat
ŋ	ring, drink	th	thin, truth
		th	the, father
ō	own, go		
ô	horn, all	u	up, bud
		ʉ	urn, fur
o͝o	look, pull		
o͞o	tool, crew		
		v	vat, have
oi	oil, toy		
ou	out, how	w	will, away
p	put, tap	y	yet, yard
r	red, far		
s	sell, toss	z	zebra, haze
sh	she, wash	zh	azure, leisure

A few explanatory notes on some of the more complex of these symbols follow.

' The apostrophe before an *l, m,* or *n* indicates that the following consonant forms the nucleus of a syllable with no appreciable vowel sound, as in *cattle* (kat''l) or *satin* (sat''n). In some persons' speech, certain syllabic consonants are replaced with syllables containing reduced vowels, as (sa'tin).

ə This symbol, called the schwa, represents the indistinct, neutral vowel sound heard in the unstressed syllables of *ago, over,* etc.

ä This symbol represents essentially the sound of *a* in *car* but may also represent the vowel sound sometimes heard in New England for *bath* (bäth). In words like *alms* and *hot,* the usual sound of the letters *a* and *o* is the same as the sound of *a* in *ah.* Many speakers, however, use a sound that approaches or is the same as the sound of the *o* in *horn.*

e This symbol represents the sound of *e* in *ten* and is also used, followed and hence colored by *r,* to represent the vowel sound of *care* (ker).

ē This symbol represents the vowel sound in *meet* and is also used for the vowel in the unstressed final syllable of such words as *fidelity* (fə del'ə tē), *pretty* (prit'ē), etc.

i This symbol represents the vowel sound in *hit* and is also used for the vowel in the unstressed syllables of such words as *garbage* (gär′bij), *reply* (ri plī′), etc. In such contexts reductions to ə (gär′bəj), (rə plī′), etc. are commonly heard and may be assumed as variants. This symbol is also used, followed and hence colored by *r*, to represent the vowel sound of *dear* (dir).

ô This symbol represents essentially the sound of *a* in *all*. When followed by *r*, as in *more* (môr), vowels ranging to ō (mōr *or* mō′ər) are often heard and may be assumed as variants.

r This symbol represents the sound of the letter *r* in *red, part*, and *far*. In words like *part* and *far*, however, the spelled *r* is usually not pronounced by speakers in the South and along the eastern seaboard.

ŋ This symbol represents the nasal sound of the *-ng* of *sing* and of the *n* before *k* and *g*, as in *drink* (driŋk) and *finger* (fiŋ′gər).

C. *Foreign Sounds*—In recording the approximate pronunciation of foreign words, it has been necessary to use the following five symbols in addition to those preceding.

ë This symbol represents the sound made by rounding the lips as for (ō) and pronouncing (e).

ö This symbol represents the sound made by rounding the lips as for (ō) and pronouncing (ā).

ü This symbol represents the sound made by rounding the lips as for (ōō) and pronouncing (ē).

kh This symbol represents the sound made by arranging the speech organs as for (k) but allowing the breath to escape in a continuous stream, as in pronouncing (h).

n This symbol indicates that the vowel immediately preceding it is given a nasal sound, as in Fr. *bonjour* (bōn zhōōr′).

D. *Styling of Pronunciation*—Pronunciations are given inside parentheses, immediately following the boldface entry. A primary, or strong, stress is indicated by a heavy stroke (′) immediately following the syllable so stressed. A secondary, or weak, stress is indicated by a lighter stroke (′) following the syllable so stressed. Some compound entries formed of words that are separately entered in the dictionary are syllabified and stressed and repronounced only in part or not repronounced at all.

hap·pi coat (hap′ē) . . .
hap·py (hap′ē) . . .
hap′py-go-luck′y . . .
happy hour . . .

E. *Variants*—Two or more pronunciations may be given for the same word. If no qualifying note (such as *also*, *chiefly Brit.*, etc.) is given, then each pronunciation shown is considered equally acceptable, regardless of the order in which it appears.

F. *Truncation*—Variant pronunciations for a main entry or a run-in entry are truncated, or shortened, whenever possible. A hyphen after the shortened variant marks it as an initial syllable or syllables; one before the variant, as terminal; and hyphens before and after the variant, as internal.

ab·jure (ab joor′, əb-) . . .
dom·i·cile (däm′ə sīl′, -sil; *also* dō′mə-) . . .
fu·tu·ri·ty (fyōō toor′ə tē, -tyoor′-) . . .

Variant pronunciations involving different parts of speech in the same entry block usually appear as follows:

a·buse (ə byōōz′; *for n.,* ə byōōs′) *vt.* . . .

III. PART-OF-SPEECH LABELS

Part-of-speech labels are given for main entry words (excluding most proper nouns) that are solid or hyphenated forms, but not for prefixes, suffixes, and abbreviations. When an entry word is used as more than one part of speech in an entry block, long dashes introduce each different part-of-speech label, which appears in boldface italic type.

round . . . ***adj.*** . . . ***—n.*** . . . ***—vt.*** . . . ***—vi.*** . . . ***—adv.*** . . . ***—prep.*** . . .

Two or more part-of-speech labels are given jointly for an entry when the definition or definitions, or the cross-reference, will suffice for both or all.

des·patch . . . ***vt., n.*** DISPATCH

IV. INFLECTED FORMS

Inflected forms regarded as irregular or offering difficulty in spelling are entered in small boldface immediately following the part-of-speech labels. They are truncated where possible, and syllabified and pronounced where necessary.

hap·py . . . ***adj.*** **-pi·er, -pi·est** . . .
cit·y . . . ***n., pl.*** **-ies** . . .
a·moe·ba . . . ***n., pl.*** **-bas** or **-bae** (-bē) . . .

Forms regarded as regular inflections, and hence not normally indicated, include:

a) plurals formed by adding *-s* to the singular (or *-es* after *s, x, z, ch,* and *sh*), as *bats, boxes*
b) present tenses formed by adding *-s* to the infinitive (or *-es* after *s, x, z, ch,* and *sh*), as *waits, searches*
c) past tenses and past participles formed by simply adding *-ed* to the infinitive, as *waited, searched*
d) present participles formed by simply adding *-ing* to the infinitive, as *waiting, searching*
e) comparatives and superlatives formed by simply adding *-er* and *-est* to the base of an adjective or adverb, as *taller, tallest* or *sooner, soonest*

Where two inflected forms are given for a verb, the first is the form for the past tense and the past participle, and the second is the form for the present participle.

make . . . ***vt.*** **made, mak'ing** . . .

Where three forms are given, the first represents the past tense, the second the past participle, and the third the present participle.

give . . . ***vt.*** **gave, giv'en, giv'ing** . . .

Where there are alternative forms for any of the principal parts, these are given and properly indicated.

bid . . . ***vt.*** **bade** or **bid, bid'den** or **bid, bid'ding** . . .

V. ETYMOLOGY

The etymology, or word derivation, appears inside open double brackets immediately before the definitions proper. The symbols, as < for "derived from," and the abbreviations of language labels, etc. used in the etymologies are dealt with in full in the list immediately preceding page 1 of the vocabulary.

di·shev·el . . . ⟦< OFr *des-,* DIS-, + *chevel,* hair⟧ . . .

No etymology is shown where one would be superfluous, as where the elements making up the word are immediately apparent.

VI. THE DEFINITIONS

A. ***Order of Senses***—The standard, general senses of a word are given first, and colloquial, slang, etc. senses come next. Technical senses requiring special field labels, as *Astron., Chem.,* etc., follow in order.

B. ***Numbering & Grouping of Senses***—Senses are numbered consecutively within any given part of speech in boldface numerals. Where a primary sense of a word can easily be subdivided into several closely related meanings, such meanings are indicated by italicized letters.

time . . . ***n.*** . . . **1** every . . . **2** a system . . . **3** the period . . . **11** *Music* *a*) rhythm . . . *b*) tempo—***vt.*** . . . **1** to arrange . . . 2 to adjust . . . —*adj.* 1 having to . . . 2 set to . . . 3 having . . . —**in time** 1 eventually 2 before . . . 3 keeping . . .

C. ***Capitalization***—If a main entry word is capitalized in all its senses, the entry word itself is printed with a capital letter. If a capitalized main entry word has a sense or senses that are uncapitalized, these are marked with the corresponding small-boldface, lower-case letter followed by a short dash and enclosed in brackets.

Pu·ri·tan . . . *n.* . . . 1 . . . 2 [**p-**] . . .

Conversely, capitalized letters are shown, where pertinent, with lower-case main entries. In some instances these designations are qualified by the self-explanatory "*often*," "*occas.*," etc.

left[1] . . . —*n.* 1 . . . 2 [*often* **L-**] . . .

D. ***Plural Forms***—In a singular noun entry, the designation "[*pl.*]" (or "[*often pl.*]," "[*usually pl.*]," etc.) before a definition indicates that it is (or *often*, *usually*, etc. is) the plural form of the entry word that has the meaning given in the definition.

look . . . *vi.* . . . —*n.* 1 . . . 2 . . . 3 [Colloq.] *a)* [*usually pl.*] appearance *b)* [*pl.*] personal appearance . . .

If a plural noun entry or sense is construed as singular, the designation [*with sing. v.*] is added.

phys·ics . . . *n.pl.* . . . [*with sing. v.*] . . .

E. ***Verbs Followed by Prepositions or Objects***—Where certain verbs are, in usage, invariably or usually followed by a specific preposition or prepositions, this has been indicated in either of the following ways: the preposition has been worked into the definition, italicized and usually enclosed in parentheses, or a note has been added after the definition indicating that the preposition is so used.

In definitions of transitive verbs, the specific or generalized object of the verb, where given, is enclosed in parentheses, since such an object is not part of the definition.

VII. USAGE LABELS

Usage labels, if they are to be useful, must be conventional words that are clearly understood by the reader. The labels used in this dictionary are given below, with an explanation of each.

Colloquial: The term or sense is in widespread use and is generally characteristic of conversation and informal writing. It is not to be regarded as substandard or illiterate.

Slang: The term or sense is not generally regarded as conventional or standard usage, but is used, even by the best speakers, in highly informal contexts. Usually, slang terms either pass into disuse in time or come to have a standard status.

Obsolete: The term or sense is no longer used but occurs in earlier writings.

Archaic: The term or sense is rarely used today except in certain restricted contexts, as in church ritual, but occurs in earlier writings.

Old Poetic: The term or sense was never part of the everyday language, but was used chiefly in earlier poetry, or in prose where a poetic quality was desired.

Dialect: The term or sense is used regularly only in some geographical areas or in a certain designated area (*South, West,* etc.) of the United States.

British: The term or sense is restricted to the British Isles as a whole. The label "Brit., etc." indicates the term or sense is found generally throughout the English-speaking world outside the U.S. The label "Brit., etc. (exc. Cdn.)" indicates the term or sense is in general use throughout the English-speaking world except North America.

Canadian (or *Irish*, etc.): The term or sense is characteristic specifically of Canadian (or Irish, etc.) English.

Historical: The term or sense refers to something that no longer exists and to which no more current term applies.

Old-fashioned: The term or sense is not yet considered archaic but seems out-of-date.
Rare: The term or sense has never been common.
Vulgar: The term or sense is regarded by most people as highly inappropriate in most social contexts. Many such terms are also slang.

In addition to the above usage labels, supplementary information is often given after the definition, indicating whether the term or sense is generally regarded as vulgar, substandard, or derogatory, used with ironic, familiar, or hyperbolic connotations, etc.

pate . . . *n.* . . . a humorous term

VIII. RUN-IN DERIVED ENTRIES

It is possible in English to form an almost infinite number of derived forms simply by adding certain prefixes or suffixes to the base word. The editors have included as run-in entries in boldface type as many of these common derived words as space permitted, but only when the meaning of such words can be immediately understood from the meanings of the base word and the affix. Thus, **greatness** and **liveliness** are run in at the end of the entries for **great** and **lively**, the suffix **-ness** being found as a separate entry meaning "state, quality, or instance of being." Many words formed with common suffixes, as **-able, -er, -less, -like, -ly, -tion,** etc. are similarly treated as run-in entries with the base word from which they are derived. All such entries are syllabified and either accented to show stress in pronunciation or, where necessary, pronounced in full or in part.

When a derived word has a meaning or meanings different from those that can be deduced from the sum of its parts, it has been given separate entry, pronounced, and fully defined (e.g., **folder**).

A

a[1] or **A** (ā) ***n.***, *pl.* **a's, A's** (āz) the first letter of the English alphabet

a[2] (ə; *stressed*, ā) ***adj., indefinite article*** ‖ < AN ‖ **1** one; one sort of **2** each; any one **3** per /once *a* day/ Before words beginning with a consonant sound, *a* is used /*a* child, *a* home, *a* uniform/ See AN

A (ā) ***n.*** **1** a blood type **2** a grade indicating excellence **3** *Music* the sixth tone in the scale of C major

a-[1] ‖ < OE ‖ *prefix* **1** in, into, on, at, to /*ashore*/ **2** in the act or state of /*asleep*/

a-[2] *prefix* **1** ‖ < OE ‖ up, out /*arise*/ **2** ‖ < OE ‖ off, of /*akin*/ **3** ‖ < Gr ‖ not, without /*amoral*/

a or **a.** **1** about **2** acre(s) **3** adjective **4** alto **5** answer

A or **A.** **1** alto **2** answer **3** April **4** August

AA or **A.A.** **1** Alcoholics Anonymous **2** Associate in (or of) Arts

aard·vark (ärd′värk′) ***n.*** ‖ Du, earth pig ‖ a nocturnal, ant-eating S African mammal

Aar·on (er′ən) *Bible* the first high priest of the Hebrews

AB ***n.*** a blood type

ab- ‖ L ‖ *prefix* away, from, from off, down /*abdicate*/

AB **1** Alberta (Canada) **2** Bachelor of Arts: also **A.B.**

a·back (ə bak′) ***adv.*** [Archaic] backward; back —**taken aback** startled and confused; surprised

ABACUS

ab·a·cus (ab′ə kəs) ***n.***, *pl.* **-cus·es** or **-ci′** (-sī′) ‖ < Gr *abax* ‖ a frame with sliding beads for doing arithmetic

a·baft (ə baft′) ***adv.*** ‖ < OE *on*, on + *be*, by + *æftan*, aft ‖ aft

ab·a·lo·ne (ab′ə lō′nē) ***n.*** ‖ < AmInd ‖ an edible sea mollusk with an oval, somewhat spiral shell

a·ban·don (ə ban′dən) ***vt.*** ‖ < OFr *mettre a bandon*, to put under (another's) ban ‖ **1** to give up completely **2** to desert —***n.*** unrestrained activity; exuberance —**a·ban′don·ment** ***n.***

a·ban′doned ***adj.*** **1** deserted **2** shamefully wicked **3** unrestrained

a·base (ə bās′) ***vt.*** **a·based′, a·bas′ing** ‖ < ML *abassare*, to lower ‖ to humble —**a·base′ment** ***n.***

a·bash (ə bash′) ***vt.*** ‖ < OFr *es-*, intens. + *baer*, gape ‖ to make ashamed and uneasy; disconcert —**a·bash′ed·ly** ***adv.***

a·bate (ə bāt′) ***vt., vi.*** **a·bat′ed, a·bat′ing** ‖ < OFr *abattre*, beat down ‖ **1** to make or become less **2** *Law* to end —**a·bate′ment** ***n.***

ab·at·toir (ab′ə twär′, ab′ə twär′) ***n.*** ‖ Fr: see prec. ‖ a slaughterhouse

ab·bé (a′bā) ***n.*** ‖ Fr: see ABBOT ‖ a French priest's title

ab·bess (ab′əs) ***n.*** ‖ see ABBOT ‖ a woman who heads a convent of nuns

ab·bey (ab′ē) ***n.*** **1** a monastery or convent **2** a church belonging to an abbey

ab·bot (ab′ət) ***n.*** ‖ < Aram *abbā*, father ‖ a man who heads a monastery

abbr. or **abbrev.** **1** abbreviated **2** abbreviation

ab·bre·vi·ate (ə brē′vē āt′) ***vt.*** **-at′ed, -at′ing** ‖ < L *ad-*, to + *brevis*, brief ‖ to make shorter; esp., to shorten (a word) by omitting letters

ab·bre′vi·a′tion (-ā′shən) ***n.*** **1** a shortening **2** a shortened form of a word or phrase, as *Mr.* for *Mister*

ABC (ā′bē′sē′) ***n.***, *pl.* **ABC's** **1** [*usually pl.*] the alphabet **2** the basic elements (of a subject); rudiments

ab·di·cate (ab′di kāt′) ***vt., vi.*** **-cat′ed, -cat′ing** ‖ < L *ab-*, off + *dicare*, to proclaim ‖ **1** to give up formally (a throne, etc.) **2** to surrender (a right, responsibility, etc.) —**ab′di·ca′tion** ***n.***

ab·do·men (ab′də mən, ab dō′-) ***n.*** ‖ L ‖ the part of the body between the diaphragm and the pelvis; belly —**ab·dom′i·nal** (-däm′ə nəl) ***adj.***

ab·duct (ab dukt′) ***vt.*** ‖ < L *ab-*, away + *ducere*, to lead ‖ to kidnap —**ab·duc′tion** ***n.*** —**ab·duc′tor** ***n.***

a·beam (ə bēm′) ***adv.*** at right angles to a ship's length or keel

a·bed (ə bed′) ***adv., adj.*** in bed

A·bel (ā′bəl) *Bible* the second son of Adam and Eve: see CAIN

ab·er·ra·tion (ab′ər ā′shən) ***n.*** ‖ < L *ab-*, from + *errare*, wander ‖ **1** a deviation from what is right, true, normal, etc. **2** mental derangement or lapse **3** *Optics* the failure of light rays from one point to converge at a single focus —**ab·er′rant** (-er′ənt) *adj.* —**ab′er·ra′tion·al** *adj.*

a·bet (ə bet′) *vt.* **a·bet′ted, a·bet′ting** ‖ < OFr *a-*, to + *beter*, to bait ‖ to urge on or help, esp. in crime —**a·bet′tor** or **a·bet′ter** *n.*

a·bey·ance (ə bā′əns) *n.* ‖ < OFr *a-*, to, at + *bayer*, wait expectantly ‖ temporary suspension, as of an activity or ruling

ab·hor (ab hôr′) *vt.* **-horred′, -hor′ring** ‖ < L *ab-*, from + *horrere*, to shudder ‖ to shrink from in disgust, hatred, etc. —**ab·hor′rence** *n.*

ab·hor′rent (-ənt) *adj.* causing disgust, hatred, etc.; detestable —**ab·hor′rent·ly** *adv.*

a·bide (ə bīd′) *vi.* **a·bode′** or **a·bid′ed, a·bid′ing** ‖ < OE *ā-*, intens. + *bīdan*, bide ‖ **1** to remain **2** [Archaic] to reside —*vt.* to put up with —**abide by 1** to live up to (a promise, etc.) **2** to submit to and carry out —**a·bid′ance** *n.*

a·bid′ing *adj.* enduring; lasting

a·bil·i·ty (ə bil′ə tē) *n., pl.* **-ties** ‖ < L *habilitas* ‖ **1** a being able; power to do **2** talent; skill

-a·bil·i·ty (ə bil′ə tē) ‖ L *-abilitas* ‖ *suffix* a (specified) ability, capacity, or tendency

ab·ject (ab′jekt′, ab jekt′) *adj.* ‖ < L *ab-*, from + *jacere*, to throw ‖ **1** miserable; wretched **2** degraded —**ab′ject′ly** *adv.* —**ab·jec′tion** *n.*

ab·jure (ab jo͝or′, əb-) *vt.* **-jured′, -jur′ing** ‖ < L *ab-*, away + *jurare*, swear ‖ to give up (rights, allegiance, etc.) on oath; renounce —**ab·ju·ra·tion** (ab′jə rā′shən) *n.* —**ab·jur′a·to′ry** (-ə tôr′ē) *adj.* —**ab·jur′er** *n.*

ab·late (ab lāt′) *vt.* **-lat′ed, -lat′ing** ‖ see fol. ‖ **1** to remove, as by surgery **2** to wear away, burn away, or vaporize —*vi.* to be ablated, as a rocket shield in reentry —**ab·la′tion** *n.*

ab·la·tive (ab′lə tiv) *n.* ‖ < L *ab-*, away + *ferre*, to bear ‖ *Gram.* the case expressing removal, cause, agency, etc., as in Latin

a·blaze (ə blāz′) *adj.* **1** flaming **2** greatly excited

a·ble (ā′bəl) *adj.* **a′bler, a′blest** ‖ < L *habere*, have ‖ **1** having enough power, skill, etc. to do something **2** skilled; talented **3** *Law* competent —**a′bly** *adv.*

-a·ble (ə bəl) ‖ < L ‖ *suffix* **1** that can or will [*perishable*] **2** capable of being _____ed [*manageable*] **3** worthy of being _____ed [*lovable*] **4** having qualities of [*comfortable*] **5** inclined to [*peaceable*]

a′ble-bod′ied *adj.* strong; healthy

able-bodied seaman a trained or skilled seaman Also **able seaman**

a·bloom (ə blo͞om′) *adj.* in bloom

ab·lu·tion (ab lo͞o′shən) *n.* ‖ < L *ab-*, off + *luere*, to wash ‖ [*usually pl.*] a washing of the body, esp. as a religious ceremony

-a·bly (ə blē) *suffix* in a way indicating a (specified) ability, tendency, etc.

ABM anti-ballistic missile

ab·ne·gate (ab′nə gāt′) *vt.* **-gat′ed, -gat′ing** ‖ < L *ab-*, from + *negare*, deny ‖ to deny and refuse; renounce (a claim, etc.) —**ab′ne·ga′tion** *n.*

ab·nor·mal (ab nôr′məl) *adj.* not normal, average, or typical; irregular —**ab·nor′mal·ly** *adv.*

ab′nor·mal′i·ty (-mal′ə tē) *n.* **1** an abnormal condition **2** *pl.* **-ties** an abnormal thing; malformation

a·board (ə bôrd′) *adv., prep.* on or in (a train, ship, etc.)

a·bode (ə bōd′) *vi., vt. alt. pt. & pp. of* ABIDE —*n.* a home; residence

a·bol·ish (ə bäl′ish) *vt.* ‖ < L *abolere*, destroy ‖ to do away with; void

ab·o·li·tion (ab′ə lish′ən) *n.* **1** complete destruction; annulment **2** [*occas.* **A-**] the abolishing of slavery in the U.S. —**ab′o·li′tion·ist** *n.*

a·bom·i·na·ble (ə bäm′ə nə bəl) *adj.* ‖ see fol. ‖ **1** disgusting; vile **2** very bad —**a·bom′i·na·bly** *adv.*

a·bom′i·nate′ (-nāt′) *vt.* **-nat′ed, -nat′ing** ‖ < L *abominari*, regard as an ill omen ‖ **1** to hate; loathe **2** to dislike —**a·bom′i·na′tion** *n.*

ab·o·rig·i·nal (ab′ə rij′ə nəl) *adj.* **1** existing (in a region) from the beginning; first; indigenous **2** of aborigines —*n.* an aborigine

ab′o·rig′i·ne′ (-ə nē′) *n., pl.* **-nes′** ‖ L < *ab-*, from + *origine*, origin ‖ any of the first known inhabitants of a region

a·born·ing (ə bôr′niŋ) *adv.* while being born or created [the plan died *aborning*]

a·bort (ə bôrt′) *vi.* ‖ < L *aboriri*, miscarry ‖ to have a miscarriage —*vt.* **1** to check before fully developed **2** to cut short (a flight, etc.), as because of an equipment failure

a·bor′tion *n.* any expulsion of a fetus before it is able to survive, esp. if induced on purpose —**a·bor′tion·ist** *n.*

a·bor′tive *adj.* **1** unsuccessful; fruitless **2** *Biol.* arrested in development

a·bound (ə bound′) *vi.* ‖ < L *ab-*, away + *undare*, rise in waves ‖ to be plentiful; teem Often with *in* or *with*

a·bout (ə bout′) *adv.* ‖ < OE *onbūtan*, around ‖ **1** all around **2** near **3** in an opposite direction **4** nearly [*about* ready] —*adj.* astir [he is up and *about*] —*prep.* **1** on all sides of **2** near to **3** with **4** on the point of **5** concerning

a·bout′-face′ (-fās′, -fās′; *for v.*, ə bout′fās′) *n.* a reversal of position or opinion —*vi.* **-faced′, -fac′ing** to turn or face in the opposite direction

a·bove (ə buv′) *adv.* ‖ OE *abūfan* ‖ **1** in a higher place; up **2** earlier (in a book, etc.) **3** higher in rank, etc. —*prep.* **1** over; on top of **2** better or more than [*above* the average] —*adj.* mentioned earlier —**above all** most of all; mainly

a·bove′board′ *adv., adj.* without dishonesty or concealment

a·brade (ə brād′) *vt., vi.* **a·brad′ed, a·brad′ing** ‖ < L *ab-*, away + *radere*, to scrape ‖ to rub off; scrape away

A·bra·ham (ā′brə ham′) *Bible* the first patriarch of the Hebrews

a·bra·sion (ə brā′zhən) *n.* **1** an abrading **2** an abraded spot

a·bra′sive (-siv) *adj.* **1** causing abrasion **2** aggressively annoying; irritating —*n.* a substance, as sandpaper, used for grinding, polishing, etc.

a·breast (ə brest′) *adv., adj.* **1** side by side **2** informed (*of*); aware

a·bridge (ə brij′) ***vt.*** **a·bridged′, a·bridg′ing** ‖< LL *abbreviare,* abbreviate‖ 1 to shorten, lessen, or curtail 2 to shorten (a piece of writing) while keeping the substance —**a·bridg′ment** or **a·bridge′ment** ***n.***

a·broad (ə brôd′) ***adv.*** 1 far and wide 2 in circulation; current 3 outdoors 4 to or in foreign lands —**from abroad** from a foreign land

ab·ro·gate (ab′rō gāt′, -rə-) ***vt.*** **-gat′ed, -gat′ing** ‖< L *ab-,* away + *rogare,* ask‖ to abolish; repeal; annul —**ab′ro·ga′tion** ***n.*** —**ab′ro·ga′tor** ***n.***

a·brupt (ə brupt′) ***adj.*** ‖< L *ab-,* off + *rumpere,* to break‖ 1 sudden; unexpected 2 brusque 3 very steep 4 disconnected, as some writing —**a·brupt′ly** ***adv.*** —**a·brupt′ness** ***n.***

Ab·sa·lom (ab′sə ləm) *Bible* David's son who rebelled against him

ab·scess (ab′ses′) ***n.*** ‖< L *ab(s)-,* from + *cedere,* go‖ a swollen area in body tissues, containing pus —***vi.*** to form an abscess —**ab′scessed′** ***adj.***

ab·scis·sa (ab sis′ə) ***n.,*** *pl.* **-sas** or **-sae** (-ē) ‖L < *ab-,* from + *scindere,* to cut‖ *Math.* the horizontal distance of a point from a vertical axis

ab·scond (ab skänd′, əb-) ***vi.*** ‖< L *ab(s)-,* from + *condere,* hide‖ to leave hastily and secretly, esp. to escape the law —**ab·scond′er** ***n.***

ab·sence (ab′səns) ***n.*** 1 a being absent 2 the time of this 3 a lack

ab·sent (ab′sənt; *for v.,* ab sent′) ***adj.*** ‖< L *ab-,* away + *esse,* be‖ 1 not present 2 not existing; lacking 3 not attentive —***vt.*** to keep (oneself) away —***prep.*** in the absence of /*absent* her testimony, our case is weak/ —**ab′sent·ly** ***adv.***

ab·sen·tee (ab′sən tē′) ***n.*** one who is absent, as from work —***adj.*** designating, of, or from one who is absent —**ab′sen·tee′ism′** ***n.***

absentee ballot a ballot to be marked and sent to a board of elections by a person (**absentee voter**) unable to be at the polls at election time

ab′sent-mind′ed ***adj.*** 1 not attentive; preoccupied 2 habitually forgetful —**ab′sent-mind′ed·ly** ***adv.*** —**ab′sent-mind′ed·ness** ***n.***

absent without leave *Mil.* absent from duty without official permission

ab·sinthe or **ab·sinth** (ab′sinth′) ***n.*** ‖< Gr‖ a green, bitter, toxic liqueur

ab·so·lute (ab′sə lo͞ot′) ***adj.*** ‖see ABSOLVE‖ 1 perfect; complete 2 not mixed; pure 3 not limited /*absolute* power/ 4 positive 5 not doubted; real /*absolute* truth/ 6 not relative —**ab′so·lute′ly** ***adv.***

absolute value the value of a real number, disregarding its positive or negative sign /the *absolute value* of -4 or +4 is 4/

absolute zero the lower limit on physically obtainable temperatures: equal to -273.15°C or -459.67°F

ab·so·lu·tion (ab′sə lo͞o′shən) ***n.*** 1 a freeing (*from* guilt); forgiveness 2 remission (*of* sin or penalty for it)

ab·so·lut·ism (ab′sə lo͞ot′iz′əm) ***n.*** government by absolute rule; despotism —**ab′so·lut′ist** ***n., adj.***

ab·solve (ab zälv′, əb-) ***vt.*** **-solved′, -solv′ing** ‖< L *ab-,* from + *solvere,* loosen‖ 1 to free from guilt, a duty, etc. 2 to give religious absolution to

ab·sorb (ab sôrb′, -zôrb′; əb-) ***vt.*** ‖< L *ab-,* from + *sorbere,* drink in‖ 1 to suck up 2 to interest greatly; engross 3 to assimilate 4 to pay for (costs, etc.) 5 to take in (a shock, etc.) without recoil 6 to take in and not reflect (light or sound) —**ab·sorb′ing** ***adj.***

ab·sorb′ent ***adj.*** capable of absorbing moisture, etc. —***n.*** a thing that absorbs —**ab·sorb′en·cy** ***n.***

ab·sorp·tion (ab sôrp′shən, -zôrp′-; əb-) ***n.*** 1 an absorbing or being absorbed 2 great interest —**ab·sorp′tive** ***adj.***

ab·stain (ab stān′, əb-) ***vi.*** ‖< L *ab(s)-,* from + *tenere,* to hold‖ to voluntarily do without; refrain (*from*) —**ab·stain′er** ***n.*** —**ab·sten′tion** (-sten′shən) ***n.***

ab·ste·mi·ous (ab stē′mē əs, əb-) ***adj.*** ‖< L *ab(s)-,* from + *temetum,* strong drink‖ moderate in eating and drinking; temperate

ab·sti·nence (ab′stə nəns) ***n.*** an abstaining from some or all food, liquor, etc. —**ab′sti·nent** ***adj.***

ab·stract (*for adj.,* ab strakt′, ab′strakt′; *for n. & vt. 2,* ab′strakt′; *for vt. 1,* ab strakt′) ***adj.*** ‖< L *ab(s)-,* from + *trahere,* to draw‖ 1 thought of apart from material objects 2 expressing a quality so thought of 3 theoretical 4 *Art* not representing things realistically —***n.*** a summary —***vt.*** 1 to take away 2 to summarize —**ab·stract′ly** ***adv.***

ab·stract′ed ***adj.*** absent-minded

ab·strac·tion (ab strak′shən) ***n.*** 1 an abstracting; removal 2 an abstract idea, thing, etc. 3 mental withdrawal 4 an abstract painting, etc.

ab·struse (ab stro͞os′) ***adj.*** ‖< L *ab(s)-,* away + *trudere,* to thrust‖ hard to understand —**ab·struse′ly** ***adv.*** —**ab·struse′ness** ***n.***

ab·surd (ab sʉrd′, -zʉrd′; əb-) ***adj.*** ‖< L *ab-,* intens. + *surdus,* dull, insensible‖ so unreasonable as to be ridiculous —**ab·surd′i·ty** ***n.*** —**ab·surd′ly** ***adv.***

a·bun·dance (ə bun′dəns) ***n.*** ‖see ABOUND‖ great plenty; more than enough —**a·bun′dant** ***adj.*** —**a·bun′dant·ly** ***adv.***

a·buse (ə byo͞oz′; *for n.,* ə byo͞os′) ***vt.*** **a·bused′, a·bus′ing** ‖< L *ab-,* away + *uti,* to use‖ 1 to use wrongly 2 to mistreat 3 to insult; revile —***n.*** 1 wrong use 2 mistreatment 3 a corrupt practice 4 insulting language —**a·bu·sive** (ə byo͞o′siv) ***adj.*** —**a·bu′sive·ly** ***adv.***

a·but (ə but′) ***vi., vt.*** **a·but′ted, a·but′ting** ‖< OFr *a-,* to + *bout,* end‖ to border (*on* or *upon*)

a·but′ment ***n.*** 1 an abutting 2 a part supporting an arch, bridge, etc.

a·bys·mal (ə biz′məl) ***adj.*** 1 of or like an abyss; not measurable 2 very bad; wretched —**a·bys′mal·ly** ***adv.***

a·byss (ə bis′) ***n.*** ‖< Gr *a-,* without + *byssos,* bottom‖ 1 a bottomless gulf 2 anything too deep for measurement /an *abyss* of shame/

Ab·ys·sin·i·a (ab′ə sin′ē ə) *old name of* ETHIOPIA —**Ab′ys·sin′i·an** ***adj., n.***

-ac (ak, ək) ‖ < Gr ‖ *suffix* 1 characteristic of [*elegiac*] 2 relating to [*cardiac*] 3 affected by [*maniac*]

Ac *Chem. symbol for* actinium

AC, A.C., ac, or **a.c.** 1 air conditioning 2 alternating current

a·ca·cia (ə kā′shə) ***n.*** ‖ < Gr *akē*, thorn ‖ 1 a tree or shrub with yellow or white flower clusters 2 the locust tree

ac·a·dem·ic (ak′ə dem′ik) ***adj.*** 1 of academies or colleges 2 having to do with liberal arts rather than technical education 3 formal; pedantic 4 merely theoretical —**ac′a·dem′i·cal·ly** ***adv.***

a·cad·e·mi·cian (ə kad′ə mish′ən, ak′ə də-) ***n.*** a member of an ACADEMY (sense 3)

a·cad·e·my (ə kad′ə mē) ***n.***, *pl.* **-mies** ‖ < Gr *akadēmeia*, place where Plato taught ‖ 1 a private secondary school 2 a school for special instruction 3 an association of scholars, writers, etc., for advancing an art or science

a·can·thus (ə kan′thəs) ***n.***, *pl.* **-thus·es** or **-thi′** (-thī′) ‖ < Gr *akē*, a point ‖ 1 a plant with lobed, often spiny leaves 2 *Archit.* a representation of these leaves

a cap·pel·la (ä′ kə pel′ə) ‖ It, in chapel style ‖ without instrumental accompaniment: said of choral singing

A·ca·pul·co (ä′kə po͞ol′kō, ak′ə-) city & seaport in S Mexico, on the Pacific: a winter resort: pop. 409,000

ac·cede (ak sēd′) ***vi.*** **-ced′ed, -ced′ing** ‖ < L *ad-*, to + *cedere*, go, yield ‖ 1 to enter upon the duties (of an office) 2 to assent; agree (*to*)

ac·cel·er·ate (ak sel′ər āt′, ək-) ***vt.*** **-at′ed, -at′ing** ‖ < L *ad-*, to + *celerare*, hasten ‖ 1 to increase the speed of 2 to cause to happen sooner —***vi.*** to go faster —**ac·cel′er·a′tion** ***n.***

ac·cel′er·a′tor ***n.*** a person or thing that accelerates; esp., the foot throttle of a motor vehicle

ac·cent (ak′sent′; *for v. also* ak sent′) ***n.*** ‖ < L *ad-*, to + *canere*, sing ‖ 1 emphasis given a spoken syllable or word 2 a mark showing such emphasis or indicating pronunciation 3 a distinguishing manner of pronunciation [an Irish *accent*] 4 special emphasis or attention 5 *Music, Prosody* rhythmic stress —***vt.*** 1 to mark with an accent 2 to emphasize; stress

ac·cen·tu·ate (ak sen′cho͞o āt′, ək-) ***vt.*** **-at′ed, -at′ing** to accent; emphasize —**ac·cen′tu·a′tion** ***n.***

ac·cept (ak sept′, ək-) ***vt.*** ‖ < L *ad-*, to + *capere*, take ‖ 1 to receive, esp. willingly 2 to approve 3 to agree to 4 to believe in 5 to agree to pay

ac·cept′a·ble ***adj.*** worth accepting; satisfactory —**ac·cept′a·bil′i·ty** or **ac·cept′a·ble·ness** ***n.***

ac·cept′ance ***n.*** 1 an accepting 2 approval 3 belief in; assent 4 a promise to pay

ac·cept′ed ***adj.*** generally regarded as true, proper, etc.; conventional; approved

ac·cess (ak′ses′) ***n.*** ‖ see ACCEDE ‖ 1 approach or means of approach 2 the right to enter, use, etc. 3 an outburst; fit [an *access* of anger] —***vt.*** to get data from, or add data to, a database

ac·ces′si·ble ***adj.*** 1 that can be approached or entered, esp. easily 2 obtainable —**ac·ces′si·bil′i·ty** ***n.*** —**ac·ces′si·bly** ***adv.***

ac·ces·sion (ak sesh′ən) ***n.*** 1 the act of attaining (a throne, power, etc.) 2 assent 3 *a*) increase by addition *b*) an addition, as to a collection

ac·ces·so·ry (ak ses′ər ē, ək-) ***adj.*** ‖ see ACCEDE ‖ 1 additional; extra 2 helping in an unlawful act —***n.***, *pl.* **-ries** 1 something extra or complementary 2 one who, though absent, helps another to break the law

ac·ci·dent (ak′sə dənt) ***n.*** ‖ < L *ad-*, to + *cadere*, to fall ‖ 1 an unintended happening 2 a mishap 3 chance

ac′ci·den′tal (-dent′'l) ***adj.*** happening by chance —**ac′ci·den′tal·ly** ***adv.***

ac′ci·dent-prone′ (-prōn′) ***adj.*** seemingly inclined to become involved in accidents

ac·claim (ə klām′) ***vt.*** ‖ < L *ad-*, to + *clamare*, to cry out ‖ to greet or announce with loud approval or applause; hail —***n.*** loud approval

ac·cla·ma·tion (ak′lə mā′shən) ***n.*** 1 loud applause or approval 2 an approving vote by voice

ac·cli·mate (ə klī′mət, ak′lə māt′) ***vt., vi.*** **-mat·ed, -mat·ing** ‖ < L *ad-*, to + Gr *klima*, region ‖ to accustom or become accustomed to a new climate or environment Also **ac·cli′ma·tize′, -tized′, -tiz′ing** —**ac′cli·ma′tion** ***n.***

ac·cliv·i·ty (ə kliv′ə tē) ***n.***, *pl.* **-ties** ‖ < L *ad-*, up + *clivus*, hill ‖ an upward slope

ac·co·lade (ak′ə lād′) ***n.*** ‖ < L *ad*, to + *collum*, neck ‖ an approving mention; award

ac·com·mo·date (ə käm′ə dāt′) ***vt.*** **-dat′ed, -dat′ing** ‖ < L *ad-*, to + *commodare*, to fit ‖ 1 to adapt 2 to do a favor for 3 to have space for; lodge

ac·com′mo·dat′ing ***adj.*** obliging

ac·com′mo·da′tion ***n.*** 1 adjustment 2 willingness to do favors 3 a help; convenience 4 [*pl.*] *a*) lodgings *b*) traveling space, as in a train

ac·com·pa·ni·ment (ə kum′pə nə mənt, -nē-; ə kump′nə-, -nē-) ***n.*** anything that accompanies something else, as an instrumental part supporting a solo voice, etc.

ac·com·pa·ny (ə kum′pə nē, ə kump′nē) ***vt.*** **-nied, -ny·ing** ‖ see AD- & COMPANION ‖ 1 to go with 2 to add to 3 to play or sing an accompaniment for or to —**ac·com′pa·nist** ***n.***

ac·com·plice (ə käm′plis) ***n.*** ‖ < ME *a* (the article) + LL *complex*, a confederate ‖ a partner in crime

ac·com·plish (ə käm′plish) ***vt.*** ‖ < L *ad-*, intens. + *complere*, fill up ‖ to succeed in doing; complete

ac·com′plished ***adj.*** 1 done; completed 2 skilled; expert

ac·com′plish·ment ***n.*** 1 completion 2 work completed; an achievement 3 a social art or skill

ac·cord (ə kôrd′) ***vt.*** ‖ < L *ad-*, to + *cor*, heart ‖ 1 to make agree 2 to grant —***vi.*** to agree; harmonize (*with*) —***n.*** mutual agreement; harmony —**of one's own accord** willingly —**with one accord** all agreeing

ac·cord′ance ***n.*** agreement; conformity —**ac·cord′ant** ***adj.***

ac·cord'ing *adj.* in harmony —**according to** 1 in agreement with 2 as stated by

ac·cord'ing·ly *adv.* 1 in a fitting and proper way 2 therefore

ACCORDION

ac·cor·di·on (ə kôr'dē ən) *n.* ‖prob. < It *accordare*, to be in tune‖ a keyed musical instrument with a bellows, which is pressed to force air through reeds

ac·cost (ə kôst') *vt.* ‖< L *ad-*, to + *costa*, side‖ to approach and speak to, esp. in a bold or forward way

ac·count (ə kount') *vt.* ‖< OFr *a-*, to + *conter*, tell‖ to judge to be —*vi.* 1 to give a financial reckoning (*to*) 2 to give reasons (*for*) —*n.* 1 a counting 2 [*often pl.*] a record of business transactions 3 *a)* BANK ACCOUNT *b)* CHARGE ACCOUNT 4 a credit customer or client 5 worth; importance 6 an explanation 7 a report —**on account** as partial payment —**on account of** because of —**on no account** under no circumstances —**take into account** to consider

ac·count'a·ble *adj.* 1 responsible; liable 2 explainable —**ac·count'a·bil'i·ty** *n.*

ac·count·ant (ə kount''nt) *n.* one whose work is accounting

ac·count'ing *n.* the figuring and recording of financial accounts

ac·cou·ter (ə ko͞ot'ər) *vt.* ‖prob. < L *consuere*, to sew‖ to outfit; equip

ac·cou·ter·ments or **ac·cou·tre·ments** (ə ko͞ot'ər mənts, -ko͞o'trə-) *n.pl.* 1 clothes 2 a soldier's equipment

ac·cred·it (ə kred'it) *vt.* ‖see CREDIT‖ 1 to authorize; certify 2 to believe in 3 to attribute —**ac·cred'i·ta'tion** (-ə tā'shən) *n.*

ac·cre·tion (ə krē'shən) *n.* ‖< L *ad-*, to + *crescere*, to grow‖ 1 growth in size, esp. by addition 2 accumulated matter 3 a growing together of parts

ac·crue (ə kro͞o') *vi.* -**crued'**, -**cru'ing** ‖see prec.‖ to come as a natural growth or periodic increase, as interest on money —**ac·cru'al** *n.*

acct. account

ac·cul·tur·ate (ə kul'chər āt') *vi., vt.* -**at'ed**, -**at'ing** to undergo, or change by, acculturation

ac·cul·tur·a·tion (ə kul'chər ā'shən) *n.* 1 adaptation to a culture, esp. a new or different one 2 mutual influence of different cultures

ac·cu·mu·late (ə kyo͞om'yo͞o lāt', -yə-) *vt., vi.* -**lat'ed**, -**lat'ing** ‖< L *ad-*, to + *cumulare*, to heap‖ to pile up or collect —**ac·cu'mu·la'tion** *n.* —**ac·cu'mu·la'tive** *adj.*

ac·cu·ra·cy (ak'yoor ə sē, -yər-) *n.* the state of being accurate; precision

ac'cu·rate (-it) *adj.* ‖< L *ad-*, to + *cura*, care‖ 1 careful and exact 2 free from errors; precise —**ac'cu·rate·ly** *adv.* —**ac'cu·rate·ness** *n.*

ac·curs·ed (ə kur'sid, -kurst') *adj.* 1 under a curse 2 damnable Also **ac·curst'** —**ac·curs'ed·ness** *n.*

ac·cu·sa·tion (ak'yo͞o zā'shən, -yə-) *n.* 1 an accusing 2 what one is accused of —**ac·cu·sa·to·ry** (ə kyo͞o'zə tôr'ē) *adj.*

ac·cu·sa·tive (ə kyo͞o'zə tiv) *n.* ‖see fol.‖ *Gram.* the case of the direct object of a verb; also, the objective case in English

ac·cuse (ə kyo͞oz') *vt.* -**cused'**, -**cus'ing** ‖< L *ad-*, to + *causa*, a cause‖ 1 to blame 2 to bring charges against —**ac·cus'er** *n.*

ac·cus·tom (ə kus'təm) *vt.* to make familiar by custom, habit, or use

ac·cus'tomed *adj.* 1 customary; usual 2 used (*to*); in the habit of

AC/DC or **A.C./D.C.** (ā'sē'dē'sē') *adj.* ‖< *a(lternating) c(urrent or) d(irect) c(urrent)*‖ [Slang] bisexual

ace (ās) *n.* ‖< L *as*, unit‖ 1 a playing card, etc. with one spot 2 a point, as in tennis, won by a single stroke 3 *Golf* a hole in one 4 an expert, esp. in combat flying —*adj.* [Colloq.] first-rate —*vt.* **aced**, **ac'ing** 1 [Slang] to defeat completely: often with *out* 2 [Colloq.] to earn a grade of A in, on, etc.

Ace bandage *trademark for* an elasticized cloth bandage used to provide support, as for a sprain

ace in the hole [Slang] any advantage held in reserve

ac·er·bate (as'ər bāt') *vt.* -**bat'ed**, -**bat'ing** ‖< L *acerbare*‖ 1 to make sour or bitter 2 to irritate; vex

a·cer·bi·ty (ə sur'bə tē) *n., pl.* -**ties** ‖< L *acerbus*, bitter‖ 1 sourness 2 sharpness of temper, words, etc. —**a·cer'bic** *adj.*

ac·e·ta·min·o·phen (as'i tə min'ə fən; ə sē'tə-) *n.* a crystalline powder used to lessen fever and pain

ac·et·an·i·lide (as'ət an'ə lid') *n.* ‖< ACETIC + ANILINE‖ a drug used to lessen pain and fever

ac·e·tate (as'i tāt') *n.* 1 a salt or ester of acetic acid 2 something, esp. a fabric, made with an acetate of cellulose

a·ce·tic (ə sēt'ik) *adj.* ‖< L *acetum*, vinegar‖ of the sharp, sour liquid (**acetic acid**) found in vinegar

ac·e·tone (as'i tōn') *n.* ‖see prec.‖ a colorless, flammable liquid used as a solvent, esp. in making rayon —**ac'e·ton'ic** (-tän'ik) *adj.*

a·cet·y·lene (ə set''l ēn') *n.* a gas used for lighting and, with oxygen, in welding

a·ce·tyl·sal·i·cyl·ic acid (ə sēt''l sal'ə sil'ik) ASPIRIN

ache (āk) *vi.* **ached**, **ach'ing** ‖< OE *acan*‖ 1 to have or give dull, steady pain 2 [Colloq.] to yearn —*n.* a dull, continuous pain —**ach'y** *adj.*

a·chene (ā kēn', ə-) *n.* ‖< Gr *a-*, not + *chainein*, to gape‖ any small, dry fruit with one seed

a·chieve (ə chēv') *vt.* **a·chieved'**, **a·chiev'ing** ‖< OFr < *a-*, to + L *caput*, head‖ 1 to do successfully 2 to get by effort —**a·chiev'a·ble** *adj.*

a·chieve'ment *n.* 1 an achieving 2 a thing achieved; feat

A·chil·les (ə kil′ēz′) a Greek hero killed in the Trojan War

Achilles' heel (one's) vulnerable spot

ach·ro·mat·ic (ak′rō mat′ik; -rə-) ***adj.*** ‖ < Gr *a-*, without + *chrōma*, color ‖ refracting white light without breaking it up into its component colors

ac·id (as′id) ***adj.*** ‖ L *acidus*, sour ‖ **1** sour; sharp; tart **2** of an acid —***n.*** **1** a sour substance **2** [Slang] LSD **3** *Chem.* any compound that reacts with a base to form a salt —**a·cid·i·ty** (ə sid′ə tē), *pl.* **-ties**, ***n.*** —**ac′id·ly** ***adv.***

a·cid·i·fy (ə sid′ə fī′) ***vt.***, ***vi.*** **-fied′**, **-fy′ing** **1** to make or become sour **2** to change into an acid

ac·i·do·sis (as′ə dō′sis) ***n.*** a condition in which there is an abnormal retention of acid or loss of alkali in the body

acid rain rain with a high concentration of acids produced by the gases from burning fossil fuels

acid test a crucial, final test

a·cid·u·lous (ə sij′o͞o ləs) ***adj.*** **1** somewhat acid or sour **2** sarcastic

-a·cious (ā′shəs) ‖ < L ‖ *suffix* inclined to, full of [*tenacious*]

-ac·i·ty (as′ə tē) ‖ < L ‖ *suffix* a (specified) characteristic, quality, or tendency [*tenacity*]

ac·knowl·edge (ak näl′ij, ək-) ***vt.*** **-edged**, **-edg·ing** ‖ see KNOWLEDGE ‖ **1** to admit as true **2** to recognize the authority or claims of **3** to respond to **4** to express thanks for **5** to state that one has received (a letter, etc.) —**ac·knowl′edg·ment** or **ac·knowl′edge·ment** ***n.***

ACLU American Civil Liberties Union

ac·me (ak′mē) ***n.*** ‖ Gr *akmē*, a point, top ‖ the highest point; peak

ac·ne (ak′nē) ***n.*** ‖ see prec. ‖ a skin disorder usually causing pimples on the face, etc.

ac·o·lyte (ak′ə līt′) ***n.*** ‖ < Gr *akolouthos*, follower ‖ **1** an altar boy **2** an attendant; helper

ac·o·nite (ak′ə nīt′) ***n.*** ‖ < Gr ‖ a plant with hoodlike flowers

a·corn (ā′kôrn′) ***n.*** ‖ < OE *æcern*, nut ‖ the nut of the oak tree

acorn squash a kind of winter squash, acorn-shaped with dark-green skin and yellow flesh

a·cous·tic (ə ko͞os′tik) ***adj.*** ‖ < Gr *akouein*, to hear ‖ **1** having to do with hearing or acoustics **2** of or using a musical instrument that is not amplified Also **a·cous′ti·cal** —**a·cous′ti·cal·ly** ***adv.***

a·cous′tics (-tiks) ***n.pl.*** **1** the qualities of a room, etc. that determine how clearly sounds can be heard in it **2** [*with sing. v.*] the branch of physics dealing with sound

ac·quaint (ə kwānt′) ***vt.*** ‖ < L *ad-*, to + *cognoscere*, know ‖ **1** to inform **2** to make familiar (*with*)

ac·quaint′ance ***n.*** **1** knowledge got from personal experience **2** a person whom one knows slightly

ac·qui·esce (ak′wē es′) ***vi.*** **-esced′**, **-esc′ing** ‖ < L *ad-*, to + *quiescere*, grow quiet ‖ to consent without protest: often with *in* —**ac′qui·es′cence** ***n.*** —**ac′qui·es′cent** ***adj.***

ac·quire (ə kwīr′) ***vt.*** **-quired′**, **-quir′ing** ‖ < L *ad-*, to + *quaerere*, to seek ‖ **1** to gain by one's own efforts **2** to get as one's own —**ac·quir′a·ble** ***adj.*** —**ac·quire′ment** ***n.***

ac·qui·si·tion (ak′wə zish′ən) ***n.*** **1** an acquiring **2** something acquired

ac·quis·i·tive (ə kwiz′ə tiv) ***adj.*** eager to acquire (money, etc.); grasping —**ac·quis′i·tive·ness** ***n.***

ac·quit (ə kwit′) ***vt.*** **-quit′ted**, **-quit′ting** ‖ < L *ad-*, to + *quietare*, to quiet ‖ **1** to release from an obligation, etc. **2** to clear (a person) of a charge **3** to conduct (oneself); behave —**ac·quit′tal** ***n.***

a·cre (ā′kər) ***n.*** ‖ OE *æcer*, field ‖ a measure of land, 43,560 sq. ft.

a′cre·age′ (-ij′) ***n.*** acres collectively

ac·rid (ak′rid) ***adj.*** ‖ < L *acris*, sharp ‖ **1** sharp or bitter to the taste or smell **2** sharp in speech, etc. —**a·crid·i·ty** (ə krid′ə tē) ***n.*** —**ac′rid·ly** ***adv.***

ac·ri·mo·ny (ak′ri mō′nē) ***n.***, *pl.* **-nies** ‖ < L *acer*, sharp ‖ bitterness or harshness of manner or speech —**ac′ri·mo′ni·ous** ***adj.***

ac·ro·bat (ak′rə bat′) ***n.*** ‖ < Gr *akrobatos*, walking on tiptoe ‖ a performer on the trapeze, tightrope, etc.; gymnast —**ac′ro·bat′ic** ***adj.***

ac′ro·bat′ics (-iks) ***n.pl.*** [*also with sing v.*] **1** an acrobat's tricks **2** any tricks requiring great skill

ac·ro·nym (ak′rə nim′) ***n.*** ‖ < Gr *akros*, at the end + *onyma*, name ‖ a word formed from the first (or first few) letters of several words, as *radar*

ac·ro·pho·bi·a (ak′rō fō′bē ə) ***n.*** ‖ < Gr *akros*, at the top + PHOBIA ‖ an abnormal fear of being in high places

A·crop·o·lis (ə kräp′ə lis) ‖ < Gr *akros*, at the top + *polis*, city ‖ the fortified hill in Athens on which the Parthenon was built

a·cross (ə krôs′) ***adv.*** **1** crosswise **2** from one side to the other —***prep.*** **1** from one side to the other of **2** on or to the other side of **3** into contact with by chance [*to come across an old friend*]

a·cross′-the-board′ ***adj.*** **1** combining win, place, and show, as a bet **2** affecting all classes or groups

a·cros·tic (ə krôs′tik) ***n.*** ‖ Gr *akrostichos* < *akros*, at the end + *stichos*, line of verse ‖ a poem, etc. in which certain letters in each line, as the first or last, spell out a word, motto, etc.

a·cryl·ic (ə kril′ik) ***adj.*** **1** designating any of a group of synthetic fibers used to make fabrics **2** designating any of a group of clear, synthetic resins used to make paints, plastics, etc.

act (akt) ***n.*** ‖ < L *agere*, to do ‖ **1** a thing done **2** a doing **3** a law **4** a main division of a drama or opera **5** a short performance, as on a variety show **6** something done merely for show —***vt.*** to perform in (a play or part) —***vi.*** **1** to perform in a play, movie, etc. **2** to behave **3** to function **4** to have an effect (*on*) **5** to appear to be —**act up** [Colloq.] to misbehave

ACTH ‖ *a*(*dreno*)*c*(*ortico*)*t*(*ropic*) *h*(*ormone*) ‖ a pituitary hormone that acts on the adrenal cortex

act·ing (ak′tiŋ) ***adj.*** temporarily doing the duties of another —***n.*** the art of an actor

ac·ti·nide series (ak′tə nīd′) a group of radioactive chemical elements from element

89 (actinium) through element 103 (lawrencium)

ac·tin·i·um (ak tin′ē əm) ***n.*** ‖ < Gr *aktis*, ray ‖ a white, metallic radioactive chemical element

ac·tion (ak′shən) ***n.*** **1** the doing of something **2** a thing done **3** [*pl.*] behavior **4** the way of working, as of a machine **5** the moving parts, as of a gun **6** the sequence of events, as in a story **7** a lawsuit **8** military combat **9** [Slang] activity

ac·ti·vate (ak′tə vāt′) ***vt.*** **-vat′ed, -vat′ing** **1** to make active **2** to put (a military unit) on active status **3** to make radioactive **4** to purify sewage by aeration —**ac′ti·va′tion** ***n.*** —**ac′ti·va′tor** ***n.***

activated carbon a form of highly porous carbon that can adsorb gases, vapors, and colloidal particles

ac·tive (ak′tiv) ***adj.*** **1** acting; working **2** causing motion or change **3** lively; agile **4** indicating the voice of a verb whose subject performs the action —**ac′tive·ly** ***adv.***

ac′tiv·ism′ (-tə viz′əm) ***n.*** the taking of direct action to achieve a political or social end —**ac′tiv·ist** ***adj.***, ***n.***

ac·tiv·i·ty (ak tiv′ə tē) ***n.***, *pl.* **-ties** **1** a being active **2** liveliness **3** a specific action [*student activities*]

ac·tor (ak′tər) ***n.*** **1** one who does a thing **2** one who acts in plays, movies, etc. —**ac′tress** ***n.fem.***

ac·tu·al (ak′cho͞o əl) ***adj.*** ‖ < L *agere*, to do ‖ **1** existing in reality **2** existing at the time —**ac′tu·al·ly** ***adv.***

ac′tu·al′i·ty (-al′ə tē) ***n.*** **1** reality **2** *pl.* **-ties** an actual thing

ac′tu·al·ize′ (-əl īz′) ***vt.*** **-ized′, -iz′ing** **1** to make actual or real **2** to make realistic

ac·tu·ar·y (ak′cho͞o er′ē) ***n.***, *pl.* **-ies** ‖ L *actuarius*, clerk ‖ one who figures insurance risks, premiums, etc. —**ac′tu·ar′i·al** ***adj.***

ac·tu·ate (ak′cho͞o āt′) ***vt.*** **-at′ed, -at′ing** **1** to put into action **2** to impel to action —**ac′tu·a′tor** ***n.***

a·cu·i·ty (ə kyo͞o′ə tē) ***n.*** ‖ < L *acus*, needle ‖ keenness of thought or vision

a·cu·men (ə kyo͞o′mən) ***n.*** ‖ < L *acuere*, sharpen ‖ keenness of mind or insight

ac·u·punc·ture (ak′yo͞o puŋk′chər) ***n.*** ‖ < L *acus*, needle + PUNCTURE ‖ the ancient practice, esp. among the Chinese, of piercing parts of the body with needles to treat disease or relieve pain —**ac′u·punc′tur·ist** ***n.***

a·cute (ə kyo͞ot′) ***adj.*** ‖ < L *acuere*, sharpen ‖ **1** sharp-pointed **2** keen of mind **3** sensitive [*acute* hearing] **4** severe, as pain **5** severe but not chronic [an *acute* disease] **6** very serious **7** less than 90° [*acute* angles] —**a·cute′ly** ***adv.*** —**a·cute′ness** ***n.***

acute accent a mark (′) showing primary stress, the quality of a vowel, etc.

-a·cy (ə sē) ‖ ult. < Gr ‖ *suffix* quality, condition, etc. [*supremacy*]

a·cy·clo·vir (ā sī′klō vir′) ***n.*** a synthetic powder used in the treatment of certain viral infections, as herpes

ad (ad) ***n.*** [Colloq.] an advertisement

ad- ‖ L ‖ *prefix* motion toward, addition to, nearness to: becomes *a-*, *ac-*, *af-*, *ag-*, *al-*, *an-*, etc. before certain consonants

A.D. or **AD** ‖ L *Anno Domini*, in the year of the Lord ‖ of the Christian era: used with dates

ad·age (ad′ij) ***n.*** ‖ < L *ad-*, to + *aio*, I say ‖ an old saying; proverb

a·da·gio (ə dä′jō, -zhō) ***adv.*** ‖ It *ad agio*, at ease ‖ *Music* slowly —***adj.*** slow —***n.***, *pl.* **-gios** **1** a slow movement in music **2** a slow ballet dance

Ad·am (ad′əm) ‖ Heb < *adam*, a human being ‖ *Bible* the first man

ad·a·mant (ad′ə mənt) ***n.*** ‖ < Gr *a-*, not + *daman*, subdue ‖ a very hard substance —***adj.*** inflexible; unyielding

Ad·ams (ad′əmz) **1 John** 1735-1826; 2d president of the U.S. (1797-1801) **2 John Quin·cy** (kwin′zē, -sē) 1767-1848; 6th president of the U.S. (1825-29): son of John

Adam's apple the projection of cartilage in the front of the throat, esp. of a man

a·dapt (ə dapt′) ***vt.*** ‖ < L *ad-*, to + *aptare*, to fit ‖ **1** to make suitable, esp. by changing **2** to adjust (oneself) to new circumstances —**ad·ap·ta·tion** (ad′əp tā′shən) ***n.***

a·dapt′a·ble ***adj.*** able to adjust or be adjusted —**a·dapt′a·bil′i·ty** ***n.***

add (ad) ***vt.*** ‖ < L *ad-*, to + *dare*, to give ‖ **1** to join (*to*) so as to increase **2** to state further **3** to combine (numbers) into a sum —***vi.*** **1** to cause an increase (*to*) **2** to find a sum —**add up** to seem reasonable —**add up to** to mean; signify —**add′a·ble** or **add′i·ble** ***adj.***

ad·dend (ad′end′) ***n.*** ‖ < fol. ‖ *Math.* a number or quantity to be added to another

ad·den·dum (ə den′dəm) ***n.***, *pl.* **-da** (-də) ‖ L ‖ a thing added, as an appendix

ad·der (ad′ər) ***n.*** ‖ < OE *nædre* ‖ **1** a poisonous snake of Europe **2** any of various other snakes, some harmless

ad·dict (ə dikt′; *for n.*, ad′ikt) ***vt.*** ‖ < L *addicere*, give assent ‖ **1** to give (oneself) up *to* a strong habit **2** to cause to become addicted —***n.*** one addicted to a habit, as to using drugs —**ad·dic′tion** ***n.*** —**ad·dic′tive** ***adj.***

Ad·dis A·ba·ba (ad′is ab′ə bə) capital of Ethiopia: pop. 1,413,000

ad·di·tion (ə dish′ən) ***n.*** **1** an adding of numbers to get a sum **2** a joining of one thing to another **3** a part added —**in addition (to)** besides

ad·di′tion·al (-əl) ***adj.*** added; more; extra —**ad·di′tion·al·ly** ***adv.***

ad·di·tive (ad′ə tiv) ***adj.*** of addition —***n.*** something added

ad·dle (ad′'l) ***vi.***, ***vt.*** **-dled, -dling** ‖ < OE *adela*, mud ‖ to make or become confused

ad·dress (ə dres′; *for n. esp. 2, 3, & 5, also* a′dres′) ***vt.*** ‖ < L *dirigere*, to direct ‖ **1** to direct (words) *to* **2** to speak or write to **3** to write the destination on (a letter, etc.) **4** to apply (oneself) *to* —***n.*** **1** a speech **2** the place where one lives or receives mail **3** the destination indicated on an envelope **4** skill; tact **5** a computer code identifying the location of an item of information

ad·dress·ee (a′dres ē′) ***n.*** the person to whom mail, etc. is addressed

ad·duce (ə do͞os′) ***vt.*** **-duced′, -duc′ing** ‖ < L *ad-*, to + *ducere*, to lead ‖ to give as a reason or proof

-ade (ād) ‖ ult. < L ‖ *suffix* **1** the act of ______ing [*blockade*] **2** participant(s) in an action /brigade/ 3 ‖after LEMONADE‖ drink made from /limeade/

Ad·e·laide (ad′'l ād′) seaport in S Australia: pop. 969,000

A·den (ăd′'n, ād′'n), **Gulf of** gulf of the Arabian Sea, south of Arabia

ad·e·nine (ad′ə nēn′) ***n.*** a purine base contained in the DNA, RNA, and ADP of all tissue

ad·e·noids (ad′'n oidz′, ad′noidz′) ***n.pl.*** ‖< Gr *adēn*, gland + -OID‖ lymphoid growths in the throat behind the nose: they can obstruct nasal breathing

a·dept (ə dept′) ***adj.*** ‖< L *ad-*, to + *apisci*, attain‖ highly skilled **—*n.* ad·ept** (ad′ept′) an expert **—a·dept′ly *adv.* —a·dept′ness *n.***

ad·e·quate (ad′i kwət) ***adj.*** ‖< L *ad-*, to + *aequus*, equal‖ enough for what is required; sufficient; suitable **—ad′e·qua·cy** (-kwə sē) ***n.*** **—ad′e·quate·ly *adv.***

ad·here (ad hir′, əd-) ***vi.*** **-hered′, -her′ing** ‖< L *ad-*, to + *haerere*, to stick‖ 1 to stick fast; stay attached 2 to give allegiance or support (*to*) **—ad·her′ence *n.***

ad·her′ent *n.* a supporter or follower (*of* a cause, etc.)

ad·he·sion (ad hē′zhən, əd-) ***n.*** 1 an adhering or a being stuck together 2 body tissues abnormally joined

ad·he′sive (-siv) ***adj.*** 1 sticking 2 sticky **—*n.*** an adhesive substance

ad hoc (ad häk′) ‖L, to this‖ for a specific purpose /an *ad hoc* committee/

a·dieu (ə dyōō′, -dōō′; *Fr* ä dyö′) ***interj., n., pl.*** **a·dieus′** or Fr. ***a·dieux′*** (-dyö′) ‖Fr‖ goodbye

ad in·fi·ni·tum (ad in′fə nīt′əm) ‖L‖ endlessly; without limit

a·di·os (a′dē ōs′, ä′-; *Sp* ä dyôs′) ***interj.*** ‖Sp‖ goodbye

ad·i·pose (ad′ə pōs′) ***adj.*** ‖ult. < Gr *aleipha*, fat‖ of animal fat; fatty

Ad·i·ron·dack Mountains (ad′ə rän′dak′) mountain range in NE New York: also **Ad′i·ron′dacks**

adj. 1 adjective 2 adjustment

ad·ja·cent (ə jā′sənt) ***adj.*** ‖< L *ad-*, to + *jacere*, to lie‖ near or close (*to*); adjoining **—ad·ja′cen·cy *n.* —ad·ja′cent·ly *adv.***

ad·jec·tive (aj′ik tiv) ***n.*** ‖< L *adjacere*, lie near‖ a word used to modify a noun or other substantive **—ad′jec·ti′val** (-tī′vəl) ***adj.*** **—ad′jec·ti′val·ly *adv.***

ad·join (ə join′, ə-) ***vt.*** ‖< L *ad-*, to + *jungere*, to join‖ to be next to **—*vi.*** to be in contact **—ad·join′ing *adj.***

ad·journ (ə jurn′) ***vt.*** ‖< OFr *a*, at + *jorn*, day‖ to suspend (a meeting, session, etc.) for a time **—*vi.*** 1 to close a meeting, etc. for a time 2 [Colloq.] to retire (*to* another room, etc.) **—ad·journ′ment *n.***

ad·judge (ə juj′) ***vt.*** **-judged′, -judg′ing** ‖< L *ad-*, to + *judicare*, to judge‖ 1 to decide by law 2 to declare, order, or award by law

ad·ju·di·cate (ə jōō′di kāt′) ***vt.*** **-cat′ed, -cat′ing** to hear and decide (a case) **—*vi.*** to serve as a judge (*in* or *on*) **—ad·ju′di·ca′tion *n.*** **—ad·ju′di·ca′tor *n.*** **—ad·ju′di·ca·to′ry** (-kə tôr′ē) ***adj.***

ad·junct (aj′uŋkt′) ***n.*** ‖see ADJOIN‖ a secondary or nonessential addition

ad·jure (ə joor′, ə-) ***vt.*** **-jured′, -jur′ing** ‖< L *ad-*, to + *jurare*, to swear‖ 1 to charge solemnly under oath 2 to ask earnestly **—ad′ju·ra′tion *n.***

ad·just (ə just′) ***vt.*** ‖< OFr *a-*, to + *joster*, to tilt‖ 1 to change so as to fit 2 to regulate (a watch, etc.) 3 to settle rightly 4 to decide the amount to be paid in settling (an insurance claim) **—*vi.*** to adapt oneself **—ad·just′a·ble *adj.* —ad·just′er** or **ad·jus′tor *n.* —ad·just′ment *n.***

ad·ju·tant (aj′ə tənt) ***n.*** ‖< L *ad-*, to + *juvare*, to help‖ 1 an assistant 2 a military staff officer who assists the commanding officer

ad-lib (ad′lib′) ***vt., vi.*** **-libbed′, -lib′bing** ‖< L *ad libitum*, at pleasure‖ [Colloq.] to improvise (words, etc. not in a prepared script, etc.) **—*n.*** [Colloq.] an ad-libbed remark: also **ad lib** **—*adj.*** [Colloq.] spoken or done extemporaneously **—*adv.*** [Colloq.] extemporizing freely: also **ad lib**

ad′man′ *n., pl.* **-men′** a man whose work is advertising

ad·min·is·ter (ad min′is tər, əd-) ***vt.*** ‖< L *ad-*, to + *ministrare*, to serve‖ 1 to manage; direct 2 to give out, as punishment 3 to apply (medicine, etc.) 4 to tender (an oath, etc.)

ad·min′is·trate′ (-trāt′) ***vt.*** **-trat′ed, -trat′ing** to administer; manage

ad·min′is·tra′tion (-trā′shən) ***n.*** 1 management 2 [*often* **A-**] the executive officials of a government, etc. and their policies 3 their term of office 4 the administering (*of* punishment, medicine, etc.) **—ad·min′is·tra′tive *adj.***

ad·min′is·tra′tor *n.* 1 one who administers 2 *Law* one appointed to settle an estate

ad·mi·ra·ble (ad′mə rə bəl) ***adj.*** deserving admiration; excellent **—ad′mi·ra·bly *adv.***

ad·mi·ral (ad′mə rəl) ***n.*** ‖< Ar *ʾamīr*, leader + *ʿālī*, high‖ 1 the commanding officer of a fleet 2 a naval officer of the highest rank

ad′mi·ral·ty (-tē) ***n., pl.*** **-ties** [*often* **A-**] the governmental department in charge of naval affairs, as in England

ad·mi·ra·tion (ad′mə rā′shən) ***n.*** 1 an admiring 2 pleased approval

ad·mire (ad mīr′, əd-) ***vt.*** **-mired′, -mir′ing** ‖< L *ad-*, at + *mirari*, to wonder‖ 1 to regard with wonder and delight 2 to esteem highly **—ad·mir′er *n.***

ad·mis·si·ble (ad mis′ə bəl, əd-) ***adj.*** that can be accepted or admitted **—ad·mis′si·bil′i·ty *n.***

ad·mis·sion (ad mish′ən, əd-) ***n.*** 1 an admitting or being admitted 2 an entrance fee 3 a conceding, confessing, etc. 4 a thing conceded, confessed, etc.

ad·mit (ad mit′, əd-) ***vt.*** **-mit′ted, -mit′ting** ‖< L *ad-*, to + *mittere*, to send‖ 1 to permit or entitle to enter or use 2 to allow; leave room for 3 to concede or confess **—*vi.*** to allow: with *of* **—ad·mit′tance *n.***

ad·mit′ted·ly *adv.* by admission or general agreement

ad·mix·ture (ad miks′chər) ***n.*** ‖< L *ad-*, to + *miscere*, to mix‖ 1 a mixture 2 a thing added in mixing

ad·mon·ish (ad män′ish, əd-) ***vt.*** ‖< L *ad-*, to + *monere*, to warn‖ 1 to warn 2 to reprove mildly **3** to exhort —**ad·mo·ni·tion** (ad′mə nish′ən) ***n.*** —**ad·mon′i·to′ry** (-i tôr′ē) ***adj.***

ad nau·se·am (ad nô′zē əm′) ‖L‖ to the point of disgust

a·do (ə do͞o′) ***n.*** fuss; trouble

a·do·be (ə dō′bē) ***n.*** ‖Sp‖ **1** unburnt, sun-dried brick **2** clay for making this brick **3** a building of adobe

ad·o·les·cence (ad′′l es′′ns) ***n.*** the time of life between puberty and maturity; youth

ad′o·les′cent ***adj.*** ‖< L *ad-*, to + *alescere*, grow up‖ of or in adolescence —***n.*** a person during adolescence

A·do·nis (ə dŏn′is, -dän′-) *Gr. Myth.* a young man loved by Aphrodite —***n.*** a handsome young man

a·dopt (ə däpt′) ***vt.*** ‖< L *ad-*, to + *optare*, to choose‖ **1** to take legally into one's own family and raise as one's own child **2** to take as one's own **3** to choose or accept —**a·dop′tion** ***n.***

a·dop·tive (ə däp′tiv) ***adj.*** that has become so by adoption

a·dor·a·ble (ə dôr′ə bəl) ***adj.*** **1** [Rare] worthy of adoration **2** [Colloq.] delightful; charming —**a·dor′a·bly** ***adv.***

ad·o·ra·tion (ad′ə rā′shən) ***n.*** **1** a worshiping **2** great love or devotion

a·dore (ə dôr′) ***vt.*** **-dored′**, **-dor′ing** ‖< L *ad-*, to + *orare*, to speak‖ **1** to worship as divine **2** to love greatly **3** [Colloq.] to like very much

a·dorn (ə dôrn′) ***vt.*** ‖< L *ad-*, to + *ornare*, fit out‖ **1** to be an ornament to **2** to put decorations on —**a·dorn′ment** ***n.***

ADP (ā′dē′pē′) ‖*a*(*denosine*) *d*(*i*)*p*(*hosphate*)‖ a basic unit of nucleic acids vital to the energy processes of all living cells

a·dre·nal (ə drē′nəl) ***adj.*** ‖AD- + RENAL‖ **1** near the kidneys **2** of two ductless glands (**adrenal glands**), just above the kidneys

A·dren·a·lin (ə dren′ə lin′) *trademark for* a hormone secreted by the adrenal glands or synthesized for use as a drug —***n.*** [a-] this hormone, which increases endurance, muscular strength, etc.

A·dri·at·ic (Sea) (ā′drē at′ik) sea between Italy and Yugoslavia

a·drift (ə drift′) ***adv.***, ***adj.*** floating without mooring or direction

a·droit (ə droit′) ***adj.*** ‖< Fr *à*, to + L *dirigere*, lay straight‖ skillful and clever —**a·droit′ly** ***adv.*** —**a·droit′ness** ***n.***

ad·sorb (ad sôrb′) ***vt.*** ‖< AD- + L *sorbere*, drink in‖ to collect (a gas, etc.) in condensed form on a surface —**ad·sorp′tion** (-sôrp′shən) ***n.***

ad·u·late (a′jo͞o lāt′, -jə-) ***vt.*** **-lat′ed**, **-lat′ing** ‖< L *adulari*, fawn upon‖ to flatter servilely —**ad′u·la′tion** ***n.***

a·dult (ə dult′, ad′ult′) ***adj.*** ‖see ADOLESCENT‖ grown up; mature —***n.*** a mature person, animal, or plant —**a·dult′hood** ***n.***

a·dul·ter·ant (ə dul′tər ənt) ***n.*** a substance that adulterates —***adj.*** adulterating

a·dul·ter·ate (ə dul′tər āt′) ***vt.*** **-at′ed**, **-at′ing** ‖< L *ad-*, to + *alter*, other‖ to make inferior, impure, etc. by adding an improper substance —**a·dul′ter·a′tion** ***n.***

a·dul·ter·y (ə dul′tər ē) ***n.***, *pl.* **-ies** sexual intercourse between a married person and another not the spouse —**a·dul′ter·er** ***n.*** —**a·dul′ter·ess** ***n.fem.*** —**a·dul′ter·ous** ***adj.***

ad·um·brate (ad um′brāt′, ad′əm brāt′) ***vt.*** **-brat′ed**, **-brat′ing** ‖< L *ad-*, to + *umbra*, shade‖ **1** to outline vaguely **2** to foreshadow —**ad′um·bra′tion** ***n.***

adv. **1** adverb **2** advertisement

ad va·lo·rem (ad′ və lôr′əm) ‖L‖ in proportion to the value: a phrase applied to duties levied on goods, etc. as a percentage of their value: abbrev. **ad val.**

ad·vance (ad vans′, əd-) ***vt.*** **-vanced′**, **-vanc′ing** ‖< L *ab-*, from + *ante*, before‖ **1** to bring forward **2** to promote **3** to suggest **4** to raise the rate of **5** to lend —***vi.*** **1** to go forward **2** to improve; progress **3** to rise in rank, price, etc. —***n.*** **1** a moving forward **2** an improvement **3** a rise in value **4** [*pl.*] approaches to get favor **5** a payment before due —***adj.*** **1** in front [*advance* guard] **2** beforehand —**in advance** **1** in front **2** ahead of time —**ad·vance′ment** ***n.***

ad·vanced′ ***adj.*** **1** in front **2** old **3** ahead or higher in progress, price, etc.

advance man a person hired to travel in advance of a theatrical company, political candidate, etc. to arrange for publicity, appearances, etc.

ad·van·tage (ad vant′ij, əd-) ***n.*** ‖< L *ab-* + *ante*: see ADVANCE‖ **1** superiority **2** a favorable circumstance, event, etc. **3** gain; benefit —***vt.*** **-taged**, **-tag·ing** to be a benefit to —**take advantage of** **1** to use for one's own benefit **2** to impose upon —**ad′van·ta′geous** (-van tā′jəs, -vən-) ***adj.***

Ad·vent (ad′vent′) ***n.*** ‖< L *ad-*, to + *venire*, to come‖ **1** the period including the four Sundays just before Christmas **2** [a-] a coming

ad·ven·ti·tious (ad′ven tish′əs) ***adj.*** ‖see prec.‖ not inherent; accidental

ad·ven·ture (ad ven′chər, əd-) ***n.*** ‖see ADVENT‖ **1** a daring, hazardous undertaking **2** an unusual, stirring, often romantic experience —***vi.*** **-tured**, **-tur·ing** to engage in adventure —**ad·ven′tur·ous** or **ad·ven′ture·some** ***adj.*** —**ad·ven′tur·ous·ly** ***adv.***

ad·ven′tur·er ***n.*** **1** one who has or looks for adventures **2** one who seeks to become rich, etc. by dubious schemes —**ad·ven′tur·ess** ***n.fem.***

ad·verb (ad′vʉrb′) ***n.*** ‖< L *ad-*, to + *verbum*, word‖ a word used to modify a verb, an adjective, or another adverb, by expressing time, place, manner, degree, etc. —**ad·ver′bi·al** ***adj.*** —**ad·ver′bi·al·ly** ***adv.***

ad·ver·sar·i·al (ad′vər ser′ē əl) ***adj.*** of or relating to adversaries, as in a lawsuit

ad′ver·sar′y ***n.***, *pl.* **-ies** ‖see ADVERT‖ an opponent; foe

ad·verse (ad vʉrs′, ad′vʉrs′) ***adj.*** ‖see ADVERT‖ **1** opposed **2** unfavorable —**ad·verse′ly** ***adv.***

ad·ver·si·ty (ad vʉr′sə tē) ***n.*** **1** misfortune; wretched or troubled state **2** *pl.* **-ties** a calamity; disaster

ad·vert (ad vʉrt′) ***vi.*** ‖< L *ad-*, to + *vertere*, to turn‖ to call attention (*to*)

ad·ver·tise (ad′vər tīz′) ***vt.*** **-tised′**, **-tis′ing** ‖see prec.‖ to describe or praise publicly, usually so as to promote sales —***vi.*** **1** to call public attention to things for sale **2** to

ask (*for*) by public notice —**ad′ver·tis′er** ***n.*** —**ad′ver·tis′ing** ***n.***
ad·ver·tise·ment (ad′vər tīz′mənt, ad′vər tīz′-, ad vʉr′tiz-) ***n.*** a public notice, usually paid for
ad·vice (ad vīs′, əd-) ***n.*** ‖ < L *ad-*, at + *videre*, to look ‖ opinion given as to what to do; counsel
ad·vis·a·ble (ad vīz′ə bəl, əd-) ***adj.*** proper to be advised; wise; sensible —**ad·vis′a·bil′i·ty** ***n.***
ad·vise (ad vīz′, əd-) ***vt.*** **-vised′**, **-vis′ing** ‖ < ML *advisum*, advice ‖ **1** to give advice to; counsel **2** to offer as advice **3** to inform —**ad·vi′sor** or **ad·vis′er** ***n.***
ad·vis′ed·ly (-id lē) ***adv.*** deliberately
ad·vise′ment ***n.*** careful consideration —**take under advisement** to consider carefully
ad·vi·so·ry (ad vī′zə rē, əd-) ***adj.*** advising or empowered to advise —***n.***, *pl.* **-ries** a report, esp. about weather conditions
ad·vo·cate (ad′və kit; *for v.*, -kāt′) ***n.*** ‖ < L *ad-*, to + *vocare*, to call ‖ one who pleads another's cause or in support of something —***vt.*** **-cat′ed**, **-cat′ing** to speak or write in support of —**ad′vo·ca·cy** (-kə sē) ***n.***
advt. advertisement

ADZ

adz or **adze** (adz) ***n.*** ‖ < OE *adesa* ‖ an axlike tool for dressing wood, etc.
Ae·ge·an (Sea) (ē jē′ən) sea between Greece and Turkey
ae·gis (ē′jis) ***n.*** ‖ < Gr *aigis*, shield of Zeus ‖ **1** protection **2** sponsorship
Ae·ne·as (i nē′əs) *Gr. & Rom. Myth.* a Trojan whose adventures are told in a poem (the **Aeneid**) by Virgil
ae·on (ē′ən, ē′än′) ***n.*** EON
a·er·ate (er′āt′, ā′ər-) ***vt.*** **-at′ed**, **-at′ing** ‖ AER(O)- + -ATE[1] ‖ **1** to expose to air **2** to charge (liquid) with gas, as to make soda water —**a·er·a′tion** ***n.*** —**a·er′a′tor** ***n.***
aer·i·al (er′ē əl) ***adj.*** ‖ < Gr *aēr*, air + -AL ‖ **1** of, in, or by air **2** unreal; imaginary **3** of aircraft or flying —***n.*** a radio or TV antenna
aer·i·al·ist (er′ē əl ist) ***n.*** an acrobat on a trapeze, high wire, etc.
a·er·ie (ā′ər ē, ē′rē, er′ē, ir′ē) ***n.*** ‖ prob. < L *ager*, field ‖ **1** the high nest of an eagle or other bird of prey **2** a house or stronghold on a high place Also **aery**
aero- ‖ < Gr *aēr*, air ‖ *combining form* **1** air **2** aircraft or flying **3** gas, gases Also **aer-** or **aeri-**
aer·o·bat·ics (er′ō bat′iks) ***n.pl.*** ‖ prec. + (ACRO)BATICS ‖ stunts done while flying an aircraft
aer·o·bic (er ō′bik) ***adj.*** ‖ < Gr *aēr*, air + *bios*, life ‖ **1** able to live or grow only where free oxygen is present **2** of exercise, as running, that conditions the heart and lungs by increasing efficient intake of oxygen by the body —***n.*** [*pl.*, *with sing. or pl. v.*] aerobic exercises
aer·o·dy·nam·ics (er′ō dī nam′iks) ***n.pl.*** [*with sing. v.*] the branch of mechanics dealing with forces exerted by air or other gases in motion —**aer′o·dy·nam′ic** ***adj.***
aer′o·nau′tics (-nôt′iks; er′ə-) ***n.pl.*** [*with sing. v.*] the science of making and flying aircraft —**aer′o·nau′ti·cal** ***adj.***
aer·o·plane (er′ə plān′) ***n.*** [Brit., etc. (exc. Cdn.)] *var. of* AIRPLANE
aer·o·sol (er′ō säl′, -sôl′; er′ə-) ***n.*** ‖ AERO- + SOL(UTION) ‖ a suspension of insoluble particles in a gas —***adj.*** of a container in which gas under pressure dispenses liquid spray through a valve
aer′o·space′ (-spās′) ***n.*** the earth's atmosphere and the space outside it —***adj.*** of missiles, etc. for flight in aerospace
Aes·chy·lus (es′ki ləs) *c.* 525-456 B.C.; Gr. writer of tragedies
Ae·sop (ē′səp, -säp′) Gr. fable writer: supposedly lived 6th c. B.C.
aes·thete (es′thēt′) ***n.*** ‖ Gr *aisthētēs*, one who perceives ‖ a person who is or pretends to be highly sensitive to art and beauty
aes·thet·ic (es thet′ik) ***adj.*** **1** of aesthetics **2** of beauty **3** sensitive to art and beauty
aes·thet′ics ***n.pl.*** [*with sing. v.*] the philosophy of art and beauty
a·far (ə fär′) ***adv.*** [Archaic] at or to a distance
af·fa·ble (af′ə bəl) ***adj.*** ‖ < L *ad-*, to + *fari*, to speak ‖ pleasant; friendly —**af′fa·bil′i·ty** ***n.*** —**af′fa·bly** ***adv.***
af·fair (ə fer′) ***n.*** ‖ < L *ad-*, to + *facere*, to do ‖ **1** a thing to do **2** [*pl.*] matters of business **3** any matter, event, etc. **4** an amorous episode
af·fect (ə fekt′; *for 3 & 4*, a fekt′) ***vt.*** ‖ < L *ad-*, to + *facere*, to do ‖ **1** to have an effect on; influence **2** to stir the emotions of **3** to like to use, wear, etc. **4** to make a pretense of being, feeling, etc.
af·fec·ta·tion (af′ek tā′shən) ***n.*** **1** a pretending to like, have, etc. **2** artificial behavior
af·fect·ed (ə fekt′id) ***adj.*** **1** afflicted **2** influenced **3** emotionally moved **4** assumed or assuming for effect **5** full of affectation
af·fect′ing ***adj.*** emotionally moving
af·fec·tion (ə fek′shən) ***n.*** **1** fond or tender feeling **2** a disease
af·fec′tion·ate (-it) ***adj.*** tender and loving —**af·fec′tion·ate·ly** ***adv.***
af·fect·less (af′ekt′lis) ***adj.*** lacking emotion
af·fer·ent (af′ər ənt) ***adj.*** ‖ < L *ad-*, to + *ferre*, to carry ‖ bringing inward to a central part, as nerves
af·fi·ance (ə fī′əns) ***vt.*** **-anced**, **-anc·ing** ‖ < ML *ad-*, to + *fidare*, to trust ‖ to betroth
af·fi·da·vit (af′ə dā′vit) ***n.*** ‖ ML, he has made oath ‖ a written statement made on oath
af·fil·i·ate (ə fil′ē āt′; *for n., usually*, -it) ***vt.*** **-at′ed**, **-at′ing** ‖ < ML *affiliare*, adopt as a son ‖ **1** to take in as a member **2** to associate (oneself) *with* a group, etc. —***vi.*** to join —***n.*** an affiliated person, club, etc. —**af·fil′i·a′tion** ***n.***
af·fin·i·ty (ə fin′i tē) ***n.***, *pl.* **-ties** ‖ < L *affinis*, adjacent ‖ **1** relationship by marriage **2** close relationship **3** a likeness implying common origin **4** a natural liking or sympathy
af·firm (ə fʉrm′) ***vt.*** ‖ < L *ad-*, to + *firmare*, make firm ‖ **1** to declare positively; assert **2** to confirm; ratify —***vi.*** *Law* to make a

formal statement, but not under oath —**af·fir·ma·tion** (af′ər mā′shən) ***n.***

af·firm·a·tive (ə fʉrm′ə tiv) ***adj.*** affirming; answering "yes" —***n.*** **1** an expression of assent **2** the side upholding the proposition being debated

affirmative action a plan to offset past discrimination in employing or educating women, blacks, etc.

af·fix (ə fiks′; *for n.* af′iks′) ***vt.*** ‖ < L *ad-*, to + *figere*, fasten ‖ **1** to fasten; attach **2** to add at the end —***n.*** **1** a thing affixed **2** a prefix or suffix

af·fla·tus (ə flāt′əs) ***n.*** ‖ < L *ad-*, to + *flare*, to blow ‖ inspiration

af·flict (ə flikt′) ***vt.*** ‖ < L *ad-*, to + *fligere*, to strike ‖ to cause pain or suffering to; distress greatly

af·flic·tion (ə flik′shən) ***n.*** **1** pain; suffering **2** any cause of suffering

af·flu·ence (af′lo͞o əns) ***n.*** ‖ < L *ad-*, to + *fluere*, to flow ‖ **1** great plenty; abundance **2** riches; wealth

af′flu·ent ***adj.*** **1** plentiful **2** wealthy; rich —**af′flu·ent·ly** ***adv.***

af·ford (ə fôrd′) ***vt.*** ‖ < OE *geforthian*, to advance ‖ **1** to spare (money, time, etc.) without much inconvenience **2** to give; yield /it *affords* pleasure/ —**af·ford′a·ble** ***adj.***

af·for·est (ə fôr′ist) ***vt.*** ‖ see AD- & FOREST ‖ to turn (land) into forest —**af·for′est·a′tion** (-əs tā′shən) ***n.***

af·fray (ə frā′) ***n.*** ‖ < OFr *esfraer*, frighten ‖ a noisy brawl

af·front (ə frunt′) ***vt.*** ‖ < ML *ad-*, to + *frons*, forehead ‖ to insult openly —***n.*** an open insult

Af·ghan (af′gan′, -gən) ***n.*** **1** a native of Afghanistan **2** [a-] a soft blanket or shawl, crocheted or knitted

Af·ghan·i·stan (af gan′i stan′) country in SW Asia, east of Iran: 250,000 sq. mi.; pop. 15,425,000

a·fi·cio·na·do (ə fish′ə nä′dō) ***n.*** ‖ Sp ‖ a devotee of some sport, art, etc.

a·field (ə fēld′) ***adv.*** **1** in or to the field **2** away (from home); astray

a·fire (ə fīr′) ***adv., adj.*** on fire

a·flame (ə flām′) ***adv., adj.*** **1** in flames **2** glowing

AFL-CIO American Federation of Labor and Congress of Industrial Organizations

a·float (ə flōt′) ***adv.*** **1** floating **2** at sea **3** flooded, as a ship's deck

a·flut·ter (ə flut′ər) ***adv., adj.*** in a flutter

a·foot (ə foot′) ***adv.*** **1** on foot **2** in motion; in progress

a·fore·men·tioned (ə fôr′men′chənd) ***adj.*** mentioned before

a·fore′said′ (-sed′) ***adj.*** spoken of before

a·fore′thought′ ***adj.*** thought out beforehand; premeditated

a·foul (ə foul′) ***adv., adj.*** in a collision or a tangle —**run** (or **fall**) **afoul of** to get into trouble with

a·fraid (ə frād′) ***adj.*** ‖ see AFFRAY ‖ feeling frightened: followed by *of, that*, or an infinitive Often used colloquially indicating regret /I'm *afraid* I must go/

Af·ri·ca (af′ri kə) second largest continent, south of Europe: *c.* 11,677,000 sq. mi.; pop. *c.* 484,000,000 —**Af′ri·can** ***adj., n.***

African violet a tropical African plant with violet, white, or pinkish flowers and hairy, dark-green leaves, often grown as a house-plant

Af·ri·kaans (af′ri käns′, -känz′) ***n.*** ‖ Afrik < *Afrika*, Africa ‖ an official language of South Africa, based on Dutch

Af·ro (af′rō′) ***adj.*** ‖ see fol. ‖ designating or of a full, bushy hair style, as worn by some blacks —***n.,*** *pl.* **-ros′** an Afro hair style

Afro- ‖ < L *Afer*, an African ‖ *combining form* African, African and

Af·ro-A·mer·i·can (af′rō ə mer′i kən) ***adj.*** of black Americans of African ancestry, their culture, etc. —***n.*** a black American of African ancestry

aft (aft) ***adv.*** ‖ < OE *æftan* ‖ at, near, or toward the stern of a ship or rear of an aircraft

af·ter (af′tər) ***adv.*** ‖ OE *æfter* ‖ **1** behind **2** later —***prep.*** **1** behind **2** later than **3** in search of **4** as a result of **5** in spite of /*after* all I've said, he's still going/ **6** lower in rank or order than **7** in imitation of **8** for /named *after* Lincoln/ —***conj.*** following the time when —***adj.*** **1** next; later **2** nearer the rear

af′ter·birth′ ***n.*** the placenta and membranes expelled after the birth of offspring

af′ter·burn′er (-bʉrn′ər) ***n.*** a device attached to some engines for burning or utilizing exhaust gases

af′ter·ef·fect′ ***n.*** an effect coming later, or as a secondary result

af′ter·life′ ***n.*** a life after death

af′ter·math′ (-math′) ***n.*** ‖ < AFTER + OE *mæth*, cutting of grass ‖ a result, esp. an unpleasant one

af·ter·noon (af′tər no͞on′) ***n.*** the time from noon to evening —***adj.*** in the afternoon

af′ter·thought′ ***n.*** **1** an idea, explanation, part, etc. coming or added later **2** a thought coming too late to be apt

af′ter·ward (-wərd) ***adv.*** later; subsequently Also **af′ter·wards**

Ag ‖ L *argentum* ‖ *Chem. symbol for* silver

a·gain (ə gen′) ***adv.*** ‖ < OE *on-*, up to + *gegn*, direct ‖ **1** back into a former condition **2** once more **3** besides **4** on the other hand —**again and again** often; repeatedly —**as much again** twice as much

a·gainst (ə genst′) ***prep.*** ‖ see prec. ‖ **1** in opposition to **2** toward so as to strike /thrown *against* the wall/ **3** next to **4** in preparation for **5** as a charge on —**over against** **1** opposite to **2** as compared with

Ag·a·mem·non (ag′ə mem′nän′) *Gr. Myth.* commander of the Greek army in the Trojan War

a·gape (ə gāp′) ***adv., adj.*** ‖ A-[1] + GAPE ‖ with the mouth wide open

a·gar (ä′gär′) ***n.*** ‖ Malay ‖ a gelatinous product made from seaweed, used in bacterial cultures Also **a′gar′-a′gar′**

ag·ate (ag′it) ***n.*** ‖ < Gr *achatēs* ‖ a hard, semiprecious stone with striped or clouded coloring

a·ga·ve (ə gä′vē) ***n.*** ‖ < proper name in Gr. myth ‖ a desert plant with thick, fleshy leaves

age (āj) ***n.*** ‖ < L *aetas* ‖ **1** the length of time that a person or thing has existed **2** a stage of life 3 old age 4 a historical or geological period 5 [*often pl.*] [Colloq.] a long time —*vi.*, *vt.* **aged, ag′ing** or **age′ing** to grow or make old, ripe, mature, etc. —**of age** having reached the age when one is qualified for full legal rights

-age (ij) ‖ < LL *-aticum* ‖ *suffix* 1 act, state, or result of /*usage*/ 2 amount or number of /*acreage*/ 3 cost of /*postage*/ 4 place of /*steerage*/

a·ged (ā′jid; *for 2* ājd) *adj.* 1 old 2 of the age of —**the aged** old people

age·ism (āj′iz′əm) *n.* ‖ AGE + (RAC)ISM ‖ discrimination against older people

age′less *adj.* 1 seemingly not growing older 2 eternal

a·gen·cy (ā′jən sē) *n.*, *pl.* **-cies** ‖ < L *agere*, to act ‖ 1 action; power 2 means 3 a firm, etc. empowered to act for another 4 an administrative government division 5 an organization that offers assistance /a social *agency*/

a·gen·da (ə jen′də) *n.*, *pl.* **-das** ‖ < L *agere*, to do ‖ a list of things to be dealt with at a meeting

a·gent (ā′jənt) *n.* ‖ < L *agere*, to do ‖ 1 an active force or substance producing an effect 2 a person, firm, etc. empowered to act for another 3 a representative of a government agency

Agent Orange ‖ military code name, from *orange*-colored containers ‖ a highly toxic defoliant

age-old (āj′ōld′) *adj.* ancient

ag·er·a·tum (aj′ər āt′əm) *n.* ‖ < Gr *agēratos*, not growing old ‖ a plant of the composite family with small, thick heads of bluish flowers

ag·glom·er·ate (ə gläm′ər āt′; *for adj. & n.*, -ər it) *vt.*, *vi.* **-at′ed, -at′ing** ‖ < L *ad-*, to + *glomerare*, form into a ball ‖ to gather into a mass or ball —*adj.* gathered into a mass or ball —*n.* a jumbled heap, mass, etc.

ag·glu·ti·nate (ə glo͞ot′′n it; *for v.*, -āt′) *adj.* ‖ < L *ad-*, to + *gluten*, glue ‖ stuck together —*vt.*, *vi.* **-nat′ed, -nat′ing** to stick together, as with glue —**ag·glu′ti·na′tion** *n.*

ag·gran·dize (ə gran′dīz′; *also*, ag′rən-) *vt.* **-dized′, -diz′ing** ‖ < Fr *a-*, to + *grandir*, to increase ‖ to make greater, more powerful, richer, etc. —**ag·gran·dize·ment** (ə gran′diz mənt, ag′rən diz′-) *n.*

ag·gra·vate (ag′rə vāt′) *vt.* **-vat′ed, -vat′ing** ‖ < L *ad-*, to + *gravis*, heavy ‖ 1 to make worse 2 [Colloq.] to annoy; vex —**ag′gra·va′tion** *n.*

ag′gra·vat′ed *adj.* *Law* designating a grave form of a specified offense

ag·gre·gate (ag′rə git; *for v.*, -gāt′) *adj.* ‖ < L *ad-*, to + *grex*, a herd ‖ total —*n.* a mass of distinct things gathered into a total or whole —*vt.* **-gat′ed, -gat′ing** 1 to gather into a mass 2 to total —**ag′gre·ga′tion** *n.*

ag·gres·sion (ə gresh′ən) *n.* ‖ < L *aggredi*, to attack ‖ 1 an unprovoked attack or warlike act 2 a being aggressive —**ag·gres′sor** *n.*

ag·gres·sive (ə gres′iv) *adj.* 1 boldly hostile; quarrelsome 2 bold and active; enterprising —**ag·gres′sive·ly** *adv.* —**ag·gres′sive·ness** *n.*

ag·grieve (ə grēv′) *vt.* **-grieved′, -griev′ing** ‖ see AGGRAVATE ‖ to cause grief or injury to; offend; slight

a·ghast (ə gast′) *adj.* ‖ < OE *gast*, ghost ‖ feeling great horror or dismay

ag·ile (aj′əl) *adj.* ‖ < L *agere*, to act ‖ quick and easy of movement —**ag′ile·ly** *adv.* —**a·gil·i·ty** (ə jil′ə tē) *n.*

ag·i·tate (aj′i tāt′) *vt.* **-tat′ed, -tat′ing** ‖ < L *agere*, to act ‖ 1 to stir up or shake up 2 to excite the feelings of —*vi.* to stir up people so as to produce changes —**ag′i·ta′tion** *n.* —**ag′i·ta′tor** *n.*

a·gleam (ə glēm′) *adv.*, *adj.* gleaming

a·glit·ter (ə glit′ər) *adv.*, *adj.* glittering

a·glow (ə glō′) *adv.*, *adj.* in a glow (of color or emotion)

ag·nos·tic (ag näs′tik) *n.* ‖ < Gr *a-*, not + base of *gignōskein*, know ‖ one who believes it impossible to know if God exists —*adj.* of an agnostic —**ag·nos′ti·cism′** (-ti siz′əm) *n.*

a·go (ə gō′) *adj.* ‖ < OE *agan*, pass away ‖ gone by; past /years *ago*/ —*adv.* in the past /long *ago*/

a·gog (ə gäg′) *adv.*, *adj.* ‖ < OFr *en*, in + *gogue*, joke ‖ with eager anticipation or excitement

ag·o·nize (ag′ə nīz′) *vi.* **-nized′, -niz′ing** 1 to struggle 2 to be in agony —*vt.* to torture

ag·o·ny (ag′ə nē) *n.*, *pl.* **-nies** ‖ < Gr *agōn*, a contest ‖ 1 great mental or physical pain 2 death pangs 3 a strong outburst (*of* emotion)

a·grar·i·an (ə grer′ē ən) *adj.* ‖ < L *ager*, field ‖ 1 of land or the ownership of land 2 of agriculture

a·gree (ə grē′) *vi.* **-greed′, -gree′ing** ‖ < L *ad*, to + *gratus*, pleasing ‖ 1 to consent (*to*) 2 to be in accord 3 to be of the same opinion (*with*) 4 to arrive at an understanding (*about* prices, etc.) 5 to be suitable, healthful, etc.: followed by *with* —*vt.* to grant /I *agree* that it's true/

a·gree′a·ble *adj.* 1 pleasing or pleasant 2 willing to consent 3 conformable 4 acceptable —**a·gree′a·bly** *adv.*

a·gree·ment (ə grē′mənt) *n.* 1 an agreeing 2 an understanding between people, countries, etc. 3 a contract

agri- *combining form* agriculture: also **agro-**

ag·ri·busi·ness (ag′rə biz′niz, -nis) *n.* ‖ see fol. + BUSINESS ‖ farming and associated businesses and industries

ag·ri·cul·ture (ag′ri kul′chər) *n.* ‖ < L *ager*, field + *cultura*, cultivation ‖ the work of producing crops and raising livestock; farming —**ag′ri·cul′tur·al** *adj.* —**ag′ri·cul′tur·al·ly** *adv.* —**ag′ri·cul′tur·ist** *n.*

a·gron·o·my (ə grän′ə mē) *n.* ‖ < Gr *agros*, field + *nemein*, govern ‖ the science and economics of crop production —**a·gron′o·mist** *n.*

a·ground (ə ground′) *adv.*, *adj.* on or onto the shore, a reef, etc.

a·gue (ā′gyo͞o′) *n.* ‖ < ML (*febris*) *acuta*, violent (fever) ‖ a fever, usually malarial, marked by chills

ah (ä, ô) *interj.* an exclamation of pain, delight, surprise, etc.

a·ha (ä hä′) *interj.* an exclamation of satisfaction, triumph, etc.

a·head (ə hed′) *adv.*, *adj.* 1 in or to the front 2 forward; onward 3 in advance 4 winning or profiting —**get ahead** to advance financially, etc.

a·hem (ə hem′) ***interj.*** a cough, etc. made to get someone's attention, etc.

-a·hol·ic (ə häl′ik) *combining form* one preoccupied with (something specified)

a·hoy (ə hoi′) ***interj.*** a call used in hailing /ship *ahoy!*/

aid (ād) ***vt., vi.*** ‖< L *ad-*, to + *juvare*, to help‖ to help; assist —***n.*** **1** help or assistance **2** a helper

aide (ād) ***n.*** ‖Fr‖ **1** an assistant **2** an aide-de-camp

aide-de-camp or **aid-de-camp** (ād′də kamp′) ***n.***, *pl.* **aides′-** or **aids′-** ‖Fr‖ a military officer serving as an assistant to a superior

AIDS (ādz) ***n.*** ‖*A*(*cquired*) *I*(*mmune*) *D*(*eficiency*) *S*(*yndrome*)‖ a condition of deficiency of certain leukocytes, resulting in infections, cancer, etc.

ai·grette or **ai·gret** (ā gret′, ā′gret′) ***n.*** ‖see EGRET‖ a bunch of the long, white, showy plumes of the egret

ail (āl) ***vt.*** ‖OE *eglian*, to trouble‖ to cause pain and trouble to —***vi.*** to be in poor health

ai·le·ron (ā′lə rän′) ***n.*** ‖Fr < L *ala*, wing‖ a pilot-controlled airfoil at the trailing edge of an airplane wing, for controlling rolling

ail·ment (āl′mənt) ***n.*** a mild illness

aim (ām) ***vi., vt.*** ‖< L *ad-*, to + *aestimare*, to estimate‖ **1** to direct (a weapon, blow, etc.) so as to hit **2** to direct (one's efforts) **3** to intend —***n.*** **1** an aiming **2** the ability to hit a target **3** intention —**take aim** to aim a weapon, etc.

aim′less ***adj.*** having no purpose —**aim′less·ly** ***adv.*** —**aim′less·ness** ***n.***

ain't (ānt) ‖< *amn't*, contr. of *am not*‖ [Colloq.] am not: also a dialectal or substandard contraction for *is not, are not, has not*, and *have not*

ai·o·li or **aï·o·li** (ī ō′lē) ***n.*** ‖ult. < L *allium*, garlic + *oleum*, oil‖ a mayonnaise containing crushed raw garlic

air (er) ***n.*** ‖< Gr *aēr*‖ **1** the invisible mixture of gases surrounding the earth **2** *a*) a breeze; wind *b*) fresh air **3** an outward appearance /an *air* of dignity/ **4** general mood **5** [*pl.*] affected, superior manners **6** public expression **7** AIR CONDITIONING **8** a tune —***adj.*** of or by aircraft —***vt.*** **1** to let air into **2** to publicize **3** to broadcast —***vi.*** to be broadcast —**in the air** prevalent —**on** (or **off**) **the air** that is (or is not) broadcasting —**up in the air** not settled

air bag a bag that inflates instantly within an automobile in a collision, to protect riders from being thrown forward

air base a base for military aircraft

air′borne′ ***adj.*** **1** carried by or through the air **2** aloft or flying

air brake a brake operated by the action of compressed air on a piston

air′brush′ ***n.*** an atomizer worked by compressed air and used for spraying on paint, etc. Also **air brush**

air′bus′ ***n.*** an extremely large passenger airplane, esp. for short trips

air conditioning a method of keeping air humidity and temperature at desired levels in buildings, cars, etc. —**air′-con·di′tion** ***vt.*** —**air conditioner**

air′-cooled′ ***adj.*** cooled by having air passed over, into, or through it

air′craft′ ***n.***, *pl.* **-craft′** any machine for traveling through the air

aircraft carrier a warship with a large, flat deck, for carrying aircraft

air′drop′ ***n.*** the dropping of supplies, troops, etc. from an aircraft in flight —**air′drop′** ***vt.***

Aire·dale (er′dāl′) ***n.*** ‖after *Airedale*, valley in England‖ a large terrier with a wiry coat

air′field′ ***n.*** a field where aircraft can take off and land

air′foil′ ***n.*** a wing, rudder, etc. of an aircraft

air force the aviation branch of a country's armed forces

air gun a gun or gunlike device operated by compressed air

air′head′ ***n.*** [Slang] a frivolous, silly, and ignorant person

air lane a route for travel by air; airway

air′lift′ ***n.*** a system of transporting troops, supplies, etc. by aircraft —***vt.*** to transport by airlift

air′line′ ***n.*** a system or company for moving freight and passengers by aircraft —***adj.*** of or on an airline

air′lin′er ***n.*** a large airline-operated aircraft for carrying passengers

air lock an airtight compartment, with adjustable air pressure, between places of unequal air pressure

air′mail′ ***n.*** mail transported by air; esp., in the U.S., mail going overseas by air Also sp. **air mail** —***adj.*** of or for mail sent by air —***vt.*** to send (mail) by air

air′man (-mən) ***n.***, *pl.* **-men** **1** an aviator **2** an enlisted person in the U.S. Air Force

air mass *Meteorol.* a huge, uniform body of air having the properties of its place of origin

air′plane′ ***n.*** a motor-driven or jet-propelled aircraft kept aloft by the forces of air upon its wings

air′play′ ***n.*** the playing of a recording over radio or TV

air pocket an atmospheric condition that causes an aircraft to make a sudden, short drop while in flight

air′port′ ***n.*** a place where aircraft can land and take off, usually with facilities for repair, etc.

air power the total capacity of a nation for air war

air pressure the pressure of the atmosphere or of compressed air

air raid an attack by aircraft, esp. bombers

air rifle a rifle operated by compressed air

air′ship′ ***n.*** a self-propelled, steerable aircraft that is lighter than air

air′sick′ ***adj.*** nauseated because of air travel —**air′sick′ness** ***n.***

air′space′ ***n.*** the space above a nation over which it can claim jurisdiction

air′strike′ ***n.*** an attack made by aircraft

air′strip′ ***n.*** a temporary airfield

air′tight′ ***adj.*** **1** too tight for air or gas to enter or escape **2** having no weaknesses /an *airtight* alibi/

air′waves′ ***n.pl.*** the medium through which radio signals are transmitted

air′way′ ***n.*** AIR LANE

air·y (er′ē) *adj.* **-i·er, -i·est** **1** of air **2** open to the air; breezy **3** unsubstantial as air **4** light as air; graceful **5** lighthearted **6** affectedly nonchalant —**air′i·ly** *adv.* —**air′i·ness** *n.*

aisle (īl) *n.* ‖ < L *ala*, wing ‖ a passageway, as between rows of seats

a·jar (ə jär′) *adv., adj.* ‖ OE *cier*, a turn ‖ slightly open, as a door

a·kim·bo (ə kim′bō) *adv., adj.* ‖ < ON *keng*, bent + *bogi*, a bow ‖ with hands on hips and elbows bent outward /with arms *akimbo*/

ARMS AKIMBO

a·kin (ə kin′) *adj.* **1** of one kin; related **2** similar

Ak·ron (ak′rən) city in N Ohio: pop. 237,000

Al *Chem. symbol for* aluminum

-al (əl, ′l) ‖ < L ‖ *suffix* **1** of, like, or suitable for /*theatrical*/ **2** the act or process of ___ing /*rehearsal*/

à la or **a la** (ä′lə, -lä) ‖ Fr ‖ in the manner or style of

Al·a·bam·a (al′ə bam′ə) Southern State of SE U.S.: 51,609 sq. mi.; pop. 3,890,000; cap. Montgomery: abbrev. **AL** or **Ala.** —**Al′a·bam′i·an** or **Al′a·bam′an** *adj., n.*

al·a·bas·ter (al′ə bas′tər) *n.* ‖ < Gr *alabastros*, perfume vase ‖ a translucent, whitish variety of gypsum, used for statues, vases, etc.

a la carte (ä′lə kärt′) ‖ Fr ‖ with a separate price for each item on the menu

a·lac·ri·ty (ə lak′rə tē) *n.* ‖ < L *alacer*, lively ‖ eager willingness, often with quick, lively action

A·lad·din (ə lad′′n) a boy in *The Arabian Nights* who finds a magic lamp

à la king (ä′lə kiŋ′) in a cream sauce containing mushrooms, pimentos, etc.

Al·a·mo (al′ə mō′) Franciscan mission at San Antonio, Tex: scene of a massacre of Texans by Mexican troops (1836)

a la mode (al′ə mōd′) ‖ < Fr ‖ **1** in fashion **2** served in a certain style, as pie with ice cream Also **à la mode**

a·lar (ā′lər) *adj.* ‖ < L *ala*, a wing ‖ **1** of a wing **2** having wings

a·larm (ə lärm′) *n.* ‖ < It *all'arme*, to arms ‖ **1** [Archaic] a sudden call to arms **2** a warning of danger **3** a mechanism that warns of danger, arouses from sleep, etc. **4** fear caused by danger —*vt.* **1** to warn of danger **2** to frighten

alarm clock a clock that can be set to buzz, flash a light, etc. at a given time, as to awaken a person

a·larm′ing *adj.* frightening

a·larm′ist *n.* one who spreads alarming rumors, exaggerated reports of danger, etc. —*adj.* of an alarmist

a·las (ə las′) *interj.* an exclamation of sorrow, pity, etc.

A·las·ka (ə las′kə) State of the U.S. in NW North America: 586,400 sq. mi.; pop. 400,000; cap. Juneau: abbrev. **AK** or **Alas.** —**A·las′kan** *adj., n.*

alb (alb) *n.* ‖ < L *albus*, white ‖ a white robe worn by a priest at Mass

al·ba·core (al′bə kôr′) *n.* ‖ < Ar *al*, the + *buko*, young camel ‖ a tuna with unusually long pectoral fins

Al·ba·ni·a (al bā′nē ə) country in the W Balkans: 11,099 sq. mi.; pop. 3,020,000 —**Al·ba′ni·an** *adj., n.*

Al·ba·ny (ôl′bə nē) capital of N.Y., on the Hudson: pop. 102,000

al·ba·tross (al′bə trôs′) *n.* ‖ < Sp < Ar *al qādūs*, a scoop ‖ **1** a large, web-footed sea bird **2** a burden

al·be·it (ôl bē′it) *conj.* ‖ ME *al be it*, al(though) it be ‖ although

Al·ber·ta (al bʉrt′ə) province of SW Canada: 255,285 sq. mi.; pop. 2,366,000; cap. Edmonton

al·bi·no (al bī′nō) *n., pl.* **-nos** ‖ < L *albus*, white ‖ a person, animal, or plant lacking normal coloration: human albinos have white skin, whitish hair, and pink eyes

al·bum (al′bəm) *n.* ‖ < L *albus*, white ‖ **1** a book with blank pages for mounting pictures, stamps, etc. **2** a single recording, as of a set of related musical works

al·bu·men (al byōō′mən) *n.* ‖ L < *albus*, white ‖ **1** the white of an egg **2** the nutritive protein in seeds, etc. **3** ALBUMIN

al·bu·min (al byōō′min) *n.* ‖ see prec. ‖ a water-soluble protein found in milk, egg, blood, vegetable tissues, etc. —**al·bu′mi·nous** *adj.*

Al·bu·quer·que (al′bə kʉr′kē) city in central N.Mex.; pop. 332,000

al·che·my (al′kə mē) *n.* ‖ < Ar < Gr *chēmeia*; infl. by Gr *cheein*, pour ‖ the chemistry of the Middle Ages, the chief aim of which was to change the baser elements into gold —**al′che·mist** *n.*

al·co·hol (al′kə hôl′) *n.* ‖ < Ar *alkuhl*, antimony powder ‖ **1** a colorless, volatile, pungent liquid, used in various forms as a fuel, an intoxicating ingredient in fermented liquors, etc. **2** any such intoxicating liquor

al′co·hol′ic *adj.* **1** of alcohol **2** suffering from alcoholism —*n.* one who has chronic alcoholism

al′co·hol′ism′ *n.* the habitual excessive drinking of alcoholic liquor, or a resulting diseased condition

al·cove (al′kōv′) *n.* ‖ < Ar *al*, the + *qubba*, an arch ‖ a recessed section of a room

al·der (ôl′dər) *n.* ‖ OE *alor* ‖ a small tree or shrub of the birch family

al·der·man (ôl′dər mən) *n., pl.* **-men** ‖ < OE *eald*, old + *man* ‖ in some U.S. cities, a municipal officer representing a certain district or ward

ale (āl) *n.* ‖ OE *ealu* ‖ a fermented drink of malt and hops, like beer

a·le·a·to·ry (ā′lē ə tôr′ē) *adj.* ‖ < L *aleatorius*, of gambling < *alea*, chance ‖ depending on chance or luck

a·lem·bic (ə lem′bik) *n.* ‖ < Ar *al-anbīq* < Gr *ambix*, a cup ‖ **1** an apparatus formerly used for distilling **2** anything that purifies

a·lert (ə lʉrt′) *adj.* ‖ < L *erigere*, to erect ‖ **1** watchful; vigilant **2** active; nimble —*n.* a warning signal; alarm —*vt.* to warn to be ready, etc. —**on the alert** vigilant —**a·lert′ly** *adv.* —**a·lert′ness** *n.*

A·leu·tian Islands (ə lōō′shən) chain of U.S.

islands off the SW tip of Alaska —**A·leu′·tian** ***adj.***, ***n.***

ale·wife (āl′wīf′) ***n.***, *pl.* **-wives′** ‖< ?‖ a NW Atlantic fish resembling the herring, used for food and in fertilizers

Al·ex·an·der the Great (al′ig zan′dər) 356-323 B.C.; military conqueror; king of Macedonia (336-323)

Al′ex·an′dri·a (-drē ə) **1** seaport in N Egypt: pop. 2,318,000 **2** city in NE Va.: pop. 103,000

al·fal·fa (al fal′fə) ***n.*** ‖Sp < Ar *al-fisfiṣa*, fodder‖ a plant of the pea family, used for fodder, pasture, and as a cover crop

Al·fred the Great (al′frəd) A.D. 849-899; Anglo-Saxon king (871-899)

al·fres·co (al fres′kō, äl-) ***adv.*** ‖It < *al*, in the + *fresco*, cool‖ outdoors —***adj.*** outdoor Also **al fresco**

al·gae (al′jē′) ***n.pl.***, *sing.* **al′ga** (-gə) ‖pl. of L *alga*, seaweed‖ a group of simple organisms, one-celled or many-celled, containing chlorophyll and found in water or damp places

al·ge·bra (al′jə brə) ***n.*** ‖< Ar *al*, the + *jabara*, to reunite‖ a mathematical system using symbols, esp. letters, to generalize certain arithmetical operations and relationships —**al′ge·bra′ic** (-brā′ik) ***adj.*** —**al′ge·bra′i·cal·ly** ***adv.***

Al·ge·ri·a (al jir′ē ə) country in N Africa: *c.* 919,000 sq. mi.; pop. 22,817,000 —**Al·ge′ri·an** ***adj.***, ***n.***

-al·gia (al′jə) ‖< Gr *algos*‖ *combining form* pain [*neuralgia*]

Al·giers (al jirz′) seaport & capital of Algeria: pop. 2,400,000

Al·gon·qui·an (al gäŋ′kē ən, -kwē-) ***adj.*** designating or of a widespread family of North American Indian languages —***n.*** this family of languages

al·go·rithm (al′gə rith′əm) ***n.*** ‖ult. < Ar‖ any systematic method of solving a certain kind of mathematical problem

a·li·as (ā′lē əs) ***n.***, *pl.* **-as·es** ‖L < *alius*, other‖ an assumed name —***adv.*** otherwise named [Bell *alias* Jones]

A·li Ba·ba (al′ə bab′ə, ä′lē bä′bə) in *The Arabian Nights*, a poor man who finds the treasure of forty thieves

al·i·bi (al′ə bī′) ***n.***, *pl.* **-bis′** ‖L < *alius ibi*, elsewhere‖ **1** *Law* the plea or fact that an accused person was elsewhere than at the scene of the crime **2** [Colloq.] an excuse —***vi.***, ***vt.*** **-bied′**, **-bi′ing** [Colloq.] to offer an excuse (for)

al·ien (āl′yən, āl′ē ən) ***adj.*** ‖< L *alius*, other‖ **1** foreign **2** not natural; strange **3** of aliens —***n.*** **1** a foreigner **2** a foreign-born resident who is not naturalized **3** a hypothetical being from outer space

al′ien·a·ble (-ə bəl) ***adj.*** capable of being transferred to a new owner

al′ien·ate′ (-āt′) ***vt.*** **-at′ed**, **-at′ing** **1** to transfer the ownership of (property) to another **2** to make unfriendly or withdrawn **3** to cause a transference of (affection) —**al′ien·a′tion** ***n.***

a·light[1] (ə līt′) ***vi.*** **a·light′ed** or **a·lit′**, **a·light′ing** ‖ME *alihtan*‖ **1** to get down or off; dismount **2** to come down after flight

a·light[2] (ə līt′) ***adj.*** lighted up; burning

a·lign (ə līn′) ***vt.*** ‖< Fr *a-*, to + *ligne*, LINE[1]‖ **1** to bring into a straight line **2** to bring (components or parts) into adjustment **3** to bring into agreement, etc. —***vi.*** to line up —**a·lign′ment** ***n.***

a·like (ə līk′) ***adj.*** ‖< OE *gelic*‖ like one another —***adv.*** **1** similarly **2** equally

al·i·ment (al′ə mənt) ***n.*** ‖< L *alere*, nourish‖ nourishment; food

al′i·men′ta·ry (-men′tə rē) ***adj.*** **1** of food or nutrition **2** nourishing

alimentary canal (or **tract**) the passage in the body (from the mouth to the anus) that food goes through

al·i·mo·ny (al′ə mō′nē) ***n.*** ‖< L *alere*, nourish‖ money a court orders paid to a person by that person's legally separated or divorced spouse

a·line (ə līn′) ***vt.***, ***vi.*** **a·lined′**, **a·lin′ing** ALIGN —**a·line′ment** ***n.***

a·lit (ə lit′) ***vi.*** *alt. pt. & pp. of* ALIGHT[1]

a·live (ə līv′) ***adj.*** ‖< OE *on*, in + *life*, life‖ **1** having life; living **2** in existence, operation, etc. **3** lively; alert —**alive to** aware of —**alive with** teeming with

a·li·yah or **a·li·ya** (ä′lē yä′) ***n.*** ‖< Heb, lit., ascent‖ immigration by Jews to Israel

al·ka·li (al′kə lī′) ***n.***, *pl.* **-lies′** or **-lis′** ‖< Ar *al-qili*, the ashes of a certain plant‖ **1** any base, as soda, that is soluble in water and gives off ions in solution **2** a mineral salt, etc. that can neutralize acids

al′ka·line′ (-lin′, -līn′) ***adj.*** of or like an alkali —**al′ka·lin′i·ty** (-lin′ə tē) ***n.***

al′ka·lin·ize′ (-lin īz′) ***vt.*** **-ized′**, **-iz′ing** ALKALIZE

al′ka·lize′ (-līz′) ***vt.*** **-lized′**, **-liz′ing** to make alkaline —**al′ka·li·za′tion** ***n.***

al′ka·loid′ (-loid′) ***n.*** a bitter, alkaline substance, such as caffeine, morphine, etc., containing nitrogen

al·kyd (al′kid′) ***n.*** ‖ult. < ALKALI + (ACI)D‖ a synthetic resin used in paints, varnishes, etc. Also **alkyd resin**

all (ôl) ***adj.*** ‖OE *eal*‖ **1** the whole quantity of [*all* the gold] **2** every one of [*all* men] **3** the greatest possible [in *all* sincerity] **4** any [beyond *all* doubt] **5** alone; only [*all* work and no play] —***pron.*** **1** [*with pl. v.*] everyone **2** everything **3** every part or bit —***n.*** **1** one's whole property, effort, etc. [gave his *all*] **2** a totality; whole —***adv.*** **1** wholly; entirely [*all* worn out] **2** apiece [a score of two *all*] —**after all** nevertheless —**all in** [Colloq.] very tired —**all in all** **1** considering everything **2** as a whole —**all out** completely —**all the better** (or **worse**) so much the better (or worse) —**all the same** **1** nevertheless **2** unimportant —**at all** **1** in the least **2** in any way **3** under any considerations —**in all** altogether

all- *combining form* **1** wholly, entirely [*all*-American] **2** for every [*all*-purpose] **3** of everything [*all*-inclusive]

Al·lah (al′ə, ä′lə) ‖< Ar *al*, the + *ilāh*, god‖ *the Muslim name for* God

all′-A·mer′i·can ***adj.*** representative of the U.S. as a whole, or chosen as the best in the U.S. —***n.*** **1** a hypothetical football team, etc. made up of U.S. college players voted the best of the year **2** a player on such a team

all′-a·round′ *adj.* having many abilities, talents, or uses; versatile

al·lay (a lā′, ə-) *vt.* **-layed′, -lay′ing** ‖ < OE *a-*, down + *lecgan*, lay ‖ **1** to calm; quiet **2** to relieve (pain, etc.)

all′-clear′ *n.* a siren or other signal that an air raid or alert is over

al·le·ga·tion (al′ə gā′shən) *n.* an assertion, esp. one without proof or to be proved

al·lege (ə lej′) *vt.* **-leged′, -leg′ing** ‖ < L *ex-*, out of + *litigare*, to dispute ‖ **1** to declare or assert, esp. without proof **2** to offer as an excuse

al·leged (ə lejd′, ə lej′id) *adj.* **1** declared, but without proof **2** so-called /*alleged* friends/ —**al·leg′ed·ly** *adv.*

Al·le·ghe·ny Mountains (al′ə gā′nē) mountain range in Pa., Md., W.Va., and Va.: also **Al′le·ghe′nies**

al·le·giance (ə lē′jəns) *n.* ‖ < OFr *liege*, liege ‖ **1** the duty of being loyal to one's ruler, country, etc. **2** loyalty; devotion, as to a cause

al·le·go·ry (al′ə gôr′ē) *n., pl.* **-ries** ‖ < Gr *allos*, other + *agoreuein*, speak in assembly ‖ a story in which people, things, and events have a symbolic meaning, often instructive —**al′le·gor′i·cal** *adj.* —**al′le·gor′i·cal·ly** *adv.* —**al′le·go′rist** *n.*

al·le·gret·to (al′ə gret′ō) *adj., adv.* ‖ It, dim. of *allegro* ‖ *Musical Direction* moderately fast

al·le·gro (ə le′grō′, -lā′-) *adj., adv.* ‖ It ‖ *Musical Direction* fast

al·lele (ə lēl′) *n.* ‖ < Gr *allēlōn*, of one another ‖ a gene transferring inherited characteristics

al·le·lu·ia (al′ə lo͞o′yə) *interj., n.* ‖ LL(Eccles.) ‖ HALLELUJAH

Al·len·town (al′ən toun′) city in E Pa.: pop. 104,000

al·ler·gen (al′ər jən) *n.* ‖ Ger ‖ a substance inducing an allergic reaction —**al′ler·gen′ic** (-jen′ik) *adj.*

al·ler·gic (ə lʉr′jik) *adj.* **1** of, caused by, or having an allergy **2** [Colloq.] averse (*to*)

al·ler·gist (al′ər jist) *n.* a doctor who specializes in treating allergies

al·ler·gy (al′ər jē) *n., pl.* **-gies** ‖ Ger < Gr *allos*, other + *ergon*, work ‖ **1** a hypersensitivity to a specific substance (as a food, pollen, dust, etc.) or condition (as heat or cold) **2** an aversion

al·le·vi·ate (ə lē′vē āt′) *vt.* **-at′ed, -at′ing** ‖ < L *ad-*, to + *levis*, light ‖ **1** to lessen or relieve (pain, etc.) **2** to decrease (poverty, etc.) —**al·le′vi·a′tion** *n.*

al·ley (al′ē) *n., pl.* **-leys** ‖ < OFr *aler*, go ‖ **1** a narrow street between or behind buildings **2** a bowling lane

alley cat a homeless, mongrel cat

al′ley·way′ *n.* an alley between buildings

all-fired (ôl′fīrd′) *adj., adv.* ‖ < *hell-fired* ‖ [Slang] extreme(ly)

al·li·ance (ə lī′əns) *n.* ‖ see ALLY ‖ **1** an allying or close association, as of nations for a common objective, families by marriage, etc. **2** an agreement for this **3** the countries, groups, etc. in such association

al·lied (ə līd′, al′īd′) *adj.* **1** united by kinship, treaty, etc. **2** closely related

ALLIGATOR

al·li·ga·tor (al′ə gāt′ər) *n.* ‖ < Sp *el*, the + L *lacerta*, lizard ‖ a large reptile of the U.S., like the crocodile but with a broad snout

alligator pear AVOCADO

all′-im·por′tant *adj.* highly important; necessary; essential

all′-in·clu′sive *adj.* including everything; comprehensive

al·lit·er·a·tion (ə lit′ər ā′shən) *n.* ‖ < L *ad-*, to + *littera*, letter ‖ repetition of an initial sound in two or more words of a phrase —**al·lit′er·a′tive** *adj.*

al·lo·cate (al′ō kāt′, al′ə-) *vt.* **-cat′ed, -cat′ing** ‖ < L *ad-*, to + *locus*, a place ‖ **1** to set apart for a specific purpose **2** to distribute or allot —**al′lo·ca′tion** *n.*

al·lot (ə lät′) *vt.* **-lot′ted, -lot′ting** ‖ < OFr *a-*, to + *lot*, lot ‖ **1** to distribute in arbitrary shares; apportion **2** to assign as one's share —**al·lot′ment** *n.*

all′-out′ *adj.* complete or wholehearted /an *all-out* effort/

all′o′ver *adj.* over the whole surface

al·low (ə lou′) *vt.* ‖ see ALLOCATE ‖ **1** to permit; let /I'm not *allowed* to go/ **2** to let have /she *allowed* herself no sweets/ **3** to acknowledge as valid **4** to provide (a certain amount), as for shrinkage, waste, etc. —**allow for** to leave room, time, etc. for —**al·low′a·ble** *adj.*

al·low′ance (-əns) *n.* **1** an allowing **2** something allowed **3** an amount of money, food, etc. given regularly to a child, soldier, etc. **4** a reduction in price, as for a trade-in —**make allowance(s) for** to excuse because of mitigating factors

al·loy (al′oi; *also, and for v. usually*, ə loi′) *n.* ‖ < L *ad-*, to + *ligare*, to bind ‖ **1** a substance that is a mixture of two or more metals **2** something that debases another thing when mixed with it —*vt.* to make into an alloy

all′-pur′pose *adj.* useful in many ways

all right **1** satisfactory **2** unhurt **3** correct **4** yes; very well

all′-round′ *adj., adv. var. of* ALL AROUND

all·spice (ôl′spīs′) *n.* a spice, combining the tastes of several spices, made from the berry of a West Indian tree of the myrtle family

all′-star′ *adj.* **1** made up of star performers **2** of or characteristic of an all-star event —*n.* a member of an all-star team

all′-time′ *adj.* unsurpassed until now

al·lude (ə lo͞od′) *vi.* **-lud′ed, -lud′ing** ‖ L *alludere*, to jest ‖ to refer indirectly (*to*)

al·lure (ə loor′) *vt., vi.* **-lured′, -lur′ing** ‖ < OFr *a-*, to + *loirer*, to lure ‖ to tempt with something desirable; attract —*n.* fascination; charm —**al·lure′ment** *n.* —**al·lur·ing** (ə loor′iŋ, a-) *adj.*

al·lu·sion (ə lo͞o′zhən) *n.* **1** an alluding **2** an indirect or casual reference

al·lu·sive (ə lo͞os′iv) *adj.* **1** containing an allusion **2** full of allusions —**al·lu′sive·ly** *adv.* —**al·lu′sive·ness** *n.*

al·lu·vi·um (ə lo͞o′vē əm) ***n.***, *pl.* **-vi·ums** or **-vi·a** (-vē ə) ‖< L *ad-*, to + *luere*, to wash‖ sand, clay, etc. deposited by moving water —**al·lu′vi·al** ***adj.***

al·ly (ə lī′; *also, and for n. usually*, al′ī) ***vt., vi.*** **-lied′**, **-ly′ing** ‖< L *ad-*, to + *ligare*, to bind‖ **1** to unite or join for a specific purpose **2** to relate by similarity of structure, etc. —***n.***, *pl.* **-lies** a country or person joined with another for a common purpose

al·ma ma·ter (al′mə māt′ər, äl′mə mät′ər) ‖L, fostering mother‖ **1** the college or school that one attended **2** its anthem

al·ma·nac (ôl′mə nak′, al′-) ***n.*** ‖< *c.* 5th-c. Gr *almenichiaka*, calendar‖ a calendar with astronomical data, weather forecasts, etc.

al·might·y (ôl mīt′ē) ***adj.*** all-powerful —**the Almighty** God

al·mond (ä′mənd; *also* am′ənd) ***n.*** ‖< Gr *amygdalē*‖ **1** the edible, nutlike kernel of a peachlike fruit **2** the tree it grows on —***adj.*** shaped like an almond; oval and pointed at one or both ends

al·most (ôl′mōst′, ôl mōst′) ***adv.*** very nearly; all but

alms (ämz) ***n.***, *pl.* **alms** ‖< Gr *eleos*, mercy‖ money, food, etc. given to poor people —**alms′giv′er** ***n.***

alms′house′ ***n.*** **1** [Historical] a poorhouse **2** [Brit.] a privately endowed home for the poor

al·oe (al′ō′) ***n.***, *pl.* **-oes′** ‖< Gr *aloē*‖ an African plant of the lily family

a·loft (ə lôft′) ***adv.*** ‖ME < *o*, on + *loft*, loft‖ **1** high up **2** in the air; flying **3** high above the deck of a ship

a·lo·ha (ä lō′hə, -hä′; ə lō′ə) ***n., interj.*** ‖Haw, love‖ a word used as a greeting or farewell

a·lone (ə lōn′) ***adj., adv.*** ‖ME < *al*, all + *one*, one‖ **1** apart from anything or anyone else **2** without any other person **3** only **4** without equal —**let alone 1** to refrain from interfering with **2** not to speak of /we hadn't a dime, *let alone* a dollar/

a·long (ə lôŋ′) ***prep.*** ‖< OE *and-*, over against + *-lang*, long‖ **1** on or beside the length of **2** in conformity with —***adv.*** **1** lengthwise **2** progressively onward or advanced **3** together (*with*) **4** with one /take me *along*/ —**all along** from the beginning —**be along** [Colloq.] to come or arrive —**get along 1** to advance **2** to manage **3** to succeed **4** to be compatible

a·long′shore′ ***adv.*** near or beside the shore

a·long′side′ ***adv.*** at or by the side; side by side —***prep.*** beside —**alongside of** at the side of

a·loof (ə lo͞of′) ***adv.*** ‖< *a-*, on & Du *loef*, windward side‖ at a distance but in view —***adj.*** cool and reserved /an *aloof* manner/ —**a·loof′ness** ***n.***

a·loud (ə loud′) ***adv.*** **1** loudly **2** with the normal voice

alp (alp) ***n.*** ‖after ALPS‖ a high mountain

al·pac·a (al pak′ə) ***n.*** ‖< AmInd‖ **1** a South American llama **2** its silky wool, or cloth woven from it

al·pha (al′fə) ***n.*** the first letter of the Greek alphabet (Α, α)

al′pha·bet′ (-bet′) ***n.*** ‖< Gr *alpha* & *bēta*, first two letters of the Gr alphabet‖ the letters used in writing a language, esp. as arranged in their usual order —**al′pha·bet′i·cal** ***adj.*** —**al′pha·bet′i·cal·ly** ***adv.***

al·pha·bet·ize (al′fə bə tīz′) ***vt.*** **-ized′**, **-iz′·ing** to arrange in the usual order of the alphabet —**al′pha·bet′i·za′tion** (-bet′i zā′shən) ***n.***

al′pha·nu·mer′ic (-no͞o mer′ik) ***adj.*** having both alphabetical and numerical symbols

alpha particle a positively charged particle given off by certain radioactive substances

alpha ray a stream of alpha particles

alpha wave an electrical brain wave indicating relaxation Also **alpha rhythm**

Al·pine (al′pīn′) ***adj.*** **1** of the Alps **2** [a-] of or like high mountains

Alps (alps) mountain system in south central Europe

al·read·y (ôl red′ē) ***adv.*** **1** by or before the given or implied time **2** even now or even then

al·right (ôl rīt′) ***adv.*** *var. sp. of* ALL RIGHT: a disputed usage

Al·sace (al sās′, al′sas′) historical region of NE France —**Al·sa′tian** (-sā′shən) ***adj., n.***

al·so (ôl′sō) ***adv.*** ‖< OE *eall*, all + *swa*, so‖ in addition; likewise; too

al′so-ran′ ***n.*** [Colloq.] a defeated contestant in a race, election, etc.

alt. *abbrev.* **1** alternate **2** altitude **3** alto

al·tar (ôl′tər) ***n.*** ‖< L *altus*, high‖ **1** a platform where sacrifices are made to a god, etc. **2** a table, etc. for sacred purposes in a place of worship

altar boy a boy or man who helps a priest at religious services, esp. at Mass

al·ter (ôl′tər) ***vt., vi.*** ‖< L *alter*, other‖ to change; make or become different —**al′ter·a′tion** ***n.***

al·ter·ca·tion (ôl′tər kā′shən) ***n.*** ‖< L *altercari*, to dispute‖ an angry or heated argument; quarrel

al·ter e·go (ôl′tər ē′gō) ‖L, other I‖ **1** another aspect of oneself **2** a constant companion

al·ter·nate (ôl′tər nit; *for v.*, -nāt′) ***adj.*** ‖< L *alternus*, one after the other‖ **1** succeeding each other **2** every other —***n.*** a substitute —***vt.*** **-nat′ed**, **-nat′ing** to do or use by turns —***vi.*** **1** to act, happen, etc. by turns **2** to take turns regularly —**al′ter·nate·ly** ***adv.*** —**al′ter·na′tion** ***n.***

alternating current an electric current reversing direction periodically

al·ter·na·tive (ôl tur′nə tiv) ***adj.*** **1** providing a choice between things **2** of an institution, etc. appealing to unconventional interests /an *alternative* school/ —***n.*** **1** a choice between things **2** one of the things to be chosen **3** something left to choose

al·ter·na·tor (ôl′tər nāt′ər) ***n.*** an electric generator producing alternating current

al·though (ôl *th*ō′) ***conj.*** ‖ME < *al*, even + THOUGH‖ in spite of the fact that; though Also sp. **al·tho**

al·tim·e·ter (al tim′ət ər) ***n.*** ‖< L *altus*, high + -METER‖ an instrument for measuring altitude

al·ti·tude (al′tə to͞od′) ***n.*** ‖< L *altus*, high‖ **1** the height of a thing, esp. above sea level **2** a high place

al·to (al′tō) ***n.***, *pl.* **-tos** ‖It < L *altus*, high‖

1 the range of a voice between tenor and mezzo-soprano 2 a singer with this range —*adj.* of, for, or in the alto

al·to·geth·er (ôl'to͞o ge*th*'ər) ***adv.*** 1 completely 2 in all 3 on the whole

al·tru·ism (al'tro͞o iz'əm) ***n.*** ‖< L *alter*, other‖ unselfish concern for the welfare of others —**al'tru·ist** ***n.*** —**al'tru·is'tic** (-is'tik) ***adj.*** —**al'tru·is'ti·cal·ly** ***adv.***

al·um (al'əm) ***n.*** ‖< L *alumen*‖ any of a group of salts of aluminum, etc., used in manufacturing and medicine

al·u·min·i·um (al'yo͞o min'ē əm) ***n.*** [Brit., etc. (exc. Cdn.)] *var. of* ALUMINUM

a·lu·mi·num (ə lo͞o'mə nəm) ***n.*** ‖< L *alumen*, alum‖ a silvery, lightweight metallic chemical element

a·lum·nus (ə lum'nəs) ***n.***, *pl.* **-ni'** (-nī') ‖L, foster son‖ a boy or man who has attended or is a graduate of a particular school, college, etc. —**a·lum'na** (-nə), *pl.* **-nae** (-nē), ***n.fem.***

al·ways (ôl'wāz, -wiz) ***adv.*** ‖OE *ealne weg*‖ 1 at all times 2 continually 3 at any time 4 in every instance

Alz·hei·mer's disease (älts'hī'mərz) ‖after A. *Alzheimer*, 20th-c. Ger doctor‖ a degenerative brain disease

am (am, əm) ***vi.*** ‖OE *eom*‖ *1st pers. sing., pres. indic., of* BE

AM 1 amplitude modulation 2 ‖L *ante meridiem*‖ before noon: used to designate the time from midnight to noon: also **A.M.**, **am**, or **a.m.** 3 ‖L *Artium Magister*‖ master of arts: also **A.M.**

Am. 1 America 2 American

AMA American Medical Association

a·mal·gam (ə mal'gəm) ***n.*** ‖< Gr *malagma*, an emollient‖ 1 any alloy of mercury with another metal [a dental filling of silver *amalgam*] 2 a mixture; blend

a·mal'ga·mate' (-gə māt') ***vt., vi.*** **-mat'ed, -mat'ing** to unite; mix; combine —**a·mal'ga·ma'tion** ***n.***

a·man·dine (ä'mən dēn') ***adj.*** ‖Fr‖ prepared with almonds

a·man·u·en·sis (ə man'yo͞o en'sis) ***n.***, *pl.* **-ses'** (-sēz') ‖L < *a-*, from + *manus*, hand + *-ensis*, relating to‖ a secretary: now a jocular usage

am·a·ranth (am'ə ranth') ***n.*** ‖< Gr *amarantos*, unfading‖ 1 any of a family of plants, some bearing showy flowers 2 [Old Poet.] an imaginary flower that never dies

a·ma·ret·to (am'ə ret'ō) ***n.*** ‖It, rather bitter‖ [*also* **A-**] a liqueur with an almond flavor

Am·a·ril·lo (am'ə ril'ō) city in NW Tex.: pop. 149,000

am·a·ryl·lis (am'ə ril'is) ***n.*** ‖< Gr *Amaryllis*, name for a shepherdess‖ a bulb plant with white, purple, pink, or red, lilylike flowers

a·mass (ə mas') ***vt.*** ‖< Fr < L *massa*, a lump‖ to pile up; accumulate

am·a·teur (am'ə chər, -cho͝or'; -ə tʉr', -ə tər) ***n.*** ‖Fr < L *amare*, to love‖ 1 one who does something for pleasure, not for money; nonprofessional 2 one who is somewhat unskillful —***adj.*** of or done by amateurs —**am'a·teur'ish** (-cho͝or'-) ***adj.*** —**am'a·teur·ism'** ***n.***

am'a·to'ry (-tôr'ē) ***adj.*** ‖< L *amare*, to love‖ of or showing sexual love

a·maze (ə māz') ***vt.*** **a·mazed', a·maz'ing** ‖OE *āmasian*‖ to fill with great surprise or wonder; astonish —**a·maze'ment** ***n.*** —**a·maz'ing** ***adj.*** —**a·maz'ing·ly** ***adv.***

Am·a·zon (am'ə zän', -zən) river in N South America: c. 4,000 mi. —***n.*** 1 *Gr. Myth.* any of a race of female warriors 2 [**a-**] a large, strong, masculine woman

am·bas·sa·dor (am bas'ə dər) ***n.*** ‖< Prov *ambaissador*‖ the highest-ranking diplomatic representative of one country to another —**am·bas'sa·do'ri·al** (-dôr'ē əl) ***adj.*** —**am·bas'sa·dor·ship'** ***n.***

am·ber (am'bər) ***n.*** ‖< Ar *'anbar*, ambergris‖ 1 a brownish-yellow fossil resin used in jewelry, etc. 2 its color —***adj.*** amberlike or amber-colored

am'ber·gris' (-grēs', -gris') ***n.*** ‖< OFr *ambre gris*, gray amber‖ a waxy substance secreted by certain whales, used in making perfumes

ambi- ‖L‖ *combining form* both [*ambidextrous*]

am·bi·dex·trous (am'bə deks'trəs) ***adj.*** ‖< earlier *ambidexter* + -OUS‖ using both hands with equal ease —**am'bi·dex·ter'i·ty** (-deks ter'ə tē) ***n.***

am·bi·ence (am'bē əns) ***n.*** ‖Fr: see fol.‖ an environment or its distinct atmosphere Also **am'bi·ance** (-əns)

am'bi·ent (-ənt) ***adj.*** ‖< L *ambi-*, around + *ire*, to go‖ surrounding

am·bi·gu·i·ty (am'bə gyo͞o'ə tē) ***n.*** 1 a being ambiguous 2 *pl.* **-ties** an ambiguous expression

am·big·u·ous (am big'yo͞o əs) ***adj.*** ‖< L *ambi-*, around + *agere*, to do‖ 1 having two or more meanings 2 not clear; vague —**am·big'u·ous·ly** ***adv.***

am·bi·tion (am bish'ən) ***n.*** ‖< L *ambitio*, a going around (to solicit votes)‖ 1 a strong desire for fame, power, etc. 2 the thing so desired

am·bi'tious (-əs) ***adj.*** 1 full of or showing ambition 2 demanding great effort —**am·bi'tious·ly** ***adv.***

am·biv·a·lence (am biv'ə ləns) ***n.*** ‖AMBI- + VALENCE‖ simultaneous conflicting feelings —**am·biv'a·lent** ***adj.*** —**am·biv'a·lent·ly** ***adv.***

am·ble (am'bəl) ***vi.*** **-bled, -bling** ‖< L *ambulare*, to walk‖ 1 to move at an easy gait, as a horse 2 to walk in a leisurely way —***n.*** 1 a horse's ambling gait 2 a leisurely walking pace

am·bro·si·a (am brō'zhə) ***n.*** ‖< Gr *a-*, not + *brotos*, mortal‖ 1 *Gr. & Rom. Myth.* the food of the gods 2 anything that tastes or smells delicious —**am·bro'si·al** ***adj.***

am·bu·lance (am'byə ləns) ***n.*** ‖< L *ambulare*, to walk‖ a vehicle equipped for carrying the sick or wounded

am·bu·late (am'byo͞o lāt', -byə-) ***vi.*** **-lat'ed, -lat'ing** to move about; walk —**am'bu·lant** (-lənt) ***adj.*** —**am'bu·la'tion** ***n.***

am'bu·la·to'ry (-lə tôr'ē) ***adj.*** 1 of or for walking 2 able to walk

am·bus·cade (am'bəs kād') ***n., vt., vi.*** **-cad'ed, -cad'ing** AMBUSH

am·bush (am'bo͝osh') ***n.*** ‖< ML *in-*, in + *boscus*, woods‖ 1 a deployment of persons in hiding to make a surprise attack 2 their hiding place —*vt., vi.* to attack from ambush

a·me·ba (ə mē′bə) ***n.***, *pl.* **-bas** or **-bae** (-bē) *alt. sp. of* AMOEBA —**a·me′bic** (-bik) ***adj.***

a·mel·io·rate (ə mēl′yə rāt′) ***vt., vi.*** **-rat′ed, -rat′ing** ⟦< Fr < L *melior,* better⟧ to make or become better; improve —**a·mel′io·ra′tion** ***n.***

a·men (ā′men′, ä′-) ***interj.*** ⟦< Heb *amen,* truly⟧ may it be so!: used after a prayer or to express approval

a·me·na·ble (ə mē′nə bəl, -men′ə-) ***adj.*** ⟦< OFr < L *minare,* to drive (animals)⟧ **1** responsible or answerable **2** able to be controlled; submissive —**a·me′na·bil′i·ty** ***n.*** —**a·me′na·bly** ***adv.***

a·mend (ə mend′) ***vt.*** ⟦< L *emendare*⟧ **1** to correct; emend **2** to improve **3** to change or revise (a law, etc.) —***vi.*** to improve one's conduct —**a·mend′a·ble** ***adj.***

a·mend′ment ***n.*** **1** a correction of errors, faults, etc. **2** improvement **3** a revision or change proposed or made in a bill, law, etc.

a·mends (ə mendz′) ***n.pl.*** ⟦see AMEND⟧ [*sometimes with sing. v.*] payment made or satisfaction given for injury, loss, etc.

a·men·i·ty (ə men′ə tē, -mēn′-) ***n.***, *pl.* **-ties** ⟦< L *amoenus,* pleasant⟧ **1** pleasantness **2** an attractive feature or convenience **3** [*pl.*] courteous acts

am·ent (am′ənt, ā′mənt) ***n.*** ⟦< L *amentum,* thong⟧ CATKIN

Am·er·a·sian (am′ər ā′zhən) ***n.*** ⟦AMER(ICAN) + ASIAN⟧ a person of both American and Asian descent

a·merce (ə murs′) ***vt.*** **a·merced′, a·merc′ing** ⟦< OFr *a merci,* at the mercy of⟧ to punish, esp. by imposing a fine —**a·merce′ment** ***n.***

A·mer·i·ca (ə mer′i kə) ⟦associated with *Amerigo* VESPUCCI⟧ **1** North America, South America, and the West Indies, considered together: also **the A·mer′i·cas** **2** North America **3** the United States of America

A·mer·i·can (ə mer′i kən) ***adj.*** **1** of or in America **2** of the U.S., its people, etc. —***n.*** **1** a native or inhabitant of North or South America **2** a citizen of the U.S.

A·mer′i·can′a (-kan′ə) ***n.pl.*** books, papers, objects, etc. having to do with the U.S., its people, and its history

American Indian a member of any of the aboriginal peoples of North or South America or the West Indies

A·mer′i·can·ism′ ***n.*** **1** a custom or belief of the U.S. **2** a word or idiom originating in American English **3** devotion to the U.S., its customs, etc.

A·mer′i·can·ize′ (-īz′) ***vt., vi.*** **-ized′, -iz′ing** to make or become American in character, manners, etc. —**A·mer′i·can·i·za′tion** ***n.***

American plan a system of hotel operation in which the price charged covers room, service, and meals

American Revolution the war (1775-83) fought by the American colonies to gain independence from Great Britain

Am·er·in·di·an (am′ər in′dē ən) ***n., adj.*** AMERICAN INDIAN —**Am′er·ind′** ***n.***

am·e·thyst (am′i thist) ***n.*** ⟦< Gr *amethystos,* not drunken: the Greeks thought the amethyst prevented intoxication⟧ **1** a purple or violet quartz or corundum, used in jewelry **2** purple or violet

a·mi·a·ble (ā′mē ə bəl) ***adj.*** ⟦< L *amicus,* friend⟧ good-natured; friendly —**a′mi·a·bil′i·ty** ***n.*** —**a′mi·a·bly** ***adv.***

am·i·ca·ble (am′i kə bəl) ***adj.*** ⟦see prec.⟧ friendly; peaceable —**am′i·ca·bil′i·ty** ***n.*** —**am′i·ca·bly** ***adv.***

a·mid (ə mid′) ***prep.*** in the middle of; among: also **a·midst** (ə midst′)

am·ide (am′īd′) ***n.*** any of several organic compounds derived from ammonia

a·mid′ships′ ***adv., adj.*** in or toward the middle of a ship

a·mi·go (ə mē′gō) ***n.***, *pl.* **-gos′** (-gōz′) ⟦Sp⟧ a friend

a·mi·no acid (ə mē′nō, am′i nō′) ⟦< AMMONIA⟧ any of the nitrogenous organic acids that form proteins necessary for all life

Am·ish (äm′ish, am′-) ***n.pl.*** ⟦after Jacob *Ammann* (or *Amen*), the founder⟧ the members of a Christian sect that favors plain living in an agrarian society —***adj.*** of this sect

a·miss (ə mis′) ***adv.*** ⟦see A-[1] & MISS[1]⟧ in a wrong way; astray —***adj.*** wrong, faulty, improper, etc. [what is *amiss?*]

am·i·ty (am′i tē) ***n.***, *pl.* **-ties** ⟦< L *amicus,* friend⟧ peaceful relations

am·me·ter (am′mēt′ər) ***n.*** ⟦AM(PERE) + -METER⟧ an instrument for measuring an electric current in amperes

am·mo (am′ō) ***n.*** [Slang] ammunition

am·mo·ni·a (ə mōn′yə) ***n.*** ⟦prob. from a salt found near Egyptian shrine of Jupiter *Ammon*⟧ **1** a colorless, pungent gas, a compound of nitrogen and hydrogen **2** a 10% water solution of this gas: in full, **ammonia water**

am·mu·ni·tion (am′yoo nish′ən) ***n.*** ⟦< L *munire,* fortify⟧ **1** bullets, gunpowder, bombs, grenades, rockets, etc. **2** any means of attack or defense

am·ne·si·a (am nē′zhə) ***n.*** ⟦< Gr *a-,* not + *mnasthai,* to remember⟧ partial or total loss of memory

am·nes·ty (am′nəs tē) ***n.***, *pl.* **-ties** ⟦< Gr *amnēstia,* a forgetting⟧ a pardon, esp. for political offenses —***vt.*** **-tied, -ty·ing** to pardon

am·ni·o·cen·te·sis (am′nē ō′sen tē′sis) ***n.*** ⟦< fol. + Gr *kentēsis,* a pricking⟧ the surgical procedure of extracting amniotic fluid from a pregnant woman to determine the sex of the fetus, detect disease, etc.

am·ni·on (am′nē ən, -än′) ***n.***, *pl.* **-ni·ons** or **-ni·a** (-ə) ⟦Gr, dim. of *amnos,* lamb⟧ the membrane enclosing the embryo of a mammal, reptile, or bird: it is filled with a watery fluid (**amniotic fluid**) —**am′ni·ot′ic** (-ät′ik) ***adj.***

a·moe·ba (ə mē′bə) ***n.***, *pl.* **-bas** or **-bae** (-bē) ⟦< Gr *ameibein,* to change⟧ a one-celled, microscopic organism reproducing by fission —**a·moe′bic** (-bik) ***adj.***

a·mok (ə muk′) ***n.*** ⟦< Malay *amuk,* attacking furiously⟧ in Indonesia and the Philippines, a state in which a person loses control and kills indiscriminately —**run** (or **go**) **amok** **1** to rush about in a frenzy to kill **2**

to lose control and behave violently 3 to become undisciplined

a·mong (ə muŋ') *prep.* ⟦< OE *on*, in + *gemang*, a crowd⟧ 1 surrounded by /*among* friends/ 2 in the group of /best *among* books/ 3 to or for each or several of /divide it *among* the crowd/ 4 by the joint action of Also **a·mongst** (ə muŋst')

A·mon-Re (ä'mən rā') the ancient Egyptian sun god

a·mon·til·la·do (ə män'tə lä'dō) *n.* ⟦< Sp, after *Montilla*, town in Spain⟧ a pale, relatively dry sherry

a·mor·al (ā môr'əl) *adj.* 1 neither moral nor immoral 2 without moral sense —**a'mo·ral'i·ty** *n.* —**a·mor'al·ly** *adv.*

am·o·rous (am'ə rəs) *adj.* ⟦< L *amor*, love⟧ 1 fond of making love 2 full of love 3 of sexual love —**am'o·rous·ly** *adv.*

a·mor·phous (ə môr'fəs) *adj.* ⟦< Gr *a-*, without + *morphē*, form⟧ 1 without definite form 2 vague or indefinite 3 *Chem.* not crystalline

am·or·tize (am'ər tīz', ə môr'-) *vt.* **-tized'**, **-tiz'ing** ⟦< ME < L *ad*, to + *mors*, death⟧ to put money aside at intervals for gradual payment of (a debt, etc.) —**am'or·ti·za'tion** *n.*

a·mount (ə mount') *vi.* ⟦< OFr *amont*, upward < L *ad*, to + *mons*, mountain⟧ 1 to add up (*to*) 2 to be equal (*to*) in value, etc. —*n.* 1 a sum total 2 the whole value or effect 3 a quantity

a·mour (ä moor', ə-) *n.* ⟦< L *amor*, love⟧ a love affair, esp. an illicit one

a·mour-pro·pre (ä mōōr prō'pr') *n.* ⟦Fr⟧ self-esteem

amp. *abbrev.* 1 amperage 2 ampere(s)

am·per·age (am'pər ij, am pir'-) *n.* the strength of an electric current in amperes

am·pere (am'pir') *n.* ⟦< A. M. *Ampère*, 19th-c. Fr physicist⟧ the standard unit for measuring an electric current, equal to one coulomb per second

am·per·sand (am'pər sand') *n.* ⟦< *and per se and*, (the sign) & by itself (is) *and*⟧ a sign (&), meaning *and*

am·phet·a·mine (am fet'ə mēn', -min) *n.* a drug used esp. as a stimulant and to lessen appetite

am·phib·i·an (am fib'ē ən) *n.* ⟦see fol.⟧ 1 any amphibious animal or plant 2 any aircraft that can take off from or land on water or land —*adj.* AMPHIBIOUS

am·phib'i·ous *adj.* ⟦Gr *amphibios*, living a double life < *amphi-*, around + *bios*, life⟧ that can live or operate on land and in water

am·phi·the·a·ter or **am·phi·the·a·tre** (am'fə thē'ət ər) *n.* ⟦< Gr *amphi-*, around + *theatron*, theater⟧ a round or oval building with rising rows of seats around an open space

am·ple (am'pəl) *adj.* **-pler**, **-plest** ⟦< L *amplus*⟧ 1 large in size, scope, etc. 2 more than enough 3 adequate —**am'ply** *adv.*

am·pli·fi·er (am'plə fī'ər) *n.* one that amplifies; esp., a device for strengthening electrical signals

am'pli·fy' (-fī') *vt.* **-fied'**, **-fy'ing** ⟦< L *amplus*, large + *facere*, to make⟧ 1 to make stronger; esp., to strengthen (electrical signals) 2 to develop more fully —**am'pli·fi·ca'tion** *n.*

am·pli·tude (am'plə tōōd') *n.* ⟦see AMPLE⟧ 1 scope, extent, breadth, etc. 2 abundance 3 range from mean to extreme, as of an alternating current

amplitude modulation the changing of the amplitude of the transmitting radio wave in accordance with the signal being broadcast

am·pul (am'pool') *n.* ⟦< L *ampulla*, bottle⟧ a small, sealed glass container for a single dose of a hypodermic medicine Also **am'·pule** (-pyōōl') or **am'poule** (-pōōl')

am·pu·tate (am'pyōō tāt') *vt.*, *vi.* **-tat'ed**, **-tat'ing** ⟦< L *am-*, AMBI- + *putare*, to prune⟧ to cut off (an arm, etc.), esp. by surgery —**am'pu·ta'tion** *n.*

am'pu·tee' (-tē') *n.* one who has had a limb or limbs amputated

Am·ster·dam (am'stər dam') constitutional capital of the Netherlands: pop. 676,000

amt. amount

Am·trak (am'trak') ⟦*Am*(*erican*) *tr*(*avel*) (*tr*)*a*(*c*)*k*⟧ a national U.S. passenger railroad system

a·muck (ə muk') *n.* AMOK

am·u·let (am'yōō lit) *n.* ⟦< L⟧ something worn to protect against evil

a·muse (ə myōōz') *vt.* **a·mused'**, **a·mus'ing** ⟦< Fr < *à*, at + OFr *muser*, to gaze⟧ 1 to keep pleasantly occupied; entertain 2 to make laugh, smile, etc. —**a·mus'ed·ly** *adv.*

a·muse'ment *n.* 1 a being amused 2 something that amuses

amusement park an outdoor place with devices for entertainment, as a merry-go-round, roller coaster, etc.

am·yl·ase (am'ə lās') *n.* ⟦< Gr *amylon*, starch⟧ an enzyme that helps change starch into sugar, found in saliva, etc.

an (an; *unstressed*, ən, 'n) *adj.*, ***indefinite article*** ⟦< OE *an*, one⟧ 1 one; one sort of 2 each; any one 3 per /two *an* hour/ *An* is used before words beginning with a vowel sound /*an* eye, *an* honor/ See also A²

-an (ən, in, 'n) ⟦< L *-anus*⟧ *suffix* 1 (one) belonging to /*diocesan*/ 2 (one) born in or living in /*Mexican*/ 3 (one) believing in /*Lutheran*/

a·nach·ro·nism (ə nak'rə niz'əm) *n.* ⟦< Gr *ana-*, against + *chronos*, time⟧ 1 anything out of its proper historical time 2 the representation of this —**a·nach'ro·nis'tic** *adj.*

an·a·con·da (an'ə kän'də) *n.* ⟦< Sinhalese *henacandāya*, a snake of Sri Lanka⟧ a South American boa that crushes its prey in its coils

an·aer·o·bic (an'ər ō'bik) *adj.* ⟦< Gr *an-*, without + *aēr*, air + *bios*, life⟧ able to live and grow without air or free oxygen, as certain bacteria

an·aes·the·sia (an'əs thē'zhə) *n.* ANESTHESIA —**an'aes·thet'ic** (-thet'ik) *adj.*, *n.*

an·a·gram (an'ə gram') *n.* ⟦< Gr *anagrammatizein*, transpose letters⟧ 1 a word, etc. made by rearranging letters (Ex.: *now* — *won*) 2 [*pl.*, *with sing. v.*] a word game based on this

An·a·heim (an'ə hīm') city in SW Calif.: pop. 222,000

a·nal (ā'nəl) *adj.* of or near the anus

an·al·ge·si·a (an''l jē'zē ə) *n.* ⟦< Gr *an-*,

without + *algēsia*, pain ‖ a fully conscious state in which pain is not felt

an'al·ge'sic (-zik) *adj.* of or causing analgesia **—*n.*** a drug that produces analgesia

an·a·log (an'ə lôg') *adj.* 1 of an analog computer 2 of electronic devices in which the signal corresponds to a physical change 3 using hands, dials, etc. to show numerical amounts, as on a clock: cf. DIGITAL (sense 2) **—*n.*** ANALOGUE

analog computer a computer for processing data represented by a continuous physical variable, as electric current: cf. DIGITAL COMPUTER

a·nal·o·gize (ə nal'ə jīz') *vi.*, *vt.* **-gized'**, **-giz'ing** to use, or explain by, analogy

a·nal'o·gous (-gəs) *adj.* ‖ see ANALOGY ‖ similar in some way **—a·nal'o·gous·ly** *adv.*

an·a·logue (an'ə lôg') *n.* something analogous

a·nal·o·gy (ə nal'ə jē) *n.*, *pl.* **-gies** ‖ < Gr *ana-*, according to + *logos*, word, reckoning ‖ 1 similarity in some ways 2 the inference that certain resemblances imply further similarity

a·nal·y·sand (ə nal'ə sand') *n.* a person undergoing psychoanalysis

a·nal'y·sis (-sis) *n.*, *pl.* **-ses'** (-sēz') ‖ < Gr *ana-*, up + *lysis*, a loosing ‖ 1 a breaking up of a whole into its parts to find out their nature, etc. 2 a statement of the results of this 3 PSYCHOANALYSIS 4 *Chem.* an analysis of compounds or mixtures **—an·a·lyt·ic** (an'ə lit'ik) or **an'a·lyt'i·cal** *adj.* **—an'a·lyt'i·cal·ly** *adv.*

an·a·lyst (an'ə list) *n.* 1 one who analyzes 2 a psychoanalyst

an'a·lyze' (-līz') *vt.* **-lyzed'**, **-lyz'ing** 1 to make an analysis of; examine in detail 2 to psychoanalyze **—an'a·lyz'a·ble** *adj.* **—an'a·lyz'er** *n.*

an·a·pest (an'ə pest') *n.* ‖ < Gr *ana-*, back + *paiein*, to strike ‖ a metrical foot of two unaccented syllables followed by an accented one

an·ar·chism (an'ər kiz'əm) *n.* 1 the theory that all forms of government interfere unjustly with individual liberty 2 resistance to all government **—an'ar·chist'** *n.* **—an'ar·chis'tic** *adj.*

an'ar·chy (-kē) *n.*, *pl.* **-chies** ‖ < Gr *an-*, without + *archos*, leader ‖ 1 the absence of government 2 political disorder and violence 3 disorder; confusion **—an·ar·chic** (an är'kik) *adj.* **—an·ar'chi·cal·ly** *adv.*

a·nath·e·ma (ə nath'ə mə) *n.*, *pl.* **-mas** ‖ Gr, thing devoted to evil ‖ 1 a thing or person accursed or damned 2 a thing or person greatly detested 3 a formal curse, as in excommunication

a·nath'e·ma·tize' (-tīz') *vt.*, *vi.* **-tized'**, **-tiz'ing** to utter an anathema (against); curse

a·nat·o·mize (ə nat'ə mīz') *vt.*, *vi.* **-mized'**, **-miz'ing** ‖ see ANATOMY ‖ 1 to dissect (an animal or plant) in order to examine the structure 2 to analyze **—a·nat'o·mist** *n.*

a·nat'o·my (-mē) *n.*, *pl.* **-mies** ‖ < Gr *ana-*, up + *temnein*, to cut ‖ 1 dissection of an organism to study its structure 2 the science of the structure of animals or plants 3 the structure of an organism 4 any analysis **—an·a·tom·i·cal** (an'ə täm'i kəl) or **an'a·tom'ic** *adj.*

-ance (əns) ‖ < L ‖ *suffix* 1 the act or process of ____ing */discontinuance/* 2 the quality or state of being */forbearance/* 3 a thing that ____s */hindrance/* 4 a thing that is ____ed */utterance/*

an·ces·tor (an'ses'tər) *n.* ‖ < L *ante-*, before + *cedere*, go ‖ 1 a person from whom one is descended; forebear 2 a precursor or forerunner **—an·ces·tral** (an ses'trəl) *adj.* **—an·ces·tress** (an'ses'trəs) *n.fem.*

an'ces'try (-trē) *n.*, *pl.* **-tries** 1 family descent 2 ancestors collectively

an·chor (aŋ'kər) *n.* ‖ < Gr *ankyra*, an anchor, hook ‖ 1 a heavy object, usually an iron weight with flukes, lowered from a vessel, as by cable, to prevent drifting 2 anything giving stability 3 one who anchors a newscast: also **an'chor·man'**, **an'chor·wom'an**, or **an'chor·per'son** **—*vt.*** 1 to hold secure as by an anchor 2 to be the final contestant on (a relay team, etc.) 3 to serve as coordinator and chief reporter for (a newscast) **—*vi.*** 1 to lower an anchor 2 to be or become fixed **—at anchor** anchored

ANCHOR

an'chor·age (-ij) *n.* 1 an anchoring or being anchored 2 a place to anchor

An·chor·age (aŋ'kər ij) seaport in S Alaska: pop. 173,000

an·cho·rite (aŋ'kə rīt') *n.* ‖ < Gr *ana-*, back + *chōrein*, retire ‖ a religious recluse; hermit

an·cho·vy (an'chō vē, an'chō-) *n.*, *pl.* **-vies** ‖ < Port *anchova* ‖ a herringlike fish, eaten as a relish

an·cient (ān'chənt) *adj.* ‖ < L *ante*, before ‖ 1 of times long past 2 very old **—*n.*** an aged person

an·cil·lar·y (an'sə ler'ē) *adj.* ‖ < L *ancilla*, maidservant ‖ 1 subordinate: often with *to* 2 auxiliary

-an·cy (ən sē) *suffix* -ANCE

and (and; *unstressed*, ənd, ən) *conj.* ‖ OE ‖ 1 also; in addition 2 plus 3 as a result 4 in contrast; but 5 [Colloq.] to */try and come today/*

an·dan·te (än dän'tā) *adj.*, *adv.* ‖ It < *andare*, to walk ‖ *Musical Direction* moderate in tempo

An·der·sen (an'dər sən), **Hans Christian** (hans, hanz) 1805-75; Dan. writer of fairy tales

An·des (Mountains) (an'dēz') mountain system of W South America

and·i·ron (and'ī'ərn) *n.* ‖ < OFr *andier* ‖ either of a pair of metal supports for logs in a fireplace

and/or either *and* or *or* */personal and/or real property/*

An·dor·ra (an dôr'ə) country in the E Pyrenees: 180 sq. mi.; pop. 49,000

an·dro·gen (an'drō jən) *n.* ‖ < Gr *andros*, of man + -GEN ‖ a type of steroid that acts as a male sex hormone **—an'dro·gen'ic** (-jen'ik) *adj.*

an·drog·y·nous (an dräj'ə nəs) *adj.* ‖ < Gr *andros*, of man + *gynē*, woman ‖ 1 both male and female in one **2** that blends male and female characteristics, etc.

an·droid (an′droid′) ***n.*** ‖< Gr *andros*, of man + -OID‖ in science fiction, an automaton made to resemble a human being

an·ec·dote (an′ik dōt′) ***n.*** ‖< Gr *anekdotos*, unpublished‖ a short, entertaining account of some event —**an′ec·dot′al** ***adj.***

a·ne·mi·a (ə nē′mē ə) ***n.*** ‖< Gr *an-*, without + *haima*, blood‖ a condition in which the blood is low in red cells or in hemoglobin, resulting in paleness, weakness, etc. —**a·ne′mic** ***adj.***

an·e·mom·e·ter (an′ə mäm′ət ər) ***n.*** ‖< Gr *anemos*, the wind + -METER‖ a gauge for determining the force or speed of the wind; wind gauge

a·nem·o·ne (ə nem′ə nē′) ***n.*** ‖< Gr *anemos*, the wind‖ **1** a plant with cup-shaped flowers of white, pink, red, or purple **2** SEA ANEMONE

a·nent (ə nent′) ***prep.*** ‖< OE *on efen*, on even (with)‖ [Now Rare] concerning; about

aneroid barometer (an′ər oid′) ‖< Gr *a-*, without + *nēros*, liquid + -OID‖ a barometer working by the bending of a thin metal disk instead of by the rise or fall of mercury

an·es·the·si·a (an′es thē′zhə) ***n.*** ‖< Gr *an-*, without + *aisthēsis*, feeling‖ a partial or total loss of the sense of pain, touch, etc.

an′es·the′si·ol′o·gist (-thē′zē äl′ə jist) ***n.*** a doctor who specializes in giving anesthetics —**an′es·the′si·ol′o·gy** ***n.***

an′es·thet′ic (-thet′ik) ***adj.*** of or producing anesthesia —***n.*** a drug, gas, etc. used to produce anesthesia, as before surgery

an·es·the·tist (ə nes′thə tist′) ***n.*** one trained to give anesthetics

an·es′the·tize′ (-tīz′) ***vt.*** **-tized′**, **-tiz′ing** to cause anesthesia in —**an·es′the·ti·za′tion** ***n.***

an·eu·rysm or **an·eu·rism** (an′yo͞o riz′əm) ***n.*** ‖< Gr *ana-*, up + *eurys*, broad‖ a sac formed by an enlargement in a weakened wall of an artery, a vein, or the heart

a·new (ə no͞o′) ***adv.*** **1** once more; again **2** in a new manner or form

an·gel (ān′jəl) ***n.*** ‖< Gr *angelos*, messenger‖ **1** *Theol. a)* a messenger of God *b)* a supernatural being with greater than human power, etc. **2** an image of a human figure with wings and a halo **3** a person regarded as beautiful, good, innocent, etc. **4** [Colloq.] a financial backer, as for a play —**an·gel·ic** (an jel′ik) or **an·gel′i·cal** ***adj.*** —**an·gel′i·cal·ly** ***adv.***

angel dust [Slang] a powerful psychedelic drug

An·ge·le·no (an′jə lē′nō) ***n.***, *pl.* **-nos** ‖AmSp‖ an inhabitant of Los Angeles

an·gel·fish (ān′jəl fish′) ***n.***, *pl.* **-fish′** or (for different species) **-fish′es** a bright-colored tropical fish with spiny fins

angel (food) cake a light, spongy, white cake made with egg whites

an·ger (aŋ′gər) ***n.*** ‖< ON *angr*, distress‖ hostile feelings because of opposition, a hurt, etc. —***vt., vi.*** to make or become angry

an·gi·na (pec·to·ris) (an jī′nə pek′tər is) ‖L, lit., squeezing of the breast‖ a condition marked by chest pain, caused by a decrease of blood to the heart

an·gi·o·plas·ty (an′jē ō plas′tē) ***n.*** any of various surgical techniques for repairing or replacing damaged blood vessels

an′gi·o·sperm′ (-spurm′) ***n.*** ‖< Gr *angos*, vessel + *sperma*, seed‖ a plant having seeds produced within a closed pod or ovary

an·gle[1] (aŋ′gəl) ***n.*** ‖< Gr *ankylos*, bent‖ **1** the shape or space made by two straight lines or plane surfaces that meet **2** this space, measured in degrees, etc. **3** a sharp corner **4** a point of view; aspect **5** [Colloq.] a tricky method for achieving a purpose —***vt., vi.*** **-gled**, **-gling** **1** to move or bend at an angle **2** [Colloq.] to give a specific aspect to (a story, etc.)

an·gle[2] (aŋ′gəl) ***vi.*** **-gled**, **-gling** ‖< OE *angul*, fishhook‖ **1** to fish with a hook and line **2** to use tricks to get something /to *angle* for a promotion/ —**an′gler** ***n.***

angle iron a piece of iron or steel bent at a right angle, used for joining or reinforcing two beams, girders, etc.

An·gles (aŋ′gəlz) ***n.pl.*** a Germanic people that settled in E England in the 5th C. A.D.

an′gle·worm′ ***n.*** an earthworm

An·gli·can (aŋ′gli kən) ***adj.*** ‖< ML *Anglicus*, of the Angles‖ of or connected with the Church of England —***n.*** an Anglican church member

An′gli·cism′ (-glə siz′əm) ***n.*** a word or trait peculiar to the English

An′gli·cize′ (-sīz′) ***vt., vi.*** **-cized′**, **-ciz′ing** to change to English idiom, pronunciation, customs, etc. —**An′gli·ci·za′tion** (-si zā′shən) ***n.***

Anglo- *combining form* **1** English **2** Anglican

An′glo-A·mer′i·can (aŋ′glō-) ***adj.*** English and American —***n.*** an American of English birth or ancestry

An′glo-French′ ***adj.*** English and French —***n.*** the French spoken in England from the Norman Conquest through the Middle Ages

An′glo-Sax′on ***n.*** **1** a member of the Germanic peoples in England at the time of the Norman Conquest **2** their language, OLD ENGLISH **3** an Englishman —***adj.*** of the Anglo-Saxons

An·go·la (aŋ gō′lə, an-) country on the SW coast of Africa: 481,351 sq. mi.; pop. 8,164,000

An·go·ra (aŋ gôr′ə) ***n.*** ‖former name of ANKARA‖ **1** a breed of animal; specif., a cat, goat, or rabbit with long, silky fur or hair **2** *a)* yarn of Angora rabbit hair *b)* mohair

an·gry (aŋ′grē) ***adj.*** **-gri·er**, **-gri·est** **1** feeling or showing anger **2** wild and stormy —**an′gri·ly** (-grə lē) ***adv.***

ang·strom (aŋ′strəm) ***n.*** ‖after A. J. *Ångström*, 19th-c. Swed physicist‖ one hundred-millionth of a centimeter: a unit used in measuring the length of light waves

an·guish (aŋ′gwish) ***n.*** ‖< L *angustia*, tightness‖ great mental or physical pain; agony —***vi., vt.*** to feel or cause to feel anguish —**an′guished** ***adj.***

an·gu·lar (aŋ′gyo͞o lər) ***adj.*** **1** having or forming an angle or angles; having sharp corners **2** lean; gaunt **3** without ease or grace; stiff —an'gu·lar'i·ty (-lar'ə tē), *pl.* -ties, *n.*

an·i·line (an'ə lin) *n.* ‖< Ar *an-nīl*, the indigo plant‖ a colorless, poisonous, oily derivative of benzene, used in making dyes, resins, etc.

an·i·mad·vert (an'i məd vurt', -mad'-) *vi.* ‖L *animadvertere*, lit., to turn the mind‖ to comment adversely (*on* or *upon*) —**an'i·mad·ver'sion** *n.*

an·i·mal (an'i məl) *n.* ‖L < *anima*, breath, soul‖ **1** any living organism, excluding plants and bacteria, typically able to move about **2** any such organism other than a human being; esp., any four-footed creature **3** a brutish or inhuman person —*adj.* **1** of or like an animal **2** gross, bestial, etc.

an·i·mal·cule (an'i mal'kyo͞ol') *n.* [Obs.] a microscopic animal; protozoan

an·i·mate (an'i māt'; *for adj.*, -mit) *vt.* **-mat'ed, -mat'ing** ‖see ANIMAL‖ **1** to give life or motion to **2** to make merry or spirited **3** to inspire —*adj.* living —**an'i·mat'ed** *adj.* —**an'i·ma'tion** *n.* —**an'i·ma'tor** *n.*

animated cartoon a film made by photographing a series of drawings so that the figures in them seem to move

an·i·mism (an'i miz'əm) *n.* ‖< L *anima*, soul‖ the belief that all life is produced by a spiritual force, or that all natural phenomena have souls —**an'i·mis'tic** *adj.*

an·i·mos·i·ty (an'ə mäs'ə tē) *n.*, *pl.* **-ties** ‖see fol.‖ a feeling of strong dislike or hatred; hostility

an·i·mus (an'ə məs) *n.* ‖L, passion‖ animosity; hostility

an·i·on (an'ī'ən) *n.* ‖< Gr *anion*, thing going up‖ a negatively charged ion: in electrolysis, anions move toward the anode

an·ise (an'is) *n.* ‖< Gr *anison*‖ **1** a dicotyledonous plant related to the umbel **2** its fragrant seed, used for flavoring: also **an'i·seed'** (-i sēd')

an·i·sette (an'i zet', -set') *n.* ‖Fr‖ a sweet, anise-flavored liqueur

An·ka·ra (aŋ'kə rə, äŋ'-) capital of Turkey: pop. 2,800,000

ankh (aŋk) *n.* ‖Egypt, life, soul‖ a cross with a loop at the top, an ancient Egyptian symbol of life

an·kle (aŋ'kəl) *n.* ‖OE *ancleow*‖ **1** the joint that connects the foot and the leg **2** the area of the leg between the foot and calf

an·klet (aŋk'lit) *n.* **1** an ornament worn around the ankle **2** a short sock

an·nals (an'əlz) *n.pl.* ‖< L *annus*, year‖ **1** a written account of events year by year **2** historical records; history —**an'nal·ist** *n.*

An·nap·o·lis (ə nap'ə lis) capital of Md.: pop. 32,000

Ann Ar·bor (an är'bər) city in SE Mich.: pop. 107,000

an·neal (ə nēl') *vt.* ‖< OE *an-*, on + *æl*, fire‖ to heat (glass, metals, etc.) and cool slowly to prevent brittleness

an·ne·lid (an'ə lid') *n.* ‖< L dim. of *anulus*, a ring‖ any of various wormlike animals having long, segmented bodies, including leeches

an·nex (ə neks'; *for n.*, an'eks') *vt.* ‖< L *ad-*, to + *nectere*, to tie‖ **1** to attach, esp. to something larger **2** to incorporate into a state the territory of (another state) —*n.* something annexed; esp., an addition to a building —**an·nex·a·tion** (an'eks ā'shən) *n.*

an·ni·hi·late (ə nī'ə lāt') *vt.* **-lat'ed, -lat'ing** ‖< L *ad*, to + *nihil*, nothing‖ to destroy completely —**an·ni'hi·la'tion** *n.* —**an·ni'hi·la'tor** *n.*

an·ni·ver·sa·ry (an'ə vur'sə rē) *n.*, *pl.* **-ries** ‖< L *annus*, year + *vertere*, to turn‖ the yearly return of the date of some event —*adj.* of an anniversary

an·no·tate (an'ō tāt') *vt.*, *vi.* **-tat'ed, -tat'ing** ‖< L *ad-*, to + *nota*, a sign‖ to provide explanatory notes for —**an'no·ta'tion** *n.* —**an'no·ta'tor** *n.*

an·nounce (ə nouns') *vt.* **-nounced', -nounc'ing** ‖< L *ad-*, to + *nuntius*, messenger‖ **1** to declare publicly **2** to make known the arrival of **3** to be an announcer for —*vi.* to serve as announcer —**an·nounce'ment** *n.*

an·nounc·er (ə noun'sər) *n.* one who announces; specif., one who introduces radio or television programs

an·noy (ə noi') *vt.* ‖< VL *in odio*, in hate‖ to irritate or bother, as by a repeated action —**an·noy'ance** *n.* —**an·noy'ing** *adj.* —**an·noy'ing·ly** *adv.*

an·nu·al (an'yo͞o əl) *adj.* ‖< L *annus*, year‖ **1** of or measured by a year **2** yearly **3** living only one year or season —*n.* **1** a periodical published once a year **2** a plant living only one year or season —**an'nu·al·ly** *adv.*

an·nu·i·ty (ə no͞o'ə tē) *n.*, *pl.* **-ties** ‖see prec.‖ **1** an investment yielding periodic payments, esp. yearly **2** such a payment —**an·nu'i·tant** *n.*

an·nul (ə nul') *vt.* **-nulled', -nul'ling** ‖< L *ad-*, to + *nullum*, nothing‖ **1** to do away with **2** to deprive of legal force; nullify —**an·nul'ment** *n.*

an·nu·lar (an'yo͞o lər) *adj.* ‖< L *anulus*, a ring‖ like or forming a ring

an·nun·ci·a·tion (ə nun'sē ā'shən) *n.* an announcing —**the Annunciation 1** the angel Gabriel's announcement to Mary that she would bear Jesus **2** the church festival commemorating this

an·ode (an'ōd') *n.* ‖< Gr *anodos*, a way up‖ **1** the positive electrode in an electrolytic cell **2** the principal electrode for collecting electrons in an electron tube **3** the negative electrode in a battery

an·o·dyne (an'ō dīn') *n.* ‖< Gr *an-*, without + *odynē*, pain‖ anything that relieves pain or soothes

a·noint (ə noint') *vt.* ‖< L *in-*, on + *unguere*, to smear‖ to put oil on, as in consecrating —**a·noint'ment** *n.*

a·nom·a·lous (ə näm'ə ləs) *adj.* ‖< Gr *an-*, not + *homos*, the same‖ **1** abnormal **2** inconsistent or odd

a·nom'a·ly (-lē) *n.*, *pl.* **-lies 1** abnormality **2** anything anomalous

an·o·mie or **an·o·my** (an'ə mē) *n.* ‖Fr < Gr *anomia*, lawlessness‖ lack of purpose, identity, etc.; rootlessness

a·non (ə nän') *adv.* ‖< OE *on an*, into one‖ **1** soon **2** at another time

anon. anonymous

a·non·y·mous (ə nän'ə məs) *adj.* ‖< Gr

an-, without + *onyma*, name ‖ **1** with no name known **2** given, written, etc. by one whose name is withheld or unknown **3** lacking individuality —**an·o·nym·i·ty** (an′ə nim′ə tē) ***n.*** —**a·non′y·mous·ly** ***adv.***

a·noph·e·les (ə näf′ə lēz′) ***n.*** ‖ < Gr *anōpheles*, harmful ‖ the mosquito that can transmit malaria

an·o·rex·i·a (an′ə reks′ē ə) ***n.*** ‖ < Gr *an-*, without + *orexis*, desire ‖ an eating disorder characterized by obsession with weight loss In full **anorexia ner·vo·sa** (nər vō′sə) —**an′o·rex′ic** ***adj., n.***

an·oth·er (ə nuth′ər) ***adj.*** **1** one more; an additional **2** a different —***pron.*** **1** one additional **2** a different one **3** one of the same kind

an·swer (an′sər) ***n.*** ‖ < OE *and-*, against + *swerian*, swear ‖ **1** a reply to a question, letter, etc. **2** any act in response **3** a solution to a problem —***vi.*** **1** to reply **2** to be sufficient **3** to be responsible or liable (*to* a person *for*) **4** to conform (*to*) /he *answers* to the description/ —***vt.*** **1** to reply or respond to **2** to serve /to *answer* the purpose/ **3** to defend oneself against (a charge) **4** to conform to /she *answers* the description/ —**answer back** [Colloq.] to reply forcefully or insolently —**an′swer·a·ble** ***adj.***

ant (ant) ***n.*** ‖ < OE *æmet(t)e* ‖ any of a family of insects, generally wingless, that live in complex colonies

-ant (ənt) ‖ ult. < L ‖ *suffix* **1** that has, shows, or does /*defiant*/ **2** one that /*occupant*/

ant·ac·id (ant′as′id) ***adj.*** counteracting acidity —***n.*** an antacid substance

an·tag·o·nism (an tag′ə niz′əm) ***n.*** ‖ see ANTAGONIZE ‖ **1** opposition or hostility **2** an opposing force, principle, etc. —**an·tag′o·nis′tic** ***adj.*** —**an·tag′o·nis′ti·cal·ly** ***adv.***

an·tag′o·nist ***n.*** an adversary; opponent

an·tag′o·nize′ (-nīz′) ***vt.*** **-nized′**, **-niz′ing** ‖ < Gr *anti-*, against + *agōn*, a contest ‖ to incur the dislike of

ant·arc·tic (ant ärk′tik, -är′-) ***adj.*** ‖ see ANTI- & ARCTIC ‖ of or near the South Pole or the region around it —**the Antarctic** ANTARCTICA

Ant·arc′ti·ca (-ti kə) land area about the South Pole, completely covered by an ice shelf: *c.* 5,500,000 sq. mi.

Antarctic Circle [*also* **a- c-**] an imaginary circle parallel to the equator, *c.* 66°34′ south of it

Antarctic Ocean popularly, the oceans surrounding Antarctica

ant bear a large anteater of Central America and tropical South America

an·te (an′tē) ***n.*** ‖ L, before ‖ *Poker* the stake that each player must put into the pot before receiving cards —***vt., vi.*** **-ted** or **-teed**, **-te·ing** *Poker* to put in (one's ante): also **ante up**

ante- ‖ see prec. ‖ *prefix* before in time or place

ant′eat′er ***n.*** a mammal with a long snout, that feeds mainly on ants

an·te·bel·lum (an′tē bel′əm) ***adj.*** ‖ L ‖ before the war; specif., before the American Civil War

an·te·ced·ent (an′tə sēd′'nt) ***adj.*** ‖ < L *ante-*, before + *cedere*, go ‖ prior; previous —***n.*** **1** any thing prior to another **2** [*pl.*] one's ancestry, past life, etc. **3** *Gram.* the word or phrase to which a pronoun refers

an·te·cham·ber (an′tē chām′bər) ***n.*** a smaller room leading into a larger or main room

an′te·date′ (-dāt′) ***vt.*** **-dat′ed**, **-dat′ing** **1** to put a date on that is earlier than the actual date **2** to come before in time

an·te·di·lu·vi·an (an′tē də lo͞o′vē ən) ***adj.*** ‖ < ANTE- + L *diluvium*, a flood + -AN ‖ **1** of the time before the Biblical Flood **2** very old or old-fashioned

an·te·lope (an′tə lōp′) ***n.*** ‖ < Gr *antholops*, deer ‖ a swift, cud-chewing, horned animal resembling the deer

ANTELOPE (IMPALA)

an·te me·ri·di·em (an′tē mə rid′ē əm) ‖ L ‖ before noon

an·ten·na (an ten′ə) ***n.*** ‖ L, sail yard ‖ **1** *pl.* **-nae** (-ē) or **-nas** either of a pair of feelers on the head of an insect, crab, etc. **2** *pl.* **-nas** *Radio, TV* an arrangement of wires, rods, etc. used in sending and receiving electromagnetic waves

an·te·ri·or (an tir′ē ər) ***adj.*** ‖ < L *ante*, before ‖ **1** at or toward the front **2** previous; earlier

an·te·room (an′tē ro͞om) ***n.*** a room leading to a larger or main room

an·them (an′thəm) ***n.*** ‖ < Gr *anti-*, over against + *phōnē*, voice ‖ **1** a religious choral song **2** a song of praise or devotion, as to a nation

an·ther (an′thər) ***n.*** ‖ < Gr *antheros*, blooming ‖ the part of a stamen that contains the pollen

ant·hill (ant′hil′) ***n.*** the soil heaped up by ants around their nest opening

an·thol·o·gize (an thäl′ə jīz′) ***vi.*** **-gized′**, **-giz′ing** to make anthologies —***vt.*** to include in an anthology —**an·thol′o·gist** (-jist) ***n.***

an·thol·o·gy (an thäl′ə jē) ***n.***, *pl.* **-gies** ‖ < Gr *anthos*, flower + *legein*, gather ‖ a collection of poems, stories, songs, etc.

An·tho·ny (an′thə nē, -tə-), **Mark** *see* ANTONY, Mark

an·thra·cite (an′thrə sīt′) ***n.*** ‖ < Gr *anthrax*, coal ‖ hard coal, which gives much heat and little smoke

an·thrax (an′thraks′) ***n.*** ‖ < Gr, coal, carbuncle ‖ an infectious disease of cattle, sheep, etc. which can be transmitted to man

anthropo- ‖ < Gr *anthrōpos*, man ‖ *combining form* man, human

an·thro·po·cen·tric (an′thrə pō′sen′trik) ***adj.*** ‖ see ANTHROPO- ‖ centering one's view of everything around man, or humans

an·thro·poid (an′thrə poid′) ***adj.*** ‖ see ANTHROPO- & -OID ‖ **1** resembling a human **2** apelike —***n.*** any of certain highly developed primates, as the chimpanzee and gorilla

an·thro·pol·o·gy (an′thrō päl′ə jē) ***n.*** ‖ ANTHROPO- + -LOGY ‖ the study of the characteristics, customs, etc. of humanity —

an'thro·po·log'i·cal (-pō läj'i kəl) ***adj.*** — an'thro·pol'o·gist ***n.***

an'thro·po'mor'phism' (-pō'môr'fiz'əm) ***n.*** the attributing of human characteristics to gods, objects, etc. —**an'thro·po'mor'phic** ***adj.*** —**an'thro·po'mor'phi·cal·ly** ***adv.***

an·ti (an'tī', -tē) ***n.***, *pl.* **-tis'** ‖ < fol. ‖ [Colloq.] a person opposed to something —***prep.*** [Colloq.] opposed to

anti- ‖ < Gr *anti*, against ‖ *prefix* **1** against, hostile to **2** that operates against **3** that prevents, cures, or neutralizes **4** opposite, reverse **5** rivaling Also **ant-**

an·ti·air·craft (an'tī er'kraft') ***adj.*** used against hostile aircraft

an'ti·bal·lis'tic missile (-bə lis'tik) a missile intended to destroy an enemy missile in flight

an'ti·bi·ot'ic (-bī ät'ik, -bē-) ***n.*** ‖ < ANTI- + Gr *bios*, life ‖ any of certain substances, as penicillin or streptomycin, produced by various microorganisms and capable of destroying or weakening bacteria, etc. —***adj.*** of antibiotics

an·ti·bod·y (an'ti bäd'ē) ***n.***, *pl.* **-bod'ies** a protein produced in the body to neutralize an antigen

an·tic (an'tik) ***adj.*** ‖ < L: see ANTIQUE ‖ odd and funny —***n.*** a playful or ludicrous act, trick, etc.

An·ti·christ (an'ti krīst') *Bible* the great opponent of Christ: 1 John 2:18

an·tic·i·pate (an tis'ə pāt') ***vt.*** **-pat'ed, -pat'ing** ‖ < L *ante-*, before + *capere*, take ‖ **1** to look forward to **2** to forestall **3** to use or deal with in advance **4** to be ahead of in doing —**an·tic'i·pa'tion** ***n.*** —**an·tic'i·pa·to'ry** (-pə tôr'ē) ***adj.***

an·ti·cli·max (an'tī klī'maks') ***n.*** **1** a sudden drop from the important to the trivial **2** a descent which is in disappointing contrast to a preceding rise —**an'ti·cli·mac'tic** (-klī mak'tik) ***adj.***

an·ti·cline (an'ti klīn') ***n.*** ‖ < ANTI- + Gr *klinein*, to lean ‖ *Geol.* a sharply arched fold of stratified rock

an·ti·co·ag·u·lant (an'tī kō ag'yoo lənt) ***n.*** a drug or substance that delays or prevents the clotting of blood

an'ti·de·pres'sant (-dē pres'ənt) ***adj.*** lessening emotional depression —***n.*** an antidepressant drug

an·ti·dote (ant'ə dōt') ***n.*** ‖ < Gr *anti-*, against + *dotos*, given ‖ **1** a remedy to counteract a poison **2** anything that works against an evil

an·ti·freeze (an'ti frēz') ***n.*** a substance used, as in the radiator of an automobile, to prevent freezing

an·ti·gen (an'tə jən) ***n.*** ‖ ANTI- + -GEN ‖ a substance to which the body reacts by producing antibodies

An·ti·gua and Bar·bu·da (an tē'gwə 'n bär boo'də) country in the E West Indies comprising three small islands: 171 sq. mi.; pop. 82,000

an·ti·he·ro (an'tī hir'ō) ***n.***, *pl.* **-roes** the protagonist of a novel, etc. who lacks the stature of a traditional hero

an·ti·his·ta·mine (an'tī his'tə mēn', -min) ***n.*** any of several drugs used in treating such allergic conditions as hay fever and hives

an·ti·knock (an'tī näk') ***n.*** a substance added to the fuel of internal-combustion engines to reduce noise resulting from too rapid combustion

An·til·les (an til'ēz') group of islands of the West Indies, including Cuba, Jamaica, etc. (**Greater Antilles**) & the Leeward Islands and Windward Islands (**Lesser Antilles**)

an·ti·log·a·rithm (an'tī lôg'ə rith'əm) ***n.*** the resulting number when a base is raised to a power by a logarithm

an·ti·ma·cas·sar (an'ti mə kas'ər) ***n.*** ‖ ANTI- + *macassar*, a hair oil ‖ a small cover on the back or arms of a chair, sofa, etc. to prevent soiling

an·ti·mat·ter (an'ti mat'ər) ***n.*** a form of matter in which the electrical charge or other property of each particle is the reverse of that in the usual matter of our universe

an·ti·mis·sile (an'tī mis'əl) ***adj.*** designed as a defense against ballistic missiles

an·ti·mo·ny (an'tə mō'nē) ***n.*** ‖ < ML ‖ a silvery-white, nonmetallic chemical element used in alloys to harden them

an·ti·pas·to (an'ti päs'tō, -pas'-) ***n.*** ‖ It < *anti-*, before + *pasto*, food ‖ an appetizer of marinated vegetables, meats, cheeses, etc.

an·tip·a·thy (an tip'ə thē) ***n.***, *pl.* **-thies** ‖ < Gr *anti-*, against + *pathein*, to suffer ‖ **1** strong dislike; aversion **2** the object of such dislike

an·ti·per·son·nel (an'tī pur'sə nel') ***adj.*** intended to destroy people rather than objects [*antipersonnel* mines]

an'ti·per'spi·rant (-pur'spə rənt) ***n.*** a substance applied to the skin to reduce perspiration

an·ti·phon (an'tə fən, -fän') ***n.*** ‖ see ANTHEM ‖ a hymn, psalm, etc. sung in responsive, alternating parts —**an·tiph·o·nal** (an tif'ə nəl) ***adj.***

an·tip·o·des (an tip'ə dēz') ***n.pl.*** ‖ < Gr *anti-*, opposite + *pous*, foot ‖ any two places directly opposite each other on the earth —**an·tip'o·dal** ***adj.***

an·ti·quar·i·an (an'ti kwer'ē ən) ***adj.*** **1** of antiques or antiquities **2** of antiquaries —***n.*** an antiquary

an·ti·quar·y (an'ti kwer'ē) ***n.***, *pl.* **-quar'ies** a collector or student of antiquities

an'ti·quate' (-kwāt') ***vt.*** **-quat'ed, -quat'ing** ‖ see fol. ‖ to make old, out-of-date, or obsolete —**an'ti·quat'ed** ***adj.*** —**an'ti·qua'tion** ***n.***

an·tique (an tēk') ***adj.*** ‖ < L *antiquus*, ancient ‖ **1** of ancient times **2** out-of-date **3** of, or in the style of, a former period **4** dealing in antiques —***n.*** **1** any ancient relic **2** a piece of furniture, etc. from a former period —***vt.*** **-tiqued', -tiqu'ing** to make look antique

an·tiq·ui·ty (an tik'wə tē) ***n.***, *pl.* **-ties** ‖ see prec. ‖ **1** the ancient period of history **2** great age **3** [*pl.*] relics, etc. of the distant past

an·ti·se·mit·ic (an'tī sə mit'ik) ***adj.*** **1** having prejudice against Jews **2** discriminating against or persecuting Jews —**an'ti·sem'ite'** (-sem'īt') ***n.*** —**an'ti·sem'i·tism'** (-ə tiz'əm) ***n.***

an·ti·sep·sis (an'tə sep'sis) ***n.*** ‖ ANTI- + SEPSIS ‖ **1** a being antiseptic **2** the use of antiseptics

an′ti·sep′tic (-tik) ***adj.*** 1 preventing infection, decay, etc.; effective against bacteria, etc. 2 using antiseptics 3 sterile —***n.*** any antiseptic substance —**an′ti·sep′ti·cal·ly** ***adv.***

an·ti·se·rum (an′ti sir′əm) ***n.***, *pl.* **-rums** or **-ra** a serum containing antibodies

an′ti·slav′er·y (an′tī-) ***adj.*** against slavery

an′ti·so′cial ***adj.*** 1 not sociable 2 harmful to the welfare of people

an′ti·tank′ ***adj.*** for use against tanks in war

an·tith·e·sis (an tith′ə sis) ***n.***, *pl.* **-ses′** (-sēz′) ‖ < Gr *anti-*, against + *tithenai*, to place ‖ 1 a contrast or opposition, as of ideas 2 the exact opposite —**an·ti·thet·i·cal** (an′tə thet′i kəl) ***adj.*** —**an′ti·thet′i·cal·ly** ***adv.***

an·ti·tox·in (an′ti täks′in) ***n.*** 1 a circulating antibody formed by the body to act against a specific toxin 2 a serum containing an antitoxin, injected into a person to prevent a disease

an·ti·trust (an′tī trust′) ***adj.*** opposed to or regulating trusts, or business monopolies

an·ti·vi·ral (an′tī vī′rəl) ***adj.*** that can check the growth of a virus

an′ti·viv′i·sec′tion·ist (-viv′ə sek′shən ist) ***n.*** one opposing vivisection

ant·ler (ant′lər) ***n.*** ‖ < OFr *antoillier* ‖ the branched, bony growth on the head of any animal of the deer family —**ant′lered** (-lərd) ***adj.***

An·to·ny (an′tə nē), **Mark** (or **Marc**) *c.* 83-30 B.C.; Rom. general

an·to·nym (an′tə nim′) ***n.*** ‖ < Gr *anti-*, opposite + *onyma*, name ‖ a word meaning the opposite of another

Ant·werp (ant′wərp′) seaport in N Belgium: pop. 487,000

a·nus (ā′nəs) ***n.***, *pl.* **a′nus·es** or **a′ni′** (-nī′) ‖ L ‖ the opening at the lower end of the alimentary canal

ANVIL

an·vil (an′vəl) ***n.*** ‖ < OE *anfilt* ‖ an iron or steel block on which metal objects are hammered into shape

anx·i·e·ty (aŋ zī′ə tē) ***n.***, *pl.* **-ties** ‖ see fol. ‖ 1 worry or uneasiness about what may happen 2 an eager but uneasy desire /*anxiety* to do well/

anx·ious (aŋk′shəs) ***adj.*** ‖ < L *angere*, to choke ‖ 1 worried 2 causing anxiety 3 eagerly wishing —**anx′ious·ly** ***adv.***

an·y (en′ē) ***adj.*** ‖ OE *ænig* ‖ 1 one, no matter which, of more than two /*any* boy may go/ 2 some /has he *any* pain?/ 3 without limit /*any* number can play/ 4 even one or the least amount of /I haven't *any* dimes/ 5 every /*any* child can do it/ —***pron.*** (*sing. & pl.*) any one or ones —***adv.*** to any degree or extent; at all /is he *any* better?/

an′y·bod′y (-bäd′ē, -bud′ē) ***pron.*** 1 any person 2 an important person

an′y·how′ ***adv.*** ANYWAY

an′y·more′ ***adv.*** now; nowadays

an′y·one′ ***pron.*** any person; anybody

any one any single (person or thing)

an′y·place′ ***adv.*** [Colloq.] ANYWHERE

an′y·thing′ ***pron.*** any object, event, fact, etc. —***n.*** a thing, no matter of what kind —***adv.*** in any way —**anything but** not at all

an′y·way′ ***adv.*** 1 in any manner 2 nevertheless; anyhow 3 haphazardly

an′y·where′ ***adv.*** 1 in, at, or to any place 2 [Colloq.] at all —**get anywhere** [Colloq.] to have any success

A/o or **a/o** account of

A-OK (ā′ō kā′) ***adj.*** ‖ A(LL) OK ‖ [Colloq.] excellent, fine, in working order, etc. Also **A′-O·kay′**

A one (ā′ wun′) first-class Also **A 1** or **A number 1**

a·or·ta (ā ôr′tə) ***n.***, *pl.* **-tas** or **-tae** (-tē) ‖ < Gr *aeirein*, to raise ‖ the main artery of the body, carrying blood from the heart —**a·or′tic** or **a·or′tal** ***adj.***

AP Associated Press

a·pace (ə pās′) ***adv.*** at a fast pace

A·pach·e (ə pach′ē) ***n.***, *pl.* **-es** or **-e** ‖ AmSp ‖ a member of a group of SW U.S. Indians

a·part (ə pärt′) ***adv.*** ‖ < L *ad*, to, at + *pars*, part ‖ 1 aside 2 away in place or time 3 in or to pieces —***adj.*** separated —**apart from** other than —**tell apart** to distinguish between

a·part·heid (ə pär′tāt′, -tīt′) ***n.*** ‖ Afrik, separateness ‖ strict racial segregation as practiced in South Africa

a·part′ment ***n.*** ‖ < It *appartare*, to separate ‖ a room or suite of rooms to live in, esp. one of a number in an **apartment building** (or **house**)

ap·a·thy (ap′ə thē) ***n.***, *pl.* **-thies** ‖ < Gr *a-*, without + *pathos*, emotion ‖ 1 lack of emotion 2 indifference; listlessness —**ap′a·thet′ic** (-thet′ik) ***adj.*** —**ap′a·thet′i·cal·ly** ***adv.***

ap·a·tite (ap′ə tīt′) ***n.*** ‖ < Ger < Gr *apatē*, deceit ‖ a mineral incorporating calcium phosphate and found in rocks, bones, and teeth

APB all-points bulletin

ape (āp) ***n.*** ‖ < OE *apa* ‖ 1 any gibbon or great ape 2 loosely, any monkey 3 a mimic 4 a person who is gross or clumsy —***vt.*** **aped, ap′ing** to mimic —**ape′like′** ***adj.***

Ap·en·nines (ap′ə nīnz′) mountain range of central Italy

a·pe·ri·tif (ə per′ə tēf′) ***n.*** ‖ Fr ‖ an alcoholic drink taken before a meal

ap·er·ture (ap′ər chər) ***n.*** ‖ < L *aperire*, to open ‖ an opening; hole

a·pex (ā′peks′) ***n.***, *pl.* **a′pex′es** or **ap·i·ces** (ap′ə sēz′) ‖ L ‖ 1 the highest point 2 the pointed end; tip 3 the climax

a·pha·si·a (ə fā′zhə) ***n.*** ‖ Gr < *a-*, not + *phanai*, to say ‖ loss of the power to use or understand words —**a·pha′sic** (-zik) ***adj.***, ***n.***

a·phe·li·on (ə fē′lē ən) ***n.***, *pl.* **-li·ons** or **-li·a** (-ə) ‖ < Gr *apo-*, from + *hēlios*, sun ‖ the point farthest from the sun in the orbit of a planet or comet, or of a man-made satellite

a·phid (ā′fid, af′id) ***n.*** ‖ < ModL *aphis* ‖ an

insect that lives on plants by sucking their juices

aph·o·rism (af′ə riz′əm) ***n.*** ‖ < Gr *apo-*, from + *horizein*, to bound ‖ a concise statement of a truth; maxim; adage **—aph′o·ris′tic** ***adj.*** **—aph′o·ris′ti·cal·ly** ***adv.***

aph·ro·dis·i·ac (af′rə diz′ē ak′) ***adj.*** ‖ ult. after fol. ‖ arousing sexual desire **—*n.*** an aphrodisiac drug, etc.

Aph·ro·di·te (af′rə dīt′ē) the Greek goddess of love and beauty

a·pi·ar·y (ā′pē er′ē) ***n.***, *pl.* **-ar′ies** ‖ < L *apis*, bee ‖ a place where bees are kept **—a′pi·a·rist** (-ə rist) ***n.***

a·piece (ə pēs′) ***adv.*** ‖ ME *a pece* ‖ for each one; each

a·plen·ty (ə plen′tē) ***adj.***, ***adv.*** [Colloq.] in abundance

a·plomb (ə plăm′, -plum′) ***n.*** ‖ Fr: see PLUMB ‖ self-possession; poise

a·poc·a·lypse (ə päk′ə lips′) ***n.*** ‖ < Gr *apokalyptein*, disclose ‖ any revelation of a violent struggle in which evil will be destroyed —[**A-**] *Bible* the book of Revelation **—a·poc′a·lyp′tic** (-lip′tik) ***adj.***

A·poc·ry·pha (ə päk′rə fə) ‖ < Gr *apo-*, away + *kryptein*, to hide ‖ fourteen books of the Septuagint rejected in Judaism and Protestantism: eleven are in the Roman Catholic Bible

a·poc′ry·phal (-fəl) ***adj.*** **1** of doubtful authenticity **2** not genuine; spurious

ap·o·gee (ap′ə jē′) ***n.*** ‖ < Gr *apo-*, from + *gē*, earth ‖ the point farthest from the earth in the orbit of a satellite

a·po·lit·i·cal (ā′pə lit′i kəl) ***adj.*** not concerned with political matters **—a′po·lit′i·cal·ly** ***adv.***

A·pol·lo (ə päl′ō) the Greek and Roman god of music, poetry, prophecy, and medicine **—*n.***, *pl.* **-los** any handsome young man

a·pol·o·get·ic (ə päl′ə jet′ik) ***adj.*** showing regret; making an apology **—a·pol′o·get′i·cal·ly** ***adv.***

a·pol·o·gist (ə päl′ə jist) ***n.*** one who defends or attempts to justify a doctrine, faith, action, etc.

a·pol′o·gize′ (-jīz′) ***vi.*** **-gized′**, **-giz′ing** to make an apology

a·pol·o·gy (ə päl′ə jē) ***n.***, *pl.* **-gies** ‖ < Gr *apo-*, from + *logos*, speech ‖ **1** a formal defense of some idea, doctrine, etc.: also **ap·o·lo·gi·a** (ap′ə lō′jē ə) **2** an expression of regret for a fault, insult, etc.

ap·o·plex·y (ap′ə plek′sē) ***n.*** ‖ < Gr *apo-*, from + *plēssein*, to strike ‖ severe hemorrhage or infarction, esp. in the brain; stroke **—ap′o·plec′tic** ***adj.***

a·pos·ta·sy (ə päs′tə sē) ***n.***, *pl.* **-sies** ‖ < Gr *apo-*, away + *stasis*, a standing ‖ an abandoning of what one has believed in, as a faith, cause, etc.

a·pos′tate′ (-tāt′) ***n.*** a person guilty of apostasy; renegade

a·pos′ta·tize′ (-tə tīz′) ***vi.*** **-tized′**, **-tiz′ing** to become an apostate

a pos·te·ri·o·ri (ā′ päs tir′ē ôr′ī′) ‖ L ‖ **1** from effect to cause **2** based on observation or experience

a·pos·tle (ə päs′əl) ***n.*** ‖ < Gr *apo-*, from + *stellein*, send ‖ **1** [*usually* **A-**] any of the disciples of Jesus, esp. the original twelve **2** the leader of a new movement

ap·os·tol·ic (ap′əs täl′ik) ***adj.*** **1** of the Apostles, their teachings, work, etc. **2** [*often* **A-**] of the pope; papal

a·pos·tro·phe (ə päs′trə fē) ***n.*** ‖ < Gr *apo-*, from + *strephein*, to turn ‖ **1** a mark (') indicating: *a*) omission of a letter or letters from a word (Ex.: *it's* for *it is*) *b*) the possessive case (Ex.: *Mary's* dress) *c*) certain plural forms (Ex.: five *o's*, dot the *i's*) **2** an exclamatory address to a person or thing

a·poth·e·car·y (ə päth′ə ker′ē) ***n.***, *pl.* **-ies** ‖ < Gr *apothēkē*, storehouse ‖ a pharmacist or druggist

ap·o·thegm (ap′ə them′) ***n.*** ‖ < Gr *apo-*, from + *phthengesthai*, to utter ‖ a short, pithy saying

a·poth·e·o·sis (ə päth′ē ō′sis, ap′ə thē′ə sis) ***n.***, *pl.* **-ses′** (-sēz′) ‖ < Gr *apo-*, from + *theos*, god ‖ **1** the deifying of a person **2** the glorification of a person or thing **3** a glorified ideal

Ap·pa·la·chi·a (ap′ə lā′chə, -chē ə; -lach′ə) the highland region of the E U.S. extending from SW Pa. through N Ala., characterized generally by poverty

Ap′pa·la′chi·an Mountains (-lā′chən, -chē ən; -lach′ən) mountain system extending from S Quebec to N Ala.: also **Ap′pa·la′chi·ans**

ap·pall or **ap·pal** (ə pôl′) ***vt.*** **-palled′**, **-pal′ling** ‖ ult. < L *ad*, to + *pallere*, to be pale ‖ to horrify, dismay, or shock

ap·pa·loo·sa (ap′ə lo͞o′sə) ***n.*** ‖ after *Palouse* Indians of NW U.S. ‖ a Western saddle horse with black and white spots on the rump and loins

ap·pa·ra·tus (ap′ə rat′əs, -rāt′-) ***n.***, *pl.* **-tus** or **-tus·es** ‖ < L *ad-*, to + *parare*, prepare ‖ **1** the materials, tools, etc. for a specific use **2** any complex device, machine, or system

ap·par·el (ə per′əl) ***n.*** ‖ ult. < L *ad-*, to + *parere*, prepare ‖ clothing; attire **—*vt.*** **-eled** or **-elled**, **-el·ing** or **-el·ling** to clothe; dress

ap·par·ent (ə per′ənt) ***adj.*** ‖ see APPEAR ‖ **1** readily seen; visible **2** evident; obvious **3** appearing real or true **—ap·par′ent·ly** ***adv.***

ap·pa·ri·tion (ap′ə rish′ən) ***n.*** ‖ see APPEAR ‖ **1** anything that appears unexpectedly or strangely **2** a ghost; phantom **3** a becoming visible

ap·peal (ə pēl′) ***vt.*** ‖ < L *ad-*, to + *pellere*, to drive ‖ to make an appeal of (a case) **—*vi.*** **1** to appeal a law case to a higher court **2** to make an urgent request (*for* help, etc.) **3** to be attractive or interesting **—*n.*** **1** a call upon some authority for a decision **2** a request for the transference of a case to a higher court for rehearing **3** a request for help, etc. **4** attraction; interest **—ap·peal′ing** ***adj.***

ap·pear (ə pir′) ***vi.*** ‖ < L *ad-*, to + *perere*, be visible ‖ **1** to come into sight **2** to become understood or obvious **3** to seem; look **4** to present oneself formally in court **5** to come before the public

ap·pear′ance ***n.*** **1** an appearing **2** the look or outward aspect of anything **3** an outward show; pretense **—keep up appearances** to maintain an outward show of being proper, etc.

ap·pease (ə pēz′) ***vt.*** **-peased′**, **-peas′ing** ‖ ult. < L *ad*, to + *pax*, peace ‖ to pacify, quiet, or satisfy, esp. by giving in to the demands of —**ap·pease′ment** ***n.*** —**ap·peas′er** ***n.***

ap·pel·lant (ə pel′ənt) ***n.*** a person who appeals to a higher court

ap·pel′late (-it) ***adj.*** *Law* having to do with appeals /an *appellate* court/

ap·pel·la·tion (ap′ə lā′shən) ***n.*** ‖see APPEAL‖ 1 a naming 2 a title

ap·pend (ə pend′) ***vt.*** ‖< L *ad-*, to + *pendere*, hang‖ to attach or affix; add as a supplement or appendix

ap·pend′age ***n.*** 1 anything appended 2 any external organ or part, as a tail

ap·pen·dec·to·my (ap′ən dek′tə mē) ***n.***, *pl.* **-mies** ‖see -ECTOMY‖ the surgical removal of the appendix

ap·pen·di·ci·tis (ə pen′də sīt′is) ***n.*** ‖see -ITIS‖ inflammation of the appendix

ap·pen·dix (ə pen′diks) ***n.***, *pl.* **-dix·es** or **-di·ces′** (-də sēz′) ‖L, appendage‖ 1 additional material at the end of a book 2 a small, saclike appendage of the large intestine

ap·per·tain (ap′ər tān′) ***vi.*** ‖< L *ad-*, to + *pertinere*, to reach‖ to belong as a function, part, etc.; pertain

ap·pe·ten·cy (ap′ə tən sē) ***n.***, *pl.* **-cies** ‖see fol.‖ 1 a craving; appetite 2 a propensity 3 a natural attraction

ap·pe·tite (ap′ə tīt′) ***n.*** ‖< L *ad-*, to + *petere*, to desire‖ 1 a desire for food 2 any strong desire or craving

ap′pe·tiz′er (-tī′zər) ***n.*** a small portion of a tasty food to stimulate the appetite

ap′pe·tiz′ing ***adj.*** 1 stimulating the appetite 2 savory; delicious

ap·plaud (ə plôd′) ***vt., vi.*** ‖< L *ad-*, to + *plaudere*, clap hands‖ 1 to show approval (of) by clapping the hands, etc. 2 to praise —**ap·plaud′er** ***n.***

ap·plause (ə plôz′) ***n.*** approval, esp. as shown by clapping hands

ap·ple (ap′əl) ***n.*** ‖< OE *æppel*, fruit, apple‖ 1 a round, firm, edible fruit 2 the tree it grows on

apple butter a thick spread made from apples stewed with spices

ap′ple·jack′ (-jak′) ***n.*** brandy distilled from fermented cider

ap′ple·sauce′ (-sôs′) ***n.*** apples cooked to a pulp in water and sweetened

ap·pli·ance (ə plī′əns) ***n.*** a device or machine, esp. one for household use

ap·pli·ca·ble (ap′li kə bəl) ***adj.*** that can be applied; appropriate —**ap′pli·ca·bil′i·ty** (-bil′ə tē) ***n.***

ap′pli·cant (-kənt) ***n.*** one who applies, as for employment, help, etc.

ap·pli·ca·tion (ap′li kā′shən) ***n.*** 1 an applying 2 anything applied, as a remedy 3 a specific use 4 a request, or a form filled out in making one /an employment *application*/ 5 continued effort; diligence 6 relevance or practicality

ap′pli·ca′tor ***n.*** any device for applying medicine or paint, polish, etc.

ap·plied (ə plīd′) ***adj.*** used in actual practice /*applied* science/

ap·pli·qué (ap′li kā′) ***n.*** ‖Fr‖ a decoration made of one material attached to another —***vt.*** **-quéd′**, **-qué′ing** to decorate with appliqué

ap·ply (ə plī′) ***vt.*** **-plied′**, **-ply′ing** ‖< L *ad-*, to + *plicare*, to fold‖ 1 to put or spread on /*apply* glue/ 2 to put to practical or specific use /*apply* your knowledge/ 3 to devote (oneself or one's faculties) diligently —***vi.*** 1 to make a formal request 2 to be suitable or relevant —**ap·pli′er** ***n.***

ap·point (ə point′) ***vt.*** ‖< L *ad*, to + *punctum*, a point‖ 1 to set (a date, place, etc.) 2 to name for an office, position, etc. 3 to furnish /well-*appointed*/ —**ap·point′ee′** ***n.***

ap·point′ive ***adj.*** of or filled by appointment /an *appointive* office/

ap·point′ment ***n.*** 1 an appointing or being appointed 2 a position filled by appointing 3 an engagement to meet someone or be somewhere 4 [*pl.*] furniture; equipment

Ap·po·mat·tox (Court House) (ap′ə mat′əks) former village in central Va., where Lee surrendered to Grant (1865)

ap·por·tion (ə pôr′shən) ***vt.*** ‖see AD- & PORTION‖ to distribute in shares according to a plan —**ap·por′tion·ment** ***n.***

ap·pose (ə pōz′) ***vt.*** **-posed′**, **-pos′ing** ‖< L *ad-*, to + *ponere*, put‖ to put side by side or opposite

ap·po·site (ap′ə zit) ***adj.*** ‖see prec.‖ appropriate; apt —**ap′po·site·ly** ***adv.*** —**ap′po·site·ness** ***n.***

ap·po·si·tion (ap′ə zish′ən) ***n.*** 1 an apposing, or the position resulting from this 2 the placing of a word or phrase beside another in explanation, as *my cousin* in "Mary, my cousin, is here" —**ap·pos·i·tive** (ə päz′ə tiv) ***adj., n.***

ap·prais·al (ə prāz′əl) ***n.*** 1 an appraising 2 an appraised value

ap·praise (ə prāz′) ***vt.*** **-praised′**, **-prais′ing** ‖< L *ad*, to + *pretium*, price‖ 1 to set a price for; estimate the value of 2 to judge the quality or worth of —**ap·prais′er** ***n.***

ap·pre·ci·a·ble (ə prē′shə bəl, -shē ə-) ***adj.*** ‖see prec.‖ enough to be perceived or estimated; noticeable —**ap·pre′ci·a·bly** ***adv.***

ap·pre·ci·ate (ə prē′shē āt′) ***vt.*** **-at′ed**, **-at′ing** ‖see APPRAISE‖ 1 to think well of; esteem 2 to recognize gratefully 3 to estimate the quality of 4 to be fully or sensitively aware of —***vi.*** to rise in value —**ap·pre′ci·a′tor** ***n.*** —**ap·pre′ci·a·to′ry** (-shə tôr′ē, -shē ə-) ***adj.***

ap·pre′ci·a′tion ***n.*** 1 grateful recognition, as of a favor 2 sensitive awareness, as of art 3 a rise in value or price

ap·pre′ci·a·tive (-shə tiv, -shē ə-) ***adj.*** feeling or showing appreciation —**ap·pre′ci·a·tive·ly** ***adv.***

ap·pre·hend (ap′rē hend′) ***vt.*** ‖< L *ad-*, to + *prehendere*, seize‖ 1 to capture or arrest 2 to perceive; understand 3 to fear; dread

ap′pre·hen′sion (-hen′shən) ***n.*** 1 capture or arrest 2 perception or understanding 3 fear; anxiety

ap′pre·hen′sive (-siv) ***adj.*** anxious; uneasy —**ap′pre·hen′sive·ly** ***adv.*** —**ap′pre·hen′sive·ness** ***n.***

ap·pren·tice (ə pren′tis) ***n.*** ‖see APPREHEND‖ 1 a person being taught a craft or trade, now usually as a member of a labor union 2 any beginner —***vt.*** **-ticed**, **-tic·ing** to place or accept as an apprentice —**ap·pren′tice·ship′** ***n.***

ap·prise or **ap·prize** (ə prīz′) *vt.* **-prised′** or **-prized′**, **-pris′ing** or **-priz′ing** ⟦see APPREHEND⟧ to notify

ap·proach (ə prōch′) *vi.* ⟦< L *ad-*, to + *propius*, nearer⟧ to come closer —*vt.* **1** to come nearer to **2** to approximate **3** to make a proposal or request to **4** to begin dealing with —*n.* **1** a coming closer **2** an approximation **3** an overture (*to* someone): *usually used in pl.* **4** a means of reaching a person or place; access **5** a means of attaining a goal —**ap·proach′a·ble** *adj.*

ap·pro·ba·tion (ap′rə bā′shən) *n.* ⟦see APPROVE⟧ approval

ap·pro·pri·ate (ə prō′prē āt′; *for adj.*, -it) *vt.* **-at′ed**, **-at′ing** ⟦< L *ad-*, to + *proprius*, one's own⟧ **1** to take for one's own use, often improperly **2** to set aside (money, etc.) for a specific use —*adj.* suitable; fit; proper —**ap·pro′pri·ate·ly** *adv.* —**ap·pro′pri·ate·ness** *n.* —**ap·pro′pri·a′tor** *n.*

ap·pro′pri·a′tion *n.* **1** an appropriating or being appropriated **2** money set aside for a specific use

ap·prov·al (ə pro͞o′vəl) *n.* **1** the act of approving **2** favorable attitude or opinion **3** formal consent —**on approval** for the customer to examine and decide whether to buy or return

ap·prove (ə pro͞ov′) *vt.* **-proved′**, **-prov′ing** ⟦< L *ad-*, to + *probus*, good⟧ **1** to give one's consent to **2** to consider to be good, satisfactory, etc. —*vi.* to have a favorable opinion (*of*) —**ap·prov′ing·ly** *adv.*

ap·prox·i·mate (ə präk′sə mit; *for v.*, -māt′) *adj.* ⟦< L *ad-*, to + *proximus*, nearest⟧ **1** much like; resembling **2** more or less correct or exact —*vt.* **-mat′ed**, **-mat′ing** to come near to; be almost the same as —**ap·prox′i·mate·ly** *adv.*

ap·prox′i·ma′tion (-mā′shən) *n.* an estimate or guess that is approximately correct

ap·pur·te·nance (ə purt′′n əns) *n.* ⟦see APPERTAIN⟧ **1** anything added to a more important thing **2** [*pl.*] apparatus or equipment **3** *Law* an incidental right attached to some thing

ap·ri·cot (ap′ri kät′, ā′pri-) *n.* ⟦< L *praecoquum*, early matured (fruit)⟧ **1** a small, yellowish-orange, peachlike fruit **2** the tree it grows on

A·pril (ā′prəl) *n.* ⟦< L⟧ the fourth month of the year, having 30 days: abbrev. **Apr.**

a pri·o·ri (ā′ prī ôr′ī) ⟦L⟧ **1** from cause to effect **2** based on theory instead of experience

a·pron (ā′prən) *n.* ⟦< L *mappa*, napkin⟧ **1** a garment worn over the front part of the body to protect one's clothes **2** any extending or protecting part **3** a paved area, as where a driveway broadens to meet the road **4** the front part of a stage

ap·ro·pos (ap′rə pō′) *adv.* ⟦Fr *à propos*, to the purpose⟧ at the right time; opportunely —*adj.* relevant; apt —**apropos of** with regard to

apse (aps) *n.* ⟦L *apsis*, an arch⟧ a semicircular or polygonal projection of a church, usually domed or vaulted

apt (apt) *adj.* ⟦< L *aptus*⟧ **1** appropriate; fitting **2** tending or inclined; likely **3** quick to learn —**apt′ly** *adv.* —**apt′ness** *n.*

apt. apartment

ap·ti·tude (ap′tə to͞od′, -tyo͞od′) *n.* ⟦see APT⟧ **1** suitability; fitness **2** a natural tendency, ability, or talent **3** quickness to learn

aq·ua (ak′wə, äk′-) *n.*, *pl.* **-uas** or **-uae′** (-wē′) ⟦L⟧ water —*adj.* ⟦< AQUAMARINE⟧ bluish-green

aq′ua·cul′ture (-kul′chər) *n.* ⟦prec. + CULTURE⟧ the cultivation of water plants and animals for human use

aq·ua·ma·rine (ak′wə mə rēn′, äk′-) *n.* ⟦L *aqua marina*, sea water⟧ bluish green —*adj.* bluish-green

aq·ua·naut (ak′wə nôt′, äk′-) *n.* ⟦AQUA + (ASTRO)NAUT⟧ one trained to use a watertight underwater chamber as a base for undersea experiments

aq′ua·plane′ (-plān′) *n.* ⟦AQUA + PLANE[1]⟧ a board on which one rides standing up as it is pulled by a motorboat —*vi.* **-planed′**, **-plan′ing** to ride on such a board as a sport

a·quar·i·um (ə kwer′ē əm) *n.*, *pl.* **-i·ums** or **-i·a** (-ə) ⟦< L *aquarius*, of water⟧ **1** a tank, etc. for keeping live water animals and plants **2** a building where such collections are exhibited

A·quar′i·us (-əs) ⟦L, water carrier⟧ the 11th sign of the zodiac

a·quat·ic (ə kwat′ik, -kwät′-) *adj.* **1** growing or living in water **2** done in or upon the water [*aquatic* sports]

aq·ua·vit (ak′wə vēt′, äk′-) *n.* ⟦< L *aqua vitae*, water of life⟧ a Scandinavian alcoholic liquor distilled from grain or potatoes and flavored with caraway

aq·ue·duct (ak′wə dukt′) *n.* ⟦< L *aqua*, water + *ductus*, leading⟧ **1** a large pipe or conduit for bringing water from a distant source **2** an elevated structure supporting this

a·que·ous (ā′kwē əs, ak′wē-) *adj.* of, like, or formed by water

aqueous humor a watery fluid filling chambers in front of the lens of the eye

aq·ui·fer (ak′wə fər, äk′-) *n.* ⟦< L *aqua*, water + *ferre*, carry⟧ an underground layer of porous rock, etc. containing water

aq·ui·line (ak′wə līn′, -lin) *adj.* ⟦< L *aquila*, eagle⟧ **1** of or like an eagle **2** curved like an eagle's beak [an *aquiline* nose]

A·qui·nas (ə kwī′nəs), Saint **Thom·as** (täm′əs) *c.* 1225-74; It. theologian & philosopher

Ar *Chem. symbol for* argon

AR Arkansas

Ar·ab (ar′əb, er′-) *n.* **1** a native of Arabia **2** any of a Semitic people orig. native to Arabia; popularly, a Bedouin

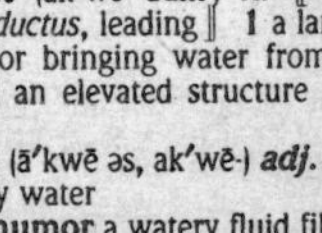

ARABESQUE

ar·a·besque (ar′ə besk′, er′-) *n.* ⟦< It *Arabo*, Arab⟧ an elaborate design of intertwined lines suggesting flowers, foliage, etc.

A·ra·bi·a (ə rā′bē ə) peninsula in SW Asia —**A·ra′bi·an** *adj.*, *n.*

Arabian camel the one-humped camel ranging from N Africa to India
Arabian Nights, The a collection of tales from Arabia, India, Persia, etc.
Arabian Peninsula ARABIA
Ar·a·bic (ar′ə bik, er′-) ***adj.*** 1 of Arabia 2 of the Arabs —***n.*** the Semitic language of the Arabs, spoken in Arabia, Syria, Jordan, Iraq, N Africa, etc.
Arabic numerals the figures 1, 2, 3, 4, 5, 6, 7, 8, 9, and the 0 (zero)
ar·a·ble (ar′ə bəl) ***adj.*** ‖ < L *arare,* to plow ‖ suitable for plowing
a·rach·nid (ə rak′nid) ***n.*** ‖ < Gr *arachnē,* spider ‖ any of a class of arthropods with four pairs of legs, including spiders and scorpions
Ar·a·ma·ic (ar′ə mā′ik) ***n.*** a Semitic language spoken during Biblical times
ar·bi·ter (är′bət ər) ***n.*** ‖ L, a witness ‖ an arbitrator; judge
ar·bit·ra·ment (är bi′trə mənt) ***n.*** 1 arbitration 2 an arbitrator's verdict or award
ar·bi·trar·y (är′bə trer′ē) ***adj.*** ‖ see ARBITER ‖ 1 left to one's judgment 2 based on one's preference or whim; capricious 3 absolute; despotic —**ar′bi·trar′i·ly** ***adv.*** —**ar′bi·trar′i·ness** ***n.***
ar·bi·trate (är′bə trāt′) ***vt., vi.*** **-trat′ed, -trat′ing** ‖ see ARBITER ‖ 1 to submit (a dispute) to an arbitrator 2 to decide (a dispute) as an arbitrator —**ar′bi·tra′tion** ***n.***
ar′bi·tra′tor ***n.*** a person selected to judge a dispute
ar·bor (är′bər) ***n.*** ‖ < L *herba,* herb ‖ a place shaded by trees, shrubs, or vines on a latticework; bower
ar·bo·re·al (är bôr′ē əl) ***adj.*** ‖ < L *arbor,* tree ‖ 1 of or like a tree 2 living in trees
ar·bo·re·tum (är′bə rēt′əm) ***n., pl.*** **-tums** or **-ta** (-ə) ‖ L ‖ a place where many kinds of trees and shrubs are grown for exhibition or study
ar·bor·vi·tae (är′bər vīt′ē) ***n.*** ‖ L, tree of life ‖ any of various cypress trees having sprays of scalelike leaves
ar·bu·tus (är byo͞ot′əs) ***n.*** ‖ L ‖ 1 a tree or shrub with dark-green leaves and strawberrylike fruit 2 a trailing plant with white or pink flower clusters
arc (ärk) ***n.*** ‖ < L *arcus,* a bow, arch ‖ 1 a bowlike curved line or object 2 the band of incandescent light formed when a current leaps a short gap between electrodes 3 any part of a curve, esp. of a circle —***vi.*** **arced** or **arcked, arc′ing** or **arck′ing** to move in a curved course or form an arc
ar·cade (är kād′) ***n.*** ‖ see prec. ‖ 1 a covered passageway, esp. one lined with shops 2 a line of arches and their supporting columns
ar·cane (är kān′) ***adj.*** ‖ < L *arcanus,* hidden ‖ secret or esoteric
arch[1] (ärch) ***n.*** ‖ see ARC ‖ 1 a curved structure used as a support over an open space, as in a doorway 2 the form of an arch 3 anything shaped like an arch —***vt.*** to span with or as an arch —***vi.*** to form an arch
arch[2] (ärch) ***adj.*** ‖ < fol. ‖ 1 chief; principal 2 gaily mischievous; pert
arch- ‖ < Gr *archos,* first, ruler ‖ *prefix* chief, principal *[archenemy]*
-arch (ärk) ‖ see prec. ‖ *suffix* ruler *[matriarch]*
arch. 1 archaic 2 architecture
ar·chae·ol·o·gy (är′kē äl′ə jē) ***n.*** ‖ < Gr *archaios,* ancient + -LOGY ‖ the study of the life of ancient peoples, as by excavation of ancient cities, etc. Also sp. **archeology** —**ar′chae·o·log′i·cal** (-ə läj′i kəl) ***adj.*** —**ar′chae·o·log′i·cal·ly** ***adv.*** —**ar′chae·ol′o·gist** ***n.***
ar·cha·ic (är kā′ik) ***adj.*** ‖ < Gr *archaios,* ancient ‖ 1 ancient 2 old-fashioned 3 no longer used except in poetry, church ritual, etc., as the word *thou* —**ar·cha′i·cal·ly** ***adv.***
ar·cha·ism (är′kā iz′m) ***n.*** an archaic word, usage, style, etc. —**ar′cha·ist** ***n.***
arch·an·gel (ärk′ān′jəl) ***n.*** an angel of high rank
arch·bish·op (ärch′bish′əp) ***n.*** a bishop of the highest rank —**arch′bish′op·ric** (-rik) ***n.***
arch′dea′con (-dē′kən) ***n.*** a church official ranking just below a bishop
arch′di′o·cese′ ***n.*** the diocese of an archbishop —**arch′di·oc′e·san** (-dī äs′ə sən) ***adj.***
arch′duke′ (-do͞ok′) ***n.*** a prince of the former Austrian imperial family —**arch′duch′ess** ***n.fem.***
arch′en′e·my ***n., pl.*** **-mies** a chief enemy —**the archenemy** Satan
arch·er (är′chər) ***n.*** ‖ < L *arcus,* bow ‖ one who shoots with bow and arrow
arch′er·y ***n.*** the sport of shooting with bow and arrow
ar·che·type (är′kə tīp′) ***n.*** ‖ < Gr *archos,* first + *typos,* a mark ‖ an original pattern, or model; prototype —**ar′che·typ′al** (-tīp′əl) or **ar′che·typ′i·cal** (-tip′i kəl) ***adj.***
ar·chi·e·pis·co·pal (är′kē ē pis′kə pəl) ***adj.*** of or related to an archbishop
Ar·chi·me·des (är′kə mē′dēz′) *c.* 287-212 B.C.; Gr. mathematician & inventor
ar·chi·pel·a·go (är′kə pel′ə gō′) ***n., pl.*** **-goes′** or **-gos′** ‖ < Gr *archi-,* chief + *pelagos,* sea ‖ 1 a sea with many islands 2 a group of many islands
ar·chi·tect (är′kə tekt′) ***n.*** ‖ < Gr *archi-,* chief + *tektōn,* carpenter ‖ 1 one who designs buildings and supervises their construction 2 any designer or planner
ar·chi·tec·ton·ics (är′kə tek tän′iks) ***n.pl.*** *[usually with sing. v.]* 1 the science of architecture 2 structural design, as of a symphony —**ar′chi·tec·ton′ic** ***adj.***
ar·chi·tec·ture (är′kə tek′chər) ***n.*** 1 the science or profession of designing and constructing buildings 2 a style of construction 3 design and construction —**ar′chi·tec′tur·al** ***adj.*** —**ar′chi·tec′tur·al·ly** ***adv.***
ar·chi·trave (är′kə trāv′) ***n.*** ‖ < L *archi-,* first + *trabs,* a beam ‖ in a classical building, the beam resting directly on the tops of the columns
ar·chive (är′kīv′) ***n.*** ‖ < Gr *archeion,* town hall ‖ *[usually pl.]* 1 a place for keeping public records, documentary material, etc. 2 the records, material, etc. kept there —**ar·chi·vist** (är′kə vist, -kī′-) ***n.***
arch·way (ärch′wā′) ***n.*** a passage under an arch, or the arch itself
-ar·chy (är kē) ‖ < Gr *archein,* to rule ‖ *combining form* ruling *[monarchy]*

arc·tic (ärk'tik, är'-) ***adj.*** ‖ < Gr *arktikos,* northern ‖ 1 of near the North Pole 2 very cold —**the Arctic** the region around the North Pole

Arctic Circle [*also* **a- c-**] an imaginary circle parallel to the equator, *c.* 66°34' north of it

Arctic Ocean ocean surrounding the North Pole

-ard (ərd) ‖ < MHG *hart,* bold ‖ *suffix* one who does something to excess [*drunkard*]

ar·dent (ärd''nt) ***adj.*** ‖ < L *ardere,* to burn ‖ 1 passionate 2 zealous 3 glowing or burning —**ar'dent·ly** ***adv.***

ar·dor (är'dər) ***n.*** ‖ < L *ardor,* a flame ‖ 1 emotional warmth; passion 2 zeal 3 intense heat Also Brit., etc. sp., **ar'dour** ***n.***

ar·du·ous (är'jo͞o əs) ***adj.*** ‖ L *arduus,* steep ‖ 1 difficult to do; laborious 2 using much energy; strenuous —**ar'du·ous·ly** ***adv.***

are (är) ***vi.*** ‖ OE *aron* ‖ *pl. & 2d pers. sing., pres. indic., of* BE

ar·e·a (er'ē ə) ***n.*** ‖ L, vacant place ‖ 1 a part of the earth's surface; region 2 the measure, in square units, of a surface 3 a location having a specific use or character [play *area*] 4 scope or extent

area code a three-digit telephone code assigned to a specific area of the U.S., Canada, etc.

a·re·na (ə rē'nə) ***n.*** ‖ L, sandy place ‖ 1 a place or building for contests, shows, etc. 2 any sphere of struggle [political *arena*]

arena theater a theater having a central stage surrounded by seats

aren't (ärnt) are not

Ar·es (er'ēz') *Gr. Myth.* the god of war

ar·gent (är'jənt) ***adj.*** ‖ L *argentum,* silver ‖ [Old Poet.] silvery

Ar·gen·ti·na (är'jən tē'nə) country in S South America: 1,070,000 sq. mi.; pop. 31,186,000 —**Ar'gen·tine'** (-tēn', -tīn') ***adj., n.***

ar·gon (är'gän') ***n.*** ‖ Gr, inert ‖ a chemical element, a nonreactive gas found in the air and used in light bulbs, radio tubes, etc.

Ar·go·naut (är'gə nôt') ***n.*** *Gr. Myth.* any of those who sail with Jason to search for the Golden Fleece

ar·go·sy (är'gə sē) ***n.,*** *pl.* **-sies** ‖ after *Ragusa,* It name of Dubrovnik in Croatia ‖ [Old Poet.] a large merchant ship or a fleet of such ships

ar·got (är'gō, -gət) ***n.*** ‖ Fr ‖ the specialized vocabulary of a particular group, as of criminals

ar·gue (är'gyo͞o) ***vi.*** **-gued, -gu·ing** ‖ < L *arguere,* prove ‖ 1 to give reasons (*for* or *against*) 2 to quarrel; dispute —***vt.*** 1 to discuss; debate 2 to maintain; contend 3 to persuade by giving reasons —**ar'gu·a·ble** ***adj.***

ar·gu·ment (är'gyo͞o mənt) ***n.*** 1 a reason or reasons offered in arguing 2 an arguing; debate 3 a summary

ar'gu·men·ta'tion (-men tā'shən) ***n.*** the process of arguing; debate

ar'gu·men'ta·tive (-men'tə tiv) ***adj.*** 1 controversial 2 apt to argue; contentious Also **ar'gu·men'tive**

ar·gyle (är'gīl') ***adj.*** ‖ after *Argyll,* Scotland ‖ knitted or woven in a diamond-shaped pattern, as socks

a·ri·a (ä'rē ə) ***n.*** ‖ It < L *aer,* air ‖ a song, as in an opera, for solo voice

-ar·i·an (er'ē ən, ar'-) ‖ < L ‖ *suffix* 1 (one) characterized by [*octogenarian*] 2 (one) believing in or associated with [*Unitarian*]

ar·id (ar'id, er'-) ***adj.*** ‖ < L *arere,* be dry ‖ 1 dry and barren 2 uninteresting; dull —**a·rid·i·ty** (ə rid'ə tē) ***n.***

Ar·i·es (er'ēz') ‖ L, the Ram ‖ the first sign of the zodiac

a·right (ə rīt') ***adv.*** correctly

a·rise (ə rīz') ***vi.*** **a·rose'** (-rōz'), **a·ris'en** (-riz'-ən), **a·ris'ing** ‖ < OE *a-,* out + *risan,* to rise ‖ 1 to get up, as from sleeping 2 to ascend 3 to come into being 4 to result (*from*)

ar·is·toc·ra·cy (ar'i stä'krə sē) ***n.,*** *pl.* **-cies** ‖ < Gr *aristos,* best + *kratos,* to rule ‖ 1 government by a privileged minority, usually of inherited wealth 2 a country with such government 3 a privileged ruling class

a·ris·to·crat (ə ris'tə krat') ***n.*** 1 a member of the aristocracy 2 one with the tastes, manners, etc. of the upper class —**a·ris'to·crat'ic** ***adj.***

Ar·is·toph·a·nes (ar'i stäf'ə nēz') *c.* 450-*c.* 388 B.C.; Greek writer of comedies

Ar·is·tot·le (ar'is tät''l, er'-) 384-322 B.C.; Gr. philosopher —**Ar·is·to·te·li·an** (ar'is tə tēl'yən) ***adj., n.***

a·rith·me·tic (ə rith'mə tik) ***n.*** ‖ < Gr *arithmos,* number ‖ the science or art of computing by positive, real numbers —**ar·ith·met·i·cal** (ar'ith met'i kəl) or **ar'ith·met'ic** ***adj.*** —**ar'ith·me·ti·cian** (-mə tish'-ən) ***n.***

arithmetic mean the average obtained by dividing a sum by the number of its addends

Ar·i·zo·na (ar'ə zō'nə, er'-) State of the SW U.S.: 113,909 sq. mi.; pop. 2,718,000; cap. Phoenix: abbrev. **Ariz.** —**Ar'i·zo'nan** ***adj., n.***

ark (ärk) ***n.*** ‖ < L *arcere,* enclose ‖ 1 ARK OF THE COVENANT 2 an enclosure in a synagogue for the scrolls of the Torah 3 *Bible* the boat in which Noah, his family, and two of every kind of creature survived the Flood

Ar·kan·sas (är'kən sô') State of the south central U.S.: 53,104 sq. mi.; pop. 2,286,000; cap. Little Rock: abbrev. **Ark.** —**Ar·kan·san** (-kan'zən) ***adj., n.***

ark of the covenant the chest containing the two stone tablets inscribed with the Ten Commandments

Ar·ling·ton (är'liŋ tən) city in NE Tex.: pop. 160,000

arm[1] (ärm) ***n.*** ‖ OE *earm* ‖ 1 an upper limb of the human body 2 anything like this in shape, function, position, etc. —**with open arms** cordially

arm[2] (ärm) ***n.*** ‖ < L *arma,* weapons ‖ 1 a weapon: *usually used in pl.* 2 any branch of the military forces —***vt.*** to provide with weapons, etc. —***vi.*** to prepare for war or any struggle —**under arms** ready for war —**up in arms** 1 prepared to fight 2 indignant

ar·ma·da (är mä'də) ***n.*** ‖ Sp < L *arma,* weapons ‖ 1 a fleet of warships 2 a fleet of military aircraft

ar·ma·dil·lo (är'mə dil'ō) ***n.,*** *pl.* **-los** ‖ Sp: see prec. ‖ a burrowing mammal of tropical America, covered with bony plates

Ar·ma·ged·don (är'mə ged''n) *n.* 1 *Bible* the site of the last, decisive battle between the forces of good and evil 2 any great, decisive battle
ar·ma·ment (är'mə mənt) *n.* ‖ < L *armare*, to arm ‖ 1 [*often pl.*] all the military forces and equipment of a nation 2 all the military equipment of a warship, tank, etc. 3 an arming or being armed for war
ar·ma·ture (är'mə chər) *n.* ‖ < L *armare*, to arm ‖ 1 any protective covering 2 the iron core wound with wire in which electromotive force is produced in a generator or motor
arm'chair' *n.* a chair with supports at the sides for one's arms
armed forces all the military, naval, and air forces of a country
Ar·me·ni·a (är mēn'yə, -mē'nē ə) former kingdom of SW Asia, now mostly a republic of the U.S.S.R. —**Ar·me'ni·an** *adj., n.*
arm·ful (ärm'fool) *n., pl.* **-fuls** as much as the arms or one arm can hold
arm'hole' *n.* an opening for the arm in a garment
ar·mi·stice (är'mə stis) *n.* ‖ < L *arma*, weapons + *stare*, to stand ‖ a truce preliminary to the signing of a peace treaty
Armistice Day VETERANS DAY
arm·let (ärm'lət) *n.* an ornamental band worn around the upper arm
ar·mor (är'mər) *n.* ‖ < L *armare*, to arm ‖ any defensive or protective covering —*vt., vi.* to put armor on —**ar'mored** (-mərd) *adj.*
armored car a vehicle covered with armor plate, as a truck for carrying money to or from a bank
ar·mo·ri·al (är môr'ē əl) *adj.* of coats of arms; heraldic
ar·mor·y (är'mər ē) *n., pl.* **-mor·ies** ‖ see ARMOR ‖ 1 an arsenal 2 a National Guard unit drill hall
arm'pit' *n.* the hollow under the arm at the shoulder
arm'rest' *n.* a support for the arm, as on the inside of an automobile door
ar·my (är'mē) *n., pl.* **-mies** ‖ ult. < L *arma*, weapons ‖ 1 a large, organized body of soldiers for waging war, esp. on land 2 a large number of persons, animals, etc. /an *army* of ants/
Ar·nold (är'nəld), **Ben·e·dict** (ben'ə dikt') 1741-1801; Am. Revolutionary general who became a traitor
a·ro·ma (ə rō'mə) *n.* ‖ < Gr *arōma*, spice ‖ a pleasant odor; fragrance
ar·o·mat·ic (ar'ə mat'ik) *adj.* of or having an aroma; fragrant or pungent —*n.* an aromatic plant, chemical, etc. —**ar'o·mat'i·cal·ly** *adv.*
a·rose (ə rōz') *vi. pt. of* ARISE
a·round (ə round') *adv.* ‖ ME ‖ 1 in a circle 2 in every direction 3 in circumference 4 to the opposite direction 5 [Colloq.] nearby /stay *around*/ —*prep.* 1 so as to encircle or envelop 2 on the border of 3 in various places in or on 4 about /*around* 1890/
a·rouse (ə rouz') *vt.* **a·roused', a·rous'ing** 1 to awaken, as from sleep 2 to stir, as to action 3 to evoke /to *arouse* pity/ —**a·rous'al** *n.*
ar·peg·gio (är pej'ō) *n., pl.* **-gios** ‖ It < *arpa*, a harp ‖ a chord whose notes are played in quick succession
ar·raign (ə rān') *vt.* ‖ < L *ad*, to + *ratio*, reason ‖ 1 to bring before a law court to answer charges 2 to call to account; accuse —**ar·raign'ment** *n.*
ar·range (ə rānj') *vt.* **-ranged', -rang'ing** ‖ < OFr *a-*, to + *renger*, to range ‖ 1 to put in the correct order 2 to classify 3 to prepare or plan 4 to arrive at an agreement about 5 *Music* to adapt (a composition) to particular instruments or voices —*vi. Music* to write arrangements, esp. as a profession —**ar·rang'er** *n.*
ar·range'ment *n.* 1 an arranging 2 a result or manner of arranging 3 [*usually pl.*] a plan 4 a settlement 5 *Music a*) an arranging of a composition *b*) the composition as thus arranged
ar·rant (ar'ənt) *adj.* ‖ var. of ERRANT ‖ out-and-out; notorious
ar·ras (ar'əs) *n.* ‖ after *Arras*, Fr city ‖ a wall hanging, esp. of tapestry
ar·ray (ə rā') *vt.* ‖ < OFr *areer* ‖ 1 to place in order 2 to dress in finery —*n.* 1 an orderly grouping, esp. of troops 2 an impressive display 3 fine clothes
ar·rears (ə rirz') *n.pl.* ‖ < L *ad*, to + *retro*, behind ‖ overdue debts —**in arrears** behind in paying a debt, doing one's work, etc.
ar·rest (ə rest') *vt.* ‖ < L *ad-*, to + *restare*, to stop ‖ 1 to stop or check 2 to seize by authority of the law 3 to catch and keep (one's attention, etc.) —*n.* an arresting or being arrested —**under arrest** in legal custody
ar·rest'ing *adj.* attracting attention; interesting
ar·rhyth·mi·a (ə rith'mē ə) *n.* ‖ < Gr *a-*, without + *rhythmos*, measure ‖ an irregularity in the heart's rhythm —**ar·rhyth'mic** or **ar·rhyth'mi·cal** (-rith'mi kəl) *adj.*
ar·riv·al (ə rī'vəl) *n.* 1 an arriving 2 a person or thing that arrives
ar·rive (ə rīv') *vi.* **-rived', -riv'ing** ‖ < L *ad-*, to + *ripa*, shore ‖ 1 to reach one's destination 2 to come /the time has *arrived*/ 3 to attain fame, etc. —**arrive at** to reach by thinking, etc.
ar·ri·ve·der·ci (är rē've der'chē) *interj.* ‖ It ‖ goodbye
ar·ro·gant (ar'ə gənt) *adj.* ‖ < L *arrogare*, to claim ‖ full of or due to pride; haughty —**ar'ro·gance** *n.* —**ar'ro·gant·ly** *adv.*
ar'ro·gate' (-gāt') *vt.* **-gat'ed, -gat'ing** ‖ < L *ad-*, for + *rogare*, to ask ‖ to claim or seize without right —**ar'ro·ga'tion** *n.*
ar·row (ar'ō) *n.* ‖ OE *arwe* ‖ 1 a pointed shaft for shooting from a bow 2 a sign (←), used to indicate direction
ar'row·head' *n.* the separable, pointed tip of an arrow
ar'row·root' *n.* ‖ from use as antidote for poisoned arrows ‖ 1 a tropical plant with starchy roots 2 a starch made from its roots
ar·roy·o (ə roi'ō) *n., pl.* **-os** ‖ Sp < L *arrugia*, mine shaft ‖ [Southwest] 1 a dry gully 2 a rivulet or stream
ar·se·nal (är'sə nəl) *n.* ‖ < Ar *dār aṣṣināʕa*, workshop ‖ 1 a place for making or storing weapons 2 a store or collection

ar·se·nic (är′sə nik′; *for adj.* är sen′ik) ***n.*** ‖ < Gr *arsenikon* ‖ a very poisonous chemical element, compounds of which are used in insecticides, etc. —***adj.*** of or containing arsenic: also **ar·sen′i·cal** (-sen′i kəl)

ar·son (är′sən) ***n.*** ‖ < L *ardere*, to burn ‖ the crime of purposely setting fire to a building or property —**ar′son·ist** ***n.***

art[1] (ärt) ***n.*** ‖ < L *ars* ‖ 1 human creativity 2 skill 3 any specific skill or its application 4 any craft or its principles 5 creative work or its principles 6 any branch of creative work, as painting or sculpture 7 products of this, as paintings or statues 8 *a*) a branch of learning *b*) [*pl.*] LIBERAL ARTS 9 cunning 10 sly trick; wile: *usually used in pl.*

art[2] (ärt) ***vi.*** *archaic 2d pers. sing., pres. indic., of* BE: used with *thou*

art. 1 article 2 artificial

art dec·o (dek′ō) a decorative style of the late 1920's and the 1930's, derived from cubism

ar·te·ri·al (är tir′ē əl) ***adj.*** 1 of or in the arteries 2 of a main road

ar·te·ri·ole (är tir′ē ōl′) ***n.*** ‖ see ARTERY ‖ any of the small blood vessels between the arteries and capillaries

ar·te·ri·o·scle·ro·sis (är tir′ē ō′sklə rō′sis) ***n.*** ‖ < Gr *artēria*, artery + SCLEROSIS ‖ a thickening and hardening of the arteries, as in old age

ar·ter·y (ärt′ər ē) ***n.***, *pl.* **-ter·ies** ‖ < Gr *aeirein*, to lift ‖ 1 any of the blood vessels that carry blood away from the heart 2 a main route

ar·te·sian well (är tē′zhən) ‖ Fr *artésien*, of Artois (in France) ‖ a deep well in which water is forced up by pressure of underground water draining from higher ground

art·ful (ärt′fəl) ***adj.*** 1 skillful or clever 2 cunning; crafty —**art′ful·ly** ***adv.*** —**art′ful·ness** ***n.***

ar·thri·tis (är thrīt′is) ***n.*** ‖ Gr < *arthron*, joint + -ITIS ‖ inflammation of a joint or joints —**ar·thrit·ic** (är thrit′ik) ***adj.***

arthro- ‖ < Gr *arthron*, joint ‖ *combining form* joint, joints

ar·thro·pod (är′thrō päd′) ***n.*** ‖ prec. + -POD ‖ any of a phylum of invertebrates with jointed legs and a segmented body

ar′thro·scope′ (-skōp′) ***n.*** ‖ ARTHRO- + -SCOPE ‖ an endoscope used inside a joint —**ar′thro·scop′ic** (-skäp′ik) ***adj.***

Ar·thur (är′thər) 1 legendary 6th-c. king of Britain 2 **Ches·ter A**(**lan**) (ches′tər) 1830-86; 21st president of the U.S. (1881-85) —**Ar·thu·ri·an** (är thoor′ē ən) ***adj.***

ar·ti·choke (ärt′ə chōk′) ***n.*** ‖ ult. < Ar *al-ḥarshaf* ‖ 1 a thistlelike plant 2 its edible flower head

ar·ti·cle (ärt′i kəl) ***n.*** ‖ < L *artus*, joint ‖ 1 one of the sections of a document 2 a complete piece of writing, as in a newspaper, magazine, etc. 3 a separate item /an *article* of luggage/ 4 *Gram.* any one of the words *a, an,* or *the*, used as adjectives

ar·tic·u·late (är tik′yoo lit; *for v.*, -lāt′) ***adj.*** ‖ see prec. ‖ 1 jointed: usually **ar·tic′u·lat′ed** 2 made up of distinct sounds, as speech 3 able to speak 4 expressing oneself clearly —***vt.*** **-lat′ed, -lat′ing** 1 to connect by joints 2 to arrange in connected sequence 3 to utter distinctly 4 to express clearly —***vi.*** 1 to speak distinctly 2 to be jointed or connected —**ar·tic′u·late·ly** ***adv.*** —**ar·tic′u·la′tion** ***n.***

ar·ti·fact (ärt′ə fakt′) ***n.*** any object made by human work

ar·ti·fice (ärt′ə fis) ***n.*** ‖ < L *ars*, art + *facere*, make ‖ 1 skill or ingenuity 2 trickery 3 an artful trick

ar·tif·i·cer (är tif′ə sər) ***n.*** 1 a skilled craftsman 2 an inventor

ar·ti·fi·cial (ärt′ə fish′əl) ***adj.*** ‖ see ARTIFICE ‖ 1 made by human work; not natural 2 simulated /*artificial* teeth/ 3 affected /an *artificial* smile/ —**ar′ti·fi′ci·al′i·ty** (-fish′ē al′ə tē), *pl.* **-ties**, ***n.*** —**ar′ti·fi′cial·ly** ***adv.***

artificial intelligence the development of computers capable of reasoning, learning, etc.

artificial respiration the maintenance of breathing by artificial means, as by forcing air into the mouth

ar·til·ler·y (är til′ər ē) ***n.*** ‖ < OFr *atillier*, equip ‖ 1 mounted guns, as cannon or missile launchers 2 gunnery —**the artillery** the branch of an army using heavy mounted guns —**ar·til′ler·y·man** (-mən), *pl.* **-men**, ***n.***

ar·ti·san (ärt′ə zən) ***n.*** ‖ ult. < L *ars*, art ‖ a skilled craftsman

art·ist (ärt′ist) ***n.*** 1 one who is skilled in any of the fine arts 2 one who does anything very well 3 a professional in any of the performing arts

ar·tis·tic (är tis′tik) ***adj.*** 1 of art or artists 2 done skillfully and tastefully 3 sensitive to beauty —**ar·tis′ti·cal·ly** ***adv.***

art·ist·ry (ärt′is trē) ***n.*** artistic quality, ability, or work

art·less (ärt′lis) ***adj.*** 1 lacking skill or art 2 simple; natural 3 without guile; ingenuous —**art′less·ly** ***adv.***

art·y (ärt′ē) ***adj.*** **art′i·er, art′i·est** [Colloq.] affectedly artistic —**art′i·ness** ***n.***

ar·um (er′əm) ***n.*** ‖ L ‖ any of a family of plants with flowers enveloped within a hoodlike leaf

Ar·y·an (ar′ē ən, er′-) ***n.*** ‖ < Sans *ārya-*, noble ‖ 1 [Obs.] the hypothetical parent language of the Indo-European family 2 a person supposed to be a descendant of the prehistoric peoples who spoke this language: *aryan* is not a valid ethnological term

as (az, əz) ***adv.*** ‖ < ALSO ‖ 1 equally /just *as* happy at home/ 2 for instance /a card game, *as* bridge/ 3 when related in a specified way /my view *as* contrasted with yours/ —***conj.*** 1 to the same amount or degree that /straight *as* an arrow/ 2 in the same manner that /do *as* you are told/ 3 while /she wept *as* she spoke/ 4 because /*as* you object, we won't go/ 5 that the consequence is /so obvious *as* to need no reply/ 6 though /tall *as* he was, he couldn't reach it/ —***pron.*** 1 a fact that /we are tired, *as* you can see/ 2 that (preceded by *such* or *the same*) /such books *as* I own/ —***prep.*** in the role or function of /he poses *as* a friend/ —**as for** (or **to**) concerning — **as if** (or **though**) as it (or one) would if —**as is** [Colloq.] just as it is —**as it were** as if it were so

As *Chem. symbol for* arsenic

as·bes·tos (as bes′təs, az-) ***n.*** ‖ < Gr *a-*, not + *sbennynai*, extinguish ‖ a nonconducting, fireproof mineral used in electrical insulation, roofing, etc.

as·cend (ə send′) ***vi.*** ‖ < L *ad-*, to + *scandere*, to climb ‖ to move upward; rise —***vt.*** **1** to move upward along; mount **2** to succeed to (a throne)

as·cend′an·cy or **as·cend′en·cy** (-ən sē) ***n.*** a position of control; domination

as·cend′ant or **as·cend′ent** (-ənt) ***adj.*** **1** rising **2** in control; dominant —**in the ascendant** at or approaching the height of power, fame, etc.

as·cen·sion (ə sen′shən) ***n.*** **1** an ascending **2** [**A-**] the 40th day after Easter, celebrating the Ascension —**the Ascension** *Bible* the bodily ascent of Jesus into heaven

as·cent (ə sent′) ***n.*** **1** an ascending **2** an upward slope

as·cer·tain (as′ər tān′) ***vt.*** ‖ see AD- & CERTAIN ‖ to find out with certainty

as·cet·ic (ə set′ik) ***adj.*** ‖ < Gr *askein*, to train the body ‖ self-denying; austere —***n.*** ‖ < Gr *awkētēs*, monk ‖ one who leads a life of strict self-denial, esp. for religious purposes —**as·cet′i·cism′** (-siz′əm) ***n.***

a·scor·bic acid (ə skôr′bik) ‖ A-[2] + SCORB(UTIC) + -IC ‖ vitamin C

ASCOT

as·cot (as′kət, -kät′) ***n.*** a necktie with very broad ends hanging from the knot

as·cribe (ə skrīb′) ***vt.*** **-cribed′**, **-crib′ing** ‖ < L *ad-*, to + *scribere*, write ‖ **1** to assign (*to* a supposed cause) **2** to regard as belonging (*to*) or coming from someone —**as·crip·tion** (ə skrip′shən) ***n.***

a·sep·tic (ā sep′tik, ə-) ***adj.*** free from disease-producing bacteria, etc.

a·sex·u·al (ā sek′sho͞o əl) ***adj.*** **1** having no sex or sexual organs **2** without the union of male and female germ cells **3** not sexual /*asexual* clothing/ —**a·sex′u·al·ly** ***adv.***

ash[1] (ash) ***n.*** ‖ < OE *æsce* ‖ **1** the grayish powder left after something has burned **2** fine, volcanic lava **3** the gray color of wood ash See also ASHES

ash[2] (ash) ***n.*** ‖ < OE *æsc* ‖ **1** a shade tree of the olive family **2** its wood

a·shamed (ə shāmd′) ***adj.*** **1** feeling shame **2** reluctant because fearing shame beforehand —**a·sham·ed·ly** (ə shām′id lē) ***adv.***

ash·en (ash′ən) ***adj.*** **1** of ashes **2** like ashes, esp. in color; pale

ash·es (ash′iz) ***n.pl.*** **1** the grayish powder and small particles left after a thing has burned **2** human remains, esp. the part left after cremation

a·shore (ə shôr′) ***adv., adj.*** **1** to or on the shore **2** to or on land

ash·ram (äsh′rəm) ***n.*** ‖ < Sans *ā*, toward + *śrama*, penance ‖ **1** a secluded place for a Hindu religious community **2** such a community

ash′tray′ ***n.*** a container for smokers' tobacco ashes, etc. Also **ash tray**

Ash Wednesday the first day of Lent: from the putting of ashes on the forehead in penitence

ash′y ***adj.*** **-i·er, -i·est** **1** of or covered with ashes **2** ashen; pale

A·sia (ā′zhə) largest continent, in the Eastern Hemisphere: *c.* 17,140,000 sq. mi.; pop. *c.* 2,633,000,000 —**A′sian** or less preferred **A·si·at·ic** (ā′zhē at′ik) ***adj., n.***

Asia Minor large peninsula in W Asia, between the Black Sea and the Mediterranean

a·side (ə sīd′) ***adv.*** **1** on or to one side **2** in reserve /put one *aside* for me/ **3** apart; notwithstanding /joking *aside*/ —***n.*** words spoken by an actor but supposedly heard only by the audience —**aside from** **1** with the exception of **2** apart from

as·i·nine (as′ə nīn′) ***adj.*** ‖ < L *asinus*, ass ‖ like an ass; stupid; silly —**as′i·nine′ly** ***adv.*** —**as′i·nin′i·ty** (-nin′ə tē) ***n.***

ask (ask) ***vt.*** ‖ OE *āscian* ‖ **1** to use words in seeking the answer to (a question) **2** to inquire of (a person) **3** to request or demand **4** to invite —***vi.*** **1** to make a request (*for*) **2** to inquire (*about* or *after*) —**ask′er** ***n.***

a·skance (ə skans′) ***adv.*** ‖ ME ‖ **1** with a sideways glance **2** with suspicion, disapproval, etc.

a·skew (ə skyo͞o′) ***adv.*** to one side; awry —***adj.*** on one side; awry

asking price the price asked by a seller, esp. as a basis for bargaining

a·slant (ə slant′) ***adv.*** on a slant —***prep.*** on a slant across —***adj.*** slanting

a·sleep (ə slēp′) ***adj.*** **1** sleeping **2** inactive; dull **3** numb **4** dead —***adv.*** into a sleeping condition

a·so·cial (ā sō′shəl) ***adj.*** **1** avoiding contact with others **2** selfish

asp (asp) ***n.*** ‖ < Gr *aspis* ‖ a poisonous snake of Africa, Arabia, etc.

as·par·a·gus (ə spar′ə gəs, -sper′-) ***n.*** ‖ < Gr *asparagos* ‖ **1** a plant of the lily family, with edible shoots **2** these shoots

as·par·tame (as pär′tām′) ***n.*** an artificial, low-calorie sweetener, used in soft drinks, candy, etc.

as·pect (as′pekt′) ***n.*** ‖ < L *ad-*, to + *specere*, to look ‖ **1** the way one appears **2** the appearance of something from a specific position or viewpoint **3** a side facing in a given direction

as·pen (as′pən) ***n.*** ‖ OE *æspe* ‖ a poplar tree whose leaves flutter in the least breeze

as·per·i·ty (ə sper′ə tē) ***n.***, *pl.* **-ties** ‖ < L *asper*, rough ‖ **1** roughness or harshness **2** sharpness of temper

as·perse (ə spurs′) ***vt.*** **-persed′**, **-pers′ing** ‖ < L *ad-*, to + *spargere*, to sprinkle ‖ to slander

as·per·sion (ə spur′zhən) ***n.*** a damaging or disparaging remark; slander

as·phalt (as′fôlt′) ***n.*** ‖ < Gr *asphaltos* ‖ a brown or black tarlike substance mixed with sand or gravel and used for paving, roofing, etc. —*vt.* to pave, roof, etc. with asphalt

as·pho·del (as′fə del′) ***n.*** ‖ < Gr *asphodelos* ‖ a plant of the lily family, having white or yellow flowers

as·phyx·i·ate (as fik′sē āt′) ***vt., vi.*** **-at′ed, -at′ing** ‖ < Gr *a-*, not + *sphyzein*, to throb ‖ **1** to make or become unconscious from lack of oxygen in the blood **2** to suffocate —**as·phyx′i·a′tion** ***n.***

as·pic (as′pik′) ***n.*** ‖ < OFr *aspe*, asp ‖ a cold jelly of meat juice, tomato juice, etc., served as a garnish or in a mold

as·pi·rant (as′pə rənt, ə spī′-) ***adj.*** aspiring —***n.*** one who aspires

as·pi·rate (as′pə rāt′; *for n.*, -pər it) ***vt.*** **-rat′ed, -rat′ing** **1** to begin (a word) with the sound of English (h) **2** to follow (a consonant) with an audible puff of breath **3** to suck in or draw in —***n.*** an aspirated sound

as·pi·ra·tion (as′pə rā′shən) ***n.*** **1** *a)* strong desire or ambition, as for advancement *b)* the thing so desired **2** a drawing in by breathing or suction

as′pi·ra′tor ***n.*** an apparatus using suction to remove air, fluids, etc.

as·pire (ə spīr′) ***vi.*** **-pired′, -pir′ing** ‖ < L *ad-*, to + *spirare*, breathe ‖ to be ambitious (*to* get or do something); seek (*after*)

as·pi·rin (as′pə rin′, -prin′) ***n.*** ‖ Ger ‖ **1** a white, crystalline powder used for reducing fever, relieving pain, etc. **2** a tablet of this

a·squint (ə skwint′) ***adv., adj.*** with a squint

ass (as) ***n.*** ‖ < L *asinus* ‖ **1** a horselike animal having long ears and a short mane **2** a stupid or silly person

as·sail (ə sāl′) ***vt.*** ‖ < L *ad-*, to + *salire*, to leap ‖ **1** to attack physically and violently **2** to attack with arguments, etc. —**as·sail′a·ble** ***adj.***

as·sail′ant (-ənt) ***n.*** an attacker

as·sas·sin (ə sas′ən) ***n.*** ‖ < Ar *ḥashshāshīn*, hashish users ‖ **1** a murderer who strikes suddenly **2** the murderer of a politically important person

as·sas′si·nate′ (-āt′) ***vt.*** **-nat′ed, -nat′ing** to murder as an assassin does —**as·sas′si·na′tion** ***n.***

as·sault (ə sôlt′) ***n.*** ‖ < L *ad-*, to + *salire*, to leap ‖ **1** a violent attack **2** *euphemism for* RAPE[1] **3** *Law* an unlawful threat or attempt to harm another physically —***vt., vi.*** to make an assault (upon)

assault and battery *Law* the carrying out of threatened physical harm

as·say (as′ā, a sā′; *for v.* a sā′) ***n.*** ‖ < OFr *essai*, trial ‖ **1** a testing **2** an analysis of the ingredients of an ore, drug, etc. —***vt.*** **1** to make an assay of; test **2** to try; attempt —***vi.*** to be shown by assay to have a specified proportion of something —**as·say′er** ***n.***

as·sem·blage (ə sem′blij′) ***n.*** **1** an assembling **2** a group of persons or things gathered together **3** *Art* things assembled in a sculptured collage

as·sem′ble (-bəl) ***vt., vi.*** **-bled, -bling** ‖ < L *ad-*, to + *simul*, together ‖ **1** to gather into a group; collect **2** to fit or put together the parts of —**as·sem′bler** ***n.***

as·sem′bly (-blē) ***n., pl.*** **-blies** **1** an assembling **2** a group of persons gathered together **3** *a)* a legislative body *b)* [A-] the lower house of some State legislatures **4** a fitting together of parts to make a whole

assembly line in many factories, a method whereby each worker performs a specific task in assembling the work as it is passed along

as·sem′bly·man (-mən) ***n., pl.*** **-men** a member of a legislative assembly —**as·sem′bly·wom′an**, *pl.* **-wom′en**, ***n.fem.***

as·sent (ə sent′) ***vi.*** ‖ < L *ad-*, to + *sentire*, to feel ‖ to express acceptance; agree (*to*) —***n.*** consent or agreement

as·sert (ə surt′) ***vt.*** ‖ < L *ad-*, to + *serere*, join ‖ **1** to declare; affirm **2** to maintain or defend (rights, etc.) —**assert oneself** to insist on one's rights, or on being recognized —**as·sert′er** or **as·ser′tor** ***n.***

as·ser·tion (ə sur′shən) ***n.*** **1** an asserting **2** a positive statement

as·ser·tive (ə surt′iv) ***adj.*** persistently positive or confident —**as·ser′tive·ly** ***adv.*** —**as·ser′tive·ness** ***n.***

as·sess (ə ses′) ***vt.*** ‖ < L *ad-*, to + *sedere*, sit ‖ **1** to set an estimated value on (property, etc.) for taxation **2** to set the amount of (a tax, fine, etc.) **3** to impose a tax, etc. on **4** to judge the worth or importance of —**as·sess′ment** ***n.*** —**as·ses′sor** ***n.***

as·set (as′et) ***n.*** ‖ < L *ad*, to + *satis*, enough ‖ **1** anything owned that has value **2** a desirable thing /charm is an *asset*/ **3** [*pl.*] the accounting entries showing the resources of a person or business **4** [*pl.*] *Law* property available to pay debts

as·sev·er·ate (ə sev′ə rāt′) ***vt.*** **-at′ed, -at′ing** ‖ < L *ad-*, to + *severus*, earnest ‖ to state positively; assert —**as·sev′er·a′tion** ***n.***

as·sid·u·ous (ə sij′o͞o əs) ***adj.*** ‖ < L *assidere*, to assist ‖ diligent; persevering; careful —**as·si·du·i·ty** (as′ə dyo͞o′ə tē), *pl.* **-ties**, ***n.*** —**as·sid′u·ous·ly** ***adv.*** —**as·sid′u·ous·ness** ***n.***

as·sign (ə sīn′) ***vt.*** ‖ < L *ad-*, to + *signare*, to sign ‖ **1** to set apart or mark for a specific purpose; designate **2** to appoint, as to a duty **3** to give out as a task; allot **4** to ascribe; attribute **5** *Law* to transfer (a right, etc.) —**as·sign′a·ble** ***adj.*** —**as·sign′er** or *Law* **as·sign·or** (ə sīn′ôr′) ***n.***

as·sig·na·tion (as′ig nā′shən) ***n.*** an appointment to meet, esp. one made secretly by lovers

as·sign′ment ***n.*** **1** an assigning or being assigned **2** anything assigned

as·sim·i·late (ə sim′ə lāt′) ***vt.*** **-lat′ed, -lat′ing** ‖ < L *ad-*, to + *similare*, make similar ‖ **1** to absorb and incorporate; digest **2** to make like or alike —***vi.*** **1** to become like or alike **2** to be absorbed and incorporated —**as·sim′i·la′tion** ***n.***

as·sist (ə sist′) ***vt., vi.*** ‖ < L *ad-*, to + *sistere*, make stand ‖ to help; aid —***n.*** an instance or act of helping —**assist at** to be present at; attend

as·sist·ance (ə sis′təns) ***n.*** help; aid

as·sist′ant (-tənt) ***adj.*** assisting; helping —***n.*** one who assists; helper; aid

as·siz·es (ə sīz′iz) ***n.pl.*** ‖ see ASSESS ‖ **1** court sessions held periodically in each county of England **2** the time or place of these

assn. association

assoc. **1** associate(s) **2** association

as·so·ci·ate (ə sō′shē āt′, -sē-; *for n. & adj.*, -it) *vt.* **-at′ed, -at′ing** ‖ < L *ad-*, to + *socius*, companion ‖ **1** to connect; combine; join **2** to bring into relationship as partner, etc. **3** to connect in the mind —*vi.* to join (*with*) as a partner, friend, etc. —*n.* **1** a friend, partner, co-worker, etc. **2** anything joined with another **3** a degree granted by a junior college —*adj.* **1** joined with others in work, etc. **2** having less than full status

as·so′ci·a′tion (-ā′shən) *n.* **1** an associating or being associated **2** fellowship; partnership **3** an organization, society, etc. **4** a mental connection between ideas, etc.

association football soccer

as·so′ci·a′tive (-āt′iv) *adj.* **1** of, by, or causing association **2** *Math.* producing the same result regardless of how the elements are grouped

as·so·nance (as′ə nəns) *n.* ‖ < L *ad-*, to + *sonare*, to sound ‖ **1** likeness of sound **2** a partial rhyme made by like vowel sounds —**as′so·nant** *adj., n.*

as·sort (ə sôrt′) *vt.* ‖ < L *ad-*, to + *sors*, lot ‖ to sort or classify

as·sort′ed *adj.* **1** various; miscellaneous **2** sorted; classified

as·sort′ment *n.* **1** an assorting **2** a miscellaneous collection; variety

asst. assistant

as·suage (ə swāj′) *vt.* **-suaged′, -suag′ing** ‖ < L *ad-*, to + *suavis*, sweet ‖ **1** to lessen (pain, distress, etc.) **2** to calm (anger, etc.) **3** to satisfy or slake (thirst, etc.)

as·sume (ə sōōm′) *vt.* **-sumed′, -sum′ing** ‖ < L *ad-*, to + *sumere*, to take ‖ **1** to take on (the appearance, role, etc. of) **2** to seize; usurp **3** to undertake **4** to take for granted; suppose **5** to pretend to have; feign —**as·sum′a·ble** *adj.*

as·sumed′ *adj.* **1** pretended; fictitious **2** taken for granted

as·sump·tion (ə sump′shən) *n.* **1** [A-] *R.C.Ch.* *a)* the ascent of the Virgin Mary into heaven *b)* a feast on Aug. 15 celebrating this **2** an assuming **3** a supposition —**as·sump′tive** *adj.*

as·sur·ance (ə shoor′əns) *n.* **1** an assuring or being assured **2** a promise, guarantee, etc. **3** self-confidence **4** [Brit., etc.] insurance

as·sure (ə shoor′) *vt.* **-sured′, -sur′ing** ‖ < L *ad-*, to + *securus*, secure ‖ **1** to make (a person) sure of something **2** to give confidence to; reassure **3** to tell or promise confidently **4** to guarantee **5** [Brit., etc.] to insure against loss

as·sured′ *adj.* **1** made sure; certain **2** confident; sure of oneself —**as·sur·ed·ly** (ə shoor′id lē) *adv.*

As·syr·i·a (ə sir′ē ə) ancient empire in SW Asia —**As·syr′i·an** *adj., n.*

as·ter (as′tər) *n.* ‖ < Gr *astēr*, star ‖ any of several plants of the composite family with variously colored daisylike flowers

as·ter·isk (as′tər isk′) *n.* ‖ < Gr dim. of *astēr*, star ‖ a starlike sign (*) used in printing to mark footnotes, etc.

a·stern (ə sturn′) *adv.* **1** behind a ship or aircraft **2** AFT **3** backward

as·ter·oid (as′tər oid′) *n.* ‖ see ASTER & -OID ‖ any of the small planets between Mars and Jupiter

asth·ma (az′mə) *n.* ‖ Gr ‖ a chronic disorder characterized by coughing, difficulty in breathing, etc. —**asth·mat′ic** (-mat′ik) *adj., n.*

a·stig·ma·tism (ə stig′mə tiz′əm) *n.* ‖ < Gr *a-*, without + *stigma*, a mark + -ISM ‖ a defect of a lens or the eyes that prevents light rays from meeting in a single focal point —**as·tig·mat·ic** (as′tig mat′ik) *adj.*

a·stir (ə stur′) *adv., adj.* **1** in motion **2** out of bed

as·ton·ish (ə stän′ish) *vt.* ‖ < L *ex-*, intens. + *tonare*, to thunder ‖ to fill with sudden wonder; amaze —**as·ton′ish·ing** *adj.* —**as·ton′ish·ing·ly** *adv.* —**as·ton′ish·ment** *n.*

as·tound (ə stound′) *vt.* ‖ see prec. ‖ to astonish greatly —**as·tound′ing** *adj.* —**as·tound′ing·ly** *adv.*

a·strad·dle (ə strad′′l) *adv.* in a straddling position

as·tra·khan (as′trə kən) *n.* ‖ after *Astrakhan*, U.S.S.R. city ‖ loosely curled fur from young lamb pelts, or a wool fabric resembling this

as·tral (as′trəl) *adj.* ‖ < Gr *astron*, star ‖ of, from, or like the stars

a·stray (ə strā′) *adv.* ‖ ME < pp. of OFr *estraier*, stray ‖ **1** off the right path **2** so as to be in error

a·stride (ə strīd′) *adv.* with a leg on either side —*prep.* **1** with a leg on either side of **2** extending over or across

as·trin·gent (ə strin′jənt) *adj.* ‖ < L *ad-*, to + *stringere*, to draw ‖ **1** that contracts body tissue **2** harsh; biting —*n.* an astringent substance —**as·trin′gen·cy** *n.*

astro- ‖ < Gr *astron*, star ‖ *combining form* star or stars [*astrophysics*]

as·tro·bi·ol·o·gy (as′trō bī äl′ə jē) *n.* the branch of biology that investigates the existence of living organisms on planets other than earth

as′tro·dy·nam′ics *n.pl.* [*with sing. v.*] the branch of dynamics dealing with the motion and gravitation of objects in space

as·trol·o·gy (ə sträl′ə jē) *n.* ‖ < Gr *astron*, star + *-logia*, -LOGY ‖ a pseudoscience claiming that the moon, sun, and stars affect human affairs and can be used to foretell the future —**as·trol′o·ger** *n.* —**as·tro·log·i·cal** (as′trə läj′i kəl) *adj.*

as·tro·naut (as′trə nôt′) *n.* ‖ < Fr < Gr *astron*, star + *nautēs*, sailor ‖ one trained to make flights in outer space —**as′tro·nau′·tics** *n.*

as·tro·nom·i·cal (as′trə näm′i kəl) *adj.* **1** of astronomy **2** very large, as numbers Also **as′tro·nom′ic** —**as′tro·nom′i·cal·ly** *adv.*

astronomical unit a unit of length based on the mean distance of the earth from the sun, *c.* 149.6 million km

as·tron·o·my (ə strän′ə mē) *n.* ‖ < Gr *astron*, star + *nomos*, law ‖ the science that deals with the origin, size, motion, etc. of stars, planets, etc. —**as·tron′o·mer** *n.*

as·tro·phys·ics (as′trō fiz′iks) *n.pl.* [*with sing v.*] the branch of astronomy dealing with the physical properties of the universe —**as′tro·phys′i·cist** (-ə sist) *n.*

As′tro·turf′ (-turf′) *trademark for* a grasslike synthetic carpet used in stadiums, etc.

as·tute (ə stōōt′) *adj.* ‖ < L *astus*, craft ‖

clever or shrewd; keen **—as·tute'ly** ***adv.*** **—as·tute'ness** ***n.***

a·sun·der (ə sun'dər) ***adv.*** ⟦< OE *on sundran*⟧ **1** into pieces **2** apart in direction or position

a·sy·lum (ə sī'ləm) ***n.*** ⟦< Gr *a-*, without + *sylon*, right of seizure⟧ **1** a place of safety; refuge **2** an old name for an institution for the mentally ill, the poor, etc.

a·sym·me·try (ā sim'ə trē) ***n.*** lack of symmetry **—a·sym·met·ri·cal** (ā'sə me'tri kəl) ***adj.***

a·symp·to·mat·ic (ā'simp tə ma'tik) ***adj.*** without symptoms

at (at, ət) ***prep.*** ⟦< OE *æt*⟧ **1** on; in; near; by /*at* the office/ **2** to or toward /look *at* her/ **3** from /visible *at* one mile/ **4** attending /*at* a party/ **5** busy with /*at* work/ **6** in the state or manner of /*at* war, *at* a trot/ **7** because of /sad *at* his death/ **8** with reference to /good *at* tennis/ **9** in the amount, etc. of /*at* five cents each/ **10** on or near the time or age of /*at* noon/

at·a·vism (at'ə viz'əm) ***n.*** ⟦< L *at-*, beyond + *avus*, grandfather⟧ resemblance or reversion to remotely ancestral characteristics **—at'a·vis'tic** ***adj.***

a·tax·i·a (ə tak'sē ə) ***n.*** ⟦< Gr *a-*, not + *tassein*, arrange⟧ an inability to coordinate one's movements, as in walking **—a·tax'ic** ***adj., n.***

ate (āt; *Brit, or U.S. dial.*, et) ***vt., vi.*** *pt. of* EAT

-ate[1] (āt; *for 2, also* it) *suffix* **1** to become, cause to become, form, provide with /*maturate, ulcerate*/ **2** of or characteristic of, characterized by, having /*passionate*/

-ate[2] (āt, it) *suffix* an office, function, agent, or official /*potentate*/

at·el·ier (at''l yā') ***n.*** ⟦Fr⟧ a studio or workshop, esp. of an artist

Ath·a·bas·kan or **Ath·a·bas·can** (ath'ə bas'kən) ***n.*** a family of North American Indian languages **—*adj.*** designating or of these languages or their native speakers

a·the·ism (ā'thē iz'əm) ***n.*** ⟦< Gr *a-*, without + *theos*, god⟧ the belief that there is no God **—a'the·ist'** ***n.*** **—a'the·is'tic** ***adj.***

A·the·na (ə thē'nə) the Greek goddess of wisdom, skills, and warfare

Ath·ens (ath'ənz) capital of Greece, in the SE part: pop. 886,000 **—A·the'ni·an** ***adj., n.***

ath·er·o·scle·ro·sis (ath'ər ō'sklə rō'sis) ***n.*** ⟦< Gr *atheroma*, grainy tumor + SCLEROSIS⟧ formation of fatty nodules on hardening artery walls

a·thirst (ə thurst') ***adj.*** **1** [Archaic] thirsty **2** eager; longing (*for*)

ath·lete (ath'lēt') ***n.*** ⟦< Gr *athlon*, a prize⟧ a person trained in exercises or games requiring strength, skill, stamina, etc.

athlete's foot ringworm of the feet

ath·let·ic (ath let'ik) ***adj.*** **1** of or like athletes or athletics **2** physically strong, active, etc. **—ath·let'i·cal·ly** ***adv.***

ath·let'ics ***n.pl.*** [*sometimes with sing. v.*] athletic sports, games, etc.

-a·thon (ə thän') ⟦< (MAR)ATHON⟧ *suffix* an event marked by length or endurance /*walkathon*/

a·thwart (ə thwôrt') ***prep.*** **1** across **2** against **—*adv.*** crosswise

a·tilt (ə tilt') ***adj., adv.*** tilted

-a·tion (ā'shən) ⟦< Fr or L⟧ *suffix* the act, condition, or result of /*alteration*/

-a·tive (ə tiv, āt'iv) ⟦< Fr or L⟧ *suffix* of or relating to, serving to /*informative*/

At·lan·ta (at lan'tə) capital of Ga.: pop. 425,000

At·lan·tic (at lan'tik) ocean touching the Americas to the west and Europe and Africa to the east **—*adj.*** of, in, on, or near this ocean

Atlantic City city in SE N.J.: an ocean resort: pop. 40,000

At·lan·tis (at lan'tis) ⟦< Gr⟧ legendary sunken continent in the Atlantic

At·las (at'ləs) *Gr. Myth.* a giant who supports the heavens on his shoulders **—*n.*** [a-] a book of maps

ATM (ā'tē em') ***n.*** ⟦a(utomated) t(eller) m(achine)⟧ a computer terminal that allows a bank customer to deposit, withdraw, or transfer funds automatically

at·mos·phere (at'məs fir') ***n.*** ⟦< Gr *atmos*, vapor + *sphaira*, sphere⟧ **1** the air surrounding the earth **2** pervading mood or spirit **3** the general tone or effect **4** a unit of pressure equal to 101,325 newtons per sq. m **—at'mos·pher'ic** (-fer'ik) ***adj.*** **—at'mos·pher'i·cal·ly** ***adv.***

ATOLL

at·oll (a'tôl') ***n.*** ⟦< Malayalam *atolu*⟧ a ring-shaped coral island surrounding a lagoon

at·om (at'əm) ***n.*** ⟦< Gr *a-*, not + *temnein*, to cut⟧ **1** a tiny particle; jot **2** *Chem., Physics* any of the smallest particles of an element that combine with similar particles of other elements **—the atom** nuclear energy

atom bomb ATOMIC BOMB

a·tom·ic (ə täm'ik) ***adj.*** **1** of an atom or atoms **2** of or using atomic energy or atomic bombs **3** tiny **—a·tom'i·cal·ly** ***adv.***

atomic bomb an extremely destructive bomb whose power results from a chain reaction of nuclear fission

atomic energy NUCLEAR ENERGY

atomic number *Chem.* a number indicating the number of protons in the nucleus of an atom of an element

atomic weight *Chem.* the weight of one atom of an element based upon the average weight of the element's isotopes

at·om·iz·er (at'əm ī zər) ***n.*** a device used to shoot out a fine spray, as of medicine or perfume

a·to·nal·i·ty (ā'tō nal'ə tē) ***n.*** *Music* the organization of tones without relation to a key **—a·ton·al** (ā tōn'əl) ***adj.***

a·tone (ə tōn') ***vi.*** **a·toned'**, **a·ton'ing** ⟦< ME *at one*, in accord⟧ to make amends (*for* wrongdoing, etc.)

a·tone'ment ***n.*** **1** an atoning **2** amends **—the Atonement** *Theol.* the redeeming of mankind by Jesus' death

a·top (ə täp′) ***adv.*** on or at the top **—*prep.*** on the top of

-a·to·ry (ə tôr′ē) ‖ < L ‖ *suffix* -ORY

ATP ‖ *a(denosine) t(ri)p(hosphate)* ‖ an organic compound present in, and vital to, all living cells

a·tri·um (ā′trē əm) ***n.***, *pl.* **a′tri·a** (-ə) or **a′tri·ums** ‖ L ‖ **1** the main room of an ancient Roman house **2** an entrance hall **3** either of the heart chambers that receive blood

a·tro·cious (ə trō′shəs) ***adj.*** ‖ < L *atrox,* fierce ‖ **1** very cruel, evil, etc. **2** very bad; offensive **—a·tro′cious·ly *adv.* —a·tro′cious·ness *n.***

a·troc·i·ty (ə träs′ə tē) ***n.***, *pl.* **-ties 1** atrocious behavior **2** an atrocious act **3** [Colloq.] a very displeasing thing

at·ro·phy (a′trə fē; *for v., also,* -fī′) ***n.*** ‖ < Gr *a-*, not + *trephein,* to feed ‖ a wasting away or failure to grow, esp. of body tissue, an organ, etc. **—*vi.* -phied, -phy·ing** to undergo atrophy **—*vt.*** to cause atrophy in

at·ro·pine (at′rə pēn′, -pin′) ***n.*** ‖ < Gr *Atropos,* one of the Fates + -INE[3] ‖ an alkaloid obtained from belladonna, used to relieve spasms, etc.

at·tach (ə tach′) ***vt.*** ‖ < OFr *estache,* a post ‖ **1** to fasten by tying, etc. **2** to join: often used reflexively **3** to connect by ties of affection, etc. **4** to add (a signature, etc.) **5** to ascribe **6** *Law* to take (property) by writ **—at·tach′a·ble *adj.***

at·ta·ché (at′ə shā′; *chiefly Brit* ə tash′ā) ***n.*** ‖ Fr: see prec. ‖ a member of an ambassador's diplomatic staff

attaché case a briefcase

at·tach′ment *n.* **1** an attaching or being attached **2** anything that attaches; fastening **3** devotion **4** anything attached **5** an accessory for an electrical appliance, etc. **6** *Law* a taking of property into custody

at·tack (ə tak′) ***vt.*** ‖ < It *attaccare* ‖ **1** to use force against in order to harm **2** to speak or write against **3** to undertake vigorously **4** to begin acting upon harmfully **—*vi.*** to make an assault **—*n.* 1** an attacking **2** an onset of a disease **3** a beginning of a task, undertaking, etc. **—at·tack′er *n.***

at·tain (ə tān′) ***vt.*** ‖ < L *ad-*, to + *tangere,* to touch ‖ **1** to gain; accomplish; achieve **2** to reach; arrive at **—at·tain′a·bil′i·ty *n.* —at·tain′a·ble *adj.***

at·tain′der (-dər) ***n.*** ‖ see prec. ‖ loss of civil rights and property of one sentenced to death or outlawed

at·tar (at′ər) ***n.*** ‖ < Ar *ʿiṭr,* perfume ‖ a perfume made from flower petals, esp. of roses (**attar of roses**)

at·tempt (ə tempt′) ***vt.*** ‖ < L *ad-*, to + *temptare,* to try ‖ to try to do, get, etc. **—*n.* 1** a try; endeavor **2** an attack, as on a person's life

at·tend (ə tend′) ***vt.*** ‖ < L *ad-*, to + *tendere,* to stretch ‖ **1** to take care of **2** to go with **3** to accompany as a result **4** to be present at **—*vi.* 1** to pay attention **2** to wait (*on* or *upon*) **3** to apply oneself (*to*) **4** to give the required care (*to*)

at·tend′ance *n.* **1** an attending **2** the number of persons attending

at·tend′ant *adj.* **1** attending or serving **2** being present **3** accompanying **—*n.*** one who attends or serves

at·ten·tion (ə ten′shən) ***n.*** ‖ see ATTEND ‖ **1** mental concentration or readiness **2** notice or observation **3** care or consideration **4** an act of courtesy or devotion: *usually used in pl.* **5** the erect posture of soldiers ready for a command

at·ten′tive (-tiv) ***adj.*** **1** paying attention **2** courteous, devoted, etc. **—at·ten′tive·ly *adv.***

at·ten·u·ate (ə ten′yo͞o āt′) ***vt.* -at′ed, -at′ing** ‖ < L *ad-*, to + *tenuis,* thin ‖ **1** to make thin **2** to dilute **3** to lessen or weaken **—*vi.*** to become thin, weak, etc. **—at·ten′u·a′tion *n.***

at·test (ə test′) ***vt.*** ‖ < L *ad-*, to + *testari,* to bear witness ‖ **1** to declare to be true or genuine **2** to certify, as by oath **3** to serve as proof of **—*vi.*** to bear witness (*to*) **—at′tes·ta′tion *n.***

at·tic (at′ik) ***n.*** ‖ < Gr *Attikos,* of Attica (ancient Gr state): with reference to architectural style ‖ the room or space just below the roof; garret

At·ti·la (at′'l ə, ə til′ə) *c.* A.D. 406-453; king of the Huns

at·tire (ə tīr′) ***vt.* -tired′, -tir′ing** ‖ < OFr *a,* to + *tire,* order ‖ to dress; clothe **—*n.*** clothes

at·ti·tude (at′ə to͞od′) ***n.*** ‖ ult. < L *aptus,* apt ‖ **1** a bodily posture showing mood, action, etc. **2** a manner showing one's feelings or thoughts **3** one's disposition, opinion, etc.

at·ti·tu·di·nize (at′ə to͞od′'n īz′) ***vi.* -nized′, -niz′ing** to pose for effect

Attn. or **attn.** attention

at·tor·ney (ə tur′nē) ***n.***, *pl.* **-neys** ‖ < OFr *a-*, to + *torner,* to turn ‖ any person legally empowered to act for another; esp., a lawyer

attorney at law a lawyer

attorney general *pl.* **attorneys general** or **attorney generals** the chief law officer of a government

at·tract (ə trakt′) ***vt.*** ‖ < L *ad-*, to + *trahere,* to draw ‖ **1** to draw to itself or oneself **2** to get the admiration, attention, etc. of; allure **—*vi.*** to be attractive **—at·tract′a·ble *adj.***

at·trac·tion (ə trak′shən) ***n.*** **1** an attracting or being attracted **2** power to attract; esp., charm **3** anything that attracts **4** *Physics* the mutual tendency of bodies to draw together

at·trac′tive (-tiv) ***adj.*** that attracts; esp., pleasing, charming, pretty, etc. **—at·trac′tive·ly *adv.* —at·trac′tive·ness *n.***

at·trib·ute (ə trib′yo͞ot; *for n.* a′trə byo͞ot′) ***vt.* -ut·ed, -ut·ing** ‖ < L *ad-*, to + *tribuere,* assign ‖ to think of as belonging *to* a certain person or thing **—*n.*** a characteristic or quality of a person or thing **—at·trib′ut·a·ble *adj.* —at·tri·bu·tion** (a′trə byo͞o′shən) ***n.***

at·trib·u·tive (ə trib′yo͞o tiv) ***adj.*** **1** attributing **2** preceding the noun it modifies: said of an adjective **—at·trib′u·tive·ly *adv.***

at·tri·tion (ə trish′ən) ***n.*** ‖ < L *ad-*, to + *terere,* to rub ‖ **1** a wearing away by or as by friction **2** a normal loss of personnel, as by retirement

at·tune (ə to͞on′) ***vt.* -tuned′, -tun′ing 1** to tune **2** to bring into harmony

ATV (ā′tē′vē′) ***n.***, *pl.* **ATVs** ‖ A(*ll*-)T(*errain*) V(*ehicle*) ‖ a small motor vehicle for traveling over rough ground, snow, and ice, and on water
a·twit·ter (ə twit′ər) ***adv., adj.*** twittering
a·typ·i·cal (ā tip′i kəl) ***adj.*** not typical; abnormal **—a·typ′i·cal·ly *adv.***
Au ‖ L *aurum* ‖ *Chem. symbol for* gold
au·burn (ô′bərn) ***adj., n.*** ‖ < L *albus*, white: infl. by ME *brun*, brown ‖ reddish brown
Auck·land (ôk′lənd) seaport of N New Zealand: pop. 890,000
auc·tion (ôk′shən) ***n.*** ‖ < L *augere*, to increase ‖ a public sale of items to the highest bidders **—*vt.*** to sell at auction **—auction off** to sell at auction **—auc′tion·eer′ *n.***
au·da·cious (ô dā′shəs) ***adj.*** ‖ < L *audax*, bold ‖ **1** bold; daring **2** too bold; brazen; insolent **—au·da′cious·ly *adv.* —au·da′cious·ness *n.***
au·dac·i·ty (ô das′ə tē) ***n.*** **1** bold courage **2** insolence; impudence **3** *pl.* **-ties** an audacious act or remark
au·di·ble (ô′də bəl) ***adj.*** ‖ < L *audire*, hear ‖ loud enough to be heard **—au′di·bil′i·ty** (-bil′ə tē) ***n.*** **—au′di·bly *adv.***
au·di·ence (ô′dē əns) ***n.*** ‖ < L *audire*, hear ‖ **1** those assembled to hear and see something **2** all those reached by a TV or radio program, book, etc. **3** a hearing, esp. a formal interview
au·di·o (ô′dē ō′) ***adj.*** ‖ < L *audire*, hear ‖ **1** of frequencies corresponding to audible sound waves **2** of sound reproduction, as of the sound phase of television
au′di·ol′o·gy (-äl′ə jē) ***n.*** the treatment of persons having hearing defects **—au′di·ol′o·gist *n.***
au′di·om′e·ter (-äm′ət ər) ***n.*** an instrument for measuring the sharpness and range of hearing **—au′di·o·met′ric** (-ō me′trik) ***adj.***
au·di·o·phile (ô′dē ō fil′) ***n.*** a devotee of high-fidelity sound reproduction, as from recordings
au·di·o·vis·u·al (ô′dē ō vizh′o͞o əl) ***adj.*** involving both hearing and sight
au·dit (ôd′it) ***n.*** ‖ < L *auditus*, a hearing ‖ a formal checking of financial records **—*vt., vi.*** **1** to check (accounts, etc.) **2** to attend (a college class) as a listener receiving no credits
au·di·tion (ô dish′ən) ***n.*** ‖ < L *audire*, hear ‖ a hearing to try out an actor, singer, etc. **—*vt., vi.*** to try out in an audition
au·di·tor (ô′dit ər) ***n.*** **1** a listener **2** one who audits accounts **3** one who audits classes
au·di·to·ri·um (ô′də tôr′ē əm) ***n.*** **1** a room where an audience sits **2** a building or hall for speeches, concerts, etc.
au·di·to·ry (ô′də tôr′ē) ***adj.*** of hearing or the sense of hearing
auf Wie·der·seh·en (ouf vē′dər zā′ən) ‖ Ger ‖ goodbye
au·ger (ô′gər) ***n.*** ‖ < OE *nafu*, hub (of a wheel) + *gar*, a spear ‖ a tool for boring holes in wood
aught (ôt) ***n.*** ‖ < OE *a*, ever + *wiht*, creature ‖ **1** anything whatever **2** ‖ < (N)AUGHT ‖ a zero
aug·ment (ôg ment′) ***vt., vi.*** ‖ < L *augere*, to increase ‖ to make or become greater **—aug′men·ta′tion *n.* —aug·ment′er *n.***
au gra·tin (ō grat′'n, -grät′-) ‖ Fr ‖ with a crust of crumbs and grated cheese
au·gur (ô′gər) ***n.*** ‖ L, priest at fertility rites ‖ a prophet; soothsayer **—*vt., vi.*** **1** to prophesy **2** to be an omen (of) **—augur ill** (or **well**) to be a bad (or good) omen
au·gu·ry (ô′gyo͞o rē) ***n.***, *pl.* **-ries** **1** the practice of divination **2** an omen
au·gust (ô gust′) ***adj.*** ‖ L *augustus* ‖ inspiring awe; imposing **—au·gust′ly *adv.* —au·gust′ness *n.***
Au·gust (ô′gəst) ***n.*** ‖ < L *Augustus* ‖ the eighth month of the year, having 31 days: abbrev. **Aug.**
Au·gus·ta (ô gus′tə, ə-) capital of Me.: pop. 22,000
Au·gus·tine (ô′gəs tēn′), Saint (A.D. 354-430); early Christian church father
Au·gus·tus (ô gus′təs) 63 B.C.-A.D. 14; 1st Rom. emperor (27 B.C.-A.D. 14)
au jus (ō zho͞o′, ō jo͞os′) ‖ Fr ‖ served in its natural juices: said of meat
auk (ôk) ***n.*** ‖ < ON *alka* ‖ a diving bird of northern seas, with webbed feet and short wings used as paddles
auld lang syne (ôld′ laŋ′ zīn′) ‖ Scot, lit., old long since ‖ the good old days
aunt (ant, änt) ***n.*** ‖ < L *amita* ‖ **1** a sister of one's mother or father **2** the wife of one's uncle
au poivre (ō pwäv′rə) ‖ Fr ‖ with crushed black peppercorns and a sauce
au·ra (ô′rə) ***n.***, *pl.* **-ras** or **-rae** (-rē) ‖ < Gr ‖ **1** an invisible emanation **2** a particular quality surrounding a person or thing
au·ral (ô′rəl) ***adj.*** ‖ < L *auris*, ear ‖ of the ear or the sense of hearing
au·re·ole (ô′rē ōl′) ***n.*** ‖ < L *aurum*, gold ‖ **1** a halo **2** a sun's corona
au re·voir (ō′rə vwär′) ‖ Fr ‖ goodbye
au·ri·cle (ô′ri kəl) ***n.*** ‖ < L dim. of *auris*, ear ‖ the outer part of the ear
Au·ro·ra (ô rôr′ə) the Rom. goddess of dawn **—*n.***, *pl.* **-ras** or **-rae** (-ē) [a-] **1** the dawn **2** either of the luminous bands sometimes seen in the night sky: in the S Hemisphere, called the **aurora aus·tra·lis** (ô strā′lis), in the N Hemisphere, the **aurora bo·re·al·is** (bôr′ē al′is)
Au·ro·ra (ô rôr′ə, ə-) city in central Colorado: pop. 159,000
aus·cul·ta·tion (ôs′kəl tā′shən) ***n.*** ‖ L *auscultare*, to listen ‖ a listening, often with a stethoscope, to sounds in the chest, abdomen, etc. so as to determine the condition of the heart, lungs, etc. **—aus′cul·tate′ *vt., vi.***
aus·pice (ôs′pis) ***n.***, *pl.* **-pi·ces** (-pə siz, -sēz′) ‖ < L *auspicium*, omen ‖ **1** an omen **2** a favorable omen or sign **3** [*pl.*] sponsorship; patronage
aus·pi·cious (ôs pish′əs) ***adj.*** **1** favorable; propitious **2** successful **—aus·pi′cious·ly *adv.***
Aus·sie (ôs′ē) ***adj., n.*** [Colloq.] Australian
Aus·ten (ôs′tən), **Jane** 1775-1817; Eng. novelist
aus·tere (ô stir′) ***adj.*** ‖ < Gr *austēros*, dry ‖ **1** stern; harsh **2** morally strict **3** unadorned; plain **—aus·tere′ly *adv.***

aus·ter·i·ty (ô ster′ə tē) ***n.**, pl.* **-ties** 1 sternness 2 an austere practice 3 tightened economy

Aus·tin (ôs′tən) capital of Tex., in the central part: pop. 345,000

aus·tral (ôs′trəl) ***adj.*** ‖< L *auster*, the south‖ southern

Aus·tral·ia (ô strāl′yə) 1 island continent between the S Pacific and Indian oceans 2 country comprising this continent & Tasmania: 2,967,907 sq. mi.; pop. 15,793,000 —**Aus·tral′i·an** ***adj., n.***

Aus·tri·a (ôs′trē ə) country in central Europe: 32,369 sq. mi.; pop. 7,546,000 —**Aus′tri·an** ***adj., n.***

au·then·tic (ô then′tik) ***adj.*** ‖< Gr *authentikos*, genuine‖ 1 credible, reliable, etc., as a report 2 genuine; real —**au·then′ti·cal·ly** ***adv.*** —**au·then·tic·i·ty** (ô′thən tis′ə tē) ***n.***

au·then′ti·cate′ (-ti kāt′) ***vt.*** **-cat′ed, -cat′·ing** 1 to make valid 2 to verify 3 to prove to be genuine —**au·then′ti·ca′tion** ***n.***

au·thor (ô′thər) ***n.*** ‖< L *augere*, to increase‖ 1 one who makes or creates something 2 a writer of books, etc. —***vt.*** to be the author of —**au′thor·ship′** ***n.***

au·thor·i·tar·i·an (ə thôr′ə ter′ē ən) ***adj.*** believing in or characterized by absolute obedience to authority —***n.*** an advocate or enforcer of such obedience —**au·thor′i·tar′i·an·ism′** ***n.***

au·thor′i·ta′tive (-tāt′iv) ***adj.*** 1 having authority; official 2 based on competent authority; reliable —**au·thor′i·ta′tive·ly** ***adv.***

au·thor′i·ty (-tē) ***n.**, pl.* **-ties** ‖see AUTHOR‖ 1 the power or right to command, act, etc. 2 [*pl.*] officials with this power 3 influence resulting from knowledge, prestige, etc. 4 a person, writing, etc. cited to support an opinion 5 an expert

au·thor·ize (ô′thər īz′) ***vt.*** **-ized′, -iz′ing** 1 to give official approval to 2 to give power or authority to 3 to justify —**au′thor·i·za′·tion** ***n.***

Authorized Version the revised English translation of the Bible published in England in 1611 with the authorization of King James I

au·tism (ô′tiz′əm) ***n.*** ‖AUT(O)- + -ISM‖ *Psychol.* a mental state marked by disregard of external reality —**au·tis′tic** (-tis′tik) ***adj.***

au·to (ôt′ō) ***n.**, pl.* **-tos** an automobile

auto- ‖< Gr *autos*, self‖ *combining form* 1 self 2 by oneself or itself

au·to·bi·og·ra·phy (ôt′ə bī ä′grə fē) ***n.**, pl.* **-phies** the story of one's own life written by oneself —**au′to·bi′o·graph′i·cal** (-bī′ə graf′i kəl) ***adj.***

au·toc·ra·cy (ô tä′krə sē) ***n.**, pl.* **-cies** ‖see fol.‖ government in which one person has absolute power

au·to·crat (ôt′ə krat′) ***n.*** ‖< Gr *autos*, self + *kratos*, power‖ 1 a ruler with absolute power 2 any domineering person —**au′to·crat′ic** ***adj.*** —**au′to·crat′i·cal·ly** ***adv.***

au·to·di·dact (ôt′ō dī′dakt′) ***n.*** ‖see AUTO- & DIDACTIC‖ a person who is self-taught

au·to·graph (ôt′ə graf′) ***n.*** ‖< Gr *autos*, self + *graphein*, write‖ a person's own signature or handwriting —***vt.*** to write one's signature on or in

au′to·mate′ (-māt′) ***vt.*** **-mat′ed, -mat′ing** ‖< AUTOMATION‖ to convert to or use automation

au′to·mat′ic (-mat′ik) ***adj.*** ‖Gr *automatos*, self-moving‖ 1 done unthinkingly, as from habit or by reflex 2 working by itself 3 using automatic equipment 4 capable of firing continuously until the trigger is released —***n.*** 1 an automatic firearm 2 a motor vehicle with a transmission that shifts gears automatically —**au′to·mat′i·cal·ly** ***adv.***

automatic pilot a gyroscopic instrument that automatically keeps an aircraft, missile, etc. to a predetermined course and position

au′to·ma′tion (-mā′shən) ***n.*** ‖AUTOMA(TIC) + -TION‖ a manufacturing system in which many or all of the processes are automatically performed or controlled, as by electronic devices

au·tom·a·tism (ô täm′ə tiz′əm) ***n.*** automatic quality, condition, or action —**au·tom′a·tize′** (-tīz′) ***vt.***

au·tom′a·ton′ (-tän′, -tən) ***n.**, pl.* **-tons′** or **-ta** (-tə) ‖see AUTOMATIC‖ 1 any automatic device, esp. a robot 2 a person acting like a robot

au·to·mo·bile (ôt′ə mə bēl′) ***n.*** ‖Fr: see AUTO- & MOBILE‖ a four-wheeled passenger car with a built-in engine

au′to·mo′tive (-mōt′iv) ***adj.*** ‖AUTO- + -MOTIVE‖ 1 self-moving 2 having to do with automobiles, trucks, etc.

au′to·nom′ic (-näm′ik) ***adj.*** of or controlled by that part of the nervous system that regulates the motor functions of the heart, lungs, etc.

au·ton·o·mous (ô tän′ə məs) ***adj.*** ‖< Gr *autos*, self + *nomos*, law‖ 1 having self-government 2 existing or functioning independently —**au·ton′o·mous·ly** ***adv.*** —**au·ton′o·my** (-mē) ***n.***

au·top·sy (ô′täp′sē) ***n.**, pl.* **-sies** ‖< Gr *autos*, self + *opsis*, a sight‖ examination of a corpse to discover the cause of death

au·tumn (ôt′əm) ***n.*** ‖< L *autumnus*‖ the season between summer and winter; fall —**au·tum·nal** (ô tum′nəl) ***adj.***

aux·il·ia·ry (ôg zil′yə rē, -ə rē) ***adj.*** ‖< L *augere*, to increase‖ 1 helping 2 subsidiary 3 supplementary —***n.**, pl.* **-ries** an auxiliary person or thing

auxiliary verb *Gram.* a verb that helps form tenses, moods, voices, etc. of other verbs, as *have* or *be*

aux·in (ôk′sin) ***n.*** ‖< Gr *auxein*, to increase‖ a plant hormone that promotes and controls growth

a·vail (ə vāl′) ***vi., vt.*** ‖< L *ad*, to + *valere*, be strong‖ to be of use, help, or worth (to) —***n.*** use or help; advantage [*to no avail*] —**avail oneself of** to take advantage of; utilize

a·vail·a·ble (ə vāl′ə bəl) ***adj.*** 1 that can be used 2 that can be got or had; handy —**a·vail′a·bil′i·ty** ***n.***

av·a·lanche (av′ə lanch′) ***n.*** ‖Fr‖ 1 a large mass of loosened snow, earth, etc. sliding down a mountain 2 an overwhelming amount

a·vant-garde (ə vänt′gärd′, ä′-) ***n.*** ‖Fr‖ the leaders in new movements, esp. in the arts —***adj.*** of such movements

av·a·rice (av′ə ris) ***n.*** ‖ < L *avere*, to desire ‖ greed for money —**av·a·ri·cious** (av′ə rish′ əs) ***adj.*** —**av′a·ri′cious·ly** ***adv.***

a·vast (ə vast′) ***interj.*** ‖ < Du *houd vast*, hold fast ‖ *Naut.* stop! cease!

av·a·tar (av′ə tär′) ***n.*** ‖ Sans *avatāra*, descent ‖ 1 *Hinduism* a god's coming to earth in bodily form 2 an embodiment, as of a quality in a person

a·vaunt (ə vônt′) ***interj.*** ‖ < L *ab*, from + *ante*, before ‖ [Archaic] go away!

avdp. avoirdupois

A·ve Ma·ri·a (ä′vā mə rē′ə) ‖ L ‖ *R.C.Ch.* 1 "Hail, Mary," the first words of a prayer 2 this prayer

a·venge (ə venj′) ***vt., vi.*** **a·venged′, a·veng′·ing** ‖ < L *ad*, to + *vindicare*, to claim ‖ 1 to get revenge for (an injury, etc.) 2 to take vengeance on behalf of —**a·veng′er** ***n.***

av·e·nue (av′ə no͞o′, -nyo͞o′) ***n.*** ‖ < L *ad-*, to + *venire*, come ‖ 1 a street, drive, etc., esp. when broad 2 a way of approach

a·ver (ə vur′) ***vt.*** **a·verred′, a·ver′ring** ‖ < L *ad-*, to + *verus*, true ‖ to declare to be true; affirm; assert

av·er·age (av′ər ij, av′rij) ***n.*** ‖ < OFr *avarie*, damage to ship or goods; hence, idea of shared losses ‖ 1 the result of dividing the sum of two or more quantities by the number of quantities 2 the usual kind, amount, etc. —***adj.*** 1 constituting an average 2 usual; normal —***vt.*** **-aged, -ag·ing** 1 to figure out the average of 2 to do, take, etc. on an average /to *average* six sales a day/ 3 to divide proportionally —**average out** to arrive at an average eventually —**on the average** as an average amount, rate, etc.

a·verse (ə vurs′) ***adj.*** ‖ see AVERT ‖ unwilling; opposed (*to*)

a·ver·sion (ə vur′zhən) ***n.*** 1 an intense dislike 2 the object arousing this

a·vert (ə vurt′) ***vt.*** ‖ < L *a-*, from + *vertere*, to turn ‖ 1 to turn (the eyes, etc.) away 2 to ward off; prevent

avg. average

a·vi·an (ā′vē ən) ***adj.*** ‖ < L *avis*, bird + -AN ‖ of or having to do with birds

a·vi·ar·y (ā′vē er′ē) ***n., pl.*** **-ar′ies** ‖ < L *avis*, bird ‖ a large cage or building for keeping many birds

a·vi·a·tion (ā′vē ā′shən) ***n.*** ‖ see prec. ‖ 1 the science of flying airplanes 2 the field of aircraft design, construction, etc.

a′vi·a′tor ***n.*** ‖ Fr *aviateur* ‖ an airplane pilot —**a′vi·a′trix** (-triks) ***n.fem.***

av·id (av′id) ***adj.*** ‖ < L *avere*, to desire ‖ very eager or greedy —**a·vid·i·ty** (ə vid′ə tē) ***n.*** —**av′id·ly** ***adv.***

a·vi·on·ics (ā′vē än′iks) ***n.pl.*** ‖ AVI(ATION) + (ELECTR)ONICS ‖ [*with sing. v.*] electronics as applied in aviation and astronautics

a·vi·ta·min·o·sis (ā′vīt′ə mi nō′sis) ***n.*** ‖ A-[2] + VITAMIN + -OSIS ‖ any disease caused by a vitamin deficiency

av·o·ca·do (av′ə kä′dō, ä′və-) ***n., pl.*** **-dos** ‖ < AmInd ‖ 1 a thick-skinned, pear-shaped tropical fruit with yellow, buttery flesh 2 the tree it grows on

av·o·ca·tion (av′ə kā′shən) ***n.*** ‖ < L *a-*, away + *vocare*, to call ‖ something done in addition to one's regular work; hobby —**av′o·ca′tion·al** ***adj.***

a·void (ə void′) ***vt.*** ‖ ME < OFr *esvuidier*, to empty ‖ to keep away from; evade; shun —**a·void′a·ble** ***adj.*** —**a·void′a·bly** ***adv.*** —**a·void′ance** ***n.***

av·oir·du·pois (av′ər də poiz′) ***n.*** ‖ < OFr *aveir de peis*, goods of weight ‖ 1 a system of weights in which 16 oz. = 1 lb.: also **avoirdupois weight** 2 [Colloq.] weight, esp. of a person

a·vouch (ə vouch′) ***vt.*** ‖ see ADVOCATE ‖ 1 to vouch for 2 to affirm

a·vow (ə vou′) ***vt.*** ‖ see ADVOCATE ‖ to declare; acknowledge —**a·vow′al** ***n.*** —**a·vowed′** ***adj.*** —**a·vow′ed·ly** ***adv.***

a·vun·cu·lar (ə vuŋ′kyo͞o lər) ***adj.*** ‖ < L *avunculus* ‖ of an uncle

aw (ô) ***interj.*** a sound of protest, etc.

a·wait (ə wāt′) ***vt., vi.*** 1 to wait for 2 to be in store for

a·wake (ə wāk′) ***vt., vi.*** **a·woke′** or **a·waked′, a·waked′** or **a·wok′en, a·wak′·ing** ‖ < OE ‖ 1 to rouse from sleep 2 to rouse from inactivity Also **a·wak′en** —***adj.*** 1 not asleep 2 active or alert

a·wak′en·ing ***n., adj.*** 1 (a) waking up 2 (an) arousing or reviving

a·ward (ə wôrd′) ***vt.*** ‖ < ME < Anglo-Fr *eswarder* ‖ 1 to give, as by legal decision 2 to give (a prize, etc.); grant —***n.*** 1 a decision, as by a judge 2 a prize

a·ware (ə wer′) ***adj.*** ‖ < OE *wær*, cautious ‖ knowing; realizing; conscious —**a·ware′·ness** ***n.***

a·wash (ə wôsh′) ***adv., adj.*** 1 at a level where the water washes over the surface 2 flooded 3 afloat

a·way (ə wā′) ***adv.*** ‖ < OE *on weg* ‖ 1 from a place /run *away*/ 2 in another place or direction /*away* from here/ 3 off; aside /turn *away*/ 4 far /*away* behind/ 5 from one's possession /give it *away*/ 6 at once /fire *away*/ 7 continuously /kept working *away*/ —***adj.*** 1 absent 2 at a distance /a mile *away*/ —***interj.*** begone! —**away with** go, come, or take away —**do away with** get rid of or kill

awe (ô) ***n.*** ‖ < ON *agi* ‖ a mixed feeling of reverence, fear, and wonder —***vt.*** **awed, aw′ing** to fill with awe —**stand** (or **be**) **in awe of** to respect and fear

a·weigh (ə wā′) ***adj.*** just clear of the bottom: said of an anchor

awe·some (ô′səm) ***adj.*** inspiring awe —**awe′some·ly** ***adv.*** —**awe′some·ness** ***n.***

awe·struck (ô′struk′) ***adj.*** filled with awe Also **awe′strick′en** (-strik′ən)

aw·ful (ô′fəl) ***adj.*** 1 inspiring awe 2 terrifying 3 very bad —***adv.*** [Colloq.] very —**aw′ful·ness** ***n.***

aw·ful·ly (ô′fə lē, ô′flē) ***adv.*** 1 in an awful way 2 [Colloq.] very

a·while (ə wīl′, -hwīl′) ***adv.*** for a short time

awk·ward (ôk′wərd) ***adj.*** ‖ < ON *ǫfugr*, turned backward ‖ 1 clumsy; bungling 2 hard to handle; unwieldy 3 uncomfortable /an *awkward* pose/ 4 embarrassed or embarrassing —**awk′ward·ly** ***adv.*** —**awk′ward·ness** ***n.***

awl (ôl) ***n.*** ‖ < OE *æl* ‖ a small, pointed tool for making holes in wood, leather, etc.

awn (ôn) ***n.*** ‖ < ON *ǫgn* ‖ the bristly fibers on a head of barley, oats, etc.

awn·ing (ôn′iŋ) ***n.*** ‖ < ? MFr *auvent*, a sloping roof ‖ a structure, as of canvas, extended before a window, door, etc. as a protection from the sun or rain

a·woke (ə wōk′) *vt., vi. pt. of* AWAKE

A·WOL or **a·wol** (ā′wôl′) ***adj., adv.*** absent without leave

a·wry (ə rī′) ***adv., adj.*** ‖see A-[1] & WRY‖ **1** with a twist to a side; askew **2** wrong; amiss /our plans went *awry*/

ax or **axe** (aks) ***n., pl.*** **ax′es** ‖< OE *æx*‖ a tool with a long handle and bladed head, for chopping wood, etc. **—*vt.*** **axed, ax′ing 1** to trim, split, etc. with an ax **2** to get rid of **—give** (or **get**) **the ax** [Colloq.] to discharge (or be discharged) from a job **—have an ax to grind** [Colloq.] to have an object of one's own to gain or promote

ax·i·al (ak′sē əl) ***adj.*** **1** of, like, or forming an axis **2** around, on, or along an axis **— ax′i·al·ly *adv.***

ax·i·om (ak′sē əm) ***n.*** ‖< Gr *axios*, worthy‖ **1** *a)* a statement universally accepted as true; maxim *b)* a self-evident truth **2** an established principle, scientific law, etc. **—ax′i·o·mat′ic** (-ə mat′ik) ***adj.*** **—ax′i·o·mat′i·cal·ly *adv.***

ax·is (ak′sis) ***n., pl.*** **ax′es** (-sēz′) ‖L‖ **1** a real or imaginary straight line on which an object rotates **2** a central line around which the parts of a thing, system, etc. are evenly arranged **—the Axis** Germany, Italy, and Japan in World War II

ax·le (ak′səl) ***n.*** ‖< ON *qxull*‖ **1** a rod on or with which a wheel turns **2** *a)* a bar connecting two opposite wheels, as of an automobile *b)* the spindle at either end of such a bar

ax′le·tree′ (-trē′) ***n.*** ‖< prec. + ON *tre*, beam‖ an axle of a wagon, carriage, etc.

Ax·min·ster (aks′min′stər) ***n.*** ‖< English town where first made‖ varicolored, patterned carpet with a cut pile

ax·o·lotl (ak′sə lät′'l) ***n.*** ‖< AmInd‖ a dark salamander of Mexico and the W U.S.

ax·on (ak′sän′) ***n.*** ‖< Gr *axōn*, axis‖ that part of a nerve cell through which impulses travel away from the cell body

a·ya·tol·lah (ī′yə tō′lə, -tō lä′) ***n.*** ‖< Ar *āyat*, sign + *Allah*, Allah‖ a leader of a Muslim sect, serving as teacher, judge, etc.

aye[1] (ā) ***adv.*** ‖< ON *ei*‖ [Old Poet.] always; ever Also **ay**

aye[2] (ī) ***adv.*** ‖prob. < *I*, pers. pron.‖ yes **— *n.*** an affirmative vote or voter Also **ay**

AZ Arizona

a·za·lea (ə zāl′yə) ***n.*** ‖< Gr *azaleos*, dry: it thrives in dry soil‖ **1** a shrub of the heath family, with flowers of various colors **2** the flower

az·i·muth (az′ə məth) ***n.*** ‖< Ar *al*, the + *samt*, way‖ *Astronomy, Surveying* distance clockwise in degrees from the north point or, in the Southern Hemisphere, south point

A·zores (ā′zôrz′, ə zôrz′) group of Portuguese islands in the N Atlantic, west of Portugal

AZT (ā′zē′tē′) ***n.*** *trademark for* an antiviral drug used to treat AIDS

Az·tec (az′tek′) ***n.*** **1** a member of an Amerindian people who had an advanced civilization in Mexico before the Spanish conquest in 1519 **2** their language **—*adj.*** of the Aztecs, their culture, etc. Also **Az′tec·an**

az·ure (azh′ər) ***adj.*** ‖< Pers *lāzhuward*, lapis lazuli‖ sky-blue **—*n.*** **1** sky blue or any similar blue color **2** [Old Poet.] the blue sky

B

b or **B** (bē) ***n., pl.*** **b's, B's** the second letter of the English alphabet

B (bē) ***n.*** **1** a blood type **2** a grade indicating above-average but not outstanding work **3** *Music* the seventh tone in the scale of C major **—*adj.*** inferior to the best /a class *B* motion picture/

b or **b. 1** bachelor **2** *Baseball a)* base *b)* baseman **3** *Music* bass **4** born Also, for 1-3, **B** or **B.**

B *Chem. symbol for* boron

Ba *Chem. symbol for* barium

BA or **B.A.** Bachelor of Arts

baa (bä) ***n., vi.*** ‖echoic‖ bleat

Ba·al (bā′əl) ***n.*** ‖< Heb‖ **1** an ancient fertility god **2** an idol

bab·ble (bab′əl) ***vi.*** **-bled, -bling** ‖echoic‖ **1** to talk like a small child; prattle **2** to talk foolishly or too much **3** to murmur, as a brook **—*vt.*** to say incoherently or foolishly **—*n.*** **1** incoherent vocal sounds **2** foolish talk **3** a murmuring sound **—bab′bler *n.***

babe (bāb) ***n.*** **1** a baby **2** a naive person: also **babe in the woods 3** [Slang] a girl or young woman

Ba·bel (bā′bəl) *Bible* a city thwarted in building a tower to heaven when God created a confusion of tongues **—*n.*** [*also* **b-**] a confusion of voices, sounds, etc. or the scene of this

BABOON

ba·boon (ba bōōn′, bə-) ***n.*** ‖< OFr *babuin*, ape, fool‖ a large, fierce, dog-faced, short-tailed monkey of Africa and Arabia

ba·bush·ka (bə bōōsh′kə) ***n.*** ‖Russ, grandmother‖ a woman's scarf worn on the head and tied under the chin

ba·by (bā′bē) ***n., pl.*** **-bies** ‖ME *babi*‖ **1** a very young child; infant **2** one who acts like an infant **3** a very young animal **4** the youngest or smallest in a group **5** [Slang] darling; honey **6** [Slang] any person or thing *—adj.* **1** of or for an infant **2** very young **3** small of its kind **4** childish *—vt.* **-bied, -by·ing** to pamper; coddle **—ba'by·hood'** *n.* **—ba'by·ish** *adj.*

baby beef meat from a prime heifer or steer that is one to two years old

baby boom·er (bōō'mər) a person born during the birthrate increase (the **baby boom**) after 1945

baby carriage a light carriage for wheeling a baby about Also **baby buggy**

baby grand a small grand piano

Bab·y·lon (bab'ə lən, -län') capital of Babylonia, famous for luxury

Bab·y·lo·ni·a (bab'ə lō'nē ə) ancient empire in SW Asia **—Bab'y·lo'ni·an** *adj., n.*

ba·by's breath (bā'bēz) a plant with small, delicate, white or pink flowers

baby sitter a person hired to take care of a child or children, as when the parents are away for the evening **—ba'by-sit', -sat', -sit'ting,** *vi.*

bac·ca·lau·re·ate (bak'ə lôr'ē it) *n.* ‖ < ML *baccalaris,* young nobleman seeking knighthood ‖ **1** the degree of bachelor of arts, bachelor of science, etc. **2** a commencement address

bac·cha·nal (bak'ə nal') *n.* **1** a worshiper of Bacchus **2** a drunken carouser **3** a drunken orgy **—bac'cha·na'li·an** (-nā'lē ən) *adj., n.*

Bac·chus (bak'əs) the Greek and Roman god of wine and revelry

Bach (bäkh), **Jo·hann Se·bas·ti·an** (yō'hän' zā bäs'tē än') 1685-1750; Ger. organist & composer

bach·e·lor (bach'ə lər) *n.* ‖ < ML *baccalaris:* see BACCALAUREATE ‖ an unmarried man **—bach'e·lor·hood'** *n.*

Bachelor of Arts (or **Science,** etc.) **1** a degree given by a college or university to one who has completed a four-year course in the humanities (or in science, etc.): also **bachelor's degree** **2** one who holds this degree

bachelor's button a plant with white, pink, or blue flowers, as the cornflower

ba·cil·lus (bə sil'əs) *n., pl.* **-cil'li'** (-ī) ‖ < L *bacillum,* little stick ‖ **1** any of a genus of rod-shaped bacteria **2** loosely, any of the bacteria **—bac·il·lar·y** (bas'ə ler'ē, bə sil'ər ē) *adj.*

back (bak) *n.* ‖ < OE *baec* ‖ **1** the rear part of the body from the nape of the neck to the end of the spine **2** the backbone **3** a part that supports or fits the back **4** the rear part or reverse of anything **5** *Sports* a player or position behind the front line *—adj.* **1** at the rear **2** remote **3** of or for the past /*back* pay/ **4** backward *—adv.* **1** at, to, or toward the rear **2** to or toward a former condition, time, etc. **3** in reserve or concealment **4** in return or requital /pay him back/ *—vt.* **1** to move backward **2** to support **3** to bet on **4** to provide or be a back for *—vi.* to go backward **—back and forth** backward and forward **—back down** to withdraw from a position or claim **—back off** (or **away,** etc.) to move back (or away, etc.) **—back out (of)** **1** to withdraw from an enterprise **2** to evade keeping a promise, etc. **—back up** **1** to support **2** to move backward **3** to accumulate because of restricted movement /traffic *backed up*/ **—go back on** [Colloq.] **1** to be disloyal to; betray **2** to fail to keep (one's word, etc.) **—turn one's back on** **1** to turn away from, as in contempt **2** to abandon

back'ache' *n.* an ache or pain in the back

back'bite' (-bīt') *vt., vi.* **-bit', -bit'ten** or **-bit', -bit'ing** to slander (someone absent) **—back'bit'er** *n.*

back'board' *n.* **1** a board at or forming the back of something **2** *Basketball* the board behind the basket

back'bone' *n.* **1** the spine **2** a main support **3** willpower, courage, etc.

back'break'ing *adj.* very tiring

back'drop' *n.* **1** a curtain, often scenic, at the back of a stage **2** background or setting

back'er *n.* **1** a patron; sponsor **2** one who bets on a contestant

back'field' *n.* *Football* the players behind the line; esp., the offensive unit

back'fire' *n.* **1** the burning out of a small area, as in a forest, to check the spread of a big fire **2** premature ignition or explosion of gases in an internal-combustion engine **3** reverse explosion in a gun *—vi.* **-fired', -fir'ing** **1** to explode as a backfire **2** to go wrong or boomerang, as a plan

back'gam'mon *n.* ‖ BACK + ME *gammen,* game ‖ a game for two, with dice governing moves of pieces on a special board

back'ground' *n.* **1** the distant part of a scene **2** surroundings, sounds, etc. behind or subordinate to something **3** one's training and experience **4** events leading up to something

back'ground'er *n.* a press briefing at which background information is provided

back'hand' *n.* **1** handwriting that slants up to the left **2** a backhand catch, stroke, etc. *—adj.* **1** done with the back of the hand turned inward, as for a baseball catch, or forward, as for a tennis stroke, and with the arm across the body **2** written in backhand *—adv.* with a backhand *—vt.* to hit, catch, swing, etc. backhand

back'hand'ed *adj.* **1** BACKHAND **2** not direct and open; devious *—adv.* with a backhand

back'ing *n.* **1** something forming a back for support **2** support given to a person or cause **3** supporters; backers

back'lash' *n.* sharp reaction; recoil

back'log' *n.* an accumulation or reserve *—vi., vt.* **-logged', -log'ging** to accumulate as a backlog

back order an order not yet filled

back'pack' *n.* a knapsack, often attached to a lightweight frame, worn by campers or hikers *—vi., vt.* to wear, or carry in, a backpack **—back'pack'er** *n.*

back'ped'al *vi.* **-ped'aled** or **-ped'alled, -ped'al·ing** or **-ped'al·ling** **1** to pedal backward, as in braking a bicycle **2** to move backward; retreat; withdraw

back'rest' *n.* a support for or at the back

back'side' *n.* **1** the back part **2** the rump

back'slap'per (-slap'ər) *n.* [Colloq.] an effusively friendly person

back'slide' *vi.* **-slid', -slid'** or **-slid'den, -slid'ing** to slide backward in morals, etc. —**back'slid'er** *n.*

back'space' *vi.* **-spaced', -spac'ing** to move a typewriter carriage, cursor, etc. one or more spaces back along the line

back'spin' *n.* a backward spin in a ball, etc., making it bound backward upon hitting the ground

back'stage' *adv., adj.* behind and off the stage, as in the wings or dressing rooms

back'stairs' *adj.* involving intrigue or scandal; secret Also **back'stair'**

back'stop' *n.* a fence, screen, etc. to keep balls from going too far, as behind the catcher in baseball

back'stretch' *n.* the part of a racetrack opposite the homestretch

back'stroke' *n.* a swimming stroke made while lying face upward

back talk [Colloq.] saucy or insolent retorts

back'-to-back' *adj.* [Colloq.] one right after another

back'track' *vi.* **1** to return by the same path **2** to retreat or recant

back'up' or **back'-up'** *adj.* **1** standing by as an alternate or auxiliary **2** supporting —*n.* a backing up; specif., *a)* an accumulation *b)* a support or help

back'ward *adv.* **1** toward the back **2** with the back foremost **3** in reverse order **4** in a way opposite to usual **5** into the past Also **back'wards** —*adj.* **1** turned toward the rear or in the opposite way **2** shy **3** slow or retarded —**back'ward·ness** *n.*

back'wash' *n.* **1** water or air moved backward, as by a ship, propeller, etc. **2** a reaction caused by some event

back'wa'ter *n.* **1** water moved or held back by a dam, tide, etc. **2** stagnant water in an inlet, etc. **3** a backward place or condition

back'woods' *n.pl.* [*occas. with sing. v.*] **1** heavily wooded remote areas **2** any remote, thinly populated area —*adj.* of or like the backwoods —**back'woods'man,** *pl.* **-men** (-mən), *n.*

ba·con (bā'kən) *n.* ⟦< OS *baco,* side of bacon⟧ salted and smoked meat from the back or sides of a hog —**bring home the bacon** [Colloq.] **1** to earn a living **2** to succeed

Ba·con (bā'kən), **Fran·cis** (fran'sis) 1561-1626; Eng. philosopher & writer

bac·te·ri·a (bak tir'ē ə) *n.pl., sing.* **-ri·um** (-əm) ⟦< Gr *baktērion,* small staff⟧ microorganisms which have no chlorophyll and multiply by simple division: some bacteria cause diseases, but others are necessary for fermentation, etc. —**bac·te'ri·al** *adj.*

bac·te'ri·cide' (-tir'ə sīd') *n.* an agent that destroys bacteria —**bac·te'ri·cid'al** *adj.*

bac·te'ri·ol'o·gy (-tir'ē äl'ə jē) *n.* the science that deals with bacteria —**bac·te'ri·o·log'i·cal** (-ē ə läj'i kəl) *adj.* —**bac·te'ri·ol'o·gist** *n.*

bad¹ (bad) *adj.* **worse, worst** ⟦ME⟧ **1** not good; not as it should be **2** inadequate or unfit **3** unfavorable [*bad* news] **4** rotten or spoiled **5** incorrect or faulty **6** *a)* wicked; immoral *b)* mischievous **7** harmful **8** severe **9** ill **10** sorry; distressed [he feels *bad* about it] **11** offensive —*adv.* [Colloq.] badly —*n.* anything bad —**in bad** [Colloq.] in trouble or disfavor —**bad'ness** *n.*

bad² (bad) *vt., vi. archaic pt. of* BID

bad blood (mutual) enmity

bade (bad) *vt., vi. alt. pt. of* BID

bad egg [Slang] a mean or dishonest person Also **bad actor, bad apple, bad hat,** or **bad lot**

bad faith insincerity; dishonesty

badge (baj) *n.* ⟦ME *bage*⟧ **1** an emblem worn to show rank, membership, etc. **2** any distinctive sign, etc.

badg·er (baj'ər) *n.* ⟦< ?⟧ **1** a burrowing animal with a broad back and thick, short legs **2** its fur —*vt.* to nag at; torment

bad·i·nage (bad''n äzh') *n.* ⟦Fr⟧ playful talk; banter

bad·lands (bad'landz') *n.pl.* **1** an area of barren land with dry soil and soft rocks eroded into odd shapes **2** [**B-**] any such W U.S. area: also **Bad Lands**

bad·ly (bad'lē) *adv.* **worse, worst 1** in a bad manner **2** [Colloq.] very much; greatly

bad'man' *n., pl.* **-men'** a cattle thief or desperado of the old West

bad·min·ton (bad'mint''n) *n.* ⟦after *Badminton,* Eng estate⟧ a game in which a feathered cork is batted back and forth with rackets across a net

bad'-mouth' *vt., vi.* [Slang] to find fault (with)

bad'-tem'pered *adj.* irritable

Bae·de·ker (bā'də kər) *n.* **1** any of a series of guidebooks to foreign countries, first published in Germany **2** loosely, any guidebook

baf·fle (baf'əl) *vt.* **-fled, -fling** ⟦< ?⟧ **1** to perplex completely; bewilder **2** to impede; check —*n.* a screen to deflect air, sound, etc. —**baf'fle·ment** *n.* —**baf'fler** *n.* —**baf'fling** *adj.*

bag (bag) *n.* ⟦< ON *baggi*⟧ **1** a nonrigid container of paper, plastic, etc., with a top opening that can be closed **2** a satchel; suitcase, etc. **3** a purse **4** game taken in hunting **5** a baglike shape or part **6** [Slang] an unattractive woman **7** [Slang] one's special interest **8** *Baseball* a base —*vt.* **bagged, bag'ging 1** to make bulge **2** to put into a bag **3** to capture **4** to kill in hunting **5** [Slang] to get —*vi.* **1** to swell **2** to hang loosely —**in the bag** [Slang] certain; assured

bag·a·telle (bag'ə tel') *n.* ⟦Fr < L *baca,* berry⟧ a trifle

ba·gel (bā'gəl) *n.* ⟦Yidd⟧ a hard bread roll shaped like a small doughnut

bag'ful' *n., pl.* **-fuls'** as much as a bag will hold

bag·gage (bag'ij) *n.* ⟦< ML *bagga,* chest, bag⟧ **1** the bags, etc. of a traveler; luggage **2** a lively girl

Bag·gie (bag'ē) *trademark for* a plastic bag, used for storing food, etc. —*n.* [**b-**] any plastic bag of this kind

bag·gy (bag'ē) *adj.* **-gi·er, -gi·est** puffy or hanging loosely, like a bag —**bag'gi·ly** *adv.* —**bag'gi·ness** *n.*

Bagh·dad (bag'dad) capital of Iraq: pop. 2,184,000: also sp. **Bag·dad**

bag lady [Slang] a homeless, poor woman who wanders city streets carrying her belongings in shopping bags

BAGPIPE

bag′pipe′ *n.* ⌊*often pl.*⌋ a wind instrument, now chiefly Scottish, played by forcing air from a bag into reed pipes and fingering the stops
bah (bä, ba) *interj.* an exclamation of con tempt, scorn, or disgust
Ba·ha·mas (bə hä′məz) country on a group of islands (**Bahama Islands**) in the West Indies: 5,380 sq. mi.; pop. 235,000
Bah·rain (bä rān′) country on a group of islands in the Persian Gulf: 260 sq. mi.; pop. 422,000: also sp. **Bah·rein**
bail[1] (bāl) *n.* ‖ < L *bajulare,* bear a burden ‖ **1** money deposited with the court to get a prisoner temporarily released **2** such a release **3** the person giving bail —*vt.* **1** to have (a prisoner) set free by giving bail **2** to help out of financial or other difficulty Often with *out* —**bail′a·ble** *adj.*
bail[2] (bāl) *n.* ‖ ME *baille,* bucket ‖ a bucket for dipping up water from a boat —*vi., vt.* to dip out (water) from (a boat): usually with *out* —**bail out** to parachute from an aircraft
bail[3] (bāl) *n.* ‖ ME *beil* ‖ a hoop-shaped han dle for a bucket, etc.
bail·iff (bāl′if) *n.* ‖ ME *bailif* ‖ **1** a deputy sheriff **2** a court officer who guards the jurors, keeps order in the court, etc. **3** in England, *a)* a district official *b)* a steward of an estate
bail·i·wick (bal′i wik′) *n.* ‖ ME < *baili,* bail-iff + *wik,* village ‖ **1** a bailiff's district **2** one's particular area of activity, authority, interest, etc.
bails·man (bālz′mən) *n., pl.* **-men** (-mən) a person who gives bail for another
bairn (bern) *n.* [Scot.] a child
bait (bāt) *vt.* ‖ < ON *beita* ‖ **1** to set dogs on for sport /to *bait* bears/ **2** to torment or harass, esp. by verbal attacks **3** to put food on (a hook or trap) as a lure for game **4** to lure; entice; tempt —*n.* **1** food, etc. put on a hook or trap as a lure **2** anything used as a lure; enticement
bait′-and-switch′ *adj.* of, or using an unethical sales technique in which a seller lures customers by advertising an often non-existent bargain item and then tries to switch their attention to more expensive items
baize (bāz) *n.* ‖ < L *badius,* brown ‖ a coarse, feltlike woolen cloth
bake (bāk) *vt.* **baked, bak′ing** ‖ < OE *bacan* ‖ **1** to cook (food) by dry heat, esp. in an oven **2** to dry and harden (pottery) by heat; fire —*vi.* **1** to bake bread, etc. **2** to become baked —*n.* **1** a baking **2** a social affair at which baked food is served
baked beans navy beans baked with salt pork, seasonings, and molasses
bak·er (bā′kər) *n.* one whose work or business is baking bread, etc.
baker's dozen thirteen
Bak·ers·field (bā′kərz fēld′) city in south central Calif.: pop. 106,000
bak·er·y (bā′kər ē) *n.* **1** *pl.* **-er·ies** a place where bread, etc. is baked or sold **2** [Colloq.] baked goods
baking powder a leavening agent contain ing baking soda and an acid forming sub-stance
baking soda sodium bicarbonate, used as a leavening agent and as an antacid
bal·a·lai·ka (bal′ə lī′kə) *n.* ‖ Russ ‖ a Russian stringed instrument somewhat like a guitar
bal·ance (bal′əns) *n.* ‖ < LL *bilanx,* having two scales ‖ **1** an instrument for weighing, esp. one with two matched hanging scales **2** a state of equilibrium in weight, value, etc. **3** bodily or mental stability **4** harmonious proportion of elements in a design, etc. **5** a weight, value, etc. that counteracts another **6** equality of debits and credits, or the differ ence between them **7** a remainder —*vt.* **-anced, -anc·ing 1** to weigh in or as in a balance **2** to compare as to relative value, etc. **3** to counteract; offset **4** to bring into proportion, harmony, etc. **5** to make or be equal to in weight, value, etc. **6** to find the difference between, or to equalize, the deb-its and credits of (an account) —*vi.* **1** to be in equilibrium **2** to be equal in weight, value, etc. **3** to have the credits and debits equal —**in the balance** not yet settled
balance sheet a statement showing the financial status of a business
bal·co·ny (bal′kə nē) *n., pl.* **-nies** ‖ < It *balcone* ‖ **1** a platform projecting from an upper story and enclosed by a railing **2** an upper floor of seats in a theater, etc. often projecting over the main floor
bald (bôld) *adj.* ‖ < ME ‖ **1** having a head with white fur, etc. growing on it **2** lacking hair on the head **3** not covered by natural growth **4** plain or blunt /*bald* truth/ —**bald′ly** *adv.* —**bald′ness** *n.*
bald eagle a large eagle of North America, with a white-feathered head
bal·der·dash (bôl′dər dash′) *n.* ‖ orig. (17th c.), an odd mixture ‖ nonsense
bald·faced (bôld′fāst′) *adj.* brazen; shame-less /a *baldfaced* lie/
bald′ing *adj.* becoming bald
bal·dric (bôl′drik′) *n.* ‖ ult. < L *balteus,* belt ‖ a belt worn over one shoulder to support a sword, etc.
bale (bāl) *n.* ‖ < OHG *balla,* ball ‖ a large bundle, esp. a standardized quantity of goods, as raw cotton compressed and bound —*vt.* **baled, bal′ing** to make into bales —**bal′er** *n.*
ba·leen (bə lēn′) *n.* ‖ ult. < Gr *phallaina,* whale ‖ WHALEBONE
bale·ful (bāl′fəl) *adj.* ‖ < OE *bealu,* evil ‖ deadly; harmful; ominous
Ba·li (bä′lē) island of Indonesia —**Ba′li·nese′** *adj., n.*
balk (bôk) *n.* ‖ OE *balca,* ridge ‖ **1** an obstruction, hindrance, etc. **2** [Obs.] a blun-der; error **3** *Baseball* an illegal motion by the pitcher entitling base runners to advance

one base —*vt.* to obstruct; foil —*vi.* 1 to stop and refuse to move or act 2 to hesitate or recoil [*at*]

Balkan Peninsula peninsula in SE Europe, east of Italy

Bal·kans (bôl′kənz) countries of Yugoslavia, Romania, Bulgaria, Albania, Greece, & the European part of Turkey, in SE Europe —**Bal′kan** *adj.*

balk·y (bôk′ē) *adj.* **-i·er, -i·est** stubbornly resisting; balking

ball[1] (bôl) *n.* ‖ ME *bal* ‖ 1 any round object; sphere; globe 2 *a)* a round or egg-shaped object used in various games *b)* any of several such games, esp. baseball 3 a throw or pitch of a ball /a fast *ball*/ 4 a missile for a cannon, rifle, etc. 5 a rounded part of the body 6 *Baseball* a pitched ball that is not hit and is not a strike —*vi., vt.* to form into a ball —**ball up** [Slang] to muddle or confuse —**be on the ball** [Slang] to be alert; be efficient

ball[2] (bôl) *n.* ‖ < Fr < Gr *ballizein,* to dance ‖ 1 a formal social dance 2 [Slang] a good time

bal·lad (bal′əd) *n.* ‖ < OFr *ballade,* dancing song ‖ 1 a sentimental song with the same melody for each stanza 2 a narrative song or poem, usually anonymous, with simple words, short stanzas, and a refrain 3 a slow, sentimental popular song —**bal′lad·eer′** *n.* —**bal′lad·ry** *n.*

ball-and-sock·et joint (bôl′ən säk′it) a joint, as of the hip, formed by a ball in a socket

bal·last (bal′əst) *n.* ‖ < MDu *bal,* bad ‖ 1 anything heavy carried in a ship or vehicle to give stability 2 crushed rock or gravel, used in railroad beds, etc. —*vt.* to furnish with ballast

ball bearing 1 a bearing in which the parts turn on freely rolling metal balls 2 one of these balls

bal·le·ri·na (bal′ə rē′nə) *n.* ‖ It ‖ a girl or woman ballet dancer

bal·let (ba lā′, bal′ā) *n.* ‖ Fr ‖ 1 an artistic dance form of graceful, precise gestures and movements used to tell a story 2 ballet dancers

ball·game (bôl′gām′) *n.* 1 a game played with a ball 2 [Colloq.] a set of circumstances /a different *ballgame*/

ballistic missile a long-range guided missile designed to fall free as it approaches its target

bal·lis·tics (bə lis′tiks) *n.pl.* [*with sing. v.*] the science dealing with the motion and impact of projectiles —**bal·lis′tic** *adj.*

ball joint a ball-and-socket joint used in automotive vehicles to connect the tie rods to the turning wheels

bal·loon (bə lo͞on′) *n.* ‖ < Fr < It *palla,* ball ‖ 1 a large, airtight bag that rises when filled with hot air or a gas lighter than air 2 an airship with such a bag 3 an inflatable rubber bag, used as a toy —*vt.* to inflate —*vi.* to swell; expand —*adj.* like a balloon —**bal·loon′ist** *n.*

bal·lot (bal′ət) *n.* ‖ < It *palla,* ball ‖ 1 a ticket, paper, etc. by which a vote is registered 2 act or right of voting, as by ballots 3 the total number of votes cast —*vi.* to vote

ball′park′ *n.* a baseball stadium

ball′play′er *n.* a baseball player

ball′point′ (**pen**) a fountain pen with a small ball bearing instead of a point Also **ball′point′** *n.*

ball′room′ *n.* a large hall for dancing

bal·lute (ba lo͞ot′) *n.* ‖ BALL(OON) + (PARA-CH)UTE ‖ a heat-resistant, balloonlike device inflated by stored gas and used to slow down a spacecraft reentering the atmosphere

bal·ly·hoo (bal′ē ho͞o′) *n.* ‖ < ? ‖ noisy talk, sensational advertising, etc. —*vt., vi.* **-hooed′, -hoo′ing** [Colloq.] to promote with ballyhoo

balm (bäm; *occas.* bälm) *n.* ‖ < Gr *balsamon* ‖ 1 a fragrant, healing ointment or oil 2 anything healing or soothing

balm′y *adj.* **-i·er, -i·est** 1 soothing, mild, etc. 2 [Slang, Chiefly Brit.] crazy

ba·lo·ney (bə lō′nē) *n.* ‖ < *bologna* ‖ 1 bologna 2 [Slang] nonsense

bal·sa (bôl′sə) *n.* ‖ Sp ‖ 1 the wood, very light in weight, of a tropical American tree 2 the tree

bal·sam (bôl′səm) *n.* ‖ see BALM ‖ 1 an aromatic resin obtained from certain trees 2 any of various aromatic, resinous oils or fluids 3 balm 4 any of various trees yielding balsam

Bal·tic Sea (bôl′tik) sea in N Europe, west of the U.S.S.R.

Bal·ti·more (bôl′tə môr) seaport in N Md.: pop. 787,000

bal·us·ter (bal′əs tər) *n.* ‖ < Gr *balaustion,* wild pomegranate flower: from the shape ‖ any of the small posts of a railing, as on a staircase

bal·us·trade (bal′əs trād′) *n.* a railing held up by balusters

Bal·zac (bäl zäk′; *E* bôl′zak), **Ho·no·ré de** (ô nô rā′də) 1799-1850; Fr. novelist

bam·boo (bam bo͞o′) *n.* ‖ Malay *bambu* ‖ a treelike tropical grass with woody, jointed, often hollow stems used for furniture, canes, etc.

BAMBOO

bamboo curtain [*often* B- C-] the political and ideological differences that separated China from the West

bam·boo·zle (bam bo͞o′zəl) *vt.* **-zled, -zling** ‖ < ? ‖ 1 to trick; cheat; dupe 2 to confuse; puzzle

ban (ban) *vt.* **banned, ban′ning** ‖ < OE *bannan,* summon ‖ to prohibit or forbid, esp. officially —*n.* 1 a condemnation by church authorities 2 a curse 3 an official prohibition 4 strong public condemnation

ba·nal (bā′nəl, bə nal′) *adj.* ‖ Fr: see prec. ‖ trite; hackneyed —**ba·nal′i·ty,** *pl.* **-ties,** *n.* —**ba′nal·ly** *adv.*

ba·nan·a (bə nan′ə) *n.* ‖ Sp & Port ‖ 1 a treelike tropical plant with large clusters of edible fruit 2 the narrow, somewhat curved fruit, having a creamy flesh and a yellow or red skin

band[1] (band) *n.* ‖ ON ‖ 1 something that binds, ties, or encircles, as a strip or ring of wood, rubber, metal, etc. 2 a strip of color or of material 3 a division of an LP phonograph record **4** a range of wavelengths —*vt.* to put a band on or around

band[2] (band) ***n.*** ‖ < Gothic *bandwa*, a sign ‖ **1** a group of people united for some purpose **2** a group of musicians playing together, esp. upon wind and percussion instruments —*vi., vt.* to unite for some purpose

band·age (ban′dij) ***n.*** ‖ Fr < *bande*, a strip ‖ a strip of cloth, etc. used to bind or cover an injury —*vt.* **-aged, -ag·ing** to put a bandage on

Band-Aid (band′ād′) ‖ prec. + AID ‖ *trademark for* a small bandage of gauze and adhesive tape —*n.* [*also* **b- a-**] such a bandage Also **band′aid′**

ban·dan·na or **ban·dan·a** (ban dan′ə) ***n.*** ‖ Hindi *bāndhnū*, a method of dyeing ‖ a large, colored handkerchief

band·box (band′bäks′) ***n.*** a light, round box to hold hats, collars, etc.

ban·deau (ban dō′) ***n.***, *pl.* **-deaux′** (-dōz′) ‖ Fr ‖ **1** a narrow ribbon **2** a narrow brassiere

ban·dit (ban′dit) ***n.*** ‖ < It ‖ a robber; highwayman —**ban′dit·ry *n.***

ban·do·leer or **ban·do·lier** (ban′də lir′) ***n.*** ‖ < Fr ‖ a broad belt with pockets for bullets, etc., worn over one shoulder and across the chest

band saw an endless toothed steel belt on pulleys, powered for sawing

bands·man (bandz′mən) ***n.***, *pl.* **-men** a member of a band of musicians

band′stand′ *n.* a platform for a band, esp. one for outdoor concerts

band′wag′on *n.* a wagon for a band to ride on, as in a parade —**on the bandwagon** [Colloq.] on the popular or apparently winning side

ban·dy[1] (ban′dē) ***vt.*** **-died, -dy·ing** ‖ Fr *bander*, bandy at tennis ‖ **1** to toss or hit back and forth **2** to pass (rumors, etc.) freely **3** to exchange (words), esp. angrily

ban·dy[2] (ban′dē) ***adj.*** ‖ Fr *bandé*, bent ‖ curved outward; bowed

ban′dy-leg′ged (-leg′id, -legd′) ***adj.*** having bandy legs; bowlegged

bane (bān) ***n.*** ‖ OE *bana* ‖ **1** ruin, death, harm, or their cause **2** [Obs.] poison —**bane′ful *adj.***

bang[1] (baŋ) ***vt.*** ‖ ON *banga*, to pound ‖ to hit, shut, etc. hard and noisily —*vi.* **1** to make a loud noise **2** to hit noisily or sharply —*n.* **1** a hard, noisy blow or impact **2** a loud, sudden noise **3** [Colloq.] a burst of vigor **4** [Slang] a thrill —*adv.* **1** hard and noisily **2** abruptly —**bang up** to damage

bang[2] (baŋ) ***n.*** ‖ < prec.: see *adv.*, 2 ‖ [*usually pl.*] hair cut to hang straight across the forehead

Bang·kok (baŋ′käk′) seaport & capital of Thailand: pop. (met. area) 5,175,000

Ban·gla·desh (bäŋ′glə desh′, baŋ′-) country in S Asia, on the Bay of Bengal: 55,598 sq. mi.; pop. 104,205,000

ban·gle (baŋ′gəl) ***n.*** ‖ Hindi *bangṛī* ‖ a decorative bracelet or anklet

bang-up (baŋ′up′) ***adj.*** [Colloq.] very good; excellent

ban·ish (ban′ish) ***vt.*** ‖ < OFr *banir* ‖ **1** to exile **2** to drive away; get rid of —**ban′ish·ment *n.***

ban·is·ter (ban′is tər) ***n.*** ‖ < BALUSTER ‖ a handrail, specif. one with balusters

ban·jo (ban′jō′) ***n.***, *pl.* **-jos′** or **-joes′** ‖ of Afr orig. ‖ a musical instrument with a long neck, circular body, and strings that are plucked —**ban′jo·ist *n.***

bank[1] (baŋk) ***n.*** ‖ ult. < OHG *bank*, bench ‖ **1** an establishment for receiving or lending money **2** a reserve supply; pool —*vt., vi.* to put into a bank —**bank on** [Colloq.] to rely on —**bank′a·ble *adj.***

bank[2] (baŋk) ***n.*** ‖ < ON *bakki* ‖ **1** a long mound or heap **2** a steep slope **3** a rise of land along a river, etc. **4** a shallow place, as in a sea **5** the lateral, slanting turn of an aircraft —*vt.* **1** to cover (a fire) with ashes and fuel so that it will burn slowly **2** to pile up so as to form a bank **3** to slope (a curve in a road, etc.) **4** to make (an aircraft) slant laterally on a turn **5** to make (a billiard ball) recoil from a cushion

bank[3] (baŋk) ***n.*** ‖ < OFr *banc*, bench ‖ **1** a row of oars **2** a row or tier, as of keys in a keyboard —*vt.* to arrange in a row or tier

bank account money deposited in a bank and credited to the depositor

bank′book′ *n.* a book recording a bank depositor's deposits; passbook

bank′er *n.* a person who owns or manages a bank

bank′ing *n.* the business of a bank

bank note a promissory note issued by a bank: a form of paper money

bank′roll′ *n.* a supply of money —*vt.* [Colloq.] to supply with money; finance

bank·rupt (baŋk′rupt′) ***n.*** ‖ < Fr < It *banca*, bench + *rotta*, broken ‖ a person legally declared unable to pay debts —*adj.* **1** that is a bankrupt; insolvent **2** lacking in some quality [*morally bankrupt*] —*vt.* to make bankrupt —**bank′rupt′cy**, *pl.* **-cies, *n.***

ban·ner (ban′ər) ***n.*** ‖ ME *banere* < OFr *baniere* ‖ **1** a flag **2** a headline running across a newspaper page —*adj.* foremost

banns (banz) ***n.pl.*** ‖ see BAN ‖ the proclamation made in church of an intended marriage

ban·quet (baŋ′kwət) ***n.*** ‖ ult. < OHG *bank*, bench ‖ **1** a feast **2** a formal dinner —*vt.* to honor with a banquet

ban·quette (baŋ ket′) ***n.*** ‖ Fr ‖ **1** a gunners' platform inside a trench, etc. **2** an upholstered bench

ban·shee or **ban·shie** (ban′shē) ***n.*** ‖ < Ir *bean*, woman + *sith*, fairy ‖ *Celt. Folklore* a female spirit whose wailing warns of impending death

ban·tam (ban′təm) ***n.*** ‖ after *Bantam*, former province in Java ‖ **1** any of various small, domestic fowls **2** a small but aggressive person —*adj.* like a bantam

ban′tam·weight′ *n.* a boxer weighing 113 to 118 lb.

ban·ter (ban′tər) ***vt.*** ‖ 17th-c. slang ‖ to tease playfully —*vi.* to exchange banter (*with* someone) —*n.* playful teasing —**ban′ter·ing·ly *adv.***

Ban·tu (ban′to͞o′) ***n.*** ‖ Bantu *ba-ntu*, the men ‖ **1** *pl.* **-tus** or **-tu** a member of a group of Negroid peoples of equatorial and southern Africa **2** any of the related languages of these people

ban·yan (ban′yən) ***n.*** ‖ ult. < Sans ‖ a fig tree of India: its branches take root and become trunks

ba·o·bab (bā′ō bab′, bä′-) ***n.*** ‖ < ? Ethiopian native name ‖ a thick-trunked tree of Africa, with edible, gourdlike fruit

bap·tism (bap′tiz′əm) ***n.*** ‖ see BAPTIZE ‖ **1** the sacrament of admitting a person into a Christian church by immersing the individual in water or by sprinkling water on the individual **2** an initiating experience —**bap·tis′mal** (-tiz′məl) ***adj.***

Bap′tist (-tist) ***n.*** a member of a Protestant denomination practicing baptism of believers by immersion

bap′tis·ter·y (-tis tər ē, -trē) ***n.***, *pl.* **-ies** a place, esp. in a church, used for baptizing Also **bap′tis·try**, *pl.* **-tries**

bap·tize (bap tīz′, bap′tīz) ***vt.*** **-tized′**, **-tiz′·ing** ‖ < Gr *baptizein,* to immerse ‖ **1** to administer baptism to **2** to initiate **3** to christen

bar (bär) ***n.*** ‖ < ML *barra* ‖ **1** any long, narrow piece of wood, metal, etc., often used as a barrier, lever, etc. **2** an oblong piece, as of soap **3** anything that obstructs or hinders **4** a band or strip **5** a law court, esp. that part, enclosed by a railing, where the lawyers sit **6** lawyers collectively **7** the legal profession **8** a counter, as for serving alcoholic drinks **9** a place with such a counter **10** *Music a)* a vertical line dividing a staff into measures *b)* a measure —***vt.*** **barred, bar′ring** **1** to fasten with a bar **2** to obstruct; close **3** to oppose **4** to exclude —***prep.*** excluding /the best, *bar* none/ —**cross the bar** to die

barb (bärb) ***n.*** ‖ < L *barba,* beard ‖ **1** a beardlike growth **2** a sharp point projecting backward from the main point of a fishhook, etc. **3** a cutting remark —***vt.*** to provide with a barb —**barbed** ***adj.***

Bar·ba·dos (bär bā′dōs, -dōz) country on an island in the West Indies: 166 sq. mi.; pop. 253,000

bar·bar·i·an (bär ber′ē ən) ***n.*** ‖ see BARBAROUS ‖ **1** a member of a people considered primitive, savage, etc. **2** a cruel person —***adj.*** uncivilized, cruel, etc. —**bar·bar′i·an·ism′** ***n.***

bar·bar′ic (-ber′ik) ***adj.*** **1** uncivilized; primitive **2** wild, crude, etc.

bar·ba·rism (bär′bə riz′əm) ***n.*** **1** a word or expression that is not standard **2** the state of being primitive or uncivilized **3** a barbarous act or custom

bar·bar·i·ty (bär ber′ə tē) ***n.***, *pl.* **-ties** **1** cruelty; brutality **2** a barbaric taste, manner, etc.

bar·ba·rize (bär′bə rīz′) ***vt.*** **-rized′**, **-riz′ing** to make or become barbarous —**bar′ba·ri·za′tion** ***n.***

bar·ba·rous (bär′bə rəs) ***adj.*** ‖ < Gr *barbaros,* foreign ‖ **1** uncivilized; primitive **2** crude, coarse, etc. **3** cruel; brutal —**bar′·ba·rous·ly** ***adv.***

bar·be·cue (bär′bə kyōō′) ***n.*** ‖ AmSp *barbacoa* ‖ **1** *a)* a hog, steer, etc. roasted whole over an open fire *b)* any meat broiled over an open fire **2** a party, picnic, or restaurant featuring this —***vt.*** **-cued′**, **-cu′ing** to roast or broil over an open fire, often with a highly seasoned sauce (**barbecue sauce**)

barbed wire wire with barbs at close intervals Also **barb′wire′** ***n.***

bar·bel (bär′bəl) ***n.*** ‖ < L *barba,* beard ‖ a threadlike growth from the lips or jaws of certain fishes

BARBELL

bar·bell (bär′bel′) ***n.*** ‖ BAR + (DUMB)BELL ‖ a metal bar with weights attached at each end, used for weight-lifting exercises Also **bar bell**

bar·ber (bär′bər) ***n.*** ‖ see BARB ‖ one whose work is cutting hair, shaving beards, etc. —***vt.***, ***vi.*** to cut the hair (of), shave, etc.

bar·ber·ry (bär′ber′ē, -bə rē) ***n.***, *pl.* **-ries** ‖ < ML *barberis* ‖ **1** a spiny shrub with sour, red berries **2** the berry

bar·bi·tu·rate (bär bich′ər it, bär′bə tyoor′it) ***n.*** ‖ < Ger ‖ a salt or ester of a crystalline acid (**barbituric acid**), used as a sedative

bar·ca·role or **bar·ca·rolle** (bär′kə rōl′) ***n.*** ‖ < Fr < It ‖ a Venetian gondolier song, or music like this

Bar·ce·lo·na (bär′sə lō′nə) seaport in NE Spain: pop. 1,757,000

bar code UNIVERSAL PRODUCT CODE

bard (bärd) ***n.*** ‖ Gael & Ir ‖ **1** an ancient Celtic poet **2** a poet

bare (ber) ***adj.*** **bar′er, bar′est** ‖ OE *bær* ‖ **1** not covered or clothed; naked **2** without furnishings; empty **3** simple; plain **4** mere /*bare* needs/ —***vt.*** **bared, bar′ing** to make bare; uncover —**lay bare** to uncover; expose —**bare′ness** ***n.***

bare′back′ ***adv.***, ***adj.*** on a horse with no saddle

bare′-bones′ ***adj.*** simple; basic

bare′faced′ ***adj.*** **1** with the face uncovered **2** open; shameless

bare′foot′ ***adj.***, ***adv.*** without shoes and stockings —**bare′foot′ed** ***adj.***

bare′hand′ed ***adj.***, ***adv.*** **1** with hands uncovered or unprotected **2** without weapons, etc.

bare′head′ed ***adj.***, ***adv.*** wearing no hat or other covering on the head

bare′leg′ged (-leg′id, -legd′) ***adj.***, ***adv.*** with the legs bare

bare·ly (ber′lē) ***adv.*** **1** plainly **2** only just; scarcely **3** scantily

bar·gain (bär′gən) ***n.*** ‖ < OFr *bargaignier,* haggle ‖ **1** a mutual agreement or contract **2** an agreement with regard to its worth /a bad *bargain*/ **3** something sold at a price favorable to the buyer —***vi.*** **1** to haggle **2** to make a bargain —**bargain for** (or **on**) to expect; count on —**into** (or **in**) **the bargain** besides —**bar′gain·er** ***n.***

bargain counter a store counter for displaying goods at reduced prices

barge (bärj) ***n.*** ‖ < ML *barga* ‖ **1** a large, flat-bottomed boat for freight on rivers, etc. **2** a large pleasure boat —***vi.*** **barged, barg′·ing** **1** to move slowly and clumsily **2** to come or go (*in* or *into*) rudely or abruptly

bar graph a graph in which the lengths of parallel bars are used to compare quantities, etc.

bar·i·tone (bar′ə tōn′, ber′-) ***n.*** ‖ < Gr *barys*, deep + *tonos*, tone ‖ **1** the range of a male voice between tenor and bass **2** a singer or instrument with this range

bar·i·um (ber′ē əm) ***n.*** ‖ < Gr *barys*, heavy ‖ a metallic chemical element

bark[1] (bärk) ***n.*** ‖ < ON *bǫrkr* ‖ the outside covering of trees and woody plants **—*vt.*** **1** to remove bark from (a tree, etc.) **2** [Colloq.] to scrape; skin (the knees, etc.)

bark[2] (bärk) ***vi.*** ‖ OE *beorcan* ‖ **1** to make the sharp, abrupt cry of a dog or a similar sound **2** to speak sharply; snap **—*n.*** the characteristic cry of a dog, or any noise like this **—bark up the wrong tree** to misdirect one's attack, energies, etc.

bark[3] (bärk) ***n.*** ‖ < LL *barca* ‖ **1** [Old Poet.] a boat **2** a sailing vessel with two forward square-rigged masts and a rear mast rigged fore-and-aft

bar′keep′er (-kē′pər) ***n.*** **1** an owner of a barroom **2** a bartender Also **bar′keep′**

bark·er (bär′kər) ***n.*** one who talks loud to attract customers to a sideshow, etc.

bar·ley (bär′lē) ***n.*** ‖ OE *bærlic* ‖ **1** a cereal grass **2** its grain, used in making barley malt, in soups, etc.

bar′maid′ ***n.*** a waitress who serves alcoholic drinks in a bar

bar mitz·vah (bär mits′və) ‖ < Yidd < Aram *bar*, son of + Heb *mitsva*, commandment ‖ [*also* **B- M-**] **1** a Jewish boy who has arrived at the age of religious responsibility, thirteen years **2** the ceremony celebrating this event **—bat mitzvah** (bät-) or **bas mitzvah** (bäs-) ***fem.***

barn (bärn) ***n.*** ‖ OE *bern* ‖ a farm building for sheltering harvested crops, livestock, machines, etc.

bar·na·cle (bär′nə kəl) ***n.*** ‖ ME *bernacle* ‖ a saltwater shellfish that attaches itself to rocks, ship bottoms, etc.

barn·storm (bärn′stôrm′) ***vi.***, ***vt.*** to tour (the country, esp. rural areas) giving speeches, plays, etc.

barn′yard′ ***n.*** the ground near a barn **—*adj.*** of, like, or fit for a barnyard

ba·rom·e·ter (bə räm′ət ər) ***n.*** ‖ < Gr *baros*, weight + -METER ‖ **1** an instrument for measuring atmospheric pressure and thus forecasting weather **2** anything that marks change **—bar·o·met·ric** (bar′ə me′trik) ***adj.***

bar·on (bar′ən, ber′-) ***n.*** ‖ ME ‖ **1** a member of the lowest rank of British nobility **2** a magnate **—bar′on·age′** (-ij′) ***n.*** **—bar′on·ess *n.fem.*** **—ba·ro·ni·al** (bə rō′nē əl) ***adj.***

bar′on·et′ (-ət′, -it) ***n.*** a man holding the lowest hereditary British title, below a baron **—bar′on·et′cy**, *pl.* **-cies, *n.***

ba·roque (bə rōk′) ***adj.*** ‖ Fr < Port *barroco*, imperfect pearl ‖ **1** [*often* **B-**] *a)* very ornate and full of curved lines, as much art and architecture of about 1550-1750 *b)* full of highly embellished melodies, fugues, etc., as much music of that time **2** fantastically ornate

bar·racks (bar′əks, ber′-) ***n.pl.*** ‖ < Sp *barro*, clay ‖ [*often with sing. v.*] a building or buildings for housing soldiers, etc.

bar·ra·cu·da (bar′ə ko͞o′də, ber′-) ***n.***, *pl.* **-da** or **-das** ‖ AmSp ‖ a fierce, pikelike fish of tropical seas

bar·rage (bə räzh′, -räj′) ***n.*** ‖ Fr < *barrer*, to stop ‖ **1** a curtain of artillery fire **2** any prolonged attack **—*vi.*, *vt.* -raged′, -rag′·ing** to subject to a barrage

barred (bärd) ***adj.*** **1** having bars or stripes **2** closed off with bars **3** not allowed

bar·rel (bar′əl, ber′-) ***n.*** ‖ < ML *barillus* ‖ **1** *a)* a large, cylindrical container with slightly bulging sides and flat ends *b)* its standard capacity ($31\frac{1}{2}$ gal.) **2** any similar container or cylinder **3** the straight tube of a gun **—*vt.*** **-reled** or **-relled, -rel·ing** or **-rel·ling** to put in barrels **—*vi.*** [Slang] to go at high speed

barrel organ a mechanical musical instrument played by turning a crank

bar·ren (bar′ən, ber′-) ***adj.*** ‖ < OFr ‖ **1** that cannot bear offspring; sterile **2** without vegetation **3** unproductive **4** boring; dull **5** devoid (*of*) **—bar′ren·ness *n.***

bar·rette (bə ret′) ***n.*** ‖ Fr ‖ a bar or clasp for holding a woman's hair in place

bar·ri·cade (bar′i kād′, ber′-; *also, esp. for v.*, bar′ə kād′) ***n.*** ‖ Fr < It *barricare*, fortify ‖ a barrier, esp. one put up hastily for defense **—*vt.*** **-cad′ed, -cad′ing** to block with a barricade

bar·ri·er (bar′ē ər, ber′-) ***n.*** ‖ < ML *barra* ‖ **1** an obstruction, as a fence **2** anything that blocks or hinders

bar·ring (bär′iŋ) ***prep.*** excepting

bar·ris·ter (bar′is tər, ber′-) ***n.*** ‖ < *bar* (law court) ‖ in England, a lawyer who pleads cases in court

bar′room′ ***n.*** a room with a bar where alcoholic drinks are sold

bar·row[1] (bar′ō, ber′-) ***n.*** ‖ < OE *beran*, to bear ‖ a handbarrow or wheelbarrow

bar·row[2] (bar′ō, ber′-) ***n.*** ‖ < OE *beorg*, hill ‖ a heap of earth or rocks covering a grave

bar′tend′er ***n.*** one who serves alcoholic drinks at a bar

bar·ter (bärt′ər) ***vi.***, ***vt.*** ‖ < OFr *barater* ‖ to trade by exchanging (goods) without money **—*n.*** **1** a bartering **2** anything bartered **—bar′ter·er *n.***

Bar·tók (bär′tôk′), **Bé·la** (bā′lä) 1881-1945; Hung. composer

bar·y·on (bar′ē än′, ber′-) ***n.*** ‖ < Gr *barys*, heavy + (ELECTR)ON ‖ any of certain heavy atomic particles

ba·sal (bā′səl) ***adj.*** **1** of or at the base **2** basic; fundamental

basal metabolism the minimum quantity of energy used by an organism at rest to sustain its life

ba·salt (bə sôlt′, bā′sôlt′) ***n.*** ‖ L *basaltes* ‖ a hard, dark volcanic rock

base[1] (bās) ***n.*** ‖ < Gr *basis* ‖ **1** the thing or part on which something rests **2** the most important element or principal ingredient **3** the part of a word to which affixes are attached **4** a basis **5** any of the four markers a baseball player must consecutively touch to score a run **6** a headquarters or a source of supply **7** *Chem.* a substance that forms a salt when it reacts with an acid —

adj. forming a base —*vt.* **based, bas'ing** 1 to make a base for 2 to establish

base² (bās) *adj.* **bas'er, bas'est** ‖ < VL *bassus,* low ‖ 1 mean; ignoble 2 menial 3 poor in quality 4 of comparatively low worth /*base* metal/ —**base'ly** *adv.* —**base'ness** *n.*

base'ball' *n.* 1 a game played with a ball and bat by two opposing teams on a field with four bases forming a diamond 2 the ball used in this game

base'board' *n.* a board or molding at the base of a wall

base hit *Baseball* a play in which the batter hits a fair ball and gets on base without an error or without forcing out a teammate

base'less *adj.* having no basis in fact; unfounded —**base'less·ness** *n.*

base line 1 a line serving as a base 2 *Baseball* the lane between any two consecutive bases 3 *Basketball, Tennis* the line at either end of the court Also **base'line'**

base'man (-mən) *n., pl.* **-men** *Baseball* an infielder stationed at first, second, or third base

base'ment *n.* the story below the main floor

base on balls *Baseball* WALK

base pay the basic rate of pay not counting overtime pay, etc.

base runner *Baseball* a player who is on base or is trying to reach a base

bash (bash) *vt.* ‖ echoic ‖ [Colloq.] to hit hard —*n.* [Slang] a party

bash'ful *adj.* ‖ (A)BASH + -FUL ‖ easily embarrassed; shy —**bash'ful·ly** *adv.* —**bash'ful·ness** *n.*

bas·ic (bā'sik) *adj.* 1 fundamental 2 *Chem.* alkaline —*n.* a basic principle, factor, etc. —**bas'i·cal·ly** *adv.*

BAS·IC (bā'sik) *n.* ‖ *B(eginner's) A(ll-purpose) S(ymbolic) I(nstruction) C(ode)* ‖ a simple computer language that uses common words and algebra

bas·il (baz'əl, bā'zəl) *n.* ‖ < Gr *basilikon* ‖ a fragrant herb of the mint family, used in cooking

ba·sil·i·ca (bə sil'i kə) *n.* ‖ < Gr *basilikē* (*stoa*), royal (portico) ‖ 1 a church with a broad nave, side aisles, and an apse 2 *R.C.Ch.* a church with certain ceremonial rights

ba·sin (bās'ən) *n.* ‖ < VL *bacca,* water vessel ‖ 1 a wide, shallow container for liquid 2 its contents 3 a sink 4 any shallow, rounded hollow, often containing water 5 RIVER BASIN

ba·sis (bā'sis) *n., pl.* **-ses'** (-sēz') ‖ < Gr, a base ‖ 1 a base or foundation 2 a principal constituent 3 a fundamental principle or theory

bask (bask) *vi.* ‖ ME *basken,* to wallow ‖ to expose oneself pleasantly to warmth, another's favor, etc.

bas·ket (bas'kit) *n.* ‖ ME ‖ 1 a container made of interwoven cane, wood strips, etc. 2 its contents 3 *Basketball a)* the goal, a round, open, hanging net *b)* a goal made by shooting the ball through this net

bas'ket·ball' *n.* ‖ invented & named (1891) by James A. Naismith (1861-1939) ‖ 1 a team game played with a bouncy, round, inflated ball on a court having a raised basket at each end 2 this ball

basket weave a weave of fabrics resembling the weave used in making baskets

bas'ket·work' *n.* work that is woven like a basket; wickerwork

Basque (bask) *n.* 1 a member of a people living in the W Pyrenees 2 their language —*adj.* of the Basques

bas-re·lief (bä'ri lēf', bas'-) *n.* ‖ Fr < It: see BASS¹ & RELIEF ‖ sculpture in which figures project slightly from a flat background

bass¹ (bās) *n.* ‖ < VL *bassus,* low ‖ 1 the range of the lowest male voice 2 a singer or instrument with this range; specif., a double bass 3 a low, deep sound —*adj.* of, for, or having the range of a bass

bass² (bas) *n., pl.* **bass** or **bass'es** ‖ OE *baers* ‖ a spiny-finned food and game fish of fresh or salt water

bas·set (bas'it) *n.* ‖ < OFr *bas,* low ‖ a hunting hound with a long body, short forelegs, and long, drooping ears

bas·si·net (bas'ə net') *n.* ‖ < Fr dim. of *berceau,* a cradle ‖ a basketlike bed for an infant, often hooded and on wheels

bas·so (bas'ō, bäs'-) *n., pl.* **-sos** or **-si** (-sē) ‖ < VL *bassus,* low ‖ a bass voice or singer

BASSOON

bas·soon (ba sōōn', bə-) *n.* ‖ < VL *bassus,* low ‖ a double-reed bass woodwind instrument

bast (bast) *n.* ‖ OE *bæst* ‖ plant fiber used in ropes, mats, etc.

bas·tard (bas'tərd) *n.* ‖ < OFr ‖ an illegitimate child —*adj.* 1 of illegitimate birth 2 inferior, sham, etc. —**bas'tar·dy** (-tər dē) *n.*

bas·tard·ize (bas'tər dīz') *vt.* **-ized', -iz'ing** 1 to make, declare, or show to be a bastard 2 to make corrupt; debase —**bas'tard·i·za'tion** *n.*

baste¹ (bāst) *vt.* **bast'ed, bast'ing** ‖ < Gmc *bastjan,* make with bast ‖ to sew temporarily with long, loose stitches until properly sewed

baste² (bāst) *vt.* **bast'ed, bast'ing** ‖ < OFr *bassin,* basin ‖ to moisten (meat) with melted butter, drippings, etc. while roasting —**bast'er** *n.*

baste³ (bāst) *vt.* **bast'ed, bast'ing** ‖ ON *beysta* ‖ 1 to beat soundly 2 to attack with words

bas·tille or **bas·tile** (bas tēl') *n.* ‖ < OFr *bastir,* to build ‖ a prison —**the Bastille** a state prison in Paris destroyed (1789) in the French Revolution

bas·tion (bas'chən, -tē ən) *n.* ‖ see BASTILLE ‖ 1 a projection from a fortification 2 any strong defense

bat¹ (bat) *n.* ‖ OE *batt* ‖ 1 a stout club 2 a club to hit the ball in baseball, etc. 3 a turn at batting 4 [Colloq.] a blow —*vt.* **bat'ted,**

bat′ting to hit, as with a bat —*vi.* to take a turn at batting
bat[2] (bat) ***n.*** ‖< Scand ‖ a furry, nocturnal flying mammal with membranous wings
bat[3] (bat) ***vt.*** **bat′ted, bat′ting** ‖< OFr *battre*, to batter ‖ [Colloq.] to wink —**not bat an eye** [Colloq.] not show surprise
batch (bach) ***n.*** ‖OE *bacan*, to bake ‖ **1** the amount (of bread, etc.) in one baking **2** one set, lot, group, etc. **3** an amount of work for processing by a computer in a single run
bate (bāt) ***vt.*** **bat′ed, bat′ing** ‖< OFr *abattre*, beat down ‖ to abate or lessen —**with bated breath** holding the breath, as in fear
bath (bath) ***n.***, *pl.* **baths** (bathz, baths) ‖OE *bæth* ‖ **1** a washing, esp. of the body, in water **2** water, etc. for bathing or for soaking or treating something **3** a bathtub **4** a bathroom **5** a BATHHOUSE (sense 1)
bathe (bāth) ***vt.*** **bathed, bath′ing** ‖OE *bæth* ‖ **1** to put into a liquid **2** to give a bath to **3** to cover as with liquid —***vi.*** **1** to take a bath **2** to soak oneself in something —**bath·er** (bā′thər) ***n.***
bath′house′ ***n.*** **1** a public building for taking baths **2** a building used by bathers for changing clothes
bathing suit a swimsuit
bath′mat′ ***n.*** a mat used in or next to a bathtub
ba·thos (bā′thäs′, -thôs′) ***n.*** ‖< Gr *bathys*, deep ‖ **1** ANTICLIMAX (sense 1) **2** excessive sentimentality **3** triteness —**ba·thet·ic** (bə thet′ik) ***adj.***
bath′robe′ ***n.*** a loose robe worn to and from the bath, etc.
bath′room′ ***n.*** a room with a bathtub, toilet, etc.
bath′tub′ ***n.*** a tub to bathe in
bath·y·scaph (bath′i skaf′, -ə-) ***n.*** ‖< Gr *bathys*, deep + *skaphē*, boat ‖ a deep-sea diving apparatus for reaching great depths without a cable Also **bath′y·scaphe′** (-skaf′, -skāf′)
ba·tik (bə tēk′) ***n.*** ‖Malay ‖ cloth with a design made by dyeing only the parts not coated with wax
ba·tiste (bə tēst′, ba-) ***n.*** ‖Fr: after supposed orig. maker, *Baptiste* ‖ a fine, thin cloth of cotton, rayon, etc.
ba·ton (bə tän′, ba-) ***n.*** ‖Fr ‖ **1** a staff serving as a symbol of office **2** a slender stick used in directing music **3** a metal rod twirled by a drum major
Bat·on Rouge (bat″n ro͞ozh′) capital of La.: pop. 219,000
bat·tal·ion (bə tal′yən) ***n.*** ‖< VL *battalia*, battle ‖ a tactical military unit forming part of a division
bat·ten[1] (bat″n) ***n.*** ‖var. of *baton* ‖ **1** a sawed strip of wood **2** a strip of wood put over a seam between boards as a fastening or covering —***vt.*** to fasten or supply with battens
bat·ten[2] (bat″n) ***vi.***, ***vt.*** ‖ON *batna*, improve ‖ to fatten; thrive
bat·ten[3] (bat″n) ***n.*** ‖< OFr *battre*, to batter ‖ in a loom, the movable frame that presses into place the threads of a woof
bat·ter[1] (bat′ər) ***vt.*** ‖< L *battuere*, to beat ‖ **1** to strike with blow after blow **2** to injure by pounding, hard wear, or use —***vi.*** to pound noisily
bat·ter[2] (bat′ər) ***n.*** *Baseball, Cricket* the player at bat
bat·ter[3] (bat′ər) ***n.*** ‖OFr *bature* ‖ a flowing mixture of flour, milk, etc. for making cakes, pancakes, etc.
battering ram a heavy beam, etc. for battering down gates, etc.
bat·ter·y (bat′ər ē) ***n.***, *pl.* **-ies** ‖< OFr *battre*, to batter ‖ **1** a battering **2** a set of things used together **3** *Baseball* the pitcher and the catcher **4** *Elec.* a cell or group of cells storing an electrical charge and able to furnish a current **5** *Law* any illegal beating of another person: see ASSAULT AND BATTERY **6** *Mil.* a set of heavy guns, rockets, etc.
bat·ting (bat″n, -iŋ) ***n.*** ‖OE *batt*, BAT[1] ‖ cotton, wool, or synthetic fiber wadded into sheets
bat·tle (bat″l) ***n.*** ‖< L *battuere*, to beat ‖ **1** a large-scale fight between armed forces **2** armed fighting **3** any fight or conflict —***vt.***, ***vi.*** **-tled, -tling** to fight —**give** (or **do**) **battle** to fight
bat′tle-ax′ or **bat′tle-axe′** ***n.*** **1** a heavy ax formerly used as a weapon **2** [Slang] a harsh, domineering woman
bat′tle·dore′ (-dôr′) ***n.*** ‖< OFr *battre*, to batter ‖ a racket used to hit a shuttlecock in a game like badminton
bat′tle·field′ ***n.*** the site of a battle Also **bat′tle·ground′**
bat′tle·ment (-mənt) ***n.*** ‖< OFr *batailler*, fortify ‖ a parapet with spaces for shooting, built atop a tower, etc.
battle royal *pl.* **battles royal** **1** a free-for-all **2** a heated dispute
bat′tle·ship′ ***n.*** a large warship with big guns and very heavy armor
bat·ty (bat′ē) ***adj.*** **-ti·er, -ti·est** ‖< BAT[2] ‖ [Slang] crazy or eccentric
bau·ble (bô′bəl) ***n.*** ‖< L *bellus*, pretty ‖ a showy trifle; trinket
baud (bôd) ***n.*** ‖after J. M. E. *Baudot* (1845-1903), Fr inventor ‖ the number of bits per second transmitted in a computer system
baux·ite (bôks′īt′) ***n.*** ‖Fr, after (*Les*) *Baux*, town in S France ‖ a claylike ore, the source of aluminum
Ba·var·i·a (bə ver′ē ə) state of S West Germany —**Ba·var′i·an** ***adj.***, ***n.***
bawd (bôd) ***n.*** ‖< ? OFr *baud*, licentious ‖ [Literary] a person, esp. a woman, who keeps a brothel
bawd·y (bô′dē) ***adj.*** **-i·er, -i·est** indecent; lewd —**bawd′i·ness** ***n.***
bawl (bôl) ***vi.***, ***vt.*** ‖< ML *baulare*, to bark ‖ **1** to shout **2** to weep loudly —***n.*** **1** an outcry **2** a noisy weeping —**bawl out** [Slang] to scold angrily
bay[1] (bā) ***n.*** ‖< ML *baia* ‖ a wide inlet of a sea or lake, along the shoreline
bay[2] (bā) ***n.*** ‖< VL *batare*, to gape ‖ **1** an alcove or recess **2** BAY WINDOW
bay[3] (bā) ***vi.*** ‖< OFr *baiier* ‖ to bark or howl in long, deep tones —***n.*** **1** the sound of baying **2** the situation of a hunted animal forced to turn and fight —**at bay** **1** cornered **2** held off —**bring to bay** to corner
bay[4] (bā) ***n.*** ‖< L *baca*, berry ‖ **1** LAUREL (*n.* 1) **2** [*pl.*] a laurel wreath
bay[5] (bā) ***adj.*** ‖< L *badius* ‖ reddish-brown

—*n.* 1 a reddish-brown horse, etc. 2 reddish brown

bay′ber′ry *n., pl.* **-ries** 1 a shrub with small, wax-coated, berrylike fruit 2 the fruit

bay leaf the dried, aromatic leaf of certain plants, as the laurel, used as a spice

bay·o·net (bā′ə net′, bā′ə nət) *n.* ⟦< Fr: after *Bayonne*, city in France⟧ a detachable blade put on a rifle muzzle, for stabbing —*vt., vi.* **-net′ed** or **-net′ted, -net′ing** or **-net′ting** to stab with a bayonet

bay·ou (bī′o͞o′) *n.* ⟦< AmInd *bayuk*, small stream⟧ in S U.S., a marshy inlet or outlet of a lake, river, etc.

bay window 1 a window or set of windows jutting out from a wall 2 [Slang] a large protruding belly

ba·zaar (bə zär′) *n.* ⟦Pers *bāzār*⟧ 1 a marketplace, esp. in the Middle East 2 a benefit sale for a church, etc.

ba·zoo·ka (bə zo͞o′kə) *n.* ⟦< name of a comic horn⟧ a portable weapon for launching armor-piercing rockets

BB (shot) ⟦designation of size⟧ a size of shot (diameter, .18 in.) for an air rifle (**BB gun**) or shotgun

BC or **B.C.** 1 before Christ 2 British Columbia

B cell any of the lymphatic leukocytes not derived from the thymus, that build antibodies: cf. T CELL

be (bē, bi) *vi.* **was** or **were, been, being** ⟦OE *beon*⟧ 1 to exist; live 2 to happen; occur 3 to remain or continue *Note*: *be* is used to link its subject to a predicate complement /she *is* nice/ or as an auxiliary: (1) with a past participle: *a*) to form the passive voice /he will *be* sued/ *b*) to form the perfect tense /Christ *is* risen/ (2) with a present participle to express continuation /he *is* running/ (3) with a present participle or infinitive to express futurity, possibility, obligation, intention, etc. /she *is* going soon, he *is* to cut it/ *Be* is conjugated in the present indicative: (I) *am*, (he, she, it) *is*, (we, you, they) *are*; in the past indicative: (I, he, she, it) *was*, (we, you, they) *were*

be- ⟦< OE *bi-*, *be-*, at⟧ *prefix* 1 around /*beset*/ 2 completely /*bedeck*/ 3 away /*betake*/ 4 about /*bemoan*/ 5 to make /*besot*/ 6 to furnish with, affect by /*becloud*/

Be *Chem. symbol for* beryllium

beach (bēch) *n.* ⟦E dial., pebbles⟧ a sandy shore —*vt., vi.* to ground (a boat) on a beach

beach′comb′er (-kōm′ər) *n.* 1 COMBER (sense 2) 2 one who lives on items found on beaches —**beach′comb′ing** *n.*

beach′head′ *n.* a position gained, specif. by invading an enemy shore

bea·con (bē′kən) *n.* ⟦< OE *beacen*, a signal⟧ 1 a light for warning or guiding 2 a radio transmitter sending guiding signals for aircraft

bead (bēd) *n.* ⟦< OE *bed*, prayer bead⟧ 1 a small ball of glass, etc., pierced for stringing 2 [*pl.*] a rosary 3 [*pl.*] a string of beads 4 any small, round object, as the front sight of a rifle 5 a drop or bubble 6 the rim edge of a rubber tire —*vt.* to decorate with beads —**draw a bead on** to take careful aim at —**say one's beads** to pray with a rosary —**bead′y, -i·er, -i·est,** *adj.*

bea·dle (bēd′'l) *n.* ⟦ME *bidel*⟧ a minor officer in the Church of England, who kept order in church

bea·gle (bē′gəl) *n.* ⟦< ? Fr *bee gueule*, wide throat⟧ a small hound with short legs and drooping ears

beak (bēk) *n.* ⟦< L *beccus*⟧ 1 a bird's bill 2 a beaklike part, as the snout of various insects

beak·er (bēk′ər) *n.* ⟦< ? Gr *bikos*, vessel with handles⟧ 1 a goblet 2 *Chem.* a glass or metal container with a beaklike lip for pouring

beam (bēm) *n.* ⟦ME⟧ 1 a long, thick piece of wood, metal, etc. 2 the crossbar of a balance 3 a ship's breadth at its widest point 4 a shaft of light, etc. 5 a radiant look, smile, etc. 6 a steady radio or radar signal for guiding aircraft or ships —*vt.* 1 to give out (shafts of light) 2 to direct (a radio signal, etc.) —*vi.* 1 to shine brightly 2 to smile warmly

bean (bēn) *n.* ⟦OE *bean*⟧ 1 a plant of the pea family, bearing kidney-shaped seeds 2 the edible, smooth seed of this plant 3 any beanlike seed /coffee *bean*/ 4 [Slang] the head or brain —*vt.* [Slang] to hit on the head —**full of beans** [Slang] lively —**spill the beans** [Colloq.] to tell a secret

bear[1] (ber) *vt.* **bore, borne** or **born, bear′ing** ⟦OE *beran*⟧ 1 to carry 2 to have or show 3 to give birth to 4 to produce or yield 5 to support or sustain 6 to withstand or endure 7 to need /this *bears* watching/ 8 to carry or conduct (oneself) 9 to give /to *bear* witness/ —*vi.* 1 to be productive 2 to lie, point, or move in a given direction 3 to have bearing (*on*) 4 to tolerate —**bear down (on)** 1 to exert pressure or effort (on) 2 to approach —**bear out** to confirm —**bear up** to endure —**bear′a·ble** *adj.* —**bear′er** *n.*

bear[2] (ber) *n.* ⟦OE *bera*⟧ 1 a large, heavy mammal with shaggy fur and a short tail 2 [B-] either of two constellations in the Northern Hemisphere (**Great Bear** and **Little Bear**) 3 one who is clumsy, rude, etc. 4 one who sells stocks, etc. hoping to buy them back later at a lower price —*adj.* falling in price —**bear′like′** *adj.*

beard (bird) *n.* ⟦OE⟧ 1 the hair on the chin and cheeks of a man 2 any beardlike part 3 an awn —*vt.* 1 to defy 2 to provide with a beard —**beard′ed** *adj.* —**beard′less** *adj.*

bear·ing (ber′iŋ) *n.* 1 way of carrying and conducting oneself 2 a supporting part 3 a producing or ability to produce 4 endurance 5 [*often pl.*] relative direction or position 6 [*pl.*] awareness of one's situation 7 relevance; relation 8 a part of a machine on which another part revolves, slides, etc.

bear′ish *adj.* 1 bearlike; rude, rough, etc. 2 falling, or causing, expecting, etc. a fall, in prices on the stock exchange —**bear′ish·ly** *adv.*

bé·ar·naise sauce (bā′är nāz′) a creamy sauce, esp. for meat or fish

bear′skin′ *n.* 1 the fur or hide of a bear 2 a rug, coat, etc. made from this

beast (bēst) ***n.*** ‖< L *bestia*‖ **1** any large, four-footed animal **2** one who is gross, brutal, etc.
beast'ly ***adj.*** **-li·er, -li·est 1** of or like a beast; brutal, etc. **2** [Colloq.] disagreeable; unpleasant **—beast'li·ness** ***n.***
beast of burden any animal used for carrying things
beast of prey any animal that hunts and kills other animals for food
beat (bēt) ***vt.*** **beat, beat'en, beat'ing** ‖OE *beatan*‖ **1** to hit repeatedly; pound **2** to punish by so hitting; whip, spank, etc. **3** to dash repeatedly against **4** *a)* to form (a path, etc.) by repeated treading or riding *b)* to keep walking on /to *beat* the pavements/ **5** to mix (eggs, etc.) by hard stirring **6** to move (esp. wings) up and down **7** to search through (a forest, etc.) **8** to defeat or outdo **9** to mark (time or rhythm) by tapping, etc. **10** [Colloq.] to baffle **11** [Colloq.] to cheat **12** [Slang] to escape the penalties of **—*vi.*** **1** to hit or dash repeatedly **2** to throb **—*n.*** **1** a beating, as of the heart **2** any of a series of strokes **3** a throb **4** a habitual route **5** the unit of musical rhythm **6** BEATNIK **—*adj.*** **1** [Colloq.] tired out **2** of a group of young persons, esp. of the 1950's, expressing social disillusionment by unconventional dress, actions, etc. **—beat down** to put or force down **—beat it!** [Slang] go away! **—beat off** to drive back **—beat up (on)** [Slang] to give a beating to **—beat'er** ***n.***
beat'en ***adj.*** **1** shaped by hammering **2** much traveled /a *beaten* path/ **3** crushed in spirit
be·a·tif·ic (bē'ə tif'ik) ***adj.*** **1** making blessed **2** showing happiness or delight
be·at·i·fy (bē at'ə fī') ***vt.*** **-fied', -fy'ing** ‖< L *beatus,* happy + *facere,* to make‖ **1** to make blissfully happy **2** *R.C.Ch.* to declare (a deceased person) to be in heaven **—be·at'i·fi·ca'tion** ***n.***
beat'ing ***n.*** **1** the act of one that beats **2** a whipping **3** a throbbing **4** a defeat
be·at·i·tude (bē at'ə to͞od') ***n.*** ‖< L *beatus,* happy‖ perfect blessedness or happiness **—the Beatitudes** the pronouncements in the Sermon on the Mount
beat·nik (bēt'nik) ***n.*** a member of the beat group
beat'-up' ***adj.*** [Slang] worn-out, dilapidated, etc.
beau (bō) ***n.,*** *pl.* **beaus** or **beaux** (bōz) ‖Fr < L *bellus,* pretty‖ [Old-fashioned] a woman's sweetheart
Beau·mont (bō'mänt') city in SE Tex.: pop. 118,000
beau·te·ous (byo͞ot'ē əs) ***adj.*** ‖ME‖ beautiful **—beau'te·ous·ly** ***adv.***
beau·ti·cian (byo͞o tish'ən) ***n.*** one who works in a beauty shop
beau·ti·ful (byo͞ot'ə fəl) ***adj.*** having beauty **—beau'ti·ful·ly** ***adv.***
beau'ti·fy' (-fī') ***vt., vi.*** **-fied', -fy'ing** to make or become beautiful **—beau'ti·fi·ca'tion** (-fi kā'shən) ***n.*** **—beau'ti·fi'er** ***n.***
beau·ty (byo͞ot'ē) ***n.,*** *pl.* **-ties** ‖< L *bellus,* pretty‖ **1** the quality of being very pleasing, as in form, color, etc. **2** a thing with this quality **3** good looks **4** a very attractive person, feature, etc.
beauty salon (or **shop, parlor,** etc.) a place where esp. women go for hair styling, manicuring, etc.

BEAVER

bea·ver (bē'vər) ***n.*** ‖< OE *beofor*‖ **1** *a)* a large amphibious rodent with soft, brown fur, webbed hind feet, and a flat, broad tail *b)* its fur **2** a man's high silk hat
be·calm (bē käm', bi-) ***vt.*** **1** to make calm **2** to make (a ship) motionless from lack of wind
be·cause (bē kôz', -kuz'; bi-) ***conj.*** ‖ME *bi,* by + *cause*‖ for the reason or cause that **—because of** by reason of
beck (bek) ***n.*** a beckoning gesture **—at the beck and call of** at the service of
beck·on (bek''n) ***vi., vt.*** ‖OE *beacnian*‖ **1** to summon by a gesture **2** to lure; entice
be·cloud (bē kloud', bi-) ***vt.*** **1** to cloud over **2** to confuse; muddle
be·come (bē kum', bi-) ***vi.*** **-came', -come', -com'ing** ‖OE *becuman*‖ to come or grow to be **—*vt.*** to befit; suit **—become of** to happen to
be·com'ing ***adj.*** **1** appropriate; fit **2** suitable to the wearer
bed (bed) ***n.*** ‖OE‖ **1** a piece of furniture for sleeping on **2** a plot of soil where plants are raised **3** the bottom of a river, lake, etc. **4** any flat surface used as a foundation **5** a stratum **—*vt.*** **bed'ded, bed'ding 1** to put to bed **2** to embed **3** to plant in a bed of earth **4** to arrange in layers **—*vi.*** **1** to go to bed; rest; sleep **2** to stratify
be·daz·zle (bē daz'əl, bi-) ***vt.*** **-zled, -zling** to dazzle thoroughly; bewilder
bed'bug' ***n.*** a small, wingless, biting insect that infests beds, etc.
bed'clothes' (-klōz', -klō*thz*') ***n.pl.*** sheets, blankets, etc. used on a bed
bed'cov'er ***n.*** a bedspread; coverlet
bed'ding (-iŋ) ***n.*** **1** mattresses and bedclothes **2** a bottom layer; base
be·deck (bē dek', bi-) ***vt.*** to adorn
be·dev·il (bē dev'əl, bi-) ***vt.*** **-iled** or **-illed, -il·ing** or **-il·ling** to plague or bewilder **—be·dev'il·ment** ***n.***
bed'fel'low ***n.*** **1** a person who shares one's bed **2** an associate, ally, etc.
be·dim (bē dim', bi-) ***vt.*** **-dimmed', -dim'ming** to make (the eyes or the vision) dim
bed·lam (bed'ləm) ***n.*** ‖after (the old London mental hospital of St. Mary of) *Bethlehem*‖ any place or condition of noise and confusion
bed of roses [Colloq.] a situation or position of ease and luxury
Bed·ou·in (bed'o͞o in') ***n.,*** *pl.* **-ins** or **-in** ‖< Ar *badāwīn,* desert dwellers‖ [*also* **b-**] **1** an Arab of the desert tribes of Arabia, Syria, or N Africa **2** any wanderer
bed'pan' ***n.*** a shallow pan for use as a toilet by one confined to bed
be·drag·gle (bē drag'əl, bi-) ***vt.*** **-gled, -gling**

to make wet, limp, and dirty, as by dragging through mire

bed'rid'den (-rid''n) ***adj.*** confined to bed by illness, infirmity, etc.

bed'rock' ***n.*** 1 solid rock beneath the soil, etc. 2 a foundation or bottom

bed'roll' ***n.*** a portable roll of bedding, as for sleeping outdoors

bed'room' ***n.*** a room for sleeping

bed'side' ***n.*** the space beside a bed —***adj.*** near a bed

bed'sore' ***n.*** a sore on the body of a bedridden person, caused by chafing

bed'spread' ***n.*** an ornamental spread covering the blanket on a bed

bed'stead' (-sted') ***n.*** a framework for the spring and mattress of a bed

bed'time' ***n.*** one's usual time for going to bed

bee[1] (bē) ***n.*** ‖ OE *beo* ‖ a broad-bodied, four-winged, hairy insect that gathers pollen and nectar and that can sting

bee[2] (bē) ***n.*** ‖ OE *ben*, compulsory service ‖ a meeting of people to work together or to compete

beech (bēch) ***n.*** ‖ OE *bece* ‖ 1 a tree with smooth, gray bark, hard wood, and edible nuts 2 its wood

beech'nut' ***n.*** the small, three-cornered, edible nut of the beech tree

beef (bēf) ***n.***, *pl.* **beeves** or **beefs** ‖ < L *bos*, ox ‖ 1 a full-grown ox, cow, bull, or steer, esp. one bred for meat 2 such animals collectively 3 their meat 4 [Colloq.] *a)* human flesh *b)* strength 5 [Slang] a complaint —***vi.*** [Slang] to complain —**beef up** [Colloq.] to reinforce

beef'cake' ***n.*** ‖ BEEF (*n.* 4*a*) + (CHEESE)CAKE ‖ [Colloq.] display of the figure of a nude or partly nude, muscular man, as in a photograph

beef'steak' ***n.*** a thick slice of beef for broiling or frying

beef'y ***adj.*** **-i·er, -i·est** brawny —**beef'i·ness** ***n.***

bee'hive' ***n.*** 1 a shelter for a colony of bees 2 a place of great activity

bee'keep'er ***n.*** one who keeps bees for producing honey —**bee'keep'ing** ***n.***

bee'line' ***n.*** a straight line or direct route

Be·el·ze·bub (bē el'zə bub') *Bible* the chief devil; Satan

been (bin, ben; *Brit* bēn) ***vi.*** *pp. of* BE

beep (bēp) ***n.*** ‖ echoic ‖ the brief, high-pitched sound of a horn or electronic signal —***vi., vt.*** to make or cause to make this sound

beer (bir) ***n.*** ‖ OE *beor* ‖ 1 an alcoholic, fermented drink made from malt and hops 2 a soft drink made from extracts of roots, etc. /ginger *beer*/

bees'wax' ***n.*** wax secreted by honeybees, used to make their honeycombs

beet (bēt) ***n.*** ‖ < L *beta* ‖ 1 a plant with edible leaves and a thick, fleshy, white or red root 2 the edible root, also a source of sugar

Bee·tho·ven (bā'tō'vən), **Lud·wig van** (loot'vikh vän) 1770-1827; Ger. composer

bee·tle[1] (bēt''l) ***n.*** ‖ OE *bītan*, to bite ‖ an insect with hard front wings that cover the membranous hind wings when these are folded

bee·tle[2] (bēt''l) ***vi.*** **-tled, -tling** ‖ prob. < fol. ‖ to overhang —***adj.*** overhanging: also **bee'tling**

bee'tle-browed' (-broud') ***adj.*** ‖ < ME < ? *bitel*, sharp + *brouwe*, brow ‖ 1 having bushy eyebrows 2 frowning

be·fall (bē fôl', bi-) ***vi., vt.*** **-fell', -fall'en, -fall'ing** ‖ < OE *be-*, BE- + *feallan*, to fall ‖ to happen or occur (to)

be·fit (bē fit', bi-) ***vt.*** **-fit'ted, -fit'ting** to be suitable or proper for; be suited to —**be·fit'ting** ***adj.***

be·fog (bē fôg', -fäg'; bi-) ***vt.*** **-fogged', -fog'ging** 1 to envelop in fog; make foggy 2 to obscure; confuse

be·fore (bē fôr', bi-) ***adv.*** ‖ OE *be-*, by + *foran*, fore ‖ 1 ahead; in front 2 previously 3 earlier; sooner —***prep.*** 1 ahead of 2 in front of 3 in or to the sight, presence, etc. of 4 earlier than 5 in preference to —***conj.*** 1 earlier than the time that /call *before* you go/ 2 rather than /I'd die *before* I'd tell/

be·fore'hand' ***adv., adj.*** ahead of time; in anticipation

be·foul (bē foul', bi-) ***vt.*** 1 to make filthy 2 to slander

be·friend (bē frend', bi-) ***vt.*** to act as a friend to; help

be·fud·dle (bē fud''l, bi-) ***vt.*** **-dled, -dling** to confuse or stupefy

beg (beg) ***vt., vi.*** **begged, beg'ging** ‖ < Du *beggaert*, religious mendicant ‖ 1 to ask for (alms) 2 to ask earnestly; entreat —**beg off** to ask to be released from —**go begging** to be available but unwanted

be·gan (bē gan', bi-) ***vi., vt.*** *pt. of* BEGIN

be·get (bē get', bi-) ***vt.*** **-got'** or [Archaic] **-gat'** (-gat'), **-got'ten** or **-got', -get'ting** ‖ < OE *begietan*, acquire ‖ 1 to be the father of 2 to produce; cause

beg·gar (beg'ər) ***n.*** 1 one who begs 2 a pauper —***vt.*** 1 to make poor 2 to make (a description, etc.) seem inadequate —**beg'gar·y**, *pl.* **-ies**, ***n.***

beg'gar·ly ***adj.*** very poor, worthless, inadequate, etc.

be·gin (bē gin', bi-) ***vi., vt.*** **-gan', -gun', -gin'ning** ‖ < OE *beginnan* ‖ 1 to start doing, acting, etc. 2 to originate

be·gin'ner ***n.*** one just beginning to do or learn something; novice

be·gin'ning ***n.*** 1 a starting 2 the time or place of starting; origin 3 the first part 4 [*usually pl.*] an early stage

be·gone (bē gôn', bi-) ***interj., vi.*** (to) be gone; go away; get out

be·gon·ia (bi gōn'yə) ***n.*** ‖ after M. *Bégon* (1638-1710), Fr patron of science ‖ a tropical plant with showy flowers and ornamental leaves

be·got (bē gät', bi-) ***vt.*** *pt. & alt. pp. of* BEGET

be·got'ten (-'n) ***vt.*** *alt. pp. of* BEGET

be·grime (bē grīm', bi-) ***vt.*** **-grimed', -grim'ing** to cover with grime; soil

be·grudge (bē gruj', bi-) ***vt.*** **-grudged', -grudg'ing** 1 to resent another's possession of (something) 2 to give with reluctance —**be·grudg'ing·ly** ***adv.***

be·guile (bē gīl', bi-) ***vt.*** **-guiled', -guil'ing** 1 to mislead or deprive (*of*) by guile; deceive 2 to pass (time) pleasantly 3 to charm or delight —**be·guile′ment** *n.* —**be·guil′er** *n.*

be·gun (bē gun′, bi-) *vi., vt. pp. of* BEGIN

be·half (bē haf′, bi-) *n.* ‖ OE *be,* by + *healf,* side ‖ support —**in** (or **on**) **behalf of** in the interest of; for

be·have (bē hāv′, bi-) *vt., vi.* **-haved′, -hav′·ing** ‖ see BE- & HAVE ‖ **1** to conduct (oneself) in a specified way **2** to conduct (oneself) properly

be·hav′ior (-yər) *n.* way of behaving; conduct or action —**be·hav′ior·al** *adj.*

behavioral science any of the sciences, as sociology, psychology, etc., that study human behavior

be·head (bē hed′, bi-) *vt.* to cut off the head of

be·held (bē held′, bi-) *vt. pt. & pp. of* BEHOLD

be·he·moth (bi hē′məth) *n.* ‖ < Heb *behema,* beast ‖ **1** *Bible* some huge animal **2** any huge or powerful animal or thing

be·hest (bē hest′, bi-) *n.* ‖ < OE *behæs,* a vow ‖ a command or earnest request

be·hind (bē hīnd′, bi-) *adv.* ‖ < OE *behindan* ‖ **1** in or to the rear **2** in a former time, place, etc. **3** in or into arrears **4** slow; late —*prep.* **1** remaining after **2** in or to the rear of **3** inferior to **4** later than /*behind* schedule/ **5** beyond **6** advocating /he is *behind* the plan/ **7** hidden by /what's *behind* this news/ —*n.* [Colloq.] the buttocks

be·hold (bē hōld′, bi-) *vt.* **-held′, -hold′ing** ‖ < OE *bihealdan* ‖ to look at; see —*interj.* look! see! —**be·hold′er** *n.*

be·hold′en (-ən) *adj.* indebted

be·hoove (bē hōōv′, bi-) *vt.* **-hooved′, -hoov′ing** ‖ < OE *behofian,* to need ‖ to be incumbent upon or proper for /it *behooves* you to go/

beige (bāzh) *n.* ‖ Fr ‖ grayish tan —*adj.* grayish-tan

Bei·jing (bā′jiŋ′) capital of the People's Republic of China, in the NE part: pop. 9,500,000

be·ing (bē′iŋ) *n.* ‖ see BE ‖ **1** existence; life **2** fundamental nature **3** one that lives or exists —**being as** (or **that**) [Colloq. or Dial.] since; because —**for the time being** for now

Bei·rut (bā rōōt′) seaport & capital of Lebanon: pop. *c.* 702,000

be·jew·el (bē jōō′əl, bi-) *vt.* **-eled** or **-elled, -el·ing** or **-el·ling** to decorate with or as with jewels

be·la·bor (bē lā′bər, bi-) *vt.* **1** to beat severely **2** to scold **3** to spend too much time on

be·lat·ed (bē lāt′id, bi-) *adj.* tardy —**be·lat′·ed·ly** *adv.*

be·lay (bi lā′) *vt., vi.* **-layed′, -lay′ing** ‖ < OE *belecgan,* make fast ‖ **1** to make (a rope) secure by winding around a cleat, etc. **2** [Colloq.] *Naut.* to hold; stop **3** to secure by a rope

bel can·to (bel′kän′tō) ‖ It ‖ a style of singing with brilliant vocal display and purity of tone

belch (belch) *vi., vt.* ‖ OE *bealcian* ‖ **1** to expel (gas) through the mouth from the stomach **2** to throw forth (its contents) violently —*n.* a belching

be·lea·guer (bē lē′gər, bi-) *vt.* ‖ < Du < *be-,* around + *leger,* a camp ‖ **1** to besiege by encircling **2** to beset or harass

Bel·fast (bel′fast; bel fast′) seaport & capital of Northern Ireland: pop. 319,000

bel·fry (bel′frē) *n., pl.* **-fries** ‖ ult. < OHG ‖ **1** a bell tower **2** the part of a tower that holds the bells

Belg. Belgium

Bel·gium (bel′jəm) kingdom in W Europe: 11,792 sq. mi.; pop. 9,868,000 —**Bel′gian** *adj., n.*

Bel·grade (bel′grād′, -gräd′) capital of Yugoslavia: pop. 1,470,000

be·lie (bē lī′, bi-) *vt.* **-lied′, -ly′ing** **1** to disguise or misrepresent **2** to leave unfulfilled **3** to prove false

be·lief (bə lēf′, bē-) *n.* ‖ < OE *geleafa* ‖ **1** conviction that certain things are true **2** religious faith **3** trust or confidence **4** creed or doctrine **5** an opinion; expectation; judgment

be·lieve (bə lēv′, bē-) *vt.* **-lieved′, -liev′ing** ‖ < OE *geliefan* ‖ **1** to take as true, real, etc. **2** to trust a statement or promise of (a person) **3** to suppose or think —*vi.* to have faith (*in*) —**be·liev′a·ble** *adj.* —**be·liev′er** *n.*

be·lit·tle (bē lit′'l, bi-) *vt.* **-tled, -tling** to make seem little, less important, etc. —**be·lit′tle·ment** *n.*

Be·lize (bə lēz′) country in Central America, on the Caribbean: 8,862 sq. mi.; pop. 160,000

bell (bel) *n.* ‖ OE *belle* ‖ **1** a hollow, cuplike object, as of metal, which rings when struck **2** the sound of a bell **3** anything shaped like a bell **4** *Naut.* a bell rung to mark the periods of the watch —*vt.* to attach a bell to —*vi.* to flare out like a bell

Bell (bel), **Alexander Gra·ham** (grā′əm) 1847 1922; U.S. inventor of the telephone, born in Scotland

bel·la·don·na (bel′ə dän′ə) *n.* ‖ < It, beautiful lady ‖ **1** a poisonous plant with purplish flowers and black berries **2** ATROPINE

bell′-bot′tom *adj.* flared at the ankles, as trousers or slacks Also **bell′-bot′tomed** —*n.* [*pl.*] bell-bottom trousers

bell′boy′ *n.* BELLHOP

belle (bel) *n.* ‖ Fr, fem. of *beau* ‖ a pretty woman or girl

belles-let·tres (bel le′tr′, -trə) *n.pl.* ‖ Fr ‖ literature as distinguished from technical writings

bell′hop′ *n.* one employed by a hotel, club, etc. to carry luggage and do errands

bel·li·cose (bel′i kōs′) *adj.* ‖ < L *bellicus,* of war ‖ quarrelsome; warlike —**bel′li·cos′i·ty** (-käs′ə tē) *n.*

bel·lig·er·ent (bə lij′ər ənt) *adj.* ‖ < L *bellum,* war + *gerere,* carry on ‖ **1** at war **2** of war **3** warlike **4** ready to fight or quarrel —*n.* a belligerent person, group, or nation —**bel·lig′er·ence** *n.* —**bel·lig′er·en·cy** *n.* —**bel·lig′er·ent·ly** *adv.*

bell jar a bell-shaped container made of glass, used to keep air, moisture, etc. in or out Also **bell glass**

bel·low (bel′ō) *vi.* ‖ < OE *bylgan* ‖ **1** to roar with a reverberating sound, as a bull **2** to cry out loudly, as in anger —*vt.* to utter loudly or powerfully —*n.* a bellowing sound

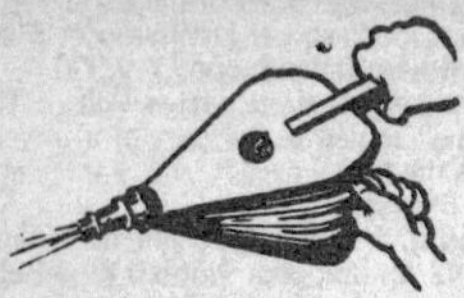

BELLOWS

bel·lows (bel′ōz′) *n.sing., n.pl.* ⟦ME *beli,* belly⟧ **1** a device that forces air out when its sides are pressed together: used in pipe organs, for blowing fires, etc. **2** anything collapsible like a bellows

bell pepper a large, sweet red pepper

Bell's palsy ⟦after C. *Bell* (1774-1842), Scot anatomist⟧ a usually temporary, sudden paralysis of the muscles on one side of the face

bell·weth·er (bel′we*th*′ər) *n.* ⟦ME⟧ **1** a male sheep, usually wearing a bell, that leads the flock **2** a leader

bel·ly (bel′ē) *n., pl.* **-lies** ⟦< OE *belg,* leather bag⟧ **1** the part of the body between the chest and thighs; abdomen **2** the underside of an animal's body **3** the stomach **4** the deep interior, as of a ship —*vt., vi.* **-lied, -ly·ing** to swell out

bel′ly·ache′ *n.* pain in the abdomen —*vi.* **-ached′, -ach′ing** [Slang] to complain

bel′ly·but′ton *n.* [Colloq.] the navel

bel′ly·ful′ *n.* **1** more than enough to eat **2** [Slang] all that one can bear

belly laugh [Colloq.] a hearty laugh

be·long (bē lôŋ′, bi-) *vi.* ⟦< ME⟧ **1** to have a proper place /it *belongs* here/ **2** to be related (*to*) **3** to be a member: with *to* **4** to be owned: with *to*

be·long′ings *n.pl.* possessions

Be·lo·rus·sian Soviet Socialist Republic (bel′ō rush′ən, bye′lō-) republic of the U.S.S.R., in the W European part: 80,300 sq. mi.; pop. 9,900,000: also **Be′lo·rus′sia** —**Be′lo·rus′sian** *adj., n.*

be·lov·ed (bi luv′id, -luvd′) *adj.* ⟦ME *biloven*⟧ dearly loved —*n.* a dearly loved person

be·low (bi lō′) *adv., adj.* ⟦see BE- & LOW[1]⟧ **1** in or to a lower place; beneath **2** later (in a book, etc.) **3** in or to hell **4** on earth **5** under in rank, amount, etc. —*prep.* **1** lower than **2** unworthy of

Bel·shaz·zar (bel shaz′ər) *Bible* the last king of Babylon

belt (belt) *n.* ⟦ult. < L *balteus*⟧ **1** a band of leather, etc. worn around the waist **2** any encircling thing like this **3** an endless band for transferring motion, as with pulleys, or conveying **4** a distinctive area /the corn *belt*/ **5** [Colloq.] a hard blow; punch **6** [Slang] *a*) a gulp, esp. of liquor *b*) a thrill —*vt.* **1** to encircle or fasten with a belt **2** to hit hard, as with a belt **3** [Colloq.] to sing loudly: usually with *out* **4** [Slang] to gulp (liquor) —**below the belt** unfair(ly) —**tighten one's belt** to live more thriftily

belt′way′ *n.* an expressway passing around an urban area

be·mire (bē mīr′, bi-) *vt.* **-mired′, -mir′ing** **1** to make dirty as with mire or mud **2** to cause to bog down in mud

be·moan (bē mōn′, bi-) *vt., vi.* to lament

be·muse (bē myōōz′, bi-) *vt.* **-mused′, -mus′·ing** ⟦BE- + MUSE⟧ **1** to muddle **2** to preoccupy

bench (bench) *n.* ⟦OE *benc*⟧ **1** a long, hard seat **2** the place where judges sit in a court **3** [*sometimes* **B-**] *a*) the status of a judge *b*) judges collectively *c*) a law court **4** WORKBENCH —*vt. Sports* to take (a player) out of a game —**on the bench** **1** serving as a judge **2** *Sports* not taking part in the game

bench mark a standard in measuring, judging quality, etc. Also **bench′mark′** *n.*

bench press a weight-lifting exercise, done while one is lying on a bench with the feet on the floor, in which a barbell is pushed upward from the chest —**bench′-press′** *vt.*

bench warrant an order issued by a judge or court for the arrest of a person

bend[1] (bend) *vt.* **bent, bend′ing** ⟦< OE *bendan,* confine with a string⟧ **1** to make curved or crooked **2** to turn, esp. from a straight line **3** to make submit —*vi.* **1** to turn, esp. from a straight line **2** to yield by curving, as from pressure **3** to curve the body; stoop (*over* or *down*) **4** to give in; yield —*n.* **1** a bending or being bent **2** a bent part —**bend′a·ble** *adj.*

bend[2] (bend) *n.* ⟦ME < prec.⟧ any of various knots for tying rope

be·neath (bē nēth′, bi-) *adv., adj.* ⟦OE *beneothan*⟧ in a lower place; underneath —*prep.* **1** below **2** under; underneath **3** unworthy of /it is *beneath* him to cheat/

ben·e·dic·tion (ben′ə dik′shən) *n.* ⟦< L *bene,* well + *dicere,* speak⟧ **1** a blessing **2** an invocation of blessing, esp. at the end of a religious service

ben·e·fac·tion (ben′ə fak′shen) *n.* ⟦< L *bene,* well + *facere,* do⟧ **1** the act of helping, esp. by charitable gifts **2** the money or help given

ben·e·fac·tor (ben′ə fak′tər) *n.* one who has given help, esp. financially; patron —**ben′e·fac′tress** *n.fem.*

ben·e·fice (ben′ə fis) *n.* ⟦< L *beneficium,* kindness⟧ an endowed church office providing a living for a vicar, etc.

be·nef·i·cence (bə nef′ə səns) *n.* ⟦see BENEFACTION⟧ **1** a being kind **2** a charitable act or gift

be·nef′i·cent (-sənt) *adj.* showing beneficence; doing or resulting in good —**be·nef′i·cent·ly** *adv.*

ben·e·fi·cial (ben′ə fish′əl) *adj.* producing benefits; advantageous; favorable —**ben′e·fi′cial·ly** *adv.*

ben′e·fi′ci·ar′y (-fish′ē er′ē, -fish′ər ē) *n., pl.* **-ar′ies** anyone receiving or to receive benefit, as funds from a will, an insurance policy, etc.

ben·e·fit (ben′ə fit, -fət) *n.* ⟦see BENEFACTION⟧ **1** anything contributing to improvement; advantage **2** [*often pl.*] payments made by an insurance company, public agency, etc. as during sickness, retirement, etc. or for death **3** a public performance, bazaar, etc. the proceeds of which are to help some person or cause —*vt.* **-fit·ed, -fit·ing** to help; aid —*vi.* to receive advantage; profit

be·nev·o·lence (bə nev′ə ləns) ***n.*** ‖< L *bene*, well + *volens*, to wish‖ 1 an inclination to do good; kindliness 2 a kindly, charitable act —**be·nev′o·lent** ***adj.*** —**be·nev′o·lent·ly** ***adv.***

Ben·gal (ben gôl′), **Bay of** part of the Indian Ocean, east of India

be·night·ed (bē nīt′id, bi-) ***adj.*** 1 surrounded by darkness 2 ignorant

be·nign (bi nīn′) ***adj.*** ‖< L *benignus*, well born‖ 1 good-natured; kindly 2 favorable; beneficial 3 *Med.* not malignant —**be·nign′ly** ***adv.***

be·nig·nant (bi nig′nənt) ***adj.*** ‖< prec‖ 1 kindly or gracious 2 BENIGN (senses 2 & 3)

be·nig′ni·ty (-nə tē) ***n.***, *pl.* **-ties** 1 kindliness 2 a kind act

Be·nin (be nēn′) country in west central Africa: 43,484 sq. mi.; pop. 4,141,000

bent[1] (bent) ***vt.***, ***vi.*** *pt. & pp. of* BEND[1] —***adj.*** 1 curved or crooked 2 strongly determined: with *on* 3 [Slang] *a)* dishonest *b)* eccentric; odd —***n.*** 1 a tendency 2 a natural leaning; propensity

bent[2] (bent) ***n.*** ‖OE *beonot*‖ a dense, low-growing grass that spreads by runners, used for lawns

bent′wood′ ***adj.*** of furniture made of wood permanently bent

be·numb (bē num′, bi-) ***vt.*** 1 to make numb 2 to deaden the mind, will, etc. of

ben·zene (ben′zēn, ben zēn′) ***n.*** ‖< Ar *lubān jāwī*, incense of Java‖ a clear, flammable, poisonous liquid used as a solvent, in plastics, etc.

ben·zo·caine (ben′zō kān′, zə-) ***n.*** ‖BENZ(ENE) + (C)OCAINE‖ a white, odorless powder used in ointments as a local anesthetic and to protect against sunburn

be·queath (bē kwēth′, kwēth′; bi-) ***vt.*** ‖< OE *be-*, BE- + *cwethan*, say‖ 1 to leave (property) to another by one's will 2 to hand down; pass on

be·quest′ (-kwest′) ***n.*** 1 a bequeathing 2 anything bequeathed

be·rate (bē rāt′, bi-) ***vt.*** **-rat′ed**, **-rat′ing** ‖BE- + RATE[2]‖ to scold severely

Ber·ber (bur′bər) ***n.*** 1 a member of a people of N Africa 2 their language —***adj.*** of the Berbers

be·reave (bē rēv′, bi-) ***vt.*** **-reaved′** or **-reft′** (-reft′), **-reav′ing** ‖< OE *be-*, BE- + *reafian*, rob‖ 1 to deprive: now usually in the pp. *bereft* /*bereft* of hope/ 2 to leave in a sad or lonely state, as by death —**be·reave′ment** ***n.***

be·ret (bə rā′) ***n.*** ‖< Fr < L *birrus*, a hood‖ a flat, round, soft cap

berg (burg) ***n.*** ICEBERG

ber·i·ber·i (ber′ē ber′ē) ***n.*** ‖Sinhalese, intens. of *beri*, weakness‖ a disease caused by lack of vitamin B_1 and characterized by nerve disorders, etc.

Ber·ing Sea (ber′iŋ) part of the N Pacific, between Siberia & Alas.

Bering Strait strait joining the Bering Sea with the Arctic Ocean

Berke·ley (burk′lē) city in Calif., near San Francisco: pop. 103,000

Ber·lin (bər lin′) city in E Germany, divided into **East Berlin**, capital of East Germany: pop. 1,197,000, & **West Berlin**, a state of West Germany that is an enclave in East Germany: pop. 1,852,000

berm (burm) ***n.*** ‖< MDu *baerm*‖ a ledge or shoulder, as along the edge of a paved road

Ber·mu·da (bər myoo′də) group of British islands in the W Atlantic

Bermuda shorts (bər myoo′də) knee-length pants Also **ber·mu′das** ***n.pl.***

Bern or **Berne** (burn) capital of Switzerland: pop. 141,000

ber·ry (ber′ē) ***n.***, *pl.* **-ries** ‖OE *berie*‖ 1 any small, juicy, fleshy fruit, as a strawberry 2 the dry seed of various plants, as a coffee bean —***vi.*** **-ried**, **-ry·ing** 1 to bear berries 2 to pick berries —**ber′ry·like′** ***adj.***

ber·serk (bər surk′, zurk′) ***adj.***, ***adv.*** ‖ON *berserkr*, warrior‖ in or into a violent rage or frenzy

berth (burth) ***n.*** ‖< BEAR[1] + -TH[1]‖ 1 a place where a ship anchors or moors 2 a position, job, etc. 3 a built-in bed, as on a ship or train —***vt.*** to put into or furnish with a berth —***vi.*** to occupy a berth —**give (a) wide berth to** to keep well clear of

ber·yl (ber′əl) ***n.*** ‖< Gr *bēryllos*‖ a very hard mineral of which emerald and aquamarine are two varieties

be·ryl·li·um (bə ril′ē əm) ***n.*** ‖< L *beryllus*, beryl‖ a hard, rare, metallic chemical element used in forming alloys

be·seech (bē sēch′, bi-) ***vt.*** **-sought′** or **-seeched′**, **-seech′ing** ‖< OE *be-* + *secan*, seek‖ to ask (for) earnestly; entreat —**be·seech′ing·ly** ***adv.***

be·seem (bē sēm′, bi-) ***vi.*** [Archaic] to be suitable or appropriate (to)

be·set (bē set′, bi-) ***vt.*** **-set′**, **-set′ting** ‖< OE *be-* + *settan*, set‖ 1 to attack from all sides; harass 2 to surround or hem in

be·set′ting ***adj.*** constantly harassing

be·side (bē sīd′, bi-) ***prep.*** ‖OE *bi sidan*‖ 1 at the side of; near 2 in comparison with /*beside* yours my share seems small/ 3 in addition to 4 other than —**beside oneself** wild or upset, as with fear, rage, etc.

be·sides′ (-sīdz′) ***adv.*** 1 in addition 2 except for that mentioned 3 moreover —***prep.*** 1 in addition to 2 other than

be·siege (bē sēj′, bi-) ***vt.*** **-sieged′**, **-sieg′ing** 1 to hem in with armed forces 2 to close in on 3 to overwhelm, harass, etc. /*besieged* with queries/

be·smear (bē smir′, bi-) ***vt.*** ‖OE *bismerian*‖ to smear over

be·smirch (bē smurch′, bi-) ***vt.*** to soil

be·som (bē′zəm) ***n.*** ‖OE *besma*‖ a broom, esp. one made of twigs tied to a handle

be·sot (bē sät′, bi-) ***vt.*** **-sot′ted**, **-sot′ting** to make a sot of; stupefy, as with liquor —**be·sot′ted** ***adj.***

be·sought (bē sôt′, bi-) ***vt.*** *alt. pt. & alt. pp. of* BESEECH

be·span·gle (bē spaŋ′gəl, bi-) ***vt.*** **-gled**, **-gling** to cover with or as with spangles

be·spat·ter (bē spat′ər, bi-) ***vt.*** to spatter, as with mud or slander

be·speak (bē spēk′, bi-) ***vt.*** **-spoke′**, **-spo′ken** or **-spoke′**, **-speak′ing** 1 to speak for in advance; reserve 2 to be indicative of; show

best (best) ***adj.*** ‖OE *betst*‖ 1 *superl. of* GOOD 2 most excellent 3 most suitable, desirable, etc. 4 largest /the *best* part of a day/ —*adv.* 1 *superl. of* WELL² 2 in the most excellent manner 3 in the highest degree —*n.* 1 the most excellent person, thing, etc. 2 the utmost —*vt.* to defeat or outdo —**all for the best** turning out to be good —**at best** under the most favorable conditions —**get** (or **have**) **the best of** 1 to defeat 2 to outwit —**make the best of** to do as well as one can with

bes·tial (bes′chəl, -tyəl; *often* bēs′) *adj.* ‖< L *bestia,* beast‖ like a beast; savage; brutal, etc. —**bes·ti·al·i·ty** (bes′chē al′ə tē, -tē-; *often* bēs′-), *pl.* **-ties,** *n.*

bes·tial·ize (bes′chəl īz′, -tyəl-; *often* bēs′) *vt.* **-ized′, -iz′ing** to make bestial

bes·ti·ar·y (bes′tē er′ē) *n., pl.* **-ies** ‖< L *bestia,* beast‖ a medieval book with fables about real or mythical animals

be·stir (bē stur′, bi-) *vt.* **-stirred′, -stir′ring** to stir to action; busy (oneself)

best man the principal attendant of the bridegroom at a wedding

be·stow (bē stō′, bi-) *vt.* ‖see BE- & STOW‖ to present as a gift: often with *on* or *upon* —**be·stow′al** *n.*

be·strew (bē strōō′, bi-) *vt.* **-strewed′, -strewed′** or **-strewn′, -strew′ing** to strew or scatter about

be·stride (bē strīd′, bi-) *vt.* **-strode′, -strid′den, -strid′ing** to sit on, mount, or stand astride

bet (bet) *n.* ‖prob. < ABET‖ 1 an agreement in which the one proved wrong about the outcome of something will do or pay what is stipulated 2 the thing or sum thus staked 3 a person or thing likely to bring about a desired result —*vt., vi.* **bet** or **bet′ted, bet′ting** 1 to declare as in a bet 2 to stake (money, etc.) in a bet with someone

be·ta (bāt′ə) *n.* the second letter of the Greek alphabet (Β, β)

beta blocker a drug used to control heart beat, treat hypertension, etc.

be·take (bē tāk′, bi-) *vt.* **-took′, -tak′en, -tak′ing** ‖ME *bitaken*‖ to go (used reflex ively)

beta particle an electron or positron ejected from the nucleus of an atom during radioac tive disintegration

beta ray a stream of beta particles

betel nut (bēt′'l) ‖Port < Malayalam *veṭṭilai*‖ the fruit of a palm (**betel palm**), chewed together with a lime and leaves of a pepper plant (**betel pepper**) by some Asians as a mild stimulant

be·think (bē thiŋk′, bi-) *vt.* **-thought′, -think′ing** [Archaic] to bring (oneself) to think of, recollect, etc.

Beth·le·hem (beth′lə hem′) ancient town in Palestine: Jesus' birthplace

be·tide (bē tīd′, bi-) *vi., vt.* **-tid′ed, -tid′ing** ‖< ME *be-,* BE- + *tiden,* happen‖ to happen (to); befall

be·times (bē tīmz′, bi-) *adv.* [Archaic] 1 early or early enough 2 promptly

be·to·ken (bē tō′kən, bi-) *vt.* ‖ME *betocnen*‖ 1 to be a token or sign of 2 to presage

be·tray (bē trā′, bi-) *vt.* ‖< L *tradere,* hand over‖ 1 to help the enemy of (one's country, etc.) 2 to expose treacherously 3 to fail to uphold /to *betray* a trust/ 4 to deceive; specif., to seduce and then desert 5 to reveal unknowingly —**be·tray′al** *n.* —**be·tray′er** *n.*

be·troth (bē trôth′, -trōth′; bi-) *vt.* ‖< ME: see BE- & TRUTH‖ to promise in marriage —**be·troth′al** *n.*

be·trothed′ (-trôtht′, -trōthd′) *adj.* engaged to be married —*n.* one engaged to be mar ried

bet·ta (bet′ə) *n.* ‖ModL‖ a brightly colored, tropical, freshwater gourami of SE Asia

bet·ter (bet′ər) *adj.* ‖OE *betera*‖ *compar. of* GOOD 1 more excellent 2 more suitable, desirable, etc. 3 larger /the *better* part of a day/ 4 improved in health —*adv.* 1 *compar. of* WELL² 2 in a more excellent manner 3 in a higher degree 4 more —*n.* 1 a person superior in authority, etc. 2 a more excellent thing, condition, etc. —*vt.* 1 to outdo; surpass 2 to improve —**better off** in a better situation —**get** (or **have**) **the better of** 1 to outdo 2 to outwit

bet′ter·ment (-mənt) *n.* a bettering; improvement

bet′tor *n.* one who bets Also **bet′ter**

be·tween (bē twēn′, bi-) *prep.* ‖OE *betweonum*‖ 1 in the space, time, etc. that separates (two things) 2 connecting /a bond *between* friends/ 3 by the joint action of 4 in the combined possession of 5 from one or the other of /choose *between* us/ 6 involving /a struggle *between* powers/ —*adv.* in an intermediate space, time, etc. —**between ourselves** as a secret: also **between you and me**

be·twixt (bē twikst′, bi-) *prep., adv.* ‖< OE *be,* by + *twegen,* twain‖ between: archaic except in **betwixt and between,** in an intermediate position

BeV or **Bev** (bev) *n., pl.* **BeV** or **Bev** ‖*b(illion) e(lectron-)v(olts)*‖ a unit of energy in the U.S., equal to one billion (10^9) electron-volts

bev·el (bev′əl) *n.* ‖< ?‖ 1 a tool for measuring or marking angles, etc. 2 an angle other than a right angle 3 angled part or surface —*adj.* beveled —*vt.* **-eled** or **-elled, -el·ing** or **-el·ling** to cut to an angle other than a right angle —*vi.* to slope at an angle

bevel gear a gearwheel meshed with another at an angle

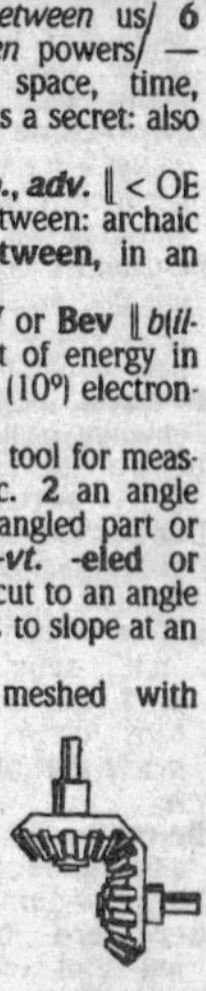
BEVEL GEARS

bev·er·age (bev′ər ij′) *n.* ‖< L *bibere,* to drink‖ any liquid for drinking, esp. one other than water

bev·y (bev′ē) *n., pl.* **-ies** ‖ME *bevey*‖ 1 a group, esp. of girls or women 2 a flock: now chiefly of quail

be·wail (bē wāl′) *vt.* to wail over; lament; mourn

be·ware (bē wer′) *vi., vt.* **-wared′, -war′ing** ‖prob. < OE *bewarian,* keep watch‖ to be wary or careful (of)

be·wigged (bē wigd′) *adj.* wearing a wig

be·wil·der (bē wil′dər) *vt.* ‖ult. < OE *wilde,* wild‖ to confuse hopelessly; befuddle —**be·wil′der·ment** *n.*

be·witch (bē wich′) *vt.* ‖< OE *wicca,* sorcerer‖ 1 to cast a spell over 2 to attract and delight greatly

bey (bā) ***n.*** ‖Turk‖ a Turkish title of respect and former title of rank

be·yond (bē änd′) ***prep.*** ‖< OE *be,* by + *geond,* yonder‖ **1** farther on than; past **2** later than **3** outside the reach of /*beyond* help/ **4** more than —***adv.*** farther away —**the (great) beyond** whatever follows death

bez·el (bez′əl) ***n.*** ‖< ?‖ **1** a sloping surface, as the cutting edge of a chisel **2** the slanting faces of a cut gem **3** the groove and flange holding a gem, watch crystal, etc. in place

Bhu·tan (bo͞o tän′) kingdom in the Himalayas, south central Asia: *c.* 18,000 mi.; pop. 1,446,000

Bi *Chem. symbol for* bismuth

bi- ‖L‖ *prefix* **1** having two **2** doubly **3** happening every two (specified periods) **4** happening twice during every (specified period) **5** using two or both **6** joining or involving two

bi·an·nu·al (bī an′yo͞o əl) ***adj.*** coming twice a year; semiannual

bi·as (bī′əs) ***n.,*** *pl.* **-as·es** ‖Fr *biais,* a slant‖ **1** a slanting or diagonal line, cut or sewn in cloth **2** partiality; prejudice —***adj.*** slanting; diagonal —***adv.*** diagonally —***vt.*** **-ased** or **-assed, -as·ing** or **-as·sing** to prejudice —**on the bias** diagonally

bi·ath·lon (bī ath′lən) ***n.*** ‖BI- + Gr *athlon,* contest‖ a winter sports event combining cross-country skiing and rifle marksmanship

bib (bib) ***n.*** ‖< L *bibere,* to drink‖ **1** a cloth or plastic cover tied under a child's chin at meals **2** the upper front part of an apron

Bib. 1 Bible **2** Biblical

bibb lettuce (bib) ‖after J. *Bibb* (1789-1884), who developed it‖ a type of lettuce with loose heads of crisp, dark-green leaves

Bi·ble (bī′b'l) ‖< Gr *biblos,* papyrus < *Byblos,* Phoenician city that exported papyrus‖ **1** the sacred book of Christianity; Old Testament and New Testament **2** the Holy Scriptures of Judaism; Old Testament —***n.*** [**b-**] any book regarded as authoritative or official —**bib·li·cal** or **Bib·li·cal** (bib′li kəl) ***adj.***

biblio- ‖< Gr *biblion,* book‖ *combining form* book, books /*bibliophile*/

bib·li·og·ra·phy (bib′lē äg′rə fē) ***n.,*** *pl.* **-phies** a list of writings on a given subject or by a given author, or of those used by the author of a given work —**bib′li·og′ra·pher** ***n.*** —**bib′li·o·graph′ic** (-ə graf′ik) ***adj.***

bib′li·o·phile′ (-ə fīl′) ***n.*** a person who loves or collects books

bib·u·lous (bib′yo͞o ləs) ***adj.*** ‖< L *bibere,* to drink‖ addicted to or fond of alcoholic beverages

bi·cam·er·al (bī kam′ər əl) ***adj.*** ‖< BI- + L *camera,* chamber‖ having two legislative chambers

bicarbonate of soda (bī kär′bən it) SODIUM BICARBONATE

bi·cen·ten·ni·al (bī′sen ten′ē əl) ***adj.*** happening once in every 200 years —***n.*** a 200th anniversary

bi·ceps (bī′seps′) ***n.,*** *pl.* **-ceps′** or **-ceps·es′** ‖< L < *bis,* two + *caput,* head‖ a muscle with two points of origin; esp., the large muscle in the front of the upper arm

bick·er (bik′ər) ***vi., n.*** ‖ME *bikeren*‖ squabble; quarrel —**bick′er·er** ***n.***

bi·con·cave (bī kän′kāv′) ***adj.*** concave on both surfaces /a *biconcave* lens/

bi·con′vex′ (-veks′) ***adj.*** convex on both surfaces /a *biconvex* lens/

bi·cus·pid (bī kus′pid) ***adj.*** ‖< BI- + L *cuspis,* pointed end‖ having two points —***n.*** any of eight adult teeth with two-pointed crowns

bi·cy·cle (bī′sik′əl) ***n.*** ‖Fr: see BI- & CYCLE‖ a vehicle consisting of a metal frame on two wheels, with handlebars and a seat —***vi.*** **-cled, -cling** to ride or travel on a bicycle —***vt.*** **1** to carry as on a bicycle **2** to travel over by bicycle —**bi′cy′clist** ***n.***

bid (bid) ***vt.*** **bade** or **bid, bid′den** or **bid, bid′ding** ‖< OE *biddan,* to urge & *beodan,* to command‖ **1** to command or ask **2** to offer (an amount) as the price one will pay or accept **3** to express /to *bid* farewell/ **4** *Card Games* to state (a number of tricks) and declare (trump) —***vi.*** to make a bid —***n.*** **1** a bidding **2** an amount bid **3** a chance to bid **4** an attempt or try (*for*) **5** [Colloq.] an invitation —**bid fair** to seem likely —**bid′der** ***n.***

bid·dy (bid′ē) ***n.,*** *pl.* **-dies** ‖< ?‖ **1** a hen **2** [Colloq.] an elderly woman regarded as annoying, gossipy, etc.: usually **old biddy**

bide (bīd) ***vi.*** **bode** or **bid′ed, bid′ed, bid′ing** ‖OE *bidan*‖ [Now Chiefly Dial.] **1** to stay; continue **2** to dwell **3** to wait —***vt.*** [Now Chiefly Dial.] to endure —**bide one's time** to wait patiently for an opportunity /she *bided* her time/

bi·det (bē dā′) ***n.*** ‖Fr‖ a low, bowl-shaped bathroom fixture, with running water, for bathing the crotch

bi·en·ni·al (bī en′ē əl) ***adj.*** ‖< L *bi-,* BI- + *annus,* year‖ **1** happening every two years **2** lasting for two years —***n.*** **1** a biennial event **2** *Bot.* a plant that lasts two years —**bi·en′ni·al·ly** ***adv.***

bier (bir) ***n.*** ‖OE *bær*‖ a portable framework on which a coffin is placed

bi·fo·cals (bī′fō′kəlz) ***n.pl.*** eyeglasses with lenses having one part ground for close focus and the other for distant focus

bi·fur·cate (bī′fər kāt′) ***vt., vi.*** **-cat′ed, -cat′ing** ‖< L *bi-,* BI- + *furca,* a fork‖ to divide into two parts or branches —**bi′fur·ca′tion** ***n.***

big (big) ***adj.*** **big′ger, big′gest** ‖ME‖ **1** of great size; large **2** great in amount or force **3** full-grown **4** elder /his *big* sister/ **5** noticeably pregnant (*with*) **6** loud **7** important **8** extravagant **9** noble /a *big* heart/ —***adv.*** [Colloq.] **1** boastfully **2** impressively —**big′ness** ***n.***

big·a·my (big′ə mē) ***n.*** ‖< L *bi-,* BI- + Gr *gamos,* marriage‖ the crime of marrying a second time when one is already legally married —**big′a·mist** ***n.*** —**big′a·mous** ***adj.***

big′-bang′ theory a theory that the expansion of the universe began with a gigantic explosion between 12 and 20 billion years ago

big game **1** large wild animals hunted for sport, as lions, tigers, moose, etc. **2** the object of any important or dangerous undertaking

big′heart′ed (-här′tid) ***adj.*** quick to give or forgive; generous

big'horn' *n.* a Rocky Mountain wild sheep with large horns

bight (bīt) *n.* ‖OE *byht*‖ 1 orig., a bend or angle 2 a slack part in a rope 3 a curve in a coastline 4 a bay

big'mouth' *n.* [Slang] a person who talks too much, esp. in an opinionated way

big·ot (big'ət) *n.* ‖Fr < ?‖ one who holds blindly and intolerantly to a particular creed, opinion, etc. —**big'ot·ed** *adj.* —**big'ot·ry** (-ə trē) *n.*

big shot [Slang] an important or influential person Also **big wheel**

bike (bīk) *n.* [Colloq.] 1 a bicycle 2 a motorcycle —**bik'er** *n.*

bi·ki·ni (bi kē'nē) *n.* ‖Fr after *Bikini*, Pacific atoll‖ 1 a very brief two-piece swimsuit for women 2 very brief legless underpants or swimming trunks

bi·lat·er·al (bī lat'ər əl) *adj.* 1 of, having, or involving two sides, factions, etc. 2 affecting both sides equally; reciprocal —**bi·lat'er·al·ly** *adv.*

bile (bīl) *n.* ‖Fr < L *bilis*‖ 1 the bitter, greenish fluid secreted by the liver: it aids digestion 2 bad temper; anger

bilge (bilj) *n.* ‖var. of BULGE‖ 1 the rounded, lower part of a ship's hold 2 stagnant water that collects there: also **bilge water** 3 [Slang] nonsense

bi·lin·gual (bī liŋ'gwəl) *adj.* ‖< L *bi-*, BI- + *lingua*, tongue‖ of, in, or using two languages —**bi·lin'gual·ism'** *n.*

bil·ious (bil'yəs) *adj.* ‖< L *bilis*, bile‖ 1 having or appearing to have some ailment of the bile or liver 2 bad tempered

bilk (bilk) *vt.* ‖? < BALK‖ to cheat or swindle; defraud —**bilk'er** *n.*

bill[1] (bil) *n.* ‖< L *bulla*, sealed document‖ 1 a statement of charges for goods or services; invoice 2 a list, as a menu or theater program 3 a poster or handbill 4 a draft of a proposed law 5 a bill of exchange 6 a piece of paper money 7 *Law* a written declaration of charges or complaints filed —*vt.* 1 to make out a bill of (items) 2 to present a statement of charges to 3 *a)* to advertise by bills *b)* to book (a performer) —**fill the bill** [Colloq.] to meet the requirements —**bill'a·ble** *adj.*

bill[2] (bil) *n.* ‖OE *bile*‖ 1 the projecting jaws of a bird, usually pointed; beak 2 a beaklike mouth part, as of a turtle —*vi.* to touch bills together —**bill and coo** to kiss, talk softly, etc. in a loving way

bill'board' *n.* a signboard, usually outdoors, for advertising posters

bil·let (bil'it) *n.* ‖see BILL[1]‖ 1 *a)* a written order to provide lodging for military personnel *b)* the lodging 2 a position, job, or situation —*vt.* to assign to lodging by billet

bil·let-doux (bē'yā do͞o') *n.*, *pl.* **bil·lets-doux** (bē'yā do͞o') ‖Fr, sweet letter‖ a love letter

bill·fold (bil'fōld') *n.* a wallet

bil·liard (bil'yərd) *adj.* of or for billiards

bil'liards (-yərdz) *n.* ‖< Fr *billard*, orig. a cue‖ a game played with hard balls moved by a cue on a table with raised, cushioned edges

bill·ing (bil'iŋ) *n.* 1 the listing of actors' names on a theater marquee, etc. 2 the order in which the names are listed

bil·lings·gate (bil'iŋz gāt') *n.* ‖< a London fish market‖ foul, vulgar, abusive talk

bil·lion (bil'yən) *n.* ‖Fr < *bi-*, two, twice + *(mi)llion*‖ 1 a thousand millions (1,000,000,000) 2 *old Brit. term for* TRILLION (a million millions) —**bil'lionth** *adj.*, *n.*

bil'lion·aire' (-yə ner') *n.* a person whose wealth comes to at least a billion dollars, pounds, francs, etc.

bill of exchange a written order to pay a certain sum of money to the person named

bill of fare a menu

bill of lading a receipt issued to a shipper by a carrier, describing the goods to be shipped

Bill of Rights the first ten amendments to the U.S. Constitution, which guarantee civil liberties

bill of sale a written statement transferring ownership of something by sale

bil·low (bil'ō) *n.* ‖ON *bylgja*‖ 1 a large wave 2 any large swelling mass or surge, as of smoke —*vi.* to surge or swell in a billow —**bil'low·y** *adj.*

bil·ly (bil'ē) *n.*, *pl.* **-lies** ‖ult. < OFr *bille*, tree trunk‖ a club, esp. a policeman's heavy stick

billy goat a male goat

bi·me·tal·lic (bī'mə tal'ik) *adj.* ‖< Fr *bi-*, BI- + *métallique*, metallic‖ 1 of, containing, or using two metals 2 of or based on bimetallism

bi·met·al·lism (bī met''l iz'əm) *n.* the use of two metals, esp. gold and silver, as the monetary standard, with fixed values in relation to each other

bi·month·ly (bī munth'lē) *adj.*, *adv.* 1 once every two months 2 [Now Rare] twice a month

bin (bin) *n.* ‖OE, crib‖ a box, crib, etc. for storing grain, coal, etc.

bi·na·ry (bī'nə rē) *adj.* ‖< L *bis*, double‖ 1 made up of two parts; double 2 designating or of a number system in which the base used is two, each number being expressed by using only two digits, specif. 0 and 1 —*n.*, *pl.* **-ries** a set of two

bi·na·tion·al (bī nash'ə nəl) *adj.* involving two nations or two nationalities

bind (bīnd) *vt.* **bound, bind'ing** ‖< OE *bindan*‖ 1 to tie together, as with rope 2 to hold or restrain 3 to encircle with a belt, etc. 4 to bandage: often with *up* 5 to constipate 6 to reinforce or ornament the edges of by a band, as of tape 7 to fasten together the pages of (a book) and protect with a cover 8 to obligate by duty, love, etc. 9 to compel, as by oath, legal restraint, or contract —*vi.* 1 to do the act of binding 2 to be or become tight or stiff 3 to stick together 4 to be obligatory or binding in force —*n.* 1 anything that binds 2 [Colloq.] a difficult or restrictive situation —**bound** *adj.* —**bind'ing** *adj.*

bind'er *n.* 1 one that binds 2 a substance that binds, as tar 3 a cover for holding sheets of paper together

bind'er·y *n.*, *pl.* **-er·ies** a place where books are bound

bind'ing *n.* a thing that binds, as a band, a tape, the covers and backing of a book, a cohesive substance, etc *adj.* that binds, obligates, etc.

binge (binj) *n.* [Colloq.] a spree *vi.* **binged, binge'ing** [Colloq.] to indulge without restraint: with *on*

bin·go (biŋ'gō) *n.* a gambling game resembling lotto

bin·na·cle (bin'ə kəl) *n.* ‖ult < L *habitaculum,* dwelling place ‖ the case holding a ship's compass

bin·oc·u·lar (bī näk'yə lər) *adj.* ‖< L *bini,* double + *oculus,* eye ‖ using, or for, both eyes —*n.* [*usually pl.*] a binocular instrument, as field glasses

bi·no·mi·al (bī nō'mē əl) *n.* ‖< L *bi-,* BI + Gr *nomos,* law ‖ **1** *Math.* an expression consisting of two terms connected by a plus or minus sign **2** a two-word scientific name of a plant or animal, indicating the genus and species

bio- ‖Gr < *bios,* life ‖ *combining form* life, of living things

bi'o·chem'is·try *n.* the study of the chemistry of life processes in plants and animals —**bi'o·chem'ist** *n.*

bi'o·de·grad'a·ble (-di grā'də bəl) *adj.* ‖BIO + *degrad(e),* decompose + ABLE ‖ capable of being readily decomposed by the action of microbes, as some detergents

bi'o·feed'back *n.* a technique of seeking to control certain emotional states by training oneself, using electronic devices, to modify autonomic body functions, such as heartbeat

biog. **1** biographical **2** biography

bi·og·ra·phy (bī äg'rə fē) *n., pl.* **-phies** ‖< Gr: see BIO- & -GRAPHY ‖ an account of a person's life written by another —**bi·og'ra·pher** *n.* —**bi·o·graph·i·cal** (bī'ə graf'i kəl) *adj.*

biol. **1** biological **2** biology

biological warfare the use of toxic microorganisms, etc. in war

bi·ol·o·gy (bī äl'ə jē) *n.* ‖see BIO- & LOGY ‖ the science that deals with the origin, history, characteristics, habits, etc. of plants and animals —**bi·o·log·i·cal** (bī'ə läj'i kəl) *adj.* —**bi'o·log'i·cal·ly** *adv.* —**bi·ol'o·gist** *n.*

bi·on·ic (bī än'ik) *adj.* ‖see fol.‖ **1** of bionics **2** having an artificial bodily part or parts, as in science fiction, so as to enhance strength, abilities, etc.

bi·on'ics (-än'iks) *n.pl.* ‖BI(O)- + (ELECTR)ONICS ‖ [*with sing. v.*] the science of designing instruments or systems modeled after living organisms

bi·o·phys·ics (bī'ō fiz'iks) *n.pl.* [*with sing. v.*] the study of biological phenomena in relation to physics —**bi'o·phys'i·cal** *adj.* —**bi'o·phys'i·cist** *n.*

bi·op·sy (bī'äp'sē) *n., pl.* **-sies** ‖< BI(O)- + Gr *opsis,* a sight ‖ *Med.* the removal of bits of living tissue for diagnosis

bi·o·rhythm (bī'ō rith'əm) *n.* any biological cycle that involves periodic changes in blood pressure, body temperature, etc.

bi·o·tin (bī'ə tin) *n.* ‖< Gr *bios,* life ‖ a factor of the vitamin B group

bi·par·ti·san (bī pär'tə zən) *adj.* of, representing, or supported by two parties —**bi·par'ti·san·ship'** *n.*

bi·par·tite (bī pär'tīt') *adj.* ‖< L *bi-,* BI- + *partire,* to divide ‖ **1** having two parts **2** involving two

bi·ped (bī'ped') *n.* ‖< L *bi-,* BI + *pes,* foot ‖ any two-footed animal

bi·plane (bī'plān') *n.* an airplane with two sets of wings, one above the other

bi·ra·cial (bī rā'shəl) *adj.* consisting of or involving two races

birch (burch) *n.* ‖OE *beorc* ‖ **1** a tree having smooth bark in thin layers, and hard, closegrained wood **2** its wood **3** a bunch of birch twigs used for whipping —*vt.* to flog

bird (burd) *n.* ‖< OE *bridd,* young bird ‖ any of a class of warmblooded vertebrates with feathers and wings —*vi.* to observe wild birds in their habitat —**birds of a feather** people with the same traits or tastes —**for the birds** [Slang] ridiculous, worthless, etc.

bird·er (burd'ər) *n.* one who engages in birding

bird·ie (burd'ē) *n.* *Golf* a score of one stroke under par for a hole

bird·ing (burd'iŋ) *n.* a hobby involving observation of wild birds in their habitat

bird's-eye (burdz'ī') *adj.* having marks resembling birds' eyes [*bird's-eye* maple]

bird's-eye view **1** a view from high above **2** an overall, but cursory, view

bi·ret·ta (bə ret'ə) *n.* ‖< LL *birrettum,* small cloak ‖ a square ceremonial hat with three or four vertical projections, worn by Roman Catholic clergy

Bir·ming·ham (bur'miŋ əm *for 1*; -ham' *for 2*) **1** city in central England: pop. 1,116,000 **2** city in N Ala.: pop. 284,000

birth (burth) *n.* ‖< ON *byrth* ‖ **1** the act of bringing forth offspring **2** a being born **3** origin or descent **4** the beginning of anything **5** natural inclination [an actress by *birth*] —*vi., vt.* to give birth (to) —**give birth to** **1** to bring forth (offspring) **2** to create

birth'day' *n.* the anniversary of the day of a person's birth —**in one's birthday suit** [Colloq.] naked

birth'mark' *n.* a skin blemish or mark present at birth

birth'place' *n.* the place of one's birth or of a thing's origin

birth'rate' *n.* the number of births per year per thousand people in a given area, group, etc. Also **birth rate**

birth'right' *n.* any right that a person has by birth

birth'stone' *n.* a gem symbolizing the month of one's birth

bis·cuit (bis'kit) *n., pl.* **-cuits** or **-cuit** ‖< L *bis,* twice + *coquere,* to cook ‖ **1** [Chiefly Brit.] a cracker or cookie **2** *a*) a quick bread baked in small pieces *b*) any of these pieces

bi·sect (bī sekt') *vt.* ‖< L *bi-,* BI- + *secare,* to cut ‖ **1** to cut in two **2** *Geom.* to divide into two equal parts —*vi.* to divide; fork —**bi·sec'tor** (-sekt'ər) *n.*

bi·sex·u·al (bī sek'shōō əl) *adj.* of, or sexually attracted by, both sexes —*n.* one who is bisexual

bish·op (bish'əp) *n.* ‖< Gr *episkopos,* overseer ‖ **1** a high-ranking member of the Christian clergy, governing a diocese or church district **2** a chess piece that can move in a diagonal direction

bish·op·ric (bish'əp rik) ***n.*** the district, office, or rank of a bishop
Bis·marck (biz'märk'), Prince **Ot·to von** (ät' ō) 1815-98; Prussian chancellor (1871-90) who unified Germany
Bismarck capital of N.Dak.: pop. 44,000
bis·muth (biz'məth) ***n.*** ‖ < Ger *wismut* ‖ a brittle, grayish white metallic chemical element used in alloys of low melting point

BISON

bi·son (bī'sən) ***n.***, *pl.* **bi'son** ‖ < L, wild ox ‖ a bovine ruminant having a shaggy mane and a humped back, as the American buffalo
bisque (bisk) ***n.*** ‖ Fr ‖ a thick, creamy soup made as from shellfish or vegetables
bis·tro (bēs'trō') ***n.*** ‖ Fr ‖ a small cafe
bit[1] (bit) ***n.*** ‖ < OE *bite,* a bite ‖ **1** the part of a bridle in the horse's mouth, used as a control **2** anything that curbs or controls **3** a drilling or boring tool for use in a brace, drill press, etc.
bit[2] (bit) ***n.*** ‖ < OE *bita,* a piece ‖ **1** *a)* a small piece or quantity *b)* small extent /a *bit* bored/ *c)* a short time **2** [Colloq.] 12½ cents: now usually in *two bits* —***adj.*** very small /a *bit* role/ —**bit by bit** gradually —**do one's bit** to do one's share
bit[3] (bit) ***n.*** ‖ *b*(*inary*) (*dig*)*it* ‖ a single digit in a binary number system
bitch (bich) ***n.*** ‖ OE *bicce* ‖ the female of the dog, fox, etc. —***vi.*** [Slang] to complain —**bitch'y** ***adj.***
bite (bīt) ***vt.*** **bit** (bit), **bit·ten** (bit''n) or **bit, bit'ing** ‖ OE *bītan* ‖ **1** to seize or pierce with or as with the teeth **2** to cut into, as with a sharp weapon **3** to sting, as an insect **4** to cause to smart **5** to eat into; corrode —***vi.*** **1** to press or snap the teeth (*into, at,* etc.) **2** to cause a biting sensation **3** to grip **4** to seize a bait **5** to be caught, as by a trick —***n.*** **1** a biting **2** biting quality; sting **3** a wound or sting from biting **4** a mouthful **5** a snack **6** [Colloq.] a sum deducted, as by a tax —**bite the bullet** to confront a painful situation bravely: from the patient's biting a bullet during battlefield surgery without an anesthetic
bit·ing (bīt'iŋ) ***adj.*** **1** cutting; sharp **2** sarcastic —**bit'ing·ly** ***adv.***
bit·ter (bit'ər) ***adj.*** ‖ OE *biter,* akin to *bītan,* to bite ‖ **1** having a sharp, often unpleasant taste **2** causing or showing sorrow, pain, etc. **3** sharp and disagreeable; harsh /a *bitter* wind/ **4** resentful; cynical —**bit'ter·ly** ***adv.*** —**bit'ter·ness** ***n.***
bit·tern (bit'ərn) ***n.*** ‖ < OFr *butor* ‖ a wading bird with a thumping cry
bit'ters ***n.pl.*** a liquor containing bitter herbs, etc. and usually alcohol, used as in some cocktails
bit'ter·sweet' ***n.*** **1** a woody vine bearing small orange fruits with bright-red fleshy seeds **2** a poisonous vine with purple flowers and red berries **3** pleasure mixed with sadness —***adj.*** **1** both bitter and sweet **2** pleasant and sad
bi·tu·men (bi tōō'mən) ***n.*** ‖ L < Celt ‖ any of several materials obtained as residue in the distillation of petroleum, coal tar, etc., or occurring as natural asphalt —**bi·tu'mi·nous** (-mə nəs) ***adj.***
bituminous coal coal that yields pitch or tar when it burns; soft coal
bi·va·lent (bī vā'lənt) ***adj.*** *Chem.* DIVALENT
bi·valve (bī'valv') ***n.*** any mollusk having a shell made of two valves hinged together, as a clam
biv·ou·ac (biv'wak') ***n.*** ‖ Fr < OHG *bi-,* by + *wahta,* watchman ‖ a temporary encampment (esp. of soldiers) in the open —***vi.*** **-acked', -ack'ing** to encamp in the open
bi·week·ly (bī wēk'lē) ***adj., adv.*** **1** once every two weeks **2** [Now Rare] semiweekly
bi·zarre (bi zär') ***adj.*** ‖ Fr < Basque *bizar,* beard ‖ **1** odd; grotesque **2** unexpected; fantastic
bk. **1** bank **2** book
bl. **1** bale(s) **2** barrel(s)
B/L or **b/l** bill of lading
blab (blab) ***vt., vi.*** **blabbed, blab'bing** ‖ ME *blabben* ‖ **1** to reveal (a secret) **2** to chatter; prattle —***n.*** gossip
black (blak) ***adj.*** ‖ OE *blæc* ‖ **1** opposite to white; of the color of coal **2** [*sometimes* **B-**] of or for the dark-skinned peoples of Africa, etc. or their descendants elsewhere, specif. Afro-Americans in the U.S. /*black* studies/ **3** without light; dark **4** dirty **5** evil; wicked **6** sad; dismal **7** sullen —***n.*** **1** black color or pigment **2** black clothes, esp. when worn in mourning **3** [*sometimes* **B-**] a member of a black people **4** darkness —***vt., vi.*** to blacken —**black out** to lose consciousness —**in the black** operating at a profit —**black'ish** ***adj.*** —**black'ly** ***adv.*** —**black'ness** ***n.***
black'-and-blue' ***adj.*** discolored, as by a bruise
black'ball' (-bôl') ***n.*** a vote against —***vt.*** **1** to vote against **2** to ostracize
black belt a black belt or sash awarded to an expert of the highest skill in judo or karate
black'ber'ry ***n.***, *pl.* **-ries** **1** the fleshy, purple or black, edible fruit of various brambles of the rose family **2** a bush or vine bearing this fruit
black'bird' ***n.*** any of various birds the male of which is almost entirely black
black'board' ***n.*** a smooth, usually dark surface on which to write with chalk
black'en (-ən) ***vi.*** to become black or dark —***vt.*** **1** to make black; darken **2** to slander; defame
black eye a discoloration of the skin around an eye, resulting from a blow or contusion
black'-eyed' Su'san (-īd' sōō'zən) a yellow, daisylike wildflower with a dark center
black·guard (blag'ərd) ***n.*** a scoundrel; villain
black·head (blak'hed') ***n.*** a dark plug of dried fatty matter in a pore of the skin
black hole a hypothetical object in space, perhaps the invisible remains of a collapsed star, with intense gravitation from which light and matter cannot escape
black'jack' (-jak') ***n.*** **1** a small, leather-covered bludgeon with a flexible handle **2** a gambling card game in which the winner

gets cards totaling 21 points or less —*vt.* to hit with a blackjack

black light ultraviolet or infrared radiation used for fluorescent effects

black'list' *n.* a list of those who are censured, refused employment, etc. —*vt.* to put on a blacklist

black lung (disease) a disease of the lungs caused by the inhalation of coal dust

black magic sorcery

black'mail' (-māl') *n.* ‖ lit., black rent < ME *male,* rent ‖ payment extorted to prevent disclosure of information that could bring disgrace —*vt.* to get or try to get blackmail from —**black'mail'er** *n.*

black mark an unfavorable item in one's record

black market a system for selling goods illegally —**black marketeer** (or **marketer**)

black'out' (-out') *n.* **1** an extinguishing of stage lights to end a scene **2** a concealing of lights that might be visible to enemy aircraft at night **3** lack of lights due to a power failure **4** temporary unconsciousness **5** suppression, as of news by censorship

black power political and economic power as sought by black Americans in the struggle for civil rights

Black Sea sea surrounded by the U.S.S.R., Asia Minor, & the Balkans

black sheep a family or group member regarded as not so respectable or successful as the others

black'smith' *n.* a smith who works in iron and makes and fits horseshoes

black'thorn' *n.* a thorny shrub with purple or black, plumlike fruit; sloe

black'top' *n.* a bituminous mixture, usually asphalt, used as a surface for roads, etc. —*vt.* **-topped', -top'ping** to cover with blacktop

black widow a black spider with a red mark underneath: the female has a poisonous bite and sometimes eats its mate

blad·der (blad'ər) *n.* ‖ OE *blæddre* ‖ **1** a sac that fills with fluid or gas, esp. one that holds urine flowing from the kidneys **2** a thing resembling this /a football *bladder*/

blade (blād) *n.* ‖ OE *blæd,* leaf ‖ **1** *a)* the leaf of a plant, esp. grass *b)* the flat part of a leaf **2** a broad, flat surface, as of an oar **3** the cutting part of a tool, knife, etc. **4** a sword or swordsman

blam·a·ble or **blame·a·ble** (blām'ə bəl) *adj.* that deserves blame —**blam'a·bly** *adv.*

blame (blām) *vt.* **blamed, blam'ing** ‖ see BLASPHEME ‖ **1** to accuse of being at fault; condemn (*for*) **2** to put the responsibility of (an error, etc.) *on* —*n.* **1** a blaming **2** responsibility for a fault —**be to blame** to be at fault —**blame'less** *adj.* —**blame'less·ly** *adv.* —**blame'less·ness** *n.*

blame'wor'thy (-wur'*thē*) *adj.* deserving to be blamed

blanch (blanch) *vt.* ‖ < OFr *blanc,* white ‖ **1** to whiten or bleach **2** to make pale **3** to process (vegetables, almonds, etc.) by scalding —*vi.* to turn pale

bland (bland) *adj.* ‖ L *blandus,* mild ‖ **1** gently agreeable **2** mild and soothing **3** insipid —**bland'ly** *adv.* —**bland'ness** *n.*

blan·dish (blan'dish) *vt., vi.* ‖ < L *blandiri,* to flatter ‖ to flatter; coax; cajole —**blan'dish·ment** *n.*

blank (blaŋk) *adj.* ‖ < OFr *blanc,* white ‖ **1** not written on **2** empty; vacant **3** empty of thought /a *blank* mind/ **4** utter; complete /a *blank* denial/ —*n.* **1** an empty space, esp. one to be filled out in a printed form **2** such a printed form **3** an empty place or time **4** a powder-filled cartridge without a bullet —*vt.* to hold (an opponent) scoreless —**blank out** to conceal by covering over —**draw a blank** [Colloq.] **1** to be unsuccessful **2** to be unable to remember a particular thing —**blank'ly** *adv.* —**blank'ness** *n.*

blank check **1** a bank check form not yet filled in **2** a signed check with no amount filled in **3** permission to use an unlimited amount of money, authority, etc.

blan·ket (blaŋ'kit) *n.* ‖ < OFr dim. of *blanc,* white ‖ **1** a large, soft piece of cloth used for warmth, esp. as a bed cover **2** anything like this /a *blanket* of leaves/ —*adj.* including many or all items /*blanket* insurance/ —*vt.* **1** to cover; overlie **2** to obscure

blank verse unrhymed verse having five iambic feet per line

blan·quette (blän ket') *n.* ‖ Fr ‖ a stew, as of chicken or veal, in cream sauce

blare (bler) *vt., vi.* **blared, blar'ing** ‖ ME *bleren,* to wail ‖ to sound or exclaim loudly —*n.* a loud, harsh sound

blar·ney (blär'nē) *n.* ‖ < *Blarney* stone in Ireland, traditionally kissed to gain skill in flattery ‖ flattery —*vt., vi.* **-neyed, -ney·ing** to flatter; coax

bla·sé (blä zā') *adj.* ‖ Fr ‖ satiated and bored

blas·pheme (blas fēm') *vt.* **-phemed', -phem'ing** ‖ < Gr *blasphēmein,* to speak evil of ‖ **1** to speak profanely of or to (God or sacred things) **2** to curse —*vi.* to utter blasphemy —**blas·phem'er** *n.*

blas'phe·my (-fə mē) *n., pl.* **-mies** profane speech, writing, or action toward God or sacred things —**blas'phe·mous** *adj.*

blast (blast) *n.* ‖ OE *blæst,* puff of wind ‖ **1** a strong rush of air **2** the sound of a sudden rush of air, as through a horn **3** a blight **4** an explosion, as of dynamite **5** an outburst, as of criticism —*vi.* **1** to make a loud, harsh sound **2** to set off explosives, etc. —*vt.* **1** to wither; ruin **2** to blow up; explode **3** to criticize sharply —**blast off** to take off: said of a rocket —**(at) full blast** at full speed

blast furnace a smelting furnace in which a blast of air forced in from below produces the intense heat

blast'off' or **blast'-off'** *n.* the launching of a rocket, spacecraft, etc.

bla·tant (blāt''nt) *adj.* ‖ prob. < L *blaterare,* to babble ‖ **1** disagreeably loud; noisy **2** boldly conspicuous or obtrusive —**bla'tan·cy** *n.*

blaze[1] (blāz) *n.* ‖ OE *blæse* ‖ **1** a bright burst of flame; fire **2** a very bright light **3** a spectacular outburst or display —*vi.* **blazed, blaz'ing** **1** to burn rapidly or shine brightly **2** to be excited, as with anger

blaze[2] (blāz) *n.* ‖ < ON *blesi* ‖ **1** a light-colored spot on an animal's face **2** a mark made on a tree by cutting off bark —*vt.*

blazed, blaz'ing to mark (a tree or trail) with blazes

blaze[3] (blāz) ***vt.*** **blazed, blaz'ing** ‖ME *blasen,* to blow < OE or ON‖ to proclaim

blaz·er (blā'zər) ***n.*** a light sports jacket usually in a solid color and with metal buttons

bla·zon (blā'zən) ***n.*** ‖OFr *blason,* a shield‖ **1** a coat of arms **2** showy display —***vt.*** **1** to proclaim **2** to adorn

bldg. building

bleach (blēch) ***vt., vi.*** ‖OE *blæcan*‖ to make or become white or colorless —***n.*** a substance for bleaching

bleach'ers ***n.pl.*** seats, usually roofless, for spectators at sporting events

bleak (blēk) ***adj.*** ‖ON *bleikr,* pale‖ **1** exposed to wind and cold; bare **2** cold; harsh **3** gloomy **4** not hopeful —**bleak'ly** ***adv.*** —**bleak'ness** ***n.***

blear·y (blir'ē) ***adj.*** **-i·er, -i·est** ‖< ME *blere*‖ dim or blurred, as the eyes by tears, fatigue, etc.: also **blear**

bleat (blēt) ***vi.*** ‖OE *blætan*‖ to make the cry of a sheep, goat, or calf —***n.*** a bleating cry or sound

bleed (blēd) ***vi.*** **bled** (bled), **bleed'ing** ‖< OE *blod,* blood‖ **1** to emit or lose blood **2** to feel pain, grief, or sympathy **3** to ooze sap, juice, etc. —***vt.*** **1** to draw blood from **2** to ooze (sap, juice, etc.) **3** [Colloq.] to extort money from —**bleed'er** ***n.***

bleep (blēp) ***n., vi.*** ‖echoic‖ beep —***vt.*** to censor (something said), as in a telecast, with a beep

blem·ish (blem'ish) ***vt.*** ‖< OFr *blesmir,* injure‖ to mar; spoil —***n.*** a flaw, defect, etc., as a spot or scar

blench[1] (blench) ***vt., vi.*** to blanch

blench[2] (blench) ***vi.*** ‖< OE *blencan,* deceive‖ to shrink back; flinch

blend (blend) ***vt.*** **blend'ed** or **blent, blend'ing** ‖OE *blendan*‖ **1** to mix or mingle (varieties of tea, etc.) **2** to mix thoroughly —***vi.*** **1** to mix; merge **2** to pass gradually into each other, as colors **3** to harmonize —***n.*** **1** a blending **2** a mixture of varieties

blend'er ***n.*** **1** a person or thing that blends **2** an electrical appliance that can chop, whip, mix, or liquefy foods

bless (bles) ***vt.*** **blessed** or **blest, bless'ing** ‖< OE *bletsian,* consecrate with blood‖ **1** to make holy **2** to ask divine favor for **3** to endow (*with*) **4** to make happy **5** to praise **6** to make the sign of the cross over

bless·ed (bles'id, blest) ***adj.*** **1** holy; sacred **2** fortunate; blissful **3** beatified —**bless'ed·ly** ***adv.*** —**bless'ed·ness** ***n.***

bless'ing ***n.*** **1** invocation or benediction **2** a grace said before or after eating **3** good wishes or approval **4** anything that gives happiness

blew (blo͞o) ***vi., vt. pt. of*** BLOW[1] & BLOW[3]

blight (blīt) ***n.*** ‖? < ON *blikja,* turn pale‖ **1** any insect, disease, etc. that destroys plants **2** anything that destroys, frustrates, etc. —***vt.*** **1** to wither **2** to destroy

blimp (blimp) ***n.*** [Colloq.] a nonrigid or semirigid airship

blind (blīnd) ***adj.*** ‖OE‖ **1** without the power of sight **2** of or for sightless persons **3** lacking insight **4** hard to see; hidden **5** closed at one end [a *blind* alley] **6** not controlled by intelligence [*blind* destiny] **7** guided only by instruments [*blind* flying] —***vt.*** **1** to make sightless **2** to dazzle **3** to deprive of insight —***n.*** **1** anything that obscures sight or keeps out light, as a window shade **2** a place of concealment **3** a decoy —**blind'ly** ***adv.*** —**blind'ness** ***n.***

blind date [Colloq.] **1** a date with a stranger, arranged by a third person **2** either person involved

blind'fold' (-fōld') ***vt.*** ‖< ME *blindfeld,* struck blind‖ to cover the eyes of, as with a cloth —***n.*** a cloth used to cover the eyes —***adj.*** **1** with the eyes covered **2** reckless

blind'side' (-sīd') ***vt.*** **-sid'ed, -sid'ing** to attack (someone) from an unexpected direction

blink (bliŋk) ***vi.*** ‖ME *blenken*‖ **1** to wink one or more times **2** to flash on and off **3** to ignore (with *at*) —***vt.*** **1** to cause (eyes, light, etc.) to blink **2** to evade or avoid —***n.*** **1** a blinking **2** a glimmer —**on the blink** [Slang] out of order

blink'er ***n.*** a flashing warning light

blintz (blints) ***n.*** ‖Yidd *blintze* < Russ *blin,* pancake‖ a thin pancake rolled with a filling of cottage cheese, fruit, etc.

blip (blip) ***n.*** ‖echoic of a brief sound‖ a luminous image on an oscilloscope

bliss (blis) ***n.*** ‖< OE *blithe,* blithe‖ **1** great happiness **2** spiritual joy —**bliss'ful** ***adj.*** —**bliss'ful·ly** ***adv.*** —**bliss'ful·ness** ***n.***

blis·ter (blis'tər) ***n.*** ‖< ?‖ **1** a raised patch of skin, filled with watery matter and caused as by a burn **2** anything like a blister —***vt.*** **1** to raise blisters on **2** to lash with words —***vi.*** to form blisters

blithe (blīth, blīth) ***adj.*** ‖OE‖ cheerful; carefree: also **blithe'some** (-səm) —**blithe'ly** ***adv.*** —**blithe'ness** ***n.***

blitz (blits) ***n.*** ‖< Ger *blitz,* lightning‖ a sudden destructive or overwhelming attack —***vt.*** to subject to a blitz

bliz·zard (bliz'ərd) ***n.*** ‖? < dial. *bliz,* violent blow‖ a violent snowstorm with very cold winds

bloat (blōt) ***vt., vi.*** ‖< ON *blautr,* soft‖ **1** to swell, as with water or air **2** to puff up, as with pride

blob (bläb) ***n.*** ‖echoic‖ a drop or a small lump or spot —***vt.*** **blobbed, blob'bing** to splash, as with blobs

bloc (bläk) ***n.*** ‖Fr < MDu *block,* log‖ a group of persons, nations, etc. combined for a common purpose

block (bläk) ***n.*** ‖< OFr *bloc* & MDu *block*‖ **1** a large, solid piece of wood, stone, metal, etc. **2** a heavy stand on which chopping, etc. is done **3** an auctioneer's platform **4** an obstruction or hindrance **5** a pulley in a frame **6** [Now Brit.] a group or row of buildings **7** an area with streets or buildings on four sides **8** a number of things regarded as a unit **9** *Printing* a piece of wood, etc. engraved with a design —***vt.*** **1** to obstruct; hinder **2** to mount or mold on a block **3** to sketch roughly (often with *out*) —**block'er** ***n.***

block·ade (blä kād') ***n.*** ‖prec. + ADE‖ **1** a shutting off of a place by troops or ships to prevent passage **2** any strategic barrier —***vt.*** **-ad'ed, -ad'ing** to subject to a blockade

block and tackle pulley blocks and ropes, used for lifting heavy objects
block'bust'ing *n.* [Colloq.] the inducing of owners to sell their homes out of fear that a minority group may move into the neighborhood —**block'bust'er** *n.*
block grant a grant of Federal funds to a State or local government to fund a block of programs
block'head' *n.* a stupid person
block'house' *n.* **1** [Historical] a wooden fort **2** a reinforced structure for observers, as of missile launchings
blond (bländ) *adj.* ‖ OFr < ? Gmc ‖ **1** having light-colored hair and skin **2** light in color Also **blonde** —*n.* a blond person —**blonde** *n.fem.* —**blond'ness** *n.*
blood (blud) *n.* ‖ OE *blod* ‖ **1** the red fluid circulating in the arteries and veins of animals **2** bloodshed **3** the essence of life; life **4** the sap of a plant **5** passion, temperament, etc. **6** parental heritage; lineage **7** kinship **8** people, esp. youthful people /new *blood* in a group/ —**bad blood** anger; hatred —**in cold blood** **1** with cruelty **2** deliberately
blood bank a supply of blood stored for future use in transfusion
blood count the number of red or white cells in a given volume of blood
blood'cur'dling (-kurd'liŋ) *adj.* frightening; terrifying
blood'ed (-id) *adj.* **1** having (a specified kind of) blood /hot-*blooded*/ **2** of fine breed
blood'hound' *n.* any of a breed of large tracking dogs with a keen sense of smell
blood'less (-lis) *adj.* **1** without bloodshed **2** anemic or pale **3** having little energy —**blood'less·ly** *adv.* —**blood'less·ness** *n.*
blood'mo·bile' (-mō bēl') *n.* a traveling unit for collecting blood from donors for blood banks
blood poisoning *nontechnical term for* SEPTICEMIA
blood pressure the pressure of the blood against the blood-vessel walls
blood relation (or **relative**) a person related by birth
blood'shed' *n.* the shedding of blood; killing
blood'shot' *adj.* tinged with red because small blood vessels are broken: said of eyes
blood'suck'er *n.* an animal that sucks blood, esp. a leech
blood'thirst'y *adj.* murderous; very cruel —**blood'thirst'i·ness** *n.*
blood vessel an artery, vein, or capillary
blood'y *adj.* **-i·er, -i·est** **1** of, like, containing, or covered with blood **2** involving bloodshed **3** bloodthirsty **4** [Brit. Slang] cursed; damned —*adv.* [Brit. Slang] very —*vt.* **-ied, -y·ing** to stain with blood —**blood'i·ly** *adv.* —**blood'i·ness** *n.*
bloom (bloom) *n.* ‖ < ON *blomi*, flowers ‖ **1** a flower; blossom **2** the state or time of flowering **3** a period of greatest health, vigor, etc. **4** a youthful, healthy glow **5** the powdery coating on some fruits and leaves —*vi.* **1** to blossom **2** to be in one's prime **3** to glow with health, etc.
bloom·ers (bloom'ərz) *n.* ‖ after Amelia *Bloomer* (1818-94), U.S. feminist ‖ baggy trousers gathered at the knee, once worn by women for athletics
bloom'ing *adj.* **1** blossoming **2** flourishing **3** [Colloq.] complete
bloop·er (bloop'ər) *n.* ‖ *bloop*, echoic + ER ‖ **1** a stupid mistake **2** *Baseball* a fly that falls just beyond the infield for a hit
blos·som (bläs'əm) *n.* ‖ OE *blostma* ‖ **1** a flower, esp. of a fruit bearing plant **2** a state or time of flowering —*vi.* **1** to have or open into blossoms **2** to begin to flourish —**blos'som·y** *adj.*
blot (blät) *n.* ‖ ME < ? ‖ **1** a spot or stain, esp. of ink **2** anything that spoils or mars **3** a moral stain —*vt.* **blot'ted, blot'ting** **1** to spot; stain **2** to disgrace **3** to erase, obscure, or get rid of: with *out* **4** to dry, as with blotting paper —*vi.* **1** to make blots **2** to become blotted **3** to be absorbent
blotch (bläch) *n.* ‖ ? < prec. ‖ **1** a discoloration on the skin **2** any large blot or stain —*vt.* to mark with blotches —**blotch'y, -i·er, -i·est,** *adj.*
blot·ter (blät'ər) *n.* **1** a piece of blotting paper **2** a book for recording events as they occur /a police *blotter*/
blotting paper a thick, soft, absorbent paper used to dry a surface freshly written on in ink
blouse (blous) *n.* ‖ Fr, workman's smock ‖ **1** a garment like a shirt, worn by women and children **2** a uniform coat worn by soldiers, etc. —*vi., vt.* **bloused, blous'ing** to gather in and drape over loosely
blow[1] (blō) *vi.* **blew, blown, blow'ing** ‖ OE *blawan* ‖ **1** to move with some force, as the wind **2** to send forth air, as with the mouth **3** to pant **4** to give sound by blowing or being blown **5** to spout water and air, as whales do **6** to be carried by the wind **7** to be stormy **8** to burst suddenly: often with *out* **9** [Colloq.] to brag **10** [Slang] to leave —*vt.* **1** to force air from, into, onto, or through **2** to drive by blowing **3** to sound by blowing **4** to form by blown air or gas **5** to burst by an explosion: often with *up* **6** to melt (a fuse, etc.) **7** [Colloq.] to spend (money) freely **8** [Slang] to leave **9** [Slang] to bungle —*n.* **1** a blowing **2** a blast of air or gale —**blow off** [Colloq.] to release emotions, as by shouting —**blow over** to pass over or by —**blow up** [Colloq.] to lose one's temper —**blow'er** *n.*
blow[2] (blō) *n.* ‖ ME *blowe* ‖ **1** a hard hit, as with the fist **2** a sudden attack **3** a sudden calamity; shock —**come to blows** to begin fighting one another
blow[3] (blō) *vi.* **blew, blown, blow'ing** ‖ OE *blowan* ‖ [Archaic] to bloom
blow'-by-blow' *adj.* detailed; full
blow'-dry' *vt.* **-dried', -dry'ing** to dry (wet hair) with hot air blown from an electric device (**blow'-dry'er**)
blow'fly' *n., pl.* **-flies'** a fly that lays its eggs on meat, in wounds, etc.
blow'gun' *n.* a long tube through which darts, etc. are blown
blow'out' *n.* **1** the bursting of a tire **2** [Slang] a party, banquet, etc.
blow'torch' *n.* a small liquid-fuel torch that shoots out a hot flame
blow'up' *n.* **1** an explosion **2** an enlarged photograph **3** [Colloq.] an angry outburst

blow'y *adj.* **-i·er, -i·est** windy
blowz·y (blou'zē) *adj.* **-i·er, -i·est** ‖ < obs. *blouze,* wench ‖ slovenly Also **blows'y**
BLT bacon, lettuce, and tomato (sandwich)
blub·ber[1] (blub'ər) *n.* ‖ ME *blober,* a bubble ‖ the fat of the whale —**blub'ber·y** *adj.*
blub·ber[2] (blub'ər) *vi.* ‖ ME *bloberen,* to bubble ‖ to weep loudly, like a child
bludg·eon (bluj'ən) *n.* ‖ ? < earlier Fr *bouge,* club ‖ a short club with a heavy end —*vt., vi.* **1** to strike with a bludgeon **2** to bully or coerce
blue (bloo) *adj.* ‖ < ? ‖ **1** of the color of the clear sky **2** livid: said of the skin **3** gloomy **4** puritanical **5** [Colloq.] indecent; risqué —*n.* **1** the color of the clear sky **2** any blue pigment **3** [*pl.*] [Colloq.] a depressed feeling: with *the* **4** [*pl.*] black folk music having, usually, slow tempo, melancholy words, etc.: often with *the* —**out of the blue** unexpectedly —**the blue 1** the sky **2** the sea
blue baby a baby born with bluish skin, esp. because of a heart defect
blue'bell' *n.* any of various plants with blue, bell-shaped flowers
blue'ber'ry *n., pl.* **-ries 1** a shrub bearing small, edible, blue-black berries **2** any of the berries
blue'bird' *n.* a small North American songbird with a bluish back
blue blood an aristocrat Also **blue'blood'** *n.* —**blue'-blood'ed** *adj.*
blue cheese any strong cheese containing bluish mold
blue'-chip' *adj.* ‖ < high-value *blue chips* of poker ‖ **1** of any high-priced stock with good earnings and a stable price **2** [Colloq.] valuable
blue'-col'lar *adj.* ‖ < color of work shirts ‖ designating or of industrial workers
blue flu ‖ < *blue* police uniforms ‖ a sickout, esp. by police officers
blue'gill' *n.* a freshwater sunfish of a bluish color
blue'grass' *n.* a type of grass with bluish-green horizontal stems
blue'jack'et *n.* an enlisted person in the navy
blue jay a common crested bird with a blue upper body and head Also **blue'jay'** *n.*
blue'jeans' (-jēnz') *n.* jeans made of blue denim Also **blue jeans**
blue law a puritanical law, esp. one prohibiting certain activities on Sunday
blue'nose' *n.* [Colloq.] a puritanical person
blue'-pen'cil *vt.* **-ciled** or **-cilled, -cil·ing** or **-cil·ling** to edit or correct with or as with a blue pencil
blue'-plate' special an inexpensive restaurant meal served at a fixed price
blue'point' *n.* ‖ after *Blue Point,* Long Island, New York ‖ a small oyster, usually eaten raw
blue'print' *n.* **1** a photographic reproduction in white on a blue background, as of architectural plans **2** any detailed plan or outline —*vt.* to make a blueprint of
blue'stock'ing *n.* a learned, bookish, or pedantic woman
blu·et (bloo'it) *n.* ‖ < Fr dim. of *bleu,* blue ‖ a small plant having little pale-blue flowers
blue whale a whalebone whale with a blue-gray back
bluff[1] (bluf) *vt., vi.* ‖ prob. < Du *bluffen,* to brag, or *verbluffen,* to baffle ‖ to mislead or frighten (a person) by a false, bold front —*n.* **1** a bluffing **2** one who bluffs: also **bluff'er**
bluff[2] (bluf) *adj.* ‖ ? < Du *blaf,* flat ‖ **1** ascending steeply with a flat front **2** having a rough, frank manner —*n.* a high, steep bank or cliff
blu·ing (bloo'iŋ) *n.* a blue rinse used on white fabrics to prevent yellowing
blu'ish (-ish) *adj.* somewhat blue Also **blue'-ish**
blun·der (blun'dər) *vi.* ‖ < ON *blunda,* shut the eyes ‖ **1** to move clumsily **2** to make a foolish mistake —*vt.* to do poorly —*n.* a foolish mistake —**blun'der·er** *n.*
blun'der·buss' (-bus') *n.* ‖ < Du *donderbus,* thunder box ‖ [Historical] a short gun with a broad muzzle
blunt (blunt) *adj.* ‖ < ? ‖ **1** having a dull edge, etc. **2** plain-spoken —*vt., vi.* to make or become dull —**blunt'ly** *adv.* —**blunt'-ness** *n.*
blur (blur) *vt., vi.* **blurred, blur'ring** ‖ < ? ‖ **1** to smear; blot **2** to make or become indistinct in shape, etc. **3** to dim —*n.* **1** an obscuring stain **2** anything indistinct —**blur'ry** *adj.* —**blur'ri·ness** *n.*
blurb (blurb) *n.* ‖ a coinage ‖ an advertisement, as on a book jacket, esp. one that is highly laudatory
blurt (blurt) *vt.* ‖ prob. echoic ‖ to say impulsively: with *out*
blush (blush) *vi.* ‖ < OE *blyscan,* to shine ‖ **1** to become red in the face, as from embarrassment **2** to be ashamed (*at* or *for*) **3** to become rosy —*n.* **1** a reddening of the face, as from shame **2** a rosy color —*adj.* rosy —**at first blush** at first sight
blush'er *n.* **1** one who blushes readily **2** a red or reddish cosmetic powder, cream, etc. for the cheeks
blush wine a dry, pale-pink wine
blus·ter (blus'tər) *vi.* ‖ ? < LowG *blüstern* ‖ **1** to blow stormily: said of wind **2** to speak in a noisy, swaggering manner —*n.* **1** noisy commotion **2** noisy or swaggering talk —**blus'ter·er** *n.* —**blus'ter·y** *adj.*
Blvd. Boulevard
BM [Colloq.] bowel movement
BO body odor
bo·a (bō'ə) *n.* ‖ L ‖ **1** a tropical snake that crushes its prey in its coils, as the anaconda **2** a woman's long scarf, as of fur or feathers
boar (bôr) *n.* ‖ OE *bar* ‖ **1** an uncastrated male pig **2** a wild hog
board (bôrd) *n.* ‖ OE *bord,* plank ‖ **1** a long, flat piece of sawed wood **2** a flat piece of wood, etc. for some special use [*bulletin board*] **3** pasteboard **4** *a*) a table for meals *b*) meals, esp. as provided regularly for pay **5** a group of administrators; council **6** the side of a ship [*overboard*] —*vt.* **1** to cover (*up*) with boards **2** to provide with meals, or room and meals, regularly for pay **3** to come onto the deck of (a ship) **4** to get on (a train, bus, etc.) —*vi.* to receive meals, or room and meals, regularly for pay —**on board** on a ship, aircraft, etc. —**the boards** the stage (of a theater) —**board'er** *n.*

board'ing·house' *n.* a house where meals, or room and meals, can be had for pay Also **boarding house**

board'walk' *n.* a walk made of thick boards, esp. one along a beach

boast (bōst) *vi.* ‖< Anglo-Fr‖ to talk, esp. about oneself, with too much pride; brag —*vt.* to brag about; glory in —*n.* 1 a boasting 2 anything boasted of —**boast'er** *n.* —**boast'ful** *adj.* —**boast'ful·ly** *adv.*

boat (bōt) *n.* ‖OE *bat*‖ 1 a small, open vehicle for traveling on water 2 loosely, a ship 3 a boat-shaped dish —**in the same boat** in the same unfavorable situation —**rock the boat** [Colloq.] to disturb the status quo —**boat'man** (-mən), *pl.* **-men,** *n.*

boat'er *n.* a stiff straw hat with a flat crown and brim

boat'ing *n.* rowing, sailing, etc.

boat·swain (bō'sən) *n.* a ship's petty officer in charge of the deck crew, the rigging, anchors, boats, etc.

bob (bäb) *n.* ‖ME *bobbe,* hanging cluster; 3 & 4 < the *v.*‖ 1 any knoblike hanging weight 2 a woman's or child's short haircut 3 a quick, jerky motion 4 a float on a fishing line —*vt.* **bobbed, bob'bing** ‖ME *bobben,* knock against‖ 1 to make move with a jerky motion 2 to cut (hair, etc.) short —*vi.* to move with a jerky motion —**bob up** to appear suddenly

bob·bin (bäb'in) *n.* ‖Fr *bobine* < ?‖ a spool for thread or yarn, used in spinning, machine sewing, etc.

bob·ble (bäb'əl) *n.* [Colloq.] *Sports* an awkward juggling of the ball —*vt.* **-bled, -bling** [Colloq.] to make a bobble with (a ball)

bob·by (bäb'ē) *n., pl.* **-bies** ‖after Sir Robert (*Bobby*) Peel (1788-1850), who reorganized the London police force‖ [Brit. Colloq.] a policeman

bobby pin ‖from use with *bobbed* hair‖ a small metal hairpin with the sides pressing close together

bobby socks (or **sox**) ‖< BOB (*vt.* 2)‖ [Colloq.] esp. in the 1940's and 1950's, girls' ankle-length socks

bob'by-sox'er or **bob'by·sox'er** (-säks'ər) *n.* [Colloq.] esp. in the 1940's, a girl in her early teens

bob'cat' *n.* a small North American lynx

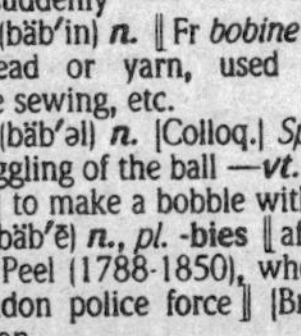

BOBSLED

bob'sled' *n.* a long racing sled —*vi.* **-sled'ded, -sled'ding** to ride or race on a bobsled

Boc·cac·cio (bō kä'chō, bō-), **Gio·van·ni** (jō vän'nē) 1313-75; It. writer

boc·cie, boc·ce, or **boc·ci** (bäch'ē) *n.* ‖It *bocce,* (wooden) balls‖ an Italian game similar to lawn bowling

bode[1] (bōd) *vt.* **bod'ed, bod'ing** ‖< OE *boda,* messenger‖ to be an omen of —**bode ill** (or **well**) to be a bad (or good) omen

bode[2] (bōd) *vi. alt. pt. of* BIDE

bod·ice (bäd'is) *n.* ‖altered < *bodies,* pl. of *body*‖ the upper part of a dress

bod·i·ly (bäd''l ē) *adj.* 1 physical 2 of, in, by, or to the body —*adv.* 1 in person 2 as a single group

bod·kin (bäd'kin) *n.* ‖ME *bodekin* < ?‖ 1 [Obs.] a dagger 2 a pointed instrument for making holes in cloth 3 a thick, blunt needle

bod·y (bäd'ē) *n., pl.* **-ies** ‖OE *bodig,* cask‖ 1 the whole physical substance of a human being, animal, or plant 2 the trunk of a human being 3 a corpse 4 [Colloq.] a person 5 a distinct group of people or things 6 the main part 7 a distinct mass [a *body* of water] 8 substance or consistency, as of liquid 9 richness of flavor

bod'y·guard' *n.* a person or persons assigned to guard someone

body language gestures, unconscious bodily movements, etc. which function as a means of communication

body politic the people who collectively constitute a political unit under a government

body stocking a tightfitting garment, usually of one piece, that covers the torso and, sometimes, the legs

bod'y·suit' *n.* a one-piece, tightfitting garment that covers the torso, usually worn with slacks, a skirt, etc. Also **body shirt**

Boer (boor, bōr) *n.* ‖Du *boer,* peasant‖ a South African of Dutch descent

bog (bäg, bôg) *n.* ‖< Gael & Ir *bog,* soft, moist‖ wet, spongy ground; a small marsh —*vt., vi.* **bogged, bog'ging** to sink in or as in a bog: often with *down* —**bog'gy** *adj.*

bo·gey (bō'gē) *n.* 1 BOGY 2 ‖after an imaginary Col. *Bogey*‖ *Golf* one stroke more than par on a hole: also **bo'gie**

bog·gle (bäg'əl) *vi.* **-gled, -gling** ‖< Scot *bogle,* specter‖ 1 to be startled (*at*) 2 to hesitate (*at*) —*vt.* to confuse (the mind, imagination, etc.)

Bo·go·tá (bō'gə tä') capital of Colombia: pop. 3,968,000

bo·gus (bō'gəs) *adj.* ‖< ?‖ not genuine; spurious

bo·gy (bō'gē, boog'ē) *n., pl.* **-gies** ‖< Scot *bogle,* specter‖ an imaginary evil spirit; goblin Also **bo'gie**

bo·gy·man or **bo·gey·man** (boog'ē man', bō'gē-) *n., pl.* **-men'** an imaginary, frightful being

Bo·he·mi·a (bō hē'mē ə) region of W Czechoslovakia: a former kingdom

Bo·he·mi·an (bō hē'mē ən) *n.* 1 CZECH (*n.* 2) 2 a native or inhabitant of Bohemia 3 [*usually* **b-**] one who lives unconventionally —*adj.* 1 of Bohemia, its people, etc. 2 [*usually* **b-**] like a bohemian —**Bo·he'mi·an·ism'** *n.*

boil[1] (boil) *vi.* ‖< L *bulla,* a bubble‖ 1 to bubble up and vaporize by being heated 2 to seethe like a boiling liquid 3 to be agitated, as with rage 4 to cook in boiling liquid —*vt.* 1 to heat to the boiling point 2 to cook in boiling liquid —*n.* the act or state of boiling —**boil down** 1 to lessen in quantity by boiling 2 to condense

boil[2] (boil) *n.* ‖OE *byle*‖ an inflamed, painful, pus-filled swelling on the skin

boil'er *n.* **1** a container in which to boil things **2** a tank in which water is turned to steam **3** a tank for heating water and storing it

boiling point the point at which one loses one's temper

Boi·se (boi'sē, -zē) capital of Ida.: pop. 102,000: also **Boise City**

bois·ter·ous (bois'tər əs) *adj.* ‖ME *boistreous,* crude‖ **1** rough and stormy; turbulent **2** loud and exuberant; rowdy —**bois'ter·ous·ly** *adv.*

bok choy (bäk' choi') ‖Chin‖ a variety of Chinese cabbage

bo·la (bō'lə) *n.* ‖< Sp, a ball‖ a long cord with heavy balls at the ends, thrown to entangle cattle, etc.

bold (bōld) *adj.* ‖OE *beald*‖ **1** daring; fearless **2** too free in manner; impudent **3** steep **4** prominent and clear —**bold'ly** *adv.* —**bold'ness** *n.*

bold'face' (-fās') *n.* a heavy, dark printing type

bold'faced' (-fāst') *adj.* impudent

bole (bōl) *n.* ‖ON *bolr*‖ a tree trunk

bo·le·ro (bō ler'ō) *n., pl.* **-ros** ‖Sp < L *bulla,* a bubble‖ **1** a lively Spanish dance, or music for it **2** a short, open vest

Bol·i·var (bäl'ə vər), **Si·món** (sī'mən) 1783-1830; South American revolutionary leader

Bo·liv·i·a (bə liv'ē ə) inland country in W South America: 424,164 sq. mi.; pop. 6,350,000 —**Bo·liv'i·an** *adj., n.*

boll (bōl) *n.* ‖ME *bolle,* BOWL[1]‖ the roundish seed pod of a plant, esp. of cotton or flax

boll weevil a small weevil whose larvae destroy cotton bolls

bo·lo·gna (bə lō'nē) *n.* ‖after *Bologna,* It city‖ a large smoked sausage of beef, pork, or veal

Bol·she·vik (bōl'shə vik') *n., pl.* **-viks'** or **-vi'ki** (-vē'kē) ‖Russ < *ból'she,* larger‖ [*also* **b-**] **1** orig., a member of a majority faction that came into power in Russia in 1917 **2** a Communist, esp. of the Soviet Union —**Bol'she·vism** *n.* —**Bol'she·vist** *n., adj.*

bol·ster (bōl'stər) *n.* ‖OE‖ **1** a long, narrow pillow **2** any bolsterlike object or support —*vt.* to prop up as with a bolster: often with *up*

bolt[1] (bōlt) *n.* ‖OE‖ **1** a short, blunt arrow shot from a crossbow **2** a flash of lightning **3** a sudden dash **4** a sliding bar for locking a door, etc. **5** a threaded metal rod used with a nut for joining parts **6** a roll (*of* cloth, paper, etc.) —*vt.* **1** to say suddenly; blurt (*out*) **2** to swallow (food) hurriedly **3** to fasten as with a bolt **4** to abandon (a party, group, etc.) —*vi.* **1** to start suddenly; spring away **2** to withdraw support from one's party, etc. —**bolt upright** straight up; erect or erectly

bolt[2] (bōlt) *vt.* ‖< OFr *buleter*‖ to sift (flour, grain, etc.)

bo·lus (bō'ləs) *n.* ‖< Gr *bōlos*‖ **1** a small, round lump **2** a mass injected into a blood vessel, as a radioactive tracer **3** a large pill

bomb (bäm) *n.* ‖prob. < Gr *bombos,* hollow sound‖ **1** a container filled as with an explosive or incendiary chemical, for dropping, hurling, etc. **2** a small container with compressed gas in it [*an aerosol bomb*] **3** [Colloq.] a complete failure —*vt.* to attack with bombs —*vi.* [Colloq.] to be a complete failure

bom·bard (bäm bärd') *vt.* ‖< Fr *bombarde,* mortar‖ **1** to attack with artillery or bombs **2** to attack with questions, etc. **3** to direct particles at (atomic nuclei) —**bom·bard'·ment** *n.*

bom'bar·dier' (-bər dir') *n.* one who releases the bombs in a bomber

bom·bast (bäm'bast') *n.* ‖< Pers *pambak,* cotton‖ high-sounding, pompous language —**bom·bas'tic** *adj.* —**bom·bas'ti·cal·ly** *adv.*

Bom·bay (bäm'bā') seaport in W India: pop. 8,227,000

bomb·er (bäm'ər) *n.* **1** an airplane for dropping bombs **2** one who bombs

bomb'shell' *n.* **1** a bomb **2** any sudden, shocking surprise

bo·na fi·de (bō'nə fīd', fī'dē) ‖L‖ in good faith; without fraud

bo·nan·za (bə nan'zə) *n.* ‖Sp, prosperity‖ **1** a rich vein of ore **2** any source of wealth

Bo·na·parte (bō'nə pärt'), **Napoleon** *see* NAPOLEON

bon·bon (bän'bän'; *Fr* bōn bōn') *n.* ‖< Fr *bon,* good‖ a small piece of candy

bond (bänd) *n.* ‖ult. < Gothic *bindan,* bind‖ **1** anything that binds, fastens, or unites **2** [*pl.*] shackles **3** a binding agreement **4** an obligation imposed by a contract, promise, etc. **5** the status of goods kept in a warehouse until taxes or duties are paid **6** an interest-bearing certificate issued by a government or business, redeemable on a specified date **7** *a*) surety against theft, absconding, etc. *b*) an amount paid as surety or bail —*vt.* **1** to join; bind **2** to furnish a surety for **3** to place or hold (goods) in bond

bond·age (bän'dij) *n.* ‖ult. < ON *bua,* inhabit‖ serfdom or slavery

bond'ing *n.* the development of a close relationship, esp. between mother and offspring

bond'man *n., pl.* **-men** **1** a serf **2** a slave —**bond'wom'an,** *pl.* **-wom'en,** *n.fem.*

bond paper ‖orig. used for bonds, etc.‖ high-quality writing paper

bonds·man (bändz'mən) *n., pl.* **-men** **1** BONDMAN **2** one who furnishes BOND (*n.* 7)

bone (bōn) *n.* ‖< OE *ban*‖ **1** any of the parts of hard tissue forming the skeleton of most vertebrates **2** this hard tissue **3** a bonelike substance or thing —*vt.* **boned, bon'ing** to remove the bones from —*vi.* [Slang] to study hard: usually with *up* —**have a bone to pick** [Colloq.] to have cause to quarrel —**make no bones about** [Colloq.] admit freely —**boneless** *adj.*

bone china translucent china made of white clay to which the ash of burned bones has been added

bone'-dry' *adj.* [Colloq.] very dry

bone meal crushed or ground bones, used as feed or fertilizer

bon·er (bōn'ər) *n.* [Slang] a blunder

bon·fire (bän'fīr') *n.* ‖ME *banefyre,* bone fire, pyre‖ an outdoor fire

bong (bôŋ, bäŋ) *n.* ‖echoic‖ a deep ringing sound, as of a large bell —*vi.* to make this sound

BONGOS

bon·go (bäŋ′gō) ***n.***, *pl.* **-gos** ⟦AmSp < ?⟧ either of a pair of small drums of different pitch struck with the fingers In full **bongo drum**

bo·ni·to (bō nēt′ō, bə-) ***n.***, *pl.* **-tos** or **-toes** ⟦Sp⟧ any of several saltwater food fishes related to the tuna

bon·jour (bōn zhōōr′) ***interj.***, ***n.*** ⟦Fr⟧ good day; hello

bonk·ers (bäŋ′kərz) ***adj.*** [Slang] crazy

bon mot (bōn′ mō′) *pl.* **bons mots** (bōn′ mōz′) ⟦Fr, lit., good word⟧ a clever or witty remark

Bonn (bän) capital of West Germany, on the Rhine: pop. 292,000

bon·net (bän′it) ***n.*** ⟦< OFr *bonet*⟧ a hat with a chin ribbon, worn by children and women

bon·ny or **bon·nie** (bän′ē) ***adj.*** **-ni·er, -ni·est** ⟦< L *bonus*, good⟧ [Now Chiefly Brit.] **1** handsome or pretty, with a healthy glow **2** pleasant

bon·sai (bän sī′) ***n.***, *pl.* **-sai′** ⟦Jpn⟧ a tree or shrub grown in a pot and dwarfed by pruning, etc.

bo·nus (bō′nəs) ***n.***, *pl.* **-nus·es** ⟦L, good⟧ anything given in addition to the customary or required amount

bon voy·age (bän′ voi äzh′) ⟦Fr⟧ pleasant journey

bon·y (bō′nē) ***adj.*** **-i·er, -i·est** **1** of, like, or having bones **2** thin; emaciated

bony fish any fish having an air bladder, covered gills, and a bony skeleton

boo (bōō) ***interj.***, ***n.***, *pl.* **boos** a sound made to express disapproval, etc., or to startle —***vi.***, ***vt.*** **booed, boo′ing** to shout "boo" (at)

boo-boo or **boo·boo** (bōō′bōō′) ***n.***, *pl.* **-boos′** [Slang] a stupid mistake

boob tube [Slang] TV or a TV set

boo·by (bōō′bē) ***n.***, *pl.* **-bies** ⟦prob. < Sp *bobo*⟧ a fool; nitwit Also **boob** (bōōb)

booby trap any scheme or device for tricking a person unawares

boo·dle (bōōd′′l) ***n.*** ⟦< Du *boedel*, property⟧ [Old Slang] **1** something given as a bribe; graft **2** loot

book (book) ***n.*** ⟦OE *boc*⟧ **1** a printed work on sheets of paper bound together, usually between protective covers **2** a main division of a literary work **3** a record or account **4** *a)* a libretto *b)* the script of a play **5** a booklike package, as of matches —***vt.*** **1** to record in a book; list **2** to engage (rooms, etc.) ahead of time **3** to record charges against on a police record —**by the book** according to the rules —**the (Good) Book** the Bible

book′bind′ing ***n.*** the art, trade, or business of binding books —**book′bind′er** ***n.*** —**book′bind′er·y,** *pl.* **-ies,** ***n.***

book′case′ (-kās′) ***n.*** a set of shelves or a cabinet for holding books

book′end′ (-end′) ***n.*** a weight or bracket that keeps a row of books upright

book′ie (-ē) ***n.*** [Slang] a bookmaker

book′ing ***n.*** an engagement, as for a lecture, performance, etc.

book′ish (-ish) ***adj.*** **1** inclined to read and study **2** pedantic

book′keep′ing ***n.*** the work of keeping a systematic record of business transactions —**book′keep′er** ***n.***

book′let (-lit) ***n.*** a small book

book′mak′er ***n.*** a person in the business of taking bets, as on horses

book′mark′ ***n.*** a thing put between the pages of a book to mark a place

book matches safety matches of paper fastened in a cardboard holder

book′mo·bile′ (-mō bēl′) ***n.*** a lending library traveling in a truck, etc.

book′plate′ ***n.*** a label pasted in a book to name its owner

book′shelf ***n.***, *pl.* **-shelves′** a shelf on which books are kept

book′store′ (-stôr′) ***n.*** a store where books are sold Also [Brit.] **book′shop′**

book′worm′ ***n.*** **1** an insect larva that feeds on the binding, paste, etc. of books **2** one who reads much

boom[1] (bōōm) ***vi.***, ***vt.*** ⟦echoic⟧ to make, or say with, a deep, hollow, resonant sound —***n.*** this sound

boom[2] (bōōm) ***n.*** ⟦Du, a beam⟧ **1** a spar extending from a mast to hold the bottom of a sail outstretched **2** a long beam extending as from an upright for supporting and guiding anything lifted **3** a barrier, as of logs, to prevent floating logs from dispersing —***vi.*** to go rapidly along

boom[3] (bōōm) ***vi.*** ⟦< ? prec. *vi.*⟧ to increase or grow rapidly —***vt.*** to cause to flourish; support —***n.*** **1** swift growth **2** a period of prosperity

boom′box′ ***n.*** [Slang] a large portable radio and tape player

boom·er·ang (bōōm′ər aŋ′) ***n.*** ⟦< Australian native name⟧ **1** a flat, curved stick that can be thrown so that it returns to the thrower **2** a scheme gone awry, to the schemer's harm —***vi.*** to act as a boomerang

boon[1] (bōōn) ***n.*** ⟦ON *bon*, a petition⟧ a welcome benefit; blessing

boon[2] (bōōn) ***adj.*** ⟦< L *bonus*, good⟧ merry; convivial: now only in **boon companion,** a close friend

boon·docks (bōōn′däks′) ***n.pl.*** ⟦< native Philippine name⟧ [Colloq.] **1** a jungle or wilderness **2** any remote rural region Used with *the*

boon·dog·gle (bōōn′dôg′əl, -däg′-) ***n.*** trifling, pointless work —***vi.*** **-gled, -gling** to engage in boondoggle —**boon′dog′gler** ***n.***

boor (boor) ***n.*** ⟦Du *boer*, a peasant⟧ a rude, awkward, or ill-mannered person —**boor′ish** ***adj.*** —**boor′ish·ly** ***adv.***

boost (bōōst) ***vt.*** ⟦< ?⟧ **1** to raise as by a push from below **2** to urge others to support **3** to increase —***n.*** **1** a push upward or forward **2** an increase —**boost′er** ***n.***

booster shot a later injection of a vaccine, for maintaining immunity

boot[1] (bōōt) ***n.*** ⟦OFr *bote*⟧ **1** a covering of leather, rubber, etc. for the foot and part of the leg **2** a patch for the inside of a tire casing 3 a kick —*vt.* 1 to put boots on 2 to kick 3 [Slang] to dismiss 4 to load, as from a disk (a program, etc.) into the memory of (a computer) —**the boot** [Slang] dismissal

boot[2] (bo͞ot) *n., vt., vi.* ‖ OE *bot,* advantage ‖ [Archaic] profit —**to boot** besides; in addition

boot′black′ *n.* one whose work is shining shoes or boots

boot·ee or **boot·ie** (bo͞o tē′; *for 2* bo͞ot′ē) *n.* 1 a short boot for women or children 2 a baby's knitted shoe

booth (bo͞oth) *n., pl.* **booths** (bo͞o*th*z) ‖ < ON *bua,* dwell ‖ 1 a stall for selling goods 2 a small enclosure for voting at elections 3 a small structure to house a public telephone, etc.

boot′leg′ *vt., vi.* **-legged′, -leg′ging** ‖ < hiding liquor in a boot ‖ to make or sell (esp. liquor) illegally —*adj.* bootlegged; illegal —*n.* bootlegged liquor —**boot′leg′ger** *n.*

boot′less *adj.* ‖ BOOT[2] + -LESS ‖ useless

boo·ty (bo͞ot′ē) *n., pl.* **-ties** ‖ LowG *bute* ‖ 1 spoils of war 2 plunder

booze (bo͞oz) *vi.* **boozed, booz′ing** ‖ < MDu *busen* ‖ [Colloq.] to drink too much liquor —*n.* [Colloq.] liquor

bop[1] (bäp) *vt.* **bopped, bop′ping** [Colloq.] to hit; punch

bop[2] (bäp) *n.* a style of jazz (*c.* 1945-55) marked by complex rhythms, harmonic experimentation, etc. —*vi.* **bopped, bop′ping** [Slang] to walk, esp. in an easy, strutting way

bo·rax (bôr′aks′) *n.* ‖ < Pers *būrah* ‖ a white crystalline salt used in the manufacture of glass, soaps, etc.

Bor·deaux (bôr dō′) *n.* ‖ after *Bordeaux,* city and region in SW France ‖ 1 a red or white wine from the Bordeaux region 2 a similar wine made elsewhere

bor·der (bôr′dər) *n.* ‖ < OFr *border,* to border ‖ 1 an edge or part near an edge; margin 2 a dividing line between two countries, etc. 3 a narrow strip along an edge —*vt.* 1 to provide with a border 2 to extend along the edge of —*adj.* of or near a border —**border on** (or **upon**) to be next to

bor′der·land′ *n.* 1 land near a border 2 a vague condition

bor′der·line′ (-līn′) *n.* a boundary —*adj.* 1 on a boundary 2 indefinite

bore[1] (bôr) *vt.* **bored, bor′ing** ‖ < OE *bor,* auger ‖ 1 to make a hole in with a drill, etc. 2 to make (a well, etc.) as by drilling 3 to weary by being dull —*vi.* to bore a hole or passage —*n.* 1 a hole made as by boring 2 *a)* the hollow part of a tube or gun barrel *b)* its inside diameter 3 a tiresome, dull person or thing

bore[2] (bôr) *vt., vi. pt. of* BEAR[1]

bore·dom (bôr′dəm) *n.* the condition of being bored or uninterested

boric acid a white crystalline compound, used as an antiseptic

born (bôrn) *vt., vi. alt. pp. of* BEAR[1] —*adj.* 1 brought into life 2 natural, as if from birth /*a born* athlete/

born-a·gain (bôrn′ə gen′) *adj.* professing a new or renewed faith or enthusiasm /*a born-again* Christian/

borne (bôrn) *vt., vi. alt. pp. of* BEAR[1]

Bor·ne·o (bôr′nē ō′) large island in the Malay Archipelago

bo·ron (bôr′än′) *n.* ‖ < BORAX ‖ a nonmetallic chemical element

bor·ough (bur′ō) *n.* ‖ OE *burg,* town ‖ 1 a self-governing, incorporated town 2 any of the five administrative units of New York City

bor·row (bär′ō, bôr′-) *vt., vi.* ‖ OE *borgian* ‖ 1 to take or receive (something) intending to return it 2 to adopt (an idea, etc.) as one's own —**bor′row·er** *n.*

borscht or **borsch** (bôrsh) *n.* ‖ Russ *borshch* ‖ a beet soup, served usually with sour cream

bor·zoi (bôr′zoi′) *n.* ‖ Russ *borzój,* swift ‖ a large dog with a narrow head, long legs, and silky coat

bosh (bäsh) *n., interj.* ‖ Turk, empty ‖ [Colloq.] nonsense

bos·om (bo͝oz′əm, bo͞o′zəm) *n.* ‖ OE *bosm* ‖ 1 the human breast 2 the breast regarded as the source of feelings 3 the inside; midst /in the *bosom* of one's family/ 4 the part of a garment that covers the breast —*adj.* close; intimate /a *bosom* friend/

bos′om·y (-əm ē) *adj.* having large breasts

bos·on (bō′sän′) *n.* ‖ after S. N. *Bose* (1894-1974), Indian physicist + -ON ‖ any of certain subatomic particles, including photons and mesons

boss[1] (bôs, bäs) *n.* ‖ Du *baas,* a master ‖ 1 an employer or manager 2 one who controls a political organization —*vt.* 1 to act as boss of 2 [Colloq.] to order (a person) about —*adj.* [Slang] excellent

boss[2] (bôs, bäs) *n.* ‖ OFr *boce,* a swelling ‖ a protruding ornament or projecting knob —*vt.* to stud

boss′ism′ *n.* control by bosses, esp. of a political machine or party

boss′y *adj.* **-i·er, -i·est** [Colloq.] domineering —**boss′i·ness** *n.*

Bos·ton (bôs′tən, bäs′-) seaport & capital of Mass.: pop. 563,000 —**Bos·to′ni·an** (-tō′nē ən) *adj., n.*

bo·sun (bō′sən) *n. alt. sp. of* BOATSWAIN

bot·a·ny (bät′′n ē) *n.* ‖ < Gr *botanē,* a plant ‖ the science that deals with plants and plant life —**bo·tan·i·cal** (bō tan′i kəl) or **bo·tan′ic** *adj.* —**bot′a·nist** *n.*

botch (bäch) *vt.* ‖ ME *bocchen,* to repair < ? ‖ 1 to patch clumsily 2 to bungle —*n.* a bungled or unskilled piece of work —**botch′er** *n.*

bot·fly (bät′flī′) *n., pl.* **-flies′** a fly resembling a small bumblebee

both (bōth) *adj., pron.* ‖ OE *ba tha,* both these ‖ the two /*both* birds sang loudly/ —*conj., adv.* together; equally /*both* tired and hungry/

both·er (bä*th*′ər) *vt., vi.* ‖ prob. < *pother* ‖ 1 to worry; harass 2 to concern (oneself) —*n.* 1 worry; trouble 2 one who gives trouble —**both′er·some** (-səm) *adj.*

Bot·swa·na (bät swä′nə) country in S Africa: 231,805 sq. mi.; pop. 1,104,000

Bot·ti·cel·li (bät′ə chel′ē), **San·dro** (sän′drō) *c.* 1445-1510; It. painter

bot·tle (bät′′l) *n.* ‖ < LL *buttis,* a cask ‖ 1 a narrow-necked container for liquids, usually of glass 2 its contents —*vt.* **-tled, -tling** to put into a bottle —**bottle up** to restrain —**hit the bottle** [Slang] to drink much alcoholic liquor —**bot'tler** *n.*

bot'tle·neck' *n.* 1 a narrow passage or road where progress, as of traffic, is slowed 2 any hindrance to movement or progress

bot·tom (bät'əm) *n.* ‖ OE *botm,* ground ‖ 1 the lowest part or place 2 the part on which something rests 3 the side underneath 4 the seat of a chair 5 the ground beneath a body of water 6 basis; cause; source 7 [Colloq.] the buttocks —*adj.* lowest; last; basic —**at bottom** fundamentally —**bot'tom·less** *adj.*

bottom line 1 [Colloq.] profits or losses, as of a business 2 [Slang] *a)* the basic factor, etc. *b)* the final statement, decision, etc.

bot·u·lism (bäch'ə liz'əm) *n.* ‖ < L *botulus,* sausage ‖ poisoning from the toxin produced by a bacillus sometimes found in foods improperly canned or preserved

bou·doir (bo͞o dwär', bo͞o'dwär') *n.* ‖ < Fr, lit., pouting room ‖ a woman's private room

bouf·fant (bo͞o fänt') *adj.* ‖ < Fr *bouffer,* puff out ‖ puffed out; full

bou·gain·vil·le·a or **bou·gain·vil·lae·a** (bo͞o'gən vil'ē ə, -vil'yə, -vē'yə) *n.* ‖ ModL ‖ a woody tropical vine having large, showy, purple or red bracts

bough (bou) *n.* ‖ OE *bog,* shoulder ‖ a main branch of a tree

bought (bôt) *vt., vi. pt. & pp. of* BUY

bouil·lon (bool'yän', -yən) *n.* ‖ < Fr *bouillir,* to boil ‖ a clear broth

boul·der (bōl'dər) *n.* ‖ < ME *bulderston,* noisy stone ‖ a large rock worn by weather and water

bou·le·vard (bool'ə värd') *n.* ‖ Fr < MDu *bolwerc,* bulwark ‖ a broad street, often lined with trees, etc.

bounce (bouns) *vi.* **bounced, bounc'ing** ‖ ME *bounsen,* to thump ‖ 1 to spring back, as upon impact; rebound 2 to spring; leap 3 [Slang] to be returned: said of a worthless check —*vt.* 1 to cause (a ball, etc.) to bounce 2 [Slang] to put (a person) out by force 3 [Slang] to fire from a job —*n.* 1 *a)* a bouncing; rebound *b)* a leap or jump 2 capacity for bouncing 3 [Colloq.] energy, zest, etc. —**the bounce** [Slang] dismissal —**bounc'y** *adj.*

bounc·er (boun'sər) *n.* [Slang] a person hired to remove disorderly people from a nightclub, restaurant, etc.

bounc'ing (-siŋ) *adj.* big, healthy, etc.

bound[1] (bound) *vi.* ‖ < OFr *bondir,* to leap ‖ 1 to move with a leap or leaps 2 to bounce; rebound —*vt.* to cause to bound or bounce —*n.* 1 a jump; leap 2 a bounce; rebound

bound[2] (bound) *vt., vi. pt. & pp. of* BIND —*adj.* 1 tied 2 closely connected 3 certain /*bound* to lose/ 4 obliged 5 having a binding, as a book 6 [Colloq.] determined; resolved

bound[3] (bound) *adj.* ‖ < ON *bua,* prepare ‖ going; headed /*bound* east/

bound[4] (bound) *n.* ‖ < ML *butina,* boundary ‖ 1 a boundary 2 [*pl.*] an area near a boundary —*vt.* 1 to limit 2 to be a limit or boundary to 3 to name the boundaries of —**out of bounds** 1 beyond the boundaries 2 forbidden

bound·a·ry (boun'də rē, -drē) *n., pl.* **-ries** anything marking a limit; bound

bound'en (-dən) *adj.* ‖ old pp. of BIND ‖ 1 [Archaic] obligated; indebted 2 obligatory /one's *bounden* duty/

bound'er (-dər) *n.* ‖ < BOUND[1] ‖ [Colloq., Chiefly Brit.] a cad

boun·te·ous (boun'tē əs) *adj.* ‖ see fol. ‖ 1 generous 2 plentiful —**boun'ti·ful** (-tə fəl) *adj.*

boun'ty (-tē) *n., pl.* **-ties** ‖ < L *bonus,* good ‖ 1 generosity 2 a generous gift 3 a reward or premium

bou·quet (bo͞o kā'; *often* bō-) *n.* ‖ Fr ‖ 1 a bunch of flowers 2 aroma, as of wine

bour·bon (bur'bən, boor'-) *n.* ‖ after *Bourbon* County, Ky. ‖ [*sometimes* **B-**] a whiskey distilled from corn mash

bour·geois (boor zhwä') *n., pl.* **-geois'** ‖ Fr < OFr *borc,* town ‖ a member of the bourgeoisie —*adj.* of the bourgeoisie: used variously to mean conventional, smug, respectable, etc.

bour·geoi·sie (boor'zhwä zē') *n.* [*with sing. or pl. v.*] the social class between the very wealthy and the working class; middle class

bout (bout) *n.* ‖ ME *bught* ‖ 1 a struggle or contest 2 a period spent in some activity; spell

bou·tique (bo͞o tēk'; *often,* bō-) *n.* ‖ Fr < L *apotheca,* storehouse ‖ a small shop where fashionable articles are sold

bou·ton·niere or **bou'ton·nière'** (bo͞o'tə nir', -tən yer') *n.* ‖ Fr, buttonhole ‖ a flower worn in a buttonhole

bo·vine (bō'vīn', vēn') *adj.* ‖ < L *bos,* ox ‖ 1 of an ox or cow 2 slow, dull, stupid, etc.

bow[1] (bou) *vi.* ‖ < OE *bugan,* to bend ‖ 1 to bend the head or body in respect, agreement, etc. 2 to yield; submit —*vt.* 1 to bend (the head or body) in respect, etc. 2 to weigh (*down*) —*n.* a bending of the head or body, as in respect, greeting, etc. —**take a bow** to acknowledge applause, etc.

bow[2] (bō) *n.* ‖ OE *boga* ‖ 1 anything curved /a *rainbow*/ 2 a curve; bend 3 a flexible, curved strip of wood with a cord connecting the two ends, for shooting arrows 4 a slender stick strung with horsehairs, for playing a violin, etc. 5 BOWKNOT —*adj.* curved —*vt., vi.* 1 to bend; curve 2 to play (a violin, etc.) with a bow

bow[3] (bou) *n.* ‖ < LowG *būg* ‖ the front part of a ship, etc.

bowd·ler·ize (boud'lər īz') *vt.* **-ized', -iz'ing** ‖ after T. *Bowdler* (1754-1825), Eng editor ‖ to expurgate —**bowd'ler·ism'** *n.* —**bowd'ler·i·za'tion** *n.*

bow·el (bou'əl) *n.* ‖ < L *botulus,* sausage ‖ 1 an intestine, esp. of a human being 2 [*pl.*] the inner part —**move one's bowels** to defecate

bow·er (bou'ər) *n.* ‖ < OE *bur,* dwelling ‖ a place enclosed by boughs or vines; arbor

bow·ie knife (bo͞o'ē, bō'-) ‖ after Col. J. *Bowie* (c. 1799-1836) ‖ a long single-edged hunting knife

bow·knot (bō'nät') *n.* a decorative knot, usually with two loops and two ends

BOWIE KNIFE

bowl[1] (bōl) ***n.*** ‖OE *bolla*‖ **1** a deep, rounded dish **2** the contents of a bowl **3** a bowllike thing or part **4** an amphitheater or stadium —**bowl′like′** ***adj.***

bowl[2] (bōl) ***n.*** ‖< L *bulla,* bubble‖ **1** the wooden ball used in the game of bowls **2** a roll of the ball in bowling —***vi.*** **1** to roll (a ball) or participate in bowling **2** to move swiftly and smoothly —**bowl over 1** to knock over **2** [Colloq.] to astonish —**bowl′er** ***n.***

bowl·der (bōl′dər) ***n.*** *alt. sp. of* BOULDER

bow·leg (bō′leg′) ***n.*** a leg with outward curvature —**bow′leg′ged** (-leg′id, -legd′) ***adj.***

bowl·ing (bōl′iŋ) ***n.*** **1** a game in which a heavy ball is bowled along a wooden lane (**bowling alley**) at ten wooden pins **2** LAWN BOWLING

bowling green a lawn for lawn bowling

bowls (bōlz) ***n.*** LAWN BOWLING

bow·man (bō′mən) ***n., pl.*** **-men** an archer

bow·sprit (bou′sprit′, bō′-) ***n.*** ‖prob. < Du‖ a tapered spar extending forward from the bow of a sailing ship

bow tie (bō) a necktie tied in a bow

box[1] (bäks) ***n.*** ‖< Gr *pyxos,* BOX[3]‖ **1** a container, usually rectangular and lidded; case **2** the contents of a box **3** a boxlike thing or space [a jury *box*] **4** a small, enclosed group of seats, as in a theater **5** a booth **6** *Baseball* an area designated for the batter, catcher, etc. —***vt.*** to put into a box —**box in** (or **up**) to shut in or keep in; surround or confine —**in a box** [Colloq.] in difficulty —**box′like′** ***adj.***

box[2] (bäks) ***n.*** ‖< ?‖ a blow struck with the hand —***vt.*** **1** to strike with such a blow **2** to fight by boxing with —***vi.*** to fight with the fists

box[3] (bäks) ***n.*** ‖< Gr *pyxos*‖ an evergreen shrub with small leathery leaves Also **box′-wood′**

box′car′ ***n.*** a fully enclosed railroad freight car

box′er ***n.*** **1** one who boxes; prizefighter **2** a medium-sized dog with a sturdy body and a smooth coat

box′ing ***n.*** the skill or sport of fighting with the fists, esp. in padded leather mittens (**boxing gloves**)

box office 1 a place where admission tickets are sold, as in a theater **2** [Colloq.] the power, as of a performer, to attract a paying audience

boy (boi) ***n.*** ‖ME *boie*‖ **1** a male child **2** any man: familiar term **3** a male servant: a patronizing term —***interj.*** [Slang] an exclamation of pleasure, surprise, etc.: often **oh, boy!** —**boy′hood′** ***n.*** —**boy′ish** ***adj.***

boy·cott (boi′kät′) ***vt.*** ‖after Capt. *Boycott,* Irish land agent so treated‖ to join together in refusing to deal with, buy, etc. so as to punish or coerce —***n.*** a boycotting

boy′friend′ ***n.*** **1** [Colloq.] a sweetheart or escort of a girl or woman **2** a boy who is one's friend

Boy Scout a member of the **Boy Scouts,** a boys' organization that stresses outdoor life and service to others

boy·sen·ber·ry (boi′zən ber′ē) ***n., pl.*** **-ries** ‖after R. *Boysen,* U.S. horticulturist‖ a berry that is a cross of the raspberry, loganberry, and blackberry

Br *Chem. symbol for* bromine

Br. 1 Britain **2** British **3** Brother

bra (brä) ***n.*** ‖< BRASSIERE‖ a brassiere

brace (brās) ***vt.* braced, brac′ing** ‖< Gr *brachiōn,* arm‖ **1** to bind **2** to strengthen by supporting the weight of, etc. **3** to make ready for an impact, shock, etc. **4** to stimulate —***n.*** **1** a couple; pair **2** a thing that clasps or connects **3** [*pl.*] [Brit.] suspenders **4** a device for setting up or maintaining tension **5** either of the signs {}, used to connect words, lines, etc. **6** any propping device **7** *a*) a device for supporting a weak part of the body *b*) [*often pl.*] a device worn for straightening the teeth **8** a tool for holding a drilling bit —**brace up** to call forth one's courage, etc.

brace and bit a tool for boring, consisting of a removable drill (*bit*) in a rotating handle (*brace*)

brace·let (brās′lit) ***n.*** ‖< Gr *brachiōn,* arm‖ an ornamental band or chain worn about the wrist or arm

brack·en (brak′ən) ***n.*** ‖ME *braken*‖ a large, coarse, weedy fern found in meadows, woods, and wastelands

brack·et (brak′it) ***n.*** ‖< Fr *brague,* knee pants‖ **1** a support projecting from a wall, etc. **2** any angle-shaped support **3** either of the signs [ ], used to enclose a word, etc. **4** a classification [high income *bracket*] —***vt.*** **1** to support with brackets **2** to enclose within brackets **3** to classify together

brack·ish (brak′ish) ***adj.*** ‖< MDu *brak*‖ **1** salty **2** nauseating

bract (brakt) ***n.*** ‖L *bractea,* thin metal plate‖ a modified leaf growing at the base of a flower or on its stalk

brad (brad) ***n.*** ‖ON *broddr,* arrow‖ a thin wire nail with a small head

brae (brā, brē) ***n.*** ‖ON *bra,* brow‖ [Scot.] a sloping bank; hillside

brag (brag) ***vt., vi.* bragged, brag′ging** ‖ME *braggen* < ?‖ to boast —***n.*** boastful talk —**brag′ger** ***n.***

brag′gart (-ərt) ***n.*** an offensively boastful person —***adj.*** boastful

Brah·ma (brä′mə) the chief member of the Hindu trinity (Brahma, Vishnu, and Siva), regarded as the creator of the universe

Brah·man (brä′mən) ***n., pl.*** **-mans** ‖Hindi < Sans, worship‖ **1** a member of the priestly Hindu caste **2** a breed of domestic cattle developed from the zebu of India and having a large hump

Brahms (brämz), **Jo·han·nes** (yō hän′əs) 1833-97; Ger. composer

braid (brād) ***vt.*** ‖< OE *bregdan,* to move quickly‖ **1** to interweave three or more strands of (hair, straw, etc.) **2** to make by such interweaving —***n.*** **1** a strip, as of hair, formed by braiding **2** a woven band of cloth, etc., used to bind or decorate clothing

Braille (brāl) ***n.*** ‖after L. *Braille* (1809-52), its Fr inventor‖ [*also* **b-**] a system of printing for the blind, using raised dots felt with the fingers

brain (brān) ***n.*** ‖OE *brægen*‖ **1** the mass of nerve tissue in the cranium of vertebrates **2** [*often pl.*] intelligence —***vt.*** to dash out the brains of

brain′child′ *n.* [Colloq.] an idea, plan, etc. produced by one's mental labor
brain drain [Colloq.] an exhausting of the intellectual or professional resources of a country, region, etc., esp. through emigration
brain′less *adj.* foolish or stupid
brain′storm′ *n.* [Colloq.] a sudden inspiration, idea, or plan —*vi.* to engage in brainstorming
brain′storm′ing *n.* the unrestrained offering of ideas by all members of a group to seek solutions to problems
brain′wash′ *vt.* [Colloq.] to indoctrinate so thoroughly as to effect a radical change of beliefs
brain wave 1 rhythmic electric impulses from the nerve centers in the brain 2 [Colloq.] a brainstorm
brain′y *adj.* **-i·er, -i·est** [Colloq.] having a good mind; intelligent
braise (brāz) *vt.* **braised, brais′ing** ‖ < Fr *braise,* live coals ‖ to brown (meat, etc.) and then simmer slowly
brake (brāk) *n.* ‖ < Ger *breken,* to break ‖ any device for slowing or stopping a vehicle or machine, as by causing a block or band to press against a moving part —*vt., vi.* **braked, brak′ing** to slow down or stop as with a brake —**brake′less** *adj.*
brake′man (-mən) *n., pl.* **-men** a railroad worker who operated the brakes on a train, but is now chiefly an assistant to the conductor
bram·ble (bram′bəl) *n.* ‖ < OE *brom,* broom ‖ a prickly shrub of the rose family, as the raspberry, blackberry, etc. —**bram′bly** *adj.*
Bramp·ton (bramp′tən) city in SE Ontario, Canada: pop. 189,000
bran (bran) *n.* ‖ OFr *bren* ‖ the husk of grains of wheat, rye, etc. separated from the flour, as by sifting
branch (branch) *n.* ‖ < LL *branca,* a claw ‖ 1 any woody extension from a tree or shrub; limb 2 a tributary stream 3 any part or extension of a main body or system, as a division of a family or a separately located unit of a business —*vi.* 1 to put forth branches 2 to come out [*from* the main part] as a branch —**branch off** 1 to separate into branches 2 to diverge —**branch out** to extend one's interests, activities, etc. —**branched** (brancht) *adj.* —**branch′like′** *adj.*
brand (brand) *n.* ‖ OE < *biernan,* to burn ‖ 1 a burning or partially burned stick 2 a mark burned on the skin, formerly used to punish criminals, now used on cattle to show ownership 3 the iron used in branding 4 a stigma 5 *a*) an identifying mark or label *b*) the make of a commodity [*a brand* of coffee] *c*) a special kind —*vt.* 1 to mark with a brand 2 to put a stigma on —**brand′er** *n.*
bran·dish (bran′dish) *vt.* ‖ < OFr *brandir* ‖ to wave menacingly or as a challenge; flourish
brand name the name by which a certain brand or make of commodity is known —**brand′-name′** *adj.*
brand′-new′ *adj.* ‖ orig., fresh from the fire: see BRAND ‖ entirely new
bran·dy (bran′dē) *n., pl.* **-dies** ‖ < Du *brandewijn,* distilled wine ‖ an alcoholic liquor distilled from wine or from fermented fruit juice —*vt.* **-died, -dy·ing** to flavor or preserve with brandy
brant (brant) *n.* ‖ < ? ‖ a wild goose of Europe and North America
brash (brash) *adj.* ‖ orig. Brit dial.; < ? ‖ 1 hasty and reckless 2 insolent; impudent —**brash′ness** *n.*
Bra·sí·lia (brä zē′lyä; *E* brə zil′yə) capital of Brazil, in the central part: pop. 411,000
brass (bras) *n., pl.* **brass′es** ‖ OE *bræs* ‖ 1 a yellowish metal, an alloy of copper and zinc 2 [*often with pl. v.*] brass instruments 3 [Colloq.] bold impudence 4 [*often with pl. v.*] [Slang] officers or officials of high rank —*adj.* of brass —**brass′y, -i·er, -i·est,** *adj.*
bras·siere or **bras·sière** (brə zir′) *n.* ‖ Fr < *bras,* an arm ‖ an undergarment worn by women to support the breasts
brass tacks [Colloq.] basic facts
brat (brat) *n.* ‖ < Gael *bratt,* cloth, rag ‖ a child, esp. an impudent, unruly child: scornful or playful term
brat·wurst (brät′voorst′) *n.* ‖ Ger < OHG, *brato,* lean meat + *wurst,* sausage ‖ highly seasoned, fresh sausage of veal and pork
braun·schwei·ger (broun′shwī′gər) *n.* ‖ after *Braunschweig,* Germany, where orig. made ‖ smoked liver sausage
bra·va·do (brə vä′dō) *n.* ‖ < Sp < *bravo,* brave ‖ pretended courage or feigned confidence
brave (brāv) *adj.* **brav′er, brav′est** ‖ Fr < It *bravo* ‖ 1 not afraid; having courage 2 having a fine appearance —*n.* 1 any brave man 2 a North American Indian warrior —*vt.* **braved, brav′ing** 1 to face with courage 2 to defy; dare —**brave′ly** *adv.* —**brave′ness** *n.*
brav·er·y (brāv′ər ē) *n.* courage; valor
bra·vo (brä′vō) *interj.* ‖ It ‖ well done! excellent! —*n., pl.* **-vos** a shout of "bravo!"
bra·vu·ra (brə vyoor′ə) *n.* ‖ It < *bravo,* brave ‖ 1 bold daring; dash 2 a brilliant musical passage or technique
brawl (brôl) *vi.* ‖ < Du *brallen,* to boast ‖ to quarrel or fight noisily —*n.* a noisy quarrel or fight
brawn (brôn) *n.* ‖ < OFr *braon,* muscle ‖ 1 strong, well-developed muscles 2 muscular strength —**brawn′y, -i·er, -i·est,** *adj.* —**brawn′i·ness** *n.*
bray (brā) *vi.* ‖ < OFr *braire* ‖ to make the loud, harsh cry of a donkey —*n.* the harsh cry of a donkey, or a sound like this
braze (brāz) *vt.* **brazed, braz′ing** ‖ Fr *braser* ‖ to solder with a metal having a high melting point
bra·zen (brā′zən) *adj.* ‖ < OE *bræsen,* brass ‖ 1 of brass 2 like brass in color, etc. 3 shameless; bold 4 harsh and piercing —**brazen it out** to act in a bold, unashamed way —**bra′zen·ly** *adv.* —**bra′zen·ness** *n.*
bra·zier[1] (brā′zhər) *n.* ‖ see BRAISE ‖ a metal container to hold burning coals
bra·zier[2] (brā′zhər) *n.* ‖ see BRASS ‖ a person who works in brass
Bra·zil (brə zil′) country in South America, on the Atlantic: 3,286,540 sq. mi.; pop. 143,277,000 —**Bra·zil′ian** *adj., n.*

Brazil nut the edible, three-sided seed of a tree of South America

breach (brēch) ***n.*** ‖ < OE *brecan*, to break ‖ **1** a failure to observe a law, promise, etc. **2** an opening made by a breakthrough **3** a break in friendly relations —***vt.*** to make a breach in —**breach of promise** a breaking of a promise to marry

bread (bred) ***n.*** ‖ OE, crumb ‖ **1** a baked food made of flour or meal mixed with water, etc. **2** livelihood /to earn one's *bread*/ —***vt.*** to coat with bread crumbs before cooking —**break bread** to eat

breadth (bredth) ***n.*** ‖ < OE *brad*, broad ‖ **1** width **2** scope; extent

bread·win·ner (bred′win′ər) ***n.*** one who supports dependents by his or her earnings

break (brāk) ***vt.* broke, bro′ken, break′ing** ‖ OE *brecan* ‖ **1** to split or crack into pieces; smash **2** to cut open the surface of (soil, the skin, etc.) **3** to make unusable by cracking, disrupting, etc. **4** to tame as with force **5** to get rid of (a habit) **6** to demote **7** to make poor, ill, bankrupt, etc. **8** to surpass (a record) **9** to violate (a law, promise, etc.) **10** to disrupt the order of /*break* ranks/ **11** to interrupt (a journey, electric circuit, etc.) **12** to reduce the force of by interrupting (a fall, etc.) **13** to bring to an end suddenly or by force **14** to penetrate (silence, darkness, etc.) **15** to disclose **16** to decipher or solve /*break* a code/ —***vi.*** **1** to split into pieces; come apart **2** to force one's way (*through* obstacles, etc.) **3** to stop associating (*with*) **4** to become unusable **5** to change suddenly /his voice *broke*/ **6** to begin suddenly /to *break* into song/ **7** to come suddenly into being, notice, etc. /the story *broke*/ **8** to stop activity temporarily **9** to suffer a collapse as of spirit —***n.*** **1** a breaking **2** a broken place **3** a beginning or appearance /the *break* of day/ **4** an interruption of regularity **5** a gap, interval, or rest **6** a sudden change **7** an escape **8** a chance piece of luck —**break down** **1** to go out of working order **2** to have a physical or nervous collapse **3** to analyze —**break in** **1** to enter forcibly **2** to interrupt **3** to train (a beginner) **4** to prepare (something new) by use or wear —**break off** to stop abruptly —**break out** **1** to become covered with pimples, etc. **2** to escape suddenly —**break up** **1** to separate; disperse **2** to stop **3** [Colloq.] to laugh or make laugh —**give (someone) a break** [Colloq.] to stop treating harshly, critically, etc. —**break′a·ble** ***adj., n.***

break′age′ (-ij′) ***n.*** **1** a breaking **2** things broken **3** loss due to breaking **4** the sum allowed for such loss

break′down′ ***n.*** **1** a breaking down **2** a failure of health **3** an analysis

break′er ***n.*** **1** a thing that breaks **2** a wave that breaks into foam

break·fast (brek′fəst) ***n.*** the first meal of the day —***vi.*** to eat breakfast

break·front (brāk′frunt′) ***adj.*** having a projecting center section in front —***n.*** a breakfront cabinet

break′-in′ ***n.*** the act of forcibly entering a building, esp. in order to rob

break·neck (brāk′nek′) ***adj.*** highly dangerous /*breakneck* speed/

break′through′ ***n.*** **1** the act of forcing a way through against resistance, as in warfare **2** a very important advance or discovery

break′up′ ***n.*** **1** a dispersion **2** a disintegration **3** a collapse

break′wa′ter ***n.*** a barrier to break the impact of waves, as before a harbor

breast (brest) ***n.*** ‖ OE *breost* ‖ **1** either of two milk-secreting glands on a woman's body **2** the upper, front part of the body **3** the part of a garment, etc. over the breast **4** the breast regarded as the center of emotions —***vt.*** to face firmly; oppose

breast′bone′ ***n.*** STERNUM

breast′-feed′ ***vt.*** **-fed′, -feed′ing** to feed (a baby) milk from the breast

breast′plate′ ***n.*** a piece of armor for the breast

breast stroke a swimming stroke in which both arms are brought out sideways from the chest

breast′work′ ***n.*** a low wall put up quickly as a defense in battle

breath (breth) ***n.*** ‖ OE *bræth*, odor ‖ **1** air taken into the lungs and then let out **2** respiration **3** the power to breathe easily **4** life; spirit **5** a fragrant odor **6** a slight breeze **7** a whisper; murmur —**catch one's breath** **1** to gasp **2** [Colloq.] to rest or pause —**out of breath** breathless, as from exertion —**take one's breath away** to thrill —**under** (or **below**) **one's breath** in a whisper

breathe (brēth) ***vi., vt.*** **breathed, breath′ing** **1** to take (air) into the lungs and let it out again; inhale and exhale **2** to live **3** to rest —**breathe again** to have a feeling of relief —**breath′a·ble** ***adj.***

breath·er (brē′thər) ***n.*** **1** one who breathes **2** [Colloq.] a pause for rest

breath·less (breth′lis) ***adj.*** **1** without breath **2** panting; gasping **3** unable to breathe easily because of emotion —**breath′less·ly** ***adv.***

breath′tak′ing (-tāk′iŋ) ***adj.*** very exciting

breath′y (-ē) ***adj.*** **-i·er, -i·est** marked by an audible emission of breath

bred (bred) ***vt., vi.*** *pt. & pp. of* BREED

breech (brēch) ***n.*** ‖ OE *brec* ‖ **1** the buttocks **2** the part of a gun behind the barrel

breech′cloth′ ***n.*** LOINCLOTH

breech·es (brich′iz) ***n.pl.*** ‖ see BREECH ‖ **1** trousers reaching to the knees **2** [Colloq.] any trousers

breed (brēd) ***vt.*** **bred, breed′ing** ‖ < OE *brod*, fetus ‖ **1** to bring forth (offspring) **2** to be the source of; produce **3** to raise (animals) **4** to rear; train —***vi.*** **1** to be produced; originate **2** to reproduce —***n.*** **1** a stock; strain **2** a sort; type —**breed′er** ***n.***

breed′ing ***n.*** **1** the producing of young **2** good upbringing **3** the producing of plants and animals, esp. for improving the stock

breeze (brēz) ***n.*** ‖ 16th-c. nautical term *brise*, prob. < Du ‖ **1** a gentle wind **2** [Colloq.] a thing easy to do —***vi.*** **breezed, breez′ing** [Colloq.] to move or go quickly

breeze′way′ ***n.*** a covered passageway, as between a house and garage

breez′y (-ē) ***adj.*** **-i·er, -i·est** **1** slightly windy 2 light and lively —**breez′i·ly** *adv.* —**breez′i·ness** *n.*

Bre·men (brem′ən) seaport in N West Germany: pop. 536,000

breth·ren (bre*th*′rən) *n.pl.* ‖ ME *bretheren* ‖ brothers: chiefly religious

bre·vet (brə vet′) *n.* ‖ < L *brevis*, brief ‖ [Historical] *Mil.* a commission giving higher honorary rank without extra pay —*vt.* **-vet′ted** or **-vet′ed, -vet′ting** or **-vet′ing** to give a brevet to

bre·vi·ar·y (brē′vē er′ē) *n.*, *pl.* **-ar′ies** ‖ < L *brevis*, brief ‖ a book of Psalms, prayers, etc. to be recited daily by priests, nuns, etc.

brev·i·ty (brev′ə tē) *n.* ‖ < L *brevis*, brief ‖ briefness

brew (bro͞o) *vt.* ‖ OE *breowan* ‖ **1** to make (beer, ale, etc.) from malt and hops by boiling and fermenting **2** to steep (tea, etc.) **3** to plot; scheme —*vi.* to begin to form —*n.* a beverage brewed —**brew′er** *n.*

brew·er·y (bro͞o′ər ē) *n.*, *pl.* **-er·ies** a place where beer, etc. is brewed

Brezh·nev (brezh′nef), **Le·o·nid** (lā ô nēd′) 1906-82; general secretary of the Communist Party of the U.S.S.R. (1964-82)

bri·ar (brī′ər) *n.* BRIER[1] or BRIER[2]

bribe (brīb) *n.* ‖ < OFr *briber*, to beg ‖ anything given or promised as an inducement, esp. to do something illegal or wrong —*vt.* **bribed, brib′ing** to offer or give a bribe to —**brib′er·y** *n.*

bric-a-brac (brik′ə brak′) *n.* ‖ < Fr *de bric et de brac*, by hook or by crook ‖ **1** small artistic objects used to ornament a room **2** knickknacks

brick (brik) *n.* ‖ MDu < *breken*, piece of baked clay ‖ **1** an oblong block of baked clay, used in building, etc. **2** anything shaped like a brick —*adj.* built or paved with brick —*vt.* to build or cover with brick

brick′bat′ *n.* **1** a piece of brick used as a missile **2** an unfavorable remark

brick′lay′er *n.* one whose work is building with bricks —**brick′lay′ing** *n.*

brid·al (brīd″l) *adj.* ‖ < OE *bryd ealu*, marriage feast ‖ **1** of a bride **2** of a wedding

bride (brīd) *n.* ‖ OE *bryd* ‖ a woman just married or about to be married

bride′groom′ *n.* ‖ < OE *bryd*, bride + *guma*, man ‖ a man just married or about to be married

brides·maid (brīdz′mād′) *n.* one of the women who attend the bride at a wedding

bridge[1] (brij) *n.* ‖ OE *brycge* ‖ **1** a structure built over a river, etc. to provide a way across **2** a thing that provides connection, contact, etc. **3** the bony part of the nose **4** a raised platform on a ship **5** a mounting for false teeth —*vt.* **bridged, bridg′ing** to build or be a bridge over —**burn one's bridges (behind one)** to follow a course from which there is no retreat —**bridge′a·ble** *adj.*

bridge[2] (brij) *n.* ‖ < ? Russ ‖ a card game, for two pairs of players, in which they bid for the right to name the trump suit or declare no-trump

bridge′head′ *n.* a fortified position established by an attacking force in enemy territory

Bridge·port (brij′pôrt′) seaport in SW Conn.: pop. 143,000

bridge′work′ *n.* a dental bridge or bridges

BRIDLE

bri·dle (brīd″l) *n.* ‖ OE *bregdan*, move quickly ‖ **1** a head harness for guiding a horse **2** anything that controls or restrains —*vt.* **bri′dled, bri′dling** **1** to put a bridle on **2** to curb or control —*vi.* to pull one's head back as an expression of anger, scorn, etc.

bridle path a path for horseback riding

brief (brēf) *adj.* ‖ < L *brevis* ‖ **1** short **2** concise —*n.* **1** a summary, specif. of the main points of a law case **2** [*pl.*] legless undershorts —*vt.* **1** to summarize **2** to supply with all pertinent information —**brief′ing** *n.* —**brief′ly** *adv.* —**brief′ness** *n.*

brief′case′ *n.* a flat, flexible case for carrying papers, books, etc.

bri·er[1] (brī′ər) *n.* ‖ OE *brer* ‖ any thorny bush, as a bramble

bri·er[2] (brī′ər) *n.* ‖ Fr *bruyère* ‖ a variety of heath, whose root is used for making tobacco pipes

brig (brig) *n.* **1** ‖ < brigantine ‖ a two-masted ship with square sails **2** ‖ < ? ‖ a prison, as on a warship

bri·gade (bri gād′) *n.* ‖ < It *briga*, strife ‖ **1** a military unit composed of two or more battalions with service and administrative units **2** a group of people organized to function as a unit in some work [a fire *brigade*]

brigadier general *pl.* **brigadier generals** a military officer ranking just above a colonel

brig·and (brig′ənd) *n.* ‖ see BRIGADE ‖ a bandit, esp. one of a roving band

brig′and·age′ (-ənd ij′) *n.* plundering by brigands

brig·an·tine (brig′ən tēn′) *n.* ‖ < It *brigantino*, pirate vessel ‖ a ship with a square-rigged foremast and a square-rigged topsail on the mainmast

bright (brīt) *adj.* ‖ OE *bryht* ‖ **1** shining with light **2** brilliant in color or sound; vivid **3** lively; cheerful **4** mentally quick; clever **5** favorable or hopeful **6** illustrious —**bright′ly** *adv.* —**bright′ness** *n.*

bright′en (-′n) *vt.*, *vi.* to make or become bright or brighter

Brigh·ton (brīt″n) resort city in S England: pop. 163,000

bril·liant (bril′yənt) *adj.* ‖ < Fr < It *brillare*, to sparkle ‖ **1** shining brightly **2** vivid **3** very splendid **4** very intelligent, talented, etc. —**bril′liance** or **bril′lian·cy** *n.* —**bril′liant·ly** *adv.*

bril·lian·tine (bril′yən tēn′) *n.* ‖ < Fr ‖ an oily dressing for the hair

brim (brim) *n.* ‖ ME *brimme* ‖ **1** the topmost edge of a cup, glass, etc. **2** a projecting rim, as of a hat —*vt., vi.* **brimmed, brim'ming** to fill or be full to the brim —**brim'less** *adj.*

brim'ful' *adj.* full to the brim

brim'stone' *n.* ‖< OE *bærnan,* to kindle + *stan,* stone‖ sulfur

brin·dle (brin'dəl) *adj.* BRINDLED —*n.* a brindled color

brin'dled (-dəld) *adj.* ‖prob. < ME *brennen,* to burn‖ having a gray or tawny coat streaked or spotted with a darker color

brine (brīn) *n.* ‖OE‖ **1** water full of salt **2** the ocean —**brin'y** *adj.*

bring (briŋ) *vt.* **brought, bring'ing** ‖OE *bringan*‖ **1** to carry or lead "here" or to the place where the speaker will be **2** to cause to happen **3** to lead to an action or belief **4** to sell for —**bring about** to cause —**bring forth** to give birth to; produce —**bring off** to accomplish —**bring out 1** to reveal **2** to offer (a play, book, etc.) to the public —**bring up 1** to rear (children) **2** to introduce, as into discussion **3** to cough or vomit up

brink (briŋk) *n.* ‖< Ger or Dan, shore‖ the edge, esp. at the top of a steep place; verge

brink'man·ship' (-mən ship') *n.* the policy of pursuing a risky course of action to the brink of disaster Also **brinks'man·ship'**

bri·oche (brē ōsh') *n.* ‖Fr‖ a light, rich roll made with flour, eggs, etc.

bri·quette or **bri·quet** (bri ket') *n.* ‖Fr < *brique,* brick‖ a small block of compressed coal dust, etc.

Bris·bane (briz'bān') seaport in E Australia: pop. 942,000

brisk (brisk) *adj.* ‖< ? Fr *brusque,* brusque‖ **1** quick in manner; energetic **2** keen, bracing, etc. —**brisk'ly** *adv.* —**brisk'ness** *n.*

bris·ket (bris'kit) *n.* ‖ME *brusket*‖ meat cut from the breast of an animal

bris·tle (bris'əl) *n.* ‖OE *byrst*‖ any short, stiff hair —*vi.* **-tled, -tling 1** to be stiff and erect **2** to have the bristles become erect **3** to become tense with fear, anger, etc **4** to be thickly covered (*with*) —**bris'tly** (-lē), **-tli·er, -tli·est,** *adj.*

bris'tle·cone pine (-kōn) a Rocky Mountain pine tree of the SW U.S.

Bris·tol (bris'təl) seaport in SW England: pop. 434,000

Brit. British

Brit·ain (brit''n) GREAT BRITAIN

britch·es (brich'iz) *n.pl.* [Colloq.] BREECHES (sense 2)

Brit·i·cism (brit'ə siz'əm) *n.* a word or idiom peculiar to British English

Brit·ish (brit'ish) *adj.* of Great Britain or its people —**the British** the people of Great Britain

British Columbia province of SW Canada: 366,255 sq. mi.; pop. 2,884,000; cap. Victoria

British Commonwealth (of Nations) *old name of* THE COMMONWEALTH

British Isles group of islands including Great Britain, Ireland, etc.

British thermal unit a unit of heat equal to about 252 calories

Brit·on (brit''n) *n.* **1** a member of an early Celtic people of S Britain **2** a native or inhabitant of Great Britain, esp. of England

brit·tle (brit''l) *adj.* ‖OE *breotan,* to break‖ easily broken or shattered —*n.* a brittle, crunchy candy with nuts in it —**brit'tle·ness** *n.*

broach (brōch) *n.* ‖< ML *brocca,* a spike‖ a tapering bit for boring holes —*vt.* **1** to make a hole in so as to let out liquid **2** to ream with a broach **3** to start a discussion of

broad (brôd) *adj.* ‖OE *brad*‖ **1** of large extent from side to side; wide **2** extending about; full /*broad* daylight/ **3** obvious /a *broad* hint/ **4** tolerant; liberal /a *broad* view/ **5** wide in range /a *broad* variety/ **6** not detailed; general /in *broad* outline/ —**broad'ly** *adv.* —**broad'ness** *n.*

broad'cast' (-kast') *vt., vi.* **-cast'** or **-cast'ed, -cast'ing 1** to scatter or spread widely **2** to transmit by radio or TV —*adj.* **1** widely scattered **2** of or for radio or TV broadcasting —*n.* **1** a sowing by broadcasting **2** a radio or TV program —*adv.* far and wide —**broad'cast'er** *n.*

broad'cloth' *n.* a fine, smooth woolen, cotton, or silk cloth

broad'en (-'n) *vt., vi.* to widen

broad jump *old name of* LONG JUMP

broad'loom' *adj.* woven on a wide loom

broad'-mind'ed *adj.* tolerant of unconventional behavior, etc.; liberal —**broad'-mind'ed·ly** *adv.* —**broad'-mind'ed·ness** *n.*

broad'side' *n.* **1** the side of a ship above the waterline **2** the firing of all guns on one side of a warship **3** a vigorous critical attack —*adv.* **1** with the side facing **2** in the side /hit *broadside*/ **3** indiscriminately

broad'-spec'trum *adj.* effective against a wide range of germs

broad'sword' *n.* a broad-bladed sword for slashing

Broad·way (brôd'wā') street in New York City, with many theaters, etc.

bro·cade (brō kād') *n.* ‖< Sp < It *broccare,* embroider‖ a rich cloth with a raised design woven into it —*vt.* **-cad'ed, -cad'ing** to weave a raised design into (cloth)

broc·co·li (bräk'ə lē) *n.* ‖It < ML *brocca,* a spike‖ a plant related to the cauliflower but bearing tender shoots with greenish buds

bro·chette (brō shet') *n.* ‖Fr‖ a skewer for broiling chunks of meat, etc.

bro·chure (brō shoor') *n.* ‖Fr < *brocher,* to stitch‖ a pamphlet

bro·gan (brō'gən) *n.* ‖Ir‖ a heavy work shoe, fitting high on the ankle

brogue[1] (brōg) *n.* ‖< ?‖ a dialectal pronunciation, esp. that of English by the Irish

brogue[2] (brōg) *n.* ‖< Ir *brōg,* a shoe‖ a man's heavy oxford shoe

broil (broil) *vt., vi.* ‖< OFr *bruillir*‖ to cook by exposure to direct heat —*n.* a broiling

broil'er *n.* **1** a pan, grill, etc. for broiling **2** a chicken fit for broiling

broke (brōk) *vt., vi. pt. of* BREAK —*adj.* [Colloq.] without money; bankrupt

bro·ken (brō'kən) *vt., vi. pp. of* BREAK —*adj.* **1** splintered, fractured, etc. **2** not in working order **3** violated /a *broken* promise/ **4** ruined **5** interrupted; discontinuous **6** imperfectly spoken **7** tamed —**bro'ken·ly** *adv.* —**bro'ken·ness** *n.*

bro'ken-down' *adj.* 1 sick or worn out 2 out of order; useless
bro'ken-heart'ed *adj.* crushed by sorrow, grief, etc.
bro·ker (brō'kər) *n.* ‖ < OFr *brokier,* to tap; orig. sense "wine dealer" ‖ a person hired as an agent in negotiating contracts, buying and selling, etc.
bro'ker·age' (-ij') *n.* 1 the business of a broker 2 a broker's fee
bro·mide (brō'mīd') *n.* 1 a compound of bromine with another element or a radical 2 potassium bromide, used as a sedative 3 a trite saying
bro·mid'ic (-mid'ik) *adj.* trite or dull
bro·mine (brō'mēn') *n.* ‖ < Gr *brōmos,* stench ‖ a chemical element, a reddish brown, corrosive liquid
bron·chi (bräŋ'kī) *n.pl., sing.* **-chus** (-kəs) ‖ < Gr *bronchos,* windpipe ‖ the two main branches of the windpipe —**bron'chi·al** (-kē əl) *adj.*
bron·chi'tis (-kīt'is) *n.* an inflammation of the bronchial tubes
bron·co (bräŋ'kō) *n., pl.* **-cos** ‖ Sp, rough ‖ a wild or only partly tamed horse or pony of the western U.S. Also **bron'cho** *n., pl.* **-chos**
bron'co·bust'er *n.* [Colloq.] a tamer of broncos —**bron'co·bust'ing** *n.*
Bron·të (brän'tē) 1 **Char·lotte** (shär'lət) 1816-55; Eng. novelist 2 **Em·i·ly** (em'ə lē) 1818-48; Eng. novelist: sister of Charlotte
bron·to·saur (brän'tō sôr', -tə-) *n.* ‖ < Gr *brontē,* thunder + *sauros,* lizard ‖ a very large, plant-eating dinosaur Also **bron'to·saur'us**
Bronx (bräŋks) borough of New York City: pop. 1,169,000
bronze (bränz) *n.* ‖ Fr, prob. ult. < Pers *birinğ,* copper ‖ 1 an alloy of copper and tin 2 a reddish-brown color —*adj.* of or like bronze —*vt.* **bronzed, bronz'ing** ‖ Fr *bronzer* < the *n.* ‖ to make bronze in color
brooch (brōch) *n.* ‖ see BROACH ‖ a large ornamental pin with a clasp
brood (broo͞d) *n.* ‖ OE *brod* ‖ 1 a group of birds hatched at one time 2 the children in a family —*vi.* 1 to sit on and hatch eggs 2 to worry: often with *on, over,* or *about*
brood'er *n.* 1 one that broods 2 a heated shelter for raising fowl
brood'mare' *n.* a mare kept for breeding
brook[1] (broo͝k) *n.* ‖ < OE *broc* ‖ a small stream
brook[2] (broo͝k) *vt.* ‖ OE *brucan,* to use ‖ to put up with; endure
Brook·lyn (broo͝k'lən) borough of New York City: pop. 2,231,000
broom (broo͞m, broo͝m) *n.* ‖ OE *brom,* brush wood ‖ 1 a flowering shrub of the pea family 2 a bundle of fibers or straws fastened to a long handle (**broom'stick'**) used for sweeping
Bros. or **bros.** brothers
broth (brôth) *n.* ‖ OE ‖ a thin soup made by boiling meat, etc. in water
broth·el (brôth'əl) *n.* ‖ < OE *broethan,* go to ruin ‖ a house of prostitution
broth·er (bru*th*'ər) *n., pl.* **-ers** or **breth'ren** ‖ OE *brothor* ‖ 1 a male related to one by having the same parents 2 a friend who is like a brother 3 a fellow member of the same race, church, profession, etc. 4 [*often* B-] a lay member of a men's religious order
broth'er·hood' *n.* 1 the bond between brothers 2 an association of men united in some interest, work, etc.
broth'er-in-law' *n., pl.* **broth'ers-in-law'** 1 the brother of one's spouse 2 the husband of one's sister 3 the husband of the sister of one's spouse
broth'er·ly *adj.* 1 of or like a brother 2 friendly, kind, loyal, etc.
brought (brôt) *vt. pt. & pp. of* BRING
brou·ha·ha (broo͞'hä hä') *n.* ‖ Fr ‖ an uproar or commotion
brow (brou) *n.* ‖ OE *bru* ‖ 1 the eyebrow 2 the forehead 3 the edge of a cliff
brow'beat' (-bēt') *vt.* **-beat', -beat'en, -beat'ing** to intimidate with harsh, stern looks and talk; bully
brown (broun) *adj.* ‖ OE *brun* ‖ 1 having the color of chocolate, a mixture of red, black, and yellow 2 tanned; dark-skinned —*n.* brown color —*vt., vi.* to make or become brown —**brown'ish** *adj.*
brown'-bag' *vt., vi.* **-bagged', -bag'ging** to carry (one's lunch) to work or school, as in a brown paper bag
brown·ie (broun'ē) *n.* 1 a small, helpful elf 2 a small bar cut from a flat chocolate cake
Brown·ing (broun'iŋ), **Rob·ert** (räb'ərt) 1812-89; Eng. poet
brown'out' *n.* a turning off of some lights in a city, as during an electric power shortage
brown rice unpolished rice
brown'stone' *n.* a reddish-brown sandstone, used for building
brown study deep thought; reverie
brown sugar sugar whose crystals retain a brown coating of syrup
browse (brouz) *n.* ‖ < OS *brustian,* to sprout ‖ leaves, shoots, etc. which animals feed on —*vt., vi.* **browsed, brows'ing** 1 to nibble at (leaves, shoots, etc.) 2 to examine (a book, articles for sale, etc.) in a casual way —**brows'er** *n.*
Bru·in (broo͞'in) ‖ Du, brown ‖ a bear
bruise (broo͞z) *vt.* **bruised, bruis'ing** ‖ < OE *brysan,* crush ‖ 1 to injure and discolor (body tissue) without breaking the skin 2 to injure the surface of, causing spoilage, denting, etc. 3 to hurt (the feelings, spirit, etc.) —*vi.* 1 to bruise tissue, etc. 2 to be or become bruised —*n.* a bruised area, as of tissue
bruis'er *n.* [Colloq.] a strong, pugnacious man
bruit (broo͞t) *vt.* ‖ < OFr, noise, rumor ‖ to spread (*about*) by rumor
brunch (brunch) *n.* [Colloq.] a combined breakfast and lunch
Bru·nei (broo nī') country on the N coast of Borneo: 2,226 sq. mi.; pop. 240,000
bru·net (broo͞ net') *adj.* ‖ < OFr, dim. of *brun,* brown ‖ having black or dark-brown hair, often with dark eyes and complexion —*n.* a brunet person
bru·nette' (-net') *adj.* BRUNET —*n.* a brunette woman or girl
Bruns·wick (brunz'wik) city in NE West Germany: pop. 255,000
brunt (brunt) *n.* ‖ ME *bront* ‖ 1 the shock

(of an attack) or impact (of a blow) **2** the hardest part

brush[1] (brush) ***n.*** ‖ < OFr *broce,* bush ‖ **1** BRUSHWOOD **2** sparsely settled country **3** a device for cleaning, painting, etc., having bristles, wires, etc. fastened into a back **4** a brushing **5** a light, grazing stroke **6** a bushy tail, as of a fox **—*vt.*** **1** to clean, paint, etc. with a brush **2** to apply, remove, etc. as with a brush **3** to touch or graze in passing **—*vi.*** to graze past something **— brush up** to refresh one's memory

brush[2] (brush) ***vi.*** ‖ ME *bruschen* ‖ to rush; hurry **—*n.*** a short, quick fight

brush'off' ***n.*** [Slang] curt dismissal, esp. in the phrase **give** (or **get**) **the brushoff**

brush'wood' ***n.*** **1** chopped-off tree branches **2** underbrush

brusque (brusk) ***adj.*** ‖ < Fr < ML *bruscus,* brushwood ‖ rough and abrupt in manner or speech; curt Also **brusk —brusque'ly *adv.* —brusque'ness *n.***

Brus·sels (brus''lz) capital of Belgium: pop. (with suburbs) 980,000

BRUSSELS SPROUTS

Brus·sels sprouts (brus''lz) **1** a plant that bears small cabbagelike heads on an erect stem **2** its edible heads

bru·tal (brōōt''l) ***adj.*** **1** like a brute; very savage, cruel, etc. **2** very harsh **—bru'tal·ly *adv.***

bru·tal·i·ty (brōō tal'ə tē) ***n.*** **1** a being brutal **2** *pl.* **-ties** a brutal act

bru·tal·ize (brōōt''l īz') ***vt.*** **-ized', -iz'ing** **1** to make brutal **2** to treat brutally **—bru'·tal·i·za'tion *n.***

brute (brōōt) ***adj.*** ‖ < L *brutus,* irrational ‖ **1** lacking the ability to reason [a *brute* beast] **2** of or like an animal; specif., savage, stupid, etc. **—*n.*** **1** an animal **2** a brutal person **—brut'ish *adj.* —brut'ish·ly *adv.***

bs or **b.s.** bill of sale

BS or **B.S.** Bachelor of Science

Btu British thermal unit(s) Also **BTU** or **btu**

bub·ble (bub'əl) ***n.*** ‖ echoic ‖ **1** a film of liquid forming a ball around air or gas **2** a tiny ball of air or gas in a liquid or solid **3** a transparent dome **4** a plausible scheme that proves worthless **—*vi.*** **-bled, -bling** **1** to rise in bubbles; boil **2** to make a gurgling sound **—bub'bly *adv.***

bubble gum a kind of chewing gum that can be blown into large bubbles

bu·bo (byōō'bō') ***n.,*** *pl.* **-boes'** ‖ < Gr *boubōn,* groin ‖ an inflamed swelling of a lymph node, esp. in the groin

bu·bon'ic plague (-bän'ik) a contagious disease characterized by buboes, fever, and delirium

buc·ca·neer (buk'ə nir') ***n.*** ‖ < Fr *boucanier* ‖ a pirate

Bu·chan·an (byōō kan'ən), **James** (jāmz) 1791-1868; 15th president of the U.S. (1857-61)

Bu·cha·rest (bōō'kə rest') capital of Romania: pop. 1,834,000

buck[1] (buk) ***n.*** ‖ OE *bucca,* male goat ‖ **1** a male deer, goat, etc.: see DOE **2** the act of bucking **3** BUCKSKIN **4** [Colloq.] a bold, vigorous young man **—*vi.*** **1** to rear upward quickly, as to throw off a rider: said of a horse **2** [Colloq.] to resist something as if plunging against it **—*vt.*** **1** to dislodge or throw by bucking **2** [Colloq.] to resist stubbornly **—buck for** [Slang] to work eagerly for (a promotion, etc.) **—buck up** [Colloq.] to cheer up

buck[2] (buk) ***n.*** ‖ < ? ‖ [Slang] a dollar **—pass the buck** [Colloq.] to throw the responsibility on another

buck'board' ***n.*** ‖ BUCK[1], *vi.* + BOARD ‖ an open carriage whose floorboards rest directly on the axles

buck·et (buk'it) ***n.*** ‖ < OE *buc,* pitcher ‖ **1** a cylindrical container with a curved handle, for carrying water, etc.; pail **2** the amount held by a bucket: also **buck'et·ful',** *pl.* **-fuls'** **3** a thing like a bucket, as a scoop on a steam shovel **—kick the bucket** [Slang] to die

bucket seat a single contoured seat with a movable back, as in sports cars

buck·eye (buk'ī') ***n.*** ‖ BUCK[1] + EYE < the appearance of the seed ‖ **1** a horse chestnut with large burs enclosing shiny brown seeds **2** the seed

buck·le[1] (buk'əl) ***n.*** ‖ < L *buccula,* cheek strap of a helmet ‖ a clasp for fastening a strap, belt, etc. **—*vt., vi.*** **-led, -ling** to fasten with a buckle **—buckle down** to apply oneself

buck·le[2] (buk'əl) ***vt., vi.*** **-led, -ling** ‖ prob. infl. by OFr *bocler,* to bulge: see prec. ‖ to bend or crumple **—*n.*** a bend, bulge, etc.

buck·ler (buk'lər) ***n.*** ‖ < OFr *bocler* ‖ a small, round shield

buck'-pass'er *n.* [Colloq.] one who regularly shifts blame or responsibility to someone else **—buck'-pass'ing *n.***

buck·ram (buk'rəm) ***n.*** ‖ ? < *Bukhara,* city in central Asia ‖ a coarse, stiff cloth used in bookbinding, etc.

buck·saw (buk'sô') ***n.*** a wood-cutting saw set in a frame

buck'shot' ***n.*** a large lead shot for shooting deer and other large game

buck'skin' ***n.*** **1** a soft leather made from the skins of deer or sheep **2** [*pl.*] clothes made of buckskin

buck'tooth' ***n.,*** *pl.* **-teeth'** a projecting front tooth **—buck'toothed' *adj.***

buck·wheat (buk'hwēt', -wēt') ***n.*** ‖ < OE *boc-,* beech + WHEAT ‖ **1** a plant with beechnut-shaped seeds **2** a dark flour made from the seeds

bu·col·ic (byōō käl'ik) ***adj.*** ‖ < Gr *boukolos,* herdsman ‖ **1** of shepherds; pastoral **2** rural; rustic **—*n.*** a pastoral poem **—bu·col'i·cal·ly *adv.***

bud (bud) ***n.*** ‖ ME *budde* ‖ **1** a small swelling on a plant, from which a shoot, leaf, or flower develops **2** an early stage of development —*vi.* **bud'ded, bud'ding** 1 to put forth buds 2 to begin to develop —**in (the) bud** 1 in a budding condition 2 in an early stage —**bud'like'** *adj.*

Bu·da·pest (bōō'də pest') capital of Hungary: pop. 2,072,000

Bud·dha (bood'ə) religious leader who lived in India *c.* 563-*c.* 483 B.C.: founder of Bud dhism

Bud·dhism (bood'iz'əm) *n.* a religion of Asia teaching that by right thinking and self denial one achieves Nirvana —**Bud'dhist** *n., adj.*

bud·dy (bud'ē) *n., pl.* **-dies** ‖ < ? ‖ [Colloq.] a comrade

budge (buj) *vt., vi.* **budged, budg'ing** ‖ < OFr *bouger,* to move ‖ to move even a little

budg·er·i·gar (buj'ər i gär') *n.* ‖ native name ‖ a greenish yellow Australian parakeet: also [Colloq.] **budg'ie**

budg·et (buj'it) *n.* ‖ < L *bulga,* bag ‖ 1 a stock of items 2 a plan adjusting expenses to income 3 estimated cost of living, oper ating, etc. —*vt.* 1 to put on a budget 2 to plan */budget* your time/ —**budg'et·ar'y** *adj.*

Bue·nos Ai·res (bwā'nəs er'ēz) capital of Argentina: pop. 2,923,000 (urban area 9,677,000)

buff (buf) *n.* ‖ < Fr < It *bufalo,* buffalo ‖ 1 a heavy, soft, brownish yellow leather 2 a military coat made of this 3 a dull brownish yellow 4 [Colloq.] a devotee; fan —*adj.* 1 made of buff 2 of the color buff —*vt.* to clean or shine with leather or a leather covered wheel —**in the buff** naked

buf·fa·lo (buf'ə lō') *n., pl.* **-loes'** or **-lo'** ‖ < It < Gr *bous,* ox ‖ 1 any of various wild oxen, as the water buffalo of India 2 popularly, the American bison —*vt.* **-loed', -lo'-ing** [Slang] to baffle, bluff, etc.

Buf·fa·lo (buf'ə lō') city in W N.Y., on Lake Erie: pop. 358,000

buff·er[1] (buf'ər) *n.* ‖ BUFF, *v.* + -ER ‖ 1 one who buffs 2 a buffing wheel, stick, block, or cloth

buff·er[2] (buf'ər) *n.* ‖ < OFr. *buffe,* a blow ‖ 1 anything that lessens shock, as of collision 2 a temporary storage area in a computer, for data being transferred to another device

buf·fet[1] (buf'it) *n.* ‖ OFr < *buffe,* a blow ‖ a blow or shock —*vt.* 1 to punch; fight 2 to thrust about

buf·fet[2] (bə fā', boo-) *n.* ‖ Fr ‖ 1 a sideboard 2 a counter or table at which guests, etc. serve themselves food 3 a meal served on such a table, etc.

buf·foon (bə fōōn') *n.* ‖ < Fr < It *buffare,* to jest ‖ one who is always clowning and trying to be funny; clown —**buf·foon'er·y** *n.* —**buf·foon'ish** *adj.*

bug (bug) *n.* ‖ prob. < ME *bugge* ‖ 1 an insect with sucking mouthparts 2 any small arthropod, as a cockroach 3 [Colloq.] a germ or virus 4 [Slang] a hidden microphone 5 [Slang] a defect, as in a machine —*vt.* **bugged, bug'ging** [Slang] 1 to hide a microphone in (a room, etc.) 2 to annoy, anger, etc.

bug'bear' *n.* ‖ ME *bugge,* a bug + BEAR[2] ‖ 1 a bogy 2 a cause of needless fear Also **bug'a·boo'** (-ə bōō') *n., pl.* **-boos'**

bug'-eyed' *adj.* [Slang] with bulging eyes

bug·gy (bug'ē) *n., pl.* **-gies** ‖ < ? ‖ 1 a light, one horse carriage with one seat 2 BABY CARRIAGE

bu·gle (byōō'gəl) *n.* ‖ < L *buculus,* young ox ‖ a brass instrument like a small trumpet, usually without valves —*vi., vt.* **-gled, -gling** to signal by blowing a bugle —**bu'-gler** *n.*

build (bild) *vt.* **built, build'ing** ‖ < OE *bold,* house ‖ 1 to make by putting together materials, parts, etc.; construct 2 to establish; base */build* a theory on facts/ 3 to create or develop: often with *up* —*vi.* 1 to put up buildings 2 to grow or intensify: often with *up* —*n.* the way a thing is built or shaped /a stocky *build*/ —**build up** to make more attractive, healthy, etc. —**build'-er** *n.*

build'ing *n.* 1 anything that is built; struc ture 2 the work or business of making houses, etc.

build'up' or **build'-up'** *n.* [Colloq.] 1 praise or favorable publicity 2 a gradual increase or expansion

built (bilt) *vt., vi. pt. & pp. of* BUILD

built'-in' *adj.* 1 made as part of the struc ture 2 inherent

built'-up' *adj.* 1 made higher, stronger, etc. with added parts */built-up* heels/ 2 hav ing many buildings on it

bulb (bulb) *n.* ‖ < Gr *bolbos* ‖ 1 an under ground bud with roots and a short, scaly stem, as in a lily or onion 2 a tuber or tuberous root resembling a bulb, as in a crocus 3 anything shaped like a bulb /an electric light *bulb*/ —**bul'bous** *adj.*

Bul·gar·i·a (bəl ger'ē ə, bool-) country in SE Europe: 42,823 sq. mi.; pop. 8,990,000 —**Bul·gar'i·an** *adj., n.*

bulge (bulj) *n.* ‖ < L *bulga,* leather bag ‖ an outward swelling; protuberance —*vi., vt.* **bulged, bulg'ing** to swell or bend outward —**bulg'y** *adj.*

bu·li·ma·rex·i·a (byōō'li mə rek'sē ə) *n.* a disorder characterized by eating large quantities of food followed by self-induced vomit ing, etc. Also **bulimia ner·vo·sa** (nər vō'sə)

bu·lim·i·a (byōō lē'mē ə, -lim'ē ə) *n.* ‖ < Gr *bous,* ox + *limos,* hunger ‖ 1 *Med.* a continuous, abnormal hunger 2 BULIMAREXIA —**bu·lim'ic** *adj.*

bulk (bulk) *n.* ‖ < ON *bulki,* a heap ‖ 1 size, mass, or volume, esp. if great 2 the main mass; largest part —*vi.* to have, or to increase in, size or importance —*adj.* 1 total; aggregate 2 not put up in individual packages —**bulk'y, -i·er, -i·est,** *adj.*

bulk·head (bulk'hed') *n.* ‖ < ON *balkr,* par tition + HEAD ‖ 1 an upright partition, as in a ship, that is watertight, fireproof, etc. 2 a retaining wall 3 a boxlike structure over an opening

bull[1] (bool) *n.* ‖ < OE *bula,* a steer ‖ 1 the adult male of any bovine animal, as the ox, or of certain other large animals, as the elephant, whale, etc. 2 a speculator who buys stocks expecting their prices to rise, or seeks to bring about such a rise 3 [Slang] insincere talk; nonsense —*adj.* 1 male 2 rising in price

bull[2] (bool) ***n.*** ‖ < LL *bulla,* a seal ‖ an official document from the pope

bull'dog' ***n.*** a short haired, square jawed, heavily built dog noted for its strong, stubborn grip —***adj.*** like a bulldog; stubborn —***vt.* -dogged', -dog'ging** to throw (a steer) by holding its horns and twisting its neck

bull'doze' (-dōz') ***vt.* -dozed', -doz'ing** ‖ < *bull,* a flogging + DOSE ‖ **1** [Colloq.] to force or frighten by threatening; bully **2** to move, make level, etc. with a bulldozer

bull'doz'er ***n.*** a tractor with a large, shovel-like blade in front, for pushing earth, debris, etc.

bul·let (bool'it) ***n.*** ‖ < L *bulla,* a knob ‖ a small, shaped piece of lead, steel, etc., to be shot from a firearm

bul·le·tin (bool'ət'n) ***n.*** ‖ < L *bulla,* a seal ‖ **1** a brief statement of late news **2** a regular publication, as of an organization, etc.

bulletin board a board or wall area on which bulletins, notices, etc. are put up

bul'let·proof' ***adj.*** that bullets cannot pierce —***vt.*** to make bulletproof

bull'fight' (-fīt') ***n.*** a spectacle in which a bull is provoked in various ways and then killed with a sword by the matador **bull'fight'er** ***n.***

bull'frog' ***n.*** a large North American frog with a deep, loud croak

bull'head'ed (-hed'id) ***adj.*** stubborn; headstrong

bull'horn' (-hôrn') ***n.*** a portable electronic voice amplifier

bul·lion (bool'yən) ***n.*** ‖ < OFr *billon,* small coin ‖ ingots, bars, etc. of gold or silver

bull'ish' ***adj.*** **1** of or like a bull **2** rising, or causing a rise, as in prices on the stock exchange **3** optimistic

bull'ock (-ək) ***n.*** ‖ < OE dim. of *bula,* steer ‖ a castrated bull; steer

bull'pen' (-pen') ***n.*** **1** [Colloq.] a temporary detention room in a jail **2** *Baseball a)* a practice area for relief pitchers *b)* the relief pitchers of one team

bull's-eye (boolz'ī') ***n.*** **1** the central mark of a target **2** a direct hit

bul·ly (bool'ē) ***n., pl.* -lies** ‖ < MHG *buole,* lover; later infl. by BULL[1] ‖ a person who hurts or browbeats those who are weaker —***vt.* -lied, -ly·ing** to act the bully (toward) —***adj., interj.*** [Colloq.] fine; good

bul·rush (bool'rush') ***n.*** ‖ < ME *bol,* stem + *rusche,* a rush ‖ a tall plant of the sedge family, found in wet places

bul·wark (bool'wərk) ***n.*** ‖ MDu *bolwerc* ‖ **1** a defensive wall; rampart **2** a defense; protection **3** [*usually pl.*] a ship's side above the deck

bum (bum) ***n.*** ‖ prob. < Ger *bummeln,* go slowly ‖ [Colloq.] **1** a vagrant **2** a loafer **3** a devotee, as of golf or skiing —***vi.* bummed, bum'ming** to live as a bum or by begging —***vt.*** [Slang] to get by begging /to *bum* a cigar/ —***adj.* bum'mer, bum'mest** [Slang] **1** poor in quality **2** false **3** lame —**bum (someone) out** [Slang] to annoy, depress, bore, etc. —**on the bum** [Colloq.] **1** living as a vagrant **2** out of repair

bum·ble (bum'b'l) ***vi.* -bled, -bling** **1** to blunder **2** to stumble ***vt.*** to bungle or botch — **bum'bler** ***n.***

bum·ble·bee (bum'bəl bē') ***n.*** ‖ < ME *bomben,* buzz ‖ a large, hairy, yellow-and-black bee

bum·mer (bum'ər) ***n.*** [Slang] an unpleasant experience, esp. with drugs

bump (bump) ***vt., vi.*** ‖ echoic ‖ **1** to collide (with); hit against **2** to move with jolts —***n.*** **1** a knock; light jolt **2** a swelling, esp. one caused by a blow — **bump into** [Colloq.] to meet unexpectedly — **bump off** [Slang] to murder —**bump'y** ***adj.***

bump'er[1] ***n.*** a device to absorb the shock of a collision; esp., a bar at the front and rear of a motor vehicle

bump'er[2] ***adj.*** ‖ prob. < *bombard,* liquor jug ‖ unusually abundant /a *bumper* crop/

bumper sticker a gummed paper with a printed slogan, witticism, etc., for sticking on an automobile bumper

bump·kin (bump'kin) ***n.*** ‖ prob. < MDu *bommekijn,* small cask ‖ an awkward or simple person from the country

bump'tious (-shəs) ***adj.*** ‖ prob. < BUMP ‖ disagreeably conceited or forward **bump'tious·ly** ***adv.***

bun (bun) ***n.*** ‖ prob. < OFr *buigne,* a swelling ‖ **1** a small roll made of bread dough, sometimes sweetened **2** hair worn in a roll or knot

bunch (bunch) ***n.*** ‖ < Fl *boudje,* little bundle ‖ **1** a cluster of similar things growing or grouped together **2** [Colloq.] a group of people —***vt., vi.*** to collect into a bunch — **bunch'y** ***adj.***

bun·combe (buŋ'kəm) ***n.*** ‖ after *Buncombe* county, N.C. ‖ [Colloq.] empty, insincere talk Also **bun'kum**

bun·dle (bun'dəl) ***n.*** ‖ MDu *bondel* ‖ **1** a number of things bound together **2** a package **3** a bunch; collection —***vt.* -dled, -dling** **1** to make into a bundle **2** to hustle (*away, off, out,* or *into*) —**bundle up** to dress warmly

bung (buŋ) ***n.*** ‖ < MDu *bonge* ‖ a stopper for a bunghole

bun·ga·low (buŋ'gə lō') ***n.*** ‖ < Hindi *bānglā,* thatched house ‖ a small, one storied house or cottage

bung·hole (buŋ'hōl') ***n.*** a hole in a barrel or keg for pouring in or drawing out liquid

bun·gle (buŋ'gəl) ***vt., vi.* -gled, -gling** ‖ < ? ‖ to do clumsily; spoil; botch —***n.*** **1** a bungling **2** a bungled piece of work — **bun'gler** ***n.***

bun·ion (bun'yən) ***n.*** ‖ < OFr: see BUN ‖ an inflamed swelling at the base of the big toe

bunk[1] (buŋk) ***n.*** ‖ prob. < Scand cognate of BENCH ‖ **1** a shelflike bed built against a wall, as in a ship **2** [Colloq.] any sleeping place —***vi.*** to sleep in a bunk —***vt.*** to provide a sleeping place for

bunk[2] (buŋk) ***n.*** [Slang] buncombe

bunk·er (buŋ'kər) ***n.*** ‖ Scot < ? ‖ **1** a large bin, as for a ship's fuel **2** an underground fortification **3** an area serving as a hazard on a golf course

bunk'house' ***n.*** a barracks for ranch hands, etc.

bun·ny (bun'ē) ***n., pl.* -nies** ‖ dim. of dial. *bun* ‖ a rabbit: a child's term

buns (bunz) ***n.pl.*** [Slang] the human buttocks

Bun·sen burner (bun'sən) ‖ after R. W.

Bunsen, 19th-c. Ger. chemist ‖ a small tubular gas burner that produces a hot, blue flame

bunt (bunt) ***vt., vi.*** ‖ < ? ME *bounten,* to return ‖ *Baseball* to bat (a pitch) lightly without swinging so that it rolls within the infield —***n.*** a bunted ball

bun·ting[1] (bun'tiŋ) ***n.*** ‖ < ? ME *bonten,* sift ‖ **1** a thin cloth for making flags, etc. **2** decorative flags

bun·ting[2] (bun'tiŋ) ***n.*** ‖ ME ‖ a small, brightly colored, short-billed bird

buoy (boi; *also,* bo͞o'ē) ***n.*** ‖ < L *boia,* fetter ‖ **1** a floating object anchored in water to warn of a hazard, etc. **2** LIFE PRESERVER —***vt.*** ‖ < Sp *boyar,* to float ‖ **1** to mark with a buoy **2** to keep afloat **3** to lift up in spirits

buoy·ant (boiy'ənt, bo͞o'yənt) ***adj.*** ‖ < ? Sp *boyar,* to float ‖ **1** having the ability or tendency to float **2** cheerful —**buoy'an·cy** ***n.***

bur (bur) ***n.*** ‖ < Scand ‖ **1** a rough, prickly seed capsule of certain plants **2** a plant with burs **3** BURR[1] & BURR[2]

Bur Bureau

bur·den[1] (burd''n) ***n.*** ‖ < OE *byrthen* ‖ **1** anything that is carried; load **2** heavy load, as of work, care, etc. **3** the carrying capacity of a ship —***vt.*** to put a burden on; oppress —**bur'den·some** ***adj.***

bur'den[2] ***n.*** ‖ < OFr *bourdon,* a humming ‖ **1** a chorus or refrain of a song **2** a repeated, central idea; theme

bur·dock (bur'däk') ***n.*** ‖ BUR + DOCK[3] ‖ a plant with large leaves and purple-flowered heads with prickles

bu·reau (byoor'ō) ***n., pl.*** **-reaus'** or **-reaux'** (-ōz') ‖ Fr, desk ‖ **1** a chest of drawers, as for clothing **2** an agency **3** a government department

bu·reauc·ra·cy (byoo rä'krə sē) ***n., pl.*** **-cies** **1** government by departmental officials following an inflexible routine **2** the officials collectively **3** governmental officialism **4** the concentration of authority in administrative bureaus —**bu·reau·crat** (byoor'ə krat') ***n.*** —**bu'reau·crat'ic** ***adj.*** —**bu'reau·crat'i·cal·ly** ***adv.***

bu·reauc'ra·tize' (-tīz') ***vt., vi.*** **-tized', -tiz'·ing** to develop into a bureaucracy —**bu·reauc'ra·ti·za'tion** ***n.***

burg (burg) ***n.*** [Colloq.] a quiet or dull town

bur·geon (bur'jən) ***vi.*** ‖ < OFr *burjon,* a bud ‖ **1** to put forth buds, etc. **2** to grow or develop rapidly

bur·ger (bur'gər) ***n.*** [Colloq.] a hamburger or cheeseburger

burgh (burg; *Scot* bu'rə) ***n.*** ‖ Scot var. of BOROUGH ‖ **1** [Brit.] a borough **2** in Scotland, a chartered town

burgh'er ***n.*** a citizen of a town

bur·glar (bur'glər) ***n.*** ‖ < OFr *burgeor* ‖ one who commits burglary

bur'glar·ize' ***vt.*** **-ized', -iz'ing** to commit burglary in

bur'gla·ry ***n., pl.*** **-ries** the act of breaking into a building to commit a felony, as theft, or a misdemeanor

bur·gle (bur'gəl) ***vt., vi.*** **-gled, -gling** [Colloq.] to burglarize or commit burglary

bur·go·mas·ter (bur'gō mas'tər, -gə-) ***n.*** ‖ < MDu *burg,* town + *meester,* master ‖ the mayor of a town in the Netherlands, Flanders, Austria, or Germany

Bur·gun·dy (bur'gən dē) ***n., pl.*** **-dies** [*often* **b-**] a red or white wine, typically dry, orig. made in Burgundy, a region in SE France —**Bur·gun'di·an** ***adj., n.***

bur·i·al (ber'ē əl) ***n.*** the burying of a dead body in a grave, tomb, etc.

Bur·ki·na Fa·so (boor kē'nə fä'sō) country in W Africa: 105,870 sq. mi.; pop. 7,094,000

burl (burl) ***n.*** ‖ < OFr *bourle,* ends of threads ‖ **1** a knot in thread or yarn that makes cloth look nubby **2** a knot on some tree trunks **3** veneer from wood with burls —**burled** ***adj.***

bur·lap (bur'lap') ***n.*** ‖ < ? ME *borel* ‖ a coarse cloth of jute or hemp

bur·lesque (bər lesk') ***n.*** ‖ Fr < It *burla,* a jest ‖ **1** any broadly comic or satirical imitation; parody **2** a sort of vaudeville with low comedy, striptease acts, etc. —***vt., vi.*** **-lesqued', -lesqu'ing** to imitate comically

bur·ley (bur'lē) ***n.*** ‖ < ? ‖ [*also* **B-**] a thin-leaved, light-colored tobacco grown in Kentucky, etc.

bur·ly (bur'lē) ***adj.*** **-li·er, -li·est** ‖ ME *borlich,* excellent ‖ **1** big and strong **2** hearty in manner

Bur·ma (bur'mə) *old name of* MYANMAR —**Bur·mese'** (-mēz') ***adj., n.***

burn (burn) ***vt.*** **burned** or **burnt, burn'ing** ‖ < OE *beornan,* to be on fire ‖ **1** to set on fire, as in order to produce heat, light, or power **2** to destroy by fire **3** to injure or damage by fire, acid, etc. **4** to consume as fuel **5** to sunburn **6** to cause (a hole, etc.) as by fire **7** to cause a sensation of heat in —***vi.*** **1** to be on fire **2** to give out light or heat **3** to be destroyed or injured by fire or heat **4** to feel hot **5** to be excited —***n.*** **1** an injury or damage caused by fire, heat, etc. **2** the process or result of burning —**burn down** to burn to the ground —**burn out** to exhaust or become exhausted from overwork, etc. —**burn up** [Slang] to make or become angry —**burn'a·ble** ***adj., n.***

burn'er ***n.*** the part of a stove, furnace, etc. from which the flame comes

bur·nish (bur'nish) ***vt., vi.*** ‖ < OFr *brunir,* make brown ‖ to make or become shiny by rubbing —***n.*** a gloss or polish —**bur'nish·er** ***n.***

bur·noose (bər no͞os') ***n.*** ‖ < Ar *burnus* ‖ a hooded cloak worn by Arabs

burn·out (burn'out') ***n.*** **1** the point at which a rocket's fuel is burned up and the rocket enters free flight or is jettisoned **2** a state of emotional exhaustion from mental stress

Burns (burnz), **Rob·ert** (räb'ərt) 1759-96; Scot. poet

burnt (burnt) ***vt., vi.*** *alt. pt. & pp. of* BURN

burp (burp) ***n., vi.*** ‖ echoic ‖ [Colloq.] belch —***vt.*** to cause (a baby) to belch

burr[1] (bur) ***n.*** ‖ var. of BUR ‖ **1** a bur **2** a rough edge left on metal, etc. by cutting or drilling —***vt.*** to form a rough edge on

burr[2] (bur) ***n.*** ‖ prob. echoic ‖ **1** the trilling of *r,* as in Scottish speech **2** a whir

bur·ro (bur'ō) *n., pl.* **-ros** ⟦Sp < LL *burricus,* small horse⟧ a donkey

bur·row (bur'ō) *n.* ⟦see BOROUGH⟧ **1** a hole dug in the ground by an animal **2** any similar hole —*vi.* **1** to make a burrow **2** to live or hide in a burrow **3** to search, as if by digging —*vt.* **1** to make burrows in **2** to make by burrowing

bur·sa (bur'sə) *n., pl.* **-sae** (-sē) or **-sas** ⟦< Gr. *byrsa,* a hide⟧ *Anat.* a sac or cavity with a lubricating fluid, as between a tendon and bone

bur·sar (bur'sər) *n.* ⟦< ML *bursa,* a purse⟧ a treasurer, as of a college

bur·si·tis (bər sīt'is) *n.* ⟦< BURSA + -ITIS⟧ inflammation of a bursa

burst (burst) *vi.* **burst, burst'ing** ⟦OE *berstan*⟧ **1** to come apart suddenly and violently; explode **2** to give sudden vent; break (*into* tears, etc.) **3** to appear, start, etc. suddenly **4** to be as full or crowded as possible —*vt.* to cause to burst —*n.* **1** a bursting **2** a break or rupture **3** a sudden action or effort; spurt **4** a volley of shots

Bu·run·di (boo roon'dē, -run'-) country in central Africa, east of Zaire: 10,747 sq. mi.; pop. 4,807,000

bur·y (ber'ē) *vt.* **-ied, -y·ing** ⟦OE *byrgan*⟧ **1** to put (a dead body) into the earth, a tomb, etc. **2** to hide or cover **3** to put away **4** to immerse

bus (bus) *n., pl.* **bus'es** or **bus'ses** ⟦< (OMNI)BUS⟧ a large motor coach for many passengers, usually following a regular route —*vt.* **bused** or **bussed, bus'ing** or **bus·sing** to transport by bus —*vi.* **1** to go by bus **2** to do the work of a busboy

bus'boy' *n.* a waiter's assistant who clears tables, brings water, etc.

bus·by (buz'bē) *n., pl.* **-bies** ⟦prob. < name *Busby*⟧ a tall fur hat worn with a full-dress uniform, as by guardsmen

bush (boosh) *n.* ⟦OE *busc*⟧ **1** a low woody plant with spreading branches; shrub **2** anything like a bush **3** uncleared land —*vi.* to grow thickly —**beat around the bush** to talk around a subject without getting to the point —**bush'y, -i·er, -i·est,** *adj.*

Bush (boosh), **George** (**Herbert Walker**) 1924- ; 41st president of the U.S. (1989-)

bushed (boosht) *adj.* [Colloq.] very tired; exhausted

bush·el (boosh'əl) *n.* ⟦< OFr *boisse,* grain measure⟧ a dry measure equal to 4 pecks or 32 quarts

bush·ing (boosh'iŋ) *n.* ⟦< MDu *busse,* box⟧ a removable metal lining for reducing friction on moving parts

bush league [Slang] a small or second-rate minor league, etc. —**bush'-league'** *adj.* —**bush leaguer**

bush'man (-mən) *n., pl.* **-men** one who lives in the Australian bush

bush'mas'ter (-mas'tər) *n.* a large poisonous snake of Central and South America

bus·i·ly (biz'ə lē) *adv.* in a busy manner

busi·ness (biz'niz, -nis) *n.* ⟦OE *bisignes*: see BUSY⟧ **1** one's work; occupation **2** a special task, duty, etc. **3** rightful concern **4** a matter or affair **5** commerce; trade **6** a commercial or industrial establishment —*adj.* of or for business —**mean business** [Colloq.] to be in earnest

business agent a representative of a labor union local

business college (or **school**) a school of typing, bookkeeping, etc.

busi'ness·like' *adj.* efficient, methodical, systematic, etc.

busi'ness·man' *n., pl.* **-men'** a man in business, esp. as an owner —**busi'ness·wom'an,** *pl.* **-wom'en,** *n.fem.*

bus·ing or **bus·sing** (bus'iŋ) *n.* the transporting of children by bus to a school outside of their neighborhood, esp. so as to desegregate the school

bus·kin (bus'kin) *n.* ⟦? < MDu *brosekin,* small boot⟧ **1** a high, laced boot worn in ancient tragedy **2** tragic drama

buss (bus) *n., vt., vi.* ⟦prob. of echoic orig.⟧ [Now Chiefly Dial.] kiss

bust[1] (bust) *n.* ⟦< It *busto*⟧ **1** a sculpture of a person's head and shoulders **2** a woman's bosom

bust[2] (bust) *vt., vi.* ⟦< BURST⟧ [Colloq.] **1** to burst or break **2** to make or become bankrupt or demoted **3** to hit **4** to arrest —*n.* [Colloq.] **1** a failure **2** financial collapse **3** a punch **4** a spree **5** an arrest —**bust'ed** *adj.*

bus·tle[1] (bus'əl) *vi., vt.* **-tled, -tling** ⟦< ME *busken,* prepare⟧ to hurry busily —*n.* busy and noisy activity

bus·tle[2] (bus'əl) *n.* ⟦< ?⟧ a padding formerly worn to fill out the upper back of a woman's skirt

BUSTLE

bus·y (biz'ē) *adj.* **-i·er, -i·est** ⟦OE *bisig*⟧ **1** active; at work **2** full of activity **3** in use, as a telephone **4** too detailed —*vt.* **bus'ied, bus'y·ing** to make or keep busy —**bus'y·ness** *n.*

bus'y·bod'y (-bäd'ē) *n., pl.* **-ies** a meddler in the affairs of others

but (but; *unstressed* bət) *prep.* ⟦OE *butan,* without⟧ except; save /nobody went *but* me/ —*conj.* **1** yet; still /it's good, *but* not great/ **2** on the contrary /I am old, *but* you are young/ **3** unless /it never rains *but* it pours/ **4** that /I don't doubt *but* you're right/ **5** that . . . not /I never gamble *but* I lose/ —*adv.* **1** only /if I had *but* known/ **2** merely /he is *but* a child/ **3** just /I heard it *but* now/ —*pron.* who . . . not; which . . . not /not a man *but* felt it/ —**but for** if it were not for

bu·tane (byoo'tān) *n.* ⟦ult. < L *butyrum,* butter⟧ a hydrocarbon used as a fuel, etc.

butch (booch) *adj.* ⟦< ? fol.⟧ **1** [Colloq.] designating a man's closely cropped haircut **2** [Slang] masculine: said of a lesbian

butch·er (booch'ər) *n.* ⟦< OFr *bouc,* he-goat⟧ **1** one whose work is killing and dressing animals for meat **2** one who cuts meat for sale **3** a brutal killer —*vt.* **1** to kill or dress (animals) for meat **2** to kill brutally or senselessly **3** to botch —**butch'er·y,** *pl.* **-ies,** *n.*

but·ler (but'lər) *n.* ⟦< OFr *bouteille,* bottle⟧ a manservant, usually the head servant of a household

butt[1] (but) *n.* ⟦< ?⟧ **1** the thick end of

anything 2 a stub or stump, as of a cigar 3 a target 4 an object of ridicule 5 [Slang] a cigarette —*vt., vi.* to join end to end

butt[2] (but) *vt., vi.* ⟦< OFr *buter,* thrust against⟧ 1 to ram with the head 2 to project —*n.* a butting —**butt in** (or **into**) [Colloq.] to mix into (another's business, etc.)

butt[3] (but) *n.* ⟦< LL *buttis,* cask⟧ a large cask for wine or beer

butte (byo͞ot) *n.* ⟦Fr, mound⟧ a steep hill standing alone in a plain

but·ter (but'ər) *n.* ⟦< Gr *bous,* cow + *tyros,* cheese⟧ 1 the solid, yellowish, edible fat that results from churning cream 2 any substance somewhat like butter —*vt.* 1 to spread with butter 2 [Colloq.] to flatter: often with *up* —**but'ter·y** *adj.*

butter bean a light-colored bean, as a lima bean or wax bean

but'ter·cup' *n.* a plant with yellow, cup-shaped flowers

but'ter·fat' *n.* the fatty part of milk, from which butter is made

but'ter·fin'gers *n.* [Colloq.] one who often fumbles and drops things

but'ter·fly' (-flī') *n., pl.* **-flies'** ⟦OE *buttorfleoge*⟧ an insect with a slender body and four broad, usually brightly colored wings

but'ter·milk' *n.* the liquid left after churning butter from milk

but'ter·nut' *n.* 1 a walnut tree of E North America 2 its edible, oily nut

but'ter·scotch' *n.* 1 a hard, sticky candy made with brown sugar, butter, etc. 2 the flavor of this candy 3 a syrup with this flavor

but·tock (but'ək) *n.* ⟦< OE *buttuc,* end⟧ 1 either of the fleshy, rounded parts of the hips 2 [*pl.*] the rump

but·ton (but''n) *n.* ⟦< OFr *boton*⟧ 1 any small disk or knob used as a fastening, ornament, etc., as on a garment 2 anything small and shaped like a button —*vt., vi.* to fasten with a button or buttons

but'ton-down' *adj.* 1 designating a collar, as on a shirt, fastened down by small buttons 2 conservative, unimaginative, etc. /a *button-down* mind/

but'ton·hole' *n.* a slit or loop through which a button is inserted —*vt.* **-holed', -hol'ing** 1 to make buttonholes in 2 to detain and talk to

but·tress (bu'tris) *n.* ⟦see BUTT[2]⟧ 1 a structure built against a wall to support or reinforce it 2 a support or prop —*vt.* to prop up; bolster

bux·om (buk'səm) *adj.* ⟦ME, humble⟧ having a shapely, full-bosomed figure: said of a woman or girl

buy (bī) *vt.* **bought, buy'ing** ⟦OE *bycgan*⟧ 1 to get by paying money; purchase 2 to get by an exchange /*buy* victory with human lives/ 3 to bribe 4 [Slang] to accept as true /I can't *buy* this excuse/ —*n.* 1 anything bought 2 [Colloq.] something worth its price —**buy off** to bribe —**buy out** to buy all the stock, rights, etc. of —**buy up** to buy all that is available of

buy'back' (-bak') *n. Finance* the buying by a corporation of its own stock to reduce the outstanding shares

buy'er *n.* 1 one who buys; consumer 2 one whose work is to buy merchandise for a retail store

buy'out' *n.* the outright purchase of a business, as by the employees or management

buzz (buz) *vi.* ⟦echoic⟧ 1 to hum like a bee 2 to gossip 3 to be filled with noisy activity or talk —*vt.* to fly an airplane low over —*n.* a sound like a bee's hum

buz·zard (buz'ərd) *n.* ⟦< L *buteo,* kind of hawk⟧ 1 a kind of hawk that is slow and heavy in flight 2 TURKEY VULTURE

buzz'er *n.* an electrical device that makes a buzzing sound as a signal

buzz saw a saw with teeth around the edge of a large disk fixed on a motor-driven shaft

bx box

by (bī) *prep.* ⟦OE *be, bi*⟧ 1 near; at /sit *by* the fire/ 2 *a*) in or during /to travel *by* day/ *b*) for a fixed time /to work *by* the hour/ *c*) not later than /be back *by* noon/ 3 *a*) through; via /to Boston *by* Route 6/ *b*) past; beyond /he walked right *by* me/ 4 in behalf of /she did well *by* me/ 5 through the agency of /gained *by* fraud/ 6 *a*) according to /to go *by* the book/ *b*) in /to die *by* degrees/ *c*) following in series /marching two *by* two/ 7 *a*) in or to the amount of /apples *by* the peck/ *b*) and in another dimension /two *by* four/ *c*) using (the given number) as multiplier or divisor —*adv.* 1 close at hand /stand *by*/ 2 away; aside /to put money *by*/ 3 past /she sped *by*/ 4 at the place specified /stop *by* on your way/ —**by and by** soon or eventually —**by and large** considering everything —**by the by** incidentally

by- *prefix* 1 near 2 secondary /*byproduct*/

by-and-by (bī''n bī') *n.* a future time

bye (bī) *n.* ⟦var. of BY⟧ the privilege, with an uneven number of participants, of not being paired with another contestant in the first round

bye-bye (bī'bī') *n., interj.* goodbye

Bye·lo·rus·sian Soviet Socialist Republic (bye'lō rush'ən) BELORUSSIAN SOVIET SOCIALIST REPUBLIC: also **Bye'lo·rus'sia** —**Bye'lo·rus'sian** *adj., n.*

by·gone (bī'gôn') *adj.* past; former —*n.* anything gone or past

by·law (bī'lô') *n.* ⟦< ME *bi,* village + *laue,* law⟧ any of a set of rules adopted by an organization or assembly for its own meetings or affairs

by'line' *n.* a line identifying the writer of a newspaper or magazine article

by'pass' *n.* 1 a way, pipe, channel, etc. between two points that avoids or is auxiliary to the main way 2 a surgical operation to allow fluid to pass around a diseased or blocked part or organ —*vt.* 1 to detour 2 to furnish with a bypass 3 to ignore

by'path' or **by'-path'** *n.* a secluded, little-used path; byway

by'play' *n.* action, gestures, etc. going on aside from the main action or conversation

by'prod'uct or **by'-prod'uct** *n.* anything produced in the course of making another thing

by'road' *n.* a road that is not a main road

By·ron (bī′rən), **George Gor·don** (gôr′d′n) 1788-1824; Eng. poet
by′stand′er ***n.*** a person who stands near but does not participate
byte (bīt) ***n.*** ‖ arbitrary formation ‖ a string of binary digits (*bits*), usually eight, operated on as a basic unit by a digital computer
by′way′ ***n.*** a secondary road or path, esp. one not much used
by′word′ ***n.*** **1** a proverb **2** one well known for some quality **3** an object of scorn or ridicule
Byz·an·tine Empire (biz′ən tēn′, tīn′; bi zan′tin) empire (A.D. 395-1453) in SE Europe & SW Asia

C

c or **C** (sē) ***n., pl.*** **c's, C's** the third letter of the English alphabet
C (sē) ***n.*** **1** a Roman numeral for 100 **2** *Educ.* a grade for average work **3** *Music* the first tone in the scale of C major
C *symbol for* **1** *Chem.* carbon **2** Celsius (or centigrade)
C or **C.** **1** carat(s) **2** catcher **3** Catholic **4** cent(s) **5** center **6** centimeter(s) **7** century; centuries **8** chapter(s) **9** circa **10** college **11** copyright **12** cup(s) **13** cycle(s) Also, except 3, **c** or **c.**
Ca *Chem. symbol for* calcium
CA California
cab (kab) ***n.*** ‖ < Fr *cabriole*, a leap ‖ **1** a carriage, esp. one for public hire **2** TAXICAB **3** the place in a truck, crane, etc where the operator sits —***vi.*** **cabbed, cab′bing** [Colloq.] to take or drive a taxicab
ca·bal (kə bal′) ***n.*** ‖ Fr, intrigue ‖ **1** a small group joined in a secret intrigue **2** the intrigue itself
cab·a·la (kab′ə lə, kə bä′lə) ***n.*** ‖ < Heb *kabala*, tradition ‖ **1** a medieval occult Jewish philosophy **2** occultism
ca·bal·le·ro (kab′ə ler′ō, -əl yer′ō) ***n., pl.*** **-ros** ‖ Sp ‖ **1** a Spanish gentleman **2** [South-west] *a)* a horseman *b)* a lady's escort
ca·ban·a (kə ban′ə, -bä′nə) ***n.*** ‖ Sp < LL *capanna* ‖ **1** a cabin or hut **2** a small shelter used as a bathhouse
cab·a·ret (kab′ə rā′) ***n.*** ‖ Fr, tavern ‖ a cafe with musical entertainment
cab·bage (kab′ij) ***n.*** ‖ OFr *caboche* < ? ‖ a vegetable with thick leaves formed into a round, compact head
cab·by or **cab·bie** (kab′ē) ***n., pl.*** **-bies** [Colloq.] one who drives a cab
ca·ber·net (kab′ər nā′) ***n.*** [*also* **C-**] a dry red wine; esp., CABERNET SAUVIGNON
cabernet sau·vi·gnon (sō vē nyōn′) [*also* **C-S-**] a fragrant, dry red wine
cab·in (kab′in) ***n.*** ‖ < LL *capanna*, hut ‖ **1** a small, crudely or simply built house; hut **2** a room on a ship or boat **3** the space for passengers, crew, or cargo in an aircraft
cab·i·net (kab′ə nit) ***n.*** ‖ Fr, prob. ult. < L *cavea*, cage ‖ **1** a case with drawers or shelves **2** a case holding a TV, radio, etc. **3** [*often* **C-**] a body of official advisors to a chief executive
cab′i·net·mak′er ***n.*** a maker of fine furniture
cab′i·net·work′ ***n.*** articles made by a cabinetmaker Also **cab′i·net·ry** (-ni trē)
cabin fever a condition of increased anxiety caused by being confined or isolated
ca·ble (kā′bəl) ***n.*** ‖ < L *capere*, to take hold ‖ **1** a thick, heavy rope, often of wire strands **2** a bundle of insulated wires to carry an electric current **3** a cablegram **4** CABLE TV —***vt.*** **-bled, -bling** **1** to fasten with a cable **2** to send a cablegram to —***vi.*** to send a cablegram
cable car a car drawn by a moving cable, as up a steep incline
ca′ble·cast′ (-kast′) ***vt.*** **-cast′, -cast′ing** to transmit to receivers by coaxial cable —***n.*** a program that is cablecast
ca′ble·gram′ (-gram′) ***n.*** a message sent by undersea cable
cable TV a TV system in which various antennas receive local and distant signals and transmit them by cable to subscribers' receivers
cab·o·chon (kab′ə shän′) ***n.*** ‖ Fr < *caboche*, head ‖ any precious stone cut in convex shape
ca·bood·le (kə bo͞od′əl) ***n.*** ‖ < BOODLE ‖ [Colloq.] lot; group [the whole *caboodle*]
ca·boose (kə bo͞os′) ***n.*** ‖ MDu *kambuis*, cabin house ‖ the trainmen's car at the rear of a freight train
ca·ca·o (kə kā′ō, -kä′-) ***n., pl.*** **-os′** ‖ Sp < AmInd (Mexico) ‖ **1** the seed of a tropical American tree from which cocoa and chocolate are made: also **cacao bean** **2** this tree
cache (kash) ***n.*** ‖ Fr < L *cogere*, to collect ‖ **1** a place in which stores of food, supplies, etc. are hidden **2** anything so hidden —***vt.*** **cached, cach′ing** to place in a cache
cache·pot (kash′pät, -pō′) ***n.*** ‖ Fr < *cacher*, to hide ‖ a decorative jar for holding potted plants Also **cache pot**
ca·chet (ka shā′) ***n.*** ‖ Fr ‖ **1** a stamp or official seal, as on a document **2** any sign of official approval, or of quality, prestige, etc. **3** a design on an envelope that marks some event
cack·le (kak′əl) ***vi.*** **-led, -ling** ‖ echoic ‖ **1** to make the shrill, broken vocal sounds of a hen **2** to laugh or chatter with similar sounds —***n.*** a cackling
ca·coph·o·ny (kə käf′ə nē) ***n., pl.*** **-nies** ‖ < Gr *kakos*, bad + *phōnē*, voice ‖ harsh, jarring sound; discord —**ca·coph′o·nous** ***adj.***
cac·tus (kak′təs) ***n., pl.*** **-tus·es** or **-ti′** (-tī′) ‖ < Gr *kaktos*, kind of thistle ‖ any of a family of desert plants with fleshy stems and spinelike leaves
cad (kad) ***n.*** ‖ < CADET ‖ a man whose behavior is not gentlemanly —**cad′dish** ***adj.*** —**cad′dish·ly** ***adv.*** —**cad′dish·ness** ***n.***

ca·dav·er (kə dav′ər) ***n.*** ‖ L, prob. < *cadere,* to fall ‖ a corpse, as for dissection

ca·dav′er·ous (-əs) ***adj.*** ‖ < L ‖ of or like a cadaver; esp., pale, ghastly, etc.

CAD/CAM (kad′kam′) ***n.*** ‖ *C(omputer)-A(ided) D(esign)/C(omputer)-A(ided) M(anufacturing)* ‖ a computer system combining design techniques and manufacturing principles

cad·die (kad′ē) ***n.*** ‖ Scot form of Fr *cadet:* see CADET ‖ one who attends a golfer, carrying the clubs **—*vi.* -died, -dy·ing** to act as a caddie

cad·dy[1] (kad′ē) ***n.***, *pl.* **-dies** ‖ < Malay *kātī,* unit of weight ‖ a small container, specif., one used for tea

cad·dy[2] (kad′ē) ***n., vi.*** CADDIE

-cade (kād) ‖ < (CAVAL)CADE ‖ *suffix* procession, parade [*motorcade*]

ca·dence (kād′′ns) ***n.*** ‖ < L *cadere,* to fall ‖ **1** fall of the voice in speaking **2** flow of rhythm **3** measured movement, as in marching

ca·den·za (kə den′zə) ***n.*** ‖ It: see prec. ‖ an elaborate passage for the solo instrument in a concerto

ca·det (kə det′) ***n.*** ‖ Fr < L dim. of *caput,* head ‖ **1** a student in training at an armed forces academy **2** any trainee, as a practice teacher

cadge (kaj) ***vt., vi.*** **cadged, cadg′ing** ‖ < ? ‖ to beg or get by begging; sponge **—cadg′er *n.***

cad·mi·um (kad′mē əm) ***n.*** ‖ < L *cadmia,* zinc ore (with which it occurs) ‖ a metallic chemical element used in alloys, pigments, etc.

ca·dre (ka′drē′, -drā′; *also,* kä′-) ***n.*** ‖ < Fr < L *quadrum,* a square ‖ a nucleus around which an expanded organization, as a military unit, can be built

ca·du·ce·us (kə do͞o′sē əs) ***n.***, *pl.* **-ce·i′** (-sē ī′) ‖ L ‖ the winged staff of Mercury: now a symbol of the medical profession

CADUCEUS

Cae·sar (sē′zər) ***n.*** ‖ after fol. ‖ **1** the title of the Roman emperors from 27 B.C. to A.D. 138 **2** [*often* **c-**] any emperor or dictator

Cae·sar (sē′zər), **Jul·ius** (jo͞ol′yəs, -ē əs) *c.* 100-44 B.C.; Rom. general & dictator (49-44)

Cae·sar·e·an section (sə zer′ē ən) ‖ from the ancient story that Julius *Caesar* was born this way ‖ [*also* **c- s-**] the delivery of a baby by cutting through the mother's abdominal and uterine walls

cae·su·ra (si zyoor′ə, -zhoor′ə) ***n.***, *pl.* **-ras** or **-rae** (-ē) ‖ L < *caedere,* to cut down ‖ a break or pause in a line of verse, usually in the middle

ca·fe or **ca·fé** (kə fā′, ka-) ***n.*** ‖ Fr, coffeehouse ‖ a small restaurant or a barroom, nightclub, etc.

caf·e·te·ri·a (kaf′ə tir′ē ə) ***n.*** ‖ AmSp, coffee store ‖ a self-service restaurant

caf·feine or **caf·fein** (kaf′ēn′) ***n.*** ‖ Ger *kaffein* ‖ the alkaloid present in coffee, tea, and kola: it is a stimulant

caf·tan (kaf′tan) ***n.*** ‖ Turk *qaftān* ‖ a long-sleeved robe, worn in eastern Mediterranean countries

cage (kāj) ***n.*** ‖ < L *cavea,* hollow place ‖ **1** a structure of wires, bars, etc., for confining animals **2** any openwork structure or frame **—*vt.* caged, cag′ing** to put or confine, as in a cage

cag·er (kāj′ər) ***n.*** [Slang] a basketball player

ca·gey or **ca·gy** (kā′jē) ***adj.*** **-gi·er, -gi·est** ‖ < ? ‖ [Colloq.] **1** sly; tricky; cunning **2** cautious **—ca′gi·ly *adv.* —ca′gi·ness *n.***

ca·hoots (kə ho͞ots′) ***n.pl.*** ‖ < ? ‖ [Slang] partnership: chiefly in phr. **in cahoots (with)** implying scheming

Cain (kān) *Bible* oldest son of Adam and Eve: he killed his brother Abel **—raise Cain** [Slang] to create a great commotion

cairn (kern) ***n.*** ‖ Scot ‖ a conical heap of stones built as a monument

Cai·ro (kī′rō) capital of Egypt: pop. 5,074,000

cais·son (kā′sən) ***n.*** ‖ Fr < L *capsa,* box ‖ **1** a two-wheeled wagon with a chest for ammunition **2** a watertight box for underwater construction work

cai·tiff (kāt′if) ***n.*** ‖ < L *captivus,* CAPTIVE ‖ a mean, evil, or cowardly person **—*adj.*** evil, mean, or cowardly

ca·jole (kə jōl′) ***vt., vi.*** **-joled′, -jol′ing** ‖ < Fr ‖ to coax with flattery and insincere talk **—ca·jol′er *n.* —ca·jol′er·y *n.***

Ca·jun or **Ca·jan** (kā′jən) ***n.*** **1** a native of Louisiana of Canadian French ancestry **2** the dialect of Cajuns

cake (kāk) ***n.*** ‖ < ON ‖ **1** a small, flat mass of baked or fried dough, batter, hashed food, etc. **2** a mixture of flour, eggs, sugar, etc. baked as in a loaf and often covered with icing **3** a shaped, solid mass, as of soap **—*vt., vi.*** **caked, cak′ing** to form into a hard mass or crust **—piece of cake** [Slang] something easy or pleasurable to do **—take the cake** [Slang] to win the prize **—cak′y** or **cak′ey *adj.***

cal. **1** caliber **2** calorie(s)

cal·a·bash (kal′ə bash′) ***n.*** ‖ < Sp *calabaza* ‖ **1** the gourdlike fruit of a tropical American tree **2** *a)* the bottle-shaped, gourdlike fruit of a tropical vine *b)* a large smoking pipe made from it **3** a gourd

cal·a·boose (kal′ə bo͞os′) ***n.*** ‖ Sp *calabozo* ‖ [Slang] a prison; jail

ca·la·ma·ri (kä′lə mä′rē) ***n.*** squid cooked as food, esp. as an Italian dish

cal·a·mine (kal′ə mīn′) ***n.*** ‖ Fr < L *cadmia,* zinc ore ‖ a zinc oxide powder used in skin lotions

ca·lam·i·ty (kə lam′ə tē) ***n.***, *pl.* **-ties** ‖ < L *calamitas* ‖ a great misfortune; disaster **—ca·lam′i·tous *adj.***

cal·car·e·ous (kal ker′ē əs) ***adj.*** ‖ < L *calx,* lime ‖ of or like limestone, calcium, or lime

cal·ci·fy (kal′sə fī′) ***vt., vi.*** **-fied′, -fy′ing** ‖ < L *calx,* lime + -FY ‖ to change into a hard, stony substance by the deposit of lime or calcium salts **—cal′ci·fi·ca′tion *n.***

cal′ci·mine′ (-mīn′) ***n.*** ‖ < L *calx,* lime ‖ a white or tinted liquid, used as a wash for plastered surfaces **—*vt.* -mined′, -min′ing** to coat with calcimine

cal·cine (kal′sīn′) ***vt., vi.*** **-cined′, -cin′ing** ‖ < L *calx,* lime ‖ to change to an ashy powder by heat

cal·cite (kal′sīt′) ***n.*** calcium carbonate, a mineral found as limestone, chalk, and marble
cal·ci·um (kal′sē əm) ***n.*** ‖ < L *calx*, lime ‖ a soft, silver-white, metallic chemical element found combined in limestone, chalk, etc.
calcium carbonate a white powder or crystalline compound found in limestone, chalk, bones, shells, etc.
cal·cu·late (kal′kyo͞o lāt′, -kyə-) ***vt.*** **-lat′ed, -lat′ing** ‖ < L *calculare*, reckon ‖ **1** to determine by using mathematics; compute **2** to determine by reasoning; estimate **3** to plan or intend for a purpose —***vi.*** **1** to reckon **2** to rely (*on*) —**cal′cu·la·ble** (-lə bəl) ***adj.***
cal′cu·lat′ed ***adj.*** deliberately planned or carefully considered
cal′cu·lat′ing ***adj.*** shrewd or cunning; scheming
cal′cu·la′tion ***n.*** **1** a calculating **2** something deduced by calculating **3** careful planning or forethought —**cal′cu·la′tive** ***adj.***
cal′cu·la′tor ***n.*** **1** one who calculates **2** a device for the rapid performance of mathematical operations
cal·cu·lus (kal′kyo͞o ləs, -kyə-) ***n.***, *pl.* **-li′** (-lī′) or **-lus·es** ‖ L, pebble used in counting ‖ **1** an abnormal stony mass in the body **2** a method of calculation or analysis in higher mathematics
Cal·cut·ta (kal kut′ə) seaport in NE India: pop. 9,166,000
cal·de·ra (kal der′ə) ***n.*** ‖ Sp < L *caldarium*, room for hot baths ‖ a broad, craterlike basin of a volcano
cal·dron (kôl′drən) ***n.*** ‖ < L *calidus*, warm ‖ **1** a large kettle or boiler **2** a state of violent agitation
cal·en·dar (kal′ən dər) ***n.*** ‖ < L *kalendarium*, account book ‖ **1** a system of determining the length and divisions of a year **2** a table that shows the days, weeks, and months of a given year **3** a schedule, as of pending court cases
cal·en·der (kal′ən dər) ***n.*** ‖ < Gr *kylindros*, cylinder ‖ a machine with rollers for giving paper, cloth, etc. a smooth or glossy finish —***vt.*** to process (paper, etc.) in a calender
calf[1] (kaf) ***n.***, *pl.* **calves** (kavz) or **calfs** ‖ < OE *cealf* ‖ **1** a young cow or bull **2** the young of some other large animals, as the elephant, seal, etc. **3** leather from a calf's hide
calf[2] (kaf) ***n.***, *pl.* **calves** ‖ ON *kalfi* ‖ the fleshy back part of the leg below the knee
calf′skin′ ***n.*** **1** the skin of a calf **2** a soft leather made from this
Cal·ga·ry (kal′gə rē) city in S Alberta, Canada: pop. 636,000
cal·i·ber (kal′ə bər) ***n.*** ‖ Fr & Sp, ult. < Gr *kalopodion*, shoemaker's last ‖ **1** the diameter of a cylindrical body, esp. of a bullet or shell **2** the diameter of the bore of a gun **3** quality or ability Also, esp. Brit., **cal′i·bre**
cal·i·brate (kal′ə brāt′) ***vt.*** **-brat′ed, -brat′ing** **1** to determine the caliber of **2** to fix or correct the graduations of (a measuring instrument) —**cal′i·bra′tion** ***n.*** —**cal′i·bra′tor** ***n.***
cal·i·co (kal′i kō′) ***n.***, *pl.* **-coes′** or **-cos′** ‖ after *Calicut*, city in India ‖ a printed cotton fabric —***adj.*** spotted like calico /*a calico cat*/
Cal·i·for·ni·a (kal′ə fôr′nyə, -nē ə) State of the SW U.S., on the Pacific: 158,693 sq. mi.; pop. 23,669,000; cap. Sacramento: abbrev. **Calif.** —**Cal′i·for′ni·an** ***adj.***, ***n.***
cal·i·per (kal′ə pər) ***n.*** ‖ var. of CALIBER ‖ **1** [*usually pl.*] an instrument consisting of a pair of hinged legs, for measuring thickness or diameter **2** a part of a braking system on a bicycle or motor vehicle —***vt.***, ***vi.*** to measure with calipers
ca·liph (kā′lif; *also*, kal′if) ***n.*** ‖ Ar *khalīfa* ‖ supreme ruler: the title taken by Mohammed's successors as heads of Islam —**ca′liph·ate** ***n.***
cal·is·then·ics (kal′is then′iks) ***n.pl.*** ‖ < Gr *kallos*, beauty + *sthenos*, strength ‖ athletic exercises
calk (kôk) ***vt.*** CAULK —**calk′er** ***n.***
call (kôl) ***vt.*** ‖ < ON *kalla* ‖ **1** to say in a loud tone; shout **2** to summon **3** to give or apply a name to **4** to describe as specified **5** to awaken **6** to telephone **7** to give orders for **8** to stop (a game, etc.) **9** to demand payment of (a loan, etc.) **10** *Poker* to equal (the preceding bet) or to equal the bet of (the last previous bettor) —***vi.*** **1** to shout **2** to visit for a short while: often with *on* **3** to telephone —***n.*** **1** a calling **2** a loud utterance **3** the distinctive cry of an animal or bird **4** a summons; invitation **5** an economic demand, as for a product **6** need /*no call for tears*/ **7** a demand for payment **8** a brief visit **9** an option to buy a stock, commodity, etc. at a specified price and time —**call down** [Colloq.] to scold —**call for** **1** to demand **2** to come and get —**call off** to cancel (a scheduled event) —**call up** **1** to recall **2** to summon for duty **3** to telephone —**on call** available when summoned —**call′er** ***n.***
cal·la (kal′ə) ***n.*** ‖ < L, a plant (of uncertain kind) ‖ a plant with a large, white leaf surrounding a yellow flower spike Also **calla lily**
call girl a prostitute who is called by telephone to assignations
cal·lig·ra·phy (kə lig′rə fē) ***n.*** ‖ < Gr *kallos*, beauty + *graphein*, write ‖ handwriting, esp. when attractive —**cal·lig′ra·pher** ***n.*** —**cal·li·graph·ic** (kal′ə graf′ik) ***adj.***
call′ing ***n.*** **1** the act of one that calls **2** one's work or profession **3** an inner urging toward some vocation
cal·li·o·pe (kə lī′ə pē′, kal′ē ōp′) ***n.*** ‖ < Gr *kallos*, beauty + *ops*, voice ‖ a keyboard instrument like an organ, having a series of steam whistles
call letters the letters, and sometimes numbers, that identify a radio or TV station
cal·lous (kal′əs) ***adj.*** ‖ < L *callum*, hard skin ‖ **1** hardened: usually **calloused** **2** unfeeling —**cal·los·i·ty** (kə läs′ə tē) ***n.*** —**cal′lous·ly** ***adv.*** —**cal′lous·ness** ***n.***
cal·low (kal′ō) ***adj.*** ‖ OE *calu*, bare, bald ‖ immature; inexperienced —**cal′low·ness** ***n.***
cal·lus (kal′əs) ***n.***, *pl.* **-lus·es** ‖ L, var. of *callum*, hard skin ‖ a hardened, thickened place on the skin
calm (käm) ***n.*** ‖ < Gr *kauma*, heat ‖ stillness; tranquillity —***adj.*** still; quiet; tranquil —***vt.***, ***vi.*** to make or become calm: often

with *down* —**calm′ly** *adv.* —**calm′ness** *n.*

ca·lor·ic (kə lôr′ik) *adj.* 1 of heat 2 of calories

cal·o·rie (kal′ə rē) *n.* ‖ Fr < L *calor*, heat ‖ a unit for measuring heat, esp. for measuring the energy produced by food when oxidized in the body

cal·o·rif·ic (kal′ə rif′ik) *adj.* ‖ < L *calor*, heat + *facere*, make ‖ producing heat

cal·u·met (kal′yə met′) *n.* ‖ CdnFr < L *calamus*, reed ‖ a long-stemmed ceremonial pipe, smoked by North American Indians, as a token of peace

ca·lum·ni·ate (kə lum′nē āt′) *vt., vi.* **-at′ed, -at′ing** ‖ see fol. ‖ to slander —**ca·lum′ni·a′tion** *n.* —**ca·lum′ni·a′tor** *n.*

cal·um·ny (kal′əm nē) *n., pl.* **-nies** ‖ < L *calumnia*, slander ‖ a false and malicious statement; slander

Cal·va·ry (kal′və rē) *Bible* the place where Jesus was crucified

calve (kav) *vi., vt.* **calved, calv′ing** to give birth to (a calf)

calves (kavz) *n. pl. of* CALF[1] & CALF[2]

Cal·vin (kal′vin), **John** 1509-64; Fr. Protestant reformer

Cal′vin·ism′ (-iz′əm) *n.* the Christian doctrines of John Calvin and his followers, esp. predestination —**Cal′vin·ist** *n., adj.* —**Cal′vin·is′tic** *adj.*

cal·vi·ti·es (kal vish′i ēz′) *n.* ‖ L ‖ a loss of hair, esp. on top of the head

ca·lyp·so (kə lip′sō) *n.* ‖ < ? ‖ a lively, topical folk song, orig. of Trinidad

ca·lyx (kā′liks′, kal′iks′) *n., pl.* **-lyx′es** or **-ly·ces′** (-lə sēz′) ‖ L, pod ‖ the outer whorl of protective leaves, or sepals, of a flower

cam (kam) *n.* ‖ Du *cam*, orig., a comb ‖ a wheel, projection on a wheel, etc. that gives irregular motion, as to a wheel or shaft, or receives such motion from it

ca·ma·ra·de·rie (kam′ə räd′ə rē, käm′-) *n.* ‖ Fr ‖ loyalty and warm, friendly feeling among comrades

cam·ber (kam′bər) *n.* ‖ OFr < L *camur*, arched ‖ a slight convex curve of a surface, as of a road —*vt., vi.* to arch slightly

cam·bi·um (kam′bē əm) *n.* ‖ < LL *cambiare*, change ‖ a layer of cells between the wood and bark in woody plants, which will eventually become wood and bark —**cam′bi·al** *adj.*

Cam·bo·di·a (kam bō′dē ə) country in S Indochina: 69,898 sq. mi.; pop. 6,388,000; cap. Phnom Penh —**Cam·bo′di·an** *adj., n.*

cam·bric (kām′brik) *n.* ‖ after *Cambrai*, Fr city ‖ a fine linen or cotton cloth

Cam·bridge (kām′brij′) 1 city in E England: pop. 100,000 2 city in E Mass.: pop. 95,000

cam·cord·er (kam′kôrd′ər) *n.* a small, portable videotape recorder and TV camera

came (kām) *vi. pt. of* COME

cam·el (kam′əl) *n.* ‖ ult. < Heb *gāmāl* ‖ a large, domesticated mammal with a humped back and long neck: because it can store water in its body, it is used in Asian and African deserts

ca·mel·li·a (kə mēl′yə, -mē′lē ə) *n.* ‖ after G. J. *Kamel* (1661 1706), missionary to the Far East ‖ 1 an Asiatic evergreen tree or shrub with glossy leaves and roselike flowers 2 the flower

Cam·em·bert (cheese) (kam′əm ber′, -bərt) ‖ after *Camembert*, Fr village ‖ a soft, creamy, rich cheese

cam·e·o (kam′ē ō′) *n., pl.* **-os′** ‖ < It < ML *camaeus* ‖ 1 a gem carved with a figure raised in relief 2 *a)* an outstanding bit role *b)* a bit of fine writing

cam·er·a (kam′ər ə) *n.* ‖ L, vault ‖ 1 the private office of a judge 2 a device for taking photographs: a closed box containing a sensitized plate or film on which an image is formed when light enters through a lens 3 *TV* the device that receives the image and transforms it into a flow of electrical impulses for transmission —**in camera** in privacy or secrecy

cam′er·a·man′ *n., pl.* **-men′** 1 an operator of a film or TV camera 2 a cinematographer

Cam·e·roon (kam′ə ro͞on′) country in central Africa, on the Atlantic: 183,568 sq. mi.; pop. 10,009,000 —**Cam′e·roon′i·an** *adj., n.*

cam·i·sole (kam′i sōl′) *n.* ‖ Fr < LL *camisia*, shirt ‖ a woman's sleeveless undergarment for the upper body

cam·o·mile (kam′ə mīl′, -mēl′) *n. alt. sp. of* CHAMOMILE

cam·ou·flage (kam′ə fläzh′, -fläj′) *n.* ‖ Fr < *camoufler*, to disguise ‖ 1 a disguising, as of ships or guns, to conceal them from the enemy 2 a disguise; deception —*vt., vi.* **-flaged′, -flag′ing** to disguise in order to conceal —**cam′ou·flag′er** *n.*

camp (kamp) *n.* ‖ < L *campus*, field ‖ 1 *a)* a place where temporary tents, huts, etc. are put up, as for soldiers *b)* a group of such tents, etc. 2 the supporters of a particular cause 3 a recreational place in the country for vacationers, esp. children 4 the people living in a camp 5 [Slang] banality, artifice, etc. so extreme as to amuse or have a perversely sophisticated appeal —*vi.* 1 to set up a camp 2 to live or stay in a camp: often with *out* —**break camp** to dismantle a camp and depart

cam·paign (kam pān′) *n.* ‖ Fr < L *campus*, field ‖ 1 a series of military operations with a particular objective 2 a series of planned actions, as for electing a candidate —*vi.* to participate in a campaign —**cam·paign′er** *n.*

cam·pa·ni·le (kam′pə nē′lē) *n., pl.* **-les** or **-li** (-lē) ‖ It < LL *campana*, a bell ‖ a bell tower

camp·er (kam′pər) *n.* 1 a vacationer at a camp 2 a motor vehicle or trailer equipped for camping out

camp′fire′ *n.* 1 an outdoor fire at a camp 2 a social gathering around such a fire

cam·phor (kam′fər) *n.* ‖ < Sans *karpuraḥ*, camphor tree ‖ a crystalline substance with a strong odor, derived from the wood of an Oriental evergreen tree (**camphor tree**): used to repel moths, in medicine as a stimulant, etc. —**cam′phor·at′ed** *adj.*

camp meeting a religious meeting held outdoors or in a tent, etc.

camp′site′ *n.* 1 any site for a camp 2 an area in a park set aside for camping

cam·pus (kam′pəs) *n., pl.* **-pus·es** ‖ L, a field ‖ the grounds, and sometimes buildings, of a school or college —*adj.* of a school or college /*campus* politics/

camp'y *adj.* **-i·er, -i·est** [Slang] characterized by CAMP (*n.* 5)

cam'shaft' *n.* a shaft having a cam, or to which a cam is fastened

can[1] (kan, kən) *v.aux., vt. pt.* **could** ‖ < OE *cunnan,* to know ‖ 1 know(s) how to 2 am, are, or is able to 3 am, are, or is likely to /*can* that be true?/ 4 have or has the right to 5 [Colloq.] am, are, or is permitted to; may —**can but** can only

can[2] (kan) *n.* ‖ OE *canne,* a cup ‖ 1 a container, usually metal, with a separate cover /a garbage *can*/ 2 a tinned metal container in which foods, etc. are sealed for preservation 3 the amount a can holds —*vt.* **canned, can'ning** 1 to put up in cans or jars for preservation 2 [Slang] to dismiss

Ca·naan (kā'nən) *Bible* the Promised Land of the Israelites

Can·a·da (kan'ə də) country in N North America: 3,849,672 sq. mi.; pop. 25,310,000; cap. Ottawa: abbrev. **Can.** —**Ca·na·di·an** (kə nā'dē ən) *adj., n.*

Canadian bacon cured, smoked pork taken from the loin

Canadian English English as spoken and written in Canada

Ca·na'di·an·ism' *n.* 1 a custom or belief of Canada 2 a word or phrase originating in Canadian English

ca·nal (kə nal') *n.* ‖ < L *canalis,* channel ‖ 1 an artificial waterway for transportation or irrigation 2 *Anat.* a tubular passage or duct

Canal Zone *former name of* a strip of land on either side of the Panama Canal: leased by the U.S. (1904-79); under U.S. control (through 1999)

ca·na·pé (kan'ə pā', kan'ə pē) *n.* ‖ Fr ‖ a small piece of bread or a cracker, spread with spiced meat, cheese, etc., served as an appetizer

ca·nard (kə närd') *n.* ‖ Fr, a duck ‖ a false, esp. malicious, report

ca·nar·y (kə ner'ē) *n., pl.* **-ies** ‖ after *Canary* Islands ‖ 1 a small, yellow finch 2 a light yellow

Canary Islands group of Spanish islands off NW Africa

ca·nas·ta (kə nas'tə) *n.* ‖ Sp, basket ‖ a card game using a double deck

Can·ber·ra (kan'bər ə, -ber'ə) capital of Australia: pop. 256,000

can·can (kan'kan') *n.* ‖ Fr ‖ a lively dance with much high kicking

can·cel (kan'səl) *vt.* **-celed** or **-celled, -cel·ing** or **-cel·ling** ‖ < L *cancellus,* lattice ‖ 1 to mark over with lines, etc., as in deleting written matter or marking a postage stamp, check, etc. as used 2 to make invalid 3 to do away with; abolish 4 to neutralize or balance: often with *out* 5 *Math.* to remove (a common factor, equivalents, etc.) —**can'cel·la'tion** *n.*

can·cer (kan'sər) ‖ < L, a crab ‖ [C-] the fourth sign of the zodiac —*n.* 1 a malignant tumor that can spread 2 any spreading evil —**can'cer·ous** *adj.*

can·de·la·brum (kan'də lä'brəm, -lā', -la'-) *n., pl.* **-bra** (-brə) or **-brums** ‖ L: see CHANDELIER ‖ a large branched candlestick Also **can'de·la'bra,** *pl.* **-bras**

can·did (kan'did) *adj.* ‖ L *candidus,* white, sincere ‖ 1 very honest or frank 2 unposed and informal /a *candid* photo/ —**can'did·ly** *adv.* —**can'did·ness** *n.*

can·di·date (kan'də dāt', -dət) *n.* ‖ L *candidatus,* white-robed, as office seekers ‖ one seeking an office, award, etc.

can·died (kan'dēd') *adj.* 1 cooked in sugar 2 sugary in expression

can·dle (kan'dəl) *n.* ‖ < L *candela* ‖ a cylinder of tallow or wax with a wick through it, which gives light when burned —*vt.* **-dled, -dling** to examine (eggs) for freshness by placing in front of a light —**can'dler** *n.*

can'dle·stick' *n.* a cupped or spiked holder for a candle or candles

can'-do' *adj.* [Colloq.] confident of one's ability

can·dor (kan'dər) *n.* ‖ L, openness ‖ honesty or frankness in expressing oneself Brit. sp. **can'dour**

can·dy (kan'dē) *n., pl.* **-dies** ‖ < Pers *qand,* cane sugar ‖ a solid confection of sugar or syrup with flavoring, fruit, nuts, etc. —*vt.* **-died, -dy·ing** 1 to cook in sugar, esp. to preserve 2 to crystallize into sugar

cane (kān) *n.* ‖ < Gr *kanna* ‖ 1 the slender, jointed stem of certain plants, as bamboo 2 a plant with such a stem, as sugar cane 3 WALKING STICK 4 split rattan —*vt.* **caned, can'ing** 1 to flog with a cane 2 to make (chair seats, etc.) with cane —**can'er** *n.*

cane·brake (kān'brāk') *n.* a dense growth of cane plants

ca·nine (kā'nīn') *adj.* ‖ < L *canis,* dog ‖ 1 of or like a dog 2 of the family of carnivores that includes dogs, wolves, and foxes —*n.* 1 a dog or other canine animal 2 any of the sharp-pointed teeth next to the incisors: in full **canine tooth**

can·is·ter (kan'is tər) *n.* ‖ < Gr *kanastron,* wicker basket ‖ a small box or can for coffee, tea, etc.

can·ker (kaŋ'kər) *n.* ‖ < L *cancer,* a crab ‖ an ulcerlike sore, esp. in the mouth —**can'ker·ous** *adj.*

can·na·bis (kan'ə bis') *n.* ‖ L, hemp ‖ 1 HEMP 2 the female flowering tops of the hemp

canned (kand) *adj.* 1 preserved, as in cans 2 [Slang] recorded for reproduction, as on radio or TV

can·ner·y (kan'ər ē) *n., pl.* **-ies** a factory where foods are canned

can·ni·bal (kan'ə bəl) *n.* ‖ Sp *canibal* ‖ 1 a person who eats human flesh 2 an animal that eats its own kind —*adj.* of or like cannibals —**can'ni·bal·ism'** *n.* —**can'ni·bal·is'tic** *adj.*

can'ni·bal·ize' (-īz') *vt., vi.* **-ized', -iz'ing** to strip (old or worn equipment) of parts for use in other units

can·non (kan'ən) *n., pl.* **-nons** or **-non** ‖ < L *canna,* cane ‖ 1 a large, mounted piece of artillery 2 an automatic gun on an aircraft

can'non·ade' (-ād') *n.* a continuous firing of artillery —*vt., vi.* **-ad'ed, -ad'ing** to fire artillery at

can·not (kan'ät', kə nät') can not —**cannot but** have no choice but to

can·ny (kan'ē) *adj.* **-ni·er, -ni·est** ‖ <

CAN¹ ‖ cautious and shrewd —**can′ni·ly** *adv.* —**can′ni·ness** *n.*

ca·noe (kə no͞o′) *n.* ‖ < Sp *canoa* < WInd ‖ a narrow, light boat moved by paddles —*vi.* **-noed′, -noe′ing** to paddle, or go in, a canoe —**ca·noe′ist** *n.*

can·on (kan′ən) *n.* ‖ OE, a rule < L ‖ 1 a law or body of laws of a church 2 *a)* a basic rule or principle *b)* a criterion 3 an official list, as of books of the Bible 4 the complete works, as of an author 5 *Music* a round 6 a clergyman serving in a cathedral

ca·ñon (kan′yən) *n. alt. sp. of* CANYON

ca·non·i·cal (kə nän′i kəl) *adj.* 1 of or according to church law 2 of or belonging to a canon

can·on·ize (kan′ən īz′) *vt.* **-ized′, -iz′ing** 1 to declare (a dead person) a saint 2 to glorify —**can′on·i·za′tion** *n.*

can·o·py (kan′ə pē) *n., pl.* **-pies** ‖ < Gr *kōnōpeion*, couch with mosquito nets ‖ 1 a drapery, etc. fastened above a bed, throne, etc., or held over a person 2 a rooflike projection —*vt.* **-pied, -py·ing** to place or form a canopy over; cover

cant¹ (kant) *n.* ‖ < L *cantus*, song ‖ 1 the secret slang of beggars, thieves, etc.; argot 2 the special vocabulary of those in a certain occupation; jargon 3 insincere talk, esp. when pious —*vi.* to use cant

cant² (kant) *n.* ‖ L *cantus*, tire of a wheel ‖ 1 an outside angle 2 a beveled edge 3 a tilt, turn, slant, etc. —*vt., vi.* to slant; tilt

can't (kant, känt) cannot

can·ta·loupe or **can·ta·loup** (kant′ə lōp′) *n.* ‖ Fr < It *Cantalupo*, estate near Rome, where first grown in Europe ‖ a muskmelon, esp. one with a rough rind and juicy, orange flesh

can·tan·ker·ous (kan taŋ′kər əs) *adj.* ‖ prob. < ME *contakour*, troublemaker ‖ bad-tempered; quarrelsome —**can·tan′ker·ous·ly** *adv.* —**can·tan′ker·ous·ness** *n.*

can·ta·ta (kän tät′ə, kən-) *n.* ‖ It < *cantare*, to sing ‖ a choral composition for a story to be sung but not acted

can·teen (kan tēn′) *n.* ‖ < Fr < It *cantina*, wine cellar ‖ 1 a recreation center for servicemen, teenagers, etc. 2 a place where food is dispensed, as in a disaster area 3 a small flask for carrying water

can·ter (kant′ər) *n.* ‖ < *Canterbury gallop*, a riding pace ‖ a moderate gallop —*vi., vt.* to ride at a canter

can·ti·cle (kan′ti kəl) *n.* ‖ < L *cantus*, song ‖ a song or chant, esp. a hymn with words from the Bible

can·ti·le·ver (kant′'l ē′vər, -ev′ər) *n.* ‖ < ? ‖ a bracket or block projecting as a support; esp., a projecting structure anchored at one end to a pier or wall —*vt.* to support by means of cantilevers —**can′ti·le′vered** *adj.*

can·to (kan′tō) *n., pl.* **-tos** ‖ It < L *cantus*, song ‖ any of the main divisions of certain long poems

can·ton (kan′tən, kan tän′) *n.* ‖ Fr < LL *cantus*, corner ‖ any of the states in the Swiss Republic

Can·ton (kan tän′) *old form of* GUANGZHOU

Can·ton·ese (kan′tə nēz′) *n.* 1 *pl.* **-ese′** a native or inhabitant of Canton, China 2 their Chinese dialect —*adj.* of Canton

can·ton·ment (kan tän′mənt, -tōn′-) *n.* ‖ Fr: see CANTON ‖ temporary quarters for troops

can·tor (kant′ər) *n.* ‖ L, singer ‖ a singer of liturgical solos in a synagogue

can·vas (kan′vəs) *n.* ‖ < L *cannabis*, hemp ‖ 1 a coarse cloth of hemp, cotton, etc., used for tents, sails, etc. 2 a sail, tent, etc. 3 an oil painting on canvas

can′vas·back′ *n.* a North American wild duck with a grayish back

can·vass (kan′vəs) *vt., vi.* ‖ < *canvas* < ? use of canvas for sifting ‖ to go through (places) or among (people) asking for votes, opinions, orders, etc. —*n.* a canvassing —**can′vass·er** *n.*

can·yon (kan′yən) *n.* ‖ Sp *cañón*, tube < L *canna*, a reed ‖ a long, narrow valley between high cliffs

cap (kap) *n.* ‖ < LL *cappa*, hooded cloak ‖ 1 any closefitting head covering, visored or brimless 2 a caplike part or thing; cover or top —*vt.* **capped, cap′ping** 1 to put a cap on 2 to cover (the end of) 3 to equal or excel

cap. 1 capacity 2 capital

ca·pa·ble (kā′pə bəl) *adj.* ‖ < L *capere*, to take ‖ having ability; skilled; competent —**capable of** 1 having the qualities necessary for 2 able or ready to —**ca′pa·bil′i·ty** (-bil′ə tē), *pl.* **-ties,** *n.* —**ca′pa·bly** *adv.*

ca·pa·cious (kə pā′shəs) *adj.* ‖ < L *capere*, to take ‖ roomy; spacious —**ca·pa′cious·ly** *adv.* —**ca·pa′cious·ness** *n.*

ca·pac·i·tor (kə pas′ə tər) *n.* a device for storing an electric charge

ca·pac′i·ty (-tē) *n., pl.* **-ties** ‖ < L *capere*, take ‖ 1 the ability to contain, absorb, or receive 2 all that can be contained; volume 3 ability 4 maximum output 5 position; function

ca·par·i·son (kə par′i sən, zən) *n.* ‖ < LL *cappa*, cloak ‖ trappings for a horse —*vt.* to cover (a horse) with trappings

cape¹ (kāp) *n.* ‖ see prec. ‖ a sleeveless garment fastened at the neck and hanging over the back and shoulders

cape² (kāp) *n.* ‖ < L *caput*, head ‖ a piece of land projecting into water

ca·per¹ (kā′pər) *vi.* ‖ ? < Fr *capriole*, a leap ‖ to skip about in a playful manner —*n.* 1 a playful leap 2 a prank —**cut a caper** (or **capers**) 1 to caper 2 to play silly tricks

ca·per² (kā′pər) *n.* ‖ < Gr *kapparis* ‖ the green flower bud of a Mediterranean bush, pickled and used as a seasoning

cape′skin′ *n.* ‖ orig. made from the skin of goats from the *Cape* of Good Hope ‖ fine leather made from sheepskin

Cape Town seaport in South Africa: seat of the legislature: pop. 214,000

Cape Verde (vʉrd) country on a group of islands in the Atlantic, west of Senegal: 1,560 sq. mi.: pop. 318,000

cap·il·lar·y (kap′ə ler′ē) *adj.* ‖ < L *capillus*, hair ‖ very slender —*n., pl.* **-ies** 1 a tube with a very small bore: also **capillary tube** 2 any of the tiny blood vessels connecting the arteries with veins

capillary attraction the action by which liquids in contact with solids, as in a capillary tube, rise or fall Also **capillary action**

cap·i·tal (kap′ət ′l) *adj.* ‖ < L *caput*, head ‖ 1 punishable by death 2 principal; chief 3 of, or being, the seat of government 4 of capital, or wealth 5 excellent —*n.* 1 CAPITAL LETTER 2 a city that is the seat of government of a state or nation 3 money or property owned or used in business 4 [*often* C-] capitalists collectively 5 the top part of a column

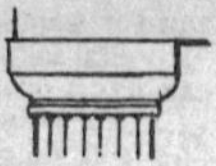

DORIC CAPITAL

capital gain profit resulting from the sale of capital investments, as stocks

cap·i·tal·ism (kap′ət 'l iz′əm) *n.* the economic system in which the means of production and distribution are privately owned and operated for profit

cap′i·tal·ist (-ist) *n.* 1 an owner of wealth used in business 2 an upholder of capitalism 3 a wealthy person —**cap′i·tal·is′tic** (-is′tik) *adj.*

cap′i·tal·ize′ (-īz′) *vt.* **-ized′**, **-iz′ing** 1 to use as or convert into capital 2 to use to one's advantage: used with *on* 3 to supply capital to or for 4 to begin (a word) with a capital letter —**cap′i·tal·i·za′tion** *n.*

capital letter the form of an alphabetical letter used to begin a sentence or proper name, as A, B, C, etc.

cap′i·tal·ly *adv.* very well

capital punishment penalty of death for a crime

Cap·i·tol (kap′ət 'l) ‖ < L *Capitolium*, temple of Jupiter in Rome ‖ the building in which the U.S. Congress meets in Washington, D.C. —*n.* [*usually* c-] the building in which a State legislature meets

ca·pit·u·late (kə pich′yoo lāt′, -pich′ə lāt′) *vi.* **-lat′ed**, **-lat′ing** ‖ < LL *capitulare*, arrange conditions ‖ 1 to give up (*to* an enemy) on prearranged conditions 2 to stop resisting —**ca·pit′u·la′tion** *n.*

cap·let (kap′lit) *n.* a pharmaceutical tablet with a tamper-resistant, capsulelike coating

ca·pon (kā′pän′, -pən) *n.* ‖ < L *capo* ‖ a castrated rooster fattened for eating

cap·puc·ci·no (kä′pə chē′nō, kap′ə-) *n.* ‖ It ‖ espresso coffee mixed with steamed milk and topped with cinnamon, etc.

ca·price (kə prēs′) *n.* ‖ Fr < It ‖ 1 a sudden, impulsive change in thinking or acting 2 a capricious quality

ca·pri·cious (kə prish′əs) *adj.* subject to caprices; erratic —**ca·pri′cious·ly** *adv.* —**ca·pri′cious·ness** *n.*

Cap·ri·corn (kap′ri kôrn′) ‖ < L *caper*, goat + *cornu*, horn ‖ the tenth sign of the zodiac

cap·size (kap′sīz′, kap sīz′) *vt.*, *vi.* **-sized′**, **-siz′ing** ‖ < ? ‖ to overturn or upset: said esp. of a boat

cap·stan (kap′stən) *n.* ‖ < L *capere*, to take ‖ an upright drum, as on ships, around which cables are wound so as to haul them in

cap·sule (kap′səl, -syool′) *n.* ‖ Fr < L *capsa*, box ‖ 1 a soluble gelatin container enclosing a dose of medicine 2 a detachable compartment to hold men, instruments, etc. in a rocket: in full **space capsule** 3 *Bot.* a seedcase —*adj.* in a concise form —**cap′su·lar** *adj.*

cap′sul·ize′ (-īz′) *vt.* **-ized′**, **-iz′ing** 1 to enclose in a capsule 2 to condense

Capt. Captain

cap·tain (kap′tən) *n.* ‖ < L *caput*, head ‖ 1 a chief; leader 2 *U.S. Mil.* an officer ranking just above first lieutenant 3 *U.S. Navy* an officer ranking just above commander 4 *a*) the master of a ship *b*) the pilot of an airplane 5 the leader of a team, as in sports —*vt.* to be captain of —**cap′tain·cy**, *pl.* **-cies**, *n.*

cap·tion (kap′shən) *n.* ‖ < L *capere*, take ‖ 1 a heading or title, as of a newspaper article or illustration 2 *Film, TV* a subtitle —*vt.* to supply a caption for

cap′tious (-shəs) *adj.* ‖ see prec. ‖ 1 made for the sake of argument, as a remark 2 quick to find fault —**cap′tious·ly** *adv.* —**cap′tious·ness** *n.*

cap·ti·vate (kap′tə vāt′) *vt.* **-vat′ed**, **-vat′ing** to capture the attention or affection of —**cap′ti·va′tion** *n.*

cap·tive (kap′tiv) *n.* ‖ < L *capere*, to take ‖ a prisoner —*adj.* 1 taken or held prisoner 2 obliged to listen —**cap·tiv′i·ty**, *pl.* **-ties**, *n.*

cap′tor (-tər) *n.* one who captures

cap′ture (-chər) *vt.* **-tured**, **-tur·ing** ‖ < L *capere*, to take ‖ 1 to take or seize by force, surprise, etc. 2 to represent in a more permanent form [to *capture* her charm on canvas] —*n.* a capturing or being captured

car (kär) *n.* ‖ < L *carrus*, chariot ‖ 1 any vehicle on wheels 2 a vehicle that moves on rails, as a streetcar 3 an automobile 4 an elevator cage

Ca·ra·cas (kə räk′əs, -rak′-) capital of Venezuela: pop. 1,163,000

car·a·cul (kar′ə kul′, -kəl) *n.* KARAKUL (esp. sense 2)

ca·rafe (kə raf′, -räf′) *n.* ‖ Fr ‖ a glass bottle for wine, water, or coffee

car·a·mel (kär′məl, kar′ə məl) *n.* ‖ Fr ‖ 1 burnt sugar used to color or flavor food 2 a chewy candy made from sugar, milk, etc.

car′a·mel·ize′ (-mə līz′) *vt.*, *vi.* **-ized′**, **-iz′ing** to turn into caramel

car·a·pace (kar′ə pās′) *n.* ‖ Fr < Sp ‖ an upper shell, as of the turtle

car·at (kar′ət) *n.* ‖ Fr < Gr *keration*, little horn ‖ 1 a unit of weight for precious stones, equal to 200 milligrams 2 KARAT

car·a·van (kar′ə van′) *n.* ‖ < Pers *kārwān* ‖ 1 a company of people traveling together for safety, as through a desert 2 VAN²

car·a·van·sa·ry (kar′ə van′sə rē) *n.*, *pl.* **-ries** ‖ < Pers *kārwān*, caravan + *sarāī*, palace ‖ in the Orient, an inn for caravans

car·a·way (kar′ə wā′) *n.* ‖ < Ar *al-karawiyā′* ‖ the spicy seeds of a plant, used to flavor bread, etc.

car·bide (kär′bīd′) *n.* a compound of a metal, with carbon

car·bine (kär′bīn′, -bēn′) *n.* ‖ < Fr *scarabée*, beetle ‖ 1 a short-barreled rifle 2 a light, semiautomatic or automatic rifle of relatively limited range

carbo- *combining form* carbon Also **carb-**

car·bo·hy·drate (kär′bō hī′drāt, -bə-) *n.* ‖ prec. + HYDRATE ‖ an organic compound composed of carbon, hydrogen, and oxygen, as a sugar or starch

car·bol·ic acid (kär bäl′ik) PHENOL

car·bon (kär′bən) *n.* ‖ < L *carbo*, coal ‖ 1 a nonmetallic chemical element found esp. in all organic compounds: diamond and graphite are pure carbon: a radioactive isotope of carbon (**carbon-14**) is used in dating fossils, etc. **2** CARBON PAPER **3** a copy made with carbon paper: in full **carbon copy** —***adj.*** of or like carbon

car'bon·ate (-bə nit; *also, and for v. always,* -nāt') ***n.*** a salt or ester of carbonic acid —***vt.*** **-at'ed, -at'ing** to charge with carbon dioxide —**car'bon·a'tion** ***n.***

carbon black carbon produced by the incomplete burning of oil or gas

car'bon-date' ***vt.*** **-dat'ed, -dat'ing** to establish the approximate age of (fossils, etc.) by measuring the amount of carbon-14 in them

carbon di·ox·ide (dī äks'īd') a heavy, colorless, odorless gas: it passes out of the lungs in respiration

car·bon·ic acid (kär bän'ik) a weak acid formed by carbon dioxide in water

car·bon·if·er·ous (kär'bə nif'ər əs) ***adj.*** containing carbon or coal

carbon mon·ox·ide (mə näks'īd') a colorless, odorless, highly poisonous gas

carbon paper thin paper coated on one side, as with a carbon preparation, used to make copies of letters, etc.

carbon tet·ra·chlo·ride (te'trə klôr'īd') a nonflammable liquid, used as a solvent for fats and oils, etc.

Car·bo·run·dum (kär'bə run'dəm) ⟦ CAR-B(ON) + (C)*orundum* ⟧ *trademark for* a hard abrasive, esp. of carbon and silicon —***n.*** [**c-**] such a substance

car·boy (kär'boi') ***n.*** ⟦ < Pers *qarābah* ⟧ a large bottle to hold corrosive liquids, enclosed in a protective container

car·bun·cle (kär'buŋ'kəl) ***n.*** ⟦ < L dim. of *carbo,* coal ⟧ a painful, pus-bearing inflammation of the tissue beneath the skin —**car·bun'cu·lar** (-kyoo lər) ***adj.***

car·bu·ret·or (kär'bə rāt'ər) ***n.*** a device for mixing air with gasoline spray to make an explosive mixture in an internal-combustion engine

car·cass (kär'kəs) ***n.*** ⟦ < Fr *carcasse* ⟧ **1** the dead body of an animal **2** a framework or shell

car·cin·o·gen (kär sin'ə jən) ***n.*** ⟦ < fol. + -GEN ⟧ any substance that produces cancer —**car·ci·no·gen·ic** (kär'sə nō jen'ik) ***adj.***

car·ci·no·ma (kär'sə nō'mə) ***n., pl.*** **-mas** or **-ma·ta** (-mə tə) ⟦ L < Gr *karkinos,* crab ⟧ any of several kinds of epithelial cancer

car coat a short overcoat

card[1] (kärd) ***n.*** ⟦ < Gr *chartēs,* layer of papyrus ⟧ **1** a flat, stiff piece of paper or pasteboard; specif., *a)* any of a pack of playing cards *b)* a card identifying a person, esp. as a member, agent, etc. *c)* a post card *d)* a card bearing a greeting *e)* any of a series of cards on which information is recorded **2** an attraction [*drawing card*] **3** [Colloq.] a witty or clowning person —**put** (or **lay**) **one's cards on the table** to reveal something frankly

card[2] (kärd) ***n.*** ⟦ < L *carrere,* to card ⟧ a metal comb or a machine with wire teeth for combing fibers of wool, cotton, etc. —***vt.*** to use a card on

card'board' ***n.*** stiff, thick paper or pasteboard, for cards, boxes, etc.

car·di·ac (kär'dē ak') ***adj.*** ⟦ < Gr *kardia,* heart ⟧ of or near the heart

cardiac arrest the complete failure of the heart to pump blood

car·di·gan (kär'di gən) ***n.*** ⟦ after 7th Earl of *Cardigan* ⟧ a sweater or jacket that opens down the front

car·di·nal (kärd''n əl) ***adj.*** ⟦ < L *cardo,* pivot ⟧ **1** principal; chief **2** bright-red —***n.*** **1** an official appointed by the pope to his council **2** bright red **3** a bright-red American songbird **4** CARDINAL NUMBER

cardinal number any number used in counting or in showing how many (e.g., two, forty, 627, etc.)

cardio- ⟦ < Gr *kardia,* heart ⟧ *combining form* of the heart

car·di·o·gram (kär'dē ō gram', -dē ə-) ***n.*** ELECTROCARDIOGRAM —**car'di·o·graph'** (-graf') ***n.***

car'di·ol'o·gy (-äl'ə jē) ***n.*** the branch of medicine dealing with the heart —**car'di·ol'o·gist** ***n.***

car·di·o·pul·mo·nar·y (kär'dē ō pool' mə ner'ē) ***adj.*** of or involving the heart and lungs

car'di·o·vas'cu·lar (-vas'kyoo lər) ***adj.*** of the heart and the blood vessels as a unified body system

cards (kärds) ***n.pl.*** any game played with a deck of playing cards, as poker

card'sharp' ***n.*** [Colloq.] a professional cheater at cards Also **card shark**

care (ker) ***n.*** ⟦ < OE *caru,* sorrow ⟧ **1** *a)* a troubled state of mind; worry *b)* a cause of such a mental state **2** close attention; heed **3** a liking or regard (*for*) **4** charge; protection **5** a responsibility —***vi.*** **cared, car'ing** **1** to feel concern **2** to feel love or a liking (*for*) **3** to look after; provide (*for*) **4** to wish (*for*); want —***vt.*** **1** to feel concern about or interest in **2** to wish —**care of** at the address of —**take care of** **1** to attend to **2** to provide for

ca·reen (kə rēn') ***vt., vi.*** ⟦ < L *carina,* keel ⟧ to lean or cause to lean sideways; tip; tilt; lurch

ca·reer (kə rir') ***n.*** ⟦ < L *carrus,* car ⟧ **1** a swift course **2** one's progress through life **3** a profession or occupation —***vi.*** to rush wildly

care'free' ***adj.*** without care

care'ful ***adj.*** **1** cautious; wary **2** accurate; thorough; painstaking —**care'ful·ly** ***adv.*** —**care'ful·ness** ***n.***

care'less ***adj.*** **1** carefree; untroubled **2** not paying enough heed; neglectful **3** done or made without enough attention, precision, etc. —**care'less·ly** ***adv.*** —**care'less·ness** ***n.***

ca·ress (kə res') ***vt.*** ⟦ ult. < L *carus,* dear ⟧ to touch lovingly or gently —***n.*** an affectionate touch, kiss, etc.

car·et (kar'it, ker'-) ***n.*** ⟦ L, there is lacking ⟧ a mark (∧) used to show where something is to be inserted in a written or printed line

care'tak'er ***n.*** **1** a person hired to take care of something or someone **2** one acting as temporary replacement

care'worn' ***adj.*** worn out by troubles and worry; haggard

car·fare (kär'fer') ***n.*** the price of a ride on a subway, bus, etc.

car·go (kär′gō) ***n.***, *pl.* **-goes** or **-gos** ‖ < Sp *cargar*, to load ‖ the load carried by a ship, truck, etc.; freight

car′hop′ ***n.*** ‖ CAR + (BELL)HOP ‖ one who serves food at a drive-in restaurant

Car·ib·be·an (Sea) (kar′ə bē′ən, kə rib′ē ən) part of the Atlantic, bounded by the West Indies, Central America, and N South America

car·i·bou (kar′ə bo͞o′) ***n.*** ‖ CdnFr ‖ a large North American reindeer

car·i·ca·ture (kar′i kə chər) ***n.*** ‖ Fr < It *caricare*, exaggerate ‖ **1** the exaggerated imitation of a person, literary style, etc. for satirical effect **2** a picture, etc. in which this is done —***vt.*** **-tured, -tur·ing** to depict as in a caricature —**car′i·ca·tur·ist** ***n.***

car·i·es (ker′ēz′) ***n.*** ‖ L, decay ‖ decay of bones or, esp., of teeth

car·il·lon (kar′ə län′) ***n.*** ‖ Fr, chime of four bells < L *quattuor*, four ‖ a set of bells tuned to the chromatic scale

ca·ri·tas (kär′ē täs′) ***n.*** love for all people

car·mine (kär′min, -mīn′) ***n.*** ‖ ult. < Ar *qirmiz*, crimson ‖ a red or purplish-red color —***adj.*** red or purplish-red

car·nage (kär′nij) ***n.*** ‖ Fr < L *caro*, flesh ‖ extensive slaughter; massacre

car′nal (-nəl) ***adj.*** ‖ < L *caro*, flesh ‖ **1** of the flesh; material; worldly **2** sensual or sexual —**car·nal′i·ty** (-nal′i tē), *pl.* **-ties, *n.*** —**car′nal·ly** ***adv.***

car·na·tion (kär nā′shən) ***n.*** ‖ < L *caro*, flesh ‖ **1** a plant of the pink family, widely cultivated for its white, pink, or red flowers **2** its flower

car·nel·ian (kär nēl′yən) ***n.*** ‖ < L *carnis*, of flesh (color) ‖ a red variety of chalcedony, used in jewelry

car·ni·val (kär′nə vəl) ***n.*** ‖ < Fr *carnaval* (or It *carnevale*) ‖ **1** the period of feasting and revelry just before Lent **2** a reveling; festivity **3** an entertainment with sideshows, rides, etc.

car·ni·vore (kär′nə vôr′) ***n.*** a carnivorous animal or plant

car·niv·o·rous (kär niv′ə rəs) ***adj.*** ‖ < L *caro*, flesh + *vorare*, to devour ‖ **1** flesh-eating **2** of the carnivores —**car·niv′o·rous·ness** ***n.***

car·ol (kar′əl) ***n.*** ‖ < OFr *carole*, kind of dance ‖ a song of joy or praise; esp., a Christmas song —***vi., vt.*** **-oled** or **-olled, -ol·ing** or **-ol·ling** to sing; warble —**car′ol·er** or **car′ol·ler** ***n.***

car·om (kar′əm) ***n.*** ‖ < Sp *carambola* ‖ **1** *Billiards* a shot in which the cue ball successively hits two balls **2** a hitting and rebounding —***vi.*** **1** to make a carom **2** to hit and rebound

ca·rot·id (kə rät′id) ***adj.*** ‖ Gr *karōtis* ‖ designating or of either of the two main arteries, one on each side of the neck, which convey blood to the head —***n.*** a carotid artery

ca·rous·al (kə rou′zəl) ***n.*** a carouse

ca·rouse (kə rouz′) ***vi.*** **-roused′, -rous′ing** ‖ < Ger *gar austrinken*, to drink ‖ to engage in a noisy drinking party —***n.*** a noisy drinking party

car·ou·sel (kar′ə sel′, zel′) ***n.*** ‖ Fr < It dial. (Naples) *carusiello*, kind of tournament ‖ a merry-go-round

carp[1] (kärp) ***n.***, *pl.* **carp** or **carps** ‖ < VL *carpa* ‖ an edible freshwater fish widely cultivated for food

carp[2] (kärp) ***vi.*** ‖ < ON *karpa*, to brag ‖ to find fault in a petty or nagging way —**carp′er** ***n.***

car·pal (kär′pəl) ***adj.*** of the carpus —***n.*** a bone of the carpus

car·pel (kär′pəl) ***n.*** ‖ < Gr *karpos*, fruit ‖ a simple pistil, regarded as a modified leaflike structure

car·pen·ter (kär′pən tər) ***n.*** ‖ < L *carpentum*, a cart ‖ one who builds and repairs wooden things, esp. buildings, ships, etc. —***vi.*** to do a carpenter's work —**car′pen·try** (-trē) ***n.***

carpenter ant any of the large, black ants that build nests by gnawing the wood in buildings, tree trunks, etc.

car·pet (kär′pət) ***n.*** ‖ < L *carpere*, to card ‖ **1** a heavy fabric for covering a floor **2** anything that covers like a carpet —***vt.*** to cover as with a carpet —**on the carpet** being reprimanded

car′pet·bag′ ***n.*** an old-fashioned traveling bag, made of carpeting —***vi.*** **-bagged′, -bag′ging** to act as a carpetbagger

car′pet·bag′ger ***n.*** a Northerner who went South to profit from unsettled conditions after the Civil War

car′pet·ing ***n.*** carpets or carpet fabric

car pool a plan by a group to rotate the use of their cars, as for going to work

car·port (kär′pôrt′) ***n.*** an automobile shelter built as a roof at the side of a building

car·pus (kär′pəs) ***n.***, *pl.* **-pi′** (-pī′) ‖ < Gr *karpos*, wrist ‖ *Anat.* the wrist, or the wrist bones

car·rel or **car′rell** (kar′əl) ***n.*** ‖ < ML *carula* ‖ a small enclosure in a library, for privacy in studying or reading

car·riage (kar′ij; *for 2, usually* kar′ē ij′) ***n.*** ‖ ult. < L *carrus*, chariot ‖ **1** a carrying; transportation **2** the manner of carrying oneself; bearing **3** *a)* a four-wheeled, horse-drawn passenger vehicle *b)* a baby carriage **4** a moving part, as on a typewriter, that supports and shifts something

car·ri·er (kar′ē ər) ***n.*** **1** one that carries **2** one in the business of transporting **3** one that transmits disease germs **4** AIRCRAFT CARRIER

carrier pigeon *old name of* HOMING PIGEON

car·ri·on (kar′ē ən) ***n.*** ‖ < L *caro*, flesh ‖ the decaying flesh of a dead body

Car·roll (kar′əl), **Lew·is** (lo͞o′is) (pseud. of *C. L. Dodgson*) 1832-98; Eng. writer

car·rot (kar′ət) ***n.*** ‖ < Gr *karōton* ‖ **1** a plant with an edible, fleshy, orange-red root **2** the root

car·rou·sel (kar′ə sel′, -zel′) ***n.*** *alt. sp. of* CAROUSEL

car·ry (kar′ē) ***vt.*** **-ried, -ry·ing** ‖ < L *carrus*, chariot ‖ **1** to hold or support **2** to take from one place to another **3** to lead or impel **4** to transmit /air *carries* sounds/ **5** to transfer or extend **6** to involve; imply /to *carry* a guarantee/ **7** to bear (oneself) in a specified way **8** *a)* to gain support for *b)* to win (an election, argument, etc.) **9** *a)* to keep in stock *b)* to keep on one's account books, etc. —***vi.*** **1** to act as a bearer, conductor, etc. 2 to cover a range, as a voice —*n.*, *pl.* **car′ries** 1 the distance covered by a gun, ball, etc. 2 a portage —**be** (or **get**) **carried away** to become very emotional or enthusiastic —**carry on** 1 to engage in 2 to go on (*with*) 3 [Colloq.] to behave wildly or childishly —**carry out** (or **through**) 1 to put (plans, etc.) into practice 2 to accomplish —**carry over** to postpone; continue

carrying charge interest paid on the balance owed in installment buying

car′ry-on′ *adj.* small enough to fit under an airplane seat or in an overhead compartment —*n.* a piece of carry-on luggage

car′ry-out′ *adj.* designating or of prepared food sold as by a restaurant to be consumed elsewhere

car′ry-o′ver *n.* something carried over, as a remainder of crops or goods

car seat a seat in an automobile; specif., a portable automobile seat used for securing a small child

car′sick′ *adj.* nauseated from riding in an automobile, bus, etc.

Car·son City (kär′sən) capital of Nev., in the W part: pop. 32,000

cart (kärt) *n.* ‖ < ON *kartr* ‖ a small wagon —*vt.*, *vi.* to carry in a cart, truck, etc.; transport

cart·age (kärt′ij) *n.* 1 the work of carting 2 the charge for this

carte blanche (kärt′ blänsh′) ‖ Fr, lit., white card ‖ full authority

car·tel (kär tel′) *n.* ‖ < Ger < Fr ‖ an association of businesses in an international monopoly; trust

Car·ter (kärt′ər), **Jim·my** (jim′ē) (legal name *James Earl Carter, Jr.*) 1924- ; 39th president of the U.S. (1977-81)

car·ti·lage (kärt′'l ij′) *n.* ‖ < L *cartilago* ‖ a tough, elastic tissue forming parts of the skeleton; gristle —**car′ti·lag′i·nous** (-aj′ə nəs) *adj.*

car·tog·ra·phy (kär täg′rə fē′) *n.* ‖ see CARD[1] & -GRAPHY ‖ the art of making maps or charts —**car·tog′ra·pher** *n.*

car·ton (kärt′'n) *n.* ‖ Fr < It *carta*, card ‖ a cardboard box or container

car·toon (kär to͞on′) *n.* ‖ < Fr: see prec. ‖ 1 a drawing caricaturing a person or event 2 *a*) COMIC STRIP *b*) ANIMATED CARTOON —*vt.*, *vi.* to draw a cartoon (of) —**car·toon′ist** *n.*

car·tridge (kär′trij) *n.* ‖ < Fr < It *carta*, card ‖ 1 a cylindrical case of cardboard, metal, etc. containing the charge and primer, and usually the projectile, for a firearm 2 a small container, as for camera film, a phonograph needle, etc.

cart′wheel′ *n.* 1 a handspring performed sideways 2 [Slang] a large coin

carve (kärv) *vt.* **carved**, **carv′ing** ‖ OE *ceorfan* ‖ 1 to make or shape by or as by cutting 2 to decorate the surface of with cut designs 3 to divide by cutting; slice —*vi.* 1 to carve statues or designs 2 to carve meat —**carv′er** *n.* —**carv′ing** *n.*

car′wash′ *n.* an establishment at which automobiles are washed

car·y·at·id (kar′ē at′id) *n.*, *pl.* **-ids** (-idz) or **-i·des′** (-ə dēz′) ‖ < Gr *karyatides*, priestesses at Karyai, in ancient Greece ‖ a supporting column having the form of a draped female figure

ca·sa·ba (kə sä′bə) *n.* ‖ after *Kasaba*, town in Asia Minor ‖ a kind of cultivated melon with a hard, yellow rind

Ca·sa·blan·ca (kas′ə blaŋ′kə, kä′sə bläŋ′kə) seaport in NW Morocco: pop. 2,158,000

Ca·sa·no·va (kaz′ə nō′və, kas′ə-) *n.* ‖ after G. *Casanova* (1725-98), It adventurer ‖ a man who has many love affairs

cas·cade (kas kād′) *n.* ‖ Fr < L *cadere*, to fall ‖ 1 a small, steep waterfall 2 a shower, as of sparks, etc. —*vt.*, *vi.* **-cad′ed**, **-cad′ing** to fall or drop in a cascade

cas·car·a (kas ker′ə) *n.* ‖ Sp *cáscara*, bark ‖ a thorny tree growing on the Pacific coast of the U.S.

case[1] (kās) *n.* ‖ < L *casus*, a chance < *cadere*, to fall ‖ 1 an example or instance /a *case* of flu/ 2 a person being helped, as by a doctor 3 any matter requiring study 4 a statement of the facts, as in a law court 5 convincing arguments /he has no *case*/ 6 a lawsuit 7 *a*) a relation shown, as in Latin, by inflection of nouns, etc. *b*) the form a word takes to show this *c*) loosely, as in English, such a relation, with or without inflection —*vt.* **cased**, **cas′ing** [Slang] to look over carefully —**in any case** anyhow —**in case** in the event that; if —**in case of** in the event of —**in no case** by no means

case[2] (kās) *n.* ‖ < L *capsa*, box ‖ 1 a container, as a box 2 a protective cover /a watch *case*/ 3 a full box or its contents /a *case* of beer/ 4 a frame, as for a window —*vt.* **cased**, **cas′ing** 1 to put in a container 2 to enclose

case′hard′en (-härd′'n) *vt.* *Metallurgy* to form a hard surface on (an iron alloy)

ca·se·in (kā′sē in, -sēn′) *n.* ‖ < L *caseus*, cheese ‖ a protein that is one of the chief constituents of milk

case′load′ *n.* the number of cases handled by a court, social agency, etc.

case·ment (kās′mənt) *n.* ‖ ult. < OFr *enchassement* ‖ a window frame that opens on hinges along the side

case′work′ *n.* social work in which guidance is given in cases of personal or family maladjustment —**case′work′er** *n.*

cash (kash) *n.* ‖ < L *capsa*, box ‖ 1 money that a person actually has; esp., ready money 2 money, a check, etc. paid at the time of purchase —*vt.* to give or get cash for —*adj.* of or for cash —**cash in** to exchange for cash

cash·ew (kash′o͞o; *also*, kə sho͞o′) *n.* ‖ < AmInd (Brazil) *acajú* ‖ 1 a tropical tree bearing kidney-shaped nuts 2 the nut

cash·ier[1] (ka shir′) *n.* ‖ Fr ‖ a person in charge of the cash transactions of a bank or store

cash·ier[2] (ka shir′) *vt.* ‖ < LL *cassare*, destroy ‖ to dismiss in dishonor

cash·mere (kash′mir′, kazh′-) *n.* ‖ after *Kashmir*, region in India ‖ 1 a fine carded wool from goats of N India and Tibet 2 a soft, twilled cloth as of this wool

cash register a device, usually with a money drawer, used for registering visibly the amount of a sale

cas·ing (kās′iŋ) *n.* 1 skin of a sausage 2 the

outer covering of a pneumatic tire **3** a frame, as for a door

ca·si·no (kə sē′nō) ***n.***, *pl.* **-nos** ‖ It < *casa*, house ‖ **1** a room or building for dancing, gambling, etc. **2** a card game for two to four players

cask (kask) ***n.*** ‖ ult. < L *quassare*, shatter ‖ **1** a barrel of any size, esp. one for liquids **2** its contents

cas·ket (kas′kit) ***n.*** ‖ < NormFr *casse*, box ‖ **1** a small box or chest, as for valuables **2** a coffin

Cas·pi·an Sea (kas′pē ən) inland salt sea between Asia and extreme SE Europe

Cas·san·dra (kə san′drə) *Gr. Myth.* a Trojan prophetess of doom whose prophecies are never believed

cas·sa·va (kə sä′və) ***n.*** ‖ < Fr < WInd *casávi* ‖ **1** a tropical American plant with starchy roots **2** a starch made from these roots, used in tapioca

cas·se·role (kas′ə rōl′) ***n.*** ‖ Fr < Gr *kyathos*, a bowl ‖ **1** a baking dish in which food can be cooked and served **2** food baked in such a dish

cas·sette (kə set′; *also*, ka-) ***n.*** ‖ < NormFr *casse*, box ‖ a case with magnetic tape or film in it, for loading a tape recorder, VCR, camera, etc. quickly

cas·si·a (kash′ə, kas′ē ə) ***n.*** ‖ ult. < Heb *qeṣī′āh*, lit., something scraped off ‖ **1** *a)* the bark of a tree of SE Asia: used as the source of cinnamon *b)* the tree **2** any of various tropical plants whose leaves yield senna

cas·si·no (kə sē′nō) ***n.*** CASINO

cas·sock (kas′ək) ***n.*** ‖ prob. < Turk *qazaq*, nomad ‖ a long, closefitting vestment worn by clergymen, etc.

cast (kast) ***vt.*** **cast, cast′ing** ‖ < ON *kasta* ‖ **1** to throw with force; hurl **2** to deposit (a ballot or vote) **3** to direct /to *cast* one's eyes/ **4** to project /to *cast* light/ **5** to throw off or shed (a skin) **6** to shape (molten metal, etc.) by pouring into a mold **7** to select (an actor) for (a role or play) —***vi.*** to throw —***n.*** **1** a casting; throw **2** something formed in a mold **3** a plaster form for immobilizing a limb **4** the set of actors in a play or movie **5** an appearance, as of features **6** a kind; quality **7** a tinge; shade —**cast about** to look (*for*) —**cast aside** (or **away**) to discard —**cast off** **1** to discard **2** to free a ship from a dock, etc. —**cast up** **1** to turn upward **2** to add up

cas·ta·nets (kas′tə nets′) ***n.pl.*** ‖ < Sp < L *castanea*, chestnut: from the shape ‖ a pair of small, hollowed pieces of hard wood or ivory, clicked together in the hand in time to music

CASTANETS

cast′a·way′ ***n.*** **1** a person or thing cast off **2** a shipwrecked person —***adj.*** **1** discarded **2** shipwrecked

caste (kast) ***n.*** ‖ Fr < L *castus*, pure ‖ **1** any of the hereditary Hindu social classes of a formerly segregated system of India **2** any exclusive group **3** rigid class distinction based on birth, wealth, etc. —**lose caste** to lose social status

cast′er ***n.*** **1** a container for vinegar, oil, etc. at the table **2** any of a set of small wheels for supporting and moving furniture

cas·ti·gate (kas′ti gāt′) ***vt.*** **-gat′ed, -gat′ing** ‖ < L *castigare* ‖ to rebuke severely, esp. by public criticism —**cas′ti·ga′tion** ***n.*** —**cas′ti·ga′tor** ***n.***

cast′ing ***n.*** a thing, esp. of metal, cast in a mold

cast iron a hard, brittle alloy of iron made by casting —**cast′-i′ron** ***adj.***

cas·tle (kas′əl) ***n.*** ‖ < L *castrum*, fort ‖ **1** a large, fortified building or group of buildings **2** any massive dwelling like this **3** *Chess* ROOK[2]

cast′off′ ***adj.*** discarded; abandoned —***n.*** a person or thing cast off

cas·tor-oil plant (kas′tər oil′) a tropical plant with large seeds which yield an oil (**castor oil**) used as a cathartic

cas·trate (kas′trāt′) ***vt.*** **-trat′ed, -trat′ing** ‖ < L *castrare* ‖ to remove the testicles of; emasculate —**cas·tra′tion** ***n.***

cas·u·al (kazh′o͞o əl) ***adj.*** ‖ < L *casus*, chance ‖ **1** happening by chance; not planned; incidental **2** occasional **3** careless or cursory **4** nonchalant **5** for informal use —**cas′u·al·ly** ***adv.*** —**cas′u·al·ness** ***n.***

cas·u·al·ty (kazh′o͞o əl tē) ***n.***, *pl.* **-ties** **1** an accident, esp. a fatal one **2** a member of the armed forces killed, wounded, captured, etc. **3** anyone hurt or killed in an accident

cas·u·ist·ry (kazh′o͞o is trē) ***n.***, *pl.* **-ries** ‖ < L *casus*, CASE[1] ‖ subtle but false reasoning, esp. about moral issues; sophistry —**cas′u·ist** ***n.***

cat (kat) ***n.*** ‖ OE ‖ **1** a small, soft-furred animal, often kept as a pet or for killing mice **2** any flesh-eating mammal related to this, as the lion, tiger, leopard, etc. **3** a spiteful woman —**let the cat out of the bag** to let a secret be found out

cat·a·clysm (kat′ə kliz′əm) ***n.*** ‖ < Gr *kata-*, down + *klyzein*, to wash ‖ any sudden, violent change, as in war —**cat′a·clys′mic** (-kliz′mik) ***adj.***

cat·a·comb (kat′ə kōm′) ***n.*** ‖ < ? L *cata*, by + *tumba*, tomb ‖ a gallery in an underground burial place

cat′a·falque′ (-falk′, -fôlk′) ***n.*** ‖ Fr < It *catafalco*, funeral canopy ‖ a wooden framework on which a body in a coffin lies in state

cat′a·lep′sy (-lep′sē) ***n.*** ‖ < Gr *katalēpsis*, a seizing ‖ a condition of muscle rigidity and sudden, temporary loss of consciousness and feeling, as in epilepsy —**cat′a·lep′tic** ***adj., n.***

cat·a·log or **cat·a·logue** (kat′ə lôg′) ***n.*** ‖ < Gr *kata-*, down + *legein*, to count ‖ a complete list, as an alphabetical card file of the books in a library, a list of articles for sale, etc. —***vt., vi.*** **-loged′** or **-logued′**, **-log′ing** or **-logu′ing** to arrange in a catalog —**cat′a·log′er** or **cat′a·logu′er** ***n.***

ca·tal·pa (kə tal′pə) ***n.*** ‖ < AmInd ‖ a tree with large, heart-shaped leaves and slender, beanlike pods

ca·tal·y·sis (kə tal′ə sis) ***n.***, *pl.* **-ses′** (-sēz′) ‖ < Gr *katalysis*, dissolution ‖ the speeding up or, sometimes, slowing down of a chemical reaction by adding a substance which itself is not changed thereby

cat·a·lyst (kat′ə list′) ***n.*** a substance serving

as the agent in catalysis —**cat'a·lyt'ic** (-lit' ik) ***adj.***

catalytic converter a chemical filter connected to the exhaust system of an automotive vehicle, so as to reduce air pollution

cat·a·ma·ran (kat'ə mə ran') ***n.*** ‖Tamil *kaṭṭumaram*‖ **1** a narrow log raft propelled by sails or paddles **2** a boat like this with two parallel hulls

cat·a·pult (kat'ə pult') ***n.*** ‖< Gr *kata-*, down + *pallein*, to hurl‖ **1** an ancient military contrivance for throwing stones, etc. **2** a device for launching an airplane, missile, etc. as from a deck or ramp —***vt.*** to shoot as from a catapult —***vi.*** to leap

cat·a·ract (kat'ə rakt') ***n.*** ‖< Gr *kata-*, down + *rhassein*, to strike or ? *arassein*, to smite‖ **1** a large waterfall **2** an eye disease in which the lens becomes opaque, causing partial or total blindness

ca·tas·tro·phe (kə tas'trə fē) ***n.*** ‖< Gr *kata-*, down + *strephein*, to turn‖ any great and sudden disaster —**cat·a·stroph·ic** (kat'ə sträf'ik) ***adj.***

cat·a·to·ni·a (kat'ə tō'nē ə) ***n.*** ‖< Gr *kata-*, down + *tonos*, tension‖ a syndrome, esp. of schizophrenia, marked by stupor or catalepsy —**cat'a·ton'ic** (-tän'ik) ***adj., n.***

cat'bird' ***n.*** a slate-gray North American songbird with a call like a cat's

cat'boat' ***n.*** a sailboat with a single sail and mast set well forward

cat'call' ***n.*** a shrill shout or whistle expressing derision, etc. —***vt., vi.*** to make catcalls (at)

catch (kach; *often*, kech) ***vt.*** **caught, catch'ing** ‖< L *capere*, to take hold‖ **1** to seize and hold; capture **2** to take by a trap **3** to deceive **4** to surprise **5** to get to in time /to *catch* a train/ **6** to lay hold of; grab /to *catch* a ball/ **7** to become infected with /he *caught* a cold/ **8** to understand **9** to get entangled **10** [Colloq.] to see, hear, etc. —***vi.*** **1** to become held, fastened, etc. **2** to take hold, as fire **3** to keep hold, as a lock —***n.*** **1** a catching **2** a thing that catches **3** something caught **4** one worth catching as a spouse **5** a snatch or fragment **6** a break in the voice **7** [Colloq.] a tricky qualification or condition —**catch at** to seize desperately —**catch on 1** to understand **2** to become popular —**catch up 1** to seize; snatch **2** to overtake

catch'all' (-ôl') ***n.*** a container or place for holding all sorts of things

catch'er ***n.*** *Baseball* the player behind home plate, who catches pitched balls

catch'ing ***adj.*** **1** contagious; infectious **2** attractive

catch'y ***adj.*** **-i·er, -i·est 1** easily caught up and remembered **2** tricky

cat·e·chism (kat'ə kiz'əm) ***n.*** ‖< Gr *kata-*, thoroughly + *ēchein*, to sound‖ **1** a handbook of questions and answers for teaching the principles of a religion **2** a close questioning

cat'e·chize' (-kīz') ***vt.*** **-chized', -chiz'ing** ‖see prec.‖ to question searchingly Also sp. **cat'e·chise'**

cat·e·gor·i·cal (kat'ə gôr'i kəl) ***adj.*** **1** positive; explicit: said of a statement, etc. **2** of, as, or in a category —**cat'e·gor'i·cal·ly** ***adv.***

cat·e·go·rize (kat'ə gə rīz') ***vt.*** **-rized', -riz'ing** to place in a category; classify

cat'e·go'ry (-gôr'ē) ***n., pl.*** **-ries** ‖< Gr *katēgorein*, to assert‖ a division in a scheme of classification

ca·ter (kāt'ər) ***vi.*** ‖< L *ad-*, to + *capere*, take hold‖ **1** to provide food and service, as for parties **2** to seek to gratify another's desires: with *to* —**ca'ter·er** ***n.***

cat·er·cor·nered (kat'ə kôr'nərd, kat'ē-) ***adj.*** ‖< OFr *catre*, four + CORNERED‖ diagonal —***adv.*** diagonally Also **cat'er-cor'ner**

cat·er·pil·lar (kat'ər pil'ər, kat'ə-) ***n.*** ‖< L *catta pilosus*, hairy cat‖ the wormlike larva of a butterfly, moth, etc.

cat·er·waul (kat'ər wôl') ***vi.*** ‖prob. echoic‖ to make a shrill sound like that of a cat; wail —***n.*** such a sound

cat'fish' ***n., pl.*** **-fish'** or (for different species) **-fish'es** a scaleless fish with long, whiskerlike feelers about the mouth

cat'gut' ***n.*** a tough thread made from dried intestines, as of sheep, and used for surgical sutures, etc.

ca·thar·sis (kə thär'sis) ***n.*** ‖< Gr *katharos*, pure‖ **1** a purging, esp. of the bowels **2** a relieving of the emotions, as through the arts or psychotherapy

ca·thar'tic ***adj.*** of catharsis; purging —***n.*** a medicine for purging the bowels; purgative

ca·the·dral (kə thē'drəl) ***n.*** ‖< Gr *kata-*, down + *hedra*, a seat‖ **1** the main church of a bishop's see **2** any large, imposing church

cath·e·ter (kath'ət ər) ***n.*** ‖< Gr *kata-*, down + *hienai*, to send‖ a slender tube inserted into a body passage, as into the bladder for drawing off urine —**cath'e·ter·ize'** (-īz'), **-ized', -iz'ing, *vt.***

cath·ode (kath'ōd') ***n.*** ‖< Gr < *kata-*, down + -ODE‖ **1** the negative electrode in an electrolytic cell **2** the electron emitter in a vacuum tube **3** the positive terminal of a battery

cathode rays streams of electrons projected from a cathode: they produce X-rays when they strike solids

cath'ode-ray' tube (-rā') a vacuum tube in which a stream of electrons can be focused on a fluorescent screen: such tubes are used as picture tubes, etc.

cath·o·lic (kath' ə lik, kath'lik) ***adj.*** ‖< Gr *kata-*, completely + *holos*, whole‖ **1** all-inclusive; universal **2** broad in sympathies, tastes, etc. **3** [C-] ROMAN CATHOLIC —***n.*** [C-] ROMAN CATHOLIC —**Ca·thol·i·cism** (kə thäl'ə siz'əm) ***n.*** —**cath·o·lic·i·ty** (kath' ə lis'i tē) ***n.***

cat·i·on (kat'ī'ən) ***n.*** ‖< Gr *kata*, down + *ienai*, to go‖ a positively charged ion: in electrolysis, cations move toward the cathode

cat·kin (kat'kin) ***n.*** ‖< Du *katte*, cat‖ a drooping, scaly spike of small flowers without petals, as on poplars, walnuts, etc.

cat'nap' ***n.*** a short nap; doze —***vi.*** **-napped', -nap'ping** to doze briefly

cat'nip' ***n.*** ‖CAT + dial. *nep*, catnip‖ an herb of the mint family: cats like its odor

cat-o'-nine-tails (kat'ə nīn'tālz') ***n., pl.***

-tails′ a whip made of nine knotted cords attached to a handle

CAT scan (kat) ‖ *c*(*omputerized*) *a*(*xial*) *t*(*omography*) ‖ 1 a diagnostic X raying of soft tissues, using many single plane X rays (*tomograms*) to form the image 2 such an image —**CAT scanner** —**CAT scanning**

cat's cradle a game in which a string looped over the fingers is transferred back and forth on the hands of the players so as to form different designs

Cats·kill Mountains (kats′kil′) mountain range in SE N.Y.: also **Cats′kills′**

cat's-paw (kats′pô′) ***n.*** a person used to do distasteful or unlawful work

cat·sup (kat′səp) ***n.*** KETCHUP

cat·tail (kat′tāl′) ***n.*** a tall marsh plant with long, brown, fuzzy spikes

cat·tle (kat′′l) ***n.pl.*** ‖ ult. < L *caput*, head ‖ 1 [Now Chiefly Dial.] livestock 2 cows, bulls, steers, or oxen —**cat′tle·man** (-mən), *pl.* **-men, *n.***

cat·ty (kat′ē) ***adj.*** **-ti·er, -ti·est** 1 of or like a cat 2 spiteful, mean, malicious, etc. —**cat′ti·ness *n.***

cat′ty-cor′nered ***adj., adv.*** CATER-CORNERED Also **cat′ty-cor′ner**

cat′walk′ ***n.*** a narrow, elevated walk

Cau·ca·sian (kô kā′zhən) ***adj.*** 1 of the Caucasus, its people, etc. 2 CAUCASOID —***n.*** 1 a native of the Caucasus 2 CAUCASOID

Cau·ca·soid (kô′kə soid′) ***adj.*** designating or of one of the major geographical varieties of human beings, loosely called the *white race* —***n.*** a member of the Caucasoid population

Cau·ca·sus (kô′kə səs) 1 region in SE European U.S.S.R., between the Black Sea and the Caspian: often called **the Caucasus** 2 mountain range in this region

cau·cus (kô′kəs) ***n.*** ‖ < ? ‖ 1 a meeting of a party or faction to decide on policy, pick candidates, etc. 2 the group attending such a meeting 3 a faction of politicians —***vi.*** **-cused** or **-cussed, -cus·ing** or **-cus·sing** to hold a caucus

cau·dal (kôd′′l) ***adj.*** ‖ < L *cauda*, tail + -AL ‖ of, like, at, or near the tail

caught (kôt) ***vt., vi.*** *pt. & pp. of* CATCH

caul·dron (kôl′drən) ***n.*** *alt. sp. of* CALDRON

cau·li·flow·er (kô′lə flou′ər) ***n.*** ‖ < It *cavolo*, cabbage + *fiore*, flower ‖ 1 a variety of cabbage with a dense white head of fleshy flower stalks 2 the head, eaten as a vegetable

caulk (kôk) ***vt.*** ‖ < L *calx*, a heel ‖ to stop up (cracks, etc.) of (a boat, etc.) as with a puttylike sealant or oakum —***n.*** a soft, puttylike compound used in caulking —**caulk′er *n.***

caus·al (kôz′əl) ***adj.*** 1 of, being, or expressing a cause 2 relating to cause and effect —**cau·sal·i·ty** (kô zal′i tē), *pl.* **-ties, *n.*** —**caus′al·ly *adv.***

cau·sa·tion (kô zā′shən) ***n.*** 1 a causing 2 a causal agency; anything producing an effect

cause (kôz) ***n.*** ‖ < L *causa* ‖ 1 anything producing an effect or result 2 a reason or motive for producing an effect 3 any objective or movement that people are interested in and support 4 *Law* a case to be resolved by a court —***vt.*** **caused, caus′ing** to be the cause of; bring about —**caus′a·tive *adj.*** —**cause′less *adj.*** —**caus′er *n.***

cau·se·rie (kō′zə rē′) ***n.*** ‖ Fr ‖ 1 a chat 2 a short, chatty composition

cause·way (kôz′wā′) ***n.*** ‖ ult. < L *calx*, lime + WAY ‖ a raised path or road, as across wet ground

caus·tic (kôs′tik) ***adj.*** ‖ < Gr *kaiein*, to burn ‖ 1 that can burn tissue by chemical action; corrosive 2 sarcastic; biting —***n.*** a caustic substance —**caus′ti·cal·ly *adv.*** —**caus·tic′i·ty** (-tis′i tē) ***n.***

cau·ter·ize (kôt′ər īz′) ***vt.*** **-ized′, -iz′ing** ‖ see prec. ‖ to burn with a hot needle, a laser, a caustic substance, etc. so as to destroy dead tissue, etc. —**cau′ter·i·za′tion *n.***

cau·tion (kô′shən) ***n.*** ‖ < L *cautio* ‖ 1 a warning 2 wariness; prudence —***vt.*** to warn —**cau′tion·ar′y *adj.***

cau·tious (kô′shəs) ***adj.*** full of caution; careful to avoid danger —**cau′tious·ly *adv.*** —**cau′tious·ness *n.***

cav·al·cade (kav′əl kād′, kav′əl kād′) ***n.*** ‖ Fr < L *caballus*, horse ‖ a procession, as of horsemen, carriages, etc.

cav·a·lier (kav′ə lir′) ***n.*** ‖ Fr: see prec. ‖ 1 an armed horseman; knight 2 a gallant gentleman, esp. a lady's escort —***adj.*** 1 casual 2 arrogant —**cav′a·lier′ly *adv.***

cav·al·ry (kav′əl rē) ***n.***, *pl.* **-ries** ‖ < Fr: see CAVALCADE ‖ combat troops mounted originally on horses but now often riding in motorized armored vehicles —**cav′al·ry·man** (-mən), *pl.* **-men, *n.***

cave (kāv) ***n.*** ‖ < L *cavus*, hollow ‖ a hollow place inside the earth; cavern —***vt., vi.*** **caved, cav′ing** to collapse or make collapse: with *in*

ca·ve·at emp·tor (kā′vē at′ emp′tôr′) ‖ L ‖ let the buyer beware

cave′-in′ *n.* 1 a caving in 2 a place where the ground, etc. has caved in

cave man a prehistoric human being of the Stone Age who lived in caves

cav·ern (kav′ərn) ***n.*** a cave, esp. a large cave —**cav′ern·ous *adj.***

cav·i·ar or **cav·i·are** (kav′ē är′) ***n.*** ‖ Fr < Pers *khāya*, egg + *-dār*, bearing ‖ the salted eggs of sturgeon, etc. eaten as an appetizer

cav·il (kav′əl) ***vi.*** **-iled** or **-illed, -il·ing** or **-il·ling** ‖ < L *cavilla*, jeering ‖ to object unnecessarily; quibble —***n.*** a trivial objection; quibble —**cav′il·er** or **cav′il·ler *n.***

cav·i·ty (kav′i tē) ***n.***, *pl.* **-ties** ‖ see CAVE ‖ a hollow place, as in a tooth

ca·vort (kə vôrt′) ***vi.*** ‖ < ? ‖ 1 to prance or caper 2 to romp; frolic

caw (kô) ***n.*** ‖ echoic ‖ the harsh cry of a crow —***vi.*** to make this sound

cay·enne (pepper) (kī en′, kā-) ‖ < AmInd (Brazil) *kynnha* ‖ very hot red pepper made from the dried fruit of a pepper plant

cay·use (kī′yōōs′, -ōōs′; kī yōōs′, -ōōs′) ***n.***, *pl.* **-us′es** ‖ < AmInd tribal name ‖ a small Western horse used by cowboys

CB (sē′bē′) ***adj.*** ‖ *c*(*itizens'*) *b*(*and*) ‖ designating or of shortwave radio frequencies set aside by the FCC for local use by private persons or businesses

cc 1 carbon copy 2 cubic centimeter(s)

CD (sē′dē′) ***n.*** compact disc

Cd *Chem. symbol for* cadmium

CDC Centers for Disease Control

Cdn. Canadian

cease (sēs) ***vt., vi.*** **ceased, ceas′ing** ⟦see CEDE⟧ to end; stop

cease′-fire′ ***n.*** a temporary cessation of warfare; truce

cease′less (-lis) ***adj.*** unceasing; continual —**cease′less·ly** ***adv.***

ce·cum (sē′kəm) ***n.***, *pl.* **-ca** (-kə) ⟦< L *caecus*, blind⟧ the pouch at the beginning of the large intestine

ce·dar (sē′dər) ***n.*** ⟦< Gr *kedros*⟧ **1** a pine tree having fragrant, durable wood **2** its wood —***adj.*** of cedar

cede (sēd) ***vt.*** **ced′ed, ced′ing** ⟦< L *cedere*, to yield⟧ **1** to surrender formally **2** to transfer the title of

ce·dil·la (sə dil′ə) ***n.*** ⟦Sp dim. of *zeda*, a zeta or *z*⟧ a hooklike mark put under *c*, as in some French words (Ex.: *façade*) to show that it has an *s* sound

ceil·ing (sēl′iŋ) ***n.*** ⟦< L *caelum*, heaven⟧ **1** the inside top part of a room, opposite the floor **2** an upper limit /a price *ceiling*/ **3** *Aeronautics* the upper limit of visibility —**hit the ceiling** [Slang] to lose one's temper

cel·e·brate (sel′ə brāt′) ***vt.*** **-brat′ed, -brat′ing** ⟦< L *celebrare*, to honor⟧ **1** to perform (a ritual, etc.) **2** to commemorate (an anniversary, holiday, etc.) with festivity **3** to honor publicly —***vi.*** [Colloq.] to have a good time —**cel′e·brant** (-brənt) ***n.*** —**cel·e·bra′tion** ***n.*** —**cel′e·bra′tor** ***n.***

cel′e·brat′ed ***adj.*** famous; renowned

ce·leb·ri·ty (sə leb′rə tē) ***n.*** **1** fame **2** *pl.* **-ties** a famous person

ce·ler·i·ty (sə ler′i tē) ***n.*** ⟦< L *celer*, swift⟧ swiftness; speed

cel·er·y (sel′ər ē, sel′rē) ***n.*** ⟦< Gr *selinon*, parsley⟧ a plant whose crisp leafstalks are eaten as a vegetable

ce·les·tial (sə les′chəl) ***adj.*** ⟦< L *caelum*, heaven⟧ **1** of or in the sky or universe **2** of heaven; divine **3** perfect

cel·i·ba·cy (sel′ə bə sē) ***n.*** **1** the state of being unmarried **2** complete sexual abstinence

cel·i·bate (sel′ə bət) ***n.*** ⟦< L *caelebs*⟧ **1** an unmarried person **2** one who abstains from sexual intercourse —***adj.*** of or in a state of celibacy

cell (sel) ***n.*** ⟦< L *cella*⟧ **1** a small room, as in a prison **2** a small hollow, as in a honeycomb **3** a small unit of protoplasm: all plants and animals are made up of one or more cells **4** a receptacle for generating electricity by chemical reactions **5** a small unit of an organization —**celled** (seld) ***adj.***

cel·lar (sel′ər) ***n.*** ⟦see prec.⟧ a room or rooms below ground and usually under a building

CELLO

cel·lo (chel′ō) ***n.***, *pl.* **-los** or **-li** (-ē) ⟦< VIOLONCELLO⟧ an instrument of the violin family, between the viola and double bass in pitch —**cel′list** ***n.***

cel·lo·phane (sel′ə fān′) ***n.*** a thin, transparent material made from cellulose, used as a wrapping

cel·lu·lar (sel′yo͞o lər) ***adj.*** of, like, or containing a cell or cells

cellular phone system a computer-controlled system connecting a telephone system to a network of mobile radiotelephones

cel·lu·lite (sel′yo͞o līt′, -lēt′; sel′yo͞o lēt′) ***n.*** ⟦Fr⟧ fatty deposits on the hips and thighs: a nonmedical term

cel·lu·loid (sel′yo͞o loid′) ***n.*** ⟦fol. + -OID⟧ a tough, flammable plastic substance made from nitrocellulose and camphor

cel·lu·lose (sel′yo͞o lōs′) ***n.*** ⟦Fr < L *cella*, cell + -OSE[1]⟧ the chief substance in the cell walls of plants, used in making paper, textiles, etc.

cellulose acetate any of several acetic esters of cellulose, used in making plastics, lacquers, etc.

ce·lo·si·a (sə lō′shə, -sī ə) ***n.*** an annual garden plant with large, plumelike clusters of tiny, brilliant red or yellow flowers; cockscomb

Cel·si·us (sel′sē əs) ***adj.*** ⟦after A. *Celsius* (1701-44), Swed astronomer, the inventor⟧ designating or of a thermometer on which 0° is the freezing point and 100° is the boiling point of water

Celt (selt, kelt) ***n.*** ⟦< L⟧ a Celtic-speaking person

Celt·ic (sel′tik, kel′-) ***adj.*** of the Celts, their languages, etc. —***n.*** a subfamily of languages including Gaelic and Welsh

ce·ment (sə ment′) ***n.*** ⟦< L *caementum*, rough stone⟧ **1** a powdered substance of lime and clay, mixed with water and sand to make mortar or with water, sand, and gravel to make concrete: it hardens upon drying **2** CONCRETE **3** anything that bonds —***vt.*** **1** to unite as with cement **2** to cover with cement —***vi.*** to become cemented —**ce·ment′er** ***n.***

cem·e·ter·y (sem′ə ter′ē) ***n.***, *pl.* **-ies** ⟦< Gr < *koiman*, to put to sleep⟧ a place for the burial of the dead

cen·o·bite (sen′ə bīt′) ***n.*** ⟦< Gr < *koinos*, common + *bios*, life⟧ a member of a religious order living in a monastery or convent

cen·o·taph (sen′ə taf′) ***n.*** ⟦< Gr *kenos*, empty + *taphos*, tomb⟧ a monument honoring a dead person whose remains are elsewhere

Ce·no·zo·ic (sē′nə zō′ik, sen′ə-) ***adj.*** ⟦*ceno-* (< Gr *kainos*, recent) + ZO(O)- + -IC⟧ designating the geologic era that includes the present, during which the various mammals have developed

cen·ser (sen′sər) ***n.*** a container in which incense is burned

cen·sor (sen′sər) ***n.*** ⟦L < *censere*, to judge⟧ an official with the power to examine literature, mail, etc. and remove or prohibit anything considered obscene, objectionable, etc. —***vt.*** to subject (a book, etc.) to censorship —**cen′sor·ship′** ***n.***

cen·so·ri·ous (sen sôr′ē əs) ***adj.*** inclined to find fault; harshly critical

cen·sure (sen′shər) ***n.*** ‖ < L *censor,* censor ‖ strong disapproval; condemnation **—*vt.* -sured, -sur·ing** to condemn as wrong **—cen′sur·a·ble *adj.***

cen·sus (sen′səs) ***n.*** ‖ L < *censere,* enroll ‖ an official count of population and recording of age, sex, economic status, etc.

cent (sent) ***n.*** ‖ < L *centum,* hundred ‖ a 100th part of a dollar, or a coin of this value; penny

cent. century; centuries

cen·taur (sen′tôr′) ***n.*** ‖ < Gr *Kentauros* ‖ *Gr. Myth.* a monster with a man's head and trunk and a horse's body

cen·ta·vo (sen tä′vō) ***n., pl.* -vos** ‖ Sp, a hundredth < L *centum,* hundred ‖ the 100th part of the monetary unit of Mexico, the Philippines, and some South American countries

cen·te·nar·i·an (sen′tə ner′ē ən) ***n.*** ‖ < fol. ‖ a person at least 100 years old

cen·te·nar·y (sen′tə ner′ē, sen ten′ər ē) ***adj.*** ‖ < L < *centum,* hundred ‖ **1** of a century **2** of a centennial **—*n., pl.* -ies** CENTENNIAL

cen·ten·ni·al (sen ten′ē əl) ***adj.*** ‖ < L *centum,* hundred + *annus,* year + -AL ‖ of or lasting 100 years **—*n.*** a 100th anniversary or its commemoration

cen·ter (sent′ər) ***n.*** ‖ < Gr *kentron,* sharp point ‖ **1** a point equally distant from all points on the circumference of a circle or surface of a sphere **2** a pivot **3** the approximate middle point or part of anything **4** a focal point of activity **5** [*often* **C-**] a group or position between the left (liberals) and right (conservatives) **6** *Sports* a player at the center of a line, floor, etc. **—*vt.* 1** to place in or near the center **2** to gather to one place **—*vi.*** to be centered

cen′ter·board′ *n.* a movable board or plate, like a keel, lowered through a slot in the floor of a shallow sailboat

cen′ter·fold′ *n.* the center facing pages of a magazine, often with an extra fold, showing a photograph, as of a nude woman or man

center of gravity that point in a body or system around which its weight is evenly balanced

cen′ter·piece′ *n.* an ornament for the center of a table

centi- ‖ L ‖ *combining form* **1** one hundred **2** a 100th part of

cen·ti·grade (sen′tə grād′) ***adj.*** ‖ Fr: see prec. & GRADE ‖ CELSIUS

cen·time (sän′tēm′) ***n.*** ‖ Fr ‖ the 100th part of a franc

cen·ti·me·ter (sen′tə mēt′ər) ***n.*** ‖ Fr: see CENTI- & METER[1] ‖ a unit of measure, $\frac{1}{100}$ meter Brit. **cen′ti·me′tre**

cen·ti·pede (sen′tə pēd′) ***n.*** ‖ Fr < L *centi-,* CENTI- + *pes,* FOOT ‖ an elongated arthropod with a pair of legs for each body segment

cen·tral (sen′trəl) ***adj.*** ‖ L *centralis* ‖ **1** in, near, or of the center **2** equally accessible from various points **3** main; basic **4** of a controlling source in a system **—cen′tral·ly *adv.***

Central African Republic country in central Africa: 240,535 sq. mi.; pop. 2,744,000

Central America part of North America between Mexico and South America **— Central American**

central city the crowded, industrial, central area of a large city

cen′tral·ize′ (-īz′) ***vt.* -ized′, -iz′ing 1** to make central; bring to a center **2** to organize under one control **—*vi.*** to become centralized **—cen′tral·i·za′tion *n.* —cen′tral·iz′er *n.***

cen·tre (sent′ər) ***n., vt., vi.* -tred, -tring** *chiefly Brit. sp. of* CENTER

centri- *combining form* CENTRO-

cen·trif·u·gal (sen trif′yo͞o gəl, -yə gəl) ***adj.*** ‖ < prec. + L *fugere,* to flee + -AL ‖ using or acted on by a force (**centrifugal force**) that tends to make rotating bodies move away from the center of rotation

cen·tri·fuge (sen′trə fyo͞oj′) ***n.*** a machine using centrifugal force to separate particles of varying density

cen·trip·e·tal (sen trip′ət′l) ***adj.*** ‖ < CENTRI- + L *petere,* rush at ‖ using or acted on by a force (**centripetal force**) that tends to make rotating bodies move toward the center of rotation

cen·trist (sen′trist) ***n.*** a person with moderate political opinions

centro- ‖ < L *centrum,* center ‖ *combining form* center

cen·tu·ri·on (sen to͝or′ē ən, -tyo͝or′-) ***n.*** ‖ see fol. ‖ the commanding officer of an ancient Roman military unit, originally of 100 men

cen·tu·ry (sen′chə rē) ***n., pl.* -ries** ‖ L < *centum,* hundred ‖ a period of 100 years, esp. as reckoned from 1 A.D.

CEO chief executive officer

ce·phal·ic (sə fal′ik) ***adj.*** ‖ < Gr < *kephalē,* head ‖ **1** of the head or skull **2** in, on, near, or toward the head

cephalo- ‖ see prec. ‖ *combining form* the head, skull, or brain

ce·ram·ic (sə ram′ik) ***adj.*** ‖ Gr < *keramos,* potter's clay ‖ **1** of pottery, porcelain, etc. **2** of ceramics **—*n.* 1** [*pl., with sing v.*] the art or work of making pottery, etc. **2** an object made of baked clay

ce·ram·ist (ser′ə mist, sə ram′ist) ***n.*** one who works in ceramics; ceramic artist Also **ce·ram·i·cist** (sə ram′ə sist)

ce·re·al (sir′ē əl) ***adj.*** ‖ < L *Cerealis,* of Ceres, Rom goddess of agriculture ‖ of grain **—*n.* 1** any grain used for food, as wheat, oats, rice, etc. **2** any grass producing such grain **3** food made from grain

cer·e·bel·lum (ser′ə bel′əm) ***n., pl.* -lums** or **-la** ‖ L, dim. of *cerebrum* ‖ the section of the brain behind and below the cerebrum

cer·e·bral (ser′ə brəl, sə rē′-) ***adj.* 1** of the brain or cerebrum **2** intellectual

cerebral palsy spastic paralysis due to brain damage

cer·e·brate (ser′ə brāt′) ***vi.* -brat′ed, -brat′·ing** ‖ < L *cerebrum,* the brain + -ATE[1] ‖ to think **—cer′e·bra′tion *n.***

cer·e·brum (ser′ə brəm, sə rē′brəm) ***n., pl.* -brums** or **-bra** ‖ L ‖ the upper, main part of the brain of vertebrates

cere·ment (ser′ə mənt, sir′mənt) ***n.*** ‖ < Gr *kēros,* wax ‖ [*usually pl.*] a shroud for a dead person

cer·e·mo·ni·al (ser′ə mō′nē əl) ***adj.*** of or consisting of ceremony; formal **—*n.* 1** a system of rites; ritual **2** a rite or ceremony **—cer′e·mo′ni·al·ly** *adv.*

cer′e·mo′ni·ous (-nē əs) *adj.* **1** full of ceremony **2** very polite or formal **—cer′e·mo′ni·ous·ly** *adv.*

cer·e·mo·ny (ser′ə mō′nē) *n., pl.* **-nies** ‖ < L *caerimonia* ‖ **1** a set of formal acts proper to a special occasion, as a religious rite **2** behavior that follows rigid etiquette **3** *a)* formality *b)* empty or meaningless formality **—stand on ceremony** to insist on formality

ce·rise (sə rēz′, -rēs′) *n., adj.* ‖ < OFr *cerise,* cherry ‖ bright red; cherry red

cer·met (sur′met′) *n.* ‖ CER(AMIC) + MET(AL) ‖ a bonded mixture of ceramic material and a metal

cer·tain (surt′'n) *adj.* ‖ < L *certus,* determined ‖ **1** fixed; settled **2** inevitable **3** reliable; dependable **4** sure; positive **5** definite, but unnamed /a *certain* person/ **6** some /to a *certain* extent/ **—for certain** without doubt

cer′tain·ly *adv.* undoubtedly; surely

cer′tain·ty (-tē) *n.* **1** the state or fact of being certain **2** *pl.* **-ties** anything certain

cer·tif·i·cate (sər tif′i kit; *for v.,* -kāt′) *n.* ‖ see CERTIFY ‖ a document attesting to a fact, qualification, etc. **—*vt.* -cat′ed, -cat′ing** to issue a certificate to

certificate of deposit a bank certificate issued for a specified large deposit of money drawing interest and requiring written notice for withdrawal

certified public accountant a public accountant certified as passing a state examination

cer·ti·fy (surt′ə fī′) *vt.* **-fied′, -fy′ing** ‖ < L *certus,* certain + -FY ‖ **1** to declare (a thing) true, accurate, etc. by formal statement **2** to declare officially insane **3** to guarantee (a check, document, etc.) **4** to issue a certificate or license to **—cer′ti·fi′a·ble** *adj.* **—cer′ti·fi·ca′tion** *n.*

cer·ti·tude (surt′ə to͞od′, -tyo͞od′) *n.* sureness; inevitability

ce·ru·le·an (sə ro͞o′lē ən) *adj.* ‖ < L < *caelum,* heaven ‖ sky-blue; azure

Cer·van·tes (sər van′tēz′), **Mi·guel de** (mē gel′ də) 1547-1616; Sp. writer

cer·vix (sur′viks′) *n., pl.* **cer·vi·ces** (sər vī′sēz′, sur′və-) or **-vix·es** ‖ L, neck ‖ a necklike part, as of the uterus **—cer′vi·cal** (-vi kəl) *adj.*

ce·si·um (sē′zē əm) *n.* ‖ ult. < L *caesius,* bluish-gray ‖ a metallic chemical element, used in photoelectric cells, radiation therapy, etc.

ces·sa·tion (se sā′shən) *n.* ‖ < L *cessare,* cease ‖ a ceasing or stopping

ces·sion (sesh′ən) *n.* ‖ < L *cedere,* to yield ‖ a ceding or giving up (of rights, property, etc.) to another

cess·pool (ses′po͞ol′) *n.* ‖ < ? It *cesso,* privy ‖ a deep hole in the ground to receive drainage or sewage from the sinks, toilets, etc. of a house

ce·ta·cean (sə tā′shən) *n.* ‖ < L *cetus,* whale ‖ a fishlike water mammal, including the whale, porpoise, and dolphin **—*adj.*** of the cetaceans

Cey·lon (sə län′, sā-, sē-) *old name of* SRI LANKA **—Cey·lo·nese** (sel′ə nēz′, sā′lə-) *n., adj.*

Cé·zanne (sā zän′), **Paul** 1839-1906; Fr. painter

cf. ‖ L *confer* ‖ compare

cg centigram(s)

Ch. or **ch.** **1** chapter **2** church

Cha·blis (sha blē′) *n.* [*occas.* **c-**] a dry, white Burgundy wine, orig. from Chablis, France

Chad (chad) country in north central Africa: 496,000 sq. mi.; pop. 5,231,000

chafe (chāf) *vt.* **chafed, chaf′ing** ‖ < L *calefacere,* make warm ‖ **1** to rub so as to make warm **2** to wear away or make sore by rubbing **3** to annoy; irritate **—*vi.*** **1** to rub (*on* or *against*) **2** to be vexed

chaff (chaf) *n.* ‖ OE *ceaf* ‖ **1** threshed or winnowed husks of grain **2** anything worthless **3** teasing; banter **—*vt., vi.*** to tease in a good-natured way

chaf·ing dish (chāf′iŋ) a pan with a heating apparatus beneath it, to cook food at the table or to keep food hot

cha·grin (shə grin′) *n.* ‖ Fr ‖ embarrassment and annoyance due to failure, disappointment, etc. **—*vt.* -grined′, -grin′ing** to cause to feel chagrin

chain (chān) *n.* ‖ < L *catena* ‖ **1** a flexible series of joined links **2** [*pl.*] *a)* bonds; shackles *b)* captivity **3** a chainlike measuring instrument, as for surveying **4** a series of things connected causally, logically, physically, etc. **5** a number of stores, etc. owned by one company **—*vt.*** **1** to fasten with chains **2** to restrain, etc.

chain gang a gang of prisoners chained together, as when working

chain reaction **1** a self-sustaining series of chemical or nuclear reactions in which the reaction products keep the process going **2** a series of events, each of which results in the following one

chain saw a portable power saw with an endless chain that carries the cutting teeth

chair (cher) *n.* ‖ < L *cathedra:* see CATHEDRAL ‖ **1** a piece of furniture with a back, for one person to sit on **2** an important or official position **3** a chairman **—*vt.*** **1** to seat **2** to preside over as chairman

chair′lift′ *n.* seats suspended from a power-driven endless cable, used to carry skiers up a slope

chair′man (-mən) *n., pl.* **-men** a person in charge of a meeting, committee, etc. Also **chair′per′son** **—chair′man·ship′** *n.* **—chair′wom′an,** *pl.* **-wom′en,** *n.fem.*

chaise (shāz) *n.* ‖ Fr ‖ a lightweight carriage, having two or four wheels

chaise longue (shāz′ lôŋ′; *often also* lounj′) *pl.* **chaise longues** (lôŋz′) ‖ Fr, lit., long chair ‖ a couchlike chair with a long seat Also **chaise lounge** (lounj′)

cha·let (shal ā′, shal′ā) *n.* ‖ Swiss-Fr ‖ **1** a Swiss house with overhanging eaves **2** any similar building

chal·ice (chal′is) *n.* ‖ < L *calix,* cup ‖ **1** a cup **2** the cup for Communion wine

chalk (chôk) *n.* ‖ < L *calx,* limestone ‖ **1** a soft, whitish limestone **2** a piece of chalk or chalklike substance used for writing on a blackboard **—*adj.*** made with chalk **—*vt.*** to mark or rub with chalk **—chalk up** **1** to score, get, or achieve **2** to charge or credit

—chalk′i·ness *n.* —chalk′y, -i·er, -i·est, *adj.*

chalk′board′ *n.* BLACKBOARD

chal·lenge (chal′ənj) *n.* ‖ < L *calumnia*, cal umny ‖ 1 a demand for identification 2 a calling into question 3 a call to a duel, contest, etc. 4 anything that calls for special effort —*vt.* **-lenged, -leng·ing** to subject to a challenge —*vi.* to make a challenge —**chal′leng·er** *n.*

chal·lis or **chal·lie** (shal′ē) *n.* ‖ < ? ‖ a soft, lightweight fabric of wool, etc.

cham·ber (chām′bər) *n.* ‖ < LL *camera*, a chamber, room ‖ 1 a room, esp. a bedroom 2 [*pl.*] a judge's office near the courtroom 3 an assembly hall 4 a legislative or judicial body 5 a council /*chamber* of commerce/ 6 an enclosed space 7 the part of a gun holding the charge or of a revolver holding the cartridge —**cham′bered** *adj.*

cham′ber·lain (-lin) *n.* ‖ < OHG *chamarlinc* ‖ 1 an officer in charge of the household of a ruler or lord; steward 2 a high official in certain royal courts 3 [Brit.] a treasurer

cham′ber·maid′ *n.* a woman whose work is taking care of bedrooms

chamber music music for performance by a small group, as a string quartet

chamber of commerce an association established to further the business interests of its community

cham·bray (sham′brā′) *n.* ‖ var. of *cambric* ‖ a smooth cotton fabric of white threads woven across a colored warp

COMMON CHAMELEON

cha·me·le·on (kə mēl′ē ən, mēl′yən) *n.* ‖ < Gr *chamai*, on the ground + *leōn*, LION ‖ any of various lizards that can change the color of their skin

cham·ois (sham′ē) *n.*, *pl.* **cham′ois** ‖ Fr ‖ 1 a small, goatlike antelope of the mountains of Europe and the Caucasus 2 a soft leather made from the skin of chamois, sheep, deer, etc.: also **cham·my** (sham′ē), *pl.* **cham′mies**

cham·o·mile (kam′ə mīl′, mēl′) *n.* ‖ < Gr *chamaimēlon*, earth apple ‖ a plant whose dried, daisylike flower heads are used in a medicinal tea

champ[1] (champ) *vt.* ‖ prob. echoic ‖ to chew hard and noisily; munch

champ[2] (champ) *n.* [Colloq.] CHAMPION (sense 2)

cham·pagne (sham pān′) *n.* an effervescent white wine, orig. from Champagne, region in NE France

cham·paign (sham pān′) *n.* ‖ < L *campus*, field ‖ flat, open country

cham·pi·on (cham′pē ən) *n.* ‖ < LL *campio*, gladiator ‖ 1 one who fights for another or for a cause; defender 2 a winner of first place in a competition —*adj.* excelling all others —*vt.* to fight for; defend; support —**cham′pi·on·ship′** *n.*

chance (chans) *n.* ‖ < L *cadere*, to fall ‖ 1 the happening of events without apparent cause; luck 2 an unpredictable event 3 a risk or gamble 4 a ticket in a lottery 5 an opportunity 6 [*often pl.*] a possibility or probability —*adj.* accidental —*vi.* **chanced, chanc′ing** to have the fortune, good or bad (*to*) —*vt.* to risk —**by chance** accidentally —**chance on** (or **upon**) to find or meet by chance —(**the**) **chances are** the likelihood is —**on the** (**off**) **chance** relying on the (remote) possibility

chan·cel (chan′səl) *n.* ‖ < L *cancelli*, lat tices ‖ the part of a church around the altar, for the clergy and the choir

chan′cel·ler·y (-ər ē) *n.*, *pl.* **-ies** ‖ < ML *cancellaria* ‖ the rank or position of a chan cellor

chan·cel·lor (chan′sə lər) *n.* ‖ < LL *cancellarius*, secretary ‖ 1 a high government offi cial, as, in certain countries, a prime minister 2 in some universities, the president or other executive officer

chance′-med′ley *n.* 1 accidental homicide 2 haphazard action

chan·cer·y (chan′sər ē) *n.*, *pl.* **-ies** ‖ < ML *cancellaria* ‖ 1 a court of equity 2 an office of public archives 3 *R.C.Ch.* the dioc esan office performing secretarial services for the bishop

chan·cre (shaŋ′kər) *n.* ‖ Fr: see CANCER ‖ a sore or ulcer of syphilis

chanc·y (chan′sē) *adj.* **-i·er, -i·est** risky; uncertain —**chanc′i·ness** *n.*

chan·de·lier (shan′də lir′) *n.* ‖ Fr < L *candela*, candle ‖ a lighting fixture hung from a ceiling, with branches for candles, light bulbs, etc.

chan·dler (chand′lər) *n.* ‖ < L *candela*, can dle ‖ 1 a maker of candles 2 a retailer of supplies, as for ships

Chang (chäŋ) river in central China, flowing into the East China Sea: old name YANGTZE

change (chānj) *vt.* **changed, chang′ing** ‖ < L *cambire*, to barter ‖ 1 to put or take (a thing) in place of something else /*change* jobs/ 2 to exchange /*change* seats/ 3 to make different; alter —*vi.* 1 to alter; vary 2 to leave one train, plane, etc. and board another 3 to put on other clothes 4 to make an exchange —*n.* 1 a substitution, alteration, or variation 2 variety 3 another set of clothes 4 *a*) money returned as the difference between the price and the greater sum presented *b*) coins or bills that together equal a single larger coin or bill *c*) small coins —**change off** to take turns —**ring the changes** to ring a set of bells with all possible variations —**change′a·ble** *adj.* —**change′less** *adj.*

change′ling (-liŋ) *n.* a child secretly put in the place of another, as by fairies

change of life MENOPAUSE

change′o′ver *n.* a complete change, as in goods produced

chan·nel (chan′əl) *n.* ‖ see CANAL ‖ 1 the bed or deeper part of a river, harbor, etc. 2 a body of water joining two larger ones 3 any means of passage 4 [*pl.*] the official course of transmission of communications 5 a groove or furrow 6 a frequency band assigned to a radio or television station —*vt.* -neled or -nelled, -nel·ing or -nel·ling 1 to make a channel in 2 to send through a channel

Channel Islands group of British islands in the English Channel

chan′nel·ize′ (-īz′) *vt.* -ized′, -iz′ing to provide a channel for

chan·son (shän sōn′) *n., pl.* ***-sons′*** (-sōn′) ‖ Fr ‖ a song

chant (chant) *n.* ‖ < L *cantare,* to sing ‖ 1 a song; esp., a liturgical song with a series of syllables or words sung to each tone 2 a singsong way of speaking —*vi., vt.* to sing or say in a chant —**chant′er** *n.*

chan·teuse (shan tʉz′) *n.* ‖ Fr ‖ a woman singer, esp. of popular ballads

chan·tey (shan′tē, chan′tē) *n., pl.* **-teys** a song formerly sung by sailors in rhythm with their motions while working Also **chan′ty,** *pl.* **-ties**

chan·ti·cleer (chan′ti klir′) *n.* ‖ < OFr *chante-cler,* lit., sing loud ‖ a rooster

Cha·nu·kah (khä′noo kä′) HANUKA

cha·os (kā′äs′) *n.* ‖ < Gr, space ‖ extreme confusion or disorder —**cha·ot·ic** (kā ät′ik) *adj.*

chap[1] (chäp, chap) *n.* ‖ < ? ‖ CHOP[2]

chap[2] (chap) *n.* ‖ < Brit *chapman,* peddler ‖ [Colloq.] a man; fellow

chap[3] (chap) *vt., vi.* **chapped** or **chapt, chap′ping** ‖ ME *chappen,* cut ‖ to crack open; split; roughen, as skin —*n.* a chapped place in the skin

chap. 1 chaplain 2 chapter

chap·ar·ral (chap′ə ral′, shap′-) *n.* ‖ Sp < *chaparro,* evergreen oak ‖ [Southwest] a thicket of shrubs, etc.

cha·peau (sha pō′) *n., pl.* **-peaus′** or **-peaux′** (-pōz′) ‖ Fr ‖ a hat

chap·el (chap′əl) *n.* ‖ < ML *cappella,* dim. of *cappa,* cape ‖ 1 a small church 2 a private place of worship, as in a hospital

chap·er·on or **chap·er·one** (shap′ər ōn′, shap′ər ōn′) *n.* ‖ < OFr, hood ‖ a person, esp. an older woman, who accompanies young unmarried people to supervise their behavior —*vt., vi.* **-oned′, -on′ing** to act as chaperon (to) —**chap′er·on′age** *n.*

chap·lain (chap′lən) *n.* ‖ see CHAPEL ‖ 1 a clergyman attached to a chapel 2 a clergyman serving in a religious capacity with the armed forces, or in a prison, hospital, etc.

chap·let (chap′lit) *n.* ‖ < LL *cappa,* cape ‖ 1 a garland for the head 2 a string of beads, esp. prayer beads

chaps (chaps, shaps) *n.pl.* ‖ < MexSp *chaparreras* ‖ leather trousers without a seat, worn over ordinary trousers by cowboys to protect their legs

chap·ter (chap′tər) *n.* ‖ < L *caput,* head ‖ 1 a main division, as of a book 2 a local branch of an organization

char (chär) *vt., vi.* **charred, char′ring** ‖ < CHARCOAL ‖ 1 to reduce to charcoal by burning 2 to burn slightly; scorch

char·ac·ter (kar′ək tər, kar′ik-) *n.* ‖ < Gr *charassein,* engrave ‖ 1 any letter, figure, or symbol used in writing and printing 2 a distinctive trait 3 kind or sort 4 behavior typical of a person or group 5 moral strength 6 reputation 7 status; position 8 a person in a play, novel, etc. 9 [Colloq.] an eccentric person

char′ac·ter·is′tic (-is′tik) *adj.* typical; distinctive —*n.* a distinguishing trait or quality —**char′ac·ter·is′ti·cal·ly** *adv.*

char′ac·ter·ize′ (-īz′) *vt.* **-ized′, -iz′ing** 1 to describe the particular traits of 2 to be a characteristic of —**char′ac·ter·i·za′tion** *n.*

cha·rade (shə rād′) *n.* ‖ Fr < Prov *charrar,* to gossip ‖ 1 [*pl.*] a game in which words to be guessed are pantomimed, often syllable by syllable 2 a pretense or fiction

char·broil or **char-broil** (chär′broil′) *vt.* to broil over a charcoal fire

char·coal (chär′kōl′) *n.* ‖ ME *char cole* ‖ a dark, porous form of carbon made by partially burning wood or other organic matter in an airless kiln or retort: used for fuel, etc.

chard (chärd) *n.* ‖ < L *carduus,* thistle ‖ a kind of beet with large, edible leaves and stalks

char·don·nay (shär′də nā′) *n.* [*also* **C-**] a dry white wine

charge (chärj) *vt.* **charged, charg′ing** ‖ ult. < L *carrus,* wagon ‖ 1 to load or fill (*with* something) 2 to add an electrical charge to (a battery, etc.) 3 to give as a duty, command, etc. to 4 to accuse 5 to make liable for (an error, etc.) 6 to ask as a price 7 to record as a debt 8 to attack vigorously —*vi.* 1 to ask payment (*for*) 2 to attack vigorously —*n.* 1 a load or burden 2 the necessary quantity, as of fuel, for a container or device 3 the amount of chemical energy stored in a battery 4 responsibility or care (*of*) 5 a person or thing entrusted to one's care 6 instruction; command 7 accusation; indictment 8 cost 9 a debt, debit, or expense 10 an onslaught —**in charge (of)** having the responsibility, control, or supervision (of) —**charge′a·ble** *adj.*

charge account an arrangement by which a customer may pay for purchases within a specified future period

charge card (or **plate**) a thin, flat, plastic card embossed with the owner's name, account number, etc., used as a stamp on bills when charging purchases

charg′er *n.* 1 a person or thing that charges 2 a horse ridden in battle

char·i·ot (char′ē ət) *n.* ‖ see CAR ‖ a horse-drawn, two-wheeled cart used in ancient times for war, racing, etc. —**char′i·ot·eer′** (-ə tir′) *n.*

cha·ris·ma (kə riz′mə) *n., pl.* **-ma·ta** (-mə tə) ‖ < Gr, favor, grace ‖ a special charm or allure that inspires allegiance or devotion

char·is·mat·ic (kar′iz mat′ik) *adj.* 1 of or having charisma 2 designating or of a religious group that stresses direct divine inspiration, manifested as in glossolalia, etc. —*n.* a member of a charismatic group

char·i·ta·ble (char′i tə bəl) *adj.* 1 generous to the needy 2 of or for charity 3 kind and forgiving —**char′i·ta·bly** *adv.*

char·i·ty (char′i tē) *n., pl.* **-ties** ‖ < L *caritas,* affection ‖ 1 *Christian Theol.* love for one's fellow men 2 leniency in judging others 3 *a)* generosity toward the needy *b)* help so given 4 a welfare institution, fund, etc.

char·la·tan (shär′lə tən) *n.* ‖ ult. < VL *cerretanus,* seller of papal indulgences ‖ a fraud; quack; impostor

Char·le·magne (shär′lə mān′) A.D. 742-814; king of the Franks (768-814): emperor of the Holy Roman Empire (800-814)

Charles·ton (chärls′tən) capital of W.Va., in the W part: pop. 64,000 —***n.*** ‖ < name of the seaport ‖ a lively dance of the 1920's, in 4/4 time

char·ley horse (chär′lē) [Colloq.] a cramp in a muscle, esp. a thigh muscle

Char·lotte (shär′lət) city in S N.C.: pop. 314,000

Char·lotte·town (shär′lət toun′) capital of Prince Edward Island, Canada: pop. 16,000

charm (chärm) ***n.*** ‖ < L *carmen* ‖ **1** an action, object, or words assumed to have magic power **2** a trinket worn on a bracelet, etc. **3** a quality that attracts or delights —***vt., vi.*** **1** to act on as if by magic **2** to fascinate; delight —**charm′er** ***n.*** —**charm′·ing** ***adj.*** —**charm′ing·ly** ***adv.***

char·nel (house) (chär′nəl) ‖ < LL *carnale*, graveyard ‖ a building or place where corpses or bones are deposited

Cha·ron (ker′ən) *Gr. Myth.* the ferryman on the river Styx

chart (chärt) ***n.*** ‖ < Gr *chartēs*, layer of papyrus ‖ **1** a map, esp. for use in navigation **2** an information sheet with tables, graphs, etc. **3** a table, graph, etc. —***vt.*** **1** to make a chart of **2** to plan (a course of action)

char·ter (chärt′ər) ***n.*** ‖ see prec. ‖ **1** a franchise granted by a government **2** a written statement of basic laws or principles; constitution **3** written permission to form a local chapter or lodge of a society —***vt.*** **1** to grant a charter to **2** to hire for exclusive use

charter member a founder or original member

char·treuse (shär trōōz′, -trōōs′) ***n.*** ‖ Fr ‖ pale, yellowish green

char·wom·an (chär′woom′ən) ***n., pl.*** **-wom′en** ‖ see CHORE ‖ a cleaning woman

char·y (cher′ē, char′-) ***adj.*** **-i·er, -i·est** ‖ < OE *cearig*, sorrowful ‖ **1** not taking chances; cautious **2** sparing —**char′i·ly** ***adv.*** —**char′i·ness** ***n.***

chase[1] (chās) ***vt.*** **chased, chas′ing** ‖ ult. < L *capere*, to take ‖ **1** to follow so as to catch **2** to run after **3** to drive away **4** to hunt —***vi.*** **1** to go in pursuit **2** [Colloq.] to rush —***n.*** **1** a chasing; pursuit **2** the hunting of game **3** anything hunted; quarry —**give chase** to pursue

chase[2] (chās) ***vt.*** **chased, chas′ing** ‖ < OFr *enchasser* ‖ to ornament (metal) as by engraving

chas′er ***n.*** [Colloq.] a mild drink, as water, taken after whiskey, etc.

chasm (kaz′əm) ***n.*** ‖ < Gr *chasma* ‖ **1** a deep crack in the earth's surface; abyss **2** any break or gap; rift

chas·sis (chas′ē, shas′-) ***n., pl.*** **-sis′** (-ēz′) ‖ Fr ‖ **1** the frame, wheels, etc. of a motor vehicle, but not the body or engine **2** *a)* a frame, as for the parts of a TV set *b)* the assembled frame and parts

chaste (chāst) ***adj.*** ‖ < L *castus*, pure ‖ **1** not indulging in unlawful sexual activity **2** decent; modest **3** simple in style; not ornate —**chaste′ly** ***adv.***

chas·ten (chās′ən) ***vt.*** ‖ < L *castigare*, punish ‖ **1** to punish so as to correct **2** to restrain or subdue

chas·tise (chas tīz′) ***vt.*** **-tised′, -tis′ing** ‖ see prec. ‖ **1** to punish, esp. by beating **2** to scold sharply —**chas·tise′ment** ***n.*** —**chas·tis′er** ***n.***

chas·ti·ty (chas′tə tē) ***n.*** a being chaste; specif., *a)* virtuousness *b)* sexual abstinence; celibacy *c)* decency or modesty

chas·u·ble (chaz′ə bəl, chas′-) ***n.*** ‖ < ML *casula* ‖ a sleeveless outer vestment worn by priests at Mass

chat (chat) ***vi.*** **chat′ted, chat′ting** ‖ < CHATTER ‖ to talk in a light, informal manner —***n.*** light, informal talk

châ·teau (sha tō′) ***n., pl.*** **-teaux′** or **-teaus′** (-tōz′, -tō′) ‖ Fr < L *castellum*, castle ‖ **1** a French feudal castle **2** a large country house and estate, esp. in France Also **cha·teau′**

chat·e·laine (shat′'l ān′) ***n.*** ‖ Fr ‖ **1** the mistress of a château **2** a woman's ornamental chain or clasp

Chat·ta·noo·ga (chat′ə nōō′gə) city in SE Tenn.: pop. 170,000

chat·tel (chat′'l) ***n.*** ‖ see CATTLE ‖ a movable item of personal property

chat·ter (chat′ər) ***vi.*** ‖ echoic ‖ **1** to make short, rapid, indistinct sounds, as apes do **2** to talk much and foolishly **3** to click together rapidly, as teeth do from cold —***n.*** **1** a chattering **2** foolish talk —**chat′ter·er** ***n.***

chat′ter·box′ ***n.*** an incessant talker

chat·ty (chat′ē) ***adj.*** **-ti·er, -ti·est** fond of chatting —**chat′ti·ness** ***n.***

Chau·cer (chô′sər), **Geof·frey** (jef′rē) *c.* 1340-1400; Eng. poet

chauf·feur (shō′fər, shō fur′) ***n.*** ‖ Fr, lit., stoker ‖ one hired to drive a private automobile for someone else —***vt.*** to act as chauffeur to

chau·vin·ism (shō′vin iz′əm) ***n.*** ‖ after N. *Chauvin*, fanatical Fr patriot ‖ **1** militant and fanatic patriotism; jingoism **2** unreasoning devotion to one's race, sex, etc. —**chau′vin·ist** ***n., adj.*** —**chau′vin·is′tic** ***adj.*** —**chau′vin·is′ti·cal·ly** ***adv.***

cheap (chēp) ***adj.*** ‖ ult. < L *caupo*, tradesman ‖ **1** low in price **2** worth more than the price **3** easily got **4** of little value **5** contemptible **6** [Colloq.] stingy —***adv.*** at a low cost —**cheap′ly** ***adv.*** —**cheap′ness** ***n.***

cheap′en ***vt., vi.*** to make or become cheap or cheaper

cheap shot [Slang] an unnecessarily rough or mean action or remark

cheap′skate′ ***n.*** [Slang] a stingy person

cheat (chēt) ***n.*** ‖ < L *ex-*, out + *cadere*, to fall ‖ **1** a fraud; swindle **2** a swindler —***vt.*** **1** to defraud; swindle **2** to foil or elude /to *cheat* death/ —***vi.*** **1** to be dishonest or deceitful **2** [Slang] to be sexually unfaithful: often with *on* —**cheat′er** ***n.***

check (chek) ***n.*** ‖ < OFr *eschec*, a check in chess ‖ **1** a sudden stop **2** any restraint **3** one that restrains **4** a supervision or test of accuracy, etc. **5** a mark (✓) to show verification **6** an identification ticket, token, etc. /a hat *check*/ **7** one's bill at a restaurant or bar **8** a written order to a bank to pay a sum of money **9** a pattern of squares, or one of the squares **10** *Chess* the state of a king that is in danger —***interj.*** [Colloq.]

agreed! right! —*vt.* 1 to stop suddenly 2 to restrain; curb; block 3 to test, verify, etc. by examination or comparison: often with *out* 4 to mark with a check (√): often with *off* 5 to mark with a pattern of squares 6 to deposit temporarily 7 to clear (esp. luggage) for shipment 8 *Chess* to place (the opponent's king) in check —*vi.* 1 to agree with one another, item for item: often with *out* 2 to investigate or verify: often with *on, up on* —**check in** 1 to register at a hotel, etc. 2 [Colloq.] to present oneself, as at work —**check out** 1 to pay and leave a hotel, etc. 2 to add up the prices of (items selected) for payment 3 to prove to be accurate, etc. —**in check** under control —**check'er** *n.*

check'book' *n.* a book of detachable forms for writing bank checks

checked (chekt) *adj.* having a pattern of squares

check'er·board' *n.* a square board with 64 squares of two alternating colors, used in checkers and chess

check·ered (chek'ərd) *adj.* 1 having a pattern of squares 2 varied

check'ers (-ərz) *n.pl.* 1 [*with sing. v.*] a game for two played with flat disks on a checkerboard 2 the disks

checking account a bank account against which the depositor can draw checks

check'list' *n.* a list of things, names, etc. to be referred to Also **check list**

check'mate' (-māt') *n.* ‖ult. < Pers *šāh māt*, the king is dead‖ 1 *Chess a)* the move that wins the game by checking the opponent's king so that it cannot be protected *b)* the condition of the king after this move 2 total defeat, frustration, etc. —*vt.* **-mat'ed, -mat'ing** 1 to place in checkmate 2 to defeat; thwart

check'off' *n.* the withholding of members' dues for the union by the employer

check'out' *n.* 1 the act or place of checking out purchases 2 the time by which one must check out of a hotel, etc.

check'point' *n.* a place on a road, etc. where traffic is inspected

check'room' *n.* a room in which hats, coats, etc. may be left until called for

check'up' *n.* a medical examination

Ched·dar (cheese) (ched'ər) ‖after *Cheddar*, England‖ [*often* **c-**] a hard, smooth cheese

cheek (chēk) *n.* ‖OE *ceoke*, jaw‖ 1 either side of the face below the eye 2 [Colloq.] sauciness; impudence —**tongue in cheek** jestingly; mockingly

cheek'bone' *n.* the bone across the upper cheek, just below the eye

cheek'y *adj.* **-i·er, -i·est** [Colloq.] saucy; impudent —**cheek'i·ness** *n.*

cheep (chēp) *n.* ‖echoic‖ the short, shrill sound made by a young bird —*vt., vi.* to make, or utter with, this sound —**cheep'er** *n.*

cheer (chir) *n.* ‖< Gr *kara*, the head‖ 1 state of mind or of feeling; spirit [be of good *cheer*] 2 gladness; joy 3 festive entertainment 4 encouragement 5 *a)* a glad, excited shout to urge on, greet, etc. *b)* a rallying cry —*vt.* 1 to gladden; comfort: often with *up* 2 to urge on, greet, or applaud with cheers —*vi.* 1 to become cheerful: usually with *up* 2 to shout cheers

cheer'ful *adj.* 1 full of cheer; gay 2 bright and attractive 3 willing [a *cheerful* helper] —**cheer'ful·ly** *adv.* —**cheer'ful·ness** *n.*

cheer'i·o' (-ē ō') *interj., n., pl.* **-os'** [Brit. Colloq.] 1 goodbye 2 good health: used as a toast

cheer'lead'er (-lē'dər) *n.* a leader of cheers, as at football games

cheer'less *adj.* not cheerful; dismal; dreary —**cheer'less·ly** *adv.* —**cheer'less·ness** *n.*

cheers (chirz) *interj.* [Chiefly Brit.] good health: used as a toast

cheer'y *adj.* **-i·er, -i·est** cheerful; lively; bright —**cheer'i·ly** *adv.* —**cheer'i·ness** *n.*

cheese (chēz) *n.* ‖OE *cyse*‖ a solid food made from milk curds

cheese'burg'er (-bur'gər) *n.* a hamburger topped with melted cheese

cheese'cake' *n.* 1 a cake made with cottage cheese or cream cheese 2 [Colloq.] photographic display of the figure, esp. the legs, of a pretty woman

cheese'cloth' *n.* ‖from its use for wrapping cheese‖ a thin cotton cloth with a very loose weave

chees'y (-ē) *adj.* **-i·er, -i·est** 1 like cheese 2 [Slang] inferior; poor

chee·tah (chēt'ə) *n.* ‖Hindi < Sans *chitraka*, spotted‖ a swift cat of Africa and S Asia, with long legs and a spotted coat

chef (shef) *n.* ‖Fr, head, chief‖ 1 a head cook 2 any cook

Che·khov (che'kôf'), **An·ton** (än tôn') 1860-1904; Russ. writer

chem. 1 chemical(s) 2 chemistry

chem·i·cal (kem'i kəl) *adj.* 1 of, made by, or used in chemistry 2 made with or operated by chemicals 3 [Slang] of or involving a drug, alcohol, etc. [*chemical* dependency] —*n.* any substance used in or obtained by a chemical process —**chem'i·cal·ly** *adv.*

chemical abuse the habitual use of a mood-altering drug, alcohol, etc. —**chemical abuser**

chemical engineering the science or profession of applying chemistry to industrial uses

chemical warfare warfare by means of poisonous gases, etc.

che·mise (shə mēz') *n.* ‖< LL *camisia*, tunic‖ 1 a woman's loose, short slip 2 a straight, loose dress

chem·ist (kem'ist) *n.* ‖ult. < Ar < ? Gr *cheein*, to pour‖ 1 a specialist in chemistry 2 [Brit.] a pharmacist, or druggist

chem·is·try (kem'is trē) *n.* ‖< prec.‖ 1 the science dealing with the composition and properties of substances, and with the reactions by which substances are produced from or converted into other substances 2 [Colloq.] rapport

chemo- *combining form* of, with, or by chemicals Also, before a vowel, **chem-**

che'mo·ther'a·py *n.* the use of chemical drugs in medicine

chem·ur·gy (kem'ər jē) *n.* chemistry dealing with the use of organic, esp. farm, products in industrial manufacture

che·nille (shə nēl') *n.* ‖Fr, lit., caterpillar‖

1 a tufted, velvety yarn **2** a fabric filled or woven with this

cheque (chek) *n. Brit. sp. of* CHECK (*n.* 8)

cher·ish (cher′ish) *vt.* ‖ < L *carus*, dear ‖ **1** to hold dear **2** to cling to the idea or feeling of

Cher·o·kee (cher′ə kē′) *n., pl.* **-kees′** or **-kee′** a member of a North American Indian people now chiefly of SW U.S.

che·root (shə ro͞ot′) *n.* ‖ < Tamil ‖ a cigar with both ends cut square

cher·ry (cher′ē) *n., pl.* **-ries** ‖ < Gr *kerasion* ‖ **1** a small, fleshy fruit with a smooth, hard pit **2** the tree that bears this fruit **3** the wood of this tree **4** a bright red

chert (churt) *n.* a fine-grained rock composed mainly of silica

cher·ub (cher′əb) *n., pl.* **-ubs, -u·bim′** (-yo͞o bim′, -ə bim′), or **-u·bims** ‖ < Heb *kerūbh* ‖ **1** any of a kind of angel, often represented as a chubby, rosy-faced child with wings **2** a child with a sweet, innocent face —**che·ru·bic** (chə ro͞o′bik) *adj.* —**che·ru′bi·cal·ly** *adv.*

cher·vil (chur′vəl) *n.* ‖ < Gr *chairephyllon* ‖ a plant like parsley, with leaves used to flavor salads, soups, etc.

Ches·a·peake (ches′ə pēk′) city in SE Va.: pop. 114,000

Chesapeake Bay arm of the Atlantic, extending into Va. and Md.

chess (ches) *n.* ‖ < OFr *eschec*, a check in chess ‖ a game played on a chessboard by two players, using a variety of pieces (**chess′-men**)

chess′board′ *n.* a checkerboard used for playing chess

chest (chest) *n.* ‖ < Gr *kistē*, a box ‖ **1** a box with a lid **2** a cabinet with drawers, as for clothes **3** a cabinet with shelves, as for medicines **4** the part of the body enclosed by the ribs, breastbone, and diaphragm

ches·ter·field (ches′tər fēld′) *n.* ‖ after a 19th-c. Earl of *Chesterfield* ‖ a single-breasted topcoat, usually with a velvet collar

chest·nut (ches′nut′, -nət) *n.* ‖ < Gr *kastaneia* ‖ **1** the edible nut of a tree of the beech family **2** this tree, or its wood **3** reddish brown **4** [Colloq.] an old, stale joke, story, etc.

chev·i·ot (chev′ē ət, shev′ē ət) *n.* ‖ after Cheviot Hills, on the Scottish-English border ‖ a rough, twilled wool fabric

chè·vre (shev′rə) *n.* a soft cheese made from goat's milk

chev·ron (shev′rən) *n.* ‖ < OFr, rafter ‖ a V-shaped bar on the sleeve of a uniform, showing rank

chew (cho͞o) *vt., vi.* ‖ OE *ceowan* ‖ to bite and crush with the teeth —*n.* **1** a chewing **2** something chewed or for chewing —**chew′er** *n.* —**chew′y, -i·er, -i·est,** *adj.*

chew′ing gum a gummy substance, as chicle, flavored for chewing

Chey·enne (shī an′, -en′) capital of Wyo., in the SE part: pop. 47,000

chg. charge

chi (kī, kē) *n.* the 22d letter of the Greek alphabet (Χ, χ)

Chi·an·ti (kē än′tē, -an′-) *n.* ‖ It ‖ a dry red wine

chi·a·ro·scu·ro (kē ä′rō sko͞o′rō′) *n., pl.* **-ros** ‖ It < L *clarus*, clear + *obscurus*, dark ‖ **1** treatment of light and shade in a painting, etc., esp. when emphasized **2** a painting, drawing, etc. notable for this

chic (shēk) *n.* ‖ Fr < Medieval LowG *schick*, skill ‖ smart elegance —*adj.* smartly stylish

Chi·ca·go (shə kä′gō, -kô′-) city and port in NE Ill.: pop. 3,005,000 (met. area 7,102,000)

chi·can·er·y (shi kān′ər ē) *n., pl.* **-ies** ‖ < Fr ‖ **1** trickery **2** a trick

Chi·ca·no (chi kä′nō) *n., pl.* **-nos** ‖ < AmSp ‖ [*also* **c-**] a U.S. citizen or inhabitant of Mexican descent

chi·chi or **chi-chi** (shē′shē) *adj.* ‖ Fr ‖ extremely chic, specif. in an affected or showy way

chick (chik) *n.* ‖ ME *chike* ‖ **1** a young chicken or bird **2** [Slang] a young woman

chick·a·dee (chik′ə dē′) *n.* ‖ echoic ‖ a kind of titmouse

chick·en (chik′ən) *n.* ‖ < OE *cycen* ‖ **1** a common farm bird raised for its edible eggs or flesh; hen or rooster, esp. a young one **2** its flesh —*adj.* [Slang] cowardly —*vi.* [Slang] to quit from fear: usually with *out*

chicken feed [Slang] a paltry sum

chick′en-fried′ *adj.* coated with seasoned flour or batter and fried

chick′en-heart′ed *adj.* cowardly; timid Also **chick′en-liv′ered**

chick′en·pox′ *n.* an acute, contagious viral disease, esp. of children, characterized by skin eruptions

chicken wire light, pliable wire fencing

chick′pea′ *n.* **1** a bushy annual plant with short, hairy pods **2** its edible seed

chick′weed′ *n.* a low-growing plant often found as a lawn weed

chic·le (chik′əl) *n.* ‖ AmSp ‖ a gumlike substance from a tropical American tree, used in chewing gum

chic·o·ry (chik′ə rē) *n., pl.* **-ries** ‖ < Gr *kichora* ‖ **1** a plant with blue flowers and with leaves used for salad **2** its root, ground for mixing with coffee or as a coffee substitute

chide (chīd) *vt., vi.* **chid′ed** or **chid** (chid), **chid′ed** or **chid** or **chid·den** (chid′′n), **chid′ing** ‖ OE *cidan* ‖ to reprove mildly —**chid′ing·ly** *adv.*

chief (chēf) *n.* ‖ < L *caput*, head ‖ a leader; head —*adj.* main; principal

chief′ly *adv.* **1** most of all **2** mainly —*adj.* of or like a chief

chief′tain (-tən) *n.* ‖ < L *caput*, head ‖ a chief, esp. of a clan or tribe

chif·fon (shi fän′) *n.* ‖ Fr ‖ a sheer, silky fabric —*adj.* **1** of chiffon **2** made fluffy as with beaten egg whites

chig·ger (chig′ər) *n.* ‖ of Afr orig. ‖ the tiny, red larva of certain mites, whose bite causes severe itching

chi·gnon (shēn′yän′) *n.* ‖ Fr < L *catena*, chain ‖ a coil of hair worn at the back of the neck

Chi·hua·hua (chi wä′wä) *n.* ‖ after *Chihuahua*, a Mex. state ‖ a breed of very small dog with large, pointed ears

chil·blain (chil′blān′) *n.* ‖ CHIL(L) + *blain* < OE *blegen*, a sore ‖ a painful swelling or sore, esp. on the fingers or toes, caused by exposure to cold

child (chīld) ***n.***, *pl.* **chil′dren** ‖ OE *cild* ‖ 1 an infant 2 a boy or girl before puberty 3 a son or daughter —**with child** pregnant —**child′hood′** ***n.*** —**child′less** ***adj.***
child′birth′ ***n.*** the act of giving birth to a child
child′ish ***adj.*** of or like a child; specif., immature, silly, etc. —**child′ish·ly** ***adv.*** —**child′ish·ness** ***n.***
child′like′ ***adj.*** of or like a child; specif., innocent, trusting etc.
chil·dren (chil′drən) ***n.*** *pl. of* CHILD
child's play any very simple task
Chi·le (chil′ē) country on the SW coast of South America: 292,258 sq. mi.; pop. 12,261,000 —**Chil·e·an** (chi lā′ən, chil′ē ən) ***adj., n.***
chil·i (chil′ē) ***n.***, *pl.* **-ies** ‖ MexSp ‖ 1 the very hot, dried pod of red pepper, often ground as a seasoning (**chili powder**) 2 any of certain other peppers used in Mexican cooking 3 a highly spiced dish of beef, chilies or chili powder, and often beans and tomatoes: in full **chili con car·ne** (kən kär′nē) Also **chil′e**
chili dog a hot dog served with chili con carne
chili sauce a spiced sauce of chopped toma toes, sweet peppers, onions, etc.
chill (chil) ***n.*** ‖ < OE *ciele* ‖ 1 coldness or coolness causing shivers 2 a moderate coldness 3 a sudden fear, etc. 4 unfriendliness —***adj.*** CHILLY —***vi., vt.*** 1 to make or become cold 2 to cause a chill (in)
chill factor the combined effect of low temperatures and high winds on exposed skin
chill′y ***adj.*** **-i·er, -i·est** 1 moderately cold 2 unfriendly —**chill′i·ness** ***n.***
chime (chīm) ***n.*** ‖ < Gr *kymbalon*, cymbal ‖ 1 [*usually pl.*] *a)* a set of tuned bells or metal tubes *b)* the musical sounds made by these 2 a single bell, as in a clock —***vi.*** **chimed, chim′ing** 1 to sound as a chime or bells 2 to agree —***vt.*** to give (the time) by chiming —**chime in** 1 to join in 2 to agree —**chim′er** ***n.***
Chi·me·ra (kī mir′ə, ki-) ‖ < Gr *chimaira*, orig., she-goat ‖ *Gr. Myth.* a monster, with a lion's head, goat's body, and serpent's tail —***n.*** [c-] an impossible fancy
chi·mer′i·cal (-mer′i kəl) ***adj.*** 1 imaginary; unreal 2 fanciful
chim·ney (chim′nē) ***n.***, *pl.* **-neys** ‖ ult. < Gr *kaminos*, oven ‖ 1 the passage or structure through which smoke escapes from a fire, often extending above the roof 2 a glass tube around the flame of a lamp
chim·pan·zee (chim′pan zē′, chim pan′zē) ***n.*** ‖ < Bantu ‖ a medium-sized great ape of Africa Also [Colloq.] **chimp** (chimp)
chin (chin) ***n.*** ‖ OE *cin* ‖ the part of the face below the lower lip —***vt.*** **chinned, chin′ning** to pull (oneself) up, while hanging by the hands from a bar, until the chin is just above the bar
Chin. Chinese
chi·na (chī′nə) ***n.*** ‖ orig. made in China ‖ 1 porcelain or any ceramic ware like porcelain 2 dishes, etc. made of china 3 any earthenware Also **chi′na·ware′**
Chi·na (chī′nə) country in E Asia: *c.* 3,707,000 sq. mi.; pop. 1,045,537,000
chin·chil·la (chin chil′ə) ***n.*** ‖ prob. dim. of Sp. *chinche*, a small bug ‖ 1 *a)* a small rodent of South America *b)* its soft, gray fur 2 a heavy wool cloth
chine (chīn) ***n.*** ‖ < OFr *eschine*, spine ‖ a cut of meat from the backbone
Chi·nese (chī nēz′, nēs′) ***n.*** 1 *pl.* **-nese′** a native or inhabitant of China 2 a language of the Chinese —***adj.*** of China, its people, language, etc.
Chinese checkers a game in which marbles are moved as checkers, on a board with holes in a star shaped pattern
Chinese lantern a paper lantern that can be folded up
chink[1] (chiŋk) ***n.*** ‖ OE *chine* ‖ a crack ***vt.*** to close up the chinks in
chink[2] (chiŋk) ***n.*** ‖ echoic ‖ a sharp, clinking sound —***vi., vt.*** to make or cause to make this sound
chi·no (chē′nō, shē′-) ***n.***, *pl.* **-nos** ‖ < ? ‖ 1 a strong, twilled cotton, khaki cloth 2 [*pl.*] pants of chino for casual wear
Chi·nook (shə no͝ok′, no͞ok′; chə-) ***n.***, *pl.* **-nooks′** or **-nook′** ‖ < AmInd name ‖ a member of a North American Indian people of Wash. and Oreg.
chintz (chints) ***n.*** ‖ < Hindi *chhīnt* ‖ a cotton cloth printed in colored designs and usually glazed
chintz′y (-ē) ***adj.*** **-i·er, -i·est** ‖ prec. + Y³ ‖ 1 like chintz 2 [Colloq.] cheap, stingy, etc.
chip (chip) ***vt.*** **chipped, chip′ping** ‖ < OE ‖ to break or cut off small pieces from —***vi.*** to break off in small pieces —***n.*** 1 a small piece of wood, etc. cut or broken off 2 a place where a small piece has been chipped off 3 a small disk used in gambling games as a counter 4 a thin slice of food [*a potato chip*] 5 INTEGRATED CIRCUIT —**chip in** [Colloq.] to contribute (money, etc.) —**chip on one's shoulder** [Colloq.] an inclination to fight
chip′munk′ (-muŋk′) ***n.*** ‖ < AmInd ‖ a small, striped North American squirrel
chipped beef dried or smoked beef sliced into shavings
chip·per (chip′ər) ***adj.*** ‖ < N Brit Dial. ‖ [Colloq.] sprightly; in good spirits
chiro- ‖ < Gr *cheir*, hand ‖ *combining form* hand
chi·rog·ra·phy (kī räg′rə fē) ***n.*** ‖ prec. + -GRAPHY ‖ handwriting
chi·rop·o·dy (kī räp′ə dē) ***n.*** ‖ CHIRO- + POD + Y⁴ ‖ PODIATRY —**chi·rop′o·dist** ***n.***
chi·ro·prac·tic (kī′rō prak′tik) ***n.*** ‖ < CHIRO- + Gr *praktikos*, practical ‖ a method of treat ing disease by manipulation of the body joints, esp. of the spine —**chi′ro·prac′tor** ***n.***
chirp (churp) ***vi., vt.*** ‖ echoic ‖ to make, or utter in, short, shrill tones, as some birds do —***n.*** this sound
chir·rup (chir′əp) ***vi.*** ‖ < prec. ‖ to chirp repeatedly —***n.*** a chirruping sound
chis·el (chiz′əl) ***n.*** ‖ < L *caedere*, to cut ‖ a sharp-edged hand tool for cutting or shaping wood, stone, etc. —***vi., vt.*** **-eled** or **-elled, -el·ing** or **-el·ling** 1 to cut or shape with a chisel 2 [Colloq.] to swindle or get by swindling —**chis′el·er** or **chis′el·ler** ***n.***
chit (chit) ***n.*** ‖ < Hindi ‖ a voucher of a small sum owed for drink, food, etc.

chit·chat (chit′chat′) ***n.*** ‖ < CHAT ‖ **1** light, informal talk **2** gossip

chi·tin (kī′tin) ***n.*** ‖ < Gr *chitōn*, tunic ‖ the tough, horny outer covering of insects, crustaceans, etc.

chi·ton (kī′tən) ***n.*** ‖ Gr *chitōn*, tunic ‖ a small marine mollusk with a dorsal shell of eight plates

chit·ter·lings, chit·lins, or **chit·lings** (chit′linz) ***n.pl.*** ‖ < Gmc base ‖ small intestines of pigs, used for food

chiv·al·rous (shiv′əl rəs) ***adj.*** **1** gallant, courteous, etc. like an ideal knight **2** of chivalry Also **chiv′al·ric′** (-rik′, shi val′rik) **—chiv′al·rous·ly** ***adv.*** **—chiv′al·rous·ness** ***n.***

chiv′al·ry (-rē) ***n.*** ‖ < OFr *chevaler*, knight < *cheval*, horse ‖ **1** medieval knighthood **2** the qualities of an ideal knight, as courage, honor, etc.

chives (chīvz) ***n.pl.*** ‖ < L *cepa*, onion ‖ [*sometimes with sing. v.*] an herb with slender, hollow leaves and a mild onion odor, used for flavoring

chla·myd·i·a (klə mid′ē ə) ***n.*** a widespread venereal disease

chloral (hydrate) (klôr′əl) a colorless, crystalline compound used as a sedative

chlo′ride′ (-īd′) ***n.*** a compound of chlorine with another element or radical

chlo′ri·nate′ (-ə nāt′) ***vt.*** **-nat′ed, -nat′ing** to combine (a substance) with chlorine; esp., to treat (water or sewage) with chlorine for purification **—chlo′ri·na′tion** ***n.***

chlo′rine′ (-ēn′) ***n.*** ‖ < Gr *chlōros*, pale green ‖ a greenish-yellow, poisonous, gaseous chemical element with a disagreeable odor, used in bleaching, water purification, etc.

chloro- ‖ < Gr *chlōros*, pale green ‖ *combining form* **1** green **2** having chlorine in the molecule

chlo·ro·form (klôr′ə fôrm′) ***n.*** ‖ < Fr: see prec. & FORMIC ‖ a colorless, volatile liquid used as a solvent and, formerly, as an anesthetic **—*vt.*** to anesthetize or kill with chloroform

chlo′ro·phyll′ or **chlo′ro·phyl′** (-fil′) ***n.*** ‖ < Fr, ult. < Gr *chlōros*, green + *phyllon*, leaf ‖ the green pigment found in plant cells, essential to photosynthesis

chock (chäk) ***n.*** ‖ NormFr *choque*, a block ‖ a block or wedge placed under a wheel, etc. to prevent motion **—*vt.*** to wedge fast as with a chock **—*adv.*** as close or tight as can be

chock′-full′ ***adj.*** as full as possible

choc·o·late (chôk′ə lət, chäk′ə-; chôk′lət, chäk′-) ***n.*** ‖ ult. < AmInd (Mexico) ‖ **1** a substance made from roasted and ground cacao seeds **2** a drink or candy made with chocolate **3** reddish brown **—*adj.*** **1** made of or flavored with chocolate **2** reddish-brown **—choc′o·lat·y** or **choc′o·lat·ey** ***adj.***

choice (chois) ***n.*** ‖ < OFr < Gothic *kausjan*, to test ‖ **1** a choosing; selection **2** the right or power to choose **3** a person or thing chosen **4** the best part **5** a variety from which to choose **6** an alternative **—*adj.*** **choic′er, choic′est** **1** of special excellence **2** carefully chosen

choir (kwīr) ***n.*** ‖ < L < Gr *choros* ‖ **1** a group of singers, esp. in a church **2** the part of a church they occupy

choke (chōk) ***vt.*** **choked, chok′ing** ‖ < OE *aceocian* ‖ **1** to prevent from breathing by blocking the windpipe; strangle; suffocate **2** to obstruct by clogging **3** to hinder the growth or action of **4** to cut off some air from the carburetor of (a gasoline engine) so as to make a richer gasoline mixture **—*vi.*** **1** to be suffocated **2** to be obstructed **—*n.*** **1** a choking **2** a sound of choking **3** the valve that chokes a carburetor **—choke back** to hold back (feelings, sobs, etc.) **—choke down** to swallow with difficulty **—choke off** to bring to an end **—choke up** [Colloq.] to be unable to perform because of fear, tension, etc.

choke collar a training collar for a dog, that tightens when the dog strains at the leash

chok′er ***n.*** a closefitting necklace

chol·er (käl′ər) ***n.*** ‖ < L *cholera*: see fol. ‖ [Now Rare] anger or ill humor

chol·er·a (käl′ər ə) ***n.*** ‖ < Gr *cholē*, bile ‖ any of several severe intestinal diseases

chol′er·ic ***adj.*** easily angered

cho·les·ter·ol (kə les′tər ôl′, -ōl′) ***n.*** ‖ < Gr *cholē*, bile + *stereos*, solid ‖ a crystalline alcohol found esp. in animal fats, blood, nerve tissue, and bile

chomp (chämp) ***vt., vi.*** **1** CHAMP[1] **2** to bite down (*on*) repeatedly

Chong·qing (choon′chiŋ′) city in south central China: pop. 2,650,000

choose (chōōz) ***vt., vi.*** **chose, cho′sen, choos′ing** ‖ OE *ceosan* ‖ **1** to take as a choice; select **2** to decide or prefer [to *choose* to go] **—cannot choose but** cannot do otherwise than **—choos′er** ***n.***

choos′y or **choos′ey** ***adj.*** **-i·er, -i·est** [Colloq.] careful or fussy in choosing

chop[1] (chäp) ***vt.*** **chopped, chop′ping** ‖ ME *choppen* ‖ **1** to cut by blows with a sharp tool **2** to cut into small bits; mince **—*vi.*** to make quick, cutting strokes **—*n.*** **1** a short, sharp stroke **2** a cut of meat and bone from the rib, loin, or shoulder **3** a short, broken movement of waves

chop[2] (chäp) ***n.*** ‖ var. of CHAP[1] ‖ **1** a jaw **2** [*pl.*] the mouth and lower cheeks

chop′house′ ***n.*** a restaurant that specializes in chops and steaks

Cho·pin (shō pan′, shō-), **Fré·dé·ric** (frā dā rēk′) 1810-49; Pol. composer, in France after 1831

chop·per (chäp′ər) ***n.*** **1** one that chops **2** [*pl.*] [Slang] teeth **3** [Colloq.] a helicopter

chop′py ***adj.*** **-pi′er, -pi·est** **1** rough with short, broken waves, as the sea **2** making abrupt starts and stops **—chop′pi·ness** ***n.***

CHOPSTICKS

chop′sticks′ ***n.pl.*** ‖ Pidgin English ‖ two small sticks held together in one hand and used, mainly in parts of Asia, to lift food to the mouth

chop su·ey (chäp′ sōō′ē) ‖ < Chin *tsa-sui*,

various pieces ‖ a Chinese-American dish of meat, bean sprouts, etc., served with rice

cho·ral (kôr′əl) ***adj.*** of, for, or sung by a choir or chorus —**cho′ral·ly** ***adv.***

cho·rale or **cho·ral** (kə ral′, -räl′) ***n.*** **1** a hymn tune **2** a choir or chorus

chord[1] (kôrd) ***n.*** ‖ altered (infl. by L *chorda*) < CORD ‖ **1** [Archaic] the string of a musical instrument **2** a straight line joining any two points on an arc

chord[2] (kôrd) ***n.*** ‖ < ME *accord*, accord ‖ *Music* a combination of three or more tones sounded together in harmony

chor·date (kôr′dāt′) ***n.*** ‖ L *chorda*, CORD + ATE[1] ‖ any of a phylum of animal having a dorsal nerve cord, including the vertebrates

chore (chôr) ***n.*** ‖ < OE *cierr*, job ‖ **1** a routine task **2** a hard task

chor·e·o·graph (kôr′ē ə graf′) ***vt., vi.*** ‖ < fol. ‖ to design or plan the movements of (a dance) —**chor′e·og′ra·pher** (-äg′rə fər) ***n.***

chor·e·og·ra·phy (kôr′ē äg′rə fē) ***n.*** ‖ Gr *choreia*, dance + -GRAPHY ‖ **1** dancing, esp. ballet dancing **2** the art of devising dances, esp. ballets —**chor′e·o·graph′ic** (-ə graf′ik) ***adj.***

chor·is·ter (kôr′is tər) ***n.*** ‖ see CHORUS ‖ a member of a choir

cho·roid (kôr′oid′) ***n.*** ‖ Gr < *chorion*, fetal membrane + *-eidēs*, -OID ‖ the dark, middle membrane of the eye

chor·tle (chôrt′′l) ***vi., vt.*** **-tled, -tling** ‖ prob. < CHUCKLE + SNORT ‖ to make, or utter with, a gleeful chuckling or snorting sound —***n.*** such a sound —**chor′tler** ***n.***

cho·rus (kôr′əs) ***n.*** ‖ < Gr *choros* ‖ **1** a group of dancers and singers performing together **2** the part of a drama, song, etc. performed by a chorus **3** a group singing or speaking something together **4** music written for group singing **5** the refrain of a song —***vt., vi.*** to sing, speak, or say in unison —**in chorus** in unison

chose (chōz) ***vt., vi.*** *pt. & obs. pp. of* CHOOSE

cho·sen (chō′zən) ***vt., vi.*** *pp. of* CHOOSE —***adj.*** selected; choice

Chou En-lai (jō′en′lī′) 1898-1976; Chin. prime minister (1949-76): Pinyin *Zhou Enlai*

chow (chou) ***n.*** ‖ < Chin ‖ **1** any of a breed of medium-sized dog, originally from China **2** [Slang] food

chow·der (chou′dər) ***n.*** ‖ Fr *chaudière*, a pot ‖ a thick soup usually of onions and potatoes and, often, clams and milk

chow mein (chou′ mān′) ‖ Chin *ch'ao*, fry + *mien*, flour ‖ a Chinese-American dish of meat, bean sprouts, etc., served with fried noodles

chrism (kriz′əm) ***n.*** ‖ < Gr *chrisma*, oil ‖ holy oil used as in baptism

Christ (krīst) ‖ < Gr *christos*, the anointed ‖ Jesus of Nazareth, regarded by Christians as the prophesied Messiah

chris·ten (kris′ən) ***vt.*** **1** to take into a Christian church by baptism; baptize **2** to give a name to, esp. at baptism —**chris′ten·ing** ***n.***

Chris′ten·dom (-dəm) ***n.*** **1** Christians collectively **2** those parts of the world where most of the inhabitants profess Christianity

Chris·tian (kris′chən) ***n.*** a believer in Jesus as the Messiah prophesied in the Old Testament, or in the religion based on the teachings of Jesus —***adj.*** **1** of Jesus Christ **2** of or professing the religion based on his teachings **3** having the qualities taught by Jesus Christ, as love, kindness, humility, etc. **4** of Christians or Christianity

Chris·ti·an·i·ty (kris′chē an′ə tē) ***n.*** **1** Christians collectively **2** the Christian religion **3** the state of being a Christian

Chris·tian·ize (kris′chən īz′) ***vt.*** **-ized′, -iz′·ing** **1** to convert to Christianity **2** to make Christian in character

Christian name the baptismal name or given name, as distinguished from the surname or family name

Christian Science a religion and system of healing: official name **Church of Christ, Scientist**

Chris·tie (kris′tē) ***n., pl.*** **-ties** ‖ after *Christiania*, former name of Oslo, Norway ‖ *Skiing* a high-speed turn with the skis parallel

Christ·mas (kris′məs) ***n.*** ‖ see CHRIST & MASS ‖ a holiday on Dec. 25 celebrating the birth of Jesus Christ

chro·mat·ic (krō mat′ik) ***adj.*** ‖ < Gr *chrōma*, color ‖ **1** of or having color or colors **2** *Music* progressing by half tones —**chro·mat′i·cal·ly** ***adv.***

chro·ma·tin (krō′mə tin′) ***n.*** ‖ < Gr *chrōma*, color ‖ a substance in cell nuclei that readily absorbs a coloring agent, as for observation under a microscope

chrome (krōm) ***n.*** ‖ Fr: see CHROMIUM ‖ chromium or chromium alloy —***adj.*** designating any of various pigments (**chrome red, chrome yellow**) made from chromium compounds —***vt.*** **chromed, chrom′ing** to plate with chromium

-chrome (krōm) ‖ < Gr *chrōma*, color ‖ *combining form* **1** color or coloring agent **2** chromium

chro·mi·um (krō′mē əm) ***n.*** ‖ < Gr *chrōma*, color ‖ a hard, metallic chemical element resistant to corrosion

chromo- ‖ < Gr *chrōma*, color ‖ *combining form* color or pigment *[chromosome]* Also **chrom-**

chro·mo·some (krō′mə sōm′) ***n.*** ‖ < prec. ‖ any of the microscopic rod-shaped bodies carrying genes

chron·ic (krän′ik) ***adj.*** ‖ < Gr *chronos*, time ‖ **1** lasting a long time or recurring: said of a disease **2** having had an ailment for a long time **3** habitual —**chron′i·cal·ly** ***adv.***

chron·i·cle (krän′i kəl) ***n.*** ‖ < Gr *chronika*, annals ‖ a historical record of events in the order in which they happened —***vt.*** **-cled, -cling** to tell the history of; recount; record —**chron′i·cler** ***n.***

chrono- ‖ < Gr *chronos*, time ‖ *combining form* time Also **chron-**

chro·nol·o·gy (krō näl′ə jē) ***n., pl.*** **-gies** ‖ prec. + -LOGY ‖ **1** the science of measuring time and of dating events **2** the arrangement of events in the order of occurrence —**chron·o·log·i·cal** (krän′ō läj′i kəl) ***adj.*** —**chron′o·log′i·cal·ly** ***adv.***

chro·nom′e·ter (-näm′ət ər) ***n.*** ‖ CHRONO- + -METER ‖ a highly accurate kind of clock or watch

chrys·a·lis (kris′ə lis) ***n.*** ‖ < Gr *chrysallis* ‖

1 the pupa of a butterfly, encased in a cocoon 2 the cocoon

chrys·an·the·mum (kri san′thə məm) ***n.*** ‖ < Gr *chrysos*, gold + *anthemon*, flower ‖ 1 a late-blooming plant of the composite family, with showy flowers 2 the flower

chub·by (chub′ē) ***adj.*** **-bi·er, -bi·est** round and plump —**chub′bi·ness *n.***

chuck[1] (chuk) ***vt.*** ‖ < ? Fr *choquer*, strike against ‖ 1 to tap playfully, esp. under the chin 2 to throw; toss 3 [Slang] to get rid of —***n.*** a chucking

chuck[2] (chuk) ***n.*** ‖ prob. var. of CHOCK ‖ 1 a cut of beef from around the neck and shoulder blade 2 a clamplike holding device, as on a lathe

chuck′-full′ ***adj.*** *var. of* CHOCK FULL

chuck′hole′ ***n.*** ‖ see CHOCK & HOLE ‖ a rough hole in pavement

chuck·le (chuk′əl) ***vi.*** **-led, -ling** ‖ ? < var. of CLUCK ‖ to laugh softly in a low tone —***n.*** a soft, low-toned laugh

chuck wagon a wagon equipped as a kitchen for feeding cowboys, etc.

chuck·wal·la (chuk′wäl′ə) ***n.*** ‖ < AmInd (Mexico) ‖ a large, edible iguana of Mexico and SW U.S.

chug (chug) ***n.*** ‖ echoic ‖ a puffing or explosive sound, as of a locomotive —***vi.*** **chugged, chug′ging** to make, or move with, such sounds

chuk·ka (boot) (chuk′ə) an ankle-high bootlike shoe

chum (chum) ***n.*** ‖ prob. < *chamber* (*mate*) ‖ [Colloq.] a close friend —***vi.*** **chummed, chum′ming** [Colloq.] to be close friends —**chum′mi·ness *n.*** —**chum′my, -mi·er, -mi·est, *adj.***

chump (chump) ***n.*** ‖ akin to MHG *kumpf*, dull ‖ [Colloq.] a stupid person; fool

Chung·king (choon′kiŋ′) *old form of* CHONGQING

chunk (chuŋk) ***n.*** ‖ < ? CHUCK[2] ‖ a short, thick piece

chunk·y (chuŋ′kē) ***adj.*** **-i·er, -i·est** 1 short and thick 2 stocky —**chunk′i·ness *n.***

church (church) ***n.*** ‖ < Gr *kyriakē* (*oikia*), Lord's (house) ‖ 1 a building for public worship, esp. Christian worship 2 religious service 3 [*usually* **C-**] *a)* all Christians *b)* a particular Christian denomination 4 ecclesiastical, as opposed to secular, government

church′go′er (-gō′ər) ***n.*** a person who attends church, esp. regularly

Church·ill (church′chil), Sir **Win·ston** (win′stən) 1874-1965; Brit. prime minister (1940-45; 1951-55)

church′man (-mən) ***n.***, *pl.* **-men** 1 a clergyman 2 a church member

Church of England the episcopal church of England; Anglican Church: it is an established church headed by the sovereign

church′war′den (-wôrd″n) ***n.*** a lay officer handling certain secular matters in a church

church′yard′ ***n.*** the ground adjoining a church, often used as a cemetery

churl (churl) ***n.*** ‖ OE *ceorl*, peasant ‖ 1 a peasant 2 a surly, ill-bred person; boor —**churl′ish *adj.*** —**churl′ish·ness *n.***

churn (churn) ***n.*** ‖ OE *cyrne* ‖ a container in which milk or cream is stirred and shaken to form butter —***vt., vi.*** 1 to stir and shake (milk or cream) in a churn 2 to make (butter) thus 3 to stir up or move vigorously

chute[1] (shōōt) ***n.*** ‖ Fr, a fall ‖ an inclined or vertical trough or passage down which things slide or drop

chute[2] (shōōt) ***n.*** *short for* PARACHUTE

chut·ney (chut′nē) ***n.***, *pl.* **-neys** ‖ Hindi *chatnī* ‖ a relish of fruits, spices, herbs, and vinegar Also **chut′nee**

chutz·pah or **chutz·pa** (hoots′pə) ***n.*** ‖ Yidd > Heb ‖ [Colloq.] impudence; brass

chyme (kīm) ***n.*** ‖ < Gr *chymos*, juice ‖ the semifluid mass formed as the stomach digests food: it passes into the small intestine

CIA Central Intelligence Agency

ci·ca·da (si kā′də) ***n.***, *pl.* **-das** or **-dae** (-dē) ‖ L ‖ a large, flylike insect with transparent wings: the male makes a loud, shrill sound

cic·a·trix (sik′ə triks′) ***n.***, *pl.* **cic·a·tri·ces** (sik′ə trī′sēz′) or **cic·a·trix·es** ‖ L ‖ a scar

Cic·e·ro (sis′ər ō′) 106-43 B.C.; Rom. statesman & orator

-cide (sīd) ‖ < L *caedere*, to kill ‖ *suffix* 1 a killer 2 a killing

ci·der (sī′dər) ***n.*** ‖ < Gr *sikera*, an intoxicant ‖ juice pressed from apples, used as a drink or for making vinegar

ci·gar (si gär′) ***n.*** ‖ Sp *cigarro* ‖ a cylindrical roll of cured tobacco wrapped in another leaf for smoking

cig·a·rette or **cig·a·ret** (sig′ə ret′) ***n.*** ‖ Fr ‖ a small roll of finely cut tobacco wrapped in thin paper for smoking

cig·a·ril·lo (sig′ə ril′ō) ***n.***, *pl.* **-los** ‖ Sp, dim. of *cigarro*, cigar ‖ a small, thin cigar

cil·i·a (sil′ē ə) ***n.pl.***, *sing.* **-i·um** (-ē əm) ‖ < L ‖ *Bot.* small hairlike projections extending from certain plant cells and forming a fringe

ci·met·i·dine (sə met′ə dēn′) ***n.*** a drug that blocks histamine receptors, reducing gastric secretion: used to treat peptic ulcers

cinch (sinch) ***n.*** ‖ < Sp < L *cingulum*, girdle ‖ 1 a saddle or pack girth 2 [Slang] a thing easy to do or sure to happen —***vt.*** 1 to fasten (a saddle) on 2 [Slang] to make sure of

cin·cho·na (sin kō′nə) ***n.*** ‖ after 17th-c. Peruvian Countess del *Chinchón* ‖ 1 a tropical tree with a bitter bark from which quinine is made 2 this bark

Cin·cin·nat·i (sin′sə nat′ē, -ə) city in SW Ohio: pop. 385,000

cinc·ture (siŋk′chər) ***n.*** ‖ L *cinctura* ‖ a belt or girdle

cin·der (sin′dər) ***n.*** ‖ OE *sinder*, slag ‖ 1 a tiny piece of partly burned wood, etc. 2 [*pl.*] ashes from coal or wood

Cin·der·el·la (sin′dər el′ə) in a fairy tale, a household drudge who eventually marries a prince

cin·e·ma (sin′ə mə) ***n.*** ‖ < Gr *kinēma*, motion ‖ [Chiefly Brit.] a film theater —**the cinema** 1 the making of films 2 films collectively —**cin′e·mat′ic *adj.***

cin·e·ma·tog·ra·phy (sin′ə mə täg′rə fē) ***n.*** the art, science, and work of photography in making films —**cin′e·ma·tog′ra·pher *n.*** —**cin′e·mat′o·graph′ic** (-mat′ə graf′ik) ***adj.***

cin·na·bar (sin′ə bär′) ***n.*** ‖ < Gr *kinnabari* ‖ mercuric sulfide, a heavy, bright-red mineral

cin·na·mon (sin′ə mən) ***n.*** ‖ < Heb *qinnāmōn* ‖ 1 the light-brown spice made from the dried inner bark of a laurel tree of the East Indies **2** this bark

ci·pher (sī′fər) ***n.*** ‖ < Ar *ṣifr* ‖ **1** the symbol 0; zero **2** a nonentity **3** secret writing based on a key; code **4** the key to such a code **—*vi.*** [Now Rare] to solve arithmetic problems

cir·ca (sur′kə) ***prep.*** ‖ L ‖ about: used before an approximate date or figure

cir·ca·di·an (sər kā′dē ən) ***adj.*** ‖ coined < L *circa,* about + *dies,* day ‖ of the behavioral or physiological rhythms associated with the 24-hour cycle of the earth's rotation

Cir·ce (sur′sē) in the *Odyssey,* an enchantress who turns men into swine

cir·cle (sur′kəl) ***n.*** ‖ < Gr *kirkos* ‖ **1** a plane figure bounded by a single curved line every point of which is equally distant from the center **2** this curved line **3** anything like a circle, as a ring **4** a complete or recurring series; cycle **5** a group of people with common interests **6** extent, as of influence; scope **—*vt.* -cled, -cling 1** to form a circle around **2** to move around, as in a circle **—*vi.*** to go around in a circle **—cir′cler *n.***

cir′clet (-klit) ***n.*** **1** a small circle **2** a circular ornament, as for the head

cir·cuit (sur′kit) ***n.*** ‖ < L *circum,* around + *ire,* go ‖ **1** a boundary line or its length **2** a going around something **3** the regular journey through a district of a person at work, as a preacher **4** a chain or association, as of theaters or resorts **5** the path or line of an electric current **—*vi.*** to go in a circuit **—*vt.*** to make a circuit about **—cir′cuit·al *adj.***

circuit breaker a device that automatically interrupts the flow of an electric current

circuit court a court that holds sessions in various places within its district

cir·cu·i·tous (sər kyo͞o′ət əs) ***adj.*** roundabout; indirect **—cir·cu′i·tous·ly *adv.* —cir·cu′i·tous·ness *n.***

cir·cuit·ry (sur′kə trē) ***n.*** the system or the elements of an electric circuit

cir·cu·lar (sur′kyə lər) ***adj.*** **1** in the shape of a circle; round **2** moving in a circle **3** circuitous **—*n.*** an advertisement, etc., intended for many readers **—cir′cu·lar′i·ty** (-ler′ə tē) ***n.***

cir′cu·lar·ize′ (-lər īz′) ***vt.* -ized′, -iz′ing 1** to make circular **2** to send circulars to **3** to canvass **—cir′cu·lar·i·za′tion *n.* —cir′cu·lar·iz′er *n.***

cir·cu·late (sur′kyo͞o lāt′) ***vi.* -lat′ed, -lat′ing** ‖ < L *circulari,* form a circle ‖ **1** to move in a circle or circuit and return, as the blood **2** to go from person to person or from place to place **—*vt.*** to make circulate **—cir′cu·lat′or *n.* —cir′cu·la·to′ry** (-lə tôr′ē) ***adj.***

cir·cu·la·tion (sur′kyo͞o lā′shən) ***n.*** **1** a circulating **2** the movement of blood through the arteries and veins **3** distribution of newspapers, magazines, etc.

circum- ‖ < L *circum* ‖ *prefix* around, about, surrounding

cir·cum·cise (sur′kəm sīz′) ***vt.* -cised′, -cis′ing** ‖ < L < *circum,* around + *caedere,* to cut ‖ to cut off all or part of the foreskin of **—cir′cum·ci′sion** (-sizh′ən) ***n.***

cir·cum·fer·ence (sər kum′fər əns) ***n.*** ‖ < L *circum,* around + *ferre,* to carry ‖ **1** the line bounding a circle, ball, etc. **2** the length of this line

cir·cum·flex (sur′kəm fleks′) ***n.*** ‖ < L *circum,* around + *flectere,* to bend ‖ a mark (^, ˜) used over a vowel letter or symbol to indicate pronunciation

cir′cum·lo·cu′tion (-lō kyo͞o′shən) ***n.*** ‖ < L: see CIRCUM- & LOCUTION ‖ a roundabout way of saying something

cir′cum·nav′i·gate′ (-nav′ə gāt′) ***vt.* -gat′ed, -gat′ing** ‖ < L: see CIRCUM & NAVIGATE ‖ to sail or fly around (the earth, etc.) **—cir′cum·nav′i·ga′tion *n.***

cir′cum·scribe′ (-skrīb′) ***vt.* -scribed′, -scrib′ing** ‖ < L: see CIRCUM- & SCRIBE ‖ **1** to trace a line around; encircle **2** to limit; confine **—cir′cum·scrip′tion** (-skrip′shən) ***n.***

cir′cum·spect′ (-spekt′) ***adj.*** ‖ < L *circumspicere,* look about ‖ cautious **—cir′cum·spec′tion *n.***

cir′cum·stance′ (-stans′) ***n.*** ‖ < L *circum,* around + *stare,* to stand ‖ **1** a fact or event accompanying another **2** [*pl.*] conditions affecting a person, esp. financial conditions **3** chance; luck **4** ceremony; show **—*vt.* -stanced′, -stanc′ing** to place in certain circumstances **—under no circumstances** never **—cir′cum·stanced′ *adj.***

cir′cum·stan′tial (-stan′shəl) ***adj.*** **1** having to do with, or depending on, circumstances **2** incidental **3** complete in detail **—cir′cum·stan′tial·ly *adv.***

circumstantial evidence *Law* indirect evidence of a fact at issue, based on attendant circumstances

cir′cum·stan′ti·ate′ (-stan′shē āt′) ***vt.* -at′ed, -at′ing** to give detailed proof or support of **—cir′cum·stan′ti·a′tion *n.***

cir′cum·vent′ (-vent′) ***vt.*** ‖ < L *circum,* around + *venire,* come ‖ to get the better of or prevent by craft or ingenuity **—cir′cum·ven′tion *n.***

cir·cus (sur′kəs) ***n.*** ‖ L, a circle ‖ **1** in ancient Rome, an amphitheater **2** a traveling show of acrobats, trained animals, clowns, etc. **3** [Colloq.] a source of great fun

ci·ré (sē rā′) ***adj.*** ‖ < Fr *cire,* wax ‖ having a smooth, glossy finish

cir·rho·sis (sə rō′sis) ***n.*** ‖ < Gr *kirrhos,* tawny + -OSIS ‖ a degenerative disease, esp. of the liver, marked by excess formation of connective tissue **—cir·rhot′ic** (-rät′ik) ***adj.***

cir·rus (sir′əs) ***n.*** ‖ L, a curl ‖ the type of cloud resembling a wispy filament and found at high altitudes

cis- ‖ < L *cis,* on this side ‖ *prefix* on this side of

cis·tern (sis′tərn) ***n.*** ‖ < L *cista,* chest ‖ a large tank for storing water

cit·a·del (sit′ə del′) ***n.*** ‖ < L *civitas,* city ‖ a fortress

cite (sīt) ***vt.* cit′ed, cit′ing** ‖ < L *citare,* summon ‖ **1** to summon before a court of law **2** to quote **3** to mention by way of example, proof, etc. **4** to mention in an official report as meritorious **—ci·ta′tion *n.***

cit·i·fied (sit′i fīd′) ***adj.*** having the manners, dress, etc. of city people

cit·i·zen (sit′ə zən) ***n.*** ‖ < L *civis,* townsman ‖ a member of a state or nation who owes allegiance to it by birth or naturalization and is entitled to certain rights, as the right to vote, etc. —**cit'i·zen·ship'** *n.*

cit'i·zen·ry (-rē) *n.* all citizens as a group

cit·ric (si'trik) *adj.* designating or of an acid obtained from citrus fruits

cit'ron (-trən) *n.* ‖ < Fr, lemon ‖ **1** a yellow, thick-skinned, lemonlike fruit **2** its candied rind

cit·ron·el·la (si'trə nel'ə) *n.* ‖ see prec. ‖ a sharp-smelling oil used in perfume, insect repellents, etc.

cit'rus (-trəs) *n.* ‖ L ‖ **1** any of the trees that bear oranges, lemons, limes, etc. **2** any such fruit —*adj.* of these trees: also **cit'-rous**

cit·y (sit'ē) *n., pl.* **-ies** ‖ < L *civis,* townsman ‖ **1** a population center larger or more important than a town **2** in the U.S., an incorporated municipality with boundaries and powers defined by State charter **3** the people of a city —*adj.* of, in, or for a city

city hall a building which houses a municipal government

civ·et (siv'it) *n.* ‖ < Ar *zabād* ‖ **1** the musky secretion of a catlike carnivore (**civet cat**) of Africa and S Asia: used in some perfumes **2** the animal, or its fur

civ·ic (siv'ik) *adj.* ‖ < L *civis,* townsman ‖ of a city, citizens, or citizenship

civ'ics (-iks) *n.pl.* [*with sing. v.*] the study of civic affairs and the duties and rights of citizenship

civ·il (siv'əl) *adj.* ‖ see CIVIC ‖ **1** of a citizen or citizens **2** civilized **3** polite **4** of citizens in matters not military or religious —**civ'il·ly** *adv.*

civil disobedience nonviolent opposition to a law through refusal to comply with it, on grounds of conscience

civil engineering engineering dealing with the construction of highways, bridges, harbors, etc. —**civil engineer**

ci·vil·ian (sə vil'yən) *n.* ‖ see CIVIC ‖ a person not in military or naval service —*adj.* of or for civilians; nonmilitary

ci·vil'i·ty (-ə tē) *n., pl.* **-ties 1** politeness **2** a civil, or polite, act

civ·i·li·za·tion (siv'ə lə zā'shən) *n.* **1** a civilizing or being civilized **2** the total culture of a people, period, etc. **3** the peoples considered to have attained a high social development

civ'i·lize' (-līz') *vt., vi.* **-lized', -liz'ing** ‖ see CIVIC ‖ **1** to bring or come out of a primitive or savage condition to a higher level of social organization and of cultural and scientific development **2** to refine —**civ'i·lized'** *adj.*

civil law the body of law having to do with private rights

civil liberties liberties guaranteed to all individuals by law, custom, court decisions, etc.; rights, as of speaking or acting as one likes, without hindrance except in the interests of the public welfare

civil rights those rights guaranteed to all individuals by the 13th, 14th, 15th, and 19th Amendments to the U.S. Constitution, as the right to vote and the right to equal treatment under the law

civil servant a civil service employee

civil service all those employed in government service, esp. through competitive public examination

civil war war between different factions of the same nation —**the Civil War** the war between the North and the South in the U.S. (1861-65)

civ·vies (siv'ēz) *n.pl.* [Colloq.] civilian clothes Also **civ'ies**

ck. check

Cl *Chem. symbol for* chlorine

cl centiliter(s)

clack (klak) *vi., vt.* ‖ prob. echoic < ON ‖ to make or cause to make a sudden, sharp sound —*n.* this sound

clad (klad) *vt. alt. pt. & pp. of* CLOTHE —*adj.* **1** clothed; dressed **2** having a bonded outer layer of another metal or an alloy /*clad* steel/

clad'ding *n.* a layer of some metal or alloy bonded to another metal

claim (klām) *vt.* ‖ < L *clamare,* cry out ‖ **1** to demand as rightfully belonging to one **2** to require; deserve /to *claim* attention/ **3** to assert —*n.* **1** a claiming **2** a right to something **3** something claimed **4** an assertion —**claim'a·ble** *adj.* —**claim'ant** or **claim'er** *n.*

clair·voy·ance (kler voi'əns) *n.* ‖ Fr < *clair,* clear + *voyant,* seeing ‖ the supposed ability to perceive things that are not in sight —**clair·voy'ant** *n., adj.*

clam (klam) *n.* ‖ < obs. *clam,* a clamp ‖ any of various hard-shelled, usually edible, bivalve mollusks —*vi.* **clammed, clam'-ming** to dig for clams —**clam up** [Colloq.] to keep silent —**clam'mer** *n.*

clam'bake' *n.* **1** a picnic at which steamed or baked clams are served **2** [Colloq.] any large, noisy party

clam·ber (klam'bər) *vi., vt.* ‖ ME *clambren* ‖ to climb clumsily, esp. by using both the hands and the feet

clam·my (klam'ē) *adj.* **-mi·er, -mi·est** ‖ ME, prob. < OE *clam,* mud ‖ moist, cold, and sticky —**clam'mi·ness** *n.*

clam·or (klam'ər) *n.* ‖ < L *clamare,* cry out ‖ **1** a loud outcry; uproar **2** a loud demand or complaint —*vi.* to make a clamor —**clam'-or·ous** *adj.*

clamp (klamp) *n.* ‖ < MDu *klampe* ‖ a device for clasping or fastening things together —*vt.* to fasten or brace, as with a clamp —**clamp down (on)** to become more strict (with)

clan (klan) *n.* ‖ < Gael < L *planta,* offshoot ‖ **1** a group of families claiming descent from a common ancestor **2** a group of people with interests in common —**clans·man** (klanz'mən), *pl.* **-men,** *n.*

clan·des·tine (klan des'tin) *adj.* ‖ < L *clam,* secret ‖ secret or hidden; furtive —**clan·des'tine·ly** *adv.*

clang (klaŋ) *vi., vt.* ‖ echoic ‖ to make or cause to make a loud, ringing sound, as by striking metal —*n.* this sound

clang'or (-ər) *n.* ‖ L < *clangere,* to sound ‖ a continuous clanging sound

clank (klaŋk) *n.* ‖ echoic ‖ a sharp, metallic sound —*vi., vt.* to make or cause to make this sound

clan·nish (klan'ish) *adj.* **1** of a clan **2** tending to associate closely with one's own group only —**clan'nish·ly** *adv.* —**clan'-nish·ness** *n.*

clap (klap) *vi.* **clapped, clap′ping** ⟦OE *clæppan,* to beat⟧ 1 to make a sudden, explosive sound, as of two flat surfaces struck together 2 to strike the hands together, as in applauding —*vt.* 1 to strike together briskly 2 to strike with an open hand 3 to put, move, etc. abruptly /*clapped* into jail/ —*n.* 1 the sound or act of clapping 2 a sharp slap

clap·board (klab′ərd) *n.* ⟦transl. of MDu *klapholt* < *klappen,* to fit + *holt,* wood⟧ a thin board with one thicker edge, used as siding —*vt.* to cover with clapboards

clap′per *n.* a thing that makes a clapping sound, as the tongue of a bell

clap′trap′ *n.* ⟦CLAP + TRAP[1]⟧ insincere, empty talk intended to get applause

claque (klak) *n.* ⟦Fr < *claquer,* to clap⟧ a group of people paid to applaud at a play, opera, etc.

clar·et (klar′it) *n.* ⟦< OFr (*vin*) *claret,* clear (wine)⟧ a dry red wine

clar·i·fy (klar′ə fī′) *vt., vi.* **-fied′, -fy′ing** ⟦< L *clarus,* clear + *facere,* to make⟧ to make or become clear —**clar′i·fi·ca′tion** *n.*

CLARINET

clar·i·net (klar′ə net′) *n.* ⟦< Fr < L *clarus,* clear⟧ a single-reed woodwind instrument played by means of holes and keys —**clar′i·net′ist** or **clar′i·net′tist** *n.*

clar·i·on (klar′ē ən) *adj.* ⟦< L *clarus,* clear⟧ clear, sharp, and ringing /a *clarion* call/

clar·i·ty (klar′ə tē) *n.* ⟦< L *clarus,* clear⟧ clear quality; clearness

clash (klash) *vi.* ⟦echoic⟧ 1 to collide with a loud, harsh, metallic noise 2 to conflict; disagree —*vt.* to strike with a clashing noise —*n.* 1 the sound of clashing 2 conflict

clasp (klasp) *n.* ⟦ME *claspe*⟧ 1 a fastening, as a hook, to hold things together 2 a grasping; embrace 3 a grip of the hand —*vt.* 1 to fasten with a clasp 2 to hold or embrace tightly 3 to grip with the hand

class (klas) *n.* ⟦< L *classis*⟧ 1 a number of people or things grouped together because of certain likenesses; kind; sort 2 social or economic rank /the working *class*/ 3 *a*) a group of students taught together *b*) a meeting of such a group *c*) a group graduating together 4 grade or quality 5 [Slang] excellence, as of style —*vt.* to classify —**class′less** *adj.*

class action (suit) a legal action brought by one or more persons on behalf of themselves and a much larger group

clas·sic (klas′ik) *adj.* ⟦< L *classis,* class⟧ 1 being an excellent model of its kind 2 CLASSICAL (senses 2 & 3) 3 balanced, formal, regular, simple, etc. 4 famous as traditional or typical —*n.* 1 a literary or artistic work of the highest excellence 2 a creator of such a work 3 [*pl.*] *a*) the works of outstanding ancient Greek and Roman authors (usually with *the*) *b*) [*with sing. v.*] the study of these works and of ancient Greek and Latin 4 a famous traditional or typical event

clas′si·cal (-i kəl) *adj.* 1 CLASSIC (senses 1 & 3) 2 of the art, literature, etc. of the ancient Greeks and Romans 3 typical of or derived from the artistic standards of the ancient Greeks and Romans 4 versed in Greek and Roman culture 5 standard and traditional /*classical* economics/ 6 designating, of, or like music conforming to certain standards of form, complexity, etc. —**clas′si·cal·ly** *adv.*

clas′si·cism′ (-ə siz′əm) *n.* 1 the aesthetic principles of ancient Greece and Rome 2 adherence to these principles 3 knowledge of classical literature and art —**clas′si·cist** *n.*

classified advertising advertising arranged according to subject, under such listings as *help wanted*

clas·si·fy (klas′ə fī′) *vt.* **-fied′, -fy′ing** 1 to arrange in classes according to a system 2 to designate (government documents) to be secret or restricted —**clas′si·fi·ca′tion** *n.* —**clas′si·fi′er** *n.*

class′mate′ *n.* a member of the same class at a school or college

class′room′ *n.* a room in a school or college in which classes are taught

class·y (klas′ē) *adj.* **-i·er, -i·est** [Slang] first-class, esp. in style; elegant —**class′i·ness** *n.*

clat·ter (klat′ər) *vi., vt.* ⟦ME *clateren*⟧ to make or cause to make a clatter —*n.* 1 a rapid succession of loud, sharp noises 2 a tumult; hubbub

clause (klôz) *n.* ⟦< L *claudere,* to close⟧ 1 a group of words containing a subject and a finite verb: see DEPENDENT CLAUSE, INDEPENDENT CLAUSE 2 a particular article or provision in a document —**claus′al** *adj.*

claus·tro·pho·bi·a (klôs′trə fō′bē ə) *n.* ⟦< L *claustrum,* enclosed place + -PHOBIA⟧ abnormal fear of enclosed places —**claus′tro·pho′bic** *adj.*

clav·i·chord (klav′i kôrd′) *n.* ⟦< L *clavis,* key + *chorda,* string⟧ a stringed musical instrument with a keyboard, predecessor of the piano

clav·i·cle (klav′i kəl) *n.* ⟦< L *clavis,* key⟧ a bone connecting the breastbone with the shoulder blade

cla·vier (klə vir′; *for 1, also* klā′vē ər) *n.* ⟦Fr < L *clavis,* key⟧ 1 the keyboard of an organ, piano, etc. 2 any stringed keyboard instrument

claw (klô) *n.* ⟦OE *clawu*⟧ 1 a sharp, hooked nail on an animal's or bird's foot 2 the pincers of a lobster, etc. —*vt., vi.* to scratch, clutch, tear, etc. with or as with claws

clay (klā) *n.* ⟦OE *clæg*⟧ 1 a firm, plastic earth, used in making bricks, etc. 2 *a*) earth *b*) the human body —**clay′ey, clay′i·er, clay′i·est,** *adj.*

clean (klēn) *adj.* ⟦OE *clæne*⟧ 1 free from dirt and impurities; unsoiled 2 morally pure 3 fair; sportsmanlike 4 neat and tidy 5 well-formed 6 free from flaws 7 clear 8 thorough —*adv.* completely —*vt., vi.* to make or be made clean —**clean up** 1 to

make neat 2 [Colloq.] to finish 3 [Slang] to make much profit —**come clean** [Slang] to confess —**clean'ly** ***adv.*** —**clean'ness** ***n.***
clean'-cut' ***adj.*** 1 clearly outlined 2 well-formed 3 trim, neat, etc.
clean'er ***n.*** a person or thing that cleans; specif., one who dry-cleans
clean·ly (klen'lē) ***adj.*** **-li·er, -li·est** 1 keeping oneself or one's surroundings clean 2 always kept clean —**clean'li·ness** ***n.***
clean room a room, as in a computer center, designed to be nearly 100% free of dust, pollen, etc.
cleanse (klenz) ***vt.*** **cleansed, cleans'ing** ⟦OE *clænsian*⟧ to make clean, pure, etc. —**cleans'er** ***n.***
clean'up' ***n.*** 1 a cleaning up 2 elimination of crime 3 [Slang] profit; gain
clear (klir) ***adj.*** ⟦< L *clarus*⟧ 1 free from clouds; bright 2 transparent 3 easily seen or heard; distinct 4 keen or logical /a *clear* mind/ 5 not obscure; obvious 6 certain; positive 7 free from guilt 8 free from deductions; net 9 free from debt 10 free from obstruction; open —***adv.*** 1 in a clear manner 2 all the way; completely —***vt.*** 1 to make clear 2 to free from impurities, blemishes, etc. 3 to make lucid; clarify 4 to open /to *clear* a path/ 5 to get rid of 6 to prove the innocence of 7 to pass or leap over, by, etc., esp. without touching 8 to be passed or approved by 9 to make as profit 10 *Banking* to pass (a check, etc.) through a clearinghouse —***vi.*** to become clear —**clear away** 1 to remove so as to leave a cleared space 2 to go away —**clear off** to clear away —**clear out** [Colloq.] to depart —**clear up** to make or become clear —**in the clear** 1 free from obstructions 2 [Colloq.] guiltless —**clear'ly** ***adv.*** —**clear'ness** ***n.***
clear'ance (-əns) ***n.*** the clear space between a moving object and that which it is passing
clear'-cut' ***adj.*** 1 clearly outlined 2 distinct; definite
clear'ing ***n.*** an area of land cleared of trees
clear'ing·house' ***n.*** 1 an office maintained by several banks for exchanging checks, balancing accounts, etc. 2 a central office, as for exchanging information
cleat (klēt) ***n.*** ⟦ME *clete*⟧ a piece of wood or metal fastened to something to strengthen it or give secure footing
cleav·age (klēv'ij') ***n.*** 1 a cleaving; dividing 2 a cleft; fissure; division
cleave[1] (klēv) ***vt., vi.*** **cleaved** or **cleft** or **clove, cleaved** or **cleft** or **clo'ven, cleav'ing** ⟦OE *cleofan*⟧ to divide by a blow; split; sever —**cleav'a·ble** ***adj.***
cleave[2] (klēv) ***vi.*** **cleaved, cleav'ing** ⟦OE *cleofian*⟧ 1 to adhere; cling (*to*) 2 to be faithful (*to*)
cleav·er (klēv'ər) ***n.*** a heavy cutting tool with a broad blade, used by butchers
clef (klef) ***n.*** ⟦Fr < L *clavis,* key⟧ a symbol used at the beginning of a musical staff to indicate the pitch of the notes
cleft[1] (kleft) ***n.*** ⟦< OE *cleofan*: see CLEAVE[1]⟧ an opening made by cleaving; crack; crevice
cleft[2] (kleft) ***vt., vi.*** *alt. pt. & pp. of* CLEAVE[1] —***adj.*** split; divided
cleft palate a cleft from front to back along the middle of the roof of the mouth, from incomplete prenatal development
clem·a·tis (klem'ə tis) ***n.*** ⟦< Gr *klēma,* vine⟧ a vine of the buttercup family, with bright-colored flowers
Clem·ens (klem'ənz), **Samuel L.** (pseud. *Mark Twain*) 1835-1910; U.S. writer & humorist
clem·ent (klem'ənt) ***adj.*** ⟦L *clemens*⟧ 1 lenient; merciful 2 mild, as weather —**clem'en·cy** (-ən sē) ***n.***
clench (klench) ***vt.*** ⟦< OE (*be*)*clencan,* to make cling⟧ 1 to close (the teeth or fist) firmly 2 to grip tightly —***n.*** a firm grip
Cle·o·pa·tra (klē'ō pa'trə, klē' ə-) *c.* 69-30 B.C.; queen of Egypt (51-49; 48-30)
clere·sto·ry (klir'stôr'ē) ***n., pl.*** **-ries** ⟦< ME *cler,* clear + *storie,* story (of a building)⟧ the upper part of a wall, as of a church, with windows for lighting the central space
cler·gy (klur'jē) ***n., pl.*** **-gies** ⟦see CLERK⟧ ministers, priests, rabbis, etc., collectively
cler'gy·man (-mən) ***n., pl.*** **-men** a member of the clergy; minister, priest, rabbi, etc. —**cler'gy·wom'an,** *pl.* **-wom'en,** ***n.fem.***
cler·ic (kler'ik) ***n.*** a member of the clergy
cler'i·cal (-i kəl) ***adj.*** 1 of the clergy or one of its members 2 of office clerks or their work
cler'i·cal·ism' (-iz'əm) ***n.*** political power of the clergy —**cler'i·cal·ist** ***n.***
clerk (klurk) ***n.*** ⟦< Gr *klērikos,* a cleric⟧ 1 a lay member of a church with minor duties 2 an office worker who types, files, etc. 3 an official who keeps the records of a court, town, etc. 4 a salesclerk —***vi.*** to work as a salesclerk
Cleve·land (klēv'lənd), **(Stephen) Gro·ver** (grō'vər) 1837-1908; 22d and 24th president of the U.S. (1885-89; 1893-97)
Cleveland city and port in NE Ohio: pop. 574,000
clev·er (klev'ər) ***adj.*** ⟦? < Norw *klöver*⟧ 1 skillful; adroit 2 intelligent; ingenious; smart —**clev'er·ly** ***adv.*** —**clev'er·ness** ***n.***
clev·is (klev'is) ***n.*** ⟦see CLEAVE[2]⟧ a U-shaped piece of iron with holes for a pin, for attaching one thing to another
clew (kloo) ***n.*** ⟦OE *cliwen*⟧ 1 a ball of thread or yarn 2 *alt. sp. of* CLUE
cli·ché (klē shā') ***n.*** ⟦Fr < pp. of *clicher,* to stereotype⟧ a trite expression or idea
cli·chéd (klē shād') ***adj.*** trite; stereotyped
click (klik) ***n.*** ⟦echoic⟧ a slight, sharp sound like that of a door latch snapping into place —***vi., vt.*** to make or cause to make a click
cli·ent (klī'ənt) ***n.*** ⟦< L *cliens,* follower⟧ 1 a person or company for whom a lawyer, accountant, etc. is acting 2 a customer
cli·en·tele (klī'ən tel') ***n.*** ⟦< Fr < L *clientela,* patronage⟧ all one's clients or customers, collectively
cliff (klif) ***n.*** ⟦OE *clif*⟧ a high, steep face of rock, esp. one on a coast
cliff'hang'er or **cliff'-hang'er** (-haŋ'ər) ***n.*** a suspenseful movie, story, situation, etc.
cli·mac·ter·ic (klī mak'tər ik, klī'mak ter'ik) ***n.*** ⟦< Gr *klimax,* ladder⟧ a crucial period in life, esp. the menopause —***adj.*** crucial
cli·mate (klī'mət) ***n.*** ⟦< Gr *klima,* region⟧ 1 the prevailing weather conditions of a place 2 a region with reference to its prevailing weather —**cli·mat'ic** (-mat'ik) ***adj.***

cli·max (klī′maks′) ***n.*** ⟦L < Gr *klimax,* ladder⟧ **1** the final, culminating element in a series; highest point of interest, excitement, etc. **2** the turning point of action in a drama, etc. —***vi., vt.*** to reach, or bring to, a climax —**cli·mac′tic** (-mak′tik) ***adj.***

climb (klīm) ***vi., vt.*** **climbed, climb′ing** ⟦OE *climban*⟧ **1** to move up by using the feet and often the hands **2** to ascend gradually **3** to move (*down, over, along,* etc.) using the hands and feet **4** to grow upward —***n.*** **1** a climbing **2** a place to be climbed —**climb′a·ble** ***adj.*** —**climb′er** ***n.***

clime (klīm) ***n.*** ⟦see CLIMATE⟧ [Old Poet.] a region, esp. with regard to climate

clinch (klinch) ***vt.*** ⟦var. of CLENCH⟧ **1** to fasten (a driven nail, etc.) by bending the projecting end **2** to settle (an argument, bargain, etc.) definitely —***vi.*** **1** *Boxing* to grip the opponent with the arms so as to hinder his punching **2** [Slang] to embrace —***n.*** a clinching

clinch′er ***n.*** **1** one that clinches **2** a decisive point, argument, act, etc.

cling (kliŋ) ***vi.*** **clung, cling′ing** ⟦OE *clingan*⟧ **1** to adhere; hold fast, as by embracing **2** to be or stay near **3** to be emotionally attached —**cling′er** ***n.***

clin·ic (klin′ik) ***n.*** ⟦< Gr *klinē,* bed⟧ **1** the teaching of medicine by treatment of patients in the presence of students **2** a place where medical specialists practice as a group **3** an outpatient department, as in a hospital **4** an intensive session of group instruction, as in a certain skill

clin′i·cal (-i kəl) ***adj.*** **1** of or connected with a clinic or sickbed **2** having to do with the treatment and observation of patients, as distinguished from theoretical study **3** purely scientific; impersonal —**clin′i·cal·ly** ***adv.***

cli·ni·cian (kli nish′ən) ***n.*** one who practices clinical medicine, psychology, etc.

clink (kliŋk) ***vi., vt.*** ⟦echoic⟧ to make or cause to make a slight, sharp sound, as of glasses striking together —***n.*** **1** such a sound **2** [Colloq.] a jail

clink′er (-ər) ***n.*** ⟦Du *klinker*⟧ **1** [Archaic] a hard brick **2** a hard mass of fused stony matter, formed as from burned coal **3** [Slang] a mistake

cli·o·met·rics (klī′ō me′triks′) ***n.pl.*** ⟦< *Clio,* Gr Muse of history + Gr *metron,* measure⟧ [*with sing. v.*] use of mathematics and statistics in the analysis of historical data —**cli′o·met′ric** ***adj.*** —**cli′o·me·tri′cian** (-mə trish′ən) ***n.***

clip[1] (klip) ***vt.*** **clipped, clip′ping** ⟦< ON *klippa*⟧ **1** to cut, as with shears **2** to cut short **3** to cut the hair of **4** [Colloq.] to hit sharply **5** [Slang] to swindle —***vi.*** **1** to clip something **2** to move rapidly —***n.*** **1** a clipping **2** a thing clipped **3** a rapid pace **4** [Colloq.] a quick, sharp blow

clip[2] (klip) ***vi., vt.*** **clipped, clip′ping** ⟦OE *clyppan,* to embrace⟧ to grip tightly; fasten —***n.*** any of various devices that clip, fasten, hold, etc.

clip′board′ ***n.*** a writing board with a hinged clip at the top to hold papers

clip joint [Slang] a nightclub, store, etc. that charges excessive prices

clipped form a shortened form of a word, as *pike* (for *turnpike*) or *fan* (for *fanatic*)

CLIPPER SHIP

clip·per (klip′ər) ***n.*** **1** [*usually pl.*] a tool for cutting or trimming **2** a sailing ship built for great speed

clip′ping ***n.*** a piece cut out or off, as an item clipped from a newspaper

clique (klēk) ***n.*** ⟦Fr < OFr *cliquer,* make a noise⟧ a small, exclusive circle of people; coterie —**cliqu′ish** ***adj.*** —**cliqu′ish·ly** ***adv.***

clit·o·ris (klit′ər is) ***n., pl.*** **clit′o·ris·es** (-is iz) or **cli·tor·i·des** (kli tôr′i dēz′) ⟦< Gr⟧ a small, sensitive, erectile organ of the vulva

clo·a·ca (klō ā′kə) ***n., pl.*** **-cae** (-sē′, -kē′) or **-cas** ⟦L < *cluere,* to cleanse⟧ a cavity, as in reptiles and birds, into which both the intestinal and the genitourinary tracts empty

cloak (klōk) ***n.*** ⟦< ML *clocca,* bell: from its shape⟧ **1** a loose, usually sleeveless outer garment **2** something that covers or conceals; disguise —***vt.*** **1** to cover with a cloak **2** to conceal

clob·ber (kläb′ər) ***vt.*** ⟦< ?⟧ [Slang] **1** to beat or hit repeatedly **2** to defeat decisively

cloche (klōsh) ***n.*** ⟦Fr, a bell⟧ a woman's closefitting, bell-shaped hat

clock[1] (kläk) ***n.*** ⟦ME *clokke,* orig., clock with bells < ML *clocca,* bell⟧ a device for measuring and indicating time, usually by means of pointers moving over a dial —***vt.*** to record the time of (a race, etc.) with a stopwatch

clock[2] (kläk) ***n.*** ⟦< ? prec., because of orig. bell shape⟧ a woven or embroidered ornament on a sock, going up from the ankle

clock radio a radio with a built-in clock that can turn it on or off

clock′wise′ ***adv., adj.*** in the direction that the hands of a clock rotate

clock′work′ (-wurk′) ***n.*** **1** the mechanism of a clock **2** any similar mechanism, with springs and gears —**like clockwork** very regularly

clod (kläd) ***n.*** ⟦OE⟧ **1** a lump, esp. of earth or clay **2** a dull, stupid person —**clod′dish** ***adj.*** —**clod′dy** ***adj.***

clod′hop′per ***n.*** ⟦prec. + HOPPER⟧ **1** a plowman **2** a clumsy, stupid person **3** a coarse, heavy shoe

clog (kläg) ***n.*** ⟦ME *clogge,* lump of wood⟧ **1** anything that hinders or obstructs **2** a shoe with a thick, usually wooden, sole —***vt.*** **clogged, clog′ging** **1** to hinder **2** to obstruct (a passage); stop up; jam —***vi.*** to become stopped up —**clog′gy** ***adj.***

cloi·son·né (kloi′zə nā′) ***adj.*** ⟦Fr, lit., partitioned⟧ designating enamel work in which the surface decoration is set in hollows formed by thin strips of wire

clois·ter (klois′tər) ***n.*** ⟦< L *claudere,* to close⟧ **1** a monastery or convent **2**

monastic life **3** a covered walk along a courtyard wall with an open colonnade —*vt.* to confine as in a cloister

clomp (klämp) *vi.* to walk heavily or noisily

clone (klōn) *n.* ⟦< Gr *klōn*, a twig⟧ **1** all the descendants derived asexually from a single organism **2** a genetically identical duplicate of an organism, produced by replacing the nucleus of an unfertilized ovum with the nucleus of a body cell from the organism **3** [Colloq.] a person or thing very much like another —*vt.* **cloned, clon′ing** to produce as a clone

clop (kläp) *n.* ⟦echoic⟧ a clattering sound, like hoofbeats —*vi.* **clopped, clop′ping** to make, or move with, such sounds

close[1] (klōs) *adj.* **clos′er, clos′est** ⟦see fol.⟧ **1** confined or confining /*close* quarters/ **2** hidden; secluded **3** secretive; reserved **4** miserly; stingy **5** warm and stuffy, as stale air **6** with little space between; near together **7** compact; dense /*close* weave/ **8** near to the surface /a *close* shave/ **9** intimate; familiar /a *close* friend/ **10** strict; careful /a *close* search/ **11** nearly alike /a *close* resemblance/ **12** nearly equal or even /a *close* contest/ **13** hard to get /credit is *close*/ —*adv.* in a close manner —**close′ly** *adv.* —**close′ness** *n.*

close[2] (klōz) *vt.* **closed, clos′ing** ⟦< L *claudere*, to close⟧ **1** to shut **2** to fill up or stop (an opening) **3** to finish —*vi.* **1** to undergo shutting **2** to come to an end **3** to come close or together —*n.* an end or conclusion —**close down** (or **up**) to shut or stop entirely —**close in** to draw near from all directions; surround —**close out** to dispose of (goods) by sale

close call (klōs) [Colloq.] a narrow escape from danger Also **close shave**

closed circuit a system for telecasting by cable only to receivers connected in the circuit —**closed′-cir′cuit** *adj.*

close-fist-ed (klōs′fis′tid) *adj.* stingy

close′fit′ting *adj.* fitting tightly

close′-knit′ *adj.* closely united

close′mouthed′ (-mouthd′, -moutht′) *adj.* not talking much; taciturn

clos-et (kläz′it) *n.* ⟦< L *claudere*, to close⟧ **1** a small room or cupboard for clothes, supplies, etc. **2** a small, private room —*vt.* to shut up in a private room for confidential talk

close-up (klōs′up′) *n.* a photograph, etc. taken at very close range

clo-sure (klō′zhər) *n.* ⟦< L *claudere*, to close⟧ **1** a closing or being closed **2** a finish; end **3** anything that closes **4** CLOTURE

clot (klät) *n.* ⟦OE⟧ a soft lump or thickened mass /a blood *clot*/ —*vt., vi.* **clot′ted, clot′ting** to form into a clot or clots; coagulate

cloth (klôth) *n., pl.* **cloths** (klôthz, klôths) ⟦OE *clath*⟧ **1** a woven, knitted, or pressed fabric of fibrous material, as cotton, wool, silk, synthetic fibers, etc. **2** a tablecloth, washcloth, etc. —*adj.* made of cloth —**the cloth** the clergy

clothe (klōth) *vt.* **clothed** or **clad, cloth′ing** ⟦see prec.⟧ **1** to provide with or dress in clothes **2** to cover

clothes (klōthz, klōz) *n.pl.* ⟦OE *clathas*⟧ articles, usually of cloth, for covering, adorning, etc. the body

clothes′pin′ *n.* a small clip for fastening clothes on a line

cloth-ier (klōth′yər) *n.* a dealer in clothes or cloth

cloth-ing (klō′thiŋ) *n.* **1** clothes; garments **2** a covering

clo-ture (klō′chər) *n.* ⟦see CLOSURE⟧ the ending of legislative debate by having the bill put to immediate vote

cloud (kloud) *n.* ⟦OE *clud*, mass of rock⟧ **1** a visible mass of condensed water droplets or ice crystals in the sky **2** a mass of smoke, dust, steam, etc. **3** a crowd; swarm /a *cloud* of locusts/ **4** anything that darkens, obscures, etc. —*vt.* **1** to darken or obscure as with clouds **2** to make gloomy **3** to sully —*vi.* to become cloudy, gloomy, etc. —**in the clouds 1** impractical **2** in a daydream —**under a cloud** under suspicion —**cloud′less** *adj.* —**cloud-y** (kloud′ē), **-i-er, -i-est,** *adj.*

cloud′burst′ *n.* a sudden, heavy rain

clout (klout) *n.* ⟦< OE *clut*, a patch⟧ **1** a blow, as with the hand **2** [Colloq.] power, esp. political power —*vt.* **1** [Colloq.] to strike, as with the hand **2** to hit (a ball) hard

clove[1] (klōv) *n.* ⟦< L *clavus*, nail: from its shape⟧ **1** the dried flower bud of a tropical evergreen tree, used as a spice **2** the tree

clove[2] (klōv) *n.* ⟦OE *clufu*⟧ a segment of a bulb, as of garlic

clove[3] (klōv) *vt., vi. alt. pt. of* CLEAVE[1]

clo-ven (klō′vən) *vt., vi. alt. pp. of* CLEAVE[1] —*adj.* divided; split

clo-ver (klō′vər) *n.* ⟦OE *clafre*⟧ any of various low-growing plants of the pea family, with leaves of three leaflets and small flowers in dense heads

clo′ver-leaf′ (-lēf′) *n., pl.* **-leafs′** a highway interchange with an overpass and curving ramps, allowing traffic to move unhindered in any of four directions

clown (kloun) *n.* ⟦< ? Scand⟧ **1** a clumsy or boorish person **2** one who entertains, as in a circus, by antics, jokes, etc. —*vi.* to act as a clown does —**clown′ish** *adj.*

cloy (kloi) *vt., vi.* ⟦< OFr *encloyer*, nail up < L *clavus*, nail⟧ to surfeit by too much that is sweet, rich, etc.

club (klub) *n.* ⟦< ON *klubba*, cudgel⟧ **1** a heavy stick used as a weapon **2** any stick used in a game, as golf **3** *a*) a group of people associated for a common purpose *b*) its meeting place **4** *a*) any of a suit of playing cards marked with a black trefoil (♣) *b*) [*pl.*] this suit —*vt.* **clubbed, club′bing** to strike as with a club —*vi.* to unite for a common purpose

club′foot′ *n., pl.* **-feet′** a congenitally misshapen, often clublike, foot

club′house′ (-hous′) *n.* **1** a building used by a club **2** a locker room used by an athletic team

club soda SODA WATER

cluck (kluk) *vi.* ⟦echoic⟧ to make a low, sharp, clicking sound, as of a hen calling her chicks —*n.* this sound

clue (klo͞o) *n.* a fact, object, etc. that helps to solve a mystery or problem —*vt.* **clued, clu′ing** to provide with clues or needed facts

clump (klump) ***n.*** ‖< LowG *klump*‖ **1** a lump; mass **2** a cluster, as of trees **3** the sound of heavy footsteps —***vi.*** **1** to walk heavily **2** to form clumps —**clump'y, -i·er, -i·est,** ***adj.***

clum·sy (klum'zē) ***adj.*** **-si·er, -si·est** ‖ME *clumsid*, numb with cold‖ **1** lacking grace or skill; awkward **2** awkwardly shaped or made —**clum'si·ly** ***adv.*** —**clum'si·ness** ***n.***

clung (kluŋ) ***vi.*** *pt. & pp. of* CLING

clunk (kluŋk) ***n.*** ‖echoic‖ a dull, heavy, hollow sound

clunk·er (kluŋk'ər) ***n.*** [Slang] an old machine or automobile in poor repair

clus·ter (klus'tər) ***n.*** ‖OE *clyster*‖ a number of persons or things grouped together —***vi., vt.*** to gather or grow in a cluster

clutch[1] (kluch) ***vt.*** ‖OE *clyccan*, clench‖ to grasp or hold eagerly or tightly —***vi.*** to snatch or seize (*at*) —***n.*** **1** [*usually pl.*] power; control **2** a grasp; grip **3** a device for engaging and disengaging a motor or engine

clutch[2] (kluch) ***n.*** ‖< ON *klekja*, to hatch‖ **1** a nest of eggs **2** a brood of chicks **3** a cluster

clut·ter (klut'ər) ***n.*** ‖< CLOT‖ **1** a number of things scattered in disorder; jumble **2** the interfering traces on a radarscope caused as by hills —***vt.*** to put into disorder; jumble: often with *up*

cm centimeter(s)

cni·dar·i·an (ni der'ē ən) ***n.*** any of a phylum of invertebrates, as jellyfishes, having stinging cells and a saclike body with only one opening

co- ‖var. of COM-‖ *prefix* **1** together **2** equally [*coextensive*] **3** joint or jointly [*copilot*]

Co *Chem. symbol for* cobalt

CO **1** Colorado **2** Commanding Officer

C/O care of

Co. or **co.** **1** company **2** county

coach (kōch) ***n.*** ‖after *Kócs*, village in Hungary‖ **1** a large, covered, four-wheeled carriage **2** a railroad passenger car **3** the lowest-priced class of airline accommodations **4** a bus **5** an instructor or trainer, as of athletes, actors, or singers —***vt., vi.*** to instruct and train (students, etc.)

coach'man (-mən) ***n., pl.*** **-men** the driver of a coach, or carriage

co·ad·ju·tor (kō aj'ə tər, kō'ə jōōt'ər) ***n.*** ‖< L *co-*, together + *adjuvare*, to help‖ an assistant, esp. to a bishop

co·ag·u·late (kō ag'yōō lāt') ***vt.*** **-lat'ed, -lat'ing** ‖< L *co-*, together + *agere*, to drive‖ to cause (a liquid) to become semisolid; clot —***vi.*** to become coagulated —**co·ag'u·lant** (-lənt) ***n.*** —**co·ag'u·la'tion** ***n.*** —**co·ag'u·la'tive** ***adj.*** —**co·ag'u·la'tor** ***n.***

coal (kōl) ***n.*** ‖OE *col*‖ **1** a black, combustible mineral solid used as fuel **2** a piece (or pieces) of this **3** an ember —***vt., vi.*** to supply or be supplied with coal —**haul** (or **rake, drag,** or **call**) **over the coals** to criticize sharply

co·a·lesce (kō'ə les') ***vi.*** **-lesced', -lesc'ing** ‖< L *co-*, together + *alescere*, grow up‖ to unite into a single body or group —**co'a·les'cence** ***n.***

co'a·li'tion (-lish'ən) ***n.*** ‖see prec.‖ a combination or alliance, as of factions, esp. a temporary one

coal tar a thick black liquid obtained from the distillation of bituminous coal: used in dyes, medicines, etc.

coarse (kôrs) ***adj.*** **coars'er, coars'est** ‖< COURSE in sense of "usual"‖ **1** of poor quality; common **2** consisting of rather large particles [*coarse* sand] **3** rough; harsh **4** unrefined; vulgar; crude —**coarse'ly** ***adv.*** —**coarse'ness** ***n.***

coars'en ***vt., vi.*** to make or become coarse

coast (kōst) ***n.*** ‖< L *costa*, rib, side‖ **1** land alongside the sea; seashore **2** a slide down an incline, as on a sled —***vi.*** **1** to sail near or along a coast **2** to go down an incline, as on a sled **3** to continue in motion on momentum —**coast·al** (kōs'təl) ***adj.***

coast'er ***n.*** **1** a person or thing that coasts **2** a small mat, etc. placed under a glass to protect a table

coaster brake a brake on a bicycle operated by reverse pressure on the pedals

coast guard **1** a governmental force employed to defend a nation's coasts, aid vessels in distress, etc. **2** [**C- G-**] such a branch of the U.S. armed forces

coast'line' ***n.*** the outline of a coast

coat (kōt) ***n.*** ‖OFr *cote*, a coat‖ **1** a sleeved outer garment opening down the front **2** the natural covering of a plant or animal **3** a layer of some substance, as paint, over a surface —***vt.*** to cover with a coat or layer

coat'ing ***n.*** a surface coat or layer

coat of arms a shield with heraldic emblems, as the insignia of some group

coat'tail' (-tāl') ***n.*** either half of the divided lower back part of a coat

co·au·thor (kō'ô'thər) ***n.*** a joint author; collaborator

coax (kōks) ***vt., vi.*** ‖< obs. slang *cokes*, a fool‖ to urge or get with soft words, flattery, etc. —**coax'er** ***n.*** —**coax'ing·ly** ***adv.***

co·ax·i·al (kō ak'sē əl) ***adj.*** **1** having a common axis **2** designating a double-conductor high-frequency transmission line, as for television

cob (käb) ***n.*** ‖prob. < LowG‖ **1** a corncob **2** a short, thickset horse

co·balt (kō'bôlt') ***n.*** ‖< Ger *kobold*, lit., goblin‖ a hard, steel-gray metallic chemical element

cob·ble (käb'əl) ***vt.*** **-bled, -bling** ‖ME < *cobelere*, cobbler‖ **1** to mend (shoes, etc.) **2** to put together clumsily

cob·bler[1] (käb'lər) ***n.*** ‖< ?‖ a kind of deep-dish fruit pie

cob·bler[2] (käb'lər) ***n.*** ‖ME *cobelere* < ?‖ one who makes or mends shoes

cob'ble·stone' ***n.*** a rounded stone formerly much used for paving streets

CO·BOL (kō'bôl') ***n.*** ‖*co*(*mmon*) *b*(*usiness*) *o*(*riented*) *l*(*anguage*)‖ a computer language using English words, for business applications

co·bra (kō'brə) ***n.*** ‖< Port‖ a very poisonous snake of Asia and Africa

cob·web (käb'web') ***n.*** ‖ME *coppe*, spider + WEB‖ **1** a web spun by a spider **2** any thing flimsy, gauzy, or ensnaring like this —**cob'web'by** ***adj.***

co·caine or **co·cain** (kō kān') ***n.*** ‖< *coca*, tropical shrub from whose leaves it is extracted ‖ an alkaloid drug used as a local anesthetic and, illegally, as a stimulant

coc·cus (käk′əs) ***n.***, *pl.* **coc′ci′** (-sī′) ‖ < Gr *kokkos*, kernel ‖ a bacterium of a spherical shape

coc·cyx (käk′siks′) ***n.***, *pl.* **coc·cy·ges** (käk sī′ jēz′) ‖ < Gr *kokkyx*, cuckoo: it is shaped like a cuckoo's beak ‖ a small, triangular bone at the base of the spine

coch·le·a (käk′lē ə) ***n.***, *pl.* **-ae′** (-ē′) or **-as** ‖ < Gr *kochlias*, snail ‖ the spiral-shaped part of the inner ear

cock[1] (käk) ***n.*** ‖ OE *coc* ‖ **1** a rooster or other male bird **2** a faucet or valve **3** *a)* the hammer of a gun *b)* its firing position **4** a jaunty tilt, as of a hat —***vt.*** **1** to tilt jauntily **2** to raise or turn alertly **3** to set (a gun's hammer) in firing position

cock[2] (käk) ***n.*** ‖ ME *cokke* ‖ a small, cone-shaped pile, as of hay

cock·ade (käk ād′) ***n.*** ‖ < OFr *coq*, COCK[1] (*n.* 1) ‖ a rosette, knot of ribbon, etc. worn on the hat as a badge

cock·a·ma·mie (käk′ə mā′mē) ***adj.*** ‖ < *decalcomania*: see DECAL ‖ [Slang] **1** poor; inferior **2** silly; ridiculous

cock-and-bull story (käk′ən bool′) an absurd, improbable story

cock·a·too (käk′ə to͞o′) ***n.***, *pl.* **-toos′** ‖ < Malay *kakatua* ‖ a crested parrot of Australia and the East Indies

cock·a·trice (käk′ə tris′) ***n.*** ‖ < L *calcare*, to tread ‖ a fabulous serpent supposedly able to kill by a look

cock·crow (käk′krō′) ***n.*** dawn

cocked hat a three-cornered hat

cock·er·el (käk′ər əl) ***n.*** a young rooster, less than a year old

cocker (spaniel) ‖ < use in hunting woodcock ‖ a small spaniel with long, silky hair and drooping ears

cock·eyed (käk′īd′) ***adj.*** ‖ < COCK[1], *v.* + EYE ‖ **1** cross-eyed **2** [Slang] *a)* crooked; awry *b)* silly; foolish *c)* drunk

cock′fight′ ***n.*** a fight between gamecocks, usually wearing metal spurs —**cock′fight′ing** ***n.***

cock·le[1] (käk′əl) ***n.*** ‖ < Gr *konchē*, mussel ‖ a mollusk, often edible, that has two heart-shaped shells —**cockles of one's heart** one's deepest emotions

cock·le[2] (käk′əl) ***n.*** ‖ OE *coccel* ‖ any of various weeds growing in fields of grain

cock·ney (käk′nē) ***n.***, *pl.* **-neys** ‖ ME *cokenei*, spoiled child, milksop ‖ [*often* **C-**] **1** a native of the East End of London, England, speaking a characteristic dialect **2** this dialect

cock′pit′ ***n.*** **1** a pit for cockfighting **2** the space in a small airplane for the pilot and passengers, or in a large airplane for the pilot, copilot, etc.

cock′roach′ (-rōch′) ***n.*** ‖ Sp *cucaracha* ‖ an insect with long feelers and a flat, soft body: a common household pest

cocks·comb (käks′kōm′) ***n.*** **1** the red, fleshy growth on a rooster's head **2** a plant with flowers like this

cock·sure (käk′shoor′) ***adj.*** ‖ COCK[1] + SURE ‖ absolutely sure or self-confident, esp. in an arrogant way

cock·tail (käk′tāl′) ***n.*** ‖ < ? ‖ **1** a mixed alcoholic drink, usually iced **2** an appetizer, as of shrimp or juice

cock·y (käk′ē) ***adj.*** **-i·er, -i·est** ‖ < COCK[1] + -Y[2] ‖ [Colloq.] jauntily conceited; aggressively self-confident —**cock′i·ly** ***adv.*** —**cock′i·ness** ***n.***

co·co (kō′kō′) ***n.***, *pl.* **-cos′** ‖ Sp < Gr *kokkos*, berry ‖ **1** the coconut palm tree **2** its fruit; coconut

co·coa (kō′kō′) ***n.*** ‖ var. of CACAO ‖ **1** powder made from roasted cacao seeds **2** a drink made of this and sugar, hot milk, etc. **3** a reddish-yellow brown

cocoa butter a yellowish-white fat prepared from cacao seeds

COCONUT AND COCONUT PALM

co·co·nut or **co·coa·nut** (kō′kō nut′, -kə-) ***n.*** the fruit of a tropical tree (**coconut palm**), a thick, brown, oval husk with edible white meat and a sweet, milky fluid (**coconut milk**) inside

co·coon (kə ko͞on′) ***n.*** ‖ < Fr < ML *coco*, shell ‖ the silky case which the larva of certain insects spins about itself for shelter during the pupa stage

cod (käd) ***n.***, *pl.* **cod** or **cods** ‖ ME ‖ a food fish of northern seas

Cod (käd), **Cape** hook-shaped peninsula in E Mass.: 64 mi. long

COD or **c.o.d.** cash, or collect, on delivery

co·da (kō′də) ***n.*** ‖ It < L *cauda*, tail ‖ *Music* an added concluding passage

cod·dle (käd″l) ***vt.*** **-dled, -dling** ‖ < ? ‖ **1** to cook (esp. eggs in shells) in water not quite boiling **2** to pamper

code (kōd) ***n.*** ‖ < L *codex*, wooden tablet ‖ **1** a systematized body of laws **2** a set of principles, as of ethics **3** a set of signals for sending messages **4** a system of symbols for secret writing, etc. —***vt.*** **cod′ed, cod′ing** to put into code —**cod′er** ***n.***

co·deine (kō′dēn′) ***n.*** ‖ < Gr *kōdeia*, poppy head ‖ an alkaloid derived from opium: used for pain relief and in cough medicines Also **co′dein′**

co·dex (kō′deks′) ***n.***, *pl.* **-di·ces′** (-də sēz′) ‖ L: see CODE ‖ a manuscript volume, esp. of the Scriptures or of a classic text

cod′fish′ (käd′-) ***n.***, *pl.* **-fish′** or (for different species) **-fish′es** a cod

codg·er (käj′ər) ***n.*** ‖ < ? ‖ [Colloq.] an elderly fellow, sometimes one who is eccentric

cod·i·cil (käd′i səl) ***n.*** ‖ see CODE ‖ an addition to a will

cod·i·fy (käd′ə fī′) ***vt.*** **-fied′, -fy′ing** to arrange (laws, rules, etc.) systematically —**cod′i·fi·ca′tion** ***n.*** —**cod′i·fi′er** ***n.***

cod′-liv′er oil oil from the liver of the cod: it is rich in vitamins A & D

co·ed or **co-ed** (kō′ed′) ***n.*** [Colloq.] a young

woman attending a coeducational college —*adj.* [Colloq.] **1** coeducational **2** of a coed

co·ed·u·ca·tion (kō'ej'ə kā'shən) ***n.*** an educational system in which students of both sexes attend classes together —**co'ed·u·ca'tion·al** ***adj.***

co·ef·fi·cient (kō'ə fish'ənt) ***n.*** [CO- + EFFICIENT] **1** a factor that contributes to a result **2** a multiplier of a variable or unknown quantity (as *6* in *6ab*) **3** a number used as a multiplier in measuring some property

coe·len·ter·ate (si len'tər it) ***n.*** [< Gr *koilos,* hollow + *enteron,* intestine] CNIDARIAN

co·e·qual (kō ē'kwəl) ***adj., n.*** equal —**co'e·qual'i·ty** (-ē kwäl'ə tē) ***n.*** —**co·e'qual·ly** ***adv.***

co·erce (kō ʉrs') ***vt.*** **-erced', -erc'ing** [< L *co-,* together + *arcere,* confine] **1** to restrain by force **2** to compel **3** to enforce —**co·er'cion** (-ʉr'shən) ***n.*** —**co·er'cive** (-siv) ***adj.***

co·e·val (kō ē'vəl) ***adj., n.*** [< L *co-,* together + *aevum,* age] contemporary

co'ex·ist' (-ig zist') ***vi.*** **1** to exist together, at the same time, or in the same place **2** to live together peacefully, despite differences —**co'ex·ist'ence** ***n.*** —**co'ex·ist'ent** ***adj.***

co'ex·ten'sive (-ik sten'siv) ***adj.*** extending equally in time or space

cof·fee (kôf'ē) ***n.*** [< Ar *qahwa*] **1** a drink made from the roasted, ground, beanlike seeds of a tall tropical shrub of the madder family **2** the seeds, whole or ground, or the shrub **3** light brown

coffee break a brief respite from work when coffee, etc. is taken

cof'fee·cake' ***n.*** a kind of cake or roll to be eaten as with coffee

cof'fee·house' ***n.*** a place where coffee is served and people gather for talk, entertainment, etc.

cof'fee·pot' ***n.*** a container with a spout, for making or serving coffee

coffee shop a small restaurant serving coffee and light refreshments or meals

coffee table a low table, usually in front of a sofa

cof·fer (kôf'ər) ***n.*** [see fol.] **1** a chest for holding money or valuables **2** [*pl.*] a treasury; funds

cof·fin (kôf'in) ***n.*** [< Gr *kophinos,* basket] the case or box in which a dead body is buried

cog (käg) ***n.*** [ME] **1** one of the teeth on the rim of a cogwheel **2** a cogwheel

co·gent (kō'jənt) ***adj.*** [< L *co-,* together + *agere,* to drive] convincingly to the point —**co'gen·cy** ***n.***

cog·i·tate (käj'ə tāt') ***vi., vt.*** **-tat'ed, -tat'ing** [< L] to think deeply (about); ponder —**cog'i·ta'tion** ***n.*** —**cog'i·ta'tive** ***adj.*** —**cog'i·ta'tor** ***n.***

co·gnac (kän'yak', kōn'-) ***n.*** [Fr] **1** a brandy from Cognac, France **2** loosely, brandy

cog·nate (käg'nāt') ***adj.*** [< L *co-,* together + *gnasci,* to be born] **1** related by family **2** from a common original form, as two words **3** related; similar —***n.*** a cognate person or thing

cog·ni·tion (käg nish'ən) ***n.*** [< L *co-,* together + *gnoscere,* know] **1** the process of knowing, perceiving, etc. **2** an idea, perception, etc.

cog·ni·za·ble (käg'ni zə bəl) ***adj.*** **1** that can be known or perceived **2** *Law* within the jurisdiction of a court

cog·ni·zance (käg'nə zəns) ***n.*** **1** perception or knowledge **2** notice; heed —**cog'ni·zant** ***adj.***

cog·no·men (käg nō'mən) ***n., pl.*** **-no'mens** [< L *co-,* with + *nomen,* name] **1** surname **2** any name; esp., a nickname

cog·wheel (käg'hwēl', wēl') ***n.*** a wheel rimmed with teeth that mesh with those of another wheel, etc., to transmit or receive motion

co·hab·it (kō hab'it) ***vi.*** [< L *co-,* together + *habitare,* dwell] to live together as husband and wife, esp. when not legally married —**co·hab'i·ta'tion** ***n.***

co·heir (kō'er', kō er') ***n.*** one who inherits jointly with another or others

co·here (kō hir') ***vi.*** **-hered', -her'ing** [< L *co-,* together + *haerere,* to stick] **1** to stick together **2** to be connected naturally or logically

co·her'ent (-ənt) ***adj.*** **1** sticking together; cohering **2** logically connected and intelligible —**co·her'ence** ***n.*** —**co·her'ent·ly** ***adv.***

co·he·sion (kō hē'zhən) ***n.*** a cohering; tendency to stick together —**co·he'sive** (-hēs'iv) ***adj.***

co·hort (kō'hôrt') ***n.*** [< L *cohors,* enclosure] **1** a band of soldiers **2** any group or band **3** an associate

coif (koif; *for 2 usually* kwäf) ***n.*** **1** [< LL *cofea,* a cap] a closefitting cap **2** [< fol.] a hairstyle

coif·fure (kwä fyoor') ***n.*** [Fr] **1** a headdress **2** a hairstyle

coil (koil) ***vt., vi.*** [< L *com-,* together + *legere,* gather] to wind into circular or spiral form —***n.*** **1** a series of rings or a spiral, or anything in this form **2** a single turn of a coil **3** *Elec.* a spiral of wire

coin (koin) ***n.*** [< L *cuneus,* a wedge] **1** a piece of stamped metal, issued by a government as money **2** such pieces collectively —***vt.*** **1** to stamp (metal) into coins **2** to invent (a new word, phrase, etc.) —**coin'age** ***n.***

co·in·cide (kō'in sīd') ***vi.*** **-cid'ed, -cid'ing** [< L *co-,* together + *incidere,* fall upon] **1** to take up the same place in space **2** to occur at the same time **3** to agree exactly

co·in·ci·dence (kō in'sə dəns) ***n.*** **1** a coinciding **2** an accidental, but seemingly planned, occurrence of events, ideas, etc. at the same time —**co·in'ci·dent** or **co·in'ci·den'tal** ***adj.*** —**co·in'ci·den'tal·ly** ***adv.***

co·i·tus (kō'it əs) ***n.*** [< L < *co-,* together + *ire,* go] sexual intercourse Also **co·i·tion** (kō ish'ən)

coke (kōk) ***n.*** [< ME *colke,* core] coal from which most of the gases have been removed by heating: used as an industrial fuel

col- *prefix* COM- Used before *l*

col. column

COL **1** Colonel: also **Col.** **2** cost of living

co·la (kō'lə) ***n.*** [< Afr name] **1** an African

tree with nuts that yield an extract used in soft drinks and medicine **2** a carbonated soft drink flavored with this extract

col·an·der (kul′ən dər, käl′-) ***n.*** ‖ prob. ult. < L *colum*, strainer ‖ a perforated pan for draining off liquids

cold (kōld) ***adj.*** ‖ OE *cald* ‖ **1** of a temperature much lower than that of the human body **2** too cool; chilly **3** unfriendly, indifferent, or depressing **4** devoid of feeling; emotionless **5** *a)* not fresh (said of a hunting scent) *b)* off the track **6** [Colloq.] unprepared /to enter a game *cold*/ **7** [Slang] perfectly memorized **8** [Slang] unconscious /knocked *cold*/ —***adv.*** [Colloq.] completely /she was stopped *cold*/ —***n.*** **1** lack of heat or warmth **2** cold weather **3** a viral infection of the respiratory tract, causing sneezing, coughing, etc. —**catch** (or **take**) **cold** to become ill with a cold —**have** (or **get**) **cold feet** [Colloq.] to be (or become) timid —**in the cold** neglected —**cold′ly** ***adv.*** —**cold′ness** ***n.***

cold′blood′ed ***adj.*** **1** having a body temperature that varies with the surrounding air, water, etc., as fish and reptiles **2** cruel or callous

cold cream a creamy preparation for softening and cleansing the skin

cold cuts sliced cold meats and, usually, cheeses

cold duck a drink made from sparkling burgundy and champagne

cold front the forward edge of a cold air mass advancing under a warmer mass

cold shoulder [Colloq.] a slight; rebuff; snub —**cold′-shoul′der** ***vt.***

cold sore **1** a viral infection characterized by little blisters in or around the mouth during a cold or fever; herpes simplex **2** any of these blisters

cold turkey [Slang] **1** the abrupt and total withdrawal from drugs or tobacco by an addict or user **2** without preparation

cold war hostility and conflict without actual warfare

cole (kōl) ***n.*** ‖ < L *caulis*, cabbage ‖ any of various plants related to the cabbage; esp., rape

cole′slaw′ (-slô′) ***n.*** ‖ < Du: see prec. & SLAW ‖ a salad of shredded raw cabbage Also **cole slaw**

co·le·us (kō′lē əs) ***n.*** ‖ < Gr *koleos*, a sheath ‖ any of various plants of the mint family with bright-colored leaves

col·ic (käl′ik) ***n.*** ‖ < Gr *kōlon*, colon ‖ acute abdominal pain —**col′ick·y** ***adj.***

col·i·se·um (käl′ə sē′əm) ***n.*** ‖ < L *colosseum* ‖ a large stadium

co·li·tis (kō lit′is) ***n.*** ‖ < COLON[2] + -ITIS ‖ inflammation of the colon

coll. **1** collect **2** college

col·lab·o·rate (kə lab′ə rāt′) ***vi.*** **-rat′ed, -rat′ing** ‖ < L *com-*, with + *laborare*, to work ‖ **1** to work together, esp. in some literary or scientific undertaking **2** to cooperate with the enemy —**col·lab′o·ra′tion** ***n.*** —**col·lab′o·ra′tor** ***n.***

col·lage (kə läzh′) ***n.*** ‖ Fr, a pasting ‖ an art form in which bits of objects are pasted together on a surface

col·lapse (kə laps′) ***vi.*** **-lapsed′, -laps′ing** ‖ < L *com-*, together + *labi*, to fall ‖ **1** to fall down or cave in **2** to break down suddenly **3** to fail suddenly in health **4** to fold together compactly —***vt.*** to make collapse —***n.*** a collapsing —**col·laps′i·ble** ***adj.***

col·lar (käl′ər) ***n.*** ‖ < L *collum*, neck ‖ **1** the part of a garment that encircles the neck **2** a band of leather, etc. for an animal's neck **3** anything like a collar —***vt.*** **1** to put a collar on **2** to seize, as by the collar

-col·lar *combining form* designating any of various categories of employed persons /pink-*collar* workers/

col′lar·bone′ ***n.*** CLAVICLE

col·lard (käl′ərd) ***n.*** ‖ < ME ‖ a kind of kale with coarse leaves

col·late (kə lāt′, käl′āt′) ***vt.*** **-lat′ed, -lat′ing** ‖ < L *com-*, together + *latus*, brought ‖ **1** to compare (texts, etc.) carefully **2** to put (pages) in proper order —**col·la′tor** ***n.***

col·lat·er·al (kə lat′ər əl) ***adj.*** ‖ < L *com-*, together + *lateralis*, lateral ‖ **1** parallel or corresponding **2** accompanying or supporting /*collateral* evidence/ **3** having the same ancestors but in a different line **4** designating or of security given as a pledge for the repayment of a loan, etc. —***n.*** **1** a collateral relative **2** collateral security

col·la·tion (kə lā′shən) ***n.*** **1** the act or result of collating **2** a light meal

col·league (käl′ēg′) ***n.*** ‖ < Fr < L *com-*, with + *legare*, appoint as deputy ‖ a fellow worker; associate in office

col·lect (kə lekt′) ***vt.*** ‖ < L *com-*, together + *legere*, gather ‖ **1** to gather together **2** to gather (stamps, etc.) as a hobby **3** to call for and receive (money) for (bills, etc.) **4** to regain control of (oneself) —***vi.*** to assemble or accumulate —***adj.***, ***adv.*** with payment to be made by the receiver /to telephone *collect*/ —**col·lect′i·ble** or **col·lect′a·ble** ***adj.***, ***n.*** —**col·lec′tor** ***n.***

col·lect′ed ***adj.*** **1** gathered together **2** in control of oneself; calm

col·lec′tion ***n.*** **1** a collecting **2** things collected **3** a mass or pile; accumulation **4** money collected

col·lec′tive ***adj.*** **1** formed by collecting **2** of or as a group /*collective* effort/ **3** designating a singular noun, as *tribe*, denoting a collection of individuals —***n.*** **1** any collective enterprise; specif., a collective farm **2** the people who work together in it **3** a collective noun —**col·lec′tive·ly** ***adv.***

collective bargaining negotiation between organized workers and their employer concerning wages, hours, etc.

col·lec′tiv·ism′ ***n.*** collective ownership and control, esp. under socialism —**col·lec′tiv·ist** ***n.***, ***adj.*** —**col·lec′tiv·ize′, -ized′, -iz′ing,** ***vt.***

col·leen (käl′ēn′, käl ēn′) ***n.*** ‖ < Ir *caile*, girl ‖ [Irish] a girl

col·lege (käl′ij) ***n.*** ‖ see COLLEAGUE ‖ **1** a group of individuals with certain powers and duties /the electoral *college*/ **2** an institution of higher education that grants degrees **3** any of the schools of a university **4** a school offering specialized instruction /a business *college*/ **5** the building or buildings of a college

col·le·gian (kə lē′jən) ***n.*** a college student

col·le′giate (-jit, -jē it) ***adj.*** of or like a college or college students

col·lide (kə līd′) ***vi.*** **-lid′ed, -lid′ing** ‖ < L *com-,* together + *laedere,* to strike ‖ **1** to come into violent contact; crash **2** to conflict; clash

COLLIE

col·lie (käl′ē) ***n.*** ‖ < ? ‖ a large, long-haired dog, orig. bred in Scotland

col·lier (käl′yər) ***n.*** ‖ < ME: see COAL & -IER ‖ [Chiefly Brit.] **1** a coal miner **2** a coal freighter

col′lier·y ***n.***, *pl.* **-ies** [Chiefly Brit.] a coal mine and its buildings, etc.

col·li·sion (kə lizh′ən) ***n.*** **1** a colliding **2** a clash or conflict

col·lo·cate (käl′ə kāt′) ***vt.*** **-cat′ed, -cat′ing** ‖ < L *com-,* together + *locare,* to place ‖ to arrange; esp., to set side by side —**col′lo·ca′tion** ***n.***

col·loid (käl′oid′) ***n.*** ‖ < Gr *kolla,* glue + -OID ‖ a substance made up of tiny, insoluble, nondiffusible particles that remain suspended in a medium of different matter —**col·loi′dal** ***adj.***

colloq. colloquial

col·lo·qui·al (kə lō′kwē əl) ***adj.*** ‖ see COLLOQUY ‖ designating or of the words, phrases, etc. characteristic of informal speech and writing; informal —**col·lo′qui·al·ism′** ***n.*** —**col·lo′qui·al·ly** ***adv.***

col·lo′qui·um ***n.***, *pl.* **-qui·a** or **-qui·ums** ‖ L: see fol. ‖ an organized conference or seminar on some subject

col·lo·quy (käl′ə kwē) ***n.***, *pl.* **-quies** ‖ < L *com-,* together + *loqui,* speak ‖ a conversation or conference

col·lu·sion (kə lo͞o′zhən) ***n.*** ‖ < L *com-,* with + *ludere,* to play ‖ a secret agreement for fraudulent or illegal purpose; conspiracy —**col·lu′sive** (-siv) ***adj.*** —**col·lu′sive·ly** ***adv.***

Colo. Colorado

co·logne (kə lōn′) ***n.*** ‖ < Fr *eau de cologne,* lit., water of Cologne, city in West Germany ‖ a perfumed toilet water made of alcohol and aromatic oils

Co·logne (kə lōn′) city in W West Germany, on the Rhine: pop. 932,000

Co·lom·bi·a (kə lum′bē ə) country in NW South America: 439,737 sq. mi.; pop. 29,956,000 —**Co·lom′bi·an** ***adj., n.***

co·lon[1] (kō′lən) ***n.*** ‖ < Gr *kōlon,* verse part ‖ a mark of punctuation (:) used before a long quotation, explanation, example, series, etc. and after the salutation of a formal letter

co·lon[2] (kō′lən) ***n.***, *pl.* **-lons** or **-la** (-lə) ‖ < Gr *kolon* ‖ that part of the large intestine extending from the cecum to the rectum

colo·nel (kur′nəl) ***n.*** ‖ < It *colonna,* (military) column ‖ a military officer ranking just above a lieutenant colonel —**colo′nel·cy,** *pl.* **-cies,** ***n.***

co·lo·ni·al (kə lō′nē əl) ***adj.*** **1** of, in, or having a colony **2** [*often* **C-**] of the thirteen British colonies that became the U.S. —***n.*** an inhabitant of a colony —**co·lo′ni·al·ly** ***adv.***

co·lo′ni·al·ism′ (-iz′əm) ***n.*** the system by which a country maintains foreign colonies, esp. for economic exploitation —**co·lo′ni·al·ist** ***n., adj.***

col·o·nist (käl′ə nist) ***n.*** a settler or inhabitant of a colony

col′o·nize′ (-nīz′) ***vt., vi.*** **-nized′, -niz′ing** **1** to found a colony (in) **2** to settle in a colony —**col′o·ni·za′tion** ***n.*** —**col′o·niz′er** ***n.***

col·on·nade (käl′ə nād′) ***n.*** ‖ < L *columna,* column ‖ *Archit.* a row of columns, as along the side of a building

col·o·ny (käl′ə nē) ***n.***, *pl.* **-nies** ‖ < L *colere,* cultivate ‖ **1** *a)* a group of settlers in a distant land, under the jurisdiction of their native land *b)* the region settled **2** any territory ruled over by a distant state **3** a community of the same nationality or pursuits, as within a city **4** *Biol.* a group living or growing together

col·o·phon (käl′ə fən, -fän′) ***n.*** ‖ LL < Gr *kolophōn,* top ‖ a publisher's emblem

col·or (kul′ər) ***n.*** ‖ L ‖ **1** the property of reflecting light of a particular visible wavelength: the *colors* of the spectrum are red, orange, yellow, green, blue, indigo, and violet **2** any coloring matter; dye; pigment **3** color of the face or skin **4** [*pl.*] a colored badge, etc. to identify the wearer **5** [*pl.*] a flag **6** outward appearance **7** vivid quality —***vt.*** **1** to give color to; paint, dye, etc. **2** to change the color of **3** to alter, as by distorting [to *color* a story] —***vi.*** **1** to become colored **2** to change color **3** to blush or flush —**show one's (true) colors** to reveal one's true self

Col·o·rad·o (kal′ə rad′ō, -rä′dō) Mountain State of the W U.S.: 104,247 sq. mi.; pop. 2,889,000; cap. Denver —**Col′o·rad′an** ***adj., n.***

col·or·ant (kul′ər ənt) ***n.*** a dye or other coloring agent

col′or·a′tion (-ər ā′shən) ***n.*** a coloring

col·o·ra·tu·ra (kul′ə rə toor′ə, -tyoor′-) ***n.*** ‖ It ‖ **1** brilliant runs, trills, etc., used to display a singer's skill **2** a soprano capable of singing such music: also **coloratura soprano**

col′or·blind′ ***adj.*** **1** unable to distinguish certain colors or any colors **2** not influenced by considerations of race —**col′or·blind′ness** ***n.***

col′ored (-ərd) ***adj.*** **1** having color **2** non-Caucasoid; specif., black

col′or·fast′ (-fast′) ***adj.*** with color not subject to fading or running

col′or·ful ***adj.*** **1** full of color **2** picturesque, vivid, etc. —**col′or·ful·ly** ***adv.*** —**col′or·ful·ness** ***n.***

col′or·ing ***n.*** **1** anything applied to impart color; pigment, etc. **2** the way a thing is colored **3** false appearance

col′or·less ***adj.*** **1** without color **2** lacking variety or interest; dull —**col′or·less·ly** ***adv.*** —**col′or·less·ness** ***n.***

color line the barrier of social, political, and economic restrictions imposed on blacks or other nonwhites Also **color bar**

co·los·sal (kə läs′əl) ***adj.*** enormous in size,

degree, etc.; astonishingly great —**co·los′sal·ly** *adv.*

co·los·sus (kə läs′əs) *n., pl.* **-si′** (ī′) or **-sus·es** ‖< Gr‖ **1** a gigantic statue **2** anything huge or important

co·los·to·my (kə läs′tə mē) *n., pl.* **-mies** surgical construction of an artificial anal opening from the colon

co·los·trum (kə läs′trəm) *n.* ‖L‖ the first fluid secreted by the mammary glands just after a birth

col·our (kul′ər) *n., vt., vi. Brit. sp. of* COLOR

colt (kōlt) *n.* ‖OE‖ a young male horse, donkey, etc.

colt′ish *adj.* of or like a colt; esp., frisky, frolicsome, etc. —**colt′ish·ly** *adv.*

Co·lum·bi·a (kə lum′bē ə, -byə) **1** capital of S.C.: pop. 102,000 **2** river flowing from Canada through Wash., & along the Wash.-Oreg. border into the Pacific

col·um·bine (käl′əm bīn′) *n.* ‖< L *columbinus,* dovelike‖ a plant of the buttercup family, having dainty flowers of various colors with petals forming backward spurs

Co·lum·bus (kə lum′bəs), **Chris·to·pher** (kris′tə fər) *c.* 1451-1506; It. explorer: discovered America (1492)

Columbus **1** capital of Ohio, in the central part: pop. 565,000 **2** city in W Ga.: pop. 169,000

col·umn (käl′əm) *n.* ‖< L *columna*‖ **1** a slender upright structure, usually a supporting member in a building **2** anything like a column /the spinal *column*/ **3** a file formation of troops, etc. **4** any of the vertical sections of printed matter on a page **5** a feature article appearing regularly in a newspaper, etc. —**co·lum·nar** (kə lum′nər) *adj.*

col·um·nist (käl′əm nist′) *n.* a writer of a COLUMN (sense 5)

com- ‖< L *com-,* with‖ *prefix* with, together Also used as an intensive

Com. **1** Commissioner **2** Committee

co·ma (kō′mə) *n.* ‖< Gr *kōma,* deep sleep‖ deep, prolonged unconsciousness caused by injury or disease

co·ma·tose (kō′mə tōs′, käm′ə-) *adj.* **1** of, like, or in a coma **2** lethargic

comb (kōm) *n.* ‖< OE *camb*‖ **1** a thin strip of hard rubber, plastic, etc., with teeth, used to arrange or clean the hair **2** any similar tool, as for cleaning and straightening wool, flax, etc. **3** a red, fleshy outgrowth on the head, as of a rooster **4** a honeycomb —*vt.* **1** to arrange, etc. with a comb **2** to search thoroughly

com·bat (*for v.* kəm bat′, käm′bat′; *for n.* käm′bat′) *vi.* **-bat′ed** or **-bat′ted, -bat′ing** or **-bat′ting** ‖< Fr < L *com-,* with + *battuere,* to fight‖ to fight, contend, or struggle —*vt.* to fight or actively oppose —*n.* **1** armed fighting; battle **2** any struggle or conflict —**com·bat·ant** (kəm bat′′nt, käm′ bə tənt) *adj., n.*

combat fatigue a psychoneurosis with anxiety, depression, etc., as after prolonged combat in warfare

com·bat·ive (kəm bat′iv, käm′bə tiv′) *adj.* ready or eager to fight

comb·er (kōm′ər) *n.* **1** one that combs **2** a wave, curling at the top

com·bi·na·tion (käm′bə nā′shən) *n.* **1** a combining or being combined **2** a thing formed by combining **3** an association of persons, firms, etc. for a common purpose **4** the series of numbers to which a dial is turned on a lock (**combination lock**) to open it

com·bine (kəm bīn′; *for n.* käm′bīn′) *vt., vi.* **-bined′, -bin′ing** ‖< L *com-,* together + *bini,* two by two‖ to join into one, as by blending; unite —*n.* **1** a machine for harvesting and threshing grain **2** an association of persons, corporations, etc. for commercial or political, often unethical, purposes —**com·bin′er** *n.*

comb·ings (kō′miŋz) *n.pl.* loose hair, wool, etc. removed in combing

combining form a word form occurring only in compounds and derivatives (Ex.: *cardio-* in *cardiograph*)

com·bo (käm′bō′) *n., pl.* **-bos′** a combination; specif., a small jazz ensemble

com·bus·ti·ble (kəm bus′tə bəl) *adj.* that can burn; flammable —**com·bus′ti·bil′i·ty** *n.* —**com·bus′ti·bly** *adv.*

com·bus′tion (-chən) *n.* ‖< L *com-,* intens. + *urere,* to burn‖ the act or process of burning

come (kum) *vi.* **came, come, com′ing** ‖< OE *cuman*‖ **1** to move from "there" to "here" **2** to arrive or appear **3** to extend; reach **4** to happen **5** to occur in a certain order /after 8 *comes* 9/ **6** to be derived or descended **7** to be caused; result **8** to become /to *come* loose/ **9** to be available /it *comes* in four sizes/ **10** to amount (*to*) —*interj.* an expression of irritation, impatience, etc. —**come about** **1** to happen **2** to turn about —**come across** (or **upon**) to meet or find by chance —**come along** **1** to appear or arrive **2** to proceed or succeed —**come around** (or **round**) **1** to recover **2** to yield —**come by** to get; gain —**come into** **1** to enter into **2** to inherit —**come off** **1** to become detached **2** to end up **3** [Colloq.] to prove effective, etc. —**come out** **1** to be disclosed **2** to make a debut **3** to end up —**come out for** to announce endorsement of —**come through** **1** to complete something successfully **2** [Colloq.] to do or give what is wanted —**come to** to recover consciousness —**come up** to arise, as a point in a discussion —**how come?** [Colloq.] why?

come′back′ *n.* **1** a return to a previous state or position, as of power **2** a witty answer; retort

co·me·di·an (kə mē′dē ən) *n.* an actor who plays comic parts —**co·me′di·enne′** (-en′) *n.fem.*

co·me′dic (-dik) *adj.* of or having to do with comedy

come′down′ *n.* a loss of status

com·e·dy (käm′ə dē) *n., pl.* **-dies** ‖< Gr *kōmos,* revel + *aeidein,* sing‖ **1** a humorous play, etc. with a nontragic ending **2** an amusing event

come·ly (kum′lē) *adj.* **-li·er, -li·est** ‖< OE *cymlic*‖ attractive; fair —**come′li·ness** *n.*

come′-on′ *n.* [Slang] an inducement

co·mes·ti·ble (kə mes′tə bəl) *n.* ‖< L *com-,* intens. + *edere,* to eat‖ [*usually pl.*] food

com·et (käm′it) *n.* ‖< Gr *komē,* hair‖ a small, frozen mass of dust and gas revolving around the sun: as it nears the sun it vaporizes, usually forming a long, luminous tail

come·up·pance (kum′up′əns) ***n.*** [Colloq.] deserved punishment

com·fit (kum′fit, käm′) ***n.*** ‖ < L *com*, with + *facere*, do ‖ a candy or sweetmeat

com·fort (kum′fərt) ***vt.*** ‖ < L *com-*, intens. + *fortis*, strong ‖ to soothe in distress or sorrow; console **—*n.*** **1** relief from distress, etc. **2** one that comforts **3** a state of, or thing that provides, ease and quiet enjoyment **—com′fort·ing** ***adj.*** **—com′fort·less** ***adj.***

com·fort·a·ble (kum′fərt ə bəl, kumf′tər bəl) ***adj.*** **1** providing comfort **2** at ease in body or mind **3** [Colloq.] sufficient to satisfy [*a comfortable* salary] **—com′fort·a·bly** ***adv.***

com·fort·er (kum′fər tər) ***n.*** **1** one that comforts **2** a quilted bed covering

comfort station a public toilet or restroom

com·fy (kum′fē) ***adj.*** **-fi·er, -fi·est** [Colloq.] comfortable

com·ic (käm′ik) ***adj.*** **1** of comedy **2** amusing; funny **—*n.*** **1** a comedian **2** the humorous element in art or life **3** *a*) COMIC STRIP *b*) [*pl.*] a section of comic strips

com′i·cal (-i kəl) ***adj.*** causing amusement; humorous; funny **—com′i·cal′i·ty** (-kal′ə tē) ***n.*** **—com′i·cal·ly** ***adv.***

comic strip a series of cartoons telling a humorous or adventurous story, as in a newspaper or in a booklet (**comic book**)

com·ing (kum′iŋ) ***adj.*** **1** approaching; next **2** showing promise of being successful, etc. **—*n.*** arrival; approach

com·i·ty (käm′ə tē) ***n.***, *pl.* **-ties** ‖ < L *comis*, polite ‖ courtesy

comm. **1** commission **2** committee

com·ma (käm′ə) ***n.*** ‖ < Gr *komma*, clause ‖ a mark of punctuation (,) used to indicate a slight separation of sentence elements

com·mand (kə mand′) ***vt.*** ‖ < L *com-*, intens. + *mandare*, entrust ‖ **1** to give an order to; direct **2** to have authority over; control **3** to have for use [*to command* a fortune] **4** to deserve and get [*to command* respect] **5** to control (a position); overlook **—*vi.*** to have authority **—*n.*** **1** an order; direction **2** controlling power or position **3** mastery **4** military or naval force, or district, under a specified authority

com·man·dant (käm′ən dant′) ***n.*** a commanding officer, as of a fort

com′man·deer′ (-dir′) ***vt.*** ‖ see COMMAND ‖ to seize (property) for military or government use

com·mand′er ***n.*** **1** one who commands **2** *U.S. Navy* an officer ranking just above a lieutenant commander

commander in chief *pl.* **commanders in chief** the supreme commander of the armed forces of a nation

com·mand′ment ***n.*** a command; specif., any of the TEN COMMANDMENTS

com·man·do (kə man′dō) ***n.***, *pl.* **-dos** or **-does** ‖ Afrik < Port ‖ a member of a small force trained to raid enemy territory

command post the field headquarters of a military unit, from which operations are directed

com·mem·o·rate (kə mem′ə rāt′) ***vt.*** **-rat′ed, -rat′ing** ‖ < L *com-*, intens. + *memorare*, remind ‖ **1** to honor the memory of, as by a ceremony **2** to serve as a memorial to **—com·mem′o·ra′tion** ***n.*** **—com·mem′o·ra′tive** ***adj.*** **—com·mem′o·ra′tor** ***n.***

com·mence (kə mens′) ***vi.***, ***vt.*** **-menced′, -menc′ing** ‖ < L *com-*, together + *initiare*, begin ‖ to begin

com·mence′ment ***n.*** **1** a beginning; start **2** the ceremony of conferring degrees or diplomas at a school

com·mend (kə mend′) ***vt.*** ‖ see COMMAND ‖ **1** to put in the care of another; entrust **2** to recommend **3** to praise **—com·mend′a·ble** ***adj.*** **—com·mend′a·bly** ***adv.*** **—com·men·da·tion** (käm′ən dā′shən) ***n.***

com·mend·a·to·ry (kə men′də tôr′ē) ***adj.*** praising or recommending

com·men·su·ra·ble (kə men′shoor ə bəl, -sər-) ***adj.*** ‖ < L *com-*, together + *mensura*, measurement ‖ measurable by the same standard or measure

com·men′su·rate (-shoor it, -sər-) ***adj.*** ‖ see prec. ‖ **1** equal in measure or size; coextensive **2** proportionate **3** commensurable

com·ment (käm′ent′) ***n.*** ‖ < L *com-*, intens. + *meminisse*, remember ‖ **1** an explanatory or critical note **2** a remark or observation **3** talk; gossip **—*vi.*** to make a comment or comments

com·men·tar·y (käm′ən ter′ē) ***n.***, *pl.* **-ies** a series of explanatory notes or remarks

com′men·tate′ (-tāt′) ***vi.*** **-tat′ed, -tat′ing** to perform as a commentator

com′men·ta′tor (-tāt′ər) ***n.*** one who reports and analyzes events, trends, etc., as on television

com·merce (käm′ərs) ***n.*** ‖ < L *com-*, together + *merx*, merchandise ‖ trade on a large scale, as between countries

com·mer·cial (kə mur′shəl) ***adj.*** **1** of commerce or business **2** made or done for profit **—*n.*** *Radio, TV* a paid advertisement **—com·mer′cial·ism′** ***n.*** **—com·mer′cial·ly** ***adv.***

com·mer′cial·ize′ (-īz′) ***vt.*** **-ized′, -iz′ing** to put on a business basis, esp. so as to make a profit **—com·mer′cial·i·za′tion** ***n.***

com·min·gle (kəm miŋ′gəl, kə-) ***vt.***, ***vi.*** **-gled, -gling** to mingle together

com·mis·er·ate (kə miz′ər āt′) ***vt.*** **-at′ed, -at′ing** ‖ < L *com-*, intens. + *miserari*, to pity ‖ to feel or show sorrow or pity for **—*vi.*** to condole or sympathize (*with*) **—com·mis′er·a′tion** ***n.*** **—com·mis′er·a′tive** ***adj.***

com·mis·sar (käm′ə sär′) ***n.*** ‖ Russ *komissar* ‖ the head of any former U.S.S.R. COMMISSARIAT (sense 2): now called *minister*

com′mis·sar′i·at (-ser′ē ət) ***n.*** ‖ Fr < L: see COMMIT ‖ **1** an army branch providing food and supplies **2** a government department in the U.S.S.R.: now called *ministry*

com·mis·sar·y (käm′ə ser′ē) ***n.***, *pl.* **-ies** ‖ see COMMIT ‖ **1** [Obs.] an army officer in charge of supplies **2** a store, as in an army camp, where food and supplies are sold **3** a restaurant in a movie or TV studio

com·mis·sion (kə mish′ən) ***n.*** ‖ see COMMIT ‖ **1** *a*) an authorization to perform certain duties or tasks *b*) a document giving such authorization *c*) the authority so granted 2 that which one is authorized to do 3 a group of people appointed to perform specified duties 4 a committing; doing 5 a percentage of money from sales, allotted to an agent, etc. 6 *Mil.* *a)* an official certificate conferring rank *b)* the rank conferred —***vt.*** 1 to give a commission to 2 to authorize 3 to put (a vessel) into service —**in** (or **out of**) **commission** in (or not in) working order

commissioned officer an officer in the armed forces holding a commission

com·mis′sion·er ***n.*** 1 a person authorized to do certain things by a commission or warrant 2 a member of a COMMISSION (*n.* 3) 3 an official in charge of a government bureau, etc. 4 a person selected to regulate and control a professional sport

com·mit (kə mit′) ***vt.*** **-mit′ted, -mit′ting** ⟦< L *com-*, together + *mittere*, send⟧ 1 to give in charge; consign 2 to put in custody or confinement /*committed* to prison/ 3 to do or perpetrate (a crime) 4 to bind, as by a promise; pledge —**com·mit′ment** ***n.*** —**com·mit′ta·ble** ***adj.*** —**com·mit′tal** ***n.***

com·mit·tee (kə mit′ē) ***n.*** ⟦see prec.⟧ a group of people chosen to report or act upon a certain matter —**com·mit′tee·man** (-mən), *pl.* **-men**, ***n.*** —**com·mit′tee·wom′an**, *pl.* **-wom′en**, ***n.fem.***

com·mode (kə mōd′) ***n.*** ⟦Fr < L: see COM- & MODE⟧ 1 a chest of drawers 2 a movable washstand 3 a toilet

com·mo·di·ous (kə mō′dē əs) ***adj.*** ⟦see prec.⟧ spacious; roomy

com·mod·i·ty (kə mäd′ə tē) ***n.***, *pl.* **-ties** ⟦see COMMODE⟧ 1 any useful thing 2 anything bought and sold 3 [*pl.*] staple products, as of agriculture

com·mo·dore (käm′ə dôr′) ***n.*** ⟦see COMMAND⟧ *U.S. Navy* [Historical] an officer ranking just above a captain

com·mon (käm′ən) ***adj.*** ⟦< L *communis*⟧ 1 belonging to or shared by each or all 2 of an entire community; public 3 general; widespread 4 familiar; usual 5 below ordinary; inferior 6 vulgar; coarse 7 designating a noun (as *book*) that refers to any of a group —***n.*** [*sometimes pl.*] land owned or used by all the inhabitants of a place —**in common** shared by each or all —**com′mon·ly** ***adv.***

com′mon·al·ty (-əl tē) ***n.***, *pl.* **-ties** the common people; public

common carrier a person or company in the business of transporting people or goods for a fee

common denominator 1 a common multiple of the denominators of two or more fractions 2 a characteristic, etc. held in common

common divisor (or **factor**) a factor common to two or more numbers

com′mon·er ***n.*** a person not of the nobility; one of the common people

common law the law based on custom, usage, and judicial decisions

com′mon-law′ marriage *Law* a marriage not solemnized by religious or civil ceremony

common market an association of countries for closer economic union

common multiple *Math.* a multiple of each of two or more quantities

com′mon·place′ ***n.*** 1 a trite remark; platitude 2 anything common or ordinary —***adj.*** trite or ordinary

common pleas *Law* in some States, a court having jurisdiction over civil and criminal trials

com·mons (käm′ənz) ***n.pl.*** 1 the common people 2 [C-] HOUSE OF COMMONS 3 [*often with sing. v.*] a dining room, as at a college

common sense good sense or practical judgment —**com′mon-sense′** ***adj.***

common stock stock in a company without the privileges of preferred stock, but usually giving its owner a vote

com′mon·weal′ (-wēl′) ***n.*** the public good; general welfare

com′mon·wealth′ (-welth′) ***n.*** 1 the people of a nation or state 2 a democracy or republic 3 a federation of states —**the Commonwealth** association of independent nations united under the British crown for purposes of consultation and mutual assistance

com·mo·tion (kə mō′shən) ***n.*** ⟦< L *com-*, together + *movere*, to move⟧ 1 violent motion 2 confusion; bustle

com·mu·nal (käm′yoo nəl, kə myoo′nəl) ***adj.*** 1 of a commune 2 of the community; public 3 marked by common ownership of property —**com′mu·nal·ize′**, **-ized′**, **-iz′·ing**, ***vt.*** —**com′mu·nal·ly** ***adv.***

com·mune[1] (kə myoon′) ***vi.*** **-muned′**, **-mun′ing** ⟦< OFr *comuner*, to share⟧ to talk together intimately

com·mune[2] (käm′yoon′) ***n.*** ⟦< L *communis*, common⟧ 1 the smallest administrative district of local government in some European countries 2 a small group of people living communally

com·mu·ni·ca·ble (kə myoo′ni kə bəl) ***adj.*** that can be communicated, as an idea, or transmitted, as a disease —**com·mu′ni·ca·bil′i·ty** ***n.***

com·mu′ni·cant (-kənt) ***n.*** one who receives Holy Communion

com·mu·ni·cate (kə myoo′ni kāt′) ***vt.*** **-cat′ed, -cat′ing** ⟦< L *communicare*⟧ 1 to impart; transmit 2 to give (information, etc.) —***vi.*** 1 to receive Holy Communion 2 to give or exchange information 3 to have a meaningful relationship 4 to be connected, as rooms —**com·mu′ni·ca′tor** ***n.***

com·mu′ni·ca′tion ***n.*** 1 a transmitting 2 *a)* a giving or exchanging of information, messages, etc. *b)* a message, letter, etc. 3 a means of communicating —**com·mu′ni·ca′tive** ***adj.***

com·mun·ion (kə myoon′yən) ***n.*** ⟦see COMMON⟧ 1 possession in common 2 a communing 3 a Christian denomination 4 [C-] HOLY COMMUNION

com·mu·ni·qué (kə myoo′ni kā′, kə myoo′ni kā′) ***n.*** ⟦Fr⟧ an official communication

com·mu·nism (käm′yoo niz′əm, -yə-) ***n.*** ⟦see COMMON⟧ 1 any theory or system of common ownership of property 2 [*often* C-] *a)* socialism as formulated by Marx, Lenin, etc. *b)* any government or political movement supporting this

com′mu·nist (-nist) ***n.*** 1 an advocate or supporter of communism 2 [C-] a member of a Communist Party —***adj.*** of, like, or supporting communism or communists —**com′mu·nis′tic *adj.***

com·mu·ni·ty (kə myo͞o′nə tē) ***n.***, *pl.* **-ties** ‖see COMMON‖ 1 *a)* any group living in the same area or having interests, work, etc. in common *b)* such an area 2 the general public 3 a sharing in common

community college a junior college serving a certain community

com·mu·ta·tive (kə myo͞ot′ə tiv, käm′yə tāt′ iv) ***adj.*** 1 involving exchange 2 *Math.* of an operation in which the order of the elements does not affect the result, as, in addition, 3 + 2 = 2 + 3

com·mute (kə myo͞ot′) ***vt.*** **-mut′ed, -mut′·ing** ‖< L *com-*, intens. + *mutare*, to change‖ 1 to exchange; substitute 2 to change (an obligation, punishment, etc.) to a less severe one —***vi.*** to travel as a commuter —***n.*** [Colloq.] the trip of a commuter —**com·mu·ta·tion** (käm′yə tā′shən) ***n.***

com·mut′er *n.* a person who travels regularly, esp. by train, bus, etc., between two points at some distance

Com·o·ro Islands (käm′ə rō′) country on a group of islands in the W Indian Ocean: 838 sq. mi.; pop. 420,000

comp. 1 comparative 2 compound

com·pact (kəm pakt′, käm′pakt; *for n.* käm′ pakt) ***adj.*** ‖< L *com-*, with, together + *pangere*, to fix‖ 1 closely and firmly packed 2 taking little space 3 terse —***vt.*** 1 to pack or join firmly together 2 to make by putting together —***n.*** 1 a small cosmetic case, usually containing face powder and a mirror 2 a relatively small car 3 an agreement; covenant —**com·pact′ly *adv.*** —**com·pact′ness *n.***

compact disc (or **disk**) a digital disc on which music, etc. has been encoded for playing on a device using a laser beam to read the encoded matter

com·pac·tor (kəm pak′tər, käm′pak′tər) ***n.*** a device that compresses trash into small bundles

com·pan·ion (kəm pan′yən) ***n.*** ‖< L *com-*, with + *panis*, bread‖ 1 an associate; comrade 2 a person paid to live or travel with another 3 one of a pair or set —**com·pan′·ion·a·ble *adj.*** —**com·pan′ion·ship′ *n.***

com·pan′ion·way′ *n.* a stairway from a ship's deck to the space below

com·pa·ny (kum′pə nē) ***n.***, *pl.* **-nies** ‖see COMPANION‖ 1 companionship; society 2 a group of people gathered or associated for some purpose 3 a guest or guests 4 an associate or associates 5 a body of troops 6 a ship's crew —**keep company** 1 to associate (*with*) 2 to go together, as a couple intending to marry —**part company** to stop associating (*with*)

com·pa·ra·ble (käm′pə rə bəl) ***adj.*** 1 that can be compared 2 worthy of comparison —**com′pa·ra·bly *adv.***

com·par·a·tive (kəm par′ə tiv) ***adj.*** 1 involving comparison 2 not absolute; relative 3 *Gram.* designating the second degree of comparison of adjectives and adverbs —***n.*** *Gram.* the comparative degree ("finer" is the *comparative* of "fine") —**com·par′a·tive·ly *adv.***

com·pare (kəm per′) ***vt.*** **-pared′, -par′ing** ‖< L *com-*, with + *parare*, make equal‖ 1 to liken (*to*) 2 to examine for similarities or differences 3 *Gram.* to form the degrees of comparison of —***vi.*** 1 to be worth comparing (*with*) 2 to make comparisons —**beyond** (or **past** or **without**) **compare** incomparably good, bad, great, etc.

com·par·i·son (kəm par′ə sən) ***n.*** 1 a comparing or being compared 2 likeness; similarity 3 *Gram.* change in an adjective or adverb to show the positive, comparative, and superlative degrees —**in comparison with** compared with

com·part·ment (kəm pärt′mənt) ***n.*** ‖< L *com-*, intens. + *partire*, divide‖ 1 any of the divisions into which a space is partitioned off 2 a separate section or category —**com·part·men·tal·ize** (käm′pärt ment′′l īz′), **-ized′, -iz′ing, *vt.***

com·pass (kum′pəs, käm′-) ***vt.*** ‖< L *com-*, together + *passus*, a step‖ 1 [Archaic] to go around 2 to surround 3 to understand 4 to achieve or contrive —***n.*** 1 [*often pl.*] an instrument with two pivoted legs, for drawing circles, for measuring, etc. 2 a boundary 3 an enclosed area 4 range; scope 5 an instrument for showing direction, esp. one with a swinging magnetic needle pointing north

DRAWING COMPASS

com·pas·sion (kəm pash′ən) ***n.*** ‖< L *com-*, together + *pati*, suffer‖ deep sympathy; pity —**com·pas′sion·ate *adj.*** —**com·pas′sion·ate·ly *adv.***

com·pat·i·ble (kəm pat′ə bəl) ***adj.*** ‖see prec.‖ 1 getting along or going well together 2 *Bot.* that can be cross-fertilized or grafted readily —**com·pat′i·bil′i·ty *n.***

com·pa·tri·ot (kəm pā′trē ət) ***n.*** ‖see COM- & PATRIOT‖ a countryman —***adj.*** of the same country

com·peer (käm′pir′, käm pir′) ***n.*** ‖see COM- & PAR‖ 1 an equal; peer 2 a comrade

com·pel (kəm pel′) ***vt.*** **-pelled′, -pel′ling** ‖< L *com-*, together + *pellere*, to drive‖ to force or get by force —**com·pel′ling·ly *adv.***

com·pen·di·um (kəm pen′dē əm) ***n.***, *pl.* **-ums** or **-a** (-ə) ‖< L *com-*, together + *pendere*, weigh‖ a concise but comprehensive summary

com·pen·sate (käm′pən sāt′) ***vt.*** **-sat′ed, -sat′ing** ‖< L *com-*, with + *pendere*, weigh‖ 1 to make up for; counterbalance 2 to pay —***vi.*** to make amends (*for*) —**com′·pen·sa′tion *n.*** —**com·pen·sa·to·ry** (kəm pen′sə tôr′ē) ***adj.***

com·pete (kəm pēt′) ***vi.*** **-pet′ed, -pet′ing** ‖< L *com-*, together + *petere*, to desire‖ to be in rivalry; contend; vie (*in* a contest, etc.)

com·pe·tence (käm′pə təns) ***n.*** 1 sufficient means for one's needs 2 ability; fitness 3 legal power, jurisdiction, etc. Also **com′pe·ten·cy** (-tən sē)

com′pe·tent (-tənt) ***adj.*** ‖see COMPETE‖ 1

capable; fit 2 sufficient; adequate 3 having legal competence —**com′pe·tent·ly** ***adv.***

com·pe·ti·tion (käm′pə tish′ən) ***n.*** ‖ L *competitio* ‖ 1 a competing; rivalry, esp. in business 2 a contest; match —**com·pet·i·tive** (kəm pet′ə tiv) ***adj.***

com·pet·i·tor (kəm pet′ət ər) ***n.*** ‖ L ‖ one who competes, as a business rival

com·pile (kəm pīl′) ***vt.*** **-piled′, -pil′ing** ‖ < L *com-*, together + *pilare*, to compress ‖ 1 to collect and assemble (data, writings, etc.) 2 to compose (a book, etc.) of materials from various sources —**com·pi·la·tion** (käm′pə lā′shən) ***n.***

com·pla·cen·cy (kəm plā′sən sē) ***n.*** ‖ < L *com-*, intens. + *placere*, to please ‖ contentment; often, specif., self-satisfaction, or smugness Also **com·pla′cence** —**com·pla′cent** ***adj.***

com·plain (kəm plān′) ***vi.*** ‖ < L *com-*, intens. + *plangere*, to strike ‖ 1 to express pain, displeasure, etc. 2 to find fault 3 to make an accusation —**com·plain′er** ***n.***

com·plain′ant (-ənt) ***n.*** a plaintiff

com·plaint′ (-plānt′) ***n.*** 1 a complaining 2 a cause for complaining 3 an ailment 4 *Law* a formal charge

com·plai·sant (kəm plā′zənt, -sənt) ***adj.*** ‖ see COMPLACENCY ‖ willing to please; obliging —**com·plai′sant·ly** ***adv.*** —**com·plai′sance** ***n.***

com·plect′ed (-plek′tid) ***adj.*** COMPLEXIONED

com·ple·ment (käm′plə mənt; *for v.*, -ment′) ***n.*** ‖ see fol. ‖ 1 that which completes or perfects 2 the amount needed to fill or complete 3 an entirety 4 *Math.* the number of degrees that must be added to a given angle to make it equal 90 degrees —***vt.*** to make complete —**com′ple·men′ta·ry** (-men′tə rē) ***adj.***

com·plete (kəm plēt′) ***adj.*** ‖ < L *com-*, intens. + *plere*, fill ‖ 1 whole; entire 2 finished 3 thorough —***vt.*** **-plet′ed, -plet′ing** 1 to finish 2 to make whole or perfect —**com·plete′ly** ***adv.*** —**com·plete′ness** ***n.*** —**com·ple′tion** (-plē′shən) ***n.***

com·plex (käm pleks′, käm′pleks′; kəm pleks′; *for n.* käm′pleks′) ***adj.*** ‖ < L *com-*, with + *plectere*, to weave ‖ 1 consisting of two or more related parts 2 complicated —***n.*** 1 a complex whole 2 an assemblage of units, as buildings 3 *Psychoanalysis a*) a group of mainly unconscious impulses, etc. strongly influencing behavior *b*) popularly, an obsession —**com·plex′i·ty** ***n.***

complex fraction a fraction with a fraction in its numerator or denominator, or in both

com·plex·ion (kəm plek′shən) ***n.*** ‖ see COMPLEX ‖ 1 the color, texture, etc. of the skin, esp. of the face 2 nature; character; aspect —**com·plex′ion·al** ***adj.***

com·plex′ioned ***adj.*** having a (specified) complexion [light-*complexioned*]

complex sentence a sentence consisting of an independent clause and one or more dependent clauses

com·pli·ance (kəm plī′əns) ***n.*** 1 a complying; acquiescence 2 a tendency to give in readily to others Also **com·pli′an·cy** —**com·pli′ant** ***adj.***

com·pli·cate (käm′pli kāt′) ***vt., vi.*** **-cat′ed, -cat′ing** ‖ < L *com-*, together + *plicare*, to fold ‖ to make or become intricate, difficult, or involved —**com′pli·ca′tion** ***n.***

com′pli·cat′ed ***adj.*** intricately involved; hard to solve, analyze, etc.

com·plic·i·ty (kəm plis′ə tē) ***n.***, *pl.* **-ties** ‖ see COMPLICATE ‖ partnership in wrongdoing

com·pli·ment (käm′plə mənt; *for v.*, -ment′) ***n.*** ‖ Fr < L: see COMPLETE ‖ 1 a formal act of courtesy; esp., something said in praise 2 [*pl.*] respects —***vt.*** to pay a compliment to

com′pli·men′ta·ry (-men′tə rē) ***adj.*** 1 paying or containing a compliment 2 given free as a courtesy

com·ply (kəm plī′) ***vt.*** **-plied′, -ply′ing** ‖ see COMPLETE ‖ to act in accordance (*with* a request, order, etc.)

com·po·nent (kəm pō′nənt) ***adj.*** ‖ see COMPOSITE ‖ serving as one of the parts of a whole —***n.*** a part, element, or ingredient

com·port (kəm pôrt′) ***vt.*** ‖ < L *com-*, together + *portare*, carry ‖ to behave (oneself) in a specified manner —***vi.*** to accord (*with*) —**com·port′ment** ***n.***

com·pose (kəm pōz′) ***vt.*** **-posed′, -pos′ing** ‖ < OFr *com-*, with + *poser*, to place ‖ 1 to make up; constitute 2 to put in proper form 3 to create (a musical or literary work) 4 to make calm 5 *a*) to set (type) *b*) to produce (printed matter) as by computer, etc. —***vi.*** to create musical works, etc. —**com·pos′er** ***n.***

com·posed′ ***adj.*** calm; self-possessed

com·pos·ite (kəm päz′it) ***adj.*** ‖ < L *com-*, together + *ponere*, to place ‖ 1 compound 2 *Bot.* designating a large family of plants with flower heads composed of dense clusters of small flowers, including the daisy and the chrysanthemum —***n.*** a composite thing —**com·pos′ite·ly** ***adv.***

com·po·si·tion (käm′pə zish′ən) ***n.*** 1 a composing, esp. of literary or musical works 2 the makeup of a person or thing 3 something composed

com·pos·i·tor (kəm päz′ət ər) ***n.*** one who sets matter for printing, esp. a typesetter

com·post (käm′pōst′) ***n.*** ‖ see COMPOSITE ‖ a mixture of decomposing vegetable refuse for fertilizing soil

com·po·sure (kəm pō′zhər) ***n.*** ‖ see COMPOSE ‖ calmness; self-possession

com·pote (käm′pōt′) ***n.*** ‖ Fr: see COMPOSITE ‖ 1 a dish of stewed fruits 2 a long-stemmed dish, as for candy

com·pound[1] (käm pound′, käm′pound′; kəm pound′; *for adj. usually & for n. always*, käm′pound′) ***vt.*** ‖ see COMPOSITE ‖ 1 to mix or combine 2 to make by combining parts 3 to compute (compound interest) 4 to intensify by adding new elements —***adj.*** made up of two or more parts —***n.*** 1 a thing formed by combining parts 2 a substance containing two or more elements chemically combined —**compound a felony** (or **crime**) to agree, for payment, not to prosecute a felony (or crime)

com·pound[2] (käm′pound′) ***n.*** ‖ Malay *kampong* ‖ an area enclosing a building or buildings

compound eye an eye made up of numerous simple eyes functioning collectively, as in insects

compound fracture a fracture in which the broken bone pierces the skin
compound interest interest paid on both the principal and the accumulated unpaid interest
compound sentence a sentence consisting of two or more independent, coordinate clauses
com·pre·hend (käm′prē hend′, pri-) ***vt.*** ‖ < L *com-*, with + *prehendere*, seize ‖ **1** to grasp mentally; understand **2** to include; take in; comprise —**com′pre·hen′si·ble** (-hen′sə bəl) ***adj.*** —**com′pre·hen′sion** ***n.***
com′pre·hen′sive ***adj.*** wide in scope; inclusive —**com′pre·hen′sive·ly** ***adv.*** —**com′pre·hen′sive·ness** ***n.***
com·press (kəm pres′; *for n.* käm′pres′) ***vt.*** ‖ < L *com-*, together + *premere*, to press ‖ to press together and make more compact —***n.*** a pad of folded cloth, often wet or medicated, applied to the skin —**com·pressed′** ***adj.*** —**com·pres′sion** ***n.***
com·pres′sor (-pres′ər) ***n.*** a machine, esp. a pump, for compressing air, gas, etc.
com·prise′ (-prīz′) ***vt.*** **-prised′**, **-pris′ing** ‖ see COMPREHEND ‖ **1** to include; contain **2** to consist of **3** to make up; form: a loose usage
com·pro·mise (käm′prə mīz′) ***n.*** ‖ < L *com-*, together + *promittere*, to promise ‖ **1** a settlement in which each side makes concessions **2** something midway —***vt.***, ***vi.*** **-mised′**, **-mis′ing** **1** to adjust by compromise **2** to lay open to suspicion, disrepute, etc.
comp·trol·ler (kən trō′lər) ***n.*** ‖ altered (infl. by Fr *compte*, an account) < CONTROLLER ‖ CONTROLLER (sense 1, esp. in government usage)
com·pul·sion (kəm pul′shən) ***n.*** a compelling or being compelled; force —**com·pul′sive** (-siv) ***adj.*** —**com·pul′sive·ly** ***adv.*** —**com·pul′sive·ness** ***n.***
com·pul′so·ry (-sə rē) ***adj.*** **1** obligatory; required **2** compelling
com·punc·tion (kəm puŋk′shən) ***n.*** ‖ < L *com-*, intens. + *pungere*, to prick ‖ an uneasy feeling prompted by guilt
com·pute (kəm pyo͞ot′) ***vt.***, ***vi.*** **-put′ed**, **-put′ing** ‖ < L *com-*, with + *putare*, reckon ‖ to determine (an amount, etc.) by arithmetic —**com·pu·ta·tion** (käm′pyo͞o tā′shən) ***n.***
com·put′er ***n.*** an electronic machine that performs rapid, complex calculations or compiles and correlates data —**com·put′er·ize′**, **-ized′**, **-iz′ing**, ***vt.***
com·rade (käm′rad′, -rəd) ***n.*** ‖ < Sp *camarada*, chamber mate < L *camera*, room ‖ **1** a friend; close companion **2** an associate —**com′rade·ship′** ***n.***
Com·sat (käm′sat′) ***n.*** ‖ < COM(MUNICATION) + SAT(ELLITE) ‖ *trademark for* any of various communications satellites for relaying microwave transmissions, as of television
con^{1} (kän) ***adv.*** ‖ < L *contra* ‖ against —***n.*** an opposing reason, vote, etc.
con^{2} (kän) ***vt.*** **conned**, **con′ning** ‖ < OE *cunnan*, know ‖ to study carefully
con^{3} (kän) ***adj.*** [Slang] CONFIDENCE /a *con* man/ —***vt.*** **conned**, **con′ning** [Slang] to swindle or trick
con^{4} (kän) ***n.*** [Slang] *short for* CONVICT
con- *prefix* COM Used before *c, d, g, j, n, q, s, t, v,* and sometimes *f*
con·cat·e·na·tion (kən kat′′n ā′shən, kän) ***n.*** ‖ < L *com-*, together + *catena*, a chain ‖ a connected series, as of events
con·cave (kän kāv′, kän′kāv′) ***adj.*** ‖ < L *com-*, intens. + *cavus*, hollow ‖ hollow and curved like the inside half of a hollow ball
con·ceal (kən sēl′) ***vt.*** ‖ < L *com-*, together + *celare*, to hide ‖ **1** to hide **2** to keep secret —**con·ceal′ment** ***n.***
con·cede (kən sēd′) ***vt.*** **-ced′ed**, **-ced′ing** ‖ < L *com-*, with + *cedere*, cede ‖ **1** to admit as true, valid, certain, etc. **2** to grant as a right
con·ceit (kən sēt′) ***n.*** ‖ see CONCEIVE ‖ **1** an exaggerated opinion of oneself, one's merits, etc.; vanity **2** a fanciful expression or notion
con·ceit′ed ***adj.*** vain
con·ceiv·a·ble (kən sēv′ə bəl) ***adj.*** that can be understood or believed —**con·ceiv′a·bil′i·ty** ***n.*** —**con·ceiv′a·bly** ***adv.***
con·ceive (kən sēv′) ***vt.*** **-ceived′**, **-ceiv′ing** ‖ < L *com-*, together + *capere*, take ‖ **1** to become pregnant with **2** to form in the mind; imagine **3** to understand —***vi.*** **1** to become pregnant **2** to form an idea (*of*)
con·cel·e·brate (kän sel′ə brāt′, kən-) ***vt.*** **-brat′ed**, **-brat′ing** ‖ < L *com-*, together + *celebrare*, to honor ‖ to celebrate (the Eucharistic liturgy) jointly, two or more priests officiating —**con′cel·e·bra′tion** ***n.***
con·cen·trate (kän′sən trāt′) ***vt.*** **-trat′ed**, **-trat′ing** ‖ < L *com-*, together + *centrum*, center + -ATE^{1} ‖ **1** to focus (one's thoughts, efforts, etc.) **2** to increase the strength, density, etc. of —***vi.*** to fix one's attention (*on* or *upon*) —***n.*** a concentrated substance —**con′cen·tra′tion** ***n.***
concentration camp a prison camp for political dissidents, members of minority ethnic groups, etc.
con·cen·tric (kən sen′trik) ***adj.*** ‖ < L *com-*, together + *centrum*, center ‖ having a center in common, as circles —**con·cen′tri·cal·ly** ***adv.***

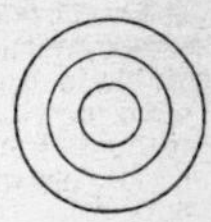
CONCENTRIC CIRCLES

con·cept (kän′sept′) ***n.*** ‖ see CONCEIVE ‖ an idea or thought; abstract notion
con·cep·tion (kən sep′shən) ***n.*** **1** a conceiving or being conceived in the womb **2** the beginning, as of a process **3** the formulation of ideas **4** a concept **5** an original idea or design
con·cep′tu·al (-cho͞o əl) ***adj.*** of conception or concepts —**con·cep′tu·al·ly** ***adv.***
con·cep′tu·al·ize′ (-cho͞o əl īz′) ***vt.*** **-ized′**, **-iz′ing** to form a concept of —**con·cep′tu·al·i·za′tion** ***n.***
con·cern (kən surn′) ***vt.*** ‖ < L *com-*, with + *cernere*, sift ‖ **1** to have a relation to **2** to engage or involve —***n.*** **1** a matter; affair **2** interest in or regard for a person or thing **3** reference **4** worry **5** a business firm —**as concerns** in regard to —**concern oneself** **1** to busy oneself **2** to be worried
con·cerned′ ***adj.*** **1** involved or interested (*in*) **2** uneasy or anxious

con·cern'ing *prep.* relating to
con·cert (kän'sərt) *n.* ‖< L *com-*, with + *certare*, strive‖ **1** mutual agreement; concord **2** a performance of music —**in concert** in unison
con·cert·ed (kən surt'id) *adj.* mutually arranged or agreed upon; combined —**con·cert'ed·ly** *adv.*
con·cer·ti·na (kän'sər tē'nə) *n.* ‖< CONCERT‖ a small accordion
con·cert·ize (kän'sər tiz') *vi.* **-ized'**, **-iz'ing** to perform as a soloist in concerts, esp. on a tour
con'cert·mas'ter *n.* the leader of the first violin section of a symphony orchestra, and often the assistant to the conductor
con·cer·to (kən cher'tō) *n., pl.* **-tos** or **-ti** (-tē) ‖It‖ a musical composition for one or more solo instruments and an orchestra
con·ces·sion (kən sesh'ən) *n.* **1** a conceding **2** a thing conceded; acknowledgment **3** a privilege granted by a government, company, etc., as the right to sell food at a park
con·ces'sion·aire' (-ə ner') *n.* ‖< Fr‖ the holder of a CONCESSION (sense 3)
conch (käŋk, känch) *n., pl.* **conchs** (käŋks) or **conch·es** (kän'chiz) ‖< Gr *konchē*‖ **1** the spiral, one-piece shell of various sea mollusks **2** the mollusk
con·ci·erge (kän'sē erzh'; *Fr* kōn syerzh') *n.* ‖Fr < L *conservus*, fellow slave‖ a custodian or head porter, as of an apartment house or hotel
con·cil·i·ar (kən sil'ē ər) *adj.* of, from, or by means of a council
con·cil'i·ate' (-āt') *vt.* **-at'ed**, **-at'ing** ‖see COUNCIL‖ to win over; make friendly; placate —**con·cil'i·a'tion** *n.* —**con·cil'i·a'tor** *n.* —**con·cil'i·a·to'ry** (-ə tôr'ē) *adj.*
con·cise (kən sīs') *adj.* ‖< L *com-*, intens. + *caedere*, to cut‖ brief and to the point; terse —**con·cise'ly** *adv.* —**con·cise'ness** *n.* —**con·ci'sion** (-sizh'ən) *n.*
con·clave (kän'klāv') *n.* ‖< L *com-*, with + *clavis*, a key‖ **1** a private meeting; specif., one held by cardinals to elect a pope **2** any large convention
con·clude (kən klo͞od') *vt., vi.* **-clud'ed**, **-clud'ing** ‖< L *com-*, together + *claudere*, to shut‖ **1** to end; finish **2** to deduce **3** to decide; determine **4** to arrange (a treaty, etc.)
con·clu'sion (-klo͞o'zhən) *n.* **1** the end **2** a judgment or opinion formed after thought **3** an outcome **4** a concluding (*of* a treaty, etc.) —**in conclusion** lastly; in closing
con·clu'sive (-siv) *adj.* final; decisive —**con·clu'sive·ly** *adv.* —**con·clu'sive·ness** *n.*
con·coct (kən käkt') *vt.* ‖< L *com-*, together + *coquere*, to cook‖ **1** to make by combining ingredients **2** to devise; plan —**con·coc'tion** *n.*
con·com'i·tant (-käm'ə tənt) *adj.* ‖< L *com-*, together + *comes*, companion‖ accompanying; attendant —*n.* a concomitant thing —**con·com'i·tant·ly** *adv.*
con·cord (kän'kôrd', käŋ'-) *n.* ‖< L *com-*, together + *cor*, heart‖ **1** agreement; harmony **2** peaceful relations, as between nations
Con·cord (*for 1* kän'kôrd; *for 2* käŋ'kərd) **1** city in W Calif.: pop. 103,000 **2** capital of N.H.: pop. 30,000
con·cord·ance (kən kôr'd'ns) *n.* **1** agreement **2** an alphabetical list of the words in a book, with references to the passages in which they occur
con·cord'ant *adj.* agreeing
con·cor·dat (kən kôr'dat') *n.* ‖Fr < L: see CONCORD‖ a formal agreement
Con·cord (grape) (käŋ'kərd) ‖after *Concord*, a town in E Mass.‖ a large, dark-blue grape used esp. for juice and jelly
con·course (kän'kôrs') *n.* ‖see CONCUR‖ **1** a crowd; throng **2** an open space for crowds, as in a park **3** a broad thoroughfare
con·crete (kän krēt'; *also, and for n. & vt. 2 usually*, kän'krēt') *adj.* ‖< L *com-*, together + *crescere*, grow‖ **1** having a material existence; real; actual **2** specific, not general **3** made of concrete —*n.* **1** anything concrete **2** a hard building material made of sand and gravel, bonded together with cement —*vt., vi.* **-cret'ed**, **-cret'ing** **1** to solidify **2** to cover with concrete —**con·crete'ly** *adv.* —**con·crete'ness** *n.*
con·cre·tion (kən krē'shən) *n.* **1** a solidifying **2** a solidified mass
con·cu·bine (kän'kyo͞o bīn', käŋ'-) *n.* ‖< L *com-*, with + *cubare*, lie down‖ in some societies, a secondary wife, having inferior social and legal status
con·cu·pis·cence (kən kyo͞op'ə səns) *n.* ‖< L *com-*, intens. + *cupiscere*, to desire‖ strong desire, esp. sexual desire; lust —**con·cu'pis·cent** *adj.*
con·cur (kən kur') *vi.* **-curred'**, **-cur'ring** ‖< L *com-*, together + *currere*, to run‖ **1** to occur at the same time **2** to act together **3** to agree (*with*) —**con·cur'rence** *n.*
con·cur'rent *adj.* **1** occurring at the same time **2** acting together **3** *Law* having equal authority —**con·cur'rent·ly** *adv.*
con·cus·sion (kən kush'ən) *n.* ‖< L *com-*, together + *quatere*, to shake‖ **1** a violent shaking; shock, as from impact **2** impaired functioning, esp. of the brain, caused by a violent blow
con·demn (kən dem') *vt.* ‖< L *com-*, intens. + *damnare*, to harm‖ **1** to disapprove of strongly **2** to declare guilty **3** to inflict a penalty upon **4** to doom **5** to appropriate (property) for public use **6** to declare unfit for use —**con·dem·na·tion** (kän'dem nā' shən, -dəm-) *n.* —**con·dem·na·to·ry** (kən dem'nə tôr'ē) *adj.* —**con·demn'er** *n.*
con·dense (kən dens') *vt.* **-densed'**, **-dens'ing** ‖< L *com-*, intens. + *densus*, dense‖ **1** to make more dense or compact **2** to express in fewer words **3** to change to a denser form, as from gas to liquid —*vi.* to become condensed —**con·den·sa·tion** (kän'dən sā'shən) *n.*
condensed milk a thick milk made by evaporating part of the water from cow's milk and adding sugar
con·dens'er *n.* one that condenses; specif., *a*) an apparatus for liquefying gases *b*) a lens for concentrating light rays *c*) *Elec.* CAPACITOR
con·de·scend (kän'di send') *vi.* ‖< L *com-*, together + *descendere*, descend‖ **1** to be gracious about doing a thing regarded as beneath one's dignity **2** to deal with others

patronizingly —**con′de·scend′ing·ly** ***adv.*** —**con′de·scen′sion** ***n.***

con·dign (kən dīn′, kän′dīn′) ***adj.*** ‖< L *com-*, intens. + *dignus,* worthy‖ deserved; suitable: said esp. of punishment

con·di·ment (kän′də mənt) ***n.*** ‖< L *condire,* to pickle‖ a seasoning or relish, as pepper, mustard, sauces, etc.

con·di·tion (kən dish′ən) ***n.*** ‖< L *com-*, together + *dicere,* to speak‖ **1** anything required for the performance, completion, or existence of something else; provision or prerequisite **2** *a)* state of being *b)* [Colloq.] an illness *c)* a healthy state **3** social position; rank —***vt.*** **1** to stipulate **2** to impose a condition on **3** to bring into fit condition **4** to make accustomed (*to*) —**on condition that** provided that; if —**con·di′tion·er** ***n.***

con·di′tion·al ***adj.*** containing, expressing, or dependent on a condition; qualified —***n.*** *Gram.* a word, clause, tense, etc. expressing a condition —**con·di′tion·al·ly** ***adv.***

con·di′tioned (-ənd) ***adj.*** **1** subject to conditions **2** in a desired condition **3** affected by conditioning **4** accustomed (*to*)

con·do (kän′dō) ***n.***, *pl.* **-dos** or **-does** *short for* CONDOMINIUM (sense 3)

con·dole (kən dōl′) ***vi.*** **-doled′**, **-dol′ing** ‖< L *com-*, with + *dolere,* grieve‖ to express sympathy; commiserate —**con·do′lence** ***n.***

con·dom (kän′dəm, kun′-) ***n.*** ‖< It *guanto,* a glove‖ a thin, elastic sheath for the penis, used as a prophylactic or contraceptive

con·do·min·i·um (kän′də min′ē əm) ***n.*** ‖ult. < L *com-*, with + *dominium,* ownership‖ **1** joint rule by two or more states **2** the territory ruled **3** one of the units in a multiunit dwelling, each separately owned

con·done (kən dōn′) ***vt.*** **-doned′**, **-don′ing** ‖< L *com-*, intens. + *donare,* give‖ to forgive or overlook (an offense) —**con·don′a·ble** ***adj.***

con·dor (kän′dər) ***n.*** ‖< Sp < AmInd (Peru)‖ **1** a large vulture of the South American Andes, with a bare head **2** a similar vulture of S Calif.

con·duce (kən do͞os′) ***vi.*** **-duced′**, **-duc′ing** ‖< L *com-*, together + *ducere,* to lead‖ to tend or lead (*to* an effect) —**con·du′cive** ***adj.***

con·duct (kän′dukt′; *for v.* kən dukt′) ***n.*** ‖< L *com-*, together + *ducere,* to lead‖ **1** management **2** behavior —***vt.*** **1** to lead **2** to manage **3** to direct (an orchestra, etc.) **4** to behave (oneself) **5** to transmit or convey —**con·duc′tion** ***n.*** —**con·duc′tive** ***adj.*** —**con′duc·tiv′i·ty** (-tiv′ə tē) ***n.***

con·duct·ance (kən dukt′əns) ***n.*** the ability to conduct electricity

con·duc′tor ***n.*** **1** the leader of an orchestra, etc. **2** one in charge of the passengers on a train **3** a thing that conducts electricity, heat, etc.

con·du·it (kän′do͞o it) ***n.*** ‖see CONDUCE‖ **1** a channel for conveying fluids **2** a tube for electric wires

RED SPRUCE CONE

cone (kōn) ***n.*** ‖< Gr *kōnos*‖ **1** a solid with a circle for its base and a curved surface tapering to a point **2** any cone-shaped object **3** the scaly fruit of evergreen trees **4** a light-sensitive cell in the retina

Co·ney Island (kō′nē) beach & amusement park in Brooklyn, N.Y.

con·fab (kän′fab′) ***n.*** ‖ult. < L *com-*, together + *fabulari,* to converse‖ [Colloq.] a chat

con·fec·tion (kən fek′shən) ***n.*** ‖< L *com-*, with + *facere,* make‖ a candy or other sweet, as ice cream

con·fec′tion·er ***n.*** one who makes or sells candy and other confections

con·fec′tion·er′y (-er′ē) ***n.***, *pl.* **-ies** a confectioner's shop; candy store

con·fed·er·a·cy (kən fed′ər ə sē) ***n.***, *pl.* **-cies** a league or alliance —**the Confederacy** the 11 Southern States that seceded from the U.S. in 1860 & 1861

con·fed·er·ate (kən fed′ər it; *for v.*, -ər āt′) ***adj.*** ‖< L *com-*, together + *foedus,* a league‖ **1** united in an alliance **2** [**C-**] of the Confederacy —***n.*** **1** an ally; associate **2** an accomplice **3** [**C-**] a Southern supporter of the Confederacy —***vt.***, ***vi.*** **-at′ed**, **-at′ing** to unite in a confederacy; ally

con·fed′er·a′tion ***n.*** a league or federation

con·fer (kən fur′) ***vt.*** **-ferred′**, **-fer′ring** ‖< L *com-*, together + *ferre,* bring‖ to give or bestow —***vi.*** to have a conference —**con·fer·ee** (kän′fər ē′) ***n.*** —**con·fer′ment** or **con·fer′ral** ***n.*** —**con·fer′rer** ***n.***

con·fer·ence (kän′fər əns) ***n.*** **1** a formal meeting for discussion **2** an association of schools, churches, etc.

con·fess (kən fes′) ***vt.***, ***vi.*** ‖< L *com-*, together + *fateri,* acknowledge‖ **1** to admit or acknowledge (a fault, crime, belief, etc.) **2** *a)* to tell (one's sins) to a priest *b)* to hear the confession of (a person) —**confess to** to acknowledge

con·fess′ed·ly (-id lē) ***adv.*** admittedly

con·fes·sion (kən fesh′ən) ***n.*** **1** a confessing **2** something confessed **3** *a)* a creed *b)* a church having a creed

con·fes′sion·al ***n.*** an enclosure in a church, where a priest hears confessions

con·fes′sor ***n.*** **1** one who confesses **2** a priest who hears confessions

con·fet·ti (kən fet′ē) ***n.pl.*** ‖It, sweetmeats‖ [*with sing. v.*] bits of colored paper scattered about at celebrations

con·fi·dant (kän′fə dant′) ***n.*** a close, trusted friend —**con′fi·dante′** ***n.fem.***

con·fide (kən fīd′) ***vi.*** **-fid′ed**, **-fid′ing** ‖< L *com-*, intens. + *fidere,* to trust‖ to trust (*in* someone), esp. by sharing secrets —***vt.*** **1** to tell about as a secret **2** to entrust

con·fi·dence (kän′fə dəns) ***n.*** **1** trust; reliance **2** assurance **3** belief in one's own abilities **4** the belief that another will keep a secret **5** something told as a secret —***adj.*** swindling or used to swindle

confidence game a swindle effected by one (**confidence man**) who first gains the confidence of the victim

con′fi·dent (-dənt) ***adj.*** full of confidence; specif., *a)* certain *b)* sure of oneself —**con′fi·dent·ly** ***adv.***

con′fi·den′tial (-den′shəl) ***adj.*** **1** secret **2** of or showing trust **3** entrusted with private matters —**con′fi·den′ti·al′i·ty** (-shē al′ə tē) ***n.*** —**con′fi·den′tial·ly** ***adv.***

con·fig·u·ra·tion (kən fig′yo͞o rā′shən) ***n.***

‖ < L *com-*, together + *figurare*, to form ‖ contour; outline

con·fine (kän′fin′; *for v.* kən fin′) ***n.*** ‖ < L *com-*, with + *finis*, an end ‖ [*usually pl.*] a boundary or bounded region —***vt.* -fined′, -fin′ing** 1 to keep within limits; restrict 2 to keep shut up, as in prison, a sickbed, etc. —**con·fine′ment *n.***

con·firm (kən furm′) ***vt.*** ‖ < L *com-*, intens. + *firmare*, strengthen ‖ 1 to make firm 2 to give formal approval to 3 to prove the truth of 4 to admit to church membership by confirmation

con·fir·ma·tion (kän′fər mā′shən) ***n.*** 1 a confirming 2 something that confirms 3 a ceremony admitting a person to full church membership

con·firmed′ ***adj.*** 1 firmly established; habitual 2 corroborated

con·fis·cate (kän′fis kāt′) ***vt.* -cat′ed, -cat′ing** ‖ < L *com-*, together + *fiscus*, treasury ‖ 1 to seize (private property) for the public treasury 2 to seize as by authority; appropriate —**con′fis·ca′tion *n.***

con·fis·ca·to·ry (kən fis′kə tôr′ē) ***adj.*** of or effecting confiscation

con·fla·gra·tion (kän′flə grā′shən) ***n.*** ‖ < L *com-*, intens. + *flagrare*, to burn ‖ a big, destructive fire

con·flict (kən flikt′; *for n.* kän′flikt′) ***vi.*** ‖ < L *com-*, together + *fligere*, to strike ‖ to be antagonistic, incompatible, etc. —***n.*** 1 a fight or war 2 sharp disagreement, as of interests or ideas 3 emotional disturbance

con·flict′ed ***adj.*** emotionally disturbed

conflict of interest a conflict between one's obligation to the public and one's self interest, as in the case of a public officeholder

con·flu·ence (kän′flo͞o əns) ***n.*** ‖ < L *com-*, together + *fluere*, to flow ‖ 1 a flowing together, esp. of streams 2 the place of this 3 a crowd —**con′flu·ent *adj.***

con·form (kən fôrm′) ***vt.*** ‖ < L *com-*, together + *formare*, to form ‖ 1 to make similar 2 to bring into agreement —***vi.*** 1 to be or become similar 2 to be in agreement 3 to act in accordance with rules, customs, etc. —**con·form′ism′ *n.*** —**con·form′ist *n.***

con·for·ma·tion (kän′fôr mā′shən) ***n.*** 1 a symmetrical arrangement of the parts of a thing 2 the shape or outline, as of an animal

con·form·i·ty (kən fôrm′ə tē) ***n.*, *pl.* -ties** 1 agreement; correspondence; similarity 2 conventional behavior

con·found (kən found′; *for 2* kän′-) ***vt.*** ‖ < L *com-*, together + *fundere*, pour ‖ 1 to confuse or bewilder 2 to damn: a mild oath —**con·found′ed *adj.***

con·fra·ter·ni·ty (kän′frə tur′nə tē) ***n.*, *pl.* -ties** ‖ see CON- & FRATERNAL ‖ 1 brotherhood 2 a religious society, usually of laymen

con·frere (kän′frer′) ***n.*** ‖ OFr ‖ a colleague or associate

con·front (kən frunt′) ***vt.*** ‖ < L *com-*, together + *frons*, forehead ‖ 1 to face, esp. boldly or defiantly 2 to bring face to face (*with*) —**con·fron·ta·tion** (kän′frən tā′shən) ***n.*** —**con′fron·ta′tion·al *adj.***

Con·fu·cius (kən fyo͞o′shəs) *c.* 551-*c.* 479 B.C.; Chin. philosopher & teacher —**Con·fu′cian** (-shən) ***adj.*, *n.***

con·fuse (kən fyo͞oz′) ***vt.* -fused′, -fus′ing** ‖ see CONFOUND ‖ 1 to mix up; put into disorder 2 to bewilder or embarrass 3 to mistake the identity of —**con·fus′ed·ly *adv.***

con·fu′sion (-fyo͞o′zhən) ***n.*** a confusing or being confused; specif., disorder, bewilderment, etc.

con·fute (kən fyo͞ot′) ***vt.* -fut′ed, -fut′ing** ‖ L *confutare* ‖ to prove to be in error or false —**con·fu·ta·tion** (kän′fyo͞o tā′shən) ***n.***

Cong. 1 Congregational 2 Congress

con·geal (kən jēl′) ***vt.*, *vi.*** ‖ < L *com-*, together + *gelare*, freeze ‖ 1 to freeze 2 to thicken; coagulate; jell —**con·geal′ment *n.***

con·ge·nial (kən jēn′yəl) ***adj.*** ‖ see CON- & GENIAL ‖ 1 kindred; compatible 2 likeminded; friendly 3 suited to one's needs; agreeable —**con·ge′ni·al′i·ty** (-jē′nē al′ə tē) ***n.*** —**con·ge′nial·ly *adv.***

con·gen·i·tal (kən jen′ə təl) ***adj.*** ‖ < L *congenitus*, born with ‖ existing as such at birth —**con·gen′i·tal·ly *adv.***

con·ger (eel) (käŋ′gər) ‖ < Gr *gongros* ‖ a large, edible saltwater eel

con·ge·ries (kän′jə rēz′) ***n.*, *pl.* -ries′** ‖ L: see fol. ‖ a heap or pile of things

con·gest (kən jest′) ***vt.*** ‖ < L *com-*, together + *gerere*, carry ‖ 1 to cause too much blood, mucus, etc. to accumulate in (a part of the body) 2 to fill to excess; overcrowd —**con·ges′tion *n.*** —**con·ges′tive *adj.***

con·glom·er·ate (kən gläm′ər āt′; *for adj. & n.*, -ər it) ***vt.*, *vi.* -at′ed, -at′ing** ‖ < L *com-*, together + *glomus*, ball ‖ to form into a rounded mass —***adj.*** 1 formed into a rounded mass 2 formed of substances collected into a single mass, esp. of rock fragments or pebbles cemented together by clay, silica, etc. —***n.*** 1 a conglomerate mass 2 a large corporation formed by merging many diverse companies 3 a conglomerate rock —**con·glom′er·a′tion *n.***

Con·go (käŋ′gō) 1 river in central Africa, flowing into the Atlantic 2 *old name of* ZAIRE 3 country in central Africa, west of Zaire: 132,046 sq. mi.; pop. 1,853,000 —**Con·go·lese** (käŋ′gə lēz′) ***adj.*, *n.***

con·grat·u·late (kən grach′ə lāt′) ***vt.* -lat′ed, -lat′ing** ‖ < L *com-*, together + *gratulari*, wish joy ‖ to express to (another) one's pleasure at that person's good fortune, etc.; felicitate [*congratulate* the winner] —**con·grat′u·la·to′ry** (-lə tôr′ē) ***adj.***

con·grat′u·la′tion *n.* 1 a congratulating 2 [*pl.*] expressions of pleasure over another's good fortune, etc.

con·gre·gate (käŋ′grə gāt′) ***vt.*, *vi.* -gat′ed, -gat′ing** ‖ < L *com-*, together + *grex*, a flock ‖ to gather into a crowd; assemble

con′gre·ga′tion *n.* 1 a gathering; assemblage 2 an assembly of people for religious worship

con′gre·ga′tion·al *adj.* 1 of or like a congregation 2 [C-] of a Protestant denomination in which each member church is self-governing

con·gress (käŋ′grəs) ***n.*** ‖ < L *com-*, together + *gradi*, to walk ‖ 1 an association or society 2 an assembly or conference 3 a legislature, esp. of a republic 4 [C-] the legislature of the U.S.; the Senate and the House of Representatives —**con·gres·sion·al** (kən gresh'ə nəl) ***adj.*** —**con·gres'sion·al·ly** ***adv.***

con'gress·man (-mən) ***n.***, *pl.* **-men** a member of Congress, esp. of the House of Representatives Also **con'gress·per'son**

con·gru·ent (käŋ'groo ənt) ***adj.*** ‖< L *congruere,* agree‖ corresponding; harmonious —**con'gru·ence *n.***

con·gru·ous (käŋ'groo əs) ***adj.*** 1 congruent 2 fitting; suitable; appropriate —**con·gru·i·ty** (kän groo'ə tē, kən-), *pl.* **-ties, *n.*** —**con'·gru·ous·ly *adv.***

con·i·cal (kän'i kəl) ***adj.*** 1 of a cone 2 resembling or shaped like a cone Also **con'ic** —**con'i·cal·ly *adv.***

con·i·fer (kän'ə fər, kō'nə-) ***n.*** ‖L < *conus,* cone + *ferre,* to bear‖ any of a class of cone-bearing trees and shrubs, mostly evergreens —**co·nif·er·ous** (kō nif'ər əs, kə-) ***adj.***

conj. 1 conjugation 2 conjunction

con·jec·ture (kən jek'chər) ***n.*** ‖< L *com-,* together + *jacere,* to throw‖ 1 an inferring, theorizing, or predicting from incomplete evidence; guesswork 2 a guess —***vt., vi.*** **-tured, -tur·ing** to guess —**con·jec'tur·al *adj.***

con·join (kən join') ***vt., vi.*** ‖< L *com-,* together + *jungere,* join‖ to join together; unite —**con·joint' *adj.***

con·ju·gal (kän'jə gəl) ***adj.*** ‖< L *conjunx,* spouse‖ of marriage or the relation between husband and wife

con·ju·gate (kän'jə gət; *also, and for v. always,* -gāt') ***adj.*** ‖< L *com-,* together + *jugare,* join‖ joined together, esp. in a pair —***vt.*** **-gat'ed, -gat'ing** 1 [Archaic] to join together 2 *Gram.* to give in order the inflectional forms of (a verb) —**con'ju·ga'tion *n.***

con·junc·tion (kən juŋk'shən) ***n.*** ‖see CONJOIN‖ 1 a joining together; union; combination 2 coincidence 3 a word used to connect words, phrases, or clauses (Ex.: *and, but, if,* etc.) —**con·junc'tive *adj.***

con·junc·ti·va (kän'jəŋk tī'və) ***n.***, *pl.* **-vas** or **-vae** (-vē) ‖see CONJOIN‖ the mucous membrane covering the inner eyelid and the front of the eyeball

con·junc·ti·vi·tis (kən juŋk'tə vīt'is) ***n.*** inflammation of the conjunctiva

con·junc·ture (kən juŋk'chər) ***n.*** ‖see CONJOIN‖ a combination of events creating a crisis

con·jure (kun'jər, kän'-; *for vt.* kən joor') ***vi.*** **-jured, -jur·ing** ‖< L *com-,* together + *jurare,* swear‖ 1 to summon a demon or spirit by magic 2 to practice magic —***vt.*** to entreat solemnly —**conjure up** to cause to appear as by magic —**con'ju·ra'tion *n.*** —**con'jur·er** or **con'ju·ror *n.***

conk (kôŋk) ***n., vt.*** ‖< CONCH‖ [Slang] hit on the head —**conk out** [Slang] 1 to fail suddenly, as a motor 2 to fall asleep from fatigue

con man [Slang] a confidence man; swindler

con·nect (kə nekt') ***vt.*** ‖< L *com-,* together + *nectere,* fasten‖ 1 to join (two things together, or one thing *with* or *to* another) 2 to show or think of as related —***vi.*** to join —**con·nec'tor** or **con·nect'er *n.***

Con·nect·i·cut (kə net'ə kət) New England State of the U.S.: 5,009 sq. mi.; pop. 3,108,000; cap. Hartford: abbrev. **Conn.**

con·nec·tion (kə nek'shən) ***n.*** 1 a connecting or being connected 2 a thing that connects 3 a relationship; association 4 *a)* a relative, as by marriage *b)* an influential associate, etc.: *usually used in pl.* 5 a transferring from one bus, plane, etc. to another

con·nec·tive (kə nekt'iv) ***adj.*** connecting —***n.*** that which connects, esp. a connecting word, as a conjunction

connective tissue body tissue, as cartilage, serving to connect and support other tissues

conniption (fit) (kə nip'shən) ‖pseudo-L‖ [Colloq.] a fit of anger, hysteria, etc.; tantrum Also **con·nip'tions *n.pl.***

con·nive (kə nīv') ***vi.*** **-nived', -niv'ing** ‖< L *conivere,* to wink, connive‖ 1 to pretend not to look (*at* crime, etc.), thus giving tacit consent 2 to cooperate secretly (*with* someone), esp. in wrongdoing; scheme —**con·niv'ance *n.*** —**con·niv'er *n.***

con·nois·seur (kän'ə sur') ***n.*** ‖< Fr < L *cognoscere,* know‖ one who has expert knowledge and keen discrimination, esp. in the fine arts

con·note (kə nōt') ***vt.*** **-not'ed, -not'ing** ‖< L *com-,* together + *notare,* to mark‖ to suggest or convey (associations, etc.) in addition to the explicit, or denoted, meaning —**con·no·ta·tion** (kän'ə tā'shən) ***n.*** —**con'·no·ta'tive** or **con'no·ta'tion·al *adj.***

con·nu·bi·al (kə noo'bē əl) ***adj.*** ‖< L *com-,* together + *nubere,* marry‖ of marriage; conjugal

con·quer (käŋ'kər) ***vt.*** ‖< L *com-,* intens. + *quaerere,* seek‖ 1 to get control of as by winning a war 2 to overcome; defeat —**con'quer·or *n.***

con·quest (käŋ'kwest', kän'-) ***n.*** 1 a conquering 2 something conquered 3 a winning of someone's affection

con·quis·ta·dor (kän kwis'tə dôr', -kēs'-) ***n.***, *pl.* **con·quis'ta·dors'** (-dôrz') or **con·quis'·ta·do'res'** (-dôr'ēz', -dôr'ās') ‖Sp, conqueror‖ any of the 16th-c. Spanish conquerors of Mexico, Peru, etc.

con·san·guin·e·ous (kän'saŋ gwin'ē əs) ***adj.*** ‖see CON- & SANGUINE‖ having the same ancestor —**con'san·guin'i·ty *n.***

con·science (kän'shəns) ***n.*** ‖< L *com-,* with + *scire,* know‖ a sense of right and wrong, with an urge to do right —**con'science·less *adj.***

con·sci·en·tious (kän'shē en'shəs) ***adj.*** ‖see prec. & -OUS‖ 1 governed by one's conscience; scrupulous 2 painstaking —**con'·sci·en'tious·ly *adv.*** —**con'sci·en'tious·ness *n.***

conscientious objector one who for reasons of conscience refuses to take part in warfare

con·scious (kän'shəs) ***adj.*** ‖< L: see CONSCIENCE‖ 1 having an awareness (*of* or *that*) 2 able to feel and think; awake 3 aware of oneself as a thinking being 4 intentional [*conscious* humor] —**con'·scious·ly *adv.***

con'scious·ness *n.* 1 the state of being conscious; awareness 2 the totality of one's thoughts and feelings

con·script (kən skript′; *for adj. & n.* kän′ skript′) ***vt.*** ⟦< L *com-*, with + *scribere*, write⟧ to enroll for compulsory service in the armed forces; draft —***n.*** a draftee —**con·scrip′tion *n.***

con·se·crate (kän′si krāt′) ***vt.*** **-crat′ed, -crat′ing** ⟦< L *com-*, together + *sacrare*, make holy⟧ to set apart as holy; devote to sacred or serious use —**con′se·cra′tion *n.***

con·sec·u·tive (kən sek′yōō tiv) ***adj.*** ⟦see CONSEQUENCE⟧ following in order, without interruption; successive —**con·sec′u·tive·ly *adv.***

con·sen·sus (kən sen′səs) ***n.*** ⟦see fol.⟧ **1** an opinion held by all or most **2** general agreement, esp. in opinion

con·sent (kən sent′) ***vi.*** ⟦< L *com-*, with + *sentire*, feel⟧ to agree, permit, or assent —***n.*** **1** permission; approval **2** agreement /by common *consent*/

con·se·quence (kän′si kwens′) ***n.*** ⟦< L *com-*, with + *sequi*, follow⟧ **1** a result; effect **2** importance —**take the consequences** to accept the results of one's actions

con′se·quent′ (-kwent′, -kwənt) ***adj.*** following as a result; resulting —**con′se·quent′ly *adv.***

con′se·quen′tial (-kwen′shəl) ***adj.*** **1** consequent **2** important

con·ser·va·tion (kän′sər vā′shən) ***n.*** **1** a conserving **2** the official care or management of natural resources —**con′ser·va′tion·ist *n.***

con·ser·va·tive (kən sur′və tiv) ***adj.*** **1** tending to conserve **2** tending to preserve established institutions, etc.; opposed to change **3** moderate; cautious —***n.*** a conservative person —**con·serv′a·tism′ *n.*** —**con·serv′a·tive·ly *adv.***

con·serv·a·to·ry (kən sur′və tôr′ē) ***n.***, *pl.* **-ries 1** a greenhouse **2** a music school

con·serve (kən surv′; *for n., usually* kän′ surv′) ***vt.*** **-served′, -serv′ing** ⟦< L *com-*, with + *servare*, keep⟧ to keep from being damaged, lost, or wasted; save —***n.*** [*often pl.*] a jam made of two or more fruits

con·sid·er (kən sid′ər) ***vt.*** ⟦< L *considerare*, observe⟧ **1** to think about in order to understand or decide **2** to keep in mind **3** to be thoughtful of (others) **4** to regard as

con·sid′er·a·ble *adj.* **1** worth considering; important **2** much or large —**con·sid′er·a·bly *adv.***

con·sid′er·ate (-it) ***adj.*** having regard for others and their feelings —**con·sid′er·ate·ly *adv.***

con·sid′er·a′tion (-ər ā′shən) ***n.*** **1** the act of considering; deliberation **2** thoughtful regard for others **3** something considered in making a decision **4** a recompense; fee **5** something given, as to make a binding contract —**take into consideration** to keep in mind —**under consideration** being thought over

con·sid′ered (-ərd) ***adj.*** arrived at after careful thought

con·sid′er·ing *prep.* in view of; taking into account

con·sign (kən sīn′) ***vt.*** ⟦< L *consignare*, to seal⟧ **1** to hand over; deliver **2** to entrust **3** to assign to an inferior place **4** to send (goods)

con·sign′ment (-mənt) ***n.*** **1** a consigning or being consigned **2** a shipment of goods sent to a dealer for sale —**on consignment** with payment due after sale of the consignment

con·sist (kən sist′) ***vi.*** ⟦< L *com-*, together + *sistere*, stand⟧ **1** to be formed or composed (*of*) **2** to be contained or inherent (*in*)

con·sis′ten·cy (-sis′tən sē) ***n.***, *pl.* **-cies 1** firmness or thickness, as of a liquid **2** agreement; harmony **3** conformity with previous practice

con·sis′tent *adj.* **1** in agreement or harmony; compatible **2** holding to the same principles or practice —**con·sis′tent·ly *adv.***

con·sis·to·ry (kən sis′tə rē) ***n.***, *pl.* **-ries** ⟦see CONSIST⟧ **1** a church council or court, as the papal senate **2** a session of such a body

con·so·la·tion (kän′sə lā′shən) ***n.*** **1** comfort; solace **2** one that consoles

con·sole[1] (kən sōl′) ***vt.*** **-soled′, -sol′ing** ⟦< L *com-*, with + *solari*, to comfort⟧ to make feel less sad or disappointed; comfort —**con·sol′ing·ly *adv.***

con·sole[2] (kän′sōl′) ***n.*** ⟦Fr⟧ **1** the desklike frame containing the keys, stops, etc. of an organ **2** a radio, television, or phonograph cabinet designed to stand on the floor **3** a control panel for operating aircraft, computers, electronic systems, etc. **4** a raised portion between automobile bucket seats

con·sol·i·date (kən säl′ə dāt′) ***vt., vi.*** **-dat′ed, -dat′ing** ⟦< L *com-*, together + *solidus*, solid⟧ **1** to combine into one; unite **2** to make or become strong or stable —**con·sol′i·da′tion *n.*** —**con·sol′i·da′tor *n.***

con·som·mé (kän′sə mā′) ***n.*** ⟦Fr⟧ a clear, strained meat soup

con·so·nance (kän′sə nəns) ***n.*** ⟦< L *com-*, with + *sonus*, sound⟧ harmony, esp. of musical sounds

con′so·nant (-nənt) ***adj.*** in harmony or accord —***n.*** **1** a speech sound made by obstructing the air stream **2** a letter representing such a sound, as *p, t, l, f*, etc.

con·sort (kän′sôrt′; *for v.* kən sôrt′) ***n.*** ⟦< L *com-*, with + *sors*, a share⟧ a wife or husband, esp. of a reigning king or queen —***vt., vi.*** to associate

con·sor·ti·um (kən sôrt′ē əm, -sôr′shē əm) ***n.***, *pl.* **-ti·a** (-ə) ⟦see prec.⟧ an international alliance, as of business firms or banks

con·spec·tus (kən spek′təs) ***n.*** ⟦L: see fol.⟧ **1** a general view **2** a summary; digest

con·spic·u·ous (kən spik′yōō əs) ***adj.*** ⟦< L *com-*, intens. + *specere*, see⟧ **1** easy to see **2** outstanding; striking —**con·spic′u·ous·ly *adv.***

con·spir·a·cy (kən spir′ə sē) ***n.***, *pl.* **-cies 1** a conspiring **2** an unlawful plot **3** a conspiring group

con·spire (kən spīr′) ***vi.*** **-spired′, -spir′ing** ⟦< L *com-*, together + *spirare*, breathe⟧ **1** to plan together secretly, esp. to commit a crime **2** to work together toward a single end —**con·spir′a·tor** (-spir′ət ər) ***n.*** —**con·spir′a·to′ri·al** (-spir′ə tôr′ē əl) ***adj.***

con·sta·ble (kän′stə bəl) ***n.*** ⟦< LL *comes stabuli*, lit., count of the stable⟧ **1** a peace officer in a small town **2** [Chiefly Brit.] a police officer

con·stab·u·lar·y (kən stab′yoo ler′ē) ***n.**, pl.* **-ies** **1** constables, collectively **2** a militarized police force

con·stant (kän′stənt) ***adj.*** ‖< L *com-*, together + *stare*, to stand‖ **1** not changing; faithful, regular, etc. **2** continual; persistent —***n.*** anything that does not change or vary —**con′stan·cy** ***n.*** —**con′stant·ly** ***adv.***

Con·stan·tine I (kän′stən tēn′, -tīn′) *c.* A.D. 280-337; first Christian emperor of Rome (306-337)

Con·stan·ti·no·ple (kän′stan tə nō′p'l) *old name* (A.D. 330-1930) *of* ISTANBUL

con·stel·la·tion (kän′stə lā′shən) ***n.*** ‖< L *com-*, with + *stella*, star‖ a group of stars thought to resemble some object, animal, etc. in outline

con·ster·na·tion (kän′stər nā′shən) ***n.*** ‖< L *consternare*, terrify‖ great fear or shock

con·sti·pate (kän′stə pāt′) ***vt.*** **-pat′ed, -pat′·ing** ‖< L *com-*, together + *stipare*, cram‖ to cause constipation in

con′sti·pa′tion (-pā′shən) ***n.*** infrequent and difficult movement of the bowels

con·stit·u·en·cy (kən stich′oo ən sē) ***n.**, pl.* **-cies** the voters in a district

con·stit′u·ent (-ənt) ***adj.*** ‖see fol.‖ **1** necessary to the whole; component /a *constituent* part/ **2** that elects **3** authorized to make or revise a constitution —***n.*** **1** a voter in a district **2** a component

con·sti·tute (kän′stə toot′) ***vt.*** **-tut′ed, -tut′·ing** ‖< L *com-*, together + *statuere*, to set‖ **1** to establish (a law, government, etc.) **2** to set up (an assembly, etc.) in a legal form **3** to appoint **4** to form; compose —**con′sti·tu′tive** ***adj.***

con′sti·tu′tion (-too′shən) ***n.*** **1** a constituting **2** structure; organization **3** *a)* the system of basic laws and principles of a government, society, etc. *b)* a document stating these *c)* [C-] such a document of the U.S.

con′sti·tu′tion·al ***adj.*** **1** of or in one's constitution or structure; basic **2** of or in accordance with the constitution of a government, society, etc. —***n.*** a walk taken for one's health —**con′sti·tu′tion·al′i·ty** (-shə nal′ə tē) ***n.*** —**con′sti·tu′tion·al·ly** ***adv.***

con·strain (kən strān′) ***vt.*** ‖< L *com-*, together + *stringere*, draw tight‖ **1** to confine **2** to restrain **3** to compel

con·straint′ ***n.*** **1** confinement or restriction **2** force; compulsion **3** forced, unnatural manner

con·strict (kən strikt′) ***vt.*** ‖see CONSTRAIN‖ to make smaller or narrower by squeezing, etc. —**con·stric′tion** ***n.***

con·stric′tor (-strik′tər) ***n.*** a snake that kills its prey by squeezing

con·struct (kən strukt′) ***vt.*** ‖< L *com-*, together + *struere*, pile up‖ to build, devise, etc. —**con·struc′tor** ***n.***

con·struc′tion (-struk′shən) ***n.*** **1** a constructing or manner of being constructed **2** a structure **3** an interpretation, as of a statement **4** the arrangement of words in a sentence

con·struc′tion·ist ***n.*** a person who interprets a law, document, etc. in a specified way

con·struc′tive ***adj.*** helping to construct; leading to improvement

con·strue (kən stroo′) ***vt.**, **vi.*** **-strued′, -stru′ing** ‖see CONSTRUCT‖ **1** to analyze the construction of (a sentence) **2** to translate **3** to explain; interpret

con·sul (kän′səl) ***n.*** ‖< L *consulere*, to deliberate‖ **1** a chief magistrate of ancient Rome **2** a government official appointed to live in a foreign city and look after his or her country's citizens and business there —**con′·sul·ar** (-ər) ***adj.***

con′sul·ate (-it) ***n.*** **1** the position, powers, etc. of a consul **2** the office or residence of a consul

con·sult (kən sult′) ***vi.*** ‖< L *consulere*, consider‖ to talk things over; confer —***vt.*** **1** to seek advice or information from **2** to consider —**con·sul·ta·tion** (kän′səl tā′shən) ***n.***

con·sult′ant ***n.*** **1** a person who consults another **2** an expert who gives professional or technical advice

con·sume′ (-soom′) ***vt.*** **-sumed′, -sum′ing** ‖< L *com-*, together + *sumere*, to take‖ **1** to destroy, as by fire **2** to use up or waste (time, money, etc.) **3** to eat or drink up; devour

con·sum′er ***n.*** one that consumes; specif., one who buys goods or services for personal needs only rather than to produce other goods

con·sum′er·ism′ ***n.*** a movement for protecting the consumer against defective products, misleading business practices, etc.

con·sum·mate (kən sum′it, kän′sə mit; *for v.* kän′sə māt′) ***adj.*** ‖< L *com-*, together + *summa*, a sum‖ perfect; supreme —***vt.*** **-mat′ed, -mat′ing** **1** to complete **2** to complete (a marriage) by sexual intercourse —**con·sum′mate·ly** ***adv.*** —**con·sum·ma·tion** (kän′sə mā′shən) ***n.***

con·sump·tion (kən sump′shən) ***n.*** **1** a consuming or being consumed **2** the using up of goods or services **3** the amount consumed **4** a wasting disease; esp., tuberculosis of the lungs

cont. or **contd.** continued

con·tact (kän′takt′) ***n.*** ‖< L *com-*, together + *tangere*, to touch‖ **1** a touching or meeting **2** the state of being in association (*with*) **3** a connection —***vt.*** **1** to come into contact with **2** to get in touch with —***vi.*** to come into contact

contact flying piloting an airplane by observing objects on the ground

contact lens a tiny, thin correctional lens worn directly over the cornea of the eye

con·ta·gion (kən tā′jən) ***n.*** ‖see CONTACT‖ **1** the spreading of disease by contact **2** a contagious disease **3** the spreading of an emotion, idea, etc.

con·ta′gious (-jəs) ***adj.*** **1** spread by contact: said of diseases **2** carrying the causative agent of a contagious disease **3** spreading from person to person —**con·ta′gious·ness** ***n.***

con·tain (kən tān′) ***vt.*** ‖< L *com-*, together + *tenere*, to hold‖ **1** to have in it; hold **2** to have the capacity for holding **3** to hold back or restrain within fixed limits —**con·tain′ment** ***n.***

con·tain′er ***n.*** a thing for containing something; box, can, etc.

con·tain′er·ize′ *vt.* **-ized′, -iz′ing** to pack (cargo) into huge, standardized containers for shipment

con·tam·i·nant (kən tam′ə nənt) *n.* a contaminating substance

con·tam′i·nate′ (-nāt′) *vt.* **-nat′ed, -nat′ing** ‖ < L *com-*, together + *tangere*, to touch ‖ to make impure, corrupt, etc. by contact; pollute; taint —**con·tam′i·na′tion** *n.*

con·temn (kən tem′) *vt.* ‖ < L *com-*, intens. + *temnere*, to scorn ‖ to treat with contempt; scorn

con·tem·plate (kän′təm plāt′) *vt.* **-plat′ed, -plat′ing** ‖ < L *contemplari*, observe ‖ **1** to look at or think about intently **2** to expect or intend —*vi.* to muse —**con′tem·pla′tion** *n.* —**con·tem·pla·tive** (kən tem′plə tiv′, kän′təm plāt′iv) *adj.*

con·tem·po·ra·ne·ous (kən tem′pə rā′nē əs) *adj.* ‖ see fol. ‖ happening in the same period —**con·tem′po·ra·ne′i·ty** (-pə rə nē′ə tē; -nā′) *n.* —**con·tem′po·ra′ne·ous·ly** *adv.*

con·tem′po·rar′y (-rer′ē) *adj.* ‖ < L *com-*, with + *tempus*, time ‖ **1** living or happening in the same period **2** of about the same age **3** modern —*n., pl.* **-ies** one living in the same period as another or others

con·tempt (kən tempt′) *n.* ‖ see CONTEMN ‖ **1** the feeling one has toward somebody or something one considers low, worthless, etc. **2** the condition of being despised **3** a showing disrespect for the dignity of a court (or legislature)

con·tempt′i·ble *adj.* deserving of contempt or scorn; despicable —**con·tempt′i·bly** *adv.*

con·temp·tu·ous (kən temp′cho͞o əs) *adj.* full of contempt; scornful —**con·temp′tu·ous·ly** *adv.* —**con·temp′tu·ous·ness** *n.*

con·tend (kən tend′) *vi.* ‖ < L *com-*, together + *tendere*, to stretch ‖ **1** to fight or argue **2** to compete —*vt.* to assert —**con·tend′er** *n.*

con·tent[1] (kən tent′) *adj.* ‖ see CONTAIN ‖ happy with one's lot; satisfied —*vt.* to satisfy —*n.* contentment

con·tent[2] (kän′tent′) *n.* ‖ see CONTAIN ‖ **1** [*usually pl.*] *a)* what is in a container *b)* what is dealt with in a book, speech, etc. **2** substance or meaning **3** amount contained

con·tent′ed *adj.* satisfied —**con·tent′ed·ly** *adv.* —**con·tent′ed·ness** *n.*

con·ten·tion (kən ten′shən) *n.* ‖ see CONTEND ‖ **1** strife, dispute, etc. **2** a point argued for —**con·ten′tious** *adj.* —**con·ten′tious·ly** *adv.* —**con·ten′tious·ness** *n.*

con·tent′ment *n.* the state or fact of being contented

con·ter·mi·nous (kən tʉrm′ə nəs) *adj.* ‖ < L *com-*, together + *terminus*, an end ‖ **1** having a common boundary **2** contained within the same boundaries —**con·ter′mi·nous·ly** *adv.*

con·test (kən test′; *for n.* kän′test′) *vt.* ‖ < L *com-*, together + *testis*, a witness ‖ **1** to dispute (a point, etc.) **2** to fight for (a position, etc.) —*vi.* to struggle (*with* or *against*) —*n.* **1** a fight; struggle **2** a competitive game, race, etc. —**con·test′a·ble** *adj.*

con·test′ant *n.* ‖ Fr ‖ a competitor in a game, etc.

con·text (kän′tekst′) *n.* ‖ < L *com-*, together + *texere*, to weave ‖ the parts just before and after a passage, that determine its meaning —**con·tex·tu·al** (kən teks′cho͞o əl) *adj.*

con·tig·u·ous (kən tig′yo͞o əs) *adj.* ‖ see CONTACT ‖ **1** in contact; touching **2** near or next —**con·ti·gu·i·ty** (kän′tə gyo͞o′ə tē) *n.*

con·ti·nence (kän′tə nəns) *n.* ‖ see CONTAIN ‖ **1** self-restraint **2** self restraint in sexual activity, esp. total abstinence

con′ti·nent (-nənt) *adj.* ‖ see CONTAIN ‖ characterized by self restraint, esp. in sexual activity —*n.* any of the main large land areas of the earth

con′ti·nen′tal (-nent′'l) *adj.* **1** of a continent **2** [*sometimes* **C-**] European **3** [**C-**] of the American colonies at the time of the American Revolution

continental drift the theory that continents slowly shift position

continental shelf submerged land sloping out gradually from the edge of a continent

con·tin·gen·cy (kən tin′jən sē) *n., pl.* **-cies** **1** dependence on chance **2** a possible or chance event

con·tin′gent *adj.* ‖ see CONTACT ‖ **1** possible **2** accidental **3** dependent (*on* or *upon* an uncertainty) —*n.* **1** a chance happening **2** a quota, as of troops **3** a part of a larger group

con·tin·u·al (kən tin′yo͞o əl) *adj.* **1** repeated often **2** continuous —**con·tin′u·al·ly** *adv.*

con·tin′u·ance *n.* **1** a continuing **2** duration **3** *Law* postponement or adjournment

con·tin′u·a′tion (-ā′shən) *n.* **1** a continuing **2** a beginning again; resumption **3** a part added; sequel

con·tin·ue (kən tin′yo͞o) *vi.* **-ued, -u·ing** ‖ < L *continuare*, join ‖ **1** to last; endure **2** to go on in a specified action or condition **3** to extend **4** to stay **5** to go on again after an interruption —*vt.* **1** to go on with **2** to extend **3** to cause to remain, as in office **4** *Law* to postpone

con·ti·nu·i·ty (kän′tə no͞o′ə tē, -nyo͞o′-) *n., pl.* **-ties** ‖ OFr < L *continuitas* ‖ **1** a continuous state or quality **2** an unbroken, coherent whole **3** the script for a film, radio or TV program, etc.

con·tin·u·ous (kən tin′yo͞o əs) *adj.* going on without interruption; unbroken —**con·tin′u·ous·ly** *adv.*

con·tin′u·um (-yo͞o əm) *n., pl.* **-u·a** (-yo͞o ə) or **-u·ums** ‖ L ‖ a continuous whole, quantity, or series

con·tort (kən tôrt′) *vt., vi.* ‖ < L *com-*, together + *torquere*, to twist ‖ to twist or wrench out of shape; distort —**con·tor′tion** *n.*

con·tor′tion·ist *n.* one who can contort his or her body into unnatural positions

con·tour (kän′to͝or′) *n.* ‖ Fr < L *com-*, intens. + *tornare*, to turn ‖ the outline of a figure, land, etc. —*vt.* to shape to the contour of something —*adj.* conforming to the shape or contour of something

con·tra (kän′trə, kōn′-) *n.* ‖ AmSp ‖ any member of those groups seeking to overthrow the Nicaraguan government established in 1979

contra- ‖< L *contra*‖ *prefix* against, opposite, opposed to

con·tra·band (kän′trə band′) ***n.*** ‖< Sp < It‖ smuggled goods —***adj.*** illegal to import or export

con·tra·cep·tion (kän′trə sep′shən) ***n.*** ‖CONTRA- + (CON)CEPTION‖ prevention of the fertilization of an ovum —**con′tra·cep′tive** ***adj., n.***

con·tract (kän′trakt′ *for n. & usually for vt. 1 & vi. 1*; kən trakt′ *for v. generally*) ***n.*** ‖< L *com-*, together + *trahere*, draw‖ an agreement between two or more people, esp. a written one enforceable by law —***vt.*** **1** to undertake by contract **2** to get or incur (a disease, debt, etc.) **3** to reduce in size; shrink —***vi.*** **1** to make a contract **2** to become smaller

con·trac·tile (kən trak′til) ***adj.*** having the power of contracting

con·trac·tion (kən trak′shən) ***n.*** **1** a contracting or being contracted **2** the shortening of a muscle of the uterus during labor **3** the shortened form of a word or phrase (Ex.: *aren't* for *are not*)

con·trac·tor (kän′trak′tər) ***n.*** a builder, etc. who contracts to supply materials or do work

con·trac·tu·al (kən trak′cho͞o əl) ***adj.*** of, or having the nature of, a contract —**con·trac′tu·al·ly** ***adv.***

con·tra·dict (kän′trə dikt′) ***vt.*** ‖< L *contra-*, against + *dicere*, speak‖ **1** to assert the opposite of **2** to deny the statement of (a person) **3** to be contrary to —**con′tra·dic′tion** ***n.*** —**con′tra·dic′to·ry** ***adj.***

con′tra·dis·tinc′tion (-dis tiŋk′shən) ***n.*** distinction by contrast

con·trail (kän′trāl′) ***n.*** ‖CON(DENSATION) + TRAIL‖ a white trail of water vapor in an airplane's wake

con·tra·in·di·cate (kän′trə in′di kāt′) ***vt.*** **-cat′ed, -cat′ing** to make (as an indicated medical treatment) inadvisable

con·tral·to (kən tral′tō) ***n.***, *pl.* **-tos** ‖It: see CONTRA- & ALTO‖ **1** the range of the lowest female voice **2** a voice or singer with this range

con·trap·tion (kən trap′shən) ***n.*** ‖< ?‖ a contrivance or gadget

con·tra·pun·tal (kän′trə punt′'l) ***adj.*** ‖< It *contrappunto*, counterpoint‖ of or characterized by counterpoint

con·trar·i·wise (kän′trer′ē wīz′) ***adv.*** **1** on the contrary **2** in the opposite way, order, etc.

con·trar·y (kän′trer′ē; *for adj. 4, often* kən trer′ē) ***adj.*** ‖< L *contra*, against‖ **1** opposed **2** opposite in nature, order, etc.; altogether different **3** unfavorable **4** always resisting; perverse —***n.***, *pl.* **-ies** the opposite —**on the contrary** as opposed to what has been said —**to the contrary** to the opposite effect —**con′tra·ri′e·ty** (-trə rī′ə tē) ***n.*** —**con′trar′i·ly** ***adv.*** —**con′trar′i·ness** ***n.***

con·trast (kən trast′; *for n.* kän′trast′) ***vt.*** ‖< L *contra*, against + *stare*, to stand‖ to compare so as to point out the differences —***vi.*** to show differences when compared —***n.*** **1** a contrasting or being contrasted **2** a striking difference between things being compared **3** a person or thing showing differences when compared with another —**con·trast′a·ble** ***adj.***

con·tra·vene (kän′trə vēn′) ***vt.*** **-vened′, -ven′ing** ‖< L *contra*, against + *venire*, come‖ **1** to go against; violate **2** to contradict

con·tre·temps (kän′trə tän′) ***n.***, *pl.* **-temps′** (-tän′) ‖Fr‖ a confusing, embarrassing, or awkward occurrence

con·trib·ute (kən trib′yo͞ot) ***vt., vi.*** **-ut·ed, -ut·ing** ‖< L: see CON- & TRIBUTE‖ **1** to give jointly with others **2** to write (an article, etc.) as for a magazine **3** to furnish (ideas, etc.) —**contribute to** to share in bringing about —**con·trib′u·tor** ***n.*** —**con·trib′u·to′ry** ***adj.***

con·tri·bu·tion (kän′trə byo͞o′shən) ***n.*** **1** a contributing **2** something contributed, as money

con·trite (kən trīt′) ***adj.*** ‖< L *com-*, together + *terere*, to rub‖ deeply sorry for having done wrong; repentant —**con·trite′ly** ***adv.*** —**con·trite′ness** ***n.*** —**con·tri′tion** (-trish′ən) ***n.***

con·triv·ance (kən trī′vəns) ***n.*** **1** the act, way, or power of contriving **2** something contrived; device, etc.

con·trive (kən trīv′) ***vt.*** **-trived′, -triv′ing** ‖ult. < VL *contropare*, compare‖ **1** to think up; devise **2** to make inventively **3** to bring about; manage —**con·triv′er** ***n.***

con·trol (kən trōl′) ***vt.*** **-trolled′, -trol′ling** ‖< ML *contrarotulus*, a register‖ **1** to regulate or direct **2** to verify (an experiment) by comparison **3** to exercise authority over; direct **4** to restrain ***n.*** **1** power to direct or regulate **2** a means of controlling; check **3** an apparatus to regulate a mechanism: *usually used in pl.* —**con·trol′la·ble** ***adj.***

controlled substance a drug whose sale is regulated by law

con·trol′ler ***n.*** **1** the person in charge of finances, as in a business **2** a person or device that controls

con·tro·ver·sial (kän′trə vʉr′shəl) ***adj.*** subject to controversy; debatable

con′tro·ver′sy (-sē) ***n.***, *pl.* **-sies** ‖< L *contra*, against + *vertere*, to turn‖ a conflict of opinion; dispute

con·tro·vert (kän′trə vʉrt′, kän′trə vʉrt′) ***vt.*** **1** to argue against; dispute **2** to argue about; debate —**con′tro·vert′i·ble** ***adj.***

con·tu·ma·cy (kän′tyo͞o mə sē) ***n.***, *pl.* **-cies** ‖< L *com-*, intens. + *tumere*, swell up‖ stubborn resistance to authority —**con′tu·ma′cious** (-mā′shəs) ***adj.***

con·tu·me·ly (kän′tyo͞o mēl′ē, kən to͞om′ə lē) ***n.***, *pl.* **-lies** ‖< L *contumelia*, abuse‖ **1** humiliating treatment **2** a scornful insult —**con′tu·me′li·ous** (-mē′lē əs) ***adj.***

con·tu·sion (kən to͞o′zhən, -tyo͞o′-) ***n.*** ‖< L *com-*, intens. + *tundere*, to beat‖ a bruise

co·nun·drum (kə nun′drəm) ***n.*** ‖pseudo-L‖ **1** a riddle whose answer contains a pun **2** any puzzling problem

con·ur·ba·tion (kän′ər bā′shən) ***n.*** ‖< CON- + L *urbs*, city + -ATION‖ a vast urban area around and including a large city

con·va·lesce (kän′və les′) ***vi.*** **-lesced′, -lesc′ing** ‖< L *com-*, intens. + *valere*, be strong‖

to regain strength and health —**con'va·les'cence** *n.* —**con'va·les'cent** *adj., n.*

con·vec·tion (kən vek'shən) *n.* ‖< L *com-,* together + *vehere,* carry‖ 1 a transmitting 2 *a)* movement of parts of a fluid within the fluid because of differences in heat, etc. *b)* heat transference by such movement —**con·vec'tion·al** *adj.* —**con·vec'tive** *adj.*

con·vene (kən vēn') *vi., vt.* **-vened', -ven'ing** ‖< L *com-,* together + *venire,* come‖ to assemble for a meeting —**con·ven'er** *n.*

con·ven·ience (kən vēn' yəns) *n.* ‖see prec.‖ 1 the quality of being convenient 2 comfort 3 anything that adds to one's comfort or saves work —**at one's convenience** at a time or place suitable to one

con·ven'ient (-yənt) *adj.* easy to do, use, or get to; handy —**con·ven'ient·ly** *adv.*

con·vent (kän'vənt, -vent') *n.* ‖see CONVENE‖ 1 the residence of a religious community, esp. of women 2 the community itself

con·ven·ti·cle (kən ven'ti kəl) *n.* ‖see CONVENE‖ a religious assembly held illegally and secretly

con·ven·tion (kən ven'shən) *n.* ‖see CONVENE‖ 1 an assembly, often periodical, or its members 2 an agreement, as between nations 3 custom; usage

con·ven'tion·al (-shə nəl) *adj.* 1 having to do with a convention 2 sanctioned by or following custom or usage; customary 3 formal 4 nonnuclear /*conventional* weapons/ —**con·ven'tion·al'i·ty** (-nal'ə tē), *pl.* **-ties,** *n.* —**con·ven'tion·al·ly** *adv.*

con·ven'tion·al·ize' (-īz') *vt.* **-ized', -iz'ing** to make conventional

con·verge (kən vurj') *vi.* **-verged', -verg'ing** ‖< L *com-,* together + *vergere,* to bend‖ to come together at a point —**con·ver'gence** *n.* —**con·ver'gent** *adj.*

con·ver·sant (kən vur'sənt, kän'vər-) *adj.* familiar or acquainted (*with*)

con·ver·sa·tion (kän'vər sā'shən) *n.* a conversing; informal talk —**con'ver·sa'tion·al** *adj.* —**con'ver·sa'tion·al·ist** *n.* —**con'ver·sa'tion·al·ly** *adv.*

conversation piece something, as an unusual article of furniture, that attracts attention or invites comment

con·verse[1] (kən vurs'; *for n.* kän'vurs') *vi.* **-versed', -vers'ing** ‖< L *conversari,* live with‖ to hold a conversation; talk —*n.* conversation

con·verse[2] (kän'vurs'; *also, for adj.,* kən vurs') *adj.* ‖see CONVERT‖ reversed in position, order, etc.; opposite; contrary —*n.* a thing related in a converse way; the opposite —**con·verse'ly** *adv.*

con·ver·sion (kən vur'zhən) *n.* a converting or being converted

con·vert (kən vurt'; *for n.* kän'vurt') *vt.* ‖< L *com-,* together + *vertere,* to turn‖ 1 to change; transform 2 to change from one religion, doctrine, etc. to another 3 to exchange for something equal in value 4 to misappropriate —*vi.* to be converted —*n.* a person converted, as to a religion —**con·vert'er** *n.*

con·vert·i·ble (kən vurt'ə bəl) *adj.* that can be converted —*n.* an automobile with a folding top

con·vex (kän veks', kän'veks') *adj.* ‖< L *com-,* together + *vehere,* bring‖ curving outward like the surface of a sphere —**con·vex'i·ty** *n.*

CONVEX LENS

con·vey (kən vā') *vt.* ‖< L *com-,* together + *via,* way‖ 1 to take from one place to another; transport; carry 2 to transmit —**con·vey'a·ble** *adj.* —**con·vey'or** or **con·vey'er** *n.*

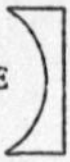

CONCAVE LENS

con·vey'ance *n.* 1 a conveying 2 a means of conveying; esp., a vehicle

con·vict (kən vikt'; *for n.* kän'vikt') *vt.* ‖see CONVINCE‖ to prove or find (a person) guilty —*n.* a convicted person serving a prison sentence

con·vic·tion (kən vik'shən) *n.* 1 a convicting or being convicted 2 a being convinced; strong belief

con·vince (kən vins') *vt.* **-vinced', -vinc'ing** ‖< L *com-,* intens. + *vincere,* conquer‖ to persuade by argument or evidence; make feel sure —**con·vinc'ing** *adj.* —**con·vinc'ing·ly** *adv.*

con·viv·i·al (kən viv'ē əl) *adj.* ‖< L *com-,* together + *vivere,* to live‖ 1 festive 2 fond of eating, drinking, and good company; sociable —**con·viv'i·al'i·ty** (-al'ə tē) *n.*

con·vo·ca·tion (kän'vō kā'shən) *n.* 1 a convoking 2 an assembly

con·voke (kən vōk') *vt.* **-voked', -vok'ing** ‖< L *com-,* together + *vocare,* to call‖ to call together; convene

con·vo·lut·ed (kän'və lo͞ot'id) *adj.* 1 having convolutions; coiled 2 involved; complicated

con'vo·lu'tion (-lo͞o'shən) *n.* ‖< L *com-,* together + *volvere,* to roll‖ 1 a twisting, coiling, or winding together 2 a fold, twist, or coil

con·voy (kän'voi') *vt.* ‖see CONVEY‖ to escort in order to protect —*n.* 1 a convoying 2 a protecting escort 3 ships, vehicles, etc. being convoyed

con·vulse (kən vuls') *vt.* **-vulsed', -vuls'ing** ‖< L *com-,* together + *vellere,* to pluck‖ 1 to shake violently; agitate 2 to cause to shake with laughter, rage, etc.

con·vul'sion (-vul'shən) *n.* 1 a violent, involuntary spasm of the muscles: *often in pl.* 2 a fit of laughter 3 a violent disturbance —**con·vul'sive** *adj.* —**con·vul'sive·ly** *adv.*

coo (ko͞o) *vi.* ‖echoic‖ to make the soft, murmuring sound of pigeons or doves —*n.* this sound

cook (ko͝ok) *n.* ‖< L *coquere,* to cook‖ one who prepares food —*vt.* to prepare (food) by boiling, baking, frying, etc. —*vi.* 1 to be a cook 2 to undergo cooking —**cook up** [Colloq.] to devise; invent —**cook'er** *n.*

cook'book' *n.* a book containing recipes and other food-preparation information

cook'er·y *n.* [Chiefly Brit.] the art or practice of cooking

cook'ie (-ē) *n.* ‖prob. < Du *koek,* cake‖ a small, sweet, flat cake, often crisp Also **cook'y,** *pl.* **-ies**

cook'out' *n.* a meal cooked and eaten outdoors
cool (ko͞ol) ***adj.*** ‖ OE *col* ‖ 1 moderately cold 2 tending to reduce the effects of heat /*cool* clothes/ 3 not excited; composed 4 showing dislike or indifference 5 calmly bold 6 [Colloq.] without exaggeration /a *cool* $1,000/ 7 [Slang] very good —***n.*** 1 a cool place, time, etc. /the *cool* of the evening/ 2 [Slang] cool, dispassionate manner —***vt., vi.*** to make or become cool —**cool'ly** ***adv.*** —**cool'ness** ***n.***
cool'ant ***n.*** a fluid or other substance for cooling engines, etc.
cool'er ***n.*** 1 a container or room for keeping things cool 2 a cold, refreshing drink 3 [Slang] jail
Coo·lidge (ko͝o'lij), **(John) Calvin** 1872-1933; 30th president of the U.S. (1923-29)
coo·lie (ko͞o'lē) ***n.*** ‖ Hindi *quli,* servant ‖ an unskilled native laborer, esp. formerly, in India, China, etc.
coon (ko͞on) ***n.*** *short for* RACCOON
coon'skin' ***n.*** the skin of a raccoon, used as a fur
coop (ko͞op) ***n.*** ‖ < L *cupa,* cask ‖ a small pen as for poultry —***vt.*** to confine as in a coop
co-op (kō'äp') ***n.*** [Colloq.] a cooperative
coop·er (ko͞op'ər) ***n.*** ‖ see COOP ‖ one whose work is making or repairing barrels and casks —**coop'er·age'** (-ij') ***n.***
co·op·er·ate or **co-op·er·ate** (kō äp'ər āt') ***vi.*** **-at'ed, -at'ing** ‖ < L *co-,* with + *opus,* work ‖ to act or work together with another or others —**co·op'er·a'tion** or **co-op'er·a'tion** ***n.***
co·op'er·a·tive or **co-op'er·a·tive** (-ər ə tiv, -ər āt'iv) ***adj.*** 1 cooperating 2 owned collectively by members who share in its benefits —***n.*** a cooperative store, etc.
co-opt (kō äpt', kō'äpt') ***vt.*** ‖ < L < *co-,* with + *optare,* choose ‖ 1 to appoint as an associate 2 to get (an opponent) to join one's side
co·or·di·nate or **co-or·di·nate** (kō ôr'də nit; *also, and for v. always,* -də nāt') ***adj.*** ‖ < L *co-,* with + *ordo,* order ‖ 1 of the same order or importance /*coordinate* clauses in a sentence/ 2 of coordination or coordinates —***n.*** a coordinate person or thing —***vt.*** **-nat'ed, -nat'ing** 1 to make coordinate 2 to bring into proper order or relation; adjust —**co·or'di·na'tor** or **co-or'di·na'tor** ***n.***
coordinating conjunction a conjunction connecting coordinate words, clauses, etc. (Ex.: *and, but, nor*)
co·or'di·na'tion or **co-or'di·na'tion** ***n.*** 1 a coordinating or being coordinated 2 harmonious action, as of muscles
coot (ko͞ot) ***n.*** ‖ ME *cote* ‖ 1 a ducklike water bird 2 [Colloq.] an eccentric
coot·ie (ko͞ot'ē) ***n.*** [Slang] a louse
cop (käp) ***vt.*** **copped, cop'ping** ‖ prob. < L *capere,* take ‖ [Slang] to seize, steal, etc. —***n.*** [Slang] a policeman —**cop out** [Slang] 1 to renege 2 to give up; quit
co·part·ner (kō pärt'nər, kō'pärt'-) ***n.*** a partner
cope[1] (kōp) ***vi.*** **coped, cop'ing** ‖ < OFr *coper,* to strike ‖ 1 to fight or contend (*with*) successfully 2 to deal with problems, etc.
cope[2] (kōp) ***n.*** ‖ < LL *cappa* ‖ 1 a large, capelike vestment worn by priests 2 any cover like this
Co·pen·hag·en (kō'pən hā'gən, -hä'-) capital of Denmark: pop. 633,000
Co·per·ni·cus (kō pur'ni kəs), **Nic·o·la·us** (nik'ə lā'əs) 1473-1543; Pol. astronomer —**Co·per'ni·can** ***adj., n.***
cop·i·er (käp'ē ər) ***n.*** 1 one who copies 2 a duplicating machine
co·pi·lot (kō'pī'lət) ***n.*** the assistant pilot of an airplane
cop·ing (kō'piŋ) ***n.*** ‖ < COPE[2] ‖ the top layer of a masonry wall
co·pi·ous (kō'pē əs) ***adj.*** ‖ < L *copia,* abundance ‖ plentiful; abundant —**co'pi·ous·ly** ***adv.*** —**co'pi·ous·ness** ***n.***
cop'-out' ***n.*** [Slang] a copping out, as by reneging or quitting
cop·per (käp'ər) ***n.*** ‖ < LL *cuprum* ‖ 1 a reddish-brown, ductile, metallic chemical element 2 a reddish brown —***adj.*** 1 of copper 2 reddish-brown —**cop'per·y** ***adj.***
cop'per·head' ***n.*** a poisonous North American snake
co·pra (kä'prə, kō'-) ***n.*** ‖ Port < Hindi *khoprā* ‖ dried coconut meat, the source of coconut oil
copse (käps) ***n.*** ‖ < OFr *coper,* to strike ‖ a thicket of small trees or shrubs Also **cop·pice** (käp'is)
cop·ter (käp'tər) ***n.*** *short for* HELICOPTER
cop·u·la (käp'yo͞o lə) ***n.,*** *pl.* **-las** ‖ L, a link ‖ a verb form, as of *be, seem, appear,* etc., that links a subject with a predicate —**cop'u·la'tive** (-lāt'iv) ***adj.***
cop·u·late (käp'yo͞o lāt') ***vi.*** **-lat'ed, -lat'ing** ‖ < L *co-,* together + *apere,* to join ‖ to have sexual intercourse —**cop'u·la'tion** ***n.***
cop·y (käp'ē) ***n.,*** *pl.* **-ies** ‖ < L *copia,* plenty ‖ 1 a thing made just like another 2 any of a number of books, magazines, etc. having the same contents 3 matter to be set in type 4 the words of an advertisement —***vt., vi.*** **cop'ied, cop'y·ing** 1 to make a copy of 2 to imitate —**cop'y·ist** ***n.***
cop'y·cat' (-kat') ***n.*** an imitator
cop'y·right' ***n.*** the exclusive right to the publication, sale, etc. of a literary or artistic work —***vt.*** to protect (a book, etc.) by copyright
cop'y·writ'er ***n.*** a writer of copy, esp. for advertisements
co·quette (kō ket') ***n.*** ‖ Fr ‖ a girl or woman flirt —***vi.*** **-quet'ted, -quet'ting** to flirt —**co·quet'tish** ***adj.***
cor- *prefix* COM- Used before *r*
cor·al (kôr'əl) ***n.*** ‖ < Gr *korallion* ‖ 1 the hard skeleton secreted by certain marine polyps: reefs and atolls of coral occur in tropical seas 2 a piece of coral 3 a yellowish red —***adj.*** of coral
coral snake a small, poisonous snake marked with coral, yellow, and black bands
cor·bel (kôr'bəl) ***n.*** ‖ < L *corvus,* raven ‖ a piece of stone, wood, etc. projecting from a wall and supporting a cornice, arch, etc.
cord (kôrd) ***n.*** ‖ < Gr *chordē* ‖ 1 a thick string 2 a measure of wood cut for fuel (128 cubic feet) 3 a rib on the surface of a fabric 4 ribbed cloth 5 [*pl.*] corduroy trou-

sers 6 *Anat.* any part like a cord 7 *Elec.* a slender cable —*vt.* to provide with cords

cord′age′ (-ij′) ***n.*** cords and ropes

cor·dial (kôr′jəl) ***adj.*** ‖< L *cor,* heart‖ warm; hearty; sincere —***n.*** a liqueur —**cor′·di·al′i·ty** (-jē al′ə tē) ***n.*** —**cor′dial·ly** ***adv.***

cor·dil·le·ra (kôr′dil yer′ə, -də ler′ə) ***n.*** ‖Sp < L *chorda,* a cord‖ a system or chain of mountains

cord·ite (kôrd′īt′) ***n.*** ‖< CORD: it is stringy‖ a smokeless explosive made of nitroglycerin, etc.

cord·less (kôrd′lis) ***adj.*** operated by batteries, as an electric shaver

cor·don (kôr′dən) ***n.*** ‖see CORD‖ **1** a line or circle of police, troops, etc. guarding an area **2** a cord or braid worn as a decoration —***vt.*** to encircle with a cordon

cor·do·van (kôr′də vən) ***n.*** ‖after *Córdoba,* Spain‖ a soft, colored leather

cor·du·roy (kôr′də roi′) ***n.*** ‖prob. < CORD + obs. *duroy,* a coarse fabric‖ a heavy, ribbed cotton fabric

core (kôr) ***n.*** ‖prob. < L *cor,* heart‖ **1** the central part of an apple, pear, etc. **2** the central part of anything **3** the most important part —***vt.*** **cored, cor′ing** to remove the core of

co·re·spond·ent (kō′ri spän′dənt) ***n.*** ‖CO- + RESPONDENT‖ *Law* a person charged with having committed adultery with the wife or husband from whom a divorce is being sought

co·ri·an·der (kôr′ē an′dər) ***n.*** ‖< Gr *koriandron*‖ an annual herb with strong-smelling, seedlike fruit used as a flavoring

cork (kôrk) ***n.*** ‖ult. < L *quercus,* oak‖ **1** the light, thick, elastic outer bark of an oak tree (**cork oak**) **2** a piece of cork; esp., a stopper for a bottle, etc. **3** any stopper —***adj.*** of cork —***vt.*** to stop with a cork

cork′screw′ ***n.*** a spiral-shaped device for pulling corks out of bottles —***adj.*** spiral —***vi., vt.*** to twist

corm (kôrm) ***n.*** ‖< Gr *kormos,* a log‖ a fleshy, underground stem of certain plants, as the gladiolus

cor·mo·rant (kôr′mə rənt) ***n.*** ‖< L *corvus,* raven + *marinus,* marine‖ a large, voracious sea bird

corn¹ (kôrn) ***n.*** ‖OE‖ **1** a small, hard seed, esp. of a cereal grass **2** *a)* an American cereal plant with kernels growing in rows along a woody, husk-enclosed core (**corncob**); maize *b)* the kernels **3** [Brit.] grain, esp. wheat **4** the leading cereal crop in a place **5** [Colloq.] ideas, humor, etc. regarded as old-fashioned, trite, etc. —***vt.*** to pickle (meat, etc.) in brine

corn² (kôrn) ***n.*** ‖< L *cornu,* horn‖ a hard, thick, painful growth of skin, esp. on a toe

corn′ball′ (-bôl′) ***adj.*** ‖CORN¹, *n.* 5 + (SCREW)BALL‖ [Slang] corny

corn bread bread made with cornmeal

cor·ne·a (kôr′nē ə) ***n.*** ‖< L *cornu,* horn‖ the transparent outer coat of the eyeball —**cor′ne·al** ***adj.***

cor·ner (kôr′nər) ***n.*** ‖< L *cornu,* horn‖ **1** the point or place where lines or surfaces join and form an angle **2** the angle formed **3** any of the angles formed at a street intersection **4** a remote, secluded place **5** a region; quarter **6** a position hard to escape from **7** a monopoly acquired on a stock or commodity so as to raise the price —***vt.*** **1** to force into a CORNER (*n.*6) **2** to get a monopoly on (a stock, etc.) —***adj.*** at, on, or for a corner —**cut corners** to cut down expenses, time, etc. —**cor′nered** ***adj.***

cor′ner·back′ ***n.*** *Football* either of two defensive backs positioned between the line of scrimmage and the safety men

cor′ner·stone′ ***n.*** **1** a stone at the corner of a building, often laid at a ceremony **2** the basic or main part; foundation

cor·net (kôr net′) ***n.*** ‖< L *cornu,* horn‖ a brass instrument similar to the trumpet but more compact

corn′flow′er ***n.*** an annual plant of the composite family, with white, pink, or blue flowers

cor·nice (kôr′nis) ***n.*** ‖< Gr *korōnis,* wreath‖ a horizontal molding projecting along the top of a wall, etc.

corn′meal′ ***n.*** meal made from corn (maize)

corn′starch′ ***n.*** a starch made from corn, used in cooking

corn syrup a syrup made from cornstarch

cor·nu·co·pi·a (kôr′nyōō kō′pē ə, -nōō-, -nə-) ***n.*** ‖L *cornu copiae,* horn of plenty‖ **1** a horn-shaped container overflowing with fruits, flowers, etc. **2** an abundance

CORNUCOPIA

corn·y (kôrn′ē) ***adj.*** **-i·er, -i·est** [Colloq.] trite, sentimental, etc.

co·rol·la (kə rōl′ə, -räl′ə) ***n.*** ‖< L, dim. of *corona,* crown‖ the petals of a flower

cor·ol·lar·y (kôr′ə ler′ē) ***n., pl.*** **-ies** ‖see prec.‖ **1** a proposition that follows from one already proved **2** a normal result

co·ro·na (kə rō′nə) ***n., pl.*** **-nas** or **-nae** (-nē) ‖L‖ **1** the layer of ionized gas surrounding the sun **2** a ring of colored light seen around a luminous body, as the sun or moon

cor·o·nar·y (kôr′ə ner′ē) ***adj.*** **1** of or like a crown **2** of the arteries supplying blood to the heart muscle —***n., pl.*** **-ies** a thrombosis in a coronary artery: in full **coronary thrombosis**

cor·o·na·tion (kôr′ə nā′shən) ***n.*** the crowning of a sovereign

cor·o·ner (kôr′ə nər) ***n.*** ‖ME, officer of the crown‖ a public officer who must determine the cause of any death not obviously due to natural causes

cor·o·net (kôr′ə net′, kôr′ə net′) ***n.*** ‖< OFr *corone,* crown‖ **1** a small crown worn by nobility **2** a band of jewels, flowers, etc. for the head

Corp. or **corp.** corporation

cor·po·ral¹ (kôr′pə rəl) ***n.*** ‖< L *caput,* head‖ the lowest-ranking noncommissioned officer, just below a sergeant

cor·po·ral² (kôr′pə rəl) ***adj.*** ‖< L *corpus,* body‖ of the body; bodily

corporal punishment bodily punishment, as flogging

cor·po·rate (kôr′pə rit) ***adj.*** ‖< L *corpus,* body‖ **1** of, like, or being a corporation **2** shared; joint

cor′po·ra′tion (-pə rā′shən) ***n.*** a legal entity,

usually a group of people, that has a charter granting it certain legal powers generally given to individuals, as to buy and sell property or to enter into contracts

cor·po·re·al (kôr pôr′ē əl) ***adj.*** ‖ < L *corpus,* body ‖ **1** of or for the body; physical **2** of a material nature; tangible

corps (kôr) ***n.,*** *pl.* **corps** (kôrz) ‖ < L *corpus,* body ‖ **1** a body of people associated under common direction **2** *Mil. a)* a specialized branch of the armed forces *b)* a tactical subdivision of an army

corpse (kôrps) ***n.*** ‖ var. of prec. ‖ a dead body, esp. of a person

cor·pu·lence (kôr′pyōō ləns, ·pyə·) ***n.*** ‖ < L *corpus,* body ‖ fatness; obesity —**cor′pu·lent** ***adj.***

cor·pus (kôr′pəs) ***n.,*** *pl.* **cor′po·ra** (·pə rə) ‖ L ‖ **1** a body, esp. a dead one **2** a complete collection, as of laws

Cor·pus Chris·ti (kôr′pəs kris′tē) city in SE Tex.: pop. 232,000

cor′pus′cle (·pus′əl , ·pə səl) ***n.*** ‖ < L dim. of *corpus,* body ‖ **1** a very small particle **2** a cell in the blood, lymph, etc. of vertebrates

corpus de·lic·ti (də lik′tī′) ‖ ModL, lit., body of the crime ‖ **1** the facts constituting a crime **2** loosely, the body of a murder victim

cor·ral (kə ral′) ***n.*** ‖ Sp < L *currere,* to run ‖ an enclosure for horses, cattle, etc.; pen —***vt.*** **-ralled′, -ral′ling** **1** to drive into or confine in a corral **2** to surround or capture

cor·rect (kə rekt′) ***vt.*** ‖ < L *com-,* together + *regere,* to rule ‖ **1** to make right **2** to mark the errors of **3** to scold or punish **4** to cure or remove (a fault, etc.) —***adj.*** **1** conforming to an established standard **2** true; accurate; right —**cor·rect′a·ble** ***adj.*** —**cor·rec′tive** ***adj., n.*** —**cor·rect′ly** ***adv.*** —**cor·rect′ness** ***n.***

cor·rec′tion (·rek′shən) ***n.*** **1** a correcting or being corrected **2** a change that corrects a mistake **3** punishment to correct faults —**cor·rec′tion·al** ***adj.***

cor·re·late (kôr′ə lāt′) ***vi., vt.*** **-lat′ed, -lat′ing** ‖ see COM- & RELATE ‖ to be in or bring into mutual relation —**cor′re·la′tion** ***n.***

cor·rel·a·tive (kə rel′ə tiv′) ***adj.*** **1** having a mutual relationship **2** *Gram.* expressing mutual relation and used in pairs, as the conjunctions *neither* and *nor* —***n.*** a correlative word, etc.

cor·re·spond (kôr′ə spänd′) ***vi.*** ‖ < L *com-,* together + *respondere,* respond ‖ **1** to be in agreement (*with* something) **2** to be similar or equal (*to* something) **3** to communicate by letters —**cor′re·spond′ing·ly** ***adv.***

cor′re·spond′ence ***n.*** **1** agreement **2** similarity **3** *a)* communication by letters *b)* the letters

cor′re·spond′ent ***adj.*** corresponding —***n.*** **1** a thing that corresponds **2** one who exchanges letters with another **3** one hired by a newspaper, radio network, etc. to furnish news, etc. from a distant place

cor·ri·dor (kôr′ə dər, ·dôr′) ***n.*** ‖ Fr < L *currere,* to run ‖ a long hall

cor·rob·o·rate (kə räb′ə rāt′) ***vt.*** **-rat′ed, -rat′ing** ‖ < L *com-,* intens. + *robur,* strength ‖ to confirm; support —**cor·rob′o·ra′tion** ***n.*** —**cor·rob′o·ra′tive** ***adj.*** —**cor·rob′o·ra′tor** ***n.***

cor·rode (kə rōd′) ***vt., vi.*** **-rod′ed, -rod′ing** ‖ < L *com-,* intens. + *rodere,* gnaw ‖ to eat into or wear away gradually, as by chemical action —**cor·ro′sion** (·rō′zhən) ***n.*** —**cor·ro′sive** (·rōs′iv) ***adj., n.*** —**cor·ro′sive·ly** ***adv.***

cor·ru·gate (kôr′ə gāt′) ***vt., vi.*** **-gat′ed, -gat′ing** ‖ < L *com-,* intens. + *rugare,* to wrinkle ‖ to shape into parallel grooves and ridges —**cor′ru·ga′tion** ***n.***

cor·rupt (kə rupt′) ***adj.*** ‖ < L *com-,* together + *rumpere,* to break ‖ **1** evil; depraved **2** taking bribes —***vt., vi.*** to make or become corrupt —**cor·rupt′i·ble** ***adj.*** —**cor·rup′tion** ***n.*** —**cor·rupt′ly** ***adv.***

cor·sage (kôr säzh′) ***n.*** ‖ see CORPS & -AGE ‖ a small bouquet for a woman to wear, as at the waist or shoulder

cor·sair (kôr′ser′) ***n.*** ‖ < Fr < L *cursus,* course ‖ a pirate or pirate ship

cor·set (kôr′sit) ***n.*** ‖ see CORPS ‖ a closefitting undergarment worn, chiefly by women, to give support or a desired figure to the body

cor·tege or **cor·tège** (kôr tezh′, ·tāzh′) ***n.*** ‖ Fr < L *cohors* ‖ **1** a retinue **2** a ceremonial procession

cor·tex (kôr′teks′) ***n.,*** *pl.* **-ti·ces′** (·tə sēz′) ‖ L, bark of a tree ‖ **1** the outer part of an internal organ; esp., the outer layer of gray matter over most of the brain **2** an outer layer of plant tissue —**cor′ti·cal** (·ti kəl) ***adj.***

cor·ti·sone (kôrt′ə sōn′, ·zōn′) ***n.*** ‖ so named by E. C. Kendall (1886-1972), U.S. physician ‖ a hormone used in adrenal insufficiency and for inflammatory diseases, etc.

co·run·dum (kə run′dəm) ***n.*** ‖ < Sans *kuruvinda,* ruby ‖ a very hard mineral used for grinding and polishing

cor·us·cate (kôr′ə skāt′) ***vi.*** **-cat′ed, -cat′ing** ‖ < L *coruscus,* vibrating ‖ to glitter; sparkle —**cor′us·ca′tion** ***n.***

cor·vette (kôr vet′) ***n.*** ‖ Fr ‖ a fast warship smaller than a destroyer and used chiefly for convoy duty

co·sign (kō′sīn′, kō′sīn′) ***vt., vi.*** **1** to sign (a promissory note) in addition to the maker, thus becoming responsible if the maker defaults **2** to sign jointly —**co′sign′er** ***n.***

co·sig′na·to′ry (·sig′nə tôr′ē) ***n.,*** *pl.* **-ries** one of two or more joint signers, as of a treaty

cos·met·ic (käz met′ik) ***adj.*** ‖ < Gr *kosmos,* order ‖ beautifying, or correcting faults in, the face, hair, etc. —***n.*** a cosmetic preparation, as lipstick —**cos·met′i·cal·ly** ***adv.***

cos′me·tol′o·gy (·mə täl′ə jē) ***n.*** the work of a beautician —**cos′me·tol′o·gist** ***n.***

cos·mic (käz′mik) ***adj.*** ‖ < Gr *kosmos,* universe ‖ **1** of the cosmos **2** vast

cosmic rays streams of high-energy charged particles from outer space

cos·mog·o·ny (käz mäg′ə nē) ***n.*** ‖ < Gr *kosmos,* universe + *-gonos,* generation ‖ **1** the study of the origin of the universe **2** *pl.* **-nies** a theory of this

cos·mol′o·gy (·mäl′ə jē) ***n.*** ‖ < ML ‖ the study of the form, evolution, etc. of the universe —**cos′mo·log′i·cal** (·mə läj′ə k′l) ***adj.***

cos·mo·naut (käz′mə nôt′) ***n.*** ‖ Russ *kosmonaut* ‖ a Soviet astronaut

cos·mo·pol·i·tan (käz′mə päl′ə tən) ***adj.*** ‖ < Gr *kosmos*, universe + *polis*, city-state ‖ **1** common to or representative of all or many parts of the world **2** not bound by local or national habits or prejudices; at home in all places —***n.*** a cosmopolitan person or thing: also **cos·mop′o·lite′** (-mäp′ə līt′)

cos·mos (käz′məs, -mōs′) ***n.*** ‖ < Gr *kosmos*, universe ‖ **1** the universe considered as an orderly system **2** any complete and orderly system

co·spon·sor (kō′spän′sər) ***n.*** a joint sponsor, as of a proposed piece of legislation —***vt.*** to be a cosponsor of —**co′spon′sor·ship′** ***n.***

Cos·sack (käs′ak′, -ək) ***n.*** a member of any of several groups of peasants that lived in autonomous communal settlements, esp. in the Ukraine, until the late 19th c.

cost (kôst) ***vt.*** **cost, cost′ing** ‖ < L *com-*, together + *stare*, to stand ‖ **1** to be obtained for (a certain price) **2** to require the expenditure, loss, etc. of —***n.*** **1** the amount of money, etc. asked or paid for a thing; price **2** loss; sacrifice —**at all costs** by any means required

co·star (kō′stär′; *for v., usually* kō′stär′) ***n.*** any featured actor or actress given equal billing with another in a movie, play, etc. —***vt., vi.*** **-starred′, -star′ring** to present as or be a costar

Cos·ta Ri·ca (käs′tə rē′kə, kôs′-, kōs′-) country in Central America: 19,575 sq. mi.; pop. 2,714,000 —**Cos′ta Ri′can**

cost-ef·fec·tive (kôst′ə fek′tiv) ***adj.*** producing good results for the amount of money spent; efficient —**cost′-ef·fec′tive·ness** ***n.***

cost′ly ***adj.*** **-li·er, -li·est** ‖ ME ‖ **1** costing much; expensive **2** magnificent —**cost′li·ness** ***n.***

cost of living the average cost of the necessities of life, as food, shelter, and clothes

cos·tume (käs′to͞om′, -tyo͞om′) ***n.*** ‖ < L *consuetudo*, custom ‖ **1** *a)* the style of dress typical of a certain country, period, profession, etc. *b)* a set of such clothes **2** a set of outer clothes —***vt.*** **-tumed′, -tum′ing** to provide with a costume

co·sy (kō′zē) ***adj.*** **-si·er, -si·est** *chiefly Brit. sp. of* COZY —***n.***, *pl.* **-sies** COZY —**co′si·ly** ***adv.*** —**co′si·ness** ***n.***

cot¹ (kät) ***n.*** ‖ < Sans *khāṭvā* ‖ a narrow, collapsible bed, as one made of canvas on a folding frame

cot² (kät) ***n.*** ‖ OE ‖ **1** a small shelter **2** a sheath, as for a hurt finger

cote (kōt) ***n.*** ‖ ME ‖ a small shelter for fowl, sheep, etc.

co·te·rie (kōt′ər ē) ***n.*** ‖ Fr ‖ a close circle of friends; clique

co·ter·mi·nous (kō tʉr′mə nəs) ***adj.*** CONTERMINOUS

co·til·lion (kō til′yən) ***n.*** ‖ < OFr *cote*, coat ‖ **1** an intricate, formal group dance **2** a formal ball Also **co·til′lon**

cot·tage (kät′ij) ***n.*** ‖ ME ‖ **1** a small house **2** a house used for vacations —**cot′tag·er** ***n.***

cottage cheese a soft, white cheese made from the curds of sour milk

cot·ter (kät′ər) ***n.*** [Scot.] a tenant farmer Also **cot′tar**

cotter pin a split pin fastened in place by spreading apart its ends after it is inserted

cot·ton (kät′′n) ***n.*** ‖ < Ar *quṭun* ‖ **1** the soft, white hairs around the seeds of certain mallow plants **2** such a plant or plants **3** thread or cloth made of cotton —**cotton to** [Colloq.] to take a liking to —**cot′ton·y** ***adj.***

cotton gin ‖ see GIN² ‖ a machine for separating cotton from the seeds

cot′ton·mouth′ ***n.*** WATER MOCCASIN

cot′ton·seed′ ***n.*** the seed of the cotton plant, yielding an oil (**cottonseed oil**) used in margarine, cooking oil, soap, etc.

cot′ton·tail′ ***n.*** a common American rabbit with a short, fluffy tail

cot′ton·wood′ ***n.*** a poplar that has seeds thickly covered with cottony or silky hairs

cot·y·le·don (kät′ə lēd′′n) ***n.*** ‖ < Gr *kotylē*, cavity ‖ the first leaf or one of the first pair of leaves produced by the embryo of a flowering plant

couch (kouch) ***n.*** ‖ < OFr *coucher*, lie down ‖ an article of furniture on which one may sit or lie down; sofa —***vt., vi.*** **1** to recline as on a couch **2** to put in words; express

cou·gar (ko͞o′gər) ***n.*** ‖ < AmInd (Brazil) ‖ a large, powerful, tawny wild cat

cough (kôf) ***vi.*** ‖ ME *coughen* ‖ to expel air suddenly and noisily from the lungs —***vt.*** to expel by coughing —***n.*** **1** the act of coughing **2** a condition causing frequent coughing —**cough up** [Slang] to hand over (money, etc.)

cough drop a small medicated tablet for the relief of coughs, etc.

could (ko͝od) ***v.aux.*** **1** *pt. of* CAN¹ **2** an auxiliary verb generally equivalent to CAN¹, expressing esp. a shade of doubt [*it could be so*]

cou·lomb (ko͞o läm′) ***n.*** ‖ after C. A. de *Coulomb* (1736-1806), Fr physicist ‖ a unit of electric charge equal to the charge of 6.28×10^{18} electrons

coun·cil (koun′səl) ***n.*** ‖ < L *com-*, together + *calere*, to call ‖ **1** a group of people called together for discussion, advice, etc. **2** an administrative, advisory, or legislative body —**coun′cil·man** (-mən), *pl.* **-men,** ***n.*** —**coun′cil·wom′an**, *pl.* **-wom′en,** ***n.fem.***

coun′ci·lor (-sə lər) ***n.*** a member of a council

coun·sel (koun′səl) ***n.*** ‖ < L *consilium* ‖ **1** a mutual exchange of ideas, etc.; discussion **2** advice **3** a lawyer or group of lawyers **4** a consultant —***vt.*** **-seled** or **-selled, -sel·ing** or **-sel·ling** **1** to give advice to **2** to recommend (an action, etc.) —***vi.*** to give or take advice

coun′se·lor or **coun′sel·lor** (-sə lər) ***n.*** **1** an advisor **2** a lawyer

count¹ (kount) ***vt.*** ‖ < L *computare*, compute ‖ **1** to name or add up, unit by unit, to get a total **2** to take account of; include **3** to believe to be; consider —***vi.*** **1** to name numbers or add up items in order **2** to be taken into account; have importance **3** to have a specified value: often with *for* **4** to rely or depend (*on* or *upon*) —***n.*** **1** a counting **2** the total number **3** a reckoning **4** *Law* any of the charges in an indictment

count² (kount) ***n.*** ‖ < L *comes*, companion ‖

a European nobleman with a rank equal to that of an English earl

count′down′ *n.* 1 the schedule of operations just before the firing of a rocket, etc. 2 the counting off, in reverse order, of time units in this schedule

coun·te·nance (koun′tə nəns, kount′′n əns) *n.* ‖< L *continentia*, bearing‖ 1 facial expression 2 the face 3 approval; support —*vt.* **-nanced, -nanc·ing** to approve or tolerate

count·er[1] (kount′ər) *n.* 1 a person, device, etc. that counts something 2 a small disk for keeping count in games 3 an imitation coin or token 4 a long table, cabinet top, etc. for the displaying of goods, serving of food, etc. —**over the counter** direct trading Said of stock sales not conducted through a stock exchange —**under the counter** in a secret manner Said of sales, etc. made illegally

coun·ter[2] (kount′ər) *adv.* ‖< L *contra*, against‖ in opposition; opposite —*adj.* contrary; opposed —*n.* the opposite; contrary —*vt., vi.* to act, do, etc. counter to; oppose

counter- ‖< L *contra-*, against‖ *combining form* 1 contrary to /*counterclockwise*/ 2 in retaliation /*counterattack*/ 3 complementary /*counterpart*/

coun′ter·act′ *vt.* to act against; neutralize —**coun′ter·ac′tion** *n.*

coun′ter·at·tack′ *n.* an attack made in opposition to another attack —*vt., vi.* to attack to offset the enemy's attack

coun′ter·bal′ance *n.* a weight, force, etc. that balances another —*vt.* **-anced, -anc·ing** to be a counterbalance to; offset

coun·ter·claim (kount′ər klām′; *for v., also* kount′ər klām′) *n.* an opposing claim —*vt., vi.* to present as a counterclaim

coun′ter·clock′wise′ (-wīz′) *adj., adv.* in a direction opposite to that in which the hands of a clock move

coun′ter·cul′ture *n.* a culture with a lifestyle that is opposed to the prevailing culture

coun′ter·es′pi·o·nage′ *n.* actions to prevent or thwart enemy espionage

coun·ter·feit (kount′ər fit′) *adj.* ‖< OFr *contre-*, counter- + *faire*, make‖ 1 made in imitation of something genuine so as to deceive; forged 2 sham; pretended —*n.* an imitation made to deceive —*vt., vi.* 1 to make an imitation of (money, etc.), usually to deceive 2 to pretend —**coun′ter·feit′er** *n.*

count′er·man′ *n., pl.* **-men′** a man who serves customers at a counter, as of a lunchroom

coun′ter·mand′ (-mand′) *vt.* ‖< L *contra*, against + *mandare*, to command‖ to cancel or revoke by a contrary order

coun′ter·pane′ (-pān′) *n.* ‖ult. < L *culcita puncta*, embroidered quilt‖ a bedspread

coun′ter·part′ *n.* 1 a person or thing that closely resembles another 2 a copy or duplicate

coun′ter·point′ *n.* ‖< It: see COUNTER- & POINT‖ 1 the technique of combining two or more distinct lines of music that sound simultaneously 2 any melody played or sung against a basic melody 3 a thing set up in contrast with another

coun′ter·poise′ *n.* ‖see COUNTER[2] & POISE‖ 1 a counterbalance 2 equilibrium —*vt.* **-poised′, -pois′ing** to counterbalance

coun′ter·pro·duc′tive *adj.* having results contrary to those intended

coun′ter·rev′o·lu′tion *n.* a political movement against a government set up by a previous revolution —**coun′ter·rev′o·lu′tion·ar′y**, *pl.* **-ies**, *n., adj.*

coun′ter·sign′ *n.* 1 a signature added to a previously signed document, as for confirmation 2 a secret signal to another, as a password —*vt.* to confirm with one's own signature

coun′ter·sink′ *vt.* **-sunk′, -sink′ing** 1 to enlarge the top part of (a hole) so that the head of a bolt, etc. will fit flush with the surface 2 to sink (a bolt, etc.) into such a hole

coun′ter·ten′or *n.* 1 the range of the highest male voice, above tenor 2 a singer or voice with such a range

coun′ter·weight′ *n.* a counterbalance

count·ess (kount′is) *n.* 1 the wife or widow of a count or earl 2 a woman of nobility with a rank equal to that of a count or earl

count·less (kount′lis) *adj.* too many to count; innumerable; myriad

coun·try (kun′trē) *n., pl.* **-tries** ‖< L *contra*, against‖ 1 an area of land; region 2 the whole land, or the people, of a nation 3 the land of one's birth or citizenship 4 land with farms and small towns

country club a social club with a clubhouse, golf course, etc.

coun′try·man (-mən) *n., pl.* **-men** a man of one's own country

country music popular music that derives from the rural folk music of the S U.S.

coun′try·side′ *n.* a rural region

coun·ty (kount′ē) *n., pl.* **-ties** ‖< ML *comitatus*, jurisdiction of a count‖ a small administrative district of a country, State, etc.

coup (ko͞o) *n., pl.* **coups** (ko͞oz) ‖Fr < L *colaphus*, a blow‖ 1 a sudden, successful action 2 COUP D'ÉTAT

coup de grâce (ko͞o′ də gräs′) ‖Fr, stroke of mercy‖ 1 the blow, shot, etc. that brings death to a sufferer 2 a finishing stroke

coup d'é·tat (ko͞o′ dā tä′) ‖Fr, stroke of state‖ the sudden, forcible overthrow as of a ruler

coupe (ko͞op) *n.* ‖< Fr *couper*, to cut‖ a closed, two-door automobile

cou·ple (kup′əl) *n.* ‖< L *copula*‖ 1 a link 2 a pair of things or persons, as a man and woman who are engaged, etc. 3 [Colloq.] a few —*vt., vi.* **-pled, -pling** to link or unite

cou′plet (-lit) *n.* two successive lines of poetry, esp. two that rhyme

cou′pling (-liŋ) *n.* 1 a joining together 2 a mechanical device for joining parts together

cou·pon (ko͞o′pän′, kyo͞o′-) *n.* ‖Fr < *couper*, to cut‖ 1 a detachable printed statement on a bond, specifying the interest due at a given time 2 a certificate entitling one to a specified right, as a discount, gift, etc.

cour·age (kur′ij) *n.* ‖< L *cor*, heart‖ the quality of being brave; valor

cou·ra·geous (kə rā′jəs) *adj.* having or showing courage; brave —**cou·ra′geous·ly** *adv.*

cou·ri·er (koor′ē ər, kur′-) ***n.*** ‖< L *currere,* to run‖ **1** a messenger **2** a person hired to take care of hotel accommodations, etc. for a traveler

course (kôrs) ***n.*** ‖< L *currere,* to run‖ **1** an onward movement; progress **2** a way, path, or channel **3** the direction taken **4** a regular manner of procedure or conduct /our wisest *course*/ **5** a series of like things in order **6** a part of a meal served at one time **7** *Educ. a)* a complete series of studies, as for a degree *b)* any of the separate units of such a series —***vi.*** **coursed, cours′ing** to run or race —**in due course** in the usual sequence (of events) —**in the course of** during —**of course 1** naturally **2** certainly

cours·er (kôr′sər) ***n.*** a graceful, spirited, or swift horse

court (kôrt) ***n.*** ‖< L *cohors,* enclosure‖ **1** a courtyard **2** a short street **3** a space for playing a game, as basketball **4** *a)* the palace, or the family, etc., of a sovereign *b)* a sovereign and councilors, etc. as a governing body *c)* a formal gathering held by a sovereign **5** courtship; wooing **6** *a)* a judge or judges *b)* a place where trials are held *c)* a judicial assembly —***vt.*** **1** to pay attention to (a person) so as to get something **2** to seek as a mate; woo **3** to try to get /to *court* favor/ —***vi.*** to carry on a courtship —**court′er *n.***

cour·te·ous (kurt′ē əs) ***adj.*** ‖see prec. & -EOUS‖ polite and gracious —**cour′te·ous·ly *adv.***

cour·te·san (kôrt′ə zən) ***n.*** ‖see COURT‖ a prostitute Also **cour′te·zan**

cour·te·sy (kurt′ə sē) ***n.***, *pl.* **-sies 1** courteous behavior **2** a polite or considerate act or remark

court′house′ ***n.*** **1** a building housing law courts **2** a building housing offices of a county government

cour·ti·er (kôrt′ē ər, -yər) ***n.*** an attendant at a royal court

court′ly ***adj.*** **-li·er, -li·est** suitable for a king's court; dignified; elegant —**court′li·ness *n.***

court′-mar′tial ***n.***, *pl.* **courts′-mar′tial**; for 2, now often **court′-mar′tials 1** a court in the armed forces for the trial of persons accused of breaking military law **2** a trial by a court-martial **3** a conviction by a court-martial —***vt.*** **-tialed** or **-tialled, -tial·ing** or **-tial·ling** to try by a court-martial

court′room′ ***n.*** a room in which a law court is held

court′ship′ ***n.*** the act, process, or period of wooing

court′yard′ ***n.*** a space enclosed by walls, adjoining or in a large building

cous·cous (kōōs′kōōs′) ***n.*** ‖Fr < Ar *kaskasa,* to grind‖ a N African dish made with crushed grain, served as with lamb in a spicy sauce

cous·in (kuz′ən) ***n.*** ‖ult. < L *com-,* with + *soror,* sister‖ **1** the son or daughter of one's uncle or aunt **2** loosely, any relative by blood or marriage

cou·tu·ri·er (kōō tü ryā′; *Eng* kōō′toor ē ā′) ***n.*** ‖Fr‖ a designer of women's fashions —***cou·tu·ri·ère*** (-ryer′; *Eng,* -ē er′) ***n.fem.***

cove (kōv) ***n.*** ‖OE *cofa,* cave‖ a small bay or inlet

cov·en (kuv′ən) ***n.*** ‖see CONVENE‖ a gathering or meeting, esp. of witches

cov·e·nant (kuv′ə nənt) ***n.*** ‖see CONVENE‖ an agreement; compact —***vt.*** to promise by a covenant —***vi.*** to make a covenant

cov·er (kuv′ər) ***vt.*** ‖< L *co-,* intens. + *operire,* to hide‖ **1** to place something on or over **2** to extend over **3** to clothe **4** to conceal; hide **5** to shield, protect, or watch (someone or something) **6** to include; deal with /to *cover* a subject/ **7** to protect financially /to *cover* a loss/ **8** to accept (a bet) **9** to travel over **10** to point a firearm at **11** *Journalism* to gather the details of (a news story) —***vi.*** **1** to spread over a surface, as a liquid does **2** to provide an alibi (*for*) —***n.*** **1** anything that covers, as a lid, top, etc. **2** a shelter for protection **3** a tablecloth and setting **4** COVER CHARGE **5** something used to hide one's real actions, etc. —**cover up** to keep blunders, crimes, etc. from being known —**take cover** to seek shelter —**under cover** in secrecy or concealment

cov′er·age′ (-ij′) ***n.*** the amount, extent, etc. covered by something

cov′er·all′ ***n.*** (*usually pl.*) a one-piece outer garment, often worn over regular clothing while working, etc.

cover charge a fixed charge added to the cost of food and drink at a nightclub, etc.

cover crop a crop, as clover, grown to keep soil fertile and uneroded

covered wagon a large wagon with an arched cover of canvas

cov′er·ing ***n.*** anything that covers

cov·er·let (kuv′ər lit) ***n.*** ‖< OFr *covrir,* to cover + *lit,* bed‖ any covering, esp. a bedspread

cover story the article in a magazine that deals with the subject depicted on the cover

cov·ert (kuv′ərt, kō′vərt) ***adj.*** ‖see COVER‖ hidden or disguised —***n.*** a protected shelter, as for game —**cov′ert·ly *adv.***

cov′er-up′ ***n.*** something used for hiding one's real activities, etc.

cov·et (kuv′it) ***vt., vi.*** ‖< L *cupiditas,* cupidity‖ to want ardently (esp., something that another person has)

cov′et·ous (-ət əs) ***adj.*** tending to covet; greedy —**cov′et·ous·ness *n.***

cov·ey (kuv′ē) ***n.***, *pl.* **-eys** ‖< OFr *cover,* to hatch‖ a small flock of birds, esp. partridges or quail

cow[1] (kou) ***n.*** ‖OE *cu*‖ **1** the mature female of domestic cattle, valued for its milk **2** the mature female of certain other mammals, as the whale

cow[2] (kou) ***vt.*** ‖< ON *kūga,* subdue‖ to make timid; intimidate

cow·ard (kou′ərd) ***n.*** ‖ult. < L *cauda,* tail‖ one who lacks courage, esp. one who is shamefully afraid —***adj.*** cowardly

cow′ard·ice′ (-ər dis′) ***n.*** lack of courage

cow′ard·ly ***adj.*** of or like a coward —***adv.*** in the manner of a coward —**cow′ard·li·ness *n.***

cow′boy′ ***n.*** a ranch worker who herds cattle Also **cow′hand′** —**cow′girl′ *n.fem.***

cow·er (kou′ər) ***vi.*** ‖ME *couren*‖ to crouch or huddle up, as from fear or cold; shrink; cringe

cow'hide' *n.* 1 the hide of a cow 2 leather from it 3 a whip made of this
cowl (koul) *n.* ‖< L *cucullus,* hood‖ a monk's hood or a monk's cloak with a hood
cow·lick (kou'lik') *n.* ‖< its looking as if licked by a cow‖ a tuft of hair that cannot easily be combed flat
cowl·ing (koul'iŋ) *n.* ‖see COWL‖ a metal covering for an airplane engine, etc.
co'-work'er *n.* a fellow worker
cow'poke' *n.* [Colloq.] COWBOY
cow pony a horse for herding cattle
cow'pox' *n.* a disease of cows: people vaccinated with its virus have temporary immunity to smallpox
cox·comb (käks'kōm') *n.* ‖for *cock's comb*‖ a silly, vain fellow; dandy
cox·swain (käk'sən, -swān') *n.* ‖< *cock,* small boat + SWAIN‖ one who steers a boat or racing shell
coy (koi) *adj.* ‖ME, quiet‖ 1 bashful; shy 2 pretending to be shy —**coy'ly** *adv.* —**coy'ness** *n.*
coy·o·te (kī ōt'ē, kī'ōt') *n.* ‖< AmInd (Mex)‖ a small, wolflike animal of North America
coz·en (kuz'ən) *vt., vi.* ‖< ME *cosin,* fraud‖ to cheat; deceive —**coz'en·age** *n.*
co·zy (kō'zē) *adj.* **-zi·er, -zi·est** ‖Scot‖ warm and comfortable; snug —*n., pl.* **-zies** a padded cover for a teapot, to keep the tea hot —**cozy up to** [Colloq.] to try to ingratiate oneself with —**co'zi·ly** *adv.* —**co'zi·ness** *n.*
CPA Certified Public Accountant
CPO Chief Petty Officer
CPR cardiopulmonary resuscitation
CPU (sē'pē'yoo') *n.* central processing unit Also **cpu**
Cr *Chem. symbol for* chromium

EDIBLE CRAB

crab (krab) *n.* ‖OE *crabba*‖ 1 a crustacean with four pairs of legs and a pair of pincers 2 a peevish person —*vi.* **crabbed, crab'bing** [Colloq.] to complain
crab apple 1 a small, very sour apple 2 a tree bearing crab apples
crab·bed (krab'id) *adj.* ‖< CRAB (APPLE)‖ 1 peevish 2 hard to read or understand, as writing —**crab'bed·ness** *n.*
crab'by *adj.* **-bi·er, -bi·est** ‖see prec.‖ cross and complaining —**crab'bi·ly** *adv.* —**crab'bi·ness** *n.*
crab grass a weedy grass, with freely rooting stems, that spreads rapidly
crack (krak) *vi.* ‖< OE *cracian,* resound‖ 1 to make a sudden, sharp noise, as in breaking 2 to break or split, usually without separation of parts 3 to rasp or shift erratically in vocal tone 4 [Colloq.] to break down, as from strain —*vt.* 1 to cause to make a sharp, sudden noise 2 to cause to break or split 3 to break down (petroleum hydrocarbons) into the lighter hydrocarbons of gasoline, etc. 4 [Colloq.] to hit hard 5 to solve 6 [Colloq.] to break into or force open 7 [Slang] to make (a joke) —*n.* 1 a sudden, sharp noise 2 a partial break; fracture 3 a chink; crevice 4 a cracking of the voice 5 [Colloq.] a sudden, sharp blow 6 [Colloq.] an attempt or try 7 [Slang] a joke —*adj.* [Colloq.] excellent; first-rate —**crack down** (on) to become strict (with) —**cracked up to be** [Colloq.] believed to be —**crack up** 1 to crash 2 [Colloq.] *a)* to break down physically or mentally *b)* to laugh or cry
crack'down' *n.* a resorting to strict or stricter discipline or punishment
cracked (krakt) *adj.* 1 having a crack or cracks 2 sounding harsh or strident 3 [Colloq.] crazy
crack'er *n.* 1 a firecracker 2 a thin, crisp wafer
crack'er·jack' *adj.* [Slang] outstanding; excellent —*n.* [Slang] an excellent person or thing
crack·le (krak'əl) *vi.* **-led, -ling** ‖ME *crakelen,* to crack‖ to make a series of slight, sharp, popping sounds —*n.* 1 a series of such sounds 2 the fine, irregular surface cracks on some pottery, etc.
crack'pot' *n.* [Colloq.] an eccentric person —*adj.* [Colloq.] eccentric
crack'up' *n.* 1 a crash 2 [Colloq.] a physical or mental breakdown
-cra·cy (krə sē) ‖< Gr *kratos,* rule‖ *combining form* a (specified) type of government; rule by *[autocracy]*
cra·dle (krād''l) *n.* ‖OE *cradol*‖ 1 a baby's small bed, usually on rockers 2 infancy 3 the place of a thing's beginning 4 anything like a cradle —*vt.* **-dled, -dling** 1 to place, rock, or hold in or as in a cradle 2 to take care of in infancy
cra'dle·song' *n.* a lullaby
craft (kraft) *n.* ‖OE *cræft,* power‖ 1 a special skill or art 2 an occupation requiring special skill 3 the members of a skilled trade 4 guile; slyness 5 *pl.* **craft** a boat, ship, or aircraft
crafts·man (krafts'mən) *n., pl.* **-men** a skilled worker; artisan —**crafts'man·ship'** *n.*
craft'y *adj.* **-i·er, -i·est** ‖ME *crafti,* sly‖ subtly deceitful; sly; cunning —**craft'i·ly** *adv.* —**craft'i·ness** *n.*
crag (krag) *n.* ‖< Celt‖ a steep, rugged rock rising from a rock mass —**crag'gy, -gi·er, -gi·est,** *adj.*
cram (kram) *vt.* **crammed, cram'ming** ‖OE *crammian*‖ 1 to pack full or too full 2 to stuff; force 3 to feed to excess —*vi.* 1 to eat too much or too quickly 2 to study a subject in a hurried, intensive way, as for an examination
cramp (kramp) *n.* ‖< OFr *crampe,* bent‖ 1 a sudden, painful, involuntary contraction of muscles from chill, strain, etc. 2 [*usually pl.*] abdominal or uterine spasms and pain —*vt.* 1 to cause a cramp or cramps in 2 ‖< MDu *krampe,* bent in‖ to hamper; restrain
cramped (krampt) *adj.* 1 confined or restricted 2 irregular and crowded, as some handwriting

cran·ber·ry (kran′ber′ē, ·bər ē) ***n.,*** *pl.* **-ries** ‖< Du *kranebere*‖ 1 a firm, sour, edible, red berry, the fruit of an evergreen shrub 2 the shrub

crane (krān) ***n.*** ‖OE *cran*‖ 1 a large wading bird with very long legs and neck 2 a machine for lifting or moving heavy weights, using a movable projecting arm or a horizontal traveling beam —***vt., vi.*** **craned, cran′ing** to stretch (the neck)

cra·ni·um (krā′nē əm) ***n.,*** *pl.* **-ni·ums** or **-ni·a** (·ə) ‖< Gr *kranion*‖ the skull, esp. the part containing the brain —**cra′ni·al** ***adj.***

crank (kraŋk) ***n.*** ‖OE *cranc-*, something twisted‖ 1 a handle or arm bent at right angles and connected to a machine shaft to transmit motion 2 [Colloq.] an eccentric or irritable person —***vt.*** to start or operate by a crank

crank′case′ ***n.*** the metal casing that encloses the crankshaft of an internal-combustion engine

crank′shaft′ ***n.*** a shaft with one or more cranks for transmitting motion

crank′y ***adj.*** **-i·er, -i·est** 1 apt to operate poorly 2 irritable 3 eccentric —**crank′i·ly** ***adv.***

cran·ny (kran′ē) ***n.,*** *pl.* **-nies** ‖< VL *crena*, a notch‖ a crevice; crack

crap (krap) ***n.*** ‖< ML *crappa*, chaff‖ [Vulgar] 1 nonsense 2 junk; trash —**crap′py, -pi·er, -pi·est,** ***adj.***

crape (krāp) ***n.*** 1 CREPE (sense 1) 2 a piece of black crepe as a sign of mourning

crap·pie (krap′ē) ***n.*** a small North American sunfish

craps (kraps) ***n.pl.*** ‖Fr *crabs*‖ a gambling game played with two dice

crap·shoot·er (krap′sho͞ot′ər) ***n.*** a gambler at craps

crash (krash) ***vi.*** ‖ME‖ 1 to fall, collide, or break with a loud noise 2 to collapse; fail —***vt.*** 1 to cause (a car, airplane, etc.) to crash 2 to force with or as with a crashing noise: with *in, out, through*, etc. 3 [Colloq.] to get into (a party, etc.) without an invitation, etc. —***n.*** 1 a loud, sudden noise 2 a crashing 3 a sudden collapse, as of business —***adj.*** [Colloq.] using all possible resources, effort, and speed [a *crash* program to build roads]

crash′-land′ ***vt., vi.*** to bring (an airplane) down in a forced landing, esp. without use of the landing gear —**crash landing**

crash pad [Slang] a place to live or sleep temporarily

crass (kras) ***adj.*** ‖L *crassus*, thick‖ tasteless, insensitive, materialistic —**crass′ly** ***adv.***

-crat (krat) ‖< Gr *kratos*, rule‖ *combining form* member or supporter of (a specified kind of) government

crate (krāt) ***n.*** ‖L *cratis*, wickerwork‖ a packing case made of slats of wood —***vt.*** **crat′ed, crat′ing** to pack in a crate

cra·ter (krāt′ər) ***n.*** ‖< Gr *kratēr*, mixing bowl‖ 1 a bowl-shaped cavity, as at the mouth of a volcano 2 a pit made by an exploding bomb, etc.

cra·vat (krə vat′) ***n.*** ‖< Fr‖ a necktie

crave (krāv) ***vt.*** **craved, crav′ing** ‖OE *crafian*‖ 1 to ask for earnestly; beg 2 to long for eagerly

cra·ven (krā′vən) ***adj.*** ‖< L *crepare*, to rattle‖ cowardly —***n.*** a coward —**cra′ven·ly** ***adv.*** —**cra′ven·ness** ***n.***

crav·ing (krā′viŋ) ***n.*** an intense and prolonged desire, as for affection or for a food or drug

craw (krô) ***n.*** ‖ME *craue*‖ 1 the crop of a bird 2 the stomach

craw·fish (krô′fish′) ***n.,*** *pl.* **-fish′** or (for different species) **-fish′es** crayfish

crawl (krôl) ***vi.*** ‖< ON *krafla*‖ 1 to move slowly by dragging the body along the ground 2 to go on hands and knees; creep 3 to move slowly 4 to move or act in a servile manner 5 to swarm (*with* crawling things) —***n.*** 1 a slow movement 2 an overarm swimming stroke

crawl space an unfinished space, as under a floor, allowing access to wiring, plumbing, etc.

crawl′y ***adj.*** **-i·er, -i·est** CREEPY

cray·fish (krā′fish′) ***n.,*** *pl.* **-fish′** or (for different species) **-fish′es** ‖< OHG *krebiz*‖ a freshwater crustacean somewhat like a little lobster

cray·on (krā′ən, ·än′) ***n.*** ‖Fr, pencil < L *creta*, chalk‖ 1 a small stick of chalk, charcoal, or colored wax, used for drawing, coloring, or writing 2 a drawing made with crayons —***vt.*** to draw or color with crayons

craze (krāz) ***vt., vi.*** **crazed, craz′ing** ‖ME *crasen*, to crack‖ to make or become insane —***n.*** a fad

cra·zy (krā′zē) ***adj.*** **-zi·er, -zi·est** ‖< prec.‖ 1 unsound of mind; insane 2 [Colloq.] foolish; not sensible 3 [Colloq.] very enthusiastic or eager —***interj.*** [Slang] an exclamation of pleasure, etc. —***n.,*** *pl.* **-zies** [Slang] a crazy person —**cra′zi·ly** ***adv.*** —**cra′zi·ness** ***n.***

crazy bone FUNNY BONE

crazy quilt a patchwork quilt with no regular design

creak (krēk) ***vi., vt.*** ‖echoic‖ to make, cause to make, or move with a harsh, squeaking sound —***n.*** such a sound —**creak′y, -i·er, -i·est,** ***adj.*** —**creak′i·ly** ***adv.*** —**creak′i·ness** ***n.***

cream (krēm) ***n.*** ‖< OFr‖ 1 the oily, yellowish part of milk 2 a cosmetic, emulsion, or food with a creamy consistency 3 the best part 4 yellowish white —***adj.*** made of or with cream —***vt.*** 1 to add cream to 2 to beat into a creamy consistency 3 [Slang] *a*) to beat or defeat soundly *b*) to hurt, etc., as by striking with great force —**cream of** creamed purée of —**cream′y, -i·er, -i·est,** ***adj.*** —**cream′·i·ness** ***n.***

cream cheese a soft, white cheese made of cream or of milk and cream

cream′er ***n.*** 1 a pitcher for cream 2 a nondairy substance used in place of cream

cream′er·y (·ər ē) ***n.,*** *pl.* **-ies** a place where dairy products are processed or sold

cream of tartar a white substance used in baking powder, medicine, etc.

crease (krēs) ***n.*** ‖< ME *creste*, crest‖ 1 a line made by folding and pressing 2 a fold or wrinkle —***vt.*** **creased, creas′ing** 1 to make a crease in 2 to wrinkle —***vi.*** to become creased

cre·ate (krē āt′) ***vt.*** **-at′ed, -at′ing** ‖< L

creare ‖ 1 to cause to come into existence; make; originate 2 to bring about; give rise to; cause

cre·a'tion (-ā'shən) ***n.*** 1 a creating or being created 2 the universe 3 anything created —**the Creation** God's creating of the world

cre·a'tive (-āt'iv) ***adj.*** 1 creating or able to create 2 inventive 3 stimulating the imagination —**cre·a'tive·ly** ***adv.*** —**cre·a'tive·ness** ***n.*** —**cre'a·tiv'i·ty** (-ā tiv'ə tē) ***n.***

cre·a'tor (-āt'ər) ***n.*** ‖ L ‖ one who creates —[C-] God

crea·ture (krē'chər) ***n.*** ‖ < L *creatura* ‖ a living being, animal or human

crèche (kresh, krāsh) ***n.*** ‖ Fr ‖ a display of the stable scene of Jesus' birth

cre·dence (krēd''ns) ***n.*** ‖ < L *credere*, believe ‖ belief, esp. in the reports or testimony of another

cre·den·tial (kri den'shəl) ***n.*** ‖ see prec. ‖ [*usually pl.*] a letter or certificate showing one's right to a certain position or authority

cre·den·za (kri den'zə) ***n.*** ‖ It ‖ a type of buffet or sideboard

credibility gap 1 a disparity between what is said and the facts 2 the inability to have one's truthfulness or honesty accepted

cred·i·ble (kred'ə bəl) ***adj.*** ‖ < L *credere*, believe ‖ that can be believed; reliable —**cred'i·bil'i·ty** ***n.*** —**cred'i·bly** ***adv.***

cred·it (kred'it) ***n.*** ‖ < L *credere*, believe ‖ 1 belief; confidence 2 favorable reputation 3 praise or approval 4 a person or thing bringing approval or honor 5 *a*) acknowledgment of work done *b*) [*pl.*] a list of such acknowledgments in a movie, book, etc. 6 a sum available to one, as in a bank account 7 the entry, in an account, of payment on a debt 8 trust in one's ability to meet payments when due 9 the time allowed for payment 10 a completed unit of study in a school —***vt.*** 1 to believe; trust 2 to give credit to or commendation for 3 to give credit in a bank account, etc. —**do credit to** to bring honor to —**on credit** agreeing to pay later

cred'it·a·ble ***adj.*** deserving some credit or praise —**cred'it·a·bly** ***adv.***

credit card a card entitling one to charge purchases, etc. at certain businesses

cred'i·tor (-it ər) ***n.*** one to whom money is owed

credit union a cooperative association for pooling savings of members and making low-interest loans to them

cre·do (krē'dō', krā'-) ***n.***, *pl.* **-dos'** ‖ L, I believe ‖ a creed

cred·u·lous (krej'oo ləs, -ə ləs) ***adj.*** ‖ < L *credere*, believe ‖ tending to believe too readily —**cre·du·li·ty** (krə dōō'lə tē, -dyōō-) ***n.*** —**cred'u·lous·ly** ***adv.***

creed (krēd) ***n.*** ‖ < L *credo*, I believe ‖ 1 a brief statement of religious belief, esp. one accepted as authoritative by a church 2 any statement of belief, principles, etc.

creek (krēk, krik) ***n.*** ‖ < ON *kriki*, a bend, winding ‖ a small stream —**up the creek** [Slang] in trouble

creel (krēl) ***n.*** ‖ < L *cratis*, wickerwork ‖ a wicker basket for holding fish

creep (krēp) ***vi.*** **crept, creep'ing** ‖ OE *creopan* ‖ 1 to move with the body close to the ground, as on hands and knees 2 to move slowly or stealthily 3 to grow along the ground or a wall, as ivy —***n.*** 1 the act of creeping 2 [Slang] an annoying or disgusting person —**make one's flesh creep** to give one a feeling of fear, disgust, etc. —**the creeps** [Colloq.] a feeling of fear, disgust, etc. —**creep'er** ***n.***

creep'y ***adj.*** **-i·er, -i·est** having or causing a feeling of fear or disgust —**creep'i·ly** ***adv.*** —**creep'i·ness** ***n.***

cre·mains (krē mānz') ***n.pl.*** the ashes remaining after cremation

cre·mate (krē'māt', kri māt') ***vt.*** **-mat'ed, -mat'ing** ‖ < L *cremare* ‖ to burn (a dead body) to ashes —**cre·ma'tion** ***n.***

cre·ma·to·ry (krē'mə tôr'ē, krem'ə-) ***n.***, *pl.* **-ries** a furnace for cremating Also **cre'ma·to'ri·um** (-ē əm), *pl.* **-ri·ums, -ri·a** (-ə), or **-ries** —***adj.*** of or for cremation

crème de menthe (krem' də mänt', mint'; krēm') ‖ Fr, cream of mint ‖ a sweet, mint flavored liqueur

crème fraîche (krem' fresh') ‖ Fr, fresh cream ‖ slightly fermented high-fat cream, served with fresh fruit, etc. and used in sauces

cren·el·ate or **cren·el·late** (kren'əl āt') ***vt.*** **-el·at'ed** or **-el·lat'ed, -el·at'ing** or **-el·lat'ing** ‖ < VL *crena*, a notch ‖ to furnish with battlements or with squared notches —**cren'el·a'tion** or **cren'el·la'tion** ***n.***

Cre·ole or **cre·ole** (krē'ōl') ***n.*** ‖ < Fr < Port *crioulo*, native ‖ 1 a person descended from the original French settlers of Louisiana 2 a person of mixed Creole and black descent 3 [c-] a language that develops when different languages remain in contact with each other —***adj.*** [*usually* **c-**] prepared with sautéed tomatoes, green peppers, onions, spices, etc.

cre·o·sote (krē'ə sōt') ***n.*** ‖ < Gr *kreas*, flesh + *sōzein*, to save ‖ an oily liquid with a pungent odor, distilled from wood tar or coal tar: used as an antiseptic and as a wood preservative

crepe or **crêpe** (krāp; *for 5, also* krep) ***n.*** ‖ < Fr < L *crispus*, curly ‖ 1 a thin, crinkled cloth of silk, rayon, wool, etc. 2 CRAPE (sense 2) 3 wrinkled soft rubber: also **crepe rubber** 4 thin paper like crepe: also **crepe paper** 5 a thin pancake, rolled and filled

crêpes su·zette (krāp' sōō zet') ‖ Fr ‖ crêpes rolled in a hot, orange-flavored sauce and served in flaming brandy

crept (krept) ***vi.*** *pt. & pp. of* CREEP

cre·scen·do (kri shen'dō') ***adj.***, ***adv.*** ‖ It < L *crescere*, grow ‖ *Music* gradually increasing in loudness —***n.***, *pl.* **-dos'** a gradual increase in loudness, force, etc.

cres·cent (kres'ənt) ***n.*** ‖ < L *crescere*, grow ‖ 1 a phase of a planet or a moon, when it appears to have one concave edge and one convex edge 2 anything shaped like this —***adj.*** shaped like a crescent

cress (kres) ***n.*** ‖ OE *cressa* ‖ a plant, as watercress, whose leaves are used in salads

crest (krest) ***n.*** ‖ < L *crista* ‖ 1 any growth on the head of an animal, as a comb or tuft 2 a heraldic device placed on seals, silverware, etc. 3 the top line or surface; summit 4 the highest point, level, degree, etc. —***vi.*** to form or reach a crest —**crest·ed** (kres'tid) ***adj.***

crest'fall'en *adj.* dejected, disheartened, or humbled

Cre·ta·ceous (kri tā'shəs, krē-) *adj.* ⟦< L *creta,* chalk⟧ of the latest period of the Mesozoic Era, marked by the dying out of dinosaurs, the rise of mammals and flowering plants, and the depositing of chalk beds

Crete (krēt) Greek island in the E Mediterranean —**Cre·tan** (krēt''n) *adj., n.*

cre·tonne (krē tän', krē'tän') *n.* ⟦Fr, after *Creton,* village in Normandy⟧ a heavy, printed cotton or linen cloth, used for curtains, slipcovers, etc.

cre·vasse (krə vas') *n.* ⟦Fr⟧ a deep crack, esp. in a glacier

crev·ice (krev'is) *n.* ⟦< L *crepare,* to rattle⟧ a narrow opening caused by a crack or split; fissure

crew[1] (kroo) *n.* ⟦< L *crescere,* grow⟧ a group of people working together /a road crew/ —**crew'man,** *pl.* **-men,** *n.*

crew[2] (kroo) *vi.* [Chiefly Brit.] *alt. pt. of* CROW[2] (sense 1)

crew cut a man's haircut in which the hair is cropped close to the head

crew·el (kroo'əl) *n.* ⟦ME *crule*⟧ a loosely twisted, worsted yarn used in embroidery —**crew'el·work'** *n.*

crib (krib) *n.* ⟦OE, ox stall⟧ **1** a rack or box for fodder **2** a small bed with high sides, for a baby **3** an enclosure for storing grain **4** an underwater structure serving as a pier, water intake, etc. **5** [Colloq.] a translation or other aid used dishonestly in doing schoolwork —*vt.* **cribbed, crib'bing 1** to confine **2** to furnish with a crib **3** [Colloq.] to plagiarize —*vi.* [Colloq.] to do schoolwork dishonestly

crib·bage (krib'ij) *n.* a card game in which the object is to form combinations for points

crib death SUDDEN INFANT DEATH SYNDROME

crick[1] (krik) *n.* ⟦< ON *kriki,* bend⟧ a painful cramp in the neck, back, etc.

crick[2] (krik) *n.* [Dial.] CREEK

crick·et[1] (krik'it) *n.* ⟦< OFr *criquer,* to creak⟧ a leaping insect similar to a grasshopper

crick·et[2] (krik'it) *n.* ⟦OFr *criquet,* a bat⟧ an outdoor game played by two teams of eleven players each, using a ball, bats, and wickets

cried (krīd) *vi., vt. pt. & pp. of* CRY

cri·er (krī'ər) *n.* **1** one who cries **2** one who shouts out announcements, news, etc.

crime (krīm) *n.* ⟦< L *crimen,* offense⟧ **1** an act committed or omitted in violation of a law **2** a sin

Cri·me·a (krī mē'ə) peninsula in SW U.S.S.R., extending into the Black Sea —**Cri·me'an** *adj.*

crim·i·nal (krim'ə nəl) *adj.* **1** having the nature of crime **2** relating to or guilty of crime —*n.* a person guilty of a crime —**crim'i·nal'i·ty** (-nal'ə tə) *n.* —**crim'i·nal·ly** *adv.*

crim'i·nol'o·gy (-näl'ə jē) *n.* the scientific study of crime and criminals —**crim'i·nol'o·gist** *n.*

crimp (krimp) *vt.* ⟦< MDu *crimpen,* to wrinkle⟧ **1** to press into narrow folds; pleat **2** to curl (hair) —*n.* **1** a crimping **2** anything crimped —**put a crimp in** [Colloq.] to hinder

crim·son (krim'zən, -sən) *n.* ⟦< Ar *qirmiz*⟧ deep red —*adj.* deep-red —*vt., vi.* to make or become crimson

cringe (krinj) *vi.* **cringed, cring'ing** ⟦< OE *cringan,* to fall (in battle)⟧ **1** to draw back, crouch, etc., as when afraid; cower **2** to fawn

crin·kle (kriŋ'kəl) *vi., vt.* **-kled, -kling** ⟦see prec.⟧ **1** to wrinkle **2** to rustle, as crushed paper —**crin'kly, -kli·er, -kli·est,** *adj.*

crin·o·line (krin'ə lin') *n.* ⟦Fr < It < *crino,* horsehair + *lino,* linen⟧ **1** a coarse, stiff cloth used as a lining in garments **2** HOOP SKIRT

crip·ple (krip'əl) *n.* ⟦< OE *creopan,* to creep⟧ one who is lame or otherwise disabled —*vt.* **-pled, -pling 1** to lame **2** to disable; impair

cri·sis (krī'sis) *n., pl.* **-ses'** (-sēz') ⟦L < Gr *krinein,* to separate⟧ **1** the turning point of a disease for better or worse **2** a decisive or crucial time, stage, or event

crisp (krisp) *adj.* ⟦< L *crispus,* curly⟧ **1** brittle; easily crumbled **2** fresh and firm **3** sharp and clear **4** fresh and invigorating **5** curled and wiry Also **crisp'y** —**crisp'ly** *adv.* —**crisp'ness** *n.*

criss·cross (kris'krôs') *n.* ⟦ME *Christcros,* Christ's cross⟧ a mark or pattern made of crossed lines —*adj.* marked by crossing lines —*vt.* to mark with crossing lines —*vi.* to move crosswise —*adv.* **1** crosswise **2** awry

cri·te·ri·on (krī tir'ē ən) *n., pl.* **-ri·a** (-ē ə) or **-ri·ons** ⟦< Gr *kritēs,* judge⟧ a standard, rule, or test by which something can be judged

crit·ic (krit'ik) *n.* ⟦< Gr *krinein,* discern⟧ **1** one who judges books, music, plays, etc., as for a newspaper **2** one who finds fault

crit'i·cal (-i kəl) *adj.* **1** tending to find fault **2** of critics or criticism **3** of or forming a crisis; decisive —**crit'i·cal·ly** *adv.*

crit'i·cism' (-ə siz'əm) *n.* **1** the act of making judgments, esp. of literary or artistic work **2** a review, article, etc. expressing such judgment **3** censure **4** the art, principles, or methods of critics

crit'i·cize' (-ə sīz') *vi., vt.* **-cized', -ciz'ing 1** to analyze and judge as a critic **2** to find fault (with) —**crit'i·ciz'a·ble** *adj.* —**crit'i·ciz'er** *n.*

cri·tique (kri tēk') *n.* ⟦Fr⟧ a critical analysis or review —*vt., vi.* **-tiqued', -tiqu'ing** to criticize (a subject, art work, etc.)

crit·ter (krit'ər) *n. dial. var. of* CREATURE

croak (krōk) *vi.* ⟦echoic⟧ **1** to make a deep, hoarse sound, as a frog does **2** [Slang] to die —*vt.* to utter in deep, hoarse tones —*n.* a croaking sound

Cro·a·tia (krō ā'shə) constituent republic of Yugoslavia —**Cro·a'tian** *adj., n.*

cro·chet (krō shā') *n.* ⟦Fr, small hook⟧ needlework done with one hooked needle —*vi., vt.* **-cheted'** (-shād'), **-chet'ing** to do, or make by, crochet —**cro·chet'er** (-shā'ər) *n.*

crock (kräk) *n.* ⟦OE *crocca*⟧ an earthenware pot or jar —**crock'er·y** *n.*

crocked (kräkt) *adj.* ⟦< *crock,* to disable⟧ [Slang] drunk

CROCODILE

croc·o·dile (kräk′ə dīl′) ***n.*** ⟦< Gr *krokodilos,* lizard⟧ a large, lizardlike reptile of tropical streams, having a long, narrow head with massive jaws

cro·cus (krō′kəs) ***n.,*** *pl.* **-cus·es** or **-ci′** (-sī′) ⟦< Gr *krokos,* saffron⟧ a spring-blooming plant of the iris family, with fleshy underground stems and a yellow, purple, or white flower

Croe·sus (krē′səs) a wealthy king of ancient times (6th c. B.C.) **—*n.*** a very rich man

crois·sant (kroo̅ sänt′, krə sänt′) ***n.*** ⟦Fr, crescent⟧ a crescent-shaped, flaky bread roll

Cro-Mag·non (krō mag′nən) ***adj.*** ⟦after *Cro-Magnon* cave in France⟧ of a Stone Age type of tall human of the European continent

Crom·well (kräm′wel), **Ol·i·ver** (äl′ə vər) 1599-1658; Eng. revolutionary leader & head (Lord Protector) of England (1653-58)

crone (krōn) ***n.*** ⟦< MDu *kronje,* old ewe⟧ an ugly, withered old woman

cro·ny (krō′nē) ***n.,*** *pl.* **-nies** ⟦< Gr *chronos,* time⟧ a close friend

crook (krook) ***n.*** ⟦< ON *krōkr,* hook⟧ **1** a hooked or curved staff, etc.; hook **2** a bend or curve **3** [Colloq.] a swindler **—*vt., vi.*** **crooked** (krookt), **crook′ing** to bend or curve

crook·ed (krookt; *for 2 & 3* krook′id) ***adj.*** **1** having a crook **2** not straight; bent **3** dishonest **—crook′ed·ly *adv.*** **—crook′ed·ness *n.***

crook′neck′ *n.* a squash with a long, curved neck

croon (kroo̅n) ***vi., vt.*** ⟦ME *cronen*⟧ to sing or hum in a low, gentle tone **—*n.*** a low, gentle singing or humming **—croon′er *n.***

crop (kräp) ***n.*** ⟦OE *croppa,* a cluster⟧ **1** a saclike part of a bird's gullet, in which food is stored before digestion **2** any agricultural product, growing or harvested **3** the yield of any product in one season or place **4** a group **5** the handle of a whip **6** a riding whip **7** hair cut close to the head **—*vt.*** **cropped, crop′ping 1** to cut or bite off the tops or ends of **2** to reap **3** to cut short **—crop out** (or **up**) to appear unexpectedly

crop′-dust′ing *n.* the spraying of crops with pesticides from an airplane **—crop′-dust′ *vi., vt.***

crop′per *n.* **1** one that crops **2** a sharecropper **—come a cropper** [Colloq.] to come to ruin; fail

cro·quet (krō kā′) ***n.*** ⟦Fr, dial. form of *crochet,* small hook⟧ an outdoor game in which the players use mallets to drive a ball through hoops in the ground

cro·quette (krō ket′) ***n.*** ⟦Fr < *croquer,* to crunch⟧ a small mass of meat, fish, etc. fried in deep fat

cro·sier (krō′zhər) ***n.*** ⟦< OFr *croce*⟧ the staff carried by a bishop or abbot

cross (krôs) ***n.*** ⟦< L *crux*⟧ **1** an upright post with a bar across it, on which the ancient Romans executed people **2** a representation of this as a symbol of the crucifixion of Jesus, hence of Christianity **3** any trouble or affliction **4** any design or mark made by two intersecting lines, bars, etc. **5** a crossing of varieties or breeds **—*vt., vi.*** **1** to make the sign of the cross (upon) **2** to place or lie across or crosswise **3** to intersect **4** to draw a line or lines across **5** to go or extend across **6** to meet and pass (each other) **7** to oppose **8** to interbreed (animals or plants) **—*adj.*** **1** lying or passing across **2** contrary; opposed **3** cranky; irritable **4** of mixed variety or breed **—cross off** (or **out**) to cancel as by drawing lines across **—cross one's mind** to come suddenly to one's mind **—cross one's path** to meet one **—cross′ly *adv.***

cross′bar′ *n.* a bar, line, or stripe placed crosswise

cross′beam′ *n.* any transverse beam in a structure

cross′bones′ *n.* a representation of two bones placed across each other, under a skull, used to symbolize death

cross′bow′ (-bō′) ***n.*** a weapon consisting of a bow set transversely on a wooden stock **—cross′bow′man,** *pl.* **-men, *n.***

cross′breed′ *vt., vi.* **-bred′** (-bred′), **-breed′ing** HYBRIDIZE **—*n.*** HYBRID (sense 1)

cross′-coun′try *adj., adv.* across open country or fields, as a race

cross′cut′ saw a saw designed to cut across the grain of wood

cross′-ex·am′ine (-ig zam′in) ***vt., vi.*** **-ined′, -in′ing** *Law* to question (a witness called by the opposing side) in order to challenge the witness's previous testimony **—cross′-ex·am′i·na′tion *n.***

cross′-eye′ *n.* an abnormal condition in which the eyes are turned toward each other **—cross′-eyed′** (-īd′) ***adj.***

cross′hatch′ (-hach′) ***vt., vi.*** to shade (a drawing) with two sets of parallel lines that cross each other

cross′ing *n.* **1** the act of passing across, interbreeding, etc. **2** an intersection, as of streets **3** a place where a street, etc. may be crossed

cross′piece′ *n.* a piece lying across another

cross′-pol′li·nate′ *vt., vi.* **-nat′ed, -nat′ing** to transfer pollen from the anther of (a flower) to the stigma of (a genetically different flower) **—cross′-pol′li·na′tion *n.***

cross′-pur′pose *n.* a contrary purpose **—at cross-purposes** having a misunderstanding as to each other's purposes

cross′-ref′er·ence *n.* a reference from one part of a book, etc. to another **—*vt.*** **-enced, -enc·ing** to provide (an index, etc.) with cross-references **—cross′-re·fer′ *vt., vi.***

cross′road′ *n.* **1** a road that crosses another **2** [*usually pl., often with sing. v.*] *a)* the place where roads intersect *b)* any center of activity, etc. *c)* a time of important changes or major decisions

cross section 1 *a)* a cutting through something *b)* a piece so cut off *c)* a representation of this **2** a representative part of a whole **—cross′-sec′tion *vt.***

cross′-town′ *adj.* going across a city [a *cross-town* bus]

cross′walk′ *n.* a lane marked off for pedestrians to use in crossing a street

cross′wise′ (-wīz′) *adv.* so as to cross; across Also **cross′ways′** (-wāz′)

cross′word′ puzzle an arrangement of numbered squares to be filled in with the letters of words whose synonyms and definitions are given as clues

crotch (kräch) *n.* ‖ ME *crucche,* crutch ‖ **1** a forked place, as on a tree **2** the place where the legs fork from the human body

crotch·et (kräch′it) *n.* ‖ < OFr *croc,* a hook ‖ a peculiar whim or stubborn notion —**crotch′et·y** (-ē) *adj.*

crouch (krouch) *vi.* ‖ < OFr *croc,* a hook ‖ **1** to stoop or bend low **2** to cringe —*n.* a crouching position

croup (kro͞op) *n.* ‖ < obs. *croup,* speak hoarsely ‖ an inflammation of the respiratory passages, with labored breathing, hoarse coughing, etc.

crou·pi·er (kro͞o′pē ā′, -ər) *n.* ‖ Fr ‖ one in charge of a gambling table

crou·ton (kro͞o′tän′, kro͞o tän′) *n.* ‖ Fr < *croûte,* a crust ‖ a small, piece of toasted bread put in soup or a salad

crow¹ (krō) *n.* ‖ OE *crawa* ‖ a large, glossy-black bird with a harsh call —**as the crow flies** in a straight, direct line —**eat crow** [Colloq.] to admit an error

crow² (krō) *vi.* **crowed** or, for 1, [Chiefly Brit.] **crew** (kro͞o), **crowed, crow′ing** ‖ OE *crawan* ‖ **1** to make the shrill cry of a rooster **2** to boast in triumph **3** to make a sound of pleasure —*n.* a crowing sound

crow′bar′ *n.* a long metal bar used as a lever for prying, etc.

crowd (kroud) *vi.* ‖ OE *crudan* ‖ **1** to push one's way (*into*) **2** to throng —*vt.* **1** to press or push **2** to fill too full; cram —*n.* **1** a large number of people or things grouped closely **2** the common people; the masses **3** [Colloq.] a set; clique —**crowd′ed** *adj.*

crow′foot′ (krō′-) *n., pl.* **-foots′** or **-feet′** a plant of the buttercup family, with leaves resembling a crow's foot

crown (kroun) *n.* ‖ < Gr *korōnē,* wreath ‖ **1** a wreath worn on the head in victory **2** a reward; honor **3** a monarch's headdress **4** [*often* **C-**] *a)* the power of a monarch *b)* the monarch **5** a British coin equal to 25 (new) pence: no longer minted **6** the top part, as of the head **7** the highest quality, state, etc. of anything **8** *a)* the part of a tooth outside the gum *b)* an artificial substitute for this —*vt.* **1** to put a crown on **2** to make (a person) a monarch **3** to honor **4** to be the highest part of **5** to complete successfully

crown prince the male heir apparent to a throne —**crown princess**

crow's-foot (krōz′fo͝ot′) *n., pl.* **-feet′** any of the wrinkles that often develop at the outer corners of the eyes of adults

crow's′-nest′ (-nest′) *n.* a lookout's platform high on a ship's mast

cro·zier (krō′zhər) *n.* CROSIER

CRT (sē′är′tē′) *n.* cathode-ray tube

cru·cial (kro͞o′shəl) *adj.* ‖ < L *crux,* a cross ‖ **1** decisive; critical **2** severe; difficult —**cru′cial·ly** *adv.*

cru·ci·ble (kro͞o′sə bəl) *n.* ‖ ML *crucibulum,* lamp ‖ **1** a heat-resistant container for melting ores, metals, etc. **2** a severe trial

cru·ci·fix (kro͞o′sə fiks′) *n.* ‖ < L *crux,* a cross + *figere,* fasten ‖ a cross with the figure of the crucified Jesus Christ on it

cru′ci·fix′ion (-fik′shən) *n.* **1** a crucifying **2** [**C-**] the crucifying of Jesus, or a representation of this

cru′ci·form′ *adj.* formed in a cross

cru′ci·fy′ (-fī′) *vt.* **-fied′, -fy′ing** ‖ see CRUCIFIX ‖ **1** to execute by nailing to a cross and leaving to die **2** to be very cruel to; torment

crude (kro͞od) *adj.* **crud′er, crud′est** ‖ < L *crudus,* raw ‖ **1** in a raw or natural condition **2** lacking grace, taste, etc. **3** roughly made —**crude′ly** *adv.* —**crude′ness** *n.* —**cru·di·ty** (kro͞o′də tē) *n.*

cru·di·tés (kro͞o′də tā′) *n.pl.* ‖ Fr, raw things ‖ raw vegetables cut up and served as hors d'oeuvres, usually with a dip

cru·el (kro͞o′əl) *adj.* ‖ see CRUDE ‖ causing pain and suffering; pitiless —**cru′el·ly** *adv.* —**cru′el·ty,** *pl.* **-ties,** *n.*

cru·et (kro͞o′it) *n.* ‖ < OFr *crue,* earthen pot ‖ a small glass bottle to hold vinegar, oil, etc. for the table

cruise (kro͞oz) *vi.* **cruised, cruis′ing** ‖ < Du *kruisen,* to cross ‖ **1** to sail or ride about from place to place, as for pleasure or in search of something **2** to move at the most efficient speed for sustained travel **3** to operate at a predetermined speed by use of a regulating mechanism (**cruise control**) —*vt.* to sail or journey over or about —*n.* a cruising voyage

cruise missile a long-range, jet-propelled winged missile that can be launched from an airplane, submarine, ship, etc. and guided by remote control

cruis′er *n.* **1** anything that cruises, as a police car **2** a fast warship smaller than a battleship

crul·ler (krul′ər) *n.* ‖ Du < *krullen,* to curl ‖ a kind of twisted doughnut

crumb (krum) *n.* ‖ < OE *cruma,* scraping from bread crust ‖ **1** a small piece broken off, as of bread **2** any bit or scrap [*crumbs of knowledge*] —*vt. Cooking* to cover with crumbs —**crumb·y** (krum′ē), **-i·er, -i·est,** *adj.*

crum·ble (krum′bəl) *vt.* **-bled, -bling** ‖ < prec. ‖ to break into crumbs —*vi.* to fall to pieces —**crum′bly** (-blē), **-bli·er, -bli·est,** *adj.*

crum·my (krum′ē) *adj.* **-mi·er, -mi·est** [Slang] shabby, mean, etc.

crum·pet (krum′pit) *n.* ‖ < OE *crump,* twisted ‖ a batter cake baked on a griddle

crum·ple (krum′pəl) *vt.* **-pled, -pling** ‖ < MDu *crimpen,* to wrinkle ‖ to crush together into wrinkles

crunch (krunch) *vi., vt.* ‖ echoic ‖ to chew, press, grind, etc. with a noisy, crackling sound —*n.* **1** the act or sound of crunching **2** [Slang] a showdown or tight situation —**crunch′y, -i·er, -i·est,** *adj.*

crup·per (krup′ər, kro͝op′-) *n.* ‖ < OFr *crope,* rump ‖ a leather strap attached to a saddle or harness and passed under a horse's tail

cru·sade (kro͞o sād′) *n.* ‖ ult. < L *crux,* a cross ‖ **1** [*sometimes* **C-**] any of the Christian military expeditions (11th-13th c.) to recover the Holy Land from the Muslims **2**

vigorous, concerted action for some cause, or against some abuse —*vi.* -sad′ed, -sad′-ing to engage in a crusade —**cru·sad′er** *n.*

cruse (kro͞os, kro͞oz) *n.* ‖OE‖ a small con tainer for water, oil, etc.

crush (krush) *vt.* ‖< OFr *croisir*, to crash, break‖ **1** to press with force so as to break or put out of shape **2** to grind or pound into small bits **3** to subdue; overwhelm **4** to extract by squeezing —*vi.* to become crushed —*n.* **1** a crushing; severe pressure **2** a crowded mass of people **3** [Colloq.] an infatuation —**crush′er** *n.*

crust (krust) *n.* ‖< L *crusta*‖ **1** the hard, outer part of bread **2** any dry, hard piece of bread **3** the pastry shell of a pie **4** any hard surface layer, as of snow **5** [Slang] insolence **6** *Geol.* the solid, outer layer of the earth —*vt., vi.* to cover or become covered with a crust —**crust′y, -i·er, -i·est,** *adj.*

crus·ta·cean (krus tā′shən) *n.* ‖see prec.‖ any of a class of arthropods, including shrimps, crabs, lobsters, etc. that have a hard outer shell

crutch (kruch) *n.* ‖< OE *crycce*, staff‖ **1** a staff with a top crosspiece that fits under the armpit, used to aid the lame in walking **2** any prop or support

crux (kruks) *n.* ‖L, a cross‖ **1** a difficult problem **2** the essential or deciding point

cry (krī) *vi.* **cried, cry′ing** ‖< L *quiritare*, to wail‖ **1** to utter a loud sound, as in pain, fright, etc. **2** to sob and shed tears; weep **3** to plead or clamor (*for*) **4** to utter its charac teristic call: said of an animal —*vt.* **1** to utter loudly; shout **2** to call out (wares for sale, etc.) —*n., pl.* **cries** **1** a loud vocal sound; call; shout **2** a plea; appeal **3** a fit of weeping **4** the characteristic call of an animal —**a far cry** a great distance or differ ence

cry′ba′by *n., pl.* **-bies** one who complains constantly, in a childish way

cry·o·gen·ics (krī′ō jen′iks, -ə-) *n.pl.* ‖< Gr *kryos*, cold + -GEN + -ICS‖ the science that deals with the production of very low tem peratures and their effect on the properties of matter

cry′o·sur′ger·y *n.* ‖< Gr *kryos*, cold + SURGERY‖ surgery that destroys tissues by freezing

crypt (kript) *n.* ‖< Gr *kryptein*, to hide‖ an underground vault, esp. one under a church, used for burial

cryp·tic (krip′tik) *adj.* **1** hidden or mysteri ous; baffling **2** obscure and curt —**cryp′ti·cal·ly** *adv.*

crypto- ‖see CRYPT‖ *combining form* **1** secret or hidden [*cryptogram*] **2** being such secretly and not publicly [*a crypto-*Fascist]

cryp·to·gram (krip′tō gram′, -tə-) *n.* ‖prec. + -GRAM‖ a message in code or cipher

cryp·tog·ra·phy (krip täg′rə fē) *n.* ‖CRYPTO- + -GRAPHY‖ the art of writing or deci phering messages in code —**cryp·tog′ra·pher** *n.*

crys·tal (kris′təl) *n.* ‖< Gr *krystallos*, crystal, ice < *kryos*, frost‖ **1** a clear, transparent quartz **2** *a*) a very clear, brilliant glass *b*) articles of such glass, as goblets **3** anything clear like crystal, as the covering over a watch face **4** a solidified form of a sub stance having plane faces arranged in a sym metrical, three-dimensional pattern —*adj.* **1** of crystal **2** like crystal; clear

crys′tal·line (-in) *adj.* **1** made of crystals **2** like crystal in clearness, structure, etc.

crys′tal·lize′ (-īz′) *vi., vt.* **-lized′, -liz′ing** **1** to become or cause to become crystalline **2** to take on or cause to take on a definite form —**crys′tal·li·za′tion** *n.*

cs. case(s)

Cs *Chem. symbol for* cesium

CST Central Standard Time

ct. **1** cent **2** court

cu. cubic

Cu ‖L *cuprum*‖ *Chem. symbol for* copper

cub (kub) *n.* ‖< ? Ir *cuib*, whelp‖ **1** a young fox, bear, lion, whale, etc. **2** a youth or novice

Cu·ba (kyo͞o′bə) country on an island in the West Indies, south of Fla.: 44,197 sq. mi.: pop. 10,221,000 —**Cu′ban** *adj., n.*

cub·by·hole (kub′ē hōl′) *n.* ‖< Brit dial. *cub*, little shed + HOLE‖ a small, enclosed space Also **cub′by**

cube (kyo͞ob) *n.* ‖< Gr *kybos*‖ **1** a solid with six equal, square sides **2** the product obtained by multiplying a given number by its square [the *cube* of 3 is 27] —*vt.* **cubed, cub′ing** **1** to obtain the cube of (a number) **2** to cut or shape into cubes —**cub′er** *n.*

cube root the quantity of which a given quantity is the cube [the *cube root* of 8 is 2]

cu·bic (kyo͞o′bik) *adj.* **1** having the shape of a cube: also **cu′bi·cal** **2** having three dimensions: a cubic foot is the volume of a cube one foot in length, width, and height

cu·bi·cle (kyo͞o′bi kəl) *n.* ‖< L *cubare*, lie down‖ a small compartment

cub·ism (kyo͞ob′iz′əm) *n.* a school of modern art characterized by the use of cubes and other geometric forms —**cub′ist** *n., adj.* —**cu·bis′tic** *adj.*

cu·bit (kyo͞o′bit) *n.* ‖< L *cubitum*‖ an ancient measure of length, about 18 to 22 inches

cuck·old (kuk′əld) *n.* ‖see fol.‖ a man whose wife has committed adultery —*vt.* to make a cuckold of —**cuck′old·ry** (-rē) *n.*

cuck·oo (ko͞o′ko͞o′, kook′o͞o) *n.* ‖< OFr *cucu*, echoic‖ **1** a gray-brown bird with a long, slender body: many species lay eggs in the nests of other birds **2** its call —*adj.* [Slang] crazy

cu·cum·ber (kyo͞o′kum′bər) *n.* ‖< L *cucumis*‖ a long, green-skinned fruit with firm, white flesh, used in salads or preserved as pickles

cud (kud) *n.* ‖OE *cudu*‖ a mouthful of swal lowed food regurgitated from the first stom ach of cattle and other ruminants and chewed again

cud·dle (kud′'l) *vt.* **-dled, -dling** ‖< ?‖ to embrace and fondle —*vi.* to lie close and snug

cud′dly (-lē) *adj.* **-dli·er, -dli·est** that invites cuddling; lovable Also **cud′dle·some** (-'l səm)

cudg·el (kuj′əl) *n.* ‖< OE *cycgel*‖ a short, thick stick or club —*vt.* **-eled** or **-elled, -el·ing** or **-el·ling** to beat with a cudgel

cue[1] (kyo͞o) *n.* ‖< *q* (? for L *quando*, when) found in 16th-c. plays‖ **1** a signal in dialogue, etc. for an actor's entrance or speech 2 any signal to do something 3 a hint —*vt.* **cued, cu'ing** or **cue'ing** to give a cue to

cue[2] (kyoo͞) *n.* ‖ var. of QUEUE ‖ a long, tapering rod used in billiards and pool to strike the ball (**cue ball**)

cuff (kuf) *n.* ‖ < ME *cuffe*, glove ‖ 1 a band at the wrist end of a sleeve 2 a turned-up fold at the bottom of a trouser leg 3 a slap —*vt.* to slap —**off the cuff** [Slang] in an offhand manner; extemporaneously —**on the cuff** [Slang] on credit

cuff link a pair of linked buttons, or any similar small device for fastening a shirt cuff

cui·sine (kwē zēn', kwi-) *n.* ‖ Fr < L *coquere*, to cook ‖ 1 a style of cooking or preparing food 2 the food prepared, as at a restaurant

cul-de-sac (kul'də sak') *n.*, *pl.* **-sacs'** ‖ Fr, bottom of a sack ‖ a blind alley

cu·li·nar·y (kyoo͞'lə ner'ē, kul'ə-) *adj.* ‖ < L *culina*, kitchen ‖ of cooking

cull (kul) *vt.* ‖ < L *colligere*, collect ‖ to pick out; select and gather —*n.* something picked out for rejection as not being up to standard

cul·mi·nate (kul'mə nāt') *vi.* **-nat'ed, -nat'ing** ‖ < L *culmen*, peak ‖ to reach its highest point or climax —**cul'mi·na'tion** *n.*

cu·lotte (kyoo͞ lät', koo͞-) *n.* ‖ Fr < L *culus*, posterior ‖ [*often pl.*] a woman's garment consisting of pants, usually knee-length, made to resemble a skirt

cul·pa·ble (kul'pə bəl) *adj.* ‖ < L *culpa*, fault ‖ deserving blame —**cul'pa·bil'i·ty** *n.* —**cul'pa·bly** *adv.*

cul·prit (kul'prit) *n.* ‖ < Anglo-Fr *culpable*, guilty + *prit*, ready (to prove) ‖ a person accused, or found guilty, of a crime

cult (kult) *n.* ‖ < L *cultus*, care, cultivation ‖ 1 a system of religious worship or ritual 2 devoted attachment to a person, principle, etc. 3 a sect —**cult'ism** *n.* —**cult'ist** *n.*

cul·ti·vate (kul'tə vāt') *vt.* **-vat'ed, -vat'ing** ‖ < L *colere*, to till ‖ 1 to prepare (land) for growing crops; till 2 to loosen the soil and kill weeds around (plants) 3 to grow (plants) 4 to develop or improve [*cultivate your mind*] 5 to seek to become familiar with —**cul'ti·va·ble** (-və bəl) or **cul'ti·vat'a·ble** *adj.* —**cul'ti·va'tor** *n.*

cul'ti·va'tion *n.* 1 the act of cultivating 2 refinement, or culture

cul·ture (kul'chər) *n.* ‖ see CULT ‖ 1 cultivation of the soil 2 a growth of bacteria, etc. in a prepared substance 3 improvement of the mind, manners, etc. 4 development by special training or care 5 the skills, arts, etc. of a given people in a given period; civilization —*vt.* **-tured, -tur·ing** to cultivate —**cul'tur·al** *adj.* —**cul'tur·al·ly** *adv.*

culture shock the alienation, confusion, etc. that may be experienced by someone encountering new surroundings, a different culture, etc.

cul·vert (kul'vərt) *n.* ‖ < ? ‖ a drain or conduit under a road or embankment

cum·ber (kum'bər) *vt.* ‖ < OFr *combre*, barrier ‖ to hinder; hamper

cum'ber·some (-səm) *adj.* burdensome; unwieldy Also **cum'brous** (-brəs)

cum·in (kum'in) *n.* ‖ < Gr *kyminon* ‖ 1 a plant related to parsley and celery 2 its aromatic fruits, used for flavoring

cum·mer·bund (kum'ər bund') *n.* ‖ < Ar Pers *kamar*, loins + Pers *band*, band ‖ a wide sash worn as a waistband, esp. with men's formal dress

cu·mu·la·tive (kyoo͞'myoo͞ lāt'iv, myə-; -lə tiv') *adj.* ‖ < L *cumulus*, a heap ‖ increasing in effect, size, etc. by successive additions

cu·mu·lus (kyoo͞'myoo͞ ləs, myə-) *n.*, *pl.* **-li'** (-lī') ‖ L, a heap ‖ a white, billowy cloud type with a dark, flat base

cu·ne·i·form (kyoo͞ nē'ə fôrm') *adj.* ‖ < L *cuneus*, a wedge + FORM ‖ wedge-shaped, as the characters in ancient Assyrian and Babylonian inscriptions —*n.* cuneiform writing

cun·ning (kun'iŋ) *adj.* ‖ < ME *cunnen*, know ‖ 1 sly; crafty 2 made with skill 3 pretty; cute —*n.* slyness; craftiness —**cun'ning·ly** *adv.*

cup (kup) *n.* ‖ < L *cupa*, tub ‖ 1 a small, bowl-shaped container for beverages, usually with a handle 2 a cup and its contents 3 a cupful 4 anything shaped like a cup —*vt.* **cupped, cup'ping** to shape like a cup

cup·board (kub'ərd) *n.* a closet or cabinet with shelves for cups, plates, food, etc.

cup'cake' *n.* a small cake

cup'ful' *n.*, *pl.* **-fuls'** as much as a cup will hold; specif., eight ounces

Cu·pid (kyoo͞'pid) *Rom. Myth.* the god of love —*n.* [c-] a representation of Cupid as a winged boy with bow and arrow

cu·pid·i·ty (kyoo͞ pid'ə tē) *n.* ‖ < L *cupere*, to desire ‖ strong desire for wealth; avarice

cu·po·la (kyoo͞'pə lə) *n.* ‖ It < L *cupa*, a tub ‖ a small dome, etc. on a roof —**cu'po·laed** (-ləd) *adj.*

CUPOLA

cur (kʉr) *n.* ‖ prob. < ON *kurra*, to growl ‖ 1 a dog of mixed breed; mongrel 2 a contemptible person

cu·rate (kyoor'it) *n.* ‖ < L *cura*, care ‖ a member of the clergy who assists a vicar or rector —**cu'ra·cy** (-ə sē), *pl.* **-cies**, *n.*

cu·ra·tive (kyoor'ət iv) *adj.* having the power to cure —*n.* a remedy

cu·ra·tor (kyoo͞ rāt'ər, kyoor'āt'ər) *n.* ‖ < L *curare*, take care of ‖ a person in charge of a museum, library, etc. —**cu·ra·to·ri·al** (kyoor'ə tôr'ē əl) *adj.*

curb (kʉrb) *n.* ‖ < L *curvus*, bent ‖ 1 a chain or strap attached to a horse's bit, used to check the horse 2 anything that checks or restrains 3 a stone or concrete edging along a street —*vt.* to restrain; control

curb service service offered to customers in parked cars, as at some restaurants

curb'stone' *n.* the stone or stones making up a curb

curd (kʉrd) *n.* ‖ < ME *crud*, coagulated substance ‖ [*often pl.*] the coagulated part of soured milk, from which cheese is made

cur·dle (kʉrd''l) *vt.*, *vi.* **-dled, -dling** to form into curd; coagulate

cure (kyoor) *n.* ‖ < L *cura*, care ‖ 1 a healing or being healed 2 a remedy 3 a method of medical treatment —*vt.* **cured, cur'ing** 1 to restore to health 2 to get rid of (an ailment, evil, etc.) 3 *a*) to preserve

(meat), as by salting or smoking *b)* to process (tobacco, leather, etc.), as by drying or aging —**cur'a·ble** *adj.* —**cur'er** *n.*
cu·ré (kyo͞o rā') *n.* ‖Fr < L *cura,* care‖ in France, a parish priest
cure'-all' *n.* something supposed to cure all ailments or evils
cu·ret·tage (kyo͞o ret'ij', kyo͞o'rə täzh') *n.* ‖Fr‖ the process of cleaning or scraping the walls of a body cavity with a spoonlike instrument
cur·few (kʉr'fyo͞o') *n.* ‖< OFr *covrefeu,* lit., cover fire: orig. a nightly signal to cover fires and retire‖ a time in the evening beyond which children, etc. may not appear on the streets
Cu·ri·a (kyo͞o'rē ə, kyoor'ē ə) *n., pl.* **-ri·ae'** (-ē') ‖L‖ the official body governing the Roman Catholic Church under the authority of the pope
Cu·rie (kyoo rē', kyoor'ē), **Ma·rie** (mə rē', ma-) 1867-1934; Pol. chemist in France
cu·ri·o (kyoor'ē ō') *n., pl.* **-os'** ‖contr. of fol.‖ an unusual or rare article
cu·ri·os·i·ty (kyoor'ē äs'ə tē) *n., pl.* **-ties** 1 a desire to learn 2 inquisitiveness 3 anything curious or rare
cu·ri·ous (kyoor'ē əs) *adj.* ‖< L *curiosus,* careful‖ 1 eager to learn or know 2 prying or inquisitive 3 unusual; strange —**cu'ri·ous·ly** *adv.*
curl (kʉrl) *vt.* ‖< ME *crul,* curly‖ 1 to twist (esp. hair) into ringlets 2 to cause to bend around —*vi.* to become curled —*n.* 1 a ringlet of hair 2 anything with a curled shape —**curl'er** *n.* —**curl'y, -i·er, -i·est,** *adj.*
cur·lew (kʉr'lo͞o', kʉrl'yo͞o') *n.* ‖echoic‖ a large, brownish wading bird with long legs
curl·i·cue (kʉrl'i kyo͞o') *n.* ‖< CURLY + CUE[2]‖ a fancy curve, flourish, etc.
curl·ing (kʉrl'iŋ) *n.* a game for two teams, played on ice by sliding a flat stone toward a mark
cur·rant (kʉr'ənt) *n.* ‖ult. < *Corinth,* ancient Gr city‖ 1 a small, seedless raisin from the Mediterranean region 2 *a)* the sour berry of several species of hardy shrubs *b)* any such shrub
cur·ren·cy (kʉr'ən sē) *n., pl.* **-cies** ‖see fol.‖ 1 circulation 2 the money in circulation in any country 3 general use or acceptance
cur·rent (kʉr'ənt) *adj.* ‖< L *currere,* to run‖ 1 now going on; of the present time 2 circulating 3 commonly accepted; prevalent —*n.* 1 a flow of water or air in a definite direction 2 a general tendency 3 the flow or rate of flow of electricity in a conductor —**cur'rent·ly** *adv.*
cur·ric·u·lum (kə rik'yo͞o ləm, -yə-) *n., pl.* **-la** (-lə) or **-lums** ‖L, course for racing‖ a course of study in a school —**cur·ric'u·lar** (-lər) *adj.*
cur·ry[1] (kʉr'ē) *vt.* **-ried, -ry·ing** ‖< OFr *correier,* to put in order‖ 1 to rub down and clean the coat of (a horse, etc.) with a comb or brush 2 to prepare (tanned leather) 3 to try to win (favor) by flattery, etc.
cur·ry[2] (kʉr'ē) *n., pl.* **-ries** ‖Tamil *kari,* sauce‖ 1 a powder prepared from various spices, or a sauce made with this 2 a stew made with curry —*vt.* **-ried, -ry·ing** to prepare with curry
cur'ry·comb' *n.* a comb with teeth or ridges, for currying a horse —*vt.* to use a currycomb on
curse (kʉrs) *n.* ‖OE *curs*‖ 1 a calling on God or the gods to bring evil on some person or thing 2 a profane or obscene oath 3 evil coming as if in answer to a curse —*vt.* **cursed** or **curst, curs'ing** 1 to call evil down on 2 to swear at 3 to afflict —*vi.* to swear; blaspheme —**be cursed with** to suffer from
curs·ed (kʉr'sid, kʉrst) *adj.* 1 under a curse 2 deserving to be cursed; evil; hateful
cur·sive (kʉr'siv) *adj.* ‖ult. < L *currere,* to run‖ designating writing in which the letters are joined
cur·sor (kʉr'sər) *n.* ‖L, runner‖ a movable indicator light on a computer video screen marking the current position at which a character may be entered
cur·so·ry (kʉr'sə rē) *adj.* ‖ult. < L *currere,* to run‖ hastily, often superficially, done —**cur'so·ri·ly** *adv.*
curt (kʉrt) *adj.* ‖L *curtus,* short‖ brief, esp. to the point of rudeness —**curt'ly** *adv.* —**curt'ness** *n.*
cur·tail (kər tāl') *vt.* ‖< L *curtus,* short‖ to cut short; reduce —**cur·tail'ment** *n.*
cur·tain (kʉrt''n) *n.* ‖< LL *cortina*‖ a piece of cloth, etc. hung at a window, in front of a stage, etc. to decorate or conceal —*vt.* to provide with or shut off as with a curtain
curtain call 1 a call, usually by applause, for performers to return to the stage 2 such a return
curt·sy (kʉrt'sē) *n., pl.* **-sies** ‖var. of COURTESY‖ a woman's bow of greeting, respect, etc. made by bending the knees and lowering the body slightly —*vi.* **-sied, -sy·ing** to make a curtsy Also **curt'sey**
cur·va·ceous (kər vā'shəs) *adj.* ‖< CURVE‖ having a full, shapely figure: said of a woman
cur·va·ture (kʉr'və chər) *n.* 1 a curving or being curved 2 a curve
curve (kʉrv) *n.* ‖< L *curvus,* bent‖ 1 a line having no straight part; bend with no angles 2 something shaped like, or moving in, a curve —*vt., vi.* **curved, curv'ing** 1 to form a curve by bending 2 to move in a curve —**curv'y, -i·er, -i·est,** *adj.*
cush·ion (koosh'ən) *n.* ‖< ML *coxinum*‖ 1 a pillow or pad 2 a thing like this in shape or use 3 anything that absorbs shock —*vt.* to provide with a cushion
cush·y (koosh'ē) *adj.* **-i·er, -i·est** ‖< Pers *khūsh,* pleasant‖ [Slang] easy; comfortable
cusp (kusp) *n.* ‖L *cuspis*‖ a point or pointed end, as on the chewing surface of a tooth
cus·pid (kus'pid) *n.* ‖see prec.‖ a tooth with one cusp; canine
cus·pi·dor (kus'pə dôr') *n.* ‖< Port *cuspir,* to spit‖ a spittoon
cuss (kus) *n., vt., vi.* [Colloq.] CURSE
cus·tard (kus'tərd) *n.* ‖< L *crusta,* crust‖ a mixture of eggs, milk, sugar, etc., boiled or baked
cus·to·di·an (kus tō'dē ən, kəs-) *n.* ‖< fol.‖ 1 one who has something in one's custody or care; caretaker 2 a person responsible for the maintenance of a building

cus·to·dy (kus′tə dē) ***n.***, *pl.* **-dies** ‖ < L *custos*, a guard ‖ a guarding or keeping safe; care —**in custody** under arrest —**cus·to′di·al** (-tō′dē əl) ***adj.***

cus·tom (kus′təm) ***n.*** ‖ < L *com-*, intens. + *suere*, be accustomed ‖ **1** a usual practice; habit **2** social conventions carried on by tradition **3** [*pl.*] duties or taxes imposed on imported goods **4** the regular patronage of a business —***adj.*** **1** made to order **2** making things to order

cus′tom·ar′y (-tə mer′ē) ***adj.*** in keeping with custom; usual; habitual —**cus′tom·ar′i·ly** ***adv.***

cus′tom-built′ ***adj.*** built to order, to the customer's specifications

cus′tom·er ***n.*** a person who buys, esp. one who buys regularly

cus′tom·house′ ***n.*** an office where customs or duties are paid

cus′tom·ize′ (-īz′) ***vt.*** **-ized′**, **-iz′ing** to make according to individual specifications

cus′tom-made′ ***adj.*** made to order, to the customer's specifications

cut (kut) ***vt.*** **cut**, **cut′ting** ‖ ME *cutten* ‖ **1** to make an opening in with a sharp-edged instrument; gash **2** to pierce sharply so as to hurt **3** to have (a new tooth) grow through the gum **4** to divide into parts with a sharp-edged instrument; sever **5** to hew **6** to reap **7** to reduce; curtail **8** to trim; pare **9** to divide (a pack of cards) **10** to make or do as by cutting **11** to hit (a ball) so that it spins **12** [Colloq.] to pretend not to recognize (a person) **13** [Colloq.] to be absent from (a school class, etc.) **14** [Slang] to stop —***vi.*** **1** to pierce, sever, gash, etc. **2** to take cutting [pine *cuts* easily] **3** to go (*across* or *through*) **4** to swing a bat, etc. (*at* a ball) **5** to change direction suddenly —***adj.*** **1** that has been cut **2** made or formed by cutting —***n.*** **1** a cutting or being cut **2** a stroke or opening made by a sharp-edged instrument **3** a piece cut off, as of meat **4** a reduction **5** a passage or channel cut out **6** the style in which a thing is cut **7** an act, remark, etc. that hurts one's feelings **8** a block or plate engraved for printing, or the impression from this **9** [Colloq.] an unauthorized absence from school, etc. **10** [Colloq.] a share, as of profits —**cut and dried** **1** arranged beforehand **2** lifeless; dull —**cut down** (**on**) to reduce; lessen —**cut it out** [Colloq.] to stop doing what one is doing —**cut off** **1** to sever **2** to stop abruptly; shut off —**cut out for** [Colloq.] suited for —**cut up** **1** to cut into pieces **2** [Slang] to clown, joke, etc.

cu·ta·ne·ous (kyo͞o tā′nē əs) ***adj.*** ‖ < L *cutis*, skin ‖ of or on the skin

cut′a·way′ ***n.*** a man's formal coat cut so as to curve back to the tails

cut′back′ ***n.*** a reduction or discontinuance, as of production

cute (kyo͞ot) ***adj.*** **cut′er**, **cut′est** ‖ < ACUTE ‖ [Colloq.] **1** clever; shrewd **2** pretty or attractive, esp. in a dainty way —**cute′ly** ***adv.*** —**cute′ness** ***n.***

cute·sy or **cute·sie** (kyo͞ot′sē) ***adj.*** **-si·er**, **-si·est** [Colloq.] cute in an affected way

cut·i·cle (kyo͞ot′i kəl) ***n.*** ‖ < L *cutis*, skin ‖ **1** the outer layer of the skin **2** hardened skin, as at the base and sides of a fingernail

cut·lass or **cut·las** (kut′ləs) ***n.*** ‖ < L *culter*, plowshare ‖ a short, thick, curved sword

cut·ler·y (kut′lər ē) ***n.*** ‖ < L *culter*, plowshare ‖ cutting implements, as knives; often, specif., eating implements

cut·let (kut′lit) ***n.*** ‖ < L *costa*, rib ‖ **1** a small slice of meat from the ribs or leg **2** a small, flat croquette of chopped meat or fish

cut′off′ ***n.*** a road, etc. that is a shortcut

cut′-rate′ ***adj.*** selling or on sale at a lower price

cut·ter (kut′ər) ***n.*** **1** a person or thing that cuts **2** a small, swift vessel

cut′throat′ ***n.*** a murderer —***adj.*** **1** murderous **2** merciless; ruthless

cut·ting (kut′iŋ) ***n.*** a shoot cut away from a plant for rooting or grafting —***adj.*** **1** that cuts; sharp **2** chilling or piercing **3** sarcastic; wounding

cut·tle·fish (kut′'l fish′) ***n.***, *pl.* **-fish′** or (for different species) **-fish′es** ‖ OE *cudele* ‖ a sea mollusk with eight sucker-bearing arms and two tentacles and a hard internal shell (**cut′tle·bone′**)

cwt. hundredweight

-cy (sē) ‖ < Gr *-kia* ‖ *suffix* **1** quality, condition, or fact of being [*hesitancy*] **2** position, rank, or office of [*captaincy*]

cy·a·nide (sī′ə nīd′) ***n.*** a highly poisonous, white, crystalline compound

cy·ber·net·ics (sī′bər net′iks) ***n.pl.*** ‖ < Gr *kybernan*, to steer + -ICS ‖ [*with sing. v.*] the comparative study of human control systems, as the brain, and complex electronic systems —**cy′ber·net′ic** ***adj.***

cy·cla·men (sī′klə mən) ***n.*** ‖ < Gr *kyklaminos* ‖ a plant of the primrose family with heart-shaped leaves

cy·cle (sī′kəl) ***n.*** ‖ < Gr *kyklos*, a circle ‖ **1** *a*) a period of time within which a round of regularly recurring events is completed *b*) a complete set of such events **2** a series of poems or songs on one theme **3** a bicycle, motorcycle, etc. **4** *Elec.* one complete period of the reversal of an alternating current from positive to negative and back again —***vi.*** **-cled**, **-cling** to ride a bicycle, etc. —**cy·clic** (sik′lik) ***adj.***

cy·clist (sik′list) ***n.*** a cycle rider

cyclo- ‖ < Gr *kyklos*, a circle ‖ *combining form* of a circle or wheel

cy·clom·e·ter (sī kläm′ət ər) ***n.*** ‖ prec. + -METER ‖ an instrument that records the revolutions of a wheel for measuring distance traveled

cy·clone (sī′klōn′) ***n.*** ‖ < Gr *kyklōma*, wheel ‖ a storm with strong winds rotating about a center of low pressure

cyclone fence a heavy-duty fence of interwoven steel links

cy·clo·pe·di·a or **cy·clo·pae·di·a** (sī′klō pē′dē ə, -klə-) ***n.*** *early term for* ENCYCLOPEDIA

Cy·clops (sī′kläps′) ***n.***, *pl.* **Cy·clo·pes** (sī klō′pēz′) *Gr. Myth.* any of a race of one-eyed giants

cy·clo·tron (sī′klō trän′, -klə-) ***n.*** ‖ CYCLO- + (ELEC)TRON ‖ a circular apparatus for giving high energy to positive ions, as protons, etc., used in atomic research

cyg·net (sig′net, -nit) ***n.*** ‖ < Gr *kyknos*, swan ‖ a young swan

cyl·in·der (sil′ən dər) ***n.*** ‖ < Gr *kylindein*, to

roll ‖ 1 a solid figure described by a line having end points in common with two equal, parallel, circular bases and moving parallel to a perpendicular axis 2 anything with this shape; specif., *a)* the turning part of a revolver *b)* the piston chamber of an engine —**cy·lin·dri·cal** (sə lin′dri kəl) ***adj.***

CYMBALS

cym·bal (sim′bəl) ***n.*** ‖ < Gr *kymbē*, hollow of a vessel ‖ *Music* a circular brass plate that makes a sharp, ringing sound when hit —**cym′bal·ist** ***n.***

cyn·ic (sin′ik) ***n.*** ‖ < Gr *kynikos*, doglike ‖ a cynical person

cyn′i·cal (-i kəl) ***adj.*** 1 denying the sincerity of people's motives and actions 2 sarcastic, sneering, etc. —**cyn′i·cal·ly** ***adv.***

cyn′i·cism′ (-ə siz′əm) ***n.*** 1 the attitude or beliefs of a cynic 2 a cynical remark, idea, etc.

cy·no·sure (sī′nə shoor′, sin′ə-) ***n.*** ‖ < Gr *kynosoura*, dog's tail ‖ a center of attention or interest

cy·pher (sī′fər) ***n.***, ***vi.*** *Brit. sp. of* CIPHER

cy·press (sī′prəs) ***n.*** ‖ < Gr *kyparissos* ‖ 1 an evergreen tree with cones and dark foliage 2 its wood

Cy·prus (sī′prəs) country on an island at the E end of the Mediterranean: 3,572 sq. mi.; pop. 673,000 —**Cyp·ri·ot** (sip′rē ət) ***adj.***, ***n.***

cyst (sist) ***n.*** ‖ < Gr *kystis*, sac ‖ a saclike structure in plants or animals, esp. one filled with diseased matter —**cyst·ic** (sis′tik) ***adj.***

cystic fibrosis a children's disease marked by fibrosis of the pancreas and frequent respiratory infections

cy·tol·o·gy (sī täl′ə jē) ***n.*** ‖ < Gr *kytos*, a hollow + -LOGY ‖ the branch of biology dealing with cells

cy·to·plasm (sīt′ō plaz′əm) ***n.*** ‖ < Gr *kytos*, a hollow + *plasma*, something molded ‖ the protoplasm of a cell that is outside the nucleus

cy·to·sine (sīt′ō sēn′) ***n.*** ‖ Ger *zytosin* ‖ one of the four bases that combine to form DNA

czar (zär) ***n.*** ‖ Russ < L *Caesar* ‖ 1 the title of any of the former emperors of Russia 2 an autocrat —**cza·ri·na** (zä rē′nə) ***n.fem.***

Czech (chek) ***n.*** 1 a member of a Slavic people of central Europe 2 the West Slavic language of the Czechs 3 loosely, a native or inhabitant of Czechoslovakia —***adj.*** of Czechoslovakia, its people, or their language

Czech·o·slo·va·ki·a (chek′ə slō vä′kē ə) country in central Europe: 49,367 sq. mi.; pop. 15,542,000 —**Czech′o·slo′vak** or **Czech′o·slo·vak′i·an** ***adj.***, ***n.***

D

d or **D** (dē) ***n.***, *pl.* **d's, D's** the fourth letter of the English alphabet

D (dē) ***n.*** 1 a Roman numeral for 500 2 a grade for below-average work 3 *Music* the second tone in the scale of C major

'd 1 had or would: a shortened form used in contractions *[I'd seen; they'd see]* 2 *old sp. of* -ED *[foster'd]*

d or **d.** 1 day(s) 2 degree 3 diameter 4 died 5 ‖ L *denarii* ‖ penny; pence

D or **D.** 1 December 2 Democrat

DA or **D.A.** District Attorney

dab (dab) ***vt.***, ***vi.*** **dabbed, dab′bing** ‖ ME *dabben*, to strike ‖ 1 to touch lightly and quickly; pat 2 to put on (paint, etc.) with light, quick strokes —***n.*** 1 a tap; pat 2 a soft or moist bit of something

dab·ble (dab′əl) ***vi.*** **-bled, -bling** ‖ Du *dabbelen*, freq. of MDu *dabben*, to strike, dab ‖ 1 to play in water, as with the hands 2 to do something superficially: with *in* or *at*

Dac·ca (dak′ə) *old sp. of* DHAKA

dachs·hund (däks′hoont′) ***n.*** ‖ Ger < *dachs*, badger + *hund*, dog ‖ a small dog with a long body, short legs, and drooping ears

Da·cron (dā′krän′, dak′rän′) *trademark for* a synthetic wrinkle-resistant fabric —***n.*** *[also* **d-***]* this fabric

dac·tyl (dak′til) ***n.*** ‖ < Gr *daktylos*, finger ‖ a metrical foot of three syllables, one accented and two unaccented —**dac·tyl′ic** (-til′ik) ***adj.***

dad (dad) ***n.*** ‖ < child's cry *dada* ‖ [Colloq.] father: also **dad·dy** (dad′ē), *pl.* **-dies**

daddy long′legs′ an arachnid with long legs

da·do (dā′dō) ***n.***, *pl.* **-does** ‖ < L *datum*, a die ‖ 1 the part of a pedestal between the cap and the base 2 the lower part of a wall if decorated differently from the upper part

dae·mon (dē′mən) ***n.*** ‖ < Gr *daimōn* ‖ 1 *Gr. Myth.* a secondary deity 2 a guardian spirit 3 DEMON (sense 1) —**dae·mon·ic** (di män′ik) ***adj.***

daf·fo·dil (daf′ə dil′) ***n.*** ‖ < Gr *asphodelos* ‖ a narcissus with long leaves and yellow flowers

daf·fy (daf′ē) ***adj.*** **-fi·er, -fi·est** ‖ < ME *dafte*, daft ‖ [Colloq.] crazy; silly —**daf′fi·ness** ***n.***

daft (daft) ***adj.*** ‖ < OE (*ge*)*dæfte*, mild ‖ 1 silly 2 insane

dag·ger (dag′ər) ***n.*** ‖ < Prov *daga* ‖ 1 a weapon with a short, pointed blade, used for stabbing 2 *Printing* a reference mark (†)

da·guerre·o·type (də ger′ō tīp′) ***n.*** ‖ after L. J. M. *Daguerre*, 19th-c. Fr inventor ‖ an early kind of photograph made on a chemically treated plate —***vt.*** **-typed′, -typ′ing** to photograph by this method

dahl·ia (dāl′yə, dal′-) ***n.*** ‖ after A. *Dahl*, 18th-

c. Swed botanist ‖ a perennial plant with large, showy flowers

dai·li·ness (dā′lē nəs) ***n.*** the ordinary, routine aspects of a way of life

dai·ly (dā′lē) ***adj.*** done, happening, or published every (week)day —***n.***, *pl.* **-lies** a daily newspaper —***adv.*** every day

daily double a bet or betting procedure in which winning depends on choosing both winners in two specified races

dain·ty (dān′tē) ***n.***, *pl.* **-ties** ‖ < OFr *deinté* ‖ a delicacy —***adj.*** **-ti·er, -ti·est** **1** delicious and choice **2** delicately pretty **3** *a)* of refined taste; fastidious *b)* squeamish —**dain′ti·ly** ***adv.*** —**dain′ti·ness** ***n.***

dai·qui·ri (dak′ər ē) ***n.*** ‖ after *Daiquirí,* Cuban village ‖ a cocktail made of rum, sugar, and lime or lemon juice

dair·y (der′ē) ***n.***, *pl.* **-ies** ‖ ME *daie,* dairymaid ‖ **1** a building or room where milk and cream are made into butter and cheese, etc. **2** a farm that produces, or a store that sells, milk and milk products —**dair′y·man** (-mən), *pl.* **-men,** ***n.***

dair′y·ing ***n.*** the business of producing or selling dairy products

da·is (dā′is) ***n.***, *pl.* **da′is·es** ‖ < ML *discus,* table ‖ a raised platform

dai·sy (dā′zē) ***n.***, *pl.* **-sies** ‖ < OE *dæges eage,* day's eye ‖ a plant of the composite family, bearing flowers with white rays around a yellow disk

dale (dāl) ***n.*** ‖ OE *dæl* ‖ a valley

Dal·las (dal′əs) city in NE Tex.: pop. 904,000

dal·ly (dal′ē) ***vi.*** **-lied, -ly·ing** ‖ < OFr *dalier,* to trifle ‖ **1** to flirt **2** to deal carelessly (*with*); trifle **3** to waste time; loiter —**dal·li·ance** (dal′yəns, -ē əns) ***n.***

DALMATIAN

Dal·ma·tian (dal mā′shən) ***n.*** a large, short-haired dog with dark spots on a white coat

dam[1] (dam) ***n.*** ‖ ME ‖ a barrier built to hold back flowing water —***vt.*** **dammed, dam′ming** **1** to build a dam in **2** to keep back or confine

dam[2] (dam) ***n.*** ‖ see DAME ‖ the female parent of any four-legged animal

dam·age (dam′ij) ***n.*** ‖ < L *damnum* ‖ **1** injury or harm resulting in a loss **2** [*pl.*] *Law* money compensating for injury, loss, etc. —***vt.*** **-aged, -ag·ing** to do damage to —**dam′age·a·ble** ***adj.***

Da·mas·cus (də mas′kəs) capital of Syria: pop. 1,251,000

dam·ask (dam′əsk) ***n.*** ‖ after prec. ‖ **1** a reversible fabric in figured weave, used for table linen, etc. **2** steel decorated with wavy lines **3** deep pink or rose —***adj.*** **1** of or like damask **2** deep-pink or rose

dame (dām) ***n.*** ‖ < L *domina,* lady ‖ **1** [D-] in Great Britain, a woman's title of honor **2** [Slang] any woman

damn (dam) ***vt.*** **damned, damn′ing** ‖ < L *damnare,* condemn ‖ **1** to condemn to an unhappy fate **2** *Theol.* to condemn to hell **3** to condemn as bad, inferior, etc. **4** to swear at by saying "damn" —***n.*** the saying of "damn" as a curse —***adj., adv.*** [Colloq.] *short for* DAMNED —***interj.*** an expression of anger, etc.

dam·na·ble (dam′nə bəl) ***adj.*** **1** deserving damnation **2** deserving to be sworn at —**dam′na·bly** ***adv.***

dam·na′tion (-nā′shən) ***n.*** a damning or being damned —***interj.*** an expression of anger, etc.

damned (damd) ***adj.*** **1** condemned, as to hell **2** [Colloq.] deserving cursing; outrageous —***adv.*** [Colloq.] very

Dam·o·cles (dam′ə klēz′) *Classical Legend* a man whose king seated him under a sword hanging by a hair to show him the perils of a ruler's life

damp (damp) ***n.*** ‖ MDu, vapor ‖ a slight wetness —***adj.*** somewhat moist or wet; humid —***vt.*** **1** to bank (a fire) **2** to check or reduce —**damp′ness** ***n.***

damp′-dry′ ***vt.*** **-dried′, -dry′ing** to dry (laundry) so that some moisture is retained —***adj.*** designating or of laundry so treated

damp·en (dam′pən) ***vt.*** **1** to make damp; moisten **2** to deaden, depress, or reduce —***vi.*** to become damp —**damp′en·er** ***n.***

damp′er (-pər) ***n.*** ‖ see DAMP ‖ **1** anything that deadens or depresses **2** a valve in a flue to control the draft **3** a device to check vibration in piano strings

dam·sel (dam′zəl) ***n.*** ‖ see DAME ‖ [Old-fashioned] a girl; maiden

dam′sel·fly′ ***n.***, *pl.* **-flies′** a slow-flying, brightly colored dragonfly

dam·son (dam′zən) ***n.*** ‖ ult. < *Damascenus,* of DAMASCUS ‖ a small, purple plum

Dan. Danish

dance (dans) ***vi.*** **danced, danc′ing** ‖ < OFr *danser* ‖ **1** to move the body and feet in rhythm, ordinarily to music **2** to move lightly, rapidly, gaily, etc. —***vt.*** **1** to perform (a dance) **2** to cause to dance —***n.*** **1** rhythmic movement, ordinarily to music **2** a particular kind of dance **3** the art of dancing **4** a party for dancing **5** a piece of music for dancing **6** rapid movement —**danc′er** ***n.***

D and C dilatation (of the cervix) and curettage (of the uterus)

dan·de·li·on (dan′də lī′ən) ***n.*** ‖ < OFr *dent,* tooth + *de,* of + *lion,* lion ‖ a common weed with yellow flowers

dan·der (dan′dər) ***n.*** ‖ < ? ‖ [Colloq.] anger or temper

dan·dle (dan′dəl) ***vt.*** **-dled, -dling** ‖ < ? ‖ to dance (a child) up and down on the knee or in the arms

dan·druff (dan′drəf) ***n.*** ‖ < earlier *dandro* + dial. *hurf,* scab ‖ little scales of dead skin on the scalp

dan·dy (dan′dē) ***n.***, *pl.* **-dies** ‖ < ? ‖ **1** a man overly attentive to his clothes and appearance **2** [Colloq.] something very good —***adj.*** **-di·er, -di·est** [Colloq.] very good; fine

Dane (dān) ***n.*** a native or inhabitant of Denmark

dan·ger (dān′jər) ***n.*** ‖ ult. < L *dominus,* a master ‖ **1** liability to injury, damage, loss, etc.; peril **2** a thing that may cause injury, pain, etc.

dan′ger·ous ***adj.*** full of danger; unsafe —**dan′ger·ous·ly** ***adv.***

dan·gle (daŋ′gəl) ***vi.*** **-gled, -gling** ‖< Scand‖ to hang swinging loosely —***vt.*** to cause to dangle —**dan′gler** ***n.***

Dan·iel (dan′yəl) *Bible* a Hebrew prophet whose faith saved him in the lions' den

Dan·ish (dān′ish) ***adj.*** of Denmark, the Danes, or their language —***n.*** **1** the language of the Danes **2** [*also* **d-**] (a) rich, flaky pastry filled with fruit, cheese, etc.: in full **Danish pastry**

dank (daŋk) ***adj.*** ‖ME‖ disagreeably damp —**dank′ly** ***adv.*** —**dank′ness** ***n.***

dan·seuse (dän so͞oz′) ***n.*** ‖Fr‖ a female ballet dancer

Dan·te (Alighieri) (dän′tā, dan′tē) 1265-1321; It. poet

Dan·ube (dan′yo͞ob) river in S Europe, flowing from SW West Germany into the Black Sea —**Da·nu·bi·an** (də nyo͞o′bē ən) ***adj.***

dap·per (dap′ər) ***adj.*** ‖MDu, nimble‖ **1** small and active **2** trim; neat

dap·ple (dap′əl) ***adj.*** ‖< ON *depill*, a spot‖ marked with spots; mottled: also **dap′pled** —***vt.*** **-pled, -pling** to cover with spots

Dar·da·nelles (där′də nelz′) strait separating the Balkan Peninsula from Asia Minor

dare (der) ***vt., vi.*** **dared** or [Now Chiefly Dial.] **durst, dared, dar′ing** ‖OE *durran*‖ **1** to have enough courage for (some act) **2** to face (something) bravely **3** to challenge (someone) to do something —***n.*** a challenge —**dare say** to think probable —**dar′er** ***n.***

dare′dev′il (-dev′əl) ***adj.*** bold and reckless —***n.*** a bold, reckless person

dar′ing ***adj.*** fearless; bold —***n.*** bold courage —**dar′ing·ly** ***adv.***

dark (därk) ***adj.*** ‖< OE *deorc*‖ **1** entirely or partly without light **2** *a*) almost black *b*) not light in color **3** hidden **4** gloomy **5** evil **6** ignorant —***n.*** **1** the state of being dark **2** night —**dark′ly** ***adv.*** —**dark′ness** ***n.***

Dark Ages ‖< prec., *adj.* 6‖ the Middle Ages, esp. the earlier part

dark′en ***vt., vi.*** to make or become dark or darker —**dark′en·er** ***n.***

dark horse [Colloq.] a little-known contestant thought unlikely to win

dark′room′ ***n.*** a darkened room for developing photographs

dar·ling (där′liŋ) ***n.*** ‖OE *deorling*‖ a person much loved by another —***adj.*** **1** very dear; beloved **2** [Colloq.] cute

darn[1] (därn) ***vt., vi.*** ‖< Fr dial. *darner*‖ to mend (cloth) by sewing a network of stitches across the gap —***n.*** a darned place in fabric

darn[2] (därn) ***vt., n., adj., adv., interj.*** [Colloq.] damn: a euphemism —**darned** ***adj., adv.***

dart (därt) ***n.*** ‖< OFr‖ **1** a small, pointed missile for throwing or shooting **2** a sudden movement **3** a short, tapered seam **4** [*pl., with sing. v.*] a game in which darts (see sense 1) are thrown at a target (**dartboard**) —***vt., vi.*** to send out or move suddenly and fast

Dar·von (där′vän′) *trademark for* an analgesic drug containing a narcotic painkiller

Dar·win (där′win), **Charles (Robert)** (chärlz) 1809-82; Eng. naturalist: originated theory of evolution

dash (dash) ***vt.*** ‖< Scand‖ **1** to smash; destroy **2** to strike violently (*against*) **3** to throw or thrust (*away, down,* etc.) **4** to splash —***vi.*** **1** to strike violently (*against*) **2** to rush —***n.*** **1** a splash **2** a bit of something added **3** a rush **4** a short, fast race **5** spirit; vigor **6** the mark of punctuation (—) used to indicate a break, omission, etc —**dash off** to do, write, etc. hastily —**dash′er** ***n.***

dash′board′ ***n.*** a panel with controls and gauges, as in an automobile

da·shi·ki (dä shē′kē) ***n.*** a loosefitting, brightly colored robe modeled after an African tribal garment

dash′ing ***adj.*** **1** full of dash or spirit; lively **2** showy; striking —**dash′ing·ly** ***adv.***

das·tard (das′tərd) ***n.*** ‖ME, a craven‖ a sneaky, cowardly evildoer

das′tard·ly ***adj.*** mean, cowardly, etc.

dat. dative

da·ta (dāt′ə, dat′ə) ***n.pl.*** [*now usually with sing. v.*] facts or figures from which conclusions can be drawn

da′ta·base′ ***n.*** a mass of data in a computer, arranged for rapid expansion, updating, and retrieval: also **data base**

data processing the handling of large amounts of information, esp. by a computer —**data processor**

date[1] (dāt) ***n.*** ‖< L *dare*, give‖ **1** the time at which a thing happens, was made, etc. **2** the day of the month **3** *a*) an appointment *b*) a social engagement with a person of the opposite sex *c*) this person —***vt.*** **dat′ed, dat′ing** **1** to mark (a letter, etc.) with a date **2** to find out or give the date of **3** to make seem old-fashioned **4** to have social engagements with —***vi.*** **1** to belong to a definite period in the past **2** to date persons of the opposite sex —**dat′er** ***n.***

date[2] (dāt) ***n.*** ‖< Gr *daktylos*, a date‖ the sweet, fleshy fruit of a desert palm tree (**date palm**)

date′line′ ***n.*** the date and place of writing or issue, as given in a line in a newspaper story, etc.

da·tive (dāt′iv) ***n.*** ‖< L *dativus*, relating to giving‖ *Gram.* the case of the indirect object of a verb

da·tum (dāt′əm, dat′-) ***n.*** ‖L, what is given‖ *sing. of* DATA

daub (dôb) ***vt., vi.*** ‖< L *de-*, intens. + *albus*, white‖ **1** to cover or smear with sticky, soft matter **2** to paint badly —***n.*** **1** anything daubed on **2** a daubing stroke **3** a poorly painted picture —**daub′er** ***n.***

daugh·ter (dôt′ər) ***n.*** ‖< OE *dohtor*‖ **1** a girl or woman as she is related to either or both parents **2** a female descendant —**daugh′ter·ly** ***adj.***

daugh′ter-in-law′ ***n., pl.*** **daugh′ters-in-law′** the wife of one's son

Dau·mier (dō myā′), **Ho·no·ré** (ô nô rā′) 1808-79; Fr. painter

daunt (dônt) ***vt.*** ‖< L *domare*, to tame‖ to frighten or dishearten

daunt′less ***adj.*** that cannot be daunted or

intimidated; fearless —**daunt′less·ly** ***adv.*** —**daunt′less·ness** ***n.***

dau·phin (dô′fin) ***n.*** ‖ Fr, dolphin ‖ the eldest son of the king of France: a title used from 1349 to 1830

dav·en·port (dav′ən pôrt′) ***n.*** ‖ < ? ‖ a large couch or sofa

Dav·en·port (dav′ən pôrt′) city in E Iowa: pop. 103,000

Da·vid (dā′vid) *Bible* the second king of Israel and Judah

da Vin·ci (də vin′chē), **Le·o·nar·do** (lē′ə när′ dō) 1452-1519; It. painter, sculptor, architect, & scientist

Da·vis (dā′vis), **Jefferson** 1808-89; president of the Confederacy (1861-65)

da·vit (dā′vit, dav′it) ***n.*** ‖ OFr dim. of *David* ‖ either of a pair of uprights on a ship for lowering or raising a small boat

daw·dle (dôd′'l) ***vi., vt.*** **-dled, -dling** ‖ < ? ‖ to waste (time) in trifling; loiter —**daw′dler** ***n.***

dawn (dôn) ***vi.*** ‖ < OE *dagian* ‖ **1** to begin to be day **2** to begin to appear, develop, etc. **3** to begin to be understood or felt —***n.*** **1** daybreak **2** the beginning (*of* something)

day (dā) ***n.*** ‖ OE *dæg* ‖ **1** the period of light between sunrise and sunset **2** the time (24 hours) that it takes the earth to rotate once on its axis **3** [*also pl.*] a period; era **4** a time of power, glory, etc. **5** daily work period /an 8-hour *day*/ —**day after day** every day: also **day in, day out**

day′bed′ ***n.*** a couch that can also be used as a bed

day′break′ ***n.*** the time in the morning when light first appears

day care daytime care given to children, as at a day nursery, or to the elderly, as at a social agency —**day′-care′** ***adj.***

day′dream′ ***n.*** **1** a pleasant, dreamy series of thoughts **2** a visionary scheme —***vi.*** to have daydreams

day′light′ ***n.*** **1** the light of day **2** dawn **3** understanding

daylight saving time [*often* **D- S- T-**] time that is one hour later than standard time

day nursery a place for daytime care of preschool children, as of working parents

Day of Atonement Yom Kippur

day′time′ ***n.*** the time between dawn and sunset

day′-to-day′ ***adj.*** daily; routine

Day·ton (dāt′'n) city in SW Ohio: pop. 204,000

daze (dāz) ***vt.*** **dazed, daz′ing** ‖ < ON *dasi*, tired ‖ to stun or bewilder —***n.*** a dazed condition —**daz′ed·ly** ***adv.***

daz·zle (daz′əl) ***vt., vi.*** **-zled, -zling** ‖ freq. of DAZE ‖ **1** to overpower or be overpowered by bright light **2** to surprise or arouse admiration with brilliant qualities, display, etc. —***n.*** a dazzling —**daz′zler** ***n.***

db or **dB** decibel(s)

DC **1** direct current: also **D.C., dc,** or **d.c.** **2** District of Columbia: also **D.C.**

DD or **D.D.** Doctor of Divinity

DDS or **D.D.S.** Doctor of Dental Surgery

DDT (dē′dē′tē′) ***n.*** ‖ < its chemical name ‖ a powerful insecticide

de- ‖ < Fr *dé-* or L *de* ‖ *prefix* **1** away from, off /*derail*/ **2** down /*decline*/ **3** entirely /*defunct*/ **4** reverse the action of /*decode*/

DE Delaware

DEA Drug Enforcement Administration

dea·con (dē′kən) ***n.*** ‖ < Gr *diakonos*, servant ‖ **1** a cleric ranking just below a priest **2** a church officer who helps the minister —**dea′con·ess** ***n.fem.***

de·ac·ti·vate (dē ak′tə vāt′) ***vt.*** **-vat′ed, -vat′ing** **1** to make (an explosive, chemical, etc.) inactive **2** *Mil.* to demobilize

dead (ded) ***adj.*** ‖ OE ‖ **1** no longer living **2** without life **3** deathlike **4** lacking warmth, interest, brightness, etc. **5** without feeling, motion, or power **6** extinguished; extinct **7** no longer used; obsolete **8** unerring /a *dead* shot/ **9** complete /a *dead* stop/ **10** [Colloq.] very tired —***n.*** the time of most cold, most darkness, etc. /the *dead* of night/ —***adv.*** **1** completely **2** directly —**the dead** those who have died

dead′beat′ ***n.*** [Slang] one who tries to evade paying debts

dead′bolt′ ***n.*** a lock for a door, with a bolt that can be moved only by turning the key

dead·en (ded′'n) ***vt.*** **1** to lessen the vigor or intensity of; dull **2** to numb **3** to make soundproof

dead end **1** a street, alley, etc. closed at one end **2** an impasse —**dead′-end′** ***adj.***

dead heat a race in which two or more contestants finish even

dead letter **1** a rule, law, etc. no longer enforced **2** an unclaimed letter

dead′line′ ***n.*** the latest time by which something must be done

dead′lock′ ***n.*** a standstill resulting from the action of equal and opposed forces —***vt., vi.*** to bring or come to a deadlock

dead′ly ***adj.*** **-li·er, -li·est** **1** causing or likely to cause death **2** implacable **3** typical of death /*deadly* pallor/ **4** extreme **5** very boring **6** very accurate —***adv.*** extremely —**dead′li·ness** ***n.***

dead′pan′ ***adj., adv.*** without expression; blank(ly)

Dead Sea inland body of salt water on the Israel-Jordan border

dead′wood′ (-wood′) ***n.*** anything useless or burdensome

deaf (def) ***adj.*** ‖ OE ‖ **1** unable to hear **2** unwilling to respond, as to a plea —**deaf′ness** ***n.***

deaf′en (-ən) ***vt.*** **1** to make deaf **2** to overwhelm with noise —**deaf′en·ing** ***adj.***

deaf′-mute′ ***n.*** a person who is deaf and has not learned to speak

deal[1] (dēl) ***vt.*** **dealt** (delt), **deal′ing** ‖ < OE *dælan* ‖ **1** to portion out or distribute **2** to give; administer (a blow, etc.) **3** [Slang] to sell (illegal drugs) —***vi.*** **1** to have to do (*with*) /science *deals* with facts/ **2** to conduct oneself /*deal* fairly with others/ **3** to do business; trade (*with* or *in*) —***n.*** **1** the distributing of playing cards **2** a business transaction **3** a bargain or agreement, esp. when secret **4** [Colloq.] treatment /a fair *deal*/ —**deal′er** ***n.***

deal[2] (dēl) ***n.*** ‖ OE *dæl*, a part ‖ an indefinite amount —**a good** (or **great**) **deal** **1** a large amount **2** very much

deal′er·ship′ ***n.*** a franchise to sell a product in a specified area

deal′ing ***n.*** **1** way of acting **2** |*usually pl.*| transactions or relations

dean (dēn) ***n.*** ‖< LL *decanus*, chief of ten (monks, etc.)‖ **1** the presiding official of a cathedral **2** a college official in charge of students or faculty **3** the senior member of a group

dean's list a list of students at a college who have earned high grades

dear (dir) ***adj.*** ‖OE *deore*‖ **1** much loved **2** esteemed: a polite form of address /*Dear* Sir/ **3** high-priced; costly **4** earnest /our *dearest* wish/ **—*n.*** a loved one; darling **—dear′ly *adv.* —dear′ness *n.***

Dear John (letter) |Colloq.| a letter, as to a fiancé, breaking off a close relationship

dearth (durth) ***n.*** ‖ME *derth*‖ scarcity or lack

death (deth) ***n.*** ‖OE‖ **1** the act or fact of dying **2** the state of being dead **3** end or destruction **4** the cause of death **—death′-like′ *adj.***

death′bed′ *n.* **1** the bed on which a person dies **2** a person's last hours

death′blow′ *n.* **1** a blow that kills **2** a thing fatal (*to* something)

death′less *adj.* that cannot die; immortal **—death′less·ly *adv.***

death′ly *adj.* **1** causing death; deadly **2** like or characteristic of death **—*adv.*** extremely /*deathly* ill/

death′trap′ *n.* any unsafe structure

Death Valley dry, hot desert basin in E Calif. & S Nev.

deb (deb) ***n.*** |Colloq.| a debutante

de·ba·cle (di bä′kəl) ***n.*** ‖Fr *débâcler*, break up‖ **1** a crushing defeat **2** a ruinous collapse

de·bar (dē bär′) ***vt.* -barred′, -bar′ring** ‖< Anglo-Fr: see DE- & BAR‖ **1** to keep (a person) *from* some right, etc. **2** to prevent or prohibit **—de·bar′ment *n.***

de·bark (dē bärk′) ***vt., vi.*** ‖< Fr: see DE- & BARK[3]‖ to unload from or leave a ship or aircraft **—de·bar·ka·tion** (dē′bär kā′shən) ***n.***

de·base (dē bās′) ***vt.* -based′, -bas′ing** ‖DE- + BASE[2]‖ to make lower in value, dignity, etc. **—de·base′ment *n.***

de·bate (dē bāt′) ***vi., vt.* -bat′ed, -bat′ing** ‖< OFr: see DE- & BATTER[1]‖ **1** to discuss reasons for and against (something) **2** to take part in a debate with (a person) or about (a question) **—*n.* 1** a discussion of opposing reasons **2** a formal contest of skill in reasoned argument **—de·bat′a·ble *adj.* —de·bat′er *n.***

de·bauch (dē bôch′) ***vt.*** ‖< OFr *desbaucher*, seduce‖ to lead astray morally; corrupt **—*n.*** an orgy **—de·bauch′er·y,** *pl.* **-ies, *n.***

deb·au·chee (deb′ô shē′, di bôch′ē′) ***n.*** a dissipated person

de·ben·ture (di ben′chər) ***n.*** ‖< L: see DEBT‖ **1** a voucher acknowledging a debt **2** an interest-bearing bond, often issued without security

de·bil·i·tate (dē bil′ə tāt′) ***vt.* -tat′ed, -tat′ing** ‖< L *debilis*, weak‖ to make weak; enervate

de·bil·i·ty (də bil′ə tē) ***n.,*** *pl.* **-ties** ‖see prec.‖ weakness; feebleness

deb·it (deb′it) ***n.*** ‖< L *debere*, owe‖ **1** an entry in an account of money owed **2** the total of such entries **—*vt.*** to enter as a debit

deb·o·nair (deb′ə ner′) ***adj.*** ‖< OFr *de bon aire*, lit., of good breed‖ **1** carefree; jaunty **2** urbane **—deb′o·nair′ly *adv.***

de·brief (dē brēf′) ***vt.*** ‖DE- + BRIEF‖ to receive information from (a pilot, etc.) about a recent mission

de·bris or **dé·bris** (də brē′) ***n.*** ‖Fr < OFr *desbrisier*, break apart‖ bits and pieces of stone, rubbish, etc.

debt (det) ***n.*** ‖< L *debere*, owe‖ **1** something owed to another **2** the condition of owing /to be in *debt*/

debt′or (-ər) ***n.*** one who owes a debt

de·bug (dē bug′) ***vt.* -bugged′, -bug′ging** ‖DE- + BUG‖ **1** to correct defects in **2** |Colloq.| to find and remove hidden electronic listening devices from

de·bunk (dē buŋk′) ***vt.*** ‖DE- + BUNK[2]‖ to expose the exaggerated or false claims, etc. of

De·bus·sy (də bü sē′; *E* deb′yoo sē′), **Claude** (klôd) 1862-1918; Fr. composer

de·but or **dé·but** (dā byōō′, də-; dā′byōō′) ***n.*** ‖Fr < *débuter*, to lead off‖ **1** a first public appearance **2** the formal introduction of a girl into society **—*vi.*** to make a debut

deb·u·tante (deb′yoo tänt′) ***n.*** ‖Fr‖ a girl making a debut into society

Dec. December

deca- ‖< Gr *deka*, ten‖ *combining form* ten Also **dec-**

dec·ade (dek′ād′) ***n.*** ‖< Gr *deka*, ten‖ a period of ten years

dec·a·dence (dek′ə dəns, di kād′′ns) ***n.*** ‖< L *de*, from + *cadere*, to fall‖ a decline, as in morals, art, etc.; deterioration **—dec′a·dent *adj., n.***

de·caf·fein·at·ed (dē kaf′ə nāt′id) ***adj.*** with caffeine removed

de·cal (dē′kal′, dē kal′) ***n.*** ‖< *decalcomania* < Fr < L *calcare*, to tread + Gr *mania*, madness‖ a picture or design transferred from prepared paper to glass, wood, etc.

Dec·a·logue or **Dec·a·log** (dek′ə lôg′) ***n.*** ‖see DECA- & -LOGUE‖ |*sometimes* **d-**| TEN COMMANDMENTS

de·camp (dē kamp′) ***vi.*** ‖< Fr: see DE- & CAMP‖ **1** to break camp **2** to go away suddenly and secretly

de·cant (dē kant′) ***vt.*** ‖< Fr < L *de-*, from + *canthus*, tire of a wheel‖ to pour gently from one container into another

de·cant′er *n.* a decorative glass bottle for serving wine, etc.

de·cap·i·tate (dē kap′ə tāt′) ***vt.* -tat′ed, -tat′ing** ‖< L *de-*, off + *caput*, head‖ to behead **—de·cap′i·ta′tion *n.***

de·cath·lon (di kath′län′) ***n.*** ‖DEC(A)- + Gr *athlon*, a prize‖ an athletic contest in which each contestant takes part in ten TRACK (sense 6*b*) events

de·cay (dē kā′) ***vi.*** ‖see DECADENCE‖ **1** to lose strength, prosperity, etc. gradually; deteriorate **2** to rot **3** to undergo radioactive disintegration **—*vt.*** to cause to decay **—*n.* 1** deterioration **2** a rotting or rottenness

de·cease (dē sēs′) ***n.*** ‖< L *de-*, from + *cedere*, go‖ death **—*vi.* -ceased′, -ceas′ing** to die

de·ceased′ (-sēst′) ***adj.*** dead —**the deceased** the dead person or persons

de·ce·dent (dē sēd′′nt) ***n.*** ‖see DECEASE‖ *Law* a deceased person

de·ceit (dē sēt′) ***n.*** **1** a deceiving or lying **2** a lie **3** deceitful quality

de·ceit′ful ***adj.*** **1** apt to lie or cheat **2** deceptive —**de·ceit′ful·ly** ***adv.***

de·ceive (dē sēv′) ***vt., vi.*** **-ceived′**, **-ceiv′ing** ‖< L *de-*, from + *capere*, take‖ to make (a person) believe what is not true; mislead —**de·ceiv′er** ***n.*** —**de·ceiv′ing·ly** ***adv.***

de·cel·er·ate (dē sel′ər āt′) ***vt., vi.*** **-at′ed**, **-at′ing** ‖DE- + (AC)CELERATE‖ to reduce the speed (of); slow down —**de·cel′er·a′tion** ***n.***

De·cem·ber (dē sem′bər) ***n.*** ‖< L *decem*, ten: tenth month in Roman calendar‖ the twelfth and last month of the year, having 31 days

de·cen·cy (dē′sən sē) ***n., pl.*** **-cies** a being decent; propriety, courtesy, etc.

de·cen·ni·al (dē sen′ē əl) ***adj.*** ‖< L *decem*, ten + *annus*, year‖ **1** happening every ten years **2** lasting ten years

de·cent (dē′sənt) ***adj.*** ‖< L *decere*, befit‖ **1** proper and fitting **2** not obscene **3** respectable **4** adequate /*decent* wages/ **5** fair and kind —**de′cent·ly** ***adv.***

de·cen·tral·ize (dē sen′trə līz′) ***vt.*** **-ized′**, **-iz′ing** to break up a concentration of (governmental authority, industry, etc.) and distribute more widely —**de·cen′tral·i·za′tion** ***n.***

de·cep·tion (dē sep′shən) ***n.*** **1** a deceiving or being deceived **2** an illusion or fraud —**de·cep′tive** ***adj.***

deci- ‖< L *decem*, ten‖ *combining form* one tenth part of

dec·i·bel (des′ə bəl) ***n.*** ‖prec. + *bel*, after BELL‖ a unit for measuring relative loudness of a sound

de·cide (dē sīd′) ***vt.*** **-cid′ed**, **-cid′ing** ‖< L *de-*, off + *caedere*, to cut‖ **1** to end (a contest, dispute, etc.) by giving one side the victory **2** to reach a decision about; resolve —***vi.*** to reach a decision —**de·cid′a·ble** ***adj.***

de·cid′ed ***adj.*** **1** definite; clear-cut **2** determined —**de·cid′ed·ly** ***adv.***

de·cid·u·ous (dē sij′o͞o əs) ***adj.*** ‖< L *de-*, off, down + *cadere*, to fall‖ **1** falling off at a certain season, as some leaves or antlers **2** shedding leaves annually

dec·i·mal (des′ə məl) ***adj.*** ‖< L *decem*, ten‖ of or based on the number 10 —***n.*** a fraction with a denominator of 10 or some power of 10, shown by a point (**decimal point**) before the numerator (Ex.: .5 = $\frac{5}{10}$)

dec·i·mate (des′ə māt′) ***vt.*** **-mat′ed**, **-mat′ing** ‖< L *decem*, ten‖ to destroy or kill a large part of (lit., a tenth part of) —**dec′i·ma′tion** ***n.***

de·ci·pher (dē sī′fər) ***vt.*** ‖DE- + CIPHER‖ **1** DECODE **2** to make out the meaning of (a scrawl, etc.)

de·ci·sion (dē sizh′ən) ***n.*** **1** the act of deciding or settling a dispute or question **2** the act of making up one's mind **3** a judgment or conclusion **4** determination; firmness of mind

de·ci′sive (-sī′siv) ***adj.*** **1** that settles a dispute, question, etc. **2** showing decision —**de·ci′sive·ly** ***adv.***

deck[1] (dek) ***n.*** ‖prob. < earlier LowG *verdeck*‖ **1** a floor of a ship **2** a pack of playing cards **3** TAPE DECK

deck[2] (dek) ***vt.*** ‖MDu *decken*, to cover‖ to array or adorn: often with *out*

de·claim (dē klām′) ***vi., vt.*** ‖< L *de-*, intens. + *clamare*, to cry‖ to recite or speak in a studied, dramatic, or impassioned way —**dec·la·ma·tion** (dek′lə mā′shən) ***n.*** —**de·clam·a·to·ry** (dē klam′ə tôr′ē) ***adj.***

dec·la·ra·tion (dek′lə rā′shən) ***n.*** **1** a declaring; announcement **2** a formal statement

de·clar·a·tive (dē kler′ə tiv) ***adj.*** making a statement or assertion

de·clare (dē kler′) ***vt.*** **-clared′**, **-clar′ing** ‖< L *de-*, intens. + *clarus*, clear‖ **1** to announce openly or formally **2** to show or reveal **3** to say emphatically

de·clar′er ***n.*** **1** one who declares **2** *Bridge* the member of the partnership which made the winning bid who plays both his own and the dummy's hand

de·clas·si·fy (dē klas′ə fī′) ***vt.*** **-fied′**, **-fy′ing** to make (secret documents, etc.) available to the public

de·clen·sion (dē klen′shən) ***n.*** ‖see fol.‖ **1** a descent **2** a decline **3** *Gram.* the inflection of nouns, pronouns, or adjectives

de·cline (dē klīn′) ***vi.*** **-clined′**, **-clin′ing** ‖< L *de-*, from + *clinare*, to bend‖ **1** to bend or slope downward **2** to deteriorate **3** to refuse something —***vt.*** **1** to cause to bend or slope downward **2** to refuse politely **3** *Gram.* to give the inflected forms of (a noun, pronoun, or adjective) —***n.*** **1** a declining; dropping, failing, decay, etc. **2** a period of decline **3** a downward slope —**dec·li·na·tion** (dek′lə nā′shən) ***n.*** —**de·clin′er** ***n.***

de·cliv·i·ty (dē kliv′ə tē) ***n., pl.*** **-ties** ‖< L *de-*, down + *clivus*, a slope‖ a downward slope

de·code (dē kōd′) ***vt.*** **-cod′ed**, **-cod′ing** to decipher (a coded message)

dé·col·le·té (dā käl′ə tā′) ***adj.*** ‖Fr < L *de*, from + *collum*, neck‖ cut low so as to bare the neck and shoulders

de·col·o·ni·za·tion (dē käl′ə nə zā′shən) ***n.*** a freeing or being freed from colonial status —**de·col′o·nize′** (-ə nīz′), **-nized′**, **-niz′ing**, ***vt., vi.***

de·com·pose (dē′kəm pōz′) ***vt., vi.*** **-posed′**, **-pos′ing** ‖< Fr: see DE- & COMPOSE‖ **1** to break up into basic parts **2** to rot —**de′com·po·si′tion** (-käm pə zish′ən) ***n.***

de·com·press (dē′kəm pres′) ***vt.*** to free from pressure, esp. from air pressure —**de′com·pres′sion** ***n.***

de·con·gest·ant (dē′kən jes′tənt) ***n.*** a medication that relieves congestion, as in the nose

de′con·tam′i·nate′ (-tam′ə nāt′) ***vt.*** **-nat′ed**, **-nat′ing** to rid of a harmful substance, as radioactive products

dé·cor or **de·cor** (dā kôr′) ***n.*** ‖Fr‖ a decorative scheme, as of a room

dec·o·rate (dek′ə rāt′) ***vt.*** **-rat′ed**, **-rat′ing** ‖< L *decus*, an ornament‖ **1** to adorn; ornament **2** to paint or wallpaper **3** to give a medal or similar honor to —**dec·o·ra·tive** (dek′rə tiv, -ə rāt′iv) ***adj.*** —**dec′o·ra′tor** ***n.***

dec'o·ra'tion *n.* 1 a decorating 2 an ornament 3 a medal, etc.
Decoration Day MEMORIAL DAY
dec·o·rous (dek'ə rəs, di kôr'əs) *adj.* having or showing decorum, good taste, etc. —**dec'o·rous·ly** *adv.*
de·co·rum (di kō'rəm, -kôr'əm) *n.* ‖< L *decorus*, proper‖ propriety and good taste in behavior, speech, etc.
de·cou·page or **dé·cou·page** (dā'ko͞o päzh') *n.* ‖< Fr *dé-*, DE + *couper*, to cut‖ the art of decorating a surface with paper cutouts
de·coy (dē koi'; *for n., also* dē'koi') *n.* ‖< Du *de kooi*, the cage‖ 1 an artificial or trained bird, etc. used to lure game within gun range 2 a thing or person used to lure into danger —*vt.* to lure into danger
de·crease (dē krēs'; *for n. also* dē'krēs') *vi., vt.* **-creased', -creas'ing** ‖< L *de-*, from + *crescere*, grow‖ to become or make less, smaller, etc.; diminish —*n.* 1 a decreasing 2 amount of decreasing
de·cree (dē krē') *n.* ‖< L *de-*, from + *cernere*, to judge‖ an official order or decision —*vt.* **-creed', -cree'ing** to order or decide by decree
de·crep·it (dē krep'it) *adj.* ‖< L *de-*, intens. + *crepare*, to creak‖ broken down or worn out by old age or long use —**de·crep'i·tude'** (-ə to͞od') *n.*
de·crim·i·nal·ize (dē krim'ə nəl īz') *vt.* **-ized', -iz'ing** to eliminate or reduce the penalties for (a crime)
de·cry (dē krī') *vt.* **-cried', -cry'ing** ‖< Fr: see DE & CRY‖ to speak out against openly; denounce
ded·i·cate (ded'i kāt') *vt.* **-cat'ed, -cat'ing** ‖< L *de-*, intens. + *dicare*, proclaim‖ 1 to set apart for, or devote to, a special purpose 2 to address (a book, etc.) to someone as a sign of honor —**ded'i·ca'tion** *n.*
ded'i·cat'ed *adj.* devoted
de·duce (dē do͞os', -dyo͞os') *vt.* **-duced', -duc'ing** ‖< L *de-*, down + *ducere*, to lead‖ to infer or decide by reasoning —**de·duc'i·ble** *adj.*
de·duct (dē dukt') *vt.* ‖see prec.‖ to take away or subtract (a quantity)
de·duct'i·ble (-ə bəl) *adj.* that can be deducted —*n.* an amount stipulated in an insurance policy to be paid by the person insured in the event of a loss, etc., with the insurer paying the remainder
de·duc'tion (-duk'shən) *n.* 1 a deducting 2 an amount deducted 3 *a)* reasoning from the general to the specific *b)* a conclusion reached by such reasoning —**de·duc'tive** *adj.*
deed (dēd) *n.* ‖< OE *ded*‖ 1 a thing done; act 2 a feat of courage, skill, etc. 3 a legal document which transfers a property —*vt.* to transfer (property) by deed
deem (dēm) *vt., vi.* ‖< OE *deman*, to judge‖ to think, believe, or judge
de·em·pha·size (dē em'fə sīz') *vt.* **-sized', -siz'ing** to lessen the importance of —**de·em'pha·sis** (-sis) *n.*
deep (dēp) *adj.* ‖OE *deop*‖ 1 extending far downward, inward, or backward 2 hard to understand; abstruse 3 serious; profound 4 dark and rich /*a deep* red/ 5 absorbed by: with *in* /*deep* in thought/ 6 great in degree; intense 7 of low pitch /*a deep* voice/ 8 large; big —*n.* a deep place —*adv.* far down, far back, etc. —**the deep** [Old Poet.] the ocean —**deep'ly** *adv.* —**deep'ness** *n.*
deep·en (dē'pən) *vt., vi.* to make or become deep or deeper
deep'freeze' *n.* a condition of suspended activity, etc. —*vt.* **-froze', -fro'zen, -freez'·ing** to subject (foods) to sudden freezing so as to preserve and store
deep'-fry' *vt.* **-fried', -fry'ing** to fry in a deep pan of boiling fat or oil
deep'-root'ed *adj.* 1 having deep roots 2 firmly fixed
deep'-seat'ed *adj.* 1 buried deep 2 firmly fixed
deep'-six' *vt.* ‖< six fathoms‖ [Slang] to get rid of, as by throwing overboard
deep space OUTER SPACE
deer (dir) *n., pl.* **deer** or **deers** ‖OE *deor*, wild animal‖ a kind of ruminant, the male of which grows and sheds antlers annually
de·es·ca·late (dē es'kə lāt') *vi., vt.* **-lat'ed, -lat'ing** to reduce in scope, magnitude, etc. —**de·es'ca·la'tion** *n.*
de·face (dē fās') *vt.* **-faced', -fac'ing** ‖see DE- & FACE‖ to spoil the look of; mar —**de·face'ment** *n.*
de fac·to (dē fak'tō) ‖L‖ actually existing but not officially approved
de·fal·cate (dē fal'kāt') *vi.* **-cat'ed, -cat'ing** ‖< L *de-*, from + *falx*, a sickle‖ to steal or misuse funds entrusted to one's care; embezzle —**de'fal·ca'tion** *n.*
de·fame (dē fām') *vt.* **-famed', -fam'ing** ‖< L *dis-*, from + *fama*, fame‖ to attack the reputation of; slander or libel —**def·a·ma·tion** (def'ə mā'shən) *n.* —**de·fam·a·to·ry** (dē fam'ə tôr'ē) *adj.* —**de·fam'er** *n.*
de·fault (dē fôlt') *n.* ‖< L *de-*, away + *fallere*, fail‖ failure to do or appear as required; specif., failure to pay money due —*vi., vt.* 1 to fail to do or pay when required 2 to lose (a contest) by default —**de·fault'er** *n.*
de·feat (dē fēt') *vt.* ‖< L *dis-*, from + *facere*, do‖ 1 to win victory over 2 to bring to nothing; frustrate —*n.* a defeating or being defeated
de·feat'ist *n.* one who too readily accepts defeat —**de·feat'ism'** *n.*
def·e·cate (def'i kāt') *vi.* **-cat'ed, -cat'ing** ‖< L *de-*, from + *faex*, dregs‖ to excrete waste matter from the bowels —**def'e·ca'·tion** *n.*
de·fect (dē'fekt'; *also, and for v. always,* dē fekt') *n.* ‖< L *de-*, from + *facere*, do‖ 1 lack of something necessary for completeness 2 an imperfection; fault —*vi.* to forsake a party, cause, etc., esp. so as to join the opposition —**de·fec'tion** *n.* —**de·fec'tor** *n.*
de·fec·tive (dē fek'tiv) *adj.* having defects; imperfect; faulty
de·fend (dē fend') *vt.* ‖< L *de-*, away + *fendere*, to strike‖ 1 to guard from attack; protect 2 to support or justify 3 *Law a)* to oppose (an action) *b)* to act as lawyer for (an accused) —**de·fend'er** *n.*
de·fend·ant (dē fen'dənt) *n.* *Law* the person sued or accused
de·fense (dē fens', dē'fens') *n.* 1 a defending against attack 2 something that defends 3 justification by speech or writing 4 *a)* the

arguments of a defendant *b)* the defendant and his counsel Brit., etc. sp. **defence** —**de·fense′less** *adj.* —**de·fen′si·ble** *adj.*

defense mechanism any thought process used unconsciously to protect oneself against painful feelings

de·fen′sive *adj.* 1 defending 2 of or for defense —*n.* a position of defense —**de·fen′sive·ly** *adv.*

de·fer[1] (dē fur′) *vt., vi.* **-ferred′, -fer′ring** ‖see DIFFER‖ 1 to postpone; delay 2 to postpone the induction of (a person) into compulsory military service —**de·fer′ment** *n.*

de·fer[2] (dē fur′) *vi.* **-ferred′, -fer′ring** ‖< L *de-*, down + *ferre*, to BEAR[1]‖ to yield with courtesy (*to*)

def·er·ence (def′ər əns) *n.* 1 a yielding in opinion, judgment, etc. 2 courteous respect

def′er·en′tial (-en′shəl) *adj.* showing deference; very respectful

de·fi·ance (dē fī′əns) *n.* a defying; open, bold resistance to authority —**de·fi′ant** *adj.* —**de·fi′ant·ly** *adv.*

de·fi·cien·cy (dē fish′ən sē) *n.* ‖< L *de-*, from + *facere*, do‖ 1 a being deficient 2 *pl.* **-cies** a shortage

deficiency disease a disease caused by a lack of vitamins, minerals, etc. in the diet

de·fi′cient (-ənt) *adj.* ‖see DEFICIENCY‖ 1 lacking in some essential; incomplete 2 inadequate in amount

def·i·cit (def′ə sit) *n.* ‖L < *deficere*, to lack‖ the amount by which a sum of money is less than the required amount

de·file[1] (dē fīl′) *vt.* **-filed′, -fil′ing** ‖< OFr *defouler*, tread underfoot‖ 1 to make filthy 2 to profane; sully —**de·file′ment** *n.* —**de·fil′er** *n.*

de·file[2] (dē fīl′, dē′fīl′) *vi.* **-filed′, -fil′ing** ‖< Fr *dé-*, from + *fil*, thread‖ to march in single file —*n.* a narrow passage, valley, etc.

de·fine (dē fīn′) *vt.* **-fined′, -fin′ing** ‖< L *de-*, from + *finis*, boundary‖ 1 to determine the limits or nature of; describe exactly 2 to state the meaning of (a word, etc.) —**de·fin′er** *n.*

def·i·nite (def′ə nit) *adj.* ‖see prec.‖ 1 having exact limits 2 precise in meaning; explicit 3 certain; positive 4 *Gram.* limiting or specifying /"the" is the *definite* article/ —**def′i·nite·ly** *adv.* —**def′i·nite·ness** *n.*

def′i·ni′tion (-nish′ən) *n.* 1 a defining or being defined 2 a statement of the meaning of a word 3 clarity of outline, sound, etc.

de·fin·i·tive (dē fin′ə tiv) *adj.* 1 conclusive; final 2 most nearly complete 3 serving to define

de·flate (dē flāt′) *vt., vi.* **-flat′ed, -flat′ing** ‖DE- + (IN)FLATE‖ 1 to collapse by letting out air or gas 2 to lessen in size, importance, etc. 3 to cause deflation of (currency, etc.)

de·fla′tion *n.* 1 a deflating 2 a lessening of the amount of money in circulation, making it rise in value

de·flect (dē flekt′) *vt., vi.* ‖< L *de-*, from + *flectere*, to bend‖ to turn or make go to one side —**de·flec′tion** *n.* —**de·flec′tive** *adj.* —**de·flec′tor** *n.*

De·foe (di fō′), **Daniel** 1660-1731; Eng. writer

de·fog·ger (dē fôg′ər) *n.* an apparatus for clearing condensed moisture, as from a car window

de·fo·li·ant (dē fō′lē ənt) *n.* a chemical substance that causes leaves to fall from growing plants

de·fo′li·ate′ (-āt′) *vt.* **-at′ed, -at′ing** ‖< L *de-*, from + *folium*, leaf‖ to strip (trees, etc.) of leaves —**de·fo′li·a′tion** *n.*

de·form (dē fôrm′) *vt.* ‖< L *de-*, from + *forma*, form‖ 1 to impair the form of 2 to make ugly —**de·for·ma·tion** (dē′fôr mā′shən, def′ər-) *n.*

de·formed′ *adj.* misshapen

de·form·i·ty (dē fôr′mə tē) *n., pl.* **-ties** 1 a deformed part, as of the body 2 ugliness or depravity

de·fraud (dē frôd′) *vt.* to take property, rights, etc. from by fraud; cheat —**de·fraud′er** *n.*

de·fray (dē frā′) *vt.* ‖Fr *défrayer*‖ to pay (the cost or expenses) —**de·fray′a·ble** *adj.* —**de·fray′al** *n.*

de·frost (dē frôst′) *vt., vi.* to rid or get rid of frost or ice —**de·frost′er** *n.*

deft (deft) *adj.* ‖see DAFT‖ skillful; dexterous —**deft′ly** *adv.*

de·funct (dē fuŋkt′) *adj.* ‖< L *defungi*, to finish‖ no longer existing; dead or extinct

de·fuse (dē fyo͞oz′) *vt.* **-fused′, -fus′ing** 1 to remove the fuse from (a bomb, etc.) 2 to make harmless, less tense, etc.

de·fy (dē fī′) *vt.* **-fied′, -fy′ing** ‖< LL *dis-*, from + *fidus*, faithful‖ 1 to resist or oppose boldly or openly 2 to dare to do or prove something

de·gen·er·ate (dē jen′ər it; *for v.*, -ər āt′) *adj.* ‖< L *de-*, from + *genus*, race‖ 1 having sunk below a former or normal condition, etc.; deteriorated 2 depraved —*n.* a degenerate person —*vi.* **-at′ed, -at′ing** to lose former normal or higher qualities —**de·gen′er·a·cy** (-ə sē) *n.* —**de·gen′er·a′tion** *n.* —**de·gen′er·a·tive** *adj.*

de·grade (dē grād′) *vt.* **-grad′ed, -grad′ing** ‖< L *de-*, down + *gradus*, a step‖ 1 to demote 2 to lower in quality, moral character, dignity, etc.; debase, dishonor, etc. —**deg·ra·da·tion** (deg′rə dā′shən) *n.*

de·gree (di grē′) *n.* ‖see prec.‖ 1 any of the successive steps in a process 2 social or official rank 3 extent, amount, or intensity 4 a rank given by a college or university to one who has completed a course of study, or to a distinguished person as an honor 5 a grade of comparison of adjectives and adverbs /the superlative *degree*/ 6 *Law* the seriousness of a crime /murder in the first *degree*/ 7 *Math.* a unit of measure for angles or arcs, one 360th of the circumference of a circle 8 *Physics* a unit of measure for temperature —**to a degree** somewhat

de·hu·man·ize (dē hyo͞o′mə nīz′) *vt.* **-ized′, -iz′ing** to deprive of human qualities; make machinelike —**de·hu′man·i·za′tion** *n.*

de·hu·mid·i·fy (dē′hyo͞o mid′ə fī′) *vt.* **-fied′, -fy′ing** to remove moisture from (air, etc.) —**de′hu·mid′i·fi′er** *n.*

de·hy·drate (dē hī′drāt′) *vt.* **-drat′ed, -drat′ing** to remove water from; dry —*vi.* to lose water —**de′hy·dra′tion** *n.* —**de·hy′dra′tor** *n.*

de·ice (dē īs′) *vt.* **-iced′**, **-ic′ing** to melt ice from —**de·ic′er** *n.*

de·i·fy (dē′ə fī′) *vt.* **-fied′**, **-fy′ing** ‖ < L *deus*, god + *facere*, make ‖ **1** to make a god of **2** to look upon as a god —**de′i·fi·ca′tion** (-fi kā′shən) *n.*

deign (dān) *vi.*, *vt.* ‖ < L *dignus*, worthy ‖ to condescend (to do or give)

de·ism (dē′iz′əm) *n.* ‖ < L *deus*, god ‖ the belief that God exists and created the world but takes no part in its functioning —**de′ist** *n.*

de·i·ty (dē′ə tē) *n.* ‖ < L *deus*, god ‖ **1** the state of being a god **2** *pl.* **-ties** a god or goddess —**the Deity** God

dé·jà vu (dā zhä vü′) ‖ Fr, already seen ‖ a feeling of having been in a place or experienced something before

de·ject (dē jekt′) *vt.* ‖ < L *de-*, down + *jacere*, throw ‖ to dishearten; depress —**de·ject′ed** *adj.* —**de·jec′tion** *n.*

Del·a·ware (del′ə wer′, -war′) Eastern State of the U.S.: 2,057 sq. mi.; pop. 595,000; cap. Dover: abbrev. **Del.** —**Del′a·war′e·an** *adj.*, *n.*

de·lay (dē lā′) *vt.* ‖ < OFr *de-*, intens. + *laier*, to leave ‖ **1** to put off; postpone **2** to make late; detain —*vi.* to linger —*n.* a delaying or being delayed

de·lec·ta·ble (dē lek′tə bəl) *adj.* ‖ see DELIGHT ‖ delightful or delicious

de·lec·ta·tion (dē′lek tā′shən) *n.* ‖ see DELIGHT ‖ delight; enjoyment

del·e·gate (del′ə gət; *also*, -gāt′; *for v.*, -gāt′) *n.* ‖ < L *de-*, from + *legare*, send ‖ a person authorized to act for others; representative —*vt.* **-gat′ed**, **-gat′ing** **1** to appoint as a delegate **2** to entrust (authority, etc.) to another

del′e·ga′tion *n.* **1** a delegating or being delegated **2** a body of delegates

de·lete (dē lēt′) *vt.* **-let′ed**, **-let′ing** ‖ < L *delere*, destroy ‖ to take out (a word, etc.); cross out —**de·le′tion** *n.*

del·e·te·ri·ous (del′ə tir′ē əs) *adj.* ‖ < Gr *dēleisthai*, injure ‖ harmful to health or well-being; injurious

delft·ware (delft′wer′) *n.* ‖ after *Delft*, city in Holland ‖ glazed earthenware, usually blue and white Also **delft**

Del·hi (del′ē) city in N India: pop. 5,714,000: see also NEW DELHI

del·i (del′ē) *n.* *short for* DELICATESSEN

de·lib·er·ate (di lib′ər it; *for v.*, -āt′) *adj.* ‖ < L *de-*, intens. + *librare*, weigh ‖ **1** carefully thought out; premeditated **2** not rash or hasty **3** unhurried —*vi.*, *vt.* **-at′ed**, **-at′ing** to consider carefully —**de·lib′er·ate·ly** *adv.* —**de·lib′er·a′tive** *adj.*

de·lib′er·a′tion *n.* **1** a deliberating **2** [*often pl.*] consideration of alternatives **3** carefulness; slowness

del·i·ca·cy (del′i kə sē) *n.*, *pl.* **-cies** **1** the quality of being delicate; fineness, weakness, sensitivity, etc. **2** a choice food

del′i·cate (-kit) *adj.* ‖ < L *delicatus*, delightful ‖ **1** pleasing in its lightness, mildness, etc. **2** beautifully fine in texture, workmanship, etc. **3** slight and subtle **4** easily damaged **5** frail in health **6** *a)* needing careful handling *b)* showing tact, consideration, etc. **7** finely sensitive —**del′i·cate·ly** *adv.* —**del′i·cate·ness** *n.*

del·i·ca·tes·sen (del′i kə tes′ən) *n.* ‖ < Ger pl. < Fr *délicatesse*, delicacy ‖ **1** prepared cooked meats, fish, cheeses, salads, etc., collectively **2** a shop where such foods are sold

de·li·cious (di lish′əs) *adj.* ‖ see fol. ‖ **1** delightful **2** very pleasing to taste or smell —**de·li′cious·ly** *adv.* —**de·li′cious·ness** *n.*

de·light (di līt′) *vt.* ‖ < L *de-*, from + *lacere*, entice ‖ to give great pleasure to —*vi.* **1** to give great pleasure **2** to be highly pleased; rejoice —*n.* **1** great pleasure **2** something giving great pleasure —**de·light′ed** *adj.*

de·light′ful *adj.* giving delight; very pleasing —**de·light′ful·ly** *adv.*

De·li·lah (di lī′lə) *Bible* the mistress and betrayer of Samson

de·lim·it (dē lim′it) *vt.* to fix the limits of —**de·lim′i·ta′tion** *n.*

de·lin·e·ate (di lin′ē āt′) *vt.* **-at′ed**, **-at′ing** ‖ < L *de-*, from + *linea*, a line ‖ **1** to draw; sketch **2** to depict in words —**de·lin′e·a′tion** *n.*

de·lin·quent (di liŋ′kwənt) *adj.* ‖ < L *de-*, from + *linquere*, leave ‖ **1** failing to do what duty or law requires **2** overdue, as taxes —*n.* a delinquent person; esp., a juvenile delinquent —**de·lin′quen·cy**, *pl.* **-cies**, *n.* —**de·lin′quent·ly** *adv.*

del·i·quesce (del′i kwes′) *vi.* **-quesced′**, **-quesc′ing** ‖ < L < *de-*, from + *liquere*, be liquid ‖ to become liquid by absorbing moisture from the air —**del′i·ques′cent** *adj.*

de·lir·i·ous (di lir′ē əs) *adj.* **1** in a state of delirium **2** of or caused by delirium **3** wildly excited —**de·lir′i·ous·ly** *adv.* —**de·lir′i·ous·ness** *n.*

de·lir′i·um (-əm) *n.* ‖ < L *de-*, from + *lira*, a line ‖ **1** a temporary mental disturbance, as during a fever, marked by confused speech and hallucinations **2** uncontrollably wild excitement

de·liv·er (di liv′ər) *vt.* ‖ < L *de-*, intens. + *liber*, free ‖ **1** to set free or rescue **2** to assist at the birth of **3** to make (a speech, etc.) **4** to hand over **5** to distribute (mail, etc.) **6** to strike (a blow) **7** to throw (a ball, etc.)

de·liv′er·ance *n.* a freeing or being freed; rescue

de·liv′er·y *n.*, *pl.* **-er·ies** **1** a handing over **2** a distributing, as of mail **3** a giving birth **4** any giving forth **5** the act or manner of delivering a speech, ball, etc. **6** something delivered

dell (del) *n.* ‖ OE *del* ‖ a small, secluded valley or glen, usually wooded

del·phin·i·um (del fin′ē əm) *n.* ‖ < Gr *delphin*, dolphin ‖ a tall plant bearing spikes of flowers, usually blue

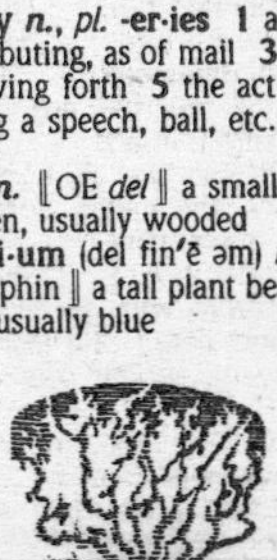

DELTA OF A RIVER

del·ta (del′tə) *n.* **1** the fourth letter of the

Greek alphabet (Δ, δ) **2** a deposit of soil, usually triangular, formed at the mouth of some rivers

de·lude (di lo͞od′) *vt.* **-lud′ed, -lud′ing** ‖ < L *de-*, from + *ludere*, to play ‖ to mislead; deceive

del·uge (del′yo͞oj′) *n.* ‖ < L *dis*, off + *luere*, to wash ‖ **1** a great flood **2** a heavy rainfall —*vt.* **-uged′, -ug′ing 1** to flood **2** to overwhelm

de·lu·sion (di lo͞o′zhən) *n.* **1** a deluding or being deluded **2** a false belief, specif. one that persists psychotically —**de·lu′sive** *adj.*

de·luxe (di luks′, -lo͝oks′) *adj.* ‖ Fr, of luxury ‖ of extra fine quality —*adv.* in a deluxe manner

delve (delv) *vi.* **delved, delv′ing** ‖ OE *delfan* ‖ **1** [Now Dial., Chiefly Brit.] to dig **2** to search (*into*) —**delv′er** *n.*

Dem. 1 Democrat **2** Democratic

de·mag·net·ize (dē mag′nə tīz′) *vt.* **-ized′, -iz′ing** to remove magnetism or magnetic properties from —**de·mag′net·i·za′tion** *n.*

dem·a·gogue or **dem·a·gog** (dem′ə gäg′) *n.* ‖ < Gr *dēmos*, the people + *agōgos*, leader ‖ one who tries to stir up people's emotions in order to win them over and so gain power —**dem′a·gog′y** (-gä′jē, -gäg′ē) or **dem′a·gogu′er·y** (-gäg′ər ē) *n.*

de·mand (di mand′) *vt.* ‖ < L *de-*, from + *mandare*, entrust ‖ **1** to ask for boldly or urgently **2** to ask for as a right **3** to require; need —*vi.* to make a demand —*n.* **1** a demanding **2** a thing demanded **3** a strong request **4** an urgent requirement **5** *Economics* the desire for a commodity together with ability to pay for it; also, the amount people are ready to buy —**in demand** wanted or sought —**on demand** when presented for payment

de·mand′ing *adj.* making difficult demands on one's patience, energy, etc.

de·mar·ca·tion (dē′mär kā′shən) *n.* ‖ < Sp *de-*, from + *marcar*, to mark ‖ **1** the act of setting and marking limits or boundaries **2** a limit or boundary

de·mean[1] (dē mēn′) *vt.* ‖ DE- + MEAN[2] ‖ to degrade; humble

de·mean[2] (dē mēn′) *vt.* ‖ see fol. ‖ to behave or conduct (oneself)

de·mean·or (di mēn′ər) *n.* ‖ < OFr *demener*, to lead ‖ outward behavior; conduct; deportment Brit. sp. **demeanour**

de·ment·ed (dē ment′id) *adj.* ‖ see fol. ‖ mentally deranged; insane

de·men·tia (di men′shə) *n.* ‖ < L *de-*, out from + *mens*, the mind ‖ severe mental deficiency or impairment

de·mer·it (dē mer′it) *n.* ‖ < L *de-*, intens. + *merere*, to deserve, with *de-* taken as negative ‖ **1** a fault; defect **2** a mark recorded against a student, etc. for poor conduct or work

de·mesne (di mān′; *also*, -mēn′) *n.* ‖ see DOMAIN ‖ a region or domain

De·me·ter (di mēt′ər) *Gr. Myth.* the goddess of agriculture

demi- ‖ < L *dimidius*, half ‖ *prefix* **1** half **2** less than usual in size, power, etc. [*demigod*]

dem·i·god (dem′i gäd′) *n.* **1** a minor deity **2** a godlike person

dem′i·john′ (-jän′) *n.* ‖ Fr *dame-jeanne* ‖ a large bottle of glass or earthenware in a wicker casing

de·mil·i·ta·rize (dē mil′ə tə rīz′) *vt.* **-rized′, -riz′ing** to free from organized military control

dem·i·monde (dem′i mänd′) *n.* ‖ Fr < *demi-* + *monde*, world ‖ the class of women who have lost social standing because of sexual promiscuity

de·mise (dē mīz′) *n.* ‖ < L *de-*, down + *mittere*, send ‖ **1** *Law* a transfer of an estate by lease **2** death —*vt.* **-mised′, -mis′ing** to transfer (an estate) by lease

dem·i·tasse (dem′i täs′, -tas′) *n.* ‖ Fr < *demi-* + *tasse*, cup ‖ a small cup of or for after dinner coffee

dem·o (dem′ō) *n.* a recording made to demonstrate a song, the talent of a performer, etc.

de·mo·bi·lize (dē mō′bə līz′) *vt.* **-lized′, -liz′ing** to disband (troops) —**de·mo′bi·li·za′tion** *n.*

de·moc·ra·cy (di mäk′rə sē) *n.*, *pl.* **-cies** ‖ < Gr *dēmos*, the people + *kratein*, to rule ‖ **1** government by the people, directly or through representatives **2** a country, etc. with such government **3** equality of rights, opportunity, and treatment

dem·o·crat (dem′ə krat′) *n.* **1** one who supports or practices democracy **2** [D-] a Democratic Party member

dem′o·crat′ic *adj.* **1** of or for democracy **2** of or for all the people **3** not snobbish **4** [D-] of the Democratic Party —**dem′o·crat′i·cal·ly** *adv.*

Democratic Party one of the two major political parties in the U.S.

de·mod·u·la·tion (dē mä′jo͞o lā′shən) *n.* *Radio* the recovery, at the receiver, of a signal that has been modulated on a carrier wave

dem·o·graph·ics (dem′ə graf′iks) *n.pl.* demographic characteristics of a population, as age, sex, income, etc., for analysis

de·mog·ra·phy (di mä′grə fē) *n.* ‖ < Gr *dēmos*, the people + -GRAPHY ‖ the statistical study of human populations —**de·mog′ra·pher** *n.* —**dem·o·graph·ic** (dem′ə graf′ik) *adj.* —**dem′o·graph′i·cal·ly** *adv.*

de·mol·ish (di mäl′ish) *vt.* ‖ < L *de-*, down + *moliri*, build ‖ to wreck —**dem·o·li·tion** (dem′ə lish′ən) *n.*

de·mon (dē′mən) *n.* ‖ < L *daemon* ‖ **1** a devil; evil spirit **2** a person or thing regarded as evil, cruel, etc. —**de·mon·ic** (di män′ik) *adj.*

de·mon·e·tize (dē män′ə tīz′) *vt.* **-tized′, -tiz′ing** to deprive (esp. currency) of its standard value

de·mo·ni·ac (dē mō′nē ak′) *adj.* of or like a demon; fiendish; frenzied Also **de·mo·ni·a·cal** (dē′mə nī′ə kəl)

de·mon·stra·ble (di män′strə bəl) *adj.* that can be demonstrated, or proved —**de·mon′stra·bly** *adv.*

dem·on·strate (dem′ən strāt′) *vt.* **-strat′ed, -strat′ing** ‖ < L *de-*, from + *monstrare*, to show ‖ **1** to show by reasoning; prove **2** to explain by using examples, etc. **3** to show how something works —*vi.* to show feelings or views publicly by meetings, etc. —**dem′on·stra′tion** *n.* —**dem′on·stra′tor** *n.*

de·mon·stra·tive (di män′strə tiv) *adj.* **1**

illustrative 2 giving proof (*of*) 3 showing feelings openly 4 *Gram.* pointing out ["this" is a *demonstrative* pronoun] —*n.* *Gram.* a demonstrative pronoun or adjective

de·mor·al·ize (dē môr′ə līz′) ***vt.*** **-ized′, -iz′·ing** 1 to lower the morale of 2 to throw into confusion —**de·mor′al·i·za′tion** ***n.***

De·mos·the·nes (di mäs′thə nēz′) 384-322 B.C.; Athenian orator

de·mote (dē mōt′) ***vt.*** **-mot′ed, -mot′ing** ⟦DE- + (PRO)MOTE⟧ to reduce to a lower rank —**de·mo′tion** ***n.***

de·mul·cent (dē mul′sənt) ***adj.*** ⟦< L *de-*, down + *mulcere*, to stroke⟧ soothing —***n.*** a soothing ointment

de·mur (dē mur′, di-) ***vi.*** **-murred′, -mur′·ring** ⟦< L *de-*, from + *mora*, a delay⟧ to hesitate, as because of doubts; have scruples; object —***n.*** a demurring: also **de·mur′ral**

de·mure (di myoor′) ***adj.*** ⟦< ME *de-* (prob. intens.) + OFr *mëur*, mature⟧ 1 decorous; modest 2 affectedly modest; coy —**de·mure′ly** ***adv.***

de·mur·rage (di mur′ij) ***n.*** 1 the compensation payable for delaying a vehicle or vessel carrying freight, as by failure to load or unload 2 the delay itself

de·mur·rer (di mur′ər) ***n.*** ⟦see DEMUR⟧ 1 a plea for dismissal of a lawsuit because statements supporting a claim are defective 2 an objection

den (den) ***n.*** ⟦OE *denn*⟧ 1 the lair of a wild animal 2 a haunt, as of thieves 3 a small, cozy room where one can be alone to read, work, etc.

de·na·ture (dē nā′chər) ***vt.*** **-tured, -tur·ing** 1 to change the nature of 2 to make (alcohol) unfit to drink

den·drite (den′drīt′) ***n.*** ⟦< Gr *dendron*, tree⟧ the part of a nerve cell that carries impulses toward the cell body

Deng Xiao·ping (duŋ′ shou′piŋ′) 1904- ; Chin. Communist leader; held various official titles from 1967-87; China's de facto ruler (*c.* 1981-87; 1989-)

de·ni·al (dē nī′əl) ***n.*** 1 a denying; saying "no" (to a request, etc.) 2 a contradiction 3 a refusal to believe or accept (a doctrine, etc.) 4 SELF-DENIAL

de·nier[1] (den′yər) ***n.*** ⟦< L *deni*, by tens⟧ a unit of weight for measuring the fineness of threads of silk, nylon, etc.

de·ni·er[2] (dē nī′ər) ***n.*** one who denies

den·i·grate (den′ə grāt′) ***vt.*** **-grat′ed, -grat′·ing** ⟦< L < *de-*, entirely + *nigrare*, blacken⟧ to belittle the character of; defame —**den′i·gra′tion** ***n.***

den·im (den′im) ***n.*** ⟦< Fr (*serge*) *de Nîmes*, (serge) of Nîmes, town in France⟧ a coarse, twilled, cotton cloth

den·i·zen (den′ə zən) ***n.*** ⟦< L *de intus*, from within⟧ an inhabitant or frequenter of a particular place

Den·mark (den′märk) country in Europe, on a peninsula & several islands in the North & Baltic seas: 16,632 sq. mi.; pop. 5,124,000

de·nom·i·nate (dē näm′ə nāt′) ***vt.*** **-nat′ed, -nat′ing** ⟦< L *de-*, intens. + *nominare*, to name⟧ to name; call

de·nom′i·na′tion (-nā′shən) ***n.*** 1 the act of naming 2 a name 3 a class or kind, as of coins, having a specific name or value 4 a particular religious body

de·nom′i·na′tion·al ***adj.*** of, or under the control of, a religious denomination

de·nom′i·na′tor (-nāt′ər) ***n.*** 1 a shared characteristic 2 *Math.* the term below the line in a fraction

de·note (dē nōt′) ***vt.*** **-not′ed, -not′ing** ⟦< L *de-*, down + *notare*, to mark⟧ 1 to indicate 2 to signify; mean —**de·no·ta·tion** (dē′nō tā′shən) ***n.***

de·noue·ment or **dé·noue·ment** (dā′no͞o män′) ***n.*** ⟦Fr⟧ the outcome or unraveling of a plot in a drama, etc.

de·nounce (dē nouns′) ***vt.*** **-nounced′, -nounc′ing** ⟦see DENUNCIATION⟧ 1 to accuse publicly; inform against 2 to condemn strongly —**de·nounce′ment** ***n.***

dense (dens) ***adj.*** **dens′er, dens′est** ⟦< L *densus*, compact⟧ 1 packed tightly together 2 difficult to get through 3 stupid —**dense′ly** ***adv.*** —**dense′ness** ***n.***

den·si·ty (den′sə tē) ***n., pl.*** **-ties** 1 a dense condition 2 stupidity 3 number per unit, as of area 4 ratio of the mass of an object to its volume

dent (dent) ***n.*** ⟦ME, var. of DINT⟧ 1 a slight hollow made in a surface by a blow 2 a slight effect —***vt., vi.*** to make or receive a dent (in)

den·tal (dent′'l) ***adj.*** ⟦< L *dens*, tooth⟧ of or for the teeth or dentistry

dental floss thread for removing food particles between the teeth

den·ti·frice (den′tə fris) ***n.*** ⟦< L *dens*, tooth + *fricare*, rub⟧ any preparation for cleaning teeth

den·tin (den′tin) ***n.*** ⟦see DENTAL⟧ the hard tissue under the enamel of a tooth Also **den′tine′** (-tēn′, -tin)

den·tist (den′tist) ***n.*** one whose profession is the care and repair of teeth —**den′tist·ry** ***n.***

den·ture (den′chər) ***n.*** ⟦see DENTAL⟧ a set of teeth

de·nu·cle·ar·ize (dē no͞o′klē ər īz′) ***vt.*** **-ized′, -iz′ing** to prohibit the possession of nuclear weapons in

de·nude (dē no͞od′) ***vt.*** **-nud′ed, -nud′ing** ⟦< L *de-*, off + *nudare*, to strip⟧ to make bare or naked; strip

de·nun·ci·a·tion (dē nun′sē ā′shən) ***n.*** ⟦< L *de-*, intens. + *nuntiare*, announce⟧ the act of denouncing

Den·ver (den′vər) capital of Colo.: pop. 491,000

de·ny (dē nī′) ***vt.*** **-nied′, -ny′ing** ⟦< L *de-*, intens. + *negare*, to deny⟧ 1 to declare (a statement) untrue 2 to refuse to accept as true or right 3 to repudiate 4 to refuse to grant or give 5 to refuse the request of —**deny oneself** to do without desired things

de·o·dor·ant (dē ō′dər ənt) ***adj.*** that can counteract undesired odors —***n.*** any deodorant preparation

de·o′dor·ize′ (-dər īz′) ***vt.*** **-ized′, -iz′ing** to counteract the odor of —**de·o′dor·iz′er** ***n.***

de·part (dē pärt′) ***vi.*** ⟦< L *dis-*, apart + *partire*, divide⟧ 1 to go away; leave 2 to die 3 to deviate (*from*) —***vt.*** to leave

de·part′ed ***adj.*** 1 gone away 2 dead —**the departed** the dead

de·part·ee (dē′pär tē′) ***n.*** one who has departed, as from a job, country, etc.

de·part·ment (dē pärt′mənt) *n.* 1 a separate part or division, as of a business 2 a field of activity —**de′part·men′tal** (-ment′'l) *adj.*

de′part·men′tal·ize′ (-men′t'l īz′) *vt.* **-ized′**, **-iz′ing** to organize into departments —**de′part·men′tal·i·za′tion** *n.*

department store a large retail store for the sale of many kinds of goods arranged in departments

de·par·ture (dē pär′chər) *n.* 1 a departing 2 a starting out, as on a trip 3 a deviation (*from*)

de·pend (dē pend′) *vi.* ‖< L *de-*, down + *pendere*, to hang‖ 1 to be determined by something else; be contingent (*on*) 2 to have trust; rely (*on*) 3 to rely (*on*) for support or aid

de·pend′a·ble *adj.* trustworthy; reliable —**de·pend′a·bil′i·ty** *n.*

de·pend′ence *n.* 1 a being dependent 2 reliance (*on*) for support or aid 3 reliance; trust 4 DEPENDENCY (sense 4)

de·pend′en·cy *n.*, *pl.* **-cies** 1 dependence 2 something dependent 3 a territory, as a possession, subordinate to its governing country 4 addiction to alcohol or drugs

de·pend′ent *adj.* 1 hanging down 2 determined by something else 3 relying (*on*) for support, etc. 4 subordinate 5 addicted —*n.* one relying on another for support, etc. Also **de·pend′ant** —**de·pend′ent·ly** *adv.*

dependent clause *Gram.* a clause that cannot function as a complete sentence by itself

de·pict (dē pikt′) *vt.* ‖< L *de-*, intens. + *pingere*, to paint‖ 1 to represent by drawing, painting, etc. 2 to describe —**de·pic′tion** *n.*

de·pil·a·to·ry (di pil′ə tôr′ē) *adj.* ‖< L *de-*, from + *pilus*, hair‖ serving to remove unwanted hair —*n.*, *pl.* **-ries** a depilatory substance or device

de·plane (dē plān′) *vi.* **-planed′**, **-plan′ing** to leave an airplane after it lands

de·plete (dē plēt′) *vt.* **-plet′ed**, **-plet′ing** ‖< L *de-*, from + *plere*, fill‖ 1 to use up (funds, etc.) 2 to use up the resources, etc. of —**de·ple′tion** *n.*

de·plor·a·ble (dē plôr′ə bəl) *adj.* regrettable, very bad, wretched, etc.

de·plore (dē plôr′) *vt.* **-plored′**, **-plor′ing** ‖< L *de-*, intens. + *plorare*, weep‖ 1 to regret deeply 2 to disapprove of

de·ploy (dē ploi′) *vt.*, *vi.* ‖< L *dis-*, apart + *plicare*, to fold‖ to spread out or place (military troops, etc.), as by a plan —**de·ploy′ment** *n.*

de·po·lar·ize (dē pō′lər īz′) *vt.* **-ized′**, **-iz′ing** to destroy or counteract the polarization of —**de·po′lar·i·za′tion** *n.*

de·po·lit·i·cize (dē′pə lit′ə sīz′) *vt.* **-cized′**, **-ciz′ing** to remove from political influence

de·pon·ent (dē pōn′ənt) *n.* ‖< L *de-*, down + *ponere*, put‖ *Law* one who gives written testimony under oath

de·pop·u·late (dē päp′yə lāt′) *vt.* **-lat′ed**, **-lat′ing** to reduce the population of —**de·pop′u·la′tion** *n.*

de·port (dē pôrt′) *vt.* ‖< L *de-*, from + *portare*, carry‖ 1 to behave (oneself) 2 to expel (an alien) —**de′por·ta′tion** *n.*

de·port′ment *n.* conduct; behavior

de·pose (dē pōz′) *vt.* **-posed′**, **-pos′ing** ‖< OFr *de-*, from + *poser*, cease‖ 1 to remove from office 2 *a*) to testify *b*) to take the deposition of

de·pos·it (dē päz′it) *vt.* ‖< L *de-*, down + *ponere*, put‖ 1 to place (money, etc.) for safekeeping, as in a bank 2 to give as a pledge or partial payment 3 to set down 4 to cause (sediment, etc.) to settle —*n.* 1 something placed for safekeeping, as money in a bank 2 a pledge or part payment 3 something deposited or left lying —**de·pos′i·tor** *n.*

dep·o·si·tion (dep′ə zish′ən) *n.* 1 a deposing or being deposed 2 testimony 3 something deposited

de·pos·i·to·ry (dē päz′ə tôr′ē) *n.*, *pl.* **-ries** a place where things are put for safekeeping

de·pot (dē′pō; *military & Brit* dep′ō) *n.* ‖< Fr: see DEPOSIT‖ 1 a warehouse 2 a railroad or bus station 3 a storage place for military supplies

de·prave (dē prāv′) *vt.* **-praved′**, **-prav′ing** ‖< L *de-*, intens. + *pravus*, crooked‖ to make morally bad; corrupt —**de·praved′** *adj.* —**de·prav′i·ty** (-prav′ə tē), *pl.* **-ties**, *n.*

dep·re·cate (dep′rə kāt′) *vt.* **-cat′ed**, **-cat′ing** ‖< L *de-*, off + *precari*, pray‖ 1 to express disapproval of 2 to belittle —**dep′re·ca′tion** *n.* —**dep′re·ca·to′ry** (-kə tôr′ē) *adj.*

de·pre·ci·ate (dē prē′shē āt′) *vt.*, *vi.* **-at′ed**, **-at′ing** ‖< L *de-*, from + *pretium*, price‖ 1 to lessen in value or price 2 to belittle —**de·pre′ci·a′tion** *n.*

dep·re·da·tion (dep′rə dā′shən) *n.* ‖< L *de-*, intens. + *praedari*, to plunder‖ a robbing or plundering

de·press (dē pres′) *vt.* ‖< L *de-*, down + *premere*, to press‖ 1 to press down 2 to sadden; deject 3 to make less active 4 to lower in value, price, etc. —**de·pressed′** *adj.*

de·pres′sant *n.* a medicine, drug, etc. that lessens nervous activity

de·pres·sion (dē presh′ən) *n.* 1 a depressing or being depressed 2 a hollow or low place 3 low spirits; dejection 4 a decrease in force, activity, etc. 5 a period of reduced business, much unemployment, etc.

de·pres·sive (dē pres′iv) *adj.* 1 tending to depress 2 characterized by psychological depression —*n.* one suffering from psychological depression

de·prive (dē prīv′) *vt.* **-prived′**, **-priv′ing** ‖< L *de-*, intens. + *privare*, to separate‖ 1 to take away from forcibly 2 to keep from having, etc. —**dep·ri·va·tion** (dep′rə vā′shən) *n.*

de·pro·gram (dē prō′gram′, -grəm) *vt.* **-grammed′** or **-gramed′**, **-gram′ming** or **-gram′ing** to cause to abandon rigidly held beliefs, etc. by undoing the effects of indoctrination

dept. 1 department 2 deputy

depth (depth) *n.* ‖< ME *dep*, deep + -TH¹‖ 1 the distance from the top downward, or from front to back 2 deepness 3 intensity 4 [*usually pl.*] the deepest or inmost part —**in depth** comprehensively

dep·u·ta·tion (dep′yo͞o tā′shən) *n.* 1 a deputing 2 a delegation
de·pute (dē pyo͞ot′) *vt.* **-put′ed, -put′ing** ⟦< L *de-*, from + *putare*, cleanse⟧ 1 to give (authority, etc.) to a deputy 2 to appoint as one's substitute, etc.
dep·u·tize (dep′yo͞o tīz′) *vt.* **-tized′, -tiz′ing** to appoint as deputy
dep·u·ty (dep′yo͞o tē) *n., pl.* **-ties** a person appointed to act for another
de·rail (dē rāl′) *vt., vi.* to run off the rails, as a train —**de·rail′ment** *n.*
de·rail·leur (də rāl′ər) *n.* ⟦Fr⟧ a gear-shifting mechanism on a bicycle for shifting the sprocket chain from one size of sprocket wheel to another
de·range (dē rānj′) *vt.* **-ranged′, -rang′ing** ⟦< OFr *des-*, apart + *rengier*, to range⟧ 1 to upset the arrangement or working of 2 to make insane —**de·range′ment** *n.*
Der·by (dur′bē; *Brit* där′-) *n., pl.* **-bies** 1 ⟦after an Earl of *Derby*, who founded the race (1780)⟧ any of various horse races, as ones held annually in England, Kentucky, etc. 2 any of various contests or races, open to anyone 3 [d-] a stiff felt hat with a round crown
de·reg·u·late (dē reg′yə lāt′) *vt.* **-lat′ed, -lat′ing** to remove regulations governing —**de·reg′u·la′tion** *n.*
der·e·lict (der′ə likt′) *adj.* ⟦< L *de-*, intens. + *relinquere*: see RELINQUISH⟧ 1 deserted by the owner; abandoned 2 negligent —*n.* 1 an abandoned ship on the open sea 2 a destitute and rejected person
der′e·lic′tion (-lik′shən) *n.* 1 a forsaking or being forsaken 2 a neglect of, or failure in, duty
de·ride (di rīd′) *vt.* **-rid′ed, -rid′ing** ⟦< L *de-*, down + *ridere*, to laugh⟧ to laugh at in scorn; ridicule —**de·ri′sion** (-rizh′ən) *n.* —**de·ri′sive** (-rī′siv) *adj.* —**de·ri′sive·ly** *adv.*
der·i·va·tion (der′ə vā′shən) *n.* 1 a deriving or being derived 2 the source or origin of something 3 the origin and development of a word
de·riv·a·tive (də riv′ə tiv) *adj.* derived —*n.* something derived
de·rive (di rīv′) *vt.* **-rived′, -riv′ing** ⟦< L *de-*, from + *rivus*, a stream⟧ 1 to get or receive (something) *from* a source 2 to deduce or infer 3 to trace from or to a source —*vi.* to be derived
der·ma·bra·sion (dur′mə brā′zhən) *n.* ⟦DERM(IS) + ABRASION⟧ the surgical procedure of scraping off upper layers of the skin with an abrasive device, to remove acne scars, blemishes, etc.
der·ma·ti·tis (dur′mə tīt′is) *n.* ⟦< Gr *derma*, skin + -ITIS⟧ inflammation of the skin
der·ma·tol·o·gy (dur′mə täl′ə jē) *n.* ⟦< Gr *derma*, skin + -LOGY⟧ the branch of medicine dealing with the skin —**der′ma·tol′o·gist** *n.*
der·mis (dur′mis) *n.* ⟦see EPIDERMIS⟧ the layer of skin just below the epidermis
der·o·gate (der′ə gāt′) *vi., vt.* **-gat′ed, -gat′ing** ⟦< L *de-*, from + *rogare*, ask⟧ to detract or disparage —**der′o·ga′tion** *n.*
de·rog·a·to·ry (di räg′ə tôr′ē) *adj.* ⟦see prec.⟧ 1 detracting 2 disparaging; belittling
der·rick (der′ik) *n.* ⟦after Thos. *Derrick*, London hangman of the early 17th c.: orig. applied to a gallows⟧ 1 a pivoted beam for lifting and moving heavy objects 2 a tall framework, as over an oil well, to support drilling machinery, etc.

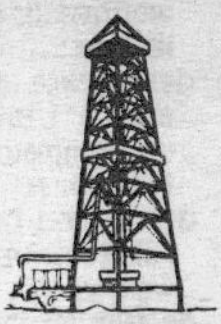

OIL DERRICK

der·ri·ère (der′yer′, der′ē er′) *n.* ⟦Fr, back part⟧ the buttocks
der·rin·ger (der′in jər) *n.* ⟦after H. *Deringer*, 19th-c. U.S. gunsmith⟧ a small, short-barreled pistol
der·vish (dur′vish) *n.* ⟦< Pers *darvēsh*, beggar⟧ a member of any of various Muslim ascetic religious groups
de·sal·i·na·tion (dē′sal′ə nā′shən) *n.* ⟦DE- + SALIN(E) + -ATION⟧ the removal of salt, esp. from sea water to make it drinkable —**de′sal′i·nate′, -nat′ed, -nat′ing,** *vt.*
des·cant (des′kant′, des kant′) *vi.* ⟦< L *dis-*, apart + *cantus*, song⟧ 1 to discourse (*on* or *upon*) 2 to sing
Des·cartes (dā kärt′), **Re·né** (rə nā′) 1596-1650; Fr. philosopher
de·scend (dē send′) *vi.* ⟦< L *de-*, down + *scandere*, climb⟧ 1 to move down to a lower place 2 to pass from an earlier to a later time, from greater to less, etc. 3 to slope downward 4 to come down (*from* a source) 5 to stoop (*to*) 6 to make a sudden attack or visit (*on*) —*vt.* to move down along
de·scend′ant *n.* an offspring of a certain ancestor, family, group, etc.
de·scent (dē sent′) *n.* 1 a coming down or going down 2 ancestry 3 a downward slope 4 a way down 5 a sudden attack 6 a decline
de·scribe (di skrīb′) *vt.* **-scribed′, -scrib′ing** ⟦< L *de-*, from + *scribere*, write⟧ 1 to tell or write about 2 to trace the outline of —**de·scrib′er** *n.*
de·scrip·tion (di skrip′shən) *n.* 1 the act or technique of describing 2 a statement or passage that describes 3 sort; kind 4 a tracing or outlining —**de·scrip′tive** (-tiv) *adj.*
de·scry (di skrī′) *vt.* **-scried′, -scry′ing** ⟦< OFr *descrier*, proclaim⟧ 1 to catch sight of; discern 2 to detect
des·e·crate (des′i krāt′) *vt.* **-crat′ed, -crat′ing** ⟦DE- (sense 4) + (CON)SECRATE⟧ to violate the sacredness of; profane —**des′e·cra′tion** *n.*
de·seg·re·gate (dē seg′rə gāt′) *vt., vi.* **-gat′ed, -gat′ing** to abolish racial segregation in (public schools, etc.) —**de·seg′re·ga′tion** *n.*
de·sen·si·tize (dē sen′sə tīz′) *vt.* **-tized′, -tiz′ing** to make less sensitive, as to an allergen
de·sert[1] (di zurt′) *vt., vi.* ⟦< L *de-*, from + *serere*, join⟧ 1 to abandon; forsake 2 to leave (one's military post, etc.) without permission and with no intent to return —**de·sert′er** *n.* —**de·ser′tion** (-zur′shən) *n.*
des·ert[2] (dez′ərt) *n.* ⟦see prec.⟧ 1 an uninhabited region; wilderness 2 a dry, barren, sandy region
de·sert[3] (di zurt′) *n.* ⟦see fol.⟧ [*often pl.*] deserved reward or punishment
de·serve (di zurv′) *vt., vi.* **-served′, -serv′-**

ing ⟦ < L *de-*, intens. + *servire*, serve ⟧ to be worthy (of); merit —**de·serv'ed·ly** (-zurʹvid lē) *adv.*

des·ic·cate (desʹi kātʹ) *vt., vi.* **-cat'ed, -cat'ing** ⟦ < L *de-*, intens. + *siccus*, dry ⟧ to dry out completely —**des'ic·ca'tion** *n.* —**des'ic·ca'tor** *n.*

de·sid·er·a·tum (di zid'ər ātʹəm) *n., pl.* **-ta** (-ə) ⟦ see DESIRE ⟧ something needed and wanted

de·sign (di zīnʹ) *vt.* ⟦ < L *de-*, out + *signum*, a mark ⟧ 1 to sketch an outline for; plan 2 to contrive 3 to plan to do; intend —*vi.* to make original plans, etc. —*n.* 1 a plan; scheme 2 purpose; aim 3 a working plan; pattern 4 arrangement of parts, form, color, etc.; artistic invention —**by design** purposely —**de·sign'er** *n.*

des·ig·nate (dezʹig nātʹ) *vt.* **-nat'ed, -nat'ing** ⟦ see prec. ⟧ 1 to point out; specify 2 to name 3 to appoint —**des'ig·na'tion** *n.*

de·sign'ing *adj.* scheming; artful —*n.* the art of creating designs, etc.

de·sir·a·ble (di zīrʹə bəl) *adj.* 1 worth having 2 pleasing —**de·sir'a·bil'i·ty** *n.* —**de·sir'a·bly** *adv.*

de·sire (di zīrʹ) *vt.* **-sired', -sir'ing** ⟦ < L *desiderare* ⟧ 1 to long for; crave 2 to ask for —*vi.* to have a desire —*n.* 1 a wish; craving 2 sexual appetite 3 a request 4 a thing desired

de·sir'ous *adj.* desiring

de·sist (di zistʹ) *vi.* ⟦ < L *de-*, from + *stare*, to stand ⟧ to cease; stop

desk (desk) *n.* ⟦ < ML *desca*, table ⟧ a table for writing, drawing, or reading —*adj.* of, for, or at a desk /a *desk* job/

Des Moines (də moinʹ) capital of Iowa: pop. 191,000

des·o·late (desʹə lit; *for v.,* -lātʹ) *adj.* ⟦ < L *de-*, intens. + *solus*, alone ⟧ 1 lonely; solitary 2 uninhabited 3 laid waste 4 forlorn —*vt.* **-lat'ed, -lat'ing** 1 to rid of inhabitants 2 to lay waste 3 to make forlorn —**des'o·late·ly** *adv.* —**des'o·late·ness** *n.*

des'o·la'tion *n.* 1 a making desolate 2 a desolate condition or place 3 misery 4 loneliness

de·spair (di sperʹ) *vi.* ⟦ < L *de-*, without + *sperare*, to hope ⟧ to lose hope —*n.* 1 loss of hope 2 a person or thing causing despair

des·patch (di spachʹ) *vt., n.* DISPATCH

des·per·a·do (des'pər äʹdō, -āʹ-) *n., pl.* **-does** or **-dos** ⟦ < 17th-c. Sp < L *desperare*: see DESPAIR ⟧ a dangerous criminal; bold outlaw

des·per·ate (desʹpər it) *adj.* 1 rash or violent because of despair 2 having a very great need 3 very serious 4 drastic —**des'per·ate·ly** *adv.*

des·per·a·tion (des'pər āʹshən) *n.* 1 the state of being desperate 2 recklessness resulting from despair

des·pi·ca·ble (desʹpi kə bəl, di spikʹə-) *adj.* deserving scorn; contemptible

de·spise (di spīzʹ) *vt.* **-spised', -spis'ing** ⟦ < L *de*, down + *specere*, look at ⟧ 1 to scorn 2 to loathe

de·spite (di spītʹ) *prep.* ⟦ see prec. ⟧ in spite of; notwithstanding

de·spoil (dē spoilʹ) *vt.* ⟦ < L *de-*, intens. + *spoliare*, to strip ⟧ to rob; plunder —**de·spoil'ment** *n.*

de·spond·en·cy (di spänʹdən sē) *n.* ⟦ < L *de-*, from + *spondere*, to promise ⟧ loss of hope; dejection Also **de·spond'ence** —**de·spond'ent** *adj.*

des·pot (desʹpət) *n.* ⟦ < Gr *despotēs*, a master ⟧ 1 an absolute ruler 2 a tyrant —**des·pot'ic** (-pätʹik) *adj.* —**des'pot·ism'** (-pət izʹəm) *n.*

des·sert (di zurtʹ) *n.* ⟦ < L *de*, from + *servire*, serve ⟧ the final course of a meal, typically cake, pie, etc.

des·ti·na·tion (des'tə nāʹshən) *n.* 1 the purpose for which something or someone is destined 2 the place toward which one is going or sent

des·tine (desʹtin) *vt.* **-tined, -tin·ing** ⟦ < L *de-*, intens. + *stare*, to stand ⟧ 1 to predetermine, as by fate 2 to intend —**destined for** 1 bound for 2 intended for

des·ti·ny (desʹtə nē) *n., pl.* **-nies** 1 the seemingly inevitable succession of events 2 (one's) fate

des·ti·tute (desʹtə to͞otʹ) *adj.* ⟦ < L *de-*, down + *statuere*, to set ⟧ 1 lacking: with *of* 2 totally impoverished —**des'ti·tu'tion** *n.*

de·stroy (di stroiʹ) *vt.* ⟦ < L *de-*, down + *struere*, to build ⟧ 1 to tear down; demolish 2 to wreck; ruin 3 to do away with 4 to kill

de·stroy'er *n.* 1 one that destroys 2 a small, fast warship

de·struct (di struktʹ, dēʹstrukt') *vi.* ⟦ < fol. ⟧ to be automatically destroyed

de·struc·tion (di strukʹshən) *n.* 1 a destroying or being destroyed 2 a cause or means of destroying —**de·struc'tive** *adj.* —**de·struc'tive·ly** *adv.* —**de·struc'tive·ness** *n.*

des·ue·tude (desʹwi to͞od') *n.* ⟦ < L *de-*, from + *suescere*, be accustomed ⟧ disuse

des·ul·to·ry (desʹəl tôr'ē) *adj.* ⟦ < L *de-*, from + *salire*, to leap ⟧ 1 aimless; disconnected 2 random

de·tach (dē tachʹ) *vt.* ⟦ < Fr: see DE- & ATTACH ⟧ 1 to unfasten and remove; disconnect; disengage 2 to send (troops, etc.) on a special mission —**de·tach'a·ble** *adj.*

de·tached' *adj.* 1 not connected 2 aloof; disinterested; impartial

de·tach'ment *n.* 1 a detaching 2 a unit of troops, etc. on a special mission 3 impartiality or aloofness

de·tail (dē tālʹ, dēʹtāl) *n.* ⟦ < Fr < *dé-*, from + *tailler*, to cut ⟧ 1 a dealing with things item by item 2 a minute account 3 a small part; item 4 *a)* one or more soldiers, etc. on special duty *b)* the duty —*vt.* 1 to tell, item by item 2 to assign to special duty —**in detail** with particulars

de·tain (dē tānʹ) *vt.* ⟦ < L *de-*, off + *tenere*, to hold ⟧ 1 to keep in custody; confine 2 to keep from going on —**de·tain'ment** *n.*

de·tect (dē tektʹ) *vt.* ⟦ < L *de-*, from + *tegere*, to cover ⟧ to discover (something hidden, not clear, etc.) —**de·tect'a·ble** or **de·tect'i·ble** *adj.* —**de·tec'tion** *n.* —**de·tec'tor** *n.*

de·tec'tive *n.* one whose work is to investigate crimes, uncover evidence, etc.

dé·tente or **de·tente** (dā tän'tʹ) *n.* ⟦ Fr ⟧ a lessening of tension, esp. between nations

de·ten·tion (dē tenʹshən) *n.* 1 a detaining

or being detained 2 the punishment of having to stay after school

detention home a place where juvenile offenders are held in custody

de·ter (dē tʉr′) *vt.* **-terred′, -ter′ring** ⟦< L *de-*, from + *terrere*, frighten⟧ to keep or discourage (a person) from doing something through fear, doubt, etc. —**de·ter′ment** *n.*

de·ter·gent (dē tʉr′jənt) *adj.* ⟦< L *de-*, off + *tergere*, wipe⟧ cleansing —*n.* a soaplike cleansing substance

de·te·ri·o·rate (dē tir′ē ə rāt′) *vt., vi.* **-rat′ed, -rat′ing** ⟦< L *deterior*, worse⟧ to make or become worse —**de·te′ri·o·ra′tion** *n.*

de·ter·mi·nant (dē tʉr′mi nənt) *n.* a thing or factor that determines

de·ter′mi·nate (-nit) *adj.* clearly determined; fixed; settled

de·ter·mi·na·tion (dē tʉr′mi nā′shən) *n.* 1 a determining or being determined 2 a firm intention 3 firmness of purpose

de·ter·mine (dē tʉr′mən) *vt.* **-mined, -min·ing** ⟦< L *de-*, from + *terminus*, a limit⟧ 1 to set limits to 2 to settle conclusively 3 to decide or decide upon 4 to be the deciding factor in; direct 5 to find out exactly —*vi.* to decide —**de·ter′mi·na·ble** *adj.*

de·ter′mined (-mənd) *adj.* 1 having one's mind made up 2 resolute; firm

de·ter·rence (dē tʉr′əns) *n.* 1 a deterring 2 the stockpiling of nuclear weapons to deter nuclear attack

de·ter′rent *adj.* deterring —*n.* something that deters

de·test (dē test′) *vt.* ⟦< L *detestari*, to curse by the gods⟧ to dislike intensely; hate —**de·test′a·ble** *adj.* —**de′tes·ta′tion** (-tes tā′shən) *n.*

de·throne (dē thrōn′) *vt.* **-throned′, -thron′·ing** to depose (a monarch)

det·o·nate (det′′n āt′) *vi., vt.* **-nat′ed, -nat′·ing** ⟦< L *de-*, intens. + *tonare*, to thunder⟧ to explode violently —**det′o·na′tion** *n.* —**det′o·na′tor** *n.*

de·tour (dē′toor′) *n.* ⟦< Fr: see DE- & TURN⟧ 1 a roundabout way 2 a substitute route —*vi., vt.* to go or route on a detour

de·tox (dē täks′, dē′täks′) *vt.* [Colloq.] *short for* DETOXIFY —*n.* [Colloq.] *short for* DETOXIFICATION

de·tox·i·fy (dē täk′si fī′) *vt.* **-fied′, -fy′ing** ⟦DE- + TOXI(N) + -FY⟧ to remove a poison or poisonous effect from —**de·tox′i·fi·ca′·tion** *n.*

de·tract (dē trakt′) *vt.* ⟦< L *de-*, from + *trahere*, to draw⟧ to take away —*vi.* to take something desirable (*from*) —**de·trac′tion** *n.* —**de·trac′tor** *n.*

det·ri·ment (de′trə mənt) *n.* ⟦< L *de-*, off + *terere*, to rub⟧ 1 damage; injury 2 anything that causes this —**det′ri·men′tal** *adj.*

de·tri·tus (dē trīt′əs) *n.* ⟦L, a rubbing away: see prec.⟧ rock fragments, etc. from disintegration

De·troit (di troit′) city & port in SE Mich.: pop. 1,203,000

deuce (do͞os) *n.* ⟦< L *duo*, two⟧ 1 a playing card or side of a die with two spots 2 *Tennis, Badminton, etc.* a tie score after which one side must score twice in a row to win

deu·te·ri·um (do͞o tir′ē əm) *n.* ⟦< Gr *deuteros*, second⟧ a hydrogen isotope used in nuclear reactors, etc.

Deu·ter·on·o·my (do͞ot′ər än′ə mē) ⟦< Gr *deuteros*, second + *nomos*, law⟧ the fifth book of the Pentateuch

deut·sche mark (doi′chə märk′) *pl.* **mark** or **marks** the monetary unit of West Germany

de·val·ue (dē val′yo͞o) *vt.* **-ued, -u·ing** 1 to lessen the value of 2 to lower the exchange value of (a currency) —**de·val′u·a′tion** *n.*

dev·as·tate (dev′əs tāt′) *vt.* **-tat′ed, -tat′ing** ⟦< L *de-*, intens. + *vastus*, empty⟧ 1 to lay waste; ravage; destroy 2 to overwhelm —**dev′as·ta′tion** *n.* —**dev′as·ta′tor** *n.*

de·vel·op (di vel′əp) *vt.* ⟦< OFr *des-*, apart + *voloper*, to wrap⟧ 1 to make fuller, bigger, better, etc. 2 to show or work out by degrees 3 to enlarge upon 4 *Photog.* to put (a film, etc.) into chemicals to make the pictures visible —*vi.* 1 to come into being or activity; occur 2 to become developed —**de·vel′op·er** *n.* —**de·vel′op·ment** *n.*

de·vi·ant (dē′vē ənt) *adj.* deviating, esp. from what is considered normal —*n.* one whose behavior is deviant

de·vi·ate (dē′vē āt′; *for adj. & n. usually*, -it) *vi.* **-at′ed, -at′ing** ⟦< L *de-*, from + *via*, road⟧ to turn aside (*from* a course, standard, etc.); diverge —*adj.* DEVIANT —*n.* a deviant, esp. in sexual behavior —**de′vi·a′tion** *n.* —**de′vi·a′tor** *n.*

de·vice (di vīs′) *n.* ⟦see DEVISE⟧ 1 a thing devised; plan, scheme, or trick 2 a mechanical contrivance 3 an ornamental design, esp. on a coat of arms —**leave to one's own devices** to allow to do as one wishes

dev·il (dev′əl) *n.* ⟦ult. < Gr *diabolos*, slanderous⟧ 1 *Theol. a)* [*often* **D-**] the chief evil spirit; Satan (with *the*) *b)* any evil spirit; demon 2 a very wicked person 3 a person who is mischievous, reckless, unlucky, etc. 4 anything hard to operate, control, etc. —*vt.* **-iled** or **-illed, -il·ing** or **-il·ling** 1 to prepare (food) with hot seasoning 2 to annoy; tease —**dev′il·ish** *adj.*

dev′il-may-care′ *adj.* reckless

dev′il·ment *n.* mischievous action

devil's advocate a person upholding the wrong side for argument's sake

dev′il's-food′ cake a rich chocolate cake

dev′il·try (-trē) *n., pl.* **-tries** reckless mischief, fun, etc. Also **dev′il·ry** (-rē)

de·vi·ous (dē′vē əs) *adj.* ⟦< L *de-*, off + *via*, road⟧ 1 not direct; roundabout or deviating 2 not straightforward —**de′vi·ous·ness** *n.*

de·vise (di vīz′) *vt., vi.* **-vised′, -vis′ing** ⟦< L *dividere*, to divide⟧ 1 to work out or create (a plan, device, etc.) 2 to bequeath (real property) by will —*n.* a bequest of property

de·vi·tal·ize (dē vīt′′l īz′) *vt.* **-ized′, -iz′ing** to deprive of vitality

de·void (di void′) *adj.* ⟦see DE- & VOID⟧ completely without; empty (*of*)

de·volve (di välv′) *vt., vi.* **-volved′, -volv′·ing** ⟦< L *de-*, down + *volvere*, to roll⟧ to pass (*on*) to another: said of duties, responsibilities, etc.

de·vote (di vōt′) *vt.* **-vot′ed, -vot′ing** ⟦< L

de-, from + *vovere*, to vow] to set apart for or give up to some purpose, activity, or person; dedicate
de·vot'ed (-id) ***adj.*** very loving, loyal, or faithful —**de·vot'ed·ly** ***adv.***
dev·o·tee (dev'ə tē', -tā') ***n.*** one strongly devoted to something
de·vo·tion (di vō'shən) ***n.*** 1 a devoting or being devoted 2 piety 3 religious worship 4 [*often pl.*] one or more prayers, etc. 5 loyalty or deep affection —**de·vo'tion·al** ***adj.***
de·vour (di vour') ***vt.*** [< L *de-*, intens. + *vorare*, swallow whole] 1 to eat hungrily 2 to swallow up 3 to take in greedily, as with the eyes
de·vout (di vout') ***adj.*** [see DEVOTE] 1 very religious; pious 2 earnest; sincere — **de·vout'ly** ***adv.***
dew (do͞o) ***n.*** [OE *deaw*] 1 atmospheric moisture condensed in drops on cool surfaces at night 2 anything refreshing, pure, etc., like dew —**dew'y**, **-i·er**, **-i·est**, ***adj.***
dew'ber'ry ***n.***, *pl.* **-ries** 1 a trailing blackberry plant 2 its berry
dew'drop' ***n.*** a drop of dew
dew'lap' ***n.*** [see DEW & LAP[1]] loose skin under the throat of cattle, etc.
dew point the temperature at which water vapor in the air starts to condense into liquid
dex·ter·i·ty (deks ter'ə tē) ***n.*** [see fol.] skill in using one's hands, body, or mind
dex·ter·ous (deks'tər əs, -trəs) ***adj.*** [< L *dexter*, right] having or showing dexterity Also **dex'trous**
dex·trose (deks'trōs) ***n.*** a glucose found in plants and animals
Dhak·a (dăk'ə, dak'ə) capital of Bangladesh: pop. 3,440,000
dho·ti (dō'tē) ***n.*** [Hindi *dhotī*] a loincloth worn by Hindu men
dhur·rie or **dur·rie** (dur'ē, dur'-) ***n.*** a coarse rug woven in India
di-[1] [Gr *di-* < *dis-*, twice] *prefix* twice, double, twofold
di-[2] *prefix* DIS-
di·a·be·tes (dī'ə bēt'ēz', -is) ***n.*** [< Gr *diabainein*, to pass through] a disease caused by an insulin deficiency and characterized by excess sugar in the blood and urine Also **sugar diabetes** —**di'a·bet'ic** (-bet'ik) ***adj.***, ***n.***
di·a·bol·ic (dī'ə băl'ik) ***adj.*** [see DEVIL] very wicked or cruel; fiendish Also **di'a·bol'i·cal**
di·a·crit·ic (dī'ə krit'ik) ***adj.*** [< Gr *dia-*, across + *krinein*, to separate] distinguishing Also **di'a·crit'i·cal** —***n.*** a mark, as a macron, added to a letter or symbol to show pronunciation, etc.: in full **diacritical mark**
di·a·dem (dī'ə dem') ***n.*** [< Gr *diadēma*, a band, fillet] 1 a crown 2 an ornamental headband
di·ag·nose (dī'əg nōs') ***vt.***, ***vi.*** **-nosed'**, **-nos'·ing** to make a diagnosis (of)
di'ag·no'sis (-nō'sis) ***n.***, *pl.* **-ses'** (-sēz') [< Gr *dia-*, through + *gignoskein*, to know] 1 the act of deciding the nature of a disease, situation, problem, etc. by examination and analysis 2 the resulting decision —**di'ag·nos'tic** (-näs'tik) ***adj.*** —**di'ag·nos·ti'cian** (-tish'ən) ***n.***
di·ag·o·nal (dī ag'ə nəl) ***adj.*** [< Gr *dia-*, through + *gōnia*, an angle] 1 extending slantingly between opposite corners 2 slanting; oblique —***n.*** a diagonal line, plane, course, part, etc. —**di·ag'o·nal·ly** ***adv.***
di·a·gram (dī'ə gram') ***n.*** [< Gr *dia-*, across + *graphein*, write] a sketch, plan, graph, etc. that explains something, as by outlining its parts —***vt.*** **-gramed'** or **-grammed'**, **-gram'ing** or **-gram'ming** to make a diagram of
di·al (dī'əl) ***n.*** [< L *dies*, day] 1 the face of a clock, etc. 2 the face of a meter, etc. for indicating, as by a pointer, an amount, direction, etc. 3 a graduated disk, strip, knob, etc., as on a radio or TV for tuning in stations, etc. 4 a rotating disk, or set of numbered push buttons, on a telephone, used to make automatic connections —***vt.***, ***vi.*** **-aled** or **-alled**, **-al·ing** or **-al·ling** 1 to show on or measure with a dial 2 to tune in (a radio station, etc.) 3 to call by using a telephone dial
dial. 1 dialect(al) 2 dialectic(al)
di·a·lect (dī'ə lekt') ***n.*** [< Gr *dia*, between + *legein*, to talk] the form of a spoken language peculiar to a region, social group, etc. —**di'a·lec'tal** ***adj.***
di·a·lec·tic (dī'ə lek'tik) ***n.*** 1 [*often pl.*] a logical test of ideas for validity 2 logical debate —***adj.*** DIALECTICAL
di'a·lec'ti·cal (-ti kəl) ***adj.*** 1 of or using dialectics 2 of a dialect
di·a·logue or **di·a·log** (dī'ə lôg', -läg') ***n.*** [see DIALECT] 1 interchange of ideas by open discussion 2 the passages of talk in a play, story, etc.
di·al·y·sis (dī al'ə sis) ***n.***, *pl.* **-ses'** (-sēz') [< Gr *dia-*, apart + *lyein*, loose] the separation of dissolved substances from colloids in a solution by diffusion through a membrane: used in purifying the blood during kidney failure
di·am·e·ter (dī am'ət ər) ***n.*** [< Gr *dia-*, through + *metron*, a measure] 1 a line segment passing through the center of a circle, sphere, etc. from one side to the other 2 its length
di·a·met·ri·cal (dī'ə me'tri kəl) ***adj.*** designating an opposite, difference, etc. that is wholly so; complete
di·a·mond (dim'ənd, dī'ə mənd) ***n.*** [< Gr *adamas*] 1 a nearly pure, brilliant, crystalline carbon, the hardest mineral known 2 a gem, etc. cut from it 3 *a*) the plane figure (◇) *b*) a playing card so marked 4 *Baseball* the infield or the whole field —***adj.*** 1 of a diamond 2 marking the 60th, or sometimes 75th, year
di'a·mond·back' ***n.*** a large, poisonous rattlesnake of the S U.S.
Di·an·a (dī an'ə) *Rom. Myth.* the goddess of the moon and of hunting
di·a·pa·son (dī'ə pā'zən) ***n.*** [< Gr *dia*, through + *pas*, all] an organ stop covering the instrument's entire range
di·a·per (dī'pər, dī'ə pər) ***n.*** [< ML *diasprum*, flowered cloth] a soft, absorbent cloth folded and arranged between the legs and around the waist of a baby —***vt.*** to put a diaper on (a baby)
di·aph·a·nous (dī af'ə nəs) ***adj.*** [< Gr *dia-*,

through + *phainein*, to show ⟧ letting much light through

di·a·phragm (dī'ə fram') ***n.*** ⟦< Gr *dia-*, through + *phragma*, fence⟧ 1 the muscular partition between the chest and abdominal cavities 2 a vibrating disk producing sound waves 3 a vaginal contraceptive device —**di'a·phrag·mat'ic** (-frag mat'ik) ***adj.***

di·ar·rhe·a or **di·ar·rhoe·a** (dī'ə rē'ə) ***n.*** ⟦< Gr *dia-*, through + *rhein*, to flow⟧ too frequent and loose bowel movements

di·a·ry (dī'ə rē) ***n.***, *pl.* **-ries** ⟦< L *dies*, day⟧ a daily written record of one's experiences, etc. —**di'a·rist** ***n.***

di·a·stase (dī'ə stās') ***n.*** ⟦< Gr *dia*, apart + *histanai*, stand⟧ an enzyme in the seed of grains and malt capable of changing starches into dextrose

di·as·to·le (dī as'tə lē') ***n.*** ⟦< Gr *dia-*, apart + *stellein*, put⟧ the usual rhythmic expansion of the heart —**di·a·stol·ic** (dī'ə stäl'ik) ***adj.***

di·a·tom (dī'ə täm', -ə təm) ***n.*** ⟦< Gr *diatomos*, cut in two⟧ any of various microscopic algae that are an important source of food for marine life

di·a·tom·ic (dī'ə täm'ik) ***adj.*** ⟦DI-[1] + ATOMIC⟧ having two atoms or radicals in the molecule

di·a·ton·ic (dī'ə tän'ik) ***adj.*** ⟦< Gr *dia-*, through + *teinein*, to stretch⟧ *Music* designating or of a scale of eight tones that is either a MAJOR SCALE or a MINOR SCALE

di·a·tribe (dī'ə trīb') ***n.*** ⟦< Gr *dia-*, through + *tribein*, to rub⟧ a bitter, abusive denunciation

dib·ble (dib'əl) ***n.*** ⟦ME *dibbel*⟧ a pointed tool used for making holes in the soil for seeds, bulbs, etc.

dice (dīs) ***n.pl.***, *sing.* **die** or **dice** ⟦see DIE[2]⟧ small cubes marked on each side with a different number of spots (from one to six), used in games of chance —***vi.*** **diced, dic'·ing** to play or gamble with dice —***vt.*** to cut (vegetables, etc.) into small cubes —**no dice** [Colloq.] 1 no: used in refusing a request 2 no luck

di·chot·o·my (dī kät'ə mē) ***n.***, *pl.* **-mies** ⟦< Gr *dicha*, in two + *temnein*, to cut⟧ division into two parts

dick (dik) ***n.*** [Slang] a detective

Dick·ens (dik'ənz), **Charles** (chärlz) (pseud. *Boz*) 1812-70; Eng. novelist

dick·er (dik'ər) ***vi.*** ⟦ult. < L *decem*, ten⟧ to bargain or haggle

dick·ey (dik'ē) ***n.***, *pl.* **-eys** ⟦< nickname *Dick*⟧ 1 a detachable shirt front 2 a small bird: also **dickey bird** Also **dick'y**, *pl.* **-ies**

Dick·in·son (dik'in s'n), **Em·i·ly** (em'ə lē) 1830-86; U.S. poet

di·cot·y·le·don (dī'kät'ə lēd''n) ***n.*** a plant with two seed leaves (cotyledons) —**di'·cot'y·le'don·ous** ***adj.***

Dic·ta·phone (dik'tə fōn') ⟦fol. + -PHONE⟧ *trademark for* a machine that records and plays back speech for typed transcripts, etc. —***n.*** this machine

dic·tate (dik'tāt'; *also, for v.* dik tāt') ***vt., vi.*** **-tat'ed, -tat'ing** ⟦< L *dicere*, to speak⟧ 1 to speak (something) aloud for someone else to write down 2 to command forcefully 3 to give (orders) with authority —***n.*** an authoritative order —**dic·ta'tion** ***n.***

dic'ta'tor ***n.*** one who dictates; esp., a ruler or tyrant with absolute power —**dic'ta·to'·ri·al** (-tə tôr'ē əl) ***adj.*** —**dic·ta'tor·ship'** ***n.***

dic·tion (dik'shən) ***n.*** ⟦< L *dicere*, say⟧ 1 manner of expression in words; choice of words 2 enunciation

dic·tion·ar·y (dik'shə ner'ē) ***n.***, *pl.* **-ar'ies** ⟦see prec.⟧ a book of alphabetically listed words in a language, with definitions, pronunciations, etc.

dic·tum (dik'təm) ***n.***, *pl.* **-tums** or **-ta** (-tə) ⟦< L *dicere*, say⟧ a formal statement of opinion; pronouncement

did (did) *pt. of* DO[1]

di·dac·tic (dī dak'tik) ***adj.*** ⟦< Gr *didaskein*, teach⟧ 1 intended for instruction 2 morally instructive

did·dle (did''l) ***vt., vi.*** **-dled, -dling** ⟦< ?⟧ [Colloq.] 1 to cheat 2 to waste (time) in trifling

di·do (dī'dō) ***n.***, *pl.* **-does** or **-dos** ⟦< ?⟧ [Colloq.] a mischievous trick; prank

die[1] (dī) ***vi.*** **died, dy'ing** ⟦< ON *deyja*⟧ 1 to stop living 2 to stop functioning; end 3 to lose force or activity 4 [Colloq.] to wish very much [I'm *dying* to go] —**die away** (or **down**) to cease gradually —**die off** to die one by one until all are gone —**die out** to stop existing

die[2] (dī) ***n.***, *pl.* for 2, **dies** (dīz) ⟦< L *dare*, give⟧ 1 *sing. of* DICE 2 a tool for shaping, punching, etc. metal or other material

die'-hard' or **die'hard'** ***n.*** a person stubbornly resistant to new ideas, reform, etc.

di·e·lec·tric (dī'i lek'trik) ***n.*** ⟦< *dia-*, across + ELECTRIC⟧ a material that does not conduct electricity

di·er·e·sis (dī er'ə sis) ***n.***, *pl.* **-ses'** (-sēz') ⟦< Gr *dia-*, apart + *hairein*, to take⟧ a mark (¨) placed over the second of two consecutive vowels to show that it is pronounced separately

die·sel (dē'zəl, -səl) ***n.*** ⟦after R. *Diesel* (1858-1913), Ger inventor⟧ [*often* D-] an internal-combustion engine that burns oil ignited by heat from air compression: also **diesel engine** (or **motor**) —***vi.*** to continue to run after the ignition is turned off: said of an internal-combustion engine

di·et[1] (dī'ət) ***n.*** ⟦< Gr *diaita*, way of life⟧ 1 what a person or animal usually eats or drinks 2 a special or limited selection of food and drink, chosen or prescribed as to bring about weight loss —***vi., vt.*** to adhere to or place on a diet —**di'et·er** ***n.*** —**di'e·tar'y** (-ə ter'ē) ***adj.***

di·et[2] (dī'ət) ***n.*** ⟦< ML *dieta*⟧ a formal assembly

di'e·tet'ic (-ə tet'ik) ***adj.*** of or for a particular diet of food and drink

di'e·tet'ics (-iks) ***n.pl.*** [*with sing. v.*] the study of the kinds and quantities of food needed for health

di·e·ti·tian (dī'ə tish'ən) ***n.*** an expert in dietetics

dif- *prefix* DIS-: used before *f*

dif·fer (dif'ər) ***vi.*** ⟦< L *dis-*, apart + *ferre*, to bring⟧ 1 to be different 2 to be of a different opinion; disagree

dif·fer·ence (dif'ər əns, dif'rəns) ***n.*** 1 a being different 2 the way in which people or things are different 3 a differing in opinion; disagreement 4 a dispute 5 the amount by which one quantity is less than another

dif'fer·ent *adj.* 1 not alike 2 not the same 3 various 4 unusual —**dif'fer·ent·ly** *adv.*

dif·fer·en·tial (dif'ər en'shəl) *adj.* of, showing, or constituting a difference —*n.* 1 a differentiating amount, degree, etc. 2 a differential gear

differential gear (or **gearing**) a gear arrangement allowing one axle to turn faster than the other

dif'fer·en'ti·ate' (-shē āt') *vt.* -at'ed, -at'ing 1 to constitute a difference in or between 2 to make unlike 3 to distinguish between —*vi.* 1 to become different or differentiated 2 to note a difference —**dif'fer·en'ti·a'tion** *n.*

dif·fi·cult (dif'i kult', -kəlt) *adj.* 1 hard to do, understand, etc. 2 hard to satisfy, deal with, etc.

dif'fi·cul'ty *n., pl.* -ties [< L *dis-*, not + *facilis*, easy] 1 a being difficult 2 something difficult, as a problem, obstacle, or objection 3 trouble

dif'fi·dent (-dənt) *adj.* [< L *dis-*, not + *fidere*, to trust] lacking self-confidence; shy —**dif'fi·dence** *n.*

dif·frac·tion (di frak'shən) *n.* [< L *dis-*, apart + *frangere*, to break] the spreading of a wave motion, as light, as it passes an obstacle and expands into the region that is behind the obstacle

dif·fuse (di fyo͞os'; *for v.*, -fyo͞oz') *adj.* [< L *dis-*, apart + *fundere*, to pour] 1 spread out; not concentrated 2 using more words than are needed —*vt., vi.* -fused', -fus'ing to pour in every direction; spread widely —**dif·fuse'ly** *adv.* —**dif·fuse'ness** *n.* —**dif·fu'sion** *n.* —**dif·fu'sive** *adj.*

dig (dig) *vt.* **dug, dig'ging** [< OFr < Du *dijk*, dike] 1 to turn up or remove (ground, etc.) as with a spade, the hands, etc. 2 to make (a hole, etc.) by digging 3 to get out by digging 4 to find out, as by careful study 5 to jab 6 [Slang] *a)* to understand *b)* to like —*vi.* to excavate —*n.* 1 [Colloq.] *a)* a poke, nudge, etc. *b)* a taunt 2 an archaeological excavation —**dig'ger** *n.*

di·gest (dī'jest'; *for v.* di jest', dī-) *n.* [< L *di-*, apart + *gerere*, to bear] a collection of condensed, systematic information; summary —*vt.* 1 to summarize 2 to change (food taken into the body) into an absorbable form 3 to absorb mentally —*vi.* to undergo digestion —**di·gest'i·ble** *adj.*

di·ges'tion *n.* 1 a digesting or being digested 2 the ability to digest —**di·ges'tive** *adj.*

dig·it (dij'it) *n.* [< L *digitus*, a finger] 1 a finger or toe 2 any number from 0 to 9

dig·i·tal (dij'i təl, -it'l) *adj.* 1 of or like a digit 2 using a row of digits, rather than numbers on a dial [a *digital* watch] 3 designating a recording technique in which sounds or images are converted into electronic bits: the bits are read electronically, as by a laser beam, for reproduction

digital computer a computer for processing data represented by physical signals, as the presence or absence of an electric current

dig·i·tal·is (dij'i tal'is) *n.* [ModL, foxglove: see DIGIT] 1 a plant with long spikes of thimblelike flowers; foxglove 2 a medicine made from the leaves of the purple foxglove, used as a heart stimulant

dig·ni·fied (dig'nə fīd') *adj.* having or showing dignity

dig·ni·fy (dig'nə fī') *vt.* -fied', -fy'ing [< L *dignus*, worthy + *facere*, to make] to give dignity to; exalt

dig'ni·tar'y (-ter'ē) *n., pl.* -tar'ies [< L *dignitas*, dignity] a person holding a high position or office

dig'ni·ty (-tē) *n., pl.* -ties [< L *dignus*, worthy] 1 honorable quality; worthiness 2 high repute or honor, or the degree of this 3 a high position, rank, or title 4 stately appearance or manner 5 self-respect

di·graph (dī'graf') *n.* a combination of two letters to represent one sound (Ex.: *read*, gra*ph*ic)

di·gress (di gres', dī-) *vi.* [< L *dis-*, apart + *gradi*, to go] to turn aside, esp. from the main subject, in talking or writing —**di·gres'sion** (-gresh'ən) *n.* —**di·gres'sive** *adj.*

Di·jon mustard (dē zhōn') [after *Dijon*, city in France] a mild mustard paste blended with white wine

dike (dīk) *n.* [OE *dic*, ditch] an embankment or dam made to prevent flooding as by the sea

di·lap·i·dat·ed (də lap'ə dāt'id) *adj.* [< L *dis-*, apart + *lapidare*, throw stones at] falling to pieces; broken down —**di·lap'i·da'tion** *n.*

di·late (dī'lāt', dī lāt') *vt., vi.* -lat'ed, -lat'ing [< L *dis-*, apart + *latus*, wide] 1 to make or become wider or larger 2 to speak or write in detail (*on* or *upon* a subject) —**di·la'tion** or **dil·a·ta·tion** (dil'ə tā'shən) *n.*

dil·a·to·ry (dil'ə tôr'ē) *adj.* [see prec.] 1 causing delay 2 inclined to delay; slow; tardy

di·lem·ma (di lem'ə; *also* dī-) *n.* [< LGr *di-*, two + *lēmma*, proposition] 1 any situation requiring a choice between unpleasant alternatives 2 any serious problem

dil·et·tante (dil'ə tant', -tan'tē; dil'ə tänt', -tän'tē; dil'ə tänt') *n., pl.* -tantes' or -tan'ti' (-tī', -tē) [It < L *delectare*, to delight] one who dabbles in art, literature, etc. in a superficial way —**dil'et·tant'ish** *adj.* —**dil'et·tant'ism'** *n.*

dil·i·gent (dil'ə jənt) *adj.* [< L *di-*, apart + *legere*, choose] 1 persevering and careful in work; hard-working 2 done carefully —**dil'i·gence** *n.* —**dil'i·gent·ly** *adv.*

dill (dil) *n.* [OE *dile*] a plant related to the parsley, with aromatic seeds and leaves, used to flavor pickles, etc.

dil·ly (dil'ē) *n., pl.* -lies [? < DEL(IGHTFUL) + -Y[2]] [Slang] a remarkable person or thing

dil·ly·dal·ly (dil'ē dal'ē) *vi.* -lied, -ly·ing [< DALLY] to waste time by hesitating; loiter or dawdle

di·lute (di lo͞ot', dī-) *vt.* -lut'ed, -lut'ing [< L *dis-*, off + *lavare*, to wash] to thin down or weaken as by mixing with water —*adj.* diluted —**di·lu'tion** *n.*

dim (dim) *adj.* **dim'mer, dim'mest** [OE] 1 not bright, clear, or distinct; dull, obscure, etc. 2 not clearly seeing, hearing, or understanding 3 [Colloq.] stupid —*vt.*, *vi.* **dimmed, dim′ming** to make or grow dim —**dim′ly** *adv.* —**dim′ness** *n.*

dim. diminutive

dime (dīm) *n.* ⟦< L *decem*, ten⟧ a U.S. and Canadian 10-cent coin

di·men·sion (də men′shən) *n.* ⟦< L *dis-*, off, from + *metiri*, to measure⟧ 1 any measurable extent, as length, width, etc. 2 [*pl.*] measurements in length, width, and often depth 3 [*often pl.*] extent; scope —**di·men′sion·al** *adj.*

dime store FIVE-AND-TEN-CENT STORE

di·min·ish (də min′ish) *vt.*, *vi.* ⟦< L *diminuere*, reduce⟧ to make or become smaller in size, degree, importance, etc.; lessen —**dim·i·nu·tion** (dim′ə no͞o′shən, -nyo͞o′-) *n.*

di·min·u·en·do (də min′yo͞o en′dō) *adj.*, *adv.* ⟦It: see prec.⟧ *Music* with gradually diminishing volume

di·min·u·tive (də min′yo͞o tiv) *adj.* ⟦see DIMINISH⟧ very small; tiny —*n.* a word having a suffix that expresses smallness, endearment, etc.

dim·i·ty (dim′ə tē) *n.*, *pl.* **-ties** ⟦< Gr *dis-*, two + *mitos*, a thread⟧ a thin, corded or patterned cotton cloth

dim′mer *n.* a device, as a rheostat, for dimming electric lights

dim·ple (dim′pəl) *n.* ⟦ME *dimpel*⟧ a small, natural hollow, as on the cheek or chin —*vi.*, *vt.* **-pled, -pling** to form dimples (in) —**dim′ply** (-plē) *adj.*

dim sum (dim′ tso͞om′) ⟦Chin⟧ small dumplings filled with meat, vegetables, etc.

dim′wit′ *n.* [Slang] a stupid person; simpleton —**dim′wit′ted** *adj.*

din (din) *n.* ⟦OE *dyne*⟧ a loud, continuous noise; confused uproar —*vt.* **dinned, din′ning** 1 to beset with a din 2 to repeat insistently or noisily

din-din (din′din′) *n.* [Colloq.] dinner

dine (dīn) *vi.* **dined, din′ing** ⟦ult. < L *dis-*, away + *jejunus*, hungry⟧ to eat dinner —*vt.* to provide a dinner for

din·er (dīn′ər) *n.* 1 a person eating dinner 2 a railroad car equipped to serve meals 3 a small restaurant built to look like such a car

di·nette (dī net′) *n.* an alcove or small space used as a dining room

ding (diŋ) *n.* ⟦< Scand⟧ the sound of a bell Also **ding′-dong′** (-dôŋ′)

din·ghy (diŋ′gē, diŋ′ē) *n.*, *pl.* **-ghies** ⟦Hindi *dĩgī*⟧ any of various small boats, as one carried on a ship

din·gle (diŋ′gəl) *n.* ⟦ME *dingel*, abyss⟧ a small, deep, wooded valley

din·go (diŋ′gō) *n.*, *pl.* **-goes** ⟦native name⟧ the Australian wild dog, usually tawny in color

ding·us (diŋ′əs) *n.* ⟦< Du *ding*, thing⟧ [Colloq.] any device; gadget

din·gy (din′jē) *adj.* **-gi·er, -gi·est** ⟦orig. dial. var. < DUNG⟧ 1 not bright or clean; grimy 2 dismal; shabby —**din′gi·ness** *n.*

dink·y (diŋ′kē) *adj.* **-i·er, -i·est** ⟦< Scot *dink*, trim⟧ [Colloq.] small

din·ner (din′ər) *n.* ⟦see DINE⟧ 1 the chief meal of the day 2 a banquet in honor of a person or event

dinner jacket a tuxedo jacket

dinner ring a woman's ring with a large stone or stones, worn on formal occasions

din′ner·ware′ (-wer′) *n.* 1 plates, cups, saucers, etc., collectively 2 a set of such dishes

DINOSAUR (TRICERATOPS)

di·no·saur (dī′nə sôr′) *n.* ⟦< Gr *deinos*, terrible + *sauros*, lizard⟧ a prehistoric, extinct reptile, often huge

dint (dint) *n.* ⟦OE *dynt*⟧ 1 force; exertion: now chiefly in **by dint of** 2 a dent

di·o·cese (dī′ə sis, -sēs′, -sēz′) *n.* ⟦< Gr *dioikein*, to keep house⟧ the district under a bishop's jurisdiction —**di·oc′e·san** (-äs′ə sən, -zən) *adj.*

di·ode (dī′ōd′) *n.* ⟦DI-[1] + -ODE⟧ an electron tube used esp. as a rectifier

Di·og·e·nes (dī äj′ə nēz′) *c.* 412-*c.* 323 B.C.; Gr. philosopher

Di·o·ny·sus or **Di·o·ny·sos** (dī′ə nī′səs) *Gr. Myth.* the god of wine

di·o·ram·a (dī′ə ram′ə) *n.* ⟦< Gr *dia-*, through + *horama*, a view⟧ a scenic display, as of three-dimensional figures against a painted background

di·ox·in (dī äks′in) *n.* a highly toxic chemical contaminant

dip (dip) *vt.* **dipped, dip′ping** ⟦OE *dyppan*⟧ 1 to immerse briefly 2 to scoop (liquid) up or out 3 to lower (a flag, etc.) and immediately raise again —*vi.* 1 to plunge into a liquid and quickly come out 2 to sink suddenly 3 to decline slightly 4 to slope down 5 to lower a container, the hand, etc. as into water 6 to read or inquire superficially: with *into* —*n.* 1 a dipping or being dipped 2 a brief plunge into water, etc. 3 a liquid, sauce, etc. into which something is dipped 4 whatever is removed by dipping 5 a downward slope or plunge

diph·the·ri·a (dif thir′ē ə; *widely* dip-) *n.* ⟦< Gr *diphthera*, leather⟧ an acute infectious disease marked by high fever and difficult breathing

diph·thong (dif′thôŋ; *often* dip′-) *n.* ⟦< Gr *di-*, two + *phthongos*, sound⟧ a sound made by gliding from one vowel to another in one syllable, as in *oil*

di·plo·ma (də plō′mə) *n.* ⟦< Gr *diplōma*, folded letter⟧ a certificate issued by a school, college, etc. indicating graduation or the conferring of a degree

di·plo′ma·cy (-sē) *n.* ⟦see fol.⟧ 1 the conducting of relations between nations 2 tact

dip·lo·mat (dip′lə mat′) *n.* 1 a representative of a government who conducts relations with another government 2 a tactful person

dip′lo·mat′ic *adj.* 1 of diplomacy 2 tactful —**dip′lo·mat′i·cal·ly** *adv.*

di·pole (dī′pōl′) *n.* a kind of radio or TV antenna with a single line separated at the center for connection to the receiver

dip·per (dip′ər) *n.* a long-handled cup, etc. for dipping —[D-] either of two groups of stars in the shape of a dipper (**Big Dipper**, **Little Dipper**)

dip·so·ma·ni·a (dip′sə mā′nē ə) ***n.*** ⟦< Gr *dipsa*, thirst + *mania*, madness⟧ an abnormal craving for alcoholic drink —**dip′so·ma′ni·ac′** (-ak′) ***n.***
dip′stick′ ***n.*** a graduated rod for measuring quantity or depth
Dir. Director
dire (dīr) ***adj.*** **dir′er, dir′est** ⟦L *dirus*⟧ **1** dreadful; terrible: also **dire′ful** **2** urgent /a *dire* need/
di·rect (də rekt′, dī-) ***adj.*** ⟦< L *di-*, apart + *regere*, to rule⟧ **1** not roundabout or interrupted; straight **2** honest; frank /a *direct* answer/ **3** with nothing between; immediate **4** in an unbroken line of descent; lineal **5** exact; complete /the *direct* opposite/ **6** in the exact words /a *direct* quote/ —***vt.*** **1** to manage; guide **2** to order; command **3** to turn or point; aim; head **4** to tell (a person) the way to a place **5** to address (a letter, etc.) **6** to plan the action and effects of (a play, etc.) —***adv.*** directly —**di·rect′ness** ***n.***
direct current an electric current flowing in one direction
di·rec·tion (də rek′shən; *also* dī-) ***n.*** **1** a directing **2** (*usually pl.*) instructions for doing, using, etc. **3** a command **4** the point toward which something faces or the line along which it moves or lies —**di·rec′tion·al** ***adj.***
di·rec′tive (-rek′tiv) ***adj.*** directing —***n.*** a general order issued authoritatively
di·rect′ly ***adv.*** **1** in a direct way or line; straight **2** with nothing or no one between **3** exactly /*directly* opposite/ **4** instantly; right away
direct object *Gram.* the word or words denoting the receiver of the action of a verb (Ex.: *me* in "he hit me")
di·rec′tor ***n.*** one who directs a school, corporation, etc. or a play, choir, etc. —**di·rec′tor·ship′** ***n.***
di·rec′tor·ate (-it) ***n.*** **1** the position of director **2** a board of directors
di·rec′to·ry (-tə rē) ***n.***, *pl.* **-ries** a book listing the names, addresses, etc. of a specific group of persons
dirge (durj) ***n.*** ⟦< L *dirige* (direct), first word of a prayer⟧ a song, poem, etc. of grief or mourning
dir·i·gi·ble (dir′ə jə bəl, də rij′ə-) ***n.*** ⟦see DIRECT & -IBLE⟧ AIRSHIP
dirk (durk) ***n.*** ⟦< ?⟧ a long dagger
dirn·dl (durn′dəl) ***n.*** ⟦< Ger *dirne*, girl⟧ a full skirt gathered at the waist
dirt (durt) ***n.*** ⟦< ON *drita*, excrement⟧ **1** any unclean matter, as mud, trash, etc.; filth **2** earth; soil **3** dirtiness, corruption, etc. **4** obscenity **5** malicious gossip
dirt′-cheap′ ***adj.***, ***adv.*** [Colloq.] very inexpensive(ly)
dirt′y ***adj.*** **-i·er, -i·est** **1** not clean **2** obscene **3** contemptible or nasty **4** unfair; dishonest **5** rough, as weather —***vt.***, ***vi.*** **dirt′ied, dirt′y·ing** to make or become dirty —**dirt′i·ness** ***n.***
dis- ⟦< L⟧ *prefix* separation, negation, reversal /*disbar, disable, disintegrate*/
dis·a·bil·i·ty (dis′ə bil′ə tē) ***n.***, *pl.* **-ties** **1** a disabled condition **2** that which disables or disqualifies
dis·a′ble (-ā′bəl) ***vt.*** **-bled, -bling** to make unable, unfit, or disqualified
dis·a·buse (dis′ə byo͞oz′) ***vt.*** **-bused′, -bus′ing** to rid of false ideas
dis·ad·van·tage (dis′əd vant′ij) ***n.*** **1** an unfavorable situation or circumstance **2** detriment —**dis′ad′van·ta′geous** (-ad′vən tā′jəs) ***adj.***
dis′ad·van′taged ***adj.*** underprivileged
dis·af·fect (dis′ə fekt′) ***vt.*** to make unfriendly, discontented, or disloyal —**dis′af·fec′tion** ***n.***
dis′af·fil′i·ate′ (-ə fil′ē āt′) ***vt.***, ***vi.*** **-at′ed, -at′ing** to end an affiliation (with) —**dis′af·fil′i·a′tion** ***n.***
dis′a·gree′ (-ə grē′) ***vi.*** **-greed′, -gree′ing** **1** to fail to agree; differ **2** to differ in opinion; quarrel **3** to give distress: with *with* —**dis′a·gree′ment** ***n.***
dis′a·gree′a·ble ***adj.*** **1** unpleasant; offensive **2** quarrelsome —**dis′a·gree′a·bly** ***adv.***
dis·al·low (dis′ə lou′) ***vt.*** to refuse to allow (a claim, etc.); reject
dis′ap·pear′ (-ə pir′) ***vi.*** **1** to cease to be seen; vanish **2** to cease existing —**dis′ap·pear′ance** ***n.***
dis′ap·point′ (-ə point′) ***vt.*** to fail to satisfy the hopes or expectations of —**dis′ap·point′ment** ***n.***
dis·ap·pro·ba·tion (dis′ap′rə bā′shən) ***n.*** a disapproving; disapproval
dis·ap·prove (dis′ə pro͞ov′) ***vt.***, ***vi.*** **-proved′, -prov′ing** **1** to have or express an unfavorable opinion (of) **2** to refuse to approve —**dis′ap·prov′al** ***n.*** —**dis′ap·prov′ing·ly** ***adv.***
dis·arm (dis ärm′, dis′-) ***vt.*** **1** to take away weapons from **2** to make harmless **3** to make friendly —***vi.*** to reduce armed forces and armaments —**dis·ar′ma·ment** (-är′mə mənt) ***n.***
dis·ar·range (dis′ə rānj′) ***vt.*** **-ranged′, -rang′ing** to undo the order of —**dis′ar·range′ment** ***n.***
dis′ar·ray′ (-ə rā′) ***vt.*** to throw into disorder —***n.*** disorder
dis′as·sem′ble (-ə sem′bəl) ***vt.*** **-bled, -bling** to take apart
dis′as·so′ci·ate′ (-ə sō′shē āt′, -sē-) ***vt.*** **-at′ed, -at′ing** to sever association with; dissociate
dis·as·ter (di zas′tər) ***n.*** ⟦< L *dis-*, away + *astrum*, a star⟧ any happening that causes great harm or damage; calamity —**dis·as′trous** (-trəs) ***adj.***
dis·a·vow (dis′ə vou′) ***vt.*** to deny any knowledge of or responsibility for; disclaim —**dis′a·vow′al** ***n.***
dis·band (dis band′) ***vt.***, ***vi.*** to break up, as an organization
dis·bar′ (-bär′) ***vt.*** **-barred′, -bar′ring** to deprive (a lawyer) of the right to practice law —**dis·bar′ment** ***n.***
dis·be·lieve (dis′bə lēv′) ***vt.***, ***vi.*** **-lieved′, -liev′ing** to refuse to believe —**dis′be·lief′** (-lēf′) ***n.***
dis·burse (dis burs′) ***vt.*** **-bursed′, -burs′ing** ⟦< OFr *desbourser*⟧ to pay out; expend —**dis·burse′ment** ***n.***
disc (disk) ***n.*** **1** DISK **2** a phonograph record
dis·card (dis kärd′; *for n.* dis′kärd′) ***vt.*** ⟦< OFr: see DIS- & CARD[1]⟧ **1** *Card Games* to remove (a card or cards) from one's hand **2** to get rid of as no longer useful —***n.*** **1** a

discarding or being discarded **2** something discarded

disc brake a brake, as on a car, with two friction pads that press on a disc rotating along with the wheel

dis·cern (di zurn′, -surn′) ***vt.*** ⟦ < L *dis-*, apart + *cernere*, to separate ⟧ to perceive or recognize clearly —**dis·cern′i·ble** ***adj.*** —**dis·cern′ment** ***n.***

dis·cern′ing ***adj.*** having good judgment; astute —**dis·cern′ing·ly** ***adv.***

dis·charge (dis chärj′; *for n., usually* dis′-chärj′) ***vt.*** **-charged′**, **-charg′ing** ⟦ < L *dis-*, from + *carrus*, wagon ⟧ **1** to release or dismiss **2** to unload (a cargo) **3** to shoot (a gun or projectile) **4** to emit /to *discharge* pus/ **5** to pay (a debt) or perform (a duty) **6** *Elec.* to remove stored energy from (a battery, etc.) —***vi.*** **1** to get rid of a load, etc. **2** to go off, as a gun —***n.*** **1** a discharging or being discharged **2** that which discharges or is discharged

dis·ci·ple (di sī′pəl) ***n.*** ⟦ < L *dis-*, apart + *capere*, to hold ⟧ **1** a pupil or follower of any teacher or school **2** an early follower of Jesus, esp. one of the Apostles —**dis·ci′ple·ship′** ***n.***

dis·ci·pli·nar·i·an (dis′ə pli ner′ē ən) ***n.*** a person who believes in or enforces strict discipline

dis·ci·pline (dis′ə plin′, -plən) ***n.*** ⟦ see DISCIPLE ⟧ **1** training that develops self-control, efficiency, etc. **2** strict control to enforce obedience **3** orderly conduct **4** a system of rules, as for a monastic order **5** treatment that corrects or punishes —***vt.*** **-plined′**, **-plin′ing** **1** to train; control **2** to punish —**dis′ci·pli·nar′y** (-pli ner′ē) ***adj.***

disc jockey one who conducts a radio program of recorded music

dis·claim (dis klām′) ***vt.*** **1** to give up any claim to **2** to repudiate

dis·claim′er ***n.*** a denial or renunciation, as of responsibility

dis·close (dis klōz′) ***vt.*** **-closed′**, **-clos′ing** to reveal —**dis·clo′sure** (-klō′zhər) ***n.***

dis·co (dis′kō) ***n.*** **1** *pl.* **-cos** *short for* DISCOTHÈQUE **2** a kind of popular dance music with a strong beat

dis·col′or ***vt., vi.*** to change in color as by fading, streaking, or staining Brit. sp. **dis·col′our** —**dis′col·or·a′tion** ***n.***

dis·com·fit (dis kum′fit) ***vt.*** ⟦ < L *dis-*, away + *conficere*, prepare ⟧ to frustrate or disconcert —**dis·com′fi·ture** (-fi chər) ***n.***

dis·com′fort ***n.*** **1** lack of comfort; uneasiness **2** anything causing this —***vt.*** to cause discomfort to

dis·com·mode (dis′kə mōd′) ***vt.*** **-mod′ed**, **-mod′ing** ⟦ < DIS- + L *commodare*, to make suitable ⟧ to cause bother to; inconvenience

dis′com·pose′ (-kəm pōz′) ***vt.*** **-posed′**, **-pos′ing** to disturb; fluster —**dis′com·po′sure** (-pō′zhər) ***n.***

dis′con·cert′ (-kən surt′) ***vt.*** to upset; embarrass; confuse

dis′con·nect′ (-kə nekt′) ***vt.*** to break the connection of; separate —**dis′con·nec′tion** ***n.***

dis′con·nect′ed ***adj.*** **1** separated **2** incoherent

dis·con·so·late (dis kän′sə lit) ***adj.*** ⟦ see DIS- & CONSOLE[1] ⟧ inconsolable; dejected —**dis·con′so·late·ly** ***adv.***

dis·con·tent (dis′kən tent′) ***adj.*** ⟦ ME ⟧ DISCONTENTED —***n.*** dissatisfaction with one's situation Also **dis′con·tent′ment** —***vt.*** to make discontented

dis′con·tent′ed ***adj.*** not contented; wanting something more or different

dis·con·tin·ue (dis′kən tin′yo͞o) ***vt., vi.*** **-ued**, **-u·ing** to stop; cease; give up —**dis′con·tin′u·ance** ***n.*** —**dis′con·tin′u·a′tion** ***n.***

dis′con·tin′u·ous ***adj.*** not continuous; having interruptions or gaps

dis·cord (dis′kôrd′) ***n.*** ⟦ < L *dis-*, apart + *cor*, heart ⟧ **1** disagreement **2** a din **3** a lack of musical harmony —**dis·cord′ant** ***adj.***

dis·co·thèque (dis′kə tek′) ***n.*** ⟦ Fr ⟧ a place for dancing to recorded music

dis·count (dis′kount′; *for v., also* dis kount′) ***n.*** ⟦ see DIS- & COMPUTE ⟧ **1** a reduction from a usual or list price **2** the rate of interest charged on a discounted bill, note, etc.: also called **discount rate** —***vt.*** **1** to pay or receive the value of (a bill, promissory note, etc.), minus a deduction for interest **2** to deduct an amount from (a bill, price, etc.) **3** to sell at less than the regular price **4** *a)* to allow for exaggeration, bias, etc. in (a story, etc.) *b)* to disregard **5** to lessen the effect of by anticipating

dis·coun·te·nance (dis kount′'n əns) ***vt.*** **-nanced**, **-nanc·ing** **1** to make ashamed or embarrassed **2** to refuse approval or support

discount house (or **store**) a retail store that sells goods for less than regular prices

dis·cour·age (di skur′ij) ***vt.*** **-aged**, **-ag·ing** **1** to deprive of courage or confidence **2** to persuade (a person) to refrain **3** to try to prevent by disapproving —**dis·cour′age·ment** ***n.***

dis·course (dis′kôrs′; *for v., usually* dis kôrs′) ***n.*** ⟦ < L *dis-*, from + *currere*, to run ⟧ **1** talk; conversation **2** a formal treatment of a subject, in speech or writing —***vi.*** **-coursed′**, **-cours′ing** to talk

dis·cour·te·ous (dis kur′tē əs) ***adj.*** impolite; rude; ill-mannered

dis·cour′te·sy (-kurt′ə sē) ***n.*** **1** lack of courtesy; rudeness **2** *pl.* **-sies** a rude or impolite act or remark

dis·cov·er (di skuv′ər) ***vt.*** ⟦ see DIS- & COVER ⟧ **1** to be the first to find out, see, etc. **2** to learn of the existence of —**dis·cov′er·er** ***n.***

dis·cov·er·y (di skuv′ər ē) ***n.***, *pl.* **-er·ies** **1** a discovering **2** anything discovered

dis·cred·it (dis kred′it) ***vt.*** **1** to disbelieve **2** to cast doubt on **3** to disgrace —***n.*** **1** loss of belief; doubt **2** disgrace —**dis·cred′it·a·ble** ***adj.***

dis·creet (di skrēt′) ***adj.*** ⟦ see DISCERN ⟧ careful about what one says or does; prudent —**dis·creet′ly** ***adv.***

dis·crep·an·cy (di skrep′ən sē) ***n.***, *pl.* **-cies** ⟦ < L *dis-*, from + *crepare*, to rattle ⟧ disagreement; inconsistency

dis·crete (di skrēt′) ***adj.*** ⟦ see DISCERN ⟧ separate and distinct; unrelated

dis·cre·tion (di skresh′ən) ***n.*** **1** the freedom to make decisions **2** the quality of being discreet; prudence —**dis·cre′tion·ar′y** (-er′ē) ***adj.***

dis·crim·i·nate (di skrim′i nāt′) *vi.* **-nat′ed, -nat′ing** ⟦see DISCERN⟧ **1** to distinguish **2** to make distinctions in treatment; show partiality or prejudice —**dis·crim′i·nat′ing** *adj.* —**dis·crim′i·na′tion** *n.*

dis·crim′i·na·to′ry (-nə tôr′ē) *adj.* showing discrimination or bias

dis·cur·sive (dis kur′siv) *adj.* ⟦see DISCOURSE⟧ wandering from one topic to another; rambling

DISCUS THROWER

dis·cus (dis′kəs) *n.* ⟦< Gr *diskos*⟧ a disk, as of metal and wood, thrown in a contest of strength and skill

dis·cuss (di skus′) *vt.* ⟦< L *dis-*, apart + *quatere*, to shake⟧ to talk or write about; consider the pros and cons of —**dis·cus′sion** (-skush′ən) *n.*

dis·cuss′ant (-ənt) *n.* a participant in an organized discussion

dis·dain (dis dān′) *vt.* ⟦< L *dis-*, DIS- + *dignari*, deign⟧ to regard as beneath one's dignity; scorn —*n.* aloof contempt —**dis·dain′ful** *adj.*

dis·ease (di zēz′) *n.* ⟦< OFr *des-*, DIS- + *aise*, ease⟧ **1** illness in general **2** a particular destructive process in an organism; specif., an illness —**dis·eased′** *adj.*

dis·em·bark (dis′im bärk′) *vi.*, *vt.* to leave, or unload from, a ship, aircraft, etc. —**dis′em·bar·ka′tion** *n.*

dis′em·bod′y (-im bäd′ē) *vt.* **-bod′ied, -bod′y·ing** to free from bodily existence —**dis′em·bod′i·ment** *n.*

dis′em·bow′el (-im bou′əl) *vt.* **-eled** or **-elled, -el·ing** or **-el·ling** to take out the entrails of

dis′en·chant′ (-in chant′) *vt.* **1** to free from an enchantment or illusion **2** DISILLUSION (sense 2) —**dis′en·chant′ment** *n.*

dis′en·cum′ber (-in kum′bər) *vt.* to relieve of a burden

dis′en·gage′ *vt.*, *vi.* **-gaged′, -gag′ing** to release or get loose from something that engages, holds, entangles, etc.; unfasten —**dis′en·gage′ment** *n.*

dis′en·tan′gle *vt.* **-gled, -gling** to free from something that entangles, confuses, etc.; extricate; untangle

dis′es·teem′ *n.* lack of esteem

dis·fa·vor (dis fā′vər) *n.* **1** an unfavorable opinion; dislike; disapproval **2** the state of being disliked, etc.

dis·fig′ure (-fig′yər) *vt.* **-ured, -ur·ing** to hurt the appearance of; mar —**dis·fig′ure·ment** *n.*

dis·fran·chise (dis fran′chīz′) *vt.* **-chised′, -chis′ing** to deprive of a right, privilege, etc., esp. the right to vote Also **dis′en·fran′chise′**

dis·gorge′ (-gôrj′) *vt.*, *vi.* **-gorged′, -gorg′ing** ⟦< OFr: see DIS- & GORGE⟧ **1** to vomit **2** to pour forth (its contents); empty (itself)

dis·grace′ (-grās′) *n.* ⟦< It *dis-*, not + *grazia*, favor⟧ **1** loss of favor or respect; shame; disrepute **2** a person or thing bringing shame —*vt.* **-graced′, -grac′ing** to bring shame or dishonor upon —**dis·grace′ful** *adj.*

dis·grun′tle (-grunt′'l) *vt.* **-tled, -tling** ⟦ult. < DIS- + GRUNT⟧ to make peevishly discontented; make sulky

dis·guise′ (-gīz′) *vt.* **-guised′, -guis′ing** ⟦< OFr: see DIS- & GUISE⟧ **1** to make appear, sound, etc. so different as to be unrecognizable **2** to hide the real nature of —*n.* **1** anything that disguises **2** a being disguised

dis·gust′ (-gust′) *n.* ⟦< DIS- + L *gustus*, a taste⟧ a sickening dislike —*vt.* to cause to feel disgust —**dis·gust′ed** *adj.* —**dis·gust′ing** *adj.*

dish (dish) *n.* ⟦see DISCUS⟧ **1** a container, generally shallow and concave, for holding food **2** as much as a dish holds **3** a particular kind of food —*vt.* to serve in a dish: with *up* or *out*

dis·ha·bille (dis′ə bēl′) *n.* ⟦< Fr *dés-*, DIS- + *habiller*, to dress⟧ the state of being dressed only partially or in night clothes

dish antenna a radio antenna consisting of a dish-shaped reflector

dis·har·mo·ny (dis här′mə nē) *n.* absence of harmony; discord —**dis′har·mo′ni·ous** (-mō′nē əs) *adj.*

dish′cloth′ *n.* a cloth for washing dishes

dis·heart·en (dis härt′'n) *vt.* to discourage; depress

di·shev·el (di shev′əl) *vt.* **-eled** or **-elled, -el·ing** or **-el·ling** ⟦< OFr *des-*, DIS- + *chevel*, hair⟧ to cause (hair, clothing, etc.) to become disarranged; rumple —**di·shev′el·ment** *n.*

dis·hon′est *adj.* not honest; lying, cheating, etc. —**dis·hon′est·ly** *adv.*

dis·hon′es·ty *n.* **1** a being dishonest **2** *pl.* **-ties** a dishonest act

dis·hon′or *n.* **1** loss of honor or respect; shame; disgrace **2** a cause of dishonor —*vt.* **1** to insult or disgrace **2** to refuse to pay (a check, etc.) —**dis·hon′or·a·ble** *adj.*

dish′pan′ *n.* a pan in which dishes, cups, etc. are washed

dish′rag′ *n.* DISHCLOTH

dish′wash′er *n.* a person or machine that washes dishes, cups, etc.

dis′il·lu′sion *vt.* **1** to free from illusion **2** to take away the idealism of and make bitter, etc. —**dis′il·lu′sion·ment** *n.*

dis·in·cline (dis′in klīn′) *vt.* **-clined′, -clin′ing** to make unwilling

dis·in·fect (dis′in fekt′) *vt.* to destroy the harmful bacteria, viruses, etc. in; sterilize —**dis′in·fect′ant** *n.*

dis′in′for·ma′tion *n.* deliberately false information leaked so as to confuse another nation's intelligence operations

dis·in·gen·u·ous (dis′in jen′yo͞o əs) *adj.* not candid or frank

dis·in·her·it (dis′in her′it) *vt.* to deprive of an inheritance

dis·in·te·grate (dis in′tə grāt′) *vt.*, *vi.* **-grat′ed, -grat′ing** to separate into parts or fragments; break up —**dis′in′te·gra′tion** *n.*

dis·in·ter (dis'in tur') *vt.* **-terred', -ter'ring** to remove from a grave, etc.

dis·in·ter·est·ed (dis in'tris tid, ·tər is-) *adj.* 1 impartial; unbiased 2 uninterested; indifferent

dis'in'ter·me'di·a'tion (-in'tər mē'dē ā' shən) *n.* the withdrawal of funds from banks to invest them at higher rates of interest, as in government securities

dis·joint' *vt.* 1 to put out of joint; dislocate 2 to dismember 3 to destroy the unity, connections, etc. of —**dis·joint'ed** *adj.*

disk (disk) *n.* ⟦L *discus*: see DISCUS⟧ 1 any thin, flat, circular thing 2 DISC 3 a thin, flat, circular plate coated with magnetic particles, for storing computer data

disk·ette (di sket') *n.* FLOPPY DISK

dis·like' *vt.* **-liked', -lik'ing** to have a feeling of not liking —*n.* a feeling of not liking; distaste

dis·lo·cate (dis'lō kāt') *vt.* **-cat'ed, -cat'ing** 1 to displace (a bone) from its proper position 2 to disarrange; disrupt —**dis'lo·ca'·tion** *n.*

dis·lodge' *vt., vi.* **-lodged', -lodg'ing** to force from or leave a place where lodged, hiding, etc.

dis·loy'al *adj.* not loyal or faithful —**dis·loy'al·ty** *n.*

dis·mal (diz'məl) *adj.* ⟦< ML *dies mali*, evil days⟧ 1 causing gloom or misery 2 dark and gloomy; dreary

dis·man·tle (dis mant''l) *vt.* **-tled, -tling** ⟦see DIS- & MANTLE⟧ 1 to strip (a house, etc.), as of furniture 2 to take apart —**dis·man'tle·ment** *n.*

dis·may' (-mā') *vt.* ⟦< Anglo-Fr⟧ to make afraid at the prospect of trouble; daunt —*n.* consternation

dis·mem'ber (-mem'bər) *vt.* ⟦see DIS- & MEMBER⟧ 1 to cut or tear the limbs from 2 to pull or cut to pieces —**dis·mem'ber·ment** *n.*

dis·miss' (-mis') *vt.* ⟦< L *dis-*, from + *mittere*, send⟧ 1 to cause or allow to leave 2 to discharge from an office, employment, etc. 3 to put aside mentally 4 *Law* to reject (a claim, etc.) —**dis·miss'al** *n.*

dis·mount' *vi.* to get off, as from a horse —*vt.* 1 to remove (a thing) from its mounting 2 to take apart

dis·o·be·di·ence (dis'ō bē'dē əns, -ə bē'-) *n.* refusal to obey; insubordination —**dis'o·be'di·ent** *adj.*

dis'o·bey' *vt., vi.* to refuse to obey

dis'o·blige' *vt.* **-bliged', -blig'ing** 1 to refuse to oblige 2 to offend

dis·or'der *n.* 1 a lack of order; confusion 2 a breach of public peace; riot 3 an ailment —*vt.* 1 to throw into disorder 2 to upset the normal functions of

dis·or'der·ly *adj.* 1 untidy 2 violating public peace, safety, etc. —**dis·or'der·li·ness** *n.*

dis·or·gan·ize (dis ôr'gə nīz') *vt.* **-ized', -iz'·ing** to break up the order or system of; throw into confusion —**dis·or'gan·i·za'·tion** *n.*

dis·o'ri·ent' (-ôr'ē ent') *vt.* ⟦see DIS- & ORIENT, *v.*⟧ 1 to cause to lose one's bearings 2 to confuse mentally —**dis·o'ri·en·ta'tion** *n.*

dis·own' *vt.* to refuse to acknowledge as one's own; repudiate

dis·par·age (di spar'ij) *vt.* **-aged, -ag·ing** ⟦< OFr *des-* (see DIS-) + *parage*, rank⟧ 1 to discredit 2 to belittle —**dis·par'age·ment** *n.*

dis·pa·rate (dis'pə rət) *adj.* ⟦< L *dis-*, not + *par*, equal⟧ distinct or different in kind; unequal —**dis·par·i·ty** (di spar'ə tē), *pl.* **-ties**, *n.*

dis·pas'sion·ate *adj.* free from passion or bias; impartial —**dis·pas'sion·ate·ly** *adv.*

dis·patch (di spach') *vt.* ⟦< L *dis-*, away + *pes*, foot⟧ 1 to send promptly, as on an errand 2 to kill 3 to finish quickly —*n.* 1 a sending off 2 a killing 3 speed; promptness 4 a message 5 a news story sent by a reporter —**dis·patch'er** *n.*

dis·pel (di spel') *vt.* **-pelled', -pel'ling** ⟦< L *dis-*, apart + *pellere*, to drive⟧ to scatter and drive away

dis·pen·sa·ble (di spen'sə bəl) *adj.* 1 that can be dealt out 2 that can be dispensed with; not important

dis·pen'sa·ry (-sə rē) *n., pl.* **-ries** a room or place where medicines and first-aid treatment are available

dis·pen·sa·tion (dis'pən sā'shən) *n.* 1 a dispensing 2 something dispensed 3 an administrative system 4 a release from an obligation 5 *Theol.* the ordering of events under divine authority

dis·pense (di spens') *vt.* **-pensed', -pens'·ing** ⟦< L *dis-*, out + *pendere*, weigh⟧ 1 to give out; distribute 2 to prepare and give out (medicines) 3 to administer (the law or justice) —**dispense with** 1 to get rid of 2 to do without —**dis·pens'er** *n.*

dis·perse' (-spurs') *vt.* **-persed', -pers'ing** ⟦< L *dis-*, out + *spargere*, scatter⟧ 1 to break up and scatter 2 to dispel (mist, etc.) —*vi.* to scatter —**dis·per'sal** *n.* —**dis·per'·sion** *n.*

dis·pir·it (di spir'it) *vt.* to depress; discourage —**dis·pir'it·ed** *adj.*

dis·place' *vt.* **-placed', -plac'ing** 1 to move from its usual place 2 to remove from office 3 to replace

displaced person one forced from one's country, esp. as a result of war

dis·place'ment *n.* 1 a displacing or being displaced 2 the weight or volume of air, water, or other fluid displaced by a floating object

dis·play (di splā') *vt.* ⟦< L *dis-*, apart + *plicare*, to fold⟧ 1 [Obs.] to spread out 2 to exhibit —*n.* 1 an exhibition 2 anything displayed

dis·please' *vt., vi.* **-pleased', -pleas'ing** to fail to please; offend

dis·pleas'ure (-plezh'ər) *n.* a being displeased; dissatisfaction

dis·port (di spôrt') *vi.* ⟦< OFr *des-* (see DIS-) + *porter*, carry⟧ to play; frolic —*vt.* to amuse (oneself)

dis·pos·al (di spō'zəl) *n.* 1 a disposing 2 a device in the drain of a kitchen sink to grind up garbage

dis·pose' (-spōz') *vt.* **-posed', -pos'ing** ⟦see DIS- & POSITION⟧ 1 to arrange 2 to settle (affairs) 3 to make willing —**dispose of** 1 to settle 2 to give away or sell 3 to get rid of —**dis·pos'a·ble** *adj.*

dis·po·si·tion (dis′pə zish′ən) ***n.*** **1** arrangement **2** management of affairs **3** a selling or giving away **4** the authority to settle, etc.; control **5** a tendency **6** one's temperament

dis′pos·sess′ ***vt.*** to deprive of the possession of land, a house, etc.; oust

dis·praise (dis prāz′) ***vt.*** **-praised′, -prais′·ing** ‖ < OFr *despreisier* ‖ to blame; censure —***n.*** blame

dis′pro·por′tion ***n.*** a lack of proportion — **dis′pro·por′tion·ate** ***adj.***

dis·prove′ ***vt.*** **-proved′, -proved′** or **-prov′·en, -prov′ing** to prove to be false —**dis·proof′** ***n.***

dis·pu·ta·tion (dis′pyo͞o tā′shən) ***n.*** **1** a disputing **2** debate

dis′pu·ta′tious (-pyo͞o tā′shəs) ***adj.*** inclined to dispute; contentious —**dis′pu·ta′tious·ly** ***adv.***

dis·pute (di spyo͞ot′) ***vi.*** **-put′ed, -put′ing** ‖ < L *dis-*, apart + *putare*, to think ‖ **1** to argue; debate **2** to quarrel —***vt.*** **1** to argue (a question) **2** to doubt **3** to oppose in any way —***n.*** **1** a disputing; debate **2** a quarrel —**in dispute** not settled —**dis·put′·a·ble** ***adj.*** —**dis·pu′tant** ***adj., n.***

dis·qual′i·fy′ ***vt.*** **-fied′, -fy′ing** to make or declare unqualified, unfit, or ineligible — **dis·qual′i·fi·ca′tion** ***n.***

dis·qui·et (dis kwī′ət) ***vt.*** to make uneasy; disturb —***n.*** restlessness: also **dis·qui′e·tude′** (-ə to͞od′)

dis·qui·si·tion (dis′kwi zish′ən) ***n.*** ‖ < L *dis-*, apart + *quaerere*, to seek ‖ a formal discussion; treatise

dis·re·gard (dis′ri gärd′) ***vt.*** **1** to pay little or no attention to **2** to treat without due respect —***n.*** **1** lack of attention **2** lack of due regard or respect —**dis′re·gard′ful** ***adj.***

dis′re·pair′ ***n.*** the condition of needing repairs; state of neglect

dis·rep′u·ta·ble ***adj.*** **1** not reputable **2** not fit to be seen

dis′re·pute′ ***n.*** lack or loss of repute; bad reputation; disgrace

dis′re·spect′ ***n.*** lack of respect; discourtesy —**dis′re·spect′ful** ***adj.***

dis·robe (dis rōb′) ***vt., vi.*** **-robed′, -rob′ing** to undress

dis·rupt (dis rupt′) ***vt., vi.*** ‖ < L *dis-*, apart + *rumpere*, to break ‖ **1** to break apart **2** to disturb or interrupt —**dis·rup′tion** ***n.*** — **dis·rup′tive** ***adj.***

dis·sat′is·fy′ ***vt.*** **-fied′, -fy′ing** to fail to satisfy; displease —**dis·sat′is·fac′tion** ***n.***

dis·sect (di sekt′) ***vt.*** ‖ < L *dis-*, apart + *secare*, to cut ‖ **1** to cut apart piece by piece, as a body for purposes of study **2** to analyze closely —**dis·sec′tion** ***n.*** —**dis·sec′tor** ***n.***

dis·sem·ble (di sem′bəl) ***vt., vi.*** **-bled, -bling** ‖ < OFr *dessembler* ‖ to conceal (the truth, one's feelings, etc.) under a false appearance —**dis·sem′blance** ***n.*** —**dis·sem′bler** ***n.***

dis·sem·i·nate (di sem′ə nāt′) ***vt.*** **-nat′ed, -nat′ing** ‖ < L *dis-*, apart + *seminare*, to sow ‖ to scatter about; spread widely —**dis·sem′i·na′tion** ***n.***

dis·sen·sion (di sen′shən) ***n.*** a dissenting; disagreement or quarreling

dis·sent (di sent′) ***vi.*** ‖ < L *dis-*, apart + *sentire*, feel ‖ **1** to disagree **2** to reject the doctrines of an established church —***n.*** a dissenting —**dis·sent′er** ***n.***

dis·ser·ta·tion (dis′ər tā′shən) ***n.*** ‖ < L *dis-*, apart + *serere*, join ‖ a formal discourse or treatise, esp. one written to fulfill the requirements for a doctorate from a university

dis·serv·ice (dis sʉr′vis) ***n.*** harm

dis·sev·er (di sev′ər) ***vt.*** **1** to sever **2** to divide into parts —***vi.*** to separate; disunite

dis·si·dence (dis′ə dəns) ***n.*** ‖ < L *dis-*, apart + *sidere*, sit ‖ disagreement —**dis′si·dent** (-dənt) ***adj., n.***

dis·sim·i·lar (dis sim′ə lər) ***adj.*** not similar; different —**dis·sim′i·lar′i·ty** (-lar′ə tē), *pl.* **-ties,** ***n.***

dis·si·mil·i·tude (dis′si mil′ə to͞od′) ***n.*** dissimilarity; difference

dis·sim·u·late (di sim′yo͞o lāt′) ***vt., vi.*** **-lat′ed, -lat′ing** ‖ see DIS- & SIMULATE ‖ to dissemble —**dis·sim′u·la′tion** ***n.*** —**dis·sim′u·la′tor** ***n.***

dis·si·pate (dis′ə pāt′) ***vt.*** **-pat′ed, -pat′ing** ‖ < L *dis-*, apart + *supare*, to throw ‖ **1** to scatter; disperse **2** to make disappear **3** to waste or squander —***vi.*** **1** to vanish **2** to indulge in pleasure to the point of harming oneself —**dis′si·pa′tion** ***n.***

dis·so·ci·ate (di sō′shē āt′) ***vt.*** **-at′ed, -at′ing** ‖ < L *dis-*, apart + *sociare*, join ‖ to break the connection between; disunite —**dis·so′·ci·a′tion** ***n.***

dis·so·lute (dis′ə lo͞ot′) ***adj.*** ‖ see DISSOLVE ‖ dissipated and immoral —**dis′so·lute′ly** ***adv.*** —**dis′so·lute′ness** ***n.***

dis·so·lu·tion (dis′ə lo͞o′shən) ***n.*** a dissolving or being dissolved; specif., *a)* a breaking up or into parts *b)* a termination *c)* death

dis·solve (di zälv′, -zôlv′) ***vt., vi.*** **-solved′, -solv′ing** ‖ < L *dis-*, apart + *solvere*, loosen ‖ **1** to make or become liquid; melt **2** to pass or make pass into solution **3** to break up **4** to end as by breaking up **5** to disappear or make disappear

dis·so·nance (dis′ə nəns) ***n.*** ‖ < L *dis-*, apart + *sonus*, a sound ‖ **1** an inharmonious combination of sounds; discord **2** any lack of harmony or agreement —**dis′so·nant** ***adj.***

dis·suade (di swād′) ***vt.*** **-suad′ed, -suad′ing** ‖ < L *dis-*, away + *suadere*, to persuade ‖ to turn (a person) aside (*from* a course, etc.) by persuasion or advice —**dis·sua′sion** ***n.***

dis·taff (dis′taf′) ***n.*** ‖ < OE *dis-*, flax + *stæf*, staff ‖ a staff on which flax, wool, etc. is wound for use in spinning —***adj.*** female

dis·tal (dis′təl) ***adj.*** ‖ DIST(ANT) + AL ‖ *Anat.* farthest from the point of attachment or origin —**dis′tal·ly** ***adv.***

dis·tance (dis′təns) ***n.*** ‖ < L *dis-*, apart + *stare*, to stand ‖ **1** a being separated in space or time; remoteness **2** an interval between two points in space or time **3** a remoteness in behavior; reserve **4** a faraway place

dis′tant (-tənt) ***adj.*** **1** far away in space or time **2** away [100 miles *distant*] **3** far apart in relationship **4** aloof; reserved **5** from or at a distance —**dis′tant·ly** ***adv.***

dis·taste (dis tāst′) *n.* dislike —**dis·taste′ful** *adj.*

dis·tem·per (dis tem′pər) *n.* ‖ < ML *distemperare*, to disorder ‖ an infectious viral disease of young dogs

dis·tend (di stend′) *vt., vi.* ‖ < L *dis-*, apart + *tendere*, to stretch ‖ **1** to stretch out **2** to make or become swollen —**dis·ten′tion** *n.*

dis·till or **dis·til** (di stil′) *vi., vt.* **-tilled′**, **-till′ing** ‖ < L *de-*, down + *stillare*, to drop ‖ **1** to fall or let fall in drops **2** to undergo, subject to, or produce by distillation —**dis·till′er** *n.*

dis·til·late (dis′tə lāt′, -lit) *n.* a liquid obtained by distilling

dis·til·la·tion (dis′tə lā′shən) *n.* **1** the process of heating a mixture and condensing the resulting vapor to produce a more nearly pure substance **2** anything distilled

dis·till′er·y *n., pl.* **-ies** a place where alcoholic liquors are distilled

dis·tinct (di stiŋkt′) *adj.* ‖ see DISTINGUISH ‖ **1** not alike **2** separate **3** clearly marked off; plain **4** unmistakable —**dis·tinct′ly** *adv.*

dis·tinc′tion (-stiŋk′shən) *n.* **1** the act of making or keeping distinct **2** difference **3** a quality or feature that differentiates **4** fame; eminence **5** the quality that makes one seem superior **6** a mark of honor

dis·tinc′tive *adj.* making distinct; characteristic —**dis·tinc′tive·ly** *adv.* —**dis·tinc′tive·ness** *n.*

dis·tin·guish (di stiŋ′gwish) *vt.* ‖ < L *dis-*, apart + *-stinguere*, to prick ‖ **1** to perceive or show the difference in **2** to characterize **3** to perceive clearly **4** to classify **5** to make famous —*vi.* to make a distinction (*between* or *among*) —**dis·tin′guish·a·ble** *adj.*

dis·tin′guished *adj.* celebrated; famous

dis·tort (di stôrt′) *vt.* ‖ < L *dis-*, intens. + *torquere*, to twist ‖ **1** to twist out of shape **2** to misrepresent (facts, etc.) —**dis·tor′tion** *n.*

dis·tract (di strakt′) *vt.* ‖ < L *dis-*, apart + *trahere*, draw ‖ **1** to draw (the mind, etc.) away in another direction; divert **2** to confuse; bewilder —**dis·tract′ed** *adj.* —**dis·tract′ing** *adj.*

dis·trac′tion *n.* **1** a distracting or being distracted **2** anything that distracts confusingly or amusingly; diversion **3** great mental distress

dis·trait (di strā′) *adj.* ‖ see DISTRACT ‖ absent-minded; inattentive

dis·traught′ (-strôt′) *adj.* ‖ var. of prec. ‖ **1** mentally confused; distracted **2** driven mad; crazed

dis·tress (di stres′) *vt.* ‖ ult. < L *dis-*, apart + *stringere*, to stretch ‖ to cause misery or suffering to —*n.* **1** pain, suffering, etc. **2** an affliction **3** a state of danger or trouble

dis·trib·ute (di strib′yo͞ot) *vt.* **-ut·ed**, **-ut·ing** ‖ < L *dis-*, apart + *tribuere*, allot ‖ **1** to give out in shares **2** to spread out **3** to classify **4** to put (things) in various distinct places —**dis′tri·bu′tion** *n.*

dis·trib′u·tor *n.* one that distributes; specif., *a)* a dealer who distributes goods to consumers *b)* a device for distributing electric current to the spark plugs of a gasoline engine

dis·trict (dis′trikt) *n.* ‖ < L *dis-*, apart + *stringere*, to stretch ‖ **1** a division of a state, city, etc. made for a specific purpose **2** any region

district attorney the prosecuting attorney for the State or the Federal government in a specified district

District of Columbia federal district of the U.S., on the Potomac: 69 sq. mi.; pop. 638,000; coextensive with the city of Washington

dis·trust′ *n.* a lack of trust; doubt —*vt.* to have no trust in; doubt —**dis·trust′ful** *adj.*

dis·turb (di sturb′) *vt.* ‖ < L *dis-*, intens. + *turbare*, to disorder ‖ **1** to break up the quiet or settled order of **2** to make uneasy; upset **3** to interrupt —**dis·turb′er** *n.*

dis·turb′ance *n.* **1** a disturbing or being disturbed **2** anything that disturbs **3** commotion; disorder

dis·u·nite (dis′yo͞o nīt′) *vt., vi.* **-nit′ed**, **-nit′ing** to divide or separate into parts, factions, etc. —**dis·u′ni·ty** *n.*

dis·use′ (-yo͞os′) *n.* lack of use

ditch (dich) *n.* ‖ OE *dic* ‖ a long, narrow channel dug into the earth, as for drainage —*vt.* **1** to make a ditch in **2** [Slang] to get rid of

dith·er (di*th*′ər) *vi.* ‖ ME *dideren* ‖ to be nervously excited or confused —*n.* a nervously excited or confused state

dit·to (dit′ō) *n., pl.* **-tos** ‖ It < L *dicere*, to say ‖ **1** the same (as above or before) **2** DITTO MARK

ditto mark a mark (") used in lists or tables to show that the item above is to be repeated

dit·ty (dit′ē) *n., pl.* **-ties** ‖ < L *dicere*, to say ‖ a short, simple song

di·u·ret·ic (dī′yo͞o ret′ik) *adj.* ‖ < Gr *dia-*, through + *ourein*, urinate ‖ increasing the flow of urine —*n.* a diuretic drug or substance

di·ur·nal (dī ʉr′nəl) *adj.* ‖ < L *dies*, day ‖ **1** daily **2** of the daytime —**di·ur′nal·ly** *adv.*

div. **1** dividend **2** division

di·va (dē′və) *n., pl.* **-vas** or **-ve** (-ve) ‖ It < L, goddess ‖ PRIMA DONNA

di·va·lent (dī′vā′lənt, dī vā′-) *adj. Chem.* having two valences or a valence of two

di·van (dī′van′, di van′) *n.* ‖ < Pers *dīwān* ‖ a large, low couch or sofa

dive (dīv) *vi.* **dived** or **dove, dived, div′ing** ‖ OE *dyfan* ‖ **1** to plunge headfirst into water **2** to submerge **3** to plunge suddenly into something **4** to make a steep descent, as an airplane —*n.* **1** a diving **2** any sudden plunge **3** a sharp descent **4** [Colloq.] a cheap, disreputable saloon, etc. —**div′er** *n.*

di·verge (dī vʉrj′, di-) *vi.* **-verged′**, **-verg′ing** ‖ < L *dis-*, apart + *vergere*, to turn ‖ **1** to go or move in different directions; branch off **2** to differ, as in opinion —**di·ver′gence** *n.* —**di·ver′gent** *adj.*

di·vers (dī′vərz) *adj.* ‖ see fol. ‖ various

di·verse (də vʉrs′, dī-) *adj.* ‖ < L *dis-*, apart + *vertere*, to turn ‖ **1** different **2** varied —**di·verse′ly** *adv.*

di·ver·si·fy (də vʉr′sə fī′) *vt.* **-fied′**, **-fy′ing** to make diverse; vary —**di·ver′si·fi·ca′tion** *n.*

di·ver·sion (də vʉr′zhən, dī-) *n.* **1** a divert

ing or turning aside **2** distraction of attention **3** a pastime

di·ver'sion·ar'y *adj.* serving to divert or distract /*diversionary* tactics/

di·ver·si·ty (də vʉr'sə tē, dī-) *n., pl.* **-ties** **1** difference **2** variety

di·vert (də vʉrt', dī-) *vt.* ‖ see DIVERSE ‖ **1** to turn (a person or thing) aside **2** to amuse

di·ver·tic·u·li·tis (dī'vər tik'yoo lit'is) *n.* ‖ < L *de-*, from + *vertere*, to turn + -ITIS ‖ inflammation of a sac (**di'ver·tic'u·lum**) opening out from a tubular organ or main cavity

di·vest (də vest', dī-) *vt.* ‖ < L *dis-*, from + *vestire*, to dress ‖ **1** to strip (*of* clothing, etc.) **2** to deprive (*of* rank, rights, etc.) **3** to rid (*of* something unwanted)

di·vide (də vīd') *vt.* **-vid'ed, -vid'ing** ‖ < L *dividere* ‖ **1** to separate into parts; sever **2** to classify **3** to make or keep separate **4** to apportion **5** to cause to disagree **6** *Math.* to separate into equal parts by a divisor —*vi.* **1** to be or become separate **2** to disagree **3** to share **4** *Math.* to do division —*n.* a ridge that divides two drainage areas —**di·vid'er** *n.*

div·i·dend (div'ə dend') *n.* **1** the number or quantity to be divided **2** *a)* a sum to be divided among stockholders, etc. *b)* a single share of this **3** a bonus

div·i·na·tion (div'ə nā'shən) *n.* ‖ see fol. ‖ **1** the practice of trying to foretell the future **2** a prophecy

di·vine (də vīn') *adj.* ‖ < L *divus*, god ‖ **1** of, like, or from God or a god; holy **2** devoted to God; religious **3** supremely great, good, etc. —*n.* a clergyman —*vt.* **-vined', -vin'ing** **1** to prophesy **2** to guess **3** to find out by intuition —**di·vine'ly** *adv.*

divining rod a forked stick alleged to dip downward when held over an underground supply of water, etc.

di·vin·i·ty (də vin'ə tē) *n., pl.* **-ties** **1** a being divine **2** a god **3** theology —**the Divinity** God

di·vis·i·ble (də viz'ə bəl) *adj.* that can be divided, esp. without leaving a remainder —**di·vis'i·bil'i·ty** *n.*

di·vi·sion (də vizh'ən) *n.* **1** a dividing or being divided **2** an apportioning **3** a difference of opinion **4** anything that divides **5** a segment, section, department, class, etc. **6** the process of finding how many times a number (the *divisor*) is contained in another (the *dividend*) **7** a major military unit

di·vi·sive (də vī'siv) *adj.* causing disagreement or dissension —**di·vi'sive·ly** *adv.* —**di·vi'sive·ness** *n.*

di·vi·sor (də vī'zər) *n.* the number by which the dividend is divided

di·vorce (də vôrs') *n.* ‖ < L *dis-*, apart + *vertere*, to turn ‖ **1** legal dissolution of a marriage **2** complete separation —*vt.* **-vorced', -vorc'ing** **1** to dissolve legally a marriage between **2** to dissolve the marriage with (one's spouse) **3** to separate —**di·vorce'ment** *n.*

di·vor·cée or **di·vor·cee** (də vôr sā', -sē') *n.* ‖ Fr ‖ a divorced woman

div·ot (div'ət) *n.* ‖ Scot ‖ *Golf* a lump of turf dislodged in making a stroke

di·vulge (də vulj') *vt.* **-vulged', -vulg'ing** ‖ < L *dis-*, apart + *vulgare*, make public ‖ to make known; reveal

div·vy (div'ē) *vt., vi.* **-vied, -vy·ing** [Slang] to share; divide (*up*)

Dix·ie (dik'sē) ‖ < *Dixie*, the minstrel song ‖ the Southern States of the U.S.

Dix'ie·land' *adj.* in, of, or like a style of jazz with a ragtime tempo

diz·zy (diz'ē) *adj.* **-zi·er, -zi·est** ‖ OE *dysig*, foolish ‖ **1** feeling giddy or unsteady **2** causing giddiness **3** confused **4** [Colloq.] silly; harebrained —**diz'zi·ly** *adv.* —**diz'zi·ness** *n.*

DJ (dē'jā') *n.* DISC JOCKEY

djel·la·ba or **djel·la·bah** (jə lä'bə) *n.* ‖ < Ar ‖ a long, loose outer garment, worn in Arabic countries

Dji·bou·ti (ji boo̅t'ē) country in E Africa: 8,500 sq. mi.; pop. *c.* 430,000

DNA ‖ < *d*(*eoxyribo*)*n*(*ucleic*) *a*(*cid*) ‖ the basic chromosomal material, containing and transmitting the hereditary pattern

Dne·pr (nē'pər) river in W U.S.S.R., flowing into the Black Sea

do[1] (doo̅) *vt.* **did, done, do'ing** ‖ OE *don* ‖ **1** to perform (an action, etc.) **2** to complete; finish **3** to cause /it *does* no harm/ **4** to exert /*do* your best/ **5** to deal with as is required /*do* the ironing/ **6** to have as one's occupation; work at **7** [Colloq.] to cheat **8** [Colloq.] to serve (a jail term) —*vi.* **1** to behave /*do* as you please/ **2** to be active /up and *doing*/ **3** to get along; fare /he is *doing* well/ **4** to be adequate /the black hat will *do*/ **5** to take place /anything *doing* tonight?/ **6** auxiliary uses of *do*: *a)* to give emphasis /*do* stay a while/ *b)* to ask a question /*did* you go?/ *c)* to serve as a substitute verb /act as I *do* (act)/ —**do in** **1** [Slang] to kill **2** [Colloq.] to tire out —**do over** [Colloq.] to redecorate —**do up** to wrap up —**do with** to make use of —**do without** to get along without —**have to do with** to be related to

do[2] (dō) *n.* ‖ It ‖ *Music* the first or last tone of the diatonic scale

do·a·ble (doo̅'ə bəl) *adj.* that can be done

Do·ber·man pin·scher (dō'bər mən pin'chər) ‖ < Ger after L. *Dobermann*, 19th-c. breeder + *pinscher*, terrier ‖ a large dog with a short, dark coat

doc (däk) *n.* [Slang] doctor

do·cent (dō'sənt) *n.* ‖ < L *docere*, to teach ‖ a lecturer or tour guide, as at a museum

doc·ile (däs'əl) *adj.* ‖ see prec. ‖ easy to discipline; submissive —**do·cil·i·ty** (dō sil'ə tē, dä-) *n.*

dock[1] (däk) *n.* ‖ < It *doccia*, canal ‖ **1** an excavated basin for receiving ships **2** a wharf; pier **3** the water between two piers **4** a platform for loading and unloading trucks, etc. —*vt.* to pilot (a ship) to a dock —*vi.* to come to a dock

dock[2] (däk) *n.* ‖ < Fl *dok*, a cage ‖ the place where the accused stands or sits in court

dock[3] (däk) *n.* ‖ OE *docce* ‖ a tall, coarse weed of the buckwheat family

dock[4] (däk) *vt.* ‖ ME *dok*, tail ‖ **1** to cut off the end of (a tail, etc.); bob **2** to deduct from (wages, etc.)

dock·et (däk'it) *n.* ‖ < ? ‖ **1** a list of cases to

be tried by a law court **2** an agenda —*vt.* to enter in a docket

dock'yard' *n.* SHIPYARD

doc·tor (däk'tər) *n.* ‖< L, teacher‖ **1** one who holds a doctorate **2** a physician or surgeon **3** one licensed to practice any of the healing arts —*vt.* [Colloq.] **1** to try to heal **2** to mend **3** to tamper with —**doc'·tor·al** *adj.*

doc'tor·ate (-it) *n.* **1** the highest degree awarded by universities **2** the status of doctor

Doctor of Philosophy the highest doctorate awarded for original research

doc·tri·naire (däk'tri ner') *adj.* ‖Fr‖ adhering to a doctrine dogmatically —**doc'tri·nair'ism'** *n.*

doc·trine (däk'trin) *n.* ‖see DOCTOR‖ something taught, esp. as the principles of a religion, political party, etc.; tenet or tenets; dogma —**doc'tri·nal** (-tri nəl) *adj.*

doc·u·ment (däk'yo͞o mənt, yə-; *for v.*, ment') *n.* ‖< L *documentum*, proof‖ anything printed, written, etc. that is relied upon to record or prove something —*vt.* to provide with or support by documents —**doc'u·men·ta'tion** *n.*

doc'u·men'ta·ry (-ment'ə rē) *adj.* **1** of or supported by documents **2** depicting news events, social conditions, etc. in nonfictional but dramatic form —*n., pl.* **-ries** a documentary film, TV show, etc.

dod·der (däd'ər) *vi.* ‖ME *daderen*‖ **1** to shake or tremble, as from old age **2** to totter —**dod'der·ing** *adj.*

dodge (däj) *vi., vt.* **dodged, dodg'ing** ‖< ?‖ **1** to move quickly aside, or avoid by so moving **2** to use tricks or evasions, or evade by so doing —*n.* **1** a dodging **2** a trick used in evading or cheating —**dodg'er** *n.*

DODO

do·do (dō'dō) *n., pl.* **-dos** or **-does** ‖Port *doudo*, lit., stupid‖ a large, flightless bird, now extinct

doe (dō) *n.* ‖OE *da*‖ the female deer, antelope, rabbit, etc.

do·er (do͞o'ər) *n.* **1** one who does something **2** one who gets things done

does (duz) *vt., vi. 3d pers. sing., pres. indic., of* DO[1]

doe'skin' *n.* **1** leather from the skin of a female deer **2** a soft wool cloth

doff (däf, dôf) *vt.* ‖see DO[1] & OFF‖ to take off (one's hat, clothes, etc.)

dog (dôg) *n.* ‖OE *docga*‖ **1** any of various canines, esp. one of a domesticated breed kept as a pet, for hunting, etc. **2** a mean, contemptible fellow **3** [*pl.*] [Slang] feet **4** [Slang] an unattractive person or unsatisfactory thing **5** *Mech.* a device for holding or grappling —*vt.* **dogged, dog'ging** to follow or hunt like a dog —**go to the dogs** [Colloq.] to deteriorate

dog'ear' *n.* a turned-down corner of the leaf of a book —**dog'eared'** *adj.*

dog'fish' *n., pl.* **-fish'** or (for different species) **-fish'es** any of various small sharks

dog·ged (dôg'id) *adj.* persistent; stubborn —**dog'ged·ly** *adv.*

dog·ger·el (dôg'ər əl) *n.* ‖ME *dogerel*‖ trivial, awkward verse, usually having a monotonous rhythm

dog·gie bag (dôg'ē) a bag supplied by a restaurant for carrying leftovers, as for one's dog

dog'gone' *interj.* damn! darn! —*vt.* **-goned', -gon'ing** [Colloq.] to damn

dog'house' *n.* a dog's shelter —**in the doghouse** [Slang] in disfavor

do·gie (dō'gē) *n.* ‖< ?‖ in the W U.S., a stray calf

dog·ma (dôg'mə) *n.* ‖< Gr, opinion‖ a doctrine; tenet; belief; esp., a body of theological doctrines strictly adhered to

dog·mat'ic (-mat'ik) *adj.* **1** of or like dogma **2** asserted without proof **3** stating opinion positively or arrogantly —**dog·mat'i·cal·ly** *adv.*

dog'ma·tism' (-mə tiz'əm) *n.* dogmatic assertion of opinion —**dog'ma·tist** *n.*

do'-good'er *n.* [Colloq.] an idealistic, but impractical person who seeks to correct social ills

dog'trot' *n.* a slow, easy trot

dog'wood' *n.* a small, flowering tree of the E U.S.

doi·ly (doi'lē) *n., pl.* **-lies** ‖after a 17th-c. London draper‖ a small mat, as of lace, put under a dish, etc. as a decoration or to protect a surface

do·ing (do͞o'iŋ) *n.* something done; action, etc.: *usually used in pl.*

do'-it-your·self' *n.* the practice of making or repairing things oneself, instead of hiring another —**do'-it-your·self'er** *n.*

Dol·by (dōl'bē) ‖after R. *Dolby*, U.S. recording engineer‖ *trademark for* an electronic system used to reduce unwanted noise in a tape recording

dol·drums (dōl'drəmz, däl'-) *n.pl.* ‖< ? DULL **1** *a)* low spirits *b)* sluggishness **2** equatorial ocean regions having little or no wind

dole (dōl) *n.* ‖OE *dal*, a share‖ **1** money or food given in charity **2** money paid by a government to the unemployed —*vt.* **doled, dol'ing** to give sparingly or as a dole

dole'ful (-fəl) *adj.* ‖< L *dolere*, suffer‖ sad; mournful —**dole'ful·ly** *adv.*

doll (däl) *n.* ‖< nickname for *Dorothy*‖ **1** a child's toy made to resemble a human being **2** [Slang] any attractive or lovable person —*vt., vi.* [Colloq.] to dress stylishly or showily: with *up*

dol·lar (däl'ər) *n.* ‖< Ger *thaler*, a coin‖ **1** the monetary unit of the U.S., equal to 100 cents **2** the monetary unit of various other countries, as of Canada **3** a piece of money worth one dollar

dol·lop (däl'əp) *n.* ‖< ?‖ **1** a soft mass **2** a quantity, often a small one

dol·ly (däl'ē) *n., pl.* **-lies** **1** a doll: child's word **2** a low, flat, wheeled frame for moving heavy objects

dol·men (dōl′mən, däl′-) ***n.*** ‖ Fr ‖ a prehistoric monument consisting of a large, flat stone laid across upright stones

do·lo·mite (dō′lə mit′, däl′ə-) ***n.*** ‖ after D. *Dolomieu*, 18th-c. Fr geologist ‖ a mineral which forms vast layers of rock

do·lor·ous (dō′lər əs, däl′ər-) ***adj.*** ‖ < L *dolere*, suffer ‖ sorrowful; sad —**do′lor·ous·ly *adv.***

dol·phin (däl′fin, dôl′-) ***n.*** ‖ < Gr *delphis* ‖ a highly intelligent toothed whale with a beak-like snout

dolt (dōlt) ***n.*** ‖ prob. < ME *dolte* ‖ a stupid person —**dolt′ish *adj.***

-dom (dəm) ‖ OE *dom*, state ‖ *suffix* **1** rank or domain of *[kingdom]* **2** fact or state of being *[martyrdom]* **3** all who are *[officialdom]*

do·main (dō mān′) ***n.*** ‖ < L *dominus*, a lord ‖ **1** territory under one government or ruler **2** field of activity or influence

dome (dōm) ***n.*** ‖ < Gr *dōma*, housetop ‖ **1** a rounded roof or ceiling **2** any dome-shaped object

do·mes·tic (dō mes′tik, də-) ***adj.*** ‖ < L *domus*, house ‖ **1** of the home or family **2** of or made in one's country **3** tame: said of animals **4** home-loving —***n.*** a maid, cook, etc. in the home —**do·mes′ti·cal·ly *adv.***

do·mes′ti·cate′ (-ti kāt′) ***vt.*** **-cat′ed, -cat′ing** **1** to accustom to home life **2** to tame for human use —**do·mes′ti·ca′tion *n.***

do·mes·tic·i·ty (dō′mes tis′ə tē) ***n.*** home life or devotion to it

dom·i·cile (däm′ə sil′, -sil; *also* dō′mə-) ***n.*** ‖ < L *domus*, home ‖ a home; residence —***vt.*** **-ciled′, -cil′ing** to establish in a domicile

dom·i·nant (däm′ə nənt) ***adj.*** dominating; ruling; prevailing —**dom′i·nance *n.*** —**dom′i·nant·ly *adv.***

dom′i·nate′ (-nāt′) ***vt., vi.*** **-nat′ed, -nat′ing** ‖ < L *dominus*, a master ‖ **1** to rule or control by superior power **2** to rise above (the surroundings) —**dom′i·na′tion *n.***

dom·i·neer (däm′ə nir′) ***vi., vt.*** ‖ < Du: see prec. ‖ to rule (*over*) in a harsh or arrogant way; tyrannize

dom′i·neer′ing *adj.* overbearing

Dom·i·ni·ca (däm′ə nē′kə, də min′i kə) island country in the West Indies: 290 sq. mi.; pop. 74,000 —**Dom′i·ni′can *adj., n.***

Do·min·i·can Republic (dō min′i kən, də-) country in the E part of Hispaniola, in the West Indies: 18,816 sq. mi.; pop. 6,785,000

do·min·ion (də min′yən) ***n.*** ‖ see DOMINATE ‖ **1** rule or power to rule **2** a governed territory or country **3** [D-] [Historical] a self-governing nation of the Commonwealth of Nations

dom·i·no (däm′ə nō′) ***n.**, pl.* **-noes′** or **-nos′** ‖ Fr & It ‖ **1** a hooded cloak and a mask, worn at masquerades **2** a mask for the eyes **3** a small, oblong tile marked with dots **4** [*pl., with sing. v.*] a game played with such tiles

domino theory the theory that if one nation falls to Communism, nearby nations will also, like a row of dominoes falling down

don[1] (dän) ***n.*** ‖ Sp < L *dominus*, master ‖ **1** [D-] Sir; Mr.: a Spanish title of respect **2** a Spanish gentleman **3** [Colloq.] a teacher at a British university **4** a Mafia leader

don[2] (dän) ***vt.*** **donned, don′ning** ‖ contr. of *do on* ‖ to put on (clothes)

Don (dän) river of the central European U.S.S.R., flowing into the Black Sea

Do·ña (dô′nyä) ***n.*** ‖ Sp ‖ Lady; Madam: a Spanish title of respect

do·nate (dō′nāt′) ***vt., vi.*** **-nat′ed, -nat′ing** ‖ < L *donum*, gift ‖ to give or contribute —**do·na′tion *n.***

done (dun) ***vt., vi.*** *pp. of* DO[1] —***adj.*** **1** completed **2** cooked —**done (for)** [Colloq.] dead, ruined, etc.

Don Juan (dän′ wän′) *Sp. Legend* a dissolute nobleman and seducer of women

don·key (däŋ′kē, dôŋ′-, duŋ′-) ***n.**, pl.* **-keys** ‖ < ? ‖ **1** a domesticated ass **2** a stupid or foolish person

don·ny·brook (dän′ē brook′) ***n.*** ‖ after a fair formerly held near Dublin ‖ [Colloq.] a rowdy fight or free-for-all

do·nor (dō′nər) ***n.*** one who donates

Don Qui·xo·te (dän′kē hōt′ē, kwik′sət) **1** a satirical novel by Cervantes **2** its chivalrous but unrealistic hero

don't (dōnt) do not

do·nut (dō′nut′) ***n.*** *colloq. sp. of* DOUGHNUT

doo·dle (do͞od′'l) ***vi.*** **-dled, -dling** ‖ Ger *dudeln*, to trifle ‖ to scribble aimlessly —***n.*** a mark made in doodling —**doo′dler *n.***

doom (do͞om) ***n.*** ‖ OE *dom* ‖ **1** a judgment; sentence **2** fate **3** ruin or death —***vt.*** **1** to pass judgment on; condemn **2** to destine to a tragic fate

dooms′day′ *n.* Judgment Day

door (dôr) ***n.*** ‖ OE *duru* ‖ **1** a movable structure for opening or closing an entrance **2** a doorway **3** a means of access —**out of doors** outdoors

door′bell′ *n.* a bell, etc. at the entrance of a building or room, sounded to alert the occupants of a visitor

door′man′ (-man′, -mən) ***n.**, pl.* **-men′** (-men′, -mən) one whose work is opening the door of a building, hailing taxicabs, etc.

door′mat′ *n.* a mat to wipe the shoes on before entering a house, etc.

door′step′ *n.* a step that leads from an outer door to a path, lawn, etc.

door′way′ *n.* **1** an opening in a wall that can be closed by a door **2** any means of access

door′yard′ *n.* a yard onto which a door of a house opens

do·pa (dō′pə) ***n.*** ‖ < chemical name ‖ an amino acid that is converted by an enzyme in the bloodstream into certain biological chemicals: one isomer (*L-dopa*) is used in treating Parkinson's disease

dope (dōp) ***n.*** ‖ Du *doop*, sauce ‖ **1** any thick liquid used as a lubricant, varnish, filler, etc. **2** [Colloq.] a drug or narcotic **3** [Colloq.] a stupid person **4** [Slang] information —***vt.*** **doped, dop′ing** to drug —**dope out** [Slang] to solve —**dop′er *n.***

dop·ey or **dop·y** (dō′pē) ***adj.*** **-i·er, -i·est** [Colloq.] lethargic or stupid

Dor·ic (dôr′ik) ***adj.*** designating or of a classical style of architecture marked by fluted columns with plain capitals

dorm (dôrm) ***n.*** [Colloq.] DORMITORY

dor·mant (dôr′mənt) ***adj.*** ‖ < L *dormire*, to

sleep ‖ 1 inactive 2 *Biol.* in a resting or torpid state —**dor′man·cy** *n.*

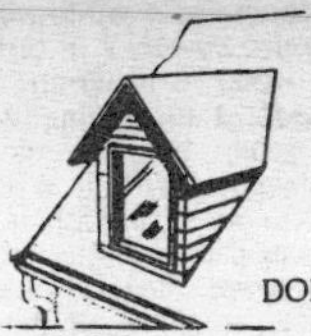

DORMER

dor·mer (dôr′mər) *n.* ‖ see prec. ‖ 1 a window set upright in a structure projecting from a sloping roof: also **dormer window** 2 such a structure

dor·mi·to·ry (dôr′mə tôr′ē) *n., pl.* **-ries** ‖ see DORMANT ‖ 1 a room with beds for a number of people 2 a building with rooms for sleeping and living in, as by students at a college

dor·mouse (dôr′mous′) *n., pl.* **-mice′** (-mīs′) ‖ ME *dormous* ‖ a small, furry-tailed European rodent

dor·sal (dôr′səl) *adj.* ‖ < L *dorsum*, the back ‖ of, on, or near the back

do·ry (dôr′ē) *n., pl.* **-ries** ‖ < ? AmInd (Central America) *dori*, dugout ‖ a small, flat-bottomed fishing boat with high sides

DOS *Comput.* disk operating system

dose (dōs) *n.* ‖ < Gr *dosis*, a giving ‖ an amount of a medicine to be taken at one time —*vt.* **dosed, dos′ing** to give doses to —**dos′age** *n.*

do·sim·e·ter (dō sim′ət ər) *n.* a device for measuring exposure to ionizing radiation

dos·si·er (däs′ē ā′) *n.* ‖ Fr ‖ a collection of documents about some person or matter

dost (dust) *vt., vi. archaic 2d pers. sing., pres. indic., of* DO[1]: used with *thou*

Dos·to·ev·ski or **Dos·to·yev·sky** (dôs′tô yef′skē), **Fe·o·dor** (fyô′dôr) 1821-81; Russ. novelist

dot (dät) *n.* ‖ OE *dott*, head of boil ‖ 1 a tiny speck or mark 2 a small, round spot —*vt.* **dot′ted, dot′ting** to mark with or as with a dot or dots —**on the dot** [Colloq.] at the exact time

dot·age (dōt′ij) *n.* ‖ ME < *doten*, DOTE ‖ childish state due to old age

dot′ard (-ərd) *n.* one in one's dotage

dote (dōt) *vi.* **dot′ed, dot′ing** ‖ ME *doten* ‖ 1 to be weak-minded, esp. because of old age 2 to be excessively fond: with *on* or *upon*

doth (duth) *vt., vi. archaic 3d pers. sing., pres. indic., of* DO[1]

dot·ing (dōt′iŋ) *adj.* foolishly or excessively fond —**dot′ing·ly** *adv.*

dot′-ma′trix *adj.* of or by printing in which characters are formed of closely spaced dots

Dou·ay Bible (do͞o ā′) an English version of the Bible for Roman Catholics: after Douai, France, where the Old Testament was published

dou·ble (dub′əl) *adj.* ‖ < L *duplus* ‖ 1 twofold 2 having two layers 3 having two of one kind 4 being of two kinds [*a double standard*] 5 twice as much, as many, etc. 6 made for two —*adv.* 1 twofold or twice 2 two together —*n.* 1 anything twice as much, as many, etc. as normal 2 a duplicate; counterpart 3 a fold 4 [*pl.*] a game of tennis, etc. with two players on each side 5 *Baseball* a hit on which the batter reaches second base 6 *Bridge* the doubling of an opponent's bid —*vt.* **-bled, -bling** 1 to make twice as much or as many 2 to fold 3 to repeat or duplicate 4 *Bridge* to increase the point value or penalty of (an opponent's bid) —*vi.* 1 to become double 2 to turn sharply backward [*to double on one's tracks*] 3 to serve as a double 4 to serve an additional purpose 5 *Baseball* to hit a double —**double up** 1 to clench (one's fist) 2 to bend over, as in pain 3 to share a room, etc. with someone

double agent a spy employed by two rival espionage organizations

dou′ble-bar′reled *adj.* 1 having two barrels, as a kind of shotgun 2 having a double purpose or meaning

double bass (bās) the largest, deepest-toned instrument of the violin family

dou′ble-blind′ *adj.* designating or of a test of the effects of a drug in which neither the subjects nor the researchers know who is receiving the drug

double boiler a cooking utensil in which one pan, for food, fits over another, for boiling water

dou′ble-breast′ed *adj.* overlapping across the breast, as a coat

dou′ble-cross′ *vt.* [Colloq.] to betray —**dou′ble-cross′er** *n.*

double date [Colloq.] a social engagement shared by two couples —**dou′ble-date′, -dat′ed, -dat′ing,** *vi., vt.*

dou′ble-deal′ing *n.* duplicity

dou′ble-deck′er *n.* 1 any structure or vehicle with an upper deck 2 [Colloq.] a two-layer sandwich made with three slices of bread

double dipping an unethical receiving of pay from two or more sources

dou·ble-en·ten·dre (dub′əl än tän′drə, do͞o′ blôn tôn′-) *n.* ‖ < Fr ‖ a term with two meanings, esp. when one is risqué

dou′ble-head′er *n.* two games played in succession on the same day

dou′ble-joint′ed *adj.* having joints that permit limbs, fingers, etc. to bend at other than the usual angles

dou′ble-knit′ *adj.* knit with a double stitch that makes the fabric extra thick

double play *Baseball* a play in which two players are put out

dou′ble-reed′ *adj.* designating or of a woodwind instrument, as the oboe, having two reeds separated by a narrow opening

dou′ble·speak′ *n.* ambiguous language, esp. if meant to deceive

double standard a system, code, etc. applied unequally; specif., a moral code stricter for women than for men

dou·blet (dub′lit) *n.* ‖ < OFr *double*, orig., something folded ‖ 1 a man's closefitting jacket of the 14th-16th c. 2 a pair, or one of a pair

double take a delayed reaction following unthinking acceptance

double talk 1 ambiguous and deceptive talk 2 meaningless syllables made to sound like talk

dou·bloon (dub lo͞on′) ***n.*** ‖< Fr < Sp < L *duplus,* double‖ an obsolete Spanish gold coin

dou·bly (dub′lē) ***adv.*** **1** twice **2** two at a time

doubt (dout) ***vi.*** ‖< L *dubius,* uncertain‖ to be uncertain or undecided —***vt.*** **1** to be uncertain about **2** to tend to disbelieve —***n.*** **1** *a)* a wavering of opinion or belief *b)* lack of trust **2** a condition of uncertainty **3** an unsettled point or matter —**beyond** (or **without**) **doubt** certainly —**no doubt** **1** certainly **2** probably —**doubt′er** ***n.*** —**doubt′ing·ly** ***adv.***

doubt′ful ***adj.*** **1** uncertain **2** causing doubt or suspicion **3** feeling doubt —**doubt′ful·ly** ***adv.***

doubt′less ***adv.*** **1** certainly **2** probably —**doubt′less·ly** ***adv.***

douche (do͞osh) ***n.*** ‖Fr < It *doccia*‖ **1** a jet of liquid applied externally or internally to the body **2** a device for douching —***vt., vi.*** **douched, douch′ing** to apply a douche (to)

dough (dō) ***n.*** ‖OE *dag*‖ **1** a mixture of flour, liquid, etc. worked into a soft mass for baking **2** [Slang] money

dough′nut′ ***n.*** a small, usually ring-shaped cake, fried in deep fat

dough·ty (dout′ē) ***adj.*** **-ti·er, -ti·est** ‖OE *dohtig*‖ [Now Rare] valiant; brave

dough·y (dō′ē) ***adj.*** **-i·er, -i·est** of or like dough; soft, pasty, etc.

Doug·las fir (dug′ləs) ‖after D *Douglas,* 19th-c. Scot botanist in U.S‖ a giant North American evergreen tree valued for its wood

dour (door, dour) ***adj.*** ‖< L *durus,* hard‖ **1** [Scot.] stern; severe **2** sullen; gloomy —**dour′ness** ***n.***

douse (dous) ***vt.*** **doused, dous′ing** ‖< ?‖ **1** to thrust suddenly into liquid **2** to drench **3** [Colloq.] to put out (a light, etc.)

dove[1] (duv) ***n.*** ‖ME *douve*‖ **1** any of the smaller species of pigeon: often used as a symbol of peace **2** an advocate of measures which avoid or end wars

dove[2] (dōv) ***vi.*** *alt. pt. of* DIVE

Do·ver (dō′vər) capital of Del.: pop. 24,000

dove·tail (duv′tāl′) ***n.*** a projecting part that fits into a corresponding cut-out space to form a joint —***vt.*** to fasten or piece together, as by means of dovetails —***vi.*** to fit together closely or logically

dow·a·ger (dou′ə jər) ***n.*** ‖< L *dotare,* endow‖ **1** a widow with a title or property derived from her dead husband **2** an elderly, wealthy woman

dow·dy (dou′dē) ***adj.*** **-di·er, -di·est** ‖< ME *doude,* plain woman‖ not neat or smart in dress —**dow′di·ness** ***n.***

dow·el (dou′əl) ***n.*** ‖ME *doule*‖ a peg of wood, etc., usually fitted into corresponding holes in two pieces to fasten them together —***vt.*** **-eled** or **-elled, -el·ing** or **-el·ling** to fasten with dowels

dow·er (dou′ər) ***n.*** ‖< L *dare,* give‖ **1** that part of a man's property which his widow inherits for life **2** a dowry —***vt.*** to endow (*with*)

down[1] (doun) ***adv.*** ‖OE *adune,* from the hill‖ **1** to, in, or on a lower place or level **2** in or to a low or lower condition, amount, etc. **3** from an earlier to a later period **4** out of one's hands /put it *down*/ **5** in a serious manner /get *down* to work/ **6** completely /loaded *down*/ **7** in cash /$5 *down* and $5 a week/ **8** in writing /take *down* notes/ —***adj.*** **1** descending **2** in a lower place **3** gone, brought, etc. down **4** dejected; discouraged **5** ill **6** finished /four *down,* six to go/ **7** in cash /a *down* payment/ **8** inoperative /the computer is *down*/ —***prep.*** down toward, along, through, into, or upon —***vt.*** to put or throw down —***n.*** **1** a misfortune /ups and *downs*/ **2** *Football* one of a series of plays in which a team tries to advance the ball —**down and out** penniless, ill, etc. —**down on** [Colloq.] angry or annoyed with —**down with!** do away with!

down[2] (doun) ***n.*** ‖< ON *dūnn*‖ **1** soft, fine feathers **2** soft, fine hair

down[3] (doun) ***n.*** ‖OE *dun,* hill‖ open, high, grassy land: *usually used in pl.*

down′beat′ ***n.*** *Music* the downward stroke of the conductor's hand indicating the first beat of each measure

down′cast′ ***adj.*** **1** directed downward **2** unhappy; dejected

Down East [Colloq.] New England, esp. Maine: also **down east**

down′er ***n.*** [Slang] any depressant or sedative

down′fall′ ***n.*** **1** *a)* a sudden fall, as from power *b)* the cause of this **2** a heavy fall, as of snow

down′fall′en ***adj.*** fallen; ruined

down′grade′ ***n.*** a downward slope —***adj., adv.*** downward —***vt.*** **-grad′ed, -grad′ing** **1** to demote **2** to belittle

down′heart′ed ***adj.*** discouraged

down′hill′ ***adv.*** toward the bottom of a hill —***adj.*** **1** going downward **2** without difficulty

Down·ing Street (doun′iŋ) street in London, location of some of the principal government offices of the United Kingdom

down′play′ ***vt.*** to play down; minimize

down′pour′ ***n.*** a heavy rain

down′right′ ***adv.*** utterly —***adj.*** **1** absolute; utter **2** plain; frank

down′scale′ ***adj.*** of or for people who are unstylish, not affluent, etc.

Down's syndrome (dounz) ‖after J. *Down,* 19th-c. Brit physician‖ a congenital condition characterized by mental deficiency, a broad face, etc

down′stage′ ***adj., adv.*** of or toward the front of the stage

down′stairs′ ***adv.*** **1** down the stairs **2** on or to a lower floor —***adj.*** on a lower floor —***n.*** a lower floor

down′state′ ***adj., adv.*** in, to, or from the southerly part of a State

down′stream′ ***adv., adj.*** in the direction of the current of a stream

down′swing′ ***n.*** **1** a downward swing, as of a golf club **2** a downward trend: also **down′turn′**

down′-to-earth′ ***adj.*** realistic or practical

down′town′ ***adj., adv.*** in or toward the main business section of a city —***n.*** the downtown section of a city

down′trod′den ***adj.*** oppressed

down′ward (-wərd) ***adv., adj.*** toward a

lower place, position, etc.: also **down′wards** ***adv.***
down′y ***adj.*** **-i·er, -i·est** 1 covered with soft, fine feathers or hair 2 soft and fluffy, like down
dow·ry (dou′rē) ***n.***, *pl.* **-ries** ‖ see DOWER ‖ the property that a woman brings to her husband at marriage
dowse (douz) ***vi.*** **dowsed, dows′ing** ‖ < ? ‖ to use a divining rod
dox·ol·o·gy (däks äl′ə jē) ***n.***, *pl.* **-gies** ‖ < Gr *doxa*, praise + *-logia*, LOGY ‖ a hymn of praise to God
doz. dozen(s)
doze (dōz) ***vi.*** **dozed, doz′ing** ‖ prob. < Scand ‖ to sleep lightly; nap —***n.*** a light sleep —**doz′er** ***n.***
doz·en (duz′ən) ***n.***, *pl.* **-ens** or **-en** ‖ < L *duo*, two + *decem*, ten ‖ a set of twelve —**doz′enth** ***adj.***
dpt. 1 department 2 deponent
Dr or **Dr.** 1 Doctor 2 Drive
drab (drab) ***n.*** ‖ < VL *drappus*, cloth ‖ a dull yellowish brown —***adj.*** **drab′ber, drab′best** 1 dull yellowish-brown 2 dull; dreary —**drab′ness** ***n.***
drach·ma (drak′mə) ***n.*** ‖ < Gr *drachmē* ‖ 1 an ancient Greek coin 2 the monetary unit of modern Greece
draft (draft) ***n.*** ‖ OE *dragan*, to draw ‖ 1 a drawing or pulling, as of a vehicle or load 2 *a)* a drawing in of a fish net *b)* the amount of fish caught in one draw 3 *a)* a drinking or the amount taken at one drink *b)* [Colloq.] a portion of beer, etc. drawn from a cask 4 an inhalation 5 a preliminary or tentative piece of writing 6 a plan or drawing of a work to be done 7 a current of air 8 a device for regulating the current of air in a heating system 9 a written order for payment of money; check 10 *a)* the choosing or taking of persons, esp. for compulsory military service *b)* those so taken 11 the depth of water that a ship needs in order to float —***vt.*** 1 to take, as for military service, by drawing from a group 2 to make a sketch of or plans for —***adj.*** 1 used for pulling loads 2 drawn from a cask */draft beer/* —**draft′er** ***n.***
draft·ee (draft ē′) ***n.*** a person drafted, esp. for military service
drafts·man (drafts′mən) ***n.***, *pl.* **-men** 1 one who draws plans, as of machinery 2 an artist skillful in drawing —**drafts′man·ship′** ***n.***
draft′y ***adj.*** **-i·er, -i·est** full of or exposed to drafts of air
drag (drag) ***vt., vi.*** **dragged, drag′ging** ‖ see DRAW ‖ 1 to pull or be pulled with effort, esp. along the ground 2 to search (a lake bottom, etc.) with a dragnet or the like 3 to draw (something) out over a period of time; move or pass too slowly: often with *on* or *out* —***n.*** 1 a dragging 2 a dragnet, grapnel, etc. 3 anything that hinders 4 [Slang] influence 5 [Slang] clothing of the opposite sex, esp. as worn by a male homosexual 6 [Slang] a puff of a cigarette, etc. 7 [Slang] street */the main drag/* 8 [Slang] a dull person, situation, etc.
drag′gy (-ē) ***adj.*** **-gi·er, -gi·est** dragging; slow-moving, dull, etc.
drag′net′ ***n.*** 1 a net dragged along a lake bottom, etc., as for catching fish 2 an organized system or network for catching criminals, etc.
drag·on (drag′ən) ***n.*** ‖ < Gr *drakōn* ‖ a mythical monster, usually shown as a large, winged reptile breathing out fire

DRAGONFLY

drag′on·fly′ ***n.***, *pl.* **-flies′** a large, long-bodied insect with transparent, net-veined wings
dra·goon (drə gōōn′) ***n.*** ‖ < Fr *dragon*, DRAGON ‖ a heavily armed cavalryman —***vt.*** to force *into* doing something; coerce
drag race a race between cars accelerating from a standstill on a short, straight course (**drag strip**) —**drag′-race′, -raced′, -rac′ing,** ***vi.***
drain (drān) ***vt.*** ‖ OE *dryge*, dry ‖ 1 to draw off (liquid) gradually 2 to draw liquid from gradually 3 to exhaust (strength, resources, etc.) gradually —***vi.*** 1 to flow off or trickle through gradually 2 to become dry by draining —***n.*** 1 a channel or pipe for draining 2 a draining —**drain′er** ***n.***
drain′age (-ij) ***n.*** 1 a draining 2 a system of drains 3 that which is drained off 4 an area drained
drain′pipe′ ***n.*** a large pipe used to carry off water, sewage, etc.
drake (drāk) ***n.*** ‖ ME ‖ a male duck
dram (dram) ***n.*** < Gr *drachmē*, handful ‖ 1 a unit of apothecaries' weight equal to 3.89 grams 2 a unit of avoirdupois weight equal to 1.77 grams 3 a small drink of alcoholic liquor
dra·ma (drä′mə, dram′ə) ***n.*** ‖ < Gr ‖ 1 a literary composition to be performed by actors; play, esp. one that is not a comedy 2 the art of writing, acting, or producing plays 3 a series of events suggestive of those of a play 4 dramatic quality
Dram·a·mine (dram′ə mēn′) *trademark for* a drug to relieve motion sickness —***n.*** [**d-**] a tablet of this drug
dra·mat·ic (drə mat′ik) ***adj.*** 1 of drama 2 like a play 3 vivid, striking, etc. —**dra·mat′i·cal·ly** ***adv.***
dra·mat′ics ***n.pl.*** 1 [*usually with sing. v.*] the performing or producing of plays 2 exaggerated emotionalism
dram·a·tist (dram′ə tist, drä′mə-) ***n.*** a playwright
dram′a·tize′ (-tīz′) ***vt.*** **-tized′, -tiz′ing** 1 to make into a drama 2 to regard or show in a dramatic manner —**dram′a·ti·za′tion** ***n.***
drank (draŋk) ***vt., vi.*** *pt. of* DRINK
drape (drāp) ***vt.*** **draped, drap′ing** ‖ < VL *drappus*, cloth ‖ 1 to cover or hang as with cloth in loose folds 2 to arrange (a garment, etc.) in folds or hangings —***n.*** cloth hanging in loose folds; esp., a heavy curtain: *usually used in pl.*
drap·er (drā′pər) ***n.*** [Brit.] a dealer in cloth and dry goods

drap′er·y ***n.***, *pl.* **-er·ies** **1** [Brit.] DRY GOODS **2** hangings or clothing arranged in loose folds **3** [*pl.*] curtains of heavy material

dras·tic (dras′tik) ***adj.*** ‖Gr *drastikos,* active‖ having a violent effect; severe; harsh —**dras′ti·cal·ly** ***adv.***

draught (draft) ***n., vt., adj.*** *now chiefly Brit. sp. of* DRAFT

draughts (drafts) ***n.pl.*** [Brit.] the game of checkers

draw (drô) ***vt.*** **drew, drawn, draw′ing** ‖OE *dragan*‖ **1** to make move toward one; pull **2** to pull up, down, back, in, or out **3** to need (a specified depth of water) to float in: said of a ship **4** to attract **5** to breathe in **6** to elicit (a reply, etc.) **7** to bring on; provoke **8** to receive /to *draw* a salary/ **9** to withdraw (money) held in an account **10** to write (a check or draft) **11** to deduce **12** to take or get (cards, etc.) **13** to stretch **14** to make (lines, pictures, etc.), as with a pencil **15** to make (comparisons, etc.) —***vi.*** **1** to draw something **2** to be drawn **3** to come; move **4** to shrink **5** to allow a draft of air, smoke, etc. to move through **6** to make a demand (*on*) —***n.*** **1** a drawing or being drawn **2** the result of drawing **3** a thing drawn **4** a tie; stalemate **5** a thing that attracts —**draw out** **1** to extend **2** to take out **3** to get (a person) to talk —**draw up** **1** to arrange in order **2** to draft (a document) **3** to stop

draw′back′ ***n.*** anything that prevents or lessens satisfaction; shortcoming

draw′bridge′ ***n.*** a bridge that can be raised or drawn aside, as to permit passage of ships

draw·er (drô′ər; *for 2* drôr) ***n.*** **1** a person or thing that draws **2** a sliding box in a table, chest, etc.

drawers (drôrz) ***n.pl.*** an undergarment for the lower part of the body

draw′ing ***n.*** **1** the act of one that draws; specif., the art of making pictures, etc., as with a pencil **2** a picture, etc. thus made **3** a lottery

drawing card an entertainer, show, etc. that draws a large audience

drawing room ‖< *withdrawing room*: guests withdrew there after dinner‖ a room where guests are received or entertained

drawl (drôl) ***vt., vi.*** ‖prob. < DRAW, *v.*‖ to speak slowly, prolonging the vowels —***n.*** a manner of speaking thus

drawn (drôn) ***vt., vi.*** *pp. of* DRAW —***adj.*** **1** disemboweled **2** tense; haggard

drawn butter melted butter

draw′string′ ***n.*** a string drawn through a hem, as to tighten a garment

dray (drā) ***n.*** ‖OE *dragan,* to draw‖ a low cart for carrying heavy loads

dread (dred) ***vt.*** ‖OE *ondrædan*‖ to anticipate with fear or distaste —***n.*** **1** intense fear **2** fear mixed with awe —***adj.*** inspiring dread

dread′ful ***adj.*** **1** inspiring dread; awesome; terrible **2** [Colloq.] very bad, offensive, etc. —**dread′ful·ly** ***adv.***

dread′locks′ (-läks′) ***n.pl.*** hair worn in long, thin braids or uncombed, twisted locks

dread′nought′ or **dread′naught′** (-nôt′) ***n.*** a large, heavily armored battleship

dream (drēm) ***n.*** ‖OE, joy, music‖ **1** a sequence of images, etc. passing through a sleeping person's mind **2** a daydream; reverie **3** a fond hope **4** anything dreamlike —***vi., vt.*** **dreamed** or **dreamt** (dremt), **dream′ing** to have a dream or remote idea (*of*) —**dream up** [Colloq.] to devise (a fanciful plan, etc.) —**dream′er** ***n.*** —**dream′less** ***adj.*** —**dream′like′** ***adj.***

dream′land′ ***n.*** **1** any lovely but imaginary place **2** sleep

dream world **1** DREAMLAND **2** the realm of fantasy

dream′y ***adj.*** **-i·er, -i·est** **1** filled with dreams **2** fond of daydreaming **3** like something in a dream **4** soothing **5** [Slang] wonderful —**dream′i·ly** ***adv.***

drear·y (drir′ē) ***adj.*** **-i·er, -i·est** ‖OE *dreorig,* sad‖ dismal: also [Old Poet.] **drear** —**drear′i·ly** ***adv.*** —**drear′i·ness** ***n.***

dredge[1] (drej) ***n.*** ‖prob. < MDu‖ an apparatus for scooping up mud, etc., as in deepening channels —***vt., vi.*** **dredged, dredg′ing** **1** to search (*for*) or gather (*up*) as with a dredge **2** to enlarge or clean out with a dredge

dredge[2] (drej) ***vt.*** **dredged, dredg′ing** ‖ME *dragge,* sweetmeat‖ to coat (food) with flour or the like

dregs (dregz) ***n.pl.*** ‖< ON *dregg*‖ **1** particles settling at the bottom in a liquid **2** the most worthless part

Drei·ser (drī′sər, -zər), **The·o·dore** (**Herman Albert**) (thē′ə dôr′) 1871-1945; U.S. novelist

drench (drench) ***vt.*** ‖OE *drincan,* to drink‖ to make wet all over; soak

Dres·den (drez′dən) city in SE East Germany: pop. 520,000

dress (dres) ***vt.*** **dressed** or **drest, dress′ing** ‖< L *dirigere,* lay straight‖ **1** to put clothes on; clothe **2** to trim; adorn **3** to arrange (the hair) in a certain way **4** to align (troops) **5** to apply medicines and bandages to (a wound, etc.) **6** to prepare for use, esp. for cooking /to *dress* a fowl/ **7** to smooth or finish (stone, wood, etc.) —***vi.*** **1** to put on clothes **2** to dress formally **3** to line up in rank —***n.*** **1** clothing **2** the usual outer garment of women, generally of one piece with a skirt —***adj.*** **1** of or for dresses **2** for formal wear —**dress down** to scold —**dress up** to dress formally, elegantly, etc.

dres·sage (dre säzh′) ***n.*** ‖Fr, training‖ horsemanship using slight movements to control the horse

dress circle a semicircle of seats in a theater, etc., usually behind and above the orchestra seats

dress′er ***n.*** **1** one who dresses (in various senses) **2** a chest of drawers for clothes, usually with a mirror

dress′ing ***n.*** **1** the act of one that dresses **2** bandages, etc. applied to wounds **3** a sauce for salads, etc. **4** a stuffing for roast fowl, etc.

dress′ing-down′ ***n.*** a sound scolding

dressing gown a loose robe for one not fully clothed, as when lounging

dress′mak′er ***n.*** one who makes dresses, etc. —**dress′mak′ing** ***n.***

dress rehearsal a final rehearsal, as of a play, with costumes, etc.

dress'y *adj.* **-i·er, -i·est** 1 showy or elaborate in dress or appearance 2 elegant; smart —**dress'i·ness** *n.*

drew (dro͞o) *vt., vi. pt. of* DRAW

drib·ble (drib'əl) *vi., vt.* **-bled, -bling** ‖< DRIP‖ 1 to flow, or let flow, in drops 2 to drool 3 *Sports* to move (a ball or puck) along by repeated bouncing, kicking, or tapping —*n.* 1 a dribbling 2 a tiny amount: also **drib'let** (-lit) —**drib'bler** *n.*

dried (drīd) *vt., vi. pt. & pp. of* DRY

dri·er (drī'ər) *n.* 1 a substance added to paint, etc. to make it dry fast 2 DRYER —*adj. compar. of* DRY

dri'est (-ist) *adj. superl. of* DRY

drift (drift) *n.* ‖OE *drifan,* to drive‖ 1 *a)* a being carried along, as by a current *b)* the course of this 2 a trend; tendency 3 general meaning 4 a heap of snow, sand, etc. piled up by wind —*vi.* 1 to be carried along, as by a current 2 to go along aimlessly 3 to pile up in drifts —*vt.* to make drift —**drift'er** *n.*

drift'wood' *n.* wood drifting in the water or washed ashore

drill[1] (dril) *n.* ‖< Du *drillen,* to bore‖ 1 a tool for boring holes 2 *a)* systematic military or physical training *b)* the method or practice of teaching by repeated exercises —*vt., vi.* 1 to bore with a drill (the tool) 2 to train in, or teach by means of, a drill —**drill'er** *n.*

drill[2] (dril) *n.* ‖< ?‖ a planting machine for making holes or furrows and dropping seeds into them

drill[3] (dril) *n.* ‖< L *trilix,* three-threaded‖ a coarse, twilled cotton cloth, used for uniforms, etc.

drill'mas'ter *n.* 1 an instructor in military drill 2 one who teaches by drilling

drill press a power-driven machine for drilling holes in metal, etc.

dri·ly (drī'lē) *adv.* DRYLY

drink (driŋk) *vt.* **drank, drunk, drink'ing** ‖OE *drincan*‖ 1 to swallow (liquid) 2 to absorb (liquid) 3 to swallow the contents of —*vi.* 1 to swallow liquid 2 to drink alcoholic liquor, esp. to excess —*n.* 1 any liquid for drinking 2 alcoholic liquor —**drink in** to take in eagerly with the senses or mind —**drink to** to drink a toast to —**drink'a·ble** *adj.* —**drink'er** *n.*

drip (drip) *vi., vt.* **dripped** or **dript, drip'ping** ‖OE *dryppan*‖ to fall, or let fall, in drops —*n.* 1 a dripping 2 [Slang] an insipid person —**drip'per** *n.*

drip'-dry' *adj.* designating garments that dry quickly when hung wet and require little or no ironing

drive (drīv) *vt.* **drove, driv·en** (driv'ən), **driv'ing** ‖OE *drifan*‖ 1 to force to go 2 to force into or from a state or act 3 to force to work, esp. to excess 4 to hit (a ball, etc.) hard 5 to make penetrate 6 *a)* to control the movement of; operate (a car, bus, etc.) *b)* to transport in a car, etc. 7 to push (a bargain, etc.) through —*vi.* 1 to advance violently 2 to try hard, as to reach a goal 3 to drive a blow, ball, etc. 4 to be driven: said of a car, bus, etc. 5 to operate, or go in, a car, etc. —*n.* 1 a driving 2 a trip in a car, etc. 3 *a)* a road for cars, etc. *b)* a driveway 4 a rounding up of animals 5 a campaign 6 energy and initiative 7 a strong impulse or urge 8 the propelling mechanism of a machine, etc. —**drive at** to mean; intend —**drive in** 1 to force in, as by a blow 2 *Baseball* to cause (a runner) to score or (a run) to be scored

drive'-in' *n.* a restaurant, movie theater, bank, etc. designed to serve people seated in their cars

driv·el (driv'əl) *vi., vt.* **-eled** or **-elled, -el·ing** or **-el·ling** ‖OE *dreflian*‖ 1 to let (saliva) drool 2 to speak or say in a silly, stupid way —*n.* silly, stupid talk —**driv'el·er** or **driv'el·ler** *n.*

driv'er *n.* a person or thing that drives, as *a)* one who drives a car, etc. *b)* one who herds cattle *c)* a golf club for hitting the ball from the tee

drive shaft a shaft that transmits motion, as to the rear axle of a car

drive'train' *n.* the system that transmits an engine's power to wheels, a propeller, etc.

drive'way' *n.* a path for cars, from a street to a garage, house, etc.

driz·zle (driz'əl) *vi., vt.* **-zled, -zling** ‖prob. < ME‖ to rain in fine, misty drops —*n.* a fine, misty rain —**driz'zly** *adj.*

drogue (drōg) *n.* ‖prob. < Scot *drug,* drag‖ a funnel-shaped device towed behind an aircraft or spacecraft, as for its drag effect, or as a target, etc.

droll (drōl) *adj.* ‖< Fr < MDu *drol,* stout fellow‖ amusing in an odd or wry way —**droll'er·y** (-ər ē), *pl.* **-ies,** *n.* —**droll'ness** *n.* —**drol'ly** *adv.*

drom·e·dar·y (dräm'ə der'ē) *n., pl.* **-ies** ‖< LL *dromedarius* (*camelus*), running (camel)‖ the one-humped camel

drone[1] (drōn) *n.* ‖OE *dran*‖ 1 a male bee that does no work 2 an idler; loafer

drone[2] (drōn) *vi.* **droned, dron'ing** ‖< prec.‖ 1 to make a continuous humming sound 2 to talk in a monotonous way —*vt.* to utter in a monotonous tone —*n.* a droning sound

drool (dro͞ol) *vi.* ‖< DRIVEL‖ 1 to let saliva flow from one's mouth 2 to flow from the mouth, as saliva

droop (dro͞op) *vi.* ‖< ON *drūpa*‖ 1 to sink, hang, or bend down 2 to lose strength or vitality 3 to become dejected —*vt.* to let hang down —*n.* a drooping —**droop'y, -i·er, -i·est,** *adj.* —**droop'i·ness** *n.*

drop (dräp) *n.* ‖OE *dropa*‖ 1 a bit of liquid rounded in shape by falling, etc. 2 anything like this in shape, etc. 3 a very small quantity 4 a sudden fall, descent, slump, etc. 5 something that drops, as a curtain or trapdoor 6 the distance between a higher and lower level —*vi.* **dropped, drop'ping** 1 to fall in drops 2 to fall 3 to fall exhausted, wounded, or dead 4 to pass into a specified state /to *drop* off to sleep/ 5 to come to an end /let the matter *drop*/ —*vt.* 1 to let or make fall 2 to utter (a hint, etc.) casually 3 to send (a letter) 4 to stop, end, or dismiss 5 to lower 6 [Colloq.] to leave at a specified place —**drop in** (or **over** or **by**) to pay a casual visit —**drop out** to stop participating —**drop'let** *n.*

drop kick *Football* a kick of a dropped ball

just as it hits the ground —**drop′-kick′** *vt., vi.* —**drop′-kick′er** *n.*
drop′-off′ *n.* 1 a very steep drop 2 a decline, as in sales, prices, etc.
drop′out′ *n.* one who withdraws from school before graduating
drop′per *n.* a small tube with a hollow rubber bulb at one end, used to measure out a liquid in drops
drop·sy (dräp′sē) *n.* ‖ < Gr *hydrōps* < *hydōr*, water ‖ *old term for* EDEMA —**drop′si·cal** (-si kəl) *adj.*
dross (drôs) *n.* ‖ OE *dros* ‖ 1 scum on molten metal 2 refuse; rubbish
drought (drout) *n.* ‖ < OE *drugoth*, dryness ‖ prolonged dry weather
drove[1] (drōv) *n.* ‖ OE *draf* ‖ 1 a number of cattle, sheep, etc. driven or moving along as a group; flock; herd 2 a moving crowd of people: *usually used in pl.*
drove[2] (drōv) *vt., vi. pt. of* DRIVE
dro·ver (drō′vər) *n.* one who herds droves of animals, esp. to market
drown (droun) *vi.* ‖ ME *drounen* ‖ to die by suffocation in water —*vt.* 1 to kill by such suffocation 2 to flood 3 to be so loud as to overcome (another sound): usually with *out*
drowse (drouz) *vi.* **drowsed, drows′ing** ‖ < OE *drusian*, become sluggish ‖ to be half asleep; doze —*n.* a doze
drows·y (drou′zē) *adj.* **-i·er, -i·est** being or making sleepy or half asleep —**drows′i·ly** *adv.* —**drows′i·ness** *n.*
drub (drub) *vt.* **drubbed, drub′bing** ‖ < Ar *daraba*, to cudgel ‖ 1 to beat as with a stick 2 to defeat soundly —**drub′ber** *n.* —**drub′bing** *n.*
drudge (druj) *n.* ‖ ME *druggen* ‖ one who does hard, menial, or tedious work —*vi.* **drudged, drudg′ing** to do such work —**drudg′er·y**, *pl.* **-ies**, *n.*
drug (drug) *n.* ‖ < OFr *drogue* ‖ 1 any substance used as or in a medicine 2 a narcotic, hallucinogen, etc. —*vt.* **drugged, drug′ging** 1 to put a harmful drug in (a drink, etc.) 2 to stupefy as with a drug —**drug on the market** a thing in plentiful supply for which there is little or no demand
drug′gie (-ē) *n.* [Slang] a habitual user of drugs Also **drug′gy**, *pl.* **-gies**
drug′gist (-ist) *n.* 1 a dealer in drugs, medical supplies, etc. 2 a pharmacist 3 a drugstore owner or manager
drug′store′ *n.* a store where drugs, medical supplies, and various items are sold and prescriptions are filled
dru·id (drōō′id) *n.* ‖ < Celt ‖ [*often* **D-**] a member of a Celtic religious order in ancient Britain, Ireland, and France —**dru′id·ism′** *n.*
drum (drum) *n.* ‖ < Du *trom* ‖ 1 a percussion instrument consisting of a hollow cylinder with a membrane stretched over the end or ends 2 the sound produced by beating a drum 3 any drumlike cylindrical object 4 the eardrum —*vi.* **drummed, drum′ming** 1 to beat a drum 2 to tap continually —*vt.* 1 to play (a rhythm, etc.) as on a drum 2 to instill (ideas, facts, etc. *into*) by continued repetition —**drum out of** to expel from in disgrace —**drum up** to get (business, etc.) by soliciting
drum·lin (drum′lin) *n.* ‖ < Ir ‖ a long ridge formed of gravel, etc. deposited by a glacier
drum major one who leads a marching band, keeping time with a baton —**drum ma′jor·ette′** (-et′) *fem.*
drum′mer *n.* 1 a drum player 2 [Colloq.] a traveling salesman
drum′stick′ *n.* 1 a stick for beating a drum 2 the lower half of the leg of a cooked fowl
drunk (druŋk) *vt., vi. pp. of* DRINK —*adj.* 1 overcome by alcoholic liquor; intoxicated 2 [Colloq.] DRUNKEN (sense 2) Usually used in the predicate —*n.* 1 [Colloq.] a drunken person 2 [Slang] a drinking spree
drunk·ard (druŋk′ərd) *n.* a person who often gets drunk
drunk′en (-ən) *adj.* 1 intoxicated 2 caused by or occurring during intoxication Used before a noun —**drunk′en·ly** *adv.* —**drunk′en·ness** *n.*
drupe (drōōp) *n.* ‖ < Gr *druppa* (*elaa*), olive ‖ any fleshy fruit with an inner stone, as a peach
dry (drī) *adj.* **dri′er, dri′est** ‖ OE *dryge* ‖ 1 not under water /*dry* land/ 2 not wet or damp 3 lacking rain or water; arid 4 thirsty 5 not yielding milk 6 solid; not liquid 7 not sweet /*dry* wine/ 8 prohibiting alcoholic beverages /a *dry* town/ 9 funny in a quiet but sharp way /*dry* wit/ 10 unproductive 11 boring; dull —*n., pl.* **drys** [Colloq.] a prohibitionist —*vt., vi.* **dried, dry′ing** to make or become dry —**dry up** 1 to make or become thoroughly dry 2 to make or become unproductive 3 [Slang] to stop talking —**dry′ly** *adv.* —**dry′ness** *n.*
dry·ad (drī′ad′) *n.* ‖ < Gr *drys*, tree ‖ [*also* **D-**] *Gr. & Rom. Myth.* a tree nymph
dry cell a voltaic cell containing a dry electrolyte which cannot spill
dry′-clean′ *vt.* to clean (garments, etc.) with a solvent other than water, as naphtha —**dry cleaner**
dry dock a dock from which the water can be emptied, used for building and repairing ships
dry′er *n.* 1 a person or thing that dries; specif., an appliance for drying clothes with heat 2 DRIER
dry farming farming without irrigation, by conserving the soil's moisture
dry goods cloth, cloth products, etc.
dry ice carbon dioxide solidified for use as a refrigerant
dry run [Colloq.] a simulated or practice performance; rehearsal
dry′wall′ *n.* PLASTERBOARD
DST daylight saving time
Du. Dutch
du·al (dōō′əl) *adj.* ‖ < L *duo*, two ‖ 1 of two 2 double; twofold —**du′al·ism′** *n.* —**du·al′i·ty** (-al′ə tē) *n.*
dub[1] (dub) *vt.* **dubbed, dub′bing** ‖ < OE *dubbian*, to strike ‖ 1 *a*) to confer a title or rank upon *b*) to name or nickname 2 to smooth by hammering, scraping, etc. 3 [Slang] to bungle (a golf stroke, etc.) —**dub′ber** *n.*
dub[2] (dub) *vt.* **dubbed, dub′bing** ‖ < DOUBLE ‖ to provide with a soundtrack, esp. one with dialogue in another language —**dub in**

to insert (dialogue, music, etc.) in the sound track —**dub'ber** *n.*

dub·bin (dub'in) *n.* ‖< DUB¹‖ a greasy preparation for waterproofing leather

du·bi·e·ty (dōō bī'ə tē) *n.* **1** a being dubious **2** *pl.* **-ties** a doubtful thing

du·bi·ous (dōō'bē əs) *adj.* ‖< L *dubius*, uncertain‖ **1** causing doubt **2** feeling doubt; skeptical **3** questionable —**du'bi·ous·ly** *adv.*

Dub·lin (dub'lən) capital of Ireland: pop 526,000

du·cal (dōō'kəl) *adj.* ‖< LL *ducalis*, of a leader‖ of a duke or dukedom

duc·at (duk'ət) *n.* ‖see DUCHY‖ any of sev eral former European coins

duch·ess (duch'is) *n.* **1** a duke's wife or widow **2** a woman ruling a duchy

duch'y (-ē) *n., pl.* **-ies** ‖< L *dux*, leader‖ the territory ruled by a duke or duchess

duck¹ (duk) *n.* ‖< OE *duce*, diver‖ **1** a small waterfowl with a flat bill, a short neck, and webbed feet **2** the flesh of a duck as food

duck² (duk) *vt., vi.* ‖ME *douken*‖ **1** to plunge or dip under water for a moment **2** to lower or bend (the head, body, etc.) sud denly, as to avoid a blow **3** [Colloq.] to avoid (a task, person, etc.) —*n.* a ducking

duck³ (duk) *n.* ‖Du *doek*‖ a cotton or linen cloth like canvas but finer and lighter in weight

duck'bill' *n.* PLATYPUS

duck'ling *n.* a young duck

duck'pins' *n.pl.* [*with sing. v.*] a game like bowling, played with smaller pins and balls

duck'y *adj.* **-i·er, -i·est** [Slang] pleasing, delightful, etc.

duct (dukt) *n.* ‖< L *ducere*, to lead‖ a tube, channel, or pipe, as for passage of a liquid —**duct'less** *adj.*

duc·tile (duk'til) *adj.* ‖see prec.‖ **1** that can be drawn or hammered thin without breaking: said of metals **2** easily led; trac table —**duc·til'i·ty** (-til'ə tē) *n.*

ductless gland an endocrine gland

dud (dud) *n.* ‖prob. < Du *dood*, dead‖ [Colloq.] **1** a bomb or shell that fails to explode **2** a failure

dude (dōōd) *n.* ‖< ?‖ **1** a dandy; fop **2** [Slang] any man or boy —*vt., vi.* **dud'ed, dud'ing** [Slang] to dress up, esp. in showy clothes: usually with *up*

dude ranch a vacation resort on a ranch, with horseback riding, etc.

due (dōō, dyōō) *adj.* ‖< L *debere*, owe‖ **1** owed or owing as a debt; payable **2** suit able; proper **3** enough /*due* care/ **4** expected or scheduled to arrive —*adv.* exactly; directly /*due* west/ —*n.* **1** deserved recognition **2** [*pl.*] fees or other charges /union *dues*/ —**due to 1** caused by **2** [Colloq.] because of —**pay one's dues** [Slang] to earn a right, etc., as by having suffered in struggle

due bill a receipt for money paid, exchange able for goods or services only

du·el (dōō'əl) *n.* ‖< medieval L *duellum*‖ **1** a prearranged fight between two persons armed with deadly weapons **2** any contest like this —*vi., vt.* **-eled** or **-elled, -el·ing** or **-el·ling** to fight a duel with —**du'el·ist** or **du'el·list, du'el·er** or **du'el·ler** *n.*

due process (of law) legal proceedings established to protect individual rights and liberties

du·et (dōō et') *n.* ‖< L *duo*, two‖ **1** a composition for two voices or instruments **2** the two performers of this

duf·fel (or **duf·fle**) **bag** (duf'əl) ‖after *Duffel*, town in Belgium‖ a large cloth bag for carrying clothing, etc

duff·er (duf'ər) *n.* ‖< thieves' slang *duff*, to fake‖ [Colloq.] **1** a slow witted or dawdling elderly person **2** a relatively unskilled golfer

dug (dug) *vt., vi. pt. & pp. of* DIG

dug'out' *n.* **1** a boat hollowed out of a log **2** a shelter, as in warfare, dug in the ground **3** *Baseball* a covered shelter for the players

du jour (dōō zhoor') offered on this day /soup *du jour*/

duke (dōōk) *n.* ‖< L *dux*, leader‖ **1** a prince ruling an independent duchy **2** a nobleman next in rank to a prince —**duke'·dom** *n.*

dul·cet (dul'sit) *adj.* ‖< L *dulcis*, sweet‖ soothing or pleasant to hear

DULCIMER

dul·ci·mer (dul'sə mər) *n.* ‖< L *dulce*, sweet + *melos*, song‖ a musical instrument with metal strings, which are struck with two small hammers or plucked with a plectrum or quill

dull (dul) *adj.* ‖OE *dol*‖ **1** mentally slow; stupid **2** physically slow; sluggish **3** bor ing; tedious **4** not sharp; blunt **5** not feel ing or felt keenly **6** not vivid or bright /a *dull* color/ —*vt., vi.* to make or become dull —**dull'ness** *n.* —**dul'ly** *adv.*

dull'ard (-ərd) *n.* a stupid person

Du·luth (də lōōth') city & port in NE Minn., on Lake Superior: pop. 93,000

du·ly (dōō'lē) *adv.* in due manner; in the proper way, at the right time, etc.

Du·mas (dü mä'), **Alexandre** 1802-70; Fr. writer

dumb (dum) *adj.* ‖OE‖ **1** lacking the power of speech; mute **2** silent **3** ‖Ger *dumm*‖ [Colloq.] stupid —**dumb'ly** *adv.* —**dumb'ness** *n.*

dumb·bell (dum'bel') *n.* **1** a device consist ing of round weights joined by a short bar, used for muscular exercise **2** [Slang] a stu pid person

dumb·found or **dum·found** (dum'found') *vt.* ‖DUMB + (CON)FOUND‖ to make speechless by shocking; amaze

dumb'wait'er *n.* a small elevator for send ing food, etc. between floors

dum·dum (bullet) (dum'dum') ‖after *Dum-dum*, arsenal in India‖ a soft-nosed bullet that expands when it hits

dum·my (dum'ē) *n., pl.* **-mies 1** a figure

made in human form, as for displaying clothing 2 an imitation; sham 3 [Slang] a stupid person 4 *Bridge* the declarer's partner, whose hand is exposed on the table and played by the declarer —*adj.* sham

dump (dump) *vt.* ‖prob. < ON‖ 1 to unload in a heap or mass 2 to throw away (rubbish, etc.) 3 to sell (a commodity) in a large quantity at a low price 4 *Comput. a)* to transfer (data) to another section of storage *b)* to make a printout of (data) —*n.* 1 a place for dumping rubbish, etc. 2 *Mil.* a temporary storage center in the field 3 an ugly, run-down place —**(down) in the dumps** in low spirits —**dump on** [Slang] to treat with contempt

dump·ling (dump′liŋ) *n.* ‖< ?‖ 1 a small piece of steamed or boiled dough served with meat or soup 2 a crust of baked dough filled with fruit

Dump·ster (dump′stər) *trademark for* a large, metal trash bin, often one emptied by a special truck —*n.* [d-] such a trash bin

dump′y *adj.* **-i·er, -i·est** 1 short and thick; squat 2 [Colloq.] ugly, run-down, etc.

dun[1] (dun) *adj., n.* ‖OE‖ dull grayish-brown

dun[2] (dun) *vt., vi.* **dunned, dun′ning** ‖? dial. var. of DIN‖ to ask (a debtor) repeatedly for payment —*n.* an insistent demand, for payment

dunce (duns) *n.* ‖after John *Duns* Scotus, 13th-c. Scot scholar‖ a dull, ignorant person

dune (do͞on) *n.* ‖Fr < MDu‖ a rounded hill or ridge of drifted sand

dung (duŋ) *n.* ‖OE‖ animal excrement; manure

dun·ga·ree (duŋ′gə rē′) *n.* ‖Hindi *dungrī*‖ 1 a coarse cotton cloth 2 [*pl.*] work trousers or overalls of this

dun·geon (dun′jən) *n.* ‖< OFr *donjon*‖ a dark underground cell or prison

dung′hill′ *n.* a heap of dung

dunk (duŋk) *vt.* ‖Ger *tunken*‖ 1 to dip (bread, etc.) into coffee, etc. before eating it 2 to immerse briefly

Dun·kirk (dun′kərk) seaport in N France: scene of the evacuation of Allied troops under fire (May, 1940)

du·o (do͞o′ō) *n., pl.* **du′os** ‖It‖ 1 DUET (esp. sense 2) 2 a pair; couple

du·o·de·num (do͞o′ō dē′nəm, do͞o äd′′n əm) *n., pl.* **-na** (-nə) or **-nums** ‖< L *duodeni*, twelve each: its length is about twelve fingers' breadth‖ the first section of the small intestine, below the stomach —**du′o·de′nal** *adj.*

dup. duplicate

dupe (do͞op) *n.* ‖< L *upupa*, stupid bird‖ a person easily tricked —*vt.* **duped, dup′ing** to deceive; fool; trick —**dup′er** *n.*

du·plex (do͞o′pleks′) *adj.* ‖L < *duo*, TWO + *-plex*, -fold‖ double —*n.* 1 an apartment with rooms on two floors 2 a house consisting of two separate family units

du·pli·cate (do͞o′pli kit; *for v.*, -kāt′) *adj.* ‖< L *duplicare*, to double‖ 1 double 2 corresponding exactly —*n.* an exact copy —*vt.* **-cat′ed, -cat′ing** 1 to make an exact copy of 2 to make or do again —**du′pli·ca′tion** *n.*

duplicating machine a machine for making copies of a letter, drawing, etc.

du·plic·i·ty (do͞o plis′ə tē) *n., pl.* **-ties** ‖< LL *duplicitas*‖ hypocritical cunning or deception

du·ra·ble (door′ə bəl) *adj.* ‖< L *durare*, to last‖ 1 lasting in spite of hard wear or frequent use 2 stable —**du′ra·bil′i·ty** *n.* —**du′ra·bly** *adv.*

du·ra ma·ter (doo′rə māt′ər) ‖< ML, lit., hard mother, transl. of Ar term‖ the tough, outermost membrane covering the brain and spinal cord

dur·ance (door′əns) *n.* ‖see DURABLE‖ imprisonment: esp. in **in durance vile**

du·ra·tion (do͞o rā′shən) *n.* ‖see DURABLE‖ the time that a thing continues or lasts

du·ress (do͞o′res′, do͞o res′) *n.* ‖< L *durus*, hard‖ 1 imprisonment 2 coercion

Dur·ham (dur′əm) city in N N.C.: pop. 101,000

dur·ing (door′iŋ, dyoor′-) *prep.* ‖see DURABLE‖ 1 throughout the entire time of 2 in the course of

durst (durst) *now chiefly dial. pt. of* DARE

du·rum (do͞o′rəm) *n.* ‖< L *durus*, hard‖ a hard wheat that yields flour for macaroni, spaghetti, etc.

dusk (dusk) *n.* ‖< OE *dox*, dark-colored‖ 1 the dim part of twilight 2 gloom —**dusk′y, -i·er, -i·est,** *adj.*

dust (dust) *n.* ‖OE‖ 1 powdery earth or any finely powdered matter 2 earth 3 disintegrated mortal remains 4 anything worthless —*vt.* 1 to sprinkle with dust, powder, etc. 2 to rid of dust, as by wiping —*vi.* to remove dust, as from furniture —**bite the dust** [Colloq.] to die, esp. in battle —**dust′less** *adj.*

dust bowl an arid region with eroded topsoil easily blown off by winds

dust′er *n.* 1 a person or thing that dusts 2 a lightweight housecoat

dust′pan′ *n.* a shovel-like receptacle into which floor dust is swept

dust′y *adj.* **-i·er, -i·est** 1 covered with or full of dust 2 powdery 3 dust-colored —**dust′i·ness** *n.*

Dutch (duch) *n.* the language of the Netherlands —*adj.* 1 of the Netherlands or its people, language, or culture 2 [Obs. or Slang] German —**go Dutch** [Colloq.] to have each pay his own expenses —**in Dutch** [Colloq.] in trouble or disfavor —**the Dutch** Dutch people

Dutch door a door with upper and lower halves opening separately

Dutch oven a heavy pot with an arched lid, for pot roasts, etc.

Dutch treat [Colloq.] any date, etc. on which each pays his own expenses

Dutch uncle [Colloq.] one who bluntly and sternly lectures another, often with benevolent intent

du·te·ous (do͞ot′ē əs) *adj.* dutiful; obedient —**du′te·ous·ly** *adv.*

du·ti·a·ble (do͞ot′ē ə bəl) *adj.* necessitating payment of a duty or tax

du·ti·ful (do͞ot′i fəl) *adj.* showing, or resulting from, a sense of duty; obedient —**du′ti·ful·ly** *adv.*

du·ty (do͞ot′ē) *n., pl.* **-ties** ‖see DUE & -TY‖ 1 obedience or respect to be shown to one's parents, elders, etc. 2 any action required by one's position or by moral or legal considerations, etc. **3** service, esp. military service [*overseas duty*] **4** a tax, as on imports —**on** (or **off**) **duty** at (or temporarily relieved from) one's work

du·vet (do͞o vā′, dyo͞o-) ***n.*** a comforter, often filled with down

dwarf (dwôrf) ***n., pl.*** **dwarfs** or **dwarves** (dwôrvz) ‖ < OE *dweorg* ‖ **1** any abnormally small person, animal, or plant **2** *Folklore* a little being in human form, with magic powers —***vt.*** **1** to stunt the growth of **2** to make seem small in comparison —***vi.*** to become dwarfed —***adj.*** undersized —**dwarf′ish** ***adj.*** —**dwarf′ism′** ***n.***

dwell (dwel) ***vi.*** **dwelt** or **dwelled, dwell′ing** ‖ < OE *dwellan*, to hinder ‖ to make one's home; reside —**dwell on** (or **upon**) to linger over —**dwell′er** ***n.***

dwell′ing (place) ‖ ME: see prec. ‖ a residence; abode

DWI ***n.*** a citation for driving while intoxicated

dwin·dle (dwin′dəl) ***vi., vt.*** **-dled, -dling** ‖ < OE *dwīnan*, waste away ‖ to keep on becoming or making smaller or less; diminish; shrink

dyb·buk (dib′ək) ***n.*** ‖ Heb *dibbūq* ‖ *Jewish Folklore* the spirit of a dead person, that enters someone living

dye (dī) ***n.*** ‖ < OE *deag* ‖ a substance or solution for coloring fabric, hair, etc.; also, the color produced —***vt.*** **dyed, dye′ing** to color with dye —**dy′er** ***n.***

dyed′-in-the-wool′ ***adj.*** thoroughgoing; unchanging

dye′stuff′ ***n.*** any substance constituting or yielding a dye

dy·ing (dī′iŋ) ***vi. prp. of*** DIE[1] —***adj.*** **1** about to die or end **2** at death —***n.*** death

dy·nam·ic (dī nam′ik) ***adj.*** ‖ < Gr *dynasthai*, be able ‖ **1** of energy or physical force in motion **2** energetic; vigorous —**dy·nam′i·cal·ly** ***adv.***

dy·nam′ics ***n.pl.*** [*with sing. v. for 1*] **1** the science dealing with motions produced by given forces **2** the forces operative in any field

dy·na·mite (dī′nə mīt′) ***n.*** ‖ see DYNAMIC ‖ a powerful explosive made with nitroglycerin —***vt.*** **-mit′ed, -mit′ing** to blow up with dynamite

dy·na·mo (dī′nə mō′) ***n., pl.*** **-mos′** ‖ see DYNAMIC ‖ **1** *early term for* GENERATOR **2** a dynamic person

dy·nas·ty (dī′nəs tē) ***n., pl.*** **-ties** ‖ < Gr *dynasteia*, rule ‖ a succession of rulers who are members of the same family —**dy·nas′·tic** (-nas′tik) ***adj.***

dys- ‖ Gr ‖ *prefix* bad, ill, difficult, etc.

dys·en·ter·y (dis′ən ter′ē) ***n.*** ‖ < Gr *dys-*, bad + *entera*, bowels ‖ an intestinal inflammation characterized by abdominal pain and bloody diarrhea

dys·func·tion (dis fuŋk′shən) ***n.*** abnormal or impaired functioning

dys·lex·i·a (dis lek′sē ə) ***n.*** ‖ < DYS- + L *lexis*, speech ‖ impairment of the ability to read —**dys·lex′ic** or **dys·lec′tic** ***adj., n.***

dys·pep·si·a (dis pep′sē ə, -shə) ***n.*** ‖ < Gr *dys-*, bad + *pepsis*, digestion ‖ indigestion —**dys·pep′tic** ***adj., n.***

dz. dozen(s)

E

e or **E** (ē) ***n., pl.*** **e's, E's** the fifth letter of the English alphabet

E (ē) ***n.*** **1** *Educ.* a grade for below-average work or, sometimes, excellence **2** *Music* the third tone in the scale of C major

e- *prefix* EX-

E *Physics symbol for* energy

E or **E.** **1** east **2** easterly **3** eastern

each (ēch) ***adj., pron.*** ‖ OE *ælc* ‖ every one of two or more considered separately —***adv.*** apiece Abbrev. ea.

ea·ger (ē′gər) ***adj.*** ‖ < L *acer* ‖ keenly desiring; impatient or anxious —**ea′ger·ly** ***adv.*** —**ea′ger·ness** ***n.***

ea·gle (ē′gəl) ***n.*** ‖ < L *aquila* ‖ **1** a large bird of prey, with sharp vision and powerful wings **2** a representation of the eagle, as the U.S. emblem **3** a former U.S. $10 gold coin **4** *Golf* a score of two under par on a hole

ea′gle-eyed′ ***adj.*** having keen vision

ea·glet (ē′glit) ***n.*** a young eagle

ear[1] (ir) ***n.*** ‖ OE *ēare* ‖ **1** the part of the body that perceives sound **2** the visible, external part of the ear **3** one's sense of hearing or hearing ability **4** anything like an ear —**be all ears** to listen attentively —**give** (or **lend**) **ear** to give attention; heed —**play by ear** to play (music) without using notation —**play it by ear** [Colloq.] to improvise

ear[2] (ir) ***n.*** ‖ < OE *ēar* ‖ the grain-bearing spike of a cereal plant, esp. of corn —***vi.*** to sprout ears

ear′ache′ ***n.*** an ache in the ear

ear′drum′ ***n.*** TYMPANIC MEMBRANE

earl (ʉrl) ***n.*** ‖ < OE *eorl*, warrior ‖ a British nobleman ranking above a viscount —**earl′·dom** ***n.***

ear·ly (ʉr′lē) ***adv., adj.*** **-li·er, -li·est** ‖ < OE *ær*, before + *-lice*, -ly ‖ **1** near the beginning **2** before the expected or usual time **3** in the distant past **4** in the near future —**early on** at an early stage —**ear′li·ness** ***n.***

ear′mark′ ***n.*** **1** a brand put on the ear of livestock **2** an identifying mark or feature —***vt.*** **1** to set such a brand or mark on **2** to reserve for a special purpose

ear′muffs′ (-mufs′) ***n.pl.*** coverings worn over the ears in cold weather

earn (ʉrn) ***vt.*** ‖ OE *earnian* ‖ **1** to receive (wages, etc.) for one's work **2** to get as deserved **3** to gain (interest, etc.) as profit —**earn′er** ***n.***

ear·nest[1] (ʉr′nist) ***adj.*** ‖ OE *eornoste* ‖ **1** serious and intense; not joking **2** important —**in earnest** **1** serious **2** in a determined

manner —**ear'nest·ly** *adv.* —**ear'nest·ness** *n.*
ear·nest[2] (ur'nist) *n.* ‖ult. < Heb *eravon*‖ money, etc. given as a pledge in binding a bargain
earn'ings *n.pl.* 1 wages or other recompense 2 profits, interest, etc.
ear'phone' *n.* a receiver for radio, etc., held to, or put into, the ear
ear'ring' *n.* a ring or other small ornament for the lobe of the ear
ear'shot' (-shät') *n.* the distance within which a sound can be heard
ear'split'ting *adj.* so loud as to hurt the ears; deafening
earth (urth) *n.* ‖OE *eorthe*‖ 1 [*often* E-] the planet we live on, the third planet from the sun: see PLANET 2 this world, as distinguished from heaven and hell 3 land, as distinguished from sea or sky 4 soil; ground —**down to earth** 1 practical; realistic 2 sincere; without affectation
earth'en *adj.* made of earth or clay
earth'en·ware' *n.* clay pottery
earth'ling *n.* a person who lives on the earth; human being
earth'ly *adj.* 1 *a*) terrestrial *b*) worldly 2 conceivable
earth'quake' *n.* a trembling of the earth's crust, caused by underground volcanic forces or shifting of rock
earth station a device for sending or receiving signals to or from communications satellites
earth'ward (-wərd) *adv., adj.* toward the earth Also **earth'wards** *adv.*
earth'work' *n.* an embankment or fortification made by piling up earth
earth'worm' *n.* a round, segmented worm that burrows in the soil
earth·y (urth'ē) *adj.* -**i·er**, -**i·est** 1 of or like earth 2 coarse; unrefined
ease (ēz) *n.* ‖< L *adjacens*, lying nearby‖ 1 freedom from pain or trouble; comfort 2 natural manner; poise 3 freedom from difficulty; facility 4 affluence —*vt.* **eased, eas'ing** 1 to free from pain or trouble; comfort 2 to lessen (pain, anxiety, etc.) 3 to facilitate 4 to reduce the strain or pressure of 5 to move by careful shifting, etc. —*vi.* to become less tense, severe, etc.
ea·sel (ē'zəl) *n.* ‖ult. < L *asinus*, ass‖ an upright frame or tripod to hold an artist's canvas, etc.
ease·ment (ēz'mənt) *n.* 1 an easing or being eased 2 *Law* a right that one may have in another's land
eas·i·ly (ē'zə lē) *adv.* 1 with ease 2 without a doubt 3 very likely
east (ēst) *n.* ‖OE‖ 1 the direction in which sunrise occurs; 90° on a compass, opposite west 2 a region in or toward this direction —*adj.* 1 in, of, to, toward, or facing the east 2 from the east —*adv.* in or toward the east —**the East** 1 the eastern part of the U.S. 2 Asia and the nearby islands; Orient
East Berlin *see* BERLIN
East China Sea part of the Pacific Ocean, between China & Japan
Eas·ter (ēs'tər) *n.* ‖< OE *Eastre*, dawn goddess‖ an annual Christian festival in the spring, celebrating the resurrection of Jesus
east'er·ly *adj., adv.* 1 in or toward the east 2 from the east
east'ern *adj.* 1 in, of, or toward the east 2 from the east 3 [E-] of the East
east'ern·er *n.* a native or inhabitant of the east
Eastern Hemisphere that half of the earth which includes Europe, Africa, Asia, and Australia
East Germany German Democratic Republic: see GERMANY
East In·dies (in'dēz') the Malay Archipelago; esp., the islands of Indonesia —**East Indian**
east'ward (-wərd) *adv., adj.* toward the east Also **east'wards** *adv.*
eas·y (ē'zē) *adj.* -**i·er**, -**i·est** ‖see EASE‖ 1 not difficult 2 free from anxiety, pain, etc. 3 comfortable; restful 4 free from constraint; not stiff 5 not strict or severe 6 *a*) unhurried *b*) gradual —*adv.* [Colloq.] easily —**take it easy** [Colloq.] 1 to refrain from anger, haste, etc. 2 to relax; rest —**eas'i·ness** *n.*
easy chair a stuffed armchair
eas'y·go'ing *adj.* dealing with things in a relaxed or lenient way
eat (ēt) *vt.* **ate, eat'en, eat'ing** ‖OE *etan*‖ 1 to chew and swallow (food) 2 to consume or ravage: with *away* or *up* 3 to destroy, as acid does; corrode 4 to make by or as by eating /acid *eats* holes in cloth/ 5 [Slang] to worry or bother —*vi.* to eat food; have a meal —**eat'a·ble** *adj.* —**eat'er** *n.*
eat·er·y (ēt'ər ē) *n., pl.* -**ies** [Colloq.] a restaurant
eats (ēts) *n.pl.* [Colloq.] food
eaves (ēvz) *n.pl., sing.* **eave** ‖< OE *efes*, edge‖ the projecting lower edge or edges of a roof
eaves'drop' (-dräp') *vi.* -**dropped'**, -**drop'ping** ‖prob. < *eavesdropper*, one who stands under eaves to listen‖ to listen secretly to a private conversation —**eaves'drop'per** *n.*
ebb (eb) *n.* ‖OE *ebba*‖ 1 the flow of the tide back toward the sea 2 a lessening; decline —*vi.* 1 to recede, as the tide 2 to lessen; decline
eb·on·y (eb'ə nē) *n., pl.* -**ies** ‖< Gr *ebenos*‖ the hard, heavy, dark wood of certain tropical trees —*adj.* 1 of ebony 2 like ebony; dark or black
e·bul·lient (i bool'yənt, -bul'-) *adj.* ‖< L *e-*, out + *bullire*, to boil‖ 1 bubbling; boiling 2 enthusiastic; exuberant —**e·bul'lience** *n.*
eb·ul·li·tion (eb'ə lish'ən) *n.* ‖see prec.‖ 1 a boiling or bubbling up 2 a sudden outburst, as of emotion
ec·cen·tric (ək sen'trik) *adj.* ‖< Gr *ek-*, out of + *kentron*, center‖ 1 not having the same center, as two circles 2 off-center 3 not exactly circular 4 odd, as in conduct; unconventional —*n.* 1 a disk set off center on a shaft, for converting circular motion into back-and-forth motion 2 an eccentric person —**ec·cen'tri·cal·ly** *adv.* —**ec·cen·tric·i·ty** (ek'sen tris'ə tē), *pl.* -**ties**, *n.*
Ec·cle·si·as·tes (e klē'zē as'tēz') ‖< Gr *ek-*, out + *kalein*, to call‖ a book of the Old Testament
ec·cle'si·as'tic (-tik) *adj.* ‖see prec.‖ ECCLESIASTICAL —*n.* a Christian clergyman

ec·cle'si·as'ti·cal (ti kəl) ***adj.*** of the church or the clergy

ech·e·lon (esh'ə län') ***n.*** ‖< Fr < L *scala*, ladder‖ **1** a steplike formation of ships, troops, or aircraft **2** a subdivision of a military force **3** any of the levels of responsibility in an organization

e·chi·no·derm (ē kī'nō durm') ***n.*** ‖< ModL‖ a marine animal with a hard, spiny skeleton and radial body, as the starfish

ech·o (ek'ō) ***n.***, *pl.* **-oes** ‖< Gr *ēchō*‖ **1** the repetition of a sound by reflection of sound waves from a surface **2** a sound so produced **3** any repetition or imitation of the words, ideas, etc. of another **—*vi.* -oed, -o·ing 1** to reverberate **2** to make an echo **—*vt.*** to repeat (another's words, ideas, etc.)

e·cho·ic (e kō'ik) ***adj.*** imitative in sound, as the word *tinkle*

é·clair (ā kler', i-, ē-) ***n.*** ‖Fr, lit., lightning‖ an oblong, frosted pastry shell filled with custard, etc.

é·clat (ā klä', i-, ē-) ***n.*** ‖Fr < *éclater*, burst (out)‖ **1** brilliant success **2** striking effect **3** acclaim; fame

ec·lec·tic (ek lek'tik) ***adj.*** ‖< Gr *ek-*, out + *legein*, choose‖ selecting or selected from various sources **—*n.*** one who uses eclectic methods **—ec·lec'ti·cal·ly *adv.* —ec·lec'ti·cism' *n.***

e·clipse (i klips') ***n.*** ‖< Gr *ek-*, out + *leipein*, leave‖ **1** the obscuring of the sun when the moon comes between it and the earth (**solar eclipse**), or of the moon when the earth's shadow is cast upon it (**lunar eclipse**) **2** any obscuring of light, or of fame, glory, etc. **—*vt.* e·clipsed', e·clips'ing 1** to cause an eclipse of **2** to surpass

e·clip·tic (i klip'tik) ***n.*** the great circle of the celestial sphere; the sun's apparent annual path, as seen from the orbiting earth

ec·logue (ek'lôg') ***n.*** ‖see ECLECTIC‖ a short pastoral poem

eco- ‖< Gr *oikos*, house‖ *combining form* environment or habitat

ec·o·cide (ek'ō sīd') ***n.*** ‖prec. + -CIDE‖ the destruction of the environment, as by pollutants

e·col·o·gy (ē käl'ə jē) ***n.*** ‖< Gr *oikos*, house + *-logia*, -LOGY‖ the branch of biology that deals with the relations between living organisms and their environment **—ec'o·log'i·cal *adj.* —ec'o·log'i·cal·ly *adv.* —e·col'o·gist *n.***

econ. 1 economic(s) **2** economy

ec·o·nom·ic (ek'ə näm'ik, ē'kə-) ***adj.*** **1** of the management of income, expenditures, etc. **2** of economics **3** of the satisfaction of the material needs of people

ec'o·nom'i·cal *adj.* **1** not wasting money, time, etc.; thrifty **2** of economics **—ec'o·nom'i·cal·ly *adv.***

ec'o·nom'ics *n.pl.* [*with sing. v.*] **1** the science that deals with the production, distribution, and consumption of wealth **2** economic factors

e·con·o·mist (i kän'ə mist, ē-) ***n.*** a specialist in economics

e·con'o·mize' (-mīz') ***vi.* -mized', -miz'ing** to avoid waste or reduce expenses **—*vt.*** to manage or use with thrift **—e·con'o·miz'er *n.***

e·con'o·my (-mē) ***n.***, *pl.* **-mies** ‖< Gr *oikos*, house + *nomos*, law‖ **1** the management of the income, expenditures, etc. of a household, government, etc. **2** careful management of wealth, etc.; thrift **3** an instance of thrift **4** a system of producing and distributing wealth

ec·o·sys·tem (ek'ō sis'təm, ē'kō-) ***n.*** ‖< Gr *oikos*, house + SYSTEM‖ a community of animals and plants, together with its environment

ec·sta·sy (ek'stə sē) ***n.***, *pl.* **-sies** ‖< Gr *ek*, out + *histanai*, to set‖ a state or feeling of overpowering joy; rapture **—ec·stat·ic** (ek stat'ik) ***adj.* —ec·stat'i·cal·ly *adv.***

-ec·to·my (ek'tə mē) ‖< Gr *ek-*, out + *temnein*, to cut‖ *combining form* a surgical excision of

Ec·ua·dor (ek'wə dôr') country on the NW coast of South America: 109,483 sq. mi.; pop. 9,647,000 **—Ec'ua·do're·an, Ec'ua·do'ri·an,** or **Ec'ua·dor'an *adj.*, *n.***

ec·u·men·i·cal (ek'yōō men'i kəl) ***adj.*** ‖< Gr *oikoumenē* (*gē*), the inhabited (world)‖ **1** general, or universal; esp., of the Christian church as a whole **2** furthering religious unity, esp. among Christian churches **—ec'u·men'i·cal·ly *adv.***

ec·u·men·ism (ek'yōō mə niz'əm, e kyōō'-) ***n.*** the ecumenical movement, esp. among Christian churches Also **ec'u·men'i·cism' —ec'u·men·ist *n.***

ec·ze·ma (ek'zə mə, eg'zə-; ig zē'-) ***n.*** ‖< Gr *ek-*, out + *zein*, to boil‖ a skin disorder characterized by inflammation, itching, and scaliness

-ed ‖OE‖ *suffix* **1** forming the past tense or past participle of certain verbs **2** forming adjectives from nouns or verbs [*cultured, bearded*]

ed. 1 edited (by) **2** *a*) edition *b*) editor **3** education

E·dam (cheese) (ē'dəm) ‖after *Edam*, Netherlands‖ a mild, yellow cheese

ed·dy (ed'ē) ***n.***, *pl.* **-dies** ‖prob. < ON *itha*‖ a little whirlpool or whirlwind **—*vi.* -died, -dy·ing** to whirl

e·del·weiss (ā'dəl vīs') ***n.*** ‖Ger < *edel*, noble + *weiss*, white‖ a small, flowering plant, esp. of the Alps, with white and woolly leaves

e·de·ma (ē dē'mə) ***n.***, *pl.* **-mas** or **-ma·ta** (-mə tə) ‖< Gr *oidēma*, swelling‖ an abnormal accumulation of fluid in body tissues or cavities

E·den (ēd''n) *Bible* the garden where Adam and Eve first lived; Paradise **—*n.*** any delightful place **—E·den·ic** (ē den'ik) ***adj.***

edge (ej) ***n.*** ‖OE *ecg*‖ **1** the sharp, cutting part of a blade **2** sharpness; keenness **3** the projecting ledge of a cliff, etc.; brink **4** the part farthest from the middle; border; margin **5** [Colloq.] advantage [*he has the edge on me*] **—*vt.*, *vi.* edged, edg'ing 1** to form an edge (on) **2** to make (one's way) sideways **3** to move gradually **—on edge 1** very tense; irritable **2** impatient **—edg'er *n.***

edge'ways' (-wāz') ***adv.*** with the edge foremost Also **edge'wise'** (-wīz')

edg'ing *n.* trimming along an edge

edg·y (ej'ē) ***adj.*** **-i·er, -i·est** irritable; on edge —**edg'i·ness** ***n.***

ed·i·ble (ed'ə bəl) ***adj.*** ‖ < L *edere*, eat ‖ fit to be eaten —***n.*** food: *usually used in pl.* —**ed'i·bil'i·ty** (-bil'ə tē) ***n.***

e·dict (ē'dikt') ***n.*** ‖ < L *e-*, out + *dicere*, speak ‖ a public order; decree

ed·i·fice (ed'i fis) ***n.*** ‖ see fol. ‖ a building, esp. a large, imposing one

ed·i·fy (ed'i fī') ***vt.*** **-fied', -fy'ing** ‖ < L *aedificare*, build ‖ to instruct so as to improve or uplift morally —**ed'i·fi·ca'tion** ***n.*** —**ed'i·fi'er** ***n.***

Ed·in·burgh (ed''n bur'ə, -ō) capital of Scotland: pop. 419,000

Ed·i·son (ed'i sən), **Thom·as (Alva)** (täm'əs) 1847-1931; U.S. inventor

ed·it (ed'it) ***vt.*** ‖ < EDITOR ‖ **1** to prepare (a manuscript) for publication by arranging, revising, etc. **2** to control the policy and publication of (a newspaper, etc.) **3** to prepare (a film, tape, etc.) for presentation by cutting, dubbing, etc. **4** to make changes in (a computer file)

edit. 1 edited (by) **2** edition **3** editor

e·di·tion (ē dish'ən, i-) ***n.*** ‖ see fol. ‖ **1** the size or form in which a book is published **2** the total number of copies of a book, etc. published at one time **3** any particular issue of a newspaper

ed·i·tor (ed'it ər) ***n.*** ‖ L < *e-*, out + *dare*, give ‖ **1** one that edits **2** a department head of a newspaper, etc.

ed·i·to·ri·al (ed'i tôr'ē əl) ***adj.*** of or by an editor —***n.*** a statement of opinion in a newspaper, etc., as by an editor, publisher, or owner —**ed'i·to'ri·al·ly** ***adv.***

ed'i·to'ri·al·ize' (-īz') ***vt., vi.*** **-ized', -iz'ing** to express editorial opinions about (something)

editor in chief *pl.* **editors in chief** the editor who heads the editorial staff of a publication

Ed·mon·ton (ed'mən tən) capital of Alberta, Canada: pop. 573,000

educ. 1 education **2** educational

ed·u·ca·ble (ej'o͞o kə bəl, ej'ə-) ***adj.*** that can be educated or trained —**ed'u·ca·bil'i·ty** ***n.***

ed·u·cate (ej'o͞o kāt', ej'ə-) ***vt.*** **-cat'ed, -cat'ing** ‖ < L *e-*, out + *ducere*, to lead ‖ **1** to develop the knowledge, skill, or character of, esp. by formal schooling; teach **2** to pay for the schooling of —**ed'u·ca'tor** ***n.***

ed'u·ca'tion ***n.*** **1** the process of educating; teaching **2** knowledge, etc. thus developed **3** formal schooling —**ed'u·ca'tion·al** ***adj.***

e·duce (ē do͞os') ***vt.*** **e·duced', e·duc'ing** ‖ see EDUCATE ‖ **1** to draw out; elicit **2** to deduce

-ee (ē) ‖ < Anglo-Fr pp. ending ‖ *suffix* **1** the recipient of an action *[appointee]* **2** one in a (specified) condition *[absentee]*

EEG electroencephalogram

eel (ēl) ***n.*** ‖ OE *æl* ‖ a long, slippery, snakelike fish

EEOC Equal Employment Opportunity Commission

e'er (er, ar) ***adv.*** *old poet. contr. of* EVER

-eer (ir) ‖ < L *-arius* ‖ *suffix* **1** *a)* one having to do with *[auctioneer]* *b)* one who writes, makes, etc. *[profiteer]* **2** to have to do with *[electioneer]*

ee·rie or **ee·ry** (ir'ē) ***adj.*** **-ri·er, -ri·est** ‖ < OE *earg*, timid ‖ mysterious, uncanny, or weird —**ee'ri·ly** ***adv.*** —**ee'ri·ness** ***n.***

ef- *prefix* EX- Used before *f*

ef·face (ə fās', i-) ***vt.*** **-faced', -fac'ing** ‖ < L *ex-*, out + *facies*, face ‖ **1** to rub out; erase **2** to make (oneself) inconspicuous —**ef·face'ment** ***n.***

ef·fect (e fekt', i-) ***n.*** ‖ < L *ex-*, out + *facere*, do ‖ **1** anything brought about by a cause; result **2** the power to cause results **3** influence **4** meaning *[spoke to this effect]* **5** an impression made on the mind, or its cause **6** a being operative or in force **7** *[pl.]* belongings; property —***vt.*** to bring about; accomplish —**in effect 1** actually **2** virtually **3** in operation —**take effect** to become operative

ef·fec'tive ***adj.*** **1** producing a desired effect; efficient **2** in effect; operative **3** impressive —**ef·fec'tive·ly** ***adv.*** —**ef·fec'tive·ness** ***n.***

ef·fec·tu·al (e fek'cho͞o əl, i-) ***adj.*** **1** producing, or able to produce, the desired effect **2** having legal force; valid —**ef·fec'tu·al·ly** ***adv.***

ef·fec'tu·ate' (-āt') ***vt.*** **-at'ed, -at'ing** to bring about; effect

ef·fem·i·nate (e fem'ə nit, i-) ***adj.*** ‖ < L *ex-*, out + *femina*, woman ‖ having qualities attributed to women, as weakness, delicacy, etc.; unmanly —**ef·fem'i·na·cy** ***n.***

ef·fer·ent (ef'ər ənt) ***adj.*** ‖ < L *ex-*, out + *ferre*, to bear ‖ carrying away from a central part, as nerves

ef·fer·vesce (ef'ər ves') ***vi.*** **-vesced', -vesc'ing** ‖ < L *ex-*, out + *fervere*, to boil ‖ **1** to give off gas bubbles; bubble **2** to be lively —**ef'fer·ves'cence** ***n.*** —**ef'fer·ves'cent** ***adj.***

ef·fete (e fēt', i-) ***adj.*** ‖ < L *ex-*, out + *fetus*, productive ‖ **1** no longer able to produce; sterile **2** decadent, soft, too refined, etc. —**ef·fete'ly** ***adv.*** —**ef·fete'ness** ***n.***

ef·fi·ca·cious (ef'i kā'shəs) ***adj.*** ‖ see EFFECT ‖ that produces the desired effect —**ef'fi·ca'cious·ly** ***adv.*** —**ef'fi·ca·cy** (-kə sē) ***n.***

ef·fi·cient (e fish'ənt, i-) ***adj.*** ‖ see EFFECT ‖ producing the desired result with a minimum of effort, expense, or waste —**ef·fi'cien·cy** ***n.*** —**ef·fi'cient·ly** ***adv.***

ef·fi·gy (ef'i jē) ***n.***, *pl.* **-gies** ‖ < L *ex-*, out + *fingere*, to form ‖ a statue or other image; often, a crude representation (for hanging or burning) of a despised person

ef·flu·ent (ef'lo͞o ənt) ***adj.*** ‖ < L *effluere*, flow out ‖ flowing out —***n.*** the outflow of a sewer, septic tank, etc. —**ef'flu·ence** ***n.***

ef·flu·vi·um (e flo͞o'vē əm) ***n.***, *pl.* **-vi·a** (-ə) or **-vi·ums** ‖ see prec. ‖ a disagreeable vapor or odor

ef·fort (ef'ərt) ***n.*** ‖ < L *ex-*, intens. + *fortis*, strong ‖ **1** the use of energy to do something **2** a try; attempt **3** a result of working or trying —**ef'fort·less** ***adj.*** —**ef'fort·less·ly** ***adv.***

ef·fron·ter·y (e frunt'ər ē, i-) ***n.*** ‖ < L *ex-*, from + *frons*, forehead ‖ impudence; audacity

ef·ful·gence (e ful'jəns, i-) ***n.*** ‖ < L *ex-*, forth

+ *fulgere*, shine ‖ radiance; brilliance —**ef·ful'gent** *adj.*

ef·fuse (e fyo͞oz', i-) *vt., vi.* **-fused', -fus'ing** ‖ < L *ex-*, out + *fundere*, pour ‖ **1** to pour out or forth **2** to spread out; diffuse

ef·fu'sion (-fyo͞o'zhən) *n.* **1** a pouring forth **2** unrestrained expression in speaking or writing —**ef·fu'sive** *adj.* —**ef·fu'sive·ly** *adv.* —**ef·fu'sive·ness** *n.*

e.g. ‖ L *exempli gratia* ‖ for example

e·gad (ē gad') *interj.* ‖ prob. < *oh God* ‖ [Archaic] a softened oath

e·gal·i·tar·i·an (ē gal'ə ter'ē ən) *adj.* ‖ < Fr *égalité*, equality ‖ advocating full political and social equality for all people —*n.* one advocating this

egg[1] (eg) *n.* ‖ ON ‖ **1** the oval body laid by a female bird, fish, etc., containing the germ of a new individual **2** a female reproductive cell; ovum **3** a hen's egg, raw or cooked

egg[2] (eg) *vt.* ‖ < ON *eggja*, give edge to ‖ to urge or incite: with *on*

egg'beat'er *n.* a kitchen utensil for beating eggs, cream, etc.

egg foo yong (or **young**) (eg' fo͞o yuŋ') a Chinese-American dish of eggs beaten and cooked with bean sprouts, onions, minced pork or shrimp, etc.

egg'head' *n.* [Slang] an intellectual

egg'nog' *n.* ‖ EGG[1] + *nog*, strong ale ‖ a drink made of beaten eggs, milk, sugar, and, often, whiskey or rum

egg'plant' *n.* **1** a plant with a large, ovoid, purple-skinned fruit eaten as a vegetable **2** the fruit

egg roll a Chinese-American dish, a roll of egg dough wrapped around minced vegetables, meat, etc. and deep-fried

e·gis (ē'jis) *n. alt. sp. of* AEGIS

eg·lan·tine (eg'lən tīn', -tēn') *n.* ‖ < L *aculeus*, a sting ‖ a European rose with sweet-scented leaves and pink flowers

e·go (ē'gō) *n., pl.* **-gos** ‖ L, I ‖ **1** the self; the individual as self-aware **2** egotism **3** *Psychoanalysis* that part of the psyche which governs action rationally

e'go·cen'tric (-sen'trik) *adj.* viewing everything in relation to oneself —**e'go·cen'tri·cal·ly** *adv.*

e'go·ism' *n.* **1** selfishness; self-interest **2** egotism; conceit —**e'go·ist** *n.* —**e'go·is'tic** or **e'go·is'ti·cal** *adj.*

e·go·tism (ē'gō tiz'əm, ē'gə-) *n.* **1** excessive reference to oneself in speaking or writing **2** self-conceit —**e'go·tist** *n.* —**e'go·tis'tic** or **e'go·tis'ti·cal** *adj.*

ego trip [Slang] an experience that gratifies or indulges the ego

e·gre·gious (ē grē'jəs, i-) *adj.* ‖ < L *e-*, out + *grex*, a herd ‖ remarkably bad; flagrant —**e·gre'gious·ly** *adv.*

e·gress (ē'gres') *n.* ‖ < L *e-*, out + *gradi*, go ‖ a way out; exit

e·gret (ē'gret', -grit) *n.* ‖ < OFr *aigrette* ‖ **1** a kind of heron with long, white plumes **2** AIGRETTE

E·gypt (ē'jipt) country in NE Africa, on the Mediterranean: 386,650 sq. mi.; pop. 50,525,000

E·gyp·tian (ē jip'shən, i-) *n.* **1** the language of the ancient Egyptians **2** a native or inhabitant of Egypt —*adj.* of Egypt, its people, etc.

eh (ā, e) *interj.* **1** an exclamation of surprise **2** an expression of doubt or inquiry

ei·der (ī'dər) *n.* ‖ ult. < ON *æthr* ‖ **1** a large sea duck of northern regions **2** EIDERDOWN

ei'der·down' *n.* the soft, fine down of the eider duck, used as a stuffing for quilts, pillows, etc.

eight (āt) *adj., n.* ‖ < OE *eahta* ‖ one more than seven; 8; VIII —**eighth** (ātth) *adj., n.*

eight ball a black ball with the number eight on it, used in playing pool —**behind the eight ball** [Slang] in a very unfavorable position

eight·een (ā'tēn') *adj., n.* eight more than ten; 18; XVIII —**eight'eenth'** (-tēnth') *adj., n.*

eight·y (āt'ē) *adj., n., pl.* **-ies** eight times ten; 80; LXXX —**the eighties** the numbers or years, as of a century, from 80 through 89 —**eight'i·eth** *adj., n.*

Ein·stein (īn'stīn'), **Al·bert** (al'bərt) 1879-1955; U.S. physicist, born in Germany: formulated theory of relativity

Eir·e (er'ə) *Gael. name of* IRELAND

Ei·sen·how·er (ī'zen hou'ər), **Dwight David** (dwīt) 1890-1969; U.S. general & 34th president of the U.S. (1953-61)

ei·ther (ē'thər, ī'-) *adj.* ‖ OE *æghwæther* ‖ **1** one or the other (of two) **2** each (of two) —*pron.* one or the other —*conj.* a correlative used with *or* to imply a choice of alternatives [*either* go *or* stay] —*adv.* any more than the other; also [if you don't go, I won't *either*]

e·jac·u·late (ē jak'yo͞o lāt', i-) *vt., vi.* **-lat'ed, -lat'ing** ‖ see fol. ‖ **1** to eject (esp. semen) **2** to utter suddenly; exclaim —**e·jac'u·la'tion** *n.*

e·ject (ē jekt', i-) *vt.* ‖ < L *e-*, out + *jacere*, to throw ‖ to throw or force out; expel; discharge —**e·jec'tion** *n.*

eke (ēk) *vt.* **eked, ek'ing** ‖ < OE *eacan*, to increase ‖ to manage to make (a living) with difficulty: with *out*

EKG electrocardiogram

e·lab·o·rate (ē lab'ə rit, i-; *for v.*, -ə rāt') *adj.* ‖ < L *e-*, out + *labor*, work ‖ developed in great detail; complicated —*vt.* **-rat'ed, -rat'ing** to work out in great detail —*vi.* to add more details: usually with *on* or *upon* —**e·lab'o·rate'ly** *adv.* —**e·lab'o·rate'ness** *n.* —**e·lab'o·ra'tion** *n.*

é·lan (ā län') *n.* ‖ Fr < *élancer*, to dart ‖ spirited self-assurance; dash

e·lapse (ē laps', i-) *vi.* **e·lapsed', e·laps'ing** ‖ < L *e-*, out + *labi*, to glide ‖ to slip by; pass: said of time

e·las·tic (ē las'tik, i-) *adj.* ‖ < Gr *elaunein*, set in motion ‖ **1** able to spring back to its original size, shape, etc. after being stretched, squeezed, etc.; flexible **2** able to recover easily, as from dejection; buoyant **3** adaptable —*n.* an elastic band or fabric —**e'las·tic'i·ty** (-tis'ə tē) *n.*

e·las'ti·cize' (-tə sīz') *vt.* **-cized', -ciz'ing** to make (fabric) elastic

e·late (ē lāt', i-) *vt.* **-lat'ed, -lat'ing** ‖ < L *ex-*, out + *ferre*, to bear ‖ to raise the spirits of; make very proud, happy, etc. —**e·la'tion** *n.*

el·bow (el'bō') *n.* ‖ see ELL[2] & BOW[2] ‖ **1** the joint between the upper and lower arm;

esp., the outer angle made by a bent arm 2 anything bent like an elbow —*vt.*, *vi.* to shove as with the elbows
elbow grease [Colloq.] vigorous physical effort
el'bow·room' *n.* ample space or room
eld·er[1] (el'dər) *adj.* ‖ < OE *eald*, old ‖ 1 older 2 of superior rank, position, etc. 3 earlier; former —*n.* 1 an older or aged person 2 an older person with some authority, as in a tribe 3 any of certain church officers
el·der[2] (el'dər) *n.* ‖ OE *ellern* ‖ a shrub or tree of the honeysuckle family, with red or purple berries
el'der·ber'ry (-ber'ē) *n., pl.* **-ries** 1 ELDER[2] 2 its berry, used for making wines, jelly, etc.
eld'er·ly *adj.* 1 somewhat old 2 in old age; aged
eld·est (el'dist) *adj.* oldest; esp., firstborn
El Do·ra·do or **El·do·ra·do** (el'də rä'dō) *n., pl.* **-dos** ‖ Sp, the gilded ‖ any place supposed to be rich in gold, opportunity, etc.
e·lect (ē lekt', i-) *adj.* ‖ < L *e-*, out + *legere*, choose ‖ 1 chosen 2 elected but not yet installed in office [mayor-*elect*] —*vt.*, *vi.* 1 to select for an office by voting 2 to choose; select —**e·lect'a·ble** *adj.* —**e·lect'a·bil'i·ty** *n.*
e·lec·tion (ē lek'shən, i-) *n.* 1 a choosing or choice 2 a choosing or being chosen by vote
e·lec'tion·eer' (-shə nir') *vi.* to canvass votes in an election
e·lec'tive (-tiv) *adj.* 1 *a)* filled by election [an *elective* office] *b)* chosen by election 2 having the power to choose 3 optional —*n.* an optional course or subject in a school curriculum
e·lec'tor (-tər) *n.* 1 one who elects; specif., a qualified voter 2 a member of the electoral college —**e·lec'tor·al** *adj.*
electoral college an assembly elected by the voters to perform the formal duty of electing the president and vice president of the U.S.
e·lec'tor·ate (-it) *n.* all those qualified to vote in an election
E·lec·tra (ē lek'trə, i-) *Gr. Myth.* a daughter of Agamemnon: she plots the death of her mother
e·lec·tric (ē lek'trik, i-) *adj.* ‖ < Gr *ēlektron*, amber: from the effect of friction upon amber ‖ 1 of or charged with electricity 2 producing, or produced by, electricity 3 operated by electricity 4 using electronic amplification [*electric* guitar] 5 very tense or exciting Also **e·lec'tri·cal** —**e·lec'tri·cal·ly** *adv.*
electric chair a chair used in electrocuting those sentenced to death
e·lec·tri·cian (ē'lek trish'ən, ē lek'-) *n.* one whose work is the construction and repair of electric apparatus
e'lec·tric'i·ty (-tris'i tē) *n.* 1 a property of certain fundamental particles of all matter, as electrons (negative charges) and protons or positrons (positive charges): electrical charge is generated by friction, induction, or chemical change 2 an electric current 3 electric current as a public utility for lighting, heating, etc.
e·lec·tri·fy (ē lek'trə fī', i-) *vt.* **-fied'**, **-fy'ing** 1 to charge with electricity 2 to excite; thrill 3 to equip for the use of electricity —**e·lec'tri·fi·ca'tion** *n.* —**e·lec'tri·fi'er** *n.*
electro- *combining form* electric, electricity
e·lec·tro·car·di·o·gram (ē lek'trō kär'dē ə gram', i-) *n.* a tracing showing the variations in electric force which trigger heart contractions
e·lec'tro·car'di·o·graph' (-graf') *n.* an instrument for making electrocardiograms
e·lec'tro·cute' (-trə kyo͞ot') *vt.* **-cut'ed**, **-cut'ing** ‖ ELECTRO- + (EXE)CUTE ‖ to kill or execute with electricity —**e·lec'tro·cu'tion** *n.*
e·lec'trode' (-trōd') *n.* ‖ ELECTR(O)- + -ODE ‖ any terminal by which electricity enters or leaves a battery, etc.
e·lec'tro·en·ceph'a·lo·gram' (-trō en sef'ə lō gram') *n.* ‖ see ENCEPHALITIS & -GRAM ‖ a tracing of the variations in electric force in the brain
e·lec'tro·en·ceph'a·lo·graph' (-graf') *n.* an instrument for making electroencephalograms
e·lec·trol·o·gist (ē'lek träl'ə jist, i-) *n.* a practitioner of ELECTROLYSIS (sense 2)
e'lec·trol'y·sis (-i sis) *n.* ‖ ELECTRO- + -LYSIS ‖ 1 the decomposition of an electrolyte by the action of an electric current passing through it 2 the eradication of unwanted hair with an electrified needle
e·lec·tro·lyte (ē lek'trō līt', i-) *n.* ‖ ELECTRO- + -LYTE ‖ any substance which in solution is capable of conducting an electric current by the movement of its dissociated ions —**e·lec'tro·lyt'ic** (-lit'ik) *adj.*
e·lec'tro·mag'net (-mag'nit) *n.* a soft iron core that becomes a magnet when an electric current flows through a surrounding coil —**e·lec'tro·mag·net'ic** (-net'ik) *adj.*
electromagnetic wave a wave generated by an oscillating electric charge
e·lec'tro·mo'tive (-mōt'iv) *adj.* producing an electric current through differences in potential
e·lec·tron (ē lek'trän', i-) *n.* ‖ see ELECTRIC ‖ a stable, negatively charged elementary particle that forms a part of all atoms
e·lec·tron·ic (ē'lek trän'ik, i-) *adj.* 1 of electrons 2 operating, produced, or done by the action of electrons —**e·lec'tron'i·cal·ly** *adv.*
electronic music music in which the sounds are originated or altered by electronic devices
e'lec·tron'ics *n.pl.* [*with sing. v.*] the science dealing with the action of electrons, and with the use of electron tubes, transistors, etc.
electron microscope a device that focuses a beam of electrons on a fluorescent screen, etc. to form a greatly enlarged image of an object
electron tube a sealed glass or metal tube with gas or a vacuum inside, used to control the flow of electrons
e·lec·tro·plate (ē lek'trō plāt', i-) *vt.* **-plat'ed**, **-plat'ing** to deposit a coating of metal on by electrolysis
e·lec'tro·scope' (-skōp') *n.* a device for detecting very small charges of electricity or radiation —**e·lec'tro·scop'ic** (-skäp'ik) *adj.*

e·lec'tro·shock' therapy (-shäk') shock therapy using electricity
e·lec'tro·type' (-tīp') ***n.*** *Printing* a plate made by electroplating a wax or plastic impression of the surface to be reproduced
el·ee·mos·y·nar·y (el'i mäs'ə ner'ē, el'ē ə-) ***adj.*** ‖ < Gr *eleēmosynē*, pity ‖ of, for, or supported by charity
el·e·gant (el'ə gənt) ***adj.*** ‖ < L *e-*, out + *legere*, choose ‖ **1** having dignified richness and grace, as of manner, design, dress, etc.; tastefully luxurious **2** cleverly apt and simple /an *elegant* solution/ **3** [Colloq.] excellent —**el'e·gance** ***n.*** —**el'e·gant·ly** ***adv.***
el·e·gi·ac (el ē'jē ak', el'ə jī'ak') ***adj.*** **1** of, like, or fit for an elegy **2** sad; mournful
el·e·gy (el'ə jē) ***n.***, *pl.* **-gies** ‖ < Gr *elegos*, a lament ‖ a mournful poem, esp. of lament and praise for the dead
el·e·ment (el'ə mənt) ***n.*** ‖ < L *elementum* ‖ **1** the natural or suitable environment for a person or thing **2** a component part or quality, often one that is basic or essential **3** *Chem.* any substance that cannot be separated into different substances except by radioactive decay or by nuclear reactions: all matter is composed of such substances —**the elements 1** the first principles; rudiments **2** wind, rain, etc.; forces of the atmosphere
el·e·men·tal (el'ə ment''l) ***adj.*** **1** of or like basic, natural forces; primal **2** ELEMENTARY (sense 2*a*) **3** being an essential part or parts
el'e·men'ta·ry (-ə rē) ***adj.*** **1** ELEMENTAL **2** *a*) of first principles or fundamentals; basic; simple *b*) of the formal instruction of children in basic subjects
elementary particle a subatomic particle, as a neutron, electron, etc.
elementary school a school of the first six (sometimes eight) grades, where basic subjects are taught

AFRICAN ELEPHANT

INDIAN ELEPHANT

el·e·phant (el'ə fənt) ***n.*** ‖ < Gr *elephas* ‖ a huge, thick-skinned mammal with a long, flexible snout, or trunk, and, usually, two ivory tusks
el·e·phan·ti·a·sis (el'ə fən tī'ə sis) ***n.*** a chronic disease causing the enlargement of certain body parts and hardening of the surrounding skin
el·e·phan·tine (el'ə fan'tin, -tīn') ***adj.*** like an elephant; huge, clumsy, etc.
el·e·vate (el'ə vāt') ***vt.*** **-vat'ed, -vat'ing** ‖ < L *e-*, out + *levare*, to lift ‖ **1** to lift up; raise **2** to raise in rank **3** to raise to a higher intellectual or moral level **4** to elate; exhilarate
el'e·va'tion ***n.*** **1** an elevating or being elevated **2** a high place or position **3** height above the surface of the earth or above sea level
el'e·va'tor ***n.*** **1** one that elevates, or lifts up **2** a suspended cage for hoisting or lowering people or things **3** a warehouse for storing and discharging grain: in full **grain elevator**
e·lev·en (ē lev'ən, i-) ***adj.***, ***n.*** ‖ OE *endleofan* ‖ one more than ten; 11; XI —**e·lev'·enth** (-ənth) ***adj.***, ***n.***
elf (elf) ***n.***, *pl.* **elves** (elvz) ‖ OE *ælf* ‖ *Folklore* a tiny, often mischievous fairy —**elf'in** or **elf'ish** ***adj.***
El Gre·co (el grek'ō) *c.* 1541-*c.* 1614; painter in Italy & Spain, born in Crete
e·lic·it (ē lis'it, i-) ***vt.*** ‖ < L *e-*, out + *lacere*, entice ‖ to draw forth; evoke (a response, etc.) —**e·lic'i·ta'tion** ***n.***
e·lide (ē līd', i-) ***vt.*** **e·lid'ed, e·lid'ing** ‖ < L *e-*, out + *laedere*, to hurt ‖ to leave out; esp., to slur over (a vowel, etc.) in pronunciation —**e·li'sion** (-lizh'ən) ***n.***
el·i·gi·ble (el'i jə bəl) ***adj.*** ‖ see ELECT ‖ fit to be chosen; qualified —**el'i·gi·bil'i·ty** ***n.***
E·li·jah (ē lī'jə, i-) *Bible* a prophet of Israel in the 9th c. B.C.
e·lim·i·nate (ē lim'ə nāt', i-) ***vt.*** **-nat'ed, -nat'ing** ‖ < L *e-*, out + *limen*, threshold ‖ **1** to remove; get rid of **2** to leave out of consideration; omit **3** to excrete —**e·lim'i·na'tion** ***n.***
El·i·ot (el'ē ət) **1 George** (pseud. of *Mary Ann Evans*) 1819-80; Eng. novelist **2 T**(homas) **S**(tearns) 1885-1965; Brit. poet, born in the U.S.
e·lite (ā lēt', i-) ***n.*** ‖ Fr < L: see ELECT ‖ [*also with pl. v.*] the group or part of a group regarded as the best, most powerful, etc.
e·lit'ism' (-iz'əm) ***n.*** government or control by an elite —**e·lit'ist** ***adj.***, ***n.***
e·lix·ir (ē liks'ir, i-) ***n.*** ‖ < Ar *al-iksīr* ‖ **1** a hypothetical substance sought by medieval alchemists to change base metals into gold or (in full **elixir of life**) to prolong life indefinitely **2** *Pharmacy* a sweetened solution used for medicine, etc.
E·liz·a·beth (ə liz'ə bəth, i-) name of two queens: **Elizabeth I** 1533-1603; queen of England (1558-1603) & **Elizabeth II** 1926- ; queen of Great Britain & Northern Ireland (1952-)
Elizabeth city in NE Ill.: pop. 106,000
E·liz·a·be·than (ē liz'ə bē'thən, -beth'ən) ***adj.*** of or characteristic of the time of Elizabeth I's reign —***n.*** an English person, esp. a writer, of that time
elk (elk) ***n.*** ‖ < OE *eolh* ‖ **1** MOOSE: the common term in Europe **2** WAPITI
ell[1] (el) ***n.*** **1** an extension or wing at right angles to the main structure **2** an L-shaped pipe, etc.
ell[2] (el) ***n.*** ‖ < OE *eln* ‖ a former English unit of measure, equal to 45 inches
el·lipse (e lips', i-) ***n.***, *pl.* **-lip'ses'** (-sēz') ‖ < Gr *elleipein*, fall short ‖ *Geom.* a closed curve in the form of a symmetrical oval
el·lip'sis (-lip'sis) ***n.***, *pl.* **-ses'** (-sēz') ‖ see prec. ‖ **1** *Gram.* the omission of a word or words understood in the context (Ex.: "if (it is) possible") **2** a mark (. . .) indicating an omission of words: in full **ellipsis points**
el·lip'ti·cal (-ti kəl) ***adj.*** **1** of, or having the form of, an ellipse **2** of or characterized by

ellipsis Also **el·lip'tic** —**el·lip'ti·cal·ly** *adv.*

elm (elm) *n.* ⟦OE⟧ 1 a tall, hardy, deciduous shade tree 2 its hard, heavy wood

El Ni·ño (el nēn'yō) a warm inshore current annually flowing south along the coast of Ecuador

el·o·cu·tion (el'ə kyōō'shən) *n.* ⟦see ELOQUENT⟧ the art of public speaking —**el'o·cu'tion·ist** *n.*

e·lo·de·a (ē lō'də ə, el'ə dē'ə) *n.* ⟦< Gr *helōdēs*, swampy⟧ a submerged water plant with whorls of short, grasslike leaves

e·lon·gate (ē lôŋ'gāt', i-) *vt., vi.* **-gat'ed, -gat'ing** ⟦< L *e-*, out + *longus*, long⟧ to make or become longer; stretch —**e'lon·ga'tion** *n.*

e·lope (ē lōp', i-) *vi.* **e·loped', e·lop'ing** ⟦prob. < OE *a-*, away + *hleapan*, to run⟧ to run away secretly, esp. in order to get married —**e·lope'ment** *n.*

el·o·quent (el'ə kwənt) *adj.* ⟦< L *e-*, out + *loqui*, speak⟧ vivid, forceful, fluent, etc. in speech or writing —**el'o·quence** *n.* —**el'o·quent·ly** *adv.*

El Pas·o (el pas'ō) city in westernmost Tex.: pop. 425,000

El Sal·va·dor (el sal'və dôr') country in Central America, on the Pacific: 8,260 sq. mi.; pop. 5,105,000

else (els) *adj.* ⟦OE *elles*⟧ 1 different; other /somebody *else*/ 2 in addition /is there anything *else*?/ —*adv.* 1 differently; otherwise /where *else* can I go?/ 2 if not /study, (or) *else* you will fail/

else'where' (-hwer', -wer') *adv.* in or to some other place; somewhere else

e·lu·ci·date (ə lōō'sə dāt') *vt., vi.* **-dat'ed, -dat'ing** ⟦< L *e-*, out + *lucidus*, clear⟧ to make (something) clear; explain —**e·lu'ci·da'tion** *n.*

e·lude (ē lōōd', i-) *vt.* **e·lud'ed, e·lud'ing** ⟦< L *e-*, out + *ludere*, to play⟧ 1 to avoid or escape from by quickness, cunning, etc.; evade 2 to escape the mental grasp of /his name *eludes* me/

e·lu'sive (-lōō'siv) *adj.* tending to elude; evasive —**e·lu'sive·ness** *n.*

elves (elvz) *n. pl. of* ELF

E·ly·si·um (ē lizh'əm, -liz'ē əm; i-) *Gr. Myth.* the dwelling place of virtuous people after death —*n.* any state of ideal bliss; paradise —**E·ly'si·an** (-lizh'ən, -liz'ē ən) *adj.*

em (em) *n.* ⟦< the letter *M*⟧ *Printing* a unit of measure, as of column width

'em (əm) *pron.* [Colloq.] them

em- *prefix* EN-: Used before *b*, *m*, or *p*

e·ma·ci·ate (ē mā'shē āt', -sē-; i-) *vt.* **-at'ed, -at'ing** ⟦< L *e-*, out + *macies*, leanness⟧ to cause to become abnormally lean —**e·ma'ci·a'tion** *n.*

em·a·nate (em'ə nāt') *vi.* **-nat'ed, -nat'ing** ⟦< L *e-*, out + *manare*, to flow⟧ to come forth; issue, as from a source —**em'a·na'tion** *n.*

e·man·ci·pate (ē man'sə pāt', i-) *vt.* **-pat'ed, -pat'ing** ⟦< L *e-*, out + *manus*, the hand + *capere*, to take⟧ 1 to set free (a slave, etc.) 2 to free from restraint —**e·man'ci·pa'tion** *n.* —**e·man'ci·pa'tor** *n.*

e·mas·cu·late (ē mas'kyōō lāt') *vt.* **-lat'ed, -lat'ing** ⟦< L *e-*, out + *masculus*, male⟧ 1 to castrate 2 to weaken —**e·mas'cu·la'tion** *n.*

em·balm (em bäm') *vt.* ⟦see EN- & BALM⟧ to preserve (a dead body) with various chemicals —**em·balm'er** *n.*

em·bank (em baŋk', im-) *vt.* to protect, support, or enclose with a bank of earth, etc. —**em·bank'ment** *n.*

em·bar·go (em bär'gō, im-) *n., pl.* **-goes** ⟦Sp < L *in-*, in + ML *barra*, a bar⟧ 1 a government order prohibiting the entry or departure of commercial ships at its ports 2 any legal restriction of commerce —*vt.* **-goed, -go·ing** to put an embargo upon

em·bark (em bärk', im-) *vt.* ⟦ult. < L *in-*, in + *barca*, small boat⟧ to put or take (goods, etc.) aboard a ship, aircraft, etc. —*vi.* 1 to go aboard a ship, aircraft, etc. 2 to begin a journey 3 to engage in an enterprise —**em'bar·ka'tion** *n.*

em·bar·rass (em bar'əs, im-) *vt.* ⟦< It *in-*, in + *barra*, a bar⟧ 1 to cause to feel self-conscious 2 to hinder 3 to cause to be in debt —**em·bar'rass·ing** *adj.* —**em·bar'rass·ment** *n.*

em·bas·sy (em'bə sē) *n., pl.* **-sies** ⟦see AMBASSADOR⟧ 1 the residence or offices of an ambassador 2 an ambassador and his or her staff 3 a group sent on an official mission

em·bat·tled (em bat''ld) *adj.* ⟦< OFr⟧ engaged in battle or conflict

em·bed (em bed', im-) *vt.* **-bed'ded, -bed'ding** to set or fix firmly in a surrounding mass —**em·bed'ment** *n.*

em·bel·lish (em bel'ish, im-) *vt.* ⟦< OFr *em-*, in + *bel*, beautiful⟧ 1 to decorate; adorn 2 to improve (a story, etc.) by adding details, often fictitious —**em·bel'lish·ment** *n.*

em·ber (em'bər) *n.* ⟦OE *æmerge*⟧ 1 a glowing piece of coal, wood, etc. 2 [*pl.*] the smoldering remains of a fire

em·bez·zle (em bez'əl, im-) *vt.* **-zled, -zling** ⟦< OFr *en-*, in + *besillier*, destroy⟧ to steal (money, etc. entrusted to one) —**em·bez'zle·ment** *n.* —**em·bez'zler** *n.*

em·bit'ter (-bit'ər) *vt.* to make bitter

em·bla'zon (-blā'zən) *vt.* ⟦EM- (see EN-) + BLAZON⟧ 1 to decorate (*with* coats of arms, etc.) 2 to display brilliantly 3 to extol —**em·bla'zon·ment** *n.*

em·blem (em'bləm) *n.* ⟦< Gr *en-*, in + *ballein*, throw⟧ a visible symbol of a thing, idea, etc.; sign; badge —**em'blem·at'ic** (-blə mat'ik) *adj.*

em·bod·y (em bäd'ē, im-) *vt.* **-ied, -y·ing** 1 to give bodily form to 2 to give definite form to 3 to bring together into an organized whole; incorporate —**em·bod'i·ment** *n.*

em·bold'en (-bōl'dən) *vt.* to give courage to; cause to be bold

em·bo·lism (em'bə liz'əm) *n.* ⟦< Gr *en-*, in + *ballein*, to throw⟧ the obstruction of a blood vessel as by a blood clot or air bubble

em·boss (em bôs', -bäs'; im-) *vt.* ⟦see EN- & BOSS[2]⟧ 1 to decorate with raised designs, patterns, etc. 2 to raise (a design, etc.) in relief —**em·boss'er** *n.*

em·bou·chure (äm'bōō shoor') *n.* ⟦Fr < L *in*, in + *bucca*, cheek⟧ the method of applying the lips to the mouthpiece of a wind instrument

em·brace (em brās′, im-) *vt.* **-braced′, -brac′ing** ⟦< L *im-*, in + *brachium*, an arm⟧ 1 to clasp in the arms lovingly; hug 2 to accept readily 3 to take up or adopt 4 to encircle 5 to include —*vi.* to clasp each other in the arms —*n.* an embracing; hug —**em·brace′a·ble** *adj.*

em·bra·sure (em brā′zhər, im-) *n.* ⟦Fr < *embraser*, widen an opening⟧ 1 an opening (for a door, window, etc.) wider on the inside than on the outside 2 an opening in a wall for a gun, with the sides slanting outward

em·broi·der (em broi′dər, im-) *vt.*, *vi.* ⟦< OFr *en-*, on + *brosder*, embroider⟧ 1 to make (a design, etc.) on (fabric) with needlework 2 to embellish (a story); exaggerate

em·broi′der·y *n.*, *pl.* **-ies** 1 the art of embroidering 2 embroidered work or fabric 3 embellishment

em·broil (em broil′, im-) *vt.* ⟦< OFr *en-*, in + *brouillier*, to dirty⟧ 1 to confuse; muddle 2 to involve in conflict or trouble —**em·broil′ment** *n.*

em·bry·o (em′brē ō′) *n.*, *pl.* **-os′** ⟦< Gr *en-*, in + *bryein*, to swell⟧ 1 an animal in the earliest stages of its development in the uterus 2 the rudimentary plant contained in a seed 3 an early stage of something —**em′bry·on′ic** (-än′ik) *adj.*

em′bry·ol′o·gy (-äl′ə jē) *n.* ⟦prec. + -LOGY⟧ the branch of biology dealing with the formation and development of embryos —**em′bry·ol′o·gist** *n.*

em·cee (em′sē′) *vt.*, *vi.* **-ceed′, -cee′ing** ⟦< MC, sense 1⟧ [Colloq.] to act as master of ceremonies (for) —*n.* [Colloq.] a master of ceremonies

e·mend (ē mend′, i-) *vt.* ⟦< L *emendare*, to correct⟧ to make scholarly corrections in (a text) —**e·men·da·tion** (ē′men dā′shən, em′ən-) *n.*

em·er·ald (em′ər əld) *n.* ⟦< Gr *smaragdos*⟧ 1 a bright-green, transparent precious stone 2 bright green

e·merge (ē murj′, i-) *vi.* **e·merged′, e·merg′·ing** ⟦< L *e-*, out + *mergere*, to dip⟧ 1 to rise as from a fluid 2 to become visible or apparent 3 to evolve —**e·mer′gence** *n.* —**e·mer′gent** *adj.*

e·mer·gen·cy (ē mur′jən sē, i-) *n.*, *pl.* **-cies** ⟦orig. sense, emergence⟧ a sudden, generally unexpected occurrence demanding immediate action

e·mer·i·tus (ē mer′i təs, i-) *adj.* ⟦< L *e-*, out + *mereri*, to serve⟧ retired from active service, usually for age, but retaining one's title [professor *emeritus*]

Em·er·son (em′ər sən), **Ralph Wal·do** (ralf wôl′dō) 1803-82; U.S. writer & philosopher

em·er·y (em′ər ē) *n.* ⟦< Gr *smyris*⟧ a dark, coarse variety of corundum used for grinding, polishing, etc.

e·met·ic (ē met′ik, i-) *adj.* ⟦< Gr *emein*, to vomit⟧ causing vomiting —*n.* an emetic substance

-e·mi·a (ē′mē ə) ⟦< Gr *haima*, blood⟧ *combining form* a (specified) condition of the blood [*leukemia*]

em·i·grate (em′i grāt′) *vt.* **-grat′ed, -grat′·ing** ⟦< L *e-*, out + *migrare*, to move⟧ to leave one country or region to settle in another —**em′i·grant** (-grənt) *adj.*, *n.* —**em′i·gra′tion** *n.*

é·mi·gré or **e·mi·gré** (em′i grā′, em′i grā′) *n.* ⟦Fr⟧ one forced to flee his country for political reasons

em·i·nence (em′i nəns) *n.* ⟦< L *eminere*, stand out⟧ 1 a high place, thing, etc. 2 superiority in rank, position, etc. 3 [E-] a title of honor of a cardinal: preceded by *Your* or *His*

em′i·nent *adj.* ⟦< L *eminens*⟧ 1 high; lofty 2 projecting; prominent 3 renowned; distinguished 4 outstanding —**em′i·nent·ly** *adv.*

eminent domain the right of a government to take or purchase private property for public use

e·mir (e mir′, ə-) *n.* ⟦< Ar *amara*, to command⟧ in Muslim countries, a ruler or prince

em·is·sar·y (em′i ser′ē) *n.*, *pl.* **-ies** ⟦see EMIT⟧ one, esp. a secret agent, sent on a specific mission

e·mis·sion (ē mish′ən, i-) *n.* 1 an emitting 2 something emitted; discharge

e·mit (ē mit′, i-) *vt.* **e·mit′ted, e·mit′ting** ⟦< L *e-*, out + *mittere*, send⟧ 1 to send out; give forth; discharge 2 to utter (words, etc.) —**e·mit′ter** *n.*

e·mol·li·ent (ē mäl′yənt, i-) *adj.* ⟦< L *e-*, out + *mollire*, soften⟧ softening; soothing —*n.* something that softens or soothes, as a medicine

e·mol′u·ment (-yoo mənt) *n.* ⟦< L *e-*, out + *molere*, grind⟧ gain from employment or position; salary, fees, etc.

e·mote (ē mōt′, i-) *vi.* **e·mot′ed, e·mot′ing** [Colloq.] to act in a theatrical manner

e·mo·tion (ē mō′shən, i-) *n.* ⟦< L *e-*, out + *movere*, move⟧ 1 strong feeling 2 any specific feeling, as love, hate, fear, anger, etc.

e·mo′tion·al *adj.* 1 of or showing emotion 2 easily aroused to emotion 3 appealing to the emotions; moving —**e·mo′tion·al·ism′** *n.* —**e·mo′tion·al·ly** *adv.*

e·mo′tion·al·ize′ *vt.* **-ized′, -iz′ing** to treat in an emotional way

em·pa·thet·ic (em′pə thet′ik) *adj.* of or showing empathy

em·pa·thize (em′pə thīz′) *vt.* **-thized′, -thiz′·ing** to feel empathy (*with*)

em′pa·thy (-thē) *n.* ⟦< Gr *en-*, in + *pathos*, feeling⟧ ability to share in another's emotions, thoughts, or feelings

em·per·or (em′pər ər) *n.* ⟦< L *in-*, in + *parare*, to set in order⟧ the supreme ruler of an empire

em·pha·sis (em′fə sis) *n.*, *pl.* **-ses′** (-sēz′) ⟦< Gr *en-*, in + *phainein*, to show⟧ 1 force of expression, action, etc. 2 special stress given to a word or phrase in speaking 3 importance; stress

em′pha·size′ (-sīz′) *vt.* **-sized′, -siz′ing** to give emphasis to; stress

em·phat·ic (em fat′ik, im-) *adj.* 1 felt or done with emphasis 2 using emphasis in speaking, etc. 3 forcible; striking —**em·phat′i·cal·ly** *adv.*

em·phy·se·ma (em′fə sē′mə, -zē′-) *n.* ⟦< Gr *en-*, in + *physaein*, to blow⟧ a condition of the lungs in which the air sacs become distended and lose elasticity

em·pire (em′pīr′) ***n.*** ‖ see EMPEROR ‖ 1 supreme rule 2 government by an emperor or empress 3 a group of states or territories under one ruler 4 an extensive organization under the control of a single person, corporation, etc.

em·pir·i·cal (em pir′i kəl) ***adj.*** ‖ < Gr *en-*, in + *peira*, trial ‖ relying or based on experiment or experience —**em·pir′i·cal·ly** ***adv.*** —**em·pir′i·cism′** (-siz′əm) ***n.***

em·place·ment (em plās′ mənt, im-) ***n.*** the prepared position from which a heavy gun or guns are fired

em·ploy (em ploi′, im-) ***vt.*** ‖ < L *in-*, in + *plicare*, to fold ‖ 1 to use 2 to keep busy or occupied 3 to engage the services of; hire —***n.*** employment

em·ploy′a·ble ***adj.*** that can be employed; specif., physically or mentally fit to be hired for work

em·ploy·ee or **em·ploy·e** (em ploi′ē, im-) ***n.*** one hired by another for wages or salary

em·ploy′er ***n.*** one who employs others for wages or salary

em·ploy′ment ***n.*** 1 an employing or being employed 2 work; occupation 3 the number or percentage of persons gainfully employed

em·po·ri·um (em pôr′ē əm) ***n.***, *pl.* **-ri·ums** or **-ri·a** (-ə) ‖ < Gr *en-*, in + *poros*, way ‖ a large store with a wide variety of things for sale

em·pow·er (em pou′ər, im-) ***vt.*** 1 to give power to; authorize 2 to enable

em·press (em′pris) ***n.*** 1 an emperor's wife 2 a woman ruler of an empire

emp·ty (emp′tē) ***adj.*** **-ti·er, -ti·est** ‖ OE *æmettig* ‖ 1 having nothing or no one in it; unoccupied 2 worthless /*empty* pleasure/ 3 insincere /*empty* promises/ —***vt.*** **-tied, -ty·ing** 1 to make empty 2 to remove (the contents) of something —***vi.*** 1 to become empty 2 to pour out; discharge —***n.***, *pl.* **-ties** an empty truck, bottle, etc. —**emp′ti·ly** ***adv.*** —**emp′ti·ness** ***n.***

emp′ty-hand′ed ***adj.*** bringing or carrying away nothing

em·py·re·an (em pir′ē ən, em′pī rē′ən) ***n.*** ‖ < Gr *en-*, in + *pyr*, fire ‖ 1 the highest heaven 2 the sky; firmament

e·mu (ē′myōō′) ***n.*** ‖ < Port *ema*, a crane ‖ a large, flightless Australian bird, like the ostrich but smaller

em·u·late (em′yōō lāt′, -yə-) ***vt.*** **-lat′ed, -lat′ing** ‖ < L *aemulus*, trying to equal or excel ‖ 1 to try to equal or surpass 2 to imitate (a person or thing admired) 3 to rival successfully —**em′u·la′tion** ***n.*** —**em′u·la′tive** ***adj.*** —**em′u·la′tor** ***n.***

e·mul·si·fy (ē mul′sə fī′, i-) ***vt., vi.*** **-fied′, -fy′ing** to form into an emulsion —**e·mul′si·fi·ca′tion** ***n.***

e·mul·sion (ē mul′shən, i-) ***n.*** ‖ < L *e-*, out + *mulgere*, to milk ‖ a fluid formed by the suspension of one liquid in another, as some medications, etc.

en- ‖ < L *in-*, in ‖ *prefix* 1 to put or get into or on /*enthrone*/ 2 to make, cause to be /*endanger*/ 3 in or into /*encase*/

-en (ən, ′n) ‖ OE ‖ *suffix* 1 *a)* to become or cause to be /*darken*/ *b)* to cause to have /*heighten*/ 2 made of /*wooden*/ 3 forming plurals /*children*/ 4 forming diminutives /*chicken*/

en·a·ble (en ā′bəl, in-) ***vt.*** **-bled, -bling** to make able; provide with means, power, etc. (*to* do something)

en·act (en akt′, in-) ***vt.*** 1 to pass (a bill, law, etc.) 2 to represent as in a play —**en·act′ment** ***n.***

en·am·el (e nam′əl, i-) ***n.*** ‖ < OFr *esmail* ‖ 1 a glassy, opaque substance fused to metal, pottery, etc. as an ornamental or protective coating 2 the hard, white coating of teeth 3 paint that dries to a smooth, glossy surface —***vt.*** **-eled** or **-elled, -el·ing** or **-el·ling** to coat with enamel —**en·am′el·er** or **en·am′el·ler** ***n.***

en·am·or (en am′ər, in-) ***vt.*** ‖ ult. < L *in-*, in + *amor*, love ‖ to fill with love; charm: now mainly in the passive voice, with *of* /*enamored* of her/

en bloc (en bläk′) ‖ Fr, lit., in a block ‖ in a mass; all together

en bro·chette (än brô shet′) ‖ Fr ‖ broiled on small skewers

en·camp (en kamp′, in-) ***vi., vt.*** to set up, or put in, a camp —**en·camp′ment** ***n.***

en·cap·su·late (en kap′sə lāt′) ***vt.*** **-lat′ed, -lat′ing** 1 to enclose in a capsule 2 to make concise; condense Also **en·cap′sule** (-səl, -syōōl′), **-suled, -sul·ing** —**en·cap′su·la′tion** ***n.***

en·case (en kās′, in-) ***vt.*** **-cased′, -cas′ing** to enclose, as in a case

en cas·se·role (en kas′ə rōl′) ‖ Fr ‖ (baked and served) in a casserole

-ence (əns, ′ns) ‖ < L ‖ *suffix* act, state, or result /*conference*/

en·ceph·a·li·tis (en sef′ə līt′is) ***n.*** ‖ < Gr *en-*, in + *kephalē*, the head + -ITIS ‖ inflammation of the brain

en·chain (en chān′) ***vt.*** to bind with chains; fetter

en·chant (en chant′, in-) ***vt.*** ‖ < L *in-*, intens. + *cantare*, sing ‖ 1 to cast a spell over 2 to charm greatly; delight —**en·chant′er** ***n.*** —**en·chant′ing** ***adj.*** —**en·chant′ment** ***n.***

en·chi·la·da (en′chi lä′də) ***n.*** ‖ AmSp ‖ a tortilla rolled with meat inside, served with a chili-flavored sauce

en·cir·cle (en sur′kəl, in-) ***vt.*** **-cled, -cling** 1 to surround 2 to move in a circle around

en·clave (en′klāv′, än′-) ***n.*** ‖ < L *in*, in + *clavis*, a key ‖ a territory surrounded by another country's territory

en·close (en klōz′, in-) ***vt.*** **-closed′, -clos′ing** 1 to shut in all around; surround 2 to insert in an envelope, etc., often along with a letter, etc.

en·clo′sure (-klō′zhər, in-) ***n.*** 1 an enclosing or being enclosed 2 something that encloses 3 something enclosed, as in an envelope or by a wall

en·code (en kōd′, in-) ***vt.*** **-cod′ed, -cod′ing** to put (a message, etc.) into code

en·co·mi·um (en kō′mē əm) ***n.***, *pl.* **-ums** or **-a** (-ə) ‖ < Gr *en-*, in + *kōmos*, a revel ‖ high praise; eulogy

en·com·pass (en kum′pəs, in-) ***vt.*** 1 to surround 2 to contain; include

en·core (än′kôr′) ***interj.*** ‖ Fr ‖ again; once

more —*n.* a further performance, etc. in answer to an audience's applause

en·coun·ter (en koun′tər, in-) *vt.* ‖ < L *in*, in + *contra*, against ‖ 1 to meet unexpectedly 2 to meet in conflict —*n.* 1 a direct meeting, as in battle 2 a meeting, esp. when unexpected

en·cour·age (en kur′ij, in-) *vt.* **-aged, -ag·ing** 1 to give courage, hope, or confidence to 2 to give support to; help —**en·cour′·age·ment** *n.*

en·croach (en krōch′, in-) *vi.* ‖ < OFr *en-*, in + *croc*, a hook ‖ to trespass or intrude (*on* or *upon*) —**en·croach′ment** *n.*

en croûte (än kro͞ot′) ‖ Fr ‖ wrapped in pastry and baked: said esp. of meats

en·crust (en krust′) *vt.* to cover as with a crust —*vi.* to form a crust —**en′crus·ta′·tion** *n.*

en·cum·ber (en kum′bər, in-) *vt.* ‖ see EN- & CUMBER ‖ 1 to hold back the motion or action of; hinder 2 to burden —**en·cum′·brance** *n.*

-en·cy (ən sē) ‖ L *-entia* ‖ *suffix* -ENCE /*dependency*/

en·cyc·li·cal (en sik′li kəl, in-) *n.* ‖ < Gr *en-*, in + *kyklos*, a circle ‖ a papal document addressed to the bishops

en·cy·clo·pe·di·a or **en·cy·clo·pae·di·a** (en sī′klō pē′dē ə, -klə-; in-) *n.* ‖ < Gr *enkyklios*, general + *paideia*, education ‖ a book or set of books with alphabetically arranged articles on all branches, or on one field, of knowledge —**en·cy′clo·pe′dic** or **en·cy′·clo·pae′dic** *adj.*

en·cyst (en sist′) *vt., vi.* to enclose or become enclosed in a cyst, capsule, or sac —**en·cyst′ment** *n.*

end (end) *n.* ‖ OE *ende* ‖ 1 a limit; boundary 2 the last part of anything; finish; conclusion 3 a ceasing to exist; death or destruction 4 the part at or near an extremity; tip 5 an object; purpose 6 an outcome; result 7 *Football* a player at either end of the line —*vt., vi.* to bring or come to an end; finish; stop —*adj.* at the end; final —**make (both) ends meet** to manage to keep one's expenses within one's income —**put an end to** 1 to stop 2 to do away with

en·dan·ger (en dān′jər, in-) *vt.* to expose to danger, harm, etc.; imperil

endangered species a species of animal or plant in danger of becoming extinct

en·dear (en dir′, in-) *vt.* to make dear or beloved —**en·dear′ing** *adj.*

en·dear′ment *n.* 1 an endearing 2 a word or act expressing affection

en·deav·or (en dev′ər, in-) *vi.* ‖ < EN- + OFr *deveir*, duty ‖ to make an earnest attempt; try Usually with an infinitive —*n.* an earnest attempt or effort Brit. sp. **en·deav′our**

en·dem·ic (en dem′ik) *adj.* ‖ < Gr *en-*, in + *dēmos*, people ‖ prevalent in or restricted to a particular locality, as a disease or plant —**en·dem′i·cal·ly** *adv.*

end·ing (en′diŋ) *n.* 1 the last part; finish 2 death

en·dive (en′dīv′, än′dēv′) *n.* ‖ < Gr *entybon* ‖ a cultivated plant with curled, narrow leaves used in salads

end′less *adj.* 1 having no end; eternal; infinite 2 lasting too long /an *endless* speech/ 3 continual /*endless* problems/ 4 with the ends joined to form a closed unit /an *endless* chain/ —**end′less·ly** *adv.* —**end′less·ness** *n.*

end′most′ *adj.* at the end; farthest

endo- ‖ < Gr *endon* ‖ *combining form* within, inner

en·do·crine (en′dō krin′, -krīn′; -də-) *adj.* ‖ prec. + Gr *krinein*, to separate ‖ designating or of any gland producing a hormone

en·dorse (en dôrs′, in-) *vt.* **-dorsed′, -dors′·ing** ‖ < L *in*, on + *dorsum*, the back ‖ 1 to write on the back of (a title, check, etc.) to transfer ownership, make a deposit, etc. 2 to sanction, approve, or support 3 to recommend (an advertised product) for a fee —**en·dorse′ment** *n.* —**en·dors′er** *n.*

en·do·scope (en′dō skōp′, -də-) *n.* an instrument for examining visually the inside of a hollow organ, as the rectum

en·dow (en dou′, in-) *vt.* ‖ < OFr *en-*, in + *dotare*, to endow ‖ 1 to provide with some talent, quality, etc. /*endowed* with courage/ 2 to give money to (a college, etc.) —**en·dow′ment** *n.*

end product the final result of a series of changes, processes, etc.

end table a small table placed at the end of a sofa, etc.

en·due (en do͞o′, in-) *vt.* **-dued′, -du′ing** ‖ < L *in-*, in + *ducere*, to lead ‖ to provide (*with* qualities)

en·dur·ance (en door′əns, in-) *n.* the ability to last, stand pain, etc.

en·dure (en door′, in-) *vt.* **-dured′, -dur′ing** ‖ < L *durus*, hard ‖ 1 to hold up under (pain, fatigue, etc.) 2 to tolerate —*vi.* 1 to continue; last 2 to bear pain, etc. without flinching —**en·dur′a·ble** *adj.*

end′ways′ (-wāz′) *adv.* 1 on end; upright 2 with the end foremost 3 lengthwise Also **end′wise′** (-wīz′)

-ene (ēn) ‖ after Gr *-enos*, adj. suffix ‖ *Chem. suffix* a certain type of hydrocarbon /*benzene*/

en·e·ma (en′ə mə) *n., pl.* **-mas** or **-ma·ta** (-mə tə) ‖ < Gr *en-*, in + *hienai*, send ‖ the forcing of a liquid, as a purgative, medicine, etc., into the colon through the anus

en·e·my (en′ə mē) *n., pl.* **-mies** ‖ < L *in-*, not + *amicus*, friend ‖ 1 one who hates and wishes to injure another 2 *a*) a nation or force hostile to another *b*) troops, ship, etc. of a hostile nation 3 one hostile to an idea, cause, etc. 4 anything injurious

en·er·get·ic (en′ər jet′ik) *adj.* having or showing energy; vigorous —**en′er·get′i·cal·ly** *adv.*

en·er·gize (en′ər jīz′) *vt.* **-gized′, -giz′ing** to give energy to; activate —**en′er·giz′er** *n.*

en·er·gy (en′ər jē) *n., pl.* **-gies** ‖ < Gr *en-*, in + *ergon*, work ‖ 1 force of expression 2 *a*) inherent power; capacity for action *b*) [*often pl.*] such power, esp. in action 3 a resource, as oil, gas, etc., from which usable energy can be produced 4 *Physics* the capacity for doing work

en·er·vate (en′ər vāt′) *vt.* **-vat′ed, -vat′ing** ‖ < L *e-*, out + *nervus*, nerve ‖ to deprive of strength, force, vigor, etc.; devitalize —**en′·er·va′tion** *n.*

en·fee·ble (en fē′bəl, in-) *vt.* **-bled, -bling** to make feeble

en·fi·lade (en′fə lād′, en′fə lād′) *n.* ⟦ Fr ⟧ gunfire directed along a line of troops

en·fold (en fōld′, in-) *vt.* 1 to wrap in folds; wrap up 2 to embrace

en·force (en fôrs′, in-) *vt.* **-forced′, -forc′ing** 1 to impose by force /to *enforce* one's will/ 2 to compel observance of (a law, etc.) —**en·force′a·ble** *adj.* —**en·force′ment** *n.*

en·fran·chise (en fran′chīz′, in-) *vt.* **-chised′, -chis′ing** 1 to free from slavery 2 to give the right to vote —**en·fran′chise·ment** (-chiz mənt) *n.*

Eng. 1 England 2 English

en·gage (en gāj′, in-) *vt.* **-gaged′, -gag′ing** ⟦ see EN- & GAGE¹ ⟧ 1 to pledge (oneself) 2 to bind by a promise of marriage 3 to hire 4 to involve or occupy 5 to attract and hold (the attention, etc.) 6 to enter into conflict with (the enemy) 7 to mesh (gears, etc.) —*vi.* 1 to pledge oneself 2 to occupy or involve oneself /to *engage* in dramatics/ 3 to enter into conflict 4 to mesh

en·gaged′ *adj.* 1 betrothed 2 occupied; employed 3 involved in combat, as troops 4 meshed

en·gage′ment *n.* an engaging or being engaged; specif., *a*) a betrothal *b*) an appointment *c*) employment *d*) a conflict; battle

en·gag′ing *adj.* attractive; charming —**en·gag′ing·ly** *adv.*

en·gen·der (en jen′dər, in-) *vt.* ⟦ < L *in-*, in + *generare*, beget ⟧ to bring into being; cause; produce

en·gine (en′jən) *n.* ⟦ < L *in-*, in + base of *gignere*, beget ⟧ 1 any machine that uses energy to develop mechanical power 2 a railroad locomotive 3 any machine

en·gi·neer (en′jə nir′) *n.* 1 one skilled in some branch of engineering 2 one who operates or supervises the operation of engines or technical equipment /a locomotive *engineer*/ —*vt.* 1 to plan, construct, etc. as an engineer 2 to manage skillfully

en′gi·neer′ing *n.* 1 the science concerned with putting scientific knowledge to practical uses 2 the planning, designing, construction, etc. of machinery, roads, bridges, etc.

Eng·land (iŋ′glənd) division of the United Kingdom in S Great Britain: 50,331 sq. mi.; pop. 46,363,000

Eng·lish (iŋ′glish) *adj.* 1 of England, its people, etc. 2 of their language —*n.* 1 the language of the people of England, the official language of the Commonwealth of Nations, the U.S., etc. 2 [*sometimes* e-] a spinning motion given to a ball —**the English** the people of England

ENGLISH HORN

English Channel arm of the Atlantic, between England & France

English horn a double-reed woodwind instrument

Eng′lish·man (-mən) *n.*, *pl.* **-men** a native or inhabitant of England —**Eng′lish·wom′an**, *pl.* **-wom′en**, *n.fem.*

en·gorge (en gôrj′, in-) *vt.* **-gorged′, -gorg′ing** ⟦ < OFr *en-*, in + *gorge*, gorge ⟧ 1 to devour greedily 2 *Med.* to congest (tissue, etc.) with fluid, as blood

en·grave (en grāv′, in-) *vt.* **-graved′, -grav′ing** ⟦ < Fr *en-*, in + *graver*, to incise ⟧ 1 to cut or etch letters, designs, etc. in or on (a metal plate, etc.) 2 to print with such a plate 3 to impress deeply —**en·grav′er** *n.*

en·grav′ing *n.* 1 the act or art of one who engraves 2 an engraved plate, drawing, etc. 3 a print made from an engraved surface

en·gross (en grōs′, in-) *vt.* ⟦ < OFr *engroissier*, become thick ⟧ to take the entire attention of; occupy wholly —**en·gross′ing** *adj.*

en·gulf (en gulf′, in-) *vt.* to swallow up

en·hance (en hans′, in-) *vt.* **-hanced′, -hanc′ing** ⟦ < L *in-*, in + *altus*, high ⟧ to make greater, better, etc.; heighten —**en·hance′ment** *n.*

e·nig·ma (i nig′mə, e-) *n.* ⟦ < Gr *ainos*, story ⟧ 1 a riddle 2 a perplexing or baffling matter, person, etc. —**en·ig·mat·ic** (en′ig mat′ik, ē′nig-) *adj.*

en·jamb·ment or **en·jambe·ment** (en jam′mənt) *n.* ⟦ < Fr *enjamber*, to encroach ⟧ the running on of a sentence from one line to the next of a poem

en·join (en join′, in-) *vt.* ⟦ < L *in-*, in + *jungere*, join ⟧ 1 to command; order 2 to prohibit, esp. by legal injunction

en·joy (en joi′, in-) *vt.* ⟦ < OFr *en-*, in + *joir*, rejoice ⟧ 1 to get pleasure from; relish 2 to have the use or benefit of —**enjoy oneself** to have a good time —**en·joy′a·ble** *adj.* —**en·joy′ment** *n.*

en·large (en lärj′, in-) *vt.* **-larged′, -larg′ing** to make larger; expand —*vi.* 1 to become larger; expand 2 to speak or write at greater length: with *on* or *upon* —**en·large′ment** *n.*

en·light·en (en līt′'n, in-) *vt.* 1 to free from ignorance, prejudice, etc. 2 to inform —**en·light′en·ment** *n.*

en·list (en list′, in-) *vt.*, *vi.* 1 to enroll in some branch of the armed forces 2 to engage in support of a cause or movement —**en·list′ment** *n.*

enlisted man any person in the armed forces who is not a commissioned officer or warrant officer

en·liv·en (en lī′vən, in-) *vt.* to make active, cheerful, etc.; liven up

en masse (en mas′) ⟦ Fr, lit., in mass ⟧ in a group; as a whole

en·mesh (en mesh′, in-) *vt.* to catch as in the meshes of a net; entangle

en·mi·ty (en′mə tē) *n.*, *pl.* **-ties** ⟦ see ENEMY ⟧ the attitude or feelings of an enemy or enemies; hostility

en·no·ble (en nō′bəl, i-) *vt.* **-bled, -bling** to give a noble quality to; dignify —**en·no′ble·ment** *n.*

en·nui (än′wē′) *n.* ⟦ Fr ⟧ a feeling of weariness and boredom

e·nor·mi·ty (ē nôr′mə tē, i-) *n.*, *pl.* **-ties** ⟦ < L *enormis*, immense ⟧ 1 great wickedness 2 an outrageous act 3 enormous size or extent

e·nor·mous (ē nôr′məs, i-) *adj.* ⟦ see prec. ⟧ of great size, number, etc.; huge; vast; immense —**e·nor′mous·ly** *adv.*

e·nough (ē nuf′, i-) *adj.* ⟦ OE *genoh* ⟧ as

much or as many as necessary; sufficient —*n.* the amount needed —*adv.* 1 sufficiently 2 fully; quite [oddly *enough*] 3 tolerably

e·now (ē nou′, i-) *adj., n., adv.* [Archaic] enough

en·plane (en plān′, in-) *vi.* **-planed′, -plan′ing** to board an airplane

en·quire (en kwīr′, in-) *vt., vi.* **-quired′, -quir′ing** INQUIRE —**en·quir′y** (-ē), *pl.* **-ies,** *n.*

en·rage (en rāj′, in-) *vt.* **-raged′, -rag′ing** to put into a rage; infuriate

en·rap·ture (en rap′chər, in-) *vt.* **-tured, -tur·ing** to fill with delight

en·rich (en rich′, in-) *vt.* to make rich or richer; give greater value, better quality, etc. to —**en·rich′ment** *n.*

en·roll or **en·rol** (en rōl′, in-) *vt., vi.* **-rolled′, -roll′ing** 1 to record or be recorded in a roll or list 2 to enlist 3 to make or become a member —**en·roll′ment** or **en·rol′ment** *n.*

en route (en ro͞ot′, än-) ‖ Fr ‖ on the way

en·sconce (en skäns′, in-) *vt.* **-sconced′, -sconc′ing** ‖ < Du *schans,* small fort ‖ to place or settle snugly or securely

en·sem·ble (än säm′bəl) *n.* ‖ Fr < L *in-*, in + *simul,* at the same time ‖ 1 total effect 2 a whole costume of matching parts 3 *a)* a small group of musicians, actors, etc. *b)* the performance of such a group

en·shrine (en shrīn′, in-) *vt.* **-shrined′, -shrin′ing** 1 to enclose in a shrine 2 to hold as sacred; cherish

en·shroud (en shroud′, in-) *vt.* to cover as if with a shroud; hide; obscure

en·sign (en′sīn′; *also, & for 2 always,* -sən) *n.* ‖ see INSIGNIA ‖ 1 a flag or banner 2 *U.S. Navy* a commissioned officer of the lowest rank

en·slave (en slāv′, in-) *vt.* **-slaved′, -slav′ing** 1 to make a slave of 2 to subjugate —**en·slave′ment** *n.*

en·snare′ *vt.* **-snared′, -snar′ing** to catch as in a snare

en·sue (en so͞o′, in-) *vi.* **-sued′, -su′ing** ‖ < L *in-*, in + *sequi,* follow ‖ 1 to come afterward 2 to result

en·sure′ *vt.* **-sured′, -sur′ing** 1 to make sure 2 to protect

-ent (ənt) ‖ < OFr *-ent,* L *-ens,* prp. ending ‖ *suffix* 1 that has, shows, or does [*insistent*] 2 a person or thing that [*superintendent, solvent*]

en·tail (en tāl′, in-) *vt.* ‖ < OFr *taillier,* to cut ‖ 1 *Law* to limit the inheritance of (real property) to a specific line of heirs 2 to make necessary; require

en·tan′gle *vt.* **-gled, -gling** 1 to involve in a tangle 2 to involve in difficulty 3 to confuse 4 to complicate —**en·tan′gle·ment** *n.*

en·tente (än tänt′) *n.* ‖ Fr < OFr *entendre,* understand ‖ 1 an understanding or agreement, as between nations 2 the parties to this

en·ter (ent′ər) *vt.* ‖ < L *intra,* within ‖ 1 to come or go into 2 to penetrate 3 to insert 4 to write down in a list, etc. 5 to become a member of or participant in 6 to get (a person, etc.) admitted 7 to begin 8 to put on record, formally or before a law court —*vi.* 1 to come or go into some place 2 to penetrate —**enter into** 1 to take part in 2 to form a part of —**enter on** (or **upon**) to begin; start

en·ter·i·tis (ent′ər īt′is) *n.* ‖ < Gr *enteron,* intestine + -ITIS ‖ inflammation of the intestine

en·ter·prise (ent′ər prīz′) *n.* ‖ ult. < L *inter,* in + *prehendere,* take ‖ 1 an undertaking, esp. a big, bold, or difficult one 2 energy and initiative

en′ter·pris′ing *adj.* showing enterprise; full of energy and initiative

en·ter·tain (ent′ər tān′) *vt.* ‖ ult. < L *inter,* between + *tenere,* to hold ‖ 1 to amuse; divert 2 to have as a guest 3 to have in mind; consider —*vi.* to give hospitality to guests

en′ter·tain′er *n.* one who entertains; esp., a popular singer, comedian, etc.

en′ter·tain′ing *adj.* interesting and pleasurable; amusing

en′ter·tain′ment *n.* 1 an entertaining or being entertained 2 something that entertains; esp., a show

en·thrall or **en·thral** (en thrôl′, in-) *vt.* **-thralled′, -thrall′ing** ‖ see EN- & THRALL ‖ to captivate; fascinate

en·throne′ *vt.* **-throned′, -thron′ing** 1 to place on a throne 2 to exalt

en·thuse (en tho͞oz′, in-) *vi.* **-thused′, -thus′ing** [Colloq.] to express enthusiasm —*vt.* [Colloq.] to make enthusiastic

en·thu·si·asm (en tho͞o′zē az′əm, in-) *n.* ‖ < Gr *en-*, in + *theos,* god ‖ intense or eager interest; zeal —**en·thu′si·ast′** (-ast′) *n.* —**en·thu′si·as′tic** *adj.* —**en·thu′si·as′ti·cal·ly** *adv.*

en·tice (en tīs′, in-) *vt.* **-ticed′, -tic′ing** ‖ < L *in,* in + *titio,* a burning brand ‖ to tempt with hope of reward or pleasure —**en·tice′ment** *n.*

en·tire (en tīr′, in-) *adj.* ‖ < L *integer,* whole ‖ not lacking any parts; whole; complete; intact —**en·tire′ly** *adv.*

en·tire′ty (-tē) *n., pl.* **-ties** 1 the state or fact of being entire; wholeness 2 an entire thing; whole

en·ti·tle (en tīt′'l, in-) *vt.* **-tled, -tling** 1 to give a title or name to 2 to give a right or claim to

en·ti′tle·ment *n.* something to which one is entitled, esp. a benefit, as Medicare, provided by certain government programs

en·ti·ty (en′tə tē) *n., pl.* **-ties** ‖ ult. < L *esse,* to be ‖ 1 existence 2 a thing that has definite existence

en·tomb (en to͞om′, in-) *vt.* to place in a tomb; bury —**en·tomb′ment** *n.*

en·to·mol·o·gy (en′tə mäl′ə jē) *n.* ‖ < Gr *entomon,* insect + -LOGY ‖ the branch of zoology that deals with insects —**en′to·mo·log′i·cal** (-mə läj′i kəl) *adj.* —**en′to·mol′o·gist** *n.*

en·tou·rage (än′too räzh′) *n.* ‖ Fr < *entourer,* surround ‖ a group of accompanying attendants, etc.; retinue

en·trails (en′trālz, -trəlz) *n.pl.* ‖ < L *interaneus,* internal ‖ the inner organs; specif., the intestines; viscera

en·trance[1] (en′trəns) *n.* 1 the act of entering **2** a place for entering; door, etc. **3** permission or right to enter; admission

en·trance[2] (en trans′, in-) ***vt.*** **-tranced′, -tranc′ing** ‖ see EN- & TRANCE ‖ to fill with delight; enchant

en·trant (en′trənt) ***n.*** one who enters

en·trap (en trap′, in-) ***vt.*** **-trapped′, -trap′ping** to catch as in a trap

en·treat (en trēt′, in-) ***vt., vi.*** ‖ < OFr *en-*, in + *traiter*, to treat ‖ to ask earnestly; beseech; implore

en·treat′y ***n.***, *pl.* **-ies** an earnest request; prayer

en·tree or **en·trée** (än′trā′) ***n.*** ‖ Fr < OFr *entrer*, enter ‖ **1** right to enter **2** the main course of a meal

en·trench (en trench′, in-) ***vt.*** **1** to surround with trenches **2** to establish securely —**en·trench′ment** ***n.***

en·tre·pre·neur (än′trə prə nʉr′) ***n.*** ‖ Fr: see ENTERPRISE ‖ one who organizes a business undertaking, assuming the risk for the sake of the profit

en·tro·py (en′trə pē) ***n.*** ‖ < Gr *entropē*, a turning toward ‖ **1** a thermodynamic measure of the energy unavailable for useful work in a system **2** the tendency of an energy system to run down

en·trust (en trust′, in-) ***vt.*** **1** to charge with a trust or duty **2** to turn over for safekeeping

en·try (en′trē) ***n.***, *pl.* **-tries** ‖ < OFr: see ENTER ‖ **1** an entering; entrance **2** a way by which to enter **3** an item or note in a list, journal, etc. **4** one entered in a race, etc.

en·twine (en twīn′, in-) ***vt., vi.*** **-twined′, -twin′ing** to twine together or around

e·nu·mer·ate (ē no͞o′mər āt′, i-) ***vt.*** **-at′ed, -at′ing** ‖ < L *e-*, out + *numerare*, to count ‖ **1** to count **2** to name one by one —**e·nu′mer·a′tion** ***n.***

e·nun·ci·ate (ē nun′sē āt′, i-) ***vt., vi.*** **-at′ed, -at′ing** ‖ < L *e-*, out + *nuntiare*, announce ‖ **1** to state definitely **2** to announce **3** to pronounce (words) —**e·nun′ci·a′tion** ***n.***

en·vel·op (en vel′əp, in-) ***vt.*** ‖ < OFr: see EN- & DEVELOP ‖ **1** to wrap up; cover completely **2** to surround **3** to conceal; hide —**en·vel′op·ment** ***n.***

en·ve·lope (än′və lōp′, en′-) ***n.*** **1** a thing that envelops; covering **2** a folded paper container for a letter, etc., usually with a gummed flap

en·ven·om (en ven′əm, in-) ***vt.*** **1** to put venom into **2** to fill with hate

en·vi·a·ble (en′vē ə bəl) ***adj.*** good enough to be envied or desired —**en′vi·a·bly** ***adv.***

en·vi·ous (en′vē əs) ***adj.*** feeling or showing envy —**en′vi·ous·ly** ***adv.***

en·vi·ron·ment (en vī′rən mənt, in-) ***n.*** ‖ see ENVIRONS ‖ **1** surroundings **2** all the conditions, etc. surrounding, and affecting the development of, an organism —**en·vi′ron·men′tal** ***adj.***

en·vi′ron·men′tal·ist ***n.*** one working to solve environmental problems, as air and water pollution

en·vi·rons (en vī′rənz, in-) ***n.pl.*** ‖ < OFr *en-*, in + *viron*, a circuit ‖ **1** the districts surrounding a city; suburbs **2** surrounding area; vicinity

en·vis·age (en viz′ij, in-) ***vt.*** **-aged, -ag·ing** ‖ see EN- & VISAGE ‖ to form an image of in the mind; visualize

en·vi·sion (en vizh′ən, in-) ***vt.*** ‖ EN- + VISION ‖ to imagine (something not yet in existence)

en·voy (än′voi′, en′-) ***n.*** ‖ < Fr < L *in*, in + *via*, way ‖ **1** a messenger **2** a diplomatic agent just below an ambassador

en·vy (en′vē) ***n.***, *pl.* **-vies** ‖ < L *in-*, in + *videre*, to look ‖ **1** discontent and ill will over another's advantages, possessions, etc. **2** desire for something that another has **3** an object of such feeling —***vt.*** **-vied, -vy·ing** to feel envy toward or because of —**en′vy·ing·ly** ***adv.***

en·zyme (en′zīm′) ***n.*** ‖ < Gr *en-*, in + *zymē*, leaven ‖ a protein, formed in plant and animal cells or made synthetically, acting as a catalyst in chemical reactions

e·on (ē′ən, ē′än′) ***n.*** ‖ < Gr *aiōn*, an age ‖ an extremely long, indefinite period of time

-e·ous (ē əs) ‖ < L *-eus* + -OUS ‖ *suffix var. of* -OUS [*gaseous*]

EPA Environmental Protection Agency

ep·au·let or **ep·au·lette** (ep′ə let′, ep′ə let′) ***n.*** ‖ < Fr dim. of *épaule*, shoulder ‖ a shoulder ornament, esp. on military uniforms

EPAULETS

e·pee or **é·pée** (ā pā′) ***n.*** ‖ Fr ‖ a fencing sword like a foil, but heavier and more rigid

e·phed·rine (e fe′drin) ***n.*** ‖ < L *ephedra*, the plant horsetail ‖ an alkaloid used to relieve nasal congestion and asthma

e·phem·er·al (e fem′ər əl, i-) ***adj.*** ‖ < Gr *epi-*, upon + *hēmera*, day ‖ **1** lasting one day **2** short-lived; transitory

epi- ‖ < Gr *epi*, at, on ‖ *prefix* on, upon, over, among [*epiglottis*]

ep·ic (ep′ik) ***n.*** ‖ < Gr *epos*, a word, song, epic ‖ a long narrative poem in a dignified style about the deeds of a hero or heroes —***adj.*** of or like an epic; heroic; grand

ep·i·cen·ter (ep′i sent′ər) ***n.*** **1** the area of the earth's surface directly above the place of origin of an earthquake **2** a focal or central point

ep·i·cure (ep′i kyoor′) ***n.*** ‖ after *Epicurus*, ancient Gr philosopher ‖ one who enjoys and has a discriminating taste for fine foods and drinks

ep·i·cu·re·an (ep′i kyo͞o rē′ən) ***adj.*** fond of sensuous pleasure, esp. that of eating and drinking —***n.*** an epicure

ep·i·dem·ic (ep′ə dem′ik) ***adj.*** ‖ < Fr < Gr *epi-*, among + *dēmos*, people ‖ spreading rapidly among many people in a community, as a disease —***n.*** **1** an epidemic disease **2** the spreading of such a disease **3** a rapid, widespread growth —**ep′i·dem′i·cal·ly** ***adv.***

ep·i·de·mi·ol·o·gy (ep′ə dē′mē äl′ə jē) ***n.*** ‖ prec. + -LOGY ‖ the branch of medicine that studies epidemics

ep·i·der·mis (ep′ə dʉr′mis) ***n.*** ‖ < Gr *epi-*, upon + *derma*, the skin ‖ the outermost layer of the skin —**ep′i·der′mal** or **ep′i·der′mic** ***adj.***

ep·i·glot·tis (ep′ə glät′is) ***n.*** ⟦see EPI- & GLOTTIS⟧ the thin cartilage lid that covers the windpipe during swallowing

ep·i·gram (ep′ə gram′) ***n.*** ⟦< Gr *epi-*, upon + *graphein*, write⟧ a terse, witty, pointed statement —**ep′i·gram·mat′ic** (-grə mat′ik) ***adj.***

e·pig·ra·phy (ē pig′rə fē, i-) ***n.*** the study of inscriptions, esp. ancient ones

ep·i·lep·sy (ep′ə lep′sē) ***n.*** ⟦< Gr *epi-*, upon + *lambanein*, seize⟧ a recurrent disorder of the nervous system, characterized by seizures causing convulsions, unconsciousness, etc.

ep′i·lep′tic (-tik) ***adj.*** of or having epilepsy —***n.*** one who has epilepsy

ep·i·logue or **ep·i·log** (ep′ə lôg′) ***n.*** ⟦< Gr *epi-*, upon + *legein*, speak⟧ a closing section added to a novel, play, etc., providing further comment, as a speech by an actor to the audience

E·piph·a·ny (ē pif′ə nē, i-) ***n.***, *pl.* **-nies** ⟦< Gr *epiphainein*, show forth⟧ a Christian feast day (Jan. 6) commemorating the revealing of Jesus as the Christ to the Gentiles

e·pis·co·pa·cy (ē pis′kə pə sē, i-) ***n.***, *pl.* **-cies** ⟦< Gr *epi-*, upon + *skopein*, to look⟧ **1** church government by bishops **2** EPISCOPATE

e·pis′co·pal (-pəl) ***adj.*** **1** of or governed by bishops **2** [**E-**] designating or of any of various churches governed by bishops

E·pis′co·pa′lian (-pāl′yən) ***adj.*** Episcopal —***n.*** a member of the Protestant Episcopal Church

e·pis′co·pate (-pit, -pāt′) ***n.*** **1** the position, rank, etc. of a bishop **2** bishops collectively

ep·i·sode (ep′ə sōd′) ***n.*** ⟦< Gr *epi-*, upon + *eisodos*, entrance⟧ **1** any part of a novel, poem, etc. that is complete in itself **2** an event or series of events complete in itself —**ep′i·sod′ic** (-säd′ik) ***adj.*** —**ep′i·sod′i·cal·ly** ***adv.***

e·pis·tle (ē pis′əl) ***n.*** ⟦< Gr *epi-*, to + *stellein*, send⟧ **1** a letter **2** [**E-**] any of the letters in the New Testament —**e·pis′to·lar′y** (-tə ler′ē) ***adj.***

ep·i·taph (ep′ə taf′) ***n.*** ⟦< Gr *epi-*, upon + *taphos*, tomb⟧ an inscription on a tomb, etc. in memory of a dead person

ep·i·the·li·um (ep′i thē′lē əm) ***n.***, *pl.* **-li·ums** or **-li·a** (-ə) ⟦< Gr *epi-*, upon + *thēlē*, nipple⟧ cellular tissue covering external body surfaces or lining internal surfaces —**ep′i·the′li·al** (-əl) ***adj.***

ep·i·thet (ep′ə thet′) ***n.*** ⟦< Gr *epi-*, on + *tithenai*, put⟧ a word or phrase characterizing some person or thing

e·pit·o·me (ē pit′ə mē, i-) ***n.***, *pl.* **-mes′** (-mēz′) ⟦< Gr *epi-*, upon + *temnein*, to cut⟧ **1** an abstract; summary **2** a person or thing that typifies a whole class

e·pit′o·mize′ (-mīz′) ***vt.*** **-mized′**, **-miz′ing** to make or be an epitome of

e plu·ri·bus u·num (ē′ ploor′ē boos′ o͞o′ no͝om) ⟦L⟧ out of many, one: a motto of the U.S.

ep·och (ep′ək) ***n.*** ⟦< Gr *epi-*, upon + *echein*, to hold⟧ **1** the start of a new period in the history of anything **2** a period of time in terms of noteworthy events, persons, etc. —**ep′och·al** ***adj.***

ep·ox·y (ē päk′sē, i-) ***adj.*** ⟦EP(I)- + OXY(GEN)⟧ designating a resin used in strong, resistant glues, enamels, etc. —***n.***, *pl.* **-ies** an epoxy resin

ep·si·lon (ep′sə län′) ***n.*** ⟦Gr *e psilon*⟧ the fifth letter of the Greek alphabet (Ε, ε)

Ep·som salts (or **salt**) (ep′səm) ⟦after *Epsom*, town in England⟧ a white, crystalline salt, magnesium sulfate, used as a cathartic

Ep·stein-Barr virus (ep′stēn bär′) a herpeslike virus that causes infectious mononucleosis and may cause various forms of cancer

eq·ua·ble (ek′wə bəl) ***adj.*** ⟦see fol.⟧ steady; uniform; even; tranquil —**eq′ua·bil′i·ty** ***n.*** —**eq′ua·bly** ***adv.***

e·qual (ē′kwəl) ***adj.*** ⟦< L *aequus*, even⟧ **1** of the same quantity, size, value, etc. **2** having the same rights, ability, rank, etc. **3** evenly proportioned **4** having the necessary ability, strength, etc.: with *to* —***n.*** any person or thing that is equal —***vt.*** **e′qualed** or **e′qualled**, **e′qual·ing** or **e′qual·ling** **1** to be equal to **2** to do or make something equal to —**e·qual·i·ty** (ē kwôl′ə tē, -kwäl′-), *pl.* **-ties**, ***n.*** —**e′qual·ly** ***adv.***

e·qual·ize (ē′kwəl īz′) ***vt.*** **-ized′**, **-iz′ing** to make equal or uniform —**e′qual·i·za′tion** ***n.*** —**e′qual·iz′er** ***n.***

equal sign (or **mark**) the sign (=), indicating that the terms on either side of it are equal or equivalent

e·qua·nim·i·ty (ek′wə nim′ə tē, ē′kwə-) ***n.*** ⟦< L *aequus*, even + *animus*, mind⟧ evenness of mind; composure

e·quate (ē kwāt′, i-) ***vt.*** **e·quat′ed**, **e·quat′ing** **1** to make equal **2** to treat, regard, or express as equal —**e·quat′a·ble** ***adj.***

e·qua·tion (ē kwā′zhən, i-) ***n.*** **1** an equating or being equated **2** a statement of equality between two quantities, as shown by the equal sign (=)

e·qua·tor (ē kwāt′ər, i-) ***n.*** an imaginary circle around the earth, equally distant from the North Pole and the South Pole —**e·qua·to·ri·al** (ē′kwə tôr′ē əl, ek′wə-) ***adj.***

Equatorial Guinea country in W Africa: 10,830 sq. mi.; pop. 359,000

eq·uer·ry (ek′wər ē, ē kwer′ē) ***n.***, *pl.* **-ries** ⟦< Fr⟧ **1** an officer in charge of royal horses **2** an officer who attends a person of royalty

e·ques·tri·an (ē kwes′trē ən, i-) ***adj.*** ⟦< L *equus*, horse⟧ **1** of horses or horsemanship **2** on horseback —***n.*** a rider or circus performer on horseback —**e·ques′tri·enne′** (-trē en′) ***n.fem.***

equi- *combining form* equal, equally [*equidistant*]

e·qui·dis·tant (ē′kwi dis′tənt) ***adj.*** equally distant

e′qui·lat′er·al (-lat′ər əl) ***adj.*** ⟦< L *aequus*, even + *latus*, side⟧ having all sides equal

e′qui·lib′ri·um (-lib′rē əm) ***n.***, *pl.* **-ri·ums** or **-ri·a** (-ə) ⟦< L *aequus*, even + *libra*, a balance⟧ a state of balance between opposing forces

e·quine (ē′kwīn′) ***adj.*** ⟦< L *equus*, horse⟧ of or like a horse

e·qui·nox (ē′kwi näks′, ek′wə näks′) ***n.*** ⟦< L *aequus*, even + *nox*, night⟧ the time when the sun crosses the equator, making night and day of equal length in all parts of the earth —**e'qui·noc'tial** (-näk'shəl) *adj.*

e·quip (ē kwip', i-) *vt.* **e·quipped', e·quip'·ping** ⟦< OFr *esquiper*, embark⟧ to provide with what is needed

eq·ui·page (ek'wi pij') *n.* a carriage with horses and liveried servants

e·quip·ment (ē kwip'mənt, i-) *n.* **1** an equipping or being equipped **2** whatever one is equipped with; supplies, furnishings, etc.

eq·ui·poise (ek'wi poiz', ē'kwi-) *n.* ⟦EQUI- + POISE⟧ **1** state of equilibrium **2** counterbalance

eq'ui·ta·ble (-wit ə bəl) *adj.* ⟦see EQUITY⟧ fair; just —**eq'ui·ta·bly** *adv.*

eq·ui·ta·tion (ek'wi tā'shən) *n.* ⟦< L *equitare*, to ride⟧ horsemanship

eq·ui·ty (ek'wit ē) *n., pl.* **-ties** ⟦< L *aequus*, even⟧ **1** fairness; impartiality; justice **2** the value of property beyond the amount owed on it **3** *Finance a)* assets minus liabilities; net worth *b)* [*pl.*] shares of stock **4** *Law* a system of doctrines supplementing common and statute law

e·quiv·a·lent (ē kwiv'ə lənt, i-) *adj.* ⟦< L *aequus*, equal + *valere*, be strong⟧ equal in quantity, value, force, meaning, etc. —*n.* an equivalent thing —**e·quiv'a·lence** *n.*

e·quiv·o·cal (ē kwiv'ə kəl, i-) *adj.* ⟦< L *aequus*, even + *vox*, voice⟧ **1** having two or more meanings; purposely ambiguous **2** uncertain; doubtful **3** suspicious —**e·quiv'o·cal·ly** *adv.* —**e·quiv'o·cal·ness** *n.*

e·quiv'o·cate' (-kāt', i-) *vi.* **-cat'ed, -cat'ing** to use equivocal terms in order to deceive or mislead —**e·quiv'o·ca'tion** *n.* —**e·quiv'o·ca'tor** *n.*

-er (ər) ⟦ME⟧ *suffix* **1** *a)* a person or thing having to do with [*hatter*] *b)* a person living in [*New Yorker*] *c)* one that ____s [*roller*] *d)* repeatedly [*flicker*] **2** forming the comparative degree [*later*]

e·ra (ir'ə, er'ə) *n.* ⟦LL *aera*⟧ **1** a period of time measured from some important event **2** a period of time having some special characteristic

ERA **1** *Baseball* earned run average: also **era** **2** Equal Rights Amendment

e·rad·i·cate (ē rad'i kāt', i-) *vt.* **-cat'ed, -cat'ing** ⟦< L *e-*, out + *radix*, root⟧ to uproot; wipe out; stamp out; destroy —**e·rad'i·ca'tion** *n.* —**e·rad'i·ca'tor** *n.*

e·rase (ē rās', i-) *vt.* **e·rased', e·ras'ing** ⟦< L *e-*, out + *radere*, scrape⟧ **1** to rub, scrape, or wipe out (esp. writing) **2** to remove (something recorded) from (magnetic tape) **3** to obliterate, as from the mind —**e·ras'a·ble** *adj.*

e·ras'er *n.* a thing that erases; specif., a rubber device for erasing ink or pencil marks, or a pad for removing chalk marks from a blackboard

E·ras·mus (i raz'məs), **Des·i·der·i·us** (des'ə dir'ē əs) *c.* 1466-1536; Du. humanist & theologian

e·ra·sure (ē rā'shər, i-) *n.* **1** an erasing **2** an erased word, mark, etc.

ere (er) *prep.* ⟦OE *ær*⟧ [Archaic] before (in time) —*conj.* [Old Poet.] **1** before **2** rather than

e·rect (ē rekt', i-) *adj.* ⟦< L *e-*, up + *regere*, make straight⟧ upright —*vt.* **1** to construct (a building, etc.) **2** to set in an upright position; raise **3** to set up; assemble —**e·rec'tion** *n.* —**e·rect'ly** *adv.* —**e·rect'·ness** *n.* —**e·rec'tor** *n.*

e·rec·tile (ē rek'til, i-) *adj.* that can become erect, as tissue that becomes rigid when filled with blood

erg (urg) *n.* ⟦< Gr *ergon*, work⟧ *Physics* a unit of work or energy

er·go (er'gō) *conj., adv.* ⟦L⟧ therefore

er·gos·ter·ol (ur gäs'tər ōl', -ôl') *n.* a steroid alcohol prepared from yeast, that produces vitamin D when exposed to ultraviolet rays

Er·ie (ir'ē) **1** city & port in NW Pa.: pop. 119,000 **2 Lake** one of the Great Lakes, between Lake Huron & Lake Ontario

Er·in (er'in) *old poet. name for* IRELAND

er·mine (ur'min) *n.* ⟦prob. < OHG *harmo*, weasel⟧ **1** a weasel whose fur is white in winter **2** its white fur

e·rode (ē rōd', i-) *vt.* **e·rod'ed, e·rod'ing** ⟦< L *e-*, out + *rodere*, gnaw⟧ **1** to wear away **2** to form by wearing away gradually [the stream *eroded* a gully] —*vi.* to become eroded

e·rog·e·nous (ē räj'ə nəs, i-) *adj.* ⟦< Gr *erōs*, love + -GEN + -OUS⟧ sensitive to sexual stimulation Also **e·ro·to·gen·ic** (er'ə tō' jen'ik)

E·ros (er'äs', ir'-) *Gr. Myth.* the god of love —*n.* [**e-**] sexual love or desire

e·ro·sion (ē rō'zhən, i-) *n.* an eroding or being eroded —**e·ro'sive** (-siv) *adj.*

e·rot·ic (ē rät'ik, i-) *adj.* ⟦< Gr *erōs*, love⟧ of or arousing sexual feelings or desires; amatory —**e·rot'i·cal·ly** *adv.*

e·rot'i·ca (-i kə) *n.pl.* [*often with sing. v.*] erotic books, pictures, etc.

err (ur, er) *vi.* ⟦< L *errare*, wander⟧ **1** to be wrong or mistaken **2** to deviate from the established moral code

er·rand (er'ənd) *n.* ⟦OE *ærende*, mission⟧ **1** a trip to do a thing, as for someone else **2** the thing to be done

er·rant (er'ənt) *adj.* ⟦see ERR⟧ **1** roving or wandering, esp. in search of adventure **2** erring **3** shifting about

er·rat·ic (er rat'ik; e rat'-, i-) *adj.* ⟦< L *errare*, wander⟧ **1** irregular; random **2** eccentric; queer —**er·rat'i·cal·ly** *adv.*

er·ra·tum (er rät'əm, -rāt'-) *n., pl.* **-ta** (-ə) ⟦see ERR⟧ an error in a work already printed

er·ro·ne·ous (ər rō'nē əs; e rō'-, i-) *adj.* containing error; mistaken; wrong —**er·ro'·ne·ous·ly** *adv.*

er·ror (er'ər) *n.* ⟦see ERR⟧ **1** the state of believing what is untrue **2** a wrong belief **3** something incorrectly done; mistake **4** a transgression **5** *Baseball* any misplay in fielding

er·satz (er'zäts', er zäts') *n., adj.* ⟦Ger⟧ substitute or synthetic and inferior

Erse (urs) *n., adj.* ⟦ME *Erish*, var. of *Irisc*, Irish⟧ GAELIC

erst (urst) *adv.* ⟦< OE *ær*, ere⟧ [Archaic] formerly

erst'while' (-hwīl') *adv.* [Archaic] formerly —*adj.* former

e·ruct (ē rukt') *vt., vi.* ⟦< L *e-*, out + *ructare*, belch⟧ to belch —**e'ruc·ta'tion** *n.*

er·u·dite (er'yoo dīt', -oo-) *adj.* ⟦< L *e-*, out

\+ *rudis*, rude ‖ learned; scholarly —**er′u·dite′ly** ***adv.***

er·u·di·tion (er′yo͞o dish′ən) ***n.*** learning acquired by reading and study

e·rupt (ē rupt′, i-) ***vi.*** ‖ < L *e-*, out + *rumpere*, to break ‖ **1** to burst forth or out /*erupting* lava/ **2** to throw forth lava, water, etc. **3** to break out in a rash —***vt.*** to cause to burst forth

e·rup·tion (ē rup′shən, i-) ***n.*** **1** a bursting forth or out **2** *a*) a breaking out in a rash *b*) a rash

-er·y (ər ē) ‖ < LL *-aria* ‖ *suffix* **1** a place to /*tannery*/ **2** a place for /*nunnery*/ **3** the practice or act of /*surgery*/ **4** the product of /*pottery*/ **5** a collection of /*greenery*/ **6** the condition of /*drudgery*/

e·ryth·ro·cyte (e rith′rō sīt′) ***n.*** ‖ < Gr *erythros*, red + *kytos*, a hollow ‖ a mature red blood cell that contains hemoglobin, which carries oxygen to the body tissues

-es (iz, əz, z) ‖ < OE ‖ *suffix* **1** forming plurals /*glasses*/ **2** forming the 3d person sing., pres. indic., of verbs /he *kisses*/

E·sau (ē′sô′) *Bible* Isaac's son who sold his birthright to his brother, Jacob

es·ca·late (es′kə lāt′) ***vi.*** **-lat′ed, -lat′ing** **1** to rise as on an escalator **2** to expand step by step **3** to increase rapidly —**es′ca·la′tion** ***n.***

es′ca·la′tor (-ər) ***n.*** ‖ ult. < L *scala*, ladder ‖ a moving stairway on an endless belt

es·ca·pade (es′kə pād′, es′kə pād′) ***n.*** ‖ Fr: see fol. ‖ a reckless adventure or prank

es·cape (e skāp′, i-) ***vi.*** **-caped′, -cap′ing** ‖ < L *ex-*, out of + *cappa*, cloak ‖ **1** to get free **2** to avoid an illness, accident, etc. **3** to leak away —***vt.*** **1** to get away from **2** to avoid /to *escape* death/ **3** to come from involuntarily **4** to be missed or forgotten by —***n.*** **1** an escaping **2** a means of escape **3** a leakage **4** a temporary mental release from reality —***adj.*** providing an escape

es·cap·ee (e skāp′ē′, -skāp′ē′; i-) ***n.*** one who has escaped, as from prison

es·cape′ment ***n.*** a notched wheel with a detaining catch that controls the action of a mechanical clock or watch

escape velocity the minimum speed required for a particle, satellite, etc. to escape permanently from the gravitational field of a planet, star, etc.

es·cap′ism′ ***n.*** a tendency to escape from reality, responsibilities, etc. through the imagination —**es·cap′ist** ***adj., n.***

es·car·got (es kär gō′) ***n.*** ‖ Fr ‖ an edible snail

es·ca·role (es′kə rōl′) ***n.*** ‖ Fr ‖ ENDIVE

es·carp·ment (e skärp′mənt) ***n.*** ‖ < Fr ‖ a steep slope or cliff

-es·cence (es′əns) ‖ see fol. ‖ *suffix* the process of becoming /*obsolescence*/

-es·cent (es′ənt) ‖ L *-escens* ‖ *suffix* **1** starting to be, being, or becoming /*obsolescent*/ **2** giving off light /*phosphorescent*/

es·chew (es cho͞o′) ***vt.*** ‖ < OHG *sciuhan*, to fear ‖ to shun; avoid

es·cort (es′kôrt′; *for v.* es kôrt′, is-) ***n.*** ‖ < L *ex-*, out + *corrigere*, set right ‖ **1** one or more persons, cars, etc. accompanying another to protect it or show honor **2** a man accompanying a woman —***vt.*** to go with as an escort

es·cri·toire (es′kri twär′) ***n.*** ‖ < L *scribere*, write ‖ a writing desk

es·crow (es′krō′) ***n.*** ‖ see SCROLL ‖ the state of a deed, etc. put in the care of a third party until certain conditions are fulfilled

es·cutch·eon (e skuch′ən, i-) ***n.*** ‖ < L *scutum*, shield ‖ a shield on which a coat of arms is displayed

-ese (ēz, ēs) ‖ < L *-ensis* ‖ *suffix* **1** of a country or place /*Javanese*/ **2** in the language of /*Cantonese*/

Es·ki·mo (es′kə mō′) ***n.*** ‖ < Fr < AmInd ‖ **1** *pl.* **-mos′** or **-mo′** a member of a people from Greenland, N Canada, or Alaska **2** any of the languages of the Eskimos —***adj.*** of the Eskimos, their language, etc.

Eskimo dog a strong breed of dog used by the Eskimos to pull sleds

e·soph·a·gus (i säf′ə gəs, ē-) ***n.***, *pl.* **-gi′** (-jī′) ‖ < Gr *oisophagos* ‖ the passage for food from the pharynx to the stomach

es·o·ter·ic (es′ə ter′ik) ***adj.*** ‖ < Gr *esōteros*, inner ‖ meant for or understood by only a chosen few

esp. especially

ESP extrasensory perception

es·pa·drille (es′pə dril′) ***n.*** ‖ Fr < Sp *esparto*, coarse grass ‖ a casual shoe with a canvas upper and a sole of twisted rope

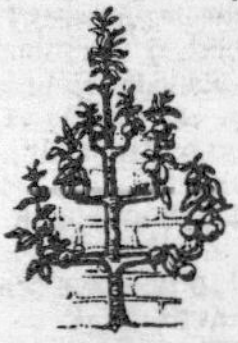

ESPALIER

es·pal·ier (es pal′yər) ***n.*** ‖ Fr < It *spalla*, shoulder ‖ **1** a lattice on which trees or shrubs are trained to grow flat **2** such a plant

es·pe·cial (e spesh′əl, i-) ***adj.*** special; particular —**es·pe′cial·ly** ***adv.***

Es·pe·ran·to (es′pə rän′tō, -ran′-) ***n.*** an invented international language based on the European word roots

es·pi·o·nage (es′pē ə näzh′) ***n.*** ‖ < Fr < It *spia*, spy ‖ the act or practice of spying

es·pla·nade (es′plə nād′, -näd′) ***n.*** ‖ < Fr < It < L *explanare*, to level ‖ a level stretch of ground, as a public walk

es·pous·al (e spou′zəl, i-) ***n.*** **1** [*often pl.*] a wedding **2** an espousing (of some cause, idea, etc.); advocacy

es·pouse (e spouz′, i-) ***vt.*** **-poused′, -pous′ing** ‖ see SPOUSE ‖ **1** to marry **2** to advocate (some cause, idea, etc.)

es·pres·so (e spres′ō) ***n.***, *pl.* **-sos** ‖ It ‖ coffee made by forcing steam through finely ground coffee beans

es·prit de corps (e sprē′ də kôr′) ‖ Fr ‖ group spirit; pride, etc. shared by those in the same group

es·py (e spī′, i-) ***vt.*** **-pied′, -py′ing** ‖ see SPY ‖ to catch sight of; spy

-esque (esk) ‖ < Fr < It *-esco* ‖ *suffix* **1** in

the manner or style of *[Romanesque]* 2 like *[statuesque]*

es·quire (es'kwīr') ***n.*** ⟦< L *scutum*, a shield⟧ 1 [Historical] a candidate for knighthood; squire 2 in England, a member of the gentry ranking just below a knight 3 [E-] a title of courtesy: in the U.S., now specif. used for lawyers: usually abbrev. **Esq.** or **Esqr.**

-ess (es, is, əs) ⟦< LL *-issa*⟧ *suffix* female *[lioness]*

es·say (e sā'; *for n. 1 usually, & for n. 2 always,* es'ā) ***vt.*** ⟦< LL *ex-*, out of + *agere*, to do⟧ to try; attempt —***n.*** 1 a trying or testing 2 a short, personal literary composition dealing with a single subject —**es·say'er** ***n.*** —**es·say·ist** (es'ā ist) ***n.***

es·sence (es'əns) ***n.*** ⟦< L *esse*, to be⟧ 1 the basic nature (of something) 2 *a)* a concentrated substance that keeps the flavor, etc. of that from which it is extracted *b)* perfume

Es·sene (es'ēn', e sēn') ***n.*** a member of an ancient Jewish ascetic sect (2d c. B.C. to the 2d c. A.D.)

es·sen·tial (e sen'shəl, i-, ə-) ***adj.*** 1 of or constituting the essence of something; basic 2 absolutely necessary; indispensable —***n.*** something necessary or fundamental —**es·sen'tial·ly** ***adv.***

-est (est, ist, əst) ⟦OE⟧ *suffix* forming the superlative degree *[greatest]*

est. 1 established 2 estimate 3 estimated

EST Eastern Standard Time

es·tab·lish (e stab'lish, i-) ***vt.*** ⟦< L *stabilis*, stable⟧ 1 to order, ordain, or enact (a law, etc.) permanently 2 to set up (a nation, business, etc.) 3 to cause to be; bring about 4 to set up in a business, etc. 5 to cause to be accepted 6 to prove; demonstrate

es·tab'lish·ment ***n.*** 1 an establishing or being established 2 a thing established, as a business —**the Establishment** an inner circle thought of as holding decisive power in a nation, institution, etc.

es·tate (e stāt', i-) ***n.*** ⟦< OFr *estat*⟧ 1 a condition or stage of life 2 property; possessions 3 a large, individually owned piece of land containing a residence

es·teem (e stēm', i-) ***vt.*** ⟦< L *aestimare*, to value⟧ 1 to value highly; respect 2 to consider —***n.*** favorable opinion

es·ter (es'tər) ***n.*** ⟦Ger < *essig*, vinegar + *äther*, ether⟧ an organic compound formed by the reaction of an acid and an alcohol

Es·ther (es'tər) *Bible* the Jewish wife of a Persian king: she saved her people from slaughter

es'thete' ***n.*** AESTHETE —**es·thet'ics** ***n.pl.***

es·ti·ma·ble (es'tə mə bəl) ***adj.*** worthy of esteem

es·ti·mate (es'tə māt'; *for n.,* -mit) ***vt.*** **-mat'ed, -mat'ing** ⟦see ESTEEM⟧ 1 to form an opinion about 2 to calculate approximately (size, cost, etc.) —***n.*** 1 a general calculation; esp., an approximate computation of probable cost 2 an opinion or judgment —**es'ti·ma'tor** ***n.***

es'ti·ma'tion ***n.*** 1 an estimate or judgment 2 esteem; regard

Es·to·ni·a (es tō'nē ə) republic (**Estonian Soviet Socialist Republic**) of the U.S.S.R., in NE Europe: 17,400 sq. mi.; pop. 1,500,000 —**Es·to'ni·an** ***adj., n.***

es·trange (e strānj', i-) ***vt.*** **-tranged', -trang'ing** ⟦< L *extraneus*, strange⟧ to turn (a person) from an affectionate attitude to an indifferent or unfriendly one —**es·trange'ment** ***n.***

es·tro·gen (es'trə jən) ***n.*** ⟦< Gr *oistros*, frenzy + -GEN⟧ any of several female sex hormones or synthetic compounds

es·trous cycle (es'trəs) the regular female reproductive cycle of most placental mammals

es·tu·ar·y (es'tyōō er'ē, -chōō-) ***n.***, *pl.* **-ies** ⟦< L *aestus*, the tide⟧ the wide mouth of a river into which the tide flows from the sea

-et (et, it, ət) ⟦< LL *-itus*⟧ *suffix* little *[islet]*

e·ta (āt'ə, ēt'ə) ***n.*** the seventh letter of the Greek alphabet (H, η)

é·ta·gère (ā tä zher') ***n.*** ⟦Fr⟧ a stand with open shelves, for displaying art objects, ornaments, etc.

et al. ⟦L *et alii*⟧ and others

et cet·er·a (et set'ər ə, se'trə) ⟦L⟧ and others; and the like: abbrev. **etc.**

etch (ech) ***vt.*** ⟦< MHG *ezzen*, eat⟧ to make (a drawing, design, etc.) on metal, glass, etc. by the action of an acid —**etch'er** ***n.***

etch'ing ***n.*** 1 the art of an etcher 2 a print made from an etched plate

e·ter·nal (ē tur'nəl, i-) ***adj.*** ⟦< L *aeturnus*⟧ 1 without beginning or end; everlasting 2 always the same; unchanging 3 seeming never to stop —**e·ter'nal·ly** ***adv.*** —**e·ter'nal·ness** ***n.***

e·ter·ni·ty (ē tur'nə tē, i-) ***n.***, *pl.* **-ties** 1 the state or fact of being eternal 2 infinite or endless time 3 a long period of time that seems endless 4 the endless time after death

eth·ane (eth'ān') ***n.*** ⟦< fol.⟧ an odorless, colorless, gaseous hydrocarbon, found in natural gas and used as a fuel

e·ther (ē'thər) ***n.*** ⟦< Gr *aithein*, to burn⟧ 1 an imaginary substance once thought to pervade space 2 the upper regions of space 3 a volatile, colorless, highly flammable liquid used as an anesthetic and solvent

e·the·re·al (ē thir'ē əl, i-) ***adj.*** 1 very light; airy; delicate 2 not earthly; heavenly; celestial —**e·the're·al·ly** ***adv.***

eth·ic (eth'ik) ***n.*** ⟦see fol.⟧ a system of moral standards

eth·i·cal (eth'i kəl) ***adj.*** ⟦< Gr *ēthos*, character⟧ 1 having to do with ethics; of or conforming to moral standards 2 conforming to professional standards of conduct —**eth'i·cal·ly** ***adv.***

eth·ics (eth'iks) ***n.pl.*** 1 [*with sing. v.*] the study of standards of conduct and moral judgment 2 the system of morals of a particular person, religion, group, etc.

E·thi·o·pi·a (ē'thē ō'pē ə) country in E Africa, on the Red Sea: 471,800 sq. mi.; pop. 43,882,000 —**E'thi·o'pi·an** ***adj., n.***

eth·nic (eth'nik) ***adj.*** ⟦< Gr *ethnos*, nation⟧ designating or of a group of people having common customs, characteristics, language, etc. —***n.*** a member of an ethnic group, esp. a minority or nationality group —**eth'ni·cal·ly** ***adv.***

eth·nic·i·ty (eth nis'ə tē) ***n.*** ethnic classification or affiliation

eth·nol·o·gy (eth näl'ə jē) ***n.*** ⟦< Gr *ethnos*,

nation + -LOGY ‖ the branch of anthropology that studies comparatively the cultures of contemporary, or recent, societies or language groups —**eth'no·log'i·cal** (-nō läj'i kəl, -nə-) ***adj.*** —**eth·nol'o·gist** ***n.***

e·thos (ē'thäs') ***n.*** ‖ Gr *ēthos*, character ‖ the characteristic attitudes, habits, etc. of an individual or group

eth·yl (eth'əl) ***n.*** ‖ < ETHER ‖ the hydrocarbon radical which forms the base of ethyl alcohol, ether, etc.

ethyl alcohol ALCOHOL (sense 1)

eth·yl·ene (eth'əl ēn') ***n.*** ‖ ETHYL + -ENE ‖ a colorless, flammable, gaseous hydrocarbon used to synthesize organic chemicals, esp. polyethylene

ethylene gly·col (glī'kôl') a colorless, viscous liquid used as an antifreeze, solvent, etc.

e·ti·ol·o·gy (ēt'ē äl'ə jē) ***n.***, *pl.* **-gies** ‖ < Gr *aitia*, cause + *logia*, description ‖ **1** the cause assigned, as for a disease **2** the science of causes or origins —**e'ti·o·log'ic** (-ə läj'ik) ***adj.***

et·i·quette (et'i kit, -ket') ***n.*** ‖ Fr *étiquette*, lit., ticket ‖ the forms, manners, etc. conventionally acceptable or required in society, a profession, etc.

Et·na (et'nə) volcanic mountain in E Sicily

E·to·bi·coke (i tō'bi kook') city within metropolitan Toronto, Canada: pop. 299,000

E·trus·can (ē trus'kən, i-) ***adj.*** of an ancient country (*Etruria*) in what is now central Italy

et seq. ‖ L *et sequens* ‖ and the following

-ette (et) ‖ Fr: see -ET ‖ *suffix* **1** little [*statuette*] **2** female [*majorette*]

é·tude (ā'tood') ***n.*** ‖ Fr, study ‖ a musical composition for a solo instrument, designed to give practice in some point of technique

et·y·mol·o·gy (et'ə mäl'ə jē) ***n.***, *pl.* **-gies** ‖ < Gr *etymos*, true + *logos*, word ‖ **1** the origin and development of a word **2** the scientific study of word origins —**et'y·mo·log'i·cal** (-mə läj'i kəl) ***adj.*** —**et'y·mol'o·gist** ***n.***

eu- ‖ Fr < Gr ‖ *prefix* good, well [*eulogy, euphony*]

eu·ca·lyp·tus (yōō'kə lip'təs) ***n.***, *pl.* **-tus·es** or **-ti'** (-tī') ‖ < Gr *eu-*, well + *kalyptos*, covered ‖ a tall, aromatic, chiefly Australian evergreen tree of the myrtle family

Eu·cha·rist (yōō'kə rist) ***n.*** ‖ < Gr *eucharistia*, gratitude ‖ **1** HOLY COMMUNION **2** the consecrated bread and wine used in this —**Eu'cha·ris'tic** ***adj.***

eu·chre (yōō'kər) ***n.*** ‖ < ? ‖ a card game played with thirty-two cards

Eu·clid (yōō'klid) 4th c. B.C.; Gr. mathematician: author of a basic work in geometry —**Eu·clid'e·an** (-ē ən) or **Eu·clid'i·an** ***adj.***

Eu·gene (yōō jēn') city in W Oreg.: pop. 106,000

eu·gen·ics (yōō jen'iks) ***n.pl.*** ‖ see EU- & GENESIS ‖ [*with sing. v.*] the movement devoted to improving the human species by controlling heredity —**eu·gen'ic** ***adj.*** —**eu·gen'i·cal·ly** ***adv.*** —**eu·gen'i·cist** (-ə sist) ***n.***

eu·lo·gize (yōō'lə jīz') ***vt.*** **-gized'**, **-giz'ing** ‖ see fol. ‖ to praise highly —**eu'lo·gist** or **eu'lo·giz'er** ***n.***

eu'lo·gy (-jē) ***n.***, *pl.* **-gies** ‖ < Gr *eulegein*, speak well of ‖ **1** speech or writing praising a person or thing; esp., a funeral oration **2** high praise —**eu'lo·gis'tic** (-jis'tik) ***adj.***

eu·nuch (yōō'nək, nuk') ***n.*** ‖ < Gr *eunē*, bed + *echein*, have ‖ a castrated man

eu·phe·mism (yōō'fə miz'əm) ***n.*** ‖ < Gr *eu-*, good + *phēmē*, voice ‖ **1** the use of a less direct word or phrase for one considered offensive **2** a word or phrase so substituted —**eu'phe·mis'tic** ***adj.*** —**eu'phe·mis'ti·cal·ly** ***adv.***

eu·pho·ni·ous (yōō fō'nē əs) ***adj.*** having a pleasant sound; harmonious —**eu·pho'ni·ous·ly** ***adv.***

eu·pho·ny (yōō'fə nē) ***n.***, *pl.* **-nies** ‖ < Gr *eu-*, well + *phōnē*, voice ‖ a pleasant combination of agreeable sounds, as in speech

eu·pho·ri·a (yōō fôr'ē ə) ***n.*** ‖ < Gr *eu-*, well + *pherein*, to bear ‖ a feeling of well-being —**eu·phor'ic** ***adj.***

Eu·phra·tes (yoo frāt'ēz) river flowing from central Turkey through Syria & Iraq into the Persian Gulf: cf. TIGRIS

Eur·a·sia (yoo rā'zhə) land mass made up of Europe & Asia

Eur·a'sian (-zhən) ***adj.*** **1** of Eurasia **2** of mixed European and Asian descent —***n.*** a person of Eurasian descent

eu·re·ka (yōō rē'kə) ***interj.*** ‖ < Gr *heurēka*, I have found (it) ‖ an exclamation of triumphant achievement

Eu·rip·i·des (yoo rip'ə dēz') 480-406 B.C.; Gr. writer of tragedies

Eu·rope (yoor'əp) continent between Asia & the Atlantic: *c.* 4,000,000 sq. mi.; pop. *c.* 688,000,000 —**Eu·ro·pe·an** (yoor'ə pē'ən) ***adj., n.***

European Community an organization of European countries to bring about the political and economic unification of western Europe

European plan a system of hotel operation in which guests are charged for rooms, and pay for meals separately

eu·ryth·mics (yōō rith'miks) ***n.pl.*** ‖ < Gr *eu-*, well + *rhythmos*, rhythm ‖ [*with sing. v.*] the art of performing bodily movements in rhythm, usually to music

eu·sta·chi·an tube (yōō stā'kē ən, -stā'shən) ‖ after B. *Eustachio*, 16th-c. It anatomist ‖ [*also* **E- t-**] a slender tube between the middle ear and the pharynx

eu·tha·na·si·a (yōō'thə nā'zhə) ***n.*** ‖ < Gr *eu-*, well + *thanatos*, death ‖ act of causing death painlessly, so as to end suffering

eu·than·ize (yōō'thə nīz') ***vt.*** **-ized'**, **-iz'ing** to put to death by euthanasia

eu·then·ics (yōō then'iks) ***n.pl.*** ‖ < Gr *euthēnein*, to flourish ‖ [*with sing. v.*] the science of improving the human species by controlling the environment

e·vac·u·ate (ē vak'yōō āt') ***vt.*** **-at'ed, -at'ing** ‖ < L *e-*, out + *vacuus*, empty ‖ **1** to make empty **2** to discharge (bodily waste, esp. feces) **3** to withdraw from; remove —***vi.*** to withdraw —**e·vac'u·a'tion** ***n.*** —**e·vac'u·ee'** (-ē') ***n.***

e·vade (ē vād') ***vi., vt.*** **e·vad'ed, e·vad'ing** ‖ < L *e-*, out, from + *vadere*, go ‖ **1** to avoid or escape (from) by deceit or cleverness **2** to avoid doing or answering directly —**e·vad'er** ***n.***

e·val·u·ate (ē val'yōō āt') ***vt.*** **-at'ed, -at'ing** ‖ ult. < L *ex-*, out + *valere*, be worth ‖ **1** to find the value or amount of 2 to judge the worth of —**e·val′u·a′tion** *n.*

ev·a·nes·cent (ev′ə nes′ənt) ***adj.*** ‖< L *e-*, out + *vanescere*, vanish‖ tending to fade from sight; fleeting; ephemeral —**ev′a·nes′-cence** ***n.***

e·van·gel·i·cal (ē′van jel′i kəl, ev′ən-) ***adj.*** ‖< Gr *euangelos*, bringing good news‖ 1 of or according to the Gospels or the New Testament 2 of those Protestant churches that emphasize salvation by faith in Jesus

e·van·ge·list (ē van′jə list) ***n.*** 1 [E-] any of the four writers of the Gospels 2 a revivalist or a preacher who holds large public services in various cities, now often televised —**e·van′ge·lism′** ***n.***

e·van′ge·lize′ (-līz′) ***vt.*** **-lized′**, **-liz′ing** to convert to Christianity —***vi.*** to preach the gospel

Ev·ans·ville (ev′ənz vil′) city in SW Ind.: pop. 130,000

e·vap·o·rate (ē vap′ə rāt′) ***vt.*** **-rat′ed**, **-rat′-ing** ‖< L *e-*, out, from + *vaporare*, emit vapor‖ 1 to change (a liquid or solid) into vapor 2 to remove moisture from (milk, etc.), as by heating, so as to get a concentrated product —***vi.*** 1 to become vapor 2 to give off vapor 3 to vanish —**e·vap′o·ra′-tion** ***n.*** —**e·vap′o·ra′tor** ***n.***

e·va·sion (ē vā′zhən) ***n.*** 1 an evading; specif., an avoiding of a duty, question, etc. by deceit or cleverness 2 a way of doing this; subterfuge

e·va′sive (-siv) ***adj.*** 1 tending or seeking to evade; tricky 2 elusive —**e·va′sive·ly** ***adv.*** —**e·va′sive·ness** ***n.***

eve (ēv) ***n.*** ‖< OE *æfen*, evening‖ 1 [Old Poet.] evening 2 [*often* E-] the evening or day before a holiday 3 the period just prior to some event

Eve (ēv) *Bible* the first woman, Adam's wife

e·ven (ē′vən) ***adj.*** ‖OE *efne*‖ 1 flat; level; smooth 2 not varying; constant /an *even* tempo/ 3 calm; tranquil /an *even* temper/ 4 in the same plane or line /*even* with the rim/ 5 owing and being owed nothing 6 equal in number, quantity, etc. 7 exactly divisible by two 8 exact /an *even* mile/ —***adv.*** 1 however improbable; indeed 2 exactly; just /it happened *even* as I expected/ 3 still; yet /he's *even* better/ —***vt.***, ***vi.*** to make or become even —**even if** though —**e′ven·ly** ***adv.*** —**e′ven·ness** ***n.***

e′ven·hand′ed ***adj.*** impartial; fair

eve·ning (ēv′niŋ) ***n.*** ‖< OE *æfnung*‖ 1 the last part of the day and early part of night 2 [Dial.] afternoon

even money equal stakes in betting, with no odds

e·vent (ē vent′) ***n.*** ‖< L *e-*, out + *venire*, come‖ 1 an occurrence, esp. when important 2 [Archaic] an outcome 3 a particular contest in a program of sports —**in any event** anyhow —**in the event of** in case of —**in the event that** if it should happen that

e′ven-tem′pered ***adj.*** not quickly angered; calm

e·vent′ful ***adj.*** 1 full of outstanding events 2 having an important outcome —**e·vent′-ful·ly** ***adv.*** —**e·vent′ful·ness** ***n.***

e·ven·tide (ē′vən tīd′) ***n.*** [Archaic] evening

e·ven·tu·al (ē ven′cho͞o əl) ***adj.*** ultimate; final —**e·ven′tu·al·ly** ***adv.***

e·ven′tu·al′i·ty (-al′ə tē) ***n.***, *pl.* **-ties** a possible event or outcome

e·ven′tu·ate′ (-āt′) ***vi.*** **-at′ed**, **-at′ing** to happen in the end; result

ev·er (ev′ər) ***adv.*** ‖< OE *æfre*‖ 1 always /*ever* the same/ 2 at any time /do you *ever* see her?/ 3 at all; by any chance /how can I *ever* repay you?/ —**ever so** [Colloq.] very

Ev·er·est (ev′ər ist, ev′rist), **Mount** peak of the Himalayas: highest known mountain in the world: 29,028 ft.

ev′er·glade′ (-glād′) ***n.*** marshy land

ev′er·green′ ***adj.*** having green leaves all year long, as most conifers —***n.*** an evergreen plant or tree

ev′er·last′ing ***adj.*** lasting forever; eternal —***n.*** eternity

ev′er·more′ ***adv.*** [Archaic] forever; constantly

ev·er·y (ev′rē) ***adj.*** ‖OE *æfre ælc*, lit., ever each‖ 1 each, individually and separately 2 the greatest possible /to make *every* effort/ 3 each interval /take a pill *every* three hours/ —**every now and then** occasionally: also [Colloq.] **every so often** —**every other** each alternate, as the first, third, fifth, etc. —**every which way** [Colloq.] in complete disorder

ev′er·y·bod′y (-bäd′ē, -bud′ē) ***pron.*** every person; everyone

ev′er·y·day′ ***adj.*** 1 daily 2 suitable for ordinary days /*everyday* shoes/ 3 usual; common

ev′er·y·one′ ***pron.*** every person

every one every person or thing of those named /*every one* of the boys/

ev′er·y·thing′ ***pron.*** every thing; all

ev′er·y·where′ ***adv.*** in or to every place

e·vict (ē vikt′) ***vt.*** ‖< L *e-*, intens. + *vincere*, conquer‖ to remove (a tenant) by legal procedure —**e·vic′tion** ***n.***

ev·i·dence (ev′ə dəns; *also, esp. for v.*, -dens′) ***n.*** 1 something that makes another thing evident; sign 2 a statement of a witness, an object, etc. bearing on or establishing the point in question in a court of law —***vt.*** **-denced**, **-denc·ing** to make evident —**in evidence** plainly seen

ev·i·dent (ev′ə dənt) ***adj.*** ‖< L *e-*, from + *videre*, see‖ easy to see or perceive; clear —**ev′i·dent·ly** ***adv.***

e·vil (ē′vəl) ***adj.*** ‖OE *yfel*‖ 1 morally bad or wrong; wicked 2 harmful; injurious 3 unlucky; disastrous —***n.*** 1 wickedness; sin 2 anything that causes harm, pain, etc. —**e′vil·ly** ***adv.***

e′vil·do′er (-do͞o′ər) ***n.*** one who does evil —**e′vil·do′ing** ***n.***

e·vince (ē vins′) ***vt.*** **e·vinced′**, **e·vinc′ing** ‖< L *e-*, intens. + *vincere*, conquer‖ to show plainly; make clear

e·vis·cer·ate (ē vis′ər āt′) ***vt.*** **-at′ed**, **-at′ing** ‖< L *e-*, out + *viscera*, viscera‖ 1 to remove the entrails from 2 to deprive of an essential part —**e·vis′cer·a′tion** ***n.***

e·voke (ē vōk′) ***vt.*** **e·voked′**, **e·vok′ing** ‖< L *e-*, out, from + *vox*, voice‖ 1 to call forth 2 to elicit (a reaction, etc.) —**ev·o·ca·tion** (ev′ə kā′shən, ē′vō-) ***n.***

ev·o·lu·tion (ev′ə lo͞o′shən) ***n.*** ‖see fol.‖ 1 an unfolding; process of development or change 2 a thing evolved 3 a movement that is part of a series 4 *Biol.* *a)* the development of a species, organism, etc. from its original to its present state *b)* the theory that all species developed from earlier forms —**ev'o·lu'tion·ar'y** *adj.* —**ev'o·lu'tion·ist** *n.*

e·volve (ē välv', ·vôlv') *vt., vi.* **e·volved', e·volv'ing** ‖ < L *e-*, out + *volvere*, to roll ‖ 1 to develop gradually; unfold 2 to develop by evolution

ewe (yo͞o) *n.* ‖ OE *eowu* ‖ a female sheep

ew·er (yo͞o'ər) *n.* ‖ < L *aqua*, water ‖ a large, wide-mouthed water pitcher

ex- ‖ < OFr or L ‖ *prefix* 1 *a)* from, out */expel/* *b)* beyond *c)* thoroughly *d)* upward 2 former, previous */ex-president/*

ex. 1 example 2 exchange

ex·ac·er·bate (eg zas'ər bāt') *vt.* **-bat'ed, -bat'ing** ‖ < L *ex-*, intens. + *acerbus*, bitter ‖ 1 to aggravate (pain, annoyance, etc.) 2 to exasperate; irritate —**ex·ac'er·ba'tion** *n.*

ex·act (eg zakt') *adj.* ‖ < L *ex-*, out + *agere*, to do ‖ 1 characterized by or requiring accuracy; methodical; correct 2 without variation; precise —*vt.* 1 to extort 2 to demand; require —**ex·act'ly** *adv.* —**ex·act'ness** *n.*

ex·act'ing *adj.* 1 making severe demands; strict 2 demanding great care, effort, etc.; arduous —**ex·act'ing·ly** *adv.*

ex·ac·tion (eg zak'shən) *n.* 1 an exacting 2 an extortion 3 an exacted fee, tax, etc.

ex·ac'ti·tude' (-tə to͞od') *n.* ‖ Fr ‖ the quality of being exact; accuracy

ex·ag·ger·ate (eg zaj'ər āt') *vt., vi.* **-at'ed, -at'ing** ‖ < L *ex-*, out + *agger*, a heap ‖ to think or tell of (something) as greater than it is; overstate —**ex·ag'ger·a'tion** *n.* —**ex·ag'ger·a'tive** *adj.* —**ex·ag'ger·a'tor** *n.*

ex·alt (eg zôlt') *vt.* ‖ < L *ex-*, up + *altus*, high ‖ 1 to raise in status, dignity, etc. 2 to praise; glorify 3 to fill with joy, pride, etc.; elate —**ex·al·ta·tion** (eg'zôl tā'shən) *n.*

ex·am·i·na·tion (eg zam'ə nā'shən) *n.* 1 an examining or being examined 2 a set of questions asked in testing: also [Colloq.] **exam'**

ex·am·ine (eg zam'ən) *vt.* **-ined, -in·ing** ‖ < L *examinare*, weigh ‖ 1 to look at critically or methodically; investigate; inspect 2 to test by questioning —**ex·am'in·er** *n.*

ex·am·ple (eg zam'pəl) *n.* ‖ < L *eximere*, take out ‖ 1 something selected to show the character of the rest; sample 2 a case that serves as a warning 3 a model; pattern 4 an instance that illustrates a principle

ex·as·per·ate (eg zas'pər āt') *vt.* **-at'ed, -at'ing** ‖ < L *ex-*, out + *asper*, rough ‖ to irritate; anger; vex —**ex·as'per·a'tion** *n.*

ex·ca·vate (eks'kə vāt') *vt.* **-vat'ed, -vat'ing** ‖ < L *ex-*, out + *cavus*, hollow ‖ 1 to make a hole or cavity in 2 to form (a tunnel, etc.) by hollowing out 3 to unearth 4 to dig out (earth, soil, etc.) —**ex'ca·va'tion** *n.* —**ex'ca·va'tor** *n.*

ex·ceed (ek sēd') *vt.* ‖ < L *ex-*, out + *cedere*, to go ‖ 1 to go or be beyond (a limit, etc.) 2 to surpass

ex·ceed'ing (-iŋ) *adj.* surpassing; extreme —**ex·ceed'ing·ly** *adv.*

ex·cel (ek sel') *vi., vt.* **-celled', -cel'ling** ‖ < L *ex*, out of + *-cellere*, to rise ‖ to be better or greater than (another or others)

ex·cel·lence (ek'sə ləns) *n.* 1 the fact or state of excelling; superiority 2 a particular virtue

ex'cel·len·cy (-lən sē) *n., pl.* **-cies** 1 [E-] a title of honor for certain dignitaries 2 EXCELLENCE

ex·cel·lent (ek'sə lənt) *adj.* ‖ see EXCEL ‖ outstandingly good of its kind; of exceptional merit —**ex'cel·lent·ly** *adv.*

ex·cel·si·or (eks sel'sē ôr'; *for n.* ek sel'sē ər) *interj.* ‖ see EXCEL ‖ always upward! —*n.* long, thin wood shavings used for packing

ex·cept (ek sept') *vt.* ‖ < L *ex-*, out + *capere*, to take ‖ to leave out or take out; exclude —*prep.* leaving out; but —*conj.* [Colloq.] were it not that; only —**except for** if it were not for

ex·cept'ing *prep., conj.* EXCEPT

ex·cep'tion *n.* 1 an excepting 2 *a)* a case to which a rule does not apply *b)* a person or thing different from others of the same class 3 an objection —**take exception** to object

ex·cep'tion·a·ble *adj.* liable to exception; open to objection

ex·cep'tion·al *adj.* 1 unusual; esp., unusually good 2 needing special education, as because mentally handicapped —**ex·cep'tion·al·ly** *adv.*

ex·cerpt (ek surpt'; *for n.* ek'surpt') *vt.* ‖ < L *ex-*, out + *carpere*, to pick ‖ to select or quote (passages from a book, etc.); extract —*n.* a passage selected or quoted; extract

ex·cess (ek ses'; *also, esp. for adj.*, ek'ses') *n.* ‖ see EXCEED ‖ 1 action that goes beyond a reasonable limit 2 an amount greater than is necessary 3 the amount by which one thing exceeds another; surplus —*adj.* extra; surplus —**in excess of** more than

ex·ces'sive *adj.* being too much; immoderate —**ex·ces'sive·ly** *adv.*

ex·change (eks chānj') *vt., vi.* **-changed', -chang'ing** ‖ see EX- & CHANGE ‖ 1 to give or receive (something) *for* another thing; barter; trade 2 to interchange (similar things) —*n.* 1 an exchanging; interchange 2 a thing exchanged 3 a place for exchanging */a stock exchange/* 4 a central office providing telephone service 5 the value of one currency in terms of another —**ex·change'a·ble** *adj.*

exchange rate the rate at which one currency can be exchanged for another

ex·cheq·uer (eks chek'ər, eks'chek'·) *n.* ‖ ME *escheker*, lit., chessboard < OFr *eschekier*: accounts of revenue were kept on a squared board ‖ 1 a national treasury 2 funds; finances

ex·cise[1] (ek'sīz', ·sīs') *n.* ‖ ult. < L *assidere*, assist (in office) ‖ a tax on various commodities, as liquor, etc., within a country Also **excise tax**

ex·cise[2] (ek sīz') *vt.* **-cised', -cis'ing** ‖ < L *ex-*, out + *caedere*, to cut ‖ to remove by cutting out —**ex·ci'sion** (-sizh'ən) *n.*

ex·cit·a·ble (ek sīt'ə bəl) *adj.* easily excited —**ex·cit'a·bil'i·ty** *n.*

ex·cite (ek sīt') *vt.* **-cit'ed, -cit'ing** ‖ < L *ex-*, out + *ciere*, to call ‖ 1 to make active; stir up **2** to arouse; provoke **3** to arouse the feelings of —**ex·ci·ta·tion** (ek'si tā'shən) ***n.*** —**ex·cit'ed·ly** ***adv.*** —**ex·cit'er** ***n.***

ex·cite'ment ***n.*** **1** an exciting or being excited; agitation **2** that which excites

ex·cit'ing ***adj.*** causing excitement; stirring, thrilling, etc.

ex·claim (ek sklām') ***vi., vt.*** ‖ < L *ex-*, out + *clamare*, to shout ‖ to cry out; say suddenly and vehemently

ex·cla·ma·tion (ek'sklə mā'shən) ***n.*** **1** an exclaiming **2** something exclaimed; inter jection —**ex·clam·a·to·ry** (ek sklam'ə tôr'ē) ***adj.***

exclamation point (or **mark**) a mark (!) used in punctuating to show surprise, strong emotion, etc.

ex·clude (eks klo͞od') ***vt.*** **-clud'ed, -clud'ing** ‖ < L *ex-*, out + *claudere*, to close ‖ **1** to refuse to admit, consider, etc.; reject **2** to put or force out —**ex·clu'sion** (klo͞o'zhən) ***n.***

ex·clu'sive (klo͞o'siv) ***adj.*** **1** excluding all others **2** not shared or divided; sole /an *exclusive* right/ **3** excluding certain people, as for social or economic reasons —**exclusive of** not including —**ex·clu'sive·ly** ***adv.*** —**ex·clu'sive·ness** ***n.***

ex·com·mu·ni·cate (eks'kə myo͞o'ni kāt') ***vt.*** **-cat'ed, -cat'ing** to exclude from com munion with a church —**ex'com·mu'ni·ca'tion** ***n.***

ex·co·ri·ate (eks kôr'ē āt') ***vt.*** **-at'ed, -at'ing** ‖ < L *ex-*, off + *corium*, the skin ‖ to denounce harshly —**ex·co'ri·a'tion** ***n.***

ex·cre·ment (eks'krə mənt) ***n.*** waste matter excreted from the bowels

ex·cres·cence (eks kres'əns) ***n.*** ‖ < L *ex-*, out + *crescere*, grow ‖ an abnormal out growth or addition

ex·cre·ta (eks krēt'ə) ***n.pl.*** waste matter excreted from the body

ex·crete (eks krēt') ***vt., vi.*** **-cret'ed, -cret'ing** ‖ < L *ex-*, out of + *cernere*, sift ‖ to eliminate (waste matter) from the body —**ex·cre'tion** ***n.*** —**ex·cre·to·ry** (eks'krə tôr' ē) ***adj.***

ex·cru·ci·at·ing (eks kro͞o'shē āt'iŋ) ***adj.*** **1** intensely painful; agonizing **2** intense or extreme

ex·cul·pate (eks'kul'pāt') ***vt.*** **-pat'ed, -pat'ing** ‖ < L *ex*, out + *culpa*, fault ‖ to free from blame; prove guiltless —**ex'cul·pa'tion** ***n.***

ex·cur·sion (eks kʉr'zhən) ***n.*** ‖ < L *ex-*, out + *currere*, to run ‖ **1** a short trip, as for pleasure **2** a round trip at reduced rates **3** a digression —***adj.*** for an excursion —**ex·cur'sion·ist** (-ist) ***n.***

ex·cur·sive (eks kʉr'siv) ***adj.*** rambling; digressive —**ex·cur'sive·ly** ***adv.*** —**ex·cur'sive·ness** ***n.***

ex·cuse (ek skyo͞oz'; *for n.*, -skyo͞os') ***vt.*** **-cused', -cus'ing** ‖ < L *ex-*, from + *causa*, a charge ‖ **1** to apologize or give reasons for **2** to overlook (an offense or fault) **3** to release from an obligation, etc. **4** to permit to leave **5** to justify —***n.*** **1** a defense of some action; apology **2** something that excuses **3** a pretext —**excuse oneself** **1** to apologize **2** to ask for permission to leave —**ex·cus'a·ble** ***adj.***

ex·e·cra·ble (ek'si krə bəl) ***adj.*** ‖ see fol. ‖ **1** detestable **2** very inferior

ex'e·crate' (krāt') ***vt.*** **-crat'ed, -crat'ing** ‖ < L *execrare*, to curse ‖ **1** to denounce scathingly **2** to loathe; abhor —**ex'e·cra'tion** ***n.***

ex·e·cute (ek'si kyo͞ot') ***vt.*** **-cut'ed, -cut'ing** ‖ see EXECUTOR ‖ **1** to carry out; do **2** to administer (laws, etc.) **3** to put to death by a legal sentence **4** to create in accordance with a plan, etc. **5** to make valid (a deed, will, etc.)

ex'e·cu'tion ***n.*** **1** an executing; specif., *a)* a carrying out, performing, etc. *b)* a putting to death by a legal sentence **2** the manner of performing

ex'e·cu'tion·er ***n.*** one who carries out a court imposed death penalty

ex·ec·u·tive (eg zek'yo͞o tiv) ***adj.*** ‖ see fol. ‖ **1** of or capable of carrying out duties, func tions, etc. **2** empowered to administer (laws, government affairs, etc.) —***n.*** **1** the branch of government administering the laws and affairs of a nation **2** one who administers or manages affairs

ex·ec·u·tor (eg zek'yo͞o tər) ***n.*** ‖ < L *ex-*, intens. + *sequi*, to follow ‖ a person appointed to carry out the provisions of a will

ex·e·ge·sis (ek'sə jē'sis) ***n.***, *pl.* **-ge'ses'** (-sēz') ‖ < Gr *ex-*, out + *hēgeisthai*, to lead ‖ inter pretation of a word, passage, etc., esp. in the Bible

ex·em·plar (eg zem'plər, -plär') ***n.*** ‖ < L *exemplum*, a pattern ‖ **1** a model; pattern **2** a typical specimen

ex·em·pla·ry (eg zem'plə rē) ***adj.*** ‖ < L *exemplum*, a pattern ‖ serving as a model or example /an *exemplary* life/

ex·em·pli·fy (eg zem'plə fī') ***vt.*** **-fied', -fy'ing** ‖ < L *exemplum*, example + *facere*, to make ‖ to show by example —**ex·em'pli·fi·ca'tion** ***n.***

ex·empt (eg zempt') ***vt.*** ‖ < L *ex-*, out + *emere*, to buy ‖ to free from a rule or obliga tion which applies to others —***adj.*** freed from a usual rule, duty, etc. —**ex·emp'tion** ***n.***

ex·er·cise (ek'sər sīz') ***n.*** ‖ < L *exercere*, put to work ‖ **1** active use or operation **2** per formance (of duties, etc.) **3** activity for developing the body or mind **4** a task to be practiced for developing some skill **5** [*pl.*] a program of speeches, etc. —***vt.*** **-cised', -cis'ing** **1** to put into action; use **2** to put into use so as to develop or train **3** to exert (influence, etc.) **4** to worry; disturb —***vi.*** to do exercises

ex·ert (eg zʉrt') ***vt.*** ‖ < L *exserere*, stretch out ‖ **1** to put into action **2** to apply (one self) with great effort

ex·er'tion ***n.*** **1** the act, fact, or process of exerting **2** effort

ex·hale (eks hāl') ***vt., vi.*** **-haled', -hal'ing** ‖ < L *ex-*, out + *halare*, breathe ‖ **1** to breathe forth (air) **2** to give off (vapor, etc.) —**ex·ha·la·tion** (eks'hə lā'shən) ***n.***

ex·haust (eg zôst') ***vt.*** ‖ < L *ex-*, out + *haurire*, to draw ‖ **1** to use up **2** to empty completely; drain **3** to tire out **4** to deal with thoroughly —***n.*** **1** the discharge of used steam, gas, etc. from an engine **2** the pipes through which it is released 3 fumes, etc. given off —**ex·haust′i·ble** *adj.*

ex·haus·tion (eg zôs′chən) *n.* 1 an exhausting 2 great fatigue

ex·haus′tive *adj.* leaving nothing out

ex·hib·it (eg zib′it) *vt.* ‖< L *ex-*, out + *habere*, to hold‖ 1 to show; display 2 to present to public view —*vi.* to put art objects, etc. on public display —*n.* 1 a display 2 a thing exhibited 3 *Law* an object produced as evidence in a court —**ex·hib′i·tor** *n.*

ex·hi·bi·tion (ek′sə bish′ən) *n.* 1 an exhibiting 2 that which is exhibited 3 a public showing, as of art

ex′hi·bi′tion·ism′ *n.* 1 a tendency to call attention to oneself or show off 2 a tendency to expose oneself sexually —**ex′hi·bi′tion·ist** *n.*

ex·hil·a·rate (eg zil′ə rāt′) *vt.* **-rat′ed, -rat′ing** ‖< L *ex-*, intens. + *hilaris*, glad‖ 1 to make cheerful or lively 2 to stimulate —**ex·hil′a·ra′tion** *n.* —**ex·hil′a·ra′tive** *adj.*

ex·hort (eg zôrt′) *vt., vi.* ‖< L *ex-*, out + *hortari*, to urge‖ to urge earnestly; advise strongly —**ex·hor·ta·tion** (eg′zôr tā′shən, ek′sər-) *n.*

ex·hume (eks hyo͞om′, eg zyo͞om′) *vt.* **-humed′, -hum′ing** ‖< L *ex-*, out + *humus*, the ground‖ to dig out of the earth; disinter —**ex·hu·ma·tion** (eks′hyo͞o mā′shən) *n.*

ex·i·gen·cy (eks′ə jən sē) *n., pl.* **-cies** ‖< L *exigere*, drive out‖ 1 urgency 2 a situation calling for immediate attention 3 [*pl.*] pressing needs —**ex′i·gent** *adj.*

ex·ig·u·ous (eg zig′yo͞o əs) *adj.* ‖see prec.‖ scanty; meager

ex·ile (eks′īl′, eg′zīl′) *n.* ‖< L *exul*, an exile‖ 1 a prolonged living away from one's country, usually enforced 2 a person in exile —*vt.* **-iled′, -il′ing** to force (a person) into exile; banish

ex·ist (eg zist′) *vi.* ‖< L *ex-*, out + *sistere*, to set, place‖ 1 to have reality or being; be 2 to occur or be present 3 to continue being; live

ex·ist′ence *n.* 1 the act or fact of being 2 life; living 3 occurrence —**ex·ist′ent** *adj.*

ex·is·ten·tial (eg′zis ten′shəl) *adj.* 1 of existence 2 of existentialism

ex′is·ten′tial·ism′ *n.* a philosophical movement stressing individual existence and holding that human beings are totally free and responsible for their acts —**ex′is·ten′tial·ist** *adj., n.*

ex·it (eks′it, eg′zit) *n.* ‖< L *ex-*, out + *ire*, to go‖ 1 an actor's departure from the stage 2 a going out; departure 3 a way out —*vi.* to leave a place

exo- ‖< Gr *exō*‖ *prefix* outside, outer, outer part

ex·o·bi·ol·o·gy (eks′ō bī äl′ə jē) *n.* the branch of biology investigating the possibility of extraterrestrial life

ex·o·dus (eks′ə dəs) *n.* ‖< Gr *ex-*, out + *hodos*, way‖ a going out or forth —[E-] 1 the departure of the Israelites from Egypt: with *the* 2 the second book of the Bible, describing this

ex of·fi·ci·o (eks′ ə fish′ē ō′, -ē ō′) ‖L, lit., from office‖ by virtue of one's position

ex·on·er·ate (eg zän′ər āt′) *vt.* **-at′ed, -at′ing** ‖< L *ex-*, out + *onerare*, to load‖ to declare or prove blameless —**ex·on′er·a′tion** *n.*

ex·or·bi·tant (eg zôr′bi tənt) *adj.* ‖< L *ex-*, out + *orbita*, a track‖ going beyond what is reasonable, just, etc.; excessive —**ex·or′bi·tance** *n.*

ex·or·cise or **ex·or·cize** (eks′ôr sīz′) *vt.* **-cised′** or **-cized′**, **-cis′ing** or **-ciz′ing** ‖< Gr *ex-*, out + *horkos*, an oath‖ 1 to drive (an evil spirit) out or away by ritual prayers, etc. 2 to free from such a spirit —**ex′or·cism′** (-siz′əm) *n.* —**ex′or·cist** *n.*

ex·o·skel·e·ton (eks′ō skel′ə tən) *n.* any hard, external supporting structure, as the shell of an oyster

ex′o·ther′mic (-thur′mik) *adj.* of a chemical change in which there is a liberation of heat

ex·ot·ic (eg zät′ik) *adj.* ‖< Gr *exō*, outside‖ 1 foreign 2 strangely beautiful, enticing, etc.

exp. experience(d)

ex·pand (ek spand′) *vt., vi.* ‖< L *ex-*, out + *pandere*, to spread‖ 1 to spread out; unfold 2 to increase in size, scope, etc.; enlarge; develop

ex·panse (ek spans′) *n.* a large area or unbroken surface; wide extent

ex·pan′si·ble *adj.* that can be expanded Also **ex·pand′a·ble**

ex·pan′sion *n.* 1 an expanding or being expanded; enlargement 2 an expanded thing or part 3 the degree or extent of expansion

expansion bolt a bolt with an attachment that expands in use to act as a wedge

ex·pan′sive *adj.* 1 that can expand 2 broad; extensive 3 effusive; demonstrative —**ex·pan′sive·ly** *adv.*

ex·pa·ti·ate (eks pā′shē āt′) *vi.* **-at′ed, -at′ing** ‖< L *ex(s)patiari*, wander‖ to speak or write at length (*on* or *upon*) —**ex·pa′ti·a′tion** *n.*

ex·pa·tri·ate (eks pā′trē āt′; *for n.*, -it) *vt., vi.* **-at′ed, -at′ing** ‖< L *ex*, out of + *patria*, fatherland‖ to exile (a person or oneself) —*n.* an expatriated person —**ex·pa′tri·a′tion** *n.*

ex·pect (ek spekt′) *vt.* ‖< L *ex-*, out + *spectare*, to look‖ 1 to look for as likely to occur or appear 2 to look for as proper or necessary 3 [Colloq.] to suppose; guess —**be expecting** [Colloq.] to be pregnant

ex·pect′an·cy *n., pl.* **-cies** 1 EXPECTATION 2 that which is expected, esp. on a statistical basis

ex·pect′ant *adj.* that expects; expecting —**ex·pect′ant·ly** *adv.*

ex·pec·ta·tion (ek′spek tā′shən) *n.* 1 an expecting; anticipation 2 a thing looked forward to 3 [*also pl.*] a reason for expecting something

ex·pec·to·rant (ek spek′tə rənt) *n.* ‖see fol.‖ a medicine that helps to bring up phlegm

ex·pec′to·rate′ (-tə rāt′) *vt., vi.* **-rat′ed, -rat′ing** ‖< L *ex-*, out + *pectus*, breast‖ to spit —**ex·pec′to·ra′tion** *n.*

ex·pe·di·en·cy (ek spē′dē ən sē) *n., pl.* **-cies** 1 a being expedient; suitability for a given purpose 2 the doing of what is selfish rather than of what is right or just; self-interest **3** an expedient Also **ex·pe′di·ence**

ex·pe′di·ent *adj.* ‖ see fol. ‖ **1** useful for effecting a desired result; convenient **2** based on or guided by self-interest —*n.* an expedient thing; means to an end

ex·pe·dite (eks′pə dit′) *vt.* **-dit′ed, -dit′ing** ‖ < L *expedire*, lit., to free the foot ‖ **1** to speed up the progress of; facilitate **2** to do quickly

ex′pe·dit′er *n.* one employed to expedite urgent or involved projects

ex·pe·di·tion (eks′pə dish′ən) *n.* ‖ see EXPEDITE ‖ **1** *a)* a voyage, march, etc., as for exploration or battle *b)* those on such a journey **2** efficient speed —**ex′pe·di′tion·ar′y** *adj.*

ex′pe·di′tious (-dish′əs) *adj.* efficient and speedy; prompt —**ex′pe·di′tious·ly** *adv.*

ex·pel (ek spel′) *vt.* **-pelled′, -pel′ling** ‖ < L *ex-*, out + *pellere*, to thrust ‖ **1** to drive out by force **2** to dismiss by authority [*expelled* from college] —**ex·pel′la·ble** *adj.* —**ex·pel′ler** *n.*

ex·pend (ek spend′) *vt.* ‖ < L *ex-*, out + *pendere*, to weigh ‖ **1** to spend **2** to use up

ex·pend′a·ble *adj.* **1** that can be expended **2** *Mil.* designating equipment (or men) expected to be used up (or sacrificed) in service

ex·pend′i·ture (-spen′di chər) *n.* **1** an expending of money, time, etc. **2** the amount of money, time, etc. expended

ex·pense (ek spens′) *n.* ‖ see EXPEND ‖ **1** financial cost; charge **2** any cost or sacrifice **3** [*pl.*] charges met with in doing one's work, etc.

ex·pen′sive *adj.* costly; high-priced

ex·pe·ri·ence (ek spir′ē əns) *n.* ‖ < L *experiri*, to try ‖ **1** the act of living through an event **2** anything or everything observed or lived through **3** *a)* training and personal participation *b)* knowledge, skill, etc. resulting from this —*vt.* **-enced, -enc·ing** to have experience of; undergo

ex·pe′ri·enced *adj.* having had or having learned from experience

ex·per·i·ment (ek sper′ə mənt; *for v., usually*, -ment′) *n.* ‖ < L *experimentum*, a trial ‖ a test or trial undertaken to discover or demonstrate something —*vi.* to make an experiment —**ex·per′i·men·ta′tion** (-mən tā′shən) *n.* —**ex·per′i·ment′er** *n.*

ex·per′i·men′tal *adj.* **1** based on or used for experiments **2** testing; trial —**ex·per′i·men′tal·ly** *adv.*

ex·pert (eks′pərt) *adj.* ‖ see EXPERIENCE ‖ very skillful —*n.* one who is very skillful or well-informed in some special field —**ex′pert·ly** *adv.* —**ex′pert·ness** *n.*

ex·per·tise (ek′spər tēz′) *n.* ‖ Fr ‖ the skill or knowledge of an expert

ex·pi·ate (eks′pē āt′) *vt.* **-at′ed, -at′ing** ‖ < L *ex-*, out + *piare*, to appease ‖ to make amends for (wrongdoing or guilt); atone for —**ex′pi·a′tion** *n.* —**ex′pi·a·to′ry** (-ə tôr′ē) *adj.*

ex·pire (ek spīr′) *vi.* **-pired′, -pir′ing** ‖ < L *ex-*, out + *spirare*, breathe ‖ **1** to exhale **2** to die **3** to come to an end —**ex·pi·ra·tion** (ek′spə rā′shən) *n.*

ex·plain (ek splān′) *vt.* ‖ < L *ex-*, out + *planus*, level ‖ **1** to make plain or understandable **2** to give the meaning of; expound **3** to account for —*vi.* to give an explanation —**ex·plain′a·ble** *adj.*

ex·pla·na·tion (eks′plə nā′shən) *n.* **1** an explaining **2** something that explains; interpretation, meaning, etc.

ex·plan·a·to·ry (ek splan′ə tôr′ē) *adj.* explaining or intended to explain

ex·ple·tive (eks′plə tiv) *n.* ‖ < L *ex-*, out, up + *plere*, to fill ‖ an oath or exclamation

ex·pli·ca·ble (eks′pli kə bəl) *adj.* ‖ see fol. ‖ that can be explained

ex′pli·cate′ (-kāt′) *vt.* **-cat′ed, -cat′ing** ‖ < L *ex-*, out + *plicare*, to fold ‖ to make clear; explain fully

ex·plic·it (eks plis′it) *adj.* ‖ see prec. ‖ **1** clearly stated or shown; definite **2** outspoken —**ex·plic′it·ly** *adv.*

ex·plode (ek splōd′) *vt.* **-plod′ed, -plod′ing** ‖ orig., to drive off the stage < L *ex-*, off + *plaudere*, applaud ‖ **1** to expose as false **2** to make burst with a loud noise **3** to cause to change suddenly and violently, as from a solid to an expanding gas —*vi.* to burst forth noisily —**ex·plod′a·ble** *adj.*

ex·ploit (eks′ploit′; *for v., usually* ik sploit′) *n.* ‖ see EXPLICATE ‖ a daring act; bold deed —*vt.* **1** to make use of **2** to make unethical use of for one's own profit —**ex′ploi·ta′tion** *n.* —**ex·ploit′a·tive** *adj.* —**ex·ploit′er** *n.*

ex·plore (ek splôr′) *vt., vi.* **-plored′, -plor′ing** ‖ < L *ex-*, out + *plorare*, cry out ‖ **1** to examine (something) carefully; investigate **2** to travel in (a little-known region) for discovery —**ex·plo·ra·tion** (eks′plə rā′shən) *n.* —**ex·plor′a·to′ry** (-ə tôr′ē) *adj.* —**ex·plor′er** *n.*

ex·plo·sion (ek splō′zhən) *n.* **1** an exploding **2** the noise made by exploding **3** a noisy outburst **4** a sudden, widespread increase

ex·plo′sive (-siv) *adj.* **1** of, causing, or like an explosion **2** tending to explode —*n.* a substance that can explode, as gunpowder —**ex·plo′sive·ly** *adv.* —**ex·plo′sive·ness** *n.*

ex·po·nent (eks pō′nənt; *for n. 3*, eks′pōn′-) *n.* ‖ see EXPOUND ‖ **1** one who expounds or promotes (principles, etc.) **2** a person or thing that is an example or symbol (*of* something) **3** *Algebra* a symbol placed at the upper right of another to show how many times the latter is to be multiplied by itself (Ex.: $b^2 = b \times b$) —**ex·po·nen·tial** (eks′pō nen′shəl) *adj.*

ex·port (eks pôrt′; *also, and for n. always*, eks′pôrt′) *vt.* ‖ < L *ex-*, out + *portare*, to carry ‖ to send (goods) to another country, esp. for sale —*n.* **1** something exported **2** an exporting —**ex′por·ta′tion** *n.* —**ex·port′er** *n.*

ex·pose (eks pōz′) *vt.* **-posed′, -pos′ing** ‖ see EXPOUND ‖ **1** to lay open (*to* danger, attack, etc.) **2** to reveal; exhibit **3** to make (a crime, etc.) known **4** *Photog.* to subject (a sensitized film or plate) to actinic rays, etc.

ex·po·sé (eks′pō zā′) *n.* ‖ Fr ‖ a public disclosure of a scandal, crime, etc.

ex·po·si·tion (eks′pə zish′ən) *n.* ‖ see EXPOUND ‖ **1** a detailed explanation **2**

writing or speaking that explains **3** a large public exhibition or show

ex·pos·i·tor (eks päz′ət ər) ***n.*** one who expounds or explains

ex·pos′i·to′ry (-ə tôr′ē) ***adj.*** of or containing exposition; explanatory

ex post fac·to (eks′ pōst fak′tō) ‖ L, from (the thing) done afterward ‖ done afterward, but retroactive

ex·pos·tu·late (eks päs′chə lāt′) ***vi.*** **-lat′ed, -lat′ing** ‖ < L *ex-*, intens. + *postulare*, to demand ‖ to reason with a person earnestly, objecting to that person's actions **—ex·pos′tu·la′tion *n.***

ex·po·sure (eks pō′zhər) ***n.*** **1** an exposing or being exposed **2** a location, as of a house, in relation to the sun, etc. /an eastern *exposure*/ **3** frequent appearance before the public **4** *Photog.* *a)* the subjection of a sensitized film or plate to actinic rays, etc. *b)* a section of a film for one picture *c)* the time during which such film is exposed

ex·pound (eks pound′) ***vt.*** ‖ < L *ex-*, out + *ponere*, to put ‖ **1** to set forth; state in detail **2** to explain

ex·press (eks pres′) ***vt.*** ‖ < L *ex-*, out + *premere*, to press ‖ **1** to squeeze out (juice, etc.) **2** to put into words; state **3** to reveal; show **4** to symbolize; signify **5** to send by express **—*adj.*** **1** expressed; stated; explicit **2** exact **3** specific **4** fast and direct /an *express* bus/ **5** marked by speed **6** having to do with an express train, bus, service, etc. **—*adv.*** by express **—*n.*** **1** an express train, bus, etc. **2** *a)* a service for transporting things rapidly *b)* the things sent by express

ex·pres·sion (eks presh′ən) ***n.*** **1** a putting into words; stating **2** a manner of expressing, esp. with eloquence **3** a particular word or phrase **4** a showing of feeling, character, etc. **5** a look, intonation, etc. that conveys meaning **6** a mathematical symbol or set of symbols **—ex·pres′sion·less *adj.***

ex·pres′sion·ism′ *n.* a 20th-c. movement in art, literature, etc. seeking to give symbolic, objective expression to inner experience **—ex·pres′sion·ist *adj., n.*** **—ex·pres′sion·is′tic *adj.***

ex·pres′sive *adj.* **1** that expresses **2** full of meaning or feeling **—ex·pres′sive·ly *adv.*** **—ex·pres′sive·ness *n.***

ex·press′ly *adv.* **1** plainly; definitely **2** especially; particularly

ex·press′way′ *n.* a divided highway for high-speed, through traffic, with grade separations at intersections

ex·pro·pri·ate (eks prō′prē āt′) ***vt.*** **-at′ed, -at′ing** ‖ < L *ex-*, out + *proprius*, one's own ‖ to take (land, etc.) from its owner, esp. for public use **—ex·pro′pri·a′tion *n.***

ex·pul·sion (eks pul′shən) ***n.*** an expelling or being expelled

ex·punge (ek spunj′) ***vt.*** **-punged′, -pung′ing** ‖ < L *ex-*, out + *pungere*, to prick ‖ to blot or strike out; erase

ex·pur·gate (eks′pər gāt′) ***vt.*** **-gat′ed, -gat′ing** ‖ < L *ex-*, out + *purgare*, cleanse ‖ to remove passages considered obscene, etc. from (a book, etc.) **—ex′pur·ga′tion *n.***

ex·qui·site (eks′kwi zit, ik skwiz′it) ***adj.*** ‖ < L *ex-*, out + *quaerere*, to ask ‖ **1** carefully or elaborately done **2** very beautiful, delicate, etc. **3** of highest quality **4** very intense; keen

ex·tant (eks′tənt, ek stant′) ***adj.*** ‖ < L *ex-*, out + *stare*, to stand ‖ still existing; not extinct

ex·tem·po·ra·ne·ous (eks′tem′pə rā′nē əs) ***adj.*** ‖ see fol. ‖ done or spoken with little preparation; offhand **—ex′tem′po·ra′ne·ous·ly *adv.***

ex·tem·po·re (eks tem′pə rē) ***adv., adj.*** ‖ < L *ex-*, out of + *tempus*, time ‖ with little preparation; offhand

ex·tem′po·rize′ (-rīz′) ***vi., vt.*** **-rized′, -riz′ing** to speak, perform, etc. extempore; improvise

ex·tend (ek stend′) ***vt.*** ‖ < L *ex-*, out + *tendere*, to stretch ‖ **1** to make longer; stretch out; prolong **2** to enlarge in area, scope, etc.; expand **3** to stretch forth **4** to offer; grant **5** to make (oneself) work very hard **—*vi.*** to be extended **—ex·tend′ed *adj.*** **—ex·tend′er *n.*** **—ex·ten′si·ble** (-sten′sə bəl) or **ex·tend′i·ble *adj.***

extended care nursing care in a facility for convalescents, the disabled, etc.

extended family a group of parents, their children, and other relatives living in close proximity or together, esp. if three generations are involved

ex·ten′sion (-sten′shən) ***n.*** **1** an extending or being extended **2** range; extent **3** a part forming a continuation or addition

ex·ten′sive (-siv) ***adj.*** having great extent; vast; far-reaching; comprehensive **—ex·ten′sive·ly *adv.*** **—ex·ten′sive·ness *n.***

ex·tent (ek stent′) ***n.*** **1** the space, amount, or degree to which a thing extends; size **2** scope; limits **3** an extended space; vast area

ex·ten·u·ate (ek sten′yōō āt′) ***vt.*** **-at′ed, -at′ing** ‖ < L *ex-*, out + *tenuis*, thin ‖ to make (an offense, etc.) seem less serious **—ex·ten′u·a′tion *n.***

ex·te·ri·or (ek stir′ē ər) ***adj.*** ‖ see EXTERNAL ‖ **1** *a)* on the outside; outer *b)* to be used on the outside /*exterior* paint/ **2** coming from without **—*n.*** an outside or outside surface **—ex·te′ri·or·ly *adv.***

ex·ter·mi·nate (ek stur′mə nāt′) ***vt.*** **-nat′ed, -nat′ing** ‖ < L *ex-*, out + *terminus*, boundary ‖ to destroy entirely; wipe out **—ex·ter′mi·na′tion *n.*** **—ex·ter′mi·na′tor *n.***

ex·ter·nal (eks tur′nəl) ***adj.*** ‖ < L *externus* ‖ **1** on or of the outside **2** existing apart from the mind; material **3** coming from without **4** superficial **5** foreign **—*n.*** an outside surface or part **—ex·ter′nal·ly *adv.***

ex·tinct (ek stiŋkt′) ***adj.*** ‖ see EXTINGUISH ‖ **1** having died down; extinguished **2** no longer in existence

ex·tinc′tion *n.* **1** an extinguishing **2** a destroying or being destroyed **3** a dying out, as a species

ex·tin·guish (ek stiŋ′gwish) ***vt.*** ‖ < L *ex-*, out + *stinguere*, extinguish ‖ **1** to put out (a fire, etc.) **2** to destroy **—ex·tin′guish·er *n.***

ex·tir·pate (ek′stər pāt′) ***vt.*** **-pat′ed, -pat′ing** ‖ < L *ex-*, out + *stirps*, root ‖ **1** to pull up by the roots **2** to destroy completely **—ex′tir·pa′tion *n.***

ex·tol or **ex·toll** (eks tōl′) *vt.* **-tolled′**, **-tol′ling** ‖ < L *ex-*, up + *tollere*, to raise ‖ to praise highly; laud

ex·tort (eks tôrt′) *vt.* ‖ < L *ex-*, out + *torquere*, to twist ‖ to get (money, etc.) from someone by force or threats

ex·tor·tion (eks tôr′shən) *n.* **1** an extorting **2** something extorted —**ex·tor′tion·ate** *adj.* —**ex·tor′tion·er** *n.* —**ex·tor′tion·ist** *n.*

ex·tra (eks′trə) *adj.* ‖ < L *extra*, more than ‖ more or better than normal, expected, etc.; additional —*n.* an extra person or thing; specif., *a*) a special edition of a newspaper *b*) an extra benefit *c*) an actor hired by the day to play a minor part *adv.* more than usually; esp., exceptionally

extra- ‖ see EXTERNAL ‖ *prefix* outside, beyond, besides

ex·tract (eks trakt′; *for n.* eks′trakt′) *vt.* ‖ < L *ex-*, out + *trahere*, to draw ‖ **1** to draw out by effort **2** to obtain by pressing, distilling, etc. **3** to deduce; derive **4** to select or quote (a passage, etc.) —*n.* something extracted; specif., *a*) a concentrate [*beef extract*] *b*) an excerpt

ex·trac′tion *n.* **1** the act or process of extracting **2** origin; descent

ex·tra·cur·ric·u·lar (eks′trə kə rik′yo͞o lər) *adj.* not part of the required curriculum

ex·tra·dite (eks′trə dīt′) *vt.* **-dit′ed**, **-dit′ing** ‖ < L *ex*, out + *traditio*, a surrender ‖ to turn over (an alleged criminal, etc.) to the jurisdiction of another country, State, etc. —**ex′tra·di′tion** (-dish′ən) *n.*

ex′tra·le′gal *adj.* outside of legal control

ex·tra·ne·ous (eks trā′nē əs) *adj.* ‖ L *extraneus*, foreign ‖ **1** coming from outside; foreign **2** not pertinent; irrelevant —**ex·tra′ne·ous·ly** *adv.*

ex·tra·or·di·nar·y (ek strôrd′′n er′ē) *adj.* ‖ < L *extra ordinem*, out of order ‖ **1** not ordinary **2** going far beyond the ordinary; unusual; remarkable

ex·trap·o·late (ek strap′ə lāt′) *vt.*, *vi.* **-lat′ed**, **-lat′ing** ‖ see EXTRA- & INTERPOLATE ‖ to estimate (something unknown) on the basis of known facts —**ex·trap′o·la′tion** *n.*

ex·tra·sen·so·ry (eks′trə sen′sə rē) *adj.* apart from, or in addition to, normal sense perception

ex′tra·ter·res′tri·al *adj.* being, of, or from outside the earth's limits —*n.* an extraterrestrial being, as in science fiction

ex·trav·a·gant (ek strav′ə gənt) *adj.* ‖ < L *extra*, beyond + *vagari*, to wander ‖ **1** going beyond reasonable limits; excessive **2** costing or spending too much; wasteful —**ex·trav′a·gance** *n.*

ex·trav·a·gan·za (ek strav′ə gan′zə) *n.* ‖ < It *estravaganza*, extravagance ‖ a spectacular theatrical production

ex·tra·ve·hic·u·lar (eks′trə vē hik′yo͞o lər) *adj.* designating activity by an astronaut outside a vehicle in space

ex·treme (ek strēm′) *adj.* ‖ < L *exterus*, outer ‖ **1** farthest away; utmost **2** very great; excessive **3** unconventional or radical, as in politics **4** harsh; drastic —*n.* **1** either of two things that are as different or far as possible from each other **2** an extreme act, state, etc. **3** *Math.* the first or last term of a proportion —**ex·treme′ly** *adv.* —**ex·treme′ness** *n.*

ex·trem′ism′ (-iz′əm) *n.* a going to extremes, esp. in politics —**ex·trem′ist** *adj.*, *n.*

ex·trem·i·ty (ek strem′ə tē) *n.*, *pl.* **-ties** **1** the outermost part; end **2** the greatest degree **3** great need, danger, etc. **4** an extreme measure **5** [*pl.*] the hands and feet

ex·tri·cate (eks′tri kāt′) *vt.* **-cat′ed**, **-cat′ing** ‖ < L *ex-*, out + *tricae*, vexations ‖ to set free (*from* a net, difficulty, etc.) —**ex′tri·ca′tion** *n.*

ex·trin·sic (eks trin′sik) *adj.* ‖ < L *exter*, without + *secus*, otherwise ‖ not essential —**ex·trin′si·cal·ly** *adv.*

ex·tro·vert (eks′trə vurt′) *n.* ‖ < L *extra-*, outside + *vertere*, to turn ‖ one whose interest is more in his environment and in other people than in himself —**ex′tro·ver′sion** (-vur′zhən) *n.* —**ex′tro·vert′ed** *adj.*

ex·trude (eks tro͞od′) *vt.* **-trud′ed**, **-trud′ing** ‖ < L *ex-*, out + *trudere*, to thrust ‖ to force out, as through a small opening —*vi.* to be extruded; esp., to protrude —**ex·tru′sion** *n.* —**ex·tru′sive** *adj.*

ex·u·ber·ant (eg zo͞o′bər ənt) *adj.* ‖ < L *ex-*, intens. + *uberare*, bear abundantly ‖ **1** growing profusely; luxuriant **2** characterized by good health and high spirits —**ex·u′ber·ance** *n.* —**ex·u′ber·ant·ly** *adv.*

ex·ude (eg zo͞od′) *vt.*, *vi.* **-ud′ed**, **-ud′ing** ‖ < L *ex-*, out + *sudare*, to sweat ‖ **1** to ooze **2** to seem to radiate [*to exude joy*] —**ex·u·da·tion** (eks′yo͞o dā′shən) *n.*

ex·ult (eg zult′) *vi.* ‖ < L *ex-*, intens. + *saltare*, to leap ‖ to rejoice greatly; glory —**ex·ult′ant** *adj.* —**ex·ul·ta·tion** (eg′zul tā′shən, eks′ul-) *n.*

ex·ur·bi·a (eks ur′bē ə) *n.* ‖ EX- + (SUB)URBIA ‖ the semirural communities beyond the suburbs, lived in by upper-income families —**ex·ur′ban** *adj.* —**ex·ur′ban·ite′** *adj.*, *n.*

eye (ī) *n.* ‖ OE *eage* ‖ **1** the organ of sight in humans and animals **2** *a*) the eyeball *b*) the iris [*brown eyes*] **3** the area around the eye [*a black eye*] **4** [*often pl.*] sight; vision **5** a look; glance **6** attention; observation **7** the power of judging, etc. by eyesight [*an eye for distances*] **8** [*often pl.*] judgment; opinion [*in the eyes of the law*] **9** a thing like an eye in appearance or function —*vt.* **eyed**, **eye′ing** or **ey′ing** to look at; observe —**have an eye for** to have a keen appreciation of —**keep an eye on** to look after —**lay** (or **set** or **clap**) **eyes on** to look at —**make eyes at** to look at amorously —**see eye to eye** to agree completely —**with an eye to** paying attention to; considering

eye′ball′ *n.* the ball-shaped part of the eye

eye′brow′ *n.* the bony arch over each eye, or the hair growing on this

eye′-catch′er *n.* something that especially attracts one's attention —**eye′-catch′ing** *adj.*

eye′ful′ (-fo͝ol′) *n.* [Slang] a person or thing that looks striking or unusual

eye′glass′ *n.* **1** a lens to help faulty vision **2** [*pl.*] a pair of such lenses in a frame; glasses

eye′lash′ *n.* any of the hairs on the edge of the eyelid

eye′let (-lit) ***n.*** **1** a small hole for receiving a cord, hook, etc. **2** a metal ring for reinforcing such a hole **3** a small hole edged by stitching in embroidery
eye′lid′ ***n.*** either of the two folds of flesh that cover and uncover the eyeball
eye′-o′pen·er (-ō′pə nər) ***n.*** a surprising piece of news, sudden realization, etc.
eye′piece′ ***n.*** in a telescope, microscope, etc., the lens or lenses nearest the viewer's eye
eye′sight′ ***n.*** **1** the power of seeing; sight **2** the range of vision
eye′sore′ ***n.*** an unpleasant sight
eye′strain′ ***n.*** a tired or strained condition of the eye muscles
eye′tooth′ ***n., pl.*** **-teeth′** a canine tooth of the upper jaw
eye′wash′ ***n.*** **1** a medicated solution for the eyes **2** [Slang] *a)* nonsense *b)* flattery
eye′wit′ness ***n.*** one who sees or has seen something happen, as an accident, etc.
ey·rie or **ey·ry** (er′ē, ir′ē) ***n., pl.*** **-ries** AERIE

F

f or **F** (ef) ***n., pl.*** **f's, F's** the sixth letter of the English alphabet
F (ef) ***n.*** **1** *Educ.* a grade for failing work or, sometimes, fair or average work **2** *Music* the fourth tone in the scale of C major
f or **f.** **1** feminine **2** folio **3** following **4** franc(s)
F *symbol for* **1** Fahrenheit **2** *Chem.* fluorine
F or **F.** **1** female **2** franc(s) **3** Friday
fa (fä) ***n.*** ‖ < ML ‖ *Music* the fourth tone of the diatonic scale
FAA Federal Aviation Administration
fa·ble (fā′bəl) ***n.*** ‖ < L *fabula,* a story ‖ **1** a fictitious story, usually about animals, meant to teach a moral lesson **2** a myth or legend **3** a falsehood
fa′bled ***adj.*** **1** mythical; legendary **2** unreal; fictitious
fab·ric (fab′rik) ***n.*** ‖ < L *fabrica,* workshop ‖ **1** a framework; structure **2** a material made from fibers, etc. by weaving, felting, etc., as cloth
fab·ri·cate (fab′ri kāt′) ***vt.*** **-cat′ed, -cat′ing** ‖ see prec. ‖ **1** to make, construct, etc.; manufacture **2** to make up (a story, lie, etc.); invent **—fab′ri·ca′tion** ***n.*** **—fab′ri·ca′tor** ***n.***
fab·u·lous (fab′yoo ləs) ***adj.*** ‖ see FABLE ‖ **1** of or like a fable; fictitious **2** incredible; astounding **3** [Colloq.] wonderful **—fab′u·lous·ly** ***adv.***
fa·çade or **fa·cade** (fə säd′) ***n.*** ‖ Fr: see fol. ‖ **1** the front or main face of a building **2** an imposing appearance concealing something inferior
face (fās) ***n.*** ‖ < L *facies* ‖ **1** the front of the head **2** the expression of the countenance **3** the main or front surface **4** the surface that is marked, as of a clock, etc., or that is finished, as of fabric, etc. **5** appearance; outward aspect **6** dignity; self-respect: usually in **lose** (or **save**) **face** **—*vt.*** **faced, fac′ing** **1** to turn, or have the face turned, toward **2** to confront with boldness, etc. **3** to cover with a new surface **—*vi.*** to turn, or have the face turned, in a specified direction **—face to face** **1** confronting each other **2** very near: with *with* **—face up to** to face with courage **—in the face of** **1** in the presence of **2** in spite of **—make a face** to grimace **—on the face of it** apparently
-faced (fāst) *combining form* having a specified kind of face /round-*faced*/
face′less ***adj.*** lacking a distinct character; anonymous
face lifting **1** plastic surgery to remove wrinkles, etc. from the face **2** an altering, repairing, etc., as of a building's exterior Also **face lift** **—face-lift** (fās′lift′) ***vt.***
face′-off′ ***n.*** *Hockey* the start or resumption of play when the referee drops the puck between two opposing players
face′-sav′ing ***adj.*** preserving one's dignity or self-respect
fac·et (fas′it) ***n.*** ‖ see FACE ‖ **1** any of the polished plane surfaces of a cut gem **2** any of a number of sides or aspects, as of a personality **—*vt.*** **-et·ed** or **-et·ted, -et·ing** or **-et·ting** to cut or make facets on
fa·ce·tious (fə sē′shəs) ***adj.*** ‖ < L *facetus,* witty ‖ joking, esp. at an inappropriate time **—fa·ce′tious·ly** ***adv.***
face value **1** the value written on a bill, bond, etc. **2** the seeming value
fa·cial (fā′shəl) ***adj.*** of or for the face **—*n.*** a cosmetic treatment, massage, etc. for the skin of the face
facial tissue a sheet of soft tissue paper used as a handkerchief, etc.
fac·ile (fas′il) ***adj.*** ‖ Fr < L *facere,* do ‖ **1** not hard to do **2** working or done easily; fluent **3** superficial
fa·cil·i·tate (fə sil′ə tāt′) ***vt.*** **-tat′ed, -tat′ing** ‖ see prec. ‖ to make easy or easier **—fa·cil′i·ta′tion** ***n.***
fa·cil′i·ty (-tē) ***n., pl.*** **-ties** **1** absence of difficulty **2** skill; dexterity **3** [*usually pl.*] the means by which something can be done **4** a building, etc. that facilitates some activity
fac·ing (fās′iŋ) ***n.*** **1** a lining on the edge of a garment **2** a covering of contrasting material on a building
fac·sim·i·le (fak sim′ə lē) ***n.*** ‖ < L *facere,* make + *simile,* like ‖ an exact reproduction or copy
fact (fakt) ***n.*** ‖ < L *facere,* do ‖ **1** a deed, esp. a criminal deed /an accessory before (or after) the *fact*/ **2** a thing that has actually happened or is really true **3** reality; truth **4** something stated to be true **—as a matter of fact** in reality: also **in fact**
fac·tion (fak′shən) ***n.*** ‖ see prec. ‖ **1** a group of people in an organization working in a common cause against the main body **2** dissension **—fac′tion·al** ***adj.*** **—fac′tion·al·ism′** ***n.***

fac'tious (-shəs) ***adj.*** producing or tending to produce faction

fac·ti·tious (fak tish'əs) ***adj.*** ‖see FACT‖ forced or artificial

fac·tor (fak'tər) ***n.*** ‖< L *facere*, do‖ **1** one who transacts business for another **2** any of the conditions, etc. that bring about a result **3** *Math.* any of the quantities which form a product when multiplied together —***vt.*** *Math.* to resolve into factors

fac·to·ry (fak'tə rē) ***n.***, *pl.* **-ries** ‖see prec.‖ a building or buildings in which things are manufactured

fac·to·tum (fak tōt'əm) ***n.*** ‖< L *facere*, do + *totum*, all‖ a handyman

fac·tu·al (fak'cho͞o əl) ***adj.*** of or containing facts; real; actual

fac·ul·ty (fak'əl tē) ***n.***, *pl.* **-ties** ‖see FACILE‖ **1** any natural or specialized power of a living organism **2** special aptitude or skill **3** all the teachers of a school or of one of its departments

fad (fad) ***n.*** ‖< Brit dial.‖ a style, etc. that interests many people for a short time; passing fashion —**fad'dish** ***adj.***

fade (fād) ***vi.*** **fad'ed, fad'ing** ‖< OFr *fade*, pale‖ **1** to lose color, brilliance, etc. **2** to lose freshness or strength **3** to disappear slowly; die out —***vt.*** to cause to fade —**fade in** (or **out**) *Film, Radio, TV* to appear (or disappear) gradually

fa·er·ie or **fa·er·y** (fā'ər ē, fer'ē) ***n.*** [Archaic] **1** fairyland **2** *pl.* **-ies** a fairy

fag (fag) ***vi.*** **fagged, fag'ging** ‖< ?‖ to make or become very tired by hard work —***n.*** [Slang] a male homosexual: a hostile term

fag·ot or **fag·got** (fag'ət) ***n.*** ‖ult. < Gr *phakelos*, a bundle‖ a bundle of sticks or twigs, esp. for use as fuel

fag·ot·ing or **fag·got·ing** (fag'ət iŋ) ***n.*** **1** a hemstitch with wide spaces **2** openwork with crisscross or barlike stitches across the open seam

Fahr·en·heit (fer'ən hīt') ***adj.*** ‖after G. D. *Fahrenheit* (1686-1736), Ger physicist‖ designating or of a thermometer on which 32° is the freezing point and 212° is the boiling point of water

fail (fāl) ***vi.*** ‖< L *fallere*, deceive‖ **1** to be insufficient; fall short **2** to weaken; die away **3** to stop operating **4** to be negligent in a duty, expectation, etc. **5** to be unsuccessful **6** to become bankrupt **7** *Educ.* to get a grade of failure —***vt.*** **1** to be of no help to; disappoint **2** to leave; abandon **3** to neglect /to *fail* to go/ **4** *Educ.* to give a grade of failure to or get such a grade in —**without fail** without failing (to occur, do, etc.)

fail'ing ***n.*** **1** a failure **2** a fault —***prep.*** without; lacking

faille (fīl, fāl) ***n.*** ‖Fr‖ a ribbed, soft fabric of silk or rayon

fail'-safe' ***adj.*** of an intricate procedure for preventing accidental operation, as of nuclear weapons

fail·ure (fāl'yər) ***n.*** **1** *a)* a falling short *b)* a weakening *c)* a breakdown in operation *d)* neglect *e)* a not succeeding *f)* a becoming bankrupt **2** one that does not succeed **3** *Educ.* a failing to pass, or a grade showing this

fain (fān) ***adj.***, ***adv.*** ‖< OE *fægen*, glad‖ [Archaic] glad(ly); willing(ly)

faint (fānt) ***adj.*** ‖see FEIGN‖ **1** weak; feeble **2** timid **3** feeling weak and dizzy **4** dim; indistinct —***n.*** a state of temporary unconsciousness —***vi.*** to fall into a faint —**faint'ly** ***adv.*** —**faint'ness** ***n.***

fair[1] (fer) ***adj.*** ‖< OE *fæger*‖ **1** attractive; beautiful **2** unblemished; clean **3** blond /*fair* hair/ **4** clear and sunny **5** easy to read /a *fair* hand/ **6** just and honest **7** according to the rules **8** moderately large **9** average /in *fair* condition/ **10** that may be hunted /*fair* game/ **11** *Baseball* that is not foul —***adv.*** **1** in a fair manner **2** squarely —**fair'ness** ***n.***

fair[2] (fer) ***n.*** ‖< L *feriae*, festivals‖ **1** a regular gathering for barter and sale of goods **2** a carnival or bazaar, often for charity **3** a competitive exhibition of farm, household, and manufactured products, with various amusements and educational displays

fair'-haired' ***adj.*** **1** having blond hair **2** [Colloq.] favorite

fair'ly ***adv.*** **1** justly; honestly **2** somewhat; moderately **3** completely or really

fair shake [Colloq.] fair or just treatment

fair'way' (-wā') ***n.*** the mowed part of a golf course between a tee and a green

fair·y (fer'ē) ***n.***, *pl.* **-ies** ‖< OFr *fée*‖ **1** a tiny, graceful imaginary being in human form, with magic powers **2** [Slang] a male homosexual: term of contempt —***adj.*** **1** of fairies **2** graceful; delicate

fair'y·land' ***n.*** **1** the imaginary land where the fairies live **2** a lovely, enchanting place

fairy tale **1** a story about fairies, magic deeds, etc. **2** an unbelievable story; lie

fait ac·com·pli (fe tä kōn plē') ‖Fr‖ something done that cannot be changed

faith (fāth) ***n.*** ‖< L *fidere*, to trust‖ **1** unquestioning belief, specif. in God, religion, etc. **2** a particular religion **3** complete trust or confidence **4** loyalty

faith'ful (-fəl) ***adj.*** **1** loyal **2** conscientious **3** accurate; reliable —**faith'ful·ly** ***adv.*** —**faith'ful·ness** ***n.***

faith'less (-lis) ***adj.*** **1** dishonest or disloyal **2** unreliable —**faith'less·ly** ***adv.*** —**faith'less·ness** ***n.***

fake (fāk) ***vt.***, ***vi.*** **faked, fak'ing** ‖< ?‖ to make (something) seem real, etc. by deception —***n.*** a fraud; counterfeit —***adj.*** **1** sham; false **2** artificial —**fak'er** ***n.***

fa·kir (fə kir') ***n.*** ‖Ar *faqīr*, lit., poor‖ **1** one of a Muslim holy sect of beggars **2** a Hindu ascetic

fa·la·fel (fə läf'əl) ***n.*** ‖< Ar‖ a deep-fried patty of ground chickpeas

fal·con (fôl'kən, fô'kən; fal'-) ***n.*** ‖ult. < L *falx*, sickle‖ any of certain birds of prey trained to hunt small game —**fal'con·er** ***n.*** —**fal'con·ry** ***n.***

fall (fôl) ***vi.*** **fell, fall'en, fall'ing** ‖OE *feallan*‖ **1** to come down by gravity; drop; descend **2** to come down suddenly from an upright position; tumble or collapse **3** to be wounded or killed in battle **4** to take a downward direction **5** to become lower, less, weaker, etc. **6** to lose power, status, etc. **7** to do wrong; sin **8** to be captured **9** to take on a sad look /my face *fell*/ **10** to take place; occur 11 to come by lot, inheritance, etc. 12 to pass into a specified condition /to *fall* ill/ 13 to be directed by chance 14 to be divided (*into*) —*n.* 1 a dropping; descending 2 a coming down suddenly from an upright position 3 a downward direction or slope 4 a becoming lower or less 5 a capture 6 a loss of status, reputation, etc. 7 a yielding to temptation 8 autumn 9 the amount of what has fallen /a six-inch *fall* of snow/ 10 the distance that something falls 11 [*pl., often with sing. v.*] water falling over a cliff, etc. 12 a long tress of hair, added to a woman's hairdo —*adj.* of, in, for, or like the fall season —**fall back** to withdraw; retreat —**fall for** [Colloq.] 1 to fall in love with 2 to be tricked by —**fall in** to line up in formation —**fall off** to become smaller, worse, etc. —**fall on** (or **upon**) to attack —**fall out** 1 to quarrel 2 to leave one's place in a formation —**fall short** to fail to reach, suffice, etc. —**fall through** to fail —**fall to** 1 to begin 2 to start eating

fal·la·cious (fə lā'shəs) *adj.* ‖see fol.‖ 1 erroneous 2 misleading or deceptive —**fal·la'cious·ly** *adv.*

fal·la·cy (fal'ə sē) *n., pl.* **-cies** ‖< L *fallere*, deceive‖ 1 a mistaken idea; error 2 a flaw in reasoning

fall·en (fôl'ən) *adj.* that fell; dropped, prostrate, ruined, dead, etc.

fal·li·ble (fal'ə bəl) *adj.* ‖< L *fallere*, deceive‖ liable to be mistaken, deceived, or erroneous —**fal'li·bil'i·ty** or **fal'li·ble·ness** *n.* —**fal'li·bly** *adv.*

fall'ing-out' *n.* a quarrel

falling star METEOR (sense 1)

fall'off' *n.* a decline

fal·lo·pi·an tube (fə lō'pē ən) ‖after G. *Fallopius*, 16th-c. It anatomist‖ either of two tubes that carry ova to the uterus Also **Fallopian tube**

fall'out' *n.* 1 the descent to earth of radioactive particles, as after a nuclear explosion 2 these particles

fal·low (fal'ō) *adj.* ‖< OE *fealh*‖ 1 left unplanted 2 inactive

false (fôls) *adj.* **fals'er, fals'est** ‖< L *fallere*, deceive‖ 1 not true; incorrect; wrong 2 untruthful; lying 3 unfaithful 4 misleading 5 not real; artificial —*adv.* in a false manner —**false'ly** *adv.* —**false'ness** *n.*

false'hood' *n.* 1 falsity 2 a lie

fal·set·to (fôl set'ō) *n., pl.* **-tos** ‖It, dim. of *falso*, false‖ an artificial way of singing in which the voice is much higher pitched than normal

fal·si·fy (fôl'sə fī') *n.* **-fied', -fy'ing** 1 to misrepresent 2 to alter (a record, etc.) fraudulently —**fal'si·fi·ca'tion** *n.* —**fal'si·fi'er** *n.*

fal'si·ty (-tē) *n.* 1 the quality of being false 2 *pl.* **-ties** a lie

Fal·staff (fôl'staf'), Sir **John** in Shakespeare's plays, a fat, witty, boastful knight

fal·ter (fôl'tər) *vi.* ‖prob. < ON‖ 1 to move unsteadily; stumble 2 to stammer 3 to act hesitantly; waver —**fal'ter·ing·ly** *adv.*

fame (fām) *n.* ‖< L *fama*‖ 1 reputation, esp. for good 2 the state of being well known —**famed** *adj.*

fa·mil·ial (fə mil'yəl) *adj.* of or common to a family

fa·mil·iar (fə mil'yər) *adj.* ‖see FAMILY‖ 1 friendly or intimate 2 too friendly; unduly intimate 3 closely acquainted (*with*) 4 common; ordinary —**fa·mil'iar·ly** *adv.*

fa·mil'i·ar'i·ty (-ē er'ə tē) *n., pl.* **-ties** 1 intimacy 2 free and intimate behavior 3 undue intimacy 4 close acquaintance (*with* something)

fa·mil'iar·ize' (-yər īz') *vt.* **-ized', -iz'ing** 1 to make commonly known 2 to make (another or oneself) fully acquainted —**fa·mil'iar·i·za'tion** *n.*

fam·i·ly (fam'ə lē, fam'lē) *n., pl.* **-lies** ‖< L *familia*‖ 1 [Obs.] household 2 parents and their children 3 relatives 4 all those descended from a common ancestor; lineage 5 a group of similar or related things

family planning the regulation, as by birth control methods, of the size, etc. of the family

family room a room in a home set apart for relaxation and recreation

fam·ine (fam'in) *n.* ‖< L *fames*, hunger‖ 1 an acute and general shortage of food 2 any acute shortage

fam'ish (-ish) *vt., vi.* ‖see prec.‖ to make or be very hungry

fa·mous (fā'məs) *adj.* 1 having fame; renowned 2 [Colloq.] excellent; very good —**fa'mous·ly** *adv.*

fan[1] (fan) *n.* ‖< L *vannus*, basket for winnowing grain‖ any device used to set up a current of air for ventilating or cooling —*vt., vi.* **fanned, fan'ning** 1 to move (air) as with a fan 2 to direct air toward as with a fan 3 to stir up; excite 4 *Baseball* to strike out —**fan out** to spread out

fan[2] (fan) *n.* ‖< FAN(ATIC)‖ a person enthusiastic about a specified sport, performer, etc.

fa·nat·ic (fə nat'ik) *adj.* ‖< L *fanum*, temple‖ unreasonably enthusiastic; overly zealous Also **fa·nat'i·cal** —*n.* a fanatic person —**fa·nat'i·cal·ly** *adv.* —**fa·nat'i·cism'** *n.*

fan·ci·er (fan'sē ər) *n.* a person with a special interest in something, esp. plant or animal breeding

fan·ci·ful (fan'sə fəl) *adj.* 1 full of fancy; imaginative 2 imaginary; not real —**fan'ci·ful·ly** *adv.*

fan·cy (fan'sē) *n., pl.* **-cies** ‖contr. < ME *fantasie*, fantasy‖ 1 imagination when light, playful, etc. 2 a mental image 3 a notion; caprice; whim 4 an inclination or fondness —*adj.* **-ci·er, -ci·est** 1 capricious; whimsical 2 extravagant /a *fancy* price/ 3 ornamental; elaborate /a *fancy* necktie/ 4 of superior skill or quality —*vt.* **-cied, -cy·ing** 1 to imagine 2 to be fond of 3 to suppose —**fan'ci·ly** *adv.* —**fan'ci·ness** *n.*

fan'cy-free' *adj.* 1 not married, engaged, etc. 2 carefree

fan'cy·work' *n.* embroidery, crocheting, and other ornamental needlework

fan·dom (fan'dəm) *n.* fans, collectively, as of a sport or entertainer

fan·fare (fan'fer') ‖Fr, prob. < *fanfaron*, braggart‖ *n.* 1 a loud flourish of trumpets 2 noisy or showy display

FANGS

fang (faŋ) ***n.*** ‖ OE < *fon*, seize ‖ **1** one of the long, pointed teeth of meat-eating mammals **2** one of the long, hollow teeth through which poisonous snakes inject venom

fan·ta·size (fant′ə sīz′) ***vt., vi.*** **-sized′, -siz′·ing** to indulge in fantasies or have daydreams (about)

fan·tas·tic (fan tas′tik) ***adj.*** ‖ see fol. ‖ **1** imaginary; unreal **2** grotesque; odd **3** extravagant **4** incredible —**fan·tas′ti·cal·ly** ***adv.*** —**fan·tas′ti·cal·ness** ***n.***

fan·ta·sy (fant′ə sē) ***n., pl.*** **-sies** ‖ < Gr *phainein*, to show ‖ **1** imagination or fancy **2** an illusion or reverie **3** fiction portraying highly IMAGINATIVE (sense 2) characters or settings

far (fär) ***adj.*** **far′ther, far′thest** ‖ OE *feorr* ‖ **1** distant in space or time **2** more distant /the *far* side/ —***adv.*** **1** very distant in space, time, or degree **2** to or from a distance in time or position **3** very much /*far* better/ —**as far as** to the distance or degree that —**by far** very much; considerably Also **far and away** —(**in**) **so far as** to the extent that —**so far** up to this place, time, or degree

far′a·way′ ***adj.*** **1** distant in time or place **2** dreamy

farce (färs) ***n.*** ‖ Fr < L *farcire*, to stuff ‖ **1** (an) exaggerated comedy based on broadly humorous situations **2** an absurd or ridiculous action, pretense, etc. —**far·ci·cal** (fär′si kəl) ***adj.***

fare (fer) ***vi.*** **fared, far′ing** ‖ < OE *faran*, go ‖ **1** to happen; result **2** to be in a specified condition /to *fare* well/ —***n.*** **1** money paid for transportation **2** a passenger who pays a fare **3** food

Far East E Asia, including China, Japan, Korea, & Mongolia

fare·well (fer wel′; *for adj.* fer′wel′) ***interj.*** goodbye —***n.*** good wishes at parting —***adj.*** parting; final /a *farewell* gesture/

far-fetched (fär′fecht′) ***adj.*** forced; strained; unlikely

far′-flung′ (-fluŋ′) ***adj.*** extending over a wide area

fa·ri·na (fə rē′nə) ***n.*** ‖ < L, meal ‖ flour or meal made from cereal grains, potatoes, etc. and eaten as a cooked cereal

far·i·na·ceous (far′ə nā′shəs) ***adj.*** ‖ see prec. ‖ **1** consisting of or made from flour or meal **2** like meal

farm (färm) ***n.*** ‖ < ML *firma*, fixed payment ‖ a piece of land (with house, barns, etc.) on which crops or animals are raised: orig., such land let out to tenants —***vt.*** **1** to cultivate (land) **2** to turn over to another for a fee —***vi.*** to work on or operate a farm

farm′er ***n.*** a person who manages or operates a farm

farm′hand′ ***n.*** a hired farm worker

farm′house′ ***n.*** a house on a farm

farm′ing ***n.*** the business of operating a farm; agriculture

farm′yard′ ***n.*** the yard surrounding or enclosed by farm buildings

far·o (fer′ō) ***n.*** ‖ Fr *pharaon*, pharaoh: from the picture of a Pharaoh on early French faro cards ‖ a gambling game played with cards

far-off (fär′ôf′) ***adj.*** distant; remote

far′-out′ ***adj.*** [Colloq.] nonconformist; esp., avant-garde

far·ra·go (fə rä′gō, -rā′-) ***n., pl.*** **-goes** ‖ < L *far*, kind of grain ‖ a jumble

far′-reach′ing ***adj.*** having a wide range, extent, influence, or effect

far·ri·er (far′ē ər) ***n.*** ‖ < L *ferrum*, iron ‖ [Brit.] a blacksmith

far·row (far′ō) ***n.*** ‖ < OE *fearh*, young pig ‖ a litter of pigs —***vt., vi.*** to give birth to (a litter of pigs)

far′sight′ed ***adj.*** **1** planning ahead; provident: also **far′see′ing** **2** seeing distant objects more clearly than near ones —**far′·sight′ed·ness** ***n.***

far·ther (fär′*th*ər) ***adj.*** **1** *compar. of* FAR **2** more distant **3** additional; more —***adv.*** **1** *compar. of* FAR **2** at or to a greater distance **3** to a greater degree Cf. FURTHER

far·thest (fär′*th*ist) ***adj.*** **1** *superl. of* FAR **2** most distant —***adv.*** **1** *superl. of* FAR **2** at or to the greatest distance or degree

far·thing (fär′*th*iŋ) ***n.*** ‖ OE *feorthing* ‖ a former British coin worth $\frac{1}{4}$ penny

fas·ci·nate (fas′ə nāt′) ***vt.*** **-nat′ed, -nat′ing** ‖ < L *fascinum*, a charm ‖ **1** to hold motionless, as by inspiring terror **2** to charm; captivate —**fas′ci·na′tion** ***n.***

fas·cism (fash′iz′əm) ***n.*** ‖ < It < L *fasces*, rods bound about an ax, ancient Roman symbol of authority ‖ [*sometimes* **F-**] a system of government characterized by dictatorship, belligerent nationalism and racism, militarism, etc.: first instituted in Italy (1922-43) —**fas′cist** ***n., adj.***

fash·ion (fash′ən) ***n.*** ‖ < L *factio*, a making ‖ **1** the form or shape of a thing **2** way; manner **3** the current style of dress, conduct, etc. —***vt.*** **1** to make; form **2** to fit; accommodate (*to*) —**after** (or **in**) **a fashion** to some extent —**fash′ion·er** ***n.***

fash′ion·a·ble ***adj.*** **1** stylish **2** of or used by people who follow fashion —**fash′ion·a·bly** ***adv.***

fast[1] (fast) ***adj.*** ‖ OE *fæst* ‖ **1** firm; firmly fastened **2** loyal; devoted **3** nonfading /*fast* colors/ **4** swift; quick **5** ahead of time /a *fast* watch/ **6** wild, promiscuous, or dissipated **7** [Colloq.] glib **8** *Photog.* allowing very short exposure time —***adv.*** **1** firmly; fixedly **2** thoroughly /*fast* asleep/ **3** rapidly

fast[2] (fast) ***vi.*** ‖ OE *fæstan* ‖ to abstain from all or certain foods —***n.*** **1** a fasting **2** a period of fasting

fast′back′ (-bak′) ***n.*** an automobile body which slopes from the roof to the rear bumper

fas·ten (fas′ən) ***vt.*** ‖ see FAST[1] ‖ **1** to attach; connect **2** to make secure, as by locking, buttoning, etc. **3** to fix (the attention, etc.) *on* something —***vi.*** to become fastened —**fas′ten·er** ***n.***

fas′ten·ing ***n.*** anything used to fasten; bolt, clasp, hook, etc.

fast′-food′ ***adj.*** designating a business that offers food, as hamburgers, prepared and served quickly

fas·tid·i·ous (fas tid′ē əs) ***adj.*** ‖< L *fastus*, disdain‖ **1** not easy to please **2** daintily refined; oversensitive —**fas·tid′i·ous·ly** ***adv.*** —**fas·tid′i·ous·ness** ***n.***

fast′ness ***n.*** **1** a being fast **2** a stronghold

fast′-talk′ ***vt.*** [Colloq.] to persuade with smooth, but often deceitful talk

fat (fat) ***adj.*** **fat′ter, fat′test** ‖< OE *fætt*‖ **1** containing fat; oily **2** *a)* fleshy; plump *b)* too plump **3** thick; broad **4** fertile /*fat* land/ **5** profitable /a *fat* job/ **6** plentiful —***n.*** **1** an oily or greasy material found in animal tissue and plant seeds **2** the richest part of anything **3** superfluous part —**chew the fat** [Slang] to chat —**fat′ly** ***adv.*** —**fat′ness** ***n.***

fa·tal (fāt′'l) ***adj.*** **1** fateful; decisive **2** resulting in death **3** destructive; disastrous —**fa′tal·ly** ***adv.***

fa′tal·ism′ ***n.*** the belief that all events are determined by fate and are hence inevitable —**fa′tal·ist** ***n.*** —**fa′tal·is′tic** ***adj.*** —**fa′tal·is′ti·cal·ly** ***adv.***

fa·tal·i·ty (fā tal′ə tē, fə-) ***n.***, *pl.* **-ties** **1** a deadly effect; deadliness **2** a death caused by a disaster or accident

fat′back′ ***n.*** fat from a hog's back, usually dried and salted in strips

fat cat [Slang] a wealthy, influential donor, esp. to a political campaign

fate (fāt) ***n.*** ‖< L *fatum*, oracle‖ **1** the power supposed to determine the outcome of events; destiny **2** one's lot or fortune **3** final outcome **4** death; destruction

fat·ed (fāt′id) ***adj.*** **1** destined **2** doomed

fate′ful (-fəl) ***adj.*** **1** prophetic **2** significant; decisive **3** controlled as if by fate **4** bringing death or destruction —**fate′ful·ly** ***adv.***

Fates (fāts) *Gr. & Rom. Myth.* the three goddesses who control human destiny and life

fa·ther (fä′*th*ər) ***n.*** ‖OE *fæder*‖ **1** a male parent **2** an ancestor **3** an originator, founder, or inventor **4** [*often* **F-**] a Christian priest: used esp. as a title —***vt.*** to be the father of —[**F-**] God —**fa′ther·hood′** ***n.*** —**fa′ther·less** ***adj.***

fa′ther-in-law′ ***n.***, *pl.* **fa′thers-in-law′** the father of one's spouse

fa′ther·land′ ***n.*** one's native land

fa′ther·ly ***adj.*** of or like a father; kind —**fa′ther·li·ness** ***n.***

fath·om (fa*th*′əm) ***n.*** ‖< OE *fæthm*, the two arms outstretched‖ a length of 6 feet, used as a nautical unit of depth or length —***vt.*** **1** to measure the depth of **2** to understand thoroughly —**fath′om·a·ble** ***adj.*** —**fath′om·less** ***adj.***

fa·tigue (fə tēg′) ***n.*** ‖Fr < L *fatigare*, to weary‖ **1** exhaustion; weariness **2** [*pl.*] soldiers' work clothing —***vt.***, ***vi.*** **-tigued′**, **-tigu′ing** to tire out

fat·ten (fat′'n) ***vt.***, ***vi.*** to make or become fat (in various senses)

fat′ty ***adj.*** **-ti·er, -ti·est** **1** of or containing fat **2** like fat; greasy

fatty acid any of a group of organic acids in animal or vegetable fats and oils

fat·u·ous (fach′o͞o əs) ***adj.*** ‖L *fatuus*‖ complacently stupid; foolish —**fa·tu·i·ty** (fə to͞o′ə tē) ***n.*** —**fat′u·ous·ly** ***adv.*** —**fat′u·ous·ness** ***n.***

fau·cet (fô′sit) ***n.*** ‖prob. < OFr *faulser*, to breach‖ a device with a valve for regulating the flow of a liquid from a pipe, etc.; tap

Faulk·ner (fôk′nər), **Wil·liam** (wil′yəm) 1897 1962; U.S. novelist

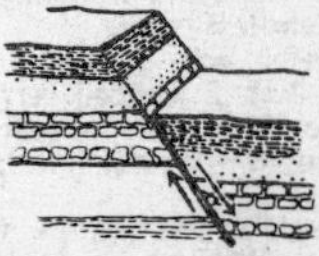

FAULT IN ROCK

fault (fôlt) ***n.*** ‖< L *fallere*, deceive‖ **1** something that mars; defect or failing **2** a misdeed or mistake **3** blame for something wrong **4** a fracture in rock strata —**at fault** deserving blame —**find fault (with)** to criticize

fault′find′ing ***n.***, ***adj.*** criticizing

fault′less ***adj.*** perfect

fault′y ***adj.*** **fault′i·er, fault′i·est** having a fault or faults; defective —**fault′i·ly** ***adv.*** —**fault′i·ness** ***n.***

faun (fôn) ***n.*** ‖< L *faunus*‖ any of a class of minor Roman deities, half man and half goat

fau·na (fô′nə) ***n.*** ‖< LL *Fauna*, Rom. goddess‖ the animals of a specified region or time

Faust (foust) a man in legend and literature who sells his soul to the devil for knowledge and power

faux pas (fō pä′) *pl.* **faux pas** (fō päz′) ‖Fr, lit., false step‖ a social blunder

fa·vor (fā′vər) ***n.*** ‖< L *favere*, to favor‖ **1** friendly regard; approval **2** partiality **3** a kind or obliging act **4** a small gift or token —***vt.*** **1** to approve or like **2** to be partial to **3** to support; advocate **4** to help **5** to do a kindness for **6** to resemble /to *favor* one's mother/ Brit. sp. **fa′vour** —**in favor of** **1** approving **2** to the advantage of —**fa′vor·er** ***n.***

fa′vor·a·ble ***adj.*** **1** approving **2** helpful **3** pleasing —**fa′vor·a·bly** ***adv.***

fa·vor·ite (fā′vər it) ***n.*** **1** a person or thing regarded with special liking **2** a contestant regarded as most likely to win —***adj.*** highly regarded; preferred

fa′vor·it·ism′ ***n.*** partiality; bias

fawn[1] (fôn) ***vi.*** ‖< OE *fægen*, glad‖ **1** to show friendliness by licking hands, etc.: said of a dog **2** to cringe and flatter —**fawn′er** ***n.***

fawn[2] (fôn) ***n.*** ‖< L *fetus*, progeny‖ **1** a deer less than one year old **2** a pale, yellowish brown —***adj.*** of this color

fay (fā) ***n.*** ‖see FATE‖ a fairy

faze (fāz) ***vt.*** **fazed, faz′ing** ‖< OE *fesian*, to drive‖ to disturb

FBI Federal Bureau of Investigation

FCC Federal Communications Commission

FDA Food and Drug Administration

FDIC Federal Deposit Insurance Corporation

Fe ‖L *ferrum*‖ *Chem. symbol for* iron

fe·al·ty (fē′əl tē) ***n.***, *pl.* **-ties** ‖< L *fidelitas*, fidelity ‖ loyalty, esp. as owed to a feudal lord

fear (fir) ***n.*** ‖ < OE *fær*, sudden attack ‖ **1** anxiety caused by real or possible danger, pain, etc.; fright **2** awe; reverence **3** apprehension; concern **4** a cause for fear —***vt., vi.*** **1** to be afraid (of) **2** to be in awe (of) **3** to expect with misgiving —**fear′less** ***adj.*** —**fear′less·ly** ***adv.***

fear′ful (-fəl) ***adj.*** **1** causing, feeling, or showing fear **2** [Colloq.] very bad, great, etc. —**fear′ful·ly** ***adv.*** —**fear′ful·ness** ***n.***

fear′some ***adj.*** **1** causing fear; frightful **2** frightened; timid

fea·si·ble (fē′zə bəl) ***adj.*** ‖ < OFr *faire*, to do ‖ **1** capable of being done; possible **2** likely; probable **3** suitable —**fea′si·bil′i·ty** ***n.*** —**fea′si·bly** ***adv.***

feast (fēst) ***n.*** ‖ < L *festus*, festal ‖ **1** a religious festival **2** a rich and elaborate meal —***vi.*** to have a feast —***vt.*** **1** to entertain at a feast **2** to delight /to *feast* one's eyes on a sight/

feat (fēt) ***n.*** ‖ < L *factum*, a deed ‖ a deed of unusual daring or skill

feath·er (feth′ər) ***n.*** ‖ OE *fether* ‖ any of the soft, light growths covering the body of a bird —***vt.*** **1** to provide or adorn with feathers **2** to turn (an oar or propeller blade) so that the edge is foremost —**feather in one's cap** a distinctive achievement —**feath′er·y** ***adj.***

feath′er·bed′ding (-bed′iŋ) ***n.*** the practice of limiting output or requiring extra, standby workers

feath′er·weight′ ***n.*** a boxer with a maximum weight of 126 pounds

fea·ture (fē′chər) ***n.*** ‖ < L *facere*, to make ‖ **1** *a)* facial form or appearance *b)* any of the parts of the face **2** a distinct or outstanding part or quality of something **3** a special attraction, sale item, newspaper article, etc. **4** a film running more than 34 minutes —***vt., vi.*** **-tured, -tur·ing** to make or be a feature of (something)

fe·brile (fē′bril, feb′ril) ***adj.*** ‖ < L *febris*, FEVER ‖ feverish

Feb·ru·ar·y (feb′ro͞o er′ē, feb′yo͞o-) ***n.***, *pl.* **-ies** ‖ < L *Februarius* (*mensis*), orig. month of expiation ‖ the second month of the year, having 28 days (or 29 days in leap years): abbrev. **Feb.**

fe·ces (fē′sēz′) ***n.pl.*** ‖ < L *faeces*, dregs ‖ excrement —**fe′cal** (-kəl) ***adj.***

feck·less (fek′lis) ***adj.*** ‖ Scot < *feck*, effect + LESS ‖ **1** weak; ineffective **2** irresponsible —**feck′less·ly** ***adv.***

fe·cund (fē′kənd, fek′ənd) ***adj.*** ‖ < L *fecundus* ‖ fertile; productive —**fe·cun·di·ty** (fē kun′də tē) ***n.***

fe·cun·date (fē′kən dāt′, fek′ən-) ***vt.*** **-dat′ed, -dat′ing** **1** to make fecund **2** to fertilize

fed (fed) ***vt., vi.*** *pt. & pp. of* FEED —**fed up** [Colloq.] having had enough to become disgusted, bored, etc.

Fed. **1** Federal **2** Federation

fed·a·yeen (fed′ä yēn′) ***n.pl.*** ‖ Ar *fidāʔiyīn*, sacrificers ‖ Arab guerrillas

fed·er·al (fed′ər əl) ***adj.*** ‖ < L *foedus*, a league ‖ **1** designating or of a union of states, etc. in which each member subordinates its power to a central authority **2** *a)* designating or of a central government in such a union *b)* [*usually* **F-**] designating or of the central government of the U.S. **3** [**F-**] of or supporting a former U.S. political party (**Federalist Party**) which favored a strong centralized government **4** [**F-**] of or supporting the Union in the Civil War —***n.*** [**F-**] a supporter or soldier of the Union in the Civil War —**fed′er·al·ism′** ***n.*** —**fed′er·al·ist** ***adj., n.*** —**fed′er·al·ly** ***adv.***

fed′er·al·ize′ (-īz′) ***vt.*** **-ized′, -iz′ing** **1** to unite (states, etc.) in a federal union **2** to put under federal authority —**fed′er·al·i·za′tion** ***n.***

fed·er·ate (fed′ər āt′) ***vt., vi.*** **-at′ed, -at′ing** to unite in a federation

fed·er·a·tion (fed′ər ā′shən) ***n.*** ‖ see FEDERAL ‖ **1** a union of states, groups, etc. in which each subordinates its power to that of the central authority **2** a federated organization

fe·do·ra (fə dôr′ə) ***n.*** ‖ Fr ‖ a soft felt hat worn by men

fee (fē) ***n.*** ‖ ult < Gmc ‖ a charge for professional services, licenses, etc.

fee·ble (fē′bəl) ***adj.*** **-bler, -blest** ‖ < L *flere*, weep ‖ **1** weak; infirm /a *feeble* old man/ **2** without force or effectiveness /a *feeble* attempt/ —**fee′ble·ness** ***n.*** —**fee′bly** ***adv.***

feed (fēd) ***vt.*** **fed, feed′ing** ‖ < OE *foda*, food ‖ **1** to give food to **2** to provide something necessary for the growth, operation, etc. of **3** to gratify /to *feed* one's vanity/ —***vi.*** to eat: said esp. of animals —***n.*** **1** food for animals; fodder **2** *a)* the material fed into a machine *b)* the part of the machine supplying this material —**feed′er** ***n.***

feed′back′ ***n.*** **1** the transfer of part of the output back to the input, as of electricity or information **2** a response

feed′stock′ ***n.*** raw material for industrial processing

feel (fēl) ***vt.*** **felt, feel′ing** ‖ OE *felan* ‖ **1** to touch; examine by handling **2** to be aware of through physical sensation **3** to experience (an emotion or condition); be affected by **4** to be aware of **5** to think or believe —***vi.*** **1** to have physical sensation **2** to appear to be to the senses /it *feels* warm/ **3** to grope **4** to be aware of being /I *feel* sad/ **5** to be moved to sympathy, pity, etc. (*for*) —***n.*** **1** the act of feeling **2** the sense of touch **3** the nature of a thing as perceived through touch —**feel like** [Colloq.] to have a desire for —**feel one's way** to advance cautiously —**feel someone out** to find out the opinions of someone cautiously —**feel up to** [Colloq.] to feel capable of

feel′er ***n.*** **1** a specialized organ of touch in an animal or insect, as an antenna **2** a remark, offer, etc. made to feel another out

feel′ing ***n.*** **1** the sense of touch **2** the ability to experience physical sensation **3** an awareness; sensation **4** an emotion **5** [*pl.*] sensibilities /hurt *feelings*/ **6** sympathy; pity **7** an opinion or sentiment

fee simple absolute and unrestricted ownership of real property

feet (fēt) ***n.*** *pl. of* FOOT

feign (fān) ***vt., vi.*** ‖ < L *fingere*, to shape ‖ **1** to make up (an excuse, etc.) **2** to pretend; dissemble

feint (fānt) ***n.*** ‖ see prec. ‖ a pretended attack intended to take the opponent off his guard, as in boxing —***vi., vt.*** to deliver (such an attack)

feld·spar (feld′spär′) ***n.*** ‖ < Ger *feld*, field + *spath*, a mineral ‖ any of several hard, crystalline minerals

fe·lic·i·tate (fə lis′i tāt′) ***vt.*** **-tat′ed, -tat′ing** ‖ < L *felix*, happy ‖ to wish happiness to; congratulate —**fe·lic′i·ta′tion** ***n.*** —**fe·lic′i·ta′tor** ***n.***

fe·lic′i·tous (-təs) ***adj.*** ‖ < fol. ‖ used or expressed in a way suitable to the occasion; appropriate

fe·lic′i·ty ***n.,*** *pl.* **-ties** ‖ < L *felix*, happy ‖ **1** happiness; bliss **2** anything producing happiness **3** apt and pleasing expression in writing, etc.

fe·line (fē′līn) ***adj.*** ‖ < L *feles*, cat ‖ **1** of a cat or the cat family **2** catlike; sly —***n.*** any animal of the cat family

fell[1] (fel) ***vi., vt.*** *pt. of* FALL

fell[2] (fel) ***vt.*** ‖ OE *fellan* ‖ **1** to knock down **2** to cut down (a tree)

fell[3] (fel) ***adj.*** ‖ < ML *fello* ‖ fierce; cruel

fel·low (fel′ō, -ə) ***n.*** ‖ Late OE *feolaga*, partner ‖ **1** an associate **2** one of the same rank; equal **3** one of a pair; mate **4** one holding a fellowship in a college, etc. **5** a member of a learned society **6** [Colloq.] a man or boy —***adj.*** **1** having the same position, work, etc. **2** associated /*fellow* workers/

fel′low·ship′ ***n.*** **1** companionship **2** a mutual sharing **3** a group of people with the same interests **4** an endowment for the support of a student or scholar doing advanced work

fellow traveler a nonmember who supports the cause of a party

fel·on[1] (fel′ən) ***n.*** ‖ < ML *felo*, villain ‖ a person guilty of a felony; criminal

fel·on[2] (fel′ən) ***n.*** ‖ ME ‖ a painful infection at the end of a finger or toe

fel·o·ny (fel′ə nē) ***n.,*** *pl.* **-nies** ‖ < ML *felonia*, treachery ‖ a major crime, as murder, arson, etc. —**fe·lo·ni·ous** (fə lō′nē əs) ***adj.***

felt[1] (felt) ***n.*** ‖ < OE ‖ a fabric of wool, often mixed with fur, hair, cotton, etc., worked together by pressure, etc. —***adj.*** made of felt —***vt.*** to make into felt

felt[2] (felt) ***vt., vi.*** *pt. and pp. of* FEEL

fe·male (fē′māl′) ***adj.*** ‖ < L *femina*, woman ‖ **1** designating or of the sex that bears offspring **2** of, like, or suitable to women or girls; feminine **3** consisting of women or girls **4** having a hollow part for receiving an inserted part (called *male*): said of electric sockets, etc. —***n.*** a female person, animal, or plant

fem·i·nine (fem′ə nin) ***adj.*** ‖ < L *femina*, woman ‖ **1** of women or girls **2** having qualities characteristic of or suitable to women; gentle, delicate, etc. **3** *Gram.* designating or of the gender of words referring to females or other words with no distinction of sex —**fem′i·nin′i·ty** ***n.***

fem′i·nism′ ***n.*** the movement to win political, economic, and social equality for women —**fem′i·nist** ***n., adj.***

fe·mur (fē′mər) ***n.,*** *pl.* **fe′murs** or **fem·o·ra** (fem′ə rə) ‖ < L, thigh ‖ the bone extending from the hip to the knee —**fem′o·ral** ***adj.***

fen (fen) ***n.*** ‖ OE ‖ an area of low, flat, marshy land; swamp; bog

fence (fens) ***n.*** ‖ < ME *defens*, defense ‖ **1** a protective or confining barrier of posts, wire mesh, etc. **2** one who deals in stolen goods —***vt.*** **fenced, fenc′ing** **1** to enclose, as with a fence: with *in, off*, etc. **2** to keep (*out*) as by a fence **3** to sell (stolen property) to a fence —***vi.*** **1** to practice the art of fencing **2** to avoid giving a direct reply —**fenc′er** ***n.***

fenc′ing ***n.*** **1** the art of fighting with a foil or other sword **2** material for making fences **3** a system of fences

fend (fend) ***vi.*** ‖ ME *fenden*, defend ‖ to resist —**fend for oneself** to manage by oneself —**fend off** to ward off

fend′er ***n.*** anything that fends off or protects something else, as the part of an automobile body over the wheel

fen·nel (fen′əl) ***n.*** ‖ < L *fenum*, hay ‖ a tall herb with aromatic seeds used to flavor foods

fe·ral (fir′əl) ***adj.*** ‖ < L *ferus*, wild ‖ **1** untamed; wild **2** savage

fer·ment (fʉr′ment′; *for v.* fər ment′) ***n.*** ‖ < L *fervere*, to boil ‖ **1** a substance causing fermentation, as yeast **2** excitement or agitation —***vt.*** **1** to cause fermentation in **2** to excite; agitate —***vi.*** **1** to be in the process of fermentation **2** to be excited or agitated; seethe

fer·men·ta·tion (fʉr′mən tā′shən) ***n.*** **1** the breakdown of complex molecules in organic compounds, caused by the influence of a ferment /bacteria cause milk to curdle by *fermentation*/ **2** excitement; agitation

fer·mi·on (fer′mē ăn′, fʉr′-) ***n.*** ‖ after E. *Fermi*, 20th-c. U.S. nuclear physicist ‖ any of certain subatomic particles, including leptons and baryons

FERN

fern (fʉrn) ***n.*** ‖ < OE *fearn* ‖ any of a large group of nonflowering plants having roots, stems, and fronds, and reproducing by spores

fe·ro·cious (fə rō′shəs) ***adj.*** ‖ < L *ferus*, wild ‖ **1** fierce; savage; violently cruel **2** [Colloq.] very great /a *ferocious* appetite/ —**fe·ro′cious·ly** ***adv.*** —**fe·roc·i·ty** (fə răs′ə tē) ***n.***

-fer·ous (fər əs) ‖ < L *ferre*, to bear ‖ *suffix forming adjectives* bearing, yielding

fer·ret (fer′ət) ***n.*** ‖ < L *fur*, thief ‖ a small European polecat, easily tamed for hunting rats, etc. —***vt.*** **1** to force out of hiding with a ferret **2** to find out by investigation: with *out*

fer·ric (fer′ik) ***adj.*** ‖ < L *ferrum*, iron ‖ of, containing, or derived from iron

Fer·ris wheel (fer′is) ‖ after G. *Ferris* (1859-

96), U.S. engineer]] a large, upright wheel revolving on a fixed axle and having suspended seats: used as an amusement ride
ferro- [[< L *ferrum*, iron]] *combining form* **1** iron **2** iron and
fer·rous (fer′əs) ***adj.*** [[< L *ferrum*, iron]] of, containing, or derived from iron
fer·rule (fer′əl, -o͞ol′) ***n.*** [[< L *viriae*, bracelets]] a metal ring or cap put around the end of a cane, tool handle, etc. to give added strength
fer·ry (fer′ē) ***vt.*** **-ried, -ry·ing** [[OE *ferian*]] **1** to take (people, cars, etc.) across a river, etc. **2** to deliver (airplanes) by flying them **3** to transport by airplane —***n.***, *pl.* **-ries** **1** a system for carrying people, goods, etc. across a river, etc. by boat **2** a boat used for this: also **fer′ry·boat′**
fer·tile (furt′'l) ***adj.*** [[< L *ferre*, to bear]] **1** producing abundantly; fruitful **2** able to produce young, seeds, fruit, pollen, spores, etc. **3** fertilized —**fer·til·i·ty** (fər til′ə tē) ***n.***
fer′til·ize′ (-īz′) ***vt.*** **-ized′, -iz′ing** **1** to make fertile **2** to spread fertilizer on **3** to make (the female cell or female) fruitful by pollinating, or impregnating, with the male gamete —**fer′til·iz′a·ble** ***adj.*** —**fer′til·i·za′tion** ***n.***
fer′til·iz′er ***n.*** manure, chemicals, etc., used to enrich the soil
fer·ule (fer′əl, -o͞ol′) ***n.*** [[< L *ferula*, a whip, rod]] a flat stick or ruler used for punishing children
fer·vent (fur′vənt) ***adj.*** [[< L *fervere*, to glow]] showing great warmth of feeling; intensely devoted or earnest —**fer′ven·cy** ***n.*** —**fer′vent·ly** ***adv.***
fer·vid (fur′vid) ***adj.*** [[see prec.]] impassioned; fervent —**fer′vid·ly** ***adv.***
fer·vor (fur′vər) ***n.*** [[see FERVENT]] great warmth of emotion; ardor; zeal
-fest (fest) [[< Ger *fest*, a feast]] *combining form* an occasion of much or many *[songfest]*
fes·tal (fes′təl) ***adj.*** [[< L *festum*, feast]] of or like a joyous celebration; festive
fes·ter (fes′tər) ***n.*** [[< L *fistula*, ulcer]] a small sore filled with pus —***vi.*** **1** to form pus **2** to rankle
fes·ti·val (fes′tə vəl) ***n.*** [[see fol.]] **1** a time or day of feasting or celebration **2** a celebration or series of performances
fes·tive (fes′tiv) ***adj.*** [[< L *festum*, feast]] **1** of or for a feast or festival **2** merry; joyous —**fes′tive·ly** ***adv.*** —**fes′tive·ness** ***n.***
fes·tiv·i·ty (fes tiv′ə tē) ***n.***, *pl.* **-ties** **1** merrymaking; gaiety **2** a festival **3** [*pl.*] things done in celebration
fes·toon (fes to͞on′) ***n.*** [[< It *festa*, feast]] a curved garland of flowers, etc. —***vt.*** to adorn with festoons
fet·a (cheese) (fet′ə) [[< ModGr < It *fetta*, a slice]] a white, soft cheese, orig. made in Greece
fe·tal (fēt′'l) ***adj.*** of a fetus
fetch (fech) ***vt.*** [[OE *feccan*]] **1** to go after and bring back; get **2** to cause to come **3** to sell for
fetch′ing ***adj.*** attractive; charming
fete or **fête** (fāt, fet) ***n.*** [[Fr *fête*: see FEAST]] a festival; entertainment, esp. outdoors —***vt.*** **fet′ed** or **fêt′ed, fet′ing** or **fêt′ing** to honor with a fete
fet·id (fet′id) ***adj.*** [[< L *foetere*, to stink]] having a bad smell; stinking; putrid —**fet′id·ness** ***n.***
fet·ish (fet′ish) ***n.*** [[< Port *feitiço*]] **1** any object believed to have magical power **2** anything to which one is irrationally devoted **3** any nonsexual object that abnormally excites erotic feelings Also **fet′ich** —**fet′ish·ism′** ***n.*** —**fet′ish·ist** ***n.***
fet·lock (fet′läk′) ***n.*** [[< ME *fet*, feet]] **1** a tuft of hair on the back of a horse's leg above the hoof **2** the joint bearing this tuft
fe·to·scope (fē′tə skōp′) ***n.*** **1** an endoscope used to examine a fetus in the womb **2** a special stethoscope used to listen to the fetal heartbeat
fet·ter (fet′ər) ***n.*** [[< OE *fot*, foot]] **1** a shackle or chain for the feet **2** any check or restraint —***vt.*** **1** to bind with fetters **2** to restrain
fet·tle (fet′'l) ***n.*** [[ME *fetlen*, make ready]] condition; state *[in fine fettle]*
fe·tus (fēt′əs) ***n.***, *pl.* **-tus·es** [[L, a bringing forth]] the unborn young of an animal, esp. in its later stages and specif., in humans, from about the eighth week after conception until birth
feud (fyo͞od) ***n.*** [[< OFr *faide*]] a deadly quarrel, esp. between clans or families —***vi.*** to carry on a feud; quarrel
feu·dal (fyo͞od′'l) ***adj.*** [[ML *feudalis*]] of or like feudalism
feu′dal·ism′ ***n.*** the economic and social system in medieval Europe, in which land, worked by serfs, was held by vassals in exchange for military and other services to overlords
fe·ver (fē′vər) ***n.*** [[< L *febris*]] **1** an abnormally increased body temperature **2** any disease marked by a high fever **3** a restless excitement —**fe′ver·ish** ***adj.*** —**fe′ver·ish·ly** ***adv.***
fever blister (or **sore**) COLD SORE
few (fyo͞o) ***adj.*** [[OE *feawe*]] not many —***pron.*** not many; a small number —**the few** the minority
fey (fā) ***adj.*** [[OE *fæge*, fated]] strange or unusual; specif., eccentric, whimsical, etc. —**fey′ness** ***n.***
fez (fez) ***n.***, *pl.* **fez′zes** [[after *Fez*, city in Morocco]] a red, tapering felt hat, worn formerly by Turkish men
ff. **1** folios **2** following (pages, etc.)
fi·an·cé (fē′än sā′) ***n.*** [[Fr < OFr *fiance*, a promise]] a man who is engaged to be married
fi·an·cée (fē′än sā′) ***n.*** [[Fr: see prec.]] a woman who is engaged to be married
fi·as·co (fē as′kō) ***n.***, *pl.* **-coes** or **-cos** [[Fr < It]] a complete, ridiculous failure
fi·at (fī′at′, -ət) ***n.*** [[L, let it be done]] **1** a decree; order **2** a sanction
fib (fib) ***n.*** [[< ? FABLE]] a small or trivial lie —***vi.*** **fibbed, fib′bing** to tell such a lie —**fib′ber** ***n.***
fi·ber (fī′bər) ***n.*** [[< L *fibra*]] **1** a threadlike structure that combines with others to form animal or vegetable tissue **2** any substance that can be separated into threadlike parts for weaving, etc. **3** texture **4** character or nature **5** ROUGHAGE —**fi′brous** (-brəs) ***adj.***
fi′ber·board′ ***n.*** a building material consist-

ing of fibers of wood, etc. pressed into stiff sheets

Fi'ber·glas' (-glas') *trademark for* finespun filaments of glass made into textiles or insulating material —*n.* [f-] this substance: also **fiberglass**

fiber optics 1 the science of transmitting light and images, as around curves, through transparent fibers 2 such fibers —**fi'ber-op'tic** *adj.*

fi·bril·la·tion (fib'ri lā'shən) *n.* ⟦< L *fibra*, fiber + -ATION⟧ very rapid contractions of part of the heart muscle, causing irregular heartbeats

fi·brin (fī'brin) *n.* a fibrous, insoluble blood protein formed in blood clots

fi·brin·o·gen (fī brin'ə jən) *n.* ⟦prec. + -GEN⟧ a protein in the blood from which fibrin is formed

fi·broid (fī'broid') *adj.* like or composed of fibrous tissue, as a tumor

fi·bro·sis (fī brō'sis) *n.* an excessive growth of fibrous connective tissue in an organ, part, etc.

fib·u·la (fib'yoo lə) *n.*, *pl.* **-lae'** (-lē') or **-las** ⟦L, a clasp⟧ the long, thin outer bone of the lower leg —**fib'u·lar** *adj.*

-fic (fik) ⟦< L *facere*, make⟧ *suffix* making [*terrific*]

FICA Federal Insurance Contributions Act

-fi·ca·tion (fi kā'shən) ⟦see -FIC⟧ *suffix* a making [*glorification*]

fich·u (fish'oo) *n.* ⟦Fr⟧ a triangular lace or muslin cape for women, worn with the ends fastened in front

fick·le (fik'əl) *adj.* ⟦< OE *ficol*, tricky⟧ changeable or unstable; capricious

fic·tion (fik'shən) *n.* ⟦< L *fingere*, to form⟧ 1 an imaginary statement, story, etc. 2 *a*) literary works, collectively, with imaginary characters or events, as novels *b*) a work of this kind —**fic'tion·al** *adj.*

fic'tion·al·ize' (-shə nəl īz') *vt.* **-ized'**, **-iz'ing** to deal with (historical events) in fictional form

fic·ti·tious (fik tish'əs) *adj.* 1 of or like fiction; imaginary 2 false 3 assumed for disguise [a *fictitious* name]

fic·tive (fik'tiv) *adj.* 1 of fiction 2 imaginary —**fic'tive·ly** *adv.*

fi·cus (fī'kəs) *n.*, *pl.* **fi'cus** ⟦< L, fig tree⟧ any of a genus of tropical shrubs, trees, etc. with glossy, leathery leaves

fid·dle (fid''l) *n.* ⟦OE *fithele*⟧ [Colloq.] a violin —*vi.* **-dled**, **-dling** 1 [Colloq.] to play a fiddle 2 to tinker (*with*) nervously —**fid'dler** *n.*

fid'dle·sticks' *interj.* nonsense!

fi·del·i·ty (fə del'ə tē) *n.*, *pl.* **-ties** ⟦< L *fides*, faith⟧ 1 faithful devotion to duty; loyalty 2 accuracy of description, sound reproduction, etc.

fidg·et (fij'it) *n.* ⟦< ME < ?⟧ a restless or nervous state: esp. in phrase **the fidgets** —*vi.* to move about restlessly or nervously —**fidg'et·y** *adj.*

fi·du·ci·ar·y (fi doo'shē er'ē) *adj.* ⟦< L *fiducia*, trust⟧ holding or held in trust —*n.*, *pl.* **-ies** TRUSTEE (sense 1)

fie (fī) *interj.* for shame!

fief (fēf) *n.* ⟦Fr: see FEE⟧ in feudalism, heritable land held by a vassal

fief'dom (-dəm) *n.* 1 FIEF 2 anything under one's complete control

field (fēld) *n.* ⟦OE *feld*⟧ 1 a stretch of open land 2 a piece of cleared land for crops or pasture 3 a piece of land used for a particular purpose [a landing *field*] 4 any wide, unbroken expanse [a *field* of ice] 5 *a*) a battlefield *b*) a battle 6 a realm of knowledge or work 7 the background, as on a flag 8 all the entrants in a contest 9 *Physics* a physical quantity specified at points throughout a region of space —*vt.* 1 to stop or catch and throw (a baseball, etc.) 2 to put (a player or team) into active play 3 [Colloq.] to answer (a question) extemporaneously —**play the field** to not confine one's activities to one object —**field'er** *n.*

field glasses a small, portable, binocular telescope

field goal 1 *Basketball* a shot made from play, scoring two points or, if from a certain distance, three points 2 *Football* a goal kicked from the field, scoring three points

field hand a hired farm laborer

field hockey HOCKEY (sense 2)

field marshal in some armies, an officer of the highest rank

field'-test' *vt.* to test (a device, method, etc.) under operating conditions

fiend (fēnd) *n.* ⟦OE *feond*⟧ 1 an evil spirit; devil 2 an inhumanly wicked person 3 [Colloq.] an addict [a dope *fiend*, fresh-air *fiend*] —**fiend'ish** *adj.*

fierce (firs) *adj.* **fierc'er**, **fierc'est** ⟦< L *ferus*, wild⟧ 1 savage 2 violent 3 intense [a *fierce* embrace] —**fierce'ly** *adv.* —**fierce'ness** *n.*

fi·er·y (fī'ər ē) *adj.* **-er·i·er**, **-er·i·est** 1 like fire; glaring, hot, etc. 2 ardent; spirited 3 excitable 4 inflamed

fi·es·ta (fē es'tə) *n.* ⟦Sp < L *festus*, festal⟧ 1 a religious festival 2 any gala celebration; holiday

fife (fīf) *n.* ⟦Ger *pfeife*⟧ a small flute used mainly with drums in playing marches

fif·teen (fif'tēn') *adj.*, *n.* ⟦OE *fiftene*⟧ five more than ten; 15; XV —**fif'teenth'** (-tēnth') *adj.*, *n.*, *adv.*

fifth (fifth) *adj.* ⟦< OE *fif*, five⟧ preceded by four others in a series; 5th —*n.* 1 the one following the fourth 2 any of the five equal parts of something; $\frac{1}{5}$ 3 a fifth of a gallon —*adv.* in the fifth place, rank, etc.

Fifth Amendment an amendment to the U.S. Constitution mainly guaranteeing certain protections in criminal cases; specif., the clause protecting persons from being compelled to testify against themselves

fif·ty (fif'tē) *adj.*, *n.*, *pl.* **-ties** ⟦OE *fiftig*⟧ five times ten; 50; L —**the fifties** the numbers or years, as of a century, from 50 through 59 —**fif'ti·eth** (-ith) *adj.*, *n.*

fif'ty-fif'ty *adj.* [Colloq.] equal; even —*adv.* [Colloq.] equally

fig (fig) *n.* ⟦< L *ficus*⟧ 1 *a*) a small, sweet, pear-shaped fruit that grows on a tree related to the mulberry *b*) the tree 2 a trifle [not worth a *fig*]

fig. 1 figurative(ly) 2 figure(s)

fight (fīt) *vi.* **fought**, **fight'ing** ⟦OE *feohtan*⟧ to take part in a struggle, contest, etc., esp. against a foe or for a cause —*vt.* 1 to oppose physically or in battle 2 to struggle against **3** to engage in (a war, etc.) **4** to gain (one's way) by struggle —*n.* **1** any struggle, contest, or quarrel **2** power or readiness to fight

fight′er *n.* **1** one that fights; esp., a prizefighter **2** a fast, highly maneuverable combat airplane

fig·ment (fig′mənt) *n.* ⟦< L *fingere,* to form⟧ something merely imagined

fig·ur·a·tive (fig′yoor ə tiv′) *adj.* **1** representing by means of a figure or symbol **2** not in its literal sense; metaphorical **3** using figures of speech —**fig′ur·a·tive′ly** *adv.*

fig·ure (fig′yər) *n.* ⟦< L *fingere,* to form⟧ **1** an outline or shape; form **2** the human form **3** a person thought of in a specified way /a historical *figure*/ **4** a likeness of a person or thing **5** an illustration; diagram **6** a design; pattern **7** the symbol for a number **8** [*pl.*] arithmetic **9** a sum of money **10** *Geom.* a surface or space bounded by lines or planes —*vt.* **-ured, -ur·ing 1** to represent in definite form **2** to imagine **3** to ornament with a design **4** to compute with figures **5** [Colloq.] to believe; consider —*vi.* **1** to appear prominently **2** to do arithmetic —**figure in** to include —**figure on** to rely on —**figure out 1** to solve **2** to understand —**figure up** to add; total

fig′ure·head′ *n.* **1** a carved figure on the bow of a ship **2** one put in a position of leadership, but having no real power or authority

figure of speech an expression, as a metaphor or simile, using words in a nonliteral or unusual sense

fig·u·rine (fig′yoo rēn′) *n.* ⟦Fr⟧ a small sculptured or molded figure

Fi·ji (fē′jē) country on a group of islands (**Fiji Islands**) in the SW Pacific: *c.* 7,000 sq. mi.; pop. 672,000

fil·a·ment (fil′ə mənt) *n.* ⟦< L *filum,* thread⟧ a very slender thread or threadlike part; specif., the fine wire in a light bulb or electron tube

fil·bert (fil′bərt) *n.* ⟦ME *filberde*⟧ HAZELNUT

filch (filch) *vt.* ⟦ME *filchen*⟧ to steal (usually something small or petty)

file¹ (fīl) *vt.* **filed, fil′ing** ⟦< L *filum,* thread⟧ **1** to put (papers, etc.) in order for future reference **2** to dispatch or register (a news story, application, etc.) **3** to put on public record —*vi.* **1** to move in a line **2** to make application (*for* divorce, etc.) —*n.* **1** a container for keeping papers in order **2** an orderly arrangement of papers, etc. **3** a line of persons or things **4** *Comput.* a collection of data stored as a single unit —**file′a·ble** *adj.* —**fil′er** *n.*

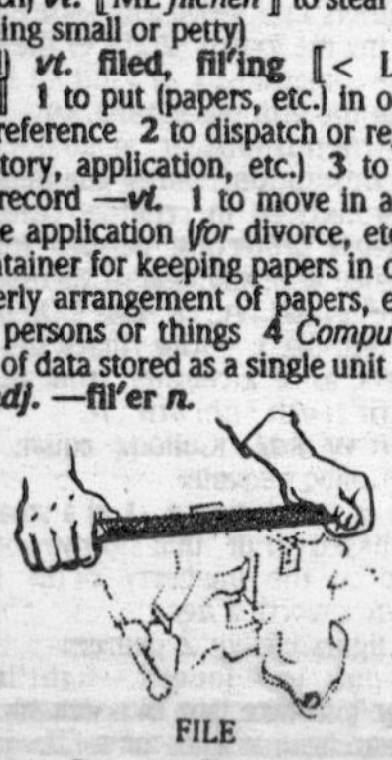

FILE

file² (fīl) *n.* ⟦OE *feol*⟧ a steel tool with a rough, ridged surface for smoothing or grinding —*vt.* **filed, fil′ing** to smooth or grind, as with a file

fi·let (fi lā′, fil′ā) *n.* ⟦Fr: see FILLET⟧ FILLET (*n.* 2) —*vt.* FILLET

fi·let mi·gnon (fē′lā mēn yōn′, -yŏn′) ⟦Fr, lit., tiny fillet⟧ a thick, round cut of lean beef tenderloin

fil·i·al (fil′ē əl, fil′yəl) *adj.* ⟦< L *filius,* son⟧ of, suitable to, or due from a son or daughter

fil·i·bus·ter (fil′i bus′tər) *n.* ⟦< Sp < MDu *vrijbuiter,* freebooter⟧ **1** the making of long speeches, etc. to obstruct a bill's passage in the Senate **2** a Senator who does this —*vt., vi.* to obstruct (a bill) by a filibuster

fil·i·gree (fil′i grē′) *n.* ⟦< L *filum,* thread + *granum,* grain⟧ lacelike ornamental work of intertwined wire of gold, silver, etc. —*vt.* **-greed′, -gree′ing** to ornament with filigree

fil·ing (fīl′iŋ) *n.* a small piece scraped off with a file: *usually used in pl.*

Fil·i·pi·no (fil′i pē′nō) *n., pl.* **-nos** ⟦Sp⟧ a native of the Philippines —*adj.* Philippine

fill (fil) *vt.* ⟦OE *fyllan*⟧ **1** to put as much as possible into **2** to occupy wholly **3** to put a person into or to occupy (a position, etc.) **4** to supply the things called for in (an order, etc.) **5** to close or plug (holes, etc.) —*vi.* to become full —*n.* **1** enough to make full or to satisfy **2** anything that fills —**fill in 1** to complete by supplying something **2** to supply for completion **3** to be a substitute —**fill out 1** to make or become larger, etc. **2** to make (a document, etc.) complete with data —**fill up** to make or become completely full —**fill′er** *n.*

fil·let (fil′it; *for n. 2 & vt., usually* fi lā′, fil′ā′) *n.* ⟦OFr *filet* < L *filum,* thread⟧ **1** a thin strip or band **2** a boneless, lean piece of meat or fish —*vt.* to bone and slice (meat or fish)

fill′-in′ *n.* one that fills a vacancy or gap, often temporarily

fill′ing *n.* a substance used to fill something, as gold in a tooth cavity

filling station SERVICE STATION

fil·lip (fil′ip) *n.* ⟦< FLIP¹⟧ **1** an outward snap of a finger from the thumb **2** something stimulating —*vt.* to strike or toss with a fillip

Fill·more (fil′môr), **Mill·ard** (mil′ərd) 1800-74; 13th president of the U.S. (1850-53)

fil·ly (fil′ē) *n., pl.* **-lies** ⟦< ON *fylja*⟧ a young female horse

film (film) *n.* ⟦OE *filmen*⟧ **1** a fine, thin skin, coating, etc. **2** a flexible cellulose material coated with an emulsion sensitive to light and used in photography **3** a haze or blur **4** a series of still pictures projected on a screen in such rapid succession as to create the illusion of moving persons and objects **5** a play, story, etc. in this form —*vt., vi.* **1** to cover or be covered as with a film **2** to photograph or make a film (of)

film′strip′ *n.* a length of film with still photographs, often of illustrations, charts, etc., for projection separately

film′y *adj.* **-i·er, -i·est 1** gauzy; sheer; thin **2** blurred; hazy

fil·ter (fil′tər) *n.* ⟦< ML *filtrum,* FELT¹⟧ **1** a device for straining out solid particles, impurities, etc. from a liquid or gas **2** a device or substance for screening out electric oscillations, light waves, etc. of certain frequencies —*vt., vi.* 1 to pass through or as through a filter 2 to remove with a filter —**fil′ter·a·ble** or **fil′tra·ble** (-trə bəl) *adj.*

filter tip 1 a cigarette with a tip of cellulose, cotton, etc. for filtering the smoke 2 such a tip

filth (filth) *n.* ‖OE *fylthe*‖ 1 foul dirt 2 obscenity —**filth′i·ness** *n.* —**filth′y, -i·er, -i·est,** *adj.*

fil·trate (fil′trāt′) *vt.* **-trat′ed, -trat′ing** to filter —*n.* a filtered liquid —**fil·tra′tion** *n.*

fin (fin) *n.* ‖OE *finn*‖ 1 any of several winglike organs on the body of a fish, dolphin, etc., used in swimming 2 anything like a fin in shape or use

fi·na·gle (fə nā′gəl) *vt., vi.* **-gled, -gling** ‖< ?‖ [Colloq.] to use, or get by, craftiness or trickery —**fi·na′gler** *n.*

fi·nal (fīn′əl) *adj.* ‖< L *finis,* end‖ 1 of or coming at the end; last 2 deciding; conclusive —*n.* 1 anything final 2 [*pl.*] the last of a series of contests 3 a final examination —**fi·nal′i·ty** (-nal′ə tē) *n.* —**fi′nal·ly** *adv.*

fi·na·le (fə nal′ē) *n.* ‖It‖ the concluding part of a musical work, etc.

fi′nal·ist *n.* a contestant in the final, deciding contest of a series

fi′nal·ize′ *vt.* **-ized′, -iz′ing** ‖FINAL + IZE‖ to make final; complete —**fi′nal·i·za′tion** *n.*

fi·nance (fī′nans′; *also* fə nans′) *n.* ‖< L *finis,* end‖ 1 [*pl.*] money resources, income, etc. 2 the science of managing money —*vt.* **-nanced′, -nanc′ing** to supply or get money for —**fi·nan′cial** (-nan′shəl) *adj.* —**fi·nan′cial·ly** *adv.*

fin·an·cier (fin′ən sir′; *also* fī′nan-) *n.* ‖Fr‖ one skilled in finance

finch (finch) *n.* ‖OE *finc*‖ any of various small, seed-eating birds, including canaries, goldfinches, etc.

find (fīnd) *vt.* **found, find′ing** ‖OE *findan*‖ 1 to discover by chance; come upon 2 to get by searching 3 to perceive; learn 4 to recover (something lost) 5 to reach; attain 6 to decide and declare to be —*vi.* to reach a decision /the jury *found* for the accused/ —*n.* 1 a finding 2 something found —**find out** to discover; learn —**find′er** *n.*

find′ing *n.* 1 discovery 2 something found 3 [*often pl.*] the verdict of a judge, scholar, etc.

fine[1] (fīn) *adj.* **fin′er, fin′est** ‖< L *finis,* end‖ 1 very good; excellent 2 with no impurities; refined 3 clear and bright /*fine* weather/ 4 not heavy or coarse /*fine* sand/ 5 very thin or small /*fine* print/ 6 sharp /a *fine* edge/ 7 subtle; delicate /a *fine* distinction/ 8 elegant —*adv.* in a fine manner —**fine′ly** *adv.* —**fine′ness** *n.*

fine[2] (fīn) *n.* ‖see prec.‖ a sum of money paid as a penalty —*vt.* **fined, fin′ing** to order to pay a fine

fine art any of the art forms that include drawing, painting, sculpture, etc.: *usually used in pl.*

fin·er·y (fīn′ər ē) *n., pl.* **-ies** elaborate clothes, jewelry, etc.

fines herbes (fēn zerb′) ‖Fr‖ a seasoning of chopped herbs, esp. parsley, chives, tarragon, and chervil

fi·nesse (fə nes′) *n.* ‖see FINE[1]‖ 1 adroitness; skill 2 the ability to handle difficult situations diplomatically 3 cunning; artfulness —*vt.* **-nessed′, -ness′ing** 1 to manage or bring about by finesse 2 to evade (a problem, etc.)

fin·ger (fiŋ′gər) *n.* ‖OE‖ 1 any of the five jointed parts extending from the palm of the hand, esp. one other than the thumb 2 anything like a finger in shape or use —*vt.* 1 to touch with the fingers; handle 2 *Music* to use the fingers in a certain way in playing —**have** (or **keep**) **one's fingers crossed** to hope for something —**put one's finger on** to ascertain exactly

fin′ger·board′ *n.* the part of a stringed instrument against which the strings are pressed to produce the desired tones

fin′ger·ling (-liŋ) *n.* a small fish

fin′ger·nail′ *n.* the horny substance at the upper end of a finger

finger painting a painting done by using the fingers, hand, or arm to spread, on wet paper, paints (**finger paints**) made of starch, glycerin, and pigments —**fin′ger-paint′** *vi., vt.*

fin′ger·print′ *n.* an impression of the lines and whorls on a finger tip, used to identify a person —*vt.* to take the fingerprints of

fin′ger·tip′ *n.* the tip of a finger —**have at one's fingertips** to have available for instant use

fin·i·al (fin′ē əl) *n.* ‖ult. < L *finis,* end‖ a decorative, terminal part at the tip of a spire, lamp, etc.

fin·ick·y (fin′ik ē) *adj.* ‖< FINE[1]‖ too particular; fussy Also **fin′i·cal** (-i kəl) or **fin′ick·ing**

fin·is (fin′is, fē nē′) *n., pl.* **-nis·es** the end; finish

fin·ish (fin′ish) *vt.* ‖< L *finis,* end‖ 1 *a)* to bring to an end *b)* to come to the end of 2 to consume all of 3 to give final touches to; perfect 4 to give (wood, etc.) a desired surface effect —*vi.* to come to an end —*n.* 1 the last part; end 2 *a)* anything used to finish a surface *b)* the finished effect 3 means or manner of completing or perfecting 4 polished manners, speech, etc. —**finish off** 1 to end 2 to kill or ruin —**finish with** to bring to an end —**fin′ished** *adj.* —**fin′ish·er** *n.*

fi·nite (fī′nīt′) *adj.* ‖< L *finis,* end‖ having definable limits; not infinite

fink (fiŋk) *n.* ‖Ger‖ [Slang] 1 an informer 2 a strikebreaker —*vi.* [Slang] to inform (*on*)

Fin·land (fin′lənd) country in N Europe: 130,119 sq. mi.; pop. 5,099,000

Finn (fin) *n.* a native or inhabitant of Finland

fin·nan had·die (fin′ən had′ē) ‖prob. < *Findhorn* (Scotland) *haddock*‖ smoked haddock

Finn·ish (fin′ish) *n.* the language spoken in Finland: abbrev. **Finn.** —*adj.* of Finland or the Finns, their language, etc.

fin·ny (fin′ē) *adj.* 1 having fins 2 like a fin 3 of, full of, or being fish

fiord (fyôrd) *n.* ‖Norw < ON *fjörthr*‖ a narrow inlet of the sea bordered by steep cliffs

fir (fur) *n.* ‖OE *fyrh*‖ 1 a cone-bearing evergreen tree of the pine family 2 its wood

fire (fīr) *n.* ‖OE *fyr*‖ 1 the flame, heat, and

light of combustion 2 something burning 3 a destructive burning /a forest *fire*/ 4 strong feeling 5 a discharge of firearms —*vt., vi.* **fired, fir'ing** 1 to start burning; ignite 2 to supply with fuel 3 to bake (bricks, etc.) in a kiln 4 to excite or become excited 5 to shoot (a gun, bullet, etc.) 6 to hurl or direct with force 7 to dismiss from a position; discharge —**catch (on) fire** to ignite —**on fire** 1 burning 2 greatly excited —**under fire** under attack —**fir'er** *n.*

fire'arm' *n.* any hand weapon from which a shot is fired by explosive force, as a rifle or pistol

fire'base' *n.* a military base in a combat zone, from which artillery, rockets, etc. are fired

fire'bomb' *n.* an incendiary bomb *vt.* to attack or damage with a firebomb

fire'brand' *n.* 1 a piece of burning wood 2 one who stirs up others to revolt or strife

fire'break' *n.* a strip of forest or prairie land cleared or plowed to stop the spread of fire

fire·brick (fīr'brik') *n.* a highly heat resistant brick for lining fireplaces, furnaces, etc.

fire'bug' *n.* [Colloq.] one who compulsively starts destructive fires

fire'crack'er *n.* a roll of paper containing an explosive, set off as a noisemaker at celebrations, etc.

fire'damp' *n.* an explosive gas, largely methane, formed in coal mines

fire engine a motor truck with equipment for fighting fires

fire escape an outside stairway for escape from a burning building

fire'fight' *n.* a short exchange of gunfire between small units of soldiers

fire'fight'er *n.* a person whose work is fighting fires —**fire'fight'ing** *n.*

fire'fly' *n., pl.* **-flies'** a winged beetle whose abdomen glows with a luminescent light

fire'man (-mən) *n., pl.* **-men** 1 FIREFIGHTER 2 a person who tends a fire in a furnace, etc.

fire'place' *n.* a place for a fire, esp. an open place built in a wall

fire'plug' *n.* a street hydrant supplying water for fighting fires

fire'proof' *adj.* not easily destroyed by fire —*vt.* to make fireproof

fire'side' *n.* 1 the space around a fireplace 2 home or home life

fire'storm' *n.* 1 an intense fire over a large area, as one caused by an atomic explosion with its high winds 2 a strong, often violent, outburst or upheaval

fire tower a tower used as a lookout for forest fires

fire'trap' *n.* a building easily set on fire or hard to get out of if on fire

fire'truck' *n.* FIRE ENGINE

fire'wa'ter *n.* alcoholic liquor: now humorous

fire'wood' *n.* wood used as fuel

fire'works' *n.pl.* 1 firecrackers, rockets, etc., for noisy effects or brilliant displays: *sometimes used in sing.* 2 a noisy quarrel or display of anger

firing line 1 the line from which gunfire is directed at the enemy 2 any vulnerable front position

firm[1] (furm) *adj.* ‖< L *firmus*‖ 1 solid; hard 2 not moved easily; fixed 3 unchanging; steady 4 resolute; constant 5 showing determination; strong 6 definite /a *firm* contract/ —*vt., vi.* to make or become firm —**firm'ly** *adv.* —**firm'ness** *n.*

firm[2] (furm) *n.* ‖< It < L *firmus*: see prec.‖ a business company

fir·ma·ment (furm'ə mənt) *n.* ‖< L *firmare*, strengthen‖ the sky, viewed poetically as a solid arch or vault

first (furst) *adj.* ‖OE *fyrst*‖ 1 before all others in a series; 1st 2 earliest 3 foremost, as in rank, quality, etc. —*adv.* 1 before any other person or thing 2 for the first time 3 sooner; preferably —*n.* 1 any person or thing that is first 2 the beginning 3 the winning place, as in a race 4 the slowest forward gear ratio of a motor vehicle transmission

first aid emergency treatment for injury, etc., before regular medical care is available —**first'-aid'** *adj.*

first'born' *adj.* born first in a family; oldest —*n.* the firstborn child

first'-class' *adj.* 1 of the highest class, quality, etc. 2 designating the most expensive accommodations 3 of the most expensive class of ordinary mail —*adv.* 1 with first-class accommodations 2 by first-class mail

first family [*often* **F- F-**] the family of the U.S. president

first'hand' *adj., adv.* from the original producer or source; direct

first lady [*often* **F- L-**] the wife of the U.S. president

first lieutenant a military officer ranking just above a second lieutenant

first'ly *adv.* in the first place; first

first person the form of a pronoun or verb that refers to the speaker

first'-rate' *adj.* highest in rank, quality, etc. —*adv.* [Colloq.] very well

first'-string' *adj.* [Colloq.] *Sports* that is the first choice for regular play at a specified position

firth (furth) *n.* ‖< ON *fjörthr*‖ a narrow inlet or arm of the sea

fis·cal (fis'kəl) *adj.* ‖< L *fiscus*, public chest‖ 1 relating to the public treasury or revenues 2 financial —**fis'cal·ly** *adv.*

fish (fish) *n., pl.* **fish** or (for different species) **fish'es** ‖OE *fisc*‖ 1 any of a large group of coldblooded vertebrate animals living in water and having gills for breathing, fins, and, usually, scales 2 the flesh of a fish used as food —*vi.* 1 to catch or try to catch fish 2 to try to get something indirectly: often with *for* —*vt.* to grope for, find, and bring to view: often with *out*

fish'er (-ər) *n.* 1 the largest marten, having very dark fur 2 this fur

fish'er·man (-ər mən) *n., pl.* **-men** 1 a person who fishes for sport or for a living 2 a commercial fishing vessel

fish'er·y *n., pl.* **-ies** 1 the business of catching fish 2 a place where fish, etc. are caught or bred

fish'hook' *n.* a hook, usually barbed, for catching fish

fish′ing *n.* the catching of fish for sport or for a living

fish meal ground, dried fish, used as fertilizer or fodder

fish′wife′ *n., pl.* **-wives′** a coarse, scolding woman

fish′y *adj.* **-i·er, -i·est** 1 like a fish in odor, taste, etc. 2 dull or expressionless /*fishy* eyes/ 3 [Colloq.] questionable; odd —**fish′i·ness** *n.*

fis·sion (fish′ən) *n.* ‖< L *findere*, to split‖ 1 a splitting apart; cleavage 2 NUCLEAR FISSION —**fis′sion·a·ble** *adj.*

fis·sure (fish′ər) *n.* ‖see prec.‖ a cleft or crack

fist (fist) *n.* ‖OE *fyst*‖ a hand with the fingers closed tightly into the palm

fist·i·cuffs (fis′ti kufs′) *n.pl.* [Old fashioned] a fight with the fists

fis·tu·la (fis′tyo͞o lə) *n., pl.* **-las** or **-lae′** (-lē′) ‖L, a pipe, ulcer‖ an abnormal passage, as from an abscess to the skin

fit[1] (fit) *vt.* **fit′ted** or **fit, fit′ted, fit′ting** ‖ME *fitten*‖ 1 to be suitable to 2 to be the proper size, shape, etc. for 3 to adjust so as to fit 4 to equip; outfit —*vi.* 1 [Archaic] to be suitable or proper 2 to have the proper size or shape —*adj.* **fit′ter, fit′test** 1 suited to some purpose, function, etc. 2 proper; right 3 healthy 4 [Colloq.] inclined /she was *fit* to scream/ —*n.* the manner of fitting /a tight *fit*/ —**fit′ly** *adv.* —**fit′ness** *n.* —**fit′ter** *n.*

fit[2] (fit) *n.* ‖OE *fitt*, conflict‖ 1 any sudden, uncontrollable attack, as of coughing 2 an outburst, as of anger 3 a seizure involving convulsions, loss of consciousness, etc. —**by fits (and starts)** in an irregular way —**have** (or **throw**) **a fit** [Colloq.] to become very angry or upset

fit′ful (-fəl) *adj.* characterized by intermittent activity; spasmodic —**fit′ful·ly** *adv.* —**fit′ful·ness** *n.*

fit′ting *adj.* suitable; proper —*n.* 1 an adjustment or trying on of clothes, etc. 2 a small part used to join or adapt other parts 3 [*pl.*] fixtures

five (fīv) *adj., n.* ‖OE *fif*‖ one more than four; 5; V

five′-and-ten′-cent′ store a store that sells a wide variety of inexpensive merchandise Also **five′-and-ten′** *n.*

fix (fiks) *vt.* **fixed, fix′ing** ‖< L *figere*, fasten‖ 1 to fasten firmly 2 to set firmly in the mind 3 to direct (one's eyes) steadily at something 4 to make rigid 5 to make permanent 6 to establish (a date, etc.) definitely 7 to set in order; adjust 8 to repair 9 to prepare (food or meals) 10 [Colloq.] to influence the result or action of (a race, jury, etc.), as by bribery 11 to punish —*vi.* 1 to become fixed 2 [Colloq. or Dial.] to prepare or intend —*n.* 1 the position of a ship, etc. determined from the bearings of two known positions 2 [Colloq.] a predicament 3 [Slang] a contest, etc. that has been fixed 4 [Slang] an injection of a narcotic by an addict —**fix up** [Colloq.] 1 to repair 2 to arrange; set in order —**fix′a·ble** *adj.* —**fix′er** *n.*

fix·a·tion (fiks ā′shən) *n.* 1 a fixing or being fixed 2 an obsession 3 a remaining at an early stage of psychosexual development

fix·a·tive (fiks′ə tiv) *adj.* that is able or tends to make permanent, prevent fading, etc. —*n.* a fixative substance

fixed (fikst) *adj.* 1 firmly in place 2 established; settled 3 resolute; unchanging 4 persistent /a *fixed* idea/ —**fix·ed·ly** (fiks′id lē) *adv.*

fix·ings (fiks′iŋz′) *n.pl.* [Colloq.] accessories or trimmings

fix·i·ty (fiks′i tē) *n.* the quality or state of being fixed or steady

fix·ture (fiks′chər) *n.* ‖see FIX‖ 1 anything firmly in place 2 any attached piece of equipment in a house, etc. 3 a person long established in a job, etc.

fizz (fiz) *n.* ‖? akin to fol.‖ 1 a hissing, sputtering sound 2 an effervescent drink —*vi.* 1 to make a hissing sound 2 to effervesce

fiz·zle (fiz′əl) *vi.* **-zled, -zling** ‖< ME‖ 1 FIZZ (*vi.* 1) 2 [Colloq.] to fail, esp. after a good start —*n.* 1 a hissing sound 2 [Colloq.] a failure

fl. 1 floor 2 ‖L *floruit*‖ (he or she) flourished 3 fluid

FL or **Fla.** Florida

flab (flab) *n.* ‖< FLABBY‖ [Colloq.] sagging flesh

flab·ber·gast (flab′ər gast′) *vt.* ‖18th-c. slang < ?‖ to dumbfound

flab·by (flab′ē) *adj.* **-bi·er, -bi·est** ‖< FLAP‖ 1 limp and soft 2 weak —**flab′bi·ly** *adv.* —**flab′bi·ness** *n.*

flac·cid (flak′sid, flas′id) *adj.* ‖< L *flaccus*‖ soft and limp; flabby

flack (flak) *n.* ‖< ?‖ [Slang] PRESS AGENT —**flack′er·y** *n.*

fla·con (flä kōn′) *n.* ‖Fr‖ a small flask with a stopper, as for perfume

flag[1] (flag) *n.* ‖< FLAG[4], to flutter‖ a cloth with colors, patterns, etc. used as a symbol of a nation, etc., or as a signal —*vt.* **flagged, flag′ging** to signal with or as with a flag; esp., to signal to stop: often with *down*

flag[2] (flag) *n.* ‖< ON *flaga*, slab of stone‖ FLAGSTONE

flag[3] (flag) *n.* ‖ME *flagge*‖ any of various irises, or a flower or leaf of one

flag[4] (flag) *vi.* **flagged, flag′ging** ‖prob. < ON *flogra*, to flutter‖ 1 to become limp; droop 2 to grow weak or tired

flag·el·late (flaj′ə lāt′) *vt.* **-lat′ed, -lat′ing** ‖< L *flagellum*, a whip‖ to whip; flog —**flag′el·la′tion** *n.*

fla·gel·lum (flə jel′əm) *n., pl.* **-la** (-ə) or **-lums** ‖L, a whip‖ a whiplike part of some cells, as of bacteria or protozoans, used as for moving about

flag·on (flag′ən) *n.* ‖< LL *flasco*‖ a container for liquids, with a handle, narrow neck, spout, and, often, a lid

flag′pole′ *n.* a pole on which a flag is raised and flown Also **flag′staff′**

fla·grant (flā′grənt) *adj.* ‖< L *flagrare*, to blaze‖ glaringly bad; outrageous —**fla′gran·cy** (-grən sē) or **fla′grance** *n.* —**fla′grant·ly** *adv.*

flag′ship′ *n.* 1 the ship that carries the commander of a fleet or other large unit 2 the largest or most important member or part, as of a group

flag′stone′ *n.* a flat paving stone

flail (flāl) *n.* ‖ < L *flagellum*, a whip ‖ a farm tool for threshing grain by hand —*vt., vi.* **1** to thresh with a flail **2** to beat **3** to move (one's arms) like flails

flair (fler) *n.* ‖ < L *fragrare*, to smell ‖ **1** a natural talent; aptitude **2** [Colloq.] a sense of style; dash

flak (flak) *n.* ‖ Ger acronym ‖ **1** the fire of antiaircraft guns **2** [Colloq.] strong criticism Also **flack**

flake (flāk) *n.* ‖ < Scand ‖ **1** a small, thin mass **2** a piece split off; chip —*vt., vi.* **flaked, flak′ing 1** to form into flakes **2** to peel off in flakes —**flak′y, -i·er, -i·est,** *adj.*

flam·bé (fläm bā′) *adj.* ‖ Fr ‖ served with a sauce of flaming brandy, rum, etc. —*n.* a dessert so served

flam·boy·ant (flam boi′ənt) *adj.* ‖ Fr < L *flamma*, a flame ‖ **1** flamelike or brilliant **2** too showy or ornate —**flam·boy′ance** *n.* —**flam·boy′ant·ly** *adv.*

flame (flām) *n.* ‖ < L *flamma* ‖ **1** the burning gas of a fire, appearing as a tongue of light **2** the state of burning with a blaze **3** a thing like a flame **4** an intense emotion **5** a sweetheart —*vi.* **flamed, flam′ing 1** to burst into flame **2** to grow red or hot **3** to become excited

fla·men·co (flə meŋ′kō) *n.* ‖ Sp ‖ a Spanish gypsy style of dance or music

flame′out′ *n.* a failure of combustion in a jet engine during flight

flame′throw′er *n.* a weapon that shoots flaming oil, napalm, etc.

fla·min·go (flə miŋ′gō′) *n., pl.* **-gos′** or **-goes′** ‖ Port ‖ a tropical wading bird with long legs and pink or red feathers

flam·ma·ble (flam′ə bəl) *adj.* easily set on fire; that will burn readily or quickly —**flam′ma·bil′i·ty** *n.*

Flan·ders (flan′dərz) region in NW Europe, in France & Belgium

flange (flanj) *n.* ‖ < ? ME ‖ a projecting rim on a wheel, etc., as to hold it in place or give it strength

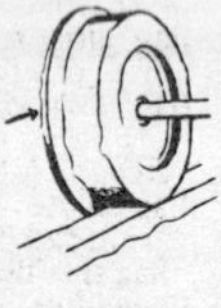

FLANGE

flank (flaŋk) *n.* ‖ < OFr *flanc* ‖ **1** the side of an animal between the ribs and the hip **2** the side of anything **3** *Mil.* the right or left side of a formation —*vt.* **1** to be at the side of **2** *Mil.* to attack, or pass around, the side of (enemy troops)

flan·nel (flan′əl) *n.* ‖ prob. < Welsh *gwlan*, wool ‖ **1** a loosely woven cloth of wool or cotton **2** [*pl.*] trousers, etc. made of this

flan·nel·ette or **flan·nel·et** (flan′əl et′) *n.* a soft, napped cotton cloth

flap (flap) *n.* ‖ ME *flappe* ‖ **1** anything flat and broad hanging loose at one end **2** the motion or sound of a swinging flap **3** [Archaic] a slap **4** [Colloq.] a commotion; stir —*vt.* **flapped, flap′ping 1** to slap **2** to move back and forth or up and down, as wings

flap′jack′ *n.* a pancake

flap′per *n.* **1** one that flaps **2** [Colloq.] in the 1920's, a bold, unconventional young woman

flare (fler) *vi.* **flared, flar′ing** ‖ ME *fleare* < ? ‖ **1** *a)* to blaze brightly *b)* to burn unsteadily **2** to burst out suddenly, as in anger: often with *up* or *out* **3** to curve outward, as a bell's rim —*n.* **1** a bright, unsteady blaze **2** a brightly flaming light for signaling, etc. **3** an outburst, as of emotion **4** a curving outward

flare′-up′ *n.* a sudden outburst of flame or of anger, trouble, etc.

flash (flash) *vi.* ‖ ME *flashen*, to splash ‖ **1** to send out a sudden, brief light **2** to sparkle **3** to come or pass suddenly —*vt.* **1** to cause to flash **2** to send (news, etc.) swiftly —*n.* **1** a sudden, brief light **2** a brief moment **3** a sudden, brief display **4** a brief news report sent by radio, etc. **5** a gaudy display —*adj.* happening swiftly or suddenly —**flash′er** *n.*

flash′back′ *n.* an interruption in the continuity of a story, etc. by telling or showing an earlier episode

flash′-for′ward *n.* an interruption in the continuity of a story, etc. by telling or showing a future episode

flash′ing *n.* sheets of metal used to weatherproof roof joints or edges

flash′light′ *n.* a portable electric light

flash point the lowest temperature at which vapor, as of an oil, will ignite with a flash

flash′y *adj.* **-i·er, -i·est 1** dazzling **2** gaudy; showy —**flash′i·ness** *n.*

flask (flask) *n.* ‖ < L *flasca*, bottle ‖ **1** any bottle-shaped container used in laboratories, etc. **2** a small, flat pocket container for liquor, etc.

flat[1] (flat) *adj.* **flat′ter, flat′test** ‖ < ON *flatr* ‖ **1** having a smooth, level surface **2** lying spread out **3** broad, even, and thin **4** absolute /a *flat* denial/ **5** not fluctuating /a *flat* rate/ **6** tasteless; insipid **7** not interesting **8** emptied of air /a *flat* tire/ **9** without gloss /*flat* paint/ **10** *Music a)* lower in pitch by a half step *b)* below true pitch —*adv.* **1** in a flat manner or position **2** exactly **3** *Music* below true pitch —*n.* **1** anything flat, esp. a surface, part, or expanse **2** a deflated tire **3** *Music a)* a note one half step below another *b)* the symbol (♭) for this —*vt.* **flat′ted, flat′ting** *Music* to make flat —*vi.* to sing or play below true pitch —**fall flat** to fail in the desired effect —**flat′ly** *adv.* —**flat′ness** *n.* —**flat′tish** *adj.*

flat[2] (flat) *n.* ‖ < Scot dial. *flet*, floor ‖ [Chiefly Brit.] an apartment or suite of rooms

flat′bed′ *n.* a truck, trailer, etc. having a bed or platform without sides or stakes

flat′boat′ *n.* a flat-bottomed boat for carrying freight on rivers, etc.

flat′car′ *n.* a railroad freight car without sides or a roof

flat′fish′ *n., pl.* **-fish′** or (for different species) **-fish′es** a fish having both eyes on the same side of a very flat body

flat′foot′ *n.* **1** a condition of the foot in which the instep arch is flattened **2** *pl.* **-foots′** or **-feet′** a policeman —**flat′-foot′ed** *adj.*

flat′i′ron *n.* an iron for clothes

flat′-out′ (-out′) *adj.* [Colloq.] **1** at full speed, with maximum effort, etc. **2** absolute; thorough

flat·ten (flat′'n) *vt., vi.* to make or become flat or flatter
flat·ter (flat′ər) *vt.* ‖< OFr *flater,* to smooth‖ 1 to praise insincerely 2 to try to please, as by praise 3 to make seem more attractive than is so 4 to gratify the vanity of —**flat′ter·er** *n.* —**flat′ter·ing·ly** *adv.* —**flat′ter·y** *n.*
flat′top′ *n.* [Slang] an aircraft carrier
flat·u·lent (flach′ə lənt) *adj.* ‖see fol.‖ 1 having or producing gas in the stomach or intestines 2 pompous —**flat′u·lence** *n.*
fla·tus (flāt′əs) *n.* ‖L < *flare,* to blow‖ gas in, or expelled from, the stomach or intestines
flat′ware′ *n.* knives, forks, and spoons
flat′worm′ *n.* any of various worms with flat bodies, as the tapeworm
Flau·bert (flō ber′), **Gus·tave** (güs täv′) 1821-80; Fr. novelist
flaunt (flônt) *vi.* ‖? < dial. *flant,* to strut‖ to make a gaudy or defiant display —*vt.* 1 to show off proudly or defiantly 2 FLOUT: usage objected to by many —**flaunt′ing·ly** *adv.*
flau·tist (flôt′ist, flout′-) *n.* ‖< It‖ *var. of* FLUTIST
fla·vor (flā′vər) *n.* ‖ult. < L *flare,* to blow‖ 1 that quality of a substance that is a mixing of its characteristic taste and smell 2 flavoring 3 characteristic quality —*vt.* to give flavor to Brit. sp. **fla′vour** —**fla′vor·ful** *adj.* —**fla′vor·less** *adj.*
fla′vor·ing *n.* an essence, extract, etc. that adds flavor to food or drink
flaw (flô) *n.* ‖ME, a flake, splinter‖ 1 a crack, as in a gem 2 a defect; fault —**flaw′less** *adj.* —**flaw′less·ly** *adv.* —**flaw′less·ness** *n.*
flax (flaks) *n.* ‖< OE *fleax*‖ 1 a slender, erect plant with delicate blue flowers: its seed (**flax′seed**) is used to make linseed oil 2 the fibers of this plant, which are spun into linen thread
flax·en (flak′sən) *adj.* 1 of or made of flax 2 pale-yellow
flay (flā) *vt.* ‖OE *flean*‖ 1 to strip off the skin of, as by whipping 2 to criticize harshly
flea (flē) *n.* ‖OE *fleah*‖ a small, wingless jumping insect that is a bloodsucking parasite as an adult
flea market an outdoor bazaar dealing mainly in cheap, secondhand goods
fleck (flek) *n.* ‖ON *flekkr*‖ a spot, speck, or flake —*vt.* to spot; speckle
fled (fled) *vi., vt. pt. & pp. of* FLEE
fledg·ling (flej′liŋ) *n.* ‖< ME *flegge,* ready to fly‖ 1 a young bird just able to fly 2 a young, inexperienced person Also, chiefly Brit., **fledge′ling**
flee (flē) *vi.* **fled, flee′ing** ‖OE *fleon*‖ 1 to go swiftly or escape, as from danger 2 to vanish —*vt.* to run away or try to escape from
fleece (flēs) *n.* ‖OE *fleos*‖ 1 the wool covering a sheep or similar animal 2 a soft, warm, napped fabric —*vt.* **fleeced, fleec′ing** 1 to shear the fleece from 2 to swindle —**fleec′er** *n.*
fleec·y (flēs′ē) *adj.* **-i·er, -i·est** of or like fleece; soft and light —**fleec′i·ness** *n.*
fleet[1] (flēt) *n.* ‖OE *fleot*‖ 1 a number of warships under one command 2 any group of ships, trucks, etc. under one control
fleet[2] (flēt) *adj.* ‖< OE *fleotan,* to float‖ swift; rapid —**fleet′ness** *n.*
fleet′ing *adj.* passing swiftly —**fleet′ing·ly** *adv.* —**fleet′ing·ness** *n.*
Flem·ish (flem′ish) *adj.* of Flanders, its people, or their language —*n.* the West Germanic language of Flanders
flesh (flesh) *n.* ‖OE *flæsc*‖ 1 the soft substance of the body; esp., the muscular tissue 2 meat 3 the pulpy part of fruits and vegetables 4 the body as distinct from the soul 5 all humankind 6 yellowish pink —**in the flesh** 1 alive 2 in person —**one's (own) flesh and blood** one's close relatives —**flesh′y, -i·er, -i·est,** *adj.*
flesh′ly *adj.* **-li·er, -li·est** 1 of the body; corporeal 2 sensual
fleur-de-lis (flur′də lē′) *n., pl.* **fleurs-de-lis** (flur′də lēz′) ‖< OFr *flor de lis,* lit., flower of the lily‖ a lilylike emblem: the coat of arms of the former French royal family
flew (flo͞o) *vi., vt. pt. of* FLY[1]
flex (fleks) *vt., vi.* ‖< L *flectere,* to bend‖ 1 to bend (an arm, knee, etc.) 2 to shorten and thicken (a muscle) in action
flex·i·ble (flek′sə bəl) *adj.* 1 able to bend without breaking; pliant 2 easily influenced 3 adjustable to change —**flex′i·bil′i·ty** *n.*
flex·time (fleks′tīm′) *n.* a system allowing individual employees some flexibility in choosing when they work
flib·ber·ti·gib·bet (flib′ər tē jib′it) *n.* ‖< ?‖ a frivolous, flighty person
flick[1] (flik) *n.* ‖echoic‖ a light, quick stroke —*vt.* to strike, remove, etc. with a light, quick stroke
flick[2] (flik) *n.* ‖< fol.‖ [Slang] a movie —**the flicks** [Slang] a showing of a movie
flick·er (flik′ər) *vi.* ‖OE *flicorian*‖ 1 to move with a quick, light, wavering motion 2 to burn or shine unsteadily —*n.* 1 a flickering 2 a dart of flame or light
fli·er (flī′ər) *n.* 1 a thing that flies 2 an aviator 3 a bus, train, etc. with a fast schedule 4 a widely distributed handbill 5 [Colloq.] a reckless gamble
flight[1] (flīt) *n.* ‖OE *flyht*‖ 1 the act, manner, or power of flying 2 the distance flown 3 a group of things flying together 4 an airplane scheduled to fly a certain trip 5 a trip by airplane 6 a soaring above the ordinary [a *flight* of fancy] 7 a set of stairs, as between landings
flight[2] (flīt) *n.* ‖< OE *fleon,* flee‖ a fleeing from or as from danger
flight attendant an airplane attendant who sees to passengers' comfort and safety
flight′less *adj.* not able to fly
flight′y *adj.* **-i·er, -i·est** 1 given to sudden whims; frivolous 2 easily excited, upset, etc. —**flight′i·ness** *n.*
flim·sy (flim′zē) *adj.* **-si·er, -si·est** ‖< ?‖ 1 easily broken or damaged; frail 2 ineffectual [a *flimsy* excuse] —**flim′si·ly** *adv.* —**flim′si·ness** *n.*
flinch (flinch) *vi.* ‖< OFr *flenchir*‖ to draw back from a blow or anything difficult or painful —*n.* a flinching

fling (fliŋ) *vt.* **flung, fling′ing** ‖< ON *flengja,* to whip‖ 1 to throw, esp. with force; hurl 2 to put abruptly or violently 3 to move (one's arms, legs, etc.) suddenly —*n.* 1 a flinging 2 a brief time of wild pleasures 3 a spirited dance 4 [Colloq.] a try

flint (flint) *n.* ‖OE‖ a very hard, siliceous rock, usually gray, that produces sparks when struck against steel —**flint′y, -i·er, -i·est,** *adj.*

Flint (flint) city in SE Mich.: pop. 160,000

flip[1] (flip) *vt.* **flipped, flip′ping** ‖echoic‖ 1 to toss with a quick jerk; flick 2 to snap (a coin) into the air with the thumb 3 to turn or turn over —*vi.* 1 to move jerkily 2 [Slang] to lose self-control —*n.* a flipping —**flip one's lid** (or **wig**) [Slang] to go berserk

flip[2] (flip) *adj.* **flip′per, flip′pest** [Colloq.] flippant

flip′pant (-ənt) *adj.* ‖prob. < FLIP[1]‖ frivolous and disrespectful; saucy —**flip′pan·cy,** *pl.* **-cies,** *n.* —**flip′pant·ly** *adv.*

flip′per (-ər) *n.* ‖< FLIP[1]‖ 1 a broad, flat limb adapted for swimming, as in seals 2 a paddlelike rubber device worn on each foot by skin divers, etc.

flirt (flurt) *vt.* ‖< ?‖ to move jerkily /the bird *flirted* its tail/ —*vi.* 1 to pay amorous attention to someone, without serious intentions 2 to trifle or toy /to *flirt* with an idea/ —*n.* 1 a quick, jerky movement 2 one who flirts with others

flir·ta·tion (flər tā′shən) *n.* a frivolous love affair —**flir·ta′tious** *adj.*

flit (flit) *vi.* **flit′ted, flit′ting** ‖< ON *flytja*‖ to move lightly and rapidly

float (flōt) *n.* ‖< OE *flota,* a ship‖ 1 anything that stays on the surface of a liquid, as a raft, a cork on a fishing line, etc. 2 a floating ball, etc. that regulates a valve, as in a water tank 3 a low, flat vehicle decorated for exhibit in a parade —*vi.* 1 to stay on the surface of a liquid 2 to drift easily on water, in air, etc. 3 to move about aimlessly —*vt.* 1 to cause to float 2 to put into circulation /to *float* a bond issue/ 3 to arrange for (a loan) —**float′er** *n.*

flock (fläk) *n.* ‖OE *flocc*‖ 1 a group of certain animals, as sheep, birds, etc., living or feeding together 2 any group, esp. a large one —*vi.* to assemble or travel in a flock or crowd

flock·ing (fläk′iŋ) *n.* ‖< L *floccus,* tuft of wool‖ 1 tiny fibers of wool, rayon, etc. applied to a fabric, wallpaper, etc. as a velvetlike surface: also **flock** 2 such a fabric, etc.

floe (flō) *n.* ‖? < Norw *flo,* layer‖ ICE FLOE

flog (fläg, flôg) *vt.* **flogged, flog′ging** ‖? < L *flagellare,* to whip‖ to beat with a stick, whip, etc. —**flog′ger** *n.*

flood (flud) *n.* ‖OE *flod*‖ 1 an overflowing of water on an area normally dry 2 the rising of the tide 3 a great outpouring, as of words —*vt.* 1 to cover or fill, as with a flood 2 to put too much water, fuel, etc. on or in —*vi.* 1 to gush out in a flood 2 to become flooded —**the Flood** *Bible* the great flood in Noah's time

flood′light′ *n.* 1 a lamp that casts a broad beam of bright light 2 such a beam of light —*vt.* **-light′ed** or **-lit′, -light′ing** to illuminate by a floodlight

flood tide the rising tide

floor (flôr) *n.* ‖OE *flor*‖ 1 the inside bottom surface of a room 2 the bottom surface of anything /the ocean *floor*/ 3 a story in a building 4 the right to speak in an assembly —*vt.* 1 to furnish with a floor 2 to knock down 3 [Colloq.] *a)* to defeat *b)* to flabbergast; astound

floor′board′ *n.* 1 a board in a floor 2 the floor of an automobile, etc.

floor exercise any gymnastic exercise done without apparatus

floor′ing *n.* 1 a floor or floors 2 material for making a floor

floor show a show presenting singers, dancers, etc., as in a nightclub

flop (fläp) *vt.* **flopped, flop′ping** ‖var. of FLAP‖ to flap or throw noisily and clumsily —*vi.* 1 to move, drop, or flap around loosely or clumsily 2 [Colloq.] to fail —*n.* 1 the act or sound of flopping 2 [Colloq.] a failure —**flop′py, -pi·er, -pi·est,** *adj.*

flop′house′ *n.* [Colloq.] a cheap hotel

floppy disk a small, flexible computer disk for storing data

flo·ra (flôr′ə) *n.* ‖L < *flos,* a flower‖ the plants of a specified region or time

flo′ral (-əl) *adj.* of or like flowers

Flor·ence (flôr′əns) city in central Italy: pop. 430,000 —**Flor′en·tine′** (-ən tēn′) *adj., n.*

flo·res·cence (flō res′əns) *n.* ‖< L *flos,* a flower‖ a blooming or flowering —**flo·res′cent** *adj.*

flor·id (flôr′id) *adj.* ‖< L *flos,* a flower‖ 1 ruddy: said of the complexion 2 gaudy; showy; ornate

Flor·i·da (flôr′ə də, flär′-) Southern State of the SE U.S.: 58,560 sq. mi.; pop. 9,740,000; cap. Tallahassee —**Flo·rid·i·an** (flô rid′ē ən) or **Flor′i·dan** *adj., n.*

flor·in (flôr′in) *n.* ‖< L *flos,* a flower‖ any of various European or South African silver or gold coins

flo·rist (flôr′ist) *n.* ‖< L *flos,* a flower‖ one who grows or sells flowers

floss (flôs, fläs) *n.* ‖ult. < L *floccus,* tuft of wool‖ 1 the short, downy waste fibers of silk 2 a soft, loosely twisted thread or yarn, as of silk, for embroidery 3 a substance like this 4 DENTAL FLOSS —*vt., vi.* to clean (the teeth) with dental floss —**floss′y, -i·er, -i·est,** *adj.*

flo·ta·tion (flō tā′shən) *n.* the act or condition of floating

flo·til·la (flō til′ə) *n.* ‖Sp, dim. of *flota,* a fleet‖ 1 a small fleet 2 a fleet of boats or small ships

flot·sam (flät′səm) *n.* ‖< MDu *vloten,* to float‖ the wreckage of a ship or its cargo floating at sea: chiefly in **flotsam and jetsam**

flounce[1] (flouns) *vi.* **flounced, flounc′ing** ‖< ? Scand‖ to move with quick, flinging motions of the body, as in anger —*n.* a flouncing

flounce[2] (flouns) *n.* ‖< OFr *froncir,* to wrinkle‖ a wide ruffle sewn to a skirt, sleeve, etc. —**flounc′y, -i·er, -i·est,** *adj.*

floun·der[1] (floun′dər) *vi.* ‖< ? FOUNDER‖ 1 to struggle awkwardly, as in deep mud 2 to speak or act in an awkward, confused manner

floun·der² (floun'dər) ***n.*** ‖ < Scand ‖ any of various flatfishes caught for food, as the halibut

flour (flour) ***n.*** ‖ orig., flower (i.e., best) of meal ‖ **1** a fine, powdery substance produced by grinding and sifting grain, esp. wheat **2** any finely powdered substance —**flour'y *adj.***

flour·ish (flur'ish) ***vi.*** ‖ < L *flos*, a flower ‖ **1** to grow vigorously; thrive **2** to be at the peak of development, etc. —***vt.*** to brandish (a sword, etc.) —***n.*** **1** anything done in a showy way **2** a brandishing **3** decorative lines in writing **4** a musical fanfare

flout (flout) ***vt., vi.*** ‖ < ? ME *flouten*, play the flute ‖ to mock or scoff —***n.*** a scornful act or remark —**flout'er *n.***

flow (flō) ***vi.*** ‖ OE *flowan* ‖ **1** to move as a liquid does **2** to move gently and smoothly **3** to pour out **4** to issue; proceed **5** to hang loose *[flowing* hair*]* **6** to be plentiful —***n.*** **1** a flowing **2** the rate of flow **3** anything that flows **4** the rising of the tide

flow'chart' ***n.*** a diagram showing steps in a sequence of operations, as in manufacturing

flow·er (flou'ər) ***n.*** ‖ < L *flos* ‖ **1** the seed-producing structure of a flowering plant; blossom **2** a plant cultivated for its blossoms **3** the best or finest part —***vi.*** **1** to produce blossoms **2** to reach the best stage —**in flower** flowering

flow'er·pot' ***n.*** a container in which to grow plants

flow'er·y ***adj.*** **-i·er, -i·est** **1** covered or decorated with flowers **2** full of ornate expressions and fine words —**flow'er·i·ness *n.***

flown (flōn) ***vi., vt. pp. of*** FLY¹

flu (flōō) ***n.*** **1** *short for* INFLUENZA **2** a respiratory or intestinal infection caused by a virus

flub (flub) ***vt., vi.*** **flubbed, flub'bing** ‖ < ? FL(OP) + (D)UB¹ ‖ [Colloq.] to bungle (a job, stroke, etc.) —***n.*** [Colloq.] a blunder

fluc·tu·ate (fluk'chōō āt') ***vi.*** **-at'ed, -at'ing** ‖ < L *fluctus*, a wave ‖ to be continually varying in an irregular way —**fluc'tu·a'tion *n.***

flue (flōō) ***n.*** ‖ < ? OFr *fluie*, a flowing ‖ a shaft for the passage of smoke, hot air, etc., esp. in a chimney

flu·ent (flōō'ənt) ***adj.*** ‖ < L *fluere*, to flow ‖ **1** flowing smoothly **2** able to write or speak easily, expressively, etc. —**flu'en·cy *n.*** —**flu'ent·ly *adv.***

fluff (fluf) ***n.*** ‖ ? blend of *flue*, soft mass + PUFF ‖ **1** soft, light down **2** a loose, soft mass, as of hair —***vt.*** **1** to shake or pat until loose or fluffy **2** to bungle (one's lines), as in acting

fluff'y ***adj.*** **-i·er, -i·est** soft and light like fluff; feathery

flu·id (flōō'id) ***adj.*** ‖ < L *fluere*, to flow ‖ **1** that can flow as a liquid or gas does **2** that can change rapidly or easily **3** available for investment or as cash —***n.*** a liquid or gas —**flu·id'i·ty *n.*** —**flu'id·ly *adv.***

fluke¹ (flōōk) ***n.*** ‖ OE *floc*, a flatfish ‖ TREMATODE

fluke² (flōōk) ***n.*** ‖ < ? ‖ **1** a pointed end of an anchor, which catches in the ground **2** a barb of a harpoon, etc. **3** a lobe of a whale's tail **4** [Colloq.] a stroke of luck

flung (fluŋ) ***vt. pt. & pp. of*** FLING

flunk (fluŋk) ***vt., vi.*** ‖ < ? ‖ [Colloq.] to fail, as in a school assignment

flunk·y (fluŋ'kē) ***n., pl.*** **-ies** ‖ orig. Scot ‖ **1** orig., a liveried manservant **2** a toady **3** a person with menial tasks Also **flunk'ey**

flu·o·resce (flōō'ə res', flōō res') ***vi.*** **-resced', -resc'ing** to produce, show, or undergo fluorescence

flu·o·res·cence (flōō'ə res'əns, flōō res'-) ***n.*** ‖ ult. < L *fluor*, flux ‖ **1** the property of producing light when acted upon by radiant energy **2** the production of such light **3** light so produced —**flu'o·res'cent *adj.***

fluorescent lamp (or **tube**) a glass tube coated on the inside with a fluorescent substance that gives off light (**fluorescent light**) when mercury vapor in the tube is acted upon by a stream of electrons

flu·o·ri·date (flôr'ə dāt', floor'-) ***vt.*** **-dat'ed, -dat'ing** to add fluorides to (a supply of drinking water) in order to reduce tooth decay —**flu'o·ri·da'tion *n.***

flu·o·ride (flôr'īd', floor'īd') ***n.*** any of various compounds of fluorine

flu·o·rine (flôr'ēn', -in; floor'-) ***n.*** ‖ < L *fluor*, flux ‖ a greenish-yellow gaseous chemical element

flu·o·rite (flôr'īt') ***n.*** ‖ < L *fluor*, flux ‖ calcium fluoride, a transparent, crystalline mineral: the principal source of fluorine

flu·o·ro·car·bon (flôr'ə kär'bən) ***n.*** any of certain compounds containing carbon, fluorine, and, sometimes, hydrogen

flu·o·ro·scope (flôr'ə skōp') ***n.*** a machine for examining internal structures by viewing the shadows cast on a fluorescent screen by objects through which X-rays are directed

flur·ry (flur'ē) ***n., pl.*** **-ries** ‖ < ? ‖ **1** a sudden gust of wind, rain, or snow **2** a sudden commotion —***vt.*** **-ried, -ry·ing** to confuse; agitate

flush¹ (flush) ***vi.*** ‖ blend of FLASH & ME *flusshen*, fly up suddenly ‖ **1** to flow rapidly **2** to blush or glow **3** to be washed out with a sudden flow of water **4** to start up from cover: said of birds —***vt.*** **1** to wash out with a sudden flow of water **2** to make blush or glow **3** to excite **4** to drive (birds) from cover —***n.*** **1** a rapid flow, as of water **2** a sudden, vigorous growth **3** sudden excitement **4** a blush; glow **5** a sudden feeling of heat, as in a fever —***adj.*** **1** well supplied, esp. with money **2** abundant **3** level or even (*with*) **4** direct; full —***adv.*** **1** so as to be level **2** directly

flush² (flush) ***n.*** ‖ < L *fluere*, to flow ‖ a hand of cards all in the same suit

flus·ter (flus'tər) ***vt., vi.*** ‖ prob. < Scand ‖ to make or become confused —***n.*** a being flustered

flute (flōōt) ***n.*** ‖ < Prov *flaut* ‖ **1** a high-pitched wind instrument consisting of a long, slender tube with finger holes and keys **2** a groove in the shaft of a column, etc. —**flut'ed *adj.*** —**flut'ing *n.*** —**flut'ist *n.***

flut·ter (flut'ər) ***vi.*** ‖ < OE *fleotan*, to float ‖ **1** to flap the wings rapidly, without flying **2** to wave, move, or beat rapidly and irregularly —*vt.* to cause to flutter —*n.* **1** a fluttering movement **2** an excited or confused state —**flut′ter·y** *adj.*

flux (fluks) *n.* ‖< L *fluere,* to flow‖ **1** a flowing **2** a continual change **3** a substance used to help metals fuse together, as in soldering

fly[1] (flī) *vi.* **flew, flown, fly′ing** ‖OE *fleogan*‖ **1** to move through the air in an aircraft or by using wings, as a bird **2** to wave or float in the air **3** to move or pass swiftly **4** to flee **5 flied, fly′ing** *Baseball* to hit a fly —*vt.* **1** to cause to float in the air **2** to operate (an aircraft) **3** to flee from —*n., pl.* **flies 1** a flap that conceals the zipper, etc. in a garment **2** a flap serving as the door of a tent **3** *Baseball* a ball batted high in the air **4** [*pl.*] *Theater* the space above a stage —**fly into** to have a violent outburst of —**let fly (at) 1** to throw (at) **2** to direct a verbal attack (at) —**on the fly** [Colloq.] while in a hurry

fly[2] (flī) *n., pl.* **flies** ‖OE *fleoge*‖ **1** any of a large group of insects with two transparent wings **2** an artificial fly used as a fish lure

fly′a·ble *adj.* suitable for flying

fly′by′ or **fly′-by′** *n., pl.* **-bys′** a flight past a designated point or place by an aircraft or spacecraft

fly′-by-night′ *adj.* financially irresponsible —*n.* an absconding debtor

fly′-by-wire′ *adj.* of a system for controlling an airplane or spacecraft electronically, as by computer

fly′-cast′ *vt.* **-cast′, -cast′ing** to fish by casting artificial flies

fly′er *n.* FLIER (esp. senses 1, 2, & 5)

flying buttress a buttress connected with a wall by an arch, serving to resist outward pressure

FLYING BUTTRESS

flying colors notable success

flying fish a fish with winglike fins used in gliding through the air

flying saucer a UFO

fly′leaf′ *n., pl.* **-leaves′** a blank leaf at the beginning or end of a book

fly′pa′per *n.* a sticky or poisonous paper set out to catch flies

fly′speck′ *n.* **1** a speck of fly excrement **2** any tiny spot or petty flaw

fly′way′ *n.* a route taken regularly by birds migrating to and from breeding grounds

fly′weight′ *n.* a boxer who weighs 112 pounds or less

fly′wheel′ *n.* a heavy wheel on a machine, for regulating its speed

FM frequency modulation

f-num·ber (ef′num′bər) *n. Photog.* a number indicating the relative aperture of a lens: a higher number means a smaller opening

foal (fōl) *n.* ‖OE *fola*‖ a young horse, mule, etc.; colt or filly —*vt., vi.* to give birth to (a foal)

foam (fōm) *n.* ‖OE *fam*‖ **1** the whitish mass of bubbles formed on or in liquids by shaking, etc. **2** something like foam, as frothy saliva **3** a rigid or spongy cellular mass, made from liquid rubber, plastic, etc. —*vi.* to produce foam —**foam′y, -i·er, -i·est,** *adj.*

fob (fäb) *n.* ‖prob. < dial. Ger *fuppe,* a pocket‖ **1** a short ribbon or chain attached to a pocket watch **2** any ornament worn on such a chain, etc.

fo·cal (fō′kəl) *adj.* of or at a focus

focal length the distance from the optical center of a lens to the point where the light rays converge

fo′c′sle or **fo′c′s′le** (fōk′s′l) *n. phonetic sp. of* FORECASTLE

fo·cus (fō′kəs) *n., pl.* **-cus·es** or **-ci′** (-sī′) ‖L, hearth‖ **1** the point where rays of light, heat, etc. come together; specif., the point where rays of reflected or refracted light meet **2** FOCAL LENGTH **3** an adjustment of this to make a clear image [move the lens into *focus*] **4** any center of activity, attention, etc. —*vt.* **-cused** or **-cussed, -cus·ing** or **-cus·sing 1** to bring into focus **2** to adjust the focal length of (the eye, a lens, etc.) so as to produce a clear image **3** to concentrate —**in focus** clear —**out of focus** blurred

fod·der (fäd′ər) *n.* ‖OE *fodor*‖ coarse food for cattle, horses, etc., as hay

foe (fō) *n.* ‖OE *fah,* hostile‖ an enemy

foe·tus (fēt′əs) *n. alt. sp. of* FETUS

fog (fôg, fäg) *n.* ‖prob. < Scand‖ **1** a large mass of water vapor condensed to fine particles, at or just above the earth's surface **2** a state of mental confusion —*vt., vi.* **fogged, fog′ging** to make or become foggy

fog′gy *adj.* **-gi·er, -gi·est 1** full of fog **2** dim; blurred **3** confused

fog′horn′ *n.* a horn blown to warn ships in a fog

fo·gy (fō′gē) *n., pl.* **-gies** ‖< ?‖ one who is old-fashioned in ideas and actions Also **fo′gey,** *pl.* **-geys**

foi·ble (foi′bəl) *n.* ‖< Fr *faible,* feeble‖ a small weakness in character

foil[1] (foil) *vt.* ‖< OFr *fuler,* trample‖ to keep from being successful; thwart

foil[2] (foil) *n.* ‖< L *folium,* leaf‖ **1** a very thin sheet of metal **2** a person or thing that sets off another by contrast **3** ‖< ?‖ a long, thin, blunted fencing sword

foist (foist) *vt.* ‖prob. < dial. Du *vuisten,* to hide in the hand‖ to get (a thing) accepted, sold, etc. by fraud, deception, etc.; palm off: with *on* or *upon*

fol. **1** folio(s) **2** following

fold[1] (fōld) *vt.* ‖OE *faldan*‖ **1** to double (material) up on itself **2** to draw together and intertwine [*fold* your arms] **3** to embrace **4** to wrap up; envelop —*vi.* **1** to be or become folded **2** [Colloq.] *a)* to fail, as a business, play, etc. *b)* to collapse —*n.* a folded part

fold[2] (fōld) *n.* ‖OE *fald*‖ **1** a pen for sheep **2** a flock of sheep **3** a group of people, as in a church

-fold (fōld) ‖< OE *-feald*‖ *suffix* **1** having (a specified number of) parts **2** (a specified number of) times as many or as much [to profit *tenfold*]

fold′a·way′ *adj.* that can be folded together for easy storage

fold′er *n.* **1** a sheet of heavy paper folded for holding loose papers **2** a pamphlet or circular of one or more folded, unstitched sheets

fo·li·age (fō′lē ij′) ***n.*** ‖ < L *folia* ‖ leaves, as of a plant or tree

fo·lic acid (fō′lik) ‖ < L *folium*, leaf ‖ a substance belonging to the vitamin B complex, used in treating anemia

fo·li·o (fō′lē ō′) ***n.***, *pl.* **-os′** ‖ < L *folium*, leaf ‖ **1** a large sheet of paper folded once **2** a large size of book, about 12 by 15 inches, made of sheets so folded **3** the number of a page in a book

folk (fōk) ***n.***, *pl.* **folk** or **folks** ‖ OE *folc* ‖ **1** *a)* a people; nation *b)* the common people of a nation **2** [*pl.*] people; persons —***adj.*** of or originating among the common people —**one's** (or **the**) **folks** one's family, esp. one's parents

folk′lore′ ***n.*** ‖ prec. + LORE ‖ the traditional beliefs, legends, etc. of a culture

folk song **1** a song made and handed down among the common people **2** a song composed in imitation of this —**folk singer**

folk′sy (-sē) ***adj.*** **-si·er, -si·est** [Colloq.] friendly or sociable

fol·li·cle (fäl′i kəl) ***n.*** ‖ < L *follis*, bellows ‖ any small sac, cavity, or gland [a hair *follicle*]

fol·low (fäl′ō) ***vt.*** ‖ < OE *folgian* ‖ **1** to come or go after **2** to pursue **3** to go along [*follow* the road] **4** to take up (a trade, etc.) **5** to result from **6** to take as a model; imitate **7** to obey **8** to watch or listen to closely **9** to understand —***vi.*** **1** to come or go after something else in place, time, etc. **2** to result —**follow out** (or **up**) to carry out fully —**follow through** to continue and complete a stroke or action

fol′low·er ***n.*** one that follows; specif., *a)* one who follows another's teachings; disciple *b)* an attendant

fol′low·ing ***adj.*** that follows; next after —***n.*** a group of followers —***prep.*** after [*following* dinner he left]

fol′low-up′ ***n.*** a letter, visit, etc. that follows as a review, addition, etc.

fol·ly (fäl′ē) ***n.***, *pl.* **-lies** ‖ see FOOL ‖ **1** a lack of sense; foolishness **2** a foolish action or belief

fo·ment (fō ment′) ***vt.*** ‖ < L *fovere*, keep warm ‖ to stir up (trouble); incite —**fo′men·ta′tion** ***n.***

fond (fänd) ***adj.*** ‖ < ME *fonnen*, be foolish ‖ **1** tender and affectionate; loving or doting **2** cherished [a *fond* hope] —**fond of** having a liking for —**fond′ly** ***adv.*** —**fond′ness** ***n.***

fon·dle (fän′dəl) ***vt.*** **-dled, -dling** ‖ < prec. ‖ to caress or handle lovingly

fon·due or **fon·du** (fän do͞o′, fän′do͞o′) ***n.*** ‖ Fr < *fondre*, melt ‖ melted cheese, etc. used as a dip for cubes of bread

font[1] (fänt) ***n.*** ‖ < L *fons*, spring ‖ **1** a basin to hold baptismal water **2** a container for holy water **3** a source

font[2] (fänt) ***n.*** ‖ see FOUND[2] ‖ *Printing* a complete assortment of type in one size and style

fon·ta·nel or **fon·ta·nelle** (fän′tə nel′) ***n.*** ‖ ME *fontinel*, a hollow ‖ a soft, boneless area in a baby's skull that later closes up

food (fo͞od) ***n.*** ‖ OE *foda* ‖ **1** any substance, esp. a solid, taken in by a plant or animal to enable it to live and grow **2** anything that nourishes

food chain *Ecology* a sequence (as grass, rabbit, fox) of organisms in a community in which each member feeds on the one below it

food poisoning sickness caused by contaminants, as bacteria, in food, or by naturally poisonous foods

food processor an electrical appliance that can blend, purée, slice, grate, chop, etc. foods rapidly

food stamp any of the Federal coupons given to qualifying low-income persons for use in buying food

food′stuff′ ***n.*** any substance used as food

fool (fo͞ol) ***n.*** ‖ < L *follis*, windbag ‖ **1** a silly person; simpleton **2** a jester **3** a dupe —***vi.*** **1** to act like a fool **2** to joke **3** [Colloq.] to meddle (*with*) —***vt.*** to trick; deceive —**fool around** [Colloq.] to trifle —**fool′er·y** ***n.***

fool′har′dy ***adj.*** **-di·er, -di·est** foolishly daring; reckless —**fool′har′di·ly** ***adv.*** —**fool′har′di·ness** ***n.***

fool′ish ***adj.*** silly; unwise; absurd —**fool′ish·ly** ***adv.*** —**fool′ish·ness** ***n.***

fool′proof′ ***adj.*** so simple, well-designed, etc. as not to be mishandled, damaged, etc. even by a fool

fools·cap (fo͞olz′kap′) ***n.*** ‖ from a watermark of a jester's cap ‖ a size of writing paper, 13 by 16 in. in the U.S.

foot (foot) ***n.***, *pl.* **feet** ‖ OE *fot* ‖ **1** the end part of the leg, on which one stands **2** the base or bottom [the *foot* of a page] **3** the muscular part of a mollusk used in burrowing, moving, etc. **4** a measure of length equal to 12 inches: symbol ′ **5** [Brit.] infantry **6** a group of syllables serving as a unit of meter in verse —***vt.*** **1** to add (a column of figures): often with *up* **2** [Colloq.] to pay (costs, etc.) —**foot it** [Colloq.] to dance or walk —**on foot** walking —**under foot** in the way

foot′age (-ij) ***n.*** measurement in feet

foot′-and-mouth′ disease a contagious disease of cloven-footed animals, causing blisters in the mouth and around the hoofs

foot′ball′ ***n.*** **1** a field game played with an inflated leather ball by two teams **2** the ball used

foot′bridge′ ***n.*** a bridge for pedestrians

foot′-can′dle ***n.*** a unit for measuring illumination

foot′ed ***adj.*** having feet of a specified number or kind [four-*footed*]

foot′fall′ ***n.*** the sound of a footstep

foot′hill′ ***n.*** a low hill at or near the foot of a mountain or mountain range

foot′hold′ ***n.*** **1** a secure place for a foot, as in climbing **2** a secure position

foot′ing ***n.*** **1** a secure placing of the feet **2** a foothold **3** a secure position **4** a basis for relationship

foot′less ***adj.*** **1** without feet **2** without basis **3** [Colloq.] clumsy; inept

foot′lights′ ***n.pl.*** a row of lights along the front of a stage floor —**the footlights** the theater or acting

foot′lock′er ***n.*** a small trunk, usually kept at the foot of a bed

foot′loose′ ***adj.*** free to go about

foot′man (-mən) ***n.***, *pl.* **-men** a male servant who assists the butler

foot′note′ *n.* 1 a note of comment or reference at the bottom of a page 2 such a note at the end of a chapter or a book 3 an additional comment —*vt.* **-not′ed, -not′ing** to add a footnote or footnotes to

foot′path′ *n.* a narrow path for use by pedestrians only

foot′-pound′ *n.* a unit of energy, the amount required to raise one pound a distance of one foot

foot′print′ *n.* 1 a mark made by a foot 2 an area, or its shape, which something affects, occupies, etc.

foot′sore′ *adj.* having sore or tender feet, as from much walking

foot′step′ *n.* 1 the distance covered in a step 2 the sound of a step 3 FOOTPRINT (sense 1)

foot′stool′ *n.* a low stool for supporting the feet of a seated person

foot′wear′ *n.* shoes, boots, etc.

foot′work′ *n.* the manner of using the feet, as in boxing or dancing

fop (făp) *n.* ‖ME *foppe*, a fool‖ DANDY (*n.* 1) —**fop′per·y**, *pl.* **-ies**, *n.* —**fop′pish** *adj.* —**fop′pish·ly** *adv.*

for (fôr, fər) *prep.* ‖OE‖ 1 in place of /use a rope *for* a belt/ 2 in the interest of /to act *for* another/ 3 in favor of /vote *for* the levy/ 4 in honor of /a party *for* her/ 5 in order to be, get, have, keep, find, etc. /walk *for* exercise, start *for* home/ 6 meant to be received by /flowers *for* a friend/ 7 suitable to /a room *for* sleeping/ 8 with regard to; concerning /an ear *for* music/ 9 as being /to know *for* a fact/ 10 considering the nature of /cool *for* July/ 11 because of /a cry *for* pain/ 12 at the price of /sold *for* $20,000/ 13 to the length, amount, or duration of —*conj.* because

for- ‖OE‖ *prefix* away, apart, off /*forbid, forgo*/

for·age (fôr′ij, făr′-) *n.* ‖< OFr *forre*, fodder‖ 1 food for domestic animals 2 a search for food —*vi.* **-aged, -ag·ing** 1 to search for food 2 to search for something one wants —*vt.* to take food from; raid —**for′ag·er** *n.*

for·ay (fôr′ā) *vt., vi.* ‖< OFr *forrer*, to forage‖ to plunder —*n.* a raid in order to seize things

for·bear[1] (fôr ber′) *vt.* **-bore′, -borne′, -bear′ing** ‖see FOR- & BEAR[1]‖ to refrain from (doing, saying, etc.) —*vi.* 1 to refrain 2 to control oneself

for′bear′[2] *n. alt. sp. of* FOREBEAR

for·bear′ance (-əns) *n.* 1 the act of forbearing 2 self-restraint

for·bid (fər bid′, fôr-) *vt.* **-bade′** (-bad′) or **-bad′, -bid′den, -bid′ding** ‖see FOR- & BID‖ 1 to order (a person) not to do (something); prohibit 2 to prevent

for·bid′ding *adj.* looking dangerous or disagreeable; repellent —**for·bid′ding·ly** *adv.*

force (fôrs) *n.* ‖< L *fortis*, strong‖ 1 strength; power 2 physical coercion against a person or thing 3 the power to control, persuade, etc.; effectiveness 4 military power 5 any group of people organized for some activity /a sales *force*/ 6 energy that causes or alters motion —*vt.* **forced, forc′ing** 1 to make do something by force; compel 2 to break open, into, or through by force 3 to take by force; extort 4 to impose by force: with *on* or *upon* 5 to produce as by force /to *force* a smile/ 6 to cause (plants, etc.) to develop faster by artificial means —**in force** 1 in full strength 2 in effect; valid —**force′less** *adj.*

forced (fôrst) *adj.* 1 compulsory /*forced* labor/ 2 not natural; strained /a *forced* smile/ —**forc·ed·ly** (fôrs′id lē) *adv.*

force′-feed′ *vt.* **-fed′, -feed′ing** to feed as by a tube through the throat to the stomach

force′ful (-fəl) *adj.* full of force; powerful, vigorous, effective, etc. —**force′ful·ly** *adv.* —**force′ful·ness** *n.*

for·ceps (fôr′seps′) *n., pl.* **-ceps′** ‖L < *formus*, warm + *capere*, to take‖ small pincers for grasping, pulling, etc.

for·ci·ble (fôr′sə bəl) *adj.* 1 done by force 2 having force —**for′ci·bly** *adv.*

ford (fôrd) *n.* ‖OE‖ a shallow place in a stream, etc. where one can cross by wading —*vt.* to cross at a ford

Ford (fôrd) 1 **Ger·ald R(udolph), Jr.** (jer′əld) 1913- ; 38th president of the U.S. (1974-77) 2 **Henry** 1863-1947; U.S. automobile manufacturer

fore (fôr) *adv., adj.* ‖OE‖ at, in, or toward the front part, as of a ship —*n.* the front —*interj. Golf* a shout warning that one is about to hit the ball

fore- ‖OE‖ *prefix* 1 before in time, place, etc. /*forenoon*/ 2 the front part of /*forehead*/

fore-and-aft (fôr′n aft′) *adj. Naut.* from the bow to the stern; set lengthwise, as sails

fore′arm′[1] *n.* the part of the arm between the elbow and the wrist

fore·arm′[2] *vt.* to arm in advance

fore′bear′ (-ber′) *n.* ‖< FORE + BE + -ER‖ an ancestor

fore·bode′ (-bōd′) *vt., vi.* **-bod′ed, -bod′ing** ‖< OE‖ 1 to foretell; predict 2 to have a presentiment of (something bad) —**fore·bod′ing** *n.*

fore′cast′ *vt.* **-cast′** or **-cast′ed, -cast′ing** 1 to predict 2 to serve as a prediction of —*n.* a prediction —**fore′cast′er** *n.*

fore·cas·tle (fōk′s′l) *n.* 1 the upper deck of a ship in front of the foremast 2 the front part of a merchant ship, where the crew's quarters are located

fore·close (fôr klōz′) *vt., vi.* **-closed′, -clos′ing** ‖< OFr *fors*, outside + *clore*, CLOSE[2]‖ to take away the right to redeem (a mortgage, etc.) —**fore·clo′sure** (-klō′zhər) *n.*

fore·doom′ *vt.* to doom in advance

fore′fa′ther *n.* an ancestor

fore′fin′ger *n.* the finger nearest the thumb

fore′foot′ *n., pl.* **-feet′** either of the front feet of an animal

fore′front′ *n.* 1 the extreme front 2 the position of most importance

fore·go′[1] *vt., vi.* **-went′, -gone′, -go′ing** to precede

fore·go′[2] *vt. alt. sp. of* FORGO

fore′go′ing *adj.* previously said, written, etc.; preceding

fore·gone′ *adj.* 1 previous 2 previously determined; inevitable

fore′ground′ *n.* 1 the part of a scene, etc. nearest to the viewer 2 the most noticeable position —*vt.* to place in the foreground; emphasize

fore′hand′ *n.* a stroke, as in tennis, made with the palm of the hand turned forward —*adj.* done as with a forehand

fore·head (fôr′ed′, hed′; fär′-) *n.* the part of the face between the eyebrows and the line where the hair normally begins

for·eign (fôr′in, fär′) *adj.* ‖ < L *foras,* out of doors ‖ 1 situated outside one's own coun try, locality, etc. 2 of, from, or having to do with other countries 3 not belonging; not characteristic

for′eign-born′ *adj.* born in some other country; not native

for′eign·er *n.* a person from another coun try; alien

foreign minister a member of a govern mental cabinet in charge of foreign affairs for the country

fore·know′ *vt.* **-knew′**, **-known′**, **-know′·ing** to know beforehand —**fore′knowl′·edge** (-näl′ij) *n.*

fore′leg′ *n.* either of the front legs of an animal

fore′lock′ *n.* a lock of hair growing just above the forehead

fore′man (-mən) *n., pl.* **-men** 1 the chair man of a jury 2 the head of a group of workers —**fore′wom′an,** *pl.* **-wom′en,** *n.fem.*

fore′mast′ *n.* the mast nearest the bow of a ship

fore′most′ (-mōst′) *adj.* first in place, time, etc. —*adv.* first

fore′noon′ *n.* the time from sunrise to noon; morning

fo·ren·sic (fə ren′sik) *adj.* ‖ < L *forum,* marketplace ‖ 1 of or suitable for public debate 2 involving the application of scien tific, esp. medical, knowledge to legal mat ters —**fo·ren′si·cal·ly** *adv.*

forensic medicine MEDICAL JURISPRUDENCE

fore′or·dain′ *vt.* to ordain beforehand; pre destine —**fore′or′di·na′tion** (-ôrd ″n ā′ shən) *n.*

fore′run′ner *n.* 1 a herald 2 a sign that tells or warns of something to follow 3 a predecessor; ancestor

fore′sail′ (-sāl′, -səl) *n.* the main sail on the foremast of a schooner

fore·see′ *vt.* **-saw′**, **-seen′**, **-see′ing** to see or know beforehand —**fore·see′a·ble** *adj.* —**fore·se′er** *n.*

fore·shad′ow *vt.* to indicate or suggest beforehand; presage

fore·short′en *vt.* in drawing, etc., to shorten some lines of (an object) to give the illusion of proper relative size

FORE-SHORTENED ARM

fore′sight′ *n.* 1 *a)* a fore seeing *b)* the power to fore see 2 prudent regard or provision for the future

fore′skin′ *n.* the fold of skin that covers the end of the penis

for·est (fôr′ist) *n.* ‖ < L *foris,* out-of-doors ‖ a thick growth of trees, etc. cover ing a large tract of land —*vt.* to plant with trees

fore·stall (fôr stôl′) *vt.* ‖ < OE *foresteall,* ambush ‖ 1 to prevent by doing something ahead of time 2 to act in advance of; antici pate

for·est·a·tion (fôr′is tā′shən) *n.* the planting or care of forests

for′est·er *n.* one trained in forestry

for′est·ry *n.* the science of planting and tak ing care of forests

fore′taste′ *n.* a taste or sample of what can be expected

fore·tell′ *vt.* **-told′**, **-tell′ing** to tell or indi cate beforehand; predict

fore′thought′ *n.* 1 a thinking or planning beforehand 2 foresight

for·ev·er (fôr ev′ər, fər-) *adv.* 1 for always; endlessly 2 at all times; always Also **for·ev′er·more′**

fore·warn′ *vt.* to warn beforehand

fore′word′ *n.* an introductory statement in a book

for·feit (fôr′fit) *n.* ‖ < OFr *forfaire,* trans gress ‖ 1 a fine or penalty for some crime, fault, or neglect 2 the act of forfeiting —*adj.* lost or taken away as a forfeit —*vt.* to lose or be deprived of as a forfeit

for′fei·ture (-fə chər) *n.* 1 the act of forfeit ing 2 anything forfeited

for·gath·er (fôr gath′ər) *vi.* to come together; meet; assemble

for·gave (fər gāv′, fôr-) *vt., vi. pt. of* FORGIVE

forge[1] (fôrj) *n.* ‖ < L *faber,* workman ‖ 1 a furnace for heating metal to be wrought 2 a place where metal is heated and wrought; smithy —*vt.* **forged, forg′ing** 1 to form or shape (metal) by heating and hammering 2 to form; shape 3 to imitate (a signature) fraudulently; counterfeit (a check) —*vi.* 1 to work at a forge 2 to commit forgery —**forg′er** *n.*

forge[2] (fôrj) *vi.* **forged, forg′ing** ‖ prob. < FORCE ‖ to move forward steadily: often with *ahead*

for′ger·y *n., pl.* **-ies** 1 the act or crime of imitating or counterfeiting documents, sig natures, etc. to deceive 2 anything forged

for·get (fər get′, fôr-) *vt., vi.* **-got′**, **-got′ten** or **-got′**, **-get′ting** ‖ OE *forgietan* ‖ 1 to be unable to remember 2 to overlook or neglect (something) —**forget oneself** to act in an improper manner —**for·get′ta·ble** *adj.*

for·get′ful *adj.* 1 apt to forget 2 heedless or negligent —**for·get′ful·ly** *adv.* —**for·get′ful·ness** *n.*

for·get′-me-not′ *n.* a marsh plant with small blue, white, or pink flowers

for·give (fər giv′, fôr-) *vt., vi.* **-gave′**, **-giv′en, -giv′ing** ‖ OE *forgiefan* ‖ to give up resentment against or the desire to punish; pardon (an offense or offender) —**for·giv′a·ble** *adj.* —**for·give′ness** *n.* —**for·giv′er** *n.*

for·giv′ing *adj.* inclined to forgive —**for·giv′ing·ly** *adv.*

for·go (fôr gō′) *vt.* **-went′**, **-gone′**, **-go′ing** ‖ OE *forgan* ‖ to do without; abstain from; give up —**for·go′er** *n.*

for·got (fər gät′) *vt., vi. pt. & alt. pp. of* FORGET

for·got′ten (-′n) *vt., vi. alt. pp. of* FORGET

fork (fôrk) *n.* ‖ < L *furca* ‖ 1 an instrument of varying size with prongs at one end, as for eating food, pitching hay, etc. **2** something like a fork in shape, etc **3** the place where a road, etc. divides into branches **4** any of these branches —*vi.* to divide into branches —*vt.* to pick up or pitch with a fork —**fork over** (or **out** or **up**) [Colloq.] to pay out; hand over —**fork'ful'**, *pl.* **-fuls'**, *n.*

fork'lift' *n.* a device for lifting heavy objects by means of projecting prongs that are slid under the load

for·lorn (fôr lôrn') *adj.* ‖< OE *forleosan*, lose utterly‖ **1** abandoned **2** wretched; miserable **3** without hope —**for·lorn'ly** *adv.*

form (fôrm) *n.* ‖< L *forma*‖ **1** shape; general structure **2** the figure of a person or animal **3** a mold **4** a particular mode, kind, type, etc. /ice is a *form* of water, the *forms* of poetry/ **5** arrangement; style **6** a way of doing something requiring skill **7** a customary or conventional way of acting; ceremony; ritual **8** a printed document with blanks to be filled in **9** condition of mind or body **10** a chart with information on horses in a race **11** a changed appearance of a word to show inflection, etc. **12** type, etc. locked in a frame for printing —*vt.* **1** to shape; fashion **2** to train; instruct **3** to develop (habits) **4** to make up; constitute —*vi.* to be formed

-form (fôrm) ‖< L‖ *combining form* having the form of /*cuneiform*/

for·mal (fôr'məl) *adj.* ‖< L *formalis*‖ **1** according to fixed customs, rules, etc. **2** stiff in manner **3** *a)* designed for wear at ceremonies, etc. *b)* requiring clothes of this kind **4** done or made in explicit, definite form /a *formal* contract/ **5** designating language usage characterized by expanded vocabulary, complex syntax, etc. —*n.* **1** a formal dance **2** a woman's evening dress —**for'mal·ly** *adv.*

form·al·de·hyde (fôr mal'də hīd') *n.* ‖FORM(IC) + *aldehyde*‖ a pungent gas used in solution as a disinfectant and preservative

for'mal·ism' *n.* strict attention to outward forms and traditions

for·mal·i·ty (fôr mal'ə tē) *n.*, *pl.* **-ties** **1** *a)* an observing of customs, rules, etc.; propriety *b)* excessive attention to convention; stiffness **2** a formal act; ceremony

for·mal·ize (fôr'mə līz') *vt.* **-ized'**, **-iz'ing** **1** to shape **2** to make formal —**for'mal·i·za'tion** *n.*

for·mat (fôr'mat') *n.* ‖< L *formatus*, formed‖ **1** the shape, size, and arrangement of a book, etc. **2** the arrangement or plan, as of a TV program

for·ma·tion (fôr mā'shən) *n.* **1** a forming or being formed **2** a thing formed **3** the way in which something is formed; structure **4** an arrangement or positioning, as of troops

form·a·tive (fôrm'ə tiv) *adj.* helping or involving formation or development

for·mer (fôr'mər) *adj.* ‖ME *formere*‖ **1** earlier; past /in *former* times/ **2** being the first mentioned of two

for'mer·ly *adv.* in the past

for·mic (fôr'mik) *adj.* ‖< L *formica*, ant‖ designating a colorless acid found in ants, spiders, etc.

For·mi·ca (fôr mī'kə) *trademark for* a laminated, heat resistant plastic used for counter tops, etc.

for·mi·da·ble (fôr'mə də bəl) *adj.* ‖< L *formidare*, to dread‖ **1** causing fear, dread, or awe **2** hard to handle

form·less (fôrm'lis) *adj.* shapeless; amorphous

form letter a standardized letter, usually one of many, with the date, address, etc. added separately

For·mo·sa (fôr mō'sə, -zə) *old (Port.) name of* TAIWAN —**For·mo'san** *adj.*, *n.*

for·mu·la (fôr'myoo lə, -myə-) *n.*, *pl.* **-las** or **-lae'** (-lē', -lī') ‖L < *forma*, form‖ **1** a fixed form of words, esp. a conventional expression **2** a conventional rule for doing something **3** a prescription or recipe **4** fortified milk for a baby **5** a set of symbols expressing a mathematical rule **6** *Chem.* an expression of the composition, as of a compound, using symbols and figures

for'mu·late' (-lāt') *vt.* **-lat'ed**, **-lat'ing** **1** to express in a formula **2** to express in a definite way —**for'mu·la'tion** *n.* —**for'mu·la'tor** *n.*

for·ni·cate (fôr'ni kāt') *vi.* **-cat'ed**, **-cat'ing** ‖< L *fornix*, a brothel‖ to commit fornication —**for'ni·ca'tor** *n.*

for'ni·ca'tion *n.* sexual intercourse between unmarried persons

for·sake (fôr sāk') *vt.* **-sook'** (-sook'), **-sak'en**, **-sak'ing** ‖< OE *for-*, FOR- + *sacan*, to strive‖ **1** to give up (a habit, etc.) **2** to leave; abandon

for·sooth (fôr sooth') *adv.* ‖ME *forsoth*‖ [Archaic] indeed

for·swear (fôr swer') *vt.* **-swore'**, **-sworn'**, **-swear'ing** to deny or renounce on oath —*vi.* to commit perjury

for·syth·i·a (fôr sith'ē ə, fər-) *n.* ‖after W. *Forsyth* (1737 1804), Eng botanist‖ a shrub with yellow, bell-shaped flowers in early spring

fort (fôrt) *n.* ‖< L *fortis*, strong‖ **1** a fortified place for military defense **2** a permanent army post

forte[1] (fôrt) *n.* ‖< OFr: see prec.‖ that which one does particularly well

for·te[2] (fôr'tā') *adj.*, *adv.* ‖It < L *fortis*, strong‖ *Musical Direction* loud

forth (fôrth) *adv.* ‖OE‖ **1** forward; onward **2** out into view

Forth (fôrth), **Firth of** long estuary of the Forth River in SE Scotland

forth'com'ing *adj.* **1** about to appear; approaching **2** ready when needed

forth'right' *adj.* direct and frank

forth'with' *adv.* at once

for·ti·fy (fôrt'ə fī') *vt.* **-fied'**, **-fy'ing** ‖< L *fortis*, strong + *facere*, to make‖ **1** to strengthen physically, emotionally, etc. **2** to strengthen against attack, as with forts **3** to support **4** to add alcohol to (wine, etc.) **5** to add vitamins, etc. to (milk, etc.) —**for'ti·fi·ca'tion** *n.* —**for'ti·fi'er** *n.*

for·tis·si·mo (fôr tis'ə mō') *adj.*, *adv.* ‖It, superl. of *forte*, strong‖ *Musical Direction* very loud

for·ti·tude (fôrt'ə tood') *n.* ‖< L *fortis*, strong‖ patient endurance of trouble, pain, etc.; courage

Fort Knox (nāks) military reservation in N Ky.: site of U.S. gold bullion depository

Fort Lau·der·dale (lô′dər dāl′) city on the SE coast of Fla.: pop. 153,000

fort·night (fôrt′nīt′) ***n.*** ‖ ME *fourte(n) niht* ‖ [Chiefly Brit.] a period of two weeks —**fort′·night′ly** ***adj., adv.***

for·tress (fôr′tris) ***n.*** ‖ < L *fortis,* strong ‖ a fortified place; fort

for·tu·i·tous (fôr to͞o′ə təs) ***adj.*** ‖ < L *fors,* luck ‖ **1** happening by chance **2** lucky —**for·tu′i·tous·ly** ***adv.***

for·tu·nate (fôr′chə nət) ***adj.*** **1** having good luck **2** coming by good luck; favorable —**for′tu·nate·ly** ***adv.***

for·tune (fôr′chən) ***n.*** ‖ < L *fors,* luck ‖ **1** luck; chance; fate **2** one's future lot, good or bad **3** good luck; success **4** wealth; riches

for′tune·tell′er ***n.*** one who professes to foretell the future of others —**for′tune·tell′ing** ***n., adj.***

Fort Wayne (wān) city in NE Ind.: pop. 172,000

Fort Worth (wurth) city in N Tex.: pop. 385,000

for·ty (fôrt′ē) ***adj., n.,*** *pl.* **-ties** ‖ OE *feowertig* ‖ four times ten; 40; XL —**the forties** the numbers or years, as of a century, from 40 through 49 —**for′ti·eth** (-ith) ***adj.***

fo·rum (fôr′əm) ***n.*** ‖ L ‖ **1** the public square of an ancient Roman city **2** an assembly, program, etc. for the discussion of public matters

for·ward (fôr′wərd) ***adj.*** ‖ OE *foreweard* ‖ **1** at, toward, or of the front **2** advanced **3** onward **4** prompt; ready **5** bold; presumptuous **6** of or for the future —***adv.*** toward the front; ahead —***n.*** *Basketball, Hockey, etc.* a player in a front position —***vt.*** **1** to promote **2** to send on

for′wards ***adv.*** FORWARD

fos·sil (fäs′əl, fôs′-) ***n.*** ‖ < L *fossilis,* dug up ‖ **1** any hardened remains of a plant or animal of a previous geologic period, preserved in the earth's crust **2** a person with outmoded ideas or ways —***adj.*** **1** of or like a fossil **2** dug from the earth /coal is a *fossil* fuel/ **3** antiquated

fos′sil·ize′ (-īz′) ***vt., vi.*** **-ized′, -iz′ing** **1** to change into a fossil **2** to make or become out of date, rigid, etc. —**fos′sil·i·za′tion** ***n.***

fos·ter (fôs′tər) ***vt.*** ‖ OE *fostrian,* to nourish ‖ **1** to bring up; rear **2** to help to develop; promote —***adj.*** having a specified standing in a family but not by birth /a *foster* brother/

fought (fôt) ***vi., vt.*** *pt. & pp. of* FIGHT

foul (foul) ***adj.*** ‖ OE *ful* ‖ **1** stinking; loathsome **2** extremely dirty **3** indecent; profane **4** wicked; abominable **5** stormy /*foul* weather/ **6** tangled /a *foul* rope/ **7** not within the limits or rules set **8** designating lines setting limits on a playing area **9** dishonest **10** [Colloq.] unpleasant, disagreeable, etc. —***adv.*** in a foul manner —***n.*** *Sports* a hit, blow, move, etc. that is FOUL (*adj.* 7) —***vt.*** **1** to make filthy **2** to dishonor **3** to obstruct /grease *fouls* drains/ **4** to entangle (a rope, etc.) **5** to make a foul against, as in a game **6** *Baseball* to bat (the ball) foul —***vi.*** to be or become fouled —**foul up** [Colloq.] to bungle —**foul′ly** ***adv.*** —**foul′ness** ***n.***

fou·lard (fo͞o lärd′) ***n.*** ‖ Fr ‖ a lightweight printed fabric of silk, etc.

foul′-up′ ***n.*** a mix-up; botch

found[1] (found) ‖ OE *funden* ‖ ***vt., vi.*** *pp. & pt. of* FIND

found[2] (found) ***vt.*** ‖ < L *fundus,* bottom ‖ **1** to set for support; base **2** to bring into being; set up; establish —**found′er** ***n.***

found[3] (found) ***vt.*** ‖ < L *fundere,* pour ‖ **1** to melt and pour (metal) into a mold **2** to make by founding metal

foun·da·tion (foun dā′shən) ***n.*** **1** a founding or being founded; establishment **2** *a)* an endowment for an institution *b)* such an institution **3** basis **4** the base of a wall, house, etc.

foun·der (foun′dər) ***vi.*** ‖ < L *fundus,* bottom ‖ **1** to stumble, fall, or go lame **2** to fill with water and sink: said of a ship **3** to break down

found·ling (found′liŋ′) ***n.*** an infant of unknown parents, found abandoned

found·ry (foun′drē) ***n.,*** *pl.* **-ries** a place where metal is cast

fount (fount) ***n.*** ‖ < L *fons* ‖ **1** [Old Poet.] a fountain or spring **2** a source

foun·tain (fount′′n) ***n.*** ‖ < L *fons* ‖ **1** a natural spring of water **2** a source **3** *a)* an artificial jet or flow of water /a drinking *fountain*/ *b)* the basin where this flows **4** a reservoir, as for ink

foun′tain·head′ ***n.*** the source, as of a stream

fountain pen a pen which is fed ink from its own reservoir

four (fôr) ***adj., n.*** ‖ OE *feower* ‖ one more than three; 4; IV

four′-flush′er (-flush′ər) ***n.*** ‖ < FLUSH[2] ‖ [Colloq.] one who bluffs in an effort to deceive

four′-in-hand′ ***n.*** a necktie tied in a slipknot with the ends left hanging

four′score′ ***adj., n.*** four times twenty; eighty

four′some (-səm) ***n.*** four people

four·square (fôr′skwer′) ***adj.*** **1** square **2** unyielding; firm **3** frank; forthright —***adv.*** in a square form or manner

four·teen (fôr′tēn′) ***adj., n.*** ‖ OE *feowertyne* ‖ four more than ten; 14; XIV —**four′teenth′** ***adj., n.***

fourth (fôrth) ***adj.*** ‖ OE *feortha* ‖ preceded by three others in a series; 4th —***n.*** **1** the one following the third **2** any of the four equal parts of something; $\frac{1}{4}$ **3** the fourth forward gear

fourth′-class′ ***adj., adv.*** of or in a class of mail consisting of merchandise, printed matter, etc. not included in first-class, second-class, or third-class; parcel post

fourth dimension in the theory of relativity, time added as a dimension to those of length, width, and depth

fourth estate [*often* **F- E-**] journalism or journalists

Fourth of July *see* INDEPENDENCE DAY

4WD four-wheel-drive (vehicle)

four′-wheel′ ***adj.*** **1** having four wheels **2** affecting four wheels /a *four-wheel* drive/

fowl (foul) ***n.*** ‖ OE *fugol* ‖ **1** any bird **2** any of the domestic birds used as food, as the chicken, duck, etc. **3** the flesh of these birds used for food

fox (fäks) ***n.*** ‖ OE ‖ **1** a small, wild animal of the dog family, considered sly and crafty **2** its fur **3** a sly, crafty person —*vt.* to trick by slyness

fox'glove' *n.* DIGITALIS

fox'hole' *n.* a hole dug in the ground as a protection against enemy gunfire

fox'hound' *n.* a hound with a keen scent, bred and trained to hunt foxes

fox terrier a small, active terrier with a smooth or wiry coat, formerly trained to drive foxes out of hiding

fox trot a dance for couples in 4/4 time, or music for it —**fox'-trot', -trot'ted, -trot'ting,** *vi.*

fox·y (fäk'sē) *adj.* **-i·er, -i·est 1** foxlike; crafty; sly **2** [Slang] attractive or sexy: used esp. of women

foy·er (foi'ər, foi yā') *n.* ‖ < L *focus*, hearth ‖ an entrance hall or lobby, as in a theater or hotel

Fr. 1 Father **2** French

frab·jous (frab'jəs) *adj.* ‖ coined by Lewis Carroll ‖ [Colloq.] splendid; fine

fra·cas (frā'kəs) *n.* ‖ Fr < It *fracassare*, to smash ‖ a noisy fight; brawl

frac·tion (frak'shən) *n.* ‖ < L *frangere*, to break ‖ **1** a small part, amount, etc. **2** *Math.* *a)* a quantity less than a whole, expressed as a decimal *b)* any quantity expressed in terms of a numerator and denominator —**frac'tion·al** *adj.*

frac·tious (frak'shəs) *adj.* ‖ < ? ‖ **1** unruly; rebellious **2** irritable; cross

frac·ture (frak'chər) *n.* ‖ < L *frangere*, to break ‖ a breaking or break, esp. of a bone —*vt., vi.* **-tured, -tur·ing** to break, crack, or split

frag·ile (fraj'əl) *adj.* ‖ < L *frangere*, to break ‖ easily broken or damaged; delicate —**fra·gil·i·ty** (frə jil'ə tē) *n.*

frag·ment (frag'mənt) *n.* ‖ < L *frangere*, to break ‖ **1** a part broken away **2** an incomplete part, as of a novel —*vt., vi.* to break up —**frag'men·ta'tion** (-mən tā'shən) *n.*

frag'men·tar'y (-mən ter'ē) *adj.* consisting of fragments; not complete

fra·grant (frā'grənt) *adj.* ‖ < L *fragrare*, to emit a (sweet) smell ‖ having a pleasant odor —**fra'grance** *n.*

frail (frāl) *adj.* ‖ see FRAGILE ‖ **1** easily broken **2** not robust; weak **3** easily tempted; morally weak —**frail'ly** *adv.*

frail'ty (-tē) *n.* **1** a being frail; esp., moral weakness **2** *pl.* **-ties** a fault arising from such weakness

frame (frām) *vt.* **framed, fram'ing** ‖ prob. < ON *frami*, profit ‖ **1** to form according to a pattern; design /to *frame* laws/ **2** to construct **3** to put into words /to *frame* an excuse/ **4** to enclose (a picture, etc.) in a border **5** [Colloq.] to falsify evidence in order to make appear guilty —*n.* **1** body structure **2** the framework, as of a house **3** the structural case enclosing a window, door, etc. **4** an ornamental border, as around a picture **5** the way anything is put together; form **6** mood; temper /good *frame* of mind/ **7** one exposure in a filmstrip or movie film **8** *Bowling, etc.* a division of a game —*adj.* having a wooden framework /a *frame* house/ —**fram'er** *n.*

frame'-up' *n.* [Colloq.] a secret, deceitful scheme, as a falsifying of evidence to make a person seem guilty

frame'work' *n.* **1** a structure to hold together or support something **2** a basic structure, system, etc.

franc (fraŋk) *n.* ‖ Fr < L *Francorum rex*, king of the French, on the coin in 1360 ‖ the monetary unit of Belgium, France, Switzerland, Chad, etc.

France (frans, fräns) country in W Europe: 212,821 sq. mi.; pop. 54,335,000

fran·chise (fran'chīz') *n.* ‖ < OFr *franc*, free ‖ **1** any special right or privilege granted by a government **2** the right to vote; suffrage **3** the right to sell a product or service —*vt.* **-chised', -chis'ing** to grant a franchise to

Franco- *combining form* French, French and

fran·gi·ble (fran'jə bəl) *adj.* ‖ < L *frangere*, to break ‖ breakable; fragile

frank (fraŋk) *adj.* ‖ < OFr *franc*, free ‖ free in expressing oneself; candid —*vt.* to send (mail) free of postage —*n.* **1** the right to send mail free **2** a mark indicating this right —**frank'ly** *adv.* —**frank'ness** *n.*

Frank (fraŋk) *n.* a member of the Germanic tribes whose 9th-c. empire extended over what is now France, Germany, and Italy

Frank·en·stein (fraŋk'ən stīn') the title character in a novel (1818), creator of a monster that destroys him —*n.* popularly, the monster

Frank·fort (fraŋk'fərt) capital of Ky.: pop. 26,000

Frank·furt (fraŋk'fərt; *Ger* fräŋk'foort) city in central West Germany: pop. 604,000

frank·furt·er (fraŋk'furt'ər) *n.* ‖ Ger: after *Frankfurt*, city in Germany ‖ a smoked sausage of beef, beef and pork, etc.; wiener Also [Colloq.] **frank**

frank·in·cense (fraŋk'in sens') *n.* ‖ see FRANK & INCENSE[1] ‖ a gum resin burned as incense

Frank·ish (fraŋk'ish) *n.* the West Germanic language of the Franks —*adj.* of the Franks or their language or culture

Frank·lin (fraŋk'lin), **Ben·ja·min** (ben'jə mən) 1706-90; Am. statesman, scientist, inventor, & writer

fran·tic (frant'ik) *adj.* ‖ < Gr *phrenitis*, delirium ‖ wild with anger, pain, worry, etc. —**fran'ti·cal·ly** *adv.*

frap·pé (fra pā') *n.* ‖ Fr < *frapper*, to strike ‖ **1** a dessert made of partly frozen fruit juices, etc. **2** a beverage poured over shaved ice **3** [New England] a milkshake Also **frappe** (frap)

fra·ter·nal (frə turn'əl) *adj.* ‖ < L *frater*, brother ‖ **1** of brothers; brotherly **2** designating or of a society organized for fellowship **3** designating twins developed from separate ova and thus not identical

fra·ter·ni·ty (frə turn'ət ē) *n., pl.* **-ties 1** brotherliness **2** a group of men joined together for fellowship, etc., as in college **3** a group of people with the same beliefs, work, etc.

frat·er·nize (frat'ər nīz') *vi.* **-nized', -niz'ing** to associate in a friendly way —**frat'er·ni·za'tion** *n.*

frat·ri·cide (fra'trə sīd') *n.* ‖ < L *frater*, brother + *caedere*, to kill ‖ **1** the killing of one's own brother or sister **2** one who commits fratricide

Frau (frou) ***n.***, *pl.* ***Frau'en*** (ən) ‖Ger‖ a wife: a title corresponding to *Mrs.*

fraud (frôd) ***n.*** ‖< L *fraus*‖ **1** deceit; trickery **2** *Law* intentional deception **3** a trick **4** an impostor

fraud·u·lent (frô'jə lənt) ***adj.*** **1** based on or using fraud **2** done or obtained by fraud —**fraud'u·lence** ***n.*** —**fraud'u·lent·ly** ***adv.***

fraught (frôt) ***adj.*** ‖< MDu *vracht*, a load‖ **1** filled or loaded (*with*) /a life *fraught* with hardship/ **2** tense, anxious, etc.

Fräu·lein (froi'lin') ***n.***, *pl.* ***-lein'*** or Eng. **-leins'** ‖Ger‖ an unmarried woman: a title corresponding to *Miss*

fray[1] (frā) ***n.*** ‖< AFFRAY‖ a noisy quarrel or fight; brawl

fray[2] (frā) ***vt., vi.*** ‖< L *fricare*, to rub‖ **1** to make or become worn or ragged **2** to make or become weak

fraz·zle (fraz'əl) ***vt., vi.*** **-zled, -zling** ‖< dial. *fazle*‖ [Colloq.] **1** to wear to tatters; fray **2** to tire out —***n.*** [Colloq.] a being frazzled

freak (frēk) ***n.*** ‖< ?‖ **1** an odd notion; whim **2** an unusual happening **3** any abnormal animal, person, or plant **4** [Slang] *a)* a drug user *b)* a devotee; buff /a chess *freak*/ —***adj.*** oddly different; abnormal —**freak out** [Slang] **1** to have hallucinations, etc., as from a psychedelic drug **2** to lose one's composure, control, etc. —**freak'ish** ***adj.***

freak'out' ***n.*** [Slang] the act or an instance of freaking out

freck·le (frek'əl) ***n.*** ‖< Scand‖ a small, brownish spot on the skin —***vt., vi.*** **-led, -ling** to make or become spotted with freckles

Fred·er·ick the Great (fred'rik, -ər ik) 1712-86; king of Prussia (1740-86)

Fred·er·ic·ton (fred'ə rik tən) capital of New Brunswick, Canada: pop. 45,000

free (frē) ***adj.*** **fre'er, fre'est** ‖< OE *freo*‖ **1** not under the control or power of another; having liberty; independent **2** having civil and political liberty **3** able to move in any direction; loose **4** not burdened by obligations, debts, discomforts, etc. **5** not confined to the usual rules /*free* verse/ **6** not exact /a *free* translation/ **7** generous; profuse /a *free* spender/ **8** frank **9** with no cost or charge **10** exempt from taxes, duties, etc. **11** clear of obstructions /a *free* road/ **12** not fastened /a rope's *free* end/ —***adv.*** **1** without cost **2** in a free manner —***vt.*** **freed, free'ing** to make free; specif., *a)* to release from bondage or arbitrary power, obligation, etc. *b)* to clear of obstruction, etc. —**free from** (or **of**) without —**make free with** to use freely —**free'ly** ***adv.*** —**free'ness** ***n.***

-free (frē) *combining form* free of or from, exempt from

free·base (frē'bās') ***n.*** a concentrated form of cocaine for smoking —***vt., vi.*** **-based', -bas'ing** to prepare or use such a form of (cocaine)

free·bie or **free'bee** (frē'bē) ***n.*** [Slang] something given or gotten free of charge, as a theater ticket

free'boot'er (-bo͞ot'ər) ***n.*** ‖< Du *vrij*, free + *buit*, plunder‖ a pirate

freed·man (frēd'mən) ***n.***, *pl.* **-men** a man legally freed from slavery

free·dom (frē'dəm) ***n.*** **1** a being free; esp., *a)* independence *b)* civil or political liberty *c)* exemption from an obligation, discomfort, etc. *d)* a being able to act, use, etc. freely *e)* ease of movement *f)* frankness **2** a right or privilege

free fall unchecked fall, as of a parachutist before the parachute opens

free flight any flight or part of a flight, as of a rocket, occurring without propulsion —**free'-flight'** ***adj.***

free'-for-all' ***n.*** a disorganized, general fight; brawl —***adj.*** open to anyone

free'hand' ***adj.*** drawn by hand without the use of instruments, etc.

free'hold' ***n.*** an estate in land held for life or with the right to pass it on through inheritance —**free'hold'er** ***n.***

free-lance or **free-lance** (frē'lans') ***n.*** a writer, artist, etc. who sells his services to individual buyers Also **free'lanc'er** or **free'-lanc'er** —***adj.*** of or working as a freelance —***vi.*** **-lanced', -lanc'ing** to work as a freelance

free'load'er (-lōd'ər) ***n.*** [Colloq.] a person who habitually imposes on others for free food, etc. —**free'load'** ***vi.***

free·man (frē'mən) ***n.***, *pl.* **-men** **1** a person not in slavery **2** a citizen

Free·ma·son (frē'mā'sən) ***n.*** a member of an international secret society based on brotherliness and mutual aid —**Free'ma'son·ry** ***n.***

free on board delivered (by the seller) aboard the train, ship, etc. at no extra charge to the buyer

free'stone' ***n.*** a peach, etc. in which the pit does not cling to the pulp

free'think'er ***n.*** one who forms his opinions about religion independently

free trade trade carried on without protective tariffs, quotas, etc.

free university a loosely organized forum for studying subjects not normally offered at universities

free verse poetry without regular meter, rhyme, etc.

free'way' ***n.*** a multiple-lane divided highway with fully controlled access

free'will' ***adj.*** voluntary

freeze (frēz) ***vi.*** **froze, fro'zen, freez'ing** ‖OE *freosan*‖ **1** to be formed into, or become covered with, ice **2** to become very cold **3** to be damaged or killed by cold **4** to become motionless **5** to be made speechless by strong emotion **6** to become formal or unfriendly —***vt.*** **1** to form into, or cover with, ice **2** to make very cold **3** to preserve (food) by rapid refrigeration **4** to kill or damage by cold **5** to make motionless **6** to make formal or unfriendly **7** *a)* to fix (prices, etc.) at a given level by authority *b)* to make (funds, etc.) unavailable to the owners —***n.*** **1** a freezing or being frozen **2** a period of freezing weather —**freeze out** **1** to die out through freezing, as plants **2** [Colloq.] to keep out by a cold manner, competition, etc. —**freeze over** to become covered with ice —**freez'a·ble** ***adj.***

freeze'-dry' *vt.* **-dried', -dry'ing** to quick freeze (food, etc.) and then dry under high vacuum

freez'er *n.* **1** a refrigerator, compartment, etc. for freezing and storing perishable foods **2** a machine for making ice cream

freezing point the temperature at which a liquid freezes: the freezing point of water is 32°F or 0°C

freight (frāt) *n.* ‖< MDu *vracht,* a load‖ **1** the transporting of goods by water, land, or air **2** the cost for this **3** the goods transported **4** a railroad train for transporting goods: in full **freight train** —*vt.* **1** to load with freight **2** to send by freight

freight'er *n.* a ship for freight

Fre·mont (frē'mänt) city in W Calif., on San Francisco Bay: pop. 132,000

French (frənch) *adj.* of France, its people, language, etc. —*n.* the language of France —**the French** the people of France — **French'man** (-mən), *pl.* **-men,** *n.*

French bread bread with a crisp crust made with white flour in a long, slender loaf

French cuff a shirt-sleeve cuff turned back and fastened with a cuff link

French doors a pair of doors hinged at the sides to open in the middle

French dressing 1 a salad dressing made of vinegar, oil, etc. **2** an orange-colored, creamy salad dressing

French fries [*often* **f- f-**] strips of potato that have been French fried

French fry [*often* **f- f-**] to fry in hot deep fat

French Gui·a·na (gē an'ə, -ä'nə) French overseas department in NE South America

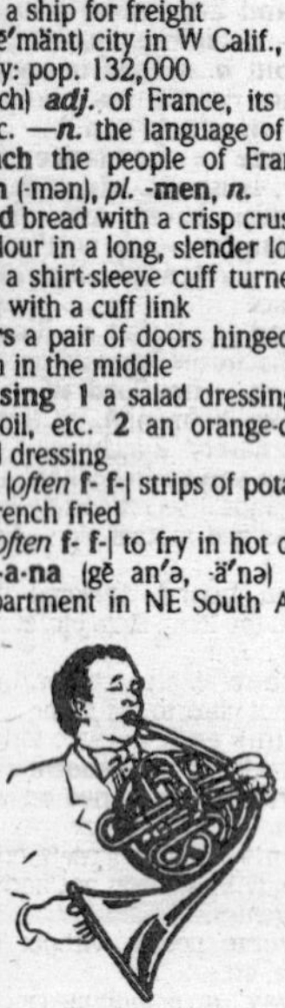

FRENCH HORN

French horn a mellow-toned brass instrument with a long spiral tube and a flaring bell: now usually *horn*

French leave an unauthorized departure

French toast sliced bread dipped in a batter of egg and milk and fried

fre·net·ic (frə net'ik) *adj.* ‖see PHRENETIC‖ frantic; frenzied —**fre·net'i·cal·ly** *adv.*

fren·zy (fren'zē) *n., pl.* **-zies** ‖< Gr *phrenitis,* madness‖ wild excitement; delirium

Fre·on (frē'än') *trademark for* any of a series of gaseous compounds of fluorine, carbon, etc.: used as refrigerants, aerosol propellants, etc.

fre·quen·cy (frē'kwən sē) *n., pl.* **-cies 1** frequent occurrence **2** the number of times any event recurs in a given period **3** *Physics* the number of oscillations or cycles per unit of time

frequency modulation the variation of the frequency of a carrier wave in accordance with the signal to be transmitted

fre·quent (frē'kwənt; *for v.* frē kwent') *adj.* ‖< L *frequens,* crowded‖ **1** occurring often **2** constant; habitual —*vt.* to go to or be at often —**fre'quent·ly** *adv.*

fres·co (fres'kō) *n., pl.* **-coes** or **-cos** ‖It, fresh‖ a painting with watercolors on wet plaster

fresh[1] (fresh) *adj.* ‖OE *fersc*‖ **1** recently made, grown, etc. [*fresh* coffee] **2** not salted, pickled, etc. **3** not spoiled **4** not tired; lively **5** not worn, soiled, faded, etc. **6** new; recent **7** inexperienced **8** cool and refreshing [*a fresh* spring day] **9** brisk: said of wind **10** not salt: said of water — **fresh'ly** *adv.* —**fresh'ness** *n.*

fresh[2] (fresh) *adj.* ‖< Ger *frech,* bold‖ [Slang] bold; saucy; impertinent

fresh'en (-ən) *vt., vi.* to make or become fresh —**freshen up** to bathe, change into fresh clothes, etc.

fresh'man (-mən) *n., pl.* **-men** ‖FRESH[1] + MAN‖ **1** a beginner **2** a person in his or her first year in college, Congress, etc.

fresh'wa'ter *adj.* **1** of or living in water that is not salty **2** sailing only on inland waters

Fres·no (frez'nō) city in central Calif.: pop. 218,000

fret[1] (fret) *vt., vi.* **fret'ted, fret'ting** ‖OE *fretan,* to devour‖ **1** to gnaw, wear away, rub, etc. **2** to ripple or ruffle **3** to irritate or be irritated; worry —*n.* irritation; worry —**fret'ter** *n.*

fret[2] (fret) *n.* ‖ME *frette*‖ a running design of interlacing small bars

fret[3] (fret) *n.* ‖< OFr *frette,* a band‖ any of the ridges on the fingerboard of a banjo, guitar, etc.

fret'ful *adj.* irritable; peevish —**fret'ful·ly** *adv.* —**fret'ful·ness** *n.*

fret'work' *n.* decorative carving or openwork, as of interlacing lines

Freud (froid), **Sig·mund** (sig'mənd) 1856-1939; Austrian physician: founder of psychoanalysis —**Freud'i·an** *adj., n.*

Freudian slip a mistake made in speaking that inadvertently reveals unconscious motives, etc.

fri·a·ble (frī'ə bəl) *adj.* ‖Fr < L *friare,* to rub‖ easily crumbled

fri·ar (frī'ər) *n.* ‖< L *frater,* brother‖ *R.C.Ch.* a member of certain religious orders

fric·as·see (frik'ə sē', frik'ə sē') *n.* ‖< Fr *fricasser,* cut up and fry‖ meat cut into pieces, stewed or fried, and served in a sauce of its own gravy —*vt.* **-seed', -see'ing** to prepare in this way

fric·tion (frik'shən) *n.* ‖< L *fricare,* to rub‖ **1** a rubbing of one object against another **2** conflict, as because of differing opinions **3** *Mech.* the resistance to motion of surfaces that touch —**fric'tion·al** *adj.*

Fri·day (frī'dā, -dē) *n.* ‖< *Frig,* Germanic goddess‖ **1** the sixth day of the week: abbrev. **Fri. 2** ‖< the devoted servant of ROBINSON CRUSOE‖ a faithful helper: usually **man** (or **girl**) **Friday**

fried (frīd) *vt., vi. pt. & pp. of* FRY[1]

fried'cake' *n.* a small cake fried in deep fat; doughnut or cruller

friend (frend) *n.* ‖OE *freond*‖ **1** a person whom one knows well and is fond of **2** an ally, supporter, or sympathizer 3 [F-] a member of the Society of Friends; Quaker —**make** (or **be**) **friends with** to become (or be) a friend of —**friend'less** ***adj.***

friend'ly ***adj.*** **-li·er, -li·est** 1 of or like a friend; kindly 2 not hostile; amicable 3 supporting; helping —**friend'li·ly** ***adv.*** —**friend'li·ness** ***n.***

friend'ship' ***n.*** 1 the state of being friends 2 friendly feeling

frieze (frēz) ***n.*** ‖ < ML *frisium* ‖ a horizontal band with designs or carvings along a wall or around a room

frig·ate (frig'it) ***n.*** ‖ < It *fregata* ‖ a fast, medium-sized sailing warship of the 18th and early 19th c.

fright (frīt) ***n.*** ‖ OE *fyrhto* ‖ 1 sudden fear; alarm 2 something unsightly

fright'en ***vt.*** 1 to make suddenly afraid; scare 2 to force (*away, off,* etc.) by scaring —**fright'en·ing·ly** ***adv.***

fright'ful ***adj.*** 1 causing fright; alarming 2 shocking; terrible 3 [Colloq.] *a*) unpleasant *b*) great —**fright'ful·ly** ***adv.***

frig·id (frij'id) ***adj.*** ‖ < L *frigus,* coldness ‖ 1 extremely cold 2 not warm or friendly 3 sexually unresponsive: said of a woman —**fri·gid'i·ty** ***n.*** —**frig'id·ly** ***adv.***

Frigid Zone either of two zones (**North Frigid Zone** or **South Frigid Zone**) between the polar circles and the poles

frill (fril) ***n.*** ‖ < ? ‖ 1 any unnecessary ornament 2 a ruffle —**frill'y, -i·er, -i·est,** ***adj.***

fringe (frinj) ***n.*** ‖ < L *fimbria* ‖ 1 a border of threads, etc. hanging loose or tied in bunches 2 an outer edge; border 3 a marginal or minor part —***vt.*** **fringed, fring'ing** to be or make a fringe for —***adj.*** 1 at the outer edge 2 additional 3 minor

fringe benefit an employee's benefit other than wages, as a pension or insurance

frip·per·y (frip'ər ē) ***n.,*** *pl.* **-ies** ‖ < OFr *frepe,* a rag ‖ 1 cheap, gaudy clothes 2 showy display in dress, etc.

Fris·bee (friz'bē) ‖ < "Mother Frisbie's" pie tins ‖ *trademark for* a plastic, saucer-shaped disk sailed back and forth in a simple game —***n.*** [*also* **f-**] such a disk

fri·sé (frē zā', fri-) ***n.*** ‖ Fr < *friser,* to curl ‖ an upholstery fabric with a thick pile of loops

Fri·sian (frizh'ən) ***n.*** the West Germanic language of an island chain, the Frisian Islands, along the coast of N Netherlands, West Germany, & Denmark

frisk (frisk) ***vi.*** ‖ < OHG *frisc,* lively ‖ to frolic —***vt.*** [Slang] to search (a person) for weapons, etc. by passing the hands quickly over his clothing

frisk·y (fris'kē) ***adj.*** **-i·er, -i·est** lively; frolicsome —**frisk'i·ly** ***adv.*** —**frisk'i·ness** ***n.***

frit·ter¹ (frit'ər) ***vt.*** ‖ < L *frangere,* to break ‖ to waste (money, time, etc.) bit by bit: usually with *away*

frit·ter² (frit'ər) ***n.*** ‖ < L *frigere,* to fry ‖ a small cake of fried batter, usually containing corn, fruit, etc.

friv·o·lous (friv'ə ləs) ***adj.*** ‖ < L *frivolus* ‖ 1 of little value; trivial 2 silly and light minded; giddy —**fri·vol·i·ty** (fri väl'ə tē), *pl.* **-ties,** ***n.*** —**friv'o·lous·ly** ***adv.***

frizz or **friz** (friz) ***vt., vi.*** **frizzed, friz'zing** ‖ Fr *friser* ‖ to form into small, tight curls —***n.*** hair, etc. that is frizzed —**friz'zly** or **friz'zy** ***adj.***

friz·zle¹ (friz'əl) ***vt., vi.*** **-zled, -zling** ‖ < FRY¹ ‖ to sizzle, as in frying

friz·zle² (friz'əl) ***n., vt., vi.*** **-zled, -zling** FRIZZ

fro (frō) ***adv.*** ‖ < ON *frā* ‖ backward; back: now only in TO AND FRO (at TO)

frock (fräk) ***n.*** ‖ < OFr *froc* ‖ 1 a robe worn by friars, monks, etc. 2 a dress

frog (frôg, fräg) ***n.*** ‖ OE *frogga* ‖ 1 a tailless, leaping amphibian with long hind legs and webbed feet 2 a fancy braided loop used to fasten clothing —**frog in the throat** hoarseness

frog'man' ***n.,*** *pl.* **-men'** one trained and equipped for underwater demolition, exploration, etc.

frol·ic (fräl'ik) ***n.*** ‖ < MDu *vrō,* merry ‖ 1 a lively party or game 2 merriment; fun —***vi.*** **-icked, -ick·ing** 1 to make merry; have fun 2 to romp about; gambol —**frol'ick·er** ***n.***

frol'ic·some (-səm) ***adj.*** playful; merry

from (frum, främ) ***prep.*** ‖ OE ‖ 1 beginning at; starting with [*from* noon to midnight] 2 out of [*from* her purse] 3 originating with [a letter *from* me] 4 out of the possibility of or use of [kept *from* going] 5 as not being like [to know good *from* evil] 6 because of [to tremble *from* fear]

frond (fränd) ***n.*** ‖ < L *frons,* leafy branch ‖ the leaf of a fern or palm

front (frunt) ***n.*** ‖ < L *frons,* forehead ‖ 1 *a*) outward behavior [a bold *front*] *b*) [Colloq.] an appearance of social standing, wealth, etc. 2 the part facing forward 3 the first part; beginning 4 a forward or leading position 5 the land bordering a lake, street, etc. 6 the advanced battle area in warfare 7 an area of activity [the home *front*] 8 a person or group used to hide another's activity 9 *Meteorol.* the boundary between two differing air masses —***adj.*** at, to, in, on, or of the front —***vt., vi.*** 1 to face 2 to serve as a front (*for*) —**in front of** before —**fron'tal** ***adj.***

front·age (frunt'ij) ***n.*** 1 the front part of a building 2 the front boundary line of a lot or the length of this line 3 land bordering a street, lake, etc.

fron·tier (frun tir') ***n.*** ‖ see FRONT ‖ 1 the border between two countries 2 the part of a country which borders an unexplored region 3 any new field of learning, etc. —***adj.*** of, on, or near a frontier —**frontiers'man** (-tirz'mən), *pl.* **-men,** ***n.***

fron·tis·piece (frunt'is pēs') ***n.*** ‖ < L *frons,* front + *specere,* to look ‖ an illustration facing the title page of a book

front office the management or administration, as of a company

front'-run'ner ***n.*** a leading contestant

front-wheel drive an automotive design in which only the front wheels receive driving power

frost (frôst, fräst) ***n.*** ‖ OE < *freosan,* freeze ‖ 1 a temperature low enough to cause freezing 2 frozen dew or vapor; rime —***vt.*** 1 to cover with frost 2 to cover with frosting 3 to give a frostlike, opaque surface to (glass) —**frost'y, -i·er, -i·est,** ***adj.***

Frost (frôst, fräst), **Robert (Lee)** (räb′ərt) 1874-1963; U.S poet

frost′bite′ *vt.* **-bit′**, **-bit′ten**, **-bit′ing** to injure the tissues of (a body part) by exposing to intense cold —*n.* injury caused by such exposure

frost′ing *n.* 1 a mixture of sugar, butter, etc. for covering a cake; icing 2 a dull finish on glass, metal, etc.

frost line the limit of penetration of soil by frost

froth (frôth, fräth) *n.* ‖ < ON *frotha* ‖ 1 foam 2 foaming saliva 3 light, trifling talk, ideas, etc. —*vi.* to foam —**froth′y**, **-i·er**, **-i·est**, *adj.*

frou·frou (fro͞o′fro͞o′) *n.* ‖ Fr ‖ [Colloq.] excessive ornateness

fro·ward (frō′wərd, -ərd) *adj.* ‖ see FRO & WARD ‖ not easily controlled; willful; contrary —**fro′ward·ness** *n.*

frown (froun) *vi.* ‖ < OFr *froigne*, sullen face ‖ 1 to contract the brows, as in displeasure 2 to show disapproval: with *on* or *upon* —*n.* a frowning

frow·zy (frou′zē) *adj.* **-zi·er**, **-zi·est** ‖ < ? ‖ dirty and untidy; slovenly —**frow′zi·ly** *adv.* —**frow′zi·ness** *n.*

froze (frōz) *vi.*, *vt. pt. of* FREEZE

fro·zen (frō′zən) *vi.*, *vt. pp. of* FREEZE —*adj.* 1 turned into or covered with ice 2 damaged or killed by freezing 3 preserved by freezing, as food 4 made motionless 5 kept at a fixed level 6 not readily convertible into cash

frozen custard a food resembling ice cream, but with a lower butterfat content

fruc·ti·fy (fruk′tə fī′) *vi.*, *vt.* **-fied′**, **-fy′ing** ‖ < L *fructificare* ‖ to bear or cause to bear fruit

fruc·tose (fruk′tōs′, fro͝ok′-) *n.* ‖ < L *fructus*, fruit + -OSE[1] ‖ a sugar found in sweet fruits and in honey

fru·gal (fro͞o′gəl) *adj.* ‖ < L *frugi*, fit for food ‖ 1 not wasteful; thrifty 2 inexpensive or meager —**fru·gal′i·ty** (-gal′ə tē), *pl.* **-ties**, *n.* —**fru′gal·ly** *adv.*

fruit (fro͞ot) *n.* ‖ < L *fructus* ‖ 1 any plant product, as grain, vegetables, etc.: *usually used in pl.* 2 *a)* a usually sweet, edible plant structure, containing the seeds inside a juicy pulp *b) Bot.* the mature, seed-bearing part of a flowering plant 3 the result or product of any action

fruit′cake′ *n.* a rich cake containing nuts, preserved fruit, citron, etc.

fruit fly any of various small flies whose larvae feed on fruits and vegetables

fruit′ful *adj.* 1 bearing much fruit 2 productive; prolific 3 profitable

fru·i·tion (fro͞o ish′ən) *n.* 1 the bearing of fruit 2 a coming to fulfillment; realization

fruit′less *adj.* 1 without results; unsuccessful 2 bearing no fruit; sterile; barren —**fruit′less·ly** *adv.*

frump (frump) *n.* ‖ prob. < Du *rompelen*, rumple ‖ a dowdy woman —**frump′ish** or **frump′y** *adj.*

frus·trate (frus′trāt′) *vt.* **-trat′ed**, **-trat′ing** ‖ < L *frustra*, in vain ‖ 1 to cause to have no effect 2 to prevent from achieving a goal or gratifying a desire —**frus·tra′tion** *n.*

fry[1] (frī) *vt.*, *vi.* **fried**, **fry′ing** ‖ < L *frigere*, to fry ‖ to cook in a pan over direct heat, usually in hot fat —*n.*, *pl.* **fries** 1 [*pl.*] fried potatoes 2 a social gathering at which food is fried and eaten

fry[2] (frī) *n.*, *pl.* **fry** ‖ < OFr *freier*, to spawn ‖ young fish —**small fry** 1 children 2 insignificant people

fry′er (-ər) *n.* 1 a utensil for deep-frying 2 a chicken for frying

FSLIC or **F.S.L.I.C.** Federal Savings and Loan Insurance Corporation

ft. foot; feet

FTC Federal Trade Commission

fuch·sia (fyo͞o′shə) *n.* ‖ after L. *Fuchs* (1501-66), Ger botanist ‖ 1 a shrubby plant with pink, red, or purple flowers 2 purplish red

fud·dle (fud″l) *vt.* **-dled**, **-dling** ‖ < ? ‖ to confuse or stupefy as with alcoholic liquor —*n.* a fuddled state

fud·dy-dud·dy (fud′ē dud′ē) *n.*, *pl.* **-dies** [Colloq.] a fussy, critical, or old fashioned person

fudge (fuj) *n.* ‖ < ? ‖ a soft candy made of butter, milk, sugar, flavoring, etc. —*vi.* **fudged**, **fudg′ing** 1 to refuse to commit oneself; hedge 2 to be dishonest; cheat

fu·el (fyo͞o′əl) *n.* ‖ ult. < L *focus*, fireplace ‖ 1 coal, oil, gas, wood, etc., burned to supply heat or power 2 material from which atomic energy can be obtained 3 anything that intensifies strong feeling —*vt.*, *vi.* **fu′eled** or **fu′elled**, **fu′el·ing** or **fu′el·ling** to supply with or get fuel

fuel injection a system for forcing fuel into combustion chambers of a diesel, gasoline, jet, or rocket engine

fu·gi·tive (fyo͞o′ji tiv) *adj.* ‖ < L *fugere*, to flee ‖ 1 fleeing, as from danger or justice 2 fleeting —*n.* one who is fleeing from justice, etc.

fugue (fyo͞og) *n.* ‖ < L *fugere*, to flee ‖ a musical work in which a theme is taken up successively and developed by the various parts in counterpoint

-ful (fəl; *for 2, usually* fo͝ol) ‖ < FULL[1] ‖ *suffix* 1 *a)* full of, having [*joyful*] *b)* having the qualities of or tendency to [*helpful*] 2 the quantity that will fill [*handful*]

ful·crum (ful′krəm, fo͝ol′-) *n.*, *pl.* **-crums** or **-cra** (-krə) ‖ L, a support ‖ the support on which a lever turns in raising something

ful·fill or **ful·fil** (fo͝ol fil′) *vt.* **-filled′**, **-fill′ing** ‖ OE *fullfyllan* ‖ 1 to carry out (a promise, etc.) 2 to do (a duty, etc.); obey 3 to satisfy (a condition) 4 to bring to an end; complete —**ful·fill′ment** or **ful·fil′ment** *n.*

full[1] (fo͝ol) *adj.* ‖ OE ‖ 1 having in it all there is space for; filled 2 having eaten all that one wants 3 having a great deal or number (*of*) 4 complete [a *full* dozen] 5 having reached the greatest size, extent, etc. 6 plump; round 7 with wide folds; flowing [a *full* skirt] —*n.* the greatest amount, extent, etc. —*adv.* 1 to the greatest degree; completely 2 directly; exactly —**full′ness** or **ful′ness** *n.*

full[2] (fo͝ol) *vt.*, *vi.* ‖ < L *fullo*, cloth fuller ‖ to shrink and thicken (wool cloth) —**full′er** *n.*

full′back′ *n. Football* an offensive back stationed behind the quarterback

full′-blood′ed *adj.* 1 of unmixed breed or race 2 vigorous

full′-blown′ *adj.* **1** in full bloom **2** fully developed; matured

full′-fledged′ *adj.* completely developed or trained; of full status

full moon the moon when it reflects light as a full disk

full′-scale′ *adj.* **1** according to the original or standard scale **2** to the utmost degree; all-out

full′-time′ *adj.* of or engaged in work, study, etc. that takes all of one's regular working hours

full′y *adv.* **1** completely; thoroughly **2** at least

ful·mi·nate (ful′mə nāt′) *vi., vt.* **-nat′ed, -nat′ing** ‖< L *fulmen*, lightning‖ **1** to explode **2** to shout forth —**ful′mi·na′tion** *n.*

ful·some (fool′səm) *adj.* ‖see FULL[1] & SOME[1], but infl. by ME *ful*, foul‖ disgusting, esp. because excessive

fum·ble (fum′bəl) *vi., vt.* **-bled, -bling** ‖prob. < ON *famla*‖ **1** to grope (*for*) or handle (a thing) clumsily **2** to lose one's grasp on (a football, etc.) —*n.* a fumbling —**fum′bler** *n.*

fume (fyoom) *n.* ‖< L *fumus*‖ [*often pl.*] a gas, smoke, or vapor, esp. if offensive or suffocating —*vi.* **fumed, fum′ing** **1** to give off fumes **2** to show anger

fu·mi·gate (fyoo′mə gāt′) *vt.* **-gat′ed, -gat′ing** ‖< L *fumus*, smoke + *agere*, do‖ to expose to fumes, esp. so as to disinfect or kill the vermin in —**fu′mi·ga′tion** *n.* —**fu′mi·ga′tor** *n.*

fum·y (fyoom′ē) *adj.* **-i·er, -i·est** full of or producing fumes; vaporous

fun (fun) *n.* ‖< ME *fonne*, foolish‖ **1** *a)* lively, joyous play or playfulness *b)* pleasure **2** a source of amusement —**make fun of** to ridicule

func·tion (funk′shən) *n.* ‖< L *fungi*, to perform‖ **1** the normal or characteristic action of anything **2** a special duty required in work **3** a formal ceremony or social occasion **4** a thing that depends on and varies with something else —*vi.* to act in a required manner; work; be used —**func′tion·less** *adj.*

func′tion·al *adj.* **1** of a function **2** performing a function **3** *Med.* affecting a function of some organ without apparent organic changes

functional illiterate a person who cannot read well enough to function properly in a complex society

func′tion·ar′y (-shə ner′ē) *n., pl.* **-ies** an official performing some function

function word a word, as an article or conjunction, serving mainly to show grammatical relationship

fund (fund) *n.* ‖L *fundus*, bottom‖ **1** a supply that can be drawn upon; stock **2** *a)* a sum of money set aside for a purpose *b)* [*pl.*] ready money —*vt.* **1** to put or convert into a long-term debt that bears interest **2** to provide funds for (a project, etc.)

fun·da·men·tal (fun′də ment′'l) *adj.* ‖see prec.‖ of or forming a foundation or basis; basic; essential —*n.* a principle, theory, law, etc. serving as a basis —**fun′da·men′tal·ly** *adv.*

fun′da·men′tal·ism′ *n.* [*sometimes* **F-**] religious beliefs based on a literal interpretation of the Bible —**fun′da·men′tal·ist** *n., adj.*

fu·ner·al (fyoo′nər əl) *n.* ‖< L *funus*‖ the ceremonies connected with burial or cremation of the dead

funeral director one who manages a funeral home

funeral home (or **parlor**) an establishment where the bodies of the dead are prepared for burial or cremation and where funeral services can be held

fu·ne·re·al (fyoo nir′ē əl) *adj.* suitable for a funeral; sad and solemn; dismal —**fu·ne′re·al·ly** *adv.*

fun·gi·cide (fun′ji sīd′) *n.* ‖see -CIDE‖ any substance that kills fungi

fun·gus (fuŋ′gəs) *n., pl.* **fun·gi** (fun′jī′) or **fun′gus·es** ‖< L‖ any of various plants, as molds, mildews, mushrooms, etc., that lack chlorophyll, stems, and leaves and reproduce by spores —**fun′gous** *adj.*

fu·nic·u·lar (fyoo nik′yoo lər) *adj.* ‖< L *funiculus*, little rope‖ worked by a rope or cable —*n.* a mountain railway with counterbalanced cable cars on parallel sets of rails

funk (fuŋk) *n.* ‖< ? Fl *fonck*, dismay‖ [Colloq.] **1** a state of great fear; panic **2** a depressed mood

funk·y (fuŋ′kē) *adj.* **-i·er, -i·est** ‖orig., earthy‖ **1** *Jazz* having an earthy style derived from early blues **2** [Slang] unconventional, eccentric, offbeat, etc.

fun·nel (fun′əl) *n.* ‖ult. < L *fundere*, to pour‖ **1** a tapering tube with a cone-shaped mouth, for pouring things into small-mouthed containers **2** the smokestack of a steamship —*vi., vt.* **-neled** or **-nelled, -nel·ing** or **-nel·ling** to move or pour as through a funnel

fun·nies (fun′ēz) *n.pl.* [Colloq.] comic strips

fun·ny (fun′ē) *adj.* **-ni·er, -ni·est** **1** causing laughter; humorous **2** [Colloq.] *a)* strange; queer *b)* tricky —**fun′ni·ly** *adv.* —**fun′ni·ness** *n.*

funny bone a place on the elbow where a sharp impact on a nerve causes a strange, tingling sensation

funny farm [Slang] an institution for the mentally ill

fur (fur) *n.* ‖< OFr *fuerre*, sheath‖ **1** the soft, thick hair covering certain animals **2** a processed skin bearing such hair —*adj.* of fur —**furred** *adj.*

fur·be·low (fur′bə lō′) *n.* ‖ult. < Fr *falbala*‖ **1** a flounce or ruffle **2** a showy, useless decorative addition

fur·bish (fur′bish) *vt.* ‖< OFr *forbir*‖ **1** to polish; burnish **2** to renovate

Fu·ries (fyoor′ēz) *Gr. & Rom. Myth.* the three terrible female spirits who punish unavenged crimes

fu·ri·ous (fyoor′ē əs) *adj.* **1** full of fury; very angry **2** very great, intense, wild, etc. —**fu′ri·ous·ly** *adv.*

furl (furl) *vt.* ‖< L *firmus*, FIRM[1] + *ligare*, to tie‖ to roll up (a sail, flag, etc.) tightly and make secure

fur·long (fur′lôŋ′) *n.* ‖< OE *furh*, a furrow + *lang*, LONG[1]‖ a measure of distance equal to $\frac{1}{8}$ of a mile

fur·lough (fur′lō) *n.* ‖< Du *verlof*‖ a leave

of absence, esp. for military personnel —*vt.* to grant a furlough to

fur·nace (fʉr′nəs) *n.* ‖ < L *fornax*, furnace ‖ an enclosed structure in which heat is produced, as by burning fuel

fur·nish (fʉr′nish) *vt.* ‖ < OFr *furnir* ‖ 1 to supply with furniture, etc.; equip 2 to supply; provide

fur′nish·ings *n.pl.* 1 the furniture, carpets, etc. as for a house 2 things to wear /men's *furnishings*/

fur·ni·ture (fʉr′ni chər) *n.* ‖ Fr *fourniture* ‖ 1 the things in a room, etc. which equip it for living, as chairs, beds, etc. 2 necessary equipment

fu·ror (fyoor′ôr′) *n.* ‖ < L ‖ 1 fury; frenzy 2 *a*) a widespread enthusiasm; craze *b*) a commotion or uproar Also [Chiefly Brit.] **fu·ro·re** (fyoo′rôr′ē)

fur·ri·er (fʉr′ē ər) *n.* one who processes furs or deals in fur garments

fur·ring (fʉr′iŋ) *n.* thin strips of wood fixed on a wall, floor, etc. before adding boards or plaster

fur·row (fʉr′ō) *n.* ‖ < OE *furh* ‖ 1 a narrow groove made in the ground by a plow 2 anything like this, as a deep wrinkle —*vt.* to make furrows in —*vi.* to become wrinkled

fur·ry (fʉr′ē) *adj.* **-ri·er, -ri·est** 1 of or like fur 2 covered with fur —**fur′ri·ness** *n.*

fur·ther (fʉr′*th*ər) *adj.* ‖ OE *furthor* ‖ 1 *alt. compar. of* FAR 2 additional 3 more distant; farther —*adv.* 1 *alt. compar. of* FAR 2 to a greater degree or extent 3 in addition 4 at or to a greater distance; farther —*vt.* to give aid to; promote In sense 3 of the *adj.* and sense 4 of the *adv.*, FARTHER is more commonly used —**fur′ther·ance** *n.*

fur′ther·more′ *adv.* in addition; besides; moreover

fur·thest (fʉr′*th*ist) *adj.* 1 *alt. superl. of* FAR 2 most distant; farthest: also **fur′ther·most′** —*adv.* 1 *alt. superl. of* FAR 2 at or to the greatest distance or degree

fur·tive (fʉr′tiv) *adj.* ‖ < L *fur*, a thief ‖ done or acting in a stealthy manner; sneaky —**fur′tive·ly** *adv.* —**fur′tive·ness** *n.*

fu·ry (fyoor′ē) *n., pl.* **-ries** ‖ < L *furere*, to rage ‖ 1 violent anger; wild rage 2 violence; vehemence

furze (fʉrz) *n.* ‖ OE *fyrs* ‖ a prickly evergreen shrub native to Europe

fuse[1] (fyōōz) *vt., vi.* **fused, fus′ing** ‖ < L *fundere*, to shed ‖ 1 to melt 2 to unite as if by melting together

fuse[2] (fyōōz) *n.* ‖ < L *fusus*, spindle ‖ 1 a tube or wick filled with combustible material, for setting off an explosive charge 2 *Elec.* a strip of easily melted metal placed in a circuit: it melts and breaks the circuit if the current becomes too strong

fu·see (fyōō zē′) *n.* ‖ Fr *fusée*, a rocket ‖ a colored flare used as a signal by trainmen, truck drivers, etc.

fu·se·lage (fyōō′sə lij′, -läzh′) *n.* ‖ Fr ‖ the body of an airplane, exclusive of the wings, tail assembly, and engines

fu·si·ble (fyōō′zə bəl) *adj.* that can be fused or easily melted

fu·si·lier or **fu·sil·eer** (fyōō′zi lir′) *n.* ‖ Fr ‖ [Historical] a soldier armed with a flintlock musket

fu·sil·lade (fyōō′sə lād′) *n.* ‖ Fr < *fusiller*, to shoot ‖ a simultaneous or rapid discharge of many firearms

fu·sion (fyōō′zhən) *n.* ‖ L *fusio* ‖ 1 a fusing or melting together 2 a blending; coalition 3 NUCLEAR FUSION 4 a style of popular music blending elements of jazz, rock, etc.

fuss (fus) *n.* ‖ prob. echoic ‖ 1 nervous, excited activity; bustle 2 a nervous state 3 a quarrel 4 a showy display of approval, etc. —*vi.* 1 to bustle about or worry over trifles 2 to whine, as a baby

fuss′budg′et (-buj′it) *n.* ‖ prec. + BUDGET ‖ [Colloq.] a fussy person Also [Colloq., Chiefly Brit.] **fuss′pot′** (-pät′)

fuss′y *adj.* **-i·er, -i·est** 1 *a*) worrying over trifles *b*) hard to please *c*) whining, as a baby 2 full of unnecessary details —**fuss′i·ly** *adv.* —**fuss′i·ness** *n.*

fus·tian (fus′chən) *n.* ‖ < L *fustis*, wooden stick ‖ pompous, pretentious talk or writing; bombast

fus·ty (fus′tē) *adj.* **-ti·er, -ti·est** ‖ < OFr *fust*, a cask ‖ 1 musty; moldy 2 old-fashioned —**fus′ti·ly** *adv.* —**fus′ti·ness** *n.*

fut. future

fu·tile (fyōōt′'l) *adj.* ‖ < L *futilis*, lit., that easily pours out ‖ useless; vain —**fu·til·i·ty** (fyōō til′ə tē), *pl.* **-ties,** *n.*

fu·ton (fōō′tän′) *n.* ‖ Sino-Jpn ‖ a thin mattress like a quilt, placed on the floor for use as a bed

fu·ture (fyōō′chər) *adj.* ‖ < L *futurus*, about to be ‖ 1 that is to be or come 2 indicating time to come /the *future* tense/ —*n.* 1 the time that is to come 2 what is going to be 3 the chance to succeed, etc. 4 [*usually pl.*] a contract for a commodity bought or sold for delivery at a later date —**fu′tur·is′tic** *adj.*

future shock ‖ after A. Toffler's book *Future Shock* (1970) ‖ the inability to cope with rapid social changes, or the distress resulting from this

fu·tu·ri·ty (fyōō toor′ə tē, -tyoor′-) *n., pl.* **-ties** 1 the future 2 a future condition or event 3 a race for two-year-old horses in which the entries are selected before birth: in full **futurity race**

fu·tur·ol·o·gy (fyōō′chər äl′ə jē) *n.* ‖ FUTUR(E) + -OLOGY ‖ the study of probable or presumed future conditions, as by making assumptions based on known facts —**fu′tur·ol′o·gist** *n.*

futz (futs) *vi.* ‖ ? < Yidd ‖ [Slang] to trifle or fool (*around*)

fuzz (fuz) *n.* ‖ < ? ‖ 1 loose, light particles of down, wool, etc.; fine hairs or fibers —**the fuzz** [Slang] a policeman or the police —**fuzz′y, -i·er, -i·est,** *adj.*

-fy (fī) ‖ < L *facere*, do ‖ *suffix* 1 to make /*liquefy*/ 2 to cause to have /*glorify*/ 3 to become /*putrefy*/

FYI for your information

G

g or **G** (jē) ***n.***, *pl.* **g's, G's** the seventh letter of the English alphabet

G (jē) ***n.*** **1** *Music* the fifth tone in the scale of C major **2** a motion-picture rating for a film considered suitable for general audiences

g gram

G or **G. 1** game(s) **2** gauge **3** German **4** guard **5** Gulf Also, for 1, 2, & 4, **g** or **g.**

Ga *Chem. symbol for* gallium

GA or **Ga.** Georgia

gab (gab) ***n.***, ***vt.*** **gabbed, gab'bing** ⟦ON *gabba*, to mock⟧ [Colloq.] chatter

gab·ar·dine (gab'ər dēn') ***n.*** ⟦< OFr *gaverdine*, kind of cloak⟧ a twilled cloth of wool, cotton, etc., with a fine, diagonal weave Brit. sp. **gab'er·dine**

gab·ble (gab'əl) ***vi.***, ***vt.*** **-bled, -bling** ⟦< GAB⟧ to talk or utter rapidly or incoherently **—*n.*** such talk

gab·by (gab'ē) ***adj.*** **-bi·er, -bi·est** [Colloq.] talkative **—gab'bi·ness *n.***

gab'fest' (-fest') ***n.*** [Colloq.] an informal gathering to talk or gab

ga·ble (gā'bəl) ***n.*** ⟦< Gmc⟧ the triangular wall enclosed by the sloping ends of a ridged roof **—ga'bled *adj.***

Ga·bon (gä bōn') country on the W coast of Africa: 103,346 sq. mi.; pop. 1,017,000

Ga·bri·el (gā'brē əl) *Bible* one of the archangels, the herald of good news

gad (gad) ***vi.*** **gad'ded, gad'ding** ⟦ME *gadden*, to hurry⟧ to wander about idly or restlessly **—gad'der *n.***

gad'a·bout' ***n.*** one who gads about, looking for fun, etc.

gad'fly' ***n.***, *pl.* **-flies'** ⟦see GOAD & FLY[2]⟧ **1** a large fly that bites livestock **2** one who annoys others

gadg·et (gaj'it) ***n.*** ⟦< ?⟧ any small mechanical contrivance or device

Gael·ic (gāl'ik) ***adj.*** of the Celtic people of Ireland, Scotland, or the Isle of Man **—*n.*** the Celtic language of Scotland

gaff (gaf) ***n.*** ⟦< OProv *gaf* or Sp *gafa*⟧ **1** a large hook on a pole for landing fish **2** a spar supporting a fore-and-aft sail **—stand the gaff** [Slang] to bear up well under punishment, ridicule, etc.

gaffe (gaf) ***n.*** ⟦Fr⟧ a blunder

gag (gag) ***vt.*** **gagged, gag'ging** ⟦echoic⟧ **1** to cause to retch **2** to keep from speaking, as by stopping up the mouth of **—*vi.*** to retch **—*n.*** **1** something put into or over the mouth to prevent talking, etc. **2** any restraint of free speech **3** a joke

gage[1] (gāj) ***n.*** ⟦< OFr, a pledge⟧ **1** something pledged; security **2** a glove, etc. thrown down as a challenge to fight **3** a challenge

gage[2] (gāj) ***n.***, ***vt.*** **gaged, gag'ing** *alt. sp. of* GAUGE

gag·gle (gag'əl) ***n.*** ⟦echoic⟧ **1** a flock of geese **2** any group or cluster

gai·e·ty (gā'ə tē) ***n.***, *pl.* **-ties 1** the quality of being gay; cheerfulness **2** merrymaking **3** showy brightness

gai·ly (gā'lē) ***adv.*** in a gay manner; specif., *a)* merrily *b)* brightly

gain (gān) ***n.*** ⟦< OFr *gaaigne*⟧ **1** an increase; specif., *a)* [*often pl.*] profit *b)* an increase in advantage **2** acquisition **—*vt.*** **1** to earn **2** to win **3** to attract **4** to get as an addition, profit, or advantage **5** to make an increase in **6** to get to; reach **—*vi.*** **1** to make progress **2** to increase in weight **—gain on** to draw nearer to (an opponent in a race, etc.)

gain'er ***n.*** **1** a person or thing that gains **2** a fancy dive forward, but with a backward somersault

gain'ful ***adj.*** producing gain; profitable **—gain'ful·ly *adv.***

gain·say (gān'sā') ***vt.*** **-said'** (-sed'), **-say'ing** ⟦< OE *gegn*, against + *secgan*, to say⟧ **1** to deny **2** to contradict **—gain'say'er *n.***

gait (gāt) ***n.*** ⟦< ON *gata*, path⟧ **1** manner of walking or running **2** any of the various foot movements of a horse, as a trot, pace, canter, etc.

gai·ter (gāt'ər) ***n.*** ⟦< Fr *guêtre*⟧ a cloth or leather covering for the instep, ankle, and lower leg

gal (gal) ***n.*** a girl

gal. gallon(s)

ga·la (gā'lə, gal'ə) ***n.*** ⟦ult. < It *gala*⟧ a celebration **—*adj.*** festive

gal·a·bi·a or **gal·a·bi·ya** (gal'ə bē'ə) ***n.*** ⟦< Ar⟧ *var. of* DJELLABA

Gal·a·had (gal'ə had') *Arthurian Legend* the knight who, because of his purity, finds the Holy Grail

gal·ax·y (gal'ək sē) ⟦< Gr *gala*, milk⟧ [*often* **G-**] MILKY WAY **—*n.***, *pl.* **-ies 1** a large, independent system of stars **2** a group of illustrious people **—ga·lac·tic** (gə lak'tik) ***adj.***

gale (gāl) ***n.*** ⟦< ?⟧ **1** a strong wind **2** an outburst /*a gale* of laughter/

ga·le·na (gə lē'nə) ***n.*** ⟦L, lead ore⟧ native lead sulfide, a lead-gray mineral with metallic luster

Gal·i·lee (gal'ə lē'), **Sea of** lake of NE Israel

Gal·i·le·o (gal'ə lē'ō, -lā'-) 1564-1642; It. astronomer & physicist

gall[1] (gôl) ***n.*** ⟦OE *galla*⟧ **1** BILE (sense 1) **2** something bitter or distasteful **3** bitter feeling **4** [Colloq.] impudence

gall[2] (gôl) ***n.*** ⟦see fol.⟧ a sore on the skin caused by chafing **—*vt.*** **1** to make sore by rubbing **2** to annoy

gall[3] (gôl) ***n.*** ⟦< L *galla*⟧ a tumor on plant tissue caused by stimulation by fungi, insects, or bacteria

gal·lant (gal'ənt; *for adj.* 3 *& n., usually* gə lant', -länt') ***adj.*** ⟦< OFr *galer*, to make merry⟧ **1** stately; imposing **2** brave and noble **3** polite and attentive to women **—*n.*** **1** [Now Rare] a high-spirited, stylish man **2** a man attentive and polite to women

gal·lant·ry (gal'ən trē) ***n.***, *pl.* **-ries 1** heroic courage 2 the behavior of a gallant 3 a courteous act or remark

gall·blad·der (gôl′blad′ər) ***n.*** a membranous sac closely attached to the liver, in which excess gall, or bile, is stored

gal·le·on (gal′ē ən) ***n.*** ⟦ult. < Gr *galeos,* shark⟧ a large sailing ship of the 15th and 16th c.

gal·le·ri·a (gal′ə rē′ə) ***n.*** a large arcade or court, sometimes with a glass roof

gal·ler·y (gal′ər ē) ***n.,*** *pl.* **-ies** ⟦< ML *galeria*⟧ 1 a covered walk or porch open at one side 2 a long, narrow, outside balcony 3 *a)* a balcony in a theater, etc.; esp., the highest balcony with the cheapest seats *b)* the people in these seats 4 the spectators at a sports event, etc. 5 an establishment for exhibitions, etc.

GALLEY

gal·ley (gal′ē) ***n.,*** *pl.* **-leys** ⟦< Gr *galeos,* shark⟧ 1 a long, low ship of ancient times, propelled by oars and sails 2 a ship's kitchen 3 *Printing a)* a shallow tray for holding composed type *b)* proof printed from such type (in full, **galley proof**)

Gal·lic (gal′ik) ***adj.*** 1 of ancient Gaul or its people 2 French

Gal·li·cism (gal′i siz′əm) ***n.*** ⟦< prec.⟧ [*also* **g-**] a French idiom, custom, etc.

gal·li·um (gal′ē əm) ***n.*** ⟦named after L *Gallia,* France⟧ a bluish-white, metallic chemical element, often a supercooled liquid at room temperature, used in semiconductors, lasers, etc.

gal·li·vant (gal′ə vant′) ***vi.*** ⟦arbitrary elaboration of GALLANT⟧ to go about in search of amusement

gal·lon (gal′ən) ***n.*** ⟦< OFr *jalon*⟧ a liquid measure equal to 4 quarts

gal·lop (gal′əp) ***vi., vt.*** ⟦< OFr *galoper*⟧ to go, or cause to go, at a gallop —***n.*** the fastest gait of a horse, etc., a succession of leaping strides

gal·lows (gal′ōz) ***n.,*** *pl.* **-lows** or **-lows·es** ⟦OE *galga*⟧ an upright frame with a crossbeam and a rope, for hanging condemned persons

gall·stone (gôl′stōn′) ***n.*** a small, solid mass sometimes formed in the gallbladder or bile duct

ga·lore (gə lôr′) ***adj.*** ⟦Ir *go leōr,* enough⟧ in abundance; plentifully

ga·losh or **ga·loshe** (gə läsh′) ***n.*** ⟦< OFr *galoche*⟧ a high, warmly lined overshoe of rubber and fabric

gal·van·ic (gal van′ik) ***adj.*** ⟦after L. *Galvani* (1737-98), It physicist⟧ 1 of or producing an electric current, esp. from a battery 2 startling

gal′va·nism′ (-və niz′əm) ***n.*** electricity produced by chemical action

gal·va·nize (gal′və nīz′) ***vt.*** **-nized′, -niz′ing** 1 to stimulate as if by electric shock; rouse; stir 2 to plate (metal) with zinc

gal′va·nom′e·ter (-năm′ət ər) ***n.*** an instrument for detecting and measuring a small electric current

Gam·bi·a (gam′bē ə) country on the W coast of Africa: 3,451 sq. mi.; pop. 695,800

gam·bit (gam′bit) ***n.*** ⟦< Sp *gambito,* a tripping⟧ 1 *Chess* an opening in which a pawn, etc. is sacrificed to get an advantage in position 2 an action intended to gain an advantage

gam·ble (gam′bəl) ***vi.*** **-bled, -bling** ⟦ME *gamen,* to play⟧ 1 to play games of chance for money, etc. 2 to take a risk for some advantage —***vt.*** to risk in gambling; bet —***n.*** an undertaking involving risk —**gam′bler *n.***

gam·bol (gam′bəl) ***n.*** ⟦< It *gamba,* leg⟧ a gamboling; frolic —***vi.*** **-boled** or **-bolled, -bol·ing** or **-bol·ling** to jump and skip about in play; frolic

gam·brel (roof) (gam′brəl) a roof with two slopes on each side

game[1] (gām) ***n.*** ⟦OE *gamen*⟧ 1 any form of play; amusement 2 *a)* amusement or sport involving competition under rules *b)* a single contest in such a competition 3 the number of points required for winning 4 a scheme; plan 5 wild birds or animals hunted for sport or food 6 [Colloq.] a business or job, esp. one involving risk —***vi.*** **gamed, gam′ing** to play cards, etc. for stakes; gamble —***adj.*** 1 designating or of wild birds or animals hunted for sport or food 2 *a)* plucky; courageous *b)* enthusiastic; ready (*for*) —**the game is up** failure is certain —**game′ly *adv.*** —**game′ness *n.***

game[2] (gām) ***adj.*** ⟦< ?⟧ lame or injured [*a game leg*]

game′cock′ ***n.*** a specially bred rooster trained for cockfighting

game′keep′er ***n.*** a person who takes care of game birds and animals, as on an estate

game plan 1 the strategy planned before a game 2 any long-range strategy

game point 1 the situation when the next point scored could win a game 2 the winning point

games·man·ship (gāmz′mən ship′) ***n.*** skill in using ploys to gain an advantage

game·ster (gām′stər) ***n.*** a gambler

gam·ete (gam′ēt, gə mēt′) ***n.*** ⟦< Gr *gamos,* marriage⟧ a reproductive cell that unites with another to form the cell that develops into a new individual

gam·in (gam′in) ***n.*** ⟦Fr⟧ 1 a neglected child who roams the streets 2 a girl with saucy charm: also **ga·mine** (ga mēn′)

gam·ma (gam′ə) ***n.*** the third letter of the Greek alphabet (Γ, γ)

gamma glob·u·lin (gläb′yoo lin) that fraction of blood serum which contains most antibodies

gamma ray an electromagnetic radiation with a very short wavelength, produced as by the reactions of nuclei

gam·ut (gam′ət) ***n.*** ⟦< Gr letter *gamma,* for the lowest note of the medieval scale⟧ 1 any complete musical scale 2 the entire range or extent

gam·y (gām′ē) ***adj.*** **-i·er, -i·est** 1 having the strong flavor of cooked game 2 slightly tainted **3** risqué **4** coarse or crude — **gam'i·ness** *n.*

gan·der (gan'dər) *n.* ⟦OE *gan(d)ra*⟧ **1** a male goose **2** [Slang] a look

Gan·dhi (gän'dē), **Mo·han·das K.** (mō hän' dəs) 1869-1948; Hindu nationalist leader: called *Mahatma Gandhi*

gang (gaŋ) *n.* ⟦< OE *gangan*, to go⟧ a group of people working or acting together; specif., a group of criminals or juvenile delinquents —**gang up on** [Colloq.] to attack as a group

Gan·ges (gan'jēz) river in N India & Bangladesh

gan·gling (gaŋ'gliŋ) *adj.* ⟦< ?⟧ thin, tall, and awkward Also **gan'gly**

gan·gli·on (gaŋ'glē ən) *n.*, *pl.* **-gli·a** (-ə) or **-gli·ons** ⟦ult. < Gr, tumor⟧ a mass of nerve cells from which nerve impulses are transmitted

gang'plank' *n.* a movable ramp by which to board or leave a ship

gan·grene (gaŋ'grēn', gaŋ grēn') *n.* ⟦< Gr *gran*, gnaw⟧ decay of body tissue when the blood supply is obstructed —**gan'gre·nous** (-grə nəs) *adj.*

gang·ster (gaŋ'stər) *n.* a member of a gang of criminals —**gang'ster·ism'** *n.*

gang'way' *n.* ⟦OE *gangweg*⟧ **1** a passageway **2** *a)* an opening in a ship's bulwarks for loading, etc. *b)* GANGPLANK —*interj.* clear the way!

gant·let (gônt'lit, gänt'-, gant'-) *n.* ⟦< Swed *gata*, lane + *lopp*, a run⟧ **1** a former punishment in which the offender ran between two rows of men who struck him **2** a series of troubles Now sp. equally *gauntlet*

gan·try (gan'trē) *n.*, *pl.* **-tries** ⟦< L *canterius*, beast of burden⟧ **1** a framework, often on wheels, for a traveling crane **2** a wheeled framework with a crane, platforms, etc., for readying a rocket to be launched

GAO General Accounting Office

gaol (jāl) *n. Brit. sp. of* JAIL

gap (gap) *n.* ⟦< ON *gapa*, to gape⟧ **1** an opening made by breaking or parting **2** a mountain pass or ravine **3** a blank space **4** a lag or disparity

gape (gāp) *vi.* **gaped, gap'ing** ⟦< ON *gapa*⟧ **1** to open the mouth wide, as in yawning **2** to stare with the mouth open **3** to open wide —*n.* **1** a gaping **2** a wide opening

gar (gär) *n.*, *pl.* **gar** or **gars** ⟦< OE *gar*, a spear⟧ a freshwater fish with a beaklike snout Also **gar'fish'**

ga·rage (gə räzh', -räj') *n.* ⟦Fr < *garer*, to protect⟧ **1** a shelter for motor vehicles **2** a business place where such vehicles are stored, repaired, etc.

garage sale a sale of used or unwanted household articles, etc.

garb (gärb) *n.* ⟦< It *garbo*, elegance⟧ clothing; style of dress [clerical *garb*] —*vt.* to clothe

gar·bage (gär'bij) *n.* ⟦ME, entrails of fowls⟧ spoiled or waste food

gar·ble (gär'bəl) *vt.* **-bled, -bling** ⟦< Ar *gharbāl*, a sieve⟧ to distort or confuse (a story, etc.)

gar·çon (gär sōn') *n.* ⟦Fr⟧ a waiter

gar·den (gärd''n) *n.* ⟦< Frankish⟧ **1** a piece of ground for growing vegetables, flowers, etc. **2** an area of fertile land: also **garden spot** **3** [*often pl.*] a public, parklike place, sometimes having displays of animals or plants —*vi.* to take care of a garden —*adj.* of, for, or grown in a garden —**gar'den·er** *n.*

Garden Grove city in SW Calif.: pop. 123,000

gar·de·ni·a (gär dēn'yə) *n.* ⟦after A. *Garden* (1730-91), Am botanist⟧ a plant with fragrant, waxy flowers

gar'den-va·ri'e·ty *adj.* ordinary; commonplace

Gar·field (gär'fēld), **James A·bram** (jāmz ā' brəm) 1831-81; 20th president of the U.S. (1881): assassinated

Gar·gan·tu·a (gär gan'cho͞o ə) a giant king in a satire by Rabelais —**Gar·gan'tu·an** or **gar·gan'tu·an** *adj.*

gar·gle (gär'gəl) *vt.*, *vi.* **-gled, -gling** ⟦< Fr *gargouille*, throat⟧ to rinse (the throat) with a liquid kept in motion by the expulsion of air from the lungs —*n.* a liquid for gargling

gar·goyle (gär'goil') *n.* ⟦see prec.⟧ a waterspout formed like a fantastic creature, projecting from a building

GARGOYLE

Gar·i·bal·di (gar'ə bôl'dē), **Giu·sep·pe** (jo͞o zep'pe) 1807-82; It. patriot & general

gar·ish (gar'ish, ger'-) *adj.* ⟦prob. < ME *gauren*, to stare⟧ too gaudy; showy —**gar'ish·ly** *adv.* —**gar'ish·ness** *n.*

gar·land (gär'lənd) *n.* ⟦< OFr *garlande*⟧ a wreath of flowers, leaves, etc. —*vt.* to decorate with garlands

Gar·land (gär'lənd) city in NE Tex.: pop. 139,000

gar·lic (gär'lik) *n.* ⟦< OE *gar*, a spear + *leac*, leek⟧ **1** an herb of the lily family **2** its strong-smelling bulb, used as seasoning —**gar'lick·y** *adj.*

gar·ment (gär'mənt) *n.* ⟦see GARNISH⟧ any article of clothing

gar·ner (gär'nər) *vt.* ⟦< L *granum*, grain⟧ to gather up and store

gar·net (gär'nit) *n.* ⟦< ML *granatum*⟧ a hard, glasslike mineral: red varieties are often used as gems

gar·nish (gär'nish) *vt.* ⟦< OFr *garnir*, furnish⟧ **1** to decorate **2** to decorate (food) with something that adds color or flavor **3** to garnishee —*n.* **1** a decoration **2** something used to garnish food, as parsley

gar·nish·ee (gär'ni shē') *vt.* **-eed', -ee'ing** ⟦< prec.⟧ *Law* to attach (a debtor's property, wages, etc.) so that it can be used to pay the debt

gar'nish·ment *n. Law* a notice ordering a person in possession of a defendant's property or money not to dispose of it

gar·ret (gar'it) *n.* ⟦< OFr *garite*, watchtower⟧ an attic

gar·ri·son (gar'ə sən) *n.* ⟦< OFr *garir*, to watch⟧ **1** troops stationed in a fort or fortified place **2** a military post or station —*vt.* to station (troops) in (a fortified place) for its defense

gar·rote (gə rōt', gə rät') *n.* ⟦Sp⟧ **1** a cord, thong, etc. used in strangling a person in a surprise attack 2 a strangling in this way —*vt.* **-rot′ed** or **-rot′ted, -rot′ing** or **-rot′ting** to execute or attack by such strangling Also **ga·rotte′** or **gar·rotte′** (-rät′, -rōt′) — **gar·rot′er** *n.*

gar·ru·lous (gar′ə ləs, gar′yoo-) *adj.* ⟦< L *garrire,* to chatter⟧ talking much, esp. about unimportant things —**gar·ru·li·ty** (gə roo′lə tē) or **gar′ru·lous·ness** *n.* —**gar′ru·lous·ly** *adv.*

gar·ter (gärt′ər) *n.* ⟦< OFr *garet,* the back of the knee⟧ an elastic band or strap for holding a stocking in place

garter snake a small, harmless snake common in North America

Gar·y (ger′ē) city in NW Ind.: pop. 152,000

gas (gas) *n., pl.* **gas′es** or **gas′ses** ⟦coined < Gr *chaos,* space⟧ 1 the fluid form of a substance in which it can expand indefinitely; vapor 2 any mixture of flammable gases used for lighting or heating 3 any gas used as an anesthetic 4 any poisonous substance dispersed in the air, as in war 5 [Colloq.] *a)* GASOLINE *b)* the accelerator in an automobile —*vt.* **gassed, gas′sing** to injure or kill by gas —**gas′e·ous** (-ē əs) *adj.*

gas chamber a room in which people are put to be killed with poison gas

gash (gash) *vt.* ⟦< Gr *charassein,* to cut⟧ to make a long, deep cut in; slash —*n.* a long, deep cut

gas·ket (gas′kit) *n.* ⟦prob. < OFr *garcete,* small cord⟧ a piece or ring of rubber, metal, etc. used to make a joint leakproof

gas mask a filtering mask to protect against breathing in poisonous gases

gas·o·hol (gas′ə hôl′) *n.* a motor fuel mixture of gasoline and alcohol

gas·o·line (gas′ə lēn′, gas′ə lēn′) *n.* ⟦< *gas* + L *oleum,* oil⟧ a volatile, flammable liquid distilled from petroleum, used chiefly as a fuel in internal-combustion engines Also **gas′o·lene′**

gasp (gasp) *vi.* ⟦< ON *geispa,* to yawn⟧ to inhale suddenly, as in surprise, or breathe with effort —*vt.* to say with gasps —*n.* a gasping

gas station SERVICE STATION

gas′sy *adj.* **-si·er, -si·est** 1 full of gas; esp., flatulent 2 like gas

gas·tric (gas′trik) *adj.* ⟦GASTR(O)- + -IC⟧ of, in, or near the stomach

gastric juice the clear, acid digestive fluid produced by glands in the stomach lining

gas·tri·tis (gas trīt′is) *n.* ⟦fol. + -ITIS⟧ inflammation of the stomach

gastro- ⟦< Gr *gastēr*⟧ *combining form* stomach (and)

gas·tron·o·my (gas trän′ə mē) *n.* ⟦< Gr *gastēr,* stomach + *nomos,* a rule⟧ the art of good eating —**gas′tro·nom′ic** (-trə näm′ik) or **gas′tro·nom′i·cal** *adj.*

gas·tro·pod (gas′trō päd′) *n.* ⟦GASTRO- + -POD⟧ a mollusk of the class including snails, slugs, etc.

gate (gāt) *n.* ⟦OE⟧ 1 a movable structure controlling passage through an opening in a fence or wall 2 a gateway 3 a movable barrier 4 a structure controlling the flow of water, as in a canal 5 the total amount or number of paid admissions to a performance —**give** (or **get**) **the gate** [Slang] to subject (or be subjected) to dismissal

-gate (gāt) ⟦< (*Water*)*gate,* political scandal, after the *Watergate,* building in Washington, D.C., site of 1972 burglary⟧ *combining form* a scandal marked by charges of corruption against public officials, etc.

gate′-crash′er *n.* [Colloq.] one who attends a social affair without an invitation or a performance without paying

gate′fold′ *n.* an oversize page, as in a magazine, bound so it can be unfolded

gate′way′ *n.* 1 an entrance as in a wall, fitted with a gate 2 a means of access

gath·er (gath′ər) *vt.* ⟦OE *gad(e)rian*⟧ 1 to bring together in one place or group 2 to get gradually; accumulate 3 to collect by picking; harvest 4 to infer; conclude 5 to draw into folds or puckers —*vi.* 1 to assemble 2 to increase —*n.* a pucker or fold

gath′er·ing *n.* 1 a meeting; crowd 2 a gather in cloth

ga·tor or **'ga·tor** (gā′tər) *n. short for* ALLIGATOR

gauche (gōsh) *adj.* ⟦Fr < MFr *gauchir,* become warped⟧ lacking social grace; awkward; tactless

gau·che·rie (gō′shə rē) *n.* gauche behavior or a gauche act

gau·cho (gou′chō) *n., pl.* **-chos** ⟦AmSp⟧ a South American cowboy

gaud·y (gôd′ē) *adj.* **-i·er, -i·est** ⟦< ME *gaude,* trinket⟧ bright and showy, but lacking in good taste —**gaud′i·ly** *adv.* —**gaud′i·ness** *n.*

gauge (gāj) *n.* ⟦Norm Fr⟧ 1 a standard measure or criterion 2 any device for measuring 3 the distance between the rails of a railroad 4 the size of the bore of a shotgun 5 the thickness of sheet metal, wire, etc. —*vt.* **gauged, gaug′ing** 1 to measure the size, amount, etc. of 2 to judge

Gaul (gôl) ancient division of the Roman Empire, in W Europe —*n.* any of the people of Gaul

Gaul′ish *n.* the Celtic language of ancient Gaul

gaunt (gônt) *adj.* ⟦ME *gawnte*⟧ 1 thin and bony; haggard, as from great hunger 2 looking grim or forbidding —**gaunt′ness** *n.*

gaunt·let[1] (gônt′lit, gänt′-) *n.* ⟦< OFr *gant,* glove⟧ 1 a knight's armored glove 2 a long glove with a flaring cuff —**throw down the gauntlet** to challenge, as to combat

gaunt·let[2] (gônt′lit, gänt′-) *n. see* GANTLET

gauze (gôz) *n.* ⟦< Fr *gaze* < Ar *kazz,* silk⟧ any very thin, transparent material, as of cotton or silk —**gauz′y, -i·er, -i·est,** *adj.*

gave (gāv) *vt., vi. pt. of* GIVE

gav·el (gav′əl) *n.* ⟦< Scot *gable,* fork⟧ a small mallet used, as by a presiding officer, to call for attention, etc.

ga·votte (gə vät′) *n.* ⟦Fr⟧ a 17th-c. dance like the minuet, but livelier

gawk (gôk) *vi.* ⟦prob. < *gowk,* stupid person⟧ to stare stupidly

gawk·y (gô′kē) *adj.* **-i·er, -i·est** ⟦see prec.⟧ clumsy; ungainly —**gawk′i·ly** *adv.* — **gawk′i·ness** *n.*

gay (gā) *adj.* ⟦OFr *gai*⟧ 1 joyous and lively; merry 2 bright; brilliant /*gay* colors/ 3 homosexual —*n.* a homosexual, esp. a male homosexual

gay·e·ty (gā′ə tē) *n. alt. sp. of* GAIETY

gay·ly (gā′lē) *adv. alt. sp. of* GAILY

gaze (gāz) *vi.* **gazed, gaz′ing** ⟦< Scand⟧ to look steadily; stare —*n.* a steady look

ga·ze·bo (gə zē′bō, -zā′-) *n., pl.* **-bos** or **-boes** ⟦< prec.⟧ a summerhouse, windowed balcony, etc. for gazing at scenery

ga·zelle (gə zel′) *n.* ⟦< Ar *ghazāl*⟧ a small, swift antelope of Africa and Asia, with large, lustrous eyes

ga·zette (gə zet′) *n.* ⟦Fr < It dial. *gazeta,* a small coin, price of the newspaper⟧ **1** a newspaper: now mainly in newspaper titles **2** in England, an official publication —*vt.* **-zet′ted, -zet′ting** [Brit.] to publish in a gazette

gaz·et·teer (gaz′ə tir′) *n.* a dictionary or index of geographical names

gaz·pa·cho (gäs pä′chō, gäz-) *n.* ⟦Sp⟧ a cold Spanish soup of tomatoes, chopped cucumbers, onions, peppers, oil, vinegar, etc.

G.B. or **GB** Great Britain

Ge *Chem. symbol for* germanium

gear (gir) *n.* ⟦< ON *gervi,* preparation⟧ **1** clothing **2** equipment, esp. for some task **3** *a)* a toothed wheel designed to mesh with another *b)* [*often pl.*] a system of such gears meshed together to pass motion along *c)* a specific adjustment of such a system *d)* a part of a mechanism with a specific function /the steering *gear*/ —*vt.* **1** to connect by or furnish with gears **2** to adapt (one thing) to conform with another /to *gear* supply to demand/ —**in** (or **out of**) **gear** **1** (not) connected to the motor **2** (not) in proper working order

gear′shift′ *n.* the lever for engaging or disengaging any of several sets of transmission gears to a motor, etc.

gear′wheel′ *n.* a toothed wheel in a system of gears; cogwheel

geck·o (gek′ō) *n., pl.* **-os** or **-oes** ⟦prob. < Malay⟧ a tropical lizard with suction pads on its feet

gee (jē) *interj.* ⟦< JE(SUS)⟧ [Slang] an exclamation of surprise, etc.

geese (gēs) *n. pl. of* GOOSE

gee·zer (gē′zər) *n.* ⟦< GUISE⟧ [Slang] an eccentric old man

ge·fil·te fish (gə fil′tə fish) ⟦Yidd⟧ chopped, seasoned fish, boiled and served in balls or cakes

Gei·ger counter (gī′gər) ⟦after H. *Geiger* (1882-1945), Ger physicist⟧ an instrument for detecting and counting ionizing particles, as from radioactive ores

gei·sha (gā′shə) *n., pl.* **-sha** or **-shas** ⟦Sino-Jpn *gei,* art + *sha,* person⟧ a Japanese girl trained as an entertainer to serve as a hired companion to men

gel (jel) *n.* ⟦< fol.⟧ a jellylike substance formed from a colloidal solution —*vi.* **gelled, gel′ling** to form a gel

gel·a·tin (jel′ə tin) *n.* ⟦< L *gelare,* freeze⟧ a tasteless, odorless substance extracted by boiling bones, horns, etc., or a similar vegetable substance: dissolved and cooled, it forms a jellylike substance used in foods, photographic film, etc. Also **gel′a·tine** —**ge·lat·i·nous** (jə lat′'n əs) *adj.*

geld (geld) *vt.* **geld′ed** or **gelt, geld′ing** ⟦< ON *geldr,* barren⟧ to castrate (esp. a horse)

geld′ing *n.* a castrated horse

gel·id (jel′id) *adj.* ⟦< L *gelu,* frost⟧ extremely cold; frozen

gem (jem) *n.* ⟦< L *gemma*⟧ **1** a cut and polished gemstone or a pearl **2** something very precious or valuable

Gem·i·ni (jem′ə nī′, -nē′) ⟦L, twins⟧ the third sign of the zodiac

gem′stone′ *n.* any mineral that can be used in a piece of jewelry when cut and polished

ge·müt·lich (gə müt′likh) *adj.* ⟦Ger⟧ agreeable, cheerful, cozy, etc.

-gen (jən, jen) ⟦< Gr *-genēs,* born⟧ *suffix* **1** something that produces /*hydrogen*/ **2** something produced (in a specified way)

Gen. **1** General **2** *Bible* Genesis

gen·darme (zhän′därm′) *n.* ⟦Fr < *gens d'armes,* men-at-arms⟧ a French police officer

gen·der (jen′dər) *n.* ⟦< L *genus,* origin⟧ **1** *Gram.* the classification by which words are grouped as masculine, feminine, or neuter **2** [Colloq.] a person's sex

gene (jēn) *n.* ⟦see -GEN⟧ any of the units in the chromosomes by which hereditary characters are transmitted

ge·ne·al·o·gy (jē′nē al′ə jē; *often,* -äl′-) *n., pl.* **-gies** ⟦< Gr *genea,* race + *-logia,* -LOGY⟧ **1** a recorded history of a person's ancestry **2** the study of family descent **3** lineage —**ge′ne·a·log′i·cal** (-ə läj′i kəl) *adj.* —**ge′ne·al′o·gist** *n.*

gen·er·a (jen′ər ə) *n. pl. of* GENUS

gen·er·al (jen′ər əl) *adj.* ⟦< L *genus,* class⟧ **1** of, for, or from all; not local, special, or specialized **2** of or for a whole genus, kind, etc. **3** widespread /*general* unrest/ **4** most common; usual **5** not specific or precise /in *general* terms/ **6** highest in rank /attorney *general*/ —*n.* a military officer ranking above a colonel, specif. one ranking above a lieutenant general —**in general** **1** usually **2** without specific details —**gen′er·al·ship′** *n.*

general assembly [*often* **G- A-**] **1** the legislative assembly in some States **2** the deliberative assembly of the United Nations

general delivery delivery of mail at the post office to addressees who call for it

gen·er·al·is·si·mo (jen′ər ə lis′i mō′) *n., pl.* **-mos′** ⟦It⟧ in some countries, the commander in chief of the armed forces

gen·er·al·i·ty (jen′ər al′ə tē) *n., pl.* **-ties** **1** the quality of being general **2** a general or vague statement, idea, etc. **3** the main body

gen·er·al·ize (jen′ər əl īz′) *vt.* **-ized′, -iz′ing** **1** to state in terms of a general law **2** to infer or derive (a general law) from (particular instances) —*vi.* **1** to formulate general principles **2** to talk in generalities

gen′er·al·ly *adv.* **1** widely; popularly **2** usually **3** not specifically

general practitioner a practicing physician who does not specialize in a particular field of medicine

gen·er·ate (jen′ər āt′) *vt.* **-at′ed, -at′ing** ⟦< L *genus,* race⟧ **1** to produce (offspring); beget **2** to bring into being —**gen′er·a′tive** *adj.*

gen′er·a′tion *n.* **1** the producing of offspring **2** production **3** a single stage in the succession of descent **4** the average period (*c.* 30 years) between human generations **5** all the people born and living at about the same time **—gen′er·a′tion·al** ***adj.***

gen′er·a′tor ***n.*** a machine for changing mechanical energy into electrical energy; dynamo

ge·ner·ic (jə ner′ik) ***adj.*** ⟦< L *genus*, race, kind⟧ **1** of a whole kind, class, or group; inclusive **2** without a trademark **—*n.*** a product without a brand name: *often used in pl.* **—ge·ner′i·cal·ly** ***adv.***

gen·er·ous (jen′ər əs) ***adj.*** ⟦< L *generosus*, noble⟧ **1** noble-minded; magnanimous **2** willing to give or share; unselfish **3** large; ample **—gen·er·os·i·ty** (jen′ər äs′ə tē) ***n.*** **—gen′er·ous·ly** ***adv.***

gen·e·sis (jen′ə sis) ***n.*** ⟦Gr⟧ the beginning; origin **—**[**G-**] the first book of the Bible

genetic code the order in which four chemical constituents are arranged in huge molecules of DNA

ge·net·ics (jə net′iks) ***n.pl.*** ⟦ult. < GENESIS⟧ [*with sing. v.*] the branch of biology dealing with heredity and variation in animal and plant species **—ge·net′ic** ***adj.*** **—ge·net′i·cal·ly** ***adv.*** **—ge·net′i·cist** (-ə sist) ***n.***

Ge·ne·va (jə nē′və) city in SW Switzerland: pop. 159,500

Gen·ghis Khan (geŋ′gis kän′, jeŋ′-) *c.* 1162-1227; Mongol conqueror

gen·i·al (jēn′yəl) ***adj.*** ⟦see GENIUS⟧ **1** good for life and growth /a *genial* climate/ **2** cheerful and friendly; amiable **—ge·ni·al·i·ty** (jē′nē al′ə tē) ***n.*** **—gen′i·al·ly** ***adv.***

ge·nie (jē′nē) ***n.*** ⟦< Fr < Ar *jinnī*⟧ JINNI

gen·i·tal (jen′i təl) ***adj.*** ⟦< L *genere*, beget⟧ of reproduction or the sexual organs

gen′i·tals ***n.pl.*** ⟦see prec.⟧ the reproductive organs; esp., the external sex organs Also **gen′i·ta′li·a** (-tā′lē ə)

gen·i·tive (jen′i tiv) ***n.*** ⟦< Gr *genos*, genus⟧ *Gram.* a case expressing possession, source, etc., or referring to a part of a whole

gen·i·to·u·ri·nar·y (jen′i tō yoor′ə ner′ē) ***adj.*** of the genital and urinary organs

gen·i·us (jēn′yəs) ***n.*** ⟦L, guardian spirit⟧ **1** particular spirit of a nation, place, age, etc. **2** natural ability; strong inclination (*for*) **3** great mental capacity and inventive ability **4** one having such capacity or ability

Gen·o·a (jen′ə wə) seaport in NW Italy: pop. 738,000

gen·o·cide (jen′ə sīd′) ***n.*** ⟦< Gr *genos*, race + -CIDE⟧ the systematic killing of a whole people or nation

gen·re (zhän′rə) ***n.*** ⟦Fr < L *genus*, a kind⟧ **1** a distinct kind, or type, as of works of literature, art, or popular fiction **2** painting in which everyday subjects are treated realistically

gent (jent) ***n.*** [Colloq.] a gentleman

gen·teel (jen tēl′) ***adj.*** ⟦< Fr *gentil*⟧ polite or well-bred; now, esp., affectedly refined, polite, etc.

gen·tian (jen′shən) ***n.*** ⟦< L *gentiana*⟧ a plant typically with blue, fringed flowers

gen·tile (jen′tīl′) ***n.*** ⟦< L *gentilis*, of the same clan⟧ [*also* **G-**] any person not a Jew **—*adj.*** not Jewish

gen·til·i·ty (jen til′i tē) ***n.*** ⟦see fol.⟧ the quality of being genteel

gen·tle (jent′'l) ***adj.*** **-tler, -tlest** ⟦< L *gentilis*, of the same clan⟧ **1** of the upper classes **2** refined, courteous, etc. **3** generous; kind **4** tame /a *gentle* dog/ **5** kindly; patient **6** not harsh or rough /a *gentle* tap/ **7** gradual /a *gentle* slope/ **—gen′tle·ness** ***n.*** **—gen′tly** ***adv.***

gen′tle·folk′ ***n.pl.*** people of good social standing Also **gen′tle·folks′**

gen′tle·man (-mən) ***n.***, *pl.* **-men** **1** a man of good family and social standing **2** a courteous, gracious, and honorable man **3** any man: a polite term, esp. as (in pl.) a form of address **—gen′tle·man·ly** ***adv.*** **—gen′tle·wom′an**, *pl.* **-wom′en**, ***n.fem.***

gen·tri·fy (jen′tri fī′) ***vt.*** **-fied′**, **-fy′ing** ⟦< fol. + -FY⟧ **1** to convert (an aging neighborhood) into a more affluent one, as by remodeling homes **2** to raise to a higher status **—gen′tri·fi·ca′tion** ***n.***

gen·try (jen′trē) ***n.*** ⟦see GENTLE⟧ **1** people of high social standing **2** people of a particular class or group

gen·u·flect (jen′yo͞o flekt′) ***vi.*** ⟦< L *genu*, knee + *flectere*, bend⟧ to bend the knee, as in worship **—gen′u·flec′tion** ***n.***

gen·u·ine (jen′yo͞o in) ***adj.*** ⟦L *genuinus*, inborn⟧ **1** not counterfeit or artificial; real; true **2** sincere **—gen′u·ine·ly** ***adv.*** **—gen′u·ine·ness** ***n.***

ge·nus (jē′nəs) ***n.***, *pl.* **gen·er·a** (jen′ər ə) or **ge′nus·es** ⟦L, race, kind⟧ **1** a class; kind; sort **2** a classification of related plants or animals

geo- ⟦< Gr *gē*⟧ *combining form* earth, of the earth

ge·o·cen·tric (jē′ō sen′trik) ***adj.*** **1** viewed as from the center of the earth **2** having the earth as a center **—ge′o·cen′tri·cal·ly** ***adv.***

ge·ode (jē′ōd′) ***n.*** ⟦< Gr *geōdēs*, earthlike⟧ a stone with a cavity lined with crystals or silica

ge·o·des·ic (jē′ō des′ik) ***adj.*** **1** GEODETIC (sense 1) **2** *a*) designating the shortest line between two points on a curved surface *b*) of the geometry of such lines **3** having a surface formed of straight bars in a grid of polygons /*geodesic* dome/

ge·o·det·ic (jē′ō det′ik) ***adj.*** **1** of or concerned with the measurement of the earth and its surface **2** GEODESIC (sense 2)

ge·og·ra·phy (jē äg′rə fē) ***n.*** ⟦< Gr *gē*, earth + *graphein*, write⟧ **1** the science dealing with the earth's surface, continents, climates, plants, animals, resources, etc. **2** the physical features of a region **—ge·og′ra·pher** ***n.*** **—ge′o·graph′i·cal** (-ə graf′i kəl) or **ge′o·graph′ic** ***adj.*** **—ge′o·graph′i·cal·ly** ***adv.***

ge·ol·o·gy (jē äl′ə jē) ***n.*** ⟦see GEO- & -LOGY⟧ the science dealing with the development of the earth's crust, its rocks and fossils, etc. **—ge′o·log′ic** (-ə läj′ik) or **ge′o·log′i·cal** ***adj.*** **—ge′o·log′i·cal·ly** ***adv.*** **—ge·ol′o·gist** ***n.***

ge·o·mag·net·ic (jē′ō mag net′ik) ***adj.*** of the magnetic properties of the earth **—ge′o·mag′ne·tism′** ***n.***

ge·om·e·try (jē äm′ə trē) ***n.*** ⟦< Gr *gē*, earth + *metrein*, to measure⟧ the branch of mathematics dealing with the properties, measurement, and relationships of points, lines, planes, and solids **—ge′o·met′ric** (-ə me′-

trik) or **ge′o·met′ri·cal** *adj.* —**ge′o·met′ri·cal·ly** *adv.*

ge·o·phys·ics (jē′ō fiz′iks) ***n.pl.*** [*with sing. v.*] the science dealing with the effects of weather, winds, tides, etc. on the earth —**ge′o·phys′i·cal** *adj.*

George III (jôrj) 1738-1820; king of Great Britain & Ireland (1760-1820)

Geor·gia (jôr′jə) 1 Southern State of the SE U.S.: 58,876 sq. mi.; pop. 5,464,000; cap. Atlanta 2 GEORGIAN SOVIET SOCIALIST REPUBLIC —**Geor·gian** (jôr′jən) ***adj., n.***

Georgian Soviet Socialist Republic republic of the U.S.S.R., on the Black Sea: 26,900 sq. mi.; pop. *c.* 5,200,000

ge·o·sta·tion·ar·y (jē′ō stā′shə ner′ē) ***adj.*** designating or of a satellite orbiting the earth at a speed which keeps it above the same point on the earth's surface Also **ge′o·syn′·chro·nous** (-siŋ′krə nəs)

ge′o·syn′cline′ (-sin′klīn′) ***n.*** a very large depression in the earth's surface

ge′o·ther′mic (-thur′mik) ***adj.*** ⟦GEO- + Gr *thermē*, heat⟧ of the heat inside the earth Also **ge′o·ther′mal**

Ger. 1 German 2 Germany

ge·ra·ni·um (jə rā′nē əm) ***n.*** ⟦< Gr *geranos*, a crane⟧ 1 a common garden plant with showy red, pink, or white flowers 2 a related wildflower

ger·bil (jur′bil) ***n.*** ⟦ult. < Ar⟧ a small rodent with long hind legs

ger·i·at·rics (jer′ē a′triks) ***n.pl.*** ⟦< Gr *gēras*, old age + -IATRICS⟧ [*with sing. v.*] the branch of medicine dealing with the diseases of old age —**ger′i·at′ric** ***adj.***

germ (jurm) ***n.*** ⟦< L *germen*⟧ 1 the rudimentary form from which a new organism is developed; seed; bud 2 any microscopic, disease-bearing organism, esp. one of the bacteria 3 an origin /the *germ* of an idea/

Ger·man (jur′mən) ***n.*** 1 a native or inhabitant of Germany 2 the language of Germany, Austria, etc. —***adj.*** of Germany, its people, language, etc.

ger·mane (jər mān′) ***adj.*** ⟦see GERM⟧ truly relevant; pertinent

Ger·man·ic (jər man′ik) ***adj.*** 1 [Now Rare] German 2 designating or of the original language of the German peoples or the languages descended from it —***n.*** the Germanic branch of languages, including English, Dutch, Danish, etc.

ger·ma·ni·um (jər mā′nē əm) ***n.*** ⟦< L *Germania*, Germany⟧ a nonmetallic chemical element used in semiconductors

German measles RUBELLA

Ger·ma·ny (jur′mə nē′) former country in north central Europe: partitioned (1949) into *a)* the **Federal Republic of Germany** country made up of the W part: 95,735 sq. mi.; pop. 61,175,000: also called **West Germany** *b)* **German Democratic Republic** country comprising the E part: *c.* 41,800 sq. mi.; pop. 16,700,000: also called **East Germany**

germ cell an ovum or sperm cell

ger·mi·cide (jur′mə sīd′) ***n.*** ⟦< GERM + -CIDE⟧ any antiseptic, etc. used to destroy germs —**ger′mi·ci′dal** ***adj.***

ger·mi·nal (jur′mə nəl) ***adj.*** 1 of or like germ cells 2 in the first stage of growth or development

ger′mi·nate′ (-nāt′) ***vi., vt.*** **-nat′ed, -nat′ing** ⟦< L *germen*, a sprout⟧ 1 to sprout, as from a seed 2 to start developing —**ger′mi·na′tion** ***n.***

ger·on·tol·o·gy (jer′ən täl′ə jē) ***n.*** ⟦< Gr *gerōn*, old man + -LOGY⟧ the study of aging and the problems of the aged —**ger′on·tol′o·gist** ***n.***

ger·ry·man·der (jer′i man′dər; *also* ger′-) ***vt., vi.*** ⟦after Elbridge *Gerry*, governor of Mass. (1812) + (SALA)MANDER (from the shape of the county redistricted then)⟧ to divide (a voting area) unfairly, as to give one political party an advantage

ger·und (jer′ənd) ***n.*** ⟦< L *gerere*, carry out⟧ *Gram.* a verbal noun ending in *-ing*

Ge·sta·po (gə stä′pō) ***n.*** ⟦< Ger *Ge(heime) Sta(ats)po(lizei)*, secret state police⟧ the terrorist secret police force of Nazi Germany

ges·ta·tion (jes tā′shən) ***n.*** ⟦< L *gerere*, to bear⟧ the act or period of carrying young in the uterus; pregnancy —**ges′tate, -tat·ed, -tat·ing,** *vt.*

ges·tic·u·late (jes tik′yo͞o lāt′) ***vi.*** **-lat′ed, -lat′ing** ⟦see fol.⟧ to make gestures —**ges·tic′u·la′tion** ***n.***

ges·ture (jes′chər) ***n.*** ⟦< L *gerere*, to bear⟧ 1 a movement of part of the body to express or emphasize ideas, emotions, etc. 2 any act or remark conveying a state of mind, intention, etc., often made merely for effect —***vi.*** **-tured, -tur·ing** to make gestures

get (get) ***vt.*** **got, got′ten** or **got, get′ting** ⟦< ON *geta*⟧ 1 to come into the state of having; receive, obtain, acquire, etc. 2 to arrive at /*get* home early/ 3 to go and bring /*get* your books/ 4 to catch 5 to persuade /*get* him to leave/ 6 to cause to be /*get* the jar open/ 7 to prepare /to *get* lunch/ 8 to manage or contrive /to *get* to do something/ 9 [Colloq.] *a)* to be obliged to (with *have* or *has*) /he's *got* to pass/ *b)* to possess (with *have* or *has*) /he's *got* red hair/ *c)* to strike, kill, baffle, defeat, etc. *d)* to understand 10 [Slang] to cause an emotional response in /her singing *gets* me/ —***vi.*** 1 to come, go, or arrive 2 to come to be /to *get* caught/ *Get* is used as an auxiliary for emphasis in passive construction [to *get* praised] —***n.*** the young of an animal —**get around** 1 to move from place to place; circulate: also **get about** 2 to circumvent 3 to influence as by flattery —**get away** 1 to go away 2 to escape —**get away with** [Slang] to do something without being discovered or punished —**get by** [Colloq.] to survive; manage —**get it** [Colloq.] 1 to understand 2 to be punished —**get off** 1 to come off, down, or out of 2 to leave or start 3 to escape or help to escape —**get on** 1 to go on or into 2 to put on 3 to proceed 4 to grow older 5 to succeed —**get out** 1 to go out or away 2 to take out 3 to be disclosed 4 to publish —**get over** 1 to recover from 2 to forget —**get through** 1 to finish 2 to manage to survive —**get together** 1 to assemble 2 [Colloq.] to reach an agreement —**get up** 1 to rise (from sleep, etc.) 2 to organize

get′a·way′ ***n.*** 1 the act of starting, as in a race 2 the act of escaping

get′-to·geth′er ***n.*** an informal social gathering or meeting

Get·tys·burg (get′iz burg′) town in S Pa.: site of a crucial Civil War battle (July, 1863)
get′-up′ *n.* [Colloq.] costume; dress
GeV *n.* giga-electron-volt; one billion electron-volts
gew·gaw (gyōō′gô′) *n.* ⟦ME⟧ a trinket
gey·ser (gī′zər) *n.* ⟦< ON *gjosa*, to gush⟧ a spring from which columns of boiling water and steam gush into the air at intervals
Gha·na (gä′nə) country on the W coast of Africa: 92,010 sq. mi.; pop. 12,200,000
ghast·ly (gast′lē) *adj.* **-li·er, -li·est** ⟦< OE *gast*, spirit⟧ 1 horrible; frightful 2 ghostlike; pale 3 [Colloq.] very bad —**ghast′li·ness** *n.*
gher·kin (gur′kin) *n.* ⟦< Pers *angārah*, watermelon⟧ a small pickled cucumber
ghet·to (get′ō) *n., pl.* **-tos** or **-toes** ⟦It⟧ 1 a section of some European cities to which Jews were restricted 2 any section of a city in which many members of a minority group live
ghet′to·ize′ (-īz′) *vt.* **-ized′, -iz′ing** 1 to restrict to a ghetto 2 to make into a ghetto
ghost (gōst) *n.* ⟦< OE *gast*⟧ 1 the supposed disembodied spirit of a dead person, appearing as a pale, shadowy apparition 2 a slight trace; shadow /not a *ghost* of a chance/ —**give up the ghost** to die —**ghost′ly** *adj.*
ghost′writ′er *n.* one who writes books, articles, etc. for another who professes to be the author —**ghost′write′** *vt., vi.*
ghoul (gōōl) *n.* ⟦< Ar *ghāla*, to seize⟧ *Muslim Folklore* an evil spirit that robs graves and feeds on the dead —**ghoul′ish** *adj.* —**ghoul′ish·ly** *adv.*
GHQ General Headquarters
GI (jē′ī′) *adj.* 1 government issue: designating clothing, etc. issued to military personnel 2 [Colloq.] of or characteristic of the U.S. armed forces /a *GI* haircut/ —*n., pl.* **GI's** or **GIs** [Colloq.] a U.S. enlisted soldier
gi·ant (jī′ənt) *n.* ⟦< Gr *gigas*⟧ 1 any imaginary being of superhuman size 2 a person or thing of great size, strength, intellect, etc. —*adj.* like a giant —**gi′ant·ess** *n.fem.*
gib·ber (jib′ər) *vi., vt.* ⟦echoic⟧ to speak rapidly and incoherently
gib′ber·ish *n.* unintelligible chatter
gib·bet (jib′it) *n.* ⟦< OFr *gibet*⟧ 1 a gallows 2 a structure from which bodies of executed criminals were hung and exposed to public scorn —*vt.* to hang on a gibbet
gib·bon (gib′ən) *n.* ⟦Fr⟧ a small, slender, long-armed ape of India, S China, and the East Indies
Gib·bon (gib′ən), **Ed·ward** (ed′wərd) 1737-94; Eng. historian
gibe (jīb) *vi., vt.* **gibed, gib′ing** ⟦< ?⟧ to jeer or taunt —*n.* a jeer or taunt
gib·let (jib′lit) *n.* ⟦< OFr *gibelet*, stew made of game⟧ any of the edible internal parts of a fowl, as the gizzard
Gi·bral·tar (ji brôl′tər) British colony occupying a peninsula consisting mostly of a rocky hill (**Rock of Gibraltar**) at the S tip of Spain
gid·dy (gid′ē) *adj.* **-di·er, -di·est** ⟦< OE *gydig*, insane⟧ 1 having or causing a whirling, unsteady sensation; dizzy 2 frivolous —**gid′di·ness** *n.*
Gid·e·on (gid′ē ən) *Bible* a judge of Israel and victorious leader in battle
gift (gift) *n.* ⟦< OE *giefan*, give⟧ 1 something given; present 2 the act of giving 3 a natural ability —*vt.* to present with or as a gift
gift′ed *adj.* 1 having a natural ability; talented 2 of superior intelligence
gig[1] (gig) *n.* ⟦ME *gigge*, whirligig⟧ 1 a light, two-wheeled, open carriage 2 a long, light ship's boat
gig[2] (gig) *n.* ⟦< ?⟧ [Slang] a job, esp. one performing jazz or rock
gi·gan·tic (jī gan′tik) *adj.* ⟦see GIANT⟧ huge; enormous; immense
gig·gle (gig′əl) *vi.* **-gled, -gling** ⟦< Du *giggelen*⟧ to laugh with high, quick sounds in a silly or nervous way —*n.* such a sound —**gig′gly** *adj.*
gig·o·lo (jig′ə lō′) *n., pl.* **-los** ⟦Fr⟧ a man paid to be a woman's escort

GILA MONSTER

Gi·la monster (hē′lə) ⟦after the *Gila* River, Ariz.⟧ a stout, poisonous lizard of the SW U.S. deserts
gild (gild) *vt.* **gild′ed** or **gilt, gild′ing** ⟦< OE *gyldan*⟧ 1 to coat with gold leaf or a gold color 2 to make seem more attractive or valuable than it is —**gild′er** *n.* —**gild′ing** *n.*
gill[1] (gil) *n.* ⟦ME *gile*⟧ the breathing organ of most water animals, as fish
gill[2] (jil) *n.* ⟦< LL *gillo*, cooling vessel⟧ a unit of liquid measure, equal to $\frac{1}{4}$ pint
gilt (gilt) *vt. alt. pt. & pp. of* GILD —*n.* gold leaf or color —*adj.* coated with gilt
gilt′-edged′ *adj.* of the highest quality /*gilt-edged* securities/ Also **gilt′-edge′**
gim·bals (gim′bəlz, jim′-) *n.pl.* ⟦< L *gemellus*, twin⟧ [*with sing. v.*] a pair of rings so pivoted that one swings freely within the other: used to keep a ship's compass level
gim·crack (jim′krak′) *adj.* ⟦< ME *gibbecrak*, an ornament⟧ showy but cheap and useless —*n.* a gimcrack thing —**gim′crack′·er·y** *n.*
gim·let (gim′lit) *n.* ⟦< MDu *wimmel*⟧ a small boring tool with a spiral cutting edge
gim·mick (gim′ik) *n.* ⟦< ?⟧ [Colloq.] 1 a tricky device 2 an attention-getting device or feature, as for promoting a product, etc.
gimp·y (gim′pē) *adj.* ⟦prob. < Norw dial. *gimpa*, to rock⟧ [Colloq.] lame; limping
gin[1] (jin) *n.* ⟦< L *juniperus*, juniper⟧ a distilled alcoholic liquor typically flavored with juniper berries
gin[2] (jin) *n.* ⟦< OFr *engin*, engine⟧ 1 a snare, as for game 2 COTTON GIN —*vt.* **ginned, gin′ning** to remove seeds from (cotton) with a gin
gin·ger (jin′jər) *n.* ⟦< Gr *zingiberi*⟧ 1 a tropical herb with rhizomes used esp. as a spice 2 this spice 3 [Colloq.] vigor; spirit —**gin′ger·y** *adj.*

ginger ale a carbonated soft drink flavored with ginger
gin′ger·bread′ *n.* 1 a cake flavored with ginger 2 showy ornamentation
gin′ger·ly *adv.* very carefully —*adj.* very careful; cautious
gin′ger·snap′ *n.* a crisp cookie flavored with ginger and molasses
ging·ham (giŋ′əm) *n.* ⟦< Malay *ginggang*⟧ a cotton cloth, usually woven in stripes, checks, or plaids
gin·gi·vi·tis (jin′jə vīt′is) *n.* ⟦< L *gingiva,* the gum + -ITIS⟧ inflammation of the gums
gink·go (giŋ′kō) *n., pl.* **-goes** ⟦Jpn *ginkyo*⟧ an Asian tree with fan-shaped leaves Also **ging′ko**
gin rummy (jin) a variety of the card game rummy Also **gin**
gip (jip) *n., vt., vi. alt. sp. of* GYP
Gip·sy (jip′sē) *n.* GYPSY
gi·raffe (jə raf′) *n.* ⟦< Ar *zarāfa*⟧ a large African ruminant with a very long neck and legs
gird (gʉrd) *vt.* **gird′ed** or **girt, gird′ing** ⟦OE *gyrdan*⟧ 1 to encircle or fasten with a belt 2 to surround 3 to prepare (oneself) for action
gird·er (gʉr′dər) *n.* a large wooden or steel beam for supporting joists, the framework of a building, etc.
gir·dle (gʉrd′'l) *n.* ⟦OE *gyrdel*⟧ 1 a belt for the waist 2 anything that encircles 3 a woman's elasticized undergarment for supporting the waist and hips —*vt.* **-dled, -dling** to encircle or bind, as with a girdle
girl (gʉrl) *n.* ⟦ME *girle,* youngster⟧ 1 a female child 2 a young, unmarried woman 3 a female servant 4 [Colloq.] a woman of any age 5 [Colloq.] a sweetheart —**girl′hood′** *n.* —**girl′ish** *adj.*
Girl Scout a member of the **Girl Scouts of the United States of America,** a girls' organization providing healthful, character-building activities
girt[1] (gʉrt) *vt. alt. pt. & pp. of* GIRD
girt[2] (gʉrt) *vt.* to fasten with a girth
girth (gʉrth) *n.* ⟦< ON *gyrtha,* encircle⟧ 1 a band put around the belly of a horse, etc. to hold a saddle or pack 2 the circumference, as of a tree trunk
gist (jist) *n.* ⟦< OFr *giste,* point at issue⟧ the essence or main point, as of an article or argument
give (giv) *vt.* **gave, giv′en, giv′ing** ⟦OE *giefan*⟧ 1 to make a gift of 2 to hand over /to *give* the porter a bag/ 3 to hand over in or for payment 4 to pass (regards, etc.) along 5 to cause to have /to *give* pleasure/ 6 to act as host or sponsor of 7 to produce; supply /cows *give* milk/ 8 to devote or sacrifice 9 to concede; yield 10 to offer /to *give* advice/ 11 to perform /to *give* a concert/ 12 to utter /to *give* a reply/ 13 to inflict (punishment, etc.) —*vi.* to bend, move, yield, etc. from force or pressure —*n.* a bending, moving, etc. under pressure —**give away** 1 to make a gift of 2 to present (the bride) to the bridegroom 3 [Colloq.] to reveal or betray —**give forth** (or **off**) to emit —**give in** to yield —**give it to** [Colloq.] to beat or scold —**give or take** plus or minus —**give out** 1 to emit 2 to make public 3 to distribute 4 to become worn out, etc. —**give up** 1 to hand over 2 to cease 3 to stop trying 4 to despair of —**giv′er** *n.*
give′-and-take′ *n.* 1 mutual concession 2 repartee or banter
give′a·way′ *n.* 1 an unintentional revelation 2 something given free or sold cheap 3 a radio or television program giving prizes
give′back′ *n.* a previously negotiated workers' benefit relinquished to management, as for some concession
giv·en (giv′ən) *vt., vi. pp. of* GIVE —*adj.* 1 accustomed (*to*) by habit, etc. 2 specified 3 assumed; granted —*n.* something assumed or accepted as fact
given name a person's first name
giz·mo (giz′mō) *n., pl.* **-mos** ⟦< ?⟧ [Slang] a gadget Also sp. **gis′mo**
giz·zard (giz′ərd) *n.* ⟦< L *gigeria,* cooked entrails of poultry⟧ the muscular second stomach of a bird
Gk. Greek
gla·cé (gla sā′) *adj.* ⟦< L *glacies,* ice⟧ 1 glossy, as silk 2 candied, as fruits —*vt.* **-céed′, -cé′ing** to glaze (fruits, etc.)
gla·cial (glā′shəl) *adj.* of or like ice or glaciers —**gla′cial·ly** *adv.*
gla·cier (glā′shər) *n.* ⟦< L *glacies,* ice⟧ a large mass of ice and snow moving slowly down a mountain or valley
glad (glad) *adj.* **glad′der, glad′dest** ⟦OE *glæd*⟧ 1 happy 2 causing joy 3 very willing 4 bright —**glad′ly** *adv.* —**glad′ness** *n.*
glad·den (glad′'n) *vt.* to make glad
glade (glād) *n.* ⟦ME⟧ an open space in a forest
glad hand [Slang] a cordial or effusive welcome —**glad′-hand′er** *n.*
glad·i·a·tor (glad′ē āt′ər) *n.* ⟦L < *gladius,* sword⟧ 1 in ancient Rome, a man, often a slave, who fought in an arena as a public show 2 any person taking part in a fight —**glad′i·a·to′ri·al** (-ə tôr′ē əl) *adj.*
glad·i·o·lus (glad′ē ō′ləs) *n., pl.* **-lus·es** or **-li′** (-lī′) ⟦L, small sword⟧ a plant of the iris family with swordlike leaves and tall spikes of funnel-shaped flowers Also **glad′i·o′la** (-lə)
glad·some (glad′səm) *adj.* joyful or cheerful —**glad′some·ly** *adv.*
Glad·stone (bag) (glad′stōn′) ⟦after W. *Gladstone,* 19th-c. Brit statesman⟧ a traveling bag hinged to open flat
glam·or·ize (glam′ər īz′) *vt.* **-ized′, -iz′ing** to make glamorous —**glam′or·i·za′tion** *n.*
glam·our or **glam·or** (glam′ər) *n.* ⟦Scot var. of *grammar,* magic⟧ seemingly mysterious allure; bewitching charm —**glam′or·ous** or **glam′our·ous** *adj.*
glance (glans) *vi.* **glanced, glanc′ing** ⟦ME *glansen*⟧ 1 to strike a surface obliquely and go off at an angle 2 to flash 3 to look quickly —*n.* 1 a glancing off 2 a flash 3 a quick look
gland (gland) *n.* ⟦< L *glans,* acorn⟧ any organ that separates certain elements from the blood and secretes them for the body to use or throw off —**glan·du·lar** (glan′jə lər) *adj.*
glans (glanz) *n.* ⟦L, lit., acorn⟧ 1 the head of the penis 2 the tip of the clitoris

glare (gler) *vi.* **glared, glar′ing** ⟦ME *glaren*⟧ 1 to shine with a steady, dazzling light 2 to stare fiercely —*n.* 1 a steady, dazzling light 2 a fierce stare 3 a bright, glassy surface, as of ice

glar′ing *adj.* 1 dazzlingly bright 2 too showy 3 staring fiercely 4 flagrant /a *glaring* error/ —**glar′ing·ly** *adv.*

Glas·gow (glas′kō) seaport in SW Scotland: pop. 762,000

glas·nost (glas′nōst′) *n.* ⟦Russ, lit., openness⟧ Soviet official policy of publicizing internal problems

glass (glas) *n.* ⟦OE *glæs*⟧ 1 a hard, brittle substance, usually transparent, made by fusing silicates with soda, lime, etc. 2 GLASSWARE 3 *a)* a glass article, as a drinking container *b)* [*pl.*] eyeglasses or binoculars 4 the amount held by a drinking glass —*vt.* to equip with glass panes —*adj.* of or made of glass —**glass′ful′** *n.*

glass′ware′ *n.* articles made of glass

glass′y *adj.* **-i·er, -i·est** 1 like glass, as in smoothness 2 expressionless /a *glassy* stare/ —**glass′i·ly** *adv.* —**glass′i·ness** *n.*

glau·co·ma (glô kō′mə) *n.* ⟦< Gr *glaukos*, gleaming⟧ an eye disorder marked by increased pressure within the eye

glaze (glāz) *vt.* **glazed, glaz′ing** ⟦ME *glasen*⟧ 1 to fit (windows, etc.) with glass 2 to give a hard, glossy finish to (pottery, etc.) 3 to cover (foods) with a coating of sugar syrup, etc. —*vi.* to become glassy or glossy —*n.* a glassy finish or coating

gla·zi·er (glā′zhər) *n.* one whose work is fitting glass in windows, etc.

gleam (glēm) *n.* ⟦OE *glæm*⟧ 1 a flash or beam of light 2 a faint light 3 a reflected brightness, as from a polished surface 4 a faint manifestation, as of hope, understanding, etc. —*vi.* 1 to shine with a gleam 2 to appear suddenly —**gleam′y** *adj.*

glean (glēn) *vt., vi.* ⟦< Celt⟧ 1 to collect (grain left by reapers) 2 to collect (facts, etc.) gradually

glee (glē) *n.* ⟦OE *gleo*⟧ lively joy; merriment —**glee′ful** *adj.*

glee club a group that sings part songs

glen (glen) *n.* ⟦Medieval Scot⟧ a narrow, secluded valley

Glen·dale (glen′dāl) city in SW Calif.: pop. 139,000

glen plaid [*also* **G- p-**] a plaid pattern with thin crossbarred stripes

glib (glib) *adj.* **glib′ber, glib′best** ⟦< or akin to Du *glibberig*, slippery⟧ speaking or spoken smoothly, often too smoothly to be convincing —**glib′ly** *adv.* —**glib′ness** *n.*

glide (glīd) *vi.* **glid′ed, glid′ing** ⟦OE *glidan*⟧ 1 to move smoothly and easily 2 *Aeronautics* to descend with little or no engine power —*vt.* to cause to glide —*n.* 1 a gliding 2 a disk or ball, as of nylon, under a furniture leg to allow easy sliding

glid·er (glīd′ər) *n.* 1 an engineless aircraft carried along by air currents 2 a porch swing suspended in a frame

glim·mer (glim′ər) *vi.* ⟦< OE *glæm*, gleam⟧ 1 to give a faint, flickering light 2 to appear faintly —*n.* 1 a faint, flickering light 2 a faint manifestation —**glim′mer·ing** *n.*

glimpse (glimps) *vt.* **glimpsed, glimps′ing** ⟦< OE *glæm*, gleam⟧ to catch a brief, quick view of —*vi.* to look quickly —*n.* a brief, quick view

glint (glint) *vi.* ⟦ME *glenten*⟧ to gleam or glitter —*n.* a glinting

glis·san·do (gli sän′dō) *n., pl.* **-di** (-dē) or **-dos** ⟦as if It < Fr *glisser*, to slide⟧ *Music* a sliding effect achieved by a rapid sounding of tones

glis·ten (glis′ən) *vi.* ⟦OE *glisnian*⟧ to shine with reflected light, as a wet surface

glitch (glich) *n.* ⟦< Ger *glitsche*, a slip⟧ [Slang] a mishap, error, etc.

glit·ter (glit′ər) *vi.* ⟦prob. < ON *glitra*⟧ 1 to shine brightly; sparkle 2 to be brilliant or showy —*n.* 1 a bright, sparkling light 2 striking or showy brilliance 3 bits of glittering material —**glit′ter·y** *adj.*

glitz (glits) *n.* ⟦< ?⟧ [Colloq.] gaudy or glittery showiness —**glitz′y, -i·er, -i·est,** *adj.*

gloam·ing (glōm′iŋ) *n.* ⟦< OE *glom*⟧ evening dusk; twilight

gloat (glōt) *vi.* ⟦prob. < ON *glotta*, grin scornfully⟧ to gaze or think with malicious pleasure

glob (gläb) *n.* ⟦prob. < GLOBULE⟧ a rounded mass or lump, as of jelly

glob·al (glō′bəl) *adj.* worldwide —**glob′al·ly** *adv.*

glob′al·ism′ (-iz′əm) *n.* a policy, outlook, etc. that is worldwide in scope

globe (glōb) *n.* ⟦< L *globus*, a ball⟧ 1 anything spherical or somewhat spherical 2 the earth, or a model of the earth

globe′-trot′ter *n.* one who travels widely about the world

glob·u·lar (gläb′yoo lər) *adj.* 1 spherical 2 made up of globules

glob′ule′ (-yōōl′) *n.* ⟦< L *globulus*⟧ a tiny ball; very small drop

glock·en·spiel (gläk′ən spēl′) *n.* ⟦Ger *glocke*, bell + *spiel*, to play⟧ a percussion instrument with tuned metal bars in a frame, played with hammers

gloom (glōōm) *n.* ⟦prob. < Scand⟧ 1 darkness; dimness 2 deep sadness; dejection —**gloom′y, -i·er, -i·est,** *adj.*

glop (gläp) *n.* ⟦< ? GL(UE) + (SL)OP⟧ [Colloq.] any soft, gluey substance —**glop′py** *adj.*

glo·ri·fy (glôr′ə fī′) *vt.* **-fied′, -fy′ing** ⟦< L *gloria*, glory + *facere*, to make⟧ 1 to give glory to 2 to exalt (God), as in worship 3 to honor; extol 4 to make seem better, greater, etc. than is so —**glo′ri·fi·ca′tion** *n.*

glo′ri·ous (-ē əs) *adj.* 1 having, giving, or deserving glory 2 splendid —**glo′ri·ous·ly** *adv.*

glo·ry (glôr′ē) *n., pl.* **-ries** ⟦< L *gloria*⟧ 1 great honor or fame, or its source 2 adoration 3 great splendor, prosperity, etc. 4 heavenly bliss —*vi.* **-ried, -ry·ing** to exult (*in*)

gloss¹ (glôs, gläs) *n.* ⟦< ? Scand⟧ 1 the shine of a polished surface 2 a deceptive outward show —*vt.* 1 to give a shiny surface to 2 to hide (an error, etc.) or make seem right or trivial —**gloss′y, -i·er, -i·est,** *adj.*

gloss² (glôs, gläs) *n.* ⟦< Gr *glōssa*, tongue⟧ a note of comment or explanation, as in a footnote —*vt.* to provide glosses for

glos·sa·ry (glôs′ə rē, gläs′-) *n., pl.* **-ries** ⟦see

prec. ⟦ a list of difficult terms with explanations, as for a book

glos·so·la·li·a (gläs'ō lā'lē ə, glôs'-) ***n.*** ⟦ < Gr *glōssa*, tongue + *lalein*, to speak ⟧ an uttering of unintelligible sounds, as in a religious ecstasy

glot·tis (glät'is) ***n.*** ⟦ < Gr *glōssa*, tongue ⟧ the opening between the vocal cords in the larynx —**glot'tal** ***adj.***

glove (gluv) ***n.*** ⟦OE *glof*⟧ **1** a covering for the hand, with separate sheaths for the fingers and thumb **2** a baseball player's mitt **3** a padded mitten worn by boxers —***vt.*** **gloved, glov'ing** to cover with a glove

glow (glō) ***vi.*** ⟦OE *glowan*⟧ **1** to give off a bright light as a result of great heat **2** to give out a steady light **3** to give out heat **4** to be elated **5** to be bright with color —***n.*** **1** a light given off, as a result of great heat **2** steady, even light **3** brightness, warmth, etc. —**glow'ing** ***adj.*** —**glow'ing·ly** ***adv.***

glow·er (glou'ər) ***vi.*** ⟦prob. < ON⟧ to stare with sullen anger; scowl

glow'worm' (glō'-) ***n.*** a wingless, luminescent female or larva of the firefly

glu·cose (glōō'kōs') ***n.*** ⟦Fr < Gr *gleúkos*, sweetness⟧ **1** a crystalline sugar occurring naturally in fruits, honey, etc. **2** a sweet syrup prepared by the hydrolysis of starch

glue (glōō) ***n.*** ⟦< LL *glus*⟧ **1** a sticky, viscous liquid made from animal gelatin, used as an adhesive **2** any similar substance —***vt.*** **glued, glu'ing** to make stick as with glue —**glu'ey, -i·er, -i·est,** ***adj.***

glum (glum) ***adj.*** **glum'mer, glum'mest** ⟦prob. < ME *glomen*, look morose⟧ gloomy; sullen —**glum'ly** ***adv.*** —**glum'ness** ***n.***

glut (glut) ***vi.*** **glut'ted, glut'ting** ⟦< L *gluttire*, to swallow⟧ to eat to excess —***vt.*** **1** to feed, fill, etc. to excess **2** to supply (the market) beyond demand —***n.*** **1** a glutting or being glutted **2** a supply greater than the demand

glu·ten (glōōt''n) ***n.*** ⟦L, glue⟧ a gray, sticky, nutritious mixture of proteins found in wheat, etc. —**glu'ten·ous** ***adj.***

glu'ti·nous (-əs) ***adj.*** ⟦see prec.⟧ gluey; sticky —**glu'ti·nous·ly** ***adv.***

glut·ton (glut''n) ***n.*** ⟦see GLUT⟧ **1** one who eats to excess **2** one with a great capacity for something —**glut'ton·ous** ***adj.*** —**glut'ton·ous·ly** ***adv.***

glut'ton·y ***n.***, *pl.* **-ies** the habit or act of eating too much

glyc·er·in (glis'ər in) ***n.*** ⟦< Gr *glykeros*, sweet⟧ *nontechnical term for* GLYCEROL Also **glyc'er·ine** (-in, -ēn')

glyc·er·ol (glis'ər ôl', -ōl') ***n.*** ⟦< prec.⟧ a colorless, syrupy liquid made from fats and oils: used in skin lotions, in making explosives, etc.

gly·co·gen (glī'kə jən) ***n.*** ⟦< Gr *glykys*, sweet + -GEN⟧ a substance in animal tissues that is changed into glucose as the body needs it

GM General Manager

Gmc. Germanic

gnarl (närl) ***n.*** ⟦< ME *knorre*⟧ a knot on a tree trunk or branch —***vt.*** to make knotted; twist —**gnarled** ***adj.***

gnash (nash) ***vt., vi.*** ⟦prob. < ON⟧ to grind (the teeth) together, as in anger —***n.*** a gnashing

gnat (nat) ***n.*** ⟦OE *gnæt*⟧ any of various small, two-winged insects, which often bite

gnaw (nô) ***vt.*** ⟦OE *gnagen*⟧ **1** to bite away bit by bit; consume **2** to harass or vex —***vi.*** to bite repeatedly

gneiss (nīs) ***n.*** ⟦< OHG *gneisto*, a spark⟧ a granitelike rock formed of layers of quartz, mica, etc.

gnome (nōm) ***n.*** ⟦< Gr *gnōmē*, thought⟧ *Folklore* a dwarf who dwells in the earth and guards its treasures —**gnom'ish** ***adj.***

GNP gross national product

WHITE-BEARDED GNU

gnu (nōō) ***n.*** ⟦< the native name⟧ a large African antelope with an oxlike head and a horselike tail; wildebeest

go (gō) ***vi.*** **went, gone, go'ing** ⟦< OE *gan*⟧ **1** to move along; travel; proceed **2** to work properly; operate /the clock is *going*/ **3** to act, sound, etc. as specified /the balloon *went* "pop"/ **4** to turn out; result /the war *went* badly/ **5** to pass: said of time **6** to become /to *go* mad/ **7** to be expressed, sung, etc. /as the saying *goes*/ **8** to harmonize; agree /blue *goes* with gold/ **9** to be accepted, valid, etc. **10** to leave; depart **11** to come to an end; fail /his eyesight is *going*/ **12** to be allotted (*to*) or sold (*for*) **13** to extend, reach, etc. **14** to be able to pass (*through*), fit (*into*), etc. **15** to be capable of being divided (*into*) /5 *goes* into 10 twice/ **16** to belong /socks *go* in that drawer/ —***vt.*** **1** to travel along /to *go* the wrong way/ **2** [Colloq.] *a*) to put up with *b*) to furnish (bail) for an arrested person —***n.***, *pl.* **goes** **1** a success /to make a *go* of marriage/ **2** [Colloq.] animation; energy **3** [Colloq.] a try; attempt —**go back on** [Colloq.] **1** to betray **2** to break (a promise, etc.) —**go for** **1** to try to get **2** [Colloq.] to attack **3** [Colloq.] to be attracted by —**go in for** [Colloq.] to engage or indulge in —**go off** **1** to depart **2** to explode —**go on** **1** to proceed; continue **2** to happen **3** [Colloq.] to chatter —**go out** **1** to be extinguished, become outdated, etc. **2** to attend social affairs, etc. —**go over** **1** to examine thoroughly **2** to do again **3** [Colloq.] to be successful —**go through** **1** to endure; experience **2** to look through —**go through with** to pursue to the end —**go together** **1** to match; harmonize **2** [Colloq.] to date only each other —**go under** to fail, as in business —**let go** **1** to let escape **2** to release one's hold —**let oneself go** to be unrestrained —**on the go** [Colloq.] in constant motion or action —**to go** [Colloq.] **1** to be taken out: said of food in a restaurant **2** still to be done, etc.

goad (gōd) ***n.*** ⟦OE *gad*⟧ **1** a sharp-pointed stick used in driving oxen **2** any driving impulse; spur —*vt.* to drive as with a goad; urge on

go'-a·head' *n.* permission or a signal to proceed: usually with *the*

goal (gōl) *n.* ⟦ME *gol,* boundary⟧ **1** the place at which a race, trip, etc. is ended **2** an end that one strives to attain **3** in some games, *a)* the line or net over or into which the ball or puck must go to score *b)* the score made

goal'keep'er *n.* in some games, a player stationed at a goal to prevent the ball or puck from entering it Also **goal'ie** (-ē) or **goal'tend'er**

goat (gōt) *n.* ⟦OE *gat*⟧ **1** a cud-chewing mammal with hollow horns, related to the sheep **2** a lecherous man **3** [Colloq.] a scapegoat —**get someone's goat** [Colloq.] to annoy someone

goat·ee (gō'tē') *n.* a small, pointed beard on a man's chin

goat'herd' *n.* one who herds goats

goat'skin' *n.* the skin of a goat, or leather made from this skin

gob[1] (gäb) *n.* ⟦< OFr *gobe,* mouthful⟧ **1** a soft lump or mass **2** [*pl.*] [Colloq.] a large quantity

gob[2] (gäb) *n.* ⟦< ?⟧ [Slang] a sailor in the U.S. Navy

gob·ble[1] (gäb'əl) *n.* ⟦echoic⟧ the throaty sound made by a male turkey —*vi.* **-bled, -bling** to make this sound

gob·ble[2] (gäb'əl) *vt., vi.* **-bled, -bling** ⟦< OFr *gobet,* mouthful⟧ **1** to eat quickly and greedily **2** to seize eagerly; snatch (*up*)

gob'ble·dy·gook' (-dē gook') *n.* ⟦? echoic of turkey cries⟧ [Slang] pompous, wordy talk or writing

gob·bler (gäb'lər) *n.* a male turkey

go-be·tween (gō'bē twēn') *n.* one who makes arrangements between each of two sides; intermediary

Go·bi (gō'bē) large desert plateau in E Asia, chiefly in Mongolia

gob·let (gäb'lit) *n.* ⟦< OFr *gobel*⟧ a drinking glass with a base and stem

gob·lin (gäb'lin) *n.* ⟦< ML *gobelinus*⟧ *Folklore* an evil or mischievous spirit

go-by (gō'bī') *n.* [Colloq.] an intentional disregard or slight

god (gäd, gôd) *n.* ⟦OE⟧ **1** any of various beings conceived of as supernatural and immortal; esp., a male deity **2** an idol **3** a person or thing deified —[**G-**] in monotheistic religions, the creator and ruler of the universe; Supreme Being —**god'like'** *adj.*

god'child' *n., pl.* **-chil'dren** the person a godparent sponsors

god'daugh'ter *n.* a female godchild

god·dess (gäd'is) *n.* **1** a female god **2** a woman of great beauty, charm, etc.

god'fa'ther *n.* a male godparent

god'head' *n.* godhood —[**G-**] God: usually with *the*

god'hood' *n.* the state of being a god; divinity

Go·di·va (gə dī'və) *Eng. Legend* an 11th-c. noblewoman who rides naked through the streets on condition that her husband will abolish a heavy tax

god'less *adj.* **1** irreligious; atheistic **2** wicked —**god'less·ness** *n.*

god'ly *adj.* **-li·er, -li·est** devoted to God; devout —**god'li·ness** *n.*

god'moth'er *n.* a female godparent

god'par'ent *n.* a person who sponsors a child, as at baptism, taking responsibility for its faith

god'send' *n.* anything unexpected and needed or desired that comes at the opportune moment, as if sent by God

god'son' *n.* a male godchild

God·win Austen (gäd'win) mountain in N India: 2d highest mountain in the world: 28,250 ft.

Goe·the (gö'tə; *Eng* gur'tə), **Jo·hann Wolf·gang von** (yō'hän vôlf'gäŋ fôn) 1749-1832; Ger. poet & dramatist

go-fer or **go-fer** (gō'fər) *n.* ⟦from being asked to *go for* something⟧ [Slang] an employee who performs menial tasks, as running errands

go-get·ter (gō'get'ər) *n.* [Colloq.] an enterprising and aggressive person who usually achieves ambitions, goals, etc.

gog·gle (gäg'əl) *vi.* **-gled, -gling** ⟦ME *gogelen*⟧ to stare with bulging eyes —*n.* [*pl.*] large spectacles to protect the eyes against dust, wind, sparks, etc. —*adj.* bulging or rolling: said of the eyes

go-go (gō'gō') *adj.* ⟦short for *à gogo* < Fr, in plenty⟧ **1** of dancing to rock music, as in discothèques **2** of a dancer performing erotic movements to rock music, as in a bar

go·ing (gō'iŋ) *n.* **1** a departure **2** the condition of the ground or land as it affects traveling, walking, etc. —*adj.* **1** moving; working **2** commonly accepted; current —**be going to** will or shall

go'ing-ov'er *n.* [Colloq.] **1** a thorough inspection **2** a severe scolding or beating

go'ings-on' *n.pl.* [Colloq.] actions or events, esp. when disapproved of

goi·ter or **goi·tre** (goit'ər) *n.* ⟦< L *guttur,* throat⟧ an enlargement of the thyroid gland, often visible as a swelling in the front of the neck

gold (gōld) *n.* ⟦OE⟧ **1** a heavy, yellow, metallic, highly malleable chemical element: it is a precious metal **2** money; wealth **3** bright yellow

gold'brick' *n.* [Mil. Slang] one who avoids work: also **gold'brick'er** —*vi.* [Mil. Slang] to shirk a duty or avoid work

gold'en *adj.* **1** made of or containing gold **2** bright-yellow **3** very valuable; excellent **4** flourishing **5** marking the 50th year [*golden* anniversary]

golden ag·er (ā'jər) [*also* **G- A-**] [Colloq.] an elderly person, specif. one 65 or older and retired

Golden Fleece *Gr. Myth.* the fleece of gold captured by Jason

Golden Gate strait between San Francisco Bay & the Pacific

gold'en·rod' *n.* a North American plant with long, branching stalks bearing clusters of small, yellow flowers

golden rule the precept that one should act toward others as one would want them to act toward oneself

gold'-filled' *adj.* made of a base metal overlaid with gold

gold'finch' *n.* ⟦OE *goldfinc*⟧ any of various yellow-and-black finches

gold'fish' *n., pl.* **-fish'** a small, golden-yellow or orange fish, often kept in ponds or aquariums

gold leaf gold beaten into very thin sheets, used for gilding

gold'smith' *n.* an artisan who makes and repairs articles of gold

gold standard a monetary standard in which the basic currency unit equals a specified quantity of gold

golf (gôlf, gälf) *n.* ⟦? < Du *kolf,* a club⟧ an outdoor game played with a small, hard ball and a set of clubs, the object being to hit the ball into each of a series of 9 or 18 holes with the fewest possible strokes —*vi.* to play golf —**golf'er** *n.*

golf course (or **links**) a tract of land for playing golf

Go·li·ath (gə lī'əth) *Bible* the Philistine giant killed by David

gol·ly (gäl'ē) *interj.* an exclamation of surprise, etc.: a euphemism for *God*

-gon (gän, gən) ⟦< Gr *gōnia,* an angle⟧ *combining form* a figure having (a specified number of) angles

go·nad (gō'nad') *n.* ⟦< Gr *gonē,* a seed⟧ an animal organ or gland that produces reproductive cells; esp., an ovary or testis

gon·do·la (gän'dō lə, -də-) *n.* ⟦It⟧ 1 a narrow boat used on the canals of Venice 2 a railroad freight car with no top and, often, with low sides 3 a cabin suspended under an airship or balloon

gon'do·lier' (-lir') *n.* a man who propels a gondola

gone (gôn, gän) *vi., vt. pp. of* GO —*adj.* ⟦ME *gon* < OE *gan*⟧ 1 departed 2 ruined 3 lost 4 dead 5 used up; consumed 6 ago; past

gon·er (gôn'ər) *n.* a person or thing certain to die, be ruined, etc.

gong (gôŋ, gäŋ) *n.* ⟦Malay *guṅ*⟧ a slightly convex metallic disk that gives a loud, resonant tone when struck

gon·or·rhe·a or **gon·or·rhoe·a** (gän'ə rē'ə) *n.* ⟦< Gr *gonos,* semen + *rheein,* to flow⟧ a venereal disease with inflammation of the genital organs

goo (go͞o) *n.* [Slang] 1 anything sticky, or sticky and sweet 2 sentimentality —**goo'ey, -i·er, -i·est,** *adj.*

goo·ber (go͞o'bər) *n.* ⟦< Afr *nguba*⟧ [Chiefly South] a peanut

good (good) *adj.* **bet'ter, best** ⟦OE *gōd*⟧ 1 having the proper qualities 2 beneficial 3 valid; real /*good* money/ 4 healthy or sound /*good* eyesight/ 5 honorable /one's *good* name/ 6 enjoyable, pleasant, etc. 7 thorough 8 virtuous, devout, kind, dutiful, etc. 9 skilled 10 considerable /a *good* many/ —*n.* something good; worth, benefit, etc. —*adv.* [Colloq. or Dial.] well; fully —**as good as** virtually; nearly —**for good (and all)** permanently —**good and** [Colloq.] very or altogether —**good for** 1 able to endure or be used for (a period of time) 2 worth 3 able to pay or give —**make good** 1 to repay or replace 2 to fulfill 3 to succeed —**no good** useless; worthless

good'bye' or **good'-bye'** (-bī') *interj., n., pl.* **-byes'** ⟦contr. of *God be with ye*⟧ farewell Also sp. **good'by', good'-by'**

good faith good intentions; sincerity

Good Friday the Friday before Easter, commemorating the Crucifixion

good'-heart'ed *adj.* kind and generous —**good'-heart'ed·ly** *adv.* —**good'-heart'ed·ness** *n.*

Good Hope, Cape of cape at the SW tip of Africa

good humor a cheerful, agreeable mood —**good'-hu'mored** *adj.* —**good'-hu'mored·ly** *adv.*

good'-look'ing *adj.* handsome

good'ly *adj.* **-li·er, -li·est** 1 of good appearance or quality 2 ample

good'-na'tured *adj.* agreeable; affable —**good'-na'tured·ly** *adv.*

good'ness *n.* the state or quality of being good; virtue, kindness, etc. —*interj.* an exclamation of surprise

goods (goodz) *n.pl.* 1 movable personal property 2 merchandise; wares 3 fabric; cloth —**get** (or **have**) **the goods on** [Slang] to discover (or know) something incriminating about

good Sa·mar·i·tan (sə mer'ət 'n) one who helps another or others unselfishly: see Luke 10:30-37

good'-sized' *adj.* ample; fairly big

good'-tem'pered *adj.* amiable

good turn a friendly, helpful act

good'will' *n.* 1 benevolence 2 willingness 3 the value of a business as a result of patronage, reputation, etc., beyond its tangible assets Also, exc. for sense 3, **good will**

good·y (good'ē) *n., pl.* **-ies** [Colloq.] something good to eat, as a piece of candy —*interj.* a child's exclamation of delight

good'y-good'y *adj.* [Colloq.] affectedly moral or pious —*n.* [Colloq.] a goody-goody person

goof (go͞of) *n.* [Slang] 1 a stupid or silly person 2 a mistake; blunder —*vi.* [Slang] 1 to err or blunder 2 to waste time, shirk duties, etc.: with *off* or *around* —**goof'y, -i·er, -i·est,** *adj.*

gook (gook, go͞ok) *n.* ⟦GOO + (GUN)K⟧ [Slang] any sticky or slimy substance

goon (go͞on) *n.* [Slang] 1 a ruffian or thug 2 a grotesque or stupid person

goop (go͞op) *n.* ⟦GOO + (SOU)P⟧ [Slang] any sticky, semiliquid substance

goose (go͞os) *n., pl.* **geese** ⟦< OE *gos*⟧ 1 a long-necked, web-footed waterfowl like a duck but larger 2 its flesh as food 3 a silly person —**cook one's goose** [Colloq.] to spoil one's chances

goose'ber'ry *n., pl.* **-ries** 1 a small, sour berry 2 the shrub it grows on

goose flesh (or **bumps** or **pimples**) a momentary roughened condition of the skin, induced by cold, fear, etc.

GOP Grand Old Party (Republican Party)

go·pher (gō'fər) *n.* ⟦< ? Fr *gaufre,* honeycomb: from its burrowing⟧ 1 a burrowing rodent with wide cheek pouches 2 a striped ground squirrel of the prairies of North America

Gor·ba·chev (gôr'bə chôf'), **Mi·kha·il S(ergeyevich)** (mē'khä ēl') 1931- ; general secretary of the Communist Party of the U.S.S.R. (1985-)

gore[1] (gôr) ***n.*** ⟦OE *gor*, filth⟧ blood from a wound, esp. when clotted

gore[2] (gôr) ***vt.* gored, gor′ing** ⟦< OE *gar*, a spear⟧ **1** to pierce as with a horn or tusk **2** to insert gores in —***n.*** a tapering piece of cloth inserted in a skirt, sail, etc. to give it fullness

gorge (gôrj) ***n.*** ⟦< L *gurges*, whirlpool⟧ **1** the gullet **2** what has been swallowed **3** resentment, disgust, etc. **4** a deep, narrow pass between steep heights —***vi., vt.* gorged, gorg′ing** to eat greedily or glut (oneself)

gor·geous (gôr′jəs) ***adj.*** ⟦< OFr *gorgias*⟧ **1** brilliantly showy; magnificent **2** [Colloq.] beautiful, delightful, etc. —**gor′geous·ly** ***adv.***

GORILLA

go·ril·la (gə ril′ə) ***n.*** ⟦< W Afr⟧ the largest, and most powerful, of the great apes, native to Africa

Gor·ki or **Gor′ky** (gôr′kē) city in E European U.S.S.R.: pop. 1,400,000

gor·mand·ize (gôr′mən dīz′) ***vi., vt.* -ized′, -iz′ing** ⟦< Fr *gourmandise*, gluttony⟧ to eat like a glutton

gorp (gôrp) ***n.*** a mix of raisins, nuts, etc. eaten for quick energy

gorse (gôrs) ***n.*** ⟦OE *gorst*⟧ FURZE

gor·y (gôr′ē) ***adj.* -i·er, -i·est 1** covered with gore; bloody **2** with much bloodshed —**gor′i·ness *n.***

gosh (gäsh, gôsh) ***interj.*** an exclamation of surprise, etc.: a euphemism for *God*

gos·ling (gäz′liŋ) ***n.*** a young goose

gos·pel (gäs′pəl) ***n.*** ⟦< OE *gōdspel*, good news⟧ **1** [*often* **G-**] the teachings of Jesus and the Apostles **2** [**G-**] any of the first four books of the New Testament **3** anything proclaimed or accepted as the absolute truth: also **gospel truth**

gos·sa·mer (gäs′ə mər) ***n.*** ⟦ME *gosesomer*, lit., goose summer⟧ **1** a filmy cobweb **2** a very thin, filmy cloth —***adj.*** light, thin, and filmy

gos·sip (gäs′əp) ***n.*** ⟦< Late OE *godsibbe*, godparent⟧ **1** one who chatters idly about others **2** such talk —***vi.*** to be a gossip —**gos′sip·y *adj.***

got (gät) ***vt., vi. pt. & alt. pp. of*** GET

Goth (gäth, gôth) ***n.*** any member of a Germanic people that conquered most of the Roman Empire in the 3d, 4th, and 5th c. A.D.

Goth·ic (gäth′ik) ***adj.*** **1** of the Goths or their language **2** designating or of a style of architecture developed in W Europe between the 12th and 16th c., with pointed arches, steep roofs, etc. **3** [*sometimes* **g-**] uncivilized **4** of a type of fiction that uses remote, gloomy settings and a sinister atmosphere to suggest mystery —***n.*** **1** the East Germanic language of the Goths **2** Gothic architecture

got·ten (gät′'n) ***vt., vi. alt. pp. of*** GET

Gou·da (cheese) (gou′də, gōō′-) ⟦after *Gouda*, Netherlands⟧ a mild cheese sometimes coated with red wax

gouge (gouj) ***n.*** ⟦< LL *gulbia*⟧ **1** a chisel for cutting grooves or holes in wood **2** such a groove or hole —***vt.* gouged, goug′ing 1** to make a groove, etc. in (something) as with a gouge **2** to scoop out **3** [Colloq.] to cheat out of money —**goug′er *n.***

gou·lash (gōō′läsh′, -lash′) ***n.*** ⟦< Hung *gulyás*⟧ a beef or veal stew seasoned with paprika

gou·ra·mi (goor′ə mē, goor′ə-) ***n., pl.* -mies** or **-mi** ⟦Malay *gurami*⟧ any of various tropical, freshwater fishes; esp., a food fish of SE Asia

gourd (gôrd, goord) ***n.*** ⟦< L *cucurbita*⟧ **1** any trailing or climbing plant of a family that includes the squash, melon, etc. **2** the fruit of one species or its dried, hollowed-out shell, used as a cup, dipper, etc.

gour·mand (goor mŏn′, -mänd′; goor′mŏn′, -mänd′) ***n.*** ⟦OFr⟧ one who likes good food and drink and tends to indulge in them to excess

gour·met (goor′mā; *Fr* gōōr me′) ***n.*** ⟦Fr < OFr, wine taster⟧ one who likes and is an excellent judge of fine foods and drinks

gout (gout) ***n.*** ⟦< L *gutta*, a drop⟧ a form of arthritis characterized by painful swelling of the joints, esp. in the big toe —**gout′y, -i·er, -i·est, *adj.***

gov. or **Gov. 1** government **2** governor

gov·ern (guv′ərn) ***vt., vi.*** ⟦< Gr *kybernan*, to steer⟧ **1** to exercise authority over; rule, control, etc. **2** to influence the action of; guide **3** to determine —**gov′ern·a·ble *adj.***

gov′ern·ance (-ər nəns) ***n.*** the action, function, or power of government

gov′ern·ess (-ər nis) ***n.*** a woman employed in a private home to train and teach the children

gov·ern·ment (guv′ərn mənt, -ər mənt) ***n.*** **1** the exercise of authority over a state, organization, etc.; control; rule **2** a system of ruling, political administration, etc. **3** those who direct the affairs of a state, etc.; administration —**gov′ern·men′tal *adj.***

gov·er·nor (guv′ər nər, -ə nər) ***n.*** **1** one who governs; esp., *a)* one appointed to govern a province, etc. *b)* the elected head of any State of the U.S. **2** a mechanical device for automatically controlling the speed of an engine —**gov′er·nor·ship′ *n.***

governor general *pl.* **governors general** or **governor generals** a governor who has subordinate or deputy governors

govt. or **Govt.** government

gown (goun) ***n.*** ⟦< LL *gunna*⟧ a long, loose outer garment; specif., *a)* a woman's formal dress *b)* a nightgown *c)* a long, flowing robe worn by judges, clergymen, scholars, etc.

GP or **G.P.** general practitioner

gr. 1 grain(s) **2** gross

Gr. 1 Greece **2** Greek

grab (grab) ***vt.* grabbed, grab′bing** ⟦prob. < MDu *grabben*⟧ **1** to snatch suddenly **2**

to get by unscrupulous methods 3 [Slang] to impress greatly —*n.* a grabbing —**grab′ber** *n.*

grace (grās) *n.* ⟦< L *gratus*, pleasing⟧ 1 beauty or charm of form, movement, or expression 2 goodwill; favor 3 a delay granted for payment of an obligation 4 a short prayer of thanks for a meal 5 [G-] a title of an archbishop, duke, or duchess 6 the love and favor of God toward man —*vt.* **graced, grac′ing** 1 to decorate 2 to dignify —**in the good** (or **bad**) **graces of** in favor (or disfavor) with

grace′ful *adj.* having beauty of form, movement, or expression —**grace′ful·ly** *adv.* —**grace′ful·ness** *n.*

grace′less *adj.* 1 lacking any sense of what is proper 2 clumsy —**grace′less·ly** *adv.* —**grace′less·ness** *n.*

gra·cious (grā′shəs) *adj.* ⟦see GRACE⟧ 1 having or showing kindness, courtesy, charm, etc. 2 compassionate 3 polite to supposed inferiors 4 marked by luxury, ease, etc. /*gracious* living/ —**gra′cious·ly** *adv.* —**gra′cious·ness** *n.*

grack·le (grak′əl) *n.* ⟦L *graculus*, jackdaw⟧ any of several blackbirds somewhat smaller than a crow

grad (grad) *n.* [Colloq.] a graduate

gra·da·tion (grā dā′shən) *n.* 1 an arranging in grades, or stages 2 a gradual change by stages 3 a step or degree in a graded series

grade (grād) *n.* ⟦< L *gradus*⟧ 1 a stage or step in a progression 2 *a*) a degree in a scale of quality, rank, etc. *b*) a group of people of the same rank, merit, etc. 3 *a*) the degree of slope *b*) a sloping part 4 any of the divisions of a school curriculum, by years 5 a mark or rating in an examination, etc. —*vt.* **grad′ed, grad′ing** 1 to classify by grades; sort 2 to give a GRADE (sense 5) to 3 to make (ground) level or evenly sloped, as for a road —**make the grade** to succeed

grade crossing the place where a railroad intersects another railroad or a roadway on the same level

grade school ELEMENTARY SCHOOL

grade separation a crossing with an overpass or underpass

gra·di·ent (grā′dē ənt) *n.* ⟦< L *gradi*, to step⟧ 1 a slope, as of a road 2 the degree of such slope

grad·u·al (gra′jo͞o əl, -jo͞o wəl) *adj.* ⟦< L *gradus*, a step⟧ taking place by degrees; developing little by little —**grad′u·al·ly** *adv.*

grad′u·al·ism′ *n.* the principle of promoting gradual rather than rapid change

grad·u·ate (gra′jo͞o it, -jo͞o wit; *for v.*, -āt′, -wāt′) *n.* ⟦< L *gradus*, a step⟧ one who has completed a course of study at a school or college —*vt.* **-at′ed, -at′ing** 1 to give a degree or diploma to upon completion of a course of study 2 [Colloq.] to become a graduate of /to *graduate* college/ 3 to mark with degrees for measuring 4 to classify into grades according to amount, size, etc. —*vi.* to become a graduate of a school, etc. —*adj.* 1 being a graduate of a school, etc. 2 of or for graduates —**grad′u·a′tor** *n.*

grad′u·a′tion *n.* 1 a graduating from a school or college 2 the ceremony connected with this

graf·fi·to (grə fēt′ō) *n.*, *pl.* **-ti** (-ē) ⟦It < L: see fol.⟧ an inscription or drawing on a wall or other public surface: the plural often takes a sing. verb

graft (graft) *n.* ⟦< Gr *grapheion*, stylus⟧ 1 *a*) a shoot or bud of one plant or tree inserted into another, where it grows permanently *b*) the inserting of such a shoot 2 the transplanting of skin, bone, etc. 3 *a*) the dishonest use of one's position to gain money, etc., as in politics *b*) anything so gained —*vt.*, *vi.* 1 to insert (a graft) 2 to obtain (money, etc.) by graft —**graft′er** *n.*

gra·ham (grā′əm) *adj.* ⟦after S. *Graham*, 19th-c. U.S. dietary reformer⟧ designating or made of whole-wheat flour /*graham* crackers/

Grail (grāl) ⟦< ML *gradalis*, cup⟧ *Medieval Legend* the cup used by Jesus at the Last Supper Also **Holy Grail**

grain (grān) *n.* ⟦< L *granum*⟧ 1 the small, hard seed of any cereal plant, as wheat, corn, etc. 2 cereal plants 3 a tiny, solid particle, as of salt or sand 4 a tiny bit 5 the smallest unit in the system of weights used in the U.S. 6 *a*) the arrangement or direction of fibers, layers, etc. of wood, leather, etc. *b*) the markings or texture due to this 7 disposition; nature

grain′y *adj.* **-i·er, -i·est** 1 having a clearly defined grain, as wood 2 coarsely textured; granular —**grain′i·ness** *n.*

gram (gram) *n.* ⟦< Gr *gramma*, small weight⟧ the basic unit of mass in the metric system, equal to about $\frac{1}{28}$ ounce

-gram (gram) ⟦< Gr *gramma*, writing⟧ *combining form* something written /*telegram*/

gram·mar (gram′ər) *n.* ⟦< Gr *gramma*, writing⟧ 1 language study dealing with the forms of words and with their arrangement in sentences 2 a system of rules for speaking and writing a given language 3 one's manner of speaking or writing as judged by such rules —**gram·mar·i·an** (grə mer′ē ən) *n.* —**gram·mat′i·cal** (-mat′i kəl) *adj.* —**gram·mat′i·cal·ly** *adv.*

grammar school [Now Rare] ELEMENTARY SCHOOL

gran·a·ry (gran′ə rē, grān′-) *n.*, *pl.* **-ries** ⟦< L *granum*, grain⟧ a building for storing threshed grain

grand (grand) *adj.* ⟦< L *grandis*, large⟧ 1 higher in rank than others /a *grand* duke/ 2 most important; main /the *grand* ballroom/ 3 imposing in size, beauty, and extent 4 distinguished; illustrious 5 complete; overall /the *grand* total/ 6 [Colloq.] excellent; delightful —*n.*, *pl.* **grand** [Slang] a thousand dollars —**grand′ly** *adv.*

grand- *combining form* of the generation older (or younger) than /*grandmother*, *grandson*/

gran·dam (gran′dam′, -dəm) *n.* ⟦see prec. & DAME⟧ [Now Rare] 1 a grandmother 2 an old woman

grand′child′ *n.*, *pl.* **-chil′dren** a child of one's son or daughter

grand′daugh′ter *n.* a daughter of one's son or daughter

grande dame (gränd däm; *Fr* gränd däm′) ⟦Fr⟧ a woman, esp. an older one, of great dignity

gran·dee (gran dē′) ***n.*** ⟦Sp & Port *grande*: see GRAND⟧ a man of high rank

gran·deur (gran′jər, -joor′; -dyoor′) ***n.*** ⟦see GRAND⟧ **1** splendor; magnificence **2** nobility; dignity

grand′fa′ther ***n.*** **1** the father of one's father or mother **2** a forefather —***vt.*** [Colloq.] to exempt (a practice, person, etc.) from a new law or regulation

grandfather (or **grandfather's**) **clock** a large clock with a pendulum, in a tall, narrow case

gran·dil·o·quent (gran dil′ə kwənt) ***adj.*** ⟦< L *grandis*, grand + *loqui*, speak⟧ using pompous, bombastic words —**gran·dil′o·quence** ***n.***

gran·di·ose (gran′dē ōs′) ***adj.*** ⟦< L *grandis*, great⟧ **1** having grandeur; imposing **2** pompous and showy —**gran′di·os′i·ty** (-äs′ə tē) ***n.***

grand jury a jury that investigates accusations and indicts persons for trial if there is sufficient evidence

grand·ma (gran′mə) ***n.*** [Colloq.] GRANDMOTHER

grand′mas′ter ***n.*** any exceptionally skilled chess player

grand′moth′er ***n.*** the mother of one's father or mother

grand opera opera in which the whole text is set to music

grand·pa (gran′pə) ***n.*** [Colloq.] GRANDFATHER

grand′par′ent ***n.*** a grandfather or grandmother

grand piano a large piano with strings set horizontally in a wing-shaped case

Grand Rapids city in SW Mich.: pop. 182,000

grand slam **1** *Baseball* a home run hit when there is a runner on each base **2** *Bridge* the winning of all the tricks in a deal

grand′son′ ***n.*** a son of one's son or daughter

grand′stand′ ***n.*** the main seating structure for spectators at a sporting event

grange (grānj) ***n.*** ⟦< L *granum*, grain⟧ a farm —[**G-**] an association of farmers or a local lodge of this

gran·ite (gran′it) ***n.*** ⟦< L *granum*, grain⟧ a hard, plutonic rock consisting chiefly of feldspar and quartz —**gra·nit·ic** (grə nit′ik) ***adj.***

gran·ny or **gran·nie** (gran′ē) ***n.***, *pl.* **-nies** [Colloq.] **1** a grandmother **2** an old woman —***adj.*** of a style like that formerly worn by elderly women [*granny* glasses]

gran·o·la (grə nō′lə) ***n.*** ⟦< ? L *granum*, grain⟧ a breakfast cereal of rolled oats, wheat germ, sesame seeds, brown sugar or honey, dried fruit or nuts, etc.

grant (grant) ***vt.*** ⟦< L *credere*, believe⟧ **1** to give (what is requested, as permission, etc.) **2** to give or transfer by legal procedure **3** to admit as true; concede —***n.*** **1** a granting **2** something granted, as property, a right, etc. —**take for granted** to consider as true, already settled, etc.

Grant (grant), **Ulysses S**(**impson**) 1822-85; 18th president of the U.S. (1869-77): Union commander in the Civil War

grant′-in-aid′ ***n.***, *pl.* **grants′-in-aid′** a grant of funds, as by the Federal government, or by a foundation to a scientist, artist, etc., to support a specific project

grants′man·ship′ ***n.*** skill in acquiring grants-in-aid

gran·u·lar (gran′yoo lər) ***adj.*** **1** containing or consisting of grains **2** like grains or granules —**gran′u·lar′·i·ty** (-ler′ə tē) ***n.***

gran′u·late′ (-lāt′) ***vt.***, ***vi.*** **-lat′ed, -lat′ing** to form into grains or granules —**gran′u·la′·tion** ***n.***

gran·ule (gran′yool) ***n.*** ⟦< L *granum*, grain⟧ a small grain or particle

grape (grāp) ***n.*** ⟦< OFr *graper*, to gather with a hook⟧ **1** a small, round, juicy berry, growing in clusters on a woody vine **2** a grapevine **3** a dark purplish red

grape′fruit′ ***n.*** a large, round, sour citrus fruit with a yellow rind

grape hyacinth a small plant of the lily family, with spikes of small, blue or white, bell-shaped flowers

grape′shot′ ***n.*** a cluster of small iron balls, formerly fired from a cannon

grape′vine′ ***n.*** **1** a woody vine bearing grapes **2** a secret means of spreading information **3** a rumor

graph (graf) ***n.*** ⟦short for *graphic formula*⟧ a diagram representing the successive changes in a variable quantity or quantities —***vt.*** to represent by a graph

-graph (graf) ⟦< Gr *graphein*, to write⟧ *combining form* **1** something that writes or records [*telegraph*] **2** something written [*monograph*]

graph·ic (graf′ik) ***adj.*** ⟦< Gr *graphein*, to write⟧ **1** described in realistic detail; vivid **2** of those arts (**graphic arts**) that include any form of visual artistic representation, esp. painting, drawing, etching, etc. Also **graph′i·cal** —**graph′i·cal·ly** ***adv.***

graph′ics ***n.pl.*** [*with sing. v.*] **1** the graphic arts **2** design as employed in the graphic arts

graph·ite (graf′īt′) ***n.*** ⟦< Gr *graphein*, to write⟧ a soft, black form of carbon used in pencils, for lubricants, etc.

graph·ol·o·gy (graf äl′ə jē) ***n.*** ⟦< Fr: see GRAPHIC & -LOGY⟧ the study of handwriting, esp. as a clue to character —**graph·ol′o·gist** ***n.***

-gra·phy (grə fē) ⟦< Gr *graphein*, to write⟧ *combining form* **1** a process or method of writing, or graphically representing [*calligraphy*] **2** a descriptive science [*geography*]

grap·nel (grap′nəl) ***n.*** ⟦< Prov *grapa*, a hook⟧ **1** a small anchor with several curved, pointed arms **2** an iron bar with claws at one end for grasping things

grap·ple (grap′əl) ***n.*** ⟦OFr *grapil*⟧ **1** GRAPNEL (sense 2) **2** a hand-to-hand fight —***vt.*** **-pled, -pling** to grip and hold —***vi.*** **1** to use a GRAPNEL (sense 2) **2** to wrestle **3** to try to cope (*with*)

grappling iron (or **hook**) GRAPNEL (sense 2)

grasp (grasp) ***vt.*** ⟦ME *graspen*⟧ **1** to grip, as with the hand **2** to take hold of eagerly; seize **3** to comprehend —***vi.*** **1** to try to seize: with *at* **2** to accept eagerly: with *at* —***n.*** **1** a grasping; grip **2** control; possession **3** the power to hold or seize **4** comprehension —**grasp′a·ble** ***adj.***

grasp′ing ***adj.*** avaricious; greedy

grass (gras, gräs) ***n.*** ⟦OE *græs*⟧ **1** a plant

with long, narrow leaves, jointed stems, and seedlike fruit, as wheat, rye, etc. **2** any of various green plants with narrow leaves, growing densely in meadows, lawns, etc. **3** pasture or lawn **4** [Slang] marijuana —**grass'y, -i·er, -i·est,** *adj.*

grass'hop'per *n.* any of various winged, plant-eating insects with powerful hind legs for jumping

grass roots [Colloq.] **1** the common people **2** the basic source or support, as of a movement —**grass'-roots'** *adj.*

grass widow a woman divorced or separated from her husband

grate[1] (grāt) *vt.* **grat'ed, grat'ing** ⟦< OFr *grater*⟧ **1** to grind into particles by scraping **2** to rub against (an object) or grind (the teeth) together with a harsh sound **3** to irritate; annoy; fret —*vi.* **1** to rub with or make a rasping sound **2** to be irritating —**grat'er** *n.*

grate[2] (grāt) *n.* ⟦< L *cratis,* a hurdle⟧ **1** GRATING[1] **2** a frame of metal bars for holding fuel in a fireplace, etc. **3** a fireplace

grate·ful (grāt'fəl) *adj.* ⟦obs. *grate* (< L *gratus*), pleasing⟧ **1** thankful **2** welcome —**grate'ful·ly** *adv.* —**grate'ful·ness** *n.*

grat·i·fy (grat'i fī') *vt.* **-fied', -fy'ing** ⟦< L *gratus,* pleasing + *-ficare,* -FY⟧ **1** to please or satisfy **2** to indulge; humor —**grat'i·fi·ca'tion** *n.*

grat·ing[1] (grāt'iŋ) *n.* a framework of bars set in a window, door, etc.

grat'ing[2] *adj.* **1** rasping **2** irritating

gra·tis (grāt'is, grat'-) *adv., adj.* ⟦L < *gratia,* a favor⟧ free of charge

grat·i·tude (grat'i to͞od') *n.* ⟦< L *gratus,* pleasing⟧ thankful appreciation for favors received

gra·tu·i·tous (grə to͞o'i təs, -tyo͞o'-) *adj.* ⟦< L *gratus,* pleasing⟧ **1** given free of charge **2** uncalled-for —**gra·tu'i·tous·ly** *adv.*

gra·tu'i·ty (-tē) *n., pl.* **-ties** a gift of money, esp. for a service; tip

gra·va·men (grə vā'mən) *n., pl.* **-mens** or **gra·vam'i·na** (-vam'i nə) ⟦LL, a burden⟧ *Law* the essential part of a complaint or accusation

grave[1] (grāv) *adj.* **grav'er, grav'est** ⟦< L *gravis,* heavy⟧ **1** important **2** serious /a *grave* illness/ **3** solemn **4** somber; dull —**grave'ly** *adv.* —**grave'ness** *n.*

grave[2] (grāv) *n.* ⟦< OE *grafan,* to dig⟧ **1** *a)* a hole in the ground in which to bury a dead body *b)* any burial place; tomb **2** death —*vt.* **graved, grav'en** or **graved, grav'ing** **1** [Archaic] to sculpture or engrave **2** to impress sharply

grave accent a mark (`) showing the quality of a vowel, stress, etc.

grav·el (grav'əl) *n.* ⟦< OFr *grave,* coarse sand⟧ a loose mixture of pebbles and rock fragments coarser than sand

grav'el·ly (-ē) *adj.* **1** full of or like gravel **2** harsh or rasping

grav·en (grāv'ən) *vt. alt. pp. of* GRAVE[2]

grave'stone' *n.* a tombstone

grave'yard' *n.* a cemetery

graveyard shift [Colloq.] a night work shift, esp. one starting at midnight

grav·id (grav'id) *adj.* ⟦< L *gravis,* heavy⟧ pregnant

gra·vim·e·ter (grə vim'ət ər) *n.* ⟦< L *gravis,* heavy + Fr *-mètre,* -METER⟧ **1** a device for determining specific gravity **2** an instrument for measuring the earth's gravitational pull

grav·i·tate (grav'i tāt') *vi.* **-tat'ed, -tat'ing** **1** to move or tend to move in accordance with the force of gravity **2** to be attracted (*toward*)

grav'i·ta'tion *n.* **1** a gravitating **2** *Physics* the force by which every mass attracts and is attracted by every other mass —**grav'i·ta'tion·al** *adj.*

grav·i·ty (grav'i tē) *n., pl.* **-ties** ⟦< L *gravis,* heavy⟧ **1** graveness; seriousness **2** weight /specific *gravity*/ **3** *Physics* gravitation; esp., the pull on all bodies in the earth's sphere toward the earth's center

gra·vy (grā'vē) *n., pl.* **-vies** ⟦< ?⟧ **1** the juice given off by meat in cooking **2** a sauce made from this juice **3** [Slang] any benefit beyond that expected

gray (grā) *n.* ⟦< OE *græg*⟧ a color that is a blend of black and white —*adj.* **1** of this color **2** having hair this color **3** *a)* darkish *b)* dreary **4** designating a vague, intermediate area —*vt., vi.* to make or become gray —**gray'ish** *adj.* —**gray'ness** *n.*

gray'beard' *n.* an old man

gray matter **1** grayish nerve tissue of the brain and spinal cord **2** [Colloq.] intellectual capacity; brains

graze[1] (grāz) *vt.* **grazed, graz'ing** ⟦< OE *græs,* grass⟧ **1** to put livestock to feed on (growing grass, etc.) **2** to tend (feeding livestock) —*vi.* to feed on growing grass, etc.

graze[2] (grāz) *vt., vi.* **grazed, graz'ing** ⟦prob. < prec.⟧ to scrape or rub lightly in passing —*n.* a grazing

Gr. Brit. or **Gr. Br.** Great Britain

grease (grēs; *for v., also* grēz) *n.* ⟦< L *crassus,* fat⟧ **1** melted animal fat **2** any thick, oily substance or lubricant —*vt.* **greased, greas'ing** to smear or lubricate with grease

grease'paint' *n.* greasy coloring matter used in making up for the stage

greas·y (grē'sē, -zē) *adj.* **-i·er, -i·est** **1** soiled with grease **2** containing or like grease; oily —**greas'i·ness** *n.*

great (grāt) *adj.* ⟦OE⟧ **1** of much more than ordinary size, extent, etc. /the *Great* Lakes/ **2** much above the average; esp., *a)* intense /*great* pain/ *b)* eminent /a *great* writer/ **3** most important; main **4** designating a relationship one generation removed /*great*-grandparent/ **5** [Colloq.] skillful: often with *at* **6** [Colloq.] excellent; fine —*n.* a distinguished person —**great'ly** *adv.* —**great'ness** *n.*

great ape any of a family of primates consisting of the gorilla, chimpanzee, and orangutan

Great Britain principal island of the United Kingdom, including England, Scotland, & Wales

Great Dane a very large, muscular dog with a short, smooth coat

great'-grand'child' *n.* a child of any of one's grandchildren

great'-grand'par'ent *n.* a parent of any of one's grandparents

great'heart'ed *adj.* **1** brave; fearless **2** generous; unselfish

Great Lakes chain of five freshwater lakes in east central North America

Great Salt Lake shallow saltwater lake in NW Utah

grebe (grēb) *n.* ⟦Fr *grèbe*⟧ a diving and swimming bird with broadly lobed webbed feet

Gre·cian (grē′shən) *adj., n.* GREEK

Greco- ⟦< L *Graecus*⟧ *combining form* Greek, Greek and /*Greco*-Roman/

Greece (grēs) country in the S Balkan Peninsula, on the Mediterranean: 50,949 sq. mi.; pop. 9,900,000

greed (grēd) *n.* ⟦< fol.⟧ excessive desire, esp. for wealth; avarice

greed·y (grēd′ē) *adj.* **-i·er, -i·est** ⟦OE *grædig*⟧ **1** desiring more than one needs or deserves **2** having too strong a desire for food and drink; gluttonous —**greed′i·ly** *adv.* —**greed′i·ness** *n.*

Greek (grēk) *n.* **1** a native or inhabitant of Greece **2** the language, ancient or modern, of the Greeks —*adj.* of Greece

green (grēn) *adj.* ⟦OE *grene*⟧ **1** of the color of growing grass **2** overspread with green plants or foliage **3** sickly or bilious **4** unripe **5** inexperienced or naive **6** not dried or seasoned **7** [Colloq.] jealous —*n.* **1** the color of growing grass **2** [*pl.*] green leafy vegetables, as spinach, etc. **3** an area of smooth turf /a putting *green*/ —**green′ish** *adj.* —**green′ness** *n.*

green′back′ *n.* any piece of U.S. paper money printed in green ink on the back

green bean the edible, immature green pod of the kidney bean

green′belt′ *n.* a beltlike area around a city, reserved for park land or farms

green′er·y *n., pl.* **-er·ies** green vegetation; verdure

green′-eyed′ *adj.* very jealous

green′gro′cer (-grō′sər) *n.* [Brit.] a retail dealer in fresh vegetables and fruit

green′horn′ *n.* **1** an inexperienced person **2** a person easily deceived

green′house′ *n.* a heated building, mainly of glass, for growing plants

greenhouse effect the warming of the earth and its lower atmosphere, caused by trapped solar radiation

Green·land (grēn′lənd) self-governing Danish island northeast of North America

green manure a crop, as of clover, plowed under to fertilize the soil

green onion an immature onion with green leaves, often eaten raw; scallion

green pepper the green, immature fruit of a red pepper, esp. the bell pepper

green power money, as the source of economic power

Greens·bor·o (grēnz′bur′ō) city in N N.C.: pop. 156,000

green′sward′ (-swôrd′) *n.* green, grassy turf

green thumb a talent for growing plants

Green·wich (gren′ich; *chiefly Brit,* grin′ij) borough of London, on the prime meridian: pop. 216,000

Green·wich Village (gren′ich) section of New York City: noted as a center for artists, writers, etc.

green′wood′ *n.* a forest in leaf

greet (grēt) *vt.* ⟦OE *gretan*⟧ **1** to address with friendliness **2** to meet or receive (a person, event, etc.) in a specified way **3** to come or appear to

greet′ing *n.* **1** the act or words of one who greets **2** [*often pl.*] a message of regards

gre·gar·i·ous (grə ger′ē əs) *adj.* ⟦< L *grex,* herd⟧ **1** living in herds **2** fond of the company of others; sociable

Gregorian calendar (grə gôr′ē ən) the calendar now widely used, introduced by Pope Gregory XIII in 1582

grem·lin (grem′lin) *n.* ⟦prob. < Dan *gram,* a devil⟧ a small imaginary creature humorously blamed for the disruption of any procedure

Gre·na·da (grə nā′də) country on an island in the West Indies: 133 sq. mi.; pop. 92,000

gre·nade (grə nād′) *n.* ⟦Fr < OFr, pomegranate⟧ a small bomb detonated by a fuse and usually thrown by hand

gren·a·dier (gren′ə dir′) *n.* **1** orig., a soldier who threw grenades **2** a member of a special regiment

gren·a·dine (gren′ə dēn′) *n.* ⟦Fr⟧ a red syrup made from pomegranate juice

grew (gro͞o) *vi., vt. pt. of* GROW

grey (grā) *adj., n., vt., vi. Brit. sp. of* GRAY

GREYHOUND

grey′hound′ *n.* a tall, slender, swift dog with a narrow head

grid (grid) *n.* ⟦short for GRIDIRON⟧ **1** a gridiron or grating **2** a metallic plate in a storage battery **3** an electrode, as of wire mesh, for controlling the flow of electrons in an electron tube

grid·dle (grid′'l) *n.* ⟦< L *craticula,* gridiron⟧ a heavy, flat, metal pan for cooking pancakes, etc.

grid′dle·cake′ *n.* a pancake

grid·i·ron (grid′ī′ərn) *n.* ⟦see GRIDDLE⟧ **1** a framework of metal bars or wires for broiling **2** anything resembling this, as a football field

grid′lock′ *n.* a traffic jam in which no vehicle can move in any direction

grief (grēf) *n.* ⟦see GRIEVE⟧ **1** intense emotional suffering caused as by a loss **2** a cause of such suffering —**come to grief** to fail or be ruined

griev·ance (grēv′əns) *n.* **1** a circumstance thought to be unjust and ground for complaint **2** complaint against a real or imagined wrong

grieve (grēv) *vi., vt.* **grieved, griev′ing** ⟦< L *gravis,* heavy⟧ to feel or cause to feel grief

griev·ous (grēv′əs) *adj.* **1** causing grief **2** showing or full of grief **3** severe **4** deplorable; atrocious

grif·fin (grif′in) *n.* ⟦< Gr⟧ a mythical monster, part lion and part eagle

grill (gril) *n.* ⟦see GRIDDLE⟧ **1** a griddle **2** grilled food **3** a restaurant that specializes in grilled foods —*vt.* **1** to broil **2** to question relentlessly

grille (gril) *n.* ⟦see GRIDDLE⟧ an open grating forming a screen

grim (grim) *adj.* **grim′mer, grim′mest** ⟦OE

grimm ⟧ 1 hard and unyielding; stern 2 appearing forbidding, harsh, etc. 3 repellent; ghastly —**grim'ly** ***adv.*** —**grim'ness** ***n.***

gri·mace (gri mās', grim'is) ***n.*** ⟦ Fr ⟧ a distortion of the face, as in expressing pain, disgust, etc. —***vi.*** **-maced', -mac'ing** to make grimaces

grime (grīm) ***n.*** ⟦ prob. < Fl *grijm* ⟧ dirt rubbed into a surface, as of the skin —**grim'y, -i·er, -i·est,** ***adj.***

Grimm (grim) **1 Ja·kob (Ludwig Karl)** (yä'kôp) 1785-1863; Ger. philologist **2 Wil·helm (Karl)** (vil'helm) 1786-1859; Ger. philologist: brother of Jakob, with whom he collected fairy tales

grin (grin) ***vi.*** **grinned, grin'ning** ⟦ < OE *grennian,* bare the teeth ⟧ 1 to smile broadly as in amusement 2 to show the teeth in pain, scorn, etc. —***n.*** the act or look of grinning

grind (grīnd) ***vt.*** **ground, grind'ing** ⟦ OE *grindan* ⟧ 1 to crush into fine particles; pulverize 2 to oppress 3 to sharpen or smooth by friction 4 to rub (the teeth, etc.) together gratingly 5 to operate by turning the crank of —***n.*** 1 a grinding 2 long, difficult work or study 3 [Colloq.] a student who studies hard —**grind out** to produce by steady or laborious effort

grind·er (grīn'dər) ***n.*** 1 a person or thing that grinds 2 [*pl.*] [Colloq.] the teeth 3 HERO SANDWICH

grind'stone' ***n.*** a revolving stone disk for sharpening tools or polishing things —**keep one's nose to the grindstone** to work hard and steadily

grip (grip) ***n.*** ⟦ < OE *gripan,* seize ⟧ 1 a secure grasp; firm hold 2 the manner of holding a club, bat, etc. 3 the power of grasping firmly 4 mental grasp 5 firm control; mastery 6 a handle 7 a small traveling bag —***vt.*** **gripped** or **gript, grip'ping** 1 to take firmly and hold fast 2 to get and hold the attention of —***vi.*** to get a grip —**come to grips** to struggle (*with*) —**grip'per** ***n.***

gripe (grīp) ***vt.*** **griped, grip'ing** ⟦ OE *grīpan,* seize ⟧ 1 [Archaic] to distress 2 to cause sharp pain in the bowels of 3 [Slang] to annoy —***vi.*** [Slang] to complain —***n.*** 1 a sharp pain in the bowels: *usually used in pl.* 2 [Slang] a complaint —**grip'er** ***n.***

grippe (grip) ***n.*** ⟦ Fr ⟧ INFLUENZA

gris-gris (grē'grē') ***n.,*** *pl.* **gris'-gris'** ⟦ of Afr orig. ⟧ an amulet, charm, or spell associated with voodoo

gris·ly (griz'lē) ***adj.*** **-li·er, -li·est** ⟦ OE *grislic* ⟧ terrifying; ghastly —**gris'li·ness** ***n.***

grist (grist) ***n.*** ⟦ OE ⟧ grain that is to be or has been ground

gris·tle (gris'əl) ***n.*** ⟦ OE ⟧ cartilage, esp. as found in meat —**gris'tly** (-lē) ***adj.***

grist'mill' ***n.*** a mill for grinding grain

grit (grit) ***n.*** ⟦ < OE *greot* ⟧ 1 rough particles, as of sand 2 coarse sandstone 3 stubborn courage; pluck —***vt.*** **grit'ted, grit'ting** to grind (the teeth) as in determination —***vi.*** to make a grating sound —**grit'ty, -ti·er, -ti·est,** ***adj.***

grits (grits) ***n.pl.*** ⟦ OE *grytte* ⟧ [*often with sing. v.*] coarsely ground grain

griz·zled (griz'əld) ***adj.*** ⟦ < OFr *gris,* gray ⟧ 1 gray or streaked with gray 2 having gray hair

griz'zly (-lē) ***adj.*** **-zli·er, -zli·est** grayish; grizzled

grizzly (bear) a large, ferocious, brown or grayish bear of W North America

groan (grōn) ***vi., vt.*** ⟦ < OE *granian* ⟧ to utter (with) a deep sound expressing pain, distress, etc. —***n.*** such a sound

gro·cer (grō'sər) ***n.*** ⟦ < OFr *grossier* ⟧ a dealer in food and household supplies

gro'cer·y ***n.,*** *pl.* **-ies** 1 a grocer's store 2 [*pl.*] the food and supplies sold by a grocer

grog (gräg) ***n.*** ⟦ after Old *Grog,* nickname of an 18th-c. Brit admiral ⟧ 1 rum diluted with water 2 any alcoholic liquor

grog'gy ***adj.*** **-gi·er, -gi·est** ⟦ < prec. + -Y[2] ⟧ 1 orig., intoxicated 2 dizzy 3 sluggish or dull —**grog'gi·ness** ***n.***

groin (groin) ***n.*** ⟦ prob. < OE *grynde,* abyss ⟧ 1 the fold where the abdomen joins either thigh 2 *Archit.* the sharp, curved edge at the junction of two vaults

grom·met (gräm'it) ***n.*** ⟦ < obs. Fr *gromette,* a curb ⟧ 1 a ring of rope 2 a metal eyelet in cloth, etc.

groom (groom, groom) ***n.*** ⟦ ME *grom,* boy ⟧ 1 one whose work is tending horses 2 a bridegroom —***vt.*** 1 to clean and curry (a horse, etc.) 2 to make neat and tidy 3 to train for a particular purpose

groove (groov) ***n.*** ⟦ < ON *grof,* a pit ⟧ 1 a long, narrow furrow cut with a tool 2 any channel or rut 3 a settled routine —***vt.*** **grooved, groov'ing** to make a groove in

groov'y ***adj.*** **-i·er, -i·est** [Slang] very pleasing or attractive

grope (grōp) ***vi.*** **groped, grop'ing** ⟦ < OE *grapian,* to touch ⟧ to feel or search about blindly or uncertainly —***vt.*** to seek or find (one's way) by groping —**grop'er** ***n.*** —**grop'ing·ly** ***adv.***

gros·beak (grōs'bēk') ***n.*** ⟦ Fr: see GROSS & BEAK ⟧ a songbird with a thick, strong, conical bill

gros·grain (grō'grān') ***n.*** ⟦ Fr, lit., coarse grain ⟧ a ribbed silk or rayon fabric for ribbons, etc.

gross (grōs) ***adj.*** ⟦ < LL *grossus,* thick ⟧ 1 fat and coarse-looking; burly 2 flagrant; very bad 3 dense; thick 4 lacking in refinement 5 vulgar; coarse 6 with no deductions; total —***n.*** 1 *pl.* **gross'es** overall total 2 *pl.* **gross** twelve dozen —***vt., vi.*** to earn (a specified total amount) before expenses are deducted —**gross'ly** ***adv.***

gross national product the total value of a nation's annual output of goods and services

gro·tesque (grō tesk') ***adj.*** ⟦ < It *grotta,* grotto: from designs found in caves ⟧ 1 distorted or fantastic in appearance, shape, etc. 2 ridiculous; absurd —**gro·tesque'ly** ***adv.***

grot·to (grät'ō) ***n.,*** *pl.* **-toes** or **-tos** ⟦ < It < L *crypta,* crypt ⟧ 1 a cave 2 a cavelike summerhouse, shrine, etc.

grouch (grouch) ***vi.*** ⟦ < ME *gruchen* ⟧ to grumble or complain sulkily —***n.*** 1 one who grouches 2 a sulky mood —**grouch'y, -i·er, -i·est,** ***adj.***

ground[1] (ground) ***n.*** ⟦ OE *grund,* bottom ⟧ 1 the solid surface of the earth 2 soil; earth

3 [*often pl.*] a tract of land /*grounds* of an estate/ 4 area, as of discussion 5 [*often pl.*] *a*) basis; foundation *b*) valid reason or motive 6 the background, as in a design 7 [*pl.*] sediment /coffee *grounds*/ 8 the connection of an electrical conductor with the ground —***adj.*** of, on, or near the ground —***vt.*** 1 to set on the ground 2 to cause to run aground 3 to base; found; establish 4 to instruct in the first principles of 5 *a*) to keep (an aircraft or pilot) from flying *b*) [Colloq.] to punish (a teenager) by not permitting him or her to leave home for dates, etc. 6 *Elec.* to connect (a conductor) with the ground —***vi.*** 1 to run ashore 2 *Baseball* to be put out on a grounder: usually with *out* —**break ground** 1 to dig; excavate 2 to plow 3 to start building —**gain (or lose) ground** to gain (or lose) in achievement, popularity, etc. —**give ground** to retreat; yield — **hold** (or **stand**) **one's ground** to remain firm, not yielding

ground[2] (ground) ***vt., vi. pt. & pp. of*** GRIND

ground control personnel and equipment on the ground, for guiding airplanes and spacecraft in takeoff, landing, etc.

ground cover low, dense-growing plants used for covering bare ground

ground crew a group of workers who maintain and repair aircraft

ground'er ***n.*** *Baseball* a batted ball that travels along the ground

ground floor that floor of a building approximately level with the ground; first floor —**in on the ground floor** [Colloq.] in at the start (of a business, etc.)

ground glass nontransparent glass, whose surface has been ground to diffuse light

ground'hog' ***n.*** WOODCHUCK

ground'less ***adj.*** without reason or cause

ground rule 1 *Baseball* a rule adapted to playing conditions in a specific ballpark 2 any basic rule

ground swell 1 a violent rolling of the ocean 2 a wave of popular feeling: usually **ground'swell'**

ground'work' ***n.*** a foundation; basis

group (gro͞op) ***n.*** ⟦< It *gruppo*⟧ a number of persons or things gathered or classified together —***vt., vi.*** to form into a group or groups

grou·per (gro͞o'pər) ***n.*** ⟦Port *garupa*⟧ a large sea bass found in warm seas

group·ie (gro͞op'ē) ***n.*** [Colloq.] a female fan of rock groups or other popular personalities, who follows them about

group therapy (or **psychotherapy**) a form of treatment for a group of patients with similar emotional problems, as by mutual criticism

grouse[1] (grous) ***n., pl.*** **grouse** ⟦< ?⟧ a game bird with a round, plump body, feathered legs, and mottled feathers

grouse[2] (grous) ***vi.*** **groused, grous'ing** ⟦< ?⟧ [Colloq.] to complain

grout (grout) ***n.*** ⟦ME⟧ a thin mortar used as between tiles

grove (grōv) ***n.*** ⟦< OE *graf*⟧ a group of trees, without undergrowth

grov·el (gruv'əl, gräv'-) ***vi.*** **-eled** or **-elled, -el·ing** or **-el·ling** ⟦< ME *grufelinge*, down on one's face⟧ 1 to lie or crawl in a prostrate position, esp. abjectly 2 to behave abjectly —**grov'el·er** or **grov'el·ler** ***n.***

grow (grō) ***vi.*** **grew, grown, grow'ing** ⟦< OE *growan*⟧ 1 to come into being or be produced naturally 2 to develop or thrive, as a living thing 3 to increase in size, quantity, etc. 4 to become /to *grow* weary/ —***vt.*** to cause to or let grow; raise; cultivate —**grow on** [Colloq.] to have an increasing effect on —**grow up** to mature —**grow'er** ***n.***

growl (groul) ***n.*** ⟦ME *groulen*⟧ a rumbling, menacing sound such as an angry dog makes —***vi., vt.*** to make, or express by, such a sound

grown (grōn) ***vi., vt. pp. of*** GROW —***adj.*** having completed its growth; mature

grown'-up' ***adj., n.*** adult Also, for ***n.***, **grown'up'**

growth (grōth) ***n.*** 1 a growing or developing 2 *a*) increase in size, etc. *b*) the full extent of this 3 something that grows or has grown 4 a tumor or other abnormal mass of tissue

grub (grub) ***vi.*** **grubbed, grub'bing** ⟦ME *grubben*⟧ 1 to dig in the ground 2 to work hard —***vt.*** 1 to clear (ground) of roots 2 to uproot —***n.*** 1 a wormlike larva, esp. of a beetle 2 a drudge 3 [Slang] food

grub'by ***adj.*** **-bi·er, -bi·est** dirty; untidy —**grub'bi·ness** ***n.***

grub'stake' (-stāk') ***n.*** ⟦GRUB, *n.* 3 + STAKE⟧ [Colloq.] money or supplies advanced, as to a prospector

grudge (gruj) ***vt.*** **grudged, grudg'ing** ⟦< OFr *grouchier*⟧ 1 BEGRUDGE 2 to give with reluctance —***n.*** resentment or ill will over some grievance —**grudg'ing·ly** ***adv.***

gru·el (gro͞o'əl) ***n.*** ⟦< ML *grutum*, meal⟧ thin porridge made by cooking meal in water or milk

gru'el·ing or **gru'el·ling** ***adj.*** ⟦prp. of obs. v. *gruel*, punish⟧ extremely trying; exhausting

grue·some (gro͞o'səm) ***adj.*** ⟦< dial. *grue*, to shudder + -SOME[1]⟧ causing horror or disgust; grisly

gruff (gruf) ***adj.*** ⟦< Du *grof*⟧ 1 rough or surly 2 harsh and throaty; hoarse —**gruff'ly** ***adv.*** —**gruff'ness** ***n.***

grum·ble (grum'bəl) ***vi.*** **-bled, -bling** ⟦prob. < Du *grommelen*⟧ 1 to growl 2 to mutter in discontent 3 to rumble —***vt.*** to express by grumbling —***n.*** a grumbling —**grum'bler** ***n.***

grump·y (grum'pē) ***adj.*** **-i·er, -i·est** ⟦prob. echoic⟧ grouchy; peevish

grun·gy (grun'jē) ***adj.*** **-gi·er, -gi·est** [Slang] dirty, messy, etc.

grun·ion (gro͞on'yən) ***n.*** ⟦prob. < Sp *gruñón*, grumbler⟧ a fish of the California coast: it spawns on sandy beaches

grunt (grunt) ***vi., vt.*** ⟦< OE *grunian*⟧ to utter (with) the deep, hoarse sound of a hog —***n.*** this sound

Gru·yère (cheese) (gro͞o yer', grē-) ⟦after *Gruyère*, Switzerland⟧ [*often* **g- c-**] a light-yellow Swiss cheese, rich in butterfat

Guam (gwäm) island in the W Pacific: an unincorporated territory of the U.S.

Guang·zhou (guäŋ'jō) seaport in SE China: pop. 3,120,000

gua·nine (gwä'nēn') ***n.*** ⟦< fol. + -INE[3]⟧ a

crystalline base contained in the nucleic acids of all tissue

gua·no (gwä′nō) *n., pl.* **-nos** ⟦Sp < AmInd (Peru)⟧ manure of sea birds, used as fertilizer

guar·an·tee (gar′ən tē′) *n.* 1 GUARANTY (sense 1) 2 *a)* a pledge to replace something if it is not as represented *b)* an assurance that something will be done as specified 3 a guarantor —*vt.* **-teed′**, **-tee′ing** 1 to give a guarantee for 2 to promise

guar·an·tor (gar′ən tôr′) *n.* one who gives a guaranty or guarantee

guar′an·ty (-tē) *n., pl.* **-ties** ⟦< OFr *garant*, a warrant⟧ 1 a pledge or security for another's debt or obligation 2 an agreement that secures the existence or maintenance of something

guard (gärd) *vt.* ⟦< OFr *garder*⟧ 1 to watch over and protect; defend 2 to keep from escape or trouble —*vi.* 1 to keep watch (*against*) 2 to act as a guard —*n.* 1 defense; protection 2 a posture of readiness for defense 3 any device to protect against injury or loss 4 a person or group that guards 5 *Basketball* either of two players who are the main ball handlers 6 *Football* either of the two players next to the center —**on (one's) guard** vigilant

guard′ed *adj.* 1 kept safe 2 cautious /a *guarded* reply/ —**guard′ed·ly** *adv.*

guard′house′ *n. Mil.* 1 a building used by a guard when not walking a post 2 a jail for temporary confinement

guard′i·an (-ē ən) *n.* 1 one who guards or protects; custodian 2 a person legally in charge of the affairs of a minor or of a person of unsound mind —*adj.* protecting —**guard′i·an·ship′** *n.*

guard′rail′ *n.* a protective railing, as on a staircase

Gua·te·ma·la (gwä′tə mä′lə) country in Central America: 42,042 sq. mi.; pop. 8,335,000

gua·va (gwä′və) *n.* ⟦< native name⟧ a yellow, pear-shaped, tropical American fruit

gu·ber·na·to·ri·al (go͞o′bər nə tôr′ē əl) *adj.* ⟦L *gubernator*, governor⟧ of a governor or the office of governor

Guern·sey (gurn′zē) *n., pl.* **-seys** ⟦after *Guernsey*, one of the Channel Islands⟧ a breed of dairy cattle, usually fawn-colored with white markings

guer·ril·la or **gue·ril·la** (gə ril′ə) *n.* ⟦Sp, dim. of *guerra*, war⟧ a member of a small defensive force of irregular soldiers, making surprise raids

guess (ges) *vt., vi.* ⟦ME *gessen*⟧ 1 to form a judgment or estimate of (something) without actual knowledge; surmise 2 to judge correctly by doing this 3 to think or suppose —*n.* 1 a guessing 2 something guessed; conjecture

guess′work′ *n.* 1 a guessing 2 a judgment, result, etc. arrived at by guessing

guest (gest) *n.* ⟦< ON *gestr*⟧ 1 a person entertained at the home, club, etc. of another 2 any paying customer of a hotel, restaurant, etc. —*adj.* 1 for guests 2 performing by special invitation /a *guest* artist/

guff (guf) *n.* ⟦echoic⟧ [Slang] 1 nonsense 2 brash or insolent talk

guf·faw (gu fô′) *n.* ⟦echoic⟧ a loud, coarse burst of laughter —*vi.* to laugh in this way

guid·ance (gīd′′ns) *n.* 1 a guiding; leadership 2 advice or assistance

guide (gīd) *vt.* **guid′ed**, **guid′ing** ⟦< OFr *guider*⟧ 1 to point out the way for; lead 2 to direct the course of; control —*n.* 1 one whose work is conducting tours, etc. 2 a controlling device 3 a book of basic instruction

guide′book′ *n.* a book containing directions and information for tourists

guided missile a military missile whose course is controlled by radar, etc.

guide′line′ *n.* a principle by which to determine a course of action

guild (gild) *n.* ⟦< OE *gieldan*, to pay⟧ an association for mutual aid and the promotion of common interests

guil·der (gil′dər) *n.* ⟦< MDu *gulden*, golden⟧ the monetary unit of the Netherlands

guile (gīl) *n.* ⟦< OFr⟧ slyness and cunning in dealing with others —**guile′ful** *adj.* —**guile′less** *adj.*

guil·lo·tine (gil′ə tēn′; *for v., usually* gil′ə tēn′) *n.* ⟦Fr: after J. *Guillotin* (1738-1814), Fr physician who advocated its use⟧ an instrument for beheading, having a heavy blade dropped between two grooved uprights —*vt.* **-tined′**, **-tin′ing** to behead with a guillotine

guilt (gilt) *n.* ⟦OE *gylt*, a sin⟧ 1 the state of having done a wrong or committed an offense 2 a feeling of self-reproach from believing that one has done a wrong —**guilt′less** *adj.*

guilt′y *adj.* **-i·er**, **-i·est** 1 having guilt 2 legally judged an offender 3 of or showing guilt /a *guilty* look/ —**guilt′i·ly** *adv.* —**guilt′i·ness** *n.*

guin·ea (gin′ē) *n.* ⟦first coined of gold from *Guinea*⟧ a former English gold coin equal to 21 shillings

Guin·ea (gin′ē) country on the W coast of Africa: 94,925 sq. mi.; pop. 5,400,000

Guin′ea-Bis·sau′ (-bi sou′) country on the W coast of Africa: 13,948 sq. mi.; pop. 859,000

guinea fowl (or **hen**) ⟦orig. imported from *Guinea*⟧ a domestic fowl with a rounded body and speckled feathers

guinea pig ⟦prob. orig. brought to England by ships plying between England, *Guinea*, and South America⟧ 1 a small, fat rodent used in biological experiments 2 any subject used in an experiment

guise (gīz) *n.* ⟦< OHG *wisa*, manner⟧ 1 manner of dress; garb 2 semblance 3 a false appearance; pretense

gui·tar (gi tär′) *n.* ⟦ult. < Gr *kithara*, lyre⟧ a musical instrument with usually six strings plucked with the fingers or a plectrum —**gui·tar′ist** *n.*

gulch (gulch) *n.* ⟦prob. < dial., to swallow greedily⟧ a deep, narrow ravine

gulf (gulf) *n.* ⟦ult. < Gr *kolpos*, bosom⟧ 1 a large area of ocean reaching into land 2 a wide, deep chasm 3 a wide gap or separation

Gulf Stream warm ocean current flowing from the Gulf of Mexico northward toward Europe

gull[1] (gul) ***n.*** ⟦< Celt⟧ a white and gray water bird with webbed feet

gull[2] (gul) ***n.*** ⟦ME, lit., unfledged bird⟧ a person easily tricked; dupe —***vt.*** to cheat or trick

gul·let (gul′ət) ***n.*** ⟦< L *gula*, throat⟧ **1** the esophagus **2** the throat

gul·li·ble (gul′ə bəl) ***adj.*** easily gulled; credulous —**gul′li·bil′i·ty** ***n.***

gul·ly (gul′ē) ***n.***, *pl.* **-lies** ⟦see GULLET⟧ a small, narrow ravine

gulp (gulp) ***vt.***, ***vi.*** ⟦prob. < Du *gulpen*⟧ **1** to swallow hastily or greedily **2** to choke back as if swallowing —***n.*** a gulping or swallowing

gum[1] (gum) ***n.*** ⟦< LL *gumma*⟧ **1** a sticky substance found in certain trees and plants **2** an adhesive **3** CHEWING GUM —***vt.*** **gummed, gum′ming** to coat or unite with gum —***vi.*** to become sticky or clogged —**gum up** [Slang] to cause to go awry —**gum′my, -mi·er, -mi·est,** ***adj.***

gum[2] (gum) ***n.*** ⟦OE *goma*⟧ [*often pl.*] the firm flesh surrounding the base of the teeth —***vt.*** **gummed, gum′ming** to chew with toothless gums

gum arabic a gum from certain acacias, used in medicine, candy, etc.

gum·bo (gum′bō) ***n.*** ⟦< Bantu name for okra⟧ a soup thickened with okra

gum′drop′ ***n.*** a small, firm candy made of sweetened gelatin, etc.

gump·tion (gump′shən) ***n.*** ⟦< Scot⟧ [Colloq.] initiative; enterprise

gun (gun) ***n.*** ⟦< ME *gonnilde*, cannon < ON⟧ **1** a weapon with a metal tube from which a projectile is discharged by the force of an explosive **2** any similar device not discharged by an explosive /an air *gun*/ **3** anything like a gun —***vi.*** **gunned, gun′ning** to shoot or hunt with a gun —***vt.*** **1** [Colloq.] to shoot (a person) **2** [Slang] to advance the throttle of (an engine) —**gun for** [Slang] to try to get —**jump the gun** [Colloq.] to begin before the proper time —**stick to one's guns** [Colloq.] to stand fast; be firm —**under the gun** [Colloq.] in a tense situation, often one involving a deadline

gun′boat′ ***n.*** a small armed ship

gun′fight′ ***n.*** a fight between persons using pistols or revolvers

gun′fire′ ***n.*** the firing of guns

gung-ho (guŋ′hō′) ***adj.*** ⟦Chin *kung-ho*, lit., work together⟧ [Colloq.] enthusiastic

gunk (guŋk) ***n.*** ⟦< ?⟧ [Slang] a viscous or thick, messy substance

gun′man ***n.***, *pl.* **-men** an armed gangster or hired killer

gun′met′al ***n.*** **1** a bronze with a dark tarnish **2** its dark-gray color

gun′ner ***n.*** **1** a soldier, etc. who helps fire artillery **2** a naval warrant officer in charge of guns, missiles, etc.

gun′ner·y ***n.*** the science of making and using heavy guns and projectiles

gun·ny (gun′ē) ***n.***, *pl.* **-nies** ⟦< Sans *gōṇī*, a sack⟧ a coarse fabric of jute or hemp

gun′ny·sack′ ***n.*** a sack made of gunny

gun′play′ ***n.*** an exchange of gunshots, as between gunmen and police

gun′pow′der ***n.*** an explosive powder used in guns, for blasting, etc.

gun′ship′ ***n.*** a heavily armed helicopter used to assault enemy ground forces

gun′shot′ ***n.*** shot fired from a gun

gun′-shy′ ***adj.*** easily frightened at the firing of a gun /a *gun-shy* dog/

gun′smith′ ***n.*** one who makes or repairs small guns

gun·wale (gun′əl) ***n.*** ⟦< bulwarks supporting a ship's guns⟧ the upper edge of the side of a ship or boat

gup·py (gup′ē) ***n.***, *pl.* **-pies** ⟦after R. J. L. *Guppy*, of Trinidad⟧ a tiny freshwater fish of the West Indies, etc.

gur·gle (gur′gəl) ***vi.*** **-gled, -gling** ⟦< L *gurgulio*, gullet⟧ to make a bubbling sound —***n.*** such a sound

gu·ru (go͞o′ro͞o′, go͞o ro͞o′) ***n.*** ⟦< Sans *guruḥ*, venerable⟧ in Hinduism, one's personal spiritual advisor or teacher

gush (gush) ***vi.*** ⟦ME *guschen*⟧ **1** to flow out plentifully **2** to have a sudden flow **3** to talk or write effusively —***vt.*** to cause to gush —***n.*** a gushing —**gush′y, -i·er, -i·est,** ***adj.***

gush′er ***n.*** **1** one who gushes **2** an oil well from which oil spouts forth

gus·set (gus′it) ***n.*** ⟦< OFr *gousset*⟧ a triangular piece inserted in a garment, etc. to make it stronger or roomier

gus·sy or **gus·sie** (gus′ē) ***vt.***, ***vi.*** **-sied, -sy·ing** [Slang] to dress (*up*) in a fine or showy way

gust (gust) ***n.*** ⟦< ON *gjosa*, to gush⟧ **1** a sudden, strong rush of air **2** a sudden outburst of rain, laughter, etc. —**gust′y, -i·er, -i·est,** ***adj.***

gus·ta·to·ry (gus′tə tôr′ē) ***adj.*** ⟦< L *gustus*, taste⟧ of the sense of taste

gus·to (gus′tō) ***n.*** ⟦see prec.⟧ **1** zest; relish **2** great vigor or liveliness

gut (gut) ***n.*** ⟦< OE *geotan*, to pour⟧ **1** [*pl.*] the bowels or the stomach **2** the intestine **3** tough cord made from animal intestines **4** [*pl.*] [Colloq.] daring; courage —***vt.*** **gut′ted, gut′ting** **1** to remove the intestines from **2** to destroy the interior of —***adj.*** [Slang] **1** basic **2** easy; simple

gut′less ***adj.*** [Colloq.] lacking courage

guts·y (gut′sē) ***adj.*** **-i·er, -i·est** [Colloq.] courageous, forceful, etc.

gut·ter (gut′ər) ***n.*** ⟦< L *gutta*, a drop⟧ a channel to carry off water, as along the eaves of a roof or the side of a street —***vi.*** to flow in a stream

gut·tur·al (gut′ər əl) ***adj.*** ⟦L *guttur*, throat⟧ **1** of the throat **2** produced in the throat; rasping

guy[1] (gī) ***n.*** ⟦< OFr *guier*, to guide⟧ a rope, chain, etc. used to steady or guide something —***vt.*** to guide or steady with a guy

guy[2] (gī) ***n.*** ⟦after *Guy* Fawkes, Eng conspirator⟧ [Slang] **1** a man or boy **2** any person —***vt.*** to tease

Guy·a·na (gī an′ə) country in NE South America: 83,000 sq. mi.; pop. 965,000

guz·zle (guz′əl) ***vi.***, ***vt.*** **-zled, -zling** ⟦< ? OFr *gosier*, throat⟧ to drink greedily or immoderately

gym (jim) ***n.*** [Colloq.] **1** *short for* GYMNASIUM **2** PHYSICAL EDUCATION

gym·na·si·um (jim nā′zē əm) ***n.***, *pl.* **-si·ums** or **-si·a** (-ə) ⟦< Gr *gymnos*, naked⟧ a room

or building equipped for physical training and sports
gym·nas·tics (jim nas′tiks) ***n.pl.*** a sport combining tumbling and acrobatic feats —**gym′nast′** ***n.*** —**gym·nas′tic** ***adj.*** —**gym·nas′ti·cal·ly** ***adv.***
gym·no·sperm (jim′nō spurm′, -nə-) ***n.*** ⟦< Gr *gymnos*, naked + *sperma*, seed⟧ any of a large division of seed plants having the ovules not enclosed within an ovary, as seed ferns, conifers, etc.
gy·ne·col·o·gy (gī′ni käl′ə jē; jin′i-, jī′ni-) ***n.*** ⟦< Gr *gynē*, woman + -LOGY⟧ the branch of medicine dealing with women's diseases, etc. —**gy′ne·col′o·gist** ***n.***
gyp (jip) ***n.*** ⟦prob. < GYPSY⟧ [Colloq.] **1** a swindle **2** a swindler: also **gyp′per** or **gyp′ster** —***vt., vi.*** **gypped, gyp′ping** [Colloq.] to swindle; cheat
gyp·sum (jip′səm) ***n.*** ⟦< Gr *gypsos*⟧ a sulfate of calcium used for making plaster of Paris, in treating soil, etc.
Gyp·sy (jip′sē) ***n.***, *pl.* **-sies** ⟦< *Egipcien*, Egyptian: orig. thought to be from Egypt⟧ **1** [*also* **g-**] a member of a wandering Caucasoid people, perhaps orig. from India, with dark skin and black hair **2** their language **3** [**g-**] one who looks or lives like a Gypsy
gypsy moth a moth in E U.S.: its larvae feed on leaves, damaging trees
gy·rate (jī′rāt′) ***vi.*** **-rat′ed, -rat′ing** ⟦< Gr *gyros*, a circle⟧ to move in a circular or spiral path; whirl —**gy·ra′tion** ***n.*** —**gy′ra′tor** ***n.***
gy·ro (yir′ō, jī′rō′) ***n.***, *pl.* **-ros** ⟦see prec.⟧ **1** layers of lamb and beef roasted and sliced **2** a sandwich of this Also **gy·ros** (yir′ōs)
gyro- ⟦see GYRATE⟧ *combining form* gyrating [*gyroscope*]
gy·ro·scope (jī′rō skōp′, -rə-) ***n.*** ⟦prec. + -SCOPE⟧ a wheel mounted in a set of rings so that its axis is free to turn in any direction: when the wheel is spun rapidly, it will keep its original plane of rotation
gyve (jīv) ***n., vt.*** **gyved, gyv′ing** ⟦ME *give*⟧ [Archaic] fetter; shackle

H

h or **H** (āch) ***n.***, *pl.* **h's, H's** the eighth letter of the English alphabet
H *Chem. symbol for* hydrogen
H, H., h, or **h.** **1** height **2** high **3** *Baseball* hit(s) **4** hour(s) **5** hundred(s) **6** husband
ha (hä) ***interj.*** ⟦echoic⟧ an exclamation of wonder, surprise, anger, triumph, etc.
ha·be·as cor·pus (hā′bē əs kôr′pəs) ⟦L, (that) you have the body⟧ *Law* a writ requiring that a detained person be brought before a court to decide the legality of the detention
hab·er·dash·er (hab′ər dash′ər) ***n.*** ⟦< ME⟧ a dealer in men's hats, shirts, neckties, etc. —**hab′er·dash′er·y** ***n.***
ha·bil·i·ment (hə bil′ə mənt) ***n.*** ⟦< MFr *habiller*, to clothe⟧ **1** [*usually pl.*] clothing; attire **2** [*pl.*] trappings
hab·it (hab′it) ***n.*** ⟦< L *habere*, to have⟧ **1** a distinctive costume, as of a nun, etc. **2** a thing done often and, hence, easily **3** a usual way of doing **4** an addiction, esp. to narcotics
hab′it·a·ble ***adj.*** fit to be lived in
hab·i·tat (hab′i tat′) ***n.*** ⟦L, it inhabits⟧ **1** the region where a plant or animal naturally lives **2** the place where a person is ordinarily found
hab′i·ta′tion ***n.*** **1** an inhabiting **2** a dwelling; home
hab′it-form′ing ***adj.*** resulting in the formation of a habit or in addiction
ha·bit·u·al (hə bich′o͞o əl) ***adj.*** **1** done or acquired by habit **2** steady; inveterate [*a habitual smoker*] **3** much seen, done, or used; usual —**ha·bit′u·al·ly** ***adv.*** —**ha·bit′u·al·ness** ***n.***
ha·bit′u·ate′ (-āt′) ***vt.*** **-at′ed, -at′ing** to accustom (*to*)
ha·bit·u·é (hə bich′o͞o ā′) ***n.*** ⟦Fr⟧ one who frequents a certain place
ha·ci·en·da (hä′sē en′də) ***n.*** ⟦Sp < L *facere*, do⟧ in Spanish America, a large estate or ranch, or its main house
hack[1] (hak) ***vt.*** ⟦OE *haccian*⟧ to chop or cut crudely, roughly, etc. —***vi.*** **1** to make rough cuts **2** to give harsh, dry coughs —***n.*** **1** a tool for hacking **2** a gash or notch **3** a harsh, dry cough —**hack′er** ***n.***
hack[2] (hak) ***n.*** ⟦< HACKNEY⟧ **1** a horse for hire **2** an old, worn-out horse **3** a literary drudge **4** a coach for hire **5** [Colloq.] a taxicab —***adj.*** **1** employed as, or done by, a hack [*hack writer*] **2** trite; hackneyed
hack′er (-ər) ***n.*** a talented amateur user of computers
hack·le (hak′əl) ***n.*** ⟦ME *hechele*⟧ **1** the neck feathers of a rooster, pigeon, etc., collectively **2** [*pl.*] the hairs on a dog's neck and back that bristle
hack·ney (hak′nē) ***n.***, *pl.* **-neys** ⟦after *Hackney*, England⟧ **1** a horse for driving or riding **2** a carriage for hire
hack′neyed′ (-nēd′) ***adj.*** made trite by overuse
hack′saw′ ***n.*** a fine-toothed saw for cutting metal Also **hack saw**
had (had) ***vt.*** *pt. & pp. of* HAVE

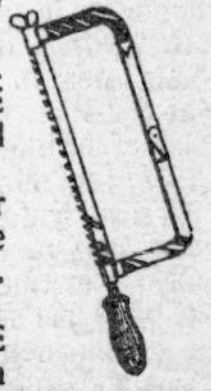
HACKSAW

had·dock (had′ək) ***n.***, *pl.* **-dock** or **-docks** ⟦ME *hadok*⟧ an Atlantic food fish, related to the cod
Ha·des (hā′dēz′) ⟦Gr *Haidēs*⟧ *Gr. Myth.* the home of the dead —***n.*** [*often* **h-**] hell
haft (haft, häft) ***n.*** ⟦OE *hæft*⟧ the handle or hilt of a knife, ax, etc.
hag (hag) ***n.*** ⟦< OE *hægtes*⟧ **1** a witch **2** an ugly, often vicious old woman —**hag′gish** ***adj.***

hag·gard (hag′ərd) ***adj.*** ⟦MFr *hagard,* untamed (hawk)⟧ having a wild, wasted, worn look; gaunt

hag·gle (hag′əl) ***vi.*** **-gled, -gling** ⟦< Scot *hag,* to hack⟧ to argue about terms, price, etc. —***n.*** a haggling —**hag′gler *n.***

Hague (hāg), **The** political capital of the Netherlands (cf. AMSTERDAM): pop. 672,000

hah (hä) ***interj., n.*** HA

hai·ku (hī′ko͞o′) ***n.*** ⟦Jpn⟧ **1** a Japanese verse form of three unrhymed lines of 5, 7, and 5 syllables, respectively **2** *pl.* **-ku′** a poem in this form

hail[1] (hāl) ***vt.*** ⟦< ON *heill,* whole, sound⟧ **1** to greet with cheers; acclaim **2** to call out to —***n.*** a greeting —***interj.*** an exclamation of tribute, greeting, etc. —**hail from** to be from

hail[2] (hāl) ***n.*** ⟦OE *hægel*⟧ **1** frozen raindrops falling during thunderstorms **2** a shower of or like hail —***vt., vi.*** to pour down like hail

hail′stone′ *n.* a pellet of hail

hail′storm′ *n.* a storm with hail

hair (her, har) ***n.*** ⟦OE *hær*⟧ **1** any of the threadlike outgrowths from the skin **2** a growth of these, as on the human head **3** a very small space, degree, etc. **4** a threadlike growth on a plant —**get in one's hair** [Slang] to annoy one —**split hairs** to quibble —**hair′less *adj.*** —**hair′like′ *adj.***

hair′ball′ *n.* a ball of hair often found in the stomach of a cow, cat, or other animal that licks its coat

hair′breadth′ (-bredth′) ***n.*** a very small space or amount —***adj.*** very narrow; close Also **hairs′breadth′**

hair′cut′ *n.* the act of, or a style of, cutting the hair

hair′do′ *n.,* *pl.* **-dos′** the style in which hair is arranged; coiffure

hair′dress′er *n.* one whose work is dressing hair

-haired (herd) having (a specified kind of) hair /short-*haired*/

hair′line′ *n.* **1** a very thin line **2** the outline of the hair on the head

hair′piece′ *n.* a toupee or wig

hair′pin′ *n.* a small, bent piece of wire, etc., for keeping the hair in place —***adj.*** U-shaped /a *hairpin* turn/

hair′-rais′ing *adj.* terrifying or shocking

hair′split′ting *adj., n.* making petty distinctions; quibbling

hair′spring′ *n.* a slender, hairlike coil spring, as in a watch

hair′y *adj.* **-i·er, -i·est** covered with hair —**hair′i·ness *n.***

Hai·ti (hāt′ē) country occupying the W portion of the island of Hispaniola, West Indies: 10,714 sq. mi.; pop. 5,250,000 —**Hai·ti·an** (hā′shən, hāt′ē ən) ***adj., n.***

hake (hāk) ***n.,*** *pl.* **hake** or **hakes** ⟦prob. < ON⟧ a marine food fish related to the cod

hal·berd (hal′bərd) ***n.*** ⟦< MHG *helmbarte*⟧ a combination spear and battle-ax of the 15th and 16th c.

hal·cy·on (hal′sē ən) ***adj.*** ⟦< Gr *alkyōn,* kingfisher (fabled calmer of the sea)⟧ tranquil, happy, idyllic, etc.

hale[1] (hāl) ***adj.*** **hal′er, hal′est** ⟦OE *hal*⟧ vigorous and healthy

hale[2] (hāl) ***vt.*** **haled, hal′ing** ⟦< OFr *haler*⟧ to force (a person) to go

half (haf, häf) ***n.,*** *pl.* **halves** ⟦OE *healf*⟧ **1** either of the two equal parts of something **2** either of the two equal parts of some games —***adj.*** **1** being a half **2** incomplete; partial —***adv.*** **1** to the extent of a half **2** partly /*half* done/ **3** at all: used with *not* /not *half* bad/

half- *combining form* **1** one half /*half*-life/ **2** partly /*half*-baked/

half′-and-half′ *n.* something that is half of one thing and half of another, as a mixture of milk and cream —***adj.*** combining two things equally —***adv.*** in two equal parts

half′back′ *n.* *Football* an offensive back stationed behind the quarterback and typically smaller and faster than a fullback

half′-breed′ *n.* one whose parents are of different ethnic types

half brother a brother through one parent only

half dollar a coin of the U.S. and Canada, worth 50 cents

half′heart′ed *adj.* with little enthusiasm, determination, interest, etc. —**half′heart′ed·ly *adv.***

half′-life′ (-līf′) ***n.*** the constant time period required for the disintegration of half of the atoms in a sample of a radioactive substance Also **half life**

half′-mast′ *n.* the position of a flag halfway down its staff, esp. as a sign of mourning

half note *Music* a note having one half the duration of a whole note

half·pen·ny (hāp′nē, hā′pən ē) ***n.,*** *pl.* **-pence** (hā′pəns) or **-pen·nies** a former British coin equal to half a penny

half sister a sister through one parent only

half sole a sole (of a shoe or boot) from the arch to the toe

half′track′ *n.* an army truck, armored vehicle, etc. with tractor treads instead of rear wheels

half′way′ *adj.* **1** midway between two points, etc. **2** partial /*halfway* measures/ —***adv.*** **1** to the midway point **2** partially —**meet halfway** to be willing to compromise with

halfway house a place for helping people adjust to society after being imprisoned, hospitalized, etc.

half′-wit′ *n.* a stupid or silly person; fool —**half′-wit′ted *adj.***

hal·i·but (hal′ə bət) ***n.,*** *pl.* **-but** or **-buts** ⟦ME *hali,* holy + *butt,* a flounder (so called because eaten on holidays)⟧ a large, edible flatfish found in northern seas

Hal·i·fax (hal′ə faks′) capital of Nova Scotia, Canada: pop. 205,000

hal·ite (hal′īt′, hā′līt′) ***n.*** rock salt

hal·i·to·sis (hal′i tō′sis) ***n.*** ⟦< L *halitus,* breath⟧ bad-smelling breath

hall (hôl) ***n.*** ⟦OE *heall*⟧ **1** the main dwelling of an estate **2** a public building with offices, etc. **3** a large room for gatherings, exhibits, etc. **4** a college building **5** a vestibule at the entrance of a building **6** a hallway

hal·le·lu·jah or **hal·le·lu·iah** (hal′ə lo͞o′yə) ***interj.*** ⟦< Heb < *hallelū,* praise + *yāh,*

Jehovah ⟧ praise (ye) the Lord! —*n.* a hymn of praise to God

hall·mark (hôl′märk′) *n.* ⟦< the mark stamped on gold and silver articles at Goldsmith's Hall in London⟧ a mark or symbol of genuineness or high quality

hal·loo (hə lo͞o′) *interj., n.* a shout to attract attention —*vi., vt.* **-looed′, -loo′ing** to shout or call

hal·low (hal′ō) *vt.* ⟦OE *halgian*⟧ to make or regard as holy

hal·lowed (hal′ōd, -ō ed′, -ō id) *adj.* holy or sacred

Hal·low·een or **Hal·low·e'en** (hal′ō ēn′, hal′ə wēn′) *n.* ⟦contr. < *all hallow even*⟧ the evening of Oct. 31, followed by All Saints' Day

hal·lu·ci·nate (hə lo͞o′si nāt′) *vi., vt.* **-nat′ed, -nat′ing** ⟦see fol.⟧ to have or cause to have hallucinations

hal·lu·ci·na·tion (hə lo͞o′si nā′shən) *n.* ⟦< L *hallucinari*, to wander mentally⟧ the apparent perception of sights, sounds, etc. that are not actually present —**hal·lu′ci·na·to′ry** (-nə tôr′ē) *adj.*

hal·lu′ci·no·gen (-nə jen, hal′yo͞o sin′ə-) *n.* a drug or other substance that produces hallucinations

hall′way′ *n.* a passageway; corridor

ha·lo (hā′lō) *n., pl.* **-los** or **-loes** ⟦< Gr *halōs*, circular threshing floor⟧ **1** a ring of light, as around the sun **2** a symbolic ring of light around the head of a saint, etc., as in pictures

hal·o·gen (hal′ō jən, -jen′; hal′ə-) *n.* ⟦< Gr *hals*, salt⟧ any of the five nonmetallic chemical elements fluorine, chlorine, bromine, astatine, and iodine

halt[1] (hôlt) *n., vi., vt.* ⟦< Ger *halt machen*⟧ stop

halt[2] (hôlt) *vi.* ⟦< OE *healt*⟧ **1** [Archaic] to limp **2** to hesitate —*adj.* lame —**the halt** those who are lame

hal·ter (hôl′tər) *n.* ⟦OE *hælftre*⟧ **1** a rope or strap for tying or leading an animal **2** a hangman's noose **3** a woman's upper garment, held up by a loop around the neck

halve (hav, häv) *vt.* **halved, halv′ing** **1** to divide into two equal parts **2** to reduce to half

halves (havz, hävz) *n. pl. of* HALF —**by halves** halfway; imperfectly —**go halves** to share expenses equally

hal·yard (hal′yərd) *n.* ⟦< ME *halier*: see HALE[2]⟧ a rope or tackle for raising or lowering a flag, sail, etc.

ham (ham) *n.* ⟦OE *hamm*⟧ **1** the back of the thigh **2** the upper part of a hog's hind leg, salted, smoked, etc. **3** [Colloq.] an amateur radio operator **4** [Slang] an actor who overacts —**ham′my, -mi·er, -mi·est,** *adj.*

Ham·burg (ham′bərg) seaport in N West Germany: pop. 1,600,000

ham·burg·er (ham′burg′ər) *n.* ⟦after *Hamburg*, Germany⟧ **1** ground beef **2** a cooked patty of such meat, often in a sandwich Also **ham′burg**

Ham·il·ton (ham′əl t'n), **Alexander** *c.* 1755-1804; Am. statesman

Hamilton city & port in SE Ontario, Canada: pop. 307,000

ham·let (ham′lit) *n.* ⟦< OFr *hamelete* < Old LowG *hamm*, enclosed area⟧ a very small village

Ham·let (ham′lit) the title hero of a tragedy by Shakespeare

ham·mer (ham′ər) *n.* ⟦OE *hamor*⟧ **1** a tool for pounding, having a metal head and a handle **2** a thing like this in shape or use, as the part of a gun that strikes the firing pin —*vt., vi.* **1** to strike repeatedly, as with a hammer **2** to drive, force, or shape, as with hammer blows —**hammer (away) at** to keep emphasizing —**ham′mer·er** *n.*

hammer and sickle the emblem of Communist parties in some countries

ham′mer·head′ *n.* **1** the head of a hammer **2** a shark with a mallet-shaped head having an eye at each end

ham′mer·toe′ *n.* a toe that is deformed, with its first joint bent downward

ham·mock (ham′ək) *n.* ⟦Sp *hamaca*, of WInd orig.⟧ a bed of canvas, etc. swung from ropes at both ends

Ham·mond (ham′ənd) city in NW Ind., near Chicago: pop. 94,000

ham·per[1] (ham′pər) *vt.* ⟦ME *hampren*⟧ to hinder; impede; encumber

ham·per[2] (ham′pər) *n.* ⟦< OFr *hanap*, a cup⟧ a large basket, usually covered

Hamp·ton (hamp′tən) seaport in SE Va.: pop. 123,000

ham·ster (ham′stər) *n.* ⟦< OHG *hamustro*⟧ a ratlike animal of Europe and Asia, used in scientific experiments

ham·string (ham′striŋ′) *n.* a tendon at the back of the knee —*vt.* **-strung′, -string′ing** to disable, as by cutting a hamstring

hand (hand) *n.* ⟦OE⟧ **1** the part of the arm below the wrist, used for grasping **2** a side or direction /at my right *hand*/ **3** possession or care /the land is in my *hands*/ **4** control /to strengthen one's *hand*/ **5** an active part /take a *hand* in the work/ **6** a promise to marry **7** skill **8** one having a special skill **9** manner of doing something **10** handwriting **11** applause **12** help /to lend a *hand*/ **13** a hired worker /a farm *hand*/ **14** a source /to get news at first *hand*/ **15** anything like a hand, as a pointer on a clock **16** the breadth of a hand **17** *Card Games a*) the cards held by a player at one time *b*) a round of play —*adj.* of, for, or controlled by the hand —*vt.* **1** to give as with the hand **2** to help or conduct with the hand —**at hand** near —**hand in hand** together —**hand it to** [Slang] to give credit to —**hand over fist** [Colloq.] easily and in large amounts —**hands down** easily —**on hand** **1** near **2** available **3** present —**on the one** (or **other**) **hand** from one (or the opposed) point of view

hand′bag′ *n.* a woman's purse

hand′ball′ *n.* a game in which players bat a small rubber ball against a wall or walls with the hand

hand′bar′row *n.* a frame carried by two people holding handles at the ends

hand′bill′ *n.* a small printed notice to be passed out by hand

hand′book′ *n.* a compact reference book; manual

hand′breadth′ *n.* the breadth of the human palm, about 4 inches

hand'car' *n.* a small, open car, orig. hand-powered, used on railroads
hand'cart' *n.* a small cart pulled or pushed by hand
hand'clasp' (-klasp') *n.* HANDSHAKE
hand'craft' *n.* HANDICRAFT —*vt.* to make skillfully by hand
hand'cuff' *n.* either of a pair of connected rings for shackling the wrists of a prisoner: *usually used in pl.* —*vt.* to put handcuffs on; manacle
-hand·ed (han'did) *combining form* having or involving (a specified kind or number of) hands /right-*handed*, two-*handed*/
Han·del (han'd'l), **George Fri·der·ic** (frē'dər ik, -drik) 1685-1759; Eng. composer, born in Germany
hand'ful' *n.*, *pl.* **-fuls'** 1 as much or as many as the hand will hold 2 a few; not many 3 [Colloq.] someone or something hard to manage
hand'gun' *n.* any firearm that is held and fired with one hand, as a pistol
hand·i·cap (han'di kap', -dē-) *n.* ⟦< *hand in cap*, former kind of lottery⟧ 1 a competition in which difficulties are imposed on, or advantages given to, the various contestants to equalize their chances 2 such a difficulty or advantage 3 *a)* any hindrance *b)* a physical disability —*vt.* **-capped'**, **-cap'·ping** 1 to give a handicap to 2 to hinder —**the handicapped** those who are physically disabled or mentally retarded
hand'i·cap'per *n.* a person, as a sportswriter, who tries to predict the winners in horse races
hand·i·craft (han'di kraft', -dē-) *n.* skill with the hands, or work calling for it
hand'i·work' *n.* 1 HANDWORK 2 work done by a particular person
hand·ker·chief (haŋ'kər chif') *n.* ⟦HAND + KERCHIEF⟧ a small cloth for wiping the nose, face, etc.
han·dle (han'dəl) *n.* ⟦OE < *hand*⟧ that part of a tool, etc. by which it is held or lifted —*vt.* **-dled**, **-dling** 1 to touch, lift, operate, etc. with the hand 2 to manage; control 3 to deal with; treat 4 to sell or deal in —*vi.* to respond to control /the car *handles* well/ —**han'dler** *n.*
han'dle·bar' *n.* [*often pl.*] a curved metal bar with handles on the ends, for steering a bicycle, etc.
hand'made' *adj.* made by hand, not by machine
hand'maid'en *n.* [Archaic] a woman or girl servant Also **hand'maid'**
hand'-me-down' *n.* [Colloq.] a used garment, etc. passed on to one
hand'out' *n.* 1 a gift of food, clothing, etc., as to a beggar 2 a leaflet handed out 3 an official news release
hand'pick' *vt.* 1 to pick by hand 2 to choose with care or for a purpose
hand'rail' *n.* a rail serving as a guard or support, as along a staircase
hand'set' *n.* a telephone mouthpiece and receiver in a single unit
hand'shake' *n.* a gripping of each other's hand in greeting, agreement, etc.
hands'-off' *adj.* designating or of a policy, etc. of not interfering
hand·some (han'səm, hand'-) *adj.* ⟦orig., easily handled⟧ 1 considerable 2 generous; gracious 3 good-looking, esp. in a manly or impressive way
hand'spring' *n.* a spring in which one turns over in midair with one or both hands touching the ground
hand'-to-hand' *adj.* at close quarters: said of fighting
hand'-to-mouth' *adj.* consuming all that is obtained
hand'work' *n.* work done by hand
hand'writ'ing *n.* 1 writing done by hand, as with a pen 2 a style of such writing —**hand'writ'ten** *adj.*
hand'y *adj.* **-i·er**, **-i·est** 1 close at hand; easily reached 2 easily used; convenient 3 clever with the hands —**hand'i·ly** *adv.* —**hand'i·ness** *n.*
hand'y·man' *n.*, *pl.* **-men'** a man who does odd jobs
hang (haŋ) *vt.* **hung**, **hang'ing**; for vt. 3 & vi. 5, **hanged** is preferred pt. & pp. ⟦OE *hangian*⟧ 1 to attach from above with no support from below; suspend 2 to attach (a door, etc.) so as to permit free motion at the point of attachment 3 to kill by suspending from a rope about the neck 4 to attach (wallpaper, etc.) to walls 5 to let (one's head) droop downward 6 to deadlock (a jury) —*vi.* 1 to be attached above with no support from below 2 to hover in the air 3 to swing freely 4 to fall or drape, as cloth 5 to die by hanging 6 to droop; bend —*n.* the way a thing hangs —**get** (or **have**) **the hang of** 1 to learn (or have) the knack of 2 to understand the meaning or idea of —**hang around** (or **about**) [Colloq.] to loiter around —**hang back** (or **off**) to be reluctant, as from shyness —**hang in** (**there**) [Colloq.] to persevere —**hang loose** [Slang] to be relaxed, easygoing, etc. —**hang on** 1 to go on; persevere 2 to depend on 3 to listen attentively to —**hang out** [Slang] to spend much time —**hang up** 1 to put on a hanger, hook, etc. 2 to end a telephone call by replacing the receiver 3 to delay
hang·ar (haŋ'ər) *n.* ⟦Fr⟧ a repair shed or shelter for aircraft
hang'dog' *adj.* abject or ashamed
hang'er *n.* 1 one who hangs things 2 that on which something is hung
hang gliding the sport of gliding through the air while hanging suspended by a harness from a large type of kite (**hang glider**)
hang'ing *adj.* that hangs —*n.* 1 a killing by hanging 2 something hung on a wall, etc., as a drapery
hang'man (-mən) *n.*, *pl.* **-men** one who hangs convicted criminals
hang'nail' *n.* ⟦OE *angnægl*, a corn (on the toe)⟧ a bit of torn skin hanging next to a fingernail
hang'o'ver *n.* 1 a survival 2 headache, nausea, etc. as an aftereffect of drinking much alcoholic liquor
hang'-up' *n.* [Slang] an emotional or psychological problem, difficulty, etc.
hank (haŋk) *n.* ⟦prob. < Scand⟧ a skein of yarn or thread
han·ker (haŋ'kər) *vi.* ⟦prob. < Du⟧ to long or yearn (*for*) —**han'ker·ing** *n.*

HANSOM CAB

han·som (cab) (han′səm) ⟦after J. A. *Hansom* (1803-82), Eng inventor⟧ a two-wheeled covered carriage pulled by one horse, with the driver's seat above and behind

Ha·nu·ka (khä′noo kä′, -kə; hä′-) ***n.*** ⟦< Heb *chanuka*, lit., dedication⟧ an 8-day Jewish festival commemorating the rededication of the Temple Also **Ha′nuk·kah′**

hap (hap) ***n.*** ⟦< ON *happ*⟧ luck

hap·haz·ard (hap′haz′ərd) ***adj.*** not planned; random —***adv.*** by chance

hap·less (hap′lis) ***adj.*** unlucky

hap·loid (hap′loid′) ***adj.*** *Biol.* having the full number of chromosomes normally occurring in the mature germ cell or half the number of the usual somatic cell —***n.*** a haploid cell or gamete

hap′ly ***adv.*** [Archaic] by chance

hap·pen (hap′ən) ***vi.*** ⟦ME *happenen*⟧ **1** to take place; occur **2** to be, occur, or come by chance **3** to have the luck or occasion /I *happened* to see it/ —**happen on** (or **upon**) to meet or find by chance

hap′pen·ing ***n.*** occurrence; event

hap′pen·stance′ (-stans′) ***n.*** [Colloq.] chance or accidental happening

hap·pi coat (hap′ē) ⟦< Jpn + COAT⟧ a short, light Japanese coat worn with a sash

hap·py (hap′ē) ***adj.*** **-pi·er, -pi·est** ⟦< HAP⟧ **1** lucky; fortunate **2** having, showing, or causing great pleasure or joy **3** suitable and clever; apt —**hap′pi·ly** ***adv.*** —**hap′pi·ness** ***n.***

hap′py-go-luck′y ***adj.*** easygoing

happy hour a time, as in the late afternoon, when a bar features drinks at reduced prices

har·a-kir·i (här′ə kir′ē) ***n.*** ⟦Jpn < *hara*, belly + *kiri*, a cutting⟧ ritual suicide by cutting the abdomen

ha·rangue (hə raŋ′) ***n.*** ⟦< OIt *aringo*, site for public assemblies⟧ a long, blustering speech; tirade —***vi.***, ***vt.*** **-rangued′**, **-rangu′ing** to speak or address in a harangue

har·ass (hə ras′, har′əs) ***vt.*** ⟦< OFr *harer*, to set a dog on⟧ **1** to worry or torment **2** to trouble by repeated raids or attacks —**har·ass′ment** ***n.***

Har·bin (här′bin) city in NE China: pop. 2,550,000

har·bin·ger (här′bin jər) ***n.*** ⟦< OFr *herberge*, a shelter⟧ a forerunner; herald

har·bor (här′bər) ***n.*** ⟦< OE *here*, army + *beorg*, shelter⟧ **1** a shelter **2** a protected inlet for anchoring ships; port —***vt.*** **1** to shelter or house **2** to hold in the mind /to *harbor* envy/ —***vi.*** to take shelter Brit. sp. **har′bour**

hard (härd) ***adj.*** ⟦OE *heard*⟧ **1** firm and unyielding to the touch; solid and compact **2** powerful /a *hard* blow/ **3** difficult to do, understand, or deal with **4** *a*) unfeeling /a *hard* heart/ *b*) unfriendly /*hard* feelings/ **5** harsh; severe **6** having mineral salts that interfere with lathering **7** energetic /a *hard* worker/ **8** containing much alcohol /*hard* liquor/ **9** addictive and harmful /heroin is a *hard* drug/ **10** *a*) of currency, not credit (said of money) *b*) readily accepted as foreign exchange /a *hard* currency/ —***adv.*** **1** energetically /work *hard*/ **2** with strength /hit *hard*/ **3** with difficulty /*hard*-earned/ **4** close; near /we live *hard* by/ **5** so as to be solid /frozen *hard*/ **6** sharply /turn *hard* right/ —**hard and fast** invariable; strict —**hard of hearing** partially deaf —**hard up** [Colloq.] in great need of money —**hard′ness** ***n.***

hard′back′ ***n.*** a hardcover book

hard′ball′ ***n.*** BASEBALL

hard′-bit′ten ***adj.*** tough; dogged

hard′-boiled′ ***adj.*** **1** boiled until solid: said of eggs **2** [Colloq.] unfeeling; tough; callous

hard copy a computer printout, often supplied along with or instead of a video screen display

hard′-core′ ***adj.*** absolute; unqualified

hard′cov′er ***adj.*** designating any book bound in a stiff cover

hard·en (härd′′n) ***vt.***, ***vi.*** to make or become hard —**hard′en·er** ***n.***

hard hat **1** a protective helmet worn by construction workers, miners, etc. **2** [Slang] such a worker

hard′head′ed ***adj.*** **1** shrewd and unsentimental; practical **2** stubborn

hard′heart′ed ***adj.*** unfeeling; cruel

har·di·hood (här′dē hood′) ***n.*** boldness

Har·ding (här′diŋ), **War·ren G(amaliel)** (wôr′ən, wär′-) 1865-1923; 29th president of the U.S. (1921-23)

hard′-line′ ***adj.*** aggressive; unyielding, as in politics, etc.

hard′-lin′er (-ər) ***n.*** one who takes a hard-line position

hard·ly (härd′lē) ***adv.*** **1** only just; scarcely **2** probably not; not likely

hard′-nosed′ ***adj.*** [Colloq.] tough and stubborn or shrewd

hard·scrab·ble (härd′skrab′əl) ***adj.*** producing or earning only a very small amount; barren /a *hardscrabble* farm, life, etc./

hard sell high-pressure salesmanship

hard′ship′ ***n.*** a thing hard to bear, as poverty, pain, etc.

hard′stand′ ***n.*** a paved area for parking aircraft or other vehicles

hard′tack′ (-tak′) ***n.*** unleavened bread made in hard, large wafers

hard′top′ ***n.*** an automobile like a sedan but having no post between the front and rear windows

hard′ware′ (-wer′) ***n.*** **1** articles made of metals, as tools, nails, fittings, etc. **2** the mechanical, magnetic, and electronic devices of a computer

hard′wood′ ***n.*** **1** any tough, heavy timber with a compact texture **2** the wood of any tree with broad, flat leaves, as the oak, maple, etc.

har·dy (här′dē) *adj.* **-di·er, -di·est** ⟦< OFr *hardir*, to make bold⟧ 1 bold and resolute 2 robust; vigorous —**har′di·ly** *adv.* —**har′di·ness** *n.*

hare (her) *n.* ⟦OE *hara*⟧ a mammal related to and resembling the rabbit

hare′brained′ *adj.* giddy, rash, etc.

Ha·re Krishna (hä′rē) ⟦< Hindi⟧ 1 a cult, founded in the U.S. in 1966, involving devotion to Krishna 2 a member of this cult

hare′lip′ *n.* a congenital deformity consisting of a cleft of the upper lip

ha·rem (her′əm, har′-) *n.* ⟦Ar *ḥarīm*, lit., prohibited (place)⟧ 1 that part of a Muslim household in which the women live 2 the women in a harem

hark (härk) *vi.* ⟦ME *herkien*⟧ to listen carefully: usually in the imperative —**hark back** to go back in thought or speech

hark·en (här′kən) *vi.* HEARKEN

Har·le·quin (här′li kwin, -kin) a comic character in pantomime, who wears a mask and diamond-patterned tights of many colors —*n.* [h-] a clown

har·lot (här′lət) *n.* ⟦< OFr, rogue⟧ PROSTITUTE —**har′lot·ry** (-lə trē) *n.*

harm (härm) *n.* ⟦OE *hearm*⟧ hurt; injury; damage —*vt.* to do harm to

harm′ful *adj.* causing harm; hurtful —**harm′ful·ly** *adv.*

harm′less *adj.* causing no harm —**harm′less·ly** *adv.*

har·mon·ic (här män′ik) *adj.* of or in harmony —*n. Music* a pure tone making up a composite tone —**har·mon′i·cal·ly** *adv.*

har·mon′i·ca (-i kə) *n.* a small wind instrument with a series of metal reeds that produce tones when air is blown or sucked across them

har·mo·ni·ous (här mō′nē əs) *adj.* 1 having parts arranged in an orderly or pleasing way 2 having similar ideas, interests, etc. 3 having musical tones combined to give a pleasing effect —**har·mo′ni·ous·ly** *adv.*

har·mo·nize (här′mə nīz′) *vi.* **-nized′, -niz′ing** 1 to be in harmony 2 to sing in harmony —*vt.* to make harmonious —**har′mo·ni·za′tion** *n.* —**har′mo·niz′er** *n.*

har·mo·ny (här′mə nē) *n., pl.* **-nies** ⟦< Gr *harmos*, a fitting⟧ 1 pleasing arrangement of parts in color, size, etc. 2 agreement in action, ideas, etc.; friendly relations 3 the pleasing combination of tones in a chord

har·ness (här′nis) *n.* ⟦< OFr *harneis*, armor⟧ 1 the leather straps and metal pieces by which a horse, etc. is fastened to a vehicle, etc. 2 something like a harness —*vt.* 1 to put a harness on 2 to control so as to use the power of

harp (härp) *n.* ⟦OE *hearpe*⟧ a musical instrument with strings stretched vertically in an open, triangular frame and played by plucking —*vi.* 1 to play a harp 2 to persist in talking or writing tediously (*on* or *upon* something) —**harp′ist** *n.*

har·poon (här po͞on′) *n.* ⟦< ON *harpa*, to squeeze⟧ a barbed spear with a line attached to it, used for spearing whales, etc. —*vt.* to strike with a harpoon

harp·si·chord (härp′si kôrd′) *n.* ⟦< It *arpa*, harp + *corda*, CORD⟧ a pianolike keyboard instrument whose strings are plucked rather than struck

Har·py (här′pē) *n., pl.* **-pies** ⟦< Gr *harpazein*, to snatch⟧ 1 *Gr. Myth.* any of several monsters, part woman and part bird 2 [h-] *a)* a greedy person *b)* a shrewish woman

har·ri·dan (har′i dən) *n.* ⟦< Fr *haridelle*, worn-out horse⟧ a nasty, bad-tempered old woman

har·ri·er (har′ē ər) *n.* ⟦< HARE + -IER⟧ 1 a small hound used for hunting hares 2 a cross-country runner

Har·ris·burg (har′is burg′) capital of Pa., in the S part: pop. 53,000

Har·ri·son (har′ə s′n) 1 **Ben·ja·min** (ben′jə mən) 1833-1901; 23d president of the U.S. (1889-93): grandson of William Henry 2 **William Henry** 1773-1841; 9th president of the U.S. (1841)

har·row (har′ō) *n.* ⟦prob. < ON⟧ a heavy frame with spikes or disks, used for breaking up and leveling plowed ground, etc. —*vt.* 1 to draw a harrow over (land) 2 to cause mental distress to —**har′row·ing** *adj.*

har·ry (har′ē) *vt.* **-ried, -ry·ing** ⟦< OE *here*, army⟧ 1 to raid and ravage or rob 2 to torment or worry

harsh (härsh) *adj.* ⟦ME *harsk*⟧ 1 unpleasantly rough to the eye, ear, taste, or touch 2 offensive to the mind or feelings 3 cruel or severe —**harsh′ly** *adv.* —**harsh′ness** *n.*

hart (härt) *n.* ⟦OE *heorot*⟧ a full-grown, male European red deer

har·te·beest (här′tə bēst′, härt′bēst′) *n.* ⟦obs. Afrik < *harte*, hart + *beest*, beast⟧ a large African antelope with long horns curved backward

Hart·ford (härt′fərd) capital of Conn., in the central part: pop. 136,000

har·um-scar·um (her′əm sker′əm) *adj.* ⟦< ?⟧ reckless or irresponsible —*adv.* in a harum-scarum way

har·vest (här′vist) *n.* ⟦OE *hærfest*⟧ 1 the time of the year when grain, fruit, etc. are gathered in 2 a season's crop 3 the gathering in of a crop 4 the outcome of any effort —*vt., vi.* to gather in (a crop, etc.) —**har′vest·er** *n.*

has (haz; *before "to"* has) *vt. 3d pers. sing., pres. indic., of* HAVE

has′-been′ *n.* [Colloq.] a person or thing whose popularity is past

hash (hash) *vt.* ⟦< Fr *hacher*, to chop⟧ to chop up (meat or vegetables) for cooking —*n.* 1 a chopped mixture of cooked meat and vegetables, usually baked 2 a mixture 3 a muddle; mess 4 [Slang] hashish —**hash out** [Colloq.] to settle by long discussion —**hash over** [Colloq.] to discuss at length

hash·ish (hash′ēsh′, -ish) *n.* ⟦Ar *ḥashīsh*, dried hemp⟧ a narcotic and intoxicant made from hemp

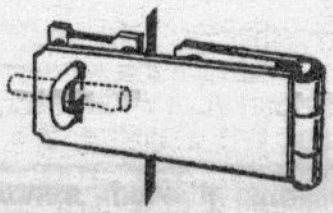

HASP

hasp (hasp, häsp) *n.* ⟦OE *hæsp*⟧ a hinged

fastening for a door, etc.; esp., a metal piece fitted over a staple and fastened as by a bolt or padlock

has·sle (has′əl) ***n.*** ⟦< ?⟧ [Colloq.] **1** a heated argument; squabble **2** a troublesome situation —***vi.*** **-sled, -sling** [Colloq.] to have a hassle —***vt.*** [Slang] to annoy, harass, etc.

has·sock (has′ək) ***n.*** ⟦OE *hassuc,* (clump of) coarse grass⟧ a firm cushion used as a footstool or seat

hast (hast) ***vt.*** *archaic 2d pers. sing., pres. indic., of* HAVE: used with *thou*

haste (hāst) ***n.*** ⟦OFr⟧ quickness of motion; rapidity —***vt., vi.*** **hast′ed, hast′ing** [Rare] HASTEN —**make haste** to hurry

has·ten (hās′ən) ***vt.*** to cause to be or come faster; speed up —***vi.*** to move or act swiftly; hurry

hast·y (hās′tē) ***adj.*** **-i·er, -i·est** **1** done with haste; hurried **2** done, made, or acting too quickly or rashly —**hast′i·ly** ***adv.*** —**hast′i·ness** ***n.***

hat (hat) ***n.*** ⟦OE *hætt*⟧ a head covering, usually with a brim and a crown —**pass the hat** to take up a collection —**talk through one's hat** [Colloq.] to talk nonsense —**throw one's hat into the ring** to enter a contest, esp. one for political office —**under one's hat** [Colloq.] strictly confidential

hatch¹ (hach) ***vt.*** ⟦ME *hacchen*⟧ **1** to bring forth (young) from (an egg or eggs) **2** to contrive (a plan, plot, etc.) —***vi.*** **1** to bring forth young: said of eggs **2** to emerge from the egg

hatch² (hach) ***n.*** ⟦OE *hæcc,* grating⟧ **1** HATCHWAY **2** a lid for a hatchway

hatch′back′ ***n.*** ⟦prec. + BACK⟧ an automobile with a rear that swings up, giving wide entry to a storage area

hat′check′ ***adj.*** of or working in a checkroom for hats, coats, etc.

hatch′er·y ***n., pl.*** **-ies** a place for hatching eggs, esp. of fish or poultry

hatch·et (hach′it) ***n.*** ⟦< OFr *hache,* an ax⟧ a small ax with a short handle —**bury the hatchet** to make peace

hatchet job [Colloq.] a biased, malicious attack on another's character

hatch′way′ ***n.*** an opening in a ship's deck, or in a floor or roof

hate (hāt) ***vt.*** **hat′ed, hat′ing** ⟦OE *hatian*⟧ **1** to have strong dislike or ill will for **2** to wish to avoid /to *hate* fights/ —***vi.*** to feel hatred —***n.*** **1** a strong feeling of dislike or ill will **2** a person or thing hated —**hat′er** ***n.***

hate′ful ***adj.*** deserving hate —**hate′ful·ly** ***adv.*** —**hate′ful·ness** ***n.***

hath (hath) ***vt.*** *archaic 3d pers. sing., pres. indic., of* HAVE

ha·tred (hā′trid) ***n.*** strong dislike or ill will; hate

hat·ter (hat′ər) ***n.*** one who makes, sells, or cleans men's hats

hau·berk (hô′bərk) ***n.*** ⟦< Frankish *hals,* neck + *bergan,* to protect⟧ a medieval coat of armor, usually of chain mail

haugh·ty (hôt′ē) ***adj.*** **-ti·er, -ti·est** ⟦< OFr *haut,* high⟧ having or showing great pride in oneself and contempt for others; arrogant —**haugh′ti·ly** ***adv.*** —**haugh′ti·ness** ***n.***

haul (hôl) ***vt.*** ⟦< OFr *haler*⟧ **1** to move by pulling; drag **2** to transport by wagon, truck, etc. —***n.*** **1** the act of hauling; pull **2** the amount gained, caught, etc. at one time **3** the distance over which something is transported —**haul off** [Colloq.] to draw the arm back before hitting —**in** (or **over**) **the long haul** over a long period of time

haunch (hônch, hänch) ***n.*** ⟦< OFr *hanche* < Gmc⟧ **1** the hip, buttock, and upper thigh together **2** an animal's loin and leg together

haunt (hônt) ***vt.*** ⟦< OFr *hanter,* to frequent⟧ **1** to visit often or continually **2** to recur repeatedly to /*haunted* by memories/ —***n.*** a place often visited

haunt′ed ***adj.*** supposedly frequented by ghosts /a *haunted* house/

haunt′ing ***adj.*** often recurring to the mind; not easily forgotten

hau·teur (hō tʉr′; *Fr* ō tër′) ***n.*** ⟦Fr < *haut,* high⟧ disdainful pride; haughtiness

Ha·van·a (hə van′ə) capital of Cuba: pop. 1,950,000 —***n.*** a cigar made of Cuban tobacco

have (hav; *before "to"* haf) ***vt.*** **had, hav′ing** ⟦OE *habban*⟧ **1** to hold; own; possess /to *have* money, a week *has* 7 days/ **2** to experience /*have* a good time/ **3** to hold mentally /to *have* an idea/ **4** to state /so rumor *has* it/ **5** to get, take, consume, etc. /*have* a drink/ **6** to bear or beget (offspring) **7** to engage in /to *have* a fight/ **8** to cause to; cause to be /*have* her leave/ **9** to permit; tolerate /I won't *have* this noise!/ **10** [Colloq.] *a*) to hold at a disadvantage *b*) to deceive; cheat *Have* is used as an auxiliary to express completed action (Ex.: I *had* left) and with infinitives to express obligation or necessity (Ex.: we *have* to go). *Have got* often replaces *have. Have* is conjugated in the present indicative: (I) *have,* (he, she, it) *has,* (we, you, they) *have* —***n.*** a wealthy person or nation —**have it out** to settle an issue by fighting or discussion —**have on** to be wearing

ha·ven (hā′vən) ***n.*** ⟦OE *hæfen*⟧ **1** a port **2** any sheltered place; refuge

have-not (hav′nät′) ***n.*** a person or nation with little or no wealth

hav·er·sack (hav′ər sak′) ***n.*** ⟦< Ger *habersack,* lit., sack of oats⟧ a canvas bag for rations, etc., worn over one shoulder, as by soldiers or hikers

hav·oc (hav′ək) ***n.*** ⟦< OFr *havot*⟧ great destruction and devastation —**play havoc with** to devastate; ruin

haw¹ (hô) ***n.*** ⟦OE *haga*⟧ **1** the berry of the hawthorn **2** HAWTHORN

haw² (hô) ***vi.*** ⟦echoic⟧ to grope for words Usually in **hem and haw** (see HEM²)

Ha·wai·i (hə wä′ē, -yē) **1** a State of the U.S., consisting of a group of islands (**Hawaiian Islands**) in the North Pacific: 6,450 sq. mi.; pop. 965,000; cap. Honolulu **2** largest of these islands —**Ha·wai′ian** (-yən) ***adj., n.***

hawk¹ (hôk) ***n.*** ⟦OE *hafoc*⟧ **1** a bird of prey with short, rounded wings, a long tail, and a hooked beak and claws **2** an advocate of war

hawk² (hôk) ***vt.*** ⟦< HAWKER⟧ to advertise or peddle (goods) in the streets by shouting

hawk³ (hôk) ***vi., vt.*** ⟦echoic⟧ to clear the throat (of) audibly

hawk·er (hôk′ər) ***n.*** ⟦< Old LowG *hoker*⟧ a peddler or huckster

hawk′-eyed′ (-īd′) ***adj.*** keen sighted

haw·ser (hô′zər) ***n.*** ⟦< OFr *haucier* < L *altus*, high⟧ a large rope used for towing or mooring a ship

haw·thorn (hô′thôrn′) ***n.*** ⟦< OE *haga*, hedge + THORN⟧ a thorny shrub or small tree of the rose family, with flowers and small, red fruits

Haw·thorne (hô′thôrn′), **Na·than·iel** (nə than′yəl) 1804-64; U.S. writer

hay (hā) ***n.*** ⟦< OE *hieg*⟧ grass, clover, etc. cut and dried for fodder —***vi.*** to mow and dry grass, etc. for hay —**hit the hay** [Slang] to go to bed to sleep

hay′cock′ ***n.*** a small, conical heap of hay drying in a field

Hay·dn (hīd′'n), **(Franz) Jo·seph** (yō′zef) 1732-1809; Austrian composer

Hayes (hāz), **Ruth·er·ford B(irchard)** (ruth′ ər fərd) 1822-93; 19th president of the U.S. (1877-81)

hay fever an acute inflammation of the eyes and respiratory tract: an allergic reaction to some kinds of pollen

hay′loft′ ***n.*** a loft, or upper story, in a barn or stable, for storing hay

hay′mow′ (-mou′) ***n.*** 1 a pile of hay in a barn 2 HAYLOFT

hay′stack′ ***n.*** a large heap of hay piled up outdoors

hay′wire′ ***adj.*** [Colloq.] 1 out of order; disorganized 2 crazy —**go haywire** [Colloq.] 1 to behave erratically 2 to become crazy

haz·ard (haz′ərd) ***n.*** ⟦< OFr *hasard*, game of dice⟧ 1 risk; danger 2 an obstacle on a golf course —***vt.*** to risk

haz′ard·ous ***adj.*** risky; dangerous

haze[1] (hāz) ***n.*** ⟦prob. < HAZY⟧ 1 a thin vapor of fog, smoke, etc. in the air 2 slight vagueness of mind —***vi., vt.*** **hazed, haz′·ing** to make or become hazy: often with *over*

haze[2] (hāz) ***vt.*** **hazed, haz′ing** ⟦< ?⟧ to force to do ridiculous or painful things, as in initiation

ha·zel (hā′zəl) ***n.*** ⟦OE *hæsel*⟧ 1 a shrub or tree of the birch family, with edible nuts 2 a reddish brown —***adj.*** light reddish-brown

ha′zel·nut′ ***n.*** FILBERT

ha·zy (hā′zē) ***adj.*** **-zi·er, -zi·est** ⟦prob. < OE *hasu*, dusky⟧ 1 somewhat foggy or smoky 2 somewhat vague —**ha′zi·ly** ***adv.*** —**ha′zi·ness** ***n.***

H-bomb (āch′bäm′) ***n.*** HYDROGEN BOMB

he (hē) ***pron.***, *pl. see* THEY ⟦OE⟧ 1 the man, boy, or male animal previously mentioned 2 anyone /*he* who laughs last laughs best/ —***n.*** a male

He *Chem. symbol for* helium

head (hed) ***n.*** ⟦OE *heafod*⟧ 1 the part of the body containing the brain, and the jaws, eyes, ears, nose, and mouth 2 the mind; intelligence 3 *pl.* **head** a unit of counting /ten *head* of cattle/ 4 the main side of a coin 5 the uppermost part or thing; top 6 the topic or title of a section, chapter, etc. 7 the foremost or projecting part; front 8 the part designed for holding, striking, etc. /the *head* of a nail/ 9 the part of a tape recorder that records or plays back the magnetic signals on the tape 10 the membrane across the end of a drum, etc. 11 the source of a river, etc. 12 froth, as on beer 13 a position of leadership or honor 14 a leader, ruler, etc. —***adj.*** 1 most important; principal 2 at the top or front 3 striking against the front /*head* current/ —***vt.*** 1 to be the chief of; command 2 to lead; precede 3 to cause to go in a specified direction —***vi.*** to set out; travel /to *head* eastward/ —**come to a head** 1 to be about to suppurate, as a boil 2 to culminate, or reach a crisis —**go to one's head** 1 to confuse or intoxicate one 2 to make one vain —**head off** to get ahead of and intercept —**head over heels** deeply; completely —**heads up!** [Colloq.] look out! —**keep** (or **lose**) **one's head** to keep (or lose) one's poise, self-control, etc. —**on** (or **upon**) **one's head** as one's responsibility or misfortune —**over one's head** 1 too difficult for one to understand 2 to a higher authority —**turn one's head** to make one vain —**head′less** ***adj.***

head′ache′ (-āk′) ***n.*** 1 a continuous pain in the head 2 [Colloq.] a cause of worry, annoyance, or trouble

head′board′ (-bôrd′) ***n.*** a board that forms the head of a bed, etc.

head cold a common cold with congestion of the nasal passages

head′dress′ ***n.*** 1 a decorative covering for the head 2 a hairdo; coiffure

-head·ed (-id) *combining form* having a head or heads /clear-*headed*, two-*headed*/

head′first′ ***adv.*** 1 with the head in front; headlong 2 recklessly; rashly

head′gear′ ***n.*** a hat, cap, etc.

head′ing ***n.*** 1 something forming the head, top, or front 2 the title, topic, etc., as of a chapter 3 the direction in which a ship, plane, etc. is moving

head′land′ ***n.*** a point of land reaching out into the water; promontory

head′light′ ***n.*** a light with a reflector and lens, at the front of a vehicle

head′line′ ***n.*** printed lines at the top of a newspaper article, giving the topic —***vt.*** **-lined′, -lin′ing** to give featured billing or publicity to

head′long′ (-lôŋ′) ***adv., adj.*** ⟦ME *hedelinge(s)*⟧ 1 with the head first 2 with uncontrolled speed or force 3 reckless(ly); rash(ly)

head′mas′ter ***n.*** the principal of a private school —**head′mis′tress** ***n.fem.***

head′-on′ ***adj., adv.*** with the head or front foremost /a *head-on* collision/

head′phone′ ***n.*** [*often pl.*] a listening device for a radio, stereo, etc. worn over the head to position its tiny speakers over the ears

head·quar·ters (hed′kwôrt′ərz) ***n.pl.*** [*often with sing. v.*] 1 the main office, or center of operations, of one in command, as in an army 2 the main office in any organization

head′rest′ ***n.*** a support for the head

head′room′ ***n.*** space overhead, as in a doorway, tunnel, etc.

head start an early start or other competitive advantage

head′stone′ ***n.*** a stone marker placed at the head of a grave

head′strong′ ***adj.*** determined to do as one pleases

head′wa′ters ***n.pl.*** the small streams that are the sources of a river

head′way′ ***n.*** **1** forward motion **2** progress or success

head·y (hed′ē) ***adj.*** **-i·er, -i·est 1** impetuous; rash **2** intoxicating /*heady* wine/

heal (hēl) ***vt., vi.*** [[OE *hælan*]] **1** to make or become well or healthy again **2** to cure (a disease) or mend, as a wound —**heal′er** ***n.***

health (helth) ***n.*** [[OE *hælth*]] **1** physical and mental well-being; freedom from disease, etc. **2** condition of body or mind /poor *health*/ **3** a wish for one's health and happiness, as in a toast **4** soundness, as of a society or culture

health food food thought to be very healthful, as food grown with natural fertilizers and free of additives

health′ful ***adj.*** helping to produce or maintain health; wholesome

health·y (hel′thē) ***adj.*** **-i·er, -i·est 1** having good health **2** showing or resulting from good health /a *healthy* color/ **3** HEALTHFUL —**health′i·ness** ***n.***

heap (hēp) ***n.*** [[< OE *heap*, a troop]] **1** a pile or mass of jumbled things **2** [*often pl.*] [Colloq.] a large amount —***vt.*** **1** to make a heap of **2** to give in large amounts **3** to fill (a plate, etc.) full or to overflowing —***vi.*** to rise in a heap

hear (hir) ***vt.*** **heard** (hurd), **hear′ing** [[OE *hieran*]] **1** to be aware of (sounds) by the ear **2** to listen to **3** to conduct a hearing of (a law case, etc.) **4** to be informed of; learn —***vi.*** **1** to be able to hear sounds **2** to be told (*of* or *about*) —**hear from** to get a letter, etc. from —**not hear of** to refuse to consider —**hear′er** ***n.***

hear′ing ***n.*** **1** the act or process of perceiving sounds **2** the ability to hear **3** an opportunity to be heard **4** an appearance before a judge, investigative committee, etc. **5** the distance a sound will carry /within *hearing*/

heark·en (härk′ən) ***vi.*** [[OE *heorknian*]] to listen carefully; pay heed

hear·say (hir′sā′) ***n.*** rumor; gossip

hearse (hurs) ***n.*** [[< L *hirpex*, a harrow]] a vehicle used in a funeral for carrying the corpse

heart (härt) ***n.*** [[OE *heorte*]] **1** the hollow, muscular organ that circulates the blood by alternate dilation and contraction **2** the central, vital, or main part; core **3** the human heart considered as the center of emotions, personality attributes, etc.; specif., *a*) inmost thought and feeling *b*) love, sympathy, etc. *c*) spirit or courage **4** a conventionalized design of a heart (♥) **5** any of a suit of playing cards marked with such symbols in red —**after one's own heart** that pleases one perfectly —**at heart** in one's innermost nature —**by heart** by or from memorization —**set one's heart on** to have a fixed desire for —**take to heart** **1** to consider seriously **2** to be troubled by

heart′ache′ ***n.*** sorrow or grief

heart attack any sudden instance of heart failure; esp., a coronary

heart′beat′ ***n.*** one full contraction and dilation of the heart

heart′break′ ***n.*** overwhelming sorrow or grief —**heart′bro′ken** ***adj.***

heart′burn′ ***n.*** a burning, acid sensation beneath the breastbone

-heart·ed (härt′id) [[ME]] *combining form* having a (specified kind of) heart /*stout-hearted*/

heart·en (härt′'n) ***vt.*** to encourage

heart failure the inability of the heart to pump enough blood to supply the body tissues adequately

heart′felt′ ***adj.*** sincere; genuine

hearth (härth) ***n.*** [[OE *heorth*]] **1** the stone or brick floor of a fireplace **2** *a*) the fireside *b*) family life; home

heart′land′ ***n.*** a geographically central area having crucial importance

heart′less ***adj.*** unkind; unfeeling —**heart′less·ly** ***adv.*** —**heart′less·ness** ***n.***

heart′-rend′ing ***adj.*** causing much grief or mental anguish

heart′sick′ ***adj.*** sick at heart; extremely unhappy or despondent

heart′strings′ ***n.pl.*** deepest feelings or affections

heart′-to-heart′ ***adj.*** intimate and candid

heart′warm′ing ***adj.*** such as to cause genial feelings

heart′y ***adj.*** **-i·er, -i·est 1** warm and friendly; cordial **2** strongly felt; unrestrained /*hearty* laughter/ **3** strong and healthy **4** nourishing and plentiful /a *hearty* meal/ —***n.***, *pl.* **heart′ies** [Archaic] a fellow sailor —**heart′i·ly** ***adv.*** —**heart′i·ness** ***n.***

heat (hēt) ***n.*** [[OE *hætu*]] **1** the quality of being hot; hotness, or the perception of this **2** much hotness **3** hot weather or climate **4** the warming of a house, etc. **5** *a*) strong feeling; ardor, anger, etc. *b*) the period of this **6** a single bout, round, or trial **7** the period of sexual excitement in animals, esp. females **8** [Slang] coercion —***vt., vi.*** **1** to make or become warm or hot **2** to make or become excited

heat′ed ***adj.*** **1** hot **2** vehement or angry —**heat′ed·ly** ***adv.***

heat′er ***n.*** an apparatus for giving heat; stove, furnace, radiator, etc.

heath (hēth) ***n.*** [[OE *hæth*]] **1** a tract of open wasteland, esp. in the British Isles **2** any of various shrubs that grow on heaths, as heather

hea·then (hē′*th*ən) ***n.***, *pl.* **-thens** or **-then** [[OE *hæthen*]] **1** anyone not a Jew, Christian, or Muslim **2** a person regarded as irreligious, uncivilized, etc. —***adj.*** **1** pagan **2** irreligious, uncivilized, etc. —**hea′then·ish** ***adj.***

heath·er (he*th*′ər) ***n.*** [[ME *haddyr*]] a plant of the heath family, esp. common in the British Isles, with small, bell-shaped, purplish-pink flowers

HEATHER

heating pad a pad consisting of an electric heating element covered with fabric, for applying heat to the body

heat lightning lightning without thunder, seen on hot evenings

heat′stroke′ ***n.*** a condition

of high fever, collapse, etc. resulting from exposure to intense heat

heat wave 1 unusually hot weather 2 a period of such weather

heave (hēv) ***vt.*** **heaved** or (esp. *Naut.*) **hove, heav′ing** ⟦OE *hebban*⟧ 1 to lift, esp. with effort 2 to lift in this way and throw 3 to utter (a sigh, etc.) with effort 4 *Naut.* to raise, haul, etc. by pulling as with a rope —***vi.*** 1 to swell up 2 to rise and fall rhythmically 3 *a)* to vomit *b)* to pant; gasp 4 *Naut.* to haul (*on* or *at* a rope, etc.) —***n.*** the act or effort of heaving —**heave to** *Naut.* to stop —**heav′er** ***n.***

heave′-ho′ (-hō′) ***n.*** [Colloq.] dismissal, as from a job: chiefly in **give** (or **get**) **the** (**old**) **heave-ho**

heav·en (hev′ən) ***n.*** ⟦OE *heofon*⟧ 1 [*usually pl.*] the visible sky; firmament 2 [*often* **H-**] *Theol. a)* a state or place of complete happiness, etc. attained by the good after death *b)* the abode of God, his angels, and the blessed *c)* God 3 any place of great beauty or state of great happiness —**heav′en·ly** ***adj.***

heav′en·ward (-wərd) ***adv., adj.*** toward heaven Also **heav′en·wards** ***adv.***

heav·y (hev′ē) ***adj.*** **-i·er, -i·est** ⟦OE *hefig*⟧ 1 hard to lift because of great weight 2 of more than the usual, expected, or defined weight 3 larger, greater, or more intense than usual /a *heavy* blow, a *heavy* vote, *heavy* applause/ 4 to an unusual extent /a *heavy* drinker/ 5 hard to do /*heavy* work/ 6 sorrowful /a *heavy* heart/ 7 burdened with sleep /*heavy* eyelids/ 8 hard to digest /a *heavy* meal/ 9 clinging; penetrating /a *heavy* odor/ 10 cloudy; gloomy /a *heavy* sky/ 11 using massive machinery to produce basic materials, as steel —***adv.*** in a heavy manner —***n.,*** *pl.* **-ies** *Theater* a villain —**heav′i·ly** ***adv.*** —**heav′i·ness** ***n.***

heav′y-du′ty ***adj.*** made to withstand great strain, bad weather, etc.

heav′y-hand′ed ***adj.*** 1 clumsy or tactless 2 oppressive or tyrannical

heav′y-heart′ed ***adj.*** sad; depressed

heav′y-set′ ***adj.*** having a stout or stocky build

heav′y·weight′ ***n.*** 1 one weighing more than average; esp., a boxer in the heaviest weight class 2 [Colloq.] a very influential or important person

Heb. 1 Hebrew 2 *Bible* Hebrews

He·bra·ic (hē brā′ik, hi-) ***adj.*** of or characteristic of the Hebrews, their language, or culture; Hebrew

He·brew (hē′bro͞o′) ***n.*** 1 *a)* a member of an ancient Semitic people; Israelite *b)* a Jew 2 *a)* the ancient Semitic language of the Israelites *b)* its modern form, the language of Israel —***adj.*** 1 of Hebrew or the Hebrews 2 JEWISH

Heb·ri·des (heb′rə dēz′) group of islands off the W coast of Scotland

heck (hek) ***interj., n.*** [Colloq.] *a euphemism for* HELL

heck·le (hek′əl) ***vt.*** **-led, -ling** ⟦ME *hechele*⟧ to harass (a speaker) with questions or taunts —**heck′ler** ***n.***

hec·tare (hek′ter′) ***n.*** ⟦Fr⟧ a metric unit of area, 10,000 square meters

hec·tic (hek′tik) ***adj.*** ⟦< Gr *hektikos*, habitual⟧ 1 feverish; flushed 2 confused, rushed, excited, etc. —**hec′ti·cal·ly** ***adv.***

Hec·tor (hek′tər) in Homer's *Iliad*, a Trojan hero, killed by Achilles —***vt.*** [**h-**] to browbeat; bully

hedge (hej) ***n.*** ⟦OE *hecg*⟧ 1 a dense row of shrubs, etc. forming a boundary 2 any fence or barrier 3 a hedging —***vt.*** **hedged, hedg′ing** 1 to put a hedge around 2 to hinder or guard as with a barrier: often with *in* 3 to try to avoid loss in (a bet, etc.) by making counterbalancing bets, etc. —***vi.*** to refuse to commit oneself or give a direct answer

hedge fund a partnership of investors who pool large sums for speculating in securities

hedge′hog′ ***n.*** 1 a small, insect-eating mammal of the Old World, with sharp spines on the back 2 the American porcupine

he·don·ism (hē′dən iz′əm, hēd′′n-) ***n.*** ⟦< Gr *hēdonē*, pleasure + -ISM⟧ the self-indulgent pursuit of pleasure as a way of life —**he′don·ist** ***n.*** —**he·do·nis·tic** (hē′də nis′tik, hēd′′n is′-) ***adj.***

-he·dron (hē′drən) ⟦< Gr⟧ *combining form* a geometric figure or crystal having (a specified number of) surfaces

heed (hēd) ***vt., vi.*** ⟦OE *hedan*⟧ to pay close attention (to) —***n.*** close attention —**heed′ful** ***adj.*** —**heed′less** ***adj.*** —**heed′less·ly** ***adv.*** —**heed′less·ness** ***n.***

hee·haw (hē′hô′) ***n., vi.*** ⟦echoic⟧ bray

heel[1] (hēl) ***n.*** ⟦OE *hela*⟧ 1 the back part of the foot, under the ankle 2 that part of a stocking, shoe, etc. at the heel 3 anything like a heel in location, shape, crushing power, etc. 4 [Colloq.] a despicable person —***vt.*** 1 to furnish with a heel 2 to follow closely 3 [Colloq.] to provide with money, etc. —***vi.*** to follow along at the heels of someone —**down at** (**the**) **heel** (or **heels**) shabby; seedy —**kick up one's heels** have fun —**on** (or **upon**) **the heels of** close behind

heel[2] (hēl) ***vi.*** ⟦OE *hieldan*⟧ to lean to one side, as a ship —***vt.*** to cause (a vessel) to heel

heft (heft) ***n.*** ⟦< base of HEAVE⟧ [Colloq.] 1 weight; heaviness 2 importance; influence —***vt.*** [Colloq.] to try to judge the weight of by lifting

heft·y (hef′tē) ***adj.*** **-i·er, -i·est** [Colloq.] 1 heavy 2 large and powerful 3 big —**heft′i·ness** ***n.***

he·gem·o·ny (hi jem′ə nē) ***n.,*** *pl.* **-nies** ⟦< Gr *hēgeisthai*, to lead⟧ leadership or dominance, esp. that of one state or nation over others

he·gi·ra (hi jī′rə) ***n.*** ⟦< Ar *hijrah*, flight⟧ 1 [*often* **H-**] Mohammed's flight from Mecca in 622 A.D. 2 a journey, esp. one made to escape

Hei·del·berg (hīd′′l burg′) city in SW West Germany: site of a famous university: pop. 133,000

heif·er (hef′ər) ***n.*** ⟦OE *heahfore*⟧ a young cow that has not borne a calf

height (hīt) ***n.*** ⟦< OE *heah*, high⟧ 1 the topmost point 2 the highest limit; extreme 3 the distance from the bottom to the top 4 elevation above a given level; altitude 5 a relatively great distance above a given level 6 [*often pl.*] an elevation; hill

height'en (-'n) ***vt., vi.*** 1 to bring or come to a higher position 2 to make or become larger, greater, etc.

Heim·lich maneuver (hīm'lik) ⟦after H. J. *Heimlich*, 20th-c. U.S. surgeon⟧ an emergency technique for dislodging an object stuck in the windpipe, using air forced out from the victim's lungs

hei·nous (hā'nəs) ***adj.*** ⟦< OFr *hair*, to hate⟧ outrageously evil —**hei'nous·ly** ***adv.*** —**hei'nous·ness** ***n.***

heir (er) ***n.*** ⟦< L *heres*⟧ one who inherits or is entitled to inherit another's property, title, etc.

heir apparent *pl.* **heirs apparent** the heir whose right to inherit cannot be denied if he outlives the ancestor

heir'ess (-is) ***n.*** a female heir, esp. to great wealth

heir'loom' ***n.*** ⟦see HEIR & LOOM[1]⟧ any treasured possession handed down from generation to generation

heist (hīst) ***n.*** ⟦< HOIST⟧ [Slang] a robbery —***vt.*** [Slang] to rob or steal

held (held) ***vt., vi.*** *pt. & pp. of* HOLD[1]

Hel·e·na (hel'i nə) capital of Mont.: pop. 24,000

Helen of Troy *Gr. Legend* the beautiful wife of the king of Sparta: the Trojan War is started because of her abduction by Paris to Troy

hel·i·cal (hel'i kəl) ***adj.*** ⟦< Gr *helix*, spiral⟧ shaped like a helix; spiral

hel·i·cop·ter (hel'i käp'tər, hē'li-) ***n.*** ⟦< Gr *helix*, spiral + *pteron*, wing⟧ a vertical-lift aircraft, capable of hovering or moving in any direction, having a motor-driven, horizontal rotor —***vi., vt.*** to travel or convey by helicopter

he·li·o·cen·tric (hē'lē ō sen'trik) ***adj.*** ⟦< Gr *hēlios*, the sun + *kentron*, a point⟧ having or regarding the sun as the center

he·li·o·trope (hē'lē ə trōp') ***n.*** ⟦< Gr *hēlios*, the sun + *trepein*, to turn⟧ 1 a plant with fragrant clusters of small, white or reddish-purple flowers 2 reddish purple —***adj.*** reddish-purple

hel·i·port (hel'i pôrt') ***n.*** ⟦HELI(COPTER) + (AIR)PORT⟧ an airport for helicopters

he·li·um (hē'lē əm) ***n.*** ⟦< Gr *hēlios*, the sun⟧ a chemical element, a colorless, odorless, very light inert gas having the lowest known boiling and melting points

he·lix (hē'liks') ***n.***, *pl.* **-lix·es'** (-iz') or **hel·i·ces** (hel'i sēz') ⟦L & Gr⟧ a spiral

hell (hel) ***n.*** ⟦< OE *helan*, to hide⟧ 1 [*often* H-] *Theol.* the state or place of total and final separation from God and so of eternal misery and suffering, arrived at by those who die unrepentant in grave sin 2 any place or condition of evil, pain, etc. —**catch** (or **get**) **hell** [Slang] to receive a severe scolding, punishment, etc.

hell'bent' ***adj.*** [Slang] 1 recklessly determined 2 moving fast

hell'cat' ***n.*** an evil, spiteful woman

hel·le·bore (hel'ə bôr') ***n.*** ⟦< Gr *helleboros*⟧ a plant of the buttercup family whose rhizomes were used in medicine

Hel·len·ic (hə len'ik, he-) ***adj.*** 1 Greek 2 of the history, language, or culture of the ancient Greeks —**Hel·len·ism** (hel'ən iz' əm) ***n.*** —**Hel'len·is'tic** ***adj.***

hel·lion (hel'yən) ***n.*** ⟦< Scot dial. *hallion*, a low fellow⟧ [Colloq.] a person fond of deviltry; troublemaker

hell'ish ***adj.*** 1 devilish; fiendish 2 [Colloq.] very unpleasant —**hell'ish·ly** ***adv.*** —**hell'ish·ness** ***n.***

hel·lo (he lō', hə lō'; hel'ō') ***interj.*** an exclamation of greeting

helm (helm) ***n.*** ⟦OE *helma*⟧ 1 the wheel or tiller by which a ship is steered 2 the control or leadership of an organization, government, etc.

hel·met (hel'mət) ***n.*** ⟦< OFr *helme*⟧ a protective, rigid head covering for use in combat, certain sports, etc.

helms·man (helmz'mən) ***n.***, *pl.* **-men** one who steers a ship

hel·ot (hel'ət) ***n.*** ⟦after *Helos*, ancient Greek town⟧ a serf or slave

help (help) ***vt.*** ⟦OE *helpan*⟧ 1 to make things easier or better for; aid; assist 2 to remedy [*to help a cough*] 3 to keep from; avoid [*can't help crying*] 4 to serve or wait on (a customer, etc.) —***vi.*** to give aid; be useful —***n.*** 1 a helping; aid; assistance 2 a remedy 3 one that helps; esp., a hired person or persons; servant(s), farmhand(s), etc. —**help oneself to** to take without asking —**help out** to help in getting or doing something —**help'er** ***n.***

help'ful (-fəl) ***adj.*** giving help; useful —**help'ful·ly** ***adv.*** —**help'ful·ness** ***n.***

help'ing (-iŋ) ***n.*** a portion of food served to one person

help'less (-lis) ***adj.*** 1 not able to help oneself; weak 2 lacking help or protection 3 incompetent —**help'less·ly** ***adv.*** —**help'less·ness** ***n.***

help'mate' ***n.*** ⟦< fol.⟧ a helpful companion; specif., a wife or husband

help'meet' ***n.*** ⟦misreading of "an *help meet* for him" (Genesis 2:18)⟧ HELPMATE

Hel·sin·ki (hel'siŋ kē) capital of Finland: pop. 485,000

hel·ter-skel·ter (hel'tər skel'tər) ***adv.*** in haste and confusion —***adj.*** disorderly

helve (helv) ***n.*** ⟦OE *helfe*⟧ the handle of a tool, esp. of an ax

Hel·ve·tian (hel vē'shən) ***adj., n.*** Swiss

hem[1] (hem) ***n.*** ⟦OE⟧ the border on a garment, etc. made by folding the edge and sewing it down —***vt.*** **hemmed, hem'ming** to fold back the edge of and sew down —**hem in** (or **around** or **about**) 1 to encircle 2 to confine

hem[2] (hem) ***interj., n.*** the sound made in clearing the throat —***vi.*** **hemmed, hem'ming** 1 to make this sound, as in trying to get attention 2 to grope about in speech for the right words: usually used in the phrase **hem and haw**

he'-man' ***n.*** [Colloq.] a strong, virile man

hem·a·tite (hem'ə tīt', hē'mə-) ***n.*** ⟦< Gr *haimatitēs*, bloodlike⟧ native ferric oxide, an important iron ore

he·ma·tol·o·gy (hē'mə täl'ə jē) ***n.*** ⟦< Gr *haima*, blood + -LOGY⟧ the study of blood and blood diseases —**he'ma·tol'o·gist** ***n.***

he'ma·to'ma (-tō'mə) ***n.***, *pl.* **-mas** or **-ma·ta**

(-mə tə) ⟦< Gr *haima*, blood + *-ōma*, a mass⟧ a tumorlike collection of blood out side a blood vessel

heme (hēm) ***n.*** ⟦ult. < Gr *haima*, blood⟧ the iron-containing pigment in hemoglobin

hemi- ⟦Gr *hēmi-*⟧ *prefix* half */hemisphere/*

Hem·ing·way (hem′iŋ wā′), **Er·nest** (ʉr′ nist) 1899-1961; U.S. writer

hem·i·sphere (hem′i sfir′) ***n.*** ⟦< Gr *hēmisphairion*⟧ **1** half of a sphere, globe, celestial body, etc. **2** any of the halves (northern, southern, eastern, or western) of the earth —**hem′i·spher′i·cal** (-sfer′i kəl) or **hem′i·spher′ic** ***adj.***

hem′line′ ***n.*** the bottom edge of a dress, skirt, coat, etc.

hem·lock (hem′läk′) ***n.*** ⟦OE *hemlic*⟧ **1** *a*) a poisonous European plant related to parsley *b*) a poison made from this plant **2** *a*) an evergreen tree of the pine family *b*) the wood of this tree

hemo- ⟦< Gr *haima*⟧ *combining form* blood Also **hema-**

he·mo·glo·bin (hē′mō glō′bin, -mə-) ***n.*** ⟦< prec. + GLOBULE⟧ the red coloring matter of the red blood corpuscles

he·mo·phil·i·a (hē′mō fil′ē ə, -mə-) ***n.*** ⟦< HEMO- + -PHILE⟧ a hereditary disorder in which the blood fails to clot normally, causing prolonged bleeding from even minor injuries —**he′mo·phil′i·ac′** (-ak′) ***n.***

hem·or·rhage (hem′ər ij′, hem′rij′) ***n.*** ⟦< Gr *haima*, blood + *rhēgnynai*, to break⟧ the escape of large quantities of blood from a blood vessel; heavy bleeding —***vi.*** **-rhaged′**, **-rhag·ing′** (-ij iŋ′) to have a hemorrhage —**hem′or·rhag′ic** (-aj′ik) ***adj.***

hem·or·rhoid (hem′ər oid′, hem′roid′) ***n.*** ⟦< Gr *haima*, blood + *rheein*, to flow⟧ a painful swelling of a vein in the region of the anus, often with bleeding: *usually used in pl.* —**hem′or·rhoi′dal** ***adj.***

he·mo·stat (hē′mō stat′) ***n.*** ⟦see HEMO- & STATIC⟧ anything used to stop bleeding, as a surgical clamp

hemp (hemp) ***n.*** ⟦OE *hænep*⟧ **1** a tall Asiatic plant having tough fiber **2** the fiber, used to make rope, sailcloth, etc. **3** a substance, as marijuana, made from its leaves and flowers

hemp·en (hemp′ən) ***adj.*** of or like hemp

hem′stitch′ ***n.*** an ornamental stitch, used esp. at a hem, made by pulling out several parallel threads and tying the cross threads into small bunches —***vt.*** to put hemstitches on

hen (hen) ***n.*** ⟦OE *henn*⟧ **1** the female of the domesticated chicken **2** the female of various other birds

hence (hens) ***adv.*** ⟦< OE *heonan*, from here⟧ **1** from this place; away */go hence/* **2** from this time */a year hence/* **3** as a result; therefore **4** [Archaic] from this origin or source

hence·forth′ ***adv.*** from this time on Also **hence′for′ward**

hench·man (hench′mən) ***n.***, *pl.* **-men** ⟦< OE *hengest*, stallion + *-man*⟧ a trusted helper or follower

hen·na (hen′ə) ***n.*** ⟦Ar *ḥinnā′*⟧ **1** an Old World plant with minute flowers **2** a dye extracted from its leaves, used to tint the hair auburn **3** reddish brown —***adj.*** reddish-brown —***vt.*** **-naed**, **-na·ing** to tint with henna

hen·peck (hen′pek′) ***vt.*** to nag and domineer over (one's husband) —**hen′pecked′** ***adj.***

Henry VIII (hen′rē) 1491 1547; king of England (1509-47)

hep (hep) ***adj.*** *early form of* HIP²

hep·a·rin (hep′ə rin) ***n.*** ⟦Gr *hēpar*, liver + -IN⟧ a substance in body tissues, esp. in the liver, that slows the clotting of blood

he·pat·ic (hi pat′ik) ***adj.*** ⟦< Gr *hēpar*, liver⟧ of or like the liver

hep·a·ti·tis (hep′ə tīt′is) ***n.*** ⟦< Gr *hēpar*, liver + -ITIS⟧ inflammation of the liver

her (hʉr) ***pron.*** ⟦OE *hire*⟧ *objective case of* SHE —***poss. pronominal adj.*** of, belonging to, or done by her

He·ra (hir′ə) *Gr. Myth.* the wife of Zeus and queen of the gods

her·ald (her′əld) ***n.*** ⟦< OFr *heralt*⟧ **1** [Historical] an official who made proclamations, carried state messages, etc. **2** one who announces significant news, etc. **3** a forerunner; harbinger —***vt.*** to announce, foretell, etc.

he·ral·dic (hə ral′dik) ***adj.*** of heraldry or heralds

her′ald·ry ***n.***, *pl.* **-ries** **1** the art or science having to do with coats of arms, genealogies, etc. **2** ceremony or pomp

herb (ʉrb, hʉrb) ***n.*** ⟦< L *herba*⟧ **1** any seed plant whose stem withers away annually **2** any plant used as a medicine, seasoning, etc. —**her·ba·ceous** (hər bā′shəs, ər-) ***adj.*** —**herb′al** ***adj.***

herb·age (ʉr′bij, hʉr′-) ***n.*** herbs collectively, esp. pasturage; grass

herb·al·ist (hʉr′bəl ist, ʉr′-) ***n.*** one who grows or deals in herbs

her·bi·cide (hʉr′bə sīd′, ʉr′-) ***n.*** any chemical substance used to destroy plants, esp. weeds —**her′bi·ci′dal** ***adj.***

her′bi·vore′ (-vôr′) ***n.*** ⟦Fr⟧ a herbivorous animal

her·biv·o·rous (hər biv′ər əs) ***adj.*** ⟦un< L *herba*, herb + *vorare*, to devour⟧ feeding chiefly on grass or other plants

her·cu·le·an (hər kyōō′lē ən, hʉr′kyōō lē′ən) ***adj.*** [*sometimes* **H-**] **1** having the great size or strength of Hercules **2** calling for great strength, size, or courage

Her·cu·les (hʉr′kyōō lēz′) *Gr. & Rom. Myth.* a hero famous for feats of strength —***n.*** [**h-**] a very strong man

herd (hʉrd) ***n.*** ⟦OE *heord*⟧ **1** a number of cattle or other large animals feeding or living together **2** *a*) a crowd *b*) the common people; masses (a contemptuous term) —***vt., vi.*** to gather or move as a herd

herds·man (hʉrdz′mən) ***n.***, *pl.* **-men** one who keeps or tends a herd

here (hir) ***adv.*** ⟦OE *her*⟧ **1** at or in this place: often used as an intensive */John here is an actor/* **2** to or into this place */come here/* **3** at this point; now **4** on earth —***n.*** this place —**neither here nor there** irrelevant

here′a·bout′ ***adv.*** in this general vicinity Also **here′a·bouts′**

here·af′ter ***adv.*** **1** from now on; in the future **2** following this —***n.*** **1** the future **2** the state after death

here·by′ *adv.* by this means

he·red·i·tar·y (hə red′i ter′ē) *adj.* **1** *a)* of, or passed down by, inheritance from an ancestor *b)* having title, etc. by inheritance **2** of, or passed down by, heredity

he·red·i·ty (hə red′i tē) *n., pl.* **-ties** ⟦< L *heres,* heir⟧ the transmission of characteristics from parent to offspring by means of genes

here·in (hir in′, hir′in′) *adv.* **1** in here **2** in this writing

here·of′ *adv.* of or concerning this

here's (hirz) here is

her·e·sy (her′i sē) *n., pl.* **-sies** ⟦< Gr *hairesis,* selection, sect⟧ **1** a religious belief opposed to the orthodox doctrines of a church **2** any opinion opposed to official or established views

her′e·tic (-tik) *n.* one who professes a heresy; esp., a church member who holds beliefs opposed to church dogma —**he·ret·i·cal** (hə ret′i kəl) *adj.*

here′to·fore′ *adv.* up until now

here′up·on′ *adv.* **1** immediately following this; at once **2** concerning this subject, etc.

here·with′ *adv.* **1** along with this **2** by this method or means

her·it·a·ble (her′it ə bəl) *adj.* that can be inherited

her·it·age (her′i tij′) *n.* **1** property that is or can be inherited **2** tradition, etc. handed down from one's ancestors or the past

her·maph·ro·dite (hər maf′rō dīt′, -rə-) *n.* ⟦after *Hermaphroditos,* son of Hermes and Aphrodite, united in a single body with a nymph⟧ a person, animal, or plant with the sexual organs of both the male and the female —**her·maph′ro·dit′ic** (-dit′ik) *adj.*

Her·mes (hʉr′mēz′) *Gr. Myth.* the god who was the messenger of the other gods

her·met·ic (hər met′ik) *adj.* ⟦after prec. (reputed founder of alchemy)⟧ airtight Also **her·met′i·cal** —**her·met′i·cal·ly** *adv.*

her·mit (hʉr′mit) *n.* ⟦< Gr *erēmos,* desolate⟧ one who lives alone in a secluded spot; recluse

her′mit·age (-mi tij) *n.* a secluded retreat, as the place where a hermit lives

hermit crab a soft-bodied crab that lives in an empty mollusk shell

her·ni·a (hʉr′nē ə) *n., pl.* **-as** or **-ae′** (-ē′, -ī′) ⟦L⟧ the protrusion of all or part of an organ through a tear in the wall of the surrounding structure; rupture —**her′ni·al** *adj.*

her′ni·ate′ (-āt′) *vi.* **-at′ed, -at′ing** to protrude so as to form a hernia —**her′ni·a′tion** *n.*

he·ro (hir′ō, hē′rō′) *n., pl.* **-roes** ⟦< Gr *hērōs*⟧ **1** any person, esp. a man, admired for courage, nobility, etc. **2** the central male character in a novel, play, etc.

He·rod·o·tus (hə räd′ə təs) *c.* 485-*c.* 425 B.C.; Gr. historian

he·ro·ic (hi rō′ik) *adj.* **1** of or like a hero **2** of or about a hero and his deeds **3** daring and risky —*n.* [*pl.*] heroic behavior, talk, or deeds —**he·ro′i·cal·ly** *adv.*

her·o·in (her′ō in) *n.* ⟦Ger, orig. a trademark⟧ a habit-forming narcotic derived from morphine

her·o·ine (her′ō in) *n.* a female hero in life or literature

her′o·ism′ (-iz′əm) *n.* the qualities and actions of a hero or heroine

her·on (her′ən) *n.* ⟦< OFr *hairon*⟧ a wading bird with a long neck, long legs, and a long, tapered bill

HERON

hero sandwich a large, sliced roll filled with meats, cheeses, etc.

her·pes (hʉr′pēz′) *n.* ⟦L < Gr *herpein,* to creep⟧ a viral disease causing small blisters on the skin and mucous membranes

herpes sim·plex (sim′·pleks′) a recurrent, incurable form of herpes usually affecting the mouth, lips, face, or genitals

herpes zos·ter (zäs′tər) ⟦< HERPES + Gr *zōstēr,* a girdle⟧ a viral infection of certain sensory nerves, causing pain and an eruption of blisters; shingles

her·pe·tol·o·gy (hʉr′pə täl′ə jē) *n.* ⟦< Gr *herpeton,* reptile⟧ the branch of zoology having to do with the study of reptiles and amphibians —**her′pe·tol′o·gist** *n.*

Herr (her) *n., pl.* ***Her′ren*** (-ən) ⟦Ger⟧ in Germany, a man; gentleman: title corresponding to *Mr.* or *Sir*

her·ring (her′iŋ) *n.* ⟦OE *hæring*⟧ a small food fish of the North Atlantic

her′ring·bone′ *n.* **1** the spine of a herring, having numerous sweptback, thin, parallel bony extensions on each side **2** such a pattern or anything having such a pattern

hers (hʉrz) *pron.* that or those belonging to her [*hers* are better]

her·self′ (hər-) *pron.* a form of the 3d pers. sing., fem. pronoun, used as an intensive [she went *herself*], as a reflexive [she hurt *herself*], or as a quasi-noun meaning "her true self" [she is not *herself* today]

hertz (herts, hʉrts) *n., pl.* **hertz** ⟦after H. R. *Hertz,* 19th-c. Ger physicist⟧ the international unit of frequency, equal to one cycle per second

Hertz·i·an waves (hert′sē ən, hʉrt′-) ⟦see prec.⟧ [*sometimes* **h- w-**] radio waves or other electromagnetic radiation resulting from the oscillations of electricity in a conductor

he's (hēz) **1** he is **2** he has

hes·i·tant (hez′i tənt) *adj.* hesitating or undecided; doubtful —**hes′i·tan·cy** *n.* —**hes′i·tant·ly** *adv.*

hes′i·tate′ (-tāt′) *vi.* **-tat′ed, -tat′ing** ⟦< L *haerere,* to stick⟧ **1** to stop because of indecision **2** to pause **3** to be reluctant [*hesitating* to ask] **4** to pause continually in speaking —**hes′i·tat′ing·ly** *adv.* —**hes′i·ta′tion** *n.*

hetero- ⟦Gr *hetero-*⟧ *combining form* other, another, different Also **heter-**

het·er·o·dox (het′ər ō däks′, -ər ə-) *adj.* ⟦< prec. + Gr *doxa,* opinion⟧ opposed to the usual beliefs, esp. in religion; unorthodox —**het′er·o·dox′y,** *pl.* **-ies,** *n.*

het·er·o·ge·ne·ous (het′ər ō′jē′nē əs, -ər ə-) *adj.* ⟦< HETERO- + Gr *genos,* a kind⟧ **1** differing in structure, quality, etc.; dissimilar **2** composed of unlike parts

het′er·o·sex′u·al (-sek′shōō əl) *adj.* **1** of or having sexual desire for those of the opposite sex 2 of different sexes —*n.* a heterosexual individual

heu·ris·tic (hyōō ris′tik) *adj.* ⟦< Gr *heuriskein*, to invent⟧ helping to learn, as by a method of education based on following rules to find answers

hew (hyōō) *vt.* **hewed, hewed** or **hewn, hew′ing** ⟦OE *heawan*⟧ **1** to chop or cut with an ax, knife, etc. **2** to make or shape in this way —*vi.* to conform (*to* a rule, principle, etc.)

hex (heks) *n.* ⟦< Ger *hexe*, witch⟧ a sign, spell, etc. supposed to bring bad luck —*vt.* [Dial.] to cause to have bad luck

hexa- ⟦< Gr *hex*, six⟧ *combining form* six Also **hex-**

hex·a·gon (hek′sə gän′) *n.* ⟦< Gr *hex*, six + *gōnia*, an angle⟧ a plane figure with six angles and six sides —**hex·ag·o·nal** (heks ag′ə nəl) *adj.*

hex·am·e·ter (heks am′ə tər) *n.* ⟦see HEXA- & METER[1]⟧ **1** a line of verse containing six metrical feet **2** verse consisting of hexameters

hey (hā) *interj.* an exclamation used to attract attention, etc.

hey·day (hā′dā′) *n.* the time of greatest health, vigor, etc.; prime

Hg ⟦L *hydrargyrum*⟧ *Chem. symbol for* mercury

HHS (Department of) Health and Human Services

hi (hī) *interj.* an informal exclamation of greeting

HI Hawaii

hi·a·tus (hī āt′əs) *n.*, *pl.* **-tus·es** or **-tus** ⟦L < *hiare*, to gape⟧ a gap or break, as where a part is missing

hi·ba·chi (hē bä′chē, hi-) *n.*, *pl.* **-chis** ⟦Jpn < *hi*, fire + *bachi*, bowl⟧ a small, charcoal-burning grill

hi·ber·nate (hī′bər nāt′) *vi.* **-nat′ed, -nat′ing** ⟦< L *hibernus*, wintry⟧ to spend the winter in a dormant state —**hi′ber·na′tion** *n.*

hi·bis·cus (hī bis′kəs, hi-) *n.* ⟦< L⟧ a plant of the mallow family, with large, colorful flowers

hic·cup (hik′up′, -əp) *n.* ⟦echoic⟧ a sudden, involuntary contraction of the diaphragm as air enters the lungs, causing the glottis to close, producing an abrupt sound —*vi.* **-cuped′** or **-cupped′, -cup′ing** or **-cup′ping** to make a hiccup Also **hic·cough** (hik′ôf; hik′up′, -əp)

hick (hik) *n.* ⟦< *Richard*⟧ an awkward, unsophisticated person regarded as typical of rural areas

hick·ey (hik′ē) *n.*, *pl.* **-eys** or **-ies** [Colloq.] any device or gadget

hick·o·ry (hik′ə rē, hik′rē) *n.*, *pl.* **-ries** ⟦< AmInd *pawcohiccora*⟧ **1** a North American tree of the walnut family **2** its hard, tough wood **3** its smooth-shelled, edible nut: usually **hickory nut**

hid·den (hid′'n) *vt.*, *vi.* ⟦OE *gehydd*⟧ *alt. pp. of* HIDE[1] —*adj.* concealed; secret

hide[1] (hīd) *vt.* **hid** (hid), **hid′den** or **hid, hid′ing** ⟦OE *hydan*⟧ **1** to put or keep out of sight; conceal **2** to keep secret **3** to keep from sight by obscuring, etc. —*vi.* **1** to be concealed **2** to conceal oneself

hide[2] (hīd) *n.* ⟦OE *hid*⟧ an animal skin or pelt, either raw or tanned

hide′a·way′ *n.* [Colloq.] a place where one can hide, be secluded, etc.

hide′bound′ *adj.* obstinately narrow-minded and conservative

hid·e·ous (hid′ē əs) *adj.* ⟦< OFr *hide*, fright⟧ horrible; very ugly —**hid′e·ous·ly** *adv.* —**hid′e·ous·ness** *n.*

hide′-out′ *n.* [Colloq.] a hiding place

hie (hī) *vi.*, *vt.* **hied, hie′ing** or **hy′ing** ⟦OE *higian*⟧ to hasten

hi·er·ar·chy (hī′ər är′kē) *n.*, *pl.* **-chies** ⟦< Gr *hieros*, sacred + *archos*, ruler⟧ **1** church government by clergy in graded ranks **2** the highest officials in such a system **3** a group of persons or things arranged in order of rank, grade, etc. —**hi′er·ar′chi·cal** (-ki kəl) *adj.*

hi·er·o·glyph·ic (hī′ər ō′glif′ik, -ər ə-; hī′rō-, -rə-) *n.* ⟦< Gr *hieros*, sacred + *glyphein*, to carve⟧ **1** a picture or symbol representing a word, syllable, or sound, used by the ancient Egyptians and others **2** a symbol, etc. hard to understand —*adj.* of or like hieroglyphics

hi·er·o·phant (hī′ər ō fant′) *n.* ⟦< Gr *hieros*, sacred + *phainein*, to show⟧ in ancient Greece, a priest of a mystery cult

hi-fi (hī′fī′) *n.* a radio, phonograph, etc. having high fidelity —*adj.* of or having high fidelity of sound reproduction

high (hī) *adj.* ⟦OE *heah*⟧ **1** lofty; tall **2** extending upward a (specified) distance **3** reaching to, situated at, or done from a height **4** above others in rank, position, etc.; superior **5** grave /*high* treason/ **6** greater in size, amount, degree, etc. than usual /*high* prices/ **7** luxurious /*high* living/ **8** acute in pitch; shrill **9** slightly tainted, as meat **10** elated /*high* spirits/ **11** [Slang] *a*) drunk *b*) under the influence of a drug —*adv.* in or to a high level, place, degree, etc. —*n.* **1** a high level, place, etc. **2** an area of high barometric pressure **3** that gear of a motor vehicle, etc. producing the greatest speed **4** [Slang] a condition of euphoria induced as by drugs —**high and low** everywhere —**high on** [Colloq.] enthusiastic about —**on high** in heaven

high′ball′ *n.* whiskey or brandy mixed with water, soda water, ginger ale, etc.

high′born′ *adj.* of noble birth

high′boy′ *n.* a high chest of drawers mounted on legs

high′brow′ *n.* [Colloq.] one having or affecting highly cultivated tastes; intellectual —*adj.* [Colloq.] of or for a highbrow

high′chair′ *n.* a baby's chair with long legs used esp. during meals

high′er-up′ *n.* [Colloq.] a person of higher rank or position

high′fa·lu′tin(g) (-fə lōōt′'n) *adj.* [Colloq.] pretentious or pompous

high fidelity in radio, sound recording, etc., nearly exact reproduction of sound

high′-flown′ *adj.* **1** extravagantly ambitious **2** bombastic

high frequency any radio frequency between 3 and 30 megahertz

High German the West Germanic dialects spoken in central and S Germany

high'hand'ed *adj.* overbearing —**high'hand'ed·ly** *adv.* —**high'hand'ed·ness** *n.*

high'-hat' *adj.* [Slang] snobbish —*vt.* **-hat'ted, -hat'ting** [Slang] to snub

high'land (-lənd) *n.* region with many hills or mountains —**the Highlands** mountainous region occupying most of the N of Scotland —**High'land·er** *n.*

high'-lev'el *adj.* 1 of or by persons of high office 2 in a high office

high'light' *n.* 1 a part on which light is brightest: also **high light** 2 the most important or interesting part, scene, etc. —*vt.* 1 to give highlights to 2 to give prominence to; emphasize

high'ly *adv.* 1 very much 2 favorably 3 at a high level, wage, etc.

high'-mind'ed *adj.* having high ideals, principles, etc. —**high'-mind'ed·ly** *adv.*

high'ness *n.* 1 height 2 [H-] a title used in speaking to or of royalty

high'-pres'sure *adj.* 1 having or withstanding high pressure 2 using forcefully persuasive or insistent methods —*vt.* **-sured, -sur·ing** [Colloq.] to urge with such methods

high'-rise' *adj.* designating or of a tall apartment house, office building, etc. —*n.* a high-rise building

high'road' *n.* 1 [Chiefly Brit.] a highway 2 an easy or direct way

high school a secondary school that includes grades 10, 11, and 12, and sometimes grade 9

high seas open ocean waters outside the territorial limits of any nation

high sign a secret signal, as in a warning

high'-spir'it·ed (-spir'i tid) *adj.* 1 courageous 2 lively; fiery

high'-strung' *adj.* highly sensitive or nervous and tense

high'-tech' (-tek') *adj.* 1 of specialized, complex technology: in full **high'-tech·nol'o·gy** 2 of furnishings, fashions, etc. industrial in design

high'-ten'sion *adj.* having or carrying a high voltage

high tide the highest level to which the tide rises

high time time beyond the proper time but before it is too late

high'way' *n.* 1 a public road 2 a main road; thoroughfare

high'way·man (-mən) *n., pl.* **-men** one who robs travelers on a highway

high wire a cable stretched high above the ground, on which aerialists perform

hi·jack (hī'jak') *vt.* [Colloq.] 1 to steal (goods in transit, etc.) by force 2 to seize control forcibly of (an aircraft, etc.), esp. to go to a nonscheduled destination —**hi'jack'er** *n.*

hike (hīk) *vi.* **hiked, hik'ing** ⟦< dial. *heik*⟧ to take a long walk —*vt.* [Colloq.] 1 to pull up; hoist 2 to raise (prices, etc.) —*n.* 1 a long walk 2 [Colloq.] a rise —**hik'er** *n.*

hi·lar·i·ous (hi ler'ē əs, hī-) *adj.* ⟦< Gr *hilaros*, cheerful⟧ noisily merry; very funny —**hi·lar'i·ty** (-i tē) *n.*

hill (hil) *n.* ⟦OE *hyll*⟧ 1 a natural raised part of the earth's surface, smaller than a mountain 2 a small pile, heap, or mound

hill'bil'ly *n., pl.* **-lies** ⟦prec. + *Billy*⟧ [Colloq.] one who lives in or comes from the mountains or backwoods, esp. of the South

hill'side' *n.* the side of a hill

hill'top' *n.* the top of a hill

hill'y *adj.* **-i·er, -i·est** 1 full of hills 2 like a hill; steep —**hill'i·ness** *n.*

hilt (hilt) *n.* ⟦OE⟧ the handle of a sword, dagger, tool, etc.

him (him) *pron.* ⟦OE⟧ *objective case of* HE

Hi·ma·la·yas (him'ə lā'əz) mountain system of central Asia, mostly in India & China —**Hi'ma·la'yan** *adj.*

him·self' *pron.* a form of the 3d pers. sing., masc. pronoun, used as an intensive [he went *himself*], as a reflexive [he hurt *himself*], and as a quasi-noun meaning "his true self" [he is not *himself* today]

hind[1] (hīnd) *adj.* **hind'er, hind'most'** or **hind'er·most'** ⟦prob. < HINDER[2]⟧ back; rear; posterior

hind[2] (hīnd) *n.* ⟦OE⟧ the female of the red deer

Hind. 1 Hindi 2 Hindu

hin·der[1] (hin'dər) *vt.* ⟦OE *hindrian*⟧ 1 to keep back; stop 2 to impede; thwart

hind·er[2] (hīn'dər) *adj.* ⟦OE⟧ [Now Rare] rear

Hin·di (hin'dē) *n.* the main (and official) language of India

hind'most' *adj.* farthest back; last

hind'quar'ter *n.* either of the two hind legs and the adjoining part of a carcass of veal, beef, etc.

hin·drance (hin'drəns) *n.* 1 the act of hindering 2 an obstacle

hind'sight' *n.* ability to see, after the event, what should have been done

Hin·du (hin'dōō') *n.* 1 [Archaic] a native or inhabitant of India 2 a follower of Hinduism —*adj.* designating or of the Hindus or Hinduism

Hin'du·ism' *n.* the religion and social system of the Hindus

Hin·du·stan (hin'dōō stan') 1 a region in N India 2 the entire Indian subcontinent 3 the republic of India

hinge (hinj) *n.* ⟦< ME *hengen*, to hang⟧ 1 a joint on which a door, lid, etc. swings 2 a natural joint, as of the shell of a clam —*vt.* **hinged, hing'ing** to attach by a hinge —*vi.* to hang as on a hinge; depend

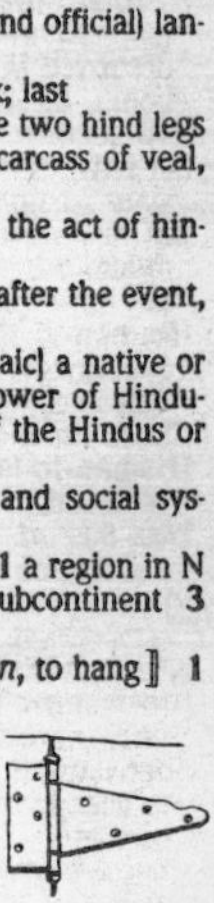

T HINGE

hint (hint) *n.* ⟦prob. < OE *hentan*, to grasp⟧ a slight indication; indirect suggestion —*vt., vi.* to give a hint (of)

hin·ter·land (hin'tər land') *n.* ⟦Ger⟧ 1 the land behind that bordering a coast or river 2 a remote area

hip[1] (hip) *n.* ⟦OE *hype*⟧ the part of the body around the joint formed by each thighbone and the pelvis

hip[2] (hip) *adj.* **hip'per, hip'pest** ⟦< ? HEP⟧ [Slang] 1 sophisticated; aware; fashionable 2 of hippies —**get** (or **be**) **hip to** [Slang] to become (or be) informed about

hip'pie *n.* [Slang] a person who, in a state of alienation from conventional society, turned variously to mysticism, psychedelic drugs, communal living, etc. Also **hip'py**, *pl.* **-pies**

hip·po (hip'ō) ***n.***, *pl.* **-pos** [Colloq.] HIPPOPOTAMUS

Hip·poc·ra·tes (hi päk'rə tēz') 460-*c.* 377 B.C.; Gr. physician

Hip·po·crat·ic oath (hip'ə krat'ik) the oath, attributed to Hippocrates, generally taken by medical graduates: it sets forth their ethical code

hip·po·drome (hip'ə drōm') ***n.*** ⟦< Gr *hippos*, horse + *dromos*, course⟧ an arena for a circus, game, etc.

hip·po·pot·a·mus (hip'ə pät'ə məs) ***n.***, *pl.* **-a·mus·es** or **-a·mi'** ⟦< Gr *hippos*, a horse + *potamos*, river⟧ a large, plant-eating mammal with a heavy, thick-skinned body and short legs: it lives chiefly in or near African rivers

hire (hīr) ***n.*** ⟦< OE *hyr*, wages⟧ **1** the amount paid in hiring **2** a hiring —***vt.*** **hired, hir'ing** to pay for the services of (a person) or the use of (a thing) —**hire out** to work for pay

hire'ling ***n.*** one who will follow anyone's orders for pay; mercenary

Hi·ro·shi·ma (hir'ə shē'mə; *occas.* hi rō'shi mə) seaport in SW Honshu, Japan: largely destroyed (Aug. 6, 1945) by a U.S. atomic bomb, the first ever used in warfare: pop. 907,000

hir·sute (hur'so͞ot', hər so͞ot') ***adj.*** ⟦L *hirsutus*⟧ hairy; shaggy

his (hiz) ***pron.*** ⟦OE⟧ that or those belonging to him /*his* are better/ —***poss. pronominal adj.*** of, belonging to, or done by him

His·pan·ic (hi span'ik) ***adj.*** **1** Spanish or Spanish-and-Portuguese **2** of or relating to Hispanics —***n.*** a Spanish-speaking person of Latin American origin who lives in the U.S.

His·pan·io·la (his'pən yō'lə) island in the West Indies, between Cuba & Puerto Rico

hiss (his) ***vi.*** ⟦echoic⟧ **1** to make a sound like that of a prolonged *s* **2** to show disapproval by hissing —***vt.*** to say or indicate by hissing —***n.*** the act or sound of hissing

hist (st; hist) ***interj.*** be quiet!

his·ta·mine (his'tə mēn', -min') ***n.*** ⟦< Gr *histos*, web + AMMONIA⟧ an ammonia derivative in all organic matter: it is released in allergic reactions, lowers the blood pressure, etc.

his·tol·o·gy (his täl'ə jē) ***n.*** ⟦< Gr *histos*, web + -LOGY⟧ *Biol.* the microscopic study of tissue structure —**his·tol'o·gist** ***n.***

his·to·ri·an (his tôr'ē ən) ***n.*** a writer of, or authority on, history

his·tor'ic (-ik) ***adj.*** historical; esp., famous in history

his·tor'i·cal (-i kəl) ***adj.*** **1** of or concerned with history **2** based on people or events of the past **3** established by history; factual —**his·tor'i·cal·ly** ***adv.***

historical present the present tense used for the narration of past events

his·to·ric·i·ty (his'tə ris'ə tē) ***n.*** historical authenticity

his·to·ri·og·ra·phy (his tôr'ē äg'rə fē) ***n.*** the study of the techniques of historical research

his·to·ry (his'tə rē, -trē) ***n.***, *pl.* **-ries** ⟦< Gr *histōr*, knowing⟧ **1** an account of what has happened, esp. in the life of a people, country, etc. **2** all recorded past events **3** the branch of knowledge that deals systematically with the past **4** a known or recorded past /the odd *history* of his coat/

his·tri·on·ic (his'trē än'ik) ***adj.*** ⟦< L *histrio*, actor⟧ **1** of acting or actors **2** overacted or overacting

his'tri·on'ics ***n.pl.*** [*sometimes with sing. v.*] **1** dramatics **2** an artificial manner, display of emotion, etc.

hit (hit) ***vt.***, ***vi.*** **hit, hit'ting** ⟦< ON *hitta*, meet with⟧ **1** to come against (something) with force; knock **2** to give a blow (to); strike **3** to strike with a missile **4** to affect strongly /a town hard *hit* by floods/ **5** to come (upon) by accident or after search **6** to arrive at /stocks *hit* a new high/ **7** *Baseball* to get (a hit) —***n.*** **1** a blow that strikes its mark **2** a collision **3** a successful and popular song, book, etc. **4** [Slang] a murder **5** [Slang] a dose of a drug, a drink of liquor, etc. **6** *Baseball* BASE HIT —**hit it off** to get along well together —**hit'ter** ***n.***

hit-and-run (hit''n run') ***adj.*** hitting a person, car, etc. with a moving vehicle and fleeing the scene immediately Also **hit'-skip'**

hitch (hich) ***vi.*** ⟦ME *hicchen*⟧ **1** to move jerkily **2** to become fastened or caught —***vt.*** **1** to move, pull, etc. with jerks **2** to fasten with a hook, knot, etc. **3** [Slang] to hitchhike —***n.*** **1** a tug; jerk **2** a limp **3** a hindrance; obstacle **4** a fastening or catch **5** [Slang] a period of time served **6** a kind of knot

hitch'hike' ***vi.*** **-hiked', -hik'ing** to travel by asking for rides from passing drivers —**hitch'hik'er** ***n.***

hith·er (hith'ər) ***adv.*** ⟦< OE *hider*⟧ to this place —***adj.*** nearer

hith'er·to' ***adv.*** until this time

Hit·ler (hit'lər), **Ad·olf** (ad'ôlf', ä'dôlf') 1889-1945; Nazi dictator of Germany (1933-45), born in Austria —**Hit·ler'i·an** (-lir'ē ən) ***adj.***

hit man [Colloq.] a hired murderer

hit'-or-miss' ***adj.*** haphazard; random

HIV ***n.*** a retrovirus that infects human T cells and causes AIDS

hive (hīv) ***n.*** ⟦< OE *hyfe*⟧ **1** a shelter for a colony of bees; beehive **2** a colony of bees; swarm **3** a crowd of busy people **4** a place of great activity —***vt.*** **hived, hiv'ing** to gather (bees) into a hive —***vi.*** to enter a hive

hives (hīvz) ***n.pl.*** ⟦orig. Scot dial.⟧ an allergic skin condition characterized by itching, burning, and the formation of smooth patches

HMO ***n.***, *pl.* **HMO's** ⟦*h*(*ealth*) *m*(*aintenance*) *o*(*rganization*)⟧ a health care system in which an organization hires medical professionals to provide services for its subscribers

HMS or **H.M.S.** **1** Her (or His) Majesty's Service **2** Her (or His) Majesty's Ship

hoa·gie or **hoa·gy** (hō'gē) ***n.***, *pl.* **-gies** HERO SANDWICH

hoard (hôrd) ***n.*** ⟦OE *hord*⟧ a supply stored up and hidden —***vi.***, ***vt.*** to accumulate and store away (money, goods, etc.) —**hoard'er** ***n.*** —**hoard'ing** ***n.***

hoar·frost (hôr'frôst') ***n.*** FROST (sense 2)

hoarse (hôrs) ***adj.*** ⟦OE *has*⟧ **1** harsh and

grating in sound **2** having a rough, husky voice —**hoarse'ness** *n.*

hoar·y (hôr'ē) *adj.* **-i·er, -i·est** ⟦< OE har⟧ **1** white or gray **2** having white or gray hair from old age **3** very old Also **hoar** —**hoar'i·ness** *n.*

hoax (hōks) *n.* ⟦< ? HOCUS-POCUS⟧ a trick or fraud; esp., a practical joke —*vt.* to deceive with a hoax

hob (häb) *n.* ⟦< *Robin* or *Robert*⟧ [Brit. Dial.] an elf or goblin —**play** (or **raise**) **hob with** to make trouble for

hob·ble (häb'əl) *vi.* **-bled, -bling** ⟦ME *hobelen*⟧ to go unsteadily; limp —*vt.* **1** to cause to limp **2** to hamper (a horse, etc.) by tying two feet together **3** to hinder —*n.* **1** a limp **2** a rope, etc. used to hobble a horse

hob·by (häb'ē) *n., pl.* **-bies** ⟦ME *hobi*⟧ **1** HOBBYHORSE **2** something that one likes to do in one's spare time —**hob'by·ist** *n.*

hob'by·horse' *n.* **1** a child's toy consisting of a stick with a horse's head **2** ROCKING HORSE **3** an idea with which one is preoccupied

hob·gob·lin (häb'gäb'lin) *n.* ⟦HOB + GOBLIN⟧ **1** an elf **2** a bugbear

hob'nail' *n.* ⟦*hob,* a peg + NAIL⟧ a short nail with a broad head, put on the soles of heavy shoes to prevent wear or slipping —*vt.* to put hobnails on

hob'nob' (-näb') *vi.* **-nobbed', -nob'bing** ⟦< ME *habben,* have + *nabben,* not to have⟧ to be on close terms

ho·bo (hō'bō') *n., pl.* **-bos'** or **-boes'** **1** a migratory worker **2** a tramp

Ho Chi Minh City (hō'chē'min') seaport in S Vietnam: formerly (as *Saigon*) capital of South Vietnam (1954-76): pop. 4,000,000

hock[1] (häk) *n.* ⟦< OE *hoh,* heel⟧ the joint bending backward in the hind leg of a horse, ox, etc.

hock[2] (häk) *vt., n.* ⟦< Du *hok,* prison⟧ [Slang] PAWN[1]

hock·ey (häk'ē) *n.* ⟦prob. < OFr *hoquet,* bent stick⟧ **1** a team game played on ice skates, with curved sticks and a hard rubber disk (*puck*) **2** a similar game played on foot on a field, with a small ball

hock'shop' *n.* [Slang] PAWNSHOP

ho·cus-po·cus (hō'kəs pō'kəs) *n.* ⟦imitation L⟧ **1** meaningless words used as a formula by conjurers **2** a magician's trick **3** trickery

hod (häd) *n.* ⟦prob. < MDu *hodde*⟧ **1** a long-handled wooden trough used for carrying bricks, mortar, etc. on the shoulder **2** a coal scuttle

hodge·podge (häj'päj') *n.* ⟦< OFr *hochepot,* a stew⟧ a jumbled mixture

Hodg·kin's disease (häj'kinz-) ⟦after T. *Hodgkin* 19th-c. Eng physician⟧ a chronic disease of unknown cause characterized by progressive enlargement of the lymph nodes

hoe (hō) *n.* ⟦< OHG *houwan,* to cut⟧ a tool with a thin blade set across the end of a long handle, for weeding, loosening soil, etc. —*vt., vi.* **hoed, hoe'ing** to cultivate with a hoe

hoe'cake' *n.* a thin bread made of cornmeal

hoe'down' *n.* **1** a lively, rollicking dance **2** a party with such dances

hog (hôg, häg) *n.* ⟦OE *hogg*⟧ **1** any swine, esp. a domesticated adult ready for market **2** [Colloq.] a selfish, greedy, or filthy person —*vt.* **hogged, hog'ging** [Slang] to take all of or an unfair share of —**go (the) whole hog** [Slang] to go all the way —**high on** (or **off**) **the hog** [Colloq.] in a luxurious or costly way —**hog'gish** *adj.* —**hog'gish·ly** *adv.*

ho·gan (hō'gôn', -gən) *n.* ⟦< AmInd⟧ a Navajo Indian dwelling, built of earth walls supported by timbers

hogs·head (hôgz'hed') *n.* **1** a large barrel or cask holding from 63 to 140 gallons **2** a liquid measure, esp. one equal to 63 gallons

hog'tie' *vt.* **-tied', -ty'ing** or **-tie'ing** **1** to tie the four feet or the hands and feet of **2** [Colloq.] to make incapable of effective action

hog'wash' *n.* **1** refuse fed to hogs; swill **2** insincere talk, writing, etc.

hoi pol·loi (hoi'pə loi') ⟦Gr, the many⟧ the common people; the masses

hoist (hoist) *vt.* ⟦< Du *hijschen*⟧ to raise aloft; lift, esp. with a pulley, crane, etc. —*n.* **1** a hoisting **2** an apparatus for lifting; elevator; tackle

hoke (hōk) *vt.* **hoked, hok'ing** ⟦< fol.⟧ [Slang] to treat in a sentimental or crudely comic way: usually with *up* —**hok'ey** *adj.*

ho·kum (hō'kəm) *n.* ⟦< HOCUS(-POCUS)⟧ [Slang] **1** trite sentiment, crude humor, etc. **2** nonsense; humbug

hold[1] (hōld) *vt.* **held, hold'ing** ⟦OE *haldan*⟧ **1** to keep in the hands, arms, etc.; grasp **2** to keep in a certain position or condition **3** to restrain or control; keep back **4** to possess; occupy /to *hold* an office/ **5** to guard; defend /*hold* the fort/ **6** to carry on (a meeting, etc.) **7** to contain /the jar *holds* a pint/ **8** to regard; consider /I *hold* the story to be true/ **9** *Law* to decide; decree —*vi.* **1** to go on being firm, loyal, etc. **2** to remain unbroken or unyielding /the rope *held*/ **3** to be true or valid /this rule *holds* for any case/ **4** to continue /the wind *held* steady/ —*n.* **1** a grasping or seizing; grip **2** a thing to hold on by **3** a thing for holding something else **4** a dominating force /she has a *hold* over him/ **5** a prison —**catch (get, lay, or take) hold of** to take, seize, acquire, etc. —**hold forth** **1** to preach; lecture **2** [Now Rare] to offer —**hold on** [Colloq.] stop! wait! —**hold out** **1** to last; endure **2** to stand firm **3** to offer **4** [Colloq.] to refuse to give (what is to be given) —**hold over** **1** to postpone **2** to stay for an additional period —**hold up** **1** to prop up **2** to show **3** to last; endure **4** to stop; delay **5** to stop forcibly and rob —**hold·er** *n.*

hold[2] (hōld) *n.* ⟦< HOLE or < MDu *hol*⟧ **1** the interior of a ship below decks, where the cargo is carried **2** the compartment for cargo in an aircraft

hold'ing *n.* **1** land, esp. a farm, rented from another **2** [*usually pl.*] property owned, esp. stocks or bonds

hold'o'ver *n.* [Colloq.] one staying on from a previous period

hold'up' *n.* **1** a delay **2** the act of stopping forcibly and robbing

hole (hōl) *n.* ⟦OE *hol*⟧ **1** a hollow place; cavity **2** an animal's burrow; den **3** a small, dingy, squalid place **4** an opening in anything; break; gap; tear **5** *Golf a)* a small cup into which a ball is to be hit *b)* the tee, the fairway, etc. leading to this **—hole up** [Colloq.] to hibernate, as in a hole **—in the hole** [Colloq.] financially embarrassed or behind

-hol·ic (häl′ik) *combining form* -AHOLIC

hol·i·day (häl′ə dā′) ***n.*** **1** a religious festival; holy day **2** a day of freedom from labor, often one set aside by law to celebrate some event **3** [*often pl.*] [Chiefly Brit.] a vacation **—*adj.*** of or for a holiday; joyous; gay

ho·li·er-than-thou (hō′lē ər *than thou*′) ***adj.*** annoyingly self-righteous

ho·li·ness (hō′lē nis) ***n.*** **1** a being holy **2** [H-] a title of the pope

ho·lis·tic (hō lis′tik) ***adj.*** of or dealing with wholes or integrated systems rather than with their parts /*holistic* health care/ **—ho·lis′ti·cal·ly *adv.***

Hol·land (häl′ənd) NETHERLANDS **—Hol′·land·er *n.***

hol·lan·daise sauce (häl′ən dāz′) ⟦Fr, of Holland⟧ a creamy sauce made of butter, egg yolks, lemon juice, etc.

hol·ler (häl′ər) ***vi., vt., n.*** [Colloq.] shout or yell

hol·low (häl′ō) ***adj.*** ⟦OE *holh*⟧ **1** having a cavity inside; not solid **2** shaped like a bowl; concave **3** sunken /*hollow* cheeks/ **4** empty or worthless /*hollow* praise/ **5** hungry **6** deep-toned and muffled **—*n.*** **1** a hollow place; cavity **2** a valley **—*vt., vi.*** to make or become hollow **—hol′low·ness *n.***

hol·ly (häl′ē) ***n., pl.* -lies** ⟦OE *holegn*⟧ an evergreen shrub or tree with stiff, glossy, sharp-pointed leaves and bright-red berries

hol′ly·hock′ *n.* ⟦< OE *halig*, holy + *hoc*, mallow⟧ a tall plant of the mallow family, with large, showy flowers

HOLLYHOCK

Hol·ly·wood (häl′ē wood′) **1** section of Los Angeles, Calif., once the site of many U.S. film studios **2** city on the SE coast of Fla.: pop. 117,000

Holmes (hōmz, hōlmz), **Ol·i·ver Wen·dell** (äl′ə vər wen′d′l) 1841-1935; associate justice, U.S. Supreme Court (1902-32)

hol·o·caust (häl′ə kôst′, hō′lə-) ***n.*** ⟦< Gr *holos*, whole + *kaustos*, burnt⟧ great destruction of life, esp. by fire **—the Holocaust** [*also* **the h-**] the killing of millions of European Jews by the Nazis

Hol·o·cene (häl′ō sēn′, hō′lə-) ***adj.*** ⟦< Gr *holos*, whole + *kainos*, recent⟧ designating the present epoch of geologic time

hol·o·graph (häl′ə graf′) ***n.*** ⟦< Gr *holos*, whole + *graphein*, to write⟧ a document, letter, etc. in the handwriting of the person under whose name it appears **—hol′o·graph′ic *adj.***

ho·log·ra·phy (hō läg′rə fē) ***n.*** ⟦< Gr *holos*, whole + -GRAPHY⟧ a method of making three-dimensional photographs using a laser beam

Hol·stein (hōl′stēn′, -stīn′) ***n.*** ⟦after the region of Schleswig-*Holstein*, Germany⟧ a breed of large, black-and-white dairy cattle

hol·ster (hōl′stər) ***n.*** ⟦Du⟧ a pistol case attached to a belt, saddle, etc.

ho·ly (hō′lē) ***adj.* -li·er** or **-li·est** ⟦OE *halig*⟧ [*often* **H-**] **1** dedicated to religious use; sacred **2** spiritually pure; sinless **3** deserving deep respect, awe, etc.

Holy Communion a Christian rite in which bread and wine are consecrated and received as the body and blood of Jesus or as symbols of them

Holy Land PALESTINE

Holy Roman Empire empire of west central Europe, from A.D. 962 until 1806

Holy Spirit (or **Ghost**) the third person of the Trinity; spirit of God

hom·age (häm′ij, äm′-) ***n.*** ⟦< L *homo*, man⟧ anything given or done to show reverence, honor, etc.

hom·burg (häm′burg′) ***n.*** ⟦after *Homburg*, Prussia⟧ a man's felt hat with a crown dented front to back and a stiff, curved brim

home (hōm) ***n.*** ⟦OE *ham*⟧ **1** the place where one lives **2** the place where one was born or reared **3** a place thought of as home **4** a household and its affairs **5** an institution for orphans, the aged, etc. **6** the natural environment of an animal, plant, etc. **7** HOME PLATE **—*adj.*** **1** of one's home or country; domestic **2** central /*home* office/ **—*adv.*** **1** at, to, or in the direction of home **2** to the point aimed at /to drive a nail *home*/ **—at home 1** in one's home **2** at ease **—bring home to** to impress upon **—home′less *adj.* —home′like′ *adj.***

home economics the science and art of homemaking, nutrition, etc.

home′land′ *n.* the country in which one was born or makes one's home

home′ly *adj.* -li·er, -li·est 1 suitable for home life; everyday **2** crude **3** plain or unattractive **—home′li·ness *n.***

home′made′ *adj.* made, or as if made, at home

home′mak′er *n.* one who manages a home

home plate *Baseball* the slab that the batter stands beside: it is the last base touched in scoring a run

Ho·mer (hō′mər) semilegendary Gr. epic poet of *c.* 8th c. B.C. **—Ho·mer·ic** (hō mer′ik) ***adj.***

home run *Baseball* a hit that allows the batter to touch all bases and score a run Also [Colloq.] **hom′er *n.***

home′sick′ *adj.* longing for home **—home′·sick′ness *n.***

home′spun′ *n.* **1** cloth made of yarn spun at home **2** coarse cloth like this **—*adj.*** **1** spun at home **2** made of homespun **3** plain; homely

home′stead′ (-sted′) ***n.*** **1** a place for a family's home, including the land and buildings **2** a tract of land granted by the U.S. government to a settler **—home′stead′er *n.***

home′stretch′ *n.* **1** the part of a racetrack between the last turn and the finish line **2** the final part

home′ward *adv., adj.* toward home Also **home′wards *adv.***

home′work′ *n.* **1** work, esp. piecework, done at home **2** lessons to be done outside the classroom 3 preparation for some project: usually in **do one's homework**

home'y (-ē) *adj.* **hom'i·er, hom'i·est** familiar, cozy, etc. —**home'y·ness** *n.*

hom·i·cide (häm'ə sīd', hō'mə-) *n.* ⟦< L *homo*, a man + *caedere*, to kill⟧ 1 the killing of one person by another 2 a person who kills another —**hom'i·ci'dal** *adj.*

hom·i·let·ics (häm'ə let'iks) *n.pl.* ⟦see fol.⟧ the art of preparing and delivering sermons

hom·i·ly (häm'ə lē) *n., pl.* **-lies** ⟦< Gr *homilos*, assembly⟧ 1 a sermon 2 a solemn, moralizing talk or writing

homing pigeon a pigeon trained to find its way home from distant places

hom·i·nid (häm'ə nid) *n.* ⟦< L *homo*, a man⟧ a human, extinct or living

hom·i·ny (häm'ə nē) *n.* ⟦< AmInd⟧ dry corn hulled and coarsely ground (**hominy grits**): it is boiled for food

homo- ⟦< Gr *homos*⟧ *combining form* same, equal, like

ho·mo·ge·ne·ous (hō'mō jē'nē əs, -mə-; häm'ō-, -ə-) *adj.* ⟦see prec. & GENUS⟧ 1 the same in structure, quality, etc.; similar 2 composed of similar parts —**ho'mo·ge·ne'i·ty** (-jə nē'ə tē; -nā'-) *n.*

ho·mog·e·nize (hə mäj'ə nīz') *vt.* **-nized', -niz'ing** to make homogeneous, or more uniform throughout; specif., to process (milk) so that fat particles are so finely emulsified that the cream does not separate

hom·o·graph (häm'ə graf', hō'mə-) *n.* ⟦HOMO- + -GRAPH⟧ a word with the same spelling as another but with a different meaning and origin

ho·mol·o·gous (hō mäl'ə gəs) *adj.* ⟦Gr *homologos*, agreeing⟧ matching in structure, position, etc.

hom·o·nym (häm'ə nim') *n.* ⟦< Gr *homos*, same + *onyma*, name⟧ a word with the same pronunciation as another but with a different meaning, origin, and, usually, spelling

ho·mo·pho·bi·a (hō'mə fō'bē ə) *n.* ⟦HOMO(SEXUAL) + -PHOBIA⟧ hatred or fear of homosexuals or homosexuality —**ho'mo·pho'bic** (-fō'bik) *adj.*

Ho·mo sa·pi·ens (hō'mō sā'pē enz') ⟦ModL *homo*, man + *sapiens*, prp. of *sapere*, to know⟧ human being

ho·mo·sex·u·al (hō'mō sek'sho͞o əl, -mə-) *adj.* of or having sexual desire for those of the same sex —*n.* a homosexual person —**ho'mo·sex'ual'i·ty** (-al'ə tē) *n.*

Hon. honorable

Hon·du·ras (hän do͞or'əs) country in Central America: 43,227 sq. mi.; pop. 4,092,000

hone (hōn) *n.* ⟦OE *han*, a stone⟧ a hard stone used to sharpen cutting tools —*vt.* **honed, hon'ing** to sharpen, as with a hone

hon·est (än'ist) *adj.* ⟦< L *honor*, honor⟧ 1 truthful; trustworthy 2 *a*) sincere or fair [*honest* effort] *b*) gained by fair means [an *honest* living] 3 frank and open [an *honest* face] —**hon'est·ly** *adv.* —**hon'es·ty** *n.*

hon·ey (hun'ē) *n., pl.* **-eys** ⟦OE *hunig*⟧ 1 a sweet, syrupy substance that bees make as food from the nectar of flowers 2 sweetness 3 darling

hon'ey·comb' *n.* 1 the structure of six-sided wax cells made by bees to hold their honey or eggs 2 anything like this —*vt.* to cause to have holes like a honeycomb —*adj.* of or like a honeycomb: also **hon'ey·combed'**

hon'ey·dew' melon a variety of melon with a smooth, whitish rind and sweet, greenish flesh

hon'ey·lo'cust *n.* a North American tree having featherlike foliage and large, twisted pods

hon'ey·moon' *n.* the vacation spent together by a newly married couple —*vi.* to have or spend a honeymoon

hon'ey·suck'le *n.* a plant with small, fragrant flowers of red, yellow, or white

Hong Kong or **Hong·kong** (häŋ'käŋ', hôŋ' kôŋ') British colony in SE China

honk (hôŋk, häŋk) *n.* ⟦echoic⟧ 1 the call of a wild goose 2 a similar sound, as of an automobile horn —*vi., vt.* to make or cause to make such a sound

hon·ky-tonk (hôŋ'kē tôŋk') *n.* [Old Slang] a cheap, noisy nightclub —*adj.* designating music played on a piano with a tinkling sound

Hon·o·lu·lu (hän'ə lo͞o'lo͞o, hō'nə-) capital of Hawaii: seaport on Oahu: pop. 365,000

hon·or (än'ər) *n.* ⟦L⟧ 1 high regard or respect; esp., *a*) glory; fame *b*) good reputation 2 adherence to principles considered right; integrity 3 chastity 4 high rank; distinction 5 [H-] a title of certain officials, as judges 6 something done or given as a token of respect 7 a source of respect and fame —*vt.* 1 to respect greatly 2 to show high regard for 3 to do or give something in honor of 4 to accept and pay [to *honor* a check] Brit. sp. **hon'our** —**do the honors** to act as host

hon'or·a·ble *adj.* 1 worthy of being honored 2 honest; upright 3 bringing honor —**hon'or·a·bly** *adv.*

hon·o·ra·ri·um (än'ə rer'ē əm) *n., pl.* **-ri·ums** or **-ri·a** (-ə) ⟦L⟧ a payment as to a professional person for services on which no fee is set

hon'or·ar'y (-ər er'ē) *adj.* 1 given as an honor 2 designating or in an office held as an honor, without service or pay —**hon'or·ar'i·ly** *adv.*

hon'or·if'ic (-ə rif'ik) *adj.* ⟦< L *honor* + *facere*, to make⟧ conferring honor [an *honorific* title]

Hon·shu (hän'sho͞o') largest of the islands forming Japan

hood (hood) *n.* ⟦OE *hod*⟧ 1 a covering for the head and neck, often part of a coat, etc. 2 anything resembling a hood, as the metal cover over an automobile engine —*vt.* to cover as with a hood —**hood'ed** *adj.*

-hood (hood) ⟦OE *had*⟧ *suffix* 1 state or quality [*childhood*] 2 the whole group of [*priesthood*]

hood·lum (hood'ləm, ho͞od'-) *n.* ⟦prob. < Ger dial. *hudilump*, wretch⟧ a lawless person, as a member of a gang

hoo·doo (ho͞o'do͞o') *n., pl.* **-doos'** ⟦var. of VOODOO⟧ 1 VOODOO 2 [Colloq.] bad luck or a person or thing that causes it

hood'wink' *vt.* ⟦HOOD + WINK⟧ to mislead by trickery; dupe

hoo·ey (ho͞o'ē) *interj., n.* ⟦echoic⟧ [Slang] nonsense; bunk

hoof (ho͞of, hoof) ***n., pl.*** **hoofs** or **hooves** (ho͞ovz, hoovz) ⟦OE *hof*⟧ the horny covering on the feet of cattle, horses, etc., or the entire foot —***vt., vi.*** [Colloq.] to walk —**hoofed** ***adj.***

hook (hook) ***n.*** ⟦OE *hoc*⟧ **1** a bent piece of metal, etc. used to catch, hold, or pull something **2** a fishhook **3** something shaped like a hook **4** something moving in a hooklike path, as a punch or pitch —***vt.*** **1** to catch, fasten, throw, etc. with a hook **2** [Colloq.] to steal —***vi.*** **1** to curve as a hook does **2** to be fastened or caught by a hook —**by hook or by crook** by any means, honest or dishonest —**hook up** to connect (a radio, etc.) —**off the hook** [Colloq.] out of trouble

hook·ah or **hook·a** (hook'ə) ***n.*** ⟦Ar *ḥuqqa*⟧ a tobacco pipe of the Middle East, with a long tube for drawing the smoke through water to cool it

hooked (hookt) ***adj.*** **1** like a hook **2** made with a hook [*hooked* rug] **3** [Slang] *a*) obsessed with or addicted to (often with *on*) *b*) married

hook'er ***n.*** [Slang] a prostitute

hook'up' ***n.*** the arrangement and connection of parts, circuits, etc., as in a radio

hook'worm' ***n.*** a small, parasitic, intestinal roundworm with hooks around the mouth

hoo·li·gan (ho͞o'li gən) ***n.*** ⟦< ? *Hooligan*, a family name⟧ [Slang] a hoodlum

hoop (ho͞op) ***n.*** ⟦OE *hop*⟧ **1** a circular band for holding together the staves of a barrel, etc. **2** anything like this, as a metal basketball rim —***vt.*** to bind or fasten as with a hoop

hoop·la (ho͞op'lä') ***n.*** ⟦< ?⟧ [Colloq.] **1** great excitement **2** showy publicity

hoop skirt a skirt worn over a framework of hoops

hoo·ray (hoo rā', hə-; ho͞o-) ***interj., n., vi., vt.*** HURRAH

hoose·gow (ho͞os'gou') ***n.*** ⟦< Sp *juzgado*, court of justice⟧ [Slang] a jail

Hoo·sier (ho͞o'zhər) ***n.*** [Colloq.] a native or inhabitant of Indiana

hoot (ho͞ot) ***n.*** ⟦echoic⟧ **1** the sound that an owl makes **2** any sound like this, as a shout of scorn —***vi.*** to utter a hoot —***vt.*** to express (scorn) of (someone) by hooting —**hoot'er** ***n.***

hoot·en·an·ny (ho͞ot''n an'ē, ho͞ot''n an'ē) ***n., pl.*** **-nies** a meeting of folk singers, as for public entertainment

Hoo·ver (ho͞o'vər), **Her·bert C(lark)** (hur'bərt) 1874-1964; 31st president of the U.S. (1929-33)

hop[1] (häp) ***vi.*** **hopped, hop'ping** ⟦OE *hoppian*⟧ **1** to make a short leap or leaps on one foot **2** to leap with both, or all, feet at once, as a frog **3** [Colloq.] to go briskly —***vt.*** **1** to jump over **2** to get aboard —***n.*** **1** a hopping **2** [Colloq.] *a*) a dance *b*) a short flight in an airplane

hop[2] (häp) ***n.*** ⟦< MDu *hoppe*⟧ **1** a twining vine with small, cone-shaped flowers **2** [*pl.*] the dried ripe cones, used for flavoring beer, ale, etc. —**hop up** **1** to stimulate, as by a drug **2** to supercharge (an automobile engine, etc.)

hope (hōp) ***n.*** ⟦OE *hopa*⟧ **1** a feeling that what is wanted will happen; desire accompanied by expectation **2** the object of this **3** a person or thing on which one may base some hope —***vt.*** **hoped, hop'ing** to want and expect —***vi.*** to have hope (*for*) —**hope'ful** ***adj.*** —**hope'ful·ly** ***adv.*** —**hope'less** ***adj.*** —**hope'less·ly** ***adv.***

hop'head' ***n.*** [Slang] a drug addict

hop·per (häp'ər) ***n.*** **1** one that hops **2** any hopping insect **3** a container from which the contents can be emptied slowly and evenly

hop·sack·ing (häp'sak'iŋ) ***n.*** a sturdy fabric resembling coarse material used for bags, that is made into coats, suits, etc. Also **hop'sack'**

hop·scotch (häp'skäch') ***n.*** a children's game in which a player hops from section to section of a figure drawn on the ground

Hor·ace (hôr'is, här'-) 65-8 B.C.; Rom. poet

horde (hôrd) ***n.*** ⟦ult. < Tatar *urdu*, a camp⟧ a crowd or throng; swarm —***vi.*** **hord'ed, hord'ing** to form or gather in a horde

hore·hound (hôr'hound') ***n.*** ⟦OE *harhune*⟧ **1** a bitter mint plant **2** medicine or candy made from its juice

ho·ri·zon (hə rī'zən) ***n.*** ⟦< Gr *horos*, boundary⟧ **1** the line where the sky seems to meet the earth **2** [*usually pl.*] the limit of one's experience, interest, etc.

hor·i·zon·tal (hôr'i zänt''l) ***adj.*** **1** parallel to the plane of the horizon; not vertical **2** flat and even; level —**hor'i·zon'tal·ly** ***adv.***

hor·mone (hôr'mōn') ***n.*** ⟦< Gr *hormē*, impulse⟧ a substance formed in some organ of the body and carried to another part, where it takes effect —**hor·mo'nal** ***adj.***

horn (hôrn) ***n.*** ⟦OE⟧ **1** a hard, bonelike projection growing on the head of a cow, goat, etc. **2** the substance horns are made of **3** anything like a horn in position, shape, etc. **4** any brass instrument; specif., FRENCH HORN **5** a device sounded to give a warning —***adj.*** made of horn —**horn in** (**on**) to intrude or meddle (in) —**horned** ***adj.*** —**horn'less** ***adj.*** —**horn'like'** ***adj.***

Horn, Cape southernmost point of South America, on an island of Chile

horn·blende (hôrn'blend') ***n.*** ⟦Ger⟧ a black, rock-forming mineral, common in some kinds of granite

horned toad a small, scaly, insect-eating lizard with hornlike spines

hor·net (hôr'nit) ***n.*** ⟦OE *hyrnet*⟧ a large, yellow and black wasp

horn of plenty CORNUCOPIA

horn'pipe' ***n.*** ⟦ME⟧ a lively dance formerly popular with sailors

horn·y (hôrn'ē) ***adj.*** **-i·er, -i·est** **1** made of horn **2** having horns **3** toughened and calloused [*horny* hands] **4** [Slang] sexually aroused

ho·rol·o·gy (hō räl'ə jē) ***n.*** ⟦< Gr *hōra*, hour + -LOGY⟧ the science of measuring time or making timepieces

hor·o·scope (hôr'ə skōp') ***n.*** ⟦< Gr *hōra*, hour + *skopos*, watcher⟧ a chart of the zodiacal signs and positions of planets, etc., esp. at the time of a person's birth, used by an astrologer to make a forecast

hor·ren·dous (hô ren'dəs) ***adj.*** ⟦see HORRID⟧ horrible; frightful

hor·ri·ble (hôr'ə bəl) ***adj.*** ⟦see fol.⟧ **1**

causing horror; terrible; dreadful **2** [Colloq.] very bad, ugly, unpleasant, etc. —**hor'ri·bly** *adv.*

hor·rid (hôr'id) *adj.* ⟦< L *horrere*, to bristle, shake, be afraid⟧ **1** causing horror; terrible **2** very bad, ugly, unpleasant, etc. —**hor'rid·ly** *adv.*

hor·rif·ic (hô rif'ik, hə-) *adj.* horrifying

hor·ri·fy (hôr'ə fī') *vt.* **-fied', -fy'ing** **1** to cause to feel horror **2** [Colloq.] to shock or disgust

hor·ror (hôr'ər) *n.* ⟦see HORRID⟧ **1** the strong feeling caused by something frightful or shocking **2** strong dislike **3** something that causes horror, etc.

hors de com·bat (ôr də kōn bä') ⟦Fr, out of combat⟧ disabled

hors d'oeu·vre (ôr'durv') *pl.* **hors d'oeu·vres** (ôr'durvz') ⟦Fr, lit., outside of work⟧ an appetizer, as olives, canapés, etc., served before a meal

horse (hôrs) *n.* ⟦OE *hors*⟧ **1** a large, four-legged, solid-hoofed animal with flowing mane and tail, domesticated for drawing loads, carrying riders, etc. **2** a frame with legs for supporting something —*vt.* **horsed, hors'ing** to supply with a horse or horses; put on horseback —*adj.* of or on horses —**hold one's horses** [Slang] to curb one's impatience —**horse around** [Slang] to engage in horseplay

horse'back' *n.* the back of a horse —*adv.* on horseback

horse chestnut **1** a flowering tree with large leaves and glossy brown seeds **2** its seed

horse'feath'ers *n.*, *interj.* [Slang] nonsense

horse'fly' *n.*, *pl.* **-flies'** a large fly that sucks the blood of horses, etc.

horse'hair' *n.* **1** hair from the mane or tail of a horse **2** a stiff fabric made from this hair

horse'hide' *n.* **1** the hide of a horse **2** leather made from this

horse'laugh' *n.* a loud, boisterous, usually derisive laugh; guffaw

horse'man (-mən) *n.*, *pl.* **-men** a man skilled in the riding or care of horses —**horse'man·ship'** *n.* —**horse'wom'an**, *pl.* **-wom'en**, *n.fem.*

horse opera [Slang] WESTERN (*n.*)

horse pistol a large pistol formerly carried by horsemen

horse'play' *n.* rough, boisterous fun

horse'pow'er *n.* a unit for measuring the power of engines, etc., equal to 746 watts or 33,000 foot-pounds per minute

horse'rad'ish *n.* **1** a plant with a pungent, white, fleshy root **2** a relish made of the grated root

horse sense [Colloq.] common sense

horse'shoe' *n.* **1** a flat, U-shaped metal plate nailed to a horse's hoof to protect the hoof **2** anything shaped like this **3** [*pl.*] a game in which players toss horseshoes at two stakes

horseshoe crab a sea arthropod shaped like the base of a horse's foot, with a long, spine-like tail

horse'tail' *n.* a common rushlike plant found in moist areas

horse'whip' *n.* a whip for driving horses —*vt.* **-whipped', -whip'ping** to lash with a horsewhip

hors·y (hôrs'ē) *adj.* **-i·er, -i·est** **1** of, like, or suggesting a horse **2** of or like people who are fond of horses, fox-hunting, horse racing, etc. Also **hors'ey**

hor·ta·to·ry (hôr'tə tôr'ē) *adj.* ⟦< L *hortari*, incite⟧ exhorting; advising

hor·ti·cul·ture (hôr'ti kul'chər) *n.* ⟦< L *hortus*, garden + *cultura*, cultivation⟧ the art or science of growing flowers, fruits, and vegetables —**hor'ti·cul'tur·al** *adj.*

ho·san·na (hō zan'ə) *n.*, *interj.* ⟦< Heb *hōshī'āh nnā*, lit., save, we pray⟧ an exclamation of praise to God

hose (hōz) *n.*, *pl.* **hose** or, for 2, usually **hos'es** ⟦OE *hosa*⟧ **1** [*pl.*] *a*) stockings *b*) socks **2** a flexible tube used to convey fluids —*vt.* **hosed, hos'ing** to water with a hose

ho·sier·y (hō'zhər ē) *n.* stockings

hos·pice (häs'pis) *n.* ⟦< L *hospes*, host, guest⟧ **1** a shelter for travelers **2** a homelike facility for the care of terminally ill patients

hos·pi·ta·ble (häs'pit ə bəl, häs pit'-) *adj.* ⟦see prec.⟧ friendly and solicitous toward guests, new arrivals, etc. —**hos'pi·ta·bly** *adv.*

hos·pi·tal (häs'pit''l) *n.* ⟦< L *hospes*, host, guest⟧ an institution providing medical treatment for people who are ill, injured, pregnant, etc.

hos·pi·tal·i·ty (häs'pi tal'ə tē) *n.*, *pl.* **-ties** the act, practice, or quality of being hospitable

hos·pi·tal·ize (häs'pit'l īz') *vt.* **-ized', -iz'ing** to put in, or admit to, a hospital —**hos'pi·tal·i·za'tion** *n.*

host[1] (hōst) *n.* ⟦< ML *hostia*⟧ a wafer of the bread used in the Eucharist

host[2] (hōst) *n.* ⟦< L *hospes*, host, guest⟧ **1** one who entertains guests, esp. at home **2** a person who keeps an inn or hotel **3** any organism on or in which a parasitic organism lives —*vi.*, *vt.* to act as host (to)

host[3] (hōst) *n.* ⟦< ML *hostis*, army⟧ **1** an army **2** a great number

hos·tage (häs'tij) *n.* ⟦< OFr⟧ a person kept or given as a pledge until certain conditions are met

hos·tel (häs'təl) *n.* ⟦< L *hospes*, host, guest⟧ an inn Also **hos'tel·ry** (-rē), *pl.* **-ries** —**hos'tel·er** *n.*

host·ess (hōs'tis) *n.* **1** a woman who entertains guests, esp. at home; sometimes, the host's wife **2** a woman employed in a restaurant to supervise serving, seating, etc.

hos·tile (häs'təl) *adj.* ⟦< L *hostis*, enemy⟧ **1** of or characteristic of an enemy **2** unfriendly; antagonistic —**hos'tile·ly** *adv.*

hos·til·i·ty (häs til'ə tē) *n.*, *pl.* **-ties** **1** a feeling of enmity, ill will, etc. **2** *a*) a hostile act *b*) [*pl.*] warfare

hos·tler (häs'lər, äs'-) *n.* ⟦contr. of HOSTELER⟧ one who takes care of horses at an inn, stable, etc.

hot (hät) *adj.* **hot'ter, hot'test** ⟦OE *hat*⟧ **1** *a*) having a temperature higher than that of the human body *b*) having a relatively high temperature **2** producing a burning sensation /*hot* pepper/ **3** characterized by strong feeling or intense activity, etc., as *a*) impetuous /a *hot* temper/ *b*) violent /a *hot* battle/

c) lustful d) very controversial **4** following closely /in *hot* pursuit/ **5** electrically charged /a *hot* wire/ **6** [Colloq.] recent; fresh /*hot* news/ **7** [Slang] a) recently stolen or smuggled b) excellent; good —**make it hot for** [Colloq.] to make things uncomfortable for —**hot′ly** *adv.* —**hot′ness** *n.*

hot air [Slang] empty talk

hot′bed′ *n.* **1** a bed of earth covered with glass and heated, as by manure, for forcing plants **2** any place that fosters rapid growth or extensive activity

hot′blood′ed *adj.* easily excited; passionate, reckless, etc.

hot′box′ *n.* an overheated bearing on an axle or shaft

hot cake a pancake —**sell like hot cakes** [Colloq.] to be sold rapidly and in large quantities

hot dog [Colloq.] a wiener, esp. one served hot in a long, soft roll

ho·tel (hō tel′) *n.* ⟦< OFr *hostel*, hostel⟧ an establishment providing lodging and, usually, meals for travelers, etc.

ho·tel·ier (hōt″l ir′, -yā′; hō′tel′-) *n.* ⟦Fr⟧ an owner or manager of a hotel

hot flash the sensation of a wave of heat passing over the body, often experienced by women during menopause

hot′head′ed *adj.* **1** quick-tempered **2** impetuous —**hot′head′** *n.*

hot′house′ *n.* GREENHOUSE

hot line a telephone line for immediate communication, as between heads of state in a crisis

hot plate a small, portable stove for cooking food

hot potato [Colloq.] a troubling problem that no one wants to handle

hot rod [Slang] an automobile, often an old one, whose engine has been supercharged —**hot rod·der**

hot seat [Slang] **1** ELECTRIC CHAIR **2** a difficult situation

hot′shot′ *n.* [Slang] one who is expert at something in an aggressive way

hot′-tem′pered *adj.* having a fiery temper

Hot·ten·tot (hät″n tät′) *n.* **1** a member of a nomadic people of SW Africa **2** their language

hot tub a large wooden tub in which several people can soak in hot water

hound (hound) *n.* ⟦OE *hund*, dog⟧ **1** any of several breeds of hunting dog **2** any dog —*vt.* **1** to hunt or chase with or as with hounds **2** to urge on

hounds·tooth check (houndz′to͞oth′) a pattern of irregular broken checks, used in woven material

hour (our) *n.* ⟦< Gr *hōra*⟧ **1** one of the twenty-four parts of a day; sixty minutes **2** the time for a particular activity /lunch *hour*/ **3** [*pl.*] a period fixed for work, etc. /office *hours*/ **4** the time of day /the *hour* is 2:30/ **5** *Educ.* a credit, equal to one hour spent in class per week —**after hours** after the regular hours for business, school, etc. —**hour after hour** every hour

hour′glass′ *n.* an instrument for measuring time by the trickling of sand, etc. from one part to another

HOURGLASS

hour hand the short hand of a clock or watch, which indicates the hours

hou·ri (ho͝o′rē, hou′-) *n.*, *pl.* **-ris** ⟦< Ar *hūrīyah*, black-eyed woman⟧ a beautiful nymph of the Muslim Paradise

hour′ly *adj.* **1** happening every hour **2** done during an hour **3** frequent —*adv.* **1** once an hour **2** often

house (hous; *for v.* houz) *n.*, *pl.* **hous·es** (hou′ziz) ⟦OE *hus*⟧ **1** a building to live in; specif., a building occupied by one family or person **2** the people who live in a house; household **3** [*often* **H-**] a family as including kin, ancestors, and descendants, esp. a royal family **4** shelter, living or storage space, etc. **5** a) a theater b) the audience in a theater **6** a business firm **7** [*often* **H-**] a legislative assembly —*vt.* **housed, hous′ing** **1** to provide a house or lodgings for **2** to cover, shelter, etc. —**keep house** to take care of a home —**on the house** at the expense of the establishment

house′boat′ *n.* a large, flat-bottomed boat used as a residence

house′break′ing *n.* the act of breaking into and entering another's house to commit theft or another felony

house′bro′ken *adj.* trained to live in a house (i.e., to urinate, etc. in a special place): said of a dog, cat, etc.

house′fly′ *n.*, *pl.* **-flies′** a two-winged fly found in and around houses

house′hold′ *n.* **1** all those living in one house **2** the home and its affairs —**house′hold′er** *n.*

household word a common saying or thing, familiar to nearly everyone

house′hus′band *n.* a married man whose job is keeping house and taking care of domestic affairs

house′keep′er *n.* one who runs a home, esp. a person hired to do this

house′maid′ *n.* a maid for housework

House of Commons the lower house of the legislature of Great Britain or Canada

House of Lords the upper house of the legislature of Great Britain

House of Representatives the lower house of the legislature of the U.S. and most of the States of the U.S.

house′plant′ *n.* an indoor plant used mainly for decoration

house′wares′ (-werz′) *n.pl.* articles for household use, esp. in the kitchen

house′warm′ing *n.* a party to celebrate moving into a new home

house′wife′ *n.*, *pl.* **-wives′** a married woman whose job is keeping house and taking care of domestic affairs

house′work′ *n.* the work involved in keeping house; cleaning, cooking, etc.

hous·ing (hou′ziŋ) *n.* **1** the providing of shelter or lodging **2** shelter or lodging **3** houses collectively **4** *Mech.* a frame, box, etc. for containing some part, mechanism, etc.

Hous·ton (hyo͞os′tən) city & port in SE Tex.: pop. 1,594,000

hove (hōv) *vt.*, *vi.* *alt. pt. & pp. of* HEAVE

hov·el (huv′əl, häv′-) ***n.*** ⟦ME⟧ any small, miserable dwelling; hut
hov·er (huv′ər, häv′-) ***vi.*** ⟦< ME *hoven*, to stay (suspended)⟧ **1** to flutter in the air near one place **2** to linger close by **3** to waver (*between*)
how (hou) ***adv.*** ⟦OE *hu*⟧ **1** in what manner or way **2** in what state or condition **3** for what reason **4** to what extent, degree, etc. *How* is also used as an intensive —**how about?** what is your thought concerning?
how·be·it (hou bē′it) ***adv.*** [Archaic] however it may be; nevertheless
how·dah (hou′də) ***n.*** ⟦Hindi *hauda*⟧ a seat for riding on the back of an elephant or camel
how·ev′er ***adv.*** **1** in whatever manner **2** to whatever degree **3** nevertheless Also [Old Poet.] **how·e′er′**
how·itz·er (hou′it sər) ***n.*** ⟦< Czech *houfnice*, orig., a sling⟧ a short cannon, firing shells in a high trajectory
howl (houl) ***vi.*** ⟦ME *hulen*⟧ **1** to utter the long, wailing cry of wolves, dogs, etc. **2** to utter a similar cry of pain, anger, etc. **3** to shout or laugh in scorn, mirth, etc. —***vt.*** **1** to utter with a howl **2** to drive by howling —***n.*** **1** the wailing cry of a wolf, dog, etc. **2** any similar sound **3** [Colloq.] a joke
howl′er ***n.*** **1** one that howls **2** [Colloq.] a ludicrous blunder
how·so·ev·er (hou′sō ev′ər) ***adv.*** **1** to whatever degree or extent **2** by whatever means
hoy·den (hoi′dən) ***n.*** ⟦< ? Du⟧ a bold, boisterous girl; tomboy
Hoyle (hoil) ***n.*** a book of rules for card games, orig. compiled by E. Hoyle (1672-1769) —**according to Hoyle** according to the rules
HP or **hp** horsepower
HQ or **hq** headquarters
hr. hour
HR or **H.R.** House of Representatives
HRH or **H.R.H.** Her (or His) Royal Highness
HS or **H.S.** high school
ht. height
Huang (hwäŋ) river in N China, flowing into the Yellow Sea: also **Hwang**
hua·ra·ches (wä rä′chēz′, -chäz′) ***n.pl.*** ⟦MexSp⟧ flat sandals with uppers made of straps or woven leather strips
hub (hub) ***n.*** ⟦< ?⟧ **1** the center part of a wheel **2** a center of activity
hub·bub (hub′bub′) ***n.*** ⟦prob. < Gael exclamation⟧ an uproar; tumult
hub′cap′ ***n.*** a tight cap over the hub of a wheel, esp. on an automobile
hu·bris (hyōō′bris) ***n.*** ⟦Gr *hybris*⟧ arrogance caused by excessive pride
huck·le·ber·ry (huk′əl ber′ē) ***n.***, *pl.* **-ries** ⟦prob. < ME *hurtilberye*⟧ **1** a shrub with blue berries **2** this berry
huck·ster (huk′stər) ***n.*** ⟦< MDu *hoeken*, peddle⟧ a peddler, esp. of fruits, vegetables, etc. —***vt.*** to peddle
HUD (Department of) Housing and Urban Development
hud·dle (hud′'l) ***vi., vt.*** **-dled, -dling** ⟦< ?⟧ **1** to crowd close together **2** to draw (oneself) up —***n.*** **1** a confused crowd or heap **2** [Colloq.] a private conference **3** *Football* a grouping of a team to get signals before a play
Hud·son (hud′s'n) river in E N.Y.
Hudson Bay inland sea in NE Canada; arm of the Atlantic
hue[1] (hyōō) ***n.*** ⟦< OE *heow*⟧ **1** color **2** a particular shade or tint of a color
hue[2] (hyōō) ***n.*** ⟦< OFr *hu*, outcry⟧ a shouting: now only in **hue and cry**
huff (huf) ***vi.*** to blow; puff —***n.*** a state of smoldering anger or resentment —**huff′y, -i·er, -i·est, *adj.***
hug (hug) ***vt.*** **hugged, hug′ging** ⟦prob. < ON *hugga*, to comfort⟧ **1** to clasp closely and fondly in the arms; embrace **2** to cling to (a belief, etc.) **3** to keep close to —***vi.*** to embrace each other —***n.*** a close embrace
huge (hyōōj) ***adj.*** **hug′er, hug′est** ⟦< OFr *ahuge*⟧ very large; gigantic; immense —**huge′ly *adv.*** —**huge′ness *n.***
Hu·go (hyōō′gō), **Vic·tor Ma·rie** (vēk tôr′ mä rē′) 1802-85; Fr. poet, novelist, & playwright
Hu·gue·not (hyōō′gə nät′) ***n.*** a 16th or 17th-c. French Protestant
huh (hu, hun) ***interj.*** an exclamation used to express contempt, surprise, etc., or to ask a question
hu·la (hōō′lə) ***n.*** ⟦Haw⟧ a native Hawaiian dance Also **hu′la-hu′la**
hulk (hulk) ***n.*** ⟦< Gr *holkas*, towed ship⟧ **1** the hull of an old, dismantled ship **2** a big, clumsy person or thing
hulk′ing *adj.* bulky and clumsy
hull (hul) ***n.*** ⟦OE *hulu*⟧ **1** the outer covering of a seed or fruit, as the husk of grain, shell of a nut, etc. **2** the frame or main body of a ship, airship, etc. **3** any outer covering —***vt.*** to take the hulls off (nuts, etc.) —**hull′er *n.***
hul·la·ba·loo (hul′ə bə lōō′) ***n.*** ⟦echoic⟧ clamor; hubbub
hum (hum) ***vi.*** **hummed, hum′ming** ⟦echoic⟧ **1** to make a low, continuous, murmuring sound **2** to sing with closed lips **3** [Colloq.] to be full of activity —***vt.*** to sing (a tune) with closed lips —***n.*** a continuous murmur
hu·man (hyōō′mən) ***adj.*** ⟦< L *humanus*⟧ of, characteristic of, or having the qualities typical of mankind —***n.*** a person: also **human being** —**hu′man·ness *n.***
hu·mane (hyōō mān′) ***adj.*** ⟦var. of prec.⟧ **1** kind, tender, merciful, etc. **2** civilizing; refining —**hu·mane′ly *adv.*** —**hu·mane′ness *n.***
hu·man·ism (hyōō′mə niz′əm) ***n.*** **1** any system of thought based on the interests and ideals of man **2** [**H-**] the intellectual movement that stemmed from the study of the Greek and Latin classics during the Middle Ages —**hu′man·ist *n., adj.*** —**hu′man·is′tic *adj.*** —**hu′man·is′ti·cal·ly *adv.***
hu·man·i·tar·i·an (hyōō man′ə ter′ē ən) ***n.*** a person devoted to promoting the welfare of humanity; philanthropist —***adj.*** helping humanity —**hu·man′i·tar′i·an·ism′ *n.***
hu·man·i·ty (hyōō man′ə tē) ***n.***, *pl.* **-ties** **1** the fact or quality of being human or humane **2** mankind; people —**the humanities** literature, philosophy, the fine

arts, etc. as distinguished from the sciences
hu·man·ize (hyōō'mə nīz') ***vt.*** **-ized', -iz'ing** to make or become human or humane —**hu'man·i·za'tion** ***n.*** —**hu'man·iz'er** ***n.***
hu'man·kind' ***n.*** mankind; people
hu'man·ly ***adv.*** **1** in a human manner **2** by human means
hu'man·oid' (-mə noid') ***adj.*** nearly human —***n.*** a nearly human creature
hum·ble (hum'b'l, um'-) ***adj.*** **-bler, -blest** ⟦< L *humilis*, low⟧ **1** having or showing a consciousness of one's shortcomings; modest **2** lowly; unpretentious —***vt.*** **-bled, -bling** **1** to lower in condition or rank **2** to lower in pride; make modest —**hum'ble·ness** ***n.*** —**hum'bly** ***adv.***
hum·bug (hum'bug') ***n.*** ⟦< ?⟧ **1** fraud; sham; hoax **2** an impostor —***vt.*** **-bugged', -bug'ging** to dupe; deceive —***interj.*** nonsense!
hum·drum (hum'drum') ***adj.*** ⟦echoic⟧ dull; monotonous
hu·mer·us (hyōō'mər əs) ***n.***, *pl.* **-mer·i'** (-ī') ⟦L⟧ the bone of the upper arm or forelimb —**hu'mer·al** ***adj.***
hu·mid (hyōō'mid) ***adj.*** ⟦< L *umere*, be moist⟧ damp; moist
hu·mid·i·fy (hyōō mid'ə fī') ***vt.*** **-fied', -fy'·ing** to make humid; dampen —**hu·mid'i·fi'er** ***n.***
hu·mid'i·ty ***n.*** **1** moistness; dampness **2** amount of moisture in the air
hu·mi·dor (hyōō'mə dôr') ***n.*** a case or jar for keeping tobacco moist
hu·mil·i·ate (hyōō mil'ē āt') ***vt.*** **-at'ed, -at'·ing** ⟦< L *humilis*, humble⟧ to hurt the pride or dignity of; mortify —**hu·mil'i·a'·tion** ***n.***
hu·mil'i·ty (-ə tē) ***n.*** the state or quality of being humble
hum·ming·bird (hum'iŋ burd') ***n.*** a very small, brightly colored bird with narrow wings that vibrate rapidly, often with a humming sound
hum·mock (hum'ək) ***n.*** ⟦< ?⟧ a low, rounded hill; knoll —**hum'mock·y** ***adj.***
hu·mon·gous (hyōō mäŋ'gəs, -muŋ'-) ***adj.*** ⟦? a blend of *huge, monstrous*, etc.⟧ [Slang] enormous
hu·mor (hyōō'mər, yōō'-) ***n.*** ⟦< L *humor*, fluid: after former belief in four body fluids (humors) held responsible for one's disposition⟧ **1** mood; state of mind **2** whim; caprice **3** a comical quality **4** *a)* the ability to appreciate or express what is funny, amusing, etc. *b)* the expression of this —***vt.*** to comply with the mood or whim of; indulge Brit. sp. **hu'mour** —**out of humor** not in a good mood; disagreeable —**hu'mor·ist** ***n.*** —**hu'mor·less** ***adj.***
hu'mor·ous ***adj.*** funny; amusing; comical —**hu'mor·ous·ly** ***adv.***
hump (hump) ***n.*** ⟦< ?⟧ a rounded, protruding lump, as on a camel's back —***vt.*** to hunch; arch —**over the hump** [Colloq.] past the most difficult part
hump'back' ***n.*** **1** a humped, deformed back **2** a person having this **3** a large whale with long flippers and a raised, rounded back —**hump'backed'** ***adj.***
hu·mus (hyōō'məs) ***n.*** ⟦L, earth⟧ the dark part of the soil, resulting from the partial decay of leaves, etc.
Hun (hun) ***n.*** a member of a warlike Asiatic people who invaded Europe in the 4th and 5th c. A.D.
hunch (hunch) ***vt.*** ⟦< ?⟧ to arch into a hump —***vi.*** to move forward jerkily —***n.*** **1** a hump **2** a feeling not based on known facts; premonition
hunch·back (hunch'bak') ***n.*** HUMPBACK (senses 1 & 2) —**hunch'backed'** ***adj.***
hun·dred (hun'drəd) ***n.***, ***adj.*** ⟦OE⟧ ten times ten; 100; C —**hun'dredth** (-drədth) ***adj.***, ***n.***
hun'dred·fold' ***adj.***, ***adv.*** a hundred times as much or as many
hun'dred·weight' ***n.*** a unit of weight equal to 100 pounds in the U.S. and 112 pounds in Great Britain
hung (huŋ) ***vt.***, ***vi.*** *pt. & pp. of* HANG —**hung over** [Slang] having a hangover —**hung up (on)** [Slang] emotionally disturbed, frustrated, or obsessed (by)
Hung. **1** Hungarian **2** Hungary
Hun·gar·i·an (huŋ ger'ē ən) ***n.*** **1** the language of Hungary **2** a native or inhabitant of Hungary —***adj.*** of Hungary
Hun·ga·ry (huŋ'gər ē) country in central Europe: 35,911 sq. mi.; pop. 10,700,000
hun·ger (huŋ'gər) ***n.*** ⟦OE *hungor*⟧ **1** discomfort caused by a need for food **2** starvation **3** a desire for food **4** any strong desire —***vi.*** **1** to be hungry **2** to desire —**hun'·gry, -gri·er, -gri·est,** ***adj.*** —**hun'gri·ly** ***adv.***
hunger strike the refusal of a prisoner, demonstrator, etc. to eat until certain demands are met
hunk (huŋk) ***n.*** ⟦Fl *hunke*⟧ [Colloq.] a large piece, lump, etc.
hun·ker (huŋ'kər) ***vi.*** ⟦< dial.⟧ to squat —***n.*** [*pl.*] haunches or buttocks
hunt (hunt) ***vt.***, ***vi.*** ⟦OE *huntian*⟧ **1** to kill or catch (game) for food or sport **2** to try to find; search **3** to chase —***n.*** **1** a hunting **2** a group of people who hunt together **3** a search —**hunt'er** or **hunts'man** (-mən), *pl.* **-men,** ***n.*** —**hunt'ress** ***n.fem.***
Hun·ting·ton Beach (hun'tiŋ tən) city in SW Calif.: pop. 171,000
Hunts·ville (hunts'vil') city in N Ala.: pop. 143,000

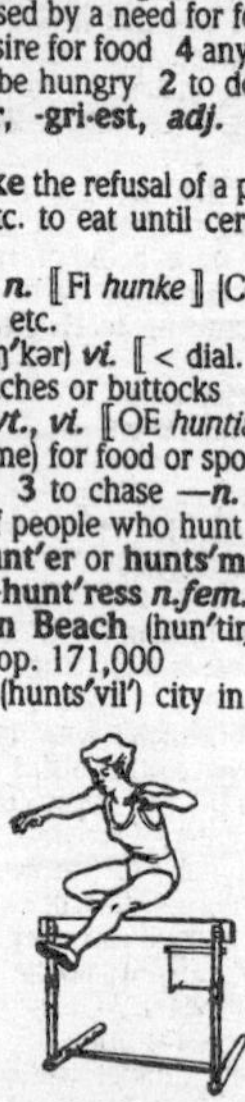

HURDLES

hur·dle (hurd''l) ***n.*** ⟦OE *hyrdel*⟧ **1** a framelike barrier which horses or runners must leap in a race **2** an obstacle —***vt.*** **-dled, -dling** **1** to jump over **2** to overcome (an obstacle) —**hur'dler** ***n.***
hur·dy-gur·dy (hur'dē gur'dē) ***n.***, *pl.* **-dies** ⟦? echoic⟧ BARREL ORGAN
hurl (hurl) ***vt.*** ⟦prob. < ON⟧ **1** to throw with force or violence **2** to cast down **3** to

utter vehemently —*vi.* [Colloq.] *Baseball* to pitch —**hurl'er** *n.*

hurl·y-burl·y (hurl'ē burl'ē) *n., pl.* **-burl'ies** a turmoil; uproar

Hu·ron (hyoor'ən), **Lake** second largest of the Great Lakes, between Mich. & Canada

hur·rah (hə rä', -rô') *interj., n.* ⟦echoic⟧ a shout of joy, approval, etc. —*vi., vt.* to shout "hurrah" (for); cheer Also **hur·ray'** (-rā')

hur·ri·cane (hur'i kān') *n.* ⟦< WInd *huracan*⟧ a violent tropical cyclone

hurricane lamp 1 an oil lamp or candlestick with a glass chimney to protect the flame 2 an electric lamp like this

hur·ry (hur'ē) *vt.* **-ried, -ry·ing** ⟦prob. akin to HURL⟧ 1 to move or send with haste 2 to cause to occur or be done more rapidly or too rapidly 3 to urge to act soon or too soon —*vi.* to move or act with haste —*n.* 1 rush; urgency 2 eagerness to do, go, etc. quickly —**hur'ried·ly** *adv.*

hurt (hurt) *vt.* **hurt, hurt'ing** ⟦< OFr *hurter*, to hit⟧ 1 to cause pain or injury to 2 to harm 3 to offend —*vi.* 1 to cause injury, pain, etc. 2 to have pain; be sore —*n.* 1 a pain or injury 2 harm; damage —*adj.* injured; damaged

hurt'ful *adj.* causing hurt; harmful

hur·tle (hurt''l) *vi., vt.* **-tled, -tling** ⟦ME *hurtlen*⟧ to move or throw with great speed or much force

hus·band (huz'bənd) *n.* ⟦< ON *hūs*, house + *bondi*, freeholder⟧ a married man —*vt.* to manage economically; conserve

hus'band·man (-mən) *n., pl.* **-men** [Archaic] a farmer

hus'band·ry *n.* 1 careful, thrifty management 2 farming

hush (hush) *vt.* ⟦< ME *huscht*, quiet (adj.)⟧ 1 to make quiet or silent 2 to soothe; lull —*vi.* to become quiet or silent —*n.* quiet; silence —*interj.* an exclamation calling for silence

hush'-hush' *adj.* [Colloq.] very secret

hush puppy a small ball of fried cornmeal dough

husk (husk) *n.* ⟦prob. < MDu *huus*, house⟧ 1 the dry outer covering of various fruits or seeds, as of an ear of corn 2 any dry, rough, or useless covering —*vt.* to remove the husk from

hus·ky[1] (hus'kē) *n., pl.* **-kies** ⟦< a var. of ESKIMO⟧ [*also* **H-**] a dog of any of several breeds for pulling sleds in the Arctic

husk·y[2] (hus'kē) *adj.* **-i·er, -i·est** 1 dry in the throat; hoarse 2 ⟦< toughness of a *husk*⟧ big and strong

hus·sar (hoo zär') *n.* ⟦< Serb *husar*⟧ a European light-armed cavalryman, usually with a brilliant dress uniform

hus·sy (huz'ē, hus'-) *n., pl.* **-sies** ⟦< ME *huswif*, housewife⟧ 1 a woman of low morals 2 a bold, saucy girl

hus·tings (hus'tiŋz) *n.pl.* ⟦< ON *hūsthing*, house council⟧ [*usually with sing. v.*] the process of, or a place for, political campaigning

hus·tle (hus'əl) *vt.* **-tled, -tling** ⟦Du *husselen*, shake up⟧ 1 to push about; jostle 2 to force in a rough, hurried manner —*vi.* 1 to move hurriedly 2 [Colloq.] to work energetically 3 [Slang] to obtain money aggressively or immorally —*n.* 1 a hustling 2 [Colloq.] energetic action; drive —**hus'tler** *n.*

hut (hut) *n.* ⟦< OHG *hutta*⟧ a very plain or crude little house or cabin

hutch (huch) *n.* ⟦< ML *hutica*, chest⟧ 1 a chest or cupboard 2 a pen or coop for small animals 3 a hut

hutz·pah (hoots'pə) *n.* CHUTZPAH

huz·zah or **huz·za** (hə zä') *interj., n., vi., vt. archaic var. of* HURRAH

hwy. highway

hy·a·cinth (hī'ə sinth') *n.* ⟦< Gr *hyakinthos*⟧ a plant of the lily family, with spikes of bell-shaped flowers

hy·brid (hī'brid) *n.* ⟦L *hybrida*⟧ 1 the offspring of two animals or plants of different varieties, species, etc. 2 anything of mixed origin —*adj.* of or like a hybrid —**hy'brid·ism'** *n.*

hy·brid·ize (hī'bri dīz') *vt., vi.* **-ized', -iz'ing** to produce or cause to produce hybrids; crossbreed

Hy·der·a·bad (hī'dər ə bad', -bäd') city in south central India: pop. 2,500,000

hy·dra (hī'drə) *n., pl.* **-dras** or **-drae'** (-drē') ⟦< Gr, water serpent⟧ a small, freshwater polyp with a soft, tubelike body

hy·dran·ge·a (hī drān'jə, -dran'-; -jē ə) *n.* ⟦< HYDR(O)- + Gr *angeion*, vessel⟧ a shrub with large, showy clusters of white, blue, or pink flowers

hy·drant (hī'drənt) *n.* ⟦< Gr *hydōr*, water⟧ a large pipe with a valve for drawing water from a water main

hy·drate (hī'drāt') *n.* ⟦HYDR(O)- + -ATE[1]⟧ a chemical compound of water and some other substance

hy·drau·lic (hī drô'lik) *adj.* ⟦ult. < Gr *hydōr*, water + *aulos*, tube⟧ 1 of hydraulics 2 operated by the movement and force of liquid /*hydraulic* brakes/ —**hy·drau'li·cal·ly** *adv.*

hy·drau'lics *n.pl.* [*with sing. v.*] the science dealing with the mechanical properties of liquids, as water, and their application in engineering

hydro- ⟦< Gr *hydōr*, WATER⟧ *combining form* 1 water /*hydrometer*/ 2 hydrogen

hy·dro·car·bon (hī'drō kär'bən) *n.* any compound containing only hydrogen and carbon

hy·dro·chlo·ric acid (hī'drō klôr'ik) a strong, highly corrosive acid that is a water solution of the gas hydrogen chloride

hy'dro·e·lec'tric (-ē lek'trik) *adj.* producing, or relating to the production of, electricity by water power —**hy'dro·e'lec'tric'i·ty** *n.*

hy·dro·foil (hī'drō foil') *n.* ⟦HYDRO- + (AIR)FOIL⟧ 1 a winglike structure that lifts and carries a watercraft just above the water at high speed 2 such a watercraft

hy·dro·gen (hī'drə jən) *n.* ⟦see HYDRO- & -GEN⟧ a flammable, colorless, odorless, gaseous chemical element: the lightest known substance

hy·drog·e·nate (hī dräj'ə nāt') *vt.* **-nat'ed, -nat'ing** to combine with or treat with hydrogen /oil is *hydrogenated* to make a solid fat/

hydrogen bomb an extremely destructive nuclear bomb in which an atomic bomb explosion starts a nuclear fusion explosion of heavy hydrogen atoms

hydrogen peroxide a colorless liquid used as a bleach or disinfectant

hy·drol·o·gy (hī dräl′ə jē) ***n.*** ⟦ see HYDRO- & -LOGY ⟧ the study of the earth's waters, their distribution, and the cycle involving evaporation, precipitation, etc.

hy·drol′y·sis (-i sis) ***n.***, *pl.* **-ses′** (-sēz′) ⟦ HYDRO- + -LYSIS ⟧ a chemical reaction in which a substance reacts with water so as to be changed into one or more other substances

hy·drom·e·ter (hī dräm′ət ər) ***n.*** ⟦ HYDRO- + -METER ⟧ an instrument for measuring the specific gravity of liquids —**hy·drom′e·try** ***n.***

hy·dro·pho·bi·a (hī′drō fō′bē ə) ***n.*** ⟦ see HYDRO- & -PHOBIA ⟧ **1** abnormal fear of water **2** ⟦ from symptomatic inability to swallow liquids ⟧ RABIES

hy·dro·phone (hī′drō fōn′) ***n.*** ⟦ HYDRO- + -PHONE ⟧ an instrument for registering the distance and direction of sound transmitted through water

hy′dro·plane′ (-plān′) ***n.*** **1** a small, high-speed motorboat with hydrofoils or a flat bottom **2** SEAPLANE

hy′dro·pon′ics (-pän′iks) ***n.pl.*** ⟦ < HYDRO- & Gr *ponos*, labor ⟧ [*with sing. v.*] the science of growing plants in nutrient-rich solutions instead of soil

hy′dro·sphere′ (-sfir′) ***n.*** ⟦ HYDRO- + *-sphere*, a layer of the earth's atmosphere ⟧ all the water on the surface of the earth, as oceans, glaciers, etc.

hy′dro·ther′a·py ***n.*** the treatment of disease, etc. by the use of water

hy·drous (hī′drəs) ***adj.*** ⟦ HYDR(O)- + -OUS ⟧ containing water, esp. in chemical combination

hy·drox·ide (hī dräks′īd′) ***n.*** ⟦ HYDR(O)- + OXIDE ⟧ a compound consisting of an element or radical combined with the radical OH

hy·e·na (hī ē′nə) ***n.*** ⟦ < Gr *hyaina* ⟧ a wolflike, flesh-eating animal of Africa and Asia, with a shrill cry

hy·giene (hī′jēn′) ***n.*** ⟦ < Gr *hygiēs*, healthy ⟧ **1** a system of principles for preserving health **2** cleanliness

hy·gi·en·ic (hī′jē en′ik; hī jēn′ik, -jen′-) ***adj.*** **1** of hygiene or health **2** sanitary —**hy′gi·en′i·cal·ly** ***adv.***

hy·grom·e·ter (hī gräm′ət ər) ***n.*** ⟦ < Gr *hygros*, wet + *metron*, a measure ⟧ an instrument for measuring humidity

hy·men (hī′mən) ***n.*** ⟦ Gr *hymēn*, membrane ⟧ the thin mucous membrane that closes part or sometimes all of the opening of the vagina

hy·me·ne·al (hī′mə nē′əl) ***adj.*** ⟦ < Gr *Hymēn*, god of marriage ⟧ of a wedding or marriage

hymn (him) ***n.*** ⟦ < Gr *hymnos* ⟧ a song of praise, esp. in honor of God

hym·nal (him′nəl) ***n.*** a collection of hymns Also **hymn′book′**

hype[1] (hīp) ***n.*** [Slang] **1** *short for* HYPODERMIC **2** a drug addict —***vt.*** **hyped, hyp′ing** [Slang] to stimulate, excite, etc. as by a drug injection: usually with *up*

hype[2] (hīp) ***n.*** ⟦ ? < HYPERBOLE ⟧ [Slang] deception, esp. excessive promotion, as of a product —***vt.*** **hyped, hyp′ing** [Slang] to promote in a sensational way

hy·per (hī′pər) ***adj.*** [Slang] high-strung; keyed up

hyper- ⟦ < Gr *hyper* ⟧ *prefix* over, above, excessive

hy·per·bo·la (hī pur′bə lə) ***n.***, *pl.* **-las** or **-lae′** (-lē′) ⟦ < Gr *hyperbolē*, a throwing beyond, excess ⟧ *Geom.* a curve formed by the intersection of a cone with a plane more steeply inclined than its side

hy·per·bo·le (hī pur′bə lē) ***n.*** ⟦ see prec. ⟧ exaggeration for effect, not meant to be taken literally —**hy·per·bol·ic** (hī′pər bäl′ik) ***adj.***

hy·per·crit·i·cal (hī′pər krit′i kəl) ***adj.*** too critical

hy′per·gly·ce′mi·a (-glī sē′mē ə) ***n.*** ⟦ < HYPER- + Gr *glykys*, sweet + -EMIA ⟧ an abnormally high amount of sugar in the blood

hy′per·sen′si·tive (-sen′sə tiv) ***adj.*** excessively sensitive —**hy′per·sen′si·tiv′i·ty** ***n.***

hy′per·ten′sion (-ten′shən) ***n.*** abnormally high blood pressure

hy′per·thy′roid·ism′ (-thī′roid iz′əm) ***n.*** excessive activity of the thyroid gland, causing nervousness, rapid pulse, etc. —**hy′per·thy′roid′** ***adj.***, ***n.***

hy·per·ven·ti·la·tion (hī′pər vent′′l ā′shən) ***n.*** extremely rapid or deep breathing that may cause dizziness, fainting, etc. —**hy′per·ven′ti·late′** (-āt′), **-lat′ed, -lat′ing,** ***vi.***, ***vt.***

hy·phen (hī′fən) ***n.*** ⟦ < Gr *hypo-*, under + *hen*, one ⟧ a mark (-) used between the parts of a compound word or the syllables of a divided word, as at the end of a line —***vt.*** HYPHENATE

hy·phen·ate (hī′fə nāt′) ***vt.*** **-at′ed, -at′ing** to connect or write with a hyphen —**hy′phen·a′tion** ***n.***

hyp·no·sis (hip nō′sis) ***n.***, *pl.* **-ses′** (-sēz′) ⟦ < Gr *hypnos*, sleep + -OSIS ⟧ a trancelike condition usually induced by another person, in which the subject responds to the suggestions of the hypnotist

hyp·not′ic (-nät′ik) ***adj.*** **1** causing sleep; soporific **2** of, like, or inducing hypnosis —***n.*** any agent causing sleep —**hyp·not′i·cal·ly** ***adv.***

hyp′no·tism′ (-nə tiz′əm) ***n.*** the act or practice of inducing hypnosis —**hyp′no·tist** ***n.***

hyp′no·tize′ (-tīz′) ***vt.*** **-tized′, -tiz′ing** to induce hypnosis in

hy·po (hī′pō) ***n.***, *pl.* **-pos** *short for* HYPODERMIC

hypo- ⟦ Gr < *hypo*, less than ⟧ *prefix* **1** under, beneath [*hypodermic*] **2** less than

hy·po·chon·dri·a (hī′pō kän′drē ə, -pə-) ***n.*** ⟦ LL, pl., abdomen (supposed seat of the condition) ⟧ abnormal anxiety over one's health, often with imaginary illnesses —**hy′po·chon′dri·ac′** (-ak′) ***adj.***, ***n.***

hy·poc·ri·sy (hi päk′rə sē) ***n.***, *pl.* **-sies** ⟦ < Gr *hypokrisis*, acting a part ⟧ a pretending to be what one is not, or to feel what one does not feel; esp., a pretense of virtue, piety, etc.

hyp·o·crite (hip′ə krit′) ***n.*** ⟦ see prec. ⟧ one who pretends to be pious, virtuous, etc.

without really being so —**hyp'o·crit'i·cal** *adj.*

hy·po·der·mic (hī'pō dur'mik, -pə-) *adj.* ⟦< HYPO- + Gr *derma*, skin⟧ injected under the skin —*n.* a hypodermic syringe or injection

hypodermic syringe a syringe attached to a hollow needle (**hypodermic needle**) and used for the injection of a medicine or drug under the skin

hy·po·gly·ce·mi·a (hī'pō glī sē'mē ə) *n.* ⟦< HYPO- + Gr *glykys*, sweet + -EMIA⟧ an abnormally low amount of sugar in the blood

hy·pot·e·nuse (hī pät'i nōōs') *n.* ⟦< Gr *hypo-*, under + *teinein*, to stretch⟧ the side of a right-angled triangle located opposite the right angle

hy·po·thal·a·mus (hī'pō thal'ə məs) *n.*, *pl.* **-mi'** (-mī') ⟦see HYPO- & THALAMUS⟧ a portion of the brain that regulates certain basic body functions, as temperature

hy'po·ther'mi·a (-thur'mē ə) *n.* ⟦< HYPO- + Gr *thermē*, heat⟧ a subnormal body temperature

hy·poth·e·sis (hī päth'ə sis, hi-) *n.*, *pl.* **-ses'** (-sēz') ⟦< Gr *hypo-*, under + *tithenai*, to place⟧ an unproved theory, etc. tentatively accepted to explain certain facts —**hy·poth'e·size'** (-sīz'), **-sized'**, **-siz'ing**, *vi.*, *vt.*

hy·po·thet·i·cal (hī'pō thet'i kəl) *adj.* based on a hypothesis; assumed; supposed —**hy'po·thet'i·cal·ly** *adv.*

hy·po·thy·roid·ism (hī'pō thī'roid iz'əm) *n.* deficient activity of the thyroid gland, causing sluggishness, puffiness, etc. —**hy'po·thy'roid** *adj.*, *n.*

hys·sop (his'əp) *n.* ⟦< Heb *ēzōbh*⟧ a fragrant, blue-flowered plant of the mint family

hys·ter·ec·to·my (his'tər ek'tə mē) *n.*, *pl.* **-mies** ⟦< Gr *hystera*, uterus + -ECTOMY⟧ surgical removal of all or part of the uterus

hys·te·ri·a (hi ster'ē ə, -stir'-) *n.* ⟦< Gr *hystera*, uterus: orig. thought to occur more often in women than in men⟧ **1** a psychiatric condition characterized by excitability, anxiety, the simulation of organic disorders, etc. **2** any outbreak of wild, uncontrolled feeling: also **hys·ter'ics** —**hys·ter'i·cal** (-ster'-) or **hys·ter'ic** *adj.* —**hys·ter'i·cal·ly** *adv.*

Hz hertz

I

i or **I** (ī) *n.*, *pl.* **i's, I's** the ninth letter of the English alphabet

I[1] (ī) *n.* a Roman numeral for 1

I[2] (ī) *pron.* ⟦OE *ic*⟧ the person speaking or writing

I *Chem. symbol for* iodine

I, I., i, or **i.** **1** island(s) **2** isle(s)

IA or **Ia.** Iowa

-i·al (ē əl, yəl) ⟦L *-ialis*⟧ *suffix* -AL

i·amb (ī'amb', -am') *n.* ⟦< Gr *iambos*⟧ a metrical foot of one unaccented syllable followed by one accented one

i·am·bic (ī am'bik) *adj.* ⟦< Gr *iambikos*⟧ of or made up of iambs —*n.* an iamb

-i·at·rics (ē a'triks') ⟦< Gr *iatros*, physician⟧ *combining form* treatment of disease *[pediatrics]*

-i·a·try (ī'ə trē) ⟦< Gr *iatreia*, healing⟧ *combining form* medical treatment *[psychiatry]*

I·be·ri·a (ī bir'ē ə) peninsula in SW Europe, comprising Spain & Portugal: also **Iberian Peninsula** —**I·be'ri·an** *adj.*, *n.*

i·bex (ī'beks') *n.*, *pl.* **i'bex'es** or **i·bi·ces** (ī'bə sēz') ⟦L⟧ a wild goat of the Old World, with large, backward-curved horns

ibid. ⟦L *ibidem*⟧ in the same place, i.e., the book, page, etc. just cited

i·bis (ī'bis) *n.* ⟦Egypt *hb*⟧ a large wading bird found chiefly in tropical regions

-i·ble (i bəl, ə bəl) ⟦L *-ibilis*⟧ *suffix* -ABLE

Ib·sen (ib'sən), **Hen·rik** (hen'rik) 1828-1906; Norw. playwright

i·bu·pro·fen (ī'byōō prō'fən) *n.* a white powder used for reducing fever and relieving pain, esp. for arthritis

-ic (ik) ⟦< Gr *-ikos*⟧ *suffix* **1** *a)* of, having to do with *[volcanic]* *b)* like *[angelic]* *c)* produced by *[anaerobic]* *d)* consisting of, containing *[dactylic]* *e)* having, showing *[lethargic]* **2** a person or thing: *a)* having *[paraplegic]* *b)* supporting *c)* producing *[hypnotic]* Also **-i·cal** (i kəl, ə kəl)

ICBM intercontinental ballistic missile

ICC Interstate Commerce Commission

ice (īs) *n.* ⟦OE *is*⟧ **1** water frozen solid by cold **2** a frozen dessert of fruit juice, sugar, etc. **3** [Slang] diamonds —*vt.* **iced, ic'ing** **1** to change into ice; freeze **2** to cool with ice **3** to cover with icing —*vi.* to freeze: often with *up* or *over* —**break the ice** to make a start, as in getting acquainted —**cut no ice** [Colloq.] to have no influence —**on thin ice** [Colloq.] in danger

Ice. **1** Iceland **2** Icelandic

ice'berg' (-burg') *n.* ⟦prob. < Du *ijsberg*, ice mountain⟧ a great mass of ice broken off from a glacier and floating in the sea

ice'bound' (-bound') *adj.* held fast or shut in by ice

ice'box' (-bäks') *n.* a refrigerator, esp. one in which ice is used

ice'break'er *n.* a sturdy boat for cutting channels through ice

ice'cap' *n.* a mass of glacial ice that spreads slowly from a center

ice cream ⟦orig., *iced cream*⟧ a sweet, frozen food made from flavored cream or milk —**ice'-cream'** *adj.*

ice floe a piece of floating sea ice

ice hockey *see* HOCKEY (sense 1)

Ice·land (īs'lənd) country on an island in the North Atlantic, southeast of Greenland: 39,768 sq. mi.; pop. 240,000 —**Ice'land·er** *n.*

Ice·lan·dic (īs lan'dik) *n.* the Germanic language of Iceland —*adj.* of Iceland

ice·man (īs'man', -mən) *n.*, *pl.* **-men'** one who sells or delivers ice

ice milk a frozen dessert like ice cream, but with less butterfat

ice skate *see* SKATE[1] (*n.* 1) —**ice′-skate′, -skat′ed, -skat′ing,** *vi.*
ich·thy·ol·o·gy (ik′thē äl′ə jē) *n.* ⟦< Gr *ichthys*, a fish + -LOGY⟧ the branch of zoology dealing with fishes —**ich′thy·ol′o·gist** *n.*
i·ci·cle (ī′sik′əl, -si kəl) *n.* ⟦< OE Is, ice + *gicel*, piece of ice⟧ a hanging piece of ice, formed by the freezing of dripping water
ic·ing (Is′iŋ) *n.* a mixture variously of sugar, butter, flavoring, egg whites, etc. for covering a cake; frosting
ick·y (ik′ē) *adj.* **-i·er, -i·est** ⟦< STICKY⟧ [Slang] **1** unpleasantly sticky or sweet **2** very distasteful
i·con (ī′kän′) *n.* ⟦< Gr *eikōn*, image⟧ **1** an image; figure **2** *Eastern Orthodox Ch.* a sacred image or picture of Jesus, Mary, etc.
i·con·o·clast (ī kän′ə klast′) *n.* ⟦< *c.* 6th-c. Gr *eikōn*, image + *klaein*, to break⟧ one who attacks widely accepted ideas, beliefs, etc. —**i·con′o·clas′tic** *adj.*
-ics (iks) ⟦-IC + -S (pl.)⟧ *suffix* [*usually with sing. v.*] art, science, study /*mathematics*/
i·cy (ī′sē) *adj.* **i′ci·er, i′ci·est** **1** full of or covered with ice **2** of or like ice; specif., *a*) slippery *b*) very cold **3** cold in manner; unfriendly —**i′ci·ly** *adv.* —**i′ci·ness** *n.*
id (id) *n.* ⟦L, it⟧ *Psychoanalysis* that part of the psyche which is the source of psychic energy
ID identification
I·da·ho (ī′də hō′) Mountain State of the NW U.S.: 83,557 sq. mi.; pop. 944,000; cap. Boise: abbrev. **ID** or **Ida.** —**I′da·ho′an** *adj., n.*
i·de·a (ī dē′ə) *n.* ⟦L < Gr, appearance of a thing⟧ **1** a thought; mental conception or image **2** an opinion or belief **3** a plan; scheme **4** meaning or significance
i·de·al (ī dē′əl, -dēl′) *adj.* ⟦see prec.⟧ **1** existing as an idea, model, etc. **2** thought of as perfect **3** existing only in the mind; imaginary —*n.* **1** a conception of something in its most excellent form **2** a perfect model **3** a goal or principle
i·de′al·ism′ *n.* **1** behavior or thought based on a conception of things as one thinks they should be **2** a striving to achieve one's ideals —**i·de′al·ist** *n.* —**i′de·al·is′tic** *adj.*
i·de·al·ize (ī dē′əl īz′) *vt.* **-ized′, -iz′ing** to regard or show as perfect or more nearly perfect than is true —**i·de′al·i·za′tion** *n.* —**i·de′al·iz′er** *n.*
i·de′al·ly *adv.* **1** in an ideal manner; perfectly **2** in theory
i·den·ti·cal (ī den′ti kəl) *adj.* ⟦< L *idem*, the same⟧ **1** the very same **2** exactly alike —**i·den′ti·cal·ly** *adv.*
i·den·ti·fi·ca·tion (ī den′tə fi kā′shən) *n.* **1** an identifying or being identified **2** anything by which one can be identified
i·den·ti·fy (ī den′tə fī′) *vt.* **-fied′, -fy′ing** **1** to make identical; treat as the same **2** to fix the identity of /to *identify* a biological specimen/ **3** to connect or associate closely
i·den·ti·ty (ī den′tə tē) *n., pl.* **-ties** **1** the state or fact of being the same **2** *a*) the state or fact of being a specific person or thing; individuality *b*) the state of being as described
identity crisis the state of being uncertain about oneself regarding character, goals, etc., esp. in adolescence
id·e·o·gram (id′ē ō gram′, ī′dē-) *n.* ⟦see IDEA & -GRAM⟧ a symbol representing an object or idea without expressing the word for it Also **id′e·o·graph′**
i·de·ol·o·gy (ī′dē äl′ə jē, id′ē-) *n., pl.* **-gies** ⟦see IDEA & -LOGY⟧ the doctrines, opinions, etc. of an individual, class, etc. —**i′de·o·log′i·cal** *adj.* —**i′de·ol′o·gist** *n.*
ides (īdz) *n.pl.* ⟦< L *idus*⟧ in the ancient Roman calendar, the 15th day of March, May, July, or October, or the 13th of the other months
id·i·o·cy (id′ē ə sē) *n.* **1** great foolishness or stupidity **2** *pl.* **-cies** an idiotic act or remark
id·i·om (id′ē əm) *n.* ⟦< Gr *idios*, one's own⟧ **1** the language or dialect of a people, region, class, etc. **2** the usual way that the words of a language are joined to express thought **3** a phrase or expression with an unusual syntactic pattern or with a meaning differing from the literal meaning of its parts **4** a characteristic style, as in art or music —**id′i·o·mat′ic** (-ə mat′ik) *adj.*
id·i·o·path·ic (id′ē ō′path′ik, -ē ə-) *adj.* ⟦< Gr *idiopatheia*, feeling for oneself alone⟧ of a disease whose cause is unknown
id·i·o·syn·cra·sy (id′ē ō′ siŋ′krə sē) *n., pl.* **-sies** ⟦< Gr *idio-*, one's own + *synkrasis*, a mixing⟧ any personal peculiarity, mannerism, etc.
id·i·ot (id′ē ət) *n.* ⟦< Gr *idiōtēs*, ignorant person⟧ **1** [Obs.] a retarded person mentally equal or inferior to a child two years old **2** a very foolish or stupid person —**id′i·ot′ic** (-ät′ik) *adj.* —**id′i·ot′i·cal·ly** *adv.*
i·dle (īd′'l) *adj.* **i′dler, i′dlest** ⟦OE *idel*, empty⟧ **1** useless; futile **2** unfounded /*idle* rumors/ **3** *a*) unemployed; not busy *b*) inactive; not in use **4** lazy —*vi.* **i′dled, i′dling** **1** to move slowly or aimlessly **2** to be unemployed or inactive **3** to operate without transmitting power /the motor *idled*/ —*vt.* **1** to waste: usually with *away* **2** to cause (a motor, etc.) to idle —**i′dle·ness** *n.* —**i′dler** *n.* —**i′dly** *adv.*
i·dol (īd′'l) *n.* ⟦< Gr *eidōlon*, image⟧ **1** an image of a god, used as an object of worship **2** any object of ardent or excessive devotion
i·dol·a·try (ī däl′ə trē) *n., pl.* **-tries** **1** worship of idols **2** excessive reverence for or devotion to a person or thing —**i·dol′a·ter** *n.* —**i·dol′a·trous** *adj.*
i·dol·ize (īd′'l īz′) *vt.* **-ized′, -iz′ing** **1** to make an idol of **2** to love or admire excessively
i·dyll or **i·dyl** (īd′'l) *n.* ⟦< Gr *eidos*, a form⟧ **1** a short poem or prose work describing a simple, peaceful scene of rural or pastoral life **2** a scene or incident suitable for such a work —**i·dyl·lic** (ī dil′ik) *adj.*
-ie (ē) ⟦earlier form of -Y[1]⟧ *suffix* **1** small or little (one, as specified) /*lassie*/ **2** *a*) one that is as specified /*softie*/ *b*) one connected with /*groupie*/
i.e. ⟦L *id est*⟧ that is (to say)
IE Indo-European
-i·er (ē′ər, yər; ir, ər) ⟦< L *-arius*⟧ *suffix* a person concerned with (a specified action or thing) /*bombardier*/
if (if) *conj.* ⟦OE *gif*⟧ **1** on condition that; in case that /*if* I were you, I would quit/ **2**

allowing that /*if* she was there, I didn't see her/ **3** whether /ask him *if* he knows her/

if·fy (if'ē) ***adj.*** [Colloq.] not definite; containing doubtful elements

IGLOO

ig·loo (ig'lōō') ***n.***, *pl.* **-loos'** ⟦Esk *igdlu*, snow house⟧ an Eskimo hut, usually dome-shaped and built of blocks of packed snow

ig·ne·ous (ig'nē əs) ***adj.*** ⟦< L *ignis*, a fire⟧ **1** of fire **2** produced by volcanic action or intense heat /*igneous* rock/

ig·nite (ig nīt') ***vt.*** **-nit'ed, -nit'ing** ⟦see prec.⟧ to set fire to —***vi.*** to catch on fire; start burning —**ig·nit'a·ble** or **ig·nit'i·ble** ***adj.***

ig·ni·tion (ig nish'ən) ***n.*** **1** an igniting or being ignited **2** a device or system for igniting the explosive mixture in the cylinder of an internal-combustion engine

ig·no·ble (ig nō'bəl) ***adj.*** ⟦< L *in-*, not + *nobilis* (< earlier *gnobilis*, known⟧ not noble; base; mean —**ig·no'bly** ***adv.***

ig·no·min·y (ig'nə min'ē) ***n.***, *pl.* **-ies** ⟦< L *in-*, no, not + *nomen*, name⟧ loss of reputation; shame; disgrace —**ig'no·min'i·ous** ***adj.*** —**ig'no·min'i·ous·ly** ***adv.***

ig·no·ra·mus (ig'nə rā'məs) ***n.***, *pl.* **-mus·es** an ignorant person

ig·no·rant (ig'nə rənt) ***adj.*** ⟦see fol.⟧ **1** lacking knowledge or experience **2** caused by or showing lack of knowledge **3** unaware (*of*) —**ig'no·rance** ***n.*** —**ig'no·rant·ly** ***adv.***

ig·nore (ig nôr') ***vt.*** **-nored', -nor'ing** ⟦< L *in-*, not + *gnarus*, knowing⟧ to disregard; pay no attention to

i·gua·na (i gwä'nə) ***n.*** ⟦Sp < WInd⟧ a large tropical American lizard

il- *prefix* **1** IN-[1] **2** IN-[2] Used before *l*

IL or **Ill.** Illinois

Il·i·ad (il'ē əd) ***n.*** ⟦< Gr *Ilios*, Troy⟧ a Greek epic poem, ascribed to Homer, about the Trojan War

ilk (ilk) ***n.*** ⟦< OE *ilca*, same⟧ kind; sort; class: only in **of that** (or **his, her,** etc.) **ilk**

ill (il) ***adj.*** **worse, worst** ⟦< ON *illr*⟧ **1** bad /*ill* repute, *ill* will, *ill* omen/ **2** not well; sick —***n.*** an evil or a disease —***adv.*** **worse, worst 1** badly **2** scarcely /I can *ill* afford it/ —**ill at ease** uneasy; uncomfortable

ill-ad·vised (il'əd vīzd') ***adj.*** showing or resulting from poor advice; unwise

ill'-bred' ***adj.*** rude; impolite

il·le·gal (il lē'gəl) ***adj.*** prohibited by law; against the law —**il·le·gal·i·ty** (il'lē gal'i tē), *pl.* **-ties,** ***n.*** —**il·le'gal·ly** ***adv.***

il·leg·i·ble (il lej'ə bəl) ***adj.*** hard or impossible to read because badly written or printed —**il·leg'i·bly** ***adv.***

il·le·git·i·mate (il'lə jit'ə mət) ***adj.*** **1** born of parents not married to each other **2** contrary to law, rules, or logic —**il'le·git'i·ma·cy** (-mə sē), *pl.* **-cies,** ***n.***

ill-fat·ed (il'fāt'id) ***adj.*** **1** certain to have an evil fate or unlucky end **2** unlucky

ill'-fa'vored ***adj.*** ugly or unpleasant

ill'-got'ten ***adj.*** obtained by evil, unlawful, or dishonest means

il·lib·er·al (il lib'ər əl) ***adj.*** **1** narrow-minded **2** not generous

il·lic·it (il lis'it) ***adj.*** ⟦< L *illicitus*, not allowed⟧ unlawful; improper —**il·lic'it·ly** ***adv.*** —**il·lic'it·ness** ***n.***

il·lim·it·a·ble (il lim'i tə bəl) ***adj.*** without limit; immeasurable

Il·li·nois (il'ə noi') Middle Western State of the U.S.: 56,400 sq. mi.; pop. 11,418,000; cap. Springfield —**Il'li·nois'an** ***adj., n.***

il·liq·uid (il lik'wid) ***adj.*** not readily convertible into cash

il·lit·er·ate (il lit'ər it) ***adj.*** uneducated; esp., not knowing how to read or write —***n.*** an illiterate person —**il·lit'er·a·cy** (-ə sē) ***n.***

ill-man·nered (il'man'ərd) ***adj.*** having bad manners; rude; impolite

ill nature a disagreeable or mean disposition —**ill-na·tured** (il'nā'chərd) ***adj.***

ill'ness ***n.*** the condition of being in poor health; sickness; disease

il·log·i·cal (il läj'i kəl) ***adj.*** not logical or reasonable —**il·log'i·cal·ly** ***adv.***

ill-starred (il'stärd') ***adj.*** unlucky

ill'-suit'ed ***adj.*** not suited or appropriate

ill'-tem'pered ***adj.*** sullen; irritable

ill'-timed' ***adj.*** inopportune

ill'-treat' ***vt.*** to treat unkindly, unfairly, etc. —**ill'-treat'ment** ***n.***

il·lu·mi·nate (i lōō'mə nāt') ***vt.*** **-nat'ed, -nat'ing** ⟦< L *in-*, in + *luminare*, to light⟧ **1** to give light to; light up **2** *a*) to make clear; explain *b*) to inform **3** to decorate as with lights —**il·lu'mi·na·ble** ***adj.***

il·lu'mi·na'tion ***n.*** **1** an illuminating **2** the intensity of light per unit of area

il·lu'mine (-mən) ***vt.*** **-mined, -min·ing** to light up

illus. **1** illustrated **2** illustration

ill-us·age (il'yōō'sij) ***n.*** unkind or cruel treatment; abuse Also **ill usage**

ill'-use' (-yōōz'; *for n.*, -yōōs') ***vt.*** **-used', -us'ing** to treat unkindly; abuse —***n.*** ILL-USAGE

il·lu·sion (i lōō'zhən) ***n.*** ⟦< L *illudere*, to mock⟧ **1** a false idea or conception **2** an unreal or misleading appearance or image —**il·lu'so·ry** (-sə rē) or **il·lu'sive** (-siv) ***adj.***

il·lus·trate (il'əs trāt') ***vt.*** **-trat'ed, -trat'ing** ⟦< L *in-*, in + *lustrare*, illuminate⟧ **1** to explain; make clear, as by examples **2** to furnish (books, etc.) with explanatory or decorative pictures, etc. —**il'lus·tra'tor** ***n.***

il'lus·tra'tion ***n.*** **1** an illustrating **2** an example, etc. used to help explain **3** a picture, diagram, etc. used to decorate or explain

il·lus·tra·tive (i lus'trə tiv) ***adj.*** serving as an illustration or example

il·lus·tri·ous (i lus'trē əs) ***adj.*** ⟦< L *illustris*, clear⟧ distinguished; famous; outstanding —**il·lus'tri·ous·ly** ***adv.*** —**il·lus'tri·ous·ness** ***n.***

ill will hostility; hate; dislike

I'm (īm) I am

im- *prefix* **1** IN-[1] **2** IN-[2] Used before *b, m,* or *p*

im·age (im'ij) ***n.*** ⟦< L *imago*⟧ **1** a representation of a person or thing; esp., a statue **2**

the visual impression of something in a mirror, through a lens, etc. 3 a copy 4 *a)* a mental picture; idea *b)* the concept of a person, product, etc. held by the general public 5 a metaphor or simile —*vt.* **-aged, -ag·ing** 1 to make a representation of 2 to reflect 3 to imagine

im·age·ry (im′ij rē) *n.* 1 mental images 2 figurative language

i·mag·i·na·ble (i maj′i nə bəl) *adj.* that can be imagined

i·mag′i·nar′y (-ner′ē) *adj.* existing only in the imagination; unreal

i·mag′i·na′tion (-nā′shən) *n.* 1 *a)* the act or power of forming mental images of what is not present *b)* the act or power of creating new ideas by combining previous experiences 2 the ability to understand the imaginative creations of others 3 resourcefulness

i·mag′i·na·tive (-nə tiv) *adj.* 1 having, using, or showing imagination 2 of or resulting from imagination —**i·mag′i·na·tive·ly** *adv.*

i·mag·ine (i maj′in) *vt., vi.* **-ined, -in·ing** ⟦< L *imago*, image⟧ 1 to make a mental image (of); conceive in the mind 2 to suppose; think

im·bal·ance (im bal′əns) *n.* lack of balance, as in proportion or force

im·be·cile (im′bə sil) *n.* ⟦< L *imbecilis*, feeble⟧ 1 [Obs.] a retarded person mentally equal to a child between three and eight years old 2 a foolish or stupid person —*adj.* foolish or stupid: also **im′be·cil′ic** (-sil′ik) —**im′be·cil′i·ty** *n.*

im·bed (im bed′) *vt.* EMBED

im·bibe (im bīb′) *vt.* **-bibed′, -bib′ing** ⟦< L *in-*, in + *bibere*, to drink⟧ 1 to drink (esp. alcoholic liquor) 2 to take into the mind and keep, as ideas —*vi.* to drink, esp. alcoholic liquor

im·bro·glio (im brōl′yō) *n., pl.* **-glios** ⟦It < *imbrogliare*, embroil⟧ 1 an involved and confusing situation 2 a confused misunderstanding

im·bue (im byōō′) *vt.* **-bued′, -bu′ing** ⟦< L *imbuere*, to wet⟧ 1 to dye 2 to permeate (*with* ideas, emotions, etc.)

im·i·tate (im′i tāt′) *vt.* **-tat′ed, -tat′ing** ⟦< L *imitari*⟧ 1 to seek to follow the example of 2 to mimic 3 to reproduce in form, color, etc. 4 to resemble —**im′i·ta′tor** *n.*

im′i·ta′tion *n.* 1 an imitating 2 the result of imitating; copy —*adj.* not real; sham [*imitation* leather] —**im′i·ta′tive** *adj.*

im·mac·u·late (im mak′yōō lit, -yə-) *adj.* ⟦< L *in-*, not + *macula*, a spot⟧ 1 perfectly clean 2 without a flaw or error 3 pure; innocent; sinless —**im·mac′u·late·ly** *adv.* —**im·mac′u·late·ness** *n.*

im·ma·nent (im′ə nənt) *adj.* ⟦< L *in-*, in + *manere*, remain⟧ 1 operating within; inherent 2 present throughout the universe: said of God —**im′ma·nence** *n.* —**im′ma·nent·ly** *adv.*

im·ma·te·ri·al (im′mə tir′ē əl) *adj.* 1 spiritual 2 unimportant

im·ma·ture (im′mə toor′, -tyoor′, -choor′) *adj.* 1 not mature; not completely developed 2 not finished or perfected —**im′ma·tu′ri·ty** *n.*

im·meas·ur·a·ble (im mezh′ər ə bəl) *adj.* that cannot be measured; boundless; vast —**im·meas′ur·a·bly** *adv.*

im·me·di·a·cy (i mē′dē ə sē) *n.* a being immediate; esp., direct relevance to the present time, purpose, etc.

im·me·di·ate (i mē′dē it) *adj.* ⟦see IN-[2] & MEDIATE⟧ 1 not separated in space; closest 2 without delay; instant 3 next in order or relation 4 direct; firsthand —**im·me′di·ate·ly** *adv.*

im·me·mo·ri·al (im′me môr′ē əl) *adj.* extending back beyond memory or record; ancient

im·mense (im mens′) *adj.* ⟦< L *in-*, not + *metiri*, to measure⟧ very large; vast; huge —**im·mense′ly** *adv.* —**im·men′si·ty** *n.*

im·merse (im murs′) *vt.* **-mersed′, -mers′·ing** ⟦< L *immergere*⟧ 1 to plunge into or as if into a liquid 2 to baptize by submerging in water 3 to absorb deeply; engross [*immersed* in study] —**im·mer′sion** (-mur′shən, -mur′zhən) *n.*

immersion heater an electric coil or rod immersed in water to heat it

im·mi·grant (im′ə grənt) *n.* one who immigrates —*adj.* immigrating

im′mi·grate′ (-grāt′) *vi.* **-grat′ed, -grat′ing** ⟦see IN-[1] & MIGRATE⟧ to come into a new country, etc., esp. to settle there —**im′mi·gra′tion** *n.*

im·mi·nent (im′ə nənt) *adj.* ⟦< L *in-*, on + *minere*, to project⟧ likely to happen without delay; impending

im·mo·bile (im mō′bəl) *adj.* 1 firmly placed; stable 2 motionless —**im′mo·bil′i·ty** *n.* —**im·mo′bi·lize′** (-bə līz′), **-lized′, -liz′ing,** *vt.*

im·mod·er·ate (im mäd′ər it) *adj.* without restraint; excessive

im·mod·est (im mäd′ist) *adj.* 1 indecent 2 not shy; forward —**im·mod′est·ly** *adv.* —**im·mod′es·ty** *n.*

im·mo·late (im′ə lāt′) *vt.* **-lat′ed, -lat′ing** ⟦< L *immolare*, sprinkle with sacrificial meal⟧ to kill as a sacrifice —**im′mo·la′tion** *n.*

im·mor·al (im môr′əl) *adj.* 1 not moral 2 lewd —**im·mor′al·ly** *adv.*

im·mo·ral·i·ty (im′mō ral′i tē, im′ə-) *n.* 1 a being immoral 2 *pl.* **-ties** an immoral act or practice; vice

im·mor·tal (im môrt′'l) *adj.* 1 not mortal; living forever 2 enduring 3 having lasting fame —*n.* an immortal being —**im·mor·tal·i·ty** (im′môr tal′i tē) *n.*

im·mor·tal·ize (im môrt′'l īz′) *vt.* **-ized′, -iz′·ing** to make immortal, as in fame

im·mov·a·ble (im mōōv′ə bəl) *adj.* 1 firmly fixed 2 unyielding; steadfast

im·mune (im myōōn′, i myōōn′) *adj.* ⟦< L *in-*, without + *munia*, duties⟧ 1 exempt from or protected against something disagreeable or harmful 2 not susceptible to some specified disease

im·mu·ni·ty (im myōōn′i tē) *n., pl.* **-ties** 1 exemption from something burdensome, as a legal obligation 2 resistance to infection or a specified disease

im·mu·nize (im′myōō nīz′) *vt.* **-nized′, -niz′·ing** to make immune, as by inoculation —**im′mu·ni·za′tion** *n.*

im·mu·nol·o·gy (im′myōō näl′ə jē) *n.* the branch of science dealing with immunity, as to infection or a disease, and with the body mechanisms producing it —**im'mu·nol'o·gist** ***n.***

im·mure (im myoor') ***vt.*** **-mured', -mur'ing** ⟦< L *in-*, in + *murus*, wall⟧ to shut up within walls; confine

im·mu·ta·ble (im myōōt'ə bəl) ***adj.*** unchangeable —**im·mu'ta·bly** ***adv.***

imp (imp) ***n.*** ⟦< Gr *em-*, in + *phyton*, growth⟧ **1** a young demon **2** a mischievous child —**imp'ish** ***adj.***

im·pact (im pakt'; *for n.* im'pakt') ***vt.*** ⟦< L *impingere*, press firmly together⟧ **1** to force tightly together **2** [Colloq.] to affect —***vi.*** **1** to hit with force **2** [Colloq.] to have an effect (*on*) —***n.*** **1** a violent contact **2** the power to move feelings, influence thinking, etc.

im·pact'ed (-pakt'id) ***adj.*** abnormally lodged in the jaw: said of a tooth

im·pair (im per') ***vt.*** ⟦< L *in-*, intens. + *pejor*, worse⟧ to make worse, less, etc. —**im·pair'ment** ***n.***

im·pa·la (im pä'lə) ***n., pl.*** **-la** or **-las** a reddish antelope of central and S Africa

im·pale (im pāl') ***vt.*** **-paled', -pal'ing** ⟦< L *in-*, on + *palus*, a pole⟧ to pierce through with, or fix on, something pointed —**im·pale'ment** ***n.***

im·pal·pa·ble (im pal'pə bəl) ***adj.*** **1** not perceptible to the touch **2** too subtle to be easily understood

im·pan·el (im pan'əl) ***vt.*** **-eled** or **-elled, -el·ing** or **-el·ling** to choose (a jury) in a law case —**im·pan'el·ment** ***n.***

im·part (im pärt') ***vt.*** ⟦see IN-[1] & PART⟧ **1** to give a share of; give **2** to make known; reveal

im·par·tial (im pär'shəl) ***adj.*** without bias; fair —**im·par'ti·al'i·ty** (-shē al'i tē) ***n.*** —**im·par'tial·ly** ***adv.***

im·pass·a·ble (im pas'ə bəl) ***adj.*** that cannot be passed or traveled over

im·passe (im'pas', im pas') ***n.*** ⟦Fr⟧ a situation offering no escape or resolution, as a deadlocked argument

im·pas·sioned (im pash'ənd) ***adj.*** passionate; fiery; ardent

im·pas·sive (im pas'iv) ***adj.*** not feeling or showing emotion; calm —**im·pas·siv·i·ty** (im'pa siv'i tē) ***n.***

im·pas·to (im päs'tō) ***n.*** ⟦It⟧ **1** painting in which the paint is laid thickly on the canvas **2** such paint

im·pa·tient (im pā'shənt) ***adj.*** lacking patience; specif., *a*) annoyed because of delay, opposition, etc. *b*) restlessly eager to do something, etc. —**im·pa'tience** ***n.***

im·peach (im pēch') ***vt.*** ⟦< L *in-*, in + *pedica*, a fetter⟧ **1** to discredit (a person's honor, etc.) **2** to try (a public official) on charges of wrongdoing —**im·peach'ment** ***n.***

im·pec·ca·ble (im pek'ə bəl) ***adj.*** ⟦< L *in-*, not + *peccare*, to sin⟧ without defect or error; flawless —**im·pec'ca·bil'i·ty** ***n.*** —**im·pec'ca·bly** ***adv.***

im·pe·cu·ni·ous (im'pi kyōō'nē əs) ***adj.*** ⟦< L *in-*, not + *pecunia*, money⟧ having no money; poor

im·ped·ance (im pēd''ns) ***n.*** ⟦< fol. + -ANCE⟧ the resistance in an electric circuit to a flow of alternating current

im·pede (im pēd') ***vt.*** **-ped'ed, -ped'ing** ⟦< L *in-*, in + *pes*, foot⟧ to hinder the progress of; obstruct

im·ped·i·ment (im ped'ə mənt) ***n.*** anything that impedes; specif., a speech defect

im·ped'i·men'ta (-men'tə) ***n.pl.*** encumbrances, as baggage or supplies

im·pel (im pel') ***vt.*** **-pelled', -pel'ling** ⟦< L *in-*, in + *pellere*, to drive⟧ **1** to drive or move forward **2** to force, compel, or urge —**im·pel'ler** ***n.***

im·pend (im pend') ***vi.*** ⟦< L *in-*, in + *pendere*, hang⟧ to be about to happen; be imminent /*impending* disaster/ —**im·pend'·ing** ***adj.***

im·pen·e·tra·ble (im pen'i trə bəl) ***adj.*** **1** that cannot be penetrated **2** that cannot be solved or understood

im·pen·i·tent (im pen'ə tənt) ***adj.*** without regret, shame, or remorse

im·per·a·tive (im per'ə tiv) ***adj.*** ⟦< L *imperare*, to command⟧ **1** indicating authority or command **2** necessary; urgent **3** designating or of the mood of a verb that expresses a command, etc. —***n.*** a command

im·per·cep·ti·ble (im'pər sep'tə bəl) ***adj.*** not easily perceived by the senses or the mind; very slight, subtle, etc. —**im'per·cep'·ti·bly** ***adv.***

im'per·cep'tive (-tiv) ***adj.*** not perceiving —**im'per·cep'tive·ness** ***n.***

im·per·fect (im pur'fikt) ***adj.*** **1** not complete **2** not perfect **3** designating a verb tense that indicates a past action or state as uncompleted or continuous —**im·per'fect·ly** ***adv.***

im·per·fec·tion (im'pər fek'shən) ***n.*** **1** a being imperfect **2** a defect; fault

im·pe·ri·al (im pir'ē əl) ***adj.*** ⟦< L *imperium*, empire⟧ **1** of an empire, emperor, or empress **2** having supreme authority **3** majestic; august **4** of great size or superior quality —***n.*** a small, pointed chin beard

imperial gallon the standard British gallon, equal to 4.546 liters

im·pe'ri·al·ism' ***n.*** **1** imperial state or authority **2** the policy of forming and maintaining an empire, as by establishing colonies, etc. **3** the policy of seeking to dominate the affairs of weaker countries —**im·pe'ri·al·ist** ***n., adj.*** —**im·pe'ri·al·is'tic** ***adj.***

im·per·il (im per'əl) ***vt.*** **-iled** or **-illed, -il·ing** or **-il·ling** to put in peril; endanger

im·pe·ri·ous (im pir'ē əs) ***adj.*** ⟦< L *imperium*, empire⟧ **1** overbearing, arrogant, etc. **2** urgent; imperative —**im·pe'ri·ous·ly** ***adv.***

im·per·ish·a·ble (im per'ish ə bəl) ***adj.*** not perishable; indestructible

im·per·ma·nent (im pur'mə nənt) ***adj.*** not permanent; temporary —**im·per'ma·nent·ly** ***adv.***

im·per·son·al (im pur'sə nəl) ***adj.*** **1** without reference to any particular person **2** not existing as a person /an *impersonal* force/ **3** designating or of a verb occurring only in the third person singular, usually with *it* as subject —**im·per'son·al·ly** ***adv.***

im·per·son·ate (im pur'sə nāt') ***vt.*** **-at'ed, -at'ing** to assume the role of, for purposes of entertainment or fraud —**im·per'son·a'tion** *n.* —**im·per'son·a'tor** *n.*

im·per·ti·nent (im purt''n ənt) *adj.* 1 not pertinent 2 insolent; impudent —**im·per'ti·nence** *n.*

im·per·turb·a·ble (im'pər tur'bə bəl) *adj.* that cannot be disconcerted, disturbed, or excited; impassive

im·per·vi·ous (im pur'vē əs) *adj.* 1 incapable of being penetrated, as by moisture 2 not affected by: with *to*

im·pe·ti·go (im'pə tī'gō) *n.* ⟦see IMPETUS⟧ a contagious skin disease with eruption of pustules

im·pet·u·ous (im pech'o͞o əs) *adj.* ⟦see fol.⟧ acting or done suddenly with little thought; rash —**im·pet'u·os'i·ty** (-äs'i tē) *n.* —**im·pet'u·ous·ly** *adv.*

im·pe·tus (im'pə təs) *n.* ⟦< L *in-*, in + *petere*, rush at⟧ 1 the force with which a body moves against resistance 2 driving force or motive

im·pi·e·ty (im pī'ə tē) *n.* 1 lack of reverence for God 2 disrespect

im·pinge (im pinj') *vi.* **-pinged'**, **-ping'ing** ⟦< L *in-*, in + *pangere*, to strike⟧ 1 to strike, hit, etc. (*on* or *upon*) 2 to encroach (*on* or *upon*) —**im·pinge'ment** *n.*

im·pi·ous (im'pē əs) *adj.* not pious; specif., lacking reverence for God

im·pla·ca·ble (im plā'kə bəl, -plak'ə-) *adj.* not to be placated or appeased; relentless —**im·pla'ca·bly** *adv.*

im·plant (im plant'; *for n.* im'plant') *vt.* 1 to plant firmly 2 to fix firmly in the mind 3 to insert surgically —*n.* an implanted organ, etc.

im·plau·si·ble (im plô'zə bəl) *adj.* not plausible —**im·plau'si·bly** *adv.*

im·ple·ment (im'plə mənt; *for v.*, -ment') *n.* ⟦< L *in-*, in + *plere*, to fill⟧ something used in a given activity; tool, instrument, etc. —*vt.* to carry into effect; accomplish —**im'ple·men·ta'tion** (-mən tā'shən) *n.*

im·pli·cate (im'pli kāt') *vt.* **-cat'ed**, **-cat'ing** ⟦see IMPLY⟧ to show to be party to a crime, etc. —**im'pli·ca'tive** *adj.*

im'pli·ca'tion *n.* 1 an implicating or being implicated 2 an implying or being implied 3 something implied

im·plic·it (im plis'it) *adj.* ⟦see IMPLY⟧ 1 suggested though not plainly expressed; implied 2 necessarily involved though not apparent; inherent 3 without reservation —**im·plic'it·ly** *adv.*

im·plode (im plōd') *vt.*, *vi.* **-plod'ed**, **-plod'ing** ⟦< IN-[1] + (EX)PLODE⟧ to burst or cause to burst inward —**im·plo'sion** (-plō'zhən) *n.* —**im·plo'sive** (-plō'siv) *adj.*

im·plore (im plôr') *vt.* **-plored'**, **-plor'ing** ⟦< L *in-*, intens. + *plorare*, cry out⟧ 1 to ask earnestly for 2 to beg (a person) to do something —**im·plor'ing·ly** *adv.*

im·ply (im plī') *vt.* **-plied'**, **-ply'ing** ⟦< L *in-*, in + *plicare*, to fold⟧ 1 to have as a necessary part, condition, etc. 2 to indicate indirectly; hint; suggest

im·po·lite (im'pə līt') *adj.* not polite; discourteous —**im'po·lite'ly** *adv.*

im·pol·i·tic (im päl'ə tik') *adj.* not politic; unwise

im·pon·der·a·ble (im pän'dər ə bəl) *adj.* that cannot be weighed or measured —*n.* anything imponderable

im·port (im pôrt', *also, and for n. always* im'pôrt') *vt.* ⟦< L *in-*, in + *portare*, carry⟧ 1 to bring in (goods) from another country, especially for sale 2 to mean; signify —*n.* 1 something imported 2 meaning; signification 3 importance —**im'por·ta'tion** *n.* —**im·port'er** *n.*

im·por·tant (im pôrt''nt) *adj.* ⟦see prec.⟧ 1 meaning a great deal; having much significance or value 2 having, or acting as if having, power, authority, etc. —**im·por'tance** *n.* —**im·por'tant·ly** *adv.*

im·por·tu·nate (im pôr'cho͞o nit) *adj.* persistent in asking or demanding

im·por·tune (im'pôr to͞on') *vt.*, *vi.* **-tuned'**, **-tun'ing** ⟦< L *importunus*, troublesome⟧ to urge or entreat persistently or repeatedly —**im'por·tu'ni·ty**, *pl.* **-ties**, *n.*

im·pose (im pōz') *vt.* **-posed'**, **-pos'ing** ⟦< L *in-*, on + *ponere*, to place⟧ 1 to place (a burden, tax, etc. *on* or *upon*) 2 to force (oneself) on others —**impose on** (or **upon**) 1 to take advantage of 2 to cheat or defraud —**im'po·si'tion** (-pə zish'ən) *n.*

im·pos'ing *adj.* impressive because of great size, strength, dignity, etc. —**im·pos'ing·ly** *adv.*

im·pos·si·ble (im päs'ə bəl) *adj.* 1 not capable of being, being done, or happening 2 not capable of being endured, used, etc. because disagreeable or unsuitable —**im·pos'si·bil'i·ty**, *pl.* **-ties**, *n.* —**im·pos'si·bly** *adv.*

im·post (im'pōst') *n.* ⟦see IMPOSE⟧ a tax; esp., a duty on imported goods

im·pos·tor or **im·post'er** (im päs'tər) *n.* ⟦see IMPOSE⟧ one who deceives or cheats others by pretending to be what he is not

im·pos'ture (-chər) *n.* the act or practice of an impostor; fraud

im·po·tent (im'pə tənt) *adj.* 1 lacking physical strength 2 ineffective; powerless 3 unable to engage in sexual intercourse: said of males —**im'po·tence** or **im'po·ten·cy** *n.* —**im'po·tent·ly** *adv.*

im·pound (im pound') *vt.* 1 to shut up (an animal) in a pound 2 to take and hold in legal custody 3 to gather and enclose (water), as for irrigation

im·pov·er·ish (im päv'ər ish) *vt.* ⟦< L *in-*, in + *pauper*, poor⟧ 1 to make poor 2 to deprive of strength, resources, etc. —**im·pov'er·ish·ment** *n.*

im·prac·ti·ca·ble (im prak'ti kə bəl) *adj.* not capable of being carried out in practice

im·prac·ti·cal (im prak'ti kəl) *adj.* not practical

im·pre·cate (im'pri kāt') *vt.* **-cat'ed**, **-cat'ing** ⟦< L *in-*, on + *precari*, pray⟧ to invoke (evil, a curse, etc.) —**im'pre·ca'tion** *n.*

im·pre·cise (im'pri sīs') *adj.* not precise; vague —**im'pre·cise'ly** *adv.* —**im'pre·ci'sion** (-sizh'ən) *n.*

im·preg·na·ble (im preg'nə bəl) *adj.* 1 that cannot be captured or entered by force 2 unyielding —**im·preg'na·bil'i·ty** *n.* —**im·preg'na·bly** *adv.*

im·preg·nate (im preg'nāt') *vt.* **-nat'ed**, **-nat'ing** 1 to make pregnant; fertilize 2 to saturate 3 to imbue (*with* ideas, etc.) —**im'preg·na'tion** *n.*

im·pre·sa·ri·o (im′prə sä′rē ō′) ***n.***, *pl.* **-os** ⟦It⟧ one who manages an opera, organizes concert series, etc.

im·press[1] (im pres′) ***vt.*** ⟦< IN-[1] + PRESS[2]⟧ **1** to force into military service **2** to seize for public use

im·press[2] (im pres′; *for n.* im′pres′) ***vt.*** ⟦see IMPRINT⟧ **1** to stamp; imprint **2** to affect strongly the mind or emotions of **3** to fix in the memory: with *on* or *upon* **—*n.*** **1** an impressing **2** an imprint

im·press′i·ble (-ə bəl) ***adj.*** that can be impressed **—im·press′i·bil′i·ty *n.***

im·pres·sion (im presh′ən) ***n.*** **1** an impressing **2** *a)* a mark, imprint, etc. *b)* an effect produced on the mind **3** a vague notion **4** an amusing impersonation; mimicking

im·pres′sion·a·ble *adj.* easily impressed or influenced; sensitive

im·pres′sion·ism′ *n.* a theory of art, music, etc. whose aim is to capture a brief, immediate impression **—im·pres′sion·ist *n.* —im·pres′sion·is′tic *adj.***

im·pres·sive (im pres′iv) ***adj.*** tending to impress the mind or emotions; eliciting wonder or admiration **—im·pres′sive·ly *adv.***

im·pri·ma·tur (im′pri māt′ər) ***n.*** ⟦ModL, lit., let it be printed⟧ permission to publish a book, etc., as granted by a Catholic bishop

im·print (im print′; *for n.* im′print′) ***vt.*** ⟦< L *in-*, on + *premere*, to press⟧ to mark or fix as by pressing or stamping **—*n.*** **1** a mark made by imprinting **2** a lasting effect **3** a note in a book giving facts of its publication

im·pris·on (im priz′ən) ***vt.*** to put in or as in prison **—im·pris′on·ment *n.***

im·prob·a·ble (im präb′ə bəl) ***adj.*** not probable; unlikely **—im′prob·a·bil′i·ty *n.* — im·prob′a·bly *adv.***

im·promp·tu (im prämp′to͞o′) ***adj., adv.*** ⟦< L *in promptu*, in readiness⟧ without preparation; offhand

im·prop·er (im präp′ər) ***adj.*** **1** not suitable; unfit **2** incorrect **3** not in good taste **— im·prop′er·ly *adv.***

im·pro·pri·e·ty (im′prō prī′ə tē) ***n.***, *pl.* **-ties** **1** a being improper **2** an improper act, word usage, etc.

im·prove (im pro͞ov′) ***vt.*** **-proved′, -prov′ing** ⟦< Anglo-Fr *en-*, in + *prou*, gain⟧ **1** to make better **2** to make (real estate) more valuable by cultivation, construction, etc. **—*vi.*** to become better **—improve on** (or **upon**) to do or make better than **—im·prov′a·ble *adj.***

im·prove′ment ***n.*** **1** an improving or being improved **2** an addition or change that improves something

im·prov·i·dent (im präv′ə dənt) ***adj.*** lacking foresight or thrift **—im·prov′i·dence *n.* — im·prov′i·dent·ly *adv.***

im·pro·vise (im′prə vīz′) ***vt., vi.*** **-vised′, -vis′ing** ⟦< L *in-*, not + *providere*, foresee⟧ **1** to compose and perform without preparation **2** to make or do with whatever is at hand **—im·prov′i·sa′tion** (-präv′i zā′shən) ***n.* —im·prov′i·sa′tion·al *adj.***

im·pru·dent (im pro͞od″nt) ***adj.*** not prudent; rash **—im·pru′dence *n.***

im·pu·dent (im′pyo͞o dənt) ***adj.*** ⟦< L *in-*, not + *pudere*, feel shame⟧ shamelessly bold; insolent **im′pu·dence *n.* —im′pu·dent·ly *adv.***

im·pugn (im pyo͞on′) ***vt.*** ⟦< L *in-*, against + *pugnare*, to fight⟧ to oppose or challenge as false

im·pulse (im′puls′) ***n.*** ⟦see IMPEL⟧ **1** *a)* a driving forward *b)* an impelling force; impetus *c)* the motion or effect caused by such a force **2** *a)* incitement to action by a stimulus *b)* a sudden inclination to act **3** a brief surge in an electric current

im·pul·sion (im pul′shən) ***n.*** **1** an impelling or being impelled **2** IMPULSE (sense 1*b*) **3** IMPULSE (sense 2)

im·pul·sive (im pul′siv) ***adj.*** **1** driving forward **2** likely to act on impulse **—im·pul′sive·ly *adv.***

im·pu·ni·ty (im pyo͞o′ni tē) ***n.*** ⟦< L *in-*, without + *poena*, punishment⟧ freedom from punishment, harm, etc.

im·pure (im pyoor′) ***adj.*** **1** unclean; dirty **2** immoral; obscene; **3** mixed with foreign matter; adulterated **—im·pure′ly *adv.* — im·pure′ness *n.***

im·pu′ri·ty (-ə tē) ***n.*** **1** a being impure **2** *pl.* **-ties** an impure thing or part

im·pute (im pyo͞ot′) ***vt.*** **-put′ed, -put′ing** ⟦< L *in-*, in, to + *putare*, to think⟧ to attribute (esp. a fault or misconduct) to another **—im′pu·ta′tion** (-pyo͞o tā′shən) ***n.***

in (in) ***prep.*** ⟦OE⟧ **1** contained by /*in* the room/ **2** wearing /dressed *in* furs/ **3** during /done *in* a day/ **4** at the end of /due *in* an hour/ **5** not beyond /*in* sight/ **6** employed, enrolled, etc. at /*in* college/ **7** out of a group of /one *in* ten/ **8** amidst /*in* a storm/ **9** affected by /*in* trouble/ **10** with regard to /to vary *in* size/ **11** using /speak *in* English/ **12** because of; for /to cry *in* pain/ **13** into /come *in* the house/ **—*adv.*** **1** to the inside /he went *in*/ **2** to or at a certain place **3** so as to be contained by a certain space, condition, etc. **—*adj.*** **1** that is in power /the *in* group/ **2** inner; inside **3** gathered, counted, etc. **4** [Colloq.] currently smart, popular, etc. **—*n.*** **1** one that is in power: *usually used in pl.* **2** [Colloq.] special influence or favor **—have it in for** [Colloq.] to hold a grudge against **—ins and outs** all the details and intricacies **—in that** because; since **—in with** associated with

in-[1] ⟦< the prep. IN or L *in*, in⟧ *prefix* in, into, within, on, toward /*inbreed*/

in-[2] ⟦L⟧ *prefix* no, not, without, NON- The following list includes some common compounds formed with *in-*, with no special meanings; they will be understood if "not" or "lack of" is used with the meaning of the base word:

inability	**inapt**
inaccessible	**inaudible**
inaccuracy	**inauspicious**
inaccurate	**incapable**
inaction	**incautious**
inactive	**incivility**
inadequacy	**incombustible**
inadequate	**incommensurate**
inadmissible	**incommunicable**
inadvisable	**incomprehensible**
inanimate	**inconceivable**
inapplicable	**inconclusive**
inappropriate	**inconsistency**

inconsistent
incorrect
incurable
indecorous
indefinable
indiscernible
indisputable
indistinct
indistinguishable
indivisible
inedible
ineffective
ineffectual
inefficacy
inelastic
ineligible
inequality
inequitable
inequity
inexact
inexcusable
inexpensive
infertile
inharmonious
inhospitable
inhumane
injudicious
inopportune
inseparable
insignificance
insignificant
insolvable
insufficient
insurmountable
insusceptible
invariable

-in (in) *combining form* a mass action or gathering of a (specified) type /pray-*in*, be-*in*/

in. inch(es)

IN Indiana

in ab·sen·ti·a (in ab sen′shə, -shē ə) ⟦L⟧ although not present /to receive an award *in absentia*/

in·ac·ti·vate (in ak′tə vāt′) *vt.* **-vat′ed, -vat′·ing** to make inactive —**in·ac′ti·va′tion** *n.*

in·ad·vert·ent (in′ad vurt′'nt, -əd-) *adj.* **1** not attentive or observant **2** due to oversight —**in′ad·vert′ence** *n.* —**in′ad·vert′·ent·ly** *adv.*

in·al·ien·a·ble (in āl′yən ə bəl) *adj.* ⟦see ALIEN⟧ that may not be taken away or transferred —**in·al′ien·a·bly** *adv.*

in·am·o·ra·ta (in am′ə rät′ə) *n.* ⟦It⟧ a sweetheart or lover: said of a woman

in·ane (in ān′) *adj.* ⟦L *inanis*⟧ **1** empty **2** lacking sense; silly —**in·an′i·ty** (-an′i tē) *n.*

in·ar·tic·u·late (in′är tik′yo͞o lit, -yə-) *adj.* **1** without the articulation of normal speech /an *inarticulate* cry/ **2** mute **3** unable to speak clearly or coherently **4** unexpressed or unexpressible

in·as·much as (in′əz much′ az′) **1** since; because **2** to the extent that

in·at·ten·tion (in′ə ten′shən) *n.* failure to pay attention; negligence —**in′at·ten′tive** *adj.*

in·au·gu·ral (in ô′gyoo rəl) *adj.* ⟦Fr⟧ **1** of an inauguration **2** first in a series —*n.* **1** a speech made at an inauguration **2** an inauguration

in·au′gu·rate′ (-rāt′) *vt.* **-rat′ed, -rat′ing** ⟦< L *inaugurare*, to practice augury⟧ **1** to induct into office with a formal ceremony **2** to make a formal beginning of **3** to dedicate formally —**in·au′gu·ra′tion** *n.*

in·au·then·tic (in′ô then′tik) *adj.* not authentic

in·board (in′bôrd′) *adv.*, *adj.* **1** inside the hull of a ship or boat **2** close to the fuselage of an aircraft —*n.* a boat with an inboard motor

in·born (in′bôrn′) *adj.* present in the organism at birth; innate

in·bound (in′bound′) *adj.* traveling or going inward —*vt.*, *vi.* *Basketball* to put (the ball) in play from out of bounds

in·bred (in′bred′) *adj.* **1** innate; inborn **2** resulting from inbreeding

in·breed (in′brēd′) *vt.* **-bred′, -breed′ing** to breed by continual mating of individuals of the same or closely related stocks —*vi.* **1** to engage in such breeding **2** to become too refined, effete, etc.

inc. **1** incorporated: also **Inc.** **2** increase

In·ca (iŋ′kə) *n.* a member of the highly civilized Indian people that dominated ancient Peru until the Spanish conquest

in·cal·cu·la·ble (in kal′kyo͞o lə bəl) *adj.* **1** that cannot be calculated; too great or too many to be counted **2** unpredictable —**in·cal′cu·la·bly** *adv.*

in·can·des·cent (in′kən des′ənt) *adj.* ⟦< L *in-*, in + *candere*, to shine⟧ **1** glowing with intense heat **2** very bright —**in′can·des′·cence** *n.*

incandescent lamp a lamp with a filament in a vacuum heated to incandescence by an electric current

in·can·ta·tion (in′kan tā′shən) *n.* ⟦< L *in-*, intens. + *cantare*, to sing⟧ words chanted in magic spells or rites

in·ca·pac·i·tate (in′kə pas′ə tāt′) *vt.* **-tat′ed, -tat′ing** **1** to make unable or unfit **2** *Law* to disqualify

in′ca·pac′i·ty *n.* **1** lack of capacity, power, or fitness **2** legal ineligibility

in·car·cer·ate (in kär′sər āt′) *vt.* **-at′ed, -at′·ing** ⟦< L *in*, in + *carcer*, prison⟧ to imprison —**in·car′cer·a′tion** *n.*

in·car·na·dine (in kär′nə dīn′) *vt.* **-dined′, -din′ing** to make red

in·car·nate (in kär′nit, -nāt′; *for v. always*, -nāt′) *adj.* ⟦< L *in-*, in + *caro*, flesh⟧ endowed with a human body; personified —*vt.* **-nat′ed, -nat′ing** **1** to give bodily form to **2** to be the type or embodiment of —**in′car·na′tion** *n.*

in·cen·di·ar·y (in sen′dē er′ē) *adj.* ⟦< L *incendium*, a fire⟧ **1** having to do with the willful destruction of property by fire **2** designed to cause fires, as certain bombs **3** willfully stirring up strife, riot, etc. —*n.*, *pl.* **-ar′ies** one who willfully stirs up strife, riot, etc.

in·cense[1] (in′sens′) *n.* ⟦< L *in-*, in + *candere*, to burn⟧ **1** any substance burned to produce a pleasant odor **2** the odor from this **3** any pleasant odor

in·cense[2] (in sens′) *vt.* **-censed′, -cens′ing** ⟦see prec.⟧ to make very angry —**in·cense′ment** *n.*

in·cen·tive (in sent′iv) *n.* ⟦< L *in-*, in, on + *canere*, sing⟧ a stimulus; motive

in·cep·tion (in sep′shən) *n.* ⟦see INCIPIENT⟧ the beginning of something; start

in·cer·ti·tude (in surt′ə to͞od′, -tyo͞od′) *n.* **1** doubt **2** insecurity

in·ces·sant (in ses′ənt) *adj.* ⟦< L *in-*, not + *cessare*, cease⟧ never ceasing; continuing without stopping; constant —**in·ces′sant·ly** *adv.*

in·cest (in′sest′) *n.* ⟦< L *in-*, not + *castus*, chaste⟧ sexual intercourse between persons too closely related to marry legally —**in·ces·tu·ous** (in ses′tyo͞o əs) *adj.* —**in·ces′tu·ous·ly** *adv.* —**in·ces′tu·ous·ness** *n.*

inch (inch) *n.* ⟦< L *uncia*, twelfth part⟧ a measure of length equal to $\frac{1}{12}$ foot: symbol, ″ —*vt.*, *vi.* to move very slowly, or by degrees —**every inch** in all respects —**inch by inch** gradually: also **by inches** —**within an inch of** very close to

in·cho·ate (in kō′it) *adj.* ⟦< L *inchoare*, begin⟧ **1** just begun; rudimentary **2** not yet clearly formed

in·ci·dence (in′sə dəns) *n.* the degree or range of occurrence or effect
in′ci·dent (-dənt) *adj.* ⟦< L *in-*, on + *cadere*, to fall⟧ 1 likely to happen as a result 2 falling upon or affecting /*incident* rays/ —*n.* 1 something that happens; an event, esp. a minor one 2 a minor conflict
in′ci·den′tal (-dent″l) *adj.* 1 happening in connection with something more important; casual 2 secondary or minor —*n.* 1 something incidental 2 [*pl.*] miscellaneous items
in′ci·den′tal·ly *adv.* 1 in an incidental manner 2 by the way
in·cin·er·ate (in sin′ər āt′) *vt., vi.* **-at′ed, -at′ing** ⟦< L *in*, in + *cinis*, ashes⟧ to burn to ashes; burn up —**in·cin′er·a′tion** *n.*
in·cin′er·a′tor *n.* a furnace for burning trash
in·cip·i·ent (in sip′ē ənt) *adj.* ⟦< L *in-*, in + *capere*, to take⟧ just beginning to exist or appear —**in·cip′i·ence** *n.*
in·cise (in sīz′) *vt.* **-cised′, -cis′ing** ⟦< L *in-*, into + *caedere*, to cut⟧ to cut into with a sharp tool; specif., to engrave or carve
in·ci·sion (in sizh′ən) *n.* 1 an incising 2 a cut; specif., one made surgically 3 incisive quality
in·ci·sive (in sī′siv) *adj.* 1 cutting into 2 sharp; penetrating —**in·ci′sive·ly** *adv.* —**in·ci′sive·ness** *n.*
in·ci·sor (in sī′zər) *n.* any of the front cutting teeth between the canines
in·cite (in sīt′) *vt.* **-cit′ed, -cit′ing** ⟦< L *in-*, on + *citare*, to urge⟧ to urge to action; rouse —**in·cite′ment** *n.*
incl. 1 including 2 inclusive
in·clem·ent (in klem′ənt) *adj.* ⟦< L *in-*, on + *clemens*, lenient⟧ 1 rough; stormy 2 lacking mercy; harsh —**in·clem′en·cy**, *pl.* **-cies**, *n.*
in·cli·na·tion (in′klə nā′shən) *n.* 1 a bending, leaning, or sloping 2 an inclined surface; slope 3 *a*) a bias; tendency *b*) a preference
in·cline (in klīn′; *for n., usually* in′klīn′) *vi.* **-clined′, -clin′ing** ⟦< L *in-*, on + *clinare*, to lean⟧ 1 to lean; slope 2 to have a tendency 3 to have a preference or liking —*vt.* 1 to cause to lean, slope, etc. 2 to make willing; influence —*n.* a slope; grade

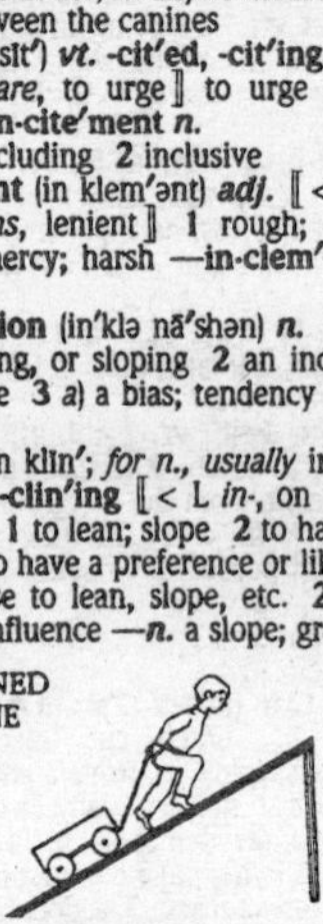

inclined plane a sloping plane surface, esp. one sloping slightly, as for raising heavy objects
in·close (in klōz′) *vt.* **-closed′, -clos′ing** ENCLOSE —**in·clo′sure** (-klō′zhər) *n.*
in·clude (in klo͞od′) *vt.* **-clud′ed, -clud′ing** ⟦< L *in-*, in + *claudere*, to close⟧ 1 to enclose 2 to have as part of a whole; contain; comprise 3 to take into account —**in·clu′sion** (-klo͞o′zhən) *n.*
in·clu′sive (-klo͞o′siv) *adj.* 1 taking everything into account 2 including the terms or limits mentioned /the third to the fifth *inclusive*/ —**inclusive of** including —**in·clu′sive·ly** *adv.*
in·cog·ni·to (in käg′ni tō′, in′käg nē′-) *adv., adj.* ⟦It < L *in-*, not + *cognitus*, known⟧ with true identity unrevealed or disguised
in·co·her·ent (in′kō hir′ənt, -her′-) *adj.* 1 not logically connected; disjointed 2 characterized by speech, etc. like this —**in′co·her′ence** *n.* —**in′co·her′ent·ly** *adv.*
in·come (in′kum′, -kəm) *n.* money, etc. received in a given period, as wages, rent, interest, etc.
in·com·mu·ni·ca·do (in′kə myo͞o′ni kä′dō) *adj., adv.* ⟦Sp⟧ not allowed to communicate with others
in·com·pa·ra·ble (in käm′pə rə bəl) *adj.* 1 having no basis of comparison 2 beyond comparison; matchless
in·com·pat·i·ble (in′kəm pat′ə bəl) *adj.* not compatible; specif., unable to live together harmoniously —**in′com·pat′i·bil′i·ty**, *pl.* **-ties**, *n.*
in·com·pe·tent (in käm′pə tənt) *adj.* without adequate ability, knowledge, fitness, etc. —*n.* an incompetent person —**in·com′pe·tence** *n.* —**in·com′pe·tent·ly** *adv.*
in·com·plete (in′kəm plēt′) *adj.* 1 lacking a part or parts 2 unfinished 3 not perfect
in·con·gru·ous (in käŋ′gro͞o əs) *adj.* 1 lacking harmony or agreement of parts, etc. 2 unsuitable; inappropriate —**in′con·gru′i·ty** (-kän gro͞o′i tē) *n.*
in·con·se·quen·tial (in kän′si kwen′shəl) *adj.* of no consequence
in·con·sid·er·a·ble (in′kən sid′ər ə bəl) *adj.* trivial; small
in′con·sid′er·ate (-it) *adj.* without thought or consideration for others; thoughtless —**in′con·sid′er·ate·ly** *adv.* —**in′con·sid′er·ate·ness** or **in′con·sid′er·a′tion** (-ər ā′shən) *n.*
in·con·sol·a·ble (in′kən sōl′ə bəl) *adj.* that cannot be consoled
in·con·spic·u·ous (in′kən spik′yo͞o əs) *adj.* attracting little attention
in·con·stant (in kän′stənt) *adj.* not constant; changeable, fickle, irregular, etc. —**in·con′stan·cy** *n.*
in·con·test·a·ble (in′kən tes′tə bəl) *adj.* unquestionable; indisputable —**in′con·test′a·bil′i·ty** *n.* —**in′con·test′a·bly** *adv.*
in·con·ti·nent (in kän′tə nənt) *adj.* 1 without self-restraint, esp. in sexual activity 2 unable to restrain a natural discharge, as of urine —**in·con′ti·nence** *n.*
in·con·ven·ience (in′kən vēn′yəns) *n.* 1 lack of comfort, ease, etc. 2 anything inconvenient —*vt.* **-ienced, -ienc·ing** to cause inconvenience to
in′con·ven′ient *adj.* not favorable to one's comfort; causing bother, etc.
in·cor·po·rate (in kôr′pə rāt′) *vt.* **-rat′ed, -rat′ing** ⟦see IN-[1] & CORPORATE⟧ 1 to combine; include; embody 2 to bring together into a single whole; merge 3 to form into a corporation —*vi.* 1 to combine into a single whole 2 to form a corporation —**in·cor′po·ra′tion** *n.*
in·cor·ri·gi·ble (in kôr′ə jə bəl) *adj.* ⟦< LL *incorrigibilis*⟧ that cannot be corrected or reformed, esp. because set in bad habits —**in·cor′ri·gi·bil′i·ty** *n.* —**in·cor′ri·gi·bly** *adv.*

in·cor·rupt·i·ble (in'kə rup'tə bəl) ***adj.*** that cannot be corrupted, esp. morally

in·crease (in krēs', in'krēs') ***vi.*** **-creased', -creas'ing** ⟦< L *in-*, in + *crescere*, grow⟧ to become greater in size, amount, degree, etc. **—*vt.*** to make greater in size, etc. **—*n.*** **1** an increasing or becoming increased **2** the result or amount of an increasing **—on the increase** increasing

in·creas'ing·ly ***adv.*** more and more

in·cred·i·ble (in kred'ə bəl) ***adj.*** **1** not credible **2** seeming too unusual to be possible **—in·cred'i·bly *adv.***

in·cred·u·lous (in krej'oo ləs) ***adj.*** **1** unwilling to believe **2** showing doubt or disbelief **—in·cre·du·li·ty** (in'krə dōō'lə tē) ***n.***

in·cre·ment (in'krə mənt, iŋ'-) ***n.*** ⟦< L *incrementum*⟧ **1** an increase **2** amount of increase

in·crim·i·nate (in krim'i nāt') ***vt.*** **-nat'ed, -nat'ing** ⟦< L *in-*, in + *crimen*, offense⟧ **1** to accuse of a crime **2** to involve in, or make appear guilty of, a crime or fault **—in·crim'i·na'tion *n.***

in·crust (in krust') ***vt., vi.*** ENCRUST **—in·crus·ta·tion** (in'krus tā'shən) ***n.***

in·cu·bate (in'kyōō bāt', iŋ'-) ***vt.*** **-bat'ed, -bat'ing** ⟦< L *in-*, on + *cubare*, to lie⟧ **1** to sit on and hatch (eggs) **2** to heat, etc. so as to hatch or grow, as in an incubator **3** to develop, as by planning **—*vi.*** to undergo incubation **—in'cu·ba'tion *n.***

in'cu·ba'tor ***n.*** **1** a heated container for hatching eggs **2** any similar device, as for protecting premature babies, growing cell cultures, etc.

in·cu·bus (in'kyōō bəs) ***n.*** ⟦LL⟧ **1** a nightmare **2** an oppressive burden

in·cul·cate (in kul'kāt', in'kul-) ***vt.*** **-cat'ed, -cat'ing** ⟦< L *in-*, in + *calcare*, trample underfoot⟧ to impress upon the mind, as by persistent urging **—in'cul·ca'tion *n.***

in·cul·pate (in kul'pāt', in'kul-) ***vt.*** **-pat'ed, -pat'ing** ⟦< L *in*, on + *culpa*, blame⟧ INCRIMINATE

in·cum·ben·cy (in kum'bən sē) ***n.,*** *pl.* **-cies** **1** a duty or obligation **2** tenure of office

in·cum'bent (-bənt) ***adj.*** ⟦< L *in-*, on + *cubare*, lie down⟧ currently in office **—*n.*** one currently in office **—incumbent on** (or **upon**) resting upon as a duty or obligation

in·cum·ber (in kum'bər) ***vt.*** ENCUMBER **—in·cum'brance *n.***

in·cu·nab·u·la (in'kyōō nab'yōō lə) ***n.pl.,*** *sing.* **-u·lum** (-ləm) ⟦< L *in-*, in + *cunabula*, pl., a cradle⟧ **1** infancy; beginnings **2** books printed before 1500

in·cur (in kur') ***vt.*** **-curred', -cur'ring** ⟦< L *in-*, in + *currere*, to run⟧ **1** to acquire (something undesirable) **2** to bring upon oneself

in·cu·ri·ous (in kyoor'ē əs) ***adj.*** not curious; uninterested

in·cur·sion (in kur'zhən) ***n.*** ⟦see INCUR⟧ an invasion or raid

ind. **1** independent **2** index

Ind. **1** India **2** Indian **3** Indiana

in·debt·ed (in det'id) ***adj.*** **1** in debt **2** owing gratitude, as for a favor

in·debt'ed·ness ***n.*** **1** a being indebted **2** the amount owed

in·de·cent (in dē'sənt) ***adj.*** not decent; specif., *a)* improper *b)* morally offensive; obscene **—in·de'cen·cy *n.*** **—in·de'cent·ly *adv.***

in·de·ci·pher·a·ble (in'dē sī'fər ə bəl) ***adj.*** that cannot be deciphered

in·de·ci·sion (in'dē sizh'ən) ***n.*** inability to decide; vacillation

in'de·ci'sive (-sī'siv) ***adj.*** **1** not conclusive or final **2** showing indecision **—in'de·ci'sive·ly *adv.*** **—in'de·ci'sive·ness *n.***

in·deed (in dēd') ***adv.*** certainly; truly **—*interj.*** an exclamation of surprise, doubt, sarcasm, etc.

in·de·fat·i·ga·ble (in'di fat'i gə bəl) ***adj.*** ⟦< L *in-*, not + *defatigare*, tire out⟧ that cannot be tired out

in·de·fen·si·ble (in'dē fen'sə bəl) ***adj.*** **1** that cannot be defended **2** that cannot be justified

in·def·i·nite (in def'ə nit) ***adj.*** not definite; specif., *a)* having no exact limits *b)* not precise in meaning; vague *c)* uncertain *d)* *Gram.* not limiting or specifying /"a" and "an" are *indefinite* articles/ **—in·def'i·nite·ly *adv.***

in·del·i·ble (in del'ə bəl) ***adj.*** ⟦< L *in-*, not + *delere*, destroy⟧ **1** that cannot be erased, blotted out, etc. **2** leaving an indelible mark

in·del·i·cate (in del'i kit) ***adj.*** lacking propriety or modesty; coarse **—in·del'i·ca·cy,** *pl.* **-cies, *n.***

in·dem·ni·fy (in dem'ni fī') ***vt.*** **-fied', -fy'ing** ⟦< L *indemnis*, unhurt + -FY⟧ **1** to insure against loss, damage, etc. **2** to repay for (loss or damage) **—in·dem'ni·fi·ca'tion *n.***

in·dem'ni·ty ***n.,*** *pl.* **-ties** **1** insurance against loss, damage, etc. **2** repayment for loss, damage, etc.

in·dent[1] (in dent') ***vt.*** ⟦< L *in*, in + *dens*, tooth⟧ **1** to notch **2** to space (a line, paragraph, etc.) in from the margin of a page **—*vi.*** **1** to form or be marked by notches or a jagged border **2** to space in from the margin

in·dent[2] (in dent') ***vt.*** ⟦IN-[1] + DENT⟧ to make a dent in

in·den·ta·tion (in'den tā'shən) ***n.*** **1** a being indented **2** a notch, cut, inlet, etc. **3** a dent **4** a spacing in from a margin, or a blank space so made: usually **in·den'tion**

in·den·ture (in den'chər) ***n.*** **1** a written contract **2** [*often pl.*] a contract binding one to work for another **3** a document listing the terms of a bond issue **—*vt.*** **-tured, -turing** to bind by indenture

in·de·pend·ence (in'dē pen'dəns) ***n.*** a being independent; freedom from the influence or control of others

In·de·pend·ence (in'dē pen'dəns) city in W Mo.: pop. 112,000

Independence Day the anniversary of the adoption of the Declaration of Independence on July 4, 1776

in'de·pend'ent (-dənt) ***adj.*** **1** free from the influence or control of others; specif., *a)* self-governing *b)* self-reliant *c)* not adhering to any political party *d)* not connected with others /an *independent* grocer/ **2** not depending on another for financial support

—*n.* one who is independent in thinking, action, etc. —**in'de·pend'ent·ly** *adv.*
independent clause a clause that can function as a complete sentence
in'-depth' *adj.* profound; thorough
in·de·scrib·a·ble (in'di skrib'ə bəl) *adj.* beyond the power of description —**in'de·scrib'a·bly** *adv.*
in·de·struct·i·ble (in'di struk'tə bəl) *adj.* that cannot be destroyed
in·de·ter·mi·nate (in'dē tur'mi nit, -di-) *adj.* **1** indefinite; vague **2** unsettled; inconclusive
in·dex (in'deks') *n., pl.* **-dex'es** or **-di·ces'** (-di sēz') ⟦L, indicator⟧ **1** forefinger: in full, **index finger** **2** a pointer or indicator **3** an indication /an *index* of ability/ **4** an alphabetical list of names, subjects, etc. indicating pages where found, as in a book **5** a number used to measure change in prices, wages, etc. —*vt.* to make or be an index of or for
In·di·a (in'dē ə) **1** region in S Asia, south of the Himalayas **2** republic in central & S India: 1,269,000 sq. mi.; pop. 783,940,000
In·di·a ink (in'dē ə) a black liquid ink
In'di·an *n.* **1** a native of India or the East Indies **2** a member of any of the aboriginal peoples of the Americas: also **American Indian** —*adj.* **1** of India, or the East Indies, their people, etc. **2** of the American Indians, their culture, etc.
In·di·an·a (in'dē an'ə) Middle Western State of the U.S.: 36,291 sq. mi.; pop. 5,490,000; cap. Indianapolis —**In'di·an'i·an** (-an'ē ən) *adj., n.*
In·di·an·ap·o·lis (in'dē ə nap'ə lis) capital of Ind., in the central part: pop. 701,000
Indian corn CORN[1] (sense 2)
Indian file SINGLE FILE
Indian Ocean ocean south of Asia, between Africa & Australia
Indian summer mild, warm weather following the first frosts of late autumn
India paper **1** a thin, absorbent paper for taking proofs from engraved plates **2** a thin, opaque printing paper, as for Bibles
in·di·cate (in'di kāt') *vt.* **-cat'ed, -cat'ing** ⟦< L *in-*, in + *dicare*, declare⟧ **1** to direct attention to; point out **2** to be a sign of; signify **3** to show the need for **4** to express briefly or generally —**in'di·ca'tion** *n.*
in·dic·a·tive (in dik'ə tiv) *adj.* **1** giving an indication **2** designating the mood of a verb used to express an act, state, etc. as actual, or to ask a question of fact —*n.* the indicative mood
in'di·ca'tor *n.* a person or thing that indicates; specif., a gauge, dial, etc. that measures something
in·dict (in dīt') *vt.* ⟦ult. < L *in*, against + *dicere*, speak⟧ to charge with a crime —**in·dict'ment** *n.*
in·dif·fer·ent (in dif'ər ənt, -dif'rənt) *adj.* **1** neutral **2** unconcerned; apathetic **3** of no importance **4** average —**in·dif'fer·ence** *n.* —**in·dif'fer·ent·ly** *adv.*
in·dig·e·nous (in dij'ə nəs) *adj.* ⟦< L *indegena*, a native⟧ existing or growing naturally in a region or country; native
in·di·gent (in'di jənt) *adj.* ⟦< L *indegere*, to be in need⟧ poor; needy —*n.* an indigent person —**in'di·gence** *n.* —**in'di·gent·ly** *adv.*
in·di·gest·i·ble (in'di jes'tə bəl) *adj.* not easily digested
in'di·ges'tion (-jes'chən) *n.* difficulty in digesting food
in·dig·nant (in dig'nənt) *adj.* ⟦< L *in-*, not + *dignus*, worthy⟧ feeling or expressing anger, esp. at unjust or mean action —**in·dig'nant·ly** *adv.*
in·dig·na·tion (in'dig nā'shən) *n.* righteous anger
in·dig·ni·ty (in dig'nə tē) *n., pl.* **-ties** an insult or affront to one's dignity or self-respect
in·di·go (in'di gō') *n., pl.* **-gos'** or **-goes'** ⟦Sp < Gr *Indikos*, Indian⟧ **1** a blue dye obtained from certain plants or made synthetically **2** a deep violet blue —*adj.* of this color
in·di·rect (in'də rekt', -di-) *adj.* **1** not straight **2** not straight to the point **3** dishonest /*indirect* dealing/ **4** not immediate; secondary /an *indirect* result/ —**in'di·rect'ly** *adv.* —**in'di·rect'ness** *n.*
indirect object the word or words denoting the person or thing indirectly affected by the action of the verb (Ex.: *him* in "give *him* the ball")
in·dis·creet (in'di skrēt') *adj.* not prudent, as in speech or action; unwise
in'dis·cre'tion (-skresh'ən) *n.* **1** lack of discretion; imprudence **2** an indiscreet act or remark
in·dis·crim·i·nate (in'di skrim'i nit) *adj.* **1** mixed or random **2** making no distinctions —**in'dis·crim'i·nate·ly** *adv.*
in·dis·pen·sa·ble (in'di spen'sə bəl) *adj.* absolutely necessary
in·dis·posed (in'di spōzd') *adj.* **1** slightly ill **2** unwilling; disinclined —**in·dis·po·si·tion** (in'dis pə zish'ən) *n.*
in·dis·sol·u·ble (in'di säl'yoo bəl) *adj.* that cannot be dissolved or destroyed; lasting
in·dite (in dīt') *vt.* **-dit'ed, -dit'ing** ⟦see INDICT⟧ to compose and write
in·di·vid·u·al (in'də vij'oo əl) *adj.* ⟦< L < *in-*, not + *dividere*, to divide⟧ **1** existing as a separate thing or being; single **2** of, for, by, or relating to a single person or thing —*n.* **1** a single thing or being **2** a person
in'di·vid'u·al·ism' *n.* **1** individuality **2** the doctrine that the state exists for the individual **3** the leading of one's life in one's own way —**in'di·vid'u·al·ist** *n., adj.* —**in'di·vid'u·al·is'tic** *adj.*
in'di·vid'u·al'i·ty (-al'ə tē) *n., pl.* **-ties** **1** the sum of the characteristics that set one person or thing apart **2** existence as an individual
in'di·vid'u·al·ize' (-əl īz') *vt.* **-ized', -iz'ing** **1** to make individual **2** to treat as an individual —**in'di·vid'u·al·i·za'tion** *n.*
in'di·vid'u·al·ly *adv.* **1** as individuals; separately **2** distinctively
In·do·chi·na (in'dō chī'nə) **1** large peninsula south of China, including Burma, Thailand, etc. **2** E part of this peninsula, consisting of Laos, Cambodia, & Vietnam
in·doc·tri·nate (in däk'trə nāt') *vt.* **-nat'ed, -nat'ing** to instruct in, or imbue with, doctrines, theories, etc. —**in·doc'tri·na'tion** *n.*
In·do-Eu·ro·pe·an (in'dō yoor'ə pē'ən) *adj.*

designating a family of languages including most of those of Europe and many of those of Asia

in·do·lent (in′də lənt) ***adj.*** ⟦< L *in-*, not + *dolere*, feel pain⟧ idle; lazy —**in′do·lence** ***n.*** —**in′do·lent·ly** ***adv.***

in·dom·i·ta·ble (in däm′i tə bəl) ***adj.*** ⟦< L *in-*, not + *domitare*, to tame⟧ not easily discouraged or defeated

In·do·ne·sia (in′də nē′zhə) republic in the Malay Archipelago, consisting of Java, Sumatra, & most of Borneo: 736,510 sq. mi.; pop. 176,764,000

In·do·ne·sian (in′də nē′zhən) ***n.*** **1** a native or inhabitant of Indonesia, the Philippines, etc. **2** the official Malay language of Indonesia —***adj.*** of Indonesia, its people, language, etc.

in′door′ ***adj.*** living, belonging, etc. in a building

in′doors′ ***adv.*** in or into a building

in·dorse (in dôrs′) ***vt.*** **-dorsed′**, **-dors′ing** ENDORSE

in·du·bi·ta·ble (in do͞o′bi tə bəl) ***adj.*** that cannot be doubted —**in·du′bi·ta·bly** ***adv.***

in·duce (in do͞os′) ***vt.*** **-duced′**, **-duc′ing** ⟦< L *in-*, in + *ducere*, to lead⟧ **1** to persuade **2** to bring on or about; cause **3** to draw (a conclusion) from particular facts **4** to bring about (an electric or magnetic effect) in a body by placing it within a field of force —**in·duc′er** ***n.***

in·duce′ment ***n.*** **1** an inducing or being induced **2** a motive; incentive

in·duct (in dukt′) ***vt.*** ⟦see INDUCE⟧ **1** to place formally in an office, a society, etc. **2** to enroll (esp. a draftee) in the armed forces

in·duct′ance (-əns) ***n.*** the property of an electric circuit by which a varying current in it produces a magnetic field that induces voltages in the same or a nearby circuit

in·duct·ee (in′duk tē′) ***n.*** a person inducted, esp. into the armed forces

in·duc′tion (-shən) ***n.*** **1** an inducting or being inducted **2** reasoning from particular facts to a general conclusion **3** the inducing of an electric or magnetic effect by a field of force —**in·duc′tive** ***adj.***

in·due (in do͞o′, -dyo͞o′) ***vt.*** **-dued′**, **-du′ing** ENDUE

in·dulge (in dulj′) ***vt.*** **-dulged′**, **-dulg′ing** ⟦L *indulgere*, be kind to⟧ **1** to satisfy (a desire) **2** to gratify the wishes of; humor —***vi.*** to give way to one's own desires —**in·dulg′er** ***n.***

in·dul·gence (in dul′jəns) ***n.*** **1** an indulging or being indulgent **2** a thing indulged in **3** a favor or privilege **4** *R.C.Ch.* remission of punishment still due for a sin committed but forgiven

in·dul′gent (-jənt) ***adj.*** indulging or inclined to indulge; kind or lenient, often to excess —**in·dul′gent·ly** ***adv.***

in·dus·tri·al (in dus′trē əl) ***adj.*** having to do with industry or its workers, products, etc. —**in·dus′tri·al·ly** ***adv.***

industrial arts the mechanical and technical skills used in industry

in·dus′tri·al·ism′ ***n.*** social and economic structure characterized by large industries, machine production, etc.

in·dus′tri·al·ist ***n.*** one who owns or controls an industrial enterprise

in·dus′tri·al·ize′ (-īz′) ***vt.*** **-ized′**, **-iz′ing** **1** to establish or develop industrialism in **2** to organize as an industry —**in·dus′tri·al·i·za′tion** ***n.***

industrial park a planned area for industrial use, usually on the outskirts of a city

in·dus·tri·ous (in dus′trē əs) ***adj.*** diligent; hard-working —**in·dus′tri·ous·ly** ***adv.*** —**in·dus′tri·ous·ness** ***n.***

in·dus·try (in′dəs trē) ***n.***, *pl.* **-tries** ⟦< L *industrius*, active⟧ **1** earnest, steady effort **2** any particular branch of productive, esp. manufacturing, enterprise, or all of these collectively **3** any large-scale business activity **4** the owners and managers of industry

-ine[1] (*variously* īn, in, ēn, ən) ⟦< L *-inus*⟧ *suffix* of, having the nature of, like *[aquiline, crystalline]*

-ine[2] (in, ən) ⟦< L *-ina*⟧ *suffix* forming abstract nouns *[discipline, doctrine]*

-ine[3] (*variously* ēn, in, īn, ən) ⟦< L *-inus*⟧ *suffix* forming chemical names, as of *a*) halogens *[iodine]* *b*) alkaloids or nitrogenous bases *[morphine]* Often forming commercial names *[Vaseline]*

in·e·bri·ate (in ē′brē āt′; *for n. also*, -it′) ***vt.*** **-at′ed**, **-at′ing** ⟦< L *in-*, intens. + *ebrius*, drunk⟧ to make drunk —***n.*** a drunkard —**in·e′bri·a′tion** ***n.***

in·ed·u·ca·ble (in ej′o͞o kə bəl) ***adj.*** thought to be incapable of being educated

in·ef·fa·ble (in ef′ə bəl) ***adj.*** ⟦< L *in-*, not + *effabilis*, utterable⟧ **1** inexpressible **2** too sacred to be spoken

in·ef·fi·cient (in′e fish′ənt) ***adj.*** **1** not producing the desired effect with a minimum use of energy, time, etc. **2** incapable —**in′ef·fi′cien·cy** ***n.*** —**in′ef·fi′cient·ly** ***adv.***

in·el·e·gant (in el′ə gənt) ***adj.*** not elegant; crude —**in·el′e·gant·ly** ***adv.***

in·e·luc·ta·ble (in′ē luk′tə bəl) ***adj.*** ⟦< L *in-*, not + *eluctari*, to struggle⟧ not to be avoided or escaped —**in′e·luc′ta·bly** ***adv.***

in·ept (in ept′) ***adj.*** ⟦< L *in-*, not + *aptus*, apt⟧ **1** unsuitable; unfit **2** foolish **3** awkward; clumsy —**in·ep′ti·tude′** (-ep′tə to͞od′) ***n.*** —**in·ept′ness** ***n.***

in·ert (in urt′) ***adj.*** ⟦< L *in-*, not + *ars*, skill⟧ **1** without power to move or to resist **2** inactive; dull; slow **3** with few or no active properties

in·er·ti·a (in ur′shə) ***n.*** ⟦see prec.⟧ **1** *Physics* the tendency of matter to remain at rest or to continue in a fixed direction unless affected by some outside force **2** a disinclination to move or act —**in·er′tial** ***adj.***

in·es·cap·a·ble (in′e skāp′ə bəl) ***adj.*** that cannot be escaped or avoided

in·es·ti·ma·ble (in es′tə mə bəl) ***adj.*** too great to be properly measured

in·ev·i·ta·ble (in ev′i tə bəl) ***adj.*** ⟦< L *in-*, not + *evitabilis*, avoidable⟧ certain to happen; unavoidable —**in·ev′i·ta·bil′i·ty** ***n.*** —**in·ev′i·ta·bly** ***adv.***

in·ex·haust·i·ble (in′eg zôs′tə bəl) ***adj.*** **1** that cannot be used up or emptied **2** tireless

in·ex·o·ra·ble (in eks′ə rə bəl) ***adj.*** ⟦< L *in-*, not + *exorare*, move by entreaty⟧ **1** that cannot be influenced by persuasion or entreaty; unrelenting **2** that cannot be altered, checked, etc. —**in·ex′o·ra·bly** ***adv.***

in·ex·pe·ri·ence (in′ek spir′ē əns) ***n.*** lack of experience or of the knowledge or skill resulting from experience —**in′ex·pe′ri·enced** ***adj.***

in·ex·pert (in ek′spərt; *also* in′ek spurt′) ***adj.*** not expert; unskillful

in·ex·pi·a·ble (in eks′pē ə bəl) ***adj.*** that cannot be expiated or atoned for

in·ex·pli·ca·ble (in eks′pli kə bəl) ***adj.*** that cannot be explained

in·ex·press·i·ble (in′eks pres′ə bəl) ***adj.*** that cannot be expressed

in·ex·tin·guish·a·ble (in′ek stiŋ′gwish ə bəl) ***adj.*** that cannot be put out or stopped

in ex·tre·mis (in′ eks trē′mis) ⟦L, in extremity⟧ at the point of death

in·ex·tri·ca·ble (in eks′tri kə bəl) ***adj.*** **1** that one cannot extricate oneself from **2** that cannot be disentangled or untied **3** insolvable

in·fal·li·ble (in fal′ə bəl) ***adj.*** ⟦see IN-[2] & FALLIBLE⟧ **1** incapable of error **2** dependable; reliable —**in·fal′li·bil′i·ty** ***n.*** —**in·fal′li·bly** ***adv.***

in·fa·mous (in′fə məs) ***adj.*** **1** having a bad reputation; notorious **2** causing a bad reputation; scandalous

in′fa·my (-mē) ***n.***, *pl.* **-mies** **1** very bad reputation; disgrace **2** great wickedness **3** an infamous act

in·fan·cy (in′fən sē) ***n.***, *pl.* **-cies** **1** the state or period of being an infant **2** the earliest stage of anything

in·fant (in′fənt) ***n.*** ⟦< L *in-*, not + *fari*, speak⟧ a very young child; baby —***adj.*** **1** of or for infants **2** in a very early stage

in·fan·ti·cide (in fan′tə sīd′) ***n.*** **1** the murder of a baby **2** a person guilty of this

in·fan·tile (in′fən tīl′) ***adj.*** **1** of infants **2** like an infant; babyish

infantile paralysis POLIOMYELITIS

in·fan·try (in′fən trē) ***n.***, *pl.* **-tries** ⟦< L *infans*, child⟧ that branch of an army consisting of soldiers trained to fight on foot —**in′fan·try·man** (-mən), *pl.* **-men,** ***n.***

in·farct (in färkt′) ***n.*** ⟦< L *in-*, in + *farcire*, to stuff⟧ an area of dying or dead tissue resulting from inadequate blood flow to that area Also **in·farc′tion** (-färk′shən)

in·fat·u·ate (in fach′o͞o āt′) ***vt.*** **-at′ed, -at′ing** ⟦< L *in-*, intens. + *fatuus*, foolish⟧ to inspire with foolish love or affection —**in·fat′u·a′tion** ***n.***

in·fect (in fekt′) ***vt.*** ⟦< L *inficere*, to stain⟧ **1** to contaminate or cause to become diseased by contact with disease-producing matter **2** to imbue with one's feelings, beliefs, etc. esp. so as to harm

in·fec·tion (in fek′shən) ***n.*** **1** an infecting or being infected **2** an infectious disease

in·fec′tious (-shəs) ***adj.*** **1** likely to cause infection **2** designating a disease caused by the presence in the body of certain bacteria, viruses, etc. **3** tending to affect others, as a laugh —**in·fec′tious·ly** ***adv.*** —**in·fec′tious·ness** ***n.***

in·fe·lic·i·tous (in′fə lis′ə təs) ***adj.*** not felicitous; unsuitable; not apt —**in′fe·lic′i·ty,** *pl.* **-ties,** ***n.***

in·fer (in fur′) ***vt.*** **-ferred′, -fer′ring** ⟦< L *in-*, in + *ferre*, to carry⟧ **1** to conclude by reasoning from something known or assumed **2** to imply: still sometimes regarded as a loose usage —**in·fer·ence** (in′fər əns) ***n.***

in·fer·en·tial (in′fər en′shəl) ***adj.*** based on or having to do with inference

in·fe·ri·or (in fir′ē ər) ***adj.*** ⟦< L *inferus*, low⟧ **1** lower in space **2** lower in order, status, etc. **3** lower in quality than: with *to* **4** poor in quality —***n.*** an inferior person or thing —**in·fe′ri·or′i·ty** (-ôr′ə tē) ***n.***

in·fer·nal (in fur′nəl) ***adj.*** ⟦< L *inferus*, below⟧ **1** of hell or Hades **2** hellish; fiendish

in·fer·no (in fur′nō′) ***n.***, *pl.* **-nos′** ⟦see prec.⟧ HELL

in·fest (in fest′) ***vt.*** ⟦< L *infestus*, hostile⟧ **1** to overrun in large numbers, usually so as to be harmful **2** to be parasitic in or on —**in′fes·ta′tion** ***n.*** —**in·fest′er** ***n.***

in·fi·del (in′fə del′) ***n.*** ⟦< L *in-*, not + *fidelis*, faithful⟧ **1** one who does not believe in a particular religion **2** one who has no religion

in·fi·del·i·ty (in′fə del′ə tē) ***n.*** unfaithfulness, esp. in marriage

in·field (in′fēld′) ***n.*** **1** the area enclosed by the four base lines on a baseball field **2** the players (**infielders**) whose field positions are there

in·fight·ing (in′fīt′iŋ) ***n.*** **1** fighting, esp. boxing, at close range **2** personal conflict within a group —**in′fight′er** ***n.***

in·fil·trate (in fil′trāt, in′fil trāt′) ***vi.***, ***vt.*** **-trat′ed, -trat′ing** **1** to filter or pass gradually through or into **2** to penetrate (enemy lines, a region, etc.) gradually or stealthily, so as to attack or to seize control from within —**in′fil·tra′tion** ***n.*** —**in′fil·tra′tor** ***n.***

in·fi·nite (in′fə nit) ***adj.*** ⟦see IN-[2] & FINITE⟧ **1** lacking limits or bounds; endless **2** very great; vast —***n.*** something infinite —**in′finite·ly** ***adv.***

in·fin·i·tes·i·mal (in′fin i tes′i məl) ***adj.*** ⟦< L *infinitus*, infinite⟧ too small to be measured; infinitely small —**in′fin·i·tes′i·mal·ly** ***adv.***

in·fin·i·tive (in fin′i tiv) ***n.*** ⟦see INFINITE⟧ the form of a verb without reference to person, number, or tense Usually with *to* as in "I want *to go*" —**in·fin′i·ti′val** (-tī′vəl) ***adj.***

in·fin′i·tude′ (-to͞od′, -tyo͞od′) ***n.*** ⟦< L *infinitus*, INFINITE, prob. infl. by MAGNITUDE⟧ **1** a being infinite **2** an infinite quantity

in·fin′i·ty (-tē) ***n.***, *pl.* **-ties** ⟦< L *infinitas*⟧ **1** the quality of being infinite **2** unlimited space, time, etc. **3** an indefinitely large quantity

in·firm (in furm′) ***adj.*** **1** weak; feeble **2** not firm; unstable; frail; shaky —**in·firm′ly** ***adv.*** —**in·firm′ness** ***n.***

in·fir·ma·ry (in fur′mə rē) ***n.***, *pl.* **-ries** a place for the care of the sick, injured, or infirm; hospital

in·fir′mi·ty (-mə tē) ***n.***, *pl.* **-ties** physical weakness or defect

in·flame (in flām′) ***vt.***, ***vi.*** **-flamed′, -flam′ing** ⟦see IN-[1] & FLAME⟧ **1** to arouse, excite, etc. or become aroused, excited, etc. **2** to undergo or cause to undergo inflammation

in·flam·ma·ble (in flam′ə bəl) ***adj.*** **1** FLAM-

MABLE 2 easily excited —**in·flam′ma·bil′i·ty** *n.*

in·flam·ma·tion (in′flə mā′shən) *n.* 1 an inflaming or being inflamed 2 redness, pain, heat, and swelling in the body, due to injury or disease

in·flam·ma·to·ry (in flam′ə tôr′ē) *adj.* 1 rousing excitement, anger, etc. 2 of or caused by inflammation

in·flate (in flāt′) *vt.* **-flat′ed, -flat′ing** ⟦< L *in-*, in + *flare*, to blow⟧ 1 to blow full as with air or gas 2 to puff up with pride 3 to increase beyond what is normal; specif., to cause inflation of (money, credit, etc.) —*vi.* to become inflated —**in·flat′a·ble** *adj.*

in·fla′tion *n.* 1 an inflating or being inflated 2 *a*) an increase in the amount of money and credit in relation to the supply of goods and services *b*) an excessive or persistent increase in the general price level as a result of this, causing a decline in purchasing power —**in·fla′tion·ar′y** *adj.*

in·flect (in flekt′) *vt.* ⟦< L *in-*, in + *flectere*, to bend⟧ 1 to vary the tone of (the voice) 2 *Gram.* to change the form of (a word) by inflection

in·flec·tion (in flek′shən) *n.* 1 a change in the tone of the voice 2 the change of form in a word to indicate number, case, tense, etc. Brit. sp. **in·flex′ion** —**in·flec′tion·al** *adj.*

in·flex·i·ble (in flek′sə bəl) *adj.* not flexible; stiff, rigid, fixed, unyielding, etc. —**in·flex′i·bil′i·ty** *n.*

in·flict (in flikt′) *vt.* ⟦< L *in-*, on + *fligere*, to strike⟧ 1 to cause (pain, wounds, etc.) as by striking 2 to impose (a punishment, etc. *on* or *upon*) —**in·flic′tion** *n.* —**in·flic′tive** *adj.*

in-flight (in′flīt′) *adj.* done, shown, etc. while an aircraft is in flight

in·flo·res·cence (in′flō res′əns, -flô-) *n.* 1 the producing of blossoms 2 the arrangement of flowers on a stem 3 a flower cluster 4 flowers collectively

in·flu·ence (in′flo͞o əns) *n.* ⟦< L *in-*, in + *fluere*, to flow⟧ 1 power to affect others 2 power to produce effects because of wealth, position, ability, etc. 3 one that has influence —*vt.* **-enced, -enc·ing** to have influence or effect on

in′flu·en′tial (-en′shəl) *adj.* exerting influence, esp. great influence

in·flu·en·za (in′flo͞o en′zə) *n.* ⟦It, an influence⟧ an acute, contagious viral disease, characterized by inflammation of the respiratory tract, fever, and muscular pain

in·flux (in′fluks′) *n.* ⟦see INFLUENCE⟧ a flowing in or streaming in

in·fo (in′fō) *n.* [Slang] *short for* INFORMATION (senses 1 & 2)

in·fold (in fōld′) *vt. var. of* ENFOLD

in·form (in fôrm′) *vt.* ⟦see IN-[1] & FORM⟧ to give knowledge of something to —*vi.* to give information, esp. in accusing another —**in·form′er** *n.*

in·for·mal (in fôr′məl) *adj.* not formal; specif., *a*) not according to fixed customs, rules, etc. *b*) casual, relaxed, etc. *c*) not requiring formal dress *d*) COLLOQUIAL —**in′for·mal′i·ty** (-mal′ə tē), *pl.* **-ties,** *n.* —**in·for′mal·ly** *adv.*

in·form·ant (in fôrm′ənt) *n.* a person who gives information

in·for·ma·tion (in′fər mā′shən) *n.* 1 an informing or being informed 2 something told or facts learned; news or knowledge 3 data stored in or retrieved from a computer

information science the science dealing with the collection, storage, and retrieval of information

in·form·a·tive (in fôrm′ə tiv) *adj.* giving information; instructive

infra- ⟦< L⟧ *prefix* below, beneath

in·frac·tion (in frak′shən) *n.* ⟦see INFRINGE⟧ a violation of a law, pact, etc.

in·fran·gi·ble (in fran′jə bəl) *adj.* ⟦see IN-[2] & FRANGIBLE⟧ unbreakable or inviolable —**in·fran′gi·bly** *adv.*

in·fra·red (in′frə red′) *adj.* designating or of those invisible rays just beyond the red of the visible spectrum: they have a penetrating heating effect

in′fra·son′ic (-săn′ik) *adj.* of a frequency of sound below the range audible to the human ear

in′fra·struc′ture (-struk′chər) *n.* basic installations and facilities, as roads, power plants, transportation and communication systems, etc.

in·fre·quent (in frē′kwənt) *adj.* not frequent; happening seldom; rare —**in·fre′quen·cy** or **in·fre′quence** *n.* —**in·fre′quent·ly** *adv.*

in·fringe (in frinj′) *vt.* **-fringed′, -fring′ing** ⟦< L *in-*, in + *frangere*, to break⟧ to break (a law or pact) —**infringe on** (or **upon**) to encroach on (the rights, etc. of others) —**in·fringe′ment** *n.*

in·fu·ri·ate (in fyoor′ē āt′) *vt.* **-at′ed, -at′ing** ⟦< L *in-*, in + *furia*, rage⟧ to make very angry; enrage

in·fuse (in fyo͞oz′) *vt.* **-fused′, -fus′ing** ⟦< L *in-*, in + *fundere*, pour⟧ 1 to instill or impart (qualities, etc.) 2 to fill; inspire 3 to steep (tea leaves, etc.) to extract the essence —**in·fus′er** *n.* —**in·fu′sion** *n.*

-ing (iŋ) ⟦< OE⟧ *suffix* used to form the present participle or verbal nouns /*talking, painting*/

in·gen·ious (in jēn′yəs) *adj.* ⟦< L *in-*, in + *gignere*, to produce⟧ 1 clever, resourceful, etc. 2 made or done in a clever or original way —**in·gen′ious·ly** *adv.*

in·gé·nue (an′zhā no͞o′, -jə-) *n.* ⟦Fr, ingenuous⟧ *Theater* the role of an inexperienced young woman, or an actress in this role

in·ge·nu·i·ty (in′jə no͞o′ə tē, -nyo͞o′-) *n.* the quality of being ingenious; cleverness

in·gen·u·ous (in jen′yo͞o əs) *adj.* ⟦< L *in-*, in + *gignere*, to produce⟧ 1 frank; open 2 simple; naive —**in·gen′u·ous·ly** *adv.* —**in·gen′u·ous·ness** *n.*

in·gest (in jest′) *vt.* ⟦< L *in-*, into + *gerere*, carry⟧ to take (food, etc.) into the body —**in·ges′tion** *n.*

in·glo·ri·ous (in glôr′ē əs) *adj.* shameful; disgraceful

in·got (iŋ′gət) *n.* ⟦prob. < OFr *lingo*, tongue⟧ a mass of metal cast into a bar or other convenient shape

in·grained (in′grānd′) *adj.* 1 firmly established, as habits 2 inveterate /an *ingrained* liar/

in·grate (in′grāt′) ***n.*** ⟦< L *in-*, not + *gratus*, grateful⟧ an ungrateful person

in·gra·ti·ate (in grā′shē āt′) ***vt.*** **-at′ed, -at′ing** ⟦< L *in-*, in + *gratia*, favor⟧ to bring (oneself) into another's favor —**in·gra′ti·a′tion** ***n.***

in·grat·i·tude (in grat′i to͞od′, -tyo͞od′) ***n.*** lack of gratitude; ungratefulness

in·gre·di·ent (in grē′dē ənt) ***n.*** ⟦see fol.⟧ any of the things that a mixture is made of; component

in·gress (in′gres′) ***n.*** ⟦< L *in-*, into + *gradi*, to go⟧ entrance

in·grown (in′grōn′) ***adj.*** grown inward, esp. into the flesh, as a toenail

in·gui·nal (iŋ′gwi nəl) ***adj.*** ⟦< L *inguen*, groin⟧ of or near the groin

in·hab·it (in hab′it) ***vt.*** ⟦< L *in-*, in + *habitare*, dwell⟧ to live in —**in·hab′it·a·ble** ***adj.***

in·hab′it·ant (-i tənt) ***n.*** a person or animal inhabiting a specified place

in·hal·ant (in hāl′ənt) ***n.*** a medicine, etc. to be inhaled

in·ha·la·tor (in′hə lāt′ər) ***n.*** **1** an apparatus used in inhaling medicinal vapors **2** RESPIRATOR (sense 2)

in·hale (in hāl′) ***vt.***, ***vi.*** **-haled′, -hal′ing** ⟦< L *in-*, in + *halare*, breathe⟧ to breathe in (air, vapor, etc.) —**in·ha·la·tion** (in′hə lā′shən) ***n.***

in·hal·er (in hāl′ər) ***n.*** **1** one who inhales **2** RESPIRATOR (sense 1) **3** INHALATOR (sense 1)

in·here (in hir′) ***vi.*** **-hered′, -her′ing** ⟦< L *in-*, in + *haerere*, to stick⟧ to be inherent

in·her·ent (in hir′ənt, -her′-) ***adj.*** existing in someone or something as a natural and inseparable quality

in·her·it (in her′it) ***vt.***, ***vi.*** ⟦< L *in*, in + *heres*, heir⟧ **1** to receive (property, etc.) as an heir **2** to have (certain characteristics) by heredity

in·her·it·ance (in her′i təns) ***n.*** **1** the action of inheriting **2** something inherited

in·hib·it (in hib′it) ***vt.*** ⟦< L *in-*, in, on + *habere*, to hold⟧ to check or repress

in·hi·bi·tion (in′hi bish′ən, in′i-) ***n.*** **1** an inhibiting or being inhibited **2** a mental process that restrains an action, emotion, or thought

in·hu·man (in hyo͞o′mən) ***adj.*** not having worthy human characteristics; heartless, cruel, brutal, etc. —**in′hu·man′i·ty** (-man′ə tē) ***n.***

in·im·i·cal (i nim′i kəl) ***adj.*** ⟦< L *in-*, not + *amicus*, friend⟧ **1** hostile; unfriendly **2** in opposition; adverse

in·im·i·ta·ble (in im′i tə bəl) ***adj.*** that cannot be imitated; matchless

in·iq·ui·ty (i nik′wi tē) ***n.*** ⟦< L *in-*, not + *aequus*, equal⟧ **1** wickedness **2** *pl.* **-ties** a wicked or unjust act —**in·iq′ui·tous** ***adj.***

in·i·tial (i nish′əl) ***adj.*** ⟦< L *in-*, into, in + *ire*, go⟧ of or at the beginning; first —***n.*** the first letter of a name, esp. when used alone —***vt.*** **-tialed** or **-tialled**, **-tial·ing** or **-tial·ling** to mark with initials —**in·i′tial·ly** ***adv.***

in·i·ti·ate (i nish′ē āt′) ***vt.*** **-at′ed, -at′ing** ⟦see prec.⟧ **1** to bring into practice or use **2** to teach the fundamentals of a subject to **3** to admit as a member into a fraternity, club, etc., esp. with a special or secret ceremony —**in·i′ti·a′tion** ***n.*** —**in·i′ti·a·to′ry** (-ə tôr′ē) ***adj.***

in·i·ti·a·tive (i nish′ə tiv, -ē ə tiv) ***n.*** **1** the action of taking the first step or move **2** ability in originating new ideas or methods **3** the introduction of proposed legislation, as to popular vote, by voters' petitions

in·ject (in jekt′) ***vt.*** ⟦< L *in-*, in + *jacere*, to throw⟧ **1** to force (a fluid) into a vein, tissue, etc. with a syringe or the like **2** to introduce (a remark, quality, etc.) —**in·jec′tion** ***n.*** —**in·jec′tor** ***n.***

in·junc·tion (in juŋk′shən) ***n.*** ⟦< L *in-*, in + *jungere*, join⟧ **1** a command; order **2** a court order prohibiting or ordering a given action

in·jure (in′jər) ***vt.*** **-jured, -jur·ing** ⟦see INJURY⟧ **1** to do harm or damage to; hurt **2** to wrong or offend

in·ju·ri·ous (in joor′ē əs) ***adj.*** injuring or likely to injure; harmful

in·ju·ry (in′jə rē) ***n.***, *pl.* **-ries** ⟦< L *in-*, not + *jus*, right⟧ **1** harm or damage **2** an injurious act

in·jus·tice (in jus′tis) ***n.*** **1** a being unjust **2** an unjust act; wrong

ink (iŋk) ***n.*** ⟦< Gr *en-*, in + *kaiein*, to burn⟧ **1** a colored liquid used for writing, printing, etc. **2** a dark, liquid secretion ejected by cuttlefish, squid, etc. —***vt.*** to cover, mark, or color with ink

ink′blot′ ***n.*** any of the patterns made by blots of ink that are used in the RORSCHACH TEST

ink·ling (iŋk′liŋ′) ***n.*** ⟦ME *ingkiling*⟧ **1** a hint **2** a vague notion

ink′well′ ***n.*** a container for ink

ink′y ***adj.*** **-i·er, -i·est** **1** like ink in color; dark; black **2** covered with ink —**ink′i·ness** ***n.***

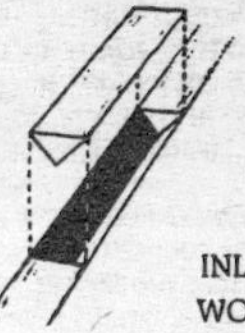

INLAID WOOD

in·laid (in′lād′, in lād′) ***adj.*** set into a surface or formed, decorated, etc. by inlaying

in·land (*for adj.* in′lənd; *for n. & adv.*, -land′, -lənd) ***adj.*** of or in the interior of a country —***n.*** inland region —***adv.*** into or toward this region

in-law (in′lô′) ***n.*** ⟦< *mother-* (or *father-*, etc.) *in-law*⟧ [Colloq.] a relative by marriage

in·lay (*for v.* in′lā′, in lā′; *for n.* in′lā′) ***vt.*** **-laid′, -lay′ing** **1** to set (pieces of wood, etc.) into a surface, specif. for decoration **2** to decorate thus —***n.***, *pl.* **-lays′** **1** inlaid decoration or material **2** a shaped filling, as of gold, cemented into the cavity of a tooth

in·let (in′let′) ***n.*** a narrow strip of water extending into a body of land

in·mate (in′māt′) ***n.*** a person confined with others in a prison or mental institution

in·most (in′mōst′) ***adj.*** 1 farthest within 2 most secret

inn (in) ***n.*** ⟦OE⟧ 1 a small hotel 2 a restaurant or tavern: now usually only in the names of such places

in·nards (in′ərdz) ***n.pl.*** ⟦< INWARDS⟧ [Colloq. or Dial.] the inner organs or parts

in·nate (in′āt′, i nāt′) ***adj.*** ⟦< L *in-*, in + *nasci*, be born⟧ inborn; natural

in·ner (in′ər) ***adj.*** 1 farther within 2 more secret

inner circle the small, exclusive, most influential part of a group

inner city the crowded or blighted central sections of a large city

inner ear the part of the ear consisting of the semicircular canal, vestibule, and cochlea

in′ner·most′ ***adj.*** INMOST

in′ner·sole′ ***n.*** INSOLE

in′ner·spring′ mat′tress a mattress with built-in coil springs

in·ner·vate (i nur′vāt′, in′ər vāt′) ***vt.*** **-vat′ed, -vat′ing** *Med.* 1 to supply (a part) with nerves 2 to stimulate (a muscle, etc.) **—in′ner·va′tion *n.***

in·ning (in′iŋ) ***n.*** ⟦< OE *innung*, getting in⟧ [*pl. for Cricket*] *Baseball, Cricket* 1 a team's turn at bat 2 a numbered round of play in which both teams have a turn at bat

inn′keep′er *n.* the owner of an inn

in·no·cent (in′ə sənt) ***adj.*** ⟦< L *in-*, not + *nocere*, to harm⟧ 1 free from sin, evil, etc.; specif., not guilty of a specific crime 2 harmless 3 knowing no evil 4 without guile **—*n.*** an innocent person, as a child **—in′no·cence *n.* —in′no·cent·ly *adv.***

in·noc·u·ous (in näk′yo͞o əs) ***adj.*** ⟦see prec.⟧ harmless **—in·noc′u·ous·ly *adv.* —in·noc′u·ous·ness *n.***

in·no·va·tion (in′ə vā′shən) ***n.*** ⟦< L *in-*, in + *novus*, new⟧ 1 the process of making changes 2 a new method, custom, device, etc. **—in′no·vate′, -vat′ed, -vat′ing, *vi., vt.* —in′no·va′tive *adj.* —in′no·va′tor *n.***

in·nu·en·do (in′yo͞o en′dō′) ***n., pl.*** **-does′** or **-dos′** ⟦< L *in-*, in + *-nuere*, to nod⟧ a hint or sly remark, usually derogatory; insinuation

in·nu·mer·a·ble (in no͞o′mer ə bəl) ***adj.*** too numerous to be counted

in·oc·u·late (i näk′yo͞o lāt′) ***vt.*** **-lat′ed, -lat′ing** ⟦< L *in-*, in + *oculus*, eye⟧ to inject a serum, vaccine, etc. into, esp. in order to create immunity **—in·oc′u·la′tion *n.***

in·of·fen·sive (in′ə fen′siv) ***adj.*** causing no harm or annoyance; not objectionable **—in′of·fen′sive·ly *adv.***

in·op·er·a·ble (in äp′ər ə bəl) ***adj.*** not operable; specif., *a*) not practical *b*) incapable of being treated by surgery

in·op·er·a·tive (in äp′ər ə tiv, -ər āt′iv) ***adj.*** not working or functioning

in·or·di·nate (in ôr′də nit, -ôrd′'n it) ***adj.*** ⟦< L *in-*, not + *ordino*, to order⟧ excessive; immoderate **—in·or′di·nate·ly *adv.***

in·or·gan·ic (in′ôr gan′ik) ***adj.*** not organic; specif., designating or of matter not animal or vegetable; not living

in·pa·tient (in′pā′shənt) ***n.*** a patient who stays in a hospital, etc. while receiving treatment

in·put (in′po͝ot′) ***n.*** 1 what is put in; specif., *a*) power into a machine, etc. *b*) data or programs into a computer 2 opinion; advice **—*vt.* -put′, -put′ting** to feed (data) into a computer

in·quest (in′kwest′) ***n.*** ⟦see INQUIRE⟧ a judicial inquiry, esp. before a jury, as a coroner's inquiry of a death

in·qui·e·tude (in kwī′ə to͞od′, -tyo͞od′) ***n.*** restlessness; uneasiness

in·quire (in kwīr′) ***vi.*** **-quired′, -quir′ing** ⟦< L *in-*, into + *quaerere*, seek⟧ 1 to ask a question or questions 2 to investigate: usually with *into* **—*vt.*** to seek information about

in·quir·y (in′kwə rē, in kwīr′ē) ***n., pl.*** **-ies** 1 an inquiring; investigation 2 a question

in·qui·si·tion (in′kwə zish′ən) ***n.*** 1 an investigation or inquest 2 [**I-**] *R.C.Ch.* the tribunal established in the 13th c. for suppressing heresy and heretics 3 any relentless questioning or harsh suppression **—in·quis′i·tor *n.***

in·quis·i·tive (in kwiz′ə tiv) ***adj.*** 1 inclined to ask many questions 2 unnecessarily curious; prying **—in·quis′i·tive·ness *n.***

in re (in rē′, -rā′) ⟦L⟧ in the matter (of)

-in-res·i·dence *combining form* appointed to work and usually residing at an institution, as a college, for a certain period

in·road (in′rōd′) ***n.*** 1 a raid 2 [*usually pl.*] any injurious encroachment

in·sane (in sān′) ***adj.*** 1 not sane; mentally ill or deranged 2 of or for insane people 3 very foolish, extravagant, etc. **—in·sane′ly *adv.* —in·san′i·ty** (-san′ə tē) ***n.***

in·sa·ti·a·ble (in sā′shə bəl, -shē ə-) ***adj.*** ⟦see IN-[2] & SATIATE⟧ that cannot be satisfied **—in·sa′ti·a·bly *adv.***

in·scribe (in skrīb′) ***vt.*** **-scribed′, -scrib′ing** ⟦< L *in-*, in + *scribere*, write⟧ 1 to mark or engrave (words, etc.) on (a surface) 2 to add (a person's name) to a list 3 *a*) to dedicate (a book, etc.) to someone *b*) to autograph 4 to fix in the mind **—in·scrip′tion** (-skrip′shən) ***n.***

in·scru·ta·ble (in skro͞ot′ə bəl) ***adj.*** ⟦< L *in-*, not + *scrutari*, examine⟧ not easily understood; enigmatic **—in·scru′ta·bly *adv.***

in·seam (in′sēm′) ***n.*** an inner seam; specif., the seam from the crotch to the bottom of a trouser leg

in·sect (in′sekt′) ***n.*** ⟦< L *insectum*, lit., notched⟧ any of a large class of small, usually winged, invertebrates, as beetles, flies, wasps, etc., having three pairs of legs

in·sec·ti·cide (in sek′tə sīd′) ***n.*** any substance used to kill insects **—in·sec′ti·ci′dal *adj.***

in·sec·ti·vore (in sek′tə vôr′) ***n.*** ⟦see fol.⟧ any of various small mammals that are active mainly at night and that feed principally on insects, as moles, shrews, etc.

in·sec·tiv·o·rous (in′sek tiv′ə rəs) ***adj.*** ⟦< INSECT + L *vorare*, devour⟧ feeding chiefly on insects

in·se·cure (in′si kyoor′) ***adj.*** 1 not safe from danger 2 feeling anxiety 3 not firm or dependable **—in′se·cure′ly *adv.* —in′se·cu′ri·ty, *pl.* -ties, *n.***

in·sem·i·nate (in sem′ə nāt′) ***vt.*** **-nat′ed, -nat′ing** ⟦< L *in-*, in + *semen*, seed⟧ 1 to sow seeds in; esp., to impregnate 2 to imbue (with ideas, etc.) —**in·sem'i·na'tion** *n.*

in·sen·sate (in sen'sāt', -sit) *adj.* 1 not feeling sensation 2 foolish; stupid 3 without regard or feeling; cold

in·sen·si·ble (in sen'sə bəl) *adj.* 1 unable to perceive with the senses 2 unconscious 3 unaware; indifferent 4 so small as to be virtually imperceptible —**in·sen'si·bil'i·ty** *n.*

in·sen'si·tive (-sə tiv) *adj.* not sensitive; not responsive —**in·sen'si·tive·ly** *adv.* —**in·sen'si·tiv'i·ty** *n.*

in·sen·ti·ent (in sen'shənt, -shē ənt) *adj.* not sentient; without life or consciousness —**in·sen'ti·ence** *n.*

in·sert (in surt'; *for n.* in'surt') *vt.* ⟦< L *in-*, in + *serere*, join⟧ to put or fit (something) into something else —*n.* anything inserted or for insertion —**in·ser'tion** *n.*

in·set (in set'; *for n.* in'set') *vt.* **-set', -set'·ting** to set in; insert —*n.* something inserted

in·shore (in'shôr', in shôr') *adv., adj.* in, near, or toward the shore

in·side (in'sīd', in'sīd', in sīd') *n.* 1 the inner side, surface, or part 2 [*pl.*] [Colloq.] the viscera —*adj.* 1 internal 2 known only to insiders; secret —*adv.* 1 on or to the inside; within 2 indoors —*prep.* in or within —**inside of** within the space or time of —**inside out** 1 reversed 2 [Colloq.] thoroughly

in'sid'er *n.* 1 one inside a given place or group 2 one having secret or confidential information

in·sid·i·ous (in sid'ē əs) *adj.* ⟦< L *insidiae*, an ambush⟧ 1 characterized by treachery or slyness 2 more dangerous than seems evident

in·sight (in'sīt') *n.* 1 the ability to see and understand clearly the inner nature of things, esp. by intuition 2 an instance of such understanding

in·sig·ni·a (in sig'nē ə) *n.pl., sing.* **in·sig'ne** (-nē) or **in·sig'ni·a** ⟦ult. < L *in-*, in + *signum*, a mark⟧ distinguishing marks, as emblems of rank, membership, etc.

in·sin·cere (in'sin sir') *adj.* not sincere; deceptive or hypocritical —**in'sin·cere'ly** *adv.* —**in'sin·cer'i·ty** (-ser'ə tē), *pl.* **-ties**, *n.*

in·sin·u·ate (in sin'yoo āt') *vt.* **-at'ed, -at'·ing** ⟦< L *in-*, in + *sinus*, a curve⟧ 1 to introduce or work into gradually, indirectly, etc. 2 to hint or suggest indirectly; imply —**in·sin'u·a'tion** *n.* —**in·sin'u·a'tive** *adj.* —**in·sin'u·a'tor** *n.*

in·sip·id (in sip'id) *adj.* ⟦< L *in-*, not + *sapidus*, savory⟧ 1 without flavor; tasteless 2 not exciting; dull

in·sist (in sist') *vi.* ⟦< L *in-*, in, on + *sistere*, to stand⟧ to take and maintain a stand: often with *on* or *upon* —*vt.* 1 to demand strongly 2 to declare firmly —**in·sist'ing·ly** *adv.*

in·sist'ent *adj.* insisting or demanding —**in·sist'ence** *n.*

in si·tu (in sī'too') ⟦L⟧ in position; in its original place

in·so·far (in'sō fär') *adv.* to such a degree or extent: usually with *as*

in·sole (in'sōl') *n.* 1 the inside sole of a shoe 2 a removable inside sole put in for comfort

in·so·lent (in'sə lənt) *adj.* ⟦< L *in-*, not + *solere*, be accustomed⟧ boldly disrespectful; impudent —**in'so·lence** *n.*

in·sol·u·ble (in säl'yoo bəl) *adj.* 1 that cannot be solved 2 that cannot be dissolved —**in·sol'u·bil'i·ty** *n.*

in·sol·vent (in säl'vənt) *adj.* not solvent; unable to pay debts; bankrupt —**in·sol'ven·cy** *n.*

in·som·ni·a (in säm'nē ə) *n.* ⟦< L *in-*, without + *somnus*, sleep⟧ abnormal inability to sleep —**in·som'ni·ac'** (-ak') *n., adj.*

in·so·much (in'sō much') *adv.* 1 to such a degree or extent; so: with *that* 2 inasmuch (*as*)

in·sou·ci·ant (in soo'sē ənt) *adj.* ⟦Fr < *in-*, not + *soucier*, to care⟧ calm and untroubled; carefree

in·spect (in spekt') *vt.* ⟦< L *in-*, at + *specere*, look at⟧ 1 to look at carefully 2 to examine or review officially —**in·spec'·tion** *n.*

in·spec'tor *n.* 1 one who inspects 2 an officer on a police force, ranking next below a superintendent

in·spi·ra·tion (in'spə rā'shən) *n.* 1 an inhaling 2 an inspiring or being inspired mentally or emotionally 3 *a)* any stimulus to creative thought or action *b)* an inspired idea, action, etc. —**in'spi·ra'tion·al** *adj.*

in·spire (in spīr') *vt.* **-spired', -spir'ing** ⟦< L *in-*, in, on + *spirare*, breathe⟧ 1 to inhale 2 to stimulate or impel, as to some creative effort 3 to motivate as by divine influence 4 to arouse (a thought or feeling) in (someone) 5 to occasion or cause —*vi.* 1 to inhale 2 to give inspiration

in·spir·it (in spir'it) *vt.* to put spirit into; cheer; hearten

Inst. 1 Institute 2 Institution

in·sta·bil·i·ty (in'stə bil'ə tē) *n.* lack of firmness, determination, etc.

in·stall or **in·stal** (in stôl') *vt.* **-stalled', -stall'ing** ⟦< ML *in-*, in + *stallum*, a place⟧ 1 to place in an office, rank, etc., with formality 2 to establish in a place 3 to fix in position for use [to *install* new fixtures] —**in·stal·la·tion** (in'stə lā'shən) *n.* —**in·stall'er** *n.*

in·stall'ment or **in·stal'ment** *n.* 1 an installing or being installed 2 any of the parts of a sum of money to be paid at regular specified times 3 any of several parts, as of a serial

installment plan a credit system by which debts, as for purchased articles, are paid in installments

in·stance (in'stəns) *n.* ⟦see fol.⟧ 1 an example; case 2 a step in proceeding; occasion [in the first *instance*] —*vt.* **-stanced, -stanc·ing** to give as an example; cite —**at the instance of** at the suggestion or instigation of

in·stant (in'stənt) *adj.* ⟦< L *in-*, in, upon + *stare*, to stand⟧ 1 urgent; pressing 2 imminent 3 immediate 4 concentrated or precooked for quick preparation, as a food or beverage 5 [Archaic] present; current —*n.* 1 a moment 2 a particular moment —**the instant** as soon as

in·stan·ta·ne·ous (in'stən tā'nē əs) *adj.*

done or happening in an instant —**in'stan·ta'ne·ous·ly** *adv.*

in·stan·ter (in stan'tər) *adv.* ⟦L⟧ *Law* immediately

in'stant·ly *adv.* immediately

in·state (in stāt') *vt.* **-stat'ed, -stat'ing** ⟦IN-[1] + STATE⟧ to put in a particular rank, etc.; install

in·stead (in sted') *adv.* ⟦IN + STEAD⟧ in place of the one mentioned —**instead of** in place of

in·step (in'step') *n.* the upper part of the arch of the foot, between the ankle and the toes

in·sti·gate (in'stə gāt') *vt.* **-gat'ed, -gat'ing** ⟦< L *in-*, on + *-stigare*, to prick⟧ 1 to urge on to some action 2 to foment (rebellion, etc.) —**in sti·ga'tion** *n.* —**in'sti·ga'tor** *n.*

in·still or **in·stil** (in stil') *vt.* **-stilled', -still'·ing** ⟦< L *in-*, in + *stilla*, a drop⟧ 1 to put in drop by drop 2 to put (an idea, etc.) *in* or *into* gradually

in·stinct (in'stiŋkt') *n.* ⟦< L *instinguere*, to impel⟧ 1 (an) inborn tendency to behave in a way characteristic of a species 2 a natural or acquired tendency; knack —**in·stinc'tive** *adj.* —**in·stinc'tu·al** *adj.*

in·sti·tute (in'stə to͞ot', -tyo͞ot') *vt.* **-tut'ed, -tut'ing** ⟦< L *in-*, in, on + *statuere*, to cause to set up⟧ 1 to set up; establish 2 to start; initiate —*n.* something instituted; specif., *a*) an organization for the promotion of art, science, etc. *b*) a school or college specializing in some field —**in'sti·tut'er** or **in'sti·tu'tor** *n.*

in·sti·tu·tion (in'stə to͞o'shən, -tyo͞o'-) *n.* 1 an instituting or being instituted 2 an established law, custom, etc. 3 *a*) an organization having a social, educational, or religious purpose *b*) the building housing it 4 a person or thing long established in a place —**in'sti·tu'tion·al** *adj.*

in'sti·tu'tion·al·ize' (-īz') *vt.* **-ized', -iz'ing** 1 to make into an institution 2 to place in an institution, as for treatment —**in'sti·tu'·tion·al·i·za'tion** *n.*

in·struct (in strukt') *vt.* ⟦< L *in-*, in + *struere*, pile up⟧ 1 to teach; educate 2 to inform 3 to order or direct

in·struc'tion (-struk'shən) *n.* 1 an instructing; education 2 something taught 3 [*pl.*] orders or directions

in·struc'tive *adj.* giving knowledge

in·struc'tor *n.* 1 a teacher 2 a college teacher of the lowest rank

in·stru·ment (in'strə mənt) *n.* ⟦see INSTRUCT⟧ 1 a thing by means of which something is done 2 a tool or implement 3 any of various devices for indicating, measuring, controlling, etc. 4 any of various devices producing musical sound 5 *Law* a formal document

in'stru·men'tal (-ment''l) *adj.* 1 serving as a means; helpful 2 of, performed on, or written for a musical instrument or instruments

in'stru·men'tal·ist *n.* a person who performs on a musical instrument

in'stru·men'tal'i·ty (-men'tal'ə tē) *n., pl.* **-ties** a means; agency

in'stru·men'ta'tion (-tā'shən) *n.* 1 the writing or scoring of music for instruments 2 the use of or equipment with instruments

instrument flying the flying of an aircraft by instruments only

in·sub·or·di·nate (in'sə bôrd''n it) *adj.* not submitting to authority; disobedient —**in'·sub·or'di·na'tion** *n.*

in·sub·stan·tial (in'səb stan'shəl) *adj.* not substantial; specif., *a*) not real; imaginary *b*) weak or flimsy

in·suf·fer·a·ble (in suf'ər ə bəl) *adj.* not sufferable; intolerable; unbearable

in·su·lar (in'sə lər; -so͞o-, -syo͞o-) *adj.* ⟦< L *insula*, island⟧ 1 of or like an island or islanders 2 narrow-minded; illiberal

in'su·late' (-lāt') *vt.* **-lat'ed, -lat'ing** ⟦< L *insula*, island⟧ 1 to set apart; isolate 2 to cover with a nonconducting material in order to prevent the escape of electricity, heat, sound, etc.

in'su·la'tion *n.* 1 an insulating or being insulated 2 material for this

in·su·lin (in'sə lin; -so͞o-, -syo͞o-) *n.* ⟦< L *insula*, island⟧ 1 a hormone vital to carbohydrate metabolism, secreted by islets of tissue in the pancreas 2 an extract from the pancreas of sheep, oxen, etc., used in the treatment of diabetes

insulin shock the abnormal condition caused by an excess of insulin: it is characterized by tremors, cold sweat, convulsions, and coma

in·sult (in sult'; *for n.* in'sult') *vt.* ⟦< L *in-*, on + *salire*, to leap⟧ to subject to an act, remark, etc. meant to hurt the feelings or pride —*n.* an insulting act, remark, etc.

in·su·per·a·ble (in so͞o'pər ə bəl) *adj.* ⟦< L *insuperabilis*⟧ that cannot be overcome

in·sup·port·a·ble (in'sə pôrt'ə bəl) *adj.* not supportable; incapable of being borne, upheld, proved, etc.

in·sur·ance (in shoor'əns) *n.* 1 an insuring or being insured 2 a contract (**insurance policy**) purchased to guarantee compensation for a specified loss by fire, death, etc. 3 the amount for which something is insured 4 the business of insuring against loss

in·sure (in shoor') *vt.* **-sured', -sur'ing** ⟦ME *ensuren*: see ENSURE⟧ 1 to take out or issue insurance on 2 ENSURE —**in·sur'a·ble** *adj.*

in·sured' *n.* a person whose life, property, etc. is insured against loss

in·sur'er *n.* a person or company that insures others against loss

in·sur·gent (in sur'jənt) *adj.* ⟦< L *in-*, upon + *surgere*, rise⟧ rising up against established authority —*n.* an insurgent person —**in·sur'gence** *n.*

in·sur·rec·tion (in'sə rek'shən) *n.* ⟦see prec.⟧ a rising up against established authority; rebellion —**in'sur·rec'tion·ist** *n.*

int. 1 interest 2 international

in·tact (in takt') *adj.* ⟦< L *in-*, not + *tactus*, touched⟧ unimpaired or uninjured; kept or left whole

in·ta·glio (in tal'yō) *n., pl.* **-glios'** ⟦It < *in-*, in + *tagliare*, to cut⟧ a design carved or engraved below the surface

in·take (in'tāk') *n.* 1 a taking in 2 amount taken in 3 the place in a pipe, etc. where a fluid is taken in

in·tan·gi·ble (in tan'jə bəl) *adj.* 1 that cannot be touched; incorporeal 2 representing value, but either without intrinsic value or without material being /goodwill is an *intangible* asset/ 3 that cannot be easily defined; vague —*n.* something intangible

in·te·ger (in′tə jər) *n.* ⟦L, whole⟧ a whole number (e.g., 5, -10) or zero

in·te·gral (in′tə grəl; *often* in teg′rəl) *adj.* ⟦see prec.⟧ 1 necessary for completeness; essential 2 whole or complete 3 made up of parts forming a whole

in′te·grate′ (-grāt′) *vt., vi.* -**grat′ed**, -**grat′ing** ⟦< L *integer*, whole⟧ 1 to make or become whole or complete 2 to bring (parts) together into a whole 3 *a)* to remove barriers imposing segregation upon (racial groups) *b)* to abolish segregation in —**in′te·gra′tion** *n.* —**in′te·gra′tive** *adj.*

integrated circuit an electronic circuit with many interconnected circuit elements formed on a single body, or chip, of semiconductor material

in·teg·ri·ty (in teg′rə tē) *n.* ⟦see INTEGER⟧ 1 completeness; wholeness 2 unimpaired condition; soundness 3 honesty, sincerity, etc.

in·teg·u·ment (in teg′yoo̅ mənt) *n.* ⟦< L *in-*, upon + *tegere*, to cover⟧ an outer covering; skin, shell, etc.

in·tel·lect (in′tə lekt′, int′'l ekt′) *n.* ⟦< L *inter-*, between + *legere*, choose⟧ 1 the ability to reason or understand 2 high intelligence 3 a very intelligent person

in·tel·lec·tu·al (in′tə lek′choo̅ əl, int′'l ek′-) *adj.* 1 of, involving, or appealing to the intellect 2 requiring intelligence 3 showing high intelligence —*n.* one with intellectual interests or tastes —**in′tel·lec′tu·al·ly** *adv.*

in′tel·lec′tu·al·ize′ (-īz′) *vt.* -**ized′**, -**iz′ing** to examine or interpret rationally, often without proper regard for emotional considerations

in·tel·li·gence (in tel′ə jəns) *n.* ⟦see INTELLECT⟧ 1 *a)* the ability to learn or understand *b)* the ability to cope with a new situation 2 news or information 3 those engaged in gathering secret, esp. military, information

intelligence quotient a number intended to indicate a person's level of intelligence, based on a test

in·tel′li·gent (-jənt) *adj.* having or showing intelligence; clever, wise, etc. —**in·tel′li·gent·ly** *adv.*

in·tel′li·gent′si·a (-jənt′sē ə) *n.pl.* ⟦< Russ⟧ [*also with sing. v.*] intellectuals collectively

in·tel·li·gi·ble (in tel′i jə bəl) *adj.* that can be understood; clear —**in·tel′li·gi·bly** *adv.*

in·tem·per·ate (in tem′pər it) *adj.* 1 not temperate or moderate; excessive 2 drinking too much alcoholic liquor —**in·tem′per·ance** *n.*

in·tend (in tend′) *vt.* ⟦< L *in-*, at + *tendere*, to stretch⟧ 1 to plan; purpose 2 to mean (something) to be or be used (*for*) 3 to mean; signify

in·tend′ed *n.* [Colloq.] one's prospective spouse; fiancé(e)

in·tense (in tens′) *adj.* ⟦see INTEND⟧ 1 very strong /an *intense* light/ 2 strained to the utmost; strenuous /*intense* thought/ 3 characterized by much action, strong emotion, etc. —**in·tense′ly** *adv.*

in·ten·si·fy (in ten′sə fī′) *vt., vi.* -**fied′**, -**fy′ing** to make or become more intense —**in·ten′si·fi·ca′tion** *n.*

in·ten′si·ty *n., pl.* -**ties** 1 a being intense 2 great energy or vehemence, as of emotion 3 the amount of force or energy of heat, light, sound, etc.

in·ten′sive *adj.* 1 of or characterized by intensity; thorough 2 designating very attentive care given to patients right after surgery, etc. 3 *Gram.* giving force or emphasis /"very" is an *intensive* adverb/ —*n. Gram.* an intensive word, prefix, etc. —**in·ten′sive·ly** *adv.* —**in·ten′sive·ness** *n.*

-in·ten·sive (in ten′siv) *combining form* intensively using or requiring large amounts of (a specified thing) /*energy-intensive*/

in·tent (in tent′) *adj.* ⟦see INTEND⟧ 1 firmly directed; earnest 2 having one's attention or purpose firmly fixed /*intent* on going/ —*n.* 1 an intending 2 something intended; purpose or meaning —**to all intents and purposes** in almost every respect; practically; virtually —**in·tent′ly** *adv.* —**in·tent′ness** *n.*

in·ten·tion (in ten′shən) *n.* 1 a determination to act in a specified way 2 anything intended; purpose

in·ten′tion·al *adj.* done purposely

in·ter (in tur′) *vt.* -**terred′**, -**ter′ring** ⟦< L *in*, in + *terra*, earth⟧ to put (a dead body) into a grave or tomb

inter- ⟦L⟧ *prefix* 1 between or among: the second element of the compound is singular in form /*interstate*/ 2 with or on each other (or one another) /*interact*/

in·ter·act (in′tər akt′) *vi.* to act on one another —**in′ter·ac′tion** *n.*

in′ter·ac′tive (-ak′tiv) *adj.* 1 acting on one another 2 designating or of programming electronic equipment, as for TV, etc., which allows viewers to participate, as by making a response, etc. 3 of or involving exchange of information between the computer and the user at a video screen

in·ter·breed (in′tər brēd′, in′tər brēd′) *vt., vi.* -**bred′**, -**breed′ing** HYBRIDIZE

in′ter·cede′ (-sēd′) *vi.* -**ced′ed**, -**ced′ing** ⟦< L *inter-*, between + *cedere*, go⟧ 1 to plead in behalf of another 2 to mediate

in′ter·cept′ (-sept′) *vt.* ⟦< L *inter-*, between + *capere*, take⟧ 1 to seize or stop in its course /to *intercept* a message/ 2 *Math.* to cut off or mark off between two points, lines, etc. —**in′ter·cep′tion** *n.*

in′ter·ces′sion (-sesh′ən) *n.* an interceding; mediation or prayer in behalf of another —**in′ter·ces′sor** (-ses′ər) *n.* —**in′ter·ces′so·ry** *adj.*

in·ter·change (in′tər chānj′; *for n.* in′tər chānj′) *vt.* -**changed′**, -**chang′ing** 1 to give and take mutually; exchange 2 to put (each of two things) in the other's place 3 to alternate —*n.* 1 an interchanging 2 a junction which allows movement on traffic between highways on different levels, as a cloverleaf —**in′ter·change′a·ble** *adj.*

in′ter·col·le′gi·ate *adj.* between or among colleges and universities

in·ter·com (in′tər käm′) *n.* a radio or telephone intercommunication system, as between rooms

in'ter·com·mu'ni·cate' *vt., vi.* **-cat'ed, -cat'ing** to communicate with or to each other or one another —**in'ter·com·mu'ni·ca'tion** *n.*
in'ter·con·nect' (-kə nekt') *vt., vi.* to connect or be connected with one another —**in'ter·con·nec'tion** *n.*
in'ter·con'ti·nen'tal *adj.* **1** between or among continents **2** able to travel from one continent to another, as a missile, etc.
in'ter·cos'tal (-käs'təl, -kôs'-) *adj.* between the ribs —*n.* an intercostal muscle, etc.
in·ter·course (in'tər kôrs') *n.* ⟦see INTER- & COURSE⟧ **1** communication or dealings between or among people, countries, etc. **2** SEXUAL INTERCOURSE
in'ter·de·nom'i·na'tion·al *adj.* between or among religious denominations
in'ter·de'part·men'tal *adj.* between or among departments
in'ter·de·pend'ence *n.* mutual dependence —**in'ter·de·pend'ent** *adj.*
in·ter·dict (in'tər dikt'; *for n.* in'tər dikt') *vt.* ⟦< L *inter-*, between + *dicere*, say⟧ **1** to prohibit (an action) **2** to restrain from doing or using something —*n.* an official prohibition —**in'ter·dic'tion** *n.*
in'ter·dis'ci·pli·nar'y *adj.* involving two or more disciplines, or branches of learning
in·ter·est (in'trist, -trəst, -tər ist) *n.* ⟦< L *inter-*, between + *esse*, be⟧ **1** a right to, or share in, something **2** anything in which one has a share **3** [*often pl.*] advantage; benefit **4** [*usually pl.*] those having a common concern or power in some industry, cause, etc. [the steel *interests*] **5** *a)* a feeling of concern, curiosity, etc. about something *b)* the power of causing this feeling *c)* something causing this feeling **6** *a)* money paid for the use of money *b)* the rate of such payment —*vt.* **1** to involve or excite the interest or attention of **2** to cause to have an interest, or share, in —**in the interest(s) of** for the sake of
in'ter·est·ed *adj.* **1** having an interest or share **2** influenced by personal interest; biased **3** feeling or showing interest
in'ter·est·ing *adj.* exciting curiosity or attention; of interest
in·ter·face (in'tər fās') *n.* **1** a plane forming the common boundary between two parts of matter or space **2** a point or means of interaction between two systems, groups, etc. —*vt., vi.* **-faced', -fac'ing** to interact with (another system, group, etc.)
in'ter·faith' *adj.* between or involving persons adhering to different religions
in·ter·fere (in'tər fir') *vi.* **-fered', -fer'ing** ⟦ult. < L *inter-*, between + *ferire*, to strike⟧ **1** to clash; collide **2** *a)* to come between; intervene *b)* to meddle **3** *Sports* to hinder an opposing player in any of various illegal ways —**interfere with** to hinder —**in'ter·fer'ence** *n.*
in·ter·fer·on (in'tər fir'än') *n.* ⟦INTERFER(E) + *-on*, arbitrary suffix⟧ a cellular protein produced in response to infection by a virus and acting to inhibit viral growth
in'ter·gen'er·a'tion·al *adj.* of or involving persons of different generations
in·ter·im (in'tər im) *n.* ⟦< L *inter*, between⟧ the period of time between; meantime —*adj.* temporary
in·te·ri·or (in tir'ē ər) *adj.* ⟦< L *inter*, between⟧ **1** situated within; inner **2** inland **3** private —*n.* **1** the interior part, as of a room, country, etc. **2** the internal, or domestic, affairs of a country
interior decoration the art or business of decorating and furnishing the interiors of houses, offices, etc. —**interior decorator**
in·te'ri·or·ize' (-īz') *vt.* **-ized', -iz'ing** to make (a concept, value, etc.) part of one's inner nature
interj. interjection
in·ter·ject (in'tər jekt') *vt.* ⟦< L *inter-*, between + *jacere*, to throw⟧ to throw in between; interrupt with
in'ter·jec'tion (-jek'shən) *n.* **1** an interjecting **2** something interjected **3** *Gram.* an exclamation
in'ter·lace' *vt., vi.* **-laced', -lac'ing** to lace or weave together
in'ter·lard' (-lärd') *vt.* ⟦see INTER- & LARD⟧ to intersperse; diversify [to *interlard* a talk with quotations]
in·ter·leu·kin (in'tər lo͞o'kin) *n.* any of several proteins derived from many cell types and having an effect on the activity of other cells, as stimulating the growth of T cells, etc.
in'ter·line'[1] *vt.* **-lined', -lin'ing** to write (something) between the lines of (a text, etc.)
in'ter·line'[2] *vt.* **-lined', -lin'ing** to put an inner lining under the ordinary lining of (a garment)
in'ter·lock' *vt., vi.* to lock together; join with one another
in·ter·loc·u·to·ry (in'tər läk'yo͞o tôr'ē, -yə-) *adj. Law* not final [an *interlocutory* divorce decree]
in·ter·lop·er (in'tər lō'pər) *n.* ⟦INTER- + *-loper* < Du *lopen*, to run⟧ one who meddles
in·ter·lude (in'tər lo͞od') *n.* ⟦< L *inter*, between + *ludus*, play⟧ anything that fills time between two events, as music between acts of a play
in'ter·mar'ry *vi.* **-ried, -ry·ing** **1** to become connected by marriage: said of different clans, races, etc. **2** to marry: said of closely related persons —**in'ter·mar'riage** *n.*
in'ter·me'di·ar'y (-mē'dē er'ē) *adj.* **1** acting as a go-between or mediator **2** intermediate —*n., pl.* **-ar'ies** a go-between; mediator
in'ter·me'di·ate (-mē'dē it) *adj.* ⟦< L *inter-*, between + *medius*, middle⟧ **1** in the middle; in between **2** of an automobile larger than a compact but smaller than the standard size —*n.* an intermediate automobile
in·ter·ment (in tʉr'mənt) *n.* the act of interring; burial
in·ter·mez·zo (in'tər met'sō') *n., pl.* **-zos'** or **-zi'** (-sē') ⟦It < L: see INTERMEDIATE⟧ a short piece of music, as between parts of a composition
in·ter·mi·na·ble (in tʉr'mi nə bəl) *adj.* lasting, or seeming to last, forever; endless —**in·ter'mi·na·bly** *adv.*
in'ter·min'gle *vt., vi.* **-gled, -gling** to mix together; mingle
in·ter·mis·sion (in'tər mish'ən) *n.* ⟦< L

inter-, between + *mittere*, send ⟧ an interval of time between periods of activity, as between acts of a play

in'ter·mit'tent (-mit''nt) ***adj.*** ⟦see prec.⟧ stopping and starting again at intervals; periodic

in·tern (*for n. & vi.* in'turn'; *for vt.* in turn', in'turn') ***n.*** ⟦< L *internus*, inward⟧ **1** a doctor serving as assistant resident in a hospital generally just after graduation from medical school **2** an apprentice teacher, journalist, etc. —***vi.*** to serve as an intern —***vt.*** to detain or confine (foreign persons, etc.), as during a war —**in·tern'ment** ***n.*** —**in'tern'ship'** ***n.***

in·ter·nal (in tur'nəl, -turn''l) ***adj.*** ⟦< L *internus*⟧ **1** of or on the inside; inner **2** to be taken inside the body /*internal* remedies/ **3** intrinsic /*internal* evidence/ **4** domestic /*internal* revenue/ —**in·ter'nal·ly** ***adv.***

in·ter'nal-com·bus'tion engine an engine, as in an automobile, powered by the explosion of a fuel-and-air mixture within the cylinders

in·ter'nal·ize' (-īz') ***vt.*** **-ized'**, **-iz'ing** to make (others' ideas, etc.) a part of one's own way of thinking

internal medicine the branch of medicine that deals with the diagnosis and nonsurgical treatment of diseases

internal revenue governmental income from taxes on income, profits, etc.

in·ter·na·tion·al (in'tər nash'ə nəl) ***adj.*** **1** between or among nations **2** concerned with the relations between nations **3** for the use of all nations **4** of or for people in various nations —**in'ter·na'tion·al·ize'**, **-ized'**, **-iz'ing**, ***vt.*** —**in'ter·na'tion·al·ly** ***adv.***

International Phonetic Alphabet a set of phonetic symbols for international use: each symbol represents a single sound, whether the sound occurs in only one language or in more than one

in·ter·ne·cine (in'tər nē'sin) ***adj.*** ⟦< L *inter-*, between + *necare*, kill⟧ deadly or harmful to both sides

in·tern·ist (in'turn'ist, in turn'ist) ***n.*** a doctor who specializes in the nonsurgical treatment of diseases

in·ter·of·fice (in'tər ôf'is) ***adj.*** between the offices of an organization

in'ter·per'son·al (-pur'sən əl) ***adj.*** between persons /*interpersonal* relationships/

in'ter·plan'e·tar'y ***adj.*** between planets

in'ter·play' ***n.*** action, effect, or influence on each other

in·ter·po·late (in tur'pə lāt') ***vt.*** **-lat'ed**, **-lat'ing** ⟦< L *inter-*, between + *polire*, to polish⟧ **1** to change (a text, etc.) by inserting new material **2** to insert between or among others —**in·ter'po·la'tion** ***n.***

in·ter·pose (in'tər pōz') ***vt.***, ***vi.*** **-posed'**, **-pos'ing** **1** to place or come between **2** to intervene (with) **3** to interrupt (with) —**in'ter·po·si'tion** (-pə zish'ən) ***n.***

in·ter·pret (in tur'prət) ***vt.*** ⟦< L *interpres*, agent, broker⟧ **1** to explain or translate **2** to construe /to *interpret* a silence as contempt/ **3** to give one's own conception of (a work of art), as in performance or criticism —***vi.*** to explain or translate —**in·ter'pre·ta'tion** ***n.*** —**in·ter'pret·er** ***n.***

in·ter'pre·tive (-prə tiv) ***adj.*** that interprets; explanatory Also **in·ter'pre·ta'tive** (-tāt'iv)

in·ter·ra·cial (in'tər rā'shəl) ***adj.*** between, among, or for members of different races Also **in'ter·race'**

in'ter·re·late' (-ri lāt') ***vt.***, ***vi.*** **-lat'ed**, **-lat'ing** to make or be mutually related —**in'ter·re·lat'ed** ***adj.***

in·ter·ro·gate (in ter'ə gāt') ***vt.***, ***vi.*** **-gat'ed**, **-gat'ing** ⟦< L *inter-*, between + *rogare*, ask⟧ to ask questions, esp. formally —**in·ter'ro·ga'tion** ***n.*** —**in·ter'ro·ga'tor** ***n.***

in·ter·rog·a·tive (in'tə räg'ə tiv) ***adj.*** asking a question Also **in'ter·rog'a·to'ry** (-ə tôr'ē)

in·ter·rupt (in'tə rupt', -tər rupt') ***vt.*** ⟦< L *inter-*, between + *rumpere*, to break⟧ **1** to break into (a discussion, etc.) or to break in upon (a speaker, worker, etc.) **2** to make a break in the continuity of —***vi.*** to interrupt an action, talk, etc. —**in'ter·rup'tion** ***n.***

in·ter·scho·las·tic (in'tər skə las'tik) ***adj.*** between or among schools

in·ter·sect (in'tər sekt') ***vt.*** ⟦< L *inter-*, between + *secare*, to cut⟧ to divide into two parts by passing through —***vi.*** to cross each other

in'ter·sec'tion (-sek'shən) ***n.*** **1** an intersecting **2** the place where two lines, roads, etc. meet or cross

in'ter·serv'ice ***adj.*** between or among branches of the armed forces

in'ter·ses'sion ***n.*** a short session between regular college sessions, for concentration on specialized projects

in·ter·sperse (in'tər spurs') ***vt.*** **-spersed'**, **-spers'ing** ⟦< L *inter-*, among + *spargere*, scatter⟧ **1** to put here and there; scatter **2** to vary with things scattered here and there

in'ter·state' ***adj.*** between or among states, esp. of the U.S.

in'ter·stel'lar ***adj.*** between or among the stars

in·ter·stice (in tur'stis) ***n.***, *pl.* **-sti·ces'** (-stə siz', -sēz') ⟦< L *inter-*, between + *sistere*, to set⟧ a crack; crevice

in'ter·twine' ***vt.***, ***vi.*** **-twined'**, **-twin'ing** to twine together

in'ter·ur'ban (-ur'bən) ***adj.*** between cities or towns

in·ter·val (in'tər vəl) ***n.*** ⟦< L *inter-*, between + *vallum*, wall⟧ **1** a space between things; gap **2** the time between events **3** the difference in pitch between two tones —**at intervals** **1** once in a while **2** here and there

in·ter·vene (in'tər vēn') ***vi.*** **-vened'**, **-ven'ing** ⟦< L *inter-*, between + *venire*, come⟧ **1** to come or be between **2** to occur between two events, etc. **3** to come between to modify, settle, or hinder some action, etc.

in'ter·ven'tion (-ven'shən) ***n.*** **1** an intervening **2** interference, esp. of one state in the affairs of another

in'ter·view' (-vyōō') ***n.*** **1** a meeting of people face to face to confer **2** *a*) a meeting in which a person is asked about personal views, etc., as by a reporter *b*) a published, taped, or filmed account of this —***vt.*** to have an interview with —**in'ter·view·ee'** ***n.*** —**in'ter·view'er** ***n.***

in'ter·weave' ***vt.***, ***vi.*** **-wove'**, **-wo'ven**,

-weav′ing 1 to weave together 2 to connect closely

in·tes·ta·cy (in tes′tə sē) *n.* the fact or state of dying intestate

in·tes·tate (in tes′tāt′, -tit) ***adj.*** ⟦< L *in-*, not + *testari*, make a will⟧ having made no will

in·tes·tine (in tes′tən) ***n.*** ⟦< L *intus*, within⟧ [*usually pl.*] the lower part of the alimentary canal, extending from the stomach to the anus and consisting of a long, winding upper part (*small intestine*) and a shorter, thicker lower part (*large intestine*); bowels —**in·tes′tin·al** ***adj.***

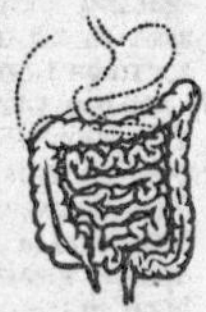

HUMAN INTESTINES

in·ti·mate (in′tə mət; *for v.*, -māt′) ***adj.*** ⟦< L *intus*, within⟧ 1 most private or personal 2 very close or familiar 3 deep and thorough —***n.*** an intimate friend —***vt.*** **-mat′ed, -mat′ing** to hint or imply —**in′ti·ma·cy** (-mə sē), *pl.* **-cies,** ***n.*** —**in′ti·mate·ly** ***adv.*** —**in′ti·ma′tion** ***n.***

in·tim·i·date (in tim′ə dāt′) ***vt.*** **-dat′ed, -dat′ing** ⟦< L *in-*, in + *timidus*, afraid⟧ to make afraid, as with threats —**in·tim′i·da′tion** ***n.***

in·to (in′to͞o, -to͝o) ***prep.*** ⟦OE⟧ 1 toward and within /*into* a room/ 2 continuing to the midst of /to talk *into* the night/ 3 to the form, substance, or condition of /divided *into* parts/ 4 so as to strike /to run *into* a wall/ 5 [Colloq.] involved in /she's *into* jazz now/

in·tol·er·a·ble (in täl′ər ə bəl) ***adj.*** unbearable; too severe, painful, etc. to be endured —**in·tol′er·a·bly** ***adv.***

in·tol′er·ant (-ənt) ***adj.*** unwilling to tolerate others' beliefs, etc. —**intolerant of** not able or willing to tolerate —**in·tol′er·ance** ***n.***

in·to·na·tion (in′tō nā′shən, -tə-) ***n.*** 1 an intoning 2 the manner of producing tones with regard to a given standard of pitch 3 variations in pitch within an utterance

in·tone (in tōn′) ***vt., vi.*** **-toned′, -ton′ing** to speak or recite in a singing tone; chant —**in·ton′er** ***n.***

in to·to (in tō′tō) ⟦L⟧ as a whole

in·tox·i·cate (in täks′i kāt′) ***vt.*** **-cat′ed, -cat′ing** ⟦< L *in-*, in + *toxicum*, poison⟧ 1 to make drunk 2 to excite greatly —**in·tox′i·cant** ***n.*** —**in·tox′i·ca′tion** ***n.***

intra- ⟦L, within⟧ *prefix* within, inside

in·tra·cit·y (in′trə sit′ē) ***adj.*** of or within a large municipality, often specif. the inner city

in·trac·ta·ble (in trak′tə bəl) ***adj.*** hard to manage; unruly or stubborn

in·tra·der·mal (in′trə dʉr′məl) ***adj.*** within the skin or between the layers of the skin

in′tra·mu′ral (-myo͝or′əl) ***adj.*** ⟦INTRA- + MURAL⟧ between or among members of the same school, college, etc. /*intramural* athletics/

in·tran·si·gent (in tran′sə jənt) ***adj.*** ⟦< L *in-*, not + *transigere*, to settle⟧ refusing to compromise —**in·tran′si·gence** ***n.***

in·tran·si·tive (in tran′sə tiv) ***adj.*** not transitive; designating a verb that does not require a direct object —**in·tran′si·tive·ly** ***adv.***

in·tra·u·ter·ine (contraceptive) device (in′trə yo͞ot′ər in) any of various devices, as a plastic loop, inserted in the uterus as a contraceptive

in′tra·ve′nous (-vē′nəs) ***adj.*** ⟦INTRA- + VENOUS⟧ directly into a vein —**in′tra·ve′nous·ly** ***adv.***

in·trench (in trench′) ***vt., vi.*** ENTRENCH

in·trep·id (in trep′id) ***adj.*** ⟦< L *in-*, not + *trepidus*, alarmed⟧ bold; fearless; brave —**in·trep′id·ly** ***adv.***

in·tri·cate (in′tri kit) ***adj.*** ⟦< L *in-*, in + *tricae*, vexations⟧ 1 hard to follow or understand because full of puzzling parts, details, etc. 2 full of elaborate detail —**in′tri·ca·cy** (-kə sē), *pl.* **-cies,** ***n.*** —**in′tri·cate·ly** ***adv.***

in·trigue (in trēg′; *for n., also* in′trēg′) ***vi.*** **-trigued′, -trigu′ing** ⟦see prec.⟧ to plot secretly or underhandedly —***vt.*** to excite the interest or curiosity of —***n.*** 1 a secret or underhanded plotting 2 a secret or underhanded plot or scheme 3 a secret love affair —**in·trigu′er** ***n.*** —**in·trigu′ing·ly** ***adv.***

in·trin·sic (in trin′sik) ***adj.*** ⟦< L *intra-*, within + *secus*, following⟧ belonging to the real nature of a thing; inherent —**in·trin′si·cal·ly** ***adv.***

intro- ⟦L⟧ *prefix* into, within, inward

in·tro·duce (in′trə do͞os′, -dyo͞os′) ***vt.*** **-duced′, -duc′ing** ⟦< L *intro-*, in + *ducere*, to lead⟧ 1 to put in; insert 2 to bring in as a new feature 3 to bring into use or fashion 4 *a)* to make acquainted; present /*introduce* me to her/ *b)* to give experience of /they *introduced* him to music/ 5 to bring forward 6 to start; begin /to *introduce* a talk with a joke/

in′tro·duc′tion (-duk′shən) ***n.*** 1 an introducing or being introduced 2 the preliminary section of a book, speech, etc.; preface

in′tro·duc′to·ry (-duk′tə rē) ***adj.*** serving to introduce; preliminary

in·tro·it (in trō′it, in′troit′) ***n.*** ⟦< L *intro-*, in + *ire*, to go⟧ 1 a psalm or hymn at the opening of a Christian worship service 2 [I-] *R.C.Ch.* the first variable part of the Mass

in·tro·spec·tion (in′trə spek′shən) ***n.*** ⟦< L *intro-*, within + *specere*, to look⟧ a looking into one's own mind, feelings, etc. —**in′tro·spec′tive** ***adj.***

in·tro·vert (in′trō vʉrt′, -trə-) ***n.*** ⟦< L *intro-*, within + *vertere*, to turn⟧ one whose interest is more in oneself than in external objects or other people —**in′tro·ver′sion** (-vʉr′zhən) ***n.*** —**in′tro·vert′ed** ***adj.***

in·trude (in tro͞od′) ***vt.*** **-trud′ed, -trud′ing** ⟦< L *in-*, in + *trudere*, to push⟧ to force (oneself) upon others unasked —**in·trud′er** ***n.***

in·tru·sion (in tro͞o′zhən) ***n.*** an intruding —**in·tru′sive** (-siv) ***adj.*** —**in·tru′sive·ly** ***adv.*** —**in·tru′sive·ness** ***n.***

in·trust (in trust′) ***vt.*** ENTRUST

in·tu·bate (in′to͞o bāt′) ***vt.*** **-bat′ed, -bat′ing** to insert a tube into (a hollow organ, etc.) to admit air, etc.

in·tu·i·tion (in′to͞o ish′ən) ***n.*** ⟦< L *in-*, in + *tueri*, look at⟧ the immediate knowing of something without the conscious use of reasoning —**in·tu·i·tive** (in to͞o′i tiv) ***adj.***

in·u·it (in′oo wit) ***n.*** ⟦Esk⟧ ESKIMO: now the preferred term, esp. in Canada
in·un·date (in′ən dāt′) ***vt.*** **-dat′ed, -dat′ing** ⟦< L *in-*, in + *unda*, a wave⟧ to cover with or as with a flood; deluge —**in′un·da′tion** ***n.***
in·ure (in yoor′) ***vt.*** **-ured′, -ur′ing** ⟦ME *in ure*, in practice⟧ to accustom to pain, trouble, etc.
in·vade (in vād′) ***vt.*** **-vad′ed, -vad′ing** ⟦< L *in-*, in + *vadere*, to go⟧ **1** to enter forcibly or hostilely **2** to intrude upon; violate —**in·vad′er** ***n.***
in·va·lid[1] (in′və lid) ***adj.*** ⟦< L *in-*, not + *validus*, strong⟧ **1** weak and sickly **2** of or for invalids —***n.*** one who is ill or disabled
in·val·id[2] (in val′id) ***adj.*** not valid
in·val′i·date′ (-ə dāt′) ***vt.*** **-dat′ed, -dat′ing** to make invalid; deprive of legal force —**in·val′i·da′tion** ***n.***
in·val·u·a·ble (in val′yoo ə bəl) ***adj.*** too valuable to be measured; priceless —**in·val′u·a·bly** ***adv.***
in·va·sion (in vā′zhən) ***n.*** an invading or being invaded, as by an army
in·vec·tive (in vek′tiv) ***n.*** ⟦see fol.⟧ a violent verbal attack; vituperation
in·veigh (in vā′) ***vi.*** ⟦< L *in-*, in + *vehere*, carry⟧ to make a violent verbal attack; rail (*against*)
in·vei·gle (in vē′g'l, -vā′-) ***vt.*** **-gled, -gling** ⟦< MFr *aveugler*, to blind⟧ to entice or trick into doing or giving something —**in·vei′gler** ***n.***
in·vent (in vent′) ***vt.*** ⟦< L *in-*, in + *venire*, come⟧ **1** to think up /to *invent* excuses/ **2** to think out or produce (a new device, process, etc.); originate —**in·ven′tor** ***n.***
in·ven′tion (-ven′shən) ***n.*** **1** an inventing **2** the power of inventing **3** something invented
in·ven′tive (-tiv) ***adj.*** **1** of invention **2** skilled in inventing —**in·ven′tive·ly** ***adv.*** —**in·ven′tive·ness** ***n.***
in·ven·to·ry (in′vən tôr′ē) ***n.***, *pl.* **-ries** ⟦see INVENT⟧ **1** an itemized list of goods, property, etc., as of a business **2** the store of goods, etc. for such listing; stock —***vt.*** **-ried, -ry·ing** to make an inventory of
in·verse (in vurs′, in′vurs′) ***adj.*** inverted; directly opposite —***n.*** any inverse thing —**in·verse′ly** ***adv.***
in·ver·sion (in vur′zhən) ***n.*** **1** an inverting or being inverted **2** something inverted; reversal **3** *Meteorol.* a temperature reversal in which a layer of warm air traps cooler air near the surface of the earth
in·vert (in vurt′) ***vt.*** ⟦< L *in-*, to + *vertere*, to turn⟧ **1** to turn upside down **2** to reverse the order, position, direction, etc. of
in·ver·te·brate (in vur′tə brit, -brāt′) ***adj.*** not vertebrate; having no backbone —***n.*** any invertebrate animal
in·vest (in vest′) ***vt.*** ⟦< L *in-*, in + *vestis*, clothing⟧ **1** to clothe **2** to install in office with ceremony **3** to furnish with power, authority, etc. **4** to put (money) into business, stocks, etc. in order to get a profit —***vi.*** to invest money —**in·ves′tor** ***n.***
in·ves·ti·gate (in ves′tə gāt′) ***vt., vi.*** **-gat′ed, -gat′ing** ⟦< L *in-*, in + *vestigare*, to track⟧ to search (into); inquire —**in·ves′ti·ga′tor** ***n.***
in·ves′ti·ga′tion ***n.*** an investigating; careful search; systematic inquiry
in·ves′ti·ture (-chər) ***n.*** a formal investing, as with an office
in·vest·ment (in vest′mənt) ***n.*** **1** an investing or being invested **2** *a*) money invested *b*) anything in which money is or may be invested
in·vet·er·ate (in vet′ər it) ***adj.*** ⟦< pp. of L *inveterare*, to age⟧ firmly established; habitual —**in·vet′er·a·cy** ***n.***
in·vid·i·ous (in vid′ē əs) ***adj.*** ⟦< L *invidia*, envy⟧ such as to excite ill will; giving offense, as by discriminating unfairly —**in·vid′i·ous·ly** ***adv.*** —**in·vid′i·ous·ness** ***n.***
in·vig·or·ate (in vig′ər āt′) ***vt.*** **-at′ed, -at′ing** to give vigor to; fill with energy —**in·vig′or·a′tion** ***n.***
in·vin·ci·ble (in vin′sə bəl) ***adj.*** ⟦< L *invincibilis*, not easily overcome⟧ that cannot be overcome; unconquerable —**in·vin′ci·bil′i·ty** ***n.***
in·vi·o·la·ble (in vī′ō lə bəl) ***adj.*** **1** not to be violated; not to be profaned or injured; sacred **2** indestructible —**in·vi′o·la·bil′i·ty** ***n.***
in·vi′o·late (-lit) ***adj.*** not violated; kept sacred or unbroken
in·vis·i·ble (in viz′ə bəl) ***adj.*** **1** not visible; that cannot be seen **2** out of sight **3** imperceptible —**in·vis′i·bil′i·ty** ***n.*** —**in·vis′i·bly** ***adv.***
in·vi·ta·tion (in′və tā′shən) ***n.*** **1** an inviting **2** a message used in inviting
in′vi·ta′tion·al ***adj.*** only for those invited to take part, as an art show
in·vite (in vīt′; *for n.* in′vīt′) ***vt.*** **-vit′ed, -vit′ing** ⟦< L *invitare*⟧ **1** to ask to come somewhere or do something **2** to ask for **3** to give occasion for /action that *invites* scandal/ **4** to tempt; entice —***n.*** [Colloq.] an invitation —**in′vit·ee′** ***n.***
in·vit′ing ***adj.*** tempting; enticing
in vi·tro (in vē′trō′) ⟦L, in glass⟧ isolated from the living organism and artificially maintained, as in a test tube
in·vo·ca·tion (in′və kā′shən) ***n.*** an invoking of God, the Muses, etc.
in·voice (in′vois′) ***n.*** ⟦prob. < ME *envoie*, message⟧ a list of goods shipped or services rendered, stating prices, etc.; bill —***vt.*** **-voiced′, -voic′ing** to present an invoice for or to
in·voke (in vōk′) ***vt.*** **-voked′, -vok′ing** ⟦< L *in-*, in, on + *vocare*, to call⟧ **1** to call on (God, the Muses, etc.) for blessing, help, etc. **2** to resort to (a law, ruling, etc.) as pertinent **3** to conjure **4** to beg for; implore
in·vol·un·tar·y (in väl′ən ter′ē) ***adj.*** **1** not done by choice **2** not consciously controlled —**in·vol′un·tar′i·ly** ***adv.*** —**in·vol′un·tar′i·ness** ***n.***
in·vo·lu·tion (in′və loo′shən) ***n.*** **1** an involving or being involved; entanglement **2** a complication; intricacy
in·volve (in välv′, -vôlv′) ***vt.*** **-volved′, -volv′ing** ⟦< L *in-*, in + *volvere*, to roll⟧ **1** to make intricate or complicated **2** to entangle in difficulty, danger, etc.; implicate **3** to affect or include /the riot *involved* thousands/ **4** to require /saving *involves*

thrift/ 5 to make busy; occupy /*involved* the class in research/ —**in·volved′** *adj.* —**in·volve′ment** *n.*

in·vul·ner·a·ble (in vul′nər ə bəl) *adj.* 1 that cannot be wounded or injured 2 proof against attack

in·ward (in′wərd) *adj.* 1 situated within; internal 2 mental or spiritual 3 directed toward the inside 4 sensitive, subtle, reticent, etc. —*adv.* 1 toward the inside 2 into the mind or soul Also **in′wards** *adv.*

in′ward·ly *adv.* 1 in or on the inside 2 in the mind or spirit 3 toward the inside

I/O input/output

i·o·dine (ī′ə dīn′, -din) *n.* ⟦< Gr *iōdēs*, violetlike⟧ 1 a nonmetallic chemical element, used in medicine, etc. 2 a tincture of iodine, used as an antiseptic

i·on (ī′ən, -än′) *n.* ⟦< Gr *ienai*, to go⟧ an electrically charged atom or group of atoms

-i·on ⟦< L *-io*⟧ *suffix* 1 the act or condition of 2 the result of

I·on·ic (ī än′ik) *adj.* designating or of a Greek or Roman style of architecture, distinguished by ornamental scrolls on the capitals

i·on·ize (ī′ən īz′) *vt.*, *vi.* -ized′, -iz′ing to dissociate into ions, as a salt dissolved in water, or become electrically charged, as a gas under radiation —**i′on·i·za′tion** *n.* —**i′on·iz′er** *n.*

IONIC CAPITAL

i·on·o·sphere (ī än′ə sfir′) *n.* the outer layers of the earth's atmosphere, with some electron and ion content

i·o·ta (ī ōt′ə) *n.* 1 the ninth letter of the Greek alphabet (Ι, ι) 2 a very small quantity; jot

IOU (ī′ō′yōō′) *n.*, *pl.* **IOU's** ⟦for *I owe you*⟧ a signed paper bearing the letters *IOU*, acknowledging a specified debt

-ious (ē əs, yəs, əs) ⟦see -OUS⟧ *suffix* characterized by /*furious*/

I·o·wa (ī′ə wə) Middle Western State of the U.S.: 56,290 sq. mi.; pop. 2,913,000; cap. Des Moines —**I′o·wan** *adj.*, *n.*

ip·e·cac (ip′i kak′) *n.* ⟦< AmInd (Brazil) name⟧ an emetic made as from the dried roots of a South American plant

ip·so fac·to (ip′sō fak′tō) ⟦L⟧ by that very fact

IQ or **I.Q.** intelligence quotient

ir- *prefix* 1 IN-[1] 2 IN-[2] Used before *r*

Ir *Chem. symbol for* iridium

Ir. 1 Ireland: also **Ire.** 2 Irish

IRA (ī′är′ā′; ī′rə) *n.*, *pl.* **IRA's** ⟦*I*(*ndividual*) *R*(*etirement*) *A*(*ccount*)⟧ a personal retirement plan with taxes on the earnings deferred until funds are withdrawn

I·ran (i ran′, ī-; ē rän′) country in SW Asia: 636,296 sq. mi.; pop. 46,604,000: former name PERSIA —**I·ra·ni·an** (i rā′nē ən, ī-; -rä′-) *adj.*, *n.*

I·raq (i räk′, -rak′) country in SW Asia, at the head of the Persian Gulf: 171,599 sq. mi.; pop. 16,019,000 —**I·ra·qi** (i rä′kē, -rak′ē) *adj.*, *n.*

i·ras·ci·ble (i ras′ə bəl, ī-) *adj.* ⟦see fol.⟧ easily angered; hot-tempered

i·rate (ī rāt′, ī′rāt′) *adj.* ⟦< L *ira*, anger⟧ angry; wrathful; incensed —**i·rate′ly** *adv.* —**i·rate′ness** *n.*

ire (īr) *n.* ⟦< L *ira*⟧ anger; wrath

Ire·land (īr′lənd) 1 one of the British Isles, west of Great Britain 2 republic comprising most of this island: 27,136 sq. mi.; pop. 3,624,000

i·ren·ic (ī ren′ik) *adj.* ⟦< Gr *eirēnē*, peace⟧ promoting peace

ir·i·des·cent (ir′i des′ənt) *adj.* ⟦< Gr *iris*, rainbow⟧ having or showing an interplay of rainbowlike colors —**ir′i·des′cence** *n.*

i·rid·i·um (i rid′ē əm) *n.* ⟦see fol.⟧ a white, metallic chemical element

i·ris (ī′ris) *n.*, *pl.* **i′ris·es** ⟦Gr, rainbow⟧ 1 the round, pigmented membrane surrounding the pupil of the eye 2 a plant with sword-shaped leaves and a showy flower

I·rish (ī′rish) *adj.* of Ireland, its people, language, etc. —*n.* 1 the Celtic language of Ireland 2 the English dialect of Ireland —**the Irish** the people of Ireland —**I′rish·man**, *pl.* -**men**, *n.* —**I′rish·wom′an**, *pl.* -**wom′en**, *n.fem.*

Irish coffee brewed coffee with Irish whiskey, topped with whipped cream

Irish Sea arm of the Atlantic between Ireland & Great Britain

irk (ʉrk) *vt.* ⟦ME *irken*, be weary of⟧ to annoy, irritate, tire out, etc.

irk′some (-səm) *adj.* that tends to irk; tiresome or annoying

i·ron (ī′ərn) *n.* ⟦OE *iren*⟧ 1 a metallic chemical element, the most common of all metals 2 any device of iron; esp., such a device with a flat undersurface, heated for pressing cloth 3 [*pl.*] iron shackles 4 firm strength; power 5 any of certain golf clubs with angled metal heads —*adj.* 1 of iron 2 like iron; strong; firm —*vt.*, *vi.* to press with a hot iron —**iron out** to smooth out; eliminate

i′ron·clad′ (-klad′) *adj.* 1 covered or protected with iron 2 difficult to change or break /an *ironclad* lease/

iron curtain a barrier of secrecy and censorship, esp. around the U.S.S.R.

i·ron·ic (ī rän′ik) *adj.* 1 meaning the contrary of what is expressed 2 using irony 3 opposite to what is or might be expected Also **i·ron′i·cal** —**i·ron′i·cal·ly** *adv.*

i′ron·ware′ *n.* things made of iron

i·ro·ny (ī′rə nē, ī′ər nē) *n.*, *pl.* -**nies** ⟦< Gr *eirōn*, dissembler in speech⟧ 1 expression in which the intended meaning of the words is the direct opposite of their usual sense 2 an event or result that is the opposite of what is expected

Ir·o·quois (ir′ə kwoi′) *n.*, *pl.* -**quois′** (-kwoi′, -kwoiz′) a member of a confederation of North American Indian peoples that lived in upstate New York —*adj.* of the Iroquois —**Ir′o·quoi′an** *n.*, *adj.*

ir·ra·di·ate (ir rā′dē āt′) *vt.* -**at′ed**, -**at′ing** 1 to shine upon; light up 2 to enlighten 3 to radiate 4 to expose to X-rays or other radiant energy —*vi.* to emit rays; shine —**ir·ra′di·a′tion** *n.*

ir·ra·tion·al (ir rash′ə nəl) *adj.* 1 lacking the power to reason 2 senseless; unreasonable; absurd —**ir·ra′tion·al′i·ty** (-ə nal′ə tē), *pl.* -**ties**, *n.* —**ir·ra′tion·al·ly** *adv.*

ir·re·claim·a·ble (ir′ri klām′ə bəl) ***adj.*** that cannot be reclaimed

ir·rec·on·cil·a·ble (ir rek′ən sīl′ə bəl) ***adj.*** that cannot be brought into agreement; incompatible

ir·re·cov·er·a·ble (ir′ri kuv′ər ə bəl) ***adj.*** that cannot be recovered, rectified, or remedied

ir·re·deem·a·ble (ir′ri dēm′ə bəl) ***adj.*** **1** that cannot be bought back **2** that cannot be converted into coin, as certain paper money **3** that cannot be changed or reformed

ir·ref·u·ta·ble (ir ref′yoo tə bəl, ir′ri fyo͞ot′ə-) ***adj.*** indisputable

ir·re·gard·less (ir′i gärd′lis) ***adj.***, ***adv.*** REGARDLESS: a nonstandard or humorous usage

ir·reg·u·lar (ir reg′yoo lər) ***adj.*** **1** not conforming to an established rule, standard, etc. **2** not straight, even, or uniform **3** *Gram.* not inflected in the usual way —**ir·reg′u·lar′i·ty**, *pl.* **-ties**, ***n.***

ir·rel·e·vant (ir rel′ə vənt) ***adj.*** not pertinent; not to the point —**ir·rel′e·vance** ***n.*** —**ir·rel′e·vant·ly** ***adv.***

ir·re·li·gious (ir′ri lij′əs) ***adj.*** **1** not religious **2** indifferent or hostile to religion **3** profane; impious

ir·re·me·di·a·ble (ir′ri mē′dē ə bəl) ***adj.*** that cannot be remedied or corrected —**ir′re·me′di·a·bly** ***adv.***

ir·rep·a·ra·ble (ir rep′ə rə bəl) ***adj.*** that cannot be repaired, mended, etc.

ir·re·place·a·ble (ir′ri plās′ə bəl) ***adj.*** that cannot be replaced

ir′re·press′i·ble (-pres′ə bəl) ***adj.*** that cannot be repressed

ir′re·proach′a·ble (-prō′chə bəl) ***adj.*** blameless; faultless

ir′re·sist′i·ble (-zis′tə bəl) ***adj.*** that cannot be resisted; too strong, fascinating, etc. to be withstood

ir·res·o·lute (ir rez′ə lo͞ot′) ***adj.*** not resolute; wavering; indecisive —**ir·res′o·lu′tion** (-lo͞o′shən) ***n.***

ir·re·spec·tive (ir′ri spek′tiv) ***adj.*** regardless (*of*)

ir′re·spon′si·ble (-spän′sə bəl) ***adj.*** **1** not responsible for actions **2** lacking a sense of responsibility —**ir′re·spon′si·bil′i·ty** ***n.***

ir′re·triev′a·ble (-trēv′ə bəl) ***adj.*** that cannot be retrieved

ir·rev·er·ence (ir rev′ər əns) ***n.*** lack of reverence; disrespect —**ir·rev′er·ent** ***adj.***

ir·re·vers·i·ble (ir′ri vur′sə bəl) ***adj.*** that cannot be reversed; esp., that cannot be annulled or turned back

ir·rev·o·ca·ble (ir rev′ə kə bəl) ***adj.*** that cannot be revoked or undone —**ir·rev′o·ca·bly** ***adv.***

ir·ri·ga·ble (ir′i gə bəl) ***adj.*** that can be irrigated

ir·ri·gate (ir′ə gāt′) ***vt.*** **-gat′ed**, **-gat′ing** ⟦< L *in-*, in + *rigare*, to water⟧ **1** to supply (land) with water, as by means of artificial ditches **2** *Med.* to wash out (a cavity, wound, etc.) —**ir′ri·ga′tion** ***n.***

ir·ri·ta·ble (ir′i tə bəl) ***adj.*** **1** easily irritated or provoked **2** *Med.* excessively sensitive to a stimulus —**ir′ri·ta·bil′i·ty** ***n.*** —**ir′ri·ta·bly** ***adv.***

ir′ri·tant (-tənt) ***adj.*** causing irritation —***n.*** a thing that irritates

ir′ri·tate′ (-tāt′) ***vt.*** **-tat′ed**, **-tat′ing** ⟦< L *irritare*, excite⟧ **1** to provoke to anger; annoy **2** to make inflamed or sore —**ir′ri·ta′tion** ***n.***

ir·rupt (ir rupt′) ***vi.*** ⟦< L *in-*, in + *rumpere*, to break⟧ to burst suddenly or violently (*into*) —**ir·rup′tion** ***n.*** —**ir·rup′tive** ***adj.***

IRS Internal Revenue Service

Ir·ving (ur′viŋ) city in NW Tex.: pop. 110,000

is (iz) ***vi.*** ⟦OE⟧ *3d pers. sing., pres. indic., of* BE

is. **1** island(s) **2** isle(s)

I·saac (ī′zək) *Bible* one of the patriarchs, son of Abraham, and father of Jacob and Esau

I·sa·iah (ī zā′ə) *Bible* **1** a Hebrew prophet of the 8th c. B.C. **2** the book containing his teachings

-ise (īz) *suffix chiefly Brit. sp. of* -IZE

-ish (ish) ⟦< OE *-isc*⟧ *suffix* **1** of (a specified people) *[Irish]* **2** somewhat *[tallish]* **3** [Colloq.] approximately *[thirtyish]*

Ish·tar (ish′tär′) the Babylonian and Assyrian goddess of fertility

i·sin·glass (ī′zin glas′; *also*, -ziŋ-) ***n.*** ⟦< MDu *huizen*, sturgeon + *blas*, bladder⟧ mica, esp. in thin sheets

I·sis (ī′sis) the Egyptian goddess of fertility

isl. **1** island **2** isle

Is·lam (is′läm′, iz′-; is läm′) ***n.*** ⟦Ar *islām*, lit., submission (to God's will)⟧ **1** the Muslim religion, a monotheistic religion founded by Mohammed **2** Muslims collectively or the lands in which they predominate —**Is·lam′ic** (-läm′ik, -lam′-) ***adj.***

Is·lam·a·bad (is läm′ə bäd′) the capital of Pakistan, in the NE part: pop. 201,000

is·land (ī′lənd) ***n.*** ⟦< OE *igland*, lit., island land: sp. after *isle*⟧ **1** a land mass smaller than a continent and surrounded by water **2** anything like this in position or isolation

is′land·er ***n.*** a native or inhabitant of an island

isle (īl) ***n.*** ⟦< L *insula*⟧ an island, esp. a small island

is·let (ī′lit) ***n.*** a very small island

islets (or **islands**) **of Lang·er·hans** (läŋ′ər häns′) ⟦after P. *Langerhans* (1847-88), Ger histologist⟧ endocrine cells in the pancreas that produce the hormone insulin

ism (iz′əm) ***n.*** a doctrine, theory, system, etc. whose name ends in *-ism*

-ism (iz′əm) ⟦< Gr *-ismos*⟧ *suffix* **1** act or result of *[terrorism]* **2** condition, conduct, or qualities of *[patriotism]* **3** theory of *[socialism]* **4** devotion to *[nationalism]* **5** an instance of *[witticism]*

is·n't (iz′ənt) is not

iso- ⟦< Gr *isos*⟧ *combining form* equal, similar, identical *[isomorph]*

i·so·bar (ī′sō bär′) ***n.*** ⟦< prec. + Gr *baros*, weight⟧ a line on a map connecting points of equal barometric pressure

i·so·late (ī′sə lāt′; *for n., usually*, -lit) ***vt.*** **-lat′ed**, **-lat′ing** ⟦< It *isola* (< L *insula*), island⟧ to set apart from others; place alone —***n.*** a person or thing that is isolated —**i′so·la′tion** ***n.*** —**i′so·la′tor** ***n.***

i′so·la′tion·ist ***n.*** one who opposes the involvement of a country in international alliances, etc. —*adj.* of isolationists —**ī'so·la'tion·ism'** *n.*

i·so·mer (ī'sō mər) *n.* ⟦< Gr *isos*, equal + *meros*, a part⟧ any of two or more chemical compounds whose molecules contain the same atoms but in different arrangements —**ī'so·mer'ic** (-mer'ik) *adj.*

ī'so·met'ric (-met'rik) *adj.* ⟦< Gr *isos*, equal + *metron*, measure⟧ **1** equal in measure **2** of isometrics —*n.* [*pl.*] exercise in which muscles are briefly tensed in opposition to other muscles or to an immovable object —**ī'so·met'ri·cal·ly** *adv.*

i·sos·ce·les (ī säs'ə lēz') *adj.* ⟦< Gr *isos*, equal + *skelos*, leg⟧ designating a triangle with two equal sides

ISOSCELES TRIANGLE

i·so·tope (ī'sə tōp') *n.* ⟦< ISO- + Gr *topos*, place⟧ any of two or more forms of an element having the same atomic number but different atomic weights

Is·ra·el (iz'rē əl) **1** *Bible* Jacob **2** ancient land of the Hebrews at the SE end of the Mediterranean **3** kingdom in the N part of this land **4** country between the Mediterranean Sea & Jordan: 7,992 sq. mi.; pop. 4,208,000

Is·rae·li (iz rā'lē) *n.* a native or inhabitant of modern Israel —*adj.* of modern Israel or its people

Is·ra·el·ite (iz'rē ə līt') *n.* any of the people of ancient Israel

is·su·ance (ish'o͞o əns) *n.* an issuing; issue

is·sue (ish'o͞o) *n.* ⟦< L *ex-*, out + *ire*, go⟧ **1** an outgoing; outflow **2** an exit; outlet **3** a result; consequence **4** offspring **5** a point under dispute **6** a sending or giving out **7** all that is put forth at one time /an *issue* of bonds, a periodical, etc./ —*vi.* **-sued**, **-su·ing** **1** to go or flow out; emerge **2** to result (*from*) or end (*in*) **3** to be published —*vt.* **1** to let out; discharge **2** to give or deal out /to *issue* supplies/ **3** to publish —**at issue** in dispute —**take issue** to disagree

-ist (ist, əst) ⟦< Gr *-istēs*⟧ *suffix* **1** one who does, makes, or practices /*satirist*/ **2** one skilled in or occupied with /*druggist, violinist*/ **3** an adherent of /*anarchist*/

Is·tan·bul (is'tan bo͞ol', -tän-) seaport in NW Turkey: pop. 2,773,000

isth·mus (is'məs) *n.*, *pl.* **-mus·es** or **-mi'** (-mī') ⟦< Gr *isthmos*, a neck⟧ a narrow strip of land having water at each side and connecting two larger bodies of land

it (it) *pron.*, *pl. see* THEY ⟦< OE *hit*⟧ **1** the animal or thing previously mentioned **2** *It* is also used as: *a*) the subject of an impersonal verb /*it* is snowing/ *b*) a subject or object of indefinite sense in various idiomatic constructions /*it's* all right, he lords *it* over us/ —*n.* the player, as in tag, who must try to catch another —**with it** [Slang] alert, informed, or hip

It. or **Ital.** **1** Italian **2** Italy

I·tal·ian (i tal'yən) *adj.* of Italy, its people, language, etc. —*n.* **1** a native or inhabitant of Italy **2** the Romance language of Italy

i·tal·ic (i tal'ik) *adj.* ⟦< its early use in *Italy*⟧ designating a type in which the characters slant upward to the right (Ex.: *this is italic type*) —*n.* [*usually pl., sometimes with sing. v.*] italic type or print: abbrev. **ital.**

i·tal·i·cize (i tal'ə sīz', ī-) *vt.* **-cized'**, **-ciz'ing** to print in italics

It·a·ly (it''l ē) country in S Europe: 116,304 sq. mi.; pop. 57,226,000

itch (ich) *vi.* ⟦OE *giccan*⟧ **1** to feel a tingling of the skin, with the desire to scratch **2** to have a restless desire —*vt.* [Colloq.] SCRATCH —*n.* **1** an itching **2** a restless desire —**itch'y**, **-i·er**, **-i·est**, *adj.*

-ite (īt) ⟦< Gr *-itēs*⟧ *suffix* **1** an inhabitant of /*Akronite*/ **2** an adherent of /*laborite*/ **3** a manufactured product /*dynamite*/

i·tem (īt'əm) *n.* ⟦< L *ita*, so, thus⟧ **1** an article; unit; separate thing **2** a bit of news or information

i'tem·ize' (-īz') *vt.* **-ized'**, **-iz'ing** to specify the items of; set down by items —**i'tem·i·za'tion** *n.*

it·er·ate (it'ər āt') *vt.* **-at'ed**, **-at'ing** ⟦< L *iterum*, again⟧ to utter or do again —**it'er·a'tion** *n.*

i·tin·er·ant (ī tin'ər ənt) *adj.* ⟦< L *iter*, a walk⟧ traveling from place to place —*n.* a traveler

i·tin'er·ar'y (-er'ē) *n.*, *pl.* **-ar'ies** **1** a route **2** a record of a journey **3** a detailed plan of a journey

-i·tis (īt'is) ⟦< Gr *-itis*⟧ *suffix* inflammation of (a specified part or organ) /*neuritis*/

its (its) *pron.* that or those belonging to it —*poss. pronominal adj.* of, belonging to, or done by it

it's (its) **1** it is **2** it has

it·self (it self') *pron.* a form of *it* used: *a*) as an intensive /the work *itself* is easy/ *b*) as a reflexive /the dog bit *itself*/ *c*) as a quasi-noun meaning "its real, true self" /the bird is not *itself* today/

it·ty-bit·ty (it'ē bit'ē) *adj.* ⟦baby talk < *little bit*⟧ [Colloq.] very small; tiny Also **it·sy-bit·sy** (it'sē bit'sē)

-i·ty (ə tē, i-) ⟦< L *-itas*⟧ *suffix* state, quality, or instance /*chastity*/

IUD intrauterine (contraceptive) device

IV intravenous

-ive (iv) ⟦< L *-ivus*⟧ *suffix* **1** of or having the nature of /*sportive*/ **2** tending to /*retrospective*/

i·vied (ī'vēd) *adj.* covered or overgrown with ivy

i·vo·ry (ī'və rē) *n.*, *pl.* **-ries** ⟦ult. < Egypt *3bw*⟧ **1** the hard, white substance forming the tusks of elephants, walruses, etc. **2** any substance like ivory **3** creamy white **4** [*pl.*] [Slang] *a*) piano keys *b*) dice —*adj.* **1** of or like ivory **2** creamy-white

Ivory Coast country on the W coast of Africa: 124,500 sq. mi.; pop. 10,500,000

ivory tower a retreat away from reality or action

i·vy (ī'vē) *n.*, *pl.* **i'vies** ⟦OE *ifig*⟧ **1** a climbing vine with a woody stem and evergreen leaves **2** any of various similar climbing plants

-ize (īz) ⟦< Gr *-izein*⟧ *suffix* **1** to cause to be /*sterilize*/ **2** to become (like) /*crystallize*/ **3** to combine with /*oxidize*/ **4** to engage in /*soliloquize*/

J

j or **J** (jā) ***n.**, pl.* **j's, J's** the tenth letter of the English alphabet

jab (jab) ***vt., vi.*** **jabbed, jab'bing** ⟦< ME *jobben,* to peck⟧ **1** to poke, as with a sharp instrument **2** to punch with short, straight blows **—*n.*** a quick thrust or blow

jab·ber (jab'ər) ***vi., vt.*** ⟦prob. echoic⟧ to speak or say quickly, incoherently, or foolishly; chatter **—*n.*** chatter **—jab'ber·er *n.***

ja·bot (zha bō') ***n.*** ⟦Fr, bird's crop⟧ a ruffle or frill down the front of a blouse, etc.

jack (jak) ***n.*** ⟦< the name *Jack*⟧ **1** [*often* **J-**] a man or boy **2** any of various machines used to lift something heavy a short distance /an automobile *jack*/ **3** a playing card with a picture of a royal male servant or soldier **4** a small flag flown on a ship's bow to show nationality **5** any of the small 6-pronged metal pieces tossed and picked up in a game (**jacks**) **6** *Elec.* a plug-in receptacle used to make electrical contact **—*vt.*** to raise by means of a jack: usually with *up* **—jack up** [Colloq.] to raise (prices, wages, etc.)

jack- ⟦see prec.⟧ *combining form* **1** male /*jackass*/ **2** large or strong /*jackknife*/ **3** boy; fellow /*jack*-in-the-box/

jack·al (jak'əl) ***n.*** ⟦< Sans⟧ a wild dog of Asia and N Africa

jack·ass (jak'as') ***n.*** ⟦JACK- + ASS⟧ **1** a male donkey **2** a fool

jack'daw' (-dô') ***n.*** ⟦JACK- + ME *dawe,* jackdaw⟧ a small European crow

jack·et (jak'it) ***n.*** ⟦< Ar *shakk*⟧ **1** a short coat **2** an outer covering, as the removable paper cover on a book, the cardboard holder of a phonograph record, the skin of a potato, etc.

Jack Frost frost or cold weather personified

jack'ham'mer *n.* a portable type of pneumatic hammer, used for breaking up concrete, rock, etc.

jack'-in-the-box' *n., pl.* -box'es a toy consisting of a box from which a figure on a spring jumps up when the lid is lifted Also **jack'-in-a-box'**

jack'-in-the-pul'pit (-pool'pit) ***n., pl.*** **-pits** a plant with a flower spike partly arched over by a hoodlike covering

JACK-IN-THE-PULPIT

jack'knife' *n., pl.* -knives' 1 a large pocketknife **2** a dive in which the diver keeps knees unbent, touches the feet, and then straightens out **—*vi., vt.*** **-knifed', -knif'ing** to bend or fold at the middle or at a connection

jack'-of-all'-trades' *n., pl.* **jacks'-** [*often* **J-**] one who can do many kinds of work acceptably

jack-o'-lan·tern (jak'ə lant'ərn) ***n., pl.*** **-terns** a hollow pumpkin cut to look like a face and used as a lantern

jack'pot' *n.* ⟦*jack,* playing card + *pot*⟧ cumulative stakes, as in poker

jack rabbit a large hare of W North America, with strong hind legs

Jack·son (jak'sən), **An·drew** (an'drōō') 1767-1845; 7th president of the U.S. (1829-37)

Jackson capital of Miss., in the SW part: pop. 203,000

Jack·son·ville (jak'sən vil') port in NE Fla.: pop. 541,000

Ja·cob (jā'kəb) *Bible* a son of Isaac

Jac·quard (jə kärd') ***n.*** ⟦after J. M. *Jacquard* (1752-1834), Fr inventor⟧ a fabric with a figured weave

Ja·cuz·zi (jə kōō'zē) ⟦< *Jacuzzi,* U.S. developers⟧ *trademark for* a kind of whirlpool bath

jade¹ (jād) ***n.*** ⟦< Sp (*piedra de*) *ijada,* (stone of) the side: supposed to cure pains in the side⟧ **1** a hard, greenish, ornamental gemstone **2** a medium green color

jade² (jād) ***n.*** ⟦< ON *jalda,* a mare⟧ **1** a worn-out, worthless horse **2** a disreputable woman **—*vt., vi.*** **jad'ed, jad'ing 1** to tire **2** to satiate **—jad'ed·ly *adv.* —jad'ed·ness *n.***

jade·ite (jād'īt) ***n.*** a hard, translucent type of jade

jade plant a thick-leaved plant native to S Africa and Asia

jag¹ (jag) ***n.*** ⟦ME *jagge*⟧ a sharp, toothlike projection

jag² (jag) ***n.*** ⟦< ?⟧ a drunken spree

jag·ged (jag'id) ***adj.*** having sharp projecting points; notched or ragged **—jag'ged·ly *adv.* —jag'ged·ness *n.***

jag·uar (jag'wär') ***n.*** ⟦Port < AmInd (Brazil)⟧ a large, leopardlike cat found from SW U.S. to Argentina

jai a·lai (hī'lī', hī'ə lī') ⟦< Basque *jai,* celebration + *alai,* merry⟧ a game like handball, played with a basketlike racket

jail (jāl) ***n.*** ⟦ult. < L *cavea,* cage⟧ a prison, esp. for minor offenders or persons awaiting trial **—*vt.*** to put or keep in jail

jail'break' *n.* a breaking out of jail

jail'er or **jail'or *n.*** a person in charge of a jail or of prisoners

Ja·kar·ta (jə kär'tə) capital of Indonesia, on Java island: pop. *c.* 6,500,000

ja·la·pe·ño (häl'ə pān'yō) ***n.*** ⟦Mex⟧ a kind of hot pepper, orig. from Mexico

ja·lop·y (jə läp'ē) ***n., pl.*** **-lop'ies** ⟦< ?⟧ [Slang] an old, ramshackle car

jal·ou·sie (jal'ə sē') ***n.*** ⟦Fr < It *gelosia,* jealousy⟧ a window, shade, or door formed of adjustable horizontal slats of wood, metal, or glass

jam¹ (jam) ***vt.*** **jammed, jam'ming** ⟦< ?⟧ **1** to squeeze into a confined space **2** to crush **3** to crowd **4** to crowd into or block (a passageway, etc.) **5** to make stick so that it cannot move or work **6** to make (radio broadcasts, etc.) unintelligible, as by sending out other signals on the same wavelength **—*vi.*** **1** *a*) to become stuck fast *b*) to become unworkable because of jammed parts 2 to become squeezed into a confined space 3 [Slang] *Jazz* to improvise, as in a gathering of musicians (**jam session**) —*n.* 1 a jamming or being jammed /a traffic *jam*/ 2 [Colloq.] a difficult situation

jam[2] (jam) *n.* ⟦< ? prec.⟧ fruit boiled with sugar to a thick mixture

Ja·mai·ca (jə mā′kə) country on an island in the West Indies, south of Cuba: 4,243 sq. mi.; pop. 2,288,000 —**Ja·mai′can** *adj., n.*

jamb (jam) *n.* ⟦< LL *gamba*, hoof⟧ a side post of a doorway

jam·bo·ree (jam′bə rē′) *n.* ⟦< ?⟧ 1 [Colloq.] a noisy revel 2 a large assembly of Boy Scouts from many places

James (jāmz), **Henry** 1843-1916; U.S. novelist, in England

James·town (jāmz′toun′) former village in Va.: the 1st permanent English colonial settlement in America (1607)

jam-packed (jam′pakt′) *adj.* [Colloq.] tightly packed

jan·gle (jaŋ′gəl) *vi.* **-gled, -gling** ⟦< OFr *jangler*⟧ to make a harsh, usually metallic sound —*vt.* 1 to cause to jangle 2 to irritate /*jangled* nerves/ —*n.* a jangling —**jan′gler** *n.*

jan·i·tor (jan′i tər) *n.* ⟦L, doorkeeper⟧ one who takes care of a building, doing routine repairs, etc. —**jan′i·to′ri·al** (-i tôr′ē əl) *adj.*

Jan·u·ar·y (jan′yo͞o er′ē) *n., pl.* **-ar′ies** ⟦< L < *Janus*, Roman god who was a patron of beginnings and endings⟧ the first month of the year, having 31 days: abbrev. **Jan.**

ja·pan (jə pan′) *n.* ⟦orig. made in Japan⟧ a lacquer giving a hard, glossy finish

Ja·pan (jə pan′) 1 island country in the Pacific, off the E coast of Asia: 143,750 sq. mi.; pop. 121,402,000 2 **Sea of** arm of the Pacific, between Japan & E Asia

Jap·a·nese (jap′ə nēz′) *adj.* of Japan, its people, language, etc. —*n.* 1 *pl.* **-nese′** a native of Japan 2 the language of Japan

Japanese beetle a shiny, green-and-brown scarab beetle, orig. from Japan, damaging to crops

jape (jāp) *vi.* **japed, jap′ing** ⟦< OFr *japer*, to howl⟧ 1 to joke 2 to play tricks —*n.* 1 a joke 2 a trick

jar[1] (jär) *vi.* **jarred, jar′ring** ⟦ult. echoic⟧ 1 to make a harsh sound; grate 2 to have an irritating effect (*on* one) 3 to vibrate from an impact 4 to clash; conflict —*vt.* to jolt —*n.* 1 a grating sound 2 a vibration due to impact 3 a jolt

jar[2] (jär) *n.* ⟦< Ar *jarrah*, earthen container⟧ 1 a container made of glass, earthenware, etc., with a large opening 2 as much as a jar will hold: also **jar′ful′**

jar·di·niere (jär′də nir′) *n.* ⟦< Fr < *jardin*, a garden⟧ an ornamental pot or stand for flowers or plants

jar·gon (jär′gən) *n.* ⟦< MFr, a chattering⟧ 1 unintelligible talk 2 the specialized vocabulary of those in the same work, way of life, etc.

jas·mine (jaz′min, jas′-) *n.* ⟦< Pers *yāsamin*⟧ any of certain plants of warm regions, with fragrant flowers of yellow, red, or white

Ja·son (jā′sən) *Gr. Myth.* the leader of the Argonauts: cf. ARGONAUT

jas·per (jas′pər) *n.* ⟦< Gr *iaspis*⟧ an opaque variety of colored quartz

ja·to or **JA·TO** (jā′tō) *n.* ⟦*j*(*et*-)*a*(*ssisted*) *t*(*ake*)*o*(*ff*)⟧ an airplane takeoff assisted by a jet-producing unit

jaun·dice (jôn′dis) *n.* ⟦< L *galbus*, yellow⟧ a diseased condition in which the eyeballs, skin, and urine become abnormally yellowish as a result of increased bile in the blood —*vt.* **-diced, -dic·ing** 1 to cause to have jaundice 2 to make bitter through envy, etc.

jaunt (jônt) *vi.* ⟦< ?⟧ to take a short pleasure trip —*n.* such a trip

jaun·ty (jônt′ē) *adj.* **-ti·er, -ti·est** ⟦< Fr *gentil*, genteel⟧ showing an easy confidence; sprightly or perky —**jaun′ti·ly** *adv.* —**jaun′ti·ness** *n.*

Ja·va (jä′və, jav′ə) large island of Indonesia —*n.* 1 a coffee grown there 2 [*often* **j-**] any coffee —**Jav·a·nese** (jav′ə nēz′) *adj., n.*

jav·e·lin (jav′lin, -ə lin) *n.* ⟦MFr *javeline*⟧ a light spear, esp. one thrown for distance in a contest

jaw (jô) *n.* ⟦< OFr *joue*, cheek⟧ 1 either of the two bony parts that hold the teeth and frame the mouth 2 either of two movable parts that grasp or crush something, as in a vise —*vi.* [Slang] to talk

jaw′bone′ *n.* a bone of a jaw, esp. of the lower jaw —*vt., vi.* **-boned′, -bon′ing** to try to persuade by using the influence of one's office

jaw′break′er (-brā′kər) *n.* 1 a hard, usually round candy 2 [Slang] a word hard to pronounce

jaw′less fish a jawless fish with an eel-like body and a circular sucking mouth, as the lamprey

jay (jā) *n.* ⟦< LL *gaius*, jay⟧ any of several birds, usually strikingly colored, as the blue jay

jay′walk′ *vi.* to walk across a street without obeying traffic rules and signals —**jay′walk′er** *n.*

jazz (jaz) *n.* ⟦< ?⟧ 1 a kind of syncopated, highly rhythmic music originated by Southern blacks in the late 19th c. 2 [Slang] talk, acts, etc. regarded disparagingly —*vt.* [Slang] to enliven or embellish: with *up*

jazz′y *adj.* **-i·er, -i·est** 1 of or like jazz 2 [Slang] lively, flashy, etc.

jeal·ous (jel′əs) *adj.* ⟦see ZEAL⟧ 1 watchful in guarding /*jealous* of one's rights/ 2 *a*) resentfully suspicious of rivalry /a *jealous* lover/ *b*) resentfully envious *c*) resulting from such feelings /a *jealous* rage/ —**jeal′ous·ly** *adv.*

jeal′ous·y *n.* 1 the quality or condition of being jealous 2 *pl.* **-ous·ies** a jealous feeling

jean (jēn) *n.* ⟦< L *Genua*, Genoa, city in Italy⟧ 1 a durable, twilled cotton cloth 2 [*pl.*] trousers of this or of denim

jeep (jēp) *n.* ⟦< creature in comic strip by E. C. Segar (1894-1938)⟧ a small, rugged military vehicle of World War II —[**J-**] *trademark for* a similar vehicle for civilian use

jeer (jir) *vt., vi.* ⟦< ? CHEER⟧ to make fun of in a rude, sarcastic manner; scoff (at) —*n.* a jeering remark

Jef·fer·son (jef′ər sən), **Thom·as** (täm′əs)

1743-1826; 3d president of the U.S. (1801-09)

Jefferson City capital of Mo.: pop. 34,000

Je·ho·vah (ji hō′və) ⟦< Heb⟧ God

je·june (ji jōōn′) ***adj.*** ⟦L *jejunus,* empty⟧ **1** not interesting or satisfying **2** not mature; childish

je·ju·num (jē jōō′nəm) ***n., pl.*** **-na** (-nə) ⟦< L *jejunus,* empty⟧ the middle part of the small intestine

jell (jel) ***vi., vt.*** ⟦< fol.⟧ **1** to become, or make into, jelly **2** [Colloq.] to crystallize /plans haven't *jelled* yet/

jel·ly (jel′ē) ***n., pl.*** **-lies** ⟦< L *gelare,* freeze⟧ **1** a soft, gelatinous food made from cooked fruit syrup or meat juice **2** any substance like this —***vi., vt.*** **-lied, -ly·ing** JELL (sense 1)

jel·ly bean a small, bean-shaped, gelatinous candy Also **jel′ly·bean′**

jel′ly·fish′ ***n., pl.*** **-fish′** or (for different species) **-fish′es** **1** a sea animal with an umbrella-shaped, jellylike body and long tentacles **2** [Colloq.] a weak-willed person

jel′ly·roll′ ***n.*** a thin sheet of sponge cake spread with jelly and rolled up

jeop·ard·ize (jep′ər dīz′) ***vt.*** **-ized′, -iz′ing** to put in jeopardy

jeop′ard·y (-dē) ***n.*** ⟦< OFr *jeu parti,* lit., a game with even chances⟧ great danger or risk

jer·e·mi·ad (jer′ə mī′ad′, -əd) ***n.*** a long lamentation or complaint: in allusion to the *Lamentations of Jeremiah*

Jer′e·mi′ah (-ə) *Bible* a Hebrew prophet of the 7th and 6th c. B.C.

Jer·i·cho (jer′i kō′) city in W Jordan: site of an ancient city in Canaan

jerk (jurk) ***n.*** ⟦< ?⟧ **1** a sharp, abrupt pull, twist, etc. **2** a sudden muscular contraction **3** [Slang] a person regarded as disagreeable, contemptible, etc. —***vi., vt.*** **1** to move with a jerk; pull sharply **2** to twitch

jer·kin (jur′kin) ***n.*** ⟦< ?⟧ a short, closefitting jacket, often sleeveless

jerk′wa′ter ***adj.*** [Colloq.] small, unimportant, etc. /a *jerkwater* town/

jerk·y[1] (jurk′ē) ***adj.*** **jerk′i·er, jerk′i·est** **1** moving by jerks; spasmodic **2** [Slang] foolish, mean, etc. —**jerk′i·ly** ***adv.***

jer·ky[2] (jur′kē) ***n.*** ⟦< Sp *charqui*⟧ meat preserved by being sliced into strips and dried in the sun

jer·ry-built (jer′ē bilt′) ***adj.*** built poorly, of cheap materials

jer·sey (jur′zē) ***n., pl.*** **-seys** ⟦after *Jersey,* one of the Channel Islands⟧ **1** [J-] any of a breed of reddish-brown dairy cattle, orig. from Jersey **2** a soft, knitted cloth **3** a closefitting, knitted upper garment

Jer·sey City (jur′zē) city in NE N.J., across the Hudson from New York City: pop. 224,000

Je·ru·sa·lem (jə rōōz′ə ləm) capital of Israel (the country): pop. *c.* 250,000

jest (jest) ***n.*** ⟦< L *gerere,* perform⟧ **1** a mocking remark; taunt **2** a joke **3** fun; joking **4** something to be laughed at —***vi.*** **1** to jeer **2** to joke

jest′er ***n.*** one who jests; esp., a man kept by a medieval ruler to amuse him by joking and clowning

Jes·u·it (jezh′ōō it, jez′-) ***n.*** a member of the Society of Jesus, a Roman Catholic religious order for men, founded in 1534

Je·sus (jē′zəz, -zəs) founder of the Christian religion: also **Jesus Christ**

jet[1] (jet) ***vt., vi.*** **jet′ted, jet′ting** ⟦< L *jacere,* to throw⟧ **1** to gush out in a stream **2** to travel or convey by jet airplane —***n.*** **1** a stream of liquid or gas suddenly emitted **2** a spout or nozzle for emitting a jet **3** a jet-propelled airplane: in full, **jet (air)plane** —***adj.*** driven by jet propulsion

jet[2] (jet) ***n.*** ⟦after *Gagas,* town in Asia Minor⟧ **1** a hard, black mineral like coal, polished and used in jewelry **2** a lustrous black —***adj.*** black

jet lag a disruption of the daily body rhythms, associated with high-speed travel by jet airplane to distant time zones

jet′port′ ***n.*** a large airport with long runways, for use by jetliners

jet propulsion propulsion of airplanes, boats, etc. by forcing compressed outside air and hot exhaust gases through a jet nozzle —**jet′-pro·pelled′** (-prō peld′) ***adj.***

jet·sam (jet′səm) ***n.*** ⟦var. of JETTISON⟧ cargo thrown overboard to lighten a ship in danger

jet set fashionable people who frequently travel, often by jet, as for pleasure —**jet′-set′ter** ***n.***

jet stream high-velocity winds moving from west to east, high above the earth

jet·ti·son (jet′ə sən) ***vt.*** ⟦< L *jactare,* to throw⟧ **1** to throw (goods) overboard so as to lighten a ship in danger **2** to discard

jet·ty (jet′ē) ***n., pl.*** **-ties** ⟦see JET[1]⟧ **1** a wall built out into the water to restrain currents, protect a harbor, etc. **2** a landing pier

Jew (jōō) ***n.*** ⟦< Heb *yehūdī,* citizen of Judah⟧ **1** a person descended, or regarded as descended, from the ancient Hebrews **2** a person whose religion is Judaism

jew·el (jōō′əl) ***n.*** ⟦ult. < L *jocus,* a joke⟧ **1** a valuable ring, necklace, etc., esp. one set with gems **2** a precious stone; gem **3** any person or thing very dear to one **4** a small gem used as a bearing in a watch —***vt.*** **-eled** or **-elled, -el·ing** or **-el·ling** to decorate or set with jewels

jew′el·er or **jew′el·ler** (-ər) ***n.*** ⟦ME *jueler* < OFr *joieleor* < *joel:* see prec.⟧ one who makes or deals in jewelry

jew′el·ry ***n.*** ornaments such as rings, bracelets, etc., collectively

Jew·ish (jōō′ish) ***adj.*** of or having to do with Jews or Judaism —***n.*** loosely, Yiddish —**Jew′ish·ness** ***n.***

Jew·ry (jōō′rē) ***n.*** the Jewish people

jew's-harp (jōōz′härp′) ***n.*** ⟦< Du *jeugd-tromp,* child's trumpet⟧ a small, metal musical instrument held between the teeth and plucked to produce twanging tones

Jez·e·bel (jez′ə bel′) *Bible* a wicked queen of Israel

jib (jib) ***n.*** ⟦Dan *gib*⟧ a triangular sail secured forward of the mast or foremast

jibe[1] (jīb) ***vi.*** **jibed, jib′ing** ⟦< Du *gijpen*⟧ **1** to shift from one side of a ship to the other, as a fore-and-aft sail **2** to change the course of a ship so that the sails jibe **3** [Colloq.] to be in agreement or accord

jibe[2] (jīb) *vi., vt., n.* GIBE
jif·fy (jif'ē) *n., pl.* **-fies** ⟦< ?⟧ a very short time Also **jiff**
jig (jig) *n.* ⟦prob. < MFr *giguer,* to dance⟧ **1** a fast, springy dance in triple time, or music for this **2** a device used to guide a tool —*vi., vt.* **jigged, jig'ging** to dance (a jig) —**in jig time** [Colloq.] very quickly —**the jig is up** [Slang] no chance is left
jig·ger (jig'ər) *n.* **1** a small glass, usually of $1\frac{1}{2}$ ounces, used to measure liquor **2** the contents of a jigger
jig·gle (jig'əl) *vt., vi.* **-gled, -gling** ⟦< JIG⟧ to move in quick, slight jerks —*n.* a jiggling
jig·saw (jig'sô') *n.* a saw with a narrow blade set in a frame, for cutting curves, etc.
jigsaw puzzle a puzzle consisting of a picture cut up into irregularly shaped pieces, which must be put together again
jilt (jilt) *vt.* ⟦< *Jill,* sweetheart⟧ to reject or cast off (a previously accepted lover, etc.)
Jim Crow ⟦name of an early black minstrel song⟧ [*also* **j- c-**] [Colloq.] discrimination against or segregation of blacks —**Jim'-Crow'** *vt., adj.*
jim·my (jim'ē) *n., pl.* **-mies** ⟦< *James*⟧ a short crowbar, used as by burglars to pry open windows, etc. —*vt.* **-mied, -my·ing** to pry open with or as with a jimmy
jim·son weed (jim'sən) ⟦< *Jamestown weed*⟧ a poisonous weed with white or purplish, trumpet-shaped flowers
jin·gle (jiŋ'gəl) *vi.* **-gled, -gling** ⟦echoic⟧ to make light, ringing sounds, as small bells —*vt.* to cause to jingle —*n.* **1** a jingling sound **2** a catchy verse or song with easy rhythm, simple rhymes, etc.
jin·go·ism (jiŋ'gō iz'əm) *n.* ⟦< phrase *by jingo* in patriotic Brit song⟧ chauvinistic advocacy of an aggressive, warlike foreign policy —**jin'go·ist** *n.* —**jin'go·is'tic** *adj.*
jin·ni (ji nē', jin'ē) *n., pl.* **jinn** ⟦Ar⟧ *Muslim Folklore* a supernatural being that can influence human affairs
jin·rik·i·sha (jin rik'shô') *n.* ⟦Jpn < *jin,* a man + *riki,* power + *sha,* carriage⟧ a small, two-wheeled carriage, pulled by a man, esp. formerly in the Orient Also sp. **jin·rick'-sha'** or **jin·rik'sha'**
jinx (jiŋks) *n.* ⟦< Gr *iynx,* the wryneck (bird used in black magic)⟧ [Colloq.] a person or thing supposed to bring bad luck —*vt.* [Colloq.] to be a jinx to
jit·ney (jit'nē) *n., pl.* **-neys** ⟦< ? Fr *jeton,* a token⟧ a small bus or a car carrying passengers for a low fare
jit·ter·bug (jit'ər bug') *n.* a fast, acrobatic dance for couples, esp. in the 1940's —*vi.* **-bugged', -bug'ging** to do this dance
jit·ters (jit'ərz) *n.pl.* [Colloq.] an uneasy, nervous feeling; fidgets: with *the* —**jit'ter·y** *adj.*
jive (jīv) *n.* ⟦< JIBE[2]⟧ [Slang] foolish, exaggerated, or insincere talk —*adj.* [Slang] insincere, fraudulent, etc.
Joan of Arc (jōn əv ärk), Saint (1412-31); Fr. military heroine: burned at the stake for witchcraft
job (jäb) *n.* ⟦< ?⟧ **1** a piece of work done for pay **2** a task; duty **3** the thing or material being worked on **4** employment; work —*adj.* hired or done by the job —*vt., vi.* **jobbed, job'bing** **1** to deal in (goods) as a jobber **2** to sublet (work, etc.) —**job'-hold'er** *n.* —**job'less** *adj.*
Job (jōb) *Bible* a man who suffered much but kept his faith in God
job action a refusal by a group of employees (esp. a group forbidden by law to strike) to perform their duties in an effort to win certain demands
job·ber (jäb'ər) *n.* **1** one who buys goods in quantity and sells them to dealers **2** one who does piecework
job lot an assortment of goods for sale as one quantity
jock (jäk) *n.* **1** *short for:* *a)* JOCKEY *b)* JOCKSTRAP **2** [Slang] a male athlete
jock·ey (jäk'ē) *n., pl.* **-eys** ⟦< Scot dim. of JACK⟧ one whose work is riding horses in races —*vt., vi.* **-eyed, -ey·ing** **1** to cheat; swindle **2** to maneuver for position or advantage
jock·strap (jäk'strap') *n.* ⟦*jock,* penis + STRAP⟧ an elastic belt with a pouch for supporting the genitals, worn by male athletes
jo·cose (jō kōs') *adj.* ⟦< L *jocus,* a joke⟧ joking or playful —**jo·cose'ly** *adv.* —**jo·cos'i·ty** (-käs'ə tē), *pl.* **-ties,** or **jo·cose'ness** *n.*
joc·u·lar (jäk'yo͞o lər) *adj.* ⟦< L *jocus,* a joke⟧ joking; full of fun —**joc'u·lar'i·ty** (-lar'ə tē), *pl.* **-ties,** *n.*
joc·und (jäk'ənd) *adj.* ⟦< L *jucundus,* pleasant⟧ cheerful; genial —**joc'und·ly** *adv.*
jodh·purs (jäd'pərz) *n.pl.* ⟦after *Jodhpur,* former state in India⟧ riding breeches made loose and full above the knees and closefitting below
jog[1] (jäg) *vt.* **jogged, jog'ging** ⟦ME *joggen,* to spur (a horse)⟧ **1** to give a little shake to; nudge **2** to rouse (the memory) —*vi.* to move along at a slow, steady, jolting pace; specif., to engage in jogging —*n.* **1** a little shake or nudge **2** a slow, steady, jolting motion —**jog'ger** *n.*
jog[2] (jäg) *n.* ⟦var. of JAG[1]⟧ **1** a projecting or notched part in a surface or line **2** a sharp change of direction
jog'ging *n.* trotting slowly and steadily as a form of exercise
jog·gle (jäg'əl) *vt., vi.* **-gled, -gling** ⟦< JOG[1]⟧ to shake or jolt slightly —*n.* a slight jolt
Jo·han·nes·burg (jō han'is burg') city in NE South Africa: pop. 1,156,000
john (jän) *n.* [Slang] **1** a toilet **2** [*also* **J-**] a prostitute's customer
John (jän) *Bible* **1** a Christian apostle, the reputed author of the fourth Gospel **2** this book
John Bull *personification of* England or an Englishman
John Doe (dō) a fictitious name used in legal papers for an unknown person
John·son (jän'sən) **1 An·drew** (an'dro͞o') 1808-75; 17th president of the U.S. (1865-69) **2 Lyn·don Baines** (lin'dən bānz') 1908-73; 36th president of the U.S. (1963-69) **3 Samuel** 1709-84; Eng. lexicographer & writer
John the Baptist *Bible* the forerunner and baptizer of Jesus
join (join) *vt., vi.* ⟦< L *jungere*⟧ **1** to bring

or come together (with); connect; unite 2 to become a part or member of (a club, etc.) 3 to participate (*in* a conversation, etc.)

join'er *n.* 1 a carpenter who finishes interior woodwork 2 [Colloq.] one who joins many organizations

joint (joint) *n.* ⟦< L *jungere*⟧ 1 a place where, or way in which, two things are joined 2 any of the parts of a jointed whole 3 a large cut of meat with the bone still in it 4 [Slang] a cheap bar, restaurant, etc., or any house, building, etc. 5 [Slang] a marijuana cigarette —*adj.* 1 common to two or more /*joint* property/ 2 sharing with another /a *joint* owner/ —*vt.* 1 to connect by or provide with a joint or joints 2 to cut (meat) into joints —**out of joint** 1 dislocated 2 disordered

joint'ly *adv.* in common

joist (joist) *n.* ⟦< OFr *giste,* a bed⟧ any of the parallel beams that hold up the planks of a floor or the laths of a ceiling

joke (jōk) *n.* ⟦L *jocus*⟧ 1 anything said or done to arouse laughter, as a funny anecdote 2 a thing done or said merely in fun 3 a person or thing to be laughed at —*vi.* **joked, jok'ing** to make jokes —**jok'ing·ly** *adv.*

jok'er *n.* 1 one who jokes: also **joke'ster** 2 a hidden provision put into a legal document, etc. to make it different from what it seems to be 3 an extra playing card

jok'ey *adj.* comical or lighthearted Also **jok'y**

jol·li·ty (jäl'ə tē) *n.* a being jolly

jol·ly (jäl'ē) *adj.* **-li·er, -li·est** ⟦OFr *joli*⟧ 1 full of high spirits and good humor; merry 2 [Colloq.] enjoyable —*vt., vi.* **-lied, -ly·ing** [Colloq.] 1 to try to make (a person) feel good, as by coaxing: often with *along* 2 to make fun of (someone) —**jol'li·ly** *adv.* —**jol'li·ness** *n.*

jolt (jōlt) *vt.* ⟦< earlier *jot*⟧ 1 to shake up, as with a bumpy ride 2 to shock or surprise —*vi.* to move along in a bumpy manner —*n.* 1 a sudden jerk, bump, etc. 2 a shock or surprise

Jo·nah (jō'nə) *Bible* a Hebrew prophet: cast overboard and swallowed by a big fish, he was later cast up unharmed —*n.* one who brings bad luck

Jones (jōnz), **John Paul** 1747-92; Am. naval officer in the Revolutionary War, born in Scotland

jon·quil (jäŋ'kwil, jän'-) *n.* ⟦< L *juncus,* a rush⟧ a species of narcissus with small, yellow flowers

Jon·son (jän'sən), **Ben** (ben) *c.* 1572-1637; Eng. dramatist & poet

Jor·dan (jôrd''n) 1 river in the Near East, flowing into the Dead Sea 2 country east of Israel: 35,000 sq. mi.; pop. 2,756,000 —**Jor·da·ni·an** (jôr dā'nē ən) *adj., n.*

Jo·seph (jō'zəf) *Bible* 1 one of Jacob's sons, who became a high official in Egypt 2 the husband of Mary, mother of Jesus

josh (jäsh) *vt., vi.* ⟦< ?⟧ [Colloq.] to tease; banter —**josh'er** *n.*

Josh·u·a (jäsh'yo͞o ə) *Bible* Moses' successor, who led the Israelites into the Promised Land

jos·tle (jäs'əl) *vt., vi.* **-tled, -tling** ⟦see JOUST⟧ to push, as in a crowd; shove roughly —*n.* a jostling

jot (jät) *n.* ⟦< Gr *iōta,* the smallest letter⟧ a very small amount —*vt.* **jot'ted, jot'ting** to make a brief note of: usually with *down* —**jot'ter** *n.*

joule (jo͞ol) *n.* ⟦after J. P. *Joule,* 19th-c. Eng physicist⟧ the unit of work or energy in the metric system

jounce (jouns) *vt., vi.* **jounced, jounc'ing** ⟦< ?⟧ to jolt or bounce —*n.* a jolt —**jounc'y** *adj.*

jour·nal (jʉr'nəl) *n.* ⟦< L *diurnalis,* daily⟧ 1 a daily record of happenings, as a diary 2 a newspaper or periodical 3 *Bookkeeping* a book of original entry for recording transactions 4 ⟦orig. Scot⟧ the part of an axle or shaft that turns in a bearing

jour·nal·ese (jʉr'nəl ēz') *n.* a facile style of writing found in many newspapers, magazines, etc.

jour'nal·ism' (-iz'əm) *n.* the work of gathering news for, or producing, a newspaper, etc. —**jour'nal·ist** *n.* —**jour'nal·is'tic** *adj.*

jour·ney (jʉr'nē) *n., pl.* **-neys** ⟦< OFr *journee;* ult. < L *dies,* day⟧ a traveling from one place to another; trip —*vi.* **-neyed, -ney·ing** to travel —**jour'ney·er** *n.*

jour'ney·man (-mən) *n., pl.* **-men** ⟦ME < *journee,* day's work + *man*⟧ 1 a worker qualified to work at a specified trade 2 any sound, experienced, but not brilliant performer

joust (joust, just) *n.* ⟦ult. < L *juxta,* close to⟧ a combat with lances between two knights on horseback —*vi.* to engage in a joust

jo·vi·al (jō'vē əl) *adj.* ⟦< LL *Jovialis,* of Jupiter: from astrological notion of planet's influence⟧ full of playful good humor —**jo'vi·al'i·ty** (-al'ə tē) *n.* —**jo'vi·al·ly** *adv.*

jowl[1] (joul) *n.* ⟦OE *ceafl,* jaw⟧ 1 the lower jaw 2 the cheek, esp. of a hog

jowl[2] (joul) *n.* ⟦OE *ceole,* throat⟧ [*usually pl.*] the fleshy hanging part under the jaw —**jowl'y** *adj.*

joy (joi) *n.* ⟦ult. < L *gaudium,* joy⟧ 1 a very glad feeling; happiness; delight 2 anything causing this

Joyce (jois), **James** 1882-1941; Ir. novelist

joy'ful *adj.* feeling, expressing, or causing joy; glad —**joy'ful·ly** *adv.*

joy'ous (-əs) *adj.* joyful; happy —**joy'ous·ly** *adv.* —**joy'ous·ness** *n.*

joy ride [Colloq.] an automobile ride, often at a reckless speed, just for pleasure —**joy rider** —**joy riding**

joy'stick' *n.* 1 [Slang] the control stick of an airplane 2 a manual device with a control lever for positioning a lighted indicator, as on a video screen

JP or **J.P.** Justice of the Peace

Jpn. 1 Japan 2 Japanese

Jr. or **jr.** junior

ju·bi·lant (jo͞o'bə lənt) *adj.* ⟦< L *jubilum,* wild shout⟧ joyful and triumphant; elated; rejoicing

ju·bi·la·tion (jo͞o'bə lā'shən) *n.* 1 a rejoicing 2 a happy celebration

ju·bi·lee (jo͞o'bə lē') *n.* ⟦< Heb *yōbēl,* a ram's horn (trumpet)⟧ 1 a 50th or 25th anniversary 2 a time of rejoicing 3 jubilation

Ju·dah (jo͞o'də) 1 *Bible* one of Jacob's sons 2 ancient kingdom in the S part of Palestine

Ju·da·ism (jo͞o′dā iz′əm, -dē-, -də-) ***n.*** the Jewish religion —**Ju·da′ic** (-dā′ik) ***adj.***

Judas (jo͞o′dəs) *Bible* the disciple who betrayed Jesus for money: in full **Judas Is·car·i·ot** (is ker′ē ət) —***n.*** a traitor or betrayer

Ju·de·a (jo͞o dē′ə) ancient region of S Palestine

Judeo- *combining form* Jewish

judge (juj) ***n.*** ⟦< L *jus,* law + *dicere,* say⟧ 1 a public official with authority to hear and decide cases in a court of law 2 a person designated to determine the winner, settle a controversy, etc. 3 a person qualified to decide on the relative worth of anything —***vt., vi.*** **judged, judg′ing** 1 to hear and pass judgment on in a court of law 2 to determine the winner of (a contest) or settle (a controversy) 3 to form an opinion about 4 to criticize or censure 5 to think; suppose —**judge′ship′** ***n.***

judg·ment (juj′mənt) ***n.*** 1 a judging; deciding 2 a legal decision; order given by a judge, etc. 3 an opinion 4 the ability to come to an opinion 5 [J-] *short for* LAST JUDGMENT Also **judge′ment**

judg·men′tal (-ment′'l) ***adj.*** making judgments as to value, etc., often, specif., judgments considered to be lacking in tolerance, objectivity, etc.

Judgment Day *Theol.* the time of God's final judgment of all people

ju·di·ca·to·ry (jo͞o′di kə tôr′ē) ***adj.*** ⟦see JUDGE⟧ having to do with administering justice —***n., pl.*** **-ries** a law court, or law courts collectively

ju′di·ca·ture (-chər) ***n.*** 1 the administering of justice 2 jurisdiction 3 judges or courts collectively

ju·di·cial (jo͞o dish′əl) ***adj.*** 1 of judges, courts, or their functions 2 allowed, enforced, etc. by a court 3 befitting a judge 4 fair; impartial

ju·di·ci·ar·y (jo͞o dish′ē er′ē) ***adj.*** of judges or courts —***n., pl.*** **-ar′ies** 1 the part of government that administers justice 2 judges collectively

ju·di′cious (-dish′əs) ***adj.*** having or showing sound judgment —**ju·di′cious·ly** ***adv.***

ju·do (jo͞o′dō) ***n.*** ⟦Jpn < *jū,* soft + *dō,* way⟧ a form of jujitsu

jug (jug) ***n.*** ⟦a pet form of *Judith* or *Joan*⟧ 1 a container for liquids, with a small opening and a handle 2 [Slang] a jail

jug·ger·naut (jug′ər nôt′) ***n.*** ⟦< Sans *Jagannātha,* lord of the world⟧ a terrible, irresistible force

jug·gle (jug′əl) ***vt.*** **-gled, -gling** ⟦< L *jocus,* a joke⟧ 1 to perform skillful tricks of sleight of hand with (balls, etc.) 2 to manipulate so as to deceive —***vi.*** to toss up balls, etc. and keep them in the air —**jug·gler** (jug′lər) ***n.*** —**jug′gler·y** ***n.***

jug·u·lar (jug′yo͞o lər, jug′lər) ***adj.*** ⟦< L *jugum,* a yoke⟧ of the neck or throat —***n.*** JUGULAR VEIN

jugular vein either of two large veins in the neck carrying blood from the head

juice (jo͞os) ***n.*** ⟦< L *jus,* broth, juice⟧ 1 the liquid part of a plant, fruit, etc. 2 a liquid in or from animal tissue 3 [Colloq.] vitality 4 [Slang] *a)* electricity *b)* alcoholic liquor *c)* power or influence —***vt.*** **juiced, juic′ing** to extract juice from —***vi.*** [Slang] to drink alcoholic beverages to excess

juiced (jo͞ost) ***adj.*** drunk; intoxicated

juic·er (jo͞o′sər) ***n.*** 1 a device for extracting juice from fruit 2 [Slang] one who drinks alcoholic beverages to excess

juic·y (jo͞o′sē) ***adj.*** **-i·er, -i·est** 1 full of juice 2 [Colloq.] *a)* very interesting *b)* highly profitable —**juic′i·ness** ***n.***

ju·jit·su (jo͞o jit′so͞o′) ***n.*** ⟦< Jpn *jū,* soft, pliant + *jutsu,* art⟧ a Japanese system of wrestling in which an opponent's strength and weight are used against him

ju·ju·be (jo͞o′jo͞o bē′) ***n.*** ⟦< Gr *zizyphon,* name of a fruit⟧ a fruit-flavored, jellylike lozenge

ju·jut·su (jo͞o jo͝ot′so͞o′, -jut′-) ***n.*** JUJITSU

juke·box (jo͞ok′bäks′) ***n.*** ⟦< Am black *juke,* wicked⟧ a coin-operated record player

ju·lep (jo͞o′ləp) ***n.*** ⟦< Pers *gul,* rose + *āb,* water⟧ MINT JULEP

ju·li·enne (jo͞o′lē en′) ***adj.*** ⟦Fr⟧ cut into strips: said of vegetables, etc.

Ju·li·et (jo͞o′lē et′, jo͞o′lē et′) the heroine of Shakespeare's tragedy *Romeo and Juliet*

Ju·ly (jo͞o lī′, jo͞o-) ***n.*** ⟦< L < *Julius* Caesar⟧ the seventh month of the year, having 31 days: abbrev. **Jul.**

jum·ble (jum′bəl) ***vt., vi.*** **-bled, -bling** ⟦? blend of JUMP + TUMBLE⟧ to mix or be mixed in a confused heap —***n.*** a confused mixture or heap

jum·bo (jum′bō) ***n., pl.*** **-bos** ⟦< Am black *jamba,* elephant⟧ a large person, animal, or thing —***adj.*** very large

jump (jump) ***vi.*** ⟦< ?⟧ 1 to spring or leap from the ground, a height, etc. 2 to jerk; bob 3 to move or act eagerly: often with *at* 4 to pass suddenly, as to a new topic 5 to rise suddenly, as prices 6 [Slang] to be lively —***vt.*** 1 *a)* to leap over *b)* to pass over 2 to cause to leap 3 to leap upon 4 to cause (prices, etc.) to rise 5 [Colloq.] *a)* to attack suddenly *b)* to react to prematurely 6 [Slang] to leave suddenly [*to jump* town] —***n.*** 1 a jumping 2 a distance jumped 3 a sudden transition 4 a sudden rise, as in prices 5 a sudden, nervous start —**get** (or **have**) **the jump on** [Slang] to get (or have) an advantage over —**jump bail** to forfeit bail by running away

jump·er¹ (jump′ər) ***n.*** 1 one that jumps 2 a short wire to make a temporary electrical connection

jump·er² (jump′ər) ***n.*** ⟦< dial. *jump,* short coat⟧ 1 a loose jacket 2 a sleeveless dress for wearing over a blouse, etc.

jumper cables a pair of thick, insulated electrical wires with clamplike terminals, used to connect a live battery to a dead one

jump′-start′ ***vt.*** to start (the engine of a motor vehicle) with jumper cables —***n.*** a starting in such a way

jump·suit (jump′so͞ot) ***n.*** 1 a coverall worn by paratroops, etc. 2 any one-piece garment like this

jump·y (jum′pē) ***adj.*** **-i·er, -i·est** 1 moving in jumps, etc. 2 easily startled —**jump′i·ly** ***adv.*** —**jump′i·ness** ***n.***

jun·co (juŋ′kō′) ***n., pl.*** **-cos′** ⟦< Sp⟧ a small bird with a gray or black head

junc·tion (juŋk′shən) ***n.*** ⟦< L *jungere,* join⟧

1 a joining or being joined 2 a place of joining, as of roads —**junc′tion·al** *adj.*

junc·ture (juŋk′chər) *n.* 1 a junction 2 a point of time 3 a crisis

June (jo͞on) *n.* ⟦< L *Junius,* of *Juno*⟧ the sixth month of the year, having 30 days: abbrev. **Jun.**

Ju·neau (jo͞o′nō′) capital of Alas.: seaport on the SE coast: pop. 20,000

jun·gle (juŋ′gəl) *n.* ⟦< Sans *jaṅgala,* wasteland⟧ 1 land densely covered with trees, vines, etc., as in the tropics 2 [Slang] a situation in which people struggle fiercely for survival

jun·ior (jo͞on′yər) *adj.* ⟦L < *juvenis,* young⟧ 1 the younger: written *Jr.* after a son's name if it is the same as his father's 2 of more recent position or lower status /a *junior* partner/ 3 of juniors —*n.* 1 one who is younger, of lower rank, etc. 2 a student in the next-to-last year, as of college

junior college a school offering courses two years beyond high school

junior high school a school usually including grades 7, 8, and 9

ju·ni·per (jo͞o′ni pər) *n.* ⟦L *juniperus*⟧ a small evergreen shrub or tree with berrylike cones

junk[1] (juŋk) *n.* ⟦< ?⟧ 1 old metal, paper, rags, etc. that might be reusable in some way 2 [Colloq.] worthless stuff; trash 3 [Slang] heroin —*vt.* [Colloq.] to scrap —**junk′y, -i·er, -i·est,** *adj.*

JUNK

junk[2] (juŋk) *n.* ⟦< Malay *adjong*⟧ a Chinese or Japanese flat-bottomed ship

junk bond [Colloq.] a speculative BOND (*n.* 6), often issued to finance the takeover of a corporation

junk·er (juŋ′kər) *n.* [Slang] an old, dilapidated car or truck

Jun·ker (yooŋ′kər) *n.* ⟦Ger⟧ [Historical] a Prussian of the militaristic landowning class

jun·ket (juŋk′it) *n.* ⟦ME *joncate,* cream cheese⟧ 1 milk sweetened, flavored, and thickened into curd 2 a picnic 3 an excursion, esp. one by an official at public expense —*vi.* to go on a junket —**jun′ket·eer′** (-i tir′) or **jun′ket·er** *n.*

junk food snack food with chemical additives and little food value

junk·ie or **junk·y** (juŋk′ē) *n., pl.* **-ies** ⟦< JUNK[1], *n.* 3⟧ [Slang] 1 a narcotics addict 2 one who is addicted to a specified activity, food, etc. /a TV *junkie*/

Ju·no (jo͞o′nō) *Rom. Myth.* the wife of Jupiter and queen of the gods

jun·ta (hoon′tə, jun′-) *n.* ⟦Sp < L *jungere,* join⟧ a group of political intriguers, esp. military men, in power after a coup d'état Also **jun·to** (jun′tō), *pl.* **-tos**

Ju·pi·ter (jo͞o′pit ər) 1 the chief Roman god 2 the largest planet of the solar system: see PLANET

Ju·ras·sic (jo͞o ras′ik) *adj.* ⟦< Fr, after *Jura* Mountains, between France and Switzerland⟧ of the geologic period characterized by the dominance of dinosaurs

ju·rid·i·cal (jo͞o rid′i kəl, joo-) *adj.* ⟦< L *jus,* law + *dicere,* declare⟧ of judicial proceedings or law

ju·ris·dic·tion (joor′is dik′shən) *n.* ⟦see prec.⟧ 1 legal authority 2 authority in general —**ju′ris·dic′tion·al** *adj.*

ju·ris·pru·dence (joor′is pro͞od′′ns) *n.* ⟦< L *jus,* law + *prudentia,* a foreseeing⟧ 1 the science or philosophy of law 2 a division of law

ju·rist (joor′ist) *n.* ⟦< L *jus,* law⟧ an expert in law or writer on law

ju·ror (joor′ər) *n.* a member of a jury

ju·ry (joor′ē) *n., pl.* **-ries** ⟦L *jurare,* to swear⟧ 1 a group of people sworn to hear evidence in a law case and to give a decision 2 a committee that decides winners in a contest

just (just) *adj.* ⟦< L *jus,* law⟧ 1 right or fair /a *just* decision/ 2 righteous /a *just* man/ 3 deserved /*just* praise/ 4 lawful 5 proper 6 correct or true 7 accurate; exact —*adv.* 1 exactly /*just* one o'clock/ 2 nearly 3 only /*just* a taste/ 4 barely /*just* missed him/ 5 a very short time ago /she's *just* left/ 6 immediately /*just* east of here/ 7 [Colloq.] really /*just* beautiful/ —**just the same** [Colloq.] nevertheless —**just′ly** *adv.* —**just′ness** *n.*

jus·tice (jus′tis) *n.* 1 a being righteous 2 fairness 3 rightfulness 4 reward or penalty as deserved 5 the use of authority to uphold what is just 6 the administration of law 7 *a)* JUDGE (*n.* 1) *b)* JUSTICE OF THE PEACE —**do justice to** to treat fairly

justice of the peace a local magistrate who decides minor cases, performs marriages, etc.

jus·ti·fy (jus′tə fī′) *vt.* **-fied′, -fy′ing** ⟦< L *justus,* just + *facere,* to do⟧ 1 to show to be just, right, etc. 2 *Theol.* to free from blame or guilt 3 to supply grounds for —**jus′ti·fi′a·ble** *adj.* —**jus′ti·fi·ca′tion** (-fi kā′shən) *n.*

Jus·tin·i·an I (jus tin′ē ən) A.D. 483-565; ruler of Byzantine Empire (527-565): codified Roman law

jut (jut) *vi., vt.* **jut′ted, jut′ting** ⟦prob. var. of JET[1]⟧ to stick out; project —*n.* a part that juts

jute (jo͞ot) *n.* ⟦< Sans *jūṭa,* matted hair⟧ 1 a strong fiber used for making burlap, rope, etc. 2 a S Asian plant yielding this fiber

ju·ve·nile (jo͞o′və nīl′, -nəl) *adj.* ⟦< L *juvenis,* young⟧ 1 young; immature 2 of or for young persons —*n.* 1 a young person 2 an actor who plays youthful roles 3 a book for children

juvenile delinquency antisocial or illegal behavior by minors, usually 18 or younger —**juvenile delinquent**

jux·ta·pose (juks′tə pōz′, juks′tə pōz′) *vt.* **-posed′, -pos′ing** ⟦< Fr < L *juxta,* beside + POSE⟧ to put side by side —**jux′ta·po·si′tion** *n.*

K

k or **K** (kā) ***n.***, *pl.* **k's, K's** the eleventh letter of the English alphabet

K *symbol for:* **1** *Baseball* strikeout **2** ⟦ModL *kalium*⟧ *Chem.* potassium **3** *Electronics* the number 1,024, or 2^{10}

K *abbrev.* **1** karat (carat) **2** kilometer **3** kindergarten Also, for 1 & 2, **k**

kad·dish (käd′ish) ***n.*** ⟦Aram *kadish,* lit., holy⟧ *Judaism* a hymn in praise of God, recited at the daily service or as a mourner's prayer

kaf·fee·klatsch (kä′fā kläch′, kô′fē klach′) ***n.*** ⟦Ger < *kaffee,* coffee + *klatsch,* gossip⟧ [*also* **K-**] an informal gathering to drink coffee and chat

Kai·ser (kī′zər) ***n.*** ⟦ME *caiser,* emperor < L *Caesar*⟧ the title of the former rulers of Austria and Germany

kale (kāl) ***n.*** ⟦var. of COLE⟧ a hardy cabbage with spreading leaves

ka·lei·do·scope (kə lī′də skōp′) ***n.*** ⟦< Gr *kalos,* beautiful + *eidos,* form + -SCOPE⟧ **1** a small tube containing bits of colored glass reflected by mirrors to form symmetrical patterns as the tube is rotated **2** anything that constantly changes —**ka·lei′do·scop′ic** (-skäp′ik) ***adj.***

ka·mi·ka·ze (kä′mə kä′zē) ***adj.*** ⟦Jpn, divine wind⟧ of a suicidal attack by a WWII Japanese airplane pilot

Kam·pu·che·a (kam′po͞o chē′ə) *a name used* (c. 1975-c. 1983) *for* CAMBODIA

kan·ga·roo (kaŋ′gə ro͞o′) ***n.*** ⟦< ?⟧ a leaping marsupial of Australia and nearby islands, with short forelegs and strong, large hind legs

kangaroo court [Colloq.] a mock court illegally passing and executing judgment, as among frontiersmen

Kan·sas (kan′zəs) Middle Western State of the U.S.: 82,264 sq. mi.; pop. 2,363,000; cap. Topeka: abbrev. **Kans.** —**Kan′san** ***adj.***, ***n.***

Kansas City **1** city in W Mo., on the Missouri River: pop. 448,000 **2** city opposite this, in NE Kans.: pop. 161,000

Kant (känt), **Im·man·u·el** (i man′yo͞o el′) 1724-1804; Ger. philosopher

ka·o·lin (kā′ə lin) ***n.*** ⟦Fr < Chin name of hill where found⟧ a white clay used in porcelain, etc.

ka·pok (kā′päk′) ***n.*** ⟦Malay⟧ the silky fibers around the seeds of certain tropical trees, used for stuffing mattresses, etc.

kap·pa (kap′ə) ***n.*** the tenth letter of the Greek alphabet (K, κ)

ka·put (kə po͝ot′, -po͞ot′) ***adj.*** ⟦Ger *kaputt*⟧ [Slang] ruined, destroyed, etc.

Ka·ra·chi (kə rä′chē) seaport in S Pakistan: former capital: pop. 5,103,000

kar·a·kul (kar′ə kul′, -kəl) ***n.*** ⟦ult. < Turkic *qara köl,* dark lake⟧ **1** a sheep native to central Asia **2** the curly black fur from the fleece of its lambs: usually sp. *caracul*

kar·at (kar′ət) ***n.*** ⟦var. of CARAT⟧ one 24th part (of pure gold)

ka·ra·te (kə rät′ē) ***n.*** ⟦Jpn⟧ a Japanese system of self-defense by sharp, quick blows with the hands and feet

kar·ma (kär′mə) ***n.*** ⟦Sans, act⟧ **1** *Buddhism, Hinduism* the totality of one's acts in each state of one's existence **2** loosely, fate

kart (kärt) ***n.*** ⟦< CART⟧ a small, flat, motorized vehicle, used in racing

ka·ty·did (kāt′ē did′) ***n.*** ⟦echoic of its shrill sound⟧ a large, green tree insect resembling the grasshopper

kay·ak (kī′ak′) ***n.*** ⟦Esk⟧ an Eskimo canoe made of skins completely covering a wooden frame except for a small opening for the paddler

kay·o (kā′ō′) ***vt.*** **-oed′, -o′ing** ⟦< KO⟧ [Slang] *Boxing* to knock out —***n.*** [Slang] *Boxing* a knockout

ka·zoo (kə zo͞o′) ***n.*** ⟦echoic⟧ a toy musical instrument consisting of a small tube with a paper-covered hole: it makes buzzing tones when hummed into

KB kilobyte(s)

kc kilocycle(s)

Keats (kēts), **John** 1795-1821; Eng. poet

ke·bab or **ke·bob** (kə bäb′) ***n.*** ⟦Ar *kabāb*⟧ any of the small pieces of marinated meat used in making shish kebab

keel (kēl) ***n.*** ⟦< ON *kjǫlr*⟧ the chief timber or piece extending along the length of the bottom of a boat or ship —**keel over** **1** to capsize **2** to fall over suddenly —**on an even keel** in an upright, level position

keen[1] (kēn) ***adj.*** ⟦OE *cene,* wise⟧ **1** having a sharp edge or point /a *keen* knife/ **2** cutting; piercing /a *keen* wind/ **3** very perceptive /*keen* eyes/ **4** shrewd **5** eager **6** strongly felt; intense —**keen′ly** ***adv.*** —**keen′ness** ***n.***

keen[2] (kēn) ***n.*** ⟦< Ir *caoinim,* I wail⟧ [Irish] a wailing for the dead —***vt.***, ***vi.*** [Irish] to lament or wail for (the dead)

keep (kēp) ***vt.*** **kept, keep′ing** ⟦OE *cœpan,* behold⟧ **1** to celebrate; observe /to *keep* the Sabbath/ **2** to fulfill (a promise, etc.) **3** to protect; guard; take care of; tend **4** to preserve **5** to provide for; support **6** to make regular entries in /to *keep* books/ **7** to maintain in a specified state, position, etc. /to *keep* prices down/ **8** to hold for the future; retain **9** to hold and not let go; detain, withhold, restrain, etc. **10** to stay in or on (a course, place, etc.) —***vi.*** **1** to stay in a specified state, position, etc. **2** to continue; go on **3** to refrain /to *keep* from eating/ **4** to stay fresh; not spoil —***n.*** **1** care or custody **2** food and shelter; support **3** the inner stronghold of a castle —**for keeps** [Colloq.] **1** with the winner keeping what he wins **2** permanently —**keep to oneself** **1** to avoid others **2** to refrain from telling —**keep up** **1** to maintain in good condition **2** to continue **3** to maintain the pace **4** to remain informed about: with *on* or *with*

keep′er *n.* one that keeps; specif., *a)* a guard *b)* a guardian *c)* a custodian

keep′ing *n.* **1** observance (of a rule, etc.) **2** care; charge —**in keeping with** in conformity or accord with

keep′sake′ *n.* something kept, or to be kept, in memory of the giver

keg (keg) *n.* ⟦< ON *kaggi,* keg⟧ **1** a small barrel **2** a unit of weight for nails, equal to 100 lb.

kelp (kelp) *n.* ⟦ME *culp*⟧ a large, coarse, brown seaweed, rich in iodine

Kelt (kelt) *n. var. of* CELT

Kel·vin (kel′vin) *adj.* ⟦after 1st Baron *Kelvin,* 19th-c. Brit physicist⟧ designating a scale of temperature measured from absolute zero (-273.15°C)

ken (ken) *vt.* **kenned, ken′ning** ⟦OE *cennan,* cause to know⟧ [Scot.] to know —*n.* range of knowledge

Ken·ne·dy (ken′ə dē), **John Fitz·ger·ald** (fits jer′əld) 1917-63; 35th president of the U.S. (1961-63): assassinated

ken·nel (ken′əl) *n.* ⟦< L *canis,* dog⟧ **1** a doghouse **2** [*often pl.*] a place where dogs are bred or kept —*vt.* **-neled** or **-nelled, -nel·ing** or **-nel·ling** to keep in a kennel

Ken·tuck·y (kən tuk′ē) east central State of the U.S.: 40,395 sq. mi.; pop. 3,661,000; cap. Frankfort —**Ken·tuck′i·an** *adj., n.*

Ken·ya (ken′yə, kēn′-) country on the E coast of Africa: 224,960 sq. mi.; pop. 21,044,000

kept (kept) *vt., vi. pt. & pp. of* KEEP —*adj.* maintained as a mistress [*a kept* woman]

ker·a·tin (ker′ə tin) *n.* ⟦< Gr *keras,* horn⟧ a tough, fibrous protein, the basic substance of hair, nails, etc.

kerb (kurb) *n. Brit. sp. of* CURB (*n.* 3)

ker·chief (kur′chif) *n.* ⟦< OFr *covrir,* to cover + *chef,* head⟧ **1** a piece of cloth worn over the head or around the neck **2** a handkerchief

ker·nel (kur′nəl) *n.* ⟦< OE *cyrnel*⟧ **1** a grain or seed, as of corn **2** the inner, softer part of a nut, etc. **3** the central, most important part; essence

ker·o·sene (ker′ə sēn′) *n.* ⟦Gr *kēros,* wax⟧ a thin oil distilled from petroleum, used as a fuel, solvent, etc. Also **kerosine**

kes·trel (kes′trəl) *n.* ⟦echoic of its cry⟧ a small European falcon

ketch (kech) *n.* ⟦ME *cache*⟧ a fore-and-aft rigged sailing vessel

ketch·up (kech′əp) *n.* ⟦? Malay *kēchap,* sauce⟧ a sauce for meat, fish, etc.; esp., a thick sauce (**tomato ketchup**) of tomatoes, onions, spices, etc.

ket·tle (ket″l) *n.* ⟦< L *catinus,* container for food⟧ **1** a metal container for boiling or cooking things **2** a teakettle

ket′tle·drum′ *n.* a hemispheric percussion instrument of copper with a parchment top that can be tightened or loosened to change the pitch

KETTLEDRUMS

Kev·lar (kev′lär′) *trademark for* a tough, light, synthetic fiber used in bulletproof vests, boat hulls, etc.

key[1] (kē) *n., pl.* **keys** ⟦OE *cæge*⟧ **1** a device for moving the bolt of a lock and thus locking or unlocking something **2** any somewhat similar device, as a lever pressed in operating a piano, typewriter, etc. **3** a thing that explains or solves something else, as a code, the legend of a map, etc. **4** a controlling person or thing **5** tone or style of expression **6** *Music* a system of related tones based on a keynote and forming a given scale —*adj.* controlling; important —*vt.* **keyed, key′ing 1** to furnish with a key **2** to regulate the tone or pitch of **3** to bring into harmony —**key in** to input (data) by means of a keyboard —**key up** to make nervous

key[2] (kē) *n., pl.* **keys** ⟦Sp *cayo*⟧ a reef or low island

key·board (kē′bôrd′) *n.* **1** the row or rows of keys of a piano, typewriter, computer terminal, etc. **2** an instrument with a keyboard —*vt., vi.* to write (text) or input (data) by means of a keyboard —**key′board′er** *n.*

key′hole′ *n.* an opening (in a lock) into which a key is inserted

key′note′ *n.* **1** the lowest, basic note or tone of a musical scale **2** the basic idea or ruling principle —*vt.* **-not′ed, -not′ing 1** to give the keynote of **2** to give the keynote speech at —**key′not′er** *n.*

keynote speech (or **address**) a speech, as at a convention, setting forth the main line of policy

key punch a machine with a keyboard for recording data by punching holes in cards for use in data processing

key′stone′ *n.* **1** the central, topmost stone of an arch **2** an essential part

key′stroke′ *n.* any of the strokes made in operating a keyboard

Key West island off S Fla., in the Gulf of Mexico

kg kilogram(s)

kha·ki (kak′ē, kä′kē) *adj.* ⟦< Pers *khāk,* dust⟧ **1** dull yellowish-brown **2** made of khaki (cloth) —*n., pl.* **-kis 1** a dull yellowish brown **2** strong, twilled cloth of this color **3** [*often pl.*] a khaki uniform or pants

khan (kän, kan) *n.* ⟦< Mongolian *qan,* lord⟧ **1** a title of Tatar or Mongol rulers in the Middle Ages **2** a title of various dignitaries in Iran, Afghanistan, etc.

Khar·kov (kär′kôf′) city in NE Ukrainian S.S.R.: pop. 1,554,000

Khar·toum (kär to͞om′) capital of Sudan, on the Nile: pop. 476,000

kHz or **khz** kilohertz

kib·butz (ki bo͞ots′, -bo͝ots′) *n., pl.* **kib·but·zim** (kē′bo͞o tsēm′) ⟦ModHeb⟧ an Israeli collective settlement, esp. a collective farm

kib·itz·er (kib′its ər) *n.* ⟦Yidd < Ger *kiebitz*⟧ [Colloq.] **1** an onlooker at a card game, etc., esp. one who volunteers advice **2** a giver of unwanted advice or meddler in others' affairs —**kib′itz** *vi.*

ki·bosh (kī′bäsh′, ki bäsh′) *n.* ⟦< ?⟧ end: now usually in **put the kibosh on,** to check, squelch, etc.

kick (kik) *vi.* ⟦ME *kiken*⟧ **1** to strike out with the foot **2** to recoil, as a gun **3** [Colloq.] to complain **4** *Football* to kick the ball —*vt.* **1** to strike with the foot **2** to drive, force, etc., as by kicking **3** to score (a goal, etc.) by kicking **4** [Slang] to get rid of (a habit) **—*n.*** **1** an act or method of kicking **2** a sudden recoil **3** a complaint **4** [Colloq.] an intoxicating effect **5** [*often pl.*] [Colloq.] pleasure **—kick in** [Slang] to pay (one's share) **—kick over** to start up, as an automobile engine **—kick′er *n.***

kick′back′ *n.* [Slang] **1** a giving back of part of money received as payment **2** the money so returned

kick′off′ *n.* **1** *Football* a kick that puts the ball into play **2** a beginning, as of a campaign

kick′stand′ *n.* a pivoted metal bar that can be kicked down to support a bicycle, etc. in an upright position

kick·y (kik′ē) ***adj.*** **-i·er, -i·est** [Slang] **1** fashionable **2** exciting

kid (kid) ***n.*** ⟦ME *kide*⟧ **1** a young goat **2** leather from the skin of young goats: also **kid′skin′** **3** [Colloq.] a child **—*vt., vi.* kid′ded, kid′ding** [Colloq.] to tease or fool playfully

kid′die or **kid′dy** (-ē) ***n.,*** *pl.* **-dies** ⟦dim. of prec., *n.* 3⟧ [Colloq.] a child

kid·nap (kid′nap′) ***vt.*** **-napped′** or **-naped′, -nap′ping** or **-nap′ing** ⟦KID, *n.* 3 + dial. *nap,* to snatch⟧ to seize and hold (a person) by force or fraud, as for ransom **—kid′nap′per** or **kid′nap′er *n.***

kid·ney (kid′nē) ***n.,*** *pl.* **-neys** ⟦< ?⟧ **1** either of a pair of glandular organs that separate waste products from the blood and excrete them as urine **2** an animal's kidney, used as food **3** *a*) disposition *b*) class; kind

kidney bean the kidney-shaped seed of the common garden bean

kidney stone a hard mineral deposit sometimes formed in the kidney

kiel·ba·sa (kēl bä′sə, kil-) ***n.,*** *pl.* **-si** (-sē) or **-sas** ⟦Pol⟧ a Polish smoked sausage

Ki·ev (kē ev′) capital of the Ukrainian S.S.R.: pop. 2,448,000

kill (kil) ***vt.*** ⟦< ? OE *cwellan*⟧ **1** to cause the death of; slay **2** to destroy; put an end to **3** to defeat or veto (legislation) **4** to spend (time) on trivial matters **5** to turn off (an engine, etc.) **6** to stop publication of **—*n.*** **1** the act of killing **2** an animal or animals killed **—kill′er *n.***

killer whale a large dolphin that hunts in packs and preys on large fish, seals, etc.

kill′ing ***adj.*** **1** causing death; deadly **2** exhausting; fatiguing **—*n.*** **1** slaughter; murder **2** [Colloq.] a sudden great profit

kill′joy′ *n.* one who destroys or lessens other people's enjoyment Also **kill-joy**

kiln (kil, kiln) ***n.*** ⟦< L *culina,* cookstove⟧ a furnace or oven for drying, burning, or baking bricks, pottery, etc.

ki·lo (kē′lō, kil′ō) ***n.,*** *pl.* **-los** ⟦Fr⟧ **1** KILOGRAM **2** KILOMETER

kilo- ⟦< Gr *chilioi*⟧ *combining form* one thousand

kil·o·byte (kil′ō bīt′, kil′ə-) ***n.*** 1,024 bytes, or, loosely, 1,000 bytes

kil′o·cy′cle (-sī′kəl) ***n.*** *old term for* KILOHERTZ

kil′o·gram′ (-gram′) ***n.*** a metric unit of weight equal to 1,000 grams

kil′o·hertz′ (-herts′, -hurts′) ***n.,*** *pl.* **-hertz′** 1,000 hertz

kil·o·me·ter (kil′ə mēt′ər, kə läm′ət ər) ***n.*** a metric unit of linear measure equal to 1,000 meters

kil·o·ton (kil′ō tun′, kil′ə-) ***n.*** the explosive force of 1,000 tons of TNT

kil′o·watt′ (-wät′) ***n.*** a unit of electrical power, equal to 1,000 watts

kilt (kilt) ***n.*** ⟦prob. < ON⟧ a knee-length, pleated tartan skirt worn sometimes by men of the Scottish Highlands

kil·ter (kil′tər) ***n.*** ⟦< ?⟧ [Colloq.] good condition; proper order: now chiefly in **out of kilter**

ki·mo·no (kə mō′nə) ***n.,*** *pl.* **-nos** ⟦Jpn⟧ **1** a robe with wide sleeves and a sash, part of the traditional Japanese costume **2** a woman's dressing gown

kin (kin) ***n.*** ⟦OE *cynn*⟧ relatives; family

-kin (kin) ⟦< MDu *-ken*⟧ *suffix* little [*lambkin*]

kind (kīnd) ***n.*** ⟦OE *cynd*⟧ **1** a natural group or division **2** essential character **3** sort; variety; class **—*adj.*** sympathetic, gentle, benevolent, etc. **—in kind** in the same way **—kind of** [Colloq.] somewhat; rather **—of a kind** alike

kin·der·gar·ten (kin′dər gärt′'n) ***n.*** ⟦Ger < *kinder,* child + *garten,* garden⟧ a school or class for young children, usually four to six years old, that develops basic skills and social behavior by games, handicraft, etc. **—kin′der·gart′ner** or **kin′der·gar′ten·er** (-gärt′nər) ***n.***

kind′heart′ed *adj.* kind

kin·dle (kin′dəl) ***vt.*** **-dled, -dling** ⟦< ON *kynda*⟧ **1** to set on fire; ignite **2** to excite (interest, feelings, etc.) **—*vi.*** **1** to catch fire **2** to become aroused or excited

kin·dling (kind′liŋ) ***n.*** material, as bits of dry wood, for starting a fire

kind·ly (kīnd′lē) ***adj.*** **-li·er, -li·est** **1** kind; gracious **2** agreeable; pleasant **—*adv.*** **1** in a kind, gracious manner **2** agreeably; favorably **3** please [*kindly* shut the door] **—kind′li·ness *n.***

kind′ness *n.* **1** the state, quality, or habit of being kind **2** a kind act

kin·dred (kin′drid) ***n.*** ⟦< OE *cynn,* kin + *ræden,* condition⟧ relatives or family **—*adj.*** similar [*kindred* spirits]

kine (kīn) ***n.pl.*** ⟦< OE *cy,* cows⟧ [Archaic] cows; cattle

ki·net·ic (ki net′ik) ***adj.*** ⟦< Gr *kinein,* to move⟧ of or resulting from motion

kin·folk (kin′fōk′) ***n.pl.*** family; relatives Also **kin′folks′**

king (kiŋ) ***n.*** ⟦< OE *cyning*⟧ **1** a male ruler of a state **2** a man who is supreme in some field **3** something supreme in its class **4** a playing card with a picture of a king on it **5** *Chess* the chief piece **—*adj.*** chief (in size, importance, etc.) **—king′ly *adj.***

King (kiŋ), **Mar·tin Luther, Jr.** (märt′'n) 1929-68; U.S. clergyman & leader in the black civil rights movement: assassinated

king′dom (-dəm) ***n.*** **1** a country headed by a king or queen; monarchy **2** a realm; domain [the *kingdom* of poetry] **3** any of three divisions into which all natural objects have been classified (the animal, vegetable, and mineral kingdoms)

king'fish'er *n.* a short-tailed diving bird that feeds chiefly on fish
King James Version AUTHORIZED VERSION
King Lear (lir) the title character of a tragedy by Shakespeare
king'pin' *n.* 1 the pin at the front of a triangle of bowling pins 2 the essential person or thing
king'-size' *adj.* larger than the regular kind Also **king'-sized'**
kink (kiŋk) *n.* ⟦< Scand⟧ 1 a short, sharp twist or curl in a rope, wire, hair, etc. 2 a painful cramp in the neck, back, etc. 3 a mental twist; eccentricity —*vi., vt.* to form or cause to form a kink or kinks —**kink'y, -i·er, -i·est,** *adj.*
kin·ship (kin'ship') *n.* 1 family relationship 2 close connection
kins·man (kinz'mən) *n., pl.* **-men** a relative; esp., a male relative —**kins'wom'an,** *pl.* **-wom'en,** *n.*
ki·osk (kē'äsk', kē äsk') *n.* ⟦< Pers *kūshk,* palace⟧ a small, open structure used as a newsstand, etc.
kip·per (kip'ər) *vt.* ⟦< ?⟧ to cure (herring, salmon, etc.) by salting and drying or smoking —*n.* a kippered herring, etc.
Kir·i·bati (kir'ə bas') country on a group of islands in the central Pacific, on the equator: 313 sq. mi.; pop. 63,000
kirk (kurk, kirk) *n.* [Scot. or North Eng.] a church
kis·met (kiz'met) *n.* ⟦< Ar *qasama,* to divide⟧ fate; destiny
kiss (kis) *vt., vi.* ⟦OE *cyssan*⟧ 1 to touch or caress with the lips as an act of affection, greeting, etc 2 to touch lightly or gently —*n.* 1 an act of kissing 2 a light, gentle touch 3 any of various candies —**kiss'a·ble** *adj.*
kit (kit) *n.* ⟦ME *kyt,* tub⟧ 1 *a)* personal equipment, esp. as packed for travel *b)* a set of tools *c)* equipment for some particular activity, etc. *d)* a set of parts to be assembled 2 a box, bag, etc. for carrying such parts, equipment, or tools —**the whole kit and caboodle** [Colloq.] the whole lot
kitch·en (kich'ən) *n.* ⟦ult. < L *coquere,* to cook⟧ a room or place for the preparation and cooking of food
Kitch·e·ner (kich'ə nər) city in SE Ontario, Canada: pop. 150,000
kitch'en·ette' or **kitch'en·et'** (-et') *n.* a small, compact kitchen
kitch'en·ware' (-wer') *n.* kitchen utensils
kite (kīt) *n.* ⟦< OE *cyta*⟧ 1 any of several long-winged birds of prey 2 a light, wooden frame covered with paper or cloth, to be flown in the wind at the end of a string
kith (kith) *n.* ⟦< OE *cyth*⟧ friends: now only in **kith and kin,** friends and relatives; also, relatives, or kin
kitsch (kich) *n.* ⟦Ger, gaudy trash⟧ pretentious but shallow art or writing —**kitsch'y** *adj.*
kit·ten (kit''n) *n.* ⟦< OFr dim. of *chat,* cat⟧ a young cat —**kit'ten·ish** *adj.*
kit·ty[1] (kit'ē) *n., pl.* **-ties** 1 a kitten 2 *a pet name for* a cat
kit·ty[2] (kit'ē) *n., pl.* **-ties** ⟦prob. < KIT⟧ 1 the stakes in a poker game 2 money pooled for some purpose
kit·ty-cor·nered (kit'ē kôr'nərd) *adj., adv.* CATER-CORNERED Also **kit'ty-cor'ner**
ki·wi (kē'wē) *n., pl.* **-wis** ⟦echoic of its cry⟧ a flightless bird of New Zealand
KKK Ku Klux Klan
Klee·nex (klē'neks') *trademark for* soft tissue paper used as a handkerchief, etc. —*n.* [*occas.* **k-**] a piece of such paper
klep·to·ma·ni·a (klep'tō mā'nē ə) *n.* ⟦< Gr *kleptēs,* thief + MANIA⟧ an abnormal, persistent impulse to steal —**klep'to·ma'ni·ac'** *n., adj.*
klieg light (klēg) ⟦after A. & J. *Kliegl,* who developed it in 1911⟧ a very bright arc light used on motion picture sets
Klon·dike (klän'dīk') gold-mining region in W Yukon Territory, Canada
klutz (kluts) *n.* ⟦< Yidd *klots,* lit., wooden block⟧ [Slang] a clumsy or stupid person
km kilometer(s)
knack (nak) *n.* ⟦ME *knak,* sharp blow⟧ 1 a clever expedient 2 ability to do something easily
knack·wurst (näk'wurst') *n.* ⟦Ger < *knacken,* to burst + *wurst,* sausage⟧ a thick, highly seasoned sausage
knap·sack (nap'sak') *n.* ⟦< Du *knappen,* eat + *zak,* a sack⟧ a leather or canvas bag for carrying equipment or supplies on the back
knave (nāv) *n.* ⟦< OE *cnafa,* boy⟧ 1 a dishonest, deceitful person; rogue 2 JACK (*n.* 3) —**knav'ish** *adj.*
knav·er·y (nāv'ər ē) *n., pl.* **-ies** rascality; dishonesty
knead (nēd) *vt.* ⟦< OE *cnedan*⟧ 1 to work (dough, clay, etc.) into a pliable mass by pressing and squeezing 2 to massage —**knead'er** *n.*
knee (nē) *n.* ⟦< OE *cneow*⟧ 1 the joint between the thigh and the lower leg 2 anything shaped like a bent knee —*vt.* **kneed, knee'ing** to hit or touch with the knee
knee'cap' *n.* a movable bone at the front of the human knee
knee'-deep' *adj.* 1 up to the knees 2 very much involved
knee'-jerk' *adj.* ⟦< the reflex when the knee is tapped⟧ [Colloq.] characterized by or reacting with an automatic, predictable response
kneel (nēl) *vi.* **knelt** or **kneeled, kneel'ing** ⟦< OE *cneow,* knee⟧ to bend or rest on one's knee or knees
knell (nel) *vi.* ⟦< OE *cnyllan*⟧ 1 to ring slowly; toll 2 to sound ominously —*vt.* to call or announce as by a knell —*n.* 1 the sound of a bell rung slowly, as at a funeral 2 an omen of death, failure, etc.
knelt (nelt) *vi. alt. pt. and pp. of* KNEEL
knew (no͞o, nyo͞o) *vt., vi. pt. of* KNOW
knick·ers (nik'ərz) *n.pl.* ⟦after D. *Knickerbocker,* fictitious Du author of W. Irving's *History of New York*⟧ loose breeches gathered just below the knees: also **knick'er·bock'ers** (-ər bäk'ərz)
knick·knack (nik'nak') *n.* ⟦< KNACK⟧ a small ornamental article
knife (nīf) *n., pl.* **knives** ⟦< OE *cnif*⟧ 1 a cutting instrument with a sharp-edged blade set in a handle 2 a cutting blade, as in a machine —*vt.* **knifed, knif'ing** 1 to cut or stab with a knife 2 [Colloq.] to injure or

defeat by treachery **—under the knife** [Colloq.] undergoing surgery

knight (nīt) ***n.*** ⟦< OE *cniht,* boy⟧ **1** in medieval times, a man formally raised to special military rank and pledged to chivalrous conduct **2** in Great Britain, a man who for some achievement is given honorary rank entitling him to use *Sir* before his given name **3** a chessman shaped like a horse's head **—*vt.*** to make (a man) a knight

knight'-er'rant (-er'ənt) ***n.,*** *pl.* **knights'-er'rant 1** a medieval knight wandering in search of adventure **2** a chivalrous or quixotic person

knight'hood' (-hood') ***n.* 1** the rank, status, or vocation of a knight **2** chivalry **3** knights collectively

knight'ly ***adj.*** of or like a knight; chivalrous, brave, etc.

knit (nit) ***vt., vi.*** **knit'ted** or **knit, knit'ting** ⟦< OE *cnotta,* a knot⟧ **1** to make (a fabric) by looping yarn or thread together with special needles **2** to join or grow together closely and firmly, as a broken bone **3** to draw or become drawn together in wrinkles, as the brows **—knit'ter *n.***

knit'wear' (-wer') ***n.*** knitted clothing

knob (näb) ***n.*** ⟦ME *knobbe*⟧ **1** a rounded lump or protuberance **2** *a)* a handle, usually round, of a door, drawer, etc. *b)* a similar device used to control a radio, TV, etc.

knob'by ***adj.*** **-bi·er, -bi·est 1** covered with knobs **2** like a knob

knock (näk) ***vi.*** ⟦< OE *cnocian*⟧ **1** to strike a blow **2** to rap on a door **3** to bump; collide **4** to make a thumping noise: said of an engine, etc. **—*vt.* 1** to hit; strike **2** to make by hitting /to *knock* a hole in a wall/ **3** [Colloq.] to find fault with **—*n.* 1** a knocking **2** a hit; rap **3** a thumping noise in an engine, etc., as because of faulty combustion **4** [Colloq.] an adverse criticism **—knock about** (or **around**) [Colloq.] to wander about **—knock down 1** to hit so as to cause to fall **2** to take apart **3** to indicate the sale of (an article) at an auction **—knock off 1** [Colloq.] to stop working **2** [Colloq.] to deduct **3** [Slang] to kill, overcome, etc. **—knock out** to make unconscious or exhausted **—knock together** to make or compose hastily

knock'er ***n.*** one that knocks; esp., a small ring, knob, etc. on a door for use in knocking

knock'-kneed' (-nēd') ***adj.*** having legs that bend inward at the knees

knock'out' (-out') ***n.* 1** a knocking out or being knocked out **2** [Slang] a very attractive person or thing **3** *Boxing* a victory won when the opponent is unable to continue to fight, as by being knocked unconscious

knock·wurst (näk'wurst') ***n.*** *alt. sp. of* KNACKWURST

knoll (nōl) ***n.*** ⟦OE *cnoll*⟧ a hillock; mound

knot (nät) ***n.*** ⟦< OE *cnotta*⟧ **1** a lump in a thread, etc., formed by a tightened loop or tangle **2** a fastening made by tying together pieces of string, rope, etc. **3** an ornamental bow of ribbon, etc. **4** a small group or cluster **5** something that ties closely; esp., the bond of marriage **6** a problem; difficulty **7** a hard lump on a tree where a branch grows out, or a cross section of such a lump in a board **8** *Naut.* a unit of speed of one nautical mile (6,076.12 feet) an hour **—*vt., vi.*** **knot'ted, knot'ting 1** to make or form a knot (in) **2** to entangle or become entangled **—tie the knot** [Colloq.] to get married

knot'hole' ***n.*** a hole in a board, etc. where a knot has fallen out

knot'ty ***adj.*** **-ti·er, -ti·est** ⟦ME⟧ **1** full of knots /*knotty* pine/ **2** hard to solve; puzzling /a *knotty* problem/

know (nō) ***vt.*** **knew, known, know'ing** ⟦< OE *cnawan*⟧ **1** to be well informed about **2** to be aware of /to *know* that one is loved/ **3** to be acquainted with **4** to recognize or distinguish /to *know* right from wrong/ **—*vi.* 1** to have knowledge **2** to be sure or aware **—in the know** [Colloq.] having confidential information

know'-how' ***n.*** [Colloq.] technical skill

know'ing ***adj.* 1** having knowledge **2** shrewd; clever **3** implying shrewd or secret understanding /a *knowing* look/ **—know'ing·ly *adv.***

know'-it-all' ***n.*** [Colloq.] one who acts as if he knows much about nearly everything

knowl·edge (näl'ij) ***n.* 1** the fact or state of knowing **2** range of information or understanding **3** what is known; learning **4** the body of facts, etc. accumulated by mankind **—to (the best of) one's knowledge** as far as one knows

knowl'edge·a·ble (-ə bəl) ***adj.*** having knowledge or intelligence **—knowl'edge·a·bly *adv.***

known (nōn) ***vt., vi.*** *pp. of* KNOW **—*adj.* 1** familiar **2** recognized, proven, etc. /a *known* expert/

Knox·ville (näks'vil') city in E Tenn.: pop. 175,000

knuck·le (nuk'əl) ***n.*** ⟦< or akin to MDu & LowG *knokel,* dim. of *knoke,* bone⟧ **1** a joint of the finger; esp., the joint connecting a finger to the rest of the hand **2** the knee or hock joint of an animal, used as food **—knuckle down** to work hard **—knuckle under** to yield; give in

knuck'le·head' (-hed') ***n.*** [Colloq.] a stupid person

knurl (nurl) ***n.*** ⟦prob. < ME *knur,* a knot + GNARL⟧ **1** a knot, knob, etc. **2** any of a series of small beads or ridges, as along the edge of a coin **—*vt.*** to make knurls on

KO (kā'ō') ***vt.*** **KO'd, KO'ing** [Slang] *Boxing* to knock out **—*n.,*** *pl.* **KO's** [Slang] *Boxing* a knockout Also **K.O.** or **k.o.**

ko·a·la (kō ä'lə) ***n.*** ⟦< native name⟧ a tree-dwelling Australian marsupial with thick, gray fur

kohl·ra·bi (kōl'rä'bē) ***n.,*** *pl.* **-bies** ⟦< It *cavolo rapa*⟧ a vegetable related to the cabbage, with an edible, turniplike stem

KOHLRABI

ko·la (kō'lə) ***n.*** COLA

kook (ko͞ok) ***n.*** ⟦prob. < CUCKOO⟧ [Slang] a person regarded as silly, eccentric, etc. **—kook'y** or **kook'ie *adj.***

kook·a·bur·ra (kook'ə bur'

ə) *n.* ⟦< native name⟧ an Australian kingfisher with a harsh cry like loud laughter

ko·peck or **ko·pek** (kō′pek′) *n.* ⟦Russ < *kopye,* a lance⟧ the 100th part of the Russian ruble

Ko·ran (kə ran′, kôr′an′) ⟦< Ar *qur'ān,* book⟧ the sacred book of Islam

Ko·re·a (kə rē′ə) peninsula & country northeast of China: divided (1948) into *a)* **Korean People's Democratic Republic (North Korea)**: 46,768 sq. mi.; pop. 20,543,000 *b)* **Republic of Korea (South Korea)**: 38,030 sq. mi.; pop. 43,285,000 —**Ko·re′an** *adj., n.*

ko·sher (kō′shər) *adj.* ⟦< Heb *kāshēr,* proper⟧ *Judaism* clean or fit to eat according to the dietary laws

kow·tow (kou′tou′) *vi.* ⟦Chin *k'o-t'ou,* lit., bump head⟧ to show great deference, respect, etc. (*to*)

KP kitchen police, a detail to assist the cooks in an army kitchen

kraal (kräl) *n.* ⟦Afrik⟧ **1** a village of South African natives **2** an enclosure for cattle or sheep in South Africa

Krem·lin (krem′lin) *n.* ⟦< Russ *kryeml'*⟧ **1** the citadel of Moscow, traditionally housing many Soviet government offices **2** the Soviet government

Krem·lin·ol·o·gy (krem′lin äl′ə jē) *n.* the study of the policies, etc. of the Soviet Union —**Krem′lin·ol′o·gist** *n.*

Krish·na (krish′nə) *n.* a Hindu god, an incarnation of Vishnu

kro·na (krō′nə) *n., pl.* **-nor′** (-nôr′) ⟦ult. < L *corona,* crown⟧ the monetary unit of Sweden

kró·na (krō′nə) *n., pl.* **-nur** (-nər) ⟦see prec.⟧ the monetary unit of Iceland

kro·ne (krō′nə) *n., pl.* **-ner** (-nər) ⟦see KRONA⟧ the monetary unit of *a)* Denmark *b)* Norway

Kru·ger·rand (krōō′gə rand′) *n.* a gold coin of South Africa

KS Kansas

ku·chen (kōō′kən) *n.* ⟦Ger, cake⟧ a kind of cake made of yeast dough, often filled with raisins, nuts, etc.

ku·dos (kyōō′däs′, kōō′-) *n.* ⟦Gr *kydos*⟧ credit for an achievement; glory; fame: often wrongly taken to be the plural (*pron.* -dōz) of an assumed word "kudo"

kud·zu (kood′zōō′) *n.* ⟦Jpn⟧ a fast-growing, perennial vine with large, three-part leaves

Ku Klux Klan (kōō′ kluks′ klan′, kyōō′-) ⟦< Gr *kyklos,* circle⟧ a U.S. secret society that is anti-black, anti-semitic, anti-Catholic, etc., and uses terrorist methods

kum·quat (kum′kwät′) *n.* ⟦< Mandarin *chin-chü,* lit., golden orange⟧ a small, orange-colored, oval fruit with a sour pulp and a sweet rind

kung fu (kooŋ′ fōō′, gooŋ′-) ⟦< Chin⟧ a Chinese system of self-defense, like karate but with circular movements

Ku·wait (kōō wāt′) independent Arab state in E Arabia: 7,000 sq. mi.; pop. 1,771,000 —**Ku·wai′ti** (-wāt′ē) *adj., n.*

kW or **kw** kilowatt(s)

Kwang·chow (kwäŋ′chō′; *Chin* gwäŋ′jō′) *old form of* GUANGZHOU

KY or **Ky.** Kentucky

Kyo·to (kē′ōt′ō) city in S Honshu, Japan: pop. 1,464,000

L

l or **L** (el) *n., pl.* **l's, L's** the 12th letter of the English alphabet

L (el) *n., pl.* **L's** **1** an extension forming an L with the main structure **2** a Roman numeral for 50

l or **l.** **1** latitude **2** left **3** length **4** line **5** long

L or **L.** **1** Lake **2** large **3** Latin **4** left **5** length **6** longitude **7** ⟦L *libra,* pl. *librae*⟧ pound(s): now usually £

l liter(s)

la (lä) *n.* ⟦< L⟧ *Music* the sixth tone of the diatonic scale

LA **1** Los Angeles: also **L.A.** **2** Louisiana: also **La.**

lab (lab) *n.* [Colloq.] a laboratory

la·bel (lā′bəl) *n.* ⟦OFr, a rag⟧ **1** a card, paper, etc. marked and attached to an object to indicate its contents, owner, destination, etc. **2** a term of generalized classification —*vt.* **-beled** or **-belled, -bel·ing** or **-bel·ling** **1** to attach a label to **2** to classify as; call

la·bi·al (lā′bē əl) *adj.* ⟦< L *labium,* lip⟧ **1** of the lips **2** *Phonetics* articulated with one or both lips, as (f), (b), and (ü)

la′bi·um (-əm) *n., pl.* **-bi·a** (-ə) ⟦L, lip⟧ any one of the liplike folds of the vulva

la·bor (lā′bər) *n.* ⟦< L⟧ **1** physical or mental exertion; work **2** a specific task **3** all wage-earning workers **4** labor unions collectively **5** the process of childbirth —*vi.* **1** to work **2** to work hard **3** to move slowly and with difficulty **4** to suffer (*under* a false idea, etc.) **5** to be in childbirth —*vt.* to develop in too great detail /*to labor* a point/

lab·o·ra·to·ry (lab′ə rə tôr′ē, lab′rə-) *n., pl.* **-ries** ⟦see prec.⟧ a room, building, etc. for scientific work or research

Labor Day the first Monday in September, a legal holiday honoring labor

la·bored (lā′bərd) *adj.* made or done with great effort; strained

la′bor·er *n.* one who labors; esp., a wage-earning worker whose work is largely hard physical labor

la·bo·ri·ous (lə bôr′ē əs) *adj.* **1** involving

much hard work; difficult 2 hard-working 3 LABORED —**la·bo′ri·ous·ly** *adv.*

labor union an association of workers to promote and protect the welfare, rights, etc. of its members

la·bour (lā′bər) *n., vi., vt. Brit. sp. of* LABOR

Lab·ra·dor (lab′rə dôr′) 1 region along the Atlantic in NE Canada: the mainland part of Newfoundland 2 large peninsula between the Atlantic & Hudson Bay, containing this region & Quebec

Labrador retriever a retriever with a short, dense, black, yellow, or brown coat

la·bur·num (lə bur′nəm) *n.* ⟦< L⟧ a small tree or shrub of the pea family, with drooping yellow flowers

lab·y·rinth (lab′ə rinth′) *n.* ⟦< Gr *labyrinthos*⟧ a structure containing winding passages hard to follow without losing one's way; maze

lac (lak) *n.* ⟦< Sans *lākṣā*⟧ a resinous substance secreted on certain Asiatic trees by a certain kind of insect: source of shellac

lace (lās) *n.* ⟦< L *laqueus*, noose⟧ 1 a string, etc. used to draw together and fasten the parts of a shoe, corset, etc. 2 a fine netting of cotton, polyester, silk, etc., woven in ornamental designs —*vt.* **laced, lac′ing** 1 to fasten with a lace 2 to weave together; intertwine 3 to thrash; whip 4 to add a dash of alcoholic liquor to (a drink)

lac·er·ate (las′ər āt′) *vt.* **-at′ed, -at′ing** ⟦< L *lacer*, lacerated⟧ to tear jaggedly; mangle —**lac′er·a′tion** *n.*

lace′work′ *n.* lace, or any openwork decoration like lace

lach·ry·mal (lak′ri məl) *adj.* ⟦< L *lacrima*, TEAR²⟧ 1 of or producing tears 2 LACRIMAL (sense 1)

lach′ry·mose′ (-mōs′) *adj.* ⟦see prec.⟧ shedding, or causing to shed, tears; tearful or sad

lack (lak) *n.* ⟦< or akin to Medieval LowG *lak*⟧ 1 the fact or state of not having enough or not having any 2 the thing that is needed —*vi., vt.* to be deficient in or entirely without

lack·a·dai·si·cal (lak′ə dā′zi kəl) *adj.* ⟦< archaic *lackaday*, an exclamation of regret, etc.⟧ showing lack of interest or spirit; listless

lack·ey (lak′ē) *n., pl.* **-eys** ⟦< Sp *lacayo*⟧ 1 a male servant of low rank, usually in some sort of livery or uniform 2 a servile follower; toady

lack·lus·ter (lak′lus′tər) *adj.* lacking brightness; dull Also, chiefly Brit. sp., **lack′lus′tre**

la·con·ic (lə kän′ik) *adj.* ⟦< Gr *Lakōn*, a Spartan⟧ terse in expression; concise —**la·con′i·cal·ly** *adv.*

lac·quer (lak′ər) *n.* ⟦< Fr < Port *laca*, lac⟧ 1 a coating substance made of shellac, gum resins, etc. dissolved in ethyl alcohol or other solvent that evaporates rapidly 2 a resinous varnish obtained from certain Oriental trees 3 a wooden article coated with this —*vt.* to coat with lacquer

lac·ri·mal (lak′ri məl) *adj.* 1 of or near the glands that secrete tears 2 LACHRYMAL (sense 1)

la·crosse (lə krôs′) *n.* ⟦CdnFr, lit., the crutch⟧ a ballgame played by two teams using long-handled, pouched rackets

LACROSSE PLAYER

lac·ta·tion (lak tā′shən) *n.* ⟦< L *lac*, milk⟧ 1 the secretion of milk by a mammary gland 2 the period during which milk is secreted

lac·te·al (lak′tē əl) *adj.* ⟦< L *lac*, milk⟧ of or like milk; milky

lac·tic (lak′tik) *adj.* ⟦< L *lac*, milk⟧ of or obtained from milk

lactic acid a clear, syrupy acid formed when milk sours

lac·tose (lak′tōs′) *n.* ⟦< L *lac*, milk⟧ a sugar found in milk: used in foods

la·cu·na (lə kyōō′nə) *n., pl.* **-nas** or **-nae** (-nē) ⟦L, a ditch⟧ a blank space; esp., a missing portion in a text, etc.

lac·y (lās′ē) *adj.* **-i·er, -i·est** of or like lace —**lac′i·ness** *n.*

lad (lad) *n.* ⟦ME *ladde*⟧ a boy; youth

lad·der (lad′ər) *n.* ⟦OE *hlæder*⟧ 1 a framework consisting of two sidepieces connected by a series of rungs, for use in climbing up or down 2 any means of climbing

lad·die (lad′ē) *n.* [Chiefly Scot.] a lad

lade (lād) *vt., vi.* **lad′ed, lad′ed** or **lad′en, lad′ing** ⟦OE *hladan*⟧ 1 to load 2 to bail; ladle

lad′en *adj.* 1 loaded 2 burdened; afflicted

la-di-da (lä′dē dä′) *adj.* ⟦imitative⟧ [Colloq.] affectedly refined

lad′ing *n.* a load; cargo; freight

la·dle (lād′'l) *n.* ⟦OE *hlædel*⟧ a long-handled, cuplike spoon —*vt.* **-dled, -dling** to dip out with a ladle

la·dy (lād′ē) *n., pl.* **-dies** ⟦< OE *hlaf*, loaf + *dæge*, kneader⟧ 1 *a*) a woman of high social position *b*) a woman who is polite, refined, etc. 2 any woman: used to address a group 3 [L-] a British title given to women of certain ranks —*adj.* [Colloq.] female

la′dy·bug′ *n.* a small, roundish beetle with a spotted back Also **la′dy·bird′**

la′dy·fin′ger *n.* a small spongecake shaped somewhat like a finger

la′dy-in-wait′ing *n., pl.* **la′dies-in-wait′ing** a woman waiting upon a queen or princess

la′dy·like′ *adj.* like or suitable for a lady; refined; well-bred

la′dy·love′ *n.* a female sweetheart

la′dy·ship′ *n.* 1 the rank or position of a lady 2 [*usually* L-] a title used in speaking to or of a titled Lady

la′dy-slip′per *n.* an orchid with flowers somewhat like slippers Also **la′dy's-slip′per**

la·e·trile (lā′ə tril′) *n.* any of several compounds obtained from certain substances, as almond seeds, and claimed to be effective in treating cancer

La·fa·yette (lä′fē et′, -fā-), Marquis de 1757-1834; Fr. general: served (1777-81) in the American Revolutionary army

lag (lag) *vi.* **lagged, lag′ging** ⟦< ?⟧ 1 to fall behind or move slowly; loiter 2 to become less intense —*n.* 1 a falling behind 2 the amount of this

la·ger (beer) (lä'gər) ⟦Ger *lagerbier,* storehouse beer⟧ a beer that has been aged for several months

lag·gard (lag'ərd) ***n.*** ⟦< LAG + -ARD⟧ a slow person, esp. one who falls behind —***adj.*** slow; falling behind

la·gniappe or **la·gnappe** (lan yap', lan'yap') ***n.*** ⟦Creole < Fr & Sp⟧ **1** [Chiefly South] a small present given to a customer with a purchase **2** a gratuity

la·goon (lə go͞on') ***n.*** ⟦< L *lacuna,* pool⟧ **1** a shallow lake or pond, esp. one connected with a larger body of water **2** the water enclosed by a circular coral reef **3** shallow water separated from the sea by sand dunes

La·hore (lə hôr') city in NE Pakistan: pop. 2,922,000

laid (lād) ***vt., vi.*** *pt. & pp. of* LAY[1]

laid'-back' (-bak') ***adj.*** [Slang] relaxed, easygoing, etc.; not hurried

lain (lān) ***vi.*** *pp. of* LIE[1]

lair (ler) ***n.*** ⟦OE *leger*⟧ a resting place of a wild animal; den

lais·sez faire (les'ā fer') ⟦Fr, allow to do⟧ noninterference; specif., absence of government control over industry and business

la·i·ty (lā'i tē) ***n., pl.*** **-ties** ⟦< LAY[3]⟧ laymen collectively

lake (lāk) ***n.*** ⟦< L *lacus*⟧ **1** a large inland body of usually fresh water **2** a pool of oil or other liquid

Lake·wood (lāk'wood') city in N Colo.: suburb of Denver: pop. 113,000

lal·ly·gag (läl'ē gag') ***vi.*** **-gagged', -gag'ging** [Colloq.] LOLLYGAG

lam (lam) ***n.*** ⟦< ?⟧ [Slang] headlong flight —***vi.*** **lammed, lam'ming** [Slang] to flee; escape —**on the lam** [Slang] in flight, as from the police

la·ma (lä'mə) ***n.*** ⟦Tibetan *blama*⟧ a priest or monk in Lamaism

La·ma·ism (lä'mə iz'əm) ***n.*** a form of Buddhism in Tibet and Mongolia

la·ma·ser·y (lä'mə ser'ē) ***n., pl.*** **-ies** a monastery of lamas

La·maze (lə mäz') ***n.*** ⟦after F. *Lamaze,* 20th-c. Fr physician⟧ a training program in natural childbirth, involving the help of the father

lamb (lam) ***n.*** ⟦OE⟧ **1** a young sheep **2** its flesh, used as food **3** a gentle, innocent, or gullible person

lam·baste (lam bāst', -bast') ***vt.*** **-bast'ed, -bast'ing** ⟦< *lam,* to beat + *baste,* to flog⟧ [Colloq.] **1** to beat soundly **2** to scold severely

lamb·da (lam'də) ***n.*** the 11th letter of the Greek alphabet (Λ, λ)

lam·bent (lam'bənt) ***adj.*** ⟦< L *lambere,* to lick⟧ **1** playing lightly over a surface: said of a flame, etc. **2** glowing softly **3** light and graceful /*lambent* wit/ —**lam'ben·cy** ***n.***

lamb'kin ***n.*** a little lamb

lame (lām) ***adj.*** ⟦OE *lama*⟧ **1** crippled; esp., having an injury that makes one limp **2** stiff and painful **3** poor; ineffectual /a *lame* excuse/ —***vt.*** **lamed, lam'ing** to make lame —**lame'ly** ***adv.*** —**lame'ness** ***n.***

la·mé (la mā', lä-) ***n.*** ⟦< Fr *lame,* metal plate⟧ a cloth interwoven with metal threads, as of gold or silver

lame duck an elected official whose term ends after someone else has been elected to the office

la·mel·la (lə mel'ə) ***n., pl.*** **-lae** (-ē) or **-las** ⟦L⟧ a thin plate, scale, or layer

la·ment (lə ment') ***vi., vt.*** ⟦< L *lamentum,* a wailing⟧ to feel or express deep sorrow (for); mourn —***n.*** **1** a lamenting **2** an elegy, dirge, etc. mourning some loss or death —**lam·en·ta·ble** (lam'ən tə bəl, lə men'-) ***adj.*** —**lam·en·ta·tion** (lam'ən tā' shən) ***n.***

lam·i·na (lam'i nə) ***n., pl.*** **-nae'** (-nē') or **-nas** ⟦L⟧ a thin scale or layer, as of metal, tissue, etc.

lam·i·nate (lam'i nāt'; *for adj. usually,* -nit) ***vt.*** **-nat'ed, -nat'ing** ⟦see prec.⟧ **1** to cover with one or more thin layers **2** to make by building up in layers —***adj.*** LAMINATED —**lam'i·na'tion** ***n.***

lam'i·nat'ed (-nāt'id) ***adj.*** **1** built in thin sheets or layers **2** covered with a thin protective layer, as of clear plastic

lamp (lamp) ***n.*** ⟦< Gr *lampein,* to shine⟧ **1** a container with a wick for burning oil, etc. to produce light or heat **2** any device for producing light or heat, as an electric light bulb **3** a holder or base for such a device

lamp'black' ***n.*** fine soot used as a black pigment

lam·poon (lam po͞on') ***n.*** ⟦< Fr *lampons,* let us drink: used as a refrain⟧ a satirical writing attacking someone —***vt.*** to attack in a lampoon

lamp·post (lamp'pōst', lam'-) ***n.*** a post supporting a street lamp

lam·prey (lam'prē) ***n., pl.*** **-preys** ⟦< ML *lampreda*⟧ an eel-like fish with a jawless, sucking mouth

la·na·i (lə nä'ē, -nī') ***n.*** ⟦Haw⟧ a veranda or open-sided living room

lance (lans, läns) ***n.*** ⟦< L *lancea*⟧ **1** a long, wooden spear with a sharp metal head **2** *a*) LANCER *b*) LANCET **3** any instrument like a lance —***vt.*** **lanced, lanc'ing** **1** to pierce with a lance **2** to cut open with a lancet

Lan·ce·lot (lăn'sə lət, -lät') the most celebrated of the Knights of the Round Table

lanc·er (lans'ər) ***n.*** a cavalry soldier armed with a lance

lan·cet (lan'sit) ***n.*** ⟦< OFr dim. of *lance,* lance⟧ a small, pointed surgical knife, usually two-edged

land (land) ***n.*** ⟦OE⟧ **1** the solid part of the earth's surface **2** a country or nation **3** ground or soil **4** real estate —***vt.*** **1** to put on shore from a ship **2** to bring to a particular place /it *landed* him in jail/ **3** to set (an aircraft) down on land or water **4** to catch /to *land* a fish/ **5** [Colloq.] to get or secure /to *land* a job/ **6** [Colloq.] to deliver (a blow) —***vi.*** **1** to leave a ship and go on shore **2** to come to a port, etc.: said of a ship **3** to arrive at a specified place **4** to come to rest

land contract a contract in which a buyer makes payments over a specified period until the full price is paid, after which the seller transfers his interest to the buyer

land·ed (lan'did) ***adj.*** owning land /*landed* gentry/

land'fall' ***n.*** **1** a sighting of land from a ship at sea **2** the land sighted

land'fill' ***n.*** disposal of garbage, rubbish, etc. by burying it in the ground

land grant a grant of land by the government for a railroad, college, etc.

land'hold'er *n.* an owner of land —**land'hold'ing** *adj., n.*

land·ing (lan'diŋ) *n.* 1 the act of coming to shore 2 a place where a ship or boat is loaded or unloaded 3 a platform at the end of a flight of stairs 4 the act of alighting

landing gear the system of parts on an aircraft or spacecraft used for support or mobility on land or water

land'locked' *adj.* 1 surrounded by land, as a bay 2 cut off from the sea and confined to fresh water /*landlocked* salmon/

land'lord' *n.* 1 a person who leases land, houses, etc. to others 2 a man who keeps a rooming house, inn, etc. —**land'la'dy,** *pl.* **-dies,** *n.fem.*

land'lub'ber (-lub'ər) *n.* one who has had little experience at sea

land'mark' *n.* 1 an object that marks the boundary of a piece of land 2 any prominent feature of the landscape, distinguishing a locality 3 an important event or turning point

land'mass' *n.* a very large area of land; esp., a continent

land office a government office that handles the sales of public lands

land'-of'fice business [Colloq.] a booming business

land'scape' (-skāp') *n.* ⟦< Du *land*, land + *-schap*, -ship⟧ 1 a picture of natural, inland scenery 2 an expanse of natural scenery seen in one view —*vt.* **-scaped', -scap'ing** to make (a plot of ground) more attractive, as by adding lawns, bushes, etc. —**land'scap'er** *n.*

land'slide' *n.* 1 the sliding of a mass of earth or rocks down a slope 2 the mass sliding down 3 an overwhelming victory, esp. in an election

land'ward (-wərd) *adv., adj.* toward the land Also **land'wards** *adv.*

lane (lān) *n.* ⟦OE *lanu*⟧ 1 a narrow way, path, road, etc. 2 a path or route designated, for reasons of safety, for ships, aircraft, automobiles, etc.

lan·guage (laŋ'gwij) *n.* ⟦< L *lingua*, tongue⟧ 1 human speech or the written symbols for speech 2 *a*) any means of communicating *b*) a special set of symbols used in a computer 3 the speech of a particular nation, etc. /the French *language*/ 4 the particular style of verbal expression characteristic of a person, group, profession, etc.

lan·guid (laŋ'gwid) *adj.* ⟦< L *languere*, be weary⟧ 1 without vigor or vitality; weak 2 listless; indifferent 3 slow; dull —**lan'guid·ly** *adv.*

lan'guish (-gwish) *vi.* ⟦see prec.⟧ 1 to become weak; droop 2 to live under distressing conditions /to *languish* in poverty/ 3 to long; pine 4 to put on a wistful air

lan·guor (laŋ'gər) *n.* ⟦see LANGUID⟧ lack of vigor or vitality; weakness; listlessness —**lan'guor·ous** *adj.*

lank (laŋk) *adj.* ⟦OE *hlanc*⟧ 1 long and slender; lean 2 straight and limp: said of hair —**lank'ness** *n.*

lank·y (laŋk'ē) *adj.* **-i·er, -i·est** awkwardly tall and lean

lan·o·lin (lan'ə lin') *n.* ⟦< L *lana*, wool + *oleum*, oil⟧ a fatty substance obtained from wool and used in ointments, cosmetics, etc.

Lan·sing (lan'siŋ) capital of Mich., in the S part: pop. 130,000

lan·tern (lan'tərn) *n.* ⟦ult. < Gr *lampein*, to shine⟧ a transparent case for holding and shielding a light

lan'tern-jawed' *adj.* having long, thin jaws and sunken cheeks

lan·yard (lan'yərd) *n.* ⟦< OFr *lasne*, noose⟧ a short rope used on board ship for holding or fastening something

La·os (lä'ōs') country in the NW part of Indochina: 91,429 sq. mi.; pop. 3,679,000 —**La·o·tian** (lā ō'shən) *adj., n.*

lap[1] (lap) *n.* ⟦OE *læppa*⟧ 1 the front part from the waist to the knees of a sitting person 2 the part of the clothing covering this 3 that in which a person or thing is cared for 4 *a*) an overlapping *b*) a part that overlaps 5 one complete circuit of a race-track —*vt.* **lapped, lap'ping** 1 to fold (*over* or *on*) 2 to wrap; enfold 3 to overlap 4 to get a lap ahead of (an opponent) in a race —*vi.* 1 to overlap 2 to extend beyond something in space or time: with *over*

lap[2] (lap) *vi., vt.* **lapped, lap'ping** ⟦OE *lapian*⟧ 1 to drink (a liquid) by dipping it up with the tongue as a dog does 2 to strike gently with a light splash: said of waves —*n.* 1 a lapping 2 the sound of lapping —**lap up** to accept eagerly

La Paz (lə päz') city & seat of government of Bolivia: pop. 881,000

lap'board' *n.* a board placed on the lap for use as a table or desk

lap dog any pet dog small enough to be held in the lap

la·pel (lə pel') *n.* ⟦dim. of LAP[1]⟧ the front part of a coat folded back and forming a continuation of the collar

lap·i·dar·y (lap'ə der'ē) *n., pl.* **-dar'ies** ⟦< L *lapis*, a stone⟧ one who cuts and polishes precious stones

lap·in (lap'in) *n.* ⟦Fr, rabbit⟧ rabbit fur, often dyed to resemble other skins

lap·is laz·u·li (lap'is laz'yo͞o lī', -lazh'-; -lē') ⟦< L *lapis*, a stone + ML *lazulus*, azure⟧ an azure, opaque, semiprecious stone

Lap·land (lap'land') region of N Europe, including the N parts of Norway, Sweden, & Finland

Lapp (lap) *n.* ⟦Swed⟧ a member of a people living in Lapland Also **Lap'land'er**

lap·pet (lap'it) *n.* ⟦dim. of LAP[1]⟧ a loose flap or fold of a garment or head covering

lap robe a heavy blanket, fur covering, etc. laid over the lap for warmth

lapse (laps) *n.* ⟦< L *labi*, to slip⟧ 1 a small error 2 *a*) a moral slip *b*) a falling into a lower condition 3 a passing, as of time 4 the termination as of a privilege through failure to meet requirements —*vi.* **lapsed, laps'ing** 1 to fall into a specified state /he *lapsed* into silence/ 2 to backslide 3 to elapse 4 to come to an end; stop 5 to become void because of failure to meet requirements

lar·board (lär'bôrd') *n.* ⟦< OE *hladan*, lade + *bord*, side⟧ port; left

lar·ce·ny (lär′sə nē) ***n.***, *pl.* **-nies** ⟦ult. < L *latro,* robber⟧ the unlawful taking of another's property; theft —**lar′ce·nist** ***n.*** —**lar′ce·nous** ***adj.***

larch (lärch) ***n.*** ⟦< L *larix*⟧ **1** a tree of the pine family that sheds its needles annually **2** its tough wood

lard (lärd) ***n.*** ⟦< L *lardum*⟧ the fat of hogs, melted and clarified —***vt.*** **1** to put strips of fat pork, bacon, etc. on (meat, etc.) before cooking **2** to embellish /a talk *larded* with jokes/

lard′er ***n.*** **1** a place where food supplies are kept **2** food supplies

la·res and pe·na·tes (lā′rēz′ ənd pē nā′tēz) the household gods of the ancient Romans

large (lärj) ***adj.*** **larg′er, larg′est** ⟦< L *largus*⟧ **1** of great extent or amount; big, bulky, spacious, etc. **2** bigger than others of its kind **3** operating on a big scale /a *large* producer/ —***adv.*** in a large way /write *large*/ —**at large 1** free; not confined **2** fully; in detail **3** representing no particular district /a congressman *at large*/ —**large′ness** ***n.*** —**larg′ish** ***adj.***

large′heart′ed ***adj.*** generous; kindly

large intestine the relatively large section of the intestines of vertebrates, including the cecum, colon, and rectum

large′ly ***adv.*** **1** much; in great amounts **2** for the most part; mainly

large′-scale′ ***adj.*** **1** drawn to a large scale **2** of wide scope; extensive

lar·gess or **lar·gesse** (lär jes′, lär′jis) ***n.*** ⟦see LARGE⟧ **1** generous giving **2** a gift generously given

lar·go (lär′gō) ***adj., adv.*** ⟦It, slow⟧ *Musical Direction* slow and stately

lar·i·at (lar′ē ət) ***n.*** ⟦Sp *la reata,* the rope⟧ **1** a rope used for tethering grazing horses, etc. **2** LASSO

lark[1] (lärk) ***n.*** ⟦< OE *læwerce*⟧ any of a large family of chiefly Old World birds, esp. the skylark

lark[2] (lärk) ***vi.*** ⟦? < ON *leika*⟧ to play or frolic —***n.*** a frolic or spree

lark·spur (lärk′spur′) ***n.*** DELPHINIUM

lar·va (lär′və) ***n.***, *pl.* **-vae′** (-vē′) or **-vas** ⟦L, ghost⟧ the early form of any animal that changes structurally when it becomes an adult /the tadpole is the *larva* of the frog/ —**lar′val** ***adj.***

lar·yn·gi·tis (lar′in jīt′is) ***n.*** an inflammation of the larynx, often with a temporary loss of voice

lar·ynx (lar′iŋks) ***n.***, *pl.* **lar′ynx·es** (-iz′) or **la·ryn·ges** (lə rin′jēz′) ⟦< Gr⟧ the structure at the upper end of the trachea, containing the vocal cords

la·sa·gna (lə zän′yə) ***n.*** ⟦It⟧ a dish of wide noodles baked in layers with tomato sauce, ground meat, and cheese

las·civ·i·ous (lə siv′ē əs) ***adj.*** ⟦< L *lascivus,* wanton⟧ **1** characterized by or expressing lust **2** exciting lust

la·ser (lā′zər) ***n.*** ⟦*l(ight) a(mplification by) s(timulated) e(mission of) r(adiation)*⟧ a device that raises the energy state of a substance so that it emits light in an intense, narrow beam

laser disc (or **disk**) a videodisc for recording audio and video data to be read by a laser beam

lash[1] (lash) ***n.*** ⟦< ?⟧ **1** the flexible striking part of a whip **2** a stroke as with a whip **3** an eyelash —***vt.*** **1** to strike or drive as with a lash **2** to switch energetically /the cat *lashed* her tail/ **3** to censure or rebuke —***vi.*** to make strokes as with a whip —**lash out 1** to strike out violently **2** to speak angrily

lash[2] (lash) ***vt.*** ⟦see LACE⟧ to fasten or tie with a rope, etc.

lass (las) ***n.*** ⟦prob. < ON *lǫskr,* weak⟧ a young woman

las·sie (las′ē) ***n.*** [Scot.] a young woman

las·si·tude (las′i to͞od′) ***n.*** ⟦< L *lassus,* faint⟧ weariness; languor

las·so (las′ō′) ***n.***, *pl.* **-sos′** or **-soes′** ⟦< Sp < L *laqueus,* noose⟧ a rope with a sliding noose used to catch cattle, etc. —***vt.*** **-soed′, -so′ing** to catch with a lasso

last[1] (last) ***adj.*** **1** *alt. superl. of* LATE **2** being or coming after all others in place or time; final **3** only remaining **4** most recent /*last* month/ **5** least likely /the *last* person to suspect/ **6** conclusive /the *last* word/ —***adv.*** **1** after all others **2** most recently **3** finally —***n.*** the one coming last —**at (long) last** finally

last[2] (last) ***vi.*** ⟦OE *læstan*⟧ to remain in existence, use, etc.; endure —***vt.*** **1** to continue during **2** to be enough for

last[3] (last) ***n.*** ⟦< OE *last,* footstep⟧ a form shaped like the foot, used in making or repairing shoes

last hurrah a final attempt or appearance, as in politics

last′ing ***adj.*** that lasts a long time —**last′ing·ly** ***adv.***

Last Judgment *Theol.* the final judgment at the end of the world

last′ly ***adv.*** in conclusion; finally

last straw ⟦< the straw that broke the camel's back⟧ a final trouble that results in a defeat, loss of patience, etc.

Las Ve·gas (läs vā′gəs) city in SE Nev.: pop. 165,000

lat. latitude

latch (lach) ***n.*** ⟦< OE *læccan*⟧ a fastening for a door, gate, or window; esp., a bar that fits into a notch —***vt., vi.*** to fasten with a latch —**latch onto** [Colloq.] to get or obtain

late (lāt) ***adj.*** **lat′er** or **lat′ter, lat′est** or **last** ⟦OE *læt*⟧ **1** happening, coming, etc. after the usual or expected time, or at a time far advanced in a period /*late* to class, *late* Victorian/ **2** recent **3** having recently died —***adv.*** **lat′er, lat′est** or **last 1** after the expected time **2** at or until an advanced time of the day, year, etc. **3** toward the end of a period **4** recently —**of late** recently —**late′ness** ***n.***

late·ly (lāt′lē) ***adv.*** recently; not long ago

la·tent (lāt′′nt) ***adj.*** ⟦< L *latere,* lurk⟧ lying hidden and undeveloped in a person or thing —**la′ten·cy** ***n.***

lat·er·al (lat′ər əl) ***adj.*** ⟦< L *latus,* a side⟧ of, at, from, or toward the side; sideways —**lat′er·al·ly** ***adv.***

la·tex (lā′teks′) ***n.*** ⟦L, a fluid⟧ a milky liquid in certain plants and trees: used esp. as the basis of rubber

lath (lath) ***n.***, *pl.* **laths** (la*th*z, laths) ⟦< ME⟧ **1** any of the thin, narrow strips of wood used as a foundation for plaster, etc. **2** any foundation for plaster

lathe (lāth) ***n.*** ⟦prob. < MDu *lade*⟧ a machine for shaping wood, metal, etc. by holding and turning it rapidly against a cutting tool —***vt.*** **lathed, lath′ing** to shape on a lathe

lath·er (lath′ər) ***n.*** ⟦OE *leathor,* soap⟧ **1** the foam formed by soap and water **2** foamy sweat **3** [Slang] an excited state —***vt., vi.*** to cover with or form lather —**lath′er·y** ***adj.***

Lat·in (lat′'n) ***adj.*** ⟦< *Latium,* ancient country in central Italy⟧ **1** of ancient Rome, its people, their language, etc. **2** designating or of the languages derived from Latin, the peoples who speak them, their countries, etc. —***n.*** **1** a native or inhabitant of ancient Rome **2** the language of ancient Rome **3** a person whose language is derived from Latin, as a Spaniard or Italian

Latin America that part of the Western Hemisphere south of the U.S. where Spanish, Portuguese, & French are the official languages

lat·ish (lāt′ish) ***adj., adv.*** somewhat late

lat·i·tude (lat′ə to͞od′) ***n.*** ⟦< L *latus,* wide⟧ **1** freedom from narrow restrictions **2** *a)* distance, measured in degrees, north or south from the equator *b)* a region with reference to this distance

la·trine (lə trēn′) ***n.*** ⟦< L *lavare,* to wash⟧ a toilet for the use of a large number of people, as in an army camp

lat·ter (lat′ər) ***adj.*** ⟦orig. compar. of LATE⟧ **1** *alt. compar. of* LATE **2** *a)* later; more recent *b)* nearer the end or close **3** being the last mentioned of two

lat·tice (lat′is) ***n.*** ⟦< OHG *latta,* lath⟧ an openwork structure of crossed strips of wood, metal, etc. used as a screen, support, etc.

lat′tice·work′ (-wurk′) ***n.*** **1** a lattice **2** lattices collectively

Lat·vi·a (lat′vē ə) republic (**Latvian Soviet Socialist Republic**) of the U.S.S.R. in NE Europe: 24,594 sq. mi.; pop. 2,600,000 —**Lat′vi·an** ***adj., n.***

laud (lôd) ***vt.*** ⟦< L *laus,* glory⟧ to praise; extol

laud′a·ble ***adj.*** praiseworthy; commendable

lau·da·num (lôd′'n əm) ***n.*** ⟦< L *ladanum,* a dark resin⟧ **1** [Archaic] any of various opium preparations **2** a solution of opium in alcohol

laud·a·to·ry (lôd′ə tôr′ē) ***adj.*** expressing praise; commendatory

laugh (laf) ***vi.*** ⟦< OE *hleahhan*⟧ to make the sounds and facial movements that express mirth, ridicule, etc. —***n.*** **1** the act or sound of laughing **2** a cause of laughter —**laugh at** **1** to be amused by **2** to make fun of

laugh′a·ble ***adj.*** amusing or ridiculous —**laugh′a·bly** ***adv.***

laughing gas nitrous oxide used as an anesthetic: inhaling it may cause a reaction of laughter

laugh′ing·stock′ (-stäk′) ***n.*** an object of ridicule

laugh′ter ***n.*** the action or sound of laughing

launch[1] (lônch) ***vt.*** ⟦< L *lancea,* a lance⟧ **1** to hurl or send forth with some force /to *launch* a rocket/ **2** to slide (a new vessel) into the water **3** to set in operation or on some course; start /to *launch* an attack/ —***vi.*** **1** to start something new: often with *out* or *forth* **2** to plunge (*into*) —***n.*** a launching —***adj.*** designating or of vehicles, sites, etc. used in launching spacecraft or missiles

launch[2] (lônch) ***n.*** ⟦Sp or Port *lancha*⟧ an open, or partly enclosed, motorboat

launch pad the platform from which a rocket, guided missile, etc. is launched Also **launching pad**

launch window a favorable time period for launching a spacecraft, etc.

laun·der (lôn′dər) ***vt.*** ⟦< L *lavare,* to wash⟧ **1** to wash, or wash and iron (clothes, etc.) **2** to exchange or invest (illegally gotten money) so as to conceal its source —**laun′der·er** ***n.*** —**laun′dress** (-dris) ***n.fem.***

Laun·dro·mat (lôn′drō mat′, -drə-) *service mark for* a self-service laundry —***n.*** [l-] such a laundry

laun·dry (lôn′drē) ***n., pl.*** **-dries** **1** a place for laundering **2** clothes, etc. laundered or to be laundered

laun′dry·man′ ***n., pl.*** **-men′** a man who works in or for a laundry, esp. one who collects and delivers laundry —**laun′dry·wom′an,** *pl.* **-wom′en,** ***n.fem.***

lau·re·ate (lôr′ē it) ***adj.*** ⟦< L *laurus,* laurel⟧ honored, as with a crown of laurel —***n.*** POET LAUREATE

lau·rel (lôr′əl) ***n.*** ⟦< L *laurus*⟧ **1** an evergreen tree or shrub of S Europe, with large, glossy leaves **2** its foliage, esp. as woven into crowns **3** [*pl.*] fame; honor **4** any of various trees and shrubs resembling the true laurel

la·va (lä′və, lav′ə) ***n.*** ⟦It < L *labi,* to slide⟧ **1** melted rock issuing from a volcano **2** such rock when solidified by cooling

La·val (lə val′) city in SW Quebec, Canada, near Montreal: pop. 284,000

lav·a·liere or **lav·a·lier** (lav′ə lir′, lä′və-) ***n.*** ⟦< Fr⟧ an ornament on a chain, worn around the neck

lav·a·to·ry (lav′ə tôr′ē) ***n., pl.*** **-ries** ⟦< L *lavare,* to wash⟧ a room with a washbowl and a toilet

lave (lāv) ***vt., vi.*** **laved, lav′ing** ⟦< L *lavare*⟧ [Old Poet.] to wash or bathe

lav·en·der (lav′ən dər) ***n.*** ⟦< ML *lavandria*⟧ **1** a fragrant European mint, with spikes of pale-purplish flowers **2** its dried flowers and leaves, used to perfume clothes, etc. **3** a pale purple —***adj.*** pale-purple

lav·ish (lav′ish) ***adj.*** ⟦< OFr *lavasse,* downpour⟧ **1** very generous; prodigal **2** very abundant —***vt.*** to give or spend generously —**lav′ish·ly** ***adv.***

law (lô) ***n.*** ⟦OE *lagu*⟧ **1** *a)* all the rules of conduct established by the authority or custom of a nation, etc. *b)* any one of such rules **2** obedience to such rules **3** the study of such rules; jurisprudence **4** the seeking of justice in courts under such rules **5** the profession of lawyers, judges, etc. **6** *a)* a sequence of natural events occurring with unvarying uniformity under the same conditions *b)* the stating of such a sequence **7** any rule expected to be observed /the *laws* of health/ —**the Law** **1** the Mosaic law, or the part of the Jewish Scriptures containing it **2** [the l-] [Colloq.] a policeman or the police

law′-a·bid′ing *adj.* obeying the law

law′break′er *n.* one who violates the law —**law′break′ing** *adj., n.*

law′ful *adj.* **1** in conformity with the law **2** recognized by law /*lawful* debts/ —**law′ful·ly** *adv.*

law′giv′er *n.* a lawmaker; legislator

law′less *adj.* **1** not regulated by the authority of law **2** not in conformity with law; illegal **3** not obeying the law; unruly —**law′less·ness** *n.*

law′mak′er *n.* one who makes or helps to make laws; esp., a legislator

lawn[1] (lôn) *n.* ⟦< OFr *launde,* heath⟧ land covered with grass kept closely mowed, esp. around a house

lawn[2] (lôn) *n.* ⟦after *Laon,* city in France⟧ a fine, sheer cloth of linen or cotton

lawn bowling a bowling game played on a smooth lawn with wooden balls

Law·rence (lôr′əns), **D(avid) H(erbert)** 1885-1930; Eng. novelist & poet

law′suit′ *n.* a suit between private parties in a law court

law·yer (lô′yər) *n.* one whose profession is advising others in matters of law or representing them in lawsuits

lax (laks) *adj.* ⟦< L *laxus*⟧ **1** loose; slack; not tight **2** not strict or exact —**lax′ly** *adv.*

lax·a·tive (laks′ə tiv) *adj.* ⟦see prec.⟧ making the bowels loose and relieving constipation —*n.* any laxative medicine

lax·i·ty (laks′i tē) *n.* lax quality or condition

lay[1] (lā) *vt.* **laid, lay′ing** ⟦< OE *lecgan*⟧ **1** to cause to fall with force; knock down **2** to place or put in a resting position: often with *on* or *in* **3** to put down (bricks, carpeting, etc.) in the correct position or way **4** to place; put; set /to *lay* emphasis on accuracy/ **5** to produce (an egg) **6** to allay, suppress, etc. **7** to bet (a specified sum, etc.) **8** to devise /to *lay* plans/ **9** to present or assert /to *lay* claim to property/ —*n.* the way or position in which something is situated /the *lay* of the land/ —**lay aside** to put away for future use; save: also **lay away** or **lay by** —**lay in** to get and store away —**lay off 1** to discharge (an employee), esp. temporarily **2** [Slang] to cease —**lay open 1** to cut open **2** to expose —**lay out 1** to spend **2** to arrange according to a plan **3** to spread out (clothes, etc.) ready for wear, etc. —**lay over** to stop a while in a place before going on —**lay up 1** to store for future use **2** to confine to a sickbed

lay[2] (lā) *vi. pt. of* LIE[1]

lay[3] (lā) *adj.* ⟦< Gr *laos,* the people⟧ **1** of a layman **2** not belonging to a given profession

lay[4] (lā) *n.* ⟦ME & OFr *lai*⟧ **1** a short poem, esp. a narrative poem, orig. for singing **2** [Obs.] a song

lay′a·way′ *n.* a method of buying by making a deposit on something which is delivered only after full payment

lay′er *n.* **1** a person or thing that lays **2** a single thickness, fold, etc.

lay·ette (lā et′) *n.* ⟦< MDu *lade,* chest⟧ a complete outfit of clothes, bedding, etc. for a newborn baby

lay·man (lā′mən) *n., pl.* **-men** a person not a clergyman or one not belonging to a given profession

lay′off′ *n.* temporary unemployment, or the period of this

lay′out′ *n.* **1** the manner in which anything is laid out; specif., the makeup of a newspaper, advertisement, etc. **2** the thing laid out

lay′o′ver *n.* a stop during a journey

Laz·a·rus (laz′ə rəs) *Bible* a man raised from the dead by Jesus

laze (lāz) *vi., vt.* **lazed, laz′ing** to idle or loaf

la·zy (lā′zē) *adj.* **-zi·er, -zi·est** ⟦prob. < Medieval LowG or MDu⟧ **1** not eager or willing to work or exert oneself **2** sluggish —*vi., vt.* **-zied, -zy·ing** LAZE —**la′zi·ly** *adv.* —**la′zi·ness** *n.*

la′zy·bones′ *n.* [Colloq.] a lazy person

Lazy Su·san (sōō′zən) a rotating tray for food

lb. ⟦L *libra,* pl. *librae*⟧ pound; pounds

l.c. ⟦L *loco citato*⟧ in the place cited

LCD ⟦*l(iquid-)c(rystal) d(isplay)*⟧ a device for alphanumeric displays, as on digital watches, using a crystalline liquid

lea (lē) *n.* ⟦OE *leah*⟧ [Old Poet.] a meadow

leach (lēch) *vt.* ⟦prob. < OE *leccan,* to water⟧ **1** to wash (some material) with a filtering liquid **2** to extract (a soluble substance) from some material —*vi.* to dissolve and be washed away

lead[1] (lēd) *vt.* **led, lead′ing** ⟦OE *lædan*⟧ **1** to direct, as by going before or along with, by physical contact, pulling a rope, etc.; guide **2** to guide by influence **3** to be the head of (an expedition, orchestra, etc.) **4** to be at the head of /to *lead* one's class/ **5** to be ahead of in a contest **6** to live; spend /to *lead* a hard life/ —*vi.* **1** to show the way, as by going before **2** to tend in a certain direction: with *to, from,* etc. **3** to bring as a result: with *to* /hate *led* to war/ **4** to be or go first —*n.* **1** the role or example of a leader **2** first or front place **3** the amount or distance ahead /to hold a safe *lead*/ **4** anything that leads, as a clue **5** the leading role in a play, etc. **6** the right of playing first in cards or the card played —**lead off** to begin —**lead on** to lure —**lead up to** to prepare the way for

lead[2] (led) *n.* ⟦OE⟧ **1** a heavy, soft, bluish-gray metallic chemical element **2** a weight for measuring depth at sea **3** bullets **4** a stick of graphite, used in pencils —*adj.* of or containing lead —*vt.* to cover, line, or weight with lead

lead·ed (led′əd) *adj.* containing a lead compound: said of gasoline

lead·en (led′′n) *adj.* **1** of lead **2** heavy **3** sluggish **4** gloomy **5** gray

lead·er (lēd′ər) *n.* one that leads; guiding head —**lead′er·ship′** *n.*

lead·ing (lēd′iŋ) *adj.* **1** that leads; guiding **2** principal; chief

leading question a question put in such a way as to suggest the answer sought

lead time (lēd) the period of time between the decision to make a product and the start of production

leaf (lēf) *n., pl.* **leaves** ⟦OE⟧ **1** any of the

flat, thin parts, usually green, growing from the stem of a plant 2 a sheet of paper 3 a very thin sheet of metal 4 a hinged or removable section of a table top —*vi.* 1 to bear leaves 2 to turn the pages of a book: with *through* —**leaf′less** *adj.*

leaf′let (-lit) *n.* 1 a small or young leaf 2 a separate sheet of printed matter, often folded

leaf′y *adj.* **-i·er, -i·est** having many or broad leaves /a *leafy* vegetable/

league[1] (lēg) *n.* ⟦< L *ligare*, bind⟧ 1 an association of nations, groups, etc. for promoting common interests 2 *Sports* a group of teams organized to play one another —*vt., vi.* **leagued, leagu′ing** to form into a league

league[2] (lēg) *n.* ⟦ult. < OE *leowe*, mile⟧ a measure of distance, about three miles

leak (lēk) *vi.* ⟦< ON *leka*, to drip⟧ 1 to let a fluid out or in accidentally 2 to pass in or out of a container thus 3 to become known gradually, by accident, etc. —*vt.* to allow to leak —*n.* 1 an accidental crack, etc. that lets something out or in 2 any accidental means of escape 3 leakage —**leak′y, -i·er, -i·est,** *adj.*

leak′age (-ij) *n.* 1 a leaking 2 that which or the amount that leaks

lean[1] (lēn) *vi.* **leaned** or **leant** (lent), **lean′·ing** ⟦OE *hlinian*⟧ 1 to bend or slant from an upright position 2 to bend the body and rest part of one's weight on something 3 to rely (*on* or *upon*) 4 to tend (*toward* or *to*) —*vt.* to cause to lean —**lean′er** *n.*

lean[2] (lēn) *adj.* ⟦OE *hlæne*⟧ 1 with little flesh or fat; thin; spare 2 meager —**lean′·ness** *n.*

lean′ing *n.* a tendency; inclination

lean′-to′ *n., pl.* **-tos′** a structure whose sloping roof abuts a wall, etc.

leap (lēp) *vi.* **leapt** (lept, lēpt) or **lept** or **leaped, leap′ing** ⟦OE *hleapan*⟧ 1 to jump; spring; bound 2 to accept eagerly something offered: with *at* —*vt.* 1 to pass over by a jump 2 to cause to leap —*n.* 1 a jump; spring 2 the distance covered in a jump 3 a sudden transition —**leap′er** *n.*

leap′frog′ *n.* a game in which each player in turn leaps over the bent backs of the other players —*vt., vi.* **-frogged′, -frog′ging** to leap or jump in or as in this way; skip (*over*)

leap year every fourth year, containing an extra day in February

learn (lurn) *vt., vi.* **learned** (lurnd) or **learnt** (lurnt), **learn′ing** ⟦OE *leornian*⟧ 1 to get knowledge of or skill in (an art, trade, etc.) by study, experience, etc. 2 to come to know; hear (*of* or *about*) 3 to memorize —**learn′er** *n.*

learn·ed (lurn′id; *for 2* lurnd) *adj.* 1 having or showing much learning 2 acquired by study, experience, etc.

learn′ing *n.* 1 the acquiring of knowledge or skill 2 acquired knowledge or skill

learning disability any of several conditions, believed to involve the nervous system, which limit the ability to read, write, etc.

lease (lēs) *n.* ⟦< L *laxus*, loose⟧ a contract by which a landlord rents lands, buildings, etc. to a tenant for a specified time —*vt.* **leased, leas′ing** to give or get by a lease —**leas′er** *n.*

lease′hold′ *n.* 1 the act of holding by lease 2 land, buildings, etc. held by lease —**lease′·hold′er** *n.*

leash (lēsh) *n.* ⟦< L *laxus*, loose⟧ a cord, strap, etc. by which a dog or the like is held in check —*vt.* to check or control as by a leash

least (lēst) *adj.* ⟦OE *læst*⟧ 1 *alt. superl. of* LITTLE 2 smallest or slightest in size, degree, etc. —*adv.* in the smallest degree —*n.* the smallest in amount, importance, etc. —**at (the) least** 1 at the lowest 2 at any rate —**not in the least** not at all

least′wise′ *adv.* [Colloq.] at least; anyway Also **least′ways′**

leath·er (leth′ər) *n.* ⟦< OE *lether-*⟧ animal skin prepared for use by removing the hair and tanning —*adj.* of leather

leath′er·neck′ *n.* ⟦< former leather-lined uniform collar⟧ [Slang] a U.S. Marine

leath′er·y *adj.* like leather; tough and flexible —**leath′er·i·ness** *n.*

leave[1] (lēv) *vt.* **left, leav′ing** ⟦OE *læfan*, let remain⟧ 1 to allow to remain /*leave* it open/ 2 to have remaining behind or after one 3 to bequeath 4 to go away from 5 to abandon 6 [Chiefly Dial.] to let /*leave* us go/ —*vi.* to go away or set out —**leave off** to stop —**leave out** to omit —**leav′er** *n.*

leave[2] (lēv) *n.* ⟦OE *leaf*⟧ 1 permission 2 *a)* permission to be absent from duty *b)* the period for which this is granted —**take leave of** to say goodbye to —**take one's leave** to depart

leave[3] (lēv) *vi.* **leaved, leav′ing** to put forth, or bear, leaves; leaf

leav·en (lev′ən) *n.* ⟦< L *levare*, raise⟧ 1 a substance, as fermenting dough from a previous baking, yeast, etc., used to make dough rise 2 a tempering or modifying quality or thing —*vt.* 1 to make (dough) rise 2 to spread through, causing gradual change

leav′en·ing (-iŋ) *n.* 1 LEAVEN 2 a causing to be leavened

leave of absence permission to be absent from work or duty, esp. for a long time; also, the period for which this is granted

leaves (lēvz) *n. pl. of* LEAF

leave′-tak′ing *n.* a parting; farewell

leav·ings (lēv′iŋz) *n.pl.* leftovers, remnants, refuse, etc.

Leb·a·non (leb′ə nän′) country in SW Asia, on the Mediterranean: *c.* 4,000 sq. mi.; pop. 2,675,000 —**Leb′a·nese′** (-nēz′) *n., adj.*

LECTERN

lech·er (lech′ər) *n.* ⟦OFr *lechier*, live debauchedly⟧ a lewd, grossly sensual man —**lech′er·ous** *adj.* —**lech′·er·y** *n.*

lec·i·thin (les′i thin) *n.* ⟦< Gr *lekithos*, egg yolk⟧ a nitrogenous, fatty compound found in animal and plant cells: used in medicine, foods, etc.

lec·tern (lek′tərn) *n.* ⟦< L *legere*, to read⟧ a reading stand

lec·ture (lek′chər) *n.* ⟦< L *legere*, read⟧ 1

an informative talk to a class, etc. 2 a lengthy scolding —*vt., vi.* -tured, -tur·ing 1 to give a lecture (to) 2 to scold —lec'tur·er *n.*

led (led) *vt., vi. pt. & pp. of* LEAD[1]

LED *n.* ⟦*l*(*ight-*)*e*(*mitting*) *d*(*iode*)⟧ a semiconductor diode that emits light when voltage is applied: used as in lamps and digital watches

ledge (lej) *n.* ⟦ME *legge*⟧ 1 a shelf 2 a projecting ridge of rocks

ledg·er (lej'ər) *n.* ⟦ME *legger*⟧ a book of final entry, in which a record of debits and credits is kept

lee (lē) *n.* ⟦OE *hleo*, shelter⟧ 1 shelter 2 *Naut.* the side or direction away from the wind —*adj.* of or on the lee

Lee (lē), **Rob·ert E**(**dward**) (räb'ərt) 1807-70; commander in chief of the Confederate Army

leech (lēch) *n.* ⟦OE *læce*⟧ 1 a bloodsucking worm living in water and used, esp. formerly, to bleed patients 2 one who clings to another for personal advantage —*vi.* to cling (*onto*) thus

leek (lēk) *n.* ⟦OE *leac*⟧ a vegetable that resembles a thick green onion

leer (lir) *n.* ⟦OE *hleor*⟧ a sly, sidelong look showing lust, malicious triumph, etc. —*vi.* to look with a leer —**leer'ing·ly** *adv.*

leer·y (lir'ē) *adj.* -i·er, -i·est wary; suspicious

lees (lēz) *n.pl.* ⟦< ML *lia*⟧ dregs or sediment, as of wine

lee·ward (lē'wərd'; *naut.* lo͞o'ərd) *adj.* away from the wind —*n.* the side or direction away from the wind —*adv.* toward the lee

Lee·ward Islands (lē'wərd) N group of islands in the Lesser Antilles of the West Indies

lee·way (lē'wā') *n.* 1 the leeward drift of a ship or aircraft from its course 2 [Colloq.] *a*) margin of time, money, etc. *b*) room for freedom of action

left[1] (left) *adj.* ⟦< OE *lyft*, weak⟧ 1 of or on the side that is toward the west when one faces north 2 closer to the left side of one facing the thing mentioned —*n.* 1 the left side 2 [*often* L-] *Politics* a liberal or radical position, party, etc.: often with *the* —*adv.* on or toward the left hand or side

left[2] (left) *vt., vi. pt. & pp. of* LEAVE[1]

left'-hand' *adj.* 1 on the left 2 of, for, or with the left hand

left'-hand'ed *adj.* 1 using the left hand more skillfully than the right 2 done with or made for use with the left hand 3 ambiguous or backhanded [*a left-handed* compliment] —*adv.* with the left hand [to write *left-handed*]

left'ist *n., adj.* liberal or radical

left'o'ver *n.* something left over

left wing the more liberal or radical section of a political party, group, etc. —**left'-wing'** *adj.* —**left'-wing'er** *n.*

left'y *n., pl.* -ies [Slang] a left-handed person: often a nickname

leg (leg) *n.* ⟦ON *leggr*⟧ 1 one of the parts of the body by means of which humans and animals stand and walk 2 the part of a garment covering the leg 3 anything like a leg in shape or use 4 a stage, as of a trip —*vi.* **legged, leg'ging** [Colloq.] to walk or run: chiefly in the phrase **leg it**

leg·a·cy (leg'ə sē) *n., pl.* -cies ⟦ult. < L *lex*, law⟧ 1 money or property left to someone by a will 2 anything handed down as from an ancestor

le·gal (lē'gəl) *adj.* ⟦< L *lex*, law⟧ 1 of or based on law 2 permitted by law 3 of or for lawyers —**le'gal·ly** *adv.*

le'gal·ese' (-ēz') *n.* the special language of legal forms, documents, etc.

legal holiday a holiday set by law

le'gal·ism' *n.* strict or too strict adherence to the law —**le'gal·is'tic** *adj.*

le·gal·i·ty (li gal'i tē) *n., pl.* -ties quality, condition, or instance of being legal or lawful

le·gal·ize (lē'gəl īz') *vt.* -ized', -iz'ing to make legal or lawful

legal tender money acceptable by law in payment of an obligation

leg·ate (leg'it) *n.* ⟦< L *lex*, law⟧ an envoy or ambassador

leg·a·tee (leg'ə tē') *n.* one to whom a legacy is bequeathed

le·ga·tion (li gā'shən) *n.* 1 a diplomatic minister and staff collectively 2 the headquarters of such a group

le·ga·to (li gät'ō) *adj., adv.* ⟦< L *ligare*, to tie⟧ *Music* in a smooth, even style, with no breaks between notes

leg·end (lej'ənd) *n.* ⟦< L *legere*, read⟧ 1 a story or body of stories handed down for generations and popularly believed to have a historical basis 2 a notable person or the stories told about his exploits 3 an inscription on a coin, etc. 4 a title, key, etc. accompanying an illustration or map

leg·end·ar·y (lej'ən der'ē) *adj.* of, based on, or presented in legends

leg·er·de·main (lej'ər di mān') *n.* ⟦< Fr *leger de main*, light of hand⟧ 1 sleight of hand 2 trickery

-leg·ged (leg'id, legd) *combining form* having (a specified number or kind of) legs [*short-legged*]

leg·ging (leg'iŋ, -in) *n.* a covering for the lower leg: *usually used in pl.*

leg·gy (leg'ē) *adj.* -gi·er, -gi·est 1 having long legs 2 [Colloq.] having long, spindly stems

leg·horn (leg'hôrn', -ərn) *n.* ⟦after *Leghorn*, It seaport⟧ [*often* L-] any of a breed of small chicken

leg·i·ble (lej'ə bəl) *adj.* ⟦< L *legere*, read⟧ that can be read, esp. easily —**leg'i·bil'i·ty** *n.* —**leg'i·bly** *adv.*

le·gion (lē'jən) *n.* ⟦< L *legere*, choose⟧ 1 a large group of soldiers; army 2 a large number; multitude —**le'gion·naire'** (-jə ner') *n.*

leg·is·late (lej'is lāt') *vi.* -lat'ed, -lat'ing ⟦see fol.⟧ to make or pass a law or laws —*vt.* to cause to be, go, etc. by making laws —**leg'is·la'tor** *n.*

leg'is·la'tion *n.* ⟦< L *lex*, law + *latio*, a bringing⟧ 1 the making of laws 2 the laws made

leg'is·la'tive *adj.* 1 of legislation or a legislature 2 having the power to make laws —**leg'is·la'tive·ly** *adv.*

leg'is·la'ture (-lā'chər) *n.* a body of persons given the power to make laws

le·git·i·mate (lə jit'ə mət; *for v.*, -māt') *adj.* ⟦< L *lex*, law⟧ 1 born of parents married to each other 2 lawful 3 *a*) reasonable *b*) justifiable **4** conforming to accepted rules, standards, etc. **5** of stage plays, as distinguished from films, vaudeville, etc. —*vt.* **-mat'ed, -mat'ing** LEGITIMIZE —**le·git'i·ma·cy** (-mə sē) *n.* —**le·git'i·mate·ly** *adv.*

le·git'i·ma·tize' (-mə tīz') *vt.* **-tized', -tiz'·ing** LEGITIMIZE

le·git'i·mize' (-mīz') *vt.* **-mized', -miz'ing** to make or declare legitimate —**le·git'i·mi·za'·tion** *n.*

leg·man (leg'man') *n., pl.* **-men'** **1** a news reporter who transmits information from the scene **2** an assistant who does routine tasks outside the office

leg'room' *n.* adequate space for the legs while seated, as in a car

leg·ume (leg'yōōm') *n.* ⟦< L *legere,* gather⟧ **1** any of an order of plants having seeds growing in pods, including peas, beans, etc. **2** the pod or seed of such a plant —**le·gu·mi·nous** (lə gyōō'mə nəs) *adj.*

leg'work' *n.* [Colloq.] necessary, routine work, typically involving walking, as part of a job

lei (lā, lā'ē) *n., pl.* **leis** ⟦Haw⟧ a garland of flowers

Leip·zig (līp'sig) city in S East Germany: pop. 556,000

lei·sure (lē'zhər, lezh'ər) *n.* ⟦< L *licere,* be permitted⟧ free time during which one may indulge in rest, recreation, etc. —*adj.* free and unoccupied

lei'sure·ly *adj.* without haste; slow —*adv.* in an unhurried manner

leit·mo·tif or **leit·mo·tiv** (līt'mō tēf') *n.* ⟦Ger *leitmotiv* < *leiten,* to guide + *motiv,* motive⟧ a dominant theme

lem·ming (lem'iŋ) *n.* ⟦< ON *læmingi*⟧ a small arctic rodent with a short tail

lem·on (lem'ən) *n.* ⟦< Pers *līmūn*⟧ **1** a small, sour, pale-yellow citrus fruit **2** the spiny, semitropical tree that it grows on **3** [Slang] something that is defective —*adj.* pale-yellow

lem'on·ade' (-ād') *n.* a drink made of lemon juice, sugar, and water

le·mur (lē'mər) *n.* ⟦< L *lemures,* ghosts⟧ a small tree-dwelling primate with large eyes

lend (lend) *vt.* **lent, lend'ing** ⟦< OE *læn,* a loan⟧ **1** to let another use or have (a thing) temporarily **2** to let out (money) at interest **3** to give; impart —*vi.* to make loans —**lend itself** (or **oneself**) **to** to be useful for or open to —**lend'er** *n.*

length (leŋkth) *n.* ⟦< OE *lang,* long⟧ **1** the distance from end to end of a thing **2** extent in space or time **3** a long stretch or extent **4** a piece of a certain length —**at length** **1** finally **2** in full

length'en *vt., vi.* to make or become longer

length'wise' *adv., adj.* in the direction of the length Also **length'ways'**

length'y *adj.* **-i·er, -i·est** long; esp., too long —**length'i·ly** *adv.*

le·ni·ent (lēn'yənt, lē'nē ənt) *adj.* ⟦< L *lenis,* soft⟧ not harsh or severe; merciful —**le'ni·en·cy** *n.* —**le'ni·ent·ly** *adv.*

Len·in (len'in), **V**(ladimir) **I**(lyich) 1870-1924; Russ. leader of the Communist revolution of 1917 —**Len'in·ism'** (-iz'əm) *n.*

Len'in·grad' (-grad') seaport in NW R.S.F.S.R.: pop. 4,867,000

len·i·tive (len'ə tiv) *adj.* ⟦< L *lenire,* to soften⟧ lessening pain or distress

lens (lenz) *n.* ⟦L, lentil: < its shape⟧ **1** a curved piece of glass, plastic, etc. for bringing together or spreading rays of light passing through it: used in optical instruments to form an image **2** any device used to focus microwaves, sound waves, etc. **3** a similar transparent part of the eye: it focuses light rays upon the retina

lent (lent) *vt., vi. pt. & pp. of* LEND

Lent (lent) *n.* ⟦OE *lengten,* the spring⟧ *Christianity* the forty weekdays of fasting and penitence from Ash Wednesday to Easter —**Lent'en** or **lent'en** *adj.*

len·til (lent''l) *n.* ⟦< L *lens*⟧ **1** a kind of legume, with small, edible seeds **2** this seed

Le·o (lē'ō) ⟦L, lion⟧ the fifth sign of the zodiac

le·o·nine (lē'ə nīn') *adj.* ⟦< L *leo,* lion⟧ of or like a lion

leop·ard (lep'ərd) *n.* ⟦< Gr *leōn,* lion + *pardos,* panther⟧ any of various large, ferocious cats, including the jaguar; esp., one with a black-spotted, tawny coat, found in Africa and Asia

le·o·tard (lē'ə tärd') *n.* ⟦after J. *Léotard,* 19th-c. Fr aerial performer⟧ a tightfitting garment for acrobats, dancers, etc.

lep·er (lep'ər) *n.* ⟦< Gr *lepros,* scaly⟧ a person having leprosy

lep·re·chaun (lep'rə kôn') *n.* ⟦< Old Ir *lu,* little + *corp,* body⟧ *Ir. Folklore* a fairy who can reveal hidden treasure

lep·ro·sy (lep'rə sē) *n.* ⟦see LEPER⟧ a progressive infectious disease of the skin, flesh, nerves, etc., characterized by ulcers, white scaly scabs, deformities, etc. —**lep'rous** *adj.*

lept (lept) *vi., vt. alt. pt. of* LEAP

lep·ton (lep'tän') *n.* ⟦< Gr *leptos,* thin⟧ any of certain light atomic particles

les·bi·an (lez'bē ən) *n.* ⟦after *Lesbos,* Gr. island home of the poetess Sappho⟧ a homosexual woman —**les'bi·an·ism'** *n.*

lèse-ma·jest·é (lez'ma'zhes tā', -maj'is tē) *n.* ⟦Fr < L *laesa majestas,* injured majesty⟧ **1** a crime against the sovereign **2** any lack of proper respect as toward one in authority

le·sion (lē'zhən) *n.* ⟦< L *laedere,* to harm⟧ an injury of an organ or tissue resulting in impairment of function

Le·sot·ho (le sut'hō', le sō'thō') country in SE Africa, surrounded by South Africa: 11,716 sq. mi.; pop. 1,552,000

less (les) *adj.* ⟦OE *læs(sa)*⟧ **1** *alt. compar. of* LITTLE **2** not so much **3** fewer —*adv.* **1** *compar. of* LITTLE **2** to a smaller extent —*n.* a smaller amount —*prep.* minus —**less and less** decreasingly

-less (lis, ləs) ⟦OE *leas,* free⟧ *suffix* **1** without **2** not able to **3** not able to be ____ed

les·see (les ē') *n.* ⟦see LEASE⟧ one to whom a lease is given; tenant

less·en (les'ən) *vt., vi.* to make or become less; decrease

less·er (les'ər) *adj.* **1** *alt. compar. of* LITTLE **2** smaller, less, or less important

les·son (les'ən) *n.* ⟦< L *legere,* to read⟧ **1** an exercise for a student to learn **2** something learned for one's safety, etc. **3** [*pl.*]

course of instruction **4** a selection read from the Bible

les·sor (les′ôr′) ***n.*** ⟦see LEASE⟧ one who gives a lease

lest (lest) ***conj.*** ⟦< OE *thy læs the*, lit., by the less that⟧ for fear that

let[1] (let) ***vt.*** **let, let′ting** ⟦OE *lætan*, leave behind⟧ **1** to leave: now only in **let alone, let be** **2** *a)* to rent *b)* to assign (a contract) **3** to cause to escape /to *let* blood/ **4** to allow; permit Also used as an auxiliary in commands or suggestions /*let* us go/ —***vi.*** to be rented —**let down 1** to lower **2** to slow up **3** to disappoint —**let off 1** to give forth **2** to deal leniently with —**let on** [Colloq.] **1** to indicate one's awareness **2** to pretend —**let out 1** to release **2** to rent out **3** to make a garment larger —**let up 1** to relax **2** to cease

let[2] (let) ***n.*** ⟦< OE *lettan*, make late⟧ an obstacle: in **without let or hindrance**

-let (lit, lət) ⟦Fr *-el* + *-et*, dim. suffixes⟧ *suffix* small /*piglet*/

let′down′ ***n.*** **1** a slowing up **2** a disappointment

le·thal (lē′thəl) ***adj.*** ⟦< L *letum*, death⟧ causing death; fatal

leth·ar·gy (leth′ər jē) ***n.***, *pl.* **-gies** ⟦< Gr *lēthē*, oblivion + *argos*, idle⟧ **1** an abnormal drowsiness **2** sluggishness, apathy, etc. —**le·thar·gic** (li thär′jik) ***adj.*** —**le·thar′gi·cal·ly** ***adv.***

let's (lets) let us

let·ter (let′ər) ***n.*** ⟦< L *littera*⟧ **1** any character in an alphabet **2** a written or printed message, usually sent by mail **3** [*pl.*] *a)* literature *b)* learning; knowledge **4** literal meaning —***vt.*** to mark with letters —**let′ter·er** ***n.***

letter carrier a postal employee who delivers mail

let′tered ***adj.*** **1** literate **2** highly educated **3** marked with letters

let′ter·head′ ***n.*** the name, address, etc. as a heading on stationery

let′ter·ing ***n.*** the act of making or inscribing letters, or such letters

let′ter-per′fect ***adj.*** entirely correct

letters patent a document granting a patent

let·tuce (let′əs) ***n.*** ⟦< L *lac*, milk⟧ **1** a plant with crisp, green leaves **2** the leaves, much used for salads

let·up (let′up′) ***n.*** [Colloq.] **1** a slackening **2** a stop or pause

leu·ke·mi·a (lo͞o kē′mē ə) ***n.*** ⟦see fol. & -EMIA⟧ a disease characterized by an abnormal increase in the number of leukocytes Also sp. **leu·kae′mi·a**

leu·ko·cyte (lo͞o′kō sīt′, -kə-) ***n.*** ⟦< Gr *leukos*, white + *kytos*, hollow⟧ a white blood cell: it destroys disease-causing organisms

lev·ee (lev′ē) ***n.*** ⟦ult. < L *levare*, to raise⟧ an embankment to prevent a river from flooding bordering land

lev·el (lev′əl) ***n.*** ⟦< L *libra*, a balance⟧ **1** an instrument for determining the horizontal **2** a horizontal plane or line /sea *level*/ **3** a horizontal area **4** normal position with reference to height /water seeks its *level*/ **5** position in a scale of values /income *level*/ —***adj.*** **1** perfectly flat and even **2** not sloping **3** even in height (*with*) **4** equal in importance, advancement, quality, etc. **5** calm or steady —***vt., vi.*** **-eled** or **-elled, -el·ing** or **-el·ling 1** to make or become level **2** to demolish **3** to aim (a gun, etc.) —**level with** [Slang] to be honest with —**lev′el·er** or **lev′el·ler** ***n.***

lev′el·head′ed ***adj.*** having an even temper and sound judgment

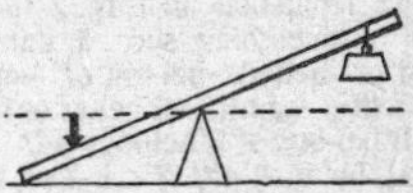

LEVER

lev·er (lev′ər, lē′vər) ***n.*** ⟦< L *levare*, to raise⟧ **1** a bar used as a pry **2** a means to an end **3** a device consisting of a bar turning about a fixed point, using force at a second point to lift a weight at a third

lev′er·age (-ij) ***n.*** the action or mechanical power of a lever

le·vi·a·than (lə vī′ə thən) ***n.*** ⟦< Heb *liwyāthān*⟧ **1** *Bible* a sea monster **2** anything huge

Le·vi's (lē′vīz′) ⟦after *Levi* Strauss, U.S. manufacturer⟧ *trademark for* closefitting trousers of heavy denim —***n.pl.*** such trousers: usually written **Le′vis** or **le′vis**

lev·i·ta·tion (lev′ə tā′shən) ***n.*** ⟦< L *levis*, light⟧ the illusion of raising a body in the air with no support —**lev′i·tate′, -tat′ed, -tat′ing, *vt., vi.***

Le·vit·i·cus (lə vit′i kəs) the third book of the Pentateuch

lev·i·ty (lev′i tē) ***n.***, *pl.* **-ties** ⟦< L *levis*, light⟧ frivolity; improper gaiety

lev·y (lev′ē) ***n.***, *pl.* **lev′ies** ⟦< L *levare*, to raise⟧ **1** an imposing and collecting of a tax, fine, etc. **2** the amount collected **3** compulsory enlistment for military service **4** a group so enlisted —***vt.*** **-ied, -y·ing 1** to impose (a tax, fine, etc.) **2** to enlist (troops) **3** to wage (war)

lewd (lo͞od) ***adj.*** ⟦OE *læwede*, unlearned⟧ indecent; lustful; obscene —**lewd′ly** ***adv.*** —**lewd′ness** ***n.***

lex·i·cog·ra·phy (leks′i käg′rə fē) ***n.*** ⟦see fol. & -GRAPHY⟧ the act, art, or work of writing a dictionary —**lex′i·cog′ra·pher** ***n.***

lex·i·con (leks′i kän′) ***n.*** ⟦< Gr *lexis*, word⟧ **1** a dictionary **2** a special vocabulary

Lex·ing·ton (leks′iŋ tən) city in N Ky.: with the county in which it is located, pop. 204,000

Li *Chem. symbol for* lithium

li·a·bil·i·ty (lī′ə bil′ə tē) ***n.***, *pl.* **-ties 1** the state of being liable **2** anything for which a person is liable **3** [*pl.*] the debts of a person or business **4** something that works to one's disadvantage

li·a·ble (lī′ə bəl) ***adj.*** ⟦< L *ligare*, bind⟧ **1** legally bound or responsible **2** subject to /*liable* to heart attacks/ **3** likely *to* /*liable* to get hurt/

li·ai·son (lē ā′zän′, -zən) ***n.*** ⟦< L *ligare*, bind⟧ **1** intercommunication as between units of a military force **2** an illicit love affair

li·ar (lī′ər) ***n.*** one who tells lies

lib (lib) ***n.*** *short for* LIBERATION

li·ba·tion (lī bā′shən) ***n.*** ⟦< L *libare*, pour out⟧ 1 the ritual of pouring out wine or oil in honor of a god 2 this liquid 3 an alcoholic drink

li·bel (lī′bəl) ***n.*** ⟦< L *liber*, book⟧ 1 any written or printed matter tending to injure a person's reputation unjustly 2 the act or crime of publishing such a thing —***vt.*** **-beled** or **-belled, -bel·ing** or **-bel·ling** to make a libel against —**li′bel·er** or **li′bel·ler** ***n.*** —**li′bel·ous** or **li′bel·lous** ***adj.***

lib·er·al (lib′ər əl) ***adj.*** ⟦< L *liber*, free⟧ 1 generous 2 ample; abundant 3 not literal or strict 4 tolerant; broad-minded 5 favoring reform or progress —***n.*** one who favors reform or progress —**lib′er·al·ism′** ***n.*** —**lib′er·al·ly** ***adv.*** —**lib′er·al·ness** ***n.***

liberal arts literature, languages, history, etc. as courses of study

lib′er·al′i·ty (-al′i tē) ***n.***, *pl.* **-ties** 1 generosity 2 broad-mindedness

lib′er·al·ize′ (-əl īz′) ***vt., vi.*** **-ized′, -iz′ing** to make or become liberal —**lib′er·al·i·za′tion** ***n.***

lib·er·ate (lib′ər āt′) ***vt.*** **-at′ed, -at′ing** ⟦< L *liber*, free⟧ 1 to release from slavery, enemy occupation, etc. 2 to secure equal rights for (women, etc.) —**lib′er·a′tion** ***n.*** —**lib′er·a′tor** ***n.***

Li·ber·i·a (lī bir′ē ə) country on the W coast of Africa: founded (1821) as settlement for freed U.S. slaves: 43,000 sq. mi.; pop. 2,307,000 —**Li·ber′i·an** ***adj., n.***

lib·er·tar·i·an (lib′ər ter′ē ən) ***n.*** an advocate of full individual freedom of thought and action

lib·er·tine (lib′ər tēn′) ***n.*** ⟦< L *liber*, free⟧ a man who is sexually promiscuous —***adj.*** licentious

lib·er·ty (lib′ər tē) ***n.***, *pl.* **-ties** ⟦< L *liber*, free⟧ 1 freedom from slavery, captivity, etc. 2 a particular right, freedom, etc. 3 an impertinent action or attitude 4 permission given to a sailor to go ashore See also CIVIL LIBERTIES —**at liberty** 1 not confined 2 permitted (to do or say something) 3 not busy or in use —**take liberties** 1 to be too familiar or impertinent 2 to deal inaccurately (*with* facts, data, etc.)

li·bid·i·nous (li bid′'n əs) ***adj.*** ⟦see fol.⟧ lustful; lascivious

li·bi·do (li bē′dō, -bī′-) ***n.*** ⟦< L, pleasure⟧ 1 the sexual urge 2 *Psychoanalysis* psychic energy generally; specif., that comprising the positive, loving instincts

Li·bra (lī′brə, lē′-) ⟦L, a balance⟧ the seventh sign of the zodiac

li·brar·i·an (lī brer′ē ən) ***n.*** one in charge of a library or trained in library management

li·brar·y (lī′brer′ē) ***n.***, *pl.* **-ies** ⟦< L *liber*, book⟧ 1 a collection of books, etc. 2 a room or building for, or an institution in charge of, such a collection

li·bret·to (li bret′ō) ***n.***, *pl.* **-tos** or **-ti** (-ē) ⟦It < L *liber*, book⟧ the words, or text, of an opera, oratorio, etc. —**li·bret′tist** ***n.***

Lib·y·a (lib′ē ə) country in N Africa, on the Mediterranean: 679,359 sq. mi.; pop. 3,876,000 —**Lib′y·an** ***adj., n.***

lice (līs) ***n.*** *pl. of* LOUSE

li·cense (lī′səns) ***n.*** ⟦< L *licere*, be permitted⟧ 1 formal or legal permission to do something specified 2 a document indicating such permission 3 freedom to deviate from rule, practice, etc. /poetic *license*/ 4 excessive freedom, constituting an abuse of liberty Brit. sp. **li′cence** —***vt.*** **-censed, -cens·ing** to permit formally

li·cen·see (lī′səns ē′) ***n.*** a person to whom a license is granted

li·cen·ti·ate (lī sen′shē it, -āt′) ***n.*** a person having a professional license

li·cen·tious (lī sen′shəs) ***adj.*** ⟦see LICENSE⟧ sexually unrestrained; lascivious —**li·cen′tious·ness** ***n.***

li·chen (lī′kən) ***n.*** ⟦< Gr *leichein*, to lick⟧ a mosslike plant growing in patches on rock, wood, soil, etc.

lic·it (lis′it) ***adj.*** ⟦< L *licitus*, permitted⟧ lawful —**lic′it·ly** ***adv.***

lick (lik) ***vt.*** ⟦OE *liccian*⟧ 1 to pass the tongue over 2 to pass lightly over like a tongue 3 [Colloq.] *a*) a whip *b*) to vanquish —***vi.*** to move lightly, as a flame —***n.*** 1 a licking with the tongue 2 a small quantity 3 *short for* SALT LICK 4 [Colloq.] *a*) a sharp blow *b*) a short, rapid burst of activity (also **lick and a promise**) —**lick up** to consume as by licking

lic·o·rice (lik′ər ish, -ə ris) ***n.*** ⟦< Gr *glykys*, sweet + *rhiza*, root⟧ 1 a black flavoring extract made from the root of a European plant 2 candy flavored with this extract

lid (lid) ***n.*** ⟦OE *hlid*⟧ 1 a movable cover, as for a box, etc. 2 *short for* EYELID 3 [Colloq.] a restraint —**lid′ded** ***adj.***

lie[1] (lī) ***vi.*** **lay, lain, ly′ing** ⟦OE *licgan*⟧ 1 to be or put oneself in a reclining or horizontal position 2 to rest on a support in a horizontal position 3 to be in a specified condition 4 to be situated /Canada *lies* to the north/ 5 to exist /love *lies* in her eyes/ —***n.*** the way in which something is situated; lay

lie[2] (lī) ***vi.*** **lied, ly′ing** ⟦OE *leogan*⟧ to make a statement that one knows is false —***vt.*** to bring, put, accomplish, etc. by lying —***n.*** a false statement made with intent to deceive

Lieb·frau·milch (lēb′frou milk′) ***n.*** ⟦Ger⟧ a white wine

Liech·ten·stein (lik′tən stīn′) country between Switzerland & Austria: 61 sq. mi.; pop. 27,000

lie detector a polygraph used on persons suspected of lying

lief (lēf) ***adv.*** ⟦< OE *leof*, dear⟧ willingly; gladly: only in **would** (or **had**) **as lief**

liege (lēj) ***adj.*** ⟦OFr⟧ loyal; faithful —***n.*** *Feudal Law* 1 a lord or sovereign 2 a subject or vassal

li·en (lēn, lē′ən) ***n.*** ⟦Fr < L *ligare*, to bind⟧ a legal claim on another's property as security for the payment of a just debt

lieu (lo͞o) ***n.*** ⟦< L *locus*⟧ place: chiefly in **in lieu of**, instead of

lieu·ten·ant (lo͞o ten′ənt) ***n.*** ⟦< Fr *lieu*, place + *tenant*, holding⟧ 1 one who acts for a superior 2 *U.S. Mil.* an officer ranking below a captain: see FIRST LIEUTENANT, SECOND LIEUTENANT 3 *U.S. Navy* an officer ranking just above a lieutenant junior grade Abbrev. **Lieut.** —**lieu·ten′an·cy** ***n.***

lieutenant colonel *U.S. Mil.* an officer ranking just above a major

lieutenant commander *U.S. Navy* an officer ranking just above a lieutenant
lieutenant general *U.S. Mil.* an officer ranking just above a major general
lieutenant governor an elected official of a State who ranks below and substitutes for the governor
lieutenant junior grade *U.S. Navy* an officer ranking just above an ensign
life (līf) ***n.***, *pl.* **lives** ⟦OE *lif*⟧ **1** that property of plants and animals (ending at death) which makes it possible for them to take in food, get energy from it, grow, etc. **2** the state of having this property **3** a human being /100 *lives* were lost/ **4** living things collectively /plant *life*/ **5** the time a person or thing is alive or exists **6** one's manner of living /a *life* of ease/ **7** the people and activities of a given time, place, etc. /military *life*/ **8** *a*) one's animate existence *b*) a biography **9** the source of liveliness /the *life* of the party/ **10** vigor; liveliness
life belt a life preserver in belt form
life′blood′ ***n.*** **1** the blood necessary to life **2** a vital element
life′boat′ ***n.*** one of the small rescue boats carried by a ship
life′guard′ ***n.*** a swimmer employed as at a beach to prevent drownings
life insurance insurance in which a stipulated sum is paid at the death of the insured
life jacket (or **vest**) a life preserver like a sleeveless jacket or vest
life′less ***adj.*** **1** without life; specif., *a*) inanimate *b*) dead **2** dull
life′like′ ***adj.*** resembling real life or a real person or thing
life′line′ ***n.*** **1** the rope for raising or lowering a diver **2** a very important commercial route
life′long′ ***adj.*** lasting or not changing during one's whole life
life net a strong net used as by firefighters to catch people jumping from a burning building
life preserver a buoyant device for saving a person from drowning by keeping the body afloat
lif′er ***n.*** [Slang] a person sentenced to prison for life
life raft a small, inflatable raft for emergency use at sea
life′sav′er ***n.*** **1** a lifeguard **2** [Colloq.] a help in time of need
life′-size′ ***adj.*** as big as the person or thing represented: said of a picture, sculpture, etc. Also **life′-sized′**
life′style′ ***n.*** an individual's whole way of living
life′time′ ***n.*** **1** the period of time that someone lives or that a thing lasts **2** a very long time
life′work′ ***n.*** the work to which a person's life is devoted
lift (lift) ***vt.*** ⟦< ON *lopt*, air⟧ **1** to bring up to a higher position; raise **2** to raise in rank, condition, etc.; exalt **3** to pay off (a mortgage, debt, etc.) **4** to end (a blockade, etc.) **5** [Slang] to steal —***vi.*** **1** to exert strength in raising something **2** to rise; go up —***n.*** **1** a lifting or rising **2** the amount lifted **3** the distance something is lifted **4** lifting power or influence **5** elevation of mood **6** elevated position or carriage **7** a ride in the direction one is going **8** help of any kind **9** [Brit.] ELEVATOR
lift′off′ ***n.*** **1** the initial vertical takeoff of a rocket, helicopter, etc. **2** the time this occurs
lig·a·ment (lig′ə mənt) ***n.*** ⟦< L *ligare*, bind⟧ a band of tissue connecting bones or holding organs in place
lig·a·ture (lig′ə chər) ***n.*** ⟦< L *ligare*, bind⟧ **1** a tying or binding together **2** a tie, bond, etc. **3** two or more letters united, as æ, *th* **4** *Surgery* a thread used to tie up an artery, etc.
light[1] (līt) ***n.*** ⟦OE *leoht*⟧ **1** *a*) the form of radiant energy acting on the retina of the eye to make sight possible *b*) ultraviolet or infrared radiation **2** brightness; illumination **3** a source of light, as the sun, a lamp, etc. **4** daylight **5** a thing used to ignite something **6** a window or windowpane **7** knowledge; enlightenment **8** public view /to bring new facts to *light*/ **9** aspect /viewed in another *light*/ **10** an outstanding person —***adj.*** **1** having light; bright **2** pale in color; fair —***adv.*** palely /a *light* blue color/ —***vt.*** **light′ed** or **lit**, **light′ing** **1** to ignite /to *light* a bonfire/ **2** to cause to give off light **3** to furnish with light **4** to brighten; animate —***vi.*** **1** to catch fire **2** to be lighted: usually with *up* —**in the light of** considering —**see the light (of day)** **1** to come into existence **2** to come to public view **3** to understand
light[2] (līt) ***adj.*** ⟦OE *leoht*⟧ **1** having little weight; not heavy, esp. for its size **2** less than usual in weight, amount, force, etc. /a *light* blow/ **3** of little importance **4** easy to bear /a *light* tax/ **5** easy to do /*light* work/ **6** gay; happy **7** dizzy; giddy **8** not serious /*light* reading/ **9** containing fewer calories **10** moderate /a *light* meal/ **11** moving with ease /*light* on one's feet/ **12** producing small products /*light* industry/ —***adv.*** LIGHTLY —***vi.*** **light′ed** or **lit**, **light′ing** **1** to come to rest after traveling through the air **2** to come or happen (*on* or *upon*) —**light into** [Colloq.] to attack —**light out** [Colloq.] to depart suddenly —**make light of** to treat as unimportant
light′en[1] ***vt.***, ***vi.*** **1** to make or become light or brighter **2** to shine; flash
light′en[2] ***vt.***, ***vi.*** **1** to make or become lighter in weight **2** to make or become more cheerful
light′er[1] ***n.*** a person or thing that starts something burning
light′er[2] ***n.*** ⟦< MDu *licht*, LIGHT[2]⟧ a large barge used to load or unload ships anchored in a harbor
light′-fin′gered ***adj.*** **1** skillful at stealing **2** likely to steal
light′-foot′ed ***adj.*** stepping lightly and gracefully
light′head′ed ***adj.*** **1** giddy; dizzy **2** flighty; frivolous
light′heart′ed ***adj.*** gay; cheerful —**light′heart′ed·ly** ***adv.*** —**light′heart′ed·ness** ***n.***
light heavyweight a boxer with a maximum weight of 175 lb.
light′house′ ***n.*** a tower with a very bright light to guide ships at night

light'ing *n.* the act or manner of giving light, or illuminating
light'ly *adv.* 1 with little weight or pressure; gently 2 to a small degree or amount 3 nimbly; deftly 4 cheerfully 5 with indifference
light meter an instrument to measure intensity of light, used in photography
light'-mind'ed *adj.* silly; frivolous
light·ness[1] (līt'nis) *n.* 1 the amount of light; brightness 2 paleness in color
light'ness[2] *n.* 1 a being light, not heavy 2 mildness, nimbleness, cheerfulness, etc.
light'ning (-niŋ) *n.* a flash of light in the sky caused by the discharge of atmospheric electricity
lightning bug FIREFLY
lightning rod a metal rod placed high on a building and grounded to divert lightning from the structure
light opera OPERETTA
light'weight' *n.* a boxer with a maximum weight of 135 lb. —*adj.* light in weight
light'-year' *n.* a unit of distance equal to the distance light travels in one year, *c.* 6 trillion miles
lig·nite (lig'nīt') *n.* ⟦< L *lignum*, wood⟧ a soft coal, brownish-black in color and retaining the texture of the original wood
lik·a·ble (līk'ə bəl) *adj.* attractive, pleasant, genial, etc. Also **lik'ea·ble** —**lik'a·ble·ness** or **lik'a·bil'i·ty** *n.*
like[1] (līk) *adj.* ⟦OE *gelic*⟧ having the same characteristics; similar; equal —*adv.* [Colloq.] likely /*like* as not, he'll go/ —*prep.* 1 similar to 2 similarly to /to sing *like* a bird/ 3 characteristic of /not *like* her to cry/ 4 in the mood for /to feel *like* sleeping/ 5 indicative of /it looks *like* rain/ 6 as for example /fruit, *like* pears and plums/ —*conj.* [Colloq.] 1 as /it's just *like* he said/ 2 as if /it looks *like* he's late/ —*n.* an equal or counterpart /I've never met her *like*/ —**and the like** and others of the same kind —**nothing like** not at all like —**something like** almost like —**the like** (or **likes**) **of** [Colloq.] any person or thing like
like[2] (līk) *vi.* **liked, lik'ing** ⟦OE *lician*⟧ to be inclined /do as you *like*/ —*vt.* 1 to be pleased with; enjoy 2 to wish /I'd *like* to go/ —*n.* [*pl.*] preferences or tastes —**lik'er** *n.*
-like (līk) *suffix forming adjectives* like, characteristic of /*homelike*, bull-*like*/
like·li·hood (līk'lē hood') *n.* a being likely to happen; probability
like·ly (līk'lē) *adj.* **-li·er, -li·est** ⟦OE *geliclic*⟧ 1 credible /a *likely* cause/ 2 reasonably to be expected /*likely* to rain/ 3 suitable /a *likely* place to swim/ —*adv.* probably /she'll *likely* go/
like'-mind'ed *adj.* having the same ideas, plans, tastes, etc. —**like'-mind'ed·ness** *n.*
lik·en (līk'ən) *vt.* to compare
like'ness *n.* 1 a being like 2 (the same) form 3 a copy, portrait, etc.
like'wise' *adv.* ⟦< *in like wise*⟧ 1 in the same manner 2 also; too
lik·ing (līk'iŋ) *n.* 1 fondness; affection 2 preference; taste; pleasure
li·lac (lī'lak', -lək, -läk') *n.* ⟦ult. < Pers *līlak*, bluish⟧ 1 a shrub with large clusters of tiny, fragrant flowers 2 pale purple —*adj.* pale-purple
Lil·li·pu·tian (lil'ə pyōō'shən) *adj.* ⟦after *Lilliput*, place in J. Swift's *Gulliver's Travels*⟧ 1 tiny 2 petty
lilt (lilt) *n.* ⟦ME *lilten*, to sound⟧ a light, swingy rhythm or tune —**lilt'ing** *adj.*
lil·y (lil'ē) *n., pl.* **lil'ies** ⟦< L *lilium*⟧ 1 a plant grown from a bulb and having typically trumpet-shaped flowers 2 its flower 3 any similar plant, as the waterlily —*adj.* like a lily, as in whiteness, purity, etc.
lil'y-liv'ered *adj.* cowardly; timid
lily of the valley *pl.* **lilies of the valley** a low plant with a spike of fragrant, white, bell-shaped flowers

LILY OF THE VALLEY

Li·ma (lē'mə) capital of Peru: pop. 5,257,000
li·ma bean (lī'mə) ⟦after *Lima*, Peru⟧ 1 a bean with broad pods 2 its broad, flat, edible seed
limb (lim) *n.* ⟦OE lim⟧ 1 an arm, leg, or wing 2 a large branch of a tree —**out on a limb** [Colloq.] in a precarious position —**limb'less** *adj.*
lim·ber (lim'bər) *adj.* ⟦< ? prec.⟧ 1 easily bent; flexible 2 able to bend the body easily; supple —*vt., vi.* to make or become limber
Lim·bo (lim'bō') ⟦< L (*in*) *limbo*, (on) the border⟧ [*often* l-] in some Christian theologies, the abode after death of unbaptized children, etc. —*n., pl.* **-bos'** [l-] 1 a vague condition 2 a place of oblivion
Lim·burg·er (cheese) (lim'burg'ər) ⟦after *Limburg*, Belgian province⟧ a semisoft cheese with a strong odor
lime[1] (līm) *n.* ⟦OE *lim*⟧ a white substance, calcium oxide, obtained from limestone, etc. and used in mortar and cement and to neutralize acid soil —*vt.* **limed, lim'ing** to treat with lime
lime[2] (līm) *n.* ⟦< Ar *līmah*⟧ a small, lemon-shaped, greenish-yellow citrus fruit with a juicy, sour pulp
lime'ade' (-ād') *n.* a drink made of lime juice, sugar, and water
lime'light' *n.* 1 a brilliant light created by the incandescence of lime, formerly used in theaters 2 a prominent position before the public
lim·er·ick (lim'ər ik) *n.* ⟦prob. after *Limerick*, Ir county⟧ a rhymed nonsense poem of five lines
lime'stone' *n.* rock consisting mainly of calcium carbonate
lim·it (lim'it) *n.* ⟦< L *limes*⟧ 1 the point, line, etc. where something ends; boundary 2 [*pl.*] bounds 3 the greatest amount allowed —*vt.* to set a limit to; restrict —**lim'i·ta'tion** *n.* —**lim'it·er** *n.* —**lim'it·less** *adj.*
lim'it·ed *adj.* 1 confined within bounds 2 making a restricted number of stops: said of a train, bus, etc.
limn (lim) *vt.* **limned, limn·ing** (lim'iŋ, -niŋ) ⟦< L *illuminare*, to illuminate⟧ 1 to paint or draw 2 to describe

lim·nol·o·gy (lim näl′ə jē) *n.* ⟦< Gr *limnē,* marsh + -LOGY⟧ the science that deals with the physical, etc. properties and features of fresh waters, esp. lakes, etc.

lim·o (lim′ō) *n., pl.* **lim′os** [Colloq.] LIMOUSINE

lim·ou·sine (lim′ə zēn′) *n.* ⟦Fr, lit., cloak⟧ a large, luxurious sedan, esp. one driven by a chauffeur

limp (limp) *vi.* ⟦< OE *limpan*⟧ to walk with or as with a lame leg —*n.* a halt or lameness in walking —*adj.* lacking firmness; wilted, flexible, etc. —**limp′ly** *adv.* —**limp′ness** *n.*

limp·et (limp′it) *n.* ⟦< ML *lempreda*⟧ a mollusk that clings to rocks, etc.

lim·pid (lim′pid) *adj.* ⟦< L *limpidus*⟧ perfectly clear; transparent —**lim·pid′i·ty** *n.* —**lim′pid·ly** *adv.*

lim·y (līm′ē) *adj.* **-i·er, -i·est** of, like, or containing lime

lin·age (līn′ij) *n.* the number of written or printed lines, as on a page

linch·pin (linch′pin′) *n.* ⟦OE *lynis,* linchpin⟧ a pin in an axle to keep the wheel from coming off

Lin·coln (liŋ′kən), **Abraham** 1809-65; 16th president of the U.S. (1861-65): assassinated

Lincoln capital of Nebr., in the SE part: pop. 172,000

lin·den (lin′dən) *n.* ⟦OE⟧ a tree with dense, heart-shaped leaves

line[1] (līn) *n.* ⟦< L *linea,* lit., linen thread⟧ 1 a cord, rope, wire, etc. 2 any wire, pipe, etc., or system of these, conducting fluid, electricity, etc. 3 a thin, threadlike mark 4 a border or boundary 5 a limit 6 outline; contour 7 a row of persons or things, as of printed letters across a page 8 a succession of persons or things 9 lineage 10 a transportation system of buses, ships, etc. 11 the course a moving thing takes 12 a course of conduct, action, explanation, etc. 13 a person's trade or occupation 14 a stock of goods 15 a piece of information 16 a short letter, note, etc. 17 [*pl.*] all the speeches of a character in a play 18 the forward combat position in warfare 19 *Football* the players in the forward row 20 *Math.* the path of a moving point —*vt.* **lined, lin′ing** 1 to mark with lines 2 to form a line along —**bring** (or **come**) **into line** to bring (or come) into alignment or conformity —**draw the** (or a) **line** to set a limit —**hold the line** to stand firm —**in line for** being considered for —**line up** to form, or bring into, a line

line[2] (līn) *vt.* **lined, lin′ing** ⟦< L *linum,* flax⟧ to put, or serve as, a lining in

lin·e·age (lin′ē ij) *n.* ⟦see LINE[1]⟧ 1 direct descent from an ancestor 2 ancestry; family

lin·e·al (lin′ē əl) *adj.* 1 in the direct line of descent from an ancestor 2 hereditary 3 of lines; linear

lin·e·a·ment (lin′ē ə mənt) *n.* ⟦< L *linea,* line⟧ a distinctive feature, esp. of the face *Usually used in pl.*

lin·e·ar (lin′ē ər) *adj.* 1 of, made, or using a line or lines 2 narrow and long 3 in relation to length only

line·back·er (līn′bak′ər) *n. Football* a defensive player directly behind the line

line drive a baseball hit in a straight line parallel to the ground

line′man (-mən) *n., pl.* **-men** 1 one who sets up and repairs telephone lines, electric power lines, etc. 2 *Football* a player in the line

lin·en (lin′ən) *n.* ⟦< OE *lin,* flax: see LINE[2]⟧ 1 thread or cloth made of flax 2 [*often pl.*] sheets, cloths, etc. of linen, or of cotton, etc.

lin·er (līn′ər) *n.* 1 a steamship, airplane, etc. in regular service for a specific line 2 a cosmetic applied in a fine line, as along the eyelid

lines·man (līnz′mən) *n., pl.* **-men** 1 *Football* an official who marks the gains or losses in ground 2 *Tennis* an official who reports whether the ball is inside or outside the lines

line′up′ *n.* an arrangement of persons or things in or as in a line

-ling (liŋ) ⟦OE⟧ *suffix* 1 small [*duckling*] 2 unimportant or contemptible [*princeling*]

lin·ger (liŋ′gər) *vi.* ⟦OE *lengan,* to delay⟧ 1 to continue to stay, esp. through reluctance to leave 2 to loiter —**lin′ger·er** *n.* —**lin′ger·ing** *adj.*

lin·ge·rie (lan′zhə rē′, -rā′; -jə-) *n.* ⟦Fr⟧ women's underwear

lin·go (liŋ′gō′) *n., pl.* **-goes′** ⟦< L *lingua,* tongue⟧ [Colloq.] a dialect, jargon, etc. that one is not familiar with

lin·gua fran·ca (liŋ′gwə fraŋ′kə) a hybrid language used for communication by speakers of different languages

lin·gual (liŋ′gwəl) *adj.* ⟦see LANGUAGE⟧ of, or pronounced with, the tongue

lin·gui·ne (liŋ gwē′nē) *n.* ⟦< It *lingua,* tongue⟧ pasta in thin, flat, narrow strips Also sp. **lin·gui′ni** (-nē)

lin·guist (liŋ′gwist) *n.* ⟦< L *lingua,* tongue⟧ 1 a specialist in linguistics 2 loosely, POLYGLOT (*n.* 1)

lin·guis′tics (-gwis′tiks) *n.pl.* [*with sing. v.*] 1 the science of language 2 the study of a particular language —**lin·guis′tic** *adj.*

lin·i·ment (lin′ə mənt) *n.* ⟦< L *linere,* to smear⟧ a soothing medicated liquid to be rubbed on the skin

lin·ing (līn′iŋ) *n.* the material covering an inner surface

link (liŋk) *n.* ⟦< Scand⟧ 1 any of the loops making up a chain 2 *a*) a section of something like a chain [*a link* of sausage] *b*) an element in a series [*a weak link* in evidence] 3 anything that connects [*a link* with the past] —*vt., vi.* to join; connect

link·age (liŋk′ij) *n.* 1 a linking 2 a series or system of links

linking verb a verb that functions chiefly as a connection between a subject and a predicate (Ex.: *be, seem, become*)

links (liŋks) *n.pl.* ⟦OE *hlinc,* a slope⟧ GOLF COURSE

link′up′ *n.* a linking together

Lin·nae·us (li nē′əs), **Car·o·lus** (kar′ə ləs) 1707-78; Swed. botanist

lin·net (lin′it) *n.* ⟦< L *linum,* flax: it feeds on flaxseed⟧ either of two small finches of the Old World or the New World

li·no·le·um (li nō′lē əm) *n.* ⟦< L *linum,* flax + *oleum,* oil⟧ 1 a smooth, washable floor covering, formerly much used, esp. in kitchens 2 any floor covering like linoleum

lin·seed (lin′sēd′) ***n.*** ⟦OE *linsæd*⟧ the seed of flax; flaxseed

linseed oil a yellowish oil extracted from flaxseed, used in oil paints, etc.

lint (lint) ***n.*** ⟦< L *linum*, flax⟧ **1** scraped and softened linen **2** bits of thread, fluff, etc. from cloth or yarn —**lint′y, -i·er, -i·est,** ***adj.***

lin·tel (lint″l) ***n.*** ⟦ult. < L *limen*, threshold⟧ the horizontal crosspiece over a door, window, etc.

lin·y (līn′ē) ***adj.*** **-i·er, -i·est** **1** like a line; thin **2** marked with lines

li·on (lī′ən) ***n.*** ⟦< Gr *leōn*⟧ **1** a large, powerful cat, found in Africa and SW Asia **2** a person of great courage or strength **3** a celebrity —**li′on·ess** ***n.fem.***

li′on·heart′ed ***adj.*** very brave

li·on·ize (lī′ən īz′) ***vt.*** **-ized′, -iz′ing** to treat as a celebrity

lip (lip) ***n.*** ⟦OE *lippa*⟧ **1** either of the two fleshy folds forming the edges of the mouth **2** anything like a lip, as the rim of a pitcher **3** [Slang] insolent talk —***adj.*** spoken, but insincere /*lip* service/ —**keep a stiff upper lip** [Colloq.] to bear pain or distress bravely

lip·id (lip′id) ***n.*** ⟦< Gr *lipos*, fat⟧ any of a group of organic compounds consisting of the fats and other similar substances Also **lip·ide** (lip′īd′, -id)

lip·py (lip′ē) ***adj.*** **-pi·er, -pi·est** [Slang] impudent; insolent —**lip′pi·ness** ***n.***

lip reading the act or skill of recognizing a speaker's words by watching the lip movements: it is taught esp. to the deaf —**lip′-read′** ***vt., vi.*** —**lip reader**

lip′stick′ ***n.*** a small stick of cosmetic paste for coloring the lips

lip′-sync′ or **lip′-synch′** (-siŋk′) ***vt., vi.*** ⟦< *lip sync*(*hronization*)⟧ to move the lips silently so as to seem to be speaking or singing (something recorded) —***n.*** a lip-syncing

liq·ue·fy (lik′wi fī′) ***vt., vi.*** **-fied′, -fy′ing** ⟦< L *liquere*, be liquid + *facere*, make⟧ to change into a liquid —**liq′ue·fac′tion** (-fak′shən) ***n.***

li·queur (lē kur′, li kur′) ***n.*** ⟦Fr⟧ a sweet, syrupy, flavored alcoholic liquor

liq·uid (lik′wid) ***adj.*** ⟦< L *liquidus*⟧ **1** readily flowing; fluid **2** clear; limpid **3** flowing smoothly and musically, as verse **4** readily convertible into cash —***n.*** a substance that, unlike a solid, flows readily but, unlike a gas, does not expand indefinitely —**liq·uid′i·ty** ***n.***

liq·ui·date (lik′wi dāt′) ***vt.*** **-dat′ed, -dat′ing** ⟦see prec.⟧ **1** to settle the accounts of (a business) by apportioning assets and debts **2** to pay (a debt) **3** to convert into cash **4** to get rid of, as by killing —**liq′ui·da′tion** ***n.*** —**liq′ui·da′tor** ***n.***

liq′uid·ize′ (-wid īz′) ***vt.*** **-ized′, -iz′ing** to cause to become liquid

liq·uor (lik′ər) ***n.*** ⟦L⟧ **1** any liquid **2** an alcoholic drink, esp. a distilled drink, as whiskey or rum

li·ra (lir′ə) ***n.,*** *pl.* **li′re** (-ā) or **li′ras** ⟦< L *libra*, a pound⟧ the monetary unit of Italy

Lis·bon (liz′bən) capital of Portugal: pop. 817,000

lisle (līl) ***n.*** ⟦after *Lisle* (now *Lille*), city in France⟧ **1** a fine, hard, extra-strong cotton thread **2** a fabric, or stockings, gloves, etc., woven of lisle

lisp (lisp) ***vi.*** ⟦< OE *wlisp*, a lisping⟧ **1** to substitute the sounds (th) and (*th*) for the sounds of *s* and *z*, respectively **2** to speak imperfectly —***vt.*** to utter with a lisp —***n.*** the act or sound of lisping

lis·some or **lis·som** (lis′əm) ***adj.*** ⟦< *lithesome*⟧ lithe, supple, limber, agile, etc.

list[1] (list) ***n.*** ⟦< OE *liste*, border⟧ a series of names, words, numbers, etc. set forth in order —***vt.*** to set forth or enter in a list, directory, etc.

list[2] (list) ***vt., vi.*** ⟦prob. ult. < OE *lust*, desire⟧ to tilt to one side, as a ship —***n.*** such a tilting

lis·ten (lis′ən) ***vi.*** ⟦< OE *hlysnan*⟧ **1** to make a conscious effort to hear **2** to give heed; take advice —**lis′ten·er** ***n.***

list·ing (lis′tiŋ) ***n.*** **1** the making of a list **2** an entry in a list

list·less (list′lis) ***adj.*** ⟦< OE *lust*, desire + -LESS⟧ indifferent because of illness, dejection, etc.; languid —**list′less·ly** ***adv.*** —**list′less·ness** ***n.***

list price retail price as given in a list or catalog

lists (lists) ***n.pl.*** ⟦< ME *liste*, border⟧ a fenced area in which knights jousted

Liszt (list), **Franz** (fränts) 1811-86; Hung. composer & pianist

lit (lit) ***vt., vi.*** *alt. pt. & pp. of* LIGHT[1]

lit. **1** literally **2** literature

lit·a·ny (lit″n ē) ***n.,*** *pl.* **-nies** ⟦< Gr *litē*, a request⟧ a series of fixed invocations and responses, used as a prayer

li·tchi (lē′chē′) ***n.*** ⟦< Chin⟧ the raisinlike fruit of a Chinese evergreen tree, enclosed in a papery shell

li·ter (lēt′ər) ***n.*** ⟦< Gr *litra*, a pound⟧ the basic metric unit of capacity equal to 1 cubic decimeter or 61.025 cubic inches Brit. sp. **li′tre**

lit·er·a·cy (lit′ər ə sē) ***n.*** the ability to read and write

lit·er·al (lit′ər əl) ***adj.*** ⟦< L *littera*, a letter⟧ **1** following exactly the wording of the original /a *literal* translation/ **2** in a basic or strict sense /the *literal* meaning/ **3** prosaic; matter-of-fact /a *literal* mind/ **4** real /the *literal* truth/ —**lit′er·al·ly** ***adv.***

lit·er·ar·y (lit′ər er′ē) ***adj.*** **1** of or dealing with literature **2** familiar with or versed in literature

lit·er·ate (lit′ər it) ***adj.*** ⟦< L *littera*, a letter⟧ **1** able to read and write **2** well-educated —***n.*** a literate person

lit·e·ra·ti (lit′ə rä′tī′, -rä′tē) ***n.pl.*** ⟦It < L *litterati*: see prec.⟧ scholarly people

lit·er·a·ture (lit′ər ə choor′) ***n.*** ⟦< L *littera*, a letter⟧ **1** *a*) all writings in prose or verse of an imaginative character *b*) all such writings having permanent value, excellence of form, etc. *c*) all the writings of a particular time, country, etc. *d*) all the writings on a particular subject **2** [Colloq.] any printed matter

lithe (līth) ***adj.*** **lith′er, lith′est** ⟦OE *lithe*, soft⟧ bending easily; flexible; supple Also **lithe′some** (-səm)

lith·i·um (lith′ē əm) ***n.*** ⟦< Gr *lithos*, stone⟧ a soft, silver-white, chemical element

lithium carbonate a white, powdery salt, used in making glass, dyes, etc. and in treating manic-depressive disorders

lith·o·graph (lith′ə graf′) *n.* a print made by lithography —*vi.*, *vt.* to make (prints or copies) by this process —**li·thog·ra·pher** (li thäg′rə fər) *n.*

li·thog·ra·phy (li thäg′rə fē) *n.* ⟦< Gr *lithos*, stone + -GRAPHY⟧ printing from a flat stone or metal plate, parts of which have been treated to repel ink —**lith·o·graph·ic** (lith′ə graf′ik) *adj.*

lith·o·sphere (lith′ō sfir′) *n.* ⟦< Gr *lithos*, stone + *sphaira*, sphere⟧ the solid, rocky part of the earth; earth's crust

Lith·u·a·ni·a (lith′o͞o ā′nē ə) republic (**Lithuanian Soviet Socialist Republic**) of the U.S.S.R., in NE Europe: 25,170 sq. mi.; pop. 3,572,000 —**Lith′u·a′ni·an** *adj.*, *n.*

lit·i·gant (lit′i gənt) *n.* ⟦see fol.⟧ a party to a lawsuit

lit′i·gate′ (-gāt′) *vt.*, *vi.* **-gat′ed**, **-gat′ing** ⟦< L *lis*, dispute + *agere*, do⟧ to contest in a lawsuit —**lit′i·ga′tion** *n.* —**lit′i·ga′tor** *n.*

li·ti·gious (li tij′əs) *adj.* ⟦see prec.⟧ 1 *a*) given to carrying on lawsuits *b*) quarrelsome 2 of lawsuits —**li·ti′gious·ness** *n.*

lit·mus (lit′məs) *n.* ⟦< ON *litr*, color + *mosi*, moss⟧ a purple coloring matter obtained from various lichens: paper treated with it (**litmus paper**) turns blue in bases and red in acids

LittD or **Litt.D.** Doctor of Letters

lit·ter (lit′ər) *n.* ⟦< L *lectus*, a couch⟧ 1 a framework enclosing a couch on which a person can be carried 2 a stretcher for carrying the sick or wounded 3 straw, hay, etc. used as bedding for animals 4 granular clay used in an indoor receptacle (**litter box**) to absorb cat waste 5 the young borne at one time by a dog, cat, etc. 6 things lying about in disorder, esp. bits of rubbish —*vt.* 1 to make untidy 2 to scatter about carelessly

lit′ter·bug′ (-bug′) *n.* one who litters public places with rubbish, etc.

lit·tle (lit′'l) *adj.* **lit′tler** or **less** or **less′er**, **lit′tlest** or **least** ⟦OE *lytel*⟧ 1 small in size, amount, degree, etc. 2 short in duration; brief 3 small in importance or power /the *little* man/ 4 narrow-minded /a *little* mind/ —*adv.* **less**, **least** 1 slightly; not much 2 not in the least —*n.* a small amount, degree, etc. —**little by little** gradually — **make** (or **think**) **little of** to consider as not very important —**lit′tle·ness** *n.*

Little Rock capital of Ark.: pop. 158,000

little slam *Bridge* the winning of all but one trick in a deal

lit·to·ral (lit′ə rəl) *adj.* ⟦< L *litus*, seashore⟧ of or along the shore

lit·ur·gy (lit′ər jē) *n.*, *pl.* **-gies** ⟦ult. < Gr *leōs*, *laos*, people + *ergon*, work⟧ prescribed ritual for public worship —**li·tur·gi·cal** (lə tur′ji kəl) *adj.* —**lit′ur·gist** *n.*

liv·a·ble (liv′ə bəl) *adj.* 1 fit or pleasant to live in /a *livable* house/ 2 endurable Also **live′a·ble**

live[1] (liv) *vi.* **lived**, **liv′ing** ⟦OE *libban*⟧ 1 to have life 2 *a*) to remain alive *b*) to endure 3 to pass one's life in a specified manner 4 to enjoy a full life 5 to feed /to *live* on fruit/ 6 to reside —*vt.* 1 to carry out in one's life /to *live* one's faith/ 2 to spend; pass /to *live* a useful life/ —**live down** to live so as to wipe out the shame of (a misdeed, etc.) —**live up to** to live or act in accordance with (one's ideals, etc.)

live[2] (līv) *adj.* ⟦< ALIVE⟧ 1 having life 2 of the living state or living beings 3 of present interest /a *live* issue/ 4 still burning /a *live* spark/ 5 unexploded /a *live* shell/ 6 carrying electrical current /a *live* wire/ 7 *a*) in person *b*) broadcast, recorded, etc. during the actual performance 8 *Sports* in play /a *live* ball/

live·bear·er (līv′ber′ər) *n.* any of various small, tropical, American, freshwater aquarium fishes, as the guppy, swordtail, etc.

-lived (līvd; *often* livd) *combining form* having (a specified kind of) life /long-*lived*/

live·li·hood (līv′lē hood′) *n.* ⟦< OE *lif*, life + *-lad*, course⟧ means of living or of supporting life

live·long (liv′lôŋ′, līv′-) *adj.* ⟦ME *lefe longe*, lit., lief long: *lief* is merely intens.⟧ long in passing; whole /the *livelong* day/

live·ly (līv′lē) *adj.* **-li·er**, **-li·est** ⟦OE *liflic*⟧ 1 full of life; vigorous 2 full of spirit; exciting 3 animated, cheerful, vivacious, etc. 4 vivid; keen 5 bounding back with great resilience /a *lively* ball/ —**live′li·ness** *n.*

liv·en (līv′ən) *vt.*, *vi.* to make or become lively; cheer Often with *up*

liv·er (liv′ər) *n.* ⟦OE *lifer*⟧ 1 the largest glandular organ in vertebrate animals: it secretes bile and is important in metabolism 2 this organ of an animal used as food

Liv·er·pool (liv′ər po͞ol′) seaport in NW England: pop. 497,000

liv·er·wurst (liv′ər wurst′) *n.* ⟦< Ger *leber*, liver + *wurst*, sausage⟧ a sausage containing ground liver

liv·er·y (liv′ər ē) *n.*, *pl.* **-er·ies** ⟦ME, gift of clothes to a servant⟧ 1 an identifying uniform as of a servant 2 *a*) the care and feeding of horses for a fee *b*) the keeping of horses or vehicles for hire

lives (līvz) *n. pl. of* LIFE

live·stock (līv′stäk′) *n.* domestic animals raised for use and sale

liv·id (liv′id) *adj.* ⟦< L *lividus*⟧ 1 discolored by a bruise; black-and-blue 2 grayish-blue or pale /*livid* with rage/

liv·ing (liv′iŋ) *adj.* 1 alive; having life 2 in active operation or use /a *living* institution/ 3 of persons alive /within *living* memory/ 4 true; lifelike 5 of life /*living* conditions/ —*n.* 1 a being alive 2 livelihood 3 manner of existence —**the living** those that are still alive

living room a room in a home, with sofas, chairs, etc., used for social activities, entertaining guests, etc.

living wage a wage sufficient to maintain a reasonable level of comfort

living will a document directing that the signer's life not be artificially supported during a terminal illness

Li·vo·ni·a (li vō′nē ə) city in SE Mich.: pop. 105,000

liz·ard (liz′ərd) *n.* ⟦< L *lacerta*⟧ any of a group of slender, scaly reptiles with four legs and a tail

'll will or shall Used in contractions /*she'll* sing/
ll. lines
LL Late Latin
lla·ma (lä'mə) ***n.*** ⟦Sp < AmInd (Peru)⟧ a South American beast of burden related to the camel but smaller
lla·no (lä'nō) ***n.***, *pl.* **-nos** ⟦Sp < L *planus*, plain⟧ any of the level, grassy plains of Spanish America
LLB or **LL.B.** Bachelor of Laws
LLD or **LL.D.** Doctor of Laws
lo (lō) ***interj.*** ⟦OE *la*⟧ look! see!
load (lōd) ***n.*** ⟦< OE *lad*, a course⟧ **1** an amount carried at one time **2** something borne with difficulty; burden **3** [*often pl.*] [Colloq.] a great amount **4** *Finance* an amount added to the price of mutual fund shares to cover costs, etc. **—*vt.*** **1** to put (a load) into or upon (a carrier) **2** to burden; oppress **3** to supply in large quantities **4** to put a charge of ammunition into (a firearm) **5** *Comput.* to transfer (a program or data) into main memory from a disk, etc. **—load'er *n.* —load'ing *n.***
load·star (lōd'stär') ***n.*** LODESTAR
load·stone (lōd'stōn') ***n.*** LODESTONE
loaf[1] (lōf) ***n.***, *pl.* **loaves** (lōvz) ⟦OE *hlaf*⟧ **1** a portion of bread baked in one piece **2** any food baked in this shape
loaf[2] (lōf) ***vi.*** ⟦prob. < fol.⟧ to spend time idly; idle, dawdle, etc.
loaf'er *n.* ⟦prob. < Ger *landläufer*, a vagabond⟧ one who loafs; idler
loam (lōm) ***n.*** ⟦OE *lam*⟧ a rich soil, esp. one composed of clay, sand, and some organic matter **—loam'y, -i·er, -i·est, *adj.***
loan (lōn) ***n.*** ⟦< ON *lān*⟧ **1** the act of lending **2** something lent, esp. money at interest **—*vt.*, *vi.*** to lend
loan'er (-ər) ***n.*** **1** one who loans something **2** an automobile, TV, etc. lent in place of one left for repair
loan shark [Colloq.] one who lends money at illegal rates of interest
loan'word' (-wurd') ***n.*** a word of one language taken into and used in another
loath (lōth) ***adj.*** ⟦< OE *lath*, hostile⟧ reluctant /to be *loath* to depart/
loathe (lō*th*) ***vt.*** **loathed, loath'ing** ⟦< OE *lathian*, be hateful⟧ to feel intense dislike or disgust for; abhor
loath'ing (-iŋ) ***n.*** intense dislike, disgust, or hatred; abhorrence
loath'some (-səm) ***adj.*** causing loathing; disgusting; abhorrent
loaves (lōvz) ***n.*** *pl. of* LOAF[1]
lob (läb) ***vt.*, *vi.*** **lobbed, lob'bing** ⟦ME *lobbe*, heavy⟧ to toss or hit (a ball) in a high curve **—lob'ber *n.***
lob·by (läb'ē) ***n.***, *pl.* **-bies** ⟦LL *lobia*⟧ **1** an entrance hall, as of a hotel, theater, etc. **2** a group of lobbyists representing the same interest **—*vi.*** **-bied, -by·ing** to act as a lobbyist
lob'by·ist (-ist) ***n.*** one who tries to get legislators to support certain measures
lobe (lōb) ***n.*** ⟦< Gr *lobos*⟧ a rounded projection, as the lower end of the ear or any of the divisions of the lung
lo·bot·o·my (lō bät'ə mē) ***n.***, *pl.* **-mies** ⟦< prec. + -TOMY⟧ a surgical operation in which a lobe of the brain is cut into or across: now rarely used

LOBSTER

lob·ster (läb'stər) ***n.*** ⟦< OE *loppe*, spider + -*estre*, -ster⟧ an edible sea crustacean with four pairs of legs and a pair of large pincers
lobster tail the edible tail of any of various crustaceans
lo·cal (lō'kəl) ***adj.*** ⟦< L *locus*, a place⟧ **1** of, characteristic of, or confined to a particular place **2** of or for a particular part of the body **3** making all stops along its run /a *local* bus/ **—*n.*** **1** a local train, bus, etc. **2** a branch, as of a labor union **—lo'cal·ly *adv.***
lo·cale (lō kal') ***n.*** ⟦OFr *local*⟧ a locality, esp. with reference to events, etc. associated with it
lo·cal·i·ty (lō kal'ə tē) ***n.***, *pl.* **-ties** **1** position with regard to surrounding objects, etc. **2** a place or district
lo·cal·ize (lō'kəl īz') ***vt.*** **-ized', -iz'ing** to limit, confine, or trace to a particular place **—lo'cal·i·za'tion *n.***
lo·cate (lō'kāt', lō kāt') ***vt.*** **-cat'ed, -cat'ing** ⟦< L *locus*, a place⟧ **1** to establish in a certain place /offices *located* downtown/ **2** to discover the position of **3** to show the position of /to *locate* Guam on a map/ **—*vi.*** [Colloq.] to settle /she *located* in Ohio/
lo·ca'tion *n.* **1** a locating or being located **2** position; place **—on location** *Film* away from the studio
loc. cit. ⟦L *loco citato*⟧ in the place cited
loch (läk, läkh) ***n.*** ⟦< Gael & OIdIr⟧ [Scot.] **1** a lake **2** an arm of the sea
lock[1] (läk) ***n.*** ⟦< OE *loc*, a bolt⟧ **1** a mechanical device for fastening a door, strongbox, etc. as with a key or combination **2** an enclosed part of a canal, etc. equipped with gates for raising or lowering the level of the water **3** the mechanism of a firearm that explodes the charge **—*vt.*** **1** to fasten with a lock **2** to shut (*up*, *in*, or *out*); confine **3** to fit; link /to *lock* arms/ **4** to jam together so as to make immovable **—*vi.*** **1** to become locked **2** to interlock
lock[2] (läk) ***n.*** ⟦OE *loc*⟧ **1** a curl of hair **2** a tuft of wool, cotton, etc.
lock'er *n.* **1** a chest, closet, etc. which can be locked **2** a large compartment for freezing and storing foods
lock·et (läk'it) ***n.*** ⟦< OFr *loc*, a lock⟧ a small, hinged case of gold, etc. for holding a picture, lock of hair, etc.: usually worn on a necklace
lock'jaw' *n.* a form of tetanus, in which the jaws become firmly closed
lock'out' *n.* the shutdown of a plant to bring the workers to terms
lock'smith' *n.* one whose work is making or repairing locks and keys
lock·up (läk'up') ***n.*** a jail
lo·co (lō'kō) ***adj.*** ⟦Sp, mad⟧ [Slang] crazy; demented

lo·co disease (lō'kō) a nervous disease of horses and cattle caused by locoweed poison

lo·co·mo·tion (lō'kə mō'shən) ***n.*** ⟦< L *locus*, a place + MOTION⟧ motion, or the power of moving, from one place to another

lo'co·mo'tive (-mōt'iv) ***adj.*** of locomotion —***n.*** an electric, steam, or diesel engine on wheels, designed to push or pull a railroad train

lo·co·weed (lō'kō wēd') ***n.*** a plant of W North America that causes the loco disease of cattle, horses, etc.

lo·cus (lō'kəs) ***n.***, *pl.* **lo'ci'** (-sī') ⟦L⟧ **1** a place **2** *Math.* a line, plane, etc. every point of which satisfies a given condition

lo·cust (lō'kəst) ***n.*** ⟦< L *locusta*⟧ **1** a large grasshopper often traveling in swarms and destroying vegetation **2** SEVENTEEN-YEAR LOCUST **3** a tree of the E or Central U.S., with clusters of fragrant white flowers

lo·cu·tion (lō kyōō'shən) ***n.*** ⟦< L *loqui*, speak⟧ a word, phrase, etc.

lode (lōd) ***n.*** ⟦< OE *lad*, course⟧ a vein, stratum, etc. of metallic ore

lode'star' ***n.*** a star by which one directs one's course; esp., the North Star

lode'stone' ***n.*** a strongly magnetic variety of iron ore

lodge (läj) ***n.*** ⟦< OFr *loge*, arbor⟧ **1** *a*) a small house for some special use /a hunting *lodge*/ *b*) a resort hotel or motel **2** the local chapter or hall of a fraternal society —***vt.*** **lodged, lodg'ing 1** to house temporarily **2** to shoot, thrust, etc. firmly (*in*) **3** to bring (a complaint, etc.) before legal authorities **4** to confer (powers) upon: with *in* —***vi.*** **1** to live in a place for a time **2** to live (*with* or *in*) as a paying guest **3** to come to rest and stick firmly (*in*)

lodg'er ***n.*** one who lives in a rented room in another's home

lodg'ing ***n.*** **1** a place to live in, esp. temporarily **2** [*pl.*] a room or rooms rented in a private home

loft (lôft, läft) ***n.*** ⟦< ON *lopt*, upper room, air⟧ **1** the space just below the roof of a house, barn, etc. **2** an upper story of a warehouse or factory; specif., a dwelling space, artist's studio, etc. in such an upper story **3** a gallery /a choir *loft*/ **4** height given to a ball hit or thrown —***vt.*** to send (a ball) into a high curve

loft bed a bed on a platform or balcony allowing the use of the floor area below as living room, etc.

loft'y ***adj.*** **-i·er, -i·est 1** very high **2** elevated; noble **3** haughty; arrogant —**loft'i·ness** ***n.***

log[1] (lôg, läg) ***n.*** ⟦ME *logge*⟧ **1** a section of the trunk or of a large branch of a felled tree **2** a device for measuring the speed of a ship **3** a record of progress, speed, etc., specif. one kept on a ship's voyage or aircraft's flight —***vt.*** **logged, log'ging 1** to saw (trees) into logs **2** to record in a log **3** to sail or fly (a specified distance) —***vi.*** to cut down trees and remove the logs —**log on** (or **off**) to enter the necessary information to begin (or end) a session on a computer terminal

log[2] (lôg, läg) ***n.*** *short for* LOGARITHM

-log (lôg, läg) *combining form* -LOGUE

lo·gan·ber·ry (lō'gən ber'ē) ***n.***, *pl.* **-ries** ⟦after J. H. *Logan*, who developed it (1881)⟧ **1** a hybrid bramble developed from the blackberry and the red raspberry **2** its purplish-red fruit

log·a·rithm (lôg'ə rith əm, läg'-) ***n.*** ⟦< Gr *logos*, ratio + *arithmos*, number⟧ *Math.* the exponent expressing the power to which a fixed number must be raised to produce a given number —**log'a·rith'mic** ***adj.***

loge (lōzh) ***n.*** ⟦OFr: see LODGE⟧ a theater box or mezzanine section

log·ger·head (lôg'ər hed', läg'-) ***n.*** ⟦dial. *logger*, block of wood + HEAD⟧ a blockhead —**at loggerheads** in sharp disagreement

log·ic (läj'ik) ***n.*** ⟦ult. < Gr *logos*, word⟧ **1** correct reasoning, or the science of this **2** way of reasoning /bad *logic*/ **3** what is expected by the working of cause and effect **4** *Comput.* the system of switching functions, circuits, or devices —**lo·gi·cian** (lō jish'ən) ***n.***

log'i·cal (-i kəl) ***adj.*** ⟦ML *logicalis*⟧ **1** based on or using logic **2** expected because of what has gone before —**log'i·cal·ly** ***adv.***

lo·gis·tics (lō jis'tiks) ***n.pl.*** ⟦< Fr *loger*, to quarter⟧ [*with sing. v.*] the military science of procuring, maintaining, and transporting materiel and personnel —**lo·gis'tic** or **lo·gis'ti·cal** ***adj.*** —**lo·gis'ti·cal·ly** ***adv.***

log'jam' ***n.*** **1** an obstacle of logs jamming together in a stream **2** piled-up work, etc. that obstructs progress **3** a deadlock

log·o·type (lôg'ə tīp', läg'-) ***n.*** ⟦< Gr *logos*, a word + -TYPE⟧ a distinctive company signature, trademark, etc. Also **log·o** (lô'gō', lō'gō, läg'ō)

log'roll'ing ***n.*** **1** mutual exchange of favors, esp. among legislators **2** the sport of balancing oneself while revolving a floating log with one's feet

-logue (lôg, läg) ⟦see LOGIC⟧ *combining form* a (specified kind of) speaking or writing /*Decalogue*/

lo·gy (lō'gē) ***adj.*** **-gi·er, -gi·est** ⟦< ? Du *log*, dull⟧ [Colloq.] dull or sluggish

-lo·gy (lə jē) ⟦see LOGIC⟧ *combining form* **1** a (specified kind of) speaking /*eulogy*/ **2** science, doctrine, or theory of /*biology*/

loin (loin) ***n.*** ⟦< L *lumbus*⟧ **1** [*usually pl.*] the lower part of the back between the hipbones and the ribs **2** the front part of the hindquarters of beef, lamb, etc. **3** [*pl.*] the hips and the lower abdomen regarded as the region of strength, etc.

loin'cloth' ***n.*** a cloth worn about the loins, as by some peoples in the tropics

loi·ter (loit'ər) ***vi.*** ⟦< MDu *loteren*⟧ **1** to spend time idly; linger **2** to move slowly and idly —**loi'ter·er** ***n.***

loll (läl) ***vi.*** ⟦< MDu *lollen*⟧ **1** to lean or lounge about lazily **2** to hang loosely; droop /the camel's tongue *lolled* out/ —***vt.*** to let hang loosely

lol·li·pop or **lol·ly·pop** (läl'ē päp') ***n.*** ⟦prob. < dial. *lolly*, the tongue + *pop*⟧ a piece of candy on the end of a stick

lol·ly·gag (läl'ē gag') ***vi.*** **-gagged', -gag'ging** ⟦var. of *lallygag* < ?⟧ [Colloq.] to waste time in trifling or aimless activity

Lon·don (lun'dən) **1** capital of England, the United Kingdom, & the Commonwealth:

pop. 6,754,000 2 city in SE Ontario, Canada: pop. 275,000

lone (lōn) ***adj.*** ⟦< *alone*⟧ 1 by oneself; solitary 2 isolated

lone′ly ***adj.*** **-li·er, -li·est** 1 solitary or isolated 2 unhappy at being alone —**lone′li·ness** ***n.***

lon·er (lōn′ər) ***n.*** [Colloq.] one who prefers to be independent of others, as by living or working alone

lone′some ***adj.*** 1 having or causing a lonely feeling 2 unfrequented

long[1] (lôŋ) ***adj.*** ⟦< OE⟧ 1 measuring much in space or time 2 in length /six feet *long*/ 3 of greater than usual length, quantity, etc. /a *long* list/ 4 tedious; slow 5 far-reaching /a *long* view of the matter/ 6 well-supplied /*long* on excuses/ —***adv.*** 1 for a long time 2 from start to finish /all day *long*/ 3 at a remote time /*long* ago/ —**as** (or **so**) **long as** 1 during the time that 2 since 3 provided that —**before long** soon

long[2] (lôŋ) ***vi.*** ⟦< OE *langian*⟧ to feel a strong yearning; wish earnestly

long. longitude

Long Beach seaport in SW Calif., on the Pacific: pop. 361,000

long distance a telephone service for calls to and from distant places —**long′-dis′tance** ***adj., adv.***

lon·gev·i·ty (län jev′ə tē, lôn-) ***n.*** ⟦< L *longus*, long + *aevum*, age⟧ long life

long′-faced′ ***adj.*** glum

long′hair′ ***adj.*** of intellectuals or intellectual tastes

long′hand′ ***n.*** ordinary handwriting, as distinguished from shorthand

long′ing ***n.*** strong desire; yearning —***adj.*** feeling or showing a yearning

Long Island island in SE N.Y., in the Atlantic south of Conn.

lon·gi·tude (län′jə to͞od′) ***n.*** ⟦< L *longus*, long⟧ distance east or west of the prime meridian, expressed in degrees or time

lon′gi·tu′di·nal (-to͞od′′n əl) ***adj.*** 1 of or in length 2 running or placed lengthwise 3 of longitude

long jump *Sports* a jump for distance made either from a stationary position or with a running start

long′-lived′ (-līvd′, -livd′) ***adj.*** having or tending to have a long life span

long′-range′ ***adj.*** reaching over a long distance or period of time

long·shore·man (lôŋ′shôr′mən) ***n., pl.*** **-men** ⟦< *alongshore* + MAN⟧ a person who works on a waterfront loading and unloading ships; stevedore

long shot [Colloq.] in betting, a choice that is little favored and, hence, carries great odds

long′-stand′ing ***adj.*** having continued for a long time

long′-suf′fer·ing ***adj.*** bearing trouble, etc. patiently for a long time

long′-term′ ***adj.*** for or extending over a long time

long ton TON (sense 2)

Lon·gueuil (lôŋ gāl′) city in S Quebec: suburb of Montreal: pop. 124,000

long′-wind′ed (-win′did) ***adj.*** 1 speaking or writing at great length 2 tiresomely long

look (lo͝ok) ***vi.*** ⟦< OE *locian*⟧ 1 to direct one's eyes in order to see 2 to search 3 to appear; seem 4 to be facing in a specified direction —***vt.*** 1 to direct one's eyes on 2 to have an appearance befitting /to *look* the part/ —***n.*** 1 a looking; glance 2 appearance; aspect 3 [Colloq.] *a*) [*usually pl.*] appearance *b*) [*pl.*] personal appearance —***interj.*** 1 see! 2 pay attention! —**look after** to take care of —**look down on** (or **upon**) to regard with contempt —**look for** to expect —**look forward to** to anticipate —**look in** (**on**) to pay a brief visit (to) —**look into** to investigate —**look out** to be careful —**look over** to examine —**look to** 1 to take care of 2 to rely on —**look up** 1 to search for as in a reference book 2 [Colloq.] to call on —**look up to** to admire —**look′er** ***n.***

look′er-on′ ***n., pl.*** **look′ers-on′** an observer or spectator; onlooker

looking glass a (glass) mirror

look′out′ ***n.*** 1 a careful watching 2 a place for keeping watch 3 a person detailed to watch 4 [Colloq.] concern

look′-see′ ***n.*** [Colloq.] a quick look

loom[1] (lo͞om) ***n.*** ⟦< OE (*ge*)*loma*, tool⟧ a machine for weaving thread or yarn into cloth —***vt.*** to weave on a loom

loom[2] (lo͞om) ***vi.*** ⟦< ?⟧ to come into sight indistinctly, esp. threateningly

loon[1] (lo͞on) ***n.*** ⟦< ON *lomr*⟧ a fish-eating, diving bird, similar to a duck

loon[2] (lo͞on) ***n.*** ⟦< ?⟧ 1 a clumsy, stupid person 2 a crazy person

loon·y (lo͞on′ē) ***adj.*** **-i·er, -i·est** ⟦< LUNATIC⟧ [Slang] crazy; demented

loop (lo͞op) ***n.*** ⟦ME *loup*⟧ 1 the figure made by a line, thread, etc. that curves back to cross itself 2 anything forming this figure 3 an intrauterine contraceptive device 4 a segment of movie film or magnetic tape —***vt.*** 1 to make a loop of 2 to fasten with a loop —***vi.*** to form a loop or loops

loop′hole′ ***n.*** ⟦prob. < MDu *lupen*, to peer + HOLE⟧ 1 a hole in a wall for looking or shooting through 2 a means of evading an obligation, etc.

loop·y (lo͞o′pē) ***adj.*** **-i·er, -i·est** [Slang] 1 slightly crazy 2 confused

loose (lo͞os) ***adj.*** **loos′er, loos′est** ⟦< ON *lauss*⟧ 1 not confined or restrained; free 2 not firmly fastened 3 not tight or compact 4 not precise; inexact 5 sexually immoral 6 [Colloq.] relaxed —***adv.*** loosely —***vt.*** **loosed, loos′ing** 1 to set free; unbind 2 to make less tight, compact, etc. 3 to relax 4 to release (an arrow, etc.) —***vi.*** to become loose —**on the loose** not confined; free —**loose′ly** ***adv.*** —**loose′ness** ***n.***

loose ends unsettled details —**at loose ends** unsettled, idle, etc.

loose′-leaf′ ***adj.*** having leaves, or sheets, that can easily be removed or replaced

loos·en (lo͞os′ən) ***vt., vi.*** to make or become loose or looser

loot (lo͞ot) ***n.*** ⟦Hindi *lūt*⟧ 1 goods stolen or taken by force; plunder 2 [Slang] money, presents, etc. —***vt., vi.*** to plunder

lop[1] (läp) ***vt.*** **lopped, lop′ping** ⟦< OE *loppian*⟧ 1 to trim (a tree, etc.) by cutting off branches, etc. 2 to remove as by cutting off —**lop′per** ***n.***

lop[2] (läp) *vi.* **lopped, lop′ping** ⟦prob. akin to LOB⟧ to hang down loosely

lope (lōp) *vi.* **loped, lop′ing** ⟦< ON *hlaupa*, to leap⟧ to move with a long, swinging stride —*n.* such a stride

lop·sid·ed (läp′sīd′id) *adj.* noticeably heavier, bigger, or lower on one side

lo·qua·cious (lō kwā′shəs) *adj.* ⟦< L *loqui*, speak⟧ very talkative —**lo·quac′i·ty** (-kwas′ə tē) *n.*

lord (lôrd) *n.* ⟦< OE *hlaf*, loaf + *weard*, keeper⟧ **1** a ruler; master **2** the head of a feudal estate **3** [L-] in Great Britain, a titled nobleman —[L-] **1** God **2** Jesus Christ —**lord it** (**over**) to be overbearing toward

lord′ly (-lē) *adj.* **-li·er, -li·est 1** noble; magnificent **2** haughty —*adv.* in the manner of a lord

Lord's Day Sunday

lord′ship′ *n.* **1** the rank or authority of a lord **2** rule; dominion **3** the territory of a lord **4** [*often* L-] a title used in speaking to or of a lord

Lord's Prayer the prayer beginning *Our Father*: Matt. 6:9-13

lore (lôr) *n.* ⟦< OE *lar*⟧ knowledge; learning, esp. of a traditional nature

lor·gnette (lôrn yet′) *n.* ⟦Fr < OFr *lorgne*, squinting⟧ eyeglasses, or opera glasses, attached to a handle

lo·ris (lō′ris, lôr′is) *n.* ⟦ult. < Du *loer*, a clown⟧ a small, slow-moving, large-eyed Asiatic lemur that lives in trees and is active at night

lorn (lôrn) *adj.* ⟦ME < *losen*, lose⟧ [Old Poet.] forsaken, forlorn, etc.

lor·ry (lôr′ē) *n., pl.* **-ries** ⟦prob. < dial. *lurry*, to pull⟧ [Brit.] a motor truck

Los An·ge·les (lôs an′jə ləs, läs an′-) city & seaport on the SW coast of Calif.: pop. 2,967,000 (met. area with Long Beach 7,477,000)

lose (lo͞oz) *vt.* **lost, los′ing** ⟦OE *losian*⟧ **1** to become unable to find /to *lose* one's keys/ **2** to have taken from one by accident, death, removal, etc. **3** to fail to keep /to *lose* one's temper/ **4** to fail to see, hear, or understand **5** to fail to have, get, etc. /to *lose* one's chance/ **6** to fail to win **7** to cause the loss of **8** to wander from (one's way, etc.) **9** to squander —*vi.* to suffer (a) loss —**lose oneself** to become absorbed —**los′er** *n.*

loss (lôs, läs) *n.* ⟦ME *los*⟧ **1** a losing or being lost **2** the damage, trouble, etc. caused by losing **3** the person, thing, or amount lost —**at a loss to** uncertain how to

lost (lôst, läst) *vt., vi. pt. & pp. of* LOSE —*adj.* **1** ruined; destroyed **2** not to be found; missing **3** no longer held, seen, heard, etc. **4** not gained or won **5** having wandered astray **6** wasted

lot (lät) *n.* ⟦< OE *hlot*⟧ **1** the deciding of a matter by chance, as by drawing counters **2** the decision thus arrived at **3** one's share by lot **4** fortune /her unhappy *lot*/ **5** a plot of ground **6** a group of persons or things **7** [*often pl.*] [Colloq.] a great amount **8** [Colloq.] sort /he's a bad *lot*/ —*adv.* very much Also **lots** —**draw** (or **cast**) **lots** to decide by lot

Lo·thar·i·o (lō ther′ē ō′) *n., pl.* **-i·os′** ⟦after the rake in the play *The Fair Penitent*⟧ [*often* l-] a seducer of women; rake

lo·tion (lō′shən) *n.* ⟦< L *lavare*, to wash⟧ a liquid preparation used, as on the skin, for cleansing, healing, etc.

lot·ter·y (lät′ər ē) *n., pl.* **-ies** ⟦< MDu *lot*, lot⟧ **1** a game of chance in which people buy numbered tickets on prizes, winners being chosen by lot **2** a drawing, event, etc. based on chance

lot·to (lät′ō) *n.* ⟦It < MDu: see LOT⟧ a game resembling bingo

lo·tus (lōt′əs) *n.* ⟦< Gr *lōtos*⟧ **1** *Gr. Legend* a plant whose fruit induced forgetfulness **2** any of several tropical waterlilies

lotus position an erect sitting position in yoga, with the legs crossed close to the body

loud (loud) *adj.* ⟦< OE *hlud*⟧ **1** strongly audible: said of sound **2** sounding with great intensity **3** noisy **4** emphatic /*loud* denials/ **5** [Colloq.] *a*) flashy *b*) vulgar —*adv.* in a loud manner —**loud′ly** *adv.* —**loud′ness** *n.*

loud′mouthed′ (-mouthd′, -moutht′) *adj.* talking in a loud, irritating voice

loud′speak′er *n.* a device for converting electrical signals to sound waves which are radiated into the air

Lou·is (lo͞o′ē; *Fr* lwē) name of eighteen French kings including **Louis XIV** (1638-1715; king 1643-1715); **Louis XV** (1710-74; king 1715-74); and **Louis XVI** (1754-93; king 1774-92: guillotined)

Lou·i·si·an·a (lo͞o ē′zē an′ə) Southern State of the U.S.: 48,523 sq. mi.; pop. 4,204,000; cap. Baton Rouge —**Lou·i′si·an′i·an** or **Lou·i′si·an′an** *adj., n.*

Lou·is·ville (lo͞o′ē vil) city in N Ky.: pop. 298,000

lounge (lounj) *vi.* **lounged, loung′ing** ⟦Scot dial. < ? *lungis*, a laggard⟧ **1** to move, sit, lie, etc. in a relaxed way **2** to spend time in idleness —*n.* **1** a room with comfortable furniture for lounging **2** a couch or sofa

louse (lous) *n., pl.* **lice** ⟦< OE *lus*⟧ **1** a small, wingless insect parasitic on man and other animals **2** any similar insect parasitic on plants **3** [Slang] a mean, contemptible person —**louse up** [Slang] to spoil; ruin

lous·y (lou′zē) *adj.* **-i·er, -i·est 1** infested with lice **2** [Slang] *a*) disgusting *b*) poor; inferior **3** well supplied (*with*) —**lous′i·ness** *n.*

lout (lout) *n.* ⟦prob. < or akin to ME *lutien*, to lurk⟧ a clumsy, stupid fellow —**lout′ish** *adj.*

lou·ver (lo͞o′vər) *n.* ⟦< MDu *love*, gallery⟧ **1** an opening, window, etc. fitted with a series of sloping slats arranged so as to admit light and air but shed rain **2** any of these slats

love (luv) *n.* ⟦< OE *lufu*⟧ **1** strong affection or liking for someone or something **2** a passionate affection of one person for another **3** the object of such affection; a sweetheart or lover **4** *Tennis* a score of zero —*vt., vi.* to feel love (for) —**in love** feeling love —**make love 1** to woo, embrace, etc. **2** to have sexual intercourse —**lov′a·ble** or **love′a·ble** *adj.* —**love′less** *adj.*

love′bird′ (-burd′) *n.* any of various small, Old World parrots often kept as cage birds

love′lorn′ *adj.* pining from love

love′ly *adj.* **-li·er, -li·est 1** beautiful **2**

[Colloq.] highly enjoyable —**love'li·ness** *n.*
lov·er (luv'ər) *n.* one who loves; specif., *a*) a sweetheart *b*) a paramour *c*) [*pl.*] a couple in love with each other *d*) a devotee, as of music
love seat a small sofa for two people
lov'ing *adj.* feeling or expressing love —**lov'ing·ly** *adv.*
loving cup a large drinking cup with two handles, often given as a prize
low[1] (lō) *adj.* ⟦< ON *lagr*⟧ 1 not high or tall 2 below the normal level /*low* ground/ 3 shallow 4 less in size, degree, etc. than usual /*low* speed/ 5 deep in pitch 6 depressed in spirits 7 not of high rank; humble 8 vulgar; coarse 9 poor; inferior 10 not loud —*adv.* in or to a low level, degree, etc. —*n.* 1 a low level, degree, etc. 2 an arrangement of gears giving the lowest speed and greatest power 3 *Meteorol.* an area of low barometric pressure —**lay low** to overcome or kill —**lie low** to keep oneself hidden —**low'ness** *n.*
low[2] (lō) *vi., n.* ⟦< OE *hlowan*⟧ MOO
low'born' *adj.* of humble birth
low'boy' *n.* a chest of drawers mounted on short legs
low'brow' *n.* [Colloq.] one considered to lack cultivated tastes
Low Countries the Netherlands, Belgium, & Luxembourg
low·down (lō'doun'; *for adj.*, -doun') *n.* [Slang] the true, pertinent facts: with *the* —*adj.* [Colloq.] mean; contemptible
low·er[1] (lō'ər) *adj.* ⟦compar. of LOW[1]⟧ 1 below in place, rank, etc. 2 less in amount, degree, etc. —*vt.* 1 to let or put down /*lower* the window/ 2 to reduce in height, amount, etc. 3 to bring down in respect, etc. —*vi.* to become lower
low·er[2] (lou'ər) *vi.* ⟦ME *louren*⟧ 1 to scowl or frown 2 to appear dark and threatening, as the sky —**low'er·ing** *adj.* —**low'er·ing·ly** *adv.*
low·er·case (lō'ər kās') *n.* small-letter type used in printing, as distinguished from capital letters —*adj.* of or in lowercase
low'er·class'man (-klas'mən) *n., pl.* **-men** a student in the freshman or sophomore class of a high school or college
low frequency any radio frequency between 30 and 300 kilohertz
Low German 1 the vernacular dialects of N Germany 2 the branch of Germanic languages including English, Dutch, Flemish, etc.
low'-grade' *adj.* of low quality, degree, etc.
low'-key' *adj.* of low intensity, tone, etc.; subdued Also **low'-keyed'**
low'land' *n.* land below the level of the surrounding land —**the Lowlands** lowland region of S Scotland
low'ly *adj.* **-li·er, -li·est** 1 of low position or rank 2 humble; meek —*adv.* humbly —**low'li·ness** *n.*
low'-mind'ed *adj.* having or showing a coarse, vulgar mind
low profile a barely noticeable presence or concealed activity
low'-spir'it·ed *adj.* sad; depressed
low tide the lowest level reached by the ebbing tide
lox[1] (läks) *n.* ⟦< Yidd < Ger *lachs*, salmon⟧ a kind of smoked salmon
lox[2] (läks) *n.* ⟦*l*(*iquid*) *ox*(*ygen*)⟧ liquid oxygen, esp. when used in rockets Also **LOX**
loy·al (loi'əl) *adj.* ⟦see LEGAL⟧ 1 faithful to one's country, friends, ideals, etc. 2 showing such faithfulness —**loy'al·ly** *adv.* —**loy'al·ty,** *pl.* **-ties,** *n.*
loy'al·ist *n.* one who supports the government during a revolt
loz·enge (läz'ənj) *n.* ⟦< OFr *losenge*⟧ a cough drop, candy, etc., orig. diamond-shaped
LP (el'pē') *n.* ⟦*L*(*ong*) *P*(*laying*)⟧ a phonograph record having microgrooves, for playing at 33⅓ revolutions per minute
LPN. or **L.P.N.** Licensed Practical Nurse
Lr *Chem.* lawrencium
LSD ⟦*l*(*y*)*s*(*ergic acid*) *d*(*iethylamide*)⟧ a chemical compound used in the study of mental disorders and as a psychedelic drug
Lt. Lieutenant
Ltd. or **ltd.** limited
lu·au (lo͞o ou') *n.* a Hawaiian feast
lub·ber (lub'ər) *n.* ⟦< ME *lobbe-*, heavy⟧ 1 a big, slow, clumsy person 2 an inexperienced, clumsy sailor
Lub·bock (lub'ək) city in NW Tex.: pop. 174,000
lube (lo͞ob) *n.* 1 a lubricating oil for machinery: also **lube oil** 2 [Colloq.] a lubrication
lu·bri·cant (lo͞o'bri kənt) *adj.* reducing friction by providing a smooth film over parts coming into contact —*n.* a lubricant oil, etc.
lu'bri·cate' (-kāt') *vt.* **-cat'ed, -cat'ing** ⟦< L *lubricus*, smooth⟧ 1 to make slippery or smooth 2 to apply a lubricant to machinery, etc. —*vi.* to serve as a lubricant —**lu'bri·ca'tion** *n.* —**lu'bri·ca'tor** *n.*
lu·cid (lo͞o'sid) *adj.* ⟦< L *lucere*, to shine⟧ 1 [Old Poet.] shining 2 transparent 3 sane 4 clear; readily understood —**lu·cid'i·ty** *n.* —**lu'cid·ly** *adv.*
Lu·ci·fer (lo͞o'sə fər) Satan
luck (luk) *n.* ⟦prob. < MDu *gelucke*⟧ 1 the seemingly chance happening of events which affect one; fortune; lot 2 good fortune —**luck out** [Colloq.] to be lucky —**luck'less** *adj.*
luck'y *adj.* **-i·er, -i·est** 1 having good luck 2 resulting fortunately 3 believed to bring good luck —**luck'i·ly** *adv.* —**luck'i·ness** *n.*
lu·cra·tive (lo͞o'krə tiv) *adj.* ⟦< L *lucrum*, riches⟧ producing wealth or profit; profitable
lu·cre (lo͞o'kər) *n.* ⟦< L *lucrum*, riches⟧ riches; money: chiefly derogatory
lu·cu·brate (lo͞o'kə brāt', -kyo͞o-) *vi.* **-brat'ed, -brat'ing** ⟦< L *lucubrare*, to work by candlelight⟧ to work, study, or write laboriously, esp. late at night —**lu'cu·bra'tion** *n.*
lu·dic (lo͞o'dik) *adj.* ⟦see fol.⟧ expressive of a playful but aimless outlook /the *ludic* uses of rhyme/
lu·di·crous (lo͞o'di krəs) *adj.* ⟦< L *ludus*, a game⟧ causing laughter because absurd or ridiculous —**lu'di·crous·ly** *adv.* —**lu'di·crous·ness** *n.*
luff (luf) *vi.* ⟦ME *lof*⟧ to turn the bow of a ship toward the wind
lug (lug) *vt.* **lugged, lug'ging** ⟦prob. <

Scand ⟧ to carry or drag with effort —*n.* 1 an earlike projection by which a thing is held or supported 2 a heavy nut for securing a wheel to an axle

lug·gage (lug′ij) *n.* ⟦ < prec. ⟧ suitcases, trunks, etc.; baggage

lu·gu·bri·ous (lə go͞o′brē əs) *adj.* ⟦ < L *lugere*, mourn ⟧ very sad or mournful, esp. in an exaggerated way —**lu·gu′bri·ous·ly** *adv.* —**lu·gu′bri·ous·ness** *n.*

Luke (lo͝ok) *Bible* 1 an early Christian, the reputed author of the third Gospel 2 this book

luke·warm (lo͝ok′wôrm′) *adj.* ⟦ < ME *luke*, tepid + *warm*, warm ⟧ 1 barely warm; tepid 2 lacking enthusiasm —**luke′·warm′ly** *adv.* —**luke′warm′ness** *n.*

lull (lul) *vt.* ⟦ ME *lullen* ⟧ 1 to calm by gentle sound or motion 2 to bring into a specified condition by soothing and reassuring —*vi.* to become calm —*n.* a short period of calm

lull′a·by′ (-ə bī′) *n., pl.* **-bies′** a song for lulling a baby to sleep

lum·ba·go (lum bā′gō) *n.* ⟦ L < *lumbus*, loin ⟧ pain in the lower back

lum·bar (lum′bər, -bär′) *adj.* ⟦ < L *lumbus*, loin ⟧ of or near the loins

lum·ber¹ (lum′bər) *n.* ⟦ < ? pawnbrokers of *Lombardy*, Italy; hence, stored articles ⟧ 1 discarded household articles, furniture, etc. 2 timber sawed into boards, etc. —*vi.* to cut down timber and saw it into lumber —**lum′·ber·er** *n.* —**lum′ber·ing** *n.*

lum·ber² (lum′bər) *vi.* ⟦ < ? Scand ⟧ to move heavily and noisily —**lum′ber·ing** *adj.*

lum′ber·jack′ (-jak′) *n.* one whose work is cutting down timber and preparing it for the sawmill

lum′ber·man (-mən) *n., pl.* **-men** one who deals in lumber

lu·mi·nar·y (lo͞o′mə ner′ē) *n., pl.* **-nar′ies** ⟦ < L *lumen*, light ⟧ 1 a body that gives off light, such as the sun 2 a famous or notable person

lu·mi·nes·cence (lo͞o′mə nes′əns) *n.* ⟦ < L *lumen*, LIGHT¹ + -ESCENCE ⟧ the giving off of light without heat, as in fluorescence or phosphorescence —**lu′mi·nes′cent** *adj.*

lu·mi·nous (lo͞o′mə nəs) *adj.* ⟦ < L *lumen*, light ⟧ 1 giving off light; bright 2 clear; readily understood —**lu′mi·nos′i·ty** (-näs′ə tē) *n.*

lum·mox (lum′əks) *n.* ⟦ < ? ⟧ [Colloq.] a clumsy, stupid person

lump¹ (lump) *n.* ⟦ ME *lompe* ⟧ 1 an indefinitely shaped mass of something 2 a swelling 3 [*pl.*] [Colloq.] hard blows, criticism, etc. —*adj.* in a lump or lumps —*vt.* 1 to put together in a lump or lumps 2 to treat or deal with in a mass —*vi.* to become lumpy —**lump′i·ness** *n.* —**lump′y, -i·er, -i·est,** *adj.*

lump² (lump) *vt.* ⟦ < ? ⟧ [Colloq.] to have to put up with (something disagreeable)

lump sum a gross, or total, sum paid at one time

lu·na·cy (lo͞o′nə sē) *n.* ⟦ < LUNATIC ⟧ 1 insanity 2 utter folly

lu·nar (lo͞o′nər) *adj.* ⟦ < L *luna*, the moon ⟧ of or like the moon

lu·na·tic (lo͞o′nə tik) *adj.* ⟦ < L *luna*, the moon ⟧ 1 insane or for the insane 2 utterly foolish —*n.* an insane person

lunch (lunch) *n.* ⟦ < ? Sp *lonja*, slice of ham ⟧ a light meal; esp., the midday meal between breakfast and dinner —*vi.* to eat lunch

lunch·eon (lunch′ən) *n.* a lunch; esp., a formal lunch

lunch·eon·ette (lun′chən et′) *n.* a place where light lunches are served

luncheon meat meat processed in loaves, sausages, etc. and ready to eat

lung (luŋ) *n.* ⟦ OE *lungen* ⟧ either of the two spongelike breathing organs in the thorax of vertebrates

lunge (lunj) *n.* ⟦ < Fr *allonger*, lengthen ⟧ 1 a sudden thrust as with a sword 2 a sudden plunge forward —*vi., vt.* **lunged, lung′ing** to move, or cause to move, with a lunge

lung·fish (luŋ′fish′) *n., pl.* **-fish′** or (for different species) **-fish′es** any of various fishes having lungs as well as gills

lunk·head (luŋk′hed′) *n.* ⟦ prob. echoic alteration of LUMP¹ + HEAD ⟧ [Colloq.] a stupid person Also **lunk**

lu·pine (lo͞o′pīn′; *for n.*, -pin) *adj.* ⟦ < L *lupus*, wolf ⟧ of or like a wolf —*n.* a plant with long spikes of white, rose, or blue flowers

lu·pus (lo͞o′pəs) *n.* ⟦ < L, a wolf ⟧ any of various diseases with skin lesions

lurch¹ (lʉrch) *vi.* ⟦ < ? ⟧ 1 to pitch or sway suddenly to one side 2 to stagger —*n.* a lurching movement

lurch² (lʉrch) *n.* ⟦ prob. < OFr *lourche*, duped ⟧ a difficult situation Only in **leave in the lurch**

lure (lo͝or) *n.* ⟦ < OFr *loirre* ⟧ 1 anything that tempts or entices 2 a bait used in fishing —*vt.* **lured, lur′ing** to attract; tempt; entice

lu·rid (lo͝or′id) *adj.* ⟦ L *luridus*, ghastly ⟧ 1 glowing through a haze, as flames enveloped by smoke 2 shocking; sensational —**lu′rid·ness** *n.*

lurk (lʉrk) *vi.* ⟦ ME *lurken* ⟧ 1 to stay hidden, ready to attack, etc. 2 to move furtively

lus·cious (lush′əs) *adj.* ⟦ ME *lucius* ⟧ 1 highly gratifying to taste or smell; delicious 2 delighting any of the senses —**lus′cious·ness** *n.*

lush¹ (lush) *adj.* ⟦ < ? OFr *lasche*, lax ⟧ 1 of or showing luxuriant growth 2 rich, abundant, extravagant, etc.

lush² (lush) *n.* [Slang] an alcoholic

lust (lust) *n.* ⟦ OE, pleasure ⟧ 1 bodily appetite; esp., excessive sexual desire 2 overmastering desire /a *lust* for power/ —*vi.* to feel an intense desire —**lust′ful** *adj.* —**lust′ful·ly** *adv.*

lus·ter (lus′tər) *n.* ⟦ < L *lustrare*, illumine ⟧ 1 gloss; sheen 2 brightness; radiance 3 brilliant beauty or fame; glory Also, chiefly Brit., **lus′tre**

lus′trous *adj.* having luster; shining

lust·y (lus′tē) *adj.* **-i·er, -i·est** full of vigor; robust —**lust′i·ly** *adv.* —**lust′i·ness** *n.*

lute (lo͞ot) *n.* ⟦ ult. < Ar *al′ūd*, the wood ⟧ an old stringed instrument like the guitar, with a rounded body

lu·te·nist (lo͞ot′′n ist) *n.* a lute player Also **lu′ta·nist**

Lu·ther (lo͞o′thər), **Mar·tin** (märt′′n) 1483-1546; Ger. Reformation leader

Lu′ther·an *adj.* of the Protestant denomination founded by Luther —*n.* a member of a Lutheran Church —**Lu′ther·an·ism′** *n.*

lut·ist (lo͞ot′ist) *n.* 1 LUTENIST 2 a maker of lutes

Lux·em·bourg (luk′səm burg′) grand duchy in W Europe, north of France: 998 sq. mi.; pop. 366,000

lux·u·ri·ant (lug zhoor′ē ənt) *adj.* ⟦see LUXURY⟧ 1 growing with vigor and in abundance 2 having rich ornamentation, etc. —**lux·u′ri·ance** *n.*

lux·u′ri·ate′ (-āt′) *vi.* **-at′ed, -at′ing** 1 to live in great luxury 2 to revel (*in*) —**lux·u′-ri·a′tion** *n.*

lux·u′ri·ous (-əs) *adj.* 1 fond of or indulging in luxury 2 constituting luxury; rich, comfortable, etc. —**lux·u′ri·ous·ly** *adv.*

lux·u·ry (luk′shə rē, lug′zhə rē) *n.*, *pl.* **-ries** ⟦< L *luxus*⟧ 1 the enjoyment of the best and most costly things 2 anything contributing to such enjoyment, usually something not necessary

Lu·zon (lo͞o zän′) main island of the Philippines

-ly[1] (lē) ⟦< OE *-lic*⟧ *suffix* 1 like or characteristic of [*manly*] 2 happening (once) every (specified period of time) [*monthly*]

-ly[2] (lē) ⟦< OE *-lic*⟧ *suffix* 1 in a (specified) manner or direction, to a (specified) extent, in or at a (specified) time or place [*harshly, inwardly, hourly*] 2 in the (specified) order [*thirdly*]

ly·ce·um (lī sē′əm) *n.* ⟦< Gr *Lykeion*, grove at Athens where Aristotle taught⟧ 1 a lecture hall 2 an organization presenting lectures, etc.

lye (lī) *n.* ⟦OE *leag*⟧ any strongly alkaline substance, used in cleaning, making soap, etc.

ly·ing[1] (lī′iŋ) *vi. prp. of* LIE[1]

ly·ing[2] (lī′iŋ) *vt.*, *vi. prp. of* LIE[2] —*adj.* false; not truthful —*n.* the telling of a lie or lies

ly′ing-in′ (-in′) *n.* confinement in childbirth —*adj.* of or for childbirth

lymph (limf) *n.* ⟦L *lympha*, spring water⟧ a clear, yellowish body fluid resembling blood plasma, found in intercellular spaces and in the lymphatic vessels

lym·phat·ic (lim fat′ik) *adj.* 1 of or containing lymph 2 sluggish

lymph node any of the small, compact structures lying in groups along the course of the lymphatic vessels

lymph·oid (limf′oid′) *adj.* of or like lymph or tissue of the lymph nodes

lym·pho·ma (lim fō′mə) *n.* any of a group of diseases resulting from the proliferation of malignant lymphoid cells

lynch (linch) *vt.* ⟦after W. *Lynch*, vigilante in Va. in 1780⟧ to murder (an accused person) by mob action and without lawful trial, as by hanging

lynx (liŋks) *n.* ⟦< Gr *lynx*⟧ a wildcat found throughout the Northern Hemisphere, having a short tail and tufted ears

lynx′-eyed′ (-īd′) *adj.* keen-sighted

Lyon (lyōn) city in central France: pop. 418,000

ly·on·naise (lī′ə nāz′) *adj.* ⟦Fr⟧ prepared with sliced onions

LYRE

lyre (līr) *n.* ⟦< Gr *lyra*⟧ a small stringed instrument of the harp family, used by the ancient Greeks

lyr·ic (lir′ik) *adj.* ⟦< Gr *lyrikos*⟧ 1 suitable for singing; specif., designating or of poetry expressing the poet's personal emotion 2 of or having a high voice with a light, flexible quality [*a lyric tenor*] —*n.* 1 a lyric poem 2 [*usually pl.*] the words of a song

lyr′i·cal (-i kəl) *adj.* 1 LYRIC 2 expressing rapture or great enthusiasm

lyr′i·cist (-ə sist) *n.* a writer of lyrics, esp. lyrics for popular songs

ly·ser·gic acid (lī sur′jik) see LSD

-ly·sis (lə sis, li-) ⟦< Gr *lysis*, a loosening⟧ *combining form* a loosening, dissolution, dissolving, destruction [*catalysis, electrolysis*]

-lyte (līt) ⟦< Gr *lyein*, dissolve⟧ *combining form* a substance undergoing decomposition [*electrolyte*]

M

m or **M** (em) *n.*, *pl.* **m's, M's** the 13th letter of the English alphabet

M (em) *n.* a Roman numeral for 1,000

m meter(s)

m or **m.** 1 married 2 masculine 3 medium 4 mile(s) 5 minute(s)

M or **M.** 1 male 2 married 3 medium 4 Monday 5 Monsieur 6 month

ma (mä) *n.* [Colloq.] mother

MA 1 Massachusetts 2 ⟦L *Magister Artium*⟧ Master of Arts: also **M.A.**

ma'am (mam, mäm, məm) *n.* [Colloq.] madam: used in direct address

ma·ca·bre (mə käb′rə, mə käb′) *adj.* ⟦< OFr (*danse*) *Macabré*, (dance) of death⟧ grim and horrible; gruesome

mac·ad·am (mə kad′əm) *n.* ⟦after J. L. *McAdam* (1756-1836), Scot engineer⟧ small broken stones, or a road made by rolling successive layers of these, often with tar or asphalt

Ma·cao (mə kou′) Chinese territory under

Portuguese administration in SE China, near Hong Kong

mac·a·ro·ni (mak'ə rō'nē) *n.* ⟦It *maccaroni,* ult. < Gr *makar,* blessed⟧ pasta in the form of tubes, etc.

mac·a·roon (mak'ə ro͞on') *n.* ⟦see prec.⟧ a small, chewy cookie made with crushed almonds or coconut

ma·caw (mə kô') *n.* ⟦prob. < AmInd (Brazil)⟧ a large, bright-colored parrot of Central and South America

Mac·beth (mək beth') the title character of a tragedy by Shakespeare

Mac·ca·bees (mak'ə bēz') a family of Jewish patriots who headed a successful revolt against the Syrians (175-164 B.C.)

mace[1] (mās) *n.* ⟦OFr *masse*⟧ **1** a heavy, spiked war club, used in the Middle Ages **2** a staff used as a symbol of authority by certain officials

mace[2] (mās) *n.* ⟦< ML *macis*⟧ a spice made from the husk of the nutmeg

Mace (mās) ⟦< MACE[1]⟧ *trademark for* a gas, sold in aerosol containers, that temporarily stuns its victims —*n.* |*often* **m-**| such a substance, or a container of it —*vt.* **Maced, Mac'ing** |*often* **m-**| to spray with Mace

Mac·e·do·ni·a (mas'ə dō'nē ə) ancient kingdom in SE Europe —**Mac'e·do'ni·an** *adj., n.*

mac·er·ate (mas'ər āt') *vt.* **-at'ed, -at'ing** ⟦< L *macerare,* soften⟧ **1** to soften and separate into parts by soaking in liquid **2** to steep (fruit or vegetables), as in wine **3** loosely, to tear, chop, etc. into bits —**mac'-er·a'tion** *n.*

ma·che·te (mə shet'ē, -chet'ē) *n.* ⟦Sp < L *marcus,* hammer⟧ a large knife used for cutting sugar cane, underbrush, etc., esp. in Central and South America

Mach·i·a·vel·li·an (mak'ē ə vel'ē ən) *adj.* ⟦after N. *Machiavelli* (1469-1527), It statesman⟧ crafty; deceitful

mach·i·na·tion (mak'ə nā'shən) *n.* ⟦< L *machinari,* to plot⟧ a plot or scheme, esp. one with evil intent

ma·chine (mə shēn') *n.* ⟦< Gr *mēchos,* contrivance⟧ **1** |Old-fashioned| a vehicle, as an automobile **2** a structure consisting of a framework with various moving parts, for doing some kind of work **3** an organization functioning like a machine **4** the controlling group in a political party **5** *Mech.* a device, as the lever, that transmits, or changes the application of, energy —*adj.* **1** of machines **2** done by machinery —*vt.* **-chined', -chin'ing** to shape, etc. by machinery

machine gun an automatic gun, firing a rapid stream of bullets

machine language a language entirely in binary digits, used directly by a computer

ma·chin·er·y (mə shēn'ər ē, -shēn'rē) *n., pl.* **-ies 1** machines collectively **2** the working parts of a machine **3** the means for keeping something going

ma·chin'ist *n.* one who makes, repairs, or operates machinery

ma·chis·mo (mä chēz'mō) *n.* ⟦Sp < *macho,* masculine + *-ismo,* -ISM⟧ overly assertive or exaggerated masculinity

Mach number (mäk) ⟦after E. *Mach* (1838-1916), Austrian physicist⟧ |*also* **m- n-**| a number indicating the ratio of an object's speed to the speed of sound in the surrounding medium

ma·cho (mä'chō) *adj.* ⟦Sp, masculine⟧ exhibiting or characterized by machismo

mack·er·el (mak'ər əl) *n., pl.* **-el** or **-els** ⟦< OFr *maquerel*⟧ an edible fish of the North Atlantic

Mack·i·naw (coat) (mak'ə nô') ⟦after *Mackinac* Island in N Lake Huron⟧ |*also* **m-**| a short, heavy, double-breasted woolen coat, usually plaid

mack·in·tosh (mak'in täsh') *n.* ⟦after C. *Macintosh,* 19th-c. Scot inventor⟧ a raincoat of rubberized cloth

Ma·con (mā'kən) city in central Ga.: pop. 117,000

mac·ra·mé (mak'rə mā') *n.* ⟦Fr, ult. < Ar *miqramah,* a veil⟧ coarse lace made as of cord knotted in designs

macro- ⟦< Gr *makros,* long⟧ *combining form* long, large, enlarged

mac·ro·bi·ot·ics (mak'rō bī ät'iks) *n.pl.* ⟦< prec. + Gr *bios,* life⟧ |*with sing. v.*| the study of prolonging life, as by special diets —**mac'ro·bi·ot'ic** *adj.*

mac'ro·cosm' (-käz'əm) *n.* ⟦see MACRO- & COSMOS⟧ **1** the universe **2** any large, complex entity

ma·cron (mā'krən) *n.* ⟦< Gr *makros,* long⟧ a mark (¯) placed over a vowel to indicate its pronunciation

mad (mad) *adj.* **mad'der, mad'dest** ⟦< OE (*ge*)*mædan,* make mad⟧ **1** mentally ill; insane **2** frantic /*mad* with fear/ **3** foolish and rash **4** infatuated /he's *mad* about her/ **5** wildly amusing **6** having rabies /a *mad* dog/ **7** angry —*n.* an angry mood —**mad'ly** *adv.* —**mad'ness** *n.*

Mad·a·gas·car (mad'ə gas'kər) an island country off the SE coast of Africa: 228,919 sq. mi.; pop. 7,604,000

mad·am (mad'əm) *n., pl.* **mad'ams**; for 1, usually **mes·dames** (mā däm', -dam') ⟦Fr *madame,* orig. *ma dame,* my lady⟧ **1** a woman; lady: a polite term of address **2** a woman in charge of a brothel

ma·dame (mə dam', -däm'; mad'əm; *Fr* mä däm') *n., pl.* **mes·dames** (mā'dam', -däm'; *Fr* mā däm') ⟦Fr: see prec.⟧ **1** a married woman: equivalent to *Mrs.* **2** a distinguished woman: a title of respect

mad·cap (mad'kap') *n.* ⟦MAD + CAP, figurative for head⟧ a reckless, impulsive person —*adj.* reckless and impulsive

mad·den (mad''n) *vt., vi.* to make or become insane, angry, or wildly excited —**mad'den·ing** *adj.*

mad·der (mad'ər) *n.* ⟦OE *mædere*⟧ **1** any of various related plants, esp. a vine with yellow flowers and a red root **2** a red dye made from this root

made (mād) *vt., vi. pt. & pp. of* MAKE

ma·de·moi·selle (mad'ə mə zel'; *Fr* mäd mwä zel') *n., pl.* Fr. ***mes·de·moi·selles*** (mād mwä zel') ⟦Fr < *ma,* my + *demoiselle,* young lady⟧ an unmarried woman or girl: equivalent to *Miss*

made'-to-or'der *adj.* made to conform to the customer's specifications

made'-up' *adj.* **1** put together **2** invented;

false /a *made-up* story/ **3** with cosmetics applied

mad′house′ *n.* **1** an insane asylum **2** any place of turmoil, noise, etc.

Mad·i·son (mad′ə sən), **James** 1751-1836; 4th president of the U.S. (1809-17)

Madison capital of Wis.: pop. 171,000

mad′man′ *n., pl.* **-men′** an insane person; lunatic —**mad′wom′an,** *pl.* **-wom′en,** *n.fem.*

Ma·don·na (mə dän′ə) ⟦It < *ma,* my + *donna,* lady⟧ Mary, mother of Jesus —*n.* a picture or statue of Mary

ma·dras (ma′drəs, mə dras′) *n.* ⟦after fol.⟧ a fine, firm cotton cloth, usually striped or plaid

Ma·dras (mə dras′, -dräs′) seaport on SE coast of India: pop. 4,277,000

Ma·drid (mə drid′) capital of Spain, in the central part: pop. 3,200,000

mad·ri·gal (ma′dri gəl) *n.* ⟦< It⟧ a part song, without accompaniment, popular in the 15th to 17th c.

mael·strom (māl′strəm) *n.* ⟦< Du *malen,* to grind + *stroom,* a stream⟧ **1** a large or violent whirlpool **2** an agitated state of mind, affairs, etc.

ma·es·tro (mīs′trō, mä es′trō′) *n., pl.* **-tros** or **-tri** (-trē) ⟦It < L *magister,* master⟧ a master in any art; esp., a great composer or conductor of music

Ma·fi·a (mä′fē ə) *n.* ⟦It *maffia*⟧ a secret society engaged in illegal activities —**Ma·fi·o·so** (mä′fē ō′sō′), *pl.* **-si** (-sē), *n.*

mag·a·zine (mag′ə zēn′) *n.* ⟦< Ar *makhzan,* storehouse⟧ **1** a warehouse or military supply depot **2** a space in which explosives are stored, as in a fort **3** a supply chamber, as in a rifle, camera, etc. **4** a periodical publication containing stories, articles, etc.

Ma·gel·lan (mə jel′ən), **Fer·di·nand** (fur′d′n and′) *c.* 1480-1521; Port. navigator in the service of Spain

ma·gen·ta (mə jen′tə) *n.* ⟦after *Magenta,* town in Italy⟧ **1** a purplish-red dye **2** purplish red —*adj.* purplish-red

mag·got (mag′ət) *n.* ⟦ME *magotte*⟧ a wormlike insect larva, as of the housefly —**mag′got·y** *adj.*

Ma·gi (mā′jī′) *n.pl., sing.* **-gus** (-gəs) ⟦< old Pers *magus,* magician⟧ the wise men who came bearing gifts to the infant Jesus

mag·ic (maj′ik) *n.* ⟦< Gr *magikos,* of the Magi⟧ **1** the use of charms, spells, etc. in seeking or pretending to control events **2** any mysterious power /the *magic* of love/ **3** the art of producing illusions by sleight of hand, etc. —*adj.* **1** of, produced by, or using magic **2** producing extraordinary results, as if by magic —**mag′i·cal** *adj.* —**mag′i·cal·ly** *adv.*

ma·gi·cian (mə jish′ən) *n.* ⟦< OFr *magicien*⟧ an expert in magic

mag·is·te·ri·al (maj′is tir′ē əl) *adj.* **1** of or suitable for a magistrate **2** authoritative —**mag′is·te′ri·al·ly** *adv.*

mag·is·trate (maj′is trāt′) *n.* ⟦< L *magister,* master⟧ **1** a civil officer empowered to administer the law **2** a minor official, as a justice of the peace

mag·ma (mag′mə) *n.* ⟦< Gr *massein,* knead⟧ liquid or molten rock in the earth, which solidifies to produce igneous rock

Mag·na Car·ta or **Mag·na Char·ta** (mag′nə kär′tə) ⟦ML, great charter⟧ the charter, granted in 1215, that guarantees certain civil and political liberties to the English people

mag·nan·i·mous (mag nan′ə məs) *adj.* ⟦< L *magnus,* great + *animus,* soul⟧ generous in overlooking injury or insult; rising above pettiness; noble —**mag′na·nim′i·ty** (-nə nim′ə tē) *n.* —**mag·nan′i·mous·ly** *adv.*

mag·nate (mag′nāt) *n.* ⟦< L *magnus,* great⟧ a very influential person, esp. in business

mag·ne·sia (mag nē′zhə, -shə) *n.* ⟦ModL, ult. < Gr *Magnēsia,* ancient Gr city⟧ magnesium oxide, a white powder, used as a mild laxative and antacid

mag·ne′si·um (-zē əm, -zhē-) *n.* ⟦ModL: see prec.⟧ a light metallic chemical element

mag·net (mag′nit) *n.* ⟦see MAGNESIA⟧ **1** any piece of iron or certain other materials that has the property of attracting similar material **2** one that attracts

mag·net·ic (mag net′ik) *adj.* **1** having the properties of a magnet **2** of, producing, or caused by magnetism **3** of the earth's magnetism **4** that can be magnetized **5** powerfully attractive —**mag·net′i·cal·ly** *adv.*

magnetic field a physical field arising from an electric charge in motion, producing a force on a moving electric charge

magnetic tape a thin plastic ribbon with a magnetized coating for recording sounds, digital computer data, etc.

mag·net·ism (mag′nə tiz′əm) *n.* **1** the property, quality, or condition of being magnetic **2** the force to which this is due **3** personal charm

mag′net·ite′ (-tīt′) *n.* ⟦< Ger⟧ black iron oxide, an important iron ore

mag′net·ize′ (-tīz′) *vt.* **-ized′, -iz′ing** **1** to give magnetic properties to (steel, iron, etc.) **2** to charm (a person) —**mag′net·i·za′tion** *n.*

mag·ne·to (mag nēt′ō) *n., pl.* **-tos** a small generator in which one or more permanent magnets produce the magnetic field

mag·ne·tom·e·ter (mag′nə täm′ət ər) *n.* **1** an instrument for measuring magnetic forces **2** such an instrument used as to detect concealed metal weapons at airports, etc.

magnet school a public school offering new and special courses to attract students from a broad urban area so as to bring about desegregation

mag·nif·i·cent (mag nif′ə sənt) *adj.* ⟦< L *magnus,* great + *facere,* do⟧ **1** splendid, stately, or sumptuous, as in form **2** exalted: said of ideas, etc. **3** [Colloq.] excellent —**mag·nif′i·cence** *n.* —**mag·nif′i·cent·ly** *adv.*

mag·ni·fy (mag′nə fī′) *vt.* **-fied′, -fy′ing** ⟦see prec.⟧ **1** to exaggerate **2** to increase the apparent size of, esp. with a lens **3** [Archaic] to praise —*vi.* to have the power of increasing the apparent size of an object —**mag′ni·fi·ca′tion** *n.* —**mag′ni·fi′er** *n.*

mag′ni·tude′ (-to͞od′, -tyo͞od′) *n.* ⟦< L *magnus,* great⟧ **1** greatness of size, extent, etc. **2** *a)* size *b)* loudness (of sound) *c)* importance **3** the degree of brightness of a star, etc.

mag·no·li·a (mag nō′lē ə, -nōl′yə) ***n.*** ⟦after P. *Magnol* (1638-1715), Fr botanist⟧ a tree with large, fragrant flowers of white, pink, or purple

mag·num (mag′nəm) ***n.*** ⟦< L *magnus,* great⟧ **1** a wine bottle holding 1.5 liters **2** [*usually* **M-**] a firearm, esp. a revolver, that fires magnum cartridges —***adj.*** of or pertaining to a cartridge having great explosive force for its size

mag·num o·pus (mag′nəm ō′pəs) ⟦L⟧ a great work; masterpiece

mag·pie (mag′pī′) ***n.*** ⟦< *Mag,* dim. of *Margaret* + *pie,* magpie⟧ **1** a noisy, black-and-white bird related to the jay **2** a person who chatters

Mag·yar (mag′yär′) ***n.*** **1** the Hungarian language **2** a member of the main ethnic group in Hungary

ma·ha·ra·jah or **ma·ha·ra·ja** (mä′hə rä′jə) ***n.*** ⟦< Sans *mahā,* great + *rājā,* king⟧ [Historical] in India, a prince, specif. the ruler of a native state —**ma′ha·ra′ni** or **ma′ha·ra′nee** (-nē) ***n.fem.***

ma·ha·ri·shi (mä′hä rish′ē) ***n.*** ⟦Hindi < *mahā,* great + *ṛshi,* sage⟧ a Hindu teacher of mysticism

ma·hat·ma (mə hat′mə, -hät′-) ***n.*** ⟦< Sans *mahā,* great + *ātman,* soul⟧ *Buddhism* any of a class of wise and holy persons held in special regard

mah-jongg or **mah-jong** (mä′jôŋ′) ***n.*** ⟦< Chin *ma-ch'iao,* sparrow, a figure on one of the tiles⟧ a game of Chinese origin played with small pieces called *tiles*

Mah·ler (mä′lər), **Gus·tav** (goos′täf′) 1860-1911; Austrian composer & conductor

ma·hog·a·ny (mə häg′ə nē, -hôg′-) ***n.***, *pl.* **-nies** ⟦< ?⟧ **1** *a*) a tropical American tree *b*) the reddish-brown wood of this tree **2** reddish brown

Ma·hom·et (mə häm′it) *var. of* MOHAMMED

ma·hout (mə hout′) ***n.*** ⟦< Hindi⟧ in India, an elephant driver or keeper

maid (mād) ***n.*** **1** MAIDEN **2** a girl or woman servant

maid′en (-′n) ***n.*** ⟦OE *mægden*⟧ [Now Rare] a girl or young unmarried woman —***adj.*** **1** of or for a maiden **2** unmarried or virgin **3** untried **4** first /a *maiden* voyage/ —**maid′en·hood′** ***n.*** —**maid′en·ly** ***adj.***

maid′en·hair′ ***n.*** a delicate fern

maid′en·head′ (-hed′) ***n.*** the hymen

maiden name the surname that a married woman had when not yet married

maid of honor an unmarried woman acting as chief attendant to a bride

maid′ser′vant ***n.*** a female servant

mail[1] (māl) ***n.*** ⟦< OHG *malaha,* wallet⟧ **1** letters, packages, etc. transported and delivered by the post office **2** a postal system —***adj.*** of mail —***vt.*** to send by mail —**mail′er** ***n.***

mail[2] (māl) ***n.*** ⟦< L *macula,* mesh of a net⟧ flexible body armor made of small metal rings, scales, etc. —**mailed** ***adj.***

SUIT OF MAIL

mail′box′ ***n.*** **1** a box into which mail is delivered **2** a box for depositing outgoing mail Also **mail box**

mail′man′ ***n.***, *pl.* **-men′** a man who carries and delivers mail

mail order an order for goods to be sent by mail —**mail′-or′der** ***adj.***

maim (mām) ***vt.*** ⟦OFr *mahaigner*⟧ to cripple; mutilate

main (mān) ***n.*** ⟦OE *mægen,* strength⟧ **1** a principal pipe in a distributing system for water, gas, etc. **2** [Old Poet.] the ocean —***adj.*** chief in size, importance, etc.; principal —**by main force** (or **strength**) by sheer force (or strength) —**in the main** mostly; chiefly —**with might and main** with all one's strength

main clause *Gram.* INDEPENDENT CLAUSE

main drag [Slang] the principal street of a city or town

Maine (mān) New England State of the U.S.: 33,215 sq. mi.; pop. 1,125,000; cap. Augusta —**Main·er** (mā′nər) ***n.***

main·frame (mān′frām′) ***n.*** **1** the central processing unit of a large computer **2** a very large computer, to which several terminals may be connected

main′land′ (-land′, -lənd) ***n.*** the principal land mass of a continent, as distinguished from nearby islands

main′line′ ***n.*** the principal road, course, etc. —***vt.*** **-lined′**, **-lin′ing** [Slang] to inject (a narcotic drug) directly into a large vein

main′ly ***adv.*** chiefly; principally

main′mast′ (-mast′, -məst) ***n.*** the principal mast of a vessel

main′sail′ (-sāl′, -səl) ***n.*** the principal sail of a vessel, set from the mainmast

main′spring′ ***n.*** **1** the principal spring in a clock, watch, etc. **2** the chief motive or cause

main′stay′ (-stā′) ***n.*** **1** the supporting line extending forward from the mainmast **2** a chief support

main′stream′ (-strēm′) ***n.*** a major trend or line of thought, action, etc. —***vt.*** to cause to undergo mainstreaming

main′stream′ing ***n.*** the placement of disabled people into regular school classes, work places, etc.

main·tain (mān tān′) ***vt.*** ⟦< L *manu tenere,* hold in the hand⟧ **1** to keep or keep up; carry on **2** to keep in continuance or in a certain state, as of repair **3** to defend **4** to affirm or assert **5** to support by providing what is needed —**main·tain′a·ble** ***adj.***

main·te·nance (mān′tə nəns) ***n.*** a maintaining or being maintained

mai tai (mī′ tī′) ⟦Tahitian, lit., good⟧ [*often* **M- T-**] a cocktail of rum, fruit juices, etc.

maî·tre d'hô·tel (me tr′ dō tel′) ⟦Fr, master of the house⟧ a supervisor of waiters and waitresses Also [Colloq.] **mai·tre d'** (māt′ər dē′)

maize (māz) ***n.*** ⟦< WInd *mahiz*⟧ **1** *chiefly Brit. name for* CORN[1] (*n.* 2) **2** yellow

Maj. Major

ma·jes·tic (mə jes′tik) ***adj.*** grand; stately —**ma·jes′ti·cal·ly** ***adv.***

maj·es·ty (maj′is tē) ***n.***, *pl.* **-ties** ⟦< L *magnus,* great⟧ **1** [**M-**] a title used in speaking to or of a sovereign **2** grandeur

ma·jol·i·ca (mə jäl′i kə) ***n.*** ⟦It⟧ Italian glazed pottery

ma·jor (mā′jər) ***adj.*** ⟦L, compar. of *magnus,* great⟧ 1 greater in size, amount, importance, etc. 2 *Music* designating an interval greater than the corresponding minor by a half tone —***vi.*** *Educ.* to specialize (*in* a field of study) —***n.*** 1 *U.S. Mil.* an officer ranking just above a captain 2 *Educ.* a principal field of study

ma′jor-do′mo (-dō′mō) ***n.***, *pl.* **-mos** ⟦< L *major,* greater + *domus,* house⟧ a man in charge of a great household

major general *pl.* **major generals** *U.S. Mil.* an officer ranking just above a brigadier general

ma·jor·i·ty (mə jôr′ə tē) ***n.***, *pl.* **-ties** ⟦see MAJOR⟧ 1 the greater number; more than half of a total 2 the number by which the votes cast for the candidate who receives more than half the votes, exceed the sum of all the other votes cast 3 full legal age 4 the military rank of a major

major scale a musical scale with half steps between the third and fourth and the seventh and eighth tones, and whole steps in all other positions

make (māk) ***vt.*** **made, mak′ing** ⟦OE *macian*⟧ 1 to bring into being; build, create, produce, etc. 2 to cause to be or become /*made* king, *made* sad/ 3 to prepare for use /*make* the beds/ 4 to amount to /two pints *make* a quart/ 5 to have the qualities of /to *make* a fine leader/ 6 to acquire; earn 7 to cause the success of /that venture *made* her/ 8 to understand /what do you *make* of that?/ 9 to execute, do, etc. /to *make* a speech/ 10 to cause or force: with an infinitive without *to* /*make* him go/ 11 to arrive at; reach /the ship *made* port/ 12 [Colloq.] to get on or in /to *make* the team/ —***vi.*** 1 to start (to do something) 2 to behave as specified /*make* bold/ 3 to cause something to be as specified /*make* ready/ —***n.*** 1 the way in which something is made; style 2 type; brand —**make away with** 1 to steal 2 to kill —**make believe** to pretend —**make one's day** [Slang] to give pleasure that will be the high point of one's day —**make do** to manage with what is available —**make for** 1 to go toward 2 to help effect —**make it** [Colloq.] to achieve a certain thing —**make off with** to steal —**make out** 1 to see with difficulty 2 to understand 3 to fill out (a blank form, etc.) 4 to (try to) show or prove to be 5 to succeed; get along 6 [Slang] *a*) to kiss and caress as lovers *b*) to have sexual intercourse —**make over** 1 to change; renovate 2 to transfer the ownership of —**make up** 1 to put together 2 to form; constitute 3 to invent 4 to complete by providing what is lacking 5 to compensate (*for*) 6 to become friendly again after a quarrel 7 to put on cosmetics, etc. 8 to decide (one's mind) —**make up to** to try to win over, as by flattering —**mak′er** ***n.***

make′-be·lieve′ ***n.*** pretense; feigning —***adj.*** pretended; feigned

make′shift′ ***n.*** a temporary substitute or expedient —***adj.*** that will do as a temporary substitute

make′up′ or **make′-up′** ***n.*** 1 the way something is put together; composition 2 nature; disposition 3 the cosmetics, etc. used by an actor 4 cosmetics generally

make′-work′ ***adj.*** that serves no other purpose than to give an idle or unemployed person something to do /a *make-work* project/

mal- ⟦< L *malus,* bad⟧ *prefix* bad or badly, wrong, ill

mal·ad·just·ed (mal′ə jus′tid) ***adj.*** poorly adjusted; esp., unable to adapt oneself psychologically to one's environment or circumstances —**mal′ad·just′ment** ***n.***

mal·a·droit (mal′ə droit′) ***adj.*** ⟦Fr: see MAL- & ADROIT⟧ awkward; clumsy; bungling —**mal′a·droit′ly** ***adv.***

mal·a·dy (mal′ə dē) ***n.***, *pl.* **-dies** ⟦< VL *male habitus,* badly kept⟧ a disease; illness

ma·laise (ma lāz′) ***n.*** ⟦Fr < *mal,* bad + *aise,* ease⟧ a vague feeling of physical discomfort or of uneasiness

mal·a·mute (mal′ə myōōt′) ***n.*** ⟦< *Malemute,* an Eskimo tribe⟧ a strong dog developed as a sled dog by Eskimos

mal·a·prop·ism (mal′ə präp′iz′əm) ***n.*** ⟦after Mrs. *Malaprop* in Sheridan's *The Rivals* (1775)⟧ a ludicrous misuse of words that sound alike

ma·lar·i·a (mə ler′ē ə) ***n.*** ⟦It < *mala aria,* bad air⟧ an infectious disease transmitted by the anopheles mosquito, characterized by severe chills and fever —**ma·lar′i·al** ***adj.***

ma·lar·key or **ma·lar·ky** (mə lär′kē) ***n.*** ⟦< ?⟧ [Slang] nonsensical talk

mal·a·thi·on (mal′ə thī′än′) ***n.*** ⟦< chemical names⟧ an organic insecticide

Ma·la·wi (mä′lä wē) country in SE Africa: 45,746 sq. mi.; pop. 7,293,000

Ma·lay (mā′lā′, mə lā′) ***n.*** 1 the language of a large group of indigenous peoples of the Malay Peninsula and the Malay Archipelago, now the official language of Malaysia and Indonesia 2 a member of any of these peoples —***adj.*** of these peoples, their language, etc.

Mal·a·ya·lam (mal′ə yä′ləm) ***n.*** a language of the SW coast of India

Malay Archipelago large group of islands between SE Asia & Australia

Malay Peninsula peninsula in SE Asia

Ma·lay·sia (mə lā′zhə) 1 MALAY ARCHIPELAGO 2 country in SE Asia, mostly on the Malay Peninsula: *c.* 129,000 sq. mi.; pop. 15,270,000 —**Ma·lay′sian** ***adj.***, ***n.***

mal·con·tent (mal′kən tent′) ***adj.*** ⟦OFr: see MAL- & CONTENT[1]⟧ dissatisfied; rebellious —***n.*** a malcontent person

Mal·dives (mal′dīvz) country on a group of islands (**Mal′dive Islands**) in the Indian Ocean: 115 sq. mi.; pop. 184,000

male (māl) ***adj.*** ⟦< L *mas,* a male⟧ 1 designating or of the sex that fertilizes the ovum 2 of, like, or suitable for men or boys; masculine 3 having a part shaped to fit into a corresponding hollow part (called *female*): said of electric plugs, etc. —***n.*** a male person, animal, or plant

mal·e·dic·tion (mal′ə dik′shən) ***n.*** ⟦see MAL- & DICTION⟧ a curse

mal′e·fac′tor (-fak′tər) ***n.*** ⟦< L *male,* evil +

facere, do ⟧ an evildoer or criminal —**mal'e·fac'tion** ***n.***

ma·lef·i·cent (mə lef'ə sənt) ***adj.*** ⟦ < L: see prec. ⟧ harmful; evil —**ma·lef'i·cence** ***n.***

ma·lev·o·lent (mə lev'ə lənt) ***adj.*** ⟦ < L *male,* evil + *velle,* to wish ⟧ wishing evil or harm to others; malicious —**ma·lev'o·lence** ***n.***

mal·fea·sance (mal fē'zəns) ***n.*** ⟦ < Fr *mal,* evil + *faire,* do ⟧ wrongdoing, esp. by a public official

mal·for·ma·tion (mal'fôr mā'shən) ***n.*** faulty or abnormal formation of a body or part —**mal·formed'** ***adj.***

mal·func'tion ***vi.*** to fail to function as it should —***n.*** an instance of malfunctioning

Ma·li (mä'lē) country in W Africa: 478,786 sq. mi.; pop. 7,898,000

mal·ice (mal'is) ***n.*** ⟦ < L *malus,* bad ⟧ **1** active ill will; desire to harm another **2** *Law* evil intent

ma·li·cious (mə lish'əs) ***adj.*** having, showing, or caused by malice; spiteful —**ma·li'cious·ly** ***adv.***

ma·lign (mə lin') ***vt.*** ⟦ < L *male,* ill + *genus,* born ⟧ to speak evil of; slander —***adj.*** **1** malicious **2** evil; baleful **3** very harmful

ma·lig·nant (mə lig'nənt) ***adj.*** ⟦ see prec. ⟧ **1** having an evil influence **2** wishing evil **3** very harmful **4** causing or likely to cause death /*a malignant* tumor/ —**ma·lig'nan·cy,** *pl.* **-cies,** ***n.*** —**ma·lig'ni·ty** (-nə tē), *pl.* **-ties,** ***n.***

ma·lin·ger (mə liŋ'gər) ***vi.*** ⟦ < Fr *malingre,* sickly ⟧ to feign illness so as to escape duty —**ma·lin'ger·er** ***n.***

mall (môl) ***n.*** ⟦ < *maul,* mallet: from use in a game on outdoor lanes ⟧ **1** a shaded walk or public promenade **2** *a)* a shop-lined street for pedestrians only *b)* an enclosed shopping center

mal·lard (mal'ərd) ***n.*** ⟦ < OFr *malart* ⟧ the common wild duck

mal·le·a·ble (mal'ē ə bəl) ***adj.*** ⟦ < L *malleus,* a hammer ⟧ **1** that can be hammered, pounded, or pressed into various shapes without breaking **2** adaptable —**mal'le·a·bil'i·ty** ***n.***

mal·let (mal'ət) ***n.*** ⟦ < L *malleus,* a hammer ⟧ **1** a short-handled hammer with a wooden head, for driving a chisel, etc. **2** any similar long-handled hammer, as for use in croquet or polo **3** a small hammer for playing a xylophone, etc.

mal·low (mal'ō) ***n.*** ⟦ < L *malva* ⟧ any of a family of plants, including the hollyhock, cotton, and okra, with large, showy flowers

mal·nour·ished (mal nur'isht) ***adj.*** improperly nourished

mal'nu·tri'tion ***n.*** faulty or inadequate nutrition; poor nourishment

mal'oc·clu'sion (-ə klōō'zhən) ***n.*** improper meeting of the upper and lower teeth

mal'o'dor·ous (-ō'dər əs) ***adj.*** having a bad odor; stinking

mal·prac'tice ***n.*** professional misconduct or improper practice, esp. by a physician

malt (môlt) ***n.*** ⟦ OE *mealt* ⟧ **1** barley or other grain soaked until it sprouts and then dried in a kiln: used in brewing and distilling **2** beer, ale, etc. —***adj.*** made with malt —**malt'y, -i·er, -i·est,** ***adj.***

Mal·ta (môl'tə) country on a group of islands in the Mediterranean, south of Sicily: 122 sq. mi.; pop. 354,000

malted milk **1** powdered malt and dried milk, used in a drink with milk, ice cream, etc. **2** this drink: also **malt'ed** ***n.***

Mal·tese (môl tēz') ***n.*** **1** the variety of Arabic spoken in Malta **2** *pl.* **Mal·tese'** a native or inhabitant of Malta —***adj.*** of Malta, its inhabitants, etc.

malt liquor beer, ale, or the like made from malt by fermentation

mal·treat (mal trēt') ***vt.*** ⟦ see MAL- & TREAT ⟧ to treat roughly or unkindly; abuse —**mal·treat'ment** ***n.***

ma·ma or **mam'ma** (mä'mə; *also* mə mä') ***n.*** *child's term for* MOTHER

mam·mal (mam'əl) ***n.*** ⟦ < L *mamma,* breast ⟧ any of a large group of vertebrates the females of which have milk-secreting glands (**mam'ma·ry glands**) for feeding their offspring —**mam·ma·li·an** (mə mā'lē ən) ***adj., n.***

mam·mo·gram (mam'ə gram') ***n.*** an X-ray obtained from mammography

mam·mog·ra·phy (mə mäg'rə fē) ***n.*** ⟦ < L *mamma,* breast + -GRAPHY ⟧ an X-ray technique for detecting breast tumors before they can be seen or felt

mam·mon (mam'ən) ***n.*** ⟦ < Aram ⟧ [*often* M-] riches regarded as an object of worship and greedy pursuit

mam·moth (mam'əth) ***n.*** ⟦ < Russ *mamont* ⟧ an extinct elephant with long tusks —***adj.*** very big; huge

man (man) ***n.,*** *pl.* **men** (men) ⟦ OE *mann* ⟧ **1** a human being; person **2** the human race; mankind **3** an adult male person **4** an adult male servant, employee, etc. **5** a husband **6** any of the pieces used in chess, checkers, etc. —***vt.*** **manned, man'ning** **1** to furnish with a labor force for work, defense, etc. **2** to strengthen; brace /to *man* oneself for an ordeal/ —**as a** (or **one**) **man** in unison; unanimously —**to a man** with no exception

Man (man), **Isle of** one of the British Isles, between Northern Ireland & England

-man (mən, man) *combining form* man or person of a (specified) kind, in a (specified) activity, etc. Now often replaced by -PERSON or -WOMAN

Man. Manitoba

man·a·cle (man'ə kəl) ***n.*** ⟦ < L *manus,* hand ⟧ a handcuff: *usually used in pl.* —***vt.*** **-cled, -cling** **1** to put handcuffs on **2** to restrain

man·age (man'ij) ***vt.*** **-aged, -ag·ing** ⟦ < L *manus,* hand ⟧ **1** to control the movement or behavior of **2** to have charge of; direct /to *manage* a hotel/ **3** to succeed in accomplishing —***vi.*** **1** to carry on business **2** to contrive to get along —**man'age·a·ble** ***adj.***

man'age·ment ***n.*** **1** a managing or being managed **2** the persons managing a business, institution, etc.

man'ag·er ***n.*** one who manages; esp., one who manages a business, etc.

man·a·ge·ri·al (man'ə jir'ē əl) ***adj.*** of a manager or management

ma·ña·na (mä nyä'nä) ***n., adv.*** ⟦ Sp ⟧ tomorrow or an indefinite future time

man·a·tee (man′ə tē′) *n.* ⟦< WInd native name⟧ a large, plant-eating aquatic mammal of tropical waters

Man·ches·ter (man′ches′tər) city & port in NW England: pop. 458,000

Man·chu (man cho͞o′, man′cho͞o) *n.* **1** *pl.* **-chus′** or **-chu′** a member of a Mongolian people of Manchuria who ruled China from 1644 to 1912 **2** their language —*adj.* of the Manchus, their language, etc.

Man·chu·ri·a (man choor′ē ə) region in NE China —**Man·chu′ri·an** *adj., n.*

man·da·rin (man′də rin) *n.* ⟦< Sans *mantrin,* counselor⟧ **1** a high official in the Chinese empire **2** [**M-**] the main dialect of Chinese

man·date (man′dāt′) *n.* ⟦< L *mandare,* to command⟧ **1** an order or command **2** [Historical] *a)* a League of Nations commission to a country to administer some region *b)* this region **3** the will of constituents expressed to their representative, legislature, etc.

man·da·to·ry (man′də tôr′ē) *adj.* **1** of or containing a mandate **2** authoritatively commanded; obligatory

man·di·ble (man′də bəl) *n.* ⟦< L *mandere,* chew⟧ the jaw; specif., *a)* the lower jaw of a vertebrate *b)* either jaw of a beaked animal —**man·dib′u·lar** (-dib′yo͞o lər) *adj.*

man·do·lin (man′də lin′) *n.* ⟦< Gr *pandoura,* kind of lute⟧ a musical instrument with four to six pairs of strings

man·drake (man′drāk′) *n.* ⟦< Gr *mandragoras*⟧ a poisonous plant of the nightshade family, with a thick, forked root suggesting the human form

man·drill (man′dril) *n.* ⟦MAN + *drill,* kind of monkey⟧ a large, strong baboon of W Africa: the male has blue and scarlet patches on the face and rump

mane (mān) *n.* ⟦OE *manu*⟧ the long hair growing on the neck of the horse, lion, etc. —**maned** *adj.*

man′-eat′er *n.* an animal that eats human flesh —**man′-eat′ing** *adj.*

ma·nège or **ma·nege** (ma nezh′) *n.* ⟦Fr < It *maneggiare,* manage⟧ the art of riding and training horses

ma·neu·ver (mə no͞o′vər) *n.* ⟦< L *manu operare,* to work by hand⟧ **1** a planned and controlled movement of troops, warships, etc. **2** a skillful or shrewd move; stratagem —*vi., vt.* **1** to perform or cause to perform a maneuver or maneuvers **2** to manage or plan skillfully **3** to move, get, make, etc. by some scheme —**ma·neu′ver·a·ble** *adj.*

man·ful (man′fəl) *adj.* manly; brave, resolute, etc. —**man′ful·ly** *adv.*

man·ga·nese (maŋ′gə nēs′, -nēz′) *n.* ⟦ult. < ML *magnesia*: see MAGNESIA⟧ a grayish-white, metallic chemical element, used in alloys

mange (mānj) *n.* ⟦< OFr *mangeue,* an itch⟧ a skin disease of mammals, causing itching, hair loss, etc.

man·ger (mān′jər) *n.* ⟦< L *mandere,* chew⟧ a box or trough to hold fodder for horses or cattle to eat

man·gle[1] (maŋ′gəl) *vt.* **-gled, -gling** ⟦prob. < OFr *mehaigner,* maim⟧ **1** to mutilate by roughly cutting, tearing, crushing, etc. **2** to spoil; botch; mar

man·gle[2] (maŋ′gəl) *n.* ⟦< Gr *manganon,* war machine⟧ a machine for pressing and smoothing sheets, etc. between rollers

man·go (maŋ′gō) *n., pl.* **-goes** or **-gos** ⟦< Tamil *mān-kāy*⟧ **1** the yellow-red, somewhat acid fruit of a tropical tree **2** this tree

man·grove (maŋ′grōv) *n.* ⟦< WInd name⟧ a tropical tree with branches that spread and send down roots, forming additional trunks

man·gy (mān′jē) *adj.* **-gi·er, -gi·est** **1** having mange **2** filthy, low, etc. —**man′gi·ly** *adv.* —**man′gi·ness** *n.*

man′han′dle (man′-) *vt.* **-dled, -dling** to handle roughly

Man·hat·tan (man hat′′n) island in SE N.Y.: a borough of New York City: pop. 1,428,000 —*n.* [*often* **m-**] a cocktail made of whiskey and sweet vermouth

man′hole′ *n.* a hole through which one can enter a sewer, conduit, etc.

man′hood′ *n.* **1** the state or time of being a man **2** manly qualities; manliness **3** men collectively

man′-hour′ *n.* a time unit equal to one hour of work done by one person

man′hunt′ *n.* a hunt for a fugitive

ma·ni·a (mā′nē ə) *n.* ⟦Gr, madness⟧ **1** wild or violent mental disorder **2** an excessive enthusiasm; obsession; craze

-ma·ni·a (mā′nē ə) ⟦see prec.⟧ *combining form* a (specified) type of mental disorder

ma·ni·ac (mā′nē ak′) *adj.* wildly insane —*n.* a violently insane person —**ma·ni·a·cal** (mə nī′ə kəl) *adj.*

man·ic (man′ik) *adj.* having, characterized by, or like mania

man′ic-de·pres′sive (-dē pres′iv) *adj.* characterized by alternating periods of extreme excitability, excessive activity, etc., and severe mental depression

man·i·cure (man′i kyoor′) *n.* ⟦< L *manus,* a hand + *cura,* care⟧ a trimming, polishing, etc. of the fingernails —*vt.* **-cured′, -cur′ing** to trim, polish, etc. (fingernails) —**man′i·cur′ist** *n.*

man·i·fest (man′ə fest′) *adj.* ⟦< L *manifestus,* lit., struck by the hand⟧ apparent to the senses or the mind; obvious —*vt.* to show plainly; reveal —*n.* an itemized list of a craft's cargo or passengers —**man′i·fest′ly** *adv.*

man′i·fes·ta′tion (-fes tā′shən) *n.* **1** a manifesting or being manifested **2** something that manifests

man′i·fes′to (-fes′tō) *n., pl.* **-toes** or **-tos** ⟦It < *manifestare,* to manifest⟧ a public declaration of intention by an important person or group

man·i·fold (man′ə fōld′) *adj.* ⟦see MANY & -FOLD⟧ **1** having many forms, parts, etc. **2** of many sorts **3** being such in many ways [*a manifold* villain] **4** operating several parts of one kind —*n.* a pipe with several outlets, as for conducting cylinder exhaust from an engine —*vt.* to make copies of, as with carbon paper

man·i·kin or **man·ni·kin** (man′i kin) *n.* ⟦Du *manneken* < *man,* man + *-ken,* -KIN⟧ **1** a little man; dwarf **2** an anatomical model of the human body, used as in art classes **3** MANNEQUIN

Ma·nil·a (mə nil′ə) capital & seaport of the

Philippines, in SW Luzon: pop. 1,630,000 (met. area 5,926,000)

Manila hemp ⟦after prec.⟧ [*often* **m- h-**] a strong fiber from the leafstalks of a Philippine plant, used for making rope, paper, etc.

Manila paper [*often* **m- p-**] a strong, buff-colored paper, orig. made of Manila hemp

man in the street the average person

ma·nip·u·late (mə nip′yo͞o lāt′, -yə-) ***vt.*** **-lat′ed, -lat′ing** ⟦ult. < L *manus,* a hand + *plere,* to fill⟧ **1** to work or handle skillfully **2** to manage artfully or shrewdly, often in an unfair way **3** to alter (figures, etc.) for one's own purposes —**ma·nip′u·la′tion** ***n.***

Man·i·to·ba (man′ə tō′bə) province of south central Canada: 251,000 sq. mi.; pop. 1,064,000; cap. Winnipeg —**Man′i·to′ban** ***adj., n.***

man·kind (man′kīnd′; *also, & for 2 always,* man′kīnd′) ***n.*** **1** the human race **2** all human males

man·ly (man′lē) ***adj.*** **-li·er, -li·est** having the qualities regarded as suitable for a man; virile, brave, etc. —***adv.*** in a manly way —**man′li·ness** ***n.***

man′-made′ ***adj.*** artificial; synthetic

Mann (män), **Thom·as** (tăm′əs; *Ger* tō′mäs) 1875-1955; Ger. novelist, in U.S. 1938-52

man·na (man′ə) ***n.*** ⟦< Heb *mān*⟧ **1** *Bible* food miraculously provided for the Israelites in the wilderness **2** any help that comes unexpectedly

man·ne·quin (man′i kin) ***n.*** ⟦see MANIKIN⟧ **1** a model of the human body, used as by tailors **2** a woman who models clothes in stores, etc.

man·ner (man′ər) ***n.*** ⟦< L *manus,* a hand⟧ **1** a way of doing something; mode of procedure **2** a way, esp. a usual way, of acting; habit **3** [*pl.*] *a*) ways of social behavior /*bad manners*/ *b*) polite ways of social behavior /*to learn manners*/ **4** kind; sort

man′nered (-ərd) ***adj.*** **1** having manners of a specified sort /*ill-mannered*/ **2** artificial, stylized, etc.

man′ner·ism′ ***n.*** **1** excessive use of some distinctive manner or style in art, literature, etc. **2** a peculiarity of manner in behavior, speech, etc.

man′ner·ly ***adj.*** polite

man·nish (man′ish) ***adj.*** like a man or man's: said of a woman having characteristics generally attributed to men

ma·noeu·vre (mə no͞o′vər) ***n., vi., vt.*** **-vred, -vring** *chiefly Brit., etc. sp. of* MANEUVER

man of letters a writer, scholar, editor, etc., esp. in the field of literature

man′-of-war′ ***n., pl.*** **men′-of-war′** an armed naval vessel; warship

ma·nom·e·ter (mə năm′ət ər) ***n.*** ⟦Fr < Gr *manos,* rare (as in "thin, sparse") + Fr *-mètre,* -METER⟧ an instrument for measuring the pressure of gases or liquids

man·or (man′ər) ***n.*** ⟦< L *manere,* remain, dwell⟧ **1** in England, a landed estate **2** the main house on an estate —**ma·no·ri·al** (mə nôr′ē əl) ***adj.***

man′pow′er ***n.*** **1** power furnished by human strength **2** the collective strength or availability for work of the people in any given area, nation, etc.

man·qué (män kā′) ***adj.*** ⟦Fr < *manquer,* be lacking⟧ unfulfilled; would-be /*a poet manqué*/

MANSARD ROOF

man·sard (roof) (man′särd) ⟦after F. *Mansard,* 17th-c. Fr architect⟧ a roof with two slopes on each of four sides, the lower slope being steeper than the upper

manse (mans) ***n.*** ⟦see MANOR⟧ the residence of a minister; parsonage

man′ser′vant ***n., pl.*** **men′ser′vants** a male servant Also **man servant**

-man·ship (mən ship) *combining form* talent or skill (esp. in gaining advantage) in /*grantsmanship*/

man·sion (man′shən) ***n.*** ⟦< L *manere,* remain, dwell⟧ a large, imposing house

man′-sized′ ***adj.*** [Colloq.] of a size fit for a man; big Also **man′-size′**

man′slaugh′ter (-slôt′ər) ***n.*** the killing of a human being by another, esp. when unlawful but without malice

man·ta (man′tə) ***n.*** ⟦Sp < LL *mantum,* a cloak⟧ a giant RAY[2], with winglike pectoral fins Also **manta ray**

man·tel (man′təl) ***n.*** ⟦var. of MANTLE⟧ **1** the facing of stone, etc. about a fireplace, including a projecting shelf **2** this shelf: also **man′tel·piece′**

man·til·la (man til′ə, -tē′ə) ***n.*** ⟦Sp: see MANTA⟧ a woman's scarf, as of lace, worn over the hair and shoulders

man·tis (man′tis) ***n., pl.*** **-tis·es** or **-tes′** (-tēz′) ⟦< Gr, prophet⟧ an insect with forelegs held up together as if praying

man·tis·sa (man tis′ə) ***n.*** ⟦L, (useless) addition⟧ the decimal part of a logarithm

man·tle (man′təl) ***n.*** ⟦< L *mantellum*⟧ **1** a loose, sleeveless cloak **2** anything that envelops or conceals **3** a small hood which when placed over a flame gives off a brilliant incandescent light —***vt.*** **-tled, -tling** to cover as with a mantle —***vi.*** **1** to be or become covered **2** to blush or flush

man·tra (man′trə, mun′-) ***n.*** ⟦Sans⟧ a chant of a Vedic hymn, text, etc.

man·u·al (man′yo͞o əl) ***adj.*** ⟦< L *manus,* a hand⟧ **1** of the hands **2** made, done, or worked by hand **3** involving skill or hard work with the hands —***n.*** **1** a handy book for use as a guide, reference, etc. **2** prescribed drill in the handling of a weapon —**man′u·al·ly** ***adv.***

man·u·fac·ture (man′yo͞o fak′chər, -yə-) ***n.*** ⟦< L *manus,* a hand + *facere,* make⟧ **1** the making of goods, esp. by machinery and on a large scale **2** the making of any product, esp. when regarded as merely mechanical —***vt.*** **-tured, -tur·ing** **1** to make, esp. by machinery **2** to make up (excuses, etc.); invent —**man′u·fac′tur·er** ***n.***

man·u·mit (man′yo͞o mit′) ***vt.*** **-mit′ted, -mit′ting** ⟦< L *manus,* a hand + *mittere,* send⟧ to free from slavery —**man′u·mis′sion** ***n.***

ma·nure (mə no͞or′, -nyo͞or′) ***vt.*** **-nured′, -nur′ing** ⟦< OFr *manouvrer,* work with the hands ⟧ to put manure on or into —*n.* animal excrement, etc. used to fertilize soil

man·u·script (man′yo͞o skript′, -yə-) ***adj.*** ⟦< L *manus,* hand + *scriptus,* written ⟧ 1 written by hand or typewritten 2 designating writing that consists of unconnected letters like print —***n.*** 1 a written or typewritten document, book, etc., as submitted to a publisher 2 writing as opposed to print

Manx (maŋks) ***n.*** the language spoken on the Isle of Man, now nearly extinct —***adj.*** of the Isle of Man, its people, etc.

man·y (men′ē) ***adj.*** **more, most** ⟦OE *manig* ⟧ numerous —***n.*** a large number (of persons or things) —***pron.*** many persons or things

Ma·o·ri (mä′ō rē, mou′rē) ***n.*** 1 *pl.* **-ris** or **-ri** a member of a Polynesian people native to New Zealand 2 their language —***adj.*** of the Maoris, their language, etc.

Mao Tse-tung (mou′ dzu′do͞oŋ′) 1893-1976; Chinese communist leader: Pinyin *Mao Zedong* —**Mao′ism′** ***n.*** —**Mao′ist** ***adj., n.***

map (map) ***n.*** ⟦< L *mappa,* napkin, cloth ⟧ 1 a representation of all or part of the earth's surface, showing countries, bodies of water, etc. 2 a representation of the sky, showing the stars, etc. —***vt.*** **mapped, map′ping** 1 to make a map of 2 to plan

ma·ple (mā′pəl) ***n.*** ⟦OE *mapel* ⟧ 1 any of a large group of trees with two-winged fruits, grown for wood, sap, or shade 2 the hard, light-colored wood 3 the flavor of the syrup or sugar made from the sap

mar (mär) ***vt.*** **marred, mar′ring** ⟦OE *mierran,* hinder ⟧ to injure so as to make imperfect, etc.; spoil

mar·a·bou (mar′ə bo͞o′) ***n.*** ⟦Fr < Ar *murābit,* hermit ⟧ 1 a large-billed African stork 2 its plumes

ma·ra·ca (mə rä′kə) ***n.*** ⟦Port *maracá* < native name in Brazil ⟧ a percussion instrument that is a dried gourd or a gourd-shaped rattle with pebbles in it

mar·a·schi·no (mar′ə skē′nō, -shē′-) ***n.*** ⟦It < *marasca,* kind of cherry ⟧ a liqueur made from a dark sour cherry

maraschino cherries cherries in a syrup flavored with maraschino or imitation maraschino

mar·a·thon (mar′ə thän′) ***n.*** ⟦after *Marathon,* plain in ancient Greece ⟧ 1 a race on foot, 26 miles and 385 yards in length 2 any endurance contest

ma·raud (mə rôd′) ***vi., vt.*** ⟦< Fr *maraud,* vagabond ⟧ to raid and plunder —**ma·raud′er** ***n.***

mar·ble (mär′bəl) ***n.*** ⟦< Gr *marmaros,* white stone ⟧ 1 a hard limestone, white or colored, which takes a high polish 2 a piece of this stone, used in sculpture, etc. 3 anything like marble in hardness, coldness, etc. 4 *a)* a little ball of stone, glass, etc. *b)* [*pl., with sing. v.*] a children's game played with such balls 5 [*pl.*] [Slang] mental soundness; wits —***adj.*** of or like marble —***vt.*** **-bled, -bling** 1 to make (book edges) look mottled like marble 2 to cause (meat) to be streaked with fat

mar′ble·ize′ (-bəl īz′) ***vt.*** **-ized′, -iz′ing** to make look like marble

march[1] (märch) ***vi.*** ⟦Fr *marcher* ⟧ 1 to walk with regular steps, as in military formation 2 to advance steadily —***vt.*** to cause to march —***n.*** 1 a marching 2 a steady advance; progress 3 a regular, steady step 4 the distance covered in marching 5 a piece of music for marching —**on the march** marching —**steal a march on** to get an advantage over secretly —**march′er** ***n.***

march[2] (märch) ***n.*** ⟦< OFr ⟧ a boundary, border, or frontier

March (märch) ***n.*** ⟦< L *Mars,* the god Mars ⟧ the third month of the year, having 31 days: abbrev. **Mar.**

March hare a hare in breeding time, proverbially an example of madness

marching orders 1 orders to march, go, or leave 2 notice of dismissal

mar·chion·ess (mär′shən is) ***n.*** 1 the wife or widow of a marquess 2 a lady of the rank of a marquess

Mar·co·ni (mär kō′nē), **Gu·gliel·mo** (go͞o lyel′mō) 1874-1937; It. physicist: developed wireless telegraphy

Mar·di Gras (mär′dē grä′) ⟦Fr, fat Tuesday ⟧ [*sometimes* **M- g-**] the last day before Lent: a day of carnival in New Orleans, etc.

mare[1] (mar, mer) ***n.*** ⟦< OE *mere* ⟧ a mature female horse, mule, donkey, etc.

ma·re[2] (mä′rā′, mar′ē) ***n.,*** *pl.* **ma·ri·a** (mä′rē ə, mar′ē ə) ⟦L, sea ⟧ a large, dark area on the moon

mare's-nest (marz′nest′, merz′-) ***n.*** 1 a hoax 2 a jumble; mess

mar·ga·rine (mär′jə rin) ***n.*** ⟦Fr ⟧ a spread or cooking fat of vegetable oils processed, often with milk or whey, to the consistency of butter

mar·gin (mär′jən) ***n.*** ⟦< L *margo* ⟧ 1 a border; edge 2 the blank border of a printed or written page 3 an amount beyond what is needed 4 provision for increase, error, etc. 5 the difference between the cost and the selling price of goods 6 collateral deposited with a broker, either to meet legal requirements or to insure against loss on contracts as for buying stocks —**mar′gin·al** ***adj.***

mar·gi·na·li·a (mär′jə nā′lē ə) ***n.pl.*** marginal notes

mar′gin·al·ize′ ***vt.*** to exclude or ignore

ma·ri·a·chi (mär′ē ä′chē) ***n.,*** *pl.* **-chis** ⟦MexSp < Fr *mariage,* marriage: from playing at wedding celebrations ⟧ 1 a member of a strolling band of musicians in Mexico 2 such a band 3 its music

Mar·i·an (mer′ē ən, mar′-) ***adj.*** of the Virgin Mary

Ma·rie An·toi·nette (mə rē′ an′twə net′) 1755-93; wife of Louis XVI: queen of France (1774-92): guillotined

mar·i·gold (mar′i gōld′) ***n.*** ⟦< *Marie* (prob. the Virgin Mary) + GOLD ⟧ a plant of the composite family, with yellow or orange flowers

mar·i·jua·na or **mar·i·hua·na** (mar′i wä′nə) ***n.*** ⟦AmSp ⟧ 1 HEMP (*n.* 1) 2 its dried leaves and flowers, smoked, esp. as cigarettes, for euphoric effects

ma·rim·ba (mə rim′bə) ***n.*** ⟦< native name

in Africa] a kind of xylophone with a resonant tube beneath each bar

ma·ri·na (mə rē′nə) *n.* [< L *mare*, sea] a small harbor with docks, services, etc. for pleasure craft

mar·i·nade (mar′ə nād′) *n.* [Fr < Sp *marinar*, to pickle] 1 a spiced pickling solution for steeping meat, fish, etc., often before cooking 2 meat or fish thus steeped —*vt.* **-nad′ed, -nad′ing** MARINATE

mar·i·nate (mar′i nāt′) *vt.* **-nat′ed, -nat′ing** [< It *marinare*, to pickle] to steep (meat, fish, etc.) in a marinade

ma·rine (mə rēn′) *adj.* [< L *mare*, sea] 1 of or found in the sea 2 *a)* maritime; nautical *b)* naval —*n.* 1 a member of a military force trained for service at sea 2 [*often* **M-**] a member of the MARINE CORPS 3 naval or merchant ships

Marine Corps a branch of the United States armed forces trained for land, sea, and aerial combat

mar·i·ner (mar′i nər) *n.* a sailor

mar·i·o·nette (mar′ē ə net′, mer′-) *n.* [Fr < *Marie*, Mary] a jointed puppet moved by strings or wires

mar·i·tal (mar′i təl) *adj.* [< L *maritus*, a husband] of marriage; matrimonial —**mar′i·tal·ly** *adv.*

mar·i·time (mar′i tīm′) *adj.* [< L *mare*, sea] 1 on, near, or living near the sea 2 of sea navigation, shipping, etc.

mar·jo·ram (mär′jə rəm) *n.* [prob. ult. < Gr *amarakos*] a fragrant plant of the mint family, used in cooking

mark[1] (märk) *n.* [OE *mearc*, boundary] 1 a line, dot, spot, scratch, etc. on a surface 2 a printed or written symbol /punctuation *marks*/ 3 a brand or label on an article showing the maker, etc. 4 an indication of some quality 5 a grade /a *mark* of B in Latin/ 6 a standard of quality 7 impression, influence, etc. 8 an object of known position, serving as a guide 9 a line, dot, etc. indicating position, as on a graduated scale 10 a target; goal —*vt.* 1 to put or make a mark or marks on 2 to identify as by a mark 3 to indicate by a mark 4 to show plainly /her smile *marked* her joy/ 5 to set off; characterize 6 to take notice of; heed /*mark* my words/ 7 to grade; rate —**make one's mark** to achieve fame —**mark down** (or **up**) to mark for sale at a reduced (or an increased) price —**mark time** 1 to keep time while at a halt by lifting the feet as if marching 2 to suspend progress for a time —**mark′er** *n.*

mark[2] (märk) *n.* [< ON *mǫrk*] 1 DEUTSCHE MARK 2 the monetary unit of East Germany

Mark (märk) *Bible* 1 one of the four Evangelists, the reputed author of the second Gospel 2 this Gospel

mark′down′ *n.* 1 a selling at a reduced price 2 the amount of reduction

marked (märkt) *adj.* 1 having a mark or marks 2 noticeable; obvious —**mark·ed·ly** (märk′id lē) *adv.*

mar·ket (mär′kit) *n.* [ult. < L *merx*, merchandise] 1 a gathering of people for buying and selling things 2 an open space or a building where goods are shown for sale: also **mar′ket·place′** 3 a shop for the sale of provisions /a meat *market*/ 4 a region in which goods can be bought and sold /the European *market*/ 5 trade; buying and selling 6 demand (for goods, etc.) /a good *market* for tea/ —*vt.* 1 to offer for sale 2 to sell —*vi.* to buy provisions —**mar′ket·a·ble** *adj.* —**mar′ket·eer′** (-kə tir′) *n.* —**mar′ket·er** *n.*

mar·ket·ing (-iŋ) *n.* 1 a buying or selling in a market 2 the total of activities involved in the moving of goods from the producer to the consumer, including selling, advertising, etc.

Mark·ham (mär′kəm) city in SE Ontario, Canada: pop. 115,000

mark′ing *n.* 1 a mark or marks 2 the characteristic arrangement of marks, as of a plant or animal

marks·man (märks′mən) *n.*, *pl.* **-men** one who shoots, esp. one who shoots well —**marks′man·ship′** *n.*

mark′up′ *n.* 1 a selling at an increased price 2 the amount of increase

mar·lin (mär′lin) *n.*, *pl.* **-lin** or **-lins** [< fol.: from the shape] a large, slender, deep-sea fish

mar·line·spike (mär′lin spīk′) *n.* [< Du *marlijn*, small cord + SPIKE[1]] a pointed metal tool for splicing rope

mar·ma·lade (mär′mə lād′) *n.* [ult. < Gr *meli*, honey + *mēlon*, apple] a jamlike preserve of oranges, etc.

mar·mo·set (mär′mə zet′) *n.* [< OFr *marmouset*, grotesque figure] a small monkey of South and Central America

mar·mot (mär′mət) *n.* [prob. < L *mus montanus*, mountain mouse] any of a group of thick-bodied rodents, as the woodchuck

ma·roon[1] (mə ro͞on′) *n.*, *adj.* [Fr *marron*, chestnut] dark brownish red

ma·roon[2] (mə ro͞on′) *vt.* [< AmSp *cimarrón*, wild] 1 to put (a person) ashore in a lonely place and abandon that person 2 to leave helpless and alone

marque (märk) *n.* [Fr, a sign] a distinctive emblem on an automobile

mar·quee (mär kē′) *n.* [< Fr *marquise*, awning] a rooflike projection over an entrance, as to a theater

mar·quess (mär′kwis) *n.* [var. of MARQUIS] 1 a British nobleman ranking above an earl 2 MARQUIS

mar·que·try (mär′kə trē) *n.* [Fr, ult. < *marque*, a mark] decorative inlaid work, as in furniture

mar·quis (mär′kwis; *Fr* mär kē′) *n.* [< ML *marchisus*, prefect] in some European countries, a nobleman ranking above an earl or count

mar·quise (mär kēz′) *n.* 1 the wife or widow of a marquis 2 a lady of the rank of a marquis

mar·qui·sette (mär′ki zet′, -kwi-) *n.* [see MARQUEE] a thin, meshlike fabric used for curtains, etc.

mar·riage (mar′ij) *n.* 1 the state of being married 2 a wedding 3 a close union —**mar′riage·a·ble** *adj.*

mar′ried *adj.* 1 being husband and wife 2 having a husband or wife 3 of marriage —*n.* a married person

mar·row (mar′ō) *n.* [OE *mearg*] the soft,

fatty tissue that fills the cavities of most bones

mar·ry (mar'ē) ***vt.*** **-ried, -ry·ing** ⟦< L *maritus*, husband⟧ **1** to join as husband and wife **2** to take as husband or wife **3** to unite —***vi.*** to get married —**marry off** to give in marriage

Mars (märz) **1** the Roman god of war **2** a planet of the solar system: see PLANET

Mar·seille (mär sā') seaport in SE France: pop. 879,000 Eng. sp. **Marseilles**

marsh (märsh) ***n.*** ⟦OE *merisc*⟧ a tract of low, wet, soft land; swamp —**marsh'y, -i·er, -i·est,** ***adj.***

mar·shal (mär'shəl) ***n.*** ⟦< OHG *marah*, horse + *scalh*, servant⟧ **1** in various foreign armies, a general officer of the highest rank **2** an official in charge of ceremonies, parades, etc. **3** in the U.S., *a)* a Federal officer appointed to a judicial district with duties like those of a sheriff *b)* the head of some police or fire departments —***vt.*** **-shaled** or **-shalled, -shal·ing** or **-shal·ling** **1** to arrange (troops, ideas, etc.) in order **2** to guide

Mar·shall (mär'shəl), **John** 1755-1835; U.S. chief justice (1801-35)

marsh·mal·low (märsh'mal'ō, -məl'ō) ***n.*** ⟦orig. made of the root of a mallow found in marshes⟧ a soft, spongy confection of sugar, gelatin, etc.

mar·su·pi·al (mär sōō'pē əl) ***adj.*** ⟦< Gr *marsypos*, pouch⟧ of a group of mammals that carry their incompletely developed young in an external abdominal pouch on the mother —***n.*** such an animal, as a kangaroo or opossum

mart (märt) ***n.*** ⟦MDu *markt*⟧ a market

mar·ten (märt''n) ***n.*** ⟦< OFr *martre*⟧ **1** a small mammal like a weasel, with soft, thick fur **2** the fur

mar·tial (mär'shəl) ***adj.*** ⟦< L *martialis*, of Mars⟧ **1** of or suitable for war **2** warlike; bold **3** military —**mar'tial·ly** ***adv.***

martial arts systems of self-defense originating in the Orient, such as karate or kung fu

martial law rule by military authorities over civilians, as during a war

Mar·tian (mär'shən) ***adj.*** of Mars —***n.*** an inhabitant of Mars, as in science fiction

mar·tin (märt''n) ***n.*** ⟦Fr⟧ any of several birds of the swallow family

mar·ti·net (märt''n et') ***n.*** ⟦after *Martinet*, 17th-c. Fr general⟧ a very strict disciplinarian

mar·ti·ni (mär tē'nē) ***n.***, *pl.* **-nis** ⟦< ?⟧ a cocktail made of gin (or vodka) and dry vermouth

mar·tyr (märt'ər) ***n.*** ⟦< Gr *martyr*, a witness⟧ **1** one who chooses to suffer or die for one's faith or principles **2** one who suffers misery for a long time —***vt.*** to kill or persecute for a belief —**mar'tyr·dom** ***n.***

mar·vel (mär'vəl) ***n.*** ⟦< L *mirari*, wonder at⟧ a wonderful or astonishing thing —***vi.*** **-veled** or **-velled, -vel·ing** or **-vel·ling** to be filled with wonder —***vt.*** to wonder at or about: followed by a clause

mar'vel·ous (-və ləs) ***adj.*** **1** causing wonder; extraordinary, etc. **2** improbable; incredible **3** [Colloq.] fine; splendid Also [Chiefly Brit.] **mar'vel·lous** —**mar'vel·ous·ly** ***adv.***

Marx (märks), **Karl** (kärl) 1818-83; Ger. founder of modern socialism

Marx'ism' ***n.*** the system of thought developed by Karl Marx and Friedrich Engels (1820-95, Ger. socialist leader & writer), serving as a basis for socialism and communism —**Marx'ist** or **Marx'i·an** ***adj., n.***

Mar·y (mer'ē) *Bible* mother of Jesus

Mar·y·land (mer'ə lənd) E State of the U.S.: 10,577 sq. mi.; pop. 4,216,000; cap. Annapolis —**Mar'y·land·er** (-lən dər, -lan-) ***n.***

Mary Mag·da·lene (mag'də lən) *Bible* a woman out of whom Jesus cast devils

mar·zi·pan (mär'zi pan') ***n.*** ⟦Ger < It *marzapane*⟧ a confection of ground almonds, sugar, and egg white

masc. or **mas.** masculine

mas·car·a (mas kar'ə) ***n.*** ⟦< It *maschera*, mask⟧ a cosmetic for coloring the eyelashes —***vt.*** **-car'aed, -car'a·ing** to put mascara on

mas·cot (mas'kät') ***n.*** ⟦< Prov *masco*, sorcerer⟧ any person, animal, or thing supposed to bring good luck

mas·cu·line (mas'kyōō lin, -kyə-) ***adj.*** ⟦< L *mas*, male⟧ **1** male; of men or boys **2** suitable to or having qualities regarded as characteristic of men; strong, vigorous, manly, etc. **3** mannish: said of women **4** *Gram.* designating or of the gender of words referring to males and many other words to which no sex is attributed —**mas'cu·lin'i·ty** ***n.***

mash (mash) ***n.*** ⟦< OE *mascwyrt*⟧ **1** crushed malt or meal soaked in hot water for making wort **2** a mixture of watered bran, meal, etc. for feeding horses, etc. **3** any soft mass —***vt.*** **1** to change into a soft mass by beating, crushing, etc. **2** to crush and injure —**mash'er** ***n.***

mask (mask) ***n.*** ⟦< Fr < It *maschera*⟧ **1** a covering to conceal or protect the face **2** anything that conceals or disguises **3** a masquerade **4** *a)* a molded likeness of the face *b)* a grotesque representation of a face, worn to amuse or frighten —***vt.*** to conceal or cover with or as with a mask —**masked** ***adj.***

SURGICAL MASK

mas·o·chism (mas'ə kiz'əm) ***n.*** ⟦after L. von Sacher-*Masoch* (1835-95), Austrian writer⟧ the getting of pleasure, often sexual, from being hurt or humiliated —**mas'o·chist** ***n.*** —**mas'o·chis'tic** ***adj.*** —**mas'o·chis'ti·cal·ly** ***adv.***

ma·son (mā'sən) ***n.*** ⟦< ML *macio*⟧ **1** one whose work is building with stone, brick, etc. **2** [M-] FREEMASON

Ma·son-Dix·on line (mā's'n dik's'n) ⟦after C. *Mason* & J. *Dixon*, who surveyed it, 1763-67⟧ boundary line between Pa. & Md., regarded as separating the North from the South

Ma·son·ic (mə sän'ik) ***adj.*** [*also* **m-**] of Freemasons or Freemasonry

ma·son·ry (mā'sən rē) ***n.*** **1** a mason's trade **2** *pl.* **-ries** something built, as by a mason, of stone, brick, etc. 3 [*usually* **M-**] FREEMASONRY

masque (mask) ***n.*** ⟦see MASK⟧ 1 MASQUERADE (*n.* 1) 2 a former kind of dramatic entertainment, with a mythical or allegorical theme —**masqu'er *n.***

mas·quer·ade (mas'kər ād') ***n.*** ⟦see MASK⟧ 1 a ball or party at which masks and fancy costumes are worn 2 *a*) a disguise *b*) an acting under false pretenses —***vi.* -ad'ed, -ad'ing** 1 to take part in a masquerade 2 to act under false pretenses

mass (mas) ***n.*** ⟦< Gr *maza*, barley cake⟧ 1 a quantity of matter of indefinite shape and size; lump 2 a large quantity or number /a *mass* of bruises/ 3 bulk; size 4 the main part 5 *Physics* the quantity of matter in a body as measured by its inertia —***adj.*** of or for the masses or for a large number —***vt., vi.*** to gather or form into a mass —**the masses** the common people; specif., the working people

Mass (mas) ***n.*** ⟦< L *missa* in the words said by the priest: *ite, missa est* (*contio*), go, (the meeting) is dismissed⟧ [*also* **m-**] *R.C.Ch.* the service that includes the Eucharist

Mas·sa·chu·setts (mas'ə cho͞o'sits) New England State of the U.S.: 8,257 sq. mi.; pop. 5,737,000; cap. Boston: abbrev. **Mass.**

mas·sa·cre (mas'ə kər) ***n.*** ⟦< OFr *maçacre*, shambles⟧ the indiscriminate, merciless killing of many people or animals —***vt.* -cred, -cring** (-kər iŋ, -kriŋ) to kill in large numbers

mas·sage (mə säzh') ***n.*** ⟦Fr < Ar *massa*, to touch⟧ a rubbing, kneading, etc. of part of the body, as to stimulate circulation —***vt.* -saged', -sag'ing** to give a massage to

mas·seur (ma sʉr', mə-) ***n.*** ⟦Fr⟧ a man whose work is giving massages —**masseuse** (ma sʉz', mə-) ***n.fem.***

mas·sive (mas'iv) ***adj.*** 1 forming or consisting of a large mass; big and solid 2 large and imposing —**mas'sive·ly *adv.*** —**mas'sive·ness *n.***

mass media those means of communication that reach large numbers of people, as newspapers, radio, etc.

mass noun a noun denoting an abstraction or something that is uncountable (Ex.: *love, news*)

mass number the number of neutrons and protons in the nucleus of an atom

mass production quantity production of goods, esp. by machinery and division of labor

mast (mast) ***n.*** ⟦OE *mæst*⟧ 1 a tall vertical spar used to support the sails, yards, radar, etc. on a ship 2 a vertical pole

mas·tec·to·my (mas tek'tə mē) ***n., pl.* -mies** the surgical removal of a breast

mas·ter (mas'tər) ***n.*** ⟦< L *magister*⟧ 1 a man who rules others or has control over something; specif., *a*) one who is head of a household *b*) an employer *c*) one who owns a slave or an animal *d*) the captain of a merchant ship 2 *a*) a person very skilled and able in some work, profession, science, etc.; expert *b*) an artist regarded as great 3 [**M-**] a title applied to a boy too young to be addressed as *Mr.* —***adj.*** 1 being a master 2 of a master 3 chief; main; controlling —***vt.*** 1 to become master of 2 to become an expert in (an art, etc.)

mas'ter·ful *adj.* 1 acting the part of a master; domineering 2 expert; skillful —**mas'ter·ful·ly *adv.***

master key a key that will open every one of a set of locks

mas'ter·ly *adj.* expert; skillful —***adv.*** in a masterly manner

mas'ter·mind' *n.* a very clever person, esp. one who plans or runs a project —***vt.*** to be the mastermind of

Master of Arts (or **Science,** etc.) a degree given by a college or university to one who has completed a prescribed course at the first level of graduate study Also **master's (degree)**

master of ceremonies one who supervises a ceremony, program, etc.

mas'ter·piece' *n.* 1 a thing made or done with masterly skill 2 the greatest work of a person or group

master sergeant *U.S. Mil.* a noncommissioned officer of high rank

mas'ter·stroke' *n.* a masterly action, move, or achievement

mas'ter·work' *n.* MASTERPIECE

mas'ter·y *n., pl.* -ies 1 rule; control 2 ascendancy or victory 3 expert skill or knowledge

mast'head' *n.* 1 the top part of a ship's mast 2 a listing of the owner, editors, etc. of a newspaper or magazine

mas·ti·cate (mas'ti kāt') ***vt.* -cat'ed, -cat'ing** ⟦ult. < Gr *mastax*, mouth⟧ to chew up —**mas'ti·ca'tion *n.***

mas·tiff (mas'tif) ***n.*** ⟦< L *mansuetus*, tame⟧ a large, powerful dog with a short, thick coat

mas·to·don (mas'tə dän') ***n.*** ⟦< Gr *mastos*, breast + *odous*, tooth: from the nipplelike processes on its molar⟧ a large, extinct mammal resembling the elephant but larger

mas·toid (mas'toid') ***adj.*** ⟦< Gr *mastos*, breast + *-eidēs*, -OID⟧ designating, of, or near a projection of the temporal bone behind the ear —***n.*** the mastoid projection

mas·tur·bate (mas'tər bāt') ***vi., vt.* -bat'ed, -bat'ing** ⟦< L *masturbari*⟧ to manipulate the genitals for sexual gratification —**mas'tur·ba'tion *n.***

mat[1] (mat) ***n.*** ⟦< LL *matta*⟧ 1 a flat piece of cloth, rubber, woven straw, etc. used for protection, as on a floor or under a vase 2 a thickly padded floor covering, esp. one used for wrestling, etc. 3 anything densely interwoven or growing in a thick tangle —***vt., vi.* mat'ted, mat'ting** 1 to cover as with a mat 2 to interweave or tangle into a thick mass —**go to the mat** [Colloq.] to engage in a struggle or dispute

mat[2] (mat) ***n.*** ⟦< OFr⟧ 1 MATTE 2 a border, as of cardboard, put around a picture —***vt.* mat'ted, mat'ting** 1 to put a dull finish on 2 to frame with a mat

mat[3] (mat) ***n.*** [Colloq.] *Printing* a matrix

mat·a·dor (mat'ə dôr') ***n.*** ⟦< Sp *matar*, to kill⟧ a bullfighter whose specialty is killing the bull

match[1] (mach) ***n.*** ⟦< OFr *mesche*⟧ a slender piece of wood, cardboard, etc. tipped with a substance that catches fire by friction

match[2] (mach) ***n.*** ⟦OE (*ge*)*mæcca*, mate⟧ 1 any person or thing equal or similar to another 2 two persons or things that go well together 3 a contest or game 4 a marriage or mating —*vt.* 1 to join in marriage; mate 2 to put in opposition (*with* or *against*) 3 to be equal or similar to 4 to make or get a counterpart or equivalent to 5 to fit (one thing) to another —*vi.* to be equal, similar, suitable, etc.

match′book′ *n.* a folder of book matches

match′less *adj.* having no equal

match′mak′ing *n.* the arranging of marriages, boxing matches, etc. —**match′mak′er** *n.*

match′stick′ *n.* a thin piece of wood, cardboard, etc., as of a match

mate (māt) *n.* ⟦< MDu⟧ 1 a companion or fellow worker 2 one of a matched pair 3 *a*) a husband or wife *b*) the male or female of paired animals 4 an officer of a merchant ship, ranking below the captain —*vt., vi.* **mat′ed, mat′ing** 1 to join as a pair 2 to couple in marriage or sexual union

ma·te·ri·al (mə tir′ē əl) *adj.* ⟦< L *materia*, matter⟧ 1 of matter; physical /a *material* object/ 2 of the body or bodily needs, comfort, etc.; not spiritual 3 important, essential, etc. —*n.* 1 what a thing is, or may be, made of; elements or parts 2 cloth; fabric 3 [*pl.*] tools, etc. needed to make or do something

ma·te′ri·al·ism′ (-iz′əm) *n.* 1 the doctrine that everything in the world, including thought, can be explained only in terms of matter 2 the tendency to be more concerned with material than with spiritual or intellectual values —**ma·te′ri·al·ist** *adj., n.* —**ma·te′ri·al·is′tic** *adj.*

ma·te′ri·al·ize′ (-īz′) *vt.* **-ized′, -iz′ing** to give material form to —*vi.* 1 to become fact; be realized 2 to take on bodily form: said of spirits, etc. —**ma·te′ri·al·i·za′tion** *n.*

ma·te′ri·al·ly *adv.* 1 physically 2 to a great extent; substantially

ma·te·ri·el or **ma·té·ri·el** (mə tir′ē el′) *n.* ⟦Fr⟧ the necessary materials and tools; specif., military weapons, equipment, etc.

ma·ter·nal (mə tur′nəl) *adj.* ⟦< L *mater*, mother⟧ 1 of, like, or from a mother 2 related through the mother's side of the family —**ma·ter′nal·ly** *adv.*

ma·ter′ni·ty (-nə tē) *n.* the state of being a mother; motherhood —*adj.* 1 for pregnant women 2 for the care of mothers and their newborn babies

math·e·mat·i·cal (math′ə mat′i kəl) *adj.* ⟦< Gr *manthanein*, learn⟧ 1 of, like, or concerned with mathematics 2 very precise, accurate, etc. Also **math′e·mat′ic** —**math′e·mat′i·cal·ly** *adv.*

math·e·mat·ics (math′ə mat′iks) *n.pl.* ⟦see prec. & -ICS⟧ [*with sing. v.*] the science dealing with quantities, forms, etc. and their relationships, by the use of numbers and symbols Also **math** —**math′e·ma·ti′cian** (-mə tish′ən; math′mə-) *n.*

mat·i·nee or **mat·i·née** (mat′'n ā′) *n.* ⟦< Fr *matin*, morning⟧ an afternoon performance of a play, etc.

mat·ins (mat′'nz) *n.pl.* ⟦< L *matutinus*, of the morning⟧ [*often* **M-**] [*usually with sing. v.*] a church service of morning prayer

Ma·tisse (mä tēs′), **Hen·ri** (än rē′) 1869-1954; Fr. painter

matri- ⟦< L *mater*⟧ *combining form* mother Also **matr-**

ma·tri·arch (mā′trē ärk′) *n.* ⟦prec. + -ARCH⟧ a woman who rules a family, tribe, etc. —**ma′tri·ar′chal** (-är′kəl) *adj.* —**ma′tri·arch′y** (-är′kē), *pl.* **-ies,** *n.*

ma·tric·u·late (mə trik′yoo lāt′, -yə-) *vt., vi.* **-lat′ed, -lat′ing** ⟦< LL: see MATRIX⟧ to enroll, esp. as a student in a college —**ma·tric′u·la′tion** *n.*

mat·ri·mo·ny (ma′trə mō′nē) *n., pl.* **-nies** ⟦< L *mater*, mother⟧ 1 the act or rite of marriage 2 married life —**mat′ri·mo′ni·al** *adj.*

ma·trix (mā′triks′) *n., pl.* **-tri·ces** (mā′trə sēz′, ma′trə-) or **-trix′es** ⟦< L *mater*, mother⟧ that within which something originates, takes form, etc., as a mold for a printing plate

ma·tron (mā′trən) *n.* ⟦< L *mater*, mother⟧ 1 a wife or widow, esp. one with a mature appearance and manner 2 a woman manager of the domestic arrangements of a hospital, prison, etc. —**ma′tron·ly** *adj.*

matron of honor a married woman acting as chief attendant to a bride

matte (mat) *n.* ⟦var. of MAT²⟧ a dull surface or finish —*adj.* not shiny Also **matt**

mat·ted (mat′id) *adj.* closely tangled in a dense mass

mat·ter (mat′ər) *n.* ⟦< L *materia*⟧ 1 what a thing is made of; material 2 whatever occupies space and is perceptible to the senses 3 any specified substance /coloring *matter*/ 4 material of thought or expression 5 an amount or quantity 6 *a*) a thing or affair *b*) cause or occasion /no laughing *matter*/ 7 importance; significance /it's of no *matter*/ 8 trouble; difficulty: with *the* /what seems to be the *matter*/ 9 mail —*vi.* to be of importance —**as a matter of fact** in fact; really —**no matter** 1 it is not important 2 regardless of

mat′ter-of-fact′ *adj.* sticking to facts; literal, unimaginative, etc.

Mat·thew (math′yoo′) *Bible* 1 a Christian apostle, reputed author of the first Gospel 2 this book: abbrev. **Matt.**

mat·ting (mat′iŋ) *n.* 1 a woven fabric of fiber, as straw, for mats, etc. 2 mats collectively

mat·tock (mat′ək) *n.* ⟦OE *mattuc*⟧ a tool like a pickax, for loosening the soil, digging roots, etc.

mat·tress (ma′trəs) *n.* ⟦< Ar *maṭraḥ*, cushion⟧ a casing of strong cloth filled with cotton, foam rubber, coiled springs, etc., used on a bed

ma·ture (mə toor′, -tyoor′, -choor′) *adj.* ⟦< L *maturus*, ripe⟧ 1 full-grown; ripe 2 fully developed, perfected, etc. 3 due: said of a note, bond, etc. —*vt., vi.* **-tured′, -tur′ing** to make or become mature —**mat·u·ra·tion** (mach′ə rā′shən) *n.* —**ma·tu′ri·ty** *n.*

mat·zo (mät′sə, -sō) *n., pl.* **mat′zot, mat′zoth** (-sōt), or **mat′zos** ⟦Heb *matstsāh*, unleavened⟧ 1 flat, thin, unleavened bread eaten during the Passover 2 a piece of this

maud·lin (môd′lin) *adj.* ⟦< ME *Maudeleyne*, (Mary) Magdalene (often represented as weeping)⟧ foolishly, often tearfully, sentimental

maul (môl) ***n.*** ⟦< L *malleus,* a hammer⟧ a heavy hammer for driving stakes, etc. —***vt.*** 1 to bruise or lacerate 2 to handle roughly; manhandle —**maul′er** ***n.***

maun·der (môn′dər) ***vi.*** ⟦< earlier *mander,* to grumble⟧ to talk or move in a confused way

Mau·ri·ta·ni·a (môr′ə tā′nē ə) country in NW Africa, on the Atlantic: 419,230 sq. mi.; pop. 1,690,000

Mau·ri·ti·us (mô rish′ē əs, -rish′əs) island country in the Indian Ocean: 787 sq. mi.; pop. 851,000

mau·so·le·um (mô′sə lē′əm, -zə-) ***n.,*** *pl.* **-le′ums** or **-le′a** (-ə) ⟦after the tomb of King *Mausolus,* in ancient Asia Minor⟧ a large, imposing tomb

mauve (mōv) ***n.*** ⟦Fr, mallow⟧ any of several shades of pale purple —***adj.*** of such a color

mav·er·ick (mav′ər ik) ***n.*** ⟦after S. *Maverick,* 19th-c. Texan whose cattle had no brand⟧ 1 an unbranded animal, esp. a lost calf 2 [Colloq.] one who takes an independent stand, as in politics

maw (mô) ***n.*** ⟦OE *maga*⟧ 1 orig., the stomach 2 the throat, gullet, jaws, or oral cavity of a voracious animal

mawk·ish (môk′ish) ***adj.*** ⟦< ON *mathkr,* maggot⟧ sentimental in a weak, insipid way —**mawk′ish·ly** ***adv.***

maxi- ⟦< MAXI(MUM)⟧ *combining form* maximum, very large, very long

max·il·la (maks il′ə) ***n.,*** *pl.* **-lae** (-ē) ⟦L⟧ the upper jawbone —**max′il·lar′y** (-i ler′ē) ***adj.***

max·im (maks′im) ***n.*** ⟦< LL *maxima* (*propositio*), the greatest (premise)⟧ a concise rule of conduct

max·i·mize (maks′i mīz′) ***vt.*** **-mized′, -miz′·ing** to increase to the maximum

max·i·mum (maks′i məm) ***n.,*** *pl.* **-mums** or **-ma** (-mə) ⟦< L superl. of *magnus,* great⟧ 1 the greatest quantity, number, etc. possible 2 the highest degree or point reached —***adj.*** greatest possible, permissible, or reached —**max′i·mal** (-məl) ***adj.***

may (mā) ***v.aux.*** *pt.* **might** ⟦OE *mæg*⟧ used to express: 1 possibility /it *may* rain/ 2 permission /you *may* go/: see also CAN[1] 3 contingency /they died that we *may* be free/ 4 a wish or hope /*may* he live!/

May (mā) ***n.*** ⟦< L *Maius*⟧ the fifth month of the year, having 31 days

Ma·ya (mä′yə, mī′ə) ***n.,*** *pl.* **Ma′yas** or **Ma′ya** ⟦Sp < native name⟧ 1 a member of a tribe of Indians of Central America that had a highly developed civilization 2 the language of the Mayas —**Ma′yan** ***adj., n.***

may·be (mā′bē) ***adv.*** ⟦ME (for *it may be*)⟧ perhaps

May Day May 1: a traditional spring festival, now also a labor holiday in many countries

may′flow′er ***n.*** an early spring flower, as the trailing arbutus —[M-] the ship on which the Pilgrims came to America (1620)

may′fly′ ***n.,*** *pl.* **-flies′** ⟦thought to be prevalent in May⟧ a delicate, soft-bodied insect with gauzy wings

may·hem (mā′hem, -əm) ***n.*** ⟦see MAIM⟧ 1 *Law* the offense of maiming a person 2 any deliberate destruction

may·o (mā′ō′) ***n.*** [Colloq.] *short for* MAYONNAISE

may·on·naise (mā′ə nāz′) ***n.*** ⟦after *Mahón,* port on a Sp island⟧ a creamy sauce of egg yolks, oil, vinegar, etc. beaten together

may·or (mā′ər) ***n.*** ⟦< L *major,* greater⟧ the chief administrative official of a city, town, etc. —**may′or·al** (-ər əl, mā ôr′əl) ***adj.***

may′or·al·ty (-əl tē) ***n.,*** *pl.* **-ties** the office or term of office of a mayor

may·pole (mā′pōl′) ***n.*** [*often* **M-**] a high pole with flowers, streamers, etc., for dancing around on May Day

maze (māz) ***n.*** ⟦< OE *amasian,* amaze⟧ 1 a confusing, intricate network of pathways 2 a confused state

MAZE

maz·el tov (mä′zəl tōv′, -tôf′) ⟦Heb⟧ good luck Also **maz′el·tov**

ma·zur·ka or **ma·zour·ka** (mə zur′kə) ***n.*** ⟦Pol⟧ a lively Polish folk dance in 3/4 or 3/8 time

MBA or **M.B.A.** Master of Business Administration

MC or **M.C.** 1 Master of Ceremonies 2 Member of Congress

Mc·Kin·ley (mə kin′lē), **William** 1843-1901; 25th president of the U.S. (1897-1901): assassinated

McKinley, Mount mountain in Alas.: highest peak in North America: 20,320 ft.

MD 1 ⟦L *Medicinae Doctor*⟧ Doctor of Medicine: also **M.D.** 2 Maryland: also **Md.**

me (mē) ***pron.*** ⟦OE⟧ *objective case of* I[2]

ME or **Me.** Maine

mead[1] (mēd) ***n.*** ⟦OE *meodu*⟧ an alcoholic liquor made of fermented honey and water

mead[2] (mēd) ***n.*** [Old Poet.] *var. of* MEADOW

mead·ow (med′ō) ***n.*** ⟦< OE *mæd*⟧ 1 a grassland where the grass is grown for hay 2 low, level grassland

mea·ger (mē′gər) ***adj.*** ⟦< L *macer,* lean⟧ 1 thin; lean 2 poor; not full or rich; inadequate Brit. sp. **mea′gre** —**mea′ger·ly** ***adv.*** —**mea′ger·ness** ***n.***

meal[1] (mēl) ***n.*** ⟦OE *mæl*⟧ 1 any of the times for eating, as lunch or dinner 2 the food served at such a time

meal[2] (mēl) ***n.*** ⟦OE *melu*⟧ 1 any edible grain, coarsely ground /*cornmeal*/ 2 any substance similarly ground —**meal′y, -i·er, -i·est,** ***adj.***

meal·y-mouthed (mēl′ē mouthd′) ***adj.*** not outspoken or blunt; euphemistic

mean[1] (mēn) ***vt.*** **meant** (ment), **mean′ing** ⟦OE *mænan*⟧ 1 to have in mind; intend /he *means* to go/ 2 to intend to express /say what you *mean*/ 3 to signify; denote /"*ja*" *means* "yes"/ —***vi.*** to have a (specified) degree of importance, effect, etc. /honors *mean* little to him/ —**mean well** to have good intentions

mean[2] (mēn) ***adj.*** ⟦OE (*ge*)*mæne*⟧ 1 low in quality or value; paltry; inferior 2 poor in appearance; shabby 3 ignoble; petty 4 stingy 5 pettily bad-tempered, disagreeable, etc. 6 [Slang] *a*) hard to cope with *b*) skillful —**mean′ly** ***adv.*** —**mean′ness** ***n.***

mean[3] (mēn) ***adj.*** ⟦< L *medius,* middle⟧ 1 halfway between extremes 2 average —***n.*** 1 what is between extremes 2 *Math.* a number between the smallest and largest values of a set of quantities; esp., an average

me·an·der (mē an′dər) ***vi.*** ⟦< Gr *Maiandros*, a winding river in Asia Minor⟧ **1** to take a winding course: said of a stream **2** to wander idly

mean·ie or **mean·y** (mēn′ē) ***n.***, *pl.* **-ies** [Colloq.] one who is mean, selfish, etc.

mean′ing ***n.*** what is meant; what is intended to be signified or understood; import; sense /the *meaning* of a word/ —**mean′ing·ful** ***adj.*** —**mean′ing·less** ***adj.***

means (mēnz) ***n.pl.*** ⟦< MEAN³, *n.*⟧ **1** [*with sing. or pl. v.*] that by which something is done or obtained; agency /a *means* of travel/ **2** resources; wealth —**by all means 1** without fail **2** certainly —**by means of** by using —**by no means** not at all

meant (ment) ***vt.***, ***vi.*** *pt. & pp. of* MEAN¹

mean′time′ ***adv.*** **1** in or during the intervening time **2** at the same time —***n.*** the intervening time Also **mean′while′**

mea·sles (mē′zəlz) ***n.pl.*** ⟦ME *maseles*⟧ [*with sing. v.*] **1** an acute, infectious, communicable viral disease, usually of children, characterized by small, red spots on the skin, high fever, etc. **2** a similar but milder disease; esp., rubella (*German measles*)

mea·sly (mēz′lē) ***adj.*** **-sli·er, -sli·est** [Colloq.] contemptibly slight or worthless

meas·ure (mezh′ər) ***n.*** ⟦< L *metiri*, to measure⟧ **1** the extent, dimensions, capacity, etc. of anything **2** a determining of this; measurement **3** *a*) a unit of measurement *b*) any standard of valuation **4** a system of measurement **5** an instrument for measuring **6** a definite quantity measured out **7** a course of action /reform *measures*/ **8** a statute; law **9** a rhythmical pattern or unit; specif., the notes and rests between two bars on a musical staff —***vt.*** **-ured, -ur·ing 1** to find out or estimate the extent, dimensions, etc. of, esp. by a standard **2** to mark off by measuring **3** to be a measure of —***vi.*** **1** to take measurements **2** to be of a specified dimension, etc. —**beyond measure** exceedingly —**for good measure** as something extra —**in a measure** to some extent —**measure up** to prove to be competent —**meas′ur·a·ble** ***adj.*** —**meas′ur·a·bly** ***adv.*** —**meas′ure·less** ***adj.***

meas′ured ***adj.*** **1** determined or marked off by a standard **2** regular or steady /*measured* steps/ **3** careful and guarded: said of speech, etc.

meas′ure·ment ***n.*** **1** a measuring or being measured **2** extent or quantity determined by measuring **3** a system of measuring or of measures

meat (mēt) ***n.*** ⟦OE *mete*⟧ **1** food: now archaic except in **meat and drink 2** the flesh of animals, esp. of mammals, used as food **3** the edible, inner part /the *meat* of a nut/ **4** the substance or essence —**meat′y**, **-i·er, -i·est,** ***adj.***

meat′pack′ing ***n.*** the process or industry of preparing the meat of animals for market

Mec·ca (mek′ə) one of the two capitals of Saudi Arabia: birthplace of Mohammed & hence a holy city of Islam: pop. *c.* 367,000 —***n.*** [*often* **m-**] **1** a place visited by many people **2** a place that one yearns to go to

me·chan·ic (mə kan′ik) ***n.*** ⟦< Gr *mēchanē*, machine⟧ a worker skilled in using tools, repairing machines, etc.

me·chan′i·cal ***adj.*** **1** having to do with machinery or tools **2** produced or operated by machinery or a mechanism **3** of the science of mechanics **4** machinelike; lacking warmth, etc. —**me·chan′i·cal·ly** ***adv.***

me·chan′ics ***n.pl.*** [*with sing. v.*] **1** the science of motion and of the action of forces on bodies **2** knowledge of machinery **3** the technical part /the *mechanics* of writing/

mech·a·nism (mek′ə niz′əm) ***n.*** ⟦< Gr *mēchanē*, machine⟧ **1** the working parts of a machine **2** any system of interrelated parts **3** any physical or mental process by which a result is produced —**mech′a·nis′tic** ***adj.***

mech′a·nize′ (-nīz′) ***vt.*** **-nized′, -niz′ing 1** to make mechanical **2** to equip (an industry) with machinery or (an army, etc.) with motor vehicles, tanks, etc. —**mech′a·ni·za′tion** ***n.***

med·al (med′'l) ***n.*** ⟦< LL *medialis*, medial⟧ **1** a small, flat piece of inscribed metal commemorating some event or awarded for some distinguished action, merit, etc. **2** a similar piece of metal with a religious figure

med′al·ist ***n.*** one awarded a medal

me·dal·lion (mə dal′yən) ***n.*** ⟦Fr *médaillon*⟧ **1** a large medal **2** a design, portrait, etc. resembling a medal

med·dle (med′'l) ***vi.*** **-dled, -dling** ⟦< L *miscere*, to mix⟧ to interfere in another's affairs —**med′dler** ***n.*** —**med′dle·some** (-səm) ***adj.***

me·di·a (mē′dē ə) ***n.*** *alt. pl. of* MEDIUM: see MEDIUM (*n.* 3) —**the media** [*usually with sing. v.*] all the means of communication, as newspapers, radio, etc.

me·di·al (mē′dē əl) ***adj.*** ⟦< L *medius*⟧ **1** middle **2** ordinary

me·di·an (mē′dē ən) ***adj.*** **1** middle; intermediate **2** designating the middle number in a series —***n.*** **1** a median number, point, line, etc. **2** the strip of land separating the lanes of opposing traffic of a divided highway: in full **median strip**

me·di·ate (mē′dē āt′) ***vi.*** **-at′ed, -at′ing** ⟦< L *medius*, middle⟧ **1** to be in an intermediate position **2** to be an intermediary —***vt.*** to settle (differences) between persons, nations, etc. by intervention —**me′di·a′tion** ***n.*** —**me′di·a′tor** ***n.***

med·ic (med′ik) ***n.*** [Colloq.] **1** a physician or surgeon **2** a medical officer who gives first aid in combat

Med′ic·aid′ (-i kād′) ***n.*** ⟦MEDIC(AL) + AID⟧ [*also* **m-**] a State and Federal health program for paying certain medical expenses of persons of low income

med′i·cal (-i kəl) ***adj.*** of or connected with the practice or study of medicine —**med′i·cal·ly** ***adv.***

medical jurisprudence the application of medical knowledge to questions of law

Med′i·care′ (-ker′) ***n.*** ⟦MEDI(CAL) + CARE⟧ [*also* **m-**] a Federal health program for paying certain medical expenses of the aged and the needy

med′i·cate′ (-kāt′) ***vt.*** **-cat′ed, -cat′ing** ⟦< L *medicari*, heal⟧ to treat with medicine —**med′i·ca′tion** ***n.***

me·dic·i·nal (mə dis′ən əl) ***adj.*** of, or having the properties of, medicine

med·i·cine (med′i sən) ***n.*** ⟦< L *medicus*, physician⟧ **1** the science and art of treating and preventing disease **2** any substance, as a drug, used in treating disease, relieving pain, etc.

medicine man among North American Indians, etc., a man supposed to have supernatural powers for healing the sick, etc.

me·di·e·val (mē′dē ē′vəl) ***adj.*** ⟦< L *medius*, middle + *aevum*, age⟧ of or characteristic of the Middle Ages

me·di·o·cre (mē′dē ō′kər) ***adj.*** ⟦< L *medius*, middle + *ocris*, peak⟧ **1** ordinary; average **2** inferior —**me′di·oc′ri·ty** (-äk′rə tē), *pl.* **-ties,** ***n.***

med·i·tate (med′ə tāt′) ***vt.*** **-tat′ed, -tat′ing** ⟦< L *meditari*⟧ to plan or intend —***vi.*** to think deeply —**med′i·ta′tion** ***n.*** —**med′i·ta′tive** ***adj.***

Med·i·ter·ra·ne·an (med′i tə rā′nē ən) ***adj.*** **1** of the large sea (**Mediterranean Sea**) surrounded by Europe, Africa, & Asia **2** designating furniture made to simulate heavy, ornately carved Renaissance furniture

me·di·um (mē′dē əm) ***n.***, *pl.* **-di·ums** or **-di·a** (-ə) ⟦L < *medius*, the middle⟧ **1** *a)* something intermediate *b)* a middle state or degree; mean **2** an intervening thing through which a force acts **3** any means, agency, etc.; specif., a means of communication that reaches the general public: a singular form **media** (*pl.* **medias**) is now sometimes used **4** any surrounding substance or environment **5** one through whom messages are supposedly sent from the dead —***adj.*** intermediate in size, quality, etc.

med·ley (med′lē) ***n.***, *pl.* **-leys** ⟦< L *miscere*, to mix⟧ **1** a mixture of dissimilar things **2** a musical piece made up of various tunes or passages

me·dul·la (mi dul′ə) ***n.***, *pl.* **-las** or **-lae** (-ē) ⟦L, marrow⟧ *Anat.* **1** a widening of the spinal cord forming the lowest part of the brain: in full **medulla ob·lon·ga·ta** (äb′läŋ gät′ə) **2** the inner substance of an organ

meek (mēk) ***adj.*** ⟦< ON *miukr*, gentle⟧ **1** patient and mild **2** too submissive; spiritless —**meek′ly** ***adv.*** —**meek′ness** ***n.***

meer·schaum (mir′shəm) ***n.*** ⟦Ger, sea foam⟧ **1** a white, claylike, heat-resistant mineral used for tobacco pipes, etc. **2** a pipe made of this

meet[1] (mēt) ***vt.*** **met, meet′ing** ⟦OE *metan*⟧ **1** to come upon; encounter **2** to be present at the arrival of /to *meet* a bus/ **3** to come into contact with **4** to be introduced to **5** to contend with; deal with **6** to experience /to *meet* disaster/ **7** to be perceived by (the eye, etc.) **8** *a)* to satisfy (a demand, etc.) *b)* to pay (a bill, etc.) —***vi.*** **1** to come together **2** to come into contact, etc. **3** to be introduced **4** to assemble —***n.*** a meeting /a track *meet*/ —**meet with** **1** to experience **2** to receive

meet[2] (mēt) ***adj.*** ⟦OE (*ge*)*mæte*, fitting⟧ [Now Rare] suitable; proper

meet′ing ***n.*** **1** a coming together **2** a gathering of people **3** a junction

mega- ⟦Gr < *megas*, great⟧ *combining form* **1** large, great, powerful **2** one million Also **meg-**

meg·a·byte (meg′ə bīt′) ***n.*** ⟦prec. + BYTE⟧ 2^{20} bytes, or, loosely, one million bytes

meg′a·hertz′ ***n.***, *pl.* **-hertz′** ⟦MEGA- + HERTZ⟧ one million hertz: formerly **meg′a·cy′cle**

meg·a·lo·ma·ni·a (meg′ə lō mā′nē ə) ***n.*** ⟦< Gr *megas*, large + -MANIA⟧ a mental disorder characterized by delusions of grandeur, power, etc.

meg·a·lop·o·lis (meg′ə läp′ə lis) ***n.***, *pl.* **-lis·es** ⟦Gr, great city⟧ a vast, continuously urban area, including any number of cities

meg·a·phone (meg′ə fōn′) ***n.*** ⟦MEGA- + -PHONE⟧ a cone-shaped device for increasing the volume of the voice

meg′a·ton′ ***n.*** ⟦MEGA- + TON⟧ the explosive force of a million tons of TNT

Me·kong (mā′käŋ′, -kôŋ′) river in SE Asia, flowing into the South China Sea

mel·a·mine (mel′ə mēn′) ***n.*** ⟦Ger *melamin*⟧ a white, crystalline compound used in making synthetic resins

mel·an·cho·li·a (mel′ən kō′lē ə) ***n.*** a mental disorder, often psychotic, characterized by extreme depression

mel′an·chol′y (-käl′ē) ***n.***, *pl.* **-ies** ⟦< Gr *melas*, black + *cholē*, bile⟧ sadness and depression of spirits —***adj.*** **1** sad and depressed **2** causing sadness

Mel·a·ne·sia (mel′ə nē′zhə) a group of islands in the South Pacific —**Mel′a·ne′sian** ***adj.***, ***n.***

mé·lange (mā lônzh′, -lônj′) ***n.*** ⟦Fr < *mêler*, to mix⟧ a mixture; medley

mel·a·nin (mel′ə nin) ***n.*** ⟦< Gr *melas*, black⟧ a blackish pigment found in skin, hair, etc.

mel′a·no′ma (-nō′mə) ***n.***, *pl.* **-mas** or **-ma·ta** (-mə tə) ⟦< Gr *melas*, black + *-ōma*, mass⟧ a skin tumor derived from cells capable of melanin formation

Melba toast (mel′bə) ⟦after N. *Melba* (1861-1931), Australian soprano⟧ [*also* **m-t-**] very crisp, thinly sliced toasted bread

Mel·bourne (mel′bərn) seaport in SE Australia: pop. 2,864,000

meld (meld) ***vt.***, ***vi.*** ⟦Ger *melden*, announce⟧ *Card Games* to show (certain cards) for a score —***n.*** the cards melded

me·lee or **mê·lée** (mā′lā′, mā lā′) ***n.*** ⟦Fr⟧ **1** a confused fight or hand-to-hand struggle **2** a confused conflict or mixture

mel·io·rate (mēl′yə rāt′) ***vt.***, ***vi.*** **-rat′ed, -rat′ing** ⟦< L *melior*, better⟧ to make or become better

mel·lif·lu·ous (mə lif′lo͞o əs) ***adj.*** ⟦< L *mel*, honey + *fluere*, to flow⟧ sounding sweet and smooth Also **mel·lif′lu·ent** —**mel·lif′lu·ence** ***n.***

mel·low (mel′ō) ***adj.*** ⟦ME *melwe*, ripe⟧ **1** soft, sweet, etc. because ripe: said of fruit **2** full-flavored: said of wine, etc. **3** full, rich, soft, etc.: said of sound, light, etc. **4** made gentle, understanding, etc. by age —***vt.***, ***vi.*** to make or become mellow

me·lo·di·ous (mə lō′dē əs) ***adj.*** **1** producing melody **2** pleasing to hear; tuneful —**me·lo′di·ous·ly** ***adv.***

mel·o·dra·ma (mel′ō drä′mə, -dram′ə; mel′ə-) ***n.*** ⟦< Fr < Gr *melos*, song + LL *drama*, drama⟧ a drama with exaggerated conflicts and emotions, stereotyped characters, etc. —**mel'o·dra·mat'ic** (-drə mat'ik) ***adj.***

mel'o·dra·mat'ics (-drə mat'iks) ***n.pl.*** melodramatic behavior

mel·o·dy (mel'ə dē) ***n., pl.* -dies** ⟦< Gr *melos,* song + *aeidein,* sing⟧ **1** pleasing sounds in sequence **2** *Music a)* a tune, song, etc. *b)* the leading part in a harmonic composition —**me·lod·ic** (mə läd'ik) ***adj.*** —**me·lod'i·cal·ly** ***adv.***

mel·on (mel'ən) ***n.*** ⟦< Gr *mēlon,* apple⟧ the large, juicy, thick-skinned, many-seeded fruit of certain trailing plants, as the watermelon or cantaloupe

melt (melt) ***vt., vi.*** ⟦OE *m(i)eltan*⟧ **1** to change from a solid to a liquid state, generally by heat **2** to dissolve **3** to disappear or cause to disappear gradually **4** to soften; become gentle, tender, etc.

melt'down' ***n.*** a dangerous situation in which a nuclear reactor begins to melt its fuel rods

melting pot a country, etc. in which people of various nationalities and races are assimilated

Mel·ville (mel'vil), **Her·man** (hur'mən) 1819-91; U.S. novelist

mem·ber (mem'bər) ***n.*** ⟦< L *membrum*⟧ **1** a limb or other part of a person, animal, or plant **2** a distinct part of a whole **3** a person belonging to some group, society, etc.

mem'ber·ship' ***n.*** **1** the state of being a member **2** members collectively, as of a group **3** the number of members

mem·brane (mem'brān') ***n.*** ⟦< L *membrum,* member⟧ a thin, soft layer, esp. of animal or plant tissue, that covers or lines an organ, part, etc. —**mem'bra·nous** (-brə nəs) ***adj.***

me·men·to (mə men'tō) ***n., pl.* -tos** or **-toes** ⟦< L *meminisse,* remember⟧ a reminder; esp., a souvenir

mem·o (mem'ō) ***n., pl.* -os** *short for* MEMORANDUM

mem·oirs (mem'wärz') ***n.pl.*** ⟦< L *memoria,* memory⟧ **1** an autobiography **2** a record of events based on the writer's personal observation or knowledge

mem·o·ra·bil·i·a (mem'ə rə bil'ē ə, -bil'yə; -bēl'-) ***n.pl.*** ⟦L⟧ things worth remembering

mem·o·ra·ble (mem'ə rə bəl) ***adj.*** worth remembering; notable; remarkable —**mem'o·ra·bly** ***adv.***

mem·o·ran·dum (mem'ə ran'dəm) ***n., pl.* -dums** or **-da** (-də) ⟦L⟧ **1** a short note written to remind one of something **2** an informal written communication, as in an office **3** *Law* a short written statement of the terms of an agreement, contract, etc.

me·mo·ri·al (mə môr'ē əl) ***adj.*** ⟦< L *memoria,* memory⟧ serving to help people remember —***n.*** anything meant to help people remember a person or event, as a monument or holiday —**me·mo'ri·al·ize'** (-īz'), **-ized', -iz'ing,** ***vt.***

Memorial Day a legal holiday in the U.S. (the last Monday in May in most States) in memory of members of the armed forces killed in war

mem·o·rize (mem'ə rīz') ***vt.* -rized', -riz'ing** to commit to memory —**mem'o·ri·za'tion** ***n.***

mem·o·ry (mem'ə rē, mem'rē) ***n., pl.* -ries** ⟦< L *memor,* mindful⟧ **1** the power or act of remembering **2** all that one remembers **3** something remembered **4** the period of remembering *[within my memory]* **5** commemoration **6** storage capacity, as of a computer

Mem·phis (mem'fis) city in SW Tenn.: pop. 646,000

men (men) ***n. pl. of*** MAN

men·ace (men'əs) ***n.*** ⟦< L *minari,* threaten⟧ **1** a threat **2** [Colloq.] one who is a nuisance —***vt., vi.* -aced, -ac·ing** to threaten —**men'ac·ing·ly** ***adv.***

mé·nage or **me·nage** (mā näzh', mə-) ***n.*** ⟦Fr < L *mansio,* house⟧ a household

me·nag·er·ie (mə naj'ər ē) ***n.*** ⟦see prec.⟧ a collection of wild animals kept in cages, etc. for exhibition

mend (mend) ***vt.*** ⟦< ME *amenden,* amend⟧ **1** to repair **2** to make better; reform —***vi.*** **1** to improve, esp. in health **2** to heal, as a fracture —***n.*** **1** a mending **2** a mended place —**on the mend** improving, esp. in health —**mend'er** ***n.***

men·da·cious (men dā'shəs) ***adj.*** ⟦< L *mendax*⟧ not truthful; lying —**men·dac'i·ty** (-das'ə tē), ***pl.* -ties,** ***n.***

Men·del (men'dəl), **Gre·gor** (grā'gôr) 1822-84; Austrian monk & geneticist

Men·dels·sohn (men'dəl sən'), **Fe·lix** (fā'liks) 1809-47; Ger. composer

men·di·cant (men'di kənt) ***adj.*** ⟦< L *mendicus,* needy⟧ begging —***n.*** **1** a beggar **2** a mendicant friar

men'folk' (-fōk') ***n.pl.*** [Colloq. or Dial.] men

men·ha·den (men hād''n) ***n., pl.* -den** or **-dens** ⟦< AmInd⟧ a common fish of the W Atlantic, used for bait or for making oil and fertilizer

me·ni·al (mē'nē əl) ***adj.*** ⟦< L *mansio,* house⟧ **1** of or fit for servants **2** servile; low —***n.*** **1** a domestic servant **2** a servile, low person —**me'ni·al·ly** ***adv.***

me·nin·ges (mə nin'jēz') ***n.pl., sing.* me·ninx** (mē'niŋks') ⟦< Gr *mēninx,* membrane⟧ the three membranes that envelop the brain and the spinal cord —**me·nin'ge·al** (-jē əl) ***adj.***

men·in·gi·tis (men'in jīt'is) ***n.*** ⟦ModL: see prec. & -ITIS⟧ inflammation of the meninges

me·nis·cus (mə nis'kəs) ***n., pl.* -nis'cus·es** or **-nis'ci'** (-nis'ī', -kī') ⟦< Gr dim. of *mēnē,* the moon⟧ **1** a crescent **2** the convex or concave upper surface of a column of liquid

Men·non·ite (men'ən īt') ***n.*** ⟦after *Menno* Simons, 16th-c. Du reformer⟧ a member of an evangelical Christian sect that opposes military service, oaths, etc., and favors plain living and dress

men·o·pause (men'ə pôz') ***n.*** ⟦< Gr *mēn,* month + *pauein,* to end⟧ the permanent cessation of menstruation

me·no·rah (mə nō'rə, -nôr'ə) ***n.*** ⟦Heb *menora,* lamp stand⟧ a candelabrum with seven (or nine) branches: a symbol of Judaism

men·ses (men'sēz') ***n.pl.*** ⟦L, pl. of *mensis,* month⟧ the periodic flow, usually monthly, of blood from the uterus

men·stru·ate (men'strāt', -stroo āt') ***vi.*** **-at'ed, -at'ing** ⟦< L *mensis,* month⟧ to have a discharge of the menses —**men′stru·al** *adj.* —**men′stru·a′tion** *n.*

men·su·ra·tion (men′shə rā′shən) *n.* ⟦< L *mensura*, measure⟧ a measuring —**men′sur·a·ble** (-shər ə bəl) *adj.*

-ment (mənt, mint) ⟦< L *-mentum*⟧ *suffix* **1** a result **2** a means [*escapement*] **3** an act **4** a state [*enchantment*]

men·tal (ment′'l) *adj.* ⟦< L *mens*, the mind⟧ **1** of, for, by, or in the mind **2** ill in mind [*mental* patients] **3** for the ill in mind —**men′tal·ly** *adv.*

men′tal·ist *n.* MIND READER

men·tal·i·ty (men tal′i tē) *n., pl.* **-ties 1** mental capacity or power **2** mental attitude or outlook

mental reservation a qualification (of a statement) that one makes to oneself but does not express

mental retardation congenital disorder characterized by subnormal intelligence

men·ta·tion (men tā′shən) *n.* ⟦< L *mens*, mind + -ATION⟧ the act or process of using the mind

men·thol (men′thôl′, -thäl′) *n.* ⟦Ger < L *mentha*, MINT[2]⟧ a white, crystalline alcohol obtained from oil of peppermint and used in medicine, cosmetics, etc. —**men′tho·lat′ed** (-thə lāt′id) *adj.*

men·tion (men′shən) *n.* ⟦< L *mens*, the mind⟧ **1** a brief reference **2** a citing for honor —*vt.* to refer to briefly or incidentally —**make mention of** to mention —**not to mention** without even mentioning

men·tor (men′tər, -tôr′) *n.* ⟦after *Mentor*, friend of Odysseus⟧ **1** a wise advisor **2** a teacher or coach

men·u (men′yōō) *n., pl.* **-us** ⟦Fr, small, detailed⟧ **1** a detailed list of the foods served at a meal or those available at a restaurant **2** a list, as on a computer screen, of the various choices available to the user

me·ow or **me·ou** (mē ou′) *n.* ⟦echoic⟧ the characteristic vocal sound made by a cat —*vi.* to make such a sound

mer·can·tile (mur′kən tīl′, -til) *adj.* ⟦Fr⟧ of or characteristic of merchants or trade

mer·ce·nar·y (mur′sə ner′ē) *adj.* ⟦< L *merces*, wages⟧ working or done for payment only —*n., pl.* **-ies** a soldier hired to serve in a foreign army

mer·cer (mur′sər) *n.* ⟦< L *merx*, wares⟧ [Brit.] a dealer in textiles

mer′cer·ize′ *vt.* **-ized′, -iz′ing** ⟦after J. *Mercer* (1791-1866), Eng calico dealer⟧ to treat (cotton thread or fabric) with an alkaline solution to strengthen it, give it a silky luster, etc.

mer·chan·dise (mur′chən dīz′, -dīs′) *n.* ⟦see fol.⟧ things bought and sold; wares —*vt., vi.* **-dised′, -dis′ing 1** to buy and sell **2** to promote the sale of (a product) Also, for v., **mer′chan·dize′** (-dīz′), **-dized′, -diz′ing** —**mer′chan·dis′er** or **mer′chan·diz′er** *n.*

mer·chant (mur′chənt) *n.* ⟦ult. < L *merx*, wares⟧ **1** one whose business is buying and selling goods **2** a retail dealer; storekeeper —*adj.* mercantile

mer′chant·man (-mən) *n., pl.* **-men** a ship used in commerce

merchant marine 1 all of a nation's commercial ships **2** their personnel

mer·ci (mer sē′) *interj.* ⟦Fr⟧ thank you

mer·ci·ful (mur′sə fəl) *adj.* having or showing mercy —**mer′ci·ful·ly** *adv.*

mer′ci·less *adj.* without mercy; pitiless —**mer′ci·less·ly** *adv.*

mer·cu·ri·al (mər kyoor′ē əl) *adj.* **1** having qualities associated with Mercury; clever, shrewd, etc. **2** of or containing mercury **3** quick, changeable, fickle, etc.

Mer·cu·ry (mur′kyoo rē) **1** *Rom. Myth.* the messenger of the gods **2** a small planet in the solar system: see PLANET —*n.* [**m-**] a heavy, silver-white metallic chemical element, liquid at ordinary temperatures, used in thermometers, etc. —**mer·cu·ric** (mər kyoor′ik) *adj.* —**mer·cu′rous** *adj.*

mer·cy (mur′sē) *n., pl.* **-cies** ⟦< L *merces*, payment⟧ **1** a refraining from harming offenders, enemies, etc. **2** imprisonment rather than death for a capital crime **3** a disposition to forgive or be kind **4** the power to forgive **5** a lucky thing; blessing —**at the mercy of** in the power of

mercy killing EUTHANASIA

mere (mir) *adj. superl.* **mer′est** ⟦< L *merus*, pure⟧ nothing more or other than [*a mere* boy]

mere′ly *adv.* only; no more than

mer·e·tri·cious (mer′ə trish′əs) *adj.* ⟦< L *meretrix*, a prostitute⟧ **1** attractive in a flashy way **2** specious

mer·gan·ser (mər gan′sər) *n.* ⟦< L *mergus*, diver (bird) + *anser*, goose⟧ a fish-eating, diving duck with a long bill

merge (murj) *vi., vt.* **merged, merg′ing** ⟦L *mergere*, to dip⟧ **1** to lose or cause to lose identity by being absorbed or combined **2** to unite

merg′er *n.* a merging; specif., a combining of two or more companies into one

me·rid·i·an (mə rid′ē ən) *n.* ⟦< L *meridies*, noon⟧ **1** the highest point of power, etc. **2** *a*) a circle on the earth's surface passing through the geographical poles and any given point *b*) any of the lines of longitude

me·ringue (mə raŋ′) *n.* ⟦Fr⟧ egg whites beaten with sugar until stiff: used as a pie covering, etc.

me·ri·no (mə rē′nō) *n., pl.* **-nos** ⟦Sp⟧ **1** any of a breed of hardy, white-faced sheep with long, fine wool **2** the wool **3** yarn or cloth made of it

mer·it (mer′it) *n.* ⟦< L *merere*, deserve⟧ **1** worth; value; excellence **2** something deserving reward, praise, etc. **3** [*pl.*] intrinsic rightness or wrongness —*vt.* to deserve

mer·i·to·ri·ous (mer′i tôr′ē əs) *adj.* having merit; deserving reward, praise, etc. —**mer′i·to′ri·ous·ly** *adv.*

Mer·lin (mur′lin) *Arthurian Legend* a magician and seer, helper of King Arthur

mer·maid (mur′mād′) *n.* ⟦< OE *mere*, sea + MAID⟧ an imaginary sea creature with the head and upper body of a woman and the tail of a fish —**mer′man′** (-man′), *pl.* **-men′**, *n.masc.*

mer·ri·ment (mer′i mənt) *n.* a merrymaking; gaiety and fun; mirth

mer·ry (mer′ē) *adj.* **-ri·er, -ri·est** ⟦< OE *myrge*, pleasing⟧ **1** full of fun; lively **2** festive —**make merry** to be festive and have fun —**mer′ri·ly** *adv.* —**mer′ri·ness** *n.*

mer′ry-go-round′ *n.* 1 a circular, revolving platform with forms of animals as seats on it, used at carnivals, etc. 2 a busy round, as of work

mer′ry·mak′ing *n.* a having fun; festivity —**mer′ry·mak′er** *n.*

me·sa (mā′sə) *n.* ⟦Sp < L *mensa,* a table⟧ a small, high plateau with steep sides

mes·cal (mes kal′) *n.* ⟦< Sp < AmInd(Mex)⟧ a small cactus of N Mexico and the SW U.S.

mes·ca·line (mes′kə lēn′, -lin) *n.* ⟦< AmInd(Mex) *mexcalli,* a spineless cactus⟧ a psychedelic drug obtained from the mescal

mes·dames (mā däm′) *n. pl. of* MADAME, MADAM (sense 1), or MRS.

mes·de·moi·selles (mād mwä zel′) *n. pl. of* MADEMOISELLE

mesh (mesh) *n.* ⟦prob. < MDu *mæsche*⟧ 1 any of the open spaces of a net, screen, etc. 2 a net or network 3 a netlike material, as for stockings 4 the engagement of the teeth of gears —*vt., vi.* 1 to entangle or become entangled 2 to engage or become engaged: said of gears 3 to interlock

mes·mer·ize (mez′mər iz′, mes′-) *vt.* **-ized′**, **-iz′ing** ⟦after F. A. *Mesmer* (1734-1815), Ger physician⟧ to hypnotize —**mes′mer·ism′** *n.* —**mes′mer·ist** *n.*

mes·on (mes′än′, mez′-) *n.* ⟦< Gr *mesos,* middle + (ELECTR)ON⟧ an unstable boson with a mass between those of an electron and a proton

Mes·o·po·ta·mi·a (mes′ə pə tā′mē ə) ancient country in SW Asia, between the Tigris & Euphrates rivers

Mes·o·zo·ic (mes′ō zō′ik, mez′-) *adj.* ⟦< Gr *mesos,* middle + ZO(O)- + -IC⟧ designating the geologic era (*c.* 225 to 65 million years ago) characterized by dinosaurs and by the appearance of flowering plants, grasses, birds, etc.

mes·quite or **mes·quit** (mes kēt′) *n.* ⟦< AmInd(Mex) *mizquitl*⟧ a thorny tree or shrub of Mexico and the SW U.S.

mess (mes) *n.* ⟦< L *missus,* course (at a meal)⟧ 1 a portion of food for a meal 2 a group of people who regularly eat together, as in the army 3 the meal they eat 4 a jumble 5 a state of trouble, disorder, or confusion —*vt.* 1 to make dirty or untidy 2 to muddle; botch: often with *up* —*vi.* 1 to eat as one of a mess 2 to make a mess 3 to putter or meddle (*in* or *with*) —**mess′y,** **-i·er,** **-i·est,** *adj.* —**mess′i·ly** *adv.* —**mess′i·ness** *n.*

mes·sage (mes′ij) *n.* ⟦< L *mittere,* send⟧ 1 a communication sent by speech, in writing, etc. 2 the chief idea that an artist, writer, etc. seeks to communicate in a work —**get the message** [Colloq.] to understand a hint, etc.

mes·sen·ger (mes′ən jər) *n.* one who carries a message or goes on an errand

messenger RNA a form of RNA, derived from DNA, that carries the genetic code needed to form a protein

mess hall a room or building where soldiers, etc. regularly have meals

Mes·si·ah (mə sī′ə) ⟦< Heb *māshīaḥ,* anointed⟧ 1 *Judaism* the expected deliverer of the Jews 2 *Christianity* Jesus —**Mes·si·an·ic** (mes′ē an′ik) *adj.*

mes·sieurs (mes′ərz; *Fr* mā syö′) *n. pl. of* MONSIEUR

Messrs. (mes′ərz) messieurs: now used chiefly as the pl. of MR.

mes·ti·zo (mes tē′zō) *n., pl.* **-zos** or **-zoes** ⟦Sp < L *miscere,* to mix⟧ a person of mixed parentage, esp. Spanish and American Indian

met (met) *vt., vi. pt. & pp. of* MEET[1]

met. metropolitan

meta- ⟦< Gr *meta,* after⟧ *prefix* 1 changed [*metathesis*] 2 after, beyond, higher [*metaphysics*]

me·tab·o·lism (mə tab′ə liz′əm) *n.* ⟦< Gr *meta,* beyond + *ballein,* throw⟧ the chemical and physical processes continuously going on in living organisms and cells, including the changing of food into living tissue and the changing of living tissue into waste products and energy —**met·a·bol·ic** (met′ə bäl′ik) *adj.* —**me·tab′o·lize′** (-līz′), **-lized′**, **-liz′ing,** *vt., vi.*

met·a·car·pus (met′ə kär′pəs) *n., pl.* **-pi** (-pī) ⟦< Gr *meta,* over + *karpos,* wrist⟧ the part of the hand between the wrist and the fingers —**met′a·car′pal** *adj., n.*

Me·tai·rie (met′ə rē) city in SE La.: suburb of New Orleans: pop. 164,000

met·al (met′'l) *n.* ⟦< Gr *metallon,* a mine⟧ 1 *a)* any of a class of chemical elements, as iron or gold, that have luster, can conduct heat and electricity, etc. *b)* an alloy of such elements, as brass or bronze 2 anything consisting of metal —**me·tal·lic** (mə tal′ik) *adj.* —**me·tal′li·cal·ly** *adv.*

met·al·lur·gy (met′ə lur′jē, met′'l ur′jē) *n.* ⟦< Gr *metallon,* metal + *ergon,* work⟧ the science of separating metals from their ores and preparing them for use, by smelting, refining, etc. —**met′al·lur′gi·cal** *adj.* —**met′al·lur′gist** *n.*

met·a·mor·phose (met′ə môr′fōz′, -fōs′) *vt., vi.* **-phosed′**, **-phos′ing** to change in form; transform

met′a·mor′pho·sis (-môr′fə sis, -môr fō′sis) *n., pl.* **-ses′** (-sēz′) ⟦< Gr *meta,* over + *morphē,* form⟧ 1 a change of form, structure, substance, or function; specif., the physical change undergone by some animals, as of the tadpole to the frog 2 a marked change of character, appearance, condition, etc. —**met′a·mor′phic** *adj.*

met·a·phor (met′ə fər, -fôr′) *n.* ⟦< Gr *meta,* over + *pherein,* to bear⟧ a figure of speech in which one thing is spoken of as if it were another (Ex.: "all the world's a stage") —**met′a·phor′ic** or **met′a·phor′i·cal** *adj.* —**met′a·phor′i·cal·ly** *adv.*

met·a·phys·i·cal (met′ə fiz′i kəl) *adj.* 1 of, or having the nature of, metaphysics 2 very abstract or subtle 3 supernatural

met′a·phys′ics (-iks) *n.pl.* ⟦< Gr *meta* (*ta*) *physika,* after (the) *Physics* (of Aristotle)⟧ [*with sing. v.*] 1 the branch of philosophy that seeks to explain the nature of being and reality 2 speculative philosophy in general

me·tas·ta·sis (mə tas′tə sis) *n., pl.* **-ses′** (-sēz′) ⟦< Gr *meta,* after + *histanai,* to place⟧ the spread of disease from one part of the body to another, esp. the spread of cancer cells by way of the bloodstream —**me·tas'ta·size'** (-sīz'), **-sized'**, **-siz'ing**, ***vi.***

met·a·tar·sus (met'ə tär'səs) ***n.***, *pl.* **-si'** (-sī') ⟦< Gr *meta,* over + *tarsos,* flat of the foot⟧ the part of the human foot between the ankle and the toes —**met'a·tar'sal** ***adj.***, ***n.***

me·tath·e·sis (mə tath'ə sis) ***n.***, *pl.* **-ses'** (-sēz') ⟦< Gr *meta,* over + *tithenai,* to place⟧ transposition, specif. of sounds in a word

mete (mēt) ***vt.*** **met'ed**, **met'ing** ⟦OE *metan*⟧ to allot; distribute: usually with *out*

me·tem·psy·cho·sis (mi tem'si kō'sis; met' əm sī-) ***n.***, *pl.* **-ses'** (-sēz') ⟦< Gr *meta,* over + *en,* in + *psychē,* soul⟧ transmigration of souls

me·te·or (mēt'ē ər, -ē ôr') ***n.*** ⟦< Gr *meta,* beyond + *eōra,* a hovering⟧ **1** the streak of light, etc. observed when a meteoroid enters the earth's atmosphere **2** a meteoroid or meteorite

me'te·or'ic (-ôr'ik) ***adj.*** **1** of a meteor **2** like a meteor; momentarily brilliant, swift, etc.

me'te·or·ite' (-ər īt') ***n.*** that part of a meteoroid that survives passage through the atmosphere

me'te·or·oid' (-ər oid') ***n.*** a small, solid body traveling through outer space, seen as a streak of light when in the earth's atmosphere

me'te·or·ol'o·gy (-ər äl'ə jē) ***n.*** ⟦see METEOR & -LOGY⟧ the science of the atmosphere and its phenomena; study of weather —**me'te·or·o·log'i·cal** (-ə läj'i kəl) ***adj.*** —**me'te·or·ol'o·gist** ***n.***

me·ter[1] (mēt'ər) ***n.*** ⟦< Gr *metron,* a measure⟧ **1** rhythm in verse; measured arrangement of syllables according to stress **2** the basic pattern of beats in music **3** ⟦Fr *mètre*⟧ the basic metric unit of length, equal to *c.* 39.37 inches

me·ter[2] (mēt'ər) ***n.*** ⟦< words ending in fol.⟧ **1** an apparatus for measuring and recording the quantity of gas, water, etc. passing through it **2** PARKING METER

-me·ter (mēt'ər, mi tər) ⟦< Gr *metron,* a measure⟧ *combining form* a device for measuring *[barometer]*

meter maid a woman employed by a police traffic department to issue tickets for illegal parking, jaywalking, etc.

meth·a·done (meth'ə dōn') ***n.*** ⟦< its chemical name⟧ a synthetic narcotic drug used in medicine to treat heroin and morphine addicts

meth·ane (meth'ān') ***n.*** ⟦< METHYL⟧ a colorless, odorless, flammable gas formed by the decomposition of vegetable matter, as in marshes

meth·a·nol (meth'ə nôl') ***n.*** ⟦< METHAN(E) + (ALCOH)OL⟧ a colorless, flammable, poisonous liquid used as a fuel, solvent, antifreeze, etc. Also **methyl alcohol**

me·thinks (mē thiŋks') ***v.impersonal*** *pt.* **-thought'** ⟦OE *me,* to me + *thyncth,* it seems⟧ [Archaic] it seems to me

meth·od (meth'əd) ***n.*** ⟦< Fr < Gr *meta,* after + *hodos,* a way⟧ **1** a way of doing anything; process **2** a system in doing things or handling ideas

me·thod·i·cal (mə thäd'i kəl) ***adj.*** characterized by method; orderly; systematic Also **me·thod'ic** —**me·thod'i·cal·ly** ***adv.***

Meth·od·ist (meth'ə dist) ***n.*** a member of a Protestant Christian denomination that developed from the teachings of John Wesley —**Meth'od·ism'** ***n.***

meth'od·ol'o·gy (-ə däl'ə jē) ***n.***, *pl.* **-gies** a system of methods, as in a science

Me·thu·se·lah (mə thōō'zə lə) *Bible* a patriarch who lived 969 years

meth·yl (meth'il) ***n.*** ⟦< Gr *methy,* wine + *hylē,* wood⟧ a hydrocarbon radical found in methanol

me·tic·u·lous (mə tik'yōō ləs, -yə-) ***adj.*** ⟦< L *metus,* fear⟧ extremely or excessively careful about details; scrupulous or finicky —**me·tic'u·lous·ly** ***adv.***

mé·tier (mā tyā') ***n.*** ⟦Fr, trade⟧ work that one is particularly suited for

me·tre (mē'tər) ***n.*** *Brit. sp. of* METER[1]

met·ric (me'trik) ***adj.*** **1** METRICAL **2** *a)* of the METER[1] (sense 3) *b)* of the metric system

met·ri·cal (me'tri kəl) ***adj.*** **1** of or composed in meter or verse **2** of or used in measurement —**met'ri·cal·ly** ***adv.***

met·ri·cate (me'tri kāt') ***vt.*** **-cat'ed**, **-cat'ing** to change over to the metric system —**met'ri·ca'tion** ***n.***

metric system a decimal system of weights and measures in which the gram (.0022046 pound), the meter (39.37 inches), and the liter (61.025 cubic inches) are the basic units

met·ro (me'trō) ***n.***, *pl.* **-ros** ⟦ult. < *metro(politan)*⟧ [*often* M-] a subway

met·ro·nome (me'trə nōm') ***n.*** ⟦< Gr *metron,* measure + *nomos,* law⟧ a device that beats time at a desired rate, as for piano practice

me·trop·o·lis (mə träp'əl is) ***n.***, *pl.* **-lis·es** ⟦< Gr *mētēr,* mother + *polis,* city⟧ **1** the main city, often the capital, of a country, state, etc. **2** any large or important city —**met·ro·pol·i·tan** (me'trō päl'i tən, -trə-) ***adj.***

met·tle (met''l) ***n.*** ⟦var. of METAL⟧ spirit; courage; ardor —**on one's mettle** prepared to do one's best

met'tle·some (-səm) ***adj.*** full of mettle; spirited; ardent, brave, etc.

mew[1] (myōō) ***vt.*** ⟦< L *mutare,* to change⟧ to confine

mew[2] (myōō) ***n.*** ⟦echoic⟧ the characteristic vocal sound made by a cat —***vi.*** to make this sound

mewl (myōōl) ***vi.*** ⟦< prec.⟧ to cry weakly, like a baby; whimper

mews (myōōz) ***n.pl.*** ⟦< MEW[1]⟧ [*usually with sing. v.*] [Chiefly Brit.] stables or carriage houses in a court or alley

Mex. **1** Mexican **2** Mexico

Mex·i·co (meks'i kō') **1** country in North America, south of the U.S.: 756,198 sq. mi.; pop. 66,846,000 **2 Gulf of** arm of the Atlantic, east of Mexico —**Mex'i·can** ***adj.***, ***n.***

Mexico City capital of Mexico: pop. 9,377,000 (met. area *c.* 14,000,000)

mez·za·nine (mez'ə nēn', mez'ə nēn') ***n.*** ⟦< It *mezzano,* middle⟧ **1** a low-ceilinged story between two main stories, as a balcony over the main floor **2** the first few rows of the balcony in some theaters

mez·zo-so·pra·no (met'sō sə pran'ō) ***n.***, *pl.* **-nos** or **-ni** (-ē) ⟦It < *mezzo,* medium +

SOPRANO] a voice or singer between soprano and contralto

mfg. manufacturing

mfr. manufacturer

Mg *Chem. symbol for* magnesium

mg milligram(s)

Mgr. manager

MHz or **Mhz** megahertz

mi (mē) ***n.*** [ML] *Music* the third tone of the diatonic scale

mi. 1 mile(s) 2 mill(s)

MI 1 Michigan 2 middle initial

Mi·am·i (mī am′ē) city on the SE coast of Fla.: pop. 347,000 —**Mi·am′i·an *n.***

mi·as·ma (mī az′mə, mē-) ***n.*** [< Gr *miainein,* pollute] 1 a vapor as from marshes, formerly supposed to poison the air 2 an unwholesome atmosphere or influence

mi·ca (mī′kə) ***n.*** [L, a crumb] a mineral that crystallizes in thin, flexible layers, resistant to heat and electricity

mice (mīs) ***n.*** *pl. of* MOUSE

Mi·chel·an·ge·lo (mī′kəl an′jə lō′, mik′əl-) 1475-1564; It. sculptor, painter, & architect

Mich·i·gan (mish′i gən) 1 Middle Western State of the U.S.: 58,216 sq. mi.; pop. 9,262,000; cap. Lansing: abbrev. **Mich.** 2 **Lake** one of the Great Lakes, between Mich. & Wis. —**Mich′i·gan′der** (-gan′dər) ***n.*** —**Mich′i·ga′ni·an** (-gā′nē ən) or **Mich′i·gan·ite′ *adj., n.***

Mick·ey Finn (mik′ē fin′) [< ?] [*also* **m- f-**] [Slang] a drink of liquor to which a narcotic, etc. has been added, given to an unsuspecting person: often shortened to **Mick′ey** or **mick′ey *n., pl.* -eys**

micro- [< Gr *mikros,* small] *combining form* 1 little, small */microcosm/* 2 enlarging */microscope/* 3 microscopic */microbiology/* 4 one millionth */microsecond/* Also **micr-**

mi·crobe (mī′krōb′) ***n.*** [< Gr *mikros,* small + *bios,* life] a microorganism, esp. one causing disease

mi·cro·bi·ol·o·gy (mī′krō bī äl′ə jē) ***n.*** the branch of biology dealing with microorganisms —**mi′cro·bi·ol′o·gist *n.***

mi′cro·chip′ *n.* INTEGRATED CIRCUIT

mi′cro·com·put′er *n.* a small, inexpensive computer having a microprocessor and used in the home, etc.

mi′cro·cosm′ (-käz′əm) ***n.*** [see MICRO- & COSMOS] something regarded as a world in miniature

mi′cro·dot′ *n.* a copy, as of written or printed matter, photographically reduced to pinhead size, used in espionage, etc.

mi′cro·ec′o·nom′ics *n.pl.* [*with sing. v.*] a branch of economics dealing with certain specific factors affecting an economy, as the behavior of individual consumers

mi′cro·fiche′ (-fēsh′) ***n., pl.* -fich′es** or **-fiche′** [Fr < *micro-,* MICRO- + *fiche,* small card] a small sheet of microfilm containing a group of microfilmed pages

mi′cro·film′ *n.* film on which documents, etc. are photographed in a reduced size for storage, etc. —***vt., vi.*** to photograph on microfilm

mi′cro·groove′ *n.* the very narrow groove in an LP phonograph record

mi·crom·e·ter (mī kräm′ət ər) ***n.*** [< Fr: see MICRO- & -METER] an instrument for measuring very small distances, angles, etc.

MICROMETER

mi·cron (mī′krän′) ***n.*** [< Gr *mikros,* small] one millionth of a meter

Mi·cro·ne·sia (mī′krə nē′zhə, -shə) the group of islands in the Pacific east of the Philippines —**Mi′cro·ne′sian *adj., n.***

mi·cro·or·gan·ism (mī′krō ôr′gən iz′əm) ***n.*** a microscopic organism, esp. a bacterium, protozoan, etc.

mi′cro·phone′ (mī′krə-) ***n.*** [MICRO- + -PHONE] an instrument for converting sound waves into an electric signal

mi′cro·proc′es′sor (mī′krō-) ***n.*** an integrated circuit that controls the operation of a microcomputer

mi′cro·scope′ (mī′krə-) ***n.*** [see MICRO- & -SCOPE] an instrument consisting of a combination of lenses, for making very small objects, as microorganisms, look larger

mi′cro·scop′ic (-skäp′ik) ***adj.*** 1 so small as to be invisible or obscure except through a microscope; minute 2 of, with, or like a microscope —**mi′cro·scop′i·cal·ly *adv.***

mi′cro·sur′ger·y (mī′krō-) ***n.*** surgery performed using a microscope and minute instruments or laser beams

mi′cro·wave′ *adj.* 1 designating equipment, etc. using microwaves for radar, communications, etc. 2 designating an oven that cooks quickly using microwaves —***vt.* -waved′, -wav′ing** to cook in a microwave oven —***n.*** 1 an electromagnetic wave with a frequency of about 300,000 megahertz to 300 megahertz 2 a microwave oven

mid[1] (mid) ***adj.*** [OE *midd-*] middle

mid[2] (mid) ***prep.*** [Old Poet.] amid Also **'mid**

mid- *combining form* middle, middle part of */mid-May/*

mid′air′ *n.* any point not in contact with the ground or any other surface

Mi·das (mī′dəs) *Gr. Myth.* a king granted the power of turning everything that he touched into gold

mid′day′ *n., adj.* [OE *middæg*] noon

mid·dle (mid′'l) ***adj.*** [OE *middel*] 1 halfway between two given points, times, etc. 2 intermediate 3 [**M-**] designating a stage in language development intermediate between *Old* and *Modern /Middle* English/ —***n.*** 1 a point or part halfway between extremes; middle point, time, etc. 2 something intermediate 3 the middle part of the body; waist

middle age the time between youth and old age —**mid′dle-aged′ *adj.***

Middle Ages the period of European history between ancient and modern times, A.D. 476-c. 1450

Middle America the American middle class, seen as being conventional or conservative

mid′dle·brow′ (-brou′) ***n.*** [Colloq.] one regarded as having conventional, middle-class tastes or opinions

middle class the social class between the aristocracy or very wealthy and the lower working class

middle ear the part of the ear including the eardrum and the adjacent cavity containing three small bones

Middle East area from Afghanistan to Libya, including Arabia, Cyprus, & Asiatic Turkey —**Middle Eastern**

Middle English the English language between *c.* 1100 and *c.* 1500

mid'dle·man' *n., pl.* **-men'** 1 a trader who buys from a producer and sells at wholesale or retail 2 a go-between

mid'dle·most' *adj.* MIDMOST

mid'dle-of-the-road' *adj.* avoiding extremes, esp. political extremes

middle school a school with, usually, grades five through eight

mid'dle·weight' *n.* a boxer with a maximum weight of 160 pounds

Middle West region of the north central U.S. between the Rocky Mountains & the E border of Ohio & the S borders of Kans. & Mo. —**Middle Western**

mid·dling (mid'liŋ) *adj.* of middle size, quality, etc.; medium —*adv.* [Colloq.] fairly; moderately

mid·dy (mid'ē) *n., pl.* **-dies** ⟦< MIDSHIPMAN⟧ a loose blouse with a sailor collar, worn by women and children

midge (mij) *n.* ⟦OE *mycg*⟧ a small, gnatlike insect

midg·et (mij'it) *n.* 1 a very small person 2 anything very small of its kind —*adj.* miniature

mid·land (mid'lənd) *n.* the middle region of a country; interior —*adj.* in or of the midland; inland

mid'most' *adj.* exactly in the middle, or nearest the middle

mid'night' (-nīt') *n.* twelve o'clock at night —*adj.* 1 of or at midnight 2 like midnight; very dark

mid'point' *n.* a point at or close to the middle or center

mid·riff (mid'rif) *n.* ⟦< OE *midd-*, MID¹ + *hrif*, belly⟧ 1 DIAPHRAGM (sense 1) 2 the middle part of the torso, between the abdomen and the chest

mid·ship·man (mid'ship'mən) *n., pl.* **-men** a student in training to be a naval officer

mid-size or **mid·size** (mid'sīz') *adj.* of a size intermediate between large and small /a *mid-size* car/

midst¹ (midst) *n.* the middle; central part —**in our** (or **your** or **their**) **midst** among us (or you or them) —**in the midst of** 1 in the middle of 2 during

midst² (midst) *prep.* [Old Poet.] in the midst of; amidst Also **'midst**

mid·stream (mid'strēm') *n.* the middle of a stream

mid'sum'mer *n.* 1 the middle of summer 2 the time of the summer solstice, about June 21

mid'term' *adj.* in the middle of the term —*n.* [Colloq.] a midterm examination, as at a college

mid'way' (-wā') *n.* that part of a fair where sideshows, etc. are located —*adj., adv.* in the middle of the way or distance; halfway

Mid·west (mid'west') MIDDLE WEST —**Mid'west'ern** *adj.*

mid'wife' (-wīf') *n., pl.* **-wives'** ⟦< ME *mid*, with + *wif*, woman⟧ a person who helps women in childbirth —**mid'wife'ry** (-wif'rē) *n.*

mid'win'ter *n.* 1 the middle of winter 2 the time of the winter solstice, about Dec. 22

mid'year' *adj.* in the middle of the year —*n.* [Colloq.] a midyear examination, as at a college

mien (mēn) *n.* ⟦short for DEMEAN²⟧ one's appearance, bearing, or manner

miff (mif) *vt.* ⟦prob. orig. cry of disgust⟧ [Colloq.] to offend

MIG (mig) ⟦after *M*ikoyan & *G*urevich, its Soviet designers⟧ a high-speed, high-altitude jet fighter plane Also **MiG**

might¹ (mīt) *v.aux.* ⟦OE *mihte*⟧ 1 *pt.* of MAY 2 used as an auxiliary generally equivalent to MAY /it *might* rain/

might² (mīt) *n.* ⟦OE *miht*⟧ strength, power, or vigor

might'y (-ē) *adj.* **-i·er, -i·est** 1 powerful; strong 2 remarkably large, etc.; great —*adv.* [Colloq.] very —**might'i·ly** *adv.* —**might'i·ness** *n.*

mi·gnon·ette (min'yə net') *n.* ⟦< Fr *mignon*, small⟧ a plant with spikes of small, fragrant flowers

mi·graine (mī'grān') *n.* ⟦< Gr *hēmi-*, half + *kranion*, skull⟧ an intense, periodic headache, usually limited to one side of the head

mi·grant (mī'grənt) *adj.* migrating —*n.* 1 one that migrates 2 a farm laborer who moves from place to place to harvest seasonal crops

mi·grate (mī'grāt') *vi.* **-grat'ed, -grat'ing** ⟦< L *migrare*⟧ 1 to settle in another country or region 2 to move to another region with the change in seasons, as many birds —**mi·gra·to·ry** (mī'grə tôr'ē) *adj.*

mi·gra·tion (mī grā'shən) *n.* 1 a migrating 2 a group of people, birds, etc. migrating together

mi·ka·do (mi kä'dō) *n., pl.* **-dos** ⟦< Jpn *mi*, an honorific title + *kado*, gate⟧ [*often* **M-**] the emperor of Japan: title no longer used

mike (mīk) *n.* [Colloq.] a microphone —*vt.* **miked, mik'ing** [Colloq.] to record, amplify, etc. with a microphone

mil (mil) *n.* ⟦L *mille*, thousand⟧ a unit of linear measure, equal to $\frac{1}{1000}$ inch

mi·la·dy or **mi·la·di** (mi lā'dē) *n., pl.* **-dies** ⟦Fr < Eng *my lady*⟧ 1 a noblewoman 2 a woman of fashion: advertisers' term

Mi·lan (mi lan') city in NW Italy: pop. 1,520,000

milch (milch) *adj.* ⟦ME *milche*⟧ kept for milking /*milch* cows/

mild (mīld) *adj.* ⟦OE *milde*⟧ 1 gentle or kind; not severe 2 having a soft, pleasant flavor /a *mild* cheese/ —**mild'ly** *adv.* —**mild'ness** *n.*

mil·dew (mil'do͞o') *n.* ⟦OE *meledeaw*, honeydew⟧ a fungus that attacks some plants or appears on damp cloth, etc. as a whitish coating —*vt., vi.* to affect or be affected with mildew

mile (mīl) *n.* ⟦< L *milia* (*passuum*), thousand (paces)⟧ a unit of linear measure equal to 5,280 feet

mile′age (-ij) *n.* 1 an allowance per mile for traveling expenses 2 total miles traveled 3 the average number of miles that can be traveled, as per gallon of fuel
mile′post′ *n.* a signpost showing the distance in miles to or from a place
mil′er (-ər) *n.* one who competes in mile races
mile′stone′ *n.* 1 a stone set up to show the distance in miles to or from a place 2 a significant event
mi·lieu (mēl yʉ′, -yoo′, -yōō′; mil-) *n.* [Fr < L *medius,* middle + *locus,* a place] environment; esp., social setting
mil·i·tant (mil′i tənt) *adj.* [< L *miles,* soldier] 1 fighting 2 ready to fight, esp. for some cause —*n.* a militant person —**mil′i·tan·cy** *n.* —**mil′i·tant·ly** *adv.*
mil·i·ta·rism (mil′ə tə riz′əm) *n.* 1 military spirit 2 a policy of aggressive military preparedness —**mil′i·ta·rist** *n.* —**mil′i·ta·ris′·tic** *adj.*
mil·i·ta·rize (mil′i tə rīz′) *vt.* **-rized′, -riz′·ing** to equip and prepare for war
mil·i·tar·y (mil′ə ter′ē) *adj.* [< L *miles,* soldier] 1 of, for, or done by soldiers 2 of, for, or fit for war 3 of the army —**the military** the armed forces
military police soldiers assigned to police duties in the army
mil·i·tate (mil′ə tāt′) *vi.* **-tat′ed, -tat′ing** [< L *militare,* be a soldier] to operate or work (*against*)
mi·li·tia (mə lish′ə) *n.* [< L *miles,* soldier] an army composed of citizens rather than professional soldiers, called up in time of emergency —**mi·li′tia·man** (-mən), *pl.* **-men,** *n.*
milk (milk) *n.* [OE *meolc*] 1 a white fluid secreted by the mammary glands of female mammals for suckling their young 2 cow's milk, etc., drunk by humans as a food or used to make butter, cheese, etc. 3 any liquid like this, as coconut milk —*vt.* 1 to squeeze milk from (a cow, goat, etc.) 2 to extract money, ideas, etc. from as if by milking —**milk′er** *n.*
milk glass a nearly opaque whitish glass
milk′maid′ *n.* a girl or woman who milks cows or works in a dairy
milk′man′ *n., pl.* **-men′** a man who sells or delivers milk for a dairy
milk of magnesia a milky-white suspension of magnesium hydroxide in water, used as a laxative and antacid
milk′shake′ *n.* a drink made of milk, flavoring, and ice cream, shaken until frothy
milk′sop′ (-säp′) *n.* one who is timid, ineffectual, effeminate, etc.
milk tooth any of the temporary, first teeth of a child or young animal
milk′weed′ *n.* any of a group of plants with a milky juice
milk′y (-ē) *adj.* **-i·er, -i·est** 1 like milk; esp., white as milk 2 of or containing milk —**milk′i·ness** *n.*
Milky Way a broad, faintly luminous band of very distant stars and interstellar gas, arching across the night sky
mill[1] (mil) *n.* [< L *mola,* millstone] 1 a building with machinery for grinding grain into flour or meal 2 any of various machines for grinding, crushing, cutting, etc. 3 a factory [a textile *mill*] —*vt.* 1 to grind, form, etc. by or in a mill 2 to raise and ridge the edge of (a coin) —*vi.* to move (*around* or *about*) confusedly —**in the mill** in preparation —**through the mill** [Colloq.] through a hard, painful, instructive experience
mill[2] (mil) *n.* [< L *mille,* thousand] $\frac{1}{10}$ of a cent: unit used in calculating
mill·age (mil′ij) *n.* taxation in mills per dollar of valuation
mil·len·ni·um (mi len′ē əm) *n., pl.* **-ni·ums** or **-ni·a** (-ə) [< L *mille,* thousand + *annus,* year] 1 a thousand years 2 *Christian Theol.* the period of a thousand years during which Christ will reign on earth: with *the* 3 any period of great happiness, peace, etc.
mill·er (mil′ər) *n.* one who owns or operates a mill, esp. a flour mill
mil·let (mil′it) *n.* [< L *milium*] 1 a cereal grass whose grain is used for food in Europe and Asia 2 any of several similar grasses used for forage
milli- [< L *mille,* thousand] *combining form* one thousandth part of [*millimeter*]
mil·li·gram (mil′i gram′) *n.* one thousandth of a gram
mil′li·me′ter (-mēt′ər) *n.* one thousandth of a meter Brit. sp. **mil′li·me′tre**
mil·li·ner (mil′i nər) *n.* [< *Milaner,* vendor of dress wares from Milan] one who makes or sells women's hats
mil·li·ner·y (mil′i ner′ē) *n.* 1 women's hats, headdresses, etc. 2 the work or business of a milliner
mil·lion (mil′yən) *n.* [< L *mille,* thousand] a thousand thousands; 1,000,000
mil′lion·aire′ (-yə ner′) *n.* a person whose wealth comes to at least a million dollars, pounds, francs, etc.
mil·li·pede (mil′i pēd′) *n.* [< L *mille,* thousand + *pes,* foot] a many-legged arthropod with an elongated body
mill′race′ *n.* the channel in which water turning a wheel that drives the machinery in a mill runs
mill′stone′ *n.* 1 either of a pair of flat, round stones used for grinding grain, etc. 2 a heavy burden
mill′stream′ *n.* water flowing in a millrace
mill′wright′ (-rīt′) *n.* a worker who builds, installs, or repairs the machinery in a mill
milt (milt) *n.* [prob. < Scand] the sex glands or sperm of male fishes
Mil·ton (mil′tən), **John** 1608-74; Eng. poet
Mil·wau·kee (mil wô′kē) city & port in SE Wis., on Lake Michigan: pop. 636,000
mime (mīm) *n.* [< Gr *mimos*] 1 the representation of an action, mood, etc. by gestures, not words 2 a mimic or pantomimist —*vt.* **mimed, mim′ing** to mimic or pantomime
mim·e·o·graph (mim′ē ə graf′) *n.* [< Gr *mimeomai,* I imitate] a machine for making copies of graphic matter by means of an inked stencil —*vt.* to make (such copies) of
mi·met·ic (mi met′ik, mī-) *adj.* [< Gr *mimeisthai,* to imitate] 1 imitative 2 characterized by mimicry
mim·ic (mim′ik) *adj.* [< Gr *mimos,* actor] 1 imitative 2 make-believe —*n.* an imitator; esp., an actor skilled in mimicry —*vt.*

-icked, -ick·ing 1 to imitate, often so as to ridicule 2 to copy or resemble closely
mim·ic·ry (mim′ik rē) ***n.***, *pl.* **-ries** the practice, art, or way of mimicking
mi·mo·sa (mi mō′sə) ***n.*** ⟦see MIME⟧ a tree, shrub, or herb growing in warm regions and usually having spikes of white or pink flowers
min. 1 minimum 2 minute(s)
min·a·ret (min′ə ret′) ***n.*** ⟦< Ar *manāra(t),* lighthouse⟧ a high, slender tower attached to a mosque

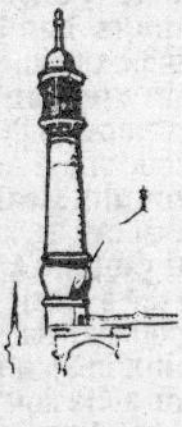
MINARET

min·a·to·ry (min′ə tôr′ē) ***adj.*** ⟦< L *minari,* threaten⟧ menacing
mince (mins) ***vt.*** **minced, minc′ing** ⟦< L *minutus,* small⟧ 1 to cut up (meat, etc.) into small pieces 2 to express or do with affected daintiness 3 to lessen the force of /to *mince* no words/ —***vi.*** to speak or act with affected daintiness —**minc′·ing** ***adj.***
mince′meat′ ***n.*** a mixture of chopped apples, spices, raisins, etc., and sometimes meat, used as a pie filling
mind (mīnd) ***n.*** ⟦< OE *(ge)mynd*⟧ 1 memory /to bring to *mind* a story/ 2 opinion /speak your *mind*/ 3 the seat of consciousness, in which thinking, feeling, etc. takes place 4 intellect 5 PSYCHE (*n.* 2) 6 reason; sanity —***vt.*** 1 to pay attention to; heed 2 to obey 3 to take care of /*mind* the baby/ 4 to be careful about /*mind* the stairs/ 5 to care about; object to /they don't *mind* the noise/ —***vi.*** 1 to pay attention 2 to be obedient 3 to be careful 4 to care; object —**bear** (or **keep**) **in mind** to remember —**change one's mind** to change one's opinion, purpose, etc. —**have in mind** to intend —**make up one's mind** to reach a decision —**on one's mind** 1 filling one's thoughts 2 worrying one —**out of one's mind** frantic
mind′ed ***adj.*** having a (specified kind of) mind: used in compounds /high-*minded*/
mind′ful (-fəl) ***adj.*** having in mind; aware or careful (*of*) —**mind′ful·ly** ***adv.*** —**mind′·ful·ness** ***n.***
mind reader one who professes ability to perceive another's thoughts
mind's eye the imagination
mine[1] (mīn) ***pron.*** ⟦OE min⟧ that or those belonging to me /this is *mine*/
mine[2] (mīn) ***n.*** ⟦< Fr⟧ 1 a large excavation made in the earth, from which to extract ores, coal, etc. 2 a deposit of ore, coal, etc. 3 any great source of supply 4 *Mil. a)* a tunnel dug under an enemy's fort, etc., in which an explosive is placed *b)* an explosive charge hidden underground or in the sea, for destroying enemy vehicles, ships, etc. —***vt., vi.*** **mined, min′ing** 1 to dig (ores, etc.) from (the earth) 2 to dig or lay military mines in or under 3 to undermine
min′er ***n.*** one whose work is digging coal, ore, etc. in a mine
min·er·al (min′ər əl) ***n.*** ⟦< ML *minera,* ore⟧ 1 an inorganic substance found naturally in the earth, as metallic ore 2 any substance that is neither vegetable nor animal —***adj.*** of or containing a mineral
min·er·al·o·gy (min′ər al′ə jē) ***n.*** the scientific study of minerals —**min′er·al′o·gist** ***n.***
mineral oil a colorless, tasteless oil from petroleum, used as a laxative
mineral water water impregnated with mineral salts or gases
Mi·ner·va (mə nur′və) *Rom. Myth.* the goddess of wisdom
mi·ne·stro·ne (min′ə strō′nē) ***n.*** ⟦It.: ult. < L *ministrare,* serve⟧ a thick vegetable soup in a meat broth
min·gle (miŋ′gəl) ***vt.*** **-gled, -gling** ⟦< OE *mengan,* to mix⟧ to mix together; blend —***vi.*** 1 to become mixed or blended 2 to join or unite with others
mini- ⟦< MINI(ATURE)⟧ *combining form* miniature, very small, very short /*miniskirt*/
min·i·a·ture (min′ē ə chər, min′i chər) ***n.*** ⟦< L *miniare,* paint red⟧ 1 a small painting, esp. a portrait 2 a copy or model on a very small scale —***adj.*** done on a very small scale
min′i·a·tur·ize′ (-īz′) ***vt.*** **-ized′, -iz′ing** to make in a small and compact form —**min′i·a·tur′i·za′tion** ***n.***
min·i·bike (min′ē bīk′) ***n.*** a compact motorcycle, usually used as an off-road vehicle
min′i·cam′ (-kam′) ***n.*** a portable TV camera for telecasting or videotaping news events, sports, etc.
min′i·com·put′er (-kəm pyo͞ot′ər) ***n.*** a computer intermediate in size, power, etc. between a mainframe and microcomputer
min·i·mal (min′i məl) ***adj.*** 1 smallest or least possible 2 of minimalism —**min′i·mal·ly** ***adv.***
min′i·mal·ism′ (-iz′əm) ***n.*** a movement in art, music, etc. in which only the simplest design, forms, etc. are used, often repetitiously —**min′i·mal·ist** ***adj., n.***
min·i·mize (min′ə mīz′) ***vt.*** **-mized′, -miz′·ing** to reduce to or estimate at a minimum
min′i·mum (-məm) ***n.***, *pl.* **-mums** or **-ma** (-mə) ⟦L, least⟧ 1 the smallest quantity, number, etc. possible 2 the lowest degree or point reached —***adj.*** smallest possible, permissible, or reached
min·ion (min′yən) ***n.*** ⟦Fr *mignon,* darling⟧ 1 a favorite, esp. one who is a servile follower: term of contempt 2 a subordinate official
min·is·cule (min′i skyo͞ol′) ***adj.*** *erroneous sp. of* MINUSCULE
min·i·se·ries (min′ē sir′ēz) ***n.***, *pl.* **-ries** a TV drama broadcast serially in a limited number of episodes
min·i·skirt (min′ē skurt′) ***n.*** a very short skirt ending well above the knee
min·is·ter (min′is tər) ***n.*** ⟦L, a servant⟧ 1 a person appointed to head a governmental department 2 a diplomat representing his or her government in a foreign nation 3 one authorized to conduct religious services in a church 4 a pastor —***vi.*** 1 to serve as a minister in a church 2 to give help (*to*) —**min′is·te′ri·al** (-tir′ē əl) ***adj.*** —**min′is·trant** (-trənt) ***adj., n.***
min′is·tra′tion (-trā′shən) ***n.*** the act of giving help or care; service
min′is·try (-is trē) ***n.***, *pl.* **-tries** 1 the act of ministering, or serving 2 *a)* the office or

function of a minister of religion *b)* ministers of religion collectively; clergy **3** *a)* the department under a minister of government *b)* the minister's term of office *c)* the ministers of a particular government as a group

mink (miŋk) ***n.*** ⟦< Scand⟧ **1** a slim, erminelike carnivore living in water part of the time **2** its valuable fur

Min·ne·ap·o·lis (min′ē ap′əl is) city in E Minn.: pop. 371,000 (met. area with St. Paul 2,114,000)

Min·ne·so·ta (min′ə sōt′ə) Middle Western State of the U.S.: 84,068 sq. mi.; pop. 4,077,000; cap. St. Paul: abbrev. **Minn.** —**Min′ne·so′tan** ***adj., n.***

min·now (min′ō) ***n.*** ⟦< OE *myne*⟧ any of various, usually small, freshwater fishes used commonly as bait

Mi·no·an (mi nō′ən) ***adj.*** ⟦after *Minos,* mythical king of Crete⟧ of an advanced prehistoric culture in Crete from *c.* 3000-*c.* 1100 B.C.

mi·nor (mī′nər) ***adj.*** ⟦< L⟧ **1** lesser in size, amount, importance, etc. **2** *Music* lower than the corresponding major by a half tone —***vi.*** *Educ.* to have a secondary field of study (*in*) —***n.*** **1** a person under full legal age **2** *Educ.* a secondary field of study

mi·nor·i·ty (mī nôr′ə tē, mi-) ***n.,*** *pl.* **-ties** **1** the lesser part or smaller number; less than half **2** a racial, religious, or political group that differs from the larger, controlling group **3** the state of being under full legal age

minor scale *Music* any of the twelve diatonic scales with a half step between the second and third tones

Min·o·taur (min′ə tôr′) *Gr. Myth.* a monster with the body of a man and the head of a bull

min·strel (min′strəl) ***n.*** ⟦see MINISTER⟧ **1** a medieval traveling singer **2** a member of a comic variety show (**minstrel show**) in which the performers blacken their faces —**min′strel·sy** (-sē), *pl.* **-sies,** ***n.***

mint[1] (mint) ***n.*** ⟦< L < Juno *Moneta,* whose temple was the mint⟧ **1** a place where money is coined by the government **2** a large amount —***adj.*** new, as if freshly minted —***vt.*** to coin (money) —**mint′age** (-ij) ***n.***

mint[2] (mint) ***n.*** ⟦< Gr *mintha*⟧ **1** an aromatic plant whose leaves are used for flavoring **2** a candy flavored with mint

mint julep an iced drink of bourbon, sugar, and mint leaves

min·u·end (min′yo͞o end′) ***n.*** ⟦< L *minuere,* lessen⟧ the number from which another is to be subtracted

min·u·et (min′yo͞o et′) ***n.*** ⟦< Fr < OFr *menu,* small⟧ **1** a slow, stately dance **2** the music for this

mi·nus (mī′nəs) ***prep.*** ⟦< L *minor,* less⟧ **1** less /four *minus* two/ **2** [Colloq.] without /*minus* a toe/ —***adj.*** **1** involving subtraction /a *minus* sign/ **2** negative **3** less than /a grade of A *minus*/ —***n.*** a sign (-), indicating subtraction or negative quantity: in full **minus sign**

mi·nus·cule (mi nus′kyo͞ol′; *commonly* min′i skyo͞ol′) ***adj.*** ⟦L *minusculus*⟧ very small; tiny

min·ute[1] (min′it) ***n.*** ⟦see fol.⟧ **1** the sixtieth part of an hour or of a degree of an arc **2** a moment **3** a specific point in time **4** [*pl.*] an official record of a meeting, etc. —**the minute (that)** just as soon as

mi·nute[2] (mī no͞ot′) ***adj.*** ⟦< L *minor,* less⟧ **1** very small **2** of little importance **3** of or attentive to tiny details; precise —**mi·nute′ly** ***adv.***

minute hand the longer hand of a clock, indicating the minutes

min′ute·man′ ***n.,*** *pl.* **-men′** [*also* **M-**] a member of the American citizen army at the time of the American Revolution

min·ute steak (min′it) a small, thin steak that can be cooked quickly

mi·nu·ti·ae (mi no͞o′shē ē′) ***n.pl.,*** *sing.* **-ti·a** (-shē ə, -shə) ⟦see MINUTE[2]⟧ small or unimportant details

minx (miŋks) ***n.*** ⟦< ?⟧ a pert girl

mir·a·cle (mir′ə kəl) ***n.*** ⟦< L *mirus,* wonderful⟧ **1** an event or action that apparently contradicts known scientific laws **2** a remarkable thing

mi·rac·u·lous (mi rak′yo͞o ləs, -yə-) ***adj.*** **1** having the nature of, or like, a miracle **2** able to work miracles —**mi·rac′u·lous·ly** ***adv.***

mi·rage (mi räzh′) ***n.*** ⟦< VL *mirare,* look at⟧ an optical illusion, caused by the refraction of light, in which a distant object appears to be nearby

mire (mīr) ***n.*** ⟦< ON *myrr*⟧ **1** an area of wet, soggy ground **2** deep mud; slush —***vt.*** **mired, mir′ing** **1** to cause to get stuck as in mire **2** to soil with mud, etc. —***vi.*** to sink in mud —**mir′y, -i·er, -i·est,** ***adj.***

mir·ror (mir′ər) ***n.*** ⟦< L *mirare,* look at⟧ **1** a smooth, reflecting surface; esp., a glass coated with silver **2** anything giving a true representation —***vt.*** to reflect, as in a mirror

mirth (murth) ***n.*** ⟦< OE *myrig,* pleasant⟧ joyfulness or gaiety, esp. with laughter —**mirth′ful** ***adj.***

MIRV (murv) ***n.,*** *pl.* **MIRV's** ⟦*m*(*ultiple*) *i*(*ndependently targeted*) *r*(*eentry*) *v*(*ehicle*)⟧ an intercontinental ballistic missile whose several warheads can be scattered

mis- ⟦< OE *mis-* or OFr *mes-*⟧ *prefix* **1** wrong(ly), bad(ly) **2** no, not

mis·ad·ven·ture (mis′əd ven′chər) ***n.*** a mishap; an instance of bad luck

mis·an·thrope (mis′ən thrōp′) ***n.*** ⟦Gr *misein,* to hate + *anthrōpos,* man⟧ a person who hates or distrusts all people Also **mis·an′thro·pist** (-an′thrə pist) —**mis′an·throp′ic** (-ən thräp′ik) ***adj.*** —**mis·an′thro·py** ***n.***

mis′ap·ply′ ***vt.*** **-plied′, -ply′ing** to apply badly or improperly

mis′ap·pre·hend′ (-ap rē hend′) ***vt.*** to misunderstand —**mis′ap·pre·hen′sion** ***n.***

mis′ap·pro′pri·ate′ ***vt.*** **-at′ed, -at′ing** to appropriate to a wrong or dishonest use —**mis′ap·pro′pri·a′tion** ***n.***

mis′be·got′ten ***adj.*** **1** wrongly or unlawfully begotten; illegitimate **2** wrongly or badly conceived

mis′be·have′ ***vt., vi.*** **-haved′, -hav′ing** to behave (oneself) wrongly —**mis′be·hav′ior** ***n.***

misc. 1 miscellaneous 2 miscellany
mis·cal'cu·late' *vt., vi.* **-lat'ed, -lat'ing** to calculate incorrectly; misjudge —**mis'cal·cu·la'tion** *n.*
mis·call' *vt.* to call by a wrong name
mis·car'ry (-kar'ē) *vi.* **-ried, -ry·ing** 1 to go wrong; fail: said of a plan, etc. 2 to fail to arrive: said of mail, etc. 3 to give birth to a fetus before it has developed enough to live —**mis·car'riage** (-ij) *n.*
mis·cast' *vt.* **-cast', -cast'ing** to cast (an actor or a play) unsuitably
mis·ce·ge·na·tion (mis'i jə nā'shən, mi sej'ə-) *n.* ⟦< L *miscere,* to mix + *genus,* race⟧ marriage or sexual relations between a man and woman of different races
mis·cel·la·ne·ous (mis'ə lā'nē əs) *adj.* ⟦< L *miscere,* to mix⟧ consisting of various kinds or qualities
mis·cel·la·ny (mis'ə lā'nē) *n., pl.* **-nies** a miscellaneous collection, esp. of literary works
mis·chance' *n.* bad luck
mis·chief (mis'chif) *n.* ⟦< OFr *mes-,* MIS- + *chief,* end⟧ 1 harm or damage 2 a cause of harm or annoyance 3 *a)* a prank *b)* playful teasing
mis·chie·vous (mis'chə vəs) *adj.* 1 causing mischief; specif., *a)* harmful *b)* prankish 2 inclined to annoy with playful tricks —**mis'chie·vous·ly** *adv.*
mis·ci·ble (mis'ə bəl) *adj.* ⟦< L *miscere,* to mix⟧ that can be mixed
mis·con·ceive (mis'kən sēv') *vt., vi.* **-ceived', -ceiv'ing** to misunderstand —**mis'con·cep'tion** (-sep'shən) *n.*
mis'con'duct' *n.* 1 bad or dishonest management 2 improper behavior
mis·con·strue (mis'kən stro͞o') *vt.* **-strued', -stru'ing** to misinterpret —**mis'con·struc'tion** *n.*
mis'count' *vt., vi.* to count incorrectly —*n.* an incorrect count
mis·cre·ant (mis'krē ənt) *adj.* ⟦< OFr *mes-,* MIS- + *croire,* believe⟧ villainous; evil —*n.* a villain
mis'deal' *vt., vi.* **-dealt', -deal'ing** to deal (playing cards) incorrectly —*n.* an incorrect deal
mis·deed (mis dēd') *n.* a wrong or wicked act; crime, sin, etc.
mis·de·mean·or (mis'di mēn'ər) *n. Law* any minor offense bringing a lesser punishment than a felony
mis'di·rect' *vt.* to direct wrongly or badly —**mis'di·rec'tion** *n.*
mis·do'ing *n.* wrongdoing
mi·ser (mī'zər) *n.* ⟦< L, wretched⟧ a greedy, stingy person who hoards money for its own sake —**mi'ser·ly** *adv.* —**mi'ser·li·ness** *n.*
mis·er·a·ble (miz'ər ə bəl) *adj.* 1 in misery 2 causing misery, discomfort, etc. 3 bad; inadequate 4 pitiable —**mis'er·a·bly** *adv.*
mis·er·y (miz'ər ē) *n., pl.* **-ies** ⟦see MISER⟧ 1 a condition of great suffering; distress 2 a cause of such suffering; pain, poverty, etc.
mis'file' *vt.* **-filed', -fil'ing** to file (papers, etc.) in the wrong place
mis'fire' *vi.* **-fired', -fir'ing** 1 to fail to go off or ignite properly 2 to fail to achieve a desired effect —*n.* a misfiring
mis·fit (mis'fit'; *for n.* mis'fit') *vt., vi.* **-fit'ted, -fit'ting** to fit badly —*n.* 1 an improper fit 2 a maladjusted person
mis'for'tune *n.* 1 ill fortune; trouble 2 a mishap, calamity, etc.
mis'giv'ing *n.* [*often pl.*] a disturbed feeling of fear, doubt, etc.
mis'gov'ern *vt.* to govern badly —**mis'gov'ern·ment** *n.*
mis'guide' (-gīd') *vt.* **-guid'ed, -guid'ing** to lead into error or misconduct; mislead —**mis'guid'ance** *n.*
mis'han'dle *vt.* **-dled, -dling** to handle badly or roughly; abuse
mis·hap (mis'hap') *n.* an unlucky or unfortunate accident
mis'hear' *vt., vi.* **-heard', -hear'ing** to hear wrongly
mish·mash (mish'mash') *n.* a jumble
mis'in·form' *vt.* to supply with false or misleading information —**mis'in'for·ma'tion** *n.*
mis'in·ter'pret *vt.* to interpret wrongly; understand or explain incorrectly —**mis'in·ter'pre·ta'tion** *n.*
mis'judge' *vt., vi.* **-judged', -judg'ing** to judge wrongly or unfairly
mis'la'bel *vt.* **-beled** or **-belled, -bel·ing** or **-bel·ling** to label incorrectly or improperly
mis'lay' (-lā') *vt.* **-laid', -lay'ing** to put in a place afterward forgotten
mis'lead' *vt.* **-led', -lead'ing** 1 to lead in a wrong direction 2 to deceive or delude 3 to lead into wrongdoing
mis'man'age *vt., vi.* **-aged, -ag·ing** to manage badly or dishonestly —**mis'man'age·ment** *n.*
mis·match (mis'mach'; *for n.* mis'mach') *vt.* to match badly or unsuitably —*n.* a bad match
mis'mate' *vt., vi.* **-mat'ed, -mat'ing** to mate badly or unsuitably
mis'name' *vt.* **-named', -nam'ing** to give an inappropriate name to
mis·no·mer (mis nō'mər) *n.* ⟦< OFr < *mes-,* MIS- + *nommer,* to name⟧ a wrong name
mi·sog·y·ny (mi säj'ə nē) *n.* ⟦< Gr *misein,* to hate + *gynē,* woman⟧ hatred of women —**mi·sog'y·nist** *n.*
mis·place (mis'plās') *vt.* **-placed', -plac'ing** 1 to put in a wrong place 2 to bestow (one's trust, etc.) unwisely 3 MISLAY
mis·play (mis plā'; *for n.* mis'plā') *vt., vi.* to play wrongly or badly, as in games or sports —*n.* a wrong or bad play
mis·print (mis print'; *for n.* mis'print') *vt.* to print incorrectly —*n.* a printing error
mis·pri'sion (-prizh'ən) *n.* ⟦< OFr *mesprendre,* take wrongly⟧ misconduct or neglect of duty by a public official
mis'pro·nounce' *vt., vi.* **-nounced', -nounc'ing** to pronounce differently from the accepted pronunciations —**mis'pro·nun'ci·a'tion** *n.*
mis'quote' *vt., vi.* **-quot'ed, -quot'ing** to quote incorrectly —**mis'quo·ta'tion** *n.*
mis'read' (-rēd') *vt., vi.* **-read'** (-red'), **-read'ing** (-rēd'iŋ) to read wrongly, esp. so as to misunderstand
mis'rep·re·sent' *vt.* to represent falsely;

give an untrue idea of —**mis′rep·re·sen·ta′·tion** *n.*

mis·rule (mis′ro͞ol′; *for n.* mis′ro͞ol′) *vt.* **-ruled′**, **-rul′ing** to rule badly; misgovern —*n.* misgovernment

miss[1] (mis) *vt.* ⟦OE *missan*⟧ **1** to fail to hit, meet, do, attend, see, hear, etc. **2** to let (a chance, etc.) go by **3** to avoid /he *missed* being hit/ **4** to notice or feel the absence or loss of **5** to lack /this book is *missing* a page/ —*vi.* **1** to fail to hit **2** to fail to be successful **3** to misfire, as an engine —*n.* a failure to hit, obtain, etc.

miss[2] (mis) *n., pl.* **miss′es** ⟦< MISTRESS⟧ **1** [M-] a title used before the name of an unmarried woman or girl **2** a young unmarried woman or girl

mis·sal (mis′əl) *n.* ⟦< LL *missa,* Mass⟧ [*often* **M-**] a book of prayers, readings, etc. authorized by the Roman Catholic Church for the celebration of Mass

mis′shape′ *vt.* **-shaped′**, **-shap′ing** to shape badly; deform —**mis·shap′en** *adj.*

mis·sile (mis′əl) *n.* ⟦< L *mittere,* send⟧ an object, as a spear, bullet, rocket, etc., designed to be thrown, fired, or launched toward a target

mis′sile·ry or **mis′sil·ry** (-rē) *n.* **1** the science of building and launching guided missiles **2** such missiles

miss·ing (mis′iŋ) *adj.* absent; lost

mis·sion (mish′ən) *n.* ⟦< L *mittere,* send⟧ **1** a sending out or being sent out to perform a special service **2** *a*) a group of persons sent by a religious body to spread its religion, esp. in a foreign land *b*) its headquarters **3** a diplomatic delegation **4** a group of technicians, specialists, etc. sent to a foreign country **5** the special duty for which one is sent **6** a special task to which one devotes one's life; calling

mis′sion·ar′y (-er′ē) *adj.* of religious missions or missionaries —*n., pl.* **-ies** a person sent on a religious mission

Mis·sis·sip·pi (mis′ə sip′ē) **1** river in central U.S., flowing from N Minn. to the Gulf of Mexico **2** Southern State of the U.S.: 47,716 sq. mi.; pop. 2,521,000; cap. Jackson: abbrev. **Miss.** —**Mis′sis·sip′pi·an** *adj., n.*

mis·sive (mis′iv) *n.* ⟦< L *mittere,* send⟧ a letter or written message

Mis·sou·ri (mi zoor′ē) **1** river in central U.S., flowing from SW Mont. into the Mississippi **2** Middle Western State of the U.S.: 69,686 sq. mi.; pop. 4,917,000; cap. Jefferson City —**Mis·sou′ri·an** *adj., n.*

mis·spell′ *vt., vi.* **-spelled′** or **-spelt′**, **-spell′ing** to spell incorrectly

mis·spend′ *vt.* **-spent′**, **-spend′ing** to spend improperly or wastefully

mis·state′ *vt.* **-stat′ed**, **-stat′ing** to state incorrectly or falsely —**mis·state′ment** *n.*

mis′step′ *n.* **1** a wrong or awkward step **2** a mistake in conduct

mist (mist) *n.* ⟦OE⟧ **1** a large mass of water vapor, less dense than a fog **2** anything that dims or obscures —*vt., vi.* to make or become misty

mis·take (mi stāk′) *vt.* **-took′**, **-tak′en**, **-tak′·ing** ⟦< ON *mistaka,* take wrongly⟧ to understand or perceive wrongly —*vi.* to make a mistake —*n.* an idea, answer, act, etc. that is wrong; error or blunder —**mis·tak′a·ble** *adj.*

mis·tak′en *adj.* **1** wrong; having an incorrect understanding **2** incorrect: said of ideas, etc.

mis·ter (mis′tər) *n.* ⟦< MASTER⟧ **1** [**M-**] a title used before the name of a man or his office and usually written *Mr.* **2** [Colloq.] sir

mis·time (mis′tīm′, mis′-) *vt.* **-timed′**, **-tim′·ing** to do or say at the wrong time

mis·tle·toe (mis′əl tō′) *n.* ⟦< OE *mistel,* mistletoe + *tan,* a twig⟧ a parasitic evergreen plant with yellowish flowers and shiny, white, poisonous berries

mis·took (mis to͝ok′) *vt., vi. pt. of* MISTAKE

mis·treat′ *vt.* to treat wrongly or badly —**mis·treat′ment** *n.*

mis·tress (mis′tris) *n.* ⟦< OFr, fem. of *maistre,* master⟧ **1** a woman who is head of a household or institution **2** a woman, nation, etc. that has control, power, etc. **3** a woman with whom a man is having a prolonged affair **4** [Chiefly Brit.] a female schoolteacher **5** [**M-**] [Obs.] a title used before the name of a woman: now replaced by *Mrs., Miss,* or *Ms.*

mis′tri′al *n. Law* a trial made void, as because of an error in the proceedings or the inability of the jury to reach a verdict

mis′trust′ *n.* lack of trust or confidence —*vt., vi.* to have no trust in; doubt —**mis·trust′ful** *adj.*

mist·y (mis′tē) *adj.* **-i·er**, **-i·est** **1** of, like, or covered with mist **2** blurred, as by mist; vague —**mist′i·ly** *adv.* —**mist′i·ness** *n.*

mis′un·der·stand′ *vt.* **-stood′**, **-stand′ing** to fail to understand correctly; misinterpret

mis′un·der·stand′ing *n.* **1** a failure to understand; mistake of meaning, etc. **2** a quarrel or disagreement

mis·use (mis′yo͞oz′; *for n.,* -yo͞os′) *vt.* **-used′**, **-us′ing** **1** to use improperly **2** to treat badly or harshly —*n.* incorrect or improper use

mite (mīt) *n.* ⟦OE⟧ **1** a tiny arachnid, often parasitic upon animals or plants **2** a very small sum of money **3** a very small creature or object

mi·ter (mīt′ər) *n.* ⟦< Gr *mitra,* headband⟧ **1** a tall, ornamented cap worn by bishops and abbots **2** *Carpentry* a joint formed by fitting together two pieces beveled to form a corner: now usually **miter joint**

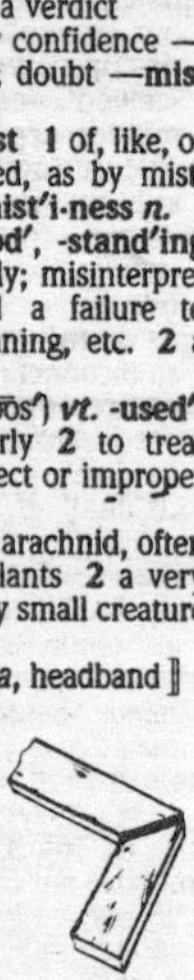
MITER JOINT

mit·i·gate (mit′ə gāt′) *vt., vi.* **-gat′ed**, **-gat′ing** ⟦< L *mitis,* soft⟧ **1** to make or become less severe, less painful, etc. **2** ⟦< confusion with MILITATE⟧ to operate or work (*against*): a loose usage —**mit′i·ga′tion** *n.*

mi·to·sis (mī tō′sis) *n.* ⟦< Gr *mitos,* thread⟧ the process by which a cell divides into two so that the nucleus of each new cell has the full number of chromosomes —**mi·tot′ic** (-tät′ik) *adj.*

mitt (mit) *n.* ⟦< fol.⟧ **1** a glove covering the hand and forearm, but only part of the fingers **2** [Slang] a hand **3** *a)* *Baseball* a padded glove, worn for protection *b)* a boxing glove

mit·ten (mit′'n) ***n.*** ⟦ < OFr *mitaine* ⟧ a glove with a thumb but no separately divided fingers

mix (miks) ***vt.*** **mixed** or **mixt, mix′ing** ⟦ < L *miscere* ⟧ **1** to blend together in a single mass **2** to make by blending ingredients /to *mix* a cake/ **3** to combine /to *mix* work and play/ **4** to blend electronically (recorded sounds, etc.) on (a tape, etc.) —***vi.*** **1** to be mixed or blended **2** to get along together —***n.*** **1** a mixture **2** a beverage for mixing with alcoholic liquor **3** the blend of sounds in a recording, etc. —**mix up 1** to mix thoroughly **2** to confuse **3** to involve or implicate (*in*): usually used in the passive —**mix′a·ble** ***adj.*** —**mix′er** ***n.***

mixed (mikst) ***adj.*** **1** blended **2** made up of different parts, classes, races, etc., or of both sexes **3** confused

mixed number a number consisting of a whole number and a fraction, as $3\frac{2}{3}$

mix·ture (miks′chər) ***n.*** **1** a mixing or being mixed **2** something mixed

mix′-up′ ***n.*** a confusion; tangle

miz·zen·mast (miz′ən mast′; *naut.*, -məst) ***n.*** ⟦ < L *medius*, middle ⟧ the mast third from the bow in a ship

ml milliliter(s)

Mlle Mademoiselle

mm millimeter(s)

MM Messieurs

Mme Madame

Mmes or **Mmes.** mesdames

Mn *Chem. symbol for* manganese

MN Minnesota

mne·mon·ic (nē män′ik) ***adj.*** ⟦ < Gr *mnēmōn*, mindful ⟧ of or helping the memory

mo. month

MO 1 Missouri: also **Mo. 2** ⟦ L *modus operandi* ⟧ mode of operation: also **m.o.**

Mo *Chem. symbol for* molybdenum

moan (mōn) ***n.*** ⟦ prob. < OE *mænan*, complain ⟧ a low, mournful sound, as of sorrow or pain —***vi., vt.*** **1** to utter or say with a moan **2** to complain (about)

moat (mōt) ***n.*** ⟦ < OFr *mote*, mound ⟧ a deep, broad ditch, often filled with water, around a fortress or castle

mob (mäb) ***n.*** ⟦ < L *mobile* (*vulgus*), movable (crowd) ⟧ **1** a disorderly, lawless crowd **2** any crowd **3** the masses: a contemptuous term **4** [Slang] a gang of criminals —***vt.*** **mobbed, mob′bing 1** to crowd around and attack, annoy, etc. **2** to throng

mo·bile (mō′bəl; *also*, -bil & *for n., usually*, -bēl′ &, *chiefly Brit & Cdn*, -bil′) ***adj.*** ⟦ < L *movere*, to move ⟧ **1** moving or movable **2** movable by means of a motor vehicle /a *mobile* X-ray unit/ **3** that can change rapidly or easily; adaptable **4** characterized by ease in change of social status —***n.*** a piece of abstract sculpture which aims to depict movement, as by an arrangement of thin forms, rings, etc. suspended and set in motion by air currents —**mo·bil′i·ty** (-bil′ə tē) ***n.***

Mo·bile (mō bēl′) seaport in SW Ala.: pop. 200,000

-mo·bile (mō bēl′) ⟦ < (AUTO)MOBILE ⟧ *combining form* motorized vehicle /*bookmobile*/

mobile home a movable dwelling set more or less permanently at a location: cf. MOTOR HOME

mo′bi·lize′ (-bə līz′) ***vt., vi.*** **-lized′, -liz′ing** to make or become organized and ready, as for war —**mo′bi·li·za′tion** ***n.***

mob·ster (mäb′stər) ***n.*** [Slang] a gangster

moc·ca·sin (mäk′ə sən) ***n.*** ⟦ < AmInd ⟧ **1** a heelless slipper of soft, flexible leather **2** any similar heeled slipper

mo·cha (mō′kə) ***n.*** a choice grade of coffee grown orig. in Arabia —***adj.*** flavored with coffee, and, often, chocolate

mock (mäk) ***vt.*** ⟦ < OFr *mocquer* ⟧ **1** to ridicule **2** to mimic, as in fun or derision **3** to defy and make futile —***vi.*** to express scorn, ridicule, etc. —***adj.*** sham; imitation; pretended —***adv.*** falsely or insincerely /*mock*-sympathetic words/

mock′er·y ***n.***, *pl.* **-ies 1** a mocking **2** one receiving or deserving ridicule **3** a false or derisive imitation

mock′ing·bird′ ***n.*** a bird of the U.S. that imitates the calls of other birds

mock′-up′ ***n.*** ⟦ < Fr *maquette* ⟧ a model built to scale, often full-sized, for teaching, testing, etc.

mod (mäd) ***adj.*** ⟦ < MOD(ERN) ⟧ up-to-date, fashionable, stylish, etc.

mode (mōd) ***n.*** ⟦ < L *modus* ⟧ **1** a manner or way of acting, doing, or being **2** customary usage or current fashion **3** *Gram.* MOOD²

mod·el (mäd′'l) ***n.*** ⟦ < L *modus*, a measure ⟧ **1** a small representation of a planned or existing object **2** a hypothetical description, often based on an analogy, used in analyzing something **3** a person or thing regarded as a standard of excellence to be imitated **4** a style or design **5** *a)* one who poses for an artist or photographer *b)* one employed to display clothes by wearing them —***adj.*** **1** serving as a model **2** representative of others of the same style, etc. /a *model* home/ —***vt.*** **-eled** or **-elled, -el·ing** or **-el·ling 1** *a)* to make a model of *b)* to plan or form after a model **2** to display (clothes) by wearing —***vi.*** to serve as a MODEL (*n.* 5)

mo·dem (mō′dem′; *also*, -dəm) ***n.*** ⟦ MO(DULATOR) + DEM(ODULATION) ⟧ a device that converts data for transmission, as by telephone, to data-processing equipment

mod·er·ate (mäd′ər it; *for v.*, -āt′) ***adj.*** ⟦ < L *moderare*, restrain ⟧ **1** within reasonable limits; avoiding extremes **2** mild; calm **3** of medium quality, amount, etc. —***n.*** one holding moderate opinions —***vt., vi.*** **-at′ed, -at′ing 1** to make or become moderate **2** to preside over (a meeting, etc.) —**mod′er·ate·ly** ***adv.***

mod′er·a′tion ***n.*** **1** a moderating **2** avoidance of extremes **3** calmness

mod′er·a′tor ***n.*** one who presides at an assembly, debate, etc.

mod·ern (mäd′ərn) ***adj.*** ⟦ < L *modo*, just now ⟧ **1** of the present or recent times; specif., up-to-date **2** [*often* **M-**] designating the most recent form of a language —***n.*** a person living in modern times, with modern ideas, etc.

Modern English the English language since about the mid-15th c.

mod′ern·ism′ ***n.*** (a) modern usage, practice, thought, etc. —**mod′ern·ist** ***n., adj.*** —**mod′ern·is′tic** ***adj.***

mod′ern·ize′ ***vt., vi.*** **-ized′, -iz′ing** to make or become modern —**mod′ern·i·za′tion** ***n.***

mod·est (mäd′ist) ***adj.*** ⟦< L *modus,* a measure⟧ **1** not vain or boastful; unassuming **2** shy or reserved **3** decorous; decent **4** not extreme; unpretentious —**mod′est·ly** ***adv.*** —**mod′es·ty** ***n.***

Mo·des·to (mə des′tō) city in central Calif.: pop. 106,000

mod·i·cum (mäd′i kəm) ***n.*** ⟦< L, moderate⟧ a small amount; bit

mod·i·fy (mäd′ə fī′) ***vt.*** **-fied′, -fy′ing** ⟦< L *modificare,* to limit⟧ **1** to change partially in character, form, etc. **2** to limit slightly **3** *Gram.* to limit in meaning; qualify —**mod′i·fi·ca′tion** ***n.*** —**mod′i·fi′er** ***n.***

mod·ish (mōd′ish) ***adj.*** fashionable; stylish —**mod′ish·ness** ***n.***

mod·u·lar (mäj′ə lər) ***adj.*** of modules

mod′u·late′ (-lāt′) ***vt.*** **-lat′ed, -lat′ing** ⟦< L *modus,* a measure⟧ **1** to regulate or adjust **2** to vary the pitch, intensity, etc. of (the voice) **3** *Radio* to vary the frequency of (radio waves, etc.) —**mod′u·la′tion** ***n.*** —**mod′u·la′tor** ***n.***

mod·ule (mäj′o͞ol′) ***n.*** ⟦Fr < L *modus,* a measure⟧ **1** a standard or unit of measurement, as of building materials **2** any of a set of units to be variously fitted together **3** a detachable unit with a specific function, as in a spacecraft

mo·gul (mō′gul′) ***n.*** ⟦Pers *Mughul,* Mongol⟧ a powerful or important person

mo·hair (mō′her′) ***n.*** ⟦< Ar *mukhayyar,* fine cloth⟧ **1** the hair of the Angora goat **2** yarn or fabric made of this

Mo·ham·med (mō ham′id) *c.* A.D. 570-632; Arab prophet: founder of Islam

Mo·ham·med·an (mō ham′i dən) ***adj.*** of Mohammed or Islam —***n.*** MUSLIM: term used mainly by non-Muslims —**Mo·ham′med·an·ism′** ***n.***

moi·e·ty (moi′ə tē) ***n.,*** *pl.* **-ties** ⟦< L *medius,* middle⟧ **1** a half **2** an indefinite part

moire (mwär, môr) ***n.*** ⟦Fr⟧ a fabric, esp. silk, etc., having a wavy pattern Also **moi·ré** (mwä rā′, mô-)

moist (moist) ***adj.*** ⟦< L *mucus,* mucus⟧ slightly wet; damp —**moist′ly** ***adv.*** —**moist′ness** ***n.***

mois·ten (mois′ən) ***vt., vi.*** to make or become moist

mois′ture (-chər) ***n.*** water or other liquid causing a slight wetness

mois′tur·ize′ (-īz′) ***vt., vi.*** **-ized′, -iz′ing** to make (the skin, air, etc.) moist —**mois′tur·iz′er** ***n.***

Mo·ja·ve Desert (mō hä′vē) desert in SE Calif.: also sp. **Mo·ha′ve Desert**

mo·lar (mō′lər) ***adj.*** ⟦< L *mola,* millstone⟧ designating a tooth or teeth adapted for grinding —***n.*** a molar tooth

mo·las·ses (mə las′iz) ***n.*** ⟦< L *mel,* honey⟧ a thick, dark syrup produced during the refining of sugar

mold¹ (mōld) ***n.*** ⟦< L *modus,* a measure⟧ **1** a hollow form for giving a certain shape to something plastic or molten **2** a frame on which something is modeled **3** a pattern; model **4** something formed in or on a mold **5** distinctive character —***vt.*** **1** to make in or on a mold **2** to form; shape

mold² (mōld) ***n.*** ⟦ME *moul*⟧ **1** a fungus producing a furry growth on the surface of organic matter **2** this growth —***vi.*** to become moldy

mold³ (mōld) ***n.*** ⟦OE *molde*⟧ loose, soft soil rich in decayed organic matter

mold·er (mōl′dər) ***vi.*** ⟦< OE *molde,* dust⟧ to crumble into dust

mold·ing (mōl′diŋ) ***n.*** **1** the act of one that molds **2** something molded **3** a shaped strip of wood, etc., as around the upper walls of a room

mold·y (mōl′dē) ***adj.*** **-i·er, -i·est** **1** covered or overgrown with mold **2** musty or stale —**mold′i·ness** ***n.***

mole¹ (mōl) ***n.*** ⟦OE *mal*⟧ a small, congenital spot on the human skin, usually dark-colored and raised

MOLE

mole² (mōl) ***n.*** ⟦ME *molle*⟧ **1** a small, burrowing mammal with soft fur **2** *a*) a spy in an enemy intelligence agency, etc. who infiltrates long before engaging in spying *b*) DOUBLE AGENT

mole³ (mōl) ***n.*** ⟦< L *moles,* dam⟧ a breakwater

mol·e·cule (mäl′i kyo͞ol′) ***n.*** ⟦< L dim. of *moles,* a mass⟧ **1** the smallest particle of an element or compound that can exist in the free state and still retain the characteristics of the substance **2** a small particle —**mo·lec·u·lar** (mō lek′yo͞o lər) ***adj.***

mole′hill′ ***n.*** a small ridge of earth, formed by a burrowing mole

mole′skin′ ***n.*** **1** the fur of the mole **2** a napped cotton fabric

mo·lest (mə lest′) ***vt.*** ⟦< L *moles,* a burden⟧ **1** to annoy or to meddle with so as to trouble or harm **2** to make improper sexual advances to **3** to assault or attack (esp. a child) sexually —**mo·les·ta·tion** (mō′les tā′shən) ***n.*** —**mo·lest′er** ***n.***

Mo·lière (mōl yer′) 1622-73; Fr. dramatist

mol·li·fy (mäl′ə fī′) ***vt.*** **-fied′, -fy′ing** ⟦< L *mollis,* soft + *facere,* make⟧ **1** to soothe; appease **2** to make less severe or violent

mol·lusk (mäl′əsk) ***n.*** ⟦< L *mollis,* soft⟧ any of a group of invertebrates, as oysters, snails, squids, etc., characterized by a soft body often enclosed in a shell

mol·ly (mäl′ē) ***n.,*** *pl.* **-lies** ⟦after F. N. *Mollien* (1758-1850), Fr statesman⟧ any of various brightly colored fishes often kept in aquariums Also **mol′lie**

mol·ly·cod·dle (mäl′ē käd′'l) ***n.*** ⟦< *Molly,* dim. of *Mary* + CODDLE⟧ a man or boy used to being coddled —***vt.*** **-dled, -dling** to pamper; coddle

molt (mōlt) ***vi.*** ⟦< L *mutare,* to change⟧ to shed hair, skin, horns, etc. prior to replacement by a new growth, as reptiles, birds, etc.

mol·ten (mōl′tən) *vt., vi.* ⟦ME⟧ *archaic pp. of* MELT —*adj.* melted by heat

mo·lyb·de·num (mə lib′də nəm) *n.* ⟦< Gr *molybdos,* lead⟧ a silvery metallic chemical element, used in alloys

mom (mäm) *n.* [Colloq.] MOTHER

mo·ment (mō′mənt) *n.* ⟦< L *momentum,* movement⟧ **1** an indefinitely brief period of time; instant **2** a definite point in time **3** a brief time of importance **4** importance

mo·men·tar·i·ly (mō′mən ter′ə lē, mō′mən ter′-) *adv.* **1** for a short time **2** in an instant **3** at any moment

mo·men·tar·y (mō′mən ter′ē) *adj.* lasting for only a moment; passing

mo·men·tous (mō men′təs) *adj.* of great moment; very important

mo·men·tum (mō men′təm) *n., pl.* **-tums** or **-ta** (-tə) ⟦L: see MOMENT⟧ the impetus of a moving object, equal to the product of its mass and its velocity

mom·my (mäm′ē) *n., pl.* **-mies** *child's term for* MOTHER

Mon·a·co (män′ə kō) country on the Mediterranean: an independent principality & an enclave in SE France: .5 sq. mi.; pop. 27,000

mon·arch (män′ərk) *n.* ⟦< Gr *monos,* alone + *archein,* to rule⟧ **1** a hereditary ruler; king, queen, etc. **2** a large butterfly of North America, having orange, black-edged wings —**mo·nar·chi·cal** (mō när′ki kəl) *adj.*

mon′ar·chist (-ər kist) *n.* one who favors monarchical government

mon′ar·chy (-kē) *n., pl.* **-chies** a government or state headed by a monarch

mon·as·ter·y (män′ə ster′ē) *n., pl.* **-ies** ⟦< Gr *monos,* alone⟧ the residence of a group of monks, etc. who have withdrawn from the world for religious reasons

mo·nas·tic (mō nas′tik) *adj.* of or like that of a monastery, monk, etc. Also **mo·nas′ti·cal** —**mo·nas′ti·cism′** (-tə siz′əm) *n.*

mon·au·ral (män ôr′əl) *adj.* of sound reproduction using a single channel to carry and reproduce sound

Mon·day (mun′dā, -dē) *n.* ⟦OE *monandæg,* moon's day⟧ the second day of the week: abbrev. **Mon.**

mon·e·tar·y (män′ə ter′ē, mun′-) *adj.* ⟦< L *moneta,* a MINT[1]⟧ **1** of the coinage or currency of a country **2** of money —**mon′e·tar′i·ly** *adv.*

mon·ey (mun′ē) *n., pl.* **-eys** or **-ies** ⟦< L *moneta,* a MINT[1]⟧ **1** stamped pieces of metal, or any paper notes, authorized by a government as a medium of exchange **2** property; wealth —**in the money** [Slang] **1** among the winners in a race, etc. **2** wealthy —**make money** to gain profits —**put money into** to invest money in

mon′ey·bag′ *n.* **1** a bag for money **2** [*pl., with sing. v.*] [Colloq.] a rich person

mon·eyed (mun′ēd) *adj.* rich; wealthy

mon′ey·mak′er *n.* **1** one good at acquiring money **2** something profitable —**mon′ey·mak′ing** *adj., n.*

money market the short-term system for lending and borrowing funds, especially by governments and large corporations

money order an order for payment of a specified sum of money, issued for a fee at one post office, bank, etc. and payable at another

mon·ger (muŋ′gər) *n.* ⟦< OE *mangere*⟧ [Chiefly Brit.] a dealer or trader

Mon·gol (mäŋ′gəl) *n., adj.* MONGOLIAN

Mon·go·li·a (mäŋ gō′lē ə) region in east central Asia, consisting of a country (**Mongolian People's Republic**: 592,280 sq. mi.; pop. 1,942,000) and a region in China (**Inner Mongolia**)

Mon·go·li·an (mäŋ gō′lē ən) *n.* **1** a native of Mongolia **2** a subfamily of languages spoken in Mongolia —*adj.* **1** of Mongolia, its peoples, or their cultures **2** [Obs.] affected with Down's syndrome

Mon·gol·ic (mäŋ gäl′ik) *adj. var. of* MONGOLIAN —*n.* Mongolian, a language spoken in Mongolia

Mon·gol·oid (mäŋ′gəl oid′) *adj.* **1** *var. of* MONGOLIAN **2** designating or of one of the major geographical varieties of human beings, including most of the peoples of Asia **3** [*often* **m-**] [Obs.] affected with Down's syndrome —*n.* **1** a member of the Mongoloid population of human beings **2** [*often* **m-**] [Obs.] one affected with Down's syndrome

mon·goose (mäŋ′gōōs′) *n., pl.* **-goos′es** ⟦< native name in India⟧ a civetlike, Old World carnivore that kills snakes, rodents, etc.

mon·grel (muŋ′grəl, mäŋ′-) *n.* ⟦< OE *gemong,* mixture⟧ an animal or plant, esp. a dog, of mixed breed —*adj.* of mixed breed, origin, character, etc.

mon·ied (mun′ēd) *adj.* MONEYED

mon·i·ker or **mon·ick·er** (män′i kər) *n.* ⟦< ?⟧ [Slang] a person's name

mo·ni·tion (mō nish′ən) *n.* ⟦< L *monere,* warn⟧ admonition; warning

mon·i·tor (män′i tər) *n.* ⟦< L *monere,* warn⟧ **1** a student chosen to help the teacher **2** any device for regulating the performance of a machine, an aircraft, etc. **3** *Radio, TV* a receiver for checking the quality of transmission —*vt., vi.* to watch or check on (a person or thing)

monk (muŋk) *n.* ⟦< Gr *monos,* alone⟧ a man devoted to a religious life, usually in retirement from the general population

mon·key (muŋ′kē) *n., pl.* **-keys** ⟦< ? Fr or Sp *mona,* ape + LowG *-ke,* -KIN⟧ **1** a primate having a flat, hairless face and a long tail **2** a gibbon or chimpanzee —*vi.* [Colloq.] to play, trifle, or meddle

monkey business [Colloq.] foolishness, mischief, or deceit

mon′key·shines′ (-shīnz′) *n.pl.* [Colloq.] playful tricks or pranks

monkey wrench a wrench with an adjustable jaw —**throw a monkey wrench into** [Colloq.] to disrupt the orderly functioning of

monk's cloth a heavy cloth with a basket weave, used for drapes, etc.

mon·o (män′ō) *adj. short for* MONOPHONIC —*n. short for* MONONUCLEOSIS

mono- ⟦< Gr *monos,* single⟧ *prefix* one, alone, single

mon·o·cle (män′ə kəl) *n.* ⟦ult. < Gr *monos,* single + L *oculus,* eye⟧ an eyeglass for one eye only

mon·o·clon·al (män'ō klōn'əl) ***adj.*** of or cloned from one cell

mon·o·cot·y·le·don (män'ō kät'l ēd''n) ***adj.*** *Bot.* a plant having an embryo with only one seed leaf (cotyledon)

mo·nog·a·my (mō näg'ə mē) ***n.*** ⟦ult. < Gr *monos,* single + *gamos,* marriage⟧ the practice or state of being married to only one person at a time —**mo·nog'a·mous** ***adj.***

mon·o·gram (män'ə gram') ***n.*** ⟦< Gr *monos,* single + *gramma,* letter⟧ the initials of a name, combined in a single design —***vt.*** **-grammed', -gram'ming** to put a monogram on

mon'o·graph' (-graf') ***n.*** ⟦MONO- + -GRAPH⟧ a book or long article, esp. a scholarly one, on a single subject

mon·o·lin·gual (män'ō liŋ'gwəl) ***adj.*** using or knowing only one language

mon·o·lith (män'ə lith') ***n.*** ⟦< Gr *monos,* single + *lithos,* stone⟧ **1** a single large block of stone, as one made into an obelisk, etc. **2** any massive, unyielding structure —**mon'o·lith'ic** ***adj.***

mon·o·logue or **mon·o·log** (män'ə lôg') ***n.*** ⟦< Gr *monos,* single + *legein,* speak⟧ **1** a long speech **2** a soliloquy **3** a skit, etc. for one actor only

mon·o·ma·ni·a (män'ō mā'nē ə) ***n.*** an excessive interest in or enthusiasm for some one thing; craze —**mon'o·ma'ni·ac'** (-mā'nē ak') ***n.*** —**mon'o·ma·ni'a·cal** (-mə nī'ə kəl) ***adj.***

mon·o·nu·cle·o·sis (män'ō nōō'klē ō'sis) ***n.*** ⟦MONO- + NUCLE(US) + -OSIS⟧ an acute disease, esp. of young people, with fever, swollen lymph nodes, etc.

mon'o·phon'ic (-fän'ik) ***adj.*** of sound reproduction using a single channel to carry and reproduce sounds

mo·nop·o·list (mə näp'ə list) ***n.*** one who has a monopoly or favors monopoly —**mo·nop'o·lis'tic** ***adj.***

mo·nop'o·lize' (-līz') ***vt.*** **-lized', -liz'ing** **1** to get, have, or exploit a monopoly of **2** to get full control of

mo·nop'o·ly (-lē) ***n.,*** *pl.* **-lies** ⟦< Gr *monos,* single + *pōlein,* sell⟧ **1** exclusive control of a commodity or service in a given market **2** such control granted by a government **3** something held as a monopoly **4** a company that has a monopoly

mon·o·rail (män'ō rāl') ***n.*** **1** a single rail that is a track for cars suspended from it or balanced on it **2** a railway with such a track

mon'o·syl'la·ble (-sil'ə bəl) ***n.*** a word of one syllable —**mon'o·syl·lab'ic** (-si lab'ik) ***adj.***

mon'o·the·ism' (-thē iz'əm) ***n.*** ⟦MONO- + THEISM⟧ the belief that there is only one God —**mon'o·the·ist'** ***n.*** —**mon'o·the·is'tic** ***adj.***

mon·o·tone (män'ə tōn') ***n.*** ⟦see MONO- & TONE⟧ **1** utterance of successive words without change of pitch or key **2** tiresome sameness of style, color, etc. **3** a single, unchanging tone

mo·not·o·nous (mə nät''n əs) ***adj.*** **1** going on in the same tone **2** having no variety **3** tiresome because unvarying —**mo·not'o·ny** ***n.***

Mon·roe (mən rō'), **James** (jāmz) 1758-1831; 5th president of the U.S. (1817-25)

mon·sieur (mə syʉr'; *Fr* mə syö') ***n.,*** *pl.* **mes·sieurs** (mes'ərz; *Fr* mā syö') ⟦Fr, lit., my lord⟧ **1** a man; gentleman **2** [**M-**] French title, equivalent to *Mr.* or *Sir*

Mon·si·gnor (män sēn'yər) ***n.*** ⟦It, lit., my lord⟧ a title given to certain Roman Catholic prelates

mon·soon (män sōōn') ***n.*** ⟦< Ar *mausim,* a season⟧ **1** a seasonal wind of the Indian Ocean and S Asia **2** the rainy season during which this wind blows from the southwest

mon·ster (män'stər) ***n.*** ⟦< L *monere,* warn⟧ **1** any grotesque imaginary creature **2** a very wicked person **3** any huge animal or thing —***adj.*** huge

mon·strance (män'strəns) ***n.*** ⟦ult. < L *monstrare,* to show⟧ *R.C.Ch.* a receptacle for displaying the consecrated Host

mon·strous (män'strəs) ***adj.*** **1** huge; enormous **2** greatly malformed **3** horrible; hideous; shocking **4** hideously evil —**mon·stros'i·ty** (-sträs'ə tē), *pl.* **-ties,** ***n.***

mon·tage (mōn täzh', män-) ***n.*** ⟦Fr < *monter,* to mount⟧ **1** a composite picture **2** a rapid sequence of film scenes, often superimposed

Mon·taigne (män tān'), **Mi·chel de** (mē shel' də) 1533-92; Fr. essayist

Mon·tan·a (män tan'ə) Mountain State of the NW U.S.: 147,138 sq. mi.; pop. 787,000; cap. Helena: abbrev. **Mont.** —**Mon·tan'an** ***adj., n.***

Mon·te Car·lo (mänt'ə kär'lō) town in Monaco: gambling resort: pop. 12,500

Mon·tes·so·ri method (mänt'ə sôr'ē) ⟦after M. *Montessori* (1870-1952), It educator⟧ a method of teaching young children, emphasizing training of the senses

Mon·te·vi·de·o (mänt'ə və dā'ō) capital & seaport of Uruguay: pop. 1,360,000

Mont·gom·er·y (munt gum'ər ē) capital of Ala.: pop. 178,000

month (munth) ***n.*** ⟦OE *monath*⟧ **1** any of the twelve divisions of the calendar year **2** a period of four weeks or 30 days **3** one twelfth of the solar year

month'ly ***adj.*** done, happening, payable, etc. every month —***n.,*** *pl.* **-lies** a periodical published once a month —***adv.*** once a month; every month

Mont·pel·ier (mänt pēl'yər) capital of Vt.: pop. 8,000

Mon·tre·al (män'trē ôl') city & seaport in SW Quebec, Canada, on an island in the St. Lawrence River: pop. 980,000

mon·u·ment (män'yōō mənt) ***n.*** ⟦< L *monere,* remind⟧ **1** something set up to keep alive the memory of a person or event, as a tablet, statue, etc. **2** a work of enduring significance

mon'u·men'tal (-ment''l) ***adj.*** **1** of or serving as a monument **2** like a monument; massive, enduring, etc. **3** very great; colossal

moo (mōō) ***n.,*** *pl.* **moos** ⟦echoic⟧ the vocal sound made by a cow —***vi.*** **mooed, moo'ing** to make this sound

mooch (mōōch) ***vi., vt.*** ⟦ult. < OFr *muchier,* to hide⟧ [Slang] to get (food, money, etc.) by begging, imposition, etc. —**mooch'er** ***n.***

mood[1] (mōōd) ***n.*** ⟦< OE *mod,* mind⟧ **1** a particular state of mind or feeling **2** a predominant or pervading feeling or spirit

mood² (mo͞od) ***n.*** ⟦< MODE⟧ a characteristic of verbs that indicates whether the action expressed is regarded as a fact, supposition, or command

mood'y ***adj.*** **-i·er, -i·est** characterized by gloomy or changing moods —**mood'i·ly** ***adv.*** —**mood'i·ness** ***n.***

moon (mo͞on) ***n.*** ⟦OE *mona*⟧ **1** the celestial body that revolves around the earth once about every 29½ days **2** anything shaped like the moon (i.e., an orb or crescent) **3** any natural satellite of a planet —***vi.*** to behave in an idle or abstracted way

moon'beam' ***n.*** a ray of moonlight

moon'light' ***n.*** the light of the moon

moon'light'ing ***n.*** the holding of a second job along with one's main job

moon'lit' ***adj.*** lighted by the moon

moon'scape' (-skāp') ***n.*** ⟦MOON + (LAND)SCAPE⟧ the surface of the moon or a representation of it

moon'shine' ***n.*** **1** MOONLIGHT **2** whiskey unlawfully distilled —**moon'shin'er** ***n.***

moon'shot' ***n.*** the launching of a spacecraft to the moon

moon'stone' ***n.*** a feldspar with a pearly luster, used as a gem

moon'struck' ***adj.*** **1** crazed; lunatic **2** romantically dreamy

moon'walk' ***n.*** a walking about by an astronaut on the surface of the moon

moor¹ (moor) ***n.*** ⟦OE *mor*⟧ [Brit.] a tract of open wasteland, usually covered with heather and often marshy

moor² (moor) ***vt.*** ⟦< ? MDu *maren,* to tie⟧ **1** to hold (a ship, etc.) in place by cables attached as to a pier, or by anchors **2** to secure —***vi.*** to moor a ship, etc.

Moor (moor) ***n.*** any of a Muslim people of NW Africa —**Moor'ish** ***adj.***

moor'ing ***n.*** **1** [*often pl.*] the cables, etc. by which a ship is moored **2** [*pl.*] a place where a ship is moored

moose (mo͞os) ***n.,*** *pl.* **moose** ⟦< AmInd⟧ a large deer of N regions, the male of which has broad, flat antlers

moot (mo͞ot) ***adj.*** ⟦< OE *mot,* a meeting⟧ **1** debatable **2** resolved and thus not worthy of discussion

mop (mäp) ***n.*** ⟦earlier *mappe*⟧ **1** a bundle of rags, or yarns, a sponge, etc. fastened to the end of a stick, as for washing floors **2** anything suggesting this, as a thick head of hair —***vt.*** **mopped, mop'ping** to wash or wipe with a mop —**mop up** [Colloq.] **1** to finish **2** to clear of remnants of beaten enemy forces

mope (mōp) ***vi.*** **moped, mop'ing** ⟦< ?⟧ to be gloomy and apathetic —**mop'ey, mop'y,** or **mop'ish** ***adj.***

mop·pet (mäp'it) ***n.*** ⟦< ME *moppe,* rag doll⟧ [Colloq.] a little child

mo·raine (mə rān') ***n.*** ⟦Fr⟧ a mass of rocks, sand, etc. left by a glacier

mor·al (môr'əl, mär'-) ***adj.*** ⟦< L *mos,* pl. *mores,* morals⟧ **1** dealing with, or capable of distinguishing between, right and wrong **2** of, teaching, or in accordance with the principles of right and wrong **3** good in conduct or character; specif., sexually virtuous **4** involving sympathy without action /*moral* support/ **5** virtually such because of effects on thoughts or attitudes /a *moral* victory/ **6** based on probability /a *moral* certainty/ —***n.*** **1** a moral lesson taught by a fable, event, etc. **2** [*pl.*] principles or standards with respect to right or wrong in conduct —**mor'al·ly** ***adv.***

mo·rale (mə ral', mô-) ***n.*** moral or mental condition with respect to courage, discipline, confidence, etc.

mor·al·ist (môr'əl ist) ***n.*** **1** a teacher of or writer on morals **2** one who seeks to impose personal morals on others —**mor'al·is'tic** ***adj.***

mo·ral·i·ty (mō ral'i tē, mə-) ***n.,*** *pl.* **-ties** **1** rightness or wrongness, as of an action **2** right or moral conduct **3** moral principles

mor·al·ize (môr'əl īz') ***vi.*** **-ized', -iz'ing** to think, write, etc. about moral questions, often in a self-righteous or tedious way

mo·rass (mə ras', mô-) ***n.*** ⟦< OFr *maresc*⟧ a bog; marsh; swamp

mor·a·to·ri·um (môr'ə tôr'ē əm) ***n.,*** *pl.* **-ri·ums** or **-ri·a** (-ə) ⟦< L *mora,* a delay⟧ **1** a legal authorization to delay payment of money due **2** any authorized delay of a specified activity

mo·ray (eel) (môr'ā) ⟦< Gr *myraina*⟧ a voracious, brilliantly colored eel

mor·bid (môr'bid) ***adj.*** ⟦< L *morbus,* disease⟧ **1** of or caused by disease; diseased **2** resulting as from a diseased state of mind **3** gruesome /*morbid* details/ —**mor·bid'i·ty** ***n.*** —**mor'bid·ly** ***adv.***

mor·dant (môr'dənt) ***adj.*** ⟦< L *mordere,* to bite⟧ caustic; sarcastic —***n.*** a substance that fixes colors in dyeing —**mor'dan·cy** ***n.*** —**mor'dant·ly** ***adv.***

more (môr) ***adj.*** ⟦OE *mara*⟧ **1** greater in amount, degree, or number: comparative of MUCH or MANY **2** additional /take *more* tea/ —***n.*** **1** a greater amount or degree **2** [*with pl. v.*] a greater number (*of*) **3** something additional —***adv.*** **1** in or to a greater degree or extent **2** in addition

more·o'ver ***adv.*** in addition to what has been said; besides

mo·res (môr'ēz', -āz') ***n.pl.*** ⟦L, customs⟧ folkways so basic as to develop the force of law

morgue (môrg) ***n.*** ⟦Fr⟧ **1** a place where the bodies of unknown dead or those dead of unknown causes are temporarily kept **2** the file of back numbers, photographs, etc. kept as in a newspaper's office

mor·i·bund (môr'i bund') ***adj.*** ⟦< L *mori,* to die⟧ dying

Mor·mon (môr'mən) ***n.*** a member of the Church of Jesus Christ of Latter-day Saints, founded (1830) in the U.S. —**Mor'mon·ism'** ***n.***

morn (môrn) ***n.*** [Old Poet.] morning

morn'ing (-iŋ) ***n.*** ⟦OE *morgen*⟧ the first or early part of the day, from midnight, or esp. dawn, to noon

morning glory a twining vine with trumpet-shaped flowers

morning sickness nausea, vomiting, etc. affecting many women early in pregnancy, occurring usually in the morning

Mo·roc·co (mə rä'kō) kingdom on the NW coast of Africa: 254,815 sq. mi.; pop. 23,667,000 —***n.*** [m-] a fine, soft leather made orig. from goatskins —**Mo·roc'can** *adj., n.*

mo·ron (môr'än') *n.* ⟦< Gr *mōros,* foolish⟧ an adult mentally equal to a child between eight and twelve years old: an obsolescent term —**mo·ron'ic** *adj.*

mo·rose (mə rōs') *adj.* ⟦< L *mos,* manner⟧ ill-tempered; gloomy, sullen, etc. —**mo·rose'ly** *adv.* —**mo·rose'ness** *n.*

mor·pheme (môr'fēm') *n.* ⟦< Gr *morphē,* form⟧ the smallest meaningful language unit, as an affix or base

mor·phine (môr'fēn') *n.* ⟦after *Morpheus,* Gr god of dreams⟧ an alkaloid derived from opium and used in medicine to relieve pain

mor·phol·o·gy (môr fäl'ə jē) *n.* ⟦Ger < Gr *morphē,* form + Ger *-logie,* -LOGY⟧ the study of form and structure, as in biology or linguistics

mor·row (mär'ō, môr'-) *n.* ⟦< OE *morgen,* morning⟧ [Archaic] **1** morning **2** the next day

Morse (môrs) *adj.* ⟦after S. *Morse,* 19th-c. U.S. inventor⟧ [*often* **m-**] designating or of a code consisting of a system of dots and dashes, used in telegraphy

mor·sel (môr'səl) *n.* ⟦< L *morsum,* a bite⟧ **1** a small bite or portion of food **2** a small piece or amount

mor·tal (môr'təl) *adj.* ⟦< L *mors,* death⟧ **1** that must eventually die **2** of man as a being who must eventually die **3** of death **4** causing physical or spiritual death; deadly; fatal **5** very intense [*mortal* terror] —*n.* a human being —**mor'tal·ly** *adv.*

mor·tal·i·ty (môr tal'ə tē) *n.* **1** the mortal nature of man **2** death on a large scale, as from war **3** the ratio of deaths to population; death rate

mor·tar (môrt'ər) *n.* ⟦< L *mortarium*⟧ **1** a bowl in which substances are pulverized with a pestle **2** a short-barreled cannon which hurls shells in a high trajectory **3** a mixture of cement or lime with sand and water, used to bind bricks or stones

mor'tar·board' *n.* **1** a square board for holding mortar **2** an academic cap with a square, flat top

mort·gage (môr'gij) *n.* ⟦< OFr *mort,* dead + *gage,* pledge⟧ **1** the pledging of property to a creditor as security for the payment of a debt **2** the deed by which this is done —*vt.* **-gaged, -gag·ing 1** to pledge (property) by a mortgage **2** to put an advance claim on [to *mortgage* one's future] —**mort'ga·gor** or **mort'gag·er** (-gi jər) *n.*

mort'ga·gee' (-gə jē') *n.* a person to whom property is mortgaged

mor·ti·cian (môr tish'ən) *n.* ⟦< L *mors,* death⟧ FUNERAL DIRECTOR

mor·ti·fy (môrt'ə fī') *vt.* **-fied', -fy'ing** ⟦< L *mors,* death + *facere,* make⟧ **1** to subdue (physical desires) by self-denial, fasting, etc. **2** to humiliate —**mor'ti·fi·ca'tion** *n.*

mor·tise (môrt'is) *n.* ⟦< Ar *murtazza,* joined⟧ a hole or recess cut in a piece of wood, to receive a projecting part (*tenon*) shaped to fit into it

mor·tu·ar·y (môr'chōō er'ē) *n., pl.* **-ies** a place where dead bodies are kept before burial or cremation

mo·sa·ic (mō zā'ik) *n.* ⟦< L *musivus,* artistic⟧ **1** the making of pictures or designs by inlaying small bits of colored stone, etc. in mortar **2** a picture or design so made

Mo·sa·ic (mō zā'ik) *adj.* of Moses or the laws, etc. attributed to him

Mos·cow (mäs'kō, -kou') capital of the U.S.S.R., in W R.S.F.S.R.: pop. 8,642,000

Mo·ses (mō'zəz, -zəs) *Bible* the leader and lawgiver who brought the Israelites out of slavery in Egypt

mo·sey (mō'zē) *vi.* ⟦prob. < VAMOOSE⟧ [Slang] to amble along

Mos·lem (mäz'ləm) *n., adj.* MUSLIM

mosque (mäsk) *n.* ⟦< Ar *masjid,* temple⟧ a Muslim place of worship

mos·qui·to (mə skēt'ō) *n., pl.* **-toes** or **-tos** ⟦Sp < L *musca,* a fly⟧ a two-winged insect, the female of which sucks blood from animals, including humans

moss (môs, mäs) *n.* ⟦OE *mos,* a swamp⟧ a very small, green plant that grows in velvety clusters on rocks, trees, etc. —**moss'y, -i·er, -i·est,** *adj.*

moss'back' *n.* [Colloq.] an old-fashioned or very conservative person

most (mōst) *adj.* ⟦OE *mast*⟧ **1** greatest in amount, degree, or number: superlative of MUCH or MANY **2** in the greatest number of instances —*n.* **1** the greatest amount or degree **2** [*with pl. v.*] the greatest number (*of*) —*adv.* in or to the greatest degree or extent

most'ly *adv.* **1** for the most part **2** chiefly **3** usually

mote (mōt) *n.* ⟦OE *mot*⟧ a speck, as of dust

mo·tel (mō tel') *n.* ⟦< MO(TOR) + (HO)TEL⟧ a hotel for motorists

moth (môth) *n., pl.* **moths** (môthz, môths) ⟦OE *moththe*⟧ a four-winged, chiefly night-flying insect, similar to the butterfly: the larvae of one kind feed on wool, etc.

moth'ball' *n.* a small ball, as of naphthalene, the fumes of which repel moths from woolens, etc. —**in mothballs** put into storage or reserve

moth·er (muth'ər) *n.* ⟦OE *modor*⟧ **1** a female parent **2** the origin or source of something **3** a woman who is the head (**mother superior**) of a religious establishment —*adj.* **1** of or like a mother **2** native [*mother* tongue] —*vt.* **1** to be the mother of **2** to be like a mother to —**moth'er·hood'** *n.* —**moth'er·less** *adj.*

Mother Goose the imaginary creator of a collection of nursery rhymes

moth'er-in-law' *n., pl.* **moth'ers-in-law'** the mother of one's husband or wife

moth'er·land' *n.* one's native land

moth'er·ly *adj.* of or like a mother; protective, nurturing, etc. —**moth'er·li·ness** *n.*

moth'er-of-pearl' *n.* the hard internal layer of the shell of the pearl oyster, etc., used to make buttons, etc.

mother tongue one's native language

mo·tif (mō tēf') *n.* ⟦Fr: see MOTIVE⟧ **1** *Art, Literature, Music* a main theme for development **2** a repeated figure in a design

mo·tile (mōt'il) *adj.* ⟦< L *movere,* to move⟧

Biol. capable of or exhibiting spontaneous motion —**mo·til′i·ty** ***n.***

mo·tion (mō′shən) ***n.*** ⟦< L *movere,* to move⟧ **1** a moving from one place to another; movement **2** a moving of a part of the body; specif., a gesture **3** a proposal formally made in an assembly —***vi.*** to make a meaningful movement of the hand, etc.; gesture —***vt.*** to direct by a meaningful gesture —**go through the motions** to do something as from habit, without enthusiasm, enjoyment, etc. —**in motion** moving —**mo′tion·less** ***adj.***

motion picture FILM (*n.* 4)

motion sickness nausea, vomiting, etc. caused by the motion of a car, boat, etc.

mo·ti·vate (mōt′ə vāt′) ***vt.*** **-vat′ed, -vat′ing** to provide with, or affect as, a motive; incite —**mo′ti·va′tion** ***n.***

mo·tive (mōt′iv) ***n.*** ⟦< L *movere,* to move⟧ **1** an inner drive, impulse, etc. that causes one to act; incentive **2** MOTIF (sense 1) —***adj.*** of or causing motion

-mo·tive (mōt′iv) *combining form* moving, of motion /*automotive*/

mot·ley (mät′lē) ***adj.*** ⟦< ?⟧ **1** of many colors **2** of many different or clashing elements /a *motley* group/

mo·to·cross (mō′tō krôs′) ***n.*** ⟦Fr⟧ a cross-country race for lightweight motorcycles

mo·tor (mōt′ər) ***n.*** ⟦L < *movere,* to move⟧ **1** anything that produces motion **2** an engine; esp., an internal-combustion engine **3** a machine for converting electric energy into mechanical energy —***adj.*** **1** producing motion **2** of or powered by a motor **3** of, by, or for motor vehicles **4** of or involving muscular movements —***vi.*** to travel by automobile

mo′tor·bike′ ***n.*** [Colloq.] **1** a motor-driven bicycle **2** a light motorcycle

mo′tor·boat′ ***n.*** a motor-driven boat, esp. a small one

mo′tor·cade′ (-kād′) ***n.*** ⟦MOTOR + -CADE⟧ an automobile procession

mo′tor·car′ ***n.*** an automobile

mo′tor·cy′cle (-sī′kəl) ***n.*** a two-wheeled vehicle propelled by an internal-combustion engine

motor home a motor vehicle with a truck chassis, outfitted as a traveling home

mo·tor·ist (mōt′ər ist) ***n.*** one who drives an automobile or travels by automobile

mo′tor·ize′ (-īz′) ***vt.*** **-ized′, -iz′ing** to equip with a motor or with motor-driven vehicles

motor vehicle an automotive vehicle, esp. an automobile, truck, or bus

mot·tle (mät′'l) ***vt.*** **-tled, -tling** ⟦< MOTLEY⟧ to mark with blotches, etc. of different colors —**mot′tled** ***adj.***

mot·to (mät′ō) ***n., pl.*** **-toes** or **-tos** ⟦It, a word⟧ a word or saying that expresses the goals, ideals, etc., as of a nation

mould (mōld) ***n., vt., vi.*** *chiefly Brit., etc. sp. of* MOLD[1], MOLD[2], MOLD[3]

mould′ing ***n.*** *chiefly Brit., etc. sp. of* MOLDING

moul·dy (mōl′dē) ***adj.*** *chiefly Brit., etc. sp. of* MOLDY

moult (mōlt) ***vi.*** *chiefly Brit. sp. of* MOLT

mound (mound) ***n.*** ⟦< ? MDu *mond,* protection⟧ a heap or bank of earth, sand, etc. —***vt.*** to heap up

mount[1] (mount) ***n.*** ⟦< L *mons*⟧ a mountain

mount[2] (mount) ***vi.*** ⟦< L *mons,* mountain⟧ **1** to climb; ascend **2** to climb up on something, as a horse **3** to increase in amount —***vt.*** **1** to go up; ascend /to *mount* stairs/ **2** to get up on (a horse, platform, etc.) **3** to provide with horses /*mounted* police/ **4** to place or fix (a jewel, picture, etc.) on or in the proper support, backing, etc. **5** to arrange (a dead animal, etc.) for exhibition **6** to place (a gun) into proper position for use **7** to prepare for and undertake (an expedition, etc.) —***n.*** **1** a mounting **2** a horse, etc. for riding **3** the support, setting, etc. on or in which a thing is mounted

moun·tain (mount′'n) ***n.*** ⟦ult. < L *mons*⟧ **1** a natural raised part of the earth, larger than a hill **2** a large pile, amount, etc. —***adj.*** of or in mountains

moun′tain·eer′ (-ir′) ***n.*** **1** one who lives in a mountainous region **2** a mountain climber

mountain goat a long-haired, goatlike antelope of the Rocky Mountains

mountain lion COUGAR

moun′tain·ous ***adj.*** **1** full of mountains **2** like a mountain; esp., huge

mountain sickness weakness, nausea, etc. caused by thin air at high altitudes

Mountain State any of the eight States of the W U.S. through which the Rocky Mountains pass; Mont., Ida., Wyo., Nev., Utah, Colo., Ariz., & N.Mex.

moun·te·bank (mount′ə baŋk′) ***n.*** ⟦It *montambanco,* lit., mounted on a bench: orig. a person on a bench selling quack medicines⟧ a charlatan or quack

mount′ing ***n.*** something serving as a backing, support, setting, etc.

mourn (môrn) ***vi., vt.*** ⟦OE *murnan*⟧ **1** to feel or express sorrow for (something regrettable) **2** to grieve for (someone who has died) —**mourn′er** ***n.***

mourn′ful ***adj.*** **1** feeling or expressing grief or sorrow **2** causing sorrow

mourn′ing ***n.*** **1** the expression of grief, esp. at someone's death **2** black clothes, etc., worn as such an expression **3** the period during which one mourns

mouse (mous; *for v. also* mouz) ***n., pl.*** **mice** ⟦OE *mus*⟧ **1** any of many small rodents, esp. a species that commonly infests buildings **2** a timid person **3** [Slang] a black eye **4** a hand-held device for controlling the video display of a computer —***vi.*** **moused, mous′ing** to hunt mice

mousse (mo͞os) ***n.*** ⟦Fr, foam⟧ **1** a light, chilled dessert made with egg white, whipped cream, etc. **2** an aerosol foam used to keep hair in place, etc.

mous·tache (mus′tash′, məs tash′) ***n.*** *var. of* MUSTACHE

mous·y (mous′ē, mouz′-) ***adj.*** **-i·er, -i·est** of or like a mouse; specif., quiet, timid, drab, etc. Also **mous′ey** —**mous′i·ness** ***n.***

mouth (mouth; *for v.* mouth) ***n., pl.*** **mouths** (mouthz) ⟦OE *muth*⟧ **1** the opening in the head through which food is taken in and sounds are made **2** any opening regarded as like this /the *mouth* of a jar, river, etc./ —***vt.*** **1** to say, esp. insincerely **2** to form (a word) with the mouth silently —**down in**

(or at) the mouth [Colloq.] unhappy —**mouth off** [Slang] to talk loudly, impudently, etc.
mouth'ful' *n., pl.* **-fuls'** 1 as much as the mouth can hold 2 as much as is usually taken into the mouth 3 a small amount 4 [Slang] a pertinent remark: chiefly in **say a mouthful**
mouth organ HARMONICA
mouth'piece' *n.* 1 a part, as of a musical instrument, held in or to the mouth 2 a person, periodical, etc. which expresses the views as of a group
mouth'wash' *n.* a flavored, often antiseptic liquid for rinsing the mouth
mouth'wa'ter·ing (-wôt'ər iŋ) *adj.* appetizing; tasty
mouth'y *adj.* **-i·er, -i·est** talkative, esp. in a bombastic or rude way —**mouth'i·ness** *n.*
mou·ton (mo͞o'tän') *n.* ⟦Fr, sheep⟧ lambskin or sheepskin made to resemble beaver, seal, etc.
mov·a·ble (mo͞ov'ə bəl) *adj.* that can be moved from one place to another —*n.* 1 something movable 2 *Law* personal property, esp. furniture: *usually used in pl.* Also **move'a·ble**
move (mo͞ov) *vt.* **moved, mov'ing** ⟦< L *movere*⟧ 1 to change the place or position of 2 to set or keep in motion 3 to cause (*to do, say*, etc.) 4 to arouse the emotions, etc. of 5 to propose formally, as in a meeting —*vi.* 1 to change place or position 2 to change one's residence 3 to be active 4 to make progress 5 to take action 6 to be, or be set, in motion 7 to make a formal application (*for*) 8 to evacuate: said of the bowels 9 to be sold: said of goods —*n.* 1 act of moving 2 an action toward some goal 3 a change of residence 4 *Chess, Checkers, etc.* the act of moving a piece, or one's turn to move —**move up** to promote or be promoted —**on the move** [Colloq.] moving about from place to place
move'ment *n.* 1 a moving or manner of moving 2 an evacuation (of the bowels) 3 a change in the location of troops, etc. 4 organized action by people working toward a goal 5 the moving parts of a mechanism, as of a clock 6 *Music a)* a principal division of a symphony, etc. *b)* rhythm
mov'er *n.* one that moves; specif., one whose work is moving furniture, etc. for those changing residence
mov·ie (mo͞ov'ē) *n.* ⟦< *moving picture*⟧ FILM (*n.* 4) —**the movies** 1 the film industry 2 a showing of a film
mow[1] (mō) *vt., vi.* **mowed, mowed** or **mown** (mōn), **mow'ing** ⟦OE *mawan*⟧ to cut down (grass, etc.) from (a lawn, etc.) —**mow down** 1 to cause to fall like cut grass 2 to overwhelm (an opponent) —**mow'er** *n.*
mow[2] (mou) *n.* ⟦OE *muga*⟧ 1 a heap of hay, etc., esp. in a barn 2 the part of a barn where hay, etc. is stored
Mo·zam·bique (mō'zəm bēk') country in SE Africa: 302,329 sq. mi.; pop. 14,022,000
Mo·zart (mō'tsärt'), **Wolf·gang A·ma·de·us** (vôlf'gäŋk' ä'mä dā'o͝os) 1756-91; Austrian composer
MP 1 Member of Parliament: also **M.P.** 2 Military Police
mpg miles per gallon
mph miles per hour
Mr. (mis'tər) mister: before a man's name or title: pl. *Messrs.*
Mrs. (mis'iz) mistress: before a married woman's name: pl. *Mmes.*
MS *abbrev.* 1 manuscript: also **ms** or **ms.** 2 Master of Science: also **M.S., MSc,** or **M.Sc.** 3 Mississippi 4 multiple sclerosis
Ms. (miz) a title, free of reference to marital status, used in place of either *Miss* or *Mrs.*
Msgr. Monsignor
MST Mountain Standard Time
MSW or **M.S.W.** Master of Social Work
MT Montana
Mt. 1 Mount 2 Mountain
mu (mo͞o, myo͞o) *n.* the 12th letter of the Greek alphabet (M, μ)
much (much) *adj.* **more, most** ⟦< OE *mycel*⟧ great in quantity, degree, etc. —*adv.* **more, most** 1 to a great degree or extent /*much* happier/ 2 nearly /*much* the same/ —*n.* 1 a great amount 2 something great or outstanding /not *much* to look at/
mu·ci·lage (myo͞o'si lij') *n.* ⟦< L *mucere*, be moldy⟧ 1 a thick, sticky substance in certain plants 2 any watery solution of gum, glue, etc. used as an adhesive
muck (muk) *n.* ⟦ME *muk*⟧ 1 moist manure 2 black earth with decaying matter, used as fertilizer 3 mud; dirt; filth —**muck'y, -i·er, -i·est,** *adj.*
muck'rake' *vi.* **-raked', -rak'ing** ⟦see prec. & RAKE[1]⟧ to search for and publicize real or alleged corruption in politics, etc. —**muck'rak'er** *n.*
mu·cous (myo͞o'kəs) *adj.* 1 of, containing, or secreting mucus 2 slimy
mucous membrane a mucus-secreting lining of certain body cavities
mu·cus (myo͞o'kəs) *n.* ⟦L⟧ the thick, slimy substance secreted by the mucous membranes for moistening and protection
mud (mud) *n.* ⟦ME⟧ 1 wet, soft, sticky earth 2 defamatory remarks
mud·dle (mud''l) *vt.* **-dled, -dling** ⟦< prec.⟧ 1 to mix up; bungle 2 to confuse mentally; befuddle —*vi.* to act or think confusedly —*n.* 1 a mess, jumble, etc. 2 mental confusion
mud'dle-head'ed *adj.* confused
mud'dy *adj.* **-di·er, -di·est** 1 full of or spattered with mud 2 not clear; cloudy /*muddy* coffee/ 3 confused, obscure, etc. /*muddy* thinking/ —*vt., vi.* **-died, -dy·ing** to make or become muddy —**mud'di·ness** *n.*
mud flat low, muddy land that floods at high tide
mud'sling'ing *n.* the making of malicious verbal attacks, as against a political opponent —**mud'sling'er** *n.*
mu·ez·zin (myo͞o ez'in) *n.* ⟦< Ar *adhana*, proclaim⟧ a Muslim crier who calls the people to prayer
muff (muf) *n.* ⟦< Fr *moufle*, mitten⟧ 1 a cylindrical covering, as of fur, to warm the hands 2 any bungle —*vt.* to bungle; specif., to miss (a catch, etc.)
muf·fin (muf'ən) *n.* ⟦< ?⟧ a quick bread baked in a cup-shaped mold

muf·fle (muf′əl) *vt.* **-fled, -fling** ⟦prob. < OFr *moufle,* mitten⟧ 1 to wrap or cover so as to keep warm, deaden sound, etc. 2 to deaden (a sound)
muf′fler (-lər) *n.* 1 a scarf worn around the throat, as for warmth 2 a device for deadening noise, esp. of a car
muf·ti (muf′tē) *n., pl.* **-tis** ⟦< Ar⟧ ordinary clothes, esp. when worn by one usually wearing a uniform
mug (mug) *n.* ⟦prob. < Scand⟧ 1 a cup made of earthenware or metal, with a handle 2 as much as a mug will hold 3 [Slang] the face 4 a police photograph of a criminal suspect: in full **mug shot** —*vt.* **mugged, mug′ging** to assault, usually with intent to rob —*vi.* [Slang] to grimace, esp. in overacting —**mug′ger** *n.*
mug·gy (mug′ē) *adj.* **-gi·er, -gi·est** ⟦< dial. *mug,* mist⟧ hot, damp, and close —**mug′gi·ness** *n.*
Mu·ham·mad (mo͞o ham′əd) *var. of* MOHAMMED
muk·luk (muk′luk′) *n.* ⟦Esk *muklok,* a seal⟧ 1 an Eskimo boot of sealskin or reindeer skin 2 any similar boot
mu·lat·to (mə lät′ō, -lat′ō) *n., pl.* **-toes** or **-tos** ⟦Sp & Port *mulato*⟧ a person who has one black parent and one white parent
mul·ber·ry (mul′ber′ē, -bər ē) *n., pl.* **-ries** ⟦< OE *morberie*⟧ 1 a tree with purplish-red, edible, berrylike fruit 2 the fruit 3 purplish red
mulch (mulch) *n.* ⟦ME *molsh,* soft⟧ leaves, straw, etc., spread around plants to prevent freezing of roots, etc. —*vt.* to apply mulch to
mulct (mulkt) *vt.* ⟦< L *mul(c)ta,* a fine⟧ 1 to fine 2 to take (money, etc.) from (someone) by fraud —*n.* a fine
mule[1] (myo͞ol) *n.* ⟦< L *mulus*⟧ 1 the (usually sterile) offspring of a jackass and a female horse 2 [Colloq.] a stubborn person
mule[2] (myo͞ol) *n.* ⟦< L *mulleus,* red shoe⟧ a lounging slipper that does not cover the heel
mu′le·teer′ (-ə tir′) *n.* ⟦OFr *muletier*⟧ a driver of mules Also [Colloq.] **mule skin·ner** (skin′ər)
mul′ish *adj.* like a mule; stubborn, obstinate, etc.
mull[1] (mul) *vt., vi.* ⟦ME *mullen,* to grind⟧ to ponder (*over*)
mull[2] (mul) *vt.* ⟦< ?⟧ to heat, sweeten, and spice (wine, cider, etc.)
mul·let (mul′it) *n.* ⟦< L *mullus*⟧ an edible, spiny-finned fish of fresh and salt waters
mul·li·gan stew (mul′i gən) a stew made of bits of meat and vegetables, esp. as by hobos
mul·li·ga·taw·ny (mul′i gə tô′nē) *n.* ⟦Tamil *milagutaṇṇir,* lit., pepper water⟧ an East Indian soup of meat, etc., flavored with curry
mul·lion (mul′yən) *n.* ⟦prob. < OFr *moien,* median⟧ a vertical dividing bar, as between windowpanes
Mul·ro·ney (mul rō′nē), **(Martin) Bri·an** (brī′ən) 1939- ; prime minister of Canada (1984-)
multi- ⟦L < *multus,* many⟧ *combining form* 1 having many 2 more than two 3 many times more than
mul·ti·far·i·ous (mul′tə far′ē əs) *adj.* ⟦< L⟧ having many kinds of parts or elements; diverse
mul′ti·lin′gual *adj.* of, in, or capable of using several languages
mul′ti·mil′lion·aire′ *n.* one whose wealth amounts to many millions of dollars, pounds, etc.
mul′ti·na′tion·al *adj.* 1 of many nations 2 designating a corporation with branches in many nations —*n.* a multinational corporation
mul·ti·ple (mul′tə pəl) *adj.* ⟦< L *multiplex*⟧ 1 having many parts, elements, etc. 2 shared by or involving many —*n.* a number which is a product of some specified number and another number
mul′ti·ple-choice′ *adj.* listing several answers from which the correct one is to be chosen
multiple sclerosis a disease of the central nervous system, with loss of muscular coordination, etc.
mul·ti·plex (mul′tə pleks′) *adj.* ⟦L, multiple⟧ designating a system for sending two or more signals simultaneously over a common circuit, etc. —**mul′ti·plex′er** or **mul′ti·plex′or** *n.*
mul′ti·pli·cand′ (-pli kand′) *n.* a number to be multiplied by another
mul′ti·pli·ca′tion (-pli kā′shən) *n.* a multiplying or being multiplied; specif., the process of finding the quantity obtained by repeating a specified quantity a specified number of times
mul′ti·plic′i·ty (-plis′ə tē) *n.* a great number or variety (*of*)
mul′ti·pli′er (-plī′ər) *n.* one that multiplies; specif., the number by which another is to be multiplied
mul′ti·ply′ (-plī′) *vt., vi.* **-plied′, -ply′ing** ⟦see MULTIPLE⟧ 1 to increase in number, degree, etc. 2 to find the product (of) by multiplication
mul·ti·proc·es·sor (mul′ti prä′ses′ər) *n.* a computer system capable of processing many programs at once
mul′ti·stage′ *adj.* having more than one stage, as a missile, process, etc.
mul·ti·tude (mul′tə to͞od′) *n.* ⟦< L *multus,* many⟧ a large number; host
mul′ti·tu′di·nous (-to͞od′′n əs) *adj.* very numerous; many
mum[1] (mum) *n.* [Colloq.] a chrysanthemum
mum[2] (mum) *adj.* ⟦ME *momme*⟧ silent; not speaking
mum·ble (mum′bəl) *vt., vi.* **-bled, -bling** ⟦ME *momelen*⟧ to speak or say indistinctly; mutter —*n.* a mumbled utterance —**mum′bler** *n.*
mum·bo jum·bo (mum′bō jum′bō) ⟦of Afr orig.⟧ 1 an idol or fetish 2 meaningless ritual, talk, etc.
mum·mer (mum′ər) *n.* ⟦< OFr *momo,* grimace⟧ one who wears a mask or costume, esp. in a pantomime
mum′mer·y *n., pl.* **-ies** 1 performance by mummers 2 any hypocritical display or ceremony
mum·mi·fy (mum′ə fī′) *vt., vi.* **-fied′, -fy′ing** to make into or become (like) a mummy
mum·my (mum′ē) *n., pl.* **-mies** ⟦ult. < Pers *mum,* wax⟧ a dead body preserved by embalming, as by the ancient Egyptians

mumps (mumps) ***n.pl.*** ⟦< obs. *mump,* a grimace⟧ [*with sing. v.*] an acute communicable disease characterized by swelling of the salivary glands
mun. municipal
munch (munch) ***vt., vi.*** ⟦ME *monchen*⟧ to chew steadily, often with a crunching sound
mun·dane (mun′dān′, mun dān′) ***adj.*** ⟦< L *mundus,* world⟧ **1** of the world; worldly **2** commonplace, ordinary, etc. —**mun′-dane′ly *adv.***
Mu·nich (myoo′nik) city in SE West Germany: pop. 1,277,000
mu·nic·i·pal (myoo nis′ə pəl) ***adj.*** ⟦< L *municeps,* inhabitant of a free town⟧ of or having to do with a city, town, etc. or its local government
mu·nic′i·pal′i·ty (-pal′ə tē) ***n.,*** *pl.* **-ties** a city, town, etc. having its own incorporated government
mu·nif·i·cent (myoo nif′ə sənt) ***adj.*** ⟦< L *munus,* a gift + *facere,* make⟧ very generous in giving; lavish —**mu·nif′i·cence *n.***
mu·ni·tions (myoo nish′ənz) ***n.pl.*** ⟦< L *munire,* fortify⟧ war supplies; esp., weapons and ammunition
mu·ral (myoor′əl) ***adj.*** ⟦< L *murus,* wall⟧ of, on, or for a wall —***n.*** a picture, esp. a large one, painted directly on a wall —**mu′-ral·ist *n.***
mur·der (mur′dər) ***n.*** ⟦OE *morthor*⟧ **1** the unlawful and malicious or premeditated killing of a person **2** [Colloq.] something very hard, unsafe, etc. to do or deal with —***vt.*** **1** to kill (a person) unlawfully and with malice **2** to spoil, as in performance [to *murder* a song] —**mur′der·er *n.*** —**mur′der·ess *n.fem.***
mur′der·ous *adj.* **1** of or characteristic of murder; brutal **2** capable or guilty of, or intending, murder —**mur′der·ous·ly *adv.***
murk (murk) ***n.*** ⟦< ON *myrkr,* dark⟧ darkness; gloom
murk′y *adj.* **-i·er, -i·est** dark or gloomy —**murk′i·ness *n.***
mur·mur (mur′mər) ***n.*** ⟦< L⟧ **1** a low, indistinct, continuous sound **2** a mumbled complaint **3** *Med.* an abnormal sound in the body, esp. in the heart —***vi.*** to make a murmur —***vt.*** to say in a murmur
mus·cat (mus′kət) ***n.*** ⟦< LL *muscus,* musk⟧ a sweet European grape
mus′ca·tel′ (-kə tel′) ***n.*** a sweet wine made from the muscat
mus·cle (mus′əl) ***n.*** ⟦< L *musculus,* lit., little mouse⟧ **1** any body organ consisting of fibrous tissue that can be contracted and expanded to produce bodily movements **2** this tissue **3** muscular strength —***vi.*** **-cled, -cling** [Colloq.] to force one's way (*in*)
mus′cle-bound′ *adj.* having some of the muscles enlarged and less elastic, as from too much exercise
mus·cu·lar (mus′kyoo lər, -kyə-) ***adj.*** **1** of, consisting of, or done by muscles **2** having well-developed muscles; strong —**mus′cu·lar′i·ty** (-lar′ə tē) ***n.***
muscular dys·tro·phy (dis′trə fē) a chronic disease characterized by a progressive wasting of the muscles
mus·cu·la·ture (mus′kyoo lə chər, -kyə-) ***n.*** ⟦Fr⟧ the arrangement of the muscles of a body, limb, etc.; muscular system
muse (myooz) ***vi.*** **mused, mus′ing** ⟦< OFr *muser,* ponder⟧ to meditate —***vt.*** to think or say meditatively
Muse (myooz) ***n.*** ⟦< Gr *mousa*⟧ **1** *Gr. Myth.* any of the nine goddesses of literature and of the arts and sciences **2** [**m-**] the spirit thought to inspire a poet, etc.
mu·sette (bag) (myoo zet′) ⟦< OFr, bagpipe⟧ a bag with a shoulder strap, worn as by soldiers to carry supplies
mu·se·um (myoo zē′əm) ***n.*** ⟦< Gr *mousa,* Muse⟧ an institution, building, etc. for preserving and exhibiting artistic or historical objects
mush[1] (mush) ***n.*** ⟦prob. var. of MASH⟧ **1** a thick porridge of boiled meal **2** any thick, soft mass **3** [Colloq.] maudlin sentimentality —**mush′y, -i·er, -i·est, *adj.***
mush[2] (mush) ***interj.*** ⟦prob. < Fr *marchons,* let's go⟧ a shout to urge on sled dogs —***vi.*** to travel on foot over snow with a dog sled
mush′room′ *n.* ⟦< LL *mussirio*⟧ any of various fleshy fungi, typically with a stalk capped by an umbrellalike top; esp., any edible variety —***adj.*** of or like a mushroom —***vi.*** to grow or spread rapidly
mu·sic (myoo′zik) ***n.*** ⟦< Gr *mousikē* (*technē*), art of the Muses⟧ **1** the art of combining tones to form expressive compositions **2** such compositions **3** any rhythmic sequence of pleasing sounds —**face the music** [Colloq.] to accept the consequences
mu′si·cal (-zi kəl) ***adj.*** **1** of or for music **2** melodious or harmonious **3** fond of or skilled in music **4** set to music —***n.*** a play or film with a musical score featuring songs and dances —**mu′si·cal·ly *adv.***
mu·si·cale (myoo′zi kal′) ***n.*** ⟦Fr⟧ a social affair featuring a musical program
mu·si·cian (myoo zish′ən) ***n.*** one skilled in music; esp., a performer
mu′si·col′o·gy (-zi käl′ə jē) ***n.*** the study of the history, forms, etc. of music —**mu′si·col′o·gist *n.***
musk (musk) ***n.*** ⟦< Sans *muṣka,* testicle⟧ a strong-smelling animal secretion, esp. from a type of male deer, used in perfume —**musk′y, -i·er, -i·est, *adj.***
mus·kel·lunge (mus′kə lunj′) ***n.*** ⟦< AmInd⟧ a very large, edible pike of North America Also **mus′kie** (-kē)
mus·ket (mus′kət) ***n.*** ⟦< L *musca,* a fly⟧ a former kind of firearm with a long barrel and smooth bore
mus·ket·eer (mus′kə tir′) ***n.*** a soldier armed with a musket
musk′mel′on *n.* any of various sweet, juicy melons, as the cantaloupe
musk ox a hardy ox of arctic North America with a long, coarse coat and a musklike odor
musk·rat (musk′rat′) ***n.*** **1** an American water rodent with webbed hind feet and a musklike odor **2** its fur
Mus·lim (muz′ləm, mooz′-; moos′-) ***n.*** ⟦Ar, true believer < *aslama,* to resign oneself (to God)⟧ an adherent of Islam —***adj.*** of Islam or the Muslims
mus·lin (muz′lin) ***n.*** ⟦after *Mosul,* city in Iraq⟧ a strong, plain-woven cotton cloth
muss (mus) ***n.*** ⟦prob. var. of MESS⟧ [Colloq.] a mess; disorder —***vt.*** to make messy or

disordered: often with *up* —**muss'y, -i·er, -i·est,** ***adj.***

mus·sel (mus'əl) ***n.*** ⟦< OE *muscle*⟧ any of various bivalve mollusks of fresh or salt waters; specif., an edible variety

must (must) ***v.aux.*** *pt.* **must** ⟦< OE *moste*⟧ used to express: **1** necessity /I *must* go/ **2** probability /it *must* be Joe/ **3** certainty /all men *must* die/ —***n.*** [Colloq.] something that must be done, had, etc.

mus·tache (mus'tash', məs tash') ***n.*** ⟦ult. < Gr *mystax*⟧ hair growing on the upper lip; esp., the hair that a man has let grow

mus·tang (mus'taŋ') ***n.*** ⟦< L *mixtus,* a mingling⟧ a small wild horse of the SW plains

mus·tard (mus'tərd) ***n.*** ⟦< OFr⟧ **1** an herb with yellow flowers and round seeds in slender pods **2** a pungent seasoning made from the ground seeds

mustard gas ⟦< its mustardlike odor⟧ an oily liquid used in warfare for its blistering and disabling effects

mus·ter (mus'tər) ***vt.*** ⟦< L *monstrare,* to show⟧ **1** to assemble (troops, etc.) **2** to collect; summon: often with *up* —***vi.*** to assemble, as troops —***n.*** **1** a gathering or assembling, as of troops for inspection **2** the persons or things assembled —**muster in** (or **out**) to enlist in (or discharge from) military service —**pass muster** to meet the required standards

mus·ty (mus'tē) ***adj.*** **-ti·er, -ti·est** ⟦< ? MOIST⟧ **1** having a stale, moldy smell or taste **2** stale or trite; antiquated —**mus'ti·ly** ***adv.*** —**mus'ti·ness** ***n.***

mu·ta·ble (myo͞ot'ə bəl) ***adj.*** ⟦< L *mutare,* to change⟧ **1** that can be changed **2** inconstant; fickle —**mu'ta·bil'i·ty** ***n.*** —**mu'ta·bly** ***adv.***

mu·tant (myo͞ot'tənt) ***adj.*** of mutation —***n.*** an animal or plant with inheritable characteristics that differ from those of the parents; sport

mu·ta·tion (myo͞o tā'shən) ***n.*** **1** a change, as in form, nature, etc. **2** a sudden variation in some inheritable characteristic of an animal or plant —**mu'tate', -tat'ed, -tat'ing,** ***vi., vt.***

TRUMPET MUTE

mute (myo͞ot) ***adj.*** ⟦< L *mutus*⟧ **1** not speaking; silent **2** unable to speak —***n.*** **1** a deaf-mute **2** a device that softens the sound of a musical instrument —***vt.*** **mut'ed, mut'ing** to soften the sound of (an instrument) —**mute'ly** ***adv.***

mu·ti·late (myo͞ot''l āt') ***vt.*** **-lat'ed, -lat'ing** ⟦< L *mutilus,* maimed⟧ to cut off, damage, or spoil an important part of —**mu'ti·la'tion** ***n.*** —**mu'ti·la'tor** ***n.***

mu·ti·ny (myo͞ot''n ē) ***n.,*** *pl.* **-nies** ⟦< L *movere,* to move⟧ revolt against constituted authority; esp., rebellion of soldiers or sailors against their officers —***vi.*** **-nied, -ny·ing** to revolt in this way —**mu'ti·neer'** ***n.*** —**mu'ti·nous** ***adj.***

mutt (mut) ***n.*** [Slang] a mongrel dog

mut·ter (mut'ər) ***vi., vt.*** ⟦ME *moteren*⟧ **1** to speak or say in low, indistinct tones **2** to grumble —***n.*** **1** a muttering **2** something muttered

mut·ton (mut''n) ***n.*** ⟦< OFr, a ram⟧ the flesh of a sheep, esp. a grown sheep, used as food

mu·tu·al (myo͞o'cho͞o əl) ***adj.*** ⟦< L *mutare,* to exchange⟧ **1** *a)* done, felt, etc. by each of two or more for or toward the other or others *b)* of each other **2** in common /our *mutual* friend/ —**mu'tu·al·ly** ***adv.***

mutual fund a corporation which manages a diversified portfolio of investments for its shareholders

muu·muu (mo͞o'mo͞o') ***n.*** ⟦< Haw⟧ a long, loose dress of Hawaiian style

Mu·zak (myo͞o'zak') *trademark for* a system of transmitting recorded background music to stores, etc. —***n.*** this music, variously regarded as unobtrusive, bland, etc.

muz·zle (muz'əl) ***n.*** ⟦< ML *musum*⟧ **1** the mouth, nose, and jaws of a dog, horse, etc. **2** a device put over the mouth of an animal to prevent its biting or eating **3** the front end of the barrel of a firearm —***vt.*** **-zled, -zling** **1** to put a muzzle on (an animal) **2** to prevent from talking

MX missile ⟦< *m(issile), (e)x(perimental)*⟧ a U.S. ICBM armed with several nuclear warheads and capable of being concealed underground

my (mī) ***poss. pronominal adj.*** ⟦< OE *min*⟧ of, belonging to, or done by me

Myan·mar (myun'mär') country in SE Asia; 261,789 sq. mi.; pop. 37,651,000

my·e·li·tis (mī'ə lit'is) ***n.*** ⟦< Gr *myelos,* marrow + -ITIS⟧ inflammation of the spinal cord or the bone marrow

My·lar (mī'lär') *trademark for* a strong, thin polyester used for recording tapes, fabrics, etc. —***n.*** [m-] this substance

my·na or **my·nah** (mī'nə) ***n.*** ⟦Hindi *mainā*⟧ any of various tropical birds of Southeast Asia: some can mimic speech

my·o·pi·a (mī ō'pē ə) ***n.*** ⟦< Gr *myein,* to close + *ōps,* eye⟧ nearsightedness —**my·op'ic** (-äp'ik) ***adj.***

myr·i·ad (mir'ē əd) ***n.*** ⟦< Gr *myrios,* countless⟧ a great number of persons or things —***adj.*** very many

myr·mi·don (mur'mə dän', -dən) ***n.*** ⟦after name of a Gr tribe led by Achilles⟧ an unquestioning follower

myrrh (mur) ***n.*** ⟦< Ar *murr*⟧ a fragrant gum resin of Arabia and E Africa, used in incense, perfume, etc.

myr·tle (murt''l) ***n.*** ⟦< Gr *myrtos*⟧ **1** an evergreen shrub with white or pink flowers and dark berries **2** any of various other plants, as the periwinkle

my·self (mī self') ***pron.*** a form of the 1st pers. sing. pronoun, used as an intensive /I went *myself*/, as a reflexive /I hurt *myself*/, or as a quasi-noun meaning "my real, true, or actual self" /I am not *myself* today/

mys·te·ri·ous (mis tir'ē əs) ***adj.*** of, containing, implying, or characterized by mystery —**mys·te'ri·ous·ly** ***adv.*** —**mys·te'ri·ous·ness** ***n.***

mys·ter·y (mis'tə rē) ***n.,*** *pl.* **-ies** ⟦< Gr *mystērion,* secret rite⟧ **1** something unexplained or secret 2 a story involving unknown persons, facts, etc. /a murder *mystery*/ 3 secrecy

mys·tic (mis′tik) ***adj.*** 1 of esoteric rites or doctrines 2 MYSTICAL 3 mysterious —***n.*** one who professes to undergo profound spiritual experiences

mys′ti·cal ***adj.*** 1 spiritually significant or symbolic 2 of mystics or mysticism 3 occult —**mys′ti·cal·ly** ***adv.***

mys·ti·cism (mis′tə siz′əm) ***n.*** 1 belief in the possibility of attaining direct communion with God or knowledge of spiritual truths, as by meditation 2 obscure thinking or belief

mys′ti·fy′ (-fī′) ***vt.*** **-fied′**, **-fy′ing** 1 to puzzle or perplex 2 to involve in mystery —**mys′ti·fi·ca′tion** ***n.***

mys·tique (mis tēk′) ***n.*** ⟦Fr, mystic⟧ a complex of quasi-mystical attitudes and feelings surrounding some person, etc.

myth (mith) ***n.*** ⟦< Gr *mythos*⟧ 1 a traditional story serving to explain some phenomenon, custom, etc. 2 mythology 3 any fictitious story, person, or thing —**myth′i·cal** ***adj.***

my·thol·o·gy (mi thäl′ə jē) ***n.***, *pl.* **-gies** 1 the study of myths 2 myths collectively, as of a specific people —**myth·o·log·i·cal** (mith′ə läj′i kəl) ***adj.***

N

n or **N** (en) ***n.***, *pl.* **n's, N's** the 14th letter of the English alphabet

N *Chem. symbol for* nitrogen

n or **n.** 1 name 2 neuter 3 new 4 nominative 5 noun 6 number

N or **N.** 1 Navy 2 north 3 northerly 4 northern 5 November

Na ⟦L *natrium*⟧ *Chem. symbol for* sodium

N.A. North America

NAACP National Association for the Advancement of Colored People

nab (nab) ***vt.*** **nabbed, nab′bing** ⟦prob. < dial. *nap*, to snatch⟧ [Colloq.] 1 to snatch or seize 2 to arrest or catch (a felon or wrongdoer)

na·bob (nā′bäb′) ***n.*** ⟦< Ar *nā'ib*, deputy⟧ a very rich or important man

na·cre (nā′kər) ***n.*** ⟦Fr < Ar *naqqārah*, small kettledrum⟧ MOTHER-OF-PEARL

na·dir (nā′dər, -dir′) ***n.*** ⟦< Ar *naẓīr*, opposite⟧ 1 the point opposite the zenith and directly below the observer 2 the lowest point

nae (nā) [Scot.] ***adv.*** no; not —***adj.*** no

nag[1] (nag) ***vt.***, ***vi.*** **nagged, nag′ging** ⟦< ON *gnaga*⟧ 1 to annoy (someone) by continual scolding, faultfinding, etc. 2 to keep troubling /*nagged* by doubts/ —***n.*** one who nags Also **nag′ger**

nag[2] (nag) ***n.*** ⟦ME *nagge*⟧ an old or inferior horse

Na·ga·sa·ki (nä′gə sä′kē) seaport in SW Japan: U.S. atomic-bomb target (1945): pop. 446,000

Na·go·ya (nä′gô yä′) seaport in S Honshu, Japan: pop. 2,066,000

nai·ad (nā′ad′, nī′-) ***n.*** ⟦< Gr *naein*, to flow⟧ [*also* **N-**] *Gr. & Rom. Myth.* a nymph living in a spring, river, etc.

nail (nāl) ***n.*** ⟦< OE *nægl*⟧ 1 the thin, horny growth at the ends of fingers and toes 2 a tapered, pointed piece of metal driven with a hammer, as to join pieces of wood —***vt.*** 1 to fasten, secure, etc. with or as with nails 2 [Colloq.] to catch or hit

Nai·ro·bi (nī rō′bē) capital of Kenya: pop. 828,000

na·ive or **na·ïve** (nä ēv′) ***adj.*** ⟦Fr < L *nativus*, natural⟧ unaffectedly simple; artless —**na·ive′ly** or **na·ïve′ly** ***adv.*** —**na·ive·té′** or **na·ïve·té′** (-tā′) ***n.***

na·ked (nā′kid) ***adj.*** ⟦OE *nacod*⟧ 1 completely unclothed; nude 2 without covering /a *naked* sword/ 3 without additions, disguises, etc.; plain /the *naked* truth/ —**na′ked·ly** ***adv.*** —**na′ked·ness** ***n.***

nam·by-pam·by (nam′bē pam′bē) ***adj.*** ⟦18th-c. play on name *Ambrose*⟧ weak, insipid, indecisive, etc. —***n.***, *pl.* **-bies** a namby-pamby person

name (nām) ***n.*** ⟦OE *nama*⟧ 1 a word or phrase by which a person, thing, or class is known; title 2 a word or words considered descriptive; epithet, often an abusive one 3 fame or reputation 4 appearance only, not reality /chief in *name* only/ —***adj.*** well-known —***vt.*** **named, nam′ing** 1 to give a name to 2 to mention by name 3 to identify by the right name /*name* the oceans/ 4 to appoint to an office, etc. 5 to specify (a date, price, etc.) —**in the name of** 1 in appeal to 2 by the authority of

name′less ***adj.*** 1 not having a name 2 left unnamed 3 indescribable

name′ly ***adv.*** that is to say; to wit

name′sake′ ***n.*** a person with the same name as another, esp. if named after the other

Nan·jing (nän′jiŋ′) city in E China, on the Chang: pop. 2,000,000

Nan·king (nan′kiŋ′, nän′-) *old form of* NANJING

nan·ny goat (nan′ē) ⟦< fem. name *Nan*⟧ a female goat

nap[1] (nap) ***vi.*** **napped, nap′ping** ⟦OE *hnappian*⟧ to sleep lightly for a short time —***n.*** a brief, light sleep

nap[2] (nap) ***n.*** ⟦ME *noppe*⟧ the downy or hairy surface of cloth or suede formed by short hairs or fibers —**nap′less** ***adj.*** —**napped** ***adj.***

na·palm (nā′päm′) ***n.*** ⟦*na(phthene)* + *palm(itate)*⟧ a jellylike substance used in flame throwers and fire bombs —***vt.*** to attack or burn with napalm

nape (nāp) ***n.*** ⟦ME⟧ the back of the neck

naph·tha (naf′thə, nap′-) ***n.*** ⟦< Pers *neft*, pitch⟧ a flammable liquid distilled from petroleum, used as a fuel, solvent, etc.

naph'tha·lene' (-lēn') ***n.*** ⟦< prec.⟧ a white, crystalline hydrocarbon distilled from coal tar, used in moth repellents, dyes, etc.

nap·kin (nap'kin) ***n.*** ⟦< L *mappa*⟧ **1** a small piece of cloth or paper used while eating to protect the clothes and wipe the lips **2** any small cloth, towel, etc.

Na·ples (nā'pəlz) seaport in S Italy: pop. 1,212,000

Na·po·le·on (nə pō'lē ən) (born *Napoleon Bonaparte*) 1769-1821; Fr. general & emperor (1804-15): in full **Napoleon I**

narc (närk) ***n.*** ⟦< NARC(OTIC)⟧ [Slang] a police agent who enforces laws dealing with narcotics Also **nark**

nar·cis·sism (när'sə siz'əm) ***n.*** ⟦< fol.⟧ self-love; specif., excessive interest in one's own appearance, etc. —**nar'cis·sist** ***n., adj.*** —**nar'cis·sis'tic** ***adj.***

Nar·cis·sus (när sis'əs) *Gr. Myth.* a youth who falls in love with his reflection in a pool and changes into the narcissus —***n.***, *pl.* **-cis'·sus, -cis'sus·es,** or **-cis'si** (-ī) [n-] any of various bulb plants whose flowers have tubelike projections

nar·co·sis (när kō'sis) ***n.***, *pl.* **-ses'** (-sēz') unconsciousness caused by a narcotic

nar·cot·ic (när kät'ik) ***n.*** ⟦< Gr *narkē*, numbness⟧ a drug, as morphine, used to relieve pain and induce sleep: narcotics are often addictive —***adj.*** of or having to do with narcotics

nar·co·tize (när'kə tīz') ***vt.*** **-tized', -tiz'ing** to subject to a narcotic —**nar'co·ti·za'tion** ***n.***

nar·rate (nar'āt', na rāt') ***vt., vi.*** **-rat'ed, -rat'ing** ⟦< L *narrare*, tell⟧ to tell (a story), relate (events), etc.

nar·ra·tion (na rā'shən) ***n.*** **1** a narrating **2** a narrative

nar·ra·tive (nar'ə tiv) ***adj.*** in story form —***n.*** **1** a story; account **2** the art or practice of narrating

nar·row (nar'ō) ***adj.*** ⟦OE *nearu*⟧ **1** small in width; not wide **2** limited in meaning, size, amount, etc. /a *narrow* majority/ **3** limited in outlook; not liberal **4** with limited margin /a *narrow* escape/ —***vi., vt.*** to decrease or limit in width, extent, etc. —***n.*** [*usually pl.*] a narrow passage; strait

nar'row·cast' (-kast') ***vt., vi.*** **-cast', -cast'·ing** to transmit by cable TV to a selected audience —***n.*** a narrowcasting

nar'row-mind'ed ***adj.*** limited in outlook; bigoted; prejudiced —**nar'row-mind'ed·ness** ***n.***

nar·whal (när'wəl) ***n.*** ⟦< ON *nahvalr*, lit., corpse whale⟧ a small arctic whale: the male has a long, spiral tusk

nar·y (ner'ē) ***adj.*** ⟦< *ne'er a*, never a⟧ [Dial.] not any; no: with *a* or *an*

NASA (nas'ə) ***n.*** National Aeronautics and Space Administration

na·sal (nā'zəl) ***adj.*** ⟦< L *nasus*, nose⟧ **1** of the nose **2** uttered so that the breath passes through the nose

na·sal·ize (nā'zəl īz') ***vt., vi.*** **-ized', -iz'ing** to pronounce or speak with a nasal sound —**na'sal·i·za'tion** ***n.***

nas·cent (nas'ənt, nā'sənt) ***adj.*** ⟦< L *nasci*, be born⟧ **1** coming into being **2** beginning to form or develop: said of ideas, etc.

Nash·ville (nash'vil) capital of Tenn.: pop. 446,000

nas·tur·tium (nə stur'shəm, na-) ***n.*** ⟦< L *nasus*, nose + *torquere*, to twist⟧ **1** a plant with red, yellow, or orange trumpet-shaped flowers **2** its flower

nas·ty (nas'tē) ***adj.*** **-ti·er, -ti·est** ⟦< ?⟧ **1** filthy **2** morally offensive; indecent **3** very unpleasant /*nasty* weather/ **4** mean; malicious —**nas'ti·ly** ***adv.*** —**nas'ti·ness** ***n.***

na·tal (nāt''l) ***adj.*** ⟦< L *nasci*, be born⟧ of or relating to one's birth

na·tes (nā'tēz') ***n.pl.*** ⟦L⟧ the buttocks

na·tion (nā'shən) ***n.*** ⟦< L *natus*, born⟧ **1** a stable community of people with a territory, history, culture, and language in common **2** people united under a single government; country

na·tion·al (nash'ə nəl) ***adj.*** of or affecting a nation as a whole —***n.*** a citizen or subject —**na'tion·al·ly** ***adv.***

National Guard the organized militia of each U.S. State: it is part of the U.S. Army

na'tion·al·ism' ***n.*** **1** devotion to one's nation; patriotism **2** the advocacy of national independence —**na'tion·al·ist** ***n., adj.*** —**na'tion·al·is'tic** ***adj.***

na'tion·al'i·ty (-nal'ə tē) ***n.***, *pl.* **-ties** **1** the status of belonging to a nation by birth or naturalization **2** a national group, esp. of immigrants

na'tion·al·ize' (-nə līz') ***vt.*** **-ized', -iz'ing** **1** to make national **2** to transfer ownership or control of (land, industries, etc.) to the government —**na'tion·al·i·za'tion** ***n.***

na'tion·wide' ***adj.*** by or throughout the whole nation; national

na·tive (nāt'iv) ***adj.*** ⟦< L *natus*, born⟧ **1** inborn **2** belonging to a locality or country by birth, production, growth **3** being, or connected with, the place of one's birth /one's *native* land or language/ **4** as found in nature; natural **5** of or characteristic of the original inhabitants of a place —***n.*** **1** a person born in the place indicated **2** an original inhabitant **3** an indigenous plant or animal

Native American AMERICAN INDIAN: now often the preferred term

na'tive-born' ***adj.*** of a specified place by birth

na·tiv·i·ty (nə tiv'ə tē) ***n.***, *pl.* **-ties** ⟦see NATIVE⟧ birth —**the Nativity** the birth of Jesus

natl. national

NATO (nā'tō) ***n.*** North Atlantic Treaty Organization

nat·ty (nat'ē) ***adj.*** **-ti·er, -ti·est** ⟦< ? NEAT⟧ trim and stylish —**nat'ti·ly** ***adv.***

nat·u·ral (nach'ər əl) ***adj.*** ⟦< L *naturalis*, by birth⟧ **1** of or dealing with nature **2** produced or existing in nature; not artificial **3** innate; not acquired **4** true to nature; lifelike **5** normal /a *natural* result/ **6** free from affectation; at ease **7** *Music* neither sharped nor flatted —***n.*** a person or thing sure to be successful —**nat'u·ral·ness** ***n.***

natural childbirth childbirth without anesthesia through prior training

natural gas a mixture of gaseous hydrocarbons, chiefly methane, occurring naturally in the earth and used as fuel

natural history the study of the animal, vegetable, and mineral world

nat'u·ral·ism' ***n.*** **1** action or thought based on natural desires **2** *Literature, Art, etc.* the portrayal of persons or things as they really are

nat'u·ral·ist ***n.*** **1** one who studies animals and plants **2** a proponent of naturalism —**nat'u·ral·is'tic** ***adj.***

nat'u·ral·ize' (-īz') ***vt.*** **-ized', -iz'ing** to confer citizenship upon (an alien) —**nat'u·ral·i·za'tion** ***n.***

nat'u·ral·ly ***adv.*** **1** in a natural manner **2** by nature **3** of course

natural number any positive integer, as 1, 2, 3, etc.

natural resources those forms of wealth supplied by nature, as land, minerals, water power, etc.

natural science the systematized knowledge of nature, including biology, chemistry, physics, etc.

natural selection the evolutionary process by which the most adaptable species survive

na·ture (nā'chər) ***n.*** ⟦< L *natus*, born⟧ **1** the essential quality of a thing; essence **2** inherent tendencies of a person **3** kind; type **4** *a)* the physical universe *b)* [*sometimes* **N-**] the power, force etc. that seems to regulate this **5** the primitive state of humans **6** natural scenery —**by nature** naturally; inherently

Naug·a·hyde (nôg'ə hīd') ⟦arbitrary coinage⟧ *trademark for* an imitation leather, used for upholstery, luggage, etc. —***n.*** [**n-**] this material

naught (nôt) ***n.*** ⟦OE *nawiht*⟧ **1** nothing **2** *alt. sp. of* NOUGHT

naugh·ty (nôt'ē) ***adj.*** **-ti·er, -ti·est** ⟦ME *naugti*⟧ **1** mischievous or disobedient **2** indelicate; improper —**naugh'ti·ly** ***adv.*** —**naugh'ti·ness** ***n.***

Na·u·ru (nä o͞o'ro͞o) country on an island in the W Pacific, south of the equator: 8 sq. mi.; pop. 7,250

nau·se·a (nô'shə, -zhə; -sē ə, -zē ə) ***n.*** ⟦< Gr *nausia*, seasickness⟧ **1** a sick feeling in the stomach, with an impulse to vomit **2** disgust; loathing

nau'se·ate' (-shē āt', -zhē-; -sē-, -zē-) ***vt.*** **-at'ed, -at'ing** to cause to feel nausea

nau·seous (nô'shəs, -zē əs, -sē-) ***adj.*** **1** causing nausea **2** [Colloq.] feeling nausea

nau·ti·cal (nôt'i kəl) ***adj.*** ⟦< Gr *naus*, ship⟧ of sailors, ships, or navigation —**nau'ti·cal·ly** ***adv.***

nautical mile a unit of linear measure used in navigation, equal to 1,852 m

NAUTILUS (CROSS SECTION)

nau·ti·lus (nôt''l əs) ***n.***, *pl.* **-lus·es** or **-li'** (-ī') ⟦< Gr *naus*, ship⟧ a tropical mollusk with a spiral shell divided into many chambers —[**N-**] *trademark for* a type of mechanical weight-lifting equipment

Nav·a·jo (nav'ə hō') ***n.*** *pl.* **-jos', -jo',** or **-joes'** a member of an American Indian people of the SW U.S. Also sp. **Navaho**

na·val (nā'vəl) ***adj.*** ⟦< L *navis*, a ship⟧ of, having, characteristic of, or for a navy, its ships, etc.

nave (nāv) ***n.*** ⟦< L *navis*, a ship⟧ the main part of a church, from the chancel to the principal entrance

na·vel (nā'vəl) ***n.*** ⟦OE *nafela*⟧ the small scar in the abdomen, marking the place where the umbilical cord was attached to the fetus

navel orange a seedless orange with a navel-like hollow at its apex

nav·i·ga·ble (nav'i gə bəl) ***adj.*** **1** wide or deep enough for the passage of ships **2** that can be steered —**nav'i·ga·bil'i·ty** ***n.***

nav·i·gate (nav'ə gāt') ***vt., vi.*** **-gat'ed, -gat'ing** ⟦< L *navis*, a ship + *agere*, to lead⟧ **1** to steer or direct (a ship or aircraft) **2** to travel through or over (water, air, etc.) in a ship or aircraft **3** [Colloq.] to walk

nav'i·ga'tion (-gā'shən) ***n.*** the science of locating the position and plotting the course of ships and aircraft

nav'i·ga'tor ***n.*** one skilled in the navigation of a ship or aircraft

na·vy (nā'vē) ***n.***, *pl.* **-vies** ⟦< L *navis*, a ship⟧ **1** all the warships of a nation **2** [*often* **N-**] a nation's entire sea force, including ships, men, stores, etc. **3** NAVY BLUE

navy bean ⟦from use in U.S. *Navy*⟧ a small, white variety of kidney bean

navy blue very dark, purplish blue

nay (nā) ***adv.*** ⟦< ON *ne*, not + *ei*, ever⟧ not that only, but also /I permit, *nay* encourage it/ —***n.*** **1** a denial **2** a negative vote or voter

nay·say·er (nā'sā ər) ***n.*** one who opposes, refuses, etc., esp. habitually

Na·zi (nät'sē) ***adj.*** ⟦Ger contr. of the party name⟧ designating or of the German fascist political party which ruled Germany under Hitler (1933-45) —***n.*** a member of this party

n.b. ⟦L *nota bene*⟧ note well

NB or **N.B.** New Brunswick

NC or **N.C.** North Carolina

NCO noncommissioned officer

ND or **N.D.** North Dakota Also **N.Dak.**

Ne *Chem. symbol for* neon

NE **1** Nebraska **2** northeast **3** northeasterly **4** northeastern Also, for 2-4, **N.E.**

Ne·an·der·thal (nē an'dər thôl') ***adj.*** ⟦after a Ger Valley⟧ **1** designating or of a widespread form of early human of the Pleistocene Epoch **2** primitive or regressive —***n.*** **1** a Neanderthal human **2** one who is crude, primitive, etc.

neap (nēp) ***adj.*** ⟦OE *nep-* in *nepflod*, neap tide⟧ designating either of the two lowest high tides in the month —***n.*** neap tide

Ne·a·pol·i·tan (nē'ə päl'ət 'n) ***adj.*** of Naples —***n.*** a native or inhabitant of Naples

Neapolitan ice cream brick ice cream in layers of different flavors

near (nir) ***adv.*** ⟦OE compar. of *neah*, nigh⟧ **1** at a short distance in space or time **2** almost /*near* right/ **3** closely; intimately —***adj.*** **1** close in distance or time **2** close in relationship; akin **3** close in friendship; intimate **4** close in degree /a *near*

escape/ 5 short or direct /the *near* way/ — ***prep.*** close to —***vt., vi.*** to draw near (to); approach —**near′ness** ***n.***
near′by′ ***adj., adv.*** near; close at hand
Near East countries near the E end of the Mediterranean, including those of SW Asia, the Arabian Peninsula, & NE Africa
near′ly ***adv.*** almost; not quite
near miss 1 a result that is nearly but not quite successful 2 a near escape
near′sight′ed ***adj.*** having better vision for near objects than for distant ones; myopic —**near′sight′ed·ness** ***n.***
neat (nēt) ***adj.*** ⟦< L *nitere,* to shine⟧ 1 unmixed; undiluted /whiskey *neat*/ 2 clean and tidy 3 skillful and precise 4 well-proportioned 5 cleverly said or done 6 [Slang] nice, pleasing, etc. —**neat′ly** ***adv.*** —**neat′ness** ***n.***
'neath or **neath** (nēth) ***prep.*** *old poet. var. of* BENEATH
Ne·bras·ka (nə bras′kə) Middle Western State of the U.S.: 77,227 sq. mi.; pop. 1,570,000; cap. Lincoln Abbrev. **Neb.** —**Ne·bras′kan** ***adj., n.***
neb·u·la (neb′yə lə) ***n.,*** *pl.* **-lae′** (-lē′) or **-las** ⟦L, mist⟧ a cloud of interstellar gas or dust, or, formerly, any hazy, distant celestial object, as a star cluster —**neb′u·lar** ***adj.***
neb′u·lous (-ləs) ***adj.*** unclear; vague
nec·es·sar·i·ly (nes′ə ser′ə lē) ***adv.*** 1 because of necessity 2 as a necessary result
nec′es·sar′y (-ser′ē) ***adj.*** ⟦< L *ne-,* not + *cedere,* give way⟧ 1 essential; indispensable 2 inevitable 3 required —***n.,*** *pl.* **-sar′ies** something necessary
ne·ces·si·tate (nə ses′ə tāt′) ***vt.*** **-tat′ed, -tat′ing** to make necessary or unavoidable
ne·ces′si·ty (-tē) ***n.,*** *pl.* **-ties** ⟦see NECESSARY⟧ 1 natural causation; fate 2 great need 3 something that cannot be done without 4 want; poverty —**of necessity** necessarily; inevitably
neck (nek) ***n.*** ⟦OE *hnecca*⟧ 1 that part of a human or animal joining the head to the body 2 that part of a garment near the neck 3 a necklike part; specif., *a*) a narrow strip of land *b*) the narrowest part of a bottle, etc. *c*) a strait —***vt., vi.*** [Slang] to hug, kiss, and caress passionately —**neck and neck** very close, as in a race
neck·er·chief (nek′ər chif, -chēf′) ***n.*** ⟦see prec. & KERCHIEF⟧ a handkerchief or scarf worn around the neck
neck′lace (-lis) ***n.*** ⟦NECK + LACE⟧ an ornamental string of beads, chain of gold, etc., worn around the neck
neck′tie′ ***n.*** a band worn around the neck under a collar and tied in front
neck′wear′ ***n.*** articles worn about the neck, as neckties, scarves, etc.
ne·crol·o·gy (ne krāl′ə jē) ***n.,*** *pl.* **-gies** ⟦ult. < Gr *nekros,* corpse + -LOGY⟧ a list of people who have died
nec·ro·man·cy (nek′rə man′sē) ***n.*** ⟦< Gr *nekros,* corpse + *manteia,* divination⟧ 1 divination by alleged communication with the dead 2 black magic; sorcery —**nec′ro·man′cer** ***n.***
ne·cro·sis (ne krō′sis) ***n.,*** *pl.* **-ses′** (-sēz′) ⟦< Gr *nekros,* corpse⟧ the death or decay of tissue in a part of the body
nec·tar (nek′tər) ***n.*** ⟦< Gr *nektar*⟧ 1 *Gr. & Rom. Myth.* the drink of the gods 2 any very delicious beverage 3 the sweetish liquid in many flowers, used by bees to make honey
nec·tar·ine (nek′tə rēn′, nek′tə rēn′) ***n.*** ⟦< prec.⟧ a kind of smooth-skinned peach
nee or **née** (nā; *now often* nē) ***adj.*** ⟦Fr⟧ born /Mrs. Helen Jones, *nee* Smith/
need (nēd) ***n.*** ⟦OE *nied*⟧ 1 necessity 2 a lack of something required or desired /the *need* of a rest/ 3 something required or desired that is lacking /your daily *needs*/ 4 *a*) a condition in which help is required /a friend in *need*/ *b*) poverty —***vt.*** 1 to have need of; require 2 to be obliged; must /I *need* to be careful/ —***vi.*** to be in need —**have need to** to be required to —**if need be** if it is required
need′ful ***adj.*** necessary; required
nee·dle (nēd′'l) ***n.*** ⟦OE *nædl*⟧ 1 a small, slender, pointed piece of steel with a hole for thread, used for sewing 2 a slender rod of steel, bone, etc. used for crocheting or knitting 3 STYLUS (sense 2*b*) 4 the pointer of a compass, gauge, etc. 5 the thin, short, pointed leaf of the pine, spruce, etc. 6 the sharp, slender metal tube at the end of a hypodermic syringe —***vt.*** **-dled, -dling** [Colloq.] 1 to goad; prod 2 to tease —**nee′dler** ***n.***
nee′dle·point′ ***n.*** 1 embroidery of woolen threads upon canvas 2 lace made on a paper pattern, with a needle: in full **needlepoint lace**
need′less ***adj.*** not needed; unnecessary —**need′less·ly** ***adv.***
nee′dle·work′ ***n.*** work done with a needle; embroidery, needlepoint, etc.
need·n't (nēd′'nt) need not
needs (nēdz) ***adv.*** ⟦OE *nedes*⟧ of necessity /he must *needs* obey/
need′y ***adj.*** **-i·er, -i·est** in need; very poor —**need′i·ness** ***n.***
ne'er (ner) ***adv.*** [Old Poet.] never
ne'er′-do-well′ ***n.*** a shiftless, irresponsible person
ne·far·i·ous (nə fer′ē əs) ***adj.*** ⟦< L *ne-,* not + *fas,* lawful⟧ very wicked; villainous —**ne·far′i·ous·ly** ***adv.*** —**ne·far′i·ous·ness** ***n.***
ne·gate (ni gāt′) ***vt.*** **-gat′ed, -gat′ing** ⟦< L *negare,* deny⟧ 1 to deny 2 to make ineffective
ne·ga·tion (ni gā′shən) ***n.*** 1 the act or an instance of denying 2 the lack or opposite of something positive
neg·a·tive (neg′ə tiv) ***adj.*** 1 expressing denial or refusal; saying "no" 2 opposite to or lacking in that which is positive /a *negative* force/ 3 *Math.* designating a quantity less than zero, or one to be subtracted 4 *Med.* not proving the presence of bacteria, a fracture, etc. 5 *Photog.* reversing the relation of light and shade of the subject 6 *Elec.* *a*) of, generating, or charged with negative electricity *b*) having an excess of electrons —***n.*** 1 a negative word, reply, etc. 2 the point of view that opposes the positive 3 the plate in a voltaic battery where the lower potential is 4 an exposed and developed photographic plate or film on which light and shadow are reversed —***vt.*** **-tived, -tiv-**

ing to reject or deny —**in the negative** in refusal or denial of a plan, etc. —**neg'a·tive·ly** *adv.*

ne·glect (ni glekt') *vt.* ⟦< L *neg-*, not + *legere*, to gather⟧ 1 to ignore or disregard 2 to fail to attend to properly 3 to leave undone —*n.* 1 a neglecting 2 lack of proper care 3 a being neglected —**ne·glect'ful** *adj.*

neg·li·gee (neg'lə zhā', neg'lə zhā') *n.* ⟦< Fr *négliger*, to neglect⟧ a woman's loosely fitting dressing gown

neg·li·gent (neg'lə jənt) *adj.* 1 habitually failing to do the required thing; neglectful 2 careless, inattentive, etc. —**neg'li·gence** *n.*

neg'li·gi·ble (-jə bəl) *adj.* that can be neglected or disregarded; trifling

ne·go·ti·ate (ni gō'shē āt') *vi.* **-at'ed, -at'ing** ⟦< L *negotium*, business⟧ to discuss with a view to reaching agreement —*vt.* 1 to settle (a business transaction, treaty, etc.) 2 to transfer or sell (bonds, stocks, etc.) 3 to succeed in crossing, passing, etc. —**ne·go'ti·a·ble** (-shē ə bəl, -shə bəl) *adj.* —**ne·go'ti·a'tion** *n.* —**ne·go'ti·a'tor** *n.*

neg·ri·tude (neg'rə to͞od', nē'grə-) *n.* ⟦Fr *négritude*⟧ [*also* **N-**] an awareness and affirmation by blacks of their distinctive cultural heritage

Ne·gro (nē'grō) *n., pl.* **-groes** ⟦Sp & Port *negro*, black⟧ a member of any of the indigenous, dark-skinned peoples of Africa, or a person having some African ancestors; a black —*adj.* of or for Negroes

Ne'groid' (-groid') *adj.* designating or of one of the major groups of human beings, including most of the peoples of Africa

Neh·ru (nā'ro͞o), **Ja·wa·har·lal** (jə wä'hər läl') 1889-1964; prime minister of India (1947-64)

neigh (nā) *vi.* ⟦OE *hnægan*⟧ to utter the characteristic cry of a horse —*n.* this cry; a whinny

neigh·bor (nā'bər) *n.* ⟦OE *neah*, nigh + *gebur*, freeholder⟧ 1 one who lives or is situated near another 2 a fellow man —*adj.* nearby —*vt., vi.* to live or be situated nearby Brit. sp. **neighbour** —**neigh'bor·ing** *adj.*

neigh'bor·hood' *n.* 1 a particular community, district, or area 2 the people living near one another —**in the neighborhood of** [Colloq.] 1 near 2 about; approximately

neigh'bor·ly *adj.* like or appropriate to neighbors; friendly, helpful, etc. —**neigh'bor·li·ness** *n.*

nei·ther (nē'*th*ər, nī'-) *adj., pron.* ⟦OE *nahwæther*, lit., not whether⟧ not one or the other (of two); not either /*neither* boy went, *neither* of them was invited/ —*conj.* not either /I could *neither* laugh nor cry/

nem·a·tode (nem'ə tōd') *n.* ⟦ult. < Gr *nēma*, thread⟧ a long, cylindrical, unsegmented worm; roundworm

nem·e·sis (nem'ə sis) *n., pl.* **-ses'** (-sēz') ⟦< Gr *nemein*, deal out⟧ 1 *a*) just punishment *b*) one who imposes it 2 anyone or anything that seems inevitably to defeat or frustrate one

neo- ⟦< Gr *neos*⟧ [*often* **N-**] *combining form* 1 new, recent 2 in a new or different way

ne·o·clas·sic (nē'ō klas'ik) *adj.* designating or of a revival of classic style and form in art, literature, etc. Also **ne'o·clas'si·cal**

ne'o·co·lo'ni·al·ism' *n.* exploitation by a foreign power of a region that has ostensibly achieved independence

ne·ol·o·gism (nē äl'ə jiz'əm) *n.* ⟦see NEO-, -LOGY, & -ISM⟧ a new word or a new meaning for an established word

ne·on (nē'än') *n.* ⟦< Gr *neos*, new⟧ a rare, inert gaseous chemical element found in the earth's atmosphere

ne·o·nate (nē'ō nāt', nē'ə-) *n.* ⟦ModL < *neo-*, NEO- + L *natus*, born⟧ a newborn infant —**ne'o·na'tal** *adj.*

neon lamp a tube containing neon, which glows red when an electric current is sent through it

ne·o·phyte (nē'ō fīt', nē'ə-) *n.* ⟦< Gr *neos*, new + *phyein*, to produce⟧ 1 a new convert 2 a beginner; novice

ne·o·plasm (nē'ō plaz'əm) *n.* ⟦< NEO- + Gr *plassein*, to form⟧ an abnormal growth of tissue, as a tumor

ne'o·prene' (-prēn') *n.* a synthetic rubber resistant to oil, heat, etc.

Ne·pal (nə pôl', -päl') country in the Himalayas: 54,300 sq. mi.; 17,422,000 —**Nep·a·lese** (nep'ə lēz') *adj., n.*

ne·pen·the (nē pen'thē, ni-) *n.* ⟦< Gr *ne-*, not + *penthos*, sorrow⟧ anything that causes forgetfulness of sorrow

neph·ew (nef'yo͞o) *n.* ⟦< L *nepos*⟧ the son of one's brother or sister, or of one's brother-in-law or sister-in-law

neph·rite (nef'rīt') *n.* ⟦< Gr *nephros*, kidney⟧ a hard, usually greenish type of jade

ne·phri·tis (nē frīt'əs, ni-) *n.* ⟦< Gr *nephros*, kidney + -ITIS⟧ a disease of the kidneys, characterized by inflammation

ne·phro·sis (nē frō'sis, ni-) *n.* ⟦< Gr *nephros*, kidney + -OSIS⟧ a degenerative disease of the kidneys, characterized by edema

ne plus ul·tra (nā plus ul'trə) ⟦L, no more beyond⟧ the ultimate

nep·o·tism (nep'ə tiz'əm) *n.* ⟦< L *nepos*, nephew⟧ favoritism shown to relatives, esp. in securing jobs

Nep·tune (nep'to͞on') 1 the Roman god of the sea 2 the planet eighth in distance from the sun: see PLANET

nep·tu·ni·um (nep to͞o'nē əm) *n.* ⟦after prec.⟧ a radioactive chemical element produced by irradiating uranium atoms

nerd (nurd) *n.* [Slang] a person regarded as dull, ineffective, etc.

Ne·ro (nir'ō) A.D. 37-68; emperor of Rome (54-68)

nerve (nurv) *n.* ⟦< L *nervus*⟧ 1 any of the cordlike fibers carrying impulses between body organs and the central nervous system 2 coolness in danger; courage 3 [*pl.*] nervousness 4 [Colloq.] impudent boldness —*vt.* **nerved, nerv'ing** to give strength or courage to —**get on someone's nerves** [Colloq.] to make someone irritable or exasperated —**nerve oneself** to collect one's energies or courage for an effort

nerve center a control center; headquarters

nerve gas a poisonous gas causing paralysis of the respiratory and nervous systems

nerve'less *adj.* 1 without strength, vigor,

etc.; weak 2 not nervous; cool; controlled —**nerve'less·ly** *adv.*

nerve'-rack'ing or **nerve'-wrack'ing** (-rak'iŋ) *adj.* very trying to one's patience or equanimity

nerv·ous (nur'vəs) *adj.* 1 animated 2 of or made up of nerves 3 emotionally tense, restless, etc. 4 fearful —**nerv'ous·ly** *adv.* —**nerv'ous·ness** *n.*

nervous system all the nerve cells and nervous tissues in an organism, including, in the vertebrates, the brain, spinal cord, nerves, etc.

nerv'y *adj.* **-i·er, -i·est** 1 bold 2 [Colloq.] brazen; impudent

-ness (nis, nəs) ⟦OE *-nes(s)*⟧ *suffix* state, quality, or instance of being [*togetherness, sadness*]

nest (nest) *n.* ⟦OE⟧ 1 the structure or place where a bird lays its eggs and shelters its young 2 the place used by insects, fish, etc. for spawning or breeding 3 a cozy place; retreat 4 *a*) a resort, haunt, etc. *b*) the people who frequent such a place [*a nest* of criminals] 5 a set of things, each fitting within the one next larger —*vi., vt.* 1 to build or settle in (a nest) 2 to fit (an object) closely within another

nest egg money, etc. put aside as a reserve or to establish a fund

nes·tle (nes'əl) *vi.* **-tled, -tling** ⟦OE *nestlian*⟧ 1 to settle down comfortably 2 to press close for comfort or in affection 3 to lie sheltered, as a house among trees —*vt.* to rest snugly

nest·ling (nest'liŋ) *n.* a young bird not yet ready to leave the nest

net[1] (net) *n.* ⟦OE *nett*⟧ 1 an openwork fabric, as of string, used to snare birds, fish, etc. 2 a trap; snare 3 a meshed fabric, esp. one used to hold, protect, etc. [*a hairnet*] —*vt.* **net'ted, net'ting** to snare or enclose, as with a net

net[2] (net) *adj.* ⟦Fr, clear⟧ remaining after deductions or allowances have been made —*n.* a net amount, profit, weight, price, etc. —*vt.* **net'ted, net'ting** to clear as profit, etc.

neth·er (neth'ər) *adj.* ⟦OE *neothera*⟧ lower or under [the *nether* world]

Neth·er·lands (neth'ər ləndz) country in W Europe: 15,770 sq. mi.; pop. 14,536,000 —**Neth'er·land'er** (-land'ər, -lən dər) *n.*

neth'er·most' *adj.* lowest

net'ting *n.* netted material

net·tle (net''l) *n.* ⟦OE *netele*⟧ a weed with stinging hairs —*vt.* **-tled, -tling** to irritate; annoy; vex

net'tle·some *adj.* that nettles or irritates

net'work' *n.* 1 an arrangement of parallel wires, etc. crossed at intervals by others so as to leave open spaces 2 anything like this, as a system of interconnected roads, individuals, computer terminals, etc. 3 *Radio, TV* a chain of transmitting stations —*adj.* broadcast over the stations of a network

net'work'ing *n.* 1 the developing of contacts or exchanging of information, as to further a career 2 the interconnection of computer systems

neu·ral (noo'rəl) *adj.* ⟦NEUR(O)- + -AL⟧ of a nerve or the nervous system

neu·ral·gi·a (noo ral'jə) *n.* ⟦see NEURO- & ALGIA⟧ severe pain along a nerve —**neu·ral'gic** (-jik) *adj.*

neu·ras·the·ni·a (noo'ras thē'nē ə) *n.* ⟦< NEURO- + Gr *asthenia*, weakness⟧ a former category of mental disorder, characterized by fatigue, anxiety, etc. —**neu'ras·then'ic** (-then'ik) *adj., n.*

neu·ri·tis (noo rīt'əs) *n.* ⟦fol. + -ITIS⟧ inflammation of a nerve or nerves —**neu·rit'ic** (-rit'ik) *adj.*

neuro- ⟦< Gr *neuron*, nerve⟧ *combining form* of a nerve or the nervous system Also **neur-**

neu·rol·o·gy (noo räl'ə jē) *n.* ⟦prec. + -LOGY⟧ the branch of medicine dealing with the nervous system and its diseases —**neu·ro·log·i·cal** (noo'rō läj'i kəl) *adj.* —**neu·rol'o·gist** *n.*

neu·ro·mus·cu·lar (noo'rō mus'kyoo lər) *adj.* of or involving both nerves and muscles

neu·ron (noo'rän') *n.* the nerve cell body and all its processes

neu·ro·sis (noo rō'sis) *n., pl.* **-ses'** (-sēz') ⟦NEURO- + -OSIS⟧ any of various mental disorders characterized by anxiety, compulsions, phobias, etc.

neu·ro·sur·ger·y (noo'rō sur'jər ē) *n.* the branch of surgery involving the brain or spinal cord —**neu'ro·sur'geon** *n.*

neu·rot·ic (noo rät'ik) *adj.* of, characteristic of, or having a neurosis —*n.* a neurotic person —**neu·rot'i·cal·ly** *adv.*

neu'ro·trans·mit'ter *n.* a biochemical substance that transmits, or inhibits, nerve impulses at a synapse

neu·ter (noot'ər) *adj.* ⟦< L *ne-*, not + *uter*, either⟧ 1 *Biol.* *a*) having no sexual organ *b*) having undeveloped sexual organs in the adult 2 *Gram.* designating or of the gender of words neither masculine nor feminine —*vt.* to castrate or spay (an animal)

neu·tral (noo'trəl) *adj.* ⟦see prec.⟧ 1 supporting neither side in a quarrel or war 2 of neither extreme in type, kind, etc.; indifferent 3 having little or no decided color —*n.* 1 a neutral person or nation 2 a neutral color 3 *Mech.* a disengaged position of gears —**neu'tral·ly** *adv.*

neu'tral·ism' (-iz'əm) *n.* a policy of remaining neutral, esp. in international conflicts —**neu'tral·ist** *adj., n.*

neu·tral'i·ty (-tral'ə tē) *n.* 1 a being neutral 2 the status or policy of a neutral nation

neu·tral·ize (noo'trə līz') *vt.* **-ized', -iz'ing** 1 to declare (a nation, etc.) neutral in war 2 to destroy or counteract the effectiveness, force, etc. of —**neu'tral·i·za'tion** *n.* —**neu'tral·iz'er** *n.*

neutral spirits ethyl alcohol of 190 proof or over, used in blended whiskeys, liqueurs, etc.

neu·tri·no (noo trē'nō) *n., pl.* **-nos** ⟦It, little neutron⟧ either of two leptons having almost no mass

neu·tron (noo'trän') *n.* ⟦< NEUTRAL⟧ one of the elementary, uncharged particles of an atom

neutron bomb a small thermonuclear bomb, that would release large numbers of neutrons that kill people without destroying buildings, etc.

neutron star a collapsed star of extremely high density composed almost entirely of neutrons

Ne·vad·a (nə vad′ə, -väd′ə) Mountain State of the W U.S.: 110,540 sq. mi.; pop. 799,000; cap. Carson City: abbrev. **Nev.** —**Ne·vad′an** *adj., n.*

nev·er (nev′ər) *adv.* ⟦< OE *ne*, not + *æfre*, ever⟧ **1** not ever; at no time **2** not at all; in no case

nev′er·more′ *adv.* never again

nev′er-nev′er land an unreal or unrealistic place or situation

nev′er·the·less′ (-*thə* les′) *adv.* in spite of that; however

Ne·vis (nē′vis, nev′is) island of the West Indies: see ST. CHRISTOPHER

ne·vus (nē′vəs) *n., pl.* **ne′vi′** (-vī′) ⟦< L *naevus*⟧ a birthmark or mole

new (no͞o) *adj.* ⟦OE *niwe*⟧ **1** appearing, thought of, developed, made, etc. for the first time **2** different from (the) one in the past /a *new* hairdo/ **3** strange; unfamiliar **4** *a*) recently grown; fresh *b*) harvested early /*new* potatoes/ **5** unused **6** modern; recent **7** more; additional **8** starting as a repetition of a cycle, series, etc. /the *new* moon/ **9** having just reached a position, rank, etc. /a *new* arrival/ —*adv.* **1** again **2** newly; recently —**new′ness** *n.*

New Age |*often* **n- a-**| **1** of or pertaining to a cultural movement variously combining belief in reincarnation, astrology, meditation, etc. **2** designating or of a style of popular instrumental music intended to effect a serene mood

New·ark (no͞o′ərk) city in NE N.J.: pop. 329,000

New Bed·ford (bed′fərd) seaport in SE Mass.: pop. 98,000

new blood new people as a potential source of new ideas, vigor, etc.

new′born′ *adj.* **1** recently born **2** reborn

New Bruns·wick (brunz′wik) province of SE Canada: 27,834 sq. mi.; pop. 709,000; cap. Fredericton

new′com′er *n.* a recent arrival

New Deal the principles and policies adopted by President F. D. Roosevelt in the 1930's to advance economic recovery and social welfare

New Delhi capital of India, adjacent to the old city of Delhi: pop. 302,000

new·el (no͞o′əl) *n.* ⟦ult. < L *nux*, nut⟧ **1** the pillar around which the steps of a winding staircase turn **2** the post that supports the handrail of a flight of stairs: also **newel post**

New England the six NE States of the U.S.: Me., Vt., N.H., Mass., R.I., & Conn. —**New Eng′land·er**

new′fan′gled (-faŋ′gəld) *adj.* ⟦ME *newe*, new + *-fangel* < OE *fon*, to take⟧ new; novel: a humorously derogatory term

new′-fash′ioned *adj.* **1** recently come into fashion **2** new in form

New·found·land (no͞o′fənd lənd, -land′) province of Canada, including an island off the E coast & Labrador: 156,185 sq. mi.; pop. 568,000; cap. St. John's: abbrev. **Newf.**

New Guinea large island in the East Indies, north of Australia

New Hamp·shire (hamp′shir) New England State of the U.S.: 9,304 sq. mi.; pop. 921,000; cap. Concord —**New Hamp′shir·ite′**

New Ha·ven (hā′vən) city in S Conn.: pop. 126,000

New Jer·sey (jur′zē) Eastern State of the U.S.: 7,836 sq. mi.; pop. 7,364,000; cap. Trenton —**New Jer′sey·ite′**

new′ly *adv.* recently; lately

new′ly·wed′ *n.* a recently married person

New Mexico Mountain State of the SW U.S.: 121,666 sq. mi.; pop. 1,300,000; cap. Santa Fe —**New Mexican**

new moon the moon when it is between the earth and the sun, with its dark side toward the earth: it is followed by a thin crescent phase

New Or·le·ans (ôr′lē ənz, -lənz, -lēnz′) city & port in SE La.: pop. 557,000

New·port News (no͞o′pôrt′) seaport in SE Va.: pop. 145,000

news (no͞oz) *n.pl.* |*with sing. v.*| **1** new information; information previously unknown **2** *a*) recent happenings *b*) reports of these **3** a newscast —**make news** to do something apt to be reported as news

news′boy′ *n.* a boy who sells or delivers newspapers

news′cast′ *n.* a radio or television news broadcast —**news′cast′er** *n.*

news′deal′er *n.* a retailer of newspapers, magazines, etc.

news′let′ter *n.* a bulletin issued regularly to subscribers, employees, or members of a group, containing news of upcoming events, etc.

news′man′ (-man′, -mən) *n., pl.* **-men′** (-men′, -mən) a newscaster or reporter, esp. a male

news′pa′per *n.* a regular publication, usually daily or weekly, containing news, opinions, advertising, etc.

news′pa′per·man′ *n., pl.* **-men′** **1** a person, esp. a man, who works for a newspaper, esp. as a reporter, editor, etc. **2** a newspaper owner or publisher —**news′pa′per·wom′an**, *pl.* **-wom′en**, *n.fem.*

news′print′ *n.* a cheap paper used chiefly for newspapers

news′stand′ *n.* a stand at which newspapers, magazines, etc. are sold

news′wor′thy (-wur′*thē*) *adj.* timely and important or interesting

news′y *adj.* **-i·er, -i·est** |Colloq.| containing much news

newt (no͞ot, nyo͞ot) *n.* ⟦by merging of ME (*a*)*n eute*, a newt⟧ any of various small amphibious salamanders

New Testament the part of the Bible that contains the life and teachings of Jesus and his followers

new·ton (no͞o′tən) *n.* ⟦after fol.⟧ a unit of force

New·ton (no͞ot′'n), Sir **Isaac** 1642-1727; Eng. mathematician & natural philosopher

New World North and South America

New Year's (Day) Jan. 1

New Year's Eve the evening before New Year's Day

New York (yôrk) **1** State of the NE U.S.:

49,576 sq. mi.; pop. 17,557,000; cap. Albany **2** city & port in SE N.Y.: pop. 7,071,000 (met. area 10,803,000): often **New York City** —**New York'er**

New Zea·land (zē'lənd) country made up of two large islands in the S Pacific, southeast of Australia: 103,736 sq. mi.; pop. 3,305,000 —**New Zea'land·er**

next (nekst) ***adj.*** ⟦OE *neahst*, superl. of *neah*, nigh⟧ nearest; immediately preceding or following —***adv.*** **1** in the nearest time, place, rank, etc. **2** on the first subsequent occasion

next'-door' ***adj.*** in or at the next house, building, etc.

nex·us (neks'əs) ***n.***, *pl.* **nex'us·es** or **nex'us** ⟦L⟧ a connection, tie, or link

NF or **Nfld.** Newfoundland

NH or **N.H.** New Hampshire

Ni *Chem. symbol for* nickel

ni·a·cin (nī'ə sin) ***n.*** ⟦NI(COTINIC) AC(ID) + *-in*⟧ NICOTINIC ACID

Ni·ag·a·ra Falls (nī ag'ə rə, -ag'rə) large waterfall on a river (**Niagara**) flowing from Lake Erie into Lake Ontario

nib (nib) ***n.*** ⟦< ME *nebb*, a bird's beak⟧ a point, esp. a pen point

nib·ble (nib'əl) ***vt., vi.*** **-bled, -bling** ⟦ME *nebyllen*⟧ **1** to eat (food) with quick, small bites **2** to bite (*at*) lightly and intermittently —***n.*** a small bite —**nib'bler** ***n.***

nibs (nibz) ***n.*** ⟦< ?⟧ [Colloq.] a self-important person: preceded by *his* or *her*

Nic·a·ra·gua (nik'ə rä'gwə) country in Central America: 54,342 sq. mi.; pop. 3,342,000 —**Nic'a·ra'guan** ***adj., n.***

nice (nīs) ***adj.*** **nic'er, nic'est** ⟦< L *nescius*, ignorant⟧ **1** fastidious; refined **2** delicate; precise; subtle /a *nice* distinction/ **3** calling for care, tact, etc. **4** finely discriminating or minutely accurate **5** pleasant, attractive, kind, good, etc.: a generalized term of approval —**nice'ly** ***adv.***

ni·ce·ty (nī'sə tē) ***n.***, *pl.* **-ties** **1** precision; accuracy **2** fastidiousness; refinement **3** a subtle or minute detail, distinction, etc. **4** something choice or dainty

niche (nich) ***n.*** ⟦Fr < L *nidus*, a nest⟧ **1** a recess in a wall, for a statue, vase, etc. **2** an especially suitable place or position

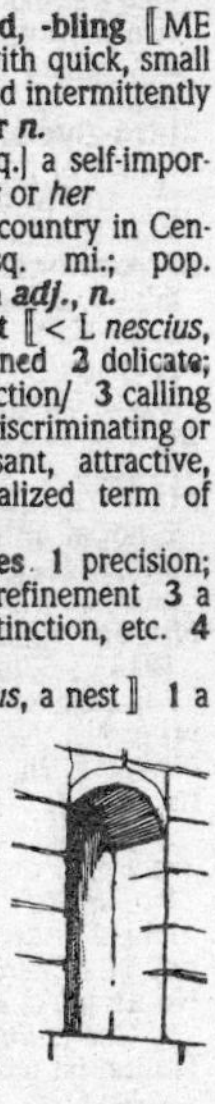
NICHE

nicht wahr? (nikht vär') ⟦Ger, not true?⟧ isn't that so?

nick (nik) ***n.*** ⟦ME *nyke*⟧ a small cut, chip, etc. made on a surface —***vt.*** **1** to make a nick or nicks in **2** to wound superficially —**in the nick of time** exactly when needed

nick·el (nik'əl) ***n.*** ⟦< Ger *kupfernickel*, copper devil: the copperlike ore contains no copper⟧ **1** a hard, silver-white, metallic chemical element, much used in alloys **2** a U.S. or Canadian coin of nickel and copper, equal to five cents

nick·el·o·de·on (nik'əl ō'dē ən) ***n.*** ⟦prec. + (*mel*)*odeon*, a small keyboard organ⟧ a coin-operated player piano or early type of jukebox

nick·er (nik'ər) ***vi., n.*** NEIGH

nick·name (nik'nām') ***n.*** ⟦by merging of ME (*a*)*n ekename*, a surname⟧ **1** a substitute, often descriptive, name given in fun, etc., as "Shorty" **2** a familiar form of a proper name, as "Dick" for "Richard" —***vt.*** **-named', -nam'ing** to give a nickname to

nic·o·tine (nik'ə tēn') ***n.*** ⟦Fr, after J. *Nicot*, 16th-c. Fr diplomat who introduced tobacco into France⟧ a poisonous alkaloid found in tobacco leaves

nic'o·tin'ic acid (-tin'ik) a member of the vitamin B complex

niece (nēs) ***n.*** ⟦< L *neptis*⟧ the daughter of one's brother or sister or of one's brother-in-law or sister-in-law

Nie·tzsche (nē'chə), **Fried·rich** (frē'drikh) 1844-1900; Ger. philosopher

nif·ty (nif'tē) ***adj.*** **-ti·er, -ti·est** ⟦prob. < *magnificent*⟧ [Slang] attractive, smart, stylish, etc.

Ni·ger (nī'jər) country in central Africa, north of Nigeria: 489,191 sq. mi.; pop. 6,715,000

Ni·ger·i·a (nī jir'ē ə) country on the W coast of Africa: 356,668 sq. mi.; pop. 105,448,000 —**Ni·ger'i·an** ***adj., n.***

nig·gard (nig'ərd) ***n.*** ⟦prob. < Scand⟧ a stingy person; miser —***adj.*** stingy; miserly —**nig'gard·ly** ***adj., adv.*** —**nig'gard·li·ness** ***n.***

nig·gle (nig'əl) ***vi.*** **-gled, -gling** ⟦prob. akin to Norw *nigla*⟧ to work fussily; be finicky —**nig'gler** ***n.*** —**nig'gling** ***adj., n.***

nigh (nī) ***adv., adj., prep.*** ⟦OE *neah*⟧ [Now Chiefly Dial.] NEAR

night (nīt) ***n.*** ⟦OE *niht*⟧ **1** the period of darkness from sunset to sunrise **2** any period or condition of darkness or gloom

night blindness imperfect vision in the dark or in dim light

night'cap' ***n.*** **1** a cap worn to bed **2** [Colloq.] an alcoholic drink taken just before going to bed

night'clothes' (-klōthz', -klōz') ***n.*** clothes to be worn in bed, as pajamas

night'club' ***n.*** a place of entertainment for drinking, dancing, etc. at night

night crawl'er a large earthworm that comes to the surface at night

night'dress' ***n.*** NIGHTGOWN

night'fall' ***n.*** the time in the evening when daylight is last visible; dusk

night'gown' ***n.*** a loose gown worn in bed by women or girls

night'hawk' ***n.*** **1** any of various nocturnal birds related to the whippoorwill **2** NIGHT OWL

night'ie (-ē) ***n.*** [Colloq.] a nightgown

night·in·gale (nīt''n gāl') ***n.*** ⟦< OE *niht*, night + *galan*, sing⟧ a small European thrush: the male sings melodiously, esp. at night

Night·in·gale (nīt''n gāl'), **Florence** 1820-1910; Eng. nurse: regarded as the founder of modern nursing

night life pleasure-seeking activity at night, as in nightclubs

night'ly ***adj.*** done or occurring every night —***adv.*** night after night; every night

night'mare' (-mer') ***n.*** ⟦ME < *niht*, night + *mare*, demon⟧ **1** a frightening dream **2** any frightening experience —**night'mar'·ish** ***adj.***

night owl a person who works at night or otherwise stays up late
night'shade' (-shād') ***n.*** 1 a chiefly tropical plant with five-lobed leaves and flowers of various colors 2 BELLADONNA
night'shirt' ***n.*** a kind of nightgown worn esp. by men or boys
night'spot' ***n.*** *colloq. var. of* NIGHTCLUB
night stand a small bedside table
night'stick' ***n.*** a policeman's club; billy
night'time' ***n.*** the time between dusk and dawn
night'wear' ***n.*** NIGHTCLOTHES
NIH National Institutes of Health
ni·hil·ism (nī'hi liz'əm, nī'ə-) ***n.*** ⟦< L *nihil*, nothing⟧ the general rejection of customary beliefs in morality, religion, etc. —**ni'hil·ist** ***n.*** —**ni'hil·is'tic** ***adj.***
Ni·hon (nē'hän') *Jpn. name for* JAPAN
nil (nil) ***n.*** ⟦L, contr. of *nihil*⟧ nothing
Nile (nīl) river in NE Africa, flowing through Egypt into the Mediterranean
nim·ble (nim'bəl) ***adj.*** **-bler, -blest** ⟦< OE *niman*, to take⟧ 1 quick-witted; alert 2 moving or acting quickly and lightly —**nim'·bly** ***adv.***
nim·bus (nim'bəs) ***n., pl.*** **-bi'** (-bī') or **-bus·es** ⟦L⟧ 1 orig., any rain-producing cloud 2 a halo around the head of a saint, etc., as on a picture
Nim·rod (nim'räd') *Bible* a mighty hunter
nin·com·poop (nin'kəm po͞op') ***n.*** ⟦< ?⟧ a stupid, silly person; fool
nine (nīn) ***adj., n.*** ⟦OE *nigon*⟧ one more than eight; 9; IX —**ninth** (nīnth) ***adj., n.***
nine'pins' ***n.pl.*** [*with sing. v.*] a British version of the game of tenpins, played with nine wooden pins
nine'teen' ***adj., n.*** nine more than ten; 19; XIX —**nine'teenth'** (-tēnth') ***adj., n.***
nine·ty (nīnt'ē) ***adj., n., pl.*** **-ties** nine times ten; 90; XC (or LXXXX) —**the nineties** the numbers or years, as of a century, from 90 through 99 —**nine'ti·eth** (-ith) ***adj., n.***
nin·ny (nin'ē) ***n., pl.*** **-nies** ⟦< (a)*n inn(ocent)*⟧ a fool; dolt
nip[1] (nip) ***vt.*** **nipped, nip'ping** ⟦prob. < earlier LowG *nippen*⟧ 1 to pinch or bite 2 to sever (shoots, etc.) by clipping 3 to check the growth of 4 to have a painful or injurious effect on because of cold —***n.*** 1 a nipping; pinch; bite 2 a stinging, as in cold air 3 stinging cold; frost —**nip and tuck** so close as to leave the outcome in doubt
nip[2] (nip) ***n.*** ⟦prob. < Du *nippen*, to sip⟧ a small drink of liquor —***vt., vi.*** **nipped, nip'·ping** to drink in nips
nip·per (nip'ər) ***n.*** 1 anything that nips 2 [*pl.*] pliers, pincers, etc. 3 the claw of a crab or lobster
nip·ple (nip'əl) ***n.*** ⟦prob. < earlier *neb*, a beak⟧ 1 the small protuberance on a breast or udder through which, in the female, the milk passes; teat 2 the teatlike part in the cap of a baby's bottle
Nip·pon (nēp'pôn'; *E* nip'än') *var. of* NIHON —**Nip'pon·ese'** (-ə nēz') ***n., adj.***
nip·py (nip'ē) ***adj.*** **-pi·er, -pi·est** 1 sharp; biting 2 cold in a stinging way
nir·va·na (nir vä'nə, nər-; -van'ə) ***n.*** ⟦< Sans⟧ [*also* **N-**] 1 *Buddhism* the state of perfect blessedness achieved by the absorption of the soul into the supreme spirit 2 great bliss
ni·sei (nē'sā') ***n., pl.*** **-sei'** or **-seis'** ⟦Jpn, second generation⟧ [*also* **N-**] a native citizen born of immigrant Japanese parents
nit (nit) ***n.*** ⟦OE *hnitu*⟧ 1 the egg of a louse or similar insect 2 a young louse, etc.
ni·ter (nīt'ər) ***n.*** ⟦< Gr *nitron*⟧ potassium nitrate or sodium nitrate, used in making explosives, fertilizers, etc.; saltpeter Also [Chiefly Brit.] **ni'tre**
nit-pick·ing (nit'pik'iŋ) ***adj., n.*** paying too much attention to petty details; niggling —**nit'-pick'er** ***n.***
ni·trate (nī'trāt') ***n.*** a salt of nitric acid, as sodium nitrate —***vt.*** **-trat'ed, -trat'ing** to combine with nitric acid or, esp., to make into a nitrate
ni·tric acid (nī'trik) a colorless, corrosive acid containing nitrogen
ni·tro·cel·lu·lose (nī'trō sel'yo͞o lōs') ***n.*** a substance obtained by treating cellulose with nitric acid, used in making explosives, lacquers, etc.
ni·tro·gen (nī'trə jən) ***n.*** ⟦< Fr: see NITER & -GEN⟧ a colorless, odorless gaseous chemical element forming nearly four fifths of the atmosphere —**ni·trog'e·nous** (-träj'ə nəs) ***adj.***
ni·tro·glyc·er·in or **ni·tro·glyc·er·ine** (nī'trō glis'ər in, -trə-) ***n.*** a thick, explosive oil, prepared by treating glycerin with nitric and sulfuric acids: used in making dynamite
ni·trous oxide (nī'trəs) a colorless gas containing nitrogen, used as an anesthetic and in aerosols
nit·ty-grit·ty (nit'ē grit'ē) ***n.*** [Slang] the actual, basic facts, issues, etc.
nit'wit' ***n.*** ⟦? NIT + WIT[1]⟧ a stupid or silly person
nix (niks) ***adv.*** ⟦Ger *nichts*⟧ [Slang] 1 no 2 not at all —***interj.*** [Slang] 1 stop! 2 I forbid, disagree, etc. —***vt.*** [Slang] to disapprove of or put a stop to
Nix·on (nik'sən), **Richard M(ilhous)** 1913- ; 37th president of the U.S. (1969-74): resigned
NJ or **N.J.** New Jersey
NM or **N.M.** New Mexico Also **N.Mex.**
no (nō) ***adv.*** ⟦< OE *ne a*, not ever⟧ 1 not at all [*no* worse] 2 nay; not so: used to deny, refuse, or disagree —***adj.*** not any; not one [*no* errors] —***n., pl.*** **noes** or **nos** 1 a refusal or denial 2 a negative vote or voter
no. ⟦L *numero*⟧ number
No·ah (nō'ə) *Bible* the patriarch commanded by God to build the ARK (sense 3)
No·bel·ist (nō bel'ist) ***n.*** one who has won a Nobel prize
No·bel prizes (nō bel') ⟦after A. B. *Nobel*, 19th-c. Swed inventor who established them⟧ annual international prizes given for distinction in physics, chemistry, economics, medicine, and literature, and for promoting peace
no·bil·i·ty (nō bil'ə tē) ***n., pl.*** **-ties** 1 a being noble 2 high rank in society 3 the class of people of noble rank
no·ble (nō'bəl) ***adj.*** **-bler, -blest** ⟦< L *nobilis*, well-known⟧ 1 famous or renowned 2 having high moral qualities 3 excellent 4 grand; stately 5 of high hereditary rank —***n.*** one having hereditary rank

or title —**no'ble·ness** *n.* —**no·bly** (nō'blē) *adv.*

no'ble·man (-mən) *n., pl.* **-men** a member of the nobility; peer

no·blesse o·blige (nō bles' ō blēzh') ⟦Fr, nobility obliges⟧ the inferred obligation of people of high rank to behave nobly toward others

no·bod·y (nō'bäd'ē; -bud'ē, -bəd ē) *pron.* not anybody; no one —*n., pl.* **-ies** a person of no importance

noc·tur·nal (näk tur'nəl) *adj.* ⟦< L *nox*, night⟧ 1 of the night 2 functioning, done, or active during the night —**noc·tur'nal·ly** *adv.*

noc·turne (näk'turn') *n.* ⟦Fr⟧ a romantic or dreamy musical composition thought appropriate to night

nod (näd) *vi.* **nod'ded, nod'ding** ⟦ME *nodden*⟧ 1 to bend the head forward quickly, as in agreement, greeting, etc. 2 to let the head fall forward because of drowsiness —*vt.* 1 to bend (the head) forward quickly 2 to signify (assent, etc.) by doing this —*n.* a nodding

node (nōd) *n.* ⟦L *nodus*⟧ 1 a knot; knob; swelling 2 that part of a stem from which a leaf starts to grow —**nod·al** (nōd''l) *adj.*

nod·ule (näj'o͞ol') *n.* ⟦L *nodulus*⟧ a small knot or rounded lump

No·el or **No·ël** (nō el') *n.* ⟦Fr < L *natalis*, natal⟧ CHRISTMAS

no'-fault' *adj.* 1 designating a form of automobile insurance in which those injured collect damages without blame being fixed 2 designating a form of divorce granted without blame being charged

nog·gin (näg'in) *n.* ⟦prob. < Brit dial. *nog*, strong ale⟧ 1 a small cup or mug 2 [Colloq.] the head

no'-good' *adj.* [Slang] contemptible

noise (noiz) *n.* ⟦< OFr⟧ 1 clamor; din 2 sound; esp., any loud, disagreeable sound —*vt.* **noised, nois'ing** to spread (a report, rumor, etc.)

noise'less *adj.* with little or no noise; very quiet —**noise'less·ly** *adv.*

noi·some (noi'səm) *adj.* ⟦see ANNOY & -SOME[1]⟧ 1 injurious to health; harmful 2 foul-smelling

nois·y (noiz'ē) *adj.* **-i·er, -i·est** 1 making noise 2 full of noise —**nois'i·ly** *adv.* —**nois'i·ness** *n.*

no-load (nō'lōd') *adj.* designating mutual funds charging no commissions on sales

no·mad (nō'mad') *n.* ⟦< Gr *nemein*, to pasture⟧ 1 any of a people having no permanent home, but moving about constantly, as in search of pasture 2 a wanderer —**no·mad'ic** *adj.*

no man's land the unoccupied region separating opposing armies

nom de plume (näm' də plo͞om') ⟦Fr⟧ a pen name

no·men·cla·ture (nō'mən klā'chər) *n.* ⟦< L *nomen*, a name + *calare*, to call⟧ the system of names used in a science, etc. or for the parts of a device

-nom·ics (näm'iks) *combining form* economics Also **-omics**

nom·i·nal (näm'ə nəl) *adj.* ⟦< L *nomen*, a name⟧ 1 of or like a name 2 in name only, not in fact /a *nominal* leader/ 3 relatively very small /a *nominal* fee/ —**nom'i·nal·ly** *adv.*

nom'i·nate' (-nāt') *vt.* **-nat'ed, -nat'ing** ⟦< L *nomen*, a name⟧ 1 to appoint to an office or position 2 to name as a candidate for election —**nom'i·na'tion** *n.*

nom'i·na·tive (-nə tiv) *n. Gram.* the case of the subject of a verb

nom'i·nee' (-ə nē') *n.* a person who is nominated

non- ⟦< L *non*, not⟧ *prefix* not: less emphatic than IN-[2] and UN-, which often give a word a strong opposite or reverse meaning The terms in the following list will be understood if "not" is used before the meaning of the base word:

nonabrasive
nonabsorbent
nonactive
nonaddictive
nonadministrative
nonaggression
nonaggressive
nonalcoholic
nonallergenic
nonallergic
nonassignable
nonathletic
nonattendance
nonautomotive
nonavailability
nonbasic
nonbeliever
nonbelligerent
nonbreakable
nonburnable
non-Catholic
nonchargeable
nonclerical
nonclinical
noncollectable
noncombustible
noncommercial
noncommunicable
non-Communist
noncompeting
noncompetitive
noncompliance
noncomplying
nonconducting
nonconforming
non-Congressional
nonconsecutive
nonconstructive
noncontagious
noncontributory
noncontroversial
nonconvertible
noncorroding
noncorrosive
noncriminal
noncritical
noncrystalline
noncumulative
nondeductible
nondelivery
nondepartmental
nondepreciating
nondestructive
nondetachable
nondisciplinary
nondiscrimination
nondramatic
nondrinker
nondrying
noneducational
noneffective
nonenforceable
non-English
nonessential
nonexchangeable
nonexclusive
nonexempt
nonexistence
nonexistent
nonexplosive
nonfactual
nonfading
nonfat
nonfatal
nonfiction
nonfictional
nonflammable
nonflowering
nonfluctuating
nonflying
nonfreezing
nonfunctional
nongovernmental
nongranular
nonhazardous
nonhereditary
nonhuman
nonidentical
noninclusive
nonindependent
nonindustrial
noninfected
noninflammatory
noninflationary
nonintellectual
noninterchangeable
noninterference
nonintoxicating
nonirritating
nonjudicial
nonlegal
nonliterary
nonmagnetic
nonmalignant
nonmember
nonmigratory
nonmilitant
nonmilitary
nonnarcotic
nonnegotiable
nonnumerical
nonobjective
nonobligatory
nonobservance
nonobservant
nonoccupational
nonoccurrence
nonofficial
nonoperational
nonoperative
nonpaying
nonpayment

nonperishable
nonphysical
nonpoisonous
nonpolitical
nonporous
nonprejudicial
nonproductive
nonprofessional
nonprofitable
nonpunishable
nonracial
nonreactive
nonreciprocal
nonreciprocating
nonrecoverable
nonrecurring
nonredeemable
nonrefillable
nonreligious
nonrenewable
nonrepresentational
nonresidential
nonresidual
nonresistant
nonreturnable
nonrhythmic
nonrigid
nonsalaried
nonscientific
nonscoring
nonseasonal
nonsecular
nonsensitive
nonsmoker
nonsocial
nonspeaking
nonspecializing
nonspiritual
nonstaining
nonstandard
nonsticking
nonstrategic
nonstriking
nonstructural
nonsuccessive
nonsupporting
nonsustaining
nonsympathizer
nontarnishable
nontaxable
nontechnical
nontheatrical
nonthinking
nontoxic
nontransferable
nontransparent
nontropical
nonuniform
nonuser
nonvenomous
nonverbal
nonvirulent
nonvocal
nonvocational
nonvoter
nonvoting
nonwhite
nonyielding

nona- *combining form* nine

non·age (nän′ij, nōn′ij) ***n.*** ⟦see NON- & AGE⟧ the state of being under full legal age

non·a·ge·nar·i·an (nän′ə jə ner′ē ən) ***n.*** ⟦< L *nonaginta*, ninety⟧ a person between the ages of 90 and 100

non′a·ligned′ ***adj.*** not aligned with either side in a conflict of power, especially power politics —**non′a·lign′ment** ***n.***

non′-book′ ***n.*** a book of little worth, published to exploit some consumer demand

nonce (näns) ***n.*** ⟦by merging of ME (*for then*) *ones*, lit., (for the) once⟧ the present use, occasion, or time: chiefly in **for the nonce**

nonce word a word coined and used for a single occasion

non·cha·lant (nän′shə länt′) ***adj.*** ⟦Fr, ult. < L *non*, not + *calere*, be warm⟧ **1** without warmth or enthusiasm **2** casually indifferent —**non′cha·lance′** ***n.*** —**non′cha·lant′ly** ***adv.***

non·com (nän′käm′) ***n.*** [Colloq.] *short for* NONCOMMISSIONED OFFICER

non·com·bat·ant (nän′käm′bə tənt) ***n.*** **1** a member of the armed forces not engaged in actual combat **2** any civilian in wartime

non′com·mis′sioned officer an enlisted person of any of various grades in the armed forces: in the U.S. Army, from corporal to sergeant major inclusive

non′com·mit′tal (-kə mit′l) ***adj.*** not committing one to a definite point of view or course of action

non com·pos men·tis (nän′ käm pōs men′tis) ⟦L⟧ *Law* not of sound mind

non′con·duc′tor ***n.*** a substance that does not readily transmit sound, heat, or, esp., electricity

non′con·form′ist ***n.*** **1** one who does not conform to prevailing attitudes, behavior, etc. **2** [N-] a British Protestant who is not Anglican —**non′con·form′i·ty** ***n.***

non·dair·y (nän′der′ē) ***adj.*** containing no milk or milk products

non·de·script (nän′di skript′, nän′di skript′) ***adj.*** ⟦< L *non*, not + *describere*, describe⟧ belonging to no definite class or type; hard to classify or describe

none (nun) ***pron.*** ⟦< OE *ne*, not + *an*, one⟧ **1** no one; not anyone **2** [*with pl. v.*] not any /there are *none* on the table/ —***n.*** not any (of); no part /I want *none* of it/ —***adv.*** not at all /*none* the worse for wear/

non·en·ti·ty (nän′en′tə tē) ***n.***, *pl.* **-ties** a person or thing of little or no importance

none·such (nun′such′) ***n.*** a person or thing unrivaled or unequaled

none·the·less (nun′*thə* les′) ***adv.*** nevertheless Also **none the less**

non·e·vent (nän′ē vent′) ***n.*** [Colloq.] an event that is boring or deliberately staged, as for publicity

non′fer′rous (-fer′əs) ***adj.*** **1** not containing iron **2** designating or of metals other than iron

non′in·ter·ven′tion (-in′tər ven′shən) ***n.*** refusal to interfere; esp., a refusal by one nation to interfere in another's affairs

non′judg·men′tal ***adj.*** objective; tolerant

non′met′al ***n.*** any chemical element, as oxygen, carbon, nitrogen, fluorine, etc., lacking the characteristics of a metal —**non′me·tal′lic** ***adj.***

no′-no′ ***n.***, *pl.* **-nos′** [Slang] something forbidden or considered unwise to do, say, etc.

no′-non′sense ***adj.*** not allowing nonsense; practical and serious

non·pa·reil (nän′pə rel′) ***adj.*** ⟦Fr < *non*, not + *pareil*, equal⟧ unequaled; unrivaled; peerless

non′par′ti·san ***adj.*** not partisan; esp., not connected with any single political party

non′per′son ***n.*** a person officially ignored by the government

non·plus (nän′plus′, nän′plus′) ***vt.*** **-plused′** or **-plussed′**, **-plus′ing** or **-plus′sing** ⟦L *non*, not + *plus*, more⟧ to greatly perplex or bewilder

non′prof′it ***adj.*** not intending or intended to earn a profit

non′res′i·dent ***adj.*** not residing in the locality where one works, attends school, etc. —***n.*** a nonresident person

non′re·stric′tive (-ri strik′tiv) ***adj.*** *Gram.* designating a clause, phrase, or word felt as not essential to the sense, usually set off by commas (Ex.: John, *who is tall*, is Bill's brother)

non′sched′uled ***adj.*** licensed for commercial air flights as demand warrants rather than on a schedule

non′sec·tar′i·an (-sek ter′ē ən) ***adj.*** not confined to any specific religion

non·sense (nän′sens′, -səns) ***n.*** words, actions, etc. that are absurd or meaningless —***interj.*** how absurd!: an exclamation —**non·sen′si·cal** ***adj.***

non se·qui·tur (nän′ sek′wi tər) ⟦L, it does not follow⟧ **1** *Logic* a conclusion which does not follow from the premises **2** a remark having no bearing on what has just been said

non′skid′ ***adj.*** having a surface made so as

to reduce slipping or skidding: said of a tire, flooring, etc.

non'-start'er *n.* [Slang] **1** an expected occurrence, etc. that fails to materialize **2** a worthless idea

non'stop' *adj., adv.* without a stop

non'sup·port' *n.* failure to provide for a legal dependent

non'un'ion *adj.* **1** not belonging to a labor union **2** not made or serviced under labor-union conditions **3** refusing to recognize a labor union

non'vi'o·lence *n.* an abstaining from violence, as in efforts to obtain civil rights —**non'vi'o·lent** *adj.*

noo·dle[1] (no͞od''l) *n.* ⟦< ?⟧ [Slang] the head

noo·dle[2] (no͞od''l) *n.* ⟦Ger *nudel*⟧ a flat, narrow strip of dry dough, usually made with egg and served in soup, etc.

nook (no͝ok) *n.* ⟦ME *nok*⟧ **1** a corner, esp. of a room **2** a small, secluded spot

noon (no͞on) *n.* ⟦< L *nona* (*hora*), ninth (hour)⟧ twelve o'clock in the daytime; midday —*adj.* of or at noon Also **noon'time'** or **noon'day'**

no one not anybody; nobody

noose (no͞os) *n.* ⟦< L *nodus*, knot⟧ a loop in a rope, etc., formed by a slipknot, the loop tightening as the rope is pulled

nor (nôr) *conj.* ⟦ME < *ne-*, not, + *or*, other⟧ and not; and not either /I can neither go *nor* stay/

Nor·dic (nôr'dik) *adj.* ⟦OE *north*, north⟧ of a Caucasoid physical type exemplified by the tall, blond Scandinavians

Nor·folk (nôr'fək) seaport in SE Va.: pop. 267,000

norm (nôrm) *n.* ⟦L *norma*, rule⟧ a standard or model; esp., the standard of achievement of a large group

nor·mal (nôr'məl) *adj.* **1** conforming with an accepted standard or norm; natural; usual **2** average in intelligence, etc. —*n.* **1** anything normal **2** the usual state, amount, etc. —**nor'mal·cy** (-sē) or **nor·mal'i·ty** (-mal'ə tē) *n.* —**nor'mal·ize'**, **-ized'**, **-iz'ing**, *vt., vi.* —**nor'mal·i·za'tion** *n.*

nor'mal·ly *adv.* **1** in a normal manner **2** under normal circumstances

Nor·man (nôr'mən) *n.* ⟦< OFr⟧ **1** any of the people of Normandy who conquered England in 1066 **2** a native of Normandy —*adj.* of Normandy, the Normans, their language, etc.

Nor·man·dy (nôr'mən dē) historical region in NW France, on the English Channel

norm·a·tive (nôr'mə tiv) *adj.* of or establishing a norm

Norse (nôrs) *adj., n.* ⟦prob. < Du *noord*, north⟧ **1** SCANDINAVIAN **2** (of) the Scandinavian group of languages

Norse'man (-mən) *n., pl.* **-men** any of the ancient Scandinavian peoples

north (nôrth) *n.* ⟦OE⟧ **1** the direction to the right of one facing the sunset (0° or 360° on the compass) **2** [*often* **N-**] a region in or toward this direction —*adj.* **1** in, of, or toward the north **2** from the north —*adv.* in or toward the north —**the North** that part of the U.S. north of Md., the Ohio River, and Mo.

North America N continent in the Western Hemisphere: 9,366,000 sq. mi.; pop. 366,628,000 —**North American**

North Car·o·li·na (kar'ə lī'nə) Southern State of the SE U.S.: 52,712 sq. mi.; pop. 5,881,000; cap. Raleigh —**North Car'o·lin'i·an** (-lin'ē ən)

North Da·ko·ta (də kō'tə) Middle Western State of the U.S.: 70,665 sq. mi.; pop. 653,000; cap. Bismarck —**North Da·ko'tan**

north'east' *n.* **1** the direction halfway between north and east **2** a region in or toward this direction —*adj.* **1** in, of, or toward the northeast **2** from the northeast —*adv.* in, toward, or from the northeast —**north'east'er·ly** *adj., adv.* —**north'east'ern** *adj.* —**north'east'ward** *adj., adv.* —**north'east'wards** *adv.*

north'er·ly (-lē) *adj., adv.* **1** toward the north **2** from the north

north·ern (nôr'*th*ərn) *adj.* **1** in, of, or toward the north **2** from the north **3** [*often* **N-**] of the north

north'ern·er *n.* a native or inhabitant of the north

Northern Hemisphere that half of the earth north of the equator

Northern Ireland division of the United Kingdom, in NE Ireland: 5,462 sq. mi.; pop. 1,573,000

northern lights [*also* **N- L-**] the aurora borealis

North Pole the northern end of the earth's axis

North Sea arm of the Atlantic, between Great Britain & the N European mainland

North Star POLARIS

north'ward' (-wərd') *adv., adj.* toward the north Also **north'wards** *adv.*

north'west' *n.* **1** the direction halfway between north and west **2** a region in or toward this direction —*adj.* **1** in, of, or toward the northwest **2** from the northwest —*adv.* in, toward, or from the northwest —**north'west'er·ly** *adj., adv.* —**north'west'ern** *adj.* —**north'west'ward** *adj., adv.* —**north'west'wards** *adv.*

Northwest Territories division of N Canada: 1,304,903 sq. mi.; pop. 52,000

North York (yôrk) city in SE Ontario, Canada: part of metropolitan Toronto: pop. 556,000

Norw. **1** Norway **2** Norwegian

Nor·way (nôr'wā') country in N Europe: 125,064 sq. mi.; pop. 4,165,000

Nor·we·gian (nôr wē'jən) *n.* **1** the language of Norway **2** a native or inhabitant of Norway —*adj.* of Norway, its people, language, etc.

nose (nōz) *n.* ⟦OE *nosu*⟧ **1** the part of the face above the mouth, having two openings for breathing and smelling; in animals, the snout, muzzle, etc. **2** the sense of smell **3** anything like a nose in shape or position —*vt.* **nosed, nos'ing** **1** to discover as by smell **2** to nuzzle **3** to push (a way, etc.) with the front forward —*vi.* **1** to pry inquisitively **2** to move forward —**nose out** **1** to defeat by a very small margin **2** to discover, as by smelling —**on the nose** [Slang] precisely; exactly

nose'bleed' *n.* a bleeding from the nose

nose cone the cone-shaped foremost part of a rocket or missile

nose dive 1 a swift, steep downward plunge of an airplane, nose first 2 any sudden, sharp drop, as in profits —**nose'-dive'**, **-dived'**, **-div'ing**, *vi.*

nose drops medication administered through the nose with a dropper

nose·gay (nōz'gā') *n.* ⟦NOSE + GAY (obs. sense "bright object")⟧ a small bouquet

nose guard *Football* the defensive lineman directly opposite the offensive center Also **nose tackle**

nosh (näsh) *vt., vi.* ⟦< Yidd < Ger *nashchen*, to nibble⟧ [Slang] to eat (a snack) —*n.* [Slang] a snack —**nosh'er** *n.*

no'-show' *n.* one who fails to claim or cancel a reservation

nos·tal·gi·a (näs tal'jə) *n.* ⟦< Gr *nostos*, a return + -ALGIA⟧ a longing for something far away or long ago —**nos·tal'gic** (-jik) *adj.*

nos·tril (näs'trəl) *n.* ⟦< OE *nosu*, the nose + *thyrel*, a hole⟧ either of the external openings of the nose

nos·trum (näs'trəm) *n.* ⟦L, ours⟧ 1 a quack medicine 2 a panacea

nos·y or **nos·ey** (nō'zē) *adj.* **-i·er**, **-i·est** [Colloq.] prying; inquisitive

not (nät) *adv.* ⟦< ME *nought*⟧ in no manner, degree, etc.: a word expressing negation or the idea of *no*

no·ta·ble (nōt'ə bəl) *adj.* ⟦< L *notare*, to note⟧ worthy of notice; remarkable; outstanding —*n.* a person of distinction —**no'ta·bly** *adv.*

no·ta·rize (nōt'ə rīz') *vt.* **-rized'**, **-riz'ing** to certify or attest (a document) as a notary public

no'ta·ry (-rē) *n., pl.* **-ries** ⟦< L *notare*, to note⟧ an official authorized to certify or attest documents, take affidavits, etc. In full **notary public**

no·ta·tion (nō tā'shən) *n.* 1 the use of signs or symbols to represent words, quantities, etc. 2 any such system of signs or symbols, as in mathematics, music, etc. 3 a brief note or noting

notch (näch) *n.* ⟦prob. < ME (*a*)*n oche*, a notch⟧ 1 a V-shaped cut in an edge or surface 2 a narrow pass with steep sides 3 [Colloq.] a step; degree —*vt.* to cut a notch or notches in

note (nōt) *n.* ⟦< L *nota*, a mark⟧ 1 a distinguishing feature /a *note* of sadness/ 2 importance, distinction, etc. /a person of *note*/ 3 a brief writing to aid the memory; memorandum 4 a comment or explanation; annotation 5 notice; heed /worthy of *note*/ 6 a short, informal letter 7 a written acknowledgment of a debt 8 a cry or call, as of a bird 9 *Music a*) a tone of definite pitch *b*) a symbol for a tone, indicating its duration and pitch —*vt.* **not'ed**, **not'ing** 1 to heed; observe 2 to set down in writing 3 to mention particularly —**compare notes** to exchange views; discuss

note'book' *n.* a book in which notes, or memorandums, are kept

not·ed (nōt'id) *adj.* distinguished; renowned; eminent

note'wor'thy *adj.* worthy of note; outstanding; remarkable

noth·ing (nuth'iŋ) *n.* ⟦OE *na thing*⟧ 1 no thing; not anything 2 nothingness 3 a thing that does not exist 4 a person or thing considered of little or no importance 5 a zero; cipher —*adv.* not at all; in no way —**for nothing** 1 free 2 in vain 3 without reason

noth'ing·ness *n.* 1 nonexistence 2 insignificance 3 unconsciousness or death

no·tice (nōt'is) *n.* ⟦see NOTE⟧ 1 announcement or warning 2 a brief article about a book, play, etc. 3 a sign giving some public information, warning, etc. 4 attention; heed 5 a formal warning of intention to end an agreement or contract at a certain time —*vt.* **-ticed**, **-tic·ing** 1 to mention; refer to 2 to observe; pay attention to —**take notice** to become aware; observe

no'tice·a·ble *adj.* readily noticed; conspicuous —**no'tice·a·bly** *adv.*

no·ti·fy (nōt'ə fī') *vt.* **-fied'**, **-fy'ing** ⟦< L *notus*, known + *facere*, make⟧ to give notice to; inform —**no'ti·fi·ca'tion** (-fi kā'shən) *n.*

no·tion (nō'shən) *n.* ⟦see NOTE⟧ 1 a general idea 2 a belief; opinion 3 an inclination; whim 4 [*pl.*] small, useful articles, as needles, thread, etc., sold in a store —**no'tion·al** *adj.*

no·to·ri·e·ty (nōt'ə rī'ə tē) *n.* a being notorious

no·to·ri·ous (nō tôr'ē əs) *adj.* ⟦see NOTE⟧ widely known, esp. unfavorably —**no·to'ri·ous·ly** *adv.*

no'-trump' *n. Bridge* a bid to play with no suit being trumps

not·with·stand·ing (nät'with stan'diŋ) *prep.* in spite of —*adv.* nevertheless —*conj.* although

nou·gat (nōō'gət) *n.* ⟦< Prov *noga*, nut⟧ a confection of sugar paste with nuts

nought (nôt) *n.* ⟦< OE *ne*, not + *awiht*, aught⟧ *Arith.* the figure zero (0)

noun (noun) *n.* ⟦< L *nomen*, a name⟧ *Gram.* a word that names or denotes a person, thing, action, etc.

nour·ish (nur'ish) *vt.* ⟦< L *nutrire*⟧ 1 to provide with substances necessary to life and growth 2 to foster; promote —**nour'ish·ing** *adj.*

nour'ish·ment (-mənt) *n.* 1 a nourishing or being nourished 2 food

nou·veau riche (nōō'vō rēsh') *pl.* **nou·veaux riches** (nōō'vō rēsh') ⟦Fr⟧ a newly rich person, esp. one lacking cultural taste, or social grace

nou·velle cuisine (nōō vel') ⟦Fr⟧ a style of French cooking using a minimum of fat and starch, and very fresh ingredients, often in unusual combinations

no·va (nō'və) *n., pl.* **-vae** (-vē) or **-vas** ⟦< L, new⟧ a star that brightens intensely and then gradually dims

No·va Sco·tia (nō'və skō'shə) province of SE Canada: 21,425 sq. mi.; pop. 873,000; cap. Halifax —**No'va Sco'tian**

nov·el (näv'əl) *adj.* ⟦< L dim. of *novus*, new⟧ new and unusual —*n.* a relatively long fictional prose narrative

nov'el·ette' (-əl et') *n.* a short novel

nov'el·ist *n.* one who writes novels

nov'el·ize' (-īz') *vt.* **-ized'**, **-iz'ing** to make into or like a novel; specif., to use (a film script) as the basis of a novel

nov'el·ty (-tē) ***n.***, *pl.* **-ties** 1 the quality of being novel; newness 2 something new, fresh, or unusual 3 a small, often cheap, cleverly made article: *usually used in pl.*

No·vem·ber (nō vem'bər) ***n.*** ⟦< L *novem*, nine: ninth month in Roman year⟧ the 11th month of the year, having 30 days: abbrev. **Nov.**

no·ve·na (nō vē'nə) ***n.*** ⟦< L *novem*, nine⟧ *R.C.Ch.* special prayers and devotions for nine days

nov·ice (näv'is) ***n.*** ⟦< L *novus*, new⟧ 1 a person on probation in a religious order before taking final vows 2 a person new to something; beginner

no·vi·ti·ate (nō vish'ē it) ***n.*** the period or state of being a novice

No·vo·cain (nō'və kān') ⟦L *nov(us)*, new + (C)OCAIN(E)⟧ *trademark for* PROCAINE Also sp. **Novocaine**

now (nou) ***adv.*** ⟦OE *nu*⟧ 1 *a)* at the present time *b)* at once 2 at that time; then 3 with things as they are /*now* we'll never know/ **—*conj.*** since; seeing that **—*n.*** the present time /that's all for *now*/ **—*adj.*** of the present time **—just now** recently **—now and then** (or **again**) occasionally

now'a·days' (-ə dāz') ***adv.*** in these days; at the present time

no·way (nō'wā') ***adv.*** by no means; not at all: now often **no way**, used with the force of an interjection

no·where (nō'hwer', -wer') ***adv.*** not in, at, or to any place **—nowhere near** not by a wide margin

no-win (nō'win') ***adj.*** designating or of a situation, policy, etc. that cannot lead to success no matter what measures are taken

no'wise' (-wīz') ***adv.*** in no manner; noway

nox·ious (näk'shəs) ***adj.*** ⟦< L *nocere*, to hurt⟧ harmful to health or morals; injurious or unwholesome

noz·zle (näz'əl) ***n.*** ⟦dim. of *nose*⟧ the spout at the end of a hose, pipe, etc.

Np *Chem. symbol for* neptunium

NS or **N.S.** Nova Scotia

-n't not Used in combination with certain verbs /*aren't*/

NT or **N.T.** New Testament

nth (enth) ***adj.*** of the indefinitely large or small quantity represented by *n*

nt. wt. net weight

nu (nōō, nyōō) ***n.*** the 13th letter of the Greek alphabet (Ν, ν)

nu·ance (nōō'äns') ***n.*** ⟦Fr < *nuer*, to shade⟧ a slight variation in tone, color, meaning, etc. **—nu'anced *adj.***

nub (nub) ***n.*** ⟦var. of *knub*, knob⟧ 1 a lump or small piece 2 [Colloq.] the main point; gist

nub·bin (nub'in) ***n.*** ⟦dim. of prec.⟧ 1 a small ear of corn 2 a small piece

nub·by (nub'ē) ***adj.*** **-bi·er, -bi·est** having a rough, knotted surface /a *nubby* fabric/

nu·bile (nōō'bil, -bīl') ***adj.*** ⟦< L *nubere*, marry⟧ 1 marriageable 2 sexually attractive Said of a young woman

nu·cle·ar (nōō'klē ər) ***adj.*** 1 of, like or forming a nucleus 2 of or relating to atomic nuclei /*nuclear* energy/ 3 of or operated by the use of atomic energy /*nuclear* weapons/ 4 of or involving nuclear weapons /*nuclear* warfare/

nuclear energy the energy released from an atom in nuclear reactions, esp. in nuclear fission or nuclear fusion

nuclear family a basic social unit consisting of parents and their children living in one household

nuclear fission the splitting of the nuclei of atoms, accompanied by conversion of part of the mass into energy: the principle of the atomic bomb

nuclear fusion the fusion of lightweight atomic nuclei into a nucleus of heavier mass with a resultant loss in the combined mass converted into energy: the principle of the hydrogen bomb

nuclear physics the branch of physics dealing with the structure of atomic nuclei, nuclear forces, etc.

nuclear reactor a device for creating a controlled nuclear chain reaction using atomic fuel, as for the production of energy

nuclear winter a hypothetical scenario following a major nuclear war in which the atmosphere will be clouded with radioactive smoke, dust, etc. for a long time causing loss of sunlight, frigid temperatures, destruction of life forms, etc.

nu·cle·ate (nōō'klē it; *for v.*, -āt') ***adj.*** having a nucleus **—*vt.*, *vi.*** **-at'ed, -at'ing** to form into a nucleus **—nu'cle·a'tion *n.***

nu·cle·ic acid (nōō klē'ik) any of a group of essential complex organic acids found in all living cells: the two major types are DNA and RNA

nucleo- *combining form* 1 nucleus 2 nuclear 3 nucleic acid Also **nucle-**

nu·cle·o·lus (nōō klē'ə ləs) ***n.***, *pl.* **-li'** (-lī') ⟦< LL, dim. of L *nucleus*⟧ a conspicuous, usually spherical, dense body in the nucleus of most cells, consisting of protein and RNA

nu·cle·us (nōō'klē əs) ***n.***, *pl.* **-cle·i'** (-ī') or **-cle·us·es** ⟦< L, kernel⟧ 1 a central thing or part around which others are grouped; core 2 any center of growth or development 3 the central part of an atom 4 the central mass of protoplasm in a cell

nude (nōōd) ***adj.*** ⟦L *nudus*⟧ naked; bare **—*n.*** 1 a nude human figure, esp. in a work of art 2 the state of being nude /in the *nude*/ **—nu'di·ty *n.***

nudge (nuj) ***vt.*** **nudged, nudg'ing** ⟦< ?⟧ to push gently, esp. with the elbow, in order to get the attention of, hint slyly, etc. **—*n.*** a gentle push

nud'ism' ***n.*** the practice or cult of going nude **—nud'ist *n.*, *adj.***

nu·ga·to·ry (nōō'gə tôr'ē) ***adj.*** ⟦< L *nugari*, to trifle⟧ 1 trifling; worthless 2 not operative; invalid

nug·get (nug'ət) ***n.*** ⟦prob. < dial. *nug*, a lump⟧ a lump; esp. of native gold

nui·sance (nōō'səns, nyōō'-) ***n.*** ⟦< L *nocere*, annoy⟧ an act, thing, or person causing trouble, annoyance, etc.

nuke (nōōk) ***n.*** ⟦< NUCLEAR⟧ [Slang] a nuclear weapon **—*vt.*** **nuked, nuk'ing** [Slang] to attack with nuclear weapons

null (nul) ***adj.*** ⟦< L *nullus*, none⟧ 1 without legal force; invalid: usually in the phrase

null and void 2 amounting to naught 3 of no value, effect, etc.

nul·li·fy (nul'ə fī') *vt.* **-fied'**, **-fy'ing** ⟦< L *nullus*, none + *facere*, to make⟧ 1 to make legally null or valueless 2 to cancel out —**nul'li·fi·ca'tion** *n.*

numb (num) *adj.* ⟦< ME *nimen*, to take⟧ deadened; insensible —*vt.* to make numb —**numb'ly** *adv.* —**numb'ness** *n.*

num·ber (num'bər) *n.* ⟦< L *numerus*⟧ 1 a symbol or word showing how many or which one in a series (Ex.: 2, 35, four, ninth) 2 [*pl.*] ARITHMETIC 3 the sum of persons or things; total 4 *a*) [*often pl.*] many *b*) [*pl.*] numerical superiority 5 quantity 6 *a*) a single issue of a periodical *b*) a single song, dance, etc. in a program of entertainment 7 [Colloq.] a person or thing singled out /a smart *number*/ 8 *Gram.* the form of a word as indicating either singular or plural —*vt.* 1 to count; enumerate 2 to give a number to 3 to include as one of a group 4 to limit the number of 5 to have or comprise; total —*vi.* to be included —**a number of** several or many; some —**beyond** (or **without**) **number** too numerous to be counted —**the numbers** an illegal lottery based on certain numbers published in newspapers: also **numbers game** (or **racket**)

num'ber·less *adj.* countless

Num·bers (num'bərz) the fourth book of the Pentateuch in the Bible: abbrev. **Num.**

nu·mer·al (no͞o'mər əl) *adj.* ⟦< L *numerus*, number⟧ of or denoting a number or numbers —*n.* a figure, letter, or word expressing a number

nu'mer·ate'[1] (-mər āt') *vt.* **-at'ed**, **-at'ing** to count one by one; enumerate

nu'mer·ate[2] (-mər it) *adj.* [Chiefly Brit.] able to understand basic mathematical concepts, etc.

nu'mer·a'tor (-mər āt'ər) *n.* the part of a fraction above the line

nu·mer·i·cal (no͞o mer'i kəl) *adj.* 1 of, or having the nature of, number 2 in or by numbers 3 expressed by numbers —**nu·mer'i·cal·ly** *adv.*

nu·mer·ol·o·gy (no͞o'mər äl'ə jē) *n.* the attributing of occult meaning to numbers, as in birth dates

nu·mer·ous (no͞o'mər əs) *adj.* 1 consisting of many persons or things 2 very many

nu·mi·nous (no͞o'mə nəs) *adj.* ⟦< L *numen*, deity⟧ having a deeply spiritual effect

nu·mis·mat·ics (no͞o'miz mat'iks, -mis-) *n.pl.* ⟦< L *numisma*, a coin⟧ [*with sing. v.*] the study or collection of coins, medals, paper money, etc. —**nu·mis'ma·tist** (-mə tist) *n.*

num·skull (num'skul') *n.* ⟦NUM(B) + SKULL⟧ a dunce

nun (nun) *n.* ⟦< LL *nonna*⟧ a woman devoted to a religious life, esp. one living in a convent under vows

nun·ci·o (nun'shē ō', -sē ō') *n.*, *pl.* **-ci·os'** ⟦< It < L *nuntius*, messenger⟧ a papal ambassador to a foreign state

nun·ner·y (nun'ər ē) *n.*, *pl.* **-ies** *old term for* CONVENT

nup·tial (nup'shəl, -chəl) *adj.* ⟦< L *nubere*, marry⟧ of marriage or a wedding —*n.* [*pl.*] a wedding

nurse (nurs) *n.* ⟦< L *nutrire*, nourish⟧ 1 a woman hired to care for another's children 2 a person trained to care for the sick, assist surgeons, etc. —*vt.* **nursed**, **nurs'ing** 1 to suckle (an infant) 2 to take care of (a child, invalid, etc.) 3 to nourish, foster, etc. 4 to try to cure /to *nurse* a cold/ 5 to use or handle so as to protect or conserve —*vi.* 1 to feed at the breast; suckle 2 to serve as a nurse

nurse'maid' *n.* a woman hired to care for a child or children

nurs·er·y (nurs'ər ē) *n.*, *pl.* **-ies** 1 a room set aside for children 2 a place where parents may temporarily leave children to be cared for 3 a place where young trees or other plants are raised for transplanting, etc.

nurs'er·y·man (-mən) *n.*, *pl.* **-men** one who owns or works in a tree nursery

nursery rhyme a poem for children

nursery school a school for children, usually three to five years of age

nursing home a residence providing care for the infirm, chronically ill, disabled, etc.

nur·ture (nur'chər) *n.* ⟦< L *nutrire*, nourish⟧ 1 food 2 training; rearing —*vt.* **-tured**, **-tur·ing** 1 to feed or nourish 2 to train, educate, rear, etc. —**nur'tur·er** *n.*

nut (nut) *n.* ⟦OE *hnutu*⟧ 1 a dry, one-seeded fruit, consisting of a kernel, often edible, in a woody shell, as the walnut 2 the kernel itself 3 any hard-shell, relatively nonperishable fruit, as the peanut 4 a small metal block with a threaded hole for screwing onto a bolt, etc. 5 [Slang] *a*) a crazy or eccentric person *b*) a devotee; fan

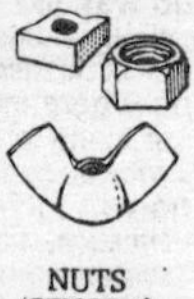

NUTS (SENSE 4)

nut case [Slang] one who is eccentric or crazy Also **nut'case'** *n.*

nut'crack'er *n.* 1 an instrument for cracking nutshells 2 a crowlike bird that feeds on nuts

nut'hatch' *n.* a small nut-eating bird with a sharp beak

nut'meat' *n.* the kernel of a nut

nut'meg' (-meg') *n.* ⟦< L *nux*, nut + LL *muscus*, musk⟧ the aromatic seed of an East Indian tree, grated and used as a spice

nut'pick' *n.* a small, sharp instrument for digging out the kernels of cracked nuts

nu·tri·a (no͞o'trē ə, nyo͞o'-) *n.* ⟦Sp < L *lutra*, otter⟧ the soft, brown fur of a South American rodent

nu·tri·ent (no͞o'trē ənt) *adj.* ⟦< L *nutrire*, nourish⟧ nourishing —*n.* anything nutritious

nu'tri·ment (-trə mənt) *n.* anything that nourishes; food

nu·tri·tion (no͞o trish'ən) *n.* ⟦see NUTRIENT⟧ 1 the process by which an organism takes in and assimilates food 2 anything that nourishes; food 3 the study of diet and health —**nu·tri'tion·al** *adj.* —**nu·tri'tion·al·ly** *adv.* —**nu'tri·tive** (-trə tiv) *adj.*

nu·tri'tious (-trish'əs) *adj.* nourishing

nuts (nuts) *adj.* [Slang] crazy; foolish —*interj.* [Slang] an exclamation of disgust, scorn, etc.: often in the phrase **nuts to**

someone (or something) —**be nuts about** [Slang] 1 to be greatly in love with 2 to be very enthusiastic about

nuts and bolts [Colloq.] the basic elements or practical aspects of something —**nuts'-and-bolts'** *adj.*

nut'shell' *n.* the shell enclosing the kernel of a nut —**in a nutshell** in concise form; in a few words

nut'ty *adj.* **-ti·er, -ti·est** 1 containing or producing nuts 2 having a nutlike flavor 3 [Slang] *a)* very enthusiastic *b)* foolish, crazy, etc. —**nut'ti·ness** *n.*

nuz·zle (nuz'əl) *vt., vi.* **-zled, -zling** ⟦< NOSE⟧ 1 to push (against) or rub with the nose, snout, etc. 2 to nestle; snuggle —**nuz'zler** *n.*

NV Nevada

NW or **N.W.** 1 northwest 2 northwesterly 3 northwestern

NWT Northwest Territories

NY or **N.Y.** New York

NYC or **N.Y.C.** New York City

ny·lon (nī'län') *n.* ⟦arbitrary coinage⟧ 1 an elastic, very strong, synthetic material made into fiber, yarn, bristles, etc. 2 [*pl.*] stockings made of this

nymph (nimf) *n.* ⟦< Gr *nymphē*⟧ 1 *Gr. & Rom. Myth.* any of a group of minor nature goddesses, living in rivers, trees, etc. 2 a lovely young woman 3 the young of an insect with incomplete metamorphosis

nym·pho·ma·ni·a (nim'fō mā'nē ə, -fə-) *n.* uncontrollable desire by a woman for sexual intercourse —**nym'pho·ma'ni·ac'** (-ak') *adj., n.*

O

o or **O** (ō) *n., pl.* **o's, O's** the 15th letter of the English alphabet

O[1] (ō) *n., pl.* **O's** 1 the numeral zero 2 a blood type

O[2] (ō) *interj.* 1 an exclamation in direct address [*O Lord!*] 2 oh

O *symbol for* 1 *Physics* ohm 2 *Chem.* oxygen

-o (ō) *suffix* 1 forming slangy words [*cheapo, freako*] 2 forming slang nouns from adjectives [*weirdo, sicko*]

O or **O.** 1 Ocean 2 Ohio 3 Old

oaf (ōf) *n.* ⟦< ON *alfr*, elf⟧ a stupid, clumsy fellow; lout —**oaf'ish** *adj.*

O·a·hu (ō ä'ho͞o) chief island of Hawaii

oak (ōk) *n.* ⟦OE *ac*⟧ 1 a large hardwood tree with nuts called *acorns* 2 its wood —*adj.* of oak —**oak'en** *adj.*

Oak·land (ōk'lənd) seaport in W Calif.: pop. 339,000

Oak Ridge city in E Tenn.: center for atomic research: pop. 28,000

oa·kum (ō'kəm) *n.* ⟦< OE *a-*, out + *camb*, a comb⟧ stringy hemp fiber gotten by taking apart old ropes, used as a caulking material

oar (ôr) *n.* ⟦OE *ar*⟧ a long pole with a broad blade at one end, used in rowing —**rest on one's oars** to stop to rest —**oars·man** (ôrz'mən), *pl.* **-men,** *n.*

oar'lock' *n.* a device, often U-shaped, for holding an oar in place in rowing

OAS Organization of American States

o·a·sis (ō ā'sis) *n., pl.* **-ses'** (-sēz') ⟦< Gr *ōasis*⟧ a fertile place in a desert, due to the presence of water

oat (ōt) *n.* ⟦OE *ate*⟧ [*usually pl.*] 1 a hardy cereal grass 2 its edible grain —**oat'en** *adj.*

oat'cake' *n.* a thin, flat cake made of oatmeal

oath (ōth) *n., pl.* **oaths** (ōthz, ōths) ⟦OE *ath*⟧ 1 a declaration based on an appeal to God that one will speak the truth, keep a promise, etc. 2 the profane use of God's name, as in anger 3 a swearword; curse

oat'meal' *n.* 1 oats crushed into meal or flakes 2 a porridge of this

ob- ⟦< L *ob*⟧ *prefix* 1 to, toward, before [*obtrude*] 2 against [*obstinate*] 3 upon, over [*obscure*] 4 completely [*obdurate*]

ob. ⟦L *obiit*⟧ he (or she) died

OB or **O.B.** 1 obstetrician 2 obstetrics

ob·bli·ga·to (äb'li gät'ō) *n., pl.* **-tos** or **-ti** (-ē) ⟦see OBLIGE⟧ an elaborate musical accompaniment, orig. thought necessary to the performance of a piece

ob·du·rate (äb'door it) *adj.* ⟦< L *obduratus* < *ob-*, intens. + *durus*, hard⟧ 1 hardhearted 2 stubborn; obstinate —**ob'du·ra·cy** (-ə sē) *n.* —**ob'du·rate·ly** *adv.*

o·be·di·ent (ō bē'dē ənt) *adj.* obeying or willing to obey —**o·be'di·ence** *n.* —**o·be'di·ent·ly** *adv.*

o·bei·sance (ō bā'səns, -bē'-) *n.* ⟦< OFr *obeir*, obey⟧ 1 a gesture of respect, as a bow 2 homage; deference —**o·bei'sant** *adj.*

ob·e·lisk (äb'ə lisk, ō'bə-) *n.* ⟦< Gr *obelos*, needle⟧ a tall, four-sided stone pillar tapering to its pyramidal top

o·bese (ō bēs') *adj.* ⟦< L *obesus* < *ob-* (see OB-) + *edere*, to eat⟧ very fat; stout —**o·be'si·ty** (-ə tē) *n.*

o·bey (ō bā', ə-) *vt.* ⟦< L *obedire* < *ob-* (see OB-) + *audire*, hear⟧ 1 to carry out the orders of 2 to carry out (an order, etc.) 3 to be guided by [*to obey one's conscience*] —*vi.* to be obedient

ob·fus·cate (äb fus'kāt', äb'fəs kāt') *vt.* **-cat'ed, -cat'ing** ⟦< L *obfuscatus* < *ob-* (see OB-) + *fuscus*, dark⟧ to obscure; confuse; bewilder —**ob'fus·ca'tion** *n.*

o·bit·u·ar·y (ō bich'o͞o er'ē) *n., pl.* **-ar'ies** ⟦< L *obire*, die⟧ a notice of someone's death, usually with a brief biography Also **o·bit** (ō'bit)

obj. 1 object 2 objective

ob·ject (äb'jikt; *for v.* əb jekt', äb-) *n.* ⟦< ML *objectum*, thing thrown in the way < L *objectus* < *ob-* (see OB-) + *jacere*, to throw⟧

1 a thing that can be seen or touched **2** a person or thing to which action, feeling, etc. is directed **3** purpose; goal **4** *Gram.* a noun or substantive that receives the action of a verb or is governed by a preposition —*vt.* to state by way of objection —*vi.* to feel or express disapproval or opposition —**ob·jec'tor** *n.*

ob·jec·tion (əb jek'shən) *n.* **1** a feeling or expression of opposition or disapproval **2** a reason for objecting

ob·jec'tion·a·ble *adj.* **1** open to objection **2** disagreeable; offensive

ob·jec'tive *adj.* **1** existing as an object or fact, independent of the mind; real **2** concerned with the realities of the thing dealt with rather than the thoughts of the artist, writer, etc. **3** without bias or prejudice **4** *Gram.* designating or of the case of an object of a preposition or verb —*n.* something aimed at —**ob·jec'tive·ly** *adv.* —**ob·jec·tiv·i·ty** (äb'jek tiv'ə tē) or **ob·jec'tive·ness** *n.*

object lesson an actual or practical demonstration or exemplification of some principle

ob·jet d'art (ôb'zhā där', äb'-) *pl.* **ob'jets d'art'** (-zhā) ⟦Fr⟧ a small object of artistic value, as a vase, etc.

ob·jur·gate (äb'jər gāt') *vt.* **-gat'ed, -gat'ing** ⟦< L *objurgatus* < *ob-* (see OB-) + *jurgare,* chide⟧ to upbraid sharply; rebuke

ob·late (äb'lāt') *adj.* ⟦ModL *oblatus,* thrust forward⟧ *Geom.* flattened at the poles /an *oblate* spheroid/

ob·la·tion (ə blā'shən) *n.* ⟦< L *oblatus,* offered⟧ an offering or sacrifice to God or a god

ob·li·gate (äb'lə gāt') *vt.* **-gat'ed, -gat'ing** ⟦see OBLIGE⟧ to bind by a contract, promise, sense of duty, etc.

ob'li·ga'tion *n.* **1** an obligating or being obligated **2** a binding contract, promise, responsibility, etc. **3** the binding power of a contract, etc. **4** a being indebted for a favor, etc.

ob·lig·a·to·ry (əb lig'ə tôr'ē, äb'lə gə-) *adj.* legally or morally binding

o·blige (ə blīj', ō-) *vt.* **o·bliged', o·blig'ing** ⟦< L *obligare* < *ob-* (see OB-) + *ligare,* to bind⟧ **1** to compel by moral, legal, or physical force **2** to make indebted for a favor; do a favor for

o·blig'ing *adj.* ready to do favors; helpful —**o·blig'ing·ly** *adv.*

ob·lique (ə blēk', ō-) *adj.* ⟦< L *obliquus* < *ob-* (see OB-) + *liquis,* awry⟧ **1** slanting **2** indirect or evasive —**ob·lique'ly** *adv.* —**ob·liq·ui·ty** (ə blik'wə tē) or **ob·lique'ness** *n.*

ob·lit·er·ate (ə blit'ər āt') *vt.* **-at'ed, -at'ing** ⟦< L *obliteratus* < *ob-* (see OB-) + *littera,* a letter⟧ **1** to blot out; efface **2** to destroy —**ob·lit'er·a'tion** *n.*

ob·liv·i·on (ə bliv'ē ən) *n.* ⟦< L *oblivisci,* to forget⟧ **1** forgetfulness **2** the condition of being forgotten

ob·liv'i·ous *adj.* forgetful or unmindful: usually with *of* or *to*

ob·long (äb'lôŋ') *adj.* ⟦< L *oblongus,* rather long < *ob-* (see OB-) + *longus,* long⟧ longer than broad; specif., rectangular and longer in one direction —*n.* an oblong figure

ob·lo·quy (äb'lə kwē) *n., pl.* **-quies** ⟦< L *obloqui* < *ob-* (see OB-) + *loqui,* speak⟧ **1** widespread censure or abuse **2** disgrace or infamy resulting from this

ob·nox·ious (əb näk'shəs, äb-) *adj.* ⟦< L *obnoxiosus* < *ob-* (see OB-) + *noxa,* harm⟧ very unpleasant; offensive —**ob·nox'ious·ly** *adv.* —**ob·nox'ious·ness** *n.*

o·boe (ō'bō) *n.* ⟦< Fr *haut,* high (pitch) + *bois,* wood⟧ a double-reed woodwind instrument having a high, penetrating tone —**o'bo·ist** *n.*

OBOE

obs. obsolete

ob·scene (äb sēn') *adj.* ⟦< L *obscenus,* filthy⟧ **1** offensive to modesty or decency; lewd **2** repulsive —**ob·scen'i·ty** (-sen'ə tē), *pl.* **-ties,** *n.*

ob·scur·ant·ism (äb'skyoor' ən tiz'əm) *n.* **1** opposition to human progress **2** a being deliberately obscure or vague

ob·scure (əb skyoor') *adj.* ⟦< L *obscurus,* covered over⟧ **1** dim; dark **2** not easily seen; faint **3** vague; ambiguous /an *obscure* answer/ **4** inconspicuous; hidden **5** not well-known /an *obscure* actor/ —*vt.* **-scured', -scur'ing** to make obscure —**ob·scure'ly** *adv.* —**ob·scu'ri·ty** *n.*

ob·se·quies (äb'si kwēz') *n.pl.* ⟦< L *obsequium,* compliance, substituted for L *exsequiae,* funeral⟧ funeral rites

ob·se·qui·ous (əb sē'kwē əs) *adj.* ⟦< L *obsequi,* to comply with⟧ much too willing to serve or obey; fawning

ob·serv·ance (əb zurv'əns) *n.* **1** the observing of a law, duty, custom, etc. **2** a customary act, rite, etc.

ob·serv'ant *adj.* **1** strict in observing a law, custom, etc. **2** paying careful attention **3** perceptive or alert

ob·ser·va·tion (äb'zər vā'shən) *n.* **1** *a)* the act or power of noticing *b)* something noticed **2** a being seen **3** a noting and recording of facts, as for research **4** a comment or remark

ob·serv·a·to·ry (əb zurv'ə tôr'ē) *n., pl.* **-ries** a building equipped for astronomical research, esp. one with a large telescope

ob·serve (əb zurv') *vt.* **-served', -serv'ing** ⟦< L *observare* < *ob-* (see OB-) + *servare,* to keep⟧ **1** to adhere to (a law, custom, etc.) **2** to celebrate (a holiday, etc.) **3** *a)* to notice (something) *b)* to pay special attention to **4** to arrive at as a conclusion **5** to say casually; remark **6** to examine scientifically —**ob·serv'a·ble** *adj.* —**ob·serv'er** *n.*

ob·sess (əb ses') *vt.* ⟦< L *obsessus* < *ob-* (see OB-) + *sedere,* sit⟧ to haunt or trouble in mind; preoccupy —**ob·ses'sive** *adj.* —**ob·ses'sive·ly** *adv.*

ob·ses'sion *n.* **1** a being obsessed **2** an idea, desire, etc. that obsesses one

ob·sid·i·an (əb sid'ē ən) *n.* ⟦after one *Obsidius,* its alleged discoverer⟧ a hard, dark, volcanic glass

ob·so·lesce (äb'sə les') *vi.* **-lesced', -lesc'ing** to be obsolescent

ob·so·les·cent (äb'sə les'ənt) *adj.* becoming obsolete —**ob'so·les'cence** *n.*

ob·so·lete (äb′sə lēt′, äb′sə lēt′) *adj.* ⟦< L *obsoletus* < *ob-* (see OB-) + *exolescere,* to grow out of use⟧ 1 no longer in use 2 out-of-date
ob·sta·cle (äb′stə kəl) *n.* ⟦< L *obstaculum* < *ob-* (see OB-) + *stare,* to stand⟧ anything that stands in the way; obstruction
ob·stet·rics (əb stet′riks) *n.pl.* ⟦< L *obstetrix,* midwife⟧ [*with sing. v.*] the branch of medicine concerned with the care and treatment of women during pregnancy and childbirth —**ob·stet′ric** or **ob·stet′ri·cal** *adj.* —**ob·ste·tri·cian** (äb′stə trish′ən) *n.*
ob·sti·nate (äb′stə nət) *adj.* ⟦< L *obstinare,* to resolve on⟧ 1 determined to have one's own way; stubborn 2 resisting treatment /an *obstinate* fever/ —**ob′sti·na·cy** (-nə sē) *n.* —**ob′sti·nate·ly** *adv.*
ob·strep·er·ous (əb strep′ər əs, äb-) *adj.* ⟦< L *obstreperus* < *ob-* (see OB-) + *strepere,* to roar⟧ noisy or unruly, esp. in resisting —**ob·strep′er·ous·ly** *adv.* —**ob·strep′er·ous·ness** *n.*
ob·struct (əb strukt′) *vt.* ⟦< L *obstructus* < *ob-* (see OB-) + *struere,* to pile up⟧ 1 to block or stop up (a passage) 2 to hinder (progress, etc.) 3 to cut off from view —**ob·struc′tive** *adj.* —**ob·struc′tive·ly** *adv.* —**ob·struc′tive·ness** *n.*
ob·struc′tion *n.* 1 an obstructing 2 anything that obstructs; hindrance
ob·struc′tion·ist *n.* one who obstructs progress —*adj.* that obstructs
ob·tain (əb tān′) *vt.* ⟦< L *obtinere* < *ob-* (see OB-) + *tenere,* to hold⟧ to get possession of by trying; procure —*vi.* to prevail /peace will *obtain*/ —**ob·tain′a·ble** *adj.* —**ob·tain′ment** *n.*
ob·trude (əb trōōd′, äb-) *vt.* **-trud′ed, -trud′ing** ⟦< L *obtrudere* < *ob-* (see OB-) + *trudere,* to thrust⟧ 1 to push out; eject 2 to force (oneself, etc.) upon others unasked or unwanted —*vi.* to obtrude oneself —**ob·tru′sion** *n.* —**ob·tru′sive** *adj.* —**ob·tru′sive·ly** *adv.* —**ob·tru′sive·ness** *n.*
ob·tuse (äb tōōs′, əb-) *adj.* ⟦< L *obtundere,* to strike upon, blunt⟧ 1 not sharp; blunt 2 greater than 90° and less than 180° /an *obtuse* angle/ 3 slow to understand or perceive —**ob·tuse′ly** *adv.* —**ob·tuse′ness** *n.*
ob·verse (äb vurs′; *for n.* äb′vurs′) *adj.* ⟦< L *obversus* < *ob-* (see OB-) + *vertere,* to turn⟧ 1 turned toward the observer 2 forming a counterpart —*n.* 1 the side, as of a coin or medal, bearing the main design 2 a counterpart
ob·vi·ate (äb′vē āt′) *vt.* **-at′ed, -at′ing** ⟦see fol.⟧ to do away with or prevent by effective measures; make unnecessary —**ob′vi·a′tion** *n.*
ob·vi·ous (äb′vē əs) *adj.* ⟦L *obvius,* in the way⟧ easy to see or understand; evident —**ob′vi·ous·ly** *adv.* —**ob′vi·ous·ness** *n.*
oc- *prefix* OB-: used before *c* /*occur*/
oc·a·ri·na (äk′ə rē′nə) *n.* ⟦It < LL *auca,* goose: from its shape⟧ a small wind instrument with finger holes and a mouthpiece
occas. occasional(ly)
oc·ca·sion (ə kā′zhən; *often* ō kā′-) *n.* ⟦< L *occasio* < *ob-* (see OB-) + *cadere,* to fall⟧ 1 a favorable time; opportunity 2 an event, etc. that makes something else possible 3 *a*) a happening *b*) a particular time 4 a special time or event 5 need arising from circumstances —*vt.* to cause —**on occasion** sometimes
oc·ca′sion·al *adj.* 1 of or for special occasions 2 happening now and then; infrequent —**oc·ca′sion·al·ly** *adv.*
oc·ci·dent (äk′sə dənt, -dent′) *n.* ⟦< L *occidere,* to fall: with reference to the setting sun⟧ [Old Poet.] the west —[O-] Europe and the Americas —**oc′ci·den′tal** or **Oc′ci·den′tal** *adj., n.*
Oc′ci·den′tal·ize′ (-den′t'l īz′) *vt., vi.* **-ized′, -iz′ing** to turn to the ways of the Occident
oc·clude (ə klōōd′) *vt.* **-clud′ed, -clud′ing** ⟦< L *occludere* < *ob-* (see OB-) + *claudere,* to shut⟧ 1 to close or block (a passage) 2 to shut in or out —*vi. Dentistry* to meet with the cusps fitting closely —**oc·clu′sion** (-klōō′zhən) *n.* —**oc·clu′sive** *adj.*
oc·cult (ə kult′, ä′kult′) *adj.* ⟦< L *occulere,* to conceal⟧ 1 hidden 2 secret 3 mysterious 4 of mystic arts, such as magic, astrology, etc.
oc·cu·pan·cy (äk′yōō pən sē) *n., pl.* **-cies** an occupying; a taking or keeping in possession
oc′cu·pant *n.* one who occupies
oc·cu·pa·tion (äk′yōō pā′shən) *n.* 1 an occupying or being occupied 2 that which occupies one's time; work; profession —**oc′cu·pa′tion·al** *adj.*
oc·cu·py (äk′yōō pī′) *vt.* **-pied′, -py′ing** ⟦< L *occupare* < *ob-* (see OB-) + *capere,* seize⟧ 1 to take possession of by settlement or seizure 2 to hold possession of; specif., *a*) to dwell in *b*) to hold (a position or office) 3 to take up (space, time, etc.) 4 to employ (oneself, one's mind, etc.)
oc·cur (ə kur′) *vi.* **-curred′, -cur′ring** ⟦< L *occurrere* < *ob-* (see OB-) + *currere,* to run⟧ 1 to be found; exist 2 to come to mind 3 to take place; happen
oc·cur′rence *n.* 1 the act or fact of occurring 2 event; incident
o·cean (ō′shən) *n.* ⟦< Gr *Ōkeanos*⟧ 1 the body of salt water that covers about 71% of the earth's surface 2 any of its four principal divisions: the Atlantic, Pacific, Indian, or Arctic Ocean 3 a great quantity —**o·ce·an·ic** (ō′shē an′ik) *adj.*
o·cean·go·ing (ō′shən gō′iŋ) *adj.* of, or made for, travel on the ocean
O·ce·an·i·a (ō′shē an′ē ə) islands in the Pacific, including Melanesia, Micronesia, & Polynesia —**O′ce·an′i·an** *adj., n.*
o·ce·an·og·ra·phy (ō′shə näg′rə fē) *n.* the study of the environment in the ocean, its plants and animals, etc. —**o′ce·an·o·graph′ic** (-nō′graf′ik) *adj.*
o′ce·an·ol′o·gy (-näl′ə jē) *n.* the study of the sea in all its aspects, including oceanography, undersea exploration, etc.
o·ce·lot (äs′ə lət, -lät′) *n.* ⟦Fr < AmInd⟧ a spotted wildcat of North and South America
o·cher or **o·chre** (ō′kər) *n.* ⟦< Gr *ōchros,* pale-yellow⟧ 1 a yellow or reddish-brown clay containing iron, used as a pigment 2 its color
o'clock (ə kläk′, ō-) *adv.* of or according to the clock /nine *o'clock* at night/
octa- ⟦< Gr *oktō,* eight⟧ *combining form* eight /*octagon*/
oc·ta·gon (äk′tə gän′) *n.* ⟦< Gr: see prec. &

-GON] a plane figure with eight angles and eight sides —**oc·tag′o·nal** (-tag′ə nəl) *adj.*
octane number (or **rating**) (äk′tān) a number representing the antiknock properties of a gasoline, etc.
oc·tave (äk′tiv, -tāv′) *n.* [< L *octavus,* eighth] **1** any group of eight **2** *Music a)* the eighth tone of a diatonic scale, or a tone seven degrees above or below a given tone *b)* the interval of seven degrees between a tone and either of its octaves *c)* the series of tones within this interval, or the keys of an instrument producing such a series
oc·ta·vo (äk tā′vō, -tä′-) *n., pl.* **-vos** [< L (*in*) *octavo,* (in) eight] **1** the page size (about 6 by 9 in.) of a book made up of printer's sheets folded into eight leaves **2** a book of such pages
oc·tet or **oc·tette** (äk tet′) *n.* [OCT(A)- + (DU)ET] **1** a composition for eight voices or instruments **2** the eight performers of this
Oc·to·ber (äk tō′bər) *n.* [< L *octo,* eight: eighth month in Rom. calendar] the 10th month of the year, having 31 days: abbrev. **Oct.**
oc·to·ge·nar·i·an (äk′tō ji ner′ē ən, -tə-) *adj.* [< L *octoginta,* eighty] between the ages of 80 and 90 —*n.* a person of this age

OCTOPUS

oc·to·pus (äk′tə pəs) *n., pl.* **-pus·es** or **-pi′** (-pī′) [< Gr *oktō,* eight + *pous,* foot] a mollusk with a soft body and eight arms covered with suckers
oc·u·lar (äk′yoo lər) *adj.* [< L *oculus,* eye] **1** of, for, or like the eye **2** by eyesight
oc′u·list (-list) *n. old term for* OPHTHALMOLOGIST
OD (ō′dē′) *n., pl.* **ODs** or **OD's** [Slang] an overdose, esp. of a narcotic —*vi.* **OD'd** or **ODed, OD'ing** or **ODing** [Slang] to take an overdose, esp. a fatal overdose of a narcotic
OD or **O.D.** [L] Doctor of Optometry
o·da·lisque or **o·da·lisk** (ō′də lisk′, ōd′′l isk′) *n.* [Fr < Turk *ōdalik,* chambermaid] a female slave or concubine in an Oriental harem
odd (äd) *adj.* [< ON *oddi*] **1** with the other of the pair missing /an *odd* glove/ **2** having a remainder of one when divided by two **3** left over after taking a round number **4** with a few more: usually in hyphenated compounds /sixty-*odd* years ago/ **5** occasional /*odd* jobs/ **6** *a)* peculiar *b)* queer; eccentric —**odd′ly** *adv.* —**odd′ness** *n.*
odd′ball′ *adj.* [Slang] strange or eccentric —*n.* [Slang] one who is oddball
odd′i·ty (-ə tē) *n.* **1** strangeness **2** *pl.* **-ties** an odd person or thing
odds (ädz) *n.pl.* **1** difference in favor of one side over the other; advantage **2** an equalized advantage in betting, based on a bettor's assumed chance of winning and expressed as a ratio /*odds* of 3 to 1/ —**at odds** quarreling —**by (all) odds** by far
odds and ends scraps; remnants
odds′mak′er *n.* an expert who estimates the odds in betting, etc.
odds′-on′ *adj.* having a very good chance of winning /an *odds-on* favorite/
ode (ōd) *n.* [< Gr *ōidē,* song] a lyric poem characterized by lofty feeling, elaborate form, and dignified style
-ode (ōd) [< Gr *hodos*] *suffix* way, path /electr*ode*/
O·des·sa (ō des′ə) seaport in S Ukrainian S.S.R., on the Black Sea: pop. 1,126,000
O·din (ō′din) *Norse Myth.* the chief deity, god of art, war, and the dead
o·di·ous (ō′dē əs) *adj.* [< L *odium,* hatred] disgusting; offensive —**o′di·ous·ly** *adv.* —**o′di·ous·ness** *n.*
o·di·um (ō′dē əm) *n.* [< L *odi,* I hate] **1** hatred **2** the disgrace brought on by hateful action
o·dom·e·ter (ō däm′ət ər) *n.* [< Gr *hodometros* < *hodos,* way + *metron,* a measure] an instrument for measuring the distance traveled by a vehicle
o·dor (ō′dər) *n.* [L] a smell; scent; aroma Brit. sp. **odour** —**be in bad** (or **ill**) **odor** to be in ill repute —**o′dor·less** *adj.* —**o′dor·ous** *adj.*
o·dor·if·er·ous (ō′dər if′ər əs) *adj.* [< L *odor,* odor + *ferre,* to bear] giving off an odor, now often, specif., a strong or offensive one
O·dys·se·us (ō dis′ē əs, ō dis′yoos′) [Gr] the hero of the *Odyssey,* one of the Greek leaders in the Trojan War
Od·ys·sey (äd′i sē) an ancient Greek epic poem, ascribed to Homer, about the wanderings of Odysseus after the fall of Troy —*n., pl.* **-seys** [*sometimes* **o-**] any extended journey
OE Old English
Oed·i·pal (ed′i pəl, ē′di-) *adj.* [*also* **o-**] of or relating to the Oedipus complex
Oed·i·pus (ed′i pəs, ē′di-) *Gr. Myth.* a king who unwittingly kills his father and marries his mother
Oedipus complex *Psychoanalysis* the unconscious tendency of a child to be attached to the parent of the opposite sex
oe·nol·o·gy (ē näl′ə jē) *n.* [< Gr *oinos,* wine + -LOGY] the science or study of wines and winemaking —**oe·nol′o·gist** *n.*
oe·no·phile (ē′nə fīl′) *n.* a connoisseur of wine
o'er (ō′ər, ôr) *prep., adv. chiefly old poet. contr. of* OVER
oeu·vre (ë′vr′) *n., pl.* ***-vres*** (-vr′) [Fr] all the works of a writer, artist, or composer
of (uv, äv, əv) *prep.* [OE] **1** from; specif., *a)* coming from /men *of* Ohio/ *b)* resulting from /to die *of* fever/ *c)* at a distance from /east *of* the city/ *d)* by /the poems *of* Poe/ *e)* separated from /robbed *of* his money/ *f)* from the whole constituting /one *of* her hats/ *g)* made from /a sheet *of* paper/ **2** belonging to **3** *a)* possessing /a man *of* wealth/ *b)* containing /a bag *of* nuts/ **4** specified as /a height *of* six feet/ **5** characterized by /a man *of* honor/ **6** concerning; about **7** during /*of* recent years/

of- *prefix* OB-: used before *f* /*offer*/

off (ôf) *adv.* ⟦ME var. of *of*⟧ 1 so as to be away, at a distance, etc. 2 so as to be no longer on, attached, etc. /take *off* your hat/ 3 (a specified distance) away in space or time /20 yards *off*/ 4 so as to be no longer in operation, etc. /turn the motor *off*/ 5 so as to be less, etc. /5% *off* for cash/ 6 away from one's work —*prep.* 1 (so as to be) no longer (or not) on, attached, etc. /*off* the road/ 2 from the substance of /live *off* the land/ 3 away from /a mile *off* shore/ 4 branching out from /an alley *off* Main Street/ 5 relieved from /*off* duty/ 6 not up to the usual standard, etc. of /*off* one's game/ —*adj.* 1 not on or attached 2 not in operation 3 on the way /*off* to bed/ 4 away from work /we are *off* today/ 5 not up to the usual standard, etc. 6 more remote /on the *off* chance/ 7 in (specified) circumstances /to be well *off*/ 8 wrong /his figures are *off*/ —*vt.* [Slang] to kill; murder —*interj.* go away! —**off and on** now and then

-off (ôf; *also* äf) *combining form* a contest of skill in a (specified) activity or field /a chili cook-*off*/

of·fal (ôf′əl) *n.* ⟦ME *ofall,* lit., off-fall⟧ 1 [*with sing. or pl. v.*] the entrails, etc. of a butchered animal 2 refuse; garbage

off′beat′ *n. Music* a beat having a weak accent —*adj.* [Colloq.] unconventional, unusual, strange, etc.

off-col·or (ôf′kul′ər) *adj.* 1 varying from the standard color 2 improper; risqué

of·fend (ə fend′) *vi.* ⟦< L *offendere,* to strike against < *ob-* (see OB-) + *fendere,* to hit⟧ 1 to commit a sin or crime 2 to create resentment, anger, etc. —*vt.* 1 to hurt the feelings of; insult 2 to be displeasing to (the taste, sense, etc.) —**of·fend′er** *n.*

of·fense (ə fens′, ô′fens′) *n.* 1 a sin or crime 2 a creating of resentment, displeasure, etc. 3 a feeling hurt, angry, etc. 4 something that causes anger, etc. 5 the act of attacking 6 the side that is attacking or seeking to score in any contest Brit. sp. **offence** —**take offense** to become offended

of·fen′sive *adj.* 1 attacking or for attack 2 unpleasant; disgusting 3 insulting 4 of the side that is seeking to score in any contest —*n.* attitude or position of attack: often with *the* —**of·fen′sive·ly** *adv.* —**of·fen′sive·ness** *n.*

of·fer (ôf′ər, äf′-) *vt.* ⟦< L *offerre* < *ob-* (see OB-) + *ferre,* to bear⟧ 1 to present in worship /to *offer* prayers/ 2 to present for acceptance /to *offer* help/ 3 to suggest; propose 4 to show or give signs of /to *offer* resistance/ 5 to bid (a price, etc.) —*vi.* to present itself —*n.* the act of offering or thing offered

of′fer·ing *n.* 1 the act of making an offer 2 something offered; specif., *a)* a gift *b)* presentation in worship

of′fer·to′ry (-tôr′ē) *n., pl.* **-ries** [*often* **O-**] 1 *a)* the part of a Eucharistic service in which the bread and wine are offered to God *b)* the prayers said, or music used, then 2 *a)* the part of a church service during which money offerings are collected *b)* the collection itself

off′hand′ *adv.* without preparation —*adj.* 1 said or done offhand 2 casual, curt, etc. Also **off′hand′ed**

of·fice (ôf′is, äf′-) *n.* ⟦< L *officium*⟧ 1 a service done for another 2 a duty, esp. as a part of one's work 3 a position of authority or trust, as in government 4 *a)* the place where the affairs of a business, etc. are carried on *b)* the people working there 5 a religious ceremony or rite

of′fice·hold′er *n.* a government official

of·fi·cer (ôf′i sər, äf′-) *n.* 1 anyone holding an office, or position of authority, in a government, business, club, etc. 2 a policeman 3 one holding a position of authority, esp. by commission, in the armed forces

officer of the day the military officer in charge of the security and guard at a military post for the day

of·fi·cial (ə fish′əl) *adj.* 1 of or holding an office, or position of authority 2 authorized or authoritative 3 formal —*n.* a person holding office —**of·fi′cial·dom** (-dəm) or **of·fi′cial·ism′** *n.* —**of·fi′cial·ly** *adv.*

of·fi·ci·ant (ə fish′ənt, -ē ənt) *n.* an officiating priest, minister, etc.

of·fi·ci·ate (ə fish′ē āt′) *vi.* **-at′ed, -at′ing** 1 to perform the duties of an office 2 to perform the functions of a priest, minister, rabbi, etc.

of·fi·cious (ə fish′əs) *adj.* ⟦see OFFICE⟧ offering unwanted advice or services; meddlesome, esp. highhandedly so —**of·fi′cious·ly** *adv.* —**of·fi′cious·ness** *n.*

off·ing (ôf′iŋ) *n.* ⟦< OFF⟧ the distant part of the sea visible from the shore —**in the offing** 1 at a distance but in sight 2 at some vague future time

off′-key′ *adj.* 1 *Music* flat or sharp 2 not harmonious

off′-lim′its (-lim′its) *adj.* ruled to be a place that cannot be entered, etc. by a specified group

off′-line′ *adj.* designating or of equipment not directly connected to and controlled by the central processing unit of a computer

off′load′ *vt., vi.* UNLOAD (1*a*, 2*b*, 4)

off′-put′ting *adj.* [Chiefly Brit.] distracting, annoying, etc.

off′-road′ *adj.* designating or of a vehicle, as a dune buggy, for use off regular highways, streets, etc.

off′-sea′son (-sē′zən) *n.* a time of the year when the usual activity is reduced or not carried on

off·set (ôf set′; *for n.* ôf′set′) *vt.* **-set′, -set′·ting** to balance, compensate for, etc. —*n.* 1 a thing that offsets another 2 OFFSET PRINTING

offset printing a printing process in which the inked impression is first made on a rubber-covered roller, then transferred to paper

off′shoot′ *n.* anything that derives from a main source; specif., a shoot growing from the main stem of a plant

off′shore′ *adj.* 1 moving away from the shore 2 at some distance from the shore 3 engaged in outside the U.S. as by U.S. banks or manufacturers /*offshore* investments/ —*adv.* 1 away from the shore 2 outside the U.S. /to borrow *offshore*/

off'side' ***adj.*** *Sports* not in the proper position for play

off'spring' ***n., pl.*** **-spring'** or **-springs'** a child or children; progeny; young

off'stage' ***n.*** the part of the stage not seen by the audience **—*adj.*** in or from this **—*adv.*** to the offstage

off'-track' ***adj.*** designating or of legalized betting on horse races, carried on away from the racetrack

off'-white' ***adj.*** grayish-white or yellowish-white

off year **1** a year in which a major election does not take place **2** a year of little production

oft (ôft) ***adv.*** ⟦OE⟧ *chiefly poet. var. of* OFTEN

of·ten (ôf'ən; *also,* -tən) ***adv.*** ⟦ME var. of prec.⟧ many times; frequently Also **of'ten·times'**

o·gle (ō'gəl) ***vi., vt.*** **o'gled, o'gling** ⟦prob. < LowG *oog,* an eye⟧ to keep looking (at) flirtatiously **—*n.*** an ogling look **—o'gler *n.***

o·gre (ō'gər) ***n.*** ⟦Fr⟧ **1** in fairy tales and folklore, a man-eating giant **2** a hideous, cruel man

oh (ō) ***interj., n., pl.*** **oh's** or **ohs** an exclamation of surprise, fear, pain, etc.

OH Ohio

O·hi·o (ō hī'ō) **1** Middle Western State of the U.S.: 41,222 sq.; pop. 10,797,000; cap. Columbus **2** river flowing from W Pa. into the Mississippi **—O·hi'o·an** (-ə wən) ***adj., n.***

ohm (ōm) ***n.*** ⟦after G. S. *Ohm* (1789-1854), Ger physicist⟧ unit of electrical resistance

o·ho (ō hō') ***interj.*** an exclamation of surprise, taunting, triumph, etc.

-o·hol·ic (ə häl'ik) *combining form* -AHOLIC */beeroholic/*

-oid (oid) ⟦< Gr *eidos,* a form⟧ *suffix* like or resembling */crystalloid/*

oil (oil) ***n.*** ⟦< L *oleum*⟧ **1** any of various greasy, combustible, liquid substances obtained from animal, vegetable, and mineral matter **2** PETROLEUM **3** *a)* OIL COLOR *b)* OIL PAINTING **—*vt.*** to lubricate or supply with oil **—*adj.*** of, from, or like oil

oil'cloth' ***n.*** cloth made waterproof by being treated with oil or paint

oil color paint made by grinding a pigment in oil Also **oil paint**

oil painting **1** a picture painted in oil colors **2** painting in oil colors

oil shale shale from which oil can be extracted by distillation

oil'skin' ***n.*** **1** cloth made waterproof by treatment with oil **2** [*often pl.*] a garment or outfit made of this

oil well a well bored through layers of rock, etc. to a supply of petroleum

oil·y (oil'ē) ***adj.*** **-i·er, -i·est** **1** of, like, or containing oil **2** greasy **3** too suave or smooth; unctuous **—oil'i·ness *n.***

oink (oiŋk) ***n.*** ⟦echoic⟧ the grunt of a pig **—*vi.*** to make this sound

oint·ment (oint'mənt) ***n.*** ⟦< L *unguentum,* a salve⟧ a fatty substance used on the skin for healing or cosmetic purposes; salve

OK or **O.K.** (ō kā'; ō'kā', ō'kā') ***adj., adv., interj.*** ⟦< "oll korrect," facetious misspelling of *all correct*⟧ all right; correct **—*n., pl.*** **OK's** or **O.K.'s** approval **—*vt.*** **OK'd** or **O.K.'d, OK'ing** or **O.K.'ing** to put an OK on; approve Also [Colloq.] **o'kay'**

o·key-doke (ō'kē dōk') ***adj., interj.*** *slang var. of* OK Also **o'key-do'key** (-dō'kē)

O·kla·ho·ma (ō'klə hō'mə) State of the south central U.S.: 69,919 sq. mi.; pop. 3,025,000; cap. Oklahoma City: abbrev. **OK** or **Okla.** **—O'kla·ho'man *adj., n.***

Oklahoma City capital of Okla.: pop. 403,000

o·kra (ō'krə) ***n.*** ⟦< WAfr name⟧ **1** a plant with sticky green pods **2** the pods, used in soups, stews, etc.

old (ōld) ***adj.*** **old'er** or **eld'er, old'est** or **eld'est** ⟦OE *ald*⟧ **1** having lived or existed for a long time **2** of aged people **3** of a certain age /two years *old*/ **4** not new **5** worn out by age or use **6** former **7** experienced /an *old* hand/ **8** ancient **9** [*often* **O-**] designating the earliest form of a language /*Old* English/ **10** designating the earlier or earliest of two or more /the *Old* World/ **—*n.*** **1** time long past /days of *old*/ **2** something old: with *the* **—old'ness *n.***

Old Church Slavonic (slə vän'ik) the South Slavic language now used only as a liturgical language by Orthodox Slavs: also called **Old Church Slavic** or **Old Bulgarian**

old country the country, esp. in Europe, from which an immigrant came

old·en (ōl'dən, old''n) ***adj.*** [Old Poet.] (of) old

Old English the Germanic language of the Anglo-Saxons, spoken in England from *c.* 400 to *c.* 1100 A.D.

old'-fash'ioned ***adj.*** suited to or favoring the styles, ideas, etc. of past times **—*n.*** [*also* **O- F-**] a cocktail made with whiskey, bitters, and bits of fruit

old fogy or **old fogey** *see* FOGY

Old French the French language from *c.* 800 to *c.* 1550 A.D.

Old Glory *name for* the flag of the United States

Old Guard ⟦transl. < Fr⟧ the conservative element of a group, party, etc.

old hat [Slang] old-fashioned or stale

Old High German the High German language before the 12th c.

old·ie or **old·y** (ōl'dē) ***n., pl.*** **-ies** [Colloq.] an old joke, saying, song, movie, etc.

old lady [Slang] **1** one's mother **2** one's wife

old'-line' ***adj.*** long-established, traditional, conservative, etc.

Old Low German the Low German language before the 12th c.

old maid **1** a woman, esp. an older woman, who has never married **2** a prim, prudish, fussy person

old man [Slang] **1** one's father **2** one's husband **3** [*usually* **O- M-**] any man in authority: with *the*

old master **1** any of the great European painters before the 18th c. **2** a painting by any of these

Old Norse the Germanic language of the Scandinavians before the 14th c.

Old Saxon the Low German dialect of the Saxons before the 10th c.

old school a group of people who cling to traditional or conservative ideas, etc.

old′ster (-stər) *n.* [Colloq.] an old or elderly person
Old Testament *Christian designation for* the Holy Scriptures of Judaism, the first of the two general divisions of the Christian Bible
old′-time′ *adj.* 1 of past times 2 of long standing
old′-tim′er *n.* [Colloq.] a long-time resident, employee, member, etc.
Old World Europe, Asia, and Africa
o·lé (ō lā′) *interj., n.* ⟦Sp⟧ a shout of approval, triumph, joy, etc.
o·le·ag·i·nous (ō′lē aj′i nəs) *adj.* ⟦< L *olea,* olive tree⟧ oily; unctuous
o·le·an·der (ō′lē an′dər) *n.* ⟦ML⟧ a poisonous evergreen shrub with fragrant white, pink, or red flowers and narrow, leathery leaves
o·le·o·mar·ga·rine or **o·le·o·mar·ga·rin** (ō′lē ō mär′jə rin) *n.* ⟦< L *oleum,* oil + MARGARINE⟧ *old term for* MARGARINE Also **o′le·o′**
ol·fac·to·ry (äl fak′tə rē, ōl-) *adj.* ⟦< L *olere,* have a smell + *facere,* make⟧ of the sense of smell
ol·i·gar·chy (äl′i gär′kē) *n., pl.* **-chies** ⟦< Gr *oligos,* few + -ARCHY⟧ 1 *a)* government in which power belongs to a few persons *b)* a state so governed 2 the ruling persons —**ol′i·gar′chic** *adj.*
ol·ive (äl′iv) *n.* ⟦< L *oliva*⟧ 1 *a)* an evergreen tree of S Europe and the Near East *b)* its small, oval fruit, eaten green or ripe as a relish or pressed, when ripe, to extract its oil (**olive oil**) 2 the yellowish-green color of the unripe fruit
olive branch the branch of the olive tree, a symbol of peace
O·lym·pi·a (ō lim′pē ə) capital of Wash.: pop. 27,000
O·lymp·ic games (ō lim′pik) ⟦< *Olympia,* plain in Greece, site of ancient games⟧ an international athletic competition generally held every four years Also **O·lym′pics** (-piks)
O·lym·pus (ō lim′pəs), **Mount** mountain in N Greece: in Greek mythology, the home of the gods —**O·lym′pi·an** (-pē ən) *n., adj.*
om (ōm) *n.* ⟦Sans⟧ *Hinduism* a word intoned as during meditation
O·ma·ha (ō′mə hô) city in E Nebr.: pop. 312,000
O·man (ō män′) country on the SE coast of Arabia: 82,000 sq. mi.; pop. 1,270,000 —**O·man′i** (-ē) *adj., n.*
om·buds·man (äm′bədz mən) *n., pl.* **-men** ⟦Swed < *ombud,* a deputy⟧ a public official appointed to investigate citizens' complaints
o·me·ga (ō mē′gə, -mā′-) *n. name of* the 24th & final letter of the Greek alphabet (Ω, ω)
om·e·let or **om·e·lette** (äm′ə lət, -lit) *n.* ⟦< L *lamella,* small plate⟧ eggs beaten and cooked flat in a pan
o·men (ō′mən) *n.* ⟦L⟧ a thing or happening supposed to foretell a future event, either good or evil
om·i·cron or **om·i·kron** (äm′i krän′, ō′mi-) *n. name of* the 15th letter of the Greek alphabet (Ο, ο)
om·i·nous (äm′ə nəs) *adj.* of or serving as an evil omen; threatening —**om′i·nous·ly** *adv.*
o·mis·sion (ō mish′ən) *n.* 1 an omitting 2 something omitted
o·mit (ō mit′) *vt.* **o·mit′ted, o·mit′ting** ⟦< L *omittere* < *ob-* (see OB-) + *mittere,* send⟧ 1 to fail to include; leave out 2 to fail to do; neglect
omni- ⟦L < *omnis,* all⟧ *combining form* all, everywhere
om·ni·bus (äm′ni bəs) *n., pl.* **-bus′es** ⟦< L, for all⟧ BUS —*adj.* dealing with many things at once
om·nip·o·tent (äm nip′ə tənt) *adj.* ⟦< L *omnis,* all + *potens,* able⟧ having unlimited power or authority; all-powerful —**the Omnipotent** God —**om·nip′o·tence** *n.*
om·ni·pres·ent (äm′ni prez′ənt) *adj.* present in all places at the same time —**om′ni·pres′ence** *n.*
om·nis·cient (äm nish′ənt) *adj.* ⟦< L *omnis,* all + *sciens,* knowing⟧ knowing all things —**the Omniscient** God —**om·nis′·cience** *n.*
om·niv·o·rous (äm niv′ə rəs) *adj.* ⟦< L *omnis,* all + *vorare,* devour⟧ 1 eating any sort of food, esp. both animal and vegetable food 2 taking in everything indiscriminately /an *omnivorous* reader/ —**om·niv′o·rous·ly** *adv.* —**om·niv′o·rous·ness** *n.*
on (än, ôn) *prep.* ⟦OE⟧ 1 in contact with, supported by, or covering 2 in the surface of /scars *on* it/ 3 *a)* near to /*on* my left/ *b)* having as its location /a house *on* Main Street/ 4 at the time of /*on* Monday/ 5 connected with /*on* the team/ 6 engaged in /*on* a trip/ 7 in a state of /*on* parole/ 8 as a result of /a profit *on* the sale/ 9 in the direction of /light shone *on* us/ 10 through the use of /live *on* bread/ 11 concerning /an essay *on* war/ 12 [Colloq.] at the expense of /a drink *on* the house/ 13 [Slang] using; addicted to /*on* drugs/ —*adv.* 1 in a situation of contacting, being supported by, or covering 2 in a direction toward /he looked *on*/ 3 forward /move *on*/ 4 without stopping /she sang *on*/ 5 into action or operation /turn *on* the light/ —*adj.* in action or operation /the TV is *on*/ —**and so on** and more like the preceding —**on and off** intermittently —**on and on** for a long time; continuously —**on to** [Slang] aware of the real nature or meaning of
once (wuns) *adv.* ⟦ME *ones*⟧ 1 one time only 2 at any time; ever 3 formerly /a *once* famous woman/ 4 by one degree /a cousin *once* removed/ —*conj.* as soon as /*once* he is tired, he will quit/ —*n.* one time /go this *once*/ —**at once** 1 immediately 2 at the same time —**once (and) for all** conclusively —**once in a while** now and then
once′-o′ver *n.* [Colloq.] a quick look
on·co·gene (äŋ′kə jēn′) *n.* ⟦< Gr *onkos,* a mass + GENE⟧ a gene that, when activated as by a virus, may cause a normal cell to become cancerous
on·col·o·gy (än käl′ə jē, äŋ-) *n.* ⟦< Gr *onkos,* a mass + -LOGY⟧ the branch of medicine dealing with tumors
on·com·ing (än′kum′iŋ) *adj.* coming nearer in position or time
one (wun) *adj.* ⟦OE *an*⟧ 1 being a single

thing or unit **2** united /with *one* accord/ **3** a certain but unnamed /take *one* path or the other, *one* day last week/ **4** the same **5** unique; only /the *one* solution/ —*n.* **1** the first and lowest cardinal number; 1; I **2** a single person or thing —*pron.* **1** a certain person or thing **2** any person or thing —**at one** in accord —**one by one** individually in succession

O'Neill (ō nēl'), **Eu·gene** (yōō jēn') 1888-1953; U.S. playwright

one'ness (-nis) *n.* **1** singleness; unity **2** unity of mind, feeling, etc.

one'-on-one' *adj., adv.* in direct personal confrontation

on·er·ous (än'ər əs) *adj.* ⟦< L *onus,* a load⟧ burdensome; oppressive

one·self (wun'self') *pron.* a person's own self Also **one's self** —**be oneself** **1** to function normally **2** to be natural —**by oneself** alone

one'-sid'ed *adj.* **1** on, having, or involving only one side **2** unfair **3** unequal /a *one-sided* race/

one'time' (-tīm') *adj.* former

one'-track' *adj.* [Colloq.] limited in scope /a *one-track* mind/

one'-up' *adj.* [Colloq.] having an advantage (over another)

one-up'man·ship' *n.* skill in seizing an advantage over others

one'-way' *adj.* moving, or allowing movement, in one direction only

on'go'ing *adj.* going on; progressing

on·ion (un'yən) *n.* ⟦< L *unus,* one⟧ **1** a plant of the lily family with an edible bulb **2** this bulb, having a strong, sharp smell and taste

on'ion·skin' *n.* a tough, thin, translucent, glossy paper

on-line (än'līn') *adj.* designating or of equipment directly connected to and controlled by the central processing unit of a computer

on'look'er *n.* a spectator

on·ly (ōn'lē) *adj.* ⟦< OE *an,* one + *-lic,* -ly⟧ **1** alone of its or their kind; sole **2** alone in superiority; best —*adv.* **1** and no other; and no more; solely **2** (but) in the end /to meet one crisis, *only* to face another/ **3** as recently as —*conj.* [Colloq.] except that; but —**only too** very; exceedingly

on·o·mat·o·poe·ia (än'ō mat'ō pē'ə, -mät'-) *n.* ⟦< Gr *onoma,* a name + *poiein,* make⟧ the formation of words by imitating sounds (Ex.: *buzz*)

on'rush' *n.* a headlong dash forward

on'set' *n.* **1** an attack **2** a start

on·slaught (än'slôt') *n.* ⟦< Du *slagen,* to strike⟧ a violent attack

On·tar·i·o (än ter'ē ō) **1** province of SE Canada: 412,582 sq. mi.; pop. 9,102,000: cap. Toronto: abbrev. **Ont.** **2** **Lake** smallest of the Great Lakes, between N.Y. & Ontario, Canada —**On·tar'i·an** *adj., n.*

on·to (än'tōō) *prep.* **1** to a position on **2** [Slang] aware of Also **on to**

on·tog·e·ny (än täj'ə nē) *n.* ⟦ult. < Gr *einai,* to be + *-genēs,* born⟧ the life cycle of a single organism

o·nus (ō'nəs) *n.* ⟦L⟧ **1** a burden, unpleasant duty, etc. **2** blame

on·ward (än'wərd) *adv.* toward or at a position ahead; forward Also **on'wards** —*adj.* advancing

on·yx (än'iks) *n.* ⟦< Gr, fingernail⟧ a type of agate with alternate colored layers

oo·dles (ōōd''lz) *n.pl.* ⟦< ?⟧ [Colloq.] a great amount; very many

ooze[1] (ōōz) *n.* ⟦OE *wos,* sap⟧ something that oozes —*vi.* **oozed, ooz'ing** to flow or leak out slowly —*vt.* to exude

ooze[2] (ōōz) *n.* ⟦OE *wase*⟧ soft mud or slime, as at the bottom of a lake

op- *prefix* OB-: used before *p* /*oppress*/

o·pal (ō'pəl) *n.* ⟦< Sans *úpalaḥ,* (precious) stone⟧ an iridescent silica of various colors: some varieties are semiprecious —**o·pal·es·cent** (ō'pəl es'ənt) *adj.*

o·paque (ō pāk') *adj.* ⟦< L *opacus,* shady⟧ **1** not transparent **2** dull or dark **3** hard to understand —**o·pac·i·ty** (ō pas'ə tē) or **o·paque'ness** *n.* —**o·paque'ly** *adv.*

op (art) (äp) a style of abstract painting creating optical illusions

op. cit. ⟦L *opere citato*⟧ in the work cited

O·PEC (ō'pek') *n.* Organization of Petroleum Exporting Countries

Op-Ed (äp'ed') *adj.* ⟦*Op*(*posite*) *Ed*(*itorial page*)⟧ designating or on a page in a newspaper featuring a wide variety of columns, articles, letters, etc.

o·pen (ō'pən) *adj.* ⟦OE⟧ **1** not closed, covered, clogged, or shut **2** not enclosed /*open* fields/ **3** spread out; unfolded /an *open* book/ **4** having gaps, holes, etc. **5** free to be entered, used, etc. /an *open* meeting/ **6** not decided /an *open* question/ **7** not closed to new ideas, etc. /an *open* mind/ **8** generous **9** free from legal or discriminatory restrictions /*open* season, *open* housing/ **10** not conventional /*open* marriage/ **11** not already taken /the job is *open*/ **12** not secret; public **13** frank; candid /an *open* manner/ —*vt., vi.* **1** to cause to be, or to become, open **2** to spread out; expand; unfold **3** to make or become available for use, etc. without restriction **4** to begin; start **5** to start operating —**open to** **1** willing to receive, discuss, etc. **2** available to —**the open** **1** the outdoors **2** public knowledge —**o'pen·er** *n.* —**o'pen·ly** *adv.* —**o'pen·ness** *n.*

open air the outdoors —**o'pen-air'** *adj.*

o'pen-and-shut' *adj.* easily decided

o'pen-end'ed (-en'did) *adj.* broad, unlimited, or unrestricted

o'pen-eyed' *adj.* with the eyes wide open, as in surprise or watchfulness

o'pen-faced' *adj.* **1** having a frank, honest face **2** designating a sandwich without a top slice of bread: also **o'pen-face'**

o'pen·hand'ed *adj.* generous

o'pen·heart'ed *adj.* **1** not reserved; frank **2** kindly; generous

o'pen-hearth' *adj.* designating or using a furnace with a wide hearth and low roof, for making steel

o'pen-heart' surgery surgery on the heart during which the blood is diverted and circulated by mechanical means

open house **1** an informal reception at one's home **2** a time when an institution is open to visitors

o'pen·ing' *n.* **1** an open place; hole; gap **2** a clearing **3** a beginning **4** start of operations **5** a favorable chance **6** an unfilled job

o'pen-mind'ed ***adj.*** having a mind open to new ideas; unprejudiced

o'pen·work' ***n.*** ornamental work, as in cloth, with openings in it

op·er·a[1] (äp'ər ə) ***n.*** ⟦< L, a work⟧ a play having its text set to music and sung to orchestral accompaniment **—op'er·at'ic** (-ə rat'ik) ***adj.***

o·pe·ra[2] (ō'pə rə, äp'ə rə) ***n. pl. of*** OPUS

op·er·a·ble (äp'ər ə bəl) ***adj.*** ⟦see OPERATE & -ABLE⟧ **1** feasible **2** that can be treated by a surgical operation

opera glasses a small binocular telescope used in theaters, etc.

op·er·ate (äp'ər āt') ***vi.*** **-at'ed, -at'ing** ⟦< L *operari,* to work⟧ **1** to be in action; act; work **2** to bring about a certain effect **3** to perform a surgical operation **—*vt.*** **1** to put or keep in action **2** to direct; manage

op'er·a'tion ***n.*** ⟦< L *operatio*⟧ **1** the act or method of operating **2** a being in action or at work **3** a process or action that is part of a series in some work **4** any surgical procedure to remedy a physical ailment

op'er·a'tion·al ***adj.*** **1** of or having to do with the operation of a device, system, process, etc. **2** *a)* that can be used or operated *b)* in use; operating

op'er·a·tive' (-ə tiv') ***adj.*** **1** in operation **2** effective **3** connected with physical work or mechanical action

op'er·a'tor (-āt'ər) ***n.*** **1** one who operates a machine [a telephone *operator*] **2** one engaged in commercial or industrial operations

op·er·et·ta (äp'ər et'ə) ***n.*** ⟦It, dim. of *opera,* OPERA[1]⟧ an amusing opera with spoken dialogue

oph·thal·mic (äf thal'mik) ***adj.*** ⟦< Gr *ophthalmos,* the eye⟧ of or involving the eye

oph·thal·mol·o·gy (äf'thal mäl'ə jē, -thəl-; äp'-) ***n.*** ⟦< Gr *ophthalmos,* the eye + -LOGY⟧ the branch of medicine dealing with the eye and its diseases **—oph'thal·mol'o·gist *n.***

o·pi·ate (ō'pē it) ***n.*** ⟦ML *opiatum*⟧ **1** a drug containing, or derived from, opium **2** anything that quiets, soothes, or deadens

o·pine (ō pin') ***vt., vi.*** **o·pined', o·pin'ing** ⟦< L *opinari,* think⟧ to hold (an opinion): usually humorous

o·pin·ion (ə pin'yən, ō-) ***n.*** ⟦< L *opinari,* think⟧ **1** a belief based not on certainty but on what seems true or probable **2** an evaluation, estimation, etc. **3** formal expert judgment

o·pin'ion·at'ed (-āt'id) ***adj.*** holding obstinately to one's opinions

o·pi·um (ō'pē əm) ***n.*** ⟦< Gr *opos,* vegetable juice⟧ a narcotic drug prepared from the seed of a certain poppy

OPOSSUMS

o·pos·sum (ə päs'əm) ***n.*** ⟦< AmInd, white beast⟧ a small, nocturnal, tree-dwelling American marsupial with a prehensile tail: it becomes motionless when frightened

op·po·nent (ə pō'nənt) ***n.*** ⟦< L *ob-* (see OB-) + *ponere,* to place⟧ one who opposes, as in a game; adversary

op·por·tune (äp'ər to͞on') ***adj.*** ⟦< L *ob-* (see OB-) + *portus,* PORT[1]⟧ **1** suitable: said of time **2** well-timed

op'por·tun'ism' ***n.*** the adapting of one's actions, thoughts, etc. to circumstances, as in politics, without regard for principles **—op'por·tun'ist *n., adj.* —op'por·tun·is'tic *adj.***

op·por·tu·ni·ty (äp'ər to͞o'nə tē) ***n., pl.* -ties** **1** a combination of circumstances favorable for the purpose **2** a good chance, as to advance oneself

op·pose (ə pōz') ***vt.*** **-posed', -pos'ing** ⟦< L *ob-* (see OB-) + *ponere,* to place⟧ **1** to place opposite **2** to contend with; resist

op·po·site (äp'ə zit) ***adj.*** ⟦< L *ob-* (see OB-) + *ponere,* to place⟧ **1** set against; in a contrary direction: often with *to* **2** entirely different; exactly contrary **—*n.*** anything opposed **—*prep.*** across from **—op'po·site·ly *adv.***

opposite number one whose position, rank, etc. parallels another's in a different place or organization

op'po·si'tion (-zish'ən) ***n.*** **1** an opposing **2** resistance, contrast, hostility, etc. **3** *a)* one that opposes *b)* [*often* **O-**] a political party opposing the party in power

op·press (ə pres') ***vt.*** ⟦< L *ob-* (see OB-) + *premere,* to press⟧ **1** to weigh heavily on the mind of; worry **2** to keep down by the cruel or unjust use of authority **—op·pres'sor *n.***

op·pres·sion (ə presh'ən) ***n.*** **1** an oppressing or being oppressed **2** a thing that oppresses **3** physical or mental distress

op·pres·sive (ə pres'iv) ***adj.*** **1** causing discomfort **2** tyrannical **3** distressing **—op·pres'sive·ly *adv.***

op·pro·bri·ous (ə prō'brē əs) ***adj.*** expressing opprobrium; abusive

op·pro'bri·um (-əm) ***n.*** ⟦< L *ob-* (see OB-) + *probrum,* a disgrace⟧ **1** the disgrace attached to shameful conduct **2** anything bringing shame

opt (äpt) ***vi.*** ⟦< L *optare,* to wish⟧ to make a choice: often with *for* **—opt out (of)** to choose not to be or continue in (some activity, organization, etc.)

op·tic (äp'tik) ***adj.*** ⟦< Gr *ōps,* an eye⟧ of the eye or sense of sight

op·ti·cal (äp'ti kəl) ***adj.*** **1** of the sense of sight; visual **2** of optics **3** for aiding vision **—op'ti·cal·ly *adv.***

op·ti·cian (äp tish'ən) ***n.*** one who makes or sells eyeglasses, etc.

op·tics (äp'tiks) ***n.pl.*** [*with sing. v.*] the branch of physics dealing with light and vision

op·ti·mism (äp'tə miz'əm) ***n.*** ⟦< L *optimus,* best⟧ **1** the belief that good ultimately prevails over evil **2** the tendency to take the most hopeful view of matters **—op'ti·mist**

(-mist) ***n.*** **—op'ti·mis'tic** (-mis'tik) ***adj.*** **—op'ti·mis'ti·cal·ly** ***adv.***

op'ti·mum (-məm) ***n.***, *pl.* **-mums** or **-ma** (-mə) ⟦see prec.⟧ the best or most favorable degree, condition, etc. **—*adj.*** most favorable; best: also **op'ti·mal** (-məl)

op·tion (äp'shən) ***n.*** ⟦< L *optare,* to wish⟧ **1** a choosing; choice **2** the right of choosing **3** something that is or can be chosen **4** the right to buy, sell, or lease at a fixed price within a specified time **—op'tion·al *adj.***

op·tom·e·try (äp täm'ə trē) ***n.*** ⟦< Gr *optikos,* optic + *metron,* a measure⟧ the profession of testing and examining the eyes and prescribing glasses to correct vision problems **—op·tom'e·trist' *n.***

op·u·lent (äp'yoo lənt, -yə-) ***adj.*** ⟦< L *ops,* riches⟧ **1** very wealthy **2** abundant **—op'u·lence *n.***

o·pus (ō'pəs) ***n.***, *pl.* **o·pe·ra** (ō'pə rə, äp'ə rə) or **o'pus·es** ⟦L, a work⟧ a work; composition; esp., any of the numbered musical works of a composer

or (ôr) ***conj.*** ⟦OE *oththe*⟧ a coordinating conjunction introducing: *a)* an alternative /red *or* blue/ or the last in a series of choices *b)* a synonymous word or phrase /oral, *or* spoken/

-or (ər, ôr) ⟦< L⟧ *suffix* **1** a person or thing that (does a specified thing) /*inventor*/ **2** quality or condition /*favor*/

OR Oregon

or·a·cle (ôr'ə kəl, är'-) ***n.*** ⟦< L *orare,* pray⟧ **1** among the ancient Greeks and Romans, *a)* the place where, or medium by which, deities were consulted *b)* the revelation of a medium or priest **2** *a)* a person of great knowledge *b)* statements of such a person **—o·rac·u·lar** (ō rak'yoo lər) ***adj.***

o·ral (ôr'əl, ōr'-) ***adj.*** ⟦< L *os,* the mouth⟧ **1** uttered; spoken **2** of or near the mouth **—o'ral·ly *adv.***

oral history **1** the gathering of personal recollections in tape recorded interviews **2** a historical account based on this

-o·ram·a (ə ram'ə, -räm'ə) *combining form* a greater-than-usual number, volume, etc. of a specified thing /*panorama*/

or·ange (ôr'inj, är'-) ***n.*** ⟦< Sans *naranga*⟧ **1** a round, edible, reddish-yellow citrus fruit, with a sweet, juicy pulp **2** the evergreen tree it grows on **3** reddish yellow

or·ange·ade (ôr'inj ād', ôrnj'ād') ***n.*** a drink made of orange juice, water, and sugar

o·rang·u·tan (ō raŋ'oo tan'; ō raŋ'-, ə-) ***n.*** ⟦< Malay *oran,* man + *utan,* forest⟧ an ape of Borneo and Sumatra with shaggy, reddish-brown hair and very long arms

o·rate (ō rāt', ô-) ***vi.*** **-rat'ed, -rat'ing** to make an oration; speak in a pompous or bombastic way

o·ra·tion (ō rā'shən, ô-) ***n.*** ⟦< L *orare,* speak⟧ a formal speech, esp. one given at a ceremony

or·a·tor (ôr'ət ər, är'-) ***n.*** an eloquent public speaker

or·a·to·ri·o (ôr'ə tôr'ē ō') ***n.***, *pl.* **-os'** ⟦It, small chapel⟧ a long, dramatic musical work, usually on a religious theme, but not acted out

or·a·to·ry (ôr'ə tôr'ē, är'-) ***n.***, *pl.* **-ries** ⟦< L *oratoria*⟧ skill in public speaking **—or'a·tor'i·cal *adj.***

orb (ôrb) ***n.*** ⟦L *orbis,* a circle⟧ a sphere, or globe

or·bit (ôr'bit) ***n.*** ⟦< L *orbis,* a circle⟧ **1** the path of a celestial body during its revolution around another **2** the path of an artificial satellite or spacecraft around a celestial body **—*vi., vt.*** to move in, or put into, an orbit **—or'bit·al *adj.***

or·chard (ôr'chərd) ***n.*** ⟦OE *ortgeard*⟧ **1** land for growing fruit trees **2** the trees

or·ches·tra (ôr'kis trə, -kes'-) ***n.*** ⟦< Gr *orcheisthai,* to dance⟧ **1** the space in front of a theater stage, where the musicians sit: in full **orchestra pit** **2** the seats on the main floor of a theater **3** *a)* a group of musicians playing together *b)* their instruments **—or·ches'tral** (-kes'trəl) ***adj.***

or'ches·trate' (-trāt') ***vt., vi.*** **-trat'ed, -trat'ing** to arrange (music) for an orchestra **—or'ches·tra'tion *n.***

or·chid (ôr'kid) ***n.*** ⟦< Gr *orchis,* testicle: from the shape of the roots⟧ **1** a perennial plant having flowers with three petals, one of which is lip-shaped **2** this flower **3** pale purple

or·dain (ôr dān') ***vt.*** ⟦< L *ordo,* an order⟧ **1** to decree; establish; enact **2** to invest with the office of minister, priest, or rabbi **—*vi.*** to command **—or·dain'ment *n.***

or·deal (ôr dēl', ôr'dēl') ***n.*** ⟦OE *ordal*⟧ any difficult or painful experience

or·der (ôr'dər) ***n.*** ⟦< L *ordo,* straight row⟧ **1** social position **2** a state of peace; orderly conduct **3** arrangement of things or events; series **4** a definite plan; system **5** a military, monastic, or social brotherhood **6** a condition in which everything is in its place and working properly **7** condition in general /in good *order*/ **8** an authoritative command, instruction, etc. **9** a class; kind **10** an established method, as of conduct in meetings, etc. **11** *a)* a request to supply something /an *order* for books/ *b)* the goods supplied **12** [*usually pl.*] the position of ordained minister, priest, etc. /to take holy *orders*/ **—*vt., vi.*** **1** to put or keep (things) in order; arrange **2** to command **3** to request (something to be supplied) **—in** (or **out of**) **order** **1** in (or not in) proper position **2** in (or not in) good condition **3** in (or not in) accordance with the rules **—in order that** so that **—in order to** for the purpose of **—in short order** quickly **—on the order of** similar to **—to order** in accordance with the buyer's specifications

or·der·ly (ôr'dər lē) ***adj.*** **1** neat or tidy **2** well-behaved; law-abiding **—*adv.*** methodically **—*n.***, *pl.* **-lies** **1** an enlisted person assigned to perform personal services for an officer **2** a male hospital attendant **—or'der·li·ness *n.***

or·di·nal (ôrd''n əl) ***adj.*** ⟦< L *ordo,* order⟧ expressing order in a series **—*n.*** any number showing order in a series (e.g., first, tenth): in full **ordinal number**

or·di·nance (ôrd''n əns) ***n.*** ⟦< L *ordo,* an order⟧ a statute or regulation, esp. a municipal one

or·di·nar·i·ly (ôrd''n er'ə lē) ***adv.*** usually; as a rule

or·di·nar·y (ôrd''n er'ē) ***adj.*** ⟦< L *ordo,* an order⟧ **1** customary; usual **2** familiar;

unexceptional; common —**out of the ordinary** unusual

or·di·nate (ôrd′'n it, -āt′) ***n.*** ⟦< L *(linea) ordinate (applicata),* line applied in ordered manner⟧ *Math.* the vertical distance of a point from a horizontal axis

or·di·na·tion (ôrd′'n ā′shən) ***n.*** an ordaining or being ordained to the clergy

ord·nance (ôrd′nəns) ***n.*** ⟦< ORDINANCE⟧ **1** artillery **2** all military weapons, ammunition, vehicles, etc.

or·do (ôr′dō) ***n.***, *pl.* **-dos** or **-di·nes′** (-də nēz′) ⟦L, order⟧ *R.C.Ch.* an annual calendar giving directions for each day's Mass and Office

or·dure (ôr′jər) ***n.*** ⟦< L *horridus,* horrid⟧ dung; filth

ore (ôr) ***n.*** ⟦OE *ar,* brass⟧ a natural combination of minerals, esp. one from which a metal or metals can be profitably extracted

o·reg·a·no (ō reg′ə nō, ə-) ***n.*** ⟦< Sp < Gr *origanon*⟧ a plant related to the mint, with fragrant leaves used for seasoning

Or·e·gon (ôr′i gən, -gän′) NW coastal State of the U.S.: 96,981 sq. mi.; pop. 2,633,000; cap. Salem: abbrev. **Oreg.** —**Or′e·go′ni·an** (-gō′nē ən) ***adj., n.***

or·gan (ôr′gən) ***n.*** ⟦< Gr *organon,* an implement⟧ **1** a keyboard musical instrument with sets of graduated pipes through which compressed air is passed, causing sound by vibration **2** in animals and plants, a part adapted to perform a specific function **3** a means for performing some action **4** a means of communicating ideas or opinions, as a periodical

or·gan·dy or **or·gan·die** (ôr′gən dē) ***n.***, *pl.* **-dies** ⟦Fr *organdi*⟧ a very sheer, crisp cotton fabric

or·gan·elle (ôr′gə nel′) ***n.*** ⟦< L *organum,* tool + dim. of *-ellus*⟧ a discrete structure within a cell, as a chloroplast, having specialized functions, a distinctive chemical composition, etc.

or·gan·ic (ôr gan′ik) ***adj.*** **1** of or having to do with a bodily organ **2** inherent; inborn **3** systematically arranged **4** designating or of any chemical compound containing carbon **5** of, like, or derived from living organisms —**or·gan′i·cal·ly** ***adv.***

or·gan·ism (ôr′gə niz′əm) ***n.*** any living thing —**or′gan·is′mic** ***adj.***

or′gan·ist ***n.*** an organ player

or·gan·i·za·tion (ôr′gə ni zā′shən) ***n.*** **1** an organizing or being organized **2** any organized group, as a club —**or′gan·i·za′tion·al** ***adj.***

or·gan·ize (ôr′gə nīz′) ***vt.*** **-ized′**, **-iz′ing** **1** to provide with an organic structure **2** to arrange for **3** to institute; establish **4** to persuade to join a cause, group, etc. —***vi.*** to become organized —**or′gan·iz′er** ***n.***

or·gan·za (ôr gan′zə) ***n.*** a thin, stiff fabric of rayon, silk, etc.

or·gasm (ôr′gaz′əm) ***n.*** ⟦< Gr *organ,* to swell⟧ the climax of a sexual act

or·gy (ôr′jē) ***n.***, *pl.* **-gies** ⟦< Gr *orgia,* secret rites⟧ **1** a wild party, esp. with sexual activity **2** unrestrained indulgence in any activity

o·ri·el (ôr′ē əl, ôr′-) ***n.*** ⟦< ML *oriolum,* porch⟧ a bay window resting on a bracket or a corbel

o·ri·ent (ôr′ē ənt; *also, esp. for v.,* -ent′) ***n.*** ⟦< L *oriri,* arise: used of the rising sun⟧ [Old Poet.] the east —***vt.*** to adjust (oneself) to a particular situation —[**O-**] the East, or Asia; esp., the Far East —**o′ri·en·ta′tion** ***n.***

O′ri·en′tal (-ent′'l) ***adj.*** of the Orient, its people, etc. —***n.*** a member of a people native to the Orient

or·i·fice (ôr′ə fis, är′-) ***n.*** ⟦< L *os,* a mouth + *facere,* make⟧ a mouth of a tube, cavity, etc.; opening

orig. **1** origin **2** original **3** originally

o·ri·ga·mi (ôr′ə gä′mē) ***n.*** ⟦Jpn⟧ the Japanese art of folding paper to form flowers, animal figures, etc.

or·i·gin (ôr′ə jin, är′-) ***n.*** ⟦< L *oriri,* to rise⟧ **1** a coming into existence or use; beginning **2** parentage; birth **3** source; root; cause

o·rig·i·nal (ə rij′i nəl) ***adj.*** **1** first; earliest **2** never having been before; new; novel **3** capable of creating something new **4** being that from which copies are made —***n.*** **1** a primary type that has given rise to varieties **2** an original work, as of art or literature —**o·rig′i·nal′i·ty** (-nal′ə tē) ***n.*** —**o·rig′i·nal·ly** ***adv.***

o·rig′i·nate′ (-nāt′) ***vt.*** **-nat′ed**, **-nat′ing** to bring into being; esp., to invent —***vi.*** to begin; start —**o·rig′i·na′tion** ***n.*** —**o·rig′i·na′tor** ***n.***

o·ri·ole (ôr′ē ōl′) ***n.*** ⟦< L *aurum,* gold⟧ a bright-orange and black American bird that builds a hanging nest

O·ri·on (ō rī′ən, ə-) a very bright equatorial constellation

Or·lon (ôr′län′) *trademark for* a synthetic acrylic fiber similar to nylon

or·mo·lu (ôr′mə lo͞o′) ***n.*** ⟦Fr *or moulu,* ground gold⟧ an imitation gold made of a copper and tin alloy, used in ornaments, moldings, etc.

or·na·ment (ôr′nə mənt; *for v.,* -ment′) ***n.*** ⟦< L *ornare,* adorn⟧ **1** anything that adorns; decoration **2** one whose character or talent adds luster to the surroundings, etc. —***vt.*** to decorate —**or′na·men′tal** ***adj.*** —**or′na·men·ta′tion** ***n.***

or·nate (ôr nāt′) ***adj.*** ⟦< L *ornare,* adorn⟧ heavily ornamented; showy —**or·nate′ly** ***adv.*** —**or·nate′ness** ***n.***

or·ner·y (ôr′nər ē) ***adj.*** ⟦< ORDINARY⟧ [Chiefly Dial.] **1** mean; nasty **2** obstinate —**or′ner·i·ness** ***n.***

or·ni·thol·o·gy (ôr′nə thäl′ə jē) ***n.*** ⟦< Gr *ornis,* bird + -LOGY⟧ the branch of zoology dealing with birds —**or′ni·thol′o·gist** ***n.***

o·ro·tund (ō′rō tund′, ôr′ə-) ***adj.*** ⟦< L *os,* mouth + *rotundas,* round⟧ **1** resonant: said of the voice **2** bombastic

or·phan (ôr′fən) ***n.*** ⟦< Gr *orphanos*⟧ a child whose parents are dead —***adj.*** **1** being an orphan **2** of or for orphans —***vt.*** to cause to become an orphan

or′phan·age (-ij) ***n.*** an institution that is a home for orphans

Or·phe·us (ôr′fē əs) *Gr. Myth.* a poet-musician with magic musical powers

or·ris (ôr′is, är′-) ***n.*** ⟦< Gr *iris,* iris⟧ a European iris, esp. one with a root (**or′ris·root′**) pulverized for perfumery, etc.

ortho- ⟦< Gr *orthos,* straight⟧ *combining form* **1** straight *[orthodontics]* **2** proper; correct *[orthography]* Also **orth-**

or·tho·don·tics (ôr'thō dän'tiks, -thə-) ***n.pl.*** ⟦< ORTH(O)- + Gr *odōn*, tooth + -ICS⟧ [*with sing. v.*] the branch of dentistry concerned with correcting tooth irregularities Also **or'tho·don'ti·a** (-dän'shə, -shē ə) —**or'tho·don'tist** ***n.***

or·tho·dox (ôr'thə däks') ***adj.*** ⟦< Gr *orthos*, straight + *doxa*, opinion⟧ conforming to the usual beliefs or established doctrines, as in religion; conventional —**or'tho·dox'y,** *pl.* **-ies,** ***n.***

Orthodox (Eastern) Church the Christian church dominant in E Europe, W Asia, and N Africa

or·thog·ra·phy (ôr thäg'rə fē) ***n.,*** *pl.* **-phies** ⟦< Gr: see ORTHO- & -GRAPHY⟧ **1** correct spelling **2** spelling as a subject for study —**or·tho·graph·ic** (ôr'thō graf'ik, -thə-) ***adj.***

or·tho·pe·dics or **or·tho·pae·dics** (ôr'thō pē'diks) ***n.pl.*** ⟦< Gr *orthos*, straight + *pais*, child⟧ [*with sing. v.*] the branch of surgery dealing with deformities, diseases, and injuries of the bones, joints, muscles, etc. —**or'tho·pe'dic** or **or'tho·pae'dic** ***adj.*** —**or'tho·pe'dist** or **or'tho·pae'dist** ***n.***

-o·ry (ôr'ē, ər ē) ⟦< L *-orius*⟧ *suffix* **1** of, having the nature of /*sensory*/ **2** a place or thing for /*crematory*/

OS Old Saxon

O·sa·ka (ō'sä kä') seaport in S Honshu, Japan: pop. 2,648,000

os·cil·late (äs'ə lāt') ***vi.*** **-lat'ed, -lat'ing** ⟦< L *oscillum*, a swing⟧ **1** to swing to and fro **2** to vacillate **3** *Physics* to vary regularly between high and low values, as an electric current —**os'cil·la'tion** ***n.*** —**os'cil·la'tor** ***n.***

os·cil·lo·scope (ə sil'ə skōp') ***n.*** ⟦< L *oscillare*, to swing + -SCOPE⟧ an instrument that visually displays an electrical wave on a fluorescent screen

os·cu·late (äs'kyoo lāt', -kyə-) ***vt., vi.*** **-lat'ed, -lat'ing** ⟦< L *osculum*, little mouth⟧ to kiss —**os'cu·la'tion** ***n.***

-ose[1] (ōs) ⟦Fr < (*gluc*)*ose*⟧ *suffix* **1** a carbohydrate /*sucrose*/ **2** the product of a protein hydrolysis

-ose[2] (ōs) ⟦L *-osus*⟧ *suffix* full of, like

o·sier (ō'zhər) ***n.*** ⟦< ML *auseria*, willow⟧ a willow with lithe branches used for baskets and furniture

-o·sis (ō'sis) ⟦< Gr⟧ *suffix* **1** condition, action /*hypnosis*/ **2** an abnormal or diseased condition /*psychosis*/

Os·lo (äs'lō, äz'-) capital of Norway: pop. 447,000

os·mo·sis (äs mō'sis, äz-) ***n.*** ⟦< Gr *ōsmos*, impulse⟧ **1** the tendency of fluids to pass through a membrane so as to equalize concentrations on both sides **2** an apparently effortless absorption of ideas, feelings, etc. —**os·mot'ic** (-mät'ik) ***adj.***

os·prey (äs'prē, -prā) ***n.,*** *pl.* **-preys** ⟦< L *os*, a bone + *frangere*, to break⟧ a large, diving, hawklike bird that feeds mainly on fish

os·si·fy (äs'ə fī') ***vt., vi.*** **-fied', -fy'ing** ⟦< L *os*, a bone + -FY⟧ **1** to change into bone **2** to fix rigidly in a custom, etc. —**os'si·fi·ca'tion** ***n.***

os·ten·si·ble (ä sten'sə bəl) ***adj.*** ⟦< L *ostendere*, to show⟧ apparent; seeming —**os·ten'si·bly** ***adv.***

os·ten·ta·tion (äs'tən tā'shən) ***n.*** ⟦< L *ostendere*, to show⟧ showy display; pretentiousness —**os'ten·ta'tious** ***adj.***

osteo- ⟦< Gr *osteon*, a bone⟧ *combining form* bone or bones

os·te·o·ar·thri·tis (äs'tē ō'är thrīt'is) ***n.*** ⟦prec. + ARTHRITIS⟧ a common form of arthritis marked by degeneration of cartilage of the joints

os·te·op·a·thy (äs'tē äp'ə thē) ***n.*** ⟦ModL: see OSTEO- & -PATHY⟧ a school of medicine and surgery that emphasizes the interrelationship of muscles and bones —**os·te·o·path** (äs'tē ō path', -tē ə-) ***n.***

os·te·o·po·ro·sis (äs'tē ō'pə rō'sis) ***n.*** ⟦OSTEO- + L *porus*, a pore + -OSIS⟧ a bone disorder marked by porous, brittle bones

os·to·my (äs'tə mē) ***n.,*** *pl.* **-mies** any surgery connecting a hollow organ to the outside of the body or to another hollow organ

os·tra·cize (äs'trə sīz') ***vt.*** **-cized', -ciz'ing** ⟦< Gr *ostrakon*, a shell (cast as a ballot)⟧ to banish from a group, society, etc. —**os'tra·cism'** ***n.***

os·trich (äs'trich, ôs'-) ***n.*** ⟦< L *avis*, bird + *struthio*, ostrich⟧ a large, swift-running bird of Africa and SW Asia

OT or **O.T.** **1** Old Testament **2** overtime

O·thel·lo (ō thel'ō) a tragedy by Shakespeare in which the title character, madly jealous, kills his wife

oth·er (uth'ər) ***adj.*** ⟦OE⟧ **1** being the remaining one or ones /Bill and the *other* boys/ **2** different or distinct from that or those implied /use your *other* foot/ **3** additional /he has no *other* coat/ —***pron.*** **1** the other one **2** some other one /to do as *others* do/ —***adv.*** otherwise /he can't do *other* than go/ —**the other day** (or **night,** etc.) not long ago; recently

oth'er·wise' ***adv.*** **1** in another manner; differently /I believe *otherwise*/ **2** in all other respects /he is *otherwise* intelligent/ **3** in other circumstances —***adj.*** different

oth'er·world'ly ***adj.*** being apart from earthly interests

o·ti·ose (ō'shē ōs') ***adj.*** ⟦< L *otium*, leisure⟧ **1** [Rare] idle **2** futile **3** useless

Ot·ta·wa (ät'ə wə, -wä') capital of Canada, in SE Ontario: pop. 567,000

ot·ter (ät'ər) ***n.*** ⟦OE *oter*⟧ **1** a furry, swimming, carnivorous mammal with webbed feet **2** its fur

ot·to·man (ät'ə mən) ***n.*** ⟦Fr *ottomane*⟧ a low, cushioned seat or footstool

ouch (ouch) ***interj.*** an exclamation of sudden pain

ought (ôt) ***v.aux.*** used with infinitives and meaning: **1** obligation, duty, or desirability /you *ought* to eat more/ **2** to be expected /it *ought* to be over soon/

oui (wē) ***adv.*** ⟦Fr⟧ yes

Oui·ja (wē'jə, -jē) ⟦< prec. + Ger *ja*, yes⟧ *trademark for* a supposedly spiritualistic device consisting of a board with the alphabet, and a sliding, three-legged pointer

ounce (ouns) ***n.*** ⟦< L *uncia*, a twelfth⟧ **1** a unit of weight, $\frac{1}{16}$ pound avoirdupois or $\frac{1}{12}$ pound troy **2** fluid ounce, $\frac{1}{16}$ pint

our (our; är) ***poss. pronominal adj.*** ⟦OE *ure*⟧ of, belonging to, or done by us

ours (ourz, ärz) ***pron.*** that or those belonging to us /a friend of *ours*/

our·selves (our selvz′) ***pron.*** 1 *the intensive form of* WE /we went *ourselves*/ 2 *the reflexive form of* WE /we hurt *ourselves*/ 3 our true selves /we are not *ourselves* when sick/

-ous (əs) ⟦< L *-osus*⟧ *suffix* having, full of, characterized by /*beauteous*/

oust (oust) ***vt.*** ⟦< L *ostare,* obstruct⟧ to force out; expel; dispossess

oust′er ***n.*** an ousting or being ousted

out (out) ***adv.*** ⟦OE *ut*⟧ 1 away or removed from a place, position, etc. 2 into the open air 3 into existence or activity /disease broke *out*/ 4 *a*) to a conclusion /argue it *out*/ *b*) completely /tired *out*/ 5 into sight or notice /the moon came *out*/ 6 from existence or activity /fade *out*/ 7 aloud /sing *out*/ 8 beyond a regular surface, condition, etc. /stand *out*/ 9 into disuse /long skirts went *out*/ 10 from a group or stock /pick *out*/ 11 [Slang] into unconsciousness 12 *Baseball* in a manner that results in an out /to fly *out*/ **—*adj.*** 1 external: usually in combination /*outpost*/ 2 beyond regular limits 3 away from work, etc. 4 in error /*out* in one's estimates/ 5 not in use, operation, etc. 6 [Colloq.] having suffered a financial loss /*out* one dollar/ 7 [Colloq.] outmoded 8 *Baseball* having failed to get on base **—*prep.*** 1 out of 2 along the way of **—*n.*** 1 something that is out 2 [Slang] a way out; excuse 3 *Baseball* the failure of a player to reach base safely **—*vi.*** to become known /the truth will *out*/ **—on the outs** [Colloq.] on unfriendly terms **—out for** making a determined effort to get or do **—out of** 1 from inside of 2 beyond 3 from (material, etc.) /made *out of* stone/ 4 because of /*out of* spite/ 5 having no /*out of* gas/ 6 so as to deprive **—out to** trying to

out- *combining form* 1 at or from a point away; outside /*outpatient*/ 2 going away or forth; outward /*outbound*/ 3 better or more than /*outdo, outsmart*/

out·age (out′ij) ***n.*** an interruption of operation, as of electric power

out′-and-out′ ***adj.*** thorough

out′back′ ***n.*** any remote, sparsely settled region viewed as uncivilized

out′bal′ance ***vt.*** **-anced, -anc·ing** to be greater than in weight, value, etc.

out′bid′ ***vt.*** **-bid′, -bid′ding** to bid or offer more than (someone else)

out′board′ ***adj.*** outside the hull of a ship or boat /an *outboard* motor/

out′bound′ ***adj.*** outward bound

out′break′ ***n.*** a breaking out; sudden occurrence, as of disease, rioting, etc.

out′build′ing ***n.*** a structure, as a barn, separate from the main building

out′burst′ ***n.*** a sudden release, as of feeling, energy, etc.

out′cast′ ***adj.*** driven out; rejected **—*n.*** a person rejected, as by society

out′class′ ***vt.*** to surpass

out′come′ ***n.*** result; consequence

out′crop′ ***n.*** 1 the emergence of a mineral at the earth's surface 2 the mineral that so emerges

out′cry′ ***n., pl.*** **-cries′** 1 a crying out 2 a strong protest

out′dat′ed ***adj.*** no longer current

out′dis′tance ***vt.*** **-tanced, -tanc·ing** to get ahead of, as in a race

out′do′ ***vt.*** **-did′, -done′, -do′ing** to exceed or surpass **—outdo oneself** to do better than one expected to do

out′door′ ***adj.*** 1 being or taking place outdoors 2 of or fond of the outdoors

out′doors′ ***adv.*** in or into the open; outside **—*n.*** any area outside a building

out′er ***adj.*** farther out or away

out′er·most′ ***adj.*** farthest out

outer space space beyond the earth's atmosphere or beyond the solar system

out′er·wear′ ***n.*** garments, as overcoats, worn over the usual clothing

out′field′ ***n.*** *Baseball* 1 the playing area beyond the infield 2 the players (**outfielders**) positioned there

out′fit′ ***n.*** 1 the equipment used in an activity 2 clothing worn together; ensemble 3 a group of people associated in an activity **—*vt.*** **-fit′ted, -fit′ting** to furnish with an outfit **—out′fit′ter** ***n.***

out′flank′ ***vt.*** to go around and beyond the flank of (enemy troops)

out′fox′ ***vt.*** to outsmart

out′go′ ***n., pl.*** **-goes′** that which is paid out; expenditure

out′go′ing ***adj.*** 1 *a*) leaving *b*) retiring from office 2 sociable

out′grow′ ***vt.*** **-grew′, -grown′, -grow′ing** 1 to grow faster or larger than 2 to lose in becoming mature /to *outgrow* one's fear/ 3 to grow too large for

out′growth′ ***n.*** 1 a growing out or that which grows out 2 a result, consequence, or development

out′guess′ ***vt.*** to outwit

out′house′ ***n.*** a small outdoor structure used as a toilet, having a seat with a hole over a deep pit

out′ing ***n.*** 1 a pleasure trip 2 an outdoor walk, ride, picnic, etc.

out′land′ish (-lan′dish) ***adj.*** very odd or strange; fantastic; bizarre

out·last′ ***vt.*** to endure longer than

out′law′ ***n.*** 1 orig., a person deprived by a court of law of legal rights and protection 2 a habitual or notorious criminal **—*vt.*** 1 orig., to declare to be an outlaw 2 to declare illegal

out′lay′ ***n.*** 1 a spending (*of* money, etc.) 2 money, etc. spent

out′let′ ***n.*** 1 a passage for letting something out 2 a means of expression /an *outlet* for anger/ 3 a retail store selling defective or surplus goods at a discount: in full **outlet store** 4 a point in a wiring system at which current may be taken

out′line′ ***n.*** 1 a line bounding the limits of an object 2 a sketch showing only contours 3 [*also pl.*] a general plan 4 a systematic summary **—*vt.*** **-lined′, -lin′ing** 1 to draw in outline 2 to make an outline of

out′live′ ***vt.*** **-lived′, -liv′ing** to live or endure longer than; outlast

out′look′ ***n.*** 1 the view from a place 2 viewpoint 3 expectation or prospect

out′ly′ing ***adj.*** relatively far out from a certain point; remote

out′ma·neu′ver or **out′ma·noeu′vre** ***vt.***

-**vered** or -**vred**, -**ver·ing** or -**vring** to outwit by maneuvering
out′match′ (-mach′) *vt.* to be superior to; outdo
out′mod′ed *adj.* no longer in fashion or accepted; obsolete
out′num′ber *vt.* to exceed in number
out′-of-date′ *adj.* no longer in style or use; old-fashioned
out′-of-door′ *adj.* OUTDOOR
out′-of-doors′ *adv., n.* OUTDOORS
out′-of-the-way′ *adj.* 1 secluded 2 not common; unusual
out′-of-town′er *n.* a visitor from another town or city
out′pa′tient *n.* a patient treated at a hospital, etc. without becoming an inpatient
out′place′ment *n.* assistance in finding a new job provided to an employee by the employer
out′play′ *vt.* to play better than
out′post′ *n.* 1 *Mil.* *a)* a small group stationed at a distance from the main force *b)* the station so occupied *c)* a foreign base 2 a frontier settlement
out′put′ *n.* 1 the work done or amount produced, esp. over a given period 2 information delivered by a computer 3 *Elec.* the useful voltage, current, or power delivered
out′rage′ *n.* ⟦ult. < L *ultra*, beyond⟧ 1 an extremely vicious or violent act 2 a deep insult or offense 3 great anger, etc. aroused by this —*vt.* -**raged′**, -**rag′ing** 1 to commit an outrage upon or against 2 to cause outrage in
out·ra′geous (-rā′jəs) *adj.* 1 involving or doing great injury or wrong 2 very offensive or shocking —**out·ra′geous·ly** *adv.*
out′rank′ *vt.* to exceed in rank
ou·tré (o͞o trā′) *adj.* ⟦Fr⟧ 1 exaggerated 2 eccentric; bizarre
out·reach (*for v.* out′rēch′; *for n. & adj.* out′rēch′) *vt., vi.* 1 to exceed; surpass 2 to reach out; extend —*n.* a reaching out —*adj.* designating or of a program extending services to those not usually accommodated
out′rid′er *n.* 1 a rider on horseback who accompanies a stagecoach, etc. 2 a cowboy riding a range, as to keep cattle from straying 3 a forerunner

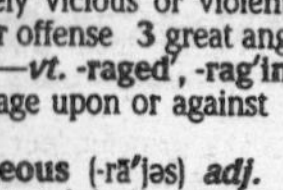
CANOE WITH OUTRIGGER

out′rig′ger (-rig′ər) *n.* 1 a timber rigged out from the side of certain canoes to prevent tipping 2 a canoe of this type
out′right′ *adj.* 1 without reservation 2 complete —*adv.* 1 entirely 2 openly 3 at once
out′run′ *vt.* -**ran′**, -**run′**, -**run′ning** 1 to run faster than 2 to exceed
out′sell′ *vt.* -**sold′**, -**sell′ing** to sell in greater amounts than
out′set′ *n.* a setting out; beginning
out′shine′ *vt.* -**shone′** or -**shined′**, -**shin′ing** 1 to shine brighter or longer than 2 to surpass; excel
out′side′ *n.* 1 the outer side or part; exterior 2 outward appearance 3 any area not inside —*adj.* 1 of or on the outside; outer 2 extreme /an *outside* estimate/ 3 slight /an *outside* chance/ —*adv.* 1 on or to the outside 2 outdoors —*prep.* 1 on or to the outer side of 2 beyond the limits of —**outside of** 1 outside 2 [Colloq.] other than
out′sid′er *n.* one who is not included in a given group
out′size′ *n.* an odd size, esp. an unusually large one
out′skirt′ *n.* a part remote from the center, as of a city: *usually used in pl.*
out′smart′ *vt.* to overcome by cunning or cleverness; outwit —**outsmart oneself** to have one's efforts at cunning or cleverness result in one's own disadvantage
out′sourc·ing (-sôr siŋ) *n.* the practice of purchasing parts, etc. from domestic nonunion shops or from foreign companies
out′spo′ken *adj.* 1 unrestrained in speech 2 spoken boldly or candidly
out′spread′ *adj.* spread out; extended
out′stand′ing *adj.* 1 projecting 2 prominent; distinguished 3 unpaid; uncollected 4 issued and sold: said of stocks and bonds
out′sta′tion *n.* a post or station in a remote or unsettled area
out′stretch′ *vt.* 1 to stretch out; extend 2 to stretch beyond
out′strip′ *vt.* -**stripped′**, -**strip′ping** 1 to go at a faster pace than 2 to excel; surpass
out′take′ *n.* a filmed scene, defective recording, etc. not used as or in the final version
out′vote′ *vt.* -**vot′ed**, -**vot′ing** to defeat in voting
out′ward (-wərd) *adj.* 1 having to do with the outside; outer 2 clearly apparent 3 away from the interior —*adv.* toward the outside: also **out′wards** —**out′ward·ly** *adv.*
out′wear′ *vt.* -**wore′**, -**worn′**, -**wear′ing** 1 to wear out 2 to outlast
out′weigh′ *vt.* 1 to weigh more than 2 to be more important than
out′wit′ *vt.* -**wit′ted**, -**wit′ting** to get the better of by cleverness
o·va (ō′və) *n. pl. of* OVUM
o·val (ō′vəl) *adj.* ⟦< L *ovum*, egg⟧ egg-shaped; elliptical —*n.* anything oval
o·va·ry (ō′və rē) *n., pl.* -**ries** ⟦< L *ovum*, egg⟧ 1 a female reproductive gland producing eggs 2 *Bot.* the enlarged, hollow part of the pistil, containing ovules —**o·var·i·an** (ō ver′ē ən) *adj.*
o·vate (ō′vāt′) *adj.* egg-shaped; oval
o·va·tion (ō vā′shən) *n.* ⟦< L *ovare*, celebrate a triumph⟧ enthusiastic applause or public welcome
ov·en (uv′ən) *n.* ⟦OE *ofen*⟧ a compartment or receptacle for baking, roasting, heating, etc.
o·ver (ō′vər) *prep.* ⟦OE *ofer*⟧ 1 *a)* in, at, or to a position above *b)* across and down from /to fall *over* a cliff/ 2 so as to cover /shutters *over* the windows/ 3 upon, as an effect /to cast a spell *over* someone/ 4 above in authority, power, etc. 5 on or to the other side of /fly *over* the lake/ 6 throughout /*over* the whole city/ 7 during

[over the years] **8** more than *[over ten cents]* **9** in preference to **10** concerning —*adv.* **1** *a)* above or across *b)* across the brim or edge **2** more *[three hours or over]* **3** from start to finish *[go over it]* **4** *a)* from an upright position *[to fall over]* *b)* upside down *[turn the cup over]* **5** again *[do it over]* **6** at, on, to, or in a specified place *[over in Spain]* **7** from one belief, etc. to another *[win him over]* —*adj.* **1** upper, outer, superior, excessive, or extra **2** finished; past **3** having reached the other side **4** [Colloq.] as a surplus

over- *combining form* **1** above in position, rank, etc. *[overlord]* **2** passing across or beyond *[overrun]* **3** excessively *[oversell]* The list below includes some common compounds formed with *over-* that can be understood if "too much" or "excessively" is added to the meaning of the base word:

overabundance
overactive
overambitious
overanxious
overbid
overburden
overcautious
overconfident
overcook
overcritical
overcrowd
overdevelop
overeager
overeat
overemphasize
overenthusiastic
overexercise
overexert
overexpose
overextend
overgenerous
overheat
overindulge
overindulgence
overload
overpay
overpopulate
overproduce
overproduction
overrefined
overripe
oversell
oversensitive
overspecialize
overspend
overstimulate
overstock
overstrict
oversupply
overtire

o′ver·a·chieve′ *vi.* **-chieved′, -chiev′ing** **1** to do better in school than might be expected from test scores **2** to drive oneself to reach unreasonable goals —**o′ver·a·chieve′ment** *n.* —**o′ver·a·chiev′er** *n.*

o′ver·act′ *vt., vi.* to act with exaggeration

o·ver·age[1] (ō′vər āj′) *adj.* over the age fixed as a standard

o·ver·age[2] (ō′vər ij) *n.* ⟦OVER + -AGE⟧ a surplus or excess

o·ver·all (*for adj.* ō′vər ôl′; *for adv.* ō′vər ôl′) *adj.* **1** from end to end **2** including everything; total —*adv.* **1** from end to end **2** in general

o′ver·alls′ (-ôlz′) *n.pl.* loose trousers extending up over the chest, worn over other clothing to protect against dirt

o′ver·awe′ *vt.* **-awed′, -aw′ing** to overcome or subdue by inspiring awe

o′ver·bal′ance *vt.* **-anced, -anc·ing** **1** OUTWEIGH **2** to throw off balance

o′ver·bear′ing *adj.* arrogant; domineering

o′ver·bite′ *n.* a dental condition in which the upper incisors and canines project abnormally over the lower ones

o′ver·blown′ (-blōn′) *adj.* **1** overdone; excessive **2** pompous or bombastic

o′ver·board′ *adv.* from a ship into the water —**go overboard** [Colloq.] to go to extremes

o′ver·book′ *vt., vi.* to issue more reservations than there are seats for

o′ver·cast′ *adj.* cloudy; dark: said of the sky

o·ver·charge (ō′vər chärj′; *also & for n.* ō′vər chärj′) *vt., vi.* **-charged′, -charg′ing** **1** to charge too much **2** to overload —*n.* **1** an excessive charge **2** too full a load

o′ver·clothes′ *n.pl.* OUTERWEAR

o′ver·cloud′ *vt., vi.* to make or become cloudy, gloomy, etc.

o′ver·coat′ *n.* a heavy coat worn over the usual clothing for warmth

o′ver·come′ *vt.* **-came′, -come′, -com′ing** **1** to get the better of in competition, etc. **2** to master, prevail over, or surmount —*vi.* to win

o′ver·de·ter′mine *vt.* to bring about through many causes or factors

o′ver·do′ *vt.* **-did′, -done′, -do′ing** **1** to do too much **2** to exaggerate **3** to overcook —*vi.* to exhaust oneself by doing too much

o′ver·dose′ *n.* too large a dose

o′ver·draw′ *vt.* **-drew′, -drawn′, -draw′·ing** to draw on in excess of the amount credited to the drawer —**o′ver·draft′** *n.*

o′ver·dress′ *vt., vi.* to dress too warmly, too showily, or too formally

o′ver·dub′ *n.* a recording of sounds, music, etc. superimposed on another recording —*vt., vi.* **-dubbed′, -dub′bing** to add (sounds, music, etc.) to (a recording)

o′ver·due′ *adj.* past the time for payment, arrival, etc.

o′ver·es′ti·mate′ *vt.* **-mat′ed, -mat′ing** to set too high an estimate on or for

o′ver·flight′ *n.* the flight of an aircraft over a foreign territory, as in reconnaissance

o·ver·flow (ō′vər flō′; *also & for n.* ō′vər flō′) *vt.* **1** to flow across; flood **2** to flow over the brim of —*vi.* **1** to run over **2** to be superabundant —*n.* **1** an overflowing **2** the amount that overflows **3** an outlet for overflowing liquids

o′ver·grow′ *vt.* **-grew′, -grown′, -grow′·ing** to overspread with foliage so as to cover —*vi.* to grow too fast or beyond normal —**o′ver·grown′** *adj.* —**o′ver·growth′** *n.*

o′ver·hand′ *adj., adv.* with the hand raised above the elbow or the arm above the shoulder

o·ver·hang (ō′vər haŋ′; *also & for n.* ō′vər haŋ′) *vt., vi.* **-hung′, -hang′ing** to hang over or project beyond (something) —*n.* the projection of one thing over another

o·ver·haul (ō′vər hôl′; *also & for n.* ō′vər hôl′) *vt.* **1** *a)* to check thoroughly, as for needed repairs *b)* to restore (a motor, etc.) to good working order **2** to catch up with —*n.* an overhauling

o·ver·head (*for adj. & adv.* ō′vər hed′, ō′vər hed′; *for n.* ō′vər hed′) *adj.* **1** above the head **2** in the sky **3** on a higher level, with reference to related objects —*n.* the general, continuing costs of a business, as of rent, taxes, etc. —*adv.* above the head; aloft

o′ver·hear′ *vt.* **-heard′, -hear′ing** to hear (something spoken or a speaker) without the speaker's knowledge

o′ver·joy′ *vt.* to give great joy to; delight

o′ver·kill′ *n.* much more of something than is necessary, appropriate, etc.

o′ver·land′ *adv., adj.* by, on, or across land

o′ver·lap′ *vt., vi.* **-lapped′, -lap′ping** to extend over a part of (something) so as to coincide with this part

o′ver·lay′ *vt.* **-laid′, -lay′ing** **1** to lay or spread over **2** to cover, as with a decorative layer

o'ver·lie' *vt.* **-lay', -lain', -ly'ing** to lie on or over

o'ver·look' *vt.* 1 to look at from above 2 to give a view of from above 3 *a)* to fail to notice *b)* to ignore; neglect 4 to excuse 5 to supervise

o'ver·lord' *n.* a lord ranking above other lords

o'ver·ly *adv.* too or too much

o'ver·mas'ter *vt.* to overcome

o'ver·much' *adj., adv., n.* too much

o·ver·night (ō'vər nīt', ō'-; ō'vər nīt') *adv.* 1 during the night 2 suddenly —*adj.* 1 done or going on during the night 2 for one night /an *overnight* guest/ 3 of or for a brief trip /an *overnight* bag/

o'ver·pass' *n.* a bridge, etc. over a road, railway, etc.

o'ver·play' *vt.* 1 to overact, overdo, or overemphasize 2 to overestimate the strength of (one's hand in cards)

o'ver·pow'er *vt.* to get the better of; subdue or overwhelm

o'ver·price' *vt.* **-priced', -pric'ing** to offer for sale at too high a price

o'ver·pro·tect' *vt.* to protect more than necessary; specif., to control excessively (one's child, etc.) in trying to shield from hurt, disappointment, etc.

o'ver·qual'i·fied *adj.* having more knowledge, education, etc. than needed to qualify

o'ver·rate' *vt.* **-rat'ed, -rat'ing** to rate or estimate too highly

o'ver·reach' *vt.* to reach beyond or above —**overreach oneself** to fail because of trying to do too much

o'ver·re·act' *vi.* to react in a highly emotional way

o'ver·ride' *vt.* **-rode', -rid'den, -rid'ing** 1 to ride over 2 to prevail over 3 to disregard or nullify

o'ver·rule' *vt.* **-ruled', -rul'ing** 1 to set aside or decide against by virtue of higher authority 2 to prevail over

o'ver·run' *vt.* **-ran', -run', -run'ning** 1 to spread out over so as to cover 2 to swarm over, as vermin 3 to extend beyond (certain limits)

o'ver·seas' *adv.* over or beyond the sea —*adj.* 1 foreign 2 over or across the sea Also [Chiefly Brit.] **o·'ver·sea'**

o'ver·see' *vt.* **-saw', -seen', -see'ing** to supervise; superintend —**o'ver·se'er** (-sir', -sē'ər) *n.*

o'ver·sexed' *adj.* having exceptional sexual drive or interest

o'ver·shad'ow *vt.* 1 *a)* to cast a shadow over *b)* to darken 2 to be more important than by comparison

o'ver·shoe' *n.* a boot of rubber, etc. worn over the regular shoe to protect against cold or dampness

o'ver·shoot' *vt.* **-shot', -shoot'ing** 1 to shoot or pass over or beyond (a target, mark, etc.) 2 to exceed

o'ver·sight' *n.* a careless mistake or omission

o'ver·sim'pli·fy' *vt., vi.* **-fied', -fy'ing** to simplify to the point of distortion —**o'ver·sim'pli·fi·ca'tion** *n.*

o'ver·size' *adj.* 1 too large 2 larger than the usual Also **o'ver·sized'**

o'ver·sleep' *vi.* **-slept', -sleep'ing** to sleep longer than intended

o'ver·spread' *vt.* **-spread', -spread'ing** to spread or cover over

o'ver·state' *vt.* **-stat'ed, -stat'ing** to exaggerate —**o'ver·state'ment** *n.*

o'ver·stay' *vt.* to stay beyond the time or limit of

o'ver·step' *vt.* **-stepped', -step'ping** to go beyond the limits of

o'ver·strung' *adj.* too highly strung; tense

o'ver·stuff' *vt.* 1 to stuff with too much of something 2 to upholster (furniture) with deep stuffing

o·vert (ō vurt', ō'vurt') *adj.* [[< L *aperire,* to open]] not hidden; apparent —**o·vert'ly** *adv.*

o'ver·take' *vt.* **-took', -tak'en, -tak'ing** 1 to catch up with 2 to come upon suddenly

o'ver·tax' *vt.* 1 to tax too heavily 2 to make excessive demands on

o'ver-the-count'er *adj.* 1 designating or of securities sold directly to buyers 2 sold legally without prescription, as some drugs

o·ver·throw (ō'vər thrō'; *also & for n.* ō'vər thrō') *vt.* **-threw', -thrown', -thow'ing** 1 to throw or turn over 2 to conquer 3 to throw beyond —*n.* 1 an overthrowing or being overthrown 2 destruction; end

o'ver·time' *n.* 1 time beyond the established limit, as of working hours 2 pay for work done in such a time —*adj., adv.* of, for, or during overtime

o'ver·tone' *n.* 1 a faint, higher tone accompanying a fundamental tone produced by a musical instrument 2 an implication; nuance: *usually in pl.*

o·ver·ture (ō'vər chər) *n.* [[< L *apertura,* aperture]] 1 an introductory proposal or offer 2 a musical introduction to an opera, etc.

o'ver·turn' *vt.* 1 to turn over 2 to conquer —*vi.* to tip over; capsize

o'ver·ween'ing (-wē'niŋ) *adj.* [[< OE *ofer,* over + *wenan,* to think]] 1 arrogant 2 excessive

o'ver·weight' *adj.* above the normal or allowed weight

o'ver·whelm' *vt.* 1 to pour down upon and bury beneath 2 to crush; overpower —**o'ver·whelm'ing** *adj.*

o'ver·work' *vt.* to work or use to excess —*vi.* to work too hard or too long —*n.* severe or burdensome work

o·ver·wrought (ō'vər rôt', ō'-) *adj.* 1 very nervous or excited 2 too elaborate

Ov·id (äv'id) 43 B.C.-*c.* A.D. 17; Rom. poet

o·vi·duct (ō'vi dukt') *n.* [[< L *ovum,* egg + DUCT]] a tube through which the ova pass from an ovary to the uterus

o·vip·a·rous (ō vip'ə rəs) *adj.* [[< L *ovum,* egg + *parere,* to bear]] producing eggs which hatch after leaving the body

o·void (ō'void') *adj.* [[< L *ovum,* egg + -OID]] egg-shaped —*n.* anything ovoid

ov·u·late (äv'yōō lāt', -yə-; ō'vyōō-, -vyə-) *vi.* **-lat'ed, -lat'ing** [[< L *ovum,* egg]] to produce and discharge ova from the ovary —**ov'u·la'tion** *n.*

ov·ule (äv'yōōl', ō'vyōōl') *n.* [[< L *ovum,* egg]] a small egg or seed, esp. one in an early stage of development —**ov'u·lar** *adj.*

o·vum (ō'vəm) ***n.***, *pl.* **o·va** (ō'və) ⟦L, egg⟧ a mature female germ cell

ow (ou) ***interj.*** a cry of pain

owe (ō) ***vt.* owed, ow'ing** ⟦OE *agan,* to own⟧ **1** to be indebted to the amount of **2** to have the need to do, give, etc., as because of gratitude **3** to be indebted *to* someone for

ow·ing (ō'iŋ) ***adj.*** ⟦ME *owynge*⟧ **1** that owes **2** due; unpaid —**owing to** because of

owl (oul) ***n.*** ⟦OE *ule*⟧ **1** a predatory night bird having a large, flat face, large eyes, and a short, hooked beak **2** a person of nocturnal habits, solemn appearance, etc. —**owl'ish *adj.***

owl'et (-it) ***n.*** a young or small owl

own (ōn) ***adj.*** ⟦OE *agan,* possess⟧ belonging or relating to oneself or itself /his *own* book/ —***n.*** that which belongs to oneself /that is her *own*/ —***vt.*** **1** to possess; have **2** to admit; acknowledge —***vi.*** to confess (*to*) —**on one's own** [Colloq.] by one's own efforts —**own'er *n.*** —**own'er·ship' *n.***

ox (äks) ***n.***, *pl.* **ox'en** ⟦OE *oxa*⟧ any of certain cud-chewing, cattlelike mammals, esp. a castrated, domesticated bull used as a draft animal

ox'blood' *n.* a deep-red color

ox'bow' (-bō') ***n.*** the U-shaped part of an ox yoke which passes under and around the animal's neck

ox·ford (äks'fərd) ***n.*** ⟦after Oxford, England⟧ [*sometimes* **O-**] **1** a low shoe laced over the instep: also **oxford shoe** **2** a cotton or rayon fabric with a basketlike weave: also **oxford cloth**

Ox·ford (äks'fərd) city in south central England; site of Oxford University: pop. 116,000

ox·i·dant (äks'i dənt) ***n.*** an oxidizing agent

ox·i·da·tion (äks'i dā'shən) ***n.*** an oxidizing or being oxidized

ox·ide (äks'īd') ***n.*** ⟦Fr⟧ a compound of oxygen with another element or a radical

ox·i·dize (äks'i dīz') ***vt.* -dized', -diz'ing** to unite with oxygen, as in burning or rusting —***vi.*** to become oxidized —**ox'i·diz'er *n.***

Ox·nard (äks'närd) city in SW Calif., near Los Angeles: pop. 108,000

ox·y·a·cet·y·lene (äks'ē ə set''l ēn') ***adj.*** of or using a mixture of oxygen and acetylene, as for producing a hot flame used in welding

ox·y·gen (äks'i jən) ***n.*** ⟦Fr *oxygène*⟧ a colorless, odorless, gaseous chemical element: it is essential to life processes and to combustion

ox'y·gen·ate' (-jə nāt') ***vt.* -at'ed, -at'ing** to treat or combine with oxygen —**ox'y·gen·a'tion *n.***

oxygen tent a transparent enclosure filled with oxygen, fitted around a bed patient to aid breathing

ox·y·mo·ron (äks'i mō'rän', -môr'än') ***n.***, *pl.* **-mo'ra** (-rə) ⟦< Gr *oxys,* sharp + *mōros,* foolish⟧ a figure of speech in which contradictory ideas, etc. are combined (Ex.: thunderous silence)

oys·ter (ois'tər) ***n.*** ⟦< Gr *ostreon*⟧ an edible bivalve mollusk with an irregular shell

oz. ounce(s)

o·zone (ō'zōn') ***n.*** ⟦Fr < Gr *ozein,* to smell⟧ **1** an unstable, pale-blue form of oxygen with a strong odor, formed by an electrical discharge in air and used as a bleaching agent, water purifier, etc. **2** [Slang] pure, fresh air

ozone layer the layer of ozone in the stratosphere that absorbs much ultraviolet radiation

P

p or **P** (pē) ***n.***, *pl.* **p's, P's** the 16th letter of the English alphabet

P *Chem. symbol for* phosphorus

p or **p.** **1** page **2** participle **3** past **4** per **5** pint

P or **P.** petite

pa (pä) ***n.*** [Colloq.] FATHER

PA **1** Pennsylvania: also **Pa.** **2** public address (system): also **P.A.**

PAC political action committee

pace (pās) ***n.*** ⟦< L *passus,* a step⟧ **1** a step in walking, etc. **2** the length of a step or stride **3** the rate of speed in walking, etc. **4** rate of progress, etc. **5** a gait **6** the gait of a horse in which both legs on the same side are raised together —***vt.* paced, pac'ing** **1** to walk back and forth across **2** to measure by paces **3** to set the pace for (a runner, etc.) —***vi.*** **1** to walk with regular steps **2** to move at a pace: said of a horse —**put through one's paces** to test one's ability, skills, etc. —**pac'er *n.***

pace'mak'er *n.* **1** one that leads the way: also **pace'set'ter** **2** an electronic device placed in the body to regulate the heartbeat

pach·y·derm (pak'ə durm') ***n.*** ⟦< Gr *pachys,* thick + *derma,* skin⟧ a large, thick-skinned, hoofed animal, as the elephant or rhinoceros

pach·y·san·dra (pak'ə san'drə) ***n.*** ⟦< ModL name of genus⟧ a low, hardy evergreen plant often used for a ground cover in the shade

pa·cif·ic (pə sif'ik) ***adj.*** ⟦see PACIFY⟧ **1** making peace **2** of a peaceful nature; tranquil; calm

Pa·cif·ic (pə sif'ik) largest of the earth's oceans, between Asia and the American continents

pac·i·fi·er (pas'ə fī'ər) ***n.*** **1** one that pacifies **2** a nipple or teething ring for babies

pac'i·fism' (-fiz'əm) ***n.*** opposition to the use of force under any circumstances; specif., refusal to participate in war —**pac'i·fist *n., adj.***

pac·i·fy (pas'ə fī') ***vt.* -fied', -fy'ing** ⟦< L *pax,* peace + *facere,* make⟧ to make peaceful, calm, nonhostile, etc. —**pac'i·fi·ca'tion** *n.*

pack[1] (pak) *n.* ⟦< MDu *pak*⟧ 1 a bundle of things tied up for carrying 2 a number of similar persons or things; specif., *a)* a group /a *pack* of lies/ *b)* a package of a standard number /a *pack* of cigarettes/ *c)* a number of wild animals living together —*vt.* 1 to make a pack of 2 *a)* to put together in a box, trunk, etc. *b)* to fill (a box, etc.) 3 to crowd; cram /the hall was *packed*/ 4 to fill in tightly, as for prevention of leaks 5 to carry in a pack 6 to send (*off*) /to *pack* him off to school/ 7 [Slang] to carry (a gun, etc.) 8 [Slang] to deliver (a punch, etc.) with force —*vi.* 1 to make up packs 2 to put one's clothes, etc. into luggage for a trip 3 to crowd together 4 to settle into a compact mass —*adj.* used for carrying packs, loads, etc. /a *pack* animal/ —**send packing** to dismiss abruptly

pack[2] (pak) *vt.* to choose (a jury, etc.) so as to get desired results

pack·age (pak'ij) *n.* 1 a wrapped or boxed thing or group of things; parcel 2 a number of items, plans, etc. offered as a unit —*vt.* **-aged, -ag·ing** to make a package of —**pack'ag·er** *n.*

package store a store where alcoholic beverages are sold by the bottle

pack'er *n.* one that packs; specif., one who operates a packing house

pack'et (-it) *n.* 1 a small package 2 a boat that travels a regular route carrying passengers, freight, and mail: in full **packet boat**

pack'ing *n.* 1 the act or process of a person or thing that packs 2 any material used to pack

pack'ing·house' *n.* a plant where meats, etc. are processed and packed for sale

pack rat a North American rat that often hides small articles in its nest

pack'sad'dle *n.* a saddle with fastenings to secure and balance the load carried by a pack animal

pact (pakt) *n.* ⟦< L *pax,* peace⟧ an agreement; compact

pad[1] (pad) *n.* ⟦echoic⟧ the dull sound of a footstep —*vi.* **pad'ded, pad'ding** to walk, esp. with a soft step

pad[2] (pad) *n.* ⟦? var. of POD⟧ 1 anything soft to protect against friction, pressure, etc.; cushion 2 the cushionlike sole of an animal's paw 3 the floating leaf of a water plant, as the waterlily 4 a number of sheets of paper glued along one edge; tablet 5 [Slang] the place where one lives —*vt.* **pad'ded, pad'ding** 1 to stuff or cover with soft material 2 to lengthen (a speech, etc.) with unnecessary material 3 to fill (an expense account, etc.) with invented or inflated entries

pad'ding *n.* anything used to pad

pad·dle[1] (pad''l) *n.* ⟦ME *padell,* small spade⟧ 1 a short pole with a wide blade at one or both ends, used in a canoe, kayak, etc. 2 an implement shaped like this, used to hit a ball, beat something, etc. —*vt., vi.* **-dled, -dling** 1 to propel (a canoe, etc.) by a paddle 2 to beat as with a paddle; spank

pad·dle[2] (pad''l) *vi.* **-dled, -dling** ⟦prob. < PAD[1]⟧ to move the hands or feet about in the water, as in playing

paddle ball a game like handball played with a short-handled paddle

paddle wheel a wheel with paddles around it for propelling a steamboat

pad·dock (pad'ək) *n.* ⟦OE *pearruc,* enclosure⟧ 1 a small enclosure near a stable, in which horses are exercised 2 an enclosure at a racetrack, where horses are saddled

pad·dy (pad'ē) *n., pl.* **-dies** ⟦Malay *padi,* rice in the husk⟧ a rice field Often **rice paddy**

pad·lock (pad'läk') *n.* a removable lock with a hinged link to be passed through a staple, chain, or eye —*vt.* to fasten or close up as with a padlock

pa·dre (pä'drā') *n.* ⟦< L *pater*⟧ 1 father: the title of a priest in Italy, Spain, etc. 2 [Colloq.] a priest or chaplain

pae·an (pē'ən) *n.* ⟦< Gr *paian,* hymn⟧ a song of joy, triumph, etc.

pa·gan (pā'gən) *n.* ⟦< L *paganus,* peasant⟧ 1 a heathen 2 one who has no religion —*adj.* of pagans —**pa'gan·ism'** *n.*

page[1] (pāj) *n.* ⟦< L *pangere,* fasten⟧ 1 *a)* one side of a leaf of a book, etc. *b)* an entire leaf in a book, etc. 2 [*often pl.*] a record of events —*vt.* **paged, pag'ing** to number the pages of

page[2] (pāj) *n.* ⟦OFr⟧ a boy attendant, esp. one who runs errands, etc., as in a hotel —*vt.* **paged, pag'ing** to try to find (a person) by calling his name, as a hotel page does

pag·eant (paj'ənt) *n.* ⟦ME *pagent,* stage scene⟧ 1 a spectacular exhibition, parade, etc. 2 an elaborate outdoor drama celebrating a historical event

pag'eant·ry (-ən trē) *n., pl.* **-ries** 1 grand spectacle; gorgeous display 2 empty show or display

pag·i·na·tion (paj'ə nā'shən) *n.* 1 the numbering of pages 2 the arrangement and number of pages

pa·go·da (pə gō'də) *n.* ⟦prob. < Pers *but,* idol + *kadah,* house⟧ in India and the Far East, a temple in the form of a pyramidal tower of several stories

paid (pād) *vt., vi. pt. & pp. of* PAY

pail (pāl) *n.* ⟦< OE *pægel,* wine vessel⟧ 1 a container, usually with a handle, for holding liquids, etc.; bucket 2 the amount held by a pail: also **pail'ful'**, *pl.* **-fuls'**

pain (pān) *n.* ⟦< Gr *poinē,* penalty⟧ 1 physical or mental suffering caused by injury, disease, grief, anxiety, etc. 2 [*pl.*] great care /take *pains* with one's work/ —*vt.* to cause pain to; hurt —**on** (or **under**) **pain of** at the risk of a penalty —**pain'ful** *adj.* —**pain'ful·ly** *adv.* —**pain'less** *adj.*

Paine (pān), **Thom·as** (täm'əs) 1737-1809; Am. Revolutionary patriot & writer

pain'kill'er *n.* [Colloq.] a medicine that relieves pain

pains·tak·ing (pānz'tā'kiŋ) *adj.* requiring or showing great care; very careful —**pains'-tak'ing·ly** *adv.*

paint (pānt) *vt.* ⟦< L *pingere*⟧ 1 *a)* to make (a picture, etc.) in colors applied to a surface *b)* to depict with paints 2 to describe vividly 3 to cover or decorate with paint —*vi.* to paint pictures —*n.* 1 a mixture of a pigment with oil, water, etc., used as a covering or coloring 2 a dried coat of paint

paint'er *n.* 1 an artist who paints pictures

2 one whose work is covering surfaces, as walls, with paint

paint′ing *n.* a painted picture

pair (per) *n., pl.* **pairs** or **pair** ⟦< L *par,* equal⟧ **1** two corresponding things associated or used together /a *pair* of shoes/ **2** a single unit of two corresponding parts /a *pair* of pants/ **3** any two persons or animals regarded as a unit —*vi., vt.* **1** to form a pair (of) **2** to mate

PAISLEY PATTERN

pais·ley (pāz′lē) *adj.* ⟦after *Paisley,* Scotland⟧ [*also* **P-**] having an intricate, multicolored pattern of swirls, etc.

pa·ja·mas (pə jä′məz, -jam′əz) *n.pl.* ⟦< Pers *pāi,* a leg + *jāma,* garment⟧ a loosely fitting sleeping or lounging suit consisting of jacket (or blouse) and trousers

Pa·ki·stan (pak′i stan′, pä′ki stän′) country in S Asia, west of India: 310,403 sq. mi.; pop. 101,855,000 —**Pak′i·stan′i** (-ē) *adj., n.*

pal (pal) *n.* ⟦Romany, brother, ult. < Sans⟧ [Colloq.] a close friend

pal·ace (pal′əs) *n.* ⟦< L *Palatium,* one of the Seven Hills of Rome⟧ **1** the official residence of a king, etc. **2** any large, magnificent building

pal·at·a·ble (pal′ə tə bəl) *adj.* pleasant or acceptable to the taste or mind

pal·ate (pal′ət) *n.* ⟦< L *palatum*⟧ **1** the roof of the mouth **2** sense of taste —**pal′a·tal** (-ə təl) *adj.*

pa·la·tial (pə lā′shəl) *adj.* ⟦see PALACE⟧ **1** of, suitable for, or like a palace **2** magnificent; stately

pal·a·tine (pal′ə tīn′, -tin) *adj.* ⟦see PALACE⟧ designating or of a count or earl who ruled in his own territory

pa·lav·er (pə lav′ər) *n.* ⟦Port *palavra,* a word⟧ talk, esp. profuse or idle talk —*vi.* to talk idly or profusely

pale[1] (pāl) *adj.* **pal′er, pal′est** ⟦< L *pallidus*⟧ **1** of a whitish or colorless complexion **2** lacking intensity, as color, light, etc.; dim —*vi., vt.* **paled, pal′ing** to become or make pale —**pale′ly** *adv.* —**pale′ness** *n.*

pale[2] (pāl) *n.* ⟦< L *palus,* a stake⟧ **1** a pointed stake used in fences **2** a boundary; restriction: now chiefly figurative

pale′face′ *n.* a white person: a term allegedly first used by North American Indians

pa·le·on·tol·o·gy (pā′lē ən täl′ə jē, -lē än-) *n.* ⟦< Fr⟧ the branch of geology studying prehistoric life by means of fossils —**pa′le·on·tol′o·gist** *n.*

Pa′le·o·zo′ic (-ō′zō′ik) *adj.* ⟦< Gr *palaios,* ancient + ZO(O)- + -IC⟧ designating the geologic era (*c.* 570-225 million years ago) characterized by the first fishes, reptiles, and land plants

Pal·es·tine (pal′əs tīn′) historical region in SW Asia at the E end of the Mediterranean, including modern Israel & Jordan —**Pal′es·tin′i·an** (-tin′ē ən) *adj., n.*

pal·ette (pal′it) *n.* ⟦Fr < L *pala,* a shovel⟧ a thin board on which an artist arranges and mixes paints

pal·frey (pôl′frē) *n., pl.* **-freys** ⟦ult. < Gr *para,* beside + L *veredus,* post horse⟧ [Archaic] a saddle horse, esp. a gentle one for a woman

pal·i·mo·ny (pal′ə mō′nē) *n.* ⟦PAL + (AL)IMONY⟧ an allowance or a property settlement claimed by or granted to one member of an unmarried couple who separate after having lived together

pal·imp·sest (pal′imp sest′) *n.* ⟦< Gr *palimpsēstos,* lit., rubbed again⟧ a parchment previously written upon that bears traces of the erased texts

pal·in·drome (pal′in drōm′) *n.* ⟦< Gr *palindromos,* running back⟧ a word, phrase, or sentence that reads the same backward or forward (Ex.: madam)

pal·ing (pāl′iŋ) *n.* a fence made of pales

pal·i·sade (pal′ə sād′) *n.* ⟦< Fr < L *palus,* a stake⟧ **1** any of a row of large pointed stakes forming a fence as for fortification **2** such a fence **3** [*pl.*] a line of steep cliffs

pall[1] (pôl) *vi.* **palled, pall′ing** ⟦ME *pallen,* appall⟧ **1** to become cloying, insipid, boring, etc. **2** to become satiated

pall[2] (pôl) *n.* ⟦< L *pallium,* a cover⟧ **1** a cloth covering for a coffin **2** a dark or gloomy covering

pall·bear·er (pôl′ber′ər) *n.* ⟦prec. + BEARER⟧ one of the persons who attend or carry the coffin at a funeral

pal·let[1] (pal′it) *n.* ⟦see PALETTE⟧ a low, portable platform used for stacking materials, as in a warehouse

pal·let[2] (pal′it) *n.* ⟦< L *palea,* chaff⟧ a small bed or a pad filled as with straw and used on the floor

pal·li·ate (pal′ē āt′) *vt.* **-at′ed, -at′ing** ⟦< L *pallium,* a cloak⟧ **1** to lessen the severity of without curing; alleviate **2** to make (an offense) appear less serious; excuse —**pal′li·a′tion** *n.* —**pal′li·a′tive** *adj., n.*

pal·lid (pal′id) *adj.* ⟦L *pallidus,* pale⟧ faint in color; pale —**pal′lid·ly** *adv.*

pal·lor (pal′ər) *n.* ⟦< L *pallere,* be pale⟧ unnatural paleness

palm[1] (päm) *n.* ⟦< L *palma*: from its handlike leaf⟧ **1** any of a large group of tropical or subtropical trees or shrubs with a branchless trunk and a bunch of large leaves at the top **2** a leaf of such a tree carried as a symbol of victory, etc.

palm[2] (päm) *n.* ⟦< L *palma*⟧ the inner surface of the hand between the fingers and wrist —*vt.* to hide (something) in the palm, as in a sleight-of-hand trick —**palm off** [Colloq.] to pass off by fraud

pal·met·to (pal met′ō) *n., pl.* **-tos** or **-toes** any of certain palms with fan-shaped leaves

palm·is·try (päm′is trē) *n.* ⟦prob. < ME *paume,* PALM[2] + *maistrie,* mastery⟧ fortunetelling by means of the lines, etc. on the palm of a person's hand —**palm′ist** *n.*

Palm Sunday *common name for* the Sunday before Easter, commemorating Jesus' entry into Jerusalem, when palm branches were strewn before him

palm·y (päm′ē) ***adj.*** **-i·er, -i·est** 1 of, like, or full of palm trees 2 prosperous

pal·o·mi·no (pal′ə mē′nō) ***n.,*** *pl.* **-nos** ⟦AmSp < Sp, dove-colored⟧ a golden or cream-colored horse with a white tail

pal·pa·ble (pal′pə bəl) ***adj.*** ⟦< L *palpare,* to touch⟧ 1 that can be touched, felt, etc. 2 easily perceived by the senses; perceptible 3 obvious; plain —**pal′pa·bly** ***adv.***

pal·pi·tate (pal′pə tāt′) ***vi.*** **-tat′ed, -tat′ing** ⟦< L *palpare,* to feel⟧ 1 to beat rapidly, as the heart 2 to throb —**pal′pi·ta′tion** ***n.***

pal·sy (pôl′zē) ***n.,*** *pl.* **-sies** ⟦ult. < L *paralysis,* paralysis⟧ paralysis of any muscle, sometimes with involuntary tremors —***vt.*** **-sied, -sy·ing** to paralyze

pal·try (pôl′trē) ***adj.*** **-tri·er, -tri·est** ⟦prob. < LowG *palte,* rag⟧ almost worthless; trifling —**pal′tri·ness** ***n.***

pam·pas (päm′pəz, -pəs) ***n.pl.*** ⟦AmSp < AmInd *pámpa,* plain, field⟧ the extensive, treeless plains of Argentina

pam·per (pam′pər) ***vt.*** ⟦ME *pampren,* to feed too much < LowG⟧ to be overindulgent with; coddle; humor

pam·phlet (pam′flit) ***n.*** ⟦< OFr *Pamphilet,* shortened name of a ML poem⟧ a thin, unbound booklet, often on some topic of current interest —**pam′phlet·eer′** (-fli tir′) ***n.***

pan[1] (pan) ***n.*** ⟦OE *panne*⟧ 1 any broad, shallow container used in cooking, etc. 2 a pan-shaped part or object —***vt.*** **panned, pan′ning** 1 [Colloq.] to criticize unfavorably 2 *Mining* to wash (gravel) in a pan, as to separate (gold) —***vi.*** *Mining* to wash gravel in a pan, searching for gold —**pan out** [Colloq.] to turn out; esp., to turn out well; succeed

pan[2] (pan) *Film, TV, etc.* ***vt., vi.*** **panned, pan′ning** ⟦< PAN(ORAMA)⟧ to move (a camera) so as to get a panoramic effect —***n.*** the act of panning

Pan (pan) *Gr. Myth.* a god of fields, forests, flocks, and shepherds, represented as having the legs of a goat

pan- ⟦< Gr *pan,* all, every⟧ *combining form* 1 all */pantheism/* 2 [**P-**] of, comprising, or uniting every */Pan-*American/

pan·a·ce·a (pan′ə sē′ə) ***n.*** ⟦< Gr *pan,* all + *akos,* healing, medicine⟧ a supposed remedy for all ills

pa·nache (pə nash′, -näsh′) ***n.*** ⟦Fr, ult. < L *pinna,* feather⟧ 1 a plume, esp. on a helmet 2 dashing elegance of manner or style

Pan·a·ma (pan′ə mä′, -mô′) country in Central America, a strip of land connecting Central & South America: 29,760 sq. mi.; pop. 2,227,000 —**Pan′a·ma′ni·an** (-mā′nē ən) ***adj., n.***

Panama Canal ship canal across Panama, connecting the Atlantic & Pacific

Panama hat [*also* **p-**] a hand-woven hat made with strawlike strips of the leaves of a tropical plant

Pan-A·mer·i·can (pan′ə mer′i kən) ***adj.*** of North, South, and Central America, collectively

pan·cake (pan′kāk′) ***n.*** a flat cake of batter fried on a griddle or in a pan

pan·chro·mat·ic (pan′krō mat′ik) ***adj.*** sensitive to light of all colors */panchromatic* film/

pan·cre·as (pan′krē əs, paŋ′-) ***n.*** ⟦< Gr *pan,* all + *kreas,* flesh⟧ a large gland that secretes a digestive juice into the small intestine and produces insulin —**pan′cre·at′ic** (-at′ik) ***adj.***

GIANT PANDA

pan·da (pan′də) ***n.*** ⟦< native name in Nepal⟧ 1 a black-and-white, bearlike mammal of China: in full **giant panda** 2 a reddish, raccoonlike mammal of the Himalayas: in full **lesser panda**

pan·dem·ic (pan dem′ik) ***adj.*** ⟦< Gr *pan,* all + *dēmos,* the people⟧ epidemic over a large region

pan·de·mo·ni·um (pan′də mō′nē əm) ***n.*** ⟦< name of demons' abode in Milton's *Paradise Lost* < Gr *pan,* all + *daimōn,* evil spirit⟧ wild disorder or noise

pan·der (pan′dər) ***n.*** ⟦< L *Pandarus,* lovers' go-between in Chaucer, etc.⟧ 1 a procurer; pimp 2 one who helps others to satisfy their vices, etc. Also **pan′der·er** —***vi.*** to act as a pander (*to*)

Pan·do·ra (pan dôr′ə) ⟦< Gr *pan,* all + *dōron,* gift⟧ *Gr. Myth.* the first mortal woman: she opens a box, letting all human ills into the world

pane (pān) ***n.*** ⟦< L *pannus,* piece of cloth⟧ a sheet of glass in a frame of a window, etc.

pan·e·gyr·ic (pan′ə jir′ik) ***n.*** ⟦< Gr *panēgyris,* public meeting⟧ 1 a formal speech or piece of writing praising a person or event 2 high praise

pan·el (pan′əl) ***n.*** ⟦see PANE⟧ 1 *a)* a section or division, usually rectangular, forming a part of a wall, door, etc. *b)* a board for instruments or controls 2 a lengthwise strip in a skirt, etc. 3 a list of persons summoned for jury duty 4 a group of persons selected for judging, discussing, etc. —***vt.*** **-eled** or **-elled, -el·ing** or **-el·ling** to provide with panels

pan′el·ing or **pan′el·ling** ***n.*** 1 panels collectively 2 sheets of plastic, wood, etc. used for panels

pan′el·ist ***n.*** a member of a PANEL (*n.* 4)

panel truck an enclosed pickup truck

pang (paŋ) ***n.*** ⟦< ?⟧ a sudden, sharp pain, physical or emotional

pan·han·dle[1] (pan′han′dəl) ***n.*** [*often* **P-**] a strip of land projecting like the handle of a pan

pan·han·dle[2] (pan′han′dəl) ***vt., vi.*** **-dled, -dling** [Colloq.] to beg (from), esp. on the streets —**pan′han′dler** ***n.***

pan·ic (pan′ik) ***n.*** ⟦< Gr *panikos,* of Pan, as inspirer of sudden fear⟧ a sudden, unreasoning fear, often spreading quickly —***vt.*** **-icked, -ick·ing** 1 to affect with panic 2 [Slang] to convulse (an audience, etc.) with laughter, etc. —*vi.* to show panic —**pan′ick·y** *adj.*

pan′ic-strick′en *adj.* badly frightened Also **pan′ic-struck′**

pan·nier or **pan·ier** (pan′yər, -ē ər) *n.* ⟦ < L *panis,* bread ⟧ a large basket for carrying loads on the back

pa·no·cha (pə nō′chə) *n.* ⟦AmSp, ult. < L *panis,* bread ⟧ **1** a coarse Mexican sugar **2** *var. of* PENUCHE

pan·o·ply (pan′ə plē) *n., pl.* **-plies** ⟦ < Gr *pan,* all + *hopla,* arms ⟧ **1** a complete suit of armor **2** any magnificent covering or array

pan·o·ram·a (pan′ə ram′ə) *n.* ⟦ < PAN- + Gr *horama,* a view ⟧ **1** a wide view in all directions **2** a constantly changing scene —**pan′o·ram′ic** *adj.*

pan·sy (pan′zē) *n., pl.* **-sies** ⟦ < Fr *penser,* think ⟧ a small plant of the violet family, with velvety petals

pant (pant) *vi.* ⟦ult. < L *phantasia,* nightmare ⟧ **1** to breathe rapidly and heavily, as from running fast **2** to yearn eagerly: with *for* or *after* —*vt.* to gasp out —*n.* any of a series of rapid, heavy breaths; gasp

pan·ta·loons (pan′tə lo͞onz′) *n.pl.* ⟦ < It: ult. after St. *Pantalone* ⟧ **1** orig., a kind of tight trousers **2** later, any trousers

pan·the·ism (pan′thē iz′əm) *n.* ⟦ < Gr *pan,* all + *theos,* a god + -ISM ⟧ **1** the doctrine that all forces, manifestations, etc. of the universe are God **2** the worship of all gods —**pan′the·ist** *n.*

pan·the·on (pan′thē än′) *n.* ⟦ < Gr *pan,* all + *theos,* a god ⟧ **1** a temple for all the gods **2** [*often* **P-**] a building in which famous dead persons of a nation are entombed or commemorated

pan·ther (pan′thər) *n.* ⟦ < Gr *panthēr* ⟧ **1** a leopard, specif. one that is black **2** a cougar or a jaguar

pant·ies (pant′ēz) *n.pl.* women's or children's short underpants Also **pant·ie** (pant′ē) or **pant′y** *n.*

pan·to·mime (pan′tə mīm′) *n.* ⟦ult. < Gr *pan,* all + *mimos,* a mimic ⟧ **1** a drama played without words, using only action and gestures **2** action or gestures without words —*vt., vi.* **-mimed′, -mim′ing** to express or act in pantomime —**pan′to·mim′ic** (-mim′ik) *adj.* —**pan′to·mim′ist** (-mīm′ist) *n.*

pan·to·then·ic acid (pan′tō then′ik) ⟦ < Gr *pantothen,* from every side ⟧ a viscous oil, part of the vitamin B complex, occurring widely in animal and plant tissues and thought essential for cell growth

pan·try (pan′trē) *n., pl.* **-tries** ⟦ < L *panis,* bread ⟧ a small room off the kitchen, where cooking ingredients and utensils, china, etc. are kept

pants (pants) *n.pl.* ⟦ < PANTALOONS ⟧ **1** trousers **2** drawers or panties

pant′suit′ *n.* matched pants and jacket for women Also **pants suit**

pant·y·hose (pan′tē hōz′) *n.* women's hose that extend to the waist, forming a one-piece garment

pant′y·waist′ (-wāst′) *n.* [Slang] a sissy

pap (pap) *n.* ⟦ME ⟧ **1** any soft food for babies or invalids **2** any oversimplified or tasteless writing, ideas, etc.

pa·pa (pä′pə) *n.* ⟦ < baby talk ⟧ *child's term for* FATHER

pa·pa·cy (pā′pə sē) *n., pl.* **-cies** ⟦LL *papa,* pope ⟧ **1** the rank of pope **2** the term of office of a pope **3** the governing of the Roman Catholic Church by the pope, its head

pa·pal (pā′pəl) *adj.* of or relating to a pope or the papacy

pa·paw (pə pô′, pô′pô′) *n.* ⟦ < fol. ⟧ **1** PAPAYA **2** *a)* a tree of central and S U.S. with an oblong, yellowish, edible fruit *b)* its fruit

pa·pa·ya (pə pī′ə) *n.* ⟦Sp < WInd name ⟧ **1** a tropical American tree with a large, oblong, yellowish-orange fruit **2** its fruit

pa·per (pā′pər) *n.* ⟦ult. < Gr *papyros,* papyrus ⟧ **1** a thin, flexible material in sheets, made from rags, wood, etc. and used for writing or printing on, for packaging, etc. **2** a single sheet of this **3** an official document **4** an essay, dissertation, etc. **5** a newspaper **6** wallpaper **7** [*pl.*] credentials —*adj.* **1** of, or made of, paper **2** like paper; thin —*vt.* to cover with wallpaper —**pa′per·y** *adj.*

pa′per·back′ *n.* a book bound in paper covers

pa′per·boy′ *n.* a boy who sells or delivers newspapers —**pa′per·girl′** *n.fem.*

paper clip a flexible clasp for holding loose sheets of paper together

pa′per·hang′er *n.* a person whose work is covering walls with wallpaper

paper tiger a person, nation, etc. that seems to pose a threat but is really powerless

pa′per·weight′ *n.* any small, heavy object set on papers to keep them from being scattered

pa′per·work′ *n.* the keeping of records, etc. incidental to some task

pa·pier-mâ·ché (pā′pər mə shā′) *n.* ⟦Fr < *papier,* paper + *mâcher,* to chew ⟧ a material made of paper pulp mixed with size, glue, etc., and molded into various objects when moist

pa·pil·la (pə pil′ə) *n., pl.* **-lae** (-ē) ⟦L < *papula,* pimple ⟧ any small nipplelike projection of tissue, as on the surface of the tongue —**pap·il·lar·y** (pap′ə ler′ē) *adj.*

pa·poose (pa po͞os′, pa-) *n.* ⟦ < AmInd ⟧ a North American Indian baby

pa·pri·ka (pə prē′kə) *n.* ⟦Hung, ult. < Gr *peperi,* pepper ⟧ a mild or hot, red, powdered condiment ground from the fruit of certain pepper plants

Pap test (pap) ⟦after G. *Papanicolaou,* 20th-c. U.S. anatomist ⟧ a test for uterine cancer

Pap·u·a New Guinea (pap′yo͞o ə) country occupying the E half of the island of New Guinea & nearby islands: *c.* 180,000 sq. mi.; pop. 3,395,000

pa·py·rus (pə pī′rəs) *n., pl.* **-ri′** (-rī′) or **-rus·es** ⟦ < Gr *papyros* ⟧ **1** a tall water plant of Egypt **2** a writing material made from the pith of this plant by the ancients

par (pär) *n.* ⟦L, an equal ⟧ **1** the established value of a currency in terms of the money of another country **2** an equal status, level, etc.: usually in **on a par (with) 3** the average state, condition, etc. [work that is above *par*] **4** the face value of stocks, etc. **5** *Golf* the number of strokes established as a skillful score for a hole or course —*adj.* 1 of or at par 2 average

par. 1 paragraph 2 parish

para- *prefix* 1 beside, beyond [*parapsychology*] 2 helping in a secondary way, accessory [*paramedical*]

par·a·ble (par′ə b'l) *n.* ⟦< Gr *parabolē*, analogy < *para-*, beside + *ballein*, to throw⟧ a short, simple story teaching a moral lesson

pa·rab·o·la (pə rab′ə lə) *n.* ⟦see prec.⟧ *Geom.* a curve formed by the intersection of a cone with a plane parallel to its side —**par·a·bol·ic** (par′ə bäl′ik) *adj.*

par·a·chute (par′ə sho͞ot′) *n.* ⟦Fr < *para-*, protecting + *chute*, a fall⟧ a cloth contrivance usually shaped like an umbrella when expanded, and used to retard the speed of one dropping from an airplane, etc. —*vt.*, *vi.* **-chut′ed**, **-chut′ing** to drop by parachute —**par′a·chut′ist** *n.*

pa·rade (pə rād′) *n.* ⟦< L *parare*, prepare⟧ 1 ostentatious display 2 a review of troops 3 any organized procession or march, as for display —*vt.* **-rad′ed**, **-rad′ing** 1 to march or walk through, as for display 2 to show off [*to parade one's knowledge*] —*vi.* 1 to march in a parade 2 to walk about ostentatiously

par·a·digm (par′ə dīm′, -dim′) *n.* ⟦< Gr *para-*, beside + *deigma*, example⟧ 1 an example or model 2 *Gram.* an example of a declension or conjugation, giving all the inflections of a word

par·a·dise (par′a dīs′) *n.* ⟦< Gr *paradeisos*, garden⟧ 1 [P-] the garden of Eden 2 heaven 3 any place or state of great happiness

par·a·dox (par′ə däks′) *n.* ⟦< Gr *para-*, beyond + *doxa*, opinion⟧ 1 a statement that seems contradictory, etc. but may be true in fact 2 a statement that is self-contradictory and, hence, false —**par′a·dox′i·cal** *adj.*

par·af·fin (par′ə fin) *n.* ⟦Ger < L *parum*, too little + *affinis*, akin: from its inertness⟧ a white, waxy substance used for making candles, sealing jars, etc. Also **par′af·fine** (-fin, -fēn′)

par·a·gon (par′ə gän′, -gən) *n.* ⟦< It *paragone*, touchstone⟧ a model of perfection or excellence

par·a·graph (par′ə graf′) *n.* ⟦< Gr *para-*, beside + *graphein*, write⟧ 1 a distinct section of a writing, begun on a new line and often indented 2 a brief item in a newspaper, etc. —*vt.* to arrange in paragraphs

Par·a·guay (par′ə gwā′, -gwī′) inland country in central South America: 157,046 sq. mi.; pop. 4,119,000 —**Par′a·guay′an** *adj.*, *n.*

par·a·keet (par′ə kēt′) *n.* ⟦prob. < MFr *perrot*, parrot⟧ a small, slender parrot with a long, tapering tail

par·a·le·gal (par′ə lē′gəl) *adj.* designating or of persons trained to aid lawyers but not licensed to practice law —*n.* such a person

par·al·lax (par′ə laks′) *n.* ⟦< Gr *para-*, beyond + *allassein*, to change⟧ the apparent change in the position of an object resulting from a change in the viewer's position

par·al·lel (par′ə lel′) *adj.* ⟦< Gr *para-*, side by side + *allēlos*, one another⟧ 1 extending in the same direction and at a constant distance apart, so as never to meet 2 similar or corresponding —*n.* 1 a parallel line, surface, etc. 2 any person or thing similar to another; counterpart 3 any comparison showing likeness 4 any of the imaginary lines parallel to the equator and representing degrees of latitude: in full **parallel of latitude** —*vt.* **-leled′** or **-lelled′**, **-lel′ing** or **-lel′ling** 1 to be parallel with [*the road parallels the river*] 2 to compare 3 to match; equal —**par′al·lel′ism′** (-iz′əm) *n.*

par′al·lel′o·gram′ (-ə gram′) *n.* a four-sided plane figure having the opposite sides parallel and equal

pa·ral·y·sis (pə ral′ə sis) *n.*, *pl.* **-ses′** (-sēz′) ⟦< Gr *paralyein*, to loosen or weaken at the side⟧ 1 partial or complete loss of voluntary motion or of sensation in part or all of the body 2 any condition of helpless inactivity —**par·a·lyt·ic** (par′ə lit′ik) *adj.*, *n.*

par·a·lyze (par′ə līz′) *vt.* **-lyzed′**, **-lyz′ing** 1 to cause paralysis in 2 to make ineffective or powerless

par·a·me·ci·um (par′ə mē′sē əm, -shē əm) *n.*, *pl.* **-ci·a** (-ə) ⟦< Gr *paramēkēs*, oval⟧ an elongated protozoan that moves by means of cilia

par·a·med·ic (par′ə med′ik) *n.* a person in paramedical work

par′a·med′i·cal (-med′i kəl) *adj.* ⟦PARA- + MEDICAL⟧ of auxiliary medical personnel, as midwives, medics, nurses' aides, etc.

pa·ram·e·ter (pə ram′ət ər) *n.* ⟦< Gr *para-*, beside + *metron*, a measure⟧ 1 any of a set of interdependent variables 2 *a*) a boundary or limit *b*) a characteristic (*usually in pl.*)

par·a·mil·i·tar·y (par′ə mil′ə ter′ē) *adj.* ⟦PARA- + MILITARY⟧ of forces working along with, or in place of, a regular military organization

par·a·mount (par′ə mount′) *adj.* ⟦< OFr *par*, by + *amont*, uphill⟧ ranking higher than any other; chief

par·a·mour (par′ə moor′) *n.* ⟦< OFr *par amour*, with love⟧ a lover or mistress, esp. in an illicit relation

par·a·noi·a (par′ə noi′ə) *n.* ⟦< Gr *para-*, beside + *nous*, the mind⟧ a mental disorder characterized by delusions, as of grandeur or, esp., persecution —**par′a·noid′** *adj.*, *n.*

par·a·pet (par′ə pet′, -pət) *n.* ⟦< It *parare*, to guard + *petto*, breast⟧ 1 a wall or bank for screening troops from enemy fire 2 a low wall or railing

par·a·pher·na·li·a (par′ə fər nāl′yə, -nā′lē ə) *n.pl.* ⟦< Gr *para-*, beyond + *phernē*, dowry⟧ 1 personal belongings 2 equipment

par·a·phrase (par′ə frāz′) *n.* ⟦< Gr *para-*, beside + *phrazein*, say⟧ a rewording of the meaning of something spoken or written —*vt.*, *vi.* **-phrased′**, **-phras′ing** to express (something) in a paraphrase

par·a·ple·gi·a (par′ə plē′jē ə, -jə) *n.* ⟦< Gr *para-*, beside + *plēgē*, a stroke⟧ paralysis of the lower half of the body —**par′a·ple′gic** (-plē′jik) *adj.*, *n.*

par′a·pro·fes′sion·al *n.* ⟦see PARA-⟧ a trained assistant to licensed professionals, as in medicine or education

par′a·psy·chol′o·gy *n.* ⟦see PARA-⟧ psychology dealing with psychic phenomena, as telepathy

par·a·site (par′ə sīt′) *n.* ⟦< Gr *para-*, beside + *sitos*, food⟧ 1 one who lives at others' expense without making any useful return 2 a plant or animal that lives on or in another organism —**par′a·sit′ic** (-sit′ik) *adj.*

par·a·sol (par′ə sôl′) *n.* ⟦< It *parare*, ward off + *sole*, sun⟧ a lightweight umbrella used as a sunshade

par·a·sym·pa·thet·ic (par′ə sim′pə thet′ik) *adj.* ⟦PARA- + SYMPATHETIC⟧ *Physiology* designating the part of the autonomic nervous system whose functions include constricting the pupils of the eyes, slowing the heartbeat, and stimulating some digestive glands

par·a·thi·on (par′ə thī′än′) *n.* ⟦PARA- + Gr *theion*, sulfur⟧ a highly poisonous insecticide

par′a·thy′roid′ (-thī′roid′) *adj.* ⟦PARA- + THYROID⟧ designating or of the small glands near the thyroid that regulate calcium and phosphorus metabolism

par·a·troops (par′ə tro͞ops′) *n.pl.* ⟦< PARA(CHUTE) + TROOP⟧ troops trained and equipped to parachute into a combat area —**par′a·troop′er** *n.*

par·boil (pär′boil′) *vt.* ⟦< L *per*, through + *bullire*, to boil: infl. by *part*⟧ to boil until partly cooked

par·cel (pär′səl) *n.* ⟦ult. < L *pars*, part⟧ 1 a small, wrapped bundle; package 2 a piece (of land) —*vt.* **-celed** or **-celled**, **-cel·ing** or **-cel·ling** to separate into parts and distribute: with *out*

parcel post a mail service for parcels of a specified total weight and size

parch (pärch) *vt.* ⟦< ?⟧ 1 to expose to great heat so as to dry or roast 2 to make very thirsty —*vi.* to become very dry, hot, thirsty, etc.

parch·ment (pärch′mənt) *n.* ⟦< L (*charta*) *Pergamena*, (paper) of Pergamum, city in Asia Minor⟧ 1 the skin of a sheep, goat, etc. prepared as a surface for writing 2 paper like parchment 3 a manuscript on parchment

par·don (pärd′′n) *vt.* ⟦< L *per-*, through + *donare*, give⟧ 1 to release from further punishment 2 to forgive (an offense) 3 to excuse (a person) for a fault, etc. —*n.* 1 forgiveness 2 an official document granting a pardon —**par′don·a·ble** *adj.* —**par′don·er** *n.*

pare (per) *vt.* **pared**, **par′ing** ⟦< L *parare*, prepare⟧ 1 to cut or trim away (the rind, skin, etc.) of; peel 2 to reduce gradually: often with *down*

par·e·gor·ic (par′ə gôr′ik) *n.* ⟦< Gr *parēgoros*, soothing⟧ a tincture of opium, used to relieve diarrhea

par·ent (per′ənt) *n.* ⟦< L *parere*, beget⟧ 1 a person in relation to his or her offspring; a mother or father 2 any organism in relation to its offspring 3 a source; origin —*adj.* of a corporation in relation to a subsidiary that it owns —**pa·ren·tal** (pə rent′′l) *adj.* —**par′ent·hood′** *n.*

par′ent·age (-ij) *n.* descent from parents or ancestors; lineage

pa·ren·the·sis (pə ren′thə sis) *n.*, *pl.* **-ses′** (-sēz′) ⟦< Gr *para-*, beside + *entithenai*, insert⟧ 1 a word, clause, etc. added as an explanation or comment within a sentence 2 either or both of the curved lines, ( ), used to set this off —**par·en·thet·i·cal** (par′ən thet′i kəl) or **par′en·thet′ic** *adj.*

par·ent·ing (per′ənt iŋ) *n.* the work or skill of a parent in raising a child or children

pa·re·sis (pə rē′sis) *n.*, *pl.* **-ses′** (-sēz′) ⟦Gr < *parienai*, relax⟧ 1 partial paralysis 2 a brain disease caused by syphilis of the central nervous system

par·fait (pär fā′) *n.* ⟦Fr, perfect⟧ a frozen dessert of cream, eggs, etc., or of ice cream with syrup, fruit, etc.

pa·ri·ah (pə rī′ə) *n.* ⟦< Tamil *paṛaiyan*, drummer⟧ 1 a member of one of the lowest social castes in India 2 any outcast

par·i·mu·tu·el (par′ə myo͞o′cho͞o əl) *n.* ⟦Fr, lit., a mutual bet⟧ a system of betting on races in which the winning bettors share the net of each pool in proportion to their wagers

par·ing (per′iŋ) *n.* a piece pared off

Par·is (par′is) *Gr. Legend* a prince of Troy: see HELEN OF TROY

Par·is (par′is; *Fr* pä rē′) capital of France: pop. 2,189,000 (urban area 8,700,000) —**Pa·ri·sian** (pə rizh′ən, -rē′zhən) *adj.*, *n.*

par·ish (par′ish) *n.* ⟦< Gr *paroikia*, diocese⟧ 1 a part of a diocese, under the charge of a priest or minister 2 the congregation of a church 3 a civil division in Louisiana, like a county

pa·rish·ion·er (pə rish′ə nər) *n.* a member of a parish

par·i·ty (par′ə tē) *n.* ⟦< L *par*, equal⟧ 1 equality in power, value, etc. 2 equality of value at a given ratio between different kinds of money, etc.

park (pärk) *n.* ⟦< ML *parricus*⟧ 1 wooded land held as part of an estate or preserve 2 an area of public land, with walks, playgrounds, etc., for recreation 3 the system in an automatic transmission that locks the drive wheels of a motor vehicle —*vt.*, *vi.* 1 to leave (a vehicle) in a place temporarily 2 to maneuver (a vehicle) into a parking space

par·ka (pär′kə) *n.* ⟦< Russ, fur coat⟧ a heavy, hooded jacket

parking meter a coin-operated device for indicating the length of time a parking space may be occupied

Par·kin·son's disease (pär′kin sənz) ⟦after J. *Parkinson* (1755-1824), Eng physician⟧ a degenerative disease of later life, causing rhythmic tremor and muscular rigidity

Parkinson's Law ⟦stated by C. *Parkinson* (1909-), Brit economist⟧ a parody of economic laws, such as that work expands to fill the allotted time

park′way′ *n.* a broad roadway landscaped with trees, bushes, etc.

par·lance (pär′ləns) *n.* ⟦< OFr *parler*, speak⟧ language or idiom

par·lay (pär′lā, -lē; *for v., also* pär lā′) *vt.*, *vi.* ⟦< It *paro*, a pair⟧ to bet (an original wager plus its winnings) on another race, etc. —*n.* a parlayed bet

par·ley (pär′lē) *vi.* ⟦< Fr *parler*, speak⟧ to confer, esp. with an enemy —*n.*, *pl.* **-leys** a conference, as to settle a dispute or discuss terms

par·lia·ment (pär′lə mənt) ***n.*** ⟦< OFr *parler,* speak⟧ **1** an official government council **2** [P-] the national legislative body of certain countries, esp. Great Britain

par′lia·men·tar′i·an (-men ter′ē ən) ***n.*** one skilled in parliamentary rules

par′lia·men′ta·ry (-men′tər ē) ***adj.*** **1** of or by a parliament **2** conforming to the rules of a parliament

par·lor (pär′lər) ***n.*** ⟦< OFr *parler,* speak⟧ **1** [Old-fashioned] any living room **2** any of certain establishments /a beauty *parlor*/ Brit., etc. sp. **par′lour**

Parmesan (cheese) (pär′mə zän′) ⟦after *Parma,* It city⟧ a very hard, dry cheese orig. of Italy

pa·ro·chi·al (pə rō′kē əl) ***adj.*** ⟦see PARISH⟧ **1** of or in a parish or parishes **2** narrow in scope; provincial

parochial school a school supported and controlled by a church

par·o·dy (par′ə dē) ***n.,*** *pl.* **-dies** ⟦< Gr *para-,* beside + *ōidē,* song⟧ a farcical imitation of a literary or musical work or style —***vt.*** **-died, -dy·ing** to make a parody of

pa·role (pə rōl′) ***n.*** ⟦< LL *parabola,* a speech⟧ the release of a prisoner whose sentence has not expired, on condition of future good behavior —***vt.*** **-roled′, -rol′ing** to release on parole

par·ox·ysm (par′əks iz′əm) ***n.*** ⟦< Gr *para-,* beyond + *oxynein,* sharpen⟧ **1** a sudden attack of a disease **2** a sudden outburst as of laughter

par·quet (pär kā′) ***n.*** ⟦Fr, < MFr *parchet,* dim. of *parc,* park⟧ **1** the main floor of a theater: usually called *orchestra* **2** a flooring of parquetry —***vt.*** **-queted′** (-kād′), **-quet′ing** (-kā′iŋ) to make of parquetry

parquet circle the part of a theater beneath the balcony and behind the parquet on the main floor

par·quet·ry (pär′kə trē) ***n.*** inlaid flooring in geometric forms

par·ri·cide (par′ə sīd′) ***n.*** ⟦< L *paricida:* see -CIDE⟧ **1** the act of murdering one's parent, close relative, etc. **2** one who does this

par·rot (par′ət) ***n.*** ⟦Fr dial. *perrot*⟧ **1** a bird with a hooked bill and brightly colored feathers: some parrots can learn to imitate human speech **2** one who parrots what others say —***vt.*** to repeat without understanding

par·ry (par′ē) ***vt.*** **-ried, -ry·ing** ⟦prob. ult. < L *parare,* prepare⟧ **1** to ward off (a blow, etc.) **2** to evade (a question, etc.) —***n.,*** *pl.* **-ries** a parrying

parse (pärs) ***vt., vi.*** **parsed, pars′ing** ⟦< L *pars* (*orationis*), part (of speech)⟧ to break (a sentence) down, giving the form and function of each part

par·si·mo·ny (pär′sə mō′nē) ***n.*** ⟦< L *parcere,* to spare⟧ stinginess; extreme frugality —**par′si·mo′ni·ous** ***adj.***

pars·ley (pärs′lē) ***n.*** ⟦< Gr *petros,* stone + *selinon,* celery⟧ a plant with aromatic, often curled leaves used to flavor or garnish some foods

pars·nip (pärs′nip′) ***n.*** ⟦< L *pastinare,* dig up⟧ **1** a plant with a long, white root used as a vegetable **2** its root

par·son (pär′sən) ***n.*** ⟦see PERSON⟧ a minister, esp. one having a parish

par′son·age (-ij) ***n.*** the dwelling provided by a church for its minister

part (pärt) ***n.*** ⟦< L *pars*⟧ **1** a portion, segment, etc. of a whole /a *part* of a book/ **2** an essential, separable element /automobile *parts*/ **3** a portion or share; specif., *a*) duty /to do one's *part*/ *b*) [*usually pl.*] talent; ability /a man of *parts*/ *c*) a role in a play *d*) any of the voices or instruments in a musical ensemble, or the score for this **4** *a*) a region *b*) [*usually pl.*] a district **5** one of the sides in a conflict, etc. **6** a dividing line formed in combing the hair —***vt.*** **1** to break or divide into parts **2** to comb (the hair) so as to leave a part **3** to break or hold apart —***vi.*** **1** to break or divide into parts **2** to separate and go different ways **3** to cease associating **4** to go away; leave: with *from* —***adj.*** partial —**for one's part** as far as one is concerned —**for the most part** mostly —**in part** partly —**part with** relinquish —**take part** to participate

par·take (pär tāk′) ***vi.*** **-took′, -tak′en, -tak′ing** ⟦< *part taker*⟧ **1** to participate (*in* an activity) **2** to eat or drink something, esp. with others: usually with *of* —**par·tak′er** ***n.***

part·ed (pärt′id) ***adj.*** separated

par·terre (pär ter′) ***n.*** ⟦Fr < *par,* on + *terre,* earth⟧ **1** a garden with flower beds and path in a pattern **2** PARQUET CIRCLE

par·the·no·gen·e·sis (pär′thə nō′jen′ə sis) ***n.*** ⟦see fol. & GENESIS⟧ reproduction from an unfertilized ovum, seed, or spore

Par′the·non′ (-nän′) ⟦< Gr *parthenos,* a virgin (i.e., Athena)⟧ the Doric temple of Athena on the Acropolis

par·tial (pär′shəl) ***adj.*** ⟦< L *pars,* a part⟧ **1** favoring one person, faction, etc. more than another; biased **2** not complete —**partial to** fond of —**par′ti·al′i·ty** (-shē al′ə tē) ***n.*** —**par′tial·ly** ***adv.***

par·tic·i·pate (pär tis′ə pāt′, pər-) ***vi.*** **-pat′ed, -pat′ing** ⟦< L *pars,* a part + *capere,* to take⟧ to have or take a share with others (*in* some activity) —**par·tic′i·pant** ***adj., n.*** —**par·tic′i·pa′tion** ***n.*** —**par·tic′i·pa′tor** ***n.*** —**par·tic′i·pa·to′ry** (-pə tôr′ē) ***adj.***

par·ti·ci·ple (pärt′i sip′əl) ***n.*** ⟦see prec.⟧ a verbal form having characteristics of both verb and adjective —**par′ti·cip′i·al** (-sip′ē əl) ***adj.***

par·ti·cle (pärt′i kəl) ***n.*** ⟦< L *pars,* a part⟧ **1** a tiny fragment or trace **2** a short, usually invariable part of speech, as an article, preposition, etc. **3** *Physics* a piece of matter of negligible size though with other attributes, as mass

par·ti·col·ored (pär′ti kul′ərd) ***adj.*** ⟦< Fr *parti,* divided + COLORED⟧ having different colors in different parts

par·tic·u·lar (pər tik′yə lər) ***adj.*** ⟦< L *particula,* particle⟧ **1** of or belonging to a single person, group, or thing **2** regarded separately; specific **3** unusual **4** exacting; fastidious —***n.*** a distinct fact, item, detail, etc. —**in particular** especially —**par·tic′u·lar′i·ty** (-lar′ə tē), *pl.* **-ties,** ***n.***

par·tic′u·lar·ize′ (-lər īz′) ***vt., vi.*** **-ized′, -iz′-**

ing to give particulars or details (of) —**par·tic′u·lar·i·za′tion** ***n.***

par·tic′u·lar·ly ***adv.*** **1** in detail **2** especially **3** specifically

par·tic′u·late (-yōō lit, -yōō lāt′) ***adj.*** of or formed of tiny, separate particles

part′ing ***adj.*** **1** dividing; separating **2** departing **3** given, spoken, etc. at parting —***n.*** **1** a breaking or separating **2** a departure

par·ti·san (pärt′i zən) ***n.*** ⟦< L *pars,* a part⟧ **1** a strong supporter of a faction, party, etc. **2** a guerrilla fighter —***adj.*** of or like a partisan Also **par′ti·zan** —**par′ti·san·ship′** ***n.***

par·ti·tion (pär tish′ən) ***n.*** ⟦< L *partitio*⟧ **1** division into parts **2** something that divides, as a wall separating rooms —***vt.*** **1** to divide into parts; apportion **2** to divide by a partition —**par·ti′tioned** ***adj.***

part′ly ***adv.*** not fully or completely

part·ner (pärt′nər) ***n.*** ⟦< ME⟧ **1** one who joins in an activity with another or others; specif., one of two or more persons jointly owning a business **2** a spouse **3** either of two persons dancing together **4** a player on the same team —**part′ner·ship′** ***n.***

part of speech any of the classes to which a word can be assigned as by form, function, or meaning, as noun, verb, etc.

par·took (pär took′) ***vi. pt. of*** PARTAKE

PARTRIDGE

par·tridge (pär′trij) ***n.*** ⟦< Gr *perdix*⟧ **1** any of several short-tailed game birds, esp. one with an orange-brown head and grayish neck **2** any of various birds resembling this

part song a song for several voices, usually without accompaniment

part′-time′ ***adj.*** designating, of, or engaged in work, study, etc. for less than the usual time

par·tu·ri·tion (pär′tōō rish′ən) ***n.*** ⟦< L *parere,* bring forth⟧ childbirth

part′way′ ***adv.*** to a degree, but not fully

par·ty (pär′tē) ***n., pl.*** **-ties** ⟦< L *pars,* a part⟧ **1** a group of people working to promote a political platform or slate, a cause, etc. **2** a group acting together to accomplish a task **3** a gathering for social entertainment **4** one concerned in an action, plan, lawsuit, etc. /a *party* to the action/ **5** [Colloq.] a person —***vi.*** **-tied, -ty·ing** to attend or hold social parties

party line **1** a single circuit connecting two or more telephone users with the exchange **2** the policies of a political party

par·ve·nu (pär′və nōō′) ***n.*** ⟦< L *pervenire,* arrive⟧ a newly rich person who is considered an upstart

Pas·a·de·na (pas′ə dē′nə) **1** city in SW Calif.: pop. 119,000 **2** city in SE Tex.: pop. 113,000

Pas·cal (pas kal′) ***n.*** ⟦after B. *Pascal* (1623-62), Fr mathematician & philosopher⟧ a computer language written in structured modules Also **PASCAL**

pas·chal (pas′kəl) ***adj.*** ⟦< LL < Gr < Heb *pesach,* Passover⟧ **1** of Passover **2** of Easter

pa·sha (pə shä′, pä′shə) ***n.*** ⟦Turk⟧ [Historical] in Turkey, a title of rank or honor placed after the name

pass (pas) ***vi.*** ⟦< L *passus,* a step⟧ **1** to go or move forward, through, etc. **2** to go or be conveyed from one place, form, condition, etc. to another **3** *a*) to cease *b*) to depart **4** to die: often with *away* or *on* **5** to go by **6** to elapse /an hour *passed*/ **7** to make a way: with *through* or *by* **8** to be accepted without question **9** to be approved, as by a legislature **10** to go through a test, course, etc. successfully **11** to give a judgment, sentence, etc. **12** *Card Games* to decline a chance to bid —***vt.*** **1** to go by, beyond, over, or through; specif., *a*) to leave behind *b*) to go through (a test, course, etc.) successfully **2** to cause or allow to go, move, or proceed; specif., *a*) to ratify; enact *b*) to spend (time) *c*) to excrete **3** to cause to move from place to place; circulate **4** to give (an opinion or judgment) —***n.*** **1** an act of passing; passage **2** a state; situation /a strange *pass*/ **3** *a*) a ticket, etc. giving permission to come or go freely or without charge *b*) *Mil.* a brief leave of absence **4** a motion of the hands **5** a tentative attempt **6** a narrow passage, etc., esp. between mountains **7** [Colloq.] an overly familiar attempt to embrace or kiss **8** *Sports* a transfer of a ball, etc. to another player during play —**come** (or **bring**) **to pass** to (cause to) happen —**pass for** to be accepted as —**pass off** to cause to be accepted through deceit —**pass out** **1** to distribute **2** to faint —**pass over** to disregard; ignore —**pass up** [Colloq.] to refuse or let go by —**pass′er** ***n.***

pass′a·ble ***adj.*** **1** that can be passed, traveled over, etc. **2** barely adequate; fair —**pass′a·bly** ***adv.***

pas·sage (pas′ij) ***n.*** **1** a passing; specif., *a*) migration *b*) transition *c*) the enactment of a law **2** permission or right to pass **3** a voyage **4** a means of passing; road, passageway, etc. **5** an exchange, as of blows **6** a portion of a book, musical composition, etc.

pas′sage·way′ ***n.*** a narrow way for passage, as a hall, alley, etc.

pass′book′ ***n.*** BANKBOOK

pas·sé (pä sā′, pa-) ***adj.*** ⟦Fr, past⟧ **1** out-of-date; old-fashioned **2** rather old

pas·sel (pas′əl) ***n.*** ⟦< PARCEL⟧ [Colloq. or Dial.] a group, esp. a fairly large one

pas·sen·ger (pas′ən jər) ***n.*** ⟦< OFr *passage,* passage⟧ a person traveling in a train, boat, car, etc.

pass′er·by′ ***n., pl.*** **pass′ers·by′** one who passes by Also **pass′er-by′**, ***pl.*** **pass′ers-by′**

pass′-fail′ ***adj.*** *Educ.* designating a grading system recording "pass" or "fail" instead of a letter or number grade

pass′ing ***adj.*** **1** going by, beyond, etc. **2** fleeting **3** casual /a *passing* remark/ **4** satisfying given requirements /a *passing* grade/

5 current —*n.* the act of one that passes; specif., death —**in passing** incidentally

pas·sion (pash′ən) *n.* ⟦< L *pati,* endure⟧ 1 any emotion, as hate, love, fear, etc. 2 intense emotional excitement, as rage, enthusiasm, lust, etc. 3 the object of any strong desire —[P-] the sufferings of Jesus, from after the Last Supper through his death on the Cross

pas′sion·ate (-ə nit) *adj.* 1 having or showing strong feelings 2 hot-tempered 3 ardent; intense 4 sensual —**pas′sion·ate·ly** *adv.*

pas·sive (pas′iv) *adj.* ⟦see PASSION⟧ 1 inactive, but acted upon 2 offering no resistance; submissive 3 *Gram.* denoting the voice of a verb whose subject is the recipient (object) of the action —**pas′sive·ly** *adv.* —**pas·siv′i·ty** *n.*

passive resistance opposition to a government, etc. by refusal to comply or by nonviolent acts, as fasting

pass′key′ *n.* 1 *a)* MASTER KEY *b)* SKELETON KEY 2 one's own key to something

Pass·o·ver (pas′ō′vər) *n.* a Jewish holiday commemorating deliverance of the ancient Hebrews from slavery in Egypt

pass′port′ *n.* a government document carried by a citizen traveling abroad, certifying identity and citizenship

pass′word′ *n.* 1 a secret term used for identification, as in passing a guard 2 any means of admission

past (past) *vi., vt. rare pp. of* PASS —*adj.* 1 gone by; ended 2 of a former time 3 immediately preceding 4 *Gram.* indicating an action completed, or a condition in existence, at a former time /the *past* tense/ —*n.* 1 time gone by 2 the history of a person, group, etc. 3 a personal background that is hidden or questionable —*prep.* beyond in time, space, amount, etc. —*adv.* to and beyond

pas·ta (päs′tə) *n.* ⟦It⟧ 1 a flour paste or dough of which spaghetti, etc. is made 2 any food made of this

paste (pāst) *n.* ⟦< Gr *pastē,* porridge⟧ 1 dough for making pastry, etc. 2 any soft, moist, smooth preparation /*toothpaste*/ 3 a mixture of flour, water, etc. used as an adhesive 4 the hard, brilliant glass of artificial gems —*vt.* **past′ed, past′ing** 1 to make adhere, as with paste 2 [Slang] to hit

paste′board′ *n.* a stiff material made as of layers of paper pasted together —*adj.*

pas·tel (pas tel′) *n.* ⟦< LL *pasta,* paste⟧ 1 a crayon of ground coloring matter 2 a picture drawn with such crayons 3 a soft, pale shade of color —*adj.* soft and pale: said of colors

pas·tern (pas′tərn) *n.* ⟦< L *pastor,* shepherd⟧ the part of the foot of a horse, dog, etc. just above the hoof or toes

Pas·teur (pas tur′), **Louis** 1822-95; Fr. chemist & bacteriologist

pas·teur·ize (pas′tər īz′, -chər-) *vt.* **-ized′, -iz′ing** ⟦after prec.⟧ to destroy bacteria in (milk, etc.) by heating to a prescribed temperature for a specified time —**pas′teur·i·za′tion** *n.*

pas·tiche (pas tēsh′) *n.* ⟦Fr⟧ 1 an artistic composition made up of bits from various sources 2 a hodgepodge

pas·time (pas′tīm′) *n.* a way of spending spare time; diversion

past master ⟦for *passed master*⟧ a person of long experience in an occupation, art, etc.; expert

pas·tor (pas′tər) *n.* ⟦L, a shepherd⟧ a priest or minister in charge of a congregation —**pas′tor·ate** (-it) *n.*

pas′to·ral *adj.* 1 of or relating to a pastor 2 of shepherds 3 of rustic life 4 peaceful; simple

past participle *Gram.* a participle used *a)* to express completed action (Ex.: *gone* in "he has gone") *b)* to form the passive voice (Ex.: *done* in "the deed was done") *c)* as an adjective (Ex.: *fried* in "fried fish")

pas·tra·mi (pə strä′mē) *n.* ⟦E Yidd, ult. < Turk *basdyrma,* dried meat⟧ highly spiced smoked beef

pas·try (pās′trē) *n., pl.* **-tries** ⟦see PASTE & -ERY⟧ 1 pies, tarts, etc. with crusts baked from flour dough made with shortening 2 broadly, all fancy baked goods

pas·tur·age (pas′chər ij) *n.* PASTURE

pas′ture *n.* ⟦< L *pascere,* to feed⟧ 1 grass, etc. used as food by grazing animals 2 ground suitable for grazing —*vt.* **-tured, -tur·ing** to put (cattle, etc.) out to graze in a pasture

past·y (pās′tē) *adj.* **-i·er, -i·est** of or like paste in color or texture

pat (pat) *n.* ⟦prob. echoic⟧ 1 a gentle tap or stroke with a flat object 2 the sound made by this 3 a small lump, as of butter —*vt.* **pat′ted, pat′ting** 1 to tap or stroke gently, esp. with the hand 2 to shape or apply by patting —*adj.* 1 exactly suitable 2 so glibly plausible as to seem contrived —**pat on the back** 1 a compliment 2 to praise —**stand pat** to refuse to change an opinion, etc.

pat. 1 patent 2 patented

patch (pach) *n.* ⟦ME *pacche*⟧ 1 a piece of material applied to mend a hole or strengthen a weak spot 2 a bandage 3 an area or spot /*patches* of blue sky/ 4 a small plot of land 5 a scrap; bit —*vt.* 1 to put a patch on 2 to produce crudely or hurriedly —**patch up** to settle (differences, a quarrel, etc.)

patch test *Med.* a test for allergy, made by attaching a sample of a substance to the skin and observing the reaction

patch′work′ *n.* needlework, as a quilt, made of odd patches of cloth

patch′y *adj.* **-i·er, -i·est** 1 made up of patches 2 not consistent or uniform; irregular —**patch′i·ness** *n.*

pate (pāt) *n.* ⟦< ?⟧ the head, esp. the top of the head: a humorous term

pâ·té (pä tā′) *n.* ⟦Fr⟧ a meat paste or pie

pa·tel·la (pə tel′ə) *n., pl.* **-las** or **-lae** (-ē) ⟦< L *patina,* a pan⟧ KNEECAP

pat·ent (pat′'nt; *also for adj. 1 & 2,* pāt′-) *adj.* ⟦< L *patere,* be open⟧ 1 open to all 2 obvious; plain 3 protected by a patent —*n.* 1 a document granting the exclusive right to produce or sell an invention, etc. for a specified time 2 *a)* the right so granted *b)* the thing protected by such a right —*vt.* to secure a patent for

patent leather (pat′'nt) leather with a hard, glossy finish: formerly patented
patent medicine (pat′'nt) a trademarked medical preparation
pa·ter·nal (pə tur′nəl) *adj.* ⟦< L *pater,* father⟧ 1 fatherly 2 inherited from a father 3 on the father's side
pa·ter′nal·ism′ *n.* the governing of a country, employees, etc. in a manner suggesting a father's relationship with his children —**pa·ter′nal·is′tic** *adj.*
pa·ter′ni·ty (-nə tē) *n.* 1 the state of being a father 2 male parentage
pa·ter·nos·ter (pät′ər nôs′tər) *n.* ⟦L, our father⟧ the Lord's Prayer, esp. in Latin Often **Pater Noster**
Pat·er·son (pat′ər s'n) city in NE N.J.: pop. 138,000
path (path) *n.* ⟦OE *pæth*⟧ 1 a way worn by footsteps 2 a walk for the use of people on foot 3 a line of movement 4 a course of conduct, thought, etc. —**path′less** *adj.*
pa·thet·ic (pə thet′ik) *adj.* ⟦see PATHOS⟧ 1 arousing pity, sorrow, etc.; pitiful 2 pitifully unsuccessful, etc. —**pa·thet′i·cal·ly** *adv.*
pathetic fallacy in literature, the attribution of human characteristics to inanimate things (Ex.: the angry sea)
patho- ⟦< Gr: see PATHOS⟧ *combining form* suffering, disease, feeling Also **path-**
path·o·gen (path′ə jən) *n.* ⟦prec. + -GEN⟧ a microorganism, etc. capable of causing disease —**path′o·gen′ic** (-jen′ik) *adj.*
pa·thol·o·gy (pə thäl′ə jē) *n., pl.* **-gies** ⟦< Gr *pathologia:* see fol. & -LOGY⟧ 1 the branch of medicine that deals with the nature of disease, esp. with structural and functional effects 2 any abnormal variation from a sound condition —**path·o·log·i·cal** (path′ə läj′i kəl) *adj.* —**pa·thol′o·gist** *n.*
pa·thos (pā′thäs′) *n.* ⟦Gr, suffering, disease, feeling⟧ the quality in something which arouses pity, sorrow, sympathy, etc.
path′way′ *n.* PATH
-pa·thy (pə thē) ⟦< Gr: see PATHOS⟧ *combining form* 1 feeling *[telepathy]* 2 (treatment of) disease *[osteopathy]*
pa·tience (pā′shəns) *n.* a being patient; calm endurance
pa′tient (-shənt) *adj.* ⟦< L *pati,* endure⟧ 1 enduring pain, trouble, etc. without complaining 2 calmly tolerating delay, confusion, etc. 3 diligent; persevering —*n.* one receiving medical care —**pa′tient·ly** *adv.*
pat·i·na (pat′'n ə, pə tē′nə) *n.* ⟦Fr < It⟧ a fine greenish crust on bronze or copper, formed by oxidation
pa·ti·o (pat′ē ō′, pät′-) *n., pl.* **-os′** ⟦Sp⟧ 1 a courtyard open to the sky 2 a paved area adjoining a house, for outdoor lounging, dining, etc.
pa·tois (pa′twä′) *n., pl.* **-tois′** (-twäz′) ⟦Fr⟧ a provincial or local dialect
pat. pend. patent pending
patri- ⟦< Gr *patēr*⟧ *combining form* father Also **patr-**
pa·tri·arch (pā′trē ärk′) *n.* ⟦< Gr *patēr,* father + *archein,* to rule⟧ 1 the father and head of a family or tribe, as Abraham, Isaac, or Jacob in the Bible 2 a man of great age and dignity 3 [*often* **P-**] a high-ranking bishop, as in the Eastern Orthodox Church —**pa′tri·ar′chal** *adj.*
pa′tri·arch′ate (-är′kit, -kāt′) *n.* the rank, jurisdiction, etc. of a patriarch
pa′tri·arch′y (-är′kē) *n., pl.* **-ies** 1 a form of social organization in which the father is head of the family, descent being traced through the male line 2 rule or domination by men
pa·tri·cian (pə trish′ən) *n.* ⟦< L *pater,* father⟧ an aristocrat
pat′ri·mo′ny (-mō′nē) *n., pl.* **-nies** ⟦< L *pater,* father⟧ property inherited from one's father or ancestors —**pat′ri·mo′ni·al** *adj.*
pa·tri·ot (pā′trē ət) *n.* ⟦< Gr *patris,* fatherland⟧ one who loves and zealously supports one's own country —**pa′tri·ot′ic** (-ät′ik) *adj.* —**pa′tri·ot′i·cal·ly** *adv.* —**pa′tri·ot·ism′** *n.*
pa·trol (pə trōl′) *vt., vi.* **-trolled′, -trol′ling** ⟦Fr *patrouiller*⟧ to make a regular, repeated circuit (of) in guarding —*n.* 1 a patrolling 2 a person or group patrolling
patrol car a police car used to patrol an area, in radio contact with headquarters
pa·trol′man (-mən) *n., pl.* **-men** a police officer who patrols a certain area
patrol wagon an enclosed truck used by police to carry prisoners
pa·tron (pā′trən) *n.* ⟦< L *pater,* father⟧ 1 a protector; benefactor 2 one who sponsors and supports some person, activity, etc. 3 a regular customer —**pa′tron·ess** *n.fem.*
pa·tron·age (pā′trən ij, pa′-) *n.* 1 support, encouragement, etc. given by a patron 2 *a)* clientele *b)* business; trade 3 *a)* the power to grant political favors *b)* such favors
pa·tron·ize (pā′trən īz′, pa′-) *vt.* **-ized′, -iz′·ing** 1 to sponsor; support 2 to be kind or helpful to, but in a haughty or snobbish way 3 to be a regular customer of
patron saint a saint looked upon as a special guardian
pat·ro·nym·ic (pa′trō nim′ik, -trə-) *n.* ⟦< Gr *patēr,* father + *onyma,* name⟧ a name showing descent from a given person (Ex.: *Johnson,* son of John)
pat·sy (pat′sē) *n., pl.* **-sies** [Slang] a person easily imposed upon
pat·ter[1] (pat′ər) *vi.* ⟦< PAT⟧ to make, or move so as to make, a patter —*n.* a series of quick, light taps
pat·ter[2] (pat′ər) *vt., vi.* ⟦< PATERNOSTER⟧ to speak rapidly or glibly —*n.* glib, rapid speech, as of salespeople
pat·tern (pat′ərn) *n.* ⟦< OFr *patrun,* patron⟧ 1 a person or thing worthy of imitation 2 a model or plan used in making things 3 a design 4 a regular way of acting or doing 5 a predictable route, movement, etc. —*vt.* to make or do in imitation of a pattern
pat·ty (pat′ē) *n., pl.* **-ties** ⟦Fr *pâté,* pie⟧ 1 a small pie 2 a small, flat cake of ground meat, fish, etc., usually fried
patty shell a small pastry case for a single portion of creamed food, etc.
pau·ci·ty (pô′sə tē) *n.* ⟦< L *paucus,* few⟧ 1 fewness 2 scarcity
Paul (pôl) (original name *Saul*) died *c.* A.D. 67: the Apostle of Christianity to the Gentiles: author of several Letters in the New Testament: also **Saint Paul**

Paul Bun·yan (bun′yən) *American Folklore* a giant lumberjack who performs superhuman feats

paunch (pônch) ***n.*** ⟦< L *pantex*, belly⟧ the abdomen, or belly; esp., a potbelly —**paunch′y** ***adj.***

pau·per (pô′pər) ***n.*** ⟦L⟧ an extremely poor person, esp. one who lives on charity —**pau′per·ism′** ***n.*** —**pau′per·ize′, -ized′, -iz′·ing,** ***vt.***

pause (pôz) ***n.*** ⟦< Gr *pauein*, to bring to an end⟧ a temporary stop or rest —***vi.*** **paused, paus′ing** to make a pause; stop

pave (pāv) ***vt.*** **paved, pav′ing** ⟦< L *pavire*, to beat⟧ to cover the surface of (a road, etc.), as with concrete —**pave the way (for)** to prepare the way (for)

pave′ment ***n.*** a paved surface, as of concrete; specif., a paved road, etc.

pa·vil·ion (pə vil′yən) ***n.*** ⟦< L *papilio*, tent⟧ **1** a large tent **2** a building, often partly open, for exhibits, etc., as at a fair or park **3** any of a group of related buildings

pav·ing (pāv′iŋ) ***n.*** a pavement

Pav·lov (pav′lôv′), **I·van** (i vän′) 1849-1936; Russ. physiologist

paw (pô) ***n.*** ⟦< OFr *poue*⟧ **1** the foot of a four-footed animal having claws **2** [Colloq.] a hand —***vt., vi.*** **1** to touch, dig, hit, etc. with paws or feet **2** to handle clumsily or roughly

pawl (pôl) ***n.*** ⟦< ?⟧ a device, as a hinged tongue which engages cogs in a wheel, allowing rotation in only one direction

pawn[1] (pôn) ***n.*** ⟦< L *pannus*, cloth⟧ **1** anything given as security, as for a debt **2** the state of being pledged —***vt.*** **1** to give as security **2** to wager or risk

pawn[2] (pôn) ***n.*** ⟦< ML *pedo*, foot soldier⟧ **1** a chess piece of the lowest value **2** a person used to advance another's purposes

pawn′bro′ker ***n.*** a person licensed to lend money at interest on personal property left as security

pawn′shop′ ***n.*** a pawnbroker's shop

paw·paw (pô′pô′) ***n.*** *var. of* PAPAW

pay (pā) ***vt.*** **paid** or obs. (except in PAY OUT) **payed, pay′ing** ⟦< L *pacare*, pacify⟧ **1** to give to (a person) what is due, as for goods or services **2** to give (what is due) in return, as for goods or services **3** to settle (a debt, etc.) **4** *a)* to give (a compliment, etc.) *b)* to make (a visit, etc.) **5** to be profitable to —***vi.*** **1** to give due compensation **2** to be profitable —***n.*** money paid; esp., wages or salary —***adj.*** **1** operated by the insertion of coins [*a pay phone*] **2** designating a service, etc. paid for by fees [*pay TV*] —**in the pay of** employed and paid by —**pay back** **1** to repay **2** to retaliate upon —**pay down** to pay (part of the price) at purchase as an installment —**pay for** to suffer or atone for (a wrong) —**pay off** **1** to pay all that is owed **2** to yield full recompense **3** [Colloq.] to succeed —**pay out** to let out (a rope, cable, etc.) —**pay up** to pay in full or on time —**pay′er** ***n.***

pay′a·ble ***adj.*** **1** that can be paid **2** due to be paid (*on* a specified date)

pay′check′ ***n.*** a check in payment of wages or salary

pay·day (pā′dā′) ***n.*** the day on which salary or wages are paid

pay dirt soil, ore, etc. rich in minerals —**hit** (or **strike**) **pay dirt** [Colloq.] to discover a source of wealth, success, etc.

pay·ee (pā ē′) ***n.*** one to whom a payment is made or owed

pay′load′ ***n.*** **1** a cargo **2** a load, as a warhead, satellite, passengers, etc., carried by an aircraft, rocket, etc. but not essential to its flight operations

pay′mas′ter ***n.*** the official in charge of paying employees

pay′ment ***n.*** **1** a paying or being paid **2** something that is paid

pay′off′ ***n.*** **1** a settlement, reckoning, or payment **2** [Colloq.] a bribe **3** [Colloq.] an unexpected climax

pay·o·la (pā ō′lə) ***n.*** [Slang] a bribe, as to a disc jockey for promoting a song unfairly

pay′out′ ***n.*** **1** a paying out; disbursement **2** an amount paid out; dividend

pay phone (or **station**) a public telephone, usually coin-operated

pay′roll′ ***n.*** **1** a list of employees to be paid, with the amount due to each **2** the total amount needed for this

Pb ⟦L *plumbum*⟧ *Chem. symbol for* lead

PBX (pē′bē′eks′) ***n.*** ⟦< *p(rivate) b(ranch) ex(change)*⟧ a telephone system within an organization, having outside lines

PC (pē′sē′) ***n.*** PERSONAL COMPUTER

pct. percent

PCV valve ⟦*p(ositive) c(rankcase) v(entilation)*⟧ a valve regulating the pollution control system of a motor vehicle

Pd *Chem. symbol for* palladium

pd. paid

pea (pē) ***n.,*** *pl.* **peas** ⟦< ME *pese*, a pea, taken as pl.; ult. < Gr *pison*⟧ **1** a climbing plant with green pods **2** its small, round seed, used as a vegetable

peace (pēs) ***n.*** ⟦< L *pax*⟧ **1** freedom from war **2** an agreement to end war **3** law and order **4** harmony; concord **5** serenity, calm, or quiet —**hold** (or **keep**) **one's peace** to be silent —**peace′a·ble** ***adj.***

peace′ful ***adj.*** **1** not quarrelsome **2** free from disturbance; calm **3** of or in a time of peace —**peace′ful·ly** ***adv.***

peace′mak′er ***n.*** a person who makes peace, as by settling disagreements or quarrels —**peace′mak′ing** ***n., adj.***

peace officer an officer entrusted with maintaining law and order, as a sheriff

peace pipe CALUMET

peace′time′ ***n.*** a time of freedom from war —***adj.*** of such a time

peach (pēch) ***n.*** ⟦< L *Persicum (malum)*, Persian (apple)⟧ **1** a tree with round, juicy, orange-yellow fruit having a fuzzy skin and a rough pit **2** its fruit **3** the color of this fruit **4** [Slang] a well-liked person or thing

pea·cock (pē′käk′) ***n.*** ⟦< L *pavo*, peacock⟧ the male of a pheasantlike bird (**pea′fowl′**), with a long, showy tail that can be spread out like a fan —**pea′hen′** ***n.fem.***

pea jacket (pē′) ⟦< Du *pijjekker*⟧ a hip-length, double-breasted coat of heavy woolen cloth, worn orig. by seamen

peak (pēk) ***n.*** ⟦var. of Brit dial. *pike*, prob. < ON *pic*⟧ **1** a pointed end or top, as of a cap, roof, etc. **2** *a)* the summit of a hill or mountain ending in a point *b)* a mountain with such a summit **3** the highest or utmost point of anything —*adj.* maximum —*vi., vt.* to come or bring to a peak

peak·ed (pēk′id) *adj.* ⟦< ?⟧ thin and drawn, as from illness

peal (pēl) *n.* ⟦ME *apele,* appeal⟧ **1** the loud ringing of a bell or bells **2** a set of tuned bells **3** a loud, prolonged sound, as of thunder, laughter, etc. —*vi., vt.* to sound in a peal; ring

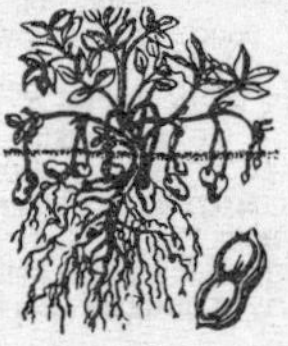

PEANUT PLANT

pea′nut′ *n.* **1** a vine related to the pea, with underground pods containing edible seeds **2** the pod or any of its seeds **3** [*pl.*] [Slang] a trifling sum

peanut butter a food paste or spread made by grinding roasted peanuts

pear (per) *n.* ⟦< L *pirum*⟧ **1** a tree with greenish-yellow, brownish, or reddish fruit **2** the juicy fruit, round at the base and narrowing toward the stem

pearl (purl) *n.* ⟦< L *perna,* sea mussel⟧ **1** a smooth, hard, usually white or bluish-gray, roundish growth, formed within the shell of some oysters and other mollusks: used as a gem **2** MOTHER-OF-PEARL **3** anything like a pearl in beauty, value, etc. **4** a bluish-gray —**pearl′y** *adj.*

Pearl Harbor inlet on the S coast of Oahu, Hawaii: site of a U.S. naval base bombed by Japan on Dec. 7, 1941

peas·ant (pez′ənt) *n.* ⟦< LL *pagus,* district⟧ **1** a small farmer or farm laborer, as in Europe or Asia **2** a person regarded as boorish, ignorant, etc. —**peas′ant·ry** *n.*

peat (pēt) *n.* ⟦< ML *peta,* piece of turf⟧ partly decayed plant matter from ancient swamps, used for fuel

peat moss peat composed of residues of mosses, used as mulch

peb·ble (peb′əl) *n.* ⟦< OE *papol-(stan),* pebble (stone), prob. echoic⟧ a small stone worn smooth and round, as by running water —**peb′bly, -bli·er, -bli·est,** *adj.*

pe·can (pē kän′, -kan′; pi-; pē′kän′, -kan′) *n.* ⟦< AmInd⟧ **1** an edible nut with a thin, smooth shell **2** the tree it grows on

pec·ca·dil·lo (pek′ə dil′ō) *n., pl.* **-loes** or **-los** ⟦< Sp < L *peccare,* to sin⟧ a small fault or offense

pec·ca·ry (pek′ə rē) *n., pl.* **-ries** ⟦< native name⟧ a piglike animal of North and South America, with sharp tusks

peck[1] (pek) *vt.* ⟦ME *picken,* to pick⟧ **1** to strike, as with a beak **2** to make by doing this /to *peck* a hole/ **3** to pick up with the beak —*vi.* to make strokes as with a pointed object —*n.* **1** a stroke so made **2** [Colloq.] a quick, casual kiss —**peck at** [Colloq.] **1** to eat very little of **2** to criticize constantly

peck[2] (pek) *n.* ⟦< OFr *pek*⟧ a unit of dry measure, ¼ bushel, or eight quarts

pecking order social organization in which status is determined by awareness of rank, income, etc.

pec·tin (pek′tin) *n.* ⟦< Gr *pēktos,* congealed⟧ a carbohydrate, obtained from certain fruits, which yields a gel that is the basis of jellies

pec·to·ral (pek′tə rəl) *adj.* ⟦< L *pectus,* breast⟧ of or located in or on the chest or breast

pec·u·late (pek′yo͞o lāt′, -yə-) *vt., vi.* **-lat′ed, -lat′ing** ⟦< L *peculari*⟧ to embezzle —**pec′u·la′tion** *n.*

pe·cu·liar (pē kyo͞ol′yər, pi-) *adj.* ⟦< L *peculium,* private property⟧ **1** of only one person, thing, etc.; exclusive **2** particular; special **3** odd; strange —**pe·cu′liar·ly** *adv.*

pe·cu·li·ar·i·ty (pē kyo͞o′lē er′ə tē, pi-) *n.* **1** a being peculiar **2** *pl.* **-ties** something that is peculiar, as a trait

pe·cu·ni·ar·y (pi kyo͞o′nē er′ē, pē-) *adj.* ⟦< L *pecunia,* money⟧ of or involving money

ped·a·gogue or **ped·a·gog** (ped′ə gäg′) *n.* ⟦< Gr *pais,* child + *agein,* to lead⟧ a teacher, esp. a pedantic one

ped′a·gog′y (-gäj′ē, -gō′jē) *n.* the art or science of teaching —**ped′a·gog′ic** or **ped′a·gog′i·cal** *adj.*

ped·al (ped′'l) *adj.* ⟦< L *pes,* FOOT⟧ of the foot or feet —*n.* a lever operated by the foot, as on a bicycle, organ, etc. —*vt., vi.* **-aled** or **-alled, -al·ing** or **-al·ling** to operate by pedals

ped·ant (ped′'nt) *n.* ⟦ult. < Gr *paidagōgos,* teacher⟧ **1** one who emphasizes trivial points of learning **2** a narrow-minded teacher who insists on exact adherence to rules —**pe·dan′tic** *adj.* —**ped′ant·ry** *n.*

ped·dle (ped′'l) *vt., vi.* **-dled, -dling** ⟦< ? ME *ped,* basket⟧ to go from place to place selling (small articles) —**ped′dler** *n.*

-pede (pēd) ⟦< L *pes*⟧ *combining form* foot or feet /*centipede*/

ped·er·as·ty (ped′ər as′tē) *n.* ⟦< Gr *paiderastēs,* lover of boys⟧ sodomy between males, esp. between a man and boy —**ped′er·ast′** *n.*

ped·es·tal (ped′əs təl) *n.* ⟦< It *piè,* foot + *di,* of + *stal,* a rest⟧ a bottom support of a pillar, statue, etc.

pe·des·tri·an (pi des′trē ən) *adj.* ⟦< L *pes,* foot⟧ **1** going or done on foot **2** of or for pedestrians **3** ordinary and dull; prosaic —*n.* a walker

pe·di·at·rics (pē′dē a′triks) *n.pl.* ⟦< Gr *pais,* child + *iatros,* physician⟧ [*with sing. v.*] the branch of medicine dealing with the care and treatment of infants and children —**pe′di·a·tri′cian** (-ə trish′ən) *n.*

ped·i·cab (ped′i kab′) *n.* ⟦< L *pes,* foot + CAB⟧ a three-wheeled carriage, esp. formerly in SE Asia, pedaled by the driver

ped·i·cure (ped′i kyoor′) *n.* ⟦< L *pes,* FOOT + *cura,* care⟧ a trimming, polishing, etc. of the toenails

ped·i·gree (ped′i grē′) *n.* ⟦< MFr *pié de grue,* lit., crane's foot: from lines in genealogical tree⟧ **1** a list of ancestors **2** descent; lineage **3** a known line of descent, esp. of a purebred animal —**ped′i·greed′** *adj.*

ped·i·ment (ped′i mənt) ***n.*** ⟦< earlier *periment,* prob. < PYRAMID⟧ an ornamental gable or triangular piece on the front of a building, over a doorway, etc.
pe·dom·e·ter (pē däm′ət ər, pi-) ***n.*** ⟦< L *pes,* foot + Gr *metron,* a measure⟧ an instrument carried to measure the distance walked
pe·dun·cle (pē duŋ′kəl, pē′duŋ′-) ***n.*** ⟦< L *pes,* foot⟧ a stalklike organ or part in some plants, animals, etc.
peek (pēk) ***vi.*** ⟦ME *piken*⟧ to look quickly and furtively —***n.*** such a look
peel (pēl) ***vt.*** ⟦< L *pilare,* make bald⟧ to cut away (the rind, skin, etc.) of —***vi.*** **1** to shed skin, etc. **2** to come off in layers or flakes —***n.*** the rind or skin of fruit
peel′ing ***n.*** a peeled-off strip
peen (pēn) ***n.*** ⟦prob. < Scand⟧ the end of a hammerhead opposite the flat striking surface, usually ball-shaped (**ball peen**) or wedge-shaped
peep¹ (pēp) ***vi.*** ⟦echoic⟧ to make the short, high-pitched cry of a young bird —***n.*** a peeping sound
peep² (pēp) ***vi.*** ⟦ME *pepen*⟧ **1** to look through a small opening or from a place of hiding **2** to show gradually or partially —***n.*** a brief look; furtive glimpse —**peep′er** ***n.***
peep′hole′ ***n.*** a hole to peep through
peeping Tom ⟦after legendary peeper at Lady Godiva⟧ one who gets sexual pleasure from furtively watching others
peer¹ (pir) ***n.*** ⟦< L *par,* an equal⟧ **1** a person or thing of the same rank, ability, etc.; an equal **2** a British noble —**peer′age** (-ij) ***n.*** —**peer′ess** ***n.fem.***
peer² (pir) ***vi.*** ⟦< ? APPEAR⟧ **1** to look closely, as in trying to see more clearly **2** to show slightly
peer′less ***adj.*** without equal
peeve (pēv) ***vt.*** **peeved, peev′ing** [Colloq.] to make peevish —***n.*** [Colloq.] an annoyance
pee·vish (pēv′ish) ***adj.*** ⟦ME *pevische*⟧ irritable; fretful; cross —**pee′vish·ly** ***adv.*** —**pee′vish·ness** ***n.***
pee·wee (pē′wē′) ***n.*** ⟦< ?⟧ [Colloq.] an unusually small person or thing
peg (peg) ***n.*** ⟦ME *pegge*⟧ **1** a short pin or bolt used to hold parts together, hang things on, etc. **2** a step or degree **3** [Colloq.] a throw —***vt.*** **pegged, peg′ging** **1** to fasten, fix, secure, mark, etc., as with pegs **2** [Colloq.] to throw —**peg away (at)** to work steadily (at)
Peg·a·sus (peg′ə səs) *Gr. Myth.* a winged horse
peign·oir (pān wär′, pen-) ***n.*** ⟦Fr⟧ a woman's loose, full dressing gown
pein (pēn) ***n.*** *alt. sp. of* PEEN
Pei·ping (bā′piŋ′) *old form of* BEIJING
pej·o·ra·tion (pej′ə rā′shən, pē′jə-) ***n.*** ⟦< L *pejor,* worse⟧ a worsening —**pe·jo·ra·tive** (pi jôr′ə tiv) ***adj.***
Pe·king (pē′kiŋ′; *Chin* bä′jiŋ′) *old form of* BEIJING
Pe·king·ese (pē′kə nēz′) ***n.***, *pl.* **-ese′** a small dog with a long, straight coat, short legs, and a short, wrinkled muzzle Also **Pe′kin·ese′** (-kə nēz′)
pe·koe (pē′kō) ***n.*** ⟦< Chin *pek-ho,* white down (on the leaves used)⟧ a black tea of Sri Lanka and India
pe·lag·ic (pi laj′ik) ***adj.*** ⟦< Gr *pelagos,* sea⟧ of the open sea or ocean
pelf (pelf) ***n.*** ⟦< ? MFr *pelfre,* booty⟧ money or wealth regarded with contempt
pel·i·can (pel′i kən) ***n.*** ⟦< Gr *pelekan*⟧ a large, web-footed water bird with an expandable pouch in the lower bill for scooping up fish
pel·la·gra (pə lā′grə, -lag′rə) ***n.*** ⟦It ult. < L *pellis,* skin + Gr *agra,* seizure⟧ a chronic disease caused by a lack of nicotinic acid in the diet, characterized by skin eruptions and mental disorders
pel·let (pel′it) ***n.*** ⟦< L *pila,* a ball⟧ **1** a little ball, as of clay or medicine **2** a bullet, small lead shot, etc.
pell-mell (pel′mel′) ***adv., adj.*** ⟦< OFr *mesler,* to mix⟧ **1** in a jumble **2** in wild, disorderly haste; headlong
pel·lu·cid (pə lo͞o′sid) ***adj.*** ⟦< L *per,* through + *lucere,* to shine⟧ **1** transparent; clear **2** easy to understand
pelt¹ (pelt) ***vt.*** ⟦ME *pelten*⟧ **1** to throw things at **2** to beat repeatedly —***vi.*** to strike heavily or steadily, as hard rain
pelt² (pelt) ***n.*** ⟦prob. < OFr *pel,* a skin⟧ the skin of a fur-bearing animal, esp. when stripped from the carcass
pel·vis (pel′vis) ***n.***, *pl.* **-vis·es** or **-ves′** (-vēz′) ⟦L, basin⟧ **1** the basinlike cavity in the posterior part of the trunk in humans and many other vertebrates **2** the bones forming this cavity —**pel′vic** ***adj.***
pem·mi·can (pem′i kən) ***n.*** ⟦< AmInd⟧ a concentrated food of dried beef, suet, dried fruit, etc.
pen¹ (pen) ***n.*** ⟦OE *penn*⟧ **1** a small enclosure for domestic animals **2** any small enclosure —***vt.*** **penned** or **pent, pen′ning** to enclose as in a pen
pen² (pen) ***n.*** ⟦< L *penna,* a feather⟧ a device used in writing, etc. with ink; specif., *a*) a device with a metal point split into two nibs *b*) BALLPOINT (PEN) *c*) FOUNTAIN PEN —***vt.*** **penned, pen′ning** to write with a pen
pen³ (pen) ***n.*** [Slang] a penitentiary
Pen. or **pen.** peninsula
pe·nal (pēn′əl) ***adj.*** ⟦< Gr *poinē,* penalty⟧ of, for, constituting, or deserving punishment
pe·nal·ize (pē′nəl īz′, pen′əl-) ***vt.*** **-ized′, -iz′·ing** to impose a penalty on; punish —**pe′·nal·i·za′tion** ***n.***
pen·al·ty (pen′əl tē) ***n.***, *pl.* **-ties** **1** a punishment **2** the handicap, etc. imposed on an offender, as a fine
pen·ance (pen′əns) ***n.*** ⟦see PENITENT⟧ voluntary self-punishment to show repentance for wrongdoing, sins, etc.
pena′tes′ *see* LARES AND PENATES
pence (pens) ***n.*** [Brit.] *pl. of* PENNY
pen·chant (pen′chənt) ***n.*** ⟦Fr < L *pendere,* hang⟧ a strong liking
pen·cil (pen′səl) ***n.*** ⟦< L *penis,* a tail⟧ a rod-shaped instrument with a core of graphite, crayon, etc. that is sharpened to a point for writing, etc. —***vt.*** **-ciled** or **-cilled, -cil·ing** or **-cil·ling** to write, etc. with a pencil

pend (pend) ***vi.*** ⟦< L *pendere,* hang⟧ to await judgment or decision

pend·ant (pen′dənt) ***n.*** ⟦see prec.⟧ a hanging ornamental object, as a locket or earring

pend·ent (pen′dənt) ***adj.*** ⟦see PEND⟧ **1** suspended **2** overhanging **3** undecided; pending

pend′ing ***adj.*** ⟦prp. of PEND, infl. by Fr *pendant,* L *pendens*⟧ **1** not decided **2** impending —***prep.*** **1** during **2** until

pen·du·lous (pen′dyo͞o ləs, -jo͞o-) ***adj.*** ⟦see PEND⟧ hanging freely; drooping

pen·du·lum (pen′dyo͞o ləm, -jo͞o-) ***n.*** ⟦see PEND⟧ a body hung so as to swing freely to and fro: used to regulate clock movements

pen·e·trate (pen′i trāt′) ***vt., vi.*** **-trat′ed, -trat′ing** ⟦< L *penitus,* inward⟧ **1** to enter by piercing **2** to have an effect throughout **3** to affect deeply **4** to understand —**pen′e·tra·ble** (-trə bəl) ***adj.*** —**pen′e·tra′tion** ***n.***

pen·e·trat·ing (pen′i trāt′iŋ) ***adj.*** **1** that penetrates **2** sharp; piercing **3** acute; discerning Also **pen′e·tra′tive** (-trāt′iv)

pen·guin (peŋ′gwin, pen′-) ***n.*** ⟦prob. < Welsh⟧ a flightless bird of the Southern Hemisphere with webbed feet and flippers for swimming

PENGUIN

pen·i·cil·lin (pen′i sil′in) ***n.*** ⟦< L *penicillus,* brush⟧ an antibiotic obtained from certain molds or produced synthetically

pen·in·su·la (pə nin′sə lə) ***n.*** ⟦< L *paene,* almost + *insula,* isle⟧ a land area almost surrounded by water —**pen·in′su·lar** ***adj.***

pe·nis (pē′nis) ***n., pl.*** **-nis·es** or **-nes′** (-nēz′) ⟦L⟧ the male organ of sexual intercourse —**pe′nile′** (-nīl′) ***adj.***

pen·i·tent (pen′i tənt) ***adj.*** ⟦< L *paenitere,* repent⟧ sorry for having done wrong and willing to atone —***n.*** a penitent person —**pen′i·tence** ***n.*** —**pen′i·ten′tial** (-ten′shəl) ***adj.*** —**pen′i·tent·ly** ***adv.***

pen·i·ten·tia·ry (pen′i ten′shə rē) ***adj.*** making one liable to imprisonment in a penitentiary —***n., pl.*** **-ries** a State or Federal prison for persons convicted of serious crimes

pen′knife′ ***n., pl.*** **-knives′** (-nīvz′) a small pocketknife

pen′light′ or **pen′lite′** ***n.*** a flashlight about the size of a fountain pen

pen′man (-mən) ***n., pl.*** **-men** one skilled in penmanship

pen′man·ship′ (-ship′) ***n.*** handwriting as an art or skill

Penn (pen), **William** 1644-1718; Eng. Quaker: founder of Pennsylvania

Penn. or **Penna.** *abbrev.* Pennsylvania

pen name a pseudonym

pen·nant (pen′ənt) ***n.*** ⟦< PENNON⟧ **1** any long, narrow flag **2** such a flag symbolizing a championship

pen·ni·less (pen′ē lis, pen′i-) ***adj.*** without even a penny; extremely poor

pen·non (pen′ən) ***n.*** ⟦< L *penna,* a feather⟧ a flag or pennant

Penn·syl·va·ni·a (pen′s′l vān′yə) State of the NE U.S.: 45,333 sq. mi.; pop. 11,867,000; cap. Harrisburg —**Penn′syl·va′ni·an** ***adj., n.***

pen·ny (pen′ē) ***n., pl.*** **-nies** or **pence** (pens) ⟦< OE *penig*⟧ **1** in the United Kingdom, *a)* one 100th of a pound *b)* before 1971, $\frac{1}{12}$ of a shilling **2** a U.S. or Canadian cent

penny arcade a public amusement hall with coin-operated games, etc.

penny pincher a miserly person —**pen′ny·pinch′ing** ***n., adj.***

pen′ny·weight′ ***n.*** a unit of weight, equal to $\frac{1}{20}$ ounce troy weight

pen′ny-wise′ ***adj.*** thrifty in small matters —**penny-wise and pound-foolish** thrifty in small matters but wasteful in major ones

pe·nol·o·gy (pē näl′ə jē) ***n.*** ⟦< Gr *poinē,* punishment + -LOGY⟧ the study of prison management and prison reform

pen pal a person, esp. one abroad, with whom one exchanges letters

pen·sion (pen′shən) ***n.*** ⟦< L *pensio,* a paying⟧ a regular payment, not wages, as to one who is retired or disabled —***vt.*** to grant a pension to —**pen′sion·er** ***n.***

pen·sive (pen′siv) ***adj.*** ⟦< L *pensare,* consider⟧ thoughtful or reflective, often in a melancholy way —**pen′sive·ly** ***adv.*** —**pen′sive·ness** ***n.***

pent (pent) ***vt.*** *alt. pt. & pp. of* PEN[1] —***adj.*** held or kept in; penned Often with *up*

penta- ⟦< Gr *pente,* FIVE⟧ *combining form* five

pen·ta·cle (pen′tə kəl) ***n.*** ⟦see prec.⟧ a symbol, usually a five-pointed star, formerly used in magic

pen·ta·gon (pen′tə gän′) ***n.*** ⟦< Gr *penta-,* five + *gōnia,* an angle⟧ **1** a plane figure with five angles and five sides **2** [**P-**] the pentagonal office building of the Defense Department, near Washington, D.C. —**pen·tag′o·nal** (-tag′ə nəl) ***adj.***

pen·tam·e·ter (pen tam′ət ər) ***n.*** ⟦see PENTA- & METER[1]⟧ a line of verse containing five metrical feet; esp., English iambic pentameter (Ex.: "Hĕ jésts ăt scárs whŏ név ĕr félt ă wóund")

Pen·ta·teuch (pen′tə to͞ok′) ***n.*** ⟦< Gr *penta-,* five + *teuchos,* book⟧ the first five books of the Bible

pen·tath·lon (pen tath′län′) ***n.*** ⟦PENTA- + Gr *athlon,* a contest⟧ a contest in which each contestant takes part in five different events —**pen·tath′lete′** (-lēt′) ***n.***

Pen·te·cost (pen′ti kôst′) ***n.*** ⟦< Gr *pentēkostē* (*hēmera*), the fiftieth (day)⟧ a Christian festival on the seventh Sunday after Easter

Pen·te·cos·tal (pen′tə kôs′təl) ***adj.*** **1** of Pentecost **2** designating or of any of various Protestant fundamentalist sects often stressing direct inspiration by the Holy Spirit —**Pen′te·cos′tal·ism′** ***n.***

pent·house (pent′hous′) ***n.*** ⟦ult. < L *appendere,* append⟧ an apartment on the roof of a building

pent-up (pent′up′) ***adj.*** held in check; curbed /*pent-up* emotion/

pe·nu·che or **pe·nu′chi** (pə no͞o′chē) ***n.*** ⟦var. of PANOCHA⟧ a fudgelike candy

pe·nul·ti·mate (pē nul′tə mət) ***adj.*** ⟦< L *paene,* almost + ULTIMATE⟧ next to the last —***n.*** the penultimate one

pe·nu·ri·ous (pe nyoor′ē əs, -noor′-) ***adj.***

[see fol.] miserly; stingy —**pe·nu′ri·ous·ly** *adv.* —**pe·nu′ri·ous·ness** *n.*

pen·u·ry (pen′yoo rē, -yə-) *n.* [< L *penuria,* want] extreme poverty

pe·on (pē′ən, -än′) *n.* [< ML *pedo,* foot soldier] 1 in Spanish America, a member of the laboring class 2 in the SW U.S., a person forced into servitude to work off a debt —**pe′on·age** *n.*

pe·o·ny (pē′ə nē) *n., pl.* **-nies** [< Gr *Paiōn,* Apollo as god of medicine: from its former medicinal use] 1 a plant with large pink, white, red, or yellow, showy flowers 2 the flower

peo·ple (pē′pəl) *n., pl.* **-ples** [< L *populus,* nation, crowd] all the persons of a racial or ethnic group; nation, race, etc. —*n.pl.* 1 the persons of a certain place, group, or class 2 one's family; relatives 3 the populace 4 persons considered indefinitely [what will *people* say?] 5 human beings —*vt.* **-pled, -pling** to populate

Pe·or·i·a (pē ôr′ē ə) city in central Ill.: pop. 124,000

pep (pep) *n.* [< fol.] [Colloq.] energy; vigor —*vt.* **pepped, pep′ping** [Colloq.] to fill with pep; invigorate: with *up* —**pep′py, -pi·er, -pi·est,** *adj.*

pep·per (pep′ər) *n.* [< Gr *peperi*] 1 *a)* a pungent condiment ground from the dried fruits of an East Indian vine *b)* this vine 2 the fruit of the red pepper plant, red, yellow, or green, sweet or hot —*vt.* 1 to season with ground pepper 2 to pelt with small objects

pep′per·corn′ *n.* the dried berry of the pepper

pepper mill a hand mill used to grind peppercorns

pep′per·mint′ *n.* 1 a plant of the mint family that yields a pungent oil used for flavoring 2 the oil 3 a candy flavored with this oil

pep·per·o·ni (pep′ər ō′nē) *n., pl.* **-nis** or **-ni** [< It *peperoni*] a hard, highly spiced Italian sausage

pepper shaker a container for ground pepper, with a perforated top

pep′per·y *adj.* 1 of, like, or highly seasoned with pepper 2 sharp or fiery, as words 3 hot-tempered

pep·sin (pep′sin) *n.* [< Gr *peptein,* to digest] a stomach enzyme, aiding in the digestion of proteins

pep talk a talk, as to an athletic team by its coach, to instill enthusiasm, determination, etc.

pep·tic (pep′tik) *adj.* [see PEPSIN] 1 of or aiding digestion 2 caused by digestive secretions [a *peptic* ulcer]

per (pur, pər) *prep.* [L] 1 through; by; by means of 2 for each [fifty cents *per* yard] 3 [Colloq.] according to

per- [< prec.] *prefix* 1 through, throughout 2 thoroughly

per·ad·ven·ture (pur′əd ven′chər) *adv.* [< OFr *par,* by + *aventure,* chance] [Archaic] possibly

per·am·bu·late (pər am′byoo lāt′) *vt., vi.* **-lat′ed, -lat′ing** [< L *per,* through + *ambulare,* to walk] to walk (through, over, etc.)

per·am′bu·la′tor (-lāt′ər) *n.* [Chiefly Brit., etc.] a baby carriage

per an·num (pər an′əm) [L] yearly

per·cale (pər kāl′) *n.* [Fr < Pers *pargāla,* scrap] fine, closely woven cotton cloth, used for sheets, etc.

per cap·i·ta (pər kap′i tə) [ML, lit., by heads] for each person

per·ceive (pər sēv′) *vt., vi.* **-ceived′, -ceiv′·ing** [< L *per,* through + *capere,* take] 1 to understand 2 to become aware (of) through the senses

per·cent (pər sent′) *adv., adj.* [< L *per centum*] in, to, or for every hundred: symbol, % Also **per cent** —*n.* [Colloq.] percentage

per·cent′age (-ij) *n.* 1 a given part in every hundred 2 part; portion 3 advantage; profit

per·cen·tile (pər sen′tīl′, -sent′′l) *n.* *Statistics* any of 100 divisions of a series, each of equal frequency

per·cep·ti·ble (pər sep′tə bəl) *adj.* that can be perceived —**per·cep′ti·bly** *adv.*

per·cep′tion (-shən) *n.* [< L *percipere,* perceive] 1 the mental grasp of objects, etc. through the senses 2 insight or intuition 3 the knowledge, etc. gotten by perceiving —**per·cep′tion·al** *adj.*

per·cep′tive *adj.* 1 of perception 2 able to perceive quickly —**per·cep′tive·ly** *adv.* —**per·cep′tive·ness** *n.*

per·cep′tu·al (-choo əl) *adj.* of or involving perception

perch[1] (purch) *n., pl.* **-es** [< Gr *perkē*] 1 a small, spiny-finned, freshwater food fish 2 any of various other spiny-finned fishes

perch[2] (purch) *n.* [< L *pertica,* pole] 1 a horizontal pole, etc. serving as a roost for birds 2 any high resting place 3 a measure of length equal to $5\frac{1}{2}$ yards —*vi., vt.* to rest or place on or as on a perch

per·chance (pər chans′) *adv.* [< OFr *par,* by + *chance,* chance] [Archaic] 1 by chance 2 perhaps

per·co·late (pur′kə lāt′) *vt.* **-lat′ed, -lat′ing** [< L *per,* through + *colare,* to strain] to pass (a liquid) through a porous substance; filter —*vi.* to ooze through a porous substance

per′co·la′tor *n.* a coffeepot in which the boiling water bubbles up through a tube and filters back down through the ground coffee

per·cus·sion (pər kush′ən) *n.* [< L *per-,* thoroughly + *quatere,* shake] the hitting of one body against another, as the hammer of a firearm against a powder cap (**percussion cap**) —*adj.* of a musical instrument producing a tone when struck, as a drum, cymbal, etc.

per·cus′sion·ist *n.* a musician who plays percussion instruments

per di·em (pər dē′əm, dī′-) [L] daily

per·di·tion (pər dish′ən) *n.* [< L *perdere,* to lose] 1 *Theol.* the loss of the soul 2 HELL

per·dure (pər door′) *vi.* **-dured′, -dur′ing** [< L *perdurare,* to endure] to remain in existence; last

per·e·gri·nate (per′ə gri nāt′) *vt., vi.* **-nat′ed, -nat′ing** [see PILGRIM] to travel (along, over, or through) —**per′e·gri·na′·tion** *n.*

per·e·grine (falcon) (per′ə grin) a swift falcon of nearly worldwide distribution, much used in falconry

per·emp·to·ry (pər emp′tə rē) ***adj.*** ⟦< L *perimere,* destroy⟧ **1** *Law* barring further action; final **2** that cannot be denied, delayed, etc., as a command **3** dogmatic; imperious

per·en·ni·al (pər en′ē əl) ***adj.*** ⟦< L *per-,* through + *annus,* year⟧ **1** lasting throughout the whole year **2** continuing for a long time **3** living more than two years: said of plants **—*n.*** a perennial plant **—per·en′ni·al·ly *adv.***

per·fect (pur′fikt; *for v. usually* pər fekt′) ***adj.*** ⟦< L *per-,* through + *facere,* do⟧ **1** complete in all respects; flawless **2** excellent, as in skill or quality **3** completely accurate **4** utter; sheer; absolute /a *perfect* fool/ **5** *Gram.* expressing a state or action completed at the time of speaking **—*vt.*** **1** to complete **2** to make perfect or nearly perfect **—*n.*** **1** the perfect tense **2** a verb form in this tense **—per′fect·ly *adv.*** **—per′fect·ness *n.***

per·fec·ta (pər fek′tə) ***n.*** ⟦Sp, perfect⟧ a bet in which one wins if one correctly picks the first and second place finishers in a race

per·fect·i·ble (pər fek′tə bəl) ***adj.*** that can become, or be made, perfect

per·fec·tion (pər fek′shən) ***n.*** **1** the act of perfecting **2** a being perfect **3** a person or thing that is the perfect embodiment of some quality

per·fec′tion·ism′ ***n.*** obsessive striving for perfection **—per·fec′tion·ist *n., adj.***

per·fi·dy (pur′fə dē) ***n.,*** *pl.* **-dies** ⟦< L *per,* through + *fides,* faith⟧ betrayal of trust; treachery **—per·fid·i·ous** (pər fid′ē əs) ***adj.***

per·fo·rate (pur′fə rāt′) ***vt., vi.*** **-rat′ed, -rat′·ing** ⟦< L *per,* through + *forare,* to bore⟧ **1** to make a hole or holes through, as by boring **2** to pierce with holes in a row, as a pattern, etc. **—per′fo·ra′tion *n.***

per·force (pər fôrs′) ***adv.*** ⟦< OFr: see PER & FORCE⟧ necessarily

per·form (pər fôrm′) ***vt.*** ⟦< OFr *parfournir*⟧ **1** to do (a task, etc.) **2** to fulfill (a promise, etc.) **3** to render or enact (a piece of music, dramatic role, etc.) **—*vi.*** to execute an action or process, esp. in a PERFORMANCE (sense 4) **—per·form′er *n.***

per·form′ance ***n.*** **1** the act of performing **2** functional effectiveness **3** deed or feat **4** *a)* a formal exhibition or presentation, as a play *b)* one's part in this

performance art an art form combining elements of several art forms, as dance, film, etc., in a presentation of juxtaposed images on various themes

performing arts arts, such as drama, for performance before an audience

per·fume (pər fyōōm′; *for n. usually* pur′ fyōōm′) ***vt.*** **-fumed′, -fum′ing** ⟦< L *per-,* intens. + *fumare,* to smoke⟧ **1** to scent **2** to put perfume on **—*n.*** a pleasing odor, or a substance producing this, as a volatile oil extracted from flowers

per·fum′er·y (-ər ē) ***n.,*** *pl.* **-ies** perfumes collectively

per·func·to·ry (pər fuŋk′tə rē) ***adj.*** ⟦< L *per-,* intens. + *fungi,* perform⟧ **1** done merely as a routine; superficial **2** without concern; indifferent **—per·func′to·ri·ly *adv.***

per·go·la (pur′gə lə) ***n.*** ⟦< L *pergula*⟧ an arbor with a latticework roof

per·haps (pər haps′) ***adv.*** ⟦PER + pl. of *hap,* chance⟧ possibly; maybe

peri- ⟦Gr⟧ *prefix* **1** around; about **2** near

per·i·car·di·um (per′i kär′dē əm) ***n.,*** *pl.* **-di·a** (-ə) ⟦< Gr *peri-,* around + *kardia,* heart⟧ in vertebrates, the thin, closed sac surrounding the heart and containing a serous liquid **—per′i·car′di·al *adj.***

Per·i·cles (per′i klēz′) *c.* 495-429 B.C.; Athenian statesman & general

per·i·gee (per′i jē′) ***n.*** ⟦< Gr *peri-,* near + *gē,* earth⟧ the point nearest to the earth in the orbit of the moon or of a man-made satellite

per·i·he·li·on (per′i hē′lē ən) ***n.,*** *pl.* **-li·ons** or **-li·a** (-ə) ⟦< Gr *peri-,* around + *hēlios,* sun⟧ the point nearest the sun in the orbit of a planet, comet, or man-made satellite

per·il (per′əl) ***n.*** ⟦< L *periculum,* danger⟧ **1** exposure to harm or injury **2** something that may cause harm **—*vt.*** **-iled** or **-illed, -il·ing** or **-il·ling** to expose to danger

per′il·ous *adj.* involving peril or risk; dangerous **—per′il·ous·ly *adv.***

pe·rim·e·ter (pə rim′ə tər) ***n.*** ⟦< Gr *peri-,* around + *metron,* measure⟧ **1** the outer boundary of a figure or area **2** the total length of this

per·i·ne·um (per′i nē′əm) ***n.,*** *pl.* **-ne′a** (-ə) ⟦< Gr *perineon*⟧ the small area between the anus and the genitals

pe·ri·od (pir′ē əd) ***n.*** ⟦< Gr *periodos,* a cycle⟧ **1** the interval between successive occurrences of an event **2** a portion of time characterized by certain processes, etc. /a *period* of change/ **3** any of the portions of time into which a game, school day, etc. is divided **4** the menses **5** an end, conclusion **6** *a)* the pause in speaking or a mark of punctuation (.) used at the end of a sentence *b)* the dot (.) following many abbreviations **—*interj.*** an exclamation used for emphasis

pe·ri·od·ic (pir′ē äd′ik) ***adj.*** **1** appearing or recurring at regular intervals **2** intermittent

pe′ri·od′i·cal *adj.* **1** PERIODIC **2** published at regular intervals, as weekly, etc. **3** of a periodical **—*n.*** a periodical publication **—pe′ri·od′i·cal·ly *adv.***

periodic table an arrangement of the chemical elements according to their atomic numbers

pe·ri·od·i·za·tion (pir′ē əd i zā′shən) ***n.*** the dividing, as of history, into chronological periods

per·i·o·don·tal (per′ē ō dänt′'l, -ē ə-) ***adj.*** ⟦< PERI- + Gr *odōn,* tooth⟧ occurring around a tooth or affecting the gums

per·i·pa·tet·ic (per′i pə tet′ik) ***adj.*** ⟦< Gr *peri-,* around + *patein,* walk⟧ walking or moving about; itinerant

pe·riph·er·al (pə rif′ər əl) ***adj.*** **1** of or forming a periphery **2** outer; external **—*n.*** a piece of equipment used with a computer to increase its range or efficiency, as a disk, etc.

pe·riph·er·y (pə rif′ər ē) ***n.,*** *pl.* **-ies** ⟦< Gr *peri-,* around + *pherein,* to bear⟧ **1** an outer boundary, esp. of a rounded object **2** surrounding space or area

pe·riph·ra·sis (pə rif′rə sis) ***n.,*** *pl.* **-ses′** (-sēz′)

⟦< Gr *peri-*, around + *phrazein*, to speak⟧ the use of many words where a few would do

per·i·scope (per′i skōp′) ***n.*** ⟦PERI- + -SCOPE⟧ an optical instrument which allows one to see around or over an obstacle: used on submarines, etc.

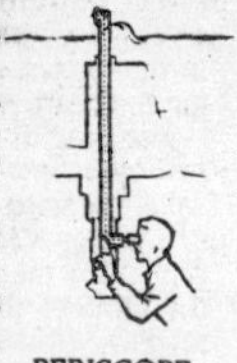

PERISCOPE

per·ish (per′ish) ***vi.*** ⟦< L *per-*, through + *ire*, go⟧ **1** to be destroyed or ruined **2** to die, esp. violently

per·ish·a·ble (per′ish ə bəl) ***adj.*** that may perish; esp., liable to spoil, as some foods **—*n.*** something perishable, esp. food

per·i·stal·sis (per′ə stal′sis, -stôl′-) ***n.**, pl.* **-ses′** (-sēz′) ⟦< Gr *peri-*, around + *stellein*, to place⟧ the contractions and dilations of the alimentary canal, moving the contents onward **—per′i·stal′tic *adj.***

per·i·to·ne·um (per′i tō nē′əm) ***n.**, pl.* **-ne′a** (-ə) or **-ne′ums** ⟦< Gr *peri-*, around + *teinein*, to stretch⟧ the serous membrane lining the abdominal cavity

per′i·to·ni′tis *n.* inflammation of the peritoneum

per·i·wig (per′i wig′) ***n.*** ⟦altered < Fr *perruque*⟧ a wig

per·i·win·kle[1] (per′i wiŋ′kəl) ***n.*** ⟦< L *pervincire*, entwine⟧ a creeping plant with blue, white, or pink flowers

per·i·win·kle[2] (per′i wiŋ′kəl) ***n.*** ⟦OE *pinewincle*⟧ a small saltwater snail with a thick, globular shell

per·jure (pur′jər) ***vt.*** **-jured, -jur·ing** ⟦< L *per*, through + *jurare*, swear⟧ to make (oneself) guilty of perjury **—per′jur·er *n.***

per·ju·ry (pur′jə rē) ***n.**, pl.* **-ries** ⟦< L *perjurus*, false⟧ the willful telling of a lie while under oath

perk[1] (purk) ***vt.*** ⟦ME *perken*⟧ **1** to raise (the head, etc.) briskly **2** to give a smart, fresh, or vivacious look to: often with *up* **—*vi.*** to become lively: with *up* **—perk′y, -i·er, -i·est, *adj.***

perk[2] (purk) ***vt.**, **vi.*** [Colloq.] *short for* PERCOLATE

perk[3] (purk) ***n.*** [Colloq.] *short for* PERQUISITE

perm (purm) ***n.*** [Colloq.] short for PERMANENT **—*vt.*** to give a permanent to

per·ma·frost (pur′mə frôst′) ***n.*** permanently frozen subsoil

per·ma·nent (pur′mə nənt) ***adj.*** ⟦< L *per*, through + *manere*, remain⟧ lasting or intended to last indefinitely or for a long time **—*n.*** a long-lasting hair wave produced by use of chemicals or heat

permanent wave PERMANENT (*n.*)

per·me·a·ble (pur′mē ə bəl) ***adj.*** that can be permeated, as by fluids **—per′me·a·bil′i·ty *n.***

per·me·ate (pur′mē āt′) ***vt.**, **vi.*** **-at′ed, -at′ing** ⟦< L *per*, through + *meare*, to glide⟧ to spread or diffuse; penetrate (*through* or *among*)

per·mis·si·ble (pər mis′ə bəl) ***adj.*** that can be permitted; allowable

per·mis·sion (pər mish′ən) ***n.*** the act of permitting; esp., formal consent

per·mis′sive (-mis′iv) ***adj.*** **1** that permits **2** allowing freedom; lenient **—per·mis′sive·ly *adv.*** **—per·mis′sive·ness *n.***

per·mit (pər mit′; *for n. usually* pur′mit′) ***vt.*** **-mit′ted, -mit′ting** ⟦< L *per*, through + *mittere*, send⟧ **1** to allow; consent to **2** to authorize **—*vi.*** to give opportunity /if time *permits*/ **—*n.*** a license

per·mu·ta·tion (pur′myoo tā′shən) ***n.*** ⟦< L *per-*, intens. + *mutare*, change⟧ **1** any radical alteration **2** any of the total number of groupings possible within a group

per·ni·cious (pər nish′əs) ***adj.*** ⟦< L < *per*, thoroughly + *necare*, kill⟧ causing great injury, destruction, etc.; fatal **—per·ni′cious·ly *adv.***

per·o·ra·tion (per′ə rā′shən) ***n.*** ⟦< L *per*, through + *orare*, speak⟧ the concluding part of a speech

per·ox·ide (pər äks′īd′, pə räk′sīd′) ***n.*** ⟦< L *per*, through + OXIDE⟧ any oxide containing the oxygen group linked by a single bond; specif., hydrogen peroxide **—*vt.*** **-id′ed, -id′ing** to bleach with hydrogen peroxide

per·pen·dic·u·lar (pur′pən dik′yoo lər, -yə-) ***adj.*** ⟦< L *perpendiculum*, plumb line⟧ **1** at right angles to a given plane or line **2** exactly upright; vertical **—*n.*** a line or plane at right angles to another line or plane

per·pe·trate (pur′pə trāt′) ***vt.*** **-trat′ed, -trat′ing** ⟦< L *per*, thoroughly + *patrare*, to effect⟧ **1** to do (something evil, criminal, etc.) **2** to commit (a blunder, etc.) **—per′pe·tra′tion *n.*** **—per′pe·tra′tor *n.***

per·pet·u·al (pər pech′oo əl) ***adj.*** ⟦< L *perpetuus*, constant⟧ **1** lasting forever or for a long time **2** continuing without interruption; constant **—per·pet′u·al·ly *adv.***

per·pet′u·ate′ (-āt′) ***vt.*** **-at′ed, -at′ing** to make perpetual; cause to continue or be remembered **—per·pet′u·a′tion *n.***

per·pe·tu·i·ty (pur′pə too′ə tē) ***n.**, pl.* **-ties** unlimited time; eternity **—in perpetuity** forever

per·plex (pər pleks′) ***vt.*** ⟦< L *per*, through + *plectere*, twist⟧ to make (a person) uncertain, doubtful, etc.; confuse **—per·plex′ing *adj.*** **—per·plex′i·ty,** *pl.* **-ties, *n.***

per·qui·site (pur′kwi zit) ***n.*** ⟦< L *per-*, intens. + *quaerere*, seek⟧ something in addition to regular pay for one's work, as a tip

per se (pur′ sā′, -sē′) ⟦L⟧ by (or in) itself; intrinsically

per·se·cute (pur′si kyoot′) ***vt.*** **-cut′ed, -cut′ing** ⟦< L *per*, through + *sequi*, follow⟧ to afflict constantly so as to injure or distress, as for reasons of religion, race, etc. **—per′se·cu′tion *n.*** **—per′se·cu′tor *n.***

per·se·vere (pur′sə vir′) ***vi.*** **-vered′, -ver′ing** ⟦< L *per-*, intens. + *severus*, severe⟧ to continue a course of action, etc. in spite of difficulty, opposition, etc. **—per′se·ver′ance *n.***

Per·sia (pur′zhə) *old name of* IRAN

Per·sian (pur′zhən, -shən) ***adj.*** of Persia, its people, language, etc.; Iranian **—*n.*** **1** a native or inhabitant of Persia **2** the Iranian language of Iran **3** a variety of domestic cat with a long, thick, glossy coat

Persian lamb the pelt of karakul lambs

per·si·flage (pur'si fläzh') *n.* ⟦Fr < L *per,* through + *sifilare,* to hiss⟧ frivolous talk or writing

per·sim·mon (pər sim'ən) *n.* ⟦< AmInd⟧ **1** a hardwood tree with plumlike fruit **2** the fruit

per·sist (pər sist', -zist') *vi.* ⟦< L *per,* through + *sistere,* cause to stand⟧ **1** to refuse to give up, esp. when faced with opposition **2** to continue insistently **3** to endure; remain

per·sist'ent *adj.* **1** continuing, esp. in the face of opposition, etc. **2** continuing to exist or endure **3** constantly repeated —**per·sist'ence** *n.*

per·snick·e·ty (pər snik'ə tē) *adj.* ⟦< Scot dial.⟧ [Colloq.] **1** too particular; fussy **2** showing or requiring careful treatment

per·son (pur'sən) *n.* ⟦< L *persona*⟧ **1** a human being **2** the human body **3** personality; self **4** *Gram.* division into three sets of pronouns and corresponding verb forms: see FIRST PERSON, SECOND PERSON, THIRD PERSON **5** *Law* any individual or incorporated group having certain legal rights and responsibilities —**in person** actually present

-per·son (pur'sən) *combining form* person in a (specified) activity Used to avoid the masculine implication of *-man [chairperson]*

per'son·a·ble (-ə bəl) *adj.* ⟦ME *personabilis*⟧ having a pleasing appearance and personality

per'son·age' (-ij') *n.* a person; esp., an important person; notable

per'son·al (-nəl) *adj.* **1** private; individual **2** done in person **3** involving human beings *[personal* relationships*]* **4** of the body or physical appearance **5** *a)* having to do with the character, conduct, etc. of a person *[a personal* remark*]* *b)* tending to make personal, esp. derogatory, remarks **6** *Gram.* indicating PERSON (sense 4) **7** *Law* of property (**personal property**) that is movable

personal computer MICROCOMPUTER

personal effects personal belongings, esp. those worn or carried

per·son·al·i·ty (pur'sə nal'ə tē) *n., pl.* **-ties** **1** the quality or fact of being a person or a particular person **2** distinctive individual qualities of a person, considered collectively **3** a notable person **4** [*pl.*] offensive remarks aimed at a person

per·son·al·ize (pur'sə nəl īz') *vt.* **-ized', -iz'·ing** **1** to apply to a particular person, esp. to oneself **2** to have marked with one's name, etc.

per'son·al·ly *adv.* **1** in person **2** as a person *[I* dislike him *personally]* **3** in one's own opinion **4** as though directed at oneself

per·so·na non gra·ta (pər sō'nə nän grät'ə) ⟦L⟧ an unwelcome person

per·son·i·fy (pər sän'i fī') *vt.* **-fied', -fy'ing** **1** to think of or represent (a thing) as a person **2** to typify; embody —**per·son'i·fi·ca'tion** *n.*

per·son·nel (pur'sə nel') *n.* ⟦Fr⟧ **1** persons employed in any work, enterprise, service, etc. **2** a personnel department or office —*adj.* of or relating to the division within a business, etc. responsible for hiring and training employees, etc.

per·spec·tive (pər spek'tiv) *n.* ⟦< L *per,* through + *specere,* look⟧ **1** the art of picturing objects so as to show relative distance or depth **2** the appearance of objects as determined by their relative distance and positions **3** sense of proportion **4** *a)* a specific point of view in understanding things or events *b)* the ability to see things in a true relationship

per·spi·ca·cious (pur'spi kā'shəs) *adj.* ⟦see prec.⟧ having keen judgment; discerning —**per'spi·ca'cious·ly** *adv.* —**per'spi·cac'i·ty** (-kas'ə tē) *n.*

per·spic·u·ous (pər spik'yo͞o əs) *adj.* ⟦see PERSPECTIVE⟧ easily understood; lucid —**per·spi·cu·i·ty** (pur'spi kyo͞o'ə tē) *n.*

per·spi·ra·tion (pur'spə rā'shən) *n.* **1** the act of perspiring **2** sweat

per·spire (pər spīr') *vt., vi.* **-spired', -spir'·ing** ⟦< L *per-,* through + *spirare,* breathe⟧ to sweat

per·suade (pər swād') *vt.* **-suad'ed, -suad'·ing** ⟦< L *per-,* intens. + *suadere,* to urge⟧ to cause to do something, esp. by reasoning, urging, etc.; convince —**per·suad'a·ble** *adj.* —**per·suad'er** *n.*

per·sua·sion (pər swā'zhən) *n.* **1** a persuading or being persuaded **2** power of persuading **3** a strong belief **4** a particular religious belief

per·sua'sive *adj.* having the power, or tending, to persuade —**per·sua'sive·ly** *adv.*

pert (purt) *adj.* ⟦< L *apertus,* open⟧ bold; impudent; saucy —**pert'ly** *adv.*

per·tain (pər tān') *vi.* ⟦< L *per-,* intens. + *tenere,* hold⟧ **1** to belong; be connected or associated **2** to be appropriate **3** to have reference

per·ti·na·cious (pur'tə nā'shəs) *adj.* ⟦< L *per-,* intens. + *tenax,* holding fast⟧ **1** holding firmly to some purpose, belief, etc. **2** hard to get rid of —**per'ti·nac'i·ty** (-nas'ə tē) *n.*

per·ti·nent (pur'tə nənt, purt''n ənt) *adj.* ⟦see PERTAIN⟧ having some connection with the matter at hand —**per'ti·nence** *n.*

per·turb (pər turb') *vt.* ⟦< L *per-,* intens. + *turbare,* disturb⟧ to cause to be alarmed, agitated, or upset —**per·tur·ba·tion** (pur'tər bā'shən) *n.*

Pe·ru (pə ro͞o') country in W South America, on the Pacific: 496,222 sq. mi.; pop. 17,000,000 —**Pe·ru'vi·an** (-vē ən) *adj., n.*

pe·ruke (pə ro͝ok') *n.* ⟦Fr *perruque*⟧ a wig

pe·ruse (pə ro͞oz') *vt.* **-rused', -rus'ing** ⟦prob. < L *per-,* intens. + ME *usen,* to use⟧ **1** to read carefully; study **2** to read in a leisurely way —**pe·rus'al** *n.*

per·vade (pər vād') *vt.* **-vad'ed, -vad'ing** ⟦< L *per,* through + *vadere,* go⟧ to spread or be prevalent throughout —**per·va'sive** *adj.*

per·verse (pər vurs') *adj.* ⟦see PERVERT⟧ **1** deviating from what is considered right or good **2** stubbornly contrary **3** obstinately disobedient —**per·verse'ly** *adv.* —**per·verse'ness** or **per·ver'si·ty** *n.*

per·ver·sion (pər vur'zhən) *n.* **1** a perverting or being perverted **2** something perverted **3** any sexual act or practice considered abnormal

per·vert (pər vurt'; *for n.* pur'vurt') ***vt.*** ⟦< L *per-*, intens. + *vertere,* turn⟧ **1** to lead astray; corrupt **2** to misuse **3** to distort **4** to debase —***n.*** one practicing sexual perversion

pe·se·ta (pə sāt'ə) ***n.*** ⟦Sp, dim. of *peso,* peso⟧ the monetary unit of Spain

pes·ky (pes'kē) ***adj.*** **-ki·er, -ki·est** ⟦prob. var. of *pesty*⟧ [Colloq.] annoying; troublesome —**pes'ki·ness *n.***

pe·so (pā'sō) ***n., pl.*** **-sos'** ⟦Sp < L *pensum,* something weighed⟧ the monetary unit of: *a)* Chile *b)* Colombia *c)* Cuba *d)* Mexico, etc.

pes·si·mism (pes'ə miz'əm) ***n.*** ⟦< L *pejor,* worse⟧ **1** the belief that the evil in life outweighs the good **2** the tendency to always expect the worst —**pes'si·mist *n.*** —**pes'si·mis'tic *adj.*** —**pes'si·mis'ti·cal·ly *adv.***

pest (pest) ***n.*** ⟦< L *pestis,* plague⟧ a person or thing that is troublesome, destructive, etc.; specif., a rat, fly, weed, etc.

pes·ter (pes'tər) ***vt.*** ⟦< OFr *empestrer,* entangle⟧ to annoy; vex

pest'hole' ***n.*** a place infested with an epidemic disease

pes·ti·cide (pes'tə sīd') ***n.*** any chemical for killing insects, weeds, etc.

pes·tif·er·ous (pes tif'ər əs) ***adj.*** ⟦< L *pestis,* plague + *ferre,* to bear⟧ **1** orig., infectious or diseased **2** noxious **3** [Colloq.] annoying

pes·ti·lence (pes'tə ləns) ***n.*** **1** a deadly epidemic disease; plague **2** anything regarded as harmful

pes·ti·lent (pes'tə lənt) ***adj.*** ⟦< L *pestis,* plague⟧ **1** likely to cause death **2** dangerous to society; pernicious /the *pestilent* threat of war/ **3** annoying

pes·tle (pes'əl) ***n.*** ⟦< L *pinsere,* to pound⟧ a tool used to pound or grind substances, esp. in a mortar

pes·to (pes'tō) ***n.*** ⟦see prec.⟧ a sauce for pasta, of ground basil and garlic mixed with olive oil

pet[1] (pet) ***n.*** ⟦orig. Scot dial.⟧ **1** an animal that is domesticated and kept as a companion **2** a person treated with particular indulgence —***adj.*** **1** kept or treated as a pet **2** especially liked **3** particular /a *pet* peeve/ **4** showing fondness /a *pet* name/ —***vt.*** **pet'ted, pet'ting** to stroke or pat gently; caress —***vi.*** [Colloq.] to kiss, embrace, etc., passionately in making love

pet[2] (pet) ***n.*** ⟦< ?⟧ a sulky mood

pet·al (pet''l) ***n.*** ⟦< Gr *petalos,* outspread⟧ any of the leaflike parts of a blossom

pe·tard (pi tärd') ***n.*** ⟦< Fr⟧ an explosive device formerly used to break down doors, walls, etc. —**hoist with (or by) one's own petard** destroyed by the very thing with which one meant to destroy others

pet·cock (pet'käk') ***n.*** ⟦< L *pedere,* break wind + *cock,* valve⟧ a small valve for draining pipes, radiators, etc.

pe·ter (pēt'ər) ***vi.*** ⟦< ?⟧ [Colloq.] to become gradually smaller, weaker, etc. and then disappear With *out*

Pe·ter (pēt'ər) **1** (original name *Simon*) died C. A.D. 64: one of the twelve Apostles, a fisherman: reputed author of two Letters: also **Saint Peter 2 Peter I** 1672-1725; czar of Russia (1682-1725): called *Peter the Great*

pet·i·ole (pet'ē ōl') ***n.*** ⟦< L *pes,* FOOT⟧ the part of a leaf supporting the blade and attached to the stem

pe·tite (pə tēt') ***adj.*** ⟦Fr⟧ small and trim in figure: said of a woman

pe·tit four (pet'ē fôr') ***pl.*** **pe'tits fours'** or **pe·tit fours** (pet'ē fôrz') ⟦Fr, lit., small oven⟧ a tiny, frosted cake

pe·ti·tion (pə tish'ən) ***n.*** ⟦< L *petere,* seek⟧ **1** a solemn, earnest request; entreaty **2** a formal document embodying such a request, often signed by many people **3** *Law* a written formal request asking for a specific court action —***vt.*** **1** to address a petition to **2** to ask for —***vi.*** to make a petition —**pe·ti'tion·er *n.***

petit jury a group of citizens picked to decide the issues of a trial in court

pet·rel (pe'trəl) ***n.*** ⟦< ?⟧ a small sea bird with long wings

pet·ri·fy (pe'tri fī') ***vt.*** **-fied', -fy'ing** ⟦< L *petra,* rock + *facere,* make⟧ **1** to turn into stone **2** to harden or deaden **3** to paralyze, as with fear

petro- ⟦< Gr *petra,* rock⟧ *combining form* **1** rock or stone **2** petroleum **3** of or relating to the petroleum business

pet·ro·chem·i·cal (pe'trō kem'i kəl) ***n.*** a chemical with a petroleum base

pet'ro·dol'lars *n.pl.* revenue from the sale of petroleum

pet·rol (pe'trəl) ***n.*** ⟦see PETROLEUM⟧ *Brit., etc. (exc. Cdn.) term for* GASOLINE

pet·ro·la·tum (pe'trə lāt'əm) ***n.*** ⟦< fol.⟧ a greasy, jellylike substance derived from petroleum and used in ointments, etc. Also **petroleum jelly**

pe·tro·le·um (pə trō'lē əm) ***n.*** ⟦< L *petra,* rock + *oleum,* oil⟧ an oily, liquid solution of hydrocarbons, occurring naturally in certain rock strata: it yields kerosene, gasoline, etc.

PET scan (pet) ⟦*p(ositron) e(mission) t(omography)*, an X-ray technique⟧ a diagnostic X-raying of the metabolism of the body, esp. the brain, using many single-plane X-rays (*tomograms*) and radioactive tracers

pet·ti·coat (pet'ē kōt', pet'i-) ***n.*** ⟦< PETTY + COAT⟧ a woman's underskirt

pet·ti·fog·ger (pet'i fäg'ər, -fôg'-; pet'ē-) ***n.*** ⟦< PETTY + *fogger* < ?⟧ a lawyer who handles petty cases, esp. unethically —**pet'ti·fog', -fogged', -fog'ging, *vi.***

pet·tish (pet'ish) ***adj.*** ⟦< PET[2]⟧ peevish; petulant —**pet'tish·ly *adv.***

pet·ty (pet'ē) ***adj.*** **-ti·er, -ti·est** ⟦< OFr *petit*⟧ **1** relatively unimportant **2** small-minded; mean **3** relatively low in rank —**pet'ti·ness *n.***

petty cash a cash fund for incidentals

petty officer *U.S. Navy* a naval enlisted person who is a noncommissioned officer

pet·u·lant (pech'ə lənt) ***adj.*** ⟦< L *petere,* to rush at⟧ impatient or irritable, esp. over a petty annoyance —**pet'u·lance *n.*** —**pet'u·lant·ly *adv.***

pe·tu·ni·a (pə tōōn'yə, -ē ə) ***n.*** ⟦ult. <

AmInd (Brazil)] a plant with showy, funnel-shaped flowers

pew (pyo͞o) ***n.*** [ult. < Gr *pous,* foot] any of the benches with a back that are fixed in rows in a church

pe·wee (pē′wē′) ***n.*** [echoic of its call] a small flycatcher

pew·ter (pyo͞ot′ər) ***n.*** [OFr *peautre*] **1** a dull, silvery-gray alloy of tin with copper, lead, etc. **2** articles made of this

pe·yo·te (pā ōt′ē) ***n.*** [AmSp < AmInd (Mexico) *peyotl,* caterpillar] the cactus plant mescal See MESCALINE

pf. or **pfd.** preferred

PFC or **Pfc.** Private First Class

PG ***n.*** a rating for a film that parents may find unsuitable for children

pg. page

PG-13 ***n.*** a film rating indicating some material may be inappropriate for children under 13

pH (pē′āch′) [< Fr *p(ouvoir) h(ydrogène),* lit., hydrogen power] a symbol for the degree of acidity or alkalinity of a solution

pha·e·ton or **pha·ë·ton** (fā′ə tən) ***n.*** [after *Phaetōn,* son of Helios, Gr sun god] **1** a light, four-wheeled carriage **2** an early type of open automobile

phag·o·cyte (fag′ō sīt′) ***n.*** [< Gr *phagein,* to eat + *kytos,* hollow] any cell, esp. a leukocyte, that destroys foreign matter in the blood and tissues

pha·lan·ger (fā lan′jər, fə-) ***n.*** [< Gr *phalanx,* bone between fingers or toes] any of various small, tree-dwelling Australian marsupials, often with bushy, prehensile tails

pha·lanx (fā′laŋks′) ***n.***, *pl.* **-lanx′es** or **pha·lan·ges** (fə lan′jēz′) [Gr, line of battle] **1** an ancient close-ranked infantry formation **2** any massed group **3** *pl.* **-lan′ges′** any of the bones forming the fingers or toes

phal·lus (fal′əs) ***n.***, *pl.* **-li′** (-ī′) or **-lus·es** [Gr *phallos*] an image of the penis —**phal′lic** ***adj.***

phan·tasm (fan′taz′əm) ***n.*** [< Gr *phantazein,* to show] **1** a figment of the mind **2** a deceptive likeness

phan·tas·ma·go·ri·a (fan taz′mə gôr′ē ə) ***n.*** [< Gr *phantasma,* phantasm + *ageirein,* assemble] a rapid sequence of images, as in a dream

phan·ta·sy (fan′tə sē) ***n.***, *pl.* **-sies** *alt. sp. of* FANTASY

phan·tom (fan′təm) ***n.*** [see PHANTASM] **1** an apparition; specter **2** an illusion —***adj.*** of or like a phantom; illusory

Phar·aoh (far′ō, fer′ō) ***n.*** the title of the kings of ancient Egypt

Phar·i·see (far′i sē′) ***n.*** **1** a member of an ancient Jewish group that observed both the written and oral law **2** [< characterization in NT] [p-] a self-righteous, hypocritical person —**phar′i·sa′ic** (-sā′ik) ***adj.***

phar·ma·ceu·ti·cal (fär′mə so͞ot′i kəl) ***adj.*** [< Gr *pharmakon,* a drug] of pharmacy or drugs Also **phar′ma·ceu′tic** —***n.*** a drug or medicine

phar′ma·ceu′tics (-iks) ***n.pl.*** [*with sing. v.*] PHARMACY (sense 1)

phar·ma·cist (fär′mə sist) ***n.*** one licensed to practice pharmacy

phar′ma·col′o·gy (-käl′ə jē) ***n.*** [< Gr *pharmakon,* a drug] the science dealing with the effect of drugs on living organisms

phar′ma·co·pe′ia or **phar′ma·co·poe′ia** (-kō pē′ə) ***n.*** [< Gr *pharmakon,* a drug + *poiein,* to make] an official book of drugs and medicines

phar·ma·cy (fär′mə sē) ***n.***, *pl.* **-cies** [< Gr *pharmakon,* a drug] **1** the art or profession of preparing drugs and medicines **2** a drugstore

phar·yn·gi·tis (far′in jīt′is) ***n.*** inflammation of the pharynx

phar·ynx (far′iŋks) ***n.***, *pl.* **phar′ynx·es** or **pha·ryn·ges** (fə rin′jēz′) [Gr *pharynx*] the cavity leading from the mouth and nasal passages to the larynx and esophagus —**pha·ryn·ge·al** (fə rin′jē əl) ***adj.***

phase (fāz) ***n.*** [< Gr *phainesthai,* to appear] **1** any stage in a series or cycle of changes, as of the moon's illumination **2** an aspect or side, as of a problem —***vt.*** **phased, phas′ing** to introduce or carry out in stages: often with *in* or *into* —**in** (or **out of**) **phase** in (or not in) a synchronized state —**phase out** to terminate (an activity) by stages

phase′out′ ***n.*** a phasing out; gradual termination or withdrawal

PhD or **Ph.D.** [L *Philosophiae Doctor*] Doctor of Philosophy

pheas·ant (fez′ənt) ***n.*** [< Gr *phasianos,* (bird) of *Phasis,* river in Asia] a large game bird with a long, sweeping tail and brilliant feathers

phe·nac·e·tin (fē nas′ə tin′, -tən; fi-) ***n.*** a white, crystalline powder used to reduce fever, relieve headaches, etc.

phe·no·bar·bi·tal (fē′nō bär′bi tôl′) ***n.*** an odorless, white, crystalline powder, used as a sedative

phe·nol (fē′nōl′, -nôl′, -näl′) ***n.*** a white crystalline compound, corrosive and poisonous, used to make synthetic resins, etc. and, in dilute solution (*carbolic acid*) as an antiseptic

phe·nol·phthal·ein (fē′nōl thal′ēn′, -ē in) ***n.*** a white to pale-yellow, crystalline powder, used as a laxative, as an acid-base indicator in chemical analysis, etc.

phe·nom (fē′näm) ***n.*** [Slang] one who is very talented or skilled, esp. a star in sports or popular music

phe·nom·e·non (fə näm′ə nən′, -nän) ***n.***, *pl.* **-na** (-nə); also, esp. for 2 and usually for 3, **-nons′** [< Gr *phainesthai,* appear] **1** any observable fact or event that can be scientifically described **2** anything very unusual **3** [Colloq.] an extraordinary person; prodigy —**phe·nom′e·nal** ***adj.***

pher·o·mone (fer′ə mōn′) ***n.*** [< Gr *pherein,* to bear + (HOR)MONE] a chemical substance secreted by certain animals, as ants, which conveys information to others of the same species

phi (fī, fē) ***n.*** the 21st letter of the Greek alphabet (Φ, ϕ)

phi·al (fī′əl) ***n.*** [< Gr *phialē,* shallow bowl] a small glass bottle; vial

Phil·a·del·phi·a (fil′ə del′fē ə) city & port in SE Pa.: pop. 1,688,000

Phil·a·del·phi·a lawyer (fil′ə del′fē ə, -fyə) [Colloq.] a shrewd or tricky lawyer

phi·lan·der (fi lan′dər, fə-) ***vi.*** [< Gr *philos,* loving + *anēr,* man] to engage lightly in love affairs: said of a man —**phi·lan′der·er** *n.*

phi·lan·thro·py (fə lan′thrə pē, fi-; -thrō-) *n.* ⟦< Gr *philein,* to love + *anthrōpos,* man⟧ 1 a desire to help mankind, esp. as shown by endowments to institutions, etc. 2 *pl.* **-pies** a philanthropic gift, institution, etc. —**phil·an·throp·ic** (fil′ən thräp′ik) *adj.* —**phi·lan′thro·pist** *n.*

phi·lat·e·ly (fə lat″l ē, fi-) *n.* ⟦< Fr < Gr *philos,* loving + *ateleia,* exemption from (further) tax (meaning "postage prepaid")⟧ the collection and study of postage stamps, postmarks, etc. —**phi·lat′e·list** *n.*

-phile (fīl, fil) ⟦< Gr *philos,* loving⟧ *combining form* one that loves, likes, etc. *[bibliophile]*

phil·har·mon·ic (fil′här män′ik) *adj.* ⟦< Gr *philos,* loving + *harmonia,* harmony⟧ devoted to music —*n.* 1 a society sponsoring a symphony orchestra 2 [Colloq.] such an orchestra

phi·lip·pic (fi lip′ik) *n.* ⟦< Gr *Philippos,* Philip, Macedonian king denounced by Demosthenes⟧ a bitter verbal attack

Phil·ip·pines (fil′ə pēnz′) country consisting of *c.* 7,100 islands (**Philippine Islands**) in the SW Pacific off the SE coast of Asia: *c.* 116,000 sq. mi.; pop. 58,000,000 —**Phil′ip·pine′** (-pēn′) *adj.*

Phil·is·tine (fi lis′tin, -tēn′; fə-; fil′is-; *also,* -tīn′) *n.* 1 any of a non-Semitic people of SW Palestine in Biblical times 2 [*often* p-] a person smugly conventional, narrow, lacking culture, etc.

Phil·lips (fil′ips) ⟦after H. F. *Phillips* (?-1958), its U.S. developer⟧ *trademark for* a screwdriver (**Phillips screwdriver**) with a cross-shaped, pointed tip

philo- ⟦< Gr *philos,* loving⟧ *combining form* loving, liking

phil·o·den·dron (fil′ō den′drən, fil′ə-) *n.* ⟦< Gr *philos,* loving + *dendron,* tree⟧ a tropical American vine

phi·lol·o·gy (fi läl′ə jē) *n.* ⟦< Gr *philein,* to love + *logos,* word⟧ *old term for* LINGUISTICS —**phil·o·log·i·cal** (fil′ō läj′i kəl, fil′ə-) *adj.* —**phi·lol′o·gist** *n.*

phi·los·o·pher (fə läs′ə fər) *n.* ⟦< Gr *philos,* loving + *sophos,* wise⟧ 1 one who is learned in philosophy 2 one who lives by or expounds a system of philosophy 3 one who meets difficulties with calm composure

phil·o·soph·ic (fil′ō säf′ik, fil′ə-) *adj.* 1 of philosophy or philosophers 2 sensibly composed or calm Also **phil′o·soph′i·cal**

phi·los·o·phize (fə läs′ə fīz′) *vi.* **-phized′, -phiz′ing** 1 to think or reason like a philosopher 2 to moralize, express truisms, etc.

phi·los·o·phy (fə läs′ə fē) *n., pl.* **-phies** ⟦see PHILOSOPHER⟧ 1 the study of the principles underlying conduct, thought, and the nature of the universe 2 the general principles or laws of a field of knowledge 3 a particular system of ethics 4 composure; calmness

phil·ter (fil′tər) *n.* ⟦< Gr *philein,* to love⟧ a magic potion, esp. one to arouse sexual love Also [Chiefly Brit.] **phil′tre** (-tər)

phle·bi·tis (flē bīt′is, fli-) *n.* ⟦< Gr *phleps,* vein + -ITIS⟧ inflammation of a vein

phlegm (flem) *n.* ⟦< Gr *phlegma,* inflammation⟧ 1 thick mucus discharged from the throat, as during a cold 2 sluggishness or apathy

phleg·mat·ic (fleg mat′ik) *adj.* ⟦see prec.⟧ sluggish or unexcited —**phleg·mat′i·cal·ly** *adv.*

phlo·em (flō′em′) *n.* ⟦< Gr *phloos,* bark⟧ the vascular tissue through which food is distributed in a plant

phlox (fläks) *n.* ⟦Gr, lit., a flame⟧ a North American plant with clusters of white, pink, or bluish flowers

-phobe (fōb) ⟦< Gr *phobos,* fear⟧ *combining form* one who fears or hates

pho·bi·a (fō′bē ə) *n.* ⟦see prec.⟧ an irrational, excessive, and persistent fear of some thing or situation

-pho·bi·a (fō′bē ə, fō′byə) ⟦Gr *-phobia* < *phobos,* fear⟧ *combining form* fear, dread, hatred *[claustrophobia]*

phoe·be (fē′bē) *n.* ⟦echoic, with sp. after *Phoebe,* Gr goddess of the moon⟧ an American bird with a grayish or brown back, that catches insects in flight

Phoe·ni·cia (fə nish′ə, -nē′shə) ancient region of city-states at the E end of the Mediterranean —**Phoe·ni′cian** *adj., n.*

phoe·nix (fē′niks) ⟦< Gr *phoinix*⟧ *Egypt. Myth.* a bird which lives for 500 years and then sets itself on fire, rising renewed from the ashes

Phoe·nix (fē′niks) capital of Ariz.: pop. 765,000

phone (fōn) *n., vt., vi.* **phoned, phon′ing** [Colloq] *short for* TELEPHONE

-phone (fōn) ⟦< Gr *phōnē,* a sound⟧ *combining form* 1 a device producing or transmitting sound 2 telephone

pho·neme (fō′nēm′) *n.* ⟦< Fr < Gr *phōnē,* voice⟧ *Linguistics* a set of language sounds with slight variations but heard as the same sound by native speakers —**pho·ne·mic** (fō nē′mik, fə-) *adj.*

pho·net·ics (fō net′iks, fə-) *n.pl.* ⟦< Gr *phōnē,* a sound⟧ [*with sing. v.*] the study of the production and written representation of speech sounds —**pho·net′ic** *adj.* —**pho·ne·ti·cian** (fō′nə tish′ən) *n.*

phon·ics (fän′iks) *n.pl.* ⟦< Gr *phōnē,* sound⟧ [*with sing. v.*] a phonetic method of teaching reading —**phon′ic** *adj.* —**phon′i·cally** *adv.*

phono- ⟦< Gr *phōnē,* a sound⟧ *combining form* sound, tone, speech *[phonology]*

pho·no·graph (fō′nə graf′) *n.* ⟦prec. + -GRAPH⟧ a device for reproducing sound recorded in a spiral groove on a revolving disk —**pho′no·graph′ic** *adj.*

pho·nol·o·gy (fō näl′ə jē, fə-) *n.* ⟦PHONO- + -LOGY⟧ 1 the study of speech sounds 2 a description of the sounds of a given language —**pho′no·log′i·cal** (-nō läj′i kəl, -nə-) *adj.* —**pho·nol′o·gist** *n.*

pho·ny (fō′nē) *adj.* **-ni·er, -ni·est** ⟦< Brit thieves' argot *fawney,* gilt ring⟧ [Colloq.] not genuine; false —*n., pl.* **-nies** [Colloq.] something or someone not genuine; fraud; fake Also sp. **phoney** —**pho′ni·ness** *n.*

phoo·ey (fo͞o′ē) *interj.* ⟦echoic⟧ an exclamation of scorn, disgust, etc.

phos·phate (fäs′fāt′) *n.* ⟦Fr⟧ 1 a salt or ester of phosphoric acid 2 a fertilizer containing phosphates **3** a flavored carbonated beverage

phos·phor (fäs′fər, -fôr′) *n.* ⟦see PHOSPHORUS⟧ a phosphorescent or fluorescent substance

phos·pho·res·cence (fäs′fə res′əns) *n.* **1** the property of giving off a lingering emission of light after exposure to radiant energy, as light **2** a continuing luminescence without noticeable heat, as from oxidizing phosphorus **—phos′pho·res′cent** *adj.*

phosphoric acid any of three colorless, crystalline acids with a phosphorus and oxygen radical

phos·pho·rus (fäs′fə rəs) *n.* ⟦< Gr *phōs,* a light + *pherein,* to bear⟧ a nonmetallic chemical element: a waxy solid that ignites spontaneously at room temperature

pho·to (fōt′ō) *n., pl.* **-tos** *short for* PHOTOGRAPH

photo- *combining form* **1** ⟦< Gr *phōs,* a light⟧ of or produced by light **2** ⟦< PHOTOGRAPH⟧ of photography

pho·to·cop·y (fōt′ō käp′ē) *n., pl.* **-ies** a photographic reproduction, as of a book page, made by a special device (**pho′to·cop′i·er**)

pho·to·e·lec·tric cell (fōt′ō ē lek′trik) any device in which light controls an electric circuit which operates a mechanical device, as for opening doors

pho′to·en·grav′ing *n.* **1** a process by which photographs are reproduced on relief printing plates **2** such a plate, or a print made from it **—pho′to·en·grave′, -graved′, -grav′ing,** *vt.* **—pho′to·en·grav′er** *n.*

photo finish a race finish so close that the winner can be determined only from a photograph of the finish

pho·to·fin·ish·ing (fōt′ō fin′ish iŋ) *n.* the process of developing photographic film, making prints, etc.

pho·to·flash (fōt′ō flash′, fōt′ə-) *adj.* designating a flashbulb, etc. electrically synchronized with the camera shutter

pho·to·gen·ic (fōt′ō jen′ik, fōt′ə-) *adj.* ⟦PHOTO- + *-genic,* suitable for⟧ likely to look attractive in photographs

pho·to·graph (fōt′ə graf′) *n.* a picture made by photography **—*vt.*** to take a photograph of **—*vi.*** to appear (as specified) in photographs **—pho·tog·ra·pher** (fə täg′rə fər) *n.*

pho·tog·ra·phy (fə täg′rə fē) *n.* ⟦PHOTO- + -GRAPHY⟧ the art or process of producing pictorial images on a surface sensitive to light or other radiant energy, as on film in a camera **—pho·to·graph·ic** (fōt′ə graf′ik) *adj.*

pho·ton (fō′tän′) *n.* ⟦PHOT(O)- + (ELECTR)ON⟧ a quantum of electromagnetic energy

pho·to·off·set (fōt′ō ôf′set′) *n.* offset printing in which the text or pictures are photographically transferred to a metal plate from which inked impressions are made on the roller

Pho·to·stat (fōt′ō stat′, fōt′ə-) *trademark for* a device for making photocopies on special paper **—*n.*** [p-] a copy so made **—*vt.*** **-stat′ed** or **-stat′ted, -stat′ing** or **-stat′ting** [p-] to make a photostat of

pho·to·syn·the·sis (fōt′ō sin′thə sis, fōt′ə-) *n.* production of organic substances, esp. sugars, from carbon dioxide and water by the action of light on the chlorophyll in green plant cells

pho′to·syn′the·size′ (-sīz′) *vi., vt.* **-sized′, -siz′ing** to carry on, or produce by, photosynthesis

phrase (frāz) *n.* ⟦< Gr *phrazein,* speak⟧ **1** a short, colorful expression **2** a group of words, not a full sentence or clause, conveying a single thought **3** a short, distinct musical passage **—*vt., vi.*** **phrased, phras′ing** to express in words or in a phrase **—phras·al** (frā′zəl) *adj.*

phra·se·ol·o·gy (frā′zē äl′ə jē) *n., pl.* **-gies** choice and pattern of words

phre·net·ic (fri net′ik) *adj.* ⟦< Gr *phrenētikos,* mad⟧ *archaic sp. of* FRENETIC

phre·nol·o·gy (fri näl′ə jē, frə-) *n.* ⟦< Gr *phrēn,* mind + -LOGY⟧ a system, now rejected, analyzing character from the shape of the skull

phy·lac·ter·y (fi lak′tər ē) *n., pl.* **-ies** ⟦< Gr *phylaktērion,* safeguard⟧ either of two small, leather cases holding Scripture texts, worn in prayer on the forehead and arm by orthodox Jewish men

phyl·lo (fē′lō, fī′-) *n.* ⟦< Gr *phyllon,* leaf⟧ dough in very thin sheets, becoming very flaky when baked

phy·log·e·ny (fī läj′ə nē) *n., pl.* **-nies** ⟦< Gr *phylon,* tribe + *-geneia,* origin⟧ the origin and evolution of a group or race of animals or plants

phy·lum (fī′ləm) *n., pl.* **-la** (-lə) ⟦< Gr *phylon,* tribe⟧ a main division of the animal kingdom or, loosely, of a plant division

phys·ic (fiz′ik) *n.* ⟦< Gr *physis,* nature⟧ a medicine, esp. a cathartic **—*vt.*** **-icked, -ick·ing** to dose with this

phys·i·cal (fiz′i kəl) *adj.* **1** of nature and all matter; material **2** of or according to the laws of nature **3** of, or produced by the forces, of, physics **4** of the body **—*n.*** a general medical examination **—phys′i·cal·ly** *adv.*

physical anthropology a major division of anthropology that deals with the physical characteristics and evolution of humans

physical education instruction in the exercise and care of the body, including sports, calisthenics, and hygiene

physical science any science dealing with nonliving matter or energy, as physics, chemistry, or astronomy

physical therapy the treatment of disease, injury, etc. by physical means, as by exercise, massage, etc.

phy·si·cian (fi zish′ən) *n.* ⟦see PHYSIC⟧ a doctor of medicine

phys·ics (fiz′iks) *n.pl.* ⟦see PHYSIC⟧ [*with sing. v.*] the science dealing with the properties, changes, interactions, etc. of matter and energy **—phys′i·cist** (-ə sist) *n.*

phys·i·og·no·my (fiz′ē äg′nə mē) *n.* ⟦< Gr *physis,* nature + *gnōmōn,* judge⟧ facial features and expression

phys′i·og′ra·phy (-äg′rə fē) *n.* ⟦see prec. & -GRAPHY⟧ the study of the earth's surface and oceans, atmosphere, etc.

phys′i·ol′o·gy (-äl′ə jē) *n.* ⟦< Gr *physis,*

nature + -LOGY]] the science dealing with the functions and vital processes of living organisms —**phys'i·o·log'i·cal** (-ō läj'i kəl) *adj.* —**phys'i·ol'o·gist** *n.*

phys·i·o·ther·a·py (fiz'ē ō'ther'ə pē) *n.* PHYSICAL THERAPY —**phys'i·o·ther'a·pist** *n.*

phy·sique (fi zēk') *n.* [[Fr]] the structure or form of the body; build

pi[1] (pī) *n., pl.* **pies** [[see PIE]] **1** jumbled printing type **2** any jumble —*vt.* **pied, pie'ing** or **pi'ing** to jumble

pi[2] (pī) *n.* **1** the 16th letter of the Greek alphabet (Π, π) **2** the symbol (π) designating the ratio of the circumference of a circle to its diameter, about 3.1416

pi·a·nis·si·mo (pē'ə nis'i mō') *adj., adv.* [[It]] *Musical Direction* very soft

pi·an·ist (pē'ə nist, pē an'ist, pyan'ist) *n.* one who plays the piano

pi·an·o[1] (pē an'ō, pyan'ō) *adj., adv.* [[It]] *Musical Direction* soft

pi·a·no[2] (pē ă'nō, pyă'-) *n., pl.* **-nos** [[< fol.]] a large, stringed keyboard instrument: each key operates a felt-covered hammer that strikes a corresponding steel wire or wires

pi·an·o·for·te (pē an'ō fôrt', -an'ō fôrt'ē) *n.* [[It < *piano*, soft + *forte*, loud]] PIANO[2]

pi·as·ter (pē as'tər) *n.* [[ult. < L *emplastrum*, plaster]] one 100th of a pound in Egypt, Lebanon, Syria, and Sudan Brit., etc. sp. **pi·as'tre**

pi·az·za (pē ät'sə, -sä'; *for 2* pē az'ə) *n., pl.* **-zas** or It. **-ze** (-tse) **1** in Italy, a public square **2** a large, covered porch

pi·broch (pē'bräk') *n.* [[< Gael *piob*, bagpipe]] music for the bagpipe, usually of a martial kind

pi·ca (pī'kə) *n.* [[< ? ML, a directory]] a size of printing type, 12 point

pic·a·resque (pik'ə resk') *adj.* [[< Sp *pícaro*, rascal]] dealing with sharp-witted vagabonds or rogues and their adventures /a *picaresque* novel/

Pi·cas·so (pi kä'sō), **Pa·blo** (pä'blō) 1881-1973; Sp. painter & sculptor in France

pic·a·yune (pik'ə yōōn', pik'ə yōōn') *adj.* [[< Fr *picaillon*, small coin]] trivial or petty

pic·ca·lil·li (pik'ə lil'ē) *n.* [[prob. < PICKLE]] a relish, of chopped vegetables, mustard, and hot spices

pic·co·lo (pik'ə lō') *n., pl.* **-los'** [[It, small]] a small flute, pitched an octave above the ordinary flute

pick[1] (pik) *n.* [[OE *pic*, PIKE[2]]] **1** any of several pointed tools or instruments for picking, esp. a heavy one used in breaking up soil, rock, etc. **2** PLECTRUM

pick[2] (pik) *vt.* [[ME *picken*]] **1** to pierce, dig up, etc. with something pointed **2** to probe, scratch at, etc. so as to remove or clear something from **3** to gather (flowers, berries, etc.) **4** to prepare (a fowl) by removing the feathers **5** to pull (fibers, rags, etc.) apart **6** to choose; select **7** to provoke (a quarrel or fight) **8** to pluck (the strings) of (a guitar, etc.) **9** to open (a lock) with a wire, etc. instead of a key **10** to steal from (another's pocket, etc.) —*vi.* **1** to use a pick **2** to select, esp. in a fussy way —*n.* **1** the act of choosing or the choice made **2** the best —**pick at** to eat sparingly of —**pick off** **1** to remove by picking **2** to hit with a carefully aimed shot —**pick on** [Colloq.] to single out for criticism or abuse; annoy; tease —**pick out** to choose —**pick up** **1** to grasp and lift **2** to get, find, or learn, esp. by chance **3** to stop for and take along **4** to gain (speed) **5** to improve **6** [Colloq.] to become acquainted with casually, esp. for lovemaking —**pick'er** *n.*

pick·a·back (pik'ə bak') *adv., adj., vt.* PIGGYBACK

pick·ax or **pick·axe** (pik'aks') *n.* [[< OFr *picquois*]] a pick with a point at one end of the head and a chisel-like edge at the other

pick·er·el (pik'ər əl) *n., pl.* **-el** or **-els** [[< PIKE[3]]] any of various small, North American freshwater fishes

pick·et (pik'it) *n.* [[< Fr *pic*, PIKE[2]]] **1** a pointed stake used in a fence, as a hitching post, etc. **2** a soldier or soldiers stationed to guard against surprise attack **3** a person, as a member of a striking labor union, stationed outside a factory, etc. to demonstrate, keep workers out, etc. —*vt.* **1** to enclose with a picket fence **2** to hitch (an animal) to a picket **3** to post as a military picket **4** to place pickets, or serve as a picket, at (a factory, etc.)

picket line a line or cordon of people serving as pickets

pick'ings *n.pl.* something picked; specif., *a*) scraps; remains *b*) something got by effort, often dishonestly

pick·le (pik'əl) *n.* [[< MDu *pekel*]] **1** any brine, vinegar, etc. used to preserve or marinate food **2** a vegetable, specif. a cucumber, preserved in this **3** [Colloq.] an awkward situation —*vt.* **-led, -ling** to put in or preserve in a pickle solution

pick'pock'et *n.* a thief who steals from pockets, as in a crowd

pick'up' *n.* **1** a picking up **2** the process or power of increasing in speed **3** a small, open delivery truck **4** [Colloq.] a casual acquaintance **5** [Colloq.] improvement **6** *a*) a device for producing electric currents from the vibrations of a phonograph needle *b*) the pivoted arm holding this device

pick·y (pik'ē) *adj.* **-i·er, -i·est** [Colloq.] overly fastidious; fussy

pic·nic (pik'nik) *n.* [[< Fr]] a pleasure outing at which a meal is eaten outdoors —*vi.* **-nicked, -nick·ing** to have a picnic —**pic'nick·er** *n.*

pi·cot (pē'kō) *n., pl.* **-cots** [[< Fr *pic*, a point]] any of the small loops forming a fancy edge as on lace

pic·to·graph (pik'tō graf', -tə-) *n.* **1** a picture or picturelike symbol used in a system of writing **2** a graph using pictures to give data

pic·to·ri·al (pik tôr'ē əl) *adj.* **1** of, containing, or expressed in pictures **2** suggesting a mental image; vivid —**pic·to'ri·al·ly** *adv.*

pic·ture (pik'chər) *n.* [[< L *pingere*, to paint]] **1** a likeness of a person, scene, etc. produced by drawing, painting, photography, etc. **2** a perfect likeness or image /the *picture* of health/ **3** anything suggestive of a beautiful painting, drawing, etc. **4** a vivid description **5** FILM (*n.* 4) **6** the image on a TV screen —*vt.* **-tured, -tur·ing** **1** to make a picture of **2** to show visibly **3** to describe 4 to imagine —**in** (or **out of**) **the picture** considered (or not considered) as involved in a situation

pic'tur·esque' (-chər esk') ***adj.*** like or suggesting a picture; beautiful, vivid, quaint, etc.

picture tube a cathode-ray tube in a TV receiver, monitor, etc., that produces visual images on its screen

picture window a large window that seems to frame the outside view

pid·dle (pid''l) ***vi., vt.*** **-dled, -dling** ⟦< ?⟧ to dawdle; trifle

pid·dling (pid'liŋ) ***adj.*** insignificant; trifling

pid·dly (pid'lē, pid''lē) ***adj.*** PIDDLING

pidg·in (pij'in) ***n.*** ⟦supposed Chin pronunciation of business⟧ a jargon for trade purposes, using words and grammar from different languages: **pidgin English** uses English words and Chinese or Melanesian syntax

pie (pī) ***n.*** ⟦ME⟧ a baked dish of fruit, meat, etc. with an under crust or upper crust, or both —**(as) easy as pie** [Colloq.] extremely easy

pie·bald (pī'bôld') ***adj.*** ⟦< *pie*, magpie + BALD⟧ covered with patches of two colors —***n.*** a piebald horse, etc.

piece (pēs) ***n.*** ⟦OFr *pece*⟧ **1** a part broken or separated from the whole **2** a section of a whole regarded as complete in itself **3** any single thing, specimen, example, etc. /a *piece* of music/ **4** a quantity, as of cloth, manufactured as a unit —***vt.*** **pieced, piec'·ing 1** to add pieces to, as in repairing **2** to join (*together*) the pieces of —**go to pieces 1** to fall apart **2** to lose self-control

pièce de ré·sis·tance (pyes də rā zēs täns') ⟦Fr, piece of resistance⟧ **1** the principal dish of a meal **2** the main item in a series

piece goods YARD GOODS

piece'meal' (-mēl') ***adv.*** ⟦< ME *pece*, a piece + *-mele*, part⟧ piece by piece —***adj.*** made or done piecemeal

piece'work' ***n.*** work paid for at a fixed rate (**piece rate**) per piece of work done

pie chart a graph in the form of a circle divided into sectors in which relative quantities are indicated by the sizes of the sectors

pied (pīd) ***adj.*** ⟦< *pie*, magpie⟧ spotted with various colors

pie'-eyed' ***adj.*** [Slang] intoxicated

pier (pir) ***n.*** ⟦< ML *pera*⟧ **1** a structure supporting the spans of a bridge **2** a structure built out over the water and supported by pillars: used as a landing place, pavilion, etc. **3** *Archit.* a heavy column used to support weight

pierce (pirs) ***vt.*** **pierced, pierc'ing** ⟦< OFr *percer*⟧ **1** to pass into or through as a pointed instrument does; stab **2** to make a hole in **3** to force a way into; break through **4** to sound sharply through **5** to penetrate with the sight or mind —***vi.*** to penetrate

Pierce (pirs), **Franklin** 1804-69; 14th president of the U.S. (1853-57)

Pierre (pir) capital of S.Dak.: pop. 12,000

pi·e·ty (pī'ə tē) ***n.***, *pl.* **-ties** ⟦< L *pius*, pious⟧ **1** devotion to religious duties, etc. **2** devotion to parents, family, etc. **3** a pious act

pif·fle (pif'əl) ***n.*** [Colloq.] anything regarded as insignificant or nonsensical —**pif·fling** (pif'liŋ) ***adj.***

pig (pig) ***n.*** ⟦ME *pigge*⟧ **1** any swine, esp. the unweaned young of the thick-bodied domesticated species; hog **2** a greedy or filthy person

pi·geon (pij'ən) ***n.*** ⟦< L *pipire*, to chirp⟧ any of various related birds with a small head, plump body, and short legs

pi'geon·hole' ***n.*** a small open compartment, as in a desk, for filing papers —***vt.*** **-holed', -hol'ing 1** to put in the pigeonhole of a desk, etc. **2** to put aside indefinitely **3** to classify

pi'geon-toed' (-tōd') ***adj.*** having the toes or feet turned in

pig·gish (pig'ish) ***adj.*** like a pig; gluttonous or filthy —**pig'gish·ness** ***n.***

pig·gy (pig'ē) ***n.***, *pl.* **-gies** a little pig —***adj.*** **-gi·er, -gi·est** PIGGISH

pig'gy·back' ***adv., adj.*** **1** on the shoulders or back **2** of or by a transportation system in which truck trailers are carried on flatcars

pig'head'ed ***adj.*** stubborn

pig iron crude iron, as it comes from the blast furnace

pig·ment (pig'mənt) ***n.*** ⟦< L *pingere*, to paint⟧ **1** coloring matter used to make paints **2** any coloring matter in the tissues of plants or animals

pig·men·ta·tion (pig'mən tā'shən) ***n.*** coloration in plants or animals due to pigment in the tissue

Pig·my (pig'mē) ***adj., n.***, *pl.* **-mies** PYGMY

pig'pen' ***n.*** a pen where pigs are kept Also **pig'sty'** (-stī'), *pl.* **-sties'**

pig'skin' ***n.*** **1** leather made from the skin of a pig **2** [Colloq.] a football

pig'tail' (-tāl') ***n.*** a long braid of hair hanging at the back of the head

pike[1] (pīk) ***n.*** [Colloq.] a highway: now chiefly in **come down the pike,** to happen or appear

pike[2] (pīk) ***n.*** ⟦Fr *pique*⟧ a former weapon consisting of a metal spearhead on a long wooden shaft (**pikestaff**)

pike[3] (pīk) ***n.***, *pl.* **pike** or **pikes** ⟦ME *pik*⟧ a slender, freshwater bony fish with a long, narrow head

pik·er (pīk'ər) ***n.*** ⟦< ? *Pike* County, Missouri⟧ [Slang] a person who does things in a petty or niggardly way

pi·laf or **pi·laff** (pi läf', pē'läf') ***n.*** ⟦Pers *pilāv*⟧ rice boiled in a seasoned liquid, and usually containing meat or fish

pi·las·ter (pi las'tər) ***n.*** ⟦< L *pila*, a pile⟧ a supporting column projecting partially from a wall

Pi·late (pī'lət), **Pon·tius** (pun'chəs) 1st c. A.D.; Rom. procurator of Judea (*c.* 26-*c.* 36) who condemned Jesus to be crucified

pil·chard (pil'chərd) ***n.*** ⟦< ?⟧ **1** a small, oily, marine fish, the commercial sardine of W Europe **2** any of several related fishes; esp., the **Pacific sardine** found off the W coast of the U.S.

pile[1] (pīl) ***n.*** ⟦< L *pila*, pillar⟧ **1** a mass of things heaped together **2** a heap of wood, etc. on which a corpse or sacrifice is burned **3** a large building **4** [Colloq.] a large amount —***vt.*** **piled, pil'ing 1** to heap up **2** to load **3** to accumulate Often with *up*

—*vi.* 1 to form a pile 2 to move confusedly in a mass: with *in, out, on, off*, etc.

pile[2] (pīl) *n.* ⟦ < L *pilus,* hair ⟧ a soft, velvety, raised surface of yarn loops, often sheared, as on a rug

pile[3] (pīl) *n.* ⟦OE *pil* ⟧ a long, heavy beam driven into the ground to support a bridge, dock, etc.

pile driver (or **engine**) a machine for driving piles by raising them and dropping a heavy weight on them

piles (pīlz) *n.pl.* ⟦ < L *pila,* a ball ⟧ hemorrhoids

pile′up′ *n.* 1 an accumulation of tasks, etc. 2 [Colloq.] a collision involving several vehicles

pil·fer (pil′fər) *vt., vi.* ⟦ < MFr *pelfre,* booty ⟧ to steal (esp. small sums, etc.) —**pil′fer·age** (-ij) *n.* —**pil′fer·er** *n.*

pil·grim (pil′grəm, -grim) *n.* ⟦ < L *peregrinus,* foreigner ⟧ 1 a wanderer 2 one who travels to a shrine or holy place as a religious act 3 [P-] any of the band of English Puritans who founded Plymouth Colony in 1620

pil′grim·age (-ij) *n.* 1 a journey made by a pilgrim, esp. to a shrine or holy place 2 any long journey

pill (pil) *n.* ⟦ < L *pila,* a ball ⟧ a small ball, tablet, etc. of medicine to be swallowed whole —**the pill** (or **Pill**) [Colloq.] any contraceptive drug for women, in the form of a pill

pil·lage (pil′ij) *n.* ⟦ < MFr *piller,* to rob ⟧ 1 a plundering 2 loot —*vt., vi.* **-laged, -lag·ing** to plunder

pil·lar (pil′ər) *n.* ⟦ < L *pila,* column ⟧ 1 a slender, vertical structure used as a support or monument; column 2 a main support of something

pill′box′ *n.* 1 a small box for holding pills 2 an enclosed gun emplacement of concrete and steel

pil·lion (pil′yən) *n.* ⟦ < L *pellis,* a skin ⟧ an extra seat behind the saddle on a horse or motorcycle

pil·lo·ry (pil′ə rē) *n., pl.* **-ries** ⟦ < OFr *pilori* ⟧ a device with holes for the head and hands, in which petty offenders were formerly locked and exposed to public scorn —*vt.* **-ried, -ry·ing** 1 to punish by placing in a pillory 2 to lay open to public scorn

pil·low (pil′ō) *n.* ⟦OE *pyle* ⟧ a cloth case filled with feathers, down, etc., used as a support, as for the head in sleeping —*vt.* to rest as on a pillow

pil′low·case′ *n.* a removable covering for a pillow Also **pil′low·slip′**

pi·lot (pī′lət) *n.* ⟦ < Gr *pēdon,* oar ⟧ 1 *a)* orig., HELMSMAN *b)* a person licensed to direct ships into or out of a harbor or through difficult waters 2 a qualified operator of aircraft 3 a guide; leader —*vt.* 1 to act as a pilot of, on, etc. 2 to guide —*adj.* serving as a trial unit in testing

pilot film (or **tape**) a film (or videotape) of a single segment of a projected television series

pi′lot·house′ *n.* an enclosure for the helmsman on the upper deck of a ship

pilot light a small gas burner which is kept burning for use in lighting a main burner when needed

pi·men·to (pə men′tō) *n., pl.* **-tos** ⟦ < Sp < L *pigmentum,* pigment ⟧ a variety of sweet red pepper Also **pi·mien′to** (-myen′-, -men′-)

pimp (pimp) *n.* ⟦ < ? ⟧ a prostitute's agent —*vi.* to act as a pimp

pim·ple (pim′pəl) *n.* ⟦ < OE *piplian,* to break out in pimples ⟧ a small, often inflamed swelling of the skin —**pim′ply, -pli·er, -pli·est,** *adj.*

pin (pin) *n.* ⟦OE *pinn* ⟧ 1 a peg, as of wood, or a pointed piece of stiff wire, for fastening things together, etc. 2 anything like a pin 3 an ornament or badge with a pin or clasp for fastening to clothing 4 *Bowling* one of the clubs at which the ball is rolled —*vt.* **pinned, pin′ning** 1 to fasten as with a pin 2 to hold firmly in one position —**pin down** 1 to get (someone) to commit himself as to his plans, etc. 2 to establish (a fact, etc.) —**pin (something) on someone** [Colloq.] to lay the blame for (something) on someone

pin·a·fore (pin′ə fôr′) *n.* ⟦prec. + archaic *afore,* before ⟧ a sleeveless garment worn over a dress

pi·ña·ta (pē nyä′tä) *n.* ⟦Sp, ult. < L *pinus,* pine tree ⟧ in Mexico, a papier-mâché container hung from the ceiling in a game in which blindfolded children take turns trying to break it open and release the toys, candy, etc. inside

pin′ball′ machine a game machine with an inclined board having pins, holes, etc. for scoring automatically the contacts of a spring-driven ball

pince-nez (pans′nā′; pins′nā′) *n.* ⟦Fr, nose-pincher ⟧ *pl.* **pince′-nez′** (-nāz′; -nā′) eyeglasses kept in place by a spring gripping the bridge of the nose

pin·cers (pin′sərz) *n.pl.* ⟦ < OFr *pincier,* to pinch ⟧ 1 a tool formed of two pivoted parts, used in gripping things 2 a grasping claw, as of a crab

PINCERS

pinch (pinch) *vt.* ⟦ME *pinchen* ⟧ 1 to squeeze between two surfaces, edges, etc. 2 to press painfully upon (a toe, etc.) 3 to make thin, cramped, etc., as by hunger 4 [Slang] *a)* to steal *b)* to arrest —*vi.* 1 to squeeze painfully 2 to be stingy or frugal —*n.* 1 a squeeze or nip 2 an amount grasped between finger and thumb 3 distress or difficulty 4 an emergency

pinch′-hit′ *vi.* **-hit′, -hit′ting** 1 *Baseball* to bat in place of the batter whose turn it is 2 to substitute in an emergency (*for*) —**pinch hitter**

pin curl a strand of hair kept curled with a bobby pin while it sets

pin′cush′ion *n.* a small cushion to stick pins in to keep them handy

pine[1] (pīn) *n.* ⟦ < L *pinus* ⟧ 1 an evergreen tree with cones and needle-shaped leaves 2 its wood

pine[2] (pīn) *vi.* **pined, pin′ing** ⟦ < L *poena,* a pain ⟧ 1 to waste (*away*) through grief, etc. 2 to yearn

pin·e·al body (pin′ē əl) ⟦ < L *pinea,* pine

cone ⟧ a small, cone-shaped body in the brain that produces a hormone

pine·ap·ple (pīn′ap′əl) *n.* ⟦ME *pinappel,* pine cone ⟧ 1 a juicy, edible tropical fruit somewhat resembling a pine cone 2 the plant it grows on

pine tar a thick, dark liquid obtained from pine wood, used in disinfectants, paints, etc.

pin′feath′er *n.* an undeveloped, emerging feather

ping (piŋ) *n.* ⟦echoic⟧ the sound made as of a bullet striking something sharply **—*vi.*, *vt.*** to strike with a ping

Ping-Pong (piŋ′pông′) ⟦echoic⟧ *trademark for* table tennis equipment **—*n.*** [p- p-] TABLE TENNIS

pin′head′ *n.* 1 the head of a pin 2 a stupid or silly person

pin′hole′ *n.* 1 a tiny hole as from a pin 2 a hole to stick a pin into

pin·ion (pin′yən) *n.* ⟦< L *pinna,* feather⟧ 1 a small cogwheel which meshes with a larger one 2 the wing of a bird **—*vt.*** 1 to bind the wings or arms of 2 to shackle

pink[1] (piŋk) *n.* ⟦< ?⟧ 1 any of certain plants with white, pink, or red flowers, often clove-scented 2 the flower 3 pale red 4 the highest degree, finest example, etc. **—*adj.*** 1 pale-red 2 [Colloq.] somewhat leftist: a derogatory term **—in the pink** [Colloq.] healthy; fit

pink[2] (piŋk) *vt.* ⟦ME *pynken*⟧ 1 to cut a saw-toothed edge on (cloth, etc.) 2 to prick or stab

pink′eye′ *n.* a contagious eye infection in which the eyeball and the lining of the eyelid are red and inflamed

pink·ie or **pink·y** (piŋk′ē) *n., pl.* **-ies** the smallest finger

pink·ing shears (piŋk′iŋ) shears with notched blades, for pinking edges of cloth

pin money a small sum of money, as for incidental minor expenses

pin·na·cle (pin′ə kəl) *n.* ⟦< L *pinna,* feather⟧ 1 a small turret or spire 2 a slender, pointed formation, as a mountain peak 3 the highest point

pin·nate (pin′āt′, -it) *adj.* ⟦< L *pinna,* feather⟧ *Bot.* with leaflets on each side of a common stem

pi·noch·le or **pi·noc·le** (pē′nuk′əl) *n.* ⟦< Fr *binocle,* pince-nez⟧ a card game played with a 48-card deck (two of every card above the eight)

pi·not noir (pē nō′ nwär) [*also* **P- N-**] 1 the main red-wine grape of the Burgundy region 2 a dry red wine made from this grape

pin′point′ *vt.* to locate precisely

pin′prick′ *n.* 1 a tiny puncture as by a pin 2 a minor annoyance

pins and needles a tingling feeling as in a numb limb **—on pins and needles** in anxious suspense

pin′set′ter *n.* a person or automatic device that sets up bowling pins on the alley Also **pin′spot′ter**

pin stripe a pattern of very narrow stripes in suit fabrics, etc.

pint (pīnt) *n.* ⟦< ML⟧ a measure of capacity equal to $\frac{1}{2}$ quart

pin·to (pin′tō) *adj.* ⟦< obs. Sp, spotted⟧ having patches of white and some other color **—*n., pl.*** **-tos** a pinto horse

pinto bean a kind of mottled kidney bean grown in the SW U.S.

pin′up′ *adj.* 1 that is or can be fastened to a wall 2 [Colloq.] designating an attractive person whose picture is often pinned up on walls

pin′wheel′ *n.* 1 a small wheel with vanes of paper, etc., pinned to a stick so as to revolve in the wind 2 a revolving firework

Pin·yin (pin yin′) *n.* ⟦Chin *pinyin,* lit., phonetic sound⟧ [*also* **p-**] system for transliterating Chinese ideograms into the Latin alphabet

pi·o·neer (pī′ə nir′) *n.* ⟦< OFr *peonier,* foot soldier⟧ one who goes before, preparing the way for others, as an early settler **—*vi.*** to be a pioneer **—*vt.*** to be a pioneer in or of

pi·os·i·ty (pī äs′ə tē) *n.* the quality of being excessively or insincerely pious

pi·ous (pī′əs) *adj.* ⟦< L *pius*⟧ 1 having or showing religious devotion 2 seemingly virtuous 3 sacred **—pi′ous·ly *adv.***

pip[1] (pip) *n.* ⟦< PIPPIN⟧ a small seed, as of an apple

pip[2] (pip) *n.* ⟦< ?⟧ any of the figures or spots on playing cards, dice, etc.

pip[3] (pip) *n.* ⟦< L *pituita,* phlegm⟧ a contagious disease of fowl

pipe (pīp) *n.* ⟦< L *pipare,* chirp⟧ 1 a tube of wood, metal, etc. for making musical sounds 2 [*pl.*] the bagpipe 3 a long tube for conveying water, gas, etc. 4 a tube with a small bowl at one end in which tobacco is smoked 5 any tubular part, organ, etc. **—*vi.* piped, pip′ing** 1 to play on a pipe 2 to utter shrill sounds **—*vt.*** 1 to play (a tune) on a pipe 2 to utter in a shrill voice 3 to bring, call, etc. by piping 4 to convey (water, gas, etc.) by pipes **—pipe down** [Slang] to shout or talk less **—pip′er *n.***

pipe dream [Colloq.] a fantastic idea, vain hope or plan, etc.

pipe fitter a mechanic who installs and maintains plumbing pipes, etc.

pipe′line′ *n.* 1 a line of pipes for conveying water, gas, etc. 2 any means whereby something is passed on

pipe organ ORGAN (sense 1)

pip·ing (pīp′iŋ) *n.* 1 music made by pipes 2 a shrill sound 3 a pipelike fold of material for trimming seams, etc. **—piping hot** so hot as to sizzle

pip·it (pip′it) *n.* ⟦echoic⟧ a small bird with a slender bill, streaked breast, and the habit of walking rather than hopping

pip·pin (pip′in) *n.* ⟦< OFr *pepin,* seed⟧ any of several varieties of apple

pip·squeak (pip′skwēk′) *n.* [Colloq.] anyone or anything regarded as small or insignificant

pi·quant (pē′kənt) *adj.* ⟦Fr < *piquer,* to prick⟧ 1 agreeably pungent to the taste 2 exciting interest; stimulating **—pi′quan·cy** (-kən sē) *n.*

pique (pēk) *n.* ⟦see prec.⟧ resentment at being slighted **—*vt.* piqued, piqu′ing** 1 to arouse such resentment in 2 to arouse; provoke

pi·qué or **pi·que** (pē kā′) *n.* ⟦see PIQUANT⟧ a cotton fabric with ribbed or corded wales

pi·ra·cy (pī′rə sē) *n., pl.* **-cies** 1 robbery of

ships on the high seas 2 the unauthorized use of copyrighted or patented work

pi·ra·nha (pə rän′yə, pi-; -rän′ə, -ran′ə) ***n.*** ⟦< Brazilian Port < Amind (Brazil) *pirá,* fish + *sainha,* tooth⟧ any of various small, voracious, freshwater South American fishes: they hunt in schools, attacking any animals

pi·rate (pī′rət) ***n.*** ⟦< Gr *peirān,* to attack⟧ one who practices piracy —***vt., vi.*** **-rat·ed, -rat·ing** 1 to take (something) by piracy 2 to publish, reproduce, etc. (a book, recording, etc.) in violation of a copyright —**pi·rat′i·cal** (-rat′ i kəl) ***adj.***

pi·ro·gi (pi rō′gē) ***n.pl.*** ⟦Russ⟧ small pastry turnovers filled with meat, cheese, etc. Also **pi·rosh′ki** (-räsh′kē)

pir·ou·ette (pir′o͞o et′) ***n.*** ⟦Fr, spinning top⟧ a whirling on one foot or the point of the toe —***vi.*** **-et′ted, -et′ting** to do a pirouette

pis·ca·to·ri·al (pis′kə tôr′ē əl) ***adj.*** ⟦< L *piscator,* fisherman⟧ of fishes, fishermen, or fishing

Pis·ces (pī′sēz′; *also* pis′ēz′) ⟦ME < L, pl. of *piscis,* FISH⟧ the 12th sign of the zodiac

pis·mire (pis′mīr′, piz′-) ***n.*** ⟦< ME *pisse,* urine + *mire,* ant⟧ [Archaic] an ant

pis·tach·i·o (pis tash′ō′, -ē ō′; -täsh′ō, -ē ō′) ***n.,*** *pl.* **-os′** ⟦< OPers *pistah*⟧ 1 a small tree of the cashew family 2 its edible, greenish seed (**pistachio nut**)

pis·til (pis′til, -təl) ***n.*** ⟦< L *pistillum,* pestle⟧ the seed-bearing organ of a flower —**pis′til·late′** ***adj.***

pis·tol (pis′təl) ***n.*** ⟦< Czech *pišt′al*⟧ a small firearm operated with one hand

pis′tol-whip′ ***vt.*** **-whipped′, -whip′ping** to beat with a pistol, esp. about the head

pis·ton (pis′tən) ***n.*** ⟦ult. < L *pinsere,* to pound⟧ the snug-fitting engine part that is forced back and forth within a cylinder by the pressure of combustion, steam, etc. and a reciprocating connecting rod (**piston rod**)

piston ring a split ring fitted into a groove around a piston to seal the cylinder, transfer heat, etc.

pit[1] (pit) ***n.*** ⟦< MDu *pitte*⟧ the hard stone, as of the plum, peach, etc. containing the seed —***vt.*** **pit′ted, pit′ting** to remove the pit from

pit[2] (pit) ***n.*** ⟦< L *puteus,* a well⟧ 1 a hole in the ground 2 an abyss 3 hell: used with *the* 4 a pitfall 5 any concealed danger 6 an enclosed area in which animals are kept or made to fight 7 a small hollow in a surface, as a scar left by smallpox 8 the section for the orchestra in front of the stage —***vt.*** **pit′ted, pit′ting** 1 to make pits or scars in 2 to set in competition (*against*) —***vi.*** to become marked with pits

pi·ta (pē′tə, -tä) ***n.*** ⟦< Heb < Modern Greek⟧ a round, flat bread of the Middle East Also **pita bread**

pit·a·pat (pit′ə pat′) ***adv.*** with rapid beating —***n.*** a rapid series of beats

pitch[1] (pich) ***n.*** ⟦< L *pix*⟧ a black, sticky substance formed from coal tar, etc. and used for roofing, etc.

pitch[2] (pich) ***vt.*** ⟦ME *picchen*⟧ 1 to set up [*pitch* a tent] 2 to throw or toss 3 to fix at a certain point, degree, key, etc. 4 *Baseball* *a)* to throw (the ball) to the batter *b)* to assign (a pitcher) *c)* to act as pitcher for (a game) —***vi.*** 1 to pitch a ball, etc. 2 to plunge forward or dip downward 3 to rise and fall, as a ship in rough water —***n.*** 1 act or manner of pitching 2 a throw or toss 3 anything pitched 4 a point or degree 5 the degree of slope 6 [Slang] a line of talk for persuading 7 *Music, etc.* the highness or lowness of a sound due to vibrations of sound waves —**pitch in** [Colloq.] 1 to begin working hard 2 to make a contribution —**pitch into** [Colloq.] to attack

pitch′-black′ ***adj.*** very black

pitch′blende′ (-blend′) ***n.*** ⟦< Ger *pech,* PITCH[1] + *blenden,* to blind⟧ a dark mineral, a major source of uranium

pitch′-dark′ ***adj.*** very dark

pitched battle (picht) 1 a battle in which troop placement is relatively fixed beforehand 2 a hard-fought battle

pitch·er[1] (pich′ər) ***n.*** ⟦< OFr *pichier*⟧ a container, usually with a handle and lip, for holding and pouring liquids —**pitch′er·ful** ***n.***

pitch·er[2] (pich′ər) ***n.*** ⟦PITCH[2] + -ER⟧ one who pitches; specif., the baseball player who pitches the ball to the batters

pitcher plant a plant with pitcherlike leaves that trap and digest insects

pitch′fork′ ***n.*** a large, long-handled fork for lifting and tossing hay, etc.

pitch′man (-mən) ***n.,*** *pl.* **-men** 1 a hawker of novelties, as at a carnival 2 [Colloq.] any high-pressure salesman

pitch pipe a small pipe which produces a fixed tone used as a standard in tuning instruments, etc.

pit·e·ous (pit′ē əs) ***adj.*** arousing or deserving pity —**pit′e·ous·ly** ***adv.***

pit′fall′ (-fôl′) ***n.*** ⟦< PIT[2] + OE *fealle,* a trap⟧ 1 a lightly covered pit for trapping animals 2 an unsuspected danger, etc.

pith (pith) ***n.*** ⟦OE *pitha*⟧ 1 the soft, spongy tissue in the center of certain plant stems 2 the essential part; gist

pith′y (-ē) ***adj.*** **-i·er, -i·est** 1 of, like, or full of pith 2 terse and full of meaning —**pith′i·ly** ***adv.***

pit·i·ful (pit′i fəl) ***adj.*** 1 arousing or deserving pity 2 contemptible Also **pit′i·a·ble** (-ē ə bəl) —**pit′i·ful·ly** ***adv.***

pit′i·less (-lis) ***adj.*** without pity

pi·ton (pē′tän′) ***n.*** ⟦Fr < MFr, a spike⟧ a metal spike with an eye for a rope, driven into rock or ice for support in mountain climbing

pit·tance (pit′′ns) ***n.*** ⟦< OFr *pitance,* food allowed a monk⟧ 1 a meager allowance of money 2 any small amount or share

pit·ter-pat·ter (pit′ər pat′ər) ***n.*** ⟦echoic⟧ a rapid succession of light tapping sounds

Pitts·burgh (pits′burg′) city in SW Pa.: pop. 424,000

pi·tu·i·tar·y (pi to͞o′ə ter′ē) ***adj.*** ⟦< L *pituita,* phlegm⟧ of a small, oval endocrine gland (**pituitary gland**) attached to the brain: it secretes hormones affecting growth, etc.

pit viper any of several poisonous vipers with a heat-sensitive pit on each side of the head, as the rattlesnake

pit·y (pit′ē) ***n.,*** *pl.* **-ies** ⟦< L *pietas,* piety⟧ 1 sorrow for another's suffering or misfortune

2 a cause for sorrow —*vt., vi.* -ied, -y·ing to feel pity (for)

piv·ot (piv'ət) *n.* ⟦Fr⟧ 1 a point, shaft, etc. on which something turns 2 a person or thing on which something depends, etc. 3 a pivoting movement —*vt.* to provide with a pivot —*vi.* to turn as on a pivot —**piv'ot·al** *adj.*

pix·el (piks'əl, -el') *n.* ⟦< *pic(ture)s* + *el(ement)*⟧ any of the dots that make up an image, as on a TV screen

pix·ie or **pix·y** (piks'ē) *n., pl.* -ies ⟦< Brit dial.⟧ a fairy, elf, or sprite

pi·zazz or **piz·zazz** (pi zaz') *n.* [Colloq.] 1 vigor 2 style, flair, etc.

piz·za (pēt'sə) *n.* ⟦It⟧ an Italian dish made by baking thin dough covered with tomatoes, cheese, etc.

piz·ze·ri·a (pēt'sə rē'ə) *n.* ⟦It⟧ a place where pizzas are made and sold

piz·zi·ca·to (pit'si kät'ō) *adj.* ⟦It⟧ *Musical Direction* plucked: a note to pluck the strings with the finger instead of bowing

pj's (pē'jāz') *n.pl. colloq. var. of* PAJAMAS

pk. 1 park 2 peck

pkg. package(s)

Pkwy. or **Pky.** Parkway

pl. 1 place: also **Pl.** 2 plural

plac·ard (plak'ärd; -ərd; *for v., also* plə kärd', pla-) *n.* ⟦< MDu *placke*, a piece⟧ a notice for display in a public place —*vt.* to place placards on or in

pla·cate (plā'kāt', plak'āt') *vt.* -cat'ed, -cat'ing ⟦< L *placare*⟧ to appease; pacify —**pla·ca'tion** *n.*

place (plās) *n.* ⟦< Gr *plateia*, a street⟧ 1 a court or short street in a city 2 space; room 3 a region 4 *a*) the part of space occupied by a person or thing *b*) situation 5 a city, town, etc. 6 a residence 7 a building or space devoted to a special purpose [a *place* of amusement] 8 a particular point, part, position, etc. [a sore *place* on the leg, a *place* in history] 9 a step or point in a sequence 10 the customary or proper position, time, etc. 11 a space, seat, etc. reserved or occupied by a person 12 an office; employment 13 the duties of any position 14 the second position at the finish of a race —*vt.* **placed, plac'ing** 1 *a*) to put in a particular place, condition, or relation *b*) to recognize or identify 2 to find employment for 3 to repose (trust) *in* a person or thing 4 to finish in (a specified position) in a race —*vi.* to finish second or among the first three in a race —**take place** to occur

pla·ce·bo (plə sē'bō) *n., pl.* -bos or -boes ⟦< L, I shall please⟧ a harmless, unmedicated preparation given as a medicine, as to humor a patient

place mat a small mat serving as an individual table cover for a person at a meal

place'ment *n.* 1 a placing or being placed 2 location or arrangement

pla·cen·ta (plə sen'tə) *n., pl.* -tas or -tae (-tē) ⟦ult. < Gr *plax*, a flat object⟧ the structure in the uterus through which the fetus is nourished: cf. AFTERBIRTH —**pla·cen'tal** *adj.*

plac·er (plas'ər) *n.* ⟦< Sp *placel*⟧ a deposit of gravel or sand containing particles of gold, platinum, etc., that can be washed out

plac·id (plas'id) *adj.* ⟦L *placidus*⟧ calm; quiet —**pla·cid·i·ty** (plə sid'ə tē) *n.* —**plac'id·ly** *adv.*

plack·et (plak'it) *n.* ⟦< ?⟧ a slit at the waist of a skirt or collar of a shirt, to make it easy to put on and take off

pla·gi·a·rize (plā'jə rīz') *vt., vi.* -rized', -riz'ing ⟦< L *plagiarius*, kidnapper⟧ to take (ideas, writings, etc.) from (another) and pass them off as one's own —**pla'gi·a·rism** (-riz'əm) *n.* —**pla'gi·a·ry** (-rē) *n.* —**pla'gi·a·rist** *n.*

plague (plāg) *n.* ⟦< Gr *plēgē*, a misfortune⟧ 1 any affliction or calamity 2 any deadly epidemic disease —*vt.* **plagued, plagu'ing** 1 to afflict with a plague 2 to vex; torment

plaid (plad) *n.* ⟦Gael *plaide*, a blanket⟧ 1 cloth with a crossbarred pattern 2 any pattern of this kind

plain (plān) *adj.* ⟦< L *planus*, flat⟧ 1 open; clear [in *plain* view] 2 clearly understood; obvious 3 outspoken; straightforward 4 not luxurious or ornate 5 not complicated; simple 6 homely 7 pure; unmixed 8 common; ordinary [a *plain* man] —*n.* an extent of level country —*adv.* clearly —**plain'ly** *adv.* —**plain'ness** *n.*

plain'clothes' man a detective or police officer who wears civilian clothes while on duty Also **plain'clothes'man**, *pl.* -men

plains·man (plānz'mən) *n., pl.* -men an American frontiersman on the western Plains

plain'song' *n.* a very old, plain kind of church music chanted in unison

plaint (plānt) *n.* ⟦< L *plangere*, to lament⟧ a complaint or lament

plain·tiff (plān'tif) *n.* ⟦see prec.⟧ one who brings a suit into a court of law

plain'tive (-tiv) *adj.* ⟦see PLAINT⟧ expressing sorrow or melancholy; mournful; sad —**plain'tive·ly** *adv.*

plait (plāt) *n.* ⟦< L *plicare*, to fold⟧ 1 PLEAT 2 a braid of hair, etc. —*vt.* 1 PLEAT 2 to braid

plan (plan) *n.* ⟦Fr, plan, foundation⟧ 1 a diagram showing the arrangement of a structure, piece of ground, etc. 2 a scheme for making, doing, or arranging something 3 any outline or sketch —*vt.* **planned, plan'ning** 1 to make a plan of (a structure, etc.) 2 to devise a scheme for doing, etc. 3 to have in mind as a project or purpose —*vi.* to make plans —**plan'ner** *n.*

plane[1] (plān) *adj.* ⟦L *planus*⟧ 1 flat; level 2 of or having to do with flat surfaces or points, lines, etc. on them [*plane* geometry] —*n.* 1 a flat, level surface 2 a level of achievement, etc. 3 *short for* AIRPLANE 4 a wing of an airplane

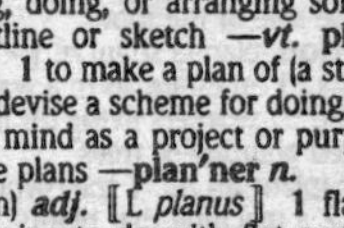

CARPENTER'S PLANE

plane[2] (plān) *n.* ⟦< L *planus*, level⟧ a carpenter's tool for leveling or smoothing wood —*vt.* **planed, plan'ing** to smooth or level with a plane

plan·et (plan'it) *n.* ⟦< Gr *planan,* wander⟧ any celestial body that revolves about a star; esp., one of the sun's nine major planets: Mercury, Venus, Earth, Mars, Jupiter, Saturn, Uranus, Neptune, and Pluto —**plan'e·tar'y** (-i ter'ē) *adj.*

plan·e·tar·i·um (plan'i ter'ē əm) *n., pl.* **-i·ums** or **-i·a** (-ə) **1** the revolving projector used to simulate the past, present, or future motions or positions of the sun, planets, etc. on the inside of a large dome **2** the room in which this is contained

plane tree any of various trees with ball-shaped fruits and bark that sheds in large patches, as the sycamore

plan·gent (plan'jənt) *adj.* ⟦< L *plangere,* to beat⟧ loud or resonant, and, often, mournful-sounding

plank (plaŋk) *n.* ⟦< LL *planca*⟧ **1** a long, broad, thick board **2** an item in the platform of a political party —*vt.* **1** to cover with planks **2** to broil and serve (steak, fish, etc.) on a board **3** [Colloq.] to set (*down*) with force

plank'ing *n.* **1** planks in quantity **2** the planks of a structure

plank·ton (plaŋk'tən) *n.* ⟦< Gr *plazesthai,* wander⟧ the microscopic animal and plant life found floating in bodies of water

plant (plant, plänt) *n.* ⟦< L *planta,* a sprout⟧ **1** a living thing that cannot move voluntarily, has no sense organs, and synthesizes food from carbon dioxide **2** an herb, as distinguished from a tree or shrub **3** the machinery, buildings, etc. of a factory, etc. —*vt.* **1** to put into the ground to grow **2** to set firmly in position **3** to settle; establish **4** [Slang] to place (a person or thing) in such a way as to trick, trap, etc.

plan·tain[1] (plan'tin) *n.* ⟦< L *plantago*⟧ a plant with basal leaves and spikes of tiny, greenish flowers

plan·tain[2] (plan'tin) *n.* ⟦< Sp *plátano,* banana tree⟧ a tropical banana plant yielding a coarse fruit

plan·tar (plan'tər) *adj.* ⟦< L *planta,* sole⟧ of or on the sole of the foot

plan·ta·tion (plan tā'shən) *n.* ⟦< L *plantare,* to plant⟧ **1** an estate, as in a warm climate, cultivated by workers living on it **2** a large, cultivated planting of trees

plant·er (plant'ər) *n.* **1** the owner of a plantation **2** a machine that plants **3** a decorative container for plants

plant louse APHID

plaque (plak) *n.* ⟦Fr < MDu *placke,* disk⟧ **1** a thin, flat piece of metal, wood, etc. with decoration or lettering on it, hung on a wall, etc. **2** a thin film of matter on uncleaned teeth

plash (plash) *vt., vi., n.* ⟦echoic⟧ SPLASH

plas·ma (plaz'mə) *n.* ⟦Ger < Gr, something molded⟧ **1** the fluid part of blood, lymph, or milk **2** a high-temperature, ionized gas that is electrically neutral

plasma membrane a very thin living membrane surrounding a plant or animal cell

plas·ter (plas'tər, pläs'-) *n.* ⟦< Gr *emplassein,* to daub over⟧ **1** a pasty mixture, as of lime, sand, and water, hard when dry, for coating walls, etc. **2** PLASTER OF PARIS **3** a pasty preparation spread on cloth and applied to the body, as a medicine —*vt.* **1** to cover as with plaster **2** to apply like a plaster /*to plaster* posters on walls/ **3** to make lie smooth and flat —**plas'ter·er** *n.*

plas'ter·board' *n.* thin board formed of layers of plaster and paper, used in wide sheets for walls, etc.

plaster of Paris ⟦from use of gypsum from *Paris,* France⟧ a thick paste of gypsum and water that sets quickly: used for casts, statuary, etc.

plas·tic (plas'tik) *adj.* ⟦< Gr *plassein,* to form⟧ **1** molding or shaping matter; formative **2** that can be molded or shaped **3** made of plastic —*n.* **1** any of various nonmetallic compounds, synthetically produced, which can be molded and hardened for commercial use **2** [Colloq.] a credit card or credit cards, or credit based on their use —**plas·tic'i·ty** (-tis'ə tē) *n.*

plas'ti·cize' (-ti sīz') *vt., vi.* **-cized', -ciz'ing** to make or become plastic

plastic surgery surgery dealing with the repair of deformed or destroyed parts of the body, as by transferring skin, bone, etc. from other parts

plat (plat) *n.* ⟦var. of PLOT⟧ **1** a small piece of ground **2** a map or plan, as of a subdivision —*vt.* **plat'ted, plat'ting** to make a map or plan of

plate (plāt) *n.* ⟦< Gr *platys,* broad⟧ **1** a smooth, flat, thin piece of metal, etc., specif. one on which an engraving is cut **2** an impression taken from an engraved surface **3** dishes, utensils, etc. of, or plated with, silver or gold **4** a shallow dish **5** the food in a dish; a course **6** a denture, specif. that part of it which fits to the mouth **7** *Baseball short for* HOME PLATE **8** *Photog.* a sheet of glass, metal, etc. coated with a film sensitive to light **9** *Printing* a cast made from a mold of set type —*vt.* **plat'ed, plat'ing 1** to coat with gold, silver, etc. **2** to cover with metal plates

pla·teau (pla tō') *n.* ⟦Fr: see prec.⟧ **1** an elevated tract of level land **2** a temporary halt in progress

plate glass polished, clear glass in thick sheets, for windows, mirrors, etc.

plat·en (plat''n) *n.* ⟦< OFr *plat,* flat⟧ **1** in a printing press, a flat metal plate which presses the paper against the type **2** in a typewriter, the roller against which the keys strike

plate tec·ton·ics (tek tän'iks) *Geol.* the theory that the earth's surface consists of plates whose constant motion explains continental drift, etc.

plat·form (plat'fôrm') *n.* ⟦Fr *plate-forme,* lit., flat form⟧ **1** a raised horizontal surface, as a stage for speakers, etc. **2** a statement of policy, esp. of a political party

plat·i·num (plat''n əm) *n.* ⟦< Sp *plata,* silver⟧ a silvery, metallic chemical element, resistant to corrosion: used for jewelry, etc.

plat·i·tude (plat'ə to͞od') *n.* ⟦Fr < *plat,* flat, after *latitude,* etc.⟧ a commonplace or trite remark

Pla·to (plā'tō) *c.* 427-*c.* 347 B.C.; Gr. philosopher

Pla·ton·ic (plə tän'ik) *adj.* **1** of Plato or his

philosophy **2** [*usually* **p-**] not sexual but purely spiritual: said of a relationship, etc.

pla·toon (plə to͞on′) ***n.*** ⟦Fr *peloton*, a group⟧ **1** a military unit composed of two or more squads **2** *Sports* any of the specialized squads making up a team —***vt.*** *Sports* to alternate (players) at a position

plat·ter (plat′ər) ***n.*** ⟦< OFr *plat*, flat⟧ a large, shallow dish, usually oval, for serving food

plat·y (plat′ē) ***n.***, *pl.* **plat′ies** ⟦clipped < ModL *Platypoecilus*, a genus of fishes⟧ a brightly colored, freshwater fish of Central America: used in aquariums

plat·y·pus (plat′i pəs) ***n.***, *pl.* **-pus·es** or **-pi′** (-pī′) ⟦< Gr *platys*, flat + *pous*, foot⟧ a small, egg-laying water mammal of Australia, with webbed feet and a ducklike bill; duckbill

plau·dit (plô′dit) ***n.*** ⟦< L *plaudere*, applaud⟧ [*usually pl.*] applause

plau·si·ble (plô′zə bəl) ***adj.*** ⟦< L *plaudere*, applaud⟧ seemingly true, trustworthy, honest, etc. —**plau′si·bil′i·ty** ***n.***

play (plā) ***vi.*** ⟦OE *plegan*⟧ **1** to move lightly, rapidly, etc. [sunlight *plays* on the water] **2** to engage in recreation **3** to take part in a game or sport **4** to trifle (*with* a thing or person) **5** to perform on a musical instrument **6** to give out sounds **7** to act in a specified way [to *play* dumb] **8** to act in a drama **9** to impose unscrupulously (*on* another's feelings) —***vt.*** **1** to take part in (a game or sport) **2** to oppose (a person, etc.) in a game **3** to do, as in fun [to *play* tricks] **4** to bet on **5** to cause to move, etc.; wield **6** to cause [to *play* havoc] **7** to perform (music, a drama, etc.) **8** to perform on (an instrument) **9** to act the part of [to *play* Hamlet] —***n.*** **1** motion or activity, esp. when free or rapid **2** freedom for motion or action **3** recreation; sport **4** fun; joking **5** the playing of a game **6** a move or act in a game **7** a dramatic composition or performance; drama —**play down** to attach little importance to —**played out** exhausted —**play up** to give prominence to —**play up to** [Colloq.] to try to please by flattery

play′act′ ***vi.*** **1** to pretend: make believe **2** to behave in an affected or dramatic manner —**play′act′ing** ***n.***

play′back′ ***n.*** **1** reproduction of sounds, images, etc. from a recorded disc, tape, etc. **2** the control or device for such reproduction on a player, recorder, etc.

play′bill′ ***n.*** a program of a play, listing the cast, etc.

play′boy′ ***n.*** a man of means who is given to pleasure-seeking

play·er (plā′ər) ***n.*** **1** one who plays a specified game, instrument, etc. **2** an actor

play′ful ***adj.*** **1** fond of play or fun **2** jocular —**play′ful·ly** ***adv.*** —**play′ful·ness** ***n.***

play′go′er ***n.*** one who goes to the theater frequently or regularly

play′ground′ ***n.*** a place, often near a school, for outdoor recreation

play′house′ ***n.*** **1** a theater for live dramatic productions **2** a small house for children to play in

playing cards cards used in playing various games, arranged in four suits

play′mate′ ***n.*** a companion in games and recreation

play·off (plā′ôf′) ***n.*** a contest to break a tie or to decide a championship

play on words a pun or punning

play′pen′ ***n.*** a portable enclosure for an infant to play or crawl in safely

play′thing′ ***n.*** toy

play′wright′ (-rīt′) ***n.*** one who writes plays; dramatist

pla·za (plä′zə, plaz′ə) ***n.*** ⟦Sp < L *platea*, street⟧ **1** a public square in a city or town **2** a shopping center **3** a service area along a superhighway

plea (plē) ***n.*** ⟦< L *placere*, to please⟧ **1** a statement in defense; excuse **2** a request; appeal **3** *Law* the response of a defendant to criminal charges

plea′-bar′gain ***vi.*** to engage in plea bargaining

plea bargaining pretrial negotiations in which the defendant agrees to plead guilty to a lesser charge if more serious charges are dropped

plead (plēd) ***vi.*** **plead′ed** or [Colloq.] **pled** or **plead** (pled), **plead′ing** ⟦see PLEA⟧ **1** to present a plea in a law court **2** to make an appeal; beg —***vt.*** **1** to argue (a law case) **2** to answer (guilty or not guilty) to a charge **3** to offer as an excuse —**plead′er** ***n.***

pleas·ant (plez′ənt) ***adj.*** ⟦< Fr *plaisir*, to please⟧ **1** agreeable to the mind or senses; pleasing **2** having an agreeable manner, look, etc. —**pleas′ant·ly** ***adv.*** —**pleas′ant·ness** ***n.***

pleas′ant·ry (-ən trē) ***n.***, *pl.* **-ries** **1** a humorous remark **2** a polite social remark [to exchange *pleasantries*]

please (plēz) ***vt.*** **pleased**, **pleas′ing** ⟦< L *placere*⟧ **1** to be agreeable to; satisfy **2** to be the wish of [it *pleased* him to go] —***vi.*** **1** to be agreeable; satisfy **2** to have the wish; like [to do as one *pleases*] *Please* is also in polite requests [*please* sit down]

pleas′ing ***adj.*** giving pleasure; agreeable —**pleas′ing·ly** ***adv.***

pleas·ur·a·ble (plezh′ər ə bəl) ***adj.*** pleasant; enjoyable

pleas·ure (plezh′ər) ***n.*** **1** a pleased feeling; delight **2** one's wish, will, or choice **3** a thing that gives delight or satisfaction —**pleas′ure·ful** ***adj.***

pleat (plēt) ***n.*** ⟦ME *pleten*⟧ a flat double fold in cloth, etc. pressed or stitched in place —***vt.*** to lay and press (cloth) in a pleat or pleats

ple·be·ian (plē bē′ən, pli-) ***n.*** ⟦< L *plebs*, common people⟧ **1** one of the common people **2** a vulgar, coarse person —***adj.*** vulgar or common

pleb·i·scite (pleb′ə sīt′) ***n.*** ⟦< L *plebs*, common people + *scitum*, decree⟧ a direct vote of the people on a political issue, such as independent nationhood, annexation, etc.

plec·trum (plek′trəm) ***n.***, *pl.* **-trums** or **-tra** (-trə) ⟦L < Gr *plēssein*, to strike⟧ a thin piece of metal, etc., for plucking the strings of a guitar, etc.

pled (pled) ***vi.***, ***vt.*** [Colloq.] *pt. & pp. of* PLEAD

pledge (plej) ***n.*** ⟦prob < OS *plegan*, to warrant⟧ **1** the condition of being given or held as security for a contract, payment, etc. **2** a person or thing given or held as such security 3 a promise or agreement 4 something promised —*vt.* **pledged, pledg′ing** 1 to give as security 2 to bind by a promise 3 to promise to give

Pleis·to·cene (plīs′tō sēn′, -tə-) *adj.* ⟦< Gr *pleistos*, most + *kainos*, recent⟧ designating an epoch in the Cenozoic Era, characterized by the appearance of modern humans

ple·na·ry (plē′nə rē, plen′ə-) *adj.* ⟦< L *plenus*, full⟧ 1 full; complete 2 for attendance by all members /a *plenary* session/

plen·i·po·ten·ti·ar·y (plen′i pō ten′shē er′ē, -shə rē; -pə-) *adj.* ⟦< L *plenus*, full + *potens*, powerful⟧ having or conferring full authority —*n., pl.* **-ar′ies** a diplomat given full authority

plen·i·tude (plen′i to͞od′) *n.* ⟦< L *plenus*, full⟧ 1 fullness; completeness 2 abundance; plenty

plen·te·ous (plen′tē əs) *adj.* plentiful

plen·ti·ful (plen′ti fəl) *adj.* 1 having or yielding plenty 2 abundant —**plen′ti·ful·ly** *adv.*

plen·ty (plen′tē) *n., pl.* **-ties** ⟦< L *plenus*, full⟧ 1 prosperity; opulence 2 a sufficient supply 3 a large number —*adv.* [Colloq.] very; quite

pleth·o·ra (pleth′ə rə) *n.* ⟦< Gr *plēthein*, to be full⟧ an overabundance

pleu·ra (plo͝or′ə) *n., pl.* **-rae** (-ē) ⟦< Gr, rib, side⟧ the thin membrane that covers a lung and lines the chest cavity in mammals

pleu·ri·sy (plo͝or′ə sē) *n.* ⟦< Gr *pleura*, rib, side⟧ inflammation of the pleura, characterized by painful breathing

Plex·i·glas (pleks′i glas′) *trademark for* a lightweight, transparent, thermoplastic substance —*n.* this material: also **plex′i·glass′**

plex·us (pleks′əs) *n., pl.* **-us·es** or **-us** ⟦< L *plectere*, to twine⟧ a network, as of blood vessels, nerves, etc.

pli·a·ble (plī′ə bəl) *adj.* ⟦< L *plicare*, to fold⟧ 1 easily bent; flexible 2 easily influenced or persuaded 3 adaptable —**pli′a·bil′i·ty** *n.*

pli·ant (plī′ənt) *adj.* 1 easily bent; pliable 2 compliant —**pli′an·cy** *n.*

pli·ers (plī′ərz) *n.pl.* ⟦< PLY[1]⟧ small pincers for gripping small objects, bending wire, etc. Often **pair of pliers**

plight[1] (plīt) *n.* ⟦< OFr *pleit*, a fold⟧ a distressing situation

plight[2] (plīt) *vt.* ⟦< OE *pliht*, danger⟧ to pledge, or bind by a pledge

plinth (plinth) *n.* ⟦< Gr *plinthos*, a brick⟧ the square block at the base of a column, pedestal, etc.

PLO Palestine Liberation Organization

plod (pläd) *vi.* **plod′ded, plod′ding** ⟦of echoic orig.⟧ 1 to move heavily and laboriously; trudge 2 to work steadily; drudge —**plod′der** *n.*

plop (pläp) *vt., vi.* **plopped, plop′ping** ⟦echoic⟧ to drop with a sound like that of something flat falling into water —*n.* such a sound

plot (plät) *n.* ⟦OE⟧ 1 a small area of ground 2 a secret, usually evil, scheme 3 the plan of action of a play, novel, etc. —*vt.* **plot′ted, plot′ting** 1 to mark or trace on a chart or map 2 to make secret plans for —*vi.* to scheme —**plot·ter** *n.*

plov·er (pluv′ər, plō′vər) *n.* ⟦< L *pluvia*, rain⟧ a shore bird with a short tail and long, pointed wings

plow (plou) *n.* ⟦OE *ploh*⟧ 1 a farm implement used to cut and turn up the soil 2 any implement like this, as a snowplow —*vt.* 1 to cut and turn up (soil) with a plow 2 to make (one's way) through as if by plowing —*vi.* 1 to use a plow 2 to move (*through*, *into*, etc.) with force 3 to plod 4 to begin work vigorously: with *into* Also, chiefly Brit., **plough** —**plow′man** (-mən), *pl.* **-men**, *n.*

plow′share′ (-sher′) *n.* the cutting blade of a plow

ploy (ploi) *n.* ⟦? < (EM)PLOY⟧ an action intended to outwit someone

pluck (pluk) *vt.* ⟦OE *pluccian*⟧ 1 to pull off or out; pick 2 to snatch 3 to pull feathers or hair from 4 to pull at (a taut string, etc.) and release quickly —*vi.* to pull: often with *at* —*n.* 1 a pulling 2 courage

pluck′y *adj.* **-i·er, -i·est** brave; spirited —**pluck′i·ness** *n.*

plug (plug) *n.* ⟦MDu *plugge*⟧ 1 an object used to stop up a hole, etc. 2 a cake of tobacco 3 an electrical device, as with prongs, for making contact or closing a circuit 4 a kind of fishing lure 5 [Colloq.] a free boost, advertisement, etc. 6 [Slang] an old, worn-out horse —*vt.* **plugged, plug′ging** 1 to fill (a hole, etc.) with a plug 2 to insert a plug of 3 [Colloq.] to advertise with a plug 4 [Slang] to shoot a bullet into —*vi.* [Colloq.] to work doggedly

plug-o′la (-ō′lə) *n.* ⟦< PLUG, *n.* 5⟧ [Slang] a bribe for underhanded promotion on radio or TV

plum (plum) *n.* ⟦OE *plume*⟧ 1 *a*) a tree bearing a smooth-skinned fruit with a flattened stone *b*) the fruit 2 a raisin 3 the bluish-red color of some plums 4 something desirable

plum·age (plo͞om′ij) *n.* ⟦Fr < *plume*, a feather⟧ a bird's feathers

plumb (plum) *n.* ⟦< L *plumbum*, LEAD[2]⟧ a lead weight (**plumb bob**) hung at the end of a line (**plumb line**), used to determine how deep water is or whether a wall, etc. is vertical —*adj.* perfectly vertical —*adv.* 1 straight down 2 [Colloq.] entirely —*vt.* 1 to test or sound with a plumb 2 to probe or fathom —**out of** (or **off**) **plumb** not vertical

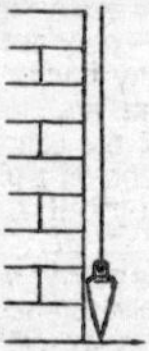

PLUMB

plumb·er (plum′ər) *n.* ⟦see prec.⟧ a skilled worker who installs and repairs pipes, fixtures, etc., as of water systems

plumber's helper [Colloq.] PLUNGER (sense 2) Also **plumber's friend**

plumb·ing (plum′iŋ) *n.* 1 the work of a plumber 2 the pipes and fixtures with which a plumber works

plume (plo͞om) *n.* ⟦< L *pluma*⟧ 1 a feather, esp. a large, showy one 2 a group of these —*vt.* **plumed, plum′ing** 1 to adorn with plumes 2 to preen —**plum′y, -i·er, -i·est,** *adj.*

plum·met (plum′it) *n.* ⟦see PLUMB⟧ 1 a

plumb 2 a thing that weighs heavily —*vi.* to fall straight downward

plump[1] (plump) *adj.* ⟦< MDu *plomp,* bulky⟧ full and rounded in form; chubby —**plump′ness** *n.*

plump[2] (plump) *vi., vt.* ⟦echoic⟧ to drop or bump suddenly or heavily —*n.* 1 a falling, bumping, etc. 2 the sound of this —*adv.* 1 suddenly; heavily 2 straight down

plun·der (plun′dər) *vt., vi.* ⟦< Ger *plunder,* baggage⟧ 1 to rob or pillage 2 to take (property) by force or fraud —*n.* 1 a plundering 2 things taken by force or fraud

plunge (plunj) *vt.* **plunged, plung′ing** ⟦see PLUMB⟧ to thrust or throw suddenly (*into* a liquid, condition, etc.) —*vi.* 1 to dive or rush 2 to move violently and rapidly downward or forward 3 [Colloq.] to gamble heavily —*n.* 1 a dive or fall 2 [Colloq.] a gamble

plung′er *n.* 1 one who plunges 2 a large, rubber suction cup used to free clogged drains 3 any cylindrical device that operates with a plunging motion, as a piston

plunk (pluŋk) *vt.* ⟦echoic⟧ 1 to strum (a banjo, etc.) 2 to throw or put down heavily —*vi.* 1 to give out a twanging sound 2 to fall heavily —*n.* the sound made by plunking —**plunk down** [Colloq.] to give in payment

plu·ral (ploor′əl) *adj.* ⟦< L *plus,* more⟧ more than one —*n. Gram.* the form of a word designating more than one (e.g., *hands, men*)

plu·ral·i·ty (ploo ral′ə tē) *n., pl.* **-ties** 1 a being plural or numerous 2 *a)* the excess of votes in an election that the leading candidate has over his nearest rival *b)* a majority

plu·ral·ize (ploor′əl īz′) *vt., vi.* **-ized′, -iz′ing** to make plural

plus (plus) *prep.* ⟦L, more⟧ 1 added to /2 *plus* 2/ 2 in addition to —*adj.* 1 indicating addition 2 positive /a *plus* quantity/ 3 somewhat higher than /a grade of B *plus*/ 4 involving extra gain /a *plus* factor/ 5 [Colloq.] and more /personality *plus*/ —*n., pl.* **plus′es** or **plus′ses** 1 a sign (**plus sign,** +) indicating addition or positive quantity 2 something added 3 an advantage; benefit

plush (plush) *n.* ⟦< L *pilus,* hair⟧ a fabric with a soft, thick pile —*adj.* [Colloq.] luxurious: also **plush′y**

Plu·tarch (plōō′tärk′) *c.* A.D. 46-*c.* 120; Gr. biographer & historian

Plu·to (plōōt′ō) 1 *Gr. & Rom. Myth.* the god of the lower world 2 the outermost planet: see PLANET

plu·toc·ra·cy (plōō täk′rə sē) *n., pl.* **-cies** ⟦< Gr *ploutos,* wealth + *kratein,* to rule⟧ 1 government by the wealthy 2 a group of wealthy people who control a government

plu·to·crat (plōōt′ō krat′, plōōt′ə-) *n.* 1 a member of a plutocracy 2 one whose wealth is the source of control or influence —**plu′to·crat′ic** *adj.*

plu·to·ni·um (plōō tō′nē əm) *n.* ⟦after PLUTO (planet)⟧ a radioactive, metallic chemical element

plu·vi·al (plōō′vē əl) *adj.* ⟦< L *pluvia,* rain⟧ of, or having much, rain

ply[1] (plī) *vt.* **plied, ply′ing** ⟦< L *plicare,* to fold⟧ [Now Rare] to twist, fold, etc. —*n., pl.* **plies** 1 a thickness or layer, as of cloth, plywood, etc. 2 any of the twisted strands in rope, yarn, etc.

ply[2] (plī) *vt.* **plied, ply′ing** ⟦contr. < APPLY⟧ 1 to use (a tool, faculty, etc.), esp. with energy 2 to work at (a trade) 3 to keep supplying, assailing, etc. (*with*) 4 to sail back and forth across —*vi.* 1 to keep busy 2 to travel regularly (*between* places)

Ply·mouth (plim′əth) town in SE Mass.: settled by the Pilgrims (1620): pop. 36,000

ply′wood′ *n.* ⟦PLY[1] + WOOD⟧ a construction material made of thin layers of wood glued together

PM, P.M., p.m., or **pm** ⟦L *post meridiem*⟧ after noon: used to designate the time from noon to midnight

PMS ⟦*p*(*re*)*m*(*enstrual*) *s*(*yndrome*)⟧ the physical and emotional disorders that may precede menstruation

pneu·mat·ic (nōō mat′ik) *adj.* ⟦< Gr *pneuma,* breath⟧ 1 of or containing wind, air, or gases 2 filled with or worked by compressed air

pneu·mo·ni·a (nōō mōn′yə) *n.* ⟦< Gr *pneumōn,* lung < *pnein,* breathe⟧ inflammation of the lungs caused as by bacteria or viruses

Po (pō) river in N Italy, flowing from the Alps into the Adriatic

PO or **P.O.** 1 Post Office 2 post office box

poach[1] (pōch) *vt.* ⟦< MFr *poche,* pocket: the yolk is "pocketed" in the white⟧ to cook (fish, an egg without its shell, etc.) in or over boiling water

poach[2] (pōch) *vt., vi.* ⟦< MHG *puchen,* to plunder⟧ 1 to trespass on (private property), esp. for hunting or fishing 2 to hunt or catch (game or fish) illegally —**poach′er** *n.*

pock (päk) *n.* ⟦OE *pocc*⟧ 1 a pustule caused by smallpox, etc. 2 POCKMARK —**pocked** *adj.*

pock·et (päk′it) *n.* ⟦< Fr *poque,* a pouch⟧ 1 a little bag or pouch, esp. one sewn into clothing, for carrying small articles 2 a pouchlike cavity or hollow 3 a small area or group /a *pocket* of poverty/ —*adj.* 1 that can be carried in a pocket 2 small —*vt.* 1 to put into a pocket 2 to envelop; enclose 3 to take (money, etc.) dishonestly 4 to suppress /*pocket* one's pride/ —**pock′et·ful′,** *pl.* **-fuls′,** *n.*

pock′et·book′ *n.* 1 a woman's purse or handbag 2 monetary resources

pock′et·knife′ *n., pl.* **-knives′** a knife with a blade or blades that fold into the handle

pock′mark′ *n.* a scar left by a pustule, as of smallpox

pod (päd) *n.* ⟦< ?⟧ a dry fruit or seed vessel, as of peas, beans, etc.

-pod (päd) ⟦< Gr *pous,* foot⟧ *combining form* 1 foot 2 (one) having (a specified number or kind of) feet Also **-pode** (pōd)

po·di·a·try (pō dī′ə trē) *n.* ⟦< Gr *pous,* foot + -IATRY⟧ the profession dealing with the care and treatment of the feet —**po·di′a·trist** *n.*

po·di·um (pō′dē əm) *n., pl.* **-di·a** (-ə) ⟦L < Gr *pous,* foot⟧ 1 a small platform, as for an orchestra conductor 2 LECTERN

Poe (pō), **Ed·gar Al·lan** (ed'gər al'ən) 1809-49; U.S. poet & short-story writer

po·em (pō'əm) ***n.*** ⟦< Gr *poiein*, to make⟧ an arrangement of words, esp. a rhythmical composition, sometimes rhymed, in a style more imaginative than ordinary speech

po·e·sy (pō'ə sē') ***n.*** *old-fashioned var. of* POETRY

po·et (pō'ət) ***n.*** 1 one who writes poems or verses: often (see -ESS) **po'et·ess** ***n.fem.*** 2 one who displays beauty of thought, language, etc. in expression

po·et·as·ter (pō'ət as'tər) ***n.*** ⟦< prec. + Gr *-aster*, dim. suffix⟧ a writer of mediocre verse

po·et·ic (pō et'ik) ***adj.*** 1 of or for poets or poetry 2 displaying the beauty, imaginative qualities, etc. found in poetry Also **po·et'i·cal** ***adj.*** —**po·et'i·cal·ly** ***adv.***

poetic license deviation from strict fact or rules, for artistic effect

poet laureate the official poet of a nation, appointed to write poems celebrating national events, etc.

po·et·ry (pō'ə trē) ***n.*** 1 the writing of poems 2 poems 3 poetic qualities

po·grom (pō gräm', pō'grəm) ***n.*** ⟦< Russ, earlier, riot, storm⟧ an organized massacre, as of Jews in czarist Russia

poi (poi) ***n.*** ⟦Haw⟧ a pastelike Hawaiian food made of taro root

poign·ant (poin'yənt) ***adj.*** ⟦< L *pungere*, to prick⟧ 1 pungent 2 *a)* sharply painful to the feelings *b)* emotionally moving 3 sharp, biting, pointed, etc. —**poign'an·cy** ***n.***

poin·ci·an·a (poin'sē an'ə) ***n.*** ⟦after M. de *Poinci*, governor of the Fr West Indies⟧ a small, tropical tree or shrub with showy red or yellow flowers

poin·set·ti·a (poin set'ē ə; *widely*, -set'ə) ***n.*** ⟦after J. R. *Poinsett*, 19th-c. U.S. ambassador to Mexico⟧ a tropical shrub with yellow flowers and petal-like, red leaves

point (point) ***n.*** ⟦< L *pungere*, to prick⟧ 1 a dot in writing, etc. [*a decimal point*] 2 a position or location 3 the exact moment 4 a condition reached [*boiling point*] 5 a detail; item [*point by point*] 6 a distinguishing feature 7 a unit, as of value, game scores, etc. 8 a sharp end 9 a projecting piece of land; cape 10 the essential fact or idea [*the point of a joke*] 11 a purpose; object 12 a convincing idea or fact 13 a helpful hint 14 a mark showing direction on a compass 15 *Finance a)* a $1 change in the price of a stock *b)* a unit or amount equal to one percent 16 *Printing* a measuring unit for type, about $\frac{1}{72}$ of an inch —***vt.*** 1 to sharpen to a point 2 to give (a story, etc.) emphasis: usually with *up* 3 to show: usually with *out* [*point out the way*] 4 to aim —***vi.*** 1 to direct one's finger (*at* or *to*) 2 to call attention (*to*) 3 to be directed (*to* or *toward*) —**at the point of** very close to —**beside the point** irrelevant —**to the point** pertinent; apt: also **in point**

point'-blank' ***adj.***, ***adv.*** ⟦prec. + *blank* (white center of a target)⟧ 1 (aimed) straight at a mark 2 direct(ly); blunt(ly)

point'ed ***adj.*** 1 having a sharp end 2 sharp; incisive 3 aimed at someone, as a remark 4 very evident —**point'ed·ly** ***adv.***

poin·telle (poin tel') ***n.*** a lacy, openwork fabric, often of acrylic, used for blouses, sweaters, etc.

point'er ***n.*** 1 a long, tapered rod for pointing to things 2 an indicator on a meter, etc. 3 a large, muscular hunting dog with a smooth coat 4 [Colloq.] a helpful hint or suggestion

poin·til·lism (pwan'tə liz'əm) ***n.*** ⟦Fr⟧ a style of painting using dots of color that blend together when seen from a distance —**poin'til·list** ***n.***, ***adj.***

point'less ***adj.*** 1 without a point 2 without meaning or force; senseless

point man 1 the soldier in the front position in a patrol 2 anyone in the forefront of attacking or supporting a political program, etc.

point of view 1 the way in which something is viewed 2 a mental attitude or opinion

point'y ***adj.*** -**i·er**, -**i·est** 1 coming to a sharp point 2 many-pointed

poise (poiz) ***n.*** ⟦< L *pendere*, weigh⟧ 1 balance; stability 2 ease and dignity of manner 3 carriage, as of the body —***vt.***, ***vi.*** **poised**, **pois'ing** to balance or be balanced

poi·son (poi'zən) ***n.*** ⟦< L *potio*, potion⟧ a substance which in small quantities can cause illness or death —***vt.*** 1 to harm or kill with poison 2 to put poison into 3 to influence wrongfully —***adj.*** poisonous

poison ivy a plant having leaves of three leaflets and ivory-colored berries: it can cause a severe rash

POISON IVY

poi'son·ous ***adj.*** that can injure or kill by or as by poison —**poi'son·ous·ly** ***adv.***

poison pill any defensive measure which makes the takeover of a corporation prohibitively expensive

poke[1] (pōk) ***vt.*** **poked**, **pok'·ing** ⟦< MDu *poken*⟧ 1 *a)* to prod, as with a stick *b)* [Slang] to hit 2 to make (a hole, etc.) by poking —***vi.*** 1 to jab (*at*) 2 to pry or search (*about* or *around*) 3 to move slowly (*along*) —***n.*** 1 a jab; thrust 2 [Slang] a blow with the fist —**poke fun (at)** to ridicule

poke[2] (pōk) ***n.*** ⟦OFr⟧ [Dial.] a sack

pok·er[1] (pōk'ər) ***n.*** ⟦< ? Ger *pochspiel*, lit., game of defiance⟧ a card game in which the players bet on the value of their hands

pok·er[2] (pōk'ər) ***n.*** a bar, usually of iron, for stirring a fire

poker face an expressionless face, as of a poker player trying to conceal the nature of his or her hand

pok·y (pōk'ē) ***adj.*** -**i·er**, -**i·est** ⟦POKE[1] + -Y[2]⟧ 1 slow, dull, etc. 2 small and uncomfortable, as a room Also **pok'ey**

pol (päl) ***n.*** [Slang] a politician

Pol. 1 Poland 2 Polish

Po·land (pō'lənd) country in central Europe, on the Baltic Sea: 120,727 sq. mi.; pop. 37,546,000

po·lar (pō′lər) ***adj.*** 1 of or near the North or South pole 2 of a pole
polar bear a large, white bear of coastal arctic regions
Po·la·ris (pō lar′is) ***n.*** the bright star almost directly above the North Pole
po·lar·i·ty (pō lar′ə tē) ***n.***, *pl.* **-ties** 1 the tendency of having opposite magnetic poles 2 the tendency to turn, grow, think, etc. in contrary directions, as if because of magnetic repulsion
po·lar·i·za·tion (pō′lər i zā′shən) ***n.*** 1 a polarizing or being polarized 2 *Optics* a condition, or the production of a condition, of electromagnetic waves in which the motion of the wave is confined to one plane or one direction
po·lar·ize (pō′lər īz′) ***vt.*** **-ized′**, **-iz′ing** to give polarity to —***vi.*** to acquire polarity; specif., to separate into opposed or antagonistic groups, viewpoints, etc.
Po·lar·oid (pō′lər oid′) *trademark for:* 1 a transparent material capable of polarizing light 2 a camera that produces a print within seconds: in full **Polaroid (Land) camera**
pole¹ (pōl) ***n.*** ⟦< L *palus*, a stake⟧ a long, slender piece of wood, metal, etc. —***vt.***, ***vi.*** **poled, pol′ing** to push along (a boat or raft) with a pole —**pol′er** ***n.***
pole² (pōl) ***n.*** ⟦< Gr *polos*⟧ 1 either end of any axis, as of the earth 2 either of two opposed forces, parts, etc., as the ends of a magnet, the terminals of a battery, etc.
Pole (pōl) ***n.*** a native or inhabitant of Poland
pole·cat (pōl′kat′) ***n.*** ⟦prob. < OFr *poule*, hen + CAT⟧ 1 a small, weasel-like Old World carnivore 2 SKUNK
po·lem·ic (pō lem′ik) ***adj.*** ⟦< Gr *polemos*, war⟧ of or involving dispute Also **po·lem′i·cal** —***n.*** (a) controversy
po·lem′ics ***n.pl.*** [*with sing. v.*] the art or practice of disputation —**po·lem′i·cist** (-i sist) ***n.***
pole′star′ Polaris, the North Star: also **Pole Star** —***n.*** a guiding principle
pole vault a leap for height by vaulting over a bar with the aid of a long pole —**pole′-vault′** ***vi.*** —**pole′-vault′er** ***n.***
po·lice (pə lēs′) ***n.*** ⟦Fr: ult. < Gr *polis*, city⟧ 1 the governmental department (of a city, state, etc.) for keeping order, detecting crime, etc. 2 [*with pl. v.*] the members of such a department —***vt.*** **-liced′**, **-lic′ing** 1 to control, protect, etc. with police or a similar force 2 to keep (a military camp, etc.) clean and orderly
po·lice′man (-mən) ***n.***, *pl.* **-men** a member of a police force —**po·lice′wom′an**, *pl.* **-wom′en**, ***n.fem.***
police officer a member of a police force
police state a government that seeks to suppress political opposition by means of police
pol·i·cy¹ (päl′ə sē) ***n.***, *pl.* **-cies** ⟦see POLICE⟧ 1 wise management 2 a principle, plan, etc., as of a government
pol·i·cy² (päl′ə sē) ***n.***, *pl.* **-cies** ⟦< Gr *apodeixis*, proof⟧ a written insurance contract In full **insurance policy**
pol′i·cy·hold′er ***n.*** a person to whom an insurance policy is issued
po·li·o·my·e·li·tis (pō′lē ō′mī′ə līt′is) ***n.*** ⟦< Gr *polios*, gray + MYELITIS⟧ an acute infectious disease caused by a virus inflammation of the gray matter of the spinal cord, often resulting in muscular paralysis Also **po′li·o′**
pol·ish (päl′ish) ***vt.*** ⟦< L *polire*⟧ 1 to smooth and brighten, as by rubbing 2 to refine (manners, style, etc.) —***vi.*** to take a polish —***n.*** 1 surface gloss 2 elegance, refinement, etc. 3 a substance used to polish —**polish off** [Colloq.] to finish (a meal, job, etc.) completely
Pol·ish (pōl′ish) ***adj.*** of Poland, its people, language, etc. —***n.*** the Slavic language of the Poles
po·lite (pə līt′) ***adj.*** ⟦< L *polire*, to polish⟧ 1 cultured; refined 2 having good manners; courteous —**po·lite′ly** ***adv.*** —**po·lite′ness** ***n.***
pol·i·tesse (päl′i tes′) ***n.*** ⟦Fr⟧ politeness
pol·i·tic (päl′i tik′) ***adj.*** ⟦see POLICE⟧ 1 having practical wisdom; prudent 2 expedient, as a plan —***vi.*** **-ticked′**, **-tick′ing** to campaign in politics
po·lit·i·cal (pə lit′i kəl) ***adj.*** 1 of, concerned with, or engaged in government, politics, etc. 2 of or characteristic of political parties or politicians —**po·lit′i·cal·ly** ***adv.***
political science the science of the principles, organization, and methods of government —**political scientist**
pol·i·ti·cian (päl′i tish′ən) ***n.*** one actively engaged in politics: often used with implications of seeking personal or partisan gain, scheming, etc.
po·lit·i·cize (pə lit′ə sīz′) ***vt.*** **-cized′**, **-ciz′ing** to make political
po·lit·i·co (pə lit′i kō′) ***n.***, *pl.* **-cos′** ⟦< Sp or It⟧ POLITICIAN
pol·i·tics (päl′i tiks) ***n.pl.*** [*with sing. or pl. v.*] 1 the science of government 2 political affairs 3 political methods, tactics, etc. 4 political opinions, etc. 5 factional scheming for power
pol′i·ty (-ə tē) ***n.***, *pl.* **-ties** ⟦see POLICE⟧ 1 governmental organization 2 a society with a government; state
Polk (pōk), **James K.** 1795-1849; 11th president of the U.S. (1845-49)
pol·ka (pōl′kə) ***n.*** ⟦Czech, Polish dance⟧ 1 a fast dance for couples 2 music for this dance
pol·ka dot (pō′kə; *also* pōl′-) any of a pattern of small, round dots on cloth
poll (pōl) ***n.*** ⟦ME *pol*⟧ 1 the head 2 a counting, listing, etc. of persons, esp. of voters 3 the number of votes recorded 4 [*pl.*] a place where votes are cast 5 a canvassing of people's opinions on some question —***vt.*** 1 to cut off or cut short the wool, hair, horns, etc. of 2 to register the votes of 3 to require each member of (a jury, etc.) to declare individual votes 4 to receive (a specified number of votes) 5 to cast (a vote) 6 to canvass in a POLL (sense 5)
pol·len (päl′ən) ***n.*** ⟦L, dust⟧ the fine, dust-like mass of grains in the anthers of seed plants
pollen count the number of grains of pollen, esp. of ragweed, in a given volume of air at a specified time and place
pol·li·nate (päl′ə nāt′) ***vt.*** **-nat′ed**, **-nat′ing** to transfer pollen to the pistil of (a flower) —**pol′li·na′tion** ***n.***

pol·li·wog (päl′ē wäg′, -wôg′) ***n.*** ⟦< ME: see POLL + WIGGLE⟧ TADPOLE Also **pol′ly·wog′**

poll·ster (pōl′stər) ***n.*** one whose work is taking public-opinion polls

pol·lute (pə lo͞ot′) ***vt.*** **-lut′ed, -lut′ing** ⟦< L *polluere*⟧ to make unclean or impure —**pol·lu′tant** ***n.*** —**pol·lu′tion** ***n.***

po·lo (pō′lō) ***n.*** ⟦ult. < Tibetan *pulu*, ball⟧ a game played on horseback by two teams, using a wooden ball and long-handled mallets

Po·lo (pō′lō), **Mar·co** (mär′kō) 1254-1324; Venetian traveler in E Asia

pol·o·naise (päl′ə nāz′) ***n.*** ⟦Fr (fem.), Polish⟧ a stately Polish dance

pol·ter·geist (pōl′tər gīst′) ***n.*** ⟦Ger < *poltern*, to rumble + *geist*, ghost⟧ a ghost supposed to be responsible for mysterious noisy disturbances

pol·troon (päl tro͞on′) ***n.*** ⟦< It *poltrone*⟧ a thorough coward

poly- ⟦< Gr⟧ *combining form* much, many

pol·y·clin·ic (päl′i klin′ik) ***n.*** ⟦POLY- + CLINIC⟧ a clinic or hospital for the treatment of various kinds of diseases

pol·y·es·ter (päl′ē es′tər) ***n.*** ⟦POLY(MER) + ESTER⟧ a polymeric resin used in making plastics, fibers, etc.

pol·y·eth·yl·ene (päl′ē eth′ə lēn′) ***n.*** ⟦POLY(MER) + ETHYLENE⟧ a thermoplastic resin used in making plastics, films, etc.

po·lyg·a·my (pə lig′ə mē) ***n.*** ⟦< Gr *poly-*, many + *gamos*, marriage⟧ the practice of having two or more spouses at the same time —**po·lyg′a·mist** ***n.*** —**po·lyg′a·mous** ***adj.***

pol·y·glot (päl′i glät′) ***adj.*** ⟦< Gr *poly-*, many + *glōtta*, tongue⟧ 1 speaking or writing several languages 2 written in several languages —***n.*** 1 a polyglot person 2 a polyglot book

pol′y·gon′ (-gän′) ***n.*** ⟦< Gr: see POLY- & -GON⟧ a plane figure, esp. one with more than four sides and angles —**po·lyg·o·nal** (pə lig′ə nəl) ***adj.***

pol′y·graph′ (-graf′) ***n.*** ⟦see POLY- & -GRAPH⟧ a device measuring changes in respiration, pulse rate, etc., used on persons suspected of lying

pol′y·math′ (-ə math′) ***n.*** ⟦< Gr *poly-*, much + *manthanein*, learn⟧ a person of great and varied learning

pol′y·mer (-mər) ***n.*** ⟦Ger < Gr *poly-*, many + *meros*, part⟧ a substance consisting of giant molecules formed from polymerization

po·lym·er·i·za·tion (pō lim′ər ə zā′shən) ***n.*** a chaining together of many simple molecules to form a more complex molecule with different properties —**po·lym′er·ize′** (-īz′), **-ized′, -iz′ing,** ***vt., vi.***

Pol·y·ne·sia (päl′ə nē′zhə) group of Pacific islands, east of Micronesia, including Hawaii, etc. —**Pol′y·ne′sian** (-i nē′zhən) ***n., adj.***

pol·y·no·mi·al (päl′i nō′mē əl) ***n.*** ⟦POLY- + (BI)NOMIAL⟧ a mathematical expression containing three or more terms (Ex: $x^3 + 3x + 2$ or $x^2 - 2xy + y^2$)

pol·yp (päl′ip) ***n.*** ⟦< Gr *poly-*, many + *pous*, foot⟧ 1 a cnidarian with many small tentacles at the top of a tubelike body 2 a growth of mucous membrane in the bladder, rectum, etc.

po·lyph·o·ny (pə lif′ə nē) ***n.*** ⟦< Gr *poly-*, many + *phōnē*, a sound⟧ *Music* a combining of independent, harmonizing tones, as in a fugue; counterpoint —**pol·y·phon·ic** (päl′i fän′ik) ***adj.*** —**pol′y·phon′i·cal·ly** ***adv.***

pol·y·rhythm (päl′i rith′əm) ***n.*** *Music* 1 the simultaneous use of strongly contrasting rhythms 2 such a rhythm: *used in pl.* —**pol′y·rhyth′mic** ***adj.***

pol·y·syl·lab·ic (päl′i si lab′ik) ***adj.*** 1 having four or more syllables 2 characterized by polysyllabic words —**pol′y·syl′la·ble** (-sil′ə bəl) ***n.***

pol′y·tech′nic (-tek′nik) ***adj.*** ⟦< Gr *poly-*, many + *technē*, art⟧ of or providing instruction in many scientific and technical subjects

pol′y·the·ism′ (-thē iz′əm) ***n.*** ⟦< Gr *poly*, many + *theos*, god⟧ belief in more than one god —**pol′y·the·ist** ***adj., n.*** —**pol′y·the·is′tic** ***adj.***

pol·y·un·sat·u·rat·ed (päl′ē un sach′ə rāt′id) ***adj.*** designating any of certain plant and animal fats and oils with a low cholesterol content

pol·y·vi·nyl (päl′i vī′nəl) ***adj.*** designating or of any of a group of polymerized vinyl compounds: see VINYL

po·made (päm ād′, *also* pō mād′; *chiefly Brit* pō mäd′) ***n.*** ⟦< It *pomo*, apple (orig. an ingredient)⟧ a perfumed ointment, as for the hair

pome·gran·ate (päm′gran′it, päm′ə-; *also* pum-) ***n.*** ⟦ult. < L *pomum*, fruit + *granum*, seed⟧ 1 a round, red fruit with a hard rind and many seeds 2 the bush or tree it grows on

pom·mel (pum′əl; *also* päm′-) ***n.*** ⟦< L *pomum*, fruit⟧ 1 the knob on the end of the hilt of some swords and daggers 2 the rounded, upward-projecting front part of a saddle —***vt.*** **-meled** or **-melled, -mel·ing** or **-mel·ling** PUMMEL

pomp (pämp) ***n.*** ⟦< Gr *pompē*, solemn procession⟧ 1 stately display 2 ostentatious show or display

pom·pa·dour (päm′pə dôr′) ***n.*** ⟦after Mme. *Pompadour*, mistress of Louis XV⟧ a hairdo in which the hair is brushed up high from the forehead

pom·pa·no (päm′pə nō′) ***n.*** ⟦< Sp⟧ a spiny-finned food fish of North America and the West Indies

pom·pom (päm′päm′) ***n.*** ⟦see POMP⟧ an ornamental tuft of silk, etc., used on clothing, etc. Also **pom′pon′** (-pän′)

pom·pous (päm′pəs) ***adj.*** 1 full of pomp 2 pretentious; self-important —**pom·pos′i·ty** (-päs′ə tē) ***n.***

pon·cho (pän′chō) ***n.,*** *pl.* **-chos** ⟦AmSp < AmInd, woolen cloth⟧ a cloak like a blanket with a hole in the middle for the head, esp. a waterproof one worn as a raincoat

pond (pänd) ***n.*** ⟦< ME *pounde*, enclosure⟧ a body of water smaller than a lake

pon·der (pän′dər) ***vt., vi.*** ⟦< L *ponderare*, weigh⟧ to think deeply (about); consider carefully

pon·der·o·sa (pine) (pän′dər ō′sə) ⟦< L

ponderosus, very heavy ⟧ a yellow pine of W North America

pon'der·ous *adj.* 1 very heavy 2 unwieldy 3 labored and dull

pone (pōn) *n.* ⟦ < AmInd ⟧ [Chiefly South] corn bread in the form of small ovals

pon·gee (pän jē', pun-) *n.* ⟦ < Mandarin Chin dial. *pen-chi*, one's own loom ⟧ a soft, thin silk cloth, usually in its natural tan

pon·iard (pän'yərd) *n.* ⟦ult. < L *pugnus*, fist ⟧ a dagger

pon·tiff (pänt'if) *n.* ⟦ < L *pontifex*, high priest ⟧ 1 a bishop 2 [P-] the pope —**pon·tif'i·cal** *adj.*

pon·tif'i·cate (-i kit; *for v.*, -kāt') *n.* the office or term of a pontiff —*vi.* **-cat'ed, -cat'ing** 1 to officiate as a pontiff 2 to be pompous or dogmatic

pon·toon (pän to͞on') *n.* ⟦ < L *pons*, a bridge ⟧ 1 a flat-bottomed boat 2 any of a row of boats or floating objects used to support a temporary bridge 3 a boatlike float on an aircraft's landing gear

po·ny (pō'nē) *n., pl.* **-nies** ⟦prob. < L *pullus*, foal ⟧ 1 a horse of any small breed 2 a small liqueur glass 3 [Colloq.] a literal translation of a foreign work, used in doing schoolwork

po'ny·tail' *n.* a hair style in which the hair is tied tightly at the back and hangs down like a pony's tail

pooch (po͞och) *n.* ⟦ < ? ⟧ [Slang] a dog

poo·dle (po͞od''l) *n.* ⟦Ger *pudel* ⟧ a dog with a thick, wiry coat of tight curls in a solid color

pooh (po͞o) *interj.* an exclamation of disdain, disbelief, or impatience

pooh-pooh (po͞o'po͞o') *vt.* to treat disdainfully; make light of

pool[1] (po͞ol) *n.* ⟦OE *pol* ⟧ 1 a small pond 2 a small collection of liquid, as a puddle 3 a tank for swimming

pool[2] (po͞ol) *n.* ⟦ < LL *pulla*, hen ⟧ 1 a game of billiards played on a table with six pockets 2 a combination of resources, funds, supplies, etc. for some common purpose 3 the parties forming such a combination —*vt., vi.* to contribute to a common fund

poop[1] (po͞op) *n.* ⟦ < L *puppis*, stern of a ship ⟧ a raised deck at the stern of a ship Also **poop deck**

poop[2] (po͞op) *vt.* [Slang] to tire

poop[3] (po͞op) *n.* [Slang] current inside information

poor (poor) *adj.* ⟦ < L *pauper*, poor ⟧ 1 having little or no means of support; needy 2 lacking in some quality; specif., *a)* inadequate *b)* inferior or worthless *c)* contemptible 3 worthy of pity; unfortunate —**the poor** poor, or needy, people —**poor'ly** *adv.*

poor'house' *n.* [Historical] a publicly supported institution for paupers

poor'-mouth' *vi.* [Colloq.] to complain about one's lack of money

pop[1] (päp) *n.* ⟦echoic ⟧ 1 a sudden, light, explosive sound 2 any carbonated, nonalcoholic beverage —*vi.* **popped, pop'ping** 1 to make, or burst with, a pop 2 to move, go, etc. suddenly 3 to bulge: said of the eyes 4 *Baseball* to hit the ball high into the infield —*vt.* 1 to cause to pop, as corn by roasting 2 to put suddenly /to *pop* one's head in/ —**pop'per** *n.*

pop[2] (päp) *n.* ⟦ < PAPA ⟧ [Colloq.] FATHER

pop[3] (päp) *adj.* 1 of music popular with the general public 2 intended for the popular taste, esp. as exploited commercially /*pop* culture/ 3 of a realistic art style using techniques and subjects adapted from commercial art, comic strips, posters, etc. —*n.* pop music

pop. 1 popular 2 popularly 3 population

pop'corn' *n.* 1 a variety of corn with hard grains which pop open into a white, puffy mass when heated 2 the popped grains

pope (pōp) *n.* ⟦ < Gr *pappas*, father ⟧ [*usually* P-] *R.C.Ch.* the bishop of Rome and head of the Church

Pope (pōp), **Alexander** 1688-1744; Eng. poet

pop'gun' *n.* a toy gun that shoots pellets by air compression, with a pop

pop·in·jay (päp'in jā') *n.* ⟦ < Ar *babghā'*, a parrot ⟧ a conceited person

pop·lar (päp'lər) *n.* ⟦ < L *populus* ⟧ 1 a tall tree of the willow family having soft, fibrous wood 2 its wood

pop·lin (päp'lin) *n.* ⟦prob. after *Poperinge*, city in Flanders ⟧ a sturdy ribbed fabric of cotton, silk, etc.

pop'o'ver *n.* a very light, puffy, hollow muffin

pop·py (päp'ē) *n., pl.* **-pies** ⟦ < L *papaver* ⟧ a plant with a milky juice and variously colored flowers

pop'py·cock' (-käk') *n.* [Colloq.] foolish talk; nonsense

poppy seed the small, dark seed of the poppy, used in baking, etc.

pops (päps) *adj.* of a symphony orchestra that plays light classical music or arrangements of popular music —*n.* a pops orchestra, concert, etc.

pop-top (päp'täp') *n.* a container with a tab or ring pulled or pushed to make an opening in the top

pop·u·lace (päp'yo͞o lis) *n.* ⟦ < L *populus* ⟧ 1 the common people; the masses 2 POPULATION (sense 1*a*)

pop·u·lar (päp'yo͞o lər) *adj.* ⟦ < L *populus*, the people ⟧ 1 of, carried on by, or intended for people generally 2 not expensive /*popular* prices/ 3 commonly accepted; prevalent 4 liked by many people —**pop'u·lar'i·ty** (-lar'ə tē) *n.* —**pop'u·lar·ly** *adv.*

pop·u·lar·ize (päp'yo͞o lə rīz') *vt.* **-ized', -iz'·ing** to make popular —**pop'u·lar·i·za'tion** *n.*

pop·u·late (päp'yo͞o lāt') *vt.* **-lat'ed, -lat'ing** ⟦ < L *populus*, the people ⟧ 1 to inhabit 2 to supply with inhabitants

pop'u·la'tion *n.* 1 *a)* all the people in a country, region, etc. *b)* the number of these 2 a populating or being populated

population explosion the great and rapid increase in human population in modern times

pop·u·list (päp'yo͞o list) *n.* a politician, etc. who claims to represent the common people: often applied to someone demagogic —*adj.* of a populist —**pop'u·lism'** *n.*

pop·u·lous (päp'yo͞o ləs) *adj.* full of people; thickly populated

por·ce·lain (pôr'sə lin) *n.* ⟦ < It *porcellana* ⟧

a hard, white, translucent variety of ceramic ware

porch (pôrch) ***n.*** ⟦< L *porta*, gate⟧ 1 a covered entrance to a building 2 an open or enclosed gallery or room on the outside of a building

por·cine (pôr′sīn′, -sin) ***adj.*** ⟦< L *porcus*, hog⟧ of or like pigs or hogs

por·cu·pine (pôr′kyoo pīn′) ***n.*** ⟦< L *porcus*, pig + *spina*, spine⟧ a rodent having coarse hair mixed with long, stiff, sharp spines

pore[1] (pôr, pōr) ***vi.*** **pored, por′ing** ⟦ME *poren*⟧ 1 to study carefully: with *over* 2 to ponder: with *over*

pore[2] (pôr, pōr) ***n.*** ⟦< Gr *poros*, passage⟧ a tiny opening, as in plant leaves or skin, for absorbing or discharging fluids

pork (pôrk) ***n.*** ⟦< L *porcus*, pig⟧ the flesh of a pig, used as food

pork barrel [Colloq.] government appropriations for political patronage

pork′y ***adj.*** **-i·er, -i·est** 1 of or like pork 2 [Slang] saucy, cocky, etc.

por·no (pôr′nō) ***n., adj.*** [Slang] *short for* PORNOGRAPHY, PORNOGRAPHIC Also **porn** (pôrn)

por·nog·ra·phy (pôr näg′rə fē) ***n.*** ⟦< Gr *pornē*, a prostitute + *graphein*, write⟧ writings, pictures, etc. intended primarily to arouse sexual desire —**por′no·graph′ic** (-nə graf′ik) ***adj.***

po·rous (pôr′əs) ***adj.*** full of pores, through which fluids, air, or light may pass —**po·ros·i·ty** (pō räs′ə tē) ***n.***

por·phy·ry (pôr′fər ē) ***n., pl.*** **-ries** ⟦< Gr *porphyros*, purple⟧ any igneous rock with large, distinct crystals

por·poise (pôr′pəs) ***n.*** ⟦< L *porcus*, pig + *piscis*, a fish⟧ 1 a small whale with a blunt snout 2 a dolphin

por·ridge (pôr′ij) ***n.*** ⟦< POTTAGE by confusion with VL *porrata*, leek broth⟧ [Chiefly Brit., etc.] a soft food of cereal or meal boiled in water or milk

por′rin·ger (-in jər) ***n.*** ⟦< Fr *potager*, soup dish: infl. by prec.⟧ a bowl for porridge, cereal, etc.

port[1] (pôrt) ***n.*** ⟦< L *portus*, haven⟧ 1 a harbor 2 a city with a harbor where ships load and unload cargo

port[2] (pôrt) ***n.*** ⟦after *Oporto*, city in Portugal⟧ a sweet, dark-red wine

port[3] (pôrt) ***vt.*** ⟦< L *portare*, carry⟧ to hold (a rifle, etc.) diagonally in front of one, as for inspection

port[4] (pôrt) ***n.*** ⟦< PORT[1]⟧ the left side of a ship, etc. as one faces forward —***adj.*** of or on this side —***vt., vi.*** to turn (the helm) to the port side

port[5] (pôrt) ***n.*** ⟦< L *porta*, door⟧ 1 PORTHOLE 2 an opening, as in a valve face, for the passage of steam, etc. 3 *Comput.* the circuit, outlet, etc. which connects a computer and its peripheral

Port. 1 Portugal 2 Portuguese

port·a·ble (pôrt′ə bəl) ***adj.*** ⟦< L *portare*, carry⟧ 1 that can be carried 2 easily carried —***n.*** something portable —**port′a·bil′i·ty** ***n.***

por·tage (pôr′tij, pôr täzh′) ***n.*** ⟦< L *portare*, carry⟧ 1 a carrying of boats and supplies overland between navigable lakes, rivers, etc. 2 any route over which this is done —***vt., vi.*** **-taged, -tag·ing** to carry (boats, etc.) over a portage

por·tal (pôrt′'l) ***n.*** ⟦< L *porta*, door⟧ a doorway, gate, or entrance

port·cul·lis (pôrt kul′is) ***n.*** ⟦< MFr *porte*, gate + *coleïce*, sliding⟧ a heavy iron grating lowered to bar the gateway of a castle or fortified town

por·tend (pôr tend′) ***vt.*** ⟦< L *por-*, forth + *tendere*, to stretch⟧ 1 to be an omen of; presage 2 to signify

por·tent (pôr′tent′) ***n.*** 1 something that portends an event 2 significance

por·ten·tous (pôr ten′təs) ***adj.*** 1 portending evil; ominous 2 amazing 3 pompous; self-important —**por·ten′tous·ly** ***adv.***

por·ter[1] (pôrt′ər) ***n.*** ⟦< L *porta*, gate⟧ a doorman or gatekeeper

por·ter[2] (pôrt′ər) ***n.*** ⟦< L *portare*, carry⟧ 1 one who carries luggage, etc. for hire 2 an employee who sweeps, cleans, etc. in a bank, store, etc. 3 a railroad attendant for passengers as on a sleeper 4 a dark-brown beer

por′ter·house′ (-hous′) ***n.*** ⟦orig. a tavern: see PORTER[2], sense 4⟧ a choice cut of beef between the tenderloin and the sirloin In full **porterhouse steak**

port·fo·li·o (pôrt fō′lē ō′) ***n., pl.*** **-li·os′** ⟦< L *portare*, carry + *folium*, leaf⟧ 1 a flat, portable case, for loose papers; briefcase 2 the office of a minister of state 3 a list of an investor's securities

port·hole (pôrt′hōl′) ***n.*** an opening in a ship's side to admit light and air

PORTICO

por·ti·co (pôr′ti kō′) ***n., pl.*** **-coes′** or **-cos′** ⟦< L *porticus*, porch⟧ a porch or covered walk, consisting of a roof supported by columns

por·tiere or **por·tière** (pôr tyer′) ***n.*** ⟦Fr < *porte*, door⟧ a curtain hung in a doorway

por·tion (pôr′shən) ***n.*** ⟦< L *portio*⟧ 1 a part, esp. that allotted to a person; share 2 a dowry 3 one's lot; destiny —***vt.*** 1 to divide into portions 2 to give as a portion to

Port·land (pôrt′lənd) city & port in NW Oreg.: pop. 366,000

port·ly (pôrt′lē) ***adj.*** **-li·er, -li·est** 1 large and stately 2 stout; corpulent —**port′li·ness** ***n.***

port·man·teau (pôrt man′tō′) ***n., pl.*** **-teaus′** or **-teaux′** (-tōz′) ⟦< Fr *porter*, carry + *manteau*, cloak⟧ a stiff suitcase that opens into two compartments

portmanteau word a word that is a combination of two other words (Ex.: *smog*, from *smoke* and *fog*)

port of entry a place where customs officials check people and goods entering a country

Por·to Ri·co (pôr′tə rē′kō) *old name of* PUERTO RICO —**Por′to Ri′can**

por·trait (pôr′trit, -trāt′) ***n.*** ⟦see PORTRAY⟧ 1 a painting, photograph, etc. of a person, esp. of the face 2 a description, portrayal, etc.

por′trai·ture (-tri chər) ***n.*** the practice or art of portraying

por·tray (pôr trā′) ***vt.*** ⟦< L *pro-*, forth + *trahere*, draw⟧ 1 to make a portrait of 2 to describe graphically 3 to play the part of as in a play or movie —**por·tray′al** ***n.***

Ports·mouth (pôrts′məth) seaport in SE Va.: pop. 105,000

Por·tu·gal (pôr′chə gəl) country in SW Europe, on the Atlantic: 35,553 sq. mi.; pop. 9,834,000

Por·tu·guese (pôr′chə gēz′, -gēs′) ***adj.*** of Portugal, its people, language, etc. —***n.*** 1 *pl.* **-guese′** a native or inhabitant of Portugal 2 a Romance language of Portugal and Brazil

por·tu·lac·a (pôr′chə lak′ə) ***n.*** ⟦< L *portula*, small door: from the opening in its seed capsule⟧ a fleshy plant with yellow, pink, or purple flowers

pose (pōz) ***vt.*** **posed, pos′ing** ⟦< L *pausare*, to stop⟧ 1 to propose (a question, etc.) 2 to put (a model, etc.) in a certain attitude —***vi.*** 1 to assume a certain attitude, as in modeling for an artist 2 to strike attitudes for effect 3 set oneself up (*as*) /to *pose* as an officer/ —***n.*** 1 a bodily attitude, esp. one held for an artist, etc. 2 behavior assumed for effect

Po·sei·don (pō sī′dən) the Greek god of the sea

pos·er (pōz′ər) ***n.*** a person who poses; esp., a poseur

po·seur (pō zur′) ***n.*** ⟦Fr⟧ one who assumes attitudes or manners merely for effect

posh (päsh) ***adj.*** ⟦< ?⟧ [Colloq.] luxurious and fashionable

pos·it (päz′it) ***vt.*** ⟦see fol.⟧ to suppose to be a fact; postulate

po·si·tion (pə zish′ən) ***n.*** ⟦< L *ponere*, to place⟧ 1 the way in which a person or thing is placed or arranged 2 one's attitude or opinion 3 the place where one is; location 4 the usual or proper place 5 rank, esp. high rank 6 a post of employment; job —***vt.*** to put in a certain position

pos·i·tive (päz′ə tiv) ***adj.*** ⟦see prec.⟧ 1 definitely set; explicit /*positive* instructions/ 2 *a*) having the mind set; confident *b*) overconfident or dogmatic 3 showing agreement; affirmative 4 constructive /*positive* criticism/ 5 regarded as having real existence /a *positive* good/ 6 based on facts /*positive* proof/ 7 *Elec.* *a*) of electricity predominating in a glass body after it has been rubbed with silk *b*) charged with positive electricity *c*) having a deficiency of electrons 8 *Gram.* of an adjective or adverb in its uncompared degree 9 *Math.* greater than zero 10 *Med.* proving the presence of a condition, bacteria, etc. 11 *Photog.* with the light and shade corresponding to those of the subject —***n.*** something positive, as a degree, quality, quantity, photographic print, etc. —**pos′i·tive·ly** ***adv.***

pos·i·tron (päz′i trän′) ***n.*** ⟦POSI(TIVE) + (ELEC)TRON⟧ the positive antiparticle of an electron, having the same mass and magnitude of charge

poss. 1 possessive 2 possibly

pos·se (päs′ē) ***n.*** ⟦< L, be able⟧ the body of men summoned to assist the sheriff in keeping the peace, etc.

pos·sess (pə zes′) ***vt.*** ⟦< L *possidere*⟧ 1 to have as belonging to one; own 2 to have as an attribute, quality, etc. 3 to gain control over /*possessed* by an idea/ —**pos·ses′sor** ***n.***

pos·sessed′ ***adj.*** 1 owned 2 controlled, as if by a demon; crazed

pos·ses′sion (-zesh′ən) ***n.*** 1 a possessing or being possessed 2 anything possessed 3 [*pl.*] wealth 4 territory ruled by an outside country

pos·ses′sive (-zes′iv) ***adj.*** 1 of possession 2 showing or desiring possession, domination, control, influence, etc. 3 *Gram.* designating or of a case, form, or construction expressing possession (Ex: *my, Bill's*) —***n.*** *Gram.* 1 the possessive case 2 a word or phrase in this case —**pos·ses′sive·ness** ***n.***

pos·si·ble (päs′ə bəl) ***adj.*** ⟦< L *posse*, be able⟧ 1 that can be or exist 2 that may or may not happen 3 that can be done, selected, etc. 4 permissible —**pos′si·bil′i·ty** (-bil′ə tē), *pl.* **-ties**, ***n.***

pos′si·bly (-blē) ***adv.*** 1 by any possible means 2 perhaps; maybe

pos·sum (päs′əm) ***n.*** [Colloq.] OPOSSUM —**play possum** to pretend to be asleep, dead, ill, etc.

post[1] (pōst) ***n.*** ⟦< L *postis*⟧ 1 a piece of wood, metal, etc. set upright to support a building, sign, etc. 2 the starting point of a horse race —***vt.*** 1 to put up (a poster, etc.) on (a wall, etc.) 2 to announce by posting notices 3 to warn against trespassing on by posted notices 4 to put (a name) on a posted or published list

post[2] (pōst) ***n.*** ⟦< Fr < It *posto*⟧ 1 the place where a soldier, guard, etc. is stationed 2 *a*) a place where troops are garrisoned *b*) the troops at such a place 3 the place assigned to one 4 a job or duty —***vt.*** 1 to assign to a post 2 to put up (a bond, etc.)

post[3] (pōst) ***n.*** ⟦< Fr < It *posta*⟧ [Chiefly Brit.] (the) mail —***vi.*** to travel fast; hasten —***vt.*** 1 [Chiefly Brit.] to mail 2 to inform /keep me *posted*/

post- ⟦L < *post*, after⟧ *prefix* 1 after in time, later (than) /*postnatal*/ 2 after in space, behind

post·age (pōst′ij) ***n.*** the amount charged for mailing a letter, etc., esp. as represented by stamps

post·al (pōs′təl) ***adj.*** ⟦Fr⟧ of mail or post offices

post′card (-kärd′) ***n.*** 1 a card with a postage stamp printed on it, for sending short messages by mail: also **postal card** 2 a similar card, usually with a picture on one side, to which a stamp is affixed

post′date′ ***vt.*** **-dat′ed, -dat′ing** 1 to assign a later date to than the actual date 2 to be subsequent to

post·er (pōs′tər) ***n.*** a large advertisement or notice posted publicly

pos·te·ri·or (päs tir′ē ər) ***adj.*** ⟦L < *post*, after⟧ 1 later; following 2 at the rear; behind —***n.*** the buttocks

pos·ter·i·ty (päs ter′ə tē) *n.* ⟦see prec.⟧ **1** all of a person's descendants **2** all suc ceeding generations

Post Exchange *trademark for* a nonprofit general store at an army post or camp

post′grad′u·ate *adj.* of or taking a course of study after graduation, esp. after receipt of the bachelor's degree

post′haste′ *adv.* with great haste

post·hu·mous (päs′tyo͞o məs, -choo-) *adj.* ⟦< L *postumus,* last⟧ **1** born after the father's death **2** published after the author's death **3** arising or continuing after one's death —**post′hu·mous·ly** *adv.*

post·hyp·not·ic (pōst′hip nät′ik) *adj.* in the time after a hypnotic trance /*posthypnotic* suggestion/

pos·til·ion or **pos·til·lion** (pōs til′yən, päs-) *n.* ⟦Fr < It *posta,* a post⟧ one who rides the leading left-hand horse of a team drawing a carriage

post′in·dus′tri·al *adj.* of a society in which the economy shifted from heavy industry to service industries, technology, etc.

post·lude (pōst′lo͞od′) *n.* ⟦POST- + (PRE)L UDE⟧ a concluding musical piece

post′man (-mən) *n. pl.* **-men** MAILMAN

post′mark′ *n.* a post-office mark stamped on mail, canceling the postage stamp and recording the date and place —*vt.* to stamp with a postmark

post′mas′ter *n.* a manager of a post office

postmaster general *pl.* **postmasters general** the head of a government's postal system

post me·ri′di·em (-mə rid′ē əm) ⟦L⟧ after noon Abbrev. *P.M., p.m., PM,* or *pm*

post′mod′ern *adj.* coming after, usually reacting to, 20th-c. modernism

post-mor·tem (pōst′môr′təm) *adj.* ⟦L⟧ **1** after death **2** of a post-mortem —*n.* **1** AUTOPSY **2** an evaluation of some event just ended

post·na·sal drip (pōst′nā′zəl) a discharge of mucus from behind the nose onto the pharynx, due to a cold, allergy, etc.

post′na′tal (-nāt′′l) *adj.* after birth

post office **1** the governmental department in charge of the mails **2** a place where mail is sorted, postage stamps are sold, etc.

post′op′er·a·tive (-äp′ər ə tiv) *adj.* occurring after a surgical operation

post′paid′ *adj.* with postage prepaid

post′par′tum (-pär′təm) *adj.* ⟦L < *post-,* after + *parere,* to bear⟧ of the time after childbirth

post·pone (pōst pōn′) *vt.* **-poned′, -pon′ing** ⟦< L *post-,* after + *ponere,* put⟧ to put off until later; delay —**post·pone′ment** *n.*

post′script′ *n.* ⟦< L *post-,* after + *scribere,* write⟧ a note added below the signature in a letter

post time the scheduled starting time of a horse race

pos·tu·late (päs′tyo͞o lāt′, -chə-; *for n.,* -lit) *vt.* **-lat′ed, -lat′ing** ⟦< L *postulare,* to demand⟧ **1** to assume to be true, real, etc., esp. as a basis for argument **2** to take for granted —*n.* **1** something postulated **2** a prerequisite

pos·ture (päs′chər) *n.* ⟦MFr < L *ponere,* to place⟧ **1** the position or carriage of the body **2** a position assumed as in posing **3** an official stand or position /our national *posture*/ —*vi.* to pose or assume an attitude

post′war′ *adj.* after the (or a) war

po·sy (pō′zē) *n., pl.* **-sies** ⟦< POESY⟧ a flower or bouquet: old fashioned term

pot[1] (pät) *n.* ⟦OE *pott*⟧ **1** a round vessel for holding liquids, cooking, etc. **2** a pot with its contents **3** [Colloq.] all the money bet at a single time —*vt.* **pot′ted, pot′ting** **1** to put into a pot **2** to cook or preserve in a pot —**go to pot** to go to ruin —**pot′ful′,** *pl.* **-fuls′,** *n.*

pot[2] (pät) *n.* ⟦< AmSp *potiguaya*⟧ [Slang] MARIJUANA

po·ta·ble (pōt′ə bəl) *adj.* ⟦< L *potare,* to drink⟧ drinkable —*n.* something drinkable —**po′ta·bil′i·ty** *n.*

pot′ash′ *n.* ⟦< Du *pot,* POT[1] + *asch,* ASH[1]⟧ a potassium compound obtained from wood ashes, etc. and used in fertilizers, soaps, etc.

po·tas·si·um (pō tas′ē əm, pə-) *n.* ⟦see prec.⟧ a soft, silver-white, metallic chemical element

po·ta·to (pə tāt′ō) *n., pl.* **-toes** ⟦< WInd⟧ **1** the starchy tuber of a widely cultivated plant, eaten as a cooked vegetable **2** this plant

potato chip a very thin slice of potato fried crisp and then salted

pot′bel′ly *n., pl.* **-lies** a protruding belly —**pot′bel′lied** *adj.*

pot′boil′er *n.* a piece of writing, etc., done quickly and for money only

po·tent (pōt′′nt) *adj.* ⟦< L *posse,* be able⟧ **1** having authority or power **2** convincing; cogent **3** effective, as a drug **4** able to have sexual intercourse: said of a male —**po′ten·cy** *n.*

po·ten·tate (pōt′′n tāt′) *n.* a person having great power; ruler; monarch

po·ten·tial (pō ten′shəl) *adj.* ⟦see POTENT⟧ that can come into being; possible; latent —*n.* **1** something potential **2** the relative voltage at a point in an electric circuit with respect to some reference point in the same circuit —**po·ten′ti·al′i·ty** (-shē al′ə tē), *pl.* **-ties,** *n.* —**po·ten′tial·ly** *adv.*

poth·er (päth′ər) *n.* ⟦< ?⟧ a fuss; commotion —*vt., vi.* to fuss or bother

pot′herb′ *n.* any herb whose leaves and stems are boiled and eaten or used as a flavoring

pot′hold′er *n.* a small pad, or piece of thick cloth, for handling hot pots, etc.

pot′hole′ *n.* **1** a deep hole or pit **2** CHUCKHOLE

pot′hook′ *n.* **1** an S-shaped hook for hanging a pot over a fire **2** a curved or S-shaped mark in writing

po·tion (pō′shən) *n.* ⟦< L *potare,* to drink⟧ a drink as of medicine, poison, or a supposedly magic substance

pot′luck′ *n.* **1** whatever the family meal happens to be /to take *potluck*/ **2** a dinner to which everyone brings a dish to share: in full, **potluck dinner**

Po·to·mac (pə tō′mək) river in the E U.S., flowing into Chesapeake Bay

pot′pie′ *n.* **1** a meat pie made in a deep dish **2** a stew with dumplings

pot·pour·ri (pō′po͞o rē′, pät′poor′ē) *n.* ⟦Fr <

pot, a pot + *pourrir*, to rot] a medley or miscellany; mixture
pot roast a large cut of beef cooked in one piece by braising
pot·sherd (pät′shurd′) *n.* [see POT[1] & SHARD] a piece of broken pottery
pot′shot′ (-shät′) *n.* 1 an easy or random shot 2 a haphazard try 3 a random attack
pot·tage (pät′ij) *n.* [< MFr *pot*, a pot] a kind of thick soup or stew
pot′ter *n.* one who makes earthenware pots, dishes, etc.
potter's field (pät′ərz) a burial ground for paupers or unknown persons

POTTER'S WHEEL

potter's wheel a rotating disk, upon which clay is molded into bowls, etc.
pot′ter·y *n.*, *pl.* **-ies** 1 a potter's workshop 2 the art of a potter; ceramics 3 pots, dishes, etc. made of clay hardened by heat
pot·ty (pät′ē) *n.*, *pl.* **-ties** 1 a small pot used as a toilet for children 2 a child's chair for toilet training using such a pot 3 a toilet: a child's word
pouch (pouch) *n.* [< MFr *poche*] 1 a small bag or sack /a tobacco *pouch*/ 2 a mailbag 3 a saclike structure, as that on the abdomen of the kangaroo, etc. for carrying young —*vt.*, *vi.* to form (into) a pouch
poul·tice (pōl′tis) *n.* [< ML *pultes*, pap] a hot, soft, moist mass applied to a sore part of the body —*vt.* **-ticed, -tic·ing** to apply a poultice to
poul·try (pōl′trē) *n.* [< L *pullus*, chicken] domestic fowls; chickens, ducks, etc.
pounce (pouns) *n.* [ME *pownce*, talon] a pouncing —*vi.* **pounced, pounc′ing** to swoop down or leap (*on*, *upon*, or *at*) as if to seize
pound[1] (pound) *n.*, *pl.* **pounds**; sometimes, after a number, **pound** [< L *pondus*, weight] 1 a unit of weight equal to 16 oz. avoirdupois or 12 oz. troy: abbrev. *lb.* 2 the monetary unit of the United Kingdom: symbol, £ 3 the monetary unit of various other countries, as Egypt, Syria, etc.
pound[2] (pound) *vt.* [OE *punian*] 1 to beat to a pulp, powder, etc. 2 to hit hard —*vi.* 1 to deliver repeated, heavy blows (*at* or *on*) 2 to move with heavy steps 3 to throb
pound[3] (pound) *n.* [< OE *pund-*] a municipal enclosure for stray animals
pound′cake′ *n.* a rich cake made (orig. with a pound each) of flour, butter, sugar, etc.
pour (pôr) *vt.* [ME *pouren*] 1 to cause to flow in a continuous stream 2 to emit, utter, etc. profusely or steadily —*vi.* 1 to flow freely, continuously, etc. 2 to rain heavily
pout (pout) *vi.* [ME *pouten*] 1 to thrust out the lips, as in sullenness 2 to sulk —*n.* a pouting —**pout′er** *n.*
pov·er·ty (päv′ər tē) *n.* [< L *pauper*, poor] 1 the condition or quality of being poor; need 2 deficiency; inadequacy 3 scarcity
pov′er·ty-strick′en *adj.* very poor
POW prisoner of war
pow·der (pou′dər) *n.* [< L *pulvis*] 1 any dry substance in the form of fine, dustlike particles, produced by crushing, grinding, etc. 2 a specific kind of powder /bath *powder*/ —*vt.* 1 to sprinkle, etc. with powder 2 to make into a powder —**pow′der·y** *adj.*
powder keg 1 a keg for gunpowder 2 an explosive situation
powder room a lavatory for women
pow·er (pou′ər) *n.* [ult. < L *posse*, be able] 1 ability to do or act 2 vigor; force; strength 3 *a*) authority; influence *b*) legal authority 4 physical force or energy /electric *power*/ 5 a person or thing having great influence, force, or authority 6 a nation with influence over other nations 7 the product of the multiplication of a quantity by itself 8 the degree of magnification of a lens —*vt.* to supply with a source of power —*adj.* 1 operated by electricity, a fuel engine, etc. /*power* tools/ 2 served by an auxiliary system that reduces effort /*power* steering/ 3 carrying electricity
pow′er·ful *adj.* strong, mighty, influential, etc. —**pow′er·ful·ly** *adv.*
pow′er·house′ *n.* 1 a building where electric power is generated 2 [Colloq.] a powerful person, team, etc.
pow·er·less (pou′ər lis) *adj.* without power; weak, unable, etc. —**pow′er·less·ly** *adv.*
power of attorney written legal authority to act for another person
pow′er·train′ *n.* DRIVETRAIN
pow·wow (pou′wou′) *n.* [< AmInd] 1 a conference of or with North American Indians 2 [Colloq.] any conference
pox (päks) *n.* [for *pocks*: see POCK] 1 a disease characterized by skin eruptions, as smallpox 2 syphilis
pp. 1 pages 2 past participle 3 postpaid 4 prepaid Also, for 3 & 4, **ppd.**
PP or **P.P.** parcel post
p.pr. or **ppr.** present participle
P.P.S., p.p.s., PPS, or **pps** [L *post postscriptum*] an additional postscript
pr. pair(s)
PR or **P.R.** 1 public relations 2 Puerto Rico
Pr. Provencal
prac·ti·ca·ble (prak′ti kə bəl) *adj.* 1 that can be put into practice; feasible 2 that can be used; usable; useful —**prac′ti·ca·bil′i·ty** *n.* —**prac′ti·ca·bly** *adv.*
prac·ti·cal (prak′ti kəl) *adj.* 1 of or obtained through practice or action 2 useful 3 concerned with the application of knowledge to useful ends /*practical* science/ 4 given to actual practice /a *practical* farmer/ 5 that is so in practice, if not in theory, law, etc. 6 matter-of-fact —**prac′ti·cal′i·ty** (-kal′ə tē), *pl.* **-ties**, *n.*
practical joke a trick played on someone in fun —**practical joker**
prac′ti·cal·ly *adv.* 1 in a practical manner

2 from a practical viewpoint 3 in effect; virtually

practical nurse a nurse with less training than a registered nurse, often one licensed by the State (**licensed practical nurse**) for specified duties

prac·tice (prak'tis) ***vt.*** **-ticed, -tic·ing** ⟦< Gr *prassein*, do⟧ 1 to do or engage in frequently; make a habit of 2 to do repeatedly so as to become proficient 3 to work at, esp. as a profession —***vi.*** to do something repeatedly so as to become proficient; drill Chiefly Brit., etc. sp. **prac'tise** —***n.*** 1 a practicing; habit, custom, etc. 2 *a)* repeated action to acquire proficiency *b)* proficiency so acquired 3 the actual doing of something 4 *a)* the exercise of a profession *b)* a business based on this

prac'ticed ***adj.*** skilled

prac·ti·cum (prak'ti kəm) ***n.*** ⟦see PRACTICE⟧ a course involving activities emphasizing the practical application of theory, as on-the-job experience in a field of study

prac·ti·tion·er (prak tish'ə nər) ***n.*** one who practices a profession

Prae·to·ri·an (prē tôr'ē ən) ***adj.*** ⟦< L *praetor*, magistrate⟧ of or belonging to the bodyguard (**Praetorian Guard**) of a Roman emperor —***n.*** a member of the Praetorian Guard

prag·mat·ic (prag mat'ik) ***adj.*** ⟦< Gr *pragma*, thing done⟧ 1 practical 2 testing the validity of all concepts by their practical results —**prag·mat'i·cal·ly** ***adv.*** —**prag'·ma·tism** (-mə tiz'əm) ***n.*** —**prag'ma·tist** ***n.***

Prague (präg) capital of Czechoslovakia: pop. 1,186,000

prai·rie (prer'ē) ***n.*** ⟦Fr < L *pratum*, meadow⟧ a large area of level or rolling grassy land

prairie dog a small, burrowing rodent of North America

prairie schooner a box-shaped covered wagon

praise (prāz) ***vt.*** **praised, prais'ing** ⟦< L *pretium*, worth⟧ 1 to commend the worth of 2 to glorify (God, a god, etc.), as in song —***n.*** a praising or being praised; commendation

praise'wor'thy ***adj.*** worthy of praise —**praise'wor'thi·ly** ***adv.*** —**praise'wor'thi·ness** ***n.***

pra·line (prä'lēn', prā'-) ***n.*** ⟦Fr⟧ any of various soft or crisp candies made of nuts, sugar, etc.

prance (prans) ***vi.*** **pranced, pranc'ing** ⟦< ?⟧ 1 to rise up, or move along, on the hind legs, as a horse 2 to caper or strut —***n.*** a prancing —**pranc'er** ***n.*** —**pranc'ing·ly** ***adv.***

prank (praŋk) ***n.*** ⟦< ?⟧ a mischievous trick —**prank'ster** ***n.***

prate (prāt) ***vi., vt.*** **prat'ed, prat'ing** ⟦< MDu *praten*⟧ to talk much and foolishly; chatter

prat·tle (prat''l) ***vi., vt.*** **-tled, -tling** ⟦LowG *pratelen*⟧ to prate or babble —***n.*** chatter or babble

prawn (prôn) ***n.*** ⟦< ?⟧ a large shrimp or other similar crustacean

pray (prā) ***vt.*** ⟦< L *prex*, prayer⟧ 1 to implore *(I) pray (you) tell me* 2 to ask for by prayer —***vi.*** to say prayers, as to God

prayer[1] (prer) ***n.*** 1 the act of praying 2 an entreaty; supplication 3 *a)* a humble request, as to God *b)* any set formula for this 4 [*often pl.*] a devotional service chiefly of prayers 5 something prayed for —**prayer'ful** ***adj.*** —**prayer'ful·ly** ***adv.***

pray·er[2] (prā'ər) ***n.*** one who prays

praying mantis MANTIS

pre- ⟦< L *prae*, before⟧ *prefix* before in time, place, rank, etc.

preach (prēch) ***vi.*** ⟦< L *prae-*, before + *dicare*, proclaim⟧ 1 to give a religious sermon 2 to give moral advice, esp. in a tiresome manner —***vt.*** 1 to urge as by preaching 2 to deliver (a sermon) —**preach'·ment** ***n.***

preach'er ***n.*** one who preaches; esp., a member of the clergy

preach'y ***adj.*** **-i·er, -i·est** [Colloq.] given to or marked by preaching

pre·am·ble (prē'am'bəl) ***n.*** ⟦< L *prae-*, before + *ambulare*, go⟧ an introduction, esp. one to a constitution, statute, etc., stating its purpose

pre'ar·range' (-ə rānj') ***vt.*** **-ranged', -rang'·ing** to arrange beforehand

pre·can·cer·ous (prē'kan'sər əs) ***adj.*** likely to become cancerous

pre·car·i·ous (prē ker'ē əs) ***adj.*** ⟦see PRAY⟧ dependent upon circumstances or chance; uncertain; risky —**pre·car'i·ous·ly** ***adv.***

pre·cau·tion (prē kô'shən) ***n.*** ⟦< L *prae-*, before + *cavere*, take care⟧ care taken beforehand, as against danger, failure, etc. —**pre·cau'tion·ar'y** ***adj.***

pre·cede (prē sēd') ***vt., vi.*** **-ced'ed, -ced'ing** ⟦< L *prae-*, before + *cedere*, to move⟧ to be, come, or go before in time, place, rank, etc.

prec·e·dence (pres'ə dəns; prē sēd''ns) ***n.*** the act, right, or fact of preceding in time, order, rank, etc.

pre·ced·ent (prē sēd''nt; *for n.* pres'ə dənt) ***adj.*** preceding —***n.*** **prec'e·dent** an act, statement, etc. that may serve as an example or justification for a later one

pre·ced'ing ***adj.*** that precedes

pre·cept (prē'sept') ***n.*** ⟦< L *prae-*, before + *capere*, take⟧ a rule of moral conduct; maxim

pre·cep·tor (prē sep'tər) ***n.*** a teacher

pre·cinct (prē'siŋkt') ***n.*** ⟦< L *prae-*, before + *cingere*, surround⟧ 1 [*usually pl.*] an enclosure between buildings, walls, etc. 2 [*pl.*] environs 3 *a)* police district *b)* a subdivision of a voting ward 4 limited area

pre·ci·os·i·ty (presh'ē äs'ə tē, pres'-) ***n.***, *pl.* **-ties** ⟦see fol.⟧ affectation, esp. in language

pre·cious (presh'əs) ***adj.*** ⟦< L *pretium*, a price⟧ 1 of great price or value; costly 2 beloved; dear 3 very fastidious, affected, etc. —**pre'cious·ly** ***adv.*** —**pre'cious·ness** ***n.***

precious stone a rare and costly gem: applied to the diamond, emerald, ruby, and sapphire

prec·i·pice (pres'i pis) ***n.*** ⟦< L *prae-*, before + *caput*, a head⟧ a vertical or overhanging rock face

pre·cip·i·tant (prē sip'i tənt) ***adj.*** ⟦see prec.⟧ PRECIPITATE

pre·cip·i·tate (prē sip'ə tāt'; *for adj. & n.*,

-tit, *also*, -tāt') *vt.* **-tat'ed, -tat'ing** ⟦see PRECIPICE⟧ 1 to hurl downward 2 to cause to happen before expected, needed, etc. 3 *Chem.* to separate (a soluble substance) out of a solution —*vi.* 1 *Chem.* to be precipitated 2 *Meteorol.* to condense and fall as rain, snow, etc. —*adj.* 1 acting or done hastily or rashly 2 very sudden or abrupt —*n.* a substance precipitated out from a solution

pre·cip'i·ta'tion *n.* 1 a headlong fall or rush 2 rash haste; impetuosity 3 a bringing on suddenly 4 *Chem.* a precipitating or being precipitated from a solution 5 *Meteorol. a)* rain, snow, etc. *b)* the amount of this

pre·cip'i·tous (-ə təs) *adj.* 1 steep like a precipice 2 rash; impetuous

pré·cis (prā sē', prā'sē') *n., pl.* **-cis'** (-sēz', -sēz') ⟦Fr: see fol.⟧ a concise abridgment; summary

pre·cise (prē sīs', pri-) *adj.* ⟦< L *prae-*, before + *caedere*, to cut⟧ 1 accurately stated; definite 2 minutely exact 3 strict; scrupulous; fastidious —**pre·cise'ly** *adv.* —**pre·cise'ness** *n.*

pre·ci·sion (prē sizh'ən) *n.* the quality of being precise; exactness —*adj.* requiring exactness /*precision* work/

pre·clude (prē klōōd') *vt.* **-clud'ed, -clud'ing** ⟦< L *prae-*, before + *claudere*, to close⟧ to make impossible, esp. in advance; prevent —**pre·clu'sion** (-klōō'zhən) *n.*

pre·co·cious (prē kō'shəs) *adj.* ⟦< L *prae-*, before + *coquere*, to cook⟧ matured earlier than usual /a *precocious* child/ —**pre·coc'i·ty** (-käs'ə tē) *n.*

pre·cog·ni·tion (prē'käg nish'ən) *n.* ⟦see PRE- & COGNITION⟧ the supposed extrasensory perception of a future event —**pre·cog'ni·tive** (-nə tiv) *adj.*

pre-Co·lum·bi·an (prē'kə lum'bē ən) *adj.* of any period in the Americas before Columbus's voyages

pre·con·ceive (prē'kən sēv') *vt.* **-ceived', -ceiv'ing** to form (an opinion) in advance —**pre'con·cep'tion** *n.*

pre'con·di'tion (-dish'ən) *vt.* to prepare to behave, react, etc. in a certain way under certain conditions —*n.* a condition required beforehand

pre·cur·sor (prē kur'sər, prē'kur'-) *n.* ⟦< L *praecurrere*, run ahead⟧ 1 a forerunner 2 a predecessor —**pre·cur'so·ry** *adj.*

pred·a·to·ry (pred'ə tôr'ē) *adj.* ⟦< L *praeda*, a prey⟧ 1 of or living by plundering or robbing 2 preying on other animals —**pred'a·tor** (-tər) *n.*

pre·de·cease (prē'dē sēs') *vt.* **-ceased', -ceas'ing** to die before (someone else)

pred·e·ces·sor (pred'ə ses'ər) *n.* ⟦< L *prae-*, before + *decedere*, go away⟧ a person preceding another, as in office

pre·des·ti·na·tion (prē des'tə nā'shən) *n.* 1 *Theol.* the doctrine that *a)* God foreordained everything that would happen *b)* God predestines souls to salvation or to damnation 2 destiny

pre·des'tine (-tin) *vt.* **-tined, -tin·ing** to destine beforehand; foreordain

pre'de·ter'mine *vt.* **-mined, -min·ing** to determine beforehand

pre·dic·a·ment (prē dik'ə mənt) *n.* ⟦see PREACH⟧ an unpleasant or embarrassing situation

pred·i·cate (pred'i kāt'; *for n. & adj.*, -kit) *vt.* **-cat'ed, -cat'ing** ⟦see PREACH⟧ 1 to affirm as a quality or attribute 2 to base (something) *on* or *upon* facts, conditions, etc. —*n. Gram.* the word or words that make a statement about the subject —*adj. Gram.* of a predicate —**pred'i·ca'tion** *n.*

pre·dict (prē dikt') *vt., vi.* ⟦< L *prae-*, before + *dicere*, tell⟧ to say in advance (what one believes will happen); foretell —**pre·dict'a·ble** *adj.* —**pre·dic'tion** *n.* —**pre·dic'tor** *n.*

pre·di·gest (prē'di jest', -dī-) *vt.* to treat (food) as with enzymes for easier digestion when eaten

pred·i·lec·tion (pred''l ek'shən, prēd'-) *n.* ⟦< L *prae-*, before + *diligere*, prefer⟧ a partiality or preference

pre·dis·pose (prē'dis pōz') *vt.* **-posed', -pos'ing** to make susceptible (*to*); incline —**pre'dis·po·si'tion** *n.*

pre·dom·i·nant (prē däm'ə nənt) *adj.* 1 having authority or influence over others; superior 2 most frequent; prevailing —**pre·dom'i·nance** *n.* —**pre·dom'i·nant·ly** *adv.*

pre·dom·i·nate (prē däm'ə nāt') *vi.* **-nat'ed, -nat'ing** 1 to have authority or influence (*over* others) 2 to be dominant in amount, number, etc.; prevail

pre·em·i·nent (prē em'ə nənt) *adj.* eminent above others; surpassing —**pre·em'i·nence** *n.* —**pre·em'i·nent·ly** *adv.*

pre·empt or **pre-empt'** (prē empt') *vt.* ⟦< L *prae-*, before + *emere*, buy⟧ 1 to gain the right to buy (public land) by settling on it 2 to seize before anyone else can 3 *Radio, TV* to replace (a scheduled program)

pre·emp'tion *n.* 1 a preempting 2 action taken to check other action beforehand —**pre·emp'tive** *adj.*

preen (prēn) *vt.* ⟦< ME *proinen*, to dress up⟧ 1 to clean and trim (the feathers) with a beak 2 to dress up or adorn (oneself) 3 to pride (oneself)

pre·ex·ist (prē'eg zist') *vt., vi.* to exist previously or before (another person or thing) —**pre'ex·ist'ence** *n.*

pref. 1 preface 2 preferred

pre·fab (prē'fab') *n.* [Colloq.] a prefabricated building

pre·fab·ri·cate (prē fab'ri kāt') *vt.* **-cat'ed, -cat'ing** to build (a house, etc.) in standardized sections for shipment and quick assembly

pref·ace (pref'is) *n.* ⟦< L *prae-*, before + *fari*, speak⟧ an introduction to a book, speech, etc. —*vt.* **-aced, -ac·ing** 1 to furnish with a preface 2 to introduce —**pref'a·to'ry** (-ə tôr'ē) *adj.*

pre·fect (prē'fekt') *n.* ⟦< L *praeficere*, to set over⟧ any of various administrators —**pre'fec'ture** (-fek'chər) *n.*

pre·fer (prē fur', pri-) *vt.* **-ferred', -fer'ring** ⟦< L *prae-*, before + *ferre*, to bear⟧ 1 to promote; advance 2 to put before a court, etc. for consideration 3 to like better

pref·er·a·ble (pref'ər ə bəl) *adj.* more desirable —**pref'er·a·bly** *adv.*

pref'er·ence (-əns) ***n.*** **1** a preferring or being preferred **2** something preferred **3** advantage given to one person, country, etc. over others —**pref'er·en'tial** (-ər en'shəl) ***adj.***

pre·fer·ment (prē fur'mənt) ***n.*** an advancement in rank, etc.; promotion

pre·fig·ure (prē fig'yər, -yoor) ***vt.*** **-ured, -ur·ing** to foreshadow

pre·fix (prē'fiks'; *also for v.* prē fiks') ***vt.*** ⟦< L *prae-*, before + *figere*, fix⟧ to fix to the beginning; esp., to add as a prefix —***n.*** a syllable, group of syllables, or word joined to the beginning of another word to alter its meaning

preg·nant (preg'nənt) ***adj.*** ⟦< L *pregnans*⟧ **1** having (an) offspring developing in the uterus; with child **2** mentally fertile; inventive **3** full of meaning, etc. /a *pregnant* silence/ **4** filled (*with*); abounding —**preg'nan·cy**, *pl.* **-cies**, ***n.*** —**preg'nant·ly** ***adv.***

pre·hen·sile (prē hen'sil, -səl) ***adj.*** ⟦< L *prehendere*, take⟧ adapted for seizing or grasping, esp. by wrapping around something, as a monkey's tail

pre·his·tor·ic (prē'his tôr'ik) ***adj.*** of the period before recorded history

pre·ig·ni·tion (prē'ig nish'ən) ***n.*** in an internal-combustion engine, ignition occurring before the intake valve is closed or before the spark plug fires

pre'judge' ***vt.*** **-judged', -judg'ing** to judge beforehand or without all the evidence —**pre'judg'ment** ***n.***

prej·u·dice (prej'ə dis) ***n.*** ⟦< L *prae-*, before + *judicium*, judgment⟧ **1** a preconceived, usually unfavorable idea **2** an opinion held in disregard of facts that contradict it; bias **3** intolerance or hatred of other races, etc. **4** injury or harm —***vt.*** **-diced, -dic·ing** **1** to injure or harm **2** to cause to have prejudice; bias —**prej'u·di'cial** (-dish'əl) ***adj.***

prel·ate (prel'it) ***n.*** ⟦< L *praelatus*, placed before⟧ a high-ranking ecclesiastic, as a bishop —**prel'a·cy**, *pl.* **-cies**, ***n.***

pre·lim·i·nar·y (prē lim'ə ner'ē, pri-) ***adj.*** ⟦< L *prae-*, before + *limen*, threshold⟧ leading up to the main action, etc.; introductory —***n.***, *pl.* **-ies** [*often pl.*] a preliminary step, procedure, etc.

pre·lit·er·ate (prē'lit'ər it) ***adj.*** of a society not having a written language

prel·ude (prel'yood', prā'lood') ***n.*** ⟦< L *prae-*, before + *ludere*, to play⟧ **1** a preliminary part **2** *Music* *a)* an introductory instrumental composition, as the overture to an opera *b)* a short, romantic composition

pre·mar·i·tal (prē mar'i təl, -it'l) ***adj.*** occurring before marriage

pre·ma·ture (prē'mə toor', -tyoor') ***adj.*** ⟦< L *prae-*, before + *maturus*, ripe⟧ happening, done, arriving, etc. before the proper or usual time; too early —**pre'ma·ture'ly** ***adv.***

pre·med'i·tate' (-med'i tāt') ***vt.***, ***vi.*** **-tat'ed, -tat'ing** to think out or plan beforehand —**pre·med'i·ta'tion** ***n.***

pre·men·stru·al (prē men'strəl) ***adj.*** occurring before a menstrual period

pre·mier (pri mir', -myir') ***adj.*** ⟦< L *primus*, first⟧ first in importance; foremost —***n.*** a chief official; specif., a prime minister —**pre·mier'ship** ***n.***

pre·mière or **pre·miere** (pri mir', -myer') ***n.*** ⟦Fr: see prec.⟧ a first performance of a play, movie, etc.

prem·ise (prem'is) ***n.*** ⟦< L *prae-*, before + *mittere*, send⟧ **1** a previous statement serving as a basis for an argument **2** [*pl.*] a piece of real estate —***vt.*** **-ised, -is·ing** to state as a premise; postulate

pre·mi·um (prē'mē əm) ***n.***, *pl.* **-ums** ⟦< L *prae-*, before + *emere*, take⟧ **1** a reward or prize, esp. as an inducement to buy **2** an additional amount paid or charged **3** a payment, as for an insurance policy **4** very high value /to put a *premium* on wit/ —**at a premium** very valuable because of scarcity

prem·o·ni·tion (prēm'ə nish'ən, prē'-) ***n.*** ⟦< L *prae-*, before + *monere*, warn⟧ **1** a forewarning **2** a foreboding —**pre·mon·i·to·ry** (prē män'i tôr'ē) ***adj.***

pre·na·tal (prē nāt''l) ***adj.*** ⟦PRE- + NATAL⟧ before birth

pre·nup·tial (prē nup'shəl) ***adj.*** before a marriage or wedding

pre·oc·cu·py (prē äk'yoo pī') ***vt.*** **-pied', -py'·ing** ⟦< L *prae-*, before + *occupare*, seize⟧ **1** to wholly occupy the thoughts of; engross **2** to take possession of before someone else or beforehand —**pre·oc'cu·pa'tion** (-pā'shən) ***n.*** —**pre·oc'cu·pied'** ***adj.***

pre·or·dain (prē'ôr dān') ***vt.*** to ordain or decree beforehand

prep (prep) ***adj.*** *short for* PREPARATORY /a *prep* school/ —***vt.*** **prepped, prep'ping** to prepare (a patient) for surgery, etc.

prep. 1 preparatory 2 preposition

pre·pack·age (prē'pak'ij) ***vt.*** **-aged, -ag·ing** to package (foods, etc.) in standard units before selling

pre·paid (prē'pād') ***vt.*** *pt. & pp. of* PREPAY

prep·a·ra·tion (prep'ə rā'shən) ***n.*** **1** a preparing or being prepared **2** a preparatory measure **3** something prepared, as a medicine, cosmetic, etc.

pre·par·a·to·ry (prē par'ə tôr'ē, pri-) ***adj.*** serving to prepare; introductory

preparatory school a private secondary school that prepares students for college

pre·pare (prē par', pri-) ***vt.*** **-pared', -par'ing** ⟦< L *prae-*, before + *parare*, get ready⟧ **1** to make ready **2** to equip or furnish **3** to put together /to *prepare* dinner/ —***vi.*** **1** to make things ready **2** to make oneself ready

pre·par'ed·ness ***n.*** the state of being prepared, esp. for waging war

pre'pay' ***vt.*** **-paid', -pay'ing** to pay or pay for in advance

pre·pon·der·ate (prē pän'dər āt', pri-) ***vi.*** **-at'ed, -at'ing** ⟦< L *prae-*, before + *ponderare*, weigh⟧ to be superior in amount, power, etc. —**pre·pon'der·ance** ***n.*** —**pre·pon'der·ant** ***adj.***

prep·o·si·tion (prep'ə zish'ən) ***n.*** ⟦< L *prae-*, before + *ponere*, to place⟧ a word, as *in*, *by*, *to*, etc. that connects a noun or pronoun to another word —**prep'o·si'tion·al** ***adj.***

pre·pos·sess (prē'pə zes') ***vt.*** **1** to bias, esp. favorably **2** to impress favorably

pre'pos·sess'ing (-iŋ) ***adj.*** that impresses favorably

pre·pos·ter·ous (prē päs'tər əs, pri-) ***adj.***

⟦< L *prae-*, before + *posterus*, following⟧ absurd; ridiculous; laughable

prep·py or **prep·pie** (prep′ē) ***n.***, *pl.* **-pies** a (former) student at a preparatory school —***adj.*** **-pi·er, -pi·est** of or like the clothes worn by such students

pre·puce (prē′pyo͞os′) ***n.*** ⟦< L *praeputium*⟧ FORESKIN

pre·re·cord (prē′ri kôrd′) ***vt.*** *Radio, TV* to record (music, a program, etc.) for later use, as for a broadcast

pre·re·cord·ed (prē′ri kôr′did) ***adj.*** designating or of a magnetic tape, as in a cassette, on which sound, etc. has been recorded before its sale

pre·req·ui·site (pri rek′wə zit) ***adj.*** required beforehand as a necessary condition —***n.*** something prerequisite

pre·rog·a·tive (prē räg′ə tiv, pri-) ***n.*** ⟦< L *prae-*, before + *rogare*, ask⟧ an exclusive right or privilege

pres. present

Pres. President

pres·age (pres′ij; *for v., usually* prē sāj′, pri-) ***n.*** ⟦< L *prae-*, before + *sagire*, perceive⟧ **1** an omen; portent **2** a foreboding —***vt.*** **-aged′, -ag′ing** to give warning of

pres·by·ter (prez′bi tər) ***n.*** ⟦see PRIEST⟧ **1** in the Presbyterian Church, an elder **2** in the Episcopal Church, a priest

Pres′by·te′ri·an (-ē ən) ***adj.*** designating or of a church of a traditionally Calvinistic denomination governed by presbyters —***n.*** a member of a Presbyterian church

pre′school′ ***adj.*** of or for a child between infancy and school age —***n.*** NURSERY SCHOOL —**pre′school′er** ***n.***

pres·ci·ence (prē′shəns, -shē əns) ***n.*** ⟦< L *prae-*, before + *scire*, know⟧ foreknowledge; foresight —**pres′ci·ent** ***adj.***

pre·scribe (prē skrīb′, pri-) ***vt.*** **-scribed′, -scrib′ing** ⟦< L *prae-*, before + *scribere*, write⟧ **1** to order; direct **2** to order or advise as a medicine or treatment: said of physicians, etc.

pre·script (prē′skript′) ***n.*** a prescribed rule —**pre·scrip′tive** ***adj.***

pre·scrip·tion (prē skrip′shən, pri-) ***n.*** **1** something prescribed **2** *a)* a written direction for the preparation and use of medicine *b)* such a medicine

pres·ence (prez′əns) ***n.*** **1** the fact or state of being present **2** immediate surroundings [*in his presence*] **3** *a)* a person's bearing or appearance *b)* impressive bearing, personality, etc.

presence of mind ability to think and act quickly in an emergency

pres·ent (prez′ənt; *for v.* prē zent′, pri-) ***adj.*** ⟦< L *prae-*, before + *esse*, be⟧ **1** being at the specified place **2** existing or happening now **3** *Gram.* indicating action or state now or action that is always true [*present tense*] —***n.*** **1** the present time or occasion **2** the present tense **3** a gift —***vt.*** **1** to introduce (a person) **2** to exhibit; show **3** to offer for consideration **4** to give (a gift, etc.) to (a person, etc.) —**present arms** to hold a rifle vertically in front of the body

pre·sent·a·ble (prē zent′ə bəl, pri-) ***adj.*** **1** suitable for presentation **2** suitably groomed for meeting people

pres·en·ta·tion (prez′ən tā′shən, prē′zən-) ***n.*** **1** a presenting or being presented **2** something presented

pres′ent-day′ ***adj.*** of the present time

pre·sen·ti·ment (prē zent′ə mənt, pri-) ***n.*** ⟦see PRE- & SENTIMENT⟧ a feeling that something, esp. of an unfortunate nature, is about to take place

pres′ent·ly ***adv.*** **1** soon; shortly **2** at present; now

pre·sent·ment (prē zent′mənt, pri-) ***n.*** presentation

present participle a participle used to express present or continuing action or existence, as in "he is *growing*"

pres·er·va·tion·ist (prez′ər vā′shən ist) ***n.*** one who advocates positive measures to preserve historic buildings, wilderness lands, etc.

pre·serv·a·tive (prē zurv′ə tiv, pri-) ***adj.*** preserving —***n.*** anything that preserves [*a preservative added to foods*]

pre·serve (prē zurv′, pri-) ***vt.*** **-served′, -serv′ing** ⟦< L *prae-*, before + *servare*, keep⟧ **1** to protect from harm, damage, etc. **2** to keep from spoiling **3** to prepare (food), as by canning, for future use **4** to carry on; maintain —***n.*** **1** [*usually pl.*] fruit preserved by cooking with sugar **2** a place where game, fish, etc. are maintained —**pres·er·va·tion** (prez′ər vā′shən) ***n.*** —**pre·serv′er** ***n.***

pre·set (prē′set′) ***vt.*** **-set′, -set′ting** to set (automatic controls) beforehand

pre·shrink (prē′shriŋk′) ***vt.*** **-shrank′** or **-shrunk′, -shrunk′** or **-shrunk′en, -shrink′ing** to shrink by a special process in manufacture, to minimize further shrinkage in laundering —**pre′shrunk′** ***adj.***

pre·side (prē zīd′, pri-) ***vi.*** **-sid′ed, -sid′ing** ⟦< L *prae-*, before + *sedere*, sit⟧ **1** to serve as chairman **2** to have control or authority (*over*)

pres·i·dent (prez′ə dənt, -dent′) ***n.*** ⟦see prec.⟧ **1** the highest executive officer of a company, club, etc. **2** [*often* **P-**] the chief executive (as in the U.S.), or the nominal head (as in Italy), of a republic —**pres′i·den·cy**, *pl.* **-cies**, ***n.*** —**pres′i·den′tial** (-den′shəl) ***adj.***

press[1] (pres) ***vt.*** ⟦< L *premere*⟧ **1** to act on with steady force or weight; push against, squeeze, compress, etc. **2** to squeeze (juice, etc.) from **3** to iron (clothes, etc.) **4** to embrace closely **5** to force; compel **6** to urge persistently; entreat **7** to try to force **8** to emphasize **9** to distress or trouble [*pressed for time*] **10** to urge on —***vi.*** **1** to weigh down **2** to go forward with determination **3** to crowd —***n.*** **1** pressure, urgency, etc. **2** a crowd **3** a machine for crushing, stamping, etc. **4** smoothness, etc. of clothes after pressing **5** *a) short for* PRINTING PRESS *b)* a printing establishment *c)* newspapers, magazines, etc., or the persons who write for them *d)* publicity, etc. in newspapers, etc. **6** an upright closet for storing clothes, etc. —**press′er** ***n.***

press[2] (pres) ***vt.*** ⟦< L *praes*, surety + *stare*, to stand⟧ to force into service, esp. military or naval service

press agent one whose work is to get publicity for a client

press box a place for reporters at sports events, etc.

press conference a group interview granted to media personnel as by a celebrity

press′ing *adj.* calling for immediate attention; urgent

press′man (-mən) *n., pl.* **-men** an operator of a printing press

press secretary one whose job is to deal with the news media on behalf of a prominent person

pres·sure (presh′ər) *n.* 1 a pressing or being pressed 2 a state of distress 3 a compelling influence /social *pressure*/ 4 urgent demands; urgency 5 *Physics* force per unit of area exerted upon a surface, etc. —*vt.* **-sured, -sur·ing** to exert pressure on

pressure cooker a container for quick cooking by steam under pressure

pres′sur·ize′ (-īz′) *vt.* **-ized′, -iz′ing** to keep nearly normal atmosphere pressure inside (an airplane, etc.), as at high altitudes —**pres′sur·i·za′tion** *n.* —**pres′sur·iz′er** *n.*

pres·ti·dig·i·ta·tion (pres′tə dij′i tā′shən) *n.* ⟦Fr < *preste*, quick + L *digitus*, finger⟧ sleight of hand

pres·tige (pres tēzh′, -tēj′) *n.* ⟦< L *praestrigiae*, deceptions⟧ 1 the power to impress or influence 2 reputation based on high achievement, character, etc. —**prestige′ful** *adj.*

pres·ti′gious (-tij′əs, -tē′jəs) *adj.* having or imparting prestige or distinction

pres·to (pres′tō) *adv., adj.* ⟦It, quick⟧ 1 fast or at once 2 *Musical Direction* in fast tempo

pre′stressed′ concrete concrete containing tensed steel cables for strength

pre·sume (prē zōōm′, pri-) *v.* **-sumed′, -sum′ing** ⟦< L *prae-*, before + *sumere*, take⟧ 1 to dare (to say or do something); venture 2 to take for granted; suppose —*vi.* to act presumptuously; take liberties —**pre·sum′a·ble** *adj.* —**pre·sum′a·bly** *adv.*

pre·sump·tion (prē zump′shən, pri-) *n.* 1 a presuming; specif., *a*) an overstepping of proper bounds *b*) a taking of something for granted 2 the thing presumed 3 a reason for presuming —**pre·sump′tive** *adj.*

pre·sump′tu·ous (-chōō əs, -chə wəs) *adj.* too bold or forward

pre·sup·pose (prē′sə pōz′) *vt.* **-posed′, -pos′·ing** 1 to suppose or assume beforehand 2 to require or imply as a preceding condition —**pre′sup·po·si′tion** (-sup ə zish′ən) *n.*

pre·teen (prē′tēn′) *n.* a child nearly a teenager

pre·tend (prē tend′, pri-) *vt.* ⟦< L *prae-*, before + *tendere*, to stretch⟧ 1 to profess /to *pretend* ignorance/ 2 to feign; simulate /to *pretend* anger/ 3 to make believe /to *pretend* to be astronauts/ —*vi.* to lay claim (*to*) —**pre·tend′er** *n.*

pre·tense (prē tens′, pri-; prē′tens′) *n.* 1 a claim; pretension 2 a false claim 3 a false show of something 4 a pretending, as at play Also [Brit., etc.] **pre·tence′**

pre·ten·sion (prē ten′shən, pri-) *n.* 1 a pretext 2 a claim 3 assertion of a claim 4 pretentiousness

pre·ten′tious (-shəs) *adj.* 1 making claims to some distinction, importance, etc. 2 affectedly grand; ostentatious —**pre·ten′tious·ly** *adv.* —**pre·ten′tious·ness** *n.*

pret·er·it or **pret·er·ite** (pret′ər it) *adj.* ⟦< L *praeter-*, beyond + *ire*, go⟧ *Gram.* expressing past action or state —*n.* the past tense

pre·ter·nat·u·ral (prēt′ər nach′ər əl) *adj.* ⟦ML *praeternaturalis*⟧ 1 differing from or beyond what is natural; abnormal 2 SUPERNATURAL

pre·test (prē′test′) *vt., vi.* to test in advance

pre·text (prē′tekst′) *n.* ⟦< L *prae-*, before + *texere*, weave⟧ a false reason put forth to hide the real one

Pre·to·ri·a (prē tôr′ē ə) a capital of South Africa: pop. 574,000

pret·ti·fy (prit′i fī′) *vt.* **-fied′, -fy′ing** to make pretty

pret·ty (prit′ē) *adj.* **-ti·er, -ti·est** ⟦OE *prættig*, crafty⟧ attractive in a dainty, graceful way —*adv.* fairly; somewhat —*vt.* **-tied, -ty·ing** to make pretty: usually with *up* —**pret′ti·ly** *adv.* —**pret′ti·ness** *n.*

pret·zel (pret′səl) *n.* ⟦< L *brachium*, an arm⟧ a hard, brittle, salted biscuit, often formed in a loose knot

PRETZEL

pre·vail (prē vāl′, pri-) *vi.* ⟦< L *prae-*, before + *valere*, be strong⟧ 1 to be victorious; triumph: often with *over* or *against* 2 to succeed 3 to be or become more widespread 4 to be prevalent —**prevail on** (or **upon** or **with**) to persuade

pre·vail′ing *adj.* 1 superior in strength or influence 2 prevalent

prev·a·lent (prev′ə lənt) *adj.* ⟦see PREVAIL⟧ widely existing; generally accepted, used, etc. —**prev′a·lence** *n.*

pre·var·i·cate (pri var′i kāt′) *vi.* **-cat′ed, -cat′ing** ⟦< L *prae-*, before + *varicare*, straddle⟧ 1 to evade the truth 2 to lie —**pre·var′i·ca′tion** *n.* —**pre·var′i·ca′tor** *n.*

pre·vent (prē vent′, pri-) *vt.* ⟦< L *prae-*, before + *venire*, come⟧ to stop or keep from doing or happening; hinder —**pre·vent′a·ble** or **pre·vent′i·ble** *adj.* —**pre·ven′tion** *n.*

pre·ven′tive (-vent′iv) *adj.* preventing or serving to prevent —*n.* anything that prevents Also **pre·vent′a·tive**

pre·view (prē′vyōō′) *n.* 1 an advance, restricted showing, as of a movie 2 a showing of scenes from a movie, etc. to advertise it Also **pre′vue** (-vyōō′)

pre·vi·ous (prē′vē əs) *adj.* ⟦< L *prae-*, before + *via*, a way⟧ occurring before; prior —**previous to** before —**pre′vi·ous·ly** *adv.*

pre·war (prē′wôr′) *adj.* before a (or the) war

prex·y (preks′ē) *n., pl.* **-ies** [Slang] the president, esp. of a college, etc.

prey (prā) *n.* ⟦< L *prehendere*, seize⟧ 1 an animal hunted for food by another animal 2 a victim 3 the mode of living by preying on other animals /a bird of *prey*/ —*vi.* 1 to plunder 2 to hunt other animals for food 3 to weigh as an obsession Generally used with *on* or *upon*

pri·ap·ic (prī ap′ik) *adj.* ⟦after *Priapos*, Gr

god of procreation] of or relating to the phallus; phallic

price (prīs) ***n.*** [< L *pretium*] **1** the amount of money, etc. asked or paid for something; cost **2** value or worth **3** the cost, as in life, labor, etc., of obtaining some benefit —***vt.*** **priced, pric′ing 1** to fix the price of **2** [Colloq.] to find out the price of

price′less ***adj.*** of inestimable value; invaluable

prick (prik) ***n.*** [OE *prica*, a point] **1** a tiny puncture made by a sharp point **2** a sharp pain caused as by being pricked —***vt.*** **1** to make (a hole) in (something) with a sharp point **2** to pain sharply —**prick up one's ears 1** to raise the ears erect **2** to listen closely

prick·le (prik′əl) ***n.*** [OE *prica*, a point] **1** a small, sharply pointed growth, as a thorn: also **prick′er 2** a tingling sensation —***vt., vi.*** **-led, -ling** to tingle —**prick′ly, -li·er, -li·est,** ***adj.***

prickly heat a skin eruption caused by inflammation of the sweat glands

pride (prīd) ***n.*** [< OE *prut*, proud] **1** *a)* an unduly high opinion of oneself *b)* haughtiness; arrogance **2** dignity and self-respect **3** satisfaction in something done, owned, etc. **4** a person or thing in which pride is taken —**pride oneself on** to be proud of —**pride′ful** ***adj.*** —**pride′ful·ly** ***adv.***

pri·er (prī′ər) ***n.*** one who pries

priest (prēst) ***n.*** [< Gr *presbys*, old] **1** a person of special rank who performs religious rites in a temple of God or a god **2** *R.C.Ch.* a clergyman ranking next below a bishop —**priest′ess** ***n.fem.*** —**priest′hood′** ***n.*** —**priest′ly, -li·er, -li·est,** ***adj.***

prig (prig) ***n.*** [< 16th-c. cant] one who smugly affects great propriety or morality —**prig′gish** ***adj.***

prim (prim) ***adj.*** **prim′mer, prim′mest** [< ?] stiffly formal, precise, or moral —**prim′ly** ***adv.*** —**prim′ness** ***n.***

pri·ma·cy (prī′mə sē) ***n., pl.*** **-cies** [< L *primus*, first] **1** a being first in time, rank, etc.; supremacy **2** the rank or office of a primate

pri·ma don·na (prē′mə dän′ə, prim′ə) *pl.* **pri′ma don′nas** [It, lit., first lady] the principal woman singer in an opera

pri·ma fa·ci·e (prī′mə fā′shē ē′, -shi ē′) [L, lit., at first sight] adequate to establish a fact unless refuted Said of evidence

pri·mal (prī′məl) ***adj.*** [< L *primus*, first] **1** first in time; original **2** first in importance; chief

pri·mar·i·ly (prī mer′ə lē, prī′mer′-) ***adv.*** **1** at first; originally **2** mainly; principally

pri·mar·y (prī′mer′ē, -mə rē) ***adj.*** [< L *primus*, first] **1** first in time or order; original **2** from which others are derived; fundamental *[primary* colors*]* **3** first in importance; chief —***n., pl.*** **-ries 1** something first in order, importance, etc. **2** a preliminary election at which candidates are chosen for the final election

primary school 1 ELEMENTARY SCHOOL **2** a school including the first three elementary grades and, sometimes, kindergarten

primary stress (or **accent**) the heaviest stress (′) in pronouncing a word

pri·mate (prī′māt′; *for 1*, -mit) ***n.*** [< L *primus*, first] **1** an archbishop, or the highest-ranking bishop in a province, etc. **2** any of the most highly developed order of animals, including man, the apes, etc.

prime (prīm) ***adj.*** [< L *primus*, first] **1** first in time; original **2** first in rank or importance; chief; principal **3** first in quality **4** fundamental **5** *Math.* that can be evenly divided by no other whole number than itself and 1 —***n.*** **1** the first or earliest part **2** the best or most vigorous period **3** the best part —***vt.*** **primed, prim′ing 1** to make ready; prepare **2** to get (a pump) into operation by pouring water into it **3** to undercoat, size, etc. before painting **4** to provide with facts, answers, etc. beforehand

prime meridian the meridian at Greenwich, England, from which longitude is measured east and west

prime minister in some countries, the chief executive of the government

prim·er[1] (prim′ər) ***n.*** [< L *primus*, first] **1** a simple book for teaching reading **2** any elementary textbook

prim·er[2] (prīm′ər) ***n.*** a thing that primes; specif., *a)* an explosive cap, etc. used to set off a main charge *b)* a preliminary coat of paint, etc.

prime rate the most favorable interest rate charged on bank loans to large corporations Also **prime interest rate** or **prime lending rate**

prime time *Radio, TV* the hours when the largest audience is available

pri·me·val (prī mē′vəl) ***adj.*** [< L *primus*, first + *aevum*, an age] of the earliest times or ages; primordial

prim·i·tive (prim′i tiv) ***adj.*** [< L *primus*, first] **1** of the earliest times; original **2** crude; simple **3** primary; basic —***n.*** a primitive person or thing

pri·mo·gen·i·ture (prī′mō jen′i chər, -mə-) ***n.*** [< L *primus*, first + *genitura*, a begetting] **1** the condition of being the firstborn of the same parents **2** the right of inheritance of the eldest son

pri·mor·di·al (prī môr′dē əl) ***adj.*** [< L *primus*, first + *ordiri*, begin] primitive; fundamental; original

primp (primp) ***vt., vi.*** [prob. < PRIM] to groom or dress up in a fussy way

prim·rose (prim′rōz′) ***n.*** [altered (after *rose*) < ML *primula*] a plant with tubelike, often yellow flowers

primrose path 1 the path of pleasure, self-indulgence, etc. **2** a course of action that seems easy but that can lead to disaster

prince (prins) ***n.*** [< L *princeps*, chief] **1** a ruler ranking below a king; head of a principality **2** a son of a sovereign **3** any preeminent person

prince consort the husband of a reigning queen

Prince Edward Island island province of SE Canada: 2,184 sq. mi.; pop. 127,000; cap. Charlottetown

prince′ly ***adj.*** **-li·er, -li·est 1** of a prince **2** magnificent; generous —**prince′li·ness** ***n.***

prin·cess (prin′sis, -ses′) ***n.*** **1** a daughter of a sovereign **2** the wife of a prince

prin·ci·pal (prin′sə pəl) ***adj.*** [see PRINCE] first in rank, importance, etc. —***n.*** **1** a principal person or thing 2 the head of a school 3 the amount of a debt, etc. minus the interest —**prin'ci·pal·ly** *adv.*

prin'ci·pal'i·ty (-pal'ə tē) *n., pl.* **-ties** the territory ruled by a prince

principal parts the principal inflected forms of a verb: in English, the infinitive, past tense, and past participle (Ex: *drink, drank, drunk*)

prin·ci·ple (prin'sə pəl) *n.* ⟦see PRINCE⟧ 1 a fundamental truth, law, etc. upon which others are based 2 *a)* a rule of conduct *b)* adherence to such rules; integrity 3 a basic part 4 *a)* the scientific law explaining a natural action *b)* the method of a thing's operation —**prin'ci·pled** *adj.*

print (print) *n.* ⟦< L *premere*, to press⟧ 1 a mark made on a surface by pressing or stamping 2 cloth printed with a design 3 the impression of letters, designs, etc. made by inked type or from a plate, block, etc. 4 a photograph, esp. one made from a negative —*vt., vi.* 1 to stamp (a mark, letter, etc.) on a surface 2 to produce on (paper, etc.) the impression of inked type, etc. 3 to produce (a book, etc.) 4 to write in letters resembling printed ones 5 to make (a photographic print) —**in** (or **out of**) **print** still (or no longer) being sold by the publisher: said of books, etc. —**print'er** *n.*

printed circuit an electrical circuit of conductive material, as in fine lines, applied to an insulating sheet

print'ing *n.* 1 the act of one that prints 2 something printed 3 all the copies printed at one time

printing press a machine for printing from inked type, plates, or rolls

print-out (print'out') *n.* the printed or typewritten output of a computer

pri·or (prī'ər) *adj.* ⟦L⟧ 1 earlier; previous 2 preceding in order or importance —*n.* the head of a priory —**prior to** before in time

pri'or·ess (-is) *n.* the woman head of a priory of nuns, etc.

pri·or·i·tize (prī ôr'ə tīz') *vt.* **-tized', -tiz'ing** to arrange (items) in order of importance

pri·or·i·ty (prī ôr'ə tē) *n., pl.* **-ties** 1 a being prior; precedence 2 a prior right to get, buy, or do something 3 something to be given prior attention

pri'o·ry *n., pl.* **-ries** a monastery governed by a prior, or a convent governed by a prioress

prism (priz'əm) *n.* ⟦< Gr *prizein*, to saw⟧ 1 *Geom.* a solid figure whose ends are parallel and equal in size and shape, and whose sides are parallelograms 2 a transparent, triangular prism used to disperse light into the spectrum —**pris·mat·ic** (priz mat'ik) *adj.*

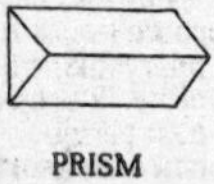

PRISM

pris·on (priz'ən) *n.* ⟦< L *prehendere*, take⟧ a place of confinement for those convicted by or awaiting trial

prison camp 1 a camp with minimum security for holding reliable prisoners 2 a camp for confining prisoners of war

pris'on·er *n.* one held captive or confined, esp. in prison

pris·sy (pris'ē) *adj.* **-si·er, -si·est** ⟦prob. PR(IM) + (S)ISSY⟧ [Colloq.] very prim or prudish —**pris'si·ness** *n.*

pris·tine (pris'tēn', pris tēn') *adj.* ⟦L *pristinus*, former⟧ 1 characteristic of the earliest period 2 unspoiled

prith·ee (prith'ē) *interj.* ⟦< *pray thee*⟧ [Archaic] I pray thee; please

pri·va·cy (prī'və sē) *n., pl.* **-cies** 1 a being private; seclusion 2 secrecy 3 one's private life

pri·vate (prī'vət) *adj.* ⟦< L *privus*, separate⟧ 1 of or concerning a particular person or group 2 not open to or controlled by the public /a *private* school/ 3 for an individual person /a *private* room/ 4 not holding public office /a *private* citizen/ 5 secret /a *private* matter/ —*n.* 1 [*pl.*] the genitals: also **private parts** 2 an enlisted man of either of the lowest ranks in the U.S. Army or of the lowest rank in the U.S. Marine Corps —**go private** to restore private corporate ownership by buying back publicly held stock —**in private** not publicly —**pri'vate·ly** *adv.*

pri·va·teer (prī'və tir') *n.* 1 a privately owned ship commissioned in war to capture enemy ships 2 a commander or crew member of a privateer

private eye [Slang] a private detective

pri·va·tion (prī vā'shən) *n.* the lack of ordinary necessities or comforts

pri·va·tize (prī'və tīz') *vt.* **-tized', -tiz'ing** to turn over (a public property, etc.) to private interests —**pri'va·ti·za'tion** *n.*

priv·et (priv'it) *n.* ⟦< ?⟧ an evergreen shrub used for hedges

priv·i·lege (priv'ə lij, priv'lij) *n.* ⟦< L *privus*, separate + *lex*, law⟧ a special right, favor, etc. granted to some person or group —*vt.* **-leged, -leg·ing** to grant a privilege to

priv·y (priv'ē) *adj.* private: now only in such phrases as **privy council**, a body of confidential advisers named by a ruler —*n., pl.* **priv'ies** an outhouse —**privy to** privately informed about

prize[1] (prīz) *vt.* **prized, priz'ing** ⟦see PRICE⟧ to value highly; esteem —*n.* 1 something given to the winner of a contest, etc. 2 anything worth striving for —*adj.* 1 that has won or is worthy of a prize 2 given as a prize

prize[2] (prīz) *n.* ⟦< L *prehendere*, to take⟧ something taken by force, as in war —*vt.* **prized, priz'ing** to pry, as with a lever

prize'fight' *n.* a professional boxing match —**prize'fight'er** *n.*

pro[1] (prō) *adv.* ⟦L, for⟧ favorably —*adj.* favorable —*n., pl.* **pros** 1 a person or vote on the affirmative side 2 an argument in favor of something

pro[2] (prō) *adj., n., pl.* **pros** *short for* PROFESSIONAL

pro-[1] ⟦Gr < *pro*, before⟧ *prefix* before in place or time

pro-[2] ⟦L < *pro*, forward⟧ *prefix* 1 moving forward or ahead of /*proclivity*/ 2 forth /*produce*/ 3 substituting for /*pronoun*/ 4 defending, supporting /*prolabor*/

pro-am (prō'am') *n.* a sports competition for both amateurs and professionals

prob. 1 probably 2 problem

prob·a·bil·i·ty (präb'ə bil'ə tē) *n., pl.* **-ties**

1 a being probable; likelihood 2 something probable

prob·a·ble (präb′ə bəl) ***adj.*** ⟦< L *probare,* prove⟧ 1 likely to occur or be 2 reasonably so, but not proved —**prob′a·bly** ***adv.***

pro·bate (prō′bāt) ***n.*** ⟦see PROBE⟧ the act or process of probating —***adj.*** having to do with probating */probate* court/ —***vt.*** **-bat′ed, -bat′ing** to establish officially that (a document, esp. a will) is genuine

pro·ba·tion (prō bā′shən) ***n.*** ⟦see PROBE⟧ 1 a testing, as of one's character, ability, etc. 2 the conditional suspension of a convicted person's sentence —**pro·ba′tion·ar′y** ***adj.***

pro·ba′tion·er (-ər) ***n.*** a person on probation

probation officer an officer who watches over persons on probation

probe (prōb) ***n.*** ⟦< L *probare,* to test⟧ 1 a surgical instrument for exploring a wound, etc. 2 a searching examination 3 a device, as a spacecraft with instruments, used to get information about an environment —***vt.*** **probed, prob′ing** 1 to explore (a wound, etc.) with a probe 2 to investigate thoroughly —***vi.*** to search

pro·bi·ty (prō′bə tē, präb′ə-) ***n.*** ⟦< L *probus,* good⟧ honesty; integrity

prob·lem (präb′ləm) ***n.*** ⟦< Gr *problēma*⟧ 1 a question proposed for solution 2 a perplexing or difficult matter, person, etc.

prob·lem·at·ic (präb′lə mat′ik) ***adj.*** 1 of the nature of a problem 2 uncertain Also **prob′lem·at′i·cal**

pro·bos·cis (prō bäs′is) ***n.,*** *pl.* **-cis·es** ⟦< Gr *pro-,* before + *boskein,* to feed⟧ an elephant's trunk, or any similar long, flexible snout

pro·caine (prō′kān′) ***n.*** ⟦PRO-[2] + (CO)CAINE⟧ a synthetic compound used as a local anesthetic

pro·ce·dure (prō sē′jər, prə-) ***n.*** the act or method of proceeding in an action —**pro·ce′dur·al** ***adj.***

pro·ceed (prō sēd′, prə-) ***vi.*** ⟦< L *pro-,* forward + *cedere,* go⟧ 1 to go on, esp. after stopping 2 to carry on some action 3 to take legal action (*against*) 4 to come forth or issue (*from*)

pro·ceed′ing ***n.*** 1 a going on with what one has been doing 2 a course of action 3 [*pl.*] a record of the business carried on, as by a learned society 4 [*pl.*] legal action

pro·ceeds (prō′sēdz′) ***n.pl.*** the sum derived from a sale, business venture, etc.

proc·ess (prä′ses′) ***n.*** ⟦see PROCEED⟧ 1 the course of being done: chiefly in **in process** 2 course (*of* time, etc.) 3 a continuing development involving many changes /the *process* of digestion/ 4 a method of doing something, with all the steps involved 5 *Biol.* a projecting part 6 *Law* a court summons —***vt.*** to prepare by or subject to a special process —**pro′cess·or** ***n.***

pro·ces·sion (prō sesh′ən, prə-) ***n.*** ⟦see PROCEED⟧ a number of persons or things moving forward, as in a parade

pro·ces′sion·al ***n.*** a hymn sung at the beginning of a church service during the entrance of the clergy

pro′-choice′ ***adj.*** advocating the right to legal abortion —**pro′-choic′er** ***n.***

pro·claim (prō klām′) ***vt.*** ⟦< L *pro-,* before + *clamare,* cry out⟧ to announce officially; announce to be

proc·la·ma·tion (präk′lə mā′shən) ***n.*** 1 a proclaiming 2 something that is proclaimed

pro·cliv·i·ty (prō kliv′ə tē) ***n.,*** *pl.* **-ties** ⟦< L *pro-,* before + *clivus,* a slope⟧ a tendency or inclination

pro·cras·ti·nate (prō kras′tə nāt′, prə-) ***vi., vt.*** **-nat′ed, -nat′ing** ⟦< L *pro-,* forward + *cras,* tomorrow⟧ to put off doing (something) until later; delay —**pro·cras′ti·na′tion** ***n.*** —**pro·cras′ti·na′tor** ***n.***

pro·cre·ate (prō′krē āt′) ***vt., vi.*** **-at′ed, -at′ing** ⟦< L *pro-,* before + *creare,* create⟧ to produce (young); beget (offspring) —**pro′cre·a′tion** ***n.***

proc·tor (präk′tər) ***n.*** ⟦see PROCURE⟧ one who supervises or monitors students, as at an examination —***vt.*** to supervise (an academic examination)

proc·u·ra·tor (präk′yoo rāt′ər, -yə-) ***n.*** ⟦see fol.⟧ in the Roman Empire, the governor of a lesser province

pro·cure (prō kyoor′) ***vt.*** **-cured′, -cur′ing** ⟦< L *pro-,* before + *curare,* attend to⟧ to obtain; get —**pro·cur′a·ble** ***adj.*** —**pro·cure′ment** ***n.***

pro·cur′er ***n.*** a pimp

prod (präd) ***vt.*** **prod′ded, prod′ding** ⟦< ?⟧ 1 to jab as with a pointed stick 2 to goad into action —***n.*** 1 a jab or thrust 2 something that prods

prod·i·gal (präd′i gəl) ***adj.*** ⟦< L *pro-,* forth + *agere,* to drive⟧ 1 exceedingly or recklessly wasteful 2 extremely abundant —***n.*** a spendthrift —**prod′i·gal′i·ty** (-gal′ə tē), *pl.* **-ties,** ***n.***

pro·di·gious (prō dij′əs, prə-) ***adj.*** ⟦see fol.⟧ 1 wonderful; amazing 2 enormous —**pro·di′gious·ly** ***adv.***

prod·i·gy (präd′ə jē) ***n.,*** *pl.* **-gies** ⟦< L *prodigium,* omen⟧ an extraordinary person, thing, or act; specif., a child of genius

pro·duce (prō do͞os′; *for n.* prä′do͞os′, prō′-) ***vt.*** **-duced′, -duc′ing** ⟦< L *pro-,* forward + *ducere,* to lead⟧ 1 to bring to view; show /to *produce* identification/ 2 to bring forth; bear 3 to make or manufacture 4 to cause 5 to get (a play, etc.) ready for presentation —***vi.*** to yield something —***n.*** something produced; esp., fruit and vegetables —**pro·duc′er** ***n.***

prod·uct (präd′ukt′, -əkt) ***n.*** 1 something produced by nature, industry, or art 2 result; outgrowth 3 *Math.* the quantity obtained by multiplying two or more quantities together

pro·duc·tion (prō duk′shən, prə-) ***n.*** a producing or something produced

pro·duc′tive ***adj.*** 1 fertile 2 marked by abundant production 3 bringing as a result (with *of*) /war is *productive* of misery/ —**pro·duc′tive·ly** ***adv.*** —**pro·duc·tiv·i·ty** (prō′dək tiv′ə tē) or **pro·duc′tive·ness** ***n.***

prof (präf) ***n.*** [Colloq.] *short for* PROFESSOR

Prof. Professor

pro·fane (prō fān′, prə-) ***adj.*** ⟦< L *pro-,* before + *fanum,* temple⟧ 1 not connected with religion; secular 2 showing disrespect or contempt for sacred things —***vt.*** **-faned′, -fan′ing** 1 to treat (sacred things) with irreverence or contempt 2 to debase; defile

—**prof·a·na·tion** (präf'ə nā'shən) ***n.*** —**pro·fane'ly** ***adv.*** —**pro·fane'ness** ***n.***

pro·fan'i·ty (-fan'ə tē) ***n.*** **1** a being profane **2** *pl.* **-ties** profane language; swearing

pro·fess (prō fes', prə-) ***vt.*** [[< L *pro-*, before + *fateri*, avow]] **1** to declare openly; affirm **2** to claim to have (some feeling, etc.): often insincerely **3** to declare one's belief in —**pro·fessed'** ***adj.***

pro·fes·sion (prō fesh'ən, prə-) ***n.*** **1** a professing, or declaring; avowal **2** an occupation requiring advanced academic training, as medicine, law, etc. **3** all the persons in such an occupation

pro·fes'sion·al ***adj.*** **1** of or engaged in a profession **2** engaged in some sport or in a specified occupation for pay —***n.*** a person who is professional (esp. in sense 2) —**pro·fes'sion·al·ly** ***adv.***

pro·fes·sor (prō fes'ər, prə-) ***n.*** **1** a college or university teacher of the highest rank **2** loosely, a teacher —**pro·fes·so·ri·al** (prō'fə sôr'ē əl) ***adj.*** —**pro·fes'sor·ship'** ***n.***

prof·fer (präf'ər) ***vt.*** [[< OFr: see PRO-[2] & OFFER]] to offer (usually something intangible) /to *proffer* friendship/ —***n.*** an offer

pro·fi·cient (prō fish'ənt, prə-) ***adj.*** [[< L *pro-*, forward + *facere*, make]] highly competent; skilled —**pro·fi'cien·cy** ***n.*** —**pro·fi'cient·ly** ***adv.***

pro·file (prō'fīl') ***n.*** [[< It *profilare*, to outline]] **1** a side view of the face **2** a drawing of this **3** an outline **4** a short, vivid biography

prof·it (präf'it) ***n.*** [[see PROFICIENT]] **1** advantage; gain **2** [*often pl.*] financial gain; esp. the sum remaining after deducting costs —***vt., vi.*** **1** to be of advantage (to) **2** to benefit —**prof'it·a·ble** ***adj.*** —**prof'it·a·bly** ***adv.*** —**prof'it·less** ***adj.***

prof·it·eer (präf'i tir') ***n.*** one who makes excessive profits by charging exorbitant prices —***vi.*** to be a profiteer

pro·fi·te·role (prə fit'ə rōl') ***n.*** a small cream puff, variously filled

prof·li·gate (präf'li git) ***adj.*** [[< L *pro-*, forward + *fligere*, to drive]] **1** dissolute **2** recklessly wasteful —**prof'li·ga·cy** (-gə sē) ***n.***

pro for·ma (prō fôr'mə) [[L]] for (the sake of) form; as a matter of form

pro·found (prō found', prə-) ***adj.*** [[< L *pro-*, forward + *fundus*, bottom]] **1** very deep /a *profound* sigh, sleep, etc./ **2** marked by intellectual depth **3** deeply felt /*profound* grief/ **4** thoroughgoing /*profound* changes/ —**pro·found'ly** ***adv.*** —**pro·fun'di·ty** (-fun'də tē), *pl.* **-ties,** ***n.***

pro·fuse (prō fyōōs', prə-) ***adj.*** [[< L *pro-*, forth + *fundere*, pour]] giving or given freely and abundantly —**pro·fuse'ly** ***adv.*** —**pro·fu'sion** (-fyōō'zhən) ***n.***

pro·gen·i·tor (prō jen'ə tər) ***n.*** [[< L *pro-*, forth + *gignere*, beget]] **1** an ancestor in direct line **2** a precursor

prog·e·ny (präj'ə nē) ***n.***, *pl.* **-nies** [[see prec.]] children; offspring

pro·ges·ter·one (prō jes'tər ōn') ***n.*** a female hormone secreted by the ovary or prepared synthetically

prog·na·thous (präg'nə thəs) ***adj.*** [[PRO-[1] + Gr *gnathos*, jaw]] having the jaws projecting beyond the upper face

prog·no·sis (präg nō'sis) ***n.***, *pl.* **-no'ses'** (-sēz') [[< Gr *pro-*, before + *gignōskein*, know]] a prediction, esp. of the course of a disease

prog'nos'tic (-näs'tik) ***n.*** [[see prec.]] **1** an omen **2** a prediction —***adj.*** foretelling

prog·nos'ti·cate' (-näs'ti kāt') ***vt.*** **-cat'ed, -cat'ing** [[see PROGNOSIS]] to foretell —**prog·nos'ti·ca'tion** ***n.*** —**prog·nos'ti·ca'tor** ***n.***

pro·gram (prō'gram', -grəm) ***n.*** [[< Gr *pro-*, before + *graphein*, write]] **1** a list of the acts, speeches, musical pieces, etc. as of an entertainment **2** a plan or procedure **3** a scheduled radio or TV broadcast **4** a logical sequence of coded instructions specifying the operations to be performed by a computer **5** a series of operations used to control an electronic device —***vt.*** **-grammed'** or **-gramed', -gram'ming** or **-gram'ing** **1** to schedule in a program **2** to prepare (a textbook, etc.) for use in programmed instruction **3** to plan a computer program for **4** to furnish (a computer) with a program Chiefly Brit., etc. sp. **pro'gramme** —**pro·gram·ma·ble** (prō'gram'ə bəl, prō gram'-) ***adj., n.*** —**pro'gram·mer** or **pro'gram·er** ***n.***

pro·gram·mat·ic (prō'grə mat'ik) ***adj.*** of or like a program; specif., predictable, mechanical, uninspired, etc.

programmed instruction instruction in which individual students answer questions about a unit of study at their own rate, checking their own answers and advancing only after answering correctly Also **programmed learning**

prog·ress (präg'res; *for v.* prō gres', prə-) ***n.*** [[< L *pro-*, before + *gradi*, to step]] **1** a moving forward or onward **2** development **3** improvement —***vi.*** **1** to move forward or onward **2** to move forward toward completion **3** to improve

pro·gres·sion (prō gresh'ən, prə-) ***n.*** **1** a moving forward **2** a succession, as of events **3** *Math.* a series of numbers increasing or decreasing by a constant difference between terms

pro·gres'sive (-gres'iv, prə-) ***adj.*** **1** moving forward **2** continuing by successive steps **3** of or favoring progress, reform, etc. **4** *Gram.* indicating continuing action or state, as certain verb forms —***n.*** one who is progressive —**pro·gres'sive·ly** ***adv.***

pro·hib·it (prō hib'it, prə-) ***vt.*** [[< L *pro-*, before + *habere*, have]] **1** to forbid by law or an order **2** to prevent; hinder —**pro·hib'i·tive** or **pro·hib'i·to'ry** ***adj.***

pro·hi·bi·tion (prō'i bish'ən) ***n.*** **1** a prohibiting **2** the forbidding by law of the manufacture or sale of alcoholic beverages —**pro'hi·bi'tion·ist** ***n.***

proj·ect (prä'jekt'; *for v.* prō jekt', prə-) ***n.*** [[< L *pro-*, before + *jacere*, to throw]] **1** a proposal; scheme **2** an organized undertaking —***vt.*** **pro·ject'** **1** to propose (a plan) **2** to throw forward **3** to cause to jut out **4** to cause (a shadow, image, etc.) to fall upon a surface —***vi.*** to jut out —**pro·jec'tion** ***n.***

pro·jec·tile (prō jek'təl, prə-) ***n.*** **1** an object designed to be shot forward, as a bullet **2** anything thrown or hurled forward

projection booth a small chamber, as in a theater, from which images on film, slides, etc. are projected

pro·jec′tion·ist *n.* the operator of a film or slide projector

pro·jec′tor *n.* a machine for projecting images on a screen

pro·le·tar·i·at (prō′lə ter′ē ət) *n.* ⟦< L *proletarius*, a citizen of the lowest class⟧ the working class; esp., the industrial working class —**pro′le·tar′i·an** *adj.*, *n.*

pro′-life′ *adj.* opposing the right to legal abortion —**pro′-lif′er** *n.*

pro·lif·er·ate (prō lif′ər āt′, prə-) *vi.* **-at′ed, -at′ing** ⟦< L *proles*, offspring + *ferre*, to bear⟧ to increase rapidly —**pro·lif′er·a′·tion** *n.*

pro·lif·ic (prō lif′ik, prə-) *adj.* ⟦< L *proles*, offspring + *facere*, make⟧ 1 producing many young or much fruit 2 turning out many products of the mind —**pro·lif′i·cal·ly** *adv.*

pro·lix (prō liks′) *adj.* ⟦< L *prolixus*, extended⟧ wordy or long-winded —**pro·lix′i·ty** *n.* —**pro·lix′ly** *adv.*

pro·logue (prō′lôg′) *n.* ⟦< Gr *pro-*, before + *logos*, discourse⟧ 1 an introduction to a poem, play, etc. 2 any preliminary act, event, etc.

pro·long (prō lôŋ′, prə-) *vt.* ⟦< L *pro-*, forth + *longus*, long⟧ to lengthen in time or space Also **pro·lon′gate′** (-gāt′), **-gat′ed, -gat′ing** —**pro·lon·ga·tion** (prō′lôŋ gā′shən) *n.*

prom (präm) *n.* ⟦< fol.⟧ a dance, as of a particular school class

prom·e·nade (präm′ə nād′, -näd′) *n.* ⟦Fr < L *pro-*, forth + *minare*, to herd⟧ 1 a leisurely walk taken for pleasure, display, etc. 2 a public place for walking 3 a ball or dance —*vi.*, *vt.* **-nad′ed, -nad′ing** to take a promenade along or through

Pro·me·the·us (prō mē′thē əs) *Gr. Myth.* a Titan who steals fire from heaven for the benefit of mankind

prom·i·nent (präm′ə nənt) *adj.* ⟦< L *prominere*, to project⟧ 1 sticking out; projecting 2 noticeable; conspicuous 3 widely and favorably known —**prom′i·nence** *n.* —**prom′i·nent·ly** *adv.*

pro·mis·cu·ous (prō mis′kyo͞o əs, prə-) *adj.* ⟦< L *pro-*, forth + *miscere*, to mix⟧ 1 consisting of different elements indiscriminately mingled 2 characterized by a lack of discrimination, esp. in sexual liaisons —**prom·is·cu·i·ty** (präm′is kyo͞o′ə tē), *pl.* **-ties**, *n.* —**pro·mis′cu·ous·ly** *adv.*

prom·ise (präm′is) *n.* ⟦< L *pro-*, forth + *mittere*, send⟧ 1 an agreement to do or not to do something 2 indication, as of a successful future 3 something promised —*vi.*, *vt.* **-ised, -is·ing** 1 to make a promise of (something) 2 to give a basis for expecting

Promised Land *Bible* Canaan, promised by God to Abraham and his descendants: Genesis 17:8

prom·is·so·ry (präm′i sôr′ē) *adj.* containing a promise

pro·mo (prō′mō) *adj.* [Colloq.] of or engaged in the promotion or advertisement of a product, etc. —*n.*, *pl.* **-mos** [Colloq.] a recorded announcement, radio or TV commercial, etc. used in advertising, etc.

prom·on·to·ry (präm′ən tôr′ē) *n.*, *pl.* **-ries** ⟦prob. < L *prominere*, to project⟧ a peak of high land that juts out into a body of water; headland

pro·mote (prō mōt′, prə-) *vt.* **-mot′ed, -mot′·ing** ⟦< L *pro-*, forward + *movere*, to move⟧ 1 to raise to a higher position or rank 2 to further the growth, establishment, sales, etc. of —**pro·mo′tion** *n.* —**pro·mo′tion·al** *adj.*

pro·mot′er *n.* one who begins, organizes, and furthers an undertaking

prompt (prämpt) *adj.* ⟦< L *pro-*, forth + *emere*, take⟧ 1 ready, punctual, etc. 2 done, spoken, etc. without delay —*vt.* 1 to urge into action 2 to remind (a person) of something he or she has forgotten; specif., to help (an actor, etc.) with a cue 3 to inspire —**prompt′er** *n.* —**prompt′ly** *adv.* —**prompt′ness** or **promp′ti·tude′** *n.*

prom·ul·gate (präm′əl gāt′, prō mul′gāt′) *vt.* **-gat′ed, -gat′ing** ⟦< L *promulgare*, publish⟧ 1 to make known officially 2 to make widespread —**prom′ul·ga′tion** *n.*

pron. 1 pronoun 2 pronunciation

prone (prōn) *adj.* ⟦< L *pronus*⟧ 1 lying face downward or prostrate 2 disposed or inclined (*to*) /*prone* to error/

prong (prôŋ) *n.* ⟦ME *pronge*⟧ 1 any of the pointed ends of a fork; tine 2 any projecting part —**pronged** *adj.*

prong′horn′ *n.* a deerlike animal of the W U.S., having curved horns: it also resembles the antelope

pro·noun (prō′noun′) *n.* ⟦< L *pro*, for + *nomen*, noun⟧ *Gram.* a word used in place of a noun (Ex.: *I, he, it*, etc.) —**pro·nom′i·nal** (-näm′i nəl) *adj.*

pro·nounce (prō nouns′, prə-) *vt.* **-nounced′, -nounc′ing** ⟦< L *pro-*, before + *nuntiare*, announce⟧ 1 to declare officially, solemnly, etc. /to *pronounce* a couple man and wife/ 2 utter or articulate (a sound or word) —**pro·nounce′a·ble** *adj.*

pro·nounced′ *adj.* clearly marked; decided /a *pronounced* change/

pro·nounce′ment *n.* a formal statement, as of an opinion

pron·to (prän′tō) *adv.* ⟦Sp: see PROMPT⟧ [Slang] at once; quickly

pro·nun·ci·a·tion (prō nun′sē ā′shən, prə-) *n.* 1 the act or manner of pronouncing words 2 the way a word is usually pronounced, esp. in phonetic symbols

proof (pro͞of) *n.* ⟦see PROBE⟧ 1 a proving or testing of something 2 evidence that establishes the truth of something 3 the relative strength of an alcoholic liquor 4 *Photog.* a trial print of a negative 5 a sheet printed from set type, for checking errors, etc. —*adj.* of tested strength in resisting: with *against*

-proof (pro͞of) ⟦< prec.⟧ *combining form* 1 impervious to /*waterproof*/ 2 protected from /*rustproof*/ 3 resistant to /*fireproof*/

proof′read′ *vt.*, *vi.* to read and mark corrections on (printers' proofs, etc.) —**proof′·read′er** *n.*

prop[1] (präp) *n.* ⟦< MDu *proppe*⟧ a support, as a pole, placed under or against something: often used figuratively —*vt.* **propped, prop′ping** 1 to support, as with

a prop: often with *up* 2 to lean (something) *against* a support
prop[2] (präp) *n.* PROPERTY (sense 4)
prop[3] (präp) *n. short for* PROPELLER
prop. 1 proper(ly) 2 property 3 proposition 4 proprietor
prop·a·gan·da (präp'ə gan'də) *n.* ⟦ModL. see fol.⟧ 1 any widespread promotion of particular ideas, doctrines, etc. 2 ideas, etc. so spread —**prop'a·gan'dist** *n., adj.* —**prop'a·gan'dize** (-dīz') *vt., vi.*
prop·a·gate (präp'ə gāt') *vt.* **-gat'ed, -gat'ing** ⟦< L *propago,* slip (of a plant)⟧ 1 to cause (a plant or animal) to reproduce itself 2 to reproduce (itself): said of a plant or animal 3 to spread (ideas, customs, etc.) —*vi.* to reproduce, as plants or animals —**prop'a·ga'tion** *n.*
pro·pane (prō'pān') *n.* a gaseous hydrocarbon from petroleum, used as a fuel
pro·pel (prō pel', prə-) *vt.* **-pelled', -pel'ling** ⟦< L *pro-,* forward + *pellere,* drive⟧ to drive onward or forward
pro·pel'lant or **pro·pel'lent** *n.* one that propels; specif., the fuel for a rocket
pro·pel'ler *n.* a device having two or more blades in a revolving hub, for propelling a ship or aircraft
pro·pen·si·ty (prə pen'sə tē) *n., pl.* **-ties** ⟦< L *propendere,* hang forward⟧ a natural inclination or tendency
prop·er (präp'ər) *adj.* ⟦< L *proprius,* one's own⟧ 1 specially suitable; appropriate; fitting 2 naturally belonging (*to*) 3 conforming to a standard; correct 4 decent; decorous 5 in the most restricted sense /Chicago *proper* (i.e., apart from its suburbs)/ 6 designating a noun that names a specific individual, place, etc. (Ex.: *Bill, Paris*) —**prop'er·ly** *adv.*
prop·er·ty (präp'ər tē) *n., pl.* **-ties** ⟦see prec.⟧ 1 ownership 2 something owned, esp. real estate 3 a characteristic or attribute 4 any of the movable articles used in a stage setting —**prop'er·tied** (-tēd) *adj.*
proph·e·cy (präf'ə sē) *n., pl.* **-cies** ⟦see PROPHET⟧ 1 prediction of the future 2 something predicted
proph'e·sy' (-sī') *vt., vi.* **-sied', -sy'ing** 1 to predict as by divine guidance 2 to predict in any way
proph·et (präf'ət, -it) *n.* ⟦< Gr *pro-,* before + *phanai,* speak⟧ 1 a religious leader regarded as, or claiming to be, divinely inspired 2 one who predicts the future —**proph'et·ess** *n.fem.*
pro·phet·ic (prō fet'ik, prə-) *adj.* 1 of or like a prophet 2 like or containing a prophecy —**pro·phet'i·cal·ly** *adv.*
pro·phy·lac·tic (prō'fə lak'tik) *adj.* ⟦< Gr *pro-,* before + *phylassein,* to guard⟧ preventive or protective; esp., preventing disease —*n.* a prophylactic medicine, device, etc.
pro'phy·lax'is (-laks'is) *n., pl.* **-lax'es'** (-ēz') prophylactic treatment; specif., in dentistry, a cleaning of the teeth to remove plaque and tartar
pro·pin·qui·ty (prō piŋ'kwə tē) *n.* ⟦< L *propinquus,* near⟧ nearness
pro·pi·ti·ate (prō pish'ē āt', prə-) *vt.* **-at'ed, -at'ing** ⟦see fol.⟧ to win the good will of; appease —**pro·pi'ti·a'tion** *n.* —**pro·pi'ti·a·to'ry** (-ē ə tôr'ē) *adj.*
pro·pi·tious (prō pish'əs, prə-) *adj.* ⟦< L *pro-,* before + *petere,* seek⟧ 1 favorably inclined 2 favorable; auspicious
pro·po·nent (prō pō'nənt, prə-) *n.* ⟦see PROPOSE⟧ one who espouses or supports a cause, etc.
pro·por·tion (prō pôr'shən, prə-) *n.* ⟦< L *pro,* for + *portio,* a part⟧ 1 the comparative relation in size, amount, etc. between things; ratio 2 a part, share, etc. in its relation to the whole 3 balance or symmetry 4 [*pl.*] dimensions —*vt.* 1 to put in proper relation with something else 2 to arrange the parts of (a whole) so as to be harmonious —**pro·por'tion·al** or **pro·por'tion·ate** (-shə nit) *adj.*
pro·pos·al (prō pōz'əl, prə-) *n.* 1 a proposing 2 a proposed plan, etc. 3 an offer of marriage
pro·pose (prō pōz', prə-) *vt.* **-posed', -pos'ing** ⟦< L *pro-,* forth + *ponere,* to place⟧ 1 to put forth for consideration, approval, etc. 2 to plan or intend 3 to present as a toast in drinking —*vi.* to offer marriage
prop·o·si·tion (präp'ə zish'ən) *n.* 1 something proposed; plan 2 [Colloq.] a proposed deal, as in business 3 [Colloq.] an undertaking, etc. to be dealt with 4 a subject to be discussed 5 *Math.* a problem to be solved
pro·pound (prō pound', prə-) *vt.* ⟦see PROPOSE⟧ to put forward for consideration
pro·pri·e·tar·y (prō prī'ə ter ē, prə-) *adj.* ⟦see PROPERTY⟧ belonging to a proprietor, as under a patent or copyright
pro·pri'e·tor *n.* an owner —**pro·pri'e·tor·ship'** *n.* —**pro·pri'e·tress** (-tris) *n.fem.*
pro·pri'e·ty (-ə tē) *n., pl.* **-ties** ⟦see PROPER⟧ 1 the quality of being proper, fitting, etc. 2 conformity with accepted standards of behavior
pro·pul·sion (prō pul'shən, prə-) *n.* ⟦see PROPEL⟧ 1 a propelling or being propelled 2 something that propels —**pro·pul'sive** *adj.*
pro·rate (prō rāt', prō'rāt') *vt., vi.* **-rat'ed, -rat'ing** ⟦< L *pro rata,* in proportion⟧ to divide or assess proportionally
pro·sa·ic (prō zā'ik) *adj.* ⟦< L *prosa,* prose⟧ commonplace; dull
pro·sce·ni·um (prō sē'nē əm) *n., pl.* **-ni·ums** or **-ni·a** (-ə) ⟦< Gr *pro-,* before + *skēnē,* tent⟧ the plane separating the stage proper from the audience and including the arch (**proscenium arch**) and the curtain within it
pro·scribe (prō skrīb') *vt.* **-scribed', -scrib'ing** ⟦< L < *pro-,* before + *scribere,* write⟧ 1 to outlaw 2 to banish; exile 3 to denounce or forbid the use, etc. of —**pro·scrip'tion** (-skrip'shən) *n.*
prose (prōz) *n.* ⟦< L *prorsus,* straight on⟧ ordinary language; not poetry
pros·e·cute (präs'i kyōōt') *vt.* **-cut'ed, -cut'ing** ⟦< L *pro-,* before + *sequi,* follow⟧ 1 to carry on 2 to conduct legal action against —**pros'e·cu'tion** *n.* —**pros'e·cu'tor** *n.*
pros·e·lyte (präs'ə līt') *n.* ⟦< Gr *prosēlytos,* a stranger⟧ one who has been converted from one religion, sect, etc. to another —*vt., vi.* **-lyt'ed, -lyt'ing** to try to make a convert (of)

pros·e·lyt·ize (präs′ə li tīz) *vi., vt.* **-ized′, -iz′ing** PROSELYTE —**pros′e·lyt·ism′** (-li tiz′əm) *n.* —**pros′e·lyt·iz′er** *n.*

pro·sim·i·an (prō sim′ē ən) *n.* any of various small, arboreal primates

pros·o·dy (präs′ə dē) *n., pl.* **-dies** ⟦< Gr *prosōidia,* accent⟧ versification; study of meter, rhyme, etc.

pros·pect (prä′spekt′) *n.* ⟦< L *pro-,* forward + *specere,* look⟧ **1** a broad view; scene **2** viewpoint; outlook **3** anticipation **4** *a)* something expected *b)* [*usually pl.*] apparent chance for success **5** a likely customer, candidate, etc. —*vt., vi.* to explore or search (*for* gold, etc.) —**pros′pec′tor** *n.*

pro·spec·tive (prō spek′tiv, prə-) *adj.* expected; likely

pro·spec·tus (prō spek′təs, prə-) *n.* ⟦L: see PROSPECT⟧ a statement of the features of a new work, enterprise, etc.

pros·per (präs′pər) *vi.* ⟦< L *prospere,* fortunately⟧ to succeed; thrive

pros·per·i·ty (prä sper′ə tē) *n., pl.* **-ties** prosperous condition; wealth

pros·per·ous (präs′pər əs) *adj.* **1** prospering; successful **2** wealthy **3** favorable —**pros′per·ous·ly** *adv.*

pros·tate (präs′tāt′) *adj.* ⟦< Gr *prostatēs,* one standing before⟧ of or designating a gland surrounding the male urethra at the base of the bladder

pros·the·sis (präs′thə sis, präs thē′-) *n., pl.* **-ses′** (-sēz′) *Med.* **1** the replacement of a missing part of the body, as a limb, by an artificial substitute **2** such a substitute —**pros·thet′ic** (-thet′ik) *adj.*

pros·ti·tute (präs′tə to͞ot′) *n.* ⟦< L *pro-,* before + *statuere,* cause to stand⟧ one who engages in promiscuous sexual activity for pay —*vt.* **-tut′ed, -tut′ing** **1** to offer (oneself) as a prostitute **2** to sell (oneself, one's talents, etc.) for base purposes —**pros′ti·tu′tion** *n.*

pros·trate (präs′trāt′) *adj.* ⟦< L *pro-,* before + *sternere,* stretch out⟧ **1** lying face downward **2** lying prone or supine **3** laid low; overcome —*vt.* **-trat′ed, -trat′ing** **1** to lay flat on the ground **2** to lay low; subjugate —**pros·tra′tion** *n.*

pros·y (prō′zē) *adj.* **-i·er, -i·est** prosaic; commonplace, dull, etc.

pro·tag·o·nist (prō tag′ə nist) *n.* ⟦< Gr *prōtos,* first + *agōnistēs,* actor⟧ the main character in a drama, novel, etc.

pro·te·an (prōt′ē ən; *also* prō tē′ən) *adj.* ⟦after *Proteus,* Gr god who changes his form at will⟧ readily taking on many forms

pro·tect (prō tekt′, prə-) *vt.* ⟦< L *pro-,* before + *tegere,* to cover⟧ to shield from injury, danger, etc.; defend —**pro·tec′tor** *n.*

pro·tec′tion *n.* **1** a protecting or being protected **2** a person or thing that protects

pro·tec′tive *adj.* **1** protecting **2** *Economics* intended to protect domestic industry from foreign competition [a *protective* tariff] —**pro·tec′tive·ly** *adv.* —**pro·tec′tive·ness** *n.*

pro·tec′tor·ate (-tek′tər it) *n.* a weak state under the protection and control of a strong state

pro·té·gé (prōt′ə zhā′) *n.* ⟦Fr: see PROTECT⟧ a person guided and helped in his career by another person

pro·te·in (prō′tēn′, prō′tē in) *n.* ⟦< Gr *prōtos,* first⟧ any of numerous nitrogenous substances occurring in all living matter and essential to diet

pro tem·po·re (prō tem′pə rē′) ⟦L⟧ for the time (being); temporarily Shortened to **pro tem**

pro·test (prō test′, prə-; *for n.,* prō′test′) *vt.* ⟦< L *pro-,* forth + *testari,* affirm⟧ **1** to state positively **2** to speak strongly against —*vi.* to express disapproval; object —*n.* **1** an objection **2** a formal statement of objection —**prot·es·ta·tion** (prät′es tā′shən) *n.*

Prot·es·tant (prät′əs tənt) *n.* ⟦see prec.⟧ any Christian not belonging to the Roman Catholic or Eastern Orthodox Church —**Prot′es·tant·ism′** *n.*

proto- ⟦< Gr *prōtos,* first⟧ *combining form* **1** first in time, original **2** first in importance, chief

pro·to·col (prōt′ō kôl′, prōt′ə-) *n.* ⟦< Gr *prōtokollon,* contents page⟧ **1** an original draft of a document, etc. **2** the ceremonial forms accepted as correct in official dealings, as between heads of states or diplomatic officials

pro·ton (prō′tän′) *n.* ⟦< Gr *prōtos,* first⟧ an elementary particle in the nucleus of all atoms, carrying a unit positive charge of electricity

pro·to·plasm (prōt′ō plaz′əm, prōt′ə-) *n.* ⟦see PROTO- & PLASMA⟧ a semifluid viscous colloid, the essential living matter of all animal and plant cells —**pro′to·plas′mic** (-plaz′mik) *adj.*

pro·to·type (prōt′ō tīp′, prōt′ə-) *n.* the first thing or being of its kind; model

pro·to·zo·an (prōt′ō zō′ən, prōt′ə-) *n.* ⟦< Gr *protos,* first + *zōion,* an animal⟧ *pl.* **-zo′a** (-ə) any of various, mostly microscopic, single-celled animals Also **pro′to·zo′on′** (-än′), *pl.* **-zo′a** (-ə)

pro·tract (prō trakt′, prə-) *vt.* ⟦< L *pro-,* forward + *trahere,* draw⟧ to draw out; prolong —**pro·trac′tion** *n.*

pro′trac′tor *n.* a graduated semicircular instrument for plotting and measuring angles

pro·trude (prō tro͞od′, prə-) *vt., vi.* **-trud′ed, -trud′ing** ⟦< L *pro-,* forth + *trudere,* to thrust⟧ to jut out; project —**pro·tru′sion** (-tro͞o′zhən) *n.*

pro·tru′sile (-tro͞o′səl) *adj.* that can be protruded, or thrust out Also **pro·trac′tile** (-trak′təl)

pro·tu·ber·ance (prō to͞o′bər əns, prə-) *n.* a part or thing that protrudes; bulge —**pro·tu′ber·ant** *adj.*

proud (proud) *adj.* ⟦< LL *prode,* beneficial⟧ **1** having a proper pride in oneself **2** arrogant; haughty **3** feeling great pride or joy **4** that is a cause of pride **5** caused by pride **6** stately; splendid [a *proud* fleet] —**proud of** highly pleased with —**proud′ly** *adv.*

proud flesh ⟦from the notion of swelling up⟧ an abnormal growth of flesh around a healing wound

Proust (pro͞ost), **Mar·cel** (mär sel′) 1871-1922; Fr. novelist

prove (pro͞ov) *vt.* **proved, proved** or **prov′en, prov′ing** ⟦< L *probare,* to test⟧

1 to test by experiment, a standard, etc. 2 to establish as true —*vi.* to be found by experience or trial —**prov'a·bil'i·ty** *n.* —**prov'a·ble** *adj.*

prov·e·nance (präv'ə nəns) *n.* ⟦< L *provenire*, come forth⟧ origin; source Also **pro·ve·ni·ence** (prō vē' nē əns)

Pro·ven·çal (prō'vän säl', -vən-; präv'ən-) *n.* the vernacular of S France, a Romance language of literary importance in the Middle Ages

prov·en·der (präv'ən dər) *n.* ⟦< L *praebere*, give⟧ 1 dry food for livestock 2 [Colloq.] food

prov·erb (präv'ʉrb') *n.* ⟦< L *pro-*, PRO-[2] + *verbum*, word⟧ a short, popular saying expressing an obvious truth —**pro·ver·bi·al** (prō vʉr'bē əl) *adj.*

Prov'erbs' a book of the Bible containing maxims

pro·vide (prō vīd') *vt.* **-vid'ed, -vid'ing** ⟦< L *pro-*, PRO-[2] + *videre*, see⟧ 1 to make available; supply 2 to furnish with 3 to stipulate —*vi.* 1 to prepare (*for* or *against* a possible situation, etc.) 2 to furnish support (*for*) —**pro·vid'er** *n.*

pro·vid'ed or **pro·vid'ing** *conj.* on the condition or understanding (*that*)

prov·i·dence (präv'ə dəns) *n.* 1 provident management 2 the benevolent guidance of God or nature —[P-] God

Prov·i·dence (präv'ə dəns) capital of R.I.: pop. 157,000

prov'i·dent *adj.* ⟦see PROVIDE⟧ 1 providing for the future 2 prudent or economical —**prov'i·dent·ly** *adv.*

prov'i·den'tial (-den'shəl) *adj.* of, by, or as if decreed by divine providence —**prov'i·den'tial·ly** *adv.*

prov·ince (präv'ins) *n.* ⟦< L *provincia*⟧ 1 an administrative division of a country; specif., of Canada 2 *a)* a district; territory *b)* [*pl.*] the parts of a country removed from the major cities 3 range of duties or work; sphere

pro·vin·cial (prō vin'shəl) *adj.* 1 of the provinces 2 having the ways, speech, etc. of a certain province 3 countrylike; rustic 4 narrow; limited —**pro·vin'cial·ism'** *n.*

proving ground a place for testing new equipment, new theories, etc.

pro·vi·sion (prō vizh'ən) *n.* 1 a providing or preparing 2 something provided for the future 3 [*pl.*] a stock of food 4 a stipulation; proviso —*vt.* to supply with provisions

pro·vi'sion·al *adj.* temporary —**pro·vi'sion·al·ly** *adv.*

pro·vi·so (prō vī'zō') *n., pl.* **-sos'** or **-soes'** ⟦see PROVIDE⟧ a condition or stipulation, or a clause making one

prov·o·ca·tion (präv'ə kā'shən) *n.* 1 a provoking 2 something that provokes; incitement

pro·voc·a·tive (prō väk'ə tiv) *adj.* provoking or tending to provoke, as to action, thought, feeling, etc. —**pro·voc'a·tive·ly** *adv.*

pro·voke (prō vōk') *vt.* **-voked', -vok'ing** ⟦< L *pro-*, forth + *vocare*, to call⟧ 1 to excite to some action or feeling 2 to anger or irritate 3 to stir up (action or feeling) 4 to evoke —**pro·vok'er** *n.* —**pro·vok'ing** *adj.*

pro·vost (prō'vōst') *n.* ⟦< L *praepositus*, chief⟧ a high executive official, as in some churches or colleges

pro'vost guard (prō'vō-) a detail of military police under the command of an officer (**provost marshal**)

prow (prou) *n.* ⟦< Gr *prōira*⟧ the forward part of a ship, etc.

prow·ess (prou'is) *n.* ⟦< OFr *prouesse*⟧ 1 bravery; valor 2 superior ability, skill, etc.

prowl (proul) *vi., vt.* ⟦< ?⟧ to roam about furtively, as in search of prey or loot —*n.* a prowling —**prowl'er** *n.*

prowl car PATROL CAR

prox·im·i·ty (präks im'ə tē) *n.* ⟦< L *prope*, near⟧ nearness

prox·y (präks'ē) *n., pl.* **-ies** ⟦< ME *procuracie*, function of a procurator⟧ 1 the authority to act for another, as in voting 2 one so authorized

prude (prōōd) *n.* ⟦Fr < *prudefemme*, excellent woman⟧ one who is overly modest or proper in behavior, dress, etc. —**prud'er·y** *n.* —**prud'ish** *adj.*

pru·dent (prōōd''nt) *adj.* ⟦< L *providens*, provident⟧ 1 exercising sound judgment in practical matters 2 cautious in conduct; not rash 3 managing carefully —**pru'dence** *n.* —**pru·den·tial** (prōō den'shəl) *adj.*

prune[1] (prōōn) *n.* ⟦< Gr *proumnon*, plum⟧ a dried plum

prune[2] (prōōn) *vt.* **pruned, prun'ing** ⟦< OFr *prooignier*⟧ 1 to trim dead or living parts from (a plant) 2 to cut out (unnecessary parts, etc.)

pru·ri·ent (proor'ē ənt) *adj.* ⟦< L *prurire*, to itch⟧ tending to excite lust; lewd —**pru'ri·ence** *n.*

Prus·sia (prush'ə) former kingdom in N Europe & the dominant state of the German Empire (1871-1919) —**Prus'sian** *adj., n.*

pry[1] (prī) *n., pl.* **pries** ⟦< PRIZE[2]⟧ a lever or crowbar —*vt.* **pried, pry'ing** 1 to raise or move with a pry 2 to obtain with difficulty

pry[2] (prī) *vi.* **pried, pry'ing** ⟦< ?⟧ to look closely and inquisitively; snoop

pry'er *n.* PRIER

PS or **P.S.** 1 postscript: also **p.s.** or **ps** 2 Public School

psalm (säm) *n.* ⟦< Gr *psallein*, to pluck (a harp)⟧ 1 a sacred song or poem 2 [*usually* **P-**] any of the songs in praise of God constituting the Book of Psalms —**psalm'ist** *n.*

Psalms (sämz) a book of the Bible consisting of 150 psalms

Psal·ter (sôl'tər) ⟦< Gr *psaltērion*, a harp⟧ Psalms —*n.* [*also* **p-**] a version of the Book of Psalms for use in religious services

pseu·do (sōō'dō) *adj.* ⟦ME: see fol.⟧ sham; false; spurious

pseudo- ⟦< Gr *pseudein*, deceive⟧ *combining form* sham, counterfeit

pseu·do·nym (sōō'də nim') *n.* ⟦< Gr *pseudēs*, false + *onyma*, a name⟧ a fictitious name, esp. one assumed by an author; pen name

pshaw (shô) *interj., n.* an exclamation of impatience, disgust, etc.

psi (sē, sī) *n.* the 23d letter of the Greek alphabet (Ψ, ψ)

psit·ta·co·sis (sit'ə kō'sis) *n.* ⟦< Gr *psit-*

takos, parrot + -OSIS ⟧ a disease of birds, esp. parrots, often transmitted to humans

pso·ri·a·sis (sō rī′ə sis, sə-) ***n.*** ⟦ ult. < Gr *psōra*, an itch ⟧ a chronic skin disease characterized by scaly, reddish patches

psst (pst) ***interj.*** sound made to get another's attention quietly

PST Pacific Standard Time

psych (sīk) ***vt.*** **psyched, psych′ing** ⟦ < PSYCHOANALYZE ⟧ [Slang] **1** to outwit, overcome, etc. by psychological means: often with *out* **2** to prepare (oneself) mentally: usually with *up*

psych. psychology

psy·che (sī′kē) ***n.*** ⟦ Gr *psychē* ⟧ **1** the soul **2** the mind regarded as an entity based ultimately upon physical processes but with its own complex processes —[**P-**] *Rom. Folklore* the wife of Cupid

psy·che·del·ic (sī′kə del′ik) ***adj.*** ⟦ < prec. + Gr *dēloun*, make manifest ⟧ **1** of or causing extreme changes in the conscious mind, as hallucinations **2** of or associated with psychedelic drugs

psy·chi·a·try (sī kī′ə trē) ***n.*** ⟦ see PSYCHO- & -IATRY ⟧ the branch of medicine dealing with disorders of the mind, including psychoses and neuroses —**psy·chi·at·ric** (sī′kē a′trik) ***adj.*** —**psy′chi′a·trist** ***n.***

psy·chic (sī′kik) ***adj.*** ⟦ see PSYCHE ⟧ **1** of the psyche, or mind **2** beyond known physical processes **3** apparently sensitive to forces beyond the physical world Also **psy′chi·cal** —**psy′chi·cal·ly** ***adv.***

psy·cho (sī′kō) ***adj., n.*** [Colloq.] *short for* PSYCHOTIC, PSYCHOPATHIC, and PSYCHOPATH

psycho- ⟦ see PSYCHE ⟧ *combining form* the mind or mental processes Also **psych-**

psy·cho·a·nal·y·sis (sī′kō ə nal′ə sis) ***n.*** a method of treating some mental disorders by discovering and analyzing repressed feelings, emotional conflicts, etc. through the use of free association, dream analysis, etc. —**psy′cho·an′a·lyst** (-an′ə list) ***n.*** —**psy′cho·an′a·lyze′** (-līz′), **-lyzed′**, **-lyz′ing**, ***vt.***

psy′cho·bab′ble (-bab′əl) ***n.*** [Colloq.] talk or writing that uses psychological terms and concepts in a trite or superficial way

psy′cho·gen′ic (-jen′ik) ***adj.*** ⟦ see PSYCHO- & GENESIS ⟧ originating in the mind or caused by mental conflicts

psy·chol·o·gy (sī käl′ə jē) ***n.***, *pl.* **-gies** ⟦ see PSYCHO- & -LOGY ⟧ **1** the science dealing with the mind and with mental and emotional processes **2** the science of human and animal behavior —**psy′cho·log′i·cal** (-kə läj′i kəl) ***adj.*** —**psy·chol′o·gist** ***n.***

psy·cho·neu·ro·sis (sī′kō no͞o rō′sis) ***n.***, *pl.* **-ro′ses′** (-sēz′) NEUROSIS

psy′cho·path′ (-path′) ***n.*** ⟦ see PSYCHO- & -PATHY ⟧ one who has a severe mental disorder with antisocial behavior —**psy′cho·path′ic** ***adj.***

psy·cho·sis (sī kō′sis) ***n.***, *pl.* **-ses′** (-sēz′) ⟦ see PSYCHO- & -OSIS ⟧ a mental disorder in which the personality is seriously disorganized and contact with reality is usually impaired —**psy·chot′ic** (-kät′ik) ***adj.***

psy′cho·so·mat′ic (-sō mat′ik) ***adj.*** ⟦ PSYCHO- + SOMATIC ⟧ designating or of a physical disorder brought on, or made worse, by one's emotional state

psy′cho·ther′a·py (-ther′ə pē) ***n.*** ⟦ PSYCHO- + THERAPY ⟧ treatment of mental disorder by counseling, psychoanalysis, etc. —**psy′cho·ther′a·pist** ***n.***

pt. **1** part **2** pint(s) **3** point

Pt *Chem. symbol for* platinum

Pt. **1** Point **2** Port

PTA Parent-Teacher Association

ptar·mi·gan (tär′mi gən) ***n.*** ⟦ < Scot *tarmachan* ⟧ a grouse of northern regions

ptero- ⟦ < Gr *pteron*, wing ⟧ *combining form* feather, wing

PTERODACTYL

pter·o·dac·tyl (ter′ō dak′təl) ***n.*** ⟦ see prec. & DACTYL ⟧ an extinct flying reptile with wings of skin stretched from the hind limbs to the long digits of each forelimb

Ptol·e·my (täl′ə mē) 2d c. A.D.; Greco-Egyptian astronomer & mathematician

pto·maine (tō′mān′) ***n.*** ⟦ < Gr *ptōma*, corpse ⟧ an alkaloid substance, often poisonous, formed in decaying matter

Pu *Chem. symbol for* plutonium

pub (pub) ***n.*** ⟦ < *pub(lic house)* ⟧ [Colloq., Chiefly Brit., etc.] a bar or tavern

pu·ber·ty (pyo͞o′bər tē) ***n.*** ⟦ < L *puber*, adult ⟧ the stage of physical development when sexual reproduction first becomes possible —**pu′ber·tal** ***adj.***

pu·bes·cent (pyo͞o bes′ənt) ***adj.*** ⟦ see prec. ⟧ reaching or having reached puberty —**pu·bes′cence** ***n.***

pu′bic (-bik) ***adj.*** of or in the region of the genitals

pub·lic (pub′lik) ***adj.*** ⟦ ult. < L *populus*, the people ⟧ **1** of people as a whole **2** for the use or benefit of all /*a public park*/ **3** acting officially for the people /*a public* prosecutor/ **4** known by, open to, or available to most or all people /to make *public*, a *public* company/ —***n.*** **1** the people as a whole **2** a specific part of the people /the reading *public*/ —**in public** openly —**pub′lic·ly** ***adv.***

pub·li·can (pub′li kən) ***n.*** **1** in ancient Rome, a tax collector **2** [Brit., etc. (exc. Cdn.)] a saloonkeeper; innkeeper

pub·li·ca·tion (pub′li kā′shən) ***n.*** ⟦ see PUBLISH ⟧ **1** public notification **2** the printing and distribution of books, magazines, etc. **3** something published, as a periodical or book

public domain the condition of being free from copyright or patent

pub·li·cist (pub′lə sist) ***n.*** a person whose business is publicity

pub·lic·i·ty (pub lis′ə tē) ***n.*** **1** *a)* any information or action that brings a person, cause, etc. to public notice *b)* work concerned with such promotional matters **2** notice by the public

pub·li·cize (pub′lə sīz′) ***vt.*** **-cized′**, **-ciz′ing** to give publicity to

public relations relations of an organization, etc. with the general public as through publicity

public school 1 in the U.S., an elementary or secondary school maintained by public taxes and supervised by local authorities 2 in England, a private boarding school

public servant a government official or a civil-service employee

pub′lic-spir′it·ed *adj.* having or showing zeal for the public welfare

public utility an organization supplying water, electricity, transportation, etc. to the public

pub·lish (pub′lish) *vt.* ⟦< L *publicare*⟧ 1 to make publicly known; announce 2 to issue (a printed work) for sale —*vi.* 1 to issue books, newspapers, printed music, etc. to the public 2 to write books, etc. that are published —**pub′lish·er** *n.*

Puc·ci·ni (po͞o chē′nē), **Gia·co·mo** (jä′kō mō′) 1858-1924; It. operatic composer

puck (puk) *n.* ⟦< dial. *puck*, to strike⟧ the hard rubber disk used in ice hockey

puck·er (puk′ər) *vt.*, *vi.* ⟦< POKE²⟧ to gather into wrinkles —*n.* a wrinkle or small fold made by puckering

puck·ish (puk′ish) *adj.* ⟦after elf in a Shakespeare play⟧ mischievous

pud·ding (pood′iŋ) *n.* ⟦ME *puddyng*⟧ a soft, sweet food variously made with flour, eggs, milk, fruit, etc.

pud·dle (pud′'l) *n.* ⟦dim. < OE *pudd*, a ditch⟧ a small pool of water, esp. stagnant, spilled, or muddy water

pud′dling (-liŋ) *n.* the making of wrought iron from pig iron melted and stirred in an oxidizing atmosphere

pudg·y (puj′ē) *adj.* **-i·er, -i·est** ⟦< Scot *pud*, belly⟧ short and fat

pueb·lo (pweb′lō) *n.*, *pl.* **-los′** (-lōz′) or **-lo** ⟦Sp < L *populus*, people⟧ an Amerindian communal village, as in SW U.S., of terraced adobe dwellings

pu·er·ile (pyo͞o′ər il) *adj.* ⟦< L *puer*, boy⟧ childish; silly —**pu′er·il′i·ty** *n.*

Puer·to Ri·co (pwer′tə rē′kō, pôr′-) island in the West Indies: a commonwealth associated with the U.S.: 3,425 sq. mi.; pop. 3,196,000; cap. San Juan —**Puer′to Ri′can** (-kən)

puff (puf) *n.* ⟦OE *pyff*⟧ 1 a short, sudden gust or expulsion of air, breath, smoke, etc. 2 a draw at a cigarette, etc. 3 a light pastry filled with whipped cream, etc. 4 a soft pad [a powder *puff*] 5 a book review, etc. giving undue praise —*vi.* 1 to blow in puffs 2 to breathe rapidly 3 to fill or swell (*out* or *up*) 4 to take puffs at a cigarette, etc. —*vt.* 1 to blow, smoke, etc. in or with puffs 2 to swell; inflate 3 to praise unduly —**puff′y**, **-i·er, -i·est**, *adj.* —**puff′i·ness** *n.*

puff′ball′ *n.* a fungus that bursts at the touch and discharges a brown powder

puff′er *n.* a small saltwater fish that can expand its body by swallowing water or air

puf·fin (puf′in) *n.* ⟦ME *poffin*⟧ a northern sea bird with a brightly colored, triangular beak

puff pastry rich, flaky pastry made of many thin layers of dough

pug (pug) *n.* ⟦< ? *Puck*, an elf⟧ any of a breed of small, short haired, snub-nosed dog

pu·gil·ism (pyo͞o′jil iz′əm) *n.* ⟦L *pugil*, boxer⟧ the sport of boxing —**pu′gil·ist** *n.* —**pu′gil·is′tic** *adj.*

pug·na·cious (pug nā′shəs) *adj.* ⟦< L *pugnare*, to fight⟧ eager and ready to fight; quarrelsome —**pug·na′cious·ly** *adv.* —**pug·nac′i·ty** (-nas′ə tē) *n.*

pug nose a short, thick, turned-up nose —**pug′-nosed′** *adj.*

puke (pyo͞ok) *n.*, *vi.*, *vt.* **puked, puk′ing** ⟦< ?⟧ [Colloq.] VOMIT

puk·ka (puk′ə) *adj.* ⟦Hindi *pakka*, ripe⟧ 1 first-rate 2 genuine; real

pul·chri·tude (pul′krə to͞od′) *n.* ⟦< L *pulcher*, beautiful⟧ beauty

pule (pyo͞ol) *vi.* **puled, pul′ing** ⟦echoic⟧ to whimper or whine, as a sick or fretful child does

pull (pool) *vt.* ⟦< OE *pullian*, to pluck⟧ 1 to exert force on so as to move toward the source of the force 2 to pluck out [to *pull* a tooth] 3 to rip; tear 4 to strain (a muscle) 5 [Colloq.] to carry out; perform [to *pull* a raid] 6 [Colloq.] to restrain [to *pull* a punch] 7 to draw out (a gun, etc.) —*vi.* 1 to exert force in dragging, tugging, or attracting 2 to be capable of being pulled 3 to move (*away, ahead*, etc.) —*n.* 1 the act or force, of pulling; a tugging, attracting, etc. 2 a difficult, continuous effort 3 something to be pulled, as a handle 4 [Colloq.] *a*) influence *b*) drawing power —**pull for** to cheer on —**pull off** [Colloq.] to accomplish —**pull oneself together** to regain one's poise, etc. —**pull out** to depart or withdraw —**pull through** [Colloq.] to get over (an illness, difficulty, etc.) —**pull up** 1 to bring or come to a stop 2 to move ahead —**pull′er** *n.*

pull′back′ *n.* a pulling back; esp., a planned military withdrawal

pul·let (pool′it) *n.* ⟦< L *pullus*, chicken⟧ a young hen

pul·ley (pool′ē) *n.*, *pl.* **-leys** ⟦< Medieval Gr *polos*, pivot⟧ a small wheel with a grooved rim in which a rope, belt, etc. runs, as to raise weights or transmit power

Pull·man (pool′mən) *n.* ⟦after G. M. *Pullman* (1831-97), U.S. inventor⟧ a railroad car with convertible berths for sleeping Also **Pullman car**

pull′out′ *n.* 1 a pulling out; esp. a removal, withdrawal, etc. 2 something to be pulled out, as a magazine insert

pull′o′ver *adj.* that is put on by being pulled over the head —*n.* a pullover sweater, shirt, etc.

pull′-up′ or **pull′up′** *n.* the act of chinning oneself

pul·mo·nar·y (pul′mə ner′ē) *adj.* ⟦< L *pulmo*, lung⟧ of the lungs

pul·mo·tor (pool′mō′tər) *n.* ⟦< L *pulmo*, lung + MOTOR⟧ an apparatus for applying artificial respiration

pulp (pulp) *n.* ⟦< L *pulpa*, flesh⟧ 1 a soft, moist, sticky mass 2 the soft, juicy part of a fruit or the pith inside a plant stem 3 the soft, sensitive tissue in the center of a tooth 4 ground-up, moistened fibers of wood, rags, etc., used to make paper —**pulp′y** *adj.*

pul·pit (pool′pit) *n.* ⟦< L *pulpitum*, a stage⟧ 1 a raised platform from which a clergyman preaches in a church **2** preachers collectively

pul·sar (pul′sär′) ***n.*** ⟦< PULSE⟧ any of several celestial objects that emit radio waves at short, regular intervals

pul·sate (pul′sāt′) ***vi.*** **-sat′ed, -sat′ing** ⟦< L *pulsare*, to beat⟧ **1** to beat or throb rhythmically **2** to vibrate; quiver —**pul·sa′tion** ***n.***

pulse (puls) ***n.*** ⟦< L *pulsus*, a beating⟧ **1** the regular beating in the arteries, caused by the contractions of the heart **2** any regular beat **3** a brief, abnormal burst or surge, as of electric current —***vi.*** **pulsed, puls′ing** to pulsate; throb

pul·ver·ize (pul′vər īz′) ***vt., vi.*** **-ized′, -iz′·ing** ⟦< L *pulvis*, powder⟧ to grind or be ground into powder

pu·ma (pyo͞o′mə) ***n.*** ⟦AmSp⟧ COUGAR

pum·ice (pum′is) ***n.*** ⟦< L *pumex*⟧ a light, porous volcanic rock used for scouring, polishing, etc.

pum·mel (pum′əl) ***vt.*** **-meled** or **-melled, -mel·ing** or **-mel·ling** ⟦< POMMEL⟧ to hit with repeated blows

pump[1] (pump) ***n.*** ⟦< Sp *bomba*⟧ a machine that forces a liquid or gas into, or draws it out of, something —***vt.*** **1** to move (fluids) with a pump **2** to remove water, etc. from **3** to drive air into with a pump **4** to draw out, move up and down, pour forth, etc. as a pump does **5** [Colloq.] to question persistently, or to elicit by this —**pump′er** ***n.***

pump[2] (pump) ***n.*** ⟦prob. < Fr *pompe*, boot⟧ a low-cut shoe without straps or ties

pum·per·nick·el (pum′pər nik′əl) ***n.*** ⟦Ger⟧ a coarse, dark, rye bread

pump·kin (pump′kin; *often* puŋ′-) ***n.*** ⟦< Gr *pepōn*, ripe⟧ a large, round, orange-yellow, edible gourdlike fruit that grows on a vine

pun (pun) ***n.*** ⟦< ? It *puntiglio*, fine point⟧ the humorous use of a word, or of different words sounded alike, so as to play on the various meanings —***vi.*** **punned, pun′ning** to make puns

punch[1] (punch) ***n.*** ⟦< ME *punchoun*, ult. < L *pungere*, to prick⟧ a tool driven against a surface that is to be stamped, pierced, etc. —***vt.*** **1** to pierce, stamp, etc. with a punch **2** to make (a hole) as with a punch

punch[2] (punch) ***vt.*** ⟦ME *punchen*⟧ **1** to prod with a stick **2** to herd (cattle) as by prodding **3** to strike with the fist —***n.*** **1** a thrusting blow with the fist **2** [Colloq.] effective force —**punch in** (or **out**) to record with a time clock one's arrival (or departure)

punch[3] (punch) ***n.*** ⟦Hindi *pañca*, five⟧ a sweet drink made with fruit juices, sherbet, etc., often mixed with wine or liquor

punch′-drunk′ ***adj.*** confused, unsteady, etc., as from many blows to the head in boxing

pun·cheon (pun′chən) ***n.*** ⟦OFr *poinçon*⟧ a large cask for beer, wine, etc.

punch line the surprise line carrying the point of a joke

punch′y ***adj.*** **-i·er, -i·est** [Colloq.] **1** forceful; vigorous **2** PUNCH-DRUNK

punc·til·i·ous (puŋk til′ē əs) ***adj.*** ⟦see fol.⟧ **1** very careful about nice points of behavior **2** very exact; scrupulous

punc·tu·al (puŋk′cho͞o əl) ***adj.*** ⟦< L *punctus*, a point⟧ on time; prompt —**punc′tu·al′i·ty** (-al′ə tē) ***n.*** —**punc′tu·al·ly** ***adv.***

punc′tu·ate′ (-cho͞o āt′) ***vt.*** **-at′ed, -at′ing** ⟦see prec.⟧ **1** to use standardized marks (**punctuation marks**), as the period and comma, in (written matter) to clarify meaning **2** to interrupt /a speech *punctuated* with applause/ **3** to emphasize —**punc′tu·a′tion** ***n.***

punc·ture (puŋk′chər) ***n.*** ⟦< L *pungere*, pierce⟧ **1** a piercing **2** a hole made by a sharp point —***vt., vi.*** **-tured, -tur·ing** to pierce or be pierced as with a sharp point

pun·dit (pun′dit) ***n.*** ⟦< Sans *paṇḍita*⟧ a person of great learning

pun·gent (pun′jənt) ***adj.*** ⟦< L *pungere*, pierce⟧ **1** producing a sharp sensation of taste and smell **2** sharp, biting, or stimulating /*pungent* wit/ —**pun′gen·cy** ***n.*** —**pun′gent·ly** ***adv.***

pun·ish (pun′ish) ***vt.*** ⟦< L *punire*⟧ **1** to cause to undergo pain, loss, etc., as for a crime **2** to impose a penalty for (an offense) —**pun′ish·a·ble** ***adj.***

pun′ish·ment ***n.*** **1** a punishing or being punished **2** the penalty imposed **3** harsh treatment

pu·ni·tive (pyo͞o′ni tiv) ***adj.*** inflicting, or concerned with, punishment

punk[1] (puŋk) ***n.*** ⟦prob. < SPUNK⟧ **1** decayed wood used as tinder **2** a fungous substance that smolders when ignited, used to light fireworks, etc.

punk[2] (puŋk) ***n.*** ⟦< ?⟧ **1** [Slang] *a)* a young hoodlum *b)* a young person regarded as inexperienced, insignificant, etc. **2** PUNK ROCK —***adj.*** **1** [Slang] poor; inferior **2** of punk rock

punk rock a loud, fast, and deliberately offensive style of rock music

pun·ster (pun′stər) ***n.*** one who is fond of making puns

punt[1] (punt) ***n.*** ⟦< ? dial. *bunt*, to kick⟧ *Football* a kick in which the ball is dropped and kicked before it hits the ground —***vt., vi.*** to kick (a football) in this way

punt[2] (punt) ***n.*** ⟦< L *pons*, a bridge⟧ a flat-bottomed boat with square ends —***vt., vi.*** to propel (a punt) with a long pole

pu·ny (pyo͞o′nē) ***adj.*** **-ni·er, -ni·est** ⟦< OFr *puis*, after + *né*, born⟧ of inferior size, strength, or importance —**pu′ni·ness** ***n.***

pup (pup) ***n.*** **1** a young dog; puppy **2** a young fox, seal, etc.

pu·pa (pyo͞o′pə) ***n.***, *pl.* **-pae** (-pē) or **-pas** ⟦< L, a doll⟧ an insect in the stage between the last larval and adult forms

pu·pil[1] (pyo͞o′pəl) ***n.*** ⟦< L *pupillus*, a ward⟧ a person taught under the supervision of a teacher or tutor

pu·pil[2] (pyo͞o′pəl) ***n.*** ⟦< L *pupilla*, figure reflected in the eye⟧ the contractile circular opening, apparently black, in the center of the iris of the eye

pup·pet (pup′ət) ***n.*** ⟦< L *pupa*, a doll⟧ **1** a small figure, as of a person, moved by strings or the hands, as in a performance (**puppet show**) **2** one whose actions, ideas, etc. are controlled by another —**pup′pet·ry** ***n.***

pup′pet·eer′ (-ə tir′) ***n.*** one who operates, designs, etc. puppets

pup·py (pup′ē) ***n.***, *pl.* **-pies** ⟦< MedievalFr *popee*, a doll⟧ PUP

pup tent a small, portable tent

pur·blind (pur′blīnd′) ***adj.*** ⟦ME *pur blind*, quite blind⟧ **1** partly blind **2** slow in understanding

pur·chase (pur′chəs) ***vt.*** **-chased, -chas·ing** ⟦< OFr *pour*, for + *chacier*, to chase⟧ to buy —***n.*** **1** anything bought **2** the act of buying **3** a firm hold applied to move something heavy or to keep from slipping —**pur′·chas·a·ble** ***adj.*** —**pur′chas·er** ***n.***

pure (pyoor) ***adj.*** ⟦< L *purus*⟧ **1** free from anything that adulterates, taints, etc.; unmixed **2** simple; mere **3** utter; absolute **4** faultless **5** blameless **6** virgin or chaste **7** abstract or theoretical */pure* physics/ —**pure′ly** ***adv.*** —**pure′ness** ***n.***

pure′bred′ ***adj.*** belonging to a recognized breed with genetic attributes maintained through generations of unmixed descent —***n.*** a purebred animal or plant

pu·rée or **pu·ree** (pyōō rā′) ***n.*** ⟦Fr: see PURE⟧ **1** cooked food pressed through a sieve or whipped in a blender to a soft, smooth consistency **2** a thick soup made of this —***vt.*** **pu·réed′** or **-reed′**, **-rée′ing** or **-ree′ing** to make a purée of

pur·ga·tive (pur′gə tiv) ***adj.*** purging —***n.*** a purging substance; cathartic

pur·ga·to·ry (pur′gə tôr′ē) ***n.***, *pl.* **-ries** ⟦see fol.⟧ [*often* **P-**] *Christian Theol.* a state or place after death for expiating sins by suffering —**pur′ga·to′ri·al** ***adj.***

purge (purj) ***vt.*** **purged, purg′ing** ⟦< L *purus*, clean + *agere*, do⟧ **1** to cleanse of impurities, etc. **2** to cleanse of sin **3** to rid (a nation, party, etc.) of (individuals held to be disloyal) **4** to empty (the bowels) —***n.*** **1** a purging **2** that which purges; esp., a cathartic —**purg′er** ***n.***

pu·ri·fy (pyoor′ə fī′) ***vt.*** **-fied′, -fy′ing** ⟦see PURE & -FY⟧ **1** to rid of impurities, etc. **2** to free from guilt, sin, etc. —***vi.*** to become purified —**pu′ri·fi·ca′tion** ***n.***

Pu·rim (poor′im) ***n.*** ⟦Heb⟧ a Jewish holiday commemorating the deliverance of the Jews by Esther from a massacre

pu·rine (pyōōr′ēn, -in) ***n.*** ⟦Ger *purin*⟧ **1** a colorless, crystalline organic compound, from which is derived a group of compounds including uric acid and caffeine **2** any of several purine derivatives, as adenine

pur·ism (pyoor′iz′əm) ***n.*** strict or excessive observance of precise usage in language, style, etc. —**pur′ist** ***n.***

Pu·ri·tan (pyoor′i tən) ***n.*** ⟦see fol.⟧ **1** a member of a group in 16th-17th-c. England which wanted to purify the Church of England from elaborate forms **2** [**p-**] a person regarded as excessively strict in morals and religion —**pu′ri·tan′i·cal** (-tan′i kəl) ***adj.*** —**Pu′ri·tan·ism′** or **pu′ri·tan·ism′** ***n.***

pu′ri·ty (-tē) ***n.*** ⟦< LL *puritas*⟧ a being pure; specif., *a)* freedom from adulterating matter *b)* cleanness *c)* freedom from sin; chastity

purl[1] (purl) ***vi.*** ⟦< ? Scand⟧ to move in ripples or with a murmuring sound —***n.*** the sound of purling water

purl[2] (purl) ***vt.***, ***vi.*** ⟦earlier *pirl*, prob. ult. < It⟧ to invert (stitches) in knitting so as to form ribbing

pur·lieu (purl′yōō′) ***n.*** ⟦< OFr *pur-*, through + *aler*, go⟧ **1** [*pl.*] environs **2** an outlying part, as of a city

pur·loin (pər loin′) ***vt.***, ***vi.*** ⟦< OFr *pur-*, for + *loin*, far⟧ to steal

pur·ple (pur′pəl) ***n.*** ⟦< Gr *porphyra*, shellfish yielding a dye⟧ **1** a dark bluish red **2** crimson cloth or clothing, esp. as a former emblem of royalty —***adj.*** **1** bluish-red **2** imperial **3** ornate */purple* prose/ **4** profane or obscene */purple* language/

pur·port (pər pôrt′; *for n.* pur′pôrt′) ***vt.*** ⟦< OFr *por-*, forth + *porter*, to bear⟧ **1** to profess or claim as its meaning **2** to give the appearance, often falsely, of being, intending, etc. —***n.*** **1** meaning; sense **2** intention —**pur·port′ed** ***adj.*** —**pur·port′·ed·ly** ***adv.***

pur·pose (pur′pəs) ***vt.***, ***vi.*** **-posed, -pos·ing** ⟦see PROPOSE⟧ to intend or plan —***n.*** **1** something one intends to get or do; aim **2** determination **3** the object for which something exists or is done —**on purpose** intentionally —**pur′pose·ful** ***adj.*** —**pur′pose·less** ***adj.***

pur′pose·ly ***adv.*** with a definite purpose; intentionally; deliberately

pur′pos·ive ***adj.*** serving or having a purpose

purr (pur) ***n.*** ⟦echoic⟧ a low, vibratory sound made by a cat at ease —***vi.***, ***vt.*** to make, or express by, such a sound

purse (purs) ***n.*** ⟦< Gr *byrsa*, a hide⟧ **1** a small bag for carrying money **2** finances; money **3** a sum of money for a present or prize **4** a woman's handbag —***vt.*** **pursed, purs′ing** to pucker

purs·er (purs′ər) ***n.*** ⟦ME, purse-bearer⟧ a ship's officer in charge of accounts, tickets, etc.

pur·su·ance (pər sōō′əns) ***n.*** a pursuing of a project, plan, etc.

pur·su′ant ***adj.*** [Now Rare] pursuing —**pursuant to** in accordance with

pur·sue (pər sōō′, -syōō′) ***vt.*** **-sued′, -su′ing** ⟦< L *pro-*, forth + *sequi*, follow⟧ **1** to follow in order to overtake or capture; chase **2** to follow (a specified course, action, etc.) **3** to strive for **4** to continue to annoy —**pur·su′er** ***n.***

pur·suit′ (-sōōt′) ***n.*** **1** a pursuing **2** an occupation; interest

pu·ru·lent (pyōō′rōō lənt, pyoor′yōō-) ***adj.*** ⟦< L *pus*, pus⟧ of, like, or discharging pus —**pu′ru·lence** ***n.***

pur·vey (pər vā′) ***vt.*** ⟦see PROVIDE⟧ to supply (esp. food) —**pur·vey′or** ***n.***

pur·view (pur′vyōō′) ***n.*** ⟦< OFr *pourveü*, provided⟧ scope or extent, as of control, activity, etc.

pus (pus) ***n.*** ⟦L⟧ the yellowish-white matter produced by an infection

push (poosh) ***vt.*** ⟦< L *pulsare*, to beat⟧ **1** to press against so as to move **2** to press or urge on **3** to urge the use, sale, etc. of —***n.*** **1** a pushing **2** a vigorous effort **3** an advance against opposition **4** [Colloq.] aggressiveness; drive

push button a small knob pushed to operate something electrically

push′er *n.* 1 one that pushes 2 [Slang] one who sells drugs, esp. narcotics, illegally

push′o′ver *n.* [Slang] 1 anything very easy to do 2 a person, group, etc. easily persuaded, defeated, etc.

push′-up′ or **push′up′** *n.* an exercise in which a prone person, with the hands under the shoulders, raises the body by pushing down with the palms

push′y *adj.* -i·er, -i·est [Colloq.] annoyingly aggressive and persistent —**push′i·ness** *n.*

pu·sil·lan·i·mous (pyo͞o′si lan′ə məs) *adj.* ⟦< L *pusillus*, tiny + *animus*, the mind⟧ timid; cowardly —**pu′sil·la·nim′i·ty** (-si lə nim′ə tē) *n.*

puss (poos) *n.* ⟦< ?⟧ a cat Also **puss′y·cat′** or **puss′y**, *pl.* -ies

puss′y·foot′ *vi.* [Colloq.] 1 to move with stealth or caution, like a cat 2 to avoid committing oneself

pussy willow a willow bearing velvetlike, silvery catkins

pus·tule (pus′tyo͞ol′) *n.* ⟦L *pustula*⟧ a pus-filled blister or pimple

put (poot) *vt.* **put, put′ting** ⟦< or akin to OE *potian*, to push⟧ 1 *a*) to thrust; drive *b*) to propel with an overhand thrust [*to put* the shot] 2 to cause to be in a certain place, condition, relation, etc.; place; set 3 to impose (a tax, etc.) 4 to attribute; ascribe 5 to express [*put* it plainly] 6 to present for decision [*put* the question] 7 to bet (money) *on* —*n. Finance* an option to sell a stock, etc. —*adj.* [Colloq.] fixed [stay *put*] —**put across** [Colloq.] to cause to be understood or accepted —**put aside** (or **by**) to reserve for later use —**put down** 1 to crush; repress 2 to write down 3 [Slang] to belittle or humiliate —**put in for** to apply for —**put it** (or **something**) **over on** [Colloq.] to deceive; trick —**put off** 1 to postpone; delay 2 to evade; divert —**put on** 1 to clothe oneself with 2 to pretend 3 to stage (a play) 4 [Slang] to hoax —**put out** 1 to expel; dismiss 2 to extinguish (a fire or light) 3 to inconvenience 4 *Baseball* to retire (a batter or runner) —**put through** 1 to carry out 2 to cause to do or undergo —**put up** 1 to offer 2 to preserve fruits, etc. 3 to build 4 to provide lodgings for 5 to provide (money) 6 to arrange (the hair) with curlers, etc. 7 [Colloq.] to incite *to* some action —**put up with** to tolerate

pu·ta·tive (pyo͞ot′ə tiv) *adj.* ⟦< L *putare*, suppose⟧ generally considered or deemed such; reputed

put′-down′ *n.* [Slang] a belittling remark or crushing retort

put′-on′ *n.* [Slang] a hoax

pu·tre·fy (pyo͞o′trə fī′) *vt.*, *vi.* -fied′, -fy′ing ⟦see PUTRID & -FY⟧ to make or become putrid; rot —**pu′tre·fac′tion** (-fak′shən) *n.*

pu·tres·cent (pyo͞o tres′ənt) *adj.* putrefying; rotting —**pu·tres′cence** *n.*

pu·trid (pyo͞o′trid) *adj.* ⟦< L *putrere*, to rot⟧ rotten and foul-smelling

putt (put) *n.* ⟦< PUT, *v.*⟧ *Golf* a shot which attempts to roll the ball into the hole —*vt.*, *vi.* to hit (the ball) with a putt

putt·er[1] (put′ər) *n.* *Golf* a short, straight-faced club used in putting

put·ter[2] (put′ər) *vi.* ⟦< OE *potian*, to push⟧ to busy oneself in an ineffective or aimless way (with *along, around*, etc.) —*vt.* to fritter (*away*)

put·ty (put′ē) *n.* ⟦Fr *potée*, lit., potful⟧ a soft, plastic mixture of powdered chalk and linseed oil, used to fill small cracks, etc. —*vt.* -tied, -ty·ing to cement or fill with putty

put′-up′ *adj.* [Colloq.] planned secretly beforehand [a *put-up* job]

puz·zle (puz′əl) *vt.* -zled, -zling ⟦< ?⟧ to perplex; bewilder —*vi.* 1 to be perplexed 2 to exercise one's mind, as over a problem —*n.* 1 something that puzzles 2 a toy or problem for testing skill or ingenuity —**puzzle out** to solve by deep study —**puz′zle·ment** *n.* —**puz′zler** *n.*

PVC (pē′vē′sē′) *n.* ⟦*p(oly)v(inyl) c(hloride)*⟧ a type of polymer used in packaging materials, plumbing, etc.

Pvt. *Mil.* Private

PX Post Exchange

Pyg·my (pig′mē) *n.*, *pl.* -mies ⟦< Gr *pygmaios*, of a forearm's length⟧ 1 a member of any of several races of small African or Asian peoples 2 [p-] a dwarf —*adj.* 1 of the Pygmies 2 [p-] very small

py·ja·mas (pə jä′məz, -jam′əz) *n.pl.* *Brit., etc. sp. of* PAJAMAS

py·lon (pī′län′) *n.* ⟦Gr *pylōn*, gateway⟧ 1 a gateway, as of an Egyptian temple 2 a towerlike structure supporting electric lines, marking a flight course, etc.

py·lo·rus (pī lō′rəs) *n.*, *pl.* -ri (-rī) ⟦< Gr *pylōros*, gatekeeper⟧ the opening from the stomach into the duodenum —**py·lor′ic** *adj.*

py·or·rhe·a (pī′ə rē′ə) *n.* ⟦< Gr *pyon*, pus + *rheein*, to flow⟧ a periodontal infection with formation of pus and loosening of teeth —**py′or·rhe′al** *adj.*

pyr·a·mid (pir′ə mid) *n.* ⟦< Gr *pyramis*⟧ 1 a huge structure with a square base and four triangular sides meeting at the top, as a royal tomb of ancient Egypt 2 *Geom.* a solid figure with a polygonal base, the sides of which form the bases of triangular surfaces meeting at a common vertex —**py·ram·i·dal** (pi ram′i dəl) *adj.*

EGYPTIAN PYRAMID

pyre (pīr) *n.* ⟦< Gr *pyr*, fire⟧ a pile of wood for burning a dead body

Pyr·e·nees (pir′ə nēz′) mountain range between France & Spain

py·ret·ic (pī ret′ik) *adj.* ⟦< Gr *pyretos*, fever⟧ of, causing, or characterized by fever

Py·rex (pī′reks′) ⟦arbitrary coinage < *pie*⟧ *trademark for* a heat-resistant glassware used for cooking, lab work, etc.

py·rite (pī′rīt′) *n.*, *pl.* **py·ri·tes** (pi rīt′ēz′, pī′rīts′) ⟦< Gr *pyritēs*, flint⟧ iron sulfide, a lustrous, yellow mineral used as a source of sulfur

pyro- ⟦< Gr *pyr*, fire⟧ *combining form* fire, heat

py·ro·ma·ni·a (pī′rō mā′nē ə) *n.* ⟦ModL: see prec. & -MANIA⟧ a compulsion to start destructive fires —**py′ro·ma′ni·ac′** *n.*, *adj.*

py·ro·tech·nics (pī′rō tek′niks) *n.pl.* ⟦< Gr

pyr, fire + *technē*, art] 1 a display of fireworks 2 a dazzling display, as of wit

Pyr·rhic victory (pir'ik) [after *Pyrrhus*, Gr king who won such a victory over Romans, 279 B.C.] a too costly victory

Py·thag·o·ras (pi thag'ə rəs) 6th c. B.C.; Gr. philosopher & mathematician —**Py·thag'o·re'an** (-ə rē'ən) ***adj., n.***

py·thon (pī'thän', -thən) ***n.*** [< Gr *Pythōn*, a serpent slain by Apollo] a large, nonpoisonous snake of Asia, Africa, and Australia, that crushes its prey to death

pyx (piks) ***n.*** [< Gr *pyxis*, a box] a container for Eucharistic wafers

Q

q or **Q** (kyōō) ***n., pl.*** **q's, Q's** the 17th letter of the English alphabet

q. 1 quart 2 question

Qa·tar (ke tär', kä'tär') country on a peninsula of E Arabia, on the Persian Gulf: *c.* 6,000 sq. mi.; pop. 305,000

Q.E.D. or **q.e.d.** [L *quod erat demonstrandum*] which was to be demonstrated or proved

qt. quart(s)

Q.T. or **q.t.** [Slang] quiet: usually in **on the Q.T.** (or **q.t.**), in secret

qua (kwā, kwä) ***adv.*** [L < *qui*, who] in the function or character of; as /the President *qua* Commander in Chief/

quack[1] (kwak) ***vi.*** [echoic] to utter the sound or cry of a duck —***n.*** this sound

quack[2] (kwak) ***n.*** [ult. < MDu *quacken*, to brag] 1 an untrained person who practices medicine fraudulently 2 one who pretends to have knowledge or skill that he does not have —***adj.*** fraudulent —**quack'er·y *n.***

quad (kwäd) ***n.*** *short for:* 1 QUADRANGLE 2 QUADRUPLET

quad *abbrev.* 1 quadrangle 2 quadrant 3 quadruplicate

quad·ran·gle (kwä'draŋ'gəl) ***n.*** [see QUADRI- & ANGLE[1]] 1 *Geom.* a plane figure with four angles and four sides 2 an area surrounded on its four sides by buildings —**quad·ran'gu·lar *adj.***

quad·rant (kwä'drənt) ***n.*** [< L *quadrans*, fourth part] 1 an arc of 90° 2 a quarter section of a circle 3 an instrument formerly used in measuring angular elevation and altitude in navigation, etc.

quad·ra·phon·ic (kwä'drə fän'ik) ***adj.*** [< QUADRI- + Gr *phōnē*, a sound] using four channels to record and reproduce sound

quad·rat·ic (kwä drat'ik) ***adj.*** *Algebra* involving a quantity or quantities that are squared but none that are raised to a higher power

quad·ren·ni·al (kwä dren'ē əl) ***adj.*** [< L *quadri-* (see fol.) + *annus*, a year] 1 happening every four years 2 lasting four years

quadri- [L < *quattuor*, four] *combining form* four, four times

quad·ri·ceps (kwä'dri seps') ***n.*** [< prec. + L *caput*, the head] a muscle with four points of origin; esp., the large muscle at the front of the thigh

quad·ri·lat·er·al (kwä'dri lat'ər əl) ***adj.*** [see QUADRI- & LATERAL] four-sided —***n.*** *Geom.* a plane figure having four sides and four angles

qua·drille (kwə dril', kwä-) ***n.*** [Fr: ult. < L *quadra*, a square] a square dance performed by four couples

quad·ri·ple·gi·a (kwä'dri plē'jē ə, -jə) ***n.*** [ModL < QUADRI- + Gr *plēgē*, a stroke] total paralysis of the body from the neck down —**quad'ri·ple'gic** (-plē'jik) ***adj., n.***

quad·ru·ped (kwä'drōō ped') ***n.*** [< L *quadru-*, four + *pes*, foot] an animal, esp. a mammal, with four feet

quad·ru·ple (kwä'droo pəl, kwä drōō'-) ***adj.*** [< L *quadru-*, four + *-plus*, -fold] 1 consisting of four 2 four times as much or as many —***n.*** an amount four times as much or as many —***vt., vi.*** **-pled, -pling** to make or become four times as much or as many

quad·ru·plet (kwä drōō'plit, -drup'lit) ***n.*** 1 any of four offspring born at a single birth 2 a collection or group of four, usually of one kind

quad·ru·pli·cate (kwä drōō'pli kāt'; *for adj. & n.*, -kit, -kāt') ***vt.*** **-cat'ed, -cat'ing** to make four identical copies of —***adj.*** 1 fourfold 2 being the last of four identical copies —***n.*** any one of such copies —**in quadruplicate** in four such copies —**quad·ru'pli·ca'tion *n.***

quaff (kwäf; *also* kwaf) ***vt., vi.*** [prob. < LowG *quassen*, overindulge] to drink deeply and heartily —***n.*** a quaffing

quag·mire (kwag'mīr') ***n.*** [*quag*, a bog + MIRE] wet, boggy ground

qua·hog or **qua·haug** (kwô'hôg'; *also* kō'-) ***n.*** [AmInd] an edible clam of the E coast

quail[1] (kwāl) ***vi.*** [prob. < L *coagulare*, coagulate] to recoil in fear

quail[2] (kwāl) ***n.*** [< OFr *quaille*] a small, short-tailed bird resembling a partridge

quaint (kwānt) ***adj.*** [< OFr *cointe* < L *cognitus*, known] 1 pleasingly odd or old-fashioned 2 unusual; curious 3 fanciful; whimsical —**quaint'ly *adv.*** —**quaint'ness *n.***

quake (kwāk) ***vi.*** **quaked, quak'ing** [< OE *cwacian*] 1 to tremble or shake 2 to shiver, as from fear or cold —***n.*** 1 a shaking or tremor 2 an earthquake —**quak'y, -i·er, -i·est, *adj.***

Quak·er (kwāk'ər) ***n.*** [< founder's admonition to "quake" at the word of the Lord] *name for* a member of the SOCIETY OF FRIENDS

qual·i·fi·ca·tion (kwôl'i fi kā'shən) ***n.*** 1 a qualifying or being qualified 2 a restriction; limiting condition 3 any skill, etc. that fits one for a job, office, etc.

qual·i·fied (kwôl'i fīd') ***adj.*** 1 fit; competent 2 limited; modified

qual'i·fi'er (-fī'ər) *n.* 1 one that qualifies 2 an adjective or adverb
qual'i·fy' (-fī') *vt.* **-fied', -fy'ing** ⟦ < L *qualis,* of what kind + *facere,* make ⟧ 1 to make fit for a job, etc. 2 to make legally capable 3 to modify; restrict 4 to moderate; soften —*vi.* to be or become qualified
qual'i·ta'tive (-tāt'iv) *adj.* having to do with quality or qualities —**qual'i·ta'tive·ly** *adv.*
qual'i·ty (-tē) *n., pl.* **-ties** ⟦ < L *qualis,* of what kind ⟧ 1 that which makes something what it is; characteristic element 2 basic nature; kind 3 the degree of excellence of a thing 4 excellence —*adj.* of high quality
quality circle a small group of workers that meet regularly to discuss ways to improve production
qualm (kwäm) *n.* ⟦ OE *cwealm,* disaster ⟧ 1 a sudden, brief feeling of sickness, faintness, etc. 2 a doubt; misgiving 3 a twinge of conscience
quan·da·ry (kwän'də rē, -drē) *n., pl.* **-ries** ⟦ prob. < L ⟧ a state of uncertainty; dilemma
quan·ti·fy (kwänt'ə fī') *vt.* **-fied', -fy'ing** ⟦ < L *quantus,* how much + *facere,* make ⟧ 1 to determine or express the quantity of 2 to express as a quantity or number
quan'ti·ta'tive (-tāt'iv) *adj.* having to do with quantity
quan'ti·ty (-tē) *n., pl.* **-ties** ⟦ < L *quantus,* how great ⟧ 1 an amount; portion 2 any indeterminate bulk or number 3 [*also pl.*] a great amount 4 that property by which a thing can be measured 5 a number or symbol expressing this property
quan·tum (kwänt'əm) *n., pl.* **-ta** (-ə) ⟦ L, how much ⟧ a fixed, elemental unit of energy: the **quantum theory** states that energy is radiated discontinuously in quanta
quar·an·tine (kwôr'ən tēn) *n.* ⟦ < L *quadraginta,* forty ⟧ 1 the period, orig. 40 days, during which a vessel suspected of carrying contagious disease is detained in port 2 any isolation imposed to keep contagious diseases, etc. from spreading 3 a place for such isolation —*vt.* **-tined', -tin'·ing** to place under quarantine
quark (kwôrk) *n.* ⟦ arbitrary coinage ⟧ any of six types of hypothetical particles assumed to be basic units of matter
quar·rel (kwôr'əl, kwär'-) *n.* ⟦ < L *queri,* complain ⟧ 1 a cause for dispute 2 a dispute, esp. an angry one —*vi.* **-reled** or **-relled, -rel·ing** or **-rel·ling** 1 to find fault 2 to dispute heatedly 3 to have a breach in friendship —**quar'rel·er** or **quar'rel·ler** *n.* —**quar'rel·some** *adj.*
quar·ry[1] (kwôr'ē) *n., pl.* **-ries** ⟦ < OFr *cuiree,* parts of prey fed to dogs ⟧ an animal, etc. being hunted down
quar·ry[2] (kwôr'ē) *n., pl.* **-ries** ⟦ < L *quadrare,* to square ⟧ a place where stone, slate, etc. is excavated —*vt.* **-ried, -ry·ing** to excavate from a quarry
quart (kwôrt) *n.* ⟦ < L *quartus,* fourth ⟧ 1 one fourth of a gallon in liquid measure 2 one eighth of a peck in dry measure
quar'ter (-ər) *n.* ⟦ < L *quartus,* fourth ⟧ 1 a fourth of something 2 one fourth of a year 3 any of the three terms of about eleven weeks each in an academic year 4 one fourth of a dollar; 25 cents, or a coin of this value 5 any leg of a four-legged animal, with the adjoining parts 6 a particular district or section 7 [*pl.*] lodgings 8 mercy 9 a particular source [news from high *quarters*] —*vt.* 1 to divide into four equal parts 2 to provide lodgings for —*adj.* constituting a quarter —**at close quarters** at close range
quar'ter·back' *n.* *Football* the back who calls the signals
quar'ter·deck' *n.* the after part of the upper deck of a ship, usually for officers
quar'ter·fi'nal *adj.* *Sports* coming just before the semifinals in a tournament —*n.* a quarterfinal match
quarter horse ⟦ < its speed in a *quarter*-mile sprint ⟧ any of a breed of muscular, solid-colored horse
quar'ter·ly *adj.* occurring regularly four times a year —*adv.* once every quarter of the year —*n., pl.* **-lies** a publication issued every three months
quar'ter·mas'ter *n.* 1 *Mil.* an officer who provides troops with quarters, clothing, equipment, etc. 2 *Naut.* a petty officer or mate involved in steering and navigating a ship
quarter note *Music* a note having one fourth the duration of a whole note
quar·tet or **quar·tette** (kwôr tet') *n.* ⟦ ult. < L *quartus,* fourth ⟧ 1 a group of four 2 *Music a*) a composition for four voices or instruments *b*) the four performers of this
quar·to (kwôrt'ō) *n., pl.* **-tos** ⟦ < L (*in*) *quarto,* (in) a fourth ⟧ 1 the page size (about 9 by 12 in.) of a book made up of sheets each of which is folded twice to form four leaves, or eight pages 2 a book with pages of this size
quartz (kwôrts) *n.* ⟦ Ger *quarz* ⟧ a crystalline mineral, a form of silica, usually colorless and transparent
qua·sar (kwā'zär') *n.* ⟦ < *quas*(*i-stell*)*ar* (*radio source*) ⟧ a distant, starlike, celestial object that emits immense quantities of light and radio waves
quash[1] (kwäsh) *vt.* ⟦ < L *cassus,* empty ⟧ *Law* to set aside (an indictment)
quash[2] (kwäsh) *vt.* ⟦ < L *quatere,* to break ⟧ to quell (an uprising)
qua·si (kwā'sī', -zī'; kwä'sē, -zē) *adv.* ⟦ L ⟧ as if; seemingly; in part —*adj.* seeming Often hyphenated as a prefix [*quasi*-legal]
quat·rain (kwä'trān') *n.* ⟦ < L *quattuor,* four ⟧ a stanza of four lines
qua·ver (kwā'vər) *vi.* ⟦ ME *cwafien* ⟧ 1 to shake or tremble 2 to be tremulous: said of the voice —*n.* a tremulous quality in a voice or tone
quay (kē) *n.* ⟦ ult. < Celt ⟧ a wharf, usually of concrete or stone
quea·sy (kwē'zē) *adj.* **-si·er, -si·est** ⟦ ME *qwesye* < Gmc ⟧ 1 affected with nausea 2 squeamish; easily nauseated
Que·bec (kwi bek') 1 province of E Canada: 594,860 sq. mi.; pop. 6,530,000: abbrev. **Que.** 2 its capital: on the St. Lawrence River: pop. 164,000
queen (kwēn) *n.* ⟦ < OE *cwen* ⟧ 1 the wife of a king 2 a female monarch in her own right 3 a woman noted for her beauty or accomplishments 4 the fully developed, reproductive female in a colony of bees,

ants, etc. 5 a playing card with a picture of a queen on it 6 *Chess* the most powerful piece —**queen'ly, -li·er, -li·est,** ***adj.***

Queens (kwēnz) borough of New York City, on W Long Island: pop. 1,891,000

queen'-size' ***adj.*** larger than usual, but less than king-size /a *queen-size* bed is 60 by 80 in./

queer (kwir) ***adj.*** ⟦ < ? Ger *quer,* crosswise ⟧ 1 different from the usual; strange 2 [Colloq.] eccentric 3 [Slang] homosexual: a derisive term —***vt.*** [Slang] to spoil the success of —***n.*** [Slang] a strange person

quell (kwel) ***vt.*** ⟦ OE *cwellan,* kill ⟧ 1 to subdue 2 to quiet; allay

quench (kwench) ***vt.*** ⟦ OE *cwencan* ⟧ 1 to extinguish /to *quench* fire with water/ 2 to satisfy /to *quench* one's thirst/ 3 to cool (hot steel, etc.) suddenly by plunging into water, etc. —**quench'less** ***adj.***

quer·u·lous (kwer'yoo̅ ləs, -ə-) ***adj.*** ⟦ < L *queri,* complain ⟧ 1 inclined to find fault 2 full of complaint; peevish —**quer'u·lous·ly** ***adv.***

que·ry (kwir'ē) ***n.,*** *pl.* **-ries** ⟦ < L *quaerere,* ask ⟧ 1 a question; inquiry 2 a question mark —***vt., vi.*** **-ried, -ry·ing** to question

quest (kwest) ***n.*** ⟦ see prec. ⟧ 1 a seeking 2 a journey for adventure

ques·tion (kwes'chən) ***n.*** ⟦ see QUERY ⟧ 1 an asking; inquiry 2 something asked 3 doubt; uncertainty 4 matter open to discussion 5 a difficult matter /not a *question* of money/ 6 a point being debated before an assembly —***vt.*** 1 to ask questions of 2 to express doubt about 3 to dispute; challenge —***vi.*** to ask questions —**out of the question** impossible

ques'tion·a·ble ***adj.*** 1 that can be questioned 2 suspected of being immoral, dishonest, etc. 3 uncertain

question mark a mark of punctuation (?) put after a sentence, word, etc. to indicate a direct question or to express doubt, uncertainty, etc.

ques'tion·naire' (-chən ner') ***n.*** a written or printed set of questions used in gathering information from people

queue (kyoo̅) ***n.*** ⟦ < L *cauda,* tail ⟧ 1 a pigtail 2 [Chiefly Brit., etc.] a line, as of persons waiting to be served 3 stored computer data or programs waiting to be processed —***vi.*** **queued, queu'ing** [Chiefly Brit., etc.] to line up in a queue: often with *up*

quib·ble (kwib'əl) ***n.*** ⟦ < L *qui,* who ⟧ a petty evasion; cavil —***vi.*** **-bled, -bling** to evade the truth of a point under discussion by caviling

quiche (kēsh) ***n.*** a custard baked in a pastry shell with various ingredients, as bacon, cheese, or spinach

quick (kwik) ***adj.*** ⟦ < OE *cwicu,* living ⟧ 1 *a)* rapid; swift /a *quick* walk/ *b)* prompt /a *quick* reply/ 2 prompt to understand or learn /a *quick* mind/ 3 easily stirred /a *quick* temper/ —***adv.*** quickly; rapidly —***n.*** 1 the living, esp. in **the quick and the dead** 2 the sensitive flesh under the nails 3 the deepest feelings /hurt to the *quick*/ —**quick'ly** ***adv.*** —**quick'ness** ***n.***

quick bread any bread leavened with baking powder, soda, etc. and baked as soon as the batter is mixed

quick'en ***vt.*** 1 to animate; enliven; revive 2 to cause to move more rapidly —***vi.*** 1 to become enlivened; revive 2 to show signs of life, as a fetus 3 to become more rapid

quick'-freeze' ***vt.*** **-froze', -fro'zen, -freez'ing** to subject (food) to sudden freezing for long storage at low temperatures

quick'ie ***n.*** [Colloq.] anything done or made quickly and, often, cheaply

quick'lime' ***n.*** unslaked lime

quick'sand' ***n.*** ⟦ < ME: see QUICK & SAND ⟧ a loose, wet, deep, sand deposit, engulfing heavy objects easily

quick'sil'ver ***n.*** mercury

quick'-tem'pered ***adj.*** easily angered

quick'-wit'ted ***adj.*** nimble of mind

quid (kwid) ***n.*** ⟦ var. of CUD ⟧ a piece, as of tobacco, to be chewed

quid pro quo (kwid' prō kwō') ⟦ L ⟧ one thing in return for another

qui·es·cent (kwī es'ənt) ***adj.*** ⟦ < L *quiescere,* become quiet ⟧ quiet; still; inactive —**qui·es'cence** ***n.***

qui·et (kwī'ət) ***adj.*** ⟦ < L *quies,* rest ⟧ 1 still; motionless 2 *a)* not noisy; hushed *b)* not speaking; silent 3 not easily excited 4 not showy /*quiet* clothes/ 5 not forward; unobtrusive 6 peaceful and relaxing —***n.*** 1 calmness, stillness, etc. 2 a quiet or peaceful quality —***vt.*** to make quiet —***vi.*** to become quiet: usually with *down* —**qui'et·ly** ***adv.***

qui·e·tude (kwī'ə to̅o̅d') ***n.*** a state of being quiet; calmness

qui·e·tus (kwī ēt'əs) ***n.*** ⟦ < ML *quietus (est),* (he is) quit ⟧ 1 discharge from debt, etc. 2 death

quill (kwil) ***n.*** ⟦ prob. < LowG or MDu ⟧ 1 a large, stiff feather 2 *a)* the hollow stem of a feather *b)* anything made from this, as a pen 3 a spine of a porcupine or hedgehog

quilt (kwilt) ***n.*** ⟦ < L *culcita,* bed ⟧ a bedcover filled with down, cotton, etc. and stitched together in lines or patterns —***vt.*** to stitch like a quilt —***vi.*** to make a quilt —**quilt'er** ***n.***

quince (kwins) ***n.*** ⟦ < Gr *kydōnion* ⟧ 1 a yellowish, apple-shaped fruit, used in preserves 2 the tree it grows on

qui·nel·la (kwi nel'ə, kē-) ***n.*** ⟦ < AmSp < L *quinque,* five ⟧ a form of betting in horseracing, in which the bettor, to win, must pick the first two finishers, in whichever order they finish Also **qui·nie·la** (kē nye'lə)

qui·nine (kwī'nīn') ***n.*** ⟦ < *quina,* cinchona bark ⟧ a bitter, crystalline alkaloid extracted from cinchona bark, used esp. for treating malaria

quin·sy (kwin'zē) ***n.*** ⟦ < Gr *kyōn,* dog + *anchein,* choke ⟧ *early term for* TONSILLITIS

quin·tes·sence (kwin tes'əns) ***n.*** ⟦ < ML *quinta essentia* ⟧ the pure essence or perfect type

quin·tet or **quin·tette** (kwin tet') ***n.*** ⟦ ult. < L *quintus,* a fifth ⟧ 1 a group of five 2 *Music a)* a composition for five voices or instruments *b)* the five performers of this

quin·tu·ple (kwin'tə pəl, kwin to̅o̅'-) ***adj.*** ⟦ < L *quintus,* a fifth + *-plex,* -fold ⟧ 1 consisting of five 2 five times as much or as many —*vt.*, *vi.* **-pled, -pling** to make or become five times as much or as many

quin·tu·plet (kwin tup′lit, -to͞o′plit) ***n.*** **1** any of five offspring born at a single birth **2** a group of five, usually of one kind

quip (kwip) ***n.*** ⟦< L *quippe,* indeed⟧ a witty or sarcastic remark; jest **—*vi.* quipped, quip′ping** to utter quips **—quip′ster *n.***

quire (kwīr) ***n.*** ⟦< L *quaterni,* four each⟧ a set of 24 or 25 sheets of paper of the same size and stock

quirk (kwurk) ***n.*** ⟦< ?⟧ **1** a sudden twist or turn **2** a peculiarity **—quirk′i·ness *n.* —quirk′y, -i·er, -i·est, *adj.***

quirt (kwurt) ***n.*** ⟦AmSp *cuarta*⟧ a riding whip with a braided leather lash and a short handle

quis·ling (kwiz′liŋ) ***n.*** ⟦after V. *Quisling,* Norw collaborator with the Nazis⟧ a traitor

quit (kwit) ***vt.* quit, quit′ted, quit′ting** ⟦< ML *quittus,* free⟧ **1** to free (oneself) *of* **2** to give up **3** to leave; depart from **4** to stop or resign from **—*vi.*** **1** to stop doing something **2** to give up one's job

quit′claim′ ***n.*** a deed relinquishing a claim, as to property

quite (kwīt) ***adv.*** ⟦see QUIT⟧ **1** completely **2** really; positively **3** very or fairly */quite* warm/ **—quite a few** (or **bit,** etc.) [Colloq.] more than a few (or bit, etc.)

Qui·to (kē′tō) capital of Ecuador: pop. 1,110,000

quits (kwits) ***adj.*** ⟦< ML *quittus,* free⟧ on even terms, as by discharge of a debt, retaliation, etc. **—call it quits** [Colloq.] **1** to stop working, etc. **2** to stop being friendly

quit·tance (kwit′'ns) ***n.*** ⟦see QUIT⟧ **1** discharge from a debt **2** recompense

quit′ter *n.* [Colloq.] one who quits or gives up easily, without trying hard

quiv·er[1] (kwiv′ər) ***vi.*** ⟦< OE *curifer-,* eager⟧ to shake tremulously; tremble **—*n.*** a quivering; tremor

quiv·er[2] (kwiv′ər) ***n.*** ⟦< OFr *coivre*⟧ a case for holding arrows

quix·ot·ic (kwiks ät′ik) ***adj.*** ⟦after DON QUIXOTE⟧ extravagantly chivalrous or foolishly idealistic

quiz (kwiz) ***n.***, *pl.* **quiz′zes** ⟦prob. < L *quis,* what⟧ a questioning; esp., a short examination to test knowledge **—*vt.* quizzed, quiz′zing** to ask questions, or test the knowledge, of **—quiz′zer *n.***

quiz′zi·cal (-i kəl) ***adj.*** **1** odd; comical **2** perplexed **—quiz′zi·cal·ly *adv.***

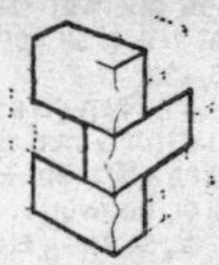

QUOINS

quoin (koin, kwoin) ***n.*** ⟦var. of COIN⟧ **1** the external corner of a building; esp., any of the large stones at such a corner **2** a wedge-shaped block

quoit (kwoit) ***n.*** ⟦prob. < OFr *coite,* a cushion⟧ **1** a ring thrown in quoits **2** [*pl., with sing. v.*] a game somewhat like horseshoes, in which rings are thrown at a peg

quon·dam (kwän′dəm) ***adj.*** ⟦L⟧ former */a quondam* companion/

Quon·set hut (kwän′sit) ⟦after *Quonset* Point, R.I., where first made⟧ *trademark for* a prefabricated, metal shelter like a half cylinder on its flat side

quo·rum (kwôr′əm) ***n.*** ⟦< L *qui,* who⟧ the minimum number of members required to be present before an assembly can transact business

quot. quotation

quo·ta (kwōt′ə) ***n.*** ⟦< L *quota pars,* how large a part⟧ a share or proportion assigned to each of a number

quotation mark either of a pair of punctuation marks (" . . . ") used to enclose a direct quotation

quote (kwōt) ***vt.* quot′ed, quot′ing** ⟦< L *quotus,* of what number⟧ **1** to repeat a passage from or statement of **2** to repeat (a passage, statement, etc.) **3** to state the price of (something) **—*n.*** [Colloq.] **1** something quoted **2** QUOTATION MARK **—quot′a·ble *adj.* —quo·ta·tion** (kwō tā′shən) ***n.***

quoth (kwōth) ***vt.*** ⟦< OE *cwethan,* speak⟧ [Archaic] said

quo·tid·i·an (kwō tid′ē ən) ***adj.*** ⟦< L *quotidie*⟧ **1** daily **2** ordinary

quo·tient (kwō′shənt) ***n.*** ⟦< L *quot,* how many⟧ *Math.* the result obtained when one number is divided by another

q.v. ⟦L *quod vide*⟧ which see

R

r or **R** (är) ***n.***, *pl.* **r's, R's** the 18th letter of the English alphabet

R (är) ***n.*** restricted: a film rating meaning that no one under seventeen will be admitted unless accompanied by a parent

r *Math. symbol for* radius

R or **R.** **1** ⟦L *Rex*⟧ king **2** ⟦L *Regina*⟧ queen **3** Republican **4** right **5** River **6** Road **7** route **8** *Baseball* run(s)

Ra *Chem. symbol for* radium

rab·bet (rab′it) ***n.*** ⟦< OFr *rabattre,* beat down⟧ a cut made in a board so that another may be fitted into it **—*vt., vi.*** to cut, or be joined by, a rabbet

rab·bi (rab′ī) ***n.***, *pl.* **-bis** ⟦< Heb *rabi,* my master⟧ an ordained teacher of the Jewish law **—rab′bin·ate** (-i nit) ***n.*** **—rab·bin·i·cal** (rə bin′i kəl) ***adj.***

rab·bit (rab′it) ***n.*** ⟦ME *rabette*⟧ a swift, burrowing mammal with soft fur, long ears, and a stubby tail

rabbit punch *Boxing* a short, sharp blow to the back of the neck

rab·ble (rab′əl) ***n.*** ⟦< ?⟧ a mob

rab′ble-rous′er ***n.*** one who tries to arouse people to violent action by appeals to emotions, prejudices, etc.

Ra·be·lais (rab′ə lā′), **Fran·çois** (frän swä′) *c.* 1494-1553; Fr. satirist & humorist

Ra·be·lai·si·an (rab′ə lā′zhən, -zē ən) ***adj.*** of or like Rabelais or his works; broadly and coarsely humorous, satirical, etc.

rab·id (rab′id) ***adj.*** ⟦< L *rabere,* to rage⟧ **1** violent; raging **2** fanatic **3** of or having rabies

ra·bies (rā′bēz) ***n.*** ⟦L, madness⟧ an infectious disease characterized by convulsions, etc., transmitted to people by the bite of an infected animal

rac·coon (ra ko͞on′) ***n.*** ⟦< AmInd *aroughcun*⟧ **1** a small, tree-climbing mammal of North America, with yellowish-gray fur and a black-ringed tail **2** its fur

race[1] (rās) ***n.*** ⟦< ON *rās,* a running⟧ **1** a competition of speed in running, etc. **2** any similar contest /the *race* for mayor/ **3** a swift current of water, or its channel **—*vi.*** **raced, rac′ing** **1** to take part in a race **2** to go or move swiftly **—*vt.*** **1** to compete with in a race **2** to enter (a horse, etc.) in a race **3** to cause to go swiftly **—rac′er *n.***

race[2] (rās) ***n.*** ⟦Fr < It *razza*⟧ **1** any of the different varieties of human beings distinguished by physical traits, blood types, etc. **2** any geographical population sharing the same habits, ideas, etc. **3** any distinct group of people

race′horse′ ***n.*** a horse bred and trained for racing

ra·ceme (rā sēm′, rə-) ***n.*** ⟦L *racemus,* cluster of grapes⟧ a flower cluster having a central stem along which individual flowers grow on small stalks

race′track′ ***n.*** a course prepared for racing, esp. an oval track for horse races

race′way′ ***n.*** **1** a narrow channel for water **2** a racetrack for harness racing, drag racing, etc.

ra·cial (rā′shəl) ***adj.*** of or characteristic of a race **—ra′cial·ly *adv.***

rac·i·ness (rā′sē nis) ***n.*** racy quality

rac·ism (rā′siz′əm) ***n.*** the practice of racial discrimination, segregation, etc. **—rac′ist *n., adj.***

rack[1] (rak) ***n.*** ⟦< LowG *rack*⟧ **1** a framework, etc. for holding or displaying various things /pipe *rack*/ **2** a toothed bar into which a pinion, etc. meshes **3** an instrument of torture which stretches the victim's limbs **4** any great torment **—*vt.*** **1** to arrange in or on a rack **2** to torture on a rack **3** to torment **—on the rack** in a difficult situation **—rack one's brains** to try hard to think of something **—rack up** [Slang] to score or achieve

rack[2] (rak) ***n.*** ⟦var. of WRACK⟧ destruction: now only in **go to rack and ruin,** to become ruined

rack·et[1] (rak′it) ***n.*** ⟦prob. echoic⟧ **1** a noisy confusion **2** *a)* an obtaining of money illegally *b)* [Colloq.] any dishonest practice

rack·et[2] (rak′it) ***n.*** ⟦< Ar *rāḥa*(*t*), palm of the hand⟧ a light bat for tennis, etc., with a network, as of catgut, in a round frame attached to a handle Also **rac′quet**

rack·et·eer (rak′ə tir′) ***n.*** one who obtains money illegally, as by fraud, extortion, etc. **—rack′et·eer′ing *n.***

rac·on·teur (rak′än tur′) ***n.*** ⟦Fr < *raconter,* to recount⟧ one skilled at telling stories or anecdotes

rac′quet·ball′ ***n.*** a game played like handball, but with a racket

rac·y (rā′sē) ***adj.*** **-i·er, -i·est** ⟦RACE[2] + -Y[2]⟧ **1** having the taste or quality of the genuine type /*racy* fruit/ **2** lively; spirited **3** pungent **4** risqué

rad (rad) ***n.*** ⟦< RAD(IATION)⟧ a dosage of absorbed ionizing radiation

ra·dar (rā′där′) ***n.*** ⟦*ra*(*dio*) *d*(*etecting*) *a*(*nd*) *r*(*anging*)⟧ a system or device that transmits radio waves to a reflecting object, as an aircraft, to determine its location, speed, etc. by the reflected waves

ra′dar·scope′ ***n.*** an oscilloscope that picks up radar waves

ra·di·al (rā′dē əl) ***adj.*** ⟦< L *radius,* ray⟧ **1** of or like a ray or rays; branching out from a center **2** of a radius

radial (ply) tire an automobile tire with plies of rubberized cords at right angles to the center line of the tread

ra·di·ant (rā′dē ənt) ***adj.*** ⟦< L *radius,* ray⟧ **1** shining brightly **2** showing pleasure, etc.; beaming **3** issuing (from a source) in or as in rays **—ra′di·ance *n.*** **—ra′di·ant·ly *adv.***

ra·di·ate (rā′dē āt′) ***vi.*** **-at′ed, -at′ing** ⟦< L *radius,* ray⟧ **1** to send out rays of heat, light, etc. **2** to branch out in lines from a center **—*vt.*** **1** to send out (heat, light, etc.) in rays **2** to spread (happiness, love, etc.)

ra′di·a′tion ***n.*** **1** a radiating **2** the rays sent out **3** nuclear particles

radiation sickness sickness produced by overexposure to X-rays, radioactive matter, etc.

ra′di·a′tor ***n.*** an apparatus for radiating heat, as into a room or from an automobile engine

rad·i·cal (rad′i kəl) ***adj.*** ⟦< L *radix,* root⟧ **1** of or from the root; fundamental **2** favoring basic change, as in the social or economic structure **—*n.*** **1** a person holding radical views **2** *Chem.* a group of two or more atoms acting as a single atom **3** *Math.* the sign (√) used with a quantity to show that its root is to be extracted **—rad′i·cal·ism′ *n.*** **—rad′i·cal·ly *adv.***

ra·dic·chio (rə dē′kyō) ***n., pl.*** **-chios** ⟦It⟧ a variety of chicory used in salads

ra·di·i (rā′dē ī′) ***n.*** *alt. pl. of* RADIUS

ra·di·o (rā′dē ō′) ***n.*** ⟦< *radio*(*telegraphy*)⟧ **1** the transmission of sounds or signals by electromagnetic waves directly through space to a receiving set **2** *pl.* **-os′** such a set **3** broadcasting by radio as an industry, entertainment, etc. **—*adj.*** of, using, used in, or sent by radio **—*vt., vi.*** **-oed′, -o′ing** to transmit, or communicate with, by radio

radio- ⟦< L *radius,* ray⟧ *combining form* **1** ray, raylike **2** by radio **3** using radiant energy **4** radioactive /*radiotherapy*/

ra′di·o·ac′tive *adj.* giving off radiant energy in the form of particles or rays by the disintegration of atomic nuclei **—ra′di·o·ac·tiv′i·ty *n.***

radio astronomy astronomy dealing with radio waves in space in order to obtain information about the universe

ra′di·o·gram′ *n.* a message sent by radio

ra′di·o·i′so·tope′ *n.* a radioactive isotope of a chemical element

ra′di·ol′o·gy (-äl′ə jē) *n.* the use of radiant energy, as X-rays, in medical diagnosis and therapy —**ra′di·ol′o·gist** *n.*

ra′di·o·paque′ (-ō pāk′) *adj.* ⟦RADIO- + (O)PAQUE⟧ not allowing the passage of X-rays, etc.

radio telescope a radio antenna for receiving and measuring radio waves from stars, spacecraft, etc.

ra′di·o·ther′a·py *n.* the treatment of disease by the use of X-rays or rays from a radioactive substance

rad·ish (rad′ish) *n.* ⟦< L *radix,* root⟧ **1** an annual plant with an edible root **2** the pungent root, eaten raw

ra·di·um (rā′dē əm) *n.* ⟦< L *radius,* ray⟧ a radioactive metallic chemical element, found in some uranium, which undergoes spontaneous atomic disintegration

ra·di·us (rā′dē əs) *n., pl.* **-di·i′** (-ī′) or **-us·es** ⟦L, ray⟧ **1** any straight line from the center to the periphery of a circle or sphere **2** the circular area limited by the sweep of such a line */within a radius of two miles/*

ra·don (rā′dän) *n.* ⟦< RADIUM⟧ a radioactive, gaseous chemical element formed in the atomic disintegration of radium

RAF Royal Air Force

raf·fi·a (raf′ē ə) *n.* ⟦< native name⟧ **1** a palm tree of Madagascar with large leaves **2** fiber from its leaves, used as string or for weaving

raff·ish (raf′ish) *adj.* ⟦(RIFF)RAFF + -ISH⟧ **1** rakish **2** vulgar; low

raf·fle (raf′′l) *n.* ⟦ME *rafle*⟧ a lottery in which each participant buys a chance to win a prize —*vt.* **-fled, -fling** to offer as a prize in a raffle: often with *off*

raft[1] (raft) *n.* ⟦< ON *raptr,* a log⟧ **1** a flat, buoyant structure of logs, etc. fastened together **2** a flat-bottomed, inflatable boat

raft[2] (raft) *n.* ⟦< Brit dial. *raff,* rubbish⟧ [Colloq.] a large quantity

raf·ter (raf′tər) *n.* ⟦OE *ræfter*⟧ any of the beams that slope from the ridge of a roof to the eaves

rag[1] (rag) *n.* ⟦< ON *rögg,* tuft of hair⟧ **1** a waste piece of cloth, esp. one old or torn **2** a small piece of cloth for dusting, etc. **3** [*pl.*] old, worn clothes

rag[2] (rag) *vt.* **ragged, rag′ging** ⟦< ?⟧ [Slang] to tease or scold

rag[3] (rag) *n.* a tune in ragtime

ra·ga (rä′gə) *n.* ⟦Sans *rāga,* color⟧ any of various melody patterns improvised on by Hindu musicians

rag·a·muf·fin (rag′ə muf′in) *n.* ⟦ME *Ragamoffyn,* name of a demon⟧ a dirty, ragged person, esp. a poor child

rag′bag′ *n.* **1** a bag for rags **2** a collection of odds and ends

rage (rāj) *n.* ⟦< LL *rabia,* madness⟧ **1** a furious, uncontrolled anger **2** a great force, violence, etc. —*vi.* **raged, rag′ing 1** to show violent anger in action or speech **2** to be forceful, violent, etc. **3** to spread unchecked, as a disease —**(all) the rage** a fad

rag·ged (rag′id) *adj.* **1** shabby or torn from wear **2** wearing shabby or torn clothes **3** uneven; imperfect **4** shaggy */ragged hair/* —**run ragged** to tire out; exhaust —**rag′ged·ness** *n.*

rag′ged·y (-i dē) *adj.* tattered

RAGLAN SLEEVES

rag·lan (rag′lən) *n.* ⟦after Lord *Raglan,* 19th-c. Brit general⟧ a loose coat with sleeves that continue in one piece to the collar —*adj.* designating such a sleeve

ra·gout (ra go͞o′) *n.* ⟦< Fr *ragoûter,* revive the appetite of⟧ a highly seasoned stew of meat and vegetables

rag′time′ *n.* ⟦prob. < *ragged time*⟧ **1** a type of American music (c. 1890-1920), with strong syncopation in even time **2** its rhythm

rag′weed′ *n.* ⟦< its ragged-looking leaves⟧ a weed whose pollen is a common cause of hay fever

rah (rä) *interj.* hurrah

raid (rād) *n.* ⟦dial. var. of ROAD⟧ **1** a sudden, hostile attack, esp. by troops or bandits **2** a sudden invasion of a place by police, for discovering violations of the law —*vt., vi.* to make a raid (on) —**raid′er** *n.*

rail[1] (rāl) *n.* ⟦< L *regula,* a rule⟧ **1** a bar of wood, metal, etc. placed between posts as a barrier or support **2** any of the parallel metal bars forming a track for a railroad, etc. **3** a railroad —*vt.* to supply with rails

rail[2] (rāl) *vi.* ⟦< LL *ragere,* to bellow⟧ to speak bitterly; complain violently

rail[3] (rāl) *n.* ⟦< Fr *raaler,* to screech⟧ a marsh bird with a harsh cry

rail′ing *n.* **1** materials for rails **2** a fence, etc. made of rails and posts

rail·ler·y (rāl′ər ē) *n., pl.* **-ies** ⟦see RAIL[2]⟧ light, good-natured ridicule

rail′road′ *n.* **1** a track of parallel steel rails for a train **2** a complete system of such tracks, trains, etc. —*vt.* **1** to transport by railroad **2** [Colloq.] to rush through quickly, so as to prevent careful consideration —*vi.* to work on a railroad —**rail′road′er** *n.* —**rail′road′ing** *n.*

rail′way′ *n.* **1** any track with rails for guiding wheels **2** RAILROAD

rai·ment (rā′mənt) *n.* ⟦see ARRAY & -MENT⟧ [Archaic] clothing; attire

rain (rān) *n.* ⟦OE *regn*⟧ **1** water falling in drops condensed from the atmosphere **2** the falling of such drops **3** a rapid falling of many small objects —*vi.* **1** to fall: said of rain **2** to fall like rain —*vt.* **1** to pour down (rain, etc.) **2** to give in large quantities —**rain out** to cause (an event) to be postponed because of rain —**rain′y, -i·er, -i·est,** *adj.*

rain'bow' (-bō') ***n.*** ⟦OE *regnboga*⟧ an arc containing the colors of the spectrum formed in the sky by the refraction, reflection, and dispersion of light in rain or fog

rain check the stub of a ticket to a ballgame, etc. allowing future admission if the event is rained out

rain'coat' ***n.*** a water-repellent coat

rain'drop' ***n.*** a single drop of rain

rain'fall' ***n.*** **1** a falling of rain **2** the amount of water falling over a given area during a given time

rain forest a dense, evergreen forest in a rainy tropical region

rain'storm' ***n.*** a storm with a heavy rain

rain'wa'ter ***n.*** water that is falling or has fallen as rain

raise (rāz) ***vt.*** **raised, rais'ing** ⟦< ON *reisa*⟧ **1** to cause to rise; lift **2** to construct; build **3** to increase in size, intensity, amount, degree, etc. /*raise* prices, *raise* one's voice/ **4** to provoke; inspire **5** to present for consideration /*raise* a question/ **6** to collect (an army, money, etc.) **7** to end /*raise* a siege/ **8** *a*) to cause to grow *b*) to rear (children) —***n.*** **1** a raising **2** an increase in salary or in a bet —**raise Cain** (or **hell,** etc.) [Slang] to create a disturbance

rai·sin (rā'zən) ***n.*** ⟦< L *racemus,* cluster of grapes⟧ a dried sweet grape

rai·son d'être (rā'zōn det', det'rə) ⟦Fr⟧ reason for being

raj (räj) ***n.*** ⟦Hindi: see fol.⟧ in India, rule; government —**the Raj** the British government in its dominion over India

ra·jah or **ra·ja** (rä'jə) ***n.*** ⟦< Sans *rāj,* to rule⟧ a prince in India

rake[1] (rāk) ***n.*** ⟦OE *raca*⟧ a long-handled tool with teeth at one end, for gathering loose hay, leaves, etc. —***vt.*** **raked, rak'ing** **1** to gather or smooth with a rake **2** to search through minutely **3** to direct gunfire along (a line of troops, etc.) —**rake in** to gather a great amount of rapidly —**rake up** to uncover facts or gossip about (the past, a scandal, etc.)

rake[2] (rāk) ***n.*** ⟦contr. of *rakehell*⟧ a dissolute, debauched man

rake[3] (rāk) ***vi., vt.*** **raked, rak'ing** ⟦< ?⟧ to slant —***n.*** a slanting

rake'-off' ***n.*** [Slang] a commission or rebate, esp. when illegitimate

rak·ish (rāk'ish) ***adj.*** ⟦< RAKE[3] + -ISH⟧ **1** having a trim appearance suggesting speed: said of a ship **2** dashing; jaunty —**rak'ish·ly** ***adv.***

Ra·leigh (rôl'ē), Sir **Wal·ter** (wôl'tər) *c.* 1552-1618; Eng. explorer & poet

Raleigh capital of N.C.: pop. 150,000

ral·ly[1] (ral'ē) ***vt., vi.*** **-lied, -ly·ing** ⟦< OFr *re-,* again + *alier,* join⟧ **1** to bring back together in, or come back to, a state of order, as troops **2** to bring or come together for a common purpose **3** to recover; revive —***n., pl.*** **-lies** **1** a rallying or being rallied; esp., a gathering of people for some purpose **2** an organized automobile run designed to test driving skills

ral·ly[2] (ral'ē) ***vt., vi.*** **-lied, -ly·ing** ⟦see RAIL[2]⟧ to tease or ridicule

ram (ram) ***n.*** ⟦OE *ramm*⟧ **1** a male sheep **2** BATTERING RAM —***vt.*** **rammed, ram'·ming** **1** to strike against with great force **2** to force into place; press down

RAM (ram) ***n.*** a computer memory that allows data to be directly accessible Also **random-access memory**

-ram·a (ram'ə) *combining form* -ORAMA /*autorama*/

ram·ble (ram'bəl) ***vi.*** **-bled, -bling** ⟦< ME *romen*⟧ **1** to roam about; esp., to stroll about idly **2** to talk or write aimlessly **3** to spread in all directions, as a vine —***n.*** a stroll

ram'bler ***n.*** a person or thing that rambles; esp., a climbing rose

ram·bunc·tious (ram buŋk'shəs) ***adj.*** ⟦alt., after RAM < earlier *rambustious*⟧ disorderly, boisterous, unruly, etc. —**ram·bunc'·tious·ness** ***n.***

ram·e·kin or **ram·e·quin** (ram'ə kin) ***n.*** ⟦< Fr < MDu⟧ a small, individual baking dish

ram·i·fy (ram'ə fī') ***vt., vi.*** **-fied', -fy'ing** ⟦< L *ramus,* a branch + *facere,* make⟧ to divide or spread out into branches or branchlike divisions —**ram'i·fi·ca'tion** ***n.***

ramp (ramp) ***n.*** ⟦< OFr *ramper,* climb⟧ **1** a sloping surface, walk, etc. joining different levels **2** a means for boarding a plane, as a movable staircase **3** a sloping runway, as for launching boats

ram·page (ram pāj'; *also, and for n.,* ram'pāj) ***vi.*** **-paged', -pag'ing** to rush about wildly; rage —***n.*** an outbreak of violent, raging behavior: chiefly in **on the** (or **a**) **rampage**

ramp·ant (ram'pənt) ***adj.*** ⟦< OFr *ramper,* climb⟧ growing unchecked; widespread

ram·part (ram'pärt', -pərt) ***n.*** ⟦< Fr *re-,* again + *emparer,* fortify⟧ an embankment of earth surmounted by a parapet for defending a fort, etc.

ram'rod' ***n.*** a rod for ramming down the charge in a muzzle-loading gun

ram·shack·le (ram'shak'əl) ***adj.*** ⟦< RANSACK⟧ loose and rickety; likely to fall to pieces

ran (ran) ***vi., vt.*** *pt. of* RUN

ranch (ranch) ***n.*** ⟦< Sp *rancho,* small farm⟧ **1** a large farm, esp. in the W U.S., for raising cattle, horses, or sheep **2** a style of house with all the rooms on one floor: in full **ranch house** —***vi.*** to work on or manage a ranch —**ranch'er** ***n.***

ran·cid (ran'sid) ***adj.*** ⟦< L *rancere,* to be rank⟧ having the bad smell or taste of stale fats or oils; spoiled

ran·cor (raŋ'kər) ***n.*** ⟦< L *rancere,* to be rank⟧ a continuing and bitter hate or ill will Brit. sp. **ran'cour** —**ran'cor·ous** ***adj.*** —**ran'cor·ous·ly** ***adv.***

R & B or **r & b** rhythm and blues

R & D research and development

ran·dom (ran'dəm) ***adj.*** ⟦< OFr *randir,* run violently⟧ purposeless; haphazard —**at random** haphazardly —**ran'dom·ly** ***adv.***

ran'dom·ize' (-īz') ***vt.*** **-ized', -iz'ing** to select or choose (items of a group) in a random order

ran·dy (ran'dē) ***adj.*** **-di·er, -di·est** [Chiefly Scot.] amorous; lustful

rang (raŋ) ***vi., vt.*** *pt. of* RING[1]

range (rānj) ***vt.*** **ranged, rang'ing** ⟦< OFr *renc,* a ring⟧ **1** to arrange in order; set in a row or rows **2** to place with others in a cause, etc. 3 to roam about —*vi.* 1 to extend in a given direction 2 to roam 3 to vary between stated limits —*n.* 1 a row, line, or series 2 a series of connected mountains 3 the distance that a weapon can fire its projectile 4 *a)* a place for shooting practice *b)* a place for testing rockets in flight 5 extent; scope 6 a large, open area for grazing livestock 7 the limits of possible variations of amount, degree, pitch, etc. /a wide *range* in price/ 8 a cooking stove

rang′er *n.* 1 *a)* a mounted trooper who patrols a region *b)* [*often* R-] a soldier trained for raiding and close combat 2 a warden who patrols forests

Ran·goon (ran go͞on′) capital of Burma: pop. 2,458,000

rang·y (rān′jē) *adj.* **-i·er, -i·est** long-limbed and slender —**rang′i·ness** *n.*

rank[1] (raŋk) *n.* ⟦< OFr *ranc*⟧ 1 a row, line, or series 2 a social class 3 high position in society 4 an official grade /the *rank* of major/ 5 a relative position in a scale /a poet of the first *rank*/ 6 *a)* a row of soldiers, etc. placed side by side *b)* [*pl.*] the army; esp., enlisted soldiers —*vt.* 1 to place in a rank 2 to assign a position to 3 to outrank —*vi.* to hold a certain position —**rank and file** 1 enlisted soldiers 2 the common people, as distinguished from leaders

rank[2] (raŋk) *adj.* ⟦OE *ranc,* strong⟧ 1 growing vigorously and coarsely /*rank* grass/ 2 strong and offensive in smell or taste 3 in bad taste 4 complete; utter /*rank* deceit/ —**rank′ness** *n.*

rank′ing *adj.* 1 of the highest rank 2 prominent or outstanding

ran·kle (raŋ′kəl) *vi., vt.* **-kled, -kling** ⟦< L dim. of *draco,* dragon⟧ 1 orig., to fester 2 to cause or cause to have long-lasting anger, rancor, etc.

ran·sack (ran′sak′) *vt.* ⟦< ON *rann,* house + *sœkja,* seek⟧ 1 to search thoroughly 2 to plunder; pillage

ran·som (ran′səm) *n.* ⟦see REDEEM⟧ 1 the redeeming of a captive by paying money or complying with demands 2 the price thus paid or demanded —*vt.* to obtain the release of (a captive, etc.) by paying the demanded price

rant (rant) *vi., vt.* ⟦< obs. Du *ranten*⟧ to talk or say in a loud, wild, extravagant way —*n.* loud, wild speech

rap (rap) *vt.* **rapped, rap′ping** ⟦prob. echoic⟧ 1 to strike quickly and sharply; tap 2 [Slang] to criticize sharply —*vi.* 1 to knock sharply 2 [Slang] to talk —*n.* 1 a quick, sharp knock 2 [Slang] blame or punishment 3 [Slang] a chat or serious discussion

ra·pa·cious (rə pā′shəs) *adj.* ⟦< L *rapere,* seize⟧ 1 greedy; voracious 2 predatory —**ra·pac′i·ty** (-pas′ə tē) *n.*

rape[1] (rāp) *n.* ⟦prob. < L *rapere,* seize⟧ 1 the crime of having sexual intercourse with a person forcibly and without consent 2 the plundering (*of* a city, etc.), as in warfare —*vt.* **raped, rap′ing** 1 to commit rape on; violate 2 to plunder or destroy —*vi.* to commit rape —**rap′ist** *n.*

rape[2] (rāp) *n.* ⟦< L *rapa,* turnip⟧ an annual plant whose leaves are used for fodder

Raph·a·el (rä′fä el′, -fī-, -fā-) 1483-1520; It. painter & architect

rap·id (rap′id) *adj.* ⟦< L *rapere,* to rush⟧ moving or occurring with speed; swift; quick —*n.* [*usually pl.*] a part of a river where the current is swift —**ra·pid·i·ty** (rə pid′ə tē) *n.* —**rap′id·ly** *adv.*

rapid transit a system of public transportation in an urban area, using electric trains along an unimpeded right of way

ra·pi·er (rā′pē ər) *n.* ⟦Fr *rapière*⟧ a light, sharp-pointed sword used only for thrusting

rap·ine (rap′in) *n.* ⟦< L *rapere,* seize⟧ plunder; pillage

rap·pel (ra pel′) *n.* ⟦Fr, lit., a recall⟧ a descent by a mountain climber, using a double rope arranged around the body to control the slide downward —*vi.* **-pelled′, -pel′ling** to make such a descent

rap·port (ra pôr′) *n.* ⟦Fr⟧ close relationship; harmony

rap·proche·ment (ra′prôsh män′) *n.* ⟦Fr⟧ an establishing of friendly relations

rap·scal·lion (rap skal′yən) *n.* ⟦< RASCAL⟧ a rascal; rogue

rap sheet [Slang] one's police record of arrests and convictions

rapt (rapt) *adj.* ⟦< L *rapere,* seize⟧ 1 carried away with joy, love, etc. 2 completely engrossed (*in* study, etc.)

rap·ture (rap′chər) *n.* the state of being carried away with joy, love, etc.; ecstasy —**rap′tur·ous** *adj.*

ra·ra a·vis (rer′ə ā′vis) *pl.* **ra·rae a·ves** (rer′ē ā′vēz) ⟦L, lit., strange bird⟧ an extraordinary person or thing

rare[1] (rer) *adj.* **rar′er, rar′est** ⟦< L *rarus*⟧ 1 not frequently encountered; scarce; unusual 2 unusually good; excellent 3 not dense /*rare* atmosphere/ —**rare′ness** *n.*

rare[2] (rer) *adj.* **rar′er, rar′est** ⟦OE *hrere*⟧ not completely cooked; partly raw: said esp. of meat —**rare′ness** *n.*

rare[3] (rer) *vi.* **rared, rar′ing** [Colloq.] to be eager: used in prp. /*raring* to go/

rare·bit (rer′bit) *n.* WELSH RABBIT

rar·e·fy (rer′ə fī′) *vt., vi.* **-fied′, -fy′ing** ⟦< L *rarus,* RARE[1] + *facere,* to make⟧ to make or become less dense —**rar′e·fac′tion** (-fak′shən) *n.*

rare·ly (rer′lē) *adv.* 1 infrequently; seldom 2 uncommonly

rar·i·ty (rer′ə tē) *n.* 1 a being rare; specif., *a)* scarcity *b)* lack of density 2 *pl.* **-ties** something remarkable or valuable because rare

ras·cal (ras′kəl) *n.* ⟦< OFr *rascaille,* rabble⟧ 1 a rogue 2 a mischievous child —**ras·cal′i·ty** (-kal′ə tē) *n.* —**ras′cal·ly** *adj., adv.*

rash[1] (rash) *adj.* ⟦ME *rasch*⟧ too hasty in acting or speaking; reckless —**rash′ly** *adv.* —**rash′ness** *n.*

rash[2] (rash) *n.* ⟦< OFr *rascaille,* rabble⟧ 1 an eruption of spots on the skin 2 a sudden appearance of a large number

rash′er *n.* ⟦< L *radere,* to scrape⟧ a thin slice of bacon, etc., or a serving of several such slices

rasp (rasp) *vt.* ⟦< OHG *raspon,* to scrape together⟧ 1 to scrape as with a file 2 to grate upon; irritate —*vi.* 1 to grate 2 to make a rough, grating sound —*n.* 1 a type of rough file 2 a rough, grating sound —**rasp′y, -i·er, -i·est,** *adj.*

rasp·ber·ry (raz′ber′ē, -bər-) ***n.***, *pl.* **-ries** ⟦< earlier *raspis*⟧ 1 a small, juicy, edible, reddish fruit related to the rose 2 a plant bearing this fruit 3 [Slang] a sound of derision

rat (rat) ***n.*** ⟦OE *ræt*⟧ 1 a long-tailed rodent, resembling, but larger than, the mouse 2 [Slang] a sneaky, contemptible person; esp., an informer **—*vi.* rat′ted, rat′ting** [Slang] to inform (*on*) **—smell a rat** to suspect a trick, plot, etc.

ratch·et (rach′it) ***n.*** ⟦< It *rocca,* distaff⟧ 1 a toothed wheel (in full **ratchet wheel**) or bar whose sloping teeth catch a pawl, preventing backward motion 2 such a pawl

rate[1] (rāt) ***n.*** ⟦< L *reri,* reckon⟧ 1 the amount, degree, etc. of anything in relation to units of something else /*rate* of pay/ 2 price, esp. per unit 3 [Now Rare] a class or rank /of the first *rate*/ **—*vt.* rat′ed, rat′ing** 1 to appraise 2 to consider; esteem 3 [Colloq.] to deserve **—*vi.*** to have value, status, etc. **—at any rate** 1 in any event 2 anyway

rate[2] (rāt) ***vt., vi.* rat′ed, rat′ing** ⟦< L *reputare,* to count⟧ to scold; chide

rath·er (ra*th*′ər) ***adv.*** ⟦OE *hræthe,* quickly⟧ 1 more willingly; preferably 2 with more justice, reason, etc. /I, *rather* than you, should pay/ 3 more accurately /my son, or *rather*, stepson/ 4 on the contrary 5 somewhat /*rather* hungry/ **—rather than** instead of

raths·kel·ler (rät′skel′ər, rath′-) ***n.*** ⟦Ger < *rat*, council + *keller*, cellar⟧ a restaurant, usually below the street level, where beer is served

rat·i·fy (rat′ə fī′) ***vt.* -fied′, -fy′ing** ⟦< L *ratus*, reckoned + *facere*, make⟧ to approve; esp., to give official sanction to **—rat′i·fi·ca′tion *n.***

rat·ing (rāt′iŋ) ***n.*** 1 a rank or grade, as of military personnel 2 a placement in a certain rank or class 3 an evaluation; appraisal 4 *Film* a classification, based on content, restricting the age of those who may attend 5 *Radio, TV* the relative popularity of a program according to sample polls

ra·tio (rā′shō, -shē ō′) ***n.***, *pl.* **-tios** ⟦L, a reckoning⟧ a fixed relation in degree, number, etc. between two similar things; proportion

ra·ti·oc·i·nate (rash′ē äs′ə nāt′) ***vi.* -nat′ed, -nat′ing** ⟦see prec.⟧ to think or argue logically; reason **—ra′ti·oc′i·na′tion *n.***

ra·tion (rash′ən, rā′shən) ***n.*** ⟦see RATIO⟧ 1 a fixed portion; share 2 a fixed allowance of food, as a daily allowance for a soldier 3 [*pl.*] food supply **—*vt.*** 1 to supply with rations 2 to distribute (food, clothing, etc.) in rations, as in times of scarcity

ra·tion·al (rash′ən əl) ***adj.*** ⟦see RATIO⟧ 1 of or based on reasoning 2 able to reason; reasoning 3 sensible or sane **—ra′tion·al′i·ty** (-ə nal′ə tē) ***n.* —ra′tion·al·ly *adv.***

ra·tion·ale (rash′ə nal′) ***n.*** ⟦< L *rationalis,* rational⟧ 1 the reasons or rational basis for something 2 an explanation of principles

ra′tion·al·ism′ *n.* the practice of accepting reason as the only authority in determining one's opinions or course of action **—ra′tion·al·ist *n., adj.* —ra′tion·al·is′tic *adj.***

ra′tion·al·ize′ *vt., vi.* -ized′, -iz′ing 1 to make or be rational or reasonable 2 to devise plausible explanations for (one's acts, beliefs, etc.), usually in self-deception **—ra′tion·al·i·za′tion *n.***

rat·line (rat′lin) ***n.*** ⟦< ?⟧ any of the horizontal ropes which join the shrouds of a ship and serve as a ladder Also **rat′lin**

rat race [Slang] a mad scramble or intense struggle, as in the business world

rat·tan (ra tan′) ***n.*** ⟦Malay *rotan*⟧ 1 a tall palm tree with long, slender, tough stems 2 its stem, used in making furniture, etc.

rat·tle (rat′'l) ***vi.* -tled, -tling** ⟦prob. echoic⟧ 1 to make a series of sharp, short sounds 2 to chatter: often with *on* **—*vt.*** 1 to cause to rattle 2 to confuse or upset **—*n.*** 1 a series of sharp, short sounds 2 a series of horny rings at the end of a rattlesnake's tail 3 a baby's toy, a percussion instrument, etc. made to rattle when shaken

rat′tle·brain′ *n.* a frivolous, talkative person **—rat′tle·brained′ *adj.***

rat′tler *n.* a rattlesnake

DIAMONDBACK RATTLESNAKE

rat′tle·snake′ *n.* a poisonous American snake with horny rings at the end of the tail that rattle when shaken

rat′tle·trap′ *n.* a rickety old car

rat′tling *adj.* 1 that rattles 2 [Colloq.] very fast, good, etc. **—*adv.*** [Colloq.] very /a *rattling* good time/

rat′trap′ *n.* 1 a trap for rats 2 [Colloq.] a dirty, run-down building

rat·ty (rat′ē) ***adj.* -ti·er, -ti·est** [Slang] shabby or run-down

rau·cous (rô′kəs) ***adj.*** ⟦L *raucus*⟧ 1 hoarse 2 loud and rowdy **—rau′cous·ly *adv.* —rau′cous·ness *n.***

raun·chy (rôn′chē, rän′-) ***adj.* -chi·er, -chi·est** ⟦< ?⟧ [Slang] 1 dirty, sloppy, etc. 2 risqué, lustful, etc.

rav·age (rav′ij) ***n.*** ⟦see RAVISH⟧ destruction; ruin **—*vt.* -aged, -ag·ing** to destroy violently; devastate; ruin **—*vi.*** to commit ravages

rave (rāv) ***vi.* raved, rav′ing** ⟦< OFr *raver,* roam⟧ 1 to talk incoherently or wildly 2 to talk with great enthusiasm (*about*) **—*n.*** [Colloq.] a very enthusiastic commendation

rav·el (rav′əl) ***vt., vi.* -eled** or **-elled, -el·ing** or **-el·ling** ⟦MDu *ravelen*⟧ to separate into its parts, esp. threads; untwist; fray **—*n.*** a raveled part in a fabric

ra·ven (rā′vən) ***n.*** ⟦OE *hræfn*⟧ the largest crow, with a straight, sharp beak **—*adj.*** black and lustrous

rav·en·ing (rav′ən iŋ) ***adj.*** ⟦ult. < L *rapere,* seize⟧ greedily searching for prey /*ravening* wolves/

rav·e·nous (rav′ə nəs) ***adj.*** ⟦< L *rapere,* seize⟧ 1 greedily hungry 2 rapacious **—rav′e·nous·ly *adv.***

ra·vine (rə vēn′) ***n.*** ⟦Fr, flood⟧ a long, deep hollow in the earth, esp. one worn by a stream; gorge

rav'ing *adj.* **1** that raves; frenzied **2** [Colloq.] exciting enthusiastic admiration /a *raving* beauty/ —*adv.* so as to cause raving /*raving* mad/

ra·vi·o·li (rav'ē ō'lē) *n.pl.* ⟦It⟧ [*usually with sing. v.*] small casings of pasta dough filled with ground meat, cheese, etc.

rav·ish (rav'ish) *vt.* ⟦< L *rapere,* seize⟧ **1** to seize and carry away forcibly **2** to rape (a woman) **3** to transport with joy or delight —**rav'ish·ment** *n.*

rav'ish·ing *adj.* causing great joy

raw (rô) *adj.* ⟦OE *hreaw*⟧ **1** not cooked **2** in its natural condition; not processed /*raw* silk/ **3** inexperienced /a *raw* recruit/ **4** abraded and sore **5** uncomfortably cold and damp /a *raw* wind/ **6** brutal, coarse, indecent, etc. **7** [Colloq.] harsh or unfair /a *raw* deal/ —**in the raw 1** in the natural state **2** naked —**raw'ness** *n.*

raw'boned' (-bōnd') *adj.* lean; gaunt

raw'hide' *n.* **1** an untanned cattle hide **2** a whip made of this

ray[1] (rā) *n.* ⟦< L *radius*⟧ **1** any of the thin lines, or beams, of light that appear to come from a bright source **2** any of several lines radiating from a center **3** a tiny amount /a *ray* of hope/ **4** a beam of radiant energy, radioactive particles, etc.

ray[2] (rā) *n.* ⟦< L *raia*⟧ a cartilaginous fish with a broad flat body, widely expanded fins on both sides, and a whiplike tail

ray·on (rā'än) *n.* ⟦< RAY[1]⟧ **1** a textile fiber made from a cellulose solution **2** a fabric of such fibers

raze (rāz) *vt.* **razed, raz'ing** ⟦< L *radere,* to scrape⟧ to tear down completely; demolish

ra·zor (rā'zər) *n.* ⟦see prec.⟧ **1** a sharp-edged cutting instrument for shaving, etc. **2** SHAVER (sense 2)

razz (raz) *vt.* ⟦< RASPBERRY⟧ [Slang] to tease, ridicule, etc.

raz·zle-daz·zle (raz'əl daz'əl) *n.* [Slang] a flashy, deceptive display

razz·ma·tazz (raz'mə taz') *n.* ⟦prob. < prec.⟧ [Slang] **1** lively spirit **2** flashy display; showiness

rbi or **RBI** *Baseball* run(s) batted in

R.C.Ch. Roman Catholic Church

rd. **1** rod **2** round

RD or **R.D.** Rural Delivery

Rd. Road

RDA Recommended Daily (*or* Dietary) Allowance: the amount of vitamins, etc. suggested for various age groups

re[1] (rā) *n.* ⟦It⟧ *Music* the second tone of the diatonic scale

re[2] (rē, rā) *prep.* ⟦L < *res,* thing⟧ in the matter of; as regards

re- ⟦< Fr or L⟧ *prefix* **1** back **2** again; anew It is sometimes hyphenated, as before a word beginning with *e* or to distinguish such forms as *re-cover* (to cover again) and RECOVER The words in the following list can be understood if "again" or "anew" is added to the meaning of the base word:

reacquaint
reacquire
readjust
readmit
reaffirm
realign
reappear
reapply
reappoint
reappraise
rearm
reassemble
reassert
reassess
reassign
reawaken
reborn
rebroadcast
rebuild
recharge
recheck
reclassify
recommence
reconquer
reconsign
reconvene
reconvert
recopy
re-cover
redecorate
rededicate
redesign
redetermine
redirect
rediscover
redistribution
redivide
redraw
reedit
reeducate
reelect
reembark
reembody
reemerge
reemphasize
reenact
reengage
reenlist
reenter
reestablish
reevaluate
reexamine
reexplain
refashion
refasten
refinance
reformulate
refuel
refurnish
rehear
reheat
rehire
reimpose
reinfect
reinoculate
reinsert
reinspect
reinvest
reissue
rekindle
relearn
reload
remake
remarry
rematch
rename
renegotiate
renominate
renumber
reoccupy
reoccur
reopen
reorder
repack
repackage
repaint
repave
rephrase
replant
replay
re-press
reprint
republish
reread
reroute
reschedule
resell
reset
resettle
reshuffle
respell
restate
restring
restudy
restyle
resubscribe
resupply
retell
retest
rethink
retrain
retrial
reunite
reupholster
reuse
revisit
revitalize
reweigh
rework
rezone

reach (rēch) *vt.* ⟦OE *ræcan*⟧ **1** to thrust out (the hand, etc.) **2** to extend to by thrusting out, etc. **3** to obtain and hand over /*reach* me the salt/ **4** to go as far as; attain **5** to influence; affect **6** to get in touch with, as by telephone —*vi.* **1** to thrust out the hand, etc. **2** to extend in influence, space, etc. **3** to carry, as sight, sound, etc. **4** to try to get something —*n.* **1** a stretching or thrusting out **2** the power of, or the extent covered in, stretching, obtaining, etc. **3** a continuous extent, esp. of water

re·act (rē akt') *vi.* **1** to act in return or reciprocally **2** to act in a reverse way; go back to a former condition, stage, etc. **3** to respond to a stimulus **4** *Chem.* to act with another substance in producing a chemical change

re·act·ant (rē ak'tənt) *n.* any substance involved in a chemical reaction

re·ac·tion (rē ak'shən) *n.* **1** a return or opposing action, etc. **2** a response, as to a stimulus or influence **3** a movement back to a former or less advanced condition **4** a chemical change

re·ac'tion·ar'y (-shə ner'ē) ***adj.*** of, characterized by, or advocating reaction, esp. in politics —***n.***, *pl.* **-ies** an advocate of reaction, esp. in politics

re·ac·ti·vate (rē ak'tə vāt') ***vt., vi.*** **-vat'ed, -vat'ing** to make or be made active again; specif., to return (a military unit, ship, etc.) to active status —**re·ac'ti·va'tion** ***n.***

re·ac'tive (-tiv) ***adj.*** **1** tending to react **2** of, from, or showing reaction —**re'ac·tiv'i·ty** ***n.***

re·ac'tor (-tər) ***n.*** NUCLEAR REACTOR

read[1] (rēd) ***vt.*** **read** (red), **read·ing** (rēd'iŋ) ⟦< OE *rædan,* to counsel⟧ **1** to get the meaning of (writing) by interpreting the characters **2** to utter aloud (written matter) **3** to understand or interpret **4** to foretell (the future) **5** to study /to *read* law/ **6** to register, as a gauge **7** *Comput.* to access (data) from (a disk, tape, etc.) **8** [Slang] to hear and understand /I *read* you/ —***vi.*** **1** to read something written **2** to learn by reading: with *about* or *of* **3** to contain certain words —**read into** (or **in**) to attribute (a particular meaning to) —**read out of** to expel from (a group) —**read'a·bil'i·ty** ***n.*** —**read'a·ble** ***adj.*** —**read'er** ***n.***

read[2] (red) ***vt., vi.*** *pt. & pp. of* READ[1] —***adj.*** informed by reading /well-*read*/

read'er·ship' ***n.*** the people who read a certain publication, author, etc.

read·ing (rēd'iŋ) ***n.*** **1** the act of one who reads **2** material to be read **3** the amount measured by a barometer, thermometer, etc. **4** a particular interpretation or performance

read'out' ***n.*** **1** the retrieving of information from a computer **2** information from a computer, thermostat, etc. displayed visually or recorded, as on tape

read·y (red'ē) ***adj.*** **-i·er, -i·est** ⟦OE *ræde*⟧ **1** prepared to act or be used immediately **2** willing **3** likely or liable; apt /*ready* to cry/ **4** dexterous **5** prompt /a *ready* reply/ **6** available at once /*ready* cash/ —***vt.*** **-ied, -y·ing** to make ready; prepare —**read'i·ly** ***adv.*** —**read'i·ness** ***n.***

read'y-made' ***adj.*** made so as to be ready for use or sale at once: also, as applied to clothing, **read'y-to-wear'**

Rea·gan (rā'gən), **Ron·ald (Wilson)** (rän'əld) 1911- ; 40th president of the U.S. (1981-89)

re·a·gent (rē ā'jənt) ***n.*** *Chem.* a substance used to detect, measure, or react with another substance

re·al (rē'əl, rēl) ***adj.*** ⟦< L *res,* thing⟧ **1** existing as or in fact; actual; true **2** authentic; genuine **3** *Law* of or relating to immovable things /*real* property/ —***adv.*** [Colloq.] very —**for real** [Slang] real or really

real estate land, including the buildings or improvements on it

re·al·ism (rē'ə liz'əm) ***n.*** **1** a tendency to face facts and be practical **2** the picturing in art and literature of people and things as they really appear to be —**re'al·ist** ***n.*** —**re'al·is'tic** ***adj.*** —**re'al·is'ti·cal·ly** ***adv.***

re·al·i·ty (rē al'ə tē) ***n.***, *pl.* **-ties** **1** the quality or fact of being real **2** a person or thing that is real; fact —**in reality** in fact; actually

re·al·ize (rē'ə līz') ***vt.*** **-ized', -iz'ing** **1** to make real **2** to understand fully **3** to convert (assets, rights, etc.) into money **4** to gain; obtain /*realize* a profit/ **5** to be sold for (a specified sum) —**re'al·i·za'tion** ***n.***

re'al-life' ***adj.*** actual; not imaginary

re'al·ly ***adv.*** **1** in reality **2** truly —***interj.*** indeed

realm (relm) ***n.*** ⟦see REGAL⟧ **1** a kingdom **2** a region; sphere

Re·al·tor (rē'əl tər, -tôr') *trademark for* a real estate broker or appraiser who is a member of the National Association of Realtors

re·al·ty (rē'əl tē) ***n.*** REAL ESTATE

ream[1] (rēm) ***n.*** ⟦< Ar *rizma,* a bale⟧ **1** a quantity of paper varying from 480 to 516 sheets **2** [*pl.*] [Colloq.] a great amount

ream[2] (rēm) ***vt.*** ⟦OE *reman*⟧ to enlarge (a hole) as with a reamer

ream'er ***n.*** **1** a sharp-edged tool for enlarging or tapering holes **2** a juicer

re·an·i·mate (rē an'ə māt') ***vt.*** **-mat'ed, -mat'ing** to give new life, power, or vigor to —**re·an'i·ma'tion** ***n.***

reap (rēp) ***vt., vi.*** ⟦OE *ripan*⟧ **1** to cut (grain) with a scythe, reaper, etc. **2** to gather (a harvest) **3** to obtain as the reward of action, etc.

reap'er ***n.*** **1** one who reaps **2** a machine for reaping grain

re·ap·por·tion (rē'ə pôr'shən) ***vt.*** to apportion again; specif., to change the representational distribution of (a legislature) —**re'ap·por'tion·ment** ***n.***

rear[1] (rir) ***n.*** ⟦< ARREARS⟧ **1** the back part **2** the position behind or at the back **3** the part of an army, etc. farthest from the enemy **4** [Slang] the buttocks —***adj.*** of, at, or in the rear —**bring up the rear** to come at the end

rear[2] (rir) ***vt.*** ⟦OE *ræran*⟧ **1** to put upright; elevate **2** to build; erect **3** to grow or breed **4** to educate, train, etc. /to *rear* a child/ —***vi.*** **1** to rise on the hind legs, as a horse **2** to rise (*up*), in anger, etc. **3** to rise high

rear admiral a naval officer ranking above a captain

rear-end' ***vt.*** to crash into, or cause the vehicle one is driving to crash into, the back end of (another vehicle)

rear'most' ***adj.*** farthest in the rear

re'ar·range' ***vt.*** **-ranged', -rang'ing** to arrange again or in a different way

rear'ward (-wərd) ***adj.*** at, in, or toward the rear —***adv.*** toward the rear: also **rear'wards**

rea·son (rē'zən) ***n.*** ⟦< L *ratio,* a reckoning⟧ **1** an explanation of an act, idea, etc. **2** a cause or motive **3** the ability to think, draw conclusions, etc. **4** good sense **5** sanity —***vi., vt.*** **1** to think logically (about); analyze **2** to argue or infer —**stand to reason** to be logical —**rea'son·ing** ***n.***

rea'son·a·ble ***adj.*** **1** able to reason **2** fair; just **3** wise; sensible **4** not excessive —**rea'son·a·bly** ***adv.***

re'as·sure' ***vt.*** **-sured', -sur'ing** **1** to assure again **2** to restore to confidence —**re'as·sur'ance** ***n.***

re·bate (rē'bāt') ***vt.*** **-bat'ed, -bat'ing** ⟦< OFr *re-,* RE- + *abattre,* beat down⟧ to give back (part of a payment) —***n.*** a return of part of a payment

Re·bek·ah or **Re·bec′ca** (ri bek′ə) *Bible* the wife of Isaac

reb·el (reb′əl; *for v.* ri bel′) *n.* ⟦< L *re-*, again + *bellare,* wage war⟧ one who resists authority —*adj.* 1 rebellious 2 of rebels —*vi.* **re·bel′, -belled′, -bel′ling** 1 to resist authority 2 to feel or show strong aversion

re·bel·lion (ri bel′yən) *n.* 1 armed resistance to one's government 2 a defiance of any authority

re·bel′lious (-yəs) *adj.* 1 resisting authority 2 opposing control; defiant

re′birth′ *n.* 1 a new or second birth 2 a reawakening; revival

re·bound (ri bound′; *for n.* rē′bound′) *vi.* to spring back, as upon impact —*n.* a rebounding, or ball, etc. that rebounds —**on the rebound** 1 after bouncing back 2 after being jilted

re·buff (ri buf′) *n.* ⟦< It *rabbuffare,* disarrange⟧ 1 an abrupt refusal of offered advice, help, etc. 2 any repulse —*vt.* 1 to snub 2 to check or repulse

re·buke (ri byo͞ok′) *vt.* **-buked′, -buk′ing** ⟦< OFr *re-*, back + *buchier,* to beat⟧ to scold in a sharp way; reprimand —*n.* a reprimand

re·bus (rē′bəs) *n.* ⟦L, lit., by things⟧ a puzzle consisting of pictures, etc. combined to suggest words or phrases

re·but (ri but′) *vt.* **-but′ted, -but′ting** ⟦< OFr *re-*, back + *buter,* to thrust⟧ to contradict or oppose, esp. in a formal manner by argument, proof, etc. —**re·but′tal** (-′l) *n.*

rec (rek) *n. short for* RECREATION: used in compounds, as **rec room**

re·cal·ci·trant (ri kal′si trənt) *adj.* ⟦< L *re-*, back + *calcitrare,* to kick⟧ 1 refusing to obey authority, etc. 2 hard to handle —**re·cal′ci·trance** *n.*

re·call (ri kôl′; *also, & for n.*, rē′kôl) *vt.* 1 to call back 2 to remember 3 to take back; revoke 4 to bring (the mind, etc.) back, as to the immediate situation —*n.* 1 a recalling 2 memory 3 the removal of, or right to remove, an official from office by popular vote

re·cant (ri kant′) *vt., vi.* ⟦< L *re-*, back + *canere,* sing⟧ to renounce formally (one's beliefs, remarks, etc.) —**re·can·ta·tion** (rē′kan tā′shən) *n.*

re·cap[1] (rē kap′; *also, and for n.*, rē′kap′) *vt.* **-capped′, -cap′ping** to put a new tread on (a worn tire) —*n.* such a tire

re·cap[2] (rē′kap′) *n.* a recapitulation, or summary —*vt., vi.* **-capped′, -cap′ping** to recapitulate

re·ca·pit·u·late (rē′kə pich′ə lāt′) *vi., vt.* **-lat′ed, -lat′ing** ⟦see RE- & CAPITULATE⟧ to repeat briefly; summarize —**re′ca·pit′u·la′tion** *n.*

re·cap′ture *vt.* **-tured, -tur·ing** 1 to capture again; retake 2 to remember —*n.* a recapturing

recd. or **rec'd** received

re·cede (ri sēd′) *vi.* **-ced′ed, -ced′ing** ⟦see RE- & CEDE⟧ 1 to go, move, or slope backward 2 to diminish

re·ceipt (ri sēt′) *n.* ⟦see RECEIVE⟧ 1 *old-fashioned var. of* RECIPE 2 a receiving or being received 3 a written acknowledgment that something has been received 4 [*pl.*] the amount received —*vt.* to write a receipt for (goods, etc.)

re·ceiv·a·ble (ri sē′və bəl) *adj.* 1 that can be received 2 due

re·ceive (ri sēv′) *vt.* **-ceived′, -ceiv′ing** ⟦< L *re-*, back + *capere,* take⟧ 1 to take or get (something given, thrown, sent, etc.) 2 to experience; undergo /to *receive* acclaim/ 3 to bear or hold 4 to react to in a specified way 5 to learn /to *receive* news/ 6 to let enter 7 to greet (visitors, etc.)

re·ceived′ *adj.* accepted; considered as standard

re·ceiv′er *n.* one that receives; specif., *a*) *Electronics* a device that converts electrical waves or signals into audible or visual signals *b*) *Football* the player designated to receive a forward pass *c*) *Law* one appointed by a court to administer or hold in trust property in bankruptcy or in a lawsuit —**re·ceiv′er·ship′** *n.*

re·cen·sion (ri sen′shən) *n.* ⟦< L *recensere,* revise⟧ a revision of a text based on a critical study of sources

re·cent (rē′sənt) *adj.* ⟦< L *recens*⟧ 1 done, made, etc. just before the present; new 2 of a time just before the present —**re′cent·ly** *adv.*

re·cep·ta·cle (ri sep′tə kəl) *n.* ⟦see RECEIVE⟧ a container

re·cep·tion (ri sep′shən) *n.* 1 *a*) a receiving or being received *b*) the manner of this 2 a social function for the receiving of guests 3 *Radio, TV* the receiving of signals with reference to the quality of reproduction

re·cep′tion·ist *n.* an office employee who receives callers, etc.

re·cep′tive *adj.* able or ready to accept new ideas, suggestions, etc.

re·cep′tor *n.* a nerve ending or group of nerve endings specialized for receiving stimuli; sense organ

re·cess (rē′ses; *also, & for v. usually,* ri ses′) *n.* ⟦< L *recedere,* recede⟧ 1 a hollow place, as in a wall 2 a hidden or inner place 3 a temporary halting as of work, a session, etc. —*vt.* 1 to place in a recess 2 to form a recess in —*vi.* to take a recess

re·ces·sion (ri sesh′ən) *n.* 1 a going back; withdrawal 2 a temporary falling off of business activity

re·ces′sion·al (-əl) *n.* a piece of music at the end of a church service played when the clergy, etc. march out

re·ces·sive (ri ses′iv) *adj.* 1 tending to recede 2 *Genetics* designating that one of any pair of hereditary factors which remains latent —*n. Genetics* a recessive character or characters

re·cher·ché (rə sher′shā, -sher′shā′) *adj.* ⟦Fr⟧ 1 rare; choice 2 refined; esp., too refined

re·cid·i·vism (ri sid′ə viz′əm) *n.* ⟦< L *re-*, back + *cadere,* to fall⟧ habitual or chronic relapse, esp. into crime

rec·i·pe (res′ə pē′) *n.* ⟦L < *recipere,* receive⟧ 1 a list of materials and directions for preparing a dish or drink 2 a way to achieve something

re·cip·i·ent (ri sip′ē ənt) *n.* ⟦see RECEIVE⟧ one that receives

re·cip·ro·cal (ri sip′rə k′l) *adj.* ⟦< L *reciprocus,* returning⟧ 1 done, given, etc.

in return 2 mutual /*reciprocal* love/ 3 corresponding but reversed 4 corresponding or complementary —*n.* 1 a complement, counterpart, etc. 2 *Math.* the quantity resulting from the division of 1 by the given quantity /the *reciprocal* of 7 is 1/7/

re·cip′ro·cate′ (-kāt′) *vt., vi.* **-cat′ed, -cat′ing** 1 to give and get reciprocally 2 to do, feel, etc. in return 3 to move alternately back and forth —**re·cip′ro·ca′tion** *n.*

rec·i·proc·i·ty (res′ə präs′ə tē) *n., pl.* **-ties** 1 reciprocal state 2 mutual exchange; esp., exchange of special privileges between two countries

re·cit·al (ri sīt′'l) *n.* 1 a reciting 2 the account, story, etc. told 3 a musical or dance program

rec·i·ta·tion (res′ə tā′shən) *n.* 1 a reciting, as of facts, events, etc. 2 *a*) a saying aloud in public of something memorized *b*) a piece so presented 3 a reciting by pupils of answers to questions on a prepared lesson

rec′i·ta·tive′ (-tə tēv′) *n.* ⟦< It: see fol.⟧ a type of declamation, as for operatic dialogue, with the rhythms of speech, but in musical tones

re·cite (ri sīt′) *vt., vi.* **-cit′ed, -cit′ing** ⟦see RE- & CITE⟧ 1 to say aloud from memory, as a poem, lesson, etc. 2 to tell in detail; relate

reck·less (rek′lis) *adj.* ⟦OE *recceleas*⟧ careless; heedless —**reck′less·ly** *adv.* —**reck′less·ness** *n.*

reck·on (rek′ən) *vt.* ⟦OE *-recenian*⟧ 1 to count; compute 2 to regard as being 3 to estimate 4 [Colloq. or Dial.] to suppose —*vi.* 1 to count up 2 [Colloq.] to rely (*on*) —**reckon with** to take into consideration

reck′on·ing *n.* 1 count or computation 2 the settlement of an account

re·claim (ri klām′) *vt.* ⟦see RE- & CLAIM⟧ 1 to bring back (a person) from error, vice, etc. 2 to make (wasteland, etc.) usable 3 to recover (useful materials) from waste products —**rec·la·ma·tion** (rek′lə mā′shən) *n.*

re·cline (ri klīn′) *vt., vi.* **-clined′, -clin′ing** ⟦< L *re-*, back + *clinare,* lean⟧ to lie or cause to lie down

re·clin′er *n.* an upholstered armchair with an adjustable back and seat for reclining Also **reclining chair**

rec·luse (rek′lo͞os, ri klo͞os′) *n.* ⟦< L *re-*, back + *claudere*, shut⟧ one who lives a secluded, solitary life

rec·og·ni·tion (rek′əg nish′ən) *n.* 1 a recognizing or being recognized 2 identification of a person or thing as having been known before

re·cog·ni·zance (ri käg′ni zəns, -kän′i-) *n.* ⟦< L *re-*, again + *cognoscere,* know⟧ *Law* a bond binding one to some act, as to appear in court

rec·og·nize (rek′əg nīz′) *vt.* **-nized′, -niz′ing** ⟦see prec.⟧ 1 to be aware of as known before 2 to know by some detail, as of appearance 3 to perceive 4 to accept as a fact /to *recognize* defeat/ 5 to acknowledge as worthy of approval 6 to acknowledge the status of (a government, etc.) 7 to grant the right to speak in a meeting —**rec′og·niz′a·ble** *adj.*

re·coil (ri koil′; *also for n.* rē′koil′) *vi.* ⟦< L *re-*, back + *culus,* buttocks⟧ 1 to draw back, as in fear, etc. 2 to spring or kick back, as a gun when fired —*n.* a recoiling

rec·ol·lect (rek′ə lekt′) *vt., vi.* ⟦see RE- & COLLECT⟧ to remember, esp. with some effort —**rec′ol·lec′tion** *n.*

re·com·bi·nant DNA (rē käm′bə nənt) DNA formed in the laboratory by splicing together pieces of DNA from different species, as to create new life forms

rec·om·mend (rek′ə mend′) *vt.* ⟦see RE- & COMMEND⟧ 1 to entrust 2 to suggest favorably as suited for some position, etc. 3 to make acceptable 4 to advise; counsel —**rec′om·men·da′tion** *n.*

re′com·mit′ *vt.* **-mit′ted, -mit′ting** 1 to commit again 2 to refer (a question, bill, etc.) back to a committee

rec·om·pense (rek′əm pens′) *vt.* **-pensed′, -pens′ing** ⟦see RE- & COMPENSATE⟧ 1 to repay or reward 2 to compensate (a loss, etc.) —*n.* 1 requital; reward 2 compensation

rec·on·cile (rek′ən sīl′) *vt.* **-ciled′, -cil′ing** ⟦see RE- & CONCILIATE⟧ 1 to make friendly again 2 to settle (a quarrel, etc.) 3 to make (ideas, accounts, etc.) consistent 4 to make content, or acquiescent (*to*) —**rec′on·cil′a·ble** *adj.* —**rec′on·cil′i·a′tion** (-sil′ē ā′shən) *n.*

rec·on·dite (rek′ən dīt′) *adj.* ⟦< L *re-*, back + *condere,* to hide⟧ beyond ordinary understanding; profound

re′con·di′tion *vt.* to put back in good condition, as by repairing

re·con·nais·sance (ri kän′ə səns) *n.* ⟦Fr: see RECOGNIZANCE⟧ a survey of a region, as in seeking out information about enemy positions

rec·on·noi·ter (rek′ə noit′ər, rē′kə-) *vt., vi.* to make a reconnaissance (of) Also [Chiefly Brit.] **rec′on·noi′tre, -tred, -tring**

re·con·sid·er (rē′kən sid′ər) *vt., vi.* to think over again, esp. with a view to changing a decision

re·con′sti·tute′ *vt.* **-tut′ed, -tut′ing** to constitute again; specif., to restore (a dried or condensed substance) to its full liquid form by adding water

re′con·struct′ *vt.* 1 to construct again; rebuild 2 to build up, as from remains, an image of the original

re′con·struc′tion *n.* a reconstructing —[R-] the process or period, after the Civil War, of reestablishing the Southern States in the Union

re·cord (ri kôrd′; *for n. & adj.* rek′ərd) *vt.* ⟦< L *recordari,* remember⟧ 1 to write down for future use 2 to register, as on a graph 3 to register (sound or visual images) on a disc, tape, etc. for later reproduction —*n.* 1 the condition of being recorded 2 anything written down and preserved; account of events 3 *a*) the known facts about anyone or anything *b*) the recorded offenses or crimes of a person 4 a grooved disc for playing on a phonograph 5 the best official performance achieved —*adj.* being the best, largest, etc. —**on** (or **off the**) **record** publicly (or confidentially) declared

re·cord′er *n.* 1 an official who keeps

records **2** a machine or device that records; esp., TAPE RECORDER **3** an early wind instrument

RECORDER

re·cord′ing *n.* **1** what is recorded, as on a disc or tape **2** the record itself

re·count[1] (ri kount′) *vt.* ⟦see RE- & COUNT[1]⟧ to tell in detail; narrate

re·count[2] (rē′kount′; *for n.* rē′kount′) *vt.* to count again —*n.* a second or additional count, as of votes

re·coup (ri ko͞op′) *vt.* ⟦< Fr *re-*, again + *couper,* to cut⟧ to make up for or regain /to *recoup* a loss/

re·course (rē′kôrs′, ri kôrs′) *n.* ⟦see RE- & COURSE⟧ **1** a turning for aid, safety, etc. **2** that to which one turns seeking aid, safety, etc.

re·cov·er (ri kuv′ər) *vt.* ⟦< L *recuperare*⟧ **1** to get back (something lost, etc.) **2** to regain (health, etc.) **3** to make up for /to *recover* losses/ **4** to save (oneself) from a fall, etc. **5** to reclaim (land from the sea, etc.) **6** *Sports* to get control of (a fumbled or wild ball, etc.) —*vi.* **1** to regain health, balance, or control **2** *Sports* to recover a ball, etc.

re·cov′er·y *n., pl.* **-ies** a recovering; specif., *a)* a regaining of something lost *b)* a return to health *c)* a retrieval of a capsule, etc. after a spaceflight

recovery room a hospital room where postoperative patients are kept for close observation and care

rec·re·ant (rek′rē ənt) *adj.* ⟦< OFr *recreire,* surrender allegiance⟧ **1** cowardly **2** disloyal —*n.* **1** a coward **2** a traitor

rec·re·a·tion (rek′rē ā′shən) *n.* ⟦< L *recreare,* refresh⟧ any play, amusement, etc. used to relax or refresh the body or mind —**rec′re·ate′, -at′ed, -at′ing,** *vt., vi.* —**rec′re·a′tion·al** *adj.*

re·crim·i·nate (ri krim′ə nāt′) *vi.* **-nat′ed, -nat′ing** ⟦< L *re-*, back + *crimen,* offense⟧ to answer an accuser by accusing that person in return —**re·crim′i·na′tion** *n.*

re·cru·desce (rē′kro͞o des′) *vi.* **-desced′, -desc′ing** ⟦< L *re-*, again + *crudus,* raw⟧ to break out again after being inactive —**re′cru·des′cence** *n.* —**re′cru·des′cent** *adj.*

re·cruit (ri kro͞ot′) *vt., vi.* ⟦< L *re-*, again + *crescere,* grow⟧ **1** to enlist (personnel) into an army or navy **2** to enlist (new members) for an organization —*n.* **1** a newly enlisted or drafted soldier, etc. **2** a new member of any group —**re·cruit′er** *n.*

rec·tal (rek′təl) *adj.* of, for, or near the rectum

rec·tan·gle (rek′taŋ′gəl) *n.* ⟦< L *rectus,* straight + *angulus,* a corner⟧ a four-sided plane figure with four right angles —**rec·tan′gu·lar** (-gyə lər) *adj.*

rec·ti·fy (rek′tə fī′) *vt.* **-fied′, -fy′ing** ⟦< L *rectus,* straight + *facere,* make⟧ **1** to put right; correct **2** *Elec.* to convert (alternating current) to direct current —**rec′ti·fi·ca′tion** *n.* —**rec′ti·fi′er** *n.*

rec·ti·lin·e·ar (rek′tə lin′ē ər) *adj.* bounded or formed by straight lines

rec·ti·tude (rek′tə to͞od′) *n.* ⟦< L *rectus,* right⟧ strict honesty; uprightness of character

rec·tor (rek′tər) *n.* ⟦< L *regere,* to rule⟧ **1** in some churches, a clergyman in charge of a parish **2** the head of certain schools, colleges, etc.

rec·to·ry (rek′tər ē) *n., pl.* **-ries** the house of a minister or priest

rec·tum (rek′təm) *n., pl.* **-tums** or **-ta** (-tə) ⟦< L *rectum* (*intestinum*), straight (intestine)⟧ the lowest, or last, segment of the large intestine

re·cum·bent (ri kum′bənt) *adj.* ⟦< L *re-*, back + *-cumbere,* lie down⟧ lying down; reclining

re·cu·per·ate (ri ko͞o′pə rāt′, -pər āt′) *vt., vi.* **-at′ed, -at′ing** ⟦< L *recuperare,* recover⟧ **1** to get well again **2** to recover (losses, etc.) —**re·cu′per·a′tion** *n.* —**re·cu′per·a′tive** (-pə rāt′iv, -per ə tiv) *adj.*

re·cur (ri kur′) *vi.* **-curred′, -cur′ring** ⟦< L *re-*, back + *currere,* run⟧ **1** to return in thought, talk, etc. **2** to occur again or at intervals —**re·cur′rence** *n.* —**re·cur′rent** *adj.*

re·cy·cle (rē sī′kəl) *vt.* **-cled, -cling** **1** to pass through a cycle again **2** to use again and again, as the same water

red (red) *n.* ⟦OE *read*⟧ **1** the color of blood **2** any red pigment **3** [*often* R-] [Colloq.] a political radical; esp., a communist —*adj.* **red′der, red′dest** **1** of the color red **2** [*often* R-] politically radical; esp., communist —**in the red** losing money —**see red** [Colloq.] to become angry —**red′dish** *adj.* —**red′ness** *n.*

re·dact (ri dakt′) *vt.* ⟦< L *redigere,* get in order⟧ to edit —**re·dac′tion** *n.* —**re·dac′tor** *n.*

red blood cell (or **corpuscle**) ERYTHROCYTE

red′-blood′ed *adj.* high-spirited and strong-willed; vigorous

red′cap′ *n.* a baggage porter, as in a railroad station

red carpet a very grand or impressive welcome and entertainment: with *the* —**red′-car′pet** *adj.*

red′coat′ *n.* a British soldier in a uniform with a red coat

Red Cross an international society for the relief of suffering in time of war or disaster

redd (red) *vt., vi.* **redd** or **redd′ed, redd′ing** ⟦< OE *hreddan,* take away⟧ [Colloq. or Dial.] to put in order; tidy: usually with *up*

red deer a deer of Europe and Asia

red·den (red′'n) *vt.* to make red —*vi.* to become red; esp., to blush

re·deem (ri dēm′) *vt.* ⟦< L *re(d)-*, back + *emere,* get⟧ **1** to buy or get back; recover **2** to pay off (a mortgage, etc.) **3** to turn in (coupons, etc.) for a premium **4** to ransom **5** to deliver from sin **6** to fulfill (a promise) **7** *a)* to make amends or atone for *b)* to restore (oneself) to favor —**re·deem′a·ble** *adj.* —**re·deem′er** *n.* —**re·demp·tion** (ri demp′shən) *n.*

re·de·ploy (rē′dē ploi′) *vt., vi.* to move (troops, etc.) from one front or area to another —**re′de·ploy′ment** *n.*

re′de·vel′op *vt.* **1** to develop again **2** to rebuild or restore —**re′de·vel′op·ment** *n.*

red′-hand′ed *adv., adj.* in the very commission of crime or wrongdoing

red'head' *n.* a person with red hair
red herring ⟦< herring drawn across the trace in hunting to divert the hounds⟧ something used to divert attention from the basic issue
red'-hot' *adj.* **1** hot enough to glow **2** very excited, angry, etc. **3** very new
re·dis'trict *vt.* to divide anew into districts
red'-let'ter *adj.* designating a memorable or joyous day or event
red'lin'ing (-lin'iŋ) *n.* ⟦from outlining such areas in red on a map⟧ the refusal by some banks or companies to issue loans or insurance on property in certain neighborhoods
re·do (rē dōō') *vt.* **-did', -done', -do'ing** **1** to do again **2** to redecorate
red·o·lent (red''l ənt) *adj.* ⟦< L *re(d)-*, intens. + *olere*, to smell⟧ **1** sweet-smelling **2** smelling (*of*) **3** suggestive (*of*) **—red'o·lence** *n.*
re·dou·ble (rē dub'əl) *vt., vi.* **-bled, -bling** to make or become twice as much or twice as great
re·doubt (ri dout') *n.* ⟦see REDUCE⟧ **1** a breastwork **2** any stronghold
re·doubt'a·ble *adj.* ⟦< L *re-*, intens. + *dubitare*, to doubt⟧ formidable **—re·doubt'a·bly** *adv.*
re·dound (ri dound') *vi.* ⟦< L *re(d)-*, intens. + *undare*, to surge⟧ **1** to have a result (*to* the credit or discredit of) **2** to come back; react (*upon*)
red pepper **1** a plant with a red, many-seeded fruit **2** the fruit, used for seasoning
re·dress (ri dres'; *for n., usually* rē'dres') *vt.* ⟦see RE- & DRESS⟧ to compensate for (a wrong, etc.) **—*n.*** **1** compensation **2** a redressing
Red Sea sea between NE Africa & W Arabia
red snapper a reddish, edible, deep-water fish
red tape ⟦< tape for tying official papers⟧ rigid adherence to regulations and routine, causing delay
red tide sea water discolored by red algae poisonous to marine life
re·duce (ri dōōs') *vt.* **-duced', -duc'ing** ⟦< L *re-*, back + *ducere*, to lead⟧ **1** to lessen, as in size, price, etc. **2** to put into a different form **3** to lower, as in rank or condition **4** to subdue or conquer **—*vi.*** to lose weight, as by dieting **—re·duc'er** *n.*
re·duc·tion (ri duk'shən) *n.* **1** a reducing or being reduced **2** anything made by reducing **3** the amount by which anything is reduced
re·dun·dant (ri dun'dənt) *adj.* ⟦see REDOUND⟧ **1** excess; superfluous **2** wordy **3** unnecessary to the meaning: said of words and affixes **—re·dun'dan·cy** *n.*
red'wood' *n.* **1** a giant evergreen of the Pacific coast **2** its reddish wood
re·ech·o or **re-ech·o** (rē ek'ō) *vt., vi.* **-oed, -o·ing** to echo back or again **—*n., pl.* -oes** the echo of an echo
reed (rēd) *n.* ⟦OE *hreod*⟧ **1** a tall, slender grass **2** a musical instrument made from a hollow stem **3** *Music* a thin strip of wood, plastic, etc. placed against the mouthpiece, as of a clarinet, and vibrated by the breath to produce a tone **—reed'y, -i·er, -i·est,** *adj.*
reef[1] (rēf) *n.* ⟦prob. < ON *rif*, a rib⟧ a ridge of rock, coral, or sand at or near the surface of the water
reef[2] (rēf) *n.* ⟦ME *riff*⟧ a part of a sail which can be folded and made fast to reduce the area exposed to the wind **—*vt., vi.*** to reduce the size of (a sail) by taking in part of it
reef'er *n.* [Slang] a marijuana cigarette
reek (rēk) *n.* ⟦OE *rec*⟧ a strong, unpleasant smell **—*vi.*** to have a strong, offensive smell **—reek'y** *adj.*
reel[1] (rēl) *n.* ⟦OE *hreol*⟧ **1** a spool on which wire, film, fishing line, etc. is wound **2** the quantity of wire, film, etc. usually wound on one reel **—*vt.*** to wind on a reel **—*vi.*** **1** to sway, stagger, etc. as from drunkenness or dizziness **2** to spin; whirl **—reel in** **1** to wind on a reel **2** to pull in (a fish) by using a reel **—reel off** to tell, write, etc. easily and quickly **—reel out** to unwind from a reel
reel[2] (rēl) *n.* ⟦prob. < prec.⟧ a lively dance
re·en·try or **re-en·try** (rē en'trē) *n., pl.* **-tries** a coming back, as of a space vehicle, into the earth's atmosphere
ref (ref) *n., vt., vi. short for* REFEREE
re·face (rē fās') *vt.* **-faced', -fac'ing** to put a new front or covering on
re·fec·tion (ri fek'shən) *n.* ⟦< L *re-*, again + *facere*, make⟧ a light meal; lunch
re·fec'to·ry (-tər ē) *n., pl.* **-ries** a dining hall, as in a monastery
re·fer (ri fur') *vt.* **-ferred', -fer'ring** ⟦< L *re-*, back + *ferre*, to bear⟧ **1** to submit (a quarrel, etc.) for settlement **2** to direct *to* someone or something for aid, information, etc. **—*vi.*** **1** to relate or apply (*to*) **2** to direct attention (*to*) **3** to turn (*to*) for information, aid, etc. **—re·fer'rer** *n.*
ref·er·ee (ref'ə rē') *n.* **1** one to whom something is referred for decision **2** an official who enforces the rules in certain sports contests **—*vt., vi.*** **-eed', -ee'ing** to act as referee (in)
ref·er·ence (ref'ər əns) *n.* **1** a referring or being referred **2** relation /in *reference* to his letter/ **3** *a)* the directing of attention to a person or thing *b)* a mention **4** *a)* an indication, as in a book, of some other source of information *b)* such a source **5** *a)* one who can offer information or recommendation *b)* a statement of character, ability, etc. by such a person
ref·er·en·dum (ref'ə ren'dəm) *n., pl.* **-dums** or **-da** (-də) ⟦L: see REFER⟧ **1** the submission of a law to a direct vote of the people **2** the vote itself
ref'er·ent *n.* the thing referred to, esp. by a word or expression
re·fer·ral (ri fur'əl) *n.* **1** a referring or being referred **2** a person who is referred to another
re·fill (rē fil'; *for n.* rē'fil) *vt., vi.* to fill again **—*n.*** **1** a unit to refill a special container **2** a refilling of a medical prescription **—re·fill'a·ble** *adj.*
re·fine (ri fīn') *vt., vi.* **-fined', -fin'ing** ⟦RE- + *fine*, make fine⟧ **1** to free or become free from impurities, etc. **2** to make or become more polished or elegant
re·fined' *adj.* **1** made free from impurities; purified **2** cultivated; elegant **3** subtle, precise, etc.
re·fine'ment *n.* **1** *a)* a refining or being

refined *b)* the result of this **2** delicacy or elegance of manners, etc. **3** an improvement **4** a subtlety

re·fin′er·y *n., pl.* **-er·ies** a plant for purifying materials, as oil, sugar, etc.

re·fin·ish (rē fin′ish) *vt.* to change or restore the finish of (furniture, etc.) —**re·fin′ish·er** *n.*

re·fit (rē fit′) *vt., vi.* **-fit′ted, -fit′ting** to make or be made fit for use again by repairing, reequipping, etc.

re·flect (ri flekt′) *vt.* ⟦< L *re-,* back + *flectere,* to bend⟧ **1** to throw back (light, heat, or sound) **2** to give back an image of **3** to bring as a result /to *reflect* honor on the city/ —*vi.* **1** to throw back light, heat, etc. **2** to give back an image **3** to think seriously (*on* or *upon*) **4** to cast blame or discredit (*on* or *upon*) —**re·flec′tive** *adj.*

re·flec′tion *n.* **1** a reflecting or being reflected **2** anything reflected **3** contemplation **4** a thoughtful idea or remark **5** blame; discredit

re·flec′tor *n.* a surface, object, etc. that reflects light, sound, heat, etc.

re·flex (rē′fleks′) *adj.* ⟦see REFLECT⟧ designating or of an involuntary action, as a sneeze, resulting from the direct transmission of a stimulus to a muscle or gland —*n.* a reflex action

re·flex·ive (ri flek′siv) *adj.* **1** designating a grammatical relation in which a verb's subject and object refer to the same person or thing (Ex.: I wash myself) **2** designating a verb, pronoun, etc. in such a relation —**re·flex′ive·ly** *adv.*

re·for·est (rē fôr′ist) *vt., vi.* to plant new trees on (land once forested) —**re′for·est·a′tion** *n.*

re·form (ri fôrm′) *vt.* ⟦see RE- & FORM⟧ **1** to make better as by stopping abuses **2** to cause (a person) to behave better —*vi.* to become better in behavior —*n.* a reforming

re-form (rē′fôrm′) *vt., vi.* to form again

ref·or·ma·tion (ref′ər mā′shən) *n.* a reforming or being reformed —**the Reformation** the 16th-c. religious movement that resulted in establishing the Protestant churches

re·form·a·to·ry (ri fôr′mə tôr′ē) *n., pl.* **-ries** an institution to which young offenders are sent to be reformed

re·form′er *n.* one who seeks to bring about political or social reform

re·fract (ri frakt′) *vt.* ⟦< L *refractus,* turned aside < *re-,* back + *frangere,* to break⟧ to cause (a ray of light, etc.) to undergo refraction

re·frac′tion *n.* the bending of a ray or wave of light, heat, or sound as it passes from one medium into another

ILLUSION CAUSED BY REFRACTION

re·frac·to·ry (ri frak′tər ē) *adj.* ⟦see REFRACT⟧ hard to manage; stubborn

re·frain¹ (ri frān′) *vi.* ⟦< L *re-,* back + *frenare,* to curb⟧ to hold back; keep oneself (*from* doing something)

re·frain² (ri frān′) *n.* ⟦see REFRACT⟧ a phrase or verse repeated at intervals in a song or poem

re·fresh (ri fresh′) *vt.* **1** to make fresh by cooling, wetting, etc. **2** to make (a person) feel cooler, stronger, etc., as by food, sleep, etc. **3** to replenish **4** to stimulate —*vi.* to revive

re·fresh′ing *adj.* **1** that refreshes **2** pleasingly new or different

re·fresh′ment *n.* **1** a refreshing or being refreshed **2** something that refreshes **3** [*pl.*] food or drink or both

re·frig·er·ate (ri frij′ə rāt′) *vt.* **-at′ed, -at′ing** ⟦< L *re-,* intens. + *frigus,* cold⟧ to make or keep cool or cold, as for preserving —**re·frig′er·ant** *adj., n.* —**re·frig′er·a′tion** *n.*

re·frig′er·a′tor *n.* a box or room in which food, drink, etc. are kept cool

ref·uge (ref′yōōj) *n.* ⟦< L *re-,* back + *fugere,* flee⟧ (a) shelter or protection from danger, difficulty, etc.

ref·u·gee (ref′yoo jē′, ref′yoo jē′) *n.* one who flees from home or country to seek refuge elsewhere

re·ful·gent (ri ful′jənt) *adj.* ⟦< L *re-,* back + *fulgere,* shine⟧ shining; radiant; glowing —**re·ful′gence** *n.*

re·fund (ri fund′; *for n.* rē′fund′) *vt., vi.* ⟦< L *re-,* back + *fundere,* pour⟧ to give back (money, etc.); repay —*n.* a refunding or the amount refunded

re·fur·bish (ri fur′bish) *vt.* ⟦RE- + FURBISH⟧ to freshen or polish up again; renovate —**re·fur′bish·ment** *n.*

re·fuse¹ (ri fyōōz′) *vt., vi.* **-fused′, -fus′ing** ⟦< L *re-,* back + *fundere,* pour⟧ **1** to decline to accept **2** to decline (to do something), to grant the request of (someone), etc. —**re·fus′al** *n.*

ref·use² (ref′yōōs, -yōōz) *n.* ⟦see prec.⟧ waste; trash; rubbish

re·fute (ri fyōōt′) *vt.* **-fut′ed, -fut′ing** ⟦L *refutare,* repel⟧ to prove to be false or wrong —**re·fut′a·ble** *adj.* —**ref·u·ta·tion** (ref′yə tā′shən) *n.*

re·gain (ri gān′) *vt.* **1** to get back; recover **2** to get back to

re·gal (rē′gəl) *adj.* ⟦< L *rex,* king⟧ of, like, or fit for a monarch

re·gale (ri gāl′) *vt.* **-galed′, -gal′ing** ⟦< Fr *re-* (see RE-) + OFr *gale,* joy⟧ to entertain as with a feast

re·ga·li·a (ri gāl′yə) *n.pl.* ⟦see REGAL⟧ **1** royal insignia **2** the insignia as of a rank or society **3** finery

re·gard (ri gärd′) *n.* ⟦see RE- & GUARD⟧ **1** a steady look; gaze **2** consideration; concern **3** respect and affection **4** reference; relation /in *regard* to your plan/ **5** [*pl.*] good wishes —*vt.* **1** to look at attentively **2** to consider **3** to hold in affection and respect **4** to concern or involve —**as regards** concerning

re·gard′ing *prep.* concerning; about

re·gard′less *adv.* [Colloq.] without regard for objections, etc.; anyway —**regardless of** in spite of

re·gat·ta (ri gat′ə, -gät′ə) *n.* ⟦< It⟧ **1** a boat race **2** a series of boat races

re·gen·er·ate (ri jen′ər it; *for v.,* -ə rāt′) *adj.* ⟦see RE- & GENERATE⟧ renewed or restored —*vt.* **-at′ed, -at′ing** **1** to cause to be spiritually reborn **2** to cause to be completely reformed 3 to bring into existence again —*vi.* to form again, or be made anew —**re·gen'er·a'tion** *n.* —**re·gen'er·a'tive** *adj.*

re·gent (rē'jənt) *n.* ⟦< L *regere*, to rule⟧ 1 a person appointed to rule when a monarch is absent, too young, etc. 2 a member of a governing board, as of a university —**re'·gen·cy** *n.*

reg·gae (reg'ā) *n.* ⟦< ?⟧ a form of popular Jamaican music influenced by rhythm and blues and calypso

reg·i·cide (rej'ə sīd') *n.* ⟦< L *regis*, of a king + *-cida* (see -CIDE)⟧ 1 one who kills a monarch 2 the killing of a monarch

re·gime or **ré·gime** (rə zhēm', rā-) *n.* ⟦see fol.⟧ 1 a political system 2 an administration

reg·i·men (rej'ə mən) *n.* ⟦< L *regere*, to rule⟧ a system of diet, exercise, etc. for improvement of health

reg·i·ment (rej'ə mənt; *for v.*, -ment') *n.* ⟦< L *regere*, to rule⟧ a military unit, smaller than a division —*vt.* 1 to organize systematically 2 to subject to strict discipline and control —**reg'i·men'tal** *adj.* —**reg'i·men·ta'tion** *n.*

Re·gi·na (ri jī'nə) capital of Saskatchewan, Canada: pop. 187,000

re·gion (rē'jən) *n.* ⟦< L *regere*, to rule⟧ 1 a large, indefinite part of the earth's surface 2 any division or part, as of an organism —**re'gion·al** *adj.*

re'gion·al·ism' *n.* 1 regional quality or character in life or literature 2 a word, etc. peculiar to some region

reg·is·ter (rej'is tər) *n.* ⟦< L *regerere*, to record⟧ 1 *a)* a list of names, items, etc. *b)* a book in which this is kept 2 a device for recording /a cash *register*/ 3 an opening into a room by which the amount of warm or cold air passing through can be controlled 4 *Music* a part of the range of a voice or instrument —*vt.* 1 to enter in a list 2 to indicate as on a scale 3 to show, as by facial expression /to *register* surprise/ 4 to protect (mail) by paying a fee to have it handled by a special postal service —*vi.* 1 to enter one's name in a list, as of voters 2 to enroll in a school 3 to make an impression —**reg'·is·trant** (-trənt) *n.*

registered nurse a trained nurse who has passed a State examination

reg·is·trar (rej'i strär') *n.* one who keeps records, as in a college

reg·is·tra·tion (rej'i strā'shən) *n.* 1 a registering or being registered 2 an entry in a register 3 the number of persons registered

reg'is·try (-is trē) *n.*, *pl.* **-tries** 1 a registering 2 an office where registers are kept 3 an official record or list

reg·nant (reg'nənt) *adj.* 1 ruling 2 predominant 3 prevalent

re·gress (rē'gres; *for v.* ri gres') *n.* ⟦< L *re-*, back + *gradi*, to go⟧ backward movement —*vi.* to go back —**re·gres'sion** *n.* —**re·gres'sive** *adj.*

re·gret (ri gret') *vt.* **-gret'ted, -gret'ting** ⟦< OFr *regreter*, mourn⟧ to feel sorry about (an event, one's acts, etc.) —*n.* remorse, esp. over one's acts or omissions —**(one's) regrets** a polite declining of an invitation —**re·gret'ful** *adj.* —**re·gret'ta·ble** *adj.*

re·group' *vt.*, *vi.* 1 to group again 2 *Mil.* to reorganize (one's forces), as after a battle

reg·u·lar (reg'yə lər) *adj.* ⟦< L *regula*, a rule⟧ 1 conforming to a rule, type, etc.; orderly; symmetrical 2 conforming to a fixed principle or procedure 3 customary or established 4 consistent /a *regular* customer/ 5 functioning in a normal way /a *regular* pulse/ 6 properly qualified /a *regular* doctor/ 7 designating or of the standing army of a country 8 [Colloq.] *a)* thorough; complete /a *regular* nuisance/ *b)* pleasant, friendly, etc. —*n.* 1 a regular soldier or player 2 [Colloq.] one who is regular in attendance 3 *Politics* a loyal party member —**reg'u·lar'i·ty** (-lar'ə tē), *pl.* **-ties**, *n.* —**reg'u·lar·ize'**, **-ized'**, **-iz'ing**, *vt.* —**reg'u·lar·ly** *adv.*

reg·u·late (reg'yə lāt') *vt.* **-lat'ed, -lat'ing** ⟦< L *regula*, a rule⟧ 1 to control or direct according to a rule, principle, etc. 2 to adjust to a standard, rate, etc. 3 to adjust so as to make operate accurately —**reg'u·la'·tor** *n.* —**reg'u·la·to'ry** (-lə tôr'ē) *adj.*

reg'u·la'tion *n.* 1 a regulating or being regulated 2 a rule or law regulating conduct —*adj.* usual; regular

re·gur·gi·tate (ri gur'jə tāt') *vi.*, *vt.* **-tat'ed, -tat'ing** ⟦< ML *re-*, back + LL *gurgitare*, to flood⟧ to bring (partly digested food) back up to the mouth —**re·gur'gi·ta'tion** *n.*

re·hab (rē'hab') *vt.* **-habbed', -hab'bing** *short for* REHABILITATE

re·ha·bil·i·tate (rē'hə bil'ə tāt') *vt.* **-tat'ed, -tat'ing** ⟦< L *re-*, back + *habere*, have⟧ 1 to restore to rank, reputation, etc. which one has lost 2 to put back in good condition 3 to bring or restore to a state of health, constructive activity, etc. —**re'ha·bil'i·ta'tion** *n.* —**re'ha·bil'i·ta'tive** *adj.*

re·hash (rē'hash'; *for v., also* rē hash') *vt.* ⟦RE- + HASH⟧ to work up again or go over again —*n.* a rehashing

re·hearse (ri hurs') *vt.*, *vi.* **-hearsed', -hears'ing** ⟦< OFr *re-*, again + *hercer*, to harrow⟧ to practice (a play, etc.) for public performance —**re·hears'al** *n.*

reign (rān) *n.* ⟦< L *regere*, to rule⟧ 1 royal power 2 dominance or sway 3 the period of rule, dominance, etc. —*vi.* 1 to rule as a sovereign 2 to prevail /peace *reigns*/

re·im·burse (rē'im burs') *vt.* **-bursed', -burs'ing** ⟦RE- + archaic *imburse*, to pay⟧ to pay back —**re'im·burse'ment** *n.*

rein (rān) *n.* ⟦see RETAIN⟧ 1 a narrow strap of leather attached in pairs to a horse's bit and manipulated to control the animal: *usually used in pl.* 2 [*pl.*] a means of controlling, etc. —*vt.* to guide or control as with reins —**give rein to** to free from restraint

re·in·car·na·tion (rē'in kär nā'shən) *n.* ⟦see RE- & INCARNATE⟧ rebirth of the soul in another body —**re'in·car'nate, -nat·ed, -nat·ing,** *vt.*

rein·deer (rān'dir') *n.*, *pl.* **-deer'** ⟦< ON *hreinn*, reindeer + *dýr*, animal⟧ a large deer found in northern regions and domesticated there as a beast of burden

re·in·force (rē'in fôrs') *vt.* **-forced', -forc'·ing** ⟦RE- + var. of ENFORCE⟧ 1 to strengthen (a military force) with more troops, ships, etc. 2 to strengthen, as by propping, adding new material, etc. —**re'in·force'ment** *n.*

re·in·state (rē'in stāt') *vt.* -stat'ed, -stat'ing to restore to a former state, position, etc. —**re'in·state'ment** *n.*

re·it·er·ate (rē it'ə rāt') *vt.* -at'ed, -at'ing ⟦< L *re-*, back + *iterare*, repeat⟧ to say or do again or repeatedly —**re·it'er·a'tion** *n.* —**re·it'er·a'tive** (-ə rāt'iv, -ər ə tiv) *adj.*

re·ject (ri jekt'; *for n.* rē'jekt) *vt.* ⟦< L *re-*, back + *jacere*, to throw⟧ 1 to refuse to take, agree to, use, believe, etc. 2 to discard —*n.* a rejected thing or person —**re·jec'tion** *n.*

re·joice (ri jois') *vi.*, *vt.* -joiced', -joic'ing ⟦< OFr *re-*, again + *joïr*, be glad⟧ to be or make glad or happy

re·join (rē join') *vt.*, *vi.* 1 to join again; reunite 2 to answer

re·join·der (ri join'dər) *n.* ⟦see RE- & JOIN⟧ an answer, esp. to a reply

re·ju·ve·nate (ri jo͞o'və nāt') *vt.* -nat'ed, -nat'ing ⟦< RE- + L *juvenis*, young⟧ to make feel or seem young again —**re·ju've·na'tion** *n.*

re·lapse (ri laps'; *for n., also* rē'laps) *vi.* -lapsed', -laps'ing ⟦see RE- & LAPSE⟧ to slip back into a former state, esp. into illness after apparent recovery —*n.* a relapsing

re·late (ri lāt') *vt.* -lat'ed, -lat'ing ⟦< L *relatus*, brought back⟧ 1 to tell the story of; narrate 2 to connect, as in thought or meaning —*vi.* to have some connection or relation (*to*)

re·lat'ed *adj.* connected, as by kinship, origin, marriage, etc.

re·la'tion *n.* 1 a narrating 2 a narrative; account 3 connection, as in thought, meaning, etc. 4 connection by blood or marriage 5 a relative 6 [*pl.*] the connections between or among persons, nations, etc. —**in** (or **with**) **relation to** concerning; regarding —**re·la'tion·ship'** *n.*

rel·a·tive (rel'ə tiv) *adj.* 1 related each to the other 2 having to do with; relevant 3 comparative /living in *relative* comfort/ 4 meaningful only in relationship /"cold" is a *relative* term/ 5 *Gram.* that refers to an antecedent /a *relative* pronoun/ —*n.* a person connected by blood or marriage —**rel'a·tive·ly** *adv.*

relative humidity the ratio of the amount of moisture in the air to the top amount possible at the temperature

rel·a·tiv·i·ty (rel'ə tiv'ə tē) *n.* 1 a being relative 2 *Physics* the theory of the relative, rather than absolute, character of motion, velocity, mass, etc., and the interdependence of matter, time, and space

re·lax (ri laks') *vt.*, *vi.* ⟦< L *re-*, back + *laxare*, loosen⟧ 1 to make or become less firm, tense, severe, etc. 2 to rest, as from work —**re·lax'er** *n.*

re·lax'ant *adj.* causing relaxation, esp. of muscles —*n.* a relaxant drug

re·lax·a·tion (rē'lak sā'shən) *n.* 1 a relaxing or being relaxed 2 *a)* rest from work or effort *b)* recreation

re·lay (rē'lā'; *for v., also* ri lā') *n.* ⟦< Fr *re-*, back + *laier*, to leave⟧ 1 a fresh supply of horses, etc., as for a stage of a journey 2 a relief crew of workers 3 a race (in full **relay race**) between teams, each member of which goes a part of the distance —*vt.* -layed', -lay'ing to convey as by relays /to *relay* news/

re·lease (ri lēs') *vt.* -leased', -leas'ing ⟦see RELAX⟧ 1 to set free, as from confinement, work, pain, etc. 2 to let go /to *release* an arrow/ 3 to permit to be issued, published, etc. —*n.* 1 a releasing, as from prison, work, etc. 2 a film, news story, etc. released to the public 3 a written surrender of a claim, etc.

rel·e·gate (rel'ə gāt') *vt.* -gat'ed, -gat'ing ⟦< L *re-*, away + *legare*, send⟧ 1 to exile or banish (*to*) 2 to consign or assign, esp. to an inferior position 3 to refer or hand over for decision —**rel'e·ga'tion** *n.*

re·lent (ri lent') *vi.* ⟦< L *re-*, again + *lentus*, pliant⟧ to become less severe, stern, or stubborn; soften

re·lent'less *adj.* 1 harsh; pitiless 2 not letting up; persistent —**re·lent'less·ly** *adv.* —**re·lent'less·ness** *n.*

rel·e·vant (rel'ə vənt) *adj.* ⟦see RELIEVE⟧ relating to the matter under consideration; pertinent —**rel'e·vance** or **rel'e·van·cy** *n.*

re·li·a·ble (ri lī'ə bəl) *adj.* that can be relied on; dependable —**re·li'a·bil'i·ty** *n.* —**re·li'a·bly** *adv.*

re·li'ance (-əns) *n.* 1 a relying 2 trust, dependence, or confidence 3 a thing relied on —**re·li'ant** *adj.*

rel·ic (rel'ik) *n.* ⟦see RELINQUISH⟧ 1 an object, custom, etc. surviving from the past 2 a souvenir 3 [*pl.*] ruins 4 the venerated remains, etc. of a saint

re·lief (ri lēf') *n.* 1 a relieving, as of pain, anxiety, a burden, etc. 2 anything that lessens tension, or offers a pleasing change 3 aid, esp. by a public agency to the needy 4 release from work or duty, or those bringing it 5 the projection of sculptured forms from a flat surface 6 the differences in height, collectively, of land forms shown as by lines on a map (**relief map**) —*adj.* *Baseball* designating a pitcher who replaces another during a game —**in relief** carved so as to project from a surface

re·lieve (ri lēv') *vt.* -lieved', -liev'ing ⟦< L *re-*, again + *levare*, to raise⟧ 1 to ease (pain, anxiety, etc.) 2 to free from pain, anxiety, a burden, etc. 3 to give or bring aid to 4 to set free from duty or work by replacing 5 to make less tedious, etc. by providing a pleasing change

re·li·gion (ri lij'ən) *n.* ⟦< L *religio*, holiness⟧ 1 belief in and worship of God or gods 2 a specific system of belief, worship, etc., often involving a code of ethics

re·li'gi·os'i·ty (-ē äs'ə tē) *n.* a being religious, esp. excessively or sentimentally religious

re·li'gious (-əs) *adj.* 1 devout; pious 2 of or concerned with religion 3 conscientiously exact; scrupulous —*n., pl.* -gious a monk or nun —**re·li'gious·ly** *adv.*

re·lin·quish (ri liŋ'kwish) *vt.* ⟦< L *re-*, from + *linquere*, to leave⟧ 1 to give up (a plan, etc.) or let go (one's grasp, etc.) 2 to renounce or surrender (property, a right, etc.) —**re·lin'quish·ment** *n.*

rel·ish (rel'ish) *n.* ⟦< OFr *relais*, something remaining⟧ 1 an appetizing flavor 2 enjoyment; zest /to listen with *relish*/ 3 pickles, raw vegetables, etc., served with a meal to add flavor —*vt.* to enjoy; like

re·live (rē liv′) *vt.* **-lived′, -liv′ing** to experience again (a past event) as in the imagination

re·lo·cate (rē lō′kāt′) *vt., vi.* **-cat′ed, -cat′ing** to move to a new location —**re′lo·ca′tion** *n.*

re·luc·tant (ri luk′tənt) *adj.* ⟦< L *re-*, against + *luctari*, to struggle⟧ 1 unwilling; disinclined 2 marked by unwillingness /*a reluctant* answer/ —**re·luc′tance** *n.* —**re·luc′tant·ly** *adv.*

re·ly (ri lī′) *vi.* **-lied′, -ly′ing** ⟦< L *re-*, back + *ligare*, bind⟧ to trust or depend: used with *on* or *upon*

rem (rem) *n., pl.* **rem** ⟦*r(oentgen) e(quivalent), m(an)*⟧ a dosage of ionizing radiation with a biological effect about equal to that of one roentgen of X-ray

REM (rem) *n., pl.* **REMs** ⟦*r(apid) e(ye) m(ovement)*⟧ the rapid, jerky movement of the eyeballs during stages of sleep associated with dreaming

re·main (ri mān′) *vi.* ⟦< L *re-*, back + *manere*, to stay⟧ 1 to be left over when the rest has been taken away, etc. 2 to stay 3 to continue /to *remain* a cynic/ 4 to be left to be dealt with, done, etc.

re·main′der *n.* 1 those remaining 2 what is left when a part is taken away 3 what is left when a smaller number is subtracted from a larger 4 what is left undivided when a number is divided by another that is not one of its factors

re·mains′ *n.pl.* 1 what is left after use, destruction, etc. 2 a dead body

re·mand (ri mand′) *vt.* ⟦< L *re-*, back + *mandare*, to order⟧ to send back, as a prisoner into custody

re·mark (ri märk′) *vt.* ⟦< Fr *re-*, again + *marquer*, to mark⟧ 1 to notice or observe 2 to say or write as a comment —*vi.* to make a comment: with *on* or *upon* —*n.* a brief comment

re·mark′a·ble *adj.* worthy of notice; extraordinary —**re·mark′a·bly** *adv.*

Rem·brandt (rem′brant′) 1606-69; Du. painter & etcher

re·me·di·al (ri mē′dē əl) *adj.* 1 providing a remedy 2 for correcting deficiencies, as some courses of study

rem·e·dy (rem′ə dē) *n., pl.* **-dies** ⟦< L *re-*, again + *mederi*, heal⟧ 1 any medicine or treatment for a disease 2 something to correct a wrong —*vt.* **-died, -dy·ing** to cure, correct, etc.

re·mem·ber (ri mem′bər) *vt.* ⟦< L *re-*, again + *memorare*, bring to mind⟧ 1 to think of again 2 to bring back to mind by an effort; recall 3 to be careful not to forget 4 to mention (a person) to another as sending regards —*vi.* to bear something in mind or call something back to mind

re·mem′brance (-brəns) *n.* 1 a remembering or being remembered 2 the power to remember 3 a souvenir

re·mind (ri mīnd′) *vt., vi.* to put (a person) in mind (*of* something); cause to remember —**re·mind′er** *n.*

rem·i·nisce (rem′ə nis′) *vi.* **-nisced′, -nisc′ing** ⟦< fol.⟧ to think, talk, or write about remembered events

rem′i·nis′cence (-əns) *n.* ⟦Fr < L *re-*, again + *memini*, remember⟧ 1 a remembering 2 a memory 3 [*pl.*] an account of remembered experiences —**rem′i·nis′cent** *adj.*

re·miss (ri mis′) *adj.* ⟦see REMIT⟧ careless; negligent —**re·miss′ness** *n.*

re·mis·sion (ri mish′ən) *n.* ⟦see fol.⟧ 1 forgiveness; pardon 2 release from a debt, tax, etc. 3 an abating of pain, a disease, etc.

re·mit (ri mit′) *vt.* **-mit′ted, -mit′ting** ⟦< L *re-*, back + *mittere*, send⟧ 1 to forgive or pardon 2 to refrain from exacting (a payment), inflicting (punishment), etc. 3 to slacken; decrease 4 to send (money) in payment —**re·mit′tance** *n.*

rem·nant (rem′nənt) *n.* ⟦see REMAIN⟧ what is left over, as a piece of cloth at the end of a bolt

re·mod·el (rē′mäd″l) *vt.* **-eled** or **-elled, -el·ing** or **-el·ling** to make over; rebuild

re·mon·strate (ri män′strāt′) *vt.* **-strat·ed, -strat·ing** ⟦< L *re-*, again + *monstrare*, to show⟧ to say in protest, objection, etc. —*vi.* to protest; object —**re·mon′strance** *n.*

re·morse (ri môrs′) *n.* ⟦< L *re-*, again + *mordere*, to bite⟧ a torturing sense of guilt for one's actions —**re·morse′ful** *adj.* —**re·morse′less** *adj.*

re·mote (ri mōt′) *adj.* **-mot′er, -mot′est** ⟦< L *remotus*, removed⟧ 1 distant in space or time 2 distant in connection, relation, etc. 3 distantly related 4 aloof 5 slight /a *remote* chance/ —**re·mote′ly** *adv.*

remote control 1 control of aircraft, missiles, etc. from a distance, as by radio waves 2 a device to control a television set, recorder, etc. from a distance

re·move (ri mo͞ov′) *vt.* **-moved′, -mov′ing** ⟦see RE- & MOVE⟧ 1 to move (something) from where it is; take away or off 2 to dismiss, as from office 3 to get rid of —*vi.* to move away, as to another residence —*n.* a step or degree away —**re·mov′a·ble** *adj.* —**re·mov′al** *n.*

re·mu·ner·ate (ri myo͞o′nə rāt′) *vt.* **-at′ed, -at′ing** ⟦< L *re-*, again + *munus*, gift⟧ to pay (a person) for (work, a loss, etc.) —**re·mu′ner·a′tion** *n.* —**re·mu′ner·a′tive** *adj.*

ren·ais·sance (ren′ə säns′) *n.* ⟦Fr⟧ a rebirth; renascence —**the Renaissance** the great revival of art and learning in Europe in the 14th, 15th, and 16th centuries

re·nal (rē′nəl) *adj.* ⟦< L *renes*, kidneys⟧ of or near the kidneys

re·nas·cence (ri nas′əns, -nās′-) *n.* ⟦< L *renasci*, be born again⟧ [*also* **R-**] RENAISSANCE

rend (rend) *vt.* **rent, rend′ing** ⟦OE *rendan*⟧ to tear apart or split with violence —*vi.* to tear; split apart

ren·der (ren′dər) *vt.* ⟦ult. < L *re(d)-*, back + *dare*, give⟧ 1 to submit, as for approval, payment, etc. 2 to give in return or pay as due /*render* thanks/ 3 to cause to be 4 to give (aid) or do (a service) 5 to depict, as by drawing 6 to play (music), act (a role), etc. 7 to translate 8 to melt down (fat) 9 to pronounce (a verdict)

ren·dez·vous (rän′dā vo͞o′) *n., pl.* **-vous′** (-vo͞oz′) ⟦< Fr *rendez-vous*, betake yourself⟧

1 a meeting place 2 an agreement to meet 3 the meeting itself —*vi.*, *vt.* **-voused′** (-vo͞od′), **-vous′ing** (-vo͞o′iŋ) to assemble as prearranged

ren·di·tion (ren dish′ən) *n.* a rendering; performance, translation, etc.

ren·e·gade (ren′ə gād′) *n.* ⟦< L *re-*, again + *negare,* deny⟧ one who abandons a party, movement, etc. to join the opposition; turncoat

re·nege (ri nig′) *vi.* **-neged′**, **-neg′ing** ⟦see prec.⟧ 1 to go back on a promise 2 *Card Games* to fail to play a card of the suit called for when able to do so

re·new (ri no͞o′) *vt.* 1 to make new or fresh again 2 to reestablish; revive 3 to resume 4 to put in a fresh supply of 5 to give or get an extension of /*renew* a lease/ —**re·new′al** *n.*

ren·net (ren′it) *n.* ⟦ME *rennen*, coagulate⟧ an extract from the stomach of calves, etc. used to curdle milk

Re·no (rē′nō) city in W Nev.: pop. 101,000

Re·noir (rən wär′, ren′wär′), **Pierre Auguste** (pyer ô güst′) 1841-1919; Fr. painter

re·nounce (ri nouns′) *vt.* **-nounced′**, **-nounc′ing** ⟦< L *re-*, back + *nuntiare*, tell⟧ 1 to give up formally (a claim, etc.) 2 to give up (a habit, etc.) 3 to disown —**renounce′ment** *n.*

ren·o·vate (ren′ə vāt′) *vt.* **-vat′ed**, **-vat′ing** ⟦< L *re-*, again + *novus*, new⟧ to make as good as new; restore —**ren′o·va′tion** *n.* —**ren′o·va′tor** *n.*

re·nown (ri noun′) *n.* ⟦< OFr *re-*, again + *nom(m)er*, to name < L *nominare*⟧ great fame or reputation —**re·nowned′** *adj.*

rent¹ (rent) *n.* ⟦< L *reddita*, paid⟧ a stated payment at fixed intervals for the use of a house, land, etc. —*vt.* to get or give use of in return for rent —*vi.* to be let for rent —**for rent** available to be rented —**rent′er** *n.*

rent² (rent) *vt.*, *vi.* *pt. & pp. of* REND —*n.* a hole or gap made by tearing

rent·al (ren′t'l) *n.* 1 an amount paid or received as rent 2 a house, car, etc. offered for rent 3 a renting —*adj.* of or for rent

re·nun·ci·a·tion (ri nun′sē ā′shən) *n.* a renouncing, as of a right

re·or·gan·ize (rē ôr′gə nīz′) *vt.*, *vi.* **-ized′**, **-iz′ing** to organize (a business, etc.) anew —**re·or′gan·i·za′tion** *n.*

rep (rep) *n.* ⟦Fr *reps* < Eng *ribs*⟧ a ribbed fabric of silk, wool, cotton, etc.

Rep. 1 Representative 2 Republican

re·paid (ri pād′) *vt.*, *vi.* *pt. & pp. of* REPAY

re·pair¹ (ri per′) *vt.* ⟦< L *re-*, again + *parare*, prepare⟧ 1 to put back in good condition; fix; renew 2 to make amends for —*n.* 1 a repairing 2 [*usually pl.*] work done in repairing 3 the state of being repaired /kept in *repair*/ —**re·pair′a·ble** *adj.*

re·pair² (ri per′) *vi.* ⟦< L *re-*, back + *patria*, native land⟧ to go (*to* a place)

re·pair′man (-mən, -man′) *n.*, *pl.* **-men** one whose work is repairing things

rep·a·ra·tion (rep′ə rā′shən) *n.* ⟦see REPAIR¹⟧ 1 a making of amends 2 [*usually pl.*] compensation, as for war damage

rep·ar·tee (rep′ər tē′, -är-; -tā′) *n.* ⟦< Fr *re-*, back + *partir*, to part⟧ a series of quick, witty retorts; banter

re·past (ri past′) *n.* ⟦< OFr *re-*, RE- + *past*, food⟧ food and drink; a meal

re·pa·tri·ate (rē pā′trē āt′) *vt.*, *vi.* **-at′ed**, **-at′ing** ⟦see REPAIR²⟧ to return to the country of birth, citizenship, etc. —**re·pa′tri·a′tion** *n.*

re·pay (ri pā′) *vt.* **-paid′**, **-pay′ing** 1 to pay back 2 to make return to for (a favor, etc.) —**re·pay′ment** *n.*

re·peal (ri pēl′) *vt.* ⟦see RE- & APPEAL⟧ to revoke; cancel; annul —*n.* revocation; abrogation

re·peat (ri pēt′) *vt.* ⟦< L *re-*, again + *petere*, to demand⟧ 1 to say again 2 to recite (a poem, etc.) 3 to say (something) as said by someone else 4 to tell to someone else /*repeat* a secret/ 5 to do or make again —*vi.* to say or do again —*n.* 1 a repeating 2 anything said or done again, as a rebroadcast of a television program 3 *Music* a) a passage to be repeated b) a symbol for this —**re·peat′er** *n.*

re·peat′ed *adj.* said, made, or done again, or often —**re·peat′ed·ly** *adv.*

re·pel (ri pel′) *vt.* **-pelled′**, **-pel′ling** ⟦< L *re-*, back + *pellere*, to drive⟧ 1 to drive or force back 2 to reject 3 to cause dislike in; disgust 4 to be resistant to (water, dirt, etc.) —**re·pel′lent** *adj.*, *n.*

re·pent (ri pent′) *vi.*, *vt.* ⟦< L *re-*, again + *poenitere*, repent⟧ 1 to feel sorry for (an error, sin, etc.) 2 to feel such regret over (an action, intention, etc.) as to change one's mind —**re·pent′ance** *n.* —**re·pent′ant** *adj.*

re·per·cus·sion (rē′pər kush′ən) *n.* ⟦see RE- & PERCUSSION⟧ 1 reverberation 2 a far-reaching, often indirect reaction to some event

rep·er·toire (rep′ər twär′) *n.* ⟦< Fr < L *reperire*, discover⟧ the stock of plays, songs, etc. that a company, singer, etc. is prepared to perform

rep′er·to′ry (-tôr′ē) *n.*, *pl.* **-ries** 1 REPERTOIRE 2 the system of alternating several plays throughout a season with a permanent acting group

rep·e·ti·tion (rep′ə tish′ən) *n.* ⟦< L *repetitio*⟧ 1 a repeating 2 something repeated —**rep′e·ti′tious** *adj.* —**re·pet·i·tive** (ri pet′ə tiv) *adj.*

re·pine (ri pīn′) *vi.* **-pined′**, **-pin′ing** ⟦RE- + PINE²⟧ to feel or express unhappiness or discontent; complain

re·place (ri plās′) *vt.* **-placed′**, **-plac′ing** 1 to put back in a former or the proper place 2 to take the place of 3 to provide an equivalent for —**re·place′a·ble** *adj.* —**re·place′ment** *n.*

re·plen·ish (ri plen′ish) *vt.* ⟦< L *re-*, again + *plenus*, full⟧ 1 to make full or complete again 2 to supply again —**re·plen′ish·ment** *n.*

re·plete (ri plēt′) *adj.* ⟦< L *re-*, again + *plere*, to fill⟧ 1 plentifully supplied 2 stuffed; gorged —**re·ple′tion** *n.*

rep·li·ca (rep′li kə) *n.* ⟦see REPLY⟧ a reproduction or close copy, as of a work of art

rep·li·cate (rep′li kāt′) *vt.* **-cat′ed**, **-cat′ing** ⟦see REPLY⟧ to repeat or duplicate

rep′li·ca′tion *n.* 1 a replicating 2 a reply; answer 3 a copy; reproduction

re·ply (ri plī′) *vi.* **-plied′**, **-ply′ing** ⟦< L *re-*, back + *plicare*, to fold ⟧ to answer or respond —*n.*, *pl.* **-plies′** an answer or response

re·port (ri pôrt′) *vt.* ⟦ < L *re-*, back + *portare*, carry ⟧ 1 to give an account of, as for publication 2 to carry and repeat (a message, etc.) 3 to announce formally 4 to make a charge about (something) or against (someone) to one in authority —*vi.* 1 to make a report 2 to present oneself, as for work —*n.* 1 rumor 2 a statement or account 3 a formal presentation of facts 4 the noise of an explosion —**re·port′ed·ly** *adv.*

re·port·age (ri pôrt′ij, rep′ər täzh′) *n.* 1 the reporting of the news 2 journalistic writings

report card a periodic written report on a pupil's progress

re·port′er *n.* one who reports; specif., one who gathers information and writes reports for a newspaper, etc. —**rep·or·to·ri·al** (rep′ər tôr′ē əl) *adj.*

re·pose[1] (ri pōz′) *vt.* **-posed′**, **-pos′ing** ⟦ < L *re-*, again + *pausare*, to rest ⟧ to lay or place for rest —*vi.* 1 to lie at rest 2 to rest from work, etc. 3 to lie dead —*n.* 1 *a*) rest *b*) sleep 2 composure 3 calm; peace —**re·pose′ful** *adj.*

re·pose[2] (ri pōz′) *vt.* **-posed′**, **-pos′ing** ⟦ see fol. ⟧ 1 to place (trust, etc.) *in* someone 2 to place (power, etc.) *in* the control of some person or group

re·pos·i·to·ry (ri päz′ə tôr′ē) *n.*, *pl.* **-ries** ⟦ < L *re-*, back + *ponere*, to place ⟧ a box, room, etc. in which things may be placed for safekeeping

re·pos·sess (rē′pə zes′) *vt.* to get possession of again —**re′pos·ses′sion** *n.*

rep·re·hend (rep′ri hend′) *vt.* ⟦ < L *re-*, back + *prehendere*, take ⟧ to rebuke, blame, or censure

rep′re·hen′si·ble (-hen′sə bəl) *adj.* deserving to be reprehended —**rep′re·hen′si·bly** *adv.*

rep·re·sent (rep′ri zent′) *vt.* ⟦ L *repraesentare* < *re-*, again + *praesentare*, to present ⟧ 1 to present to the mind 2 to present a likeness of 3 to describe 4 to stand for; symbolize 5 to be the equivalent of 6 to act (a role) 7 to act in place of, esp. by conferred authority 8 to serve as a specimen, example, etc. of

rep′re·sen·ta′tion *n.* 1 a representing or being represented, as in a legislative assembly 2 legislative representatives, collectively 3 a likeness, image, picture, etc. 4 [*often pl.*] a statement of facts, arguments, etc. meant to influence action, make protest, etc. —**rep′re·sen·ta′tion·al** *adj.*

rep′re·sent′a·tive *adj.* 1 representing 2 of or based on representation of the people by elected delegates 3 typical —*n.* 1 an example or type 2 one authorized to act for others; delegate, agent, salesman, etc. 3 [R-] a member of the lower house of Congress or of a State legislature

re·press (ri pres′) *vt.* ⟦ see RE- & PRESS[1] ⟧ 1 to hold back; restrain 2 to put down; subdue 3 *Psychiatry* to force (painful ideas, etc.) into the unconscious —**re·pres′sion** *n.* —**re·pres′sive** *adj.*

re·prieve (ri prēv′) *vt.* **-prieved′**, **-priev′ing** ⟦ < Fr *reprendre*, take back ⟧ 1 to postpone the execution of (a condemned person) 2 to give temporary relief to —*n.* a reprieving or being reprieved

rep·ri·mand (rep′rə mand′) *n.* ⟦ < L *reprimere*, repress ⟧ a severe or formal rebuke —*vt.* to rebuke severely or formally

re·pris·al (ri prī′zəl) *n.* ⟦ see REPREHEND ⟧ injury done for injury received

re·proach (ri prōch′) *vt.* ⟦ < L *re-*, back + *prope*, near ⟧ to accuse of a fault; rebuke —*n.* 1 shame, disgrace, etc. or a cause of this 2 rebuke or censure —**re·proach′ful** *adj.*

rep·ro·bate (rep′rə bāt′) *adj.* ⟦ LL *reprobare*, reprove ⟧ unprincipled or depraved —*n.* a reprobate person

re·pro·duce (rē′prə do͞os′) *vt.* **-duced′**, **-duc′ing** to produce again; specif., *a*) to produce by propagation *b*) to make a copy of —*vi.* to produce offspring —**re′pro·duc′i·ble** *adj.*

re′pro·duc′tion (-duk′shən) *n.* 1 a copy, imitation, etc. 2 the process by which animals and plants produce new individuals —**re′pro·duc′tive** *adj.*

re·proof (ri pro͞of′) *n.* a reproving; rebuke Also **re·prov′al** (-pro͞o′v′l)

re·prove (ri pro͞ov′) *vt.* **-proved′**, **-prov′ing** ⟦ see RE- & PROVE ⟧ 1 to rebuke 2 to express disapproval of

rep·tile (rep′təl, -tīl′) *n.* ⟦ < L *repere*, to creep ⟧ a coldblooded, crawling vertebrate, as a snake, lizard, turtle, etc. —**rep·til·i·an** (rep til′ē ən) *adj.*

re·pub·lic (ri pub′lik) *n.* ⟦ < L *res*, thing + *publica*, public ⟧ a state or government, specif. one headed by a president, in which the power is exercised by officials elected by the voters

re·pub′li·can (-li kən) *adj.* 1 of or like a republic 2 [R-] of or belonging to the Republican Party —*n.* 1 one who favors a republic 2 [R-] a member of the Republican Party

Republican Party one of the two major political parties in the U.S.

re·pu·di·ate (ri pyo͞o′dē āt′) *vt.* **-at′ed**, **-at′ing** ⟦ < L *repudium*, separation ⟧ 1 to refuse to have anything to do with 2 to refuse to accept or support (a belief, treaty, etc.) —**re·pu′di·a′tion** *n.*

re·pug·nant (ri pug′nənt) *adj.* ⟦ < L *re-*, back + *pugnare*, fight ⟧ 1 contradictory 2 distasteful; offensive —**re·pug′nance** *n.*

re·pulse (ri puls′) *vt.* **-pulsed′**, **-puls′ing** ⟦ see REPEL ⟧ 1 to drive back (an attack, etc.) 2 to refuse or reject with discourtesy, etc.; rebuff —*n.* a repelling or being repelled

re·pul′sion *n.* 1 a repelling or being repelled 2 strong dislike 3 *Physics* the mutual action by which bodies tend to repel each other

re·pul′sive *adj.* causing strong dislike or aversion; disgusting —**re·pul′sive·ly** *adv.* —**re·pul′sive·ness** *n.*

rep·u·ta·ble (rep′yoo tə bəl) *adj.* having a good reputation —**rep′u·ta·bil′i·ty** *n.* —**rep′u·ta·bly** *adv.*

rep·u·ta·tion (rep′yoo tā′shən) *n.* ⟦ see fol. ⟧ 1 estimation in which a person or thing is commonly held 2 favorable estimation 3 fame

re·pute (ri pyo͞ot′) *vt.* **-put′ed, -put′ing** ⟦< L *re-*, again + *putare*, think⟧ to consider or regard /*reputed* to be rich/ —*n.* REPUTATION (senses 1 & 3)

re·put′ed *adj.* generally supposed to be such /the *reputed* owner/ —**re·put′ed·ly** *adv.*

re·quest (ri kwest′) *n.* ⟦see REQUIRE⟧ **1** an asking for something **2** something asked for **3** the state of being asked for; demand —*vt.* **1** to ask for **2** to ask (a person) to do something

Re·qui·em (rek′wē əm, rā′kwē-) *n.* ⟦< L, rest⟧ [*also* **r-**] **1** *R.C.Ch.* a Mass for a dead person or persons **2** a musical setting for this

re·quire (ri kwīr′) *vt.* **-quired′, -quir′ing** ⟦< L *re-*, again + *quaerere*, ask⟧ **1** to insist upon; demand **2** to order **3** to need —**re·quire′ment** *n.*

req·ui·site (rek′wə zit) *adj.* ⟦see prec.⟧ required; necessary; indispensable —*n.* something requisite

req·ui·si·tion (rek′wə zish′ən) *n.* **1** a requiring; formal demand **2** a formal written order, as for equipment —*vt.* **1** to demand or take, as by authority **2** to submit a written request for

re·quite (ri kwīt′) *vt.* **-quit′ed, -quit′ing** ⟦RE- + *quite*, obs. var. of QUIT⟧ to repay (someone) for (a benefit, service, etc. or an injury, wrong, etc.) —**re·quit′al** *n.*

re·run (rē′run′) *n.* the showing of a film or TV program after the first run or showing

re′sale′ *n.* a selling again, specif. to a third party

re·scind (ri sind′) *vt.* ⟦< L *re-*, back + *scindere*, to cut⟧ to revoke or cancel (a law, etc.) —**re·scis′sion** (-sizh′ən) *n.*

res·cue (res′kyo͞o) *vt.* **-cued, -cu·ing** ⟦ult. < L *re-*, again + *ex-*, off + *quatere*, to shake⟧ to free or save from danger, imprisonment, evil, etc. —*n.* a rescuing —**res′cu·er** *n.*

re·search (rē′surch′, ri surch′) *n.* ⟦see RE- & SEARCH⟧ careful, systematic study and investigation in some field of knowledge —*vi., vt.* to do research (on or in) —**re′search′er** *n.*

re·sec·tion (ri sek′shən) *n.* ⟦< L *re-*, back + *secare*, to cut⟧ *Surgery* the removal of part of an organ, bone, etc.

re·sem·blance (ri zem′bləns) *n.* a similarity of appearance; likeness

re·sem·ble (ri zem′bəl) *vt.* **-bled, -bling** ⟦ult. < L *re-*, again + *simulare*, feign⟧ to be like or similar to

re·sent (ri zent′) *vt.* ⟦ult. < L *re-*, again + *sentire*, to feel⟧ to feel or show hurt or indignation at —**re·sent′ful** *adj.* —**re·sent′ful·ly** *adv.* —**re·sent′ment** *n.*

re·ser·pine (ri sur′pin, -pēn) *n.* ⟦Ger⟧ a crystalline alkaloid used in treating hypertension, mental illness, etc.

res·er·va·tion (rez′ər vā′shən) *n.* **1** a reserving or that which is reserved; specif., *a*) a withholding *b*) public land set aside for a special use, as for Indians *c*) holding of a hotel room, etc. until called for **2** a limiting condition

re·serve (ri zurv′) *vt.* **-served′, -serv′ing** ⟦< L *re-*, back + *servare*, to keep⟧ **1** to keep back or set apart for later or special use **2** to keep back for oneself —*n.* **1** something kept back or stored up, as for later use **2** a limitation /without *reserve*/ **3** the keeping one's thoughts, feelings, etc. to oneself **4** reticence; silence **5** [*pl.*] troops, players, etc. kept out of action for use as replacements **6** land set apart for a special purpose —**in reserve** reserved for later use

re·served′ *adj.* **1** kept in reserve; set apart **2** self-restrained; reticent

re·serv′ist *n.* a member of a country's military reserves

res·er·voir (rez′ər vwär′) *n.* ⟦< Fr: see RESERVE⟧ **1** a place where water is collected and stored for use **2** a receptacle for holding a fluid **3** a large supply

re·side (ri zīd′) *vi.* **-sid′ed, -sid′ing** ⟦< L *re-*, back + *sedere*, sit⟧ **1** to dwell for a long time; live (*in* or *at*) **2** to be present or inherent (*in*): said of qualities, etc.

res·i·dence (rez′i dəns) *n.* **1** a residing **2** the place where one resides —**res′i·den′tial** (-ə den′shəl) *adj.*

res′i·den·cy (-dən sē) *n., pl.* **-cies** **1** RESIDENCE **2** a period of advanced, specialized medical or surgical training at a hospital

res′i·dent *adj.* residing; esp., living in a place while working, etc. —*n.* **1** one who lives in a place, not a visitor **2** a doctor who is serving a residency

re·sid·u·al (ri zij′o͞o əl) *adj.* of or being a residue; remaining —*n.* **1** something remaining **2** [*pl.*] the fee paid for reruns on television, etc.

res·i·due (rez′ə do͞o′) *n.* ⟦< L *residuus*, remaining⟧ that which is left after part is taken away; remainder

re·sid·u·um (ri zij′o͞o əm) *n., pl.* **-u·a** (-ə) RESIDUE

re·sign (ri zīn′) *vt., vi.* ⟦< L *re-*, back + *signare*, to sign⟧ to give up (a claim, or an office, position, etc.) —**resign oneself (to)** to become reconciled (to)

res·ig·na·tion (rez′ig nā′shən) *n.* **1** *a*) the act of resigning *b*) formal notice of this **2** patient submission

re·signed (ri zīnd′) *adj.* feeling or showing resignation; submissive —**re·sign′ed·ly** (-zīn′id lē) *adv.*

re·sil·ient (ri zil′yənt) *adj.* ⟦< L *re-*, back + *salire*, to jump⟧ **1** springing back into shape, etc. **2** recovering strength, spirits, etc. quickly —**re·sil′ience** or **re·sil′ien·cy** *n.*

res·in (rez′ən) *n.* ⟦< L *resina*⟧ **1** a substance exuded from various plants and trees and used in varnishes, plastics, etc. **2** ROSIN —**res′in·ous** *adj.*

re·sist (ri zist′) *vt.* ⟦< L *re-*, back + *sistere*, to set⟧ **1** to withstand; fend off **2** to oppose actively; fight against —*vi.* to oppose or withstand something —**re·sist′er** *n.* —**re·sist′i·ble** *adj.*

re·sist′ance *n.* **1** a resisting **2** power to resist, as to ward off disease **3** opposition of some force, thing, etc. to another, as to the flow of an electric current —**re·sist′ant** *adj.*

re·sist′less *adj.* **1** irresistible **2** unable to resist; unresisting

re·sis′tor *n.* a device used in an electrical circuit to provide resistance

re′sole′ *vt.* **-soled′, -sol′ing** to put a new sole on (a shoe, etc.)

res·o·lute (rez′ə lo͞ot′) *adj.* ⟦see RE- & SOLVE⟧ fixed and firm in purpose; determined —**res′o·lute′ly** *adv.*

res′o·lu′tion *n.* 1 the act or result of resolving something 2 a thing determined upon; decision as to future action 3 a resolute quality of mind 4 a formal statement of opinion or determination by an assembly, etc.

re·solve (ri zälv′) *vt.* **-solved′**, **-solv′ing** ⟦see RE- & SOLVE⟧ 1 to break up into separate parts; analyze 2 to change: used reflexively 3 to reach as a decision; determine 4 to solve (a problem) 5 to decide by vote —*vi.* 1 to be resolved, as by analysis 2 to come to a decision; determine —*n.* 1 firm determination 2 a formal resolution —**re·solv′a·ble** *adj.*

re·solved′ *adj.* determined; resolute

res·o·nant (rez′ə nənt) *adj.* ⟦< L *resonare*, resound⟧ 1 resounding 2 intensifying sound /*resonant* walls/ 3 sonorous; vibrant /a *resonant* voice/ —**res′o·nance** *n.* —**res′o·nate′** (-nāt′), **-nat′ed**, **-nat′ing**, *vi.*, *vt.*

res′o·na′tor *n.* a device that produces, or increases sound by, resonance

re·sort (ri zôrt′) *vi.* ⟦< OFr *re-*, again + *sortir*, go out⟧ to have recourse; turn (*to*) for help, etc. /to *resort* to lies/ —*n.* 1 a place to which people go often, as on vacation 2 a source of help, support, etc.; recourse —**as a last resort** as the last available means

re·sound (ri zound′) *vi.* ⟦< L *resonare*⟧ 1 to reverberate 2 to make a loud, echoing sound —**re·sound′ing** *adj.* —**re·sound′ing·ly** *adv.*

re·source (rē′sôrs′, ri sôrs′) *n.* ⟦< OFr *re-*, again + *sourdre*, spring up⟧ 1 something that lies ready for use or can be drawn upon for aid 2 [*pl.*] wealth; assets 3 resourcefulness

re·source′ful *adj.* able to deal effectively with problems, etc. —**re·source′ful·ness** *n.*

re·spect (ri spekt′) *vt.* ⟦< L *re-*, back + *specere*, look at⟧ 1 to feel or show honor or esteem for 2 to show consideration for —*n.* 1 honor or esteem 2 consideration or regard 3 [*pl.*] expressions of regard 4 a particular detail 5 reference; relation /with *respect* to the problem/ —**re·spect′ful** *adj.* —**re·spect′ful·ly** *adv.*

re·spect′a·ble *adj.* 1 worthy of respect or esteem 2 proper; correct 3 fairly good in quality or size 4 presentable —**re·spect′a·bil′i·ty** *n.*

re·spect′ing *prep.* concerning; about

re·spec′tive *adj.* as relates individually to each one

re·spec′tive·ly *adv.* in regard to each, in the order named

res·pi·ra·tion (res′pə rā′shən) *n.* ⟦see RESPIRE⟧ act or process of breathing —**res·pi·ra·to·ry** (res′pər ə tôr′ē, ri spī′rə-) *adj.*

res′pi·ra′tor *n.* 1 a mask, as of gauze, to prevent the inhaling of harmful substances 2 an apparatus to maintain breathing by artificial means

re·spire (ri spīr′) *vi.*, *vt.* **-spired′**, **-spir′ing** ⟦< L *re-*, back + *spirare*, breathe⟧ to breathe

res·pite (res′pit) *n.* ⟦see RESPECT⟧ 1 a delay or postponement 2 temporary relief, as from pain or work

re·splend·ent (ri splen′dənt) *adj.* ⟦< L *re-*, again + *splendere*, to shine⟧ shining brightly; dazzling —**re·splend′ence** *n.* —**re·splend′ent·ly** *adv.*

re·spond (ri spänd′) *vi.* ⟦< L *re-*, back + *spondere*, to pledge⟧ 1 to answer; reply 2 to react 3 to have a favorable reaction

re·spond′ent *adj.* responding —*n.* *Law* a defendant

re·sponse (ri späns′) *n.* ⟦see RESPOND⟧ 1 something said or done in answer; reply 2 words sung or spoken by the congregation or choir replying to the clergyman 3 any reaction to a stimulus

re·spon·si·bil·i·ty (ri spän′sə bil′ə tē) *n.*, *pl.* **-ties** 1 a being responsible; obligation 2 a thing or person that one is responsible for

re·spon′si·ble (-bəl) *adj.* 1 expected or obliged to account (*for*); answerable (*to*) 2 involving obligation or duties 3 that is the cause of something 4 able to distinguish between right and wrong 5 dependable; reliable —**re·spon′si·bly** *adv.*

re·spon′sive *adj.* reacting readily, as to suggestion —**re·spon′sive·ness** *n.*

rest[1] (rest) *n.* ⟦OE⟧ 1 sleep or repose 2 ease or inactivity after exertion 3 relief from anything distressing, tiring, etc. 4 absence of motion 5 a resting place 6 a supporting device 7 *Music* a measured interval of silence between tones, or a symbol for this —*vi.* 1 to get ease and refreshment by sleeping or by ceasing from work 2 to be at ease 3 to be or become still 4 to lie, sit, or lean 5 to be placed or based (*in*, *on*, etc.) 6 to be found /the fault *rests* with him/ 7 to rely; depend —*vt.* 1 to give rest to 2 to put for ease, support, etc. /*rest* your head here/ 3 *Law* to stop introducing evidence in (a case) —**lay to rest** to bury

rest[2] (rest) *n.* ⟦< L *restare*, remain⟧ 1 what is left 2 [*with pl. v.*] the others —*vi.* to go on being /*rest* assured/

res·tau·rant (res′tə ränt′) *n.* ⟦Fr: see RESTORE⟧ a place where meals can be bought and eaten

res·tau·ra·teur (res′tər ə tur′, -to͞or′) *n.* ⟦Fr⟧ one who owns or operates a restaurant Also **res·tau·ran·teur** (res′tə rän tur′, -to͞or′)

rest·ful (rest′fəl) *adj.* 1 full of or giving rest 2 quiet; peaceful

rest home a residence that provides care for aged persons or convalescents

res·ti·tu·tion (res′tə to͞o′shən) *n.* ⟦< L *re-*, again + *statuere*, set up⟧ 1 a giving back of something that has been lost or taken away; restoration 2 reimbursement, as for loss

res·tive (res′tiv) *adj.* ⟦< OFr *rester*, remain⟧ 1 unruly or balky 2 nervous under restraint; restless —**res′tive·ly** *adv.* —**res′tive·ness** *n.*

rest′less *adj.* 1 unable to relax; uneasy 2 giving no rest; disturbed /*restless* sleep/ 3 rarely quiet or still; active 4 discontented —**rest′less·ly** *adv.* —**rest′less·ness** *n.*

res·to·ra·tion (res′tə rā′shən) *n.* 1 a restoring or being restored 2 something restored, as by rebuilding

re·stor·a·tive (ri stôr′ə tiv) *adj.* able to restore health, consciousness, etc. —*n.* something that is restorative

re·store (ri stôr′) *vt.* **-stored′, -stor′ing** ⟦< L *re-*, again + *-staurare,* to erect⟧ 1 to give back (something taken, lost, etc.) 2 to return to a former or normal state, or to a position, rank, use, etc. 3 to bring back to health, strength, etc.

re·strain (ri strān′) *vt.* ⟦< L *re-*, back + *stringere,* draw tight⟧ 1 to hold back from action; check; suppress 2 to limit; restrict

re·straint (ri strānt′) *n.* 1 a restraining or being restrained 2 a means of restraining 3 confinement 4 control of emotions, impulses, etc.; reserve

re·strict (ri strikt′) *vt.* ⟦see RESTRAIN⟧ to keep within limits; confine —**re·strict′ed** *adj.* —**re·stric′tion** *n.*

re·stric′tive *adj.* 1 restricting 2 *Gram.* designating a subordinate clause or phrase that limits the reference of the word it modifies and is not set off by punctuation

rest·room (rest′ro͞om′) *n.* a room in a public building, equipped with toilets, washbowls, etc. Also **rest room**

re·struc·ture (rē struk′chər) *vt.* **-tured, -tur·ing** to plan or provide a new structure or organization for

re·sult (ri zult′) *vi.* ⟦< L *resultare,* to rebound⟧ 1 to happen as an effect 2 to end as a consequence (*in* something) —*n.* 1 *a)* anything that comes about as an effect *b)* [*pl.*] the desired effect 2 the number, etc. obtained by mathematical calculation —**re·sult′ant** *adj.*, *n.*

re·sume (ri zo͞om′) *vt.* **-sumed′, -sum′ing** ⟦< L *re-*, again + *sumere,* take⟧ 1 to take or occupy again 2 to continue after interruption —*vi.* to proceed after interruption —**re·sump·tion** (ri zump′shən) *n.*

ré·su·mé (rez′ə mā′) *n.* ⟦Fr: see prec.⟧ a summary, esp. of employment experience: also sp. **re′su·me′** or **re′su·mé′**

re·sur·face (rē sʉr′fis) *vt.* **-faced, -fac·ing** to put a new surface on —*vi.* to come to the surface again

re·sur·gent (ri sʉr′jənt) *adj.* ⟦see fol.⟧ tending to rise again —**re·sur′gence** *n.*

res·ur·rec·tion (rez′ə rek′shən) *n.* ⟦< L *resurgere,* rise again⟧ 1 a rising from the dead 2 a coming back into notice, use, etc.; revival —**the Resurrection** *Theol.* the rising of Jesus from the dead —**res′ur·rect′** *vt.*

re·sus·ci·tate (ri sus′ə tāt′) *vt.*, *vi.* **-tat′ed, -tat′ing** ⟦< L *re-*, again + *suscitare,* revive⟧ to revive when apparently dead or in a faint, etc. —**re·sus′ci·ta′tion** *n.* —**re·sus′ci·ta′tor** *n.*

re·tail (rē′tāl′) *n.* ⟦< OFr *re-*, again + *tailler,* to cut⟧ the sale of goods in small quantities directly to the consumer —*adj.* of or engaged in such sale —*adv.* at a retail price —*vt.*, *vi.* to sell or be sold directly to the consumer —**re′tail′er** *n.*

re·tain (ri tān′) *vt.* ⟦< L *re-*, back + *tenere,* to hold⟧ 1 to keep in possession, use, etc. 2 to hold in 3 to keep in mind 4 to hire by paying a retainer

re·tain′er *n.* 1 something that retains 2 a servant, attendant, etc. 3 a fee paid to engage a lawyer's services

retaining wall a wall for keeping earth from sliding or water from flooding

re·take (rē tāk′; *for n.* rē′tāk′) *vt.* **-took′, -tak′en, -tak′ing** 1 to take again; recapture 2 to photograph again —*n.* a scene, etc. rephotographed

re·tal·i·ate (ri tal′ē āt′) *vi.* **-at′ed, -at′ing** ⟦< L *re-*, back + *talio,* punishment in kind⟧ to return like for like, esp. injury for injury —**re·tal′i·a′tion** *n.* —**re·tal′i·a·to′ry** *adj.*

re·tard (ri tärd′) *vt.* ⟦< L *re-*, back + *tardare,* make slow⟧ to hinder, delay, or slow the progress of —**re·tar·da·tion** (rē′tär dā′shən) *n.*

re·tard′ant *n.* something that retards; esp., a substance that delays a chemical reaction —*adj.* that retards

re·tard′ed *adj.* slowed or delayed in development, esp. mentally

retch (rech) *vi.* ⟦OE *hræcan,* clear the throat⟧ to strain to vomit, esp. without bringing anything up

re·ten·tion (ri ten′shən) *n.* 1 a retaining or being retained 2 capacity for retaining —**re·ten′tive** *adj.*

ret·i·cent (ret′ə sənt) *adj.* ⟦< L *re-*, again + *tacere,* be silent⟧ disinclined to speak; taciturn —**ret′i·cence** *n.*

ret·i·na (ret′′n ə) *n.*, *pl.* **-nas** or **-nae′** (-ē′) ⟦prob. < L *rete,* a net⟧ the innermost coat lining the eyeball, containing light-sensitive cells which receive the visual image

ret·i·nue (ret′′n o͞o′) *n.* ⟦< OFr, ult. < L: see RETAIN⟧ a group of persons attending a person of rank or importance

re·tire (ri tīr′) *vi.* **-tired′, -tir′ing** ⟦< Fr *re-*, back + *tirer,* draw⟧ 1 to withdraw to a secluded place 2 to go to bed 3 to retreat, as in battle 4 to give up one's work, business, etc., esp. because of age —*vt.* 1 to withdraw (troops, etc.) 2 to pay off (bonds, etc.) 3 to cause to retire from a position, office, etc. 4 to withdraw from use 5 *Baseball* to put out (a batter, side, etc.) —**re·tir′ee′** *n.* —**re·tire′ment** *n.*

re·tired′ *adj.* 1 secluded 2 *a)* no longer working, etc. as because of age *b)* of or for such retired persons

re·tir′ing *adj.* reserved; modest; shy

re·tool (rē′to͞ol′) *vt.*, *vi.* to adapt (factory machinery) for a different product

re·tort[1] (ri tôrt′) *vt.* ⟦< L *re-*, back + *torquere,* to twist⟧ 1 to turn (an insult, etc.) back upon its originator 2 to say in reply —*vi.* to make a sharp, witty reply —*n.* a sharp, witty reply

re·tort[2] (ri tôrt′) *n.* ⟦< ML *retorta:* see prec.⟧ a glass container with a long tube in which substances are distilled

re·touch (rē′tuch′) *vt.* to touch up details in (a painting, essay, etc.) so as to improve or change it

re·trace (ri trās′) *vt.* **-traced′, -trac′ing** ⟦see RE- & TRACE[1]⟧ to go back over again [to *retrace* one's steps]

re·tract (ri trakt′) *vt.*, *vi.* ⟦< L *re-*, back + *trahere,* draw⟧ 1 to draw back or in 2 to withdraw (a statement, charge, etc.) —**re·tract′a·ble** or **re·trac′tile** (-trak′təl, -tīl′) *adj.* —**re·trac′tion** *n.*

re·tread (rē′tred′; *for n.* rē′tred′) *vt.*, *n.* RECAP[1]

re·treat (ri trēt′) *n.* ⟦< L *retrahere:* see RETRACT⟧ 1 a withdrawal, as from danger 2 a safe, quiet place 3 a period of seclusion, esp. for spiritual renewal **4** *a)* the forced withdrawal of troops under attack *b)* a signal for this *c)* a signal, as by bugle, or a ceremony at sunset for lowering the national flag —*vi.* to withdraw; go back

re·trench (rē trench′) *vt., vi.* ⟦< Fr: see RE- & TRENCH⟧ to cut down (esp. expenses); economize —**re·trench′ment** *n.*

ret·ri·bu·tion (re′trə byōō′shən) *n.* ⟦< L *re-*, back + *tribuere,* to pay⟧ punishment for evil done or reward for good done —**re·trib·u·tive** (ri trib′yoo tiv) *adj.*

re·trieve (ri trēv′) *vt.* **-trieved′**, **-triev′ing** ⟦< OFr *re-*, again + *trouver*, find⟧ **1** to get back; recover **2** to restore **3** to make good (a loss, error, etc.) **4** to access (data) stored in a computer **5** to find and bring back (killed or wounded game): said of dogs —*vi.* to retrieve game —**re·triev′al** *n.*

re·triev′er *n.* a dog trained to retrieve game

retro- ⟦< L⟧ *combining form* backward, back, behind

ret·ro·ac·tive (re′trō ak′tiv) *adj.* having an effect on things that are already past —**ret′ro·ac′tive·ly** *adv.*

ret·ro·fire (re′trə fīr′) *vt.* **-fired′**, **-fir′ing** to ignite (a retrorocket)

ret′ro·fit′ (-fit′) *n.* a change in design or equipment, as of an aircraft already in operation, so as to incorporate later improvements —*vt., vi.* **-fit′ted, -fit′ting** to modify with a retrofit

ret′ro·grade′ (-grād′) *adj.* ⟦< L: see RETRO- & GRADE⟧ **1** moving backward **2** going back to a worse condition —*vi.* **-grad′ed, -grad′ing 1** to go backward **2** to become worse

ret′ro·gress′ (-gres′) *vi.* ⟦< L: see prec.⟧ to move backward, esp. into a worse condition —**ret′ro·gres′sive** *adj.* —**ret′ro·gres′sion** *n.*

ret·ro·rock·et or **ret·ro-rock·et** (re′trō räk′ it) *n.* a small rocket, as on a spacecraft, producing thrust opposite to the direction of flight to reduce speed, as for landing

ret·ro·spect (re′trə spekt′) *n.* ⟦< L *retro-*, back + *specere,* to look⟧ contemplation of the past —**ret′ro·spec′tion** *n.*

ret′ro·spec′tive *adj.* looking back on the past —*n.* a representative show of an artist's lifetime work

ret·si·na (ret sē′nə) *n.* ⟦Modern Greek, prob. < It *resina*, resin⟧ a Greek wine flavored with pine resin

re·turn (ri turn′) *vi.* ⟦< OFr: see RE- & TURN⟧ **1** to go or come back **2** to reply —*vt.* **1** to bring, send, or put back **2** to do in reciprocation [to *return* a visit] **3** to yield (a profit, etc.) **4** to report officially **5** to elect or reelect —*n.* **1** a coming or going back **2** a bringing, sending, or putting back **3** something returned **4** a recurrence **5** repayment; requital **6** [*often pl.*] yield or profit, as from investments **7** a reply **8** *a)* an official report [election *returns*] *b)* a form for computing (income) tax —*adj.* **1** of or for a return [*return* postage] **2** given, done, etc. in return —**in return** as a return —**re·turn′a·ble** *adj.*

re·turn′ee′ *n.* one who returns, as home from military service or to school after dropping out

Reu·ben (sandwich) (rōō′bən) a sandwich of rye bread, corned beef, sauerkraut, Swiss cheese, etc. served hot

re·u·ni·fy (rē yōō′nə fī′) *vt., vi.* **-fied′**, **-fy′·ing** to unify again after being divided —**re·u′ni·fi·ca′tion** *n.*

re·un·ion (rē yōōn′yən) *n.* a coming together again, as after separation

re-up (rē′up′) *vi.* **-upped′**, **-up′ping** ⟦RE- + (*sign*) *up*⟧ [Mil. Slang] to reenlist

rev (rev) *vt.* **revved, rev′ving** ⟦< REV(OLUTION)⟧ [Colloq.] to increase the speed of (an engine): usually with *up*

Rev. Reverend

re·vamp (rē vamp′) *vt.* to vamp again; specif., to revise; redo

re·veal (ri vēl′) *vt.* ⟦< L *re-*, back + *velum,* veil⟧ **1** to make known (something hidden or secret) **2** to show; exhibit; display

rev·eil·le (rev′ə lē) *n.* ⟦< Fr < L *re-*, again + *vigilare,* to watch⟧ a signal on a bugle, drum, etc. in the morning to waken soldiers, etc.

rev·el (rev′əl) *vi.* **-eled** or **-elled, -el·ing** or **-el·ling** ⟦< MFr < L *rebellare,* to rebel: see REBEL⟧ **1** to make merry **2** to take much pleasure (*in*) —*n.* merrymaking —**rev′el·er** or **rev′el·ler** *n.* —**rev′el·ry,** *pl.* **-ries,** *n.*

rev·e·la·tion (rev′ə lā′shən) *n.* **1** a revealing **2** something disclosed; esp., a striking disclosure **3** *Theol.* God's disclosure to humanity of himself —[**R-**] the last book of the New Testament

re·venge (ri venj′) *vt.* **-venged′**, **-veng′ing** ⟦< OFr: see RE- & VENGEANCE⟧ to inflict harm in return for (an injury, etc.) —*n.* **1** the act or result of revenging **2** desire to take vengeance —**re·venge′ful** *adj.*

rev·e·nue (rev′ə nōō′) *n.* ⟦< MFr, returned⟧ **1** return, as from investment; income **2** the income from taxes, licenses, etc., as of a city, state, or nation

re·ver·ber·ate (ri vur′bə rāt′) *vi., vt.* **-at′ed, -at′ing** ⟦< L *re-*, again + *verberare,* to beat⟧ to reecho or cause to reecho —**re·ver′ber·a′tion** *n.*

re·vere (ri vir′) *vt.* **-vered′**, **-ver′ing** ⟦< L *re-*, again + *vereri,* to fear⟧ to regard with deep respect, love, etc.

Re·vere (rə vir′), **Paul** 1735-1818; Am. silversmith & patriot

rev·er·ence (rev′ər əns) *n.* a feeling of deep respect, love, and awe —*vt.* **-enced, -enc·ing** to venerate —**rev′er·ent** or **rev′er·en′·tial** (-ə ren′shəl) *adj.* —**rev′er·ent·ly** *adv.*

rev·er·end (rev′ər ənd) *adj.* worthy of reverence: used with *the* as a title of respect for a member of the clergy [the *Reverend* A. B. Smith]

rev·er·ie or **rev·er·y** (rev′ər ē) *n., pl.* **-ies** ⟦< Fr⟧ daydreaming or a daydream

re·vers (ri vir′, -ver′) *n., pl.* **-vers′** (-virz′, -verz′) ⟦Fr: see REVERT⟧ a part (of a garment) turned back to show the reverse side, as a lapel Also **re·vere′** (-vir′)

re·verse (ri vurs′) *adj.* ⟦see fol.⟧ **1** turned backward; opposite or contrary **2** causing movement in the opposite direction —*n.* **1** the opposite or contrary **2** the back of a coin, medal, etc. **3** a change from good fortune to bad **4** a mechanism for reversing, as a gear on a machine —*vt.* **-versed′**,

-vers′ing 1 to turn backward, in an opposite position or direction, upside down, or inside out 2 to change to the opposite 3 *Law* to revoke or annul (a decision, etc.) —*vi.* to go or turn in the opposite direction —**re·ver′sal** (-vur′səl) *n.* —**re·vers′i·ble** *adj.* —**re·vers′i·bly** *adv.*

re·vert (ri vurt′) *vi.* ⟦< L *re-*, back + *vertere*, to turn⟧ 1 to go back, as to a former practice, state, subject, etc. 2 *Biol.* to return to a former or primitive type 3 *Law* to go back to a former owner or his or her heirs —**re·ver′sion** (-vur′zhən) *n.* —**re·vert′i·ble** *adj.*

re·vet·ment (ri vet′mənt) *n.* ⟦< Fr⟧ 1 a facing of stone, cement, etc., as to protect an embankment 2 RETAINING WALL

re·view (ri vyōō′) *n.* ⟦< L *re-*, again + *videre*, see⟧ 1 a looking at or looking over again 2 a general survey or report 3 a looking back on (past events, etc.) 4 reexamination, as of the decision of a lower court 5 a critical evaluation of a book, play, etc. 6 a formal inspection, as of troops on parade —*vt.* 1 to look back on 2 to survey in thought, speech, etc. 3 to inspect (troops, etc.) formally 4 to give a critical evaluation of (a book, etc.) 5 to study again —**re·view′er** *n.*

re·vile (ri vīl′) *vt.*, *vi.* **-viled′**, **-vil′ing** ⟦< OFr: see RE- & VILE⟧ to use abusive language (to or about) —**re·vile′ment** *n.* —**re·vil′er** *n.*

re·vise (ri vīz′) *vt.* **-vised′**, **-vis′ing** ⟦< L *re-*, back + *visere*, to survey⟧ 1 to read over carefully and correct, improve, or update 2 to change or amend —**re·vi′sion** (-vizh′ən) *n.*

Revised Standard Version a 20th-c. version of the Bible

re·viv·al (ri vī′vəl) *n.* 1 a reviving or being revived 2 a bringing or coming back into use, being, etc. 3 a new presentation of an earlier play, etc. 4 restoration to vigor or activity 5 a meeting led by an evangelist to stir up religious feeling —**re·viv′al·ist** *n.*

re·vive (ri vīv′) *vi.*, *vt.* **-vived′**, **-viv′ing** ⟦< L *re-*, again + *vivere*, to live⟧ 1 to return to life or consciousness 2 to return to health or vigor 3 to come or bring back into use, attention, popularity, exhibition, etc.

re·viv·i·fy (ri viv′ə fī′) *vt.* **-fied′**, **-fy′ing** to put new life or vigor into —*vi.* to revive —**re·viv′i·fi·ca′tion** *n.*

re·voke (ri vōk′) *vt.* **-voked′**, **-vok′ing** ⟦< L *re-*, back + *vocare*, to call⟧ to withdraw, repeal or cancel (a law, etc.) —**rev·o·ca·ble** (rev′ə kə bəl) *adj.* —**rev′o·ca′tion** (-kā′shən) *n.*

re·volt (ri vōlt′) *n.* ⟦< Fr: see REVOLVE⟧ a rebelling against the government or any authority —*vi.* 1 to rebel against authority 2 to turn (*from* or *against*) in revulsion; be shocked (*at*) —*vt.* to disgust —**re·volt′ing** *adj.*

rev·o·lu·tion (rev′ə lōō′shən) *n.* ⟦see REVOLVE⟧ 1 the movement of a body in an orbit 2 a turning around an axis; rotation 3 a complete cycle of events 4 a complete change 5 overthrow of a government, social system, etc. —**rev′o·lu′tion·ar′y** (-er′ē), *pl.* **-ies**, *n.*, *adj.* —**rev′o·lu′tion·ist** *n.*

Revolutionary War *see* AMERICAN REVOLUTION

rev′o·lu′tion·ize′ (-īz′) *vt.* **-ized′**, **-iz′ing** to make a fundamental change in

re·volve (ri välv′) *vt.* **-volved′**, **-volv′ing** ⟦< L *re-*, back + *volvere*, to roll⟧ 1 to turn over in the mind 2 to cause to travel in a circle or orbit 3 to cause to rotate —*vi.* 1 to move in a circle or orbit 2 to rotate 3 to recur at intervals —**re·volv′a·ble** *adj.*

re·volv′er *n.* a handgun with a revolving cylinder containing cartridges

re·vue (ri vyōō′) *n.* ⟦Fr, review⟧ a musical show with skits, dances, etc., often parodying recent events, etc.

re·vul·sion (ri vul′shən) *n.* ⟦< L *re-*, back + *vellere*, to pull⟧ an abrupt, strong reaction; esp., disgust

re·ward (ri wôrd′) *n.* ⟦< OFr *regarde*: see REGARD⟧ 1 something given in return for something done 2 money offered, as for capturing a criminal —*vt.* to give a reward to (someone) for (service, etc.)

re·ward′ing *adj.* giving a sense of reward or worthwhile return

re·wind (rē wīnd′) *vt.* **-wound′**, **-wind′ing** to wind again; specif., to wind (film or tape) back on the original reel

re·word′ *vt.* to change the wording of

re·write′ *vt.*, *vi.* **-wrote′**, **-writ′ten**, **-writ′ing** 1 to write again 2 to revise (something written) 3 to write (news turned in) in publishable form

Rey·kja·vik (rā′kyə vēk′, -vik′) capital of Iceland: pop. 89,000

RFD or **R.F.D.** Rural Free Delivery

rhap·so·dize (rap′sə dīz′) *vi.*, *vt.* **-dized′**, **-diz′ing** to speak or write in a rhapsodic manner

rhap′so·dy (-dē) *n.*, *pl.* **-dies** ⟦< Gr *rhaptein*, stitch together + *ōidē*, song⟧ 1 any ecstatic or enthusiastic speech or writing 2 an instrumental composition of free, irregular form, suggesting improvisation —**rhap·sod′ic** (-säd′ik) or **rhap·sod′i·cal** *adj.*

rhe·a (rē′ə) *n.* ⟦< Gr⟧ a large, flightless South American bird, like an ostrich but smaller

rhe·o·stat (rē′ə stat′) *n.* ⟦< Gr *rheos*, current + -STAT⟧ a device for varying the resistance of an electric circuit, used as for dimming or brightening electric lights

rhesus (monkey) (rē′səs) ⟦< Gr proper name⟧ a brownish-yellow monkey of India: used in medical research

RHESUS MONKEY

rhet·o·ric (ret′ər ik) *n.* ⟦< Gr *rhētōr*, orator⟧ 1 the art of using words effectively; esp., the art of prose composition 2 artificial eloquence —**rhe·tor·i·cal** (ri tôr′i kəl) *adj.* —**rhet′o·ri′cian** (-ə rish′ən) *n.*

rhetorical question a question asked only for rhetorical effect, no answer being expected

rheum (rōōm) *n.* ⟦< Gr *rheuma*, a flow⟧ watery discharge from the eyes, nose, etc., as in a cold

rheumatic fever an acute or chronic disease, usually of children, with fever, swelling of the joints, inflammation of the heart, etc.

rheu·ma·tism (ro͞o′mə tiz′əm) ***n.*** ⟦see RHEUM⟧ *nontechnical term for* a painful condition of the joints and muscles —**rheu·mat′ic** (-mat′ik) ***adj., n.*** —**rheu′ma·toid′** (-mə toid′) ***adj.***

rheumatoid arthritis a chronic disease with painful swelling of joints, often leading to deformity

Rh factor (är′āch′) ⟦first discovered in RH(ESUS) monkeys⟧ a group of antigens, usually present in human blood: people who have this factor are **Rh positive**; those who do not are **Rh negative**

Rhine (rīn) river in W Europe, flowing from E Switzerland through Germany & the Netherlands into the North Sea

rhine·stone (rīn′stōn′) ***n.*** an artificial gem of hard glass, often cut in imitation of a diamond

Rhine wine a light white wine, esp. one produced in the valley of the Rhine

rhi·ni·tis (rī nīt′is) ***n.*** ⟦< Gr *rhis,* nose + -ITIS⟧ inflammation of the nasal mucous membrane

rhi·no (rī′nō) ***n., pl.*** **-nos** or **-no** *short for* RHINOCEROS

rhi·noc·er·os (rī näs′ər əs) ***n.*** ⟦< Gr *rhis,* nose + *keras,* horn⟧ a large, thick-skinned, plant-eating mammal of Africa and Asia, with one or two upright horns on the snout

rhi·zome (rī′zōm′) ***n.*** ⟦< Gr *rhiza,* a root⟧ a horizontal stem on or under soil, bearing leaves near its tips and roots from its undersurface

rho (rō) ***n.*** *name of* the 17th letter of the Greek alphabet (P, ρ)

Rhode Island (rōd) New England State of the U.S.: 1,214 sq. mi.; pop. 947,000; cap. Providence —**Rhode Islander**

Rhodes (rōdz) large Greek island in the Aegean

rho·do·den·dron (rō′də den′drən) ***n.*** ⟦< Gr *rhodon,* rose + *dendron,* tree⟧ a tree or shrub, mainly evergreen, with pink, white, or purple flowers

rhom·boid (räm′boid′) ***n.*** ⟦< Fr: see fol. & -OID⟧ a parallelogram with oblique angles and only the opposite sides equal

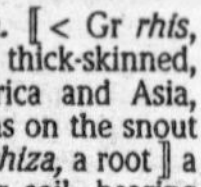

RHOMBOID

rhom·bus (räm′bəs) ***n., pl.*** **-bus·es** or **-bi′** (-bī′) ⟦L < Gr *rhombos,* turnable object⟧ an equilateral parallelogram, esp. one with oblique angles

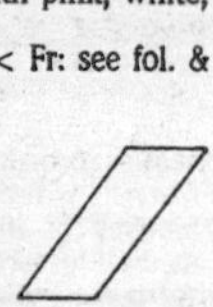

RHOMBUS

Rhone or **Rhône** (rōn) river flowing through SW Switzerland & France into the Mediterranean

rhu·barb (ro͞o′bärb′) ***n.*** ⟦< Gr *rhēon,* rhubarb + *barbaron,* foreign⟧ **1** a plant with long, thick stalks that are cooked into a sauce, etc. **2** [Slang] a heated argument

rhyme (rīm) ***n.*** ⟦< OFr⟧ **1** a poem or verse with recurring correspondence of end sounds, esp. at ends of lines **2** such verse or poetry or such correspondence of sounds **3** a word corresponding with another in end sound —***vi.*** **rhymed, rhym′ing** **1** to make (rhyming) verse **2** to form a rhyme ["more" *rhymes* with "door"] —***vt.*** **1** to put into rhyme **2** to use as a rhyme

rhym′er or **rhyme′ster** ***n.*** a maker of rhymes, esp. of trivial rhyming verse

rhythm (rith′əm) ***n.*** ⟦< Gr *rhythmos,* measure⟧ **1** movement, flow, etc. characterized by regular recurrence of beat, accent, etc. **2** the pattern of this in music, verse, etc. —**rhyth′mic** (-mik) or **rhyth′mi·cal** ***adj.*** —**rhyth′mi·cal·ly** ***adv.***

rhythm and blues the form of American popular music from which rock-and-roll derives

rhythm method a method of seeking birth control by abstaining from intercourse during the woman's probable ovulation period

RI or **R.I.** Rhode Island

rib (rib) ***n.*** ⟦OE⟧ **1** any of the arched bones attached to the spine and enclosing the chest cavity **2** anything like a rib in appearance or function —***vt.*** **ribbed, rib′bing** **1** to provide or form with ribs **2** [Slang] to tease or make fun of; kid

rib·ald (rib′əld) ***adj.*** ⟦< OHG *riban,* to rub⟧ coarse or vulgar in joking, speaking, etc. —**rib′ald·ry** ***n.***

rib·bon (rib′ən) ***n.*** ⟦< MFr *ruban*⟧ **1** a narrow strip of silk, rayon, etc. used for decoration, tying, etc. **2** [*pl.*] torn shreds **3** a strip of cloth inked for printing, as in a typewriter

ri·bo·fla·vin (rī′bə flā′vin) ***n.*** ⟦< *ribose,* a sugar + L *flavus,* yellow⟧ a factor of the vitamin B complex found in milk, eggs, fruits, etc.

rice (rīs) ***n.*** ⟦< Gr *oryza*⟧ **1** an aquatic cereal grass grown widely in warm climates, esp. in the Orient **2** the starchy grains of this grass, used as food —***vt.*** **riced, ric′ing** to make ricelike granules from (cooked potatoes, etc.) —**ric′er** ***n.***

rich (rich) ***adj.*** ⟦< OFr⟧ **1** owning much money or property; wealthy **2** well-supplied (*with*); abounding (*in*) **3** valuable or costly **4** full of choice ingredients, as butter, sugar, etc. [*rich* pastries] **5** *a)* full and mellow (said of sounds) *b)* deep; vivid (said of colors) *c)* very fragrant **6** abundant **7** yielding in abundance, as soil **8** [Colloq.] very amusing —**the rich** wealthy people collectively —**rich′ly** ***adv.*** —**rich′ness** ***n.***

Rich·ard I (rich′ərd) 1157-99; king of England (1189-99): called **Richard Coeur de Li·on** (kur′ də lē′ən)

rich·es (rich′iz) ***n.pl.*** ⟦< OFr *richesse, n. sing.*⟧ wealth

Rich·mond (rich′mənd) capital of Va.: pop. 219,000

Rich·ter scale (rik′tər) ⟦devised by C. *Richter* (1900-), U.S. geologist⟧ a scale for measuring earthquakes, with each step about ten times greater than the preceding one

rick (rik) ***n.*** ⟦OE *hreac*⟧ a stack of hay, straw, etc.

rick·ets (rik′its) ***n.*** ⟦< ? Gr *rhachis,* spine⟧ a disease, chiefly of children, characterized by a softening and, often, bending of the bones

rick·et·y (rik′it ē) ***adj.*** **1** of or having rickets **2** feeble; weak; shaky

rick·rack (rik′rak′) ***n.*** ⟦< RACK[1]⟧ flat, zigzag braid for trimming dresses, etc.
rick·shaw or **rick·sha** (rik′shô′) ***n.*** JINRIKISHA
ric·o·chet (rik′ə shā′) ***n.*** ⟦Fr⟧ the oblique rebound of a bullet, etc. after striking a surface at an angle —***vi.*** **-cheted′** (-shād′), **-chet′ing** (-shā′iŋ) to make a ricochet
ri·cot·ta (ri kät′ə) ***n.*** ⟦It < L *recocta,* recooked⟧ a soft cheese made from whey or whole milk
rid (rid) ***vt.*** **rid** or **rid′ded, rid′ding** ⟦< ON *rythja,* to clear (land)⟧ to free or relieve, as of something undesirable —**get rid of** to give or throw away or to destroy
rid·dance (rid′'ns) ***n.*** a ridding or being rid; clearance or removal
rid·den (rid′'n) ***vi., vt. pp. of*** RIDE
rid·dle[1] (rid′'l) ***n.*** ⟦OE *rædels*⟧ **1** a puzzling question, etc. requiring some ingenuity to answer **2** any puzzling person or thing
rid·dle[2] (rid′'l) ***vt.*** **-dled, -dling** ⟦< OE *hriddel,* a sieve⟧ to make many holes in; puncture throughout
ride (rīd) ***vi.*** **rode, rid′den, rid′ing** ⟦OE *ridan*⟧ **1** to be carried along by a horse, in a vehicle, etc. **2** to be supported in motion (*on* or *upon*) /tanks *ride* on treads/ **3** to admit of being ridden /the car *rides* smoothly/ **4** to move or float on water **5** [Colloq.] to continue undisturbed /let the matter *ride*/ —***vt.*** **1** to sit on or in and control so as to move along **2** to move over, along, or through (a road, area, etc.) by horse, car, etc. **3** to control, dominate, etc. /*ridden* by doubts/ **4** [Colloq.] to tease with ridicule, etc. —***n.*** **1** a riding **2** a thing to ride at an amusement park
rid′er ***n.*** **1** one who rides **2** an addition or amendment to a document
rid′er·ship′ ***n.*** the passengers of a particular transportation system
ridge (rij) ***n.*** ⟦< OE *hrycg,* animal's spine⟧ **1** the long, narrow crest of something **2** a long, narrow elevation of land **3** any raised narrow strip **4** the horizontal line formed by the meeting of two sloping surfaces —***vt., vi.*** **ridged, ridg′ing** to mark or be marked with, or form into, ridges
ridge′pole′ ***n.*** the horizontal beam at the ridge of a roof, to which the rafters are attached
rid·i·cule (rid′i kyo͞ol′) ***n.*** ⟦< L *ridere,* to laugh⟧ **1** the act of making someone the object of scornful laughter **2** words or actions intended to produce such laughter —***vt.*** **-culed′, -cul′ing** to make fun of; deride; mock
ri·dic·u·lous (ri dik′yə ləs) ***adj.*** deserving ridicule —**ri·dic′u·lous·ly** ***adv.*** —**ri·dic′u·lous·ness** ***n.***
rife (rīf) ***adj.*** ⟦OE *ryfe*⟧ **1** widespread **2** abounding /*rife* with error/
riff (rif) ***n.*** ⟦prob. altered < REFRAIN[2]⟧ *Jazz* a constantly repeated musical phrase —***vi.*** *Jazz* to perform a riff
rif·fle (rif′əl) ***n.*** ⟦< ?⟧ **1** a ripple in a stream, produced by a reef, etc. **2** a certain way of shuffling cards —***vt., vi.*** **-fled, -fling** to shuffle (playing cards) by letting a divided deck fall together as the corners are slipped through one's thumbs
riff·raff (rif′raf′) ***n.*** ⟦< OFr⟧ those people regarded as worthless, disreputable, etc.
ri·fle[1] (rī′fəl) ***vt.*** **-fled, -fling** ⟦Fr *rifler,* to scrape⟧ to cut spiral grooves within (a gun barrel, etc.) —***n.*** a gun, fired from the shoulder, with a rifled barrel to spin the bullet for greater accuracy
ri·fle[2] (rī′fəl) ***vt.*** **-fled, -fling** ⟦< OFr *rifler*⟧ to ransack and rob —**ri′fler** ***n.***
ri′fle·man (-mən) ***n., pl.*** **-men** a soldier armed with a rifle
ri·fling (rī′fliŋ) ***n.*** **1** the cutting of spiral grooves within a gun barrel to make the projectile spin **2** a system of such grooves
rift (rift) ***n.*** ⟦< Dan, fissure⟧ an opening caused by splitting; cleft —***vt., vi.*** to burst open; split
rig (rig) ***vt.*** **rigged, rig′ging** ⟦< Scand⟧ **1** to fit (a ship, mast, etc.) with (sails, shrouds, etc.) **2** to assemble **3** to equip **4** to arrange dishonestly **5** [Colloq.] to dress: with *out* —***n.*** **1** the way sails, etc. are rigged **2** equipment; gear **3** oil-drilling equipment **4** a tractor-trailer
rig·a·ma·role (rig′ə mə rōl′) ***n. var. of*** RIGMAROLE
rig′ging ***n.*** the ropes, chains, etc. for a vessel's masts, sails, etc.
right (rīt) ***adj.*** ⟦< OE *riht,* straight⟧ **1** with a straight line or plane perpendicular to a base /a *right* angle/ **2** upright; virtuous **3** correct **4** fitting; suitable **5** designating the side or surface meant to be seen **6** mentally or physically sound **7** *a)* designating or of that side of the body toward the east when one faces north *b)* designating or of the corresponding side of anything *c)* closer to the right side of a person facing the thing mentioned —***n.*** **1** what is right, just, etc. **2** power, privilege, etc. belonging to one by law, nature, etc. **3** the right side **4** the right hand **5** [*often* **R-**] *Politics* a conservative or reactionary position, party, etc.: often with *the* —***adv.*** **1** straight; directly /go *right* home/ **2** properly; fittingly **3** completely **4** exactly /*right* here/ **5** according to law, justice, etc. **6** correctly **7** on or toward the right side **8** very: in certain titles /the *right* reverend/ —***interj.*** agreed! OK! —***vt.*** **1** to put upright **2** to correct **3** to put in order —**right away** (or **off**) at once —**right on!** [Slang] that's right! —**right′ly** ***adv.*** —**right′ness** ***n.***
right′a·bout′-face′ ***n.*** ABOUT-FACE
right angle an angle of 90 degrees
right·eous (rī′chəs) ***adj.*** **1** acting in a just, upright manner; virtuous **2** morally right or justifiable —**right′eous·ly** ***adv.*** —**right′eous·ness** ***n.***
right′ful ***adj.*** **1** fair and just; right **2** having a lawful claim —**right′ful·ly** ***adv.*** —**right′ful·ness** ***n.***
right′-hand′ ***adj.*** **1** on or toward the right **2** of, for, or with the right hand **3** most helpful or reliable /the president's *right-hand* man/
right′-hand′ed ***adj.*** **1** using the right hand more skillfully than the left **2** done with or made for use with the right hand —***adv.*** with the right hand —**right′-hand′ed·ness** ***n.***
right′ist ***n., adj.*** conservative or reactionary —**right′ism′** ***n.***

right′-mind′ed *adj.* having correct views or sound principles
right of way 1 the right to move first at intersections 2 land over which a road, power line, etc. passes Also **right′-of-way′**
right′-to-life′ *adj.* designating any movement, party, etc. opposed to abortion —**right′-to-lif′er** *n.*
right triangle a triangle with a right angle
right wing the more conservative or reactionary section of a political party or group —**right′-wing′** *adj.* —**right′-wing′er** *n.*
rig·id (rij′id) *adj.* ⟦< L *rigere,* be stiff⟧ 1 not bending or flexible; stiff 2 not moving; fixed 3 severe; strict 4 having a rigid framework: said of a dirigible —**ri·gid·i·ty** (ri jid′ə tē) or **rig′id·ness** *n.* —**rig′id·ly** *adv.*
rig·ma·role (rig′mə rōl′) *n.* ⟦< ME *rageman rolle,* long list⟧ 1 nonsense 2 a foolishly complicated procedure
rig·or (rig′ər) *n.* ⟦< L *rigere:* see RIGID⟧ 1 severity; strictness 2 hardship Brit., etc. sp. **rig′our** —**rig′or·ous** *adj.* —**rig′or·ous·ly** *adv.*
rig·or mor·tis (rig′ər môr′tis, rī′gôr′) ⟦L, stiffness of death⟧ the stiffening of the muscles after death
rile (rīl) *vt.* **riled, ril′ing** ⟦var. of ROIL⟧ [Colloq. or Dial.] to anger; irritate
rill (ril) *n.* ⟦< Du *ril*⟧ a rivulet
rim (rim) *n.* ⟦OE *rima*⟧ 1 an edge, border, or margin, esp. of something circular 2 the outer part of a wheel —*vt.* **rimmed, rim′ming** to put a rim or rims on or around —**rim′less** *adj.*
rime[1] (rīm) *n., vi., vt.* **rimed, rim′ing** RHYME
rime[2] (rīm) *n.* ⟦OE *hrim*⟧ hoarfrost
rind (rīnd) *n.* ⟦OE⟧ a hard outer layer or covering, as of fruit or cheese
ring[1] (riŋ) *vi.* **rang** or [Now Chiefly Dial.] **rung, rung, ring′ing** ⟦OE *hringan*⟧ 1 to give forth a resonant sound, as a bell 2 to seem /to *ring* true/ 3 to sound a bell, esp. as a summons 4 to resound /to *ring* with laughter/ 5 to have a ringing sensation, as the ears —*vt.* 1 to cause (a bell, etc.) to ring 2 to signal, announce, etc., as by ringing 3 to call by telephone —*n.* 1 the sound of a bell 2 a characteristic quality /the *ring* of truth/ 3 the act of ringing a bell 4 a telephone call —**ring a bell** to stir up a memory
ring[2] (riŋ) *n.* ⟦OE *hring*⟧ 1 an ornamental circular band worn on a finger 2 any similar band /a key *ring*/ 3 a circular line, mark, figure, or course 4 a group of people or things in a circle 5 a group working to advance its own interests, esp. by dishonest means 6 an enclosed area for contests, exhibitions, etc. /a circus *ring*/ 7 prizefighting: with *the* —*vt.* **ringed, ring′ing** 1 to encircle 2 to form into a ring —**run rings around** [Colloq.] 1 to run much faster than 2 to excel greatly
ring′er[1] *n.* a horseshoe, etc. thrown so that it encircles the peg
ring′er[2] *n.* 1 one that rings a bell, etc. 2 [Slang] *a*) a person or thing closely resembling another *b*) a fraudulent substitute in a competition
ring′lead′er *n.* one who leads others, esp. in unlawful acts, etc.
ring′let (-lit) *n.* 1 a little ring or circle 2 a curl of hair
ring′mas′ter *n.* a person who directs the performances in a circus ring
ring′side′ *n.* the place just outside the ring, as at a boxing match
ring′worm′ *n.* a contagious skin disease caused by a fungus
rink (riŋk) *n.* ⟦< OFr *renc,* a rank⟧ 1 an expanse of ice for skating 2 a smooth floor for roller-skating
rinse (rins) *vt.* **rinsed, rins′ing** ⟦ult. < L *recens,* fresh⟧ 1 to wash or flush lightly 2 to remove soap, etc. from with clear water —*n.* 1 a rinsing or the liquid used 2 a solution used to rinse or tint hair
Ri·o de Ja·nei·ro (rē′ō dā′ zhə ner′ō) city & seaport in SE Brazil: pop. 5,090,000
Ri·o Gran·de (rē′ō grand′, -gran′dē) river flowing from S Colo. into the Gulf of Mexico: the S border of Tex.
ri·ot (rī′ət) *n.* ⟦< OFr *riote,* dispute⟧ 1 wild or violent disorder, confusion, etc.; esp., a violent public disturbance 2 a brilliant display /a *riot* of color/ 3 [Colloq.] something very funny —*vi.* to take part in a riot —**read the riot act to** to give very strict orders to so as to make obey —**run riot** 1 to act wildly 2 to grow wild in abundance —**ri′ot·er** *n.* —**ri′ot·ous** *adj.*
rip (rip) *vt.* **ripped, rip′ping** ⟦ME *rippen*⟧ 1 *a*) to cut or tear apart roughly *b*) to remove in this way (with *off, out,* etc.) *c*) to sever the threads of (a seam) 2 to saw (wood) along the grain —*vi.* 1 to become ripped 2 [Colloq.] to rush; speed —*n.* a ripped place —**rip into** [Colloq.] to attack, esp. verbally —**rip off** [Slang] 1 to steal 2 to cheat or exploit —**rip′per** *n.*
rip cord a cord, etc. pulled to open a parachute during descent
ripe (rīp) *adj.* ⟦OE⟧ 1 ready to be harvested, as grain or fruit 2 of sufficient age, etc. to be used /*ripe* cheese/ 3 fully developed; mature 4 fully prepared; ready /*ripe* for action/ —**ripe′ly** *adv.* —**ripe′ness** *n.*
rip·en (rī′pən) *vi., vt.* to become or make ripe; mature, age, etc.
rip′-off′ *n.* [Slang] the act or an instance of stealing, cheating, etc.
ri·poste or **ri·post** (ri pōst′) *n.* ⟦Fr < L *respondere,* to answer⟧ a sharp, swift response; retort
rip·ple (rip′əl) *vi., vt.* **-pled, -pling** ⟦prob. < RIP⟧ to have or form little waves on the surface (of) —*n.* 1 a small wave 2 a rippling
ripple effect the spreading effects caused by a single event
rip′-roar′ing (-rôr′iŋ) *adj.* [Slang] boisterous; uproarious
rip′saw′ *n.* a saw with coarse teeth, for cutting wood along the grain
rip′tide′ *n.* a current opposing other currents, esp. along a seashore Also **rip tide**
rise (rīz) *vi.* **rose, ris·en** (riz′ən), **ris′ing** ⟦< OE *risan*⟧ 1 to stand or sit up after sitting, kneeling, or lying 2 to rebel; revolt 3 to go up; ascend 4 to appear above the horizon, as the sun 5 to attain a higher level, rank,

etc. **6** to extend, slant, or move upward **7** to increase in amount, degree, etc. **8** to expand and swell, as dough with yeast **9** to originate; begin **10** *Theol.* to return to life **—*n.*** **1** upward movement; ascent **2** an advance in status, rank, etc. **3** a slope upward **4** an increase in degree, amount, etc. **5** beginning; origin **—give rise to** to bring about

ris′er ***n.*** **1** one that rises **2** a vertical piece between the steps in a stairway

ris·i·ble (riz′ə bəl) ***adj.*** ⟦< L *ridere,* to laugh⟧ causing laughter; funny **—ris′i·bil′i·ty,** *pl.* **-ties,** ***n.***

ris′ing ***adj.*** advancing to adult years; growing /the *rising* generation/ **—*n.*** an uprising; revolt

risk (risk) ***n.*** ⟦< Fr < It *risco*⟧ the chance of injury, damage, or loss **—*vt.*** **1** to expose to risk /to *risk* one's life/ **2** to incur the risk of /to *risk* a war/ **—risk′y, -i·er, -i·est, *adj.***

ris·qué (ris kā′) ***adj.*** ⟦Fr < *risquer,* to risk⟧ very close to being improper or indecent; suggestive

rite (rīt) ***n.*** ⟦L *ritus*⟧ a ceremonial, solemn act, as in religious use

rite of passage a significant event, ceremony, etc. in a person's life

rit·u·al (rich′ōō əl) ***adj.*** of, like, or done as a rite **—*n.*** a set form or system of rites, religious or otherwise **—rit′u·al·ism′ *n.*** **—rit′u·al·ly *adv.***

ri·val (rī′vəl) ***n.*** ⟦< L *rivalis*⟧ one who tries to get or do the same thing as another, or to equal or surpass another; competitor **—*adj.*** acting as a rival; competing **—*vt.*** **-valed** or **-valled, -val·ing** or **-val·ling** **1** to try to equal or surpass **2** to equal in some way **—ri′val·ry,** *pl.* **-ries,** ***n.***

rive (rīv) ***vt., vi.*** **rived, rived** or **riv·en** (riv′ən), **riv′ing** ⟦< ON *rifa*⟧ **1** to tear apart; rend **2** to split

riv·er (riv′ər) ***n.*** ⟦< L *ripa,* a bank⟧ a natural stream of water flowing into an ocean, a lake, etc. **—riv′er·like′ *adj.***

river basin the area drained by a river and its tributaries

riv′er·side′ ***n.*** the bank of a river

Riv·er·side (riv′ər sīd′) city in S Calif.: pop. 171,000

riv·et (riv′it) ***n.*** ⟦Fr < *river,* to clinch⟧ a metal bolt with a head and a plain end that is flattened after the bolt is passed through parts to be held together **—*vt.*** to fasten with or as with rivets **—riv′·et·er *n.***

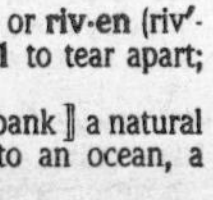

RIVET

Riv·i·er·a (riv′ē er′ə) strip of the Mediterranean coast of SE France & NW Italy: a resort area

riv·u·let (riv′yoo lit) ***n.*** ⟦< L *rivus,* brook⟧ a little stream

rm. **1** ream **2** room

Rn *Chem. symbol for* radon

RN or **R.N.** Registered Nurse

RNA ⟦*r*(*ibo*)*n*(*ucleic*) *a*(*cid*)⟧ an essential component of all living matter: one form carries genetic information

roach[1] (rōch) ***n.*** *short for* COCKROACH

roach[2] (rōch) ***n.,*** *pl.* **roach** or **roach′es** ⟦< OFr *roche*⟧ a freshwater fish of the carp family

road (rōd) ***n.*** ⟦OE *rad,* a ride⟧ **1** a way made for traveling; highway **2** a way; course /the *road* to fortune/ **3** [*often pl.*] a place near shore where ships can ride at anchor **—on the road** traveling, as a salesman

road′bed′ ***n.*** the foundation laid for railroad tracks or for a highway, etc.

road′block′ ***n.*** **1** a blockade set up in a road to prevent movement of vehicles **2** any hindrance

road runner a long-tailed, swift-running desert bird of the SW U.S. and N Mexico

road′show′ ***n.*** **1** a touring theatrical show **2** a reserved-seat film showing

road′side′ ***n.*** the side of a road **—*adj.*** on or at the side of a road

road′way′ ***n.*** a road; specif., the part of a road used by vehicles

road′work′ ***n.*** distance running or jogging as an exercise, esp. by a boxer

roam (rōm) ***vi., vt.*** ⟦ME *romen*⟧ to wander aimlessly (over or through) **—roam′er *n.***

roan (rōn) ***adj.*** ⟦< OSp *roano*⟧ bay, black, etc. thickly sprinkled with white **—*n.*** a roan horse

roar (rôr) ***vi.*** ⟦OE *rarian*⟧ **1** to make a loud, deep, rumbling sound **2** to laugh boisterously **—*vt.*** to express with a roar **—*n.*** a loud, deep, rumbling sound

roast (rōst) ***vt.*** ⟦< OFr *rostir*⟧ **1** to cook (meat, etc.) with little or no moisture, as in an oven or over an open fire **2** to process (coffee, etc.) by exposure to heat **3** to expose to great heat **4** [Colloq.] to criticize severely **—*vi.*** **1** to undergo roasting **2** to be or become very hot **—*n.*** **1** roasted meat **2** a cut of meat for roasting **3** a picnic at which food is roasted **—*adj.*** roasted /*roast* pork/ **—roast′er *n.***

rob (räb) ***vt.*** **robbed, rob′bing** ⟦< OFr *rober*⟧ **1** to take money, etc. from unlawfully by force; steal from **2** to deprive *of* something unjustly or injuriously **—*vi.*** to commit robbery **—rob′ber *n.*** **—rob′ber·y,** *pl.* **-ies,** ***n.***

robe (rōb) ***n.*** ⟦< OFr⟧ **1** a long, loose outer garment **2** such a garment worn to show rank or office, as by a judge **3** a bathrobe or dressing gown **4** a covering or wrap /a lap *robe*/ **—*vt., vi.*** **robed, rob′ing** to dress in a robe

rob·in (räb′ən) ***n.*** ⟦< OFr dim. of *Robert*⟧ a North American thrush with a dull-red breast

Robin Hood *Eng. Legend* the leader of a band of outlaws who robs the rich to help the poor

Ro·bin·son Cru·soe (räb′ən sən krōō′sō′) the title hero of Defoe's novel (1719) about a shipwrecked sailor

ro·bot (rō′bät′, -bət, -but′) ***n.*** ⟦< Czech < OSlav *rabu,* servant⟧ **1** a mechanical device operating automatically, in a seemingly human way **2** a person acting like a robot

ro·bot′ics ***n.pl.*** [*with sing. v.*] the science or technology of robots, their design, use, etc.

ro·bust (rō bust′, rō′bust′) ***adj.*** ⟦< L *robur,* oak⟧ strong and healthy **—ro·bust′ly *adv.*** **—ro·bust′ness *n.***

Roch·es·ter (räch′əs tər) city in W N.Y.: pop. 242,000

rock[1] (räk) ***n.*** ⟦ < ML *rocca* ⟧ **1** a large mass of stone **2** broken pieces of stone **3** mineral matter formed in masses in the earth's crust **4** anything like a rock; esp., a firm support **5** [Colloq. or Dial.] any stone —**on the rocks** [Colloq.] **1** ruined; bankrupt **2** served over ice cubes, as whiskey

rock[2] (räk) ***vt., vi.*** ⟦ OE *roccian* ⟧ **1** to move back and forth or from side to side **2** to sway strongly; shake —***n.*** **1** a rocking motion **2** ROCK-AND-ROLL

rock′a·bil′ly (-ə bil′ē) ***n.*** ⟦ ROCK(-AND-ROLL) + -*a*- + (HILL)BILLY ⟧ an early form of rock-and-roll with a strong country music influence

rock′-and-roll′ ***n.*** a form of popular music that evolved from rhythm and blues, characterized by a strong rhythm with an accent on the offbeat and youth-oriented lyrics

rock bottom the lowest level

rock′bound′ ***adj.*** surrounded or covered by rocks

rock candy large, hard, clear crystals of sugar formed on a string

rock′er ***n.*** **1** either of the curved pieces on which a cradle, etc. rocks **2** a chair mounted on such pieces: also **rocking chair**

rocker panel any panel section below the doors of an automotive vehicle

rock·et (räk′it) ***n.*** ⟦ It *rocchetta,* spool ⟧ any device driven forward by gases escaping through a rear vent, as a firework, a projectile weapon, or the propulsion mechanism of a spacecraft —***vi.*** to move in or like a rocket; soar

rock′et·ry (-ə trē) ***n.*** the science of building and launching rockets

Rock·ford (räk′fərd) city in N Ill.: pop. 140,000

rock garden a garden of flowers, etc. in ground studded with rocks

rocking horse a toy horse on rockers or springs, for a child to ride

rock lobster SPINY LOBSTER

rock′-ribbed′ ***adj.*** **1** having rocky ridges **2** firm; unyielding

rock salt common salt in masses

rock wool a fibrous material made from molten rock, used for insulation

rock·y[1] (räk′ē) ***adj.*** **-i·er, -i·est** **1** full of rocks **2** consisting of rock **3** like a rock; firm, hard, etc. —**rock′i·ness** ***n.***

rock·y[2] (räk′ē) ***adj.*** **-i·er, -i·est** inclined to rock; unsteady —**rock′i·ness** ***n.***

Rocky Mountains mountain system in W North America, extending from N.Mex. to N Alas.: also **Rock′ies**

Rocky Mountain sheep BIGHORN

ro·co·co (rə kō′kō) ***n.*** ⟦ Fr < *rocaille,* shell work ⟧ [*occas.* **R-**] a style of architecture, decorative art, music, etc. marked by profuse and delicate ornamentation, reduced scale, etc. —***adj.*** **1** of or in rococo **2** too elaborate

rod (räd) ***n.*** ⟦ < OE *rodd,* straight shoot or stem ⟧ **1** a straight stick or bar **2** a stick for beating as punishment **3** a scepter carried as a symbol of office **4** a pole for fishing **5** a measure of length equal to $5\frac{1}{2}$ yards **6** [Slang] a pistol

rode (rōd) ***vi., vt.*** *pt. & archaic pp. of* RIDE

ro·dent (rōd′'nt) ***n.*** ⟦ < L *rodere,* gnaw ⟧ any of an order of gnawing mammals, as rats, mice, beavers, etc.

ro·de·o (rō′dē ō′, rō dā′ō) ***n.***, *pl.* **-os′** ⟦ Sp < L *rotare,* to turn ⟧ a public exhibition of the skills of cowboys, as broncobusting, lassoing, etc.

Ro·din (rô dan′), **(François) Au·guste (René)** (ô güst′) 1840-1917; Fr. sculptor

roe[1] (rō) ***n.*** ⟦ ME *rowe* ⟧ fish eggs

roe[2] (rō) ***n.***, *pl.* **roe** or **roes** ⟦ < OE *ra* ⟧ a small, agile deer of Europe and Asia

roe′buck′ ***n.*** the male roe deer

roent·gen (rent′gən) ***n.*** ⟦ after W. K. *Roentgen* (1845-1923), Ger physicist ⟧ the unit for measuring the radiation of X-rays or gamma rays

Rog·er (rä′jər) ***interj.*** ⟦ < name of signal flag for *R* ⟧ [*also* **r-**] **1** received: used to indicate reception of a radio message **2** [Colloq.] right! OK!

rogue (rōg) ***n.*** ⟦ < ? ⟧ **1** a scoundrel **2** a mischievous person —**ro·guer·y** (rō′gər ē), *pl.* **-ies,** ***n.*** —**ro·guish** (rō′gish) ***adj.***

roil (roil) ***vt.*** ⟦ < L *robigo,* rust ⟧ **1** to make (a liquid) cloudy, muddy, etc. by stirring up sediment **2** to vex

roist·er (rois′tər) ***vi.*** ⟦ see RUSTIC ⟧ to revel noisily —**roist′er·er** ***n.***

role or **rôle** (rōl) ***n.*** ⟦ Fr ⟧ **1** the part played by an actor **2** a function assumed by someone /an advisory *role*/

role model a person so effective or inspiring in some social role, job, etc. as to be a model for others

role′-play′ing ***n.*** *Psychol.* a technique in which participants assume and act out roles so as to resolve conflicts, improve behavior, etc.

roll (rōl) ***vi.*** ⟦ < L *rota,* a wheel ⟧ **1** to move by turning around or over and over **2** to move on wheels **3** to pass /the years *roll* by/ **4** to extend in gentle swells **5** to make a loud rising and falling sound /thunder *rolls*/ **6** to rock from side to side —***vt.*** **1** to make move by turning around or over and over **2** to make move on wheels **3** to utter with full, flowing sound **4** to pronounce with a trill /to *roll* one's r's/ **5** to give a swaying motion to **6** to move around or from side to side /to *roll* one's eyes/ **7** to make into a ball or cylinder /*roll* up the rug/ **8** to flatten or spread with a roller, etc. —***n.*** **1** a rolling **2** a scroll **3** a list of names **4** something rolled into a cylinder **5** a small portion of bread, etc. **6** a swaying motion **7** a loud, reverberating sound, as of thunder **8** a slight swell on a surface —**on a roll** [Slang] at a high point —**roll back** to reduce (prices) to a previous level —**roll with a** (or **the**) **punch** [Colloq.] to ease a misfortune by not resisting much —**strike off** (or **from**) **the rolls** to expel from membership

roll′back′ ***n.*** a moving back, esp. of prices to a previous level

roll call the reading aloud of a roll to find out who is absent

roll·er (rōl′ər) ***n.*** **1** one that rolls **2** a cylinder of metal, wood, etc. on which something is rolled, or one used to crush, smooth, or spread something

roller bearing a bearing in which the shaft turns on rollers in a circular track
roller coaster an amusement ride in which small, open cars move on tracks that dip and curve sharply
roller skate SKATE[1] (sense 2) —**roll'er-skate'**, **-skat'ed**, **-skat'ing**, *vi.* —**roller skater**
rol·lick (räl'ik) *vi.* [[< ? FROLIC]] to play or behave in a lively, carefree way —**rol'lick·ing** *adj.*
rolling pin a heavy, smooth cylinder of wood, etc. used to roll out dough
roll'-top' *adj.* having a flexible, sliding top of parallel slats /a *roll-top* desk/
ro·ly-po·ly (rō'lē pō'lē) *adj.* [[< ROLL]] short and plump; pudgy
ROM (räm) *n.* [[*r(ead-)o(nly) m(emory)*]] computer memory whose contents can be read but not altered; also, a memory chip like this
Rom. Roman
ro·maine (rō mān') *n.* [[Fr, ult. < L *Romanus*, Roman]] a type of lettuce with long leaves forming a slender head
Ro·man (rō'mən) *adj.* 1 of or characteristic of ancient or modern Rome, its people, etc. 2 of the Roman Catholic Church 3 [*usually* **r-**] designating or of the usual upright style of printing types —*n.* 1 a native or inhabitant of ancient or modern Rome 2 [*usually* **r-**] roman type or characters
Roman candle a firework consisting of a tube shooting balls of fire, etc.
Roman Catholic 1 of the Christian church (**Roman Catholic Church**) headed by the pope 2 a member of this church
ro·mance (rō mans', rō'mans') *adj.* [[ult. < L *Romanicus*, Roman]] [**R-**] designating or of any of the languages derived from Vulgar Latin, as Italian, Spanish, French, etc. —*n.* 1 a long poem or tale, orig. written in a Romance dialect, about the adventures of knights 2 a novel of love, adventure, etc. 3 excitement, love, etc. of the kind found in such literature 4 a love affair —*vi.*, *vt.* **-manced'**, **-manc'ing** [Colloq.] to make love (to)
Roman Empire empire of the ancient Romans (27 B.C.-A.D. 395), including W & S Europe, N Africa, & SW Asia
Ro·ma·ni·a (rō mā'nē ə) country in SE Europe: 91,700 sq. mi.; pop. 22,830,000 —**Ro·ma'ni·an** *adj.*, *n.*
Roman numerals Roman letters used as numerals: I = 1, V = 5, X = 10, L = 50, C = 100, D = 500, and M = 1,000
ro·man·tic (rō man'tik) *adj.* 1 of, like, or characterized by romance 2 fanciful or fictitious 3 not practical; visionary 4 full of thoughts, feelings, etc. of romance 5 suited for romance 6 [*often* **R-**] of a 19th-c. cultural movement characterized by freedom of form and spirit, emphasis on feeling and originality, etc. —*n.* a romantic person —**ro·man'ti·cal·ly** *adv.* —**ro·man'ti·cism'** (-tə siz'əm) *n.*
ro·man'ti·cize' (-tə sīz') *vt.* **-cized'**, **-ciz'ing** to treat or regard romantically —*vi.* to have romantic ideas, etc.
Rom·a·ny (räm'ə nē, rō'mə-) *n.* the language of the Gypsies
Rome (rōm) capital of Italy &, formerly, of the Roman Empire: pop. 2,840,000
Ro·me·o (rō'mē ō') the young lover in Shakespeare's *Romeo and Juliet* (c. 1595)
romp (rämp) *n.* [[prob. < OFr *ramper*, climb]] boisterous, lively play —*vi.* to play in a boisterous, lively way
romp'er *n.* 1 one who romps 2 [*pl.*] a loose, one-piece outer garment with bloomerlike pants, for a small child
Rom·u·lus (räm'yoo ləs) *Rom. Myth.* founder and first king of Rome: he and his twin brother Remus are suckled by a female wolf
rood (rōōd) *n.* [[OE *rod*]] 1 a crucifix 2 [Brit., etc. (exc. Cdn.)] an old unit of area equal to $\frac{1}{4}$ acre
roof (rōōf, roof) *n.*, *pl.* **roofs** [[OE *hrof*]] 1 the outside top covering of a building 2 anything like this /the *roof* of the mouth/ —*vt.* to cover with or as with a roof —**roof'less** *adj.*
roof'er *n.* a roof maker or repairer
roof'ing *n.* material for roofs
roof'top' *n.* the roof of a building
rook[1] (rook) *n.* [[OE *hroc*]] a European crow —*vt.*, *vi.* to swindle; cheat
rook[2] (rook) *n.* [[< Pers *rukh*]] a chess piece moving horizontally or vertically
rook'er·y *n.*, *pl.* **-ies** a breeding place or colony of rooks
rook·ie (rook'ē) *n.* [Slang] 1 an inexperienced army recruit 2 any novice
room (rōōm, room) *n.* [[OE *rum*]] 1 space to contain something 2 suitable scope /*room* for doubt/ 3 an interior space enclosed or set apart by walls 4 [*pl.*] living quarters 5 the people in a room —*vi.*, *vt.* to have or provide with lodgings —**room'ful'** *n.* —**room'y**, **-i·er**, **-i·est**, *adj.* —**room'i·ness** *n.*
room and board lodging and meals
room'er *n.* one who rents a room or rooms to live in; lodger
room·ette (rōō met') *n.* a small room in a railroad sleeping car
rooming house a house with furnished rooms for rent
room'mate' *n.* a person with whom one shares a room or rooms
Roo·se·velt (rō'zə velt') 1 **Franklin Del·a·no** (del'ə nō') 1882-1945; 32d president of the U.S. (1933-45) 2 **Theodore** 1858-1919; 26th president of the U.S. (1901-09)
roost (rōōst) *n.* [[OE *hrost*]] 1 a perch on which birds, esp. domestic fowls, can rest 2 a place with perches for birds 3 a place for resting, sleeping, etc. —*vi.* 1 to perch on a roost 2 to stay or settle down, as for the night
roost'er *n.* a male chicken
root[1] (rōōt, root) *n.* [[< ON *rot*]] 1 the part of a plant, usually underground, that anchors the plant, draws water from the soil, etc. 2 the embedded part of a tooth, a hair, etc. 3 a source or cause 4 a supporting or essential part 5 a quantity that, multiplied by itself a specified number of times, produces a given quantity 6 the basic element of a word or form, without affixes or phonetic changes —*vi.* to take root —*vt.* 1 to fix the roots of in the ground 2 to establish; settle —**take root**

1 to begin growing by putting out roots 2 to become fixed, settled, etc.

root[2] (ro͞ot, ro͝ot) ***vt.*** ⟦< OE *wrot*, snout⟧ to dig (*up* or *out*) as with the snout —***vi.*** 1 to search about; rummage 2 [Colloq.] to encourage a team, etc.: usually with *for*

root beer a carbonated drink made or flavored with certain plant root extracts

root canal 1 a tubular channel in a tooth's root 2 a treatment involving filling, etc. such a channel

root'let (-lət) ***n.*** a little root

rope (rōp) ***n.*** ⟦OE *rap*⟧ 1 a thick, strong cord made of intertwisted strands of fiber, etc. 2 a ropelike string, as of beads —***vt.*** **roped, rop'ing** 1 to fasten or tie with a rope 2 to mark off or enclose with a rope 3 to catch with a lasso —**know the ropes** [Colloq.] to be acquainted with a procedure —**rope in** [Slang] to entice or trick into doing something

Roque·fort (cheese) (rōk'fərt) ⟦after *Roquefort,* France, where made⟧ *trademark for* a strong French cheese with a bluish mold

Ror·schach test (rôr'shäk') ⟦after H. *Rorschach* (1884-1922), Swiss psychiatrist⟧ *Psychol.* a personality test in which the subject's interpretations of standard inkblot designs are analyzed

ro·sa·ry (rō'zər ē) ***n.***, *pl.* **-ries** ⟦ML *rosarium*⟧ *R.C.Ch.* a string of beads used to keep count in saying prayers

rose[1] (rōz) ***n.*** ⟦< L *rosa* < Gr *rhodon*⟧ 1 a shrub with prickly stems and with flowers of red, pink, white, yellow, etc. 2 its flower 3 pinkish red or purplish red —***adj.*** of this color

rose[2] (rōz) ***vi.*** *pt. of* RISE

ro·sé (rō zā') ***n.*** ⟦Fr, pink⟧ a pink wine, tinted by the grape skins during early fermentation

ro·se·ate (rō'zē it) ***adj.*** rose-colored

rose'bud' ***n.*** the bud of a rose

rose'bush' ***n.*** a shrub that bears roses

rose'-col'ored ***adj.*** 1 pinkish-red or purplish-red 2 optimistic —**through rose-colored glasses** with optimism

rose·mar·y (rōz'mer'ē) ***n.*** ⟦< L *ros marinus*, sea dew⟧ an evergreen herb of the mint family, with fragrant leaves used in perfumes, in cooking, etc.

ro·sette (rō zet') ***n.*** a roselike ornament or arrangement, as of ribbon

rose water a preparation of water and attar of roses, used as a perfume

rose window a circular window with a roselike pattern of tracery

rose'wood' ***n.*** ⟦< its odor⟧ 1 a hard, reddish wood, used in furniture, etc. 2 a tropical tree yielding this wood

ROSE WINDOW

Rosh Ha·sha·na (rōsh' hə shō'nə, -shä'-) the Jewish New Year

ros·in (räz'ən) ***n.*** ⟦see RESIN⟧ the hard resin left after the distillation of crude turpentine: it is rubbed on violin bows, used in making varnish, etc.

ros·ter (räs'tər) ***n.*** ⟦< Du *rooster*⟧ a list or roll, as of military personnel

ros·trum (räs'trəm) ***n.***, *pl.* **-trums** or **-tra** (-trə) ⟦L, beak⟧ a platform for public speaking

ros·y (rō'zē) ***adj.*** **-i·er, -i·est** ⟦ME⟧ 1 rose in color 2 bright, promising, etc. —**ros'i·ly** ***adv.*** —**ros'i·ness** ***n.***

rot (rät) ***vi., vt.*** **rot'ted, rot'ting** ⟦OE *rotian*⟧ to decompose; decay —***n.*** 1 a rotting or something rotten 2 a disease characterized by decay 3 [Slang] nonsense

ro·ta·ry (rōt'ər ē) ***adj.*** ⟦< L *rota,* wheel⟧ 1 turning around a central axis, as a wheel 2 having rotating parts /a *rotary* press/ —***n.***, *pl.* **-ries** 1 a rotary machine 2 TRAFFIC CIRCLE

ro·tate (rō'tāt) ***vi., vt.*** **-tat·ed, -tat·ing** ⟦< L *rota,* wheel⟧ 1 to turn around an axis 2 to change or cause to change in regular succession —**ro·ta'tion** ***n.***

ROTC Reserve Officers' Training Corps

rote (rōt) ***n.*** ⟦ME⟧ a fixed, mechanical way of doing something —**by rote** by memory alone, without thought

rot·gut (rät'gut') ***n.*** [Slang] raw, low-grade whiskey or other liquor

ro·tis·ser·ie (rō tis'ər ē) ***n.*** ⟦Fr < MFr *rostir,* to roast⟧ a grill with an electrically turned spit

ro·to·gra·vure (rōt'ə grə vyoor') ***n.*** ⟦< L *rota*, wheel + Fr *gravure*, engraving⟧ 1 a printing process using a rotary press with cylinders etched from photographic plates 2 a newspaper pictorial section printed by this process

ro·tor (rōt'ər) ***n.*** 1 the rotating part of a motor, etc. 2 a system of rotating airfoils, as on a helicopter

ro·to·till·er (rōt'ə til'ər) ***n.*** a motorized machine with rotary blades, for loosening the earth around growing plants

rot·ten (rät''n) ***adj.*** ⟦< ON *rotinn*⟧ 1 decayed; spoiled 2 foul-smelling 3 morally corrupt 4 unsound, as if decayed within 5 [Slang] very bad, unpleasant, etc. —**rot'ten·ness** ***n.***

Rot·ter·dam (rät'ər dam') seaport in SW Netherlands: pop. 571,000

ro·tund (rō tund') ***adj.*** ⟦L *rotundus*⟧ round or rounded out; plump —**ro·tun'di·ty** or **ro·tund'ness** ***n.***

ro·tun·da (rō tun'də) ***n.*** ⟦see prec.⟧ a round building, hall, or room, esp. one with a dome

rou·é (ro͞o ā') ***n.*** ⟦Fr < L *rota,* wheel⟧ a dissipated man; rake

rouge (ro͞ozh) ***n.*** ⟦Fr, red⟧ 1 *old name for* BLUSHER (sense 2) 2 a reddish powder for polishing jewelry, etc. —***vt., vi.*** **rouged, roug'ing** to use cosmetic rouge (on)

rough (ruf) ***adj.*** ⟦OE *ruh*⟧ 1 not smooth or level; uneven 2 shaggy /a *rough* coat/ 3 stormy /*rough* weather/ 4 disorderly /*rough* play/ 5 harsh or coarse 6 lacking comforts and conveniences 7 not polished or finished; crude 8 approximate /a *rough* guess/ 9 [Colloq.] difficult /a *rough* time/ —***n.*** 1 rough ground, material, condition, etc. 2 *Golf* any part of the course with grass, etc. left uncut —***adv.*** in a rough way —***vt.*** 1 to roughen: often with *up* 2 to treat roughly: usually with *up* 3 to sketch, shape, etc. roughly: usually with *in* or *out* —

rough it to live without customary comforts, etc. —**rough'ly** *adv.* —**rough'ness** *n.*

rough'age (-ij) *n.* rough or coarse food or fodder, as bran, straw, etc.

rough'en *vt., vi.* to make or become rough

rough'-hew' *vt.* **-hewed'**, **-hewed'** or **-hewn'**, **-hew'ing** 1 to hew (timber, stone, etc.) roughly, or without smoothing 2 to form roughly Also **rough'hew'**

rough'house' *n.* [Slang] rough, boisterous play, fighting, etc. —*vt., vi.* **-housed'**, **-hous'ing** [Slang] to treat or act roughly or boisterously

rough'neck' *n.* 1 [Colloq.] a rowdy 2 a worker on an oil rig —*vi.* to work as a roughneck

rough'shod' *adj.* shod with horseshoes having metal points —**ride roughshod over** to treat harshly

rou·lette (ro͞o let') *n.* ⟦Fr < L *rota,* wheel⟧ a gambling game played with a small ball in a whirling shallow bowl (**roulette wheel**) with red and black, numbered compartments

round (round) *adj.* ⟦< L *rotundus*, rotund⟧ 1 shaped like a ball, circle, or cylinder 2 plump 3 full; complete /a *round* dozen/ 4 expressed by a whole number or in tens, hundreds, etc. 5 large; considerable /a *round* sum/ 6 brisk; vigorous /a *round* pace/ —*n.* 1 something round, as the rung of a ladder 2 the part of a beef animal between the rump and the leg 3 movement in a circular course 4 a series or succession /a *round* of parties/ 5 [*often pl.*] a regular, customary circuit, as by a watchman 6 a single shot from a gun, or from several guns together; also, the ammunition for this 7 a single outburst, as of applause 8 a single period of action, as in boxing 9 a short song which one group begins singing when another reaches the second phrase, etc. —*vt.* 1 to make round 2 to make plump 3 to express as a round number 4 to complete; finish 5 to go or pass around —*vi.* 1 to make a circuit 2 to turn; reverse direction 3 to become plump: often with *out* —*adv.* 1 in a circle 2 through a recurring period of time /to work the year *round*/ 3 from one to another 4 in circumference /ten feet *round*/ 5 on all sides 6 about; near 7 in a roundabout way 8 here and there 9 with a rotating movement 10 in the opposite direction —*prep.* 1 so as to encircle 2 on all sides of 3 in the vicinity of 4 in a circuit through In the U.S., *round* (*adv. & prep.*) is generally superseded by *around* —**in the round** 1 in an arena theater 2 in full, rounded form: said of sculpture 3 in full detail —**round about** in or to the opposite direction —**round up** to collect in a herd, group, etc. —**round'ness** *n.*

round'a·bout' *adj.* 1 indirect; circuitous 2 encircling; enclosing

roun·de·lay (roun'də lā') *n.* ⟦< OFr *rondel*, a short lyrical poem⟧ a simple song in which some phrase, line, etc. is continually repeated

round'house' *n.* a circular building, with a turntable in the center, for storing and repairing locomotives

round'ly *adv.* 1 in a round form 2 vigorously 3 fully; completely and thoroughly

round'-shoul'dered *adj.* having the shoulders bent forward

round steak a steak cut from a round of beef

Round Table the circular table around which King Arthur and his knights sit —[r- t-] a group gathered for an informal discussion

round'-the-clock' *adj., adv.* throughout the day and night; continuous(ly)

round trip a trip to a place and back again —**round'-trip'** *adj.*

round'-trip'per *n.* [Slang] *Baseball* a home run

round'up' *n.* 1 a driving together of cattle, etc. on the range, as for branding 2 any similar collecting 3 a summary, as of news

round'worm' *n.* NEMATODE

rouse (rouz) *vt., vi.* **roused, rous'ing** ⟦prob. < OFr⟧ 1 to stir up; excite or become excited 2 to wake

Rous·seau (ro͞o sō'), **Jean Jacques** (zhän zhäk') 1712-78; Fr. philosopher & writer, born in Switzerland

roust·a·bout (roust'ə bout') *n.* ⟦< ROUSE + ABOUT⟧ an unskilled or transient laborer, as on wharves

rout[1] (rout) *n.* ⟦< L *rupta*, broken⟧ 1 a disorderly flight 2 an overwhelming defeat —*vt.* 1 to put to flight 2 to defeat overwhelmingly

rout[2] (rout) *vt.* ⟦< ROOT[2]⟧ to force out —**rout out** 1 to gouge out 2 to make (a person) get out

route (ro͞ot, rout) *n.* ⟦< L *rupta* (*via*), broken (path)⟧ a road or course for traveling; often, a regular course, as in delivering mail —*vt.* **rout'ed, rout'ing** 1 to send by a certain route 2 to arrange the route for

rou·tine (ro͞o tēn') *n.* ⟦see prec.⟧ a regular procedure, customary or prescribed —*adj.* like or using routine —**rou·tine'ly** *adv.*

rou·tin'ize (-tē'nīz) *vt.* **-ized, -iz·ing** to make routine; reduce to a routine —**rou'·tin·i·za'tion** *n.*

rove (rōv) *vi., vt.* **roved, rov'ing** ⟦ME *roven*⟧ to roam —**rov'er** *n.*

row[1] (rō) *n.* ⟦OE *ræw*⟧ 1 a number of people or things in a line 2 any of the lines of seats in a theater, etc. —**in a row** in succession; consecutively

row[2] (rō) *vt., vi.* ⟦OE *rowan*⟧ 1 to propel (a boat) with oars 2 to carry in a rowboat —*n.* a trip by rowboat

row[3] (rou) *n., vi.* ⟦< ? ROUSE⟧ quarrel, squabble, or brawl

row'boat' (rō'-) *n.* a small boat made for rowing

row·dy (rou'dē) *n., pl.* **-dies** ⟦< ? ROW[3]⟧ a rough, quarrelsome, and disorderly person —*adj.* **-di·er, -di·est** rough, quarrelsome, etc. —**row'di·ness** *n.* —**row'dy·ism'** *n.*

row·el (rou'əl) *n.* ⟦ult. < L *rota*, wheel⟧ a small wheel with sharp points, forming the end of a spur

row house (rō) any of a line of identical houses joined by common walls

roy·al (roi'əl) *adj.* ⟦< L *regalis*⟧ 1 of a king or queen 2 like, or fit for, a king or queen; magnificent, majestic, etc. 3 of a kingdom, its government, etc. —**roy'al·ly** *adv.*

roy'al·ist *n.* one who supports a monarch or a monarchy
roy'al·ty *n., pl.* **-ties** 1 the rank or power of a king or queen 2 a royal person or persons 3 royal quality 4 a share of the proceeds from a patent, book, etc. paid to the owner, author, etc.
rpm revolutions per minute
rps revolutions per second
RR or **R.R.** 1 railroad 2 Rural Route
RSFSR or **R.S.F.S.R.** Russian Soviet Federated Socialist Republic
RSV or **R.S.V.** Revised Standard Version (of the Bible)
R.S.V.P. or **r.s.v.p.** ⟦Fr *répondez s'il vous plaît*⟧ please reply Also **RSVP** or **rsvp**
Rte. Route
rub (rub) *vt.* **rubbed, rub'bing** ⟦ME *rubben*⟧ 1 to move (one's hand, a cloth, etc.) over (something) with pressure and friction 2 to apply (polish, etc.) in this way 3 to move (things) over each other with pressure and friction 4 to make sore by rubbing 5 to remove by rubbing (*out, off*, etc.) —*vi.* 1 to move with pressure and friction (*on*, etc.) 2 to rub something —*n.* 1 a rubbing 2 an obstacle, difficulty, or source of irritation —**rub down** 1 to massage 2 to smooth, polish, etc. by rubbing —**rub elbows with** to associate or mingle with: also **rub shoulders with** —**rub the wrong way** to irritate or annoy
ru·ba·to (ro͞o bät'ō) *adj., adv.* ⟦It, stolen⟧ *Music* intentionally and temporarily not in strict tempo
rub·ber[1] (rub'ər) *n.* 1 one that rubs 2 ⟦< use as an eraser⟧ an elastic substance made from the milky sap of various tropical plants, or synthetically 3 something made of this substance; specif., *a*) a low-cut overshoe *b*) [Slang] a condom —*adj.* made of rubber —**rub'ber·y** *adj.*
rub·ber[2] (rub'ər) *n.* ⟦< ?⟧ the deciding game in a series Also **rubber game**
rubber band a narrow, continuous band of rubber as for holding small objects together
rubber cement an adhesive of unvulcanized rubber in a solvent that quickly evaporates when exposed to air
rubber check ⟦from the notion that it "bounces": see BOUNCE (*vi.* 3)⟧ [Slang] a check that is worthless because of insufficient funds in the drawer's account
rub'ber·ize' (-īz') *vt.* **-ized', -iz'ing** to impregnate with rubber
rub'ber·neck' (-nek') *vi.* to look at things or gaze about in curiosity by stretching the neck or turning the head, as a sightseer
rubber plant 1 any plant yielding latex 2 a house plant with large, glossy, leathery leaves
rubber stamp 1 a stamp of rubber, inked for printing dates, signatures, etc. 2 [Colloq.] *a*) a person, bureau, etc. that gives routine or automatic approval *b*) such approval —**rub'ber-stamp'** *vt.*
rub·bish (rub'ish) *n.* ⟦ME *robous*⟧ 1 any material thrown away as worthless; trash 2 nonsense
rub·ble (rub'əl) *n.* ⟦ME *robel*⟧ rough, broken pieces of stone, brick, etc.
rub'down' *n.* a brisk rubbing of the body, as in massage
rube (ro͞ob) *n.* ⟦< name *Reuben*⟧ [Slang] an unsophisticated rustic
ru·bel·la (ro͞o bel'ə) *n.* ⟦< L *ruber*, red⟧ an infectious disease causing small red spots on the skin
Ru·bens (ro͞o'bənz), **Peter Paul** 1577-1640; Fl. painter
ru·bi·cund (ro͞o'bə kund') *adj.* ⟦< L *ruber*, red⟧ reddish; ruddy
ru·ble (ro͞o'bəl) *n.* ⟦Russ *rubl'*⟧ the monetary unit of the U.S.S.R.
ru·bric (ro͞o'brik) *n.* ⟦< L *ruber*, red⟧ 1 a section heading, direction, etc., often in red (as in a prayer book) 2 any rule, explanatory comment, etc.
ru·by (ro͞o'bē) *n., pl.* **-bies** ⟦ult. < L *rubeus*, reddish⟧ 1 a clear, deep-red precious stone: a variety of corundum 2 deep red —*adj.* deep-red
ruck·sack (ruk'sak', ro͝ok'-) *n.* ⟦Ger, back sack⟧ a kind of knapsack
ruck·us (ruk'əs) *n.* ⟦prob. merging of RUMPUS & *ruction*, uproar⟧ [Colloq.] noisy confusion; disturbance
rud·der (rud'ər) *n.* ⟦OE *rother*⟧ a broad, flat, movable piece hinged to the rear of a ship or aircraft, used for steering —**rud'der·less** *adj.*
rud·dy (rud'ē) *adj.* **-di·er, -di·est** ⟦OE *rudig*⟧ 1 having a healthy red color 2 reddish —**rud'di·ness** *n.*
rude (ro͞od) *adj.* **rud'er, rud'est** ⟦< L *rudis*⟧ 1 crude; rough 2 barbarous 3 unrefined; uncouth 4 discourteous 5 primitive; unskillful —**rude'ly** *adv.* —**rude'ness** *n.*
ru·di·ment (ro͞o'də mənt) *n.* ⟦see RUDE⟧ [*usually pl.*] 1 a first principle or element, as of a subject to be learned 2 a first slight beginning of something —**ru'di·men'ta·ry** (-men'tər ē) *adj.*
rue[1] (ro͞o) *vt., vi.* **rued, ru'ing** ⟦OE *hreowan*⟧ 1 to feel remorse for (a sin, fault, etc.) 2 to regret (an act, etc.) —*n.* [Archaic] sorrow —**rue'ful** *adj.* —**rue'ful·ly** *adv.*
rue[2] (ro͞o) *n.* ⟦< Gr *rhytē*⟧ a strong-scented shrub with bitter leaves

RUFF

ruff (ruf) *n.* ⟦< RUFFLE⟧ 1 a high, frilled, starched collar of the 16th and 17th c. 2 a band of colored or protruding feathers or fur about an animal's neck
ruf·fi·an (ruf'ē ən) *n.* ⟦< It *ruffiano*, a pimp⟧ a rowdy or hoodlum
ruf·fle (ruf'əl) *vt.* **-fled, -fling** ⟦< ON or LowG⟧ 1 to disturb the smoothness of 2 to gather into ruffles 3 to make (features, etc.) stand up 4 to disturb or annoy —*vi.* 1 to become uneven 2 to become disturbed, irritated, etc. —*n.* 1 a strip of cloth, lace, etc. gathered along one edge 2 a disturbance 3 a ripple
rug (rug) *n.* ⟦< Scand⟧ 1 a piece of thick

fabric used as a floor covering 2 *chiefly Brit. term for* LAP ROBE

rug·by (rug'bē) ***n.*** ⟦first played at *Rugby* School in England⟧ a game from which American football developed

rug·ged (rug'id) ***adj.*** ⟦ME⟧ 1 uneven; rough 2 stormy 3 severe; harsh; hard 4 not polished or refined 5 strong; robust —**rug'ged·ly** ***adv.*** —**rug'ged·ness** ***n.***

Ruhr (roor) 1 river in central West Germany, flowing into the Rhine 2 major coal-mining & industrial region along this river: also called **Ruhr Basin**

ru·in (rōō'ən, -in') ***n.*** ⟦< L *ruere,* to fall⟧ 1 [*pl.*] the remains of something destroyed, decayed, etc. 2 anything destroyed, etc. 3 downfall, destruction, etc. 4 anything causing this —***vt.*** to bring to ruin; destroy, spoil, bankrupt, etc. —***vi.*** to go or come to ruin —**ru'in·a'tion** ***n.*** —**ru'in·ous** ***adj.***

rule (rōōl) ***n.*** ⟦< L *regere,* to rule⟧ 1 an established regulation or guide for conduct, procedure, usage, etc. 2 custom 3 the customary course 4 government; reign 5 RULER (sense 2) —***vt., vi.*** **ruled, rul'ing** 1 to have an influence (over); guide 2 to govern 3 to determine officially 4 to mark lines (on) as with a ruler —**as a rule** usually —**rule out** to exclude

rule of thumb a practical, though crude or unscientific, method

rul'er ***n.*** 1 one who governs 2 a strip of wood, etc. with a straight edge, used in drawing lines, measuring, etc.

rul·ing (rōōl'iŋ) ***adj.*** that rules —***n.*** an official decision, as of a court

rum (rum) ***n.*** ⟦< ?⟧ 1 an alcoholic liquor distilled from fermented sugar cane, etc. 2 any alcoholic liquor

Ru·ma·ni·a (rōō mā'nē ə) *var. of* ROMANIA —**Ru·ma'ni·an** ***adj., n.***

rum·ba (room'bə, rum'-) ***n.*** ⟦AmSp⟧ a dance of Cuban origin, or music for it —***vi.*** to dance the rumba

rum·ble (rum'bəl) ***vi., vt.*** **-bled, -bling** ⟦ME *romblen*⟧ 1 to make or cause to make a deep, continuous, rolling sound 2 to move with such a sound —***n.*** 1 a rumbling sound 2 [Slang] a fight between teenage gangs

rumble strip a series of closely spaced grooves or bumps across a paved road that cause vehicle tires to vibrate audibly: used as warning of approaching hazard

ru·mi·nant (rōō'mə nənt) ***adj.*** ⟦see RUMINATE⟧ 1 of or belonging to the group of cud-chewing animals 2 meditative —***n.*** any of a group of cud-chewing mammals, as cattle, deer, camels, etc., having a stomach with three or four chambers

ru'mi·nate' (-nāt') ***vt., vi.*** **-nat'ed, -nat'ing** ⟦< L *ruminare*⟧ 1 to chew (the cud) 2 to meditate or reflect (on) —**ru'mi·na'tion** ***n.***

rum·mage (rum'ij) ***n.*** ⟦< Fr *rum,* ship's hold⟧ 1 odds and ends 2 a rummaging —***vt., vi.*** **-maged, -mag·ing** to search through (a place, etc.) thoroughly

rummage sale a sale of contributed miscellaneous articles, as for charity

rum·my (rum'ē) ***n.*** ⟦< ?⟧ any of certain card games whose object is to match sets and sequences

ru·mor (rōō'mər) ***n.*** ⟦L, noise⟧ 1 general talk not based on definite knowledge 2 an unconfirmed report, story, etc. in general circulation —***vt.*** to tell or spread by rumor Brit., etc. sp. **ru'mour**

rump (rump) ***n.*** ⟦< ON *rumpr*⟧ 1 the hind part of an animal, where the legs and back join 2 the buttocks

rum·ple (rum'pəl) ***n.*** ⟦< MDu *rompe*⟧ an uneven crease; wrinkle —***vt., vi.*** **-pled, -pling** to wrinkle; muss

rum·pus (rum'pəs) ***n.*** ⟦< ?⟧ [Colloq.] noisy disturbance; uproar

run (run) ***vi.*** **ran, run, run'ning** ⟦< ON & OE⟧ 1 to go by moving the legs faster than in walking 2 to go, move, etc. easily and freely 3 to flee 4 to make a quick trip (*up to, down to,* etc.) 5 to compete in a race, election, etc. 6 to ply (between two points), as a train 7 to climb or creep, as a vine 8 to ravel, as a stocking 9 to operate, as a machine 10 to flow 11 to spread over cloth, etc. when moistened, as colors 12 to discharge pus, etc. 13 to extend in time or space; continue 14 to pass into a specified condition, etc. /to *run* into trouble/ 15 to be written, etc. in a specified way 16 to be at a specified size, price, etc. /eggs *run* high/ —***vt.*** 1 to follow (a specified course) 2 to perform as by running /to *run* a race/ 3 to incur (a risk) 4 to get past /to *run* a blockade/ 5 to cause to run, move, compete, etc. 6 to drive into a specified condition, place, etc. 7 to drive (an object) into or against (something) 8 to make flow in a specified way, place, etc. 9 to manage (a business, etc.) 10 to trace 11 to undergo (a fever, etc.) 12 to publish (a story, etc.) in a newspaper —***n.*** 1 an act or period of running 2 the distance covered in running 3 a trip; journey 4 a route /a delivery *run*/ 5 *a*) movement onward, progression, or trend /the *run* of events/ *b*) a continuous course or period /a *run* of good luck/ 6 a continuous course of performances, etc., as of a play 7 a continued series of demands, as on a bank 8 a brook 9 a kind or class; esp., the average kind 10 the output during a period of operation 11 an enclosed area for domestic animals 12 freedom to move about at will /the *run* of the house/ 13 a large number of fish migrating together 14 a ravel, as in a stocking 15 *Baseball* a scoring point, made by a successful circuit of the bases —**in the long run** ultimately —**on the run** running or running away —**run across** to encounter by chance: also **run into** —**run down** 1 to stop operating 2 to run against so as to knock down 3 to pursue and capture or kill 4 to speak of disparagingly —**run out** to come to an end; expire —**run out of** to use up —**run over** 1 to ride over 2 to overflow 3 to examine, rehearse, etc. rapidly —**run through** 1 to use up quickly or recklessly 2 to pierce —**run up** 1 to raise, rise, or accumulate rapidly 2 to sew rapidly

run'a·round' ***n.*** [Colloq.] a series of evasions

run'a·way' ***n.*** 1 a fugitive 2 a horse, etc. that runs away —***adj.*** 1 escaping, fleeing, etc. 2 easily won, as a race 3 rising rapidly, as prices

run'down' ***n.*** a concise summary

run'-down' *adj.* 1 not wound and therefore not running, as a watch 2 in poor physical condition, as from overwork 3 fallen into disrepair
rune (ro͞on) *n.* ⟦OE *run*⟧ 1 any of the characters of an ancient Germanic alphabet 2 [Old Poet.] a mystical or obscure poem or song
rung[1] (ruŋ) *n.* ⟦OE *hrung,* staff⟧ a rod forming a step of a ladder, a crosspiece on a chair, etc.
rung[2] (ruŋ) *vi., vt. pp. of* RING[1]
run'-in' *n.* 1 *Printing* matter added without a break or new paragraph: also **run'-on'** 2 [Colloq.] a quarrel, fight, etc.
run·nel (run'əl) *n.* ⟦OE *rynel*⟧ a small stream; brook Also **run'let**
run'ner *n.* 1 one that runs, as a racer, messenger, etc. 2 a long, narrow cloth or rug 3 a ravel, as in hose 4 a long, trailing stem, as of a strawberry 5 either of the long, narrow pieces on which a sled, etc. slides
run'ner-up' *n., pl.* **-ners-up'** a person or team that finishes second, etc. in a contest
run'ning *n.* the act of one that runs; racing, managing, etc. **—*adj.*** 1 that runs (in various senses) 2 measured in a straight line 3 continuous /a *running* commentary/ **—*adv.*** in succession /for five days *running*/ **—in** (or **out of**) **the running** having a (or no) chance to win
running lights the lights that a ship or aircraft must display at night
running mate a candidate for the lesser of two closely associated offices in his relationship to the candidate for the greater office
run'ny *adj.* **-ni·er, -ni·est** 1 flowing, esp. too freely 2 discharging mucus /a *runny* nose/
run'off' *n.* 1 something that runs off, as rain that is not absorbed into the ground 2 a deciding, final contest
run'-of-the-mill' *adj.* not selected or special; ordinary; average
runt (runt) *n.* ⟦< ?⟧ a stunted animal, plant, or (contemptuously) person **—runt'y, runt'i·er, runt'i·est,** *adj.*
run'-through' *n.* a complete rehearsal, from beginning to end
run'way' *n.* a channel, track, etc. in, on, or along which something moves; esp., a strip of leveled ground used by airplanes in taking off and landing
ru·pee (ro͞o'pē, ro͞o pē') *n.* ⟦< Sans *rūpyah,* wrought silver⟧ the monetary unit of: *a)* India *b)* Nepal *c)* Pakistan *d)* Sri Lanka
rup·ture (rup'chər) *n.* ⟦< L *rumpere,* to break⟧ 1 a breaking apart or being broken apart; breach 2 a hernia **—*vt., vi.*** **-tured, -tur·ing** to cause or suffer a rupture
ru·ral (roor'əl) *adj.* ⟦< L *rus,* the country⟧ of, like, or living in the country; rustic **—ru'ral·ism'** *n.*
ruse (ro͞oz) *n.* ⟦< OFr *reuser,* deceive⟧ a stratagem, trick, or artifice
rush[1] (rush) *vi., vt.* ⟦< Fr *ruser,* repel⟧ 1 to move, push, drive, etc. swiftly or impetuously 2 to make a sudden attack (*on*) 3 to pass, go, send, act, do, etc. with unusual haste; hurry **—*n.*** 1 a rushing 2 an eager movement of many people to get to a place 3 busyness; haste /the *rush* of modern life/ 4 a press, as of business, necessitating unusual haste
rush[2] (rush) *n.* ⟦OE *risc*⟧ a grasslike marsh plant with round stems used in making mats, etc.
rush hour a time of the day when business, traffic, etc. are heavy
rusk (rusk) *n.* ⟦Sp *rosca,* twisted bread roll⟧ 1 sweet, raised bread or cake toasted until browned and crisp 2 a piece of this
Russ. 1 Russia 2 Russian
rus·set (rus'it) *n.* ⟦< L *russus,* reddish⟧ 1 yellowish (or reddish) brown 2 a winter apple with a mottled skin
Rus·sia (rush'ə) 1 former empire (**Russian Empire**) in E Europe & N Asia, 1547-1917 2 loosely, the USSR
Rus·sian (rush'ən) *adj.* of Russia, its people, language, etc. **—*n.*** 1 a native or inhabitant of Russia 2 the East Slavic language of the Russians
Russian Soviet Federated Socialist Republic largest republic of the U.S.S.R., stretching from the Baltic Sea to the Pacific: 6,501,500 sq. mi.; pop. 143,078,000
rust (rust) *n.* ⟦OE⟧ 1 the reddish-brown coating formed on iron or steel during exposure to air and moisture 2 any stain resembling this 3 a reddish brown 4 a plant disease caused by fungi, spotting stems and leaves **—*vi., vt.*** 1 to form rust (on) 2 to deteriorate, as through disuse
rus·tic (rus'tik) *adj.* ⟦< L *rus,* the country⟧ 1 of the country; rural 2 simple or artless 3 rough or uncouth **—*n.*** a country person **—rus'ti·cal·ly** *adv.* **—rus·tic'i·ty** (-tis'ə tē) *n.*
rus·ti·cate (rus'tə kāt') *vi., vt.* **-cat'ed, -cat'ing** 1 to go or send to live in the country 2 to become or make rustic **—rus'ti·ca'tion** *n.*
rus·tle[1] (rus'əl) *vi., vt.* **-tled, -tling** ⟦ult. echoic⟧ to make or cause to make soft sounds, as of moving leaves, etc. **—*n.*** a series of such sounds
rus·tle[2] (rus'əl) *vi., vt.* **-tled, -tling** ⟦< ?⟧ [Colloq.] to steal (cattle, etc.) **—rustle up** [Colloq.] to collect or get together **—rus'tler** *n.*
rust'proof' *adj.* resistant to rust
rust·y (rus'tē) *adj.* **-i·er, -i·est** 1 coated with rust, as a metal 2 *a)* impaired by disuse, neglect, etc. *b)* having lost facility through lack of practice **—rust'i·ly** *adv.* **—rust'i·ness** *n.*
rut[1] (rut) *n.* ⟦< ? Fr *route,* route⟧ 1 a groove, track, etc., as made by wheels 2 a fixed, routine procedure, course of action, etc. **—*vt.*** **rut'ted, rut'ting** to make ruts in **—rut'ty, -ti·er, -ti·est,** *adj.*
rut[2] (rut) *n.* ⟦< L *rugire,* to roar⟧ the periodic sexual excitement of certain male mammals **—*vi.*** **rut'ted, rut'ting** to be in rut **—rut'tish** *adj.*
ru·ta·ba·ga (ro͞ot'ə bā'gə) *n.* ⟦Swed dial. *rotabagge*⟧ 1 a turniplike plant with a large, yellow root 2 this root
Ruth (ro͞oth) 1 *Bible* a woman deeply devoted to her mother-in-law, Naomi, for whom she left her own people 2 **George Her·man** (hʉr'mən) (called *Babe*) 1895-1948; U.S. baseball player
ruth'less (-lis) *adj.* ⟦OE *hreowan,* to rue⟧

without pity or compassion —**ruth'less·ly** *adv.* —**ruth'less·ness** *n.*

RV (är'vē') *n., pl.* **RVs** ⟦*R*(*ecreational*) *V*(*ehicle*)⟧ a camper, trailer, motor home, etc. outfitted as a place to live, as when camping out

Rwan·da (ro͞o än'də) country in central Africa, east of Zaire: 10,169 sq. mi.; pop. 4,819,000

Rwy. or **Ry.** Railway

-ry (rē) *suffix* -ERY */foundry/*

ry·a rug (rē'ə) ⟦< Swed⟧ a thick, decorative, hand-woven area rug of Scandinavian origin

rye (rī) *n.* ⟦OE *ryge*⟧ **1** a hardy cereal grass **2** its grain or seeds, used for making flour, etc. **3** whiskey distilled from this grain

S

s or **S** (es) *n., pl.* **s's, S's** the 19th letter of the English alphabet —*adj.* shaped like S

's **1** is */he's a sailor/* **2** has */she's asked them both/* **3** [Colloq.] does */what's it matter?/* **4** us */let's go/*

-s ⟦alt. of -ES⟧ *suffix* **1** forming the plural of most nouns */hips/* **2** forming the 3d pers. sing., pres. indic., of certain verbs */shouts/*

-'s ⟦OE⟧ *suffix* forming the possessive singular of nouns and some pronouns, and the possessive plural of nouns not ending in *s* */boy's, men's/*

s or **s.** **1** second(s) **2** shilling(s) **3** small

S *Chem. symbol for* sulfur

S or **S.** **1** Saturday **2** small **3** south **4** southern **5** Sunday

S.A. South America

Saar (sär, zär) rich coal-mining region in a river valley of SW West Germany: also called **Saar Basin**

Sab·bath (sab'əth) *n.* ⟦< Heb *shabat*, to rest⟧ **1** the seventh day of the week (Saturday), set aside in Jewish scripture for rest and worship **2** Sunday as the usual Christian day of rest and worship

Sab·bat·i·cal (sə bat'i kəl) *adj.* **1** of the Sabbath **2** [**s-**] bringing a period of rest —*n.* [**s-**] SABBATICAL LEAVE

sabbatical leave a period of absence with pay, for study, travel, etc., given as to teachers, orig. every seven years Also **sabbatical year**

sa·ber (sā'bər) *n.* ⟦< Hung *szablya*⟧ a heavy cavalry sword with a slightly curved blade Also **sa'bre**

Sa·bin vaccine (sā'bin) ⟦after Dr. A. B. *Sabin* (1906-), its U.S. developer⟧ a polio vaccine taken orally

sa·ble (sā'bəl) *n.* ⟦< Russ *sobol'*⟧ **1** any marten **2** its costly fur pelt

sa·bot (sa bō', sab'ō) *n.* ⟦Fr, ult. < Ar *sabbāṭ*, sandal⟧ a shoe shaped from a single piece of wood

sab·o·tage (sab'ə täzh') *n.* ⟦Fr < *sabot*, wooden shoe + -AGE: from damage done to machinery by sabots⟧ deliberate destruction of machines, etc. by employees in labor disputes or of railroads, bridges, etc. by enemy agents or by an underground resistance —*vt., vi.* **-taged', -tag'ing** to commit sabotage (on) —**sab'o·teur'** (-tur') *n.*

sa·bra (sä'brə) *n.* ⟦Heb *sabra*, a native cactus fruit⟧ a native-born Israeli

sabre saw a portable electric saw with a narrow, oscillating blade

sac (sak) *n.* ⟦see SACK¹⟧ a pouchlike part in a plant or animal

sac·cha·rin (sak'ə rin') *n.* ⟦< Gr *sakcharon*⟧ a white, crystalline coal-tar compound used as a sugar substitute

sac'cha·rine' (-rin') *adj.* **1** of or like sugar **2** too sweet */a saccharine voice/*

sac·er·do·tal (sas'ər dōt''l; *occas.* sak'-) *adj.* ⟦< L *sacerdos*, priest⟧ of priests or the office of priest; priestly

sa·chem (sā'chəm) *n.* ⟦AmInd⟧ among some North American Indian tribes, the chief

sa·chet (sa shā') *n.* ⟦Fr⟧ a small perfumed packet used to scent clothes

sack¹ (sak) *n.* ⟦ult. < Heb *saq*⟧ **1** a bag, esp. a large one of coarse cloth **2** [Slang] dismissal: with *the* **3** [Slang] a bed **4** *Football* a sacking a quarterback —*vt.* **1** to put into sacks **2** [Slang] to fire (a person) **3** *Football* to tackle (a quarterback) behind the line of scrimmage

sack² (sak) *n.* ⟦see prec.⟧ the plundering of a city, etc. —*vt.* to plunder

sack³ (sak) *n.* ⟦< Fr (*vin*)*sec*, dry (wine) < L⟧ a dry, white Spanish wine popular in England during the 16th and 17th c.

sack'cloth' *n.* **1** SACKING **2** coarse cloth worn as a symbol of mourning

sack'ful' *n., pl.* **-fuls'** the amount that a sack will hold

sack'ing *n.* a cheap, coarse cloth used for making sacks

sac·ra·ment (sak'rə mənt) *n.* ⟦< L *sacer*, holy⟧ any of certain Christian rites, as baptism, the Eucharist, etc. —**sac'ra·men'tal** *adj.*

Sac·ra·men·to (sak'rə men'tō) capital of Calif.: pop. 276,000

sa·cred (sā'krid) *adj.* ⟦< L *sacer*, holy⟧ **1** consecrated to a god or God; holy **2** having to do with religion **3** venerated; hallowed **4** inviolate —**sa'cred·ly** *adv.* —**sa'cred·ness** *n.*

sac·ri·fice (sak'rə fīs') *n.* ⟦< L *sacrificium* < *sacer*, sacred + *facere*, make⟧ **1** an offering, as of a life or object, to a deity **2** a giving up of one thing for the sake of another —*vt., vi.* **-ficed', -fic'ing** **1** to offer as a sacrifice to a deity **2** to give up one thing for the sake of another **3** to sell at less than the supposed value —**sac'ri·fi'cial** (-fish'əl) *adj.*

sac·ri·lege (sak'rə lij) *n.* ⟦< L *sacer*, sacred + *legere*, take away⟧ desecration of what is sacred —**sac'ri·le'gious** (-lij'əs, -lē'jəs) *adj.*

sac·ris·tan (sak'ris tən) *n.* a person in charge of a sacristy

sac'ris·ty (-tē) *n., pl.* **-ties** ⟦ult. < L *sacer*,

sacred]] a room in a church for sacred vessels, etc.

sac·ro·il·i·ac (sak'rō il'ē ak', sā'krō-) ***n.*** the joint between the top part (**il'i·um**) of the hipbone and the fused bottom vertebrae (**sa'crum**)

sac·ro·sanct (sak'rō saŋkt') ***adj.*** [[< L *sacer*, sacred + *sanctus*, holy]] very sacred, holy, or inviolable

sad (sad) ***adj.*** **sad'der, sad'dest** [[OE *sæd*, sated]] **1** having or expressing low spirits; unhappy; sorrowful **2** causing dejection, sorrow, etc. **3** [Colloq.] very bad; deplorable —**sad'ly** ***adv.*** —**sad'ness** ***n.***

sad'den ***vt., vi.*** to make or become sad

sad·dle (sad''l) ***n.*** [[OE *sadol*]] **1** a seat for a rider on a horse, bicycle, etc., usually padded and of leather **2** a cut of lamb, etc., including part of the backbone and the two loins —***vt.*** **-dled, -dling 1** to put a saddle upon **2** to encumber or burden —**in the saddle** in control

sad'dle·bag' ***n.*** **1** a bag hung behind the saddle of a horse, etc. **2** a similar bag carried on a bicycle, etc.

saddle horse a horse for riding

saddle shoes white oxford shoes with a contrasting band across the instep

Sad·du·cee (saj'oo sē') ***n.*** a member of an ancient Jewish party that accepted only the written law

sad·ism (sad'iz'əm, sā'diz'əm) ***n.*** [[after Marquis de *Sade* (1740-1814), Fr writer]] the getting of pleasure from mistreating others —**sad'ist** ***n.*** —**sa·dis'tic** ***adj.*** —**sa·dis'ti·cal·ly** ***adv.***

sad·o·mas·o·chism (sad'ō mas'ə kiz'əm, sā'dō-) ***n.*** the getting of pleasure, esp. sexual pleasure, from sadism or masochism, or both —**sad'o·mas'o·chist** ***n.*** —**sad'o·mas'o·chis'tic** ***adj.***

sa·fa·ri (sə fär'ē) ***n., pl.*** **-ris** [[< Ar *safar*, to journey]] a journey or hunting expedition, esp. in Africa

safe (sāf) ***adj.*** **saf'er, saf'est** [[< L *salvus*]] **1** *a)* free from damage, danger, etc.; secure *b)* having escaped injury; unharmed **2** *a)* giving protection *b)* trustworthy **3** prudent; cautious —***n.*** a locking metal container for valuables —**safe'ly** ***adv.*** —**safe'ness** ***n.***

safe'-con'duct ***n.*** permission to travel safely through enemy regions

safe'-de·pos'it ***adj.*** designating or of a box or vault, as in a bank, for storing valuables: also **safe'ty-de·pos'it**

safe'guard' ***n.*** a protection; precaution —***vt.*** to protect or guard

safe house a house, apartment, etc. used as a refuge or hiding place, as by an underground organization

safe'keep'ing ***n.*** protection; care

safe·ty (sāf'tē) ***n., pl.*** **-ties 1** a being safe; security **2** any device for preventing an accident **3** *Football a)* the grounding of the ball by the offense behind its own goal line that scores two points for the defense *b)* a defensive back farthest from the line of scrimmage (also **safety man**) —***adj.*** giving safety

safety glass shatterproof glass

safety match a match that strikes only on a prepared surface

safety net 1 a net suspended as beneath aerialists **2** any protection against loss, esp. financial loss

safety pin a pin bent back on itself and having the point held in a guard

safety razor a razor with a detachable blade held between guards

safety valve an automatic valve which releases steam if the pressure in a boiler, etc. becomes excessive

saf·flow·er (saf'flou'ər) ***n.*** [[ult. < Ar *aṣfar*, yellow]] a thistlelike, annual plant with large, orange flowers and seeds yielding an edible oil

saf·fron (saf'rən) ***n.*** [[< Ar *za'farān*]] **1** a plant having orange stigmas **2** the dried stigmas, used as a dye and flavoring **3** orange yellow

sag (sag) ***vi.*** **sagged, sag'ging** [[prob. < Scand]] **1** to sink, esp. in the middle, from weight or pressure **2** to hang down unevenly **3** to weaken through weariness, age, etc. —***n.*** **1** a sagging **2** a sagging place

sa·ga (sä'gə) ***n.*** [[ON, a tale]] **1** a medieval Scandinavian story of battles, legends, etc. **2** any long story of heroic deeds

sa·ga·cious (sə gā'shəs) ***adj.*** [[< L *sagax*, wise]] keenly perceptive; shrewd —**sa·gac'i·ty** (-gas'ə tē) ***n.***

sage[1] (sāj) ***adj.*** **sag'er, sag'est** [[ult. < L *sapere*, know]] **1** wise, discerning, etc. **2** showing wisdom /*a sage* comment/ —***n.*** a very wise man

sage[2] (sāj) ***n.*** [[< L *salvus*, safe: from its reputed healing powers]] **1** a plant of the mint family with leaves used for seasoning meats, etc. **2** SAGEBRUSH

sage'brush' ***n.*** a plant with aromatic leaves, in the dry areas of the W U.S.

sag'gy ***adj.*** **-gi·er, -gi·est** tending to sag

Sag·it·tar·i·us (saj'ə ter'ē əs) [[L, archer]] the ninth sign of the zodiac

sa·gua·ro (sə gwär'ō) ***n., pl.*** **-ros** [[< native name]] a giant cactus of the SW U.S. and N Mexico

Sa·ha·ra (sə har'ə) vast desert region extending across N Africa

sa·hib (sä'ib') ***n.*** [[Hindi < Ar]] sir; master: title used in colonial India when speaking to or of a European

said (sed) ***vt., vi. pt. & pp. of*** SAY —***adj.*** aforesaid

Sai·gon (sī gän') *old name of* HO CHI MINH CITY

sail (sāl) ***n.*** [[OE *segl*]] **1** a sheet, as of canvas, spread to catch the wind, so as to drive a vessel forward **2** sails collectively **3** a trip in a ship or boat **4** anything like a sail —***vi.*** **1** to be moved forward by means of sails **2** to travel on water **3** to begin a trip by water **4** to manage a sailboat **5** to glide or move smoothly, like a ship in full sail —***vt.*** **1** to move upon (a body of water) in a vessel **2** to manage or navigate (a vessel) —**set sail** to begin a trip by water —**under sail** sailing

sail'boat' ***n.*** a boat that is propelled by means of a sail or sails

sail'cloth' ***n.*** canvas or other cloth for making sails, tents, etc.

SAILFISH

sail'fish' *n.*, *pl.* **-fish'** or (for different species) **-fish'es** a large, marine fish with a sail-like dorsal fin
sail'or *n.* 1 a person whose work is sailing 2 an enlisted man in the navy
sail'plane' *n.* a light glider
saint (sānt) *n.* ⟦< L *sanctus*, holy⟧ 1 a holy person 2 a person who is exceptionally charitable, patient, etc. 3 in certain Christian churches, a person officially recognized and venerated for having attained heaven after an exceptionally holy life —**saint'li·ness** *n.* —**saint'ly**, **-li·er**, **-li·est**, *adj.*
Saint Ber·nard (bər närd') a large dog of a breed once used in the Swiss Alps to rescue lost travelers
Saint Pat·rick's Day (pa'triks) March 17, observed by the Irish in honor of the patron saint of Ireland
Saint Valentine's Day Feb. 14, observed in honor of a martyr of the 3d c. and as a day for sending valentines
saith (seth) *vt.*, *vi.* [Archaic] says
sake[1] (sāk) *n.* ⟦OE *sacu*, suit at law⟧ 1 motive; cause /for the *sake* of money/ 2 behalf /for my *sake*/
sa·ke[2] (sä'kē) *n.* ⟦Jpn⟧ a Japanese alcoholic beverage made from rice Also sp. **sa'ki**
sa·laam (sə läm') *n.* ⟦Ar *salām*, peace⟧ an Oriental greeting, etc. made by bowing low in respect or obeisance
sal·a·ble (sāl'ə bəl) *adj.* that can be sold; marketable Also sp. **sale'a·ble**
sa·la·cious (sə lā'shəs) *adj.* ⟦< L *salire*, to leap⟧ 1 lustful 2 obscene —**sa·la'cious·ly** *adv.* —**sa·la'cious·ness** *n.*
sal·ad (sal'əd) *n.* ⟦< L *sal*, salt⟧ a dish, usually cold, of fruits, vegetables (esp. lettuce), meat, eggs, etc. usually mixed with salad dressing
salad bar a buffet in a restaurant, at which diners make their own salads
salad dressing a preparation of oil, vinegar, spices, etc. put on a salad
sa·lade niçoise (sal'əd nē swäz') a salad of tuna, tomatoes, black olives, etc. with a garlic vinaigrette
sal·a·man·der (sal'ə man'dər) *n.* ⟦< Gr *salamandra*⟧ 1 a mythological reptile said to live in fire 2 a scaleless, tailed amphibian
sa·la·mi (sə lä'mē) *n.* ⟦It < L *sal*, salt⟧ a spiced, salted sausage
sal·a·ry (sal'ə rē) *n.*, *pl.* **-ries** ⟦< L *salarium*, orig. part of a soldier's pay for buying salt < *sal*, salt⟧ a fixed payment at regular intervals for work —**sal'a·ried** (-rēd) *adj.*
sale (sāl) *n.* ⟦< ON *sala*⟧ 1 a selling 2 opportunity to sell; market 3 an auction 4 a special offering of goods at reduced prices 5 [*pl.*] receipts in business 6 [*pl.*] the work, department, etc. of selling /a job in *sales*/ —**for sale** to be sold —**on sale** for sale, esp. at a reduced price
Sa·lem (sā'ləm) capital of Oreg., in the NW part: pop. 89,000
sales·clerk (sālz'klurk') *n.* a person employed to sell goods in a store
sales'girl' *n.* a girl or woman employed as a salesclerk
sales'la'dy *n.*, *pl.* **-dies** [Colloq.] a saleswoman employed as a salesclerk
sales'man (-mən) *n.*, *pl.* **-men** 1 a man employed as a salesclerk 2 SALES REPRESENTATIVE
sales'man·ship' *n.* the skill or technique of selling
sales'per'son *n.* a person employed to sell goods or services —**sales'peo'ple** *n.pl.*
sales representative a salesperson, esp. one employed as a traveling agent for a manufacturer, etc.
sales slip a receipt or bill of sale
sales tax a tax on sales
sales'wom'an *n.*, *pl.* **-wom'en** a woman salesclerk or sales representative
sal·i·cyl·ic acid (sal'ə sil'ik) ⟦< *salicin* (substance from certain willows)⟧ a crystalline compound, as in aspirin, for relieving pain, etc.
sa·lient (sāl'yənt) *adj.* ⟦< L *salire*, to leap⟧ 1 pointing outward; jutting 2 conspicuous; prominent —*n.* a salient angle, part, etc. —**sa'lience** *n.*
sa·line (sā'līn, -lēn) *adj.* ⟦< L *sal*, salt⟧ of, like, or containing salt —*n.* a saline solution used in medicine, etc. —**sa·lin·i·ty** (sə lin'ə tē) *n.*
sa·li·va (sə lī'və) *n.* ⟦L⟧ the watery fluid secreted by glands in the mouth: it aids in digestion —**sal·i·var·y** (sal'ə ver'ē) *adj.*
sal·i·vate (sal'ə vāt') *vi.* **-vat'ed**, **-vat'ing** ⟦< L *salivare*⟧ to secrete saliva —**sal'i·va'tion** *n.*
sal·low (sal'ō) *adj.* ⟦ME *salou*⟧ of a sickly, pale-yellowish complexion
sal·ly (sal'ē) *n.*, *pl.* **-lies** ⟦< L *salire*, to leap⟧ 1 a sudden rushing forth, as to attack 2 a quick witticism; quip 3 an excursion —*vi.* **-lied**, **-ly·ing** to rush or set (*forth* or *out*) on a sally
salm·on (sam'ən) *n.*, *pl.* **-on** or **-ons** ⟦< L *salmo*⟧ 1 a game and food fish with yellowish pink flesh, that lives in salt water and spawns in fresh water 2 yellowish pink: also **salmon pink**
sal·mo·nel·la (sal'mə nel'ə) *n.*, *pl.* **-nel'lae** (-ē), **-nel'la**, or **-nel'las** ⟦after D. E. *Salmon* (1850-1914), U.S. doctor⟧ any of a genus of bacilli that cause typhoid fever, food poisoning, etc.
sa·lon (sə län') *n.* ⟦Fr: see fol.⟧ 1 a large reception hall or drawing room 2 a regular gathering of distinguished guests 3 a parlor /beauty *salon*/
sa·loon (sə lo͞on') *n.* ⟦< Fr < It *sala*⟧ 1 any large room or hall for receptions, etc. 2 [Old-fashioned] a place where alcoholic drinks are sold; bar
sal·sa (säl'sə) *n.* ⟦AmSp, sauce < L, salted food⟧ a kind of Latin American dance music influenced by jazz and rock, and usually played at fast tempos

salt (sôlt) ***n.*** ⟦OE *sealt*⟧ **1** a white, crystalline substance, sodium chloride, found in natural beds, in sea water, etc., and used for seasoning food, etc. **2** a chemical compound derived from an acid by replacing hydrogen with a metal **3** piquancy; esp., pungent wit **4** [*pl.*] mineral salts used as a cathartic or restorative **5** [Colloq.] a sailor —***adj.*** containing, preserved with, or tasting of salt —***vt.*** to sprinkle, season, or preserve with salt —**salt away** [Colloq.] to store or save (money, etc.) —**salt of the earth** any person or persons regarded as the finest, etc. —**with a grain of salt** with allowance for exaggeration, etc. —**salt′ed** ***adj.***

SALT (sôlt) Strategic Arms Limitation Talks

salt′cel′lar (-sel′ər) ***n.*** ⟦< SALT + Fr *salière*, saltcellar⟧ **1** a small dish for holding salt **2** a saltshaker

salt·ine (sôl tēn′) ***n.*** ⟦SALT + -INE³⟧ a flat, crisp, salted cracker

Salt Lake City capital of Utah: pop. 163,000

salt lick a natural deposit or a block of rock salt which animals lick

salt′pe′ter (-pēt′ər) ***n.*** ⟦< L *sal*, salt + *petra*, rock⟧ NITER

salt pork pork cured in salt

salt′shak′er ***n.*** a container for salt, with a perforated top

salt′wa′ter ***adj.*** of or living in salt water or the sea

salt′y ***adj.*** **-i·er, -i·est** **1** of or having salt **2** suggesting the sea **3** *a*) sharp; witty *b*) coarse *c*) cross or caustic

sa·lu·bri·ous (sə lo͞o′brē əs) ***adj.*** ⟦< L *salus*, health⟧ healthful; wholesome

sal·u·tar·y (sal′yoo ter′ē) ***adj.*** ⟦see prec.⟧ **1** healthful **2** beneficial

sal·u·ta·tion (sal′yoo tā′shən) ***n.*** ⟦see fol.⟧ **1** the act of greeting, addressing, etc. **2** a form of greeting, as the "Dear Sir" of a letter

sa·lute (sə lo͞ot′) ***vt., vi.*** **-lut′ed, -lut′ing** ⟦< L *salus*, health⟧ **1** to greet with friendly words or ceremonial gesture **2** to honor by performing a prescribed act, such as raising the right hand to the head, in military and naval practice **3** to commend —***n.*** an act or remark made in saluting

sal·vage (sal′vij) ***n.*** ⟦see SAVE¹⟧ **1** *a*) the rescue of a ship and cargo from shipwreck, etc. *b*) compensation paid for such rescue **2** *a*) the rescue of any property from destruction or waste *b*) the property saved —***vt.*** **-vaged, -vag·ing** to save or rescue from shipwreck, fire, etc.

sal·va·tion (sal vā′shən) ***n.*** ⟦< L *salvare*, save⟧ **1** a saving or being saved **2** a person or thing that saves **3** *Theol.* deliverance from sin and from the penalties of sin; redemption

salve (sav) ***n.*** ⟦OE *sealf*⟧ **1** any soothing or healing ointment for wounds, burns, etc. **2** anything that soothes —***vt.*** **salved, salv′ing** to soothe

sal·ver (sal′vər) ***n.*** ⟦ult. < L *salvare*, save⟧ a tray

sal·vo (sal′vō′) ***n., pl.*** **-vos** or **-voes** ⟦< It < L *salve*, hail!⟧ a discharge of a number of guns, in salute or at a target

SAM (sam) ***n.*** surface-to-air missile

sam·ba (sam′bə, säm′-) ***n.*** ⟦Port⟧ a Brazilian dance of African origin, or music for it —***vi.*** to dance the samba

same (sām) ***adj.*** ⟦< ON *samr*⟧ **1** being the very one; identical **2** alike in kind, quality, amount, etc. **3** unchanged [to keep the *same* look] **4** before-mentioned —***pron.*** the same person or thing —***adv.*** in like manner —**same′ness** ***n.***

sam·iz·dat (säm′iz dät′) ***n.*** ⟦Russ, self-published⟧ **1** in the U.S.S.R., a system by which writings officially disapproved of are circulated secretly **2** such writings

Sa·mo·a (sə mō′ə) group of islands in the South Pacific, seven of which constitute a U.S. possession (**American Samoa**) —**Sa·mo′an** ***n., adj.***

sam·o·var (sam′ə vär′) ***n.*** ⟦Russ⟧ a Russian metal urn with an internal tube for heating water in making tea

sam·pan (sam′pan′) ***n.*** ⟦< Chin dial.⟧ a small boat used in China and Japan, rowed with a scull from the stern

sam·ple (sam′pəl) ***n.*** ⟦see EXAMPLE⟧ **1** a part taken as representative of a whole thing, group, etc.; specimen **2** an example —***vt.*** **-pled, -pling** to take or test a sample of

sam′pler ***n.*** **1** one who samples **2** a collection of representative selections **3** a cloth embroidered with designs, mottoes, etc. in different stitches

Sam·son (sam′sən) *Bible* an Israelite with great strength

Sam·u·el (sam′yoo əl) *Bible* a Hebrew judge and prophet

sam·u·rai (sam′ə rī′) ***n., pl.*** **-rai′** ⟦Jpn⟧ a member of a military class in feudal Japan

San An·to·ni·o (san′ an tō′nē ō′) city in S Tex.: site of the Alamo: pop. 785,000

san·a·to·ri·um (san′ə tôr′ē əm) ***n., pl.*** **-ri·ums** or **-ri·a** (-ə) *chiefly Brit. var. of* SANITARIUM

San Ber·nar·di·no (bur′nər dē′nō) city in S Calif.: pop. 118,000

sanc·ti·fy (saŋk′tə fī′) ***vt.*** **-fied′, -fy′ing** ⟦see SAINT & -FY⟧ **1** to set apart as holy; consecrate **2** to make free from sin —**sanc′ti·fi·ca′tion** ***n.***

sanc·ti·mo·ni·ous (saŋk′tə mō′nē əs) ***adj.*** pretending to be pious —**sanc′ti·mo′ni·ous·ly** ***adv.***

sanc′ti·mo′ny ***n.*** ⟦< L *sanctus*, holy⟧ pretended piety

sanc·tion (saŋk′shən) ***n.*** ⟦see SAINT⟧ **1** authorization **2** support; approval **3** a coercive measure, as an official trade boycott, against a nation defying international law: *often used in pl.* —***vt.*** **1** to confirm **2** to authorize; permit

sanc·ti·ty (saŋk′tə tē) ***n., pl.*** **-ties** ⟦< L *sanctus*, holy⟧ **1** holiness **2** sacredness

sanc·tu·ar·y (saŋk′choo er′ē) ***n., pl.*** **-ies** ⟦< L *sanctus*, sacred⟧ **1** a holy place; specif., a church, temple, etc. **2** a place of refuge or protection

sanc·tum (saŋk′təm) ***n.*** ⟦L⟧ **1** a sacred place **2** a private room where one is not to be disturbed

sand (sand) ***n.*** ⟦OE⟧ **1** loose, gritty grains of disintegrated rock, as on beaches, in deserts, etc. **2** [*usually pl.*] a tract of sand —***vt.*** **1** to sprinkle or fill with sand **2** to smooth or polish, as with sandpaper — **sand'er** *n.*

san·dal (san'dəl) *n.* ⟦< Gr *sandalon*⟧ **1** a shoe made of a sole fastened to the foot by straps **2** any of various low slippers or shoes

san'dal·wood' *n.* ⟦ult. < Sans⟧ **1** the hard, sweet-smelling wood at the core of an Asiatic tree **2** this tree

sand'bag' *n.* a bag filled with sand, used for ballast, protecting levees, etc. —*vt.* **-bagged'**, **-bag'ging** **1** to put sandbags in or around **2** to hit with a sandbag **3** [Colloq.] to force into doing something

sand'bar' *n.* a ridge of sand, as one formed in a river or along a shore: also **sand'bank'**

sand'blast' *n.* a current of air or steam carrying sand at a high velocity, used in cleaning stone, etc. —*vt.* to clean with a sandblast

sand'box' *n.* a box containing sand for children to play in

sand'hog' *n.* a laborer in underground or underwater construction

San Di·e·go (san' dē ā'gō) seaport in S Calif.: pop. 876,000

S & L savings and loan (association)

sand'lot' *adj.* of or having to do with games, esp. baseball, played by amateurs, orig. on a sandy lot

sand'man' *n.* a mythical person supposed to make children sleepy by dusting sand in their eyes

sand'pa'per *n.* paper coated on one side with sand, used for smoothing and polishing —*vt.* to rub with sandpaper

sand'pip'er (-pī'pər) *n.* a small shorebird with a long, soft-tipped bill

sand'stone' *n.* a sedimentary rock composed of sand grains cemented together, as by silica

sand'storm' *n.* a windstorm in which large quantities of sand are blown about in the air

sand trap a hollow filled with sand, serving as a hazard on a golf course

sand·wich (san'dwich', -wich) *n.* ⟦after 4th Earl of *Sandwich* (1718-92)⟧ slices of bread with meat, cheese, etc. between them —*vt.* to place between other persons, things, etc.

sand·y (san'dē) *adj.* **-i·er, -i·est** **1** of or like sand **2** pale reddish-yellow

sane (sān) *adj.* ⟦L *sanus*, healthy⟧ **1** mentally healthy; rational **2** sound; sensible —**sane'ly** *adv.*

San Fran·cis·co (san' frən sis'kō) seaport on the coast of central Calif.: pop. 679,000

San Francisco Bay an inlet of the Pacific in W Calif.: the harbor of San Francisco

sang (saŋ) *vi., vt. alt. pt. of* SING

sang-froid (sän frwä') *n.* ⟦Fr, lit., cold blood⟧ cool self-possession

san·gui·nar·y (saŋ'gwi ner'ē) *adj.* ⟦see fol.⟧ **1** accompanied by much bloodshed or murder **2** bloodthirsty

san·guine (saŋ'gwin) *adj.* ⟦< L *sanguis*, blood⟧ **1** of the color of blood; ruddy **2** cheerful; confident

san·i·tar·i·um (san'ə ter'ē əm) *n., pl.* **-i·ums** or **-i·a** (-ə) ⟦ModL < L *sanitas*, health⟧ **1** a resort where people go to regain health **2** an institution for the care of invalids or convalescents

san·i·tar·y (san'ə ter'ē) *adj.* ⟦< L *sanitas*, health⟧ **1** of or bringing about health and healthful conditions **2** in a clean, healthy condition

sanitary napkin an absorbent pad worn by women during menstruation

san·i·ta·tion (san'ə tā'shən) *n.* **1** the science and practice of effecting hygienic conditions **2** drainage and disposal of sewage

san·i·tize (san'ə tīz') *vt.* **-tized', -tiz'ing** to make sanitary

san·i·ty (san'ə tē) *n.* **1** the state of being sane **2** soundness of judgment

San Jo·se (san' hō zā') city in W Calif.: pop. 637,000

San Juan (san' hwän') capital of Puerto Rico: pop. 445,000

sank (saŋk) *vi., vt. alt. pt. of* SINK

San Ma·ri·no (san' mə rē'nō) independent country within E Italy: 23 sq. mi.; pop. 21,000

sans (sanz; *Fr* sän) *prep.* ⟦Fr < L *sine*⟧ without

San·skrit (san'skrit') *n.* the classical literary language of ancient India Also **San'scrit**

San·ta An·a (san'tə an'ə) **1** hot desert wind from the east or northeast in S Calif. **2** city in SW Calif.: pop. 204,000

San·ta Claus or **San·ta Klaus** (san'tə klôz') ⟦< Du *Sant Nikolaas*, St. Nicholas⟧ *Folklore* a fat, white-bearded, jolly old man in a red suit, who distributes gifts at Christmas

San·ta Fe (san'tə fā') capital of N.Mex.: pop. 49,000

San·ti·a·go (san'tē ä'gō) capital of Chile: pop. 3,615,000

São Pau·lo (soun pou'loo) city in SE Brazil: pop. 7,032,000

São To·mé and Prín·ci·pe (tô me' ənd prin'sə pē') country off the W coast of Africa, comprising two islands (**São Tomé** and **Príncipe**): 372 sq. mi.; pop. 74,000

sap¹ (sap) *n.* ⟦OE *sæp*⟧ **1** the juice that circulates through a plant, bearing water, food, etc. **2** vigor; energy **3** [Slang] a fool —**sap'less** *adj.*

sap² (sap) *vt.* **sapped, sap'ping** ⟦< Fr *sappe*, a hoe⟧ **1** to dig beneath; undermine **2** to weaken; exhaust

sa·pi·ent (sā'pē ənt) *adj.* ⟦< L *sapere*, to taste, know⟧ full of knowledge; wise —**sa'pi·ence** *n.*

sap·ling (sap'liŋ) *n.* a young tree

sap·phire (saf'īr) *n.* ⟦< Sans *śanipriya*⟧ a precious stone of a clear, deep-blue corundum

sap·py (sap'ē) *adj.* **-pi·er, -pi·est** **1** full of sap; juicy **2** [Slang] foolish; silly —**sap'pi·ness** *n.*

sap·ro·phyte (sap'rə fīt') *n.* ⟦< Gr *sapros*, rotten + *phyton*, a plant⟧ any plant that lives on dead or decaying organic matter, as some fungi

sap'suck'er *n.* an American woodpecker that often drills holes in certain trees for the sap

Sar·a·cen (sar'ə sən) *n.* [Historical] any Arab or any Muslim, esp. at the time of the Crusades

Sar·ah (ser'ə) *Bible* the wife of Abraham and mother of Isaac

sa·ran (sə ran') *n.* ⟦a coinage⟧ a thermoplastic substance used in various fabrics, wrapping material, etc.

sar·casm (sär′kaz′əm) ***n.*** ⟦< Gr *sarkazein*, to tear flesh⟧ **1** a taunting or caustic remark, generally ironic **2** the making of such remarks

sar·cas·tic (sär kas′tik) ***adj.*** **1** of, like, or full of sarcasm; sneering **2** using sarcasm —**sar·cas′ti·cal·ly** ***adv.***

sar·co·ma (sär kō′mə) ***n.***, *pl.* **-mas** or **-ma·ta** (-mə tə) ⟦< Gr *sarx*, flesh⟧ a malignant tumor in connective tissue

sar·coph·a·gus (sär käf′ə gəs) ***n.***, *pl.* **-gi′** (-jī′) or **-gus·es** ⟦< Gr *sarx*, flesh + *phagein*, to eat: limestone coffins hastened disintegration⟧ a stone coffin, esp. one exposed to view, as in a tomb

sar·dine (sär dēn′) ***n.*** ⟦< L *sarda*, a fish⟧ any of various small ocean fishes preserved in cans for eating

sar·don·ic (sär dän′ik) ***adj.*** ⟦< Gr *sardonios*⟧ scornfully or bitterly sarcastic —**sar·don′i·cal·ly** ***adv.***

sa·ri (sä′rē) ***n.*** ⟦< Sans⟧ an outer garment of Hindu women, a long cloth wrapped around the body

SARI

sa·rong (sə rôŋ′, -räŋ′) ***n.*** ⟦Malay *sarung*⟧ a garment of men and women in the East Indies, etc., consisting of a cloth worn like a skirt

sar·sa·pa·ril·la (sär′sə pə ril′ə, särs′pə-, sas′pə-) ***n.*** ⟦< Sp *zarza*, bramble + *parra*, vine⟧ **1** a tropical American vine with fragrant roots **2** a carbonated drink flavored with the dried roots

sar·to·ri·al (sär tôr′ē əl) ***adj.*** ⟦< LL *sartor*, tailor⟧ **1** of tailors or their work **2** of men's dress

SASE self-addressed, stamped envelope

sash¹ (sash) ***n.*** ⟦Ar *shāsh*, muslin⟧ an ornamental band, ribbon, etc. worn over the shoulder or around the waist

sash² (sash) ***n.*** ⟦< Fr *châssis*, a frame⟧ a frame for holding the glass pane of a window or door, esp. a sliding frame

sa·shay (sa shā′) ***vi.*** ⟦< Fr *chassé*, a dance step⟧ [Colloq.] **1** to walk or go, esp. casually **2** to move, walk, etc. so as to attract attention

Sas·katch·e·wan (sas kach′ə wän′) province of SW Canada: 251,700 sq. mi.; pop. 1,010,000; cap. Regina: abbrev. **Sask.**

sass (sas) ***n.*** ⟦var. of SAUCE⟧ [Colloq.] impudent talk —***vt.*** [Colloq.] to talk impudently to

sas·sa·fras (sas′ə fras′) ***n.*** ⟦Sp *sasafras*⟧ **1** a small tree having small, bluish fruits **2** its dried root bark used for flavoring

sass·y (sas′ē) ***adj.*** **-i·er, -i·est** ⟦var. of SAUCY⟧ [Colloq.] impudent; saucy

sat (sat) ***vi., vt.*** *pt. & pp. of* SIT

Sat. Saturday

Sa·tan (sāt′'n) ⟦< Heb *satan*, adversary⟧ the Devil

sa·tan·ic (sā tan′ik, sə-) ***adj.*** like Satan; wicked —**sa·tan′i·cal·ly** ***adv.***

satch·el (sach′əl) ***n.*** ⟦< L *saccus*, a bag⟧ a small bag for carrying clothes, books, etc.

sate (sāt) ***vt.*** **sat′ed, sat′ing** ⟦prob. < L *satiare*, fill full⟧ **1** to satisfy (an appetite, etc.) completely **2** to satiate

sa·teen (sa tēn′) ***n.*** ⟦< SATIN⟧ a cotton cloth made to imitate satin

sat·el·lite (sat′'l īt′) ***n.*** ⟦< L *satelles*, an attendant⟧ **1** an attendant of some important person **2** *a*) a moon revolving around a larger planet *b*) a man-made object rocketed into orbit around the earth, moon, etc. **3** a small state economically dependent on a larger one

sa·ti·ate (sā′shē āt′) ***vt.*** **-at′ed, -at′ing** ⟦< L *satis*, enough⟧ to provide with more than enough, so as to weary or disgust; glut

sa·ti·e·ty (sə tī′ə tē) ***n.*** a being satiated

sat·in (sat′'n) ***n.*** ⟦< Ar *zaitūnī*, of *Zaitūn*, former name of a Chinese seaport⟧ a fabric of silk, nylon, rayon, etc. with a smooth, glossy finish on one side —**sat′in·y** ***adj.***

sat′in·wood′ ***n.*** **1** a smooth wood used in fine furniture **2** any of a number of trees yielding such a wood

sat·ire (sa′tīr′) ***n.*** ⟦< L *satira*⟧ **1** a literary work in which vices, follies, etc. are held up to ridicule and contempt **2** the use of ridicule, sarcasm, etc. to attack vices, follies, etc. —**sa·tir·i·cal** (sə tir′i kəl) ***adj.*** —**sat·i·rist** (sat′ə rist) ***n.***

sat·i·rize (sat′ə rīz′) ***vt.*** **-rized′, -riz′ing** to attack with satire

sat·is·fac·tion (sat′is fak′shən) ***n.*** **1** a satisfying or being satisfied **2** something that satisfies; specif., *a*) anything that brings pleasure or contentment *b*) settlement of debt

sat′is·fac′to·ry (-tə rē) ***adj.*** good enough to fulfill a need, wish, etc.; satisfying —**sat′is·fac′to·ri·ly** ***adv.***

sat·is·fy (sat′is fī′) ***vt.*** **-fied′, -fy′ing** ⟦< L *satis*, enough + *facere*, make⟧ **1** to fulfill the needs or desires of; content **2** to fulfill the requirements of **3** to free from doubt; convince **4** *a*) to give what is due to *b*) to discharge (a debt, etc.)

sa·to·ri (sä tôr′ē) ***n.*** ⟦Jpn⟧ spiritual enlightenment: term in Zen Buddhism

sa·trap (sā′trap′, sa′-) ***n.*** ⟦< Pers⟧ a petty tyrant

sat·u·rate (sach′ə rāt′) ***vt.*** **-rat′ed, -rat′ing** ⟦< L *satur*, full⟧ **1** to make thoroughly soaked **2** to cause to be filled, charged, etc. with the most it can absorb —**sat′u·ra′tion** ***n.***

Sat·ur·day (sat′ər dā′; *occas.*, -dē′) ***n.*** ⟦< OE *Sæterdæg*, Saturn's day⟧ the seventh and last day of the week

Saturday night special ⟦from their use in weekend crimes⟧ [Slang] any small, cheap handgun

Sat·urn (sat′ərn) **1** the Roman god of agriculture **2** the second largest planet of the solar system with thin, icy rings of particles around its equator: see PLANET

sat·ur·nine (sat′ər nīn′) ***adj.*** ⟦< supposed influence of planet Saturn⟧ sluggish, gloomy, grave, etc.

sat·yr (sat′ər, sāt′-) ***n.*** ⟦< Gr *satyros*⟧ **1** *Gr. Myth.* a lecherous woodland deity represented as a man with a goat's legs, ears, and horns **2** a lecherous man

sat·y·ri·a·sis (sat′ə rī′ə sis) ***n.*** ⟦< Gr: see prec.⟧ uncontrollable desire by a man for sexual intercourse

sauce (sôs) ***n.*** ⟦< L *sal,* salt⟧ **1** a liquid or soft mixture served with food to add flavor **2** stewed or preserved fruit **3** [Colloq.] impudence

sauce′pan′ ***n.*** a small pot with a projecting handle, used for cooking

sau·cer (sô′sər) ***n.*** ⟦see SAUCE⟧ a small, round, shallow dish, esp. one designed to hold a cup

sau·cy (sô′sē) ***adj.*** **-ci·er, -ci·est** ⟦SAUC(E) + -Y²⟧ **1** rude; impudent **2** pert; sprightly —**sau′ci·ly** ***adv.*** —**sau′ci·ness** ***n.***

Sa·u·di Arabia (sou′dē, sô-) kingdom occupying most of Arabia: 849,400 sq. mi.; pop. *c.* 12,400,000

sau·er·bra·ten (sour′brät′'n, zou′ər-) ***n.*** ⟦Ger *sauer,* sour + *braten,* roast⟧ beef marinated before cooking

sau·er·kraut (sour′krout′) ***n.*** ⟦Ger *sauer,* sour + *kraut,* cabbage⟧ chopped cabbage fermented in brine

Saul (sôl) *Bible* first king of Israel

sau·na (sô′nə; *also* sou′-) ***n.*** ⟦Finnish⟧ a bath involving exposure to hot, dry air

saun·ter (sôn′tər) ***vi.*** ⟦ME *santren,* to muse⟧ to walk about idly; stroll —***n.*** a leisurely walk; stroll

sau·ri·an (sôr′ē ən) ***adj.*** ⟦< Gr *sauros,* lizard⟧ of or like lizards

sau·ro·pod (sôr′ə päd′) ***n.*** ⟦< Gr *sauros,* lizard + -POD⟧ a gigantic dinosaur with a long neck and tail and a small head, as a brontosaur

sau·sage (sô′sij) ***n.*** ⟦see SAUCE⟧ pork or other meat, chopped fine, seasoned, and often stuffed into a casing

sau·té (sô tā′, sō-) ***vt.*** **-téed′, -té′ing** ⟦Fr < *sauter,* to leap⟧ to fry quickly with a little fat

sau·ternes (sō turn′) ***n.*** ⟦after *Sauternes,* town in France⟧ any of various white wines, of varying sweetness: also **sau·terne** (sō turn′, -tern′; sô-)

sav·age (sav′ij) ***adj.*** ⟦< L *silva,* a wood⟧ **1** wild; uncultivated /a *savage* jungle/ **2** fierce; untamed /a *savage* tiger/ **3** primitive; barbarous **4** cruel; pitiless —***n.*** **1** [Archaic] a member of a preliterate, often tribal, culture **2** a brutal or crude person —**sav′age·ly** ***adv.*** —**sav′age·ry** ***n.***

sa·van·na or **sa·van·nah** (sə van′ə) ***n.*** ⟦Sp *sabana*⟧ a treeless plain or a grassland with scattered trees

Sa·van·nah (sə van′ə) seaport in SE Ga.: pop. 142,000

sa·vant (sə vänt′; *also* sav′ənt) ***n.*** ⟦Fr < *savoir,* know⟧ a learned person

save¹ (sāv) ***vt.*** **saved, sav′ing** ⟦< L *salvus,* safe⟧ **1** to rescue or preserve from harm or danger **2** to preserve for future use **3** to prevent loss or waste of /to *save* time/ **4** to prevent or lessen /to *save* expense/ **5** *Theol.* to deliver from sin —***vi.*** **1** to avoid expense, waste, etc. **2** to store (*up*) money or goods —***n.*** *Sports* an action that keeps an opponent from scoring or winning —**sav′er** ***n.***

save² (sāv) ***prep., conj.*** ⟦< OFr *sauf,* safe⟧ except; but

sav·ing (sā′viŋ) ***adj.*** that saves; specif., *a*) economizing or economical *b*) redeeming —***n.*** **1** [*often pl., with sing. v.*] any reduction in expense, time, etc. **2** [*pl.*] sums of money saved

sav·ior or **sav·iour** (sāv′yər) ***n.*** ⟦< L *salvare,* to save⟧ one who saves —**the Savior** (or **Saviour**) Jesus Christ

sa·voir-faire (sav′wär fer′) ***n.*** ⟦Fr, to know (how) to do⟧ ready knowledge of what to do or say in any situation

sa·vor (sā′vər) ***n.*** ⟦< L *sapor*⟧ **1** a particular taste or smell **2** distinctive quality —***vi.*** to have the distinctive taste, smell, or quality (*of*) —***vt.*** to taste with delight Brit. sp. **savour**

sa′vor·y ***adj.*** **-i·er, -i·est** **1** pleasing to the taste or smell **2** pleasant, agreeable, etc. Brit. sp. **savoury**

sav·vy (sav′ē) ***n.*** ⟦< Port *saber,* to know⟧ [Slang] shrewdness or understanding

saw¹ (sô) ***n.*** ⟦OE *sagu*⟧ a cutting tool consisting of a thin metal blade or disk with sharp teeth —***vt.*** to cut or shape with a saw —***vi.*** **1** to cut with or as with a saw **2** to be cut with a saw

saw² (sô) ***n.*** ⟦OE *sagu*⟧ a maxim

saw³ (sô) ***vt., vi.*** *pt. of* SEE¹

saw′dust′ ***n.*** fine particles of wood formed in sawing wood

sawed′-off′ ***adj.*** short or shortened

saw′horse′ ***n.*** a rack on which wood is placed while being sawed

saw′mill′ ***n.*** a factory where logs are sawed into boards

saw′-toothed′ ***adj.*** having notches along the edge like the teeth of a saw

saw·yer (sô′yər) ***n.*** one whose work is sawing wood

sax (saks) ***n.*** [Colloq.] *short for* SAXOPHONE

Sax·on (sak′sən) ***n.*** **1** any of an ancient Germanic people, some of whom settled in England **2** an Anglo-Saxon **3** any dialect of the Saxons

sax·o·phone (sak′sə fōn′) ***n.*** ⟦Fr, after A. J. *Sax,* 19th-c. Belgian inventor + -PHONE⟧ a single-reed, keyed woodwind instrument with a metal body —**sax′o·phon′ist** (-fōn′ ist) ***n.***

say (sā) ***vt.*** **said, say′ing** ⟦OE *secgan*⟧ **1** to utter or speak **2** to express in words; state **3** to state positively or as an opinion **4** to recite /to *say* one's prayers/ **5** to estimate; assume /he is, I'd *say,* forty/ —***n.*** **1** a chance to speak /I had my *say*/ **2** authority, as to make a final decision: often with *the* —**that is to say** in other words

say′ing ***n.*** something said; esp. an adage, proverb, or maxim

say′-so′ ***n.*** [Colloq.] **1** (one's) word, assurance, etc. **2** right of decision

Sb ⟦L *stibium*⟧ *Chem. symbol for* antimony

s.c. *Printing* small capitals

SC or **S.C.** South Carolina

scab (skab) ***n.*** ⟦< ON *skabb*⟧ **1** a crust forming over a sore during healing **2** a worker who refuses to join a union, or who replaces a striking worker —***vi.*** **scabbed, scab′bing** **1** to become covered with a scab **2** to work or act as a scab —**scab′by, -bi·er, -bi·est,** ***adj.*** —**scab′bi·ness** ***n.***

scab·bard (skab′ərd) ***n.*** ⟦< ? OHG *scar,* sword⟧ a sheath for the blade of a sword, dagger, etc.

sca·bies (skā′bēz) ***n.*** ⟦L, the itch⟧ a contagious, itching skin disease caused by a mite that burrows under the skin to lay its eggs

scab·rous (skab′rəs, skā′brəs) ***adj.*** ⟦< L *scabere,* to scratch⟧ 1 scaly or scabby 2 indecent, shocking, etc.

scads (skadz) ***n.pl.*** ⟦< ?⟧ [Colloq.] a very large number or amount

scaf·fold (skaf′əld, -ōld′) ***n.*** ⟦< OFr *escafalt*⟧ 1 a temporary framework for supporting workers during the repairing, painting, etc. of a building, etc. 2 a raised platform on which criminals are executed

scaf′fold·ing′ (-əl diŋ′) ***n.*** 1 the materials forming a scaffold 2 a scaffold

scal·a·wag (skal′ə wag′) ***n.*** ⟦< ?⟧ [Colloq.] a scamp; rascal

scald (skôld) ***vt.*** ⟦< L *ex-,* intens. + *calidus,* hot⟧ 1 to burn with hot liquid or steam 2 to heat almost to the boiling point 3 to use boiling liquid on —***n.*** a burn caused by scalding

scale[1] (skāl) ***n.*** ⟦< L *scala,* ladder⟧ 1 *a)* a series of marks along a line used in measuring /the *scale* of a thermometer/ *b)* any instrument so marked 2 the proportion that a map, etc. bears to the thing it represents /a *scale* of one inch to a mile/ 3 *a)* a series of degrees classified by size, amount, etc. /a wage *scale*/ *b)* any degree in such a series 4 *Music* a series of tones, rising or falling in pitch, according to a system of intervals —***vt.*** **scaled, scal′ing** 1 to climb up or over 2 to make according to a scale —**scale down** (or **up**) to reduce (or increase) according to a fixed ratio

scale[2] (skāl) ***n.*** ⟦< OFr *escale,* shell⟧ 1 any of the thin, flat horny plates covering many fishes, reptiles, etc. 2 any thin, platelike layer or piece —***vt.*** **scaled, scal′ing** to scrape scales from —***vi.*** to flake or peel off in scales —**scal′y, -i·er, -i·est,** ***adj.***

scale[3] (skāl) ***n.*** ⟦< ON *skāl,* bowl⟧ 1 either pan of a balance 2 [*often pl.*] *a)* a balance *b)* any weighing machine —***vt.*** **scaled, scal′ing** to weigh —**turn the scales** to decide or settle

scale insect any of various small insects destructive to plants: the females secrete a waxy scale

sca·lene (skā′lēn′, skā lēn′) ***adj.*** ⟦< Gr *skalēnos,* uneven⟧ having unequal sides /a *scalene* triangle/

scal·lion (skal′yən) ***n.*** ⟦< L (*caepa*) *Ascalonia,* (onion of) Ascalon (Philistine city)⟧ any of various onions or onionlike plants, as the shallot, green onion, or leek

SHELL OF A SCALLOP

scal·lop (skäl′əp, skal′-) ***n.*** ⟦< OFr *escalope*⟧ 1 *a)* any of various edible mollusks with two curved, hinged shells *b)* one of the shells 2 any of a series of curves, etc. forming an ornamental edge —***vt.*** 1 to cut the edge of in scallops 2 to bake with a milk sauce and bread crumbs

scalp (skalp) ***n.*** ⟦< Scand⟧ the skin on the top and back of the head, usually covered with hair —***vt.*** 1 to cut or tear the scalp from 2 [Colloq.] to buy (theater tickets, etc.) and resell them at higher prices —**scalp′er** ***n.***

scal·pel (skal′pəl) ***n.*** ⟦< L *scalprum,* a knife⟧ a small, sharp, straight knife used in surgery, etc.

scam (skam) ***n.*** ⟦prob. < *scheme*⟧ [Slang] a swindle or fraud, esp. a CONFIDENCE GAME —***vt.*** **scammed, scam′ming** [Slang] to cheat or swindle, as in a confidence game

scamp (skamp) ***n.*** ⟦< It *scampare,* to flee⟧ a mischievous fellow; rascal

scam·per (skam′pər) ***vi.*** ⟦see prec.⟧ to run or go quickly —***n.*** a scampering

scam·pi (skäm′pē, skam′-) ***n., pl.*** **-pi** or **-pies** ⟦It⟧ a large, greenish, edible prawn

scan (skan) ***vt.*** **scanned, scan′ning** ⟦< L *scandere,* to climb⟧ 1 to analyze (verse) by marking the metrical feet 2 to look at closely 3 to glance at quickly —***vi.*** to conform to metrical principles: said of poetry —***n.*** the act or an instance of scanning

Scan. or **Scand.** Scandinavia(n)

scan·dal (skan′dəl) ***n.*** ⟦< Gr *skandalon,* a snare⟧ 1 anything that offends moral feelings and leads to disgrace 2 shame, outrage, etc. caused by this 3 disgrace 4 malicious gossip

scan′dal·ize′ ***vt.*** **-ized′, -iz′ing** to outrage the moral feelings of by improper conduct —**scan′dal·iz′er** ***n.***

scan′dal·mon′ger (-muŋ′gər, -mäŋ′-) ***n.*** one who spreads scandal or gossip

scan′dal·ous (-də ləs) ***adj.*** 1 causing scandal; shameful 2 spreading slander —**scan′dal·ous·ly** ***adv.***

Scan·di·na·vi·a (skan′də nā′vē ə) region in N Europe, including Norway, Sweden, & Denmark and, sometimes, Iceland

Scan·di·na·vi·an (skan′də nā′vē ən) ***adj.*** of Scandinavia, its people, languages, etc. —***n.*** 1 a native or inhabitant of Scandinavia 2 the subbranch of the Germanic languages spoken by Scandinavians

scant (skant) ***adj.*** ⟦< ON *skammr,* short⟧ 1 inadequate; meager 2 not quite up to full measure

scant′y ***adj.*** **-i·er, -i·est** 1 barely sufficient 2 insufficient; not enough —**scant′i·ly** ***adv.*** —**scant′i·ness** ***n.***

scape·goat (skāp′gōt′) ***n.*** ⟦< ESCAPE + GOAT; see Lev. 16:7-26⟧ one who bears the blame for the mistakes of others —***vt., vi.*** to make a scapegoat (of)

scape·grace (skāp′grās′) ***n.*** ⟦< ESCAPE + GRACE⟧ a graceless, rogue; scamp

scap·u·la (skap′yə lə) ***n., pl.*** **-lae′** (-lē′) or **-las** ⟦< L⟧ the shoulder blade

scar (skär) ***n.*** ⟦< Gr *eschara,* orig., fireplace⟧ a mark left after a wound, burn, etc. has healed —***vt.*** **scarred, scar′ring** to mark as with a scar —***vi.*** to form a scar in healing

scar·ab (skar′əb) ***n.*** ⟦< L *scarabaeus*⟧ 1 a large, black beetle 2 a carved image of such a beetle

scarce (skers) ***adj.*** ⟦ult. < L *excerpere,* pick out⟧ 1 not common; rarely seen 2 not plentiful; hard to get —**make oneself scarce** [Colloq.] to go or stay away —**scarce′ness** ***n.***

scarce′ly ***adv.*** **1** hardly; only just **2** probably not or certainly not

scar·ci·ty (sker′sə tē) ***n.,*** *pl.* **-ties** **1** a being scarce; inadequate supply; dearth **2** rarity; uncommonness

scare (sker) ***vt.*** **scared, scar′ing** ⟦< ON *skjarr,* timid⟧ to fill with sudden fear —***vi.*** to become frightened —***n.*** a sudden fear —**scare away** (or **off**) to drive away (or off) by frightening —**scare up** [Colloq.] to produce or gather quickly

scare·crow (sker′krō′) ***n.*** a human figure made with sticks, old clothes, etc., put in a field to scare birds from crops

scarf (skärf) ***n.,*** *pl.* **scarves** (skärvz) or **scarfs** ⟦< OFr *escharpe,* purse hung from the neck⟧ **1** a piece of cloth worn about the neck, head, etc. **2** a long, narrow covering for a table, etc.

scar·i·fy (skar′ə fī′) ***vt.*** **-fied′, -fy′ing** ⟦< L *scarifare*⟧ to make small cuts in (the skin, etc.) —**scar′i·fi·ca′tion** ***n.***

scar·let (skär′lit) ***n.*** ⟦< ML *scarlatum*⟧ very bright red —***adj.*** **1** of this color **2** sinful; specif., whorish

scarlet fever an acute contagious disease characterized by sore throat, fever, and a scarlet rash

scar·y (sker′ē) ***adj.*** **-i·er, -i·est** [Colloq.] **1** frightening **2** easily frightened —**scar′i·ness** ***n.***

scat[1] (skat) ***vi.*** **scat′ted, scat′ting** ⟦? short for SCATTER⟧ [Colloq.] to go away: usually in the imperative

scat[2] (skat) ***adj.*** ⟦< ?⟧ *Jazz* using improvised, meaningless syllables in singing —***n.*** such singing —***vi.*** **scat′ted, scat′ting** to sing scat

scath·ing (skā′thiŋ) ***adj.*** ⟦< ON *skathi,* harm⟧ harsh or caustic [*scathing* remarks] —**scath′ing·ly** ***adv.***

sca·tol·o·gy (skə täl′ə jē) ***n.*** ⟦< Gr *skōr,* excrement⟧ obsession with excrement or excretion, as in literature —**scat·o·log·i·cal** (skat′ə läj′i kəl) ***adj.***

scat·ter (skat′ər) ***vt.*** ⟦ME *skateren*⟧ **1** to throw here and there; sprinkle **2** to separate and drive in many directions; disperse —***vi.*** to separate and go off in several directions

scat′ter·brain′ ***n.*** one who is incapable of concentrated thinking

scatter rug a small rug

scav·eng·er (skav′in jər) ***n.*** ⟦< NormFr *escauwer,* to inspect⟧ **1** one who gathers things discarded by others **2** any animal that eats refuse and decaying matter —**scav′enge** (-inj), **-enged, -eng·ing,** ***vt., vi.***

sce·nar·i·o (sə ner′ē ō′; -när′-) ***n.,*** *pl.* **-i·os′** ⟦see fol.⟧ **1** *a)* an outline of a play, etc. *b)* the script of a film **2** an outline for any planned series of events, real or imagined —**sce·nar′ist** ***n.***

scene (sēn) ***n.*** ⟦< Gr *skēnē,* stage⟧ **1** the place where an event occurs **2** the setting of a play, story, etc. **3** a division of a play, usually part of an act **4** *a)* a unit of action in a play, film, etc. *b)* a section of film having a number of shots **5** SCENERY (sense 1) **6** a display of strong feeling [to make a *scene*] **7** [Colloq.] the locale for a specified activity

sce·ner·y (sēn′ər ē) ***n.,*** *pl.* **-ies** **1** painted screens, backdrops, etc., used on the stage to represent places, as in a play, etc. **2** the features of a landscape

sce·nic (sēn′ik) ***adj.*** **1** of stage scenery **2** *a)* of natural scenery *b)* having beautiful scenery —**sce′ni·cal·ly** ***adv.***

scent (sent) ***vt.*** ⟦ult. < L *sentire,* to feel⟧ **1** to smell **2** to get a hint of **3** to fill with an odor; perfume —***n.*** **1** an odor **2** the sense of smell **3** a perfume **4** an odor left by an animal, by which it is tracked —**scent′ed** ***adj.***

scep·ter (sep′tər) ***n.*** ⟦< Gr *skēptron,* staff⟧ a staff held by a ruler as a symbol of sovereignty Chiefly Brit. sp. **sceptre**

scep·tic (skep′tik) ***n., adj.*** *chiefly Brit. sp. of* SKEPTIC —**scep′ti·cal** ***adj.*** —**scep′ti·cism** ***n.***

sched·ule (ske′jool; *Brit & often Cdn* shed′yōōl) ***n.*** ⟦< L *scheda,* a strip of papyrus⟧ **1** a list of details **2** a list of times of recurring events, projected operations, etc.; timetable **3** a timed plan for a project —***vt.*** **-uled, -ul·ing** **1** to place in a schedule **2** to plan for a certain time

sche·mat·ic (skē mat′ik) ***adj.*** of, or like a scheme, diagram, etc.

scheme (skēm) ***n.*** ⟦< Gr *schēma,* a form⟧ **1** *a)* a systematic program for attaining some object *b)* a secret plan; plot **2** an orderly combination of things on a definite plan **3** a diagram —***vt.*** **schemed, schem′ing** to devise or plot —**schem′er** ***n.***

scher·zo (sker′tsō) ***n.,*** *pl.* **-zos** or **-zi** (-tsē) ⟦It, a jest⟧ *Music* a lively composition, usually in 3/4 time, as the third movement of a symphony, etc.

schism (siz′əm) ***n.*** ⟦< Gr *schizein,* to cleave⟧ a split, as in a church, because of difference of opinion, doctrine, etc. —**schis·mat′ic** (-mat′ik) ***adj.***

schist (shist) ***n.*** ⟦< Gr *schistos,* easily cleft⟧ a crystalline rock easily split into layers

schiz·o·phre·ni·a (skit′sə frē′nē ə, skiz′ə-) ***n.*** ⟦< Gr *schizein,* cleave + *phrēn,* the mind⟧ a mental disorder characterized by separation between thought and emotions, by delusions, bizarre behavior, etc. —**schiz′oid** (-soid) or **schiz′o·phren′ic** (-fren′ik) ***adj., n.***

schle·miel (shlə mēl′) ***n.*** ⟦Yidd⟧ [Slang] a bungling person who habitually fails or is easily victimized

schlep or **schlepp** (shlep) ***vt.*** **schlepped, schlep′ping** ⟦via Yidd < LowG *slepen,* to drag⟧ [Slang] to carry, haul, etc. —***vi.*** [Slang] to go or move with effort —***n.*** [Slang] an ineffectual person

schlock (shläk) ***n.*** ⟦< ? Ger *schlacke,* dregs⟧ [Slang] anything cheap or inferior; trash —***adj.*** [Slang] cheap; inferior: also **schlock′y, -i·er, -i·est**

schmaltz (shmälts, shmôlts) ***n.*** ⟦? via Yidd < Ger *schmaltz,* rendered fat⟧ [Slang] highly sentimental music, literature, etc.

schmo (shmō) ***n.,*** *pl.* **schmoes** or **schmos** ⟦< Yidd⟧ [Slang] a foolish or stupid person Also sp. **schmoe**

schnapps (shnäps) ***n.,*** *pl.* **schnapps** ⟦Ger, a nip < Du *snaps,* a gulp⟧ a strong alcoholic liquor Also sp. **schnaps**

schnau·zer (shnou′zər) ***n.*** ⟦Ger <

schnauzen, to snarl⟧ a small dog with a wiry coat and bushy eyebrows

schnoz·zle (shnäz'əl) ***n.*** ⟦via Yidd < Ger *schnauze*⟧ [Slang] the nose Also **schnoz**

schol·ar (skäl'ər) ***n.*** ⟦< L *schola*, a school⟧ **1** a learned person **2** a student or pupil —**schol'ar·ly** ***adj.***

schol'ar·ship' ***n.*** **1** the quality of knowledge a student shows **2** the systematized knowledge of a scholar **3** a gift of money, etc. as by a foundation, to help a student

scho·las·tic (skə las'tik) ***adj.*** ⟦see fol.⟧ of schools, colleges, students, etc.; educational; academic

school[1] (sko͞ol) ***n.*** ⟦< Gr *scholē*⟧ **1** a place or institution, with its buildings, etc., for teaching and learning **2** all of its students and teachers **3** a regular session of teaching **4** formal education; schooling **5** a particular division of a university **6** a group following the same beliefs, methods, etc. —***vt.*** **1** to train; teach **2** to discipline or control —***adj.*** of a school or schools

school[2] (sko͞ol) ***n.*** ⟦Du, a crowd⟧ a group of fish, etc. swimming together

school board an elected or appointed group of people in charge of public or private schools

school'book' ***n.*** a textbook

school'boy' ***n.*** a boy attending school —**school'girl'** ***n.fem.***

school'house' ***n.*** a building used as a school

school'ing ***n.*** training or education; esp., formal instruction at school

school'marm' (-'märm', -mäm') ***n.*** **1** [Old-fashioned] a woman schoolteacher **2** [Colloq.] any person who tends to be prudish, pedantic, etc.

school'mas'ter ***n.*** [Old-fashioned] a man who teaches in a school

school'mate' ***n.*** a companion or acquaintance at school

school'mis'tress ***n.*** [Old-fashioned] a woman schoolteacher

school'room' ***n.*** a room in which pupils are taught, as in a school

school'teach'er ***n.*** one who teaches in a school

school'work' ***n.*** lessons worked on in classes or done as homework

school'yard' ***n.*** the ground around a school, used as a playground, etc.

school year the part of a year when school is in session

SCHOONER

schoon·er (sko͞on'ər) ***n.*** ⟦< ?⟧ **1** a ship with two or more masts, rigged fore and aft **2** a large beer glass

Schu·bert (sho͞o'bərt), **Franz** (fränts) 1797-1828; Austrian composer

schuss (sho͝os) ***n.*** ⟦Ger, lit., shot⟧ a straight run down a hill in skiing —***vi.*** to do a schuss

schuss'boom'er (-bo͞om'ər) ***n.*** a skier, esp. one who schusses expertly

schwa (shwä) ***n.*** ⟦Ger < Heb *sheva*⟧ **1** the neutral vowel sound of most unstressed syllables in English, as of *a* in *ago* **2** the symbol (ə) for this

sci·at·ic (sī at'ik) ***adj.*** ⟦see fol.⟧ of or in the hip or its nerves

sci·at·i·ca (sī at'i kə) ***n.*** ⟦< Gr *ischion*, the hip⟧ any painful condition in the hip or thigh; esp., neuritis of the long nerve (**sciatic nerve**) passing down the back of the thigh

sci·ence (sī'əns) ***n.*** ⟦< L *scire*, to know⟧ **1** systematized knowledge derived from observation, study, etc. **2** a branch of knowledge, esp. one that systematizes facts, principles, and methods **3** skill or technique

science fiction highly imaginative fiction typically involving some actual or projected scientific phenomenon

sci·en·tif·ic (sī'ən tif'ik) ***adj.*** **1** of or dealing with science **2** based on, or using, the principles and methods of science; systematic and exact —**sci'en·tif'i·cal·ly** ***adv.***

sci'en·tist ***n.*** a specialist in science, as in biology, chemistry, etc.

sci-fi (sī'fī') ***adj.***, ***n.*** [Colloq.] *short for* SCIENCE FICTION

scim·i·tar (sim'ə tər) ***n.*** ⟦It *scimitarra*⟧ a short, curved sword used chiefly by Turks and Arabs

scin·til·la (sin til'ə) ***n.*** ⟦L⟧ **1** a spark **2** a particle; the least trace

scin·til·late (sint''l āt') ***vi.*** **-lat'ed, -lat'ing** ⟦< L *scintilla*, a spark⟧ **1** to sparkle or twinkle **2** to be brilliant and witty —**scin'til·la'tion** ***n.***

sci·on (sī'ən) ***n.*** ⟦< OFr *cion*⟧ **1** a shoot or bud of a plant, esp. one for grafting **2** a descendant; heir

scis·sor (siz'ər) ***vt.*** ⟦< fol.⟧ to cut, cut off, or cut out with scissors —***n.*** SCISSORS, esp. in adjectival use

scis·sors (siz'ərz) ***n.pl.*** ⟦< LL *cisorium*, cutting tool⟧ [*also with sing. v.*] a cutting instrument with two opposing blades pivoted together so that they can work against each other: also called **pair of scissors**

scle·ra (sklir'ə) ***n.***, *pl.* **-ras** or **-rae** ⟦< Gr *sklēros*, hard⟧ the tough, white, membrane covering all of the eyeball except the area covered by the cornea

scle·ro·sis (skli rō'sis) ***n.***, *pl.* **-ses** (-sēz') ⟦< Gr *sklēros*, hard⟧ an abnormal hardening of body tissues —**scle·rot'ic** (-rät'ik) ***adj.***

scoff (skäf, skôf) ***n.*** ⟦prob. < Scand⟧ an expression of scorn or derision —***vt.***, ***vi.*** to mock or jeer (at) —**scoff'er** ***n.***

scoff'law' ***n.*** [Colloq.] one who flouts traffic laws, liquor laws, etc.

scold (skōld) ***n.*** ⟦< ON *skald*, poet (prob. of satirical verses)⟧ a woman who habitually uses abusive language —***vt.*** to find fault with angrily; to rebuke —***vi.*** **1** to find fault angrily **2** to use abusive language habitually —**scold'ing** ***adj.***, ***n.***

sco·li·o·sis (skō'lē ō'sis) ***n.*** ⟦< Gr *skolios*, crooked⟧ lateral curvature of the spine

sconce (skäns) ***n.*** ⟦ult. < L *absconcus*, hidden⟧ a wall bracket for candles

scone (skōn, skän) ***n.*** ⟦Scot⟧ a light cake, often quadrant-shaped and like a biscuit

scoop (sko͞op) ***n.*** ⟦< MDu *schope*, bailing vessel, *schoppe*, a shovel⟧ 1 any of various small, shovel-like utensils, as for taking up flour, ice cream, etc. 2 the deep shovel of a dredge, etc. 3 the act or motion of scooping 4 the amount scooped up at one time 5 [Colloq.] *a*) advantage gained by being first, as in publishing a news item *b*) such a news item **—*vt.*** 1 to take up or out as with a scoop 2 to hollow (*out*) 3 [Colloq.] to publish news before (a competitor)

scoot (sko͞ot) ***vi., vt.*** ⟦prob. < ON *skjōta*, to shoot⟧ [Colloq.] to hurry (off)

scoot'er ***n.*** ⟦< prec.⟧ 1 a child's two-wheeled vehicle moved by pushing one foot against the ground 2 a similar vehicle propelled by a motor: in full **motor scooter**

scope (skōp) ***n.*** ⟦< Gr *skopos*, watcher⟧ 1 the extent of the mind's grasp 2 the range or extent of action, inclusion, inquiry, etc. 3 room or opportunity for freedom of action or thought

-scope (skōp) ⟦< Gr *skopein* to see⟧ *combining form* an instrument, etc. for seeing or observing [*telescope, kaleidoscope*]

scor·bu·tic (skôr byo͞ot'ik) ***adj.*** ⟦ModL < Russ *skrobotŭ*, wither⟧ of, like, or having scurvy

scorch (skôrch) ***vt.*** ⟦< ? Scand⟧ 1 to burn slightly or superficially 2 to parch by intense heat **—*vi.*** to become scorched **—*n.*** a superficial burn

score (skôr) ***n.*** ⟦< ON *skor*⟧ 1 a scratch, mark, notch, incision, etc. 2 an account or debt 3 a grievance one seeks to settle 4 a reason or motive 5 the number of points made, as in a game 6 a grade, as on a test 7 *a*) twenty people or things *b*) [*pl.*] very many 8 a copy of a musical composition showing all parts for the instruments or voices 9 [Colloq.] the basic facts [*to know the score*] **—*vt.* scored, scor'ing** 1 to mark with notches, cuts, lines, etc. 2 *a*) to make (runs, points, etc.) in a game *b*) to record the score of 3 to achieve [*score a success*] 4 to evaluate, as in testing 5 *Music* to arrange in a score **—*vi.*** 1 to make points, as in a game 2 to keep the score of a game 3 to gain an advantage, a success, etc. **—scor'er *n.***

score'board' ***n.*** a large board posting scores, etc., as in a stadium

score'less ***adj.*** having scored no points

scorn (skôrn) ***n.*** ⟦< OFr *escharnir*, to scorn⟧ extreme, often indignant, contempt **—*vt.*** 1 to regard with scorn 2 to refuse or reject with scorn **—scorn'ful *adj.* —scorn'ful·ly *adv.***

Scor·pi·o (skôr'pē ō') ⟦L, scorpion⟧ the eighth sign of the zodiac

scor'pi·on (-ən) ***n.*** ⟦< Gr *skorpios*⟧ an arachnid with a long tail ending in a poisonous sting

Scot (skät) ***n.*** a native or inhabitant of Scotland

Scot. 1 Scotland 2 Scottish

scotch (skäch) ***vt.*** ⟦prob. < OFr *coche*, a nick⟧ 1 to maim 2 to put an end to; stifle [*to scotch a rumor*]

Scotch (skäch) ***adj.*** of Scotland: cf. SCOTTISH **—*n.*** 1 SCOTTISH 2 [*often* **s-**] whiskey distilled in Scotland from malted barley: in full **Scotch whisky**

Scotch grain a coarse, pebble-grained finish given to heavy leather

Scotch'man (-mən) ***n., pl.* -men** *var. of* SCOTSMAN

Scotch tape ⟦< *Scotch*, a trademark⟧ a thin, transparent adhesive tape

scot-free (skät'frē') ***adj.*** ⟦< earlier *scot*, a tax⟧ unharmed or unpunished

Scot·land (skät'lənd) division of the United Kingdom: the N half of Great Britain: 30,410 sq. mi.; pop. 5,130,000

Scotland Yard the London police headquarters, esp. its detective bureau

Scots (skäts) ***adj., n.*** SCOTTISH

Scots'man (-mən) ***n., pl.* -men** a native or inhabitant of Scotland, esp. a man: *Scotsman* or *Scot* is preferred to *Scotchman* in Scotland **—Scots'wom'an, *pl.* -wom'en, *n.fem.***

Scot·tie or **Scot·ty** (skät'ē) ***n., pl.* -ties** *short for* SCOTTISH TERRIER

Scot·tish (skät'ish) ***adj.*** of Scotland, its people, their English dialect, etc.: *Scottish* is formal usage, but with some words, *Scotch* is used (e.g., tweed, whisky), with others, *Scots* (e.g. law) **—*n.*** the English spoken in Scotland **—the Scottish** the Scottish people

Scottish terrier a short-legged terrier with a wiry coat

scoun·drel (skoun'drəl) ***n.*** ⟦prob. ult. < L *ab(s)-*, from + *condere*, to hide⟧ a mean, immoral, or wicked person

scour[1] (skour) ***vt., vi.*** ⟦< ? L *ex-*, intens. + *cura*, care⟧ 1 to clean by rubbing hard, as with abrasives 2 to clean or clear out as by a flow of water

scour[2] (skour) ***vt.*** ⟦< L *ex-*, out + *currere*, to run⟧ to pass over quickly, or range over, as in search [*to scour a library for a book*]

scourge (skurj) ***n.*** ⟦< L *ex*, off, + *corrigia*, a whip⟧ 1 a whip 2 any cause of serious affliction **—*vt.* scourged, scourg'ing** 1 to whip or flog 2 to punish or afflict severely

scout (skout) ***n.*** ⟦< L *auscultare*, to listen⟧ 1 a person, plane, etc. sent to spy out the enemy's strength, actions, etc. 2 a person sent out to survey a competitor, find new talent, etc. 3 [**S-**] a Boy Scout or Girl Scout **—*vt., vi.*** 1 to reconnoiter 2 to go in search of (something)

scout'ing ***n.*** 1 the act of one who scouts 2 [*often* **S-**] the activities of the Boy Scouts or Girl Scouts

scout'mas'ter ***n.*** the adult leader of a troop of Boy Scouts

scow (skou) ***n.*** ⟦Du *schouw*⟧ a large, flat-bottomed boat used for carrying loads, often towed by a tug

scowl (skoul) ***vi.*** ⟦prob. < Scand⟧ to look angry, sullen, etc., as by contracting the eyebrows **—*n.*** a scowling look **—scowl'er *n.***

scrab·ble (skrab'əl) ***vi.* -bled, -bling** ⟦< Du *schrabben*, to scrape⟧ 1 to scratch, scrape, etc. as though looking for something 2 to struggle

scrag·gly (skrag'lē) ***adj.* -gli·er, -gli·est**

[prob. < ON] uneven, ragged, etc. in growth or form

scram (skram) *vi.* **scrammed, scram′ming** [< fol.] [Slang] to get out

scram·ble (skram′bəl) *vi.* **-bled, -bling** [< ?] 1 to climb, crawl, etc. hurriedly 2 to scuffle or struggle for something —*vt.* 1 to mix haphazardly 2 to stir and cook (slightly beaten eggs) 3 to make (transmitted signals) unintelligible without special receiving equipment —*n.* 1 a hard climb or advance 2 a disorderly struggle, as for something prized

scrap[1] (skrap) *n.* [< ON *skrap*] 1 a small piece; fragment 2 discarded material 3 [*pl.*] bits of food —*adj.* 1 in the form of pieces, leftovers, etc. 2 used and discarded —*vt.* **scrapped, scrap′ping** 1 to make into scrap 2 to discard; junk —**scrap′per** *n.*

scrap[2] (skrap) *n.*, *vi.* **scrapped, scrap′ping** [< ? SCRAPE] [Colloq.] fight or quarrel —**scrap′per** *n.* —**scrap′py, -pi·er, -pi·est,** *adv.*

scrap′book′ *n.* a book in which to mount clippings, pictures, etc.

scrape (skrāp) *vt.* **scraped, scrap′ing** [< ON *skrapa*] 1 to make smooth or clean by rubbing with a tool or abrasive 2 to remove in this way: with *off, out,* etc. 3 to scratch or abrade 4 to gather slowly and with difficulty /to *scrape* up some money/ —*vi.* 1 to rub against something harshly; grate 2 to manage to get by: with *through, along, by* —*n.* 1 a scraping 2 a scraped place 3 a harsh, grating sound 4 a predicament —**scrap′er** *n.*

scrap′heap′ (-hēp′) *n.* a pile of discarded material, as of scrap iron —**throw** (or **toss, cast,** etc.) **on the scrapheap** to get rid of as useless

scratch (skrach) *vt.* [ME *scracchen*] 1 to scrape or cut the surface of slightly 2 to tear or dig with the nails or claws 3 to scrape lightly to relieve itching 4 to scrape with a grating noise 5 to write hurriedly or carelessly 6 to strike out (writing, etc.) 7 *Sports* to withdraw (a contestant, etc.) —*vi.* 1 to use nails or claws in digging, wounding, etc. 2 to scrape —*n.* 1 a scratching 2 a mark, tear, etc. made by scratching 3 a grating or scraping sound —*adj.* used for hasty notes, figuring etc. /*scratch* paper/ —**from scratch** from nothing; without advantage, etc. —**up to scratch** [Colloq.] up to standard —**scratch′y, -i·er, -i·est,** *adj.* —**scratch′i·ly** *adv.* —**scratch′i·ness** *n.*

scrawl (skrôl) *vt., vi.* [< ?] to write or draw hastily, carelessly, etc. —*n.* sprawling, often illegible handwriting

scraw·ny (skrô′nē) *adj.* **-ni·er, -ni·est** [prob. < Scand] very thin; skinny —**scraw′ni·ness** *n.*

scream (skrēm) *vi.* [ME *screamen*] 1 to utter a shrill, piercing cry in fright, pain, etc. 2 to shout, laugh, etc. wildly —*vt.* to utter as with a scream —*n.* 1 a sharp, piercing cry or sound 2 [Colloq.] a very funny person or thing

screech (skrēch) *vi., vt.* [< ON *skraekja*] to utter with a shrill, high-pitched sound —*n.* such a sound —**screech′y, -i·er, -i·est,** *adj.*

screen (skrēn) *n.* [< OFr *escren*] 1 a curtain or partition used to separate, conceal, etc. 2 anything that shields, conceals, etc. /a smoke *screen*/ 3 a coarse mesh of wire, etc., used as a sieve 4 a frame covered with a mesh /a window *screen*/ 5 *a*) a surface on which films, slides, etc. are projected *b*) the film industry *c*) the surface area of a TV set, etc. on which images are formed —*vt.* 1 to conceal or protect, as with a screen 2 to sift through a screen 3 to separate according to skills, etc. 4 to show (a film, etc.) to critics, the public, etc.

screen′play′ *n.* the script from which a film is produced

screen′writ′er *n.* the writer of a script for a film —**screen′writ′ing** *n.*

screw (skrōō) *n.* [< Fr *escroue*, hole in which the screw turns] 1 a cylindrical or conical piece of metal threaded in an advancing spiral, for fastening things by being turned 2 any spiral thing like this 3 anything operating or threaded like a screw, as a screw propeller —*vt.* 1 to twist; turn 2 to fasten, tighten, etc. as with a screw 3 to contort —*vi.* 1 to go together or come apart by being turned like a screw /the lid *screws* on/ 2 to twist or turn —**put the screws on** (or **to**) to subject to great pressure —**screw up** [Slang] to bungle

screw′ball′ *n.* [Slang] an erratic, irrational or unconventional person

screw′driv′er *n.* a tool used for turning screws

screw·worm (skrōō′wurm′) *n.* the larva of an American blowfly that infests wounds, and the nostrils, navel, etc. of animals

screw·y (skrōō′ē) *adj.* **-i·er, -i·est** [Slang] 1 crazy 2 peculiar, eccentric

scrib·ble (skrib′əl) *vt., vi.* **-bled, -bling** [< L *scribere*, write] 1 to write carelessly, hastily, etc. 2 to make meaningless or illegible marks (on) —*n.* scribbled writing

scribe (skrīb) *n.* [< L *scribere*, to write] 1 one who copied manuscripts before the invention of printing 2 a writer

scrim (skrim) *n.* [< ?] 1 a light, sheer, loosely woven cotton or linen cloth 2 such a cloth used as a stage backdrop or semi-transparent curtain

scrim·mage (skrim′ij) *n.* [< SKIRMISH] 1 *Football* the play that follows the snap from center 2 a practice game —*vi.* **-maged, -mag·ing** to take part in a scrimmage

scrimp (skrimp) *vt., vi.* [< ? Scand] to be sparing or frugal (with)

scrim′shaw′ (-shô′) *n.* [< ?] an intricate carving of bone, ivory, etc. done esp. by sailors on long voyages —*vt., vi.* to carve (bones, shells, etc.) in making scrimshaw

scrip (skrip) *n.* [< fol.] a certificate of a right to receive something, as money

script (skript) *n.* [< L *scribere*, to write] 1 handwriting 2 a copy of the text of a play, film etc.

scrip·ture (skrip′chər) *n.* [see prec.] any sacred writing —[**S-**] [*often pl.*] 1 the sacred writings of the Jews: see OLD TESTAMENT 2 the Christian Bible; Old and New Testaments —**scrip′tur·al** *adj.*

script′writ′er *n.* one who writes scripts for films, TV, etc.

scrod (skräd) *n.* [prob. < MDu *schrode*,

strip ⟧ a young codfish or haddock, esp. one prepared for cooking

scrof·u·la (skräf′yə lə) ***n.*** ⟦ < L *scrofa*, a sow ⟧ tuberculosis of the lymphatic glands, esp. of the neck —**scrof′u·lous** ***adj.***

scroll (skrōl) ***n.*** ⟦ < ME *scrowle* ⟧ **1** a roll of parchment, paper, etc., usually with writing on it **2** an ornamental design in coiled or spiral form —***vi.*** to move lines of text, etc. vertically on a video screen

scro·tum (skrōt′əm) ***n.***, *pl.* **-ta** (-ə) or **-tums** ⟦ L ⟧ the pouch of skin holding the testicles

scrounge (skrounj) ***vt.*** **scrounged, scroung′ing** ⟦ < ? ⟧ [Colloq.] **1** to get by begging or sponging; mooch **2** to pilfer —***vi.*** [Colloq.] to seek (*around*) for something —**scroung′er** ***n.***

scroung′y ***adj.*** **-i·er, -i·est** [Slang] shabby, dirty, unkempt, etc. —**scroung′i·ness** ***n.***

scrub[1] (skrub) ***n.*** ⟦ ME, var. of *shrubbe*, shrub ⟧ **1** a thick growth of stunted trees or bushes **2** any person or thing smaller than the usual, or inferior **3** *Sports* a substitute player —***adj.*** small, stunted, inferior, etc. —**scrub′by, -bi·er, -bi·est,** ***adj.***

scrub[2] (skrub) ***vt., vi.*** **scrubbed, scrub′bing** ⟦ prob. < Scand ⟧ **1** to clean or wash by rubbing hard **2** to rub hard —***n.*** a scrubbing

scrub′wom′an ***n.***, *pl.* **-wom′en** CHARWOMAN

scruff (skruf) ***n.*** ⟦ < ON *skrufr*, a tuft of hair ⟧ the nape of the neck

scruff·y (skruf′ē) ***adj.*** **-i·er, -i·est** ⟦ < SCURF + -Y[2] ⟧ shabby; unkempt

scrump·tious (skrump′shəs) ***adj.*** ⟦ < SUMPTUOUS ⟧ [Colloq.] very pleasing, etc., esp. to the taste

scrunch (skrunch) ***vt., vi.*** ⟦ < CRUNCH ⟧ **1** to crunch, crush, etc. **2** to huddle, squeeze, etc. —***n.*** a crunching or crumpling sound

scru·ple (skro͞o′pəl) ***n.*** ⟦ < L *scrupulus*, small stone ⟧ **1** a very small quantity **2** doubt arising from difficulty in deciding what is right, proper, etc. —***vt., vi.*** **-pled, -pling** to hesitate (at) from doubt

scru′pu·lous (-pyə ləs) ***adj.*** **1** having or showing scruples; conscientiously honest **2** careful of details; precise —**scru′pu·los′i·ty** (-läs′ət ē), *pl.* **-ties,** ***n.*** —**scru′pu·lous·ly** ***adv.***

scru·ti·nize (skro͞ot′′n īz′) ***vt.*** **-nized′, -niz′·ing** to examine closely

scru·ti·ny (skro͞ot′′n ē) ***n.***, *pl.* **-nies** ⟦ < L *scrutari*, to examine ⟧ **1** a close examination or watch **2** a lengthy, searching look

scu·ba (sko͞o′bə) ***n.*** ⟦ *s*(*elf*-)*c*(*ontained*) *u*(*nderwater*) *b*(*reathing*) *a*(*pparatus*) ⟧ a diver's equipment with compressed-air tanks for breathing underwater

scud (skud) ***vi.*** **scud′ded, scud′ding** ⟦ prob. < ON ⟧ to move swiftly —***n.*** a scudding

scuff (skuf) ***vt., vi.*** ⟦ prob. < ON *skufa*, to shove ⟧ **1** to wear or get a rough place on the surface (of) **2** to drag (the feet) —***n.*** **1** a worn or rough spot **2** a flat-heeled house slipper with no back upper part

scuf·fle (skuf′əl) ***vi.*** **-fled, -fling** ⟦ < prec. ⟧ **1** to struggle or fight in rough confusion **2** to drag the feet —***n.*** **1** a confused fight **2** a shuffling of feet

scull (skul) ***n.*** ⟦ ME *skulle* ⟧ **1** an oar worked from side to side over the stern of a boat **2** a light row·boat for racing —***vt., vi.*** to propel with a scull

scul·ler·y (skul′ər ē) ***n.***, *pl.* **-ies** ⟦ < L *scutella*, tray ⟧ a room near the kitchen, where pots, pans, etc. are cleaned and stored

scul·lion (skul′yən) ***n.*** ⟦ ult. < L *scopa*, a broom ⟧ [Archaic] a servant doing the rough kitchen work

sculpt (skulpt) ***vt., vi.*** SCULPTURE

sculp·tor (skulp′tər) ***n.*** an artist who creates work of sculpture

sculp·ture (skulp′chər) ***n.*** ⟦ < L *sculpere*, to carve ⟧ **1** the art of shaping stone, clay, wood, etc. into statues, figures, etc. **2** a work or works of sculpture —***vt., vi.*** **-tured, -tur·ing** **1** to cut, carve, chisel, etc. (statues, figures, etc.) **2** to make or form like sculpture —**sculp′tur·al** ***adj.***

scum (skum) ***n.*** ⟦ < MDu *schum* ⟧ **1** a thin layer of impurities on the top of a liquid **2** refuse **3** [Colloq.] despicable people —***vi.*** to become covered with scum —**scum′my, -mi·er, -mi·est,** ***adj.***

scup·per (skup′ər) ***n.*** ⟦ < OFr *escopir*, to spit ⟧ an opening in a ship's side to allow water to run off the deck

scurf (skʉrf) ***n.*** ⟦ < ON ⟧ **1** little, dry scales shed by the skin, as dandruff **2** any scaly coating —**scurf′y, -i·er, -i·est,** ***adj.***

scur·ri·lous (skʉr′ə ləs) ***adj.*** ⟦ < L *scurra*, buffoon ⟧ vulgarly abusive —**scur·ril·i·ty** (skə ril′ə tē), *pl.* **-ties,** ***n.*** —**scur′ri·lous·ly** ***adv.***

scur·ry (skʉr′ē) ***vi.*** **-ried, -ry·ing** ⟦ < ? ⟧ to scamper —***n.*** a scampering

scur·vy (skʉr′vē) ***adj.*** **-vi·er, -vi·est** ⟦ < SCURF ⟧ low; mean —***n.*** a disease resulting from a deficiency of vitamin C, characterized by weakness, anemia, spongy gums, etc. —**scur′vi·ly** ***adv.***

scutch·eon (skuch′ən) ***n.*** *var. of* ESCUTCHEON

scut·tle[1] (skut′′l) ***n.*** ⟦ < L *scutella*, salver ⟧ a bucket for carrying coal

scut·tle[2] (skut′′l) ***vi.*** **-tled, -tling** ⟦ ME *scutlen* ⟧ to scamper —***n.*** a scamper

scut·tle[3] (skut′′l) ***n.*** ⟦ < Sp *escotilla*, an indentation ⟧ an opening fitted with a cover, as in the hull or deck of a ship —***vt.*** **-tled, -tling** to cut holes through the lower hull of (a ship, etc.) to sink it

scut·tle·butt (skut′′l but′) ***n.*** ⟦ < *scuttled butt*, lidded cask ⟧ **1** a drinking fountain on shipboard **2** [Colloq.] rumor

scuz·zy (skuz′ē) ***adj.*** **-zi·er, -zi·est** ⟦ < ? ⟧ [Slang] dirty, shabby, etc.

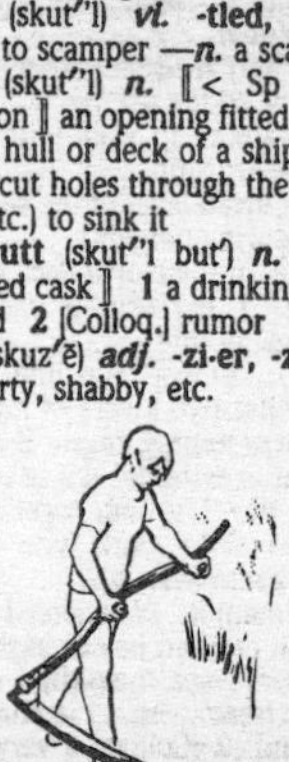

SCYTHE

scythe (sī*th*) ***n.*** ⟦ OE *sithe* ⟧ a tool with a

long, single-edged blade on a long, curved handle, for cutting grass, etc.

SD or **S.D.** South Dakota Also **S.Dak.**

Se *Chem. symbol for* selenium

SE or **S.E.** 1 southeast 2 southeastern

sea (sē) ***n.*** ⟦OE *sæ*⟧ 1 the ocean 2 any of various smaller bodies of salt water /the Red *Sea*/ 3 a large body of fresh water /*Sea* of Galilee/ 4 the state of the surface of the ocean /a calm *sea*/ 5 a heavy wave 6 a very great amount /a *sea* of debt/ **—at sea** 1 on the open sea 2 uncertain; bewildered

sea anemone a sea polyp with a gelatinous body and petal-like tentacles

sea′board′ ***n.*** ⟦SEA + BOARD⟧ land bordering on the sea **—*adj.*** bordering on the sea

sea′coast′ ***n.*** land bordering on the sea

sea cow a large sea mammal with a cigar-shaped body and a blunt snout, as the manatee

sea′far′er (-fer′ər) ***n.*** a sea traveler; esp., a sailor **—sea′far′ing *adj., n.***

sea′food′ ***n.*** food prepared from or consisting of saltwater fish or shellfish

sea′go′ing *adj.* 1 made for use on the open sea 2 SEAFARING

sea gull GULL[1]

sea horse a small, semitropical, plated fish with a head somewhat like that of a horse

seal[1] (sēl) ***n.*** ⟦< L *sigillum*⟧ 1 *a*) a design or initial impressed, often over wax, on a letter or document as a mark of authenticity *b*) a stamp or ring for making such an impression 2 a piece of paper, etc. bearing an impressed design recognized as official 3 something that seals or closes tightly 4 anything that guarantees; pledge 5 an ornamental paper stamp /Easter *seals*/ **—*vt.*** 1 to mark with a seal, as to authenticate or certify 2 to close or shut tight as with a seal 3 to confirm the truth of (a promise, etc.) 4 to decide finally

seal[2] (sēl) ***n.*** ⟦OE *seolh*⟧ 1 a sea mammal with a torpedo-shaped body and four flippers 2 the fur of some seals **—*vi.*** to hunt seals **—seal′er *n.***

seal·ant (sēl′ənt) ***n.*** a substance, as a wax, plastic, etc., used for sealing

sea legs the ability to walk without loss of balance on board ship

sea level the mean level of the sea's surface: used in measuring heights

sea lion a seal of the North Pacific

seal′skin′ ***n.*** 1 the skin of the seal 2 a garment made of this

seam (sēm) ***n.*** ⟦OE⟧ 1 a line formed by sewing together two pieces of material 2 a line that marks joining edges 3 a mark like this, as a scar or wrinkle 4 a stratum of ore, coal, etc. **—*vt.*** 1 to join together so as to form a seam 2 to mark with a seamlike line, etc. **—seam′less *adj.***

sea·man (sē′mən) ***n., pl.* -men** 1 a sailor 2 *U.S. Navy* an enlisted person ranking below a petty officer **—sea′man·ship′ *n.***

seam·stress (sēm′stris) ***n.*** a woman whose occupation is sewing

seam′y *adj.* -i·er, -i·est unpleasant or sordid /the *seamy* side of life/

se·ance (sā′äns) ***n.*** ⟦Fr < L *sedere*, sit⟧ a meeting at which a medium tries to communicate with the dead

sea′plane′ ***n.*** an airplane designed to land on or take off from water

sea′port′ ***n.*** a port or harbor used by ocean ships

sear (sir) ***vt.*** ⟦OE⟧ 1 to wither 2 to burn the surface of 3 to brand

search (surch) ***vt.*** ⟦< LL *circare*, go about⟧ 1 to look through in order to find something 2 to examine (a person) for something concealed 3 to examine carefully; probe **—*vi.*** to make a search **—*n.*** a searching **—in search of** making a search for **—search′er *n.***

search′ing *adj.* 1 examining thoroughly 2 piercing; penetrating

search′light′ ***n.*** 1 an apparatus on a swivel that projects a strong beam of light 2 such a beam

search warrant a legal document authorizing a police search

sea′scape′ (-skāp′) ***n.*** ⟦SEA + (LAND)SCAPE⟧ 1 a view of the sea 2 a drawing, painting, etc. of such a scene

sea′shell′ ***n.*** a saltwater mollusk shell

sea′shore′ ***n.*** land along the sea

sea′sick′ness ***n.*** nausea, dizziness, etc. caused by the rolling of a ship or boat at sea **—sea′sick′ *adj.***

sea′side′ ***n.*** SEASHORE

sea·son (sē′zən) ***n.*** ⟦< VL *satio*, season for sowing⟧ 1 any of the four divisions of the year; spring, summer, fall, or winter 2 the time when something takes place, is popular, permitted, etc. 3 the fitting time **—*vt.*** 1 to make (food) more tasty by adding salt, spices, etc. 2 to add zest to 3 to make more usable, as by aging 4 to make used to; accustom **—*vi.*** to become seasoned

sea′son·a·ble *adj.* 1 suitable to the season 2 opportune; timely

sea′son·al *adj.* of or depending on the season **—sea′son·al·ly *adv.***

sea′son·ing *n.* anything that adds zest; esp., salt, etc. added to food

season ticket a ticket or set of tickets as for a series of concerts, baseball games, etc.

seat (sēt) ***n.*** ⟦ON *sæti*⟧ 1 *a*) a place to sit *b*) a thing to sit on; chair, etc. 2 *a*) the buttocks *b*) the part of a chair, garment, etc. that one sits on 3 the right to sit as a member /a *seat* on the council/ 4 the chief location, or center /the *seat* of government/ **—*vt.*** 1 to set in or on a seat 2 to have seats for /the car *seats* six/ 3 to put or fix in a place, position, etc. **—be seated** to sit down: also **take a seat**

seat belt anchored straps that buckle across the hips, to protect a seated passenger from an abrupt jolt

Se·at·tle (sē at′'l) seaport in west central Wash.: pop. 494,000

sea urchin a small sea animal with a round body in a shell covered with sharp spines

sea′ward (-wərd) ***adj., adv.*** toward the sea Also **sea′wards *adv.***

sea′way′ ***n.*** an inland waterway to the sea for ocean ships

sea′weed′ ***n.*** a sea plant, esp. an alga

sea′wor′thy (-wur′thē) ***adj.*** fit to travel on the sea: said of a ship

se·ba·ceous (sə bā′shəs) ***adj.*** ⟦< L *sebum*,

tallow ⟧ of, like, or secreting fat, etc. /*sebaceous* glands/

seb·or·rhe·a or **seb·or·rhoe·a** (seb′ə rē′ə) ***n.*** ⟦ < L *sebum*, tallow & Gr *rheein*, flow ⟧ excessive discharge from the sebaceous glands causing abnormally oily skin

sec. 1 second(s) 2 secretary 3 section(s)

SEC Securities and Exchange Commission

se·cede (si sēd′) ***vi.*** **-ced′ed, -ced′ing** ⟦ < L *se-*, apart + *cedere*, to go ⟧ to withdraw formally from a group, organization, federation, etc.

se·ces·sion (si sesh′ən) ***n.*** a seceding —[*often* **S-**] the withdrawal of the Southern States from the Federal Union (1860-61) —**se·ces′sion·ist *n.***

se·clude (si klo͞od′) ***vt.*** **-clud′ed, -clud′ing** ⟦ < L *se-*, apart + *claudere*, to close ⟧ to shut off from others; isolate

se·clu·sion (si klo͞o′zhən) ***n.*** a secluding or being secluded; retirement; isolation —**se·clu′sive *adj.***

sec·ond[1] (sek′ənd) ***adj.*** ⟦ < L *sequi*, follow ⟧ 1 coming next after the first; 2d or 2nd 2 another of the same kind; other /a *second* chance/ 3 next below the first in rank, value, etc. —***n.*** 1 one that is second 2 [*pl.*] *a*) an article of merchandise not of first quality *b*) a second helping of food 3 an aide or assistant, as to a boxer 4 the gear next after low gear —***vt.*** 1 to assist 2 to indicate formal support of (a motion) before discussion or a vote —***adv.*** in the second place, group, etc.

sec·ond[2] (sek′ənd) ***n.*** ⟦ < ML (*pars minuta*) *secunda*, second (small part): from being a further division ⟧ 1 $\frac{1}{60}$ of a minute of time or of angular measure 2 a moment; instant

sec·ond·ar·y (sek′ən der′ē) ***adj.*** 1 second in order, rank, importance, place, etc. 2 subordinate; minor 3 derived, not primary; derivative —***n.***, *pl.* **-ar′ies** 1 a secondary person or thing 2 *Football* the defensive backfield —**sec′ond·ar′i·ly *adv.***

secondary school a school, as a high school, coming after elementary school

secondary stress (or **accent**) a weaker stress (′) than the primary stress of a word

sec′ond-class′ ***adj.*** 1 of the class, rank, etc. next below the highest, best, etc. 2 of a cheaper mail class, as for periodicals, etc. 3 inferior, inadequate, etc. —***adv.*** by second-class mail or travel accommodations

sec′ond-guess′ ***vt., vi.*** [Colloq.] to use hindsight in criticizing (someone), remaking (a decision), etc.

sec′ond·hand′ ***adj.*** 1 not from the original source 2 used before; not new 3 of or dealing in used merchandise

second lieutenant *Mil.* a commissioned officer of the lowest rank

sec′ond·ly ***adv.*** in the second place

second nature an acquired habit, etc. deeply fixed in one's nature

second person that form of a pronoun (as *you*) or verb (as *are*) that refers to the person spoken to

sec′ond-rate′ ***adj.*** 1 second in quality, rank, etc. 2 inferior

sec′ond-source′ ***adj.*** of an arrangement whereby one company's products are also manufactured by another company —***vt.*** **-sourced, -sourc′ing** to manufacture (another company's products) under such an arrangement

sec′ond-string′ ***adj.*** [Colloq.] *Sports* that is a substitute player at a specified position —**sec′ond-string′er *n.***

second thought a change in thought after reconsidering —**on second thought** after reconsideration

second wind 1 the return of easy breathing after initial exhaustion, as while running 2 any fresh ability to continue

se·cre·cy (sē′krə sē) ***n.***, *pl.* **-cies** 1 a being secret 2 a tendency to keep things secret

se·cret (sē′krit) ***adj.*** ⟦ < L *se-*, apart + *cernere*, sift ⟧ 1 kept from, or acting without, the knowledge of others 2 beyond general understanding; mysterious 3 concealed from sight; hidden —***n.*** a secret fact, cause, process, etc. —**se′cret·ly *adv.***

sec·re·tar·i·at (sek′rə ter′ē ət) ***n.*** a secretarial staff; specif., an administrative staff, as in a government

sec·re·tar·y (sek′rə ter′ē) ***n.***, *pl.* **-tar′ies** ⟦ < ML *secretarius*, one entrusted with secrets ⟧ 1 one who keeps records, handles correspondence, etc. for an organization or person 2 the head of a government department 3 a writing desk —**sec′re·tar′i·al *adj.***

se·crete (si krēt′) ***vt.*** **-cret′ed, -cret′ing** ⟦ see SECRET ⟧ 1 to hide; conceal 2 to form and release (a substance) as a gland, etc. does

se·cre·tion (si krē′shən) ***n.*** 1 a secreting 2 a substance secreted by an animal or plant

se·cre·tive (sē′krə tiv) ***adj.*** concealing one's thoughts, etc.; not frank or open —**se′cre·tive·ly *adv.*** —**se′cre·tive·ness *n.***

se·cre·to·ry (si krēt′ər ē) ***adj.*** having the function of secreting, as a gland

Secret Service a division of the U.S. Treasury Department for uncovering counterfeiters, guarding the President, etc.

sect (sekt) ***n.*** ⟦ < L *sequi*, follow ⟧ 1 a religious denomination 2 a group of people having a common philosophy, set of beliefs, etc.

sec·tar·i·an (sek ter′ē ən) ***adj.*** 1 of or devoted to some sect 2 narrow-minded —***n.*** a sectarian person —**sec·tar′i·an·ism′ *n.***

sec·tion (sek′shən) ***n.*** ⟦ < L *secare*, to cut ⟧ 1 a cutting apart 2 a part cut off; portion 3 any distinct part, group, etc. 4 a drawing, etc. of a thing as it would appear if cut straight through —***vt.*** to cut into sections

sec′tion·al ***adj.*** 1 of or characteristic of a given section or district 2 made up of sections —**sec′tion·al·ism′ *n.***

sec·tor (sek′tər) ***n.*** ⟦ < L *secare*, to cut ⟧ 1 part of a circle bounded by any two radii and the included arc 2 any of the districts into which an area is divided for military operations

sec·u·lar (sek′yə lər) ***adj.*** ⟦ < LL *saecularis*, worldly ⟧ not religious; not connected with a church —**sec′u·lar·ism′ *n.***

sec′u·lar·ize′ (-lə rīz′) ***vt.*** **-ized′, -iz′ing** to change from religious to civil use or control —**sec′u·lar·i·za′tion *n.***

se·cure (si kyoor′) ***adj.*** ⟦ < L *se-*, free from + *cura*, care ⟧ 1 free from fear, care, etc. 2

free from danger, risk, etc.; safe **3** firm /make the knot *secure*/ —*vt.* **-cured′, -cur′ing 1** to make secure; protect **2** to make certain, as with a pledge **3** to make firm, fast, etc. **4** to obtain —**se·cure′ly** *adv.*

se·cu·ri·ty (si kyoor′ə tē) *n., pl.* **-ties 1** a feeling secure; freedom from fear, doubt, etc. **2** protection; safeguard **3** something given as a pledge of repayment, etc. **4** [*pl.*] bonds, stocks, etc.

secy. or **sec′y.** secretary

se·dan (si dan′) *n.* ⟦< ? L *sedere*, to sit⟧ an enclosed automobile with two or four doors, posts between the front and rear windows, and seats for four to six people

se·date[1] (si dāt′) *adj.* ⟦< L *sedare*, to settle⟧ calm or composed; esp., serious and unemotional —**se·date′ly** *adv.*

se·date[2] (si dāt′) *vt.* **-dat′ed, -dat′ing** to dose with a sedative —**se·da′tion** *n.*

sed·a·tive (sed′ə tiv) *adj.* ⟦see SEDATE[1]⟧ tending to soothe or quiet; lessening excitement, irritation, etc. —*n.* a sedative medicine

sed·en·tar·y (sed″n ter′ē) *adj.* ⟦< L *sedere*, to sit⟧ marked by much sitting

Se·der (sā′dər) *n.* ⟦Heb lit., arrangement⟧ *Judaism* the feast of Passover as observed in the home on the eve of the first (by some also of the second) day of the holiday

sedge (sej) *n.* ⟦OE *secg*⟧ a coarse, grasslike plant growing in wet ground

sed·i·ment (sed′ə mənt) *n.* ⟦< L *sedere*, sit⟧ **1** matter that settles to the bottom of a liquid **2** *Geol.* matter deposited by water or wind

sed′i·men′ta·ry (-men′tər ē) *adj.* **1** of or containing sediment **2** formed by the deposit of sediment, as certain rocks

sed′i·men·ta′tion (-men tā′shən, -men-) *n.* the depositing of sediment

se·di·tion (si dish′ən) *n.* ⟦< L *sed-*, apart + *itio*, a going⟧ a stirring up of rebellion against the government —**se·di′tion·ist** *n.* —**se·di′tious** *adj.*

se·duce (si do͞os′) *vt.* **-duced′, -duc′ing** ⟦< L *se-*, apart + *ducere*, to lead⟧ **1** to tempt to wrongdoing **2** to entice into unlawful sexual intercourse, esp. for the first time —**se·duc′er** *n.* —**se·duc′tion** (-duk′shən) *n.* —**se·duc′tive** *adj.* —**se·duc′tress** (-tris) *n.fem.*

sed·u·lous (sej′o͝o ləs) *adj.* ⟦L *sedulus*⟧ **1** diligent **2** persistent

se·dum (sē′dəm) *n.* ⟦< L⟧ a perennial plant found on rocks or walls, with white, yellow, or pink flowers

see[1] (sē) *vt.* **saw, seen, see′ing** ⟦OE *seon*⟧ **1** to get knowledge of through the eyes; look at **2** to understand **3** to learn; find out **4** to experience **5** to make sure /*see* that he goes/ **6** to escort /*see* her home/ **7** to encounter **8** to call on; consult **9** to receive /too ill to *see* anyone/ —*vi.* **1** to have the power of sight **2** to think /let me *see*, who's next?/ —**see after** to take care of —**see through 1** to perceive the true nature of **2** to finish **3** to help through difficulty —**see to** (or **about**) to attend to

see[2] (sē) *n.* ⟦< L *sedes*, a seat⟧ the official seat or jurisdiction of a bishop

seed (sēd) *n., pl.* **seeds** or **seed** ⟦OE *sæd*⟧ **1** *a*) the part of a plant, containing the embryo, from which a new plant can grow *b*) such seeds collectively **2** the source of anything **3** [Archaic] descendants; posterity **4** sperm or semen —*vt.* **1** to plant with seeds **2** to remove the seeds from **3** to distribute (contestants in a tournament) so that the best players are not matched in early rounds —*vi.* to produce seed —**go** (or **run**) **to seed 1** to shed seeds after flowering **2** to deteriorate, weaken, etc. —**seed′er** *n.* —**seed′less** *adj.*

seed′ling (-liŋ) *n.* **1** a plant grown from a seed **2** a young tree

seed money money to begin a long-term project or get more funds for it

seed vessel any dry, hollow fruit containing seeds Also **seed′case′** *n.*

seed′y *adj.* **-i·er, -i·est 1** full of seed **2** gone to seed **3** shabby, rundown, etc. —**seed′i·ness** *n.*

seek (sēk) *vt.* **sought, seek′ing** ⟦OE *secan*⟧ **1** to try to find; search for **2** to try to get **3** to aim at **4** to try; attempt /to *seek* to please/

seem (sēm) *vi.* ⟦prob. < ON *sœma*, conform to⟧ **1** to appear to be /to *seem* happy/ **2** to appear /*seems* to know/ **3** to have the impression (with an infinitive) /I *seem* to have lost it/

seem′ing *adj.* that seems real, true, etc.; apparent —**seem′ing·ly** *adv.*

seem′ly *adj.* **-li·er, -li·est** suitable, proper, etc. —**seem′li·ness** *n.*

seen (sēn) *vt., vi. pp. of* SEE[1]

seep (sēp) *vi.* ⟦OE *sipian*, to soak⟧ to leak through small openings; ooze —**seep′age** (-ij) *n.*

seer (sir) *n.* one who supposedly foretells the future —**seer′ess** *n.fem.*

seer·suck·er (sir′suk′ər) *n.* ⟦< Pers *shir u shakar*, lit., milk and sugar⟧ a crinkled fabric of linen, cotton, etc.

see·saw (sē′sô′) *n.* ⟦< SAW[1]⟧ **1** a plank balanced at the middle on which children at play, riding the ends, rise and fall alternately **2** any up-and-down or back-and-forth motion or change —*vt., vi.* to move up and down or back and forth

seethe (sēth) *vi.* **seethed, seeth′ing 1** to boil, surge, or bubble **2** to be violently agitated

seg·ment (seg′mənt; *for v.*, -ment) *n.* ⟦< L *secare*, to cut⟧ any of the parts into which something is separated; section —*vt., vi.* to divide into segments —**seg′men·ta′tion** *n.*

seg·re·gate (seg′rə gāt′) *vt.* **-gat′ed, -gat′ing** ⟦< L *se-*, apart + *grex*, a flock⟧ to set apart from others; specif., to impose racial segregation on

seg′re·ga′tion *n.* the policy of compelling racial groups to live apart and use separate schools, facilities, etc. —**seg′re·ga′tion·ist** *n.*

se·gue (seg′wā, sā′gwā) *vi.* **-gued, -gue·ing** ⟦It, (it follows) < L sequi, to follow⟧ to continue without break (*to* or *into* the next part) —*n.* an immediate transition to the next part

sei·gnior (sān′yər, sān yôr′) *n.* ⟦< OFr *seignor* < L *senior*⟧ a feudal lord

seine (sān) *n.* ⟦< Gr *sagēnē*⟧ a large fishing net weighted along the bottom —*vt., vi.*

seined, sein′ing to fish with a seine —**sein′er** *n.*

Seine (sān; *Fr* sen) river in N France, flowing through Paris

seis·mic (sīz′mik) *adj.* ⟦< Gr *seismos,* earthquake⟧ of or caused by an earthquake —**seis′mi·cal·ly** *adv.*

seis′mo·graph′ (-mə graf′) *n.* ⟦see prec. & -GRAPH⟧ an instrument that records the intensity and duration of earthquakes —**seis′mo·graph′ic** *adj.*

seis·mol·o·gy (sīz mäl′ə jē, sīs-) *n.* ⟦see SEISMIC & -LOGY⟧ the science dealing with earthquakes —**seis′mo·log′ic** (-mə läj′ik) or **seis′mo·log′i·cal** *adj.*

seize (sēz) *vt.* **seized, seiz′ing** ⟦< ML *sacire*⟧ 1 *a)* to take legal possession of *b)* to capture; arrest 2 to take forcibly and quickly 3 to grasp suddenly 4 to attack or afflict suddenly /*seized* with pain/ —**sei·zure** (sē′zhər) *n.*

sel·dom (sel′dəm) *adv.* ⟦OE *seldan,* strange⟧ rarely; infrequently

se·lect (sə lekt′) *adj.* ⟦< L *se-,* apart + *legere,* to choose⟧ 1 chosen in preference to others 2 choice; excellent 3 careful in choosing 4 exclusive —*vt., vi.* to choose or pick out —**se·lect′ness** *n.* —**se·lec′tor** *n.*

se·lec′tion (-lek′shən) *n.* 1 a selecting or being selected 2 that or those selected —**se·lec′tive** *adj.* —**se·lec′tiv′i·ty** *n.*

selective service compulsory military service set by age, fitness, etc.

se·lect′man (-mən) *n., pl.* **-men** one of a board of governing officers in most New England towns

se·le·ni·um (sə lē′nē əm) *n.* ⟦ModL < Gr *selēnē,* the moon⟧ a gray, nonmetallic chemical element: used in photoelectric devices

sel·e·nog·ra·phy (sel′ə näg′rə fē) *n.* ⟦< Gr *selēnē,* moon + -GRAPHY⟧ the study of the physical features of the moon —**sel′e·nog′ra·pher** *n.*

self (self) *n., pl.* **selves** ⟦OE⟧ 1 the identity, character, etc. of any person or thing 2 one's own person as distinct from all others 3 one's own welfare or interest —*pron.* [Colloq.] myself, himself, etc. /for *self* and wife/ —*adj.* of the same kind, color, etc. /*self* trim/

self- *prefix* of, by, in, to, or with oneself or itself The following list includes some common compounds formed with *self-* that do not have special meanings:

self-abasement	**self-improvement**
self-advancement	**self-incrimination**
self-appointed	**self-induced**
self-assertion	**self-indulgence**
self-command	**self-indulgent**
self-complacent	**self-inflicted**
self-deceit	**self-knowledge**
self-deception	**self-love**
self-defeating	**self-perpetuating**
self-delusion	**self-pity**
self-destruction	**self-pollination**
self-discipline	**self-preservation**
self-effacement	**self-protection**
self-employed	**self-reproach**
self-examination	**self-sealing**
self-fertilization	**self-support**
self-help	**self-supporting**
self-imposed	**self-sustaining**

self′-ad·dressed′ *adj.* addressed to oneself /a *self-addressed* envelope/

self′-as·sur′ance *n.* confidence in oneself —**self′-as·sured′** *adj.*

self′-cen′tered *adj.* concerned only with one's own affairs; selfish

self′-con·ceit′ *n.* too high an opinion of oneself; vanity

self′-con′fi·dence *n.* confidence in one's own abilities, etc. —**self′-con′fi·dent** *adj.*

self′-con′scious *adj.* unduly conscious of oneself as an object of notice; ill at ease —**self′-con′scious·ly** *adv.* —**self′-con′scious·ness** *n.*

self′-con·tained′ *adj.* 1 keeping one's affairs to oneself 2 showing self-control 3 complete within itself

self′-con′tra·dic′tion *n.* 1 contradiction of oneself or itself 2 any statement containing elements that contradict each other —**self′-con′tra·dic′to·ry** *adj.*

self′-con·trol′ *n.* control of one's own emotions, desires, actions, etc. —**self′-con·trolled′** *adj.*

self′-de·fense′ *n.* defense of oneself or of one's rights, beliefs, actions, etc.

self′-de·ni′al *n.* denial or sacrifice of one's own desires or pleasures

self′-de·struct′ *vi.* DESTRUCT

self′-de·ter′mi·na′tion *n.* 1 determination according to one's own mind; free will 2 the right of a people to choose its own form of government —**self′-de·ter′mined** *adj.*

self′-dis·cov′er·y *n.* a becoming aware of one's true potential, character, motives, etc.

self′-ed′u·cat′ed *adj.* educated by oneself, with little formal schooling

self′-es·teem′ *n.* 1 belief in oneself 2 undue pride in oneself; conceit

self′-ev′i·dent *adj.* evident without need of proof or explanation

self′-ex·plan′a·to′ry *adj.* explaining itself; obvious

self′-ex·pres′sion *n.* expression of one's own personality, esp. in the arts

self′-ful·fill′ing *adj.* 1 bringing about one's personal goals 2 brought about chiefly as an effect of having been expected or predicted

self′-gov′ern·ment *n.* government of a group by the action of its own members —**self′-gov′ern·ing** *adj.*

self′-im′age *n.* one's conception of oneself, one's own abilities, worth, etc.

self′-im·por′tant *adj.* having an exaggerated opinion of one's own importance —**self′-im·por′tance** *n.*

self′-in′ter·est *n.* 1 one's own interest or advantage 2 an exaggerated regard for this

self′ish *adj.* overly concerned with one's own interests, etc. and having little concern for others —**self′ish·ly** *adv.* —**self′ish·ness** *n.*

self′less *adj.* devoted to others' welfare; unselfish —**self′less·ly** *adv.* —**self′less·ness** *n.*

self′-made′ *adj.* 1 made by oneself or itself 2 successful through one's own efforts

self′-pos·ses′sion *n.* full control of one's feelings, actions, etc. —**self′-pos·sessed′** *adj.*

self′-pro·pelled′ *adj.* propelled by its own motor or power

self′-reg′u·lat′ing *adj.* regulating oneself or itself, so as to function automatically or without outside control

self′-re·li′ance *n.* reliance on one's own judgment, abilities, etc. —**self′-re·li′ant** *adj.*

self′-re·spect′ *n.* proper respect for oneself —**self′-re·spect′ing** *adj.*

self′-re·straint′ *n.* restraint imposed on oneself by oneself; self-control

self′-right′eous *adj.* filled with a conviction of being morally superior to others; smugly virtuous —**self′-right′eous·ly** *adv.* —**self′-right′eous·ness** *n.*

self′-sac′ri·fice′ *n.* sacrifice of oneself or one's own interests for the benefit of others —**self′-sac′ri·fic′ing** *adj.*

self′same′ *adj.* identical

self′-sat′is·fied′ *adj.* feeling or showing an often smug satisfaction with oneself —**self′-sat′is·fac′tion** *n.*

self′-seek′er *n.* one who seeks mainly to further his or her own interests —**self′-seek′ing** *n., adj.*

self′-serve′ *adj.* *short for* SELF-SERVICE

self′-serv′ice *n.* the practice of serving oneself in a store, cafeteria, service station, etc.

self′-serv′ing *adj.* serving one's own selfish interests

self′-styled′ *adj.* so called only by oneself

self′-suf·fi′cient *adj.* be able to to get along without help; independent —**self′-suf·fi′cien·cy** *n.*

self′-taught′ *adj.* having taught oneself through one's own efforts

self′-willed′ *adj.* stubborn; obstinate

self′-wind′ing *adj.* wound automatically, as some wristwatches

sell (sel) *vt.* **sold, sell′ing** ⟦OE *sellan*, to give⟧ **1** to exchange (goods, services, etc.) for money, etc. **2** to offer for sale **3** to promote the sale of —*vi.* **1** to engage in selling **2** to be sold (*for* or *at*) **3** to attract buyers —**sell out 1** to get rid of completely by selling **2** [Colloq.] to betray —**sell′er** *n.*

sell′out′ *n.* [Colloq.] **1** a selling out; betrayal **2** a show, game, etc. for which all the seats have been sold

selt·zer (selt′sər) *n.* ⟦< *Niederselters*, Germany⟧ **1** [*often* **S-**] natural, effervescent mineral water **2** any carbonated water, often flavored

sel·vage or **sel·vedge** (sel′vij) *n.* ⟦< SELF + EDGE⟧ a specially woven edge that prevents cloth from raveling

selves (selvz) *n. pl. of* SELF

se·man·tics (sə man′tiks) *n.pl.* ⟦< Gr *sēmainein*, to show⟧ the study of the development and changes of the meanings of words —**se·man′tic** *adj.*

sem·a·phore (sem′ə fôr′) *n.* ⟦< Gr *sēma*, sign + *pherein*, to bear⟧ any apparatus for signaling, as by lights, flags, etc.

sem·blance (sem′bləns) *n.* ⟦< L *similis*, like⟧ **1** outward appearance **2** resemblance **3** a likeness or copy

se·men (sē′mən) *n., pl.* **sem·i·na** (sem′ə nə) or **-mens** ⟦L, seed⟧ the fluid secreted by the male reproductive organs

se·mes·ter (sə mes′tər) *n.* ⟦< L *sex*, six + *mensis*, month⟧ either of the two terms usually making up a school year

sem·i (sem′ī′) *n.* *short for* SEMITRAILER: used loosely for a TRACTOR (sense 2) with an attached semitrailer

semi- ⟦L⟧ *prefix* **1** half **2** partly, not fully **3** twice in a (specified period)

sem·i·an·nu·al (sem′ē an′yo͞o əl) *adj.* **1** happening, coming, etc. every half year **2** lasting half a year

sem′i·au′to·mat′ic *adj.* designating an automatic weapon requiring a trigger pull for each round fired —*n.* a semiautomatic firearm

sem·i·cir·cle (sem′i sur′kəl) *n.* a half circle —**sem′i·cir′cu·lar** (-kyə lər) *adj.*

sem′i·co′lon *n.* a mark of punctuation (;) indicating a degree of separation greater than that marked by the comma

sem′i·con·duc′tor *n.* a substance, as germanium, used as in transistors

sem′i·con′scious *adj.* not fully conscious or awake

sem·i·fi·nal (sem′i fīn′əl; *for n.*, sem′i fīn′əl) *adj.* coming just before the final match, as of a contest —*n.* a semifinal match, etc.

sem·i·month·ly (sem′i munth′lē) *adj.* done, happening, etc. twice a month —*adv.* twice monthly

sem·i·nal (sem′ə nəl) *adj.* ⟦see SEMEN⟧ **1** of seed or semen **2** that is a source **3** of essential importance; specif., *a*) basic; principal *b*) crucial; critical

sem·i·nar (sem′ə när′) *n.* ⟦see fol.⟧ **1** a group of supervised students doing research **2** a course for such a group

sem·i·nar·y (sem′ə ner′ē) *n., pl.* **-nar′ies** ⟦< L *seminarium*, nursery⟧ **1** a school, esp. a private school for young women **2** a school where priests, ministers, or rabbis are trained —**sem′i·nar′i·an** *n.*

Sem·i·nole (sem′ə nōl′) *n., pl.* **-noles′** or **-nole′** a member of an American Indian people of S Florida & Oklahoma

se·mi·ot·ics (sē′mē ät′iks) *n.pl.* ⟦< Gr *sēmeion*, sign⟧ *Philos.* a general theory of signs and symbols; esp., the analysis of signs in language

sem·i·pre·cious (sem′i presh′əs) *adj.* designating gems, as the garnet, turquoise, etc., of lower value than precious stones

sem′i·pri′vate *adj.* of a hospital room with two, three, or sometimes four beds

sem′i·pro·fes′sion·al *n.* one who engages in a sport for pay but not as a regular occupation Also **sem′i·pro′**

sem′i·skilled′ *adj.* of or doing manual work requiring only limited training

Sem·ite (sem′īt′) *n.* ⟦< Heb *Shem*, son of Noah⟧ a member of any of the peoples speaking a Semitic language

Se·mit·ic (sə mit′ik) *adj.* designating or of the Semites or their languages, etc. —*n.* a major group of African and Asian languages, including Hebrew, Arabic, etc.

sem·i·tone (sem′i tōn′) *n.* *Music* the difference in pitch between any two immediately adjacent keys on the piano

sem·i·trail·er (sem′i trāl′ər) *n.* a detachable trailer attached to a coupling at the rear of a TRACTOR (sense 2)

sem′i·trans·par′ent *adj.* not perfectly or completely transparent

sem′i·trop′i·cal *adj.* partly tropical

sem'i·week'ly *adj.* done, happening, etc. twice a week —*adv.* twice weekly
Sen. 1 Senate 2 Senator 3 [*also* s-] senior
sen·ate (sen'it) *n.* ⟦< L *senex*, old⟧ 1 a legislative assembly 2 [S-] the upper house of the U.S. Congress or of most of the State legislatures
sen·a·tor (sen'ət ər) *n.* a member of a senate —**sen·a·to·ri·al** (sen'ə tôr'ē əl) *adj.*
send (send) *vt.* **sent, send'ing** ⟦OE *sendan*⟧ 1 to cause to go or be transmitted; dispatch; transmit 2 to cause (a person) to go 3 to impel; drive 4 to cause to happen, come, etc. 5 [Slang] to thrill —**send for** 1 to summon 2 to place an order for —**send'er** *n.*
send'-off' *n.* [Colloq.] 1 a farewell demonstration for someone starting out on a trip, career, etc. 2 a start given to someone or something
Sen·e·gal (sen'i gôl') country on the W coast of Africa: 75,750 sq. mi.; pop. 6,540,000
se·nile (sē'nīl') *adj.* ⟦< L *senex*, old⟧ 1 of or resulting from old age: now chiefly medical 2 showing the deterioration accompanying old age, esp. confusion, memory loss, etc. —**se·nil·i·ty** (si nil'ə tē) *n.*
sen·ior (sēn'yər) *adj.* ⟦< L *senex*, old⟧ 1 older: written *Sr.* after a father's name if his son's name is the same 2 of higher rank or longer service 3 of or for seniors —*n.* 1 one who is older, of higher rank, etc. 2 a student in the last year of high school or college
senior citizen an elderly person, esp. one who is retired
senior high school high school, usually grades 10, 11, and 12
sen·ior·i·ty (sēn yôr'ə tē) *n., pl.* **-ties** 1 a being senior 2 status, priority, etc. achieved by length of service in a given job
sen·na (sen'ə) *n.* ⟦< Ar *sanā*, cassia plant⟧ the dried leaflets of a tropical cassia plant used, esp. formerly, as a laxative
se·ñor (se nyôr') *n., pl.* ***se·ño'res*** (-nyô'res) ⟦Sp⟧ a man; gentleman: as a title, equivalent to *Mr.* or *Sir*
se·ño·ra (se nyô'rä) *n.* ⟦Sp⟧ a married woman: as a title, equivalent to *Mrs.* or *Madam*
se·ño·ri·ta (se'nyô rē'tä) *n.* ⟦Sp⟧ an unmarried woman or girl: as a title, equivalent to *Miss*
sen·sa·tion (sen sā'shən) *n.* ⟦< L *sensus*, sense⟧ 1 the receiving of sense impressions through hearing, seeing, etc. 2 a conscious sense impression 3 a generalized feeling /a *sensation* of joy/ 4 a feeling of excitement or its cause /the play is a *sensation*/
sen·sa'tion·al *adj.* 1 arousing intense interest 2 intended to shock, thrill, etc. —**sen·sa'tion·al·ism'** *n.*
sense (sens) *n.* ⟦< L *sentire*, to feel⟧ 1 any faculty of receiving impressions through body organs; sight, touch, taste, smell or hearing 2 *a)* feeling, perception, etc. through the senses *b)* a generalized feeling or awareness 3 an ability to understand some quality /a *sense* of humor/ 4 normal intelligence and judgment 5 meaning, as of a word —*vt.* **sensed, sens'ing** 1 to perceive 2 to detect as by sensors —**in a sense** to a limited extent or degree —**make sense** to be intelligible or logical
sense'less *adj.* 1 unconscious 2 stupid; foolish 3 meaningless
sen·si·bil·i·ty (sen'sə bil'ə tē) *n., pl.* **-ties** 1 the capacity for physical sensation 2 [*often pl.*] delicate, sensitive awareness or feelings
sen'si·ble *adj.* 1 that can cause physical sensation 2 easily perceived 3 aware 4 having or showing good sense; wise —**sen'si·bly** *adv.*
sen·si·tive (sen'sə tiv') *adj.* 1 sensory 2 very keenly susceptible to stimuli 3 tender; raw 4 having keen sensibilities 5 easily offended; touchy —**sen'si·tiv'i·ty** or **sen'si·tive·ness** *n.*
sen'si·tize' (-tīz') *vt.* **-tized', -tiz'ing** to make sensitive
sen·sor (sen'sər) *n.* a device to detect, measure, or record physical phenomena, as radiation, heat, etc.
sen·so·ry (sen'sər ē) *adj.* of the senses or sensation
sen·su·al (sen'shoo əl) *adj.* ⟦< L *sensus*, sense⟧ 1 of the body and the senses as distinguished from the intellect 2 connected or preoccupied with sexual pleasure —**sen'su·al'i·ty** (-al'ə tē) *n.* —**sen'su·al·ly** *adv.*
sen·su·ous (sen'shoo əs) *adj.* 1 of, derived from, or perceived by the senses 2 enjoying sensation
sent (sent) *vt., vi. pt. & pp. of* SEND
sen·tence (sen'təns) *n.* ⟦< L *sententia*, opinion⟧ 1 *a)* a decision as of a court; esp., the determination by a court of a punishment *b)* the punishment 2 a group of words stating something, usually containing a subject and predicate —*vt.* **-tenced, -tenc·ing** to pronounce punishment upon (a convicted person)
sen·ten·tious (sen ten'shəs) *adj.* 1 full of, or fond of using, maxims, proverbs, etc. 2 ponderously trite
sen·tient (sen'shənt) *adj.* ⟦see SENSE⟧ of or capable of feeling; conscious
sen·ti·ment (sen'tə mənt) *n.* ⟦see SENSE⟧ 1 a complex combination of feelings and opinions 2 an opinion, etc., often colored by emotion 3 appeal of the emotions, or sensitivity to this 4 maudlin emotion
sen·ti·men·tal (sen'tə ment''l) *adj.* 1 having or showing tender or delicate feelings 2 maudlin; mawkish 3 of or resulting from sentiment —**sen'ti·men'tal·ism'** *n.* —**sen'ti·men'tal·ist** *n.* —**sen'ti·men·tal'i·ty** (-tal'ə tē) *n.* —**sen'ti·men'tal·ly** *adv.*
sen'ti·men'tal·ize' *vi., vt.* **-ized', -iz'ing** to be sentimental or treat in a sentimental way
sen·ti·nel (sen'ti nəl) *n.* ⟦< L *sentire*, to sense⟧ a guard or sentry
sen·try (sen'trē) *n., pl.* **-tries** ⟦< ? obs. *centrinell*, var. of prec.⟧ a sentinel; esp., a soldier posted to guard against danger
Seoul (sōl) capital of South Korea: pop. 9,500,000
se·pal (sē'pəl) *n.* ⟦< Gr *skepē*, a covering + *petalon*, petal⟧ any of the leaflike parts of the calyx
sep·a·ra·ble (sep'ər ə bəl) *adj.* that can be separated —**sep'a·ra·bly** *adv.*

sep·a·rate (sep′ə rāt′; *for adj.*, -ər it) *vt.* **-rat′ed, -rat′ing** ⟦< L *se-*, apart + *parare*, arrange⟧ **1** to set apart into sections, groups, etc.; divide **2** to keep apart by being between —*vi.* **1** to withdraw **2** to part, become disconnected, etc. **3** to go in different directions —*adj.* **1** to set apart from the rest or others **2** not associated or connected with others; distinct **3** not shared /*separate* beds/ —**sep′a·rate·ly** *adv.* —**sep′a·ra′tor** *n.*

sep·a·ra·tion (sep′ə rā′shən) *n.* **1** a separating or being separated **2** the place this occurs; break; division **3** something that separates

sep′a·ra·tism (-ər ə tiz′əm) *n.* the advocacy of separation, racially, politically, etc. —**sep′a·ra·tist** *n.*

se·pi·a (sē′pē ə) *n.*, *adj.* ⟦< Gr *sēpia*, cuttlefish secreting inky fluid⟧ (of) dark reddish-brown

sep·sis (sep′sis) *n.* ⟦see SEPTIC⟧ a poisoning caused by the absorption of pathogenic microorganisms into the blood

Sep·tem·ber (sep tem′bər) *n.* ⟦< L *septem*, seven: seventh month in Rom. calendar⟧ the ninth month of the year, having 30 days: abbrev. **Sept.**

sep·tet or **sep·tette** (sep tet′) *n.* ⟦< L *septem*, seven⟧ *Music* **1** a composition for seven voices or instruments **2** the seven performers of this

sep·tic (sep′tik) *adj.* ⟦< Gr *sēpein*, to make putrid⟧ causing, or resulting from, sepsis or putrefaction

sep·ti·ce·mi·a (sep′tə sē′mē ə) *n.* ⟦see prec.⟧ a disease caused by infectious microorganisms in the blood

septic tank an underground tank in which waste matter is putrefied and decomposed through bacterial action

Sep·tu·a·gint (sep′to͞o ə jint′) ⟦< L *septuaginta*, seventy: in tradition, done in 70 days⟧ a translation into Greek of the Old Testament

sep·tum (sep′təm) *n.*, *pl.* **-tums** or **-ta** (-tə) ⟦< L *saepire*, enclose⟧ *Biol.* a dividing wall or part, as in the nose, a fruit, etc.

sep·ul·cher (sep′əl kər) *n.* ⟦< L *sepelire*, bury⟧ a vault for burial; tomb

se·pul·chral (sə pul′krəl) *adj.* **1** of sepulchers, burial, etc. **2** suggestive of the grave or burial; gloomy **3** deep and melancholy: said of sound

seq. ⟦L *sequentes*⟧ the following

se·quel (sē′kwəl) *n.* ⟦< L *sequi*, follow⟧ **1** something that follows; continuation **2** something coming as a result of something else; aftermath; effect **3** any literary work continuing a story begun in an earlier work

se·quence (sē′kwəns) *n.* ⟦< L *sequi*, follow⟧ **1** *a*) the coming of one thing after another; succession *b*) the order in which this occurs **2** a series **3** a resulting event **4** *Film* a succession of scenes forming a single episode

se·ques·ter (si kwes′tər) *vt.* ⟦< L *sequester*, trustee⟧ **1** to set off or apart **2** to withdraw; seclude —**se·ques·tra·tion** (sē′kwə strā′shən) *n.*

se·quin (sē′kwin) *n.* ⟦Fr; ult. < Ar *sikka*, a stamp⟧ a spangle, esp. one of many sewn on fabric for decoration —**se′quined** or **se′quinned** *adj.*

se·quoi·a (si kwoi′ə) *n.* ⟦after *Sequoyah*, Indian inventor of Cherokee writing⟧ REDWOOD

se·ra (sir′ə) *n. alt. pl. of* SERUM

se·ra·glio (si ral′yō) *n.*, *pl.* **-glios** ⟦< L *sera*, a lock⟧ HAREM (sense 1)

se·ra·pe (sə rä′pē) *n.* ⟦MexSp⟧ a bright-colored woolen blanket used as a garment by men in Mexico, etc.

ser·aph (ser′əf) *n.*, *pl.* **-aphs** or **-a·phim′** (-ə fim′) ⟦< Heb *serafim*, pl.⟧ *Theol.* a heavenly being, or any of the highest order of angels —**se·raph·ic** (sə raf′ik) *adj.* —**se·raph′i·cal·ly** *adv.*

Serb (surb) *n.* a native or inhabitant of Serbia; esp., any of a Slavic people of Serbia —*adj.* SERBIAN

Ser·bi·a (sur′bē ə) constituent republic of Yugoslavia —**Ser′bi·an** *adj.*, *n.*

Ser·bo-Cro·a·tian (sur′bō krō ā′shən) *n.* the major Slavic language of Yugoslavia

sere (sir) *adj.* ⟦var. of SEAR⟧ [Old Poet.] dried up; withered

ser·e·nade (ser′ə nād′) *n.* ⟦ult. < L *serenus*, clear⟧ music played or sung at night, esp. by a lover under his sweetheart's window —*vt.*, *vi.* **-nad′ed, -nad′ing** to play or sing a serenade (to)

ser·en·dip·i·ty (ser′ən dip′ə tē) *n.* ⟦after Pers tale *The Three Princes of Serendip*⟧ a seeming gift for finding good things accidentally —**ser′en·dip′i·tous** *adj.*

se·rene (sə rēn′) *adj.* ⟦L *serenus*⟧ **1** clear; unclouded **2** undisturbed; calm —**se·rene′ly** *adv.* —**se·ren′i·ty** (-ren′ə tē) or **se·rene′ness** *n.*

serf (surf) *n.* ⟦< L *servus*, slave⟧ a person in feudal servitude, bound to his master's land and transferred with it to a new owner —**serf′dom** *n.*

serge (surj) *n.* ⟦< L *sericus*, silken⟧ a strong twilled fabric

ser·geant (sär′jənt) *n.* ⟦< L *servire*, serve⟧ **1** a noncommissioned officer ranking above a corporal **2** a police officer ranking next below a captain or a lieutenant

ser′geant-at-arms′ *n.*, *pl.* **ser′geants-at-arms′** an officer appointed to keep order, as in a court

sergeant major *pl.* **sergeants major** the highest ranking noncommissioned officer

se·ri·al (sir′ē əl) *adj.* ⟦< L *series*, an order⟧ appearing in a series of continuous parts at regular intervals —*n.* a story, etc. presented in serial form —**se′ri·al·i·za′tion** *n.* —**se′ri·al·ize′, -ized′, -iz′ing,** *vt.*

serial number one of a series of numbers given for identification

se·ries (sir′ēz) *n.*, *pl.* **-ries** ⟦L < *serere*, join together⟧ number of similar things or persons arranged in a row or coming one after another

se·ri·ous (sir′ē əs) *adj.* ⟦< L *serius*⟧ **1** earnest, grave, sober, etc. **2** not joking; sincere **3** requiring careful consideration; important **4** dangerous /a *serious* wound/ —**se′ri·ous·ly** *adv.* —**se′ri·ous·ness** *n.*

ser·mon (sur′mən) *n.* ⟦< L *sermo*, discourse⟧ **1** a speech on religion or morals, esp. by a member of the clergy **2** any serious talk on behavior, duty, etc., esp. a tedious one —**ser′mon·ize′**, **-ized′**, **-iz′ing**, *vi.*

Sermon on the Mount the sermon delivered by Jesus to his disciples

se·rous (sir′əs) *adj.* **1** of or containing serum **2** thin and watery

ser·pent (sur′pənt) *n.* ⟦< L *serpere*, to creep⟧ a snake

ser′pen·tine′ (-pən tēn′, -tīn′) *adj.* of or like a serpent; esp., *a*) cunning; treacherous *b*) coiled; winding

ser·rate (ser′āt′) *adj.* ⟦< L *serra*, a saw⟧ having sawlike notches along the edge, as some leaves Also **ser·rat′ed** —**ser·ra′tion** *n.*

ser·ried (ser′ēd) *adj.* ⟦< LL *serare*, to lock⟧ placed close together

se·rum (sir′əm) *n.*, *pl.* **-rums** or **-ra** (-ə) ⟦L, whey⟧ **1** any watery animal fluid, as the yellowish fluid (**blood serum**) separating from a blood clot after coagulation **2** blood serum used as an antitoxin, taken from an animal inoculated for a specific disease

serv·ant (sur′vənt) *n.* ⟦ult. < L *servire*, serve⟧ **1** a person employed by another, esp. to do household duties **2** a person devoted to another or to a cause, creed, etc.

serve (surv) *vt.* **served**, **serv′ing** ⟦< L *servus*, slave⟧ **1** to work for as a servant **2** to do services for; aid; help **3** to do military or naval service for **4** to spend (a term of imprisonment, etc.) /to *serve* ten years/ **5** to provide (customers, etc.) with goods or services **6** to set food, etc. before (a person) **7** to meet the needs of **8** to be used by /one hospital *serves* the city/ **9** to function for /if memory *serves* me well/ **10** to deliver (a summons, etc.) to (someone) **11** to hit (a tennis ball, etc.) in order to start play —*vi.* **1** to work as a servant **2** to do service /to *serve* in the navy/ **3** to carry out the duties of an office **4** to be of service **5** to meet needs **6** to provide guests with food or drink **7** to be favorable: said of weather, etc. —*n.* a serving of the ball in tennis, etc. —**serve someone right** to be what someone deserves —**serv′er** *n.*

serv·ice (sur′vis) *n.* ⟦< L *servus*, slave⟧ **1** the occupation of a servant **2** *a*) public employment /diplomatic *service*/ *b*) a branch of this; specif., the armed forces **3** work done for others /repair *service*/ **4** any religious ceremony **5** *a*) benefit; advantage *b*) [*pl.*] friendly help; also, professional aid **6** the act or manner of serving food **7** a set of articles used in serving /a tea *service*/ **8** a system of providing people with some utility, as water or gas **9** the act or manner of serving in tennis, etc. —*vt.* **-iced**, **-ic·ing** **1** to furnish with a service **2** to make fit for service, as by repairing —**at one's service** **1** ready to serve with one **2** ready for one's use —**in service** functioning —**of service** helpful

serv′ice·a·ble *adj.* **1** that can be of service; useful **2** that will give good service; durable

serv′ice·man′ *n.*, *pl.* **-men′** **1** a member of the armed forces **2** a person whose work is repairing something /a TV *serviceman*/: also **service man**

service mark a word, etc. used like a trademark by a supplier of a service

service station a place selling gasoline, oil, etc., for motor vehicles

ser·vile (sur′vəl, -vīl) *adj.* ⟦< L *servus*, slave⟧ **1** of slaves **2** like that of slaves **3** humbly submissive —**ser·vil·i·ty** (sər vil′ə tē) *n.*

ser·vi·tor (sur′və tər) *n.* a servant

ser·vi·tude (sur′və to͞od′) *n.* ⟦see SERF⟧ **1** slavery or bondage **2** work imposed as punishment for crime

ser·vo (sur′vō) *n.*, *pl.* **-vos** *short for:* **1** SERVOMECHANISM **2** SERVOMOTOR

ser′vo·mech′a·nism *n.* an automatic control system of low power, used to exercise remote but accurate mechanical control

ser′vo·mo′tor *n.* a device, as an electric motor, for changing a small force into a large force, as in a servomechanism

ses·a·me (ses′ə mē′) *n.* ⟦of Semitic origin⟧ **1** a plant whose edible seeds yield an oil **2** its seeds

ses·qui·cen·ten·ni·al (ses′kwi sen ten′ē əl) *adj.* ⟦< L *sesqui-*, more by a half + CENTENNIAL⟧ of a period of 150 years —*n.* a 150th anniversary

ses·sion (sesh′ən) *n.* ⟦< L *sedere*, sit⟧ **1** *a*) the meeting of a court, legislature, etc. *b*) a series of such meetings *c*) the period of these **2** a school term **3** a period of activity of any kind

set (set) *vt.* **set**, **set′ting** ⟦OE *settan*⟧ **1** to cause to sit; seat **2** to put in a specified place, condition, etc. /*set* books on a shelf, *set* slaves free/ **3** to put in a proper condition; fix (a trap for animals), adjust (a clock or dial), arrange (a table for meal), fix (hair) in a desired style, etc., put (a broken bone, etc.) into normal position, etc. **4** to make settled, rigid, or fixed /pectin *sets* jelly/ **5** to mount (gems) **6** to direct **7** to appoint; establish; fix (boundaries, the time for an event, a rule, a quota, etc.) **8** to furnish (an example) for others **9** to fit (words *to* music or music *to* words) **10** to arrange (type) for printing —*vi.* **1** to sit on eggs: said of a fowl **2** to become firm, hard, or fixed /the cement *set*/ **3** to begin to move (*out, forth, off*, etc.) **4** to sink below the horizon /the sun *sets*/ **5** to have a certain direction; tend —*adj.* **1** fixed; established /a *set* time/ **2** intentional **3** fixed; rigid; firm **4** obstinate **5** ready /get *set*/ —*n.* **1** a setting or being set **2** the way in which a thing is set /the *set* of his jaw/ **3** direction; tendency **4** the scenery for a play, etc. **5** a group of persons or things classed or belonging together **6** assembled equipment for radio or TV reception, etc. **7** *Tennis* a group of six or more games won by a margin of at least two —**set about** (or **in** or **to**) to begin —**set down** **1** to put in writing **2** to establish (rules, etc.) —**set forth** **1** to publish **2** to state —**set off** **1** to make prominent or enhance by contrast **2** to make explode —**set on** (or **upon**) to attack —**set up** **1** to erect **2** to establish; found

set′back′ *n.* a reversal in progress

set′screw′ *n.* a screw used in regulating the tension of a spring, etc.

set·tee (se tē′) *n.* **1** a seat or bench with a back **2** a small sofa

set′ter *n.* a long-haired bird dog trained to hunt game

set′ting *n.* **1** the act of one that sets **2** the

position of a dial, etc. that has been set 3 a mounting, as of a gem 4 the time, place, etc., as of a story 5 actual physical surroundings

set·tle (set''l) *vt.* **-tled, -tling** ⟦OE *setl,* a seat⟧ 1 to put in order; arrange /to *settle* one's affairs/ 2 to set in place firmly or comfortably 3 to colonize 4 to cause to sink and become more compact 5 to free (the nerves, etc.) from disturbance 6 to decide (a dispute) 7 to pay (a debt, etc.) —*vi.* 1 to stop moving and stay in one place 2 to descend, as fog over a landscape, or gloom over a person 3 to become localized, as pain 4 to take up permanent residence 5 to sink /the house *settled*/ 6 to become more dense by sinking, as sediment 7 to become more stable 8 to reach an agreement or decision (*with* or *on*) —**set'tler** *n.*

set'tle·ment *n.* 1 a settling or being settled 2 a new colony 3 a village 4 an agreement

set'-to' *n., pl.* **-tos'** (-to͞oz') [Colloq.] 1 a fight 2 an argument

set'up' *n.* 1 *a*) the plan, makeup, etc. of equipment, an organization, etc. *b*) the details of a situation, plan, etc. 2 [Colloq.] a contest, etc. arranged to result in an easy victory

sev·en (sev'ən) *adj., n.* ⟦OE *seofon*⟧ one more than six; 7; VII —**sev'enth** *adj., n.*

sev'en·teen' (-tēn') *adj., n.* seven more than ten; 17; XVII —**sev'en·teenth'** (-tēnth') *adj., n.*

sev'en·teen'-year' locust a cicada which lives underground for 13-17 years before emerging as an adult

seventh heaven perfect happiness

sev·en·ty (sev'ən tē) *adj., n., pl.* **-ties** seven times ten; 70; LXX —**the seventies** the years, from 70 through 79, as of a century —**sev'en·ti·eth** (-ith) *adj., n.*

sev·er (sev'ər) *vt., vi.* ⟦< L *separare*⟧ to separate, divide, or divide off —**sev'er·ance** *n.*

sev·er·al (sev'ər əl) *adj.* ⟦< L *separ*⟧ 1 separate; distinct 2 different; respective 3 more than two but not many; few —*n.* [*with pl. v.*] a small number (*of*) —*pron.* [*with pl. v.*] a few —**sev'er·al·ly** *adv.*

se·vere (sə vir') *adj.* **-ver'er, -ver'est** ⟦< L *severus*⟧ 1 harsh or strict, as in treatment 2 serious, grave, as in expression 3 rigidly accurate or demanding 4 extremely plain /a dress with *severe* lines/ 5 intense /*severe* pain/ 6 rigorous; trying —**se·vere'ly** *adv.* —**se·vere'ness** or **se·ver'i·ty** (-ver'ə tē) *n.*

Se·ville (sə vil') city in SW Spain: pop. 654,000

Sè·vres (sev'rə; *Fr* se'vr') *n.* ⟦after *Sèvres,* SW suburb of Paris, where made⟧ a type of fine French porcelain

sew (sō) *vt., vi.* **sewed, sewn** (sōn) or **sewed, sew'ing** ⟦OE *siwian*⟧ 1 to fasten with stitches made with needle and thread 2 to make, mend, etc. by sewing —**sew up** 1 [Colloq.] to get full control 2 to make sure of success in —**sew'er** *n.*

sew·age (so͞o'ij) *n.* the waste matter carried off by sewers

sew·er (so͞o'ər) *n.* ⟦ult. < L *ex,* out + *aqua,* water⟧ a pipe or drain, usually underground, used to carry off water and waste matter

sew'er·age *n.* 1 a system of sewers 2 SEWAGE

sew·ing (sō'iŋ) *n.* 1 the act of one who sews 2 something to be sewn

sewing machine a machine with a mechanically driven needle used for sewing

sex (seks) *n.* ⟦< L *sexus*⟧ 1 either of two divisions, male or female, into which persons, animals, or plants are divided 2 the character of being male or female 3 the attraction between the sexes 4 sexual intercourse —*adj.* SEXUAL

sex- ⟦< L *sex,* six⟧ *combining form* six

sex·a·ge·nar·i·an (seks'ə ji ner'ē ən) *adj.* ⟦< L⟧ between the ages of 60 and 70 —*n.* a person of this age

sex appeal the physical charm that attracts members of the opposite sex

sex chromosome a sex-determining chromosome in the germ cells: eggs carry an X chromosome and spermatozoa either an X or Y chromosome, with a female resulting from an XX pairing and a male from an XY

sex'ism' *n.* discrimination against people, esp. women, on the basis of sex —**sex'ist** *adj., n.*

SEXTANT

sex·tant (seks'tənt) *n.* ⟦< L *sextans,* a sixth part (of a circle)⟧ an instrument for measuring the angular distance of the sun, a star, etc. from the horizon, as to determine position at sea

sex·tet or **sex·tette** (seks tet') *n.* ⟦< L *sex,* six⟧ 1 a group of six 2 *Music* a composition for six voices or instruments, or the six performers of this

sex·ton (seks'tən) *n.* ⟦ult. < L *sacer,* sacred⟧ a church officer or employee in charge of the maintenance of church property

sex·u·al (sek'sho͞o əl) *adj.* of or involving sex, the sexes, the sex organs, etc. —**sex'u·al·ly** *adv.* —**sex'u·al'i·ty** (-al'ə tē) *n.*

sexual intercourse a joining of the sexual organs of a male and a female human being

sex'y *adj.* **-i·er, -i·est** [Colloq.] exciting or intended to excite sexual desire —**sex'i·ly** *adv.* —**sex'i·ness** *n.*

Sey·chelles (sā shel', -shelz') country on a group of islands in the Indian Ocean, northeast of Madagascar: *c.* 100 sq. mi.; pop. 64,000

sf or **SF** science fiction

Sgt. Sergeant

sh (sh) *interj.* hush! be quiet!

shab·by (shab'ē) *adj.* **-bi·er, -bi·est** ⟦OE *sceabb,* scab⟧ 1 rundown; dilapidated 2 *a*) ragged; worn *b*) wearing worn clothing 3 mean; shameful [shabby behavior] —**shab'bi·ly** *adv.* —**shab'bi·ness** *n.*

shack (shak) *n.* ⟦< ?⟧ a small, crudely built house or cabin; shanty

shack·le (shak'əl) *n.* ⟦OE *sceacel*⟧ 1 a metal fastening, usually in pairs, for the wrist or ankle of a prisoner; fetter 2 anything that restrains freedom, as of expression 3 a device for coupling, etc. —*vt.* **-led, -ling** 1 to put shackles on 2 to restrain in freedom of expression or action

shad (shad) *n., pl.* **shad** or **shads** ⟦OE *sceadd*⟧ an American coastal food fish

shade (shād) *n.* ⟦OE *sceadu*⟧ 1 comparative darkness caused by cutting off rays of light 2 an area with less light than its surroundings 3 degree of darkness of a color 4 *a*) a small difference [*shades* of opinion] *b*) a slight amount or degree 5 [Chiefly Literary] a ghost 6 device used to screen from light [a window *shade*] 7 [*pl.*] [Slang] sunglasses —*vt.* **shad'ed, shad'ing** 1 to screen from light 2 to darken; dim 3 to represent shade in (a painting, etc.) —*vi.* to change slightly or by degrees

shad·ing (shād'iŋ) *n.* 1 a shielding against light 2 the representation of shade in a picture 3 a small variation

shad·ow (shad'ō) *n.* ⟦< OE *sceadu*, shade⟧ 1 (a) shade cast by a body intercepting light rays 2 gloom or that which causes gloom 3 a shaded area in a picture 4 a ghost 5 a remnant; trace —*vt.* 1 to throw a shadow upon 2 to follow closely, esp. in secret —**shad'ow·y** *adj.*

shad'ow·box' *vi.* *Boxing* to spar with an imaginary opponent in training

shad·y (shā'dē) *adj.* **-i·er, -i·est** 1 giving shade 2 shaded; full of shade 3 [Colloq.] of questionable character —**on the shady side of** beyond (a given age) —**shad'i·ness** *n.*

shaft (shaft) *n.* ⟦OE *sceaft*⟧ 1 an arrow or spear, or its stem 2 anything hurled like a missile [*shafts* of wit] 3 a long, slender part or object, as a pillar, either of the poles between which an animal is harnessed to a vehicle, a bar transmitting motion to a mechanical part, etc. 4 a long, narrow passage sunk into the earth 5 a vertical opening passing through a building, as for an elevator —*vt.* [Slang] to cheat, trick, exploit, etc.

shag[1] (shag) *n.* ⟦< OE *sceacga*, rough hair⟧ a heavy, rough nap, as on some cloth

shag[2] (shag) *vt.* **shagged, shag'ging** ⟦< ?⟧ to chase after and retrieve (baseballs hit in batting practice)

shag'gy *adj.* **-gi·er, -gi·est** 1 covered with long, coarse hair or wool 2 unkempt, straggly, etc. 3 having a rough nap

shah (shä) *n.* ⟦Pers *šāh*⟧ the title of former rulers of Iran

shake (shāk) *vt., vi.* **shook, shak'en, shak'ing** ⟦OE *sceacan*⟧ 1 to move quickly up and down, back and forth, etc. 2 to bring, force, mix, etc. by brisk movement 3 to tremble or cause to tremble 4 *a*) to become or cause to become unsteady *b*) to unnerve or become unnerved 5 to clasp (another's hand), as in greeting —*n.* 1 an act of shaking 2 a wood shingle 3 *short for* MILKSHAKE 4 [*pl.*] [Colloq.] a convulsive trembling: usually with *the* —**no great shakes** [Colloq.] not outstanding —**shake down** 1 to cause to fall by shaking 2 [Slang] to extort money from —**shake off** to get rid of

shake'down' *n.* 1 an extortion of money, as by blackmail 2 a thorough search —*adj.* for testing new equipment, etc. [a *shakedown* cruise]

shake'out' *n.* a drop in economic activity that eliminates unprofitable businesses, etc.

shak'er *n.* 1 a person or thing that shakes 2 a device used in shaking 3 [S-] a member of a religious sect that lived in celibate communities in the U.S.

Shake·speare (shāk'spir), **William** 1564-1616; Eng. poet & dramatist —**Shake·spear'e·an** or **Shake·spear'i·an** *adj., n.*

shake'-up' *n.* a shaking up; specif., an extensive reorganization

shak'y *adj.* **-i·er, -i·est** 1 not firm; weak or unsteady 2 *a*) trembling *b*) nervous 3 not reliable; questionable —**shak'i·ness** *n.*

shale (shāl) *n.* ⟦< OE *scealu*, shell⟧ a rock formed of hard clay: it splits easily into thin layers

shale oil oil distilled from a hard shale containing veins of a greasy organic solid

shall (shal) *v.aux. pt.* **should** ⟦OE *sceal*⟧ 1 used in the first person to indicate simple future time 2 used in the second or third person, esp. in formal speech or writing, to express determination, compulsion, obligation, or necessity See usage note at WILL[2]

shal·lot (shə lät') *n.* ⟦< OFr *eschaloigne*, scallion⟧ 1 a small onion whose clustered bulbs are used for flavoring 2 GREEN ONION

shal·low (shal'ō) *adj.* ⟦ME *shalow*⟧ 1 not deep 2 lacking depth of character, intellect, etc. —*n.* [*usually pl., often with sing. v.*] a shoal

shalt (shalt) *archaic 2d pers. sing., pres. indic., of* SHALL: used with *thou*

sham (sham) *n.* ⟦< ? shame⟧ something false or fake; person or thing that is a fraud —*adj.* false or fake —*vt., vi.* **shammed, sham'ming** to pretend; feign

sham·ble (sham'bəl) *vi.* **-bled, -bling** ⟦< obs. use in "shamble legs," bench legs⟧ to walk clumsily; shuffle —*n.* a shambling walk

sham'bles (-bəlz) *n.pl.* ⟦ME *schamel*, butcher's bench; ult. < L⟧ [*with sing. v.*] 1 a slaughterhouse 2 a scene of great slaughter, destruction, or disorder

shame (shām) *n.* ⟦OE *scamu*⟧ 1 a painful feeling of guilt for improper behavior, etc. 2 dishonor or disgrace 3 something regrettable or outrageous —*vt.* **shamed, sham'ing** 1 to cause to feel shame 2 to dishonor or disgrace 3 to force by a sense of shame —**put to shame** 1 to cause to feel shame 2 to surpass —**shame'ful** *adj.* —**shame'ful·ly** *adv.* —**shame'ful·ness** *n.*

shame'faced' *adj.* showing shame; ashamed

shame'less *adj.* having or showing no shame, modesty, or decency; brazen

sham·poo (sham po͞o') *vt.* **-pooed', -poo'ing** ⟦Hindi *chāmpnā*, to press⟧ 1 to wash (the hair) 2 to wash (a rug, sofa, etc.) —*n.* 1 a shampooing 2 a liquid soap, etc. used for this

sham·rock (sham′räk′) ***n.*** ⟦Ir *seamar*, clover⟧ a cloverlike plant with leaflets in groups of three: the emblem of Ireland

shang·hai (shaŋ′hī′, shaŋ hī′) ***vt.*** ⟦< such kidnapping for crews on the China run⟧ to kidnap, usually by drugging, for service aboard ship

Shang·hai (shaŋ′hī′) seaport in E China: pop. *c.* 6,270,000 (met. area 12,000,000)

shank (shaŋk) ***n.*** ⟦OE *scanca*⟧ **1** the part of the leg between the knee and ankle in humans, or a corresponding part in animals **2** the whole leg **3** the part between the handle and the working part (of a tool, etc.) **—shank of the evening** early evening

shan't (shant) shall not

shan·tung (shan′tuŋ′) ***n.*** ⟦after *Shantung*, Chin province⟧ a silk or silky fabric with an uneven surface

shan·ty (shan′tē) ***n.***, *pl.* **-ties** ⟦< CdnFr *chantier*, workshop⟧ a small, shabby dwelling; shack; hut

shape (shāp) ***n.*** ⟦< OE (*ge*)*sceap*, a form⟧ **1** that quality of a thing which depends on the relative position of all the points on its surface; physical form **2** the contour of the body **3** definite or regular form /to begin to take *shape*/ **4** [Colloq.] physical condition **—*vt.* shaped, shap′ing 1** to give definite shape to **2** to arrange, express, etc. (a plan, etc.) in definite form **3** to adapt /*shaped* to our needs/ **—shape up** [Colloq.] to develop to a definite or satisfactory form, etc. **—take shape** to begin to have definite form **—shape′less *adj.* —shape′less·ness *n.***

shape′ly *adj.* -li·er, -li·est having a pleasing figure: used esp. of a woman

shard (shärd) ***n.*** ⟦OE *sceard*⟧ a broken piece, esp. of pottery

share[1] (sher) ***n.*** ⟦OE *scearu*⟧ **1** a portion that belongs to an individual **2** any of the equal parts of capital stock of a corporation **—*vt.* shared, shar′ing 1** to distribute in shares **2** to receive, use, etc. in common with others **—*vi.*** to have a share (*in*)

share[2] (sher) ***n.*** ⟦OE *scear*⟧ a plowshare

share′crop′ *vi.*, *vt.* -cropped′, -crop′ping to work (land) for a share of the crop **—share′crop′per *n.***

share′hold′er *n.* a person who owns shares of stock in a corporation

shark[1] (shärk) ***n.*** ⟦prob. < Ger *schurke*, scoundrel⟧ **1** a swindler **2** [Slang] an expert in a given activity

GREAT WHITE SHARK

shark[2] (shärk) ***n.*** ⟦< ?⟧ a large, predatory sea fish with a tough, gray skin

shark′skin′ *n.* a smooth, silky cloth of cotton, rayon, etc.

sharp (shärp) ***adj.*** ⟦OE *scearp*⟧ **1** having a fine edge or point for cutting or piercing **2** having a point or edge; not rounded **3** not gradual; abrupt **4** clearly defined; distinct /a *sharp* contrast/ **5** quick in perception; clever **6** attentive; vigilant **7** crafty; underhanded **8** harsh; severe /a *sharp* temper/ **9** violent, as an attack **10** brisk; active **11** intense, as a pain **12** pungent **13** nippy, as a wind **14** [Slang] smartly dressed **15** *Music* above the true pitch **—*adv.* 1** in a sharp manner; specif., *a*) abruptly or briskly *b*) attentively or alertly *c*) *Music* above the true pitch **2** precisely /one o'clock *sharp*/ **—*n.* 1** [Colloq.] an expert or adept **2** *Music a*) a tone one half step above another *b*) the symbol (♯) for such a note **—*vt.*, *vi.*** *Music* to make or become sharp **—sharp′ly *adv.* —sharp′ness *n.***

sharp′en *vt.*, *vi.* to make or become sharp **—sharp′en·er *n.***

sharp′er *n.* a swindler or cheat

sharp′-eyed′ *adj.* having keen sight or perception Also **sharp′-sight′ed *adj.***

sharp·ie (shär′pē) ***n.*** [Colloq.] a shrewd, cunning person, esp. a sharper

sharp′shoot′er *n.* a good marksman

sharp′-tongued′ *adj.* using sharp or harshly critical language

sharp′-wit′ted (-wit′id) ***adj.*** thinking quickly and effectively

shat·ter (shat′ər) ***vt.*** ⟦ME *schateren*, scatter⟧ **1** to break or burst into pieces suddenly with a blow **2** to damage or be damaged severely

shat′ter·proof′ *adj.* that will resist shattering

shave (shāv) ***vt.* shaved, shaved** or **shav′en, shav′ing** ⟦OE *sceafan*⟧ **1** to cut away thin slices or sections from **2** *a*) to cut off (hair) at the surface of the skin *b*) to cut the hair to the surface of (the face, etc.) *c*) to cut the beard of (a person) **3** to barely touch in passing; graze **—*vi.*** to cut off a beard with a razor, etc. **—*n.*** the act or an instance of shaving

shav′er *n.* 1 a person who shaves **2** an instrument used in shaving, esp. one with electrically operated cutters **3** [Colloq.] a boy; lad

shav·ing (shā′viŋ) ***n.* 1** the act of one who shaves **2** a thin piece of wood, metal, etc. shaved off

Shaw (shô), **George Ber·nard** (bər närd′, bʉr′nərd) 1856-1950; Brit. dramatist & critic, born in Ireland **—Sha·vi·an** (shā′vē ən) ***adj.*, *n.***

shawl (shôl) ***n.*** ⟦prob. < Pers *shāl*⟧ an oblong or square cloth worn as a covering for the head or shoulders

shay (shā) ***n.*** ⟦< CHAISE, assumed as pl.⟧ [Dial.] a light carriage; chaise

she (shē) ***pron.***, *pl. see* THEY ⟦< OE *seo*⟧ the woman, girl, or female animal previously mentioned **—*n.*, *pl.* shes** a woman, girl, or female animal

sheaf (shēf) ***n.***, *pl.* **sheaves** ⟦OE *sceaf*⟧ **1** a bundle of cut stalks of grain, etc. **2** a collection, as of papers, bound in a bundle

shear (shir) ***vt.* sheared, sheared** or **shorn, shear′ing** ⟦OE *scieran*⟧ **1** to cut as with shears **2** to clip (hair) from (the head), (wool) from (sheep), etc. **3** to divest (someone) *of* a power, etc. **—*n.*** a shearing **—shear′er *n.***

shears *n.pl.* 1 large scissors **2** a large tool or machine with two opposed blades, used to cut metal, etc.

sheath (shēth) *n., pl.* **sheaths** (shēthz, shēths) ⟦OE *sceath*⟧ 1 a case for the blade of a knife, sword, etc. 2 a covering resembling this 3 a woman's closefitting dress
sheathe (shēth) *vt.* **sheathed, sheath′ing** 1 to put into a sheath 2 to enclose in a case or covering
sheath·ing (shē′thiŋ) *n.* something that sheathes, as boards, etc. forming the base for roofing or siding
she·bang (shə baŋ′) *n.* [Colloq.] an affair, business, contrivance, etc. Chiefly in **the whole shebang**
shed[1] (shed) *n.* ⟦OE *scead*⟧ a small structure for shelter or storage
shed[2] (shed) *vt.* **shed, shed′ding** ⟦< OE *sceadan*, to separate⟧ 1 to pour out 2 to cause to flow /to *shed* tears/ 3 to radiate /to *shed* confidence/ 4 to cause to flow off /oilskin *sheds* water/ 5 to cast off or lose (a natural growth, as hair, etc.) —*vi.* to shed hair, etc. —**shed blood** to kill violently
sheen (shēn) *n.* ⟦< OE *sciene*, beautiful⟧ brightness; luster —**sheen′y, -i·er, -i·est,** *adj.*
sheep (shēp) *n., pl.* **sheep** ⟦< OE *sceap*⟧ 1 a cud-chewing mammal related to the goats, with heavy wool and edible flesh called mutton 2 one who is meek, timid, submissive, etc.
sheep dog a dog trained to herd sheep
sheep′fold′ *n.* a pen or enclosure for sheep Also **sheep′cote′** (-kōt′) *n.*
sheep′ish *adj.* 1 embarrassed or chagrined 2 shy or bashful —**sheep′ish·ly** *adv.* —**sheep′ish·ness** *n.*
sheep′skin′ *n.* 1 the skin of a sheep 2 parchment or leather made from it 3 [Colloq.] a diploma
sheer[1] (shir) *vi., vt.* ⟦var. of SHEAR⟧ to turn aside or cause to turn aside from a course; swerve
sheer[2] (shir) *adj.* ⟦< ON *skærr*, bright⟧ 1 very thin; transparent: said of textiles 2 absolute; utter /*sheer* folly/ 3 extremely steep —*adv.* 1 completely; utterly 2 very steeply
sheet[1] (shēt) *n.* ⟦OE *sceat*⟧ 1 a large piece of cotton, linen, etc., used on a bed 2 *a*) a single piece of paper *b*) [Colloq.] a newspaper 3 a broad, continuous surface or expanse, as of flame, ice, etc. 4 a broad, thin piece of any material, as glass, plywood, metal, etc.
sheet[2] (shēt) *n.* ⟦short for OE *sceatline*⟧ a rope for controlling the set of a sail
sheet′ing *n.* 1 cotton or linen material used for making sheets 2 material used to cover or line a surface /copper *sheeting*/
sheet metal metal rolled thin in the form of a sheet
sheet music music printed on unbound sheets of paper
sheik or **sheikh** (shēk, *also* shāk) *n.* ⟦Ar *shaikh*, lit., old man⟧ the chief of an Arab family, tribe, or village
shek·el (shek′əl) *n.* ⟦Heb < *shakal*, weigh⟧ 1 a gold or silver coin of the ancient Hebrews 2 the monetary unit of Israel 3 [*pl.*] [Slang] money
shelf (shelf) *n., pl.* **shelves** ⟦prob. < MLowG *schelf*⟧ 1 a thin, flat board fixed horizontally to a wall, used for holding things 2 something like a shelf; specif., *a*) a ledge *b*) a sandbar —**on the shelf** out of use, activity, etc.
shell (shel) *n.* ⟦OE *sciel*⟧ 1 a hard outer covering, as of a turtle, egg, nut, etc. 2 something like a shell in being hollow, empty, a covering, etc. 3 a light, narrow racing boat rowed by a team 4 an explosive artillery projectile 5 a small-arms cartridge —*vt.* 1 to remove the shell or covering from /to *shell* peas/ 2 to bombard with shells from a large gun —**shell out** [Colloq.] to pay out (money)
shel·lac or **shel·lack** (shə lak′) *n.* ⟦< SHELL & LAC⟧ 1 a resin usually produced in thin, flaky layers or shells 2 a thin varnish containing this resin and alcohol —*vt.* **-lacked′, -lack′ing** 1 to apply shellac to 2 [Slang] *a*) to beat *b*) to defeat decisively
-shelled (sheld) *combining form* having a (specified kind of) shell
Shel·ley (shel′ē) 1 **Mary Woll·stone·craft** (wool′stən kraft′) 1797-1851; Eng. novelist: second wife of Percy 2 **Per·cy Bysshe** (pur′sē bish) 1792-1822; Eng. poet
shell′fire′ *n.* the firing of artillery shells
shell′fish′ *n., pl.* **-fish′** or (for different species) **-fish′es** any aquatic animal, esp. an edible one, with a shell, as the clam, lobster, etc.
shel·ter (shel′tər) *n.* ⟦< ? OE *scield*, shield + *truma*, a troop⟧ 1 something that protects, as from the elements, danger, etc. 2 a being covered, protected, etc.; refuge —*vt.* to provide shelter for; protect —*vi.* to find shelter
shelve (shelv) *vt.* **shelved, shelv′ing** 1 to equip with shelves 2 to put on a shelf 3 to put aside; defer
shelves (shelvz) *n. pl. of* SHELF
shelv·ing (shel′viŋ) *n.* 1 material for shelves 2 shelves collectively
she·nan·i·gan (shi nan′i gən) *n.* ⟦altered < ? Ir *sionnachuighim*, I play the fox⟧ [*usually pl.*] [Colloq.] trickery; mischief
Shen·yang (shun′yäŋ′) city in NE China: pop. 4,020,000
shep·herd (shep′ərd) *n.* ⟦see SHEEP & HERD⟧ 1 one who herds sheep 2 a clergyman —*vt.* to herd, lead, etc. as a shepherd —**shep′herd·ess** *n.fem.*
sher·bet (shur′bət) *n.* ⟦< Ar *sharba*(*t*), a drink⟧ a frozen dessert like an ice but with gelatin and, often, milk added: also, erroneously, **sher′bert** (-burt)
sher·iff (sher′if) *n.* ⟦< OE *scir*, shire + *gerefa*, chief officer⟧ the chief law-enforcement officer of a county
Sher·pa (shur′pə, sher′-) *n. pl.* **-pas** or **-pa** any of a Tibetan people of Nepal, famous as mountain climbers
sher·ry (sher′ē) *n., pl.* **-ries** ⟦after *Jerez*, Spain⟧ 1 a yellow or brown Spanish fortified wine 2 any similar wine
shib·bo·leth (shib′ə leth′, -ləth) *n.* ⟦< Heb *shibolet*, a stream⟧ 1 *Bible* the test word used to distinguish the enemy: Judg. 12:4-6 2 any phrase, custom, etc. peculiar to a certain party, class, etc.
shied (shīd) *vi., vt. pt. & pp. of* SHY[1], SHY[2]
shield (shēld) *n.* ⟦OE *scield*⟧ 1 a flat piece of metal, etc. worn on the forearm to ward

off blows, etc. **2** one that guards, protects, etc. **3** anything shaped like a shield **—*vt., vi.*** to defend; protect

SHIELD

shift (shift) ***vt.*** ⟦OE *sciftan,* divide⟧ **1** to move from one person or place to another **2** to replace by another or others **3** to change the arrangement of (gears) **—*vi.*** **1** to change position, direction, etc. **2** to get along /to *shift* for oneself/ **—*n.*** **1** a shifting; transfer **2** a plan of conduct, esp. for an emergency **3** an evasion; trick **4** a gearshift **5** *a*) a group of people working in relay with another *b*) their regular work period **— make shift** to manage (*with* the means at hand)
shift′less ***adj.*** incapable, inefficient, lazy, etc. **—shift′less·ness *n.***
shift′y ***adj.*** **-i·er, -i·est** of a tricky or deceitful nature; evasive **—shift′i·ly *adv.* — shift′i·ness *n.***
Shih Tzu (shē′ dzōō′) *pl.* **Shih Tzus** or **Shih Tzu** ⟦Mandarin *shihtzu,* lion⟧ a small dog with long, silky hair and short legs
shill (shil) ***n.*** [Slang] a confederate of a gambler, auctioneer, etc. who pretends to bet, bid, etc. so as to lure others **—*vi.*** [Slang] to act as a shill
shil·le·lagh or **shil·la·lah** (shi lā′lē, -lə) ***n.*** ⟦after *Shillelagh,* Ir village⟧ a cudgel
shil·ling (shil′iŋ) ***n.*** ⟦OE *scylling*⟧ a former British monetary unit and coin, equal to $\frac{1}{20}$ of a pound
shil·ly-shal·ly (shil′ē shal′ē) ***vi.*** **-lied, -ly·ing** ⟦< *shall I?*⟧ to vacillate, esp. over trifles
shim (shim) ***n.*** ⟦< ?⟧ a thin, wedge of wood, metal, etc. used as for filling space
shim·mer (shim′ər) ***vi.*** ⟦OE *scymrian*⟧ to shine with an unsteady light; glimmer **—*n.*** a shimmering light
shim·my (shim′ē) ***n.*** ⟦< a jazz dance < CHEMISE⟧ a marked vibration or wobble, as in a car's front wheels **—*vi.*** **-mied, -my·ing** to vibrate or wobble
shin (shin) ***n.*** ⟦OE *scinu*⟧ the front part of the leg between the knee and the ankle **—*vt., vi.*** **shinned, shin′ning** to climb (a pole, etc.) by gripping with hands and legs: also **shin′ny**
shin′bone′ ***n.*** TIBIA
shin·dig (shin′dig′) ***n.*** ⟦< old colloq. *shindy,* commotion⟧ [Colloq.] a dance, party, or other informal gathering
shine (shīn) ***vi.*** **shone** or, esp. for vt. 2, **shined, shin′ing** ⟦OE *scinan*⟧ **1** to emit or reflect light **2** to stand out; excel **3** to exhibit itself clearly /love *shining* from her face/ **—*vt.*** **1** to direct the light of **2** to make shiny by polishing /to *shine* shoes/ **—*n.*** **1** brightness; light **2** luster; gloss
shin′er (-ər) ***n.*** [Slang] BLACK EYE
shin·gle (shiŋ′gəl) ***n.*** ⟦OE *scindel*⟧ **1** a thin, wedge-shaped piece of wood, slate, etc. laid with others in overlapping rows, as for roofs **2** a short haircut, tapered at the nape **3** a small signboard, as of a doctor **—*vt.*** **-gled, -gling** to cover (a roof, etc.) with shingles
shin·gles (shiŋ′gəlz) ***n.*** ⟦< L *cingere,* to gird⟧ *nontechnical name for* HERPES ZOSTER
shin′guard′ ***n.*** a padded guard worn to protect the shins in some sports
shin′splints′ ***n.pl.*** ⟦< SHIN & SPLINT, growth on bone of a horse's leg⟧ [*with sing. v.*] painful strain of muscles of the lower leg
Shin·to (shin′tō) ***n.*** ⟦Jpn < Chin *shen,* god + *tō, dō,* way⟧ a religion of Japan, emphasizing ancestor worship
shin·y (shīn′ē) ***adj.*** **-i·er, -i·est** **1** bright; shining **2** highly polished **—shin′i·ness *n.***
ship (ship) ***n.*** ⟦OE *scip*⟧ **1** any large vessel navigating deep water **2** a ship's officers and crew **3** an aircraft **—*vt.*** **shipped, ship′ping** **1** to put or take on board a ship **2** to send or transport by any carrier /to *ship* coal by rail/ **3** to take in (water) over the side in a heavy sea **4** to put (an object) in place on a vessel /*ship* the oars/ **—*vi.*** to go aboard ship; embark **—[S-]** the constellation Argo **—ship′per *n.***
-ship (ship) ⟦OE *-scipe*⟧ *suffix* **1** the quality or state of being /*friendship*/ **2** *a*) the rank or office of /*professorship*/ *b*) one having the rank of /*lordship*/ **3** skill as /*leadership*/ **4** all persons (of a specified group) collectively /*readership*/
ship′board′ ***n.*** a ship: chiefly in **on shipboard,** aboard a ship
ship′build′er ***n.*** one whose business is building ships **—ship′build′ing *n.***
ship′mate′ ***n.*** a fellow sailor
ship′ment ***n.*** **1** the shipping of goods **2** goods shipped
ship′ping ***n.*** **1** the act or business of transporting goods **2** ships collectively, as of a nation, port, etc.
shipping clerk an employee who prepares goods for shipment, and keeps records of shipments made
ship′shape′ ***adj.*** having everything neatly in place; trim
ship′wreck′ ***n.*** **1** the remains of a wrecked ship **2** the loss of a ship through storm, etc. **3** ruin; failure **—*vt.*** to cause to undergo shipwreck
ship′yard′ ***n.*** a place where ships are built and repaired
shire (shīr) ***n.*** ⟦OE *scir,* office⟧ in England, a county
shirk (shurk) ***vt., vi.*** ⟦< ?⟧ to neglect or evade (a duty, etc.) **—shirk′er *n.***
Shirley Temple ⟦after *Shirley Temple,* child movie star⟧ a nonalcoholic drink made like a cocktail
shirr (shur) ***n.*** ⟦< ?⟧ SHIRRING **—*vt.*** **1** to make shirring in (cloth) **2** to bake (eggs) in buttered dishes
shirr′ing ***n.*** a gathering made in cloth by drawing the material up on parallel rows of short stiches
shirt (shurt) ***n.*** ⟦OE *scyrte*⟧ **1** a garment worn on the upper part of the body, usually with a collar and a buttoned front **2** an undershirt **—keep one's shirt on** [Slang] to remain patient or calm
shirt′tail′ ***n.*** the part of a shirt extending below the waist
shirt′waist′ ***n.*** a woman's blouse tailored like a shirt
shish ke·bab (shish′ kə bäb′) ⟦< Ar *shish,*

skewer + *kabāb*, kebab]] a dish of kebabs, esp. lamb, stuck on a skewer, often with vegetables, and broiled

shiv (shiv) ***n.*** [[prob. < Romany *chiv*, blade]] [Slang] a knife

shiv·er[1] (shiv′ər) ***n.*** [[ME *schievere*]] a fragment or splinter —***vt.***, ***vi.*** to break into fragments or splinters

shiv·er[2] (shiv′ər) ***vi.*** [[< ? OE *ceafl*, jaw]] to shake or tremble, as from fear or cold —***n.*** a shaking, trembling, etc. —**shiv′er·y** ***adj.***

shlep or **shlepp** (shlep) ***n.*** *alt. sp. of* SCHLEP

shmaltz (shmôlts, shmälts) ***n.*** [Slang] *alt. sp. of* SCHMALTZ

shoal[1] (shōl) ***n.*** [[OE *scolu*]] **1** a large group; crowd **2** a school of fish

shoal[2] (shōl) ***n.*** [[< OE *sceald*, shallow]] **1** a shallow place in a river, sea, etc. **2** a sand bar forming a shallow place

shoat (shōt) ***n.*** [[ME *schote*]] a young, weaned pig

shock[1] (shäk) ***n.*** [[< MFr *choquer*, to collide]] **1** a sudden, powerful blow, shake, etc. **2** *a*) a sudden emotional disturbance *b*) the cause of this **3** an extreme stimulation of the nerves by the passage of electric current through the body **4** [Colloq.] *short for* SHOCK ABSORBER **5** a disorder of the blood circulation produced by hemorrhage, disturbance of heart function, etc. —***vt.*** **1** to astonish, horrify, etc. **2** to produce electrical shock in

shock[2] (shäk) ***n.*** [[ME *schokke*]] bundles of grain stacked together

shock[3] (shäk) ***n.*** [[< ? prec.]] a thick, bushy or tangled mass, as of hair

shock absorber a device, as on a motor vehicle, that absorbs the force of bumps and jarring

shock′er ***n.*** **1** anything that shocks **2** a sensational story, play, etc.

shock′ing ***adj.*** **1** causing great surprise and distress **2** disgusting

shock′proof′ ***adj.*** able to absorb shock without being damaged

shock therapy the treatment of certain mental disorders by using electricity, drugs, etc., producing convulsions or coma

shock troops troops trained to lead an attack

shod (shäd) ***vt.*** *alt. pt. & pp. of* SHOE

shod·dy (shäd′ē) ***n.***, *pl.* **shod′dies** [[< ?]] **1** an inferior woolen cloth made from used fabrics **2** anything worth less than it seems to be —***adj.*** **-di·er, -di·est 1** made of inferior material **2** poorly done or made **3** sham —**shod′di·ly** ***adv.*** —**shod′di·ness** ***n.***

shoe (sho͞o) ***n.*** [[OE *sceoh*]] **1** an outer covering for the foot **2** a horseshoe **3** the part of a brake that presses against a wheel —***vt.*** **shod** or **shoed, shoe′ing** to furnish with shoes —**fill one's shoes** to take one's place

shoe′horn′ ***n.*** an implement used to help slip one's heel into a shoe —***vt.*** to force or squeeze into a narrow space

shoe′lace′ ***n.*** a length of cord, etc. used for lacing and fastening a shoe

shoe′mak′er ***n.*** one whose business is making or repairing shoes

shoe′shine′ ***n.*** the cleaning and polishing of a pair of shoes

shoe′string′ ***n.*** **1** a shoelace **2** a small amount of capital /a business started on a shoestring/ —***adj.*** at or near the ankles /a *shoestring* catch/

shoe tree a form inserted in a shoe to stretch it or preserve its shape

sho·gun (shō′gun′) ***n.*** [[< Chin *chiang-chun*]] any of the hereditary governors of Japan who, until 1867, were absolute rulers —**sho′gun·ate** (-gə nit) ***n.***

shone (shōn) ***vi.***, ***vt.*** *alt. pt. & pp. of* SHINE

shoo (sho͞o) ***interj.*** go away! get out! —***vt.*** **shooed, shoo′ing** to drive away, as by crying "shoo"

shoo′-in′ ***n.*** [Colloq.] one expected to win easily in a race, etc.

shook (sho͝ok) ***vt.***, ***vi.*** *pt. and dial. pp. of* SHAKE —**shook up** [Slang] upset; agitated

shoot (sho͞ot) ***vt.*** **shot, shoot′ing** [[OE *sceotan*]] **1** to move swiftly over, by, etc. /to *shoot* the rapids/ **2** to variegate (*with* another color, etc.) **3** to thrust or put forth **4** to discharge or fire (a bullet, arrow, etc.) **5** to send forth swiftly or with force **6** to hit, wound, etc. with a bullet, arrow, etc. **7** to photograph **8** *Sports a*) to throw or drive (a ball, etc.) toward the objective *b*) to score (a goal, points, etc.) —***vi.*** **1** to move swiftly **2** to be felt suddenly, as pain **3** to grow rapidly **4** to jut out **5** to send forth a missile; discharge bullets, etc. **6** to use guns, etc. as in hunting —***n.*** **1** a shooting trip, contest, etc. **2** a new growth; sprout —**shoot at** (or **for**) [Colloq.] to strive for —**shoot′er** ***n.***

shooting star METEOR

shoot′out′ or **shoot′-out′** ***n.*** a battle with handguns, etc., as between police and criminals

shop (shäp) ***n.*** [[OE *sceoppa*, booth]] **1** a place where certain things are offered for sale; esp., a small store **2** a place where a particular kind of work is done —***vi.*** **shopped, shop′ping** to visit shops to examine or buy goods —**talk shop** to discuss one's work

shop′keep′er ***n.*** one who owns or operates a shop, or small store

shop′lift′er ***n.*** one who steals articles from a store during shopping hours —**shop′lift′** ***vt.***, ***vi.***

shoppe (shäp) ***n.*** *old sp. of* SHOP (*n.* 1): now used only in shop names

shop′per ***n.*** **1** one who shops **2** one hired by a store to shop for others **3** one hired by a store to compare competitors' prices, etc.

shopping center a complex of stores, restaurants, etc. with a common parking area

shop′talk′ ***n.*** **1** the specialized words and idioms of those in the same work **2** talk about work, esp. after hours

shop′worn′ ***adj.*** soiled, faded, etc. from having been displayed in a shop

shore[1] (shôr) ***n.*** [[ME *schore*]] land at the edge of a body of water

shore[2] (shôr) ***n.*** [[ME *schore*]] a prop, beam, etc. used for support, etc. —***vt.*** **shored, shor′ing** to support as with shores; prop (*up*)

shore′line′ ***n.*** the edge of a body of water

shore patrol a detail of the U.S. Navy, Coast Guard, or Marine Corps acting as military police on shore

shorn (shôrn) ***vt., vi.*** *alt. pp. of* SHEAR

short (shôrt) ***adj.*** ⟦OE *scort*⟧ 1 not measuring much from end to end in space or time 2 not great in range or scope 3 not tall 4 brief; concise 5 not retentive /a *short* memory/ 6 curt; abrupt 7 less than a sufficient or correct amount 8 crisp or flaky, as pastry rich in shortening 9 designating a sale of securities, etc. which the seller does not yet own but expects to buy later at a lower price —***n.*** 1 something short 2 [*pl.*] *a*) short trousers *b*) a man's undergarment like these 3 SHORTSTOP 4 SHORT CIRCUIT —***adv.*** 1 abruptly; suddenly 2 briefly; concisely 3 so as to be short in length —***vt., vi.*** 1 to give less than what is needed or usual 2 SHORTCHANGE 3 SHORT-CIRCUIT —**in short** briefly —**run short** to have less than enough —**short of** less than or lacking —**short′ness** ***n.***

short′age (-ij) ***n.*** a deficiency in the amount needed or expected; deficit

short′bread′ ***n.*** a rich, crumbly cake or cookie made with much shortening

short′cake′ ***n.*** a light biscuit or a sweet cake served with fruit, etc.

short′change′ ***vt., vi.*** **-changed′, -chang′ing** [Colloq.] to give less money than is due in change

short circuit 1 a connection between two points in an electric circuit, resulting in a side circuit that deflects current or in excessive current flow causing damage 2 popularly, a disrupted electric circuit caused by this —**short′-cir′cuit** ***vt., vi.***

short′com′ing ***n.*** a defect or deficiency

short′cut′ ***n.*** 1 a shorter route 2 any way of saving time, effort, etc.

short′en ***vt., vi.*** to make or become short or shorter

short·en·ing (shôrt′'n iŋ, -niŋ) ***n.*** edible fat used to make pastry, etc. crisp or flaky

short′fall′ ***n.*** a falling short, or the amount of the shortage

short′hand′ ***n.*** any system of speed writing using symbols for words

short′-hand′ed ***adj.*** short of workers

short′horn′ ***n.*** any of a breed of cattle with short, inward-curving horns

short′-lived′ (-līvd′, -livd′) ***adj.*** having a short life span or existence

short′ly ***adv.*** 1 briefly 2 soon 3 abruptly and rudely; curtly

short order any food that can be cooked or served quickly when ordered

short′-range′ ***adj.*** reaching over a short distance or period of time

short ribs the rib ends of beef from the forequarter

short shrift very little care or attention —**make short shrift of** to dispose of quickly and impatiently

short′sight′ed ***adj.*** 1 NEARSIGHTED 2 lacking in foresight —**short′sight′ed·ly** ***adv.*** —**short′sight′ed·ness** ***n.***

short′-spo′ken ***adj.*** using few words, esp. to the point of rudeness; curt

short′stop′ ***n.*** *Baseball* the infielder between second and third base

short story a piece of prose fiction shorter than a short novel

short subject a short film, as that shown with a film feature

short′-tem′pered ***adj.*** easily or quickly angered

short′-term′ ***adj.*** for or extending over a short time

short ton 2,000 pounds: see TON

short′-waist′ed (-wās′tid) ***adj.*** unusually short between shoulders and waistline

short′wave′ ***n.*** a radio wave 60 meters or less in length

short′-wind′ed (-win′did) ***adj.*** easily put out of breath by exertion

shot[1] (shät) ***n.*** ⟦OE *sceot*⟧ 1 the act of shooting 2 range; scope 3 an attempt or try 4 a pointed, critical remark 5 the path of an object thrown, etc. 6 *a*) a projectile for a gun *b*) projectiles collectively 7 small pellets of lead or steel for a shotgun 8 the heavy metal ball used in the shot put 9 a marksman 10 a photograph or a continuous film sequence 11 a hypodermic injection, as of vaccine 12 a drink of liquor —**call the shots** to direct or control what is done

shot[2] (shät) ***vt., vi.*** *pt. & pp. of* SHOOT —***adj.*** [Colloq.] ruined or worn out

shot′gun′ ***n.*** 1 a gun for firing a charge of shot at short range 2 *Football* a formation in which the quarterback stands several yards behind the line of scrimmage to receive the ball

shot put a contest in which a heavy metal ball is propelled with an overhand thrust from the shoulder —**shot′-put′ter** ***n.*** —**shot′-put′ting** ***n.***

should (shood) ***v.aux.*** ⟦OE *sceolde*⟧ 1 *pt. of* SHALL 2 used to express: *a*) obligation, duty, etc. /you *should* help/ *b*) expectation or probability /he *should* be here soon/ *c*) a future condition /if I *should* die tomorrow/

shoul·der (shōl′dər) ***n.*** ⟦OE *sculdor*⟧ 1 *a*) the joint connecting the arm or forelimb with the body *b*) the part of the body including this joint 2 [*pl.*] the two shoulders and the part of the back between them 3 a shoulderlike projection 4 the land along the edge of a paved road —***vt.*** 1 to push along or through, as with the shoulder 2 to carry upon the shoulder 3 to assume the burden of —**straight from the shoulder** without reserve; frankly — **turn** (or **give**) **a cold shoulder to** to snub or shun

shoulder blade either of the two flat bones in the upper back

shoulder harness an anchored strap passing across the chest, used with a seat belt, as in a car

shout (shout) ***n.*** ⟦ME *schoute*⟧ a loud cry or call —***vt., vi.*** to utter or cry out in a shout —**shout′er** ***n.***

shove (shuv) ***vt., vi.*** **shoved, shov′ing** ⟦OE *scufan*⟧ 1 to push, as along a surface 2 to push roughly —***n.*** a push —**shove off** 1 to push (a boat) away from shore 2 [Colloq.] to leave

shov·el (shuv′əl) ***n.*** ⟦OE *scofl*⟧ a tool with a broad scoop or blade and a long handle, for lifting and moving loose material —***vt.*** **-eled** or **-elled, -el·ing** or **-el·ling** 1 to move with a shovel 2 to dig out with a shovel

shov′el·ful′ ***n.***, *pl.* **-fuls′** as much as a shovel will hold

show (shō) ***vt.*** **showed, shown** or **showed, show'ing** ⟦< OE *sceawian*⟧ **1** to bring or put in sight **2** to guide; conduct **3** to point out **4** to reveal, as by behavior **5** to prove; demonstrate **6** to bestow (favor, mercy, etc.) **—*vi.*** **1** to be or become seen; appear **2** to be noticeable **3** to finish third or better in a horse race **—*n.*** **1** a showing or demonstration **2** pompous display **3** pretense /sorrow that was mere *show*/ **4** a public display or exhibition **5** a presentation of entertainment **—show off** to make a display of, esp. a vain display **—show up 1** to expose **2** to be seen **3** to arrive

show'boat' ***n.*** a boat with a theater and actors who play river towns

show'case' ***n.*** a glass-enclosed case for displaying things, as in a store **—*vt.*** **-cased', -cas'ing** to display to good advantage

show'down' ***n.*** [Colloq.] an action that brings matters to a climax

show·er (shou'ər) ***n.*** ⟦OE *scur*⟧ **1** a brief fall of rain, sleet, etc. **2** a sudden, abundant fall, as of sparks **3** a party at which gifts are presented to the guest of honor **4** a bath in which the body is sprayed from overhead with fine streams of water **—*vt.*** **1** to spray with water, etc. **2** to pour forth as in a shower **—*vi.*** **1** to fall or come as a shower **2** to bathe under a shower **—show'er·y** ***adj.***

show'ing ***n.*** **1** a bringing to view or notice; exhibition **2** a performance, appearance, etc. /a good *showing* in the contest/

show·man (shō'mən) ***n.***, *pl.* **-men 1** one whose business is producing shows **2** a person skilled at presenting anything in a striking manner **—show'man·ship'** ***n.***

shown (shōn) ***vt.***, ***vi.*** *alt. pp. of* SHOW

show'off' ***n.*** one who shows off

show of hands a raising of hands, as in voting or volunteering

show'piece' ***n.*** **1** something displayed or exhibited **2** something that is a fine example of its kind

show'place' ***n.*** **1** a place displayed to the public for its beauty, etc. **2** any beautiful place

show'room' ***n.*** a room where merchandise is displayed for advertising or sale

show window a store window in which merchandise is displayed

show'y ***adj.*** **-i·er, -i·est 1** of striking appearance **2** attracting attention in a gaudy way **—show'i·ness** ***n.***

shpt. shipment

shrank (shraŋk) ***vt.***, ***vi.*** *alt. pt. of* SHRINK

shrap·nel (shrap'nəl) ***n.*** ⟦after Gen. *Shrapnel* (1761-1842), its Brit inventor⟧ **1** an artillery shell filled with an explosive charge and small metal balls **2** these balls **3** any fragments scattered by an exploding shell, bomb, etc.

shred (shred) ***n.*** ⟦OE *screade*⟧ **1** a narrow strip cut, torn off, etc. **2** a fragment **—*vt.*** **shred'ded** or **shred, shred'ding** to cut or tear into shreds **—shred'da·ble** ***adj.*** **—shred'der** ***n.***

Shreve·port (shrēv'pôrt') city in NW La.: pop. 206,000

shrew (shrōō) ***n.*** ⟦< OE *screawa*⟧ **1** a small, mouselike mammal with a long snout **2** a nagging, evil-tempered woman **—shrew'ish** ***adj.***

shrewd (shrōōd) ***adj.*** ⟦see prec.⟧ clever or sharp in practical affairs; astute **—shrewd'ly** ***adv.*** **—shrewd'ness** ***n.***

shriek (shrēk) ***vi.***, ***vt.*** ⟦ME *schriken*⟧ to make or utter with a loud, piercing cry; screech **—*n.*** such a cry

shrift (shrift) ***n.*** ⟦ult. < L *scribere*, write⟧ [Archaic] confession to and absolution by a priest See also SHORT SHRIFT

shrike (shrīk) ***n.*** ⟦OE *scric*⟧ a shrill-voiced bird of prey with a hooked beak

shrill (shril) ***adj.*** ⟦echoic⟧ producing a high, thin, piercing sound **—*vi.***, ***vt.*** to utter (with) a shrill sound **—shril'ly** ***adv.*** **—shrill'ness** ***n.***

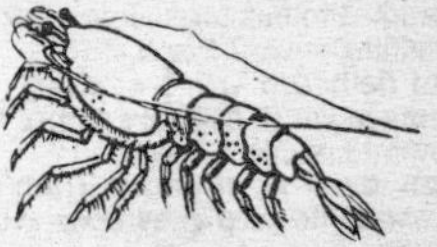

SHRIMP

shrimp (shrimp) ***n.*** ⟦OE *scrimman*, shrink⟧ **1** a small, long-tailed crustacean, valued as food **2** [Colloq.] a small or insignificant person

shrine (shrīn) ***n.*** ⟦< L *scrinium*, box⟧ **1** a container holding sacred relics **2** a saint's tomb **3** a place of worship **4** any hallowed place

shrink (shriŋk) ***vi.*** **shrank** or **shrunk, shrunk** or **shrunk'en, shrink'ing** ⟦OE *scrincan*⟧ **1** to contract, as from heat, cold, moisture, etc. **2** to lessen, as in amount **3** to draw back; flinch **—*vt.*** to make shrink **—shrink'a·ble** ***adj.***

shrink'age ***n.*** **1** a shrinking **2** the amount of shrinking

shrinking violet a very shy person

shrink'-wrap' *vt.* **-wrapped', -wrap'ping** to wrap in a plastic material shrunk by heating to fit tightly **—*n.*** a wrapping of such material

shrive (shrīv) ***vt.*** **shrived** or **shrove, shriv·en** (shriv'ən) or **shrived, shriv'ing** ⟦OE *scrifan*⟧ [Archaic] to hear the confession of and absolve

shriv·el (shriv'əl) ***vt.***, ***vi.*** **-eled** or **-elled, -el·ing** or **-el·ling** ⟦prob. < Scand⟧ to shrink and wrinkle or wither

shroud (shroud) ***n.*** ⟦OE *scrud*⟧ **1** a cloth used to wrap a corpse for burial **2** something that covers, veils, etc. **3** any of the ropes from a ship's side to a masthead **—*vt.*** to hide; cover

Shrove Tuesday ⟦see SHRIVE⟧ the last day before Lent

shrub (shrub) ***n.*** ⟦OE *scrybb*, brushwood⟧ a low, woody plant with several stems; bush **—shrub'by** ***adj.***

shrub'ber·y (-ər ē) ***n.*** shrubs collectively

shrug (shrug) ***vt.***, ***vi.*** **shrugged, shrug'ging** ⟦ME *schruggen*⟧ to draw up (the shoulders), as in indifference, doubt, etc. **—*n.*** the gesture so made

shrunk (shruŋk) ***vi.***, ***vt.*** *alt. pt. & pp. of* SHRINK

shrunk'en *vi.*, *vt. alt. pp. of* SHRINK —*adj.* contracted in size; shriveled

shtg. shortage

shtick (shtik) *n.* ⟦Yidd⟧ a comic bit or special gimmick

shuck (shuk) *n.* ⟦< ?⟧ a shell, pod, or husk —*vt.* to remove shucks from

shucks (shuks) *interj.* ⟦prob. < prec.⟧ an exclamation of disappointment, embarrassment, etc.

shud·der (shud'ər) *vi.* ⟦ME *schoderen*⟧ to shake or tremble, as in horror —*n.* a shuddering

shuf·fle (shuf'əl) *vt.*, *vi.* **-fled, -fling** ⟦prob. < LowG *schuffeln*⟧ **1** to move (the feet) with a dragging gait **2** to mix (playing cards) **3** to mix together in a jumble —*n.* a shuffling —**shuf'fler** *n.*

shuf'fle·board' *n.* ⟦< *shovel board*⟧ a game in which disks are pushed with a cue toward numbered squares

shun (shun) *vt.* **shunned, shun'ning** ⟦OE *scunian*⟧ to keep away from; avoid scrupulously

shunt (shunt) *vt.*, *vi.* ⟦ME *schunten*⟧ **1** to move or turn to one side **2** to switch, as a train, from one track to another —*n.* **1** a shunting **2** a railroad switch **3** a surgically created channel allowing flow from one organ, etc. to another

shush (shush) *interj.* ⟦echoic⟧ hush! be quiet! —*vt.* to say "shush" to

shut (shut) *vt.* **shut, shut'ting** ⟦OE *scyttan*⟧ **1** to move (a door, lid, etc.) so as to close (an opening, container, etc.) **2** *a)* to prevent entrance to or exit from *b)* to confine *in* a room, etc. **3** to bring together the parts of (an umbrella, book, etc.) —*vi.* to be or become shut —*adj.* closed, fastened, etc. —**shut down** to cease or cause to cease operating —**shut off** to prevent passage of or through —**shut out** **1** to deny entrance to **2** to prevent from scoring —**shut up** **1** to confine **2** [Colloq.] to stop or make stop talking

shut'down' *n.* a stoppage of work or activity, as in a factory

shut'-eye' *n.* [Slang] sleep

shut'-in' *adj.* confined indoors by illness —*n.* an invalid who is shut-in

shut'out' *n.* a preventing of the opposing team from scoring in a game

shut·ter (shut'ər) *n.* **1** a person or thing that shuts **2** a movable cover for a window **3** a device for opening and closing the aperture of a camera lens —*vt.* to close or furnish with a shutter

shut·tle (shut''l) *n.* ⟦< OE *scytel*, missile⟧ **1** a device that carries thread back and forth, as in weaving **2** *a)* a traveling back and forth over a short route *b)* an airplane, bus, etc. used in a shuttle —*vt.*, *vi.* **-tled, -tling** to move back and forth rapidly

shut'tle·cock' (-käk') *n.* a rounded piece of cork having a flat end stuck with feathers: used in badminton

shy[1] (shī) *adj.* **shy'er** or **shi'er, shy'est** or **shi'est** ⟦OE *sceoh*⟧ **1** easily frightened; timid **2** not at ease with others; bashful **3** distrustful; wary **4** [Slang] lacking —*vi.* **shied, shy'ing** **1** to move suddenly as when startled **2** to be or become cautious, etc. —**shy'ly** *adv.* —**shy'ness** *n.*

shy[2] (shī) *vt.*, *vi.* **shied, shy'ing** ⟦< ?⟧ to fling, esp. sideways

shy·ster (shī'stər) *n.* ⟦prob. < Ger *scheisser*, one who defecates⟧ [Slang] a lawyer who uses unethical or tricky methods

Si *Chem. symbol for* silicon

Si·am (sī am') *old name of* THAILAND

Si·a·mese (sī'ə mēz') *n.*, *pl.* **-mese'** **1** *old name for* THAI **2** a domestic cat with blue eyes and a light-colored coat —*adj. old name for* THAI

Siamese twins ⟦after such a pair born in Siam⟧ any pair of twins born with bodies joined together

Si·ber·i·a (sī bir'ē ə) region in N Asia, between the Urals & the Pacific: Asiatic section of the R.S.F.S.R. —**Si·ber'i·an** *adj.*, *n.*

sib·i·lant (sib'əl ənt) *adj.* ⟦< L *sibilare*, to hiss⟧ having or making a hissing sound —*n.* a sibilant consonant, as (s) or (z) —**sib'i·late'** (-āt'), **-lat'ed, -lat'ing,** *vt.*, *vi.*

sib·ling (sib'liŋ) *n.* ⟦< OE *sib*, kinsman + -LING⟧ a brother or sister

sib·yl (sib'əl) *n.* ⟦< Gr *sibylla*⟧ a prophetess of ancient Greece or Rome —**sib'yl·line'** (-īn', -ēn') *adj.*

sic (sik) *vt.* **sicked, sick'ing** ⟦< SEEK⟧ to incite (a dog) to attack

sic (sik, sēk) *adv.* ⟦L⟧ thus; so: used within brackets, [*sic*], to show that a quoted passage, esp. one containing an error, is precisely reproduced

Sic·i·ly (sis'əl ē) island of Italy, off its S tip —**Si·cil·i·an** (si sil'yən) *adj.*, *n.*

sick[1] (sik) *adj.* ⟦OE *seoc*⟧ **1** suffering from disease; ill **2** having nausea **3** of or for sick people /*sick* leave/ **4** deeply disturbed, as by grief **5** disgusted by an excess /*sick* of excuses/ **6** [Colloq.] sadistic, morbid, etc. /a *sick* joke/ —**the sick** sick people —**sick'ish** *adj.*

sick[2] (sik) *vt.* SIC (incite)

sick bay a hospital and dispensary, esp. on board ship

sick'bed' *n.* the bed of a sick person

sick'en *vt.*, *vi.* to make or become ill, disgusted, etc. —**sick'en·ing** *adj.*

sick'ie (-ē) *n.* [Slang] a sick person, esp. one who is emotionally disturbed, etc.

sick·le (sik'əl) *n.* ⟦ult. < L *secare*, to cut⟧ a tool having a crescent-shaped blade on a short handle, for cutting tall grasses and weeds

sickle cell anemia an inherited chronic anemia found chiefly among blacks, in which red blood cells become sickle-shaped due to defective hemoglobin

sick·ly (sik'lē) *adj.* **-li·er, -li·est** **1** in poor health **2** produced by sickness /a *sickly* pallor/ **3** faint; feeble **4** weak; mawkish

sick'ness *n.* **1** a being sick or diseased **2** a malady **3** nausea

sick'o (-ō) *n.*, *pl.* **-os** [Slang] SICKIE

sick'out' *n.* a staying out of work on the claim of illness, as by a group of employees trying to win demands

sick'room' *n.* the room of a sick person

side (sīd) *n.* ⟦OE⟧ **1** the right or left half, as of the body **2** a position beside one **3** *a)* any of the lines or surfaces that bound something *b)* either of the two bounding surfaces of an object that are not the front, back, top, or bottom **4** either of the two surfaces of paper, cloth, etc. **5** an aspect /his cruel *side*/ **6** any location, etc. with reference to a central point **7** the position or attitude of one person or faction opposing another **8** one of the parties in a contest, conflict, etc. **9** a line of descent —*adj.* **1** of, at, or on a side **2** to or from one side /a *side* glance/ **3** secondary /a *side* issue/ —*vi.* to align oneself (*with* a faction, etc.) —**side by side** together —**take sides** to support a faction

side'arm' *adj., adv.* with a forward arm motion at or below shoulder level

side arms weapons worn at the side or waist, as swords, pistols, etc.

side'bar' *n.* a short article about a sidelight of a major news story and printed alongside it

side'board' *n.* a piece of furniture for holding linen, china, etc.

side'burns' *n.pl.* ⟦< *burnsides,* side whiskers worn by A. E. *Burnside,* Civil War general⟧ the hair growing on the sides of a man's face, just in front of the ears

side'car' *n.* a small car attached to the side of a motorcycle

side dish any food served along with the main course, as in a separate dish

side'kick' *n.* [Slang] **1** a close friend **2** a partner; confederate

side'light' *n.* a bit of incidental knowledge or information

side'line' *n.* **1** either of two lines marking the side limits of a playing area, as in football **2** a secondary line of merchandise, work, etc.

side'long' *adv.* toward the side —*adj.* directed to the side, as a glance

side'man' *n., pl.* **-men'** a band member other than the leader or soloist

side'piece' *n.* a piece forming, or attached to, the side of something

si·de·re·al (sī dir'ē əl) *adj.* ⟦< L *sidus,* star⟧ with reference to the stars

side'sad'dle *n.* a saddle designed for a rider sitting with both legs on the same side of the animal —*adv.* on or as if on a sidesaddle

side'show' *n.* a small show in connection with the main show, as of a circus

side'slip' *vi.* **-slipped', -slip'ping** to slip or skid sideways —*vt.* to make sideslip —*n.* a slip or skid to the side

side'split'ting *adj.* **1** very hearty: said of laughter **2** very funny

side'step' *vt., vi.* **-stepped', -step'ping** to dodge as by stepping aside

side'swipe' *vt.* **-swiped', -swip'ing** to hit along the side in passing —*n.* such a glancing blow

side'track' *vt., vi.* **1** to switch (a train) to a siding **2** to turn away from the main issue

side'walk' *n.* a path for pedestrians, usually paved, along the side of a street

side'wall' *n.* the side of a tire between the tread and the wheel rim

side'ways' (-wāz') *adv., adj.* **1** toward or from one side **2** with one side forward Also **side'wise'** (-wīz')

sid·ing (sīd'iŋ) *n.* **1** a covering, as of overlapping boards, for the outside of a frame building **2** a short railroad track connected with a main track by a switch and used for unloading, etc.

si·dle (sīd''l) *vi.* **-dled, -dling** ⟦< *sideling,* sideways⟧ to move sideways, esp. in a shy or stealthy manner

siege (sēj) *n.* ⟦< L *sedere,* sit⟧ **1** the encirclement of a fortified place by an enemy intending to take it **2** any persistent attempt to gain control, etc. —**lay siege to** to subject to a siege

si·er·ra (sē er'ə) *n.* ⟦Sp < L *serra,* a saw⟧ a range of hills or mountains with a saw-toothed appearance

Si·er·ra Le·one (sē er'ə lē ōn') country in W Africa, on the Atlantic: 27,925 sq. mi.; pop. 3,354,000; cap. Freetown

si·es·ta (sē es'tə) *n.* ⟦Sp < L *sexta* (*hora*), sixth (hour), noon⟧ a brief nap or rest after the noon meal

sieve (siv) *n.* ⟦OE *sife*⟧ a utensil with many small holes for straining liquids or fine particles; strainer

sift (sift) *vt.* ⟦OE *siftan*⟧ **1** to pass (flour, etc.) through a sieve **2** to examine (evidence, etc.) with care **3** to separate /to *sift* fact from fable/ —*vi.* to pass as through a sieve —**sift'er** *n.*

sigh (sī) *vi.* ⟦< OE *sican*⟧ **1** to take in and let out a long, deep, audible breath, as sorrow, relief, etc. **2** to feel longing or grief (*for*) —*n.* the act or sound of sighing

sight (sīt) *n.* ⟦< OE *seon,* to see⟧ **1** something seen or worth seeing **2** the act of seeing **3** a device to aid the eyes in aiming a gun, etc. **4** aim or an observation taken, as on a sextant **5** the power or range of seeing; eyesight **6** [Colloq.] anything that looks unpleasant, odd, etc. —*vt.* **1** to observe **2** to glimpse **3** to aim at **4** to adjust the sights of —*vi.* to look carefully /*sight* along the line/ —**at** (or **on**) **sight** as soon as seen —**by sight** by appearance —**not by a long sight** **1** not nearly **2** not at all —**out of sight** **1** not in sight **2** far off **3** [Colloq.] beyond reach **4** [Slang] excellent; wonderful

sight'ed *adj.* **1** having sight; not blind **2** having (a specified kind of) sight /*farsighted*/

sight'less *adj.* blind

sight'ly *adj.* **-li·er, -li·est** pleasant to the sight —**sight'li·ness** *n.*

sight reading the skill of performing written music on sight, without previous study —**sight'-read'** *vt., vi.*

sight'see'ing *n.* a visiting of places of interest —**sight'seer** (-sē'ər) *n.*

sig·ma (sig'mə) *n.* the eighteenth letter of the Greek alphabet (Σ, σ, ς)

sign (sīn) *n.* ⟦< L *signum*⟧ **1** something that indicates a fact, quality, etc.; token **2** a gesture that conveys information, etc. **3** a mark or symbol having a specific meaning /a dollar *sign* ($)/ **4** a placard, etc. bearing information, advertising, etc. **5** any trace or indication —*vt.* **1** to write (one's name) on (a letter, check, contract, etc.) **2** to engage by written contract —*vi.* to write one's signature —**sign in** (or **out**) to sign a register on arrival (or departure) —**sign off** to stop broadcasting, as for the day

sign·age (sī'nij) *n.* public signs collectively, often, specif., when graphically coordinated

sig·nal (sig'nəl) *n.* ⟦< L *signum,* a sign⟧ **1**

a sign or event that initiates action /a bugle *signal* to attack/ 2 a gesture, device, etc. that conveys command, warning, etc. 3 in radio, etc., the electrical impulses transmitted or received —*adj.* 1 remarkable; notable 2 used as a signal —*vt., vi.* **-naled** or **-nalled, -nal·ing** or **-nal·ling** 1 to make a signal or signals (to) 2 to communicate by signals

sig'nal·ize' (-īz') *vt.* **-ized', -iz'ing** 1 to make noteworthy 2 to make known or draw attention to

sig'nal·ly *adv.* in a signal way; notably

sig·na·to·ry (sig'nə tôr'ē) *adj.* having joined in signing something —*n., pl.* **-ries** a signatory person, nation, etc.

sig·na·ture (sig'nə chər) *n.* ⟦< L *signare*, to sign⟧ 1 a person's name written by that person 2 *Music* a staff sign showing key or time

sign·board (sīn'bôrd') *n.* a board bearing a sign or advertisement

sig·net (sig'nit) *n.* ⟦< Fr *signe*, a sign⟧ a seal, as on a ring, used in marking documents as official, etc.

sig·nif·i·cance (sig nif'ə kəns) *n.* 1 that which is signified; meaning 2 the quality of being significant; expressiveness 3 importance

sig·nif'i·cant (-kənt) *adj.* ⟦< L *significare*, signify⟧ 1 having or expressing a meaning, esp. a special or hidden one 2 full of meaning 3 important —**sig·nif'i·cant·ly** *adv.*

sig·ni·fy (sig'nə fī') *vt.* **-fied', -fy'ing** ⟦< L *signum*, a sign + *facere*, make⟧ 1 to be an indication of; mean 2 to make known, as by a sign, words, etc. —*vi.* to be important —**sig'ni·fi·ca'tion** *n.*

sign of the cross an outline of a CROSS (sense 2) made symbolically by moving the hand or fingers

sign of the zodiac any of the twelve divisions of the zodiac, each represented by a symbol

si·gnor (sē nyôr') *n., pl.* ***-gno'ri*** (-nyô'rē) ⟦It⟧ 1 [S-] Mr.: Italian title 2 a gentleman; man

si·gno·ra (sē nyô'rä) *n., pl.* ***-gno're*** (-re) ⟦It⟧ 1 [S-] Mrs., Madam: Italian title 2 a married woman

si·gno·ri·na (sē'nyô rē'nä) *n., pl.* ***-ri'ne*** (-ne) ⟦It⟧ 1 [S-] Miss: Italian title 2 an unmarried woman or girl

sign'post' *n.* 1 a post bearing a sign 2 an obvious clue, symptom, etc.

si·lage (sī'lij) *n.* green fodder preserved in a silo

sild (sild) *n., pl.* **sild** or **silds** ⟦Norw, herring⟧ a small or young herring canned as a Norwegian sardine

si·lence (sī'ləns) *n.* 1 a keeping silent 2 absence of sound 3 omission of mention —*vt.* **-lenced, -lenc·ing** 1 to make silent 2 to put down; repress —*interj.* be silent!

si'lenc·er *n.* 1 one that silences 2 a device to muffle the sound of a gun

si·lent (sī'lənt) *adj.* ⟦< L *silere*, be silent⟧ 1 making no vocal sound; mute 2 not talkative 3 still; noiseless 4 not expressed; tacit 5 not active /a *silent* partner/ —**si'lent·ly** *adv.*

sil·hou·ette (sil'o͞o et') *n.* ⟦Fr, after E. de *Silhouette*, 18th-c. Fr statesman⟧ 1 a solid, usually black, outline drawing, esp. a profile 2 any dark shape seen against a light background —*vt.* **-et'ted, -et'ting** to show in silhouette

SILHOUETTE

sil·i·ca (sil'i kə) *n.* ⟦< L *silex*, flint⟧ a hard, glassy mineral found in a variety of forms, as in quartz, sand, etc. —**si·li·ceous** (sə lish'əs) *adj.*

sil'i·cate (-kit, -kāt') *n.* a salt or ester derived from silica

sil·i·con (sil'i kän', -kən) *n.* ⟦< L *silex*, flint⟧ a nonmetallic chemical element found always in combination

sil'i·cone' (-kōn') *n.* an organic silicon compound highly resistant to heat, water, etc.

Silicon Valley ⟦after the principal material used for electronic chips⟧ *name for* a valley in California, southeast of San Francisco, a center of high-technology activities

sil'i·co'sis (-kō'sis) *n.* ⟦see SILICON & -OSIS⟧ a chronic lung disease caused by inhaling silica dust

silk (silk) *n.* ⟦ult. < ? L *sericus*, (fabric) of the *Seres*, the Chinese⟧ 1 *a*) the fine, soft fiber produced by silkworms *b*) thread or fabric made from this 2 any silklike filament or substance —**silk'en** *adj.* —**silk·y** (sil'kē), **-i·er, -i·est,** *adj.* —**silk'i·ness** *n.*

silk-screen process a stencil method of printing a color design through a piece of silk or other fine cloth on which parts of the design not to be printed have been blocked up —**silk'-screen'** *vt.*

silk'worm' *n.* any of certain moth caterpillars that produce cocoons of silk fiber

sill (sil) *n.* 1 a heavy, horizontal timber or line of masonry supporting a house wall, etc. 2 a horizontal piece forming the bottom frame of a window or door opening

sil·ly (sil'ē) *adj.* **-li·er, -li·est** ⟦< OE *sælig*, happy⟧ having or showing little sense, judgment, or sobriety; foolish, absurd, etc. —**sil'li·ness** *n.*

si·lo (sī'lō) *n., pl.* **-los** ⟦< Gr *siros*⟧ 1 an airtight pit or tower in which green fodder is preserved 2 an underground facility for a long-range ballistic missile

silt (silt) *n.* ⟦prob. < Scand⟧ a fine-grained, sandy sediment carried or deposited by water —*vt., vi.* to fill or choke up with silt

sil·ver (sil'vər) *n.* ⟦< OE *seolfer*⟧ 1 a white, precious, metallic chemical element that is very ductile and malleable 2 *a*) silver coin *b*) money; riches 3 silverware 4 a lustrous, grayish white —*adj.* 1 of, containing, or plated with silver 2 silvery 3 marking the 25th anniversary —*vt.* to cover as with silver

sil'ver·fish' *n., pl.* **-fish'** a wingless insect with silvery scales and long feelers, found in damp places

silver lining some basis for hope or comfort in the midst of despair

silver nitrate a colorless, crystalline salt, used in photography, as an antiseptic, etc.

sil'ver·smith' *n.* an artisan who makes and repairs silver articles

sil′ver-tongued′ (-tuŋd′) ***adj.*** eloquent
sil′ver·ware′ ***n.*** **1** articles, esp. tableware, made of or plated with silver **2** any metal tableware
sil′ver·y ***adj.*** **1** of, like, or containing silver **2** soft and clear in tone
sim·i·an (sim′ē ən) ***adj.*** ⟦< L *simia*, an ape⟧ of or like an ape or monkey —***n.*** an ape or monkey
sim·i·lar (sim′ə lər) ***adj.*** ⟦< L *similis*⟧ nearly but not exactly the same or alike —**sim′i·lar′i·ty** (-ler′ə tē), *pl.* **-ties,** ***n.*** —**sim′i·lar·ly** ***adv.***
sim·i·le (sim′ə lē′) ***n.*** ⟦< L, a likeness⟧ a figure of speech likening one thing to another by the use of *like, as,* etc. (Ex.: tears flowed like wine)
si·mil·i·tude (sə mil′ə to͞od′) ***n.*** ⟦< L *similitudo*⟧ likeness; resemblance
sim·mer (sim′ər) ***vi.*** ⟦echoic⟧ **1** a remain at or just below the boiling point **2** to be about to break out, as in anger —***vt.*** to keep at or just below the boiling point —***n.*** a simmering
si·mon-pure (sī′mən pyoor′) ***adj.*** ⟦after *Simon Pure*, a character in an 18th-c. play⟧ genuine; authentic
si·mo·ny (sī′mə nē, sim′ə-) ***n.*** ⟦after *Simon* Magus: Acts 8:9-24⟧ the buying or selling of sacraments or benefices
sim·pa·ti·co (sim pät′i kō, -pat′-) ***adj.*** ⟦< It or Sp⟧ compatible or congenial
sim·per (sim′pər) ***vi.*** ⟦Early Modern Eng⟧ to smile in a silly or affected way —***n.*** such a smile
sim·ple (sim′pəl) ***adj.*** **-pler, -plest** ⟦< L *simplus*⟧ **1** having only one or a few parts; uncomplicated **2** easy to do or understand **3** without additions /the *simple* facts/ **4** not ornate or luxurious; plain **5** without guile or deceit **6** without ostentation; natural **7** of low rank or position **8** stupid or foolish —**sim′ple·ness** ***n.***
simple interest interest computed on principal alone, and not on principal plus interest
sim′ple-mind′ed ***adj.*** **1** artless; unsophisticated **2** foolish **3** mentally retarded
sim′ple·ton (-tən) ***n.*** a fool
sim·plic·i·ty (sim plis′ə tē) ***n.***, *pl.* **-ties** **1** a simple state or quality; freedom from complexity **2** absence of elegance, luxury, etc.; plainness **3** artlessness **4** foolishness
sim·pli·fy (sim′plə fī′) ***vt.*** **-fied′, -fy′ing** to make simpler or less complex —**sim′pli·fi·ca′tion** ***n.***
sim·plis·tic (sim plis′tik) ***adj.*** making complex problems unrealistically simple —**sim·plis′ti·cal·ly** ***adv.***
sim·ply (sim′plē) ***adv.*** **1** in a simple way **2** merely /*simply* trying/ **3** completely /*simply* furious/
sim·u·late (sim′yo͞o lāt′) ***vt.*** **-lat′ed, -lat′ing** ⟦< L *simulare*⟧ **1** to give a false appearance of; feign **2** to look or act like —**sim′u·la′tion** ***n.***
si·mul·cast (sī′məl kast′) ***vt.*** **-cast′** or **-cast′ed, -cast′ing** to broadcast (a program) simultaneously by radio and television —***n.*** a program so broadcast
si·mul·ta·ne·ous (sī′məl tā′nē əs) ***adj.*** ⟦< L *simul*, together⟧ occurring, done, etc. at the same time —**si′mul·ta·ne′i·ty** (-tə nē′ə tē) ***n.*** —**si′mul·ta′ne·ous·ly** ***adv.***
sin (sin) ***n.*** ⟦OE *synne*⟧ **1** the willful breaking of religious or moral law **2** any offense or fault —***vi.*** **sinned, sin′ning** to commit a sin —**sin′ful** ***adj.*** —**sin′ner** ***n.***
Si·nai (sī′nī′), **Mount** *Bible* the mountain where Moses received the law from God
since (sins) ***adv.*** ⟦ult. < OE *sith*, after + *thæt*, that⟧ **1** from then until now /been here ever *since*/ **2** at some time between then and now /has *since* recovered/ **3** before now; ago /long *since* gone/ —***prep.*** **1** continuously from (then) until now /*since* noon/ **2** during the period between (then) and now /twice *since* May/ —***conj.*** **1** after the time that /two years *since* they met/ **2** continuously from the time when /lonely ever *since* he left/ **3** because /*since* you are finished, let's go/
sin·cere (sin sir′) ***adj.*** **-cer′er, -cer′est** ⟦< L *sincerus*, pure⟧ **1** truthful; honest **2** genuine /*sincere* grief/ —**sin·cere′ly** ***adv.*** —**sin·cer′i·ty** (-ser′ə tē) ***n.***
si·ne·cure (sī′nə kyoor′, sin′ə-) ***n.*** ⟦< L *sine*, without + *cura*, care⟧ any position providing an income but requiring little or no work
si·ne di·e (sī′nē dī′ē) ⟦LL, without a day⟧ for an indefinite period
si·ne qua non (sī′nē kwā nän′, sin′ā kwä nōn′) ⟦L, without which not⟧ an indispensable condition or thing
sin·ew (sin′yo͞o) ***n.*** ⟦OE *seonwe*⟧ **1** a tendon **2** muscular power; strength —**sin′ew·y** (-yo͞o ē) ***adj.***
sing (siŋ) ***vi.*** **sang, sung, sing′ing** ⟦OE *singan*⟧ **1** to produce musical sounds with the voice **2** to use song or verse in praise, etc. /of thee I *sing*/ **3** to make musical sounds, as a songbird **4** to hum, buzz, etc., as a bee —***vt.*** **1** to render (a song, etc.) by singing **2** to extol, etc. in song **3** to bring or put by singing /to *sing* a baby to sleep/ —***n.*** [Colloq.] group singing —**sing′er** ***n.***
sing. *abbrev.* singular
sing′-a·long′ ***n.*** [Colloq.] an informal gathering of people to sing songs
Sin·ga·pore (siŋ′ə pôr′) **1** island country off the S tip of the Malay Peninsula: 238 sq. mi.; pop. 2,558,000 **2** its capital, a seaport on the S coast: pop. *c.* 2,000,000
singe (sinj) ***vt.*** **singed, singe′ing** ⟦OE *sengan*⟧ **1** to burn superficially or slightly **2** to expose (a carcass) to flame in removing feathers, etc. —***n.*** **1** a singeing **2** a superficial burn
sin·gle (siŋ′gəl) ***adj.*** ⟦< L *singulus*⟧ **1** *a)* one only *b)* separate and distinct /every *single* time/ **2** solitary **3** of or for one person or family **4** between two persons only /*single* combat/ **5** unmarried **6** having only one part; not multiple, etc. **7** whole; unbroken /a *single* front/ —***vt.*** **-gled, -gling** to select from others: usually with *out* —***vi.*** *Baseball* to hit a single —***n.*** **1** a single person or thing **2** *Baseball* a hit by which the batter reaches first base **3** [*pl.*] *Racket Sports* a match with only one player on each side —**sin′gle·ness** ***n.***
sin′gle-breast′ed (-bres′tid) ***adj.*** overlapping the front of the body just enough to fasten /a *single-breasted* coat/

single file a single line of people or things, one behind another

sin′gle-hand′ed *adj., adv.* 1 using only one hand 2 without help —**sin′gle-hand′ed·ly** *adv.*

sin′gle-mind′ed *adj.* with only one aim or purpose —**sin′gle-mind′ed·ly** *adv.*

sin′gle·ton (-gəl tən) *n.* 1 a playing card that is the only one of its suit held by a player 2 a single thing

sin′gle-track′ *adj.* ONE-TRACK

sin′gle·tree′ (-trē′) *n.* ⟦< ME *swingle*, rod + *tre*, tree⟧ the crossbar on a wagon, etc. to which the traces of a horse's harness are hooked

sin·gly (siŋ′glē) *adv.* 1 alone 2 one by one 3 unaided

sing′song′ *n.* a monotonous rise and fall of tone in an unvarying cadence

sin·gu·lar (siŋ′gyə lər) *adj.* ⟦< L *singulus*, single⟧ 1 unique 2 extraordinary; remarkable 3 peculiar; odd 4 *Gram.* designating only one —*n. Gram.* the singular number or form of a word —**sin′gu·lar′i·ty** (-ler′ə tē) *n.* —**sin′gu·lar·ly** *adv.*

Sin·ha·lese (sin′hə lēz′, -lēs′) *adj.* of Sri Lanka (island country of S Asia), its principal people, or their language, etc. —*n.* 1 *pl.* **-lese′** a member of the Sinhalese people 2 their language

sin·is·ter (sin′is tər) *adj.* ⟦< L *sinister*, left-hand⟧ 1 orig., on or to the left-hand side 2 threatening harm, evil, etc. 3 wicked; evil

sink (siŋk) *vi.* **sank** or **sunk, sunk, sink′ing** ⟦OE *sincan*⟧ 1 to go beneath the surface of water, etc. 2 to go down slowly 3 to appear to descend, as the sun 4 to become lower, as in level, value, or rank 5 to subside, as wind or sound 6 to become hollow, as the cheeks 7 to pass gradually (*into* sleep, etc.) 8 to approach death —*vt.* 1 to make sink 2 to make (a mine, engraving, etc.) by digging, cutting, etc. 3 to invest 4 to defeat; undo —*n.* 1 a cesspool or sewer 2 a basin, as in a kitchen, with a drainpipe 3 an area of sunken land —**sink in** [Colloq.] to be understood in full —**sink′a·ble** *adj.*

sink′er *n.* 1 one that sinks 2 a lead weight used in fishing

sink′hole′ *n.* a surface depression resulting when ground collapses

sinking fund a fund built up over time to pay off a future debt, as of a corporation

Sino- ⟦< Gr *Sinai*⟧ *combining form* Chinese and

sin·u·ous (sin′yo͞o əs) *adj.* ⟦< L *sinus*, a bend⟧ 1 bending or winding in and out; wavy 2 devious; crooked —**sin′u·os′i·ty** (-äs′ə tē) *n.*

si·nus (sī′nəs) *n.* ⟦L, a bend⟧ a cavity, hollow, etc.; specif., any of the air cavities in the skull opening into the nasal cavities

si′nus·i′tis (-īt′is) *n.* inflammation of the sinuses, esp. of the skull

Sioux (so͞o) *n., pl.* **Sioux** (so͞o, so͞oz) a member of a group of Indian tribes of the N U.S. and S Canada —*adj.* of these tribes

sip (sip) *vt., vi.* **sipped, sip′ping** ⟦ME *sippen*⟧ to drink a little at a time —*n.* 1 the act of sipping 2 a quantity sipped —**sip′per** *n.*

si·phon (sī′fən) *n.* ⟦< Gr *siphōn*, tube⟧ 1 a bent tube for carrying liquid out over the edge of a container to a lower level, through the force of air pressure 2 a sealed bottle from which carbonated water is released: in full **siphon bottle** —*vt.* to draw off as through a siphon

sir (sʉr) *n.* ⟦< ME *sire*, SIRE⟧ 1 [*sometimes* S-] a respectful term of address used to a man: not followed by the name 2 [S-] the title used before the name of a knight or baronet

sire (sīr) *n.* ⟦< L *senior*, compar. of *senex*, old⟧ 1 [S-] a title of respect used in addressing a king 2 [Old Poet.] a father or forefather 3 the male parent of a four-legged mammal —*vt.* **sired, sir′ing** to beget: said esp. of animals

si·ren (sī′rən) *n.* ⟦< Gr *Seirēn*⟧ 1 *Gr. & Rom. Myth.* any of several sea nymphs whose singing lures sailors to their death on rocky coasts 2 a seductive woman 3 a warning device producing a loud, wailing sound

sir·loin (sʉr′loin′) *n.* ⟦< OFr *sur*, over + *loigne*, loin⟧ a choice cut of beef from the loin end in front of the rump

si·roc·co (sə räk′ō) *n., pl.* **-cos** ⟦It < Ar *sharq*, the east⟧ a hot, oppressive wind blowing from the deserts of N Africa into S Europe

sir·ree or **sir·ee** (sə rē′) *interj.* ⟦< SIR⟧ an interjection used for emphasis after *yes* or *no*

sir·up (sʉr′əp, sir′-) *n. alt. sp. of* SYRUP

sis (sis) *n.* [Colloq.] *short for* SISTER

si·sal (sī′səl) *n.* ⟦after *Sisal*, in SE Mexico⟧ a strong fiber obtained from the leaves of an agave

sis·sy (sis′ē) *n., pl.* **-sies** ⟦dim. of SIS⟧ [Colloq.] 1 an effeminate boy or man 2 a timid person —**sis′si·fied′** (-ə fīd′) *adj.*

sis·ter (sis′tər) *n.* ⟦< ON *systir*⟧ 1 a woman or girl as she is related to the other children of her parents 2 a half sister or stepsister 3 a female friend who is like a sister 4 a female fellow member of the same race, organization, etc. 5 a nun 6 one of the same kind, model, etc. —**sis′ter·hood′** *n.* —**sis′ter·ly** *adj.*

sis′ter-in-law′ *n., pl.* **sis′ters-in-law′** 1 the sister of one's spouse 2 the wife of one's brother 3 the wife of the brother of one's spouse

Sis·y·phus (sis′ə fəs) *Gr. Myth.* a greedy king doomed in Hades to roll uphill a stone which always rolls down again

sit (sit) *vi.* **sat, sit′ting** ⟦OE *sittan*⟧ 1 *a*) to rest oneself upon the buttocks, as on a chair *b*) to rest on the haunches with the forelegs braced (said of a dog, etc.) *c*) to perch (said of a bird) 2 to cover and warm eggs for hatching; brood 3 *a*) to occupy a seat as a judge, legislator, etc. *b*) to be in session, as a court 4 to pose, as for a portrait 5 to be located 6 to rest or lie as specified /*cares sit* lightly on him/ 7 BABY-SIT —*vt.* 1 to cause to sit; seat 2 to keep one's seat on (a horse, etc.) —**sit down** to take a seat —**sit in (on)** to attend —**sit out** to take no part in (a dance, etc.) —**sit up** 1 to sit erect 2 to postpone going to bed 3 [Colloq.] to become suddenly alert —**sit′ter** *n.*

SITAR

si·tar (si tär′) ***n.*** ⟦Hindi *sitār*⟧ a lutelike instrument of India with a long, fretted neck
sit·com (sit′käm′) ***n.*** [Colloq.] *short for* SITUATION COMEDY
sit′-down′ ***n.*** a strike in which the strikers refuse to leave the premises
site (sīt) ***n.*** ⟦< L *situs*, position⟧ a location or scene
sit′-in′ ***n.*** a method of protest in which demonstrators sit in, and refuse to leave, a public place
sit′ting ***n.*** **1** the act or position of one that sits **2** a session, as of a court **3** a period of being seated
sitting duck [Colloq.] a person or thing especially vulnerable to attack; easy target
sit·u·ate (sich′o͞o āt′) ***vt.*** **-at′ed, -at′ing** ⟦see SITE⟧ to put in a certain place or position; place; locate
sit′u·a′tion ***n.*** **1** location; position **2** condition with regard to circumstances **3** state of affairs **4** a position of employment
situation comedy a comic television series made up of episodes involving the same group of characters
sit′-up′ or **sit′up′** ***n.*** an exercise in which a person lying supine rises to a sitting position without using his hands
sitz bath (sits, zits) ⟦< Ger⟧ a therapeutic bath in which only the hips and buttocks are immersed
Si·va (sē′və, shē′-) Hindu god of destruction and reproduction
six (siks) ***adj., n.*** ⟦OE *sex*⟧ one more than five; 6; VI —**sixth** ***adj., n.***
six′-pack′ ***n.*** a package of six units, as one with six cans of beer
six′-shoot′er ***n.*** [Colloq.] a revolver firing six shots without reloading
six′teen′ (-tēn′) ***adj.*** ⟦OE *syxtene*⟧ six more than ten; 16; XVI —**six′teenth′** ***adj., n.***
sixth sense intuitive power
six·ty (siks′tē) ***adj., n., pl.*** **-ties** ⟦OE *sixtig*⟧ six times ten; 60; LX —**the sixties** the numbers or years, as of a century, from 60 through 69 —**six′ti·eth** (-ith) ***adj., n.***
siz·a·ble (sī′zə bəl) ***adj.*** quite large or bulky Also sp. **size′a·ble**
size[1] (sīz) ***n.*** ⟦ult. < L *sedere*, sit⟧ **1** that quality of a thing which determines how much space it occupies; dimensions or magnitude **2** any of a series of graded classifications of measure into which merchandise is divided —***vt.*** **sized, siz′ing** to make or grade according to size —**size up** [Colloq.] **1** to make an estimate or judgment of **2** to meet requirements
size[2] (sīz) ***n.*** ⟦ME *syse*⟧ a pasty substance used as a glaze or filler on plaster, paper, cloth, etc. —***vt.*** **sized, siz′ing** to fill, stiffen, or glaze with size
-sized (sīzd) *combining form* having a (specified) size /medium-*sized*/ Also **-size**
siz·ing (sī′ziŋ) ***n.*** **1** SIZE[2] **2** the act or process of applying size
siz·zle (siz′əl) ***vi.*** **-zled, -zling** ⟦echoic⟧ **1** to make a hissing sound when in contact with heat **2** to be extremely hot —***vt.*** to make sizzle —***n.*** a sizzling sound
S.J. Society of Jesus
skate[1] (skāt) ***n.*** ⟦< OFr *eschace*, stilt⟧ **1** a metal runner in a frame, fastened to a shoe for gliding on ice **2** a similar frame or shoe with two pairs of small wheels, for gliding on a floor, sidewalk, etc. —***vi.*** **skat′ed, skat′ing** to glide or roll on or as on skates —**skat′er** ***n.***
skate[2] (skāt) ***n.*** ⟦< ON *skata*⟧ any ray fish
skate′board′ ***n.*** a short, oblong board with two wheels at each end, ridden, as down an incline —***vi.*** **-board′ed, -board′ing** to ride on a skateboard
ske·dad·dle (ski dad′'l) ***vi.*** **-dled, -dling** ⟦< ?⟧ [Colloq.] to run away
skeet (skēt) ***n.*** ⟦< ON *skeyti*, projectile⟧ trapshooting in which the shooter fires from different angles
skein (skān) ***n.*** ⟦< MFr *escaigne*⟧ a quantity of thread or yarn in a coil
skel·e·ton (skel′ə tən) ***n.*** ⟦< Gr *skeletos*, dried up⟧ **1** the hard framework of bones of an animal body **2** a supporting framework **3** an outline, as of a book —***adj.*** greatly reduced /a *skeleton* crew/ —**skel′e·tal** ***adj.***
skeleton key a key with a slender bit that can open many simple locks
skep·tic (skep′tik) ***adj.*** ⟦L < Gr *skeptikos*, inquiring⟧ *var. of* SKEPTICAL —***n.*** **1** an adherent of skepticism **2** one who habitually questions matters generally accepted **3** one who doubts religious doctrines
skep′ti·cal (-ti kəl) ***adj.*** doubting; questioning —**skep′ti·cal·ly** ***adv.***
skep′ti·cism′ (-siz′əm) ***n.*** **1** the doctrine that the truth of all knowledge must always be in question **2** skeptical attitude **3** doubt about religious doctrines
sketch (skech) ***n.*** ⟦ult. < Gr *schedios*, extempore⟧ **1** a rough drawing or design, done rapidly **2** a brief outline **3** a short, light story, play, etc. —***vt., vi.*** make a sketch (of) —**sketch′y, -i·er, -i·est,** ***adj.***
skew (skyo͞o) ***vi., vt.*** ⟦< OFr *eschiver*, shun < OHG⟧ to slant or set at a slant —***adj.*** slanting —***n.*** a slant or twist
skew·er (skyo͞o′ər) ***n.*** ⟦< ON *skifa*, a slice⟧ a long pin used to hold meat together while cooking —***vt.*** to fasten or pierce with skewers
ski (skē) ***n., pl.*** **skis** or **ski** ⟦Norw < ON *skith*, snowshoe⟧ either of a pair of long runners of wood, etc. fastened to shoes for gliding over snow —***vi.*** **skied, ski′ing** to glide on skis —**ski′er** ***n.***
skid (skid) ***n.*** ⟦prob. < ON *skith*, snowshoe⟧ **1** a plank, log, etc., often used as a track upon which to slide a heavy object **2** a low, wooden platform for holding loads **3** a runner on aircraft landing gear **4** a sliding wedge used to brake a wheel **5** the act of skidding —***vt., vi.*** **skid′ded, skid′ding** to

slide or slip, as a vehicle on ice —**be on** (or **hit**) **the skids** [Slang] to be on the decline, or to fail
skid row ⟦altered < *skid road*, trail to skid logs along⟧ a section of a city frequented by vagrants, derelicts, etc.
skiff (skif) ***n.*** ⟦< It *schifo*⟧ any light, open boat propelled by oars, motor, or sail
ski lift an endless cable with seats, for carrying skiers up a slope
skill (skil) ***n.*** ⟦< ON *skil*, distinction⟧ **1** great ability or proficiency **2** *a)* an art, craft, etc., esp. one involving the hands or body *b)* ability in such an art, etc. —**skilled *adj.*** —**skill′ful** or **skil′ful *adj.***
skil·let (skil′it) ***n.*** ⟦< ? L *scutra*, dish⟧ a pan for frying
skim (skim) ***vt., vi.*** **skimmed, skim′ming** ⟦ME *skimen*⟧ **1** to remove (floating matter) from (a liquid) **2** to glance through (a book, etc.) without reading word for word **3** to glide lightly (over)
skim milk milk with the cream removed Also **skimmed milk**
skimp (skimp) ***vi., vt.*** SCRIMP
skimp′y *adj.* **-i·er, -i·est** [Colloq.] barely enough; scanty
skin (skin) ***n.*** ⟦< ON *skinn*⟧ **1** the outer covering of the animal body **2** a pelt **3** something like skin, as fruit rind, etc. —***vt.*** **skinned, skin′ning 1** to remove skin from **2** to injure by scraping (one's knee, etc.) **3** [Colloq.] to swindle —**skin′less *adj.***
skin diving underwater swimming with such gear as a face mask, flippers, scuba equipment, etc. —**skin′-dive′, -dived′, -div′ing, *vi.*** —**skin diver**
skin′flick′ *n.* [Slang] a film emphasizing nudity or explicit sexual activity
skin′flint′ *n.* ⟦lit., one who would skin a flint for economy⟧ a miser
-skinned *combining form* having (a specified kind of) skin /dark-*skinned*/
skin′ny *adj.* **-ni·er, -ni·est** without much flesh; very thin —**skin′ni·ness *n.***
skin′ny-dip′ *vi.* **-dipped′, -dip′ping** [Colloq.] to swim nude —***n.*** [Colloq.] a swim in the nude
skin′tight′ *adj.* tightfitting /*skintight* jeans/
skip (skip) ***vi., vt.*** **skipped, skip′ping** ⟦ME *skippen*⟧ **1** to leap lightly (over) **2** to ricochet or bounce **3** to pass from one point to another, omitting or ignoring (what lies between) **4** [Colloq.] to leave (town, etc.) hurriedly —***n.*** a skipping; specif., a gait alternating light hops on each foot —**skip it!** [Colloq.] never mind!
skip·per (skip′ər) ***n.*** ⟦< MDu *schip*, a ship⟧ the captain of a ship
skir·mish (skur′mish) ***n.*** ⟦< It *schermire* < Gmc⟧ **1** a brief fight between small groups, as in a battle **2** any slight, unimportant conflict —***vi.*** to take part in a skirmish
skirt (skurt) ***n.*** ⟦< ON *skyrt*, shirt⟧ **1** that part of a dress, coat, etc. that hangs below the waist **2** a woman's garment that hangs from the waist **3** something like a skirt —***vt., vi.*** to be on, or move along, the edge (of)
ski run a slope or course for skiing
skit (skit) ***n.*** ⟦prob. ult. < ON *skjōta*, to shoot⟧ a short, humorous sketch, as in the theater
ski touring the sport of cross-country skiing
ski tow a kind of ski lift for pulling skiers up a slope on their skis
skit·ter (skit′ər) ***vi.*** ⟦< Scand⟧ to skip along quickly and lightly, esp. over water
skit·tish (skit′ish) ***adj.*** ⟦see SKIT & -ISH⟧ **1** lively; playful **2** easily frightened; jumpy **3** fickle
skiv·vy (skiv′ē) ***n., pl.*** **-vies** ⟦< ?⟧ [Slang] **1** a man's, esp. a sailor's, short-sleeved undershirt: usually **skivvy shirt 2** [*pl.*] men's underwear
skoal (skōl) ***interj.*** ⟦< ON *skāl*, a bowl⟧ to your health! A toast
skul·dug·ger·y or **skull·dug·ger·y** (skul dug′ər ē) ***n.*** ⟦< obs. Scot⟧ [Colloq.] sneaky behavior; trickery
skulk (skulk) ***vi.*** ⟦ME *sculken*⟧ to move in a stealthy manner; slink
skull (skul) ***n.*** ⟦< Scand⟧ **1** the bony framework of the head, enclosing the brain **2** the head; mind
skull′cap′ *n.* a light, closefitting, brimless cap, usually worn indoors
skunk (skuŋk) ***n.*** ⟦< AmInd⟧ **1** a small, bushy-tailed mammal having black fur with white stripes down the back: it ejects a foul-smelling liquid when molested **2** its fur **3** [Colloq.] a despicable person
sky (skī) ***n., pl.*** **skies** ⟦< ON, a cloud⟧ **1** [*often pl.*] the upper atmosphere /blue *skies*, a cloudy *sky*/ **2** the firmament **3** heaven
sky′cap′ *n.* a porter at an airport terminal
sky diving parachute jumping involving free-fall maneuvers
sky′-high′ *adj.* very high —***adv.*** **1** very high **2** in or to pieces
sky′jack′ *vt.* [Colloq.] to hijack (an aircraft) —**sky′jack′er *n.***
sky′lark′ *n.* a Eurasian lark famous for the song it utters as it soars —***vi.*** to romp or frolic
sky′light′ *n.* a window in a roof or ceiling
sky′line′ *n.* **1** the visible horizon **2** the outline, as of a city, seen against the sky
sky marshal a Federal officer assigned to guard against skyjacking
sky′rock′et *n.* a fireworks rocket that explodes aloft —***vi., vt.*** to rise or cause to rise rapidly
sky′scrap′er *n.* a very tall building
sky′ward (-wərd) ***adv., adj.*** toward the sky Also **sky′wards *adv.***
sky′ways′ *n.pl.* routes of air travel
sky′writ′ing *n.* the tracing of words, etc. in the sky by trailing smoke from an airplane —**sky′writ′er *n.***
slab (slab) ***n.*** ⟦ME *sclabbe*⟧ a flat, broad, and fairly thick piece
slack[1] (slak) ***adj.*** ⟦< OE *slæc*⟧ **1** slow; sluggish **2** not busy; dull /a *slack* period/ **3** loose; not tight **4** careless /a *slack* workman/ —***vt., vi.*** to slacken —***n.*** **1** a part that hangs loose **2** a lack of tension **3** a dull period; lull —**slack off** to slacken —**slack up** to go more slowly —**slack′ness *n.***
slack[2] (slak) ***n.*** ⟦ME *sleck*⟧ a mixture of small pieces of coal, coal dust, etc. left from screening coal
slack·en (slak′ən) ***vt., vi.*** **1** to make or

become less active, brisk, etc. **2** to loosen or relax, as rope
slack'er ***n.*** one who shirks
slacks (slaks) ***n.pl.*** trousers for men or women
slag (slag) ***n.*** ⟦< earlier LowG *slagge*⟧ the fused refuse separated from metal in smelting
slain (slān) ***vt. pp. of*** SLAY
slake (slāk) ***vt.*** **slaked, slak'ing** ⟦< OE *slæc,* SLACK[1]⟧ **1** to satisfy (thirst, etc.) **2** to produce a chemical change in (lime) by mixing with water
sla·lom (slä'ləm) ***n.*** ⟦Norw⟧ a downhill ski race over a zigzag course —***vi.*** to take part in a slalom
slam[1] (slam) ***vt.*** **slammed, slam'ming** ⟦prob. < Scand⟧ **1** to shut, hit, throw, or put with force and noise **2** [Colloq.] to criticize severely —***n.*** **1** a slamming **2** [Colloq.] a severe criticism
slam[2] (slam) ***n.*** ⟦< ?⟧ *Bridge short for* GRAND SLAM or LITTLE SLAM
slam'-bang' ***adv.*** [Colloq.] **1** swiftly or abruptly and recklessly **2** noisily —***adj.*** [Colloq.] lively, noisy, etc.
slam'-dunk' ***n.*** *Basketball* a hard shot from directly above the basket
slam·mer (slam'ər) ***n.*** [Slang] a prison or jail
slan·der (slan'dər) ***n.*** ⟦see SCANDAL⟧ **1** the utterance of a falsehood that damages another's reputation **2** such a spoken statement —***vt.*** to utter a slander about —**slan'der·er** ***n.*** —**slan'der·ous** ***adj.***
slang (slaŋ) ***n.*** ⟦< ?⟧ highly informal speech that is outside standard usage and consists of both coined words and phrases and of new meanings given to established terms —**slang'y, -i·er, -i·est,** ***adj.***
slant (slant) ***vt., vi.*** ⟦< Scand⟧ **1** to incline; slope **2** to tell so as to express a particular bias —***n.*** **1** an oblique surface, line, etc. **2** a point of view or attitude —***adj.*** sloping
slap (slap) ***n.*** ⟦echoic⟧ **1** a blow with something flat, as the palm of the hand **2** an insult or rebuff —***vt.*** **slapped, slap'ping** **1** to strike with something flat **2** to put, hit, etc. with force
slap'dash' ***adj., adv.*** hurried(ly), careless(ly), haphazard(ly), etc.
slap'-hap'py ***adj.*** [Slang] **1** dazed, as by blows **2** silly or giddy
slap'stick' ***n.*** crude comedy full of horseplay —***adj.*** characterized by such comedy
slash (slash) ***vt.*** ⟦< ? OFr *esclachier,* to break⟧ **1** to cut with sweeping strokes, as of a knife **2** to cut slits in **3** to reduce drastically /*slash* prices/ —***vi.*** to make a sweeping stroke as with a knife —***n.*** **1** a slashing **2** a cut made by slashing **3** a virgule —**slash'er** ***n.***
slash'-and-burn' ***adj.*** of a method of clearing fields by cutting down and burning vegetation
slash pocket a pocket (in a garment) with a finished diagonal opening
slat (slat) ***n.*** ⟦< OFr *esclat,* fragment⟧ a narrow strip of wood, etc.
slate (slāt) ***n.*** ⟦see prec.⟧ **1** a hard, fine-grained rock that cleaves into thin, smooth layers **2** a thin piece of slate or slatelike material, as a roofing tile or writing tablet **3** the bluish-gray color of most slate: also **slate blue** —***vt.*** **slat'ed, slat'ing** **1** to cover with slate **2** to designate, as for candidacy —**a clean slate** a record showing no marks of discredit, dishonor, etc.
slath·er (sla*th*'ər) ***vt.*** ⟦< ?⟧ [Colloq. or Dial.] to cover or spread on thickly
slat·tern (slat'ərn) ***n.*** ⟦< dial. *slatter,* to slop⟧ a slovenly or sluttish woman —**slat'tern·ly** ***adj.***
slaugh·ter (slôt'ər) ***n.*** ⟦< ON *slātr,* lit., slain flesh⟧ **1** the killing of animals for food; butchering **2** the brutal killing of a person **3** the killing of many people, as in battle —***vt.*** **1** to kill (animals) for food; butcher **2** to kill (people) brutally or in large numbers —**slaugh'ter·er** ***n.***
slaugh'ter·house' ***n.*** a place where animals are butchered for food
Slav (släv, slav) ***n.*** a member of a group of peoples of E and SE Europe, including Russians, Serbs, Czechs, Poles, etc. —***adj. var. of*** SLAVIC
slave (slāv) ***n.*** ⟦< Gr *Sklabos,* ult. < OSlav *Slovĕne,* first used of captive Slavs⟧ **1** a human being who is owned as property by another; a person having no freedom or personal rights **2** one dominated by some influence, etc. **3** one who slaves —***vi.*** **slaved, slav'ing** to work like a slave; drudge
slave driver **1** one who oversees slaves **2** any merciless taskmaster
slav·er (slav'ər) ***vi.*** ⟦< Scand⟧ to drool
slav·er·y (slā'vər ē) ***n.*** **1** the owning of slaves as a practice **2** the condition of a slave; bondage **3** drudgery; toil
Slav·ic (släv'ik, slav'-) ***adj.*** of the Slavs, their languages, etc. —***n.*** a family of languages, including Russian, Polish, Czech, Bulgarian, etc.
slav·ish (slā'vish) ***adj.*** **1** of or like slaves; servile **2** blindly dependent or imitative —**slav'ish·ly** ***adv.***
slaw (slô) ***n.*** ⟦Du *sla* < Fr *salade,* salad⟧ *short for* COLESLAW
slay (slā) ***vt.*** **slew, slain, slay'ing** ⟦OE *slean*⟧ to kill in a violent way —**slay'er** ***n.***
sleaze (slēz) ***n.*** ⟦< fol.⟧ [Slang] **1** sleaziness **2** anything cheap, vulgar, shoddy, etc.
slea·zy (slē'zē) ***adj.*** **-zi·er, -zi·est** ⟦< *silesia,* orig. cloth made in central Europe⟧ **1** flimsy or thin in substance **2** shoddy, shabby, etc. —**slea'zi·ly** ***adv.*** —**slea'zi·ness** ***n.***
sled (sled) ***n.*** ⟦ME *sledde*⟧ a vehicle on runners for moving over snow, ice, etc. —***vt., vi.*** **sled'ded, sled'ding** to carry or ride on a sled —**sled'der** ***n.***
sledge[1] (slej) ***n.*** ⟦OE *slecge*⟧ SLEDGEHAMMER
sledge[2] (slej) ***n.*** ⟦MDu *sleedse*⟧ a sled or sleigh
sledge'ham'mer ***n.*** ⟦see SLEDGE[1]⟧ a long, heavy hammer, usually held with both hands
sleek (slēk) ***adj.*** ⟦var. of SLICK⟧ **1** smooth and shiny; glossy **2** of well-fed or well-groomed appearance **3** suave, elegant, etc. —***vt.*** to make sleek —**sleek'ly** ***adv.*** —**sleek'ness** ***n.***
sleep (slēp) ***n.*** ⟦OE *slæp*⟧ **1** the natural, regularly recurring rest for the body, during

which there is little or no conscious thought 2 any state like this —*vi.* **slept, sleep'ing** to be in a state of or like sleep —**sleep off** to rid oneself of by sleeping —**sleep'less** *adj.* —**sleep'less·ness** *n.*

sleep'er *n.* 1 one who sleeps 2 a railroad car with berths for sleeping: also **sleeping car** 3 a beam laid flat to support something 4 something that achieves an unexpected success

sleeping bag a warmly lined, zippered bag for sleeping outdoors

sleeping sickness an infectious disease, esp. in Africa, characterized by lethargy, prolonged coma, etc.

sleep'walk'ing *n.* the act of walking while asleep —**sleep'walk'er** *n.*

sleep'wear' *n.* NIGHTCLOTHES

sleep'y *adj.* **-i·er, -i·est** 1 ready or inclined to sleep; drowsy 2 dull; idle /a *sleepy* town/ —**sleep'i·ly** *adv.* —**sleep'i·ness** *n.*

sleet (slēt) *n.* ⟦ME *slete*⟧ 1 partly frozen rain 2 the icy coating when rain freezes on trees, etc. —*vi.* to shower in the form of sleet —**sleet'y** *adj.*

sleeve (slēv) *n.* ⟦OE *sliefe*⟧ 1 that part of a garment that covers the arm 2 a tubelike part fitting over or around another part —**up one's sleeve** hidden but ready at hand —**sleeve'less** *adj.*

sleigh (slā) *n.* ⟦Du *slee*⟧ a light vehicle on runners for travel on snow, ice, etc.

sleight of hand (slīt) ⟦< ON *slœgr*, crafty⟧ 1 skill with the hands, esp. in deceiving onlookers, as in magic 2 a trick thus performed

slen·der (slen'dər) *adj.* ⟦ME *s(c)lendre* < ?⟧ 1 long and thin 2 slim of figure 3 small in amount, size, etc. 4 of little force; feeble —**slen'der·ness** *n.*

slen'der·ize' *vt., vi.* **-ized', -iz'ing** to make or become slender

slept (slept) *vi., vt. pt. & pp. of* SLEEP

sleuth (slo͞oth) *n.* ⟦< ON *slóth*, a trail⟧ [Colloq.] a detective

slew[1] (slo͞o) *n.* ⟦Ir *sluagh*, a host⟧ [Colloq.] a large number or amount

slew[2] (slo͞o) *vt. pt. of* SLAY

slice (slīs) *n.* ⟦< OFr *esclicier*⟧ 1 a relatively thin, broad piece cut from something 2 a part or share —*vt.* **sliced, slic'ing** 1 to cut into slices 2 to cut off as in a slice or slices: often with *off, from, away,* etc. 3 to hit (a ball) so that it curves to the right if right-handed or the left if left-handed —**slic'er** *n.*

slick (slik) *vt.* ⟦OE *slician*⟧ 1 to make smooth 2 [Colloq.] to make smart, neat, etc.: usually with *up* —*adj.* 1 sleek; smooth 2 slippery 3 adept; clever 4 [Colloq.] smooth but superficial, tricky, etc. —*n.* 1 a smooth area on the water, as from a layer of oil 2 a slippery, oily area on the surface of a road —**slick'ly** *adv.* —**slick'ness** *n.*

slick'er *n.* 1 a loose, waterproof coat 2 [Colloq.] a tricky person

slide (slīd) *vi.* **slid** (slid), **slid'ing** ⟦OE *slidan*⟧ 1 to move along in constant contact with a smooth surface, as on ice 2 to glide 3 to slip /it *slid* from his hand/ —*vt.* 1 to cause to slide 2 to place quietly or deftly (*in* or *into*) —*n.* 1 a sliding 2 a smooth, often inclined surface for sliding 3 something that works by sliding 4 a photographic transparency for use with a viewer or projector 5 a small glass plate on which objects are mounted for microscopic study 6 the fall of a mass of rock, snow, etc. down a slope —**let slide** to fail to attend to properly

slide fastener a zipper or a zipperlike device with two grooved plastic edges joined or separated by a sliding tab

slid'er *n.* 1 one that slides 2 *Baseball* a curve ball that breaks only slightly

sliding scale a schedule, as of costs, wages, etc., that varies with given conditions, as cost of living, etc.

slight (slīt) *adj.* ⟦OE *sliht*⟧ 1 *a)* light in build; slender *b)* frail; fragile 2 lacking strength, importance, etc. 3 small in amount or extent —*vt.* 1 to neglect 2 to treat with disrespect 3 to treat as unimportant —*n.* a slighting or being slighted —**slight'ly** *adv.* —**slight'ness** *n.*

slim (slim) *adj.* **slim'mer, slim'mest** ⟦< Du, bad⟧ 1 small in girth; slender 2 small in amount, degree, etc. —*vt., vi.* **slimmed, slim'ming** to make or become slim —**slim'ness** *n.*

slime (slīm) *n.* ⟦OE *slim*⟧ any soft, moist, slippery, often sticky matter —**slim'y, -i·er, -i·est,** *adj.*

sling (sliŋ) *n.* ⟦prob. < ON *slyngua*, to throw⟧ 1 a primitive instrument whirled by hand for throwing stones 2 a cast; throw; fling 3 *a)* a supporting band, etc. as for raising a heavy object *b)* a cloth looped from the neck under an injured arm for support —*vt.* **slung, sling'ing** 1 to throw as with a sling 2 to hang in a sling

sling'shot' *n.* a Y-shaped piece of wood, etc. with an elastic band attached to it for shooting stones, etc.

slink (sliŋk) *vi.* **slunk, slink'ing** ⟦OE *slincan*, to creep⟧ to move in a furtive or sneaking way; sneak

slink'y *adj.* **-i·er, -i·est** 1 sneaking 2 [Slang] sinuous in movement or line

slip[1] (slip) *vi.* **slipped, slip'ping** ⟦ME *slippen*, ult. < Ger⟧ 1 to go quietly or secretly /to *slip* out of a room/ 2 to pass smoothly or easily 3 to escape from one's memory, grasp, etc. 4 to slide, lose footing, etc. 5 to make a mistake; err 6 to become worse —*vt.* 1 to cause to slip 2 to put, pass, etc. quickly or deftly /to *slip* one's shoes on/ 3 to escape from (the memory) —*n.* 1 a space between piers for docking ships 2 a woman's undergarment the length of a skirt 3 a pillow case 4 a slipping or falling down 5 an error or mistake —**let slip** to say without intending to —**slip up** to make a mistake

slip[2] (slip) *n.* ⟦< MDu *slippen*, to cut⟧ 1 a stem, root, etc. of a plant, used for planting or grafting 2 a young, slim person 3 a small piece of paper

slip'case' *n.* a boxlike container for a book or books, open at one end

slip'cov'er *n.* a removable, fitted cloth cover for a chair, sofa, etc.

slip'knot' *n.* a knot that will slip along the rope around which it is tied

slip noose a noose made with a slipknot
slip·page (slip′ij) *n.* a slipping, as of one gear past another
slipped disk a ruptured cartilaginous disk between vertebrae
slip·per (slip′ər) *n.* a light, low shoe easily slipped on the foot, esp. one for indoor wear —**slip′pered** *adj.*
slip·per·y (slip′ər ē) *adj.* **-i·er, -i·est** 1 liable to cause slipping, as a wet surface 2 tending to slip away, as from a grasp 3 unreliable; deceitful
slip′shod′ (-shäd′) *adj.* ⟦< obs. *slip-shoe,* a slipper⟧ careless or slovenly
slip′-up′ *n.* [Colloq.] an error
slit (slit) *vt.* **slit, slit′ting** ⟦ME *slitten*⟧ 1 to cut or split open, esp. by a lengthwise incision 2 to cut into strips —*n.* a straight, narrow cut, opening, etc.
slith·er (slith′ər) *vi.* ⟦< OE *slidan,* to slide⟧ to slip, slide, or glide along
sliv·er (sliv′ər) *n.* ⟦< OE *slifan,* to split⟧ a thin, sharp piece cut or split off; splinter —*vt., vi.* to cut or break into slivers
slob (släb) *n.* ⟦Ir *slab,* mud⟧ [Colloq.] a sloppy or coarse person
slob·ber (släb′ər) *vi.* ⟦prob. < LowG *slubberen,* to swig⟧ 1 to drool 2 to speak, etc. in a maudlin way
sloe (slō) *n.* ⟦OE *sla*⟧ 1 the blackthorn 2 its small, plumlike fruit
sloe′-eyed′ *adj.* 1 having large, dark eyes 2 having almond-shaped eyes
sloe gin a liqueur of gin flavored with sloes
slog (släg) *vt., vi.* **slogged, slog′ging** ⟦ME *sluggen,* go slowly⟧ 1 to make (one's way) with great effort; plod 2 to toil (at)
slo·gan (slō′gən) *n.* ⟦< Gael *sluagh,* a host + *gairm,* a call: orig., a battle cry⟧ 1 a motto associated with a political party, etc. 2 a catchy phrase used in advertising
sloop (slo͞op) *n.* ⟦< LowG *slupen,* to glide⟧ a sailing vessel having a single mast with a mainsail and a jib
slop (släp) *n.* ⟦OE *sloppe*⟧ 1 watery snow or mud; slush 2 a puddle of spilled liquid 3 unappetizing, watery food 4 [*often pl.*] liquid waste of any kind —*vi., vt.* **slopped, slop′ping** to spill or splash
slope (slōp) *n.* ⟦< OE *slupan,* to glide⟧ 1 rising or falling ground 2 any inclined line, surface, etc.; slant 3 the amount or degree of deviation from the horizontal or vertical —*vi.* **sloped, slop′ing** to have an upward or downward inclination; incline; slant —*vt.* to cause to slope
slop·py (släp′ē) *adj.* **-pi·er, -pi·est** 1 splashy; slushy 2 *a)* slovenly *b)* slipshod 3 [Colloq.] gushingly sentimental —**slop′pi·ness** *n.*
sloppy Joe (jō) ground meat cooked with tomato sauce, spices, etc. and served on a bun
slop sink a deep sink for filling scrub pails, washing out mops, etc.
slosh (släsh) *vi.* ⟦var. of SLUSH⟧ 1 to splash through water, mud, etc. 2 to splash about: said of a liquid
slot (slät) *n.* ⟦< OFr *esclot,* hollow between the breasts⟧ 1 a narrow opening, as for a coin in a vending machine 2 [Colloq.] a position in a group, etc. —*vt.* **slot′ted, slot′ting** 1 to make a slot in 2 [Colloq.] to place in a series or sequence

THREE-TOED SLOTH

sloth (slōth, slôth) *n.* ⟦< OE *slaw,* slow⟧ 1 laziness; idleness 2 a slow-moving, tree-dwelling mammal of tropical America that hangs, back down, from branches —**sloth′ful** *adj.* —**sloth′ful·ness** *n.*
slot machine a machine, specif. a gambling device, worked by inserting a coin in a slot
slouch (slouch) *n.* ⟦< ON *slōka,* to droop⟧ 1 a lazy or incompetent person 2 a drooping or slovenly posture —*vi.* to sit, stand, walk, etc. in a slouch —**slouch′y, -i·er, -i·est,** *adj.*
slough[1] (sluf) *n.* ⟦ME *slouh,* a skin⟧ a cast-off layer or covering, as the skin of a snake —*vt.* to throw off; discard
slough[2] (slou) *n.* ⟦OE *sloh*⟧ 1 a place full of soft, deep mud 2 deep, hopeless dejection
Slo·vak (slō′väk′, -vak′) *n.* 1 any of a Slavic people living chiefly in E Czechoslovakia 2 their language —*adj.* of the Slovaks
slov·en (sluv′ən) *n.* ⟦prob. < MDu *slof,* lax⟧ a careless, untidy person —**slov′en·ly, -li·er, -li·est,** *adj.*
Slo·ve·ni·a (slō vē′nē ə) constituent republic of Yugoslavia —**Slo·ve′ni·an** or **Slo′vene** (-vēn) *adj., n.*
slow (slō) *adj.* ⟦OE *slaw*⟧ 1 not quick in understanding 2 taking a longer time than is usual 3 marked by low speed, etc.; not fast 4 behind the correct time, as a clock 5 passing tediously; dull —*vt., vi.* to make or become slow or slower: often with *up* or *down* —*adv.* in a slow manner —**slow′ly** *adv.* —**slow′ness** *n.*
slow burn [Slang] a gradual working up of anger: often in **do a slow burn**
slow′down′ *n.* a slowing down, as of production
slow motion an effect using slow-motion photography or video techniques
slow′-mo′tion *adj.* 1 moving slowly 2 designating a film or taped TV sequence showing the action slowed down
slow′poke′ (-pōk′) *n.* [Slang] a person who acts or moves slowly
slow′-wit′ted *adj.* mentally slow; dull
SLR *n.* ⟦*s*(*ingle*) *l*(*ens*) *r*(*eflex*)⟧ a camera allowing the photographer to see the subject through the same lens that brings the image to the film
slub (slub) *vt.* **slubbed, slub′bing** ⟦< ?⟧ to draw out (fibers of wool, cotton, etc.) and twist slightly for use in spinning
sludge (sluj) *n.* ⟦var. of *slutch,* mud⟧ 1 mud, mire, or ooze 2 any heavy, slimy deposit, sediment, etc.
slue (slo͞o) *vt., vi.* **slued, slu′ing** ⟦< ?⟧ to turn or swing around

slug[1] (slug) ***n.*** ⟦ME *slugge*, clumsy one⟧ a small mollusk like a shell-less snail

slug[2] (slug) ***n.*** ⟦prob. < prec.⟧ a small piece of metal; specif., a bullet or false coin

slug[3] (slug) ***n.*** ⟦prob. < Dan *sluge*, to gulp⟧ [Slang] a drink of liquor

slug[4] (slug) ***vt.*** **slugged, slug′ging** ⟦< ON *slag*⟧ [Colloq.] to hit hard, esp. with the fist or a bat —***n.*** [Colloq.] a hard blow or hit —**slug′ger** ***n.***

slug·gard (slug′ərd) ***n.*** ⟦< ME *sluggen*, be lazy⟧ a lazy person

slug′gish (-ish) ***adj.*** ⟦< SLUG[1]⟧ 1 lacking energy; lazy 2 slow or slow-moving 3 not functioning with normal vigor —**slug′gish·ness** ***n.***

sluice (slo͞os) ***n.*** ⟦< L *excludere*, to shut out⟧ 1 an artificial channel for water, with a gate to regulate the flow 2 such a gate: also **sluice gate** 3 any channel for excess water 4 a sloping trough, as for washing gold ore —***vt.*** **sluiced, sluic′ing** 1 to draw off through a sluice 2 to wash with water from a sluice

slum (slum) ***n.*** ⟦< ?⟧ a populous area characterized by poverty, poor housing, etc. —***vi.*** **slummed, slum′ming** to visit slums, esp. for reasons held to be condescending —**slum′my, -mi·er, -mi·est,** ***adj.***

slum·ber (slum′bər) ***vi.*** ⟦OE *sluma*⟧ 1 to sleep 2 to be inactive —***n.*** 1 sleep 2 an inactive state

slum′lord′ ***n.*** [Slang] an absentee landlord who exploits slum property

slump (slump) ***vi.*** ⟦prob. < Ger⟧ 1 to fall or sink suddenly 2 to have a drooping posture —***n.*** 1 a sudden fall 2 a decline in activity, prices, performance, etc.

slung (sluŋ) ***vt.*** *pt. & pp. of* SLING

slunk (sluŋk) ***vi.*** *pt. & pp. of* SLINK

slur (slur) ***vt.*** **slurred, slur′ring** ⟦prob. < MDu *sleuren*, to drag⟧ 1 to pass over lightly: often with *over* 2 to pronounce indistinctly 3 to disparage 4 *Music* to produce (successive notes) by gliding without a break —***n.*** 1 a slurring 2 something slurred 3 an aspersion 4 *Music* a symbol (‿) or (⁀) connecting notes to be slurred

slurp (slurp) ***vt., vi.*** ⟦Du *slurpen*, to sip⟧ [Slang] to drink or eat noisily —***n.*** [Slang] a loud sipping or sucking sound

slur·ry (slur′ē) ***n.,*** *pl.* **-ries** ⟦< MDu *slore*, thin mud⟧ a thin, watery mixture of clay, cement, soil, etc.

slush (slush) ***n.*** ⟦prob. < Scand⟧ 1 partly melted snow 2 soft mud 3 sentimentality; drivel —**slush′y, -i·er, -i·est,** ***adj.***

slush fund money used for bribery, political pressure, etc.

slut (slut) ***n.*** ⟦ME *slutte*⟧ 1 a dirty, slovenly woman 2 a sexually promiscuous woman —**slut′tish** ***adj.***

sly (slī) ***adj.*** **sli′er** or **sly′er, sli′est** or **sly′est** ⟦< ON *slœgr*⟧ 1 skillful at trickery; crafty 2 cunningly underhanded 3 playfully mischievous —**on the sly** secretly —**sly′ly** or **sli′ly** ***adv.*** —**sly′ness** ***n.***

smack[1] (smak) ***n.*** ⟦OE *smæc*⟧ 1 a slight taste or flavor 2 a small amount; trace —***vi.*** to have a smack (*of*)

smack[2] (smak) ***n.*** ⟦< ?⟧ 1 a sharp noise made by parting the lips suddenly 2 a loud kiss 3 a slap —***vt.*** 1 to part (the lips) with a smack 2 to kiss or slap loudly —***adv.*** 1 with a smack 2 directly; precisely

smack[3] (smak) ***n.*** ⟦prob. < Du *smak*⟧ a fishing boat with a well for keeping fish alive

smack[4] (smak) ***n.*** ⟦< ?⟧ [Slang] heroin

smack′er ***n.*** [Slang] a dollar bill

small (smôl) ***adj.*** ⟦OE *smæl*⟧ 1 comparatively little in size; not big 2 little in quantity, extent, duration, etc. 3 of little importance; trivial 4 young /*small* children/ 5 mean; petty —***n.*** the small part /the *small* of the back/ —**feel small** to feel shame —**small′ness** ***n.***

small arms firearms of small caliber, as pistols, rifles, etc.

small intestine the narrow section of the intestines, extending from the stomach to the large intestine

small′-mind′ed ***adj.*** mean, narrow-minded, or selfish

small′pox′ ***n.*** an acute, contagious virus disease characterized by fever and pustular eruptions

small talk light conversation about common, everyday things; chitchat

small′-time′ ***adj.*** [Colloq.] minor or petty

smart (smärt) ***vi.*** ⟦OE *smeortan*⟧ 1 *a*) to cause sharp, stinging pain, as a slap *b*) to feel such pain 2 to feel mental distress or irritation —***n.*** 1 a stinging sensation 2 [*pl.*] [Slang] intelligence —***adj.*** 1 causing sharp pain 2 sharp, as pain 3 brisk; lively /a *smart* pace/ 4 intelligent 5 neat; trim 6 stylish —**smart′ly** ***adv.*** —**smart′ness** ***n.***

smart al·eck or **smart al·ec** (al′ik) ⟦prec. + *Aleck*, dim. of *Alexander*⟧ [Colloq.] an offensively conceited person

smart bomb [Mil. Slang] a guided missile directed to its target by electronic means

smart′en ***vt., vi.*** to make or become smart or smarter: usually with *up*

smash (smash) ***vt., vi.*** ⟦prob. < MASH⟧ 1 to break into pieces with noise or violence 2 to hit, collide, or move with force 3 to destroy or be destroyed —***n.*** 1 a hard, heavy hit 2 a violent, noisy breaking 3 a violent collision 4 a popular success

smash′ing ***adj.*** [Colloq.] extraordinary

smash′up′ ***n.*** 1 a violent wreck or collision 2 total failure; ruin

smat·ter·ing (smat′ər iŋ) ***n.*** ⟦ME *smateren*, to chatter⟧ 1 superficial knowledge 2 a small number

smear (smir) ***vt.*** ⟦< OE *smerian*, to anoint⟧ 1 to cover or soil with something greasy, sticky, etc. 2 to apply (something greasy, etc.) 3 to slander —***vi.*** to be or become smeared —***n.*** 1 a mark made by smearing 2 slander —**smear′y, -i·er, -i·est,** ***adj.***

smell (smel) ***vt.*** **smelled** or [Chiefly Brit., etc.] **smelt, smell′ing** ⟦ME *smellen*⟧ 1 to be aware of through the nose; detect the odor of 2 to sense the presence of /to *smell* trouble/ —***vi.*** 1 to use the sense of smell; sniff 2 to have an odor /flowers that do not *smell*/ —***n.*** 1 the sense by which odors are perceived 2 odor; scent 3 a smelling

smelling salts an ammonia compound sniffed to relieve faintness

smell′y ***adj.*** **-i·er, -i·est** having an unpleasant smell

smelt[1] (smelt) ***n.*** ⟦OE⟧ a small, silvery food fish found esp. in northern seas
smelt[2] (smelt) ***vt.*** ⟦< MDu *smelten*⟧ 1 to melt (ore, etc.) so as to extract the pure metal 2 to refine (metal) in this way
smelt[3] (smelt) ***vt., vi.*** *chiefly Brit., etc. pt. & pp. of* SMELL
smelt'er ***n.*** 1 one whose work is smelting 2 a place for smelting
smidg·en (smij'ən) ***n.*** ⟦prob. < dial. *smidge,* particle⟧ [Colloq.] a small amount; bit Also sp. **smidg'in** or **smidg'eon**
smile (smīl) ***vi.*** **smiled, smil'ing** ⟦ME *smilen*⟧ to show pleasure, amusement, affection, etc. by an upward curving of the mouth —***vt.*** to express with a smile —***n.*** the act or expression of smiling —**smil'ing·ly** ***adv.***
smirch (smurch) ***vt.*** ⟦prob. < OFr *esmorcher,* to hurt⟧ 1 to soil or stain 2 to dishonor —***n.*** 1 a smudge; smear 2 a stain on reputation, etc.
smirk (smurk) ***vi.*** ⟦< OE *smearcian,* to smile⟧ to smile in a conceited or complacent way —***n.*** such a smile
smite (smīt) ***vt.*** **smote, smit'ten** or **smote, smit'ing** ⟦OE *smitan*⟧ 1 to strike with powerful effect 2 to affect or impress strongly
smith (smith) ***n.*** 1 one who makes or repairs metal objects; metalworker 2 *short for* BLACKSMITH
Smith (smith), Captain **John** *c.* 1580-1631; Eng. colonist in America
smith·er·eens (smith'ər ēnz') ***n.pl.*** ⟦Ir *smidirin*⟧ [Colloq.] fragments; bits
smith·y (smith'ē) ***n., pl.*** **-ies** the workshop of a smith, esp. a blacksmith
smock (smäk) ***n.*** ⟦OE *smoc*⟧ a loose, shirtlike outer garment worn to protect the clothes
smock'ing ***n.*** decorative stitching used to gather cloth and make it hang in folds
smog (smäg, smôg) ***n.*** ⟦SM(OKE) + (F)OG⟧ a low-lying, perceptible layer of polluted air
smoke (smōk) ***n.*** ⟦OE *smoca*⟧ 1 the vaporous matter arising from something burning 2 any vapor, etc. like this 3 an act of smoking tobacco, etc. 4 a cigarette, cigar, etc. —***vi.*** **smoked, smok'ing** 1 to give off smoke 2 *a*) to draw in and exhale the smoke of tobacco, etc. *b*) to be a habitual user of cigarettes, etc. —***vt.*** 1 to cure (meat, etc.) with smoke 2 to use (a pipe, cigarette, etc.) in smoking 3 to drive out or stupefy as with smoke —**smoke out** to force out of hiding —**smoke'less** ***adj.*** —**smok'er** ***n.***
smoke detector a warning device that sets off a loud signal when excessive smoke or heat is detected
smoke'house' ***n.*** a building where meats, fish, etc. are cured with smoke
smoke screen 1 a cloud of smoke for hiding troop movements, etc. 2 anything said or done to conceal or mislead
smoke'stack' ***n.*** a pipe for discharging smoke from a factory, etc.
smok·y (smō'kē) ***adj.*** **-i·er, -i·est** 1 giving off smoke 2 of, like, or of the color of, smoke 3 filled with smoke —**smok'i·ness** ***n.***
smol·der (smōl'dər) ***vi.*** ⟦ME *smoldren*⟧ 1 to burn and smoke without flame 2 to exist in a suppressed state —***n.*** a smoldering Brit., etc. sp. **smoul·der**
smooch (smōōch) ***n., vt., vi.*** [Slang] kiss
smooth (smōōth) ***adj.*** ⟦OE *smoth*⟧ 1 having an even surface, with no roughness 2 without lumps 3 even or gentle in movement /a *smooth* voyage/ 4 free from interruptions, obstacles, etc. 5 pleasing to the taste; bland 6 having an easy, flowing rhythm or sound 7 polished or ingratiating, esp. in an insincere way —***vt.*** 1 to make level or even 2 to remove lumps or wrinkles from 3 to free from difficulties, etc.; make easy 4 to make calm; soothe 5 to polish or refine —***adv.*** in a smooth manner —**smooth'ly** ***adv.*** —**smooth'ness** ***n.***
smooth muscle involuntary muscle tissue occurring in the uterus, stomach, blood vessels, etc.
smooth'-spo'ken ***adj.*** speaking in a pleasing, persuasive, or polished manner
smor·gas·bord or **smör·gås·bord** (smôr'gəs bôrd', smur'-) ***n.*** ⟦Swed⟧ 1 a wide variety of appetizers, cheeses, meats, etc., served buffet style 2 a restaurant serving these
smote (smōt) ***vt., vi.*** *pt. & alt. pp. of* SMITE
smoth·er (smuth'ər) ***vt.*** ⟦< ME *smorther,* dense smoke⟧ 1 to keep from getting air; suffocate 2 to cover over thickly 3 to stifle /to *smother* a yawn/ —***vi.*** to be suffocated
smudge (smuj) ***vt., vi.*** **smudged, smudg'ing** ⟦ME *smogen*⟧ to make or become dirty; smear —***n.*** 1 a dirty spot 2 *a*) a fire made to produce dense smoke *b*) such smoke, used to protect plants from frost, etc. —**smudg'y, -i·er, -i·est,** ***adj.***
smug (smug) ***adj.*** **smug'ger, smug'gest** ⟦prob. < LowG *smuk,* trim, neat⟧ annoyingly self-satisfied; complacent —**smug'ly** ***adv.*** —**smug'ness** ***n.***
smug·gle (smug'əl) ***vt.*** **-gled, -gling** ⟦< LowG *smuggeln*⟧ 1 to bring into or take out of a country secretly or illegally 2 to bring, take, etc. secretly —***vi.*** to practice smuggling —**smug'gler** ***n.***
smut (smut) ***n.*** ⟦< LowG *smutt*⟧ 1 sooty matter 2 a soiled spot 3 indecent talk, writing, etc. 4 a fungous disease of plants —**smut'ty, -ti·er, -ti·est,** ***adj.***
Sn ⟦L *stannum*⟧ *Chem. symbol for* tin
snack (snak) ***n.*** ⟦< ME *snaken,* to bite⟧ a light meal between regular meals —***vi.*** to eat a snack
snack bar a lunch counter, cafeteria, etc. serving snacks
snaf·fle (snaf'əl) ***n.*** ⟦prob. < Du *snavel,* horse's muzzle⟧ a bit for a horse's mouth, having a joint in the middle and no curb
snag (snag) ***n.*** ⟦< Scand⟧ 1 a sharp point or projection 2 an underwater tree stump or branch 3 a tear, as in cloth, made by a snag, etc. 4 an unexpected or hidden difficulty, etc. —***vt.*** **snagged, snag'ging** 1 to damage on a snag 2 to impede with a snag
snail (snāl) ***n.*** ⟦OE *snægl*⟧ a slow-moving mollusk having a wormlike body and a spiral protective shell
snake (snāk) ***n.*** ⟦OE *snaca*⟧ 1 a long, scaly limbless reptile with a tapering tail 2 a treacherous or deceitful person —***vi.***

snaked, snak'ing to move, twist, etc. like a snake —snake'like' *adj.*

snak'y *adj.* **-i·er, -i·est** 1 of or like a snake or snakes 2 winding; twisting 3 cunningly treacherous or evil

snap (snap) *vi., vt.* **snapped, snap'ping** ⟦< MDu *snappen*⟧ 1 to bite or grasp suddenly: with *at* 2 to speak or utter sharply: with *at* 3 to break suddenly 4 to make or cause to make a sudden, cracking sound 5 to close, fasten, etc. with this sound 6 to move or cause to move suddenly and smartly /to *snap* to attention/ 7 to take a snapshot (of) —*n.* 1 a sudden bite, grasp, etc. 2 a sharp cracking sound /the *snap* of a whip/ 3 a short, angry utterance 4 a brief period of cold weather 5 a fastening that closes with a click 6 a hard, thin cookie 7 *short for* SNAPSHOT 8 [Colloq.] alertness or vigor 9 [Slang] an easy job, problem, etc. —*adj.* 1 made or done quickly /a *snap* decision/ 2 that fastens with a snap 3 [Slang] easy —**snap out of it** to improve or recover quickly —**snap'per** *n.* —**snap'pish** *adj.*

snap bean a green bean or wax bean

snap'drag'on *n.* ⟦SNAP + DRAGON: from the mouth-shaped flowers⟧ a plant with saclike, two-lipped flowers

snap'py *adj.* **-pi·er, -pi·est** 1 cross; irritable 2 that snaps 3 [Colloq.] *a*) brisk or lively *b*) sharply chilly 4 [Colloq.] stylish; smart

snap'shot' *n.* an informal photograph taken quickly with a hand camera

snare (snar) *n.* ⟦< ON *snara*⟧ 1 a trap for small animals 2 anything dangerous, etc. that tempts or attracts 3 a length of wire or gut across the bottom of a drum —*vt.* **snared, snar'ing** to catch as in a snare; trap

snarl[1] (snärl) *vi.* ⟦< earlier *snar*, to growl⟧ 1 to growl, baring the teeth, as a dog 2 to speak sharply, as in anger —*vt.* to utter with a snarl —*n.* 1 a fierce growl 2 an angry utterance —**snarl'ing·ly** *adv.*

snarl[2] (snärl) *n., vt., vi.* ⟦< SNARE⟧ tangle; disorder —**snarl'y, -i·er, -i·est,** *adj.*

snatch (snach) *vt.* ⟦ME *snacchen*⟧ to take suddenly, without right, etc.; grab —*vi.* 1 to try to seize; grab (*at*) 2 to take advantage of a chance, etc. eagerly: with *at* —*n.* 1 a snatching 2 a brief period 3 a fragment; bit

sneak (snēk) *vt., vi.* **sneaked** or **snuck, sneak'ing** ⟦prob. < OE *snican*, to crawl⟧ to move, act, give, put, take, etc. secretly or stealthily —*n.* 1 one who sneaks 2 a sneaking —*adj.* without warning /a *sneak* attack/ —**sneak'y, -i·er, -i·est,** *adj.*

sneak'er *n.* a shoe with a cloth upper and a soft rubber sole

sneak preview an advance showing of a film, as for evaluating audience reaction

sneer (snir) *vi.* ⟦ME *sneren*⟧ 1 to show scorn as by curling the upper lip 2 to express derision, etc. in speech or writing —*n.* a sneering

sneeze (snēz) *vi.* **sneezed, sneez'ing** ⟦ME *snesen*⟧ to exhale breath from the nose and mouth in an involuntary, explosive action —*n.* a sneezing

snick·er (snik'ər) *vi.* ⟦echoic⟧ to laugh in a sly, partly stifled way —*n.* a snickering

snide (snīd) *adj.* ⟦prob. < Du dial.⟧ slyly malicious or derisive

sniff (snif) *vi., vt.* ⟦ME *sniffen*⟧ 1 to draw in (air) forcibly through the nose 2 to express (disdain, etc.) by sniffing 3 to smell by sniffing —*n.* 1 an act or sound of sniffing 2 something sniffed

snif·fle (snif'əl) *vi.* **-fled, -fling** to sniff repeatedly, as in checking mucus running from the nose —*n.* an act or sound of sniffling —**the sniffles** [Colloq.] a head cold

snif·ter (snif'tər) *n.* ⟦< *snift*, var. of SNIFF⟧ a goblet tapering to a small opening to concentrate the aroma, as of brandy

snig·ger (snig'ər) *vi., vt., n.* ⟦echoic⟧ SNICKER

snip (snip) *vt., vi.* **snipped, snip'ping** ⟦Du *snippen*⟧ to cut or cut off in a short, quick stroke, as with scissors —*n.* 1 a small piece cut off 2 [Colloq.] a small or young person

snipe (snīp) *n.* ⟦< ON *snipa*⟧ a long-billed wading bird —*vi.* **sniped, snip'ing** 1 to hunt snipe 2 to shoot from a hidden position, as at individuals —**snip'er** *n.*

snip·pet (snip'it) *n.* ⟦dim. of SNIP⟧ a small, snipped piece; scrap, specif. of information, a book, etc.

snip'py *adj.* **-pi·er, -pi·est** [Colloq.] insolently curt, sharp, etc.

snit (snit) *n.* ⟦< ? prec. + (F)IT[2]⟧ a fit of anger, pique, etc. Usually **in** (or **into**) **a snit**

snitch (snich) *vt.* [Slang] to steal; pilfer —*vi.* [Slang] to tattle (*on*) —*n.* [Slang] an informer

sniv·el (sniv'əl) *vi.* **-eled** or **-elled, -el·ing** or **-el·ling** ⟦ME *snivelen*⟧ 1 to cry and sniffle 2 to complain and whine 3 to make a tearful, often false display of grief, etc.

snob (snäb) *n.* ⟦< ?⟧ one who thinks that money and rank are very important, and has contempt for those he considers inferior —**snob'bish** *adj.* —**snob'bish·ness** or **snob'ber·y** *n.*

snood (snood) *n.* ⟦OE *snod*⟧ a baglike net worn at the back of a woman's head to hold the hair

snoop (snoop) *vi.* ⟦Du *snoepen*, eat snacks on the sly⟧ [Colloq.] to pry about in a sneaking way —*n.* [Colloq.] one who snoops —**snoop'y, -i·er, -i·est,** *adj.*

snoot (snoot) *n.* ⟦see SNOUT⟧ 1 [Colloq.] the nose 2 the face

snoot'y *adj.* **-i·er, -i·est** [Colloq.] haughty; snobbish —**snoot'i·ness** *n.*

snooze (snooz) *n.* ⟦< LowG *snusen*, to snore⟧ [Colloq.] a brief sleep; nap —*vi.* **snoozed, snooz'ing** [Colloq.] to nap; doze —**snooz'er** *n.*

snore (snôr) *vi.* **snored, snor'ing** ⟦see SNARL[1]⟧ to breathe, while asleep, with harsh sounds —*n.* the act or sound of snoring —**snor'er** *n.*

SNORKEL

snor·kel (snôr'kəl) *n.* ⟦Ger *schnorchel*,

inlet] a breathing tube extending above the water, used in swimming just below the surface —*vi.* **-keled, -kel·ing** to swim underwater using a snorkel —**snor′kel·er** *n.*
snort (snôrt) *vi.* [prob. < SNORE] 1 to force breath audibly through the nostrils 2 to express contempt, etc. by a snort —*vt.* 1 to express with a snort 2 [Slang] to inhale (a drug) through the nose —*n.* 1 a snorting 2 [Slang] a quick drink of liquor
snot (snät) *n.* [OE (*ge*)*snot,* mucus] [Slang] 1 nasal mucus: considered mildly vulgar 2 an impudent young person —**snot′ty, -ti·er, -ti·est,** *adj.*
snout (snout) *n.* [prob. < MDu *snute*] the projecting nose and jaws of an animal
snow (snō) *n.* [OE *snaw*] 1 frozen particles of water vapor that fall to earth as soft, white flakes 2 a falling of snow —*vi.* to fall as or like snow —*vt.* 1 to cover or obstruct with snow: usually with *in, up, under,* etc. 2 [Slang] to deceive or mislead —**snow under** 1 to overwhelm with work, etc. 2 to defeat decisively —**snow′y, -i·er, -i·est,** *adj.*
snow′ball′ *n.* a mass of snow packed into a ball —*vi.* to grow rapidly like a ball of snow rolling downhill
snow′bank′ *n.* a large mass of snow
Snow′belt′ the NE and Midwestern U.S., characterized by cold, snowy winters Also **Snow Belt**
snow′bound′ *adj.* shut in or blocked off by snow
snow′drift′ *n.* a heap of snow piled up by the wind
snow′drop′ *n.* a small plant with small, bell-shaped, white flowers
snow′fall′ *n.* a fall of snow or the amount of this in a given area or time
snow fence a light fence of lath and wire to control the drifting of snow
snow′flake′ *n.* a single snow crystal
snow′man′ *n., pl.* **-men′** a crude human figure made of snow packed together
snow′mo·bile′ *n.* a motor vehicle with steerable runners at the front and tractor treads at the rear
snow′plow′ *n.* a plowlike machine used to clear snow off a road, etc.
snow′shoe′ *n.* one of a pair of racket-shaped wooden frames crisscrossed with leather strips, etc., worn on the feet to prevent sinking in deep snow
snow′storm′ *n.* a storm with a heavy snowfall
snow′suit′ *n.* a child's heavily lined, hooded garment, for cold weather
snow tire a tire with a deep tread for added traction on snow or ice
snub (snub) *vt.* **snubbed, snub′bing** [< ON *snubba,* chide] 1 to treat with scorn, disdain, etc. 2 to check suddenly the movement of (a rope, etc.) —*n.* scornful treatment —*adj.* short and turned up, as a nose
snub′-nosed′ *adj.* having a snub nose
snuck (snuk) *vi., vt. alt. pt. & pp. of* SNEAK
snuff[1] (snuf) *vt.* [ME] 1 to trim off the charred end of (a wick) 2 to put out (a candle) —**snuff out** 1 to extinguish 2 to destroy —**snuff′er** *n.*
snuff[2] (snuf) *vt., vi.* [< MDu *snuffen*] to sniff or smell —*n.* 1 a sniff 2 powdered tobacco taken up into the nose or put on the gums —**up to snuff** [Colloq.] up to the usual standard
snuff′box′ *n.* a small box for snuff
snuf·fle (snuf′əl) *n., vi.* **-fled, -fling** [< SNUFF[2]] SNIFFLE
snug (snug) *adj.* **snug′ger, snug′gest** [prob. < Scand] 1 warm and cozy 2 neat; trim /a *snug* cottage/ 3 tight in fit /a *snug* coat/ 4 hidden /to lie *snug*/ —**snug′ly** *adv.*
snug′gle (-əl) *vi., vt.* **-gled, -gling** [< prec.] to nestle; cuddle
so (sō) *adv.* [OE *swa*] 1 as shown or described /hold the bat just *so*/ 2 *a*) to such an extent /why are you *so* late?/ *b*) very /they are *so* happy/ *c*) [Colloq.] very much /she *so* wants to go/ 3 therefore /they were tired, and *so* left/ 4 more or less /fifty dollars or *so*/ 5 also; likewise /I am going and *so* are you/ 6 then /and *so* to bed/ —*conj.* 1 in order (*that*) 2 [Colloq.] with the result that —*pron.* that which has been specified or named /he is a friend and will remain *so*/ —*interj.* an exclamation of surprise, triumph, etc. —*adj.* true /that's *so*/ —**and so on** (or **forth**) and the rest; et cetera —**so as** with the purpose or result —**so what?** [Colloq.] even if so, what then?
soak (sōk) *vt.* [OE *socian*] 1 to make thoroughly wet 2 to take in; absorb: usually with *up* 3 [Colloq.] to overcharge —*vi.* 1 to stay in a liquid for wetting, softening, etc. 2 to penetrate —*n.* 1 a soaking or being soaked 2 [Slang] a drunkard
so′-and-so′ *n., pl.* **so′-and-sos′** [Colloq.] an unspecified person or thing: often used euphemistically
soap (sōp) *n.* [OE *sape*] 1 a substance, usually a salt derived from fatty acids, used with water to produce suds for washing 2 [Slang] SOAP OPERA: also **soap′er** —*vt.* to scrub, etc. with soap —**no soap** [Slang] (it is) not acceptable —**soap′y, -i·er, -i·est,** *adj.*
soap′box′ *n.* any improvised platform used in speaking to a street audience
soap opera [Colloq.] a radio or television serial melodrama
soap′stone′ *n.* a soft, impure talc in rock form, used as an abrasive, etc.
soap′suds′ *n.pl.* foamy, soapy water
soar (sôr) *vi.* [ult. < L *ex-,* out + *aura,* air] 1 to rise or fly high into the air 2 to glide along high in the air 3 to rise above the usual level
So·a·ve (sə wä′vā, swä′-) *n.* [It] an Italian dry white wine
sob (säb) *vi.* **sobbed, sob′bing** [ME *sobben*] to weep aloud with short, gasping breaths —*vt.* to utter with sobs —*n.* the act or sound of sobbing
so·ber (sō′bər) *adj.* [< L *sobrius*] 1 temperate, esp. in the use of liquor 2 not drunk 3 serious, reasonable, sedate, etc. 4 not flashy; plain, as color, clothes, etc. —*vt., vi.* to make or become sober: often with *up* or *down* —**so′ber·ly** *adv.* —**so′ber·ness** *n.*
so·bri·e·ty (sə brī′ə tē) *n.* a being sober; specif., *a*) temperance, esp. in the use of liquor *b*) seriousness

so·bri·quet (sō′brə kā′) *n.* ⟦Fr⟧ **1** a nickname **2** an assumed name
soc. 1 socialist 2 society
so′-called′ *adj.* **1** known by this term **2** inaccurately or questionably designated as such /a *so-called* liberal/
soc·cer (säk′ər) *n.* ⟦alt. < (*as*)*soc*(*iation foot-ball*)⟧ a kind of football played by kicking a round ball
so·cia·ble (sō′shə bəl) *adj.* ⟦see fol.⟧ **1** friendly; gregarious **2** characterized by informal conversation and companionship —*n.* a social —**so′cia·bil′i·ty**, *pl.* **-ties**, *n.* —**so′cia·bly** *adv.*
so·cial (sō′shəl) *adj.* ⟦< L *socius*, companion⟧ **1** of or having to do with human beings in their living together **2** living with others; gregarious /man as a *social* being/ **3** of or having to do with society, esp. fashionable society **4** sociable **5** of or for companionship **6** of or doing welfare work —*n.* an informal gathering —**so′cial·ly** *adv.*
social disease any venereal disease
so′cial·ism′ (-iz′əm) *n.* **1** a theory by which the means of production and distribution are owned by society rather than by individuals **2** [*often* **S-**] a political movement for establishing such a system —**so′cial·ist** *n., adj.* —**so′cial·is′tic** *adj.*
so·cial·ite (sō′shəl īt′) *n.* a person prominent in fashionable society
so′cial·ize′ (-īz′) *vt.* **-ized′**, **-iz′ing** **1** to make social **2** to subject to governmental ownership or control —*vi.* to take part in social activity —**so′cial·i·za′tion** *n.*
socialized medicine a system supplying complete medical and hospital care to all through public funds
social science a field of study, as economics or anthropology, dealing with the structure, etc. of society —**social scientist**
social security [*often* **S- S-**] a Federal system of old-age, unemployment, or disability insurance
social work the promotion of the welfare of the community and the individual, as through counseling services, etc. —**social worker**
so·ci·e·ty (sə sī′ə tē) *n., pl.* **-ties** ⟦< L *socius*, companion⟧ **1** a group of persons forming a single community **2** the system of living together in such a group **3** all people, collectively **4** companionship **5** an organized group with some interest in common **6** the wealthy, dominant class —**so·ci′e·tal** (-təl) *adj.*
Society of Friends a Christian denomination that believes in plain worship, pacifism, etc. See QUAKER
so·ci·o·e·co·nom·ic (sō′sē ō ē′kə näm′ik, -ek′ə-) *adj.* of or involving both social and economic factors
so·ci·ol·o·gy (sō′sē äl′ə jē, -shē-) *n.* ⟦see SOCIAL & -LOGY⟧ the science of social relations, organization, and change —**so′ci·o·log′i·cal** (-ə lä′ji kəl) *adj.* —**so′ci·ol′o·gist** *n.*
so·ci·o·path (sō′sē ə path′, -shē-) *n.* an aggressively antisocial psychopath
sock[1] (säk) *n., pl.* **socks** or **sox** ⟦< L *soccus*, type of light shoe⟧ a short stocking
sock[2] (säk) *vt.* [Slang] to hit with force —*n.* [Slang] a blow
sock·et (säk′it) *n.* ⟦< OFr *soc*, plowshare⟧ a hollow part into which something fits /an eye *socket*/
sock·eye salmon (säk′ī) a red-fleshed salmon of the N Pacific
Soc·ra·tes (säk′rə tēz′) *c.* 470-399 B.C.; Athenian philosopher & teacher —**So·crat·ic** (sə krat′ik) *adj., n.*
sod (säd) *n.* ⟦prob. < MDu *sode*⟧ **1** a surface layer of earth containing grass; turf **2** a piece of this —*vt.* **sod′ded, sod′ding** to cover with sod
so·da (sō′də) *n.* ⟦ML⟧ **1** *a*) SODIUM BICARBONATE *b*) SODA WATER *c*) SODA POP **2** a drink made with soda water, syrup, and ice cream
soda biscuit **1** a biscuit made with baking soda and sour milk or buttermilk **2** [Chiefly Brit.] SODA CRACKER
soda cracker a light, crisp cracker made from flour, water, and leavening, orig. baking soda
soda fountain a counter for making and serving soft drinks, sodas, etc.
soda pop a flavored, carbonated soft drink
soda water **1** water charged under pressure with carbon dioxide gas **2** SODA POP
sod·den (säd′'n) *adj.* **1** soaked through **2** soggy from improper cooking **3** dull or stupefied, as from liquor —**sod′den·ly** *adv.*
so·di·um (sō′dē əm) *n.* ⟦< *soda*⟧ an alkaline metallic chemical element
sodium bicarbonate a white crystalline compound, $NaHCO_3$, used in baking powder, as an antacid, etc.
sodium chloride common salt
sodium hydroxide a caustic lye used in oil refining, etc.
sodium nitrate a clear, crystalline salt used in explosives, fertilizers, etc.
sodium pen·to·thal (pen′tə thôl′) a yellowish substance injected as a general anesthetic
Sod·om and Go·mor·rah (säd′əm and gə môr′ə) *Bible* two sinful cities destroyed by fire
sod′om·y (-ē) *n.* ⟦after *Sodom*⟧ any sexual intercourse held to be abnormal, as between two men —**sod′om·ite′** (-īt′) *n.*
so·ev·er (sō ev′ər) *adv.* **1** in any way **2** of any kind; at all
so·fa (sō′fə) *n.* ⟦< Ar *ṣuffa*, a platform⟧ an upholstered couch with fixed back and arms
sofa bed a sofa that can be opened into a bed
So·fi·a (sō′fē ə) capital of Bulgaria: pop. 1,173,000
soft (sôft) *adj.* ⟦OE *softe*, gentle⟧ **1** giving way easily under pressure **2** easily cut, marked, shaped, etc. /a *soft* metal/ **3** not as hard as is normal, desirable, etc. /*soft* butter/ **4** smooth to the touch **5** easy to digest: said of a diet **6** nonalcoholic: said of drinks **7** having few of the mineral salts that keep soap from lathering **8** mild, as a breeze **9** weak; not vigorous **10** easy /a *soft* job/ **11** kind or gentle **12** not bright: said of color or light **13** gentle; low: said of sound —*adv.* gently; quietly —**soft′ly** *adv.* —**soft′ness** *n.*
soft′ball′ *n.* **1** a game like baseball played with a larger and softer ball **2** this ball
soft′-boiled′ *adj.* boiled a short time to keep the yolk soft: said of an egg

soft coal BITUMINOUS COAL
soft drink a nonalcoholic drink, esp. one that is carbonated
soft·en (sôf′ən) ***vt., vi.*** to make or become soft or softer —**soft′en·er** ***n.***
soft′heart′ed ***adj.*** 1 full of compassion 2 not strict or severe; lenient
soft landing a landing of a spacecraft without damage to the craft or its contents
soft palate the soft, fleshy part at the rear of the roof of the mouth; velum
soft′-ped′al ***vt.*** **-aled** or **-alled**, **-al·ing** or **-al·ling** ⟦from pedal action in a piano, etc.⟧ [Colloq.] to make less emphatic; tone down; play down
soft sell selling that relies on subtle inducement or suggestion
soft soap [Colloq.] flattery or smooth talk —**soft′-soap′** ***vt.***
soft′ware′ ***n.*** the programs, routines, etc. for a computer
soft′wood′ ***n.*** 1 any light, easily cut wood 2 the wood of any tree bearing cones, as the pine
soft′y ***n., pl.*** **soft′ies** [Colloq.] one who is too sentimental or trusting
sog·gy (säg′ē) ***adj.*** **-gi·er, -gi·est** ⟦prob. < ON *sog*, a sucking⟧ soaked; moist and heavy —**sog′gi·ness** ***n.***
soil^1 (soil) ***n.*** ⟦< L *solum*⟧ 1 the surface layer of earth, supporting plant life 2 land; country /native *soil*/ 3 ground or earth /barren *soil*/
soil^2 (soil) ***vt.*** ⟦ult. < L *sus*, pig⟧ 1 to make dirty; stain 2 to disgrace —***vi.*** to become soiled or dirty —***n.*** a soiled spot; stain
soi·ree or **soi·rée** (swä rā′) ***n.*** ⟦< Fr *soir*, evening⟧ an evening party
so·journ (sō′jurn; *also, for v.*, sō jurn′) ***vi.*** ⟦< L *sub-*, under + *diurnus*, of a day⟧ to live somewhere temporarily —***n.*** a brief stay; visit
sol (sōl) ***n.*** ⟦< ML⟧ *Music* the fifth tone of the diatonic scale
Sol (säl) ⟦L⟧ 1 *Rom. Myth.* the sun god 2 the sun personified
sol·ace (säl′is) ***n.*** ⟦< L *solacium*⟧ 1 an easing of grief, loneliness, etc. 2 a comfort or consolation —***vt.*** **-aced, -ac·ing** to comfort; console
so·lar (sō′lər) ***adj.*** ⟦< L *sol*, the sun⟧ 1 of or having to do with the sun 2 produced by or coming from the sun
solar battery an assembly of cells (**solar cells**) used to convert solar energy into electric power
so·lar·i·um (sō ler′ē əm) ***n., pl.*** **-i·a** (-ē ə) ⟦L < *sol*, sun⟧ a glassed-in porch, room, etc. for sunning
solar plexus a network of nerves in the abdomen behind the stomach
solar system that portion of our galaxy subject to the sun's gravity; specif., the sun and its planets
sold (sōld) ***vt., vi.*** *pt. & pp. of* SELL
sol·der (säd′ər) ***n.*** ⟦< L *solidus*, solid⟧ a metal alloy used when melted to join or patch metal parts, etc. —***vt., vi.*** to join with solder
sol·dier (sōl′jər) ***n.*** ⟦< LL *solidus*, a coin⟧ 1 a member of an army 2 an enlisted person, as distinguished from an officer 3 one who works for a specified cause —***vi.*** 1 to serve as a soldier 2 to shirk one's duty, as by feigning illness, etc. —**sol′dier·ly** ***adj.***
soldier of fortune a mercenary or any adventurer
sole^1 (sōl) ***n.*** ⟦< L *solum*, a base⟧ 1 the bottom surface of the foot 2 the part of a shoe, etc. corresponding to this —***vt.*** **soled, sol′ing** to furnish (a shoe, etc.) with a sole
sole^2 (sōl) ***adj.*** ⟦< L *solus*⟧ without another; single; one and only
sole^3 (sōl) ***n., pl.*** **sole** or **soles** ⟦< L *solea*, SOLE^1: from its shape⟧ a sea flatfish valued as food
sol·e·cism (säl′ə siz′əm) ***n.*** ⟦< Gr *soloikos*, speaking incorrectly⟧ a violation of the conventional usage, grammar, etc. of a language
sole·ly (sōl′lē) ***adv.*** 1 alone 2 only, exclusively, or merely
sol·emn (säl′əm) ***adj.*** ⟦< L *sollus*, all + *annus*, year⟧ 1 sacred 2 formal 3 serious; grave; earnest 4 awe-inspiring —**sol′emn·ly** ***adv.***
so·lem·ni·ty (sə lem′nə tē) ***n., pl.*** **-ties** 1 solemn ceremony, ritual, etc. 2 seriousness; gravity; impressiveness
sol·em·nize (säl′əm nīz′) ***vt.*** **-nized′, -niz′·ing** 1 to celebrate formally or according to ritual 2 to perform the ceremony of (marriage, etc.)
so·le·noid (sō′lə noid′, säl′ə-) ***n.*** ⟦< Gr *sōlēn*, tube + *eidos*, a form⟧ a coil of wire that acts like a bar magnet when carrying a current
so·lic·it (sə lis′it) ***vt., vi.*** ⟦see SOLICITOUS⟧ 1 to appeal to (persons) for (aid, donations, etc.) 2 to entice or lure —**so·lic′i·ta′tion** ***n.***
so·lic′i·tor ***n.*** 1 one who solicits trade, contributions, etc. 2 in England, a lawyer other than a barrister 3 the law officer for a city, etc.
so·lic·i·tous (sə lis′ə təs) ***adj.*** ⟦< L *sollus*, whole + *ciere*, set in motion⟧ 1 showing care or concern /*solicitous* for her welfare/ 2 desirous; eager
so·lic′i·tude′ (-to͞od′) ***n.*** a being solicitous; care, concern, etc.
sol·id (säl′id) ***adj.*** ⟦< L *solidus*⟧ 1 relatively firm or compact; neither liquid nor gaseous 2 not hollow 3 having three dimensions 4 firm; strong; substantial 5 having no breaks or divisions 6 of one color, material, etc. throughout 7 showing unity; unanimous 8 reliable or dependable —***n.*** 1 a solid substance, not a liquid or gas 2 an object having length, breadth, and thickness —**sol′id·ly** ***adv.*** —**sol′id·ness** ***n.***
sol·i·dar·i·ty (säl′ə dar′ə tē) ***n.*** complete unity, as of opinion, feeling, etc.
so·lid·i·fy (sə lid′ə fī′) ***vt., vi.*** **-fied′, -fy′ing** to make or become solid, hard, etc. —**so·lid′i·fi·ca′tion** ***n.***
so·lid′i·ty (-tē) ***n.*** a being solid
sol′id-state′ ***adj.*** 1 of the branch of physics dealing with the structure, properties, etc. of solids 2 equipped with transistors, etc.
so·lil·o·quy (sə lil′ə kwē) ***n., pl.*** **-quies** ⟦< L *solus*, alone + *loqui*, speak⟧ 1 a talking to oneself 2 lines in a drama spoken by a character as if to himself —**so·lil′o·quize′** (-kwīz′), **-quized′, -quiz′ing, *vi., vt.***
sol·i·taire (säl′ə ter′) ***n.*** ⟦Fr: see fol.⟧ 1 a

diamond or other gem set by itself 2 a card game for one player

sol'i·tar'y (-ē) *adj.* ⟦< L *solus*, alone⟧ 1 living or being alone 2 single; only /a *solitary* example/ 3 lonely; remote 4 done in solitude

sol·i·tude (säl'ə to͞od') *n.* ⟦see prec.⟧ 1 a being solitary, or alone; seclusion 2 a secluded place

so·lo (sō'lō) *n., pl.* **-los** or **-li** (-lē) ⟦It < L *solus*, alone⟧ 1 a musical piece or passage to be performed by one person 2 any performance by one person alone —*adj.* for or by a single person —*adv.* alone —*vi.* **-loed, -lo·ing** to perform a solo —**so'lo·ist** *n.*

Sol·o·mon (säl'ə mən) *Bible* king of Israel noted for his wisdom

Solomon Islands country on a group of islands in the SW Pacific, east of New Guinea: *c.* 11,500 sq. mi.; pop. 283,000

So·lon (sō'lən, -län') *c.* 640-*c.* 559 B.C.; Athenian statesman & lawgiver

so long [Colloq.] GOODBYE

sol·stice (säl'stis) *n.* ⟦< L *sol*, sun + *sistere*, to stand⟧ the time of the year when the sun reaches the point farthest north (June 21 or 22) or farthest south (Dec. 21 or 22) of the equator: in the Northern Hemisphere, the **summer solstice** and **winter solstice**, respectively

sol·u·ble (säl'yo͞o bəl) *adj.* ⟦see SOLVE⟧ 1 that can be dissolved 2 capable of being solved —**sol'u·bil'i·ty** *n.*

sol·ute (säl'yo͞ot') *n.* the substance dissolved in a solution

so·lu·tion (sə lo͞o'shən) *n.* ⟦see fol.⟧ 1 the solving of a problem 2 an answer, explanation, etc. 3 the dispersion of one substance in another, usually a liquid, so as to form a homogeneous mixture 4 the mixture so produced

solve (sälv) *vt.* **solved, solv'ing** ⟦< L *se-*, apart + *luere*, let go⟧ to find the answer to (a problem, etc.); explain —**solv'a·ble** *adj.* —**solv'er** *n.*

sol·vent (säl'vənt) *adj.* ⟦see prec.⟧ 1 able to pay all one's debts 2 that can dissolve another substance —*n.* a substance that can dissolve another substance —**sol'ven·cy** *n.*

So·ma·li·a (sō mä'lē ə) country of E Africa, on the Indian Ocean: 246,201 sq. mi.; pop. 7,825,000

so·mat·ic (sō mat'ik) *adj.* ⟦< Gr *sōma*, body⟧ of the body; physical

somatic cell any of the cells that form the tissues and organs of the body: opposed to GERM CELL

som·ber (säm'bər) *adj.* ⟦< L *sub*, under + *umbra*, shade⟧ 1 dark and gloomy or dull 2 dismal; sad Chiefly Brit. sp. **som'bre** —**som'ber·ly** *adv.*

som·bre·ro (säm brer'ō) *n., pl.* **-ros** ⟦Sp < *sombra*, shade: see prec.⟧ a broad-brimmed, tall-crowned hat worn in Mexico, the Southwest, etc.

some (sum) *adj.* ⟦OE *sum*⟧ 1 certain but not specified or known /open *some* evenings/ 2 of a certain unspecified quantity, degree, etc. /have *some* candy/ 3 about /*some* ten of them/ 4 [Colloq.] remarkable, striking, etc. /it was *some* fight/ —*pron.* a certain unspecified number, quantity, etc. /*some* of them agree/ —*adv.* 1 approximately /*some* ten men/ 2 [Colloq.] to some extent; somewhat /slept *some*/ 3 [Colloq.] to a great extent or at a great rate /must run *some* to catch up/ —**and then some** [Colloq.] and more than that

-some[1] (səm) ⟦OE *-sum*⟧ *suffix* tending to be /*tiresome*/

-some[2] (sōm) ⟦< Gr *sōma*, body⟧ *combining form* body /*chromosome*/

some·bod·y (sum'bäd'ē, -bud'ē) *pron.* a person unknown or not named; some person; someone —*n., pl.* **-bod'ies** a person of importance

some'day' *adv.* at some future day or time

some'how' *adv.* in a way or by a method not known or stated Often in **somehow or other**

some'one' *pron.* SOMEBODY

som·er·sault (sum'ər sôlt') *n.* ⟦< L *supra*, over + *saltus*, a leap⟧ an acrobatic stunt performed by turning the body one full revolution, heels over head —*vi.* to perform a somersault

some'thing *n.* 1 a thing not definitely known, understood, etc. /*something* went wrong/ 2 a definite but unspecified thing /have *something* to eat/ 3 a bit; a little 4 [Colloq.] an important or remarkable person or thing —*adv.* 1 somewhat /looks *something* like me/ 2 [Colloq.] really; quite /sounds *something* awful/ —**make something of** 1 to find a use for 2 to treat as of great importance 3 [Colloq.] to make an issue of —**something else** [Slang] one that is quite remarkable

some'time' *adv.* at some unspecified or future time —*adj.* 1 former 2 occasional

some'times' *adv.* occasionally

some'way' *adv.* somehow or other Also **some'ways'**

some'what' *n.* some degree, amount, part, etc. —*adv.* to some extent or degree; a little

some'where' *adv.* 1 in, to, or at some place not known or specified 2 at some time, degree, age, figure, etc. (with *about, around, near, in, between*, etc.)

som·nam·bu·lism (säm nam'byo͞o liz'əm) *n.* ⟦< L *somnus*, sleep + *ambulare*, to walk⟧ sleepwalking —**som·nam'bu·list** *n.*

som·no·lent (säm'nə lənt) *adj.* ⟦< L *somnus*, sleep⟧ 1 sleepy 2 inducing drowsiness —**som'no·lence** *n.*

son (sun) *n.* ⟦OE *sunu*⟧ 1 a boy or man in his relationship to his parents 2 a male descendant —**the Son** Jesus

so·nar (sō'när') *n.* ⟦*so(und) n(avigation) a(nd) r(anging)*⟧ an apparatus that transmits sound waves in water, used in finding submarines, depths, etc.

so·na·ta (sə nät'ə) *n.* ⟦It < L *sonare*, to sound⟧ a musical composition for one or two instruments, usually consisting of several movements

song (sôŋ) *n.* ⟦OE *sang*⟧ 1 the act or art of singing 2 a piece of music for singing 3 *a)* [Old Poet.] poetry *b)* a ballad or simple lyric set to music 4 a singing sound —**for a song** for a small sum; cheap

song'bird' *n.* a bird that makes vocal sounds that are like music

song'fest' *n.* ⟦SONG + -FEST⟧ an informal

gathering of people for singing, esp. folk songs

song′ster (-stər) ***n.*** a singer —**song′stress** (-stris) ***n.fem.***

son·ic (sän′ik) ***adj.*** ⟦< L *sonus*, a sound⟧ of or having to do with sound or the speed of sound

sonic barrier the large increase of air resistance met when flying near the speed of sound

sonic boom the explosive sound of a supersonic jet passing overhead

son′-in-law′ ***n.***, *pl.* **sons′-in-law′** the husband of one's daughter

son·net (sän′it) ***n.*** ⟦< L *sonus*, a sound⟧ a poem normally of fourteen lines in any of several rhyme schemes

son·ny (sun′ē) ***n.***, *pl.* **-nies** little son Used as a familiar term of address to a young boy

so·no·rous (sə nôr′əs, sän′ər əs) ***adj.*** ⟦< L *sonor*, a sound⟧ **1** producing sound; resonant **2** full, deep, or rich in sound —**so·nor′i·ty** (-ə tē) ***n.***

soon (so͞on) ***adv.*** ⟦OE *sona*, at once⟧ **1** in a short time /will *soon* be there/ **2** promptly; quickly /as *soon* as possible/ **3** ahead of time; early /we left too *soon*/ **4** readily; willingly /as *soon* go as stay/ —**sooner or later** inevitably; eventually

soot (soot) ***n.*** ⟦OE *sot*⟧ a black substance consisting chiefly of carbon particles, in the smoke of burning matter —**soot′y, -i·er, -i·est,** ***adj.***

sooth (so͞oth) ***n.*** ⟦OE *soth*⟧ [Archaic] truth

soothe (so͞oth) ***vt.*** **soothed, sooth′ing** ⟦OE *sothian*, prove true⟧ **1** to make calm or composed, as by gentleness, flattery, etc. **2** to relieve (pain, etc.) —**sooth′er** ***n.*** —**sooth′ing** ***adj.***

sooth·say·er (so͞oth′sā′ər) ***n.*** ⟦ME *soth-seyere*, one who speaks the truth⟧ a person who claims to predict the future —**sooth′-say′ing** ***n.***

sop (säp) ***n.*** ⟦OE *sopp*⟧ **1** a piece of food, as bread, soaked in milk, etc. **2** *a)* something given to appease *b)* a bribe —***vt., vi.*** **sopped, sop′ping** **1** to soak, steep, etc. **2** to take (*up*), as water, by absorption

SOP or **S.O.P.** standard operating procedure

soph·ism (säf′iz′əm) ***n.*** ⟦< Gr *sophos*, clever⟧ a clever and plausible but fallacious argument

soph′ist ***n.*** one who uses clever, specious reasoning

so·phis·ti·cate (sə fis′tə kāt′; *for n., usually,* -kit) ***vt.*** **-cat′ed, -cat′ing** ⟦ult. < Gr *sophistēs*, wise man⟧ to change from a natural or simple state; make worldly-wise —***n.*** a sophisticated person

so·phis′ti·cat′ed ***adj.*** **1** not simple, naive, etc.; worldly-wise or knowledgeable, subtle, etc. **2** for sophisticated people **3** highly complex or developed in form, technique, etc. —**so·phis′ti·ca′tion** ***n.***

soph·ist·ry (säf′is trē) ***n.***, *pl.* **-tries** misleading but clever reasoning

Soph·o·cles (säf′ə klēz′) *c.* 496-406 B.C.; Gr. writer of tragic dramas

soph·o·more (säf′ə môr′) ***n.*** ⟦< obs. *sophumer*, sophism⟧ a student in the second year of college or the tenth grade in high school

soph′o·mor′ic ***adj.*** of or like sophomores; seen as opinionated, immature, etc.

-so·phy (sə fē) ⟦< Gr *sophia*, wisdom⟧ *combining form* knowledge

sop·o·rif·ic (säp′ə rif′ik, sō′pə-) ***adj.*** ⟦< L *sopor*, sleep + -FIC⟧ causing sleep —***n.*** a soporific drug, etc.

sop·py (säp′ē) ***adj.*** **-pi·er, -pi·est** **1** very wet: also **sop′ping** **2** [Colloq.] sentimental; maudlin

so·pra·no (sə pran′ō) ***n.***, *pl.* **-nos** ⟦It < *sopra*, above⟧ **1** the range of the highest voice of women or boys **2** a singer with such a range **3** a part for a soprano —***adj.*** of or for a soprano

sor·bet (sôr′bət, sôr bā′) ***n.*** ⟦Fr < Ar *sharba(t)*, a drink⟧ a tart ice, as of fruit juice, served mainly as a dessert

sor·cer·y (sôr′sər ē) ***n.***, *pl.* **-ies** ⟦< L *sors*, lot, share⟧ the supposed use of an evil supernatural power over people; witchcraft —**sor′cer·er** ***n.*** —**sor′cer·ess** ***n.fem.***

sor·did (sôr′did) ***adj.*** ⟦< L *sordes*, filth⟧ **1** dirty; filthy **2** squalid; wretched **3** base; ignoble; mean —**sor′did·ly** ***adv.*** —**sor′-did·ness** ***n.***

sore (sôr) ***adj.*** **sor′er, sor′est** ⟦OE *sar*⟧ **1** giving or feeling pain; painful **2** *a)* filled with grief *b)* causing sadness, misery, etc. /a *sore* task/ **3** causing irritation /a *sore* point/ **4** [Colloq.] angry; offended —***n.*** a sore, usually infected spot on the body —***adv.*** [Archaic] greatly —**sore′ness** ***n.***

sore′head′ ***n.*** [Colloq.] a person easily angered, made resentful, etc.

sore′ly ***adv.*** **1** grievously; painfully **2** urgently /*sorely* needed/

sor·ghum (sôr′gəm) ***n.*** ⟦< It *sorgo*⟧ **1** a cereal grass grown for grain, syrup, fodder, etc. **2** syrup made from its juices

so·ror·i·ty (sə rôr′ə tē) ***n.***, *pl.* **-ties** ⟦< L *soror*, sister⟧ a group of women or girls joined together for fellowship, etc., as in some colleges

sor·rel¹ (sôr′əl, sär′-) ***n.*** ⟦< OFr *surele*⟧ any of various plants with sour, edible leaves

sor·rel² (sôr′əl, sär′-) ***n.*** ⟦< OFr *sor*, light brown⟧ **1** light reddish brown **2** a horse, etc. of this color

sor·row (sär′ō, sôr′ō) ***n.*** ⟦OE *sorg*⟧ **1** mental suffering caused by loss, disappointment, etc.; grief **2** that which causes grief —***vi.*** to grieve —**sor′row·ful** ***adj.*** —**sor′row·ful·ly** ***adv.***

sor·ry (sôr′ē, sär′ē) ***adj.*** **-ri·er, -ri·est** ⟦< OE *sar*, sore⟧ **1** full of sorrow, pity, or regret **2** inferior; poor **3** wretched —**sor′ri·ly** ***adv.*** —**sor′ri·ness** ***n.***

sort (sôrt) ***n.*** ⟦< L *sors*, chance⟧ **1** any group of related things; kind; class **2** quality or type **3** [Archaic] manner; way —***vt.*** to arrange according to class or kind —**of sorts** of an inferior kind: also **of a sort** —**out of sorts** [Colloq.] not in good humor or health —**sort of** [Colloq.] somewhat

sor·tie (sôrt′ē) ***n.*** ⟦Fr < *sortir*, go out⟧ **1** a quick raid by forces of a besieged place **2** one mission by a single military plane

SOS (es′ō′es′) ***n.*** a signal of distress, as in wireless telegraphy

so-so (sō′sō′) ***adv., adj.*** just passably or passable; fair Also **so so**

sot (sät) *n.* ⟦< ML *sottus,* a fool⟧ a drunkard —**sot'tish** *adj.*

sot·to vo·ce (sät'ō vō'chē) ⟦It, under the voice⟧ in a low voice, so as not to be overheard

souf·flé (so͞o flā') *n.* ⟦Fr < L *sufflare,* puff out⟧ a baked food made light and puffy by beaten egg whites added before baking

sough (sou, suf) *n.* ⟦OE *swogan,* to sound⟧ a soft sighing or rustling sound —*vi.* to make a sough

sought (sôt) *vt., vi. pt. & pp. of* SEEK

soul (sōl) *n.* ⟦OE *sawol*⟧ **1** an entity without material reality, regarded as the spiritual part of a person **2** the moral or emotional nature of a person **3** spiritual or emotional warmth, force, etc. **4** vital or essential part, quality, etc. **5** a person /I didn't see a *soul*/ **6** the deep spiritual and emotional quality of black American culture; also, the expression of this, as in music —*adj.* of, for, or like American blacks

soul food [Colloq.] certain foods, as chitterlings or ham hocks, popular orig. in the S U.S., esp. among blacks

soul'ful *adj.* full of deep feeling —**soul'ful·ly** *adv.* —**soul'ful·ness** *n.*

sound[1] (sound) *n.* ⟦< L *sonus*⟧ **1** that which is heard, resulting from stimulation of auditory nerves by vibrations (**sound waves**) in the air **2** the distance within which a sound may be heard **3** the mental impression produced /the *sound* of his report/ —*vi.* **1** to make a sound **2** to seem upon being heard /to *sound* troubled/ —*vt.* **1** to cause to sound **2** to signal, express, etc. **3** to utter distinctly /to *sound* one's r's/ —**sound'less** *adj.*

sound[2] (sound) *adj.* ⟦OE (*ge*)*sund*⟧ **1** free from defect, damage, or decay **2** healthy /a *sound* body/ **3** safe; stable /a *sound* bank/ **4** based on valid reasoning; sensible **5** thorough; forceful /a *sound* defeat/ **6** deep and undisturbed: said of sleep **7** honest, loyal, etc. —*adv.* deeply /*sound* asleep/ —**sound'ly** *adv.* —**sound'ness** *n.*

sound[3] (sound) *n.* ⟦< OE & ON *sund*⟧ **1** a wide channel linking two large bodies of water or separating an island from the mainland **2** a long arm of the sea

sound[4] (sound) *vt., vi.* ⟦< L *sub,* under + *unda,* a wave⟧ **1** to measure the depth of (water), esp. with a weighted line **2** to try to find out the opinions of (a person), usually subtly: often with *out* —**sound'ing** *n.*

sound barrier SONIC BARRIER

sounding board **1** something to increase resonance or reflect sound: often **sound'board'** *n.* **2** a person on whom one tests one's ideas, etc.

sound'proof' *adj.* that keeps sound from coming through —*vt.* to make soundproof

sound'track' *n.* the sound record along one side of a film

soup (so͞op) *n.* ⟦Fr *soupe*⟧ a liquid food made by cooking meat, vegetables, etc. in water, milk, etc. —**soup up** [Slang] to increase the capacity for speed of (an engine, etc.)

soup·çon (so͞op sōn') *n.* ⟦Fr < L *suspicio,* suspicion⟧ **1** a slight trace, as of a flavor **2** a tiny bit

soup·y (so͞o'pē) *adj.* **-i·er, -i·est** **1** watery like soup **2** [Colloq.] foggy

sour (sour) *adj.* ⟦OE *sur*⟧ **1** having the sharp, acid taste of vinegar, etc. **2** spoiled by fermentation **3** cross; bad-tempered **4** distasteful or unpleasant —*vt., vi.* to make or become sour —**sour'ly** *adv.* —**sour'ness** *n.*

source (sôrs) *n.* ⟦< L *surgere,* to rise⟧ **1** a spring, etc. from which a stream arises **2** place of origin; prime cause **3** a person, book, etc. that provides information

sour·dough (sour'dō') *n.* **1** [Dial.] fermented dough saved for use as leaven **2** a lone prospector for gold, etc., as in the W U.S.

sour grapes a scorning of something only because it cannot be had or done

sour'puss' (-poos') *n.* [Slang] a gloomy or disagreeable person

souse (sous) *n.* ⟦< OHG *sulza,* brine⟧ **1** a pickled food, as pigs' feet **2** liquid for pickling; brine **3** a plunging into a liquid **4** [Slang] a drunkard —*vt., vi.* **soused, sous'ing** **1** to pickle (a food) **2** to plunge into a liquid **3** to make or become soaking wet

south (south) *n.* ⟦OE *suth*⟧ **1** the direction to the left of one facing the sunset (180° on the compass) **2** [*often* **S-**] a region in or toward this direction —*adj.* **1** in, of, or toward the south **2** from the south —*adv.* in or toward the south —**the South** that part of the U.S. south of Pa., the Ohio River, and generally east of the Mississippi; specif., the States that formed the Confederacy

South Africa country in southernmost Africa: 472,358 sq. mi.; pop. 33,241,000

South America S continent in the Western Hemisphere: *c.* 6,881,000 sq. mi.; pop. 241,000,000 —**South American**

South Bend city in N Ind.: pop. 110,000

South Car·o·li·na (kar'ə lī'nə) Southern State of the SE U.S.: 31,055 sq. mi.; pop. 3,121,000; cap. Columbia —**South Car'o·lin'i·an** (-lin'ē ən)

South China Sea arm of the W Pacific, between SE Asia & the Philippines

South Da·ko·ta (də kōt'ə) Middle Western State of the U.S.: 77,047 sq. mi.; pop. 690,000; cap. Pierre —**South Da·ko'tan**

south'east' *n.* **1** the direction halfway between south and east **2** a region in or toward this direction —*adj.* **1** in, of, or toward the southeast **2** from the southeast —*adv.* in, toward, or from the southeast —**south'east'er·ly** *adj., adv.* —**south'east'ern** *adj.* —**south'east'ward** (-wərd) *adv., adj.* —**south'east'wards** *adv.*

south·er·ly (su*th*'ər lē) *adj., adv.* **1** toward the south **2** from the south

south·ern (su*th*'ərn) *adj.* **1** in, of, or toward the south **2** from the south **3** [*often* **S-**] of the south

south'ern·er *n.* a native or inhabitant of the south

Southern Hemisphere the half of the earth south of the equator

southern lights [*also* **S- L-**] aurora australis

south·paw (south'pô') *n.* [Slang] a left-handed person; esp., a left-handed baseball pitcher

South Pole the southern end of the earth's axis

South Sea Islands the islands in the South Pacific

south′ward (-wərd) ***adv., adj.*** toward the south Also **south′wards** ***adv.***

south′west′ ***n.*** **1** the direction halfway between south and west **2** a region in or toward this direction —***adj.*** **1** in, of, or toward the southwest **2** from the southwest —***adv.*** in, toward, or from the southwest —**south′west′er·ly** ***adj., adv.*** —**south′west′ern** ***adj.*** —**south′west′ward** (-wərd) ***adv., adj.*** —**south′west′wards** ***adv.***

sou·ve·nir (so͞o′və nir′) ***n.*** ⟦Fr < L *subvenire*, come to mind⟧ something kept as a reminder; memento

sov·er·eign (säv′rən, -ər in) ***adj.*** ⟦< L *super*, above⟧ **1** above all others; chief; supreme **2** supreme in power, rank, etc. **3** independent of all others /a *sovereign* state/ —***n.*** **1** a monarch or ruler **2** a British gold coin worth one pound: no longer minted

sov′er·eign·ty ***n.*** **1** the status, rule, etc. of a sovereign **2** supreme and independent political authority

so·vi·et (sō′vē et′) ***n.*** ⟦Russ *sovyet*, council⟧ **1** in the Soviet Union, any of the various elected governing councils, local, intermediate, and national /the Supreme *Soviet*/ **2** any similar council in a socialist governing system —***adj.*** [S-] of or connected with the Soviet Union —**so′vi·et′ism′** ***n.***

Soviet Union UNION OF SOVIET SOCIALIST REPUBLICS

sow[1] (sou) ***n.*** ⟦OE *sugu*⟧ an adult female pig

sow[2] (sō) ***vt.*** **sowed, sown** (sōn) or **sowed, sow′ing** ⟦OE *sawan*⟧ **1** to scatter (seed) for growing **2** to plant seed in (a field, etc.) **3** to spread or scatter —***vi.*** to sow seed —**sow′er** ***n.***

sox (säks) ***n.*** *alt. pl. of* SOCK[1]

soy (soi) ***n.*** ⟦Jpn⟧ **1** a dark, salty sauce made from fermented soybeans: in full **soy sauce** **2** the soybean plant or its seeds Also [Chiefly Brit.] **soy·a** (soi′ə)

soy′bean′ ***n.*** **1** a plant widely grown for its seeds, which contain much protein and oil **2** its seed

Sp. **1** Spain **2** Spanish

spa (spä) ***n.*** ⟦after *Spa*, resort in Belgium⟧ **1** a health resort having a mineral spring **2** a commercial establishment with exercise rooms, sauna baths, etc.

space (spās) ***n.*** ⟦< L *spatium*⟧ **1** *a)* the three-dimensional, continuous expanse in which all things are contained *b)* OUTER SPACE **2** *a)* distance, area, etc. between or within things *b)* room for something /a parking *space*/ **3** an interval of time —***vt.*** **spaced, spac′ing** to arrange with spaces between

space′craft′ ***n., pl.*** **-craft′** any vehicle designed for orbiting the earth, sun, etc., as a satellite or spaceship

spaced′-out′ ***adj.*** [Slang] under or as if under the influence of a drug, marijuana, etc. Also **spaced**

space′flight′ ***n.*** a flight through outer space

space heater a small heating unit for a room or other confined area

space′man′ ***n., pl.*** **-men′** an astronaut or any of the crew of a spaceship

space′port′ ***n.*** a center for assembling, testing, and launching spacecraft

space′ship′ ***n.*** a spacecraft, esp. if manned

space shuttle a spacecraft designed to carry personnel and equipment between earth and a space station

space station (or **platform**) a spacecraft in long-term orbit serving as a launch pad, research center, etc.

space′suit′ ***n.*** a garment pressurized for use by astronauts

space′walk′ ***n.*** an astronaut's moving about in space outside a spacecraft —***vi.*** to engage in a spacewalk

space·y or **spac·y** (spā′sē) ***adj.*** **-i·er, -i·est** [Slang] **1** SPACED-OUT **2** *a)* eccentric or unconventional *b)* flighty, irresponsible, neurotic, etc. —**spac′i·ness** ***n.***

spa·cious (spā′shəs) ***adj.*** having more than enough space; vast —**spa′cious·ly** ***adv.*** —**spa′cious·ness** ***n.***

Spack·le (spak′əl) ⟦prob. < Ger *spachtel*, spatula⟧ *trademark for* a powder mixed with water to form a paste that dries hard, used to fill holes, cracks, etc. in wood, etc. —***n.*** [s-] this substance —***vt.*** **-led, -ling** [s-] to fill or cover with spackle

spade[1] (spād) ***n.*** ⟦OE *spadu*⟧ a flat-bladed, long-handled digging tool, like a shovel —***vt., vi.*** **spad′ed, spad′ing** to dig with a spade —**spade′ful** ***n.***

spade[2] (spād) ***n.*** ⟦ult. < Gr *spathē*, flat blade⟧ **1** the black figure (♠) marking one of the four suits of playing cards **2** a card of this suit

spade′work′ ***n.*** preparatory work for some main project, esp. when tiresome

spa·dix (spā′diks) ***n., pl.*** **-dix·es** or **-di·ces′** (-də sēz′) ⟦< Gr⟧ a spike of tiny flowers, usually enclosed in a spathe

SPADIX

spa·ghet·ti (spə get′ē) ***n.*** ⟦It < *spago*, small cord⟧ pasta in long, thin strings, cooked by boiling or steaming

Spain (spān) country in SW Europe: 194,346 sq. mi.; pop. 39,000,000

spake (spāk) ***vi., vt.*** *archaic pt. of* SPEAK

span (span) ***n.*** ⟦OE *sponn*⟧ **1** the distance (about 9 in.) between the tips of the extended thumb and little finger **2** *a)* the full extent between any two limits *b)* the distance between ends or supports /the *span* of an arch/ *c)* the full duration (of) /*span* of attention/ **3** a part between two supports —***vt.*** **spanned, span′ning** **1** to measure, esp. by the span of the hand **2** to extend over

Span. Spanish

span·dex (span′deks′) ***n.*** ⟦< EXPAND⟧ an elastic synthetic fiber used in girdles, etc.

span·gle (spaŋ′gəl) ***n.*** ⟦< OE *spang*, a clasp⟧ a small piece of bright metal sewn on fabric for decoration —***vt.*** **-gled, -gling** to decorate as with spangles

Span·iard (span′yərd) ***n.*** a native or inhabitant of Spain

span·iel (span′yəl) ***n.*** ⟦< MFr *espagnol*, lit., Spanish⟧ any of several breeds of dog with large, drooping ears and a dense, wavy coat

Span·ish (span′ish) ***adj.*** of Spain, its people, their language, etc. —***n.*** the language of Spain and Spanish America —**the Spanish** the people of Spain

Spanish America those countries south of the U.S. in which Spanish is the chief language —**Span′ish-A·mer′i·can** ***adj., n.***

Spanish moss a rootless plant that grows in long, graceful strands from tree branches in the SE U.S.

spank (spaŋk) ***vt.*** ⟦echoic⟧ to strike with the open hand, etc., esp. on the buttocks, as in punishment —***n.*** a smack given in spanking

spank′ing ***adj.*** **1** swiftly moving **2** brisk: said of a breeze —***adv.*** [Colloq.] completely *[spanking new]*

spar[1] (spär) ***n.*** ⟦< ON *sparri* or MDu *sparre*⟧ any pole, as a mast or yard, supporting a sail of a ship

spar[2] (spär) ***vi.*** **sparred, spar′ring** ⟦prob. < It *parare,* to parry⟧ **1** to box with feinting movements, landing few heavy blows **2** to wrangle

spare (sper) ***vt.*** **spared, spar′ing** ⟦OE *sparian*⟧ **1** to refrain from killing, hurting, etc. **2** to save or free a person from (something) **3** to avoid using or use frugally **4** to part with conveniently —***adj.*** **1** not in regular use; extra **2** free *[spare time]* **3** meager; scanty **4** lean; thin —***n.*** **1** a spare, or extra, thing **2** *Bowling* a knocking down of all the pins with two rolls of the ball —**spare′ly** ***adv.***

spare′ribs′ ***n.pl.*** a cut of pork consisting of the thin end of the ribs

spar′ing ***adj.*** **1** careful; frugal **2** scanty or meager —**spar′ing·ly** ***adv.***

spark (spärk) ***n.*** ⟦OE *spearca*⟧ **1** a glowing bit of matter, esp. one thrown off by a fire **2** any flash or sparkle **3** a particle or trace **4** a brief flash of light accompanying an electric discharge as through air —***vi.*** to make sparks —***vt.*** to stir up; activate

spar·kle (spär′kəl) ***vi.*** **-kled, -kling** **1** to throw off sparks **2** to glitter **3** to effervesce —***n.*** **1** a sparkling **2** brilliance —**spar′kler** (-klər) ***n.***

spark plug an electrical device fitted into a cylinder of an engine to ignite the fuel mixture by making sparks

spar·row (spar′ō) ***n.*** ⟦OE *spearwa*⟧ any of numerous small, perching songbirds

sparse (spärs) ***adj.*** ⟦< L *spargere,* scatter⟧ thinly spread; not dense —**sparse′ly** ***adv.*** —**sparse′ness** or **spar′si·ty** (-sə tē) ***n.***

Spar·ta (spärt′ə) ancient city in S Greece: a military power

Spar′tan ***adj.*** **1** of ancient Sparta, its people, or their culture **2** like the Spartans; warlike, hardy, disciplined, etc. —***n.*** a Spartan person

spasm (spaz′əm) ***n.*** ⟦< Gr *spasmos*⟧ **1** a sudden, involuntary muscular contraction **2** any sudden, violent, temporary activity, feeling, etc.

spas·mod·ic (spaz măd′ik) ***adj.*** ⟦see prec. & -OID⟧ of or like spasms; fitful —**spas·mod′i·cal·ly** ***adv.***

spas·tic (spas′tik) ***adj.*** of or characterized by muscular spasms —***n.*** one having spastic paralysis

spat[1] (spat) ***n.*** ⟦prob. echoic⟧ [Colloq.] a brief, petty quarrel —***vi.*** **spat′ted, spat′ting** [Colloq.] to engage in a spat

spat[2] (spat) ***n.*** ⟦< *spatterdash,* a legging⟧ a gaiterlike covering for the instep and ankle

spat[3] (spat) ***vt., vi.*** *alt. pt. & pp. of* SPIT[2]

spat[4] (spat) ***n.*** ⟦< ?⟧ a young oyster or young oysters collectively

spate (spāt) ***n.*** ⟦< ?⟧ an unusually large outpouring, as of words

spathe (spāth) ***n.*** ⟦< L *spatha,* a flat blade⟧ a large, leaflike part enclosing a flower cluster

spa·tial (spā′shəl) ***adj.*** ⟦< L *spatium,* space⟧ of, or existing in, space

spat·ter (spat′ər) ***vt., vi.*** ⟦< ?⟧ **1** to scatter or spurt out in drops **2** to splash —***n.*** **1** a spattering **2** a mark caused by spattering

spat·u·la (spach′ə lə) ***n.*** ⟦L < Gr *spathē,* flat blade⟧ an implement with a flat, flexible blade for spreading or blending foods, paints, etc.

spav·in (spav′in) ***n.*** ⟦< MFr *esparvain*⟧ a disease that lames horses in the hock joint —**spav′ined** ***adj.***

spawn (spôn) ***vt., vi.*** ⟦< L *expandere:* see EXPAND⟧ **1** to produce or deposit (eggs, sperm, or young) **2** to bring forth or produce prolifically —***n.*** **1** the mass of eggs or young produced by fish, mollusks, etc. **2** something produced, esp. in great quantity, as offspring

spay (spā) ***vt.*** ⟦< Gr *spathē,* flat blade⟧ to sterilize (a female animal) by removing the ovaries

speak (spēk) ***vi.*** **spoke, spo′ken, speak′ing** ⟦OE *sp(r)ecan*⟧ **1** to utter words; talk **2** to communicate as by talking **3** to make a request *(for)* **4** to make a speech —***vt.*** **1** to make known as by speaking **2** to use (a given language) in speaking **3** to utter (words) orally —**so to speak** that is to say — **speak out** (or **up**) to speak clearly or freely —**speak well for** to say or indicate something favorable about

speak′-eas′y (-ē′zē) ***n., pl.*** **-ies** [Slang] a place where alcoholic drinks are sold illegally

speak′er ***n.*** **1** one who speaks; esp., *a)* an orator *b)* the presiding officer of various lawmaking bodies *c)* [S-] the presiding officer of the U.S. House of Representatives **2** *short for* LOUDSPEAKER

spear (spir) ***n.*** ⟦OE *spere*⟧ **1** a weapon with a long shaft and a sharp point, for thrusting or throwing **2** ⟦var. of SPIRE⟧ a long blade or shoot, as of grass —***vt.*** to pierce or stab with or as with a spear

spear′fish′ ***n., pl.*** **-fish′** or (for different species) **-fish′es** any of a group of large food and game fishes of the open seas —***vi.*** to fish with a spear, etc.

spear′head′ ***n.*** **1** the pointed head of a spear **2** the leading person or group, as in an attack —***vt.*** to take the lead in (an attack, etc.)

spear′mint′ ***n.*** ⟦prob. from the shape of its flowers⟧ a fragrant plant of the mint family, used for flavoring

spec (spek) ***n.*** [Colloq.] *short for:* **1** SPECIFICATION (sense 1) **2** SPECULATION —**on spec** [Colloq.] **1** according to specification(s) **2** as a speculation or gamble

spe·cial (spesh′əl) ***adj.*** ⟦< L *species,* kind⟧ 1 distinctive or unique 2 exceptional; unusual 3 highly valued 4 of or for a particular purpose, etc. 5 not general; specific —***n.*** a special person or thing —**spe′cial·ly** ***adv.***

special delivery mail delivery by a special messenger, for a special fee

spe′cial·ist ***n.*** one who specializes in a particular study, work, etc.

spe′cial·ize′ ***vi.*** **-ized′, -iz′ing** to concentrate on a special branch of study, work, etc. —**spe′cial·i·za′tion** ***n.***

spe′cial·ty (-tē) ***n., pl.*** **-ties** 1 a special quality, feature, etc. 2 a special interest, study, etc. 3 an article with special features, etc.

spe·cie (spē′shē) ***n.*** ⟦< L *species,* kind⟧ coin, rather than paper money

spe·cies (spē′shēz) ***n., pl.*** **-cies** ⟦L, appearance⟧ 1 a distinct kind; sort 2 any of the groups of related plants or animals that make up a genus

specif. specifically

spe·cif·ic (spə sif′ik) ***adj.*** ⟦< L *species,* kind + *-ficus,* -FIC⟧ 1 definite; explicit 2 peculiar to or characteristic of something 3 of a particular kind 4 specially indicated as a cure for some disease —***n.*** a specific cure —**spe·cif′i·cal·ly** ***adv.***

-spe·cif′ic *combining form* limited or specific to

spec·i·fi·ca·tion (spes′ə fi kā′shən) ***n.*** 1 [*usually pl.*] a statement or enumeration of particulars, as to size, quality, terms, etc. 2 something specified

specific gravity the ratio of the weight or mass of a given volume of a substance to that of an equal volume of another substance (as water) used as a standard

spec·i·fy (spes′ə fī′) ***vt.*** **-fied′, -fy′ing** ⟦< LL *specificus,* specific⟧ 1 to mention or describe in detail 2 to state explicitly as a condition

spec·i·men (spes′ə mən) ***n.*** ⟦L < *specere,* see⟧ 1 a part or individual used as a sample of a whole or group 2 *Med.* a sample, as of urine, for analysis

spe·cious (spē′shəs) ***adj.*** ⟦< L *species,* appearance⟧ seeming to be good, sound, correct, etc. without really being so —**spe′cious·ly** ***adv.***

speck (spek) ***n.*** ⟦OE *specca*⟧ 1 a small spot, mark, etc. 2 a very small bit —***vt.*** to mark with specks

speck·le (spek′əl) ***n.*** a small speck —***vt.*** **-led, -ling** to mark with speckles

specs (speks) ***n.pl.*** [Colloq.] 1 spectacles; eyeglasses 2 specifications

spec·ta·cle (spek′tə kəl) ***n.*** ⟦< L *specere,* see⟧ 1 a remarkable sight 2 a large public show 3 [*pl.*] *a)* [Old-fashioned] a pair of eyeglasses *b)* something like a pair of eyeglasses

spec·tac·u·lar (spek tak′yə lər) ***adj.*** unusual to a striking degree —***n.*** an elaborate show or display —**spec·tac′u·lar·ly** ***adv.***

spec·ta·tor (spek′tāt′ər) ***n.*** ⟦L < *spectare,* behold⟧ one who watches without taking an active part

spec·ter (spek′tər) ***n.*** ⟦< L *spectare,* behold⟧ a ghost; apparition Brit., etc. sp. **spec′tre**

spec′tral (-trəl) ***adj.*** 1 of or like a specter 2 of a spectrum

spec·tro·scope (spek′trō skōp′) ***n.*** ⟦< Ger, ult. < L *spectare,* behold⟧ an optical instrument used for forming spectra for study —**spec′tro·scop′ic** (-skäp′ik) ***adj.*** —**spec·tros′co·py** (-träs′kə pē) ***n.***

spec·trum (spek′trəm) ***n., pl.*** **-tra** (-trə) or **-trums** ⟦< L: see SPECTER⟧ 1 a series of colored bands separated and arranged in order of their respective wavelengths by the passage of white light through a prism, etc. 2 a continuous range or entire extent

spec·u·late (spek′yoo lāt′) ***vi.*** **-lat′ed, -lat′ing** ⟦< L *specere,* see⟧ 1 to think seriously; ponder; esp., to conjecture 2 to take part in any risky venture (as buying or selling certain stocks, etc.) on the chance of making huge profits —**spec′u·la′tion** ***n.*** —**spec′u·la′tive** ***adj.*** —**spec′u·la′tor** ***n.***

speech (spēch) ***n.*** ⟦< OE *sprecan,* speak⟧ 1 the act of speaking 2 the power to speak 3 that which is spoken; utterance, remark, etc. 4 a talk given to an audience 5 the language of a certain people

speech′less ***adj.*** 1 incapable of speech 2 silent, as from shock

speed (spēd) ***n.*** ⟦OE *spæd,* success⟧ 1 swiftness; quick motion 2 rate of movement; velocity 3 an arrangement of gears, as for the drive of an engine 4 [Slang] any of various amphetamine compounds —***vi.*** **sped** (sped) or **speed′ed, speed′ing** to move rapidly, esp. too rapidly —***vt.*** 1 to help to succeed; aid 2 to cause to speed —**speed up** to increase in speed —**speed′er** ***n.***

speed′boat′ ***n.*** a fast motorboat

speed·om·e·ter (spi däm′ət ər) ***n.*** a device attached to a motor vehicle, etc. to indicate speed

speed·ster (spēd′stər) ***n.*** a very fast driver, runner, etc.

speed′way′ ***n.*** a track for racing automobiles or motorcycles

speed′y ***adj.*** **-i·er, -i·est** 1 rapid; fast; swift 2 without delay; prompt /a *speedy* reply/ —**speed′i·ly** ***adv.***

spe·le·ol·o·gy (spē′lē äl′ə jē) ***n.*** ⟦< Gr *spēlaion,* cave⟧ the scientific study and exploration of caves —**spe′le·ol′o·gist** ***n.***

spell[1] (spel) ***n.*** ⟦OE, a saying⟧ 1 a word or formula thought to have some magic power 2 irresistible influence; charm; fascination

spell[2] (spel) ***vt.*** **spelled** or **spelt, spell′ing** ⟦< OFr *espeller,* explain⟧ 1 to name in order the letters of (a word) 2 to make up (a word, etc.): said of specified letters 3 to mean /red *spells* danger/ —***vi.*** to spell words —**spell out** to explain in detail

spell[3] (spel) ***vt.*** **spelled, spell′ing** ⟦OE *spelian*⟧ [Colloq.] to work in place of (another) for an interval; relieve —***n.*** 1 a period of work, duty, etc. 2 a period of anything /a *spell* of brooding/ 3 [Colloq.] a fit of illness

spell′bind′ ***vt.*** **-bound′, -bind′ing** to cause to be spellbound; fascinate —**spell′bind′er** ***n.***

spell′bound′ ***adj.*** held by or as by a spell; fascinated

spell′down′ ***n.*** SPELLING BEE

spell′er ***n.*** 1 one who spells words 2 a textbook for teaching spelling

spell′ing *n.* 1 the act of one who spells words 2 the way a word is spelled

spelling bee a spelling contest, esp. one in which a contestant is eliminated after misspelling a word

spe·lunk·er (spi luŋ′kər) *n.* ⟦< Gr *spēlynx,* a cave⟧ a cave explorer

spend (spend) *vt.* **spent, spend′ing** ⟦< L *expendere:* see EXPEND⟧ 1 to use up, exhaust, etc. /his fury was *spent*/ 2 to pay out (money) 3 to devote (time, labor, etc.) to something 4 to pass (time) —*vi.* to pay out or use up money, etc. —**spend′a·ble** *adj.* —**spend′er** *n.*

spend′thrift′ *n.* one who wastes money —*adj.* wasteful

spent (spent) *vt., vi. pt. & pp. of* SPEND —*adj.* 1 tired out; physically exhausted 2 used up; worn out

sperm (spʉrm) *n.* ⟦< Gr *sperma,* seed⟧ 1 the male generative fluid; semen 2 SPERMATOZOON

sper·ma·to·zo·on (spʉr′mə tə zō′än′, -ən) *n., pl.* **-zo′a** (-zō′ə) ⟦< Gr *sperma,* seed + *zōion,* animal⟧ the male germ cell, found in semen, which penetrates the egg of the female to fertilize it

sperm·i·cide (spʉr′mə sīd′) *n.* ⟦SPERM + *-i-* + -CIDE⟧ an agent that kills spermatozoa

sperm whale a large toothed whale found in warm seas: its head contains a valuable lubricating oil (**sperm oil**)

spew (spyōō) *vt., vi.* ⟦OE *spiwan*⟧ 1 to throw up (something) from or as from the stomach; vomit 2 to flow or cause to flow or gush forth —*n.* something spewed

sp. gr. specific gravity

sphere (sfir) *n.* ⟦< Gr *sphaira*⟧ 1 any round body having the surface equally distant from the center at all points; globe; ball 2 the place, range, or extent of action, existence, knowledge, experience, etc. —**spher·i·cal** (sfer′i kəl, sfir′-) *adj.*

sphe·roid (sfir′oid) *n.* a body that is almost but not quite a sphere —*adj.* of this shape: also **sphe·roi′dal**

sphinc·ter (sfiŋk′tər) *n.* ⟦< Gr *sphingein,* to draw close⟧ a ring-shaped muscle at a body orifice

THE EGYPTIAN SPHINX

sphinx (sfiŋks) *n.* ⟦< Gr, strangler⟧ 1 *Gr. Myth.* a winged monster with a lion's body and a woman's head 2 one who is difficult to know or understand —[S-] 1 a statue with a lion's body and a man's head, near Cairo, Egypt 2 *Gr. Myth.* a sphinx at Thebes that strangles passersby unable to guess its riddle

spice (spīs) *n.* ⟦< L *species,* kind⟧ 1 an aromatic vegetable substance, as cinnamon, nutmeg, pepper, etc., used to season food 2 that which adds zest or interest —*vt.* **spiced, spic′ing** 1 to season with spice 2 to add zest to —**spic′y, -i·er, -i·est,** *adj.*

spick-and-span (spik′'n span′) *adj.* ⟦< *spike,* nail + ON *spānn,* a chip⟧ 1 new or fresh 2 neat and clean

spic·ule (spik′yōōl′) *n.* ⟦< L *spica,* a point⟧ a hard, needlelike part

spi·der (spī′dər) *n.* ⟦< OE *spinnan,* to spin⟧ 1 any of various arachnids that spin webs 2 a cast-iron frying pan

spi′der·y (-ē) *adj.* like a spider

spiel (spēl) *n.* ⟦Ger, play⟧ [Slang] a talk or harangue, as in selling

spiff·y (spif′ē) *adj.* **-i·er, -i·est** ⟦< dial. *spiff,* well-dressed person⟧ [Slang] spruce, smart, or dapper

spig·ot (spig′ət) *n.* ⟦ME *spigote*⟧ 1 a plug to stop the vent in a barrel, etc. 2 a faucet

spike[1] (spīk) *n.* ⟦< ON *spīkr* or MDu *spiker*⟧ 1 a long, heavy nail 2 a sharp-pointed projection, as on the sole of a shoe to prevent slipping —*vt.* **spiked, spik′ing** 1 to fasten or fit as with spikes 2 to pierce with, or impale on, a spike 3 to thwart (a scheme, etc.) 4 [Slang] to add alcoholic liquor to (a drink)

spike[2] (spīk) *n.* ⟦L *spica*⟧ 1 an ear of grain 2 a long flower cluster

spill (spil) *vt.* **spilled** or **spilt** (spilt), **spill′ing** ⟦OE *spillan,* destroy⟧ 1 to allow or cause, esp. unintentionally, to run, scatter, or flow over from a container 2 to shed (blood) 3 [Colloq.] to throw off (a rider, etc.) —*vi.* to be spilled; overflow —*n.* 1 a spilling 2 a fall or tumble —**spill′age** *n.*

spill′way′ *n.* a channel to carry off excess water, as around a dam

spin (spin) *vt.* **spun, spin′ning** ⟦OE *spinnan*⟧ 1 *a*) to draw out and twist fibers of (wool, cotton, etc.) into thread *b*) to make (thread, etc.) thus 2 to make (a web, cocoon, etc.), as a spider 3 to draw *out* (a story) to a great length 4 to rotate swiftly —*vi.* 1 to spin thread or yarn 2 to form a web, cocoon, etc. 3 to whirl 4 to seem to be spinning from dizziness 5 to move along swiftly and smoothly —*n.* 1 a spinning or rotating movement 2 a ride in a motor vehicle 3 a descent of an airplane, nose first along a spiral path —**spin off** to produce as an outgrowth or secondary development, etc. —**spin′ner** *n.*

spi·na bi·fi·da (spī′nə bif′i də) a congenital defect in which part of the spinal column is exposed, causing paralysis, etc.

spin·ach (spin′ich) *n.* ⟦ult. < Pers *aspanākh*⟧ 1 a plant with dark-green, juicy, edible leaves 2 these leaves

spi·nal (spī′nəl) *adj.* of or having to do with the spine or spinal cord

spinal column the series of joined vertebrae forming the axial support for the skeleton; spine; backbone

spinal cord the thick cord of nerve tissue in the spinal column

spin·dle (spin′dəl) *n.* ⟦< OE *spinnan,* to spin⟧ 1 a slender rod used in spinning for twisting, winding, or holding thread 2 a spindlelike thing 3 any rod or pin that revolves or serves as an axis for a revolving part

spin·dly (spind′lē) *adj.* **-dli·er, -dli·est** long or tall and very thin

spine (spīn) *n.* ⟦< L *spina,* thorn⟧ **1** *a*) a sharp, stiff projection, as on a cactus *b*) anything like this **2** *a*) SPINAL COLUMN *b*) anything like this, as the back of a book —**spin′y, -i·er, -i·est,** *adj.*

spine′less *adj.* **1** having no spine or spines **2** lacking courage or willpower

spin·et (spin′it) *n.* ⟦< It *spinetta*⟧ a small upright piano

spin·ner·et (spin′ə ret′) *n.* the organ in spiders, caterpillars, etc., that spins thread for webs or cocoons

spinning wheel a simple machine for spinning thread with a spindle driven by a large wheel spun as by a treadle

spin-off (spin′ôf′) *n.* a secondary benefit, product, development, etc.

spin·ster (spin′stər) *n.* ⟦ME < *spinnen,* to spin⟧ an unmarried woman, esp. an elderly one —**spin′ster·hood′** *n.*

spiny lobster a sea crustacean similar to the common lobster but lacking large pincers and having a spiny shell

spi·ra·cle (spir′ə kəl) *n.* ⟦< L < *spirare,* breathe⟧ an opening for breathing, as on the sides of an insect's body or on the top of a whale's head

spi·ral (spī′rəl) *adj.* ⟦< Gr *speira,* a coil⟧ circling around a point in constantly increasing (or decreasing) curves, or in constantly changing planes —*n.* a spiral curve or coil —*vi., vt.* **-raled** or **-ralled, -ral·ing** or **-ral·ling** to move in or form a spiral —**spi′ral·ly** *adv.*

spire (spīr) *n.* ⟦OE *spir*⟧ **1** the top part of a pointed, tapering object **2** anything tapering to a point, as a steeple

spi·re·a (spī rē′ə) *n.* ⟦< Gr *speira,* a coil⟧ a plant of the rose family, with dense clusters of small flowers Also sp. **spi·rae′a**

spir·it (spir′it) *n.* ⟦< L *spirare,* breathe⟧ **1** *a*) the life principle, esp. in human beings *b*) SOUL (sense 1) **2** [*also* **S-**] life, will, thought, etc., regarded as separate from matter **3** a supernatural being, as a ghost, angel, etc. **4** an individual /a brave *spirit*/ **5** [*usually pl.*] disposition; mood /high *spirits*/ **6** vivacity, courage, etc. **7** enthusiastic loyalty /school *spirit*/ **8** real meaning /the *spirit* of the law/ **9** a pervading animating principle; essential quality /the *spirit* of the times/ **10** [*usually pl.*] distilled alcoholic liquor —*vt.* to carry (*away, off,* etc.) secretly and swiftly —**spir′it·less** *adj.*

spir′it·ed *adj.* lively; animated

spir·it·u·al (spir′i chōō əl) *adj.* **1** of the spirit or the soul **2** of or consisting of spirit; not corporeal **3** of religion; sacred —*n.* a folk hymn originating among S U.S. blacks —**spir′it·u·al′i·ty** (-al′ə tē) *n.* —**spir′it·u·al·ly** *adv.*

spir′it·u·al·ism′ *n.* the belief that the dead survive as spirits which can communicate with the living —**spir′it·u·al·ist** *n.* —**spir′it·u·al·is′tic** *adj.*

spir·it·u·ous (spir′i chōō əs) *adj.* of or containing distilled alcohol

spi·ro·chete (spī′rō kēt′) *n.* ⟦< Gr *speira,* a coil + *chaitē,* hair⟧ any of various spiral-shaped bacteria

spit[1] (spit) *n.* ⟦OE *spitu*⟧ **1** a thin, pointed rod on which meat is roasted over a fire, etc. **2** a narrow point of land extending into the water —*vt.* **spit′ted, spit′ting** to fix as on a spit

spit[2] (spit) *vt.* **spit** or [Chiefly Brit.] **spat, spit′ting** ⟦OE *spittan*⟧ **1** to eject from the mouth **2** to eject explosively —*vi.* to eject saliva from the mouth —*n.* **1** a spitting **2** saliva —**spit and image** [Colloq.] perfect likeness

spit′ball′ *n.* **1** paper chewed up into a wad for throwing **2** *Baseball* a pitch, now illegal, made to curve by wetting one side of the ball as with spit

spite (spīt) *n.* ⟦see DESPITE⟧ **1** ill will; malice **2** a grudge —*vt.* **spit′ed, spit′ing** to vent one's spite upon by hurting, frustrating, etc. —**in spite of** regardless of —**spite′ful** *adj.*

spit′fire′ *n.* a woman or girl easily aroused to violent anger

spit·tle (spit′'l) *n.* saliva; spit

spit·toon (spi tōōn′) *n.* a jarlike container to spit into; cuspidor

splash (splash) *vt.* ⟦echoic⟧ **1** to cause (a liquid) to scatter **2** to dash a liquid, mud, etc. on, so as to wet or soil —*vi.* to move, strike, etc. with a splash —*n.* **1** a splashing **2** a spot made by splashing —**make a splash** [Colloq.] to attract great attention

splash′down′ *n.* a spacecraft's soft landing on the sea

splash′y *adj.* **-i·er, -i·est** **1** splashing or apt to splash; wet, muddy, etc. **2** [Colloq.] spectacular —**splash′i·ly** *adv.* —**splash′i·ness** *n.*

splat[1] (splat) *n.* ⟦< SPLIT⟧ a thin slat of wood, as in a chair back

splat[2] (splat) *n., interj.* ⟦echoic⟧ a splattering or wet, slapping sound

splat·ter (splat′ər) *n., vt., vi.* spatter or splash

splay (splā) *vt., vi.* ⟦ME *splaien*⟧ to spread out —*adj.* spreading outward

splay′foot′ *n., pl.* **-feet′** a foot that is flat and turned outward —**splay′foot′ed** *adj.*

spleen (splēn) *n.* ⟦< Gr *splēn*⟧ **1** a large lymphatic organ in the upper left part of the abdomen: it modifies the blood structure **2** malice; spite

splen·did (splen′did) *adj.* ⟦< L *splendere,* to shine⟧ **1** shining; brilliant **2** magnificent; gorgeous **3** grand; illustrious **4** [Colloq.] very good; fine —**splen′did·ly** *adv.*

splen·dor (splen′dər) *n.* ⟦see prec.⟧ **1** great luster; brilliance **2** pomp; grandeur Brit., etc. sp. **splen′dour**

sple·net·ic (spli net′ik) *adj.* **1** of the spleen **2** bad-tempered; irritable

splice (splīs) *vt.* **spliced, splic′ing** ⟦MDu *splissen*⟧ **1** to join (ropes) by weaving together the end strands **2** to join the ends of (timbers) by overlapping **3** to fasten the ends of (wire, film, etc.) together, as by soldering, etc. —*n.* a joint made by splicing

SHORT SPLICE

splint (splint) *n.* ⟦prob. < MDu *splinte*⟧ **1** a thin strip of wood, etc.

woven with others to make baskets, etc. 2 a thin, rigid strip of wood, etc. used to hold a broken bone in place

splin·ter (splin'tər) ***vt., vi.*** ⟦see prec.⟧ to break or split into thin, sharp pieces —***n.*** a thin, sharp piece, as of wood, made by splitting, etc.

split (split) ***vt., vi.*** **split, split'ting** ⟦MDu *splitten*⟧ 1 to separate lengthwise into two or more parts 2 to break or tear apart 3 to divide into shares 4 to disunite 5 *a)* to break (a molecule) into atoms *b)* to produce nuclear fission in (an atom) —***n.*** 1 a splitting 2 a break; crack 3 a division in a group, etc. —***adj.*** divided; separated

split'-lev'el ***adj.*** having floor levels staggered about a half story apart

split pea a green or yellow pea shelled, dried, and split: used esp. for soup

split'ting ***adj.*** 1 that splits 2 severe, as a headache

splotch (spläch) ***n.*** ⟦prob. < SPOT + BLOTCH⟧ an irregular spot, splash, or stain —***vt., vi.*** to mark or be marked with splotches —**splotch'y, -i·er, -i·est,** ***adj.***

splurge (splurj) ***n.*** ⟦echoic⟧ [Colloq.] 1 any very showy display or effort 2 a spell of extravagant spending —***vi.*** **splurged, splurg'ing** [Colloq.] 1 to show off 2 to spend money freely

splut·ter (splut'ər) ***vi.*** ⟦var. of SPUTTER⟧ 1 to make hissing or spitting sounds 2 to speak hurriedly and confusedly —***n.*** a spluttering

spoil (spoil) ***vt.*** **spoiled** or **spoilt, spoil'ing** ⟦< L *spolium,* plunder⟧ 1 to damage so as to make useless, etc. 2 to impair the enjoyment, etc. of 3 to cause to expect too much by overindulgence 4 [Archaic] to rob; plunder —***vi.*** to become spoiled; decay, etc., as food —***n.*** [*usually pl.*] plunder; booty —**spoil'age** ***n.*** —**spoil'er** ***n.***

spoil'sport' ***n.*** one whose actions ruin the pleasure of others

spoils system the treating of public offices as the booty of a successful political party

Spo·kane (spō kan') city in E Wash.: pop. 171,000

spoke[1] (spōk) ***n.*** ⟦OE *spaca*⟧ any of the braces or bars extending from the hub to the rim of a wheel

spoke[2] (spōk) ***vi., vt.*** *pt. & archaic pp. of* SPEAK

spo·ken (spō'kən) ***vi., vt.*** *pp. of* SPEAK —***adj.*** 1 uttered; oral 2 having a (specified) kind of voice [*soft-spoken*]

spokes·man (spōks'mən) ***n., pl.*** **-men** one who speaks for another or for a group —**spokes'wom'an,** *pl.* **-wom'en,** ***n.fem.***

spokes'per'son ***n.*** SPOKESMAN: used to avoid the masculine implication of *spokesman*

spo·li·a·tion (spō'lē ā'shən) ***n.*** ⟦< L *spoliatio*⟧ robbery; plundering

sponge (spunj) ***n.*** ⟦< Gr *spongia*⟧ 1 a stationary aquatic animal with a porous structure 2 the highly absorbent skeleton of such animals, used for washing surfaces, etc. 3 any substance like this, as a piece of spongy rubber, etc. —***vt.*** **sponged, spong'ing** 1 to dampen, wipe, absorb, etc. as with a sponge 2 [Colloq.] to get as by begging, imposition, etc. —***vi.*** [Colloq.] to live as a parasite upon other people —**spong'er** ***n.*** —**spon'gy, -gi·er, -gi·est,** ***adj.***

sponge bath a bath taken by using a wet sponge or cloth without getting into water

sponge'cake' ***n.*** a light, spongy cake without shortening Also **sponge cake**

spon·sor (spän'sər) ***n.*** ⟦L < *spondere,* promise solemnly⟧ 1 one who assumes responsibility as surety for, or endorser of, some person or thing 2 a godparent 3 a business firm, etc. that pays for a radio or TV program advertising its product —***vt.*** to act as sponsor for —**spon'sor·ship'** ***n.***

spon·ta·ne·i·ty (spän'tə nē'ə tē) ***n.*** 1 a being spontaneous 2 *pl.* **-ties** spontaneous behavior, action, etc.

spon·ta·ne·ous (spän tā'nē əs) ***adj.*** ⟦< L *sponte,* of free will⟧ 1 acting or resulting from a natural feeling or impulse, without constraint, effort, etc. 2 occurring through internal causes

spontaneous combustion the process of catching fire through heat generated by internal chemical action

spoof (spōōf) ***n.*** 1 a hoax or joke 2 a light satire —***vt., vi.*** 1 to fool; deceive 2 to satirize (something) playfully

spook (spook) ***n.*** ⟦Du⟧ [Colloq.] a ghost —***vt., vi.*** [Colloq.] to frighten or become frightened —**spook'y, -i·er, -i·est,** ***adj.***

spool (spōōl) ***n.*** ⟦< MDu *spoele*⟧ 1 a cylinder on which thread, wire, etc. is wound 2 the material so wound

spoon (spōōn) ***n.*** ⟦< OE *spon,* a chip⟧ 1 a utensil consisting of a small, shallow bowl and a handle, used for eating, stirring, etc. 2 something shaped like a spoon, as a shiny, curved fishing lure —***vt.*** to take up with a spoon —**spoon'ful',** *pl.* **-fuls',** ***n.***

spoon'bill' ***n.*** a wading bird whose flat bill is spoon-shaped at the tip

spoon·er·ism (spōōn'ər iz'əm) ***n.*** ⟦after Rev. W. A. *Spooner* (1844-1930), of England, who made such slips⟧ an unintentional interchange of the initial sounds of words (Ex.: "a well-boiled icicle" for "a well-oiled bicycle")

spoon'-feed' ***vt.*** **-fed', -feed'ing** 1 to feed with a spoon 2 to pamper; coddle

spoor (spoor) ***n.*** ⟦Afrik⟧ the track or trail of a wild animal

spo·rad·ic (spə rad'ik) ***adj.*** ⟦< Gr *sporas,* scattered⟧ happening or appearing in isolated instances [*sporadic* storms] —**spo·rad'i·cal·ly** ***adv.***

spore (spôr, spôr) ***n.*** ⟦< Gr *spora,* a seed⟧ a small reproductive body produced by algae, ferns, etc. and capable of giving rise to a new individual —***vi.*** **spored, spor'ing** to bear spores

sport (spôrt) ***n.*** ⟦< DISPORT⟧ 1 any recreational activity; specif., a game, competition, etc. requiring bodily exertion 2 fun or play 3 a thing joked about 4 [Colloq.] a sportsmanlike person 5 [Colloq.] a showy, flashy fellow 6 *Biol.* a plant or animal markedly different from the normal type —***vt.*** [Colloq.] to display [to *sport* a loud tie] —***vi.*** 1 to play 2 to joke —***adj.*** 1 of or for sports 2 suitable for casual wear [a *sport* coat]: also **sports** —**in** (or **for**) **sport** in jest —**make sport of** to mock or ridicule

sport'ing *adj.* 1 of or interested in sports 2 sportsmanlike; fair 3 of games, races, etc. involving gambling or betting

spor'tive *adj.* 1 full of sport or fun 2 done in fun —**spor'tive·ly** *adv.*

sports car a low, small automobile with a high-compression engine

sports'cast' *n.* a broadcast of sports news on radio or TV —**sports'cast'er** *n.*

sports'man *n., pl.* **-men** 1 a man who takes part in sports, esp. hunting, fishing, etc. 2 one who plays fair and can lose without complaint or win without gloating —**sports'man·like'** *adj.* —**sports'man·ship'** *n.*

sport'y *adj.* **-i·er, -i·est** [Colloq.] 1 sporting or sportsmanlike 2 flashy or showy

spot (spät) *n.* ⟦prob. < MDu *spotte*⟧ 1 *a*) a small area differing in color, etc. from the surrounding area *b*) a stain, speck, etc. 2 a flaw or defect 3 a locality; place —*vt.* **spot'ted, spot'ting** 1 to mark with spots 2 to stain; blemish 3 to place; locate 4 to see; recognize 5 [Colloq.] to allow as a handicap —*vi.* 1 to become marked with spots 2 to make a stain, as ink —*adj.* 1 ready /*spot* cash/ 2 made at random /a *spot* survey/ —**hit the spot** [Colloq.] to satisfy a craving —**in a (bad) spot** [Slang] in trouble —**on the spot** [Slang] in a bad or demanding situation —**spot'less** *adj.* —**spot'ted** *adj.*

spot'-check' *vt.* to check or examine at random —*n.* such a checking

spot'light' *n.* 1 *a*) a strong beam of light focused on a particular person, thing, etc. *b*) a lamp used to project such a light 2 public notice or prominence —*vt.* to draw attention to, as by a spotlight

spot·ter (spät'ər) *n.* one who spots, as an assistant in the stands who reports on plays at a football game

spot'ty *adj.* **-ti·er, -ti·est** 1 having, occurring in, or marked with spots 2 not uniform or consistent

spouse (spous) *n.* ⟦< L *sponsus*, betrothed⟧ (one's) husband or wife —**spous·al** (spou'zəl) *adj.*

spout (spout) *n.* ⟦< ME *spouten*, to spout⟧ 1 a projecting tube or orifice by which a liquid is poured 2 a stream, etc. as of liquid from a spout —*vt., vi.* 1 to shoot out (liquid, etc.) as from a spout 2 to speak or utter (words, etc.) in a loud, pompous manner

sprain (sprān) *vt.* ⟦< ? L *ex-*, out + *premere*, press⟧ to wrench a ligament or muscle of (a joint) without dislocating the bones —*n.* an injury resulting from this

sprang (spraŋ) *vi., vt. alt. pt. of* SPRING

sprat (sprat) *n.* ⟦OE *sprott*⟧ a small European herring

sprawl (sprôl) *vi.* ⟦< OE *spreawlian*, move convulsively⟧ 1 to sit or lie with the limbs in a relaxed or awkward position 2 to spread out awkwardly or unevenly, as handwriting, etc. —*n.* a sprawling movement or position

spray[1] (sprā) *n.* ⟦prob. < MDu *spraeien*⟧ 1 a mist of fine liquid particles 2 *a*) a jet of such particles, as from a spray gun *b*) a device for spraying 3 something likened to a spray —*vt., vi.* 1 to direct a spray (on) 2 to shoot out in a spray —**spray'er** *n.*

spray[2] (sprā) *n.* ⟦ME⟧ a small branch or sprig of a tree, etc., with leaves, flowers, etc.

spray can a can in which gas under pressure sprays out the contents

spray gun a device that shoots out a spray of liquid, as paint, etc.

spread (spred) *vt., vi.* **spread, spread'ing** ⟦OE *sprædan*⟧ 1 to open or stretch out; unfold 2 to move (the fingers, wings, etc.) apart 3 to distribute or be distributed over an area 4 to extend in time 5 to make or be made widely known, felt, etc. 6 to cover or be covered (*with* something), as in a fine layer 7 to set (a table) for a meal 8 to push or be pushed apart —*n.* 1 the act or extent of spreading 2 an expanse 3 a cloth cover for a table, bed, etc. 4 jam, butter, etc. used on bread 5 [Colloq.] a meal with many different foods

spread'-ea'gle *adj.* having the figure of an eagle with wings and legs spread —*vt.* **-gled, -gling** to stretch out in this form, as for a flogging

spread'sheet' *n.* a computer program that organizes numerical data into rows and columns on a video screen

spree (sprē) *n.* ⟦< earlier *spray*⟧ 1 a noisy frolic 2 a period of drunkenness 3 a period of uninhibited activity /a shopping *spree*/

sprig (sprig) *n.* ⟦ME *sprigge*⟧ a little twig or spray

spright·ly (sprīt'lē) *adj.* **-li·er, -li·est** ⟦< *spright*, var. of SPRITE⟧ full of energy and spirit; lively —*adv.* in a sprightly manner —**spright'li·ness** *n.*

spring (spriŋ) *vi.* **sprang** or **sprung, sprung, spring'ing** ⟦OE *springan*⟧ 1 to leap; bound 2 to come, appear, etc. suddenly 3 to bounce 4 to arise as from some source; grow or develop 5 to become warped, split, etc. 6 to rise up above surrounding objects Often followed by *up* —*vt.* 1 to cause to leap forth suddenly 2 to cause (a trap, etc.) to snap shut 3 to cause to warp, split, etc. 4 to make known suddenly 5 [Slang] to get (someone) released from jail —*n.* 1 a leap, or the distance so covered 2 a sudden flying back 3 elasticity; resilience 4 a device, as a coil of wire, that returns to its original form after being forced out of shape 5 a flow of water from the ground 6 a source or origin 7 *a*) that season of the year following winter, in which plants begin to grow *b*) any period of beginning —*adj.* 1 of, for, appearing in, or planted in the spring 2 having, or supported on, springs 3 coming from a spring /*spring* water/ —**spring a leak** to begin to leak suddenly

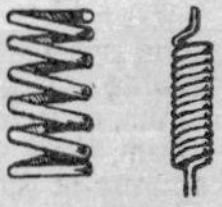
HELICAL SPRINGS

spring'board' *n.* a springy board used as a takeoff in leaping or diving

spring fever a laziness that many people feel in the early days of spring

Spring·field (spriŋ'fēld') 1 city in SW Mass.: pop. 152,000 2 city in SW Mo.: pop. 133,000 3 capital of Ill.: pop. 100,000

spring'time' *n.* the season of spring
spring'y *adj.* **-i·er, -i·est** having spring; elastic, resilient, etc. —**spring'i·ness** *n.*
sprin·kle (spriŋ'kəl) *vt., vi.* **-kled, -kling** ⟦ME *sprinklen*⟧ 1 to scatter or fall in drops or particles 2 to scatter drops or particles (upon) 3 to rain lightly —*n.* 1 a sprinkling 2 a light rain —**sprin'kler** *n.*
sprin'kling (-kliŋ) *n.* a small, scattered number or amount
sprint (sprint) *vi., n.* ⟦ME *sprenten*⟧ run or race at full speed for a short distance —**sprint'er** *n.*
sprite (sprīt) *n.* ⟦< L *spiritus,* spirit⟧ an imaginary being, as an elf
spritz (sprits, shprits) *vt., vi., n.* ⟦< Ger *spritze*⟧ squirt or spray
spritz'er *n.* a drink of white wine and soda water
sprock·et (spräk'it) *n.* ⟦< ?⟧ 1 any of the teeth, as on a wheel, arranged to fit the links of a chain 2 such a wheel: in full **sprocket wheel**
sprout (sprout) *vi.* ⟦OE *sprutan*⟧ to begin to grow; give off shoots —*vt.* to cause to sprout —*n.* 1 a young growth on a plant; shoot 2 a new growth from a bud, etc.
spruce[1] (sprōōs) *n.* ⟦ME *Spruce,* Prussia⟧ 1 an evergreen tree with slender needles 2 its wood
spruce[2] (sprōōs) *adj.* **spruc'er, spruc'est** ⟦< *Spruce* leather (see prec.)⟧ neat and trim in a smart way —*vt., vi.* **spruced, spruc'ing** to make or become spruce: usually with *up*
sprung (spruŋ) *vi., vt. pp. & alt. pt. of* SPRING
spry (sprī) *adj.* **spri'er** or **spry'er, spri'est** or **spry'est** ⟦< Scand⟧ full of life; active, esp. though elderly —**spry'ly** *adv.* —**spry'ness** *n.*
spud (spud) *n.* [Colloq.] a potato
spume (spyōōm) *n.* ⟦< L *spuma*⟧ foam, froth, or scum —*vi.* **spumed, spum'ing** to foam; froth
spu·mo·ni (spə mō'nē) *n.* ⟦It < L *spuma,* foam⟧ Italian ice cream in variously flavored layers
spun (spun) *vt., vi. pt. & pp. of* SPIN
spunk (spuŋk) *n.* ⟦Ir *sponc,* tinder⟧ [Colloq.] courage; spirit —**spunk'y, -i·er, -i·est,** *adj.*
spur (spur) *n.* ⟦OE *spura*⟧ 1 a pointed device worn on the heel by a rider, used to urge a horse forward 2 anything that urges; stimulus 3 any spurlike projection 4 a short railroad track connected with the main track —*vt.* **spurred, spur'ring** 1 to prick with spurs 2 to urge or incite —*vi.* to hurry; hasten —**on the spur of the moment** abruptly and impulsively
spurge (spurj) *n.* ⟦< Fr *espurger,* to purge⟧ any of a group of plants with milky juice and tiny flowers
spu·ri·ous (spyoor'ē əs) *adj.* ⟦L *spurius,* illegitimate⟧ not genuine; false —**spu'ri·ous·ly** *adv.* —**spu'ri·ous·ness** *n.*
spurn (spurn) *vt.* ⟦OE *spurnan*⟧ to reject with contempt; scorn
spurt (spurt) *vt.* ⟦prob. < OE *sprutan,* to sprout⟧ to expel in a stream or jet —*vi.* 1 to gush forth in a stream or jet 2 to show a sudden, brief burst of energy, etc. —*n.* 1 a sudden shooting forth; jet 2 a sudden, brief burst of energy, etc.
sput·nik (spoot'nik, sput'-) *n.* ⟦Russ, lit., co-traveler⟧ SATELLITE (sense 2*b*)
sput·ter (sput'ər) *vi.* ⟦< MDu *spotten,* to spit⟧ 1 to spit out drops, etc. explosively, as when talking excitedly 2 to speak in a confused, explosive way 3 to make sharp, sizzling sounds, as frying fat —*vt.* 1 to spit or throw out (bits or drops) explosively 2 to utter by sputtering —*n.* a sputtering
spu·tum (spyōōt'əm) *n., pl.* **-ta** (-ə) ⟦< L *spuere,* to spit⟧ saliva, usually mixed with mucus, spat out
spy (spī) *vt.* **spied, spy'ing** ⟦< OHG *spehōn,* examine⟧ 1 to watch closely and secretly: often with *out* 2 to catch sight of; see —*vi.* to watch closely and secretly; act as a spy —*n., pl.* **spies** 1 one who keeps close and secret watch on others 2 one employed by a government to get secret information about the affairs, armed forces, etc. of another government
spy'glass' (-glas') *n.* a small telescope
sq. 1 sequence 2 squadron 3 square
sqq. ⟦L *sequentes; sequentia*⟧ the following ones; what follows
squab (skwäb) *n.* ⟦prob. < Scand⟧ a nestling pigeon
squab·ble (skwäb'əl) *vi.* **-bled, -bling** ⟦< Scand⟧ to quarrel noisily over a small matter; wrangle —*n.* a noisy, petty quarrel —**squab'bler** *n.*
squad (skwäd) *n.* ⟦prob. < Sp *escuadra,* a square⟧ 1 a small group of soldiers, often a subdivision of a platoon 2 any small group of people working together
squad car PATROL CAR
squad'ron (-rən) *n.* ⟦< It *squadra,* a square⟧ a unit of warships, armored cavalry, military aircraft, etc.
squal·id (skwäl'id) *adj.* ⟦< L *squalere,* be foul⟧ 1 foul or unclean 2 wretched
squall[1] (skwôl) *n.* ⟦< Scand⟧ a brief, violent windstorm, usually with rain or snow —**squall'y, -i·er, -i·est,** *adj.*
squall[2] (skwôl) *vi., vt.* ⟦< ON *skvala*⟧ to cry or scream loudly and harshly —*n.* a harsh, loud cry or scream
squal·or (skwäl'ər) *n.* a being squalid; filth and wretchedness
squa·mous (skwā'məs) *adj.* ⟦< L *squama,* a scale⟧ like, formed of, or covered with scales
squan·der (skwän'dər) *vt.* ⟦prob. < dial. *squander,* to scatter⟧ to spend or use wastefully or extravagantly
square (skwer) *n.* ⟦< L *ex,* out + *quadrare,* to square⟧ 1 *a)* a plane figure having four equal sides and four right angles *b)* anything of or approximating this shape 2 BLOCK (*n.* 7) 3 an open area bounded by several streets, used as a park, etc. 4 an instrument for drawing or testing right angles 5 the product of a number multiplied by itself 6 [Slang] a person who is SQUARE (*adj.* 10) —*vt.* **squared, squar'ing** 1 to make into a SQUARE (sense 1) 2 to make straight, even, right-angled, etc. 3 to settle; adjust /to *square* accounts/ 4 to make conform /to *square* a statement with the facts/ 5 to multiply (a quantity) by itself —*vi.* to fit; agree; accord (*with*) —*adj.* **squar'er, squar'est** 1 having four equal

sides and four right angles **2** forming a right angle **3** straight, level, even, etc. **4** leaving no balance; even **5** just; fair **6** direct; straightforward **7** designating a unit of surface measure in the form of a square /a *square* foot/ **8** solid; sturdy /a *square* joint/ **9** [Colloq.] satisfying; substantial /a *square* meal/ **10** [Slang] old-fashioned; unsophisticated, etc. —***adv.*** in a square manner —**square off** (or **away**) to assume a posture of attack or self-defense —**square oneself** [Colloq.] to make amends —**square′ly** ***adv.*** —**square′ness** ***n.*** —**squar′ish** ***adj.***

square dance a dance with various steps, in which couples are grouped in a given form, as a square —**square′-dance′, -danced′, -danc′ing,** ***vi.***

square′-rigged′ ***adj.*** rigged with square sails as the principal sails

square root the quantity which when squared will produce a given quantity /3 is the *square root* of 9/

squash[1] (skwôsh, skwäsh) ***vt.*** ⟦< L *ex-*, intens. + *quatere*, to shake⟧ **1** to crush into a soft or flat mass; press **2** to suppress; quash —***vi.*** **1** to be squashed **2** to make a sound of squashing —***n.*** **1** something squashed **2** the act or sound of squashing **3** a game played in a walled court with rackets and a rubber ball —**squash′y, -i·er, -i·est,** ***adj.***

squash[2] (skwôsh, skwäsh) ***n.*** ⟦< AmInd⟧ the fleshy fruit of various plants of the gourd family, eaten as a vegetable

squat (skwät) ***vi.*** **squat′ted, squat′ting** ⟦< L *ex-*, intens. + *cogere*, to force⟧ **1** to sit on the heels with the knees bent **2** to crouch close to the ground **3** to settle on land without right or title **4** to settle on public land in order to get title to it —***adj.*** short and heavy or thick Also **squat′ty, -ti·er, -ti·est** —***n.*** the act or position of squatting —**squat′ness** ***n.*** —**squat′ter** ***n.***

squaw (skwô) ***n.*** ⟦< AmInd⟧ [Now Rare] a North American Indian woman or wife: now considered offensive

squawk (skwôk) ***vi.*** ⟦echoic⟧ **1** to utter a loud, harsh cry **2** [Colloq.] to complain loudly —***n.*** **1** a loud, harsh cry **2** [Colloq.] a raucous complaint

squeak (skwēk) ***vi.*** ⟦ME *squeken*⟧ to make or utter a sharp, high-pitched sound or cry —***vt.*** to say in a squeak —***n.*** a thin, sharp sound or cry —**narrow** (or **close** or **near**) **squeak** [Colloq.] a narrow escape —**squeak through** (or **by**, etc.) [Colloq.] to succeed, get through, etc. with difficulty —**squeak′y, -i·er, -i·est,** ***adj.***

squeak′er ***n.*** [Colloq.] a narrow escape, victory, etc.

squeal (skwēl) ***vi.*** ⟦ME *squelen*⟧ **1** to utter or make a long, shrill cry or sound **2** [Slang] to act as an informer —***vt.*** to utter in a squeal —***n.*** a squealing —**squeal′er** ***n.***

squeam·ish (skwēm′ish) ***adj.*** ⟦ME *squaimous*⟧ **1** easily nauseated **2** easily shocked; prudish **3** fastidious —**squeam′ish·ness** ***n.***

squee·gee (skwē′jē) ***n.*** ⟦prob. < fol.⟧ a rubber-edged tool for scraping water from a flat surface

squeeze (skwēz) ***vt.*** **squeezed, squeez′ing** ⟦< OE *cwysan*⟧ **1** to press hard, esp. from two or more sides **2** to extract (juice, etc.) from (fruit, etc.) **3** to force (*into, out*, etc.) by pressing **4** to embrace closely; hug —***vi.*** **1** to yield to pressure **2** to exert pressure **3** to force one's way by pushing —***n.*** **1** a squeezing or being squeezed **2** a close embrace; hug **3** the state of being closely pressed or packed; crush **4** a period of scarcity, hardship, etc.

squeeze bottle a plastic bottle that is squeezed to eject its contents

squelch (skwelch) ***n.*** ⟦< ?⟧ [Colloq.] a crushing retort, rebuke, etc. —***vt.*** [Colloq.] to suppress or silence completely

squib (skwib) ***n.*** ⟦prob. echoic⟧ **1** a firecracker that burns with a hissing noise before exploding **2** a short, witty verbal attack; lampoon

SQUID

squid (skwid) ***n.*** ⟦prob. < *squit*, dial. for SQUIRT⟧ a long, slender sea mollusk with eight arms and two long tentacles

squig·gle (skwig′əl) ***n.*** ⟦SQU(IRM) + (W)IGGLE⟧ a short, wavy line or illegible scrawl —***vt., vi.*** **-gled, -gling** to write as, or make, a squiggle or squiggles

squint (skwint) ***vi.*** ⟦< ASQUINT⟧ **1** to peer with the eyes partly closed **2** to look sideways or askance **3** to be cross-eyed —***n.*** **1** a squinting **2** a being cross-eyed **3** [Colloq.] a quick look or sidelong glance

squire (skwīr) ***n.*** ⟦see ESQUIRE⟧ **1** in England, the owner of a large, rural estate **2** a title of respect for a justice of the peace, etc. **3** an attendant, esp. a man escorting a woman —***vt.*** **squired, squir′ing** to act as a squire to

squirm (skwurm) ***vi.*** **1** to twist and turn the body; wriggle **2** to show or feel distress —***n.*** a squirming —**squirm′y** ***adj.***

squir·rel (skwur′əl, skwurl) ***n.*** ⟦< Gr *skia*, shadow + *oura*, tail⟧ **1** a small, tree-dwelling rodent with heavy fur and a long, bushy tail **2** its fur

squirt (skwurt) ***vt.*** ⟦prob. < LowG *swirtjen*⟧ **1** to shoot out (a liquid) in a jet; spurt **2** to wet with liquid so shot out —***n.*** **1** a jet of liquid **2** [Colloq.] a small or young person, esp. an impudent one

squish (skwish) ***vi.*** ⟦echoic var. of SQUASH[1]⟧ to make a soft, splashing sound when squeezed, etc. —***vt.*** [Colloq.] to squash —***n.*** **1** a squishing sound **2** [Colloq.] a squashing —**squish′y, -i·er, -i·est,** ***adj.***

Sr *Chem. symbol for* strontium

Sr. *abbrev.* **1** Senior **2** Sister

Sri Lan·ka (srē läŋ′kə) country coextensive with an island off the SE tip of India: 24,959 sq. mi.; pop. 14,850,000 —**Sri Lan′kan**

SRO **1** single room occupancy **2** standing room only

SS or **S.S.** steamship

SST supersonic transport
St. 1 Saint 2 Strait 3 Street
stab (stab) ***n.*** ⟦prob. < ME *stubbe,* stub⟧ 1 a wound made by stabbing 2 a thrust, as with a knife 3 a sharp pain 4 an attempt —***vt., vi.*** **stabbed, stab′bing** 1 to pierce or wound as with a knife 2 to thrust (a knife, etc.) into something 3 to pain sharply
sta·bil·i·ty (stə bil′ə tē) ***n.*** 1 a being stable; steadiness 2 firmness of purpose, etc. 3 permanence
sta·bi·lize (stā′bə līz′) ***vt.*** **-lized′, -liz′ing** 1 to make stable 2 to keep from changing 3 to give stability to (a plane or ship) —***vi.*** to become stabilized —**sta′bi·li·za′tion** ***n.*** —**sta′bi·liz′er** ***n.***
sta·ble¹ (stā′bəl) ***adj.*** **-bler, -blest** ⟦< L *stare,* to stand⟧ 1 not likely to give way; firm; fixed 2 firm in character, purpose, etc.; steadfast 3 not likely to change; lasting
sta·ble² (stā′bəl) ***n.*** ⟦see prec.⟧ 1 a building in which horses or cattle are sheltered and fed 2 all the racehorses belonging to one owner —***vt., vi.*** **-bled, -bling** to lodge, keep, or be kept in a stable
stac·ca·to (stə kät′ō) ***adj.*** ⟦It < *distaccare,* detach⟧ *Music* with distinct breaks between successive tones
stack (stak) ***n.*** ⟦< ON *stakkr*⟧ 1 a large, neatly arranged pile of straw, hay, etc. 2 any orderly pile 3 SMOKESTACK 4 [*pl.*] a series of bookshelves, as in a library —***vt.*** 1 to arrange in a stack 2 to rig so as to predetermine the outcome —**stack up** to stand in comparison (*with* or *against*)
stack′up′ ***n.*** an arrangement of circling aircraft at various altitudes awaiting their turn to land
sta·di·um (stā′dē əm) ***n.*** ⟦< Gr *stadion,* ancient unit of length, *c.* 607 ft.⟧ a large structure as for football or baseball, with tiers of seats for spectators
staff (staf) ***n., pl.*** **staffs** or **staves** ⟦OE *stæf*⟧ 1 a stick or rod used as a support, a symbol of authority, etc. 2 a group of people assisting a leader 3 a specific group of workers /a teaching *staff*/ 4 *Music* the horizontal lines on and between which notes are written —***vt.*** to provide with a staff, as of workers
staff′er ***n.*** a member of a staff, as of a newspaper
stag (stag) ***n.*** ⟦OE *stagga*⟧ a full-grown male deer —***adj.*** for men only /a *stag* dinner/ —**go stag** [Colloq.] to go unaccompanied by a date
stage (stāj) ***n.*** ⟦< L *stare,* to stand⟧ 1 a platform 2 *a*) an area or platform on which plays, etc. are presented *b*) the theater, or acting as a profession (with *the*) 3 the scene of an event 4 a stopping place, or the distance between stops, on a journey 5 *short for* STAGECOACH 6 a period or level in a process of development /the larval *stage*/ 7 any of the propulsion units used in sequence to launch a missile, spacecraft, etc. —***vt.*** **staged, stag′ing** 1 to present as on a stage 2 to plan and carry out /to *stage* an attack/
stage′coach′ ***n.*** a horse-drawn public coach that traveled a regular route
stage′hand′ ***n.*** one who sets up scenery, furniture, lights, etc. for a stage play
stage′-struck′ ***adj.*** intensely eager to become an actor or actress
stag·ger (stag′ər) ***vi.*** ⟦< ON *stakra,* totter⟧ to totter, reel, etc. as from a blow or fatigue —***vt.*** 1 to cause to stagger, as with a blow 2 to affect strongly as with grief 3 to set or arrange alternately, as on either side of a line; make zigzag 4 to arrange so as to come at different times /to *stagger* vacations/ —***n.*** 1 a staggering 2 [*pl., with sing. v.*] a nervous disease of horses, etc. causing this
stag·nant (stag′nənt) ***adj.*** ⟦see fol.⟧ 1 not flowing or moving 2 foul from lack of movement, as water 3 dull; sluggish
stag′nate′ (-nāt′) ***vi., vt.*** **-nat′ed, -nat′ing** ⟦< L *stagnare*⟧ to become or make stagnant —**stag·na′tion** ***n.***
staid (stād) ***vi., vt.*** *archaic pt. & pp. of* STAY³ —***adj.*** sober; sedate —**staid′ly** ***adv.***
stain (stān) ***vt.*** ⟦ult. < L *dis-,* from + *tingere,* to tinge⟧ 1 to spoil by discoloring or spotting 2 to disgrace; dishonor 3 to color (wood, etc.) with a dye —***n.*** 1 a color or spot resulting from staining 2 a moral blemish 3 a dye for staining wood, etc.
stain′less steel steel alloyed with chromium, etc., virtually immune to rust and corrosion
stair (ster) ***n.*** ⟦OE *stæger*⟧ 1 [*usually pl.*] a staircase 2 a single step, as of a staircase
stair′case′ ***n.*** a stairway in a building, usually with a handrail
stair′way′ ***n.*** a means of access, as from one level of a building to another, consisting of a series of stairs
stair′well′ ***n.*** a vertical shaft (in a building) containing a staircase
stake (stāk) ***n.*** ⟦OE *staca*⟧ 1 a pointed length of wood or metal for driving into the ground 2 the post to which a person was tied for execution by burning 3 [*often pl.*] money risked, as in a wager, business venture, etc. 4 [*often pl.*] the winner's prize in a race, etc. —***vt.*** **staked, stak′ing** 1 to mark the boundaries of /to *stake* out a claim/ 2 to fasten to stakes 3 to gamble 4 [Colloq.] to furnish with money or resources —**at stake** being risked —**pull up stakes** [Colloq.] to change one's residence, etc. —**stake out** to put under police surveillance
stake′out′ ***n.*** 1 the putting of a suspect or place under police surveillance 2 an area under such surveillance
sta·lac·tite (stə lak′tīt) ***n.*** ⟦< Gr *stalaktos,* trickling⟧ an icicle-shaped mineral deposit hanging from a cave roof
sta·lag (shtä′läg) ***n.*** ⟦Ger⟧ a German prisoner-of-war camp, esp. in World War II
sta·lag·mite (stə lag′mīt′) ***n.*** ⟦< Gr *stalagmos,* a dropping⟧ a cone-shaped mineral deposit built up on a cave floor by dripping water
stale (stāl) ***adj.*** **stal′er, stal′est** ⟦prob. < OFr *estale,* quiet⟧ 1 no longer fresh; flat, dry, etc. 2 trite /a *stale* joke/ 3 out of condition, bored, etc. —***vt., vi.*** **staled, stal′ing** to make or become stale —**stale′ness** ***n.***
stale′mate′ ***n.*** ⟦< OFr *estal,* fixed location⟧ 1 *Chess* any situation in which a player cannot move, resulting in a draw 2 any

deadlock —**vt.** -**mat'ed, -mat'ing** to bring into a stalemate

Sta·lin (stä'lin), **Joseph** 1879-1953; Soviet premier (1941-53) —**Sta'lin·ism'** *n.* —**Sta'lin·ist** *adj., n.*

stalk[1] (stôk) *vi., vt.* ⟦OE *stealcian*⟧ 1 to walk (through) in a stiff, haughty manner 2 to advance grimly 3 to pursue (game, etc.) stealthily —*n.* 1 a slow, stiff, haughty stride 2 a stalking

stalk[2] (stôk) *n.* ⟦ME *stalke*⟧ 1 any stem or stemlike part 2 the main stem of a plant

stall[1] (stôl) *n.* ⟦OE *steall*⟧ 1 a section for one animal in a stable 2 *a*) a booth, etc. as at a market *b*) a pew in a church 3 a stop or standstill, as a result of some malfunction —*vt., vi.* 1 to keep or be kept in a stall 2 to bring or be brought to a standstill, esp. unintentionally

stall[2] (stôl) *vi., vt.* ⟦< *stall,* decoy⟧ to act evasively so as to deceive or delay —*n.* any action used in stalling

stal·lion (stal'yən; *also* stal'ē ən) *n.* ⟦< OFr *estalon*⟧ an uncastrated male horse

stal·wart (stôl'wərt) *adj.* ⟦< OE *stathol,* foundation + *wyrthe,* worth⟧ 1 strong; sturdy 2 brave; valiant 3 resolute; firm —*n.* a stalwart person

sta·men (stā'mən) *n.* ⟦< L, thread⟧ the pollen-bearing organ in a flower

Stam·ford (stam'fərd) city in SW Conn.: pop. 102,000

stam·i·na (stam'ə nə) *n.* ⟦L, pl. of STAMEN⟧ resistance to fatigue, illness, hardship, etc.; endurance

stam·mer (stam'ər) *vt., vi.* ⟦OE *stamerian*⟧ to speak with involuntary pauses and rapid repetitions of some sounds —*n.* a stammering —**stam'mer·er** *n.*

stamp (stamp) *vt.* ⟦ME *stampen*⟧ 1 to bring (the foot) down forcibly 2 to crush or pound with the foot 3 to imprint or cut out (a design, etc.) 4 to cut (*out*) by pressing with a die 5 to put a stamp on 6 to characterize —*vi.* 1 to bring down the foot forcibly 2 to walk with loud, heavy steps —*n.* 1 a stamping 2 *a*) a machine, tool, or die for stamping *b*) a mark or form made by stamping 3 any of various seals, gummed pieces of paper, etc. used to show that a fee, as for postage, has been paid 4 any similar stamp /trading *stamp*/ 5 class; kind —**stamp out** 1 to crush by treading on forcibly 2 to suppress, or put down —**stamp'er** *n.*

stam·pede (stam pēd') *n.* ⟦< Sp *estampar,* to stamp⟧ a sudden, headlong rush or flight, as of a herd of cattle —*vi.* **-ped'ed, -ped'ing** to move, or take part, in a stampede

stamping ground [Colloq.] a regular or favorite gathering place

stance (stans) *n.* ⟦< L *stare,* to stand⟧ 1 the way one stands, esp. the placement of the feet 2 the attitude taken in a given situation

stanch (stônch, stanch) *vt., vi., adj. see* STAUNCH

stan·chion (stan'chən) *n.* ⟦see STANCE⟧ 1 an upright post or support 2 a device to confine a cow

stand (stand) *vi.* **stood, stand'ing** ⟦OE *standan*⟧ 1 to be in, or assume, an upright position on the feet 2 to be supported on a base, pedestal, etc. 3 to take or be in a (specified) position, attitude, etc. 4 to have a (specified) height when standing 5 to be placed or situated 6 to gather and remain, as water 7 to remain unchanged 8 to make resistance 9 *a*) to halt *b*) to be stationary —*vt.* 1 to place upright 2 to endure 3 to withstand 4 to undergo /to *stand* trial/ —*n.* 1 a standing; esp., a halt or stop 2 a position; station 3 a view, opinion, etc. 4 a structure to stand or sit on 5 a place of business 6 a rack, small table, etc. for holding things 7 a growth of trees, etc. —**stand by** 1 to be near and ready if needed 2 to aid —**stand for** 1 to represent 2 [Colloq.] to tolerate —**stand off** to keep at a distance —**stand on** 1 to be founded on 2 to insist upon —**stand out** 1 to project 2 to be distinct, prominent, etc. —**stand up** 1 to rise to a standing position 2 to prove valid, durable, etc. 3 [Slang] to fail to keep a date with —**take the stand** to testify in court —**stand'er** *n.*

stand·ard (stan'dərd) *n.* ⟦< OFr *estendard*⟧ 1 a flag or banner used as an emblem of a military unit, etc. 2 something established for use as a rule or basis of comparison in measuring quantity, quality, etc. 3 an upright support —*adj.* 1 used as, or conforming to, a standard, rule, model, etc. 2 generally accepted as reliable or authoritative 3 typical; ordinary

stand'ard-bear'er *n.* 1 one who carries the flag 2 the leader of a movement, political party, etc.

stand'ard·ize' *vt.* **-ized', -iz'ing** to make standard or uniform —**stand'ard·i·za'tion** *n.*

standard time the time in any of the 24 time zones, each an hour apart, into which the earth is divided, based on distance east or west of Greenwich, England

stand'by' *n., pl.* **-bys'** a person or thing that is dependable or a possible substitute

stand·ee (stan dē') *n.* one who stands, as in a theater, bus, etc.

stand'-in' *n.* a temporary substitute, as for an actor at rehearsals

stand'ing *n.* 1 status or reputation /in good *standing*/ 2 duration /a rule of long *standing*/ —*adj.* 1 upright or erect 2 from a standing position /a *standing* jump/ 3 stagnant, as water 4 lasting; permanent /a *standing* order/ 5 not in use

stand'off' *n.* a tie in a contest

stand'off'ish *adj.* reserved; aloof

stand'out' *n.* [Colloq.] one outstanding in performance, quality, etc.

stand'pipe' *n.* a high vertical pipe or cylindrical tank, as in a town's water-supply system, for storing water at a desired pressure

stand'point' *n.* point of view

stand'still' *n.* a stop or halt

stand'-up' *adj.* 1 in a standing position 2 specializing in monologues made up of jokes, as a comedian

stank (staŋk) *vi. alt. pt. of* STINK

stan·za (stan'zə) *n.* ⟦It: ult. < L *stare,* to stand⟧ a group of lines of verse forming a division of a poem or song

staph (staf) *n. short for* STAPHYLOCOCCUS

staph·y·lo·coc·cus (staf'ə lō käk'əs) *n., pl.*

-coc′ci′ (-käk′sī′) ⟦< Gr *staphylē*, bunch of grapes + *kokkos*, kernel⟧ any of certain spherical bacteria, in clusters or chains

sta·ple¹ (stā′pəl) ***n.*** ⟦< MDu *stapel*, mart⟧ **1** a chief commodity made or grown in a particular place **2** raw material **3** a regularly stocked item of trade, as flour, salt, etc. **4** the fiber of cotton, wool, etc. —***adj.*** **1** regularly stocked, produced, or used **2** most important; principal

sta·ple² (stā′pəl) ***n.*** ⟦OE *stapol*, a post⟧ a U-shaped piece of metal with sharp ends, driven into wood, etc. as to hold a hook, wire, etc., or through papers as a binding —***vt.*** **-pled, -pling** to fasten or bind with a staple or staples —**sta′pler** ***n.***

star (stär) ***n.*** ⟦OE *steorra*⟧ **1** any of the luminous celestial objects seen as points of light in the sky; esp., any far-off, self-luminous one **2** such an object regarded as influencing one's fate **3** a conventionalized figure with five or six points, or anything like this **4** ASTERISK **5** one who excels, as in a sport **6** a leading actor or actress —***vt.*** **starred, star′ring** **1** to mark with stars as a decoration, etc. **2** to present (an actor or actress) in a leading role —***vi.*** **1** to perform brilliantly **2** to perform as a star, as in films —***adj.*** **1** having great skill; outstanding **2** of a star —**star′less** ***adj.***

star·board (stär′bərd, -bôrd′) ***n.*** ⟦< OE *steoran*, to steer (rudder formerly on right side) + *bord*, side (of ship)⟧ the right-hand side of a ship, etc. as one faces forward —***adj.*** of or on this side

starch (stärch) ***n.*** ⟦< OE *stearc*, stiff⟧ **1** a white, tasteless, odorless food substance found in potatoes, cereals, etc. **2** a powdered form of this, used in laundering for stiffening cloth, etc. —***vt.*** to stiffen as with starch —**starch′y, -i·er, -i·est,** ***adj.***

star·dom (stär′dəm) ***n.*** the status of a star, as of films

stare (ster) ***vi.*** **stared, star′ing** ⟦OE *starian*⟧ to gaze steadily and intently —***vt.*** to look fixedly at —***n.*** a steady, intent look —**star′er** ***n.***

star′fish′ ***n.***, *pl.* **-fish′** or (for different species) **-fish′es** a small, star-shaped sea animal

STARFISH

star′gaze′ ***vi.*** **-gazed′, -gaz′ing** **1** to gaze at the stars **2** to indulge in dreamy thought —**star′gaz′er** ***n.***

stark (stärk) ***adj.*** ⟦OE *stearc*⟧ **1** rigid, as a corpse **2** sharply outlined **3** bleak; desolate **4** sheer; downright —***adv.*** utterly; wholly

stark′-nak′ed ***adj.*** entirely naked

star·let (stär′lit) ***n.*** a young actress being promoted as a future star

star′light′ ***n.*** light given by the stars —**star′lit′** (-lit′) ***adj.***

star·ling (stär′liŋ) ***n.*** ⟦OE *stær*⟧ any of an Old World family of birds; esp., the **common starling** with iridescent plumage, introduced into the U.S.

star′ry ***adj.*** **-ri·er, -ri·est** **1** shining; bright **2** lighted by or full of stars

star′ry-eyed′ ***adj.*** with sparkling eyes

Stars and Stripes *name for* the U.S. flag

star′-span′gled ***adj.*** studded or spangled with stars

Star-Spangled Banner the U.S. national anthem

start (stärt) ***vi.*** ⟦OE *styrtan*⟧ **1** to make a sudden or involuntary move **2** to go into action or motion; begin; commence **3** to spring into being, activity, etc. —***vt.*** **1** to flush (game) **2** to displace, loosen, etc. /to *start* a seam/ **3** *a*) to begin to play, do, etc. *b*) to set into motion, action, etc. **4** to cause to be an entrant in a race, etc. —***n.*** **1** a sudden, startled reaction or movement **2** a starting, or beginning **3** *a*) a place or time of beginning *b*) a lead or other advantage **4** an opportunity of beginning a career —**start out** (or **off**) to start a journey, project, etc. —**start′er** ***n.***

star·tle (stärt′'l) ***vt.*** **-tled, -tling** ⟦< ME *sterten*, to start⟧ to surprise, frighten, or alarm suddenly; esp., to cause to start —***vi.*** to be startled

starve (stärv) ***vi.*** **starved, starv′ing** ⟦< OE *steorfan*, to die⟧ **1** to die from lack of food **2** to suffer from hunger **3** to suffer great need: with *for* —***vt.*** **1** to cause to starve **2** to force by starvation —**star·va·tion** (stär vā′shən) ***n.***

starve′ling (-liŋ) ***n.*** a person or animal that is weak from lack of food

Star Wars ⟦from a film title⟧ [Colloq.] a proposed defense system of space-based weapons for destroying missiles

stash (stash) ***vt.*** ⟦< ?⟧ [Colloq.] to put or hide away (money, etc.) —***n.*** [Colloq.] **1** a place for hiding things **2** something hidden away

-stat (stat) *combining form* a device or agent that keeps something (specified) stationary /*thermostat*/

state (stāt) ***n.*** ⟦< L *stare*, to stand⟧ **1** a set of circumstances, etc. characterizing a person or thing; condition **2** condition as regards structure, form, etc. **3** rich display; pomp **4** [*sometimes* **S-**] a body of people politically organized under one government; nation **5** [*usually* **S-**] any of the political units forming a federal government, as in the U.S. **6** civil government /church and *state*/ —***adj.*** **1** formal; ceremonial **2** [*sometimes* **S-**] of the government or of a state —***vt.*** **stat′ed, stat′ing** **1** to establish by specifying **2** *a*) to set forth in words *b*) to express nonverbally —**in a state** [Colloq.] in an excited condition —**lie in state** to be displayed formally before burial —**the States** the United States

state′hood′ (-hood′) ***n.*** the condition of being a state

state′house′ ***n.*** [*often* **S-**] the official legislative meeting place of each U.S. State

state′less ***adj.*** having no state or nationality

state′ly ***adj.*** **-li·er, -li·est** **1** imposing; majestic **2** slow, dignified, etc. —**state′li·ness** ***n.***

state′ment ***n.*** **1** *a*) a stating *b*) a declaration, assertion, etc. **2** *a*) a financial account *b*) a bill; invoice

Stat·en Island (stat′'n) island borough of New York City: pop. 352,000

state of the art the current level of sophistication of a developing technology, as of computer science —**state'-of-the-art'** *adj.*

state'room' *n.* a private room on a ship or train

state'side' *adj.* [Colloq.] of or in the U.S. (as viewed from abroad) —*adv.* [Colloq.] in or to the U.S.

states'man *n., pl.* **-men** one who is wise or experienced in the business of government —**states'man·ship'** *n.*

stat·ic (stat'ik) *adj.* ⟦< Gr *statikos,* causing to stand⟧ 1 of masses, forces, etc. at rest or in equilibrium 2 at rest; inactive 3 of or producing stationary electrical charges, as from friction 4 of or having to do with static —*n.* 1 atmospheric electrical discharges causing noise on radio or TV 2 such noise 3 [Slang] adverse criticism —**stat'i·cal·ly** *adv.*

sta·tion (stā'shən) *n.* ⟦< L *stare,* to stand⟧ 1 the place where a person or thing stands or is located, esp. an assigned post 2 a regular stopping place, as on a bus line or railroad 3 social standing 4 *a)* a place equipped for radio or TV transmission *b)* its assigned frequency or channel —*vt.* to assign to a station

sta·tion·ar·y (stā'shə ner'ē) *adj.* 1 not moving; fixed 2 unchanging

station break a pause in radio or TV programs for station identification

sta·tion·er (stā'shə nər) *n.* ⟦< ML *stationarius,* shopkeeper⟧ a dealer in stationery, office supplies, etc.

sta'tion·er'y (-ner'ē) *n.* writing materials; specif., paper and envelopes

station wagon an automobile with extra space for cargo or seating and a rear door for loading

sta·tis·tics (stə tis'tiks) *n.pl.* ⟦< L *status,* standing⟧ 1 numerical data assembled and classified so as to present significant information 2 [*with sing. v.*] the science of compiling such data —**sta·tis'ti·cal** *adj.* —**stat·is·ti·cian** (stat'is tish'ən) *n.*

stats (stats) *n.pl.* [Colloq.] *short for* STATISTICS (sense 1)

stat·u·ar·y (stach'o͞o er'ē) *n.* statues collectively

stat·ue (stach'o͞o) *n.* ⟦< L *statuere,* to set⟧ a figure, as of a person, or an abstract form carved in stone, cast in bronze, etc.

stat'u·esque' (-esk') *adj.* of or like a statue; specif., *a)* tall *b)* dignified

stat'u·ette' (-et') *n.* a small statue

stat·ure (stach'ər) *n.* ⟦< L *statura*⟧ 1 standing height, esp. of a person 2 level of attainment /moral *stature*/

sta·tus (stat'əs, stāt'-) *n., pl.* **-tus·es** ⟦L, standing⟧ 1 legal condition /the *status* of a minor/ 2 position; rank 3 state, as of affairs

status quo (kwō') ⟦L, the state in which⟧ the existing state of affairs

status symbol a possession regarded as a mark of (high) social status

stat·ute (stach'o͞ot) *n.* ⟦see STATUE⟧ 1 an established rule 2 a law passed by a legislative body

statute of limitations a statute limiting the time for legal action

stat·u·to·ry (stach'o͞o tôr'ē) *adj.* 1 fixed or authorized by statute 2 punishable by statute, as an offense

staunch (stônch, stänch) *vt.* ⟦< L *stare,* to stand⟧ to check the flow of (blood, etc.) from (a cut, etc.) —*vi.* to stop flowing —*adj.* 1 seaworthy 2 steadfast; loyal 3 strong; solid Also, esp. for v., **stanch** —**staunch'ly** *adv.*

stave (stāv) *n.* ⟦< *staves,* pl. of STAFF⟧ 1 any of the shaped strips of wood forming the wall of a barrel, bucket, etc. 2 a stick or staff 3 a stanza —*vt.* **staved** or **stove, stav'ing** to puncture, as by breaking in staves —**stave off** to hold off or put off

staves (stāvz) *n.* 1 *alt. pl. of* STAFF 2 *pl. of* STAVE

stay[1] (stā) *n.* ⟦OE *stæg*⟧ a heavy rope or cable, used as a brace or support

stay[2] (stā) *n.* ⟦Fr *estaie*⟧ 1 a support or prop 2 a strip of stiffening material used in a corset, shirt collar, etc. —*vt.* to support, or prop up

stay[3] (stā) *vi.* **stayed, stay'ing** ⟦< L *stare,* to stand⟧ 1 to continue in the place or condition specified; remain 2 to live; dwell 3 to stop; halt 4 to pause; delay 5 [Colloq.] to continue; last —*vt.* 1 to stop or check 2 to hinder or detain 3 to postpone (legal action) 4 to satisfy (thirst, etc.) for a time 5 *a)* to remain to the end of *b)* to be able to last through —*n.* 1 *a)* a stopping or being stopped *b)* a halt or pause 2 a postponement in legal action 3 the action of remaining, or the time spent, in a place —**stay put** [Colloq.] to remain in place or unchanged

staying power ability to last or endure; endurance

St. Cath·ar·ines (kath'ər inz) city in SE Ontario, Canada: pop. 124,000

St. Chris·to·pher (kris'tə fər) island country (together with Nevis) of the West Indies: 104 sq. mi.; pop. 45,000: also **St. Christopher-Nevis**

STD sexually transmitted disease

Ste. ⟦Fr *Sainte*⟧ Saint (female)

stead (sted) *n.* ⟦OE *stede*⟧ the place of a person or thing as filled by a substitute —**stand someone in good stead** to give someone good service

stead·fast (sted'fast') *adj.* ⟦OE *stedefæste*⟧ 1 firm; fixed 2 constant —**stead'fast'ly** *adv.*

stead·y (sted'ē) *adj.* **-i·er, -i·est** ⟦STEAD + -Y[2]⟧ 1 firm; stable; not shaky 2 constant, regular, or uniform 3 constant in behavior, loyalty, etc. 4 calm and controlled /*steady* nerves/ 5 sober; reliable —*vt., vi.* **-ied, -y·ing** to make or become steady —*n.* [Colloq.] a sweetheart —*adv.* in a steady manner —**go steady** [Colloq.] to date someone exclusively —**stead'i·ly** *adv.*

steady-state theory the theory that new matter is continuously being created, thus keeping the density of the expanding universe constant

steak (stāk) *n.* ⟦< ON *steikja,* to roast on a spit⟧ a slice of meat, esp. beef, or of fish, for broiling or frying

steal (stēl) *vt.* **stole, stol'en, steal'ing** ⟦OE *stælan*⟧ 1 to take (another's property, etc.) dishonestly, esp. in a secret manner 2 to take (a look, etc.) slyly 3 to gain insidiously or artfully /he *stole* her heart/ 4 to move, put, etc. stealthily (*in, from,* etc.) 5 *Baseball* to gain (a base), as by running to it from another base while the pitch is being delivered —*vi.* 1 to be a thief 2 to move, etc. stealthily —*n.* [Colloq.] an extraordinary bargain

stealth (stelth) *n.* ⟦< ME *stelen,* to steal⟧ secret or furtive action —**stealth'y** *adj.* —**stealth'i·ly** *adv.*

steam (stēm) *n.* ⟦OE⟧ 1 water as converted into a vapor by being heated to the boiling point 2 the power of steam under pressure 3 condensed water vapor 4 [Colloq.] vigor; energy —*adj.* using, or operated by, steam —*vi.* 1 to give off steam 2 to become covered with condensed steam 3 to move by steam power —*vt.* to expose to steam, as in cooking —**steam'y, -i·er, -i·est,** *adj.*

steam'boat' *n.* a small steamship

steam engine an engine using steam under pressure to supply mechanical energy

steam'er *n.* 1 something operated by steam, as a steamship 2 a container for cooking, cleaning, etc. with steam

steam'fit'ter *n.* one whose work is installing boilers, pipes, etc. in steam-pressure systems —**steam'fit'ting** *n.*

steam'roll'er *n.* a heavy, steam-driven roller used in building roads —*vt., vi.* to move, crush, override, etc. as (with) a steamroller

steam'ship' *n.* a ship driven by steam power

steam shovel a large, mechanically operated digger, powered by steam

steed (stēd) *n.* ⟦OE *steda*⟧ a horse

steel (stēl) *n.* ⟦OE *stiele*⟧ 1 a hard, tough alloy of iron with carbon 2 a thing of steel 3 great strength or hardness —*adj.* of or like steel —*vt.* to make hard, tough, etc. —**steel'y, -i·er, -i·est,** *adj.*

steel wool long, thin shavings of steel in a pad, used for scouring, polishing, etc.

steel'yard' (-yärd') *n.* ⟦STEEL + obs. *yard,* rod⟧ a balance or scale consisting of a metal arm suspended from above

steep[1] (stēp) *adj.* ⟦OE *steap,* lofty⟧ 1 having a sharp rise or slope; precipitous 2 [Colloq.] excessive; extreme —**steep'ly** *adv.* —**steep'ness** *n.*

steep[2] (stēp) *vt.* ⟦ME *stepen*⟧ to soak, saturate, imbue, etc.

stee·ple (stē'pəl) *n.* ⟦OE *stepel*⟧ 1 a tower rising above the main structure, as of a church 2 a spire

stee'ple·chase' *n.* a horse race run over a course obstructed with ditches, hedges, etc.

stee'ple·jack' *n.* one who builds or repairs steeples, smokestacks, etc.

steer[1] (stir) *vt., vi.* ⟦OE *stieran*⟧ 1 to guide (a ship, etc.) with a rudder 2 to direct the course of (an automobile, etc.) 3 to follow (a course) —**steer clear of** to avoid —**steer'a·ble** *adj.*

steer[2] (stir) *n.* ⟦OE *steor*⟧ 1 a full-grown, castrated male of cattle 2 loosely, any male of beef cattle

steer·age (stir'ij) *n.* 1 a steering 2 [Historical] a section in a ship for the passengers paying the lowest fare

steers·man (stirz'mən) *n., pl.* **-men** one who steers a ship; helmsman

steg·o·sau·rus (steg'ə sôr'əs) *n., pl.* **-ri** (-ī) ⟦< Gr *stegos,* roof + *sauros,* lizard⟧ a large dinosaur with pointed, bony plates along the backbone

stein (stīn) *n.* ⟦Ger⟧ a beer mug

stel·lar (stel'ər) *adj.* ⟦< L *stella,* a star⟧ 1 of a star 2 excellent 3 leading; chief /a *stellar* role/

stem[1] (stem) *n.* ⟦OE *stemn*⟧ 1 the main stalk of a plant 2 any stalk or part supporting leaves, flowers, or fruit 3 a stemlike part, as of a pipe, goblet, etc. 4 the prow of a ship; bow 5 the part of a word to which inflectional endings are added —*vt.* **stemmed, stem'ming** to make headway against /to *stem* the tide/ —*vi.* to derive

stem[2] (stem) *vt.* **stemmed, stem'ming** ⟦< ON *stemma*⟧ to stop or check by or as if by damming up

stem'ware' *n.* goblets, wineglasses, etc. having stems

stench (stench) *n.* ⟦< OE *stincan,* to stink⟧ an offensive smell; stink

sten·cil (sten'səl) *vt.* **-ciled** or **-cilled, -cil·ing** or **-cil·ling** ⟦ult. < L *scintilla,* a spark⟧ to make or mark with a stencil —*n.* 1 a thin sheet, as of paper, cut through so that when ink, etc. is applied, designs, letters, etc. form on the surface beneath 2 a design, etc. so made

ste·nog·ra·phy (stə näg'rə fē) *n.* shorthand writing, as of dictation, testimony, etc., for later transcription —**ste·nog'ra·pher** *n.* —**sten·o·graph·ic** (sten'ə graf'ik) *adj.*

sten·to·ri·an (sten tôr'ē ən) *adj.* ⟦after *Stentor,* Gr herald in the *Iliad*⟧ very loud

step (step) *n.* ⟦OE *stepe*⟧ 1 a single movement of the foot, as in walking 2 the distance covered by such a movement 3 a short distance 4 a manner of stepping 5 the sound of stepping 6 a rest for the foot in climbing, as a stair 7 a degree; level; stage 8 any of a series of acts, processes, etc. —*vi.* **stepped, step'ping** 1 to move by executing a step 2 to walk a short distance 3 to move briskly (*along*) 4 to enter (*into* a situation, etc.) 5 to press the foot down (*on*) —*vt.* to measure by taking steps: with *off* —**in** (or **out of**) **step** (not) conforming to a rhythm, a regular procedure, etc. —**step up** 1 to advance 2 to increase, as in rate —**take steps** to do the things needed —**step'per** *n.*

step'broth'er *n.* one's stepparent's son by a former marriage

step'child' *n., pl.* **-chil'dren** ⟦< OE *steop-,* orphaned + *cild,* child⟧ one's spouse's child (**stepdaughter** or **stepson**) by a former marriage

step'-down' *n.* a decrease, as in amount, intensity, etc.

step'lad'der *n.* a four-legged ladder with broad, flat steps

step'par'ent *n.* the person (**stepfather** or **stepmother**) who has married one's parent after the death of or divorce from the other parent

steppe (step) *n.* ⟦Russ *styep'*⟧ any of the great plains of SE Europe and Asia, having few trees

step'ping·stone' *n.* 1 a stone to step on, as in crossing a stream 2 a means of bettering oneself

step'sis'ter *n.* one's stepparent's daughter by a former marriage

step′-up′ *n.* an increase, as in amount, intensity, etc.

-ster (stər) ⟦OE *-estre*⟧ *suffix* one who is, does, creates, or is associated with (something specified) /*trickster, gangster*/

ster·e·o (ster′ē ō′) *n., pl.* **-os′** **1** a stereophonic device, system, effect, etc. **2** a stereoscopic system, effect, picture, etc. —*adj. short for* STEREOPHONIC

stereo- ⟦< Gr *stereos,* solid⟧ *combining form* solid, firm, three-dimensional /*stereoscope*/

ster·e·o·phon·ic (ster′ē ə fän′ik) *adj.* designating or of sound reproduction using two or more channels to carry a blend of sounds from separate sources through separate speakers

ster′e·o·scope′ (-skōp′) *n.* an instrument with two eyepieces that gives a three-dimensional effect to photographs viewed through it

ster′e·o·type′ (-tīp′) *n.* ⟦see STEREO- & -TYPE⟧ **1** a printing plate cast from a mold, as a page of set type **2** a fixed or conventional notion or conception —*vt.* **-typed′, -typ′ing** to make a stereotype of —**ster′e·o·typed′** *adj.*

ster′e·o·typ′i·cal (-tip′i k′l) *adj.* stereotyped; hackneyed

ster·ile (ster′əl) *adj.* ⟦L *sterilis*⟧ **1** incapable of producing offspring, fruit, etc.; barren **2** free from living microorganisms —**ste·ril·i·ty** (stə ril′ ə tē) *n.*

ster′i·lize′ (-ə līz′) *vt.* **-lized′, -liz′ing** to make sterile; specif., *a*) to make incapable of reproduction *b*) to free from living microorganisms —**ster′i·li·za′tion** *n.* —**ster′i·liz′er** *n.*

ster·ling (stur′liŋ) *n.* ⟦ME *sterlinge,* Norman coin⟧ **1** sterling silver **2** British money —*adj.* **1** of silver that is at least 92.5 percent pure **2** of British money **3** made of sterling silver **4** excellent /*sterling* principles/

Ster·ling Heights (stur′liŋ) city in SE Mich.: suburb of Detroit: pop. 109,000

stern¹ (sturn) *adj.* ⟦OE *styrne*⟧ **1** severe; strict /*stern* measures/ **2** grim /a *stern* face/ **3** relentless; firm —**stern′ly** *adv.* —**stern′ness** *n.*

stern² (sturn) *n.* ⟦< ON *styra,* to steer⟧ the rear end of a ship, etc.

ster·num (stur′nəm) *n., pl.* **-nums** or **-na** (-nə) ⟦< Gr *sternon*⟧ a flat, bony structure to which most of the ribs are attached in the front of the chest; breastbone

ster·oid (stir′oid′, ster′-) *n.* ⟦< (CHOLE)S-TER(OL) + -OID⟧ any of a group of compounds including the bile acids, sex hormones, etc.,

ster·to·rous (stur′tər əs) *adj.* ⟦< L *stertere,* to snore⟧ characterized by raspy, labored breathing

stet (stet) *v.* ⟦L⟧ let it stand: printer's term indicating that matter marked for deletion is to remain —*vt.* **stet′ted, stet′ting** to mark with "stet"

steth·o·scope (steth′ə skōp′) *n.* ⟦< Gr *stēthos,* chest + -SCOPE⟧ *Med.* an instrument used to examine the heart, lungs, etc. by listening to the sounds they make

ste·ve·dore (stē′və dôr′) *n.* ⟦ult. < L *stipare,* cram⟧ one whose work is loading and unloading ships

stew (stōō, styōō) *vt., vi.* ⟦ult. < L *ex-,* out + Gr *typhos,* steam⟧ **1** to cook by simmering or boiling slowly **2** to worry —*n.* **1** a dish, esp. of meat and vegetables, cooked by stewing **2** a state of worry

stew·ard (stōō′ərd, styōō′-) *n.* ⟦< OE *stig,* hall + *weard,* keeper⟧ **1** a person put in charge of a large estate **2** an administrator, as of finances and property **3** one responsible for the food and drink, etc. in a club, restaurant, etc. **4** an attendant, as on a ship or airplane —**stew′ard·ship′** *n.*

stew′ard·ess (-ər dis) *n.* a woman steward, esp. on an airplane

stick (stik) *n.* ⟦OE *sticca*⟧ **1** a twig or small branch broken or cut off **2** a long, slender piece of wood, as a club, cane, etc. **3** any sticklike piece /a *stick* of gum/ —*vt.* **stuck, stick′ing** **1** to pierce, as with a pointed instrument **2** to pierce with (a knife, pin, etc.) **3** to thrust (*in, into, out,* etc.) **4** to attach as by gluing, pinning, etc. **5** to obstruct, detain, etc. /the wheels were *stuck*/ **6** [Colloq.] to place; put; set **7** [Colloq.] to puzzle; baffle **8** [Slang] *a*) to impose a burden, etc. upon *b*) to defraud —*vi.* **1** to be fixed by a pointed end, as a nail **2** to adhere; cling; remain **3** to persevere /to *stick* at a job/ **4** to remain firm and resolute /he *stuck* with us/ **5** to become embedded, jammed, etc. **6** to be puzzled **7** to hesitate; scruple /he'll *stick* at nothing/ **8** to protrude or project (*out, up,* etc.) —**stick by** to remain loyal to —**stick up for** [Colloq.] to uphold; defend —**the sticks** [Colloq.] the rural districts

stick′er *n.* a person or thing that sticks; specif., a gummed label

stick′-in-the-mud′ *n.* [Colloq.] one who resists change, new ideas, etc.

stick·le·back (stik′əl bak′) *n.* a small, bony-plated fish with sharp dorsal spines: the male builds a nest for the female's eggs

stick·ler (stik′lər) *n.* ⟦prob. < ME *stightlen,* to order⟧ **1** one who insists on a certain way of doing things /a *stickler* for discipline/ **2** [Colloq.] something difficult to solve

stick′pin′ *n.* an ornamental pin worn in a necktie, on a lapel, etc.

stick shift a gearshift, as on a car, operated manually

stick′um (-əm) *n.* ⟦STICK + *'em,* short for THEM⟧ [Colloq.] any sticky, or adhesive, substance

stick′up′ *n. slang term for* HOLDUP (sense 2)

stick′y *adj.* **-i·er, -i·est** **1** that sticks; adhesive **2** [Colloq.] hot and humid **3** [Colloq.] troublesome

stiff (stif) *adj.* ⟦OE *stif*⟧ **1** hard to bend or move; rigid; firm **2** sore or limited in movement: said of joints and muscles **3** not fluid; thick **4** strong; powerful /a *stiff* wind/ **5** harsh /*stiff* punishment/ **6** difficult /a *stiff* climb/ **7** very formal or awkward **8** [Colloq.] high /a *stiff* price/ —**stiff′ly** *adv.* —**stiff′ness** *n.*

stiff′-arm′ *vt.* to push (someone) away with one's arm out straight

stiff′en *vt., vi.* to make or become stiff or stiffer —**stiff′en·er** *n.*

stiff′-necked′ (-nekt′) *adj.* stubborn

sti·fle (stī′fəl) *vt.* **-fled, -fling** ⟦< Fr *estouffer*⟧ 1 to suffocate; smother 2 to suppress; hold back; stop /to *stifle* a sob/ —*vi.* to die or suffer from lack of air —**sti′fling·ly** *adv.*

stig·ma (stig′mə) *n., pl.* **-mas** or **stig·ma′ta** (-mät′ə) ⟦< Gr, lit., a puncture made with a sharp instrument⟧ 1 a mark of disgrace or reproach 2 a spot on the skin, esp. one that bleeds under certain conditions of nervous tension 3 the upper tip of the pistil of a flower, on which pollen falls and develops —**stig·mat′ic** (-mat′ik) *adj.*

stig′ma·tize′ (-tīz′) *vt.* **-tized′, -tiz′ing** 1 to mark with a stigma 2 to mark as disgraceful

stile (stīl) *n.* ⟦< OE *stigan,* to climb⟧ a step or set of steps used in climbing over a fence or wall

sti·let·to (sti let′ō) *n., pl.* **-tos** or **-toes** ⟦It < L *stilus,* pointed tool⟧ a small dagger with a slender blade

still[1] (stil) *adj.* ⟦OE *stille*⟧ 1 without sound; silent 2 not moving; stationary 3 tranquil; calm 4 designating or of a single photograph taken from a movie film —*n.* 1 silence; quiet 2 a still photograph —*adv.* 1 at or up to the time indicated 2 even; yet /*still* colder/ 3 nevertheless; yet /rich but *still* unhappy/ —*conj.* nevertheless; yet —*vt., vi.* to make or become still —**still′ness** *n.*

still[2] (stil) *n.* ⟦< obs. *still,* to distill⟧ an apparatus used for distilling liquids, esp. alcoholic liquors

still′birth′ *n.* 1 the birth of a stillborn fetus 2 such a fetus

still′born′ *adj.* dead when born

still life a picture of inanimate objects, as fruit, flowers, etc.

stilt (stilt) *n.* ⟦ME *stilte*⟧ 1 either of a pair of poles fitted with a footrest along its length and used for walking, as in play 2 any of a number of long posts used to hold a building, etc. above ground or out of water

stilt·ed (stil′tid) *adj.* artificially formal or dignified; pompous

stim·u·lant (stim′yo͞o lənt) *n.* anything, as a drug, that stimulates

stim′u·late′ (-lāt′) *vt.* **-lat′ed, -lat′ing** ⟦see fol.⟧ to rouse or excite to activity or increased activity —**stim′u·la′tion** *n.*

stim′u·lus (-ləs) *n., pl.* **-li′** (-lī′) ⟦L, a goad⟧ 1 an incentive 2 any action or agent that causes an activity in an organism, organ, etc.

sting (stiŋ) *vt.* **stung, sting′ing** ⟦OE *stingan*⟧ 1 to prick or wound with a sting 2 to cause sudden, pricking pain to 3 to cause to suffer mentally 4 to stimulate suddenly and sharply 5 [Slang] to cheat —*vi.* to cause or feel sharp, smarting pain —*n.* 1 a stinging 2 a pain or wound resulting from stinging 3 a sharp-pointed organ, as in insects and plants, that pricks, wounds, etc. —**sting′er** *n.*

sting′ray′ *n.* a large ray with one or more poisonous spines that can inflict painful wounds

stin·gy (stin′jē) *adj.* **-gi·er, -gi·est** ⟦< dial. form of STING⟧ 1 giving or spending grudgingly; miserly 2 less than needed; scanty —**stin′gi·ly** *adv.* —**stin′gi·ness** *n.*

stink (stiŋk) *vi.* **stank** or **stunk, stunk, stink′ing** ⟦OE *stincan*⟧ to give off a strong, unpleasant smell —*n.* a strong, unpleasant smell; stench —**stink′er** *n.*

stint (stint) *vt.* ⟦< OE *styntan,* to blunt⟧ to restrict to a certain quantity, often small —*vi.* to be sparing in giving or using —*n.* 1 restriction; limit 2 an assigned task or period of work —**stint′er** *n.*

sti·pend (stī′pənd) *n.* ⟦< L *stips,* small coin + *pendere,* to pay⟧ a regular or fixed payment, as a salary

stip·ple (stip′əl) *vt.* **-pled, -pling** ⟦< Du *stippel,* a speckle⟧ to paint, draw, or engrave in small dots

stip·u·late (stip′yo͞o lāt′) *vt.* **-lat′ed, -lat′ing** ⟦< L *stipulari,* to bargain⟧ 1 to arrange definitely 2 to specify as an essential condition of an agreement —**stip′u·la′tion** *n.*

stir[1] (stur) *vt., vi.* **stirred, stir′ring** ⟦OE *styrian*⟧ 1 to move, esp. slightly 2 to rouse from sleep, lethargy, etc.; to make or be active 3 to mix (a liquid, etc.) as by agitating with a spoon 4 to excite the feelings (of) 5 to incite: often with *up* —*n.* 1 a stirring 2 movement; activity 3 excitement; tumult —**stir′rer** *n.*

stir[2] (stur) *n.* ⟦19th-c. thieves' slang⟧ [Slang] a prison

stir′-cra′zy *adj.* [Slang] neurotically affected by long, close confinement, specif. in prison

stir′-fry′ *vt.* **-fried′, -fry′ing** to fry (diced or sliced vegetables, meat, etc.) quickly in a wok while stirring constantly

stir′ring *adj.* 1 active; busy 2 rousing; exciting /*stirring* music/

stir·rup (stur′əp) *n.* ⟦OE *stigrap*⟧ a flat-bottomed ring hung from a saddle and used as a footrest

stitch (stich) *n.* ⟦OE *stice,* a puncture⟧ 1 *a)* a single complete in-and-out movement of a needle in sewing, etc. *b)* a suture 2 a loop, knot, etc. made by stitching 3 a particular kind of stitch or style of stitching 4 a sudden, sharp pain 5 a bit —*vi., vt.* to make stitches (in); sew —**in stitches** laughing uproariously

stitch′er·y (-ər ē) *n.* ornamental needlework

St. John's capital of Newfoundland: pop. 76,000

St. Lawrence river flowing from Lake Ontario into the Atlantic: the main section of an inland waterway (**St. Lawrence Seaway**) connecting the Great Lakes with the Atlantic

St. Lou·is (lo͞o′is, lo͞o′ē) city & port in E Mo., on the Mississippi: pop. 453,000

St. Lu·ci·a (lo͞o′shē ə, -sē′ə) island country of the West Indies: 238,000 sq. mi.; pop. 120,000

stoat (stōt) *n.* ⟦ME *stote*⟧ a large European ermine, esp. in its brown summer coat

stock (stäk) *n.* ⟦OE *stocc*⟧ 1 the trunk of a tree 2 *a)* descent; lineage *b)* a strain, race, etc. of animals or plants 3 a supporting or main part of an implement, etc., as the wooden handle to which the barrel of a rifle is attached 4 [*pl.*] a wooden frame with holes for confining the ankles or wrists, formerly used for punishment 5 raw material 6 water in which meat, fish, etc. has been boiled, used in soups 7 livestock 8 a supply of goods on hand in a store, etc. 9 a certificate representing a share or shares of corporate ownership 10 a stock company or its repertoire —*vt.* 1 to furnish (a farm, shop, etc.) with stock 2 to keep a supply of, as for sale or for future use —*vi.* to put in a stock, or supply: with *up* —*adj.* 1 kept in stock [*stock* sizes] 2 common or trite [a *stock* excuse] 3 that deals with stock 4 relating to a stock company —**in** (or **out of**) **stock** (not) available for sale or use —**take stock** 1 to inventory the stock on hand 2 to make an appraisal — **take** (or **put**) **stock in** to have faith in

stock·ade (stä kād′) *n.* ⟦< Prov *estaca,* a stake⟧ 1 a barrier of stakes driven into the ground side by side, for defense 2 an enclosure, as a fort, made with such stakes

stock′bro′ker *n.* a broker who buys and sells stocks, bonds, etc.

stock car a standard automobile, modified for racing

stock company a theatrical company presenting a repertoire of plays

stock exchange 1 a place where stocks and bonds are bought and sold 2 an association of stockbrokers Also **stock market**

stock′hold′er *n.* one owning stock in a given company

Stock·holm (stäk′hōm′, -hōlm′) capital of Sweden: pop. 635,000

stock·ing (stäk′iŋ) *n.* ⟦< obs. sense of *stock*⟧ a closefitting covering, usually knitted, for the foot and leg

stocking cap a long, tapered knitted cap, often with a tassel at the end

stock′pile′ *n.* a reserve supply of goods, raw material, etc. —*vt., vi.* **-piled′, -pil′ing** to accumulate a stockpile (of)

stock′-still′ *adj.* motionless

Stock·ton (stäk′tən) city in central Calif.: pop. 150,000

stock′y *adj.* **-i·er, -i·est** heavily built; short and thickset —**stock′i·ness** *n.*

stock′yard′ *n.* an enclosure where cattle, hogs, etc. are kept before slaughtering

stodg·y (stä′jē) *adj.* **-i·er, -i·est** ⟦< *stodge,* heavy food⟧ 1 dull; uninteresting 2 old-fashioned; conventional —**stodg′i·ness** *n.*

sto·gie or **sto·gy** (stō′gē) *n., pl.* **-gies** ⟦after *Conestoga* Valley, Pa.⟧ a long, thin, inexpensive cigar

Sto·ic (stō′ik) *n.* ⟦< Gr *stoa,* a colonnade: where first Stoics met⟧ 1 a member of an ancient Greek school of philosophy 2 [s-] a stoical person —*adj.* [s-] STOICAL —**sto′i·cism′** (-i siz′əm) *n.*

sto′i·cal (-i kəl) *adj.* showing indifference to joy, grief, pleasure, or pain; impassive —**sto′i·cal·ly** *adv.*

stoke (stōk) *vt., vi.* **stoked, stok′ing** ⟦< Du *stoken,* to poke⟧ 1 to stir up and feed fuel to (a fire) 2 to tend (a furnace, boiler, etc.) —**stok′er** *n.*

STOL (stōl) *adj.* ⟦*s*(*hort*) *t*(*ake*)*o*(*ff and*) *l*(*anding*)⟧ designating or of an aircraft that can take off and land on a short airstrip —*n.* a STOL aircraft, airstrip, etc.

stole[1] (stōl) *n.* ⟦< Gr *stolē,* garment⟧ 1 a long strip of cloth worn about the neck by clergymen at various rites 2 a woman's long scarf of cloth or fur worn around the shoulders

stole[2] (stōl) *vt., vi. pt. of* STEAL

stol·en (stō′lən) *vt., vi. pp. of* STEAL

stol·id (stäl′id) *adj.* ⟦L *stolidus,* slow⟧ having or showing little or no emotion; unexcitable —**sto·lid·i·ty** (stə lid′ə tē) *n.* —**stol′id·ly** *adv.*

sto·lon (stō′län′) *n.* ⟦< L *stolo,* a shoot⟧ a creeping stem lying above the soil surface and bearing leaves, as in the strawberry

stom·ach (stum′ək) *n.* ⟦ult. < Gr *stoma,* mouth⟧ 1 the saclike digestive organ into which food passes from the esophagus 2 the abdomen, or belly 3 appetite for food 4 desire or inclination —*vt.* 1 to be able to eat or digest 2 to tolerate; bear

stom′ach·ache′ *n.* pain in the stomach or abdomen

stom′ach·er *n.* an ornamented piece of cloth formerly worn over the chest and abdomen, esp. by women

stomp (stämp) *vt., vi. var. of* STAMP (*vt.* 1, 2; *vi.* 1, 2)

stone (stōn) *n.* ⟦OE *stan*⟧ 1 the hard, solid, nonmetallic mineral matter of rock 2 a piece of rock 3 the seed of certain fruits 4 *short for* PRECIOUS STONE 5 *pl.* **stone** [Brit.] 14 pounds avoirdupois 6 an abnormal stony mass formed in the kidney, gall bladder, etc. —*vt.* **stoned, ston′ing** 1 to pelt or kill with stones 2 to remove the stone from (a peach, etc.)

stone- ⟦< prec.⟧ *combining form* completely [*stone*-blind]

Stone Age the period in human culture when stone tools were used

stoned *adj.* [Slang] drunk or under the influence of a drug

stone's throw a short distance

stone′wall′ *vi.* [Colloq.] to behave in an obstructive manner, as by withholding information, etc.

stone′ware′ *n.* a dense, opaque, glazed or unglazed pottery

ston′y (-ē) *adj.* **-i·er, -i·est** 1 full of stones 2 of or like stone; specif., unfeeling; pitiless —**ston′i·ness** *n.*

stood (stood) *vi., vt. pt. & pp. of* STAND

stooge (stōōj) *n.* ⟦< ?⟧ [Colloq.] 1 an actor who serves as the victim of a comedian's jokes, pranks, etc. 2 anyone who acts as a foil or underling

stool (stōōl) *n.* ⟦OE *stol*⟧ 1 a single seat having no back or arms 2 feces

stool pigeon [Colloq.] a spy or informer, esp. for the police

stoop[1] (stōōp) *vi.* ⟦OE *stupian*⟧ 1 to bend the body forward 2 to carry the head and shoulders habitually bent forward 3 to degrade oneself —*n.* the act or position of stooping

stoop[2] (stōōp) *n.* ⟦Du *stoep*⟧ a small porch at the door of a house

stop (stäp) *vt.* **stopped, stop′ping** ⟦< L *stuppa,* stop up⟧ 1 to close by filling, shutting off, etc. 2 to cause to cease motion, activity, etc. 3 to block; intercept; prevent 4 to cease; desist from [*stop* talking] —*vi.* 1 to cease moving, etc.; halt 2 to leave off doing something 3 to cease operating 4 to become clogged 5 to tarry or stay —*n.* 1 a stopping or being stopped 2 a finish; end 3 a stay or sojourn 4 a place stopped at, as on a bus route 5 an obstruction, plug, etc. 6 a finger hole in a wind instrument, closed to produce a desired tone **7** a pull, lever, etc. for controlling a set of organ pipes —**stop off** to stop for a while en route to a place —**stop over** to visit for a while: also **stop in** (or **by**)

stop′cock′ *n.* a cock or valve to stop or regulate the flow of a fluid

stop′gap′ *n.* a person or thing serving as a temporary substitute

stop′light′ *n.* **1** a traffic light, esp. when red to signal vehicles to stop **2** a light at the rear of a vehicle, that lights up when the brakes are applied

stop′o′ver *n.* a brief stop or stay at a place in the course of a journey

stop′page (-ij) *n.* **1** a stopping or being stopped **2** an obstructed condition; block

stop′per *n.* something inserted to close an opening; plug

stop′ple (-əl) *n.* a stopper or plug —*vt.* **-pled, -pling** to close with a stopple

stop′watch′ *n.* a watch that can be started and stopped instantly, as for timing races

stor·age (stôr′ij) *n.* **1** a storing or being stored **2** a place for, or the cost of, storing goods **3** computer memory

storage battery a battery producing electric current, with cells that can be recharged

store (stôr) *vt.* **stored, stor′ing** ⟦< L *instaurare,* restore⟧ **1** to put aside for use when needed **2** to furnish with a supply **3** to put, as in a warehouse, for safekeeping —*n.* **1** a supply (*of* something) for use when needed; stock **2** [*pl.*] supplies, esp. of food, clothing, etc. **3** a retail establishment where goods are offered for sale **4** a storehouse —**in store** set aside for the future; in reserve —**set** (or **put** or **lay**) **store by** to value

store′front′ *n.* a front room on the ground floor of a building, designed for use as a retail store

store′house′ *n.* a place where things are stored; esp., a warehouse

store′keep′er *n.* **1** a person in charge of military or naval stores **2** a retail merchant

store′room′ *n.* a room where things are stored

sto·rey (stôr′ē) *n., pl.* **-reys** *Brit., etc. sp. of* STORY²

sto·ried (stôr′ēd) *adj.* famous in story or history

stork (stôrk) *n.* ⟦OE *storc*⟧ a large, long-legged wading bird with a long neck and bill

ADJUTANT STORK

storm (stôrm) *n.* ⟦OE⟧ **1** a strong wind, with rain, snow, thunder, etc. **2** any heavy fall of snow, rain, etc. **3** a strong emotional outburst **4** any strong disturbance **5** a sudden, strong attack on a fortified place —*vi.* **1** to blow rain, snow, etc. violently **2** to rage; rant **3** to rush violently /to *storm* into a room/ —*vt.* to attack vigorously

storm door (or **window**) a door (or window) placed outside the regular one as added protection

storm′y *adj.* **-i·er, -i·est** **1** of or characterized by storms **2** violent, raging, etc. —**storm′i·ly** *adv.* —**storm′i·ness** *n.*

sto·ry¹ (stôr′ē) *n., pl.* **-ries** ⟦< Gr *historia,* narrative⟧ **1** the telling of an event or events; account; narration **2** a joke **3** a fictitious narrative shorter than a novel **4** the plot of a novel, play, etc. **5** [Colloq.] a falsehood **6** a news report

sto·ry² (stôr′ē) *n., pl.* **-ries** ⟦< prec.⟧ a horizontal division of a building, from a floor to the ceiling above it

sto′ry·board′ *n.* a large board on which sketches, etc. for shots or scenes of a film are arranged in sequence —*vt.* to make a storyboard of (a shot or scene) for (a film)

sto′ry·book′ *n.* a book of stories, esp. one for children

sto′ry·tell′er (-tel′ər) *n.* one who narrates stories —**sto′ry·tell′ing** *n.*

stoup (sto͞op) *n.* ⟦< ON *staup,* cup⟧ a font for holy water

stout (stout) *adj.* ⟦< OFr *estout,* bold⟧ **1** courageous **2** strong; sturdy; firm **3** powerful; forceful **4** fat; thickset —*n.* a heavy, dark-brown beer —**stout′ly** *adv.* —**stout′ness** *n.*

stout′heart′ed *adj.* courageous; brave

stove¹ (stōv) *n.* ⟦< MDu, heated room⟧ an apparatus for heating, cooking, etc.

stove² (stōv) *vt., vi. alt. pt. & pp. of* STAVE

stove′pipe′ *n.* a metal pipe used to carry off smoke from a stove

stow (stō) *vt.* ⟦< OE *stowe,* a place⟧ to pack in an orderly way —**stow away** **1** to put or hide away **2** to be a stowaway —**stow′age** *n.*

stow′a·way′ *n.* one who hides aboard a ship, airplane, etc. to get free passage, evade port officials, etc.

St. Paul capital of Minn.: pop. 270,000

St. Pe·ters·burg (pēt′ərz burg′) **1** *old name* (1703-1914) *of* LENINGRAD **2** city in W Fla.: pop. 237,000

strad·dle (strad′'l) *vt.* **-dled, -dling** ⟦< STRIDE⟧ **1** to stand or sit astride of, or stand with the legs wide apart **2** to appear to take both sides of (an issue) —*n.* a straddling —**strad′dler** (-lər) *n.*

strafe (strāf) *vt.* **strafed, straf′ing** ⟦< Ger *Gott strafe England* (God punish England)⟧ to attack with machine-gun fire from low-flying aircraft

strag·gle (strag′'l) *vi.* **-gled, -gling** ⟦prob. < ME *straken,* roam⟧ **1** to wander from the main group **2** to be scattered over a wide area; ramble **3** to hang in an unkempt way, as hair —**strag′gler** *n.* —**strag′gly** *adj.*

straight (strāt) *adj.* ⟦< ME *strecchen,* to stretch⟧ **1** having the same direction throughout its length; not crooked, bent, etc. **2** direct; undeviating, etc. **3** in order; properly arranged, etc. **4** honest; sincere **5** unmixed; undiluted /*straight* whiskey/ **6** [Slang] normal or conventional —*adv.* **1** in a straight line **2** upright; erectly **3** without detour, delay, etc. —*n.* *Poker* a hand of five cards in sequence —**straight away** (or **off**) without delay —**straight′ness** *n.*

straight arrow [Slang] one who is proper, righteous, conscientious, etc. and often regarded as stodgy, dull, etc. —**straight′ar′row** *adj.*

straight′a·way′ *n.* a straight section of a

racetrack, highway, etc. —*adv.* without delay
straight′edge′ *n.* a strip of wood, etc. having a perfectly straight edge, used in drawing straight lines, etc.
straight′en *vt., vi.* to make or become straight —**straighten out** 1 to make or become less confused, easier to deal with, etc. 2 to reform —**straight′en·er** *n.*
straight face a facial expression showing no amusement or other emotion —**straight′-faced′** *adj.*
straight′for′ward *adj.* 1 moving or leading straight ahead; direct 2 honest; frank —*adv.* in a straightforward manner Also **straight′for′wards**
straight time 1 the standard number of working hours, as per week 2 the rate of pay for these hours
straight′way′ *adv.* [Archaic] at once
strain[1] (strān) *vt.* ⟦< L *stringere*⟧ 1 to draw or stretch tight 2 to exert or use to the utmost 3 to injure by overexertion /to *strain* a muscle/ 4 to stretch beyond normal limits 5 to pass through a screen, sieve, etc.; filter —*vi.* 1 to make violent efforts; strive hard 2 to filter, ooze, etc. —*n.* 1 a straining or being strained 2 great effort, exertion, etc. 3 a bodily injury from overexertion 4 stress or force 5 a great demand on one's emotions, resources, etc.
strain[2] (strān) *n.* ⟦< OE *strynan,* to produce⟧ 1 ancestry; lineage 2 race; stock; line 3 a line of individuals differentiated from its species or race 4 an inherited tendency 5 a musical tune
strained *adj.* not natural or relaxed
strain′er *n.* a device for straining, sifting, or filtering; sieve, filter, etc.
strait (strāt) *adj.* ⟦< L *stringere,* draw tight⟧ [Archaic] narrow or strict —*n.* 1 [*often pl.*] a narrow waterway connecting two large bodies of water 2 [*usually pl.*] difficulty; distress
strait′en *vt.* 1 [Now Rare] to make strait or narrow 2 to bring into difficulties: usually in **in straitened circumstances,** lacking enough money
strait′jack′et *n.* a coatlike device for restraining violent persons
strait′-laced′ *adj.* narrowly strict in behavior or moral views
strand[1] (strand) *n.* ⟦OE⟧ shore, esp. ocean shore —*vt., vi.* 1 to run or drive aground, as a ship 2 to put or be put into a helpless position /*stranded* abroad with no money/
strand[2] (strand) *n.* ⟦ME *stronde*⟧ 1 any one of the threads, wires, etc. that are twisted together to form a string, cable, etc. 2 a ropelike length of anything /a *strand* of pearls/
strange (strānj) *adj.* **strang′er, strang′est** ⟦< L *extraneus,* foreign⟧ 1 not previously known, seen, etc.; unfamiliar 2 unusual; extraordinary 3 peculiar; odd 4 reserved or distant 5 unaccustomed (*to*) —**strange′ly** *adv.* —**strange′ness** *n.*
stran·ger (strān′jər) *n.* 1 a newcomer 2 a person not known to one
stran·gle (straŋ′gəl) *vt., vi.* **-gled, -gling** ⟦< Gr *strangos,* twisted⟧ 1 to choke to death 2 to suppress, stifle, or repress —**stran′gler** *n.*
stran′gle·hold′ *n.* 1 an illegal wrestling hold that chokes an opponent 2 a force or action that suppresses freedom
stran·gu·late (straŋ′gyə lāt′) *vt.* **-lat′ed, -lat′ing** *Med.* to block (a tube, etc.) by constricting
strap (strap) *n.* ⟦dial. form of STROP⟧ a narrow strip of leather, etc., as for binding or securing things —*vt.* **strapped, strap′ping** to fasten with a strap
strap′less *adj.* having no straps; specif., having no shoulder straps
strapped (strapt) *adj.* [Colloq.] in utter need; penniless
strap′ping *adj.* [Colloq.] tall and well-built; robust
stra·ta (strāt′ə, strat′ə) *n. alt. pl. of* STRATUM
strat·a·gem (strat′ə jəm) *n.* ⟦< Gr *stratos,* army + *agein,* to lead⟧ 1 a trick, plan, etc. for deceiving an enemy in war 2 any tricky scheme
strat·e·gy (strat′ə jē) *n., pl.* **-gies** 1 the science of planning and directing military operations 2 skill in managing or planning, esp. by using stratagems 3 a stratagem, plan, etc. —**stra·te·gic** (strə tē′jik) *adj.* —**stra·te′gi·cal·ly** *adv.* —**strat′e·gist** *n.*
strat·i·fy (strat′ə fī′) *vt., vi.* **-fied′, -fy′ing** ⟦< L *stratum,* layer + *facere,* make⟧ to form in layers or strata —**strat′i·fi·ca′tion** *n.*
strat′o·sphere′ (-ə sfir′) *n.* ⟦< ModL *stratum,* stratum + Fr *sphère,* sphere⟧ the atmospheric zone at an altitude of *c.* 20 to 50 km
stra·tum (strāt′əm, strat′-) *n., pl.* **-ta** (-ə) or **-tums** ⟦ModL < L *stratus,* a spreading⟧ 1 a horizontal layer of matter, as of sedimentary rock or a level of the atmosphere 2 any of the socioeconomic groups of a society
stra′tus (-əs) *n., pl.* **-ti** (-ī) ⟦see prec.⟧ a uniform, low, gray cloud layer
Strauss (strous), **Jo·hann** (yō′hän) 1825-99; Austrian composer, esp. of waltzes
Stra·vin·sky (strə vin′skē), **I·gor** (ē′gôr) 1882-1971; U.S. composer & conductor, born in Russia
straw (strô) *n.* ⟦OE *streaw*⟧ 1 hollow stalks of grain after threshing 2 a single one of these 3 a tube used for sucking beverages 4 a trifle —*adj.* 1 straw-colored; yellowish 2 made of straw 3 worthless
straw′ber′ry (-ber′ē, -bər ē) *n., pl.* **-ries** ⟦prob. from the strawlike particles on the fruit⟧ 1 the small, red, fleshy fruit of a vinelike plant of the rose family 2 this plant
straw boss [Colloq.] one having subordinate authority
straw vote (or **poll**) an unofficial vote taken to determine general group opinion
stray (strā) *vi.* ⟦< LL *strata,* street⟧ 1 to wander from a given place, course, etc. 2 to deviate (*from* what is right) —*n.* one that strays; esp., a lost domestic animal —*adj.* 1 having strayed; lost 2 isolated /a few *stray* words/
streak (strēk) *n.* ⟦< OE *strica*⟧ 1 a long, thin mark or stripe 2 a layer, as of fat in meat 3 a tendency in behavior, etc. /a nervous *streak*/ 4 a period, as of luck —*vt.* to mark with streaks —*vi.* 1 to become streaked 2 to go fast 3 to dash naked for a

short distance in public as a prank —**streak'er** *n.* —**streak'y, -i·er, -i·est,** *adj.*

stream (strēm) *n.* ⟦OE⟧ 1 a current of water; specif., a small river 2 a steady flow, as of air, light, etc. 3 a continuous series /a *stream* of cars/ —*vi.* 1 to flow as in a stream 2 to flow (*with*) 3 to move swiftly

stream'er *n.* 1 a long, narrow, flag 2 any long, narrow, flowing strip

stream'line' *vt.* **-lined', -lin'ing** to make streamlined —*adj.* STREAMLINED

stream'lined' *adj.* 1 having a contour designed to offer the least resistance in moving through air, water, etc. 2 efficient, trim, simplified, etc.

street (strēt) *n.* ⟦< L *strata* (*via*), paved (road)⟧ 1 a public road in a town or city, esp. a paved one 2 such a road with its sidewalks, buildings, etc. 3 the people living, working, etc. along a given street

street'car' *n.* a car on rails for public transportation along the streets

street'-smart' *adj.* STREETWISE

street smarts cunning or shrewdness needed to live in an urban environment characterized by poverty, crime, etc.

street'walk'er *n.* a prostitute

street'wise' *adj.* [Colloq.] experienced in dealing with the people in urban poverty areas where vice and crime are common

strength (streŋkth) *n.* ⟦OE *strengthu*⟧ 1 the state or quality of being strong; force 2 toughness; durability 3 the power to resist attack 4 potency or concentration, as of drugs, etc. 5 intensity, as of sound, etc. 6 force of an army, etc., as measured in numbers —**on the strength of** based or relying on

strength'en *vt., vi.* to make or become stronger —**strength'en·er** *n.*

stren·u·ous (stren'yo͞o əs) *adj.* ⟦L *strenuus*⟧ requiring or characterized by great effort or energy —**stren'u·ous·ly** *adv.* —**stren'u·ous·ness** *n.*

strep (strep) *n. short for* STREPTOCOCCUS

strep throat (strep) [Colloq.] a sore throat caused by a streptococcus, with inflammation and fever

strep·to·coc·cus (strep'tə käk'əs) *n., pl.* **-coc'ci'** (-käk'sī') ⟦< Gr *streptos,* twisted + COCCUS⟧ any of various spherical bacteria that occur in chains: some cause serious diseases

strep'to·my'cin (-mī'sin) *n.* ⟦< Gr *streptos,* bent + *mykēs,* fungus⟧ an antibiotic drug obtained from a soil bacterium and used in treating various diseases

stress (stres) *n.* ⟦< L *strictus,* strict⟧ 1 strain; specif., force that strains or deforms 2 emphasis; importance 3 *a*) mental or physical tension *b*) urgency, pressure, etc. causing this 4 the relative force of utterance given a syllable or word; accent —*vt.* 1 to put stress or pressure on 2 to accent 3 to emphasize

stress fracture a leg fracture caused by repetitive stress, as in marathon running

stretch (strech) *vt.* ⟦OE *streccan*⟧ 1 to reach out; extend 2 to draw out to full extent or to greater size 3 to cause to extend too far; strain 4 to strain in interpretation, scope, etc. —*vi.* 1 *a*) to spread out to full extent or beyond normal limits *b*) to extend over a given distance or time 2 *a*) to extend the body or limbs to full length *b*) to lie down (usually with *out*) 3 to become stretched —*n.* 1 a stretching or being stretched 2 an unbroken period /a ten-day *stretch*/ 3 an unbroken length, tract, etc. 4 *short for* HOMESTRETCH —*adj.* made of elasticized fabric so as to stretch easily —**stretch'a·ble** *adj.* —**stretch'y, -i·er, -i·est,** *adj.*

stretch'er *n.* 1 one that stretches 2 a light frame covered with canvas, etc. for carrying the sick, injured, etc.

strew (stro͞o) *vt.* **strewed, strewed** or **strewn, strew'ing** ⟦OE *streawian*⟧ 1 to spread here and there; scatter 2 to cover as by scattering

stri·at·ed (strī'āt'id) *adj.* ⟦< L *striare,* to groove⟧ marked with parallel lines, bands, furrows, etc.

strick·en (strik'ən) *vt., vi. alt. pp. of* STRIKE —*adj.* 1 struck or wounded 2 afflicted, as by something painful

strict (strikt) *adj.* ⟦< L *stringere,* draw tight⟧ 1 exact or precise 2 perfect; absolute 3 *a*) enforcing rules carefully *b*) closely enforced —**strict'ly** *adv.* —**strict'ness** *n.*

stric·ture (strik'chər) *n.* ⟦see prec.⟧ 1 adverse criticism 2 an abnormal narrowing of a passage in the body

stride (strīd) *vi., vt.* **strode, strid'den, strid'ing** ⟦OE *stridan*⟧ 1 to walk with long steps 2 to cross with a single, long step —*n.* 1 a long step 2 the distance covered by such a step 3 [*usually pl.*] progress /to make *strides*/

stri·dent (strīd''nt) *adj.* ⟦< L *stridere,* to rasp⟧ harsh-sounding; shrill; grating —**stri'dent·ly** *adv.*

strife (strīf) *n.* ⟦< OFr *estrif*⟧ 1 contention 2 fight or quarrel; struggle

strike (strīk) *vt.* **struck, struck** or, esp. for *vt.* 7 & 10, **strick'en, strik'ing** ⟦OE *strican,* to go⟧ 1 to hit with the hand, a tool, etc. 2 to make by stamping, etc. /to *strike* coins/ 3 to announce (time), as with a bell: said of clocks, etc. 4 to ignite (a match) or produce (a light, etc.) by friction 5 to collide with or cause to collide /he *struck* his head on a beam/ 6 to attack 7 to afflict, as with disease, pain, etc. 8 to come upon; notice, find, etc. 9 to affect as if by contact, etc.; occur to /an idea *struck* me/ 10 to remove (*from* a list, record, etc.) 11 to make (a bargain, truce, etc.) 12 to lower (a sail, flag, etc.) 13 to assume (an attitude, pose, etc.) —*vi.* 1 to hit (*at*) 2 to attack 3 to make sounds as by being struck: said of a bell, clock, etc. 4 to collide; hit (*against, on,* or *upon*) 5 to seize bait: said of a fish 6 to come suddenly (*on* or *upon*) 7 to refuse to continue to work until certain demands are met 8 to proceed, esp. in a new direction —*n.* 1 the act of striking; specif., a military attack 2 a refusal by employees to go on working, in an attempt to gain better working conditions, etc. 3 the discovery of a rich deposit of oil, etc. 4 *Baseball* a pitched ball missed, or fouled off, by the batter or called a good pitch by the umpire 5 *Bowling* a knocking down of all the pins on the first roll —**strike out** 1 to erase 2 to start out 3 *Baseball* to put out, or be put out, on three strikes —**strike up** to begin —**strik'er** *n.*

strik'ing *adj.* very impressive; outstanding, remarkable, etc.

string (striŋ) *n.* ⟦OE *streng*⟧ 1 a thin line of fiber, leather, etc. used for tying, pulling, etc. 2 a group of like things on a string /a *string* of pearls/ 3 a row, series, etc. of like things /a *string* of houses/ 4 *a*) a slender cord of wire, gut, etc. bowed, plucked, or struck to make a musical sound *b*) [*pl.*] all the stringed instruments of an orchestra 5 a fiber of a plant 6 [Colloq.] a condition attached to a plan, offer, etc.: *usually used in pl.* —*vt.* **strung, string'ing** 1 to provide with strings 2 to thread on a string 3 to tie, hang, etc. with a string 4 to remove the strings from (beans, etc.) 5 to arrange in a row 6 to extend /*string* a cable/ —**pull strings** to get someone to use influence in one's behalf, often secretly —**string'y, -i·er, -i·est,** *adj.*

string bean SNAP BEAN

stringed instrument (striŋd) an instrument with a vibrating string, as a violin or guitar

strin·gent (strin'jənt) *adj.* ⟦see STRICT⟧ strict; severe —**strin'gen·cy** *n.*

string'er *n.* 1 a long horizontal piece in a structure 2 a part-time, local correspondent for a newspaper, magazine, etc.

strip[1] (strip) *vt.* **stripped, strip'ping** ⟦OE *stripan*⟧ 1 to remove (the clothing, etc.) from (a person) 2 to dispossess of (honors, titles, etc.) 3 to plunder; rob 4 to take off (a covering, etc.) from (a person or thing) 5 to make bare by taking away removable parts, etc. 6 to break the thread of (a nut, bolt, etc.) or the teeth of (a gear) —*vi.* to take off all clothing

strip[2] (strip) *n.* ⟦< STRIPE⟧ 1 a long, narrow piece, as of land, tape, etc. 2 *short for* AIRSTRIP

strip cropping crop planting in alternate rows to lessen erosion, as on a hillside

stripe (strīp) *n.* ⟦< MDu *stripe*⟧ 1 a long, narrow band differing from the surrounding area 2 a strip of cloth on a uniform to show rank, years served, etc. 3 kind; sort /a man of his *stripe*/ —*vt.* **striped, strip'ing** to mark with stripes

strip·ling (strip'liŋ) *n.* a grown boy

strip mining mining, esp. for coal, by laying bare a mineral deposit near the surface of the earth

strip'-search' *vt.* to search (a person) by requiring removal of the clothes —*n.* such a search Also **strip search**

strip'tease' *n.* an entertainment in which the performer undresses slowly, usually to musical accompaniment

strive (strīv) *vi.* **strove** or **strived, striv·en** (striv' ən) or **strived, striv'ing** ⟦< OFr *estrif,* effort⟧ 1 to make great efforts; try very hard 2 to struggle /*strive* against oppression/

strobe (light) (strōb) ⟦< Gr *strobus,* a twisting around⟧ an electronic tube emitting rapid, brief, and brilliant flashes of light: used in photography, etc.

strode (strōd) *vi., vt. pt. of* STRIDE

stroke (strōk) *n.* ⟦ME⟧ 1 a striking of one thing against another 2 a sudden action or event /a *stroke* of luck/ 3 a sudden loss of consciousness with paralysis, caused by a cerebral hemorrhage, blood clot, etc. 4 a single strong effort 5 the sound of striking, as of a clock 6 *a*) a single movement, as with a tool, racket, etc. *b*) any of a series of repeated motions made in rowing, swimming, etc. 7 a mark made by a pen, etc. —*vt.* **stroked, strok'ing** to draw one's hand, a tool, etc. gently over the surface of

stroll (strōl) *vi.* ⟦prob. < Ger *strolch,* vagabond⟧ 1 to walk about leisurely; saunter 2 to wander —*vt.* to stroll along or through —*n.* a leisurely walk

stroll'er *n.* 1 one who strolls 2 a light, chairlike baby carriage

strong (strôŋ) *adj.* ⟦OE *strang*⟧ 1 *a*) physically powerful *b*) healthy; hearty 2 morally or intellectually powerful /a *strong* will/ 3 firm; durable /a *strong* fort/ 4 powerful in wealth, numbers, etc. 5 of a specified number /troops 6,000 *strong*/ 6 having a powerful effect 7 intense in degree or quality /*strong* coffee, a *strong* light, *strong* smell, etc./ 8 forceful; vigorous, etc. —**strong'ly** *adv.*

strong'-arm' *adj.* [Colloq.] using physical force —*vt.* [Colloq.] to use force upon

strong'box' *n.* a heavily made box or safe for storing valuables

strong'hold' *n.* a place having strong defenses; fortress

strong'-mind'ed *adj.* unyielding; determined Also **strong'-willed'**

stron·ti·um (strän'shəm, -shē əm; stränt'ē əm) *n.* ⟦ult. after *Strontian,* Scotland, where first found⟧ a metallic chemical element resembling calcium in properties

strop (sträp) *n.* ⟦OE⟧ a leather band for sharpening razors —*vt.* **stropped, strop'ping** to sharpen on a strop

stro·phe (strō'fē) *n.* ⟦Gr *strophē,* a turning⟧ a stanza of a poem

strove (strōv) *vi. alt. pt. of* STRIVE

struck (struk) *vt., vi. pt. & pp. of* STRIKE —*adj.* closed or otherwise affected by a labor strike

struc·ture (struk'chər) *n.* ⟦< L *struere,* arrange⟧ 1 something built or constructed, as a building or dam 2 the arrangement of all the parts of a whole 3 something composed of related parts —*vt.* **-tured, -tur·ing** to put together systematically —**struc'tur·al** *adj.*

stru·del (stro͞od''l) *n.* ⟦Ger⟧ a pastry made of a thin sheet of dough filled with apples, etc., rolled up, and baked

strug·gle (strug'əl) *vi.* **-gled, -gling** ⟦ME *strogelen*⟧ 1 to fight violently with an opponent 2 to make great efforts; strive; labor —*n.* 1 great effort 2 conflict; strife

strum (strum) *vt., vi.* **strummed, strum'ming** ⟦echoic⟧ to play (a guitar, etc.) casually or unskillfully

strum·pet (strum'pit) *n.* ⟦ME⟧ a prostitute

strung (struŋ) *vt., vi. pt. & alt. pp. of* STRING

strut (strut) *vi.* **strut'ted, strut'ting** ⟦OE *strutian,* stand rigid⟧ to walk in a swaggering manner —*n.* 1 a swaggering walk 2 a brace fitted into a framework to stabilize the structure

strych·nine (strik′nin, -nēn, -nīn) ***n.*** ⟦< Gr *strychnos,* nightshade⟧ a highly poisonous, colorless, crystalline alkaloid: used in small doses as a stimulant

stub (stub) ***n.*** ⟦OE *stybb*⟧ 1 a tree or plant stump 2 a short piece left over 3 any short or blunt projection or thing 4 the part of a ticket, bank check, etc. kept as a record —***vt.* stubbed, stub′bing** 1 to strike (one's toe, etc.) against something 2 to put out (a cigarette, etc.) by pressing the end against a surface: often with *out*

stub·ble (stub′əl) ***n.*** ⟦< L *stipula,* a stalk⟧ 1 short stumps of grain, corn, etc., left after harvesting 2 any short, bristly growth, as of beard

stub·born (stub′ərn) ***adj.*** ⟦ME *stoburn*⟧ 1 refusing to yield or comply; obstinate 2 done in an obstinate or persistent way 3 hard to handle —**stub′born·ness *n.***

stub·by (stub′ē) ***adj.* -bi·er, -bi·est** 1 covered with stubs or stubble 2 short and dense 3 short and thickset

stuc·co (stuk′ō) ***n., pl.* -coes** or **-cos** ⟦It⟧ plaster or cement for surfacing walls, etc. —***vt.* -coed, -co·ing** to cover with stucco

stuck (stuk) ***vt., vi.*** *pt. & pp. of* STICK

stuck′-up′ ***adj.*** [Colloq.] snobbish

stud[1] (stud) ***n.*** ⟦OE *studu,* post⟧ 1 any of a series of small knobs, etc. used to ornament a surface 2 a small, buttonlike device for fastening collars, etc. 3 an upright piece in the wall of a building, to which panels, laths, etc. are nailed —***vt.* stud′ded, stud′ding** 1 to set or decorate with studs, etc. 2 to be set thickly on /rocks *stud* the hill/

stud[2] (stud) ***n.*** ⟦OE⟧ a male animal, esp. a horse (**stud′horse′**), kept for breeding

stud′book′ ***n.*** a register of purebred animals, esp. racehorses Also **stud book**

stud′ding ***n.*** 1 studs, esp. for walls 2 material for studs

stu·dent (sto͞od′′nt) ***n.*** ⟦< L *studere,* to study⟧ 1 one who studies, or investigates 2 one who is enrolled for study at a school, college, etc.

stud·ied (stud′ēd) ***adj.*** 1 prepared by careful study 2 deliberate

stu·di·o (sto͞o′dē ō) ***n., pl.* -os′** ⟦It⟧ 1 a place where an artist, etc. works or where dancing lessons, etc. are given 2 a place where films, radio or TV programs, etc. are produced

studio couch a couch that can be opened into a full-sized bed

stu·di·ous (sto͞o′dē əs) ***adj.*** ⟦< L *studiosus*⟧ 1 fond of study 2 zealous; attentive

stud·y (stud′ē) ***n., pl.* -ies** ⟦< L *studere,* to study⟧ 1 the acquiring of knowledge, as by reading 2 careful examination of a subject, event, etc. 3 a branch of learning 4 [*pl.*] formal education; schooling 5 an essay, thesis, etc. containing the results of a particular investigation 6 an earnest effort or deep thought 7 a room for study, etc. —***vt.* -ied, -y·ing** 1 to try to learn or understand by reading, etc. 2 to investigate carefully 3 to read (a book, etc.) intently 4 to take a course in, as at a school or college —***vi.*** 1 to study something 2 to be a student 3 to meditate

stuff (stuf) ***n.*** ⟦< OFr *estoffe*⟧ 1 the material out of which anything is made 2 essence; character 3 matter in general 4 cloth, esp. woolen cloth 5 objects; things 6 worthless objects; junk 7 [Colloq.] ability, skill, etc. —***vt.*** 1 to fill or pack; specif., *a)* to fill the skin of (a dead animal) in taxidermy *b)* to fill (a turkey, etc.) with seasoning, bread crumbs, etc. before roasting 2 to fill too full; cram 3 to plug; block —***vi.*** to eat too much

stuffed shirt [Slang] a pompous, pretentious person

stuff′ing ***n.*** something used to stuff, as padding in cushions, a seasoned mixture for stuffing fowl, etc.

stuff′y ***adj.* -i·er, -i·est** 1 poorly ventilated; close 2 having the nasal passages stopped up, as from a cold 3 [Colloq.] dull, conventional, or pompous

stul·ti·fy (stul′tə fī′) ***vt.* -fied′, -fy′ing** ⟦< L *stultus,* foolish + *facere,* make⟧ 1 to make seem foolish, stupid, etc. 2 to make worthless, etc.

stum·ble (stum′bəl) ***vi.* -bled, -bling** ⟦ME *stumblen*⟧ 1 to trip in walking, running, etc. 2 to walk unsteadily 3 to speak, act, etc. in a blundering way 4 to do wrong 5 to come by chance —***n.*** a stumbling —**stum′bler *n.***

stumbling block a difficulty

stump (stump) ***n.*** ⟦ME *stumpfe*⟧ 1 the end of a tree or plant left in the ground after the upper part has been cut off 2 the part of a limb, tooth, etc. left after the rest has been removed 3 the place where a political speech is made —***vt.*** 1 to travel over (a district), making political speeches 2 [Colloq.] to puzzle or perplex —***vi.*** 1 to walk heavily 2 to travel about, making political speeches —**stump′y, -i·er, -i·est,** ***adj.***

stun (stun) ***vt.* stunned, stun′ning** ⟦< L *ex-,* intens. + *tonare,* to crash⟧ 1 to make unconscious, as by a blow 2 to daze; shock

stung (stuŋ) ***vt., vi.*** *pt. & pp. of* STING

stunk (stuŋk) ***vi.*** *pp. & alt. pt. of* STINK

stun·ning (stun′iŋ) ***adj.*** [Colloq.] remarkably attractive, excellent, etc.

stunt[1] (stunt) ***vt.*** ⟦OE, stupid⟧ 1 to check the growth or development of 2 to hinder (growth, etc.)

stunt[2] (stunt) ***n.*** ⟦< ?⟧ something done to show one's skill or daring, get attention, etc. —***vi.*** to do a stunt

stu·pe·fy (sto͞o′pə fī′, styo͞o′-) ***vt.*** ⟦< L *stupere,* be stunned + *facere,* make⟧ 1 to produce stupor in; stun 2 to astound; bewilder —**stu′pe·fac′tion** (-fak′shən) ***n.***

stu·pen·dous (sto͞o pen′dəs, styo͞o-) ***adj.*** ⟦< L *stupere,* be stunned⟧ 1 astonishing 2 astonishingly great

stu·pid (sto͞o′pid, styo͞o′-) ***adj.*** ⟦see prec.⟧ 1 lacking normal intelligence 2 foolish; silly /a *stupid* idea/ 3 dull and boring —**stu·pid′i·ty,** *pl.* **-ties, *n.***

stu·por (sto͞o′pər, styo͞o′-) ***n.*** ⟦see STUPENDOUS⟧ a state in which the mind and senses are dulled; loss of sensibility

stur·dy (stur′dē) ***adj.* -di·er, -di·est** ⟦< OFr *estourdi,* stunned⟧ 1 firm; resolute 2 strong; vigorous —**stur′di·ly *adv.*** —**stur′di·ness *n.***

stur·geon (stur′jən) ***n.*** ⟦< OFr *esturjon*⟧ a

large food fish valuable as a source of caviar

stut·ter (stut′ər) *n., vt., vi.* ⟦< ME *stutten*⟧ STAMMER

Stutt·gart (stut′gärt) city in S West Germany: pop. 563,000

St. Vin·cent and the Gren·a·dines (sānt vin′sənt ənd *thə* gren′ə dēnz) country consisting of the island of St. Vincent and the N Grenadines, in the West Indies: 150 sq. mi.; pop. 123,000

sty[1] (stī) *n., pl.* **sties** ⟦< OE *sti*, hall⟧ 1 a pen for pigs 2 any foul place

sty[2] or **stye** (stī) *n., pl.* **sties** ⟦ult. < OE *stigan*, to rise⟧ a small, inflamed swelling on the rim of an eyelid

Styg·i·an (stij′ē ən, stij′ən) *adj.* 1 of the Styx 2 [*also* s-] *a)* infernal *b)* dark or gloomy

style (stīl) *n.* ⟦< L *stilus*, pointed writing tool⟧ 1 a stylus 2 *a)* manner of expression in language *b)* characteristic manner of expression, design, etc. in any art, period, etc. *c)* excellence of artistic expression 3 *a)* fashion *b)* something stylish —*vt.* **styled, styl′ing** 1 to name; call 2 to design the style of

styl·ish (stīl′ish) *adj.* conforming to current style, as in dress; fashionable

styl′ist *n.* a writer, etc. whose work has style and distinction —**sty·lis′tic** *adj.* —**sty·lis′ti·cal·ly** *adv.*

styl·ize (stīl′īz′) *vt.* **-ized, -iz·ing** to design or represent according to a style rather than nature

sty·lus (stī′ləs) *n., pl.* **-lus·es** or **-li** (-lī) ⟦L, for *stilus*, pointed instrument⟧ 1 a sharp, pointed marking device 2 *a)* a sharp, pointed device for cutting the grooves of a phonograph record *b)* a phonograph needle

sty·mie (stī′mē) *n.* ⟦prob. < Scot, person partially blind⟧ *Golf* a situation in which a ball to be putted has another ball between it and the hole —*vt.* **-mied, -mie·ing** to block; impede Also **sty′my, -mied, -my·ing**

styp·tic (stip′tik) *adj.* ⟦< Gr *styphein*, to contract⟧ tending to halt bleeding; astringent —**styp′sis** *n.*

styptic pencil a piece of a styptic substance to stop minor bleeding

Sty·ro·foam (stī′rə fōm′) *trademark for* a rigid, lightweight, spongelike plastic —*n.* [s-] this substance

Styx (stiks) *Gr. Myth.* the river crossed by dead souls entering Hades

sua·sion (swā′zhən) *n.* ⟦< L *suadere*, to persuade⟧ PERSUASION: now chiefly in **moral suasion**, a persuading by appealing to one's sense of morality

suave (swäv) *adj.* ⟦< L *suavis*, sweet⟧ smoothly gracious or polite; polished —**suave′ly** *adv.* —**suav′i·ty** *n.*

sub (sub) *n. short for:* 1 SUBMARINE 2 SUBSTITUTE —*vi.* **subbed, sub′bing** [Colloq.] to be a substitute (*for* someone)

sub- ⟦< L *sub*, under⟧ *prefix* 1 under [*submarine*] 2 lower than; inferior to [*subhead*] 3 to a lesser degree than [*subhuman*]

sub. *abbrev.* 1 substitute(s) 2 suburb(an)

sub·a·tom·ic (sub′ə täm′ik) *adj.* smaller than an atom

sub′branch′ *n.* a division of a branch

sub′com·mit′tee *n.* a small committee chosen from a main committee

sub′com′pact′ *n.* a model of automobile smaller than a compact

sub·con′scious *adj.* occurring with little or no conscious perception on the part of the individual: said of mental processes —**the subconscious** subconscious mental activity —**sub·con′scious·ly** *adv.*

sub′con′ti·nent *n.* a large land mass smaller than a continent

sub·con·tract (sub′kän′trakt; *also, for v.* sub′kən trakt′) *n.* a secondary contract undertaking some or all obligations of another contract —*vt., vi.* to make a subcontract (for) —**sub′con′trac·tor** (-trak tər) *n.*

sub′cul′ture *n.* 1 a distinctive social group within a larger social group 2 its cultural patterns

sub′cu·ta′ne·ous *adj.* beneath the skin

sub′dea′con *n.* a cleric ranking just below a deacon

sub′deb′ *n.* a girl not quite of debutante age

sub′dis′trict *n.* a subdivision of a district

sub′di·vide′ *vt., vi.* **-vid′ed, -vid′ing** 1 to divide further 2 to divide (land) into small parcels —**sub′di·vi′sion** *n.*

sub·due (səb dōō′, -dyōō′) *vt.* **-dued′, -du′ing** ⟦< L *subducere*, take away⟧ 1 to conquer 2 to overcome; control 3 to make less intense; diminish

sub·fam·i·ly (sub′fam′ə lē) *n., pl.* **-lies** a main subdivision of a family, as of plants, language, etc.

sub′head′ *n.* a subordinate heading or title, as of a magazine article

subj. 1 subject 2 subjunctive

sub·ject (sub′jikt, -jekt′; *for v.* səb jekt′) *adj.* ⟦< L *sub-*, under + *jacere*, throw⟧ 1 under the authority or control of another 2 having a tendency [*subject* to anger] 3 exposed [*subject* to censure] 4 contingent upon [*subject* to approval] —*n.* 1 one under the authority or control of another 2 one made to undergo a treatment, experiment, etc. 3 something dealt with in discussion, study, etc.; theme 4 a course of study in a school or college 5 *Gram.* the noun, etc. in a sentence about which something is said —*vt.* 1 to bring under the authority or control of 2 to cause to undergo something [to *subject* one to questioning] —**sub·jec′tion** *n.*

sub·jec·tive (səb jek′tiv) *adj.* of or resulting from the feelings of the person thinking; not objective; personal —**sub·jec·tiv·i·ty** (sub′jek tiv′ə tē) *n.*

sub·join (səb join′) *vt.* ⟦see SUB- & JOIN⟧ to append

sub·ju·gate (sub′jə gāt′) *vt.* **-gat′ed, -gat′ing** ⟦< L *sub-*, under + *jugum*, a yoke⟧ to bring under control; conquer —**sub′ju·ga′tion** *n.*

sub·junc·tive (səb juŋk′tiv) *adj.* ⟦< L *subjungere*, subjoin⟧ designating or of the mood of a verb that is used to express supposition, desire, possibility, etc., rather than to state an actual fact

sub·lease (sub′lēs′; *for v.* sub lēs′) *n.* a lease granted by a lessee —*vt.* **-leased′, -leas′ing** to grant or hold a sublease of

sub·let (sub let′) *vt.* **-let′, -let′ting** 1 to let to another (property which one is renting) 2 to let out (work) to a subcontractor

sub·li·mate (sub′lə māt′) *vt.* **-mat′ed, -mat′ing** 1 to sublime (a solid) 2 to express (unacceptable impulses) in acceptable forms, often unconsciously —**sub′li·ma′tion** *n.*

sub·lime (sə blīm′) *adj.* ⟦< L *sub-*, up to + *limen*, lintel⟧ 1 noble; exalted 2 inspiring awe or admiration —*vt.* **-limed′, -lim′ing** to change (a solid) to gaseous state without going through an intermediate liquid state —**sub·lim·i·ty** (sə blim′ə tē) *n.*

sub·lim·i·nal (sub lim′ə nəl) *adj.* ⟦< SUB- + L *limen*, threshold + -AL⟧ below the threshold of consciousness

sub′ma·chine′ gun a portable, automatic firearm

sub·mar·gin·al (sub mär′jə nəl) *adj.* below minimum requirements or standards

sub·ma·rine (sub′mə rēn′; *for n. usually* sub′mə rēn′) *adj.* being, living, etc. underwater —*n.* a ship, esp. a warship, that can operate under water

submarine sandwich HERO SANDWICH

sub·merge (sub murj′, səb-) *vt., vi.* **-merged′, -merg′ing** ⟦< L *sub-*, under + *mergere*, to plunge⟧ to place or sink beneath the surface, as of water —**sub·mer′gence** (-mur′jəns) *n.*

sub·merse′ (-murs′) *vt.* **-mersed′, -mers′ing** SUBMERGE —**sub·mers′i·ble** *adj.* —**sub·mer′sion** *n.*

sub·mis·sion (sub mish′ən, səb-) *n.* 1 a submitting or surrendering 2 obedience; resignation —**sub·mis′sive** *adj.*

sub·mit′ (-mit′) *vt.* **-mit′ted, -mit′ting** ⟦< L *sub-*, under + *mittere*, send⟧ 1 to present to others for consideration, etc. 2 to yield to the control or power of another 3 to offer as an opinion —*vi.* to yield; give in

sub·nor·mal (sub nôr′məl) *adj.* below normal, esp. in intelligence

sub·or′bit·al (-ôr′bit′l, -bə təl) *adj.* designating a flight in which a rocket, spacecraft, etc. follows a trajectory of less than one orbit

sub·or·di·nate (sə bôrd′′n it, -bôr′də nit; *for v.*, -bôrd′′n āt′, -bôr′də nāt′) *adj.* ⟦< L *sub-*, under + *ordinare*, to order⟧ 1 below another in rank, importance, etc. 2 under the authority of another 3 *Gram.* having the function of a noun, adjective, or adverb within a sentence /a *subordinate* phrase/ —*n.* a subordinate person or thing —*vt.* **-nat′ed, -nat′ing** to place in a subordinate position —**sub·or′di·na′tion** *n.*

subordinate clause *Gram.* DEPENDENT CLAUSE

sub·orn (sə bôrn′) *vt.* ⟦< L *sub-*, under + *ornare*, adorn⟧ to induce (another) to commit perjury —**sub·or·na·tion** (sub′ôr nā′shən) *n.*

sub′plot′ *n.* a secondary plot in a play, novel, etc.

sub·poe·na (sə pē′nə) *n.* ⟦< L *sub poena*, under penalty⟧ a written legal order directing a person to appear in court to testify, etc. —*vt.* **-naed, -na·ing** to summon with such an order Also **sub·pe′na**

sub·pro·fes·sion·al (sub′prō fesh′ə nəl) *n.* PARAPROFESSIONAL

sub ro·sa (sub rō′zə) ⟦L, under the rose⟧ secretly; privately

sub·scribe (səb skrīb′) *vt., vi.* **-scribed′, -scrib′ing** ⟦< L *sub-*, under + *scribere*, write⟧ 1 to sign (one's name) on a document, etc. 2 to give support or consent (to) 3 to promise to contribute (money) 4 to agree to receive and pay for a periodical, service, etc. (with *to*) —**sub·scrib′er** *n.*

sub·script (sub′skript′) *n.* ⟦see prec.⟧ a figure, letter, or symbol written below and to the side of another

sub·scrip·tion (səb skrip′shən) *n.* 1 a subscribing 2 money subscribed 3 a formal agreement to receive and pay for a periodical, etc.

sub·se·quent (sub′si kwənt) *adj.* ⟦< L *sub-*, after + *sequi*, follow⟧ coming after; following —**subsequent to** after —**sub′se·quent·ly** *adv.*

sub·serve (səb surv′) *vt.* **-served′, -serv′ing** ⟦< L *sub-*, under + *servire*, to serve⟧ to be useful or helpful to (a purpose, cause, etc.)

sub·ser·vi·ent (səb sur′vē ənt) *adj.* 1 that is of service, esp. in a subordinate capacity 2 submissive —**sub·ser′vi·ence** *n.*

sub·set (sub′set′) *n.* a mathematical set containing some or all of the elements of a given set

sub·side (səb sīd′) *vi.* **-sid′ed, -sid′ing** ⟦< L *sub-*, under + *sidere*, settle⟧ 1 to sink to the bottom or to a lower level 2 to become less active, intense, etc. —**sub·sid′ence** *n.*

sub·sid·i·ar·y (səb sid′ē er′ē) *adj.* ⟦see SUBSIDY⟧ 1 giving aid, service, etc.; auxiliary 2 being in a subordinate relationship —*n., pl.* **-ies** one that is subsidiary; specif., a company controlled by another company

sub·si·dize (sub′sə dīz′) *vt.* **-dized′, -diz′ing** to support with a subsidy —**sub′si·di·za′tion** *n.*

sub·si·dy (sub′sə dē) *n., pl.* **-dies** ⟦< L *subsidium*, auxiliary forces⟧ a grant of money, as from a government to a private enterprise

sub·sist (səb sist′) *vi.* ⟦< L *sub-*, under + *sistere*, stand⟧ 1 to continue to be or exist 2 to continue to live; remain alive (*on* or *by*)

sub·sist′ence *n.* 1 existence 2 the act of providing sustenance 3 means of support or livelihood, esp. the barest means

sub·soil (sub′soil′) *n.* the layer of soil beneath the topsoil

sub·son′ic (-sän′ik) *adj.* designating, of, or moving at a speed less than that of sound

sub·stance (sub′stəns) *n.* ⟦< L *substare*, exist⟧ 1 the real or essential part of anything; essence 2 the physical matter of which a thing consists 3 *a)* solid or substantial quality *b)* consistency; body 4 the real meaning; gist 5 wealth 6 a drug: see CONTROLLED SUBSTANCE

sub·stand′ard *adj.* below standard

sub·stan·tial (səb stan′shəl) *adj.* 1 having substance 2 real; true 3 strong; solid 4 ample; large 5 important 6 wealthy 7 with regard to essential elements —**sub·stan′tial·ly** *adv.*

sub·stan′ti·ate′ (-shē āt′) *vt.* **-at′ed, -at′ing** ⟦see SUBSTANCE⟧ to show to be true or real by giving evidence —**sub·stan′ti·a′tion** *n.*

sub·stan·tive (sub′stən tiv) *adj.* ⟦see SUBSTANCE⟧ of or dealing with essentials —*n. Gram.* a noun or any word or group of words used as a noun

sub′sta′tion *n.* a small post-office station, as in a store

sub·sti·tute (sub′stə to͞ot′) *n.* ⟦< L *sub-*,

under + *statuere,* put ⟧ a person or thing serving or used in place of another —*vt., vi.* **-tut'ed, -tut'ing** to put, use, or serve in place of (another) —**sub'sti·tu'tion** *n.*

sub·stra·tum (sub'strāt'əm, -strat'-) *n., pl.* **-ta** (-ə) or **-tums** a part, substance, etc. which lies beneath and supports another

sub'struc'ture *n.* a part or structure that is a support, base, etc.

sub·sume (sub so͞om', səb-) *vt.* **-sumed', -sum'ing** ⟦< L *sub-,* under + *sumere,* take ⟧ to include within a larger class

sub'teen' *n.* a child nearly a teenager

sub'ten'ant *n.* a person who rents from a tenant —**sub·ten'an·cy** *n.*

sub·ter·fuge (sub'tər fyo͞oj') *n.* ⟦< L *subter,* secretly + *fugere,* flee ⟧ any plan or action used to hide or evade

sub·ter·ra·ne·an (sub'tə rā'nē ən) *adj.* ⟦< L *sub-,* under + *terra,* earth ⟧ **1** underground **2** secret; hidden

sub·text (sub'tekst') *n.* an underlying meaning, theme, etc.

sub'ti'tle *n.* **1** a secondary or explanatory title **2** one or more lines of translated dialogue at the bottom of a movie screen, etc. —*vt.* **-ti'tled, -ti'tling** to add a subtitle or subtitles to

sub·tle (sut''l) *adj.* **-tler** (-lər, -'l ər), **-tlest** ⟦< L *subtilis,* fine, thin ⟧ **1** thin; not dense **2** mentally keen **3** delicately skillful **4** crafty **5** not obvious —**sub'tle·ty,** *pl.* **-ties,** *n.* —**sub'tly** *adv.*

sub'to'tal *n.* a total that is part of a complete total —*vt., vi.* **-taled** or **-talled, -tal·ing** or **-tal·ling** to add up so as to form a subtotal

sub·tract (səb trakt') *vt., vi.* ⟦< L *sub-,* under + *trahere,* to draw ⟧ to take away or deduct (one quantity from another) —**sub·trac'tion** *n.*

sub·tra·hend (sub'trə hend') *n.* a quantity to be subtracted from another

sub·trop·i·cal (sub trä'pi kəl) *adj.* of, characteristic of, or bordering on the tropics Also **sub·trop'ic**

sub·urb (sub'ərb) *n.* ⟦< L *sub-,* near + *urbs,* town ⟧ a district, town, etc. on the outskirts of a city —**sub·ur·ban** (sə bur'bən) *adj.*

sub·ur·ban·ite (sə bur'bən īt') *n.* a person living in a suburb

sub·ur'bi·a (-bē ə) *n.* the suburbs or suburbanites collectively

sub·ven·tion (sub ven'shən, səb-) *n.* ⟦< LL *subventio,* aid ⟧ a subsidy

sub·ver·sive (səb vur'siv) *adj.* tending to subvert —*n.* a subversive person

sub·vert (səb vurt') *vt.* ⟦< L *sub-,* under + *vertere,* to turn ⟧ **1** to overthrow or destroy (something established) **2** to corrupt, as in morals —**sub·ver'sion** (-vur'zhən) *n.*

sub'way' *n.* an underground, metropolitan electric railway

suc- *prefix* SUB-: used before *c /succumb/*

suc·ceed (sək sēd') *vi.* ⟦< L *sub-,* under + *cedere,* to go ⟧ **1** to follow, as in office **2** to be successful —*vt.* to come after; follow

suc·cess (sək ses') *n.* **1** a favorable result **2** the gaining of wealth, fame, etc. **3** a successful person a thing

suc·cess'ful *adj.* **1** turning out as was hoped for **2** having gained wealth, fame, etc. —**suc·cess'ful·ly** *adv.*

suc·ces·sion (sək sesh'ən) *n.* **1** *a)* the act of succeeding another, as to an office *b)* the right to do this **2** a number of persons or things coming one after another

suc·ces'sive (-ses'iv) *adj.* coming one after another —**suc·ces'sive·ly** *adv.*

suc·ces'sor *n.* one that succeeds another, as to an office

suc·cinct (suk siŋkt', sək-) *adj.* ⟦< L *sub-,* under + *cingere,* gird ⟧ clear and brief; terse —**suc·cinct'ly** *adv.* —**suc·cinct'ness** *n.*

suc·cor (suk'ər) *vt.* ⟦< L *sub-,* under + *currere,* to run ⟧ to help in time of need or distress —*n.* aid; relief

suc·co·tash (suk'ə tash') *n.* ⟦< AmInd ⟧ a dish consisting of lima beans and corn kernels cooked together

suc·cu·lent (suk'yo͞o lənt) *adj.* ⟦< L *sucus,* juice ⟧ full of juice; juicy —**suc'cu·lence** or **suc'cu·len·cy** *n.*

suc·cumb (sə kum') *vi.* ⟦< L *sub-,* under + *cumbere,* to lie ⟧ **1** to give way (*to*); yield **2** to die

such (such) *adj.* ⟦OE *swilc* ⟧ **1** *a)* of the kind mentioned *b)* of the same or a similar kind **2** whatever /at *such* time as you go/ **3** so extreme, so much, etc. /*such* an honor/ —*adv.* to so great a degree /*such* good news/ —*pron.* **1** such a person or thing **2** the person or thing mentioned /*such* was her nature/ —**as such 1** as being what is indicated **2** in itself —**such as** for example

such and such (being) something particular but not named or specified /*such and such* a place/

such'like' *adj.* of such a kind —*pron.* persons or things of such a kind

suck (suk) *vt.* ⟦< OE *sucan* ⟧ **1** to draw (liquid) into the mouth **2** to take in as by sucking **3** to suck liquid from (fruit, etc.) **4** to hold (ice, etc.) in the mouth and lick so as to dissolve **5** to place (the thumb, etc.) in the mouth and draw on —*vi.* to suck something —*n.* the act of sucking

suck'er *n.* **1** one that sucks **2** a freshwater, bony fish with a mouth adapted for sucking **3** a part used for sucking or for holding fast by suction **4** LOLLIPOP **5** [Slang] one easily cheated **6** *Bot.* a subordinate shoot on the root or stem of a plant

suck·le (suk'əl) *vt.* **-led, -ling** ⟦ME *sokelen* ⟧ **1** to cause to suck at the breast or udder; nurse **2** to bring up; rear —*vi.* to suck at the breast or udder

suck'ling *n.* an unweaned child or young animal

su·crose (so͞o'krōs') *n.* ⟦< Fr *sucre,* sugar + -OSE[1] ⟧ a a sugar extracted from sugar cane or sugar beets

suc·tion (suk'shən) *n.* ⟦< L *sugere,* to suck ⟧ **1** a sucking **2** production of a vacuum in a cavity or over a surface so that external atmospheric pressure forces fluid in or causes something to adhere to the surface

Su·dan (so͞o dan') country in NE Africa: 967,500 sq. mi.; pop. 20,000,000 Often preceded by *the* —**Su·da·nese** (so͞o'də nēz') *adj., n.*

sud·den (sud''n) *adj.* ⟦< L *sub-,* under + *ire,* go ⟧ **1** *a)* happening or coming unexpectedly *b)* sharp or abrupt **2** quick or hasty —**all of a sudden** unexpectedly —**sud'den·ly** *adv.* —**sud'den·ness** *n.*

sudden death *Sports* an extra period added to a tied game: the game ending as soon as one side scores Usually **sud'den-death' overtime**

sudden infant death syndrome the sudden death of an apparently healthy infant, possibly caused by a breathing problem

suds (sudz) ***n.pl.*** ⟦prob. < MDu *sudse,* marsh water⟧ **1** soapy, frothy water **2** foam —**suds'y, -i·er, -i·est,** ***adj.***

sue (so͞o) ***vt., vi.*** **sued, su'ing** ⟦< L *sequi,* follow⟧ **1** to appeal (to); petition **2** to prosecute in a court in seeking justice, etc.

suede or **suède** (swād) ***n.*** ⟦< Fr *gants de Suède,* Swedish gloves⟧ **1** tanned leather with the flesh side buffed into a nap **2** a cloth like this

su·et (so͞o'it) ***n.*** ⟦< L *sebum,* tallow⟧ the hard fat of cattle and sheep: used in cooking and as tallow

Su·ez Canal (so͞o ez') ship canal joining the Mediterranean & the Red seas

suf- *prefix* SUB- Used before *f*

suf·fer (suf'ər) ***vt., vi.*** ⟦< L *sub-,* under + *ferre,* to bear⟧ **1** to undergo (pain, injury, grief, etc.) **2** to experience (any process) **3** to permit; tolerate —**suf'fer·er** ***n.***

suf'fer·ance ***n.*** **1** the capacity to endure pain, etc. **2** consent, permission, etc. implied by failure to prohibit

suf'fer·ing ***n.*** **1** the bearing of pain, distress, etc. **2** something suffered

suf·fice (sə fīs') ***vi.*** **-ficed', -fic'ing** ⟦< L *sub-,* under + *facere,* make⟧ to be enough or adequate

suf·fi·cient (sə fish'ənt) ***adj.*** as much as is needed; enough —**suf·fi'cien·cy** ***n.*** —**suf·fi'cient·ly** ***adv.***

suf·fix (suf'iks) ***n.*** ⟦< L *sub-,* under + *figere,* fix⟧ a syllable or syllables added at the end of a word to alter its meaning, etc. (Ex.: *-ness* in *darkness*)

suf·fo·cate (suf'ə kāt') ***vt.*** **-cat'ed, -cat'ing** ⟦< L *sub-,* under + *fauces,* throat⟧ **1** to kill by cutting off the supply of air for breathing **2** to smother, suppress, etc. —***vi.*** **1** to die by being suffocated **2** to choke; stifle —**suf'fo·ca'tion** ***n.***

suf·fra·gan (suf'rə gən) ***n.*** ⟦see SUFFRAGE⟧ a bishop who is an assistant to another bishop

suf·frage (suf'rij) ***n.*** ⟦< L *suffragium*⟧ **1** a vote or voting **2** the right to vote; franchise —**suf'fra·gist** ***n.***

suf·fra·gette (suf'rə jet') ***n.*** ⟦< prec. + -ETTE⟧ a woman who advocates female suffrage

suf·fuse (sə fyo͞oz') ***vt.*** **-fused', -fus'ing** ⟦< L *sub-,* under + *fundere,* pour⟧ to overspread so as to fill with a glow, etc. —**suf·fu'sion** ***n.***

sug- *prefix* SUB- Used before *g*

sug·ar (shoog'ər) ***n.*** ⟦< Sans *śárkarā*⟧ any of a class of sweet, soluble carbohydrates, as sucrose, glucose, etc.; specif., sucrose used as a food and sweetening agent —***vt.*** to sweeten, etc. with sugar —***vi.*** to form sugar —**sug'ar·less** ***adj.*** —**sug'ar·y** ***adj.***

sugar beet a beet having a white root with a high sugar content

sugar cane a very tall tropical grass cultivated as the main source of sugar

sug'ar·coat' ***vt.*** **1** to coat with sugar **2** to make (something disagreeable) seem more pleasant

sugar diabetes DIABETES

sug'ar·plum' ***n.*** a round piece of sugary candy

sug·gest (səg jest', sə-) ***vt.*** ⟦< L *sub-,* under + *gerere,* carry⟧ **1** to bring to the mind for consideration **2** to call to mind by association of ideas **3** to propose as a possibility **4** to show indirectly; imply

sug·gest'i·ble ***adj.*** readily influenced by suggestion —**sug·gest'i·bil'i·ty** ***n.***

sug·ges'tion (-jes'chən) ***n.*** **1** a suggesting or being suggested **2** something suggested **3** a hint or trace

sug·ges'tive ***adj.*** **1** that tends to suggest ideas **2** tending to suggest something considered improper or indecent —**sug·ges'tive·ly** ***adv.***

su·i·cide (so͞o'ə sīd') ***n.*** ⟦L *sui,* of oneself + -CIDE⟧ **1** the act of killing oneself intentionally **2** one who commits suicide —**su'i·ci'dal** ***adj.***

su·i ge·ne·ris (so͞o'ē jen'ər is) ⟦L, of his own kind⟧ without equal; unique

suit (so͞ot) ***n.*** ⟦< L *sequi,* follow⟧ **1** a set of clothes; esp., a coat and trousers (or skirt) **2** any of the four sets of playing cards **3** action to secure justice in a court of law **4** an act of suing, pleading, etc. **5** courtship —***vt.*** **1** to be appropriate to **2** to make right or appropriate; fit **3** to please; satisfy /nothing *suits* him/ —**follow suit** to follow the example set —**suit oneself** to act according to one's own wishes —**suit up** to put on an athletic uniform, spacesuit, etc. in preparation for a particular activity

suit'a·ble ***adj.*** that suits a given purpose, etc.; appropriate —**suit'a·bil'i·ty** ***n.*** —**suit'a·bly** ***adv.***

suit'case' ***n.*** a travel case for clothes, etc.

suite (swēt) ***n.*** ⟦Fr: see SUIT⟧ **1** a group of attendants; staff **2** a set of connected rooms, as an apartment **3** a set of matched furniture for a given room

suit'ing ***n.*** cloth for making suits

suit'or ***n.*** a man courting a woman

su·ki·ya·ki (so͞o'kē yä'kē) ***n.*** ⟦Jpn⟧ a Japanese dish of thinly sliced meat and vegetables, cooked quickly

Suk·kot or **Suk·koth** (sook'ōt, sook'ōs) ***n.*** ⟦Heb, lit., tabernacles⟧ a Jewish fall festival commemorating the wandering of the Hebrews during the Exodus

sul·fa (sul'fə) ***adj.*** designating or of a family of drugs used in combating certain bacterial infections

sul·fate (sul'fāt') ***n.*** a salt or ester of sulfuric acid

sul'fide' (-fīd') ***n.*** a compound of sulfur with another element or a radical

sul·fur (sul'fər) ***n.*** ⟦< L *sulphur*⟧ a pale-yellow, nonmetallic chemical element: it burns with a blue flame and a stifling odor

sul·fu·ric (sul fyoor'ik) ***adj.*** of or containing sulfur

sulfuric acid an oily, colorless, corrosive liquid used in making dyes, explosives, fertilizers, etc.

sul·fu·rous (sul'fər əs, sul fyoor'əs) ***adj.*** **1** of or containing sulfur **2** like burning sulfur in odor, color, etc.

sulk (sulk) *vi.* ⟦< fol.⟧ to be sulky —*n.* a sulky mood Also **the sulks**

sulk·y (sul′kē) *adj.* **-i·er, -i·est** ⟦prob. < OE *-seolcan,* become slack⟧ sullenly aloof, silent, etc.; moody; glum —*n., pl.* **-ies** a light, two-wheeled carriage for one person —**sulk′i·ly** *adv.* —**sulk′i·ness** *n.*

sul·len (sul′ən) *adj.* ⟦< L *solus,* alone⟧ **1** showing resentment and ill humor by morose, unsociable withdrawal **2** gloomy; sad —**sul′len·ly** *adv.* —**sul′len·ness** *n.*

sul·ly (sul′ē) *vt.* **-lied, -ly·ing** ⟦prob. < OFr *soillier*⟧ to soil, tarnish, etc., esp. by disgracing

sul·phur (sul′fər) *n. chiefly Brit., etc. sp. of* SULFUR

sul·tan (sult′′n) *n.* ⟦Fr < Ar *sulṭān*⟧ a Muslim ruler

sul·tan·a (sul tan′ə) *n.* a sultan's wife, mother, sister, or daughter

sul·tan·ate (sult′′n it, -āt′) *n.* a sultan's authority, office, or domain

sul·try (sul′trē) *adj.* **-tri·er, -tri·est** ⟦< SWELTER⟧ **1** oppressively hot and moist **2** inflamed, as with passion

sum (sum) *n.* ⟦< L *summus,* highest⟧ **1** an amount of money **2** gist; summary **3** the result obtained by adding quantities; total **4** a problem in arithmetic —*vt.* **summed, sum′ming** to get the sum of by adding —**sum up** to summarize

su·mac or **su·mach** (so͞o′mak′, sho͞o′-) *n.* ⟦< Ar *summāq*⟧ **1** any of numerous nonpoisonous plants with cone-shaped clusters of red fruit **2** any of several poisonous plants, as poison sumac

Su·ma·tra (so͞o mä′trə) large island of Indonesia

sum·ma·rize (sum′ə rīz′) *vt.* **-rized′, -riz′ing** to make or be a summary of

sum′ma·ry (-rē) *adj.* ⟦< L *summa,* a sum⟧ **1** summarizing; concise **2** prompt and without formality **3** hasty and arbitrary —*n., pl.* **-ries** a brief report covering the main points; digest —**sum·mar·i·ly** (sə mer′ə lē) *adv.*

sum·ma·tion (sə mā′shən) *n.* a final summary of arguments, as in a trial

sum·mer (sum′ər) *n.* ⟦< OE *sumor*⟧ the warmest season of the year, following spring —*adj.* of or typical of summer —*vi.* to pass the summer —**sum′mer·y** *adj.*

sum′mer·house′ *n.* a small, open structure in a garden, park, etc.

summer sausage a type of hard, dried and smoked sausage

sum′mer·time′ *n.* summer

sum·mit (sum′it) *n.* ⟦< L *summus,* highest⟧ **1** the highest point; top **2** the highest degree or state; acme

sum·mit·ry (sum′i trē) *n., pl.* **-ries** the use of conferences between heads of state to resolve problems of diplomacy

sum·mon (sum′ən) *vt.* ⟦< L *sub-,* under + *monere,* warn⟧ **1** to call together; order to meet **2** to call or send for with authority **3** to call forth; rouse /*summon* up one's strength/ —**sum′mon·er** *n.*

sum′mons (-ənz) *n., pl.* **-mons·es** ⟦see prec.⟧ **1** an order or command to come, attend, etc. **2** *Law* an official order to appear in court

su·mo (**wrestling**) (so͞o′mō) ⟦Jpn *sumō,* compete⟧ [*sometimes* **S- w-**] Japanese wrestling by large, extremely heavy men

sump (sump) *n.* ⟦ME *sompe,* swamp⟧ a pit, cistern, cesspool, etc. for draining, collecting, or storing liquids

sump·tu·ous (sump′cho͞o əs) *adj.* ⟦< L *sumptus,* expense⟧ **1** costly; lavish **2** magnificent or splendid

sun (sun) *n.* ⟦OE *sunne*⟧ **1** the gaseous, self-luminous central star of the solar system **2** the heat or light of the sun **3** any star that is the center of a planetary system —*vt.* **sunned, sun′ning** to expose to the sun's rays

sun′bathe′ *vi.* **-bathed′, -bath′ing** to expose the body to direct sunlight —**sun bath**

sun′beam′ *n.* a beam of sunlight

Sun′belt′ in the U.S., the S and SW States having a sunny climate and an expanding economy Also **Sun Belt**

sun′bon′net *n.* a bonnet for shading the face and neck from the sun

sun′burn′ *n.* inflammation of the skin from exposure to the sun's rays or to a sunlamp —*vi., vt.* **-burned′** or **-burnt′, -burn′ing** to get or cause to get a sunburn

sun′burst′ *n.* **1** sudden sunlight **2** a decorative device representing the sun with spreading rays

sun·dae (sun′dā, -dē) *n.* ⟦prob. < fol.⟧ a serving of ice cream covered with a syrup, fruit, nuts, etc.

Sun·day (sun′dā; *occas.,* -dē) *n.* ⟦OE *sunnandæg,* sun day⟧ the first day of the week: it is the Sabbath for most Christians Abbrev. **Sun.**

sun·der (sun′dər) *vt., vi.* ⟦< OE *sundor,* asunder⟧ to break apart; split

SUNDIAL

sun′di′al *n.* an instrument that shows time by the shadow of a pointer cast by the sun on a dial

sun′down′ *n.* SUNSET

sun′dries (-drēz) *n.pl.* sundry items

sun′dry (-drē) *adj.* ⟦< OE *sundor,* apart⟧ miscellaneous

sun′fish′ *n., pl.* **-fish′** or (for different species) **-fish′es** **1** any of a family of North American freshwater fishes **2** a large, sluggish ocean fish

sun′flow′er *n.* a tall plant having large, yellow, daisylike flowers

sung (suŋ) *vi., vt. pp. & rare pt. of* SING

sun′glass′es *n.pl.* eyeglasses with tinted lenses to shade the eyes

sunk (suŋk) *vi., vt. pp. & alt. pt. of* SINK

sunk′en (-ən) *adj.* **1** submerged **2** below the general level /a *sunken* patio/ **3** hollow /*sunken* cheeks/

sun'lamp' *n.* an ultraviolet-ray lamp, used for tanning the body, etc.
sun'light' *n.* the light of the sun
sun'lit' *adj.* lighted by the sun
sun'ny (-ē) *adj.* **-ni·er, -ni·est** 1 full of sunshine 2 bright; cheerful 3 of or like the sun —**sun'ni·ness** *n.*
sunny side 1 the sunlit side 2 the brighter aspect —**on the sunny side of** younger than (a given age) —**sunny side up** fried upturned and with unbroken yolk /eggs *sunny side up*/
sun'rise' *n.* 1 the daily appearance of the sun above the eastern horizon 2 the time of this
sun'roof' *n.* a car roof with a panel that opens to let in light and air Also **sun roof**
sun'screen' *n.* a chemical used in lotions, creams, etc. to block certain ultraviolet rays of the sun, to reduce sunburn
sun'set' *n.* 1 the daily disappearance of the sun below the western horizon 2 the time of this
sun'shine' *n.* 1 the shining of the sun 2 the light and heat from the sun 3 cheerfulness, happiness, etc. —**sun'shin'y** *adj.*
sun'spot' *n.* any of the temporarily cooler regions appearing cyclically as dark spots on the sun
sun'stroke' *n.* a form of heatstroke caused by excessive exposure to the sun
sun'suit' *n.* short pants with a bib and shoulder straps, worn by babies and young children
sun'tan' *n.* darkened skin resulting from exposure to the sun
sun'up' *n.* SUNRISE
Sun Yat-sen (so͝on' yät'sen') 1866-1925; Chin. revolutionary leader
sup (sup) *vi.* **supped, sup'ping** ⟦< OFr *soupe,* soup⟧ to have supper
sup- *prefix* SUB- Used before *p*
su·per (so͞o'pər) *n.* ⟦< fol.⟧ *short for:* 1 SUPERNUMERARY (esp. sense 2) 2 SUPERINTENDENT (esp. sense 2) —*adj.* 1 outstanding; exceptionally fine 2 great, extreme, or excessive
super- ⟦L < *super,* above⟧ *prefix* 1 over, above /*superstructure*/ 2 superior to /*superintendent*/ 3 *a*) surpassing /*superabundant*/ *b*) greater than others of its kind /*supermarket*/ 4 additional /*supertax*/
su'per·a·bun'dant *adj.* being more than enough —**su'per·a·bun'dance** *n.*
su·per·an·nu·at·ed (so͞o'pər an'yo͞o āt'id) *adj.* ⟦< L *super,* above + *annus,* year⟧ 1 too old for work 2 retired, esp. with a pension, because of old age
su·perb (sə purb'; soo-, so͞o-) *adj.* ⟦see SUPER-⟧ 1 noble or majestic 2 rich or magnificent 3 extremely fine; excellent —**su·perb'ly** *adv.*
su'per·car'go *n., pl.* **-goes** or **-gos** an officer on a merchant ship in charge of the cargo
su'per·charge' *vt.* **-charged', -charg'ing** to increase the power of (an engine), as with a device (**supercharger**) that forces air into the cylinders
su·per·cil·i·ous (so͞o'pər sil'ē əs) *adj.* ⟦< L *super-,* above + *cilium,* eyelid, hence (in allusion to raised eyebrows) haughtiness⟧ disdainful or contemptuous; haughty
su'per·cit'y *n., pl.* **-ies** MEGALOPOLIS
su'per·con'duc·tiv'i·ty *n. Physics* the lack of resistance to electrical current in certain metals, etc. when cooled to low temperatures
su'per·e'go *n., pl.* **-gos** *Psychoanalysis* that part of the psyche which enforces moral standards
su'per·em'i·nent *adj.* supremely remarkable, distinguished, etc.
su'per·er'o·ga'tion (-er'ə gā'shən) *n.* ⟦< L *super-,* above + *erogare,* pay out⟧ a doing more than is needed or expected —**su'per·e·rog'a·to'ry** (-i räg'ə tôr'ē) *adj.*
su'per·fi'cial (-fish'əl) *adj.* ⟦< L *super-,* above + *facies,* face⟧ 1 of or being on the surface 2 concerned with and understanding only the obvious; shallow 3 quick and cursory 4 merely apparent —**su'per·fi'ci·al'i·ty** (-ē al'ə tē), *pl.* **-ties,** *n.* —**su'per·fi'cial·ly** *adv.*
su·per·flu·ous (sə pur'flo͞o əs, soo-) *adj.* ⟦< L *super-,* above + *fluere,* to flow⟧ excessive or unnecessary —**su·per·flu·i·ty** (so͞o'pər flo͞o'ə tē), *pl.* **-ties,** *n.*
su'per·high'way' *n.* EXPRESSWAY
su'per·hu'man *adj.* 1 having a nature above that of man; divine 2 greater than that of a normal human being
su'per·im·pose' *vt.* **-posed', -pos'ing** to put, lay, or stack on top of something else
su·per·in·tend (so͞o'pər in tend') *vt.* to act as superintendent of; supervise —**su'per·in·tend'ence** or **su'per·in·tend'en·cy** *n.*
su'per·in·tend'ent (-ten'dənt) *n.* ⟦< LL *superintendere,* superintend⟧ 1 a person in charge of a department, institution, etc.; director 2 a person responsible for the maintenance of a building
su·pe·ri·or (sə pir'ē ər) *adj.* ⟦see SUPER-⟧ 1 higher in space, order, rank, etc. 2 greater in quality or value than: with *to* 3 above average in quality; excellent 4 refusing to give in to or be affected by: with *to* 5 showing a feeling of being better than others; haughty —*n.* 1 a superior person or thing 2 the head of a religious community —**su·pe'ri·or'i·ty** (-ôr'ə tē) *n.*
Su·pe·ri·or (sə pir'ē ər), **Lake** largest of the Great Lakes, between Mich. & Ontario, Canada
superl. superlative
su·per·la·tive (sə pur'lə tiv, soo-) *adj.* ⟦< L *super-,* above + *latus,* pp. of *ferre,* to bear, carry⟧ 1 superior to all others; supreme 2 *Gram.* designating the extreme degree of comparison of adjectives and adverbs —*n.* 1 the highest degree; peak 2 *Gram.* the superlative degree —**su·per'la·tive·ly** *adv.*
su'per·man' *n., pl.* **-men'** an apparently superhuman man
su'per·mar'ket *n.* a large, self-service, retail food store or market
su·per·nal (sə purn'əl, soo-) *adj.* ⟦< L *supernus,* upper⟧ celestial or divine
su'per·nat'u·ral *adj.* not explainable by the known forces or laws of nature; specif., of or involving God, ghosts, spirits, etc.
su'per·no'va *n., pl.* **-vae** (-vē) or **-vas** a rare, extremely bright nova
su·per·nu·mer·ar·y (so͞o'pər no͞o'mə rer'ē, -nyo͞o'-) *n., pl.* **-ies** ⟦< L *super,* above +

numerus, number] 1 an extra person or thing 2 *Theater* a person with a small, nonspeaking part

su'per·pose' *vt.* **-posed', -pos'ing** [see SUPER- & POSE] to place on or above something else —**su'per·pos'a·ble** *adj.* —**su'per·po·si'tion** *n.*

su'per·sat'u·rate' *vt.* **-rat'ed, -rat'ing** to make more highly concentrated than in normal saturation —**su'per·sat'u·ra'tion** *n.*

su'per·scribe' *vt.* **-scribed', -scrib'ing** [see SUPER- & SCRIBE] to write (something) at the top or on an outer surface of (something) —**su'per·scrip'tion** (-skrip'shən) *n.*

su'per·script' *n.* [see prec.] a figure, letter, or symbol written above and to the side of another

su·per·sede (so͞o'pər sēd') *vt.* **-sed'ed, -sed'ing** [< L *supersedere,* sit over] to replace or succeed

su'per·son'ic *adj.* [SUPER- + SONIC] 1 designating, of, or moving at a speed greater than that of sound 2 ULTRASONIC

su'per·star' *n.* a star performer, as in sports or entertainment

su·per·sti·tion (so͞o'pər stish'ən) *n.* [< L *superstitio,* lit., a standing (in awe) over] 1 any belief that is inconsistent with known facts or rational thought, esp. such a belief in omens, the supernatural, etc. 2 any action or practice based on such a belief —**su'per·sti'tious** *adj.*

su'per·struc'ture *n.* 1 a structure built on top of another, as above the main deck of a ship 2 that part of a building above the foundation

su'per·tank'er *n.* an extremely large oil tanker, of 300,000 tons or more

su·per·vene (so͞o'pər vēn') *vi.* **-vened', -ven'ing** [< L *super-,* over + *venire,* come] to come or happen as something additional or unexpected

su·per·vise (so͞o'pər vīz') *vt., vi.* **-vised', -vis'ing** [< L *super-*, over + *videre*, see] to oversee or direct (work, workers, etc.); superintend —**su'per·vi'sion** (-vizh'ən) *n.* —**su'per·vi'sor** *n.* —**su'per·vi'so·ry** *adj.*

su·pine (so͞o'pīn', so͞o pīn') *adj.* [L *supinus*] 1 lying on the back, face upward 2 inactive; sluggish; listless

supp. or **suppl.** 1 supplement 2 supplementary

sup·per (sup'ər) *n.* [see SUP] an evening meal

supper club an expensive nightclub

sup·plant (sə plant') *vt.* [< L *sub-*, under + *planta,* sole of the foot] 1 to take the place of, esp. by force or plotting 2 to remove in order to replace with something else

sup·ple (sup'əl) *adj.* **-pler, -plest** [< L *supplex,* submissive] 1 easily bent; flexible 2 lithe; limber 3 easily influenced 4 adaptable: said of the mind, etc.

sup·ple·ment (sup'lə mənt; *for v.,* -ment') *n.* [see SUPPLY] 1 something added, esp. to make up for a lack 2 a section of additional material in a book, newspaper, etc. —*vt.* to provide a supplement to —**sup'ple·men'tal** or **sup'ple·men'ta·ry** *adj.*

sup·pli·ant (sup'lē ənt) *n.* one who supplicates —*adj.* supplicating

sup'pli·cant (-lə kənt) *adj., n.* SUPPLIANT

sup·pli·cate (sup'lə kāt') *vt., vi.* **-cat'ed, -cat'ing** [< L *sub-,* under + *plicare,* to fold] 1 to ask for (something) humbly 2 to make a humble request (of) —**sup'pli·ca'tion** *n.*

sup·ply (sə plī') *vt.* **-plied', -ply'ing** [< L *sub-,* under + *plere,* fill] 1 to furnish or provide (what is needed) to (someone) 2 to compensate for (a deficiency, etc.); make good —*n., pl.* **-plies'** 1 the amount available for use or sale; stock 2 [*pl.*] needed materials, provisions, etc. —**sup·pli'er** *n.*

sup·ply-side (sə plī'sīd') *adj.* designating or of an economic theory that an increase in money for investment, as supplied by lowering taxes, will increase productivity

sup·port (sə pôrt') *vt.* [< L *sub-,* under + *portare,* carry] 1 to carry the weight of; hold up 2 encourage; help 3 to advocate; uphold 4 to maintain (a person, institution, etc.) with money or subsistence 5 to help prove, vindicate, etc. 6 to bear; endure 7 to keep up; maintain 8 to have a role subordinate to (a star) in a play —*n.* 1 a supporting or being supported 2 a person or thing that supports 3 a means of support —**sup·port'a·ble** *adj.* —**sup·port'er** *n.*

sup·port'ive *adj.* giving support or help

sup·pose (sə pōz') *vt.* **-posed', -pos'ing** [< L *sub-,* under + *ponere,* put] 1 to assume to be true, as for argument's sake 2 to believe, think, etc. 3 to consider as a possibility [*suppose* I go] 4 to expect [I'm *supposed* to sing] —*vi.* to conjecture —**sup·posed'** *adj.* —**sup·pos'ed·ly** *adv.*

sup·po·si·tion (sup'ə zish'ən) *n.* 1 a supposing 2 something supposed

sup·pos·i·to·ry (sə päz'ə tôr'ē) *n., pl.* **-ries** [see SUPPOSE] a small piece of medicated substance placed in the rectum or vagina, where it melts

sup·press (sə pres') *vt.* [< L *sub-,* under + *premere,* to press] 1 to put down by force; quell 2 to keep from being known, published, etc. 3 to keep back; restrain 4 *Psychiatry* to consciously dismiss from the mind —**sup·pres'sion** (-presh'ən) *n.*

sup·pres'sant (-ənt) *n.* a drug, etc. that tends to suppress an action, condition, etc. [a cough *suppressant*]

sup·pu·rate (sup'yo͞o rāt') *vi.* **-rat'ed, -rat'ing** [< L *sub-*, under + *pus,* pus] to form or discharge pus

supra- [< L *supra,* above] *prefix* above, over, beyond

su·pra·na·tion·al (so͞o'prə nash'ə nəl) *adj.* of, for, or above all or a number of nations [*supranational* authority]

su·prem·a·cist (sə prem'ə sist; *also* soo-, so͞o-) *n.* one who believes in the supremacy of a particular group

su·prem'a·cy (-sē) *n., pl.* **-cies** supreme condition or power

su·preme' (-prēm') *adj.* [< L *superus,* that is above] 1 highest in rank, power, etc. 2 highest in quality, achievement, etc. 3 highest in degree 4 final; ultimate —**su·preme'ly** *adv.*

Supreme Being God

Supreme Court 1 the highest Federal court 2 the highest court in most States

Supreme Soviet the parliament of the U.S.S.R.

Supt. Superintendent
sur-[1] ⟦< L *super*, over⟧ *prefix* over, upon, above, beyond
sur-[2] *prefix* SUB- Used before *r*
sur·cease (sʉr′sēs′) *n.* ⟦< L *supersedere,* refrain from⟧ an end, or cessation
sur·charge (sʉr′chärj′; *also, for v.*, sər chärj′) *vt.* **-charged′**, **-charg′ing** ⟦see SUR-[1] & CHARGE⟧ 1 to overcharge 2 to mark (a postage stamp) with a surcharge —*n.* 1 an additional charge 2 a new valuation printed over the original valuation on a postage stamp
sur·cin·gle (sʉr′siŋ′gəl) *n.* ⟦< OFr *sur-*, over + L *cingulum,* a belt⟧ a strap passed around a horse's body to bind on a saddle, pack, etc.
sure (shoor) *adj.* **sur′er, sur′est** ⟦< L *securus*⟧ 1 that will not fail /a *sure* method/ 2 that cannot be doubted or questioned 3 having no doubt; confident /*sure* of the facts/ 4 bound to be or happen /a *sure* defeat/ 5 bound (to do, be, etc.) /*sure* to lose/ —*adv.* [Colloq.] surely —**for sure** certain(ly) —**sure enough** [Colloq.] without doubt —**sure′ness** *n.*
sure′-fire′ (-fīr′) *adj.* [Colloq.] sure to be successful or as expected
sure′-foot′ed *adj.* not likely to stumble, slip, fall, or err
sure′ly *adv.* 1 with confidence 2 without a doubt; certainly
sur·e·ty (shoor′ə tē, shoor′tē) *n., pl.* **-ties** 1 a being sure 2 something that gives assurance, as against loss, etc. 3 one who takes responsibility for another
surf (surf) *n.* ⟦prob. var. of SOUGH⟧ the waves of the sea breaking on the shore or a reef —*vi.* to engage in surfing —**surf′er** *n.*
sur·face (sʉr′fis) *n.* ⟦< Fr *sur-*, over + *face,* a face⟧ 1 *a)* the exterior of an object *b)* any of the faces of a solid 2 superficial features —*adj.* 1 of, on, or at the surface 2 external; superficial —*vt.* **-faced**, **-fac·ing** to give a surface to, as in paving —*vi.* to rise to the surface of the water
surf′board′ *n.* a long, narrow board used in the sport of surfing
surf′-cast′ *vi.* **-cast′**, **-cast′ing** to fish by casting into the surf from or near the shore
sur·feit (sʉr′fit) *n.* ⟦< OFr *sorfaire,* overdo⟧ 1 too great an amount 2 overindulgence, esp. in food or drink 3 disgust, nausea, etc. resulting from excess —*vt.* to feed or supply to excess
surf·ing (surf′iŋ) *n.* the sport of riding in toward shore on the crest of a wave, esp. on a surfboard
surge (surj) *n.* ⟦< L *surgere,* to rise⟧ 1 a large wave of water, or its motion 2 a sudden, strong increase, as of power —*vi.* **surged, surg′ing** to move in or as in a surge
sur·geon (sʉr′jən) *n.* a doctor who specializes in surgery
sur·ger·y (sʉr′jər ē) *n., pl.* **-ger·ies** ⟦< Gr *cheir*, the hand + *ergein*, to work⟧ 1 the treatment of disease, injury, etc. by manual or instrumental operations 2 the operating room of a surgeon or hospital
sur′gi·cal (-ji kəl) *adj.* 1 of surgeons or surgery 2 very accurate, precisely targeted, etc. —**sur′gi·cal·ly** *adv.*
Su·ri·name (soor′i näm′) country in NE South America: 63,036 sq. mi.; pop. 381,000: earlier **Su′ri·nam′**
sur·ly (sʉr′lē) *adj.* **-li·er**, **-li·est** ⟦earlier *sirly,* imperious < *sir,* sir⟧ bad-tempered; sullenly rude; uncivil
sur·mise (sər mīz′) *n.* ⟦OFr *sur-*, upon + *mettre,* put⟧ a conjecture —*vt., vi.* **-mised′**, **-mis′ing** to guess
sur·mount (sər mount′) *vt.* ⟦SUR-[1] & MOUNT[2]⟧ 1 to overcome (a difficulty) 2 to be at the top of; rise above 3 to climb up and across (a height, etc.) —**sur·mount′a·ble** *adj.*
sur·name (sʉr′nām′) *n.* ⟦< OFr *sur-* (see SUR-[1]) + *nom,* name⟧ the family name, or last name
sur·pass (sər pas′) *vt.* ⟦< Fr *sur-* (see SUR-[1]) + *passer,* to pass⟧ 1 to excel or be superior to 2 to go beyond the limit, capacity, etc. of

SURPLICE

sur·plice (sʉr′plis) *n.* ⟦< L *super-*, above + *pelliceum,* fur robe⟧ a loose, white outer ecclesiastical vestment for some services
sur·plus (sʉr′plus′) *n.* ⟦< OFr *sur-*, above (see SUR-[1]) + L *plus,* more⟧ a quantity over and above what is needed or used —*adj.* forming a surplus
sur·prise (sər prīz′) *vt.* **-prised′**, **-pris′ing** ⟦< OFr *sur-* (see SUR-[1]) + *prendre,* to take⟧ 1 to come upon suddenly or unexpectedly; take unawares 2 to attack without warning 3 to amaze; astonish —*n.* 1 a being surprised 2 something that surprises
sur·re·al (sər rē′əl, sə-; -rēl′) *adj.* 1 surrealistic 2 bizarre; fantastic
sur·re′al·ism′ (-iz′əm) *n.* ⟦see SUR-[1] & REAL⟧ a modern movement in the arts trying to depict the workings of the unconscious mind —**sur·re′al·is′tic** *adj.* —**sur·re′al·ist** *adj., n.*
sur·ren·der (sə ren′dər) *vt.* ⟦< Fr *sur-*, up + *rendre,* render⟧ 1 to give up possession of; yield to another on compulsion 2 to give up or abandon —*vi.* to give oneself up, esp. as a prisoner —*n.* the act of surrendering
sur·rep·ti·tious (sʉr′əp tish′əs) *adj.* ⟦< L *sub-*, under + *rapere,* seize⟧ done, got, acting, etc. in a stealthy way
sur·rey (sʉr′ē) *n., pl.* **-reys** ⟦after *Surrey,* county in England⟧ a light, four-wheeled carriage with two seats
sur·ro·gate (sʉr′ə git, -gāt′) *n.* ⟦< L *sub-*, in place of + *rogare,* ask⟧ 1 a deputy or substitute 2 in some States, a probate court judge 3 a woman who substitutes for another unable to become pregnant
sur·round (sə round′) *vt.* ⟦< L *super-*, over + *undare,* to rise⟧ to encircle on all or nearly all sides
sur·round′ings *n.pl.* the things, conditions, etc. around a person or thing

sur·tax (sur′taks′) *n.* an extra tax on top of the regular tax

sur·veil·lance (sər vā′ləns) *n.* ⟦Fr < *sur-* (see SUR-[1]) + *veiller*, to watch⟧ watch kept over someone, esp. a suspect

sur·vey (sər vā′; *for n.* sur′vā′) *vt.* ⟦< OFr *sur-* (see SUR-[1]) + *veoir*, see⟧ 1 to examine or consider in detail or comprehensively 2 to determine the location, form, or boundaries of (a tract of land) —*n., pl.* **-veys** 1 a detailed study, as by gathering information and analyzing it 2 a general view 3 *a*) the process of surveying an area *b*) a written description of the area —**sur·vey′or** *n.*

sur·vey′ing *n.* the science or work of making land surveys

sur·viv·al·ist (sər vī′vəl ist) *n.* one who takes measures, as storing food and weapons, to ensure survival after an economic collapse, nuclear war, etc.

sur·vive (sər vīv′) *vt.* **-vived′**, **-viv′ing** ⟦< L *super-*, above + *vivere*, to live⟧ to remain alive or in existence after —*vi.* to continue living or existing —**sur·viv′al** *n.*

sur·vi′vor (-ər) *n.* 1 one that survives 2 someone capable of surviving changing conditions, misfortune, etc.

sus- *prefix* SUB- Used before *c, p,* and *t*

sus·cep·ti·ble (sə sep′tə bəl) *adj.* ⟦< L *sus-*, under + *capere*, take⟧ easily affected emotionally —**susceptible of** admitting; allowing /testimony *susceptible of* error/ —**susceptible to** easily influenced or affected by —**sus·cep′ti·bil′i·ty** *n.*

su·shi (so͞o′shē) *n.* ⟦Jpn⟧ a dish consisting of small cakes of cold rice garnished with raw or cooked fish, vegetables, etc.

sus·pect (sə spekt′; *for adj. & n.* sus′pekt′) *vt.* ⟦< L *sus-*, under + *spicere*, to look⟧ 1 to believe to be guilty on little or no evidence 2 to believe to be bad, wrong, etc.; distrust 3 to guess; surmise —*adj.* suspected —*n.* one suspected of a crime, etc.

sus·pend (sə spend′) *vt.* ⟦< L *sus-*, under + *pendere*, hang⟧ 1 to exclude as a penalty from an office, school, etc., for a time 2 to make inoperative for a time 3 to hold back (judgment, etc.) 4 to hang by a support from above 5 to hold (dust in the air, etc.) without attachment —*vi.* to stop temporarily

sus·pend′ed animation a temporary cessation of the vital functions resembling death

sus·pend′ers *n.pl.* 1 a pair of straps passed over the shoulders to hold up the trousers 2 [Brit., etc. (exc. Cdn.)] garters

sus·pense (sə spens′) *n.* ⟦< L *suspendere*, suspend⟧ 1 a state of uncertainty 2 the growing excitement felt while awaiting a climax of a novel, play, etc. —**sus·pense′·ful** *adj.*

sus·pen·sion (sə spen′shən) *n.* 1 a suspending or being suspended 2 a supporting device upon or from which something is suspended 3 the system of springs, etc. supporting a vehicle upon its undercarriage or axles 4 a substance whose particles are dispersed through a fluid but not dissolved in it

suspension bridge a bridge suspended from cables anchored at either end and supported by towers at intervals

sus·pi·cion (sə spish′ən) *n.* ⟦< L *suspicere*, suspect⟧ 1 a suspecting or being suspected 2 the feeling or state of mind of one who suspects 3 a very small amount; trace —*vt.* [Colloq. or Dial.] to suspect

sus·pi′cious *adj.* 1 arousing suspicion 2 showing or feeling suspicion —**sus·pi′·cious·ly** *adv.*

sus·tain (sə stān′) *vt.* ⟦< L *sus-*, under + *tenere*, to hold⟧ 1 to keep in existence; maintain or prolong 2 to provide sustenance for 3 to carry the weight of; support 4 to endure; withstand 5 to suffer (an injury, loss, etc.) 6 to uphold the validity of 7 to confirm; corroborate

sus·te·nance (sus′tə nəns) *n.* 1 a sustaining 2 means of livelihood 3 that which sustains life; food

sut·ler (sut′lər) *n.* ⟦< 16th-c. Du *soeteler*⟧ [Historical] a person following an army to sell things to its soldiers

su·ture (so͞o′chər) *n.* ⟦< L *suere*, sew⟧ 1 the line of junction of two parts, esp. of bones of the skull 2 *a*) the stitching together of the two edges of a wound or incision *b*) the thread, etc. or any of the stitches so used

su·ze·rain (so͞o′zə rin′, -rān′) *n.* ⟦Fr < L *sursum*, above⟧ 1 a feudal lord 2 a state in relation to another over which it has some political control

svelte (svelt) *adj.* ⟦Fr⟧ 1 slender; lithe 2 suave

SW or **S.W.** 1 southwest 2 southwesterly 3 southwestern

Sw. 1 Sweden 2 Swedish

swab (swäb) *n.* ⟦< Du *zwabben*, do dirty work⟧ 1 a mop 2 a small piece of cotton, etc. used to medicate or clean the throat, mouth, etc. —*vt.* **swabbed**, **swab′bing** to use a swab on

swad·dle (swäd′′l) *vt.* **-dled**, **-dling** ⟦prob. < OE *swathian*, swathe⟧ to wrap (a newborn baby) in long, narrow bands of cloth, as was formerly the custom

swag (swag) *vt.* **swagged**, **swag′ging** ⟦see fol.⟧ to hang in a swag —*n.* 1 a valance, garland, etc. hanging decoratively in a curve 2 [Slang] loot

swag·ger (swag′ər) *vi.* ⟦prob. < Norw *svagga*, sway⟧ 1 to walk with a bold, arrogant stride 2 to boast or brag loudly —*n.* swaggering walk or manner

Swa·hi·li (swä hē′lē) *n.* ⟦< Ar *sawāḥil*, the coasts⟧ the Bantu language of the east coast of Africa

swain (swān) *n.* ⟦< ON *sveinn*, boy⟧ [Archaic] 1 a country youth 2 a lover

swal·low[1] (swäl′ō) *n.* ⟦OE *swealwe*⟧ a small, swift-flying bird with long, pointed wings and a forked tail

swal·low[2] (swäl′ō) *vt.* ⟦OE *swelgan*⟧ 1 to pass (food, etc.) from the mouth into the stomach 2 to absorb: often with *up* 3 to retract (words said) 4 to put up with /to *swallow* insults/ 5 to suppress /to *swallow* one's pride/ 6 [Colloq.] to accept as true without question —*vi.* to perform the actions of swallowing something, esp. in emotion —*n.* 1 a swallowing 2 the amount swallowed at one time

swal′low-tailed′ coat CUTAWAY Also **swal′low-tail′** *n.*

swam (swam) *vi., vt. pt. of* SWIM[1] & SWIM[2]

swa·mi (swä'mē) *n., pl.* **-mis** ⟦< Sans *svāmin,* lord⟧ **1** lord; master: title of respect for a Hindu religious teacher **2** a learned man; pundit

swamp (swämp, swômp) *n.* ⟦prob. < LowG⟧ a piece of wet, spongy land; marsh; bog —*vt.* **1** to plunge in a swamp, water, etc. **2** to flood as with water **3** overwhelm /*swamped* by debts/ **4** to sink (a boat) by filling with water —**swamp'y, -i·er, -i·est,** *adj.*

swan (swän, swôn) *n.* ⟦OE⟧ a large web-footed waterfowl, usually white, with a long, graceful neck

swank (swaŋk) *n.* ⟦akin to OE *swancor,* pliant⟧ [Colloq.] ostentatious display —*adj.* [Colloq.] ostentatiously stylish Also **swank'y** *adj.* **-i·er, -i·est**

swan's'-down' *n.* **1** the soft down of the swan, used for trimming clothes, etc. **2** a soft, thick flannel Also **swans'down'**

swan song ⟦after the song sung, in ancient fable, by a dying swan⟧ the last act, final work, etc. of a person

swap (swäp, swôp) *n., vt., vi.* **swapped, swap'ping** ⟦ME *swappen,* to strike⟧ [Colloq.] trade; barter

sward (swôrd) *n.* ⟦< OE *sweard,* a skin⟧ grass-covered soil; turf

swarm (swôrm) *n.* ⟦OE *swearm*⟧ **1** a large number of bees, with a queen, leaving a hive to start a new colony **2** a colony of bees in a hive **3** a moving mass, crowd, or throng —*vi.* **1** to fly off in a swarm: said of bees **2** to move, be present, etc. in large numbers **3** to be crowded

swarth·y (swôr*th*ē, -thē) *adj.* **-i·er, -i·est** ⟦< OE *sweart*⟧ dark-skinned

swash (swäsh, swôsh) *vi.* ⟦echoic⟧ to dash, strike, etc. with a splash

swash'buck'ler (-buk'lər) *n.* ⟦< *swash,* to swagger + *buckler,* a shield⟧ a blustering, swaggering fighting man —**swash'buck'ling** *n., adj.*

swas·ti·ka (swäs'ti kə) *n.* ⟦< Sans *svasti,* well-being⟧ **1** an ancient design in the form of a cross with four equal arms, each bent in a right angle **2** this design with the arms bent clockwise, used as a Nazi emblem

swat (swät) *vt.* **swat'ted, swat'ting** ⟦echoic⟧ to hit with a quick, sharp blow —*n.* a quick, sharp blow —**swat'ter** *n.*

SWAT (swät) *n.* ⟦S(*pecial*) W(*eapons*) a(*nd*) T(*actics*)⟧ a special police unit trained to deal with violence, riots, terrorism, etc. In full **SWAT team**

swatch (swäch) *n.* ⟦orig., a cloth tally⟧ a sample piece of cloth, etc.

swath (swäth, swôth) *n.* ⟦OE *swathu,* a track⟧ **1** the width covered with one cut of a scythe or other mowing device **2** a strip, row, etc. mowed

swathe (swä*th*, swā*th*) *vt.* **swathed, swath'ing** ⟦OE *swathian*⟧ **1** to wrap up in a bandage **2** to envelop; enclose

sway (swā) *vi.* ⟦< ON *sveigja*⟧ **1** to swing or move from side to side or to and fro **2** to lean to one side; veer —*vt.* **1** to cause to sway **2** to influence or divert /*swayed* by promises/ —*n.* **1** a swaying or being swayed **2** influence or control /the *sway* of passion/

sway'backed' (-bakt') *adj.* having a sagging spine, as some horses

Swa·zi·land (swä'zē land') country in SE Africa: 6,705 sq. mi.; pop. 626,000

swear (swer) *vi.* **swore, sworn, swear'ing** ⟦OE *swerian*⟧ **1** to make a solemn declaration with an appeal to God to confirm it **2** to make a solemn promise; vow **3** to use profane language; curse —*vt.* **1** to declare, pledge, or vow on oath **2** to administer a legal oath to —**swear off** to renounce —**swear out** to obtain (a warrant for arrest) by making a charge under oath —**swear'er** *n.*

swear'word' *n.* a profane word or phrase

sweat (swet) *vi., vt.* **sweat** or **sweat'ed, sweat'ing** ⟦OE *swat,* sweat⟧ **1** to give forth or cause to give forth a salty moisture through the pores of the skin; perspire **2** to give forth or condense (moisture) on its surface **3** to work hard enough to cause sweating —*n.* **1** the salty liquid given forth in perspiration **2** moisture collected in droplets on a surface **3** a sweating or being sweated **4** a condition of eagerness, anxiety, etc. **5** [*pl.*] clothes worn for exercising, etc. —**sweat out** [Colloq.] **1** to get rid of by sweating /to *sweat out* a cold/ **2** to wait anxiously for or through —**sweat'y, -i·er, -i·est,** *adj.*

sweat'er *n.* a knitted or crocheted outer garment for the upper body

sweat shirt a heavy cotton jersey worn to absorb sweat, as after exercise

sweat'shop' *n.* a shop where employees work long hours at low wages under poor working conditions

Swed. **1** Sweden **2** Swedish

Swede (swēd) *n.* a native or inhabitant of Sweden

Swe·den (swē'd'n) country in N Europe: 173,620 sq. mi.; pop. 8,320,000

Swed·ish (swēd'ish) *adj.* of Sweden, its people, language, etc. —*n.* the Germanic language of the Swedes

sweep (swēp) *vt.* **swept, sweep'ing** ⟦OE *swapan*⟧ **1** to clean (a floor, etc.) as by brushing with a broom **2** to remove (dirt, etc.) as with a broom **3** to strip, carry away, or destroy with a forceful movement **4** to touch in moving across /hands *sweeping* the keyboard/ **5** to pass swiftly over or across **6** to win overwhelmingly —*vi.* **1** to clean a floor, etc. as with a broom **2** to move steadily with speed, force, or gracefulness **3** to extend in a long curve or line /a road *sweeping* up the hill/ —*n.* **1** the act of sweeping **2** a steady sweeping movement **3** range or scope **4** extent, as of land; stretch **5** a line, curve, etc. that seems to flow or move **6** one whose work is sweeping —**sweep'er** *n.* —**sweep'ing** *adj.* —**sweep'ing·ly** *adv.*

sweep'ings *n.pl.* things swept up, as dirt from a floor

sweep'stakes' *n., pl.* **-stakes'** a lottery in which each participant puts up money in a common fund which is given as the prize to the winner or winners of a horse race or other contest

sweet (swēt) *adj.* ⟦OE *swete*⟧ **1** having a taste of, or like that of, sugar **2** *a*) agreeable taste, smell, sound, etc. *b*) gratifying *c*) friendly, kind, etc. 3 *a)* not rancid or sour *b)* not salty or salted —*n.* [*pl.*] sweet foods —**sweet'ish** *adj.* —**sweet'ly** *adv.* —**sweet'ness** *n.*

sweet'bread' (-bred') *n.* the thymus or sometimes the pancreas of a calf, lamb, etc., when used as food: *usually used in pl.*

sweet'bri'er or **sweet'bri'ar** (-brī'ər) *n.* EGLANTINE

sweet corn a variety of Indian corn eaten unripe as a table vegetable

sweet'en *vt.* 1 to make sweet 2 to make pleasant or agreeable 3 [Colloq.] to increase the value of (collateral, an offer, etc.)

sweet'en·er *n.* a sweetening agent, esp. a synthetic one, as saccharin

sweet'heart' *n.* a loved one; lover

sweetheart contract a contract arranged by collusion between union officials and an employer without consulting the union membership

sweet'meat' *n.* a candy

sweet pea a climbing plant with butterfly-shaped, fragrant flowers

sweet pepper 1 a red pepper producing a large, mild fruit 2 the fruit

sweet potato 1 a tropical, trailing plant with a fleshy, brownish root used as a vegetable 2 its root

sweet'-talk' *vt., vi.* [Colloq.] to flatter

sweet tooth [Colloq.] a fondness or craving for sweets

swell (swel) *vi., vt.* **swelled, swelled** or **swol'len, swell'ing** ⟦OE *swellan*⟧ 1 to expand as a result of pressure from within 2 to curve out; bulge 3 to fill (*with* pride, etc.) 4 to increase in size, force, intensity, etc. —*n.* 1 a part that swells; specif., a large, rolling wave 2 an increase in size, amount, degree, etc. 3 a crescendo 4 [Colloq.] one who is strikingly stylish —*adj.* 1 [Colloq.] stylish 2 [Slang] excellent

swell'head' *n.* [Colloq.] a conceited person —**swell'head'ed** *adj.*

swell'ing *n.* 1 an increase in size, volume, etc. 2 a swollen part

swel·ter (swel'tər) *vi.* ⟦< OE *sweltan,* to die⟧ to feel uncomfortably hot; sweat, etc. from great heat

swel'ter·ing *adj.* very hot; sultry

swept (swept) *vt., vi. pt. & pp. of* SWEEP

swept'back' *adj.* having a backward slant, as the wings of an aircraft

swerve (swurv) *vi., vt.* **swerved, swerv'ing** ⟦< OE *sweorfan,* to scour⟧ to turn aside from a straight line, course, etc. —*n.* a swerving

swift (swift) *adj.* ⟦OE⟧ 1 moving with great speed; fast 2 coming, acting, etc. quickly —*n.* a swift-flying, swallowlike bird —**swift'ly** *adv.* —**swift'ness** *n.*

Swift (swift), **Jon·a·than** (jän'ə thən) 1667-1745; Eng. satirist, born in Ireland

swig (swig) *vt., vi.* **swigged, swig'ging** ⟦< ?⟧ [Colloq.] to drink in gulps —*n.* [Colloq.] a deep draft, as of liquor

swill (swil) *vt., vi.* ⟦OE *swilian*⟧ 1 to drink greedily 2 to feed swill to (pigs, etc.) —*n.* 1 liquid garbage fed to pigs 2 garbage

swim[1] (swim) *vi.* **swam, swum, swim'ming** ⟦OE *swimman*⟧ 1 to move through water by moving arms, legs, fins, etc. 2 to move along smoothly 3 to float on or in a liquid 4 to overflow /eyes *swimming* with tears/ —*vt.* to swim in or across —*n.* the act of swimming —*adj.* [Colloq.] of or for swimming /*swim* trunks/ —**in the swim** active in what is popular at the moment —**swim'mer** *n.*

swim[2] (swim) *n.* ⟦OE *swima*⟧ a dizzy spell —*vi.* **swam, swum, swim'ming** to be dizzy

swimming hole a deep place in a river, creek, etc. used for swimming

swim'suit' (-so͞ot') *n.* a garment worn for swimming

swin·dle (swin'dəl) *vt., vi.* **-dled, -dling** ⟦< Ger *schwindeln*⟧ to defraud (another) of money or property; cheat —*n.* an act of swindling; trick; fraud —**swin'dler** *n.*

swine (swīn) *n., pl.* **swine** ⟦OE *swin*⟧ 1 a pig or hog: usually used collectively 2 a vicious, contemptible person

swing (swiŋ) *vi.* **swung, swing'ing** ⟦OE *swingan*⟧ 1 to sway or move backward and forward 2 to walk, trot, etc. with relaxed movements 3 to strike (*at*) 4 to turn, as on a hinge 5 to move in a curve 6 to hang; be suspended 7 [Slang] *a)* to be ultra-fashionable, esp. in seeking pleasure *b)* to engage in casual sexual relations —*vt.* 1 to move, lift, etc. with a sweeping motion 2 to cause to move backward and forward 3 to cause to turn, as on a hinge 4 to cause to move in a curve /*swing* the car around/ 5 [Colloq.] to cause to come about successfully /to *swing* an election/ —*n.* 1 a swinging 2 the arc through which something swings 3 the manner of swinging a golf club, etc. 4 a relaxed motion, as in walking 5 a sweeping blow or stroke 6 the course of some activity, etc. 7 rhythm, as of music 8 a seat hanging from ropes, etc. on which one can swing 9 a trip or tour 10 jazz (*c.* 1935-45) characterized by large bands, fast tempos, and written arrangements —*adj.* having decisive power, as in determining an election /the *swing* vote/

swing'er *n.* 1 one that swings 2 a person who swings (see SWING, *vi.* 7*b*)

swing shift [Colloq.] the work shift from 4:00 P.M. to midnight

swipe (swīp) *n.* ⟦prob. var. of SWEEP⟧ [Colloq.] a hard, sweeping blow —*vt.* **swiped, swip'ing** 1 [Colloq.] to hit with a swipe 2 [Slang] to steal

swirl (swurl) *vi., vt.* ⟦ME *swyrl*⟧ to move or cause to move with a whirling motion —*n.* 1 a whirl; eddy 2 a twist; curl —**swirl'y** *adj.*

swish (swish) *vi.* ⟦echoic⟧ 1 to move with a sharp, hissing sound, as a cane swung through the air 2 to move with a light, brushing sound, as skirts in walking —*vt.* 1 to cause to swish 2 to move (liquid), esp. in the mouth, with a gurgling sound —*n.* a swishing sound or movement

Swiss (swis) *adj.* of Switzerland, its people, etc. —*n., pl.* **Swiss** a native or inhabitant of Switzerland

Swiss chard CHARD

Swiss (cheese) a pale-yellow, hard cheese with many large holes

Swiss steak a thick cut of round steak pounded with flour and braised

switch (swich) *n.* ⟦Early ModE *swits*⟧ 1 a thin, flexible stick used for whipping 2 a sharp lash, as with a whip 3 a separate tress of hair, used as part of a coiffure 4 a device used to open, close, or divert an electric circuit 5 a device used in transferring a train from one track to another 6 a shift; change —*vt.* 1 to whip as with a switch 2 to jerk sharply 3 to shift; change 4 to turn (an electric light, etc.) *on* or *off* 5 to transfer (a train, etc.) to another track 6 [Colloq.] to change or exchange —*vi.* to shift —**switch'er** *n.*

switch'back' *n.* a road or railroad following a zigzag course up a steep grade

switch'blade' (knife) (-blād') a large jackknife that snaps open when a release button on the handle is pressed

switch'board' (-bôrd') *n.* a panel for controlling a system of electric circuits, as in a telephone exchange

switch'-hit'ter *n.* a baseball player who bats right-handed and left-handed

Swit·zer·land (swit'sər lənd) country in west central Europe: 15,941 sq. mi.; pop. 6,365,000

swiv·el (swiv'əl) *n.* ⟦< OE *swifan,* to revolve⟧ a coupling device that allows free turning of the parts attached to it —*vi., vt.* **-eled** or **-elled, -el·ing** or **-el·ling** to turn or cause to turn as on a swivel or pivot

swiz·zle stick (swiz'əl) ⟦< ?⟧ a small rod for stirring mixed drinks

swob (swäb) *n., vt.* **swobbed, swob'bing** *alt. sp. of* SWAB

swol·len (swōl'ən) *vi., vt. alt. pp. of* SWELL —*adj.* blown up; distended; bulging

swoon (swo͞on) *vi., n.* ⟦< OE *geswogen,* unconscious⟧ FAINT

swoop (swo͞op) *vi.* ⟦< OE *swapan,* sweep along⟧ to pounce or sweep (*down* or *upon*), as a bird in hunting —*n.* the act of swooping

swop (swäp) *n., vt., vi.* **swopped, swop'ping** *alt. sp. of* SWAP

sword (sôrd) *n.* ⟦OE *sweord*⟧ a hand weapon with a long, sharp-pointed blade set in a hilt —**at swords' points** ready to quarrel or fight

SWORDFISH

sword'fish' *n., pl.* **-fish'** a large, marine food fish with the upper jawbone extending in a swordlike point

sword'play' (-plā') *n.* the act or skill of using a sword, as in fencing

swords·man (sôrdz'mən) *n., pl.* **-men** 1 one who uses a sword in fencing or fighting 2 one skilled in using a sword

swore (swôr) *vi., vt. pt. of* SWEAR

sworn (swôrn) *vi., vt. pp. of* SWEAR —*adj.* bound, pledged, etc. by an oath

swum (swum) *vi., vt. pp. of* SWIM[1] & SWIM[2]

swung (swuŋ) *vi., vt. pp. & pt. of* SWING

syb·a·rite (sib'ə rīt') *n.* ⟦after *Sybaris,* ancient Gr city in Italy⟧ anyone very fond of luxury and pleasure —**syb'a·rit'ic** (-rit'ik) *adj.*

syc·a·more (sik'ə môr') *n.* ⟦< Gr *sykomoros*⟧ 1 a maple tree of Europe and Asia 2 an American tree with bark that sheds in patches

syc·o·phant (sik'ə fənt) *n.* ⟦< Gr *sykophantēs,* informer⟧ one who seeks favor by flattering people of wealth or influence —**syc'o·phan·cy** *n.*

Syd·ney (sid'nē) seaport in SE Australia: pop. (met. area) 3,300,000

syl·lab·i·cate (si lab'i kāt') *vt.* **-cat'ed, -cat'ing** SYLLABIFY —**syl·lab'i·ca'tion** *n.*

syl·lab·i·fy (si lab'ə fī') *vt.* **-fied', -fy'ing** ⟦< L *syllaba,* syllable + *facere,* make⟧ to form or divide into syllables —**syl·lab'i·fi·ca'tion** *n.*

syl·la·ble (sil'ə bəl) *n.* ⟦< Gr *syn-,* together + *lambanein,* to hold⟧ 1 a word or part of a word pronounced with a single, uninterrupted sounding of the voice 2 one or more letters written to represent a spoken syllable —**syl·lab·ic** (si lab'ik) *adj.*

syl·la·bus (sil'ə bəs) *n., pl.* **-bus·es** or **-bi'** (-bī') ⟦< Gr *sittybos,* strip of leather⟧ a summary or outline, esp. of a course of study

syl·lo·gism (sil'ə jiz'əm) *n.* ⟦< Gr *syn-,* together + *logizesthai,* to reason⟧ a form of reasoning in which two premises are made and a logical conclusion drawn from them

sylph (silf) *n.* ⟦Mod L *sylphus,* a spirit⟧ 1 any of a class of imaginary beings supposed to inhabit the air 2 a slender, graceful woman or girl —**sylph'like'** *adj.*

syl·van (sil'vən) *adj.* ⟦< L *silva,* forest⟧ 1 of, characteristic of, or living in, the woods or forest 2 wooded

sym·bi·o·sis (sim'bī ō'sis, -bē-) *n.* ⟦< Gr *symbioun,* to live together⟧ the living together of two kinds of organisms to their mutual advantage —**sym'bi·ot'ic** (-ät'ik) *adj.*

sym·bol (sim'bəl) *n.* ⟦< Gr *syn-,* together + *ballein,* to throw⟧ 1 an object used to represent something abstract /the dove is a *symbol* of peace/ 2 a mark, letter, etc. standing for a quality, process, etc., as in music or chemistry —**sym·bol'ic** (-bäl'ik) or **sym·bol'i·cal** *adj.* —**sym·bol'i·cal·ly** *adv.*

sym·bol·ism (sim'bəl iz'əm) *n.* 1 representation by symbols 2 a system of symbols 3 symbolic meaning

sym'bol·ize' (-iz') *vt.* **-ized', -iz'ing** 1 to be a symbol of; stand for 2 to represent by a symbol or symbols

sym·me·try (sim'ə trē) *n., pl.* **-tries** ⟦< Gr *syn-,* together + *metron,* a measure⟧ 1 correspondence of opposite parts in size, shape, and position 2 balance or beauty of form resulting from this —**sym·met·ri·cal** (si me'tri kəl) *adj.* —**sym·met'ri·cal·ly** *adv.*

sym·pa·thet·ic (sim'pə thet'ik) *adj.* 1 of, feeling, or showing sympathy 2 in agreement with one's tastes, mood, etc. 3 *Physiology* designating or of that part of the autonomic nervous system for communicating the involuntary response to alarm, as by speeding the heart rate —**sym'pa·thet'i·cal·ly** *adv.*

sym'pa·thize' (-thīz') *vi.* **-thized'**, **-thiz'ing** 1 to share the feelings or ideas of another 2 to feel or express sympathy —**sym'pa·thiz'er** *n.*

sym·pa·thy (sim'pə thē) *n., pl.* **-thies** ⟦< Gr *syn-*, together + *pathos,* feeling⟧ 1 sameness of feeling 2 mutual liking or understanding 3 *a)* ability to share another's ideas, emotions, etc. *b)* [*often pl.*] pity or compassion

sym·pho·ny (sim'fə nē) *n., pl.* **-nies** ⟦< Gr *syn-*, together + *phōnē,* sound⟧ 1 harmony, as of sounds, color, etc. 2 an extended musical composition in several movements, for full orchestra 3 a large orchestra for playing symphonic works: in full **symphony orchestra** 4 [Colloq.] a symphony concert —**sym·phon'ic** (-fän'ik) *adj.*

sym·po·si·um (sim pō'zē əm) *n., pl.* **-si·ums** or **-si·a** (-ə) ⟦< Gr *syn-*, together + *posis,* a drinking⟧ 1 a conference to discuss a topic 2 a published group of opinions on a topic

symp·tom (simp'təm) *n.* ⟦< Gr *syn-*, together + *piptein,* to fall⟧ any circumstance or condition that indicates the existence, as of a particular disease —**symp'to·mat'ic** (-tə mat'ik) *adj.*

syn- ⟦Gr⟧ *prefix* with, together, at the same time

syn. 1 synonym 2 synonymy

syn·a·gogue (sin'ə gäg', -gôg') *n.* ⟦< Gr *syn-*, together + *agein,* do⟧ 1 an assembly of Jews for worship and religious study 2 a building or place for such assembly —**syn'a·gog'al** *adj.*

syn·apse (sin'aps', si naps') *n.* ⟦< Gr *syn-*, together + *apsis,* a joining⟧ the space between nerve cells through which nerve impulses are transmitted

sync or **synch** (siŋk) *vt., vi.* **synced** or **synched, sync'ing** or **synch'ing** *short for* SYNCHRONIZE —*n. short for* SYNCHRONIZATION —**in** (or **out of**) **sync** in (or out of) synchronization or harmony (*with*)

syn·chro·nize (siŋ'krə nīz') *vi.* **-nized'**, **-niz'·ing** ⟦< Gr *syn-*, together + *chronos,* time⟧ to move or occur at the same time or rate —*vt.* to cause to agree in time or rate of speed —**syn'chro·ni·za'tion** *n.*

syn'chro·nous *adj.* happening at the same time or at the same rate

syn·co·pate (siŋ'kə pāt') *vt.* **-pat'ed**, **-pat'·ing** ⟦< Gr *syn-*, together + *koptein,* cut⟧ *Music* to begin a tone on an unaccented beat and continuing it through the next accented beat —**syn'co·pa'tion** *n.*

syn·di·cate (sin'də kit; *for v.,* -kāt') *n.* ⟦< Gr *syn-*, together + *dikē,* justice⟧ 1 an association of individuals or corporations formed for a project requiring much capital 2 any group, as of criminals, organized for some undertaking 3 an organization selling articles or features to many newspapers, etc. —*vt.* **-cat'ed**, **-cat'ing** 1 to manage as or form into a syndicate 2 *a)* to sell (an article, etc.) through a syndicate *b)* to sell (a program, etc.) to a number of radio or TV stations —*vi.* to form a syndicate —**syn'di·ca'tion** *n.*

syn·drome (sin'drōm') *n.* ⟦< Gr *syn-*, with + *dramein,* run⟧ a set of symptoms characterizing a disease or condition

syn·er·gism (sin'ər jiz'əm) *n.* ⟦< Gr *syn-*, together + *ergon,* work⟧ combined action, as of several drugs, greater in total effect than the sum of their effects —**syn'er·gis'·tic** *adj.*

syn·fu·el (sin'fyo͞o'əl) *n.* ⟦SYN(THETIC) + FUEL⟧ a fuel, as oil or gas made from coal, used as a substitute for petroleum or natural gas

syn·od (sin'əd) *n.* ⟦< Gr *syn-*, together + *hodos,* way⟧ 1 an ecclesiastical council 2 a high governing body in certain Christian churches 3 any council

syn·o·nym (sin'ə nim) *n.* ⟦< Gr *syn-*, together + *onyma,* a name⟧ a word having the same or nearly the same meaning as another in the same language —**syn·on·y·mous** (si nän'ə məs) *adj.*

syn·op·sis (si näp'sis) *n., pl.* **-ses** (-sēz) ⟦< Gr *syn-*, together + *opsis,* a seeing⟧ a brief, general review or condensation; summary

syn·tax (sin'taks') *n.* ⟦< Gr *syn-*, together + *tassein,* arrange⟧ the arrangement of and relationships among words, phrases, and clauses forming sentences —**syn·tac'tic** (-tak'tik) or **syn·tac'ti·cal** *adj.*

syn·the·sis (sin'thə sis) *n., pl.* **-ses'** (-sēz') ⟦< Gr *syn-*, together + *tithenai,* to place⟧ the combining of parts or elements so as to form a whole, a compound, etc. —**syn'the·size'** (-sīz'), **-sized'**, **-siz'ing**, *vt.*

syn'the·siz'er *n.* an electronic device producing sounds unobtainable from ordinary musical instruments or imitating instruments and voices

syn·thet'ic (-thet'ik) *adj.* 1 of or involving synthesis 2 produced by chemical synthesis, rather than of natural origin 3 not real; artificial —*n.* something synthetic —**syn·thet'i·cal·ly** *adv.*

syph·i·lis (sif'ə lis) *n.* ⟦after *Syphilus,* hero of a L poem (1530)⟧ an infectious venereal disease —**syph'i·lit'ic** *adj., n.*

Syr·a·cuse (sir'ə kyo͞os', -kyo͞oz') city in central N.Y.: pop. 170,000

Syr·i·a (sir'ē ə) country in SW Asia, at the E end of the Mediterranean: 71,227 sq. mi.; pop. 10,900,000 —**Syr'i·an** *adj., n.*

sy·ringe (sə rinj', sir'inj) *n.* ⟦< Gr *syrinx,* a pipe⟧ a device consisting of a tube with a rubber bulb or piston at one end for drawing in a liquid and then ejecting it in a stream: used to inject fluids into the body, etc. —*vt.* **-ringed'**, **-ring'ing** to cleanse, inject, etc. by using a syringe

syr·up (sʉr'əp, sir'-) *n.* ⟦< OFr *sirop* < ML *sirupus* < Ar *sharāb,* a drink⟧ any sweet, thick liquid; specif., a solution of sugar and water boiled together

syr·up·y (sʉr'ə pē, sir'-) *adj.* 1 like syrup 2 overly sentimental; cloyingly sweet

sys·tem (sis'təm) *n.* ⟦< Gr *syn-*, together + *histanai,* to set⟧ 1 a set or arrangement of things so related as to form a whole [*a solar system, school system*] 2 a set of facts, rules, etc. arranged to show a plan 3 a method or plan 4 an established, orderly way of doing something 5 the body, or a

number of bodily organs, functioning as a unit
sys'tem·at'ic (-tə mat'ik) ***adj.*** **1** constituting or based on a system **2** according to a system; orderly —**sys'tem·at'i·cal·ly** ***adv.***
sys'tem·a·tize' (-təm ə tīz') ***vt.*** **-tized', -tiz'ing** to arrange according to a system; make systematic
sys·tem·ic (sis tem'ik) ***adj.*** of or affecting the body as a whole
sys·to·le (sis'tə lē') ***n.*** ⟦< Gr *syn-*, together + *stellein*, to set up⟧ the usual rhythmic contraction of the heart —**sys·tol'ic** (-täl'ik) ***adj.***

T

t or **T** (tē) ***n.***, *pl.* **t's, T's** the 20th letter of the English alphabet —**to a T** to perfection; exactly
't it *['twas]*
t or **t. 1** teaspoon(s) **2** temperature **3** ton(s) **4** transitive
T or **T. 1** tablespoon(s) **2** temperature **3** Thursday **4** Tuesday
tab[1] (tab) ***n.*** ⟦< ?⟧ **1** a small, flat loop or strap fastened to something **2** a projecting piece as of a file folder, used in filing
tab[2] (tab) ***n.*** ⟦prob. < TABULATION⟧ [Colloq.] **1** a bill, as for expenses **2** total cost —**keep tabs** (or **a tab**) **on** [Colloq.] to keep a check on
tab·bou·leh (tə bōō'lē, -le) ***n.*** ⟦Ar⟧ a salad of coarsely ground wheat, parsley, tomatoes, scallions, etc. Also **ta·bou'li** or **ta·bu'li**
tab·by (tab'ē) ***n.***, *pl.* **-bies** ⟦ult. < Ar⟧ a domestic cat, esp. a female
tab·er·nac·le (tab'ər nak'əl) ***n.*** ⟦< L *taberna*, hut⟧ a large place of worship —[T-] the portable sanctuary carried by the Jews during the Exodus
tab·la (täb'lä') ***n.*** ⟦< Ar *ṭabla*, drum⟧ a set of two small drums whose pitch can be varied, used esp. in India and played with the hands
ta·ble (tā'bəl) ***n.*** ⟦< L *tabula*, a board⟧ **1** orig., a thin slab of metal, stone, etc. **2** *a)* a piece of furniture having a flat top set on legs *b)* such a table set with food *c)* food served *d)* the people seated at a table **3** *a)* a systematic list of details, contents, etc. *b)* an orderly arrangement of facts, figures, etc. **4** any flat, horizontal surface, piece, etc. —***vt.*** **-bled, -bling** to postpone indefinitely consideration of (a legislative bill, etc.) —**at table** at a meal —**turn the tables** to reverse a situation
tab·leau (tab'lō', ta blō') ***n.***, *pl.* **-leaux'** (-lōz') or **-leaus** ⟦Fr < OFr, dim. of *table*⟧ a representation of a scene, etc. by a group posed in costume
ta'ble·cloth' ***n.*** a cloth for covering a table, esp. at meals
ta·ble d'hôte (tä'bəl dōt') ⟦Fr, table of the host⟧ a complete meal served at a restaurant for a set price
ta'ble-hop' (-häp') ***vi.*** **-hopped', -hop'ping** to leave one's table, as at a nightclub, and visit about at other tables —**ta'ble-hop'per** ***n.***
ta'ble·land ***n.*** a plateau
ta'ble·spoon' ***n.*** a large spoon holding ½ fluid ounce —**ta'ble·spoon'ful**, *pl.* **-fuls**, ***n.***
tab·let (tab'lit) ***n.*** ⟦see TABLE⟧ **1** a flat, thin piece of stone, metal, etc. with an inscription **2** a writing pad of paper sheets glued together at one edge **3** a small, flat piece of compressed material, as of medicine
table tennis a game somewhat like tennis played on a table, with a small, hollow celluloid ball
ta'ble·ware' (-wer') ***n.*** dishes, glassware, silverware, etc. for use at a meal
tab·loid (tab'loid') ***n.*** ⟦TABL(ET) + -OID⟧ a newspaper, usually half size, with many pictures and short, often sensational, news stories
ta·boo (tə bōō', ta-) ***n.*** ⟦< a Polynesian language⟧ **1** among some Polynesian peoples, a sacred prohibition making certain people or things untouchable, etc. **2** any conventional social restriction —***adj.*** prohibited by taboo —***vt.*** **1** to put under taboo **2** to prohibit or forbid Also **ta·bu'**
tab·u·lar (tab'yōō lər) ***adj.*** ⟦see TABLE⟧ **1** flat **2** of, arranged in, or computed from a table or list
tab'u·late' (-lāt') ***vt.*** **-lat'ed, -lat'ing** to put (facts, statistics, etc.) in a table —**tab'u·la'tion** ***n.*** —**tab'u·la'tor** ***n.***
ta·chom·e·ter (ta käm'ət ər, tə-) ***n.*** ⟦< Gr *tachos*, speed + -METER⟧ a device that measures the rate of rotation of a revolving shaft
tac·it (tas'it) ***adj.*** ⟦< L *tacere*, be silent⟧ **1** unspoken; silent **2** not expressed openly, but implied —**tac'it·ly** ***adv.*** —**tac'it·ness** ***n.***
tac·i·turn (tas'ə turn') ***adj.*** ⟦see prec.⟧ almost always silent; not liking to talk —**tac'i·tur'ni·ty** ***n.***
tack (tak) ***n.*** ⟦< MDu *tacke*, twig⟧ **1** a short nail with a sharp point and a large, flat head **2** a temporary stitch **3** a zigzag course **4** a course of action **5** *a)* the direction a ship goes in relation to the position of the sails *b)* a change of a ship's direction —***vt.*** **1** to fasten with tacks **2** to attach or add **3** to change the course of (a ship) —***vi.*** to change course suddenly
tack·le (tak'əl) ***n.*** ⟦< MDu *takel*⟧ **1** equipment; gear **2** a system of ropes and pulleys for moving weights **3** a tackling, as in football **4** *Football* a player next to the end on the line —***vt.*** **tack'led, tack'ling 1** to take hold of; seize **2** to try to do; undertake **3** *Football* to throw (the ball carrier) to the ground —**tack'ler** ***n.***
tack·y (tak'ē) ***adj.*** **-i·er, -i·est 1** sticky, as glue **2** dowdy or shabby **3** in poor taste —**tack'i·ness** ***n.***
ta·co (tä'kō) ***n.***, *pl.* **-cos** ⟦Sp, light lunch⟧ a

fried tortilla filled with chopped meat, lettuce, etc.

Ta·co·ma (tə kō'mə) seaport in W Wash.: pop. 159,000

tact (takt) ***n.*** ⟦< L *tangere,* to touch⟧ delicate perception of the right thing to say or do without offending —**tact'ful** ***adj.*** —**tact'ful·ly** ***adv.*** —**tact'less** ***adj.*** —**tact'less·ly** ***adv.***

tac·tics (tak'tiks) ***n.pl.*** ⟦< Gr *tassein,* arrange⟧ **1** [*with sing. v.*] the science of maneuvering military and naval forces **2** any skillful methods to gain an end —**tac'ti·cal** ***adj.*** —**tac·ti'cian** (-tish'ən) ***n.***

tac·tile (tak'təl) ***adj.*** ⟦< L *tangere,* to touch⟧ of, having, or perceived by the sense of touch

tad (tad) ***n.*** ⟦prob. < TADPOLE⟧ **1** a little child, esp. a boy **2** a small amount or degree /a *tad* tired/

tad·pole (tad'pōl') ***n.*** ⟦ME *tadde,* toad + *poll,* head⟧ the larva of a frog or toad, having gills and a tail and living in water

taf·fe·ta (taf'i tə) ***n.*** ⟦< Pers *tāftan,* to weave⟧ a fine, stiff fabric of silk, nylon, etc., with a sheen

taff·rail (taf'rāl') ***n.*** ⟦< Du⟧ the rail around the stern of a ship

taf·fy (taf'ē) ***n.*** ⟦< ?⟧ a chewy candy made of sugar or molasses

Taft (taft), **Wil·liam How·ard** (wil'yəm hou'ərd) 1857-1930; 27th president of the U.S. (1909-13): chief justice of the U.S. (1921-30)

tag (tag) ***n.*** ⟦prob. < Scand⟧ **1** a hanging end or part **2** a hard-tipped end on a cord or lace **3** a card, etc. attached as a label **4** an epithet **5** the last line or lines of a story, speech, etc. **6** a children's game in which one player chases the others with the object of touching one of them —***vt.*** **tagged, tag'ging** **1** to provide with a tag; label **2** to choose or select **3** to touch in playing tag —***vi.*** [Colloq.] to follow closely: with *along, after,* etc. —**tag'ger** ***n.***

Ta·ga·log (tä gä'lôg') ***n.*** **1** *pl.* **-logs'** or **-log'** a member of the ethnic group native to the Manila region in the Philippines **2** their language, an official language of the Republic of the Philippines

tag·board (tag'bôrd') ***n.*** sturdy cardboard used for tags, posters, etc.

Ta·hi·ti (tə hēt'ē) French island in the South Pacific —**Ta·hi'ti·an** (-hēsh'ən) ***adj., n.***

Tai (tī) ***n.*** **1** a group of languages spoken in central and SE Asia **2** a member of a group of peoples of SE Asia who speak these languages —***adj.*** of these languages or peoples

tai chi (tī' jē') ⟦Mandarin⟧ a system of exercise developed in China, consisting of a series of slow, ritual movements In full **t'ai chi ch'uan** (chwän')

tai·ga (tī'gə) ***n.*** ⟦Russ⟧ a type of transitional plant community in the far north, having scattered trees

tail (tāl) ***n.*** ⟦OE *tægel*⟧ **1** the rear end of an animal's body, esp. when a distinct appendage **2** anything like an animal's tail in form or position **3** the hind, bottom, last, or inferior part of anything **4** [*often pl.*] the reverse side of a coin **5** [*pl.*] [Colloq.] full-dress attire for men **6** [Colloq.] a person that follows another, esp. in surveillance —***adj.*** **1** at the rear or end **2** from the rear /a *tail* wind/ —***vt.*** [Slang] to follow stealthily —***vi.*** [Colloq.] to follow close behind

tail'back' ***n.*** *Football* the offensive back farthest from the line

tail'gate' ***n.*** the hinged or removable gate at the back of a wagon, truck, etc. —***vi., vt.*** **-gat'ed, -gat'ing** to drive too closely behind (another vehicle)

tail'ings ***n.pl.*** waste or refuse left in various processes of milling, mining, etc.

tail'light' ***n.*** a light, usually red, at the rear of a vehicle to warn vehicles coming from behind

tai·lor (tā'lər) ***n.*** ⟦< VL *taliare,* to cut⟧ one who makes, repairs, or alters clothes —***vi.*** to work as a tailor —***vt.*** **1** to make by tailor's work **2** to form, alter, etc. for a certain purpose /a novel *tailored* for TV/

tail'pipe' ***n.*** the exhaust pipe coming from the muffler of a motor vehicle

tail'spin' ***n.*** SPIN (*n. 3*)

taint (tānt) ***vt.*** ⟦< ?⟧ **1** to affect with something injurious, unpleasant, etc.; infect, spoil, etc. **2** to make morally corrupt —***n.*** a trace of contamination, corruption, etc.

Tai·pei or **Tai·peh** (tī pā') capital of Taiwan: pop. 2,500,000

Tai·wan (tī wän') island province of China, off the SE coast: together with nearby islands it forms the Republic of China, the Nationalist government since 1949: 13,885 sq. mi.; pop. 14,118,000

take (tāk) ***vt.*** **took, tak'en, tak'ing** ⟦< ON *taka*⟧ **1** to get possession of; capture, seize, etc. **2** to get hold of **3** to capture the fancy of **4** to obtain, acquire, assume, etc. **5** to use, consume, etc. **6** to buy, rent, subscribe to, etc. **7** to join with (one side in a disagreement, etc.) **8** to choose; select **9** to travel by /to *take* a bus/ **10** to deal with; consider **11** to occupy /*take* a chair/ **12** to require; demand /it *takes* money/ **13** to derive (a name, quality, etc.) from **14** to excerpt **15** to study **16** to write down /*take* notes/ **17** to make by photographing **18** to win (a prize, etc.) **19** to undergo /*take* punishment/ **20** to engage /*take* a nap/ **21** to accept (an offer, bet, etc.) **22** to react to /*take* a joke in earnest/ **23** to contract (a disease, etc.) **24** to understand **25** to suppose; presume **26** to feel /*take* pity/ **27** to lead, escort, etc. **28** to carry **29** to remove, as by stealing **30** to subtract **31** [Slang] to cheat, trick **32** *Gram.* to be used with /the verb "hit" *takes* an object/ —***vi.*** **1** to take root: said of a plant **2** to catch /the fire *took*/ **3** to gain favor, success, etc. **4** to be effective /the vaccination *took*/ **5** to go /to *take* to the hills/ **6** [Colloq.] to become (sick) —***n.*** **1** a taking **2** *a*) the amount taken *b*) [Slang] receipts or profit —**on the take** [Slang] taking bribes, etc. —**take after** to be, act, or look like —**take back** to retract (something said, etc.) —**take down** to put in writing; record —**take in** **1** to admit; receive **2** to make smaller **3** to understand **4** to cheat; trick —**take off** **1** to leave the ground, etc. in flight **2** [Colloq.] to start **3** [Colloq.] to imitate in a burlesque manner: with *on* —**take on** **1** to acquire; assume **2** to employ **3** to undertake (a task, etc.) **—take over** to assume control or possession of **—take to** to become fond of **—take up** 1 to make tighter or shorter 2 to become interested in (an occupation, study, etc.) **—tak'er** ***n.***

take'off' ***n.*** 1 the act of leaving the ground, as in jumping, flight, etc. 2 [Colloq.] a caricature; burlesque

take'out' ***adj.*** designating or of prepared food sold as by a restaurant to be eaten away from the premises

take'o'ver ***n.*** the usurpation of power in a nation, organization, etc.

tak·ing (tāk'iŋ) ***adj.*** attractive; winning **—*n.*** 1 the act of one that takes 2 [*pl.*] earnings; profits

talc (talk) ***n.*** ⟦< Ar *ṭalq*⟧ 1 a soft mineral used to make talcum powder, etc. 2 *short for* TALCUM (POWDER)

tal·cum (powder) (tal'kəm) a powder for the body made of purified talc

tale (tāl) ***n.*** ⟦OE *talu*⟧ 1 a true or fictitious story; narrative 2 idle or malicious gossip 3 a fiction; lie

tale'bear'er (-ber'ər) ***n.*** a gossip

tal·ent (tal'ənt) ***n.*** ⟦< Gr *talanton,* a weight⟧ 1 an ancient unit of weight or money 2 any natural ability or power 3 a superior ability in an art, etc. 4 people, or a person, with talent **—tal'ent·ed** ***adj.***

tal·is·man (tal'is mən, -iz-) ***n.,*** *pl.* **-mans** ⟦< 5th-c. Medieval Gr *telesma,* religious rite⟧ 1 a ring, stone, etc. bearing engraved figures thought to bring good luck, avert evil, etc. 2 a charm

talk (tôk) ***vi.*** ⟦prob. < OE *talian,* reckon⟧ 1 to put ideas into words; speak 2 to express ideas by speech substitutes /*talk* by signs/ 3 to chatter; gossip 4 to confer; consult 5 to confess or inform on someone **—*vt.*** 1 to use in speaking /to *talk* French/ 2 to discuss 3 to put into a specified condition, etc. by talking **—*n.*** 1 the act of talking 2 conversation 3 a speech 4 a conference 5 gossip 6 the subject of conversation, gossip, etc. 7 speech; dialect **—talk back** to answer impertinently **—talk down to** to talk patronizingly to, as by simple speech **—talk up** to promote in discussion **—talk'er** ***n.***

talk'a·tive (-ə tiv) ***adj.*** talking a great deal; loquacious Also TALKY

talking book a recording of a reading of a book, etc. for use esp. by the blind

talk·ing-to (tôk'iŋ to͞o') ***n.*** [Colloq.] a scolding

talk show *Radio, TV* a program in which a host talks with guest celebrities, experts, etc.

talk'y ***adj.*** **-i·er, -i·est** 1 talkative 2 containing too much talk, or dialogue

tall (tôl) ***adj.*** ⟦< OE (*ge*)*tæl,* swift⟧ 1 higher in stature than the average 2 having a specified height 3 [Colloq.] exaggerated /a *tall* tale/ 4 [Colloq.] large /a *tall* drink/ **—*adv.*** in an upright, dignified manner /to stand *tall*/ **—tall'ness** ***n.***

Tal·la·has·see (tal'ə has'ē) capital of Fla.: pop. 82,000

tal·low (tal'ō) ***n.*** ⟦prob. < LowG *talg*⟧ the solid fat taken from the natural fat of cattle, sheep, etc., used to make candles, soaps, etc.

tal·ly (tal'ē) ***n.,*** *pl.* **-lies** ⟦< L *talea,* a stick (notched to keep accounts)⟧ 1 anything used as a record for an account or score 2 an account, score, etc. 3 a tag or label **—*vt.*** **-lied, -ly·ing** 1 to put on or as on a tally 2 to add (*up*) **—*vi.*** 1 to score a point 2 to agree; correspond

tal·ly·ho (tal'ē hō') ***interj.*** the cry of a hunter on sighting the fox

Tal·mud (täl'mood, tal'məd) ⟦Heb, learning⟧ the body of early Jewish civil and religious law

tal·on (tal'ən) ***n.*** ⟦< L *talus,* an ankle⟧ the claw of a bird of prey

tam (tam) ***n.*** *short for* TAM-O'-SHANTER

ta·ma·le (tə mä'lē) ***n.*** ⟦< MexSp⟧ a Mexican food of minced meat, red peppers, etc. cooked in corn husks

tam·a·rack (tam'ə rak') ***n.*** ⟦< AmInd⟧ 1 an American larch tree usually found in swamps 2 its wood

tam·a·rind (tam'ə rind') ***n.*** ⟦< Ar *tamr hindī,* date of India⟧ 1 a tropical tree with yellow flowers and brown, acid pods 2 its edible fruit

tam·bou·rine (tam'bə rēn') ***n.*** ⟦prob. < Ar *ṭanbūr,* stringed instrument⟧ a shallow, single-headed hand drum with jingling metal disks in the rim: played by shaking, hitting, etc.

tame (tām) ***adj.*** **tam'er, tam'est** ⟦OE *tam*⟧ 1 changed from a wild state and trained for human use 2 gentle; docile 3 without spirit or force; dull **—*vt.*** **tamed, tam'ing** 1 to make tame 2 to make gentle; subdue **—tam'a·ble** or **tame'a·ble** ***adj.*** **—tame'ly** ***adv.*** **—tame'ness** ***n.*** **—tam'er** ***n.***

Tam·il (tam'əl, tum'-) ***n.*** the non-Indo-European language of the Tamils, a people of S India and N Sri Lanka

TAM-O'-SHANTER

tam-o'-shan·ter (tam'ə shan'tər) ***n.*** ⟦< title character of Burns's poem⟧ a Scottish cap with a round, flat top

tamp (tamp) ***vt.*** ⟦< ? Fr *tampon,* a plug⟧ to pack firmly or pound (*down*) by a series of blows or taps

Tam·pa (tam'pə) seaport in central Fla., on the Gulf of Mexico: pop. 272,000

tam·per (tam'pər) ***vi.*** ⟦< TEMPER⟧ 1 to make secret, illegal arrangements (*with*) 2 to interfere (*with*) or meddle (*with*)

tam·pon (tam'pän') ***n.*** ⟦Fr⟧ a plug of cotton, etc. put into a body cavity or wound to stop bleeding, etc.

tan (tan) ***n.*** ⟦< ML *tanum,* a bark used to tan hides⟧ 1 a yellowish-brown color 2 the color of suntan **—*adj.*** **tan'ner, tan'nest** yellowish-brown **—*vt.*** **tanned, tan'ning** 1 to change (hide) into leather by soaking in tannin 2 to produce a suntan in 3 [Colloq.] to whip severely **—*vi.*** to become tanned

tan·a·ger (tan'ə jər) ***n.*** ⟦< AmInd (Brazil)

tangara] any of various small, American songbirds with brightly colored males

tan·bark (tan′bärk′) ***n.*** any bark containing tannic acid, used to tan hides, etc.

tan·dem (tan′dəm) ***adv.*** [< punning use of L, at length] one behind another; in single file

tang (taŋ) ***n.*** [< ON *tangi,* a sting] **1** a prong on a file, etc., that fits into the handle **2** a strong, penetrating taste or odor —**tang′y, -i·er, -i·est,** ***adj.***

tan·ge·lo (tan′jə lō′) ***n., pl.*** **-los′** [TAN-G(ERINE) + (*pom*)*elo,* grapefruit] a fruit produced by crossing a tangerine with a grapefruit

tan·gent (tan′jənt) ***adj.*** [< L *tangere,* to touch] **1** touching **2** *Geom.* touching a curved surface at one point but not intersecting it —***n.*** a tangent line, curve, or surface —**go off at** (or **on**) **a tangent** to change suddenly to another line of action, etc. —**tan·gen′tial** (-jen′shəl) ***adj.***

tan·ge·rine (tan′jə rēn′) ***n.*** [after *Tangier,* city in N Africa] a small, loose-skinned, reddish-yellow orange with easily separated segments

tan·gi·ble (tan′jə bəl) ***adj.*** [< L *tangere,* to touch] **1** that can be touched or felt **2** definite; objective —***n.*** [*pl.*] assets having real substance and able to be appraised for value —**tan′gi·bil′i·ty** ***n.***

tan·gle (taŋ′gəl) ***vt.*** **-gled, -gling** [< ? Sw] **1** to catch as in a snare; trap **2** to make a snarl of; intertwine —***vi.*** **1** to become tangled **2** [Colloq.] to argue —***n.*** **1** an intertwined, confused mass **2** a confused condition

tan·go (taŋ′gō) ***n., pl.*** **-gos** [AmSp] **1** a South American dance for couples with long gliding steps **2** music for this dance in 2/4 or 4/4 time —***vi.*** to dance the tango

tank (taŋk) ***n.*** [in sense 1 < Sans] **1** any large container for liquid or gas **2** an armored vehicle with guns and full tractor treads —**tank′ful′** ***n.***

tank·ard (taŋk′ərd) ***n.*** [< OFr *tanquart*] a large drinking cup with a handle

tank·er (taŋk′ər) ***n.*** **1** a ship equipped to transport oil or other liquids **2** a plane designed to refuel another plane in flight **3** a truck, etc. equipped to transport liquids or dry commodities in bulk

tank top [orig. worn in swimming tanks] a casual shirt like an undershirt but with wider shoulder straps

tank truck a motor truck built to transport gasoline, oil, etc.

tan·ner (tan′ər) ***n.*** a person whose work is making leather by tanning hides

tan′ner·y ***n., pl.*** **-ner·ies** a place where leather is made by tanning hides

tannic acid a yellowish, astringent substance used in tanning hides, dyeing, etc. Also **tan′nin** (-in) ***n.***

tan·sy (tan′zē) ***n., pl.*** **-sies** [< LL *tanacetum*] a plant with a strong smell and small, yellow flowers

tan·ta·lize (tan′tə līz′) ***vt.*** **-lized′, -liz′ing** [after *Tantalus,* in Gr Myth, a king doomed in Hades to stand in water that always recedes when he wishes to drink and under fruit he cannot reach] to promise or show something desirable and then withhold it; tease

tan·ta·mount (tant′ə mount′) ***adj.*** [< OFr *tant,* so much + *amont,* upward] equal (*to*) in value, effect, etc.

tan·tra (tun′trə, tän′-) ***n.*** [Sans] [*often* **T-**] any of a group of Hindu or Buddhist mystical writings

tan·trum (tan′trəm) ***n.*** [< ?] a violent, willful outburst of rage, etc.

Tan·za·ni·a (tan′zə nē′ə) country in E Africa: 362,820 sq. mi.; pop. 19,730,000 —**Tan′za·ni′an** ***adj., n.***

Tao·ism (dou′iz′əm, tou′-) ***n.*** [Chin *tao,* the way] a Chinese religion and philosophy advocating simplicity, selflessness, etc. —**Tao′ist** ***n., adj.***

tap[1] (tap) ***vt., vi.*** **tapped, tap′ping** [echoic] **1** to strike lightly **2** to make or do by tapping [*to tap a message*] **3** to choose, as for membership in a club —***n.*** a light, rapid blow

tap[2] (tap) ***n.*** [OE *tæppa*] **1** a faucet or spigot **2** a plug, cork, etc. for stopping a hole in a cask, etc. **3** a tool used to cut threads in a female screw **4** the act or an instance of wiretapping **5** *Elec.* a place in a circuit where a connection can be made —***vt.*** **tapped, tap′ping 1** to put a tap or spigot on **2** to make a hole in, or pull the plug from, for drawing off liquid **3** to draw off (liquid) **4** to make use of [*to tap new resources*] **5** to make a connection with (a pipe, circuit, etc.); specif., to wiretap

tap dance a dance done with sharp taps of the foot, toe, or heel at each step —**tap′-dance′, -danced′, -danc′ing,** ***vi.*** —**tap′-danc′er** ***n.***

tape (tāp) ***n.*** [OE *tæppe,* a fillet] **1** a strong, narrow strip of cloth, paper, etc. used for binding, tying, etc. **2** *short for* MAGNETIC TAPE **3** *short for* TAPE MEASURE —***vt.*** **taped, tap′ing 1** to bind, tie, etc. with tape **2** to record on magnetic tape

tape deck a component of an audio system that records and plays back magnetic tapes

tape measure a tape with marks in inches, feet, etc. for measuring

ta·per (tā′pər) ***n.*** [OE *tapur*] **1** a slender candle **2** a gradual decrease in width or thickness —***vt., vi.*** **1** to decrease gradually in width or thickness **2** to lessen; diminish Often with *off*

tape recorder a device for recording on magnetic tape and for playing back what has been recorded

tap·es·try (tap′əs trē) ***n., pl.*** **-tries** [< Gr *tapes,* a carpet] a heavy woven cloth with decorative designs and pictures, used as a wall hanging, etc.

tape′worm′ ***n.*** a tapelike worm that lives as a parasite in the intestines

tap·i·o·ca (tap′ē ō′kə) ***n.*** [< AmInd (Brazil)] a starchy substance from cassava roots, used for puddings, etc.

ta·pir (tā′pər) ***n.*** [< AmInd (Brazil)] a large, hoglike mammal of tropical America and the Malay Peninsula

tap′room′ ***n.*** BARROOM

tap·root (tap′ro͞ot′) ***n.*** [TAP[2] + ROOT[1]] a main root, growing downward, from which small branch roots spread out

taps (taps) ***n.*** [< TAP[1], because orig. a drum

signal⟧ a bugle call to put out lights in retiring for the night

tar[1] (tär) ***n.*** ⟦OE *teru*⟧ a thick, sticky, black liquid obtained by the destructive distillation of wood, coal, etc. —***vt.*** **tarred, tar′ring** to cover or smear with tar —**tar′ry, -ri·er, -ri·est,** ***adj.***

tar[2] (tär) ***n.*** ⟦< TAR(PAULIN)⟧ [Colloq.] a sailor

HAIRY TARANTULA

ta·ran·tu·la (tə ran′cho͞o lə) ***n.*** ⟦after *Taranto,* city in S Italy⟧ any of several large, hairy somewhat poisonous spiders of S Europe and tropical America

tar·dy (tär′dē) ***adj.*** **-di·er, -di·est** ⟦< L *tardus,* slow⟧ **1** slow in moving, acting, etc. **2** late, delayed, or dilatory —**tar′di·ly** ***adv.*** —**tar′di·ness** ***n.***

tare[1] (ter) ***n.*** ⟦ME⟧ **1** the vetch **2** *Bible* an undesirable weed

tare[2] (ter) ***n.*** ⟦< Ar *ṭaraḥa,* to reject⟧ the weight of a container, etc. deducted from the total weight to determine the weight of the contents or load

tar·get (tär′git) ***n.*** ⟦< Medieval Fr *targe,* a shield⟧ **1** a board, etc. marked as with concentric circles, aimed at in archery, rifle practice, etc. **2** any object that is shot at **3** an objective; goal **4** an object of attack, criticism, etc.

tar·iff (tar′if) ***n.*** ⟦< Ar *taʕrīf,* information⟧ **1** a list or system of taxes upon exports or, esp., imports **2** a tax of this kind, or its rate **3** any list or scale of prices, charges, etc. **4** [Colloq.] any bill, charge, etc.

tar·nish (tär′nish) ***vt.*** ⟦< Fr *ternir,* make dim⟧ **1** to dull the luster of **2** to sully or mar —***vi.*** **1** to lose luster **2** to become sullied —***n.*** **1** dullness **2** a stain —**tar′nish·a·ble** ***adj.***

ta·ro (ter′ō, tär′ō) ***n.,*** *pl.* **-ros** ⟦< a Polynesian language⟧ a tropical Asiatic plant with a starchy, edible root

tar·ot (tar′ō, -ət; ta rō′) ***n.*** ⟦Fr < Ar *ṭaraḥa,* to reject⟧ [*often* **T-**] any of a set of 22 fortunetelling cards

tarp (tärp) ***n.*** [Colloq.] *short for* TARPAULIN

tar·pau·lin (tär pô′lin, tär′pə-) ***n.*** ⟦< TAR[1] + PALL[2], a covering⟧ canvas coated with a waterproofing compound, or a protective cover to this

tar·pon (tär′pən) ***n.*** ⟦< ?⟧ a large, silvery game fish of the W Atlantic

tar·ra·gon (tar′ə gän′) ***n.*** ⟦< Sp < Ar < Gr *drakōn,* a dragon⟧ an Old World plant with fragrant leaves used for seasoning

tar·ry (tar′ē) ***vi.*** **-ried, -ry·ing** ⟦< OE *tergan,* to vex & prob. OFr *targer,* to delay⟧ **1** to delay; linger **2** to stay for a time **3** to wait

tart[1] (tärt) ***adj.*** ⟦OE *teart*⟧ **1** sharp in taste; sour; acid **2** sharp in meaning; cutting /a *tart* answer/ —**tart′ly** ***adv.*** —**tart′ness** ***n.***

tart[2] (tärt) ***n.*** ⟦< OFr *tarte*⟧ a small pastry shell filled with jam, jelly, etc.

tart[3] (tärt) ***n.*** ⟦< prec., orig., slang term of endearment⟧ [Colloq.] a prostitute

tar·tan (tär′tən, tärt′′n) ***n.*** ⟦prob. < Medieval Fr *tiretaine,* a cloth of mixed fibers⟧ a woolen cloth in any of various woven plaid patterns, worn esp. in the Scottish Highlands

tar·tar (tär′tər) ***n.*** ⟦< Medieval Gr *tartaron*⟧ **1** cream of tartar, esp. the crude form present in grape juice and forming a crustlike deposit in wine casks **2** a hard deposit on the teeth

Tar·tar (tär′tər) ***n.*** TATAR

tar·tar sauce (tär′tər) ⟦Fr⟧ a sauce of mayonnaise with chopped pickles, olives, capers, etc. Also **tartare sauce**

task (task) ***n.*** ⟦ult. < L *taxare,* to rate⟧ **1** a piece of work to be done **2** any difficult undertaking —***vt.*** to burden; strain —**take to task** to scold

task force a group, esp. a military unit, assigned a specific task

task′mas′ter ***n.*** one who assigns tasks to others, esp. when severe

Tas·ma·ni·a (taz mā′nē ə) island of Australia, off its SE coast —**Tas·ma′ni·an** ***adj., n.***

tas·sel (tas′əl) ***n.*** ⟦OFr, knob⟧ **1** an ornamental tuft of threads, etc. hanging loosely from a knob **2** something resembling this, as a tuft of corn silk

taste (tāst) ***vt.*** **tast′ed, tast′ing** ⟦< OFr *taster*⟧ **1** to test the flavor of by putting a little in one's mouth **2** to detect the flavor of by the sense of taste **3** to eat or drink a small amount of **4** to experience /to *taste* success/ —***vi.*** to have a specific flavor —***n.*** **1** the sense by which flavor is perceived through the taste buds on the tongue **2** the quality so perceived; flavor **3** a small amount tasted as a sample **4** a bit; trace **5** the ability to appreciate what is beautiful, appropriate, etc. **6** a specific preference **7** a liking; inclination —**in bad** (or **good**) **taste** in a style showing a bad (or good) sense of beauty, fitness, etc. —**taste′less** ***adj.*** —**tast′er** ***n.***

taste bud any of the cells, esp. in the tongue, that are the organs of taste

taste′ful ***adj.*** having or showing good TASTE (*n.* 5) —**taste′ful·ly** ***adv.***

tast·y (tās′tē) ***adj.*** **-i·er, -i·est** that tastes good; flavorful —**tast′i·ness** ***n.***

tat (tat) ***vt.*** **tat′ted, tat′ting** to make by tatting —***vi.*** to do tatting

ta·ta·mi (tə tä′mē) ***n.,*** *pl.* **-mi** or **-mis** ⟦Jpn⟧ a floor mat of rice straw, used in Japanese homes for sitting on

Ta·tar (tät′ər) ***n.*** **1** a member of any of the E Asiatic peoples who invaded W Asia and E Europe in the Middle Ages **2** a Turkic language

tat·ter (tat′ər) ***n.*** ⟦< ON *tǫturr,* rags⟧ **1** a torn and hanging piece, as of a garment **2** [*pl.*] torn, ragged clothes —***vt., vi.*** to make or become ragged —**tat′tered** ***adj.***

tat′ter·de·mal′ion (-di māl′yən) ***n.*** ⟦< prec. + ?⟧ a person in torn, ragged clothes

tat·ting (tat′iŋ) ***n.*** ⟦prob. < Brit dial. *tat,* to tangle]] 1 a fine lace made by looping and knotting thread 2 the act or process of making this

tat·tle (tat''l) *vi.* **-tled, -tling** [[prob. < MDu *tatelen*]] 1 to talk idly 2 to reveal others' secrets —*vt.* to reveal (a secret) by gossiping —**tat'tler** *n.*

tat'tle·tale' *n.* an informer; talebearer

tat·too¹ (ta to͞o') *vt.* **-tooed', -too'ing** [[< a Polynesian language]] to make (permanent designs) on (the skin) by puncturing it and inserting indelible color —*n., pl.* **-toos'** a tattooed design

tat·too² (ta to͞o') *n., pl.* **-toos'** [[< Du *tap toe,* tap to (shut): a signal for closing barrooms]] 1 a signal on a drum or bugle, summoning military personnel to their quarters at night 2 a drumming, rapping, etc.

tau (tou, tô) *n.* the 19th letter of the Greek alphabet (Τ, τ)

taught (tôt) *vt., vi. pt. & pp. of* TEACH

taunt (tônt, tänt) *vt.* [[< ? Fr *tant pour tant,* tit for tat]] to reproach scornfully or sarcastically; mock —*n.* a scornful or jeering remark

taupe (tōp) *n.* [[Fr < L *talpa,* mole]] a dark, brownish gray

Tau·rus (tô'rəs) [[< L, a bull]] the second sign of the zodiac

taut (tôt) *adj.* [[ME *toght,* tight]] 1 tightly stretched, as a rope 2 tense /a *taut* smile/ 3 trim, tidy, etc. —**taut'ly** *adv.* —**taut'ness** *n.*

tau·tol·o·gy (tô täl'ə jē) *n., pl.* **-gies** [[< Gr < *to auto,* the same + -LOGY]] needless repetition of an idea in a different word, etc. —**tau'to·log'i·cal** *adj.*

tav·ern (tav'ərn) *n.* [[< L *taberna*]] 1 a saloon; bar 2 an inn

taw·dry (tô'drē) *adj.* **-dri·er, -dri·est** [[after *St. Audrey laces,* sold at St. Audrey's fair in Norwich, England]] cheap and showy; gaudy

taw·ny (tô'nē) *adj.* **-ni·er, -ni·est** [[< OFr *tanner,* to tan]] brownish-yellow; tan —**taw'ni·ness** *n.*

tax (taks) *vt.* [[< L *taxare,* appraise]] 1 to require to pay a tax 2 to assess a tax on (income, purchases, etc.) 3 to put a strain on 4 to accuse; charge —*n.* 1 a compulsory payment of a percentage of income, property value, etc. for the support of a government 2 a heavy demand; burden —**tax'a·ble** *adj.* —**tax·a'tion** *n.*

tax·i (tak'sē) *n., pl.* **-is** *short for* TAXICAB —*vi.* **-ied, -i·ing** or **-y·ing** 1 to go in a taxicab 2 to move along the ground or on the water as after landing: said of an airplane

tax'i·cab' *n.* [[< *taxi(meter) cab*]] an automobile in which passengers are carried for a fare

tax·i·der·my (taks'i dur'mē) *n.* [[< Gr *taxis,* arrangement + *derma,* skin]] the art of preparing, stuffing, etc. the skins of animals to make them appear lifelike —**tax'i·der'mist** *n.*

tax·i·me·ter (tak'sē mēt'ər) *n.* [[< Fr, ult. < ML *taxa,* tax + *-meter,* -METER]] a device in taxicabs that registers the fare due

tax·on·o·my (taks än'ə mē) *n., pl.* **-mies** [[< Gr *taxis,* arrangement + *nomos,* law]] classification, esp. of animals and plants —**tax·on'o·mist** *n.*

tax'pay'er *n.* one who pays a tax

tax·us (taks'əs) *n.* [[ModL]] YEW (*n.* 1)

Tay·lor (tā'lər), **Zach·a·ry** (zak'ə rē) 1784-1850; U.S. general: 12th president of the U.S. (1849-50)

tb or **TB** tuberculosis Also **t.b.** or **T.B.**

T-bone steak (tē'bōn') a beefsteak with a T-shaped bone, containing some tenderloin

tbs. or **tbsp.** 1 tablespoon(s) 2 tablespoonful(s)

T cell any of the lymphatic leukocytes affected by the thymus, that regulate immunity: cf. B CELL

Tchai·kov·sky (chī kôf'skē), **Peter** 1840-93; Russ. composer

TD touchdown Also **td**

tea (tē) *n.* [[< Chin dial. *t'e*]] 1 an evergreen plant grown in Asia 2 its dried leaves, used to make a beverage 3 the beverage made by soaking such leaves in boiling water 4 a tealike beverage made from other plants or from a meat extract 5 [Chiefly Brit., etc.] a meal in the late afternoon at which tea is the drink 6 an afternoon party at which tea, etc. is served

tea·ber·ry (tē'ber'ē) *n., pl.* **-ries** 1 WINTERGREEN (sense 1) 2 the berry of the wintergreen

teach (tēch) *vt.* **taught, teach'ing** [[OE *tæcan*]] 1 to show or help (a person) to learn (*how*) to do something 2 to give lessons to (a student, etc.) 3 to give lessons in (a subject) 4 to provide with knowledge, insight, etc. —*vi.* to give lessons or instruction —**teach'a·ble** *adj.*

teach·er (tē'chər) *n.* one who teaches, esp. as a profession

teach'ing *n.* 1 the profession of a teacher 2 something taught; precept, doctrine, etc.: *usually used in pl.*

tea'cup' *n.* a cup for drinking tea, etc. —**tea'cup·ful'**, *pl.* **-fuls'**, *n.*

teak (tēk) *n.* [[< Malayalam *tēkka*]] 1 a large East Indian tree with hard, yellowish-brown wood 2 its wood

tea'ket'tle *n.* a kettle with a spout, for boiling water to make tea, etc.

teal (tēl) *n.* [[ME *tele*]] 1 a small, short-necked, freshwater wild duck 2 a dark grayish or greenish blue: also **teal blue**

team (tēm) *n.* [[OE, offspring]] 1 two or more horses, oxen, etc. harnessed to the same plow, etc. 2 a group of people working or playing together —*vi.* to join in cooperative activity: often with *up* —*adj.* of or done by a team

team'mate' *n.* one on the same team

team'ster (-stər) *n.* one whose work is hauling loads with a team or truck

team'work' *n.* joint action by a group of people

tea'pot' *n.* a pot with a spout and handle, for brewing and pouring tea

tear¹ (ter) *vt.* **tore, torn, tear'ing** [[OE *teran,* rend]] 1 to pull apart into pieces by force; rip 2 to make by tearing /to *tear* a hole/ 3 to lacerate 4 to disrupt; split /ranks *torn* by dissensions/ 5 to divide with doubt, etc. 6 to pull with force: with *up, out, away, off,* etc. —*vi.* 1 to be torn 2 to move with force or speed —*n.* 1 a tearing

2 a torn place; rent —**tear down** 1 to wreck 2 to dismantle

tear² (tir) *n.* ⟦OE *tēar*⟧ a drop of the salty fluid which flows from the eye, as in weeping —**in tears** crying; weeping —**tear′ful** *adj.* —**tear′ful·ly** *adv.* —**tear′y, -i·er, -i·est,** *adj.*

tear′drop′ *n.* a tear

tear gas (tir) a gas that causes irritation of the eyes, a heavy flow of tears, etc. —**tear′-gas′, -gassed′, -gas′sing,** *vt.*

tea′room′ *n.* a restaurant that serves tea, coffee, light lunches, etc.

tease (tēz) *vt.* **teased, teas′ing** ⟦OE *tæsan*⟧ 1 *a)* to card or comb (flax, wool, etc.) *b)* to fluff (the hair) by combing toward the scalp 2 to raise a nap on (cloth) by brushing with teasels 3 to annoy by mocking, poking fun, etc. 4 to beg; importune 5 to tantalize —*vi.* to indulge in teasing —*n.* one who teases

tea·sel (tē′zəl) *n.* ⟦see prec.⟧ 1 a bristly plant with prickly flowers 2 the dried flower, or any device, used to raise a nap on cloth

teas′er *n.* 1 a person or thing that teases 2 a puzzling problem

tea′spoon′ *n.* a spoon for stirring tea, etc., holding 1⅓ fluid drams —**tea′spoon·ful′**, *pl.* **-fuls′**, *n.*

teat (tēt) *n.* ⟦< OFr *tete*⟧ the nipple on a breast or udder

tech. 1 technical(ly) 2 technology

tech·ni·cal (tek′ni kəl) *adj.* ⟦< Gr *technē*, an art⟧ 1 dealing with the industrial or mechanical arts or the applied sciences 2 of a specific science, art, craft, etc. 3 of, in or showing technique 4 concerned with minute details —**tech′ni·cal·ly** *adv.*

tech′ni·cal′i·ty (-kal′ə tē) *n.*, *pl.* **-ties** 1 the state or quality of being technical 2 a technical point, detail, etc. 3 a minute point, detail, etc. brought to bear upon a main issue

tech·ni·cian (tek nish′ən) *n.* one skilled in the technique of some art, craft, or science

Tech·ni·col·or (tek′ni kul′ər) *trademark for* a process of making color movies —*n.* [t-] this process

tech·nique (tek nēk′) *n.* ⟦Fr⟧ 1 the method of procedure in artistic work scientific activity, etc. 2 the degree of expertness in following this

tech·noc·ra·cy (tek näk′rə sē) *n.* ⟦< Gr *technē*, an art + -CRACY⟧ government by scientists and engineers —**tech′no·crat′** (-nə krat′) *n.*

tech·nol·o·gy (tek näl′ə jē) *n.* ⟦Gr *technologia*, systematic treatment⟧ 1 the science of the practical or industrial arts 2 applied science —**tech′no·log′i·cal** (-nə läj′i kəl) *adj.*

ted·dy bear ⟦after *Teddy* (Theodore) Roosevelt⟧ a child's stuffed toy made to look like a bear cub

te·di·ous (tē′dē əs) *adj.* full of tedium; long and dull —**te′di·ous·ly** *adv.*

te′di·um (-əm) *n.* ⟦< L *taedet*, it offends⟧ the condition or quality of being tiresome, wearisome, etc.

tee (tē) *n.* ⟦prob. < Scot dial. *teaz*⟧ *Golf* 1 a small peg from which the ball is driven 2 the place from which a player makes the first stroke on each hole —*vt., vi.* **teed, tee′ing** to place (a ball) on a tee —**tee off** 1 to play a golf ball from a tee 2 [Slang] to make angry or disgusted

teem (tēm) *vi.* ⟦< OE *team*, progeny⟧ to be prolific; abound; swarm

teen (tēn) *n.* ⟦OE *tien*, ten⟧ 1 [*pl.*] the years from 13 through 19, as of a person's age 2 TEENAGER

teen·age (tēn′āj′) *adj.* 1 in one's teens 2 of or for people in their teens —**teen′ag′er** *n.*

tee·ny (tē′nē) *adj.* **-ni·er, -ni·est** *colloq. var. of* TINY Also **teen·sy** (tēn′zē, -sē), **-si·er, -si·est**

teen·y·bop·per (tē′nē bäp′ər) *n.* [Slang] a faddish young teenager

tee·ny-wee·ny (tē′nē wē′nē) *adj.* [Colloq.] tiny Also **teen·sy-ween·sy** (tēn′zē wēn′zē, tēn′sē wēn′sē)

tee·pee (tē′pē) *n. alt. sp. of* TEPEE

tee shirt *var. of* T-SHIRT

tee·ter (tēt′ər) *vi., vt., n.* ⟦< ON *titra*, to tremble⟧ seesaw or wobble

tee′ter-tot′ter (-tôt′ər, -tät′-) *n., vi.* SEESAW

teeth (tēth) *n. pl. of* TOOTH

teethe (tēth) *vi.* **teethed, teeth′ing** to grow teeth; cut one's teeth

tee·to·tal·er or **tee·to·tal·ler** (tē tōt′′lər) *n.* ⟦< doubling of initial *t* in *total*⟧ one who practices total abstinence from alcoholic liquor

Tef·lon (tef′län′) *trademark for* a tough polymer, used for nonsticking coatings as for cookware

Teh·ran (te rän′) capital of Iran: pop. 4,530,000: also **Te·he·ran′**

tek·tite (tek′tīt′) *n.* ⟦< Gr *tēktos*, molten⟧ a small, dark, glassy body thought to be from outer space

tel. 1 telegram 2 telephone

Tel A·viv (tel′ ə vēv′) seaport in W Israel: pop. 394,000

tele- *combining form* 1 ⟦< Gr *tēle*, far off⟧ at, over, etc. a distance [*telegraph*] 2 ⟦< TELE(VISION)⟧ of, in, or by television [*telecast*]

tel·e·cast (tel′i kast′) *vt., vi.* **-cast′** or **-cast′ed, -cast′ing** to broadcast by television —*n.* a television broadcast —**tel′e·cast′er** *n.*

tel′e·com·mu′ni·ca′tion *n.* [*also pl., with sing. or pl. v.*] communication by electronic or electrical means, as through radio, TV, computers, etc.

tel′e·con′fer·ence *n.* a conference of persons in different locations, as by telephone, TV, etc.

tel·e·gram (tel′ə gram′) *n.* a message transmitted by telegraph

tel′e·graph′ (-graf′) *n.* ⟦see TELE- & -GRAPH⟧ an apparatus or system that transmits messages by electrical impulses sent by wire or radio —*vt., vi.* to send (a message) to (a person) by telegraph —**tel′e·graph′ic** *adj.*

te·leg·ra·phy (tə leg′rə fē) *n.* the operation of telegraph apparatus —**te·leg′ra·pher** *n.*

tel·e·ki·ne·sis (tel′i ki nē′sis) *n.* ⟦see TELE- & KINETIC⟧ the causing of an object to move by unexplainable means, as by the mind

tel·e·mar·ket·ing (tel′ə mär′kət iŋ) *n.* the use of the telephone in marketing for sales research, promotion, etc.

tel·e·me·ter (tel′ə mēt′ər, tə lem′ət ər) ***n.*** a device for measuring and transmitting data about radiation, temperature, etc. from a remote point —**te·lem·e·try** (tə lem′ə trē) ***n.***

te·lep·a·thy (tə lep′ə thē) ***n.*** ⟦TELE- + -PATHY⟧ supposed communication between minds by means other than the normal sensory channels —**tel·e·path·ic** (tel′ə path′ik) ***adj.***

tel·e·phone (tel′ə fōn′) ***n.*** ⟦TELE- + -PHONE⟧ an instrument or system for conveying speech over distances by converting sound into electrical impulses sent through a wire —***vt., vi.*** **-phoned′, -phon′ing** to convey (a message) to (a person) by telephone —**tel′e·phon′ic** (-fän′ik) ***adj.***

te·leph·o·ny (tə lef′ə nē) ***n.*** the making or operation of telephones

tel·e·pho·to (tel′ə fōt′ō) ***adj.*** designating or of a camera lens that produces a large image of a distant object

tel′e·pho′to·graph′ ***n.*** **1** a photograph taken with a telephoto lens **2** a photograph transmitted by telegraph or radio —***vt., vi.*** to take or transmit (telephotographs) —**tel′e·pho·tog′ra·phy** (-fə täg′rə fē) ***n.***

tel′e·proc′ess·ing ***n.*** data processing with computer terminals, over communication lines

Tel·e·Promp·Ter (tel′ə prämp′tər) *trademark for* an electronic device that unrolls a speech, script, etc. line by line, as an aid to a speaker, etc. on TV —***n.*** this device: written **tel′e·promp′ter**

REFRACTING TELESCOPE

tel·e·scope (tel′ə skōp′) ***n.*** ⟦see TELE- & -SCOPE⟧ an optical instrument for making distant objects appear nearer and larger —***vi., vt.*** **-scoped′, -scop′ing** to slide one into another like the tubes of a collapsible telescope —**tel′e·scop′ic** (-skäp′ik) ***adj.***

tel′e·thon′ (-thän′) ***n.*** ⟦TELE(VISION) + (MARA)THON⟧ a campaign, as on a lengthy telecast, seeking donations

Tel·e·type (tel′ə tīp′) ***n.*** *trademark for* a former kind of telegraphic apparatus that printed messages typed on the keyboard of the transmitter —**tel′e·type′writ′er** ***n.***

tel·e·vise (tel′ə vīz′) ***vt., vi.*** **-vised′, -vis′ing** to transmit by television

tel′e·vi′sion (-vizh′ən) ***n.*** **1** the process of transmitting images by converting light rays into electrical signals: the receiver reconverts the signals to reproduce the images on a screen **2** television broadcasting **3** a television receiving set **4** a television program or programs

tel·ex (tel′eks′) ***n.*** ⟦TEL(ETYPEWRITER) + EX(CHANGE)⟧ **1** a teletypewriter which sends messages over telephone lines **2** a message sent in this way —***vt.*** to send by telex

tell (tel) ***vt.*** **told, tell′ing** ⟦OE *tellan,* calculate⟧ **1** orig., to count **2** to narrate; relate /to *tell* a story/ **3** to express in words; say /to *tell* the truth/ **4** to reveal; disclose **5** to recognize; distinguish /to *tell* twins apart/ **6** to inform /*tell* me later/ **7** to order /*tell* him to go/ —***vi.*** **1** to give an account or evidence (*of* something) **2** to be effective /each blow *told*/ —**tell off** [Colloq.] to rebuke severely —**tell on** **1** to tire **2** [Colloq.] to inform against

tell·er (tel′ər) ***n.*** **1** one who tells (a story, etc.) **2** one who counts, as a bank clerk who pays out or receives money

tell′ing ***adj.*** forceful; striking —**tell′ing·ly** ***adv.***

tell′tale′ ***adj.*** revealing what is meant to be kept secret or hidden

tel·ly (tel′ē) ***n.,*** *pl.* **-lies** *Brit., etc.* (*exc. Cdn.*) *colloq. term for* TELEVISION

tem·blor (tem′blôr′, -blər) ***n.*** ⟦Sp < *temblar,* to tremble⟧ EARTHQUAKE

te·mer·i·ty (tə mer′ə tē) ***n.*** ⟦< L *temere,* rashly⟧ foolish or rash boldness

temp. **1** temperature **2** temporary

Tem·pe (tem′pē) city in central Ariz.: pop. 107,000

tem·per (tem′pər) ***vt.*** ⟦< L *temperare,* regulate⟧ **1** to moderate, as by mingling with something else /to *temper* blame with praise/ **2** to bring to the proper condition by some treatment /to *temper* steel/ **3** to toughen —***n.*** **1** the degree of hardness and resiliency of a metal **2** frame of mind; disposition **3** calmness of mind: in **lose** (or **keep**) **one's temper** **4** anger; rage

tem·per·a (tem′pər ə) ***n.*** ⟦It: see prec.⟧ a process of painting with pigments mixed with size, casein, or egg

tem·per·a·ment (tem′pər ə mənt; *often,* -prə-) ***n.*** ⟦see TEMPER⟧ **1** one's natural disposition; nature **2** a nature that is excitable, moody, etc. —**tem′per·a·men′tal** ***adj.***

tem·per·ance (tem′pər əns) ***n.*** **1** self-restraint in conduct, indulgence of the appetites, etc.; moderation **2** moderation in drinking alcoholic liquors or total abstinence from them

tem·per·ate (tem′pər it) ***adj.*** ⟦see TEMPER⟧ **1** moderate, as in eating or drinking **2** self-restrained in actions, speech, etc. **3** neither very hot nor very cold: said of climate, etc.

Temperate Zone either of the two zones of the earth (**North Temperate Zone** and **South Temperate Zone**) between the tropics and the polar circles

tem·per·a·ture (tem′pər ə chər; *often,* -prə chər) ***n.*** ⟦< L *temperatus,* temperate⟧ **1** the degree of hotness or coldness of anything **2** excess of body heat over the normal; fever

tem·pered (tem′pərd) ***adj.*** **1** having been given the desired TEMPER (*n.* 1) **2** having a (specified) TEMPER (*n.* 2)

tem·pest (tem′pist) ***n.*** ⟦< L *tempus,* time⟧ a violent storm with high winds, esp. one accompanied by rain, etc.

tem·pes·tu·ous (tem pes′cho͞o əs, -chə wəs) ***adj.*** of or like a tempest; violent

tem·plate (tem′plit) ***n.*** ⟦< L *templum,* small timber⟧ a pattern, as a thin metal plate, for making an exact copy

tem·ple[1] (tem′pəl) ***n.*** ⟦< L *templum*⟧ **1** a

building for the worship of God or gods 2 a large building for some special purpose /a *temple* of art/

tem·ple[2] (tem′pəl) ***n.*** ⟦< L *tempus*⟧ 1 the flat surface alongside the forehead, in front of each ear 2 either of the sidepieces of a pair of glasses

tem·po (tem′pō) ***n.***, *pl.* **-pos** or **-pi** (-pē) ⟦It < L *tempus,* time⟧ 1 the speed at which a musical composition is performed 2 rate of activity

tem·po·ral[1] (tem′pə rəl) ***adj.*** ⟦< L *tempus,* time⟧ 1 transitory; temporary 2 of this world; worldly 3 secular 4 of or limited by time

tem·po·ral[2] (tem′pə rəl) ***adj.*** of or near the temples (of the head)

tem′po·rar′y (-rer′ē) ***adj.*** ⟦< L *tempus,* time⟧ lasting only a while; not permanent —**tem′po·rar′i·ly** ***adv.***

tem′po·rize′ (-rīz′) ***vi.*** **-rized′**, **-riz′ing** to give temporary compliance, evade decision, etc., so as to gain time or avoid argument

tempt (tempt) ***vt.*** ⟦< L *temptare,* to test⟧ 1 to induce or entice, as to something immoral 2 to be inviting to; attract 3 to provoke or risk provoking (fate, etc.) 4 to incline strongly /to be *tempted* to accept/ —**temp·ta·tion** (temp tā′shən) ***n.*** —**tempt′er** ***n.*** —**tempt′ress** ***n.fem.***

tem·pu·ra (tem′poo rä′, tem poor′ə) ***n.*** ⟦Jpn⟧ a Japanese dish of deep-fried shrimp, fish, vegetables, etc.

ten (ten) ***adj., n.*** ⟦OE⟧ one more than nine; 10; X

ten·a·ble (ten′ə bəl) ***adj.*** ⟦< L *tenere,* to hold⟧ that can be held, defended, or maintained —**ten′a·bil′i·ty** ***n.***

te·na·cious (tə nā′shəs) ***adj.*** ⟦< L *tenere,* to hold⟧ 1 holding firmly /a *tenacious* grip/ 2 retentive /a *tenacious* memory/ 3 strongly cohesive or adhesive 4 persistent; stubborn /*tenacious* courage/ —**te·na′cious·ly** ***adv.*** —**te·nac·i·ty** (tə nas′ə tē) ***n.***

ten·ant (ten′ənt) ***n.*** ⟦see prec.⟧ 1 one who pays rent to occupy land, a building, etc. 2 an occupant —***vt.*** to hold as a tenant —**ten′an·cy** ***n.***

tenant farmer one who farms land owned by another and pays rent

Ten Commandments *Bible* the ten laws of moral and religious conduct given to Moses by God: Exodus 20:2-17

tend[1] (tend) ***vt.*** ⟦see ATTEND⟧ 1 to take care of 2 to manage or operate

tend[2] (tend) ***vi.*** ⟦< L *tendere,* to stretch⟧ 1 to be inclined, disposed, etc. (*to*) 2 to be directed (*to* or *toward*)

tend·en·cy (ten′dən sē) ***n.***, *pl.* **-cies** ⟦see prec.⟧ 1 an inclination to move or act in a particular direction or way 2 a course toward some object

ten·den·tious (ten den′shəs) ***adj.*** ⟦< Ger *tendenz,* TENDENCY⟧ advancing a definite point of view /*tendentious* writings/ —**ten·den′tious·ly** ***adv.***

ten·der[1] (ten′dər) ***adj.*** ⟦< L *tener,* soft⟧ 1 soft and easily chewed, broken, cut, etc. 2 physically weak 3 immature 4 that requires careful handling 5 gentle or light 6 acutely sensitive, as to pain 7 sensitive to emotions, others' feelings, etc. —**ten′der·ly** ***adv.*** —**ten′der·ness** ***n.***

ten·der[2] (ten′dər) ***vt.*** ⟦see TEND[2]⟧ to offer formally —***n.*** 1 a formal offer 2 money, etc. offered in payment

tend·er[3] (ten′dər) ***n.*** 1 one who tends something 2 a small ship for supplying a larger one 3 a railroad car, attached behind, and carrying fuel and water for a steam locomotive

ten′der·foot′ ***n.***, *pl.* **-foots′** or **-feet′** 1 a newcomer to ranching in the West, unused to hardships 2 any novice

ten′der·heart′ed ***adj.*** quick to feel pity or compassion

ten·der·ize (ten′dər īz′) ***vt.*** **-ized′**, **-iz′ing** to make (meat) tender

ten′der·loin′ ***n.*** the tenderest part of a loin of beef, pork, etc.

ten·di·ni·tis (ten′də nīt′is) ***n.*** inflammation of a tendon

ten·don (ten′dən) ***n.*** ⟦< Gr *teinein,* to stretch⟧ any of the inelastic cords of tough, connective tissue by which muscles are attached to bones, etc.

ten·dril (ten′drəl) ***n.*** ⟦prob. ult. < L *tener,* delicate⟧ a threadlike, clinging part of a climbing plant

ten·e·ment (ten′ə mənt) ***n.*** ⟦< L *tenere,* to hold⟧ 1 a room or suite tenanted as a separate dwelling 2 a building divided into tenements; now specif., one that is run-down, overcrowded, etc.: also **tenement house**

ten·et (ten′it) ***n.*** ⟦L, he holds⟧ a principle, doctrine, or belief held as a truth, as by some group

Ten·nes·see (ten′ə sē′) State of the east central U.S.: 42,244 sq. mi.; pop. 4,591,000; cap. Nashville: abbrev. **Tenn.** —**Ten′nes·se′an** ***adj., n.***

ten·nis (ten′is) ***n.*** ⟦prob. < OFr *tener,* hold (imperative)⟧ a game in which players in a marked area (**tennis court**) hit a ball back and forth with rackets over a net

tennis elbow inflammation of the elbow tendons, caused by strain

tennis shoe a sneaker

Ten·ny·son (ten′i sən), **Al·fred** (al′frəd) 1809-92; Eng. poet

ten·on (ten′ən) ***n.*** ⟦ult. < L *tenere,* to hold⟧ a projecting part cut on the end of a piece of wood for insertion into a mortise to make a joint

ten·or (ten′ər) ***n.*** ⟦< L *tenere,* to hold⟧ 1 general tendency 2 general meaning; drift 3 *a)* the highest regular adult male singing voice *b)* a singer with such a voice *c)* a part for a tenor

ten′pins′ ***n.pl.*** 1 [*with sing. v.*] the game of bowling in which ten pins are used 2 the pins

tense[1] (tens) ***adj.*** **tens′er**, **tens′est** ⟦< L *tendere,* to stretch⟧ 1 stretched tight; taut 2 feeling or showing tension —***vt., vi.*** **tensed**, **tens′ing** to make or become tense —**tense′ly** ***adv.*** —**tense′ness** or **ten·si·ty** (ten′sə tē) ***n.***

tense[2] (tens) ***n.*** ⟦< L *tempus,* time⟧ any of the forms of a verb that show the time of its action or existence

ten·sile (ten′sil; *also,* -sīl′) ***adj.*** 1 of, undergoing, or exerting tension 2 capable of being stretched

ten·sion (ten′shən) ***n.*** 1 a tensing or being

tensed 2 mental or nervous strain 3 a state of strained relations due to mutual hostility 4 VOLTAGE 5 stress on a material produced by the pull of forces causing extension

tent (tent) ***n.*** ⟦< L *tendere,* to stretch⟧ a portable shelter made of canvas, etc. stretched over poles **—*vi.*, *vt.*** to lodge in a tent or tents

ten·ta·cle (ten′tə kəl) ***n.*** ⟦< L *tentare,* to touch⟧ a long, slender, flexible growth about the head of some invertebrates, used to grasp, feel, etc.

ten·ta·tive (ten′tə tiv) ***adj.*** ⟦< L *tentare,* to try⟧ made, done, etc. as a test or experiment **—ten′ta·tive·ly *adv.***

ten·ter·hook (ten′tər ho͝ok′) ***n.*** ⟦< L *tendere,* to stretch + HOOK⟧ any of the hooked nails holding cloth stretched on a drying frame (**tenter**) **—on tenterhooks** in anxious suspense

tenth (tenth) ***adj.*** ⟦OE *teogotha*⟧ preceded by nine others in a series; 10th **—*n.*** 1 the one following the ninth 2 any of the ten equal parts of something; $\frac{1}{10}$ 3 a tenth of a gallon

ten·u·ous (ten′yo͞o əs, -yə wəs) ***adj.*** ⟦< L *tenuis,* thin⟧ 1 slender or fine, as a fiber 2 rare, as air at high altitudes 3 not substantial; flimsy /*tenuous* evidence/

ten·ure (ten′yər, -yoor) ***n.*** ⟦< Medieval Fr < *tenir,* to hold⟧ 1 the act or right of holding property, an office, etc. 2 the length of time, or the conditions under which, something is held 3 the status of holding one's position on a permanent basis, granted to teachers, etc.

TEPEE

te·pee (tē′pē) ***n.*** ⟦< AmInd *t^hípi,* dwelling⟧ a cone-shaped tent used by some North American Indians

tep·id (tep′id) ***adj.*** ⟦< L *tepidus*⟧ 1 lukewarm 2 lacking enthusiasm

te·qui·la (tə kē′lə) ***n.*** ⟦< AmInd (Mexico) *Tuiquila,* region in Mexico⟧ an alcoholic liquor of Mexico, distilled from an agave mash

ter·cen·te·nar·y (tər sen′tə ner′ē, tʉr′sen ten′ər ē) ***adj., n., pl.* -ies** ⟦L *ter,* three times + CENTENARY⟧ TRICENTENNIAL

term (tʉrm) ***n.*** ⟦< L *terminus,* a limit⟧ 1 a set date, as for payment, etc. 2 a set period of time /school *term, term* of office/ 3 [*pl.*] conditions of a contract, etc. 4 [*pl.*] mutual relationship between persons /on speaking *terms*/ 5 a word or phrase, esp. as used in some science, art, etc. 6 [*pl.*] words; speech /unkind *terms*/ 7 *Math.* *a*) either quantity of a fraction or a ratio *b*) each quantity in a series or algebraic expression **—*vt.*** to call by a term; name **—bring** (or **come**) **to terms** to force into (or arrive at) an agreement

ter·ma·gant (tʉr′mə gənt) ***n.*** ⟦< OFr *Tervagant,* imaginary Muslim deity⟧ a quarrelsome, scolding woman

ter·mi·na·ble (tʉr′mi nə bəl) ***adj.*** that can be, or is, terminated

ter·mi·nal (tʉr′mə nəl) ***adj.*** ⟦L *terminalis*⟧ 1 of, at, or forming the end or extremity 2 concluding; final 3 close to causing death /*terminal* cancer/ 4 of or at the end of a transportation line **—*n.*** 1 an end; extremity 2 a connective point on an electric circuit 3 either end of a transportation line, or a main station on it 4 a device, usually with a keyboard and video display, for putting data in, or getting it from, a computer

ter·mi·nate (tʉr′mə nāt′) ***vt.* -nat′ed, -nat′·ing** ⟦< L *terminus,* a limit⟧ 1 to form the end of 2 to put an end to; stop 3 to dismiss from employment; fire **—*vi.*** 1 to come to an end 2 to have its end (*in* something) **—ter′mi·na′tion *n.***

ter·mi·nol·o·gy (tʉr′mə näl′ə jē) ***n., pl.* -gies** the terms used in a specific science, art, etc.

term insurance life insurance that expires after a specified period

ter·mi·nus (tʉr′mə nəs) ***n., pl.* -ni′** (-nī′) or **-nus·es** ⟦L, a limit⟧ 1 a limit 2 an end; extremity or goal 3 [Chiefly Brit., etc.] either end of a transportation line

ter·mite (tʉr′mīt′) ***n.*** ⟦< L *tarmes,* woodboring worm⟧ a social insect very destructive to wooden structures

tern (tʉrn) ***n.*** ⟦< ON *therna*⟧ a gull-like seabird with webbed feet and a straight bill

ter·race (ter′əs) ***n.*** ⟦< L *terra,* earth⟧ 1 a raised, flat mound of earth with sloping sides, esp. one in a series on a hillside 2 an unroofed, paved area, between a house and lawn 3 a row of houses on ground above street level **—*vt.* -raced, -rac·ing** to form into a terrace or terraces

ter·ra cot·ta (ter′ə kät′ə) ⟦It, lit., baked earth⟧ a hard, brown-red earthenware, or its color

ter·ra fir·ma (ter′ə fʉr′mə) ⟦L⟧ firm earth

ter·rain (ter′rān′, tə rān′) ***n.*** ⟦< L *terra,* earth⟧ a tract of ground, esp. with regard to its fitness for some use

ter·ra·pin (ter′ə pin) ***n.*** ⟦< Algonquian⟧ 1 any of various terrestrial, freshwater, or tidewater turtles 2 its edible flesh

ter·rar·i·um (tə rer′ē əm) ***n., pl.* -i·ums** or **-i·a** (-ə) ⟦< L *terra,* earth + *-arium,* as in *aquarium*⟧ an enclosure, as of glass, in which small plants are grown or small land animals are kept

ter·raz·zo (tə rät′sō, te-; tə raz′ō) ***n.*** ⟦It⟧ flooring of small chips of marble set in cement and polished

ter·res·tri·al (tə res′trē əl) ***adj.*** ⟦< L *terra,* earth⟧ 1 worldly; mundane 2 of the earth 3 consisting of land, not water 4 living on land

ter·ri·ble (ter′ə bəl) ***adj.*** ⟦< L *terrere,* frighten⟧ 1 causing terror; dreadful 2 extreme; intense 3 [Colloq.] very unpleasant, etc. **—ter′ri·bly *adv.***

ter·ri·er (ter′ē ər) ***n.*** ⟦< Medieval Fr (*chien*) *terrier,* hunting (dog)⟧ any of several breeds of small and typically aggressive dog

ter·rif·ic (tə rif′ik) ***adj.*** ⟦< L *terrere,*

frighten ⟧ 1 causing great fear 2 [Colloq.] *a)* very great, intense, etc. *b)* unusually fine, admirable, etc.

ter·ri·fy (ter′ə fī′) ***vt.*** **-fied′, -fy′ing** to fill with terror; frighten greatly

ter·ri·to·ry (ter′ə tôr′ē) ***n., pl.*** **-ries** ⟦< L *terra,* earth⟧ 1 an area under the jurisdiction of a nation, ruler, etc. 2 a part of a country or empire that does not have full status 3 any large tract of land 4 an assigned area 5 a sphere of action, thought, etc. —**ter′ri·to′ri·al** ***adj.***

ter·ror (ter′ər) ***n.*** ⟦< L *terrere,* frighten⟧ 1 intense fear 2 *a)* one that causes intense fear *b)* the quality of causing such fear

ter′ror·ism′ ***n.*** the use of force or threats to intimidate, etc., esp. as a political policy —**ter′ror·ist** ***n., adj.***

ter′ror·ize′ (-īz′) ***vt.*** **-ized′, -iz′ing** 1 to terrify 2 to coerce, make submit, etc. by filling with terror

ter·ry (ter′ē) ***n.*** ⟦prob. < Fr *tirer,* to draw⟧ cloth having a pile of uncut loops, esp. cotton cloth used for toweling Also **terry cloth**

terse (turs) ***adj.*** **ters′er, ters′est** ⟦L *tersus,* wiped off⟧ free of superfluous words; concise; succinct —**terse′ly** ***adv.*** —**terse′ness** ***n.***

ter·ti·ar·y (tur′shē er′ē) ***adj.*** ⟦< L *tertius,* third⟧ third in order

tes·sel·late (tes′ə lāt′) ***vt.*** **-lat′ed, -lat′ing** ⟦< L *tessella,* little square stone⟧ to lay out in a mosaic pattern of small, square blocks

test (test) ***n.*** ⟦< OFr, assaying cup⟧ 1 *a)* an examination or trial, as of something's value *b)* the method or a criterion used in this 2 an event, etc. that tries one's qualities 3 a set of questions, etc. for determining one's knowledge, etc. 4 *Chem.* a trial or reaction for identifying a substance —***vt.*** to subject to a test; try —***vi.*** to be rated by a test —**test′er** ***n.***

tes·ta·ment (tes′ tə mənt) ***n.*** ⟦< L *testis,* a witness⟧ 1 [T-] either of the two parts of the Bible, the *Old Testament* and the *New Testament* 2 *a)* a testimonial *b)* an affirmation of beliefs 3 *Law* a will —**tes′ta·men′ta·ry** (-men′tə rē) ***adj.***

tes·tate (tes′tāt′) ***adj.*** ⟦< L *testari,* make a will⟧ having left a legally valid will

tes·ta·tor (tes′tāt′ər, tes tāt′-) ***n.*** one who has made a will

tes·ti·cle (tes′ti kəl) ***n.*** ⟦< L *testis*⟧ either of two male sex glands

tes·ti·fy (tes′tə fī′) ***vi.*** **-fied′, -fy′ing** ⟦< L *testis,* a witness + *facere,* to make⟧ 1 to give evidence, esp. under oath in court 2 to serve as evidence —***vt.*** 1 to affirm; declare, esp. under oath in court 2 to indicate

tes·ti·mo·ni·al (tes′tə mō′nē əl) ***n.*** 1 a statement recommending a person or thing 2 something given or done to show gratitude or appreciation

tes·ti·mo·ny (tes′tə mō′nē) ***n., pl.*** **-nies** ⟦< L *testis,* a witness⟧ 1 a statement made under oath to establish a fact 2 any declaration 3 any form of evidence; proof

tes·tis (tes′tis) ***n., pl.*** **-tes′** (-tēz′) ⟦L⟧ TESTICLE

tes·tos·ter·one (tes täs′tər ōn′) ***n.*** ⟦see TESTICLE⟧ a male sex hormone

test tube a tube of thin, transparent glass closed at one end, used in chemical experiments, etc.

tes·ty (tes′tē) ***adj.*** **-ti·er, -ti·est** ⟦< L *testa,* the head⟧ irritable; touchy

tet·a·nus (tet′′n əs) ***n.*** ⟦< Gr *tetanos,* spasm⟧ an acute infectious disease, often fatal, caused by a toxin and characterized by spasmodic contractions and rigidity of muscles

tête-à-tête (tāt′ə tāt′) ***n.*** ⟦Fr, lit., head-to-head⟧ a private conversation between two people

teth·er (teth′ər) ***n.*** ⟦< ON *tjōthr*⟧ 1 a rope or chain fastened to an animal to keep it from roaming 2 the limit of one's abilities, resources, etc. —***vt.*** to fasten with a tether

tet·ra (te′trə) ***n.*** ⟦< ModL⟧ a brightly colored, tropical American fish

tetra- ⟦Gr < *tettares,* four⟧ *combining form* four

tet·ra·cy·cline (te′trə sī′klin, -klīn′) ***n.*** a yellow, crystalline compound, used as an antibiotic

tet·ra·he·dron (te′trə hē′drən) ***n., pl.*** **-drons** or **-dra** (-drə) ⟦see TETRA- & -HEDRON⟧ a solid figure with four triangular faces

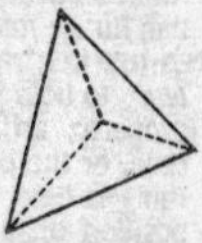

TETRAHEDRON

te·tram·e·ter (te tram′ət ər, tə-) ***n.*** ⟦see TETRA- & METER[1]⟧ 1 a line of verse containing four metrical feet 2 verse consisting of tetrameters

Teu·ton·ic (too̅ tän′ik) ***adj.*** designating or of a group of north European peoples, esp. the Germans —**Teu·ton** (too̅t′ən, too̅t′′n) ***n.***

Tex·as (teks′əs) SW State of the U.S.: 267,339 sq. mi.; pop. 14,228,000; cap. Austin: abbrev. **Tex.** —**Tex′an** ***adj., n.***

text (tekst) ***n.*** ⟦< L *texere,* to weave⟧ 1 the actual words of an author, as distinguished from notes, etc. 2 any form in which a written work exists 3 the principal matter on a printed page, as distinguished from notes, headings, etc. 4 *a)* a Biblical passage used as the topic of a sermon, etc. *b)* any topic or subject 5 *short for* TEXTBOOK —**tex·tu·al** (teks′cho̅o̅ əl) ***adj.***

text′book′ ***n.*** a book giving instructions in a subject of study

tex·tile (teks′tīl′, -til) ***adj.*** ⟦see TEXT⟧ 1 having to do with weaving 2 that has been or can be woven —***n.*** 1 a woven or knitted fabric; cloth 2 raw material suitable for this

tex·ture (teks′chər) ***n.*** ⟦< L *texere,* to weave⟧ 1 the character of a fabric, determined by the arrangement, size, etc. of its threads 2 the arrangement of the constituent parts of anything —**tex′tur·al** ***adj.***

-th[1] ⟦OE⟧ *suffix* 1 the act of _____ing *[growth]* 2 the state or quality of being or having *[wealth]*

-th[2] ⟦< OE⟧ *suffix* forming ordinal numerals *[fourth, ninth]*

Th *Chem. symbol for* thorium

Thai (tī) ***n.*** 1 *pl.* **Thais** or **Thai** a native or inhabitant of Thailand 2 the language of Thailand 3 *alt. sp. of* TAI —***adj.*** of Thailand, its people, culture, etc.

Thai·land (tī′land′) country in SE Asia: 198,456 sq. mi.; pop. 50,100,000
thal·a·mus (thal′ə məs) ***n., pl.*** **-mi′** (-mī′) ⟦< Gr *thalamos*, inner chamber⟧ a mass of gray matter at the base of the brain, involved in the transmission of certain sensations
tha·lid·o·mide (thə lid′ə mīd′) ***n.*** a drug formerly used as a sedative, but found to cause severe birth deformities when taken in pregnancy
thal·lo·phyte (thal′ə fīt′) ***n.*** ⟦< Gr *thallos*, young shoot + *phyton*, a plant⟧ any of a large group of plants lacking true roots, leaves, or stems, as the fungi, lichens, and most algae
Thames (temz) river in S England, flowing through London into the North Sea
than (*th*an; *unstressed*, *th*ən) ***conj.*** ⟦OE *thenne*⟧ introducing the second element in a comparison /A is taller *than* B/
thank (thaŋk) ***vt.*** ⟦OE *thancian*⟧ **1** to give one's thanks to **2** to hold responsible; blame: an ironic use —**thank you** *short for* I thank you
thank′ful ***adj.*** feeling or expressing thanks —**thank′ful·ly** ***adv.***
thank′less ***adj.*** **1** not feeling or expressing thanks, ungrateful **2** unappreciated —**thank′less·ly** ***adv.***
thanks ***n.pl.*** an expression of gratitude —***interj.*** I thank you —**thanks to 1** thanks be given to **2** on account of; because of
thanks′giv′ing ***n.*** **1** a formal public expression of thanks to God **2** [T-] an annual U.S. holiday observed on the fourth Thursday of November
that (*th*at) ***pron., pl.*** **those** ⟦OE *thæt*⟧ **1** the person or thing mentioned /*that* is John/ **2** the farther one or other one /this is better than *that*/ **3** who, whom, or which /the road *that* we took/ **4** where /the place *that* I saw her/ **5** when /the year *that* I was born/ —***adj., pl.*** **those 1** designating the one mentioned /*that* man is John/ **2** designating the farther one or other one /this house is larger than *that* one/ —***conj.*** *used to introduce:* **1** a noun clause /*that* she's gone is obvious/ **2** an adverbial clause expressing purpose /they died *that* we might live/, result /he ran so fast *that* I lost him/, or cause /I'm sorry *that* I won/ **3** an elliptical sentence expressing surprise, desire, etc. /oh, *that* she were here!/ —***adv.*** to that extent; so /I can't see *that* far/ —**at that** [Colloq.] **1** at that point: also **with that 2** even so —**that is 1** to be specific **2** in other words
thatch (thach) ***n.*** ⟦OE *thæc*⟧ **1** a roof of straw, rushes, etc. **2** material for such a roof: also **thatch′ing** —***vt.*** to cover as with thatch
thaw (thô) ***vi.*** ⟦OE *thawian*⟧ **1** *a)* to melt (said of ice, snow, etc.) *b)* to pass to a state that is not frozen (said of frozen foods) **2** to become warmer so that snow, etc. melts **3** to lose one's coldness of manner —***vt.*** to cause to thaw —***n.*** **1** a thawing **2** a spell of weather warm enough to allow thawing
THC ⟦t(etra)h(ydro)c(annabinol)⟧ the principal and most active chemical in marijuana
ThD or **Th.D.** ⟦L *Theologiae Doctor*⟧ Doctor of Theology
the (*th*ə; *before vowels th*ē, *th*i) ***adj., definite article*** ⟦< OE *se* with *th-* from other forms⟧ *the* (as opposed to *a, an*) refers to: **1** a particular person or thing /*the* story ended, *the* President/ **2** a person or thing considered generically /*the* cow is a domestic animal, *the* poor/ —***adv.*** **1** that much /*the* better to see you/ **2** by how much . . . by that much /*the* sooner *the* better/
the·a·ter or **the·a·tre** (thē′ə tər) ***n.*** ⟦< Gr *theasthai*, to view⟧ **1** a place or building where plays, operas, films, etc. are presented **2** any similar place with banked rows of seats **3** any scene of events **4** *a)* the dramatic art *b)* the theatrical world
the·at·ri·cal (thē a′tri kəl) ***adj.*** **1** having to do with the theater **2** dramatic; esp. (in disparagement), melodramatic —**the·at′ri·cal·ly** ***adv.***
thee (*th*ē) ***pron.*** ⟦OE *the*⟧ *the objective case of* THOU
theft (theft) ***n.*** ⟦OE *thiefth*⟧ the act or an instance of stealing; larceny
their (*th*er) ***poss. pronominal adj.*** ⟦< ON *theirra*⟧ of, belonging to, made by, or done by them
theirs (*th*erz) ***pron.*** that or those belonging to them /*theirs* are better/
the·ism (thē′iz′əm) ***n.*** ⟦< Gr *theos*, god⟧ **1** belief in a god or gods **2** MONOTHEISM —**the′ist** ***n., adj.*** —**the·is′tic** ***adj.***
them (*th*em) ***pron.*** ⟦< ON *theim*⟧ *objective case of* THEY
theme (thēm) ***n.*** ⟦< Gr *thema*, what is laid down⟧ **1** a topic, as of an essay **2** a short essay **3** a short melody used as the subject of a musical composition **4** a recurring or identifying song in a film, musical, radio or TV series, etc.: also **theme song** —**the·mat·ic** (thē mat′ik) ***adj.***
them·selves (*th*em selvz′) ***pron.*** **1** *intesive form of* THEY /they went *themselves*/ **2** *reflexive form of* THEY /they hurt *themselves*/
then (*th*en) ***adv.*** ⟦see THAN⟧ **1** at that time /he was young *then*/ **2** next in time or order /he took his hat and *then* left/ **3** in that case; accordingly /if she read it, *then* she knows/ **4** besides; moreover /he likes to walk, and *then* it's good exercise/ **5** at another time /now it's warm, *then* freezing/ —***adj.*** being such at that time /the *then* director/ —***n.*** that time /by *then*, they were gone/
thence (*th*ens, thens) ***adv.*** ⟦OE *thanan*⟧ [Archaic] **1** from that place **2** from that time; thenceforth **3** therefore
thence′forth′ ***adv.*** from that time onward; thereafter Also **thence′for′ward**
the·oc·ra·cy (thē äk′rə sē) ***n., pl.*** **-cies** ⟦< Gr *theos*, god + *kratos*, power⟧ (a) government by a person or persons claiming to rule with divine authority
the·o·lo·gi·an (thē′ə lō′jən, -jē ən) ***n.*** a student of or specialist in theology
the·ol·o·gy (thē äl′ə jē) ***n., pl.*** **-gies** ⟦< Gr *theos*, god + *logos*, word⟧ the study of God and of religious doctrines and matters of divinity —**the′o·log′i·cal** (-ə läj′i kəl) ***adj.***
the·o·rem (thē′ə rəm) ***n.*** ⟦< Gr *theōrein*, to view⟧ **1** a proposition that can be proved from accepted premises; law or principle **2**

Math., Physics a proposition embodying something to be proved

the·o·ret·i·cal (thē'ə ret'i kəl) *adj.* 1 limited to or based on theory; hypothetical 2 tending to theorize; speculative Also **the'o·ret'ic** —**the'o·ret'i·cal·ly** *adv.*

the·o·rize (thē'ə rīz') *vi.* **-rized', -riz'ing** to form a theory or theories; speculate —**the'o·re·ti'cian** (-rə tish'ən) or **the'o·rist** (-rist) *n.*

the·o·ry (thē'ə rē, thir'ē) *n., pl.* **-ries** ⟦< Gr *theōrein*, to view⟧ 1 a speculative plan 2 a formulation of underlying principles of certain observed phenomena which has been verified to some degree 3 the principles of an art or science rather than its practice 4 a conjecture; guess

the·os·o·phy (thē äs'ə fē) *n.* ⟦< Gr *theos*, god + *sophos*, wise⟧ [*also* **T-**] a religious or semireligious set of occult beliefs rejecting Christian theology, and held to be based on a special mystical insight —**the'o·soph'ic** (-ə säf'ik) *adj.* —**the'o·soph'i·cal·ly** *adv.* —**the·os'o·phist** *n.*

ther·a·peu·tic (ther'ə pyōōt'ik) *adj.* ⟦< Gr *therapeuein*, to nurse⟧ serving to cure or heal or to preserve health

ther'a·peu'tics *n.pl.* [*with sing. v.*] the branch of medicine that deals with the treatment of disease; therapy

ther'a·py (-pē) *n., pl.* **-pies** ⟦see THERAPEUTIC⟧ the treatment of any physical or mental disorder by medical or physical means, usually excluding surgery —**ther'a·pist** *n.*

there (*th*er) *adv.* ⟦OE *ther*⟧ 1 at or in that place: often used as an intensive /Mary *there* is a good player/ 2 to or into that place /go *there*/ 3 at that point; then /*there* I paused/ 4 in that respect /*there* you are wrong/ *There* is also used in impersonal constructions in which the real subject follows the verb /*there* is little time/ —*n.* that place /we left *there* at six/ —*interj.* an exclamation of defiance, satisfaction, sympathy, etc. —**(not) all there** [Colloq.] (not) mentally sound

there'a·bouts' (-ə bouts') *adv.* 1 near that place 2 near that time, number, degree, etc. Also **there'a·bout'**

there·af'ter *adv.* from then on

there·at' *adv.* 1 at that place; there 2 at that time 3 for that reason

there·by' *adv.* 1 by that means 2 connected with that

there·for' *adv.* for this or that; for it

there'fore' (-fôr') *adv.* for this or that reason; hence

there·in' *adv.* 1 in or into that place 2 in that matter, detail, etc.

there·of' *adv.* 1 of that 2 from that as a cause, reason, etc.

there·on' *adv.* 1 on that or it 2 THEREUPON

there·to' *adv.* to that place, thing, etc. Also **there·un'to** (-un'tōō; *th*er'un tōō')

there'to·fore' *adv.* until that time

there'up·on' *adv.* 1 immediately following that 2 as a consequence of that 3 concerning that subject, etc.

there·with' *adv.* 1 along with that 2 immediately thereafter

ther·mal (thur'məl) *adj.* ⟦< Gr *thermē*, heat⟧ 1 having to do with heat 2 designating a loosely knitted material with air spaces for insulation —*n. Meteorol.* a rising column of warm air

thermal pollution the discharge of heated liquid or air into lakes, rivers, etc., as by industries, that is harmful to the ecosystems

thermo- ⟦< Gr *thermē*, heat⟧ *combining form* heat

ther·mo·dy·nam·ics (thur'mō dī nam'iks) *n.pl.* [*with sing. v.*] the branch of physics dealing with the transformation of heat to and from other forms of energy —**ther'mo·dy·nam'ic** *adj.*

ther·mom·e·ter (thər mäm'ət ər) *n.* ⟦see THERMO- & -METER⟧ an instrument for measuring temperatures, as a graduated glass tube in which mercury, etc. rises or falls as it expands or contracts from changes in temperature

ther·mo·nu·cle·ar (thur'mō nōō'klē ər) *adj. Physics* 1 designating a reaction in which isotopes of a light element fuse, at extreme heat, into heavier nuclei 2 of or using the heat released in nuclear fusion

ther·mo·plas·tic (thur'mō plas'tik) *adj.* soft and moldable when subjected to heat: said of certain plastics —*n.* a thermoplastic substance

ther·mos (thur'məs) *n.* ⟦orig. a trademark < Gr *thermos*, hot⟧ a bottle or jug for keeping liquids at almost their original temperature: in full **thermos bottle** (or **jug**)

ther·mo·stat (thur'mə stat') *n.* ⟦THERMO- + -STAT⟧ an apparatus for regulating temperature, esp. one that automatically controls a heating or cooling unit

the·sau·rus (thi sô'rəs) *n., pl.* **-ri'** (-rī') or **-rus·es** ⟦< Gr *thēsauros*, a treasure⟧ a book of synonyms and antonyms

these (*th*ēz) *pron., adj. pl. of* THIS

The·se·us (thē'sē əs) *Gr. Legend* a hero who kills the Minotaur

the·sis (thē'sis) *n., pl.* **-ses'** (-sēz') ⟦< Gr *tithenai*, to put⟧ 1 a proposition to be defended in argument 2 a research paper, esp. one written by a candidate for a master's degree

Thes·pi·an (thes'pē ən) *adj.* ⟦after *Thespis*, ancient Gr poet⟧ [*often* **t-**] having to do with the drama; dramatic —*n.* [*often* **t-**] an actor or actress

the·ta (thāt'ə, thēt'-) *n.* the eighth letter of the Greek alphabet (Θ, θ, ϑ)

thews (thyōōz) *n.pl., sing.* **thew** ⟦< OE *theaw*, habit⟧ muscles or sinews

they (*th*ā) *pron., sing.* **he, she,** or **it** ⟦< ON *thei-r*⟧ 1 the persons, animals, or things previously mentioned 2 people generally or indefinitely /*they* say it's so/

thi·a·mine (thī'ə mēn', -min) *n.* ⟦ult. < Gr *theion*, brimstone + (VIT)AMIN⟧ a white, crystalline B vitamin, found in cereal, egg yolk, liver, etc.; vitamin B_1 Also **thi'a·min** (-min)

thick (thik) *adj.* ⟦OE *thicce*⟧ 1 of relatively great extent from side to side 2 measured between opposite surfaces /one inch *thick*/ 3 close and abundant /*thick* hair/ 4 viscous /*thick* oil/ 5 dense /*thick* smoke/ 6 husky; hoarse; blurred /*thick* speech/ 7 [Colloq.] stupid 8 [Colloq.] very friendly —*n.* the thickest part —**thick'ly** *adv.* —**thick'ness** *n.*

thick'en *vt., vi.* 1 to make or become thick or thicker 2 to make or become more complex —**thick'en·ing** *n.*

thick·et (thik'it) *n.* ⟦see THICK⟧ a thick growth of shrubs or small trees

thick'set' *adj.* 1 planted thickly or closely 2 thick in body; stocky

thick'-skinned' *adj.* 1 having a thick skin 2 insensitive, as to insult

thief (thēf) *n., pl.* **thieves** (thēvz) ⟦OE *theof*⟧ one who steals

thieve (thēv) *vt., vi.* **thieved, thiev'ing** to steal —**thiev'ish** *adj.*

thiev'er·y (-ər ē) *n., pl.* **-ies** the act or an instance of stealing; theft

thigh (thī) *n.* ⟦OE *theoh*⟧ that part of the leg between the knee and the hip

thigh'bone' *n.* the bone extending from the hip to the knee

thim·ble (thim'bəl) *n.* ⟦< OE *thuma,* a thumb⟧ a small cap worn to protect the finger that pushes the needle in sewing —**thim'ble·ful'**, *pl.* **-fuls'**, *n.*

thin (thin) *adj.* **thin'ner, thin'nest** ⟦OE *thynne*⟧ 1 of relatively little extent from side to side 2 lean; slender 3 not dense or compact /*thin* hair, *thin* smoke/ 4 very fluid or watery /*thin* soup/ 5 high-pitched and weak /a *thin* voice/ 6 sheer, as fabric 7 flimsy or unconvincing /a *thin* excuse/ 8 lacking substance, depth, etc.; weak —*vt., vi.* **thinned, thin'ning** to make or become thin or thinner —**thin'ly** *adv.* —**thin'ness** *n.*

thine (*th*īn) *pron.* ⟦OE *thin*⟧ *poss. form of* THOU —*poss. pronominal adj.* [Archaic] thy: used esp. before a vowel

thing (thiŋ) *n.* ⟦OE, council⟧ 1 any matter, affair, or concern 2 a happening, act, incident, event, etc. 3 a tangible or an inanimate object 4 an item, detail, etc. 5 *a*) [*pl.*] personal belongings *b*) a garment 6 [Colloq.] a person /poor *thing*/ 7 [Colloq.] a point of contention; issue 8 [Colloq.] an irrational liking, fear, etc. 9 [Colloq.] what one wants to do or is adept at /do one's own *thing*/ —**see things** [Colloq.] to have hallucinations

think (thiŋk) *vt.* **thought, think'ing** ⟦OE *thencan*⟧ 1 to form or have in the mind /*thinking* good thoughts/ 2 to judge; consider /many *think* her charming/ 3 to believe; expect /I *think* I can come/ —*vi.* 1 to use the mind; reason 2 to have an opinion, judgment, etc.: with *of* or *about* 3 to remember or consider: with *of* or *about* 4 to conceive (*of*) —**think up** to invent, plan, etc. by thinking —**think'er** *n.*

think tank (or **factory**) [Slang] a group or center organized to do intensive research and problem-solving

thin·ner (thin'ər) *n.* a substance added to paint, shellac, etc. to thin it

thin'-skinned' *adj.* 1 having a thin skin 2 sensitive, as to insult

third (thurd) *adj.* ⟦OE *thridda*⟧ preceded by two others in a series; 3d or 3rd —*adv.* in the third place, etc.: also **third'ly** —*n.* 1 the one following the second 2 any of the three equal parts of something; $\frac{1}{3}$ 3 the third forward gear of a transmission, providing more speed than second

third'-class' *adj.* 1 of the class, rank, etc. next below the second 2 of a low-cost mail class, as for advertisements —*adv.* by third-class mail or travel accommodations

third degree [Colloq.] cruel treatment and questioning to force a confession

third dimension 1 depth or solidity 2 the quality of seeming real

third person that form of a pronoun (as *she*) or verb (as *is*) that refers to the person(s) or thing(s) spoken of

third'-rate' *adj.* 1 third in quality or other rating 2 very poor

third world [*often* **T- W-**] the underdeveloped countries of the world

thirst (thurst) *n.* ⟦OE *thurst*⟧ 1 the discomfort caused by a need for drink 2 a strong desire; craving —*vi.* 1 to feel thirst 2 to have a strong desire or craving —**thirst'y, -i·er, -i·est,** *adj.* —**thirst'i·ly** *adv.*

thir·teen (thur'tēn') *adj., n.* ⟦OE *threotyne*⟧ three more than ten; 13; XIII —**thir'-teenth'** *adj., n.*

thir·ty (thurt'ē) *adj., n., pl.* **-ties** ⟦OE *thritig*⟧ three times ten; 30; XXX —**the thirties** the numbers or years, as of a century, from 30 through 39 —**thir'ti·eth** (-ith) *adj., n.*

this (*th*is) *pron., adj., pl.* **these** ⟦OE *thes*⟧ 1 (designating) the person or thing mentioned /*this* (man) is John/ 2 (designating) the nearer one or another one /*this* (desk) is older than that/ 3 (designating) something about to be presented /hear *this* (news)/ —*adv.* to this extent /it was *this* big/

THISTLE

this·tle (this'əl) *n.* ⟦OE *thistel*⟧ a plant with prickly leaves and white, purple, etc. flowers

this'tle·down' *n.* the down growing from the flowers of a thistle

thith·er (*thith*'ər, thith'-) *adv.* ⟦OE *thider*⟧ to or toward that place; there

tho or **tho'** (*th*ō) *conj., adv. short for* THOUGH

thole (thōl) *n.* ⟦OE *thol*⟧ one of a pair of pins set as an oarlock into the gunwale of a boat: also **thole'pin'**

-thon (thän) *suffix* -ATHON: used after a vowel /*radiothon*/

thong (thôŋ) *n.* ⟦OE *thwang*⟧ a narrow strip of leather, etc. used as a lace, strap, etc.

Thor (thôr) *Norse Myth.* the god of thunder, war, and strength

tho·rax (thôr'aks') *n., pl.* **-rax'es** or **-ra·ces'** (-ə sēz') ⟦< Gr⟧ 1 the part of the body between the neck and the abdomen; chest 2 the middle segment of an insect's body —**tho·rac·ic** (thō ras'ik, thô-) *adj.*

Tho·reau (thôr'ō, thə rō'), **Henry David** 1817-62; U.S. writer

tho·ri·um (thôr′ē əm, thō′rē-) ***n.*** ⟦< THOR⟧ a rare, grayish, radioactive chemical element, used as a nuclear fuel

thorn (thôrn) ***n.*** ⟦OE⟧ **1** *a)* a very short, hard, leafless stem with a sharp point *b)* any small tree or shrub bearing thorns **2** a source of constant trouble or irritation —**thorn′y, -i·er, -i·est,** ***adj.***

thor·ough (thur′ō) ***adj.*** ⟦var. of THROUGH⟧ **1** done or proceeding through to the end; complete **2** absolute /a *thorough* rascal/ **3** very exact, accurate, or painstaking —**thor′ough·ly** ***adv.*** —**thor′ough·ness** ***n.***

thor·ough·bred (thur′ō bred′, thur′ə-) ***adj.*** of pure stock; pedigreed —***n.*** [T-] any of a breed of light racehorses

thor′ough·fare′ (-fer′) ***n.*** a public street open at both ends, esp. a main highway

thor′ough·go′ing ***adj.*** very thorough

those (*th*ōz) ***adj., pron.*** *pl. of* THAT

thou (*th*ou) ***pron.*** ⟦OE *thu*⟧ you: in poetic or religious use

though (*th*ō) ***conj.*** ⟦OE *theah*⟧ **1** in spite of the fact that /*though* it rained, he went/ **2** and yet; however /they did it, *though* badly/ **3** even if /*though* he may fail, he will have tried/ —***adv.*** however; nevertheless /she sings well, *though*/

thought[1] (thôt) ***n.*** ⟦OE *thoht*⟧ **1** the act or process of thinking **2** the power of reasoning **3** an idea, concept, etc. **4** attention; consideration **5** a little; trifle /be a *thought* more careful/

thought[2] (thôt) ***vt., vi.*** *pt. & pp. of* THINK

thought′ful ***adj.*** **1** full of thought; meditative **2** considerate —**thought′ful·ly** ***adv.*** —**thought′ful·ness** ***n.***

thought′less ***adj.*** **1** not stopping to think; careless **2** ill-considered; rash **3** inconsiderate —**thought′less·ly** ***adv.*** —**thought′less·ness** ***n.***

thou·sand (thou′zənd) ***adj., n.*** ⟦OE *thusend*⟧ ten hundred; 1,000; M —**thou′sandth** (-zəndth) ***adj., n.***

thrall (thrôl) ***n.*** ⟦< ON *thræll*⟧ **1** a slave **2** slavery —**thrall′dom** or **thral′dom** (-dəm) ***n.***

thrash (thrash) ***vt., vi.*** ⟦OE *therscan*⟧ **1** THRESH **2** to beat; flog **3** to toss about violently **4** to defeat overwhelmingly —**thrash out** to settle by detailed discussion —**thrash′er** ***n.***

thrash′er ***n.*** ⟦E dial. *thresher*⟧ a thrushlike American songbird

thread (thred) ***n.*** ⟦OE *thræd*⟧ **1** a fine, stringlike length of spun cotton, silk, nylon, etc. used in sewing **2** any thin line, vein, etc. **3** something like a thread in its length, sequence, etc. /the *thread* of a story/ **4** the spiral ridge of a screw, nut, etc. —***vt.*** **1** to put a thread through (a needle, etc.) **2** to make (one's way) by twisting, weaving, etc. **3** to fashion a THREAD (sense 4) on or in —**thread′y, -i·er, -i·est,** ***adj.***

thread′bare′ ***adj.*** **1** worn down so that the threads show **2** wearing worn clothes; shabby **3** stale; trite

threat (thret) ***n.*** ⟦OE *threat,* pressure⟧ **1** an expression of intention to hurt, destroy, punish, etc. **2** an indication of, or a source of, imminent danger, harm, etc.

threat′en ***vt., vi.*** **1** to make threats, as of injury (against) **2** to indicate (danger, etc.) **3** to be a source of danger (to)

three (thrē) ***adj., n.*** ⟦OE *threo*⟧ one more than two; 3; III

three′-deck′er (-dek′ər) ***n.*** anything having three levels, layers, etc.

three′-di·men′sion·al ***adj.*** having or seeming to have depth or thickness

three′fold′ (-fōld′) ***adj.*** **1** having three parts **2** having three times as much or as many —***adv.*** three times as much or as many

three R's reading, writing, and arithmetic, regarded as the fundamentals of an education

three·score (thrē′skôr′) ***adj., n.*** sixty

thren·o·dy (thren′ə dē) ***n.,*** *pl.* **-dies** ⟦< Gr *thrēnos,* lamentation + *ōidē,* song⟧ a song of lamentation; dirge

thresh (thresh) ***vt., vi.*** ⟦ME *threschen*⟧ **1** to beat out (grain) from (husks), as with a flail **2** THRASH —**thresh′er** ***n.***

thresh·old (thresh′ōld′, -hōld′) ***n.*** ⟦OE *therscwold*⟧ **1** a length of wood, stone, etc. along the bottom of a doorway **2** the beginning point

threw (thrōō) ***vt.*** *pt. of* THROW

thrice (thrīs) ***adv.*** ⟦OE *thriwa*⟧ **1** three times **2** threefold

thrift (thrift) ***n.*** ⟦< ON *thrifa,* to grasp⟧ economy; frugality —**thrift′less** ***adj.*** —**thrift′y, -i·er, -i·est,** ***adj.*** —**thrift′i·ly** ***adv.*** —**thrift′i·ness** ***n.***

thrift shop a store where castoff clothes, etc. are sold, as for charity

thrill (thril) ***vi., vt.*** ⟦< OE, *thurh,* through⟧ **1** to feel or cause to feel emotional excitement **2** to quiver or cause to quiver; tremble —***n.*** **1** a thrilling or being thrilled **2** a tremor; quiver —**thrill′er** ***n.***

thrive (thrīv) ***vi.*** **thrived** or **throve, thrived** or **thriv·en** (thriv′′n), **thriv′ing** ⟦< ON *thrifa,* to grasp⟧ **1** to prosper or flourish; be successful **2** to grow vigorously or luxuriantly

throat (thrōt) ***n.*** ⟦OE *throte*⟧ **1** the front part of the neck **2** the upper passage from the mouth to the stomach and lungs **3** any narrow passage

throat′y ***adj.*** **-i·er, -i·est** produced in the throat, as some sounds; husky

throb (thräb) ***vi.*** **throbbed, throb′bing** ⟦ME *throbben*⟧ **1** to beat, pulsate, vibrate, etc., esp. strongly or fast **2** to feel excitement —***n.*** **1** a throbbing **2** a strong beat or pulsation

throe (thrō) ***n.*** ⟦prob. < OE *thrawu,* pain⟧ a spasm or pang of pain: *usually used in pl.* /the *throes* of childbirth, death *throes*/

throm·bo·sis (thräm bō′sis) ***n.*** ⟦< Gr *thrombos,* a clot⟧ coagulation of the blood in the heart or a blood vessel, forming a clot

throm′bus (-bəs) ***n.*** **-bi′** (-bī′) ⟦see prec.⟧ the clot attached at the site of thrombosis

throne (thrōn) ***n.*** ⟦< Gr *thronos,* a seat⟧ **1** the chair on which a king, cardinal, etc. sits on formal occasions **2** the power or rank of a king, etc. **3** a sovereign, ruler, etc.

throng (thrôŋ) ***n.*** ⟦OE *thringan,* to crowd⟧ **1** a crowd **2** any great number of things considered together —***vi.*** to gather together in a throng —***vt.*** to crowd into

throt·tle (thrät′′l) ***n.*** ⟦prob. dim. of THROAT⟧ the valve, or its control lever or pedal, that regulates the amount of fuel vapor entering an engine —*vt.* **-tled, -tling** 1 to choke; strangle 2 to censor or suppress 3 *a)* to reduce the flow of (fuel vapor, etc.) by means of a throttle *b)* to slow by this means

through (thro͞o) *prep.* ⟦OE *thurh*⟧ 1 in one side and out the other side of 2 in the midst of; among 3 by way of 4 around /touring *through* France/ 5 *a)* from the beginning to the end of *b)* up to and including 6 by means of 7 as a result of /done *through* error/ —*adv.* 1 in one side and out the other 2 from the beginning to the end 3 completely to the end /to see something *through*/ 4 completely /soaked *through*/ —*adj.* 1 extending from one place to another /a *through* street/ 2 traveling to the destination without stops /a *through* train/ 3 finished

through·out' *prep.* all the way through —*adv.* in every part; everywhere

through'way' *n. alt. sp. of* THRUWAY: see EXPRESSWAY

throve (thrōv) *vi. alt. pt. of* THRIVE

throw (thrō) *vt.* **threw, thrown, throw'·ing** ⟦OE *thrawan*, to twist⟧ 1 to send through the air by a rapid motion of the arm, etc. 2 to cause to fall; upset 3 to send rapidly /to *throw* troops into battle/ 4 to put suddenly into a specified state, etc. /*throw* into confusion/ 5 to move (a switch, etc.) so as to connect, disconnect, etc. 6 to direct, cast, etc. /*throw* a glance/ 7 [Colloq.] to lose (a game, etc.) deliberately 8 [Colloq.] to give (a party, etc.) 9 [Colloq.] to confuse or disconcert /the question *threw* him/ 10 [Colloq.] to have (a tantrum, etc.) —*vi.* to cast or hurl something —*n.* 1 the act of one who throws 2 the distance something is or can be thrown 3 a spread for a bed, etc. —**throw away** 1 to discard 2 to waste —**throw in** to add extra or free —**throw off** 1 to rid oneself of 2 to mislead or confuse 3 to expel, emit, etc. —**throw oneself at** to try very hard to win the love of —**throw out** 1 to discard 2 to reject or remove —**throw over** 1 to give up; abandon 2 to jilt —**throw together** to assemble hurriedly —**throw up** 1 to abandon 2 to vomit —**throw'er** *n.*

throw'a·way' *n.* a leaflet, handbill, etc. given out on the streets, at houses, etc. —*adj.* for discarding after use

throw'back' *n.* (a) reversion to an earlier or more primitive type

throw rug SCATTER RUG

thru (thro͞o) *prep., adv., adj. colloq. sp. of* THROUGH

thrum (thrum) *vt., vi.* **thrummed, thrum'·ming** ⟦echoic⟧ STRUM

thrush (thrush) *n.* ⟦OE *thrysce*⟧ any of a family of songbirds, including robins

thrust (thrust) *vt., vi.* **thrust, thrust'ing** ⟦< ON *thrysta*⟧ 1 to push with sudden force 2 to stab 3 to force or impose —*n.* 1 a sudden, forceful push 2 a stab 3 continuous pressure, as of a rafter against a wall 4 *a)* the driving force of a propeller *b)* the forward force produced by a jet or rocket engine 5 forward movement 6 the basic meaning; point

thru·way (thro͞o'wā') *n.* EXPRESSWAY

Thu·cyd·i·des (tho͞o sid'i dēz') *c.* 460-*c.* 400 B.C.; Athenian historian

thud (thud) *vi.* **thud'ded, thud'ding** ⟦prob. < OE *thyddan*, to strike⟧ to hit with a dull sound —*n.* a dull sound, as of an object dropping on a soft surface

thug (thug) *n.* ⟦Hindi *ṭhag*, swindler⟧ a brutal hoodlum, gangster, etc.

thumb (thum) *n.* ⟦OE *thuma*⟧ the short, thick digit of the hand —*vt.* 1 to handle, soil, etc. as with the thumb 2 [Colloq.] to solicit or get (a ride) in hitchhiking by signaling with the thumb —**all thumbs** clumsy —**under someone's thumb** under someone's influence

thumb'nail' *n.* the nail of the thumb —*adj.* very small, brief, or concise

thumb'screw' *n.* a screw that can be turned by the thumb and forefinger

thumb'tack' *n.* a tack with a wide, flat head that can be pressed into a board, etc. with the thumb

thump (thump) *n.* ⟦echoic⟧ 1 a blow with something heavy and blunt 2 the dull sound made by such a blow —*vt.* to strike with a thump —*vi.* 1 to hit or fall with a thump 2 to make a dull, heavy sound

thump'ing *adj.* 1 that thumps 2 [Colloq.] very large; whopping

thun·der (thun'dər) *n.* ⟦OE *thunor*⟧ 1 the sound following a flash of lightning 2 any similar sound —*vi.* to produce thunder or a sound like this —*vt.* to utter, etc. with a thundering sound —**thun'der·ous** *adj.*

thun'der·bolt' (-bōlt') *n.* 1 a flash of lightning and the accompanying thunder 2 something sudden and shocking, as bad news

thun'der·clap' *n.* a clap, or loud crash, of thunder

thun'der·cloud' *n.* a storm cloud charged with electricity and producing lightning and thunder

thun'der·head' *n.* a round mass of cumulus clouds appearing before a thunderstorm

thun'der·show'er *n.* a shower accompanied by thunder and lightning

thun'der·storm' *n.* a storm accompanied by thunder and lightning

thun'der·struck' *adj.* struck with amazement, terror, etc. Also **thun'der·strick'en** (-strik'ən)

Thurs·day (thurz'dā, -dē) *n.* ⟦< ON *Thorsdagr*, Thor's day⟧ the fifth day of the week Abbrev. **Thur.** or **Thurs.**

thus (*th*us) *adv.* ⟦OE⟧ 1 in this or that manner 2 to this or that degree or extent 3 therefore

thwack (thwak) *vt., n.* ⟦prob. echoic⟧ WHACK

thwart (thwôrt) *n.* ⟦< ON *thvert*, transverse⟧ a seat across a boat —*vt.* to obstruct, frustrate, or defeat (a person, plans, etc.)

thy (*th*ī) *poss. pronominal adj.* ⟦< ME *thin*⟧ of, belonging to, or done by thee: archaic or poetic var. of *your*

thyme (tīm) *n.* ⟦< Gr *thymon*⟧ a plant of the mint family, with leaves used for seasoning

thy·mo·sin (thī'mə sin) *n.* ⟦< Gr *thymos*, thymus & IN⟧ a hormone secreted by the thymus that stimulates the immune system

thy·mus (thī'məs) *n.* ⟦Gr *thymos*⟧ a ductless gland situated near the throat Also **thymus gland**

thy·roid (thī'roid') *adj.* ⟦< Gr *thyreos,* large shield⟧ designating or of a large ductless gland near the trachea, secreting a hormone which regulates growth —*n.* 1 the thyroid gland 2 an animal extract of this gland, used in treating goiter

thy·self (*th*ī self') *pron. reflexive or intensive form of* THOU

ti (tē) *n. Music* the seventh tone of the diatonic scale

Ti *Chem. symbol for* titanium

Ti·a Jua·na (tē'ə wän'ə, -hwän'ə) *old name of* TIJUANA

Tian·jin (tyen jin') seaport in NE China: pop. 5,100,000

ti·ar·a (tē er'ə, -ar'-, -är'-) *n.* ⟦< Gr⟧ 1 the pope's triple crown 2 a woman's crownlike headdress

Ti·ber (tī'bər) river in central Italy, flowing through Rome

Ti·bet (ti bet') plateau region of SW China, north of the Himalayas —**Ti·bet'an** *adj., n.*

tib·i·a (tib'ē ə) *n., pl.* **-i·ae'** (-ē ē') or **-i·as** ⟦L⟧ the inner and thicker of the two bones of the lower leg

tic (tik) *n.* ⟦Fr < ?⟧ any involuntary, regularly repeated, spasmodic contraction of a muscle

tick[1] (tik) *n.* ⟦prob. echoic⟧ 1 a light clicking sound, as of a clock 2 a mark made to check off items —*vi.* to make a tick or ticks —*vt.* to record, mark, or check by ticks

tick[2] (tik) *n.* ⟦OE *ticia*⟧ a wingless, bloodsucking insect that infests humans, cattle, etc.

tick[3] (tik) *n.* ⟦< ? L *theca,* a cover⟧ the cloth case of a mattress or pillow

tick'er *n.* 1 one that ticks 2 a telegraphic device that records stock market quotations, etc. on a paper tape (**ticker tape**) 3 [Slang] the heart

tick·et (tik'it) *n.* ⟦< obs. Fr *etiquet,* etiquette⟧ 1 a printed card, etc. that gives one a right, as to attend a theater 2 a license or certificate 3 a label on merchandise giving size, price, etc. 4 the list of candidates nominated by a political party 5 [Colloq.] a summons to court for a traffic violation —*vt.* 1 to label with a ticket 2 to give a ticket to

tick'ing *n.* strong cloth, often striped, used for casings of pillows, etc.

tick·le (tik'əl) *vt.* **-led, -ling** ⟦ME *tikelen*⟧ 1 to please, gratify, delight, etc. 2 to stroke lightly so as to cause involuntary twitching, laughter, etc. —*vi.* to have or cause a twitching or tingling sensation —*n.* a sensation of being tickled

tick·ler (tik'lər) *n.* a pad, file, etc. for noting terms to be remembered

tick'lish (-lish) *adj.* 1 sensitive to tickling 2 needing careful handling; precarious; delicate

tick-tack-toe or **tic-tac-toe** (tik'tak tō') *n.* a game for two, each marking X (or O) in turn in a nine-square block so as to complete any one row before the other can

tick·tock (tik'täk') *n.* the sound made by a clock or watch

tid·al (tīd''l) *adj.* of, having, or caused by, a tide or tides

tidal wave 1 *nontechnical term for* a tsunami or a similar huge wave caused by strong winds 2 any widespread movement, feeling, etc.

tid·bit (tid'bit') *n.* ⟦dial. *tid,* small object⟧ a choice bit of food, gossip, etc.

tid·dly·winks (tid'lē wiŋks') *n.pl.* ⟦< ?⟧ [*with sing. v.*] a game in which little disks are popped into a cup by pressing their edges with a larger disk

tide (tīd) *n.* ⟦OE *tid,* time⟧ 1 a period of time *[Eastertide]* 2 the alternate rise and fall, about twice a day, of the surface of oceans, seas, etc. caused by the attraction of the moon and sun 3 something that rises and falls like the tide 4 a stream, trend, etc. —*vi.* **tid'ed, tid'ing** to help along temporarily: with *over*

tide'land' *n.* 1 land covered when the tide is in 2 [*pl.*] land under the sea within territorial waters of a country

tide'wa'ter *n.* 1 water that is affected by the tide 2 a seaboard —*adj.* of or along a tidewater

ti·dings (tīd'iŋz) *n.pl.* ⟦OE *tidung*⟧ news; information

ti·dy (tīd'ē) *adj.* **-di·er, -di·est** ⟦<OE *tid,* time⟧ 1 neat in appearance, arrangement, etc.; orderly 2 [Colloq.] rather large *[a tidy sum]* —*vt., vi.* **-died, -dy·ing** to make tidy: often with *up* —**ti'di·ness** *n.*

tie (tī) *vt.* **tied, ty'ing** or **tie'ing** ⟦< OE *teag,* a rope⟧ 1 to bind, as with string, rope, etc. 2 to knot the laces, etc. of 3 to make (a knot) in 4 to bind in any way 5 to equal the score of, as in a contest —*vi.* to make an equal score, as in a contest —*n.* 1 a string, cord, etc. used to tie things 2 something that connects, binds, etc. 3 a necktie 4 a beam, rod, etc. that holds parts together 5 any of the crossbeams to which the rails of a railroad are fastened 6 *a)* an equality of scores, etc. *b)* a contest in which this occurs —*adj.* that has been made equal *[a tie score]* —**tie down** to confine; restrict —**tie up** 1 to wrap up and tie 2 to moor to a dock 3 to obstruct; hinder 4 to cause to be already in use, committed, etc.

tie'back' *n.* a band or ribbon used to tie curtains, etc. to one side

tie'break'er *n.* an additional game, period of play, etc. used to establish a winner from among those tied at the end of a contest

tie clasp a decorative clasp for fastening a necktie to the shirt Also **tie clip**

tie'-dye' (-dī') *n.* a method of dyeing designs on cloth by tying bunches of it so that the dye affects only exposed parts —*vt.* **-dyed', -dye'ing** to dye in this way

tie'-in' *n.* a connection or relationship

Tien·tsin (tyen tsin') *old form of* TIANJIN

tier (tir) *n.* ⟦< OFr *tire,* order⟧ any of a series of rows, as of seats, arranged one above or behind another

tie rod a rod connecting certain parts in the steering linkage of a motor vehicle

tie tack or **tie tac** a decorative pin fitted into a snap to fasten a necktie to a shirt

tie-up (tī'up') *n.* 1 a temporary stoppage of production, traffic, etc. 2 connection or relation

tiff (tif) ***n.*** ⟦< ?⟧ 1 a slight fit of anger 2 a slight quarrel; spat

ti·ger (tī′gər) ***n.*** ⟦< Gr *tigris*⟧ a large, fierce Asian cat, having a tawny coat striped with black

tight (tīt) ***adj.*** ⟦< OE *-thight*, strong⟧ 1 so compact in structure that water, air, etc. cannot pass through 2 drawn, packed, etc. closely together 3 fixed securely; firm 4 fully stretched; taut 5 fitting so closely as to be uncomfortable 6 difficult: esp. in **a tight corner** (or **squeeze,** etc.), a difficult situation 7 difficult to get; scarce 8 [Colloq.] stingy 9 [Slang] drunk —***adv.*** 1 securely 2 [Colloq.] soundly /sleep *tight*/ —**sit tight** to keep one's opinion or position and wait —**tight′ly** ***adv.*** —**tight′ness** ***n.***

tight′en ***vt., vi.*** to make or become tight or tighter —**tight′en·er** ***n.***

tight′fist′ed ***adj.*** stingy

tight′fit′ting ***adj.*** fitting very tight

tight′-lipped′ ***adj.*** secretive

tight′rope′ ***n.*** a tightly stretched rope on which acrobats perform

tights ***n.pl.*** a tightly fitting garment for the lower half of the body, as worn by acrobats, dancers, etc.

tight ship [Colloq.] an organization as efficient as a well-run ship

tight′wad′ ***n.*** ⟦TIGHT + *wad*, roll of money⟧ [Slang] a stingy person

ti·gress (tī′gris) ***n.*** a female tiger

Ti·gris (tī′gris) river flowing from east central Turkey to a juncture with the Euphrates in SE Iraq

Ti·jua·na (tē wän′ə, ·hwän′ə) city in NW Mexico, on the U.S. border: pop. 461,000

til·de (til′də) ***n.*** ⟦Sp < L *titulus*, a sign⟧ a diacritical mark (˜)

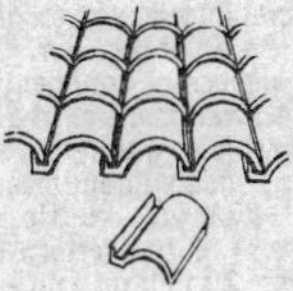

ROOFING TILES

tile (tīl) ***n.*** ⟦< L *tegula*⟧ 1 a thin piece of stone, fired clay, etc. used for roofing, flooring, walls, etc. 2 a similar piece of plastic, etc. 3 a drain of earthenware pipe —***vt.*** **tiled, til′ing** to cover with tiles

til′ing ***n.*** tiles collectively

till[1] (til) ***prep., conj.*** ⟦OE *til*⟧ UNTIL

till[2] (til) ***vt., vi.*** ⟦< OE *tilian*, lit., strive for⟧ to prepare (land) for raising crops, as by plowing, etc.

till[3] (til) ***n.*** ⟦< ? ME *tillen*, to draw⟧ a drawer for keeping money

till′age (-ij) ***n.*** 1 the tilling of land 2 land that is tilled

till·er (til′ər) ***n.*** ⟦< ML *telarium*, weaver's beam⟧ a bar or handle for turning a boat's rudder

tilt (tilt) ***vt.*** ⟦ME *tilten*, totter⟧ to cause to slope; tip —***vi.*** 1 to slope; incline 2 to charge (*at* an opponent) 3 to take part in a tilt —***n.*** 1 a medieval contest in which two horsemen fight with lances 2 any spirited contest 3 a slope —**(at) full tilt** at full speed

tilt′-top′ ***adj.*** of a table with a hinged top that can be tipped vertically

tim·bale (tim′bəl) ***n.*** ⟦Fr⟧ 1 chicken, lobster, etc. in a cream sauce, baked in a drum-shaped mold 2 a pastry shell, filled with a cooked food

tim·ber (tim′bər) ***n.*** ⟦OE⟧ 1 wood for building houses, ships, etc. 2 a wooden beam used in building 3 trees collectively —**tim′bered** ***adj.***

tim′ber·line′ ***n.*** the line above or beyond which trees do not grow, as on mountains or in polar regions

tim·bre (tam′bər, tim′-) ***n.*** ⟦< OFr, kind of drum⟧ the quality of sound that distinguishes one voice or musical instrument from another

time (tīm) ***n.*** ⟦OE *tima*⟧ 1 every moment there has ever been or ever will be 2 a system of measuring duration /standard *time*/ 3 the period during which something exists, happens, etc. 4 [*often pl.*] a period of history; age, era, etc. 5 [*usually pl.*] prevailing conditions /*times* are good/ 6 a set period or term, as of work, confinement, etc. 7 standard rate of pay 8 rate of speed in marching, driving, etc. 9 a precise or designated instant, moment, day, etc. 10 an occasion or repeated occasion /the fifth *time* it's been on TV/ 11 *Music a*) rhythm as determined by the grouping of beats into measures *b*) tempo —***vt.*** **timed, tim′ing** 1 to arrange the time of so as to be suitable, opportune, etc. 2 to adjust, set, etc. so as to coincide in time /*time* our watches/ 3 to record the pace, speed, etc. of —***adj.*** 1 having to do with time 2 set to explode, open, etc. at a given time /a *time* bomb/ 3 having to do with paying in installments —**ahead of time** early —**at the same time** however —**at times** occasionally —**do time** [Colloq.] to serve a prison term —**for the time being** temporarily —**from time to time** now and then —**in time** 1 eventually 2 before it is too late 3 keeping the set tempo, pace, etc. —**make time** to travel, work, etc. rapidly —**on time** 1 at the appointed time 2 for or by payment by installments —**time after time** again and again: also **time and again**

time clock a clock with a mechanism for recording the time an employee begins and ends a work period

time exposure a photograph taken by exposure of a film or plate for a relatively long period

time′-hon′ored ***adj.*** honored because of long existence or usage

time′keep′er ***n.*** one who keeps account of hours worked by employees or of the elapsed time in races, games, etc.

time′-lapse′ ***adj.*** of filming a slow process by exposing single frames at long intervals: the film is projected at regular speed, showing the process greatly speeded up

time′less ***adj.*** eternal

time′ly ***adj.*** **-li·er, -li·est** well-timed; opportune —**time′li·ness** ***n.***

time′out′ ***n.*** *Sports* any temporary suspension of play

time'piece' ***n.*** any device for measuring and recording time, as a clock or watch
tim·er (tīm'ər) ***n.*** a device for controlling the timing of some mechanism
times (tīmz) ***prep.*** multiplied by
time sharing 1 a system for simultaneous computer use at many remote sites 2 a system for sharing ownership of a vacation home, etc., with each joint purchaser occupying the unit at a specific time each year: also **time share**
time sheet a sheet on which are recorded the hours an employee works
time'ta'ble (-tā'bəl) ***n.*** a schedule of the times of arrival and departure of airplanes, trains, buses, etc.
time'-test'ed (-test'id) ***adj.*** having value proved by long use or experience
time warp the condition or process of being displaced from one point in time to another, as in science fiction
time'worn' ***adj.*** 1 worn out by long use 2 hackneyed; trite
time zone *see* STANDARD TIME
tim·id (tim'id) ***adj.*** ⟦< L *timere*, to fear⟧ lacking poise or self-confidence; shy; fearful; hesitant —**ti·mid·i·ty** (tə mid'ə tē) ***n.*** —**tim'id·ly** ***adv.***
tim·ing (tīm'iŋ) ***n.*** the regulation of time or speed to improve performance
tim·or·ous (tim'ər əs) ***adj.*** ⟦< L *timor*, fear⟧ full of fear; timid; afraid
tim·o·thy (tim'ə thē) ***n.*** ⟦after a *Timothy* Hanson, *c.* 1720⟧ a perennial grass with dense spikes, grown for hay
tim·pa·ni (tim'pə nē) ***n.pl.***, *sing.* **-pa·no'** (-nō') ⟦It: see TYMPANUM⟧ [*often with sing. v.*] kettledrums; esp., a set of them played by one performer
tin (tin) ***n.*** ⟦OE⟧ 1 a soft, silver-white, metallic chemical element 2 TIN PLATE 3 *a)* a pan, box, etc. made of tin plate *b)* [Chiefly Brit., etc.] CAN² (*n.* 2, 3) Variously used to connote cheapness, etc. of something —***vt.*** **tinned, tin'ning** 1 to plate with tin 2 [Chiefly Brit., etc.] CAN² (*vt.* 1)
tin can CAN² (*n.* 2)
tinc·ture (tiŋk'chər) ***n.*** ⟦< L *tingere*, to dye⟧ 1 a light color; tinge 2 a slight trace 3 a medicinal substance in an alcoholic solution —***vt.*** **-tured, -tur·ing** to tinge
tin·der (tin'dər) ***n.*** ⟦OE *tynder*⟧ any dry, easily flammable material
tin'der·box' ***n.*** 1 [Obs.] a box to hold tinder 2 a highly flammable building, etc. 3 a potential source of war, rebellion, etc.
tine (tīn) ***n.*** ⟦OE *tind*⟧ a slender, projecting point; prong [*fork tines*]
tin'foil' ***n.*** a thin sheet of tin or a tin alloy used as wrapping
tinge (tinj) ***n.*** ⟦see TINT⟧ 1 a slight coloring; tint 2 a slight trace, flavor, etc. —***vt.*** **tinged, tinge'ing** or **ting'ing** to give a tinge of to
tin·gle (tiŋ'gəl) ***vi.*** **-gled, -gling** ⟦var. of TINKLE⟧ to have a prickling or stinging feeling, as from cold, excitement, etc. —***n.*** this feeling
tin·ker (tiŋk'ər) ***n.*** ⟦ME *tinkere*⟧ 1 one who mends pots, pans, etc. 2 a bungler —***vt.*** 1 to attempt clumsily to mend something 2 to putter
tin·kle (tiŋk'əl) ***vi.*** **-kled, -kling** ⟦echoic⟧ to make a series of light sounds as of a small bell —***vt.*** to cause to tinkle —***n.*** a tinkling sound
tin·ny (tin'ē) ***adj.*** **-ni·er, -ni·est** 1 of tin 2 like tin, as in appearance, sound, value, etc. —**tin'ni·ness** ***n.***
tin plate thin sheets of iron or steel plated with tin
tin·sel (tin'səl) ***n.*** ⟦< L *scintilla*, a spark⟧ 1 thin strips of tin, metal foil, etc., as for decoration 2 something of little worth that glitters
tin·smith (tin'smith') ***n.*** one who works in tin or tin plate
tint (tint) ***n.*** ⟦< L *tingere*, to dye⟧ 1 a delicate color 2 a gradation of a color; shade 3 a hair dye —***vt.*** to give a tint to
tin·tin·nab·u·la·tion (tin'ti nab'yoo lā'shən) ***n.*** ⟦< L *tintinnabulum*, little bell⟧ the ringing sound of bells
tin·type (tin'tīp') ***n.*** an old kind of photograph taken directly as a positive print on a treated plate of tin or iron
ti·ny (tī'nē) ***adj.*** **-ni·er, -ni·est** ⟦< ME *tine*, *n.*, a little⟧ very small
-tion (shən) ⟦< Fr < L⟧ *suffix* 1 the act of _____ing 2 the state of being _____ed 3 the thing that is _____ed
-tious (shəs) *suffix* of, having, or characterized by
tip¹ (tip) ***n.*** ⟦ME *tippe*⟧ 1 the point or end of something 2 something attached to the end, as a cap, etc. —***vt.*** **tipped, tip'ping** 1 to form a tip on 2 to cover the tip of
tip² (tip) ***vt.*** **tipped, tip'ping** ⟦< ?⟧ 1 to strike lightly and sharply 2 to give a gratuity to (a waiter, etc.) 3 [Colloq.] to give secret information to: often with *off* —***vi.*** to give a tip or tips —***n.*** 1 a light, sharp blow 2 a piece of confidential information 3 a hint, warning, etc. 4 a gratuity —**tip one's hand** [Slang] to reveal a secret, one's plans, etc., often without meaning to —**tip'per** ***n.***
tip³ (tip) ***vt.***, ***vi.*** **tipped, tip'ping** ⟦ME *tipen*⟧ 1 to overturn or upset: often with *over* 2 to tilt or slant —***n.*** a tilt; slant
tip'-off' ***n.*** a tip; confidential disclosure, hint, or warning
tip·ple (tip'əl) ***vi.***, ***vt.*** **-pled, -pling** ⟦< ?⟧ to drink (alcoholic liquor) habitually —**tip'pler** ***n.***
tip·ster (tip'stər) ***n.*** [Colloq.] one who sells tips, as on horse races
tip·sy (tip'sē) ***adj.*** **-si·er, -si·est** 1 that tips easily; not steady 2 somewhat drunk —**tip'si·ly** ***adv.***
tip'toe' ***n.*** the tip of a toe —***vi.*** **-toed', -toe'ing** to walk carefully on one's tiptoes —**on tiptoe** 1 on one's tiptoes 2 eager(ly) 3 silently
tip'top' ***n.*** ⟦TIP¹ + TOP¹⟧ the highest point —***adj.***, ***adv.*** 1 at the highest point 2 [Colloq.] at the highest point of excellence, health, etc.
ti·rade (tī'rād', ti rād') ***n.*** ⟦< It *tirare*, to fire⟧ a long, vehement speech or denunciation; harangue
tire¹ (tīr) ***vt.***, ***vi.*** **tired, tir'ing** ⟦OE *tiorian*⟧ to make or become weary, exhausted, bored, etc.
tire² (tīr) ***n.*** ⟦ME *tyre*⟧ 1 a hoop of iron or

rubber around the wheel of a vehicle **2** an inflatable, vulcanized rubber or synthetic casing sealed to a wheel rim by air pressure

tired (tīərd) ***adj.*** **1** weary **2** hackneyed —**tired'ly** ***adv.*** —**tired'ness** ***n.***

tire'less ***adj.*** that does not become tired —**tire'less·ly** ***adv.*** —**tire'less·ness** ***n.***

tire'some (-səm) ***adj.*** tiring; boring —**tire'some·ly** ***adv.*** —**tire'some·ness** ***n.***

Ti·rol (ti rōl', -räl') E Alpine region in W Austria & N Italy —**Ti·ro·le·an** (ti rō'lē ən, tī-) ***adj., n.***

'tis (tiz) [Old Poet.] it is

tis·sue (tish'o͞o) ***n.*** ⟦< L *texere*, to weave⟧ **1** light, thin cloth **2** an interwoven mass; mesh; web **3** a piece of soft, absorbent paper, used as a disposable handkerchief, etc. **4** TISSUE PAPER **5** the substance of an organic body, consisting of cells and intercellular material

tissue paper very thin, unsized paper, as for wrapping things, etc.

tit[1] (tit) ***n.*** a titmouse

tit[2] (tit) ***n.*** ⟦OE⟧ **1** NIPPLE (sense 1) **2** a breast: in this sense now vulgar

ti·tan (tīt''n) ***n.*** ⟦< Gr *Titan*, a giant deity⟧ any person or thing of great size or power

ti·tan·ic (tī tan'ik) ***adj.*** of great size, strength, or power

ti·ta·ni·um (tī tā'nē əm, ti-) ***n.*** ⟦see TITAN⟧ a silvery or dark-gray, metallic chemical element used as a cleaning and deoxidizing agent in molten steel, etc.

tit for tat ⟦var. of earlier *tip for tap*⟧ blow for blow

tithe (tīth) ***n.*** ⟦OE *teothe*, a tenth⟧ a tenth of one's income paid to a church —***vt., vi.*** **tithed, tith'ing** to pay a tithe of (one's income, etc.)

ti·tian (tish'ən) ***n.*** ⟦after *Titian* (c. 1490-1576), Venetian painter⟧ reddish gold; auburn

tit·il·late (tit''l āt') ***vt.*** **-lat'ed, -lat'ing** ⟦< L *titillare*, to tickle⟧ to excite pleasurably —**tit'il·la'tion** ***n.***

ti·tle (tīt''l) ***n.*** ⟦< L *titulus*⟧ **1** the name of a book, poem, picture, etc. **2** an epithet **3** an appellation indicating one's rank, profession, etc. **4** a claim **5** *Law* *a)* a right to ownership, esp. of real estate *b)* a deed **6** *Film, TV* a subtitle, credit, etc. **7** in sports and other competition, a championship —***vt.*** **-tled, -tling** to give a title to

ti·tled (tīt''ld) ***adj.*** having a title, esp. of nobility

ti'tle·hold'er ***n.*** the holder of a title; specif., the champion in some sport

title role (or **part** or **character**) the character in a play, film, etc. whose name is used as or in its title

ti·tlist (tīt''l ist) ***n.*** a champion in some sport

tit·mouse (tit'mous') ***n.***, *pl.* **-mice'** (-mīs') ⟦ME *titemose*⟧ a small bird with ashy-gray feathers

tit·ter (tit'ər) ***vi.*** ⟦echoic⟧ to laugh in a half-suppressed way; giggle —***n.*** a tittering; giggle

tit·tle (tit''l) ***n.*** ⟦ME *title*⟧ a very small particle; jot

tit·u·lar (tich'o͞o lər, tich'ə-) ***adj.*** ⟦see TITLE⟧ **1** of a title **2** having a title **3** in name only /a *titular* sovereign/

tiz·zy (tiz'ē) ***n.***, *pl.* **-zies** ⟦< ?⟧ [Colloq.] a state of frenzied excitement

TLC tender, loving care

TM trademark

tn. ton(s)

TN Tennessee

TNT (tē'en'tē') ***n.*** ⟦*t(ri)n(itro)t(oluene)*⟧ a high explosive used for blasting, etc.

to (to͞o, too, tə) ***prep.*** ⟦OE⟧ **1** toward /turn *to* the left/ **2** so as to reach /she went *to* Boston/ **3** as far as /wet *to* the skin/ **4** into a condition of /a rise *to* fame/ **5** on, onto, at, etc. /tied *to* a post/ **6** *a)* until /from noon *to* night/ *b)* before /the time is ten *to* six/ **7** for the purpose of /he came *to* my aid/ **8** in regard to /open *to* attack/ **9** so as to produce /torn *to* bits/ **10** along with /add this *to* the rest/ **11** belonging with /a key *to* the house/ **12** as compared with /a score of 10 *to* 0/ **13** in agreement with /not *to* my taste/ **14** constituting /four quarts *to* a gallon/ **15** with (a specified person or thing) as the recipient of the action /give it *to* me/ **16** in honor of /a toast *to* you/ *To* is also a sign of the infinitive (Ex.: I want *to* stay) —***adv.*** **1** forward /wrong side *to*/ **2** shut; closed /pull the door *to*/ **3** into a state of consciousness /the boxer came *to*/ **4** at hand /we were close *to* when it happened/ —**to and fro** first in one direction and then in the opposite

toad (tōd) ***n.*** ⟦OE *tadde*⟧ a froglike animal that lives on moist land

toad'stool' (-sto͞ol') ***n.*** a mushroom, esp. any poisonous mushroom

toad·y (tōd'ē) ***n.***, *pl.* **-ies** ⟦short for *toad-eater*, quack doctor's assistant⟧ a servile flatterer —***vt., vi.*** **-ied, -y·ing** to be a toady (to)

toast[1] (tōst) ***vt.*** ⟦< L *torrere*, parch⟧ **1** to brown the surface of (bread, etc.) by heating **2** to warm thoroughly —***vi.*** to become toasted —***n.*** sliced bread made brown and crisp by heat —**toast'er** ***n.***

toast[2] (tōst) ***n.*** ⟦from the use of toasted spiced bread to flavor the wine⟧ **1** a person, thing, idea, etc. in honor of which persons raise their glasses and drink **2** a drink, or a proposal to drink, in honor of some person, etc. —***vt., vi.*** to propose or drink a toast (to)

toast'mas'ter ***n.*** the person at a banquet who proposes toasts, introduces after-dinner speakers, etc.

toast'y ***adj.*** **-i·er, -i·est** warm and comfortable or cozy

to·bac·co (tə bak'ō) ***n.***, *pl.* **-cos** ⟦Sp *tabaco* < ?⟧ **1** a plant with large leaves that are prepared for smoking, chewing, etc. **2** cigars, cigarettes, snuff, etc.

to·bac·co·nist (tə bak'ə nist) ***n.*** [Chiefly Brit., etc.] a dealer in tobacco

to·bog·gan (tə bäg'ən) ***n.*** ⟦< AmInd⟧ a long, flat sled without runners, for coasting downhill —***vi.*** **1** to coast on a toboggan **2** to decline rapidly

toc·sin (täk'sin) ***n.*** ⟦Fr < Prov *toc*, a stroke + *senh*, a bell⟧ an alarm bell

to·day (tə dā') ***adv.*** ⟦OE *to dæg*⟧ **1** on or during the present day **2** in the present time —***n.*** **1** the present day **2** the present time

tod·dle (täd''l) ***vi.*** **-dled, -dling** ⟦? < *totter*⟧

to walk with short, uncertain steps, as a child —**tod′dler** ***n.***

tod·dy (täd′ē) ***n.***, *pl.* **-dies** ⟦< Hindi⟧ a drink of whiskey, etc. mixed with hot water, sugar, etc. Also **hot toddy**

to-do (tə do͞o′) ***n.***, *pl.* **-dos** [Colloq.] a commotion; stir; fuss

toe (tō) ***n.*** ⟦OE *ta*⟧ **1** *a)* any of the digits of the foot *b)* the forepart of the foot **2** anything like a toe in location, shape, or use —***vt.*** **toed, toe′ing** to touch, kick, etc. with the toes —***vi.*** to stand, walk, etc. with the toes in a specified position /he *toes* in/ —**on one's toes** [Colloq.] alert —**toe the line** (or **mark**) to follow orders, rules, etc. strictly

toed (tōd) ***adj.*** having (a specified kind or number of) toes: usually in hyphenated compounds /two-*toed*/

toe dance a dance performed on the tips of the toes, as in ballet —**toe′-dance′, -danced′, -danc′ing,** ***vi.*** —**toe′-danc′er** ***n.***

toe′hold′ ***n.*** **1** a small space to support the toe in climbing, etc. **2** a slight footing or advantage

toe′less ***adj.*** having the toe open or uncovered /a *toeless* shoe/

toe′nail′ ***n.*** the nail of a toe

tof·fee or **tof·fy** (tôf′ē, täf′-) ***n.*** ⟦< TAFFY⟧ a hard, chewy candy, a kind of taffy

to·fu (tō′fo͞o) ***n.*** a Japanese cheeselike food made from soybeans

to·ga (tō′gə) ***n.***, *pl.* **-gas** or **-gae** (-jē, -gē) ⟦L < *tegere,* to cover⟧ in ancient Rome, a loose outer garment worn in public by citizens

ROMAN TOGA

to·geth·er (to͞o geth′ər, tə-) ***adv.*** ⟦< OE *to,* to + *gædre,* together⟧ **1** in or into one group, place, etc. /we ate *together*/ **2** in or into contact, union, etc. /the cars skidded *together*/ **3** considered collectively /he lost more than all of us *together*/ **4** at the same time /shots fired *together*/ **5** in succession /sulking for three whole days *together*/ **6** in or into agreement, cooperation, etc. /to get *together* on a deal/ —***adj.*** [Slang] having an integrated personality

to·geth′er·ness ***n.*** the spending of much time together, as by family members, when regarded as resulting in a more unified, stable relationship

tog·gle switch (täg′əl) a switch consisting of a lever moved back and forth to open or close an electric circuit

To·go (tō′gō) country on the W coast of Africa: 21,853 sq. mi.; pop. 2,700,000

togs (tägz, tôgz) ***n.pl.*** ⟦ult. < L *toga,* toga⟧ [Colloq.] clothes

toil (toil) ***vi.*** ⟦< L *tudiculare,* to stir about⟧ **1** to work hard and continuously **2** to proceed laboriously —***n.*** hard, tiring work —**toil′er** ***n.***

toi·let (toi′lit) ***n.*** ⟦< OFr *toile,* cloth < L *tela,* a web⟧ **1** the act of dressing or grooming oneself **2** dress; attire **3** *a)* a room with a bowl-shaped fixture for defecation or urination *b)* such a fixture

toilet paper (or **tissue**) soft paper for cleaning oneself after evacuation

toi′let·ry (-lə trē) ***n.***, *pl.* **-ries** soap, lotion, etc. used in grooming oneself

toi·lette (twä let′, toi-) ***n.*** ⟦Fr⟧ **1** the process of grooming oneself **2** dress; attire

toilet water a lightly scented liquid with a high alcohol content, applied to the skin after bathing, etc.

toils (toilz) ***n.pl.*** ⟦< L *tela,* web⟧ any snare suggestive of a net

toil·some (toil′səm) ***adj.*** laborious

toke (tōk) ***n.*** ⟦? < fol.⟧ [Slang] a puff on a cigarette, esp. one of marijuana or hashish —***vi.*** **toked, tok′ing** [Slang] to take such a puff

to·ken (tō′kən) ***n.*** ⟦OE *tacn*⟧ **1** a sign, indication, symbol, etc. /a *token* of one's affection/ **2** a keepsake **3** a metal disk to be used in place of currency, for transportation fares, etc. —***adj.*** **1** symbolic **2** merely simulated; of no real account /*token* resistance/ —**by the same token** following from this

to′ken·ism′ (-iz′əm) ***n.*** the making of small, often merely formal concessions to a demand, etc.; specif., token integration of blacks, as in jobs, etc.

To·ky·o (tō′kē ō′) capital of Japan, on S Honshu: pop. 8,991,000 (met. area 11,620,000)

told (tōld) ***vt., vi.*** *pt. & pp. of* TELL —**all told** all (being) counted

tole (tōl) ***n.*** ⟦Fr *tôle,* sheet iron⟧ a type of lacquered or enameled metalware, usually dark-green, ivory, or black, used for lamps, trays, etc.

To·le·do (tə lēd′ō) city & port in NW Ohio: pop. 355,000

tol·er·a·ble (täl′ər ə bəl) ***adj.*** **1** endurable **2** fairly good; passable —**tol′er·a·bly** ***adv.***

tol′er·ance (-əns) ***n.*** **1** a being tolerant of others' views, beliefs, practices, etc. **2** the amount of variation allowed from a standard **3** *Med.* the ability to resist the effects of a drug, poison, etc.

tol′er·ant ***adj.*** having or showing tolerance of others' beliefs, etc.

tol·er·ate (täl′ər āt′) ***vt.*** **-at′ed, -at′ing** ⟦< L *tolerare,* to bear⟧ **1** to allow **2** to respect (others' beliefs, practices, etc.) without sharing them **3** to put up with **4** *Med.* to have tolerance for —**tol′er·a′tion** ***n.***

toll[1] (tōl) ***n.*** ⟦ult. < Gr *telos,* tax⟧ **1** a tax or charge for a privilege, as for the use of a bridge **2** a charge for service, as for a long-distance telephone call **3** the number lost, etc. /the tornado took a heavy *toll* of lives/

toll[2] (tōl) ***vt.*** ⟦ME *tollen,* to pull⟧ **1** to ring (a church bell, etc.) with slow, regular strokes **2** to announce, summon, etc. by this —***vi.*** to ring slowly: said of a bell —***n.*** the sound of a bell tolling

toll′booth′ ***n.*** a booth at which a toll is collected, as before entering a toll road

toll′gate′ ***n.*** a gate for stopping travel at a point where a toll is collected

toll road a road on which a toll must be paid Also **toll′way′** (-wā′) ***n.***

Tol·stoy or **Tol·stoi** (täl′stoi′, tōl′-), Count **Le·o** (lē′ō) 1828-1910; Russ. novelist

tol·u·ene (täl′yo͞o ēn′) ***n.*** ⟦Sp *tolu,* after *Tolú,* seaport in Colombia + (BENZ)ENE⟧ a colorless, poisonous liquid obtained from coal tar or petroleum, and used in making dyes, explosives, etc.

tom (täm) ***adj.*** ⟦after the name *Tom*⟧ male /a *tomcat*, a *tom* turkey/

tom·a·hawk (täm′ə hôk′) ***n.*** ⟦< AmInd⟧ a light ax used by North American Indians as a tool and a weapon

to·ma·to (tə māt′ō, -mät′ō) ***n.***, *pl.* **-toes** ⟦< AmInd (Mexico)⟧ 1 a red or yellowish fruit with a juicy pulp, used as a vegetable 2 the plant it grows on

tomb (to͞om) ***n.*** ⟦< Gr *tymbos*⟧ a vault or grave for the dead

tom·boy (täm′boi′) ***n.*** a girl who behaves like a boisterous boy

tomb·stone (to͞om′stōn′) ***n.*** a stone or monument marking a tomb or grave

tom·cat (täm′kat′) ***n.*** a male cat

tome (tōm) ***n.*** ⟦< Gr *tomos*, piece cut off⟧ a book, esp. a large one

tom·fool·er·y (täm′fo͞ol′ər ē) ***n.***, *pl.* **-ies** foolish behavior; silliness

tommy gun [*sometimes* **T- g-**] a submachine gun

to·mor·row (tə mär′ō, -môr′-) ***adv.*** ⟦OE *to morgen*⟧ on the day after today —***n.*** the day after today

tom·tit (täm tit′, täm′tit′) ***n.*** [Chiefly Brit., etc.] a titmouse or other small bird

tom-tom (täm′täm′) ***n.*** ⟦Hindi *ṭamṭam*⟧ a primitive drum, usually beaten with the hands

-to·my (tə mē) ⟦< Gr < *tomē*, a cutting⟧ *combining form* a surgical operation

ton (tun) ***n.*** ⟦var. of TUN⟧ 1 a unit of weight equal to 2,000 pounds 2 in Great Britain, a unit of weight equal to 2,240 pounds

ton·al (tō′nəl) ***adj.*** of a tone —**ton′al·ly** ***adv.***

to·nal·i·ty (tō nal′ə tē) ***n.***, *pl.* **-ties** *Music* 1 KEY[1] (*n.* 6) 2 tonal character, as determined by the relationship of the tones to the keynote

tone (tōn) ***n.*** ⟦< Gr *teinein*, to stretch⟧ 1 a vocal or musical sound, or its quality as to pitch, intensity, etc. 2 a manner of expression showing a certain attitude /a friendly *tone*/ 3 style, character, spirit, etc. 4 elegant style 5 a quality of color; shade 6 normal, healthy condition of a muscle, organ, etc. 7 *Music a)* a sound of distinct pitch *b)* any of the full intervals of a diatonic scale —***vt.*** **toned, ton′ing** to give a tone to —**tone down** (or **up**) to give a less (or more) intense tone to —**tone′less** ***adj.***

tone′arm′ ***n.*** the pivoted arm beside a phonograph turntable, holding the CARTRIDGE (*n.* 2)

tone′-deaf′ ***adj.*** not able to distinguish differences in musical pitch

ton·er (tōn′ər) ***n.*** 1 the ink powder mixture used to form images in xerography 2 a facial cleanser

tone row (or **series**) see TWELVE-TONE

tong (tôŋ, täŋ) ***n.*** ⟦Mandarin *t'ang*, meeting place⟧ a Chinese association, society, etc.

Ton·ga (täŋ′gə) kingdom on a group of islands (**Tonga Islands**) in the SW Pacific, east of Fiji: 289 sq. mi.; pop. 98,700 —**Ton′gan** ***n.***

tongs (tôŋz, täŋz) ***n.pl.*** ⟦OE *tange*⟧ [*sometimes with sing. v.*] a device for seizing or lifting objects, having two long arms pivoted or hinged together

tongue (tuŋ) ***n.*** ⟦OE *tunge*⟧ 1 the movable, muscular structure in the mouth, used in eating, tasting, and (in humans) speaking 2 talk; speech 3 the act, power, or manner of speaking 4 a language or dialect 5 something like a tongue in shape, position, use, etc., as the flap under the laces of a shoe —**hold one's tongue** to keep from speaking —**speak in tongues** to utter unintelligible sounds, as while in a religious trance —**tongue′less** ***adj.***

tongue-and-groove joint (tuŋ′ 'n gro͞ov′) a kind of joint in which a projection on one board fits into a groove in another

tongue′-lash′ing ***n.*** [Colloq.] a harsh scolding or reproving; reprimand

tongue′-tied′ ***adj.*** speechless from amazement, embarrassment, etc.

tongue twister a phrase or sentence hard to speak fast (Ex: six sick sheiks)

ton·ic (tän′ik) ***adj.*** ⟦see TONE⟧ 1 of or producing good muscular tone 2 *Music* designating or based on a keynote —***n.*** 1 anything that invigorates, as a drug or medicine 2 a quinine-flavored beverage served with gin, vodka, etc. 3 *Music* a keynote

to·night (tə nīt′, too-, to͞o-) ***adv.*** ⟦OE *to niht*⟧ on or during the present or coming night —***n.*** the present or coming night

ton·nage (tun′ij) ***n.*** 1 the total amount of shipping of a country or port, calculated in tons 2 the carrying capacity of a ship, calculated in tons

ton·sil (tän′səl) ***n.*** ⟦L *tonsillae*, pl.⟧ either of a pair of oval masses of tissue at the back of the mouth

ton·sil·lec·to·my (tän′sə lek′tə mē) ***n.***, *pl.* **-mies** ⟦prec. + -ECTOMY⟧ the surgical removal of the tonsils

ton′sil·li′tis (-līt′is) ***n.*** ⟦ModL < L *tonsillae*, tonsils + -ITIS⟧ inflammation of the tonsils

ton·so·ri·al (tän sôr′ē əl) ***adj.*** ⟦see fol.⟧ of a barber or barbering: often humorous /a *tonsorial* artist/

ton·sure (tän′shər) ***n.*** ⟦< L *tondere*, to clip⟧ 1 a clipping off or shaving off of part or all of the hair of the head, done as a sign of entrance into the clerical or monastic state 2 the head area so clipped or shaved

to·nus (tō′nəs) ***n.*** ⟦ModL, ult. < Gr *teinein*, to stretch⟧ the slight, continuous contraction characteristic of a normal relaxed muscle

ton·y (tōn′ē) ***adj.*** **-i·er, -i·est** [Slang] very elegant

too (to͞o) ***adv.*** ⟦stressed form of TO⟧ 1 in addition; also 2 more than enough /the hat is *too* big/ 3 extremely; very /it was just *too* delicious!/

took (took) ***vt.***, ***vi.*** *pt. of* TAKE

tool (to͞ol) ***n.*** ⟦OE *tol*⟧ 1 any hand implement, instrument, etc. used for some work 2 any similar instrument that is the working part of a machine, as a drill 3 anything that serves as a means 4 a stooge —***vt.*** 1 to form or shape with a tool 2 to impress designs on (leather, etc.) with a tool —***vi.*** to install the tools, equipment, etc. needed: often with *up*

toot (to͞ot) ***vi., vt.*** ⟦echoic⟧ to sound (a horn, whistle, etc.) in short blasts —***n.*** a short blast of a horn, whistle, etc.

tooth (to͞oth) ***n., pl.*** **teeth** (tēth) ⟦OE *toth*⟧ **1** any of the hard, bonelike structures in the jaws, used for biting, chewing, etc. **2** a toothlike part, as on a saw, comb, gearwheel, etc.; tine, prong, cog, etc. **3** [*pl.*] effective means of enforcing /a law with *teeth*/ —**in the teeth of** **1** directly against **2** defying —**tooth and nail** with all one's strength —**toothed** ***adj.*** —**tooth'less** ***adj.***

tooth'ache' ***n.*** pain in a tooth

tooth'brush' ***n.*** a small brush for cleaning the teeth

tooth'paste' ***n.*** a paste used for brushing the teeth

tooth'pick' ***n.*** a very small, pointed stick for getting bits of food free from between the teeth

tooth powder a powder used like toothpaste

tooth'some (-səm) ***adj.*** tasty; savory

tooth'y ***adj.*** **-i·er, -i·est** having or exposing teeth that show prominently /a *toothy* smile/ —**tooth'i·ly** ***adv.***

top[1] (täp) ***n.*** ⟦OE⟧ **1** the head or crown **2** the highest point or surface of anything **3** the part of a plant above ground **4** the uppermost part or covering, as a lid, cap, etc. **5** the highest degree /at the *top* of his voice/ **6** the highest rank /the *top* of the class/ —***adj.*** of, at, or being the top; highest or foremost —***vt.*** **topped, top'ping** **1** to take off the top of (a plant, etc.) **2** to provide with a top **3** to be a top for **4** to reach the top of **5** to exceed in amount, etc. **6** to surpass; outdo —**blow one's top** [Slang] to lose one's temper —**on top** successful —**on top of** **1** resting upon **2** besides **3** controlling successfully —**top off** to complete by adding a finishing touch —**top'per** ***n.***

top[2] (täp) ***n.*** ⟦OE⟧ a cone-shaped toy with a point upon which it is spun

to·paz (tō'paz') ***n.*** ⟦< Gr *topazos*⟧ any of various yellow gems, esp. a variety of aluminum silicate

top brass [Slang] important officials

top'coat' ***n.*** a lightweight overcoat

top-draw·er (täp'drôr') ***adj.*** of first importance

top'-dress'ing ***n.*** **1** material applied to a surface, as fertilizer on land **2** the applying of such material

To·pe·ka (tə pē'kə) capital of Kans.: pop. 115,000

top·er (tōp'ər) ***n.*** ⟦< archaic *tope*, to drink (much liquor)⟧ a drunkard

top'-flight' ***adj.*** [Colloq.] first-rate

top hat a man's tall, black, cylindrical silk hat, worn in formal dress

top'-heav'y ***adj.*** too heavy at the top, so as to be unstable

top·ic (täp'ik) ***n.*** ⟦ult. < Gr *topos*, place⟧ the subject of an essay, speech, discussion, etc.

top'i·cal ***adj.*** dealing with topics of the day; of current or local interest

top'knot' ***n.*** a tuft of hair or feathers on the top of the head

top'less (-lis) ***adj.*** without a top, as a costume exposing the breasts

top-lev·el (täp'lev'əl) ***adj.*** of or by persons of the highest office or rank

top'mast' ***n.*** the second mast above the deck of a sailing ship

top'most' ***adj.*** at the very top

top'-notch' ***adj.*** [Colloq.] first-rate; excellent

to·pog·ra·phy (tə päg'rə fē) ***n., pl.*** **-phies** ⟦see TOPIC & -GRAPHY⟧ **1** the science of representing surface features of a region on maps and charts **2** these surface features —**top·o·graph·ic** (täp'ə graf'ik) or **top'o·graph'i·cal** ***adj.***

top·ping (täp'iŋ) ***n.*** something put on top of something else

top·ple (täp'əl) ***vi.*** **-pled, -pling** ⟦< TOP[1]⟧ to fall top forward; fall (*over*) because top-heavy, etc. —***vt.*** to cause to topple; overturn

top·sail (täp'sāl'; *naut.*, -səl) ***n.*** in a square-rigged vessel, the square sail next above the lowest sail on a mast

top'-se'cret ***adj.*** designating or of the most secret information

top·side (täp'sīd') ***adv.*** on or to an upper deck or the main deck of a ship

top'soil' ***n.*** the upper layer of soil, usually richer than the subsoil

top·sy-tur·vy (täp'sē tur'vē) ***adv., adj.*** ⟦prob. < *top*, highest part + ME *terven*, to roll⟧ **1** upside down; in a reversed condition **2** in disorder

toque (tōk) ***n.*** ⟦Fr⟧ a woman's small, round, usually brimless hat

to·rah or **to·ra** (tō'rə, tôr'ə, tō rä') ***n., pl.*** **-roth** or **-rot** (-rəs, -rōt') ⟦< Heb, law⟧ [*usually* **T-**] a scroll containing the Pentateuch —[*usually* **T-**] **1** the body of Jewish religious literature **2** the Pentateuch

torch (tôrch) ***n.*** ⟦see TORQUE⟧ **1** a portable flaming light **2** a source of enlightenment, etc. **3** a device for producing a very hot flame, as in welding **4** [Brit., etc. (exc. Cdn.)] a flashlight —***vt.*** [Slang] to set fire to, as in arson

torch'bear'er ***n.*** **1** one who carries a torch **2** *a*) one who brings enlightenment, truth, etc. *b*) an inspirational leader, as in some movement

torch'light' ***n.*** the light of a torch or torches —***adj.*** done by torchlight

tore (tôr) ***vt., vi.*** *pt. of* TEAR[1]

tor·e·a·dor (tôr'ē ə dôr') ***n.*** ⟦Sp < L *taurus*, a bull⟧ a bullfighter

tor·ment (tôr'ment'; *for v.* tôr ment') ***n.*** ⟦OFr < L: see TORQUE⟧ **1** great pain or anguish **2** a source of pain, anxiety, etc. —***vt.*** **1** to cause great physical pain or mental anguish in **2** to annoy; harass —**tor·ment'ing·ly** ***adv.*** —**tor·men'tor** or **tor·ment'er** ***n.***

torn (tôrn) ***vt., vi.*** *pp. of* TEAR[1]

tor·na·do (tôr nā'dō) ***n., pl.*** **-does** or **-dos** ⟦< Sp < L *tonare*, to thunder⟧ a violently whirling column of air seen as a funnel-shaped cloud that usually destroys everything in its narrow path

To·ron·to (tə ränt'ō) capital of Ontario, Canada: pop. 633,000 (met. area 3,000,000)

tor·pe·do (tôr pē'dō) ***n., pl.*** **-does** ⟦< L: see fol.⟧ **1** a large, cigar-shaped, self-propelled, underwater projectile containing explosives **2** any of various explosive devices —***vt.***

-doed, -do·ing to attack, destroy, etc. as with a torpedo

tor·pid (tôr′pid) ***adj.*** ⟦< L *torpere,* be numb⟧ **1** without sensation or motion; dormant **2** dull; sluggish

tor′por (-pər) ***n.*** ⟦L⟧ **1** a torpid state; stupor **2** dullness; apathy

torque (tôrk) ***n.*** ⟦< L *torquere,* to twist⟧ **1** *Physics* a measure of the tendency of a force to cause rotation **2** popularly, the force that acts to produce rotation, as in an automotive vehicle

Tor·rance (tôr′əns) city in SW Calif.: pop. 131,000

tor·rent (tôr′ənt, tär′-) ***n.*** ⟦< L *torrens,* rushing⟧ **1** a swift, violent stream, esp. of water **2** a flood or rush of words, mail, etc. **—tor·ren·tial** (tô ren′shəl) ***adj.***

tor·rid (tôr′id, tär′-) ***adj.*** ⟦< L *torrere,* to dry⟧ **1** subjected to intense heat, esp. of the sun; parched **2** very hot; scorching **3** passionate; ardent

Torrid Zone the area of the earth's surface between the Tropic of Cancer & the Tropic of Capricorn and divided by the equator

tor·sion (tôr′shən) ***n.*** ⟦see TORQUE⟧ **1** a twisting or being twisted **2** the stress produced in a rod, wire, etc. by twisting along a longitudinal axis

tor·so (tôr′sō) ***n.,*** *pl.* **-sos** or **-si** (-sē) ⟦< Gr *thyrsos,* a stem⟧ the trunk of the human body

tort (tôrt) ***n.*** ⟦< L *torquere,* to twist⟧ *Law* a wrongful act or damage (not involving a breach of contract), for which a civil action can be brought

torte (tôrt; *Ger* tôr′tə) ***n.,*** *pl.* **tortes;** Ger. ***tor·ten*** (tôr′tən) ⟦Ger < It < LL *torta,* a twisted bread⟧ a rich cake, as one made of eggs, finely chopped nuts, crumbs, etc.

tor·tel·li·ni (tôr′tə lē′nē) ***n.*** ⟦It⟧ pasta in tiny ring-shaped pieces, filled with meat, etc.

tor·til·la (tôr tē′ə, -yə) ***n.*** ⟦Sp, dim. of *torta,* a cake⟧ a flat, round cake of unleavened cornmeal, or of flour

tor·toise (tôr′təs, -tis) ***n.*** ⟦< ? *c.* 4th-c. Gr *tartarouchos,* evil demon⟧ a turtle, esp. one that lives on land

tortoise shell **1** the hard, mottled, yellow-and-brown shell of some turtles **2** a synthetic substance resembling this **—tor′toise-shell′** ***adj.***

tor·to·ni (tôr tō′nē) ***n.*** ⟦prob. alt. < It *tortone,* lit., big pastry tart⟧ an ice cream made with heavy cream, maraschino cherries, almonds, etc.

tor·tu·ous (tôr′cho͞o əs) ***adj.*** ⟦see TORQUE⟧ **1** full of twists, turns, etc.; crooked **2** deceitful or tricky

tor·ture (tôr′chər) ***n.*** ⟦see TORQUE⟧ **1** the inflicting of severe pain, as to force information or confession **2** any severe physical or mental pain; agony **—*vt.*** **-tured, -tur·ing** **1** to subject to torture **2** to twist or distort (meaning, etc.) **—tor′tur·er *n.***

To·ry (tôr′ē) ***n.,*** *pl.* **-ries** ⟦Ir *tōruidhe,* robber⟧ **1** after 1689, a member of the major conservative party of England **2** in the American Revolution, one loyal to Great Britain **3** [*often* t-] any extreme conservative

toss (tôs, täs) ***vt.*** ⟦prob. < Scand⟧ **1** to throw about /waves *tossed* the boat/ **2** to throw lightly from the hand **3** to jerk upward /to *toss* one's head/ **—*vi.*** **1** to be thrown about **2** to fling oneself about in sleep, etc. **—*n.*** a tossing or being tossed **— toss up** to toss a coin for deciding something according to which side lands uppermost

toss′up′ ***n.*** **1** the act of tossing up **2** an even chance

tot[1] (tät) ***n.*** ⟦prob. < ON⟧ **1** a young child **2** [Chiefly Brit., etc.] a small drink of alcoholic liquor

tot[2] (tät) ***vt., vi.*** **tot′ted, tot′ting** [Colloq., Chiefly Brit., etc.] to total: with *up*

to·tal (tōt′'l) ***adj.*** ⟦< L *totus,* all⟧ **1** constituting a whole **2** complete; utter /a *total* loss/ **—*n.*** the whole amount; sum **—*vt.*** **-taled** or **-talled, -tal·ing** or **-tal·ling** **1** to find the total of **2** to add up to **3** [Slang] to demolish **—*vi.*** to amount (*to*) as a whole **— to′tal·ly *adv.***

to·tal·i·tar·i·an (tō tal′ə ter′ē ən) ***adj.*** ⟦prec. + (AUTHOR)ITARIAN⟧ designating or of a government in which one political group maintains complete control, esp. under a dictator **—*n.*** one who favors such a government **—to·tal′i·tar′i·an·ism′ *n.***

to·tal·i·ty (tō tal′ə tē) ***n.,*** *pl.* **-ties** the total amount or sum

to·tal·i·za·tor (tōt′'l i zāt′ər) ***n.*** a machine for registering bets and computing the odds and payoffs, as at a horse race Also **to′tal·iz′er** (-ī′zər) ***n.***

tote (tōt) ***vt.*** **tot′ed, tot′ing** ⟦< ?⟧ [Colloq.] to carry or haul **—*n.*** a small piece of baggage

to·tem (tōt′əm) ***n.*** ⟦< Algonquian⟧ **1** among some peoples, an animal or natural object taken as the symbol of a family or clan **2** an image of this

totem pole a pole carved and painted with totems by Indian tribes of NW North America

tot·ter (tät′ər) ***vi.*** ⟦prob. < Scand⟧ **1** to rock as if about to fall **2** to be unsteady on one's feet; stagger

TOUCAN

tou·can (to͞o′kan′) ***n.*** ⟦< AmInd (Brazil)⟧ a brightly colored bird of tropical America, with a very large beak

touch (tuch) ***vt.*** ⟦< OFr *tochier*⟧ **1** to put the hand, etc. on, so as to feel **2** to bring (something), or come, into contact with (something else) **3** to border on **4** to strike lightly **5** to give a light tint, aspect, etc. to /*touched* with pink/ **6** to stop at (a port) **7** to handle; use **8** to come up to; reach **9** to compare with; equal **10** to affect; concern **11** to arouse sympathy, gratitude, etc. in **12** [Slang] to seek a loan or gift of money from **—*vi.*** **1** to touch a person or thing **2**

to be or come in contact **3** to verge (*on* or *upon*) **4** to pertain; bear (*on* or *upon*) **5** to treat in passing: with *on* or *upon* —*n.* **1** a touching or being touched; specif., a light tap **2** the sense by which physical objects are felt **3** a special quality or skill **4** a subtle change or addition in a painting, story, etc. **5** a trace, tinge, etc. **6** a slight attack /a *touch* of the flu/ **7** contact or communication /keep in *touch*/ **8** [Slang] the act of seeking or getting a loan or gift of money **9** *Music* the manner of striking the keys of a piano, etc. —**touch down** to land: said of an aircraft or spacecraft —**touch up** to improve or finish (a painting, story, etc.) by minor changes

touch-and-go (tuch'ən gō') *adj.* uncertain, risky, or precarious

touch'down' *n.* **1** the moment at which an aircraft or spacecraft lands **2** *Football* a play, scoring six points, in which a player carries, catches, or recovers the ball past the opponent's goal line

tou·ché (to͞o shā') *interj.* ⟦Fr⟧ touched: said when one's opponent in fencing scores a point, or to acknowledge a point in debate or a witty retort

touched (tucht) *adj.* **1** emotionally affected; moved **2** slightly demented

touch·ing (tuch'iŋ) *adj.* arousing tender emotions; moving

touch'stone' *n.* **1** a stone formerly used to test the purity of gold or silver **2** any test of genuineness

touch'-type' *vi.* **-typed', -typ'ing** to type without looking at the keyboard by regularly touching a given key with a specific finger

touch'y *adj.* **-i·er, -i·est** **1** easily offended; oversensitive; irritable **2** very risky or precarious

tough (tuf) *adj.* ⟦OE *toh*⟧ **1** that will bend, etc. without tearing or breaking **2** not easily cut or chewed /*tough* steak/ **3** strong; hardy **4** stubborn **5** brutal or rough **6** very difficult; laborious —*n.* a tough person; thug

tough'en *vt., vi.* to make or become tough or tougher —**tough'en·er** *n.*

tou·pee (to͞o pā') *n.* ⟦< Fr < OFr *toup*, tuft of hair⟧ a man's small wig

tour (toor) *n.* ⟦< OFr *tourner*, to turn⟧ **1** a turn, period, etc., as of military duty **2** a long trip, as for sightseeing **3** any trip, as for inspection, for giving performances, etc. —*vt., vi.* to go on a tour (through)

tour de force (toor' də fôrs') *pl.* **tours de force** (toor') ⟦Fr⟧ an unusually skillful or ingenious creation or performance, sometimes a merely clever one

tour'ism' *n.* tourist travel

tour'ist *n.* one who tours, esp. for pleasure —*adj.* of or for tourists

tour·ma·line (to͝or'mə lin, -lēn') *n.* ⟦Fr⟧ a crystalline mineral, used as a gemstone, etc.

tour·na·ment (tur'nə mənt, toor'-) *n.* ⟦< OFr *tourner*, to turn⟧ **1** in the Middle Ages, a contest between knights on horseback who tried to unseat one another with lances **2** a series of contests in competition for a championship Also **tour'ney** (-nē) *n., pl.* **-neys**

tour·ni·quet (tur'ni kit, -ket'; toor'-) *n.* ⟦Fr < L *tunica*, tunic⟧ a device for compressing a blood vessel to stop bleeding, as a bandage twisted about a limb and released at intervals

tou·sle (tou'zəl) *vt.* **-sled, -sling** ⟦< ME *tusen*, to pull⟧ to disorder, dishevel, muss, etc.

tout (tout) *vi., vt.* ⟦OE *totian*, to peep⟧ [Colloq.] **1** to praise highly **2** to sell betting tips on (racehorses) —*n.* [Colloq.] one who touts

tow (tō) *vt.* ⟦OE *togian*⟧ to pull, as by a rope or chain —*n.* **1** a towing or being towed **2** something towed **3** TOWLINE —**in tow** **1** being towed **2** in one's company or charge

to·ward (tôrd) *prep.* ⟦see TO & -WARD⟧ **1** in the direction of **2** facing **3** along a likely course to /steps *toward* peace/ **4** concerning **5** just before /*toward* noon/ **6** for /save *toward* a car/ Also **to·wards**

tow·el (tou'əl) *n.* ⟦< OFr *toaille*⟧ a piece of cloth or paper for wiping or drying things —*vt.* **-eled** or **-elled, -el·ing** or **-el·ling** to wipe or dry with a towel —**throw** (or **toss,** etc.) **in the towel** [Colloq.] to admit defeat

tow'el·ing or **tow'el·ling** *n.* material for making towels

tow·er (tou'ər) *n.* ⟦< L *turris*⟧ **1** a high structure, often part of a building **2** such a structure used as a fortress, etc. —*vi.* to rise high like a tower —**tow'er·ing** *adj.*

tow·head (tō'hed') *n.* ⟦< *tow*, fibers of flax, etc.⟧ **1** a head of pale-yellow hair **2** a person with such hair —**tow'head'ed** *adj.*

tow·hee (tō'hē, -ē) *n.* ⟦echoic⟧ any of various small North American sparrows

tow·line (tō'lin') *n.* a rope, etc. used for towing

town (toun) *n.* ⟦OE *tun*⟧ **1** a concentration of houses, etc. somewhat larger than a village **2** a city **3** a township **4** the business center of a city **5** the people of a town —**go to town** [Slang] to act fast and efficiently —**on the town** [Colloq.] out for a good time

town crier one who formerly cried public announcements through the streets of a village or town

town hall a building in a town, housing the offices of officials, etc.

town house a two-story or three-story dwelling, a unit in a complex of such dwellings

town meeting a meeting of the voters of a town, as in New England

town'ship *n.* a division of a county, constituting a unit of local government

towns·man (tounz'mən) *n., pl.* **-men** **1** one who lives in, or has been reared in, a town **2** a fellow resident of one's town

towns'peo'ple *n.pl.* the people of a town Also **towns'folk'** (-fōk')

tow·path (tō'path') *n.* a path along a canal, used by men or animals towing freight-carrying boats

tow'rope' *n.* a rope used in towing

tox·e·mi·a (täks ē'mē ə) *n.* ⟦see fol. & -EMIA⟧ a condition in which the blood contains poisonous substances, esp. toxins produced by pathogenic bacteria

tox·ic (täks'ik) *adj.* ⟦< Gr *toxicon*, a poison⟧ **1** of, affected by, or caused by a toxin **2** poisonous

tox·i·col·o·gy (täks′i käl′ə jē) ***n.*** ⟦see prec. & -LOGY⟧ the science of poisons and their effects, antidotes, etc. —**tox′i·col′o·gist** ***n.***

tox·in (täks′in) ***n.*** ⟦< TOXIC⟧ **1** any of various poisons produced by microorganisms and causing certain diseases **2** any poison secreted by plants or animals

toy (toi) ***n.*** ⟦< ? MDu *toi*, finery⟧ **1** a trifle **2** a bauble; trinket **3** a plaything for children —***adj.*** **1** like a toy in size, use, etc. **2** made as a toy —***vi.*** to trifle (*with* a thing, an idea, etc.)

tr. **1** transpose **2** treasurer

trace[1] (trās) ***n.*** ⟦< L *trahere*, to draw⟧ **1** a mark, track, sign, etc. left by a person, animal, or thing **2** a barely perceptible amount —***vt.*** **traced, trac′ing** **1** to follow the trail of; track **2** *a*) to follow the development or history of *b*) to determine (a source, etc.) by this procedure **3** to draw, outline, etc. **4** to copy (a drawing, etc.) by following its lines on a superimposed transparent sheet —**trace′a·ble** ***adj.*** —**trac′er** ***n.***

trace[2] (trās) ***n.*** ⟦see TRAIT⟧ either of two straps, etc. connecting a draft animal's harness to the vehicle drawn

trace element a chemical element, as copper, zinc, etc., essential in nutrition, but only in minute amounts

trac·er·y (trās′ər ē) ***n.***, *pl.* **-ies** ⟦< TRACE[1] + -ERY⟧ ornamental work of interlacing or branching lines

tra·che·a (trā′kē ə) ***n.***, *pl.* **-che·ae′** (-ē′) or **-che·as** ⟦< Gr *tracheia* (*arteria*), rough (windpipe)⟧ the passage that conveys air from the larynx to the bronchi; windpipe —**tra′che·al** ***adj.***

tra·che·ot·o·my (trā′kē ät′ə mē) ***n.***, *pl.* **-mies** ⟦see prec. & -TOMY⟧ an incision of the trachea to aid breathing in an emergency

trac·ing (trās′iŋ) ***n.*** something traced; specif., *a*) a copy of a drawing, etc. *b*) a traced line of a recording instrument

track (trak) ***n.*** ⟦< Fr *trac*⟧ **1** a mark left in passing, as a footprint, wheel rut, etc. **2** a path or trail **3** a sequence of ideas, events, etc. **4** a path or circuit laid out for racing, etc. **5** a pair of parallel metal rails on which trains, etc. run **6** *a*) sports performed on a track, as running, hurdling, etc. *b*) these sports along with other contests in jumping, throwing, etc. **7** *a*) a band on a phonograph record, compact disc, etc. *b*) any of the separate, parallel recording surfaces along a magnetic tape —***vt.*** **1** to follow the track of **2** to trace by means of evidence, etc. **3** to plot the path of, as with radar **4** to leave tracks of (mud, etc.) on: often with *up* —**in one's tracks** where one is at the moment —**keep** (or **lose**) **track of** to stay (or fail to stay) informed about —**track′less** ***adj.***

tract[1] (trakt) ***n.*** ⟦< L *trahere*, to draw⟧ **1** a continuous expanse of land **2** a system of organs having some special function [the digestive *tract*]

tract[2] (trakt) ***n.*** ⟦< LL *tractatus*, treatise⟧ a propagandizing pamphlet, esp. one on a religious subject

trac·ta·ble (trak′tə b′l) ***adj.*** ⟦< L *trahere*, to draw⟧ **1** easily managed; docile **2** easily worked; malleable

trac·tion (trak′shən) ***n.*** ⟦< L *trahere*, to draw⟧ **1** *a*) a pulling or drawing *b*) a being pulled or drawn *c*) the kind of power used for pulling [electric *traction*] **2** the power, as of tires on pavement, to hold to a surface without slipping

trac·tor (trak′tər) ***n.*** ⟦see prec.⟧ **1** a powerful, motor-driven vehicle for pulling farm machinery, etc. **2** a truck with a driver's cab and no body, for hauling large trailers

trac′tor-trail′er ***n.*** a TRACTOR (sense 2) combined with a trailer or semitrailer, used for transporting goods

trade (trād) ***n.*** ⟦< LowG, a track⟧ **1** occupation; esp., skilled work **2** all the persons in a particular business **3** buying and selling; commerce **4** customers **5** a purchase or sale **6** an exchange; swap —***vi.*** **trad′ed, trad′ing** **1** to carry on a business **2** to have business dealings (*with*) **3** to make an exchange (*with*) **4** [Colloq.] to be a customer (*at* a certain store) —***vt.*** to exchange; barter —**trade on** (or **upon**) to take advantage of

trade′-in′ ***n.*** a thing given or taken as part payment for something else

trade journal (or **magazine**) a magazine devoted to a specific trade or industry

trade′mark′ ***n.*** a symbol, word, etc. used by a manufacturer or dealer to distinguish a product: usually protected by law

trade name **1** the name by which a commodity is commonly known by those who deal in it **2** a name used as a trademark **3** the business name of a company

trade′-off′ ***n.*** an exchange in which one benefit is given up for another considered more desirable Also **trade′off′**

trad′er ***n.*** **1** one who trades; merchant **2** a ship used in trade

trades·man (trādz′mən) ***n.***, *pl.* **-men** [Chiefly Brit., etc.] a storekeeper —**trades′wom′an**, *pl.* **-wom′en**, ***n.fem.***

trade union LABOR UNION

trade wind a wind that blows toward the equator from either side of it

trading post a store in an outpost, settlement, etc., where trading is done

tra·di·tion (trə dish′ən) ***n.*** ⟦< L *tradere*, deliver⟧ **1** the handing down orally of beliefs, customs, etc. from generation to generation **2** a story, belief, etc. handed down in this way

tra·di′tion·al ***adj.*** of, handed down by, or conforming to tradition

tra·di′tion·al·ism′ ***n.*** adherence to tradition; sometimes, specif., excessive devotion to tradition —**tra·di′tion·al·ist** ***n.***

tra·duce (trə do͞os′, -dyo͞os′) ***vt.*** **-duced′, -duc′ing** ⟦< L *trans*, across + *ducere*, to lead⟧ to slander

traf·fic (traf′ik) ***n.*** ⟦< It *traffico* < L *trans*, across + It *ficcare*, bring⟧ **1** buying and selling; trade **2** dealings (*with* someone) **3** the movement or number of automobiles, pedestrians, etc. along a street, etc. **4** the business done by a transportation company —***adj.*** of or having to do with traffic —***vi.*** **-ficked, -fick·ing** **1** to carry on traffic (*in* a commodity) **2** to have dealings (*with* someone)

traffic circle a circular road at the intersection of several streets: vehicles move on it in one direction only

traffic light (or **signal**) a set of signal lights at a street intersection to regulate traffic

tra·ge·di·an (trə jē′dē ən) ***n.*** an actor or writer of tragedy

trag·e·dy (traj′ə dē) ***n.***, ***pl.*** **-dies** ⟦< Gr *tragos*, goat + *ōidē*, song⟧ **1** a serious play with an unhappy ending **2** a very sad or tragic event; disaster

trag·ic (traj′ik) ***adj.*** **1** of, or having the nature of, tragedy **2** disastrous, fatal, etc. —**trag′i·cal·ly** ***adv.***

trail (trāl) ***vt.*** ⟦< L *trahere*, to draw⟧ **1** to drag or let drag behind one **2** to follow the tracks of; track **3** to hunt by tracking **4** to follow behind —***vi.*** **1** to drag along on the ground, etc. **2** to grow along the ground, etc., as some plants **3** to flow behind, as smoke **4** to follow or lag behind; straggle **5** to grow weaker, dimmer, etc.: with *off* or *away* —***n.*** **1** something that trails behind **2** a mark, scent, etc. left by a person, animal, or thing that has passed **3** a beaten path

trail′blaz′er ***n.*** **1** one who blazes a trail **2** a pioneer in any field

trail′er ***n.*** **1** one that trails **2** *a)* a wagon, van, etc. designed to be pulled by an automobile, truck, etc. *b)* such a vehicle designed to be lived in

trailer park an area, usually with piped water, electricity, etc., for trailers, esp. mobile homes

train (trān) ***n.*** ⟦< L *trahere*, to pull⟧ **1** something that drags along behind, as a trailing skirt **2** a group of followers; retinue **3** a procession; caravan **4** any connected order; sequence [a *train* of thought] **5** a line of connected railroad cars pulled by a locomotive —***vt.*** **1** to guide the growth of (a plant) **2** to guide the mental, moral, etc. development of; rear **3** to instruct so as to make proficient **4** to make fit for an athletic contest, etc. **5** to aim (a gun, etc.) —***vi.*** to undergo training —**train·ee** (trān ē′) ***n.*** —**train′er** ***n.*** —**train′ing** ***n.***

traipse (trāps) ***vi.***, ***vt.*** **traipsed**, **traips′ing** ⟦< ?⟧ [Colloq. or Dial.] to walk, wander, or tramp

trait (trāt) ***n.*** ⟦< L *trahere*, to draw⟧ a distinguishing characteristic

trai·tor (trāt′ər) ***n.*** ⟦< L *tradere*, betray⟧ one who betrays one's country, friends, etc. —**trai′tor·ous** ***adj.***

tra·jec·to·ry (trə jek′tə rē) ***n.***, ***pl.*** **-ries** ⟦< L *trans*, across + *jacere*, to throw⟧ the curved path of something hurtling through space

tram (tram) ***n.*** ⟦prob. < LowG *traam*, a beam⟧ [Brit., etc. (exc. Cdn.)] a streetcar

tram·mel (tram′əl) ***n.*** ⟦< L *tres*, three + *macula*, a mesh⟧ [*usually pl.*] something that confines or restrains —***vt.*** **-meled** or **-melled**, **-mel·ing** or **-mel·ling** to confine, restrain, etc.

tramp (tramp) ***vi.*** ⟦ME *trampen*⟧ **1** to walk or step heavily **2** to travel about on foot —***vt.*** **1** to step on heavily **2** to walk through —***n.*** **1** a hobo; vagrant **2** the sound of heavy steps **3** a journey on foot; hike **4** a freight ship that picks up cargo, etc. wherever it may be **5** [Slang] a sexually promiscuous woman

tram·ple (tram′pəl) ***vi.*** **-pled**, **-pling** ⟦see prec.⟧ to tread heavily —***vt.*** to crush, as by treading heavily on

tram·po·line (tram′pə lēn′, -lin) ***n.*** ⟦< It⟧ a sheet of strong canvas stretched tightly on a frame, used in acrobatic tumbling

trance (trans) ***n.*** ⟦< L *transire*, to die⟧ **1** a state of altered consciousness, resembling sleep, as in hypnosis **2** a daze; stupor **3** a state of great mental abstraction

tran·quil (tran′kwil, traŋ′-) ***adj.*** **-quil·er** or **-quil·ler**, **-quil·est** or **-quil·lest** ⟦L *tranquillus*⟧ calm, serene, placid, etc. —**tran·quil′li·ty** or **tran·quil′i·ty** (-kwil′ə tē) ***n.*** —**tran′quil·ly** ***adv.***

tran′quil·ize′ or **tran′quil·lize′** (-īz′) ***vt.***, ***vi.*** **-ized′** or **-lized′**, **-iz′ing** or **-liz′ing** to make or become tranquil

tran′quil·iz′er or **tran′quil·liz′er** ***n.*** a drug used as a calming agent in treating various emotional disturbances, etc.

trans- ⟦L < *trans*, across⟧ *prefix* over, across, beyond

trans. **1** translated **2** translation

trans·act (tran zakt′, -sakt′) ***vt.*** ⟦< L *trans-*, over + *agere*, to drive⟧ to carry on or complete (business, etc.)

trans·ac′tion ***n.*** **1** a transacting **2** something transacted; specif., *a)* a business deal *b)* [*pl.*] a record of the proceedings of a society, etc.

trans·ac′tion·al analysis a form of popular psychotherapy dealing with hypothetical states of the ego

trans·at·lan·tic (trans′at lan′tik, tranz′-) ***adj.*** **1** crossing the Atlantic **2** on the other side of the Atlantic

trans·ceiv·er (tran sē′vər) ***n.*** a radio transmitter and receiver in a single housing

tran·scend (tran send′) ***vt.*** ⟦< L *trans-*, over + *scandere*, climb⟧ **1** to go beyond the limits of; exceed **2** to surpass; excel —**tran·scend′ent** ***adj.***

tran·scen·den·tal (tran′sen dent′'l) ***adj.*** **1** supernatural **2** abstract —**tran′scen·den′tal·ly** ***adv.***

tran′scen·den′tal·ism′ ***n.*** a philosophy based on a search for reality through spiritual intuition

trans′con·ti·nen′tal (trans′-) ***adj.*** **1** that crosses a continent **2** on the other side of a continent

tran·scribe (tran skrīb′) ***vt.*** **-scribed′**, **-scrib′ing** **1** to write out or type out in full (shorthand notes, etc.) **2** to represent (speech sounds) in symbols

tran·script (tran′skript′) ***n.*** **1** a written or typewritten copy **2** a copy, esp. an official copy, as of a student's record

tran·scrip′tion (-skrip′shən) ***n.*** **1** a transcribing **2** a transcript; copy **3** an arrangement of a piece of music for an instrument or voice other than that for which it was written

trans·duc·er (trans do͞os′ər, tranz-) ***n.*** ⟦< L *trans-*, over + *ducere*, to lead⟧ a device that transmits energy from one system to another, sometimes converting the energy to a different form

tran·sept (tran′sept′) ***n.*** ⟦< L *trans-*, across + *septum*, enclosure⟧ the part of a cross-shaped church at right angles to the nave, or either arm of this part

trans·fer (*for v.* trans fur′, trans′fər; *for n.*

trans'fər) *vt.* **-ferred'**, **-fer'ring** ⟦< L *trans-*, across + *ferre*, to bear⟧ 1 to carry, send, etc. to another person or place 2 to make over (property, etc.) to another 3 to convey (a picture, etc.) from one surface to another —*vi.* 1 to transfer oneself or be transferred 2 to change to another school, etc. or to another bus, etc. —*n.* 1 a transferring or being transferred 2 one that is transferred 3 a ticket entitling the bearer to change to another bus, etc. —**trans·fer'a·ble** *adj.*

trans·fer·ence (trans'fər əns, trans fur'-) *n.* a transferring or being transferred

trans·fig·ure (trans fig'yər) *vt.* **-ured**, **-ur·ing** ⟦< L *trans-*, across + *figura*, figure⟧ 1 to change the form or appearance of 2 to transform so as to glorify —**trans·fig'u·ra'·tion** *n.*

trans·fix (trans fiks') *vt.* ⟦< L *trans-*, through + *figere*, to fix⟧ 1 to pierce through; impale 2 to make motionless, as if impaled

trans·form (trans fôrm') *vt.* ⟦< L *trans-*, over + *forma*, a form⟧ 1 to change the form or appearance of 2 to change the condition, character, or function of —**trans'·for·ma'tion** *n.*

trans·form'er *n.* 1 one that transforms 2 a device for changing electrical energy to a different voltage

trans·fuse' (-fyōōz') *vt.* **-fused'**, **-fus'ing** ⟦< L *trans-*, across + *fundere*, pour⟧ 1 to instill; imbue 2 to transfer (blood, etc.) into a blood vessel —**trans·fu'sion** *n.*

trans·gress (trans gres', tranz-) *vt.*, *vi.* ⟦< L *trans-*, over + *gradi*, to step⟧ 1 to break (a law, command, etc.); sin (against) 2 to go beyond (a limit, etc.) —**trans·gres'sion** (-gresh'ən) *n.* —**trans·gres'sor** *n.*

tran·si·ent (tran'shənt) *adj.* ⟦< L *trans-*, over + *ire*, to go⟧ 1 passing away with time; temporary 2 passing quickly; fleeting —*n.* a transient person; esp., a temporary lodger —**tran'si·ence** or **tran'si·en·cy** *n.* —**tran'si·ent·ly** *adv.*

tran·sis·tor (tran zis'tər, -sis'-) *n.* ⟦TRAN(S-FER) + (RE)SISTOR⟧ a compact electronic device, composed of semiconductor material, that controls current flow —**tran·sis'tor·ize'**, **-ized'**, **-iz'ing**, *vt.*

trans·it (trans'it, tranz'it) *n.* ⟦< L *trans-*, over + *ire*, go⟧ 1 passage through or across 2 *a*) a carrying through or across; conveyance *b*) a system of urban public transportation 3 a surveying instrument for measuring horizontal angles

tran·si·tion (tran zish'ən) *n.* a passing from one condition, place, etc. to another —**tran·si'tion·al** *adj.*

tran·si·tive (tran'sə tiv, -zə-) *adj.* designating a verb taking a direct object

tran·si·to·ry (tran'sə tôr'ē, -zə-) *adj.* not enduring; temporary; fleeting

transl. 1 translated 2 translation

trans·late (trans lāt', tranz-) *vt.* **-lat'ed**, **-lat'·ing** ⟦< L *translatus*, transferred⟧ 1 to move from one place or condition to another 2 to put into the words of a different language 3 to put into different words —**trans·la'tor** *n.*

trans·la'tion *n.* 1 a translating 2 writing or speech translated into another language

trans·lit·er·ate (trans lit'ər āt', tranz-) *vt.* **-at'ed**, **-at'ing** ⟦< TRANS- + L *litera*, letter⟧ to write (words, etc.) in the characters of another alphabet

trans·lu·cent (trans lōō'sənt, tranz-) *adj.* ⟦< L *trans-*, through + *lucere*, to shine⟧ letting light pass through but not transparent

trans·mi·grate (trans mī'grāt', tranz-) *vi.* **-grat'ed**, **-grat'ing** ⟦see TRANS- & MIGRATE⟧ to pass into another body at death: said of the soul, as in Hindu religious belief —**trans'mi·gra'tion** *n.*

trans·mis·sion (trans mish'ən, tranz-) *n.* 1 a transmitting 2 something transmitted 3 the part of a motor vehicle, etc. that transmits power to the wheels, as by gears

trans·mit' (-mit') *vt.* **-mit'ted**, **-mit'ting** ⟦< L *trans-*, over + *mittere*, send⟧ 1 to cause to go to another person or place; transfer 2 to hand down by heredity, inheritance, etc. 3 *a*) to pass (light, heat, etc.) through some medium *b*) to conduct 4 to convey (force, movement, etc.) to 5 to send out (radio or television signals) —**trans·mis'si·ble** (-mis'ə bəl) *adj.* —**trans·mit'ta·ble** *adj.* —**trans·mit'tal** or **trans·mit'·tance** *n.*

trans·mit'ter *n.* one that transmits; specif., the apparatus that transmits signals in telephony, radio, etc.

trans·mute (trans myōōt', tranz-) *vt.*, *vi.* **-mut'ed**, **-mut'ing** ⟦< L *trans-*, over + *mutare*, to change⟧ to change from one form, nature, substance, etc. into another —**trans'mu·ta'tion** *n.*

trans·na'tion·al *adj.* transcending the interests, etc. of a single nation

trans·o·ce·an·ic (trans'ō'shē an'ik) *adj.* crossing the ocean

tran·som (tran'səm) *n.* ⟦prob. < L *transtrum*, crossbeam⟧ 1 a horizontal crossbar, as across the top of a door or window 2 a small window just above a door or window

trans·pa·cif·ic (trans'pə sif'ik) *adj.* 1 crossing the Pacific 2 on the other side of the Pacific

trans·par·en·cy (trans per'ən sē) *n.*, *pl.* **-cies** a transparent film or slide that can be projected on a screen

trans·par'ent *adj.* ⟦< L *trans-*, through + *parere*, appear⟧ 1 transmitting light rays so that objects on the other side may be seen 2 so fine in texture as to be seen through 3 easily understood or detected; obvious —**trans·par'ent·ly** *adv.*

tran·spire (tran spīr') *vi.* **-spired'**, **-spir'ing** ⟦< L *trans-*, through + *spirare*, breathe⟧ 1 to give off vapor, moisture, etc., as through pores 2 to become known 3 to happen: regarded by some as a loose usage —**tran'·spi·ra'tion** (-spə rā'shən) *n.*

trans·plant (*for v.* trans plant', trans'plant'; *for n.* trans'plant') *vt.* 1 to remove from one place and plant, resettle, etc. in another 2 *Surgery* to transfer (tissue or an organ) from one to another; graft —*n.* a transplanting or something transplanted, as a body organ or seedling —**trans'plan·ta'tion** (-plan tā'shən) *n.*

tran·spon·der (tran spän'dər) *n.* ⟦< TRANS-

MITTER & RESPOND]] a transceiver that automatically transmits signals

trans·port (*for v.* trans pôrt'; *for n.* trans'·pôrt') ***vt.*** [[< L *trans-*, over + *portare*, carry]] 1 to carry from one place to another 2 to carry away with emotion —***n.*** 1 a transporting; transportation 2 rapture 3 a vehicle for transporting

trans'por·ta'tion (-pər tā'shən) ***n.*** 1 a transporting or being transported 2 a means of conveyance 3 fare or a ticket for being transported

trans·pose (trans pōz') ***vt., vi.* -posed', -pos'ing** [[see TRANS- & POSE]] 1 to change the usual order or position of; interchange 2 to rewrite or play (a musical composition) in another key —**trans'po·si'tion** (-pə zish'·ən) ***n.***

trans·sex·u·al (trans sek'shōō əl) ***n.*** a person who is predisposed to identify with the opposite sex, sometimes so strongly as to undergo sex-change surgery

trans·ship (trans ship', tran-) ***vt., vi.* -shipped', -ship'ping** to transfer from one ship, train, truck, etc. to another for further shipment —**trans·ship'ment *n.***

tran·sub·stan·ti·a·tion (trans'səb stan'shē ā'shən) ***n.*** [[< L *trans-*, over + *substantia*, substance]] *R.C.Ch., Eastern Orthodox Ch.* the doctrine that, in the Eucharist, the whole substances of the bread and wine are changed into the body and blood of Christ

trans·verse (trans vurs', tranz-; *esp. for n.*, trans'vurs', tranz'-) ***adj.*** [[< L *trans-*, across + *vertere*, to turn]] situated across; crosswise —***n.*** a transverse part, etc.

trans·ves·tite (trans ves'tīt', tranz-) ***n.*** [[< TRANS- + L *vestire*, to dress]] a person who gets sexual pleasure from dressing in the clothes of the opposite sex

trap[1] (trap) ***n.*** [[< OE *træppe*]] 1 a device for catching animals, as one that snaps shut tightly when stepped on 2 any stratagem designed to catch or trick 3 a device, as in a drainpipe, for preventing the escape of gas, etc. 4 [*pl.*] percussion instruments, as in a band —***vt.* trapped, trap'ping** to catch as in a trap —***vi.*** to trap animals, esp. for their furs

trap[2] (trap) ***vt.* trapped, trap'ping** [[< OFr *drap*, cloth]] to cover, equip, or adorn with trappings

trap'door' ***n.*** a hinged or sliding door in a roof, ceiling, or floor

tra·peze (tra pēz', trə-) ***n.*** [[see fol.]] a short horizontal bar, hung high by two ropes, on which gymnasts, etc. swing

tra·pe·zi·um (trə pē'zē əm, tra-) ***n.***, *pl.* **-zi·ums** or **-zi·a** (-ə) [[< Gr *trapeza*, table]] a plane figure with four sides, no two of which are parallel

trap·e·zoid (trap'i zoid') ***n.*** [[see prec.]] a plane figure with four sides, only two of which are parallel —**trap'e·zoi'dal *adj.***

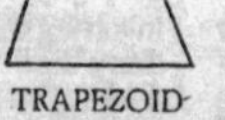
TRAPEZOID

trap·pings (trap'iŋz) ***n.pl.*** [[see TRAP[2]]] 1 an ornamental covering for a horse 2 adornments

trap'shoot'ing ***n.*** the sport of shooting at clay disks sprung into the air from throwing devices

trash (trash) ***n.*** [[prob. < Scand]] 1 worthless or waste things; rubbish 2 a disreputable person or people —***vt.*** [Slang] 1 to destroy (property) as by vandalism 2 to criticize or insult (a person, etc.) sharply or maliciously —**trash'y, -i·er, -i·est, *adj.***

trau·ma (trô'mə; *also* trä'-, trou'-) ***n.***, *pl.* **-mas** or **-ma·ta** (-mə tə) [[Gr]] 1 a bodily injury or shock 2 an emotional shock, often having a lasting psychic effect —**trau·mat·ic** (trô mat'ik; *also* trə-, trä-, trou-) ***adj.***

trau'ma·tize' (-tīz') ***vt.* -tized', -tiz'ing** to subject to a physical or mental trauma

trav·ail (trə vāl', trav'āl') ***n.*** [[< L *tri-*, three + *palus*, stake: referring to a torture device]] 1 very hard work 2 intense pain; agony

trav·el (trav'əl) ***vi.* -eled** or **-elled, -el·ing** or **-el·ling** [[var. of prec.]] 1 to go from one place to another 2 to move, pass, or be transmitted —***vt.*** to make a journey over or through —***n.*** a traveling; trip —**trav'el·er** or **trav'el·ler *n.***

traveler's check a check, issued by a bank, etc., sold to a traveler who signs it at issuance and again when cashing it

trav·e·logue or **trav·e·log** (trav'ə lôg') ***n.*** 1 an illustrated lecture on travels 2 a short film about a place, esp. one that is foreign, unusual, etc.

tra·verse (*for v.* trə vurs', tra-; *for n. & adj.* trav'ərs) ***vt.* -versed', -vers'ing** [[< L *trans-*, across + *vertere*, to turn]] to pass over, across, or through —***n.*** something that traverses or crosses, as a crossbar —***adj.*** 1 extending across 2 designating or of draperies drawn by pulling a cord at the side

trav·es·ty (trav'is tē) ***n.***, *pl.* **-ties** [[< L *trans-*, over + *vestire*, to dress]] 1 a farcical imitation in ridicule 2 a ridiculous representation —***vt.* -tied, -ty·ing** to make a travesty of

trawl (trôl) ***n.*** [[< ? MDu *traghel*, dragnet]] 1 a large net dragged along the bottom of a fishing bank 2 a long line supported by buoys, from which fishing lines are hung —***vi., vt.*** to fish or catch with a trawl

trawl'er *n.* a boat used in trawling

tray (trā) ***n.*** [[< OE *treg*, wooden board]] a flat receptacle with raised edges, for holding or carrying things

treach·er·ous (trech'ər əs) ***adj.*** 1 characterized by treachery 2 untrustworthy —**treach'er·ous·ly *adv.***

treach·er·y (trech'ər ē) ***n.***, *pl.* **-ies** [[< OFr *trichier*, to cheat]] 1 betrayal of trust; disloyalty 2 treason

trea·cle (trē'kəl) ***n.*** [[< Gr (*antidotos*) *thēriakē*, (remedy) for venom]] [Brit., etc. (exc. Cdn.)] 1 molasses 2 anything very sweet or cloying —**trea'cly** (-klē) ***adj.***

tread (tred) ***vt.* trod, trod'den** or **trod, tread'ing** [[OE *tredan*]] 1 to walk on, in, along, etc. 2 to do or follow by walking, dancing, etc. 3 to press or beat with the feet —***vi.*** 1 to walk 2 to set one's foot (*on, across*, etc.) 3 to trample (*on* or *upon*) —***n.*** 1 the manner or sound of treading 2 something on which a person or thing treads or moves, as a shoe sole, wheel, surface of a stair, etc. 3 the thick outer layer of an automotive tire —**tread water** *pt. & pp. usually*

tread'ed to stay upright in swimming by moving the legs up and down
trea·dle (tred''l) *n.* ⟦< OE *tredan*, to tread⟧ a lever moved by the foot as to turn a wheel
tread'mill' *n.* a mill wheel turned by an animal treading an endless belt
treas. 1 treasurer 2 treasury
trea·son (trē'zən) *n.* ⟦< L *trans-*, over + *dare*, give⟧ betrayal of one's country to an enemy —**trea'son·a·ble** or **trea'son·ous** *adj.*
treas·ure (trezh'ər) *n.* ⟦< Gr *thēsauros*⟧ 1 accumulated wealth, as money, jewels, etc. 2 any person or thing considered valuable —*vt.* **-ured, -ur·ing** 1 to save up for future use 2 to value greatly
treas·ur·er (trezh'ər ər) *n.* one in charge of a treasury, as of a government, club, etc.
treas'ure-trove' (-trōv') *n.* ⟦*trove* < OFr *trover*, find⟧ treasure found hidden, the original owner of which is unknown
treas'ur·y (-ē) *n., pl.* **-ies** 1 a place where treasure or funds are kept 2 the funds or revenues of a state, corporation, etc. 3 [T-] the department of government in charge of revenue, taxation, etc.
treat (trēt) *vi.* ⟦ult. < L *trahere*, to draw⟧ 1 to discuss terms (*with*) 2 to speak or write (*of*) —*vt.* 1 to deal with (a subject) in writing, music, etc. in a specified manner 2 to act toward (someone or something) in a specified manner 3 to pay for the food, etc. of (another) 4 to subject to some process, chemical, etc. 5 to give medical care to —*n.* 1 a meal, drink, etc. paid for by another 2 anything that gives great pleasure
trea·tise (trēt'is) *n.* ⟦see prec.⟧ a formal writing on some subject
treat·ment (trēt'mənt) *n.* 1 act, manner, method, etc. of treating 2 medical or surgical care
trea·ty (trēt'ē) *n., pl.* **-ties** ⟦< L *trahere*, to draw⟧ a formal agreement between two or more nations
tre·ble (treb'əl) *adj.* ⟦< L *triplus*, triple⟧ 1 threefold; triple 2 of, for, or performing the treble —*n.* 1 the highest part in musical harmony; soprano 2 a high-pitched voice or sound —*vt., vi.* **-bled, -bling** to make or become threefold
tree (trē) *n.* ⟦OE *trēow*⟧ 1 a large, woody perennial plant with one main trunk and many branches 2 anything resembling a tree; specif., a diagram of family descent (**family tree**) —*vt.* **treed, tree'ing** to chase up a tree —**tree'less** *adj.* —**tree'like'** *adj.*
treen (trēn) *n.* ⟦< obs. pl. of prec.⟧ decorative objects, esp. antiques, made of wood
tre·foil (trē'foil') *n.* ⟦< L *tri-*, three + *folium*, leaf⟧ 1 a plant with leaves divided into three leaflets, as the clover 2 a design, etc. shaped like such a leaf
trek (trek) *vi.* **trekked, trek'king** ⟦Afrik < Du *trekken*, to draw⟧ 1 to travel slowly or laboriously 2 [Colloq.] to go on foot —*n.* 1 a journey 2 a migration
trel·lis (trel'is) *n.* ⟦< L *trilix*, triple-twilled⟧ a lattice on which vines are trained
trem·a·tode (trem'ə tōd', trē'mə-) *n.* ⟦< Gr *trēmatōdēs*, perforated⟧ a parasitic flatworm with muscular suckers; fluke
trem·ble (trem'bəl) *vi.* **-bled, -bling** ⟦< L *tremere*⟧ 1 to shake or shiver, as from cold, fear, etc. 2 to feel great fear or anxiety 3 to quiver, vibrate, etc. —*n.* 1 a trembling 2 [*sometimes pl.*] a fit or state of trembling
tre·men·dous (tri men'dəs) *adj.* ⟦< L *tremere*, tremble⟧ 1 terrifying; dreadful 2 *a*) very large; great *b*) [Colloq.] wonderful, amazing, etc. —**tre·men'dous·ly** *adv.*
trem·o·lo (trem'ə lō') *n., pl.* **-los'** ⟦It⟧ *Music* a tremulous effect produced by rapid reiteration of the same tone
trem·or (trem'ər) *n.* ⟦< L *tremere*, tremble⟧ 1 a trembling, shaking, etc. 2 a trembling sensation
trem·u·lous (trem'yoo ləs) *adj.* ⟦< L *tremere*, to tremble⟧ 1 trembling; quivering 2 fearful; timid —**trem'u·lous·ly** *adv.* —**trem'u·lous·ness** *n.*
trench (trench) *vt.* ⟦< OFr *trenchier*, to cut⟧ to dig a ditch or ditches in —*n.* 1 a deep furrow 2 a long, narrow ditch dug by soldiers for cover, with earth heaped up in front
trench·ant (trench'ənt) *adj.* ⟦see prec.⟧ 1 sharp; keen; incisive /*trenchant* words/ 2 forceful; vigorous; effective /a *trenchant* argument/ —**trench'ant·ly** *adv.*
trench coat a belted raincoat in a military style
trench'er *n.* ⟦see TRENCH⟧ [Archaic] a wooden platter for meat
trench'er·man (-mən) *n., pl.* **-men** an eater; esp., one who eats much
trench foot a diseased condition of the feet from prolonged exposure to wet and cold, as in trenches
trench mouth an infectious disease of the mucous membranes of the mouth and throat
trend (trend) *vi.* ⟦OE *trendan*⟧ to have a general direction or tendency —*n.* 1 the general tendency or course; drift 2 a current style
trend·y (tren'dē) *adj.* **-i·er, -i·est** [Colloq.] of or in the latest style, or trend
Tren·ton (trent''n) capital of N.J.: pop. 92,000
trep·i·da·tion (trep'ə dā'shən) *n.* ⟦< L *trepidus*, disturbed⟧ 1 trembling movement 2 fearful uncertainty
tres·pass (tres'pəs, -pas') *vi.* ⟦< L *trans-*, across + *passus*, a step⟧ 1 to go beyond the limits of what is considered right; do wrong; transgress 2 to enter another's property without permission or right —*n.* a trespassing; specif., a moral offense —**tres'pass·er** *n.*
tress (tres) *n.* ⟦< OFr *tresse*, braid of hair⟧ 1 a lock of human hair 2 [*pl.*] a woman's or girl's hair, esp. when long
tres·tle (tres'əl) *n.* ⟦< L *transtrum*, a beam⟧ 1 a horizontal beam fastened to two pairs of spreading legs, used as a support 2 a framework of uprights and crosspieces, supporting a bridge, etc.
trey (trā) *n.* ⟦< L *tres*, three⟧ a playing card, etc. with three spots
tri- ⟦< Fr, L, or Gr⟧ *prefix* 1 having or involving three 2 three times, into three 3 every third
tri·ad (trī'ad') *n.* ⟦< Gr *treis*, three⟧ a group of three
tri·age (trē äzh') *n.* ⟦< Fr *trier*, sift⟧ a sys-

tem of establishing the order in which acts of esp. medical assistance are to be carried out in an emergency

tri·al (trī′əl) ***n.*** ⟦ see TRY ⟧ **1** the act or process of trying, testing, etc.; test; probation **2** a hardship, suffering, etc. **3** a source of annoyance **4** a formal examination to decide a case by a court of law **5** an attempt; effort —***adj.*** **1** of a trial **2** for the purpose of trying, testing, etc.

trial and error the process of making repeated trials, tests, etc. until the right result is found

trial balloon something said or done to test public opinion on an issue

tri·an·gle (trī′aŋ′gəl) ***n.*** ⟦ see TRI- & ANGLE¹ ⟧ **1** a plane figure having three angles and three sides **2** anything with three sides or corners **3** a situation involving three persons /a love *triangle*/ —**tri·an′gu·lar** (-gyo͞o lər) ***adj.*** —**tri·an′gu·lar·ly** ***adv.***

tri·an′gu·late′ (-gyo͞o lāt′) ***vt.*** **-lat′ed, -lat′ing** to divide into triangles to compute distance or relative positions —**tri·an′gu·la′tion** ***n.***

tri·ath·lon (trī ath′län′, -lən) ***n.*** ⟦ TRI- + Gr *athlon,* a contest ⟧ an endurance race combining events in swimming, bicycling, and running

tribe (trīb) ***n.*** ⟦ < L *tribus* ⟧ **1** a group of persons or clans descended from a common ancestor and living under a leader or chief **2** a natural group of plants or animals —**trib′al** ***adj.*** —**trib′al·ly** ***adv.*** —**tribes′-man** (-mən), *pl.* **-men,** ***n.***

trib·u·la·tion (trib′yo͞o lā′shən) ***n.*** ⟦ < L *tribulare,* to press ⟧ great misery or distress, or the cause of it

tri·bu·nal (trī byo͞o′nəl, tri-) ***n.*** ⟦ see fol. ⟧ **1** a seat for a judge in a court **2** a court of justice

trib·une (trib′yo͞on′, tri byo͞on′) ***n.*** ⟦ < L *tribus,* tribe ⟧ **1** in ancient Rome, a magistrate appointed to protect the rights of plebeians **2** a champion of the people: often a newspaper name

trib·u·tar·y (trib′yo͞o ter′ē) ***adj.*** **1** paying tribute **2** subject /a *tributary* nation/ **3** *a)* making additions *b)* flowing into a larger one /a *tributary* stream/ —***n.***, *pl.* **-ies** **1** a tributary nation **2** a tributary river

trib·ute (trib′yo͞ot) ***n.*** ⟦ < L *tribuere,* allot ⟧ **1** money paid regularly by one nation to another as acknowledgment of subjugation, for protection, etc. **2** any forced payment **3** something given, done, or said to show gratitude, respect, honor, or praise

trice (trīs) ***n.*** ⟦ < MDu *trisen,* to pull ⟧ an instant: now only in **in a trice**

tri·cen·ten·ni·al (trī′sen ten′ē əl) ***adj.*** happening once every 300 years —***n.*** a 300th anniversary

tri·ceps (trī′seps′) ***n.***, *pl.* **-ceps′** or **-ceps′es** ⟦ L < *tri-,* three + *caput,* head ⟧ a muscle with three points of origin; esp., the muscle on the back of the upper arm

tri·cer·a·tops (trī ser′ə täps′) ***n.*** ⟦ < TRI- + Gr *keras,* horn + *ōps,* eye ⟧ a plant-eating dinosaur with three horns

tri·chi·na (tri kī′nə) ***n.***, *pl.* **-nae** (-nē) ⟦ < Gr *trichinos,* hairy ⟧ a very small worm whose larvae cause trichinosis

trich·i·no·sis (trik′i nō′sis) ***n.*** ⟦ < Gr *trichinos,* hairy ⟧ a disease caused by intestinal worms, and acquired by eating pork from an infested hog

trick (trik) ***n.*** ⟦ < OFr *trichier,* to cheat ⟧ **1** something designed to deceive, cheat, etc. **2** a practical joke; prank **3** a clever act intended to amuse **4** any feat requiring skill **5** a personal mannerism **6** a round of duty; shift **7** *Card Games* the cards won in a single round —***vt.*** to deceive or swindle —***adj.*** apt to malfunction /a *trick* knee/ —**do** (or **turn**) **the trick** [Colloq.] to produce the desired result —**trick′er·y,** *pl.* **-ies,** ***n.*** —**trick′ster** ***n.***

trick·le (trik′əl) ***vi.*** **-led, -ling** ⟦ ME *triklen* < ? ⟧ **1** to flow slowly in a thin stream or fall in drops **2** to move slowly /the crowd *trickled* away/ —***n.*** a slow, small flow

trick′le-down′ ***adj.*** of an economic theory holding that government aid to big business will ultimately benefit the poor

trick·sy (trik′sē) ***adj.*** **-si·er, -si·est** **1** full of tricks; playful **2** TRICKY

trick′y ***adj.*** **-i·er, -i·est** **1** given to or characterized by trickery **2** like a trick in deceptiveness or intricacy

tri·col·or (trī′kul′ər) ***n.*** a flag having three colors in large areas; esp., the flag of France

tri·cy·cle (trī′sik′əl, -si kəl) ***n.*** ⟦ Fr: see TRI- & CYCLE ⟧ a child's three-wheeled vehicle operated by pedals

tri·dent (trīd′′nt) ***n.*** ⟦ < L *tri-,* three + *dens,* tooth ⟧ a three-pronged spear —***adj.*** three-pronged

tried (trīd) ***vt.***, ***vi.*** *pt. & pp. of* TRY —***adj.*** **1** tested; proved **2** trustworthy

tri·en·ni·al (trī en′ē əl) ***adj.*** ⟦ < L *tri-,* three + *annus,* year ⟧ **1** happening every three years **2** lasting three years —**tri·en′ni·al·ly** ***adv.***

Tri·este (trē est′) seaport in NE Italy: pop. 243,000

tri·fle (trī′fəl) ***n.*** ⟦ < OFr *truffe,* deception ⟧ **1** something of little value or importance **2** a small amount of money —***vi.*** **-fled, -fling** **1** to talk or act jokingly **2** to toy (*with*) —***vt.*** to waste /to *trifle* the hours away/ —**tri′fler** ***n.***

tri′fling ***adj.*** **1** frivolous; shallow **2** of little importance; trivial

tri·fo·cals (trī′fō′kəlz) ***n.pl.*** eyeglasses like bifocals, but with a third area in the lens ground for intermediate distance

trig (trig) ***n.*** *short for* TRIGONOMETRY

trig·ger (trig′ər) ***n.*** ⟦ < Du *trekken,* to pull ⟧ a lever pulled to release a catch, etc., esp. one pressed to activate the firing mechanism on a firearm —***vt.*** to initiate (an action)

trig′ger-hap′py ***adj.*** **1** tending to resort to force rashly or irresponsibly **2** ready to start a war for the slightest cause

tri·glyc·er·ide (trī glis′ər īd′) ***n.*** ⟦ TRI- + Gr *glykeros,* sweet ⟧ an ester derived from glycerol, the chief component of fats and oils

trig·o·nom·e·try (trig′ə näm′ə trē) ***n.***, *pl.* **-tries** ⟦ < Gr *trigōnon,* triangle + *-metria,* measurement ⟧ the branch of mathematics analyzing, and making calculations from, relations between the sides and angles of triangles —**trig′o·no·met′ric** (-nə me′trik) ***adj.***

trill (tril) *n.* ⟦ult. echoic⟧ **1** a rapid alternation of a musical tone with a slightly higher tone **2** a warble **3** a rapid vibration of the tongue or uvula —*vt., vi.* to sound, speak, or play with a trill

tril·lion (tril′yən) *n.* **1** 1 followed by 12 zeros **2** [Brit.] 1 followed by 18 zeros —**tril′lionth** *adj., n.*

TRILLIUM

tril·li·um (tril′ē əm) *n.* ⟦ModL < L *tri-*, three⟧ a woodland plant having a single flower with three petals and three sepals

tril·o·gy (tril′ə jē) *n., pl.* **-gies** ⟦see TRI- & -LOGY⟧ a set of three related plays, novels, etc.

trim (trim) *vt.* **trimmed, trim′ming** ⟦< OE *trymman*, make firm⟧ **1** to put in proper order; make neat or tidy [to *trim* hair] **2** to clip, lop, cut, etc. **3** to decorate, as by adding ornaments, etc. **4** *a)* to balance (a ship) by ballasting, etc. *b)* to put (sails) in order for sailing **5** to balance (a flying aircraft) **6** [Colloq.] to beat, punish, defeat, cheat, etc. —*vi.* to adjust according to expediency —*n.* **1** order; arrangement **2** good condition **3** a trimming **4** decorative parts or borders —*adj.* **trim′mer, trim′mest** **1** orderly; neat **2** well-proportioned **3** in good condition —**trim′ly** *adv.* —**trim′mer** *n.* —**trim′ness** *n.*

tri·ma·ran (trī′mə ran′) *n.* a boat like a catamaran, but with three hulls

tri·mes·ter (trī mes′tər, trī′mes′-) *n.* ⟦< L *tri-*, three + *mensis*, month⟧ in some colleges, any of the three periods of the academic year

trim·ming (trim′iŋ) *n.* **1** decoration; ornament **2** [*pl.*] *a)* the side dishes of a meal *b)* parts trimmed off **3** [Colloq.] a beating, defeat, cheating, etc.

Trin·i·dad and To·ba·go (trin′i dad′ ənd tō bā′gō) island country in the West Indies: 1,980 sq. mi.; pop. 1,055,000

trin·i·ty (trin′i tē) *n., pl.* **-ties** ⟦< L *trinitas*⟧ a set of three —**the Trinity** *Christian Theol.* the union of Father, Son, and Holy Spirit in one Godhead

trin·ket (triŋ′kit) *n.* ⟦ME *trenket*⟧ **1** a small ornament, piece of jewelry, etc. **2** a trifle or toy

tri·o (trē′ō) *n., pl.* **-os** ⟦< L *tres*, three⟧ **1** a group of three **2** *Music a)* a composition for three voices or three instruments *b)* the three performers of such a composition

trip (trip) *vi., vt.* **tripped, trip′ping** ⟦< OFr *treper*⟧ **1** to move or perform with light, rapid steps **2** to stumble or cause to stumble **3** to make or cause to make a mistake **4** to release or run past (a spring, wheel, etc.) —*n.* **1** a light, quick tread **2** a journey, jaunt, etc. **3** a stumble or a causing to stumble **4** [Slang] *a)* an experience induced by a psychedelic drug, esp. LSD *b)* an experience that is pleasing, exciting, etc. —**trip up** to catch in a lie, error, etc. —**trip′per** *n.*

tri·par·tite (trī pär′tīt′) *adj.* ⟦< L *tri-*, three + *partire*, to part⟧ **1** having three parts **2** made between three parties, as an agreement

tripe (trīp) *n.* ⟦prob. ult. < Ar *tharb*, layer of fat lining the intestines⟧ **1** part of the stomach of an ox, etc., used as food **2** [Slang] anything worthless, etc.; nonsense

trip′ham′mer *n.* a heavy, power-driven hammer, alternately raised and allowed to fall by a tripping device

tri·ple (trip′əl) *adj.* ⟦< L *triplus*⟧ **1** consisting of three; threefold **2** three times as much or as many —*n.* **1** an amount three times as much or as many **2** *Baseball* a hit on which the batter reaches third base —*vt., vi.* **tri′pled, tri′pling** **1** to make or become three times as much or as many **2** *Baseball* to hit a triple —**tri′ply** *adv.*

tri·plet (trip′lit) *n.* any of three offspring born at a single birth

trip·li·cate (trip′li kit; *for v.*, -kāt′) *adj.* ⟦< L *triplex*⟧ **1** threefold **2** being the last of three identical copies —*n.* any one of such copies —*vt.* **-cat′ed, -cat′ing** to make three copies of —**in triplicate** in three copies

tri·pod (trī′päd′) *n.* ⟦< Gr *tri-*, three + *pous*, foot⟧ a three-legged caldron, stool, support, etc.

trip·tych (trip′tik) *n.* ⟦< Gr *tri-*, three + *ptychē*, a fold⟧ a set of three panels with pictures, etc., often hinged, used as an altarpiece

tri·sect (trī sekt′, trī′sekt′) *vt.* ⟦< TRI- + L *secare*, to cut⟧ to cut or divide into three equal parts

trite (trīt) *adj.* **trit′er, trit′est** ⟦< L *terere*, wear out⟧ worn out by constant use; stale —**trite′ness** *n.*

trit·i·um (trit′ē əm) *n.* a radioactive isotope of hydrogen having an atomic weight of 3

tri·umph (trī′əmf, -umf′) *n.* ⟦< L *triumphus*⟧ **1** a victory; success **2** exultation or joy over a victory, etc. —*vi.* **1** to gain victory or success **2** to rejoice over victory, etc. —**tri·um′phal** (-um′fəl) *adj.*

tri·um′phant (-um′fənt) *adj.* **1** successful; victorious **2** rejoicing for victory —**tri·um′phant·ly** *adv.*

tri·um·vir (trī um′vir′) *n., pl.* **-virs′** or **-vi·ri′** (-vi rī′) ⟦L: see fol.⟧ in ancient Rome, any of three administrators sharing authority

tri·um·vi·rate (trī um′vi rit) *n.* ⟦< L *trium virum*, of three men⟧ government by three persons or parties

tri·va·lent (trī vā′lənt) *adj. Chem.* having three valences or a valence of three

triv·et (triv′it) *n.* ⟦< L *tripes*, tripod⟧ **1** a three-legged stand for holding pots, etc. near a fire **2** a short-legged stand for hot dishes to rest on

triv·i·a (triv′ē ə) *n.pl.* [*often with sing. v.*] unimportant matters

triv·i·al (triv′ē əl) *adj.* ⟦< L *trivialis*, commonplace⟧ unimportant; insignificant —**triv′i·al′i·ty** (-al′ə tē) *n.*

triv′i·al·ize′ (-īz′) *vt.* **-ized′, -iz′ing** to regard or treat as trivial; make seem unimportant

-trix (triks) ⟦L⟧ *suffix* forming feminine nouns of agency

tro·chee (trō′kē) ***n.*** ⟦< Gr *trechein,* to run⟧ a metrical foot of one accented syllable followed by one unaccented syllable —**tro·cha′ic** (-kā′ik) ***adj.***

trod (träd) ***vt., vi. pt. & alt. pp. of*** TREAD

trod·den (träd′′n) ***vt., vi. alt. pp. of*** TREAD

trog·lo·dyte (träg′lō dīt′, -lə-) ***n.*** ⟦< Gr *trōglē,* hole + *dyein,* enter⟧ **1** any of the prehistoric people who lived in caves **2** a recluse

troi·ka (troi′kə) ***n.*** ⟦Russ⟧ **1** a vehicle drawn by three horses abreast **2** an association of three in authority

Tro·jan (trō′jən) ***adj.*** of Troy, its people, etc. —***n.*** **1** a native or inhabitant of ancient Troy (city in Asia Minor) **2** a strong, hardworking, determined person

Trojan horse *Gr. Legend* a huge, hollow wooden horse with Greek soldiers inside: it is brought into Troy, the soldiers creep out and open the gates, and the Greek army destroys the city

troll[1] (trōl) ***vt., vi.*** ⟦ME *trollen,* to roll⟧ **1** to sing the parts of (a round, etc.) in succession **2** to sing in a full voice **3** to fish (in) with a baited line trailed behind a slowly moving boat

troll[2] (trōl) ***n.*** ⟦ON⟧ *Scand. Folklore* a supernatural being, as a giant or dwarf, living in a cave

trol·ley (träl′ē) ***n.,*** *pl.* **-leys** ⟦< TROLL[1]⟧ **1** a wheeled basket, etc. that runs suspended from an overhead track **2** a grooved wheel at the end of a pole, for transmitting electric current from an overhead wire to a streetcar, etc. **3** a trolley car

trolley bus an electric bus powered by trolleys

trolley car an electric streetcar that gets its power from a trolley

trol·lop (träl′əp) ***n.*** ⟦prob. < Ger *trolle,* wench⟧ a prostitute

TROMBONE

trom·bone (träm′bōn′, träm bōn′) ***n.*** ⟦It < *tromba,* a trumpet⟧ a large brass instrument, usually with a slide, or movable section Also **slide trombone**

troop (trōōp) ***n.*** ⟦< ML *troppus,* flock⟧ **1** a group of persons or animals **2** [*pl.*] soldiers **3** a subdivision of a cavalry regiment **4** a unit of Boy Scouts or Girl Scouts —***vi.*** **1** to gather or go together in a group **2** to walk or go

troop′er ***n.*** ⟦prec. + -ER⟧ **1** a soldier in the mounted cavalry **2** a mounted police officer **3** a State police officer

trope (trōp) ***n.*** ⟦< Gr *tropos,* a turning⟧ figurative language or a word used in a figurative sense

tro·phy (trō′fē) ***n.,*** *pl.* **-phies** ⟦< Gr *tropaion*⟧ a memorial of victory in war, sports competition, etc.; prize

trop·ic (träp′ik) ***n.*** ⟦< Gr *tropikos,* of a turn (of the sun at the solstices)⟧ **1** either of two parallels of latitude, one, the **Tropic of Cancer,** *c.* 23° 26′ north, and the other, the **Tropic of Capricorn,** *c.* 23° 26′ south **2** [*also* **T-**] [*pl.*] the region between these latitudes —***adj.*** of the tropics; tropical

trop′i·cal (-i kəl) ***adj.*** **1** of, in, characteristic of, or suitable for the tropics **2** very hot; sultry; torrid

tro·pism (trō′piz′əm) ***n.*** ⟦< Gr *tropē,* a turn⟧ the tendency of a plant or animal to grow or turn toward, or away from, a stimulus, as light

tro·po·sphere (trō′pō sfir′; *also* träp′ō-) ***n.*** ⟦Fr < Gr *tropos,* a turning + Fr *sphère,* sphere⟧ the atmospheric zone characterized by water vapor, weather, and decreasing temperatures with increasing altitude

trot (trät) ***vt., vi.*** **trot′ted, trot′ting** ⟦< OHG *trottōn,* to tread⟧ **1** to move, ride, go, etc. at a trot **2** to hurry; run —***n.*** **1** a gait, as of a horse, in which a front leg and the opposite hind leg are lifted at the same time **2** a jogging gait of a person —**trot′ter** ***n.***

troth (trôth, trōth) ***n.*** ⟦ME *trouthe*⟧ [Archaic] **1** faithfulness; loyalty **2** truth **3** a promise, esp. to marry

trou·ba·dour (trōō′bə dôr′) ***n.*** ⟦Fr < Prov *trobar,* compose⟧ **1** any of a class of lyric poets and poet-musicians in S France and N Spain and Italy in the 11th to 13th c. **2** a minstrel or singer

trou·ble (trub′əl) ***vt.*** **-bled, -bling** ⟦< L *turba,* crowd⟧ **1** to disturb or agitate **2** to worry; harass **3** to cause inconvenience to /don't *trouble* yourself/ —***vi.*** to take pains; bother —***n.*** **1** a state of mental distress; worry **2** a misfortune; calamity **3** a person, event, etc. causing annoyance, distress, etc. **4** public disturbance **5** effort; bother /take the *trouble* to listen/

trou′ble·mak′er ***n.*** one who incites others to quarrel, rebel, etc.

trou′ble·shoot′er ***n.*** one whose work is to locate and eliminate the source of trouble in any flow of work

trou′ble·some (-səm) ***adj.*** characterized by or causing trouble

trough (trôf, träf) ***n.*** ⟦OE *trog*⟧ **1** a long, narrow, open container, esp. one to hold water or food for animals **2** a channel or gutter for carrying off rainwater **3** a long, narrow hollow, as between waves **4** a long, narrow area of low barometric pressure

trounce (trouns) ***vt.*** **trounced, trounc′ing** ⟦< ?⟧ **1** to beat; flog **2** [Colloq.] to defeat —**trounc′er** ***n.***

troupe (trōōp) ***n.*** ⟦Fr⟧ a group of actors, singers, etc. —***vi.*** **trouped, troup′ing** to travel as a member of a troupe —**troup′er** ***n.***

trou·sers (trou′zərz) ***n.pl.*** ⟦< Gael *triubhas*⟧ a two-legged outer garment, esp. for men and boys, extending from the waist to the ankles

trous·seau (trōō sō′, trōō′sō) ***n.,*** *pl.* **-seaux′** (-sōz′) or **-seaus′** ⟦Fr < OFr *trousse,* a bundle⟧ a bride's clothes, linens, etc.

trout (trout) ***n.***, *pl.* **trout** or **trouts** ⟦< Gr *trōgein*, gnaw⟧ a food and game fish, related to the salmon, found chiefly in fresh water

trow (trō, trou) ***vi.***, ***vt.*** ⟦< OE *treow*, faith⟧ [Archaic] to believe

trow·el (trou′əl) ***n.*** ⟦< L *trua*, ladle⟧ 1 a flat hand tool for smoothing plaster or applying mortar 2 a scooplike tool for loosening soil, etc. —***vt.*** **-eled** or **-elled, -el·ing** or **-el·ling** to spread, smooth, dig, etc. with a trowel

troy (troi) ***adj.*** ⟦after *Troyes*, city in France, where first used⟧ of or by a system of weights (**troy weight**) for gold, silver, gems, etc.

Troy (troi) ancient city in NW Asia Minor

tru·ant (trōō′ənt) ***n.*** ⟦< OFr, beggar⟧ 1 a pupil who stays away from school without permission 2 one who shirks his or her duties —***adj.*** 1 that is a truant 2 errant; straying —**tru′an·cy**, *pl.* **-cies**, ***n.***

truce (trōōs) ***n.*** ⟦< OE *treow*, faith⟧ 1 a temporary cessation of warfare by agreement between the belligerents 2 respite from conflict, trouble, etc.

truck[1] (truk) ***n.*** ⟦< Gr *trochos*, wheel⟧ 1 a kind of two-wheeled barrow or low, wheeled frame, for carrying heavy articles 2 an automotive vehicle for hauling loads 3 a swiveling, wheeled frame under each end of a railroad car, etc. —***vt.*** to carry on a truck —***vi.*** to drive a truck —**truck′er** ***n.***

truck[2] (truk) ***vt.***, ***vi.*** ⟦< Fr *troquer*⟧ to exchange; barter —***n.*** 1 small articles of little value 2 vegetables raised for market 3 [Colloq.] dealings 4 [Colloq.] trash; rubbish

truck farm a farm where vegetables are grown to be marketed

truck·le (truk′əl) ***n.*** ⟦< Gr *trochos*, wheel⟧ TRUNDLE BED: in full **truckle bed** —***vi.*** **-led, -ling** to be servile; submit (*to*)

truc·u·lent (truk′yōō lənt, -yə-) ***adj.*** ⟦< L *trux*⟧ 1 fierce; cruel; savage 2 pugnacious —**truc′u·lence** ***n.*** —**truc′u·lent·ly** ***adv.***

trudge (truj) ***vi.*** **trudged, trudg′ing** ⟦< ?⟧ to walk, esp. wearily or laboriously —***n.*** a wearying walk

true (trōō) ***adj.*** **tru′er, tru′est** ⟦OE *treowe*⟧ 1 faithful; loyal 2 in accordance with fact; not false 3 conforming to standard, etc.; correct 4 rightful; lawful 5 accurately fitted, shaped, etc. 6 real; genuine —***adv.*** 1 truly 2 *Biol.* without variation from type —***vt.*** **trued, tru′ing** or **true′ing** to fit, place, or shape accurately: often with *up* —***n.*** that which is true: with *the*

true believer a dedicated follower or disciple, esp. one who follows without doubts or questions

true bill a bill of indictment endorsed by a grand jury

true′-blue′ ***adj.*** very loyal; staunch

truf·fle (truf′əl) ***n.*** ⟦ult. < L *tuber*, knob⟧ a fleshy, edible underground fungus

tru·ism (trōō′iz′əm) ***n.*** a statement the truth of which is obvious

tru′ly ***adv.*** 1 in a true manner; accurately, genuinely, etc. 2 really; indeed 3 sincerely *[yours truly]*

Tru·man (trōō′mən), **Har·ry S** (har′ē) 1884-1972; 33d president of the U.S. (1945-53)

trump (trump) ***n.*** ⟦< TRIUMPH⟧ 1 any playing card of a suit ranked higher than any other suit for a given hand 2 such a suit —***vt.***, ***vi.*** to play a trump on (a trick, etc.) —**trump up** to devise fraudulently

trump·er·y (trump′ər ē) ***n.***, *pl.* **-ies** ⟦< Fr *tromper*, deceive⟧ 1 something showy but worthless 2 nonsense

trum·pet (trum′pət) ***n.*** ⟦< OFr *trompe*⟧ 1 a brass instrument consisting of a looped tube with a flared bell and three valves 2 a trumpetlike device for channeling sound, as an early kind of hearing aid 3 a sound like that of a trumpet —***vi.*** to make the sound of a trumpet —***vt.*** to proclaim loudly —**trum′pet·er** ***n.***

trun·cate (truŋ′kāt′) ***vt.*** **-cat′ed, -cat′ing** ⟦< L *truncus*, stem⟧ to cut off a part of —**trun·ca′tion** ***n.***

trun·cheon (trun′chən) ***n.*** ⟦< L *truncus*, stem⟧ [Chiefly Brit., etc.] a policeman's stick or billy

trun·dle (trun′dəl) ***vt.***, ***vi.*** **-dled, -dling** ⟦< OE *trendan*, to roll⟧ to roll along —**trun′dler** ***n.***

trundle bed a low bed on small wheels, that can be rolled under another bed when not in use

trunk (truŋk) ***n.*** ⟦< L *truncus*⟧ 1 the main stem of a tree 2 a human or animal body, not including the head and limbs 3 a long snout, as of an elephant 4 a large, reinforced box to hold clothes, etc. in travel 5 [*pl.*] shorts worn by men for athletics 6 a compartment in a car, usually in the rear, for luggage, etc.

trunk line a main line of a railroad, telephone system, etc.

truss (trus) ***vt.*** ⟦< OFr *trousser*⟧ 1 orig., to bundle 2 to tie; bind (*up*) 3 to support with a truss —***n.*** 1 a bundle or pack 2 a framework for supporting a roof, bridge, etc. 3 a padded device for giving support in cases of rupture or hernia

trust (trust) ***n.*** ⟦< ON *traust*⟧ 1 *a)* firm belief in the honesty, reliability, etc. of another; faith *b)* the one trusted 2 confident expectation, hope, etc. 3 responsibility resulting from confidence placed in one 4 care; custody 5 something entrusted to one 6 faith in a buyer's ability to pay; credit 7 a combination of corporations to establish a monopoly 8 *Law a)* the fact of having nominal ownership of property to keep, use, or administer for another *b)* such property —***vi.*** to be confident —***vt.*** 1 to have confidence in 2 to commit (something) *to* a person's care 3 to allow to do something without misgivings 4 to believe 5 to hope; expect 6 to grant business credit to —***adj.*** 1 relating to a trust 2 acting as trustee —**in trust** entrusted to another's care

trust·ee (trus tē′) ***n.*** 1 one to whom another's property or its management is entrusted 2 a member of a board managing the affairs of a college, hospital, etc. —**trust·ee′ship** ***n.***

trust′ful ***adj.*** full of trust; ready to confide —**trust′ful·ly** ***adv.*** —**trust′ful·ness** ***n.***

trust fund money, securities, etc. held in trust

trust′ing ***adj.*** that trusts; trustful

trust territory a territory placed under the

administrative authority of a country by the United Nations

trust′wor′thy ***adj.*** **-thi·er, -thi·est** worthy of trust; reliable —**trust′wor′thi·ness** ***n.***

trust·y (trus′tē) ***adj.*** **-i·er, -i·est** dependable; trustworthy —***n.***, *pl.* **-ies** a convict granted special privileges as a trustworthy person

truth (tro͞oth) ***n.*** ⟦OE *treowth*⟧ **1** a being true; specif., *a*) sincerity; honesty *b*) conformity with fact *c*) reality; actual existence *d*) correctness; accuracy **2** that which is true **3** an established fact —**in truth** truly

truth′ful ***adj.*** **1** telling the truth; honest **2** corresponding with fact or reality —**truth′ful·ly** ***adv.*** —**truth′ful·ness** ***n.***

try (trī) ***vt.*** **tried, try′ing** ⟦< OFr *trier*⟧ **1** to melt out or render (fat, etc.) **2** to conduct the trial of in a law court **3** to put to the proof; test **4** to subject to trials, etc.; afflict **5** to experiment with /to *try* a recipe/ **6** to attempt; endeavor —***vi.*** to make an effort, attempt, etc. —***n.***, *pl.* **tries** an attempt; effort; trial —**try on** to test the fit of (something to wear) by putting it on —**try out 1** to test by putting into use **2** to test one's fitness, as for a place on a team

try′ing ***adj.*** that tries one's patience; annoying; irksome —**try′ing·ly** ***adv.***

try′out′ ***n.*** [Colloq.] a test to determine fitness, qualifications, etc.

tryst (trist) ***n.*** ⟦< OFr *triste*, hunting station⟧ **1** an appointment to meet, esp. one made by lovers **2** an appointed meeting or meeting place

tsar (tsär, zär) ***n.*** *alt. sp. of* CZAR (sense 1) —**tsa·ri·na** (tsä rē′nə, zä-) ***n.fem.***

tset·se fly (tset′sē, tsēt′-) ⟦< Bantu name⟧ a small fly of central and S Africa: one kind carries sleeping sickness

T-shirt (tē′shurt′) ***n.*** a collarless pullover knit shirt with short sleeves

tsp. **1** teaspoon(s) **2** teaspoonful(s)

T square a T-shaped ruler for drawing parallel lines

tsu·na·mi (tso͞o nä′mē) ***n.*** ⟦Jpn < *tsu*, a harbor + *nami*, a wave⟧ a huge sea wave caused by an undersea earthquake, volcanic eruption, etc.

tub (tub) ***n.*** ⟦< MDu *tubbe*⟧ **1** a round wooden container, usually with staves and hoops **2** any large, open container, as of metal **3** a bathtub

tu·ba (to͞o′bə) ***n.*** ⟦L, trumpet⟧ a large, low-pitched brass musical instrument

TUBA

tub·al (to͞o′bəl) ***adj.*** of or in a tube, esp. a fallopian tube /a *tubal* pregnancy/

tub·by (tub′ē) ***adj.*** **-bi·er, -bi·est** **1** shaped like a tub **2** fat and short

tube (to͞ob) ***n.*** ⟦< L *tubus*, pipe⟧ **1** a slender pipe of metal, glass, etc. for conveying fluids **2** a tubelike part, organ, etc. **3** a pliable cylinder with a screw cap, for holding paste, etc. **4** *short for*: *a*) ELECTRON TUBE *b*) VACUUM TUBE **5** [Brit.] a subway —**the tube** [Colloq.] television —**tube′less** ***adj.***

tu·ber (to͞o′bər) ***n.*** ⟦L, lit., a swelling⟧ a short, thick part of an underground stem, as a potato —**tu′ber·ous** ***adj.***

tu′ber·cle (-kəl) ***n.*** ⟦see prec.⟧ **1** a small, rounded projection, as on a bone or a plant root **2** any abnormal hard nodule or swelling; specif., the typical lesion of tuberculosis

tu·ber·cu·lin (to͞o bur′kyo͞o lin) ***n.*** a solution injected into the skin as a test for tuberculosis

tu·ber′cu·lo′sis (-lō′sis) ***n.*** ⟦see TUBERCLE & -OSIS⟧ an infectious disease characterized by the formation of tubercles in body tissue; specif., tuberculosis of the lungs —**tu·ber′cu·lar** or **tu·ber′cu·lous** ***adj.***

tube sock a stretchable sock in the form of a long tube with no shaped heel

tube top a stretchable, one-piece, sleeveless and strapless women's garment for the upper body

tub·ing (to͞ob′iŋ) ***n.*** **1** a series or system of tubes **2** material in the form of a tube **3** a piece of tube

tu·bu·lar (to͞o′byo͞o lər, -byə-) ***adj.*** ⟦< L *tubus*, pipe⟧ **1** of or like a tube **2** made with a tube or tubes

tu′bule′ (-byo͞ol′) ***n.*** a small tube

tuck (tuk) ***vt.*** ⟦< MDu *tucken*⟧ **1** to pull or gather (*up*) in a fold or folds **2** to sew a fold or folds in (a garment) **3** to fold the edges of (a sheet, etc.) under or in, to make secure **4** to press snugly into a small space —***n.*** a sewed fold in a garment

tuck·er (tuk′ər) ***vt.*** ⟦prob. < prec., in obs. sense "to punish, rebuke"⟧ [Colloq.] to tire (*out*); weary

Tuc·son (to͞o′sän′) city in S Ariz.: pop. 331,000

-tude (to͞od, tyo͞od) ⟦< L *-tudo*⟧ *suffix* state, quality, or instance of being

Tues·day (to͞oz′dā, -dē) ***n.*** ⟦OE *Tiwes dæg*, day of the god of war *Tiu*⟧ the third day of the week Abbrev. **Tues.**

tuft (tuft) ***n.*** ⟦< OFr *tufe*⟧ **1** a bunch of hairs, grass, etc. growing closely together **2** any cluster, as the fluffy ball forming the end of a cluster of threads drawn through a mattress, etc. —***vt.*** **1** to provide with tufts **2** to secure the padding of (a mattress, etc.) with tufts —**tuft′ed** ***adj.*** —**tuft′er** ***n.***

tug (tug) ***vi.***, ***vt.*** **tugged, tug′ging** ⟦prob. < ON *toga*, to pull⟧ **1** to pull hard; drag; haul **2** to tow with a tugboat —***n.*** **1** a hard pull **2** a tugboat

tug·boat (tug′bōt′) ***n.*** a sturdy, powerful boat for towing or pushing ships, barges, etc.

tug of war **1** a contest in which two teams pull at opposite ends of a rope **2** any struggle for power

tu·i·tion (to͞o ish′ən) ***n.*** ⟦< L *tueri*, protect⟧ the charge for instruction, as at a college

tu·la·re·mi·a (to͞o′lə rē′mē ə) ***n.*** ⟦after *Tulare* County, Calif.⟧ an infectious disease of rodents, esp. rabbits, transmissible to man

tu·lip (to͞o′lip) ***n.*** ⟦< Turk *tülbend*, turban: from its shape⟧ **1** a bulb plant with a large, cup-shaped flower **2** the flower

tulle (to͞ol) ***n.*** ⟦after *Tulle*, city in France⟧ a fine netting of silk, rayon, nylon, etc., used as for veils and scarves

Tul·sa (tul′sə) city in NE Okla.: pop. 361,000

tum·ble (tum′bəl) ***vi.*** **-bled, -bling** ⟦< OE *tumbian*, to jump⟧ **1** to do somersaults or similar acrobatic feats **2** to fall suddenly or helplessly **3** to toss or roll about **4** to move in a hasty, disorderly manner —*vt.* 1 to cause to tumble 2 to put into disorder; disarrange —*n.* 1 a fall 2 disorder

tum'ble·down' *adj.* dilapidated

tum'bler (-blər) *n.* 1 an acrobat who does somersaults, etc. 2 a drinking glass 3 a part of a lock whose position must be changed by a key in order to release the bolt

tum'ble·weed' *n.* a plant that breaks off near the ground in autumn and is blown about by the wind

tum·brel or **tum·bril** (tum'brəl) *n.* ⟦< Fr *tomber*, to fall⟧ a cart, esp. one that can be tilted for emptying

tu·mes·cence (to͞o mes'əns) *n.* ⟦see fol.⟧ 1 a swelling; distention 2 a swollen or distended part —**tu·mes'cent** *adj.*

tu·mid (to͞o'mid) *adj.* ⟦< L *tumere*, to swell⟧ 1 swollen; bulging 2 inflated or pompous —**tu·mid'i·ty** *n.*

tum·my (tum'ē) *n., pl.* **-mies** [Colloq.] the stomach or abdomen

tu·mor (to͞o'mər) *n.* ⟦L, a swelling⟧ an abnormal growth of new tissue, independent of its surrounding structures Brit., etc. sp. **tu'mour**

tu·mult (to͞o'mult') *n.* ⟦< L *tumere*, to swell⟧ 1 noisy commotion; uproar 2 confusion; disturbance

tu·mul·tu·ous (to͞o mul'cho͞o əs) *adj.* full of tumult, uproar, etc.

tun (tun) *n.* ⟦OE *tunne*⟧ a large cask

tu·na (to͞o'nə) *n., pl.* **-na** or **-nas** ⟦AmSp⟧ 1 a large ocean fish of the mackerel group, as the albacore 2 the flesh of the tuna, canned for food: also **tuna fish**

tun·dra (tun'drə) *n.* ⟦Russ⟧ a vast, treeless arctic plain

tune (to͞on) *n.* ⟦ME, var. of *tone*, tone⟧ 1 a rhythmic succession of musical tones; melody 2 correct musical pitch 3 agreement; concord /out of *tune* with the times/ —*vt.* **tuned, tun'ing** 1 to adjust (a musical instrument) to some standard of pitch 2 to adapt to some condition, mood, etc. 3 to adjust (a motor, circuit, etc.) for proper performance —**to the tune of** [Colloq.] to the sum, price, or extent of —**tune in** to adjust a radio or TV receiver so as to receive (a station, etc.) —**tun'er** *n.*

tune'ful *adj.* full of music; melodious

tune'less *adj.* 1 not melodious 2 not producing music —**tune'less·ly** *adv.* —**tune'less·ness** *n.*

tune'up' or **tune'-up'** *n.* an adjusting, as of an engine, to the proper condition

tung·sten (tuŋ'stən) *n.* ⟦Swed < *tung*, heavy + *sten*, stone⟧ a hard, heavy metallic chemical element, used in steel, etc.

tu·nic (to͞o'nik, tyo͞o'-) *n.* ⟦L *tunica*⟧ 1 a loose, gownlike garment worn by men and women in ancient Greece and Rome 2 a blouselike garment extending to the hips, often belted

tuning fork a two-pronged steel instrument which when struck sounds a certain fixed tone in perfect pitch

Tu·nis (to͞o'nis) seaport & capital of Tunisia: pop. 557,000

Tu·ni·si·a (to͞o nizh'ə, -nē'zhə) country in N Africa, on the Mediterranean: 48,332 sq. mi.; pop. 7,424,000 —**Tu·ni'si·an** *adj., n.*

tun·nel (tun'əl) *n.* ⟦< Fr *tonnelle*, a vault⟧ 1 an underground passageway, as for autos, etc. 2 any tunnel-like passage, as in a mine —*vt., vi.* **-neled** or **-nelled, -nel·ing** or **-nel·ling** to make a tunnel (through or under) —**tun'nel·er** or **tun'nel·ler** *n.*

tunnel vision a narrow outlook, as on a particular problem

tun·ny (tun'ē) *n., pl.* **-nies** TUNA (sense 1)

tur·ban (tur'bən) *n.* ⟦< Pers *dulbänd*⟧ 1 a headdress worn by men in parts of Asia, consisting of cloth wound in folds about the head 2 any similar headdress

tur·bid (tur'bid) *adj.* ⟦< L *turba*, a crowd⟧ 1 muddy or cloudy from having the sediment stirred up 2 thick, dense, or dark, as clouds 3 confused

tur·bine (tur'bin, -bīn') *n.* ⟦< L *turbo*, a whirl⟧ an engine driven as by the pressure of steam, water, or air against the curved vanes of a wheel

tur·bo·charge (tur'bō chärj') *vt.* **-charged', -charg'ing** to increase the power of (an engine) by the use of a type of compressor (**tur'bo·charg'er**) driven by a turbine powered by exhaust gases

tur'bo·fan' (-fan') *n.* a turbojet engine developing extra thrust from air that bypasses the engine and is accelerated by a fan: in full **turbofan engine**

tur'bo·jet' (-jet') *n.* 1 a jet engine in which the energy of the jet spins a turbine which drives the air compressor: in full **turbojet engine** 2 an aircraft with such an engine

tur'bo·prop' (-präp') *n.* 1 a turbojet engine whose turbine shaft drives a propeller: in full **turboprop engine** 2 an aircraft with such an engine

tur·bot (tur'bət) *n., pl.* **-bot** or **-bots** ⟦< OFr *tourbout*⟧ any of various flounders highly regarded as food

tur·bu·lent (tur'byo͞o lənt, -byə-) *adj.* ⟦< L *turba*, a crowd⟧ 1 wild or disorderly 2 full of violent motion —**tur'bu·lence** *n.* —**tur'bu·lent·ly** *adv.*

tu·reen (to͞o rēn') *n.* ⟦< Fr *terrine*, earthen vessel⟧ a large, deep serving dish with a lid, for soups, etc.

turf (turf) *n.* ⟦OE⟧ 1 *a*) a top layer of earth containing grass with its roots; sod *b*) [Chiefly Brit.] a piece of this 2 peat 3 a track for horse racing; also, horse racing: usually with *the* 4 [Slang] *a*) an area seen by a street gang as its territory to be defended *b*) one's own territory —*vt.* to cover with turf —**turf'y** *adj.*

tur·gid (tur'jid) *adj.* ⟦< L *turgere*, to swell⟧ 1 swollen; distended 2 bombastic; pompous —**tur·gid'i·ty** or **tur'gid·ness** *n.* —**tur'gid·ly** *adv.*

Tu·rin (toor'in) city in NW Italy: pop. 1,117,000

Turk (turk) *n.* a native or inhabitant of Turkey

Turk. 1 Turkey 2 Turkish

tur·key (tur'kē) *n.* ⟦< similarity to a fowl formerly imported through *Turkey*⟧ 1 a large North American bird with a spreading tail 2 its flesh, used as food

Tur·key (tur'kē) country occupying Asia Minor & a SE part of the Balkan Peninsula: 301,381 sq. mi.; pop. 51,819,000

turkey vulture a dark-colored vulture of

temperate and tropical America Also **turkey buzzard**

Turk·ic (tʉrk'ik) ***adj.*** designating or of a subfamily of languages including Turkish, Tatar, etc.

Turk·ish (tʉrk'ish) ***adj.*** of Turkey, its people, or their language —***n.*** the language of Turkey

Turkish bath a bathhouse with steam rooms, showers, massage, etc.

Turkish towel [*also* **t- t-**] a towel of cotton terry cloth

tur·mer·ic (tʉr'mər ik) ***n.*** ⟦< ML *terra merita,* deserved earth⟧ an East Indian plant whose powdered root is used as a yellow dye, a seasoning, etc.

tur·moil (tʉr'moil') ***n.*** ⟦< ?⟧ tumult; commotion; confusion

turn (tʉrn) ***vt.*** ⟦ult. < Gr *tornos,* lathe⟧ **1** to rotate (a wheel, etc.) **2** to move around or partly around /*turn* the key/ **3** to give form to, as in a lathe **4** to change the position or direction of **5** to reverse /to *turn* pages/ **6** to wrench /*turn* one's ankle/ **7** to upset (the stomach) **8** to deflect; divert **9** to cause to change actions, beliefs, aims, etc. **10** to go around (a corner, etc.) **11** to pass (a certain age, amount, etc.) **12** to repel (an attack, etc.) **13** to drive, set, let go, etc. /to *turn* the dog loose/ **14** to direct, point, aim, etc. **15** to change /to *turn* cream into butter/ **16** to make sour **17** to affect in some way —***vi.*** **1** to rotate or revolve; pivot **2** to move around or partly around **3** to reel; whirl **4** to become curved or bent **5** to become upset: said of the stomach **6** to change or reverse course, direction, etc., or one's feelings, allegiance, etc. **7** to refer (*to*) **8** to apply (*to*) for help **9** to shift one's attention /he *turned* to music/ **10** to make a sudden attack (*on*) **11** to be contingent or depend (*on* or *upon*) **12** to become /to *turn* cold/ **13** to change to another form /the rain *turned* to snow/ **14** to become rancid, sour, etc. —***n.*** **1** a turning around; rotation; revolution **2** a single twist, winding, etc. **3** a change or reversal of course or direction **4** a short walk, ride, etc. **5** a bend; curve /a *turn* in the road/ **6** a change in trend, events, etc. **7** a sudden shock or fright **8** an action or deed /a good *turn*/ **9** the right, duty, or chance to do something in regular order /my *turn* to go/ **10** a distinctive form, detail, etc. /an odd *turn* of speech/ **11** natural inclination —**in** (or **out of**) **turn** (not) in proper sequence —**turn down** to reject (a request, etc.) —**turn in 1** to deliver; hand in **2** [Colloq.] to go to bed —**turn off 1** to shut off **2** to make (an electrical device) stop functioning **3** [Slang] to cause to be bored, depressed, etc. —**turn on 1** to start the flow of **2** to make (an electrical device) start functioning **3** [Slang] to make or become elated, euphoric, etc. —**turn out 1** to put out (a light, etc.) **2** to put outside **3** to dismiss **4** to come or go out **5** to produce **6** to result **7** to prove to be **8** to become —**turn over 1** to ponder **2** to hand over; transfer —**turn up** to happen, appear, arrive, etc. —**turn'er *n.***

turn'a·bout' ***n.*** a shift or reversal of position, allegiance, opinion, etc.

turn'a·round' ***n.*** **1** TURNABOUT **2** a wide area, as in a driveway, to allow turning a vehicle around

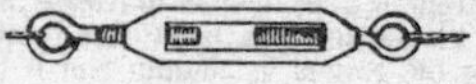

TURNBUCKLE

turn'buck'le (-buk'əl) ***n.*** an adjustable coupling for two rods, etc., consisting of a metal sleeve with opposite internal threads at each end

turn'coat' ***n.*** a renegade; traitor

turn'ing ***n.*** **1** the action of one that turns **2** a place where a road, etc. turns

turning point a point in time at which a decisive change occurs

tur·nip (tʉr'nip) ***n.*** ⟦prob. < Fr *tour,* round + ME *nepe,* turnip⟧ **1** a plant related to mustard, with a roundish, light-colored, edible root **2** the root

turn'key' ***n.,*** *pl.* **-keys'** a jailer

turn'off' ***n.*** **1** a turning off **2** a place to turn off, as a road ramp

turn'out' ***n.*** **1** a gathering of people, as for a meeting **2** a wider part of a narrow road, for vehicles to pass

turn'o'ver ***n.*** **1** a turning over; upset **2** a small pie with half the crust folded back over the other half **3** *a)* the selling out and replenishing of a stock of goods *b)* the amount of business done during a given period **4** the rate of replacement of workers

turn'pike' (-pīk') ***n.*** ⟦ME *turnpyke,* a spiked road barrier⟧ a toll road, esp. one that is an expressway

turn'stile' (-stīl') ***n.*** a device, as a post with revolving horizontal bars, placed in an entrance to allow the passage of persons one at a time

turn'ta'ble ***n.*** a circular rotating platform, as for supporting a phonograph record being played

tur·pen·tine (tʉr'pən tīn') ***n.*** ⟦< Gr *terebinthos,* tree yielding this substance⟧ a colorless, volatile oil distilled from a substance extracted from various coniferous trees: used in paints, etc.

tur·pi·tude (tʉr'pi to͞od') ***n.*** ⟦< L *turpis,* vile⟧ baseness; vileness

tur·quoise (tʉr'kwoiz', -koiz') ***n.*** ⟦< OFr *turqueis,* Turkish⟧ **1** a greenish-blue semiprecious stone **2** its color

tur·ret (tʉr'it) ***n.*** ⟦see TOWER⟧ **1** a small tower projecting from a building, usually at a corner **2** a dome or revolving structure for guns, as on a warship, tank, or airplane **3** a rotating attachment for a lathe, etc. holding cutting tools for successive use

tur·tle (tʉrt''l) ***n.*** ⟦< Fr *tortue,* tortoise⟧ any of various land or water reptiles having a soft body encased in a tough shell —**turn turtle** to turn upside down

tur'tle·dove' ***n.*** ⟦< L echoic *turtur*⟧ a wild dove with a plaintive call

tur'tle·neck' ***n.*** **1** a high, snug, turned-down collar, as on a sweater **2** a sweater, etc. with such a collar

tusk (tusk) ***n.*** ⟦OE *tucs*⟧ a long, large,

pointed tooth projecting outside the mouth, as of the elephant

tus·sle (tus′əl) ***n., vi.*** **-sled, -sling** ⟦< ME *tusen*, to pull⟧ struggle; scuffle

tus·sock (tus′ək) ***n.*** ⟦< ?⟧ a thick tuft or clump of grass, sedge, etc.

tu·te·lage (to͞ot′'l ij, tyo͞ot′-) ***n.*** ⟦< L *tutela*, protection⟧ **1** guardianship; care, protection, etc. **2** instruction —**tu′te·lar′y** (-er′ē) ***adj.***

tu·tor (to͞ot′ər, tyo͞ot′-) ***n.*** ⟦< L *tueri*, to guard⟧ a private teacher —***vt., vi.*** to act as a tutor (to); teach —**tu·to·ri·al** (to͞o tôr′ē əl, tyo͞o-) ***adj., n.***

tut·ti-frut·ti (to͞ot′ē fro͞ot′ē) ***n.*** ⟦It, all fruits⟧ ice cream, candy, etc. made or flavored with mixed fruits

tu·tu (to͞o′to͞o′) ***n.*** ⟦Fr⟧ a very short, full, projecting skirt worn by ballerinas

Tu·va·lu (to͞o′və lo͞o′) country on a group of islands in the W Pacific, north of Fiji: 10 sq. mi.; pop. 8,000

tux (tuks) ***n.,*** *pl.* **tux′es** *short for* TUXEDO

tux·e·do (tuk sē′dō) ***n.,*** *pl.* **-dos** ⟦after a country club near *Tuxedo* Lake, N.Y.⟧ a man's semiformal suit with a tailless jacket

TV (tē′vē′) ***n.*** **1** television **2** *pl.* **TVs** or **TV's** a television receiving set

TVA Tennessee Valley Authority

TV dinner a frozen, precooked dinner packaged in a divided tray for heating and serving

twad·dle (twäd′'l) ***n.*** ⟦prob. var. of TATTLE⟧ foolish, empty talk or writing; nonsense —**twad′dler** ***n.***

twain (twān) ***adj., n.*** ⟦OE *twegen*, two⟧ *archaic var. of* TWO

Twain (twān), **Mark** *pseud. of* Samuel L. CLEMENS

twang (twaŋ) ***n.*** ⟦echoic⟧ **1** a sharp, vibrating sound, as of a plucked string **2** a sharply nasal way of speaking —***vi., vt.*** **1** to make or cause to make a twang **2** to speak or say with a twang —**twang′y, -i·er, -i·est,** ***adj.***

'twas (twuz, twäz) [Old Poet.] it was

tweak (twēk) ***vt.*** ⟦OE *twiccan*, to twitch⟧ to give a twisting pinch to (the nose, ear, etc.) —***n.*** such a pinch

tweed (twēd) ***n.*** ⟦< misreading of *tweel*, Scot form of TWILL⟧ **1** a rough wool fabric in a weave of two or more colors **2** [*pl.*] clothes of tweed

tweed′y ***adj.*** **-i·er, -i·est** **1** of, like, or wearing tweeds **2** of an informal, outdoor type

'tween (twēn) ***prep.*** ⟦ME *twene*⟧ [Old Poet.] between

tweet (twēt) ***n., interj.*** ⟦echoic⟧ the chirping sound of a small bird, or a similar sound —***vi.*** to make this sound

tweet′er ***n.*** a small, high-fidelity speaker for reproducing high-frequency sounds Cf. WOOFER

tweez·ers (twē′zərz) ***n.pl.*** ⟦< obs. *tweeze*, surgical set⟧ [*with sing. or pl. v.*] small nippers for plucking out hairs, etc. Often **pair of tweezers**

twelfth (twelfth) ***adj.*** ⟦OE *twelfta*⟧ preceded by eleven others; 12th —***n.*** **1** the one following the eleventh **2** any of the twelve equal parts of something; $\frac{1}{12}$

Twelfth Day Epiphany, the twelfth day after Christmas: **Twelfth Night** is the evening before, or of, Epiphany

twelve (twelv) ***adj., n.*** ⟦OE *twelf*⟧ two more than ten; 12; XII

twelve′-tone′ ***adj.*** *Music* of composition in which the twelve tones of the chromatic scale are fixed in some arbitrary succession (*tone row*)

twen·ty (twent′ē) ***adj., n.,*** *pl.* **-ties** ⟦OE *twegentig*⟧ two times ten; 20; XX —**the twenties** the numbers or years, as of a century, from 20 through 29 —**twen′ti·eth** (-ith) ***adj., n.***

twen′ty-one′ ***n.*** the gambling game BLACKJACK (*n.* 2)

twen′ty-twen′ty (or **20/20**) **vision** normal visual ability, i.e., seeing clearly at 20 feet what the normal eye sees at 20 feet

twerp (twʉrp) ***n.*** ⟦ult. < ? Dan *tver*, perverse⟧ [Slang] a person regarded as insignificant, contemptible, etc.

twice (twīs) ***adv.*** ⟦OE *twiga*⟧ **1** two times **2** two times as much or as many

twid·dle (twid′'l) ***vt., vi.*** **-dled, -dling** ⟦prob. < TW(IST) + (*d*)*iddle*, move back and forth rapidly⟧ to twirl or play with lightly or idly —**twiddle one's thumbs** to be idle

twig (twig) ***n.*** ⟦OE *twigge*⟧ a small branch of a tree or shrub

twi·light (twī′līt′) ***n.*** ⟦ME⟧ **1** the subdued light just after sunset or, sometimes, just before sunrise **2** the period from sunset to dark **3** a gradual decline —***adj.*** of twilight

twill (twil) ***n.*** ⟦OE *twilic*, woven of double thread⟧ a cloth woven in parallel diagonal lines —**twilled** ***adj.***

twin (twin) ***adj.*** ⟦OE *twinn*, double⟧ **1** consisting of, or being one of a pair of, two similar things **2** being a twin or twins —***n.*** **1** either of two born at the same birth **2** either of two persons or things that are very much alike

twine (twīn) ***n.*** ⟦OE *twin*⟧ strong thread, string, etc. of strands twisted together —***vt., vi.*** **twined, twin′ing** **1** to twist together **2** to wind around

twinge (twinj) ***vi., vt.*** **twinged, twing′ing** ⟦OE *twengan*, to squeeze⟧ to have or cause to have a sudden, sharp pain, qualm, etc. —***n.*** such a pain, etc.

twi-night or **twi·night** (twī′nīt′) ***adj.*** ⟦TWI(LIGHT) + NIGHT⟧ *Baseball* designating a double-header starting in late afternoon and going into evening

twin·kle (twiŋk′əl) ***vi.*** **-kled, -kling** ⟦OE *twinclian*⟧ **1** to shine with quick, intermittent gleams **2** to light up, as with amusement: said of the eyes **3** to move to and fro quickly, as a dancer's feet —***n.*** **1** a glint in the eye **2** a gleam; sparkle **3** an instant

twin′kling ***n.*** an instant

twirl (twʉrl) ***vt., vi.*** ⟦prob. < Scand⟧ **1** to rotate rapidly; spin **2** to whirl in a circle —***n.*** **1** a twirling **2** a twist, coil, etc. —**twirl′er** ***n.***

twist (twist) ***vt.*** ⟦< OE *-twist*, a rope⟧ **1** to wind (strands, etc.) around one another **2** to wind (rope, etc.) around something **3** to give spiral shape to **4** *a*) to subject to torsion *b*) to wrench; sprain **5** to contort or distort **6** to confuse **7** to pervert the meaning of **8** to revolve or rotate **9** to break (*off*) by turning the end —*vi.* **1** to undergo twisting **2** to spiral, twine, etc. (*around* or *about*) **3** to revolve or rotate **4** to turn to one side **5** to wind, as a path **6** to squirm; writhe —*n.* **1** something twisted, as cord or thread, a roll of tobacco, etc. **2** a twisting or being twisted **3** stress produced by twisting **4** a contortion **5** a wrench or sprain **6** a turn; bend **7** distortion, as of meaning **8** an unexpected or different direction, method, slant, etc.

twist′er *n.* **1** a person or thing that twists **2** [Colloq.] a tornado or cyclone

twit (twit) *vt.* **twit′ted, twit′ting** ⟦< OE *æt*, at + *witan*, accuse⟧ to reproach, taunt, etc. —*n.* a taunt

twitch (twich) *vt., vi.* ⟦< OE *twiccian*, to pluck⟧ to pull (at) or move with a quick, slight jerk —*n.* **1** a twitching **2** a sudden, quick motion, esp. a spasmodic one

twitch′y *adj.* **-i·er, -i·est** [Colloq.] nervous; jittery

twit·ter (twit′ər) *vi.* ⟦ME *twiteren*⟧ **1** to chirp rapidly **2** *a*) to chatter *b*) to giggle **3** to tremble with excitement —*n.* **1** a twittering **2** a condition of trembling excitement

'twixt (twikst) *prep.* [Old Poet.] betwixt; between

two (to͞o) *adj., n.* ⟦OE *twa*⟧ one more than one; 2; II —**in two** in two parts

two′-bit′ (-bit′) *adj.* [Slang] cheap

two bits [Colloq.] twenty-five cents

two′-by-four′ *n.* a piece of lumber two inches thick and four inches wide when untrimmed ($1\frac{1}{2}$ by $3\frac{1}{2}$ inches trimmed)

two′-edged′ *adj.* **1** having two cutting edges **2** that can be taken two ways, as a remark

two′-faced′ *adj.* **1** having two faces **2** deceitful; hypocritical

two·fer (to͞o′fər) *n.* ⟦altered < *two for*⟧ [Colloq.] a pair of (theater tickets, etc.) sold for the price of one

two′-fist′ed *adj.* [Colloq.] **1** able to use both fists **2** vigorous; virile

two′fold′ *adj.* **1** having two parts **2** having twice as much or as many —*adv.* twice as much or as many

two′-hand′ed *adj.* **1** requiring the use of both hands **2** operated, played, etc. by two persons

two·pence (tup′əns) *n.* two pence

two′-ply′ *adj.* having two layers, strands, etc.

two′some (-səm) *n.* **1** two people; a couple **2** a golf match for two

two′-time′ *vt.* **-timed′, -tim′ing** [Slang] to be unfaithful to —**two′-tim′er** *n.*

two′-way′ *adj.* **1** allowing passage in either direction **2** involving two or used in two ways

Twp. township

TX Texas

-ty (tē, ti) ⟦< L *-tas*⟧ *suffix* quality of, condition of

ty·coon (tī ko͞on′) *n.* ⟦< Jpn < Chin *tai*, great + *kuan*, official⟧ a wealthy, powerful industrialist, financier, etc.

ty·ing (tī′iŋ) *vt., vi. prp. of* TIE

tyke (tīk) *n.* ⟦< ON *tik*, a bitch⟧ [Colloq.] a small child

Ty·ler (tī′lər), **John** 1790-1862; 10th president of the U.S. (1841-45)

tym·pa·ni (tim′pə nē) *n.pl. alt. sp. of* TIMPANI —**tym′pa·nist** *n.*

tym·pan·ic membrane (tim pan′ik) a thin membrane inside the ear that vibrates when struck by sound waves

tym·pa·num (tim′pə nəm) *n., pl.* **-nums** or **-na** (-nə) ⟦L, a drum⟧ **1** MIDDLE EAR **2** TYMPANIC MEMBRANE

type (tīp) *n.* ⟦< Gr *typos*, a mark⟧ **1** the characteristic form, plan, style, etc. of a class or group **2** a class, group, etc. with characteristics in common **3** a person, animal, or thing representative of a class **4** a perfect example; model **5** *a*) a piece of metal or wood with a raised letter, etc. in reverse on its top, used in printing *b*) such pieces collectively *c*) a printed or photographically reproduced character or characters —*vt.* **typed, typ′ing 1** to classify **2** to typewrite —*vi.* to typewrite

-type (tīp) *combining form* **1** type, representative form, example [*stereotype*] **2** print, printing type

type′cast′ *vt.* **-cast′, -cast′ing** to cast (an actor) repeatedly in the same type of part

type′script′ *n.* typewritten matter

type′set′ *vt.* **-set′, -set′ting** to set in type; compose

type′set′ter *n.* **1** a person who sets type **2** a machine for setting type

type′write′ *vt., vi.* **-wrote′, -writ′ten, -writ′ing** to write with a typewriter: now usually *type*

type′writ′er *n.* a writing machine with a keyboard for reproducing letters resembling printed ones

ty·phoid (tī′foid′) *n.* ⟦TYPH(US) + -OID⟧ an acute infectious disease caused by a bacillus and acquired by ingesting contaminated food or water: characterized by fever, intestinal disorders, etc. In full **typhoid fever**

ty·phoon (tī fo͞on′) *n.* ⟦< Chin *tai-fung*, great wind⟧ a violent tropical cyclone originating in the W Pacific

ty·phus (tī′fəs) *n.* ⟦< Gr *typhos*, fever⟧ an acute infectious disease caused by certain bacteria, transmitted by fleas, lice, etc., and characterized by fever, skin rash, etc. In full **typhus fever**

typ·i·cal (tip′i kəl) *adj.* **1** serving as a type **2** having the distinguishing characteristics of a class, group, etc.; representative **3** belonging to a type; characteristic —**typ′i·cal·ly** *adv.*

typ·i·fy (tip′i fī′) *vt.* **-fied′, -fy′ing 1** to be a type of; symbolize **2** to have the characteristics of; be typical of; exemplify —**typ′i·fi·ca′tion** *n.*

typ·ist (tīp′ist) *n.* a person who operates a typewriter

ty·po (tī′pō) *n., pl.* **-pos** [Colloq.] an error made in setting type or in typing

ty·pog·ra·phy (tī päg′rə fē) *n.* ⟦see TYPE & -GRAPHY⟧ **1** setting, and printing with, type **2** the arrangement, style, etc. of matter printed from type —**ty·pog′ra·pher** *n.* —**ty′po·graph′i·cal** (-pō graf′i kəl, -pə-) *adj.* —**ty′po·graph′i·cal·ly** *adv.*

ty·ran·ni·cal (tə ran′i kəl, ti-; tī-) *adj.* **1** of or suited to a tyrant **2** harsh, cruel, unjust, etc. Also **ty·ran′nic** —**ty·ran′ni·cal·ly** *adv.*

tyr·an·nize (tir′ə nīz′) *vi.* **-nized′**, **-niz′ing** 1 to govern as a tyrant 2 to govern or use authority harshly or cruelly —*vt.* to treat tyrannically

ty·ran·no·saur (tə ran′ə sôr′, ti-; tī-) *n.* ⟦< Gr *tyrannos*, tyrant + *sauros*, lizard⟧ a huge, two-footed, flesh-eating dinosaur Also **ty·ran′no·saur′us** (-əs)

tyr·an·ny (tir′ə nē) *n.*, *pl.* **-nies** 1 the authority, government, etc. of a tyrant 2 cruel and unjust use of power 3 a tyrannical act —**tyr′an·nous** *adj.*

ty·rant (tī′rənt) *n.* ⟦< Gr *tyrannos*⟧ 1 an absolute ruler 2 a cruel, oppressive ruler, master, etc.

ty·ro (tī′rō) *n.*, *pl.* **-ros** ⟦< L *tiro*, young soldier⟧ a beginner in learning something; novice

Ty·rol (ti rōl′, -räl′) *alt. sp. of* TIROL

tzar (tsär, zär) *n. alt. sp. of* CZAR —**tza·ri·na** (tsä rē′nə, zä-) *n.fem.*

U

u or **U** (yo͞o) *n.*, *pl.* **u's, U's** the 21st letter of the English alphabet

U *Chem. symbol for* uranium

u or **u.** unit(s)

U or **U.** 1 Union 2 University

UAW United Automobile Workers (of America)

u·biq·ui·tous (yo͞o bik′wə təs) *adj.* ⟦< L *ubique*, everywhere⟧ (seemingly) present everywhere at the same time —**u·biq′ui·tous·ly** *adv.* —**u·biq′ui·ty** *n.*

U-boat (yo͞o′bōt′) *n.* ⟦< Ger *Unterseeboot*, undersea boat⟧ a German submarine

U bolt a U-shaped bolt with threads and a nut at each end

ud·der (ud′ər) *n.* ⟦OE *udr*⟧ a baglike, milk-secreting organ with two or more teats, as in cows

UFO (yo͞o′fō′, yo͞o′ef ō′) *n.*, *pl.* **UFOs** or **UFO's** an unidentified flying object

u·fol·o·gy (yo͞o fäl′ə jē) *n.* the study of UFOs, esp. as supposed spacecraft from another planet —**u·fol′o·gist** *n.*

U·gan·da (yo͞o gan′də, -gän′-) country in east central Africa: 93,981 sq. mi.; pop. 15,158,000 —**U·gan′dan** *adj.*, *n.*

ugh (ookh, oo, ug, *etc.*) *interj.* an exclamation of disgust, horror, etc.

ug·ly (ug′lē) *adj.* **-li·er**, **-li·est** ⟦< ON *uggr*, fear⟧ 1 unpleasing to look at 2 bad, vile, repulsive, etc. 3 ominous; dangerous 4 [Colloq.] cross; quarrelsome —**ug′li·ness** *n.*

uh (u, un) *interj.* 1 HUH 2 a sound indicating hesitation

UHF or **uhf** ultrahigh frequency

UK United Kingdom

u·kase (yo͞o′kās′, yo͞o kāz′) *n.* ⟦Russ *ukaz*, edict⟧ an official decree

U·kraine (yo͞o krān′) UKRAINIAN SOVIET SOCIALIST REPUBLIC: used with *the*

U·krain·i·an Soviet Socialist Republic (yo͞o krā′nē ən) republic of the U.S.S.R., in the SW European part: 231,990 sq. mi.; pop. 50,000,000

u·ku·le·le (yo͞o′kə lā′lē) *n.* ⟦Haw, leaping flea⟧ a small, four-stringed, guitarlike musical instrument

ul·cer (ul′sər) *n.* ⟦L *ulcus*⟧ 1 an open sore on the skin or some mucous membrane, discharging pus 2 any corrupt condition —**ul′cer·ous** *adj.*

ul′cer·ate′ (-āt′) *vt.*, *vi.* **-at′ed**, **-at′ing** to make or become ulcerous —**ul′cer·a′tion** *n.*

ul·na (ul′nə) *n.*, *pl.* **-nae** (-nē) or **-nas** ⟦L, the elbow⟧ the larger of the two bones of the forearm —**ul′nar** *adj.*

ul·ster (ul′stər) *n.* ⟦after *Ulster*, in N Ireland⟧ a long, loose, heavy overcoat

ult. ultimate(ly)

ul·te·ri·or (ul tir′ē ər) *adj.* ⟦L: see ULTRA-⟧ 1 lying beyond or on the farther side 2 beyond what is expressed or implied; undisclosed

ul·ti·mate (ul′tə mit) *adj.* ⟦< L *ultimus*, last⟧ 1 beyond which it is impossible to go 2 final; conclusive 3 beyond further analysis; fundamental 4 greatest possible —*n.* a final point or result —**ul′ti·mate·ly** *adv.*

ul·ti·ma·tum (ul′tə māt′əm) *n.*, *pl.* **-tums** or **-ta** (-ə) ⟦see prec.⟧ a final offer or demand, as in negotiations

ul·tra (ul′trə) *adj.* ⟦< fol.⟧ going beyond the usual limit; extreme

ultra- ⟦L < *ultra*, beyond⟧ *prefix* 1 beyond *[ultrasonic]* 2 extremely *[ultraconservative]*

ul·tra·con·serv·a·tive (ul′trə kən sur′və tiv) *adj.* extremely conservative

ul·tra·high frequency (ul′trə hī′) any radio frequency between 300 and 3,000 megahertz

ul′tra·ma·rine′ (-mə rēn′) *adj.* deep-blue —*n.* deep blue

ul′tra·son′ic (-sän′ik) *adj.* above the range of sound audible to the human ear —**ul′tra·son′i·cal·ly** *adv.*

ul′tra·sound′ *n.* ultrasonic waves, used in medical diagnosis and therapy, in surgery, etc.

ul′tra·vi′o·let *adj.* of or designating those rays that are just beyond the violet end of the visible spectrum

ul·u·late (yo͞ol′yoo lāt′, ul′-) *vi.* **-lat′ed**, **-lat′ing** ⟦< L *ululare*, to howl⟧ to howl, hoot, or wail loudly —**ul′u·la′tion** *n.*

U·lys·ses (yoo lis′ēz′) ⟦ML⟧ ODYSSEUS

um·bel (um′bəl) *n.* ⟦L *umbella*, parasol: see UMBRELLA⟧ a cluster of flowers with stalks of nearly equal length which spring from the same point

um·ber (um′bər) *n.* ⟦< It (*terra d′*)*ombra*, (earth of) shade⟧ 1 a kind of earth used as a yellowish-brown or reddish-brown pigment **2** a yellowish-brown or reddish-brown color

um·bil·i·cal (um bil′i kəl) ***adj.*** ⟦< L *umbilicus*, navel⟧ of a cordlike structure (**umbilical cord**) connecting a fetus's navel to the placenta and conveying nourishment to the fetus

um·bil·i·cus (um bil′i kəs) ***n.***, *pl.* **-ci′** (-sī′) ⟦L⟧ NAVEL

um·bra (um′brə) ***n.***, *pl.* **-brae′** (-brē′) or **-bras** ⟦L, a shade⟧ **1** shade or a shadow **2** the dark cone of shadow from a planet or satellite on the side opposite the sun

um·brage (um′brij) ***n.*** ⟦< L *umbra*, a shade⟧ **1** [Obs.] shade **2** foliage **3** offense or resentment

um·brel·la (um brel′ə) ***n.*** ⟦< L *umbra*, a shade⟧ **1** a screen, usually of cloth on a folding frame, carried for protection against rain or sun **2** any comprehensive, protective alliance, strategy, device, etc.

UMIAK

u·mi·ak (o͞o′mē ak′) ***n.*** ⟦Esk⟧ a large, open boat made of skins on a wooden frame, used by Eskimos

um·laut (o͝om′lout) ***n.*** ⟦Ger < *um*, about + *laut*, a sound⟧ *Linguistics* **1** a vowel changed in sound by its assimilation to another vowel **2** the mark (¨) placed over such a vowel

ump (ump) ***n.***, ***vt.***, ***vi.*** *short for* UMPIRE

um·pire (um′pīr′) ***n.*** ⟦< Fr *nomper*, uneven, hence a third person⟧ **1** a person chosen to judge a dispute **2** an official who administers the rules in certain sports —***vt.***, ***vi.*** **-pired′**, **-pir′ing** to act as umpire (in or of)

ump·teen (ump′tēn′) ***adj.*** [Slang] very many —**ump′teenth′** ***adj.***

un- *prefix* **1** ⟦OE⟧ not, lack of, the opposite of *[unconcern]* **2** ⟦OE *un-*, *on-*⟧ back: indicating a reversal of action *[unfold]* The following list includes some common compounds formed with *un-* (either sense) that do not have special meanings:

unabashed
unable
unabridged
unaccented
unacceptable
unaccompanied
unacquainted
unadorned
unadulterated
unafraid
unaided
unaltered
unambiguous
unannounced
unanswerable
unashamed
unasked
unassailable
unassisted
unattainable
unattractive
unauthorized
unavailable
unavoidable
unbearable
unbeaten
unbiased
unbleached
unblemished
unbreakable
unbroken
unbuckle
unbutton
uncap
unceasing
uncensored
unchain
unchallenged
unchanged
unchanging
unchecked
uncivilized
unclassified
unclean
unclear
uncomplaining
uncompleted
uncomplimentary
unconcealed
unconfirmed
unconnected
uncontrollable
uncontrolled
unconventional
unconvinced
uncooked
uncooperative
uncultivated
undamaged
undefeated
undefined
undemocratic
undependable
undeserved
undesirable
undeveloped
undifferentiated
undiminished
undisciplined
undiscovered
undiscriminating
undisguised
undisputed
undistinguished
undisturbed
undivided
uneducated
unemotional
unending
unenlightened
unenviable
uneventful
unexpired
unexplained
unexplored
unexpressed
unexpurgated
unfair
unfashionable
unfasten
unfavorable
unfit
unflattering
unforeseen
unforgivable
unforgotten
unfulfilled
unfurnished
ungrammatical
ungrateful
unhampered
unhandy
unharmed
unhealthful
unheeded
unhesitating
unhitch
unhook
unhurried
unhurt
unidentified
unimaginable
unimaginative
unimpaired
unimportant
unimproved
unincorporated
uninformed
uninhabited
uninhibited
uninjured
uninspired
uninsured
unintelligent
unintelligible
unintentional
uninteresting
uninterrupted
uninvited
uninviting
unjustifiable
unjustified
unknowing
unlace
unlatch
unleavened
unlicensed
unlined
unlisted
unloved
unmanageable
unmannerly
unmarked
unmarried
unmatched
unmerited
unmoved
unnamed
unnaturalized
unnoticed
unobserved
unobstructed
unobtainable
unobtrusive
unoccupied
unofficial
unopened
unopposed
unorthodox
unpaid
unpalatable
unpardonable
unpaved
unpin
unplanned
unpolished
unpolluted
unpredictable
unprejudiced
unpremeditated
unprepared
unpretentious
unprofitable
unpromising
unprotected
unprovoked
unpunished
unquenchable
unquestioned
unquestioning
unreadable
unrealistic
unrealized
unrecognizable
unrecognized
unrecorded
unrefined
unregulated
unrelated
unreliable
unrelieved
unrepentant
unrequited
unresponsive
unrestricted
unsafe
unsanitary
unsatisfactory
unsatisfied
unsaturated
unscientific
unseasoned
unseeing
unseen
unsegmented
unselfish
unshackle
unshakable

unshaken
unshaven
unsociable
unsold
unsolicited
unsought
unspoiled
unsportsmanlike
unsuccessful
unsuitable
unsullied
unsupervised
unsupported
unsure
unsurpassed
unsuspected
unsweetened
unswerving
unsympathetic
untainted
untamed
untarnished
untasted
untenable
unthankful
untiring
untouched
untrained
untried
untroubled
untrue
untrustworthy
unvarying
unverified
unwanted
unwarranted
unwavering
unwed
unworkable
unworldly
unyielding
unzip

UN United Nations

un·ac·count·a·ble (un'ə kount'ə bəl) ***adj.*** 1 that cannot be explained; strange 2 not responsible

un'ac·cus'tomed ***adj.*** 1 not accustomed (*to*) 2 not usual; strange

un'ad·vised' ***adj.*** 1 without counsel or advice 2 indiscreet; rash

un'af·fect'ed ***adj.*** 1 not affected or influenced 2 without affectation; sincere

un'-A·mer'i·can ***adj.*** regarded as not properly American; esp., regarded as opposing the U.S., its institutions, etc.

u·nan·i·mous (yo͞o nan'ə məs) ***adj.*** ⟦< L *unus*, one + *animus*, the mind⟧ agreeing completely; without dissent —**u·nan·im·i·ty** (yo͞o'nə nim'ə tē) ***n.*** —**u·nan'i·mous·ly** ***adv.***

un'ap·proach'a·ble ***adj.*** 1 not to be approached; inaccessible; aloof 2 having no equal; unmatched

un·armed' ***adj.*** having no weapons

un'as·sum'ing ***adj.*** not assuming, pretentious, or forward; modest

un'at·tached' ***adj.*** 1 not attached 2 not engaged or married

un'at·tend'ed ***adj.*** 1 not waited on 2 unaccompanied (*by*) 3 neglected

un'a·vail'ing (-ə vāl'iŋ) ***adj.*** futile; useless —**un'a·vail'ing·ly** ***adv.***

un'a·ware' ***adj.*** not aware or conscious —***adv.*** UNAWARES

un'a·wares' (-werz') ***adv.*** 1 unintentionally 2 unexpectedly

un·backed' ***adj.*** 1 not backed, supported, etc. 2 without a back or backing

un·bal'anced ***adj.*** 1 not in balance 2 *a*) mentally deranged *b*) erratic

un·bar' ***vt.*** **-barred'**, **-bar'ring** to unbolt; unlock; open

un'be·com'ing ***adj.*** not appropriate or suited to one's appearance, character, etc.; unattractive, indecorous, etc.

un'be·known' ***adj.*** without one's knowledge; unknown: usually with *to* Also **un'be·knownst'** (-nōnst')

un'be·lief' ***n.*** lack of belief, esp. in religion

un'be·liev'a·ble ***adj.*** beyond belief; astounding; incredible

un'be·liev'er ***n.*** 1 one who does not believe 2 one who does not accept any, or any particular, religious belief

un·bend' ***vt., vi.*** **-bent'** or **-bend'ed**, **-bend'ing** 1 to release or be released from tension 2 to relax, as from formality 3 to straighten

un·bend'ing ***adj.*** 1 rigid; stiff 2 firm; resolute 3 aloof; austere

un·bid'den ***adj.*** 1 not commanded 2 not invited

un·blush'ing ***adj.*** 1 not blushing 2 shameless —**un·blush'ing·ly** ***adv.***

un·bolt' ***vt., vi.*** to withdraw the bolt or bolts of (a door, etc.); open

un·born' ***adj.*** 1 not born 2 still in the mother's uterus 3 yet to be

un·bos'om (-bo͝oz'əm) ***vt., vi.*** to tell or reveal (feelings, secrets, etc.) —**unbosom oneself** to reveal one's feelings, secrets, etc.

un·bound'ed ***adj.*** 1 without bounds or limits 2 not restrained

un'bowed' (-boud') ***adj.*** not yielding or giving in

un·bri'dled ***adj.*** 1 having no bridle on: said of a horse, etc. 2 uncontrolled

un·bur'den ***vt.*** 1 to free from a burden 2 to relieve (one's soul, mind, etc.) by disclosing (guilt, etc.)

un'but'toned ***adj.*** 1 with buttons unfastened 2 free and easy; casual

un·called'-for' ***adj.*** 1 not called for 2 unnecessary and out of place

un·can·ny (un kan'ē) ***adj.*** 1 mysterious and eerie; weird 2 so good, acute, etc. as to seem preternatural

un·cared'-for' ***adj.*** not cared for or looked after; neglected

un'cer·e·mo'ni·ous ***adj.*** 1 not ceremonious; informal 2 curt; abrupt

un·cer'tain ***adj.*** 1 *a*) not surely or certainly known *b*) not sure or certain in knowledge; doubtful 2 vague 3 not dependable or reliable 4 varying —**un·cer'tain·ty**, *pl.* **-ties**, ***n.***

un·char'i·ta·ble ***adj.*** harsh or severe, as in opinion —**un·char'i·ta·bly** ***adv.***

un·chart'ed ***adj.*** not marked on a chart or map; unexplored or unknown

un·chris'tian ***adj.*** 1 not Christian 2 [Colloq.] outrageous; dreadful

un·ci·al (un'shē əl, -shəl) ***adj.*** ⟦L *uncialis*, inch-high⟧ designating or of the large, rounded letters of Greek and Latin manuscripts between A.D. 300 and 900 —***n.*** uncial script or letter

un·cir'cum·cised' ***adj.*** 1 not circumcised; gentile 2 [Archaic] heathen

un·clasp' ***vt.*** 1 to unfasten the clasp of 2 to release from a clasp or grasp

un·cle (uŋ'kəl) ***n.*** ⟦< L *avunculus*⟧ 1 the brother of one's father or mother 2 the husband of one's aunt

Uncle Sam ⟦< abbrev. *U.S.*⟧ [Colloq.] the U.S. (government or people), personified as a tall man with whiskers, dressed in red, white, and blue

Uncle Tom ⟦after main character in novel *Uncle Tom's Cabin* (1852)⟧ [Colloq.] a black regarded as servile toward whites: a term of contempt

un·cloak' ***vt., vi.*** 1 to remove a cloak (from) 2 to reveal; expose

un·clothe' ***vt.*** **-clothed'** or **-clad'**, **-cloth'ing** to undress, uncover, etc.

un·coil' ***vt., vi.*** to unwind

un·com′fort·a·ble *adj.* 1 feeling discomfort 2 causing discomfort 3 ill at ease —**un·com′fort·a·bly** *adv.*
un′com·mit′ted *adj.* 1 not committed or pledged 2 not taking a stand
un·com′mon *adj.* 1 rare; not common or usual 2 strange; remarkable
un′com·mu′ni·ca′tive *adj.* not communicative; reserved; taciturn
un·com′pro·mis′ing *adj.* not yielding; firm; inflexible
un′con·cern′ *n.* 1 apathy; indifference 2 lack of concern, or worry
un′con·cerned′ *adj.* 1 indifferent 2 not solicitous or anxious
un′con·di′tion·al *adj.* without conditions or reservations; absolute
un·con·scion·a·ble (un kän′shən ə bəl) *adj.* 1 not guided or restrained by conscience 2 unreasonable or excessive 3 not fair or just —**un·con′scion·a·bly** *adv.*
un·con′scious *adj.* 1 deprived of consciousness 2 not aware (*of*) 3 not realized or intended /an *unconscious* habit/ —**the unconscious** *Psychoanalysis* the sum of all thoughts, impulses, etc. of which the individual is not conscious but which influence the emotions and behavior
un′con·sti·tu′tion·al *adj.* not in accordance with a constitution
un·cork′ *vt.* to pull the cork out of
un·count′ed *adj.* 1 not counted 2 inconceivably numerous
un·cou′ple *vt.* -pled, -pling to unfasten (things coupled together)
un·couth (un ko͞oth′) *adj.* ⟦OE < *un-*, not + *cunnan*, know⟧ 1 awkward; ungainly 2 uncultured; crude
un·cov′er *vt.* 1 to disclose 2 to remove the cover from 3 to remove the hat, etc. from (the head) —*vi.* to bare the head, as in respect
unc·tion (uŋk′shən) *n.* ⟦< L *ungere*, anoint⟧ 1 *a*) the act of anointing, as for medical or religious purposes *b*) the oil, ointment, etc. used for this 2 anything that soothes or comforts
unc·tu·ous (uŋk′cho͞o əs) *adj.* ⟦see prec.⟧ 1 oily or greasy 2 characterized by a smooth pretense of fervor or earnestness; too suave or oily —**unc′tu·ous·ness** *n.*
un·cut′ *adj.* not cut; specif., *a*) not ground to shape (said of a gem) *b*) not abridged or shortened
un·daunt′ed *adj.* not daunted; fearless, undismayed, etc.
un′de·ceive′ *vt.* -ceived′, -ceiv′ing to cause to be no longer deceived or misled
un′de·cid′ed *adj.* 1 not decided 2 not having come to a decision
un′de·mon′stra·tive *adj.* not demonstrative; not showing feelings openly; reserved —**un′de·mon′stra·tive·ly** *adv.*
un′de·ni′a·ble *adj.* 1 that cannot be denied; indisputable 2 unquestionably good —**un′de·ni′a·bly** *adv.*
un·der (un′dər) *prep.* ⟦OE⟧ 1 in, at, or to a position down from; below 2 beneath the surface of 3 below and to the other side of /drive *under* the bridge/ 4 covered by /a vest *under* his coat/ 5 *a*) lower in rank, position, amount, etc. than *b*) lower than the required degree of /*under* age/ 6 subject to the control, limitations, etc. of /*under* oath/ 7 undergoing /*under* repair/ 8 with the disguise of /*under* an alias/ 9 in (the designated category) 10 during the rule of /*under* Elizabeth I/ 11 being the subject of /*under* discussion/ 12 because of /*under* the circumstances/ 13 authorized by —*adv.* 1 in or to a lower position or state 2 so as to be covered, concealed, etc. —*adj.* lower in position, authority, amount, etc.
under- *prefix* 1 in, on, to, or from a lower place; beneath /*undertow*/ 2 in a subordinate position /*underling*/ 3 too little; insufficiently /*underdeveloped*/
un′der·a·chieve′ *vi.* -chieved′, -chiev′ing to fail to do as well in school as might be expected from intelligence tests —**un′der·a·chiev′er** *n.*
un′der·act′ *vt., vi.* to act (a theatrical role) with insufficient emphasis or too great restraint
un′der·age′ *adj.* 1 not of mature age 2 below the age required by law
un·der·arm (un′dər ärm′) *adj.* 1 of, for, in, or used on the area under the arm, or the armpit 2 UNDERHAND (sense 1) —*adv.* UNDERHAND (sense 1)
un′der·bel′ly *n.* 1 the lower, posterior part of an animal's belly 2 any vulnerable area, point, etc.
un′der·bid′ *vt., vi.* -bid′, -bid′ding 1 to bid lower than (another person) 2 to bid less than the worth of (a thing, as one's hand in bridge)
un′der·brush′ *n.* small trees, shrubs, etc. growing in woods or forests
un′der·car′riage *n.* a supporting frame, as of an automobile
un′der·charge′ *vt., vi.* -charged′, -charg′ing 1 to charge too low a price (to) 2 to load insufficiently
un′der·class′ *n.* the class with incomes below subsistence level, including esp. the underprivileged
un′der·class′man (-mən) *n., pl.* **-men** a freshman or sophomore in high school or college
un′der·clothes′ *n.pl.* UNDERWEAR Also **un′der·cloth′ing** *n.sing.*
un′der·coat′ *n.* 1 a tarlike coating applied to the underside of a motor vehicle to retard rust, etc. 2 a coat of paint, etc. applied before the final coat Also **un′der·coat′ing** —*vt.* to apply an undercoat to
un′der·cov′er *adj.* acting or carried out in secret
un′der·cur′rent *n.* 1 a current flowing beneath the surface 2 an underlying tendency, opinion, etc.
un′der·cut′ *vt.* -cut′, -cut′ting 1 to make a cut below or under 2 to undersell or work for lower wages than
un′der·de·vel′oped *adj.* inadequately developed, esp. economically and industrially
un′der·dog′ *n.* 1 a person or team that is losing or expected to lose 2 one who is underprivileged
un′der·done′ *adj.* not cooked enough
un′der·em·ployed′ *adj.* 1 working less than full time 2 working at low-skilled, poorly paid jobs when capable of doing

more skilled work —**un′der·em·ploy′ment** *n.*

un′der·es′ti·mate′ *vt.* **-mat′ed, -mat′ing** to set too low an estimate on or for —**un′der·es′ti·ma′tion** *n.*

un′der·foot′ *adv., adj.* 1 under the foot or feet 2 in the way

un′der·gar′ment (-gär′mənt) *n.* a piece of underwear

un′der·go′ *vt.* **-went′, -gone′, -go′ing** to experience; go through

un′der·grad′u·ate *n.* a college student who has not yet earned a degree

un′der·ground′ *adj.* 1 under the earth's surface 2 secret; hidden 3 of noncommercial newspapers, movies, etc. that are unconventional, radical, etc. —*adv.* 1 under the earth's surface 2 in or into secrecy —*n.* 1 the region under the earth's surface 2 a secret movement in a country to oppose the government or occupying enemy forces 3 [Brit., etc. (exc. Cdn.)] a subway

un′der·growth′ *n.* UNDERBRUSH

un′der·hand′ *adj.* 1 done with the hand below the level of the elbow or shoulder 2 UNDERHANDED —*adv.* 1 with an underhand motion 2 underhandedly

un′der·hand′ed *adj.* sly, deceitful, etc. —**un′der·hand′ed·ly** *adv.*

un′der·lie′ *vt.* **-lay′, -lain′, -ly′ing** 1 to lie beneath 2 to be the basis for; form the foundation of

un′der·line′ *vt.* **-lined′, -lin′ing** 1 to draw a line beneath 2 to stress

un·der·ling (un′dər liŋ) *n.* ⟦OE: see UNDER- & -LING⟧ a person in a subordinate position; inferior

un′der·ly′ing *adj.* 1 lying under 2 fundamental; basic

un′der·mine′ *vt.* **-mined′, -min′ing** 1 to dig beneath, so as to form a tunnel or mine 2 to wear away at the supports of 3 to injure or weaken, esp. by subtle or insidious means

un′der·most′ *adj., adv.* lowest in place, position, rank, etc.

un·der·neath (un′dər nēth′) *adv., prep.* ⟦< OE *under,* UNDER + *neothan,* below⟧ under; below; beneath

un′der·nour′ished *adj.* not getting the food needed for health and growth

un′der·pants′ *n.pl.* an undergarment of long or short pants

un′der·pass′ *n.* a passage under something, as a road under a railway

un′der·pin′ning (-pin′iŋ) *n.* 1 a support or prop 2 [*pl.*] [Colloq.] the legs

un·der·play (un′dər plā′) *vt., vi.* 1 UNDERACT 2 to make seem not too important

un′der·priv′i·leged *adj.* deprived of basic social rights and security through poverty, discrimination, etc.

un′der·pro·duce′ *vt., vi.* **-duced′, -duc′ing** to produce less than is needed or wanted

un′der·rate′ *vt.* **-rat′ed, -rat′ing** to rate or estimate too low

un·der·score (un′dər skôr′) *vt.* **-scored′, -scor′ing** UNDERLINE

un′der·sea′ *adj., adv.* beneath the surface of the sea Also **un′der·seas′** *adv.*

un′der·sec′re·tar′y *n., pl.* **-ies** an assistant secretary

un′der·sell′ *vt.* **-sold′, -sell′ing** 1 to sell at a lower price than 2 to publicize or promote in a restrained or inadequate manner

un′der·shirt′ *n.* a collarless undergarment worn under an outer shirt

un′der·shorts′ *n.pl.* short underpants worn by men and boys

un′der·shot′ *adj.* 1 with the lower part extending past the upper [an *undershot* jaw] 2 driven by water flowing along the lower part

un′der·side′ *n.* the side or surface that is underneath

un′der·signed′ *adj.* 1 signed at the end 2 whose name is signed at the end —**the undersigned** the person or persons having signed at the end

un′der·skirt′ *n.* a skirt worn under another

un′der·staffed′ *adj.* having fewer workers on the staff than are needed

un′der·stand′ *vt.* **-stood′** (-stood′), **-stand′ing** ⟦< OE *understandan,* lit., to stand among⟧ 1 to perceive the meaning of 2 to assume from what is heard, etc.; infer 3 to take as meant; interpret 4 to take as a fact 5 to learn 6 to know the nature, character, etc. of 7 to be sympathetic with —*vi.* 1 to have understanding, comprehension, etc. 2 to be informed; believe —**un′der·stand′a·ble** *adj.* —**un′der·stand′a·bly** *adv.*

un′der·stand′ing *n.* 1 comprehension 2 the power to think and learn; intelligence 3 a specific interpretation 4 mutual agreement, esp. one that settles differences —*adj.* that understands; sympathetic

un′der·state′ *vt.* **-stat′ed, -stat′ing** 1 to state too weakly 2 to state in a restrained style —**un′der·state′ment** *n.*

un′der·stud′y *n., pl.* **-ies** an actor prepared to substitute for another —*vt., vi.* **-ied, -y·ing** to learn (a part) as an understudy (to)

un′der·take′ *vt.* **-took′, -tak′en, -tak′ing** 1 to take upon oneself (a task, etc.) 2 to promise; guarantee

un′der·tak′er *n.* FUNERAL DIRECTOR: a somewhat old-fashioned usage

un′der·tak′ing *n.* 1 something undertaken; task; enterprise 2 a promise; guarantee

un′der-the-count′er *adj.* [Colloq.] done secretly in an unlawful way Also **un′der-the-ta′ble**

un′der·things′ *n.pl.* women's or girls' underwear

un′der·tone′ *n.* 1 a low tone of voice 2 a subdued color 3 an underlying quality, factor, etc.

un′der·tow′ *n.* a current of water moving beneath the surface water and in a different direction

un′der·wa′ter *adj.* being, done, etc. beneath the surface of the water

un′der·way′ *adj. Naut.* not anchored or moored or aground

un′der·wear′ *n.* clothing worn under one's outer clothes, usually next to the skin, as undershirts

un′der·weight′ (-wāt′; *also* un′dər wāt′) *adj.* below the normal, desirable, or allowed weight

un′der·world′ *n.* 1 Hades; hell 2 criminals as an organized group

un′der·write′ *vt.* **-wrote′, -writ′ten,**

-writ'ing 1 to agree to market (an issue of securities), guaranteeing to buy any part remaining unsubscribed 2 to agree to finance (an undertaking, etc.) 3 to sign one's name to (an insurance policy), thus assuming liability —un'der·writ'er *n.*

un·dies (un'dēz') *n.pl.* [Colloq.] women's or girls' underwear

un·do' *vt.* **-did', -done', -do'ing** 1 to untie, open, etc. 2 to do away with; annul 3 to bring to ruin

un·doc'u·ment'ed *adj.* not having a proper visa for U.S. residence /an *undocumented* alien/

un·do'ing *n.* 1 an annulling 2 a bringing to ruin 3 the cause of ruin

un·done' *adj.* 1 not done; not performed, accomplished, etc. 2 ruined 3 emotionally upset

un·doubt'ed *adj.* that cannot be doubted; certain —**un·doubt'ed·ly** *adv.*

un·dreamed' *adj.* not even dreamed (*of*) or thought (*of*) as possible Also **un·dreamt'** (-dremt')

un·dress' *vt.* to take off the clothing of —*vi.* to take off one's clothes

un·due' *adj.* 1 not appropriate; improper 2 excessive; immoderate

un·du·lant (un'dyoo lənt) *adj.* undulating

un'du·late' (-lāt') *vi., vt.* ⟦< L *unda,* a wave⟧ 1 to move or cause to move in waves 2 to have or cause to have a wavy form or surface —**un'du·la'tion** *n.*

un·du·ly (un dōō'lē) *adv.* 1 improperly; unjustly 2 excessively

un·dy'ing *adj.* immortal or eternal

un·earned' *adj.* not earned by work or service; specif., obtained as a return on an investment /*unearned* income/

un·earth' *vt.* 1 to dig up from the earth 2 to bring to light; disclose

un·earth'ly *adj.* 1 supernatural 2 weird; mysterious 3 [Colloq.] fantastic, outlandish, etc.

un·eas'y *adj.* **-i·er, -i·est** 1 having, showing, or allowing no ease of body or mind; uncomfortable, disturbed, perturbed, etc. 2 awkward; constrained —**un·eas'i·ly** *adv.* —**un·eas'i·ness** *n.*

un'em·ploy'a·ble *adj.* not employable, esp. because of severe physical or mental handicaps, outmoded skills, etc.

un'em·ployed' *adj.* 1 not employed; without work 2 not being used; idle —**un'em·ploy'ment** *n.*

un·e'qual *adj.* 1 not equal, as in size, strength, ability, value, etc. 2 not balanced, even, regular, etc. 3 not adequate (*to*)

un·e'qualed or **un·e'qualled** *adj.* not equaled; unmatched; unrivaled

un'e·quiv'o·cal *adj.* not equivocal; plain; clear

un·err·ing (un ʉr'iŋ, -er'-) *adj.* 1 free from error 2 not missing or failing; sure; exact

UNESCO (yōō nes'kō) United Nations Educational, Scientific, and Cultural Organization

un·e'ven *adj.* 1 not even, level, smooth, regular, etc. 2 unequal 3 *Math.* odd —**un·e'ven·ly** *adv.*

un'ex·am'pled *adj.* having no parallel or precedent; unprecedented

un'ex·cep'tion·a·ble *adj.* not exceptionable; without fault; beyond criticism —**un'ex·cep'tion·a·bly** *adv.*

un'ex·cep'tion·al *adj.* ordinary —**un'ex·cep'tion·al·ly** *adv.*

un'ex·pect'ed *adj.* not expected; unforeseen —**un'ex·pect'ed·ly** *adv.*

un·fail'ing *adj.* 1 not failing 2 never ceasing or falling short; inexhaustible 3 always reliable

un·faith'ful *adj.* 1 lacking or breaking faith or loyalty 2 not true, accurate, etc. 3 adulterous

un·fa·mil·iar (un'fə mil'yər) *adj.* 1 not well-known; strange 2 not acquainted (*with*)

un·feel'ing *adj.* 1 incapable of feeling; insensible 2 hardhearted; cruel —**un·feel'ing·ly** *adv.*

un·feigned' (-fānd') *adj.* genuine

un·fin'ished *adj.* 1 not finished; incomplete 2 having no finish, or final coat, as of paint

un·flap'pa·ble (-flap'ə bəl) *adj.* ⟦< UN- + FLAP, *n.* 4 + -ABLE⟧ [Colloq.] not easily excited; imperturbable

un·flinch'ing *adj.* steadfast; firm

un·fold' *vt.* 1 to open and spread out (something folded) 2 to lay open to view; reveal, explain, etc. —*vi.* 1 to become unfolded 2 to develop fully

un'for·get'ta·ble *adj.* so important, forceful, etc. as never to be forgotten

un'for·giv'ing *adj.* not willing or not able to forgive

un·for'tu·nate *adj.* 1 having or bringing bad luck; unlucky 2 not suitable —*n.* an unfortunate person —**un·for'tu·nate·ly** *adv.*

un·found'ed *adj.* 1 not founded on fact or truth 2 not established

un·friend'ly *adj.* 1 not friendly or kind 2 not favorable

un·frock' *vt.* to deprive of the rank of priest or minister

un·furl' *vt., vi.* to open or spread out from a furled state

un·gain'ly (-gān'lē) *adj.* ⟦< ME *un-,* not + ON *gegn,* ready⟧ awkward; clumsy

un·god'ly *adj.* 1 not godly or religious 2 [Colloq.] outrageous

un·gov'ern·a·ble *adj.* that cannot be governed or controlled; unruly

un·gra'cious *adj.* 1 not gracious; rude 2 unpleasant; unattractive

un·guard'ed *adj.* 1 unprotected 2 guileless 3 careless; imprudent

un·guent (uŋ'gwənt) *n.* ⟦< L *unguere,* anoint⟧ a salve or ointment

un·gu·late (uŋ'gyōō lit, -lāt') *adj.* ⟦< L *unguis,* a nail⟧ having hoofs —*n.* a mammal having hoofs

un·hand' *vt.* to loose or release from the hand or hands; let go of

un·hap'py *adj.* **-pi·er, -pi·est** 1 unfortunate 2 sad; wretched 3 not suitable —**un·hap'pi·ly** *adv.* —**un·hap'pi·ness** *n.*

un·health'y *adj.* **-i·er, -i·est** 1 sickly; not well 2 harmful to health 3 harmful to morals 4 dangerous

un·heard' *adj.* 1 not perceived by the ear 2 not given a hearing

un·heard'-of' *adj.* 1 not heard of before; unprecedented or unknown 2 unacceptable or outrageous

un·hinge' *vt.* **-hinged', -hing'ing** 1 to remove from the hinges 2 to dislodge 3 to unbalance (the mind)

un·ho'ly *adj.* **-li·er, -li·est** 1 not sacred, hallowed, etc. 2 wicked; profane 3 [Colloq.] outrageous; dreadful

un·horse' *vt.* **-horsed', -hors'ing** to throw (a rider) from a horse

uni- ⟦L < *unus,* one⟧ *prefix* one; having only one

u·ni·cam·er·al (yo͞on'i kam'ər əl) *adj.* ⟦< prec. + L *camera,* chamber⟧ of or having a single legislative chamber

UNICEF (yo͞on'ə sef') United Nations Children's Fund: formerly, *United Nations International Children's Emergency Fund*

UNICORN

u·ni·corn (yo͞on'i kôrn') *n.* ⟦< L *unus,* one + *cornu,* horn⟧ a mythical horselike animal with a single horn growing from its forehead

u·ni·cy·cle (yo͞on'ə sī'kəl) *n.* ⟦UNI- + (BI)CYCLE⟧ a one-wheeled vehicle straddled by the rider who pushes its pedals

u·ni·form (yo͞on'ə fôrm') *adj.* ⟦< L *unus,* one + *-formis,* -FORM⟧ 1 not varying in form, rate, degree, etc. 2 like others of the same class —*n.* the distinctive clothes of a particular group, as soldiers —*vt.* to supply with a uniform —**u'ni·form'i·ty** *n.* —**u'ni·form'ly** *adv.*

u·ni·fy (yo͞on'ə fī') *vt., vi.* **-fied', -fy'ing** ⟦see UNI- & -FY⟧ to become or make united —**u'ni·fi·ca'tion** *n.*

u·ni·lat·er·al (yo͞on'ə lat'ər əl) *adj.* 1 of, occurring on, or affecting one side only 2 involving one only of several parties; not reciprocal

un·im·peach·a·ble (un'im pē'chə bəl) *adj.* that cannot be doubted or discredited; irreproachable

un·in'ter·est·ed *adj.* not interested; indifferent

un·ion (yo͞on'yən) *n.* ⟦< L *unus,* one⟧ 1 a uniting or being united; combination 2 a grouping together of nations, etc. for some specific purpose 3 marriage 4 something united 5 *short for* LABOR UNION 6 a device symbolizing political union, used as in a flag 7 a device for uniting parts —**the Union** the United States

un'ion·ize' (-īz') *vt., vi.* **-ized', -iz'ing** to organize into a labor union

union jack a flag, esp. a national flag, consisting only of a UNION (sense 6) —[U- J-] the flag of the United Kingdom

Union of Soviet Socialist Republics country in E Europe & N Asia: it is a union of 15 constituent republics: 8,649,000 sq. mi.; pop. 280,000,000

u·nique (yo͞o nēk') *adj.* ⟦< L *unus,* one⟧ 1 one and only; sole 2 without like or equal 3 very unusual

u·ni·sex (yo͞on'ə seks') *adj.* suitable for both sexes, as a haircut

u·ni·son (yo͞on'ə sən, -zən) *n.* ⟦< L *unus,* one + *sonus,* a sound⟧ 1 identity of musical pitch, as of two or more tones 2 agreement —**in unison** with all the voices or instruments performing the same part

u·nit (yo͞on'it) *n.* ⟦< UNITY⟧ 1 the smallest whole number; one 2 a standard basic quantity, measure, etc. 3 a single person or group, esp. as a part of a whole 4 a distinct part or object with a specific purpose

U·ni·tar·i·an (yo͞on'ə ter'ē ən) *n.* a member of a Christian sect holding that God is a single being

u·ni·tar·y (yo͞on'ə ter'ē) *adj.* 1 of a unit or units 2 of or based on unity

u·nite (yo͞o nīt') *vt., vi.* **-nit'ed, -nit'ing** ⟦< L *unus,* one⟧ 1 to put or join together so as to make one; combine 2 to bring or come together in common cause, action, etc.

United Arab E·mir·ates (e mir'əts) country in E Arabia, on the Persian Gulf: *c.* 32,000 sq. mi.; pop. 1,326,000

United Arab Republic *old name of* Egypt (1961-71)

United Kingdom country in W Europe, consisting of Great Britain & Northern Ireland: 94,217 sq. mi.; pop. 56,458,000

United Nations an international organization of nations for world peace and security: formed in 1945 and having, in 1988, a membership of 159

United States of America country including 49 States in North America, & Hawaii: 3,615,211 sq. mi.; pop. 240,856,000; cap. Washington: also called **the United States**

u·nit·ize (yo͞on'ə tīz') *vt.* **-ized', -iz'ing** to make into a single unit

unit pricing a system of showing prices in terms of standard units

u·ni·ty (yo͞on'ə tē) *n., pl.* **-ties** ⟦< L *unus,* one⟧ 1 a being united; oneness 2 a single, separate thing 3 harmony; agreement 4 a complex that is a union of related parts 5 a harmonious, unified arrangement of parts in an artistic work 6 continuity of purpose, action, etc. 7 *Math.* any quantity, etc. identified as a unit, or 1

u·ni·va·lent (yo͞on'ə vā'lənt) *adj. Chem.* 1 having one valence 2 having a valence of one

u·ni·valve (yo͞on'ə valv') *n.* a mollusk with a one-piece shell, as a snail

u·ni·ver·sal (yo͞on'ə vur'səl) *adj.* 1 of the universe; present everywhere 2 of, for, or including all or the whole 3 used, or intended to be used, for all kinds, sizes, etc. or by all people —**u'ni·ver·sal'i·ty** (-vər sal'ə tē) *n.*

u'ni·ver'sal·ize' *vt.* **-ized', -iz'ing** to make universal

universal joint (or **coupling**) a joint or coupling that permits a swing of limited angle in any direction

u'ni·ver'sal·ly *adv.* 1 in every instance 2 in every part or place

Universal Product Code a patterned series of vertical bars printed on consumer products: it can be read by computerized scanners for pricing, etc.

u·ni·verse (yōōn′ə vurs′) ***n.*** ⟦< L *unus,* one + *vertere,* to turn⟧ 1 the totality of all things that exist 2 the world

u·ni·ver·si·ty (yōōn′ə vur′sə tē) ***n.,*** *pl.* **-ties** ⟦see prec.⟧ an educational institution offering bachelor's and advanced degrees

un·just (un just′) ***adj.*** not just or right; unfair —**un·just′ly** ***adv.***

un·kempt′ (-kempt′) ***adj.*** ⟦UN- + *kempt* < dial. *kemben,* to comb⟧ 1 tangled, disheveled, etc. 2 not tidy; slovenly

un·kind′ ***adj.*** not kind; specif., *a*) not considerate of others *b*) harsh, severe, cruel, etc. —**un·kind′ness** ***n.***

un·kind′ly ***adj.*** UNKIND —***adv.*** in an unkind way

un·known′ ***adj.*** not known; specif., *a*) unfamiliar (*to*) *b*) not identified, etc. —***n.*** an unknown person or thing

un·law′ful ***adj.*** 1 against the law; illegal 2 immoral —**un·law′ful·ly** ***adv.*** —**un·law′ful·ness** ***n.***

un·lead′ed ***adj.*** not containing lead compounds: said of gasoline

un·learn′ ***vt., vi.*** to forget or try to forget (something learned)

un·learn′ed (-lurn′id; *for 2,* -lurnd′) ***adj.*** 1 not learned or educated 2 not learned */unlearned* lessons/

un·leash′ ***vt.*** to release from or as from a leash

un·less (un les′, ən-) ***conj.*** ⟦< ME *on lesse that,* at less than⟧ in any case other than that; except that

un·let·tered (un let′ərd) ***adj.*** 1 ignorant; uneducated 2 illiterate

un·like′ ***adj.*** not alike; different —***prep.*** 1 not like; different from 2 not characteristic of

un·like′ly ***adj.*** 1 not likely; improbable 2 not likely to succeed —**un·like′li·hood′** ***n.***

un·lim′ber (-lim′bər) ***vt., vi.*** to get ready for use or action

un·lim′it·ed ***adj.*** 1 without limits or restrictions 2 vast; illimitable

un·load′ ***vt., vi.*** 1 *a*) to remove (a load) *b*) to take a load from 2 *a*) to tell (one's troubles, etc.) without restraint *b*) to relieve of something that troubles 3 to remove the charge from (a gun) 4 to get rid of

un·lock′ ***vt.*** 1 *a*) to open (a lock) *b*) to open the lock of (a door, etc.) 2 to let loose; release 3 to reveal

un·looked′-for′ ***adj.*** not expected

un·loose′ ***vt.*** **-loosed′**, **-loos′ing** to set loose; loosen, release, etc. Also **un·loos′en**

un·luck′y ***adj.*** **-i·er**, **-i·est** having or bringing bad luck; unfortunate

un·make′ ***vt.*** **-made′**, **-mak′ing** 1 to cause to be as before; undo 2 to ruin; destroy 3 to depose from a position or rank

un·man′ ***vt.*** **-manned′**, **-man′ning** to deprive of manly courage, nerve, etc.

un·man′ly ***adj.*** **-li·er**, **-li·est** not manly; specif., *a*) cowardly, weak, etc. *b*) effeminate; womanish

un·manned′ ***adj.*** without people aboard and operating by remote control

un·mask′ ***vi., vt.*** 1 to remove a mask or disguise (from) 2 to disclose the true nature or character (of)

un·mean′ing ***adj.*** lacking in meaning or sense

un·men′tion·a·ble ***adj.*** not fit to be mentioned in polite conversation

un·mer′ci·ful ***adj.*** having or showing no mercy; cruel; pitiless

un′mis·tak′a·ble ***adj.*** that cannot be mistaken or misinterpreted; clear —**un′mis·tak′a·bly** ***adv.***

un·mit′i·gat′ed ***adj.*** 1 not lessened or eased 2 out-and-out; absolute

un·mor′al ***adj.*** AMORAL

un·nat′u·ral (-nach′ər əl) ***adj.*** 1 contrary to nature; abnormal 2 artificial 3 very cruel —**un·nat′u·ral·ly** ***adv.***

un·nec′es·sar′y ***adj.*** not necessary; needless —**un·nec′es·sar′i·ly** ***adv.***

un·nerve′ (-nurv′) ***vt.*** **-nerved′**, **-nerv′ing** to cause to lose one's self-confidence, courage, etc.

un·num′bered ***adj.*** 1 not counted 2 innumerable 3 not numbered

un·or′gan·ized′ ***adj.*** not organized; specif., not belonging to a labor union

un·pack′ ***vt., vi.*** 1 to remove (the contents of a trunk, suitcase, etc.) 2 to take things out of (a trunk, etc.)

un·par′al·leled′ ***adj.*** that has no parallel, equal, or counterpart

un·pleas′ant ***adj.*** not pleasant; offensive; disagreeable —**un·pleas′ant·ly** ***adv.*** —**un·pleas′ant·ness** ***n.***

un·plumbed′ ***adj.*** 1 not measured with a plumb 2 not fully understood

un·pop′u·lar ***adj.*** not liked by the public or by the majority —**un′pop·u·lar′i·ty** (-lar′ə tē) ***n.***

un·prac′ticed (-prak′tist) ***adj.*** 1 not habitually or repeatedly done, etc. 2 not skilled or experienced

un·prec′e·dent′ed ***adj.*** having no precedent or parallel; unheard-of

un·prin′ci·pled ***adj.*** lacking moral principles; unscrupulous

un·print′a·ble ***adj.*** not fit to be printed, as because of obscenity

un′pro·fes′sion·al ***adj.*** not professional; esp., violating the ethical code of a given profession

un·qual′i·fied′ ***adj.*** 1 lacking the necessary qualifications 2 not limited or modified; absolute

un·ques′tion·a·ble ***adj.*** not to be questioned, doubted, or disputed; certain —**un·ques′tion·a·bly** ***adv.***

un′quote′ ***interj.*** I end the quotation

un·rav′el ***vt.*** **-eled** or **-elled**, **-el·ing** or **-el·ling** 1 to separate the threads of (something woven, tangled, etc.) 2 to make clear; solve —***vi.*** to become unraveled

un·read′ (-red′) ***adj.*** 1 not read, as a book 2 having read little or nothing

un·re′al ***adj.*** not real or actual; imaginary, fanciful, false, etc.

un·rea′son·a·ble ***adj.*** 1 not reasonable or rational 2 excessive; immoderate —**un·rea′son·a·bly** ***adv.***

un·rea′son·ing ***adj.*** not reasoning or reasoned; irrational

un′re·con·struct′ed ***adj.*** 1 not reconstructed 2 holding to an earlier, outmoded practice or point of view

un′re·gen′er·ate *adj.* 1 not spiritually reborn 2 stubbornly defiant
un′re·lent′ing *adj.* 1 inflexible; relentless 2 without mercy; cruel 3 not relaxing in effort, speed, etc.
un′re·mit′ting *adj.* not stopping, relaxing, etc.; incessant; persistent
un′re·served′ *adj.* not reserved; specif., *a*) frank or open in speech *b*) not restricted or qualified —**un′re·serv′ed·ly** (-zur′vid lē) *adv.*
un·rest′ *n.* 1 restlessness; disquiet 2 angry discontent verging on revolt
un·ripe′ *adj.* not ripe or mature; green
un·ri′valed or **un·ri′valled** (-rīv′əld) *adj.* having no rival, equal, or competitor
un·roll′ *vt.* 1 to open (something rolled up) 2 to display —*vi.* to become unrolled
un·ruf·fled (un ruf′əld) *adj.* not ruffled or disturbed; calm; smooth; serene
un·rul·y (un ro͞ol′ē) *adj.* **-i·er, -i·est** hard to control, restrain, or keep in order; disobedient —**un·rul′i·ness** *n.*
un·sad′dle *vt.* **-dled, -dling** to take the saddle off (a horse, etc.)
un·said′ *adj.* not expressed
un·sa′vor·y *adj.* 1 unpleasant to taste or smell 2 morally offensive
un·scathed′ (-skāthd′) *adj.* ⟦< *un-* + ON *skathi*, harm⟧ unharmed
un·schooled′ *adj.* not educated or trained, esp. by formal schooling
un·scram′ble *vt.* **-bled, -bling** to cause to be no longer scrambled, mixed up, or unintelligible
un·screw′ *vt.* to detach or loosen by removing screws, or by turning
un·scru′pu·lous *adj.* not restrained by moral scruples; unprincipled
un·seal′ *vt.* to break the seal of; open
un·sea′son·a·ble *adj.* 1 not usual for the season 2 at the wrong time
un·seat′ *vt.* 1 to dislodge from a seat 2 to remove from office
un·seem′ly *adj.* not seemly; not decent or proper; unbecoming
un·set′tle *vt., vi.* **-tled, -tling** to make or become unstable; disturb or displace
un·set′tled *adj.* 1 not settled; not fixed, orderly, stable, calm, decided, etc. 2 not paid 3 having no settlers
un·sheathe′ (-shēth′) *vt.* **-sheathed′, -sheath′ing** to remove (a sword, etc.) from a sheath
un·sight′ly (-sīt′lē) *adj.* not sightly or pleasant to look at; ugly
un·skilled′ *adj.* having or requiring no special skill or training
un·skill′ful *adj.* having little or no skill; awkward
un·snap′ *vt.* **-snapped′, -snap′ping** to undo the snaps of, so as to detach
un·snarl′ (-snärl′) *vt.* to untangle
un′so·phis′ti·cat′ed *adj.* not sophisticated; simple; ingenuous, etc.
un·sound′ *adj.* not sound; specif., *a*) not healthy, safe, firm, etc. *b*) not reliable, sensible, etc.
un·spar′ing *adj.* 1 not sparing; lavish 2 not merciful; severe
un·speak′a·ble *adj.* 1 that cannot be spoken 2 so bad, evil, etc. as to defy description —**un·speak′a·bly** *adv.*
un·sta′ble *adj.* not stable; specif., *a*) easily upset *b*) changeable *c*) unreliable *d*) emotionally unsettled *e*) *Chem.* tending to decompose
un·stead′y *adj.* not steady; specif., *a*) not firm; shaky *b*) changeable; inconstant *c*) erratic in habits, purpose, etc.
un·stop′ *vt.* **-stopped′, -stop′ping** 1 to remove the stopper from 2 to clear (a pipe, etc.) of an obstruction
un·struc′tured *adj.* not formally organized; loose, free, open, etc.
un·strung′ *adj.* 1 nervous or upset 2 with the strings loosened or detached, as a bow, racket, etc.
un·stuck′ *adj.* loosened or freed from being stuck
un·stud′ied *adj.* not got by study or conscious effort; spontaneous; natural
un′sub·stan′tial *adj.* 1 having no material substance 2 not solid; flimsy 3 unreal; visionary
un·sung′ (-suŋ′) *adj.* not honored or celebrated, as in song or poetry
un·tan′gle *vt.* **-gled, -gling** 1 to free from a snarl or tangle 2 to free from confusion; put in order
un·taught′ *adj.* 1 not taught; uneducated 2 acquired without being taught
un·think′a·ble *adj.* not to be considered or thought of; impossible
un·think′ing *adj.* 1 thoughtless; heedless 2 unable to think
un·ti′dy *adj.* **-di·er, -di·est** not tidy; slovenly; messy
un·tie′ *vt.* **-tied′, -ty′ing** or **-tie′ing** 1 to unfasten (a thing tied or knotted) 2 to free, as from restraint
un·til (un til′, ən-) *prep.* ⟦ME *untill*⟧ 1 up to the time of /*until* death/ 2 before /not *until* tomorrow/ —*conj.* 1 up to the time when or that /*until* you leave/ 2 to the point, degree, etc. that /cook *until* it is done/ 3 before /not *until* I die/
un·time′ly *adj.* 1 before the proper time; premature 2 at the wrong time; inopportune —*adv.* 1 prematurely 2 inopportunely —**un·time′li·ness** *n.*
un·to (un′to͞o, -too) *prep.* ⟦ME⟧ *old poet. var. of:* 1 to 2 until
un·told′ *adj.* 1 not told or revealed 2 too many to be counted; vast
un·touch′a·ble *adj.* that cannot or should not be touched —*n.* in India, formerly, a member of the lowest caste
un·to·ward (un tō′ərd, -tôrd′) *adj.* 1 improper, unseemly, etc. 2 not favorable; adverse
un·trav′eled or **un·trav′elled** *adj.* 1 not used or frequented by travelers 2 not having done much traveling
un·truth′ *n.* 1 falsity 2 a falsehood; lie —**un·truth′ful** *adj.*
un·tu′tored (-to͞ot′ərd) *adj.* uneducated
un·twist′ *vt., vi.* to separate, as something twisted together; unwind
un·used′ *adj.* 1 not in use 2 never used before 3 unaccustomed (*to*)
un·u′su·al *adj.* not usual or common; rare —**un·u′su·al·ly** *adv.*
un·ut′ter·a·ble *adj.* inexpressible

un·var′nished *adj.* 1 not varnished 2 plain; simple; unadorned

un·veil′ *vt.* to reveal as by removing a veil from —*vi.* to take off one's veil

un·voiced′ *adj.* not expressed; not spoken

un·war′y *adj.* not wary or cautious

un′wea′ried (-wir′ēd) *adj.* ⟦ME *unweried* (see UN- & WEARY)⟧ never wearying; tireless; indefatigable

un·well′ *adj.* not well; sick

un·whole′some *adj.* 1 harmful to body or mind 2 of unsound health or unhealthy appearance 3 morally harmful —**un·whole′some·ness** *n.*

un·wield′y *adj.* hard to wield, manage, etc., as because of large size

un·will′ing *adj.* 1 not willing; reluctant 2 done, said, etc. reluctantly —**un·will′ing·ly** *adv.*

un·wind′ *vt.* **-wound′**, **-wind′ing** 1 to wind off or undo (something wound) 2 to untangle (something involved) —*vi.* 1 to become unwound 2 to become relaxed

un·wise′ *adj.* having or showing a lack of wisdom or sound judgment

un·wit′ting (-wit′iŋ) *adj.* 1 not knowing; unaware 2 unintentional

un·wont′ed (-wän′tid, -wōn′-) *adj.* not common or usual; rare

un·wor′thy *adj.* **-thi·er**, **-thi·est** 1 lacking merit or value; worthless 2 not deserving (*of*) 3 not fit or becoming: with *of* —**un·wor′thi·ness** *n.*

un·wrap′ *vt.* **-wrapped′**, **-wrap′ping** to take off the wrapping of

un·writ′ten (-rit′'n) *adj.* 1 not in writing 2 operating only through custom or tradition /an *unwritten* rule/

up[1] (up) *adv.* ⟦OE⟧ 1 to, in, or on a higher place or level 2 to a later period 3 to or into a higher condition, amount, etc. 4 in or into a standing position 5 in or into action, view, consideration, etc. 6 aside; away /lay *up* wealth/ 7 so as to be even with in time, degree, etc. 8 so as to be tightly closed, bound, etc. /tie *up* the package/ 9 completely; thoroughly 10 *Baseball* to one's turn at batting 11 used with verbs: *a*) to form idioms with meanings different from the simple verb /look *up* this word/ *b*) as an intensive /dress *up*/ —*prep.* up to, toward, along, through, into, or upon —*adj.* 1 directed toward a higher position 2 in a higher place or position 3 advanced in amount, degree, etc. /rents are *up*/ 4 in a standing position 5 in an active or excited state 6 at an end; over /time's *up*/ 7 available for use, as a computer 8 [Colloq.] going on /what's *up*/ 9 *Baseball* at bat —*n.* 1 an upward slope 2 an upward movement, etc. —*vi.* **upped**, **up′ping** [Colloq.] to get up; rise —*vt.* [Colloq.] 1 to put up, lift up, etc. 2 to cause to rise /to *up* prices/ —**on the up and up** [Slang] honest —**up against** [Colloq.] confronted with —**up on** (or **in**) [Colloq.] well-informed concerning —**ups and downs** good periods and bad periods —**up to** [Colloq.] 1 doing or scheming 2 capable of (doing, etc.) 3 as many as 4 as far as 5 dependent upon —**up with!** give or restore power, favor, etc. to!

up[2] (up) *adv.* ⟦phonetic respelling of *ap(iece)*⟧ apiece /a score of two *up*/

up- *combining form* up

up-and-com·ing (up′ən kum′iŋ) *adj.* 1 enterprising, promising, etc. 2 gaining in prominence

up′beat′ *n. Music* an unaccented beat, esp. when on the last note of a bar —*adj.* [Colloq.] cheerful; optimistic

up·braid (up brād′) *vt.* ⟦< OE *up-*, up + *bregdan*, to pull⟧ to rebuke severely; censure; scold

up′bring′ing *n.* the training and education received while growing up

UPC Universal Product Code

up′chuck′ (-chuk′) *vi.*, *vt.*, *n.* [Slang] VOMIT

up′com′ing *adj.* coming soon

up′coun′try *adj.*, *adv.* in or toward the interior of a country

up·date′ (-dāt′; *also, and for n. always*, up′-dāt′) *vt.* **-dat′ed**, **-dat′ing** to make up-to-date; make conform to the most recent facts, methods, etc. —*n.* 1 an updating 2 an updated report, etc.

up·end′ *vt.*, *vi.* to set, turn, or stand on end

up′front′ *adj.* 1 forthright 2 in advance /*upfront* money/ Also **up′-front′**

up′grade′ (-grād′; *for v. usually* up grād′) *n.* an upward slope —*adj.*, *adv.* uphill; upward —*vt.* **-grad′ed**, **-grad′ing** to raise in value, grade, rank, quality, etc.

up·heav·al (up hē′vəl) *n.* 1 a heaving up 2 a sudden, violent change

up′hill′ *adv.* 1 toward the top of a hill; upward 2 with difficulty —*adj.* 1 going or sloping up 2 laborious; tiring

up·hold′ *vt.* **-held′**, **-hold′ing** 1 to hold up 2 to keep from falling; support 3 to confirm; sustain

up·hol·ster (up hōl′stər) *vt.* ⟦ult. < ME *upholder*, tradesman⟧ to fit out (furniture, etc.) with coverings, padding, springs, etc. —**up·hol′ster·er** *n.*

up·hol′ster·y *n.*, *pl.* **-ies** 1 the material used in upholstering 2 the work of an upholsterer

UPI United Press International

up′keep′ *n.* 1 maintenance 2 state of repair 3 the cost of maintenance

up′land (-lənd, -land′) *n.* land elevated above other land —*adj.* of or situated in upland

up·lift′ (-lift′; *for n.* up′lift′) *vt.* 1 to lift up 2 to raise to a higher moral, social, or cultural level —*n.* 1 a lifting up 2 a movement for moral, social, or cultural betterment

up′-mark′et *adj.* UPSCALE

up·on (ə pän′, ə pôn′) *prep.* on, or up and on: used interchangeably with *on* —*adv.* on

up·per (up′ər) *adj.* 1 higher in place 2 higher in rank, etc. —*n.* 1 the part of a shoe above the sole 2 [Slang] any drug that is a stimulant —**on one's uppers** [Colloq.] 1 wearing worn-out shoes 2 poor

up·per·case (up′ər kās′) *n.* capital-letter type used in printing, as distinguished from small letters —*adj.* of or in uppercase

upper class the rich or aristocratic social class

up′per·class′man (-mən) *n.*, *pl.* **-men** a junior or senior in high school or college

up'per·cut' *n. Boxing* a short, swinging blow directed upward
upper hand the position of advantage or control
up'per·most' *adj.* highest in place, power, authority, etc. —*adv.* in the highest place, rank, etc.
Upper Vol·ta (väl'tə) *old name of* BURKINA FASO
up·pi·ty (up'ə tē) *adj.* [Colloq.] haughty, arrogant, snobbish, etc. Also [Brit. Colloq.] **up'pish**
up·raise' *vt.* **-raised', -rais'ing** to raise up; lift
up·rear' *vt.* 1 to raise or lift up 2 to exalt 3 to bring up; rear
up·right (up'rīt'; *also, for adv.,* up rīt') *adj.* 1 standing, pointing, etc. straight up; erect 2 honest and just —*adv.* in an upright position or direction —*n.* something having an upright position
upright piano a piano with a vertical, rectangular body
up'ris'ing (-rī'ziŋ) *n.* a revolt
up·roar (up'rôr') *n.* ⟦Du *oproer,* a stirring up⟧ 1 violent disturbance; tumult 2 loud, confused noise
up·roar·i·ous (up rôr'ē əs) *adj.* 1 making, or full of, an uproar 2 loud and boisterous, as laughter
up·root' *vt.* 1 to tear up by the roots 2 to destroy or remove utterly
up'scale' *adj.* of or for people who are affluent, stylish, etc.
up·set (up set'; *for n.* up'set') *vt.* **-set', -set'·ting** 1 *a)* to tip over; overturn *b)* to defeat unexpectedly 2 *a)* to disturb the functioning of [to *upset* a schedule] *b)* to disturb emotionally or physically —*vi.* to become overturned or upset —*n.* 1 an upsetting 2 an unexpected defeat 3 a disturbance —*adj.* 1 tipped over 2 overthrown or defeated 3 disturbed or disordered
up'shot' *n.* ⟦orig., final shot in an archery match⟧ the conclusion; result
up'side' *n.* the upper side or part
upside down 1 with the top side or part underneath or turned over; inverted 2 in disorder —**up'side'-down'** *adj.*
up·si·lon (ōōp'sə län', up'-) *n.* the twentieth letter of the Greek alphabet (Υ, υ)
up·stage (up'stāj'; *for v.,* up stāj') *adv., adj.* toward or at the rear of a stage —*vt.* **-staged', -stag'ing** to draw attention away from another, as by moving upstage
up'stairs' *adv.* 1 up the stairs 2 on or to an upper floor or higher level 3 [Colloq.] in the mind —*adj.* on an upper floor —*n.* an upper floor
up'stand'ing *adj.* 1 erect 2 upright in character; honorable
up'start' *n.* one who has recently come into wealth, power, etc., esp. one who is presumptuous, aggressive, etc. —*adj.* of or like an upstart
up'state' *adj., adv.* in, to, or from the northerly part of a State
up'stream' *adv., adj.* in the direction against the current of a stream
up'surge' *n.* a surge upward
up'swing' *n.* a swing, trend, or movement upward
up'take' *n.* a taking up —**quick** (or **slow**) **on the uptake** [Colloq.] quick (or slow) to comprehend
up'tight' *adj.* [Slang] very tense, nervous, etc. Also **up-tight**
up'-to-date' *adj.* 1 extending to the present time 2 keeping up with what is most recent
up'town' *adj., adv.* of, in, or toward the higher or residential part of a city or town —*n.* the uptown section of a city or town
up·turn' (-turn'; *for n.* up'turn') *vt., vi.* to turn up or over —*n.* an upward turn or trend —**up'turned'** *adj.*
up'ward (-wərd) *adv., adj.* toward a higher place, position, etc. Also **up'wards** *adv.* —**upwards** (or **upward**) **of** more than —**up'ward·ly** *adv.*
upward mobility movement to a higher social and economic status
up'wind' *adv., adj.* in the direction from which the wind is blowing or usually blows
u·ra·cil (yoor'ə sil') *n.* a colorless, crystalline base that is a constituent of RNA
U·rals (yoor'əlz) mountain system in the R.S.F.S.R., regarded as the boundary between Europe & Asia: also **Ural Mountains**
u·ra·ni·um (yōō rā'nē əm) *n.* ⟦after fol.⟧ a very hard, heavy, radioactive metallic chemical element: used in work on atomic energy
U·ra·nus (yoor'ə nəs, yōō rān'əs) ⟦< Gr *Ouranos,* heaven⟧ a planet of the solar system: see PLANET
ur·ban (ur'bən) *adj.* ⟦< L *urbs,* city⟧ 1 of, in, or constituting a city 2 characteristic of cities
ur·bane (ur bān') *adj.* ⟦see prec.⟧ polite in a smooth, polished way; refined —**ur·ban'i·ty** (-ban'ə tē) *n.*
ur·ban·ize (ur'bən īz') *vt.* **-ized', -iz'ing** to change from rural to urban —**ur'ban·i·za'·tion** *n.*
ur'ban·ol'o·gist (-äl'ə jist) *n.* a specialist in urban problems —**ur'ban·ol'o·gy** *n.*
urban renewal rehabilitation of deteriorated urban areas, as by slum clearance and housing construction
urban sprawl the spread of urban congestion into surrounding areas
ur·chin (ur'chin) *n.* ⟦< L *ericius,* hedgehog⟧ a small child; esp., a mischievous boy
-ure (ər) ⟦Fr < L *-ura*⟧ *suffix* 1 act, process, or result [*exposure*] 2 agent of 3 state of being ____ed [*composure*] 4 office, rank, or collective body [*legislature*]
u·re·a (yōō rē'ə) *n.* ⟦< Gr *ouron,* urine⟧ a soluble, crystalline solid found in urine or made synthetically
u·re·mi·a (yōō rē'mē ə) *n.* ⟦< Gr *ouron,* urine + *haima,* blood⟧ a toxic condition caused by the presence in the blood of waste products normally eliminated in the urine —**u·re'mic** *adj.*
u·re·ter (yōō rēt'ər) *n.* ⟦< Gr *ourein,* urinate⟧ a tube carrying urine from a kidney to the bladder
u·re·thane (yoor'ə thān') *n.* ⟦< Fr⟧ a white, crystalline compound used as a hypnotic and sedative, a solvent, etc.
u·re·thra (yōō rē'thrə) *n., pl.* **-thrae** (-thrē') or **-thras** ⟦< Gr *ouron,* urine⟧ the canal

through which urine is discharged from the bladder: in males, also the duct for semen

urge (urj) *vt.* **urged, urg′ing** ⟦L *urgere,* press hard⟧ 1 *a)* to press upon the attention; advocate *b)* to plead with; ask earnestly 2 to incite; provoke 3 to drive or force onward —*n.* 1 an urging 2 an impulse

ur·gent (ur′jənt) *adj.* ⟦see prec.⟧ 1 calling for haste, immediate action, etc. 2 insistent —**ur′gen·cy,** *pl.* **-cies,** *n.* —**ur′gent·ly** *adv.*

-ur·gy (ur′jē) ⟦< Gr *ergon,* work⟧ *combining form* a working with or by means of (something specified) /*chemurgy*/

u·ric (yoor′ik) *adj.* of, contained in, or derived from urine

u·ri·nal (yoor′ə nəl) *n.* 1 a portable receptacle for urinating 2 a place for urinating

u·ri·nal·y·sis (yoor′ə nal′ə sis) *n., pl.* **-ses′** (-sēz′) chemical or microscopic analysis of the urine

u·ri·nar·y (yoor′ə ner′ē) *adj.* 1 of urine 2 of the organs that secrete and discharge urine

u·ri·nate (yoor′ə nāt′) *vi.* **-nat′ed, -nat′ing** to discharge urine from the body —**u′ri·na′tion** *n.*

u·rine (yoor′in) *n.* ⟦< L *urina*⟧ the yellowish liquid containing waste products secreted by the kidneys and discharged through the urethra

urn (urn) *n.* ⟦< L *urna*⟧ 1 *a)* a vase with a pedestal *b)* such a vase used to hold ashes after cremation 2 a metal container with a faucet, for making or serving hot coffee, tea, etc.

u·ro·gen·i·tal (yoor′ō jen′ə təl) *adj.* of the urinary and genital organs

u·rol·o·gy (yoo räl′ə jē) *n.* ⟦< Gr *ouron,* urine + -LOGY⟧ the branch of medicine dealing with the urinary and genital organs and their diseases —**u·rol′o·gist** *n.*

ur·sine (ur′sīn′, -sin) *adj.* ⟦< L *ursus,* a bear⟧ of or like a bear

ur·ti·car·i·a (urt′i ker′ē ə) *n.* ⟦< L *urtica,* a nettle⟧ HIVES

U·ru·guay (yoor′ə gwā′, -gwī′) country in SE South America: 72,171 sq. mi.; pop. 2,974,000 —**Ur′u·guay′an** *adj., n.*

us (us) *pron.* ⟦OE⟧ *objective case of* WE

US or **U.S.** United States

USA 1 United States of America: also **U.S.A.** 2 United States Army

us·a·ble or **use·a·ble** (yōō′zə bəl) *adj.* that can be used; fit for use —**us′a·bil′i·ty** (-bil′ə tē) or **use′a·bil′i·ty** *n.*

USAF United States Air Force

us·age (yōō′sij) *n.* 1 the act, way, or extent of using; treatment 2 established practice; custom; habit 3 the way in which a word, phrase, etc. is used to express a particular idea

USDA United States Department of Agriculture

use (yōōz; *for n.* yōōs) *vt.* **used, us′ing** ⟦< L *uti*⟧ 1 to put into action or service 2 to exercise /*use* your judgment/ 3 to deal with; treat /to *use* a friend badly/ 4 to consume, expend: often with *up* 5 to consume habitually /to *use* drugs/ —*n.* 1 a using or being used 2 the ability to use 3 the right to use 4 the need or opportunity to use 5 a way of using 6 usefulness 7 the purpose for which something is used 8 function —**used to** (yōōs′tə, -too) 1 did at one time /I *used to* live here/ 2 accustomed to —**us′er** *n.*

used (yōōzd) *vt. pt. & pp. of* USE —*adj.* not new; secondhand

use·ful (yōōs′fəl) *adj.* that can be used; serviceable; helpful —**use′ful·ly** *adv.* —**use′ful·ness** *n.*

use′less (-lis) *adj.* 1 having no use 2 to no purpose —**use′less·ly** *adv.* —**use′less·ness** *n.*

us′er-friend′ly *adj.* easy to use or understand: said esp. of computer hardware, programs, etc.

ush·er (ush′ər) *n.* ⟦< L *ostiarius,* doorkeeper⟧ 1 one who shows people to their seats in a theater, church, etc. 2 a bridegroom's attendant —*vt.* 1 to escort (others) to seats, etc. 2 to be a forerunner of: often with *in*

USMC United States Marine Corps

USN United States Navy

USO United Service Organizations

USP or **U.S.P.** United States Pharmacopoeia

USS United States Ship

USSR or **U.S.S.R.** Union of Soviet Socialist Republics

u·su·al (yōō′zhoo əl) *adj.* ⟦see USE⟧ such as is most often seen, used, etc.; common; customary —**u′su·al·ly** *adv.*

u·surp (yōō zurp′, -surp′) *vt., vi.* ⟦< L *usus,* a use + *rapere,* to seize⟧ to take (power, a position, etc.) by force —**u·sur·pa·tion** (yōō′zər pā′shən, -sər-) *n.* —**u·surp′er** *n.*

u·su·ry (yōō′zhər ē) *n., pl.* **-ries** ⟦see USE⟧ 1 the lending of money at an excessive rate of interest 2 an excessive interest rate —**u′su·rer** *n.* —**u·su·ri·ous** (yōō zhoor′ē əs) *adj.*

U·tah (yōō′tô′) Mountain State of the W U.S.: 84,916 sq. mi.; pop. 1,461,000; cap. Salt Lake City: abbrev. **UT** or **Ut.** —**U′tah·an** *adj., n.*

u·ten·sil (yōō ten′səl) *n.* ⟦< L *uti,* to use⟧ an implement or container, esp. one for use in a kitchen

u·ter·us (yōōt′ər əs) *n., pl.* **-ter·i′** (-ī′) ⟦L⟧ a hollow organ of female mammals in which the embryo and fetus are developed; womb —**u′ter·ine** (-in, -īn′) *adj.*

u·til·i·tar·i·an (yōō til′ə ter′ē ən) *adj.* 1 of or having to do with utility 2 stressing usefulness over beauty or other considerations

u·til′i·tar′i·an·ism′ *n.* 1 the doctrine that worth or value is determined solely by utility 2 the doctrine, developed by J. Bentham (1748-1832) and J.S. Mill (1806-73), that the purpose of all action should be to bring about the greatest happiness of the greatest number

u·til·i·ty (yōō til′ə tē) *n., pl.* **-ties** ⟦< L *uti,* to use⟧ 1 usefulness 2 something useful, as the service to the public of gas, water, etc. 3 a company providing such a service

utility room a room containing laundry appliances, heating equipment, etc.

u·ti·lize (yōōt′'l īz′) *vt.* **-lized′, -liz′ing** to put to profitable use; make use of —**u′ti·li·za′tion** *n.*

ut·most (ut′mōst′) *adj.* ⟦< OE superl. of *ut,*

out ⟧ 1 most extreme; farthest 2 of the greatest degree, amount, etc. —*n.* the most possible

U·to·pi·a (yōō tō′pē ə) ⟦< Gr *ou,* not + *topos,* a place ⟧ an imaginary island with a perfect political and social system, described in *Utopia* (1516) by Sir Thomas More, Eng. statesman —*n.* [*often* **u-**] 1 any idealized place of perfection 2 any visionary scheme for a perfect society —**U·to′pi·an** or **u·to′pi·an** *adj., n.*

ut·ter[1] (ut′ər) *adj.* ⟦< OE compar. of *ut,* out ⟧ 1 complete; total 2 unqualified; absolute; unconditional —**ut′ter·ly** *adv.*

ut·ter[2] (ut′ər) *vt.* ⟦< ME *utter,* outward ⟧ 1 to speak or express audibly (sounds, words, etc.) 2 to express in any way

ut′ter·ance *n.* 1 an uttering 2 the power or style of speaking 3 that which is uttered

ut′ter·most′ (-mōst′) *adj., n.* UTMOST

U-turn (yōō′turn′) *n.* a turn by a car made so as to head in the opposite direction

UV or **uv** ultraviolet

u·vu·la (yōō′vyōō lə) *n., pl.* **-las** or **-lae′** (-lē′) ⟦< L *uva,* grape ⟧ the small, fleshy process hanging down from the soft palate above the back of the tongue —**u′vu·lar** *adj.*

ux·o·ri·ous (uk sôr′ē əs, -zôr′-) *adj.* ⟦< L < *uxor,* wife ⟧ dotingly fond of or submissive to one's wife

V

v or **V** (vē) *n., pl.* **v's, V's** the 22d letter of the English alphabet

V (vē) *n.* a Roman numeral for 5

v. 1 ⟦L *vide* ⟧ see 2 verb 3 versus 4 volume

V *symbol for* 1 *Chem.* vanadium 2 velocity 3 volt(s) Also, for 2 & 3, **v**

VA 1 Veterans Administration 2 Virginia: also **Va.**

va·can·cy (vā′kən sē) *n., pl.* **-cies** 1 a being vacant 2 empty or vacant space 3 an unoccupied position, office, quarters, etc.

va·cant (vā′kənt) *adj.* ⟦< L *vacare,* be empty ⟧ 1 having nothing in it 2 not held, filled, etc., as a seat, house, etc. 3 free from work; leisure 4 foolish or stupid —**va′cant·ly** *adv.*

va′cate′ (-kāt′) *vt.* **-cat′ed, -cat′ing** 1 to cause (an office, house, etc.) to be vacant 2 to make void; annul

va·ca·tion (vā kā′shən, və-) *n.* ⟦< L *vacatio* ⟧ a period of rest from work, study, etc. —*vi.* to take one's vacation —**va·ca′tion·er** or **va·ca′tion·ist** *n.*

vac·ci·nate (vak′sə nāt′) *vt., vi.* **-nat′ed, -nat′ing** to inoculate with a vaccine to prevent disease —**vac′ci·na′tion** *n.*

vac·cine (vak sēn′; vak′sēn) *n.* ⟦< L *vacca,* cow ⟧ 1 a substance containing the cowpox virus, used in vaccination against smallpox 2 any preparation so used to produce immunity to a specific disease

vac·il·late (vas′ə lāt′) *vi.* **-lat′ed, -lat′ing** ⟦< L *vacillare* ⟧ 1 to sway to and fro; waver 2 to fluctuate 3 to show indecision —**vac′il·la′tion** *n.*

va·cu·i·ty (va kyōō′ə tē) *n., pl.* **-ties** ⟦< L *vacuus,* empty ⟧ 1 emptiness 2 an empty space 3 emptiness of mind 4 an inane or senseless thing, remark, etc.

vac·u·ous (vak′yōō əs) *adj.* ⟦L *vacuus* ⟧ 1 empty 2 stupid; senseless —**vac′u·ous·ly** *adv.*

vac·u·um (vak′yōō əm, -yōōm′, -yoom) *n., pl.* **-ums** or **-a** (-ə) ⟦L⟧ 1 space with nothing at all in it 2 a space from which most of the air or gas has been taken 3 any void —*adj.* 1 of or used to make a vacuum 2 having or working by a vacuum —*vt., vi.* to clean with a vacuum cleaner

vacuum cleaner a machine for cleaning carpets, floors, etc. by suction

vacuum-packed *adj.* packed in an airtight container to maintain freshness

vacuum tube an electron tube from which most of the air has been evacuated, containing one or more grids, used as an amplifier, etc.

vag·a·bond (vag′ə bänd′) *adj.* ⟦< L *vagari,* wander ⟧ 1 wandering 2 living a drifting or irresponsible life; shiftless —*n.* 1 one who wanders from place to place 2 a wandering beggar 3 an idle or shiftless person —**vag′a·bond′age** *n.*

va·gar·y (və ger′ē, vā′gər ē) *n., pl.* **-ies** ⟦see prec.⟧ 1 an odd or eccentric action 2 a whimsical or freakish notion; caprice —**va·gar′i·ous** *adj.*

va·gi·na (və jī′nə) *n., pl.* **-nas** or **-nae** (-nē) ⟦L, sheath ⟧ in female mammals, the canal from the vulva to the uterus —**vag·i·nal** (vaj′ə nəl) *adj.*

va·grant (vā′grənt) *n.* ⟦prob. < OFr *walcrer,* wander ⟧ one who wanders from place to place, esp. without a regular job, supporting oneself by begging, etc. —*adj.* 1 wandering; nomadic 2 of or like a vagrant 3 wayward, erratic, etc. —**va′gran·cy,** *pl.* **-cies,** *n.*

vague (vāg) *adj.* **va′guer, va′guest** ⟦< L *vagus,* wandering ⟧ 1 indefinite in shape or form 2 not sharp, certain, or precise in thought or expression —**vague′ly** *adv.* —**vague′ness** *n.*

vain (vān) *adj.* ⟦< L *vanus,* empty ⟧ 1 having no real value; worthless /*vain* pomp/ 2 without effect; futile /a *vain* endeavor/ 3 having an excessively high regard for one's self, looks, etc.; conceited —**in vain** 1 fruitlessly 2 profanely —**vain′ly** *adv.*

vain′glo′ry (-glôr′ē) *n.* ⟦< L *vana gloria,* empty boasting ⟧ excessive vanity —**vain′glo′ri·ous** *adj.*

val. 1 valuation 2 value

val·ance (val′əns, vāl′-) *n.* ⟦ME < ?⟧ a short curtain forming a border, esp. across the top of a window

vale (vāl) *n.* [Old Poet.] VALLEY

val·e·dic·to·ri·an (val'ə dik tôr'ē ən) *n.* the student who delivers the valedictory at graduation

val'e·dic'to·ry (-tər ē) *n., pl.* **-ries** ⟦< L *vale,* farewell + *dicere,* to say⟧ a farewell speech, esp. at graduation

va·lence (vā'ləns) *n.* ⟦< L *valere,* be strong⟧ *Chem.* the combining capacity of an element or radical as measured by the number of hydrogen or chlorine atoms which one radical or atom of the element will combine with or replace Also **va'len·cy,** *pl.* **-cies**

Va·len·ci·a (və len'shē ə, -shə) seaport in E Spain: pop. 752,000

val·en·tine (val'ən tīn') *n.* **1** a sweetheart chosen or greeted on Saint Valentine's Day **2** a greeting card or gift sent on this day

val·et (val'it, və lā', va lā', val'ā) *n.* ⟦Fr, a groom⟧ **1** a personal manservant who takes care of a man's clothes, helps him dress, etc. **2** an employee, as of a hotel, who cleans or presses clothes, etc.

val·e·tu·di·nar·i·an (val'ə to͞o'də ner'ē ən) *n.* ⟦< L *valetudo,* state of health, sickness⟧ **1** a person in poor health **2** one who worries about one's health —*adj.* **1** sickly **2** anxious about one's health

Val·hal·la (val hal'ə) *Norse Myth.* the great hall where Odin feasts the souls of heroes slain in battle

val·iant (val'yənt) *adj.* ⟦< L *valere,* be strong⟧ brave; courageous —**val'iance** *n.* —**val'iant·ly** *adv.*

val·id (val'id) *adj.* ⟦< L *valere,* be strong⟧ **1** having legal force **2** based on evidence or sound reasoning —**val'id·ly** *adv.* —**val'id·ness** *n.*

val·i·date (val'ə dāt') *vt.* **-dat'ed, -dat'ing** **1** to make legally valid **2** to prove to be valid

va·lid·i·ty (və lid'ə tē) *n., pl.* **-ties** the quality or fact of being valid in law or in argument, proof, etc.

va·lise (və lēs') *n.* ⟦Fr < L *valesium* < ?⟧ [Old-fashioned] a piece of hand luggage

Val·i·um (val'ē əm) *trademark for* a tranquilizing drug

Val·kyr·ie (val kir'ē, val'ki rē) *n. Norse Myth.* any of the maidens of Odin who conduct the souls of heroes slain in battle to Valhalla

val·ley (val'ē) *n., pl.* **-leys** ⟦< L *vallis*⟧ **1** low land lying between hills or mountains **2** the land drained by a river system **3** any valleylike dip

Valley Forge village in SE Pa.: scene of Washington's winter encampment (1777-78)

val·or (val'ər) *n.* ⟦< L *valere,* be strong⟧ marked courage or bravery Brit., etc. sp. **val'our** —**val'or·ous** *adj.*

Val·pa·rai·so (val'pə rā'zō, -rī'sō) seaport in central Chile: pop. 267,000

val·u·a·ble (val'yo͞o ə bəl, -yə bəl) *adj.* **1** *a)* having material value *b)* of great monetary value **2** highly important, esteemed, etc. —*n.* an article of value: *usually used in pl.*

val·u·a·tion (val'yo͞o ā'shən) *n.* **1** the determining of the value of anything **2** determined or estimated value

val·ue (val'yo͞o) *n.* ⟦< L *valere* be worth⟧ **1** the worth of a thing in money or goods **2** estimated worth **3** purchasing power **4** that quality of a thing which makes it more or less desirable, useful, etc. **5** a thing or quality having intrinsic worth **6** [*pl.*] beliefs or standards **7** relative duration, intensity, etc. —*vt.* **val'ued, val'u·ing** **1** to estimate the value of; appraise **2** to place a certain estimate of worth on /to *value* health above wealth/ **3** to think highly of —**val'ue·less** *adj.*

val'ue-add'ed tax a tax based and paid on products, etc. at each stage of production or distribution, and included in the cost to the consumer

val'ued *adj.* highly thought of

value judgment an estimate made of the worth, goodness, etc. of a person, action, etc., esp. when making such a judgment is not called for or desired

valve (valv) *n.* ⟦< L *valva,* leaf of a folding door⟧ **1** *Anat.* a membranous structure which permits body fluids to flow in one direction only, or opens and closes a tube, etc. **2** any device in a pipe, etc. that regulates the flow by means of a flap, lid, etc. **3** *Music* a device, as in the trumpet, that changes the tube length so as to change the pitch **4** *Zoology* one of the parts making up the shell of a mollusk, clam, etc.

va·moose (va mo͞os') *vi., vt.* **-moosed', -moos'ing** ⟦< Sp *vamos,* let us go⟧ [Old Slang] to leave quickly

vamp (vamp) *n.* ⟦< OFr *avant,* before + *pié,* foot⟧ **1** the part of a boot or shoe covering the instep **2** a simple, improvised introduction or interlude, as between songs in popular music —*vt.* to put a vamp on —*vi. Music* to play a vamp

vam·pire (vam'pīr') *n.* ⟦< Slavic⟧ **1** in folklore, a reanimated corpse that sucks the blood of sleeping persons **2** one who preys ruthlessly on others

vampire bat a tropical American bat that lives on the blood of animals

van[1] (van) *n. short for* VANGUARD

van[2] (van) *n.* ⟦< CARAVAN⟧ a large, closed truck used as for moving, or a small one used for deliveries, fitted out as a vacation vehicle, etc.

va·na·di·um (və nā'dē əm) *n.* ⟦< ON *Vanadis,* goddess of love⟧ a ductile metallic chemical element used in steel alloys, etc.

Van Al·len radiation belt (van al'ən) ⟦after J. *Van Allen* (1914-), U.S. physicist⟧ a broad belt of radiation encircling the earth at varying levels

Van Bu·ren (van byoor'ən), **Mar·tin** (märt''n) 1782-1862; 8th president of the U.S. (1837-41)

Van·cou·ver (van ko͞o'vər) seaport in SW British Columbia, Canada: pop. 410,000

Van·dal (van'dəl) *n.* **1** a member of a Germanic people who sacked Rome (455 A.D.) **2** [v-] one who maliciously destroys property, esp. works of art

van'dal·ize' (-īz') *vt.* **-ized', -iz'ing** to destroy or damage (property) maliciously —**van'dal·ism'** *n.*

Van·dyke (beard) (van dīk') a closely trimmed, pointed beard

vane (vān) *n.* ⟦< OE *fana,* a flag⟧ **1** a free-swinging piece of metal, etc. that shows which way the wind is blowing; weather vane 2 any of the flat pieces set around an axle and rotated about it by moving air, water, etc. or rotated to move the air or water

van Gogh (van gō′, -gôkh′), **Vin·cent** (vin′sənt) 1853-90; Du. painter

van·guard (van′gärd′) ***n.*** ⟦< OFr *avant,* before + *garde,* guard⟧ 1 the part of an army which goes ahead of the main body 2 the leading position or persons in a movement

VANILLA PLANT WITH BEANS

va·nil·la (və nil′ə) ***n.*** ⟦< Sp *vaina,* pod⟧ 1 a climbing orchid with podlike capsules (**vanilla beans**) 2 a flavoring made from these capsules

van·ish (van′ish) ***vi.*** ⟦see EVANESCENT⟧ 1 to pass suddenly from sight; disappear 2 to cease to exist

van·i·ty (van′ə tē) ***n., pl.*** **-ties** ⟦< L *vanus,* vain⟧ 1 anything vain or futile 2 worthlessness; futility 3 a being vain, or too proud of oneself 4 a small table with a mirror for use while putting on cosmetics, etc.

vanity case a woman's small traveling case for carrying cosmetics, toilet articles, etc.

van·quish (vaŋ′kwish, van′-) ***vt.*** ⟦< L *vincere*⟧ to conquer or defeat

van·tage (van′tij) ***n.*** ⟦see ADVANTAGE⟧ 1 a favorable position 2 a position allowing a clear view, understanding, etc.: also **vantage point**

Va·nua·tu (vän′wä to͞o′) country on a group of islands in the SW Pacific, west of Fiji: 5,700 sq. mi.; pop. 136,000

vap·id (vap′id) ***adj.*** ⟦L *vapidus*⟧ tasteless; flavorless; dull —**va·pid·i·ty** (va pid′ə tē) or **vap′id·ness** ***n.***

va·por (vā′pər) ***n.*** ⟦L⟧ 1 *a)* visible particles of moisture floating in the air, as fog or steam *b)* smoke, fumes, etc. 2 the gaseous form of any substance normally a liquid or solid Brit sp. **vapour**

va′por·ize′ (-pər īz′) ***vt., vi.*** **-ized′, -iz′ing** to change into vapor —**va′por·i·za′tion** ***n.*** —**va′por·iz′er** ***n.***

va·por·ous (vā′pər əs) ***adj.*** 1 forming or full of vapor; foggy; misty 2 like vapor

vapor trail CONTRAIL

va·que·ro (vä ker′ō) ***n., pl.*** **-ros** ⟦Sp < *vaca,* cow⟧ [Southwest] a man who herds cattle; cowboy

var. 1 variant(s) 2 various

var·i·a·ble (ver′ē ə bəl) ***adj.*** 1 apt to change or vary; changeable, inconstant, etc. 2 that can be changed or varied —***n.*** anything changeable; a thing that varies —**var′i·a·bil′i·ty** ***n.***

var·i·ance (ver′ē əns, var′-) ***n.*** 1 a varying or being variant 2 degree of change or difference; discrepancy 3 official permission to bypass regulations —**at variance** not in agreement or accord

var′i·ant (-ənt) ***adj.*** varying; different in some way from others of the same kind —***n.*** anything variant, as a different spelling of the same word

var′i·a′tion (-ā′shən) ***n.*** 1 a varying; change in form, extent, etc. 2 the degree of such change 3 a thing somewhat different from another of the same kind 4 *Music* the repetition of a theme with changes in rhythm, key, etc.

var·i·col·ored (ver′i kul′ərd) ***adj.*** of several or many colors

var·i·cose (var′ə kōs′) ***adj.*** ⟦< L *varix,* enlarged vein⟧ abnormally and irregularly swollen /*varicose* veins/

var·ied (ver′ēd) ***adj.*** 1 of different kinds; various 2 changed; altered

var·i·e·gat·ed (ver′ē ə gāt′id) ***adj.*** ⟦< L *varius,* various⟧ 1 marked with different colors in spots, streaks, etc. 2 having variety; varied

va·ri·e·tal (və rī′ə təl) ***adj.*** 1 of or characterizing a variety 2 designating a wine that bears the name of the kind of grape from which it is made —***n.*** a varietal wine

va·ri′e·ty (-tē) ***n., pl.*** **-ties** 1 a being various or varied 2 a different form of some thing, condition, etc.; kind /*varieties* of cloth/ 3 a collection of different things

variety store a retail store selling many small, inexpensive items

var·i·ous (ver′ē əs) ***adj.*** ⟦L *varius,* diverse⟧ 1 differing one from another; of several kinds 2 several or many 3 individual —**var′i·ous·ly** ***adv.***

var·let (vär′lit) ***n.*** ⟦OFr, a page⟧ [Archaic] a scoundrel; knave

var·mint or **var′ment** (vär′mənt) ***n.*** ⟦var. of VERMIN⟧ [Colloq. or Dial.] a person or animal regarded as objectionable

var·nish (vär′nish) ***n.*** ⟦< ML *veronix,* resin⟧ 1 a preparation of resinous substances dissolved in oil, alcohol, etc., used to give a hard, glossy surface to wood, metal, etc. 2 this surface 3 a surface smoothness, as of manner —***vt.*** 1 to cover with varnish 2 to make superficially attractive

var·si·ty (vär′sə tē) ***n., pl.*** **-ties** ⟦< UNIVERSITY⟧ the main team representing a university, school, etc., as in a sport

var·y (ver′ē) ***vt.*** **var′ied, var′y·ing** ⟦< L *varius,* various⟧ 1 to change; alter 2 to make different from one another 3 to give variety to /to *vary* one's reading/ —***vi.*** 1 to undergo change 2 to be different 3 to deviate, diverge, or depart (*from*)

vas·cu·lar (vas′kyə lər) ***adj.*** ⟦< L *vas,* vessel⟧ of or having vessels or ducts for conveying blood, sap, etc.

vase (vās, vāz) ***n.*** ⟦< L *vas,* vessel⟧ an open container used for decoration, displaying flowers, etc.

vas·ec·to·my (va sek′tə mē, və-) ***n., pl.*** **-mies** ⟦< L *vas,* vessel + -ECTOMY⟧ the surgical removal or tying of the duct carrying sperm from the testicle

Vas·e·line (vas′ə lēn′) ⟦< Ger *was(ser),*

water + Gr *el(aion),* oil ⟧ *trademark for* petrolatum —*n.* [v-] petrolatum

vas·o·mo·tor (vas′ō mōt′ər) ***adj.*** ⟦ < L *vas,* vessel + MOTOR ⟧ regulating the diameter of blood vessels: said of a nerve, drug, etc.

vas·sal (vas′əl) ***n.*** ⟦ < ML *vassus,* servant ⟧ **1** under feudalism, one who held land, owing fealty to an overlord **2** a subordinate, servant, slave, etc. —**vas′sal·age** (-ij) ***n.***

vast (vast) ***adj.*** ⟦ L *vastus* ⟧ very great in size, extent, number, degree, etc. —**vast′ly** ***adv.*** —**vast′ness** ***n.***

vat (vat) ***n.*** ⟦ < OE *fæt,* cask ⟧ a large container for holding liquids

Vat·i·can (vat′i kən) **1** the papal palace in Vatican City **2** the papal government

Vatican City independent papal state, an enclave in Rome (Italy), including the Vatican: 108 acres; pop. *c.* 1,000

vaude·ville (vôd′vil, vô′də-) ***n.*** ⟦ Fr, after *Vau-de-Vire,* a valley in Normandy, famous for convivial songs ⟧ a stage show consisting of various acts

vault[1] (vôlt) ***n.*** ⟦ < L *volvere,* to roll ⟧ **1** an arched roof or ceiling **2** an arched chamber or space **3** a cellar room used for storage **4** a burial chamber **5** a room for the safekeeping of valuables, as in a bank —***vt.*** to cover with, or build as, a vault —***vi.*** to curve like a vault

vault[2] (vôlt) ***vi., vt.*** ⟦ < OIdIt *voltare* ⟧ to jump, leap, etc. over (a barrier), esp. with the hands supported on the barrier or holding a long pole —***n.*** a vaulting —**vault′er** ***n.***

vault′ing ***adj.*** **1** leaping **2** unduly confident /*vaulting* ambition/

vaunt (vônt) ***vi., n.*** ⟦ < L *vanus,* vain ⟧ boast —**vaunt′ed** ***adj.***

VCR (vē′sē′är′) ***n.*** VIDEOCASSETTE RECORDER

VD venereal disease

VDT (vē′dē′tē′) ***n.*** a video display terminal

've have: used in contractions /*we've* seen it/

veal (vēl) ***n.*** ⟦ < L *vitulus,* calf ⟧ the flesh of a young calf, used as food

vec·tor (vek′tər) ***n.*** ⟦ < L *vehere,* to carry ⟧ an animal that transmits a disease-producing organism

Ve·da (vā′də, vē′-) ***n.*** ⟦ Sans *veda,* knowledge ⟧ any of four ancient sacred books of Hinduism —**Ve′dic** ***adj.***

Veep (vēp) ***n.*** [*also* v-] vice-president

veer (vir) ***vi., vt.*** ⟦ < Fr *virer,* turn around ⟧ to change in direction; shift; turn —***n.*** a change of direction

veg·e·ta·ble (vej′ə tə bəl, vej′tə-) ***adj.*** ⟦ see VEGETATE ⟧ **1** of plants in general **2** of, from, or like edible vegetables —***n.*** **1** any plant, as distinguished from animal or inorganic matter **2** a plant eaten whole or in part, raw or cooked

veg′e·tar′i·an (-ter′ē ən) ***n.*** one who eats no meat —***adj.*** **1** of vegetarians **2** consisting only of vegetables

veg·e·tate (vej′ə tāt′) ***vi.*** **-tat′ed, -tat′ing** ⟦ < L *vegere,* quicken ⟧ **1** to grow as plants **2** to lead a dull, inactive life —**veg′e·ta′tive** ***adj.***

veg′e·ta′tion ***n.*** **1** a vegetating **2** plant life in general

ve·he·ment (vē′ə mənt) ***adj.*** ⟦ < L *vehere,* carry ⟧ **1** violent; impetuous **2** full of intense or strong passion —**ve′he·mence** or **ve′he·men·cy** ***n.*** —**ve′he·ment·ly** ***adv.***

ve·hi·cle (vē′ə kəl) ***n.*** ⟦ < L *vehere,* to carry ⟧ **1** any device for carrying or conveying persons or objects **2** a means of expressing thoughts, etc. —**ve·hic′u·lar** (-hik′yoo lər) ***adj.***

veil (vāl) ***n.*** ⟦ < L *velum,* cloth ⟧ **1** a piece of light fabric, as of net, worn, esp. by women, over the face or head **2** anything used to conceal, cover, separate, etc. /a *veil* of silence/ **3** a part of a nun's headdress —***vt.*** **1** to cover with a veil **2** to hide or disguise —**take the veil** to become a nun

veiled (vāld) ***adj.*** **1** wearing, or covered with, a veil **2** concealed, hidden, etc. **3** not openly expressed

vein (vān) ***n.*** ⟦ < L *vena* ⟧ **1** any blood vessel carrying blood to the heart **2** any of the ribs of an insect's wing or of a leaf blade **3** a body of minerals occupying a fissure in rock **4** a lode **5** a streak of a different color, etc., as in marble **6** a distinctive quality in one's character, speech, etc. **7** a mood —***vt.*** to mark as with veins

Vel·cro (vel′krō) *trademark for* a nylon material for fastenings, made up of matching strips with tiny hooks and adhesive pile, that are easily pressed together or pulled apart

veld or **veldt** (velt) ***n.*** ⟦ Afrik < MDu *veld,* field ⟧ in South Africa, open grassy country, with few bushes or trees

vel·lum (vel′əm) ***n.*** ⟦ < L *vitulus,* calf ⟧ **1** a fine parchment prepared from calfskin, lambskin, etc. used for writing on or for binding books **2** a strong paper made to resemble this

ve·loc·i·ty (və läs′ə tē) ***n.***, *pl.* **-ties** ⟦ < L *velox,* swift ⟧ **1** quickness of motion; swiftness **2** rate of motion in a particular direction in relation to time

ve·lour or **ve·lours** (və loor′) ***n.***, *pl.* **-lours′** (-loorz′, -loor′) ⟦ Fr < L *villus,* shaggy hair ⟧ a fabric with a soft nap like velvet

ve·lum (vē′ləm) ***n.***, *pl.* **-la** (-lə) ⟦ L, a veil ⟧ SOFT PALATE

vel·vet (vel′vət) ***n.*** ⟦ < L *villus,* shaggy hair ⟧ **1** a rich fabric of silk, rayon, etc. with a soft, thick pile **2** anything like velvet in texture —***adj.*** **1** made of velvet **2** like velvet —**vel′vet·y** ***adj.***

vel′vet·een′ (-və tēn′) ***n.*** a cotton cloth with a short, thick pile like velvet

ve·nal (vēn′əl) ***adj.*** ⟦ L *venalis,* for sale ⟧ open to, or characterized by, bribery or corruption —**ve·nal·i·ty** (vi nal′ə tē) ***n.*** —**ve′nal·ly** ***adv.***

vend (vend) ***vt., vi.*** ⟦ < L *venum dare,* offer for sale ⟧ to sell (goods) —**ven′dor** or **vend′er** ***n.***

ven·det·ta (ven det′ə) ***n.*** ⟦ It < L *vindicta,* vengeance ⟧ a bitter quarrel or feud, as between families

vending machine a coin-operated machine for selling certain small articles

ve·neer (və nir′) ***vt.*** ⟦ < Fr *fournir,* furnish ⟧ to cover with a thin layer of more costly material; esp., to cover (wood) with wood of finer quality —***n.*** **1** a thin surface layer, as of fine wood, laid over a base of common material 2 superficial appearance /a *veneer* of culture/

ven·er·a·ble (ven′ər ə bəl) ***adj.*** worthy of respect or reverence because of age, dignity, etc. —**ven′er·a·bil′i·ty *n.***

ven·er·ate (ven′ər āt′) ***vt.*** **-at′ed, -at′ing** ⟦< L *venerari,* to worship⟧ to look upon with feelings of deep respect; revere —**ven′er·a′·tion *n.***

ve·ne·re·al (və nir′ē əl) ***adj.*** ⟦< L *venus,* love⟧ 1 of sexual intercourse 2 transmitted by sexual intercourse /*venereal* disease/

Ve·ne·tian (və nē′shən) ***adj.*** of Venice, its people, etc. —***n.*** a native or inhabitant of Venice

Venetian blind [*also* **v- b-**] a window blind of thin, horizontal slats that can be set at any angle

Ven·e·zue·la (ven′ə zwā′lə) country in N South America: 352,143 sq. mi.; pop. 17,791,000 —**Ven′e·zue′lan *adj., n.***

venge·ance (ven′jəns) ***n.*** ⟦< L *vindicare,* avenge⟧ the return of an injury for an injury, as in retribution; revenge —**with a vengeance** 1 with great force or fury 2 excessively

venge·ful (venj′fəl) ***adj.*** seeking vengeance; vindictive —**venge′ful·ly *adv.***

ve·ni·al (vēn′yəl, vē′nē əl) ***adj.*** ⟦< L *venia,* a grace⟧ that may be forgiven; pardonable /a *venial* sin/

Ven·ice (ven′is) seaport in N Italy: pop. 346,000

ve·ni·re·man (və nī′rē mən) ***n.,*** *pl.* **-men** ⟦< ML *venire facias,* cause to come⟧ one of a group of people from among whom a jury will be selected

ven·i·son (ven′i zən, -sən) ***n.*** ⟦< L *venari,* to hunt⟧ the flesh of a deer, used as food

ven·om (ven′əm) ***n.*** ⟦< L *venenum,* a poison⟧ 1 the poison secreted by some snakes, spiders, etc. 2 malice

ven′om·ous *adj.* 1 full of venom; poisonous 2 spiteful; malicious

ve·nous (vēn′əs) ***adj.*** ⟦L *venosus*⟧ 1 of veins 2 designating blood carried in veins

vent[1] (vent) ***n.*** ⟦< L *ventus,* wind⟧ 1 expression; release /giving *vent* to emotion/ 2 a small opening to permit passage or escape, as of a gas —***vt.*** 1 to make a vent in or for 2 to give release to; let out

vent[2] (vent) ***n.*** ⟦< L *findere,* to split⟧ a vertical slit in a garment

ven·ti·late (vent′'l āt′) ***vt.*** **-lat′ed, -lat′ing** ⟦< L *ventus,* wind⟧ 1 to circulate fresh air in (a room, etc.) 2 to provide with an opening for the escape of air, gas, etc. —**ven′ti·la′tion *n.***

ven′ti·la′tor *n.* an opening or a device used to bring in fresh air and drive out foul air

ven·tral (ven′trəl) ***adj.*** ⟦< L *venter,* belly⟧ of, near, or on the belly

ven·tri·cle (ven′tri kəl) ***n.*** ⟦see prec.⟧ either of the two lower chambers of the heart —**ven·tric′u·lar** (-trik′yə lər) ***adj.***

ven·tril·o·quism (ven tril′ə kwiz′əm) ***n.*** ⟦< L *venter,* belly + *loqui,* speak⟧ the art of speaking so that the voice seems to come from a source other than the speaker —**ven·tril′o·quist *n.***

ven·ture (ven′chər) ***n.*** ⟦see ADVENTURE⟧ 1 a risky undertaking, as in business 2 something on which a risk is taken —***vt.*** **-tured, -tur·ing** 1 to expose to danger or chance of loss 2 to express at the risk of criticism /to *venture* an opinion/ —***vi.*** to do or go at some risk

ven′ture·some (-səm) ***adj.*** 1 inclined to venture; daring 2 risky; hazardous Also **ven′tur·ous** (-əs)

ven·ue (ven′yōō′) ***n.*** ⟦< L *venire,* come⟧ 1 *Law a*) the locality in which a cause of action or a crime occurs *b*) the locality in which a jury is drawn and a case is tried 2 the scene of a large gathering for some event

Ve·nus (vē′nəs) 1 the Roman goddess of love and beauty 2 the brightest planet in the solar system: see PLANET

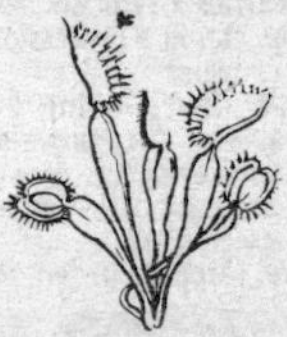

VENUS' FLYTRAP

Venus' fly′trap′ a swamp plant with hinged leaves that snap shut, trapping insects

Ve·nu·si·an (vi nōō′shən) ***adj.*** of the planet Venus —***n.*** an imaginary inhabitant of Venus

ve·ra·cious (və rā′shəs) ***adj.*** ⟦< L *verus,* true⟧ 1 habitually truthful; honest 2 true; accurate

ve·rac′i·ty (-ras′ə tē) ***n.*** 1 honesty 2 accuracy 3 truth

ve·ran·da or **ve·ran·dah** (və ran′də) ***n.*** ⟦< Port *varanda,* balcony⟧ an open porch or portico, usually roofed, along the outside of a building

verb (vʉrb) ***n.*** ⟦L *verbum,* a word⟧ a word expressing action, existence, or occurrence

ver·bal (vʉr′bəl) ***adj.*** 1 of, in, or by means of words 2 in speech; oral 3 of, like, or derived from a verb —**ver′bal·ly *adv.***

ver′bal·ize′ (-īz′) ***vi.*** **-ized′, -iz′ing** to use words for communication —***vt.*** to express in words

verbal noun *Gram.* a noun derived from a verb (Ex.: *swimming* is fun)

ver·ba·tim (vər bāt′əm) ***adv., adj.*** ⟦< L *verbum,* a word⟧ word for word

ver·be·na (vər bē′nə) ***n.*** ⟦L, foliage⟧ an ornamental plant with spikes or clusters of showy red, white, or purplish flowers

ver·bi·age (vʉr′bē ij′) ***n.*** ⟦Fr < L *verbum,* a word⟧ an excess of words; wordiness

ver·bose (vər bōs′) ***adj.*** ⟦< L *verbum,* a word⟧ using too many words; wordy —**ver·bos′i·ty** (-bäs′ə tē) ***n.***

ver·dant (vʉrd′'nt) ***adj.*** ⟦prob. VERD(URE) + -ANT⟧ 1 green 2 covered with green vegetation

Ver·di (ver′dē), **Giu·sep·pe** (jōō zep′pe) 1813-1901; It. operatic composer

ver·dict (vʉr′dikt) ***n.*** ⟦< L *vere,* truly + *dictum,* a thing said⟧ 1 the formal finding of a judge or jury 2 any decision or judgment

ver·di·gris (vʉr′di grēs′, -gris) ***n.*** ⟦< OFr *vert de Grece,* lit., green of Greece⟧ a greenish coating that forms on brass, bronze, or copper

ver·dure (vur′jər) ***n.*** ⟦< OFr *verd,* green⟧ 1 the fresh-green color of growing things 2 green vegetation

verge[1] (vurj) ***n.*** ⟦< L *virga,* rod⟧ the edge, brink, or margin (*of* something) —***vi.*** **verged, verg′ing** to be on the verge: usually with *on* or *upon*

verge[2] (vurj) ***vi.*** **verged, verg′ing** ⟦L *vergere,* to bend, turn⟧ 1 to tend or incline (*to* or *toward*) 2 to change or pass gradually (*into*) /dawn *verging* into daylight/

verg·er (vur′jər) ***n.*** ⟦ME, ult. < L *virga,* rod⟧ 1 one who carries a symbolic rod or staff before a bishop, etc. in a procession 2 a church caretaker or usher

ver·i·fy (ver′ə fī′) ***vt.*** **-fied′, -fy′ing** ⟦< L *verus,* true + *-ficare,* -FY⟧ 1 to prove to be true by demonstration, evidence, etc.; confirm 2 to test the accuracy of —**ver′i·fi′a·ble** ***adj.*** —**ver′i·fi·ca′tion** ***n.***

ver·i·ly (ver′ə lē) ***adv.*** [Archaic] in very truth; truly

ver·i·si·mil·i·tude (ver′ə si mil′ə to͞od′, -tyo͞od′) ***n.*** ⟦< L *verus,* true + *similis,* like⟧ the appearance of being true or real

ver·i·ta·ble (ver′i tə bəl) ***adj.*** ⟦see fol.⟧ true; actual

ver·i·ty (ver′ə tē) ***n.*** ⟦< L *verus,* true⟧ 1 truth; reality 2 *pl.* **-ties** a principle, belief, etc. taken to be fundamentally true; a truth

ver·mi·cel·li (vur′mə sel′ē, -chel′ē) ***n.*** ⟦It < L *vermis,* a worm⟧ pasta like spaghetti, but in thinner strings

ver·mic·u·lite (vər mik′yə līt′) ***n.*** ⟦< L *vermis,* a worm⟧ a hydrous silicate mineral that expands when heated, used as in insulation

ver·mi·form (vurm′ə fôrm′) ***adj.*** ⟦< L *vermis,* a worm + -FORM⟧ shaped like a worm

vermiform appendix the appendix extending from the cecum of the large intestine

ver·mil·ion (vər mil′yən) ***n.*** ⟦< L *vermis,* a worm⟧ 1 a bright-red pigment 2 a bright red or scarlet

ver·min (vur′mən) ***n.,*** *pl.* **-min** ⟦< L *vermis,* a worm⟧ 1 [*pl.*] various destructive insects or small animals regarded as pests, as lice or rats 2 a vile person

Ver·mont (vər mänt′) New England State of the U.S.: 9,609 sq. mi.; pop. 511,000; cap. Montpelier —**Ver·mont′er** ***n.***

ver·mouth (vər mo͞oth′) ***n.*** ⟦< Ger *wermut,* wormwood⟧ a white fortified wine flavored with herbs, used in cocktails and as an aperitif

ver·nac·u·lar (vər nak′yə lər) ***adj.*** ⟦< L *vernaculus,* indigenous⟧ 1 of, in, or using the native language of a place 2 native to a country —***n.*** 1 the native language or dialect of a country or place 2 the common, everyday language of a people 3 the jargon of a profession or trade

ver·nal (vurn′əl) ***adj.*** ⟦< L *ver,* spring⟧ 1 of or in the spring 2 springlike 3 youthful

ver·ni·er (vur′nē ər) ***n.*** ⟦after P. *Vernier,* 17th-c. Fr mathematician⟧ a short graduated scale sliding along a longer graduated instrument to indicate parts of divisions: also **vernier scale**

Ver·sailles (vər sī′) city in N France, near Paris: site of a palace built by Louis XIV: pop. 95,000

ver·sa·tile (vur′sə təl) ***adj.*** ⟦< L *vertere,* to turn⟧ competent in many things —**ver′sa·til′i·ty** (-til′ə tē) ***n.***

verse (vurs) ***n.*** ⟦< L *vertere,* to turn⟧ 1 a single line of poetry 2 poetry 3 a particular form of poetry 4 a poem 5 a stanza 6 *Bible* any of the short divisions of a chapter

versed (vurst) ***adj.*** ⟦< L *versari,* be busy⟧ skilled or learned (*in* a subject)

ver·si·fy (vur′sə fī′) ***vi.*** **-fied′, -fy′ing** ⟦< L *versus,* a verse + *facere,* make⟧ to compose verses —***vt.*** 1 to tell about in verse 2 to put into verse form —**ver′si·fi·ca′tion** (-fi kā′shən) ***n.*** —**ver′si·fi′er** ***n.***

ver·sion (vur′zhən) ***n.*** ⟦see VERSE⟧ 1 a translation, esp. of the Bible 2 an account showing one point of view 3 a particular form of something

ver·sus (vur′səs) ***prep.*** ⟦ML < L, toward⟧ 1 against 2 in contrast with

ver·te·bra (vur′tə brə) ***n.,*** *pl.* **-brae′** (-brē′, -brā′) or **-bras** ⟦L < *vertere,* to turn⟧ any of the single bones of the spinal column —**ver′te·bral** ***adj.***

ver′te·brate (-brit, -brāt′) ***adj.*** 1 having a backbone, or spinal column 2 of the vertebrates —***n.*** any of a large division of animals having a spinal column, as mammals, birds, etc.

ver·tex (vur′teks′) ***n.,*** *pl.* **-tex′es** or **-ti·ces′** (-tə sēz′) ⟦L⟧ 1 the highest point; top 2 *Geom.* the point of intersection of the two sides of an angle

ver·ti·cal (vur′ti kəl) ***adj.*** 1 of or at the vertex 2 upright, straight up or down, etc. —***n.*** a vertical line, plane, etc. —**ver′ti·cal·ly** ***adv.***

ver·tig·i·nous (vər tij′ə nəs) ***adj.*** of, having, or causing vertigo

ver·ti·go (vur′ti gō′) ***n.,*** *pl.* **-goes′** or **ver·tig·i·nes** (vər tij′ə nēz′) ⟦L < *vertere,* to turn⟧ a sensation of dizziness

verve (vurv) ***n.*** ⟦Fr < OFr, manner of speech⟧ vigor; energy; enthusiasm

ver·y (ver′ē) ***adj.*** ⟦< L *verus,* true⟧ 1 complete; absolute /the *very* opposite/ 2 same /the *very* hat I lost/ 3 being just what is needed 4 actual /caught in the *very* act/: often an intensive /the *very* rafters shook/ —***adv.*** 1 extremely 2 truly; really /the *very* same man/

very high frequency any radio frequency between 30 and 300 megahertz

very low frequency any radio frequency between 10 and 30 kilohertz

ves·i·cant (ves′i kənt) ***adj.*** ⟦< L *vesica,* a blister⟧ causing blisters —***n.*** a vesicant agent, as mustard gas used in chemical warfare to burn and blister the skin and lungs

ves′i·cle (-kəl) ***n.*** ⟦< L *vesica,* bladder⟧ a small, membranous cavity, sac, or cyst —**ve·sic·u·lar** (və sik′yə lər) or **ve·sic′u·late** (-lit) ***adj.***

ves·pers (ves′pərz) ***n.*** ⟦L, evening⟧ [*usually with sing v.*] an evening prayer or service Also **Vespers**

Ves·puc·ci (ves po͞ot′chē), **A·me·ri·go** (ä′me rē′gô) (L. name *Americus Vespucius*) 1454-1512; It. navigator & explorer

ves·sel (ves′əl) ***n.*** ⟦< L *vas*⟧ **1** a utensil for holding something, as a bowl, kettle, etc. **2** a boat or ship **3** a tube or duct of the body, as a vein, containing or circulating a fluid

vest (vest) ***n.*** ⟦< L *vestis,* garment⟧ a short, sleeveless garment, esp. one worn under a suit coat by men —***vt.*** **1** to dress, as in clerical robes **2** to place (authority, etc.) in someone **3** to put (a person) in control of, as power, etc. —***vi.*** to pass to a person; become vested (*in* a person), as property

ves·tal (ves′təl) ***adj.*** ⟦< L *Vesta,* goddess of the hearth⟧ chaste; pure —***n.*** a virgin priestess of the Roman goddess Vesta: in full **vestal virgin**

vest·ed (ves′tid) ***adj.*** ⟦pp. of VEST⟧ **1** clothed, esp. in vestments **2** *Law* fixed; settled; absolute /a *vested* right/

vested interest **1** an established right, as to some future benefit **2** [*pl.*] a number of groups cooperating or competing in pursuing selfish goals and exerting controlling influence

ves·ti·bule (ves′tə byo͞ol′) ***n.*** ⟦L *vestibulum*⟧ a small entrance hall, as to a building

ves·tige (ves′tij) ***n.*** ⟦< L *vestigium,* footprint⟧ **1** a trace, mark, or sign, esp. of something that has passed away **2** *Biol.* a degenerate part, more fully developed in an earlier stage —**ves·tig′i·al** (-tij′ē əl, -tij′əl) ***adj.***

vest′ing ***n.*** the retention by an employee of all or part of pension rights regardless of change of employers, early retirement, etc.

vest·ment (vest′mənt) ***n.*** ⟦< L *vestire,* clothe⟧ a garment or robe, esp. one worn by a clergyman

vest′-pock′et ***adj.*** very small, or unusually small for its kind

ves·try (ves′trē) ***n.,*** *pl.* **-tries** ⟦< L *vestis,* garment⟧ **1** a room in a church where vestments, etc. are kept **2** a room in a church, used as a chapel **3** a group of church members managing the temporal affairs of the church

Ve·su·vi·us (və so͞o′vē əs) active volcano in S Italy, near Naples

vet *abbrev.* **1** veteran **2** veterinarian **3** veterinary

vetch (vech) ***n.*** ⟦< L *vicia*⟧ a leafy, climbing or trailing plant of the pea family, grown for fodder

vet·er·an (vet′ər ən) ***adj.*** ⟦< L *vetus,* old⟧ **1** old and experienced **2** of veterans —***n.*** **1** one who has served in the armed forces **2** one who has served long in some position

Veterans Day a legal holiday in the U.S. honoring all veterans of the armed forces: observed on ARMISTICE DAY

vet·er·i·nar·i·an (vet′ər ə ner′ē ən) ***n.*** one who practices veterinary medicine or surgery

vet′er·i·nar′y (-ē) ***adj.*** ⟦< L *veterina,* beasts of burden⟧ designating or of the branch of medicine dealing with animals —***n.,*** *pl.* **-ies** VETERINARIAN

ve·to (vē′tō) ***n.,*** *pl.* **-toes** ⟦L, I forbid⟧ **1** *a)* an order prohibiting some act *b)* the power to prohibit action **2** *a)* the power of one branch of government to reject bills passed by another *b)* the exercise of this power —***vt.*** **-toed, -to·ing** **1** to prevent (a bill) from becoming law by a veto **2** to forbid

vex (veks) ***vt.*** ⟦< L *vexare,* agitate⟧ **1** to disturb; annoy, esp. in a petty way **2** to distress; afflict

vex·a·tion (veks ā′shən) ***n.*** **1** a vexing or being vexed **2** something that vexes —**vex·a′tious** (-shəs) ***adj.***

VHF or **vhf** very high frequency

VHS (vē′āch′es′) ⟦*v*(*ideo*) *h*(*ome*) *s*(*ystem*)⟧ *trademark for* an electronic system for recording video and audio information on videocassettes

vi. or **v.i.** intransitive verb

VI or **V.I.** Virgin Islands

vi·a (vī′ə, vē′ə) ***prep.*** ⟦L, way⟧ by way of

vi·a·ble (vī′ə bəl) ***adj.*** ⟦< L *vita,* life⟧ **1** sufficiently developed to be able to live outside the uterus **2** workable /*viable* ideas/ —**vi′a·bil′i·ty** ***n.***

vi·a·duct (vī′ə dukt′) ***n.*** ⟦< VIA + (AQUE)DUCT⟧ a bridge consisting of a series of short spans, supported on piers or towers

vi·al (vī′əl) ***n.*** ⟦< OFr *fiole*⟧ a small vessel or bottle, for liquids

vi·and (vī′ənd) ***n.*** ⟦< L *vivere,* to live⟧ an article of food

vibes (vībz) ***n.pl.*** **1** [Colloq.] VIBRAPHONE **2** [Slang] qualities, as in a person, thought of as being like vibrations which produce an emotional reaction

vi·bra·harp (vī′brə härp′) ***n.*** VIBRAPHONE

vi·brant (vī′brənt) ***adj.*** **1** quivering or vibrating **2** produced by vibration: said of sound **3** vigorous, vivacious, etc. —**vi′bran·cy** ***n.*** —**vi′brant·ly** ***adv.***

vi·bra·phone (vī′brə fōn′) ***n.*** a musical instrument like the marimba, with electrically operated resonators —**vi′bra·phon′ist** ***n.***

vi·brate (vī′brāt′) ***vt.*** **-brat′ed, -brat′ing** ⟦< L *vibrare*⟧ to set in to-and-fro motion —***vi.*** **1** to swing back and forth; oscillate **2** to move rapidly back and forth; quiver **3** to resound **4** to be emotionally stirred —**vi·bra′tion** ***n.*** —**vi′bra·tor** ***n.***

vi·bra·to (vi brät′ō) ***n.,*** *pl.* **-tos** ⟦It⟧ a pulsating effect produced by rapid alternation of a given tone with a barely perceptible variation in pitch

vi·bra·to·ry (vī′brə tôr′ē) ***adj.*** **1** of, like, or causing vibration **2** vibrating or capable of vibrating

vi·bur·num (vī bur′nəm) ***n.*** ⟦L, wayfaring tree⟧ a plant of the honeysuckle family, with white flowers

vic·ar (vik′ər) ***n.*** ⟦< L *vicis,* a change⟧ **1** *Anglican Ch.* a parish priest receiving a stipend instead of the tithes **2** *R.C.Ch.* a church officer acting as a deputy of a bishop —**vic′ar·age** ***n.***

vi·car·i·ous (vī ker′ē əs) ***adj.*** ⟦< L *vicis,* a change⟧ **1** taking the place of another **2** endured or performed by one person in place of another **3** shared in by imagined participation in another's experience /a *vicarious* thrill/ —**vi·car′i·ous·ly** ***adv.***

vice[1] (vīs) ***n.*** ⟦< L *vitium*⟧ **1** *a)* an evil action or habit *b)* evil conduct *c)* prostitution **2** a trivial fault or failing

vi·ce[2] (vī′sē) ***prep.*** ⟦L < *vicis,* a change⟧ in the place of

vice- ⟦see prec.⟧ *prefix* a subordinate; deputy /*vice*-president/

vice·ge·rent (vīs'jir'ənt) *n.* ⟦< VICE- + L *gerere*, to direct⟧ a deputy

vice'-pres'i·dent *n.* an officer next in rank below a president, acting during the president's absence or incapacity: for the U.S. official, usually **Vice President** —**vice'-pres'i·den·cy** *n.*

vice·roy (vīs'roi') *n.* ⟦MFr < *vice-* (see VICE-) + *roy*, king⟧ a person ruling a region as the deputy of a sovereign

vi·ce ver·sa (vī'sə vur'sə, vīs' vur'-) ⟦L⟧ the relation being reversed

vi·chys·soise (vē'shē swäz', vish'ē-) *n.* a thick soup of potatoes, leeks, and cream, usually served cold

vi·cin·i·ty (və sin'ə tē) *n., pl.* **-ties** ⟦< L *vicus*, village⟧ **1** nearness; proximity **2** the surrounding area

vi·cious (vish'əs) *adj.* ⟦< L *vitium*, vice⟧ **1** characterized by vice; evil or depraved **2** faulty; flawed **3** unruly /a *vicious* horse/ **4** malicious; spiteful /a *vicious* rumor/ **5** very intense, forceful, etc. /a *vicious* blow/ —**vi'cious·ly** *adv.* —**vi'cious·ness** *n.*

vicious circle a situation in which the solution of one problem gives rise to another, eventually bringing back the first problem Also **vicious cycle**

vi·cis·si·tudes (vi sis'ə to͞odz') *n.pl.* ⟦< L *vicis*, a turn⟧ unpredictable changes in life; ups and downs

vic·tim (vik'təm) *n.* ⟦L *victima*⟧ **1** someone or something killed, destroyed, sacrificed, etc. **2** one who suffers some loss, esp. by being swindled

vic'tim·ize' (-īz') *vt.* **-ized'**, **-iz'ing** to make a victim of

vic·tor (vik'tər) *n.* ⟦< L *vincere*, conquer⟧ the winner in a battle, struggle, etc.

Vic·to·ri·a (vik tôr'ē ə) 1819-1901; queen of Great Britain & Ireland (1837-1901)

Vic·to'ri·an *adj.* **1** of or characteristic of the period of the reign of Queen Victoria **2** showing the respectability, prudery, etc. attributed to the Victorians —*n.* a person of that time —**Vic·to'ri·an·ism'** *n.*

vic·to·ri·ous (vik tôr'ē əs) *adj.* **1** having won a victory; triumphant **2** of or bringing about victory

vic·to·ry (vik'tər ē, -trē) *n., pl.* **-ries** ⟦< L *vincere*, conquer⟧ the winning of a battle, war, or any struggle

vict·uals (vit''lz) *n.pl.* ⟦< L *victus*, food⟧ [Dial. or Colloq.] articles of food

vi·cu·ña (vī kyo͞on'ə, -ko͞on'yə) *n.* ⟦Sp⟧ **1** a small llama of South America with soft, shaggy wool **2** this wool

vi·de (vī'dē) *v.* ⟦L⟧ see; refer to (a certain page, etc.)

vid·e·o (vid'ē ō') *adj.* ⟦L, I see⟧ **1** of television **2** of the picture portion of a telecast **3** of data display on a computer terminal —*n.* **1** TELEVISION **2** *short for* VIDEOCASSETTE, VIDEOTAPE, etc.

vid'e·o'cas·sette' *n.* a cassette containing videotape

videocassette recorder a device for recording on and playing back videocassettes Also **video recorder**

vid'e·o·disc' (-disk') *n.* a disc on which images and sounds can be recorded for reproduction on a TV set

video game any of various games involving images, controlled by players, on a TV screen

vid'e·o·tape' *n.* a magnetic tape on which images and sounds can be recorded for reproduction on TV —*vt.* **-taped'**, **-tap'ing** to record on videotape

vie (vī) *vi.* **vied**, **vy'ing** ⟦< L *invitare*, invite⟧ to struggle for superiority (*with* someone); compete

Vi·en·na (vē en'ə) capital of Austria: pop. 1,531,000 —**Vi·en·nese** (vē'ə nēz') *adj., n.*

Vi·et·nam (vē'et näm', -nam') country on the E coast of Indochina: partitioned into two republics (**North Vietnam** & **South Vietnam**) in 1954, and reunified in 1976 as **Socialist Republic of Vietnam**: 127,300 sq. mi.; pop. 61,994,000 —**Vi'et·nam·ese'** (-nə mēz') *n., adj.*

view (vyo͞o) *n.* ⟦< L *videre*, to see⟧ **1** a seeing or looking, as in inspection **2** range of vision **3** mental survey /a correct *view* of a situation/ **4** a scene or prospect /a room with a *view*/ **5** manner of regarding something; opinion —*vt.* **1** to inspect; scrutinize **2** to see; behold **3** to survey mentally; consider —**in view 1** in sight **2** under consideration **3** as a goal or hope —**in view of** because of —**on view** displayed publicly —**with a view to** with the purpose or hope of

view'er *n.* **1** one who views something **2** an optical device for individual viewing of slides

view'find'er *n.* a camera device for viewing what will appear in the photograph

view'point' *n.* the mental position from which things are viewed and judged; point of view

vig·il (vij'əl) *n.* ⟦< L, awake⟧ **1** *a)* a watchful staying awake *b)* a watch kept **2** the eve of a church festival

vig·i·lant (vij'ə lənt) *adj.* ⟦< L *vigil*, awake⟧ staying watchful and alert to danger or trouble —**vig'i·lance** *n.*

vig·i·lan·te (vij'ə lan'tē) *n.* ⟦Sp, watchman⟧ one of an unauthorized group organized professedly to keep order and punish crime —**vig'i·lan'tism'** *n.* —**vig'i·lan'tist** *adj.*

vi·gnette (vin yet') *n.* ⟦Fr < *vigne*, vine⟧ **1** an ornamental design used on a page of a book, magazine, etc. **2** a picture shading off gradually at the edges **3** a short, delicate literary sketch, scene in a film, etc. —**vi·gnet'tist** *n.*

vig·or (vig'ər) *n.* ⟦< L *vigere*, be strong⟧ active force or strength; vitality; energy Brit., etc. sp. **vig'our** —**vig'or·ous** *adj.* —**vig'or·ous·ly** *adv.*

vik·ing (vī'kiŋ) *n.* ⟦ON *vikingr*⟧ [also **V-**] any of the Scandinavian pirates of the 8th to the 10th c.

vile (vīl) *adj.* ⟦< L *vilis*, cheap, base⟧ **1** morally evil; wicked **2** repulsive; disgusting **3** degrading; mean **4** highly disagreeable; very bad /*vile* weather/ —**vile'ness** *n.*

vil·i·fy (vil'ə fī') *vt.* **-fied'**, **-fy'ing** ⟦see prec. & -FY⟧ to use abusive language about or of; defame —**vil'i·fi·ca'tion** *n.*

vil·la (vil'ə) *n.* ⟦It < L, a farm⟧ a country house or estate, esp. a large one used as a retreat

vil·lage (vil′ij) ***n.*** ⟦see prec.⟧ **1** a community smaller than a town **2** the people of a village, collectively —**vil′lag·er *n.***

vil·lain (vil′ən) ***n.*** ⟦< VL *villanus,* a farm servant⟧ a wicked or evil person, or such a character in a play, etc. —**vil′lain·ous *adj.***

vil′lain·y *n., pl.* -ies′ **1** wickedness; evil **2** a villainous act

vil·lein (vil′ən) ***n.*** ⟦see VILLAIN⟧ a feudal serf who had become a freeman, except in relation to his lord

vim (vim) ***n.*** ⟦prob. echoic⟧ vigor

vin (van; *Anglicized* vin) ***n.*** ⟦Fr⟧ wine

vin·ai·grette (vin′ə gret′) ***n.*** ⟦Fr < *vinaigre,* vinegar⟧ a dressing, as for salads, of vinegar, oil, herbs, etc.

Vinci, Leonardo da *see* DA VINCI, Leonardo

vin·di·cate (vin′də kāt′) ***vt.* -cat′ed, -cat′ing** ⟦< L *vis,* force + *dicere,* say⟧ **1** to clear from criticism, blame, etc. **2** to defend against opposition **3** to justify —**vin′di·ca′tion *n.*** —**vin′di·ca′tor *n.***

vin·dic·tive (vin dik′tiv) ***adj.*** ⟦see prec.⟧ **1** revengeful in spirit **2** said or done in revenge —**vin·dic′tive·ly *adv.*** —**vin·dic′tive·ness *n.***

vine (vīn) ***n.*** ⟦< L *vinum,* wine⟧ **1** *a*) a plant with a long, thin stem that grows along the ground or climbs a support *b*) the stem of such a plant **2** a grapevine

vin·e·gar (vin′ə gər) ***n.*** ⟦< MFr *vin,* wine + *aigre,* sour⟧ a sour liquid made by fermenting cider, wine, etc. and used as a condiment and preservative —**vin′e·gar·y *adj.***

vine·yard (vin′yərd) ***n.*** land devoted to cultivating grapevines

vi·no (vē′nō) ***n.*** ⟦It & Sp⟧ wine

vin ro·sé (rō zā′) ⟦Fr⟧ ROSÉ

vin·tage (vin′tij) ***n.*** ⟦< L *vinum,* wine + *demere,* remove⟧ **1** the grape crop of a single season **2** the wine of a particular region and year **3** the model of a particular period /a car of prewar *vintage*/ —***adj.*** **1** of a particular vintage: said of wine **2** representative of the best /*vintage* Hemingway/ **3** of a past period /*vintage* clothes/

vint·ner (vint′nər) ***n.*** ⟦< ME < L *vinum,* wine⟧ one who sells or makes wine

vi·nyl (vī′nəl) ***n.*** ⟦< L *vinum,* wine⟧ any of various compounds polymerized to form resins and plastics (**vinyl plastics**)

vi·ol (vī′əl) ***n.*** ⟦< VL *vitula,* a fiddle⟧ any of an early family of stringed instruments, usually having six strings, frets, and a flat back

vi·o·la (vē ō′lə, vī-) ***n.*** ⟦It⟧ a stringed instrument of the violin family, slightly larger than a violin

vi·o·la·ble (vī′ə lə bəl) ***adj.*** that can be, or is likely to be, violated

vi·o·late (vī′ə lāt′) ***vt.* -lat′ed, -lat′ing** ⟦< L *violare,* use violence⟧ **1** to fail to obey or keep (a law, promise, etc.) **2** to rape **3** to desecrate (something sacred) **4** to break in upon; disturb —**vi′o·la′tor *n.***

vi′o·la′tion (-lā′shən) ***n.*** a violating or being violated; specif., *a*) infringement, as of a law *b*) rape *c*) desecration of something sacred *d*) disturbance

vi′o·lence (-ləns) ***n.*** ⟦< L *violentus,* violent⟧ **1** physical force used so as to injure **2** powerful force, as of a hurricane **3** harm done by violating rights, etc. **4** violent act or deed

vi′o·lent *adj.* **1** acting with or having great physical force **2** caused by violence **3** furious /*violent* language/ **4** extreme; intense; very strong /a *violent* storm/ —**vi′o·lent·ly *adv.***

vi·o·let (vī′ə lit) ***n.*** ⟦< L *viola*⟧ **1** a plant with white, blue, purple, or yellow flowers **2** a bluish-purple color —***adj.*** bluish-purple

VIOLIN

vi·o·lin (vī′ə lin′) ***n.*** ⟦< VIOLA⟧ any of the modern family of four-stringed musical instruments played with a bow; specif., the smallest and highest-pitched one of this family —**vi′o·lin′ist *n.***

vi·ol·ist (vī′əl ist; *for 2* vē ō′list) ***n.*** **1** a viol player **2** a viola player

vi·o·lon·cel·lo (vē′ə län chel′ō, vī′ə lən-) ***n., pl.* -los** CELLO

VIP (vē′ī pē′) ***n.*** ⟦*v*(*ery*) *i*(*mportant*) *p*(*erson*)⟧ a high-ranking official or important guest

vi·per (vī′pər) ***n.*** ⟦OFr < L *vipera*⟧ **1** a venomous snake **2** a malicious or treacherous person —**vi′per·ous *adj.***

vi·ra·go (vi rā′gō) ***n., pl.* -goes** or **-gos** ⟦< L *vir,* a man⟧ a quarrelsome, shrewish woman; scold

vi·ral (vī′rəl) ***adj.*** of, involving, or caused by a virus

vir·e·o (vir′ē ō′) ***n., pl.* -os′** ⟦L, a type of finch⟧ a small American songbird, with olive-green or gray feathers

Vir·gil (vʉr′jəl) 70-19 B.C.; Rom. poet: author of the *Aeneid*: also sp. **Ver′gil**

vir·gin (vʉr′jən) ***n.*** ⟦< L *virgo,* a maiden⟧ one, esp. a young woman, who has never had sexual intercourse —***adj.*** **1** being a virgin **2** chaste; modest **3** untouched, unused, pure, etc. —**the Virgin** Mary, the mother of Jesus

vir′gin·al *adj.* VIRGIN

Vir·gin·ia (vər jin′yə) Southern State of the U.S.: 40,815 sq. mi.; pop. 5,346,000; cap. Richmond —**Vir·gin′i·an *adj., n.***

Virginia Beach city in SE Va.: pop. 262,000

Virginia creeper WOODBINE (sense 2)

Virginia reel an American variety of reel danced by couples in two parallel rows

Virgin Islands group of islands in the West Indies, divided between those forming a British colony & those constituting a U.S. territory

vir·gin·i·ty (vər jin′ə tē) ***n.*** a virgin state; chastity, etc.

Virgin Mary Mary, the mother of Jesus

Vir·go (vʉr′gō′) ⟦L, virgin⟧ the sixth sign of the zodiac

vir·gule (vʉr′gyōōl′) ***n.*** ⟦< L *virgula,* small rod⟧ a diagonal line (/) used in dates or fractions (3/8) and also standing for "or" (and/or), "per" (feet/second), etc.

vir·ile (vir′əl) ***adj.*** ⟦< L *vir,* a man⟧ **1** of or characteristic of a man; masculine **2** having manly strength or vigor 3 capable of copulation —**vi·ril·i·ty** (və ril′ə tē) ***n.***

vi·rol·o·gy (vī räl′ə jē) ***n.*** ⟦ < VIR(US) + -O- + -LOGY ⟧ the study of viruses and virus diseases —**vi·rol′o·gist** ***n.***

vir·tu·al (vʉr′choo əl) ***adj.*** being so in effect, although not in actual fact or name —**vir′tu·al·ly** ***adv.***

vir·tue (vʉr′choo) ***n.*** ⟦ < L *virtus,* worth ⟧ 1 general moral excellence 2 a specific moral quality regarded as good 3 chastity 4 *a)* excellence in general *b)* a good quality 5 efficacy, as of a medicine —**by** (or **in**) **virtue of** because of

vir·tu·o·so (vʉr′choo ō′sō) ***n.,*** *pl.* **-sos** or **-si** (-sē) ⟦ It, skilled ⟧ one with great technical skill in some fine art, esp. in playing music —**vir′tu·os′i·ty** (-äs′ə tē) ***n.***

vir·tu·ous (vʉr′choo əs) ***adj.*** 1 having, or characterized by, moral virtue 2 chaste: said of a woman —**vir′tu·ous·ly** ***adv.*** —**vir′tu·ous·ness** ***n.***

vir·u·lent (vir′yoo lənt, -oo-) ***adj.*** ⟦ see fol. ⟧ 1 *a)* extremely poisonous; deadly *b)* bitterly antagonistic; full of hate 2 *Med. a)* violent and rapid in its course (said of a disease) *b)* highly infectious —**vir′u·lence** ***n.***

vi·rus (vī′rəs) ***n.*** ⟦ L, a poison ⟧ 1 any of a large group of tiny infective agents causing various diseases 2 any harmful influence

vi·sa (vē′zə, -sə) ***n.*** ⟦ < L *videre,* see ⟧ an endorsement on a passport, granting entry into a country

vis·age (viz′ij) ***n.*** ⟦ see prec. ⟧ 1 the face; countenance 2 aspect; look

vis-à-vis (vē′zə vē′) ***adj., adv.*** ⟦ Fr ⟧ face to face; opposite —***prep.*** 1 opposite to 2 in relation to

vis·cer·a (vis′ər ə) ***n.pl.,*** *sing.* **vis′cus** (-kəs) ⟦ L ⟧ the internal organs of the body, as the heart, lungs, intestines, etc.

vis′cer·al ***adj.*** 1 of the viscera 2 intuitive, emotional, etc. rather than intellectual /a *visceral* reaction/

vis·cid (vis′id) ***adj.*** ⟦ < LL *viscidus,* sticky ⟧ thick, syrupy, and sticky

vis·cose (vis′kōs′) ***n.*** ⟦ see VISCID ⟧ a syruplike solution of cellulose, used in making rayon and cellophane

vis·cos·i·ty (vis käs′ə tē) ***n.,*** *pl.* **-ties** 1 a viscous quality 2 *Physics* the resistance of a fluid to flowing freely, caused by friction of its molecules

vis·count (vī′kount′) ***n.*** ⟦ see VICE- & COUNT[2] ⟧ a nobleman next below an earl or count and above a baron —**vis′count′ess** ***n.fem.***

vis·cous (vis′kəs) ***adj.*** ⟦ see VISCID ⟧ 1 syrupy; viscid 2 *Physics* having viscosity

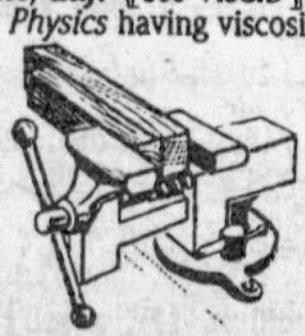

VISE

vise (vīs) ***n.*** ⟦ < L *vitis,* vine, lit., that which winds ⟧ a device having two jaws closed by a screw, used for holding firmly an object being worked on

Vish·nu (vish′noo) the second member of the Hindu trinity (Brahma, Vishnu, and Siva), called the "Preserver"

vis·i·bil·i·ty (viz′ə bil′ə tē) ***n.,*** *pl.* **-ties** 1 a being visible 2 *a)* the relative possibility of being seen under the prevailing conditions of distance, light, etc. /red has good *visibility*/ *b)* range of vision

vis·i·ble (viz′ə bəl) ***adj.*** ⟦ < L *videre,* to see ⟧ 1 that can be seen 2 apparent —**vis′i·bly** ***adv.***

vi·sion (vizh′ən) ***n.*** ⟦ see prec. ⟧ 1 the power of seeing 2 something seen in a dream, trance, etc., or supernaturally revealed 3 a mental image 4 the ability to perceive or foresee something, as through mental acuteness 5 something or someone of great beauty

vi′sion·ar′y (-er′ē) ***adj.*** 1 seen in a vision 2 not realistic; impractical /a *visionary* scheme/ —***n.,*** *pl.* **-ies** 1 one who sees visions 2 one whose ideas, etc. are impractical

vis·it (viz′it) ***vt.*** ⟦ < L *videre,* to see ⟧ 1 to go or come to see 2 to stay with as a guest 3 to afflict or trouble —***vi.*** 1 to make a visit, esp. a social call 2 [Colloq.] to chat —***n.*** a visiting, as, *a)* a social call *b)* a stay as a guest

vis′it·ant (-ənt) ***n.*** a visitor

vis·it·a·tion (viz′ə tā′shən) ***n.*** 1 an official visit, as to inspect 2 a reward or punishment, as sent by God 3 the legal right to visit one's children, as after divorce 4 the visiting of a family in mourning

vis′i·tor ***n.*** a person making a visit

vi·sor (vī′zər) ***n.*** ⟦ < OFr *vis,* a face ⟧ 1 the movable part of a helmet, covering the face 2 a projecting brim, as of a cap, for shading the eyes

vis·ta (vis′tə) ***n.*** ⟦ < L *videre,* to see ⟧ 1 a view, esp. one seen through a long passage 2 a mental view of events

vis·u·al (vizh′oo əl) ***adj.*** ⟦ < L *videre,* to see ⟧ 1 of or used in seeing 2 based on the use of sight 3 that can seen; visible

vis′u·al·ize′ ***vt., vi.*** **-ized′**, **-iz′ing** to form a mental image of (something not present to the sight) —**vis′u·al·i·za′tion** ***n.***

vi·ta (vīt′ə, vēt′ə) ***n.*** ⟦ < *curriculum vitae* < L, course of life ⟧ a summary of one's personal history and professional qualifications, as that submitted by a job applicant; résumé

vi·tal (vīt′′l) ***adj.*** ⟦ < L *vita,* life ⟧ 1 of or concerned with life 2 essential to life /*vital* organs/ 3 fatal /a *vital* wound/ 4 *a)* essential; indispensable *b)* very important 5 full of life; energetic —***n.*** [*pl.*] 1 the vital organs, as the heart, brain, etc. 2 any essential parts —**vi′tal·ly** ***adv.***

vi·tal·i·ty (vī tal′ə tē) ***n.,*** *pl.* **-ties** 1 power to live 2 power to endure 3 mental or physical vigor

vi·tal·ize (vīt′′l īz′) ***vt.*** **-ized′**, **-iz′ing** to make vital; give life or vigor to

vital signs the pulse, respiration, and body temperature

vital statistics data on births, deaths, marriages, etc.

vi·ta·min (vīt′ə min) ***n.*** ⟦ < L *vita,* life ⟧ any of certain complex substances found vari-

ously in foods and essential to good health
vitamin A a fat-soluble alcohol found in fish-liver oil, egg yolk, carrots, etc.: a deficiency of this results in imperfect vision in the dark
vitamin B (complex) a group of unrelated water-soluble substances including *a)* **vitamin B$_1$** (*see* THIAMINE) *b)* **vitamin B$_2$** (*see* RIBOFLAVIN) *c)* NICOTINIC ACID *d)* **vitamin B$_{12}$** a vitamin containing cobalt, used in treating anemia
vitamin C a compound occurring in citrus fruits, tomatoes, etc.: a deficiency of this produces scurvy
vitamin D any of several fat-soluble vitamins found esp. in fish-liver oils, milk, etc.: a deficiency of this produces rickets
vitamin E a substance occurring in wheat germ, etc., vital to the reproductive processes in some animals
vitamin K a substance occurring in green vegetables, fish meal, etc. that clots blood
vi·ti·ate (vish′ē āt′) ***vt.*** **-at′ed, -at′ing** ⟦< L *vitium,* a vice⟧ **1** to spoil; corrupt; pervert **2** to invalidate (a contract, etc.) **—vi′ti·a′tion** ***n.***
vit·i·cul·ture (vit′ə kul′chər) ***n.*** ⟦< L *vitis,* vine⟧ cultivation of grapes
vit·re·ous (vi′trē əs) ***adj.*** ⟦< L *vitrum,* glass⟧ **1** of or like glass **2** derived from or made of glass
vitreous body (or **humor**) the transparent, jellylike substance filling the eyeball between the retina and the lens
vit·ri·fy (vi′trə fī′) ***vt., vi.*** **-fied′, -fy′ing** ⟦< L *vitrum,* glass + Fr *-fier,* -FY⟧ to change into glass or a glasslike substance by heat
vit·rine (vi′trin) ***n.*** ⟦see VITREOUS⟧ a glass-paneled cabinet or display case
vit·ri·ol (vi′trē ôl′) ***n.*** ⟦< L *vitreus,* glassy⟧ **1** *a)* any of several sulfates of metals, as of copper (*blue vitriol*) or iron (*green vitriol*) *b)* SULFURIC ACID **2** sharp or bitter speech, etc. **—vit′ri·ol′ic** (-äl′ik) ***adj.***
vi·tu·per·ate (vī too͞′pər āt′, vi-) ***vt.*** **-at′ed, -at′ing** ⟦< L *vitium,* a fault, + *parare,* prepare⟧ to speak abusively to or about **—vi·tu′per·a′tion** ***n.*** **—vi·tu′per·a′tive** ***adj.***
vi·va (vē′vä) ***interj.*** ⟦It & Sp⟧ (long) live (someone specified)!
vi·va·ce (vē vä′chā) ***adj., adv.*** ⟦It⟧ *Music* in a lively, spirited manner
vi·va·cious (vī vā′shəs, vi-) ***adj.*** ⟦< L *vivere,* to live⟧ full of animation; lively **—vi·va′cious·ly** ***adv.*** **—vi·vac′i·ty** (-vas′ə tē) or **vi·va′cious·ness** ***n.***
vive (vēv) ***interj.*** ⟦Fr⟧ (long) live (someone specified)!
viv·id (viv′id) ***adj.*** ⟦< L *vivere,* to live⟧ **1** full of life; vigorous **2** bright; intense, as colors **3** strong and clear; active /a *vivid* imagination/ **—viv′id·ly** ***adv.*** **—viv′id·ness** ***n.***
viv·i·fy (viv′ə fī′) ***vt.*** **-fied′, -fy′ing** ⟦< L *vivus,* alive + *facere,* make⟧ to give life to; animate
vi·vip·a·rous (vī vip′ər əs) ***adj.*** ⟦< L *vivus,* alive + *parere,* produce⟧ bearing living young instead of laying eggs
viv·i·sec·tion (viv′ə sek′shən) ***n.*** ⟦< L *vivus,* alive + SECTION⟧ surgery performed on a living animal in medical research **—viv′i·sect′** ***vt., vi.*** **—viv′i·sec′tion·ist** ***n.***
vix·en (vik′sən) ***n.*** ⟦OE *fyxe,* female fox⟧ an ill-tempered, shrewish, or malicious woman **—vix′en·ish** ***adj.*** **—vix′en·ish·ly** ***adv.***
viz. or **viz** ⟦< L *videlicet*⟧ that is; namely
vi·zier (vi zir′, viz′yər) ***n.*** ⟦< Ar *wazara,* bear a burden⟧ a high government official in the Turkish empire (*c.* 1300-1918) Also sp. **vi·zir′**
viz·or (vī′zər) ***n.*** *alt. sp. of* VISOR
VLF or **vlf** very low frequency
vo·cab·u·lar·y (vō kab′yo͞o ler′ē) ***n., pl.*** **-ies** ⟦ult. < L *vocare,* to call⟧ **1** a list of words, etc. as in a dictionary or glossary **2** all the words used in a language or by a person, group, etc.
vo·cal (vō′kəl) ***adj.*** ⟦< L *vox,* voice⟧ **1** of or produced by the voice **2** sung **3** capable of making oral sounds **4** speaking freely **—vo′cal·ly** ***adv.***
vocal cords membranous folds in the larynx that vibrate to produce voice
vo·cal·ic (vō kal′ik) ***adj.*** of, like, or involving a vowel or vowels
vo·cal·ist (vō′kəl ist) ***n.*** a singer
vo′cal·ize′ (-īz′) ***vt.*** **-ized′, -iz′ing** to utter, speak, or sing
vo·ca·tion (vō kā′shən) ***n.*** ⟦< L *vocare,* to call⟧ **1** the career to which one feels one is called **2** any trade or occupation **—vo·ca′tion·al** ***adj.***
voc·a·tive (väk′ə tiv) ***n.*** ⟦see prec.⟧ *Gram.* a case indicating the person or thing addressed
vo·cif·er·ate (vō sif′ər āt′) ***vt., vi.*** **-at′ed, -at′ing** ⟦< L *vox,* voice + *ferre,* to bear⟧ to shout loudly; clamor **—vo·cif′er·a′tion** ***n.***
vo·cif·er·ous (vō sif′ər əs) ***adj.*** noisy; clamorous **—vo·cif′er·ous·ly** ***adv.***
vod·ka (väd′kə) ***n.*** ⟦Russ < *voda,* water⟧ a colorless alcoholic liquor distilled from rye, wheat, etc.
vogue (vōg) ***n.*** ⟦Fr⟧ **1** the fashion at any particular time **2** popularity **—*adj.*** in vogue: also **vogu·ish** (vō′gish)
voice (vois) ***n.*** ⟦< L *vox*⟧ **1** sound made through the mouth, esp. by human beings **2** the ability to make such sounds **3** anything regarded as like vocal utterance **4** an expressed wish, opinion, etc. **5** the right to express one's wish, etc.; vote **6** utterance or expression **7** a verb form showing the relation of the subject to the action: see ACTIVE (*adj.* 4), PASSIVE (*adj.* 3) **8** *Music a)* singing ability *b)* any of the parts in a composition **—*vt.*** **voiced, voic′ing** to give utterance or expression to **—with one voice** unanimously **—voice′less** ***adj.***
voice box LARYNX
voice′-o·ver ***n.*** the voice of an unseen announcer or narrator, as on TV
void (void) ***adj.*** ⟦< L *vacare,* be empty⟧ **1** containing nothing **2** devoid (*of*) /*void* of sense/ **3** ineffective; useless **4** of no legal force **—*n.*** **1** an empty space **2** a feeling of emptiness **—*vt.*** **1** to empty out **2** to make void; annul **—void′a·ble** ***adj.***
voi·là (vwä lä′) ***interj.*** ⟦Fr⟧ behold; there it is
voile (voil) ***n.*** ⟦Fr, a veil⟧ a thin, sheer fabric, as of cotton
vol. volume
vol·a·tile (väl′ə təl) ***adj.*** ⟦< L *volare,* to fly⟧

1 evaporating quickly 2 *a)* unstable; explosive *b)* fickle —**vol'a·til'i·ty** (-til'ə tē) *n.* —**vol'a·til·ize'** (-īz'), **-ized', -iz'ing,** *vt., vi.*

vol·can·ic (väl kan'ik) *adj.* 1 of or caused by a volcano 2 like a volcano; violently explosive

vol·ca·no (väl kā'nō) *n., pl.* **-noes** or **-nos** ⟦< L *Volcanus,* Vulcan⟧ 1 a vent in the earth's crust through which molten rock, ashes, etc. are ejected 2 a cone-shaped mountain of this material built up around the vent

vole (vōl) *n.* ⟦< earlier *vole mouse* < Scand, as in ON *vǫllr,* meadow⟧ any of various small rodents with a stout body and short tail

Vol·ga (väl'gə, vōl'-) river in W R.S.F.S.R., flowing into the Caspian Sea

vo·li·tion (vō lish'ən) *n.* ⟦ult. < L *velle,* be willing⟧ the act or power of using the will —**vo·li'tion·al** *adj.*

vol·ley (väl'ē) *n., pl.* **-leys** ⟦< L *volare,* to fly⟧ 1 *a)* the simultaneous discharge of a number of weapons *b)* the bullets, etc., so charged 2 a burst of words or acts 3 *Sports a)* a returning of a ball, etc. before it touches the ground *b)* an extended exchange of shots, as in tennis —*vt., vi.* **-leyed, -ley·ing** 1 to discharge or be discharged as in a volley 2 *Sports* to return (the ball, etc.) as a volley

vol'ley·ball' *n.* 1 a team game played by hitting a large, light, inflated ball back and forth over a net with the hands 2 this ball

volt (vōlt) *n.* ⟦after A. *Volta* (1745-1827), It physicist⟧ the unit of electromotive force

volt·age (vōl'tij) *n.* electromotive force expressed in volts

vol·ta·ic (väl tā'ik) *adj.* of or by electricity produced by chemical action

Vol·taire (väl ter') 1694-1778; Fr. writer & philosopher

volt'me'ter *n.* an instrument for measuring voltage

vol·u·ble (väl'yoo͞ bəl) *adj.* ⟦< L *volvere,* to roll⟧ characterized by a great flow of words; talkative —**vol'u·bil'i·ty** *n.* —**vol'u·bly** *adv.*

vol·ume (väl'yoo͞m) *n.* ⟦< L *volumen,* a scroll⟧ 1 *a)* a book *b)* one of a set of books 2 the amount of space occupied in three dimensions 3 *a)* a quantity, bulk, or amount *b)* a large quantity 4 the loudness of sound

vo·lu·mi·nous (və lo͞om'ə nəs) *adj.* 1 producing or consisting of enough to fill volumes 2 large; bulky; full —**vo·lu'mi·nous·ly** *adv.*

vol·un·ta·rism (väl'ən tər iz'əm) *n.* voluntary participation in a course of action, or a system based on this

vol'un·tar'y (-ter'ē) *adj.* ⟦< L *voluntas,* free will⟧ 1 brought about by one's own free choice 2 acting of one's own accord 3 intentional; not accidental 4 controlled by one's mind or will —**vol'un·tar'i·ly** *adv.*

vol·un·teer (väl'ən tir') *n.* one who chooses freely to do something, as entering military service —*adj.* 1 serving as a volunteer 2 of a volunteer or volunteers —*vt.* to offer or give of one's own free will —*vi.* to offer to enter into any service of one's own free will

vo·lup·tu·ar·y (və lup'cho͞o er'ē) *n., pl.* **-ar·ies** ⟦< L *voluptas,* pleasure⟧ one devoted to sensual pleasures

vo·lup'tu·ous (-cho͞o əs) *adj.* full of, producing, or fond of sensual pleasures —**vo·lup'tu·ous·ness** *n.*

vo·lute (və lo͞ot') *n.* ⟦< L *volvere,* to roll⟧ a spiral or whorl

vom·it (väm'it) *n.* ⟦< L *vomere,* to vomit⟧ matter ejected from the stomach through the mouth —*vt., vi.* 1 to eject (the contents of the stomach) through the mouth; throw up 2 to discharge or be discharged with force —**vom'i·tous** (-ə təs) *adj.*

voo·doo (vo͞o'do͞o') *n., pl.* **-doos'** ⟦of WAfr orig.⟧ 1 a primitive religion based on a belief in sorcery, etc. 2 a charm, fetish, etc. used in voodoo —*vt.* to affect by voodoo magic —**voo'doo·ism'** *n.*

vo·ra·cious (vô rā'shəs) *adj.* ⟦< L *vorare,* devour⟧ 1 greedy in eating; ravenous; gluttonous 2 very eager /a *voracious* reader/ —**vo·rac'i·ty** (-ras'ə tē) *n.*

vor·tex (vôr'teks') *n., pl.* **-tex'es** or **-ti·ces'** (-tə sēz') ⟦< L *vertere,* to turn⟧ 1 a whirlpool 2 a whirlwind 3 anything like a whirl in its rush, catastrophic power, etc.

vo·ta·ry (vōt'ə rē) *n., pl.* **-ries'** ⟦< L *vovere,* to vow⟧ 1 one bound by a vow, esp. by religious vows 2 one devoted to a cause, study, etc.

vote (vōt) *n.* ⟦< L *votum,* a vow⟧ 1 a decision on a proposal, etc., or a choice between candidates for office 2 *a)* the expression of such a decision or choice *b)* the ballot, etc. by which it is expressed 3 the right to vote 4 votes collectively —*vi.* **vot'ed, vot'ing** to give or cast a vote —*vt.* to decide or enact by vote —**vot'er** *n.*

vo·tive (vōt'iv) *adj.* ⟦see prec.⟧ designed to fulfill a promise, express devotion, etc.

vouch (vouch) *vi.* ⟦< L *vocare,* to call⟧ to give, or serve as, assurance, a guarantee, etc. *(for)* /to *vouch* for one's honesty/

vouch'er *n.* 1 one who vouches 2 a paper serving as evidence or proof; specif., a receipt

vouch·safe (vouch sāf') *vt.* **-safed', -saf'ing** ⟦< ME *vouchen safe,* vouch as safe⟧ to condescend to give or grant

vow (vou) *n.* ⟦< L *votum*⟧ 1 a solemn promise, esp. one made to God 2 a promise of love and fidelity /marriage *vows*/ —*vt.* to promise or declare solemnly —*vi.* to make a vow —**take vows** to enter a religious order

vow·el (vou'əl) *n.* ⟦< L *vocalis,* vocal⟧ 1 a speech sound in which the air passes in a continuous stream through the open mouth 2 a letter representing such a sound, as *a, e, i, o, u*

voy·age (voi'ij) *n.* ⟦< L *via,* way⟧ 1 a relatively long journey, esp. by water 2 a journey by aircraft or spacecraft —*vi., vt.* **-aged, -ag·ing** to make a voyage (over or on) —**voy'ag·er** *n.*

vo·ya·geur (vwä yä zhėr') *n., pl.* **-geurs'** (-zhėr') ⟦Fr, traveler⟧ a woodsman or boatman in Canada

voy·eur (voi ʉr', vwä yʉr') *n.* ⟦< L *videre,* see⟧ one who has an exaggerated interest in viewing sexual objects or activities —**voy·eur'ism'** *n.* —**voy'eur·is'tic** *adj.*

VP or **V.P.** Vice-President

V/STOL (vē′stôl′) ***n.*** ⟦*v*(*ertical or*) *s*(*hort*) *t*(*ake*)*o*(*ff and*) *l*(*anding*)⟧ an aircraft that can take off and land either vertically or on a short airstrip

vt. or **v.t.** transitive verb

VT or **Vt.** Vermont

VTOL (vē′tôl′) ***n.*** ⟦*v*(*ertical*) *t*(*ake*)*o*(*ff and*) *l*(*anding*)⟧ an aircraft that can take off and land vertically

Vul·can (vul′kən) the Roman god of fire and of metalworking

vul·can·ize (vul′kən īz′) ***vt.* -ized′, -iz′ing** to treat (crude rubber) with sulfur under heat to increase its strength and elasticity —***vi.*** to undergo vulcanization —**vul′can·i·za′·tion *n.***

Vulg. Vulgate

vul·gar (vul′gər) ***adj.*** ⟦< L *vulgus*, common people⟧ **1** of people in general; popular **2** vernacular **3** lacking culture, taste, etc.; crude; boorish **4** indecent or obscene —**vul′gar·ly *adv.***

vul·gar′i·an (-ger′ē ən) ***n.*** a rich person with coarse, vulgar tastes

vul′gar·ism′ *n.* **1** a word, phrase, etc. used widely but regarded as nonstandard, coarse, or obscene **2** vulgarity

vul·gar′i·ty (-ger′ə tē) ***n.*** **1** a being vulgar **2** *pl.* **-ties** a vulgar act, habit, usage in speech, etc.

vul′gar·ize′ (-gər īz′) ***vt.* -ized′, -iz′ing** **1** to popularize **2** to make vulgar, coarse, obscene, etc. —**vul′gar·iz′er *n.***

Vulgar Latin the everyday Latin spoken by ancient Romans as distinguished from standard written Latin

Vul·gate (vul′gāt′) ⟦ML *vulgata* (*editio*), popular (edition)⟧ a Latin version of the Bible, used in the Roman Catholic Church

vul·ner·a·ble (vul′nər ə bəl) ***adj.*** ⟦< L *vulnus*, a wound⟧ **1** that can be wounded or injured **2** open to, or easily hurt by, criticism or attack **3** *Bridge* subject to increased penalties and bonuses —**vul′ner·a·bil′i·ty *n.*** —**vul′ner·a·bly *adv.***

vul·pine (vul′pīn) ***adj.*** ⟦< L *vulpes*, a fox⟧ of or like a fox; cunning

TURKEY VULTURE

vul·ture (vul′chər) ***n.*** ⟦< L, akin to *vellere*, to tear⟧ **1** a large bird that lives chiefly on carrion **2** a greedy, ruthless person —**vul′·tur·ous *adj.***

vul·va (vul′və) ***n.*** ⟦L, womb⟧ the external genital organs of the female

vy·ing (vī′iŋ) ***adj.*** that vies

W

w or **W** (dub′əl yo͞o′) ***n.**, pl.* **w's, W's** the 23d letter of the English alphabet

w or **w.** **1** week(s) **2** weight **3** wide **4** width **5** wife **6** with **7** win(s)

W **1** ⟦*w*(*olfram*), alt. name of tungsten⟧ *Chem. symbol for* tungsten **2** watt(s): also **w**

W or **W.** **1** Wednesday **2** weight **3** west **4** westerly **5** western **6** wide **7** width

WA Washington (State)

wab·ble (wä′bəl) ***n., vt., vi.* -bled, -bling** *alt. sp. of* WOBBLE

Wac (wak) ***n.*** a member of the Women's Army Corps (WAC)

wack·o (wak′ō) ***adj.*** [Slang] *var. of* WACKY —***n.**, pl.* **-os** [Slang] one who is wacko

wack·y (wak′ē) ***adj.* -i·er, -i·est** ⟦< ?⟧ [Slang] erratic, eccentric, or irrational —**wack′i·ness *n.***

wad (wäd) ***n.*** ⟦ML *wadda*, wadding⟧ **1** a small, soft mass, as of cotton or paper **2** a lump or small, firm mass —***vt.* wad′ded, wad′ding** **1** to compress, or roll up, into a wad **2** to plug or stuff with a wad or wadding

wad′ding *n.* any soft material for use in padding, packing, etc.

wad·dle (wäd′əl) ***vi.* -dled, -dling** ⟦< fol.⟧ to walk with short steps, swaying from side to side, as a duck —***n.*** a waddling gait

wade (wād) ***vi.* wad′ed, wad′ing** ⟦OE *waden*, go⟧ **1** to walk through any resisting substance, as water, mud, etc. **2** to proceed with difficulty /to *wade* through a dull book/ **3** [Colloq.] to attack with vigor: with *in* or *into* —***vt.*** to cross by wading

wad′er *n.* **1** one that wades **2** [*pl.*] high waterproof boots, often with trousers

wa·di (wä′dē) ***n.**, pl.* **-dis** or **-dies** ⟦Ar *wādī*⟧ in N Africa, etc., a river valley that is usually dry

wading bird a long-legged shore bird that wades the shallows and marshes for food

wa·fer (wā′fər) ***n.*** ⟦< MDu *wafel*⟧ **1** a thin, flat, crisp cracker or cookie **2** any disklike thing resembling this

waf·fle[1] (wä′fəl) ***n.*** ⟦see prec.⟧ a crisp batter cake baked in a waffle iron

waf·fle[2] (wä′fəl) ***vi.* -fled, -fling** ⟦< echoic *waff*, to yelp⟧ to speak or write in a wordy, vague, or indecisive manner

waffle iron a utensil with two flat, studded plates pressed together so that a waffle bakes between them

waft (wäft, waft) ***vt., vi.*** ⟦< Du *wachter*, watcher⟧ to carry or move (sounds, odors, etc.) lightly through the air or over water —***n.*** **1** an odor, sound, etc. carried through the air **2** a gust of wind **3** a wafting movement

wag[1] (wag) *vt., vi.* **wagged, wag'ging** [ME *waggen*] to move rapidly back and forth, up and down, etc. —*n.* a wagging

wag[2] (wag) *n.* [prob. < obs. *waghalter*, joker] a comical person; wit —**wag'ger·y**, *pl.* **-ies**, *n.*

wage (wāj) *vt.* **waged, wag'ing** [< OFr *gage*, a pledge] to engage in or carry on (a war, etc.) —*n.* 1 [*often pl.*] money paid for work done 2 [*usually pl.*] what is given in return

wa·ger (wā'jər) *n.* [see prec.] a bet —*vt., vi.* to bet

wag·gish (wag'ish) *adj.* 1 of or like a wag; roguishly merry 2 playful; jesting

wag·gle (wag'əl) *vt., vi.* **-gled, -gling** [< WAG[1]] to wag, esp. with short, quick movements —*n.* a waggling

Wag·ner (väg'nər), **Rich·ard** (rikh'ärt) 1813-83; Ger. composer

wag·on (wag'ən) *n.* [Du *wagen*] 1 a four-wheeled vehicle, esp. one for hauling heavy loads 2 *short for* STATION WAGON —**on** (or **off**) **the wagon** [Slang] no longer (or once again) drinking alcohol

waif (wāf) *n.* [< NormFr] 1 anything found that is without an owner 2 a homeless person, esp. a child

wail (wāl) *vi.* [< ON *væ*, woe] to make a long, loud, sad cry, as in grief or pain —*n.* such a cry

wain (wān) *n.* [OE *wægn*] [Archaic] a wagon

wain·scot (wān'skät', -skət) *n.* [< MDu *wagenschot*] a wood paneling on the walls of a room, sometimes on the lower part only —*vt.* **-scot'ed** or **-scot'ted, -scot'ing** or **-scot'ting** to line (a wall) with wood, etc.

wain'scot'ing or **wain'scot'ting** *n.* 1 WAINSCOT 2 material used to wainscot

wain·wright (wān'rīt') *n.* [WAIN + WRIGHT] one who builds or repairs wagons

waist (wāst) *n.* [OE *weaxan*, grow] 1 the part of the body between the ribs and the hips 2 the part of a garment that covers the body from the shoulders to the waistline 3 the narrow part of any object that is wider at the ends 4 [Archaic] a blouse

waist'band' *n.* a band encircling the waist, as on slacks or a skirt

waist·coat (wāst'kōt', wes'kət) *n.* [Brit., etc. (exc. Cdn.)] a man's vest

waist'line' *n.* the line at the narrowest part of the waist

wait (wāt) *vi.* [< NormFr *waitier*] 1 to remain (until something expected happens) 2 to be ready 3 to remain undone /it can wait/ 4 to serve food at a meal: with *at* or *on* —*vt.* 1 to await 2 [Colloq.] to delay serving (a meal) —*n.* act or period of waiting —**lie in wait (for)** to wait so as to catch after planning a trap (*for*) —**wait on** (or **upon**) 1 to act as a servant to 2 to serve (a customer) —**wait table** to serve food to people at a table —**wait up** to delay going to bed until someone arrives, etc.

wait'er *n.* one who waits; esp. a man who waits on tables in a restaurant

wait'ing *adj.* 1 that waits 2 of or for a wait —*n.* 1 the act of one that waits 2 a period of waiting —**in waiting** in attendance, as on a king

waiting game a scheme by which one wins out over another by delaying action until one has an advantage

waiting list a list of applicants, in the order of their application

waiting room a room in which people wait, as in a bus station or dentist's office

wait·ress (wā'tris) *n.* a woman or girl who waits on tables, as in a restaurant

waive (wāv) *vt.* **waived, waiv'ing** [< ON *veifa*, fluctuate] 1 to give up or forgo (a right, etc.) 2 to postpone; defer

waiv·er (wā'vər) *n.* *Law* a waiving of a right, claim, etc.

wake[1] (wāk) *vi.* **woke** or **waked, waked** or **wok'en, wak'ing** [< OE *wacian*, be awake & *wacan*, arise] 1 to come out of sleep; awake: often with *up* 2 to stay awake 3 to become active: often with *up* 4 to become alert (*to* a realization, etc.) —*vt.* 1 to cause to wake: often with *up* 2 to arouse (passions, etc.) —*n.* a viewing of a corpse before burial

wake[2] (wāk) *n.* [< ON *vök*, hole] the track left in water by a moving ship —**in the wake of** following closely

wake'ful *adj.* 1 alert; watchful 2 unable to sleep —**wake'ful·ness** *n.*

wak·en (wā'kən) *vi., vt.* to awake

Wal·dorf salad (wôl'dôrf) [after the old *Waldorf*-Astoria Hotel in New York City] a salad made of diced raw apples, celery, and walnuts, with mayonnaise

wale (wāl) *n.* [OE *walu*, weal] 1 a welt raised by a whip, etc. 2 a ridge on the surface of cloth, as corduroy —*vt.* **waled, wal'ing** to mark with wales

Wales (wālz) division of the United Kingdom: a peninsula of W Great Britain: 8,016 sq. mi.; pop. 2,792,000

walk (wôk) *vi.* [OE *wealcan*, to roll] 1 to go on foot at a moderate pace 2 to follow a certain course /*walk* in peace/ 3 *Baseball* to go to first base after the pitching of four balls (see BALL[1], *n.* 6) —*vt.* 1 to go over, along, etc. on foot 2 to cause (a dog, etc.) to walk, as for exercise 3 to accompany on a walk or stroll /to *walk* you home/ 4 *Baseball* to advance (a batter) to first base by pitching four balls (see BALL[1], *n.* 6) —*n.* 1 the act of walking 2 a stroll or hike 3 a distance walked /an hour's *walk*/ 4 a sphere of activity, occupation, etc. /people from all *walks* of life/ 5 a path for walking 6 *Baseball* the walking of a batter —**walk (all) over** [Colloq.] to domineer over —**walk away** (or **off**) **with** 1 to steal 2 to win easily —**walk out** to go on strike —**walk out on** [Colloq.] to leave; desert; abandon

walk'a·way' *n.* an easily won victory

walk'er *n.* 1 one that walks 2 a tubular frame with wheels used by babies who are learning to walk 3 a somewhat similar frame used as a support in walking, as by the lame

walk·ie-talk·ie (wôk'ē tôk'ē) *n.* a compact radio transmitter and receiver that can be carried by one person

walking stick a stick carried when walking; cane

Walk·man (wôk'mən, wôk'man') *trademark*

for a portable, pocket-size radio or tape player with headphones

walk′-on′ *n.* a minor role in which the actor has few or no lines

walk′out′ *n.* a labor strike

walk′-up′ *n.* an apartment house, etc. of several stories without an elevator

walk′way′ *n.* a path, passage, etc. for pedestrians, esp. one that is sheltered

wall (wôl) *n.* ⟦< L *vallus*, palisade⟧ **1** an upright structure of wood, stone, etc., serving to enclose, divide, or protect **2** something like a wall in appearance or function —*vt.* **1** to enclose, divide, etc. with or as with a wall **2** to close up (an opening) with a wall: usually with *up* —**drive** (or **push**) **to the wall** to place in a desperate position —**off the wall** [Slang] **1** insane; crazy **2** very odd or unconventional

wal·la·by (wäl′ə bē) *n., pl.* **-bies** ⟦< Australian native name *wolabā*⟧ a small kangaroo

wall·board (wôl′bôrd′) *n.* fibrous material in thin slabs for making or covering walls and ceilings

wal·let (wôl′it) *n.* ⟦ME *walet*⟧ a flat case or folder, as of leather, for paper money, cards, etc.

wall′eye′ *n.* ⟦< ON *vagl*, a beam + *eygr*, eye⟧ **1** an eye that turns outward, showing much white **2** a fish with large, glossy eyes, esp. a North American freshwater perch: in full **wall′eyed′ pike**

wall′flow′er *n.* [Colloq.] a person who merely looks on at a dance, etc. as from shyness

Wal·loon (wä lo͞on′) *n.* ⟦< OHG *walh*, foreigner⟧ **1** any of a chiefly Celtic people in S Belgium **2** their French dialect

wal·lop (wäl′əp) *vt.* ⟦< OFr *galoper*, to gallop⟧ [Colloq.] **1** to beat or defeat soundly **2** to strike hard —*n.* [Colloq.] **1** a hard blow **2** a thrill

wal·low (wäl′ō) *vi.* ⟦OE *wealwian*, roll around⟧ **1** to roll about, as in mud, etc. **2** to indulge oneself fully (*in* a specified thing) —*n.* **1** a wallowing **2** a muddy or dusty place

wall′pa′per *n.* a decorative material, in sheets, for covering the walls of a room —*vt.* to hang wallpaper on or in

Wall Street **1** street in New York City; financial center of the U.S. **2** U.S. financiers and their power, influence, policies, etc., or the U.S. securities market

wall′-to-wall′ *adj.* **1** covering a floor completely **2** [Colloq.] *a*) pervasive *b*) comprehensive

wal·nut (wôl′nut′) *n.* ⟦< OE *wealh*, foreign + *hnutu*, nut⟧ **1** a shade tree valued for its nuts and wood **2** its edible nut with a two-lobed seed **3** its dark wood, used in making furniture, etc.

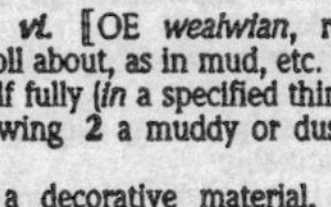

WALRUS

wal·rus (wôl′rəs) *n.* ⟦< Dan *hvalros*⟧ a massive arctic sea mammal somewhat like a seal, having two tusks projecting from the upper jaw

waltz (wôlts) *n.* ⟦< Ger *walzen*, dance about⟧ **1** a ballroom dance for couples, in 3/4 time **2** music for this —*vi.* **1** to dance a waltz **2** to move lightly

wam·pum (wäm′pəm) *n.* ⟦< AmInd⟧ small beads made of shells and used by North American Indians as money, for ornament, etc.

wan (wän) *adj.* **wan′ner, wan′nest** ⟦OE *wann*, dark⟧ **1** sickly pale **2** feeble or weak [a *wan* smile]

wand (wänd) *n.* ⟦< ON *vǫndr*⟧ **1** a staff symbolizing authority **2** a rod regarded as having magical powers

wan·der (wän′dər) *vi.* ⟦OE *wandrian*⟧ **1** to roam aimlessly; ramble **2** to stray (*from* a path, etc.) **3** to go astray in mind or purpose **4** to meander, as a river —*vt.* to roam in or over —**wan′der·er** *n.*

wan′der·lust′ *n.* ⟦Ger⟧ an urge to wander or travel

wane (wān) *vi.* **waned, wan′ing** ⟦OE *wanian*, to decrease⟧ **1** to grow gradually less in extent, as the moon after it is full **2** to grow dim, as a light **3** to decline in power, etc. **4** to approach the end —*n.* a waning

wan·gle (waŋ′gəl) *vt.* **-gled, -gling** ⟦< ? WAGGLE⟧ [Colloq.] to get or cause by persuasion, tricks, etc.

want (wänt, wônt) *vt.* ⟦< ON *vanta*⟧ **1** to lack **2** to crave [to *want* adventure] **3** to desire [to *want* to travel] **4** to wish to see or apprehend [*wanted* by the police] **5** [Chiefly Brit., etc.] to require —*vi.* **1** to have a need or lack: usually with *for* **2** to be destitute —*n.* **1** a shortage; lack **2** poverty **3** a craving **4** something needed

want ad [Colloq.] an advertisement for something wanted, as a job

want′ing *adj.* **1** lacking **2** not up to standard —*prep.* without; minus —**wanting in** deficient in

wan·ton (wän′tən, wänt′′n) *adj.* ⟦< OE *wan*, lacking + *teon*, educate⟧ **1** sexually unrestrained **2** [Old Poet.] playful **3** unprovoked or malicious **4** recklessly ignoring justice, etc. —*n.* a wanton person; esp., a sexually unrestrained woman —*vi.* to be wanton —**wan′ton·ness** *n.*

wap·i·ti (wäp′ət ē) *n.* ⟦< AmInd⟧ a large, North American deer with widely branching antlers; elk

war (wôr) *n.* ⟦< NormFr *werre*⟧ **1** open armed conflict as between nations **2** any active hostility or struggle **3** military operations as a science —*adj.* of, in, or from war —*vi.* **warred, war′ring** **1** to carry on war **2** to contend; strive —**at war** in a state of active armed conflict

war·ble (wôr′bəl) *vt., vi.* **-bled, -bling** ⟦< NormFr *werbler*⟧ to sing (a song, etc.) melodiously, with trills, quavers, etc., as a bird —*n.* a warbling; trill

war·bler (wôr′blər) *n.* a bird or person that warbles

ward (wôrd) *vt.* ⟦OE *weardian*, to guard⟧ to turn aside; fend (*off*) —*n.* **1** a being under guard **2** one under the care of a guardian or

court 3 a division of a jail, hospital, etc. 4 a division of a city or town, for purposes of voting, etc.
-ward (wərd) [OE *-weard*] *suffix* in a (specified) direction */inward/* Also **-wards** (wərdz)
war·den (wôrd′'n) *n.* [< NormFr *wardein*] 1 one who guards, or has charge of, something */game warden/* 2 the chief official of a prison
ward′er *n.* a watchman
ward heeler a follower of a politician, who solicits votes, etc.: often a contemptuous term
ward·robe (wôr′drōb′) *n.* 1 a closet, cabinet, etc. for holding clothes 2 one's supply of clothes
ward′room′ *n.* in a warship, a room used for eating, etc. by commissioned officers, except, usually, the captain
ware (wer) *n.* [OE *waru*] 1 anything for sale: *usually used in pl.* 2 pottery
ware′house′ *n.* a building where goods are stored —*vt.* **-housed′**, **-hous′ing** to store in a warehouse
war·fare (wôr′fer′) *n.* 1 the action of waging war 2 conflict of any kind
war′head′ (-hed′) *n.* the front part of a torpedo, etc. containing the explosive
war′horse′ *n.* [Colloq.] one who has been through many struggles; veteran
war·i·ly (wer′ə lē) *adv.* cautiously —**war′i·ness** (-ē nis) *n.*
war′like′ *adj.* 1 fond of or ready for war 2 of war 3 threatening war
war·lock (wôr′läk′) *n.* [OE *wærloga*, liar] a man who practices black magic
war′lord′ *n.* 1 a high military officer in a warlike nation 2 a local ruler or bandit leader, as formerly in China
warm (wôrm) *adj.* [OE *wearm*] 1 *a)* having or giving off a moderate degree of heat *b)* hot */a warm night/* 2 that keeps body heat in */a warm hat/* 3 ardent; enthusiastic 4 lively, vigorous, etc. 5 quick to anger 6 *a)* genial; cordial */a warm welcome/* *b)* sympathetic or loving 7 newly made; fresh, as a trail 8 [Colloq.] close to discovering something —*vt., vi.* to make or become warm —**warm up** to practice or exercise, as before going into a game, contest, etc. —**warm′er** *n.* —**warm′ish** *adj.* —**warm′ly** *adv.*
warm′blood′ed *adj.* having a body temperature that is relatively constant and usually higher than that of the surroundings, as mammals and birds
warmed-o·ver (wôrmd′ō′vər) *adj.* 1 reheated 2 presented again, without significant change, as ideas
warm front the forward edge of a warm air mass advancing into a colder mass
warm′heart′ed *adj.* kind, sympathetic, friendly, loving, etc.
war′mon′ger (-muŋ′gər, -mäŋ′-) *n.* one who advocates, or tries to cause, war —**war′mon′ger·ing** *adj., n.*
warmth (wôrmth) *n.* 1 *a)* the state of having heat *b)* mild heat 2 *a)* enthusiasm, ardor, etc. *b)* affectionate feelings
warm′-up′ *n.* the act of warming up
warn (wôrn) *vt., vi.* [OE *wearnian*] 1 to tell of a danger, coming evil, etc. 2 to caution about certain acts 3 to notify in advance; inform
warn′ing *n.* 1 the act of one that warns 2 something that serves to warn —*adj.* that warns
warp (wôrp) *n.* [OE *weorpan*, to throw] 1 *a)* a distortion, as a twist or bend, in wood *b)* any similar distortion 2 a mental quirk, bias, etc. 3 *Weaving* the threads running lengthwise in the loom —*vt.* 1 to bend or twist out of shape 2 to distort, pervert, etc. */a warped mind/* —*vi.* to become bent or twisted
war′path′ *n.* the path taken by American Indians on a warlike expedition —**on the warpath** 1 ready for war 2 actively angry; ready to fight
war·rant (wôr′ənt, wär′-) *n.* [< NormFr *warant*] 1 *a)* authorization, as by law *b)* justification for some act, belief, etc. 2 something serving as a guarantee of some event or result 3 *Law* a writ authorizing an arrest, search, etc. —*vt.* 1 to authorize 2 to serve as justification for (an act, belief, etc.) 3 to guarantee
warrant officer a military officer ranking above a noncommissioned officer but below a commissioned officer
war·ran·ty (wôr′ən tē, wär′-) *n., pl.* **-ties** an assurance by a seller that goods or property will be repaired or replaced if not as represented; guarantee
war·ren (wôr′ən, wär′-) *n.* [< NormFr *warir*, to preserve] 1 an area in which rabbits breed or are numerous 2 any crowded building or buildings
War·ren (wôr′ən, wär′-) city in SE Mich.: pop. 161,000
war·ri·or (wôr′yər, -ē ər) *n.* [see WAR] a person experienced in conflict, esp. war; soldier
War·saw (wôr′sô′) capital of Poland: pop. 1,628,000
war′ship′ *n.* any ship for combat use, as a battleship
wart (wôrt) *n.* [OE *wearte*] 1 a small, usually hard, tumorous growth on the skin, caused by a virus 2 a small protuberance, as on a plant —**wart′y**, **-i·er**, **-i·est**, *adj.*

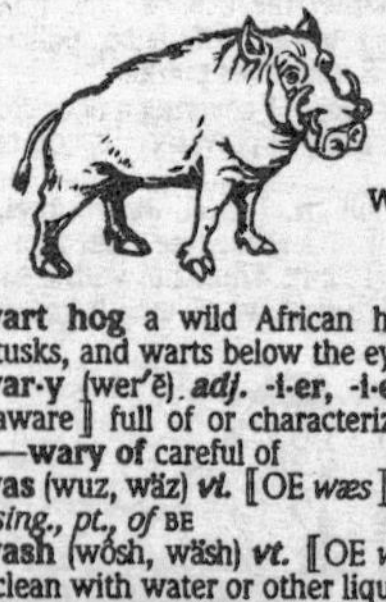
WART HOG

wart hog a wild African hog with large tusks, and warts below the eyes
war·y (wer′ē) *adj.* **-i·er**, **-i·est** [OE *wær*, aware] full of or characterized by caution —**wary of** careful of
was (wuz, wäz) *vi.* [OE *wæs*] *1st & 3d pers. sing., pt., of* BE
wash (wôsh, wäsh) *vt.* [OE *wæscan*] 1 to clean with water or other liquid 2 to purify 3 to wet or moisten 4 to flow over, past, or against: said of a sea, waves, etc. 5 to soak (*out*), flush (*off*), or carry (*away*) with water 6 to erode; wear (*out* or *away*) by flowing

over /the flood *washed* out the road/ —*vi.* 1 to wash oneself 2 to wash clothes 3 to undergo washing 4 to be removed by washing: usually with *out* or *away* 5 to be worn or carried (*out* or *away*) by the action of water /the bridge had *washed* out/ —*n.* 1 a washing 2 a quantity of clothes, etc. washed, or to be washed 3 the rush or surge of water 4 the eddy of water or air caused by a propeller, etc. 5 silt, mud, etc. carried and dropped by running water 6 a liquid for cosmetic or medicinal use /*mouthwash*/ —*adj.* that can be washed without damage; washable —**wash down** to follow (food, etc.) with a drink —**wash'a·ble** *adj.*, *n.*

wash'-and-wear' *adj.* of fabrics that need little or no ironing after washing

wash'board' *n.* a ridged board for scrubbing dirt out of clothes

wash'bowl' *n.* a bowl, esp. a bathroom fixture, for use in washing one's hands, etc. Also **wash'ba'sin**

wash'cloth' *n.* a small cloth used in washing the body Also **wash'rag'**

washed'-out' *adj.* 1 faded 2 [Colloq.] tired; spiritless; pale and wan

washed'-up' *adj.* 1 [Colloq.] tired; exhausted 2 [Slang] finished; done for; having failed

wash'er *n.* 1 one who washes 2 a flat ring of metal, rubber, etc., used with a nut, faucet valve, bolt, etc. 3 a machine for washing

wash'er·wom'an *n.*, *pl.* **-wom'en** a woman whose work is washing clothes

wash'ing *n.* 1 the act of one that washes 2 clothes, etc. to be washed

washing machine a machine for washing clothes, etc.

Wash·ing·ton (wôsh'iŋ tən, wäsh'-), **George** 1732-99; 1st president of the U.S. (1789-97)

Washington 1 NW coastal State of the U.S.: 68,192 sq. mi.; pop. 4,130,000; cap. Olympia: abbrev. **Wash.** 2 capital of the U.S., coextensive with the District of Columbia: pop. 638,000 —**Wash'ing·to'ni·an** (-tō'nē ən) *adj.*, *n.*

wash'out' *n.* 1 the washing away of soil, etc. by water 2 [Slang] a failure

wash'room' *n.* 1 a room for washing 2 RESTROOM

wash'stand' *n.* a table or plumbing fixture with a washbowl, etc.

wash'tub' *n.* a tub, often with faucets and a drain, for washing clothes, etc.

wash'y *adj.* **-i·er, -i·est** 1 watery; weak 2 feeble; insipid

wasp (wäsp, wôsp) *n.* ⟦OE *wæsp*⟧ a winged insect with a slender body and, in the females and workers, a vicious sting

WASP or **Wasp** (wäsp, wôsp) *n.* a white Anglo-Saxon Protestant

wasp'ish *adj.* bad-tempered; snappish

was·sail (wäs'əl, -āl') *n.* ⟦< ON *ves heill*, be hearty⟧ 1 a toast formerly used to drink to the health of a person 2 the spiced ale, etc. with which such toasts were drunk 3 a drinking party —*vi.*, *vt.* to drink a wassail (to)

wast·age (wāst'ij) *n.* 1 loss by use, decay, etc. 2 anything wasted

waste (wāst) *vt.* **wast'ed, wast'ing** ⟦< L *vastare*⟧ 1 to devastate; ruin 2 to wear away 3 to make weak or emaciated /*wasted* by age/ 4 to use up needlessly; squander 5 to fail to take advantage of 6 [Slang] to kill —*vi.* 1 to lose strength, etc., as by disease 2 to be used up or worn down gradually —*adj.* 1 uncultivated or uninhabited; desolate 2 left over or superfluous 3 excreted from the body 4 used for waste —*n.* 1 uncultivated or uninhabited land 2 a devastated area 3 a wasting or being wasted 4 discarded material, as ashes 5 excretions from the body, as urine —**go to waste** to be wasted —**lay waste (to)** to destroy —**wast'er** *n.*

waste'bas'ket *n.* a container for wastepaper, etc. Also **wastepaper basket**

wast·ed (wās'təd) *adj.* [Slang] 1 intoxicated by a drug 2 drunk

waste'ful *adj.* using more than is necessary —**waste'ful·ly** *adv.* —**waste'ful·ness** *n.*

waste'land' *n.* 1 barren land 2 an unproductive activity, endeavor, etc.

waste'pa'per *n.* paper thrown away after use Also **waste paper**

wast·rel (wās'trəl) *n.* one who wastes; esp., a spendthrift

watch (wäch, wôch) *n.* ⟦OE *wæcce*⟧ 1 a keeping awake, esp. in order to guard 2 close observation for a time 3 a guard, or the period of duty of a guard 4 a small timepiece carried in the pocket or worn on the wrist 5 *a*) any of the periods of duty (usually four hours) on shipboard *b*) the crew on duty during such a period —*vi.* 1 to stay awake, esp. at night; keep vigil 2 to be on the alert 3 to look or observe 4 to be looking or waiting attentively: with *for* —*vt.* 1 to guard or tend 2 to observe carefully 3 to wait and look for —**watch oneself** to be careful —**watch out** to be alert or careful —**watch'er** *n.*

watch'band' *n.* a band of leather, metal, etc. to hold a watch on the wrist

watch'dog' *n.* 1 a dog kept to guard property 2 one that keeps watch in order to prevent waste, unethical practices, etc.

watch'ful *adj.* watching closely; vigilant; alert —**watch'ful·ly** *adv.* —**watch'ful·ness** *n.*

watch'man (-mən) *n.*, *pl.* **-men** a person hired to guard property

watch'tow'er *n.* a high tower from which watch is kept, as for forest fires

watch'word' *n.* 1 a password 2 a slogan or cry of a group, etc.

wa·ter (wôt'ər, wät'-) *n.* ⟦OE *wæter*⟧ 1 the colorless liquid of rivers, lakes, etc., which falls as rain 2 water with reference to its depth, surface, or level /above *water*/ 3 a body secretion, as urine 4 a wavy, lustrous finish given to linen, silk, metal, etc. —*vt.* 1 to give (animals) water to drink 2 to supply (crops, etc.) with water 3 to moisten, soak, or dilute with water 4 to give a wavy luster to (silk, etc.) —*vi.* 1 to fill with tears: said of the eyes 2 to secrete saliva /his mouth *watered*/ 3 to take on a supply of water 4 to drink water —*adj.* of, for, in, on, near, from, or by water —**hold water** to remain sound, logical, etc.

water bed a heavy vinyl bag filled with water and used as a bed or as a mattress in a special bed frame Also **wa′ter·bed′** *n.*
water buffalo a slow, powerful buffalo of S Asia used as a draft animal
Wa·ter·bur·y (wôt′ər ber′ē, wät′-) city in W Conn.: pop. 103,000
water chestnut **1** a Chinese sedge with a nutlike tuber **2** this tuber
water closet TOILET (*n.* 3)
wa′ter·col′or *n.* **1** a pigment mixed with water for use as a paint **2** a painting done with such paints
wa′ter-cooled′ *adj.* cooled by water circulated around or through it
wa′ter·course′ *n.* **1** a stream, river, etc. **2** a channel for water, as a canal
wa′ter·craft′ *n., pl.* **-craft′** a boat, ship, or other water vehicle
wa′ter·cress′ (-kres′) *n.* a white-flowered water plant: its leaves are used in salads, etc.
wa′ter·fall′ *n.* a steep fall of water, as of a stream, from a height
wa′ter·fowl′ *n.* a water bird, esp. one that swims
wa′ter·front′ *n.* land or docks at the edge of a stream, harbor, etc.
water glass **1** a drinking glass **2** a silicate of sodium or potassium, dissolved in water to form a syrupy liquid used as an adhesive, etc. Also **wa′ter·glass′** *n.*
water hole a pond or pool

WATERLILY

wa′ter·lil′y *n., pl.* **-ies** **1** a water plant with large, flat, floating leaves and showy flowers **2** the flower
wa′ter·line′ *n.* the line to which the surface of the water comes on the side of a ship or boat
wa′ter·logged′ (-lôgd′) *adj.* soaked or filled with water so as to be heavy and sluggish: said of boats, etc.
Wa·ter·loo (wôt′ər lo͞o′, wät′-) town in central Belgium: scene of Napoleon's final defeat (1815) —*n.* any disastrous or decisive defeat
water main a main pipe in a system of water pipes
wa′ter·mark′ *n.* **1** a mark showing the limit to which water has risen **2** a mark in paper, produced by pressure of a design, as in the mold —*vt.* to mark (paper) with a watermark
wa′ter·mel′on *n.* a large, green melon with sweet, juicy, red pulp
water moccasin a large, poisonous water snake of the SE U.S.
water pipe **1** a pipe for water **2** a smoking pipe using water, as a hookah
water polo a water game played with a ball by two teams of swimmers
water power the power of running or falling water, used to drive machinery, etc. Also **wa′ter·pow′er** *n.*
wa′ter·proof′ *adj.* that keeps out water, as by being treated with rubber, etc. —*vt.* to make waterproof
water rat any of various rodents living on the banks of streams and ponds
wa′ter-re·pel′lent *adj.* that repels water but is not fully waterproof
wa′ter·shed′ (-shed′) *n.* **1** a ridge dividing the areas drained by different river systems **2** the area drained by a river system
wa′ter·side′ (-sīd′) *n.* land at the edge of a body of water —*adj.* of, at, or on the waterside
wa′ter-ski′ *vi.* **-skied′**, **-ski′ing** to be towed on skilike boards (**water skis**) by a line attached to a speedboat
wa′ter·spout′ *n.* **1** a pipe for spouting water **2** a whirling funnel-shaped column of air full of spray occurring over water, usually in tropical areas
water table the level below which the ground is saturated with water
wa′ter·tight′ *adj.* **1** so tight that no water can get through **2** that cannot be misconstrued, nullified, etc.; flawless /a *watertight* plan/
water tower an elevated tank for water storage
wa′ter·way′ *n.* **1** a channel through which water runs **2** any body of water suitable for boats, ships, etc., as a canal or river
water wheel a wheel turned by running water, as for power
water wings an inflated device to keep one afloat as while swimming
wa′ter·works′ *n.pl.* [*often with sing. v.*] a system of reservoirs, pumps, etc. supplying water to a city
wa′ter·y *adj.* **1** of or like water **2** full of water **3** thin; diluted **4** tearful **5** weak —**wa′ter·i·ness** *n.*
WATS (wäts) *n.* ⟦*w*(*ide*) *a*(*rea*) *t*(*elecommunications*) *s*(*ervice*)⟧ a telephone service that ties a customer into the long-distance network through special lines, at special rates
watt (wät) *n.* ⟦after James *Watt* (1736-1819), Scot inventor of steam engine⟧ a unit of electrical power, equal to the power developed in a circuit by a current of one ampere flowing through a potential difference of one volt; $\frac{1}{746}$ of a horsepower
watt′age (-ij) *n.* amount of electrical power, expressed in watts
wat·tle (wät′'l) *n.* ⟦OE *watul*⟧ **1** a woven work of sticks intertwined with twigs or branches **2** a fleshy flap of skin hanging from the throat of certain birds or lizards —*vt.* **-tled**, **-tling** **1** to intertwine (sticks, twigs, etc.) **2** to build of or with wattle
wave (wāv) *vi.* **waved**, **wav′ing** ⟦OE *wafian*⟧ **1** to move or sway to and fro **2** to signal by moving a hand, arm, etc. to and fro **3** to have the form of a series of curves —*vt.* **1** to cause to wave **2** to brandish (a weapon) **3** *a*) to move or swing (something) as a signal *b*) to signal (something) to (someone) by doing this **4** to give an undulating form to (hair, etc.) —*n.* **1** a ridge or swell moving along the surface of the ocean, etc. **2** an undulation or curve, as in the hair **3** a motion to and fro, as with the hand in

signaling 4 a thing like a wave in action or effect; specif., an upsurge /a crime *wave*/ 5 *Physics* a periodic motion or disturbance, as in the propagation of sound or light —**wave′like′** *adj.*

Wave (wāv) *n.* ⟦< *W(omen) A(ppointed for) V(oluntary) E(mergency) S(ervice)* ⟧ a member of the women's branch of the U.S. Navy (**WAVES**)

wave′length′ *n. Physics* the distance measured along a wave from any given point to the next similar point, as from crest to crest

wave′let (-lit) *n.* a little wave

wa·ver (wā′vər) *vi.* ⟦< ME *waven*, to wave⟧ 1 to sway to and fro 2 to show indecision; vacillate 3 to falter, flicker, or tremble —*n.* a wavering

wav·y (wā′vē) *adj.* **-i·er, -i·est** 1 having or like waves 2 moving in a wavelike motion —**wav′i·ness** *n.*

wax[1] (waks) *n.* ⟦OE *weax*⟧ 1 a plastic, dull-yellow substance secreted by bees; beeswax 2 any plastic substance like this; specif., *a)* paraffin *b)* a substance exuded by the ears —*vt.* to rub, polish, cover, or treat with wax

wax[2] (waks) *vi.* **waxed, wax′ing** ⟦OE *weaxan*, grow⟧ 1 to increase in strength, size, etc. 2 to become gradually full: said of the moon 3 [Now Rare] to become /to *wax* angry/

wax bean a variety of the common garden bean with long, edible, yellow pods

wax·en (wak′sən) *adj.* 1 made of wax 2 like wax; pale, plastic, etc.

wax museum an exhibition of wax figures, as of famous persons

wax myrtle an evergreen shrub with grayish-white, wax-coated berries

wax paper a paper made moisture-proof by a wax coating Also **waxed paper**

wax′wing′ *n.* a fruit-eating bird with brown or gray silky plumage and scarlet waxlike tips on the wings

wax′works′ *n.pl.* [*with sing. v.*] an exhibition of wax figures

wax′y *adj.* **-i·er, -i·est** of, full of, or like wax —**wax′i·ness** *n.*

way (wā) *n.* ⟦ME < OE *weg*⟧ 1 a road, street, path, etc. 2 space for passing 3 a route or course 4 course of life or conduct /avoid evil *ways*/ 5 a method of doing something 6 a manner of living, acting, etc. /the *way* of the world/ 7 distance /a long *way* off/ 8 direction of movement 9 movement forward 10 respect; specific point /right in some *ways*/ 11 wish; will /get one's own *way*/ 12 [Colloq.] *a)* a condition /he's in a bad *way*/ *b)* a locality /out our *way*/ 13 [*pl.*] a timber framework on which a ship is built —*adv.* [Colloq.] away; far /*way* behind/ —**by the way** incidentally —**by way of** 1 passing through 2 as a method, etc. of —**give way** 1 to yield 2 to break down —**lead the way** to be a guide or example —**make way** 1 to clear a passage 2 to make progress —**under way** moving; advancing

way′far′er (-fer′ər) *n.* a traveler, esp. on foot —**way′far′ing** *adj., n.*

way·lay (wā′lā′, wā′lā′) *vt.* **-laid′, -lay′ing** 1 to lie in wait for and attack 2 to wait for and accost (a person) on the way

way′-out′ *adj.* [Colloq.] very unusual or unconventional

-ways (wāz) ⟦ME < *way* (see WAY)⟧ *suffix* in a (specified) direction, position, or manner /*sideways*/

ways and means methods of raising money; specif., such methods, including legislation, in government

way′side′ *n.* the edge of a road

way′ward (-wərd) *adj.* ⟦see AWAY & -WARD⟧ 1 headstrong, willful, disobedient, etc. 2 unpredictable; erratic —**way′ward·ly** *adv.* —**way′ward·ness** *n.*

wd. 1 word 2 would

we (wē) *pron., sing.* I ⟦OE⟧ 1 the persons speaking or writing 2 I: used by a monarch, editor, etc. when speaking for others

weak (wēk) *adj.* ⟦< ON *veikr*⟧ 1 lacking physical strength; feeble 2 lacking moral strength or willpower 3 lacking mental power 4 lacking power, authority, force, etc. 5 easily torn, broken, etc. /a *weak* railing/ 6 lacking intensity, etc. /a *weak* voice/ 7 diluted /*weak* tea/ 8 unconvincing /a *weak* argument/

weak′en *vt., vi.* to make or become weak or weaker

weak′-kneed′ (-nēd′) *adj.* lacking in courage, determination, resistance, etc.

weak′ling *n.* one that is low in physical or moral strength

weak′ly *adj.* **-li·er, -li·est** sickly; feeble —*adv.* in a weak manner

weak′ness *n.* 1 state of being weak 2 a weak point; fault 3 an immoderate fondness (*for* something)

weal[1] (wēl) *n.* ⟦< WALE⟧ a mark raised on the skin, as by a blow; welt

weal[2] (wēl) *n.* ⟦< OE *wela*, wealth, well-being⟧ well-being; welfare /the public *weal*/

wealth (welth) *n.* ⟦< prec.⟧ 1 much money or property; riches 2 a large amount /a *wealth* of ideas/ 3 valuable products, contents, etc. 4 everything having value in money

wealth·y (wel′thē) *adj.* **-i·er, -i·est** having wealth; rich —**wealth′i·ness** *n.*

wean (wēn) *vt.* ⟦OE *wenian*, to accustom, train⟧ 1 to accustom (a child or young animal) to take food other than by suckling 2 to withdraw (a person) as from a habit

weap·on (wep′ən) *n.* ⟦OE *wæpen*⟧ 1 any instrument used to injure or kill 2 any means of attack or defense —**weap′on·less** *adj.*

weap′on·ry (-rē) *n.* 1 the design and production of weapons 2 weapons collectively

wear (wer) *vt.* **wore, worn, wear′ing** ⟦OE *werian*⟧ 1 to bear (clothing, etc.) on the body 2 to show in one's appearance /to *wear* a smile/ 3 to impair or diminish by use, friction, etc. 4 to make by rubbing, flowing, etc. /to *wear* a hole in the rug/ 5 to tire or exhaust —*vi.* 1 to become impaired or diminished, as by use 2 to hold up in use /that suit *wears* well/ 3 to have an irritating effect (*on*) —*n.* 1 a wearing or being worn 2 things worn; clothes /men's *wear*/ 3 impairment or loss, as from use, friction, etc. —**wear off** to diminish by degrees —**wear′a·ble** *adj.* —**wear′er** *n.*

wear and tear loss and damage resulting from use

wea·ri·some (wir′i səm) ***adj.*** causing weariness; tiresome or tedious —**wea′ri·some·ly** ***adv.***

wea·ry (wir′ē) ***adj.*** **-ri·er, -ri·est** ⟦OE *werig*⟧ **1** tired; worn out **2** without further patience, zeal, etc. **3** tiring /*weary* work/ —***vt., vi.*** **-ried, -ry·ing** to make or become weary —**wea′ri·ly** ***adv.*** —**wea′ri·ness** ***n.***

wea·sel (wē′zəl) ***n.*** ⟦OE *wesle*⟧ an agile flesh-eating mammal with a long, slender body and short legs —***vi.*** [Colloq.] to avoid or evade a commitment: with *out* —**wea′sel·ly** ***adj.***

weath·er (weth′ər) ***n.*** ⟦OE *weder*⟧ **1** the condition of the atmosphere with regard to temperature, moisture, etc. **2** storm, rain, etc. —***vt.*** **1** to expose to the action of weather **2** to pass through safely /to *weather* a storm/ **3** *Naut.* to pass to the windward of —***vi.*** to become discolored, worn, etc. by exposure to the weather —**under the weather** [Colloq.] ill

weath′er-beat′en ***adj.*** showing the effect of exposure to sun, rain, etc.

weath′er·cock′ ***n.*** a weather vane in the shape of a rooster

weath′er·ing ***n.*** the effects of the forces of weather on rock surfaces

weath′er·ize′ ***vt.*** **-ized′, -iz′ing** to weatherstrip, insulate, etc. (a building)

weath′er·man′ ***n.***, *pl.* **-men′** one whose work is forecasting the weather, or, esp., reporting it, as on TV

weath′er·proof′ ***adj.*** that can be exposed to wind, snow, etc. without being damaged —***vt.*** to make weatherproof

weath′er·strip′ ***n.*** a thin strip of metal, felt, etc. covering the joint between a door or window and the casing, to keep out drafts, etc.: also **weath′er·strip′ping** —***vt.*** **-stripped′, weath′er·strip′ping** to provide with weatherstrips

weather vane a vane for showing which way the wind is blowing

weave (wēv) ***vt.*** **wove** or, chiefly for *vt.* 5 & *vi.* 2, **weaved, wo′ven** or **wove** or, chiefly for *vt.* 5 & *vi.* 2, **weaved, weav′ing** ⟦OE *wefan*⟧ **1** to make (a fabric, basket, etc.) by interlacing (threads, straw, etc.), as on a loom **2** to construct in the mind **3** to twist (something) into or through **4** to spin (a web), as spiders do **5** to make (one's way) by moving from side to side or in and out —***vi.*** **1** to do weaving **2** to move from side to side or in and out —***n.*** a method or pattern of weaving —**weav′er** ***n.***

web (web) ***n.*** ⟦OE *webb*⟧ **1** any woven fabric **2** the network spun by a spider, etc. **3** a carefully woven trap **4** a network **5** a membrane joining the digits of various water birds, etc. —***vt.*** **webbed, web′bing** to join by, or cover as with, a web

web′bing ***n.*** a strong fabric woven in strips and used for belts, etc.

web′foot′ ***n.***, *pl.* **-feet′** a foot with the toes webbed —**web′-foot′ed** ***adj.***

Web·ster, No·ah (web′stər) 1758-1843; U.S. lexicographer

wed (wed) ***vt., vi.*** **wed′ded, wed′ded** or **wed, wed′ding** ⟦OE *weddian*⟧ **1** to marry **2** to unite or join

Wed. Wednesday

wed·ded (wed′id) ***adj.*** **1** married **2** of marriage /*wedded* bliss/ **3** devoted /*wedded* to one's work/ **4** joined

wed′ding ***n.*** **1** the marriage ceremony **2** a marriage anniversary

wedge (wej) ***n.*** ⟦OE *wecg*⟧ **1** a piece of wood, metal, etc. tapering to a thin edge: used to split wood, lift a weight, etc. **2** anything shaped like a wedge **3** any act serving to open the way for change, etc. —***vt.*** **wedged, wedg′ing** **1** to force apart, or fix in place, with a wedge **2** to crowd together or pack (*in*) —***vi.*** to push or be forced as or like a wedge

WEDGE

wedg′ie (-ē) ***n.*** a shoe having a wedge-shaped piece under the heel, which forms a solid sole, flat from heel to toe

wed′lock′ ***n.*** ⟦OE *wedlac*⟧ the state of being married

Wednes·day (wenz′dā, -dē) ***n.*** ⟦< *Woden*, Germanic god⟧ the fourth day of the week

wee (wē) ***adj.*** **we′er, we′est** ⟦OE *wege*⟧ **1** very small; tiny **2** very early /*wee* hours of the morning/

weed (wēd) ***n.*** ⟦OE *weod*⟧ any undesired, uncultivated plant, esp. one that crowds out desired plants —***vt., vi.*** **1** to remove weeds from (a garden, etc.) **2** to remove as useless, harmful, etc.: often with *out* —**weed′er** ***n.*** —**weed′less** ***adj.***

weeds (wēdz) ***n.pl.*** ⟦< OE *wæde*, garment⟧ black mourning clothes

weed′y ***adj.*** **-i·er, -i·est** **1** full of weeds **2** of or like a weed

week (wēk) ***n.*** ⟦OE *wicu*⟧ **1** a period of seven days, esp. one from Sunday through Saturday **2** the hours or days of work in this period

week′day′ ***n.*** any day of the week except Sunday and, often, Saturday

week′end′ or **week′-end′** ***n.*** the period from Friday night or Saturday to Monday morning: also **week end** —***vi.*** to spend the weekend (*at* or *in*)

week′ly ***adj.*** **1** done, happening, etc. once every week **2** of a week, or of each week —***adv.*** once a week; every week —***n.***, *pl.* **-lies** a periodical published once a week

ween (wēn) ***vi., vt.*** ⟦OE *wenan*⟧ [Archaic] to think; suppose; imagine

weep (wēp) ***vi., vt.*** **wept, weep′ing** ⟦OE *wepan*⟧ **1** to shed (tears) **2** to mourn (*for*) **3** to drip or exude (water, etc.) —**weep′er** ***n.***

weep′ing ***n.*** the act of one who weeps —***adj.*** **1** that weeps **2** having graceful, drooping branches

weeping willow an ornamental willow tree with drooping branches

weep·y (wē′pē) ***adj.*** **-i·er, -i·est** weeping or inclined to weep

wee·vil (wē′vəl) ***n.*** ⟦OE *wifel*⟧ a beetle whose larvae feed on grain, cotton, etc.

weft (weft) ***n.*** ⟦< OE *wefan*, to weave⟧ *Weaving* the woof

weigh (wā) ***vt.*** ⟦OE *wegan*, carry⟧ **1** to determine the weight of **2** to have (a specified) weight **3** to consider and choose carefully /*weigh* one's words/ **4** to hoist (an anchor) **—*vi.*** **1** to have significance, importance, etc. **2** to be a burden **—weigh down** to burden or bear down on

weight (wāt) ***n.*** ⟦OE *wiht*⟧ **1** a quantity weighing a definite amount **2** *a*) heaviness *b*) *Physics* the force of gravity acting on a body **3** amount of heaviness **4** *a*) any unit of heaviness *b*) any system of such units *c*) a piece having a specific amount of heaviness, placed on a balance or scale in weighing **5** any mass used for its heaviness /a *paperweight*/ **6** a burden, as of sorrow **7** importance or consequence **8** influence; power **—*vt.*** **1** to add weight to **2** to burden

weight′less *adj.* having little or no apparent weight, as an astronaut in orbit **— weight′less·ness *n.***

weight lifting the athletic exercise or sport of lifting barbells

weight′y *adj.* -i·er, -i·est **1** very heavy **2** burdensome **3** significant; important **— weight′i·ness *n.***

weir (wir) ***n.*** ⟦OE *wer*⟧ **1** a low dam built to back up water, as for a mill **2** a fence, as of brushwood, in a stream, etc., for catching fish

weird (wird) ***adj.*** ⟦< OE *wyrd*, fate⟧ **1** of or about ghosts, etc.; mysterious, eerie, etc. **2** strange; bizarre **—weird′ly *adv.* — weird′ness *n.***

weird·o (wir′dō) ***n.***, *pl.* **-os** [Slang] one that is weird, bizarre, etc. Also **weird′ie** (-dē)

wel·come (wel′kəm) ***adj.*** ⟦OE *wilcuma*, welcome guest⟧ **1** gladly received /a *welcome* guest/ **2** freely permitted /he is *welcome* to use my car/ **3** under no obligation /you're *welcome*/ **—*n.*** a welcoming **—*vt.*** **-comed, -com·ing** to greet or receive with pleasure, etc.

weld (weld) ***vt.*** ⟦< obs. *well*⟧ **1** to unite (pieces of metal, etc.) by heating until fused or until soft enough to hammer together **2** to unite closely **—*vi.*** to be welded **—*n.*** **1** a welding **2** the joint formed by welding **— weld′a·ble *adj.* —weld′er *n.***

wel·fare (wel′fer′) ***n.*** ⟦ME: see WELL[2] & FARE⟧ **1** condition of health, happiness, prosperity, etc.; well-being **2** *a*) the organized efforts of government agencies granting aid to the poor, the unemployed, etc. *b*) such aid **—on welfare** receiving government aid because of poverty, etc.

wel·kin (wel′kin) ***n.*** ⟦< OE *wolcen*, cloud⟧ [Archaic] the vault of the sky

well[1] (wel) ***n.*** ⟦OE *wella*⟧ **1** a natural spring and pool **2** a hole sunk into the earth to get water, oil, etc. **3** a source of abundant supply **4** a shaft, etc. resembling a well **5** a container for a liquid, as an inkwell **—*vi.*, *vt.*** to gush or flow as from a well

well[2] (wel) ***adv.* bet′ter, best** ⟦OE *wel*⟧ **1** in a satisfactory, proper, or excellent manner /treat her *well*, to sing *well*/ **2** prosperously /to live *well*/ **3** with good reason /one may *well* ask/ **4** to a considerable degree /*well* advanced/ **5** thoroughly /stir it *well*/ **6** with certainty; definitely **7** familiarly /I know her *well*/ **—*adj.*** **1** suitable, proper, etc. **2** in good health **3** favorable; comfortable **—*interj.*** an exclamation of surprise, agreement, etc. **—as well (as)** **1** in addition (to) **2** equally (with)

well-ad·vised (wel′əd vīzd′) ***adj.*** showing or resulting from careful consideration or sound advice; prudent

well′-ap·point′ed *adj.* excellently furnished or equipped

well′-bal′anced *adj.* **1** precisely adjusted **2** sane, sensible, etc.

well′-be·haved′ *adj.* behaving well; displaying good manners

well′-be′ing *n.* the state of being well, happy, or prosperous; welfare

well′-born′ *adj.* born into a family of high social position

well′-bred′ *adj.* showing good breeding; courteous and considerate

well′-dis·posed′ *adj.* friendly (*toward* a person) or receptive (*to* an idea, etc.)

well-done′ *adj.* **1** performed with skill **2** thoroughly cooked, as meat

well′-fed′ *adj.* plump or fat

well′-fixed′ *adj.* [Colloq.] wealthy

well′-found′ed *adj.* based on facts, good evidence, or sound judgment

well′-groomed′ *adj.* clean and neat

well′-ground′ed *adj.* having a thorough basic knowledge of a subject

well′head′ *n.* **1** a source; fountainhead **2** the top of a well, as an oil or gas well

well′-heeled′ *adj.* [Slang] rich; prosperous

well′-in·formed′ *adj.* having considerable knowledge of a subject or of many subjects

Wel·ling·ton (wel′iŋ tən) capital of New Zealand: pop. 135,000

well′-in·ten′tioned *adj.* having or showing good or kindly intentions

well′-knit′ *adj.* **1** well-constructed **2** sturdy in body build

well′-known′ *adj.* **1** widely known; famous **2** thoroughly known

well′-made′ *adj.* skillfully and soundly put together

well′-man′nered *adj.* having good manners; polite; courteous

well′-mean′ing *adj.* **1** having good intentions **2** said or done with good intentions: also **well′-meant′**

well′-nigh′ *adv.* very nearly; almost

well′-off′ *adj.* **1** in a fortunate condition **2** prosperous

well′-pre·served′ *adj.* in good condition or looking good, in spite of age

well′-read′ (-red′) ***adj.*** having read much

well′-round′ed *adj.* **1** well-planned for proper balance **2** showing diverse talents **3** shapely

well′-spo′ken *adj.* **1** speaking easily, graciously, etc. **2** properly or aptly spoken

well′spring′ *n.* **1** the source of a stream, etc. **2** a source of abundant supply

well′-tak′en *adj.* apt and sound or cogent

well′-thought′-of′ *adj.* having a good reputation

well′-timed′ *adj.* timely; opportune

well′-to-do′ *adj.* prosperous; wealthy

well′-turned′ *adj.* **1** gracefully shaped /a *well-turned* ankle/ **2** expressed well /a *well-turned* phrase/

well′-wish′er *n.* one who wishes well to another or to a cause, etc.

well'-worn' ***adj.*** much worn or used

welsh (welsh) ***vi.*** [Slang] to fail to pay a debt, fulfill an obligation, etc.: often with *on* —**welsh'er** ***n.***

Welsh (welsh) ***n.*** ⟦OE *Wealh*, foreigner⟧ the Celtic language of Wales —***adj.*** of Wales, its people, etc. —**the Welsh** the people of Wales —**Welsh'man** (-mən), *pl.* **-men,** ***n.***

Welsh rabbit a dish of melted cheese served on crackers or toast Also **Welsh rarebit**

welt (welt) ***n.*** ⟦ME *welte*⟧ **1** a strip of leather in the seam between the sole and upper of a shoe **2** a ridge produced on the skin by a slash or blow

wel·ter (wel'tər) ***vi.*** ⟦< MDu *welteren*⟧ to roll about or wallow —***n.*** a confusion; turmoil

wel·ter·weight (wel'tər wāt') ***n.*** ⟦prob. < *welt*, to beat⟧ a boxer weighing 136 to 147 pounds

wen (wen) ***n.*** ⟦OE *wenn*⟧ a benign skin tumor, esp. of the scalp

wench (wench) ***n.*** ⟦OE *wencel*, child⟧ **1** a young woman: derogatory or jocular term **2** [Archaic] a female servant

wend (wend) ***vt.*** **wend'ed, wend'ing** ⟦OE *wendan*, to turn⟧ to go on (one's way)

went (went) ***vi.***, ***vt.*** *pt. of* GO

wept (wept) ***vi.***, ***vt.*** *pt. & pp. of* WEEP

were (wʉr) ***vi.*** ⟦OE *wæron*⟧ *pl. & 2d pers. sing., past indic., and the past subjunctive, of* BE

we're (wir) we are

were·wolf (wir'woolf', wʉr'-) ***n.***, *pl.* **-wolves'** ⟦OE *wer*, man + *wulf*, wolf⟧ *Folklore* a person changed into a wolf Also sp. **werwolf**

Wes·ley, John (wes'lē, wez'-) 1703-91; Eng. clergyman; founder of Methodism —**Wes'·ley·an** ***adj.***, ***n.***

west (west) ***n.*** ⟦OE⟧ **1** the direction in which sunset occurs (270° on the compass; opposite east) **2** a region in or toward this direction —***adj.*** **1** in, of, or toward the west **2** from the west —***adv.*** in or toward the west —**the West 1** the western part of the U.S. **2** Europe and the Western Hemisphere

West Berlin *see* BERLIN

west'er·ly ***adj.***, ***adv.*** **1** toward the west **2** from the west

west'ern ***adj.*** ⟦OE *westerne*⟧ **1** in, of, or toward the west **2** from the west **3** [**W-**] of the West —***n.*** a movie, book, etc. about life in the western U.S., esp. during the frontier period

west'ern·er ***n.*** a native or inhabitant of the west

Western Hemisphere that half of the earth which includes North & South America

west'ern·ize' ***vt.*** **-ized', -iz'ing** to make western in habits, ideas, etc.

Western Samoa country in the South Pacific, consisting of two large islands & several small ones: 1,132 sq. mi.; pop. 165,000

West Germany *see* GERMANY

West In·dies (in'dēz') large group of islands on the Atlantic between North America & South America —**West Indian**

West Point military reservation in SE N.Y.: site of the U.S. Military Academy

West Virginia E state of the U.S.: 24,181 sq. mi.; pop. 1,950,000; cap. Charleston —**West Virginian**

west'ward (-wərd) ***adv.***, ***adj.*** toward the west Also **west'wards** ***adv.***

wet (wet) ***adj.*** **wet'ter, wet'test** ⟦OE *wæt*⟧ **1** covered or saturated with water or other liquid **2** rainy; misty **3** not yet dry /*wet* paint/ **4** permitting the sale of alcoholic beverages —***n.*** **1** water or other liquid **2** rain or rainy weather **3** one who favors the sale of alcoholic beverages —***vt.***, ***vi.*** **wet** or **wet'ted, wet'ting** to make or become wet —**all wet** [Slang] wrong —**wet'ly** ***adv.*** —**wet'ness** ***n.*** —**wet'ter** ***n.***

wet'back' ***n.*** [Colloq.] a Mexican who illegally enters the U.S. to work

wet blanket one whose presence lessens the enthusiasm of others

wet'land' ***n.*** [*usually pl.*] **1** swamps or marshes **2** an area preserved for wildlife

wet nurse a woman hired to suckle another's child —**wet'-nurse', -nursed', -nurs'ing,** ***vt.***

wet suit a closefitting suit of rubber worn by skin divers for warmth

whack (hwak) ***vt.***, ***vi.*** ⟦echoic⟧ to strike or slap with a sharp, resounding blow —***n.*** **1** a sharp, resounding blow **2** the sound of this —**have** (or **take**) **a whack at** [Colloq.] **1** to aim a blow at **2** to make an attempt at —**out of whack** [Colloq.] not in proper condition —**whack'er** ***n.***

whack'y ***adj.*** **-i·er, -i·est** [Slang] *alt. sp. of* WACKY

whale[1] (hwāl) ***n.*** ⟦OE *hwæl*⟧ a large, warm-blooded sea mammal that breathes air —***vi.*** **whaled, whal'ing** to hunt whales —**a whale of a** [Colloq.] an exceptionally large, fine, etc. example of

whale[2] (hwāl) ***vt.*** **whaled, whal'ing** ⟦prob. < WALE⟧ [Colloq.] to thrash

whale'bone' ***n.*** the horny, elastic material hanging from the upper jaw of some whales (**whalebone whales**)

whal'er ***n.*** **1** a whaling ship **2** one whose work is whaling

wham (hwam) ***interj.*** a sound imitating a heavy blow, explosion, etc. —***n.*** a heavy blow, etc. —***vt.***, ***vi.*** **whammed, wham'·ming** to strike, explode, etc. loudly

wham'my ***n.***, *pl.* **-mies** [Slang] a jinx

wharf (hwôrf) ***n.***, *pl.* **wharves** or **wharfs** ⟦OE *hwerf*, a dam⟧ a structure on a shore, at which ships are loaded or unloaded

what (hwut, hwät) ***pron.*** ⟦OE *hwa*, who⟧ **1** which thing, event, etc. /*what* is that object?/ **2** that or those which /know *what* one wants/ —***adj.*** **1** which or which kind of: used interrogatively or relatively **2** as much, or as many, as /take *what* men you need/ **3** how great, surprising, etc. /*what* nonsense!/ —***adv.*** **1** in what way? how? /*what* does it matter?/ **2** partly /*what* with the singing, the time passed/ **3** how greatly, etc. /*what* tragic news!/ —***interj.*** an exclamation of surprise, anger, etc. —**what about** what do you think, feel, etc. concerning? —**what for** why?

what·ev·er (hwut ev'ər) ***pron.*** what: an emphatic variant; specif., *a*) which thing, event, etc. *b*) anything that /say *whatever* you like/ c) no matter what /*whatever* you do, don't hurry/ —*adj.* 1 of any kind /no plans *whatever*/ 2 being who it may be /*whatever* man said that, it is not true/

what'not' (-nät') *n.* 1 a nondescript thing 2 a set of open shelves, as for bric-a-brac

what's (hwuts) 1 what is 2 what has 3 [Colloq.] what does /*what's* he want?/

what·so·ev·er (hwut'sō ev'ər) *pron., adj.* whatever: an emphatic form

wheal¹ (hwēl) *n.* ⟦ME *whele*⟧ a small, itching elevation of the skin, as from an insect bite

wheal² (hwēl) *n.* WEAL¹

wheat (hwēt) *n.* ⟦OE *hwæte*⟧ a cereal grass having spikes containing grains used in making flour, cereals, etc.

wheat germ the highly nutritious embryo of the wheat kernel

whee·dle (hwēd''l) *vt., vi.* **-dled, -dling** ⟦< ?⟧ to influence, persuade, or get by flattery, coaxing, etc.

wheel (hwēl) *n.* ⟦OE *hweol*⟧ 1 a circular disk or frame turning on a central axis 2 anything like a wheel in shape, movement, etc. 3 the steering wheel of a motor vehicle 4 [*pl.*] [Slang] an automobile 5 [*usually pl.*] the moving forces /the *wheels* of progress/ 6 a turning movement 7 [Slang] an important person —*vt., vi.* 1 to move on or in a wheeled vehicle 2 to turn, revolve, etc. 3 to turn so as to change direction —**at** (or **behind**) **the wheel** steering a motor vehicle, etc.

wheel'bar'row *n.* a shallow, open box for moving small loads, having a wheel in front, and two handles in back for moving the vehicle

wheel'base' *n.* the length of a motor vehicle between the centers of the front and rear wheels

wheel'chair' *n.* a chair mounted on wheels, for persons unable to walk

wheeled (hwēld) *adj.* having wheels

wheel·er-deal·er (hwēl'ər dēl'ər) *n.* [Slang] one who is showily aggressive, as in arranging business deals

wheel'house' *n.* PILOTHOUSE

wheel'wright' *n.* one who makes and repairs wheels and wheeled vehicles

wheeze (hwēz) *vi.* **wheezed, wheez'ing** ⟦< ON *hvæsa*, to hiss⟧ to breathe hard with a whistling, breathy sound, as in asthma —*n.* a wheezing —**wheez'y, -i·er, -i·est,** *adj.*

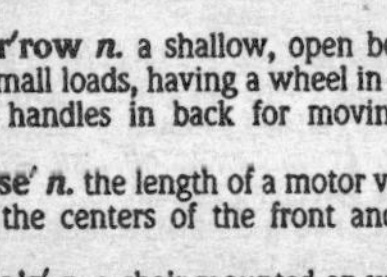

WHELK

whelk (hwelk) *n.* ⟦OE *wioluc*⟧ a large, edible marine snail

whelm (hwelm) *vt.* ⟦ME *welmen*⟧ 1 to submerge 2 to overpower or crush

whelp (hwelp) *n.* ⟦OE *hwelp*⟧ a young dog, etc. —*vt., vi.* to give birth to (young): said of some animals

when (hwen) *adv.* ⟦OE *hwænne*⟧ 1 at what time? /*when* did they leave?/ 2 on what occasion? —*conj.* 1 at what time /tell me *when* to go/ 2 at the time that /*when* we were young/ 3 at which /a time *when* people must work/ 4 as soon as /we will eat *when* he comes/ 5 although —*pron.* what or which time /until *when* will you stay?/ —*n.* the time (*of* an event)

whence (hwens) *adv.* ⟦ME *whennes*⟧ from what place, cause, etc.; from where /*whence* do you come?/

when·ev'er *adv.* [Colloq.] when: an emphatic form —*conj.* at whatever time /leave *whenever* you like/

where (hwer) *adv.* ⟦OE *hwær*⟧ 1 in or at what place? /*where* is it?/ 2 to or toward what place? /*where* did he go?/ 3 in what respect? /*where* is he to blame?/ 4 from what place or source? /*where* did he learn it?/ —*conj.* 1 at what place /I see *where* it is/ 2 at which place /I came home, *where* I ate/ 3 wherever 4 to the place to which /we go *where* you go/ —*pron.* 1 the place at which /a mile to *where* I live/ 2 what place /*where* are you from?/ —*n.* the place (*of* an event)

where'a·bouts' (-ə bouts') *adv.* near or at what place? —*n.* [*with sing. or pl. v.*] the place where one is

where·as' *conj.* 1 in view of the fact that 2 while on the contrary /she is slim, *whereas* he is fat/

where·at' *conj.* [Archaic] at which point

where·by' *conj.* by which

where'fore' (-fôr') *adv.* [Archaic] for what reason? why? —*conj.* 1 for which 2 because of which —*n.* the reason; cause

where·in' *conj.* in which

where·of' *adv., conj.* of what, which, or whom /the things *whereof* he spoke/

where·on' *conj.* on which

where'up·on' *conj.* 1 upon which 2 at which

wher·ev·er (hwer ev'ər) *adv.* [Colloq.] where: an emphatic form —*conj.* in, at, or to whatever place or situation /go *wherever* you like/

where·with' *conj.* with which

where'with·al' (-wi*th* ôl') *n.* the necessary means, esp. money

wher·ry (hwer'ē) *n., pl.* **-ries** ⟦ME *whery*⟧ a light rowboat

whet (hwet) *vt.* **whet'ted, whet'ting** ⟦< OE *hwæt*, keen⟧ 1 to sharpen by rubbing or grinding, as a knife 2 to stimulate /to *whet* the appetite/

wheth·er (hwe*th*'ər) *conj.* ⟦OE *hwæther*⟧ 1 if it be the case that /ask *whether* she sings/ 2 in case; in either case that: introducing alternatives /*whether* it rains or snows/

whet·stone (hwet'stōn') *n.* an abrasive stone for sharpening knives, etc.

whew (hyo͞o) *interj.* ⟦echoic⟧ an exclamation of relief, surprise, etc.

whey (hwā) *n.* ⟦OE *hwæg*⟧ the watery part of milk, that separates from the curds

which (hwich) *pron.* ⟦OE *hwylc*⟧ 1 what one (or ones) of several? /*which* do you want?/ 2 the one (or ones) that /he knows *which* he wants/ 3 that /the boat *which* sank/ 4 any that /take *which* you like/ —

adj. what one or ones *[which* man (or men) left?*]*

which·ev′er *pron., adj.* 1 any one *[take whichever* (desk) you like*]* 2 no matter which *[whichever* (desk) he chooses, they won't be pleased*]*

whiff (hwif) *n.* ⟦echoic⟧ 1 a light puff or gust of air, etc. 2 a slight odor

whif·fle·tree (hwif′əl trē′) *n. var. of* WHIPPLETREE

Whig (hwig) *n.* ⟦< *whiggamore* (contemptuous term for Scot Presbyterians)⟧ 1 a member of a former English political party which championed reform 2 a supporter of the American Revolution 3 a member of a U.S. political party (c. 1834-56)

while (hwīl) *n.* ⟦OE *hwil*⟧ a period of time *[a* short *while]* —*conj.* 1 during the time that *[I* read *while* I eat*]* 2 although; whereas *[while* not poor, she's not rich*]* —*vt.* **whiled, whil′ing** to spend (time) in a pleasant way: often with *away*

whi·lom (hwī′ləm) *adj.* ⟦< OE⟧ former

whilst (hwīlst) *conj.* [Now Chiefly Brit., etc.] WHILE

whim (hwim) *n.* a sudden fancy; idle and passing notion

whim·per (hwim′pər) *vi., vt.* ⟦? akin to WHINE⟧ to cry or utter with low, whining, broken sounds —*n.* a whimpering sound or cry

whim·si·cal (hwim′zi kəl) *adj.* 1 full of whims or whimsy 2 oddly out of the ordinary —**whim′si·cal′i·ty** (-kal′ə tē) *n.* —**whim′si·cal·ly** *adv.*

whim·sy (hwim′zē) *n., pl.* **-sies′** ⟦< ?⟧ 1 an odd fancy; idle notion; whim 2 quaint or fanciful humor Also sp. **whim·sey,** *pl.* **-seys**

whine (hwīn) *vi.* **whined, whin′ing** ⟦OE *hwinan*⟧ 1 *a)* to utter a high-pitched, nasal sound, as in complaint *b)* to make a prolonged sound like this 2 to complain in a childish way —*n.* 1 a whining 2 a complaint uttered in a whining tone —**whin′y, -i·er, -i·est,** *adj.*

whin·ny (hwin′ē) *vi.* **-nied, -ny·ing** ⟦prob. echoic⟧ to neigh in a low, gentle way: said of a horse —*n., pl.* **-nies** a whinnying

whip (hwip) *vt.* **whipped** or **whipt, whip′·ping** ⟦< MDu *wippen,* to swing⟧ 1 to move, pull, throw, etc. suddenly *[to whip* out a knife*]* 2 to strike, as with a strap; lash 3 to wind (cord, etc.) around (a rope, etc.) so as to prevent fraying 4 to beat into a froth *[to whip* cream*]* 5 [Colloq.] to defeat —*vi.* 1 to move quickly and suddenly 2 to flap about —*n.* 1 a flexible instrument for striking or flogging 2 a blow, etc. as with a whip 3 an officer of a political party in a legislature who maintains discipline, etc. 4 a whipping motion —**whip up** 1 to rouse (interest, etc.) 2 [Colloq.] to prepare quickly

whip′cord′ *n.* 1 a hard, twisted or braided cord 2 a strong worsted cloth with a diagonally ribbed surface

whip hand control or advantage

whip′lash′ *n.* 1 the lash of a whip 2 a sudden, severe jolting of the neck back and forth, as caused by the impact of an automobile collision

whip′per·snap′per *n.* an insignificant but presumptuous person

whip·pet (hwip′it) *n.* ⟦< WHIP⟧ a swift dog resembling a small greyhound, used in racing

whip·ple·tree (hwip′əl trē′) *n.* ⟦< WHIP + TREE⟧ SINGLETREE

whip·poor·will (hwip′ər wil′) *n.* ⟦echoic⟧ a grayish bird of E North America, active at night

whir or **whirr** (hwur) *vi., vt.* **whirred, whir′ring** ⟦ME *quirren*⟧ to fly, revolve, vibrate, with a buzzing sound —*n.* such a sound

whirl (hwurl) *vi.* ⟦< ON *hvirfla*⟧ 1 to move rapidly in a circle or orbit 2 to rotate or spin fast 3 to seem to spin *[my* head is *whirling]* —*vt.* to cause to move, rotate, revolve, etc. rapidly —*n.* 1 a whirling or whirling motion 2 a tumult; uproar 3 a confused or giddy condition —**give it a whirl** [Colloq.] to make an attempt

whirl·i·gig (hwurl′i gig′) *n.* any child's toy that whirls or spins

whirl′pool′ *n.* water in violent, whirling motion tending to draw floating objects into its center

whirlpool bath a bath in which an agitating device propels a current of warm water with a swirling motion

whirl′wind′ *n.* 1 a forward moving current of air whirling violently in a vertical spiral 2 anything like a whirlwind —*adj.* impetuous; speedy

whisk (hwisk) *n.* ⟦< ON *visk,* a brush⟧ 1 a brushing with a quick, light, sweeping motion 2 such a motion —*vt., vi.* to move, carry, brush (*away, off, out,* etc.) with a quick, sweeping motion

whisk broom a small, short-handled broom for brushing clothes, etc.

whisk·er (hwis′kər) *n.* 1 [*pl.*] the hair growing on a man's face, esp. on the cheeks 2 any of the long, bristly hairs on the upper lip of a cat, rat, etc. 3 a very small amount

whis·key (hwis′kē) *n., pl.* **-keys** or **-kies** ⟦< Ir *uisce,* water + *beathadh,* life⟧ a strong alcoholic liquor distilled from the fermented mash of grain Also sp., esp. for Brit. and Cdn. usage, **whis·ky,** *pl.* **-kies**

whis·per (hwis′pər) *vi., vt.* ⟦< OE *hwisprian*⟧ 1 to speak or say very softly, esp. without vibrating the vocal cords 2 to talk or tell furtively, as in gossiping 3 to make a rustling sound —*n.* 1 a whispering 2 something whispered 3 a soft, rustling sound

whist (hwist) *n.* ⟦< earlier *whisk*⟧ a card game: forerunner of bridge

whis·tle (hwis′əl) *vi.* **-tled, -tling** ⟦OE *hwistlian*⟧ 1 to make a clear, shrill sound as by forcing breath through the contracted lips 2 to move with a shrill sound, as the wind 3 *a)* to blow a whistle *b)* to have its whistle blown, as a train —*vt.* 1 to produce (a tune, etc.) by whistling 2 to signal, etc. by whistling —*n.* 1 an instrument for making whistling sounds 2 a whistling —**whis′tler** *n.*

whis′tle-blow′er *n.* one who informs on a wrongdoer

whis′tle-stop′ *n.* 1 a small town 2 a brief stop in a small town on a tour

whit (hwit) ***n.*** ⟦< OE *wiht*, a wight⟧ the least bit; jot; iota
white (hwit) ***adj.*** **whit′er, whit′est** ⟦OE *hwit*⟧ **1** having the color of pure snow or milk; opposite to black **2** of a light or pale color **3** pale; wan **4** lacking color **5** pure; innocent **6** having a light-colored skin —***n.*** **1** *a)* white color *b)* a white pigment **2** a white or light-colored part, as the albumen of an egg or the white part of the eyeball **3** a person with a light-colored skin —**white′-ness** ***n.***
white blood cell (or **corpuscle**) LEUKOCYTE
white′cap′ ***n.*** a wave with its crest broken into white foam
white′-col′lar ***adj.*** designating or of office or professional workers
white-collar crime fraud, embezzlement, etc., committed by a person in business, government, or a profession
white elephant **1** an albino elephant **2** something of little use, but expensive to maintain **3** any object not wanted by its owner, but useful to another
white feather symbol of cowardice
white′fish′ ***n.***, *pl.* **-fish′** or (for different species) **-fish′es** a white or silvery edible fish, found in cool lakes of the Northern Hemisphere
white flag a white banner or cloth hoisted as a signal of truce or surrender
white gold a gold alloy that looks like platinum
white goods **1** household linens, as sheets, towels, etc. **2** large household appliances, as refrigerators, stoves, etc.
white heat **1** a temperature at which material glows white **2** a state of intense emotion, etc. —**white′-hot′** ***adj.***
White House, the **1** official residence of the President of the U.S. in Washington, D.C. **2** the executive branch of the U.S. government
white lead a poisonous, white powder, lead carbonate, used in paint
white lie a lie about a trivial matter, often told to spare someone's feelings
white metal any of various light-colored alloys, esp. one containing much lead or tin, as pewter
whit·en (hwit′'n) ***vt.***, ***vi.*** to make or become white or whiter —**whit′en·er** ***n.*** —**whit′-en·ing** ***n.***
white paper **1** an official government report **2** any in-depth, authoritative report
white rat an albino rat, esp. one used in biological experiments
white sale a sale of household linens
white slave a woman forced into prostitution for the profit of others —**white′-slave′** ***adj.*** —**white slavery**
white′wall′ ***adj.*** designating or of a tire with a white band on the outer sidewall —***n.*** a whitewall tire
white′wash′ ***n.*** **1** a mixture of lime, chalk, water, etc., as for whitening walls, etc. **2** a concealing of faults in order to exonerate —***vt.*** **1** to cover with whitewash **2** to conceal the faults of **3** [Colloq.] *Sports* to defeat (an opponent) soundly
white water foaming water, as in rapids, etc.
whith·er (hwith′ər) ***adv.*** ⟦OE *hwider*⟧ to what place, condition, result, etc.? where? —***conj.*** **1** to which place, result, etc. **2** wherever
whit·ing¹ (hwit′iŋ) ***n.*** ⟦MDu *wit*, white⟧ any of various unrelated food fishes of North America, Europe, etc.
whit·ing² (hwit′iŋ) ***n.*** ⟦ME *hwiting*⟧ powdered chalk used in paints, etc.
whit′ish ***adj.*** somewhat white
Whit·man (hwit′mən, wit′-), **Walt(er)** 1819-92; U.S. poet
Whit·ney (hwit′nē, wit′-), **Mount** mountain in east central Calif.: 14,495 ft.
Whit·sun·day (hwit′sun′dā, -dē) ***n.*** ⟦OE *Hwita Sunnandæg*, lit., white Sunday⟧ PENTECOST
whit·tle (hwit′'l) ***vt.*** **-tled, -tling** ⟦< OE *thwitan*, to cut⟧ **1** *a)* to cut thin shavings from (wood) with a knife *b)* to carve (an object) thus **2** to reduce gradually —***vi.*** to whittle wood
whiz or **whizz** (hwiz) ***vi.*** **whizzed, whiz′-zing** ⟦echoic⟧ **1** to make the hissing sound of something rushing through the air **2** to speed by with this sound —***n.*** **1** this sound **2** [Slang] an expert /a *whiz* at football/
who (hōō) ***pron.*** obj. **whom**, poss. **whose** ⟦OE *hwa*⟧ **1** what or which person or persons /*who* is he? I asked *who* he was/ **2** (the, or a, person or persons) that /a man *who* knows/
WHO World Health Organization
whoa (hwō) ***interj.*** stop!: used esp. in directing a horse to stand still
who·dun·it (hōō dun′it) ***n.*** [Colloq.] a mystery novel, play, etc.
who·ev·er (hōō ev′ər) ***pron.*** **1** any person that **2** no matter who /*whoever* said it, it's not so/ **3** who?: an emphatic usage /*whoever* told you that?/
whole (hōl) ***adj.*** ⟦OE *hal*⟧ **1** healthy; not diseased or injured **2** not broken, damaged, etc.; intact **3** containing all the parts; complete **4** not divided up; in a single unit **5** not a fraction —***n.*** **1** the entire amount **2** a thing complete in itself —**on the whole** all things considered; in general —**whole′-ness** ***n.***
whole′heart′ed ***adj.*** with all one's energy, enthusiasm, etc.; sincere
whole′-hog′ ***adj.***, ***adv.*** [Slang] without reservation; complete(ly)
whole milk milk from which no butterfat, etc. has been removed
whole note *Music* a note having four times the duration of a quarter note
whole′sale′ ***n.*** the selling of goods in large quantities and at lower prices, esp. to retailers —***adj.*** **1** of or having to do with such selling **2** extensive or indiscriminate /*wholesale* criticism/ —***adv.*** **1** at wholesale prices **2** extensively or indiscriminately —***vt.***, ***vi.*** **-saled′, -sal′ing** to sell wholesale —**whole′sal′er** ***n.***
whole′some (-səm) ***adj.*** ⟦ME *holsom*⟧ **1** promoting good health or well-being; healthful **2** improving the mind or character **3** having health and vigor —**whole′some-ness** ***n.***
whole′-wheat′ ***adj.*** ground from whole

kernels of wheat or made of flour so ground

whol·ly (hōl′lē) ***adv.*** to the whole amount or extent; totally; entirely

whom (ho͞om) ***pron.*** *objective case of* WHO

whom·ev′er (-ev′ər) ***pron.*** *objective case of* WHOEVER

whoop (hwo͞op; ho͞op) ***n.*** ⟦< ? OFr *houper,* cry out⟧ 1 a loud shout, cry, etc., as of joy 2 the convulsive intake of air following a fit of coughing in whooping cough —***vt., vi.*** to utter (with) a whoop or whoops

whoop′ing cough an acute infectious disease, esp. of children, with coughing fits that end in a whoop

whop·per (hwäp′ər) ***n.*** ⟦< colloq. *whop,* to beat⟧ [Colloq.] 1 anything extraordinarily large 2 a great lie

whop′ping ***adj.*** [Colloq.] extraordinarily large or great

whore (hôr) ***n.*** ⟦OE *hore*⟧ a prostitute —**whor′ish *adj.***

who're (ho͞o′ər) who are

whorl (hwôrl, hwurl) ***n.*** ⟦ME *whorwyl*⟧ anything with a coiled or spiral appearance, as any of the circular ridges that form the patterns of a fingerprint —**whorled *adj.***

who's (ho͞oz) 1 who is 2 who has

whose (ho͞oz) ***pron.*** ⟦OE *hwæs*⟧ that or those belonging to whom —***poss. pronominal adj.*** of, belonging to, or done by whom or which

who·so·ev·er (ho͞o′sō ev′ər) ***pron.*** whoever: an emphatic form

why (hwī) ***adv.*** ⟦OE *hwæt,* what⟧ for what reason, cause, or purpose? /*why* eat?/ —***conj.*** 1 because of which /no reason *why* you shouldn't go/ 2 the reason for which /that is *why* he went/ —***n., pl.*** **whys** the reason; cause —***interj.*** an exclamation of surprise, impatience, etc.

WI Wisconsin

Wich·i·ta (wich′ə tô′) city in S Kans.: pop. 279,000

wick (wik) ***n.*** ⟦OE *weoca*⟧ a piece of cord, tape, etc., as in a candle or oil lamp, that absorbs the fuel and, when lighted, burns

wick·ed (wik′id) ***adj.*** ⟦ME < *wikke,* evil⟧ 1 morally bad; evil 2 generally bad, unpleasant, etc. /a *wicked* storm/ 3 mischievous 4 [Slang] showing great skill —**wick′ed·ly *adv.*** —**wick′ed·ness *n.***

wick·er (wik′ər) ***n.*** ⟦< Scand⟧ 1 a thin, flexible twig 2 *a)* such twigs or long, woody strips woven together, as in making baskets *b)* WICKERWORK (sense 1) —***adj.*** made of wicker

wick′er·work′ *n.* 1 things made of wicker 2 WICKER (*n.* 2*a*)

wick·et (wik′it) ***n.*** ⟦ME *wiket*⟧ 1 a small door or gate, esp. one in or near a larger one 2 a small window, as in a box office 3 *Croquet* any of the small wire arches through which the balls must be hit

wide (wīd) ***adj.*** **wid′er, wid′est** ⟦OE *wid*⟧ 1 extending over a large area, esp. from side to side 2 of a specified extent from side to side 3 of great extent /a *wide* variety/ 4 open fully /eyes *wide* with fear/ 5 far from the point, etc. aimed at: usually with *of* /*wide* of the target/ —***adv.*** 1 over a relatively large area 2 to a large or full extent /*wide* open/ 3 so as to miss the point, etc. aimed at; astray —**wide′ly *adv.*** —**wide′ness *n.***

-wide (wīd) *combining form* existing or extending throughout /*statewide*/

wide′-an′gle *adj.* having a wider angle of view than usual

wide′-a·wake′ *adj.* 1 completely awake 2 alert

wide′-eyed′ *adj.* 1 with the eyes opened widely, as in surprise or fear 2 naive or unsophisticated

wid·en (wīd′'n) ***vt., vi.*** to make or become wide or wider

wide′-o′pen *adj.* 1 opened wide 2 having no or few legal restrictions against prostitution, gambling, etc. /a *wide-open* city/

wide′spread′ *adj.* occurring over a wide area or extent

widg·eon (wij′ən) ***n.*** *alt. sp. of* WIGEON

wid·ow (wid′ō) ***n.*** ⟦OE *widewe*⟧ a woman whose husband has died and who has not remarried —***vt.*** to cause to become a widow —**wid′ow·hood′ *n.***

wid′ow·er *n.* a man whose wife has died and who has not remarried

width (width) ***n.*** 1 distance from side to side 2 a piece of a certain width /two *widths* of cloth/

wield (wēld) ***vt.*** ⟦OE *wealdan*⟧ 1 to handle (a tool, etc.), esp. with skill 2 to exercise (power, influence, etc.)

wie·ner (wē′nər) ***n.*** ⟦< Ger *Wiener wurst,* Vienna sausage⟧ a smoked link sausage; frankfurter

wie·nie (wē′nē) ***n.*** [Colloq.] WIENER

wife (wīf) ***n., pl.*** **wives** ⟦OE *wif,* woman⟧ a married woman —**wife′less *adj.*** —**wife′ly *adj.***

wig (wig) ***n.*** ⟦< PERIWIG⟧ a false covering of real or synthetic hair for the head —***vt.*** **wigged, wig′ging** 1 to furnish with a wig 2 [Slang] *a)* to annoy, upset, etc. *b)* to make excited, crazy, etc. (often with *out*) —***vi.*** [Slang] to be or become upset, excited, etc.: often with *out*

wi·geon (wij′ən) ***n.*** ⟦prob. < L *vipio,* small crane⟧ any of certain wild, freshwater ducks

wig·gle (wig′əl) ***vt., vi.*** **-gled, -gling** ⟦ME *wigelen*⟧ to move or cause to move with short, jerky motions from side to side —***n.*** a wiggling —**wig′gler *n.*** —**wig′gly, -gli·er, -gli·est, *adj.***

wight (wīt) ***n.*** ⟦OE *wiht*⟧ [Archaic] a human being

wig·let (wig′lit) ***n.*** a small wig

wig·wag (wig′wag′) ***vt., vi.*** **-wagged′, -wag′ging** ⟦< obs. *wig,* to move + WAG[1]⟧ 1 to move back and forth; wag 2 to send (a message) by waving flags, lights, etc. according to a code —***n.*** the sending of messages in this way

wig·wam (wig′wäm′) ***n.*** ⟦< Algonquian⟧ an American Indian dwelling consisting of a dome-shaped framework of poles covered with rush mats or bark

wild (wīld) ***adj.*** ⟦OE *wilde*⟧ 1 living or growing in its original, natural state 2 not lived in or cultivated; waste 3 not civilized; savage 4 not easily controlled /a *wild* child/ 5 lacking social or moral restraint; dissolute /a *wild* time/ 6 turbulent; stormy 7 enthusiastic /*wild* about golf/ 8 fantastically impractical; reckless 9 missing the target /a *wild* shot/ **10** *Card Games* having any desired value: said of a card —*adv.* in a wild manner —*n.* [*usually pl.*] a wilderness or wasteland —**wild′ly** *adv.* —**wild′ness** *n.*

wild′cat′ *n.* **1** any fierce, medium-sized, undomesticated cat, as the bobcat, ocelot, etc. **2** a productive oil well in an area not previously know to have oil —*adj.* **1** unsound or risky **2** illegal or unauthorized /a *wildcat* strike/ —*vi.* **-cat′ted, -cat′ting** to drill for oil in an area previously considered unproductive

wil·de·beest (wil′də bēst′, vil′-) *n.* ⟦Afrik⟧ GNU

wil·der·ness (wil′dər nis) *n.* ⟦< OE *wilde*, wild + *deor*, animal⟧ an uncultivated, uninhabited region; waste

wild′-eyed′ *adj.* **1** staring in a wild or demented way **2** very foolish or impractical

wild′fire′ *n.* a fire that spreads widely and rapidly

wild′flow′er *n.* **1** any flowering plant growing wild in fields, etc. **2** its flower Also **wild flower**

wild′fowl′ *n.*, *pl.* **-fowls′** or **-fowl′** a wild bird, esp. a game bird Also **wild fowl**

wild′-goose′ chase a futile search, pursuit, or endeavor

wild′life′ *n.* wild animals and birds

wild oats a wild grass common in the W U.S. —**sow one's wild oats** to be promiscuous or dissolute in one's youth

wild rice **1** an aquatic grass of the U.S. and Canada **2** its edible grain

Wild West [*also* **w- W-**] the western U.S. in its early, lawless, frontier period

wile (wīl) *n.* ⟦< OE *wigle*, magic⟧ **1** a sly trick; stratagem **2** a beguiling trick: *usually used in pl.* —*vt.* **wiled, wil′ing** to beguile; lure —**wile away** to while away (time, etc.)

wil·ful (wil′fəl) *adj. alt. sp. of* WILLFUL

will[1] (wil) *n.* ⟦OE *willa*⟧ **1** the power of making a reasoned choice or of controlling one's own actions **2** determination **3** attitude toward others /a man of good *will*/ **4** *a*) a particular desire, choice, etc. of someone *b*) mandate /the *will* of the people/ **5** a legal document directing the disposal of one's property after death —*vt.* **1** to desire; want /to *will* to live/ **2** to control by the power of the will **3** to bequeath by a will —*vi.* to wish, desire, or choose —**at will** when one wishes

will[2] (wil) *v.aux. pt.* **would** ⟦OE *willan*, to desire⟧ **1** used to indicate simple future time /when *will* she arrive?/ **2** used to express determination, obligation, etc. /you *will* listen to me/ **3** used in polite questions /*will* you have some wine?/ **4** used to express habit, expectation, etc. /they *will* talk for hours/ **5** used to express possibility *USAGE*—the distinction between **will** (for second and third person subjects) and **shall** (for the first person) in expressing simple future time or determination, etc. is today virtually nonexistent in North American English; **will** and **shall** and their respective past tenses **would** and **should** are usually used interchangeably, with **will** (and **would**) being the preferred form in all persons

will′ful (-fəl) *adj.* **1** said or done deliberately **2** doing as one pleases —**will′ful·ly** *adv.* —**will′ful·ness** *n.*

William I (wil′yəm) *c.* 1027-87; duke of Normandy who invaded England: king of England (1066-87): called *William the Conqueror*

wil·lies (wil′ēz) *n.pl.* ⟦< ?⟧ [Slang] a nervous feeling; jitters: with *the*

will′ing *adj.* **1** favorably disposed; consenting /*willing* to play/ **2** acting, giving, etc. or done, given, etc. readily and cheerfully —**will′ing·ly** *adv.* —**will′ing·ness** *n.*

wil·li·waw or **wil′ly·waw′** (wil′i wô′) *n.* **1** a violent, cold wind blowing from mountain toward the coast in far northern or southern latitudes **2** confusion; turmoil

will-o'-the-wisp (wil′ə *th*ə wisp′) *n.* **1** a light seen over marshes at night, believed to be marsh gas burning **2** a delusive hope or goal

wil·low (wil′ō) *n.* ⟦OE *welig*⟧ **1** a tree with narrow leaves, and flexible twigs used in weaving baskets, etc. **2** its wood

wil′low·y *adj.* like a willow; slender, lithe, etc.

will′pow′er *n.* strength of will, mind, or determination; self-control

wil·ly-nil·ly (wil′ē nil′ē) *adv.*, *adj.* ⟦contr. < *will I, nill I*: *nill* < OE *nyllan*, be unwilling⟧ (happening) whether one wishes it or not

Wil·son (wil′s′n), **(Thomas) Wood·row** (wood′rō) 1856-1924; 28th president of the U.S. (1913-21)

wilt (wilt) *vi.* ⟦< obs. *welk*, to wither⟧ **1** to become limp, as from heat or lack of water; droop: said of plants **2** to become weak or faint; lose strength or courage —*vt.* to cause to wilt

Wil·ton (carpet or **rug)** (wilt′'n) ⟦after *Wilton*, England⟧ a kind of carpet with a velvety pile of cut loops

wil·y (wīl′ē) *adj.* **-i·er, -i·est** full of wiles; crafty; sly —**wil′i·ness** *n.*

wimp (wimp) *n.* ⟦< ?⟧ [Slang] a weak, ineffectual, or insipid person —**wimp′y** or **wimp′ish** *adj.*

wim·ple (wim′pəl) *n.* ⟦OE *wimpel*⟧ a nun's head covering so arranged as to leave only the face exposed

win (win) *vi.* **won, win′ning** ⟦< OE *winnan*, to fight⟧ **1** *a*) to gain a victory *b*) to finish first in a race, etc. **2** to succeed in reaching a specified condition or place; get /to *win* back to health/ —*vt.* **1** to get by labor, struggle, etc. **2** to be victorious in (a contest, etc.) **3** to get to with effort /they *won* the camp by noon/ **4** to prevail upon; persuade: often with *over* **5** to gain (the sympathy, favor, etc.) of (someone) **6** to persuade to marry one —*n.* [Colloq.] a victory

wince (wins) *vi.* **winced, winc′ing** ⟦< OFr *guenchir*⟧ to shrink or draw back slightly, usually with a grimace, as in pain —*n.* a wincing

winch (winch) *n.* ⟦OE *wince*⟧ **1** a crank with a handle for transmitting motion **2** a machine for hoisting or hauling, having a cylinder upon which is wound the rope, etc. attached to the object to be moved

Win·ches·ter (rifle) (win′ches′tər) ⟦after O. F. *Winchester* (1810-80), the manufacturer⟧ *trademark for* a type of repeating rifle

wind[1] (wīnd) *vt.* **wound** or [Rare] **wind′ed, wind′ing** ⟦OE *windan*⟧ 1 to turn /to *wind* a crank/ 2 to coil into a ball or around something else; twine 3 to cover by entwining 4 *a)* to make (one's way) in a twisting course *b)* to cause to move in a twisting course 5 to tighten the spring of (a clock, etc.) as by turning a stem: often with *up* —*vi.* 1 to move or go in a curving or sinuous manner 2 to take a devious course 3 to coil (*about* or *around* something) —*n.* a turn; twist —**wind up** 1 to wind into a ball, etc. 2 to bring to an end; settle 3 to make very tense, excited, etc. 4 *Baseball* to swing the arm preparatory to pitching —**wind′er** *n.*

wind[2] (wind) *n.* ⟦OE⟧ 1 air in motion 2 a strong current of air; gale 3 air bearing a scent, as in hunting 4 air regarded as bearing information, etc. /a rumor in the *wind*/ 5 breath or the power of breathing 6 empty talk 7 [*pl.*] the wind instruments of an orchestra —*vt.* 1 to get the scent of 2 to put out of breath —**break wind** to expel gas from the bowels —**get wind of** to hear of —**in the wind** happening or about to happen

wind·bag (wind′bag′) *n.* [Colloq.] one who talks much but says little of importance

wind′break′ *n.* a hedge, fence, etc. serving as a protection from wind

wind′burn′ *n.* a roughened, reddened, sore condition of the skin, caused by overexposure to the wind

wind′chill′ factor CHILL FACTOR

wind chimes (or **bells**) a cluster of small chimes or pendants hung so that they strike one another and tinkle when blown by the wind

wind·ed (win′did) *adj.* out of breath

wind·fall (wind′fôl′) *n.* 1 something blown down by the wind, as fruit from a tree 2 an unexpected stroke of good luck

wind·ing sheet (wīn′diŋ) a shroud

wind instrument (wind) a musical instrument sounded by blowing air through it, as a flute

wind·jam·mer (wind′jam′ər) *n.* a large sailing ship or one of its crew

wind·lass (wind′ləs) *n.* ⟦< ON *vinda*, to WIND[1] + *ass*, a beam⟧ a winch, esp. one worked by a crank

wind′mill′ *n.* a mill operated by the wind's rotation of large vanes radiating from a shaft

win·dow (win′dō) *n.* ⟦< ON *vindr*, WIND[2] + *auga*, an eye⟧ 1 an opening in a building, vehicle, etc. for letting in light or air or for looking through, usually having a pane of glass in a movable frame 2 a windowpane 3 an opening resembling a window

WINDMILL

window box a long, narrow box on or outside a window ledge, for growing plants

window dressing 1 the display of goods in a store window 2 that which is meant to make something seem better than it really is —**win′dow-dress′** *vt.* —**window dresser**

win′dow·pane′ *n.* a pane of glass in a window

win′dow-shop′ *vi.* **-shopped′, -shop′ping** to look at goods in store windows without entering to buy

win′dow·sill′ *n.* the sill of a window

wind·pipe (wind′pīp′) *n.* TRACHEA

wind′row′ (-rō′) *n.* a row of hay, etc. raked together to dry

wind shear a sudden change in wind direction, esp., dangerous vertical wind shifts encountered by aircraft

wind′shield′ *n.* in automobiles, etc., a glass screen, in front, to protect from wind, etc.

wind′sock′ *n.* a long, cloth cone flown at an airfield to show wind direction Also called **wind sleeve**

Wind·sor (win′zər) port in SE Ontario, Canada: pop. 193,000

Wind·sor knot (win′zər) a double slipknot in a four-in-hand necktie

wind′storm′ *n.* a storm with a strong wind but little or no rain, hail, etc.

wind′surf′ing *n.* the sport of sailing a kind of surfboard with a sail attached to a pivoting mast

wind tunnel a tunnel-like chamber through which air is forced, for testing the effects of wind pressure on aircraft, motor vehicles, etc.

wind-up (wīnd′up′) *n.* 1 a conclusion; end 2 *Baseball* the swinging of the arm preparatory to pitching

wind·ward (wind′wərd) *n.* the direction from which the wind blows —*adv.* toward the wind —*adj.* 1 moving windward 2 on the side from which the wind blows

Windward Islands S group of islands in the West Indies, south of the Leeward Islands

wind·y (win′dē) *adj.* **-i·er, -i·est** 1 with much wind /a *windy* city/ 2 stormy, blustery, etc. 3 *a)* flimsy, intangible, etc. *b)* long-winded, pompous, etc. —**wind′i·ness** *n.*

wine (wīn) *n.* ⟦< L *vinum*⟧ 1 the fermented juice of grapes, used as an alcoholic beverage 2 the fermented juice of other fruits or plants —*vt.*, *vi.* **wined, win′ing** to provide with or drink wine: usually in the phrase **wine and dine**, to entertain lavishly

wine′-col′ored *adj.* having the color of red wine; dark purplish-red

win′er·y (-ər ē) *n.*, *pl.* **-ies** an establishment where wine is made

wing (wiŋ) *n.* ⟦ON *vaengr*⟧ 1 either of the paired organs of flight of a bird, bat, insect, etc. 2 something like a wing in use, position, etc., esp., *a)* a (or the) main lateral supporting surface of an airplane *b)* a subordinate, projecting part of a building *c)* either side of the stage out of sight of the audience 3 the section of an army, fleet, etc. to the right (or left) of the center 4 a section, as of a political party, with reference to its radicalism or conservatism 5 a unit in an air force —*vt.* 1 to provide with wings 2 *a)* to send swiftly as on wings *b)* to make (one's way) by flying *c)* to pass through or over, as by flying 3 to wound in the wing, arm, etc. —*vi.* to fly —**on the wing** (while) flying —**take wing** to fly away —**under one's wing** under one's protection, etc. —

wing it [Colloq.] to improvise in acting, speaking, etc. —**winged** (wiŋd; *poet.* wiŋ′id) *adj.* —**wing′less** *adj.*
wing′ding′ (-diŋ′) *n.* ⟦< ?⟧ [Slang] an event, party, etc. that is very festive, lively, etc.
wing′span′ *n.* the distance between the tips of an airplane's wings
wing′spread′ *n.* 1 the distance between the tips of fully spread wings 2 WINGSPAN
wink (wiŋk) *vi.* ⟦OE *wincian*⟧ 1 to close the eyelids and open them again quickly 2 to close and open one eyelid quickly, as a signal, etc. 3 to twinkle —*vt.* to make (an eye) wink —*n.* 1 a winking 2 an instant 3 a signal given by winking 4 a twinkle —**wink at** to pretend not to see
win·ner (win′ər) *n.* one that wins
win·ning (win′iŋ) *adj.* 1 victorious 2 attractive; charming —*n.* 1 a victory 2 [*pl.*] money that is won
Win·ni·peg (win′ə peg′) capital of Manitoba, Canada: pop. 564,000
win·now (win′ō) *vt., vi.* ⟦< OE *wind,* WIND²⟧ 1 to blow (the chaff) from (grain) 2 to scatter 3 to sift out
win·o (win′ō) *n., pl.* **-os** [Slang] an alcoholic who drinks cheap wine
win·some (win′səm) *adj.* ⟦OE *wynsum,* pleasant⟧ sweetly attractive; charming —**win′some·ly** *adv.*
Win·ston-Sa·lem (win′stən sā′ləm) city in N N.C.: pop. 132,000
win·ter (win′tər) *n.* ⟦OE⟧ 1 the coldest season of the year, following autumn 2 a period of decline, distress, etc. —*adj.* of, during, or for winter —*vi.* to pass the winter —*vt.* to keep, feed, etc. during winter
win′ter·green′ *n.* 1 an evergreen plant with white flowers and red berries 2 an aromatic oil (**oil of wintergreen**) made from its leaves and used as a flavoring 3 the flavor
win′ter·ize′ *vt.* **-ized′**, **-iz′ing** to put into condition for winter
win′ter·kill′ *vt., vi.* to kill or die by exposure to winter cold or excessive snow and ice —*n.* the process or an instance of winterkilling
win′ter·time′ *n.* the winter season
win·try (win′trē) *adj.* **-tri·er**, **-tri·est** of or like winter; cold, bleak, etc. /a *wintry* day/
win·y (win′ē) *adj.* **-i·er**, **-i·est** like wine in taste, smell, color, etc.
wipe (wīp) *vt.* **wiped**, **wip′ing** ⟦OE *wipian*⟧ 1 to clean or dry by rubbing with a cloth, etc. 2 to rub (a cloth, etc.) over something 3 to apply or remove by wiping —*n.* a wiping —**wipe out** 1 to remove; erase 2 to kill off 3 to destroy —**wip′er** *n.*
wire (wīr) *n.* ⟦OE *wir*⟧ 1 metal drawn into a long thread 2 a length of this 3 *a*) telegraph *b*) a telegram 4 the finish line of a horse race —*adj.* made of wire —*vt.* **wired**, **wir′ing** 1 to furnish, connect, bind, etc. with wire 2 to telegraph —*vi.* to telegraph
wired (wīrd) *adj.* [Slang] 1 provided with concealed electronic listening or recording equipment 2 extremely excited, nervous, etc.
wire′hair′ *n.* a fox terrier with a wiry coat Also called **wire-haired terrier**
wire′less (-lis) *adj.* without wire; specif., operating by electromagnetic waves, not with conducting wire —*n.* 1 wireless telegraphy or telephony 2 [Chiefly Brit.] RADIO
wire service an agency sending news by wire or electronic means to its subscribers, as newspapers
wire′tap′ *vi., vt.* **-tapped′**, **-tap′ping** to tap (a telephone wire, etc.) to get information secretly —*n.* 1 a wiretapping 2 a device for wiretapping
wir′ing *n.* a system of wires, as to provide a house with electricity
wir·y (wīr′ē) *adj.* **-i·er**, **-i·est** 1 of wire 2 like wire; stiff 3 lean and strong —**wir′i·ness** *n.*
Wis·con·sin (wis kän′sən) Middle Western State of the U.S.: 56,154 sq. mi.; pop. 4,705,000; cap. Madison: abbrev. **Wis.** —**Wis·con′sin·ite′** *n.*
wis·dom (wiz′dəm) *n.* ⟦OE: see WISE¹ & -DOM⟧ 1 the quality of being wise; good judgment 2 learning; knowledge
wisdom tooth the back tooth on each side of each jaw
wise¹ (wīz) *adj.* **wis′er**, **wis′est** ⟦OE *wis*⟧ 1 having or showing good judgment 2 informed /none the *wiser*/ 3 learned 4 shrewd; cunning 5 [Slang] conceited, impudent, fresh, etc. —**wise′ly** *adv.*
wise² (wīz) *n.* ⟦OE⟧ way; manner
-wise (wīz) ⟦< prec.⟧ *suffix* 1 in a (specified) direction, position, or manner /*lengthwise*/ 2 in a manner characteristic of /*clockwise*/ 3 with regard to /*budgetwise*/
wise·a·cre (wīz′ā′kər) *n.* ⟦ult. < OHG *wizzago,* prophet⟧ one who makes annoyingly conceited claims to knowledge
wise′crack′ *n.* [Slang] a flippant or facetious remark —*vi.* [Slang] to make wisecracks
wish (wish) *vt.* ⟦OE *wyscan*⟧ 1 to have a longing for; want 2 to express a desire concerning /I *wish* you well/ 3 to request /I *wish* you to go/ —*vi.* 1 to long; yearn 2 to make a wish —*n.* 1 a wishing 2 something wished for /to get one's *wish*/ 3 a polite request, almost an order 4 [*pl.*] expressed desire for a person's health, etc. /best *wishes*/ —**wish′er** *n.*
wish′bone′ *n.* the forked bone in front of a bird's breastbone
wish′ful (-fəl) *adj.* having or showing a wish; desirous —**wish′ful·ly** *adv.*
wish·y-wash·y (wish′ē wôsh′ē) *adj.* [Colloq.] 1 watery; thin 2 *a*) weak; feeble *b*) vacillating; indecisive
wisp (wisp) *n.* ⟦prob. < Scand⟧ 1 a small bundle, as of straw 2 a thin or filmy piece, strand, etc. /a *wisp* of smoke/ 3 something delicate, frail, etc. —**wisp′y**, **-i·er**, **-i·est**, *adj.*
wis·te·ri·a (wis tir′ē ə) *n.* ⟦after C. *Wistar* (1761-1818), U.S. anatomist⟧ a twining vine with showy clusters of flowers Also **wis·tar′i·a** (-ter′-)
wist·ful (wist′fəl) *adj.* ⟦< earlier *wistly,* attentive⟧ showing or expressing vague yearnings —**wist′ful·ly** *adv.* —**wist′ful·ness** *n.*
wit¹ (wit) *n.* ⟦OE⟧ 1 [*pl.*] powers of thinking; mental faculties 2 good sense 3 *a*) the ability to make clever remarks in a sharp,

amusing way *b)* one characterized by wit

wit[2] (wit) ***vt., vi.* wist** (wist), **wit′ting** ⟦OE *witan*⟧ [Archaic] to know or learn —**to wit** that is to say; namely

witch (wich) ***n.*** ⟦OE *wicce*⟧ **1** a woman supposedly having supernatural power by a compact with evil spirits **2** an ugly, old shrew **3** [Colloq.] a fascinating woman or girl

witch′craft′ ***n.*** the power or practices of witches

witch doctor a person who practices medicine involving the use of magic, as among primitive societies

witch′er·y (-ər ē) ***n., pl.* -ies** **1** witchcraft; sorcery **2** bewitching charm

witch hazel ⟦< OE *wice*⟧ **1** a shrub with yellow flowers **2** a lotion made from its leaves and bark

witch hunt ⟦so named in allusion to persecutions of persons alleged to be witches⟧ an investigation carried out ostensibly to uncover disloyalty, etc., usually highly publicized and often relying upon little evidence

with (with, with) ***prep.*** ⟦OE⟧ **1** in opposition to /to argue *with* a friend/ **2** *a)* alongside of; near to *b)* in the company of *c)* into; among /mix blue *with* yellow/ **3** as a member of /to play *with* a string quartet/ **4** concerning /happy *with* his lot/ **5** compared to **6** as well as /she rides *with* the best/ **7** in the opinion of /it's OK *with* me/ **8** as a result of /faint *with* hunger/ **9** by means of **10** having received /*with* your consent, I'll go/ **11** having as a possession, attribute, etc. **12** in the keeping, care, etc. of /leave it *with* me/ **13** in spite of **14** at the same time as **15** in proportion to /wages that vary *with* skill/ **16** to; onto /join one end *with* the other/ **17** from /to part *with* one's gains/ —**with that** after, or as a consequence of, that

with- *combining form* **1** away, back /*withdraw*/ **2** against, from /*withhold*/

with·al (with ôl′, with-) ***adv.*** **1** besides **2** despite that

with·draw′ (-drô′) ***vt.* -drew′, -drawn′, -draw′ing** **1** to take back; remove **2** to retract or recall (a statement, etc.) —***vi.*** **1** to move back; go away; retreat **2** to remove oneself (*from* an organization, activity, etc.)

with·draw′al (-əl) ***n.*** **1** the act of withdrawing **2** the process of giving up a narcotic drug, typically accompanied by distressing physical and mental effects (**withdrawal symptoms**)

with·drawn′ ***vt., vi. pp. of*** WITHDRAW —***adj.*** shy, reserved, etc.

withe (with, with) ***n.*** ⟦< OE *withthe*⟧ a tough, flexible twig of willow, osier, etc., used for binding things —***vt.* withed, with′ing** to bind with withes

with·er (with′ər) ***vi.*** ⟦< ME *wederen*, to weather⟧ **1** to dry up; wilt, as plants **2** to become wasted or decayed **3** to weaken; languish —***vt.*** **1** to cause to wither **2** to cause to feel abashed

with·ers (with′ərz) ***n.pl.*** ⟦< OE *wither*, against⟧ the part of a horse's back between the shoulder blades

with·hold (with hōld′, with-) ***vt.* -held′, -hold′ing** **1** *a)* to hold back; restrain *b)* to deduct (taxes, etc.) from wages **2** to refrain from granting

withholding tax the amount of estimated income tax withheld by an employer from an employee's pay, for direct payment to the government

with·in (with in′, with-) ***adv.*** ⟦OE *withinnan*⟧ **1** on or into the inside **2** indoors **3** inside the body, mind, etc. —***prep.*** **1** in the inner part of **2** not beyond **3** inside the limits of —***n.*** the inside /from *within*/

with′-it (-it) ***adj.*** [Slang] **1** sophisticated, up-to-date, etc. **2** fashionable; stylish

with·out′ ***adv.*** ⟦OE *withutan*⟧ **1** on the outside **2** out-of-doors —***prep.*** **1** [Now Rare] at, on, or to the outside of **2** lacking **3** free from **4** with avoidance of /to pass by *without* speaking/

with·stand′ (-stand′) ***vt., vi.* -stood′, -stand′ing** to oppose, resist, or endure, esp. successfully

wit·less (wit′lis) ***adj.*** lacking wit; foolish —**wit′less·ly** ***adv.***

wit·ness (wit′nis) ***n.*** ⟦< OE *witan*, know⟧ **1** evidence; testimony **2** one who saw, or can give a firsthand account of, something **3** one who testifies in court **4** one who observes, and attests to, a signing, etc. —***vt.*** **1** to testify to **2** to serve as evidence of **3** to act as witness of **4** to be present at —**bear witness** to testify

wit·ti·cism (wit′ə siz′əm) ***n.*** ⟦< WITTY⟧ a witty remark

wit·ting (wit′iŋ) ***adj.*** ⟦ME *wytting*⟧ intentional —**wit′ting·ly** ***adv.***

wit·ty (wit′ē) ***adj.* -ti·er, -ti·est** ⟦OE *wittig*⟧ having or showing wit; cleverly amusing —**wit′ti·ly** ***adv.*** —**wit′ti·ness** ***n.***

wive (wīv) ***vi., vt.* wived, wiv′ing** ⟦OE *wifian*⟧ [Archaic] to marry (a woman)

wives (wīvz) ***n. pl. of*** WIFE

wiz·ard (wiz′ərd) ***n.*** ⟦ME *wisard*⟧ **1** a magician; sorcerer **2** [Colloq.] one very skilled at a specified activity

wiz′ard·ry ***n.*** magic; sorcery

wiz·ened (wiz′ənd) ***adj.*** ⟦< OE *wisnian*, wither⟧ dried up; withered

wk. **1** week **2** work

wkly. weekly

wob·ble (wä′bəl) ***vi.* -bled, -bling** ⟦prob. < LowG *wabbeln*⟧ **1** to move unsteadily from side to side **2** to shake **3** to vacillate —***vt.*** to cause to wobble —***n.*** wobbling motion —**wob′bly, -bli·er, -bli·est,** ***adj.*** —**wob′bli·ness** ***n.***

woe (wō) ***n.*** ⟦OE *wa*⟧ **1** great sorrow; grief **2** trouble —***interj.*** alas!

woe′be·gone′ (-bē gôn′, -bi-) ***adj.*** of woeful appearance; looking sad or wretched

woe′ful (-fəl) ***adj.*** **1** full of woe; sad **2** of, causing, or involving woe **3** pitiful; wretched —**woe′ful·ly** ***adv.***

wok (wäk, wôk) ***n.*** ⟦Chin⟧ a bowl-shaped cooking pan used, as in a ringlike stand, for frying, steaming, etc.

woke (wōk) ***vi., vt. alt. pt. of*** WAKE[1]

wok·en (wō′kən) ***vi., vt. alt. pp. of*** WAKE[1]

wolf (woolf) ***n., pl.* wolves** (woolvz) ⟦OE *wulf*⟧ **1** a wild, flesh-eating, doglike mammal of the Northern Hemisphere **2** *a)* a cruel or greedy person *b)* [Slang] a man who flirts with many women —***vt.*** to eat greedily —**cry wolf** to give a false alarm —**wolf'ish** *adj.*

wolf'hound' (-hound') *n.* a breed of large dog, once used for hunting wolves

wol·ver·ine (wool'vər ēn') *n.* [[< WOLF]] a stocky, flesh-eating mammal of N North America and N Eurasia

wolves (woolvz) *n. pl. of* WOLF

wom·an (woom'ən) *n., pl.* **wom·en** (wim'·ən) [[< OE *wif,* a female + *mann,* human being]] **1** *a)* an adult female human being *b)* women collectively **2** a female servant **3** womanly qualities

-wom·an (woom'ən) *combining form* woman of a (specified) kind, in a (specified) activity, etc.: sometimes used to avoid the masculine implications of -MAN

wom'an·hood' *n.* **1** the state of being a woman **2** womanly qualities **3** women collectively

wom'an·ish *adj.* like a woman

wom'an·ize' *vt.* **-ized', -iz'ing** to make effeminate —*vi.* [Colloq.] to be sexually promiscuous with women —**wom'an·iz'er** *n.*

wom'an·kind' *n.* women in general

wom'an·like' *adj.* womanly

wom'an·ly *adj.* **1** womanish **2** characteristic of or fit for a woman

womb (wōōm) *n.* [[OE *wamb*]] UTERUS

wom·bat (wäm'bat') *n.* [[< native name]] a burrowing Australian marsupial resembling a small bear

wom·en (wim'in) *n. pl. of* WOMAN

wom'en·folk' *n.pl.* [Colloq. or Dial.] womankind Also **wom'en·folks'**

won (wun) *vi., vt. pt. & pp. of* WIN

won·der (wun'dər) *n.* [[OE *wundor*]] **1** a person, thing, or event causing astonishment and admiration; marvel **2** the feeling aroused by something strange, unexpected, etc. —*vi.* **1** to be filled with wonder; marvel **2** to have curiosity, sometimes mingled with doubt —*vt.* to have curiosity or doubt about /he *wondered* what happened/

won'der·ful *adj.* **1** that causes wonder; marvelous **2** [Colloq.] excellent, fine, etc. —**won'der·ful·ly** *adv.*

won'der·land' *n.* an imaginary land full of wonders, or a real place like this

won'der·ment *n.* amazement

won·drous (wun'drəs) *adj.* wonderful —*adv.* surprisingly Now only literary —**won'drous·ly** *adv.*

wont (wänt, wōnt) *adj.* [[< OE *wunian,* dwell]] accustomed /he was *wont* to rise early/ —*n.* usual practice; habit

won't (wōnt) will not

wont·ed (wänt'id, wōnt'-) *adj.* customary; accustomed

won ton (wän' tän') a Chinese dish of noodle casings filled with meat, etc., often served in a broth (**won-ton soup**)

woo (wōō) *vt.* [[OE *wogian*]] **1** to seek the love of, usually in order to propose marriage **2** to seek /to *woo* fame/ —*vi.* to woo a person —**woo'er** *n.*

wood (wood) *n.* [[OE *wudu*]] **1** [*usually pl.*] a thick growth of trees; forest **2** the hard, fibrous substance beneath the bark of trees and shrubs **3** lumber or timber **4** *Golf* any of certain clubs, originally with wooden heads —*adj.* **1** made of wood; wooden **2** growing or living in woods —**out of the woods** [Colloq.] out of difficulty, danger, etc. —**wood'ed** *adj.*

wood alcohol METHANOL

wood'bine' (-bīn') *n.* [[< OE *wudu,* wood + *binde,* to bind]] **1** a climbing honeysuckle **2** a climbing vine with dark-blue berries

wood'carv'ing (-kär'viŋ) *n.* **1** the art of carving wood by hand **2** an object so made —**wood'carv'er** *n.*

wood'chuck' (-chuk') *n.* [[< AmInd name]] a burrowing and hibernating marmot of North America

WOODCHUCK

wood'cock' (-käk') *n.* a small game bird with short legs and a long bill

wood'craft' *n.* **1** matters relating to the woods, as camping, hunting, etc. **2** WOODWORKING

wood'cut' (-kut') *n.* **1** a wooden block engraved with a design, etc. **2** a print from this

wood'cut'ter *n.* one who fells trees, cuts wood, etc. —**wood'cut'ting** *n.*

wood'en (-'n) *adj.* **1** made of wood **2** stiff, lifeless, etc. **3** dull; insensitive —**wood'en·ly** *adv.*

wood'land' (-lənd, -land') *n.* land covered with woods —*adj.* of the woods

wood'man (-mən) *n., pl.* **-men** WOODSMAN

wood'peck'er (-pek'ər) *n.* a climbing bird with a strong, pointed bill used to peck holes in bark to get insects

wood'pile' *n.* a pile of wood, esp. of firewood

wood screw a screw with a sharp point, for use in wood

wood'shed' *n.* a shed for firewood

woods·man (woodz'mən) *n., pl.* **-men** **1** one who lives or works in the woods **2** one skilled in woodcraft

wood'sy (-zē) *adj.* **-si·er, -si·est** of or like the woods —**wood'si·ness** *n.*

wood·wind (wood'wind') *n.* any of a family of wind instruments made, esp. orig., of wood: flute, clarinet, oboe, English horn, and bassoon —*adj.* composed of or for such an instrument

wood'work' *n.* **1** work done in wood **2** things made of wood, esp. the moldings, doors, etc. of a house

wood'work'ing *n.* the art or work of making things of wood

wood'y *adj.* **-i·er, -i·est** **1** covered with trees **2** consisting of or forming wood **3** like wood —**wood'i·ness** *n.*

woof (wōōf) *n.* [[ult. < OE *wefan,* to weave]] WEFT

woof·er (woof'ər) *n.* a large, high-fidelity speaker for reproducing low-frequency sounds

wool (wool) *n.* [[OE *wull*]] **1** the soft, curly hair of sheep or of some other animals, as the goat **2** woolen yarn, cloth, clothing, etc. **3** anything that looks or feels like wool

wool'en (-ən) *adj.* **1** made of wool **2** relating to wool or woolen cloth —*n.* [*pl.*] woolen goods Also, chiefly Brit., **wool'len**

Woolf (woolf), **Vir·gin·ia** (vər jin′yə) 1882-1941; Eng. novelist & critic
wool′gath′er·ing (-gath′ər iŋ) ***n.*** absent-mindedness or daydreaming
wool·ly (wool′ē) ***adj.*** **-li·er, -li·est** 1 of or like wool 2 bearing or covered with wool 3 rough and uncivilized: used chiefly in **wild and woolly** 4 confused /*woolly* ideas/ Also sp. **wool′y**
wooz·y (wōō′zē, wooz′ē) ***adj.*** **-i·er, -i·est** [Colloq.] dizzy or befuddled, as from drink —**wooz′i·ness** ***n.***
Worces·ter (woos′tər) city in central Mass.: pop. 162,000
word (wurd) ***n.*** ⟦OE⟧ 1 *a)* a speech sound, or series of them, having meaning as a unit of language *b)* the written or printed representation of this 2 a brief remark /a *word* of advice/ 3 a promise /he gave his *word*/ 4 news; information 5 *a)* a password or signal *b)* a command, order, etc. 6 [*usually pl.*] *a)* talk; speech *b)* lyrics; text 7 [*pl.*] a quarrel; dispute —***vt.*** to express in words; phrase —**in a word** briefly —**in so many words** exactly and plainly —**the Word** the Bible —**word for word** in precisely the same words
word′age (-ij) ***n.*** quantity of words
word′ing ***n.*** choice of words; diction
word of honor solemn promise
word′-of-mouth′ ***adj.*** communicated orally
word processor a computerized device consisting of an electronic typewriter, video screen, printer, etc., used to generate, edit, store, or duplicate documents, as letters, etc. for a business —**word processing**
Words·worth (wurdz′wərth), **William** 1770-1850; Eng. poet
word·y (wur′dē) ***adj.*** **-i·er, -i·est** containing or using many or too many words; verbose —**word′i·ness** ***n.***
wore (wôr) ***vt., vi.*** *pt. of* WEAR
work (wurk) ***n.*** ⟦OE *weorc*⟧ 1 effort exerted to do or make something; labor; toil 2 employment; occupation 3 something one is making or doing; task 4 something made or done; specif., *a)* an act; deed (*usually used in pl.*) /good *works*/ *b)* [*pl.*] collected writings *c)* [*pl.*] engineering structures, as bridges, etc. 5 [*pl., with sing. v.*] a place where work is done, as a factory 6 workmanship —***adj.*** of, for, or used in work —***vi.*** **worked** or **wrought, work′ing** 1 to do work; labor; toil 2 to be employed 3 to function or operate, esp. effectively 4 to ferment 5 to move, proceed, etc. slowly and with difficulty 6 to come or become, as by repeated movement /the door *worked* loose/ —***vt.*** 1 to cause; bring about /his idea *worked* wonders/ 2 to mold; shape 3 to sew, embroider, etc. 4 to solve (a mathematical problem, etc.) 5 to manipulate; knead 6 to bring into a specified condition /to *work* a nail loose/ 7 to cultivate (soil) 8 to operate; use 9 to cause to work /to *work* a crew hard/ 10 to make (one's way, etc.) by effort 11 to provoke; rouse /to *work* oneself into a rage/ —**at work** working —**out of work** unemployed —**the works** 1 the working parts (*of* a watch, etc.) 2 [Colloq.] everything: also **the whole works** —**work off** to get rid of —**work on** (or **upon**) 1 to influence 2 to try to persuade —**work out** 1 to accomplish 2 to solve 3 to calculate 4 to result 5 to develop 6 to have a workout —**work up** 1 to advance 2 to develop 3 to excite
work′a·ble ***adj.*** 1 that can be worked 2 practicable; feasible
work·a·day (wurk′ə dā′) ***adj.*** 1 of workdays; everyday 2 ordinary
work·a·hol·ic (wurk′ə hôl′ik) ***n.*** ⟦WORK + -AHOLIC⟧ a person having a compulsive need to work
work′bench′ (-bench′) ***n.*** a table at which work is done, as by a carpenter
work′book′ ***n.*** a book of questions, exercises, etc. for use by students
work′day′ ***n.*** 1 a day on which work is done 2 the part of a day during which work is done
work·er (wurk′ər) ***n.*** 1 one who works for a living 2 one who works for a cause, etc. 3 a sterile ant, bee, etc. that does work for the colony
work′fare′ ***n.*** ⟦WORK + (WEL)FARE⟧ a government program requiring employable recipients of welfare to register for work, training, etc.
work′horse′ ***n.*** 1 a horse used for working 2 a steady, responsible worker
work′house′ ***n.*** a prison where petty offenders are confined and made to work
work′ing ***adj.*** 1 that works 2 of, for, or used in work 3 sufficient to get work done /a *working* majority/ —***n.*** the act of one that works
work′ing·man′ ***n.***, *pl.* **-men′** a worker, esp. an industrial worker
work′load′ ***n.*** the amount of work assigned for completion within a given time period
work′man (-mən) ***n.***, *pl.* **-men** 1 WORKINGMAN 2 a craftsman
work′man·like′ ***adj.*** skillful Also **work′man·ly**
work′man·ship′ ***n.*** skill of a workman or the quality of the work done
work′out′ ***n.*** a session of physical exercises or any strenuous work
work′place′ ***n.*** the office, factory, etc. where one works
work sheet a paper sheet used for work records, working notes, etc., or with problems, etc. to be worked on
work′shop′ ***n.*** 1 a room or building where work is done 2 a seminar for specified intensive study, work, etc.
work′sta′tion ***n.*** a person's work area, including furniture, etc. and often, a microcomputer
work′-up′ ***n.*** a complete medical study of a patient, including tests
work′week′ ***n.*** the total number of hours or days worked in a week
world (wurld) ***n.*** ⟦OE *werold*⟧ 1 *a)* the earth *b)* the universe 2 *a)* mankind *b)* people generally; the public 3 *a)* [*also* **W-**] some part of the earth /the Old *World*/ *b)* any sphere or domain /the animal *world*/ 4 individual experience, outlook, etc. /her *world* is narrow/ 5 secular life and interests, or people concerned with these 6 [*often pl.*] a large amount /a *world* of good/ —**for all the world** exactly

world'-class' *adj.* of the highest class, as in international competition

world'ly *adj.* **-li·er, -li·est** 1 of this world; secular 2 devoted to the affairs, pleasures, etc. of this world 3 worldly-wise —**world'·li·ness** *n.*

world'ly-wise' *adj.* wise in the ways or affairs of the world; sophisticated

world'-shak'ing *adj.* of great significance, effect, or influence; momentous

world'view *n.* a comprehensive, esp. personal, philosophy of the world and of human life

World War I the war (1914-18) involving Great Britain, France, Russia, the U.S., etc. on one side and Germany, Austria-Hungary, etc. on the other

World War II the war (1939-45) involving Great Britain, France, the Soviet Union, the U.S., etc. on one side and Germany, Italy, Japan, etc. on the other

world'-wea'ry *adj.* weary of the world; bored with living

world'wide' *adj.* extending throughout the world

worm (wurm) *n.* ⟦< OE *wyrm,* serpent⟧ 1 a long, slender, soft-bodied animal 2 an abject or contemptible person 3 something wormlike or spiral in shape, etc., as the thread of a screw 4 [*pl.*] any disease caused by parasitic worms in the intestines, etc. —*vi.* to proceed like a worm, in a winding or devious manner —*vt.* 1 to bring about, make, etc. in a winding or devious manner 2 to purge of intestinal worms —**worm'y, -i·er, -i·est,** *adj.*

worm gear a gear consisting of a rotating screw meshed with a toothed wheel

WORM GEAR

worm'wood' (-wood') *n.* ⟦< OE *wermod*⟧ a strong-smelling plant that yields a bitter-tasting oil formerly used in making absinthe

worn (wôrn) *vt., vi. pp. of* WEAR —*adj.* 1 damaged by use or wear 2 exhausted

worn'-out' *adj.* 1 used until no longer effective, usable, etc. 2 exhausted; tired out

wor·ri·ment (wur'i mənt) *n.* 1 worry; anxiety 2 a cause of worry

wor'ri·some (-səm) *adj.* causing worry or tending to worry

wor·ry (wur'ē) *vt.* **-ried, -ry·ing** ⟦< OE *wyrgan,* to strangle⟧ 1 to bite and shake with the teeth /a dog *worrying* a bone/ 2 to annoy, bother, etc. 3 to make troubled or uneasy —*vi.* 1 to bite or tear (*at* an object) 2 to be anxious, troubled, etc. —*n., pl.* **-ries** 1 a troubled state of mind; anxiety 2 a cause of this —**wor'ri·er** *n.*

wor'ry·wart' (-wôrt') *n.* ⟦prec. + WART⟧ [Colloq.] one who tends to worry much

worse (wurs) *adj.* ⟦OE *wiersa*⟧ 1 *compar. of* BAD[1] & ILL 2 *a)* bad, evil, harmful, etc. in a greater degree *b)* of inferior quality 3 in poorer health; more ill 4 in a less satisfactory condition —*adv.* 1 *compar. of* BADLY & ILL 2 in a worse manner 3 to a worse extent —*n.* that which is worse —**worse off** in worse circumstances

wor·sen (wur'sən) *vt., vi.* to make or become worse

wor·ship (wur'ship) *n.* ⟦< OE *weorthscipe*⟧ 1 a service or rite showing reverence for a deity 2 intense love or admiration 3 [W-] [Chiefly Brit., etc.] a title of honor: used in addressing magistrates, etc. —*vt.* **-shiped** or **-shipped, -ship·ing** or **-ship·ping** 1 to show religious reverence for 2 to have intense love or admiration for —*vi.* to engage in worship —**wor'ship·er** or **wor'ship·per** *n.*

wor'ship·ful (-fəl) *adj.* 1 [Chiefly Brit.] honorable; respected 2 worshiping

worst (wurst) *adj.* ⟦OE *wyrsta*⟧ 1 *superl. of* BAD[1] & ILL 2 *a)* bad, evil, harmful, etc. in the highest degree *b)* of the lowest quality 3 in the least satisfactory condition —*adv.* 1 *superl. of* BADLY & ILL 2 in the worst manner 3 to the worst extent —*n.* that which is worst —*vt.* to defeat —**at worst** under the worst circumstances —**if (the) worst comes to (the) worst** if the worst possible thing happens —**(in) the worst way** [Slang] very much; greatly —**make the worst of** to be pessimistic about

wor·sted (woos'tid, wur'stid) *n.* ⟦after *Worstead,* England⟧ 1 a smooth, hard-twisted wool thread or yarn 2 fabric made from this

wort (wurt) *n.* ⟦OE *wyrt-*⟧ a liquid produced from malt which, after fermenting, becomes beer, ale, etc.

worth (wurth) *n.* ⟦OE *weorth*⟧ 1 material value, esp. as expressed in terms of money 2 importance, value, merit, etc. 3 the quantity to be had for a given sum /a dollar's *worth*/ —*adj.* 1 deserving or worthy of 2 equal in value to 3 having wealth amounting to

worth'less *adj.* without worth or merit; useless —**worth'less·ness** *n.*

worth'while' *adj.* worth the time or effort spent; of true value

wor·thy (wur'thē) *adj.* **-thi·er, -thi·est** 1 having worth, value, or merit 2 meriting —*n., pl.* **-thies** a person of outstanding worth, etc. —**wor'thi·ly** *adv.* —**wor'thi·ness** *n.*

would (wood) *v.aux.* ⟦OE *wolde*⟧ 1 *pt. of* WILL[2] 2 used to express a supposition or condition /he *would* write if he knew you *would* answer/ 3 used to make a polite request /*would* you please open the window?/ —*vt.* [Old Poet.] I wish /*would* that she were here/ See usage note at WILL[2]

would'-be' *adj.* 1 wishing or pretending to be 2 intended to be

wound[1] (wōōnd) *n.* ⟦OE *wund*⟧ 1 an injury in which tissue is cut, torn, etc. 2 any hurt to the feelings, honor, etc. —*vt., vi.* to inflict a wound (on or upon); hurt; injure

wound[2] (wound) *vt., vi. pt. & pp. of* WIND[1]

wove (wōv) *vt., vi. pt. & alt. pp. of* WEAVE

wo·ven (wō'vən) *vt., vi. alt. pp. of* WEAVE

wow (wou) *interj.* an exclamation of surprise, pleasure, etc. —*vt.* [Slang] to arouse enthusiasm in

wpm words per minute

wrack (rak) *n.* ⟦< MDu *wrak,* a wreck⟧ *alt. sp. of* RACK[2]

wraith (rāth) *n.* ⟦Scot⟧ a ghost

wran·gle (raŋ′gəl) *vi.* **-gled, -gling** ⟦< OE *wringan,* to press⟧ to argue; quarrel, esp. angrily and noisily —*n.* an angry, noisy dispute —**wran′gler** *n.*

wran′gler (-glər) *n.* ⟦< AmSp *caballerango,* a groom⟧ a cowboy who herds livestock, esp. saddle horses —**wran′gle, -gled, -gling,** *vt.*

wrap (rap) *vt.* **wrapped** or **wrapt, wrap′·ping** ⟦ME *wrappen*⟧ **1** to wind or fold (a covering) around something **2** to enclose and fasten in paper, etc. —*vi.* to twine, coil, etc.: usually with *over, around,* etc. —*n.* **1** an outer covering or garment **2** [*pl.*] secrecy; censorship —**wrapped up in** absorbed in —**wrap up** [Colloq.] to conclude; settle

wrap′per *n.* **1** one that wraps **2** that in which something is wrapped **3** a woman's dressing gown

wrap′ping *n.* [*often pl.*] the material in which something is wrapped

wrapt (rapt) *vt., vi. alt. pt. & pp. of* WRAP

wrap′-up′ *n.* [Colloq.] a concluding, summarizing statement, report, etc.

wrath (rath) *n.* ⟦OE, angry⟧ **1** intense anger; rage; fury **2** any action of vengeance —**wrath′ful** *adj.*

wreak (rēk) *vt.* ⟦OE *wrecan,* to revenge⟧ **1** to give vent to (one's anger, etc.) **2** to inflict (vengeance, etc.)

wreath (rēth) *n., pl.* **wreaths** (rēthz) ⟦OE *writha*⟧ **1** a twisted ring of leaves, flowers, etc. **2** something like this in shape /*wreaths* of smoke/

wreathe (rēth) *vt.* **wreathed, wreath′ing** **1** to form into a wreath **2** to coil or twist around; encircle **3** to decorate with wreaths

wreck (rek) *n.* ⟦< ON *vrek,* driftwood⟧ **1** a shipwreck **2** the remains of something destroyed **3** a run-down person **4** a wrecking or being wrecked —*vt.* **1** to destroy or damage badly; ruin **2** to tear down (a building, etc.) **3** to overthrow; thwart

wreck′age (-ij) *n.* **1** a wrecking or being wrecked **2** the remains of something wrecked

wreck′er *n.* **1** one who wrecks **2** one that salvages or removes wrecks

wren (ren) *n.* ⟦OE *wrenna*⟧ a small songbird with a stubby, erect tail

wrench (rench) *n.* ⟦OE *wrenc,* a trick⟧ **1** a sudden, sharp twist or pull **2** an injury caused by a twist, as to the back **3** a sudden feeling of grief, etc. **4** a tool for turning nuts, bolts, pipes, etc. —*vt.* **1** to twist or jerk violently **2** to injure with a twist **3** to distort (a meaning, etc.)

wrest (rest) *vt.* ⟦OE *wræstan*⟧ **1** to pull or force away violently with a twisting motion **2** to take by force; usurp —*n.* a wresting; a twist

wres·tle (res′əl; *often* ras′-) *vi., vt.* **-tled, -tling** ⟦see prec.⟧ **1** to struggle hand to hand with (an opponent) in an attempt to throw him **2** to contend (with) —*n.* a wrestling —**wres′tler** *n.*

wres′tling *n.* a sport in which the opponents wrestle, or struggle hand to hand

wretch (rech) *n.* ⟦OE *wrecca,* an outcast⟧ **1** a miserable or unhappy person **2** a person despised or scorned

wretch′ed (-id) *adj.* **1** very unhappy; miserable **2** distressing; dismal **3** poor in quality **4** contemptible; despicable —**wretch′·ed·ly** *adv.* —**wretch′ed·ness** *n.*

wrig·gle (rig′əl) *vi.* **-gled, -gling** ⟦Medieval Low G *wriggeln*⟧ **1** to twist and turn; squirm **2** to move along with a twisting motion **3** to make one's way by shifty means —*n.* a wriggling —**wrig′gler** *n.* —**wrig′gly, -gli·er, -gli·est,** *adj.*

wright (rīt) *n.* ⟦< OE *wyrcan,* to work⟧ one who makes or constructs

wring (riŋ) *vt.* **wrung, wring′ing** ⟦OE *wringan*⟧ **1** *a*) to squeeze, press, or twist *b*) to force out (water, etc.) by this means (usually with *out*) **2** to clasp and twist (the hands) in distress **3** to clasp (another's hand) in greeting **4** to extract by force, threats, etc. —*n.* a wringing

wring′er *n.* a machine with rollers to squeeze water from wet clothes

wrin·kle[1] (riŋ′kəl) *n.* ⟦ME *wrinkel*⟧ **1** a small furrow in a normally smooth surface **2** a crease in the skin —*vt., vi.* **-kled, -kling** to form wrinkles (in); pucker; crease —**wrin′kly, -kli·er, -kli·est,** *adj.*

wrin·kle[2] (riŋ′kəl) *n.* ⟦< OE *wrenc,* a trick⟧ [Colloq.] a clever trick, idea, or device

wrist (rist) *n.* ⟦OE⟧ the joint between the hand and forearm —**a slap** (or **tap**) **on the wrist** a token punishment

wrist′band′ *n.* a band that goes around the wrist, as on a cuff

wrist′watch′ *n.* a watch worn on a strap or band around the wrist

writ (rit) *n.* ⟦OE < *writan,* write⟧ a formal legal document ordering or prohibiting some action

write (rīt) *vt.* **wrote, writ′ten, writ′ing** ⟦OE *writan*⟧ **1** to form (words, letters, etc.) on a surface, as with a pen **2** to compose (literary or musical material) **3** to communicate (with) in writing /she *wrote* (me) that she was ill/ **4** to record (information) in a computer —*vi.* to write words, books, a letter, etc. —**write off** **1** to remove from accounts (bad debts, etc.) **2** to drop from consideration **3** to amortize —**write out** **1** to put into writing **2** to write in full —**write up** to write an account of

write′-in′ *n.* a candidate whose name is not on the ballot, but is written in by a voter

write′-off′ *n.* something written off, amortized, etc.

writ′er *n.* one who writes, esp. as an occupation; author

write′-up′ *n.* [Colloq.] a written report, specif. a favorable one

writhe (rīth) *vt.* **writhed, writh′ing** ⟦OE *writhan,* to twist⟧ to cause to twist or turn; contort —*vi.* **1** to twist or turn; squirm **2** to suffer great emotional distress —*n.* a writhing

writ·ing (rīt′iŋ) *n.* **1** the act of one who writes **2** something written **3** written form **4** *short for* HANDWRITING

writ·ten (rit′'n) *vt., vi. pp. of* WRITE

wrong (rôŋ) *adj.* ⟦< ON *rangr,* twisted⟧ **1** not in accordance with justice, law, morality, an established standard, etc. **2** not suitable or appropriate **3** *a*) contrary to fact, etc.; incorrect *b*) mistaken **4** not functioning properly **5** not meant to be seen /the *wrong* side of a fabric/ **—*adv.*** in a wrong manner, direction, etc. **—*n.*** something wrong; esp., an unjust, immoral, or illegal act **—*vt.*** to treat badly or unjustly **—in the wrong** not on the side supported by truth, justice, etc. **—wrong'ly *adv.* —wrong'ness *n.***

wrong'do'ing *n.* any wrong act or behavior **—wrong'do'er *n.***

wrong'ful *adj.* **1** unjust, unfair, or injurious **2** unlawful **—wrong'ful·ly *adv.* —wrong'ful·ness *n.***

wrong'head'ed *adj.* stubborn or perverse **—wrong'head'ed·ly *adv.* —wrong'head'ed·ness *n.***

wrote (rōt) ***vt., vi.*** *pt. of* WRITE

wroth (rôth) ***adj.*** ⟦OE *wrath*⟧ angry; wrathful; incensed

wrought (rôt) ***vi., vt.*** *alt. pt. & pp. of* WORK **—*adj.*** **1** formed; made **2** shaped by hammering, etc.: said of metals

wrought iron tough, ductile iron containing very little carbon **—wrought'-i'ron *adj.***

wrought'-up' *adj.* very disturbed or excited

wrung (ruŋ) ***vt., vi.*** *pt. & pp. of* WRING

wry (rī) ***adj.*** **wri'er** or **wry'er, wri'est** or **wry'est** ⟦< OE *wrigian,* to turn⟧ **1** twisted; distorted **2** distorted in a grimace /a *wry* face/ **3** perverse, ironic, etc. /*wry* humor/ **—wry'ly *adv.* —wry'ness *n.***

wt. weight

Wu·han (wo͞o'hän') city in east central China: pop. 3,200,000

WV or **W.V.** West Virginia: also **W.Va.**

WWI World War I

WWII World War II

WY or **Wyo.** Wyoming

Wy·o·ming (wī ō'miŋ) Mountain State of the W U.S.: 97,914 sq. mi.; pop. 471,000; cap. Cheyenne **—Wy·o'ming·ite' *n.***

X

x or **X** (eks) ***n., pl.*** **x's, X's** the 24th letter of the English alphabet

X (eks) ***n.*** **1** the Roman numeral 10 **2** a film rating meaning that no one under seventeen is to be admitted

x (eks) *Math. symbol for* **1** an unknown quantity **2** times (in multiplication)

X chromosome *see* SEX CHROMOSOME

xe·non (zē'nän') ***n.*** a colorless, gaseous chemical element: symbol, **Xe**

xen'o·pho'bi·a (zen'ō-, zē'nə-) ***n.*** ⟦< Gr *xenos,* foreign + -PHOBIA⟧ fear or hatred of strangers or foreigners **—xen'o·phobe'** (-fōb') ***n.*** **—xen'o·pho'bic** (-fō'bik) ***adj.***

xe·rog·ra·phy (zir äg'rə fē) ***n.*** ⟦< Gr *xēros,* dry + -GRAPHY⟧ a process for copying printed material, etc. by the action of light on an electrically charged surface **—xe·ro·graph·ic** (zir'ō graf'ik) ***adj.***

Xe·rox (zir'äks') *trademark for* a process of xerography **—*vt., vi.*** [x-] to reproduce by this process **—*n.*** [x-] a copy so made

Xer·xes I (zurk'sēz') *c.* 519-465 B.C.; king of Persia (486-465)

xi (zī, sī) ***n.*** ⟦Gr *xi,* earlier *xei*⟧ the 14th letter of the Greek alphabet (Ξ, ξ)

XL extra large

X·mas (eks'məs) ***n.*** *colloq. var. of* CHRISTMAS

X-ray (eks'rā') ***n.*** **1** a ray or radiation of very short wavelength, that can penetrate solid substances: used to study internal body structures and treat various disorders **2** a photograph made by means of X-rays **—*adj.*** of or by X-rays **—*vt.*** to examine, treat, or photograph with X-rays Also **X ray, x-ray,** or **x ray**

XS extra small

xy·lem (zī'ləm) ***n.*** ⟦< Gr *xylon,* wood⟧ the woody tissue of a plant

xy·lo·phone (zī'lə fōn') ***n.*** ⟦< Gr *xylon,* wood + -PHONE⟧ a musical percussion instrument consisting of a series of graduated wooden bars struck with small, wooden mallets **—xy'lo·phon'ist** (-fō'nist, zī läf'ə nist) ***n.***

Y

y or **Y** (wī) ***n., pl.*** **y's, Y's** the 25th letter of the English alphabet

-y[1] (ē, i) ⟦ME⟧ *suffix* little one, dear /*kitty, daddy*/

-y[2] (ē, i) ⟦OE *-ig*⟧ *suffix* **1** full of, like /*dirty*/ **2** somewhat /*yellowy*/ **3** tending to /*sticky*/

-y[3] (ē, i) ⟦< L *-ia*⟧ *suffix* **1** quality or condition /*jealousy*/ **2** a (specified) kind of shop, goods, or group /*bakery*/

-y[4] (ē, i) ⟦< L *-ium*⟧ *suffix* action of /*inquiry*/

Y *Chem. symbol for* yttrium

yacht (yät) ***n.*** ⟦Du *jacht*⟧ a small ship for pleasure cruises, racing, etc.

yacht'ing (-iŋ) ***n.*** the sport of sailing a yacht **—yachts'man** (-mən), ***pl.*** **-men, *n.***

Ya·hoo (yä'ho͞o') ***n.*** in Swift's *Gulliver's Travels,* any of a race of brutish, degraded creatures

Yah·weh or **Yah·we** (yä'we, -wā) ⟦Heb: see JEHOVAH⟧ God

yak[1] (yak) ***n.*** ⟦< Tibet *g-yag*⟧ a long-haired wild ox of Tibet and central Asia

yak[2] (yak) ***vi.*** **yakked, yak'king** ⟦echoic⟧ [Slang] to talk much or idly **—*n.*** [Slang] **1** a yakking **2** a loud laugh

yam (yam) ***n.*** ⟦< WAfr native name⟧ **1** the

edible, starchy, tuberous root of a tropical climbing plant 2 [South] a large variety of sweet potato

yam·mer (yam′ər) *vi.* ⟦< OE *geomor,* sad⟧ [Colloq.] 1 to whine, whimper, or complain 2 to shout, yell, etc. —*vt.* [Colloq.] to say complainingly —**yam′mer·er** *n.*

yang (yäŋ, yaŋ) *n.* ⟦Chin⟧ in Chinese philosophy, the masculine force or principle in the universe: cf. YIN

Yang·tze (yaŋk′sē) *a name for the* CHANG

yank (yaŋk) *n., vt., vi.* ⟦< ?⟧ [Colloq.] jerk

Yank (yaŋk) *n.* [Slang] a Yankee; esp., a U.S. soldier in World Wars I and II

Yan·kee (yaŋ′kē) *n.* ⟦< ? Du *Jan Kees,* a disparaging nickname⟧ 1 a New Englander 2 a native of a Northern State 3 a citizen of the U.S. —*adj.* of or like Yankees

yap (yap) *vi.* **yapped, yap′ping** ⟦echoic⟧ 1 to make a sharp, shrill bark 2 [Slang] to talk noisily and stupidly —*n.* 1 a sharp, shrill bark 2 [Slang] *a)* jabber *b)* the mouth

yard[1] (yärd) *n.* ⟦OE *gierd,* rod⟧ 1 a measure of length, 3 feet or 36 inches 2 *Naut.* a slender rod or spar fastened across a mast to support a sail

yard[2] (yärd) *n.* ⟦OE *geard,* enclosure⟧ 1 the ground around or next to a house or other building 2 an enclosed place for a particular purpose [*shipyard*] 3 a railroad center where trains are switched, etc.

yard·age (yärd′ij) *n.* 1 measurement in yards 2 the extent so measured

yard′arm′ *n. Naut.* either half of a yard supporting a square sail, etc.

yard goods textiles made in standard width, usually sold by the yard

yard·man (yärd′man′, -mən) *n., pl.* **-men′** a person who works in a yard, esp. a railroad yard

yard′stick′ *n.* 1 a graduated measuring stick one yard in length 2 any standard used in judging, etc.

yar·mul·ke (yär′məl kə, yä′-) *n.* ⟦Yidd < Pol⟧ a skullcap variously worn by Jewish men, as at prayer Also **yar′mel·ke**

yarn (yärn) *n.* ⟦OE *gearn*⟧ 1 fibers of wool, cotton, etc. spun into strands for weaving, knitting, etc. 2 [Colloq.] a tale or story

yat·ter (yat′ər) *vi.* ⟦prob. < YA(K)[2] + (CHA)TTER⟧ [Slang] to chatter continuously —*n.* [Slang] idle talk; chatter

yaw (yô) *vi.* ⟦ON *jaga,* to sway⟧ 1 to swing back and forth across its course, as a ship 2 to rotate or oscillate about the vertical axis: said of a spacecraft, etc. —*n.* a yawing

yawl (yôl) *n.* ⟦< Du *jol*⟧ a small, two-masted sailboat rigged fore-and-aft

yawn (yôn) *vi.* ⟦ME *yanen*⟧ 1 to open the mouth wide involuntarily, as a result of fatigue, drowsiness, etc. 2 to open wide; gape —*n.* a yawning

yaws (yôz) *n.pl.* ⟦of WInd origin⟧ [*with sing. v.*] a tropical infectious skin disease

yay (yā) *adv.* 1 YEA (sense 1) 2 [Colloq.] this; so: often with a gesture indicating size [*yay* high]

Y chromosome *see* SEX CHROMOSOME

y·clept or **y·clept′** (ē klept′) *vt.* ⟦<OE *clipian,* to call⟧ [Archaic] called; named Also **y·cleped′**

yd. yard(s)

ye[1] (*thə, thi, thē; now often erroneously or facetiously* yē) ***adj., definite article*** *archaic var. of* THE

ye[2] (yē) ***pron.*** ⟦OE *ge*⟧ *archaic var. of* YOU

yea (yā) *adv.* ⟦OE *gea*⟧ 1 yes 2 indeed; truly —*n.* 1 an affirmative vote 2 a person voting in the affirmative

yeah (ya, ye) *adv.* [Colloq.] yes

year (yir) *n.* ⟦OE *gear*⟧ 1 a period of 365 days (366 days in leap year), divided into 12 months beginning Jan. 1 2 the period (365 days, 5 hours, 48 minutes, and 46 seconds) of one revolution of the earth around the sun: also **solar year** 3 a period of 12 calendar months reckoned from any date 4 an annual period of less than 365 days [*a school year*] 5 [*pl.*] *a)* age [*old for his years*] *b)* a long time [*he died years ago*] —**year after year** every year

year′book′ *n.* an annual book; specif., *a)* a book giving data of the preceding year *b)* a publication of the graduating class of a school or college

year′ling (-liŋ) *n.* an animal one year old or in its second year

year′ly *adj.* 1 done, happening, appearing, etc. once a year, or every year [*a yearly event*] 2 of a year, or of each year —*adv.* every year

yearn (yurn) *vi.* ⟦< OE *georn,* eager⟧ 1 to be filled with longing or desire 2 to be deeply moved, esp. with tenderness —**yearn′ing** *n.*

year′-round′ *adj.* open, in use, operating, etc. throughout the year

yea′say′er *n.* one having a positive attitude toward life

yeast (yēst) *n.* ⟦OE *gist*⟧ 1 a yellowish, moist mass of fungi that cause fermentation: used in making beer, etc., and as leavening 2 yeast dried in flakes or granules or compressed into cakes 3 foam; froth 4 ferment; agitation

yeast·y (yēs′tē) *adj.* **-i·er, -i·est** 1 of, like, or containing yeast 2 frothy; light

yegg (yeg) *n.* ⟦< ?⟧ [Old Slang] a criminal; esp., a burglar, etc.

yell (yel) *vi., vt.* ⟦OE *giellan*⟧ to cry out loudly; scream —*n.* 1 a loud outcry 2 a rhythmic cheer in unison

yel·low (yel′ō) *adj.* ⟦OE *geolu*⟧ 1 of the color of ripe lemons 2 having a somewhat yellow skin 3 [Colloq.] cowardly 4 sensational, as a newspaper —*n.* 1 a yellow color 2 an egg yolk —*vt., vi.* to make or become yellow —**yel′low·ish** *adj.*

Yel·low (yel′ō) *a name for the* HUANG

yellow fever an infectious tropical disease caused by a virus transmitted by the bite of a certain mosquito

yellow jacket a wasp or hornet having bright-yellow markings

Yellow Sea arm of the East China Sea, between China & Korea

yelp (yelp) *vi., vt.* ⟦OE *gielpan,* to boast⟧ to utter or express in a short, sharp cry or bark, as a dog —*n.* a short, sharp cry or bark

Yem·en (yem′ən) 1 country in S Arabia, on the Red Sea: *c.* 75,000 sq. mi.; pop. 6,339,000: in full **Yemen Arab Republic** 2 country east of this: 124,698 sq. mi.; pop. 2,275,000: in full **People's Democratic**

Republic of Yemen —**Yem′en·ite′** or **Yem′e·ni** (-ə nē) ***adj., n.***

yen[1] (yen) ***n., pl.* yen** ⟦Jpn⟧ the monetary unit of Japan

yen[2] (yen) ***n.*** ⟦prob. < Chin *yan,* opium⟧ [Colloq.] a strong longing or desire

yeo·man (yō′mən) ***n., pl.* -men** ⟦ME *yeman*⟧ **1** [Historical] a freeholder of a class below the gentry **2** *U.S. Navy* a petty officer assigned to clerical duty

yeo′man·ry ***n.*** yeomen collectively

yes (yes) ***adv.*** ⟦OE *gese*⟧ **1** aye; yea; it is so: expressing agreement, consent, etc. **2** not only that, but more /ready, *yes,* eager to help/ —***n., pl.* yes′es** an affirmative reply, vote, etc. —***vt., vi.* yessed, yes′sing** to say *yes* (to)

ye·shi·va (yə shē′və) ***n., pl.* -vas** or **-vot′** (-vōt′) ⟦Heb, lit., act of sitting⟧ a kind of Jewish school, as one combining religious and secular studies

yes man [Slang] one who is always approving what is said by a superior

yes·ter·day (yes′tər dā′, -dē) ***n.*** ⟦OE *geostran,* yesterday + *dæg,* day⟧ **1** the day before today **2** a recent day or time —***adv.*** **1** on the day before today **2** recently

yes′ter·year′ (-yir′) ***n., adv.*** **1** last year **2** (in) recent years

yet (yet) ***adv.*** ⟦OE *giet*⟧ **1** up to now; thus far /he hasn't gone *yet*/ **2** at the present time; now /we can't go just *yet*/ **3** still /there is *yet* a chance/ **4** in addition; even /he was *yet* more kind/ **5** nevertheless /she's kind, *yet* shy/ —***conj.*** nevertheless; however /she seems well, *yet* she is ill/ —**as yet** up to now

yew (yo͞o) ***n.*** ⟦OE *iw*⟧ **1** an evergreen tree with needle leaves **2** its wood

Yid·dish (yid′ish) ***n.*** ⟦< Ger *jüdisch,* < L *Judaeus,* Jew⟧ a language derived from medieval High German, written in the Hebrew alphabet and spoken esp. by East European Jews

yield (yēld) ***vt.*** ⟦OE *gieldan,* to pay⟧ **1** to produce as a crop, result, profit, etc. **2** to surrender **3** to concede —***vi.*** **1** to produce **2** to surrender **3** to give way to physical force **4** to lose precedence, etc.: often with *to* —***n.*** the amount yielded

yield′ing ***adj.*** flexible; submissive

yin (yin) ***n.*** ⟦Chin⟧ in Chinese philosophy, the feminine force or principle in the universe: cf. YANG

yip (yip) ***n.*** ⟦echoic⟧ [Colloq.] a yelp or bark —***vi.* yipped, yip′ping** [Colloq.] to yelp or bark

yip·pie (yip′ē) ***n.*** [Slang] a person in the U.S. belonging to a loosely organized group of young radicals

YMCA Young Men's Christian Association

YMHA Young Men's Hebrew Association

yo·del (yōd′′l) ***vt., vi.* -deled** or **-delled, -del·ing** or **-del·ling** ⟦Ger *jodeln*⟧ to sing with abrupt alternating changes to the falsetto —***n.*** a yodeling

yo·ga (yō′gə) ***n.*** ⟦Sans, union⟧ a mystic Hindu discipline for achieving union with the supreme spirit through intense concentration, meditation, prescribed postures, controlled breathing, etc.

yo·gi (yō′gē) ***n., pl.* -gis** one who practices yoga Also **yo′gin** (-gin)

yo·gurt (yō′gərt) ***n.*** ⟦Turk *yoğurt*⟧ a thick, somewhat solid food made from fermented milk Also **yo′ghurt**

YOKE ON OXEN

yoke (yōk) ***n.*** ⟦OE *geoc*⟧ **1** a wooden frame for harnessing together a pair of oxen, etc. **2** such a pair harnessed **3** bondage; servitude **4** anything like a yoke, as something that binds, unites, etc., or a part of a garment fitted to the shoulders or hips as a support for the gathered parts below —***vt.* yoked, yok′ing** **1** to put a yoke on **2** to harness (an animal) to (a plow, etc.) **3** to join together

yo·kel (yō′kəl) ***n.*** a person from the country; bumpkin: a contemptuous term

Yo·ko·ha·ma (yō′kə hä′mə) seaport in S Honshu, Japan: pop. 2,915,000

yolk (yōk) ***n.*** ⟦OE *geolca*⟧ the yellow, principal substance of an egg

Yom Kip·pur (yäm kip′ər; *Heb* yōm′ kē po͞or′) the Day of Atonement, a Jewish holiday and day of fasting

yon (yän) ***adj., adv.*** ⟦OE *geon*⟧ [Now Chiefly Dial.] yonder

yon·der (yän′dər) ***adj., adv.*** ⟦ME⟧ (being) at or in that (specified or relatively distant) place; over there

Yon·kers (yaŋ′kərz) city in SE N.Y.: pop. 195,000

yoo-hoo (yo͞o′ho͞o′) ***interj., n.*** a shout or call for attracting attention

yore (yôr) ***adv.*** ⟦OE *geara*⟧ [Obs.] long ago —**of yore** formerly

you (yo͞o) ***pron.*** ⟦OE *eow* < *ge,* YE[2]⟧ **1** the person or persons spoken to **2** a person or people generally /*you* can never tell!/

young (yuŋ) ***adj.*** ⟦OE *geong*⟧ **1** being in an early period of life or growth; not old **2** youthful; fresh; vigorous **3** in an early stage **4** inexperienced; immature —***n.*** **1** young people **2** offspring, esp. young offspring —**with young** pregnant —**young′ish** ***adj.***

young blood **1** young people; youth **2** youthful strength, vigor, etc.

young·ster (yuŋ′stər) ***n.*** a child or youth

Youngs·town (yuŋz′toun′) city in NE Ohio: pop. 115,000

your (yo͝or; *often* yôr) ***poss. pronominal adj.*** ⟦OE *eower*⟧ of, belonging to, or done by you Also used before some titles /*your* Honor/

you're (yo͝or, yo͞or) you are

yours (yo͝orz; *often* yôrz) ***pron.*** that or those belonging to you /that book is *yours*/

your·self (yo͝or self′, yər-) ***pron., pl.* -selves′** (-selvz′) a form of the second pers. sing. pronoun, used as an intensive /you *yourself* said so/, as a reflexive /you hurt *yourself*/, and as a quasi-noun meaning "your real, true, or actual self" (Ex.: you are not *yourself* today)

yours truly 1 a phrase used in ending a letter 2 [Colloq.] I or me
youth (yo͞oth) ***n.***, *pl.* **youths** (yo͞othz, yo͞oths) ⟦OE *geoguthe*⟧ 1 the state or quality of being young 2 the period of adolescence 3 an early stage of growth or existence 4 young people collectively 5 a young person; esp., a young man
youth'ful ***adj.*** 1 not yet old or mature; young 2 of, like, or fit for youth 3 fresh; vigorous 4 new; early —**youth'ful·ly** ***adv.*** —**youth'ful·ness** ***n.***
yowl (youl) ***vi., n.*** ⟦< ON *gaula*⟧ howl or wail
yo-yo (yō'yō') ***n.***, *pl.* **yo'-yos'** ⟦< ?⟧ 1 a spool-like toy reeled up and let down by a string 2 [Slang] one regarded as stupid, inept, etc. —***vi.*** [Colloq.] to move up and down; fluctuate
yr. 1 year(s) 2 your
yrs. 1 years 2 yours
YT Yukon Territory
yt·tri·um (i'trē əm) ***n.*** a rare, silvery, metallic chemical element: used in color TV tubes, etc.
yuc·ca (yuk'ə) ***n.*** ⟦< AmSp *yuca*⟧ 1 a desert plant with stiff leaves and white flowers 2 its flower
yuck (yuk) ***n.*** [Slang] something unpleasant, disgusting, etc. —***interj.*** [Slang] an expression of distaste, disgust, etc. —**yuck'y, -i·er, -i·est,** ***adj.***
Yu·go·slav·i·a (yo͞o'gō slä'vē ə, -gə-) country in the NW Balkan Peninsula: 98,766 sq. mi.; pop. 23,284,000 —**Yu'go·slav'** or **Yu'go·sla'vi·an** ***adj., n.***
yuk (yuk) ***n.*** ⟦echoic⟧ [Slang] a loud laugh of amusement, or something causing such a laugh —***vi.*** **yukked, yuk'king** [Slang] to laugh loudly
Yu·kon (yo͞o'kän') territory of NW Canada, east of Alas.: *c.* 207,076 sq. mi.; pop. 22,000: usually used with *the*: in full **Yukon Territory**
yule (yo͞ol) ***n.*** ⟦OE *geol*⟧ [*often* **Y-**] Christmas or the Christmas season
yule'tide' (-tīd') ***n.*** [*often* **Y-**] Christmastime
yum·my (yum'ē) ***adj.*** **-mi·er, -mi·est** [Colloq.] very tasty; delectable
yup (yup) ***adv.*** [Slang] yes: an affirmative reply
yup·pie (yup'ē) ***n.*** ⟦< *y(oung) u(rban) p(rofessional)*⟧ [Colloq.] any of those young professionals regarded as affluent, ambitious, materialistic, etc.
YWCA Young Women's Christian Association
YWHA Young Women's Hebrew Association

Z

z or **Z** (zē; *Brit, etc.* zed) ***n.***, *pl.* **z's, Z's** the 26th and last letter of the English alphabet
Za·ire or **Za·ïre** (zä ir') country in central Africa, on the equator: 905,563 sq. mi.; pop. 31,330,000
Zam·bi·a (zam'bē ə) country in S Africa: 290,585 sq. mi.; pop. 7,054,000
za·ny (zā'nē) ***n.***, *pl.* **-nies** ⟦< It dial. *zanni*, < *Giovanni*, John⟧ 1 a clown or buffoon 2 a silly person —***adj.*** **-ni·er, -ni·est** funny in a crazy or silly way —**za'ni·ness** ***n.***
Zan·zi·bar (zan'zə bär') island off the E coast of Africa: part of Tanzania
zap (zap) ***vt., vi.*** **zapped, zap'ping** ⟦echoic⟧ [Slang] to move, strike, smash, kill, etc. with sudden speed —***n.*** [Slang] energy, pep, etc. —***interj.*** an exclamation expressing sudden swift action or change
zeal (zēl) ***n.*** ⟦< Gr *zēlos*⟧ intense enthusiasm; ardor; fervor
zeal·ot (zel'ət) ***n.*** one who is zealous, esp. to a fanatic degree
zeal·ous (zel'əs) ***adj.*** of or showing zeal; fervent —**zeal'ous·ly** ***adv.***
ze·bra (zē'brə) ***n.*** ⟦Port⟧ an African mammal related to the horse and having dark stripes on a white or tawny body
ze·bu (zē'byo͞o') ***n.*** ⟦Fr *zébu* < ?⟧ a domesticated ox of Asia and Africa
zed (zed) ***n.*** ⟦< Gr *zēta*⟧ [Brit., etc.] the letter Z, z
Zeit·geist (tsīt'gīst') ***n.*** ⟦Ger, time spirit⟧ trend of thought and feeling in a period of history
Zen (zen) ***n.*** ⟦Jpn ult. < Sans *dhyāna*, thinking⟧ a variety of Buddhism in which enlightenment is sought through introspection and intuition
ze·nith (zē'nith) ***n.*** ⟦< L *semita*, path⟧ 1 the point in the sky directly overhead 2 the highest point
zeph·yr (zef'ər) ***n.*** ⟦< Gr *zephyros*⟧ 1 the west wind 2 a gentle breeze
zep·pe·lin (zep'ə lin) ***n.*** ⟦after Count F. von *Zeppelin* (1838-1917), its Ger designer⟧ [*often* **Z-**] a type of rigid airship designed around 1900
ze·ro (zir'ō, zē'rō) ***n.***, *pl.* **-ros** or **-roes** ⟦< Ar *ṣifr*, cipher⟧ 1 the symbol 0; cipher; naught 2 the point, marked 0, from which quantities are reckoned on a graduated scale 3 nothing 4 the lowest point —***adj.*** of or at zero —**zero in on** to concentrate attention on; focus on
zero hour 1 the time set for beginning an attack, etc. 2 any crucial moment
zero (population) growth a condition in a given population in which the birthrate equals the death rate
ze'ro-sum' (-sum') ***adj.*** of or being a situation in which a gain for one must result in a loss for another
zest (zest) ***n.*** ⟦Fr *zeste*, orange peel⟧ 1 something that gives flavor or relish 2 stimulating quality 3 keen enjoyment /a *zest* for life/ —**zest'ful** ***adj.***
ze·ta (zāt'ə) ***n.*** ⟦Gr *zēta*⟧ the sixth letter of the Greek alphabet (Z, ζ)
Zeus (zyo͞os, zo͞os) *Gr. Myth.* the chief deity
zig·gu·rat (zig'oo rat') ***n.*** ⟦< Assyr *ziqquratu*⟧ an ancient Assyrian or Babylonian

temple tower in the form of a terraced pyramid

zig·zag (zig′zag′) ***n.*** ⟦Fr⟧ 1 a series of short, sharp angles in alternate directions 2 a design, path, etc. in this form ***—adj.*** having the form of a zigzag ***—adv.*** in a zigzag course ***—vt., vi.*** **-zagged′, -zag′ging** to move or form in a zigzag

zilch (zilch) ***n.*** ⟦nonsense syllable⟧ [Slang] nothing; zero

zil·lion (zil′yən) ***n.*** ⟦< MILLION⟧ [Colloq.] a very large, indefinite number

Zim·ba·bwe (zim bä′bwā′, -bwē′) country in S Africa, north of South Africa: 151,000 sq. mi.; pop. 8,984,000

zinc (ziŋk) ***n.*** ⟦Ger *zink*⟧ a bluish-white, metallic chemical element, used in alloys, as a protective coating for iron, etc.

zinc oxide a white powder used in making rubber articles, cosmetics, ointments, etc.

zin·fan·del (zin′fən del′) ***n.*** ⟦< ?⟧ a dry red wine made chiefly in California

zing (ziŋ) ***n.*** ⟦echoic⟧ [Slang] 1 a shrill whizzing sound 2 zest, vigor, etc.

zing′er ***n.*** [Slang] something with zing, as a retort, punch line, etc.

zin·ni·a (zin′ē ə, zin′yə) ***n.*** ⟦after J. G. *Zinn* (1727-59), Ger botanist⟧ a plant having colorful, composite flowers

Zi·on (zī′ən) 1 a hill in Jerusalem, site of Solomon's Temple 2 Jerusalem 3 Israel ***—n.*** 1 the Jewish people 2 heaven

Zi′on·ism′ (-iz′əm) ***n.*** an international movement formerly for reestablishing, now for supporting, the state of Israel **—Zi′on·ist *n., adj.***

zip (zip) ***n.*** ⟦echoic⟧ 1 a short, sharp hissing sound, as of a passing bullet 2 [Colloq.] energy; vigor ***—vi.*** **zipped, zip′ping** 1 to make, or move with, a zip 2 [Colloq.] to move with speed ***—vt.*** to fasten with a zipper

ZIP Code (zip) ⟦*z(oning) i(mprovement) p(lan)*⟧ *trademark for* a system of code numbers assigned by the postal service: each code designates a delivery point

zip·per (zip′ər) ***n.*** a device used to fasten and unfasten two edges of material: it consists of two rows of interlocking tabs worked by a sliding part

zip′py ***adj.*** **-pi·er, -pi·est** [Colloq.] full of vim and energy; brisk

zir·con (zur′kän′) ***n.*** ⟦ult. < Pers *zar,* gold⟧ a crystalline silicate mineral, used as a gem

zir·co·ni·um (zər kō′nē əm) ***n.*** a ductile, metallic chemical element used in alloys, nuclear reactors, etc.: symbol, **Zr**

zit (zit) ***n.*** [Slang] a pimple, esp. one on the face

zith·er (zith′ər, zith′-) ***n.*** ⟦< Gr *kithara,* lute⟧ any of various musical instruments with strings stretched across a flat soundboard and plucked, bowed, struck with mallets, etc., as the dulcimer, etc.

Zn *Chem. symbol for* zinc

zo·di·ac (zō′dē ak′) ***n.*** ⟦< Gr *zōdiakos* (*kyklos*), (circle) of animals⟧ 1 an imaginary belt in the heavens extending on either side of the apparent path of the sun and divided into twelve equal parts, or signs, named for constellations 2 a diagram representing this **—zo·di′a·cal** (-dī′ə kəl) ***adj.***

zom·bie (zäm′bē) ***n.*** ⟦of Afr orig.⟧ 1 in West Indian superstition, a supernatural power through which a corpse may be reanimated 2 such a corpse Also **zom′bi**

zone (zōn) ***n.*** ⟦Fr < Gr *zōnē*⟧ 1 an encircling band, stripe, etc. 2 any of the five great latitudinal divisions of the earth's surface: see TORRID ZONE, TEMPERATE ZONE, and FRIGID ZONE 3 any area with reference to a specified use or restriction [a canal *zone*, postal *zone*] ***—vt.*** **zoned, zon′ing** 1 to mark off into zones 2 to encircle; surround **—zon′al *adj.* —zoned *adj.***

zonked (zôŋkt, zäŋkt) ***adj.*** [Slang] 1 drunk or under the influence of a drug 2 exhausted

zoo (zo͞o) ***n.*** ⟦< *zoo(logical garden)*⟧ 1 a place where a collection of wild animals is kept for public showing 2 [Slang] a place marked by confusion, disorder, etc.

zoo- ⟦< Gr *zōion*, animal⟧ *combining form* animal(s) [*zoology*]

zo·ol·o·gy (zō äl′ə jē) ***n.*** ⟦ModL *zoologia*: see prec. & -LOGY⟧ the science that deals with animals and animal life **—zo′o·log′i·cal** (-ə läj′i kəl) ***adj.*** **—zo·ol′o·gist *n.***

zoom (zo͞om) ***vi.*** ⟦echoic⟧ 1 to make a loud, buzzing sound 2 to climb in an airplane sharply 3 to rise rapidly [prices *zoomed*] 4 to focus with a zoom lens ***—vt.*** to cause to zoom ***—n.*** a zooming

zoom lens a system of lenses, as in a film or TV camera, that can be rapidly adjusted for close-up or distant shots while keeping the image in focus

zo·o·phyte (zō′ō fīt′, zō′ə-) ***n.*** ⟦< ZOO- + Gr *phyton*, a plant⟧ any animal, as a coral or sponge, that looks and grows somewhat like a plant **—zo′o·phyt′ic** (-fit′ik) ***adj.***

Zo·ro·as·ter (zō′rō as′tər) *c.* 6th or 7th c. B.C.; Pers. founder of Zoroastrianism

Zo·ro·as·tri·an·ism (zō′rō as′trē ən iz′əm) ***n.*** the religion of the ancient Persians

zuc·chi·ni (zo͞o kē′nē) ***n.,*** *pl.* **-ni** or **-nis** ⟦It⟧ a cucumberlike summer squash

Zu·lu (zo͞o′lo͞o) ***n.*** 1 *pl.* **-lus** or **-lu** a member of a people living in South Africa 2 their language ***—adj.*** of the Zulus, their language, etc.

Zu·ni (zo͞o′nē) ***n.*** 1 *pl.* **-nis** or **-ni** a member of a pueblo-dwelling North American Indian people of W New Mexico 2 their language Also, formerly, **Zu·ñi** (zo͞on′yē)

Zur·ich (zoor′ik) city in N Switzerland: pop. 440,000

zwie·back (tsvē′bäk′, swē′-; swī′bak′) ***n.*** ⟦Ger < *zwie-*, twice + *backen*, to bake⟧ a kind of biscuit that is sliced and toasted after baking

zy·de·co (zī′də kō) ***n.*** a heavily syncopated dance music of S Louisiana, containing elements of blues, white Cajun music, etc.

zy·gote (zī′gōt′) ***n.*** ⟦< Gr *zygon,* yoke⟧ a cell formed by the union of male and female gametes

zymo- ⟦< Gr *zymē*, a leaven⟧ *combining form* fermentation Also **zym-**

zy·mur·gy (zī′mər jē) ***n.*** ⟦prec. + -URGY⟧ the chemistry of fermentation, as applied in brewing, etc.

TABLE OF MEASURES

The International Metric System

Listed here are all the base units of the International System and all the prefixes, plus the most common derived units that have special names and other common units that are not part of the International System but are used with it. The International System is also called "the SI," for its official name, *Système international d'unités* (International System of Units).

SI base units

name	*symbol*	*quantity*
meter	m	length
kilogram	kg	mass
second	s	time
ampere	A	electric current
kelvin	K	thermodynamic temperature
mole	mol	amount of substance
candela	cd	luminous intensity

SI prefixes

name	*symbol*	*multiplying factor**
exa-	E	$\times 10^{18}$
peta-	P	$\times 10^{15}$
tera-	T	$\times 10^{12}$
giga-	G	$\times 10^{9}$
mega-	M	$\times 10^{6}$
kilo-	k	$\times 10^{3}$
hecto-	h	$\times 10^{2}$
deca-	da	$\times 10$
deci-	d	$\times 10^{-1}$
centi-	c	$\times 10^{-2}$
milli-	m	$\times 10^{-3}$
micro-	μ	$\times 10^{-6}$
nano-	n	$\times 10^{-9}$
pico-	p	$\times 10^{-12}$
femto-	f	$\times 10^{-15}$
atto-	a	$\times 10^{-18}$

Common SI derived units with special names

name	*symbol*	*quantity*
hertz	Hz	frequency
pascal	Pa	pressure, stress
watt	W	power, radiant flux
volt	V	electric potential, electromotive force
gram	g	mass (= 1/1000 of a kilogram; note that the base unit is the kilogram, not the gram)

Common units used with the SI

name	*symbol*	*quantity*
liter	l or L	volume or capacity (= 1 dm^3)
degree Celsius	°C	temperature (= 1 K; 0°C = 273.15 K)
hectare	ha	area (= 10 000 m^2)
ton	t	mass (= 1000 kg)
nautical mile	M	distance (navigation) (= 1852 m)
knot	kn	speed (navigation) (= 1 M/h)
standard atmosphere	atm	atmospheric pressure (= 101.3 kPa)

* $10^2 = 100$, $10^3 = 1000$; $10^{-1} = 0.1$, $10^{-2} = 0.01$.
Thus, 2 km = 2 x 1000 = 2000 m and 3 cm = 3 x 0.01 = 0.03 m.
Any prefix may be used with any base or derived unit (e.g. mm = millimeter, MHz = megahertz).
Some common prefixes are also used with the liter (e.g. ml = milliliter).

TABLE OF MEASURES

Common Conversion Factors

1 centimeter	= 0.39 in	1 gram	= 0.04 oz
1 meter	= 39.4 in	1 kilogram	= 2.20 lb
1 kilometer	= 0.62 mi	1 ton	= 1.10 short tons
1 square centimeter	= 0.16 sq in	1 liter	= 0.88 qt
1 square meter	= 1.20 sq yd	1 cubic centimeter	= 0.06 cu in
		1 cubic meter	= 1.31 cu yd

Length

inch		(2.54 cm)
foot	12 in	(0.3048 m)
yard	3 ft	(0.9144 m)
rod	5½ yd	(5.029 m)
statute mile	1,760 yd	(1.6093 km)

Volume or Capacity

Liquid Measure

fluid ounce		(29.57 ml)
pint	16 fl oz	(0.4732 l)
quart	2 pt	(0.9464 l)
gallon	4 qt	(3.7854 l)

Dry Measure

pint		(0.5506 l)
quart	2 pt	(1.1012 l)
peck	8 qt	(8.8098 l)
bushel	4 pecks	(35.2390 l)

Area

square inch		(6.452 cm²)
square foot	144 sq in	(929.03 cm²)
square yard	9 sq ft	(0.8361 m²)
acre	4,840 sq yd	(0.4047 ha)
square mile	640 acres	(2.590 km²)

Weight

Avoirdupois Weight

ounce		(28.3495 g)
pound	16 oz	(453.59 g)
hundredweight	100 lb	(45.36 kg)
ton	20 short hundredweight	(907.18 kg)

Troy Weight

grain		(0.0648 g)
carat	3.086 grains	(200.00 mg)
pennyweight	24 grains	(1.5552 g)
ounce	20 pennyweights	(31.1035 g)
pound	12 oz	(373.24 g)

SPECIAL SIGNS AND SYMBOLS

SCIENCE

□, ♂	male
○, ♀	female
×	crossed with: for a hybrid
+	1. plus 2. positive
−	1. minus 2. negative
±	plus or minus
× ·	multiplied by
÷	divided by
=	equal to
≠	not equal to
>	greater than
<	less than
≡	identical with
≈	approximately equal to
≅	congruent to (in geometry)
:	is to: the ratio of
∞	infinity
∴	therefore
∵	since
⊥	perpendicular to
√‾ √	square root
°	degree
′	1. minute(s) of arc 2. foot, feet
″	1. second(s) of arc 2. inch(es)
∅	empty set

NUMERATION

Arabic	Roman	Arabic	Roman
0		17	XVII
1	I	18	XVIII
2	II	19	XIX
3	III	20	XX
4	IV or IIII	30	XXX
5	V	40	XL
6	VI	50	L
7	VII	60	LX
8	VIII	70	LXX
9	IX	80	LXXX
10	X	90	XC
11	XI	100	C
12	XII	400	CD
13	XIII	500	D
14	XIV	900	CM
15	XV	1,000	M
16	XVI	2,000	MM

SPECIAL SIGNS AND SYMBOLS

COMMERCE AND FINANCE

- $ dollar(s)
- ¢ cent(s)
- £ pound(s) sterling
- ¥ yen
- @ at the rate of
- ℔ per
- % percent
- per thousand

PROOFREADING

- ¶ new paragraph
- ∧ insert
- ₰ delete
- ⁐ close up space
- ₰ delete and close up
- # leave space

SUITS OF PLAYING CARDS

- ♠ spade
- ♦ diamond
- ♣ club
- ♥ heart

SIGNS OF THE ZODIAC

♈	Aries (the Ram)
♉	Taurus (the Bull)
Ⅱ, □, ♊	Gemini (the Twins)
♋, ⊗	Cancer (the Crab)
♌	Leo (the Lion)
♍	Virgo (the Virgin)
♎	Libra (the Balance)
♏	Scorpio (the Scorpion)
♐	Sagittarius (the Archer)
♑, ♑	Capricorn (the Goat)
♒	Aquarius (the Water Bearer)
♓	Pisces (the Fishes)

MISCELLANEOUS

&, &	and
&c.	and so forth
©	copyright(ed)
®	registered: said of a trademark
†	death: died
℞	take: used at beginning of a prescription
#	1. number (before a figure) 2. pound(s) (after a figure) 3. space (in printing)
w/	with
w/o	without
§	section (of a text)
"	ditto marks: repeat the word or sign located directly above
☠	poison
☢	radioactive: radiation

ABBREVIATIONS USED IN THIS DICTIONARY

abbrev.	abbreviated: abbreviation
adj.	adjective
adv.	adverb
Afr	African
Afrik	Afrikaans
alt.	alternative
Am	American
AmInd	American Indian
AmSp	American Spanish
Anat.	Anatomy
Anglo-Fr	Anglo-French
Ar	Arabic
Aram	Aramaic
Archit.	Architecture
Biol.	Biology
Bot.	Botany
Brit	British
C	Celsius
c.	circa
c.	century
cap.	capital city
Cdn	Canadian
Celt	Celtic
cf.	compare
Ch.	Church
Chem.	Chemistry
Chin	Chinese
Colloq.	colloquial
compar.	comparative
Comput.	Computer Science
conj.	conjunction
contr.	contraction (grammar)
Dan	Danish
Dial., dial.	dialectal
dim.	diminutive
Du	Dutch
E	eastern
Eccles.	Ecclesiastical
Educ.	Education
e.g.	for example
Egypt	Egyptian
Elec.	Electricity
Eng	English
Esk	Eskimo
esp.	especially
etc.	and/or the like
Ex.	example
exc.	except
F	Fahrenheit
fem.	feminine
Fl	Flemish
fol.	following entry
Fr	French
ft.	foot, feet
Gael	Gaelic
Geol.	Geology
Geom.	Geometry
Ger	German
Gmc	Germanic
Gr	classical Greek
Gram.	Grammar
Haw	Hawaiian
Heb	Hebrew
Hung	Hungarian
IE	Indo-European
i.e.	that is
in.	inch(es)
indic.	indicative
infl.	influenced
intens.	intensive
interj.	interjection
Ir	Irish
It	Italian
Jpn	Japanese
km	kilometer(s)
L	classical Latin
lb.	pound(s)
lit.	literally
LL	Late Latin
LowG	Low German
m	meter(s)
masc.	masculine
Math.	Mathematics
MDu	Middle Dutch
ME	Middle English
Mech.	Mechanics
Med.	Medicine
Mex	Mexican
MHG	Middle High German
mi.	mile(s)
Mil.	Military
ML	Middle Latin
ModGr	Modern Greek
ModL	modern scientific Latin
Myth.	Mythology
N	northern
n.	noun
Naut.	nautical usage
NE	northeastern
NormFr	Norman French
Norw	Norwegian
n.pl.	plural noun
n.sing.	singular noun
NW	northwestern
Obs., obs.	obsolete
occas.	occasionally
OE	Old English
OFr	Old French
OHG.	Old High German
ON	Old Norse
orig.	origin; originally
OS	Old Saxon
OSlav	Old Church Slavonic
pers.	person (grammar)
Pers	Persian
Photog.	Photography
pl.	plural
Poet.	poetic
Pol	Polish
pop.	population
Port	Portuguese
poss.	possessive
pp.	past participle
prec.	preceding entry
prep.	preposition
pres.	present tense
prob.	probably
pron.	pronoun
Prov	Provencal
prp.	present participle
pseud.	pseudonym
Psychol.	Psychology
pt.	past tense
R.C.Ch.	Roman Catholic Church
Rom.	Roman
Russ	Russian
S	southern
Sans	Sanskrit
Scand	Scandinavian
Scot.	Scottish
SE	southeastern
sing.	singular
Sp	Spanish
sp.	spelling, spelled
specif.	specifically
sq.	square
superl.	superlative
SW	southwestern
Swed	Swedish
Theol.	Theology
transl.	translated, translation
Turk	Turkish
ult.	ultimately
v.	verb
var.	variant
v.aux.	auxiliary verb
vi.	intransitive verb
VL	Vulgar Latin
vt.	transitive verb
W	western
WInd	West Indian
Yidd	Yiddish

<	derived from
?	uncertain or unknown
+	plus
&	and